THE ROMAN LAW OF SLAVERY

THE CONDITION OF THE SLAVE IN PRIVATE LAW FROM AUGUSTUS TO JUSTINIAN

BY

W. W. BUCKLAND

AMS PRESS
NEW YORK

Reprinted from the edition of 1908, Cambridge
First AMS EDITION published 1969
Manufactured in the United States of America

Library of Congress Catalogue Card Number: 70-94318

AMS PRESS, INC.
NEW YORK, N.Y. 10003

PREFACE

THE following chapters are an attempt to state, in systematic form, the most characteristic part of the most characteristic intellectual product of Rome. There is scarcely a problem which can present itself, in any branch of the law, the solution of which may not be affected by the fact that one of the parties to the transaction is a slave, and, outside the region of procedure, there are few branches of the law in which the slave does not prominently appear. Yet, important as the subject is, for the light it might be expected to throw on legal conceptions, there does not exist, so far as I know, any book which aims at stating the principles of the Roman Law of slavery as a whole. Wallon's well-known book covers so much ground that it cannot treat this subject with fulness, and indeed it is clear that his interest is not mainly in the law of the matter. The same is true of Blair's somewhat antiquated but still readable little book.

But though there exists no general account, there is a large amount of valuable literature, mostly foreign. Much of this I have been unable to see, but without the help of continental writers, chiefly German, I could not possibly have written this book. Indeed there are branches of the subject in which my chapters are little more than compilation. I have endeavoured to acknowledge my indebtedness in footnotes, but in some cases more than this is required. It is perhaps otiose to speak of Mommsen, Karlowa, Pernice among those we have lost, or of Gradenwitz, Krüger, Lenel among the living, for to these all students of the Roman Law owe a heavy debt, but I must mention here my special obligations to Erman, Girard, Mandry, Salkowski and Sell, whose valuable monographs on branches of the Law of Slavery have been of the greatest possible service. Where it has been necessary to touch on subjects not directly connected with Slavery I have made free use of Girard's " Manuel " and Roby's "Roman Private Law." I greatly regret that the second edition of Lenel's " Edictum Perpetuum " and the first volume of Mitteis' " Römisches Privatrecht " appeared too late to be utilised except in the later chapters of the book.

In dealing with the many problems of detail which have presented themselves, I have, of course, here and there, had occasion to differ from views expressed by one or other of these writers, whose authority is so much greater than my own. I have done so with extreme diffidence, mindful of a certain couplet which speaks of

> "What Tully wrote and what Justinian,
> And what was Pufendorf's opinion."

I have not dealt, except incidentally, with early law or with the law affecting *libertini*. The book is already too large, and only the severest compression has kept it within its present limits. To have included these topics would have made it unmanageable. It was my original intention not to deal with matter of procedure, but at an early stage I found this to be impracticable, and I fear that the only result of that intention is perfunctory treatment of very difficult questions.

Technical terms, necessarily of very frequent occurrence in a book of this kind, I have usually left in the original Latin, but I have not thought it necessary to be at any great pains to secure consistency in this matter. In one case, that of the terms *Iussum* and *Iussus*, I have felt great difficulty. I was not able to satisfy myself from the texts as to whether the difference of form did or did not express a difference of meaning. In order to avoid appearing to accept either view on the matter I have used only the form *Iussum*, but I am not sure that in so doing I may not seem to have implied an opinion on the very question I desired not to raise.

I have attempted no bibliography: for this purpose a list confined to books and articles dealing, *ex professo*, with slave law would be misleadingly incomplete, but anything more comprehensive could be little less than a bibliography of Roman Law in general. I have accordingly cited only such books as I have been able to use, with a very few clearly indicated exceptions.

To Mr H. J. Roby of St John's College, to Mr Henry Bond of Trinity Hall, to Mr P. Giles of Emmanuel College, and to Mr J. B. Moyle of New College, Oxford, I am much indebted for many valuable suggestions and criticisms. I desire to express my sincere thanks to the Syndics of the Cambridge University Press for their liberality in undertaking the publication of the book, to Mr R. T. Wright and Mr A. R. Waller, the Secretaries of the Syndicate, for their unfailing kindness, and to the Staff of the Press for the care which they have bestowed on the production of the book.

This book, begun at the suggestion of a beloved and revered Scholar, now dead, had, so long as he lived, his constant encouragement. I hope to be excused for quoting and applying to him some words which he wrote of another distinguished teacher: "What encouragement was like when it came from him his pupils are now sorrowfully remembering."

W. W. B.

September 2nd, 1908.

TABLE OF CONTENTS

PART II.

ENSLAVEMENT AND RELEASE FROM SLAVERY.

Table of Contents

LIST OF PRINCIPAL ABBREVIATIONS

In. = Institutiones Iustiniani.

D. = Digesta   „

C. = Codex   „

N. = Novellae   „

Numeral references with no initial letter are to the Digest.

C. Th. = Codex Theodosianus.

G. = Gai institutiones.

U. or Ulp. = Ulpiani Regulae.

P. = Pauli Sententiae.

Fr. D. or Fr. Dos. = Fragmenta Dositheiana.

Fr. V. or Fr. Vat. =   „   Vaticana.

Coll. = Mosaicarum et Romanarum legum collatio.

Citations of the Corpus Iuris Civilis are from the stereotyped edition of Krüger, Mommsen, Schoell and Kroll.

Citations of the Codex Theodosianus are from Mommsen's edition.

Citations of earlier juristic writings are from the Collectio librorum iuris ante-iustiniani.

Z.S.S. = Zeitschrift der Savigny Stiftung für Rechtsgeschichte.

N.R.H. = Nouvelle Revue Historique de Droit français et étranger.

ERRATA ET ADDENDA

p. 7, n. 4.   *For* 32. 60. 1. 99. 2 *read* 32. 60. 1, 99. 2.
p. 9, n. 6.   *For* der Juden *read* den Juden.
p. 12, n. 4.   *For* 5. 1. 20 *read* 6. 1. 20.
p. 18, n. 9.   *For* xxiv. *read* xxv.
,,   n. 10.   *Add* In. 1. 20. 10.
p. 32, n. 3.   *For* op. cit. *read* Inst. Jurid.
p. 68, n. 9.   *Add* See also D. 8. 4. 13.
p. 100, n. 4.   *Add* But see Naber, Mélanges Gerardin, 467.
p. 108, n. 5.   *For* 9. 4. 3. 3 *read* 9. 4. 4. 3.
p. 129, n. 7.   *For* P. 2. 31. 37 *read* P. 2. 31, 37.
p. 130, n. 13. *Add* See also *post*, pp. 338, 666.
p. 156, n. 3.   *For* 44. 3, 46. 3 *read* 44. 3 ; 46. 3.
p. 215, l. 16. *For sponsis read sponsio.*
p. 248, n. 7.   *For* mere *read* is mere.
p. 291, n. 8.   *Add* See on the whole subject, Marchand, Du Captif Romain.
p. 318, n. 1.   *For* Mommsen *read* Mommsen, Staatsr. (3) 2. 2. 998 sqq.
                Add See, however, now, as to the relations and nomenclature of all these funds, Mitteis, Röm. Privatr., 1. 349 sqq.
p. 322, n. 5.   *For* Mommsen *read* Mommsen, Staatsr. (3) 2. 2. 1000 sqq.
p. 324, n. 3.   *For* Mommsen *read* Mommsen, Staatsr. (3) 2. 2. 836.
p. 354, n. 10. *For* Eisele, Z. S. S. 7 *read* Appleton, H. Interpolations, 65.
p. 403, n. 2.   *For* congruent *read* congruunt.
p. 422, n. 6.   *Add* A study of this institution by Bonfante, Mélanges Fadda, was not available when this chapter was printed.

PART I.

CONDITION OF THE SLAVE.

CHAPTER I.

DEFINITION AND GENERAL CHARACTERISTICS.

THE Institutes tell us that all men are either slaves or free[1], and both liberty and slavery are defined by Justinian in terms borrowed from Florentinus. "Libertas," he tells us, "est naturalis facultas eius quod cuique facere libet nisi si quid vi aut iure prohibetur[2]." No one has defined liberty well: of this definition, which, literally understood, would make everyone free, the only thing to be said at present for our purpose is that it assumes a state of liberty to be "natural."

"Servitus," he says, "est constitutio iuris gentium qua quis dominio alieno contra naturam subicitur[3]." Upon this definition two remarks may be made[4].

i. Slavery is the only case in which, in the extant sources of Roman law, a conflict is declared to exist between the *Ius Gentium* and the *Ius Naturale*. It is of course inconsistent with that universal equality of man which Roman speculations on the Law of Nature assume[5], and we are repeatedly told that it is a part of the *Ius Gentium*, since it originates in war[6]. Captives, it is said, may be slain: to make them slaves is to save their lives; hence they are called *servi, ut servati*[7], and thus both names, *servus* and *mancipium*, are derived from capture in war[8].

---

[1] In. 1. 3. *pr.*   [2] In. 1. 3. 1; D. 1. 1. 4. *pr.*; 1. 5. 4. *pr.*
[3] In. 1. 3. 2; D. 1. 5. 4. 1; D. 12. 6. 64.
[4] Girard, Manuel, Bk 2, Ch. I. gives an excellent account of these matters.
[5] See the texts cited in the previous notes.   [6] In. 1. 5. *pr.*; D. 1. 1. 4; 1. 5. 4.
[7] 50. 16. 139. 1.
[8] 1. 5. 4. For the purpose of statement of the Roman view, the value of the historical, moral and etymological theories involved in these propositions is not material.

ii. The definition appears to regard subjection to a *dominus* as the essential fact in slavery. It is easy to shew that this conception of slavery is inaccurate, since Roman Law at various times recognised types of slaves without owners. Such were

(*a*) The slave abandoned by his owner. He was a *res nullius*. He could be acquired by *usucapio*, and freed by his new owner[1].

(*b*) *Servi Poenae*. Till Justinian's changes, convicts or some types of them were *servi*: they were strictly *sine domino*; neither *Populi* nor *Caesaris*[2].

(*c*) Slaves manumitted by their owner while some other person had a right in them[3].

(*d*) A freeman who allowed a usufruct of himself to be given by a fraudulent vendor to an innocent buyer. He was a *servus sine domino* while the usufruct lasted[4].

It would seem then that the distinguishing mark of slavery in Rome is something else, and modern writers have found it in rightlessness. A slave is a man without rights, i.e. without the power of setting the law in motion for his own protection[5]. It may be doubted whether this is any better, since, like the definition which it purports to replace, it does not exactly fit the facts. Indeed, it is still less exact. At the time when Florentinus wrote, Antoninus Pius had provided that slaves ill treated by their owner might lodge a complaint, and if this proved well founded, the magistrate must take certain protective steps[6]. So far as it goes, this is a right. *Servi publici Populi Romani* had very definite rights in relation to their *peculia*[7]. In fact this definition is not strictly true for any but *servi poenae*[8]. Nor does it serve, so far as our authorities go, to differentiate between slaves and alien enemies under arms. But even if it were true and distinctive, it would still be inadmissible, for it has a defect of the gravest kind. It looks at the institution from an entirely non-Roman point of view. The Roman law of slavery, as we know it, was developed by a succession of practical lawyers who were not great philosophers, and as the main purpose of our definition is to help in the elucidation of their writings, it seems unwise to base it on a highly abstract conception which they would hardly have understood and with which they certainly never worked[9]. Modern writers on jurisprudence usually make the conception of a right the basis of

---

[1] 41. 7. 8.   [2] *Post*, Ch. xii.
[3] Fr. Dosith. 11; Ulp. 1. 19; C. 7. 15. 1. 2; *post*, Ch. xxv.
[4] 40. 12. 23. *pr.*; *post*, Ch. xviii.
[5] Warnkoenig, Inst. Rom. Jur. priv. § 121; Moyle, *ad* Inst. 1. 3. 2; Accarias, Précis de Dr. Rom. i, p. 89.
[6] G. 1. 53; *post*, p. 37 where an earlier right of the same kind is mentioned.
[7] *Post*, Ch. xv.
[8] Other equivocal cases may be noted; 2. 4. 9; 5. 1. 53; 48. 10. 7.
[9] See however 50. 17. 32.

their arrangement of legal doctrines[1]. The Romans did not, though they were, of course, fully aware of the characteristic of a slave's position on which this definition rests. "Servile caput," says Paul, "nullum ius habet[2]." But they recognised another characteristic of the slave which was not less important. Over a wide range of law the slave was not only rightless, he was also dutiless. "In personam servilem nulla cadit obligatio[3]." Judgment against a slave was a nullity: it did not bind him or his master[4]. In the same spirit we are told that slavery is akin to death[5]. If a man be enslaved his debts cease to bind him, and his liability does not revive if he is manumitted[6]. The same thing is expressed in the saying that a slave is *pro nullo*[7]. All this is much better put in the Roman definition. The point which struck them, (and modern writers also do not fail to note it,) was that a slave was a *Res*, and, for the classical lawyers, the only human *Res*. This is the meaning of Florentinus' definition. *Dominus* and *dominium* are different words. The statement that slaves as such are subject to *dominium* does not imply that every slave is always owned[8]. Chattels are the subject of ownership: it is immaterial that a slave or other chattel is at the moment a *res nullius*[9].

From the fact that a slave is a *Res*, it is inferred, apparently as a necessary deduction[10], that he cannot be a person. Indeed the Roman slave did not possess the attributes which modern analysis regards as essential to personality. Of these, capacity for rights is one[11], and this the Roman slave had not, for though the shadowy rights already mentioned constitute one of several objections to the definition of slaves as "rightless men," it is true that rights could not in general vest in slaves. But many writers push the inference further, and lay it down that a slave was not regarded as a person by the Roman lawyers[12]. This view seems to rest on a misconception, not of the position of the slave, but of the meaning attached by the Roman lawyers to the word *persona*. Few legal terms retain their significance unchanged for ever, and this particular term certainly has not done so. All modern writers agree, it seems, in requiring capacity for right. The most recent philosophy seems indeed to go near divorcing the idea of personality from its human elements. For this is the effect of the theory which sees in the Corporation a real, and not a fictitious

---

[1] Hearn (Legal Duties and Rights) alone among recent English writers bases his scheme on Duties. But this is no better from the Roman point of view.
[2] 5. 3. 1. [3] 50. 17. 22. *pr.* [4] 5. 1. 44. 1.
[5] 50. 17. 209. Nov. 22. 9; G. 3. 101. [6] 44. 7. 30. [7] 28. 8. 1. *pr.*
[8] Justinian swept away nearly all the exceptional cases. C. 7. 15. 1. 2b; Nov. 22. 8; 22. 12.
[9] The objection, that slavery is an "absolute," not a "relative," status, is thus of no force against the Roman definition.
[10] Girard, Manuel, p. 92.
[11] Girard, *op. cit.* p. 90, "L'aptitude à être le sujet de droits et devoirs légaux."
[12] Girard, *loc. cit.*; Moyle, *op. cit.* Introd. to Bk 1; etc.

person[1]. If, now, we turn to the Roman texts, we find a very different conception. A large number of texts speak of slaves as persons[2]. There does not seem to be a single text in the whole Corpus Iuris Civilis, or in the Codex Theodosianus, or in the surviving classical legal literature which denies personality to a slave. It is clear that the Roman lawyers called a slave a person, and this means that, for them, "persona" meant human being[3].

It must however be borne in mind that the word has more than one meaning. Its primary meaning is not the man, but the part he plays, and thus a number of texts, including many of those above cited, speak not of the man, but of the *persona* of the man. The distinction is not material, but it may have suggested a further distinction made in modern books. It is the usage of some writers to speak of two senses in which the word is used: one technical, in which it means "man capable of rights"; the other wide, in which it means simply "man[4]." But if the texts be examined on which this distinction is based, it will be found that, so far as Roman law is concerned, this means no more than that in some texts the topic in question is such that rights are necessarily contemplated, while in others this is not the case.

A doctrine which purports to be really Roman law must necessarily be somehow rested on the texts. It is desirable to note what sort of authority has been found for the view that a slave was not a person for the Roman lawyers. One group of texts may be shortly disposed of: they are the texts which say that a slave is *pro nullo*, and that slavery is akin to death[5]. These are, as they profess to be, mere analogies: they shew, indeed, that from some points of view a slave was of no legal importance, but to treat them as shewing that *persona* means someone of legal importance is a plain begging of the question. The others are more serious. There is a text in the Novellae of Theodosius[6], (not reproduced in Justinian's Code,) which explains the slave's incapacity to take part in legal procedure

---

[1] See Maitland, Political Theories of the Middle Age (Gierke), Introd. p. xxxiv.

[2] G. 1. 120; 1. 121; 3. 189; 4. 135. Vat. Fr. 75. 2, 75. 5, 82 (drawing legal inferences from his personality); C. Th. 14. 7. 2 (rejected by Mommsen); C. 4. 36. 1. *pr.*; C. 7. 32. 121; Inst. 1. 8. *pr.*; 3. 17. 2; 4. 4. 7 (all independent of each other and of Gaius); D. 7. 1. 6. 2; 7. 2. 1. 1; 9. 4. 29; 11. 1. 20. *pr.*; 30. 86. 2 (twice); 31. 82. 2; 39. 6. 23; 45. 3. 1. 4; 47. 10. 15. 44; 47. 10. 17. 3; 48. 19. 10. *pr.*; 48. 19. 16. 3; 50. 16. 2. 215; 50. 17. 22. *pr.* See also Bas. 44. 1. 11, and Sell, Noxalrecht, p. 28, n. 2.

[3] It would not be surprising if there were some looseness, since a slave, while on the one hand an important conscious agent is on the other hand a mere thing. But the practice is unvarying. It is commonly said that the personality of the slave was gradually recognised in the course of the Empire. What were recognised were the claims of humanity, cp. 21. 1. 35. To call it a recognition of personality (Pernice, Labeo, 1. pp. 113 *sqq.*, and many others) is to use the word personality in yet another sense, for it still remained substantially true that the slave was incapable of legal rights.

[4] See Brissonius, De Verb. Sign., sub v. *persona*.   [5] nn. 4, 5, 6 on p. 3.

[6] Nov. Theod. 17. 1. 2: *quasi nec personam habentes.*

by the fact that he has no *persona*. This seems weighty, as it draws legal consequences from the absence of a *persona*. But it must be noted that similar language is elsewhere used about young people without curators[1], and the true significance of these words is shewn by a text which observes that a slave is not a *persona qui in ius vocari potest*[2]. A text in the Vatican Fragments (also in the Digest[3]) says that a *servus hereditarius* cannot stipulate for a usufruct because *ususfructus sine persona constitui non potest*. This is nearer to classical authority, but in fact does not deny personality to a slave. That is immaterial: the usufruct could never vest in him. The point is that a *hereditas iacens* is not a *persona*, though, for certain purposes, *personae vicem sustinet*[4]. Thus in another text the same language is used on similar facts, but the case put is that of *filius vel servus*[5]. A text of Cassiodorus[6] has exactly the same significance[7]. There are however two texts of Theophilus[8] (reproducing and commenting on texts of the Institutes) in which a slave is definitely denied a *persona*. He explains the fact that a slave has only a derivative power of contracting or of being instituted heir by the fact that he has no *persona*. The reason is his own: it shews that in the sixth century the modern technical meaning was developing. But to read it into the earlier sources is to misinterpret them: *persona*, standing alone, did not mean *persona civilis*[9].

Slavery has of course meant different things at different times and places[10]. In Rome it did not necessarily imply any difference of race or language. Any citizen might conceivably become a slave: almost any slave might become a citizen. Slaves were, it would seem, indistinguishable from freemen, except so far as some enactments of late date slightly restricted their liberty of dress[11]. —The fact that all the civil degrees known to the law contained persons of the same speech, race, physical habit and language, caused a prominence of rules dealing with the results of errors of Status, such as would otherwise be unaccountable. Such are the rules as to *erroris causae probatio*[12], as to the freeman who lets himself be sold as a slave[13], as to error in status

① *war captive*
② *born into*

---

[1] C. Th. 3. 17. 1; C. 5. 34. 11.   [2] 2. 7. 3. *pr.*   [3] 45. 3. 26; V. Fr. 55.
[4] 9. 2. 13. 2; In. 3. 17. *pr.*
[5] 36. 2. 9. It was only in case of legacy, not of stipulation, that the usufruct depended in any way on the life of the slave, *post*, Ch. vi.   [6] Var. 6. 8. 2.
[7] 36. 1. 57. 1 (Papinian) may be understood as denying personality, but it is really of the same type: *rescripsit non esse repraesentandam hereditatis restitutionem quando persona non est cui restitui potest.*   [8] *Ad* In. 2. 14. 2; 3. 17. *pr.*
[9] A correct decision on this matter is necessary before we can say what Gaius meant by *Ius quod ad personas pertinet.*
[10] Wallon, Histoire de l'Esclavage; Winter, Stellung der Sklaven bei d. Juden; Cobb, Slavery (in America).
[11] C. Th. 14. 10. 1; 14. 10. 4. As to the cautious abstention from such restrictions in earlier law, see Seneca, De Clementia, 1. 24; Lampridius, Alex. Severus, 27. 1.
[12] G. 1. 67–75; Ulp. 7. 4.   [13] In. 1. 3. 4, *post*, Ch. xviii.

of the witness of a will[1], and other well known cases[2]. There was
also a rule that where a man, who afterwards turned out to be a slave,
had given security *iudicatum solvi*, there was *restitutio in integrum*[3].
To the same cause are expressly set down the rules as to acquisition
through a *liber homo bona fide serviens*[4], and the rule that the *bona-fide*
sale of a freeman as a slave was valid, as a contract, *quia difficile potest
dignosci liber homo a servo*[5]. The well-known rule that *error communis
facit ius* had more striking illustrations than those already mentioned.
Thus, though a slave could not validly be appointed to decide an
arbitration[6], yet an arbitral decision by one apparently free was declared to be valid though he ultimately proved to be a slave[7]. And
where a fugitive slave was appointed Praetor, his official acts were
declared by Ulpian to be valid[8].

Slavery did not necessarily mean manual labour: the various services
involved in the maintenance of an establishment in town or country
were all rendered by troops of slaves, having their appropriate official
names, derived from the nature of their service. It is not necessary
to recite these names: numbers of them will be found in the texts
dealing with the interpretation of legacies and contracts[9]. A broad
distinction is repeatedly drawn between Urban and Rustic slaves, as
it was customary to make legacies of the one or the other class generally, probably with other property. *Mancipia rustica* were, broadly,
those engaged in the cultivation of land and other rural pursuits;
urbana were those whom *paterfamilias circum se ipsius sui cultus causa
habet*[10], elsewhere defined as *quae totius suppellectilis notitiam gerunt*[11].
The cook and the philosopher were alike urban, the land-agent (*villicus*)
and the labourer were alike rustic. The distinction is founded partly
on mode and place of maintenance, partly on nature of service, and
partly on direct statement in the owner's register of slaves[12]. Indeed
in the construction of legacies, as the testator's intention was the point
to be determined, this register was conclusive where it was available[13].
Place of residence was not conclusive; *non loco sed usus genere dis-*

---

[1] In. 2. 10. 7.
[2] The person *de statu suo incertus* (Ulp. 20. 11, etc.); institution of *servus alienus* as a
freeman (the case of Parthenius), *post*, Ch. VI.; position of child of *ancilla* supposed to be free,
post, Ch. XXVII. There are other cases in the title *De iure dotium*, e.g. 23. 3. 59. 2.
[3] 2. 8. 8. 2.   [4] 45. 3. 34.
[5] 18. 1. 4. 5. 6; 34. 2. 70. As often, the rule was severer in stipulation. Here the agreement
was void for impossibility, 44. 7. 1. 9; 45. 1. 83. 5. 103. In 18. 2. 14. 3 we are told that sale to
servus alienus thought free was valid, while one to my own slave was in any case void, *post*,
Ch. XXIX.
[6] 4. 8. 9. *pr.*   [7] C. 7. 45. 2. *Post*, p. 84.
[8] 1. 14. 3. This extreme view may be peculiar to Ulpian. Cp. Dio Cassius, 48. 34. In
England analogous cases have needed express legislation. See e.g. 51 & 52 Vict. c. 28.
[9] 32. 61; 33. 7. 8. 12 *sqq.*; P. 3. 6. 35 *sqq.*; Wallon, *op. cit.* Bk 2, Ch. III.; Blair, Slavery in
Rome, 131.   [10] 32. 60. 1.
[11] C. 5. 37. 22. 2.   [12] 32. 99. *pr.*; 33. 7. 27. 1.   [13] 50. 16. 166.

tinguuntur[1]. Residence might be temporary: a child put out to nurse in the country was not on that account rustic[2]. Even nature of service was not conclusive. Some forms of service were equivocal, e.g. those of *venatores* and *aucupes*[3], *agasones* or *muliones*[4], or even *dispensatores*, who, if they were managing town properties were urban, but if they were in charge of a farm were rustic, differing little from *villici*[5].

For many of their employments special skill and training were necessary, and a slave so trained (*arte praeditus*) acquired, of course, an added value, especially if he had several *artificia*[6]. In some texts a distinction is drawn, in this connexion, between *officium* and *artificium*[7]. The language of Marcian suggests, as do other applications of the word, that an *officium* was an occupation having reference to the person or personal enjoyments of the *dominus*[8]. The distinction is not prominent and was probably of no legal importance, except in the construction of legacies and the like.

Work of the most responsible kinds was left in the hands of slaves. Among the more important functions may be mentioned those of *negotiator, librarius, medicus, actor, dispensator, villicus, paedagogus, actuarius*[9]. They managed businesses of all kinds[10]. We find a slave carrying on the trade of a banker without express orders[11]. A slave rents a farm and cultivates it as tenant, not as a mere steward[12]. Aulus Gellius[13] gives a list of philosophers who were slaves among the Greeks and Romans. Broadly, it may be said that in private life there was scarcely an occupation in which a slave might not be employed: almost any industry in which freemen are now engaged might be carried on in Rome by slaves. It must however be remembered that all this is not true in the greater part of the Republican period. In that period the evidence shews that slaves were relatively few and unimportant[14]. And in the decline of the Empire there was a tendency to exclude slaves from responsible classes of employment, and to leave these in the hands of freemen[15].

It is obvious that slaves so differently endowed would differ greatly in value. It is improbable that the increase in number involved any

---

[1] 33. 7. 12; 33. 10. 12, etc. [2] 50. 16. 210. [3] 32. 99. 1; P. 3. 6. 71.
[4] 32. 60. 1. 99. 2; P. 3. 6. 72. [5] 50. 16. 166.
[6] 32. 65. 2; C. 5. 37. 22. Teaching slaves *artes* was among *utiles impensae* for the purpose of *Dos*. 25. 1. 6.
[7] 32. 65. 1; 40. 4. 24; 50. 15. 4. 5; etc.
[8] 32. 65. 1. See Brissonius, De Verb. Sign., sub v. *officium*.
[9] 9. 2. 22; 32. 64; 38. 1. 25; *h. t.* 49; 40. 5. 41. 6; 40. 7. 1. 21. *pr.*; 40. 12. 44. 2; P. 3. 6. 70; G. 1. 19, 39, etc.
[10] 14. 3. 5. 7. [11] 2. 13. 4. 3. [12] 33. 7. 12. 3. 20. 1. Cp. 33. 7. 18. 4.
[13] Noct. Att. 2. 18. For further reff. see Girard, Manuel, 93 *sqq.*
[14] For further details as to the number of slaves at different epochs and as to their varied and independent employments, see Wallon, *op. cit.* ii. Ch. III.; Sell, Noxalrecht, pp. 129 *sqq.*; Friedlaender, Sittengesch. ii. 228 (ed. 7); Voigt, Röm. R. G. 1. 118 *sqq.*; Marquardt, *loc. cit.*; Blair, State of Slavery among the Romans, Ch. VI. [15] *Post*, Ch. XIV.

diminution in exchange value of individual similarly qualified slaves, for it was accompanied by a great increase in quantity of other forms of convertible wealth. Changes in economic conditions and repeated alterations in the intrinsic value of coins called by a particular name, make the task of tracing the changes in value of slaves too difficult to be attempted here. It is clear however that they were of considerable value. In A.D. 139 a female child of six years of age was sold for 205 *denarii*[1]. This seems a high price, and the presence in the contract note of the unexplained expression, "sportellaria empta," leads Mommsen[2] to suppose that she was thrown in, "sportulae causa," in the purchase of her mother. But the price seems too low for this. In general, in classical times, the prices for ordinary slaves seem to have varied from 200 to 600 *denarii*[3]. These are ordinary commercial prices. Of course, for slaves with special gifts, very much higher prices might be given, and occasional enormous prices are recorded by the classical writers[4]. The prices in Justinian's time seem a little, but not much, higher. Two enactments of his fix judicial valuations, one for application in case of dispute where there is a joint legacy of *Optio Servi*, the other for the case of manumission of common slaves[5], and they are almost identical. The prices range from 10 *solidi* for ordinary children to 70 for slaves with special skill who were also eunuchs. From another enactment of his it appears that 15 *solidi* was a rather high price[6]. Other prices are recorded in the Digest[7], ranging from 2 to 100 *solidi*. But these are of little use: nearly all are imaginary cases, and even if we can regard them as rough approximations to value, we cannot tell whether the figures are of the age of Justinian or were in the original text. Another indication of price is contained in the fact that 20 *solidi* was taken as about the mean value of a slave by legislation of the classical age[8].

It may be well to make some mention of the more important terms which are used as equivalent to *servus*, or to describe particular classes of slaves, in the sources. *Servus* appears to be used generally, without reference to the point of view from which the man is regarded. *Mancipium* is usually confined to cases in which the slave is regarded as a chattel. Thus it is common in such titles as that on the Aedilician Edict[9], but not in such as that on the *Actio de peculio*[10]. *Ancilla* is

<hr/>

[1] Bruns, Fontes i. 289. [2] C. I. L. 3. 937.
[3] See the documents in Bruns, *op. cit.* 288. 29, 315—317, 325. See also Girard, Textes, 806 *sqq.* For the manumission of an adult woman 2200 *drachmae* were paid in Egypt in A.D. 221. Girard, *op. cit.* Append.
[4] Marquardt, Vie privée, i. Ch. IV. [5] C. 6. 43. 3; 7. 7. 1.
[6] C. 6. 47. 6. [7] See for some of them, Marquardt, *loc. cit.*
[8] For these and other details as to the price of slaves at various times, see Wallon, *op. cit.* Bk 2, Ch. IV.; Sell, Noxalrecht, 147.
[9] D. 21. 1. E.g., *h. t.* 51. *pr. mancipium vitiosum...servus emat.*
[10] 15. 1.

the usual term for an adult female slave, though *mulier* is of course found, and *serva* more rarely[1]. Children are called *puer* and *puella*. *Puer*, for an adult, though it is common in general literature, is found only occasionally in the legal texts[2]. *Puella* seems never to be used there without the implication of youth. A *verna* is a slave born and reared in the house of his master, and occupies a somewhat privileged position, but in law his position is not different from that of any other slave. A *novicius*[3] is an untrained slave, as opposed to a *veterator*, an experienced hand, or, more exactly, a man trained for a particular function. The edict of the Aediles contained a provision that a *veterator* was not to be sold as a *novicius*, the point apparently being that, at least for certain purchasers, a man not trained to a particular kind of work was more valuable, as being more readily trained to the work for which the purchaser wanted him. The provision seems to be mentioned only twice[4]: the surviving contract notes shew that it was not necessary to state which he was; indeed, in none of them is the slave's employment mentioned. It was a secondary provision of the edict[5]; in fact it seems to have been found necessary to declare that the statement that a man was untrained was a warranty, because, while it was plain that to sell, as a trained man, one who was untrained, was a fraud, it was not so obvious that any material wrong was done in the converse case.

The morality of slaves is not within our scope. It is clear on the literary tradition that they had notoriously a bad reputation. The special legislation which we shall have to notice will sufficiently shew the state of things at Rome. But we need not go into details to prove for Rome what is likely to be a concomitant of all slavery[6].

---

[1] E.g. P. 2. 24. 1; D. 11. 3. 1. *pr.* (the words of the Edict); 23. 3. 39; 48. 5. 6. *pr. Homo* is of course common. *Famulus* is rare in legal texts.
[2] E.g. 32. 81. *pr.*; 50. 16. 204.   [3] Brissonius, *op. cit.* sub v. *Novicius.*
[4] 21. 1. 37; *h. t.* 65. 2. The latter text tells us that a liberal education did not necessarily make him a *veterator. Post,* p. 57. *Veteranus* in 39. 4. 16. 3 seems not to mean quite the same thing. For the purpose of *professio* (*post,* p. 38) *novicius* is one who has served for less than a year.
[5] Lenel, E. Perp., p. 443.
[6] See for instance, Wallon, *op. cit.* Bk 2, Ch. vii.; Winter, Stellung der Sklaven bei der Juden, pp. 59—61. Cobb, Slavery, pp. 49—52, takes a different view, as to negro slavery. He is a determined apologist of the "peculiar institution" in America. He says at the beginning of his introduction, "No organized government has been so barbarous as not to introduce it," (i.e. Slavery,) "among its customs."

CHAPTER II.

THE SLAVE AS *RES*.

THIS aspect of the Slave was necessarily prominent in the Law. He was the one human being who could be owned. There were men in many inferior positions which look almost like slavery: there were the *nexus*, the *auctoratus*, the *addictus*, and others. But none of these was, like the slave, a *Res*. *Potestatis verbo plura significantur: in persona magistratuum imperium...in persona servi dominium*[1]. The slave is a chattel, frequently paired off with money as a *res*[2]. Not only is he a chattel: he is treated constantly in the sources as the typical chattel. The Digest contains a vast number of texts which speak of the slave, but would be equally significant if they spoke of any other subject of property. With these we are not concerned: to discuss them would be to deal with the whole law of property, but we are to consider only those respects in which a slave as a chattel is distinguished in law from other chattels[3]. From their importance follows the natural result that the rules relating to slaves are stated with great fulness, a fulness also in part due to the complexity of the law affecting them. This special complexity arises mainly from five causes. (i) Their issue were neither *fructus* nor accessories, though they shared in the qualities of both. (ii) They were capable of having *fructus* of kinds not conceivable in connexion with other *res*, i.e. gifts and earnings. (iii) The fact that they were human forced upon the Romans of the Empire some merciful modifications of the ordinary rules of sale. (iv) They had mental and moral qualities, a fact which produced several special rules. (v) There existed in regard to them a special kind of *interitus rei*, i.e. Manumission[4].

Slaves were *res mancipi* and it does not appear that there was in their case any question of maturity or taming such as divided the schools, in relation to cattle, upon the point as to the moment at

---

[1] 50. 16. 215. [2] See 18. 1. 1. 1; C. 4. 5. 10; 4. 38. 6, 7; 4. 46. 3; 8. 53. 1.
[3] As to the right of preemption in the case of a new-born slave (C. Th. 5. 10. 1) see *post*, Ch. xviii.
[4] The special rules as to possession of slaves are considered, *post*, Ch. xii.

which they became *res mancipi*[1]. No taming or educating process
was necessary to give their owner control over them. Most of the
few surviving records of actual sales in the classical age refer to
slaves. The silence of the sources, on the use of the *actio* Publiciana
by the "bonitary owner," makes it hard to say when *traditio* superseded *mancipatio*, in practice, for moveables, but this very silence,
coupled with the fact that in nearly all these cases there was a
mancipatio, leads to the conclusion that it was after the age of the
classical lawyers; for most of these cases fall between A.D. 140 and
A.D. 160[2]. On the other hand one of A.D. 166 was by *traditio*, but
this was in Asia Minor, as also was one of A.D. 359[3]. There is, indeed,
a record of a conveyance of *land* in Egypt by *traditio* as early as
A.D. 154[4].

The slave, like any other chattel, might be the subject of all ordinary
transactions[5], and these transactions gave rise to many questions owing
to the special characteristics and powers of the slave. Most of these,
however, result from the slave's powers of acquisition, of contracting,
and of wrong-doing, and will therefore be most conveniently considered
in the chapters which deal with the slave considered as a man. A few
points may, however, be taken here.

The difficult questions concerning the liability for *Custodia*, and the
various meanings of this obscure word in different connexions and at
different epochs have no special connexion with slaves and may be
omitted[6]. It is necessary, however, to note that certain texts deal
specially with *custodia* in connexion with *commodatum* of a slave.
They shew that a *commodatarius* of a slave might be liable *ex commodato*, if he was stolen[7]. But they shew also that this liability did
not arise if the slave ran away[8], unless he was of such a kind that he
needed special guarding (as might appear from his age, or his being
handed over in chains), or there was a special agreement[9]. The texts
bear marks of rehandling[10], but there is no reason to doubt that the rule
they lay down is that of the classical law. It seems to be independent

---

[1] G. 1. 120; G. 2. 15.
[2] Bruns, Fontes, i. 288 *sqq.*; Girard, Textes, 806 *sqq.* In old Jewish law slaves were
similarly grouped with land, Winter, Stellung der Sklaven, 25—26. The whole Talmudic law of
slavery is much affected by Roman Law.
[3] Bruns, *op. cit.* 325; Girard, *op. cit.* 809.
[4] Bruns, *op. cit.* i. 322. The *emptio areae* on the same page is doubtful.
[5] 21. 1. *pass.*; 13. 6. 5. 13; C. 4. 23. 2; 4. 24. 2. In late law *servi aratores* might not be
seized (by *pignoris captio*) under a judgment. C. Th. 2. 30. 1; C. 8. 16. 7.
[6] Lusignani (Studi sulla Responsibilità per *Custodia*, i. ii.) gives a full account of the texts
affecting this matter in relation to sale and *locatio*. His introductory section gives an account
of the views of Hasse, Baron, and Pernice. See also for discussion and references, Windscheid,
Pand. § 264, n. 9.
[7] 47. 2. 14. 5. His right to sue implies the liability.
[8] 13. 6. 5. 13; 13. 6. 18. *pr.*   [9] 13. 6. 5. 6; 6. 1. 21; 50. 17. 23 *in fin.*
[10] See especially 13. 6. 5. 13, *Cartilius ait periculum ad te respicere...quare culpam in eam
quoque praestandam.* Can hardly be genuine, since if the risk is with a man his *culpa* is not
material.

of the above-mentioned difficulties. If, or in the cases in which, the liability for *custodia* involves something more than liability for *culpa*, no breach of the obligation is committed by the slave's running away, though he is *fur sui*[1]. And such a flight is no proof of *culpa* in the *commodatarius*. Even an agreement for *custodia* would not impose this liability, unless expressly. All this turns on the fact that a slave is necessarily left at large, and thus it does not apply in the case of those who would not be left at large in any case by a careful man.

Like other chattels slaves were recoverable by *vindicatio* and by the *actio* Publiciana[2], and, in consequence of the equivocal character of their offspring, and of the fact that slaves could be the medium of acquisition, there were special rules as to what was recoverable in a *vindicatio* of a slave. Inasmuch as the rules of retention by the possessor will call for full discussion hereafter[3], the only point which need here be considered is the fate of those acquisitions which were made after *litis contestatio* in the real action.

The well-known rule is that the defendant must restore the thing itself *cum omni causa*, which is explained, by Gaius, as meaning everything the plaintiff would have had, if restitution had been made at *litis contestatio*[4]. It may be that defendant has usucapted the man *pendente lite*: in that case he must, besides restoring, give security against *dolus*, since it is possible that he may have pledged or freed him[5]. So too he must give up all acquisitions *post litem contestatam* except those *in re sua*, i.e. in connexion with the possessor's affairs. Thus he must give up inheritances, legacies and the like, the child of an *ancilla* who is being claimed, even though born after she was usucapted[6]. If, pending the action, he has become entitled to *fructus* which had been received by some other possessor, and has recovered them, these too must be accounted for[7]. If he has usucapted the man *pendente lite* he must cede any action which he may have acquired on his account, e.g. an *actio* Aquilia[8]. He must restore all *fructus*, which, in the case of a slave, means earnings and results of labour, such as, we are told, even an *impubes* may make[9]. Conversely, a *bonae fidei possessor* could make certain deductions, as even could a *malae fidei possessor*, so far as actual benefit had accrued to the thing[10]. He could

---

[1] Though he is still possessed, *post*, Ch. XII.
[2] 6. 1. 1; 6. 1. 5. 5; 6. 2. 11.   [3] *Post*, Ch. XV.   [4] 5. 1. 20.   [5] 6. 1. 18. 21.
[6] 6. 1. 20. He must give, in respect of the child, the same security as in the case of the woman herself.
[7] 6. 1. 17. 1.
[8] *Ibid.*; 6. 1. 21. This cannot be needed in any other case, for though the possessor may have an *actio utilis*, the owner has an *actio* Aquilia on his own title.
[9] 6. 1. 20; 6. 1. 31.
[10] 5. 3. 38, 39. The form of these texts suggests that the right of a *malae fidei possessor* to make these deductions was of late origin.

not set off ordinary costs of education and maintenance, but for such expenditure, before *litis contestatio*, as was necessary to preserve the man, e.g. paying damages in a noxal action, he might claim allowance by an *exceptio doli*[1].

In relation to merely *utiles impensae*, there is a difficulty. The general rule was that the plaintiff had the alternative of paying for them or allowing the possessor to take away the result[2]. But this could not be applied to special training given to a slave. This could not be undone, and the strict rule was that no account was taken of it[3]. This harsh rule was subject, however, to three exceptions. (*a*) Allowance was made, *si venalem habeas et plus ex pretio eius consecuturus sis propter artificium*[4]. The plain meaning of this is that if the claimant proposes to sell him, and he has a higher market value, by reason of the teaching, the cost of it must be allowed. This has an unpractical look, though it is the usual explanation of the text. In another text, on another point, a plaintiff's claim is made to depend on his intention to sell, but here the proof is the other way, and it is not easy to see how the possessor could prove the claimant's intention[5]. In practice it probably meant little more than that, if the market price was increased, the training must be allowed for. (*b*) If the possessor, knowing that a claim was on foot, notified the intending claimant that he intended to incur this expense, it would have to be allowed, if the claimant did not at once take steps. (*c*) The cost of the training could in any case be deducted from the earnings made by it. A text of Modestinus[6] following that in which this is said, adds: *Quodsi artificem fecerit post vicesimum quintum annum eius qui artificium consecutus est impensae factae poterunt pensari.* These words seem to mean that by the time the man is twenty-five these costs will have been compensated for by earnings, and no account of them need be taken in any *vindicatio*[7].

We are told that if a slave is handed over, *post conventionem*, security must be given by a *bonae fidei possessor* against *dolus*, but by *malae fidei possessor* against *culpa* too, and that, after *litis contestatio*, a *bonae fidei possessor* is on the same footing so far as this is concerned[8]. This too is obscure: how can a man be guilty of *dolus* in respect of a thing which he regards as his own[9]? According to one view the *dolus*

---

[1] *Ibid.* 6. 1. 27. 5.   The same is no doubt true of unusual medical expenses.
[2] 6. 1. 27. 5; Greg. Wisig. 6. 1 (Krüger).
[3] 6. 1. 27. 5.   [4] 6. 1. 29.   [5] 6. 1. 15. 3.   [6] 6. 1. 30—32.
[7] It has been suggested that 25 is a misprint for 5, the meaning being that these expenses may be taken into account if the slave is 5—that being the age at which a slave's services are regarded as of some value.   Pellat, de rei vindicatione *ad* 6. 1. 32, citing 7. 7. 6. 1.   Justinian seems to regard 10 as the minimum age for an *artifex*.   C. 6. 43. 32; 7. 7. 1.
[8] 6. 1. 45; 21. 2. 21. 3.
[9] It has been shewn that the text was written of the Interdict, *Quam Hereditatem*. (Lenel, E. Perp. 363.)   But this is immaterial since this interdict gave a remedy where the defendant refused the security required in a real action. Vat. Fr. 92.

contemplated is any misconduct of the possessor in relation to the slave[1], such as lessens his value and is plainly contrary to public morality. But this is extremely artificial. Another view is that the text refers to one who, having been a *bonae fidei possessor*, has learnt that the thing belongs to another[2]. But such a person is now a *malae fidei possessor*, and there is no reason to confine the rules of *malae fidei possessio* to the case of one who was so *ab initio*, a *praedo*. But the true solution may be not far from this. A *bonae fidei possessor* is one not proved to know that he was not entitled. The formal notice of claim, involved in the word *conventio*[3], is not enough to saddle him with this knowledge, but it has definitely altered his position, and the rule seems to say that if a person so notified wilfully exposes the slave to dangers which result in damage he is not to be heard to say—"So far as I knew, it was my own slave, with whom, so far as you are concerned, I could do what I liked." It may be that a man would not readily expose to risk a slave he thought his own, but it is not so clear that he would not risk one as to whom his knowledge to the contrary was not yet proved. And there are steps between belief that one is owner and knowledge that one is not.

If the man die pending the action, without fault or *mora* of the possessor, his value is not due[4], but the case must still go on to judgment, on account of *fructus* and *partus*, and because on the question of title may depend the further question, whether either party has a claim on eviction against some third party[5]. The defendant, if judgment goes against him, must account for fruits up to the death. It may be impossible to tell what the actual earnings were, and they are therefore estimated so that for any period during which the man was so ill that he could earn nothing, nothing can be charged[6]. If, now, the defendant was already in *mora* at the time of death, he must account, of course, for *omnis causa*, and for fruits up to the day on which judgment was given, estimated in the same way[7]. It is not clear when a *bonae fidei possessor* is *in mora*. The expression seems to belong to the law of *obligatio* and to be out of place in real actions. Its use is further evidence of the insufficiency of the distinction between *bonae* and *malae fidei* possessors. Pellat thinks he is *in mora* from the time when he knew or ought to have known that his title was bad[8]. This is a rather indeterminable time and a person so convinced is a *malae fidei possessor*. All that is certain is that it was not *litis contestatio*[9].

---

[1] Pellat, *op. cit. ad* 6. 1. 45.   [2] This view is as old as Azo.
[3] Pellat, *loc. cit.*   [4] 6. 1. 15. 3; 6. 1. 27. 2.   [5] 6. 1. 16. *pr.*; 46. 7. 11.
[6] 6. 1. 79.   [7] 6. 1. 17. 1.   [8] *Op. cit. ad h. l.*
[9] The possessor is not necessarily liable if the man die after *litis contestatio*. See n. 1 and 6. 1. 27. 2. Savigny thinks that *bonae fidei possessor* is in *mora* only from the time of *pronuntiatio* which imposes an obligation in him. The texts in the *Basilica* which seem to confirm this are shewn by Pellat to contemplate *mora* before the *pronuntiatio*, and there is usually no material delay between *pronuntiatio* and *condemnatio*.

If the possessor lessens the value of the slave, *dolo*, during the action, he is of course liable, but if the slave is afterwards killed by some cause in no way imputable to him, the effect is to end the plaintiff's interest, and, therefore, the liability for the damage, in that action[1].

If the slave has run away, *pendente lite*, the *bonae fidei possessor* is free from liability, unless he has usucapted him, in which case he must cede his actions, or unless the slave was one of such a sort that he ought to have been carefully looked after, in which case his value is due. In any case he must give security to hand over the man, if he recovers him[2]. If the possessor connived at the flight he is liable as if he still possessed[3], and on the same principle if he sell the man, *pendente lite*, and the vendee kill him, he must pay the value[4]. In relation to all these rules it must be remembered that if the possessor was really owner before the action, he can proceed with his defence and get absolution. These rules suppose the claimant to prove his title.

Most of these points have nothing to do specially with slaves. They are therefore very shortly treated, and many difficulties have been ignored, especially in relation to the liability of possessor for the value of the man if he cease to exist during the action. It must, however, be noted that, to the ordinary cases of *interitus rei* which release the *bonae fidei possessor*, noxal surrender must be added[5].

In the *actio furti*, *condictio furtiva* and *actio* Aquilia on account of a slave, the only points which require notice, are, that the *interesse* included the value of an inheritance upon which, owing to the slave's death or absence, his entry had been prevented[6], and that the *condictio furtiva* was necessarily extinguished if from any cause he became free or was expropriated : *domino solo competit*.

The case of legacy of a slave gives occasion for many rules, the development of which cannot well be made out, owing to the suppression by Justinian of the differences due to form[7]. In the case of simple legacy, the heir must hand over with him any acquisitions through him, any earnings the legatee could have gained if the slave had been in his possession and, in the case of an *ancilla*, any *partus*[8]. It may be assumed that, if the legacy was conditional, the legatee was entitled to such profits only from *dies cedens*. This is sufficiently clear

---

[1] 6. 1. 27. 2. *Actio* Aquilia *durat*.   [2] 6. 1. 21.
[3] 6. 1. 22.   Or if he fled through *culpa* of the possessor (21. 2. 21. 3).
[4] 6. 1. 17. *pr*.   Though the claimant can in appropriate cases, (e.g. if the price is not paid,) take cession of actions instead.
[5] 6. 1. 58.
[6] G. 3. 212; Inst. 4. 3. 10; D. 13. 1. 3; 47. 2. 52. 28.
[7] The texts give no real help on the question whether, or how far, legacies *per vindicationem* and *per damnationem* were on the same footing, in the classical law, in relation to the questions now to be considered.   See for a discussion and references Pernice, Labeo 2. 2. 113.
[8] 30. 39; 30. 86. 2.

on the texts[1], and the enactment of Justinian which gave the fulfilment a certain retrospective effect does not appear to have touched
this point[2].

If a specific slave is left, in either form, he must be taken *talis
qualis*[3], and any promise of quality the *heres* may make is void[4]. But
if there is a general gift of "a slave," *per damnationem,* (and probably
per vindicationem,) then, as it is the duty of the *heres* to give a good
title, he must warrant the slave given to be free from noxal liability,
though he need not promise that he is *sanus,* since he is not obliged to
give one of good quality[5]. But he must not give one of the very worst
quality, and thus, if he gave one whom he knew to be on the point of
death, this would be a case of *Dolus.* Where he gave one whom he
knew to be a thief, and the slave stole from the legatee, there was an
actio doli by which he could be compelled to give another, and he must
leave the bad slave *pro noxae dedito*[6].

If a *servus heredis,* or *alienus,* is legated, and has run away, Paul
tells us that, if the flight were after the testator's death, the *heres* must
give security for his production, and pay the expenses involved in his
recovery, but not if the flight had been before the death[7]. Africanus
lays down this latter rule for all slaves (left apparently in any form),
giving the reason that the *heres* can only be bound to give him as the
testator left him[8]. This seems to imply that Africanus would impose
the duty of recovery on the *heres,* even though it were the slave of the
testator, if the flight were after the death. Ulpian says that if the
slave were in flight or at a distance the *heres* must *operam praestare,* in
order that the slave be handed over, and adds that he, Julian and
Africanus, are agreed that the expense must be borne by the *heres*[9].
As it stands the text gives no restriction as to the time of flight, the
origin of the slave, or the form of the gift. In view of the texts just
cited[10] it seems that this extreme generality must be an error, even for
the time of Justinian, but, as to the liability of the *heres* to incur
expense, if the flight is after the death, the texts are explicit. It must
be noted that he is not liable for the value of the slave but only to
incur reasonable expense in recovering him[11].

If a *servus alienus legatus* is freed by his owner, the *heres* is no

---

[1] *Arg.* 32. 3. 1; 6. 1. 66; 29. 5. 1. 4.   For other texts see Bufnoir, Conditions, 379 *sqq.*
[2] C. 6. 43. 3.   [3] 30. 45. 2.
[4] 30. 56.   The same is presumably true of a *legatum optionis servi.*
[5] 36. 45. 1.   [6] 30. 110.   *Post,* Ch. v.
[7] 31. 8. *pr.*
[8] 30. 108. *pr.*   [9] 30. 39. *pr.*
[10] And of the rules in other legacies 30. 47. *pr.*; 30. 108. 12.
[11] It might be urged on the one hand that the *heres* is in general only liable for *culpa* and on
the other that he has a certain obligation and that difficulty is not impossibility.   But the
question is not of the imposition of a legal duty, but as to the testator's intention, and analogies
from the law of obligation are of little use.

longer liable[1], unless he was already *in mora* or was in some way privy to the manumission, which is a case of *dolus*[2]. The same is true, *a fortiori*, if the slave was the property of the testator and was freed by him[3]. In one text Celsus tells us that if a *servus legatus* is freed *interim*, and becomes again a slave, the legacy is good[4]. *Interim* seems to mean during the testator's life, since the case is coupled with one in which the expression *medium tempus* is used; the ordinary term for the interval between the making of the will and the death. The reenslavement may, so far as the words go, have been either before or after the death, the manumission cannot have been by the *heres* or after alienation by him, for, as we shall see, this case was differently dealt with. But the rule given by Celsus seems very doubtful. If applied to a case in which both manumission and reenslavement occurred before the death, it is not in conflict with the principles of *legatum per vindicationem—media tempora non nocent*. But the manumission was a complete ademption[5]. In later law this was not necessarily so in case of sale[6] of the *res legata*, but manumission is on a different footing: a testator cannot be regarded as having contemplated reenslavement[7]. And the rule cannot be harmonised with the principle that a slave freed is a new man, and if reenslaved is a new man again[8].

For the case of a *servus alienus* it is certainly not the law. In these matters the rules as to promise of a slave can be applied to legacy[9], and elsewhere we learn that where a *servus alienus* was promised, and was freed by his owner, the promisor was released, and that, if the man again became a slave, the promise was not enforceable: the obligation once destroyed is gone for ever, and the new slave is another man. The text expressly repudiates the view, which it credits to Celsus, that the obligation was revived by reenslavement[10]. Our case differs, in that, since the manumission preceded the death, there was never an obligation on the *heres*, but this is not material, and it is evident that Celsus held views more favourable to the validity of such gifts than were generally current[11].

If the slave belonged to the *heres*, and he freed him, (or alienated him, and the new owner freed him,) he was liable to pay his value

---

[1] 30. 35.
[2] 46. 3. 92. *pr.*; In. 2. 20. 16. So if he has become a *statu liber*, the *heres* is discharged by handing him over as such.
[3] *Post*, Ch. xx. The texts there discussed deal only with manumission by will, but manumission *inter vivos* is a stronger case, since the gift cannot in any case have been adeemed.
[4] 32. 79. 3.   [5] 33. 8. 1.   [6] In. 2. 20. 12.
[7] 34. 4. 26. 1; 45. 1. 83. 5.   [8] 46. 3. 98. 8.   [9] 30. 46.
[10] 46. 3. 98. 8.
[11] He first expressed the view which Severus and Caracalla enacted and Justinian accepted that sale of the thing legated did not adeem the gift, unless so intended. Gaius was still in doubt (G. 2. 198 ; In. 2. 20. 12). See also an exceptional view of his, in 34. 7. 1. 2.

whatever the state of his knowledge, and the same rule applies no doubt to the case of a *servus hereditarius*[1]. His knowledge is immaterial because this is true in general of all obligations under an inheritance : he was not the less liable to pay a debt because he was not aware of its existence. Other circumstances not of his creating might make it impossible to deliver the slave, and so discharge him. Thus if the *servus legatus* gains his freedom by discovering the murderer of his master, the *heres* is released[2]. So if the slave is justly killed for crime, either under judicial process, or by the *heres*, or by a third person, or if he dies before the *heres* is *in mora*[3]. But if the *heres* induced him to commit the crime, and so is guilty of *dolus*, he is liable under the legacy[4]. If the *heres* noxally surrenders him he is not released, since he could have paid the damages and can redeem him : the liability to hand over the slave with a clear title being, as it were, a debt imposed upon him[5].

A legacy giving the legatee an absolute choice (*legatum optionis*[6]) was not confined to legacies of slaves, but this seems to be the commonest case[7]. Such a legacy is said by Justinian to have been conditional in earlier law ; selection by the legatee being the fulfilment of the condition[8]. There are some signs of difference of opinion, and it may be doubted whether it is not more correct to say that to have been chosen by the *heres* was part of the definition of the slave, and thus that, if he did not choose, no slave satisfied the definition[9]. Nothing in the present connexion seems to turn on the distinction : the rules are in the main those of a conditional legacy. We are told that *optio servi* is an *actus legitimus*[10], and thus not susceptible of modalities. It is practically convenient that the choice should leave no doubt that one man has been finally chosen, since the moment of choice determines to whom he acquires. The principles of condition give the same result : a condition partially satisfied is not satisfied at all[11]. Conversely it follows that a conditional choice

---

[1] In. 2. 20. 16. So if he killed him without reason but not knowing of the gift, 36. 1. 26. 2; 45. 1. 91. 2.

[2] *Arg.* 29. 5. 3. 13.   [3] 29. 5. 3. 13; 30. 53. 3; 46. 3. 92. *pr.*

[4] 30. 53. 8. So though torture of the man under the *Sc.* Silanianum, by which he was destroyed, released the *heres* if it were lawfully done, it did not if he was not legally liable to it. 29. 5. 3. 13. So if *servus alienus legatus* is captured, apart from *dolus* of *heres*, but he will be liable if and when the slave returns. 30. 53. 9; 46. 3. 98. 8. This is the effect of *postliminium*.

[5] 30. 53. 4. As to the effect of a gift of "my slaves," see 32. 73.

[6] U. 24. 14; D. 33. 5. 2. *pr.* They varied in form (cp. 33. 5. 9. *pr.*). There might be *optio servorum*, which, so Pius decided, gave a right to choose three (33. 5. 1).

[7] 33. 5. *passim.* And see C. 6. 43. 3 in which Justinian after laying down a rule for all cases adds without comment a tariff applicable only to slaves.

[8] In. 2. 20. 23.   [9] *Post*, Ch. xxiv.

[10] 50. 17. 77. If indeed the words *Servi optio datio tutoris* were not originally *optio tutoris*. If the allusion is to exercise of the right we are considering, it is not easy to see why it is confined to *servi*. And *tutoris datio* could certainly be conditional and *ad diem.* In. 1. 14. 3; D. 26. 1. 14.

[11] 35. 1. 23.

would not bind the chooser[1]. So if the legatee choose a *servus alienus* or a *liber homo*, this is a nullity, and does not consume his right of choice[2]. If the legatee chose a man who had conditional liberty, Julian held that the testator must be understood not to have included him; the choice being a nullity was not exercised. If, however, the condition on the gift of liberty failed, then, says Julian, following Q. Mucius, he may be chosen: the exclusion is only for the event of his being free[3]. It follows that a real exercise of the option was decisive: in the case of gift *per vindicationem*, it vested the man in the legatee, and an act of his will could not substitute another for him.

The Institutes say that under the older law, if the legatee died without choosing, the gift could not take effect: the *heredes* could not choose[4]. This is confirmed by the authority of Labeo, Proculus and Gaius, in another case. They say that if a thing is left to X, "if he likes," and he does not himself accept, the right does not pass to his *heres*—*conditio personae injuncta videtur*[5]. Another text emphasises the need of personal choice by saying that the *curator* of a lunatic legatee could not choose[6].

All this puts the matter on the level of condition, but it is clear that there were doubts. Paul in one text gives the *heres* of legatee the right of choice[7], and Justinian in his constitution[8], in which he regulates the matter, tells us that the point was doubtful not only where the legatee was to choose, but where the choice was with a third party. He settles the matter by the decision that the right of choice may be exercised by the *heres* of a legatee directed to choose, and that, if a third party so directed died, or became incapable, or neglected to do it for a year, the legatee might choose. But since the third party was given the ˙choice in order to choose fairly, the legatee must not choose the best.

In a joint legacy of *optio* there had also been doubts. Clearly the condition required˙actual agreement[9]. The doubt may have been whether, in case of failure to agree, the thing was void, or each was owner in part of the man he chose[10]. It is clear that the dominant view was that, till all had agreed, there was no choice. Thus if one chooses he is free to change his mind, but if, before he does so, the

---

[1] So, as in conditions involving an act, anticipatory choice was null: it must be after *aditio*. 33. 5. 16, cp. 35. 1. 11. 1. So the legatee's declaration that he will not choose a certain man does not bar him from doing so. 33. 5. 18.
[2] 33. 5. 2. 2.   [3] 33. 5. 9. 1, 2.   [4] In. 2. 20. 23.
[5] 35. 1. 69.   [6] 33. 5. 8. 2.   [7] 33. 5. 9, 19.
[8] C. 6. 43. 3, cp. In. 2. 20. 23.
[9] 33. 5. 8. 2. In Justinian's time at least *heredes* of a legatee of choice are in the same position. C. 4. 43. 3.
[10] 35. 1. 23; In. *loc. cit.*

other fixes on the same man, he is at once common. How if the first chooser has died or gone mad in the meantime? Pomponius decides that the man cannot become common as there can be no common consent. The compilers add that the humaner view is that he does become common, the original assent being regarded as continuing. Justinian also lays down the rule that in such gifts the choice is to be exercised by one chosen by lot: the man will be his and he must compensate the others on a scale varying with the kind of slave and following a tariff laid down by the constitution[1].

As in the case of *aditio*, the law fixed no limit of time for choice. To avoid inconvenience, the Praetor could fix a limit on the application of *heres*, or of a legatee who had a right subsequent to the right of choice, or even of a buyer of the *hereditas*[2]. The time would no doubt not exceed a year. If it were past, the *heres* was free to sell, free, or pledge the slave, and the acquisition of rights by third parties barred the legatee *pro tanto*. Apart from such transfer, his right was unaffected. But if some have been sold, while Pomponius thinks he may still choose among the rest, Paul thinks him barred, since to allow him to choose now that the *heres*, having disposed of those he did not need, has reorganised his household, would impose great inconvenience on him. No doubt the inconvenience would have to be proved. The passage of Paul is from his *Quaestiones*: it may be that the compilers have made a rule where he expressed a doubt[3].

The rules in the case of promise of a slave are much the same as in legacy. If a *servus alienus promissus* is freed by his *dominus* without *dolus* or *culpa* of the *promissor*, he is released, and the obligation is not revived by reenslavement. Paul points out on the authority of Julian, that *culpa* could not arise in such a case unless there was *mora*[4]. So too the *promissor* is released if any slave promised dies before there is *mora*, even though the death is caused by neglect, since the *promissor* is bound *ad dandum*, not *ad faciendum*[5]. So too if the slave become a *statu-liber*, without act or complicity of the *promissor*, he is released by handing him over as such[6]. If he was promised as a *statu-liber* and the condition is satisfied, the *promissor* is released[7]. So too if he was duly killed for wrongdoing, or by torture under the *Sc. Silanianum*, or earned liberty by discovering crime. But if the torture is wrongly inflicted, the *promissor* is still liable : it seems to be assumed that he could, and ought to, have prevented it[8]. If the man is *alienus* and is captured by the enemy,

1 C. 6. 43. 3. 1, cp. In. *loc. cit.*
3 33. 5. 6, 7.
5 45. 1. 91. *pr.*; 46. 3. 92. *pr.*
7 45. 1. 91. 1.

2 33. 5. 6, 8. *pr.*, 13. 1.
4 45. 1. 51; 46. 3. 92. *pr.*, 98. 8; 45. 1. 91. 1.
6 46. 3. 92. 1.
8 29. 5. 3. 13; 45. 1. 96.

Paul says he can be sued for on his return[1]. Elsewhere, he seems to say that if it were the *promissor's* own slave who fell into enemy hands, he was not released. The case is put on a level with manumission by the *promissor*, and it seems that the very fact of not preventing capture is treated as *culpa*[2]. In one text, Paul raises, but does not answer, the question: what is the result if the *promissor* kill the slave, not under such circumstances as clearly release him, but in ignorance that he is the subject of the promise[3]? If the text lays down a rule, it is the same. In fact, it leaves the matter open[4].

A slave like any other *res* might have *fructus*, and, in his case, the *fructus* were of a very distinct kind. Not only did they include earnings[5], which might arise equally well in connexion with other things, but there might be gifts and profits on transactions, which are not exactly earnings, and could not arise in connexion with other chattels. Conversely it is important to observe that *partus* are not fruits[6]. Two reasons are given: *quia non temere ancillae eius rei causa comparantur ut pariant*[7], and that it is absurd to regard man as a fruit, since all things are made for him[8]. The first compares oddly with the rule that sterility might be a redhibitory defect[9], and still more oddly with the counsels of the writers on *res rusticae*[10]. The second must have seemed somewhat ironical to a slave. Both of them however express, somewhat obscurely, the real reason, which was respect for human dignity[11], rather than any legal principle. Nor were *partus* accessories. These distinctions had several important results. Thus a gift of an *ancilla cum natis* did not fail if she were dead, as would one of *servus cum peculio*[12]. They did not, like fruits, vest in the *bonae fidei possessor*[13]. *Partus* of dotal *ancillae* did not go to the *vir*, except where the *dos* was given at a valuation (*dos aestimata*), in which case only the agreed sum had to be returned[14]. Nevertheless they share in the qualities of fruits and accessories in many respects.

[1] 46. 3. 98. 8.   [2] 45. 1. 91. 1.   [3] 45. 1. 91. 2.

[4] Pernice, Labeo, 2. ii. 116, thinks he expressed the contrary view and the compilers have cut out his conclusion. These are really cases of a wider problem, beyond our scope: i.e. how far supervening impossibility discharged from liability to *condictio*, or, what is much the same thing, what is the theory of *culpa* in such cases? Pernice gives a full discussion and references.

[5] C. 6. 47. 1.

[6] 6. 1. 16. *pr.*, 17. 1; 23. 3. 10. 2, 3; 36. 1. 23. 3; 41. 3. 36. 1; 47. 2. 48. 6; C. 5. 13. 1. 9. In. 2. 1. 37; Cicero, de Fin. 1. 4. 12. It was not usual to call the children of *ancillae, liberi.* Sueton. Fragm. s.v. *liberi.*

[7] 5. 3. 27. *pr.*   [8] 22. 1. 28.   In. 2. 1. 37.

[9] 21. 1. 14. 3.   *Post*, p. 55.   [10] See Wallon, *op. cit.* 3, Ch. II.

[11] Accordingly it is late in developing. See Girard, Manuel, 247.   [12] 30. 62, 63.

[13] 47. 2. 48. 6; cp. 24. 1. 28. 5, 17. *pr.*; or in the fructuary, who had not even a usufruct of them. P. 3. 6. 19; D. 7. 1. 68 (where it is said to have been disputed among early lawyers); 22. 1. 28. 1; 41. 3. 36. 1. See also Cicero, *loc. cit.*

[14] Vat. Fr. 114; C. 5. 13. 1. 9; 5. 15. 1; D. 23. 3. 10. 2; *h. l.* 3; *h. t.* 69. 9; 24. 3. 31. 4; 31. 48. *pr.*

A *heres* handing over an *ancilla* to fidei-commissary or legatee after *mora* must hand over her *partus*[1], but not those born before *dies cedens* or even before *mora*[2]. And the beneficiary could get *missio in possessionem* as of fruits[3].

Where the sale of an *ancilla* was voidable as being in fraud of creditors, the transferee had a good title in the meantime, and thus, though she was recoverable, and *partus* born *post iudicium acceptum* were included as a matter of course, those born *medio tempore* were not recoverable, as they were never *in bonis venditoris*[4]. Proculus however held that if she were pregnant of them at the time of the transaction, they must be restored[5]. The materiality of conception before the transaction was one on which there were differences of opinion, as will be seen in relation to some of the more difficult cases now to be considered. If the child conceived be regarded as already existing, it must be considered (since it certainly passed by the sale[6]) as a sort of accessory. Further, it could be pledged, sold and even freed before it was born[7]. The first two cases prove nothing, since pledge and sale were possible of slaves not yet conceived[8]. In the last this is not so clear, since it is a gift to the child. But this case loses its significance, in view of the well-known principle that a child in the womb is regarded as already existing, so far as this makes to his benefit, but not for the advantage of others, nor to his own detriment[9]: *alii antequam nascatur nequaquam prosit*[10]; *aliis non prodest nisi natus*[11]. A modification of this in favour of the owner of the *ancilla* at the time of conception is not surprising, and we shall see other signs of this[12].

According to several texts[13], one of which is an enactment of A.D. 230[14], and assumes the rule as a standing one, children born to a pledged *ancilla* are included in the pledge, as future crops might be. In one of the Digest texts[15] it is Paul who tells us the same thing. But, in his

---

[1] 15. 1. 57. 2; 22. 1. 14; 30. 84. 10; 33. 8. 8. 8; 36. 1. 23. 3.

[2] 22. 1. 14; 33. 5. 21; 35. 2. 24. 1. Two texts seem to contradict this by saying that where the thing is to be handed over after a time, *partus* born in the meantime must be handed over as not being fruits; 36. 1. 23. 3, 60. 4. (Buhl, Salvius Julianus, p. 189). In 23. 3 the allusion is apparently interpolated, for it is out of place, but it does not clearly exclude *mora* in the sense of undue delay. 60. 4 is still more suspicious, as an authority on this point. It says of *fetus*, and seems to imply of *partus*, that they must be handed over only in so far as they have been *summissi*, i.e. used to replace those who have died. It may refer to a legacy of a whole *familia*.

[3] 36. 4. 5. 8. For further illustrations, see 4. 2. 12. *pr.*; 5. 3. 20. 3, 27. *pr.*; 6. 1. 16. *pr.*, 17. 1, 20; 12. 4. 7. 1, 12; 12. 6. 15. *pr.*, 65. 5; 30. 91. 7; 43. 26. 10.

[4] 42. 8. 10. 19—21; *h. t.* 25. 4.   [5] 42. 8. 25. 5.

[6] 13. 7. 18. 2.   [7] 20. 1. 15; 18. 1. 8. *pr.*; P. 4. 14. 1.

[8] The texts express no limitation. A child unborn is not in the *hereditas, pro Falcidia* 35. 2. 9. 1.

[9] 1. 5. 7; 1. 5. 26; 38. 17. 2. 3; 50. 16. 231.   [10] 1. 5. 7.

[11] 50. 16. 231. It is however sometimes stated more generally, 1. 5. 26. But this expresses only the fact that the principle applies over a wide field.

[12] But *partus* conceived before the sale and born after went to the buyer, 13. 7. 18. 2; 41. 1. 66; C. 3. 32. 12.

[13] 20. 1. 29. 1; 43. 33. 1. *pr.*   [14] C. 8. 24. 1.   [15] 20. 1. 29. 1.

Sententiae[1], he lays down the opposite rule, not as special to *partus*, but as applying to *fetus* also. Many attempts have been made to explain away this sharp conflict. Dernburg[2] thinks the rule of inclusion was introduced by the enactment of 230[3], after the *Sententiae* were written. But the enactment clearly treats the rule as well known. Huschke[4], observing that the MSS. give various readings, some of which agree with the general doctrine, and following the *interpretatio*, proposes to amend, so as to make Paul say, merely, that, though there was a right in a gratuitous lender, who had taken a pledge, to keep fruits in lieu of interest[5], this did not apply to *partus* and *fetus*. It should be noted that *fetus* and *partus* differ from ordinary fruits in that they bear a much less constant ratio in value to the thing itself: it is not so plainly fair that they might go in lieu of interest. Ordinary fruits, as we have seen, might often go to the creditor, and indeed it is far from certain that they were covered by the pledge[6]. The language of the enactment of Alexander[3] indicates that the inclusion of *partus* was not based on any notion of identity, but on a tacit convention which came to be presumed, and it may be that, as Dernburg[7] also suggests, this is all Paul means by his requirement of a *conventio*.

Acceptance of this rule does not end the difficulty. If a debtor sell the pledged thing, it is still subject to the pledge[8]. What is the position of *partus* born to the woman after the sale? A text which lays down the general rule of inclusion does not advert to any distinction[9]. One, from Julian[10], implies that they are not strictly pledged, but adds that there will be a *utile interdictum* to recover them. Another text, from Paul, lays it down that if the *partus* is born after the sale, it is not subject to the pledge[11]. The texts are sometimes[12] harmonised by the suggestion that, while Julian is dealing with a case in which the *partus* was conceived before the sale, Paul writes of one conceived after it. But as Vangerow says[13], this distinction is arbitrary and inconsistent with the language of the concluding part of Paul's text. He thinks the rule was that the *partus* (and *fetus*) were not included, if born *apud emptorem*, since a pledge can cover only property which is in, or grows into, the property

---

[1] P. 2. 5. 2. *Fetus vel partus eius rei quae pignori data est pignoris iure non retinetur nisi hoc inter contrahentes convenerit.*
[2] Dernburg, Pandekten i. § 273 n. 8.   [3] C. 8. 24. 1.
[4] Huschke, Jurispr. Antejust. *ad* P. 2. 5. 2.   [5] 20. 2. 8.
[6] Windscheid, Lehrbuch, § 226a, n. 10.
[7] Pfandrecht, 448, *cit.* Vangerow, Pandekten, § 370.
[8] 13. 7. 18. 2.   [9] C. 8. 24. 1.   [10] 43. 33. 1. *pr.*
[11] 20. 1. 29. 1. Another text of Paul, sometimes said to lay down the rule that such *partus* is pledged, is not in point: it merely says, allusively, that sale of an *ancilla* includes her unborn *partus*, 13. 7. 18. 2.
[12] Buhl, Salvius Julianus, 188.   [13] Pandekten, § 370.

of the pledgor[1]. This does not explain why Julian[2] allows an interdict, even *utile*, in this case. Vangerow[3] supposes it to be due to a special importance attaching to a pledge for rent. It seems more probable that it is an individual view of Julian (who holds other individual views on connected topics[4]), that he held that *partus* were included, wherever born, but that the direct interdict applied only to the crops etc. bound by tacit hypothec, and not to express hypothec[5].

Usucapio of *partus ancillae* gives rise to many conflicts of opinion in the texts, which have been the subject of much discussion by commentators[6]. The differences are not surprising, in view of the many questions of theory to which the possible facts may lead. Is the child a part of the mother? If not, when does its existence begin, and is it acquired by the same *causa*? Is it affected by *vitium* in the mother? The matter is further complicated by the fact that the rules as to *bona fides* were not the same in all the *causae*. *Emptio* had, and *donatio* may have had, special rules, and in the cases discussed this point is material. And in some of the texts the transaction under which the mother is held was between a slave and his master, and there is the further question how far the latter is affected by the *mala fides* of the slave. It will be convenient to deal first with the case in which the mother was capable of being usucapted, i.e. was not subject to any *vitium*.

As we are told by Ulpian[7], the issue are not fruits, and so do not vest in the *bonae fidei possessor*, though some texts dealing with these matters group *partus* with *fetus*[8], which are in turn grouped with fruits, and declared to vest in the *bonae fidei possessor*[9]. They are not a part of the mother[10]. As they do not vest in the *possessor*, they must be usucapted independently. If the mother is usucapted before the *partus* is born, no question arises, for as in the case of any other alienation, the new owner of the woman owns the child[11]. If it is born before that date it must be independently acquired, and possession of it does not begin till it is born[12]. So far the texts agree. But there is disagreement as to the *titulus* or *causa* by which it is

---

[1] See the reff. in Windscheid, Lehrbuch, § *cit.* n. 7.　　　　[2] 43. 33. 1. *pr.*
[3] *loc. cit.* Lenel has shewn ground for thinking that the passage was originally written of the *actio Serviana* (Ed. Perp. § 266).
[4] See next page.
[5] This is Salvianum *utile*, but not the *quasi* Salvianum which has been supposed to have existed.
[6] See e.g. Buhl, Salvius Julianus, 190—198; Appleton, Propriété Prétorienne i. 116 *sqq.*, 250—277, 318 *sqq.*
[7] 47. 2. 48. 6.
[8] 41. 3. 4. 5; *h. t.* 10. 2; 47. 2. 48. 5.　　　　[9] 41. 1. 48. 2.
[10] 18. 2. 4. 1; 21. 2. 42; 41. 3. 10. 2; 50. 16. 26. In one text we are told that till born the child is a *portio matris* (25. 4. 1. 1), but this has no general bearing: it means only that till the child has an independent existence, the interdict *de liberis agnoscendis* has no application.
[11] 41. 1. 66.　　　　[12] 41. 3. 4. 16; *h. t.* 44. 2.

acquired. According to Julian, and apparently Papinian, the *titulus* is the same as that of the mother[1]: if the mother was being usucapted, *pro emptore*, so is the child. According to Paul it is by an independent *titulus, pro suo*[2]. The latter view necessarily leads to the rule that *bona fides* is necessary at the birth, which is clearly the *initium possessionis*. And so Paul lays it down[3]. Papinian however holds that good faith at the time of acquisition of the mother is enough[4]. This is perhaps, as Buhl says, an expression of Julian's view, but it goes beyond the logical implications of identity of *titulus*. This of itself would not do away with the need for good faith when possession began. Appleton regards it as treating the *partus* as an accessory, the destination of which is governed by that of the principal thing, subject only to the need for actual possession. As we have seen, this is contrary to the general attitude of the law towards *partus*, and there is no other textual authority for it. Regarded as an expression of Julian's opinion[5] and resting on his rule that the *titulus* is the same, it may be related with his view that a *bonae fidei possessor* did not cease to acquire through the slave, by learning that he was not entitled: supervening bad faith was, for Julian, immaterial[6]. Other texts shew that this view did not prevail[7], and it would appear that, in our case too, the other view prevailed[8], so that in the case of an *ancilla non furtiva*, the conditions for *usucapio* of *partus* were the same as those for acquisition of fruits by a *bonae fidei possessor*. If that be so we get the result that the requirement of good faith at birth prevailed, while acquisition by the same *titulus* as that of the mother also prevailed. It seems to be supposed, by Appleton[9], that if this part of Julian's view prevailed, the other must. But there is no logical connexion. Two things acquired by the same *titulus* may be first possessed at different times, and good faith be necessary for each at the time of taking. It was only the conception of *partus* as an accessory that led to the view that good faith when the mother was received was sufficient[10].

The case is somewhat different where the mother has been stolen, and is thus an *ancilla furtiva,* incapable of usucapion. The first point

---

[1] 6. 2. 11. 4; 41. 3. 33. *pr.*; 30. 82. 4; cp. 31. 73.
[2] 41. 10. 2. See Buhl, *op. cit.* 191. Pomponius seems obscurely to express the same view (41. 10. 4), but it is not clear that he denies the possibility of claiming by the same *titulus*. One who possesses by any title also possesses *pro suo*.
[3] 41. 3. 4. 18. Appleton (*op. cit.* § 139) discusses this text and cites the more important earlier literature upon it.
[4] 41. 3. 44. 2.
[5] In view of his treatment of the case of *partus* born of *ancilla furtiva, apud b. f. possessorem*, it may be doubted whether Julian held this view (*post*, p. 27).
[6] 22. 1. 25. 2.   [7] 41. 1. 23. 1; *h. t.* 48.
[8] 6. 2. 7. 17 (Ulp.); 41. 3. 4. 18 (Paul).   [9] *op. cit.* i. 263.
[10] It hardly need be said that bad faith after the birth is not material, 41. 2. 6. *pr.*, 40. 2.

to notice is that the *partus* itself may be *vitiosus*, and thus incapable of *usucapio* by any one. If it is conceived before the theft or *apud furem*, it is *furtivus* wherever born : it is grouped in this respect with *fetus*[1]. There appears to be no disagreement as to the rule in the case in which the *ancilla* is pregnant when stolen ; it is stated by Julian as an application of the rule that a child conceived is regarded as already existing[2]. It is an extension, for the benefit of the owner, of a rule in general applied only for the benefit of the slave.

As to *partus* conceived *apud furem*, there is more difficulty. Ulpian tells us in one text that this too is *furtivus*, wherever born[3]. Elsewhere he reports a view of Marcellus, that if conceived *apud furem* or *furis heredem*, and born *apud furis heredem*, it cannot be usucapted by a buyer from him. In the same text he reports Scaevola as holding that on such facts the *partus* could be usucapted, as basing the view that it could not, on the idea that the *partus* is part of the *ancilla*, and as shewing that this would lead to the view that it could not be usucapted even if born *apud bonae fidei possessorem*[4]. This Scaevola seems to regard as a *reductio ad absurdum* : it is however exactly the view at which, as we have seen, Ulpian himself arrived, in the case of conception *apud furem*[3]. It does not seem to rest on the notion that the *partus* is a part, but to follow necessarily from the view on which the *partus* conceived before the theft was treated as *furtiva*, i.e. that it was to be regarded as already existing. For the thief is still " contrecting," and therefore still committing theft.

The case is different with conception *apud heredem furis*, (assuming, as we must, that he is in good faith). Here the view of Marcellus, that it is *furtivus*, cannot rest on continued contrectation, nor is it clear that it rests, as Scaevola thinks, on the view that *partus* is a part of the *ancilla*[5]. It seems, indeed, to involve a confusion. The *heres* succeeds to the defects of his predecessor's possession, but he does not succeed to his guilt as a thief, yet this is what seems to underlie the view that *partus* conceived *apud heredem furis* is *furtivus*. He could acquire no more right in the thing than his predecessor could have acquired, but there is no reason why possession by him should affect the thing itself with any disability[6], and the language of Paul and Ulpian in other texts is inconsistent with any such notion[7]. They treat conception *apud heredem furis* as being *apud bonae fidei possessorem*, and only exclude *usucapio* by him because he inherits the defects of his predecessor's possession.

---

[1] 1. 5. 26 ; 41. 3. 10. 2 ; 47. 2. 48. 5.   [2] 1. 5. 26.   [3] 47. 2. 48. 5.
[4] 41. 3. 10. 2.   [5] 41. 3. 10. 2 ; 50. 16. 26.
[6] It may be that the words *vel apud furis heredem* are inserted by the compilers.
[7] 6. 2. 11. 2 ; 41. 3. 4. 1.

If the child is conceived *apud bonae fidei possessorem* it is not *furtivus*, and can be usucapted by him on the same *titulus* as that of the mother[1]. It is clear on these texts that the possessor must have been in good faith at the time of conception. Some texts speak of good faith only at this time[2]. But none says that this is enough, and most of the texts say that good faith at the time of birth is necessary. It is noticeable that Julian takes this view[3]. Thus we arrive at the rule that good faith is necessary both at conception and birth, so that provided the child is not *furtivus* the fact that the mother was stolen makes little difference[4]. One text, indeed, from Pomponius, citing the opinion of Trebatius that bad faith supervening after the birth was immaterial, expresses disagreement, and says that, in such a case, there will be no *usucapio* unless the possessor either does or cannot give notice to the person entitled[5]. This view is so contrary to the general rule that any isolated text expressing it is suspicious. When we see that the opinion is based on the proposition that if he does not take steps his possession becomes clandestine our doubts are increased, for nothing can be clearer than that a possession *ab initio iusta* cannot become *clam*[6]. The text cannot represent the law.

The case is different where the *bonae fidei possessor* is a donee. Here we are told that he must continue in good faith up to the time of bringing the *actio* Publiciana[7], i.e. for the period of usucapion. Of this principle, that in *usucapio ex lucrativa causa* good faith must continue through the period, there are other scanty but unmistakeable traces[8].

In another text we are told that a *bonae fidei possessor* can bring the *actio* Publiciana, for the *partus* conceived *apud eum*, even though he never possessed it[9]. This has been explained[10] as meaning that not only was the *causa* of the mother extended to the child, but also the possession. This conflicts with the conclusions at which we have arrived above, and has no other text in its favour. It is argued by Appleton[11] that for recovery in the Publician it was not necessary, on the words of the Edict, to have possessed, but only to shew that your

---

[1] 6. 2. 11. 2; 41. 3. 33. *pr.*; 41. 10. 4. *pr.*; 41. 4. 9, 10; 47. 2. 48. 5; C. 7. 26. 3.
[2] 6. 2. 11. 2; C. 7. 26. 3.
[3] 41. 3. 33. *pr.* (and see 6. 2. 11. 3); 41. 10. 4. *pr.*; 47. 2. 48. 5.
[4] As to Paul's view in 41. 3. 4. 17, *post* p. 28.
[5] 41. 10. 4. pr.   [6] 41. 2. 6. pr.; *h. t.* 40.   [7] 6. 2. 11. 3.
[8] C. 7. 31. 1. 3a; C. 7. 33. 11 ; Bas. Heimb. Zach. p. 45, Sch. 14. For discussion of these texts see Pellat, La Propriété, *ad* 6. 2. 11. 3; Appleton, *op. cit.* § 182. References to suggested explanations and emendations will there be found. Pernice (Labeo, 2. i. 457) thinks that 6. 2. 11. 3 is interpolated, and rejects any inference from the texts in the Code for the classical law. He thinks that Justinian means only that a donee may claim *accessio possessionum*, as well as a buyer, and that knowledge acquired by the transferor after the transfer, that the thing was not his, shall not make it *furtiva*. But this requires that the word *ea* in the text shall not refer to the *detentio* which is under discussion, but to the possession of the successor which has not yet been mentioned.
[9] 6. 2. 11. 2.   [10] Pellat, *op. cit.*, *ad h. l.*   [11] Appleton, *op. cit.* § 134.

causa was such that if you had possessed you would have usucapted. This would certainly be the case in the supposed hypothesis, and it may be that this is the true solution of the difficulty[1].

Another text in the same extract says that the principle is the same in the case of *partus partus*, and in that in which the child is not born in the natural way, but is extracted from the body of the mother after her death, by Caesarian section. The first point is simple: the rules applied to the non-furtive *partus* are applicable to the issue of *partus furtivus*. The reason for the statement of the second proposition is not so clear. The principle which is declared to be applicable to this case too, is that of extension to the *partus* of the mother's *causa*. The remark may be intended to negative the conceivable doubt whether the connexity may not be excluded by the fact that the mother was non-existent for a certain interval of time[2]. But it may be merely that a doubt might arise as to whether a thing never actually born could be called *partus*[3].

Another group of texts raises a fresh hypothesis. It was common for a slave to provide another in lieu of himself, as the price of his freedom[4]. If the *ancilla* provided was only possessed in bad faith by the slave, we are told by Paul, on the authority of Celsus, that the master cannot usucapt her because *prima causa durat*[5]. The slave's acquisition was the master's: the intervening quasi-sale was immaterial. The slave's *vitium* would clearly affect the master. For the same reason it must be supposed that he could not usucapt *partus* even conceived *apud eum*. And so, for the case where the slave stole the *ancilla*, Paul tells us, on the authority of Sabinus and Cassius, and for the same reason[6]. But Julian appears as accepting another view of Urseius and Minicius, who say that the transaction between slave and master is tantamount to a sale, and is thus a *causa* under which the master as a *bonae fidei possessor* can usucapt *partus* conceived *apud eum*[7]. The effect of this is to avoid the difficulty that a master is affected by a *vitium* in his slave's possession. It can hardly be doubted that the other view represents the accepted law. In another text, adjoining that last cited from him[8], Paul applies the same rule even if the substitute were given by a third person for the freedom of the slave: the master cannot usucapt her *partus*. One would suppose the master was an ordinary *bonae fidei possessor* in such a case. The simplest explanation is to treat Paul as still dealing with the case of theft by the slave[9]. But the text gives little warrant for this, and its conclusion is that the same is true if

---

1 We shall not consider the questions arising out of repeated and conflicting Publician claims.
2 6. 2. 11. 5; Appleton, *op. cit.* § 146.
3 See 28. 2. 12; 38. 17. 1. 5; Macbeth, Act v, Sc. vii, ll. 40 *sqq.*   4 *Post*, Ch. xxv.
5 41. 4. 2. 14.   6 41. 3. 4. 16.   7 41. 4. 9, 10.
8 41. 3. 4. 17.   9 Appleton, *op. cit.* § 139. He cites other suggestions.

the stolen *ancilla* is handed to us in exchange, or by way of payment or as a gift. These cases can have no relation to the procuring of manumission, and the notion of a slave stealing an *ancilla* and giving it to a third person in order that he may make a present of it to the slave's master seems a little improbable: it is more likely that Paul contemplates the slave as knowing of the defect in title[1]. It may be remarked that a slave is *suis nummis emptus* for the purpose of manumission even though the price is actually provided by a third person[2], and it may be that Paul has in his mind this assimilation, and declares that for this purpose too the whole thing must be imputed to the slave.

For injuries to slaves delictal actions lay as for injury to other chattels. Thus there was an *actio* Aquilia for hurting or killing a slave, unlawfully, i.e. unless it were in self-defence, or the slave were caught in adultery or the like[3]. This action being available to the owner lay even where he had pledged the slave[4], and even though he were a buyer about to redhibit[5]. If he were freed after the wound and then died, the wounder was liable to the late owner, *de occiso*, the injury having been done while he was owner[6]. If on the same facts he had been freed and made heir by his late owner, he could presumably sue for the wounding, but if he died his heir could not sue *de occiso*, since an heir could not inherit an action which could not have belonged to the person he succeeded. If, however, the slave had been made part heir, and died, his co-heir could sue *ex* Aquilia[7]. Castrating a slave, and so increasing his value, did not give rise to an *actio* Aquilia, though it might to other proceedings[8].

The case of a slave injured twice and dying after the second injury gave rise to some interesting distinctions. The rules laid down in the texts appear to be the following:

(1) If he is mortally injured by A and afterwards dies of a certainly fatal stroke by B, B has killed, A has only wounded. This is laid down by Celsus, Marcellus, Ulpian and Julian[9].

(2) Julian lays down an analogous rule for the case in which having been mortally wounded by A he dies in a shipwreck or *ruina*[10].

(3) If having been wounded by several at once or at different times he dies and it is clear which killed him, that one alone is liable for killing, but if it is uncertain which killed him, all are liable. This is laid down by Julian (as an ancient rule) and by Ulpian[11].

---

[1] The remark perhaps only puts these transactions on a level with sale.
[2] 40. 1. 4. 1, *post*, Ch. xxvii.   [3] P. 1. 13a. 6; D. 9. 2. 3, 5. 3, 30. *pr.*; C. 3. 35. 3.
[4] 9. 2. 30. 1.   [5] 9. 2. 11. 7. On redhibiting he must cede his actions.
[6] 9. 2. 15. 1; *h. t.* 16; *h. t.* 36. 1.   [7] 9. 2. 36. 1.
[8] 9. 2. 27, 28, *post*, Ch. iv.   [9] 9. 2. 11. 3, 15. 1.
[10] 9. 2. 15. 1.   [11] 9. 2. 11. 2, 51. 1.

(4) If it is certain that A's blow would have killed, but not certain whether B's would or would not apart from A's, both are liable. So says Julian. *Ita vulneratus est servus ut eo ictu certum esset moriturum ...postea ab alio ictus decessit: quaero an cum utroque de occiso agi possit. respondit...igitur si quis servo mortiferum vulnus inflixerit eundemque alius ex intervallo ita percusserit ut maturius interficeretur quam ex priore vulnere moriturus fuerat, statuendum est utrumque eorum lege* Aquilia *teneri*[1].

(5) For the purpose of this last rule it is immaterial whether the death does or does not immediately follow the second injury. The fact that it follows at once does not prove that the second injury was of itself mortal. In the actual case the death occurred at once since Julian, while laying down the rule that the year, the highest value during which is payable, dates from the injury backward, says also that here it dates from the death[2]. The slightly adverse inference which might be drawn from the words *maturius interficeretur* is negatived by the use of a similar expression where the second event was *naufragium vel ruina*[3].

(6) Where two persons are thus liable, the damages may not be the same. In the case supposed the slave was instituted *heres* by someone between the two injuries. The loss resulting from his failure to enter is imputable to the second injurer, not to the first[4].

These texts have given rise to much controversy: it has been supposed that in 9. 2. 51. *pr.* Julian is in at least apparent conflict with Marcellus, Celsus, Ulpian and himself in 9. 2. 11. 3, 15. 1. This opinion seems to rest on the assumption that the cases in 11. 3. and 51. *pr.* are the same, i.e. that the words *alius postea examinaverit, ex alio vulnere periit* (11. 3) mean the same as *ab alio ictus decessit, alius...ita percusserit ut maturius interficeretur.* It is plain that they do not: the latter formula leaves uncertain the question whether the second injury was itself mortal. It is noticeable that Julian expresses his rule as an inference from the old rule already laid down for the case where there was doubt as to the fatal character of both of the injuries[5]. Thus the contradiction, improbable in itself, appears to be non-existent. The discussions also contain the assumption that if the death follows immediately on the second injury, this shews that the second injury was mortal. In a certain sense it does so, but not in Julian's sense. It does not shew that it was mortal apart from the first[6].

---

[1] 9. 2. 51. *pr.*   [2] Pacchioni, Law Quarterly Rev. 4. 180, *arg.* 9. 2. 51. 2.
[3] 9. 2. 11. 3. Pernice, Sachbeschädigungen, 180.   [4] 9. 2. 51. *pr.*, 2.
[5] 9. 2. 51. 1. *Idque est consequens auctoritati veterum qui cum a pluribus idem servus ita vulneratus est ut non appareret cuius ictu perisset omnes teneri iudicaverunt.*
[6] It seems unnecessary to set out the various hypotheses which all start from one or both of these assumptions. The views of Vangerow, Pernice, Grueber and Ferrini are set out by Pacchioni (*loc. cit.*) who gives also an explanation of his own.

The title *De furtis* in the Digest[1] is full of cases of theft of slaves, but so far as it is merely theft, they give rise to few special questions. The rules as to *fugitivi* will be more conveniently treated at a later stage: here it may be remarked that a *fugitivus* was regarded as a thief of himself[2]. If, however, two slaves persuade each other to run away, they have not stolen each other[3]. The reason no doubt is that there is no contrectation, and theft at your mere suggestion is not *ope et consilio tuo*. This was certainly the law for Justinian[4]. *Consilium*, to make a man liable, must be more than advice to steal; it requires advice how to do it: it must be in some way helpful, though not necessarily in the nature of material help[5]. But it is not clear that early law took the same view. Its principles were not so strictly defined, and this very extract suggests a broader liability. Pomponius says, with Sabinus, (who is known to have taken a wide view of liability for theft,) that if the runaway took anything with him the man who advised the flight was liable for *furtum*[6]. If this is so he ought to be a thief in the simpler case of the *fur sui*. There was no doubt a change of view. Again, if I urge a slave to run away intending that he shall fall into the hands of a third person, this is *furtum* in me, for I have helped the thief. Here, too, Pomponius thinks that if he actually does fall into a thief's hands I am liable, though I did not intend this[7]. According to Gaius this was not theft, but gave rise to an *actio in factum* presumably for an indemnity[8].

It must be observed that, in relation to delict, it is impossible to ignore, absolutely, the human aspect of the slave. Some acts assume distinct characters according as they are done to a slave or to some other thing. Thus, killing a slave was not only a delict: it was also a crime[9]. The Twelve Tables impose, for breaking a slave's bone, a penalty half that in the case of a freeman[10]. The *Lex Cornelia*, which made it capital to kill a man, included slaves in the term *homo*[11]. The connexion of the slave with the wrong may be somewhat different. Thus goods in his custody may be stolen: whether they are or are not *peculiares* they are stolen from the master[12]. In the same way if a third person's property is stolen from the slave, the master has *actio furti*, if the slave's holding imposed on him the duty of *custodia*, as if stolen from himself. There was, however, one limitation: if the thing had come into the slave's custody through his contract, the master's

---

[1] 47. 2. [2] 47. 2. 61; C. 6. 1. 1; *post*, Ch. XII.
[3] 47. 2. 36. 3. [4] In. 4. 1. 11. [5] 47. 2. 50.
[6] Aul. Gell., Noct. Att. xi. 18; D. 11. 3. 11. 2; 47. 2. 36. 2. [7] 47. 2. 36. *pr.*
[8] G. 3. 202; cp. 47. 2. 50. 4. [9] G. 3. 213; In. 4. 3. 11.
[10] See Bruns, Fontes, i. 29.
[11] Coll. 1. 3. 2; D. 48. 8. 1. 2; C. 3. 35. 3. If the creditor prostituted a pledged slave, she was free of the pledge—a rule in the interest of the master, but in which that of the slave is also considered, 13. 7. 24. 3; 1. 12. 1. 8.
[12] *Arg.* 47. 8. 4. 13, 14.

liability on the contract would be only *de peculio,* and his *interesse,* being measured by his liability, would be similarly limited[1].

Some wrongs might be committed in relation to slaves, which were inconceivable in relation to other things. Thus, if my slave, falsely accused, was acquitted after torture, I had an action for double damages, apart from the remedy for *calumnia*[2]. Two cases require fuller statement.

Abduction of slaves, by force or by solicitation, was punishable by the *Lex* Fabia[3], apart from the civil remedy. Mere receiving of a runaway did not suffice : there must be complicity, and of course, there was no *plagium* if the owner consented[4]. It is described as consisting in chaining, hiding, buying or selling, *dolo malo,* inducing to flight from their master, or being in any way interested in such transactions[5]. We are told on the authority of a rescript of Hadrian, that *furtum* of a slave was not necessarily *plagium*[6]. Indeed many well known kinds of theft are such that it is impossible to suppose the heavy penalties of the *lex,* or the capital punishment of later law, to have applied to them[7]. To take away, and have intercourse with, an *ancilla aliena non meretrix* was *furtum* but not *plagium,* but, *si suppressit, poena legis Fabiae coercetur*[8]. Here there was concealment ; in fact, *plagium* seems to be such a *furtum* as amounts to repudiation of the owner's right[9]

It required *dolus* and thus the act of hiring persons who were in fact *fugitivi* was not in itself *plagium* where they had been letting themselves out before[10]. But though bona fide claim of right was a defence, the mere allegation of ownership did not suffice, and if this point was raised it must be decided before the criminal charge was tried. Death of the abducted slave did not end the charge[11].

The *lex* fixed large money penalties payable to the treasury[12]. Mommsen thinks that in its first stage the proceeding was an *actio*

---

[1] 15. 1. 5. 1.   [2] 3. 6. 9.

[3] C. 9. 20. *passim* ; D. 48. 15. *passim.* This provision was in the second *caput* of the *lex* : the first dealt with abduction of freemen. Coll. 14. 3. 5. Mommsen thinks, on the authority of this text and Coll. 14. 2. 1, that the *lex* did not cover provincials and their slaves. (Strafrecht 780.) The restriction has disappeared in later law. The date of the *lex* Fabia is uncertain. It is mentioned by Cicero, Pro Rabirio 3. See Cuq, *op. cit.* 1. 587.

[4] C. 9. 20. 10, 14 ; D. 48. 15. 3. *pr.*

[5] Coll. 14. 2 ; 14. 3. 5 ; C. 9. 20. 9 ; D. 48. 15. 6. 2. Mommsen, *loc. cit.,* shews reason (see Suetonius, Aug. 32) for holding that the words *qui in eas res socius fuerit* (Coll. 14. 3. 4, 5 ; D. 48. 15. 6. 2) refer not to participation, but to forming part of unlawful organisations the object of which was the commission of these and similar offences.

[6] 48. 5. 6. *pr.*

[7] e.g. the act of a depositee who uses the slave, or the *commodatarius* who uses him in an unauthorised way, 47. 2. 40, 77.

[8] 47. 2. 39, 83. 2 ; 48. 15. 3. 5 ; C. 9. 20. 2.

[9] Mommsen (*op. cit.* 781) defines it as "Anmassung des Herrenrechts" : it is clear that many thefts would not amount to this. He thinks *furtum usus* practically the only case which was not *plagium,* but the texts he cites shew only that *furtum servi* and *plagium* go commonly together (C. Th. 9. 20. 1 ; C. 9. 31. 1). It may be doubted whether any evidence can be produced for *furtum usus* as a definite category in the classical law. Monro, De Furtis, App. I.

[10] 48. 15. 6. 1.

[11] 48. 15. 3. 1, 5 ; C. 9. 20. 8. The proceedings were cumulative with *furti* and *servi corrupti.* C. 9. 20. 2 and see n. 9.

[12] P. 1. 6a. 2 ; Coll. 14. 3. 5 ; C. 9. 20. 6.

popularis, tried before the ordinary civil courts[1]. In the later empire it has become an ordinary criminal proceeding[2], a *iudicium publicum* tried by *Praefectus Urbi* in Rome, *Praefectus Praetorio* in Italy, *Praeses* in a province[3].

The punishment is capital, varying in form according as the criminal is *ingenuus, honestior, humilior, libertinus* or *servus*, the commonest punishment being apparently *in metallum datio*[4]. An enactment in the Code speaks of a penalty payable to the *fisc*, at least for dealing in fugitives[5]. The extreme penalty is thus reserved for the actual abductor[6], if we can assume that this text was originally written of the *lex* Fabia, but this is far from certain. There was much legislation on *fugitivi*, though it seems to be all based on the *lex*[7].

The exact date of the change is not known. It must be as early as Caracalla, if the Collatio is to be trusted, since he dealt with the jurisdiction in ways which shew that he is dealing with a *iudicium publicum*[8]. It cannot be much earlier since Ulpian and Paul both speak of money penalties[9]. It is noticeable that the same writers are made in the Collatio to treat it also as a *iudicium publicum*[10], which would mean that the change was made in their time, and the closing words of the title, in the Collatio[11], which deals with this matter, are, (the compiler being the authority,) that *novellae constitutiones* have made it capital, *quamvis et Paulus crucis et metalli huiusmodi reis inrogaverit poenam.* It is clear that there was legislation with this effect after Paul, and indeed the Code contains enactments of Diocletian which seem to lay down the capital and public nature of the proceeding as a new thing[12]. It may be that this was an extension of legislation which had not covered the whole field of the *Lex*, or that, till the time of this later legislation, the *actio popularis* was an admissible alternative, and was commonly used. It no doubt had the advantage of entitling the informer to a certain share of the penalty, though we do not know how much.

For certain forms of damage to a slave, the Edict provided a special remedy by an action called *iudicium de servo corrupto.* It was an *actio in factum*, for double damages. The Edict gives it against one who is shewn *servum(am) recepisse persuasisseve quid ei dolo malo quo eum(am) deteriorem faceret*[13]. The word *corruptio* is not in the Edict,

---

[1] *loc. cit.*   [2] C. 9. 20. 13.
[3] Coll. 14. 2; 14. 3. 1; C. 9. 20. 4. *Procuratores Caesaris*, though they usurped the jurisdiction, had no right to it except when acting as *praeses*. After decision they carried out the sentence. Caracalla relaxed the rules. Coll. 14. 3; D. 1. 19. 3. *pr.*
[4] Coll. 14. 2. 2; C. Th. 9. 18. 1; C. 9. 20. 7, 16.   [5] C. 9. 20. 6.
[6] Mommsen, *loc. cit.*   [7] *Post*, Ch. XII.
[8] Coll. 14. 3. 3; Mommsen, *loc. cit.*   [9] Coll. 14. 3. 5; P. 1. 6a. 2; 5. 6. 14.
[10] Coll. 14. 2. 2; 14. 3. 2.   [11] Coll. 14. 3. 6.   [12] C. 9. 20. 6, 13.
[13] 11. 3. 1. *pr.*

and was probably not in the *formula*[1]. The title dealing with the matter gives many instances of the kind of wrong which was met by it[2]. Knowingly receiving a *fugitivus* was enough, though mere charitable shelter with innocent intent was not. In general it was no defence that the man corrupted was thought to be free, (except, of course, in receiving a *fugitivus*, in which case this belief would negative the *dolus*,) for the necessary *dolus* is the intention to make him worse, which can be done to a free man[3]. The words of the Edict are very comprehensive, but it is clear from this list, and the language of some of the texts, that the harm contemplated is usually moral[4]. The facts may often, however, amount to another delict as well, and as the corruption of the slave is a distinct wrong, the two actions would be cumulative[5]. The action is in *duplum* even *contra fatentem*, *i.e.* for twice the damage to the slave and loss immediately consequent on the wrong[6]. Thus if a slave were incited to flight or taken away, it covered the value of anything he took with him, but not the loss and liability from subsequent thefts caused by the habit formed[7]. So if he was induced to destroy documents, the loss caused was chargeable, but not that from later similar acts[8]. This might lead to severity in some cases, for it was theft in the adviser as to what the man took·with him, and the offender would thus be liable to pay twice the value for the *corruptio*, and twice or four times for the theft[9].

The death, alienation or manumission of the slave, or the return of the property does not extinguish the action[10]. Like other rights of action it passes to the *heres*, though the slave is legated[11], but, as it is penal, it does not lie against the *heres*[12]. Though it is Praetorian and penal, it is perpetual, a characteristic found in some other such actions[13].

---

[1] Lenel, Ed. Perp. § 62.

[2] 11. 3. Among them are receiving clandestinely the slave of another, making such a slave do anything which lessens his value, encouraging one, already badly inclined, to steal, corrupt others, commit *iniuria*, or ruin his *peculium* by debauchery or otherwise, leading him into vice, idleness, neglect of business, prodigality, flight, disobedience, contempt of his master, trickery or intrigue, inducing him to run to the statue of the Emperor to the shame of his master, inducing him to copy, alter or destroy private documents or contract notes. P. 1. 13a. 5; 2. 31. 33; D. 11. 3. 1, 2, 11. 2, 15; 47. 2. 52. 24; 47. 10. 26.

[3] 1. 3. 5. *pr*. 1.   [4] 11. 3. 15; C. 6. 2. 4.

[5] 11. 3. 11. 2; G. 3. 198. Thus to induce a man to run away was *furtum ope consilio*, in the adviser, if it was done with the intent that he should fall into the hands of a third person, and similar cases might arise under the *l*. Aquilia, 11. 3. 3, 4.

[6] 11. 3. 9. 2; *h. t.* 14. 5; *h. t.* 14. 8.   [7] 11. 3. 11. *pr*.

[8] 11. 3. 11. 1. It covered liability for any wrong or breach of contract he was induced to commit to third persons.

[9] 47. 2. 36. 2. As to theft in this case, *ante*, p. 31. As to the literature on cumulation, Dernburg, Pandekten, 1. § 135.

[10] 11. 3. 5. 4—7; *h. t.* 16.   [11] 11. 3. 8, 13. *pr*.

[12] 11. 3. 13. *pr*. Except as to actual profit.

[13] 11. 3. 13. *pr*. Contrary to the rule expressed in 44. 7. 35. *pr*. *Furti manifesti* is *perpetua*, but it is only a modification of a civil law liability. Our action is purely Praetorian. The *actio iniuriarum* was *annua* though not *contra ius civile* (C. 9. 35. 5). *Doli* though purely indemnificatory was *annua* (44. 7. 35; C. 2. 20. 3). *De rebus effusis* was *perpetua in duplum* (9. 3. 5. 5). Some were fourfold or twofold for a year and single after: *Calumnia*, 3. 6. 1; *damnum in turba*, 47. 8. 4. *pr*.; wrongs by *familia publicani*, 39. 4. 1; wrongs on occasion of *incendium, ruina* etc. 47. 9. 1. *pr*. *De sepulchro violato* was apparently *perpetua*, though praetorian and penal, 47. 12.

It may be noted that Ulpian says of our case, *haec actio perpetua est, non temporaria*[1], a pleonastic way of putting the matter which is unusual if not unique. It may be that this betrays a change and that, like some other of the actions[2], to which it is closely analogous, it was originally in *simplum* after a year.

The action was available to the owner, even though he had pledged the slave, and against anyone, even a usufructuary[3]. In strictness it was not available to anyone but the owner, but it was allowed in the case of corruption of a *servus hereditarius*, and, as an *actio utilis*, to the fructuary even against the owner[4]. It was not available either to or against the *bonae fidei possessor*[5].

The words of the Edict[6] are so wide as to include any kind of wrong done by persuasion, but we have seen that it was used, in practice, mainly in case of moral damage (often with material consequences), such as could not otherwise be reached by existing law. One case is peculiar: we are told, by Ulpian, that, if you persuaded a man, *dolo malo*, to a dangerous feat in which he suffered bodily harm, this action lay. Paul adds that an *actio utilis* Aquilia is better[7]. The case is clearly not within the *lex* Aquilia, and it is likely that our action was applied to such cases, (the Edict being an old one[8],) before the subsidiary actions analogous to the *actio* Aquilia were fully developed.

In general, actual damage had to be shewn: indeed to no other hypothesis could double damages be fitted. There was, however, a case in which there seem to have been doubts, hardly justified on logical grounds, but inspired by considerations of expediency. A tries to induce B's slave to steal from him. The slave tells B who, in order to catch A, tells the slave to do as A suggests. Was there any liability? Gaius is clear that there was no *furtum*, because of the consent, and no *iudicium servi corrupti* because the slave was not corrupted. He seems indeed, though his text is uncertain, to treat the doubt as obsolete. Justinian treats it as an open question, and, observing that there had been doubts, decides that both actions shall lie, to prevent a wicked act from going unpunished[9]. It is not to be supposed that there was any intention to do away with the general rule requiring actual deterioration.

One remarkable text attributed to Paul remains for discussion in connexion with this action[10]. It provides for a choice in the master, if

---

[1] 11. 3. 13. *pr.*; cp. 4. 9. 7. 6; 9. 3. 5. 5; 38. 5. 3. 1.
[2] See note 13, p. 34.   [3] 11. 3. 9. 1, 14. 3.   [4] *Ibid.* and *h. t.* 13. 1.
[5] 11. 3. 1. 1. So far the text is clear, but its form is obscure and its reasoning futile. Pernice, Labeo, 2. 1. 439.
[6] 11. 3. 1. 1.   [7] 11. 3. 3. 1, 4.
[8] It is commented by Alfenus Varus. See Cuq, Institutions Juridiques, 2. 478. Another text tells us (48. 5. 6. *pr.*) that seduction of an *ancilla* might give rise to *actio* Aquilia and to *servi corrupti*. Cp. In. 4. 1. 8. *fin.*
[9] G. 3. 198; C. 6. 2. 20; In. 4. 1. 8. In the Code Justinian treats *furtum* as admitted, the doubt being as to *servi corrupti*. In the Institutes doubt is stated as to *furti*: none are said to have allowed *servi corrupti*.   [10] 11. 3. 14. 9.

the slave *inutilis sit* (? *fit*) *ut non expediat eum habere*, either to keep
the man with double damages for his deterioration, or to receive his
original value and hand him over (or if the man is absent, his rights of
action). The latter alternative is destroyed if the slave be dead or
freed. The rule is no doubt Tribonian's[1]. On the assumption in the
text that the slave is made worthless, the damage is his value, and the
choice is absurd: it is a choice between value and double value. Indeed
there is no case in which surrender and taking his original value would
be as profitable a course as the other[2].

Even if the slave be regarded purely as a chattel, it does not
follow, according to our modern ideas, that the owner's rights are quite
unlimited, and this may excuse the treatment in this chapter of
the restrictions which were imposed on the *dominus*.

During the Republic there was no legal limitation to the power of
the *dominus*: *iure gentium* his rights were unrestricted[3]. It must not,
however, be supposed that there was no effective protection. The
number of slaves was relatively small, till late in that era, and the
relation with the master far closer than it afterwards was. Moreover,
the power of the Censor was available to check cruelty to slaves, as
much as other misconduct. Altogether there is no reason to doubt
that slaves were on the whole well treated, during the Republic[4]. But
with the enormous increase of wealth and in number of slaves and the
accompanying degeneracy of private life, which characterised the early
empire, the case was changed. Legislation to prevent abuse of dominical power was inevitable, and the steps by which full protection for
the slave was reached are fairly fully recorded[5].

As early as A.D. 20 rules were laid down by senatusconsult, as to
trial of criminal slaves; the same procedure being ordered as in the
case of freemen[6].

By a *lex* Petronia[7], supplemented by *senatus consulta*, masters
were forbidden to punish their slaves by making them fight with
beasts even when they were plainly guilty, unless the cause had
been approved as sufficient by a magistrate. Rules of a kind similar
to those of our *lex* were laid down, later, by Divi Fratres: perhaps
only then was the rule applied to slaves whose guilt was manifest[8].

Claudius provided that if a master, to avoid the expense and trouble
of cure, exposed sick slaves on the island of Aesculapius, the slaves, if

---

[1] Lenel, Palingenesia, *ad h. l.*   [2] *Iniuria* to a slave, *post*, p. 79.
[3] 1. 6. 1. 1; G. 1. 52; In. 1. 8. 1. The Jewish law was more favourable to slaves: a result
of the " relative " nature of Jewish slavery. Winter, Stellung der Sklaven bei der Juden, 33.
[4] See Willems, Droit Public Romain, 288.
[5] See Blair, Slavery amongst the Romans, 83 *sqq.*   [6] 48. 2. 12. 3.
[7] 48. 8. 11. 1, 2; 12. 4. 15. As old as A.D. 79, since a record of it was found in Pompeii.
There was a Consul, Petronius, in A.D. 6. Karlowa identifies the law with a *lex* Junia Petronia
of A.D. 19, which provided that on equality of opinion in a *causa liberalis*, the claimant should
be declared free. Rom. Rechtsg. 1. 624.   [8] 18. 1. 42.

they recovered, should be free and Latins. From the language of the Code and Digest, it seems that mere abandonment in sickness had, at least in later usage, the same effect. Suetonius adds that if he killed such a slave, he was liable *caedis crimine*. But he is not a very exact writer and may have antedated this legislation[1].

Domitian forbade the castration of slaves for commercial purposes, and seems to have lessened the temptation to infringe the law, by fixing a low maximum price for *spadones*[2]. Later events shew that this legislation was ineffective[3].

Hadrian appears to have dealt frequently with these matters. He punished by five years *relegatio* a woman who cruelly treated her slaves for slight faults. He forbade masters to kill their slaves except after judgment by a magistrate. He forbade the torture of slaves, for evidence, until there was some case against the accused, and limited torture under the *Sc. Silanianum* to those slaves who were near enough to have heard what was doing. He suppressed private prisons (*ergastula*) both for slaves and freemen. He forbade the sale of men or women to *lenones* or to *lanistae* (purveyors for gladiatorial shows), without cause. He increased the severity of the laws against castration, by bringing it under the *lex* Cornelia, with a penalty of *publicatio*. It was immaterial whether it was *libidinis* or *promercii causa*: consent was no defence and the slave might lodge the complaint. It was capital in the surgeon and the slave who consented. Emasculation by other means was put on the same level, to prevent what had probably been a common way of evading the earlier law[4].

Antoninus Pius provided that a master who killed his slave was as liable for homicide as if it had been a third person's, a rule which seems to state only existing law except that it defines the penalty more clearly[5]. On the occasion of a complaint of ill-treatment reported to him by the *praeses*, from the *familia* of one Iulus Sabinus, he laid down a general rule for such cases. If a slave complaining of ill-treatment fled to *fana deorum* or the statue of the Emperor for sanctuary, the complaint must be enquired into, and, if it were true the slave was to be sold so that he should not return to the old master[6]. The ground might be either cruelty or *infamis iniuria*, which probably means attempt to debauch an *ancilla*. It was to go before *Pr. Urbi*, *Pr. Praetorio* or *Praeses*, according to locality. The

---

[1] 40. 8. 2; C. 7. 6. 1. 3. Suetonius, Claudius, 25.

[2] Suetonius, Domitian, 7. The penalty was apparently forfeiture of half the offender's goods. See 48. 8. 6, as to a *Sc.* on the matter. Other references, Blair, *op. cit.* 87.

[3] See *post*, p. 80, for an edict of the Aediles as to castration. See also *post*, Ch. xxvi.

[4] P. 5. 23. 13; Coll. 3. 3. 4; D. 1. 6. 2; 48. 8. 3. 4, 4. 2, 5; 48. 18. 3, 4; Spartian, Hadrianus, 18; Seneca, De Ira, 3. 40. *Ergastula* reappeared. Gothofredus, *ad* C. Th. 7. 13. 8.

[5] G. 1. 53. Paul, commenting presumably on this law, says that it must be *dolo malo*: killing is not always imputable but *modum castigandi et in servorum coercitione placuit temperari.* Coll. 3. 2. 1; P. 5. 23. 6; cp. P. 5. 23. 13.

[6] *Bonis conditionibus.* Not clear whether sale by master or public officers.

complaint was not to be considered as an *accusatio* of the master[1],
a rule which saved the master's reputation on the one hand, and
on the other prevented the institution from being an exception to the
rules that a slave cannot formally "accuse" anyone or be heard against
his master[2]. The rules as to jurisdiction may be due to later legislation by Severus[3].

Alexander expressed the tendency of legislation by a rescript[4] which,
in a case in which a master had in anger directed that a slave should be
perpetually bound, provided that the *arbiter familiae erciscundae* was
to ignore the provision, if the master could be shewn in any way to
have repented.

Diocletian and Maximian issued a rescript, in itself unimportant,
but suggesting that at that time (A.D. 285) immoderate chastisement
was a ground of accusation[5]. Constantine declared the master not
liable for killing in course of *bona fide* punishment, but guilty of
homicide if the death was caused by a wantonly cruel mode of
punishment, or the killing was merely wilful[6]. He also forbade the
exposure of infant slaves[7].

The *Codex Theodosianus* contains several enactments of about the
end of the fourth century, dealing with the right of sanctuary, and with
abuses and misuses which had crept in. They shew that Christian
churches had superseded *fana deorum* and also the statue of the
Emperor for this purpose[8], and they systematise the procedure.

Leo forbade slaves to be made actors against their will, and Justinian
forbade masters to prevent them from abandoning the stage if they wished
to do so. It is clear from the language of the Institutes that the power
of the master was in Justinian's time limited to reasonable castigation[9].

It is not necessary to give details as to the taxes to which slaves,
as chattels, were subject[10].

---

[1] G. 1. 53; In. 1. 8. 2; D. 1. 6. 1, 2; Coll. 3. 3. 1, 2.
[2] *Post*, p. 85. Except in claims to liberty and the above case of castration, this was the only
case in which a slave had access to the tribunals.
[3] 1. 12. 1. *pr.*, 1. 8. He also laid down rules against prostitution of slaves, *Ibid.* As to these
and sales with proviso against prostitution and as to torture of slaves as witnesses, *post*,
Chh. III *in fine*, XXVI. Prohibition of sale to go *ad bestias*, 18. 1. 42.
[4] C. 3. 36. 5.   [5] Coll. 3. 4.
[6] C. Th. 9. 12, 1. *h. t.* 2; C. 9. 14. 1. There were also ecclesiastical penalties.
[7] C. Th. 5. 9. 1. Abrogated and superseded by Justinian, who enacts similar rules, C. 8. 51.
[8] C. Th. 9. 44. 1, modified in C. 1. 25. 1; C. Th. 9. 45. 3, 4; C. 1. 12. 3.
[9] C. 1. 4. 14, 33; In. 1. 8. 2.
[10] Marquardt, Organisation Financière, Part 3. The old *tributum* applied to them as long as it
lasted. A similar *tributum* was exacted in the Empire from the provinces: there must be
professio of slaves as of other taxable property. Failure to make it involved forfeiture: torture
of slaves might be used to discover the truth. Forfeiture did not cover *peculia*, and a procurator
or one who had committed offences against his master, was not forfeited, for plain but different
reasons, but the Fisc took his value. The tax was due on those used in any business. The
professio must state nation, age and employment, misdescription involving forfeiture. A minor
was excused, and error might be compensated for by double tax (Caracalla, who also excused non
report of a trade carried on unlawfully by the man *insciente domino*). Succession duty was
payable on slaves as on other property. There were duties on sales, and on manumissions, and
there were customs dues, imperial and provincial, import and export, full *professio* being
needed with various exemptions. See 39. 4. *passim*; 50. 15. 4. 3, 5; 50. 16. 203; C. Th. 11. 3. 2;
13. 1. 18; 13. 4. 4; C. I. L. 8. 4508.

CHAPTER III.

THE SLAVE AS *RES* (CONT.). SALE OF SLAVES.

As Sale is, in practical life, the most frequent and important contract, it is not surprising that it figures largely in the texts in connexion with slaves, and is the subject, in that relation, of many special rules.

Slave-dealing was a recognised industry, carried on, apparently, by men of poor reputation[1]. It seems to have been on account of their tendency to fraud, which they may have shared with dealers in cattle and horses, that the Edict of the Aediles was introduced, with which we shall shortly deal. As being men, slaves were not included in the term *merces* and thus slave-dealers were not *mercatores*, but *venaliciarii*, their stock being called *venalicii*[2]. Where slaves were so numerous, the traffic in them must have been a most important industry[3]. There is indeed plenty of evidence of this, and of the fact that it was often carried on on a very large scale[4]. Wallon[5] gives a lively account of the usages of this trade, of the tricks of the dealers, of sale *de catasta*[6], and of other similar matters, too remotely connected with the law of the subject for mention here.

Such a business would require large capital, and thus it was frequently carried on by firms of partners. A text of Paul[7], speaking of the practice of these firms, says that *plerumque ita societatem coeunt ut quicquid agunt in commune videantur agere.* The sense of this is not altogether clear. Though expressed as an understanding among themselves, it seems from Paul's further language to have been treated as affecting outsiders[8]. The contract was to be construed as if they had

---

[1] 21. 1. 37; *h. t.* 44. 1.

[2] 14. 4. 1. 1; 50. 16. 207 (in some literary texts the dealer is called *venalicius*). The distinction is not important: the *actio tributoria* though it applied only to slaves who traded with *merx peculiaris* was extended to *omnes negotiationes*, including slave-dealing. 14. 4. 1. 1. It may be noted that a legacy of "my slaves" would not *prima facie* include stock-in-trade though it would slaves let on hire. 32. 73. 3. In 21. 1. 65. 2 and some literary texts *venalicium* occurs as a collective term.

[3] Blair, *op. cit.* 25, gives an account of the chief centres of the slave-trade.

[4] 17. 2. 60. 1.   [5] Wallon, Histoire de l'esclavage, 2. 51 *sqq.*; Blair, *op. cit.* 144 *sqq.*

[6] *i.e.* of slaves exposed for sale on a platform or in a sort of open cage so that they might be thoroughly examined by intending buyers.

[7] 21. 1. 44. 1.   [8] *ne cogeretur emptor cum multis litigare, etc.*

all made it, the effect being that the *actio ex empto* would lie, on the general principles of joint obligation, only *pro parte* against each partner[1]. It may be that, when introduced, this was of use to the buyer, for it may have antedated the *actio ad exemplum institoriae,* by which alone an ordinary mandator could be made directly liable[2]. Apparently the plan did not work very well, for the Aediles provided that, so far as the Edictal actions were concerned, a claimant might proceed *in solidum* against any partner whose share was as great as that of any other partner[3].

The rules as to *periculum rei venditae* were the same as in other cases[4]. There are, however, some cases of *interitus rei* which call for special treatment in connexion with slaves.

(*a*) Manumission of the slave. If he were a *servus alienus,* the manumission was presumably a discharge of the vendor, unless it was in some way due to him, in which case his *actio ex vendito* would be met by *exceptio doli*[5]. If the slave were the property of the vendor, the vendee could recover his value, and anything he would have acquired if the slave had been delivered. Thus if he had been sold, *cum peculio,* acquisitions and accretions to that fund could be claimed by the buyer. Julian adds that the vendor would have to give security to hand over whatever he might acquire from the *hereditas* of the *libertus.* Marcellus remarks that he need not hand over what he would not have acquired if the slave had not been freed[6]. As, in that case, there would clearly have been no *hereditas,* it has been said[7] that this correction or limitation by Marcellus of Julian's too general statement is meant to exclude, *inter alia,* the *hereditas.* Certainly Julian's rule would involve the reckoning of some property twice, since part of the *hereditas* would come from the *peculium* which was already charged. There seems to be some confusion. The right of succession as patron is independent of the gift of *peculium,* and thus if a claim to the *hereditas* exists at all, in the vendee, it exists whether the *peculium* were sold with the man or not. The vendor has made away with the slave, and is bound to account for any reversionary right in him. But this reversionary right would be deductible from the value of the slave, for which he was responsible. Difficulties would arise when the patron's share exceeded

---

[1] 21. 1. 44. 1.

[2] This action seems to date only from the time of Papinian (17. 1. 10. 5; 19. 1. 13. 25). See Accarias, Précis, § 637. It involved solidary liability, 14. 3. 13. 2.

[3] 21. 1. 44. 1. If he sued *ex empto,* the inconvenience, which Paul notes, of divided actions still continued. Paul gives as the reason of the exceptional rule the habitual sharp practice of these dealers.

[4] Death of slave after the contract was perfect released the vendor apart from *culpa,* but the price was due. But if the death resulted from his shewing less care than a *bonus paterfamilias* would, the vendor was liable. 18. 5. 5. 2. See Moyle, Law of Sale, 107.

[5] It may be that if the buyer did not know that the slave was a third person's this was enough to give him an *exceptio doli.*

[6] 19. 1. 23.   [7] Mackintosh, Law of Sale, *ad h. l.*

the value of the slave.   It is not easy to think this excess was claimable, but it may be that Julian is applying the rule that a vendor must hand over all acquisitions through what is sold.

(*b*) Noxal Surrender.   This could ordinarily create no difficulty, for as we shall shortly see, the vendor was bound to warrant the slave not liable on any delict, and thus there was an obvious remedy[1].   If, on the other hand, he had expressly excluded this warranty, he would be liable, if he had known of the fact, and intentionally concealed it, on account of the fraud.   If he did not know of it, there could be no liability, except under the Edictal rules which will be considered shortly.

(*c*) Flight or Theft of the slave.   This is not exactly *interitus rei*, but, as it prevents delivery, it is analogous thereto.   The mere fact of his running away would be no breach of the warranty that he was not given to doing so; that refers to the time of the contract; this was later, and did not shew that he had ever fled before[2].   But flight or theft of the man may be a breach of the duty of the vendor to keep him safely.   Justinian tells us that, in such events, there is no liability in the vendor unless he has undertaken the duty of *custodia* till delivery[3].   This means, apparently, liability for all but *damnum fatale*, and thus does not render him liable if the man is seized by force, though he will have to cede his actions, as always when he is not liable[4].   Justinian applies this rule to all subjects of sale[5].

It is a general rule of sale that, apart from agreement, the vendor must hand over, with the thing sold, all its accessories existing at the time of sale[6].   In relation to slaves it is only necessary to say that this would not include children already born since they are not accessories[7].   On the other hand though the *peculium* was an accessory[8], it was said to be *exceptum*, and did not pass unless expressly agreed for; if the man took *res peculiares* with him, these could be recovered[9].

Acquisitions after the sale are on a somewhat different position. The general rule was that a vendor might not enrich himself through the man after the sale, whether delivery was due or not[10].   Hence, from that day, *fructus* of all kinds and *partus* must be given to the buyer[11]. Everything acquired by him must go, including rights of action for theft, *vi bonorum raptorum*, damage, and the like, and any actions

---

[1] *Post*, p. 56.
[2] 21. 1. 54, 58. 2; 21. 2. 3.   But see Windscheid, Lehrbuch, § 389.
[3] In. 3. 23. 3.
[4] 19. 1. 31. *pr.*; 18. 1. 35, 4; 47. 2. 14. *pr.*; In. 3. 23. 3.   Accarias, Précis, § 612.
[5] Cp. 19. 1. 31. *pr.*   We have seen (p. 11) that in earlier law the limits of the duty of *custodia* where the subject of the transaction was a slave were not necessarily the same as in other cases. On the general rules as to the liability of the vendor for *custodia* see Windscheid, *op. cit.* § 389; Lusignani, Custodia, pt. II.
[6] 18. 1. 67.   [7] 30. 62, 63.   [8] *Ibid.*
[9] 18. 1. 29; 21. 2. 3.   If the *peculium* did pass accessories to it passed as of course, 19. 1. 13. 13.
[10] 28. 5. 38. 5; V. Fr. 15.   [11] P. 2. 17. 7.

relative to property which goes with him[1]. Anything the vendor has given him, since the sale, must go too, and legacies and inheritances which have fallen to him, irrespective of the question on whose account he was instituted[2]. If the *peculium* was sold with him, the buyer is entitled to all accessions to it[3]. On these points the only restrictions to note are, that, though acquisitions *ex operis* pass, that which is acquired *ex re venditoris* does not, and that an agreement might be made, where delivery was deferred, that the buyer should have no right to *fructus*, etc., accruing in the interval[4]. If a sale was conditional, the occurrence of the condition had a retrospective effect in relation to these profits[5].

Neratius tells us that the vendor must make good not only what he has received, but also what the buyer would have received through the man if he had been delivered[6]. As this seems to impose a penalty on the vendor, it is commonly understood as applying only to the case in which the vendor has made default in delivery[7], and must therefore account for the buyer's whole *interesse*, which would naturally cover what the slave might have acquired[8]. The limitation is probably correct, for though the text might be applied to the case of a vendor who, for instance, prevents the man from accepting a legacy, this seems to be sufficiently provided for by the general rule against *dolus*.

A somewhat complex case is discussed by Julian, Marcian and Marcellus[9]. A slave, having been sold, was instituted by the buyer, equally with X. The buyer died before the slave was delivered. The vendor made the slave enter, and X also entered. This would vest in X half the inheritance, including half the vendee's right to the slave and his acquisitions. The slave's entry makes the vendor owner of half the inheritance, and he is still owner of the slave. What is to be the ultimate adjustment? The solution reached is stated by Marcellus. As the vendor is bound to hand over all that he would not have acquired if the slave had been delivered, he must hand over the whole. Julian, however, after observing that the vendor may not enrich himself through such a slave, had added that he need only hand over the proportion for which X was instituted, *i.e.* as Marcian says, half the slave and a quarter of the *hereditas*, this being what X could claim through the right to half the slave which he acquired as heir. But this view ignores the

---

[1] 47. 2. 14. *pr.*; In. 3. 23. 3.   [2] 19. 1. 13. 18.
[3] 19. 1. 13. 13.   [4] *Ibid.*; *h. t.* 13. 18.
[5] 18. 3. 4. *pr.*, *h. t.* 6. *pr.*   In two texts (19. 1. 13. 10; V. Fr. 15) we are told that fruits passed though they were ripe at the time of the contract. This would not cover earnings made but not paid to the *dominus* at the time of the sale. They were not attached to the slave as a crop is to the land. The right of action being already in the *dominus* there is no enrichment after the sale. Paul says the *operae* belong to the buyer after the sale. This cannot mean proceeds of earlier *operae*. P. 2. 17. 7.
[6] 19. 1. 31. 1.   [7] Mackintosh, Sale, *ad h. l.*
[8] 19. 1. 1. 1.   [9] 28. 5. 38. 5—40.

fact that if the slave had been delivered, his institution would have been void, and all would have gone to X[1].

The rule that he acquires to his *dominus* (though the acquisitions will have to be handed over to the buyer) was applied rigidly in cases in which another rule would have seemed simpler. If the buyer receives the slave but it is agreed that he shall hold him only as conductor till the price is paid, the man acquires to his *dominus* in the interval[2].

As the vendor has to hand over all *fructus,* he is entitled to deduct expenses. Thus he may charge such costs of training as the vendee would be likely to have incurred, and the cost of medical treatment[3]. Ordinary cost of maintenance he may not charge unless the non-delivery is imputable to the buyer[4].

Africanus discusses a case of debt from the slave to the master[5]. The slave has stolen something from the master. If he is not yet delivered and the *peculium* is included in the sale, the vendor may retain the value of the stolen thing, and, if the *peculium* has been handed over, he may recover it as paid in excess, the *peculium* having been *ipso facto* reduced by that amount. If there was no *peculium,* or it did not pass, there would be no debt, for that was essential to all debt between *dominus* and slave[6]. If the theft were after the slave was delivered, then, on general principle, the buyer would be liable to *condictio furtiva* only in so far as he or the *peculium* had received the thing[7].

Except as to eviction and the Aedilician actions[8], the texts do not lay down many principles, as to liability under the contract, which are peculiar to slaves, though there are illustrations of ordinary principle. Thus we know that the vendor must take care of the thing, and the question is raised whether he is liable if, after the sale, he orders the man to do some dangerous work by which he is injured. Labeo says that he is, if it is a thing he was not in the habit of doing. Paul points out that the vendor's previous treatment may have been negligent, and that the question is, whether the direction was negligent or dolose[9].

---

[1] The facts are insufficiently recorded, but the institution can hardly have been accompanied by a gift of liberty. The will may or may not have been made before the purchase. The difficulties are analogous to those in Jones *v.* Hensler, 19 Ch. D. 612.

[2] 18. 6. 17. It may be, though the text is not explicit, that such an agreement implied an understanding that the buyer was to have no right in these interim acquisitions.

[3] Cp. 19. 1. 13. 18. We are told that, if the slave die without fault of the vendor, the buyer may be charged with cost of funeral.

[4] 19. 1. 38. 1. In other cases he may be expected to set off this with the services he can still claim from the man. For though he must hand over *fructus,* it does not appear that he need charge himself with the value of services rendered to himself.

[5] 19. 1. 30. *pr.*   [6] *Post,* Ch. xxix.   [7] 19. 1. 30. *pr.*

[8] The Edict of the Aediles may have contained a provision that on sale of a slave his dress passed, but not *ornamenta.* The chief text is 50. 16. 74, compared with 34. 2. 25. 10. Lenel, Paling. 2. 1177; Ed. Perp. § 293, 12 (Fr. Edit.). Bremer (Jurisp. Antehad. 2. 546) thinks the rule connected with a corresponding rule in Jewish law. The Jews were great slave-dealers. There was a somewhat similar rule in sales of cattle, 21. 1. 38. *pr.* Lenel cites also 34. 2. 23, 24, 25. 9; 15. 1. 25.   [9] 19. 1. 54. *pr.*

Apart from the Edict of the Aediles the vendor was not liable for defects unless he had warranted or was guilty of *dolus*[1]. Several texts illustrate this *dolus*. It was dolose to sell, knowing of a serious defect, of which the buyer was ignorant, *e.g.* that the man was *fur aut noxius*[2]. The text adds that the buyer can sue at once, though before he could sue on the *stipulatio duplae* actual damage must have occurred[3]. It was dolose to say recklessly of a man, who was in fact a thief, that he was worthy of entire confidence[4]. Liability is, in the text, based on the view that one who recklessly makes statements which are not true, is in much the same moral position as one who is silent as to defects of which he is aware. It would seem simpler to treat it as a binding *dictum*[5].

Where a vendor sold a *mulier* knowing that the buyer supposed the woman a *virgo*, this was *dolus*, a rule severer than that of English law[6].

One case is somewhat remarkable. Paul tells us that if a woman, whose *partus* is sold, is over 50, or is sterile, the vendor is liable *ex empto* if the buyer did not know that this was so[7]. Whether this is sale of a *spes* or of a *res sperata* the agreement is void, but it is not easy to see why the vendor should be under any liability unless he knew the facts, which is not stated, and is certainly not a matter of course. It may be that the price has been paid, and all that is meant is that he can recover this. For that, a *condictio indebiti* would suffice[8], and there is some contradiction in allowing *ex empto* when there is no contract. But this was allowed at least as early as Julian's time, in some other cases[9]. Even if the vendor knew the facts, there was no sale[10], so that in this case, too, the contradiction remains. But here the buyer could no doubt recover any expenses incurred.

It is clear on the evidence of many texts that at least some of the duties created by the Aediles, and therefore, strictly, enforceable only by the Aedilician actions, were nevertheless brought within the action *ex empto* in the classical law[11]. The course of ideas seems to have been that these edicts imposed certain duties and it was the duty of a vendor to act in good faith. It was not good faith to fail in duties which were

---

[1] Or perhaps if the defect was so great that the buyer would not have bought, if he had known of it. See 19. 1. 11. 3, 5. But these texts may be affected by the rules of the Edict. Cp. *post*, p. 45, and *h. t.* 13. *pr.*

[2] 19. 1. 4. *pr.* The words *fur* and *noxius* are usually understood to mean "under some present liability for delict." But they may well mean no more than that he is given to such things. Anything more is not necessary for the rule. In 19. 1. 13. 1, *fur* certainly means only given to stealing. *Post*, p. 45.

[3] Cf. 19. 1. 31.

[4] 19. 1. 13. 3. It is not obvious why there was doubt, unless on the ground that it was mere puffery not binding on the vendor (21. 1. 19. 3). But this is difficult to reconcile with the strong word *adseverare*.

[5] *Ibid.*   [6] 19. 1. 11. 5.   Smith *v.* Hughes, L.R. 6 Q. B. 597.

[7] 19. 1. 21. *pr.*   [8] 12. 6. 37; *h. t.* 54; 18. 1. 57. *pr.*

[9] Pernice, Labeo, 2. 1. 181.   [10] 18. 1. 57. 1.

[11] *e.g.* 19. 1. 11. 7. See Moyle, Sale, 191, 213.

notorious, and therefore, the action *ex empto* being *bonae fidei*, neglect of these duties was actionable therein[1]. When this step was taken is uncertain. It is at least as old as Neratius[2], and may be older, since a corresponding extension of the Aedilician actions to sales other than those contemplated in the Edict is held by some writers to be as old as Labeo[3]. The one extension does not imply the other : it is likely that the one with which we are concerned was the later, that it was a gradual development, and that it was never complete. It probably never went so far as to give redhibition in the *actio ex empto*, wherever the *actio redhibitoria* would have lain[4]. It is sometimes held, on logical grounds, that in these extended cases, the claim was subject to the short term of limitation prescribed by the Aediles[5]. In support of this view it may be noted that the vendor's liability, *ex empto*, for defects of which he was ignorant, was applied only to defects covered by the Edict[6]. But there is no direct evidence that the time-limit was the same.

The texts give us many cases of sales of slaves in which the Edictal liabilities are made the basis of the *actio ex empto*[7]. Neratius tells us that a vendor, even in good faith, is liable *ex empto* to deliver a slave who is not *fugitivus*[8], which here means *fugax*, not one who is at this moment a runaway from his master. This merely expresses the fact that this was one of the warranties required by the Aediles. In another text, of Ulpian, it is said that if one sells, in ignorance, a slave who is, in fact, given to stealing or running away, one is not liable *ex empto* for his stealing propensity, but is for his tendency to flight. The reason given by the text is that *fugitivum habere non licet et quasi evictionis nomine tenetur dominus*[9]. The reason is unintelligible, and is in fact omitted by the Basilica[10]. There is nothing like eviction. It is as lawful to have a slave who is in the habit of running away as any other slave. There is a confusion between a *fugax* and an actual runaway. The reasoning given is probably Tribonian's: the true explanation is that the Aediles gave a remedy where a slave sold was fugacious[11], but not, apart from special agreement, where he was addicted to theft[12].

The *actio ex empto* may be left with the remark that in such actions the plaintiff recovered *quanti interest*, and that in the case of slaves this might be damages of a kind not possible in other cases[13].

---

[1] 21. 1. 31. 20. For references to the extensive literature hereon, see Windscheid, *op. cit.* § 393, n. 1.   [2] 19. 1. 11. 7, 8.
[3] Moyle, *op. cit.* 194. Also at p. 213, as to a text which seems to carry this extension back to Labeo.
[4] Moyle, *loc. cit.*   [5] Windscheid, *op. cit.* § 393, n. 12.
[6] 21. 1. 1. 10 *fin.* is explained by *h. l.* 9.   [7] *Post*, p. 63.
[8] 19. 1. 11. 7. In the next text he tells us that the vendor must give him *furtis noxiisque solutus*, being bound *ex empto*, even in the sale of a *servus alienus*, to give security covering this. The point is the same : the Aediles required a warranty.
[9] 19. 1. 13. 1.   [10] Bas. 19. 8. 13. 1.   [11] *Post*, p. 55.
[12] 21. 1. 1. 1, 17. 1, 17. 17, 52. See as to measure of damages, in these cases, *post*, p. 63.
[13] Thus it would cover costs and damages in a noxal action and the value of what he took with him and of others he induced to run away, 19. 1. 11. 12, 13. 2.

In connexion with eviction we shall consider in detail only those points which are of special importance in relation to slaves. The duty of a vendor, to give the buyer effective possession, implies a duty to compensate him, if the title proves defective. Before and after the development of the consensual contract of sale, it was the custom to guarantee this by a stipulation for twice the value (*stipulatio duplae*). This stipulation was from early times compulsory in all sales of importance, and, in the classical law, it was implied where it had been omitted[1]. The eviction contemplated in this liability is deprivation of the thing by one with a better title. The buyer is bound to give the vendor notice of the adverse claim, and to take all reasonable steps in defence of his right. Failure to satisfy these requirements will deprive him of his claim against the vendor.

In sale of slaves the *stipulatio duplae* in case of eviction was expressly required by the Edict of the Aediles[2]. This did not prevent its exclusion by agreement: it might be excluded altogether[3], or made for less or more than *duplum*[4], or limited to the acts of the vendor and those claiming under him[5]. A question of some difficulty arose where the eviction penalty was wholly or partly excluded. The liability to compensate, enforced by the *actio ex empto*, existed apart from the stipulation, *e.g.* in minor[6] sales. It is not clear whether it was excluded by the existence of the *stipulatio duplae* : but there seems no reason why they should not be alternatives[7]. If there was an agreement excluding the eviction penalty, or limiting it to eviction by the vendor, and eviction by a third person took place, there was disagreement whether anything could be claimed by the action *ex empto*[8]. Julian appeared to think the price must be refunded : the convention by which a man bound himself to pay, though he got nothing, being inconsistent with a *bonae fidei* transaction. But it is easy to see cases in which a buyer might take the risk, and Julian answers his own objection by citing the case of an *emptio spei*. Accordingly Ulpian decides that the *actio ex empto* will not lie, clearly the fairer view. For the risk was reckoned in the price, and there is no good faith in charging the vendor indirectly with what has been expressly excluded.

---

[1] On the history of the institution, see Moyle, Sale, 110—115; Mackintosh, Sale, Ed. 2, App. C; Lenel, Ed. Perp. (French Edition), 2. 288 *sqq.*; Girard, Manuel, 553, and articles there mentioned. As to eviction of a part or of a usufruct in the thing, *post*, p. 50.

[2] 21. 2. 37. 1. No *fideiussor* needed except by express agreement, 21. 2. 4; *h. t.* 37. As to apparent contradiction in 19. 1. 11. 9, see Accarias, Précis, § 606.

[3] 21. 2. 37. *pr.*   [4] 21. 2. 56. *pr.*

[5] 19. 1. 11. 18.   [6] C. 8. 44. 6.

[7] Cuq, *op. cit.* 2. 411, thinks the liability to action *ex empto* a gradual development. It seems essential to the conception of the consensual contract of Sale, 21. 2. 60; cp. 21. 1. 19. 2; C. 8. 44. 6, 8. See also 21. 2. 26 and *post*, p. 47, n. 9.

[8] 19. 1. 11. 15, 18. In 15 the agreement was to promise, if asked within 30 days, which was not demanded. Of course the vendor is liable for *dolus*, if he knew the slave was *alienus*.

The two actions differ in nature and effect in many ways[1]. Here it is enough to note a few points. The action on the stipulation could be brought only when eviction had actually occurred[2], while the *actio ex empto* might anticipate the interference[3]. The *actio* on the stipulation is for a certain sum, usually twice the price : that *ex empto* is for *quanti interest*. This will include *partus* born of an *ancilla*, a *hereditas* left to the slave and other accessions[4]. Moreover if the thing alters in value, its value at the time of the eviction is the measure of the *interesse*, whether it be more or less than the price[5].

We have seen that, to give a basis for the action on stipulation, an actual eviction must have occurred. This means, in general, that some person has substantiated a claim to take the slave from the buyer, and he has in some way satisfied the claim so that he is deprived of what he bargained for[6]. The usual case is that of adverse ownership, but, where the subject was a slave, eviction might occur in special ways. Thus, if a *statuliber* were sold without notice of his status, the occurrence of the condition would be an eviction[7]. So if the slave sold were one whom the vendor was under a *fideicommissum* to free[8]. So, if he proved to have been free at the time of the sale[9]. It might be supposed that a noxal claim was an eviction, and there is no doubt that it gave rise to an *actio ex empto* to recover the minimum sum by which the liability could be discharged[10]. The text adds that the same is true of the action *ex stipulatu*. This cannot refer to the *stipulatio* relative to eviction, since that was for a certain sum. The stipulation referred to is the action on the warranty against certain defects, of which noxal liability was one, which, as we shall shortly see, a buyer could exact. It seems therefore that, as the noxal claim did not necessarily lead to eviction, but involved damages of uncertain amount[11], it was the practice to proceed *ex empto*, or under the warranty last mentioned. This could not be done in the case of crime, for the Edict as to *noxae* did not cover crimes[12]. A somewhat similar state of things arose where the property

---

[1] Roby, Rom. Priv. Law, 2. 156 *sqq.*
[2] 21. 2. 16. 1; C. 8. 44. 3. [3] *Arg.* 19. 1. 4. *pr.*, 30. 1, 35. [4] 21. 2. 8.
[5] 19. 1. 45. If the value had greatly increased, *e.g.* a slave had been expensively trained, Paul thought a limit should be imposed, perhaps a *taxatio*, 19. 1. 43. Julian and Africanus had discussed the matter: Africanus is credited with the view that the maximum should be double the price, the result being thus brought into line with that of the action of stipulation. This does not seem to have been law till Justinian laid it down in a text which says there had been disputes. *h. t.* 45. *pr.*, *h. t.* 44; C. 7. 47. 1.
[6] Moyle, *op. cit.* 112. [7] 21. 2. 39. 4, 51. 1. Fuller treatment *post*, Ch. XIII.
[8] 21. 2. 26. *Post*, Chh. XIII, XXII. *Ex empto*, but perhaps no *actio duplae*, because the manumission though compelled was the buyer's own act.
[9] 21. 2. 19. 1; *h. t.* 39. 3, 69. *pr.*; C. 8. 44. 12, 18, 25. If the slave sold had been guilty of some capital offence, his condemnation would not be an eviction, but, whenever it occurred, it would entitle the buyer, under the *Sc.* Pisonianum, to a return of the price. 29. 5. 8. *pr.* As to sale of *statuliber*, *post*, Ch. XIII.
[10] 19. 1. 11. 12.
[11] *Post*, p. 98. Cf. 19. 1. 4. *pr.*, *antequam mihi quid abesset.*
[12] 21. 1. 17. 18, *post*, p. 99.

was taken by a pledge creditor, by an *actio* Serviana. Here, however, recovery was held to be eviction[1]. The difference is remarkable, since the creditor's action does not affect the buyer's ownership, and indeed we are told that, if the debtor pays the debt, since the buyer is now entitled to have the slave again, his action on eviction against his vendor, (the debtor,) will be met by an *exceptio doli*[2]. Thus the difference of treatment seems to be due to the fact that there is no liability on the buyer to pay, as there is in noxal cases. No doubt he could do so if he wished, and recover *ex empto*, up to the value of the slave.

It was essential to any claim that the buyer had taken proper steps to defend his title. Thus the right was lost if he had colluded with the claimant[3]. Moreover if the *condemnatio* was due to *iniuria iudicis* there was no claim against the vendor[4]. On the other hand, if there was no doubt about the justice of the claim, it does not appear to have been necessary to incur costs, in fighting the matter through: the buyer would not lose his right by admitting the plaintiff's claim[5]. Failure to recover the man from one who had taken him was equivalent to deprival[6]. If, however, he paid for the man, not under pressure of litigation, but buying him from the real owner, he has not been evicted and is thrown back on his remedy *ex empto*[7]. So also, if after the sale he acquires an independent title to the slave, there has technically been no eviction, and the only remedy is *ex empto*[8].

It has been pointed out that these requirements lead to odd results[9]. To claim, as a slave, a man you know to be free, is an *iniuria*, but if it be done to preserve an eviction claim this is a defence[10]. And while a promise to give a man who is in fact free is null[11], a promise to compensate for eviction on sale of one is good[12]. The reason seems to be that the rule of nullity, being *iuris civilis*, was not extended to collateral transactions connected with valid contracts. The sale being valid, the validity of the dependent obligation necessarily followed[13]. If, while

---

[1] 21. 2. 35.

[2] *Ibid.* The right of action is not destroyed: *semel commissa stipulatio resolvi non potest.*

[3] Vat. Fr. 8. Or neglected the defence (21. 2. 27) or failed to notify the vendor or his successors of the claim (21. 2. 51. 1, 53. 1) a reasonable time before the condemnation (21. 1. 29. 2). This text shews that the stipulation contained a proviso for notice. But as this is inconsistent with the rule that not to give notice was *dolus* and thus barred the claim (29. 2. 53. 1) it may be that the proviso was inserted in that particular case. For detail as to notice, Moyle, Sale, 117 *sqq.* Lenel thinks the Edict expressly required notice (Ed. Perp. § 296, Fr. Edit.). It applied equally in *ex empto*, C. 8. 44. 8, 20, 29.

[4] Vat. Fr. 8, 10; 21. 2. 51. *pr.*, etc.

[5] 19. 1. 11. 12. See however 47. 10. 12. Conversely the fact of his retaining the slave did not bar his claim if he paid damages in lieu of delivery 21. 2. 16. 1; *h. t.* 21. 2.

[6] 21. 2. 16. 1. [7] 21. 2. 29. *pr.*

[8] 19. 1. 13. 15; 21. 1. 41. 1. If the vendor himself acquire the title and sue on it, he can presumably be met by an *exceptio doli*, or the buyer can let judgment go and sue for *duplum* 21. 2. 17.

[9] Accarias, Précis, § 607 *bis.* [10] 47. 10. 12.

[11] In. 3. 19. 2. [12] *Ante*, p. 47, n. 9.

[13] Different reason, Accarias, *loc. cit.*

the claim against the buyer is pending, the slave runs away through his *culpa*, he will be condemned[1], but Ulpian quotes Julian to the effect that he cannot yet claim on eviction, for he lost the slave through his own fault. When he gets the fugitive back he can proceed, for it is now true that he has lost the value of the slave through defect of title.

Apart from agreement the liability for eviction is subject to no limit of time[2]. There are, however, certain circumstances which end it.

(*a*) After the buyer has usucapted the slave there can be no further liability for eviction so far as outstanding ownership is concerned[3], and if he has failed so to acquire the slave, when he could have done so, it is his own fault, and he has no claim against the vendor[4]. But, as we have seen, this was no protection against liability for eviction on other grounds, nor could it occur where the slave was *furtivus*.

(*b*) Death of the slave before eviction. Here Ulpian, following Julian, says that, as the loss is not due to the defect of title, the liability on the *stipulatio duplae* does not arise[5]. In fact there has been no eviction, and as no loss resulted from the defect of title, there could be no *actio ex empto* either. This appears from the concluding words of the text, which give *actio doli* if the vendor was in bad faith, implying that there was no other action[6]. There is damage in the sense in which this action requires it. The *actio ex empto* is to put the buyer so far as possible where he would be if the vendor had kept his contract. The *actio doli* puts him where he would be if the dolose act had not occurred: *i.e.*, he can recover the price. If the death occurs after *litis contestatio* in an action against the buyer, the action will proceed, and if the judgment is against the buyer, he will have the eviction claim[7].

(*c*) Manumission after the sale by the buyer. He cannot now claim on the stipulation, since he has abandoned his right to the slave, and so did not lose him by the eviction. So far the law is clear[8]. And the same result follows if the slave became free by any act of the buyer's, whether it was intended to have that effect or not[9]. There was disagreement as to whether the *actio ex empto* was still available. Paul quotes Ulpian's view that it was lost, but himself adopts that of Julian,

[1] 6. 1. 45. If the flight was not through his *culpa* and he was absolved on giving security, the right to claim would not arise till he had recovered the man and given him or damages instead, 21. 2. 21. 3.
[2] C. 8. 44. 21. If he has undertaken to promise *duplum*, he can be required to do so at any time, by the *actio ex empto*. So if the man sold was a *statuliber*, the liability for eviction arises however long it is before the condition is satisfied, 21. 2. 56; 21. 2. 39. 4.
[3] 21. 2. 54. *pr.*   [4] 21. 2. 56. 3.
[5] 21. 2. 21; C. 8. 44. 26.   [6] 4. 3. 1. 1.
[7] 6. 1. 16. *pr.* If the claim were one of liberty, Justinian allowed the buyer to call on the vendor to shew that the dead man was a slave: if he did not the eviction claim arose, C. 7. 17. 2. 3.
[8] 19. 1. 43; 21. 2. 25; 21. 1. 47. *pr.*
[9] *e.g.* where the sale was with a condition against prostitution (*post*, p. 70) and the buyer prostituted her, 21. 2. 34. We have seen that eviction did not always turn on defect of title.

i.e. that it was still available[1]. It may be that, as Paul elsewhere says, the remedy is still extant, but only so far as to enable the buyer to recover his *interesse* in the man as a *libertus*[2]. This he has in no way abandoned. It is hardly necessary to say that sale of the man does not destroy the right. If the original buyer is evicted after he has sold, he is liable for non-delivery, which is enough to entitle him[3]. On the other hand, abandonment of the man (*pro derelicto habere*) is abandonment of the right[4].

We have now to consider cases in which the eviction is not deprivation of ownership. If all that was sold was a right less than ownership, and this was evicted, the foregoing rules apply[5]. More detail is necessary where what is evicted is not the buyer's whole right. Several cases must be considered.

(i) Where a pledge creditor claims the slave, by *actio* Serviana (or presumably, by *actio quasi* Serviana). Here, as we have already seen, there was an eviction, and the action on the stipulation was available[6].

(ii) Where an outstanding usufruct is claimed from the buyer. Here, too, the texts make it clear that it was an ordinary case of eviction, giving the *actio ex stipulatione duplae*, with the ordinary requirement of notice[7]. Here, as in many parts of the law, usufruct and pledge are placed on the same level. The conditions are indeed much the same : though the deprival may not be permanent, there is for the time being a breach of the duty, *habere frui licere praestare*, out of which these rules as to eviction grew. The case of outstanding *Usus* is not discussed : on principle the decision should be the same[8]. It must be added that the amount recovered would be arrived at by considering what proportion of the total value would be represented by the usufruct, and doubling that proportion of the price[9].

(iii) Where, of several slaves sold, one is evicted. No difficulty arises : each is regarded as the subject of a separate stipulation[10]. We do not hear how the price is fixed if they had been sold at a lump price[11].

(iv) Where an undivided part is evicted. It seems clear on the texts that where a divided part of a piece of land sold was evicted the *actio ex stipulatione duplae* lay[12]. This rule looks rational, but it is not

---

[1] 19. 1. 43. [2] 21. 2. 26, read *ex empto*. [3] 21. 2. 33.
[4] 21. 2. 76. [5] 21. 2. 10; *h. t.* 46. 2. [6] 21. 2. 34. 2, 35. *Ante*, p. 48.
[7] 21. 2. 43, 46, 49, 62. 2. So where the existence of a usufruct was stated but the name of fructuary was wrongly given, 21. 2. 39. 5.
[8] It is a breach of the duty *habere licere praestare*. Accarias, Précis, § 608, thinks eviction of usufruct did not give rise to the action on stipulation as of course but only if specially agreed for.
[9] 21. 2. 15. 1. Mode of estimation 35. 2. 68; Roby, de usufructu, 188 *sqq*. If after this eviction there was an eviction of the ownership, the amount already recovered would be deducted, 21. 2. 48.
[10] 21. 2. 32. *pr.*, 72. [11] As to this, cp. p. 67.
[12] The amount recoverable would be double the part of the total price which the part represented, by division if sold at *per iugerum*, quality being taken into account in other cases, 21. 2. 1, 13, 53.

a necessary result of principle, and it may be a late development. All the texts which explicitly lay it down are from Paul, Ulpian, and Papinian[1]. It is possible on the language of a text from Callistratus that there may still have been doubts[2].

In the case of an undivided part, there is difficulty. Ulpian appears to put all and either kind of part on the same level[3]. Papinian gives the *actio duplae* on eviction of an undivided part[4]. Pomponius[5] says what comes to the same thing. A buys a slave. X brings *iudicium communi dividundo*, and the slave, proving common, is adjudicated to him. Pomponius gives A the *actio duplae*. It is clear that he has lost only a half; for he must have received an equivalent for the other half. Julian says that a liability for eviction arises, but it is possible that this refers only to *actio ex empto*[6], though in other parts of the text he is speaking of the *actio duplae*. On the other hand Paul expressly says that as eviction of an undivided part is not eviction of the man, it is necessary to provide expressly for eviction of the part[7]. It may be noticed that in all the mancipations of slaves by way of sale, of which a record has come down to us[8], the stipulation says *partemve*. It is clear that the case differs from that of a divided part in that there is no necessary loss of actual possession, and it is possible to harmonise the texts, by assuming that in all the cases in which *actio duplae* is here mentioned, the clause *partemve* was inserted. This may be regarded as partly borne out by the fact, otherwise surprising, that we have much earlier authority than in the other case: *i.e.* Pomponius, and perhaps Julian. But it must be admitted that nothing in the form of the texts suggests this. On the whole it seems more likely that the jurists were not agreed, and that their disagreement has been allowed to survive into the Digest.

(v) Accessories, fruits and *partus*. The rule seems to be that so far as they are expressly mentioned the ordinary liability arises. But, if they are not mentioned, there is no liability. Thus where a slave was sold *cum peculio*, and a *vicarius* was evicted, the buyer had no claim, since if he did not belong to the man he was not covered by the words *cum peculio*[9]. As to acquisitions and *partus* of the slave coming into existence *apud emptorem*, it is clear that the *stipulatio* can give no right if the slave is evicted, for no more than *duplum pretium* can be recovered by it in any case. But the question may arise where, for instance, the slave is dead

---

pr., 64. 3.   Materials of a house in existence form an apparent exception: we are told that as they are not sold eviction of them is not *partis evictio* (21. 2. 36). This view of the house and the materials as distinct led to difficulty in other matters (In. 2. 1. 29 *sq.*). We are told elsewhere that *ex empto* is available (41. 3. 23. 1). This implies that they are sold and puts them on a level with those accessories that pass with a house (19. 1. 13, 31. 15).

[1] 21. 2. 1, 13, 14, 15, 53. *pr.*, 64.   *H. t.* 45 is from Alfenus, epitomised and noted by Paul.
[2] 21. 2. 72.   [3] 21. 2. 1.   [4] 21. 1. 64. *pr.*
[5] 21. 2. 34. 1.   [6] 21. 2. 39. 2.   [7] 21. 2. 56. 2.
[8] Bruns, Fontes, i. 288 *sqq.*; Girard, Textes, 806 *sqq.*   [9] 21. 2. 5.

or has been freed before the question of title crops up. It is clear, on Julian's authority, that eviction of later acquisitions gave a right of action *ex empto*, because the vendor was bound *praestare* what could be acquired through the slave. Julian applies this to *partus* and such things as *hereditas*[1]. No doubt it is equally true of earnings, for the vendor is bound to hand over all he has received[2]; and one whose delivery has been vitiated by eviction is as if he had not delivered at all[3]. He holds this view though Ulpian quotes him as not holding that the *partus* and *fructus* were sold[4]. We have seen, however, that for some purposes at least he puts them on the same level as if they were sold: for him and Papinian they are acquired by the same *titulus* both for usucapion and in relation to the rule in legacy as to *duae lucrativae causae*[5]. But it does not appear that either he or any other jurist allowed the *actio duplae* for *partus* and *fructus*; though it seems that some had taken the not very hopeful line that as eviction of *usus-fructus* gave the right, eviction of *fructus* ought to do so as well. But Julian observes that the word *fructus* here denotes not a right but a physical thing[6].

The law as to liability of the vendor for defects in the thing sold was completely remodelled by the Edict of the Aediles. The comprehensive enactments stated in the Digest were undoubtedly a gradual development. In its earliest known form the rule of the Edict was a much simpler matter. It was a direction that on sales of slaves an inscription should be affixed setting forth any *morbus* or *vitium* of the slave, and announcing the fact, if the slave was *fugitivus* or *erro* or *noxa non solutus*, allowing redhibition or *actio quanto minoris* according to circumstances[7]. It applied apparently only to sales in open market. As recorded by Ulpian, perhaps from Labeo[8], the Edict is not limited in application to sales in open market, and the requirement of inscription is replaced by one of declaration. Moreover it enumerates certain other kinds of defect and it makes the vendor equally liable for any express warranty whether it refers to one of

---

[1] 21. 2. 8.   [2] *Ante*, pp. 41 *sqq.*   [3] 19. 1. 3. *pr.*
[4] 18. 2. 4. 1.   [5] 30. 82. 4; 31. 73. *Ante*, p. 24.
[6] 21. 2. 42, 43. In discussing eviction we have said nothing of its connexion with the *actio in duplum* against the *auctor*, the *actio auctoritatis* of commentators. The connexion is certain: the use of the stipulation spread from *traditio* to *mancipatio* (Varro, de Re Rust. 2. 10. 5). As Lenel shews (Ed. Perp. § 290), the *actio auctoritatis* survived into classical law, and several of the texts were originally written of it. But it seems to belong to an earlier state of the law: in all the classical mancipations by way of sale, of which we have a record, the stipulation was relied on. For the same reason we have said nothing of the *satisdatio secundum mancipium*. Bechmann, Kauf, 1. 123, 375 *sqq*. The rules of eviction were applied to transactions analogous to sale, *e.g.* giving *in solutum* (C. 8. 44. 4); satisfaction of *legatum generis* (21. 2. 58); *permutatio* (C. 8. 44. 29) etc. But not to mere *donatio*, apart from agreement (C. 8. 44. 2).
[7] Aul. Gell., Noct. Att. 4. 2.
[8] 21. 1. 1. 1. As to the development of this Edict: Karlowa, R.R.G. 2. 1290 *sqq*. Bechmann, Kauf, 1. 397.

the specified defects or not. It contains rules as to the conditions under which and the time within which the actions are available, and it ends with the statement that an action lies, *si quis adversus ea sciens dolo malo vendidisse dicetur*[1].

We are told that the vendor might be required to give a formal promise relative to all these matters, and that, if he refused, the *actio redhibitoria* could be brought against him within two months and the *actio quanto minoris* within six[2]. As, without the promise the actions were already available for longer terms, if any defect appeared, this is of no great value. It is possible that this may have been the original rule, and that when the other came into existence this was little more than a survival[3]. The promise gave a *strictum iudicium*, but there is no evidence that action under it differed in any other way from the action on the implied warranty. Probably it was subject to the same limit as to time[4].

The warranty could of course be expressly excluded, in part or completely[5], and Aulus Gellius tells us[6] that in sales in market overt it was customary for owners, who would not warrant, to sell the slave *pileatus, i.e.* with a cap on his head, a recognised sign that no warranty was given. Moreover the liability might always be avoided by pact, either *in continenti* or after[7]. We are told that there was no redhibition in *simplariae venditiones*[8]. This epithet is obscure : the Syro-Roman Law-book seems to shew that it refers not to trifling sales but to cases in which the buyer takes the slave, for good or ill, irrespective of his quality. Thus the text refers to these pacts, and means that agreements were usual under which the buyer could not redhibit though he could bring *quanto minoris*[9]. Of course he could expressly renounce both rights. These preliminary remarks may be concluded by the observations that no liability existed for defects which had no existence at the time of sale, whether they had ceased to exist[10], or had not yet come into existence[11], that it did not arise where the defect was one which was so obvious that the buyer ought to have seen it[12], or where in fact the buyer was aware of it[13], and that the actions did not arise

---

[1] The point of this may be that if there was *dolus* the damages were not limited as they may have been in the other case, but all damage was recoverable. But even this adds nothing to the liability under the *actio ex empto*. Pothier, *ad* 21. 1. 1. 1; C. 4. 58. 1. But the limitation is doubtful, *Post*, p. 63. Karlowa (*loc. cit.*) thinks it refers to fraud on the Edict, *post*, p. 59.
[2] 21. 1. 28. *i.e.* to compel him to promise and thus be liable *ex stipulatu.*
[3] It survived into the Digest, 19. 1. 11. 4; 21. 1. 28; C. 4. 49. 14. Some texts cited to shew this shew merely that such stipulations were made—a different matter, 21. 2. 31, 32. Some refer to the stipulation on eviction, 21. 1. 31. 20. Bechmann, *op. cit.* 1. 404, thinks it is the compilers who supersede this system.
[4] See however Accarias, *op. cit.* § 609 *bis*; Bechmann, *op. cit.* 1. 407.
[5] 21. 1. 14. 9 ; 2. 14. 31. He must conceal nothing.   [6] Noct. Att. 7. 4.
[7] 2. 14. 31 ; 21. 1. 14. 9.   [8] 21. 1. 48. 8.
[9] Bruns at pp. 207, 8 of his edition of the Syro-Roman Law-book.
[10] 21. 1. 16, 17. 17.   [11] 21. 1. 54 ; C. 4. 58. 3.   [12] 21. 1. 1. 6 ; *h. t.* 14. 10.
[13] *Ibid.*; *h. t.* 48. 4. The texts are not agreed as to whether even an express warranty was binding if the buyer knew the facts, 16. 1. 43. 1 ; 44. 4. 4. See Moyle, Sale, 197.

where the defect was not such as to affect the value of the slave[1]. On the other hand it was immaterial that the vendor had no knowledge of the defect[2], and thus the redhibitory actions do not necessarily exclude *ex empto*[3].

We have now to consider the defects and other matters non- or misstatement of which rendered the vendor liable to the Aedilician actions.

I. *Morbus* or *Vitium* in the slave. It is not necessary to go through the long list of diseases mentioned in the Digest, under this head: it will be enough to state the general principles and to discuss one or two disputed points. At first sight it might seem that *morbus* meant a case for the doctor, and *vitium* some permanent defect or deformity. But the actual nature of the distinction was unknown to the classical lawyers themselves. Aulus Gellius[4] remarks that it was an old matter of dispute, and that Caelius Sabinus (who wrote on these Edicts) reported Labeo as holding that *vitium* was a wider term, including *morbus*, and that *morbus* meant any *habitus corporis contra naturam*, by which its efficiency was lessened, either affecting the whole body (*e.g.* fever), or a part (*e.g.* blindness or lameness). Later on he quotes similar language from Masurius Sabinus[5]. The remark which Gellius describes Caelius as quoting from Labeo is credited by Ulpian to Sabinus himself[6]. It seems, however, that Labeo must have been using the word *vitium* in a very general sense, not confined to the cases covered by the Edict, for the illustrations given of *vitia*, which are not *morbi*, are those which appear not to have been contemplated by the Edict[7]. Aulus Gellius[8] gives another attempt to distinguish the meanings of the words. Some of the Veteres held, he says, that *morbus* was a disorder that came and went, while *vitium* was a permanent defect. This is a close approximation to what is suggested above as the most obvious meaning of the words, but Gellius notes that it would upset Labeo's view that blindness was a *morbus*. Ulpian remarks that it is useless to look for a distinction: the Aediles use the words side by side, and only in order to be perfectly comprehensive[9]. The texts do not usually distinguish: they say that a defect does or does not prevent a man from being *sanus*[10].

The ill must be such as to affect efficiency[11], and it must be serious, more than a trifling wound or a cold or toothache or a boil[12]. On the

---

[1] 21. 1. 1. 8, 4. 6, 6. 1, 10. 2, 10. 5, 12. 1, *etc.*   [2] 21. 1. 1. 2.
[3] 21. 1. 19. 2.   [4] Noct. Att. 4. 2. 2.
[5] *Id.* 4. 2. 15.   [6] 21. 1. 1. 7.
[7] 21. 1. 1. 9 to 4. 1; *h. t.* 10. 5. Cf. Aul. Gell. *op. cit.* 4. 2. 5.
[8] *loc. cit.*   [9] 21. 1. 1. 7.
[10] The expression *morbus sonticus* from the XII Tables is considered in two texts and its meaning discussed (see 21. 1. 65. 1; see also 42. 1. 60; 50. 16. 113). But as Ulpian and Pomponius say, the matter is one of procedure: it does not concern the Edict in which the word *sonticus* does not occur, 21. 1. 4. 5.
[11] 21. 1. 10. *pr.*   [12] 21. 1. 1. 8; *h. t.* 4. 6.

other hand it need not be permanent[1]. Thus fevers and agues, gout or epilepsy are enough[2]. A mere difficulty or hesitation in speech was not a redhibitory defect[3], though incapacity to speak intelligibly was[4]. It is clear on these texts that the limits had been matter of dispute. Shortsightedness was another subject of dispute. A man who cannot see far is as sound, says Sabinus, as one who cannot run fast[5]. But some had held that it was always a redhibitory defect; others only if it was caused by disease[6]. Ulpian says that *myops* and *luscitiosus* might be redhibited[7]. No doubt it is a question of degree[8]. The defect must be physical[9]: mental and moral faults were not enough. Thus fanaticism, even amounting to permanent religious mania, and idle or lying habits were not enough[10]. This no doubt indicates the fact that the Edict only embodies the usual practice and that the word commonly employed, *i.e. sanus,* referred, in ordinary speech, only to bodily defects[11]. It is due to this limitation that *erro* and *fugitivus* are specially mentioned[12]. On the other hand, madness caused by bodily disease was redhibitory, as shewing a bodily *vitium*[13]. It should be added that some things might be *vitia* in a man which would not be in stock, and that defects not covered by the Edict might nevertheless give *actio ex empto* if the vendor knew, and was silent as to them[14].

II. *Fugitivus* and *Erro.* The vendor must declare if the slave has either of these defects[15]. *Fugitivus* here means one who has run away at least once from his master[16]. What is involved in " running away " will be considered when we are discussing *fugitivi* in detail[17] : here we must note that the case is not one of an actual present fugitive, but of one who has shewn that he is *fugax*—inclined to run away. An *erro* is one who is given to wandering about without cause and loitering on errands[18]. The practice has a certain similarity to flight, and Labeo defines them as greater and less degrees of the same offence[19]. So,

---

[1] 21. 1. 6.   [2] 21. 1. 1. 7; *h. t.* 53.
[3] Aul. Gell. *op. cit.* 4. 2. 2; D. 21. 1. 10. 5.
[4] 21. 1. 9.   [5] Aul. Gell. *op. cit.* 4. 2. 15.
[6] Aul. Gell. *loc. cit.* 11.   [7] 21. 1. 10. 3, 4.
[8] Labeo held sterility in a woman always a redhibitory defect. But the view of Trebatius (quoted by Ulpian from Caelius Sabinus) prevailed: it was redhibitory only if resulting from disease (Aul. Gell. 4. 2. 9, 10; 21. 1. 14. 3). Servius held lack of a tooth redhibitory, but this was rejected, the reason being presumably that it is immaterial, though this is disguised under the odd proposition, that, if this were a defect, all babies and old men would be unsound. Labeo and Paul are responsible for this (Aul. Gell. 4. 2. 12; 21. 1. 11). To be a *castratus* or a *spado* was a *vitium* (21. 1. 6. 2, 7, 38. 7) though it might increase his value (9. 2. 2, 7. 28). See *ante*, p. 8.
[9] *Habitus corporis.*   [10] 21. 1. 1. 9—10; *h. t.* 65. *pr.*
[11] Pomponius suggests that an utterly useless imbecile might be redhibited. Ulpian rejects this, 21. 1. 4. 3.   Cf. *h. t.* 43. 6.   *Post*, p. 59.
[12] 21. 1. 4. 3.
[13] 21. 1. 1. 9, 4. 1, 4. 4.   In Aul. Gell. (4. 2. 15) Masurius Sabinus appears as holding that a *furiosus* is *morbosus*: it is presumably this last form of insanity he has in mind.
[14] 21. 1. 38. 7; *h. t.* 4. *pr.*   As to eunuch and *castratus*, Karlowa, R.R.G. 2. 1301.
[15] 21. 1. 1.
[16] 21. 1. 17, *passim*; *h. t.* 48. 4, 54, 58. *pr.*; C. Th. 3. 4. 1 (C. 4. 58. 5); C. 4. 58. 3; C. 4. 49. 14.
[17] *Post*, Ch. xii.   [18] 21. 1. 17. 14.   [19] *Ibid.*

Arrius Menander, speaking of military discipline, says that to be an *erro* is a *levius delictum*, while to be a *fugitivus* is a *gravius*[1]. But there is something misleading in this: the attitude of mind is different[2].

III. *Noxa non solutus*[3]. The vendor must declare if the slave is subject to any present liability for delict, *i.e.* not any delict that the man has ever committed, but only those as to which the liability is still outstanding[4]. As we have seen, the word *noxa* refers to private delicts sounding in damages, not to criminal offences[5].

IV. *Quod dictum promissumve cum veniret fuisset*[6]. The vendor is bound, by liability to the Edictal actions, to make good any representations made at the time of sale. The position of this rule in the Edict suggests that it is a somewhat later development; but it must be as old as Labeo[7]. The difference between *dictum* and *promissum* is that the former is a purely unilateral declaration, while the latter is, or may be, an actionable contract, giving an *actio ex stipulatu* as well as the Edictal actions. The *dictum* need not be made at the moment of the sale: it will bind though it was made some days before, if it was substantially one transaction[8]. The preceding text seems to contemplate its being made after the sale.

Mere general words of commendation or "puffery" do not constitute binding *dicta*: it is therefore necessary to decide on the facts whether it really is a definite statement, intended to be binding[9]. Where it is binding it is to be construed reasonably and *secundum quid*. To say that a man is *constans* and *gravis* does not mean that he has the *constantia et gravitas* of a philosopher[10]. The *dictum* might be the denial of bad qualities, or the affirmation of good[11]. It might cover any sort of quality, and was obviously most useful in relation to mental and moral qualities[12]. Many *dicta* are mentioned in the title, besides those already instanced[13]. In one text we have the curious warranty that he was not a body-snatcher, due no doubt to temporary and local conditions[14]. In some of the recorded cases of actual sales, we find a warranty

---

[1] 49. 16. 4. 14.
[2] We are told by Ulpian that the crime of concealing *fugitivi* covers that of concealing *errones* (11. 4. 1. 5). But this is more intelligible: the attitude of mind of the offender is the same.
[3] 21. 1. 1. 1.   [4] 21. 1. 17. 17.
[5] *Ante*, p. 47; 21. 1. 17. 18. While the Edict says only *noxa*, express agreements usually said *furtis noxisque*. See the mancipations recorded in Bruns and Girard, *locc. citt.* There is indeed some evidence for it in the Edict, 21. 1. 46. *Post*, p. 98.
[6] 21. 1. 1. 1.   [7] 21. 1. 18. *pr.*   [8] 21. 1. 19. 2.
[9] 21. 1. 19. *pr.*, 23. If intended to deceive they might give *a. doli*.
[10] 21. 1. 18. *pr.*, where there are other illustrations. So also *cocus* does not mean a first class cook (*h. l.* 1). The statement that he has a *peculium* is satisfied however small the *peculium* may be (*h. l.* 2). An *artifex* is a trained man, not necessarily highly skilled (21. 1. 19. 4).
[11] 21. 1. 17. 20.   [12] 21. 1. 4. 4.
[13] Laborious, active, watchful, careful, saving, not a gambler, had never fled to the statue of the Emperor, not a *fur*, which means that he had never stolen even from his master, 21. 1. 18. *pr.*, 19. 1, 31. 1, 52.
[14] 21. 2. 31. Cp. Nov. Valent. xxiii.

that the slave is not epileptic[1], though there is an independent warranty against disease. We know that the ancients hardly regarded this as a bodily disorder. We see from these notes that it was usual to stipulate even as to the defects covered by the Edict[2]. In the sale of a girl of six, in A.D. 139, it is stipulated that she is *furtis noxisque soluta*, which looks as if it was "common form[3]."

V. *Si quod mancipium capitalem fraudem admiserit*[4]. This is one of a group which appear almost as an afterthought in the Edict. They are probably a later addition, but they too must be as old as the Empire, since, as Ulpian tells us, *fraus* in the general sense of offence is an old use[5]. There is little comment on this rule. Ulpian tells us that it involves *dolus* and wickedness and that, therefore, Pomponius says that the rule could not apply to *furiosi* and *impuberes*[6]. It may be remembered that, under the *Sc.* Pisonianum, the price could be recovered on conviction[7]. The two remedies overlap, but while the remedy under the Senatusconsult was perpetual, that under the Edict was temporary. On the other hand the latter gave the better redress while it existed[8].

VI. *Si mortis consciscendae causa quid fecerit*. Ulpian gives some obvious illustrations, and suggests as the reason of the rule, the view that the man is a bad slave, who is likely to try on other men's lives what he has attempted on his own[9]. It seems hardly necessary to go so far to find a reason for not wanting to give money for a slave who was likely to kill himself[10].

VII. One who had been sent into the arena to fight with beasts[11] This does not seem to have been commented. The silence may mean only that the comment has been cut out, for masters had been long since forbidden to send their slaves into the arena, and condemnation *ad bestias* was obsolete[12].

VIII. One sold as a *novicius* who was in fact a *veterator*[13]. This case has already been considered[14]: here it is enough to say that the fact gave the Aedilician actions, and that this was in all probability laid down in a separate part of the Edict[15].

---

[1] *caducum*, Bruns, Fontes, i. 288; "ἱερὰ νόσος" *ib.* 326.
[2] See also 21. 2. 31, 32.
[3] Bruns, *op. cit.* 289. Girard, Textes, 807. But it is omitted in some sales of older persons. Girard, *op. cit.* 808, 809.
[4] 21. 1. 1. 1.   [5] 21. 1. 23. 2.   Cicero, Pro Rab. 9. 26.
[6] 21. 1. 23. 2.   [7] 29. 5. 8. *pr.*
[8] It may have covered old offences which have been *e.g.* pardoned, since these equally affect the reliability of the slave, which is clearly the point in this warranty.
[9] 21. 1. 1. 1, 23. 3.
[10] Paul observes that attempted suicide on account of misconduct is within this rule, but not from bodily anguish, 21. 1. 43. 4.
[11] 21. 1. 1. 1.   [12] *Ante*, p. 37; *Post*, Ch. XII.
[13] 21. 1. 37.   [14] *Ante*, p. 9.
[15] Lenel, Ed. Perp. § 293.

We pass now to a group of cases of which it cannot be said with
certainty·that they were mentioned in the Edict, or even that they gave
the Edictal actions.   It is said that it is *aequissimum* to declare the
facts, and in reference to one of them the Edict is mentioned[1]: it is
commonly assumed that they were on the same footing as the others.
They are:

IX.   One who under existing law cannot be manumitted[2].

X.   One who has either been sold previously, on the terms that
he is to be kept in chains, or has been condemned to *vincula* by some
competent authority[3].

XI.   One who has been sold *ut exportetur*[4].

All these are facts which shew that the slave is undesirable, but
they do not exhaust the list of bad qualities, and the principle of selection is not clear.   It may be noted that they have the common quality
that they involve more or less restriction on manumission owing to the
fault of the man, and they may be all that is left in Justinian's time of
a rule requiring declaration where there was such a restriction due to
his fault.   If that is so, it is in all probability a juristic development.
In Justinian's law past *vincula* no longer restricted manumission[5], but
the survival of this rule is not surprising.

XII.   Nationality.   The vendor must state the nationality of the
slave, on pain of liability to the Aedilician actions[6].   The reason assigned
in the text is that nationality has a good deal to do with the desirability
of slaves.   There is plenty of evidence that this was so[7]: it was, in
particular, presumptive evidence of their fitness or unfitness for certain
employments[8].   The requirement is no doubt connected with the rule
that it was necessary to insert in the *professio* of your fortune, required
during the Empire for revenue purposes, the nationality of your slaves[9].
It is assumed by Lenel[10] that the rule we are considering was expressly
laid down in the Edict.   But this is in no way proved: it may well
have been a juristic development.   In support of this view it may be
remarked that this is the only one of the cases in which it was found
necessary to assign reasons for the rule.   In the other cases nothing is
said as to reasons beyond the general proposition with which the whole
discussion opens, that the Edict was for the protection of buyers[11].

---

[1] 21. 1. 48. 3.   [2] *Post*, Ch. xxv; 21. 1. 17. 19.
[3] 21. 1. 48. 3, 4.   [4] *Post*, p. 69.
[5] *Post*, Ch. xxv.   [6] 21. 1. 31. 21.   [7] Wallon, *op. cit.* 2. 61.
[8] Marquardt, Vie Privée, 1. 200.   Many slaves were *captivi* and the possibility of *postliminium* might be important.
[9] 50. 15. 4. 5.   In most of the recorded sales of slaves the nationality of the slave is stated.
There is an exception in A.D. 139 (Bruns, *op. cit.* 288 *sqq.*, 325; Girard, Textes, 805 *sqq.*).   The
rules of *professio* were a gradual development, and may not have been fully developed at
that time.   It may be that at some date the nation had to be stated only in the case of *barbari*.
Cf. C. Th. 13. 4. 4; 3. 4. 1.
[10] Ed. Perp. § 93.   It is not clear whether he thinks the same of those last discussed.
[11] 21. 1. 1. 2.

In the foregoing statement it has been assumed that the sale was of one or more slaves as individuals. But this was not necessarily the form of the transaction. The slave might be sold with something else: a *hereditas*, a *fundus* with its *mancipia*, a slave with his *peculium* which included *vicarii*. Here if the main thing is redhibitable, so is the slave, though he be in no way defective[1]. But, for a defect in an accessory slave, the right of redhibition arises only if he was expressly mentioned, and not where he was included in a general expression such as *peculium* or *instrumentum* (sold with a *fundus*)[2]. So Ulpian, agreeing with Pomponius; and Gaius, in saying that if *omnia mancipia* are to go with a *fundus* they must be guaranteed[3], means only that this amounts to express mention. It is by reason of this rule that the Aediles provided that slaves might not be accessories to things of less value, lest a fraud be committed on the Edict[4]. Any thing however may accede to a man, *e.g.* the *vicarius* may be worth more than the principal slave[5]. Presumably where the right of redhibition did arise in respect of an accessory slave, it applied to him alone. It should be added that if a *peculium* was sold without a slave, similar rules applied as to slaves contained in it[6].

The Edict applied to other transactions resembling sale, *e.g. permutatio*[7], but not to *donationes* or *locationes*[8]. It did not apply to sales by the Fisc, by reason of privilege[9]. The text adds that it applied to sales of the property of persons under wardship[10], the point being, perhaps, that it might be doubted whether the liabilities should be imposed on an owner who was *incapax*.

The actions given by the Edict are the *actio redhibitoria*, and the *actio quanto minoris* (otherwise called *aestimatoria*)[11], the former involving return of the slave, owing its name to that fact, and available for six months; the latter, (which lay on the same defects and was in no way limited to minor cases,) claiming damages and being available for a year[12]. But if the slave were quite worthless, *e.g.* a hopeless imbecile, it was the duty of the *iudex* to order refund of the price and return of the man even in this case[13]. The actions are available, on the words of

---

[1] 21. 1. 33. 1.   [2] *h. l. pr.*   [3] 21. 1. 32.   Existing defects to be mentioned.
[4] 21. 1. 44. *pr.* It hardly seems necessary to appeal, as Pedius does, to *dignitas hominum*. At the time when this rule was laid down the Edict probably dealt only with slaves.
[5] *Ibid.*
[6] 21. 1. 33. *pr.* As to the case of sale of several slaves together, *post*, p. 67.
[7] 21. 1. 19. 5.
[8] 21. 1. 62, 63.   In the latter case apparently only because these transactions not being ordinarily carried out in open market had not come within the purview of the Aediles.
[9] 21. 1. 1. 3, 4. It applied to sales by municipalities.   [10] 21. 1. 1. 5.
[11] For a hypothesis as to the early history of this action, Karlowa, R.R.G. 2. 1291 *sqq.*
[12] 21. 1. 21; P. 2. 17. 5; 21. 1. 18. *pr.* On these points a somewhat different rule was in operation in Asia Minor in the fifth century. Bruns, Syro-Roman Law-book, 206.
[13] 21. 1. 43. 6. The periods were *utiles*. According to one text the time runs from the sale, or in the case of express *dicta*, from any later time at which they were made, 21. 1. 19. 6, 20. But another corrects this so far as to make it run from the time at which the defect was or ought to have been discovered, 21. 1. 55.

the Edict, to the heirs and all universal successors, and, though they are
in a sense penal, they lie against the heirs[1]. This is because they are
purely contractual, (for they do not depend on any wrongdoing,) and for
the same reason the action is *de peculio* if the vendor was a slave or
person in *potestas* (the slave returned being reckoned in the *peculium* at
his real value[2]).

On the *actio quanto minoris* there is not much to be said. It is not
actually mentioned in the Edict as cited by Ulpian[3]. During the six
months the buyer has his choice between the two actions; thereafter he
is confined to *quanto minoris*, which leaves the contract standing, but
entitles him to recover the difference between the price he paid, and
what he would have given had he known the facts[4]. As we have seen
above, this might be the whole price, in which case the *iudex* would
order return of the man. There is a separate action on each defect, and
it can therefore be repeated, care being taken that the buyer does not
profit, by getting compensation twice over for the same wrong. In like
manner, if there were an express warranty, it was regarded as so many
stipulations as there were defects[5].

It was for the buyer to prove the defect[6]. In such a matter the
evidence of the slave himself, taken in the ordinary way, by torture, was
admissible[7], and if there were other evidence, even the slave's declaration
made without torture in the presence of credible persons, might be
used in confirmation[8]. As the *actio redhibitoria* was for return of the
man, it would be needed ordinarily only once. But it might fail, and
it was permitted to insert a *praescriptio* limiting it to the particular
vitium, so that it could be brought again on another[9].

The action was not available so long as the contract was still conditional: the *iudex* could not set aside an obligation which did not yet
exist. Indeed an action brought prematurely in this way was a nullity,
and *litis contestatio* therein would in no way bar later action. Sometimes,
even if the sale were *pura*, a condition of law might suspend the action.
Thus if a slave in usufruct bought, no *actio redhibitoria* would lie, till
it was known out of whose *res* the price would be paid, for in the
meanwhile the *dominium* was in suspense[10]

---

[1] 21. 1. 19. 5, 23. 5, 48. 5.
[2] 21. 1. 23. 4, 57. 1. If a slave bought and his master brought *redhibitoria*, he had to
perform *in solidum* what was required of the buyer in the action—an application of a wider rule,
21. 1. 57. *pr. Post*, Ch. IX.
[3] 21. 1. 1. 1.   [4] P. 2. 17. 6; D. 21. 1. 48. 1, 48. 2, 61. See Lenel, Ed. Perp. § 293. 3.
[5] 21. 1. 31. 16; 21. 2. 32. 1.
[6] 22. 3. 4.
[7] P. 2. 17. 12; D. 21. 1. 58. 2; 22. 3. 7. All from Paul, who says that though he may not
give evidence for or against his master, this is rather against himself. The case is one of proof
of *fuga*, and it may be that the rule is no wider. It is *factum suum. Post*, p. 86.
[8] 21. 1. 58. 2.   [9] 21. 1. 48. 7.
[10] 21. 1. 43. 9, 10. *Post*, Ch. xv.

The general effect of the action is to put an end to the transaction: the man is returned, and the price repaid, and thus it is spoken of in several texts as being a sort of *restitutio in integrum* on both sides[1]. Both parties, it is said, are to be in the position in which they would have been had there been no sale[2]. But this is subject to some limitations. It did not, in fact, make the sale as if it had never been, for it would not entitle the buyer to a noxal action for any theft done to him by the slave[3], nor could a redhibited slave ever give evidence against the buyer[4]. And, as we shall see in discussing the results of the action, the vendor might often be a serious loser, and the buyer a gainer. Moreover the restitution so far as it went was only between the parties: if, for instance, the buyer redhibited merely to defraud creditors, the vendor was liable to them on account of the slave[5].

In considering the working of the action it will be assumed, for the present, that there are one seller, one buyer and one slave, who is still in the possession of the buyer. The Edict expresses in outline the duties of the parties. It provides that the buyer must give back the slave and any acquisitions, accessions and products, and must account for any deteriorations caused by himself, his *familia* or *procurator*[6]. The duties are further detailed in the commenting texts. He must be able to restore the man, and therefore if he has pledged, alienated, or created a usufruct in him, these rights must be released before the vendor can be made to refund[7]. The duty to restore accessions covered all that went with him and all acquired since the transfer[8], including what, by negligence, the buyer had failed to receive; in general any acquisition not *ex re emptoris*[9]. Thus he must give up any damages he may have received for theft of the man, but not for *iniuria*. The reason for this exception is that the action on ordinary *iniuria* to a slave depended on intent to insult the master, and accordingly the text suggests with doubt that even these must be restored in those cases of extreme insult in which this intent was not necessary[10].

---

[1] 21. 1. 23. 7, 60.
[2] 21. 1. 23. 1, 60.
[3] 47. 2. 17. 2.
[4] 48. 18. 11.
[5] 21. 1. 43. 7. *Actio* Pauliana.
[6] 21. 1. 1. 1.
[7] 21. 1. 43. 8; C. Th. 3. 4. 1 (= C. 4. 58. 5). The text says the rule is to apply *non solum in barbaris sed etiam in provincialibus servis*. The doubt might have been the other way. Perhaps it had been expressly laid down for *barbari*, in consequence of doubts as to effect of *post-liminium*, and it had been argued, *a silentio*, that it was not so with *provinciales*. He gives him back *talis qualis*: he need not warrant him *noxa solutus* except so far as he or those claiming under him had authorised the wrongful act, 21. 1. 46. *Post*, p. 66. It may be that if redemption was impossible he might give his value. Eck, Festgabe für Beseler, 169.
[8] 21. 1. 33. 1.
[9] 21. 1. 24. Instances are: earnings while in possession of buyer or recovered by him from some other possessor, legacies and *hereditates*, whether they could have been acquired by vendor or not and irrespective of the person in view of whom they were given, *partus*, usufructs which have fallen in, and *peculium* other than that given by the buyer, 21. 1. 23. 9, 31. 2, 3, 4.
[10] 21. 1. 43. 5, *post*, p. 80.

The deterioration for which he is to account must, by the Edict, be after delivery[1]. It may be physical or moral[2]. *Familia*, for this purpose, includes slaves, *bona fide servientes* and children[3], and no doubt, in classical times, persons *in mancipio*. *Procurator* means either a person with general authority or with authority in the matter in connexion with which the harm was done. It includes *tutor, curator* and any person having administration[4]. It is immaterial to the liability whether it were *dolo* or only *culpa*[5]. It might conceivably be something which would have happened equally if the sale had not occurred. In this case he was equally liable for his own act, as he would have been if there had been no sale, but if it were by a *procurator* he need only cede his actions, and if it were his slave he could surrender him noxally[6]. But if the man acquired the bad habit merely by imitation of the buyer's ill-conducted slaves, this was not so far done by them that there could be any question of noxal surrender[7]. He may have to give security for certain purposes, *e.g.* against liability on any charge he may have created, or on any wrong committed on his *iussum*, and, generally, against *dolus*[8], and for the handing over of anything receivable in future, *e.g.* damages in any pending action about the slave, whether he receive them, or, *dolo* or *culpa*, fail to do so[9].

The vendor must hand over to the buyer the price and any accessions to it, and all the properly incurred expenses of the purchase, though not any money wantonly spent; an instance of what may be recovered being overdue taxes which the buyer had to pay[10]. If the price is not yet paid he must release the buyer and his sureties. What is meant by accessions to the price is not clear, but they certainly cover interest, which he must in fairness pay, since he is recovering the *fructus* with the slave[11]. It may be conjectured that the word originally covered cases in which the price or part of it was not in money.

Other expenses are on rather a different footing. There is a right to receive all damages and expenses, such as the value of things the slave, now redhibited, had made away with, or taken with him on running away[12], expenses of medical treatment[13], cost of training[14], damages paid in a noxal action, and the value of any thing he had

---

[1] 21. 1. 1. 1, 25. *pr.*
[2] Debauching an *ancilla*, cruel treatment so that the man becomes a *fugitivus*, leading him into vicious courses, 21. 1. 23. *pr.*, 25. 6.
[3] 21. 1. 1. 1, 2, 31. 15.   [4] 21. 1. 25. 3, 31. 14.   [5] *h. t.* 25. 5, 31. 14.
[6] *h. t.* 25. 4. The rule is from Pedius. He does not expressly speak of *filiifamilias*. In later law they could not be surrendered: the *pater* would be liable *in solidum*, but in the conditions of that time might have an effective claim against the son.
[7] 21. 1. 25. 7. Must be expressly claimed if accrued before *litis contestatio*: if after, came in *officio iudicis*, 21. 1. 25. 8.
[8] 21. 1. 21. 1.   [9] *h. t.* 21. 2.   [10] 21. 1. 25. 9, 27.
[11] *h. t.* 29. 1, 2.   [12] P. 2. 17. 11; D. 21. 1. 58. *pr.*
[13] 21. 1. 30. 1.   [14] 21. 1. 1. 1. *Si quas accessiones ipse praestiterit ut recipiat.*

stolen from the buyer[1], but not the cost of maintenance, since he had the man's services in return for that[2]. But all this last group of claims the vendor can evade by refusing the slave and leaving him with the buyer by a sort of noxal surrender[3], being then liable only for the price and those things which are reckoned with it. If however he knew of the defect at the time of sale he is in any case liable *in solidum*[4].

The Aediles require the buyer to do his part first[5]: the render being made *in iudicio* and under the supervision of the *iudex*, who will issue no condemnation till it is done[6]. But since it might happen that the vendor could not fulfil his part, and the buyer would be left with a useless *actio iudicati*, the *iudex* might authorise the buyer to give security for his part of the render without actually paying it[7].

The general effect of the *actio redhibitoria* being to undo the transaction as far as possible, no prominence is given to the distinction between a vendor who knows and one who is ignorant[8]. In the *actio quanto minoris* the buyer recovers the difference between price and value at the time of sale[9]. It seems however that in classical law it was usual to enforce these Edictal duties in the *actio ex empto*, and the rule is expressed in the texts that the vendor if ignorant was liable only for the difference in value, while, if he knew, he was liable for the *interesse*. This is clearly Julian's view. In one text[10] there is no warranty, so that an innocent vendor would have been under no liability, apart from the Edict, and the defects mentioned are *morbus* and *vitium*. In another there certainly was a warranty: *tenetur ut aurum quod vendidit praestet*[11] In another text Pomponius[12] makes the warranting vendor liable for the whole *interesse* whether he knew or not. And in the text last above cited[11], he is quoted as laying down the same rule with Labeo and Trebatius in opposition to Julian. The texts may be harmonised on the view that where the duty is entirely edictal, Julian's distinction applies. Where there was a warranty there was a liability *ex empto* for the *interesse*, apart from the Edict. In support of this it may be noted that in Marcian's text dealing with warranty, Julian's remark has rather the air of being out of place. In a text of Paul[13], the innocent vendor is made liable for the whole *interesse*, though

---

[1] 21. 1. 23. 8.
[2] 21. 1. 30. 1. These claims, as well as those expressly stated in the Edict, must appear in the *formula* if accrued at time of action: if later, they come in, *officio iudicis*.
[3] 21. 1. 23. 8, 29. 3, 31. *pr.*, 58. 1. This rule suggests that the whole of this later liability is a juristic development: the power of surrender seems to date from Julian.
[4] C. 4. 58. 1. Like the buyer he may be required to give security for possible future liabilities, *e.g.* damages in a pending noxal action on account of the slave. 21. 1. 21. 2, 30. *pr.*
[5] 21. 1. 25. 10. [6] 21. 1. 29. *pr.* [7] 21. 1. 26, 29. *pr.*
[8] See however, above *n.* 4 and *post*, p. 65.
[9] *Ante*, p. 60. Lenel, Ed. Perp. § 293. 3. [10] 19. 1. 13. *pr.* Ulp. citing Julian.
[11] 18. 1. 45. Marcian, citing Julian and others. As to the presence of a warranty in this case, see Vangerow, Pandekten, § 604. The text is obscure.
[12] 19. 1. 6. 4. [13] 19. 1. 21. 2.

warranty is not expressly stated: it is however suggested by the words, hardly otherwise explicable in relation to an innocent vendor, *venditor teneri debet quanti interest non esse deceptum*[1]. Another difficulty is more striking. We have seen that the general aim of the *actio redhibitoria* is to undo the transaction as far as possible. It may result in a loss to the vendor, as he has to indemnify, and the buyer may even gain, since he gets interest and he might not have invested the money. But in general it is an equal adjustment. One text, however, speaks of the actions as penal[2], though, so far, they are no more penal than other contractual actions. And while we are told in one text by Ulpian[3] that the vendor is condemned unless he pays what is ordered by the Edict, another, by Gaius[4], says that if he does not pay he is condemned *in duplum*, while if he does make the necessary payments and releases he is condemned *in simplum*. Lenel[5] accepts this text, and assumes that the action was always penal. In each case he will have to pay double, either before or after judgment. It has been pointed out[6] that this jars with the whole nature of the action as elsewhere recorded, and with the fact that the *stipulatio* as to *vitia* says nothing about *duplum*[7]. Moreover it is an absurd way of putting the matter. It is only a roundabout way of saying that the action was *in duplum*: of course he could pay part before judgment if he liked. And in the case where there was an agreement for redhibition at pleasure, we are told that the action was the same[8]. Yet it is incredible that if, when sued under such an agreement, he took the man back and paid the price and accessions he should still have been liable even *in simplum*[9].

Karlowa[10], starting from the view, probably correct, that the rule was originally one of police, and only gradually became contractual, fully accepts the penal character of the action, and the text of Gaius. But his argument is not convincing. He treats the expression *stipulatio duplae*, which of course recurs frequently in this connexion, as correctly used, and rejects the current view that its duplex character relates to eviction, and that it became merely a collective name for the obligations required by the Edict[11]. To reach this result, he repudiates the directly contrary evidence of the existing recorded sales[7], in all of which the undertaking as to defects is simple, while the stipulation on eviction is *in duplum* in all cases but one. He passes in silence the significant rubric of the title on eviction[12], (*de evictionibus et duplae stipulatione*),

---

[1] See on these texts Pernice, Labeo, 2. 2. 245 *sqq.*; Dernburg, Pandekten, 2. § 100.
[2] 21. 1. 23. 4.   [3] 21. 1. 29. *pr., si autem venditor ista non praestat, condemnabitur ei.*
[4] 21. 1. 45.   [5] Ed. Perp. § 293.
[6] Eck, Festgabe für Beseler, 187 *sqq.*
[7] 21. 1. 28. See Bruns, Fontes, ii. Chh. 3, 8; Girard, Textes, 806 *sqq.*
[8] C. 4. 58. 4; cp. 21. 1. 31. 22 *sqq.*
[9] The *a. redhibitoria* is available against *heres*, 21. 1. 23. 5.   [10] R.R.G. 2. 1293 *sqq.*
[11] See *e.g.* Girard, Manuel, 562.   [12] 21. 1.

and the evidence from Varro[1] as to usage: indeed he holds that there is no reason to think the edict followed usage. He quotes two texts in which Ulpian[2] and Julian[3] say that, if the vendor refused to take back the man, he need pay no more than the price and accessions, as shewing that, if he did take him back, he would have to pay double, whereas what they mean is, as the context shews with certainty, that, if he took him back, he would have to pay both price and any *damna*.

Pernice[4] thinks that the concluding words of the text of Gaius[5] mean no more than that if he paid, under the judge's preliminary decision, this amounted to condemnation *in simplum*, and he paid no more, but, if he did not, he was condemned *in duplum*. But this does not explain the opening statement of Gaius that there is a *duplex condemnatio* and that *modo in duplum modo in simplum condemnatur venditor*. Here the word *condemnatio* must be used in a technical sense, while the explanation offered of the ending words is clearly untechnical. Accordingly he speaks with no confidence.

Probably the solution of the problem lies in some detail, as yet undetected, in the history of the actions. The suggestion lies ready to hand that in the classical law they were *in duplum* in case of actual fraud. This would account for the enigmatic words about fraud at the end of the Edict[6], the words *in duplum* having been struck out. It would also justify the statement that the actions were penal, and Gaius' *duplex condemnatio*. But it leaves the rest of his text unexplained, unless, here too, a reference to *dolus* has been dropped.

If the slave is handed back without action or before *iudicium acceptum*, there is no *actio redhibitoria*, but the buyer has an *actio in factum* to recover the price. The merits of the redhibition are not considered: the vendor has acknowledged the slave to be defective by taking him back[7]. It is essential that he have been actually taken back: a mere agreement for return is not enough[8]. Conversely the vendor can bring an ordinary action *ex vendito*, to recover any damage[9]. We are told that in the buyer's action he must have handed back all accessions before he could claim[10]. It is also said that the fact that the slave is redhibitable is a defence to any action for the price[11]. If there was an agreement for return on disapproval at any time or within a fixed time this was valid[12]. The claims are the same as in the ordinary *actio redhibitoria*[13]: indeed the action is called by that name[14].

---

[1] Varro, R.R. 2. 10. 5. [2] 21. 1. 29. 3. [3] 21. 1. 23. 8.
[4] Labeo, 2. 2. 249; Eck, *loc. cit.* [5] 21. 1. 45. [6] 21. 1. 1. 1 *in fine.*
[7] 21. 1. 31. 17. [8] *h. l.* 18. [9] 21. 1. 23. *pr.*
[10] 21. 1. 31. 19. [11] 21. 1. 59. *pr.*
[12] 21. 1. 31. 22. If no time was si .ted, there was an *actio in factum* within 60 days, which might be extended, *causa cognita*, if the vendor was in *mora* or there was no one to whom it could be returned or for other good cause, *h. l.* 23.
[13] 21. 1. 31. 24. [14] C. 4. 58. 4.

We have said that the buyer, desirous of recovering the price, must restore the slave[1]. But impossibility of this restoration may result from different causes, and the legal effect is not always the same. The case of the slave in actual present flight is not fully discussed: the starting point seems to be that as he must be restored there can ordinarily be no redhibition[2]. But the rule developed that if there was no *culpa* in the buyer, and the vendor had sold *sciens*, there might be an *actio redhibitoria*, the buyer giving security that he would take steps to recover the slave and hand him over[3]. Manumission of the slave by the buyer, says Paul, at once ended the aedilician actions[4]. This rule is remarkable and is elsewhere contradicted—such rights were not destroyed *ex post facto*[5]. It is commonly set down to the fact that he is now a freeman, incapable of estimation[6], but this did not destroy other such actions, *e.g.* the *Iudicium de servo corrupto*[7]. It might end the *a. redhibitoria*, as the buyer has wilfully put it out of his power to restore, but it ought not to affect the *a. quanto minoris* since there is no need to estimate his present value.

Another question arose where the slave was evicted. How, it is asked, could his defects matter if the buyer has no interest, having been evicted by a third person? But all the conditions of *actio redhibitoria* are present except the power of restoration, and as the absence of this is the vendor's fault, how should this release him? Unfortunately the texts do not really answer the question: they assume a stipulation and allow the action as not being destructible *ex post facto*. The buyer will recover his *interesse*, which is nothing if the eviction was before delivery, and will vary according to the time of actual use of the defective slave[8]. The rule as to the requirement of restoration may be more exactly stated in the form that the buyer cannot sue, *ex edicto*, unless he restore or the failure is without fault or privity of him or his[9].

Death of the man does not, as of course, destroy the actions. We are told that they survive[10] unless the death was due to *culpa* of the buyer, his *familia*, or *procurator*, etc., which means any *culpa* however slight, as by providing no doctor, or an inefficient one. If there is *culpa* we are told that it is as if he were alive, and all is to be handed over which would be handed over in that case[11]. The meaning of this statement is not

---

[1] *Ante*, p. 61.   [2] 21. 1. 21. *pr.*; C. Th. 3. 4. 1; C. 4. 58. 5.   See however Eck, *loc. cit.*
[3] 21. 1. 21. 3. And that neither he nor his *heres* would do anything to prevent the vendor from having the slave, *h. t.* 22.
[4] 21. 1. 47. *pr.*, including claims on *dicta promissa*.
[5] 21. 1. 44. 2; 21. 2. 16. 2. It will be remembered that though the action on the stipulation for eviction was lost by manumission, this was because there was in fact no eviction.
[6] Eck, *op. cit.* 173.   [7] *Ante*, p. 34.
[8] 21. 1. 44. 2; 21. 2. 16. 2. In which Pomponius states obscurely the view of Proculus and sums it up in the sense here indicated. The rule may have been the same if there was no stipulation, for the rule that rights of action are not destroyed *ex post facto* has no necessary connexion with stipulation.   [9] *e.g.* he has been robbed of the slave. 21. 1. 43. 5.
[10] 21. 1. 31. 6, 31. 24, 47. 1.   [11] 21. 1. 31. 11, 12, 14, 48. *pr.*

too clear. It is sometimes said that the rule is that he must give the value of the slave in his stead[1]. This is in itself rational and may be what is meant. But it is not precisely what the text says, and it is more favourable to the buyer than the rule in the case of flight, *culpa eius*, apart from *scientia* of the vendor[2].

We have hitherto assumed a single slave, buyer, and vendor. In each case more than one might be concerned, and the cases must be taken separately.

(*a*) More than one slave is sold. If all are defective no question arises. But there is a question how far, on the defect of one, he can be redhibited separately. It is clear that a right of redhibition arises on defect of only one: our question is: what are its limits? The fact that they were sold at a lump sum may have been the sole point for Labeo and Africanus[3] as it certainly was one of the first to be considered[4]. But it was not the decisive point in classical law. Africanus[5] himself observes that even where there were several prices the right to redhibit all may arise on defect of one, *e.g.* where they were of no use for their special function separately. Troupes of actors are mentioned and, for other reasons, persons related as parents, children or brothers[6]. Ulpian and Paul lay down the rule that sale in a lump sum does not exclude *redhibitio* of one, apart from these special cases[7]. Where one is redhibited in this way, his relative value is taken into account in fixing the price returnable, if there was a lump price, but not otherwise[8]. It may be added that if there was an express warranty that the slaves were *sanos*, and one was not, Labeo is reported as saying that there can be redhibition *de omnibus*, but these words are generally rejected[9].

(*b*) More than one person entitled as buyer. The case most discussed in the texts is that of a buyer who has left several heirs. The general rule is laid down by Pomponius, quoted by Ulpian, that there can be no redhibition unless all consent, lest the vendor find himself paying damages in *quanto minoris* to one, and part owner by redhibition from another. He adds that they ought to appoint the same *procurator ad agendum*[10]. If one of the heirs has done *damnum* he is of course liable *in solidum* for it, *arbitrio iudicis*, and if it has been paid by a

---

[1] Moyle, Sale, 206.
[2] *Ante*, p. 66. The Basilica treat the text as denying the right of action altogether. Bas. 19. 10. 43. If the death occurs after *litis contestatio* it is within the *officium iudicis* to decide whether it was by chance or *culpa*, 21. 1. 31. 13.
[3] Dernburg, *loc. cit.* But the texts hardly justify this.
[4] 21. 1. 34. *pr.*, 64. *pr.*   [5] 21. 1. 34. 1.
[6] *Ibid.* The text adds *contubernales*, but the change of case indicates that this is an addition of Justinian's, 21. 1. 35. Such persons could be legated separately, *post*, p. 77.
[7] 21. 1. 38. 14—40.   [8] 21. 1. 36, 64. *pr.*
[9] 21. 1. 64. 1. If one is redhibitable there is an *exceptio* if the price of all is sued for, but not in an action for the price of part, except where all are redhibitable for the defect of one, 21. 1. 59. 1.
[10] 21. 1. 31. 5.

common *procurator* there will be an adjustment by *iudicium familiae erciscundae*[1]. The various things due to them from the vendor can be paid *pro rata*, except indivisibles, such as *partus ancillae*, which must be given *in solidum* in common[2]. Similar rules apply to an original purchase in common : neither can redhibit alone[3]. To this, however, there are two obvious exceptions: if the contract were solidary, any buyer could redhibit *in solidum*, and if there was nothing in common in the contract, but there were quite separate contracts for parts, each could redhibit as to his share[4].

(c) More than one person entitled as vendor. Here, if there are several heirs to the vendor, or there were common owners, there may be redhibition *pro rata*, and if the vendors were selling, separately, distinct shares, the rule is the same, so that there may be redhibition in respect of one, and *actio quanto minoris* in respect of another. But if they were solidary vendors there may be redhibition *in solidum* against any[5].

Restrictive covenants are somewhat prominent in the sale of slaves. These are not conditions on the sale in the sense that breach of them avoids it : they are, for the most part, directions as to what is to be done with the slave, breach of which does not produce in all cases the same effect, since some are imposed for the benefit of the slave, some for the protection of the late owner, and some by way of mere punishment. Some of them also present exceptions to the general rule that obligations could not be assigned, and that one could not attach permanent incidents to the holding of property, except within the conception of servitudes. It is clearly laid down that a man cannot validly promise that another shall do or not do[6]. As in English law the inconvenience was felt, and one instructive text shews that the Romans took advantage of the rules of usufruct to lay down a rule which, within a very narrow field, presents a close analogy to the rule in Tulk *v.* Moxhay[7]. A. held property, subject to restrictions, which he had bound himself under a penalty to observe. On his death he left a usufruct of this to X. X., who had notice, was bound to observe the restrictions, (which were purely negative,) not on the impossible ground of an assignment of the obligation, but because to disregard them was not enjoying the property *bono viri arbitratu*[8]. The cases must be taken separately[9].

---

[1] 21. 1. 31. 9. It seems from the language of this text which Ulpian gives on the authority of Pomponius that the single procurator was matter of convenience not of absolute rule.
[2] 21. 1. 31. 6.
[3] 21. 1. 31. 7, 8. Nor could one alone compel delivery : the vendor has a lien till he is wholly paid.
[4] 21. 1. 31. 10.   [5] *Ibid.*
[6] 45. 1. 38. 1. Stipulations are found in which the promisor undertakes for himself *et eos ad quos ea res pertinebit* (*e.g.* 32. 37. 3). The reference is to the *heres.*
[7] Tulk *v.* Moxhay, 2. Ph. 774.
[8] 7. 1. 27. 5. Probably even here the grantor to A. could not have enforced it.
[9] As to 'real' effect, Ihering, Études Complém. 8. 62.

I. The slave sold *ut exportetur*, or the like. This condition was regarded as imposed entirely in the interest of the vendor, who could therefore remit it[1]. If a penalty was agreed on by stipulation, this was clearly enforceable, but only from the promisor, even though there was a second buyer who allowed him to be in the forbidden place[2]: it was the second sale, which was his act, that made this possible. He could of course impose a similar penalty on the buyer from him, and so protect himself.

If the agreement for a penalty had been informal, there was a difficulty. The older lawyers could find no *interesse*. The mere desire to inflict a hardship on the slave was no *interesse*: in enforcing this there was no *rei persecutio*, but a *poena*. This could not figure in an *actio ex vendito*. This is Papinian's earlier view[3], but in an adjoining text[4] he declares himself converted to the view of Sabinus, *i.e.* that the lower price at which he was sold was a sufficient *interesse*. The result is convenient but not free from logical difficulty. The reduction in the price is *causa* rather than *interesse*. The real *interesse* is the value to him of the man's absence[5]. If a vendor had himself promised a penalty, this would, on any view, be a sufficient *interesse*, for any agreement for a penalty, with a buyer from him: it would indeed form the measure of its enforceability[6]. One would have expected to find some necessary relation between the amount of the penalty in our case and the reduction in the price[7].

The penalty was not incurred at all in the case of a fugitive, or one who was in the place without leave of his master[8]: a slave could not impose liabilities on his master in that way.

The restriction was a bar to any manumission in the place before export: such an act was therefore void[9]. But it did not prevent manumission, *ante fidem ruptam*, elsewhere[10], and it appears that if the man returned after manumission, the Fisc seized and sold him into perpetual slavery under the same condition[11].

The mere imposition of a penalty gave the late owner no right to seize the slave: he went to the Fisc[12]. But it was usual to agree for a

[1] Vat. Fr. 6; D. 18. 7. 1.   [2] 18. 7. 9; C. 4. 55. 1, 2.
[3] 18. 7. 7.   [4] 18. 7. 6.
[5] The question of *interesse* gave rise to difficulties in case of will. A testator directs that a slave be sold for export. Who can enforce this? By what right? Ulpian says doubtfully that it will enter into the *officium iudicis* in *familiae erciscundae*, a rule which was reached in the case of a direction to keep a slave chained, 10. 2. 18. 2; C. 3. 36. 5. But what if there were nothing else in dispute? In any case *affectionis ratione recte agetur*—a penalty informally agreed on was enforceable if the covenant was *ne exportaretur* or the like: the benefit intended was enough, 18. 7. 7.
[6] *Ibid.*   [7] Ihering (French trans.), Œuvres choisies, 2. 150.
[8] 18. 7. 9; C. 4. 55. 2.   [9] C. 4. 55. 3.   [10] *h. t.* 1.
[11] *Ibid. Post*, Ch. xxv. The restriction was construed rather against the slave: one sold to be out of his province might not go to Italy. C. 4. 55. 5. If the *pomerium* was barred, the town was barred, *a fortiori*. But one sold to be out of Italy might be in any province not expressly barred, 18. 7. 2, 5.
[12] C. 4. 55. 2. The vendor has *actio ex vendito*.

power of seizure on return (*manus iniectio*): the right to seize arose on return by consent of owner, and could be remitted, as the penalty could[1]. It applied though the slave had been transferred to another person[2]; the incapacity and liability to seizure being impressed on the slave. But any buyer could manumit him elsewhere before breach of the condition, and, if he then returned, he was seized by the Fisc and dealt with as above[3]. Though the condition bound the slave in the hands of third parties the buyer selling would be liable, *ex empto*, if he did not communicate it. Thus it was usual to give notice on any resale. The resale might be subject to the same condition. If, in that case, he returned with the consent of his owner, it was the original vendor who had the right of seizure, as *auctor legis*. The intermediate owner's restriction was merely regarded as notice and for self-protection: he could not supersede his vendor's right of seizure[4].

II. An *ancilla* sold *ne prostituatur*. This restriction is imposed in the interest of morality, and of the *ancilla*, and is therefore somewhat different in its effects from the foregoing. Breach of the provision involved freedom of the woman, according to rules which varied from time to time, and will require full discussion hereafter[5]. The Digest tells us nothing as to the effect, in classical law, of a mere proviso, *ne prostituatur*, without more. After Marcus Aurelius the woman became free[6]. If there were an express agreement that she was to be free she became so, under earlier law, however informal the agreement was[7]: it was a quasi-manumission depriving the buyer of his rights on the sale[8]. The vendor was her patron[9]. The effect was the same, by a provision of Vespasian, even though she had been resold without notice of the proviso[10].

If there had been merely a stipulation for a penalty, then, apart from the question of liberty, this could always be recovered[11]. So could a penalty informally agreed for: there seems to have been no doubt as to the sufficiency of the *interesse*, where what was aimed at was benefit to the slave[12]. The penalty was recoverable only from the promisor, but it applied even where the actual wrongdoer was a second assignee, even without notice[13]. If a right of *manus iniectio* had been reserved, this was effective, at any rate after Hadrian, as against any owner of the *ancilla*[14]. If on a first sale the agreement was that she was to be free,

---

[1] 18. 7. 9; C. 4. 55. 2; Vat. Fr. 6.   [2] C. 4. 55. 1; Vat. Fr. 6.
[3] C. 4. 55. 1.
[4] 18. 7. 9. He could recover a penalty if he had agreed for one, and was liable under any promise he might have made, since it was his sale which had led to the wrongful return.
[5] *Post*, Ch. xxv.
[6] 18. 7. 6. 1; 40. 8. 6. Prostitution under colour of service at an inn was a "fraud on the law." C. 4. 56. 3.
[7] C. 4. 56. 1. 2.   [8] 21. 2. 34. *pr.*   [9] 2. 4. 10. 1.
[10] 37. 14. 7. *pr.*   [11] 18. 7. 6.   [12] *h. l.* 1.   [13] *Arg.* 37. 14. 7. *pr.*
[14] 18. 1. 56; C. 4. 56. 1. If the prostitution was by, or with the connivance of, the imposer,

and, on the second, for *manus iniectio*, or *vice versa*, she was always free. In the first case this is a necessary result of the fact that the second vendor could not undo the condition, but in the second case it is clear that to free the woman is to undo the condition imposed by the first vendor. Paulus explains the rule as a case of *favor libertatis*, which hardly justifies what is in effect an act of confiscation. Accordingly he supplements this, by saying that such a condition was in any case not imposed with a view of getting her back, but in her interest, which is equally served by giving her freedom[1]. It will be seen that in the case of a provision against prostitution there was no power to remit the condition: it was not imposed in the interest of the vendor[2].

III.   One sold *ut manumittatur, ne alterius servitutem patiatur*, etc. As by a constitution of about A.D. 176, breach of this condition involved the slave's becoming free, *ipso facto*, it follows that it was never really broken, and a penalty, however formally agreed on, was never incurred[3]. Even if there was a condition of *manus iniectio* the result was the same: the slave was free; the right of seizure was only *auxilii causa*[4]. A text of Scaevola's seems at first sight in direct conflict with this principle[5]. A slave is given, with a declaration that it is with a view to manumission, and a stipulation for a penalty if he is not freed, *vindicta*. Scaevola says, giving as usual no reasons, that the penalty is recoverable, though the person liable can always evade it by freeing. He adds that if no action is taken liberty is still due. Nothing turns on its being a donation, for the rule that liberty took effect *ipso facto* applied equally there[6]. Nor is it likely that the fact, that the agreement was for manumission *vindicta*, has anything to do with it, though this would not strictly be satisfied by freedom acquired in another way. It is more probable that the text represents an earlier state of the law. Scaevola's Digest seems to have been written under Marcus Aurelius[7] at the end of whose reign the constitution mentioned was passed. The language shews that the writer contemplates liberty as not taking effect *ipso facto*, though it is clear that he considers the penalty as at once recoverable. He says, in the end of the text, that the liberty requires to be conferred. It is clear that this was the earlier state of the law. In one text[8] Hadrian appears as saying that in such cases the slave was not free until manumitted[9].

Hadrian required the magistrate to declare the woman free, the vendor being still her patron but with limited rights, 2. 4. 10. 1; C. 4. 56. 1.   On similar principles Severus and Caracalla provided that, if a right of *manus iniectio* reserved were released, for money, the woman was free, 40. 8. 7.

[1] 18. 7. 9.   [2] p. 70, n. 14.
[3] 40. 1. 20. 2; C. 4. 57. 6.   *Post*, Ch. xxvii.   [4] 40. 1. 20. 2.
[5] 45. 1. 122. 2.   [6] C. 4. 57. 1.
[7] Roby, Introd. to Dig. clxxxvi.   [8] 18. 7. 10.
[9] As to vendor's power of withdrawal, *post*, Ch. xxvii.

IV.   One sold *ne manumittatur*[1].   As we shall see later, the effect of such a provision was to make the slave incapable of manumission[2]. As in the last case, therefore, the proviso cannot be disobeyed, and the penalty cannot be recoverable.   And so Papinian, and Alexander in the Code, lay it down[3].   It seems, however, that Sabinus thought that, if the form were gone through, this was breach of the condition and entitled to the penalty.   Others thought that the claim on such ground though formally correct should be met by an *exceptio doli.*   But Papinian is clear that what the stipulator meant was actual manumission, not the form, and that thus there has not been even a formal breach of the condition[4].

---

[1] The rule covered gifts and devises, 29. 5. 3. 15; 40. 1. 9; C. 7. 12. 2, *etc.*

[2] *Post*, Ch. xxv.   It "*cohaeret personae*," and cannot be removed by the holder, 40. 1. 9; 40. 9. 9. 2; C. 4. 57. 5.

[3] 18. 7. 6. 1; C. 4. 57. 5. 1.

[4] In another text, on another point it is said *quamvis si manumiserit nihil agat, tamen heres erit : verum est enim eum manumisisse.*   But this is a case of satisfying a condition on institution : it was conditional on his freeing a *servus hereditarius*, 28. 7. 20. 1.   Labeo is doubtless influenced by *favor libertatis*, and the desire to save an institution.   The text continues: *Post aditionem, libertas...convalescit.*   It may be doubted whether this is from Labeo.

CHAPTER IV.

THE SLAVE AS MAN. NON-COMMERCIAL RELATIONS.

In political life, it need hardly be said, the slave had no share. He could hold no office: he could sit in no public assembly. He might not serve in the legions: it was indeed a capital offence for him to enrol himself[1]. Such service was the duty and privilege of citizens, and though, in times of pressure, both during the Republic and late in the Empire, slaves were occasionally enrolled, the exceptional nature of the step was always indicated, and the slaves so enrolled were rewarded with liberty, if indeed they were not usually freed with a view to their enrolment[2]. In like manner they were excluded from the decurionate in any town, and it was criminal in a slave to aspire in any way to the position[3]. But though they never occupied the highest positions in the public service, they were largely employed in clerical and manual work in different departments, and even in work of a higher kind[4].

Both at civil and praetorian law, slaves *pro nullis habentur*[5]. This is not so at natural law, *quia quod ad ius naturale attinet omnes homines aequales sunt*[6]. We have already noted some results of this conception[7], and have now to consider some others.

The decay of the ancient Roman religion under the emperors makes it unnecessary to say more than a few words as to the position of the slave in relation thereto. The exclusion of slaves from many cults is not due to any denial of their claim to divine protection, but to the circumstance that the divinities, the worship of whom was most prominent, had special groups under their protection to which slaves did not belong. A slave did not belong to the *gens* of his master, and therefore had no share in its *sacra*, or in the united worship of *Iuno Quiris*, and similar propositions might be laid down as to other

---

[1] Pliny, Ep. Traj. 30.
[2] Livy, 22. 57; 24. 14; Iul. Capit., M. Anton. 21. 6, *volones*; Val. Max. v. 6 § 8; C. Th. 7. 13. 16. For other cases, J. Gothofredus *ad h. l.* See also Halkin, Esclaves Publics, 45. In general they volunteered and owners were compensated.
[3] C. 10. 33.   [4] 2. 11. 7; 50. 17. 211. As to this see *post*, Ch. xiv.
[5] *Ante*, p. 4; D. 28. 1. 20. 7; 28. 8. 1; 48. 10. 7.   [6] 50. 17. 32.   [7] Ch. i.

worships[1]. On the other hand slaves had a special cult of Diana. They figured prominently in the *Saturnalia* (a main feature of which was the recognition of their equality with other men[2]), and they shared in other observances. Within the household they shared in some degree in the observances connected with the *Lares* and the *Penates*, and there was even a cult of the *Manes serviles*[3]. Moreover slaves were of many races, each with its own cult or cults, and it need not be supposed that their enslavement took away from them the protection of their racial divinities[4]. When Christianity became the religion of the state, there could be no question of the exclusion of slaves from religious worship. There are indeed many Constitutions regulating the religion of slaves, some of which are referred to, later, in other connexions[5]. They are mainly directed against Judaism and heresy, and their dates and characteristics shew that they were enacted rather in the interest of the section of the Church that was then dominant, than in that of the slave[6].

Within the law itself, there are not wanting traces of this recognition of the fact that a slave was a man like any other, before the Gods. Though slaves could not be bound by contract, it was usual to impose an oath on them before manumission, in order that after the manumission they might be under a religious obligation to make a valid promise of *operae*[7], and they could offer, and take, effectively, a conventional extrajudicial oath[8].

Burial customs are closely related to religious life, and here the claims of the slave are fully recognised. Memorials to slaves are among the commonest of surviving inscriptions, and the place at which a slave was buried was *religiosum*[9]. Decent burial for a slave was regarded as a necessary. The *actio funeraria*, available to one who had reasonably spent money in burying a body, against the heir or other person on whom the duty of burial lay[10], was available even where the person buried was a *servus alienus*[11]. In this state of the law it is not surprising to find that slaves appear as members of burial clubs or *collegia*. With the general organisation of these and other *collegia* we are not concerned[12], but it is necessary to say something as to the connexion of

---

[1] See Marquardt, Culte, 1. 259. They were freely employed in the services of the various colleges of priests.
[2] As to the *Saturnalia*, Wallon, *op. cit.* 2. 231 *sqq*.
[3] On all these points, Sell, Aus der Noxalrecht der Römer, 31. n. 2; Blair, *op. cit.* 65 *sqq*. For Jewish practice, Winter, Stellung der Sklaven, 53.
[4] Tacitus, Ann. 14. 44.   [5] *Post*, Ch. xxvi.
[6] See C. Th. 16. 4. 5; 16. 5. 40. 6, 52. 4, 54. 8, 65. 3, 4.
[7] 40. 12. 44. *pr.* Ulpian says, in the Digest, that they could contract by *votum* so as to bind their master if authorised by him. This was essentially a promise to the divinity. 50. 12. 2. 1. The allusion to slaves may be an addition of the compilers: how far was *votum* a living form of contract in Justinian's time?
[8] 12. 2. 23.
[9] 11. 7. 2. *pr.* Thus the Praetor speaking of unlawful burial says *ossa hominis*, not *liberi hominis*, 11. 7. 2. 2.
[10] 11. 7. 14. 6 *sqq*.   [11] 11. 7. 31. 1.
[12] Daremberg et Saglio, Dictionnaire des Antiquités, *s.v. Lex Collegii*.

slaves with them. It was essential to a slave's entry into such a society that he have the authorisation of his master[1], who would then be bound by the *lex collegii*. Some of these *leges* have come down to us: one of them, the *lex collegii* Lanuvini[2] of A.D. 133, shews slaves as members.

In this case there was an entrance fee, (which included a bottle of good wine,) and a monthly subscription. Breaches of the statutes were penalised by fine, and in some cases by exclusion from the benefits. The members' rights were, mainly, to share in periodical banquets, and to the provision, out of the property of the college, of a fixed sum for the expenses of burial, out of which sum a certain proportion was distributed among the members present on the occasion of the funeral. There was a provision that if a slave member was freed he was to give the society a bottle of wine. If the deceased member had left no directions, the funeral was carried out by the officers of the society, but it was open to him to give directions as to the person who was to do it. The forms of the society were ordinarily modelled on those of a town. Thus the members were the *populus*, the directions were regarded as a will, and the person charged was looked on as a *heres*, in which character he took any part of the fixed sum which was not needed for the funeral. In the absence of any such claim, it seems to have remained with the society[3]. In the society at Lanuvium there was a rule, (and it may have been general,) that if the *dominus* would not hand over the slave's body for burial, and the man had left no *tabellae*, the rites were gone through without the body; *funus imaginarium fiet*[4]. The statutes of this *collegium* contain a provision that no creditor, patron or *dominus* is to have any claim on the funds of the college except as the *heres* of a member. This no doubt refers to the dispositions just mentioned, and seems to imply that the *dominus* could claim nothing, unless so made heir, and that if another person were named, it would go to him. There is nothing very surprising in this in view of the fact that all this needed initial authority of the *dominus*, and that very large powers of absolute alienation of *peculium* were commonly conferred on slaves. It must be presumed that any money received by the slave out of the funds was on the level of ordinary *peculium*[5].

Of protection to the morality of slaves there is in early law little or no trace. Probably it was not needed. But in the Empire, when it certainly was needed, it was slow to develop. We have already seen[6] that from the time of Domitian onwards there was legislation limiting

---

[1] 47. 22. 3. 2. [2] Printed in Bruns, Fontes, i. 345.
[3] Daremberg et Saglio, *loc. cit.*; Marquardt, Vie Privée, 1. 222.
[4] *Ibid.* In the Empire all these *collegia* were regulated by a *Sc.* which seems to have given them a corporate character, 3. 4. 1. *pr.* The funds were thus the property of the corporation.
[5] Bruns, *loc. cit.* 348; Wallon, *op. cit.* 3. 453. [6] *Ante*, p. 37.

the power of the *dominus* in the direction of protection of personal chastity. But it did not go very far. Not till A.D. 428 was it made penal for *lenones* to employ their slaves in prostitution, and Justinian confirmed this[1]. We have seen that the classical law regarded sale to a *leno* as a reasonable mode of punishment[2]. Debauching a man's *ancilla* was an *iniuria* to him, and might be *furtum*[3], but the injured woman does not seem to have been considered. The rules already discussed as to the effect of sale with a condition against prostitution[4] date from classical times, and do actually regard the woman herself, since the restriction could not be remitted, but the protection depends on the initial goodwill of the owner[5]. Rape of an *ancilla aliena* was made a capital offence by Justinian, but it did not involve forfeiture, as that of a freewoman did[6]. There is no penalty for seduction by the *dominus*. It is clear that, throughout, the morality of a slave woman was much less regarded than that of a freewoman[7].

Far more important in law and more fully recorded is the gradual recognition of servile cognation. In no other branch of law is the distinction so marked as here, between the rules of law and the practice of every day life. It is well-known, on the evidence of memorial inscriptions and lay literature[8], that slaves lived together in permanent union as man and wife, and were regarded, and regarded themselves, as married, and as sharing all the ordinary family relations.

But the law takes a very different view. In law, slaves were incapable of marriage[9]: any connexion between them, or between slave and free could be no more than *contubernium*[10], and thus enslavement of either party to a marriage ended it[11]. Accordingly, infidelity between slaves could not be adultery[12], and though a slave could be guilty of adultery with a married freewoman[13], it was not possible for an *ancilla* to commit the offence, or for it to be committed with her[14]. Nevertheless the names of legal relationship were freely applied to the parties to, and issue of, such connexions: we hear of *uxor, pater, filius, frater*, and so forth, even in legal texts[15], but Paul warns us that though these names, and the expression " cognation," are used, they are without

---

[1] C. Th. 15. 8. 2 ; C. 11. 41. 6. [2] *Ante*, p. 37.
[3] 47. 10. 9. 4; 47. 2. 83. 2. It might give rise to *actio* Aquilia and even *servi corrupti*, and both would lie in the same case, 48. 5. 6. *pr.*
[4] *Ante*, p. 70. [5] *Ibid.*
[6] C. 9. 13. 1e. In earlier law it was dealt with as *vis*, 48. 5. 30. 9.
[7] 47. 10. 15. 15.
[8] Wallon, *op. cit.* 2. 180; Marquardt, Vie Privée, 1. 205; Erman, Servus Vicarius, 442 *sqq.*
[9] Ulp. 5. 5. [10] P. 2. 19. 6 ; C. 9. 9. 23. *pr.*
[11] 23. 2. 45. 6; C. 5. 16. 27. As to *Captivi, post*, Ch. xiii. [12] C. 9. 9. 23. *pr.*
[13] 48. 2. 5 ; 48. 5. 34; C. 9. 9. 24.
[14] 48. 5. 6. *pr.*; C. Th. 9. 7. 1; C. 9. 9. 28. Adultery was essentially interference with a wife's chastity. Similarly corruption of an *ancilla* though called *stuprum* was not punishable as such, P. 2. 26. 16 ; C. 9. 9. 24.
[15] P. 3. 6. 38; D. 32. 41. 2; 33. 7. 12. 7, 12. 33 ; C. Th. 4. 6. 3 = C. 5. 27. 1; Nov. Marc. 4. 1.

significance for the law of succession[1]. So Ulpian tells us that the rules of cognatic succession apply to non-servile cognation, *nec enim facile ulla servilis videtur esse cognatio*[2]. Diocletian says shortly that *servus successores habere non potest*, and applies the principle in two cases[3]. So, even in late law, the title on legitimation makes it clear that an *ancilla* could not be a *concubina* for this purpose[4]. This is an enactment of Constantine, who had already made it severely punishable for *decuriones* to cohabit in any way with *ancillae*[5]: it was important that *decuriones* should have legitimate successors on whom the civic burden should descend. Both enactments were adopted by Justinian. Apart from this, cohabitation with slave women was not in any way punishable[6].

Even at law, however, these connexions between slaves were not a mere nullity. So long as all parties were slaves there was of course no great room for recognition, though it went some way; much further indeed than seems to have been the case in other systems[7]. In a legacy of *fundus cum instrumento* or *fundus instructus*, the slaves who worked it were included unless there was some special indication that the testator did not so intend[8]. Paul tells us that it must be understood to include the *uxores* of such slaves[9], and Ulpian lays down the same rule for wives and children on the ground that the testator cannot be supposed to have intended such a cruel separation[10]. It must be noted that all this turns on presumed intent. There was nothing to prevent the legacy of a single slave away from his connexions. Thus, where a business manager employed in town was legated, Paul saw no reason to suppose that the testator meant the legacy to include his wife and children[11]. And where a certain *ancilla* was left to a daughter, to be given to her on her marriage, Scaevola was clear that this did not entitle the legatee to claim a child, born to the *ancilla* before the marriage took place on which the gift was conditional[12].

There were, however, cases which had nothing to do with intent. Thus it can hardly be doubted that the rules we have already stated, according to which the issue of an *ancilla* do not belong as fruits to the

---

[1] 38. 10. 10. 5.　　　　　[2] 38. 8. 1. 2.

[3] C. 6. 59. 4. The master of an *ancilla* can claim no right of succession to a freeman who cohabited with her; there is no doubt an underlying mistake as the effect of the *Sc.* Claudianum; *h. t.* 9; a child born of a freewoman and a slave is a *spurius* and cannot rank as his father's son, though the father be freed and become a *decurio*, C. 6. 55. 6.

[4] C. 5. 27. 1; C. Th. 4. 6. 3.

[5] C. Th. 12. 1. 6; C. 5. 5. 3.

[6] In A.D. 554 Justinian seems to be undoing, but without penalties, some unions between slaves and free which had been authorised by the invading "*tyranni.*" See Pragm. Const., C. I. C. (Berlin) 3. 801. The unions were to have no legal effects.

[7] Jews, Winter, *op. cit.* 44, 45; America, Cobb, Slavery, 245, 246.

[8] 33. 7. 18. 11. Even the *vilicus*, 33. 7. 18. 4. But not a slave who rented the land from his master, *h. t.* 20. 1.

[9] P. 3. 6. 38.　　　　[10] 33. 7. 12. 7, 12. 33.　　　　[11] 33. 7. 20. 4.

[12] 33. 5. 21.

bonae fidei possessor, or to the usufructuary, or, in the case of dotal slaves, to the *vir*, are largely based on recognition of the claims of nature[1]. So, too, it was laid down by Constantine that in *iudicium familiae erciscundae*, or *communi dividundo*, the slaves were to be so distributed that those related as parent and child, or brother and sister, or husband and wife were to be kept together[2]. It is noticeable that in nearly all these cases, the recognition extends to the tie of marriage as well as to that of blood. So, too, in the *actio redhibitoria* we have seen that if several were sold together who were related as parent or child or brother, they could be redhibited only together[3].

The same recognition is brought out in a very different connexion by Venuleius. He tells us that though the *lex* Pompeia *de parricidiis* applies on its terms to lawful relationships only, yet, *cum natura communis est, similiter animadvertetur*, in the case of slaves[4].

When the slave becomes free the question of the importance which the law will attach to these previous relations becomes more important. It should be noted that there are two distinct questions: how far do they restrict the man's liberty of action? How far can they create rights?

Restrictively the recognition was fairly complete. Labeo held, in opposition to Servius, that the rule forbidding *in ius vocatio* of a father, without leave of the Praetor, applied to fathers who were slaves at the time of the birth[5]. We are told by Paul that servile relationship was a bar to marriage—the cases mentioned being child, sister, and sister's child, and, though the parentage were doubtful, the rule applied on the father's side as well as on the mother's[6].

So far as giving rights is concerned, the classical law went no further than, in construing wills, to extend such words as *filius* to children born in slavery. The earliest case is that of a man who, having no son, but one who was born a slave, instituted him heir, (he having been freed,) and then said, "If I have no son who reaches full age, let D be free." Labeo took the strict view, that D was free. Trebatius held, and Javolenus accepted the view, that in such a case the intent being clear, the word *filius* must be held to denote this son[7]. Scaevola and Tryphoninus lay

---

[1] *Ante*, pp. 21 *sq*.
[2] C. Th. 2. 25. 1; C. 3. 38. 11. The text speaks of *agnatio*, but not of course in a technical sense. So also '33. 5. 21.
[3] 21. 1. 35, 39. Here too the rule is applied to *contubernales*: the form of the text suggests compiler's work, though the rule itself would not be out of place in classical law. A slave concubine and her child were not to be seized in *bonorum venditio*. P. 1. 13a. 1g; D. 42. 5. 38. *pr*.
[4] 48. 2. 12. 4. References to cases in which slaves were allowed a *de facto* power of testation within the *familia* are not illustrations of the present point: such wills had no legal force. See Marquardt, Vie Privée, 1. 222.
[5] 2. 4. 4. 3. Severus in the text, but Servius seems more probable. See however, Roby, Introd. to Digest, clviii.
[6] 23. 2. 14. 2. As to *affinitas* Paul is less clear. He says that in so doubtful a case it is best to abstain: this must be taken as law in the time of Justinian, 23. 2. 14. 3.
[7] 28. 8. 11.

down a similar rule in a case of which the facts are rather complex, but of which the gist, for our purpose, is that in construing wills *filius* includes such children: it does not seem to be thought material that there should be no other children[1].

Justinian took a more decided step. He observes that the rules of proximity in *bonorum possessio* do not apply to servile relationships, but that he, in adjusting the hitherto confused law of patronal relations, provides that if a slave has children by a slave or freewoman, or an *ancilla* has children by a slave or freeman, and he or she is or becomes free, the children shall succeed to the parents and to each other and to other children of the whole or half blood with themselves[2]. The enactment here referred to is in the Code, more shortly expressed, in the form that children are to exclude the patron whether freed before or after or with the father, or born after his manumission[3].

Later on, while preserving the rule that slavery and marriage are incompatible[4], he allows, by a series of Novels, a right of legitimation of children of a freeman by a slave, if he had freed her and them, and obtained for them the *ius regenerationis*[5]. Most of these provisions deal with *oblatio curiae*, and are part of the machinery for keeping the lists of *decuriones* full.

The fact that an *actio iniuriarum* may lie on account of insult to a slave is, again, a recognition of his human character. The matter presents some difficulties: the chief point to note is that though the action is necessarily acquired to the *dominus*, it is brought sometimes for the insult intended to the *dominus*, sometimes without reference thereto: it may be either *suo nomine* or *servi nomine*[6].

The Edict contained a provision that for *verberatio contra bonos mores* or for subjecting the man to *quaestio*, without the owner's consent, an action would lie in any case[7]. Even a municipal magistrate

---

[1] 31. 88. 12. At the time of the *fc.* in the text, donee is still a slave, but it is *post mortem legatarii*, and donee is to be freed by *heres*: she is thus free at *dies cedens* of the *fc.* The point of the allusion to the *l.* Falcidia is that if she claimed under the second will she would suffer a deduction of ¼, as this land was all the *heres* took.

[2] In. 3. 6. 10.

[3] C. 6. 4. 4. See also C. 6. 57. 6. This contemplates a quasimarital relation before manumission, and is not designed to give rights to those who would have been *spurii* had their parents been free. The enactment of Diocletian still held good (C. 6. 59. 4, *ante*, p. 77). But while the classical lawyers contemplated only interpretation of wills, Justinian gives rights on intestacy. And though he is discussing patronal rights, the words of the In. are wide enough to cover the case of *ingenui* cohabiting with slaves.

[4] Nov. 22. 9, 10.

[5] Nov. 18. 11, 38. 2. 1, 89. Details seem unnecessary. In 23. 3. 39. *pr.* we are told that if a quasi *dos* has been given by *ancilla* to *servus*, and being freed they continue together and *peculium* is not adeemed, the connexion is marriage and the fund a *dos*. This merely shews that if two free persons were living together the question—marriage or not—was one of fact: the facts stated are evidence of *affectio maritalis*.

[6] 47. 10. 15. 35.

[7] 6. 1. 15. *pr.*; 47. 1. 2. 4; 47. 10. 15. 34. Authorisation by *tutor curator* or *procurator* was enough, 47. 10. 17. 1. To exceed *iussum* was to act *iniussu*, *h. l.* 42.

might be liable if the flogging were excessive[1]. But any reasonable beating, *corrigendi vel emendandi animo*, was not *contra bonos mores*, and so was not within the Edict[2]. Intention to insult the owner was not needed: it is incorrect to say that it was presumed: it was not required. The action lay *servi nomine*[3]. It seems probable, however, that intention to insult the *dominus* might be alleged in the formula, and proved[4], with a view to increased damages.

There is more difficulty as soon as we pass to less definite forms of *iniuria*. The Edict continues: *Si quid aliud factum esse dicetur causa cognita iudicium dabo*[5], a provision which besides covering all other kinds of insult appears to include the contrivance of *verberatio* by a third person[6]. The system of rules of which this text is the origin is not easily to be made out. The texts give indications of conflict of opinion, but the matter may be simplified by striking out two classes of case in which a slave is concerned in an *iniuria*, but which are governed by principles independent of our present question. These are:

(1) Cases in which an insult is committed to the slave, but is actually expressed to be *in contumeliam domini*. Here the slave is merely the medium through which the wrong is done: the master's action is *suo nomine*, governed by the ordinary law of *iniuria*.

(2) Cases in which the *iniuria* does not take the form of an "insult," in the ordinary sense, but is a wilful infringement of right[7]. The wanton disregard of a man's proprietary and other rights is a form of *iniuria* too well known to need illustration. Such wanton wrongs might be committed in relation to a slave. But they have no relation to our problem, even where the wrong done was one which could not be done except to a human being.

The question remains: under what circumstances, apart from the Edict as to *Verberatio*, did an action lie for an insult to a slave, and was it in any way material that there should be intention to insult the *dominus*? It is clear that, if intention to insult the *dominus* was present, the action was *suo nomine* and not *servi nomine*, the latter action being available if there was no such intention. This is expressly stated in one text[8], and appears from others, which, comparing the case in which the person insulted is a slave with that in which he is a *liber homo bona fide serviens*, state that if there was no intention to insult the

---

[1] 47. 10. 15. 39. Details, *h. t.* 32.　　　　　　[2] 47. 10. 15. 38.

[3] 47. 10. 15. 35; C. Th. 12. 1. 39. Thus while a redhibiting buyer need not return ordinary damages for *iniuria*, since they were for the *iniuria* to him, he must where it was for *verberatio* or *quaestio*: it is, in relation to the slave, an acquisition through him, 21. 1. 43. 5; 47. 10. 29. *ante*, p. 61.

[4] *Arg.* 47. 10. 15. 35, 48; Coll. 2. 6. 5.　　　　　[5] 47. 10. 15. 34.　　　　[6] 47. 10. 17. 2.

[7] *e.g.* castration of a slave, 9. 2. 27. 28. The Edict of the Aediles gave an alternative remedy, apparently *in quadruplum*. Lenel, Ed. Perp. § 293. 11.

[8] 47. 10. 15. 35.

dominus, he has no action at all in the latter case and none *suo nomine* in the other[1].

It was not, however, every insult to a slave which gave an *actio iniuriarum*, *servi nomine*. It must be something serious; not a mere *levis percussio* or *levis maledictio*, but real defamation or serious insult[2]. This restriction is part of the application of the words, *causa cognita*, in the Edict[3]. The quality of the slave would affect the question : to a common sort of slave or to one of bad fame, or careless, a greater insult would be needed to cause the Praetor to grant a formula, and perhaps it would be altogether refused (except in case of *verberatio*, etc.), where the slave was of a very low order. The matter was wholly in the hands of the Praetor[4].

If intention to insult the *dominus* were alleged, the words A[i]. A[i] *infamandi causa* were inserted in the *formula*[5]. It does not appear that any other legal result necessarily followed. The texts dealing with the matter seem to shew that no action lay *suo* or *servi nomine*, for *iniuria* to a slave, apart from the edict as to *verberatio*, unless the insult were *atrox* of a serious kind[6]. There are, however, some remarks to make on this.

(i) The granting of the *formula* being left by the Edict to the discretion of the Praetor, it is unlikely that *iniuria atrox* had in this connexion, (if anywhere,) a very precise meaning. On the other hand it is likely that where intention to insult the *dominus* was alleged in the *intentio,* and so made a condition of the *condemnatio*, the *formula* would be issued more readily than where no such intention was alleged, and damages would be on a higher scale.

(ii) The fact that an insult expressed to be an insult to the master need not be *atrox*, while one so intended, but not so expressed, must be, to give an action, is not surprising. In the former case the tendency to lessen the respect in which the insulted person is held appears directly from the facts : there can be no difference between different words but one of degree, sufficiently represented in the amount of damages awarded. In the latter case the difference may be one of kind. Contumelious treatment of a trusted steward may well have a defamatory effect on his master, and, if it be shewn to have been done with the intent of insulting him, will give rise to an action *suo* not *servi nomine*. But an abusive epithet thrown at a humble slave cannot really affect the respect in which his master is held, no

---

[1] 47. 10. 15. 45. *Si pro libero se gerentem…non caesurus eum si meum scisset, non posse eum quasi mihi iniuriam fecerit sic conveniri Mela scribit.* See also *h. l.* 48—if the slave is *bonae fidei* possessed, and there was no intent to insult any but the slave, the *dominus* has an *actio servi nomine.*
[2] 47. 10. 15. 44.   [3] *h. l.* 43. See also C. Th. 12. 1. 39; C. 9. 35. 1, 8.
[4] 47. 10. 15. 44.   The Inst. say *minuitur* in the case of these inferior slaves. In. 4. 4. 7.
[5] Lenel, Ed. Perp. § 194.   [6] G. 3. 222; In. 4. 4. 3; C. 9. 35. 8.

matter what may have been the intention of the speaker.   It follows
that the master will have no action *suo* or *servi nomine*.

(iii) These considerations explain why the master had an action
servi nomine when there was no intention to insult him, and why it
was limited to the case of *atrox iniuria*.   There can be no ordinary
actio iniuriarum under the general Edict, because there was no intention to insult[1].   But under the large words of the special Edict there
was plainly a power to give an action in the case, not so much on the
general principles of the *actio iniuriarum*, as on the ground that injury
is in fact caused to the plaintiff's reputation, and justice requires that
compensation be given for the harm done.   There is no sign that the
action was in any practical sense a recognition of the slave as having a
reputation to lose : it is the damage to the master that is considered[2].
The case is different with *verberatio* and *quaestio* : there, at least in the
opinion of the later jurists, the feelings of the slave himself are considered[3].   The difference in conception is probably an accidental result
of the fact that under the special Edict the action was not given as a
matter of course : *causa cognita iudicium dabo*.

(iv) The action *servi nomine* was the last to develop.   The Edict does
not distinguish it.   Gaius shews no knowledge of two types of action
resulting from insult to a slave[4].   All the texts which expressly mention
it are from Ulpian[5].   It has all the marks of a purely juristic creation[6].

Of the slave's civil position it may almost be said that he had none.
In commerce he figures largely, partly on account of the *peculium*, and
partly on account of his employment, as servant or agent.   His capacity
here is almost purely derivative, and the texts speak of him as un-
qualified in nearly every branch of law.   They go indeed beyond the
mark.   General propositions are laid down expressing his nullity and
incapacity in ways that are misleading unless certain correctives are
borne in mind.   We are told that he could have no *bona*, but the text
itself reminds us that he could have *peculium*[7].   The liability of slaves
on their delicts was recognised at civil law[8].   But we are told that they

---

[1] 47. 10. *pass.*
[2] 47. 10. 1. 3, *spectat ad nos*; C. 9. 35. 8, *damni haberi rationem*. The action did not pass on
alienation or manumission of the slave, 47. 10. 29.
[3] C. Th. 12. 1. 39, *iniuria corporis quod etiam in servis probrosum*; 47. 10. 15. 35, *haec enim et
servum sentire palam est*.
[4] G. 3. 222; In. 4. 4. 3.   [5] *locc. citt.*
[6] Condemnation produced *infamia* even where the person directly insulted was a slave (C. 2.
11. 10). If both insulter and insulted are slaves, noxal liability and no *infamia* (47. 10. 18. 1).
The *actio iniuriarum* was in some cases concurrent with one under the *lex* Cornelia. But this
was not available where the wrong was done to a slave (47. 10. 5. 6). As to the concurrence of
the *actio iniuriarum* with one for *damnum*, there was dispute among the jurists. See 47. 10. 15.
46; 44. 7. 32, 34. *pr.*, 41. 1, 53; 9. 2. 5. 1; 19. 5. 14. 1; 48. 5. 6. *pr.* etc. The matter has no
special connexion with the case of slaves. See Girard, Manuel, 396 ; Pernice, Labeo, 2. 1. 45.
The dominant view seems to be that the actions were cumulative.
   50. 16. 182.   [8] 44. 7. 14.

could not be bound by contract, (*in persona**n servilem nulla cadit obligatio*,)[1] and that they could be neither creditors nor debtors: if expressions contradictory of this are found (and they are common), the legal reference is to the *dominus*". But this ignores the fact that they were capable of natural right and obligation and the true rule is expressed in a text which says *ex contractu civiliter non obligantur, sed naturaliter obligant et obligantur*[3].

The exclusion of slaves from a number of *actus legitimi* seems to rest rather on the absence of *civitas* than on their slavery. Thus a slave could not be witness or *libripens* in mancipation: such a person must be a *civis*[4]. He could not be or have a tutor[5]. He could make no will, and if he became free a will made in slavery was still void. We are, however, told that slaves have *testamenti factio*[6]. This means that they may be instituted, either for their masters, or, with a gift of liberty, on their own account. But this employment of the expression *testamenti factio* puts the lawyers in some difficulty when they have to explain why a slave cannot witness a will. They put it down to his not having *iuris civilis communionem in totum, nec praetoris quidem edicti*[7]. This curiously guarded expression is no doubt due to the fact that the writer was face to face with the awkward fact that a slave could be *heres*. But illogical compromises of this kind are inherent in the Roman conception of slavery.

In relation to procedure the incapacity of slaves is strongly accentuated[8]. They could not be in any way concerned in civil proceedings, which must be, from beginning to end, in the name of the master[9]. As they could neither sue nor be sued, they could not validly stipulate or promise, in the procedural contracts *iudicio sisti* or *iudicatum solvi*, and so they could not bind a *fideiussor* by such a promise[10]. Judgment against a slave was null and void: it gave rise to no *actio iudicati de peculio*, since it was not a *negotium* of the slave. In the same way absolution of a defendant, where the plaintiff was a slave, did not in any way bar his *dominus*[11]. A slave's pact, *ne a se peteretur*, was in strictness void, though it might give the *dominus*, if he were sued,

---

[1] 44. 7. 43; 50. 17. 22. *pr.*   [2] 15. 1. 41.
[3] 44. 7. 14; 12. 6. 13. *pr.* The fact that the obligation was not *civilis* made it worthless in many cases. A master's promise to free his slave meant nothing (C. 7. 16. 36). A promise to give surety was not satisfied by offering a slave unless the circumstances made the master liable *in solidum*, 46. 1. 3, *post*, Chh. IX, XXIX.
[4] G. 1. 119.   [5] 26. 1. 14, 15.   [6] 28. 1. 16, 19.
[7] 28. 1. 20. 7. This is subject to the rule already mentioned as to *error communis* (C. 6. 23. 1). They could of course write the will at the testator's direction, 28. 1. 28.
[8] 2. 11. 13; 4. 5. 7. 2; 49. 1. 28. *pr.*; G. 3. 179.   [9] 2. 8. 8. 2; 2. 11. 13; 50. 17. 107.
[10] 2. 11. 9. *pr.*, 13. If they did so promise when supposed to be free, fresh security could be demanded: it was no case for the rule *error communis facit ius*: to make the master wholly liable was unfair to him. To have a liability only *de peculio* was unfair to the other. To make the slave liable was meaningless, 2. 8. 8. 2.
[11] 5. 1. 44. 1; C. 3. 41. 5; C. 3. 1. 6, 7. Similarly *compromissum* by *servus* is null, 15. 1. 3. 8—11.

an *exceptio doli*[1]. On the other hand if the pact had been *ne peteretur*, or *ne a domino peteretur*, then, whether the original transaction had been the slave's or not, the *pact* gave an *exceptio pacti conventi*[2]. The distinction is not unmeaning: whether there had or had not been a pact was a question of fact: whether there had been *dolus* or not left more to the *iudex*. They could not *interrogare in iure* or be interrogated to any purpose[3]. As they could not be parties, so they could not sit in judgment. We are told that they could not act as *iudices*, not, it is said, for lack of ability, but because, as in the case of women, *moribus receptum est*[4]. Similarly they could not be arbitrators: if a slave were appointed we are told that as a matter of convenience, if he became free before decision, the parties might agree to accept his decision. But this depends on his freedom, and is only a way of avoiding the trouble of a new appointment[5].

There were other less obvious cases. Slaves could not be *custodes ventris* against supposititious children[6], though they might accompany the person responsible. This is an express provision of the Edict: its reason is that such a *custos* is likely to be required to give evidence, and the evidence of slaves was not readily admitted. They could not *opus novum nuntiare*, their *nuntiatio* being a nullity. This seems to be due to the fact that the *nuntiatio* was a procedural act specially prescribed in the Edict as the first step in a process, aiming at an injunction[7]. On the other hand, *nuntiatio* could be made to a slave. The receipt of the notice was no formal act: we are indeed told that it may be made to anyone, provided it be *in re presenti operis* so that the *dominus* may hear of it[8].

There are some exceptions to this rule of exclusion, but they are only such as to throw the rule itself into relief, for the exceptional nature of the case is always either obvious, or expressly indicated. Thus though they could not be *custodes ventris*[9], yet, if a slave were instituted *si nemo natus erit*, he was allowed to take some of the formal precautions against supposititious children: the exception being expressly based on his potential freedom[10]. For similar reasons, though they could not have procurators in lawsuits, they might have *adsertores*

---

[1] 2. 14. 21. 1.   [2] 2. 14. 17. 7—19, 21. 1.
[3] 11. 1. 9. 2. They could not have procurators for lawsuits as they could not be concerned therein, 3. 3. 33.
[4] 5. 1. 12. 2.
[5] 4. 8. 9. *pr.* As to error, *ante*, p. 6. So they could not consent to the choice of an arbitrator, and the decision of one so appointed was not binding on either party, 4. 8. 32. 8.
[5] 25. 4. 1. 10.   [7] 39. 1. 5. 1.
[8] *Ibid., h. t.* 5. 2. The trespasses mentioned by Cicero (Pro Caecina, 8. 11; Pro Tullio, 8) were mere trespasses, not procedural acts, though they had procedural effects.
[9] 25. 4. 1. 10.
[10] 25. 4. 1. 13. The act does not create obligation; thus no question arises of acts done in slavery profiting after liberty, *post*, Ch. xxix.

(and later *procuratores*) in *causae liberales*[1]. One set of texts raises an apparent difficulty. A slave could offer, and take if it were offered to him, an extra-judicial oath, with the usual obligatory results, subject to some restrictions not here material[2]. There was nothing exceptional in this. But the extra-judicial oath, being purely matter of agreement, could always be refused, and one to whom it was offered had not the right, which existed in case of the judicial oath, to offer it back again: *iusiurandum quod ex conventione extra iudicium defertur referri non potest*[3]. Another text says: *si servus meus delato vel relato ei iure-iurando iuravit......puto dandam mihi actionem vel exceptionem propter conventionem*[4]. The last words shew that the reference is to an extra-judicial oath: the word *relato* is explained by the fact that the rule against *relatio* in such cases means only that if it were offered back, the offeree need not take it. The case supposed in the text is that the slave has offered an oath: the offeree has returned it and the slave has then voluntarily taken it.

As incapable of taking part in procedure slaves could not be formal *accusatores* in criminal charges[5]. It is no doubt partly on account of this exclusion that Hadrian enacted that complaints by slaves of ill-treatment by their masters were not to be regarded as accusations[4]. But it was in general as open to them as it was to freemen to "inform," *i.e.* to make *delationes* to the fisc of cases in which property is claimable by the fisc, and also of criminal offences. Both kinds of information are called *delatio*, though in legal texts the term is more commonly applied to fiscal cases[6], *i.e.* to notifications to the fisc of property to which it has a claim (such as *bona vacantia*), which someone is holding without right. The two classes may indeed overlap, since the right of the fisc may be due to the commission of a crime involving forfeiture. Informers were entitled to a reward, a fact which produced a class of professional *delatores*, the evil results compelling a number of enactments punishing false delations to the fisc, and, in some cases, true ones[7]. *Delatio* of crime was a form of blackmailing, which called for

---

[1] *Post*, Ch. xxviii. A slave could formally begin proceedings for a *libellus* to the Emperor on murder of his master. The case is exceptional, and moreover, the denouncing slave could claim his liberty, C. 1. 19. 1. Slaves could not appeal on behalf of absent master, but where possession was held on behalf of an absentee, and was invaded by force, the case being urgent, the judges were to hear even his slaves, C. Th. 4. 22. 1 = C. 8. 5. 1; C. Th. 4. 22. 4 (396). Slaves could apply for *bonorum possessio* for the master, but this could be given without application, 37. 1. 7.

[2] 12. 2. 20—23. *Post*, Ch. ix.   [3] 12. 2. 17. *pr.*   [4] 12. 2. 25.
[5] This had advantages: one who accuses a will as *falsum* loses any gift, 34. 9. 5. A slave with a gift of liberty by *fc.* induced a *heres*, on whom his liberty was not charged, to attack the will as *falsum*. He failed and lost his gift: the *fc.* was not affected, the slave not being an *accusator*, 48. 10. 24.

[6] For cases of its application to criminal charges, see p. 86, n. 2. See however, Mommsen, Strafrecht, 879.

[7] General prohibitions, P. 5. 13. 1; False delations, 49. 14. 24, C. Th. 10. 10 *passim*, C. 10. 11. 5; True delations, 34. 9. 1, C. Th. 10. 10 *passim*, C. 10. 11. 5, 7. Rein, Criminalrecht, 824; Mommsen, Strafrecht, 877 *sqq.*

repression as early as A.D. 20[1], but an information, if proved, does not seem to have been punishable in ordinary cases[2]. But even for crimes slaves were forbidden to inform against their *domini*. It seems that Constantine allowed no exceptions, but ordered the slaves to be in all cases crucified unheard[3]. Several enactments toward the close of the century except *maiestas*[4], and Justinian's Code omits this prohibition in Constantine's enactment[5]. And the Digest, laying down the general prohibition as to fiscal causes, and crediting it to Severus[6], allows slaves to accuse their masters for *maiestas*, for suppressing wills giving them liberty, for frauds on the *annona publica*, for coining, regrating, and revenue offences[7].

The capacity of slaves as witnesses requires fuller treatment. As a rule their evidence was not admissible in civil cases[8]. But the exclusion of such evidence, besides being a sort of self-denying ordinance, must have led to miscarriages of justice. Accordingly, convenience suggested a number of exceptions. Of these the most important is that they might give evidence in matters in which they were concerned—*de suo facto*—in the absence of other modes of proof, *e.g.* in case of transactions with them without witnesses[9]. We have no limitative enumeration of the cases in which their evidence was admitted[10]. Justinian adverts to a distinction drawn by earlier *leges* in the case of *hereditas*, according as the question is of the *hereditas* itself or of *res* in it, and provides that, whatever the form of the action, slaves shall be put to question only as to *res corporales*, and only those slaves who had charge of the thing, but in that case even if they had freedom by the will. Probably the older law allowed no "examination" of slaves given freedom unless the will was disputed, and then allowed it freely[11]. A text in the Digest may be read as saying that slaves may be tortured in any *res pecuniaria* if the truth cannot otherwise be reached[12], but it probably means rather that it is not to be done in any *res pecuniaria* if the truth can otherwise be reached. If understood in the former sense, it would render meaningless the texts which speak of torture of slaves as admissible in certain

---

1 Coll. 8. 7. 2, 3.
2 Delation of crime, 34. 9. 1; 37. 14. 1, 5; C. Th. 9. 5. 1; 9. 7. 2; 9. 16. 1; 10. 10. 1, 2. Rein, *loc. cit.*; Mommsen, *op. cit.* 493 *sqq.* C. 10. 11. 4, *notissimum est eos solos exsecrabiles nuntiatores esse qui fisco deferunt.*
3 C. Th. 9. 5. 1. Bruns, *op. cit.* i. 249 for a fragment of the original of this *lex.* See also C. 10. 11. 8. 2.
4 C. Th. 9. 6. 2, 3; C. 9. 1. 20; 10. 11. 6.
5 C. 9. 8. 3; C. Th. 10. 10. 17.　　　　　　　6 49. 14. 2. 6.
7 P. 5. 13. 3; 48. 4. 7. 2; 48. 10. 7; 48. 12. 1; 5. 1. 53; C. 10. 11. 7, 8. 2. The rule as to suppression of wills dates from M. Aurelius. The rules are somewhat similar to those as to evidence of slaves against their masters.
8 Nov. 90. 6.　　　　　9 P. 5. 16. 1, 2; D. 22. 5. 7; C. 9. 41. 15.
10 Cases as to ownership of them (C. 3. 32. 10; 9. 41. 12), *tutela*, disputed *hereditas* (P. 5. 15. 6; 5. 16. 2; D. 34. 9. 5. 15; 48. 10. 24; C. 9. 41. 13), *edictum* Carbonianum (37. 10. 3. 5). Justinian allowed them to be examined as to the correctness of the inventory made by the *heres* (N. 1. 2).
11 C. 9. 41. 18; *post*, Ch. XI.　　　　12 48. 18. 9. *pr.*, Pius and Severus.

urgent cases, and subject to the same restriction[1], and would be inconsistent with another text which implies that the evidence of slaves was admissible only in a limited class of cases[2].

In cases in which the evidence of slaves was admissible it was taken normally by torture[3]; indeed it appears that it could not be received in any other form[2]. It should be added that, while the evidence of slaves was not to be used except where proof was lacking, on the other hand recourse was not to be had to it, at least in later law[4], unless there was already some evidence[5].

In criminal matters also the examination of slaves was, normally, by torture[6]. But evidence so obtained is always doubtful: scorn of the torture and hope to placate the torturers were possibilities to be considered before it was applied[7]. It was therefore subject to some restrictions, in the framing of which no doubt humanity had some place[8]. There must be no torture unless there is on the one hand, need of further evidence, and on the other. at least, one witness, already[9]. As early as Augustus it was enacted that torture was not to be resorted to except in serious crime[10], and Hadrian provided that those slaves were first to be tortured who were most likely to be informed on the matter[11]. A third person's slaves could be tortured without his offering them, but only singly, and only when security or promise had been given for their value, with a double penalty if it were *per calumniam accusatoris*[12]. The value could be recovered by an action *praescriptis verbis* though the agreement were informal[13]. A slave manumitted to avoid the torture could still be tortured[14]. On the other hand slaves *ex domo accusatoris* were not to be too readily accepted for torture[15]. Slaves were not to be killed under torture, *ut salvi sint innocentiae aut supplicio*[16]. It is clear that the officer in charge of the *tormenta* had a very wide discretion. But the torture

---

[1] *e.g.* C. 9. 41. 12.   [2] 23. 5. 21. 2.
[3] P. 5. 16. 2; C. 3. 32. 10; D. 48. 18. 9. *pr.*, 20. Mommsen, *op. cit.* 412 *sqq.*
[4] 22. 3. 7; P. 2. 17. 12, wrongful admission of it was ground of appeal, 48. 19. 20.
[5] 21. 1. 58. 2.   [6] 48. 19. 1, 9. 1; C. 4. 20. 8.
[7] 48. 18. 1. 23, and adjoining texts. In one case torture was preferred to a cruel master, 48. 18. 1. 27. Similar case Val. Max. 8. 4. Mommsen, Strafrecht, 416, says that the object being to see if he changes his language under torture, there would be none if the facts were not contradicted. But the court might wish to satisfy itself. Cp. p. 96, n. 2.
[8] But a slave might be tortured many times: Val. Max. *loc. cit.* speaks of *octies tortus.*
[9] P. 5. 14. 4; C. 9. 41. 8; D. 48. 18. 1. 1, 2, 10. 3, 18. 3, 20. No judgment on sole evidence of a tortured slave.
[10] 48. 18. 8.
[11] 48. 18. 1. 2. Women to be tortured only in extreme cases and on suspicion: pregnant women not at all, D. 48. 19. 3; P. 1. 12. 4; C. 9. 41. 3. Pius seems to have laid down the same rule for children under 14, but the texts suggest that in later law the rule did not apply to *maiestas* and was not absolute, 48. 18. 10, 15. 1.
[12] C. 9. 41. 7; C. 9. 46. 6; P. 5. 16. 3; D. 48. 18. 13.
[13] 19. 5. 8. The text deals with a suspected slave, but the rule is probably general.
[14] 48. 18. 1. 13; P. 5. 16. 9; Coll. 4. 12. 8; the rule is attributed to Pius. *Post*, Ch. xxv. Slaves sometimes deposited with *sequester, ut quaestio habeatur.* 16. 3. 7. *pr.*
[15] 48. 18. 1. 3, 10. 4.   [16] 48. 18. 7.

was to be in reason and this was for the judge to determine[1]. It seems indeed that the question whether a man should be tortured at all was always in the discretion of the court, and not of a party[2].

It is frequently laid down that a slave is not to be examined for[3] or against[4] his *dominus*, or one jointly owned for or against either master[5]. As to evidence against *domini* this is a very ancient rule. Tacitus, speaking of A.D. 16, alludes to it as based on *vetus senatus-consultum*[6]. According to Dio Cassius[7], Julius Caesar solemnly confirmed the rule. Cicero in several passages[8] refers to it, basing it not on the doubtfulness of the evidence, but on the reason that it exposes the master to an ignominy worse than death. Augustus and Tiberius evaded the rule (in *maiestas*), by ordering the slave to be sold to an *actor publicus*[9]. Tiberius even disregarded it altogether[10].

The exclusion of evidence on behalf of the master seems a much later notion. From the language of Tacitus it does not seem to have existed in A.D. 20[11]. A text from Papinian quotes Hadrian as holding such evidence admissible[12]. On the other hand Paul speaks of the evidence as excluded[13], and an enactment of A.D. 240 speaks of this as an old established rule[14]. It is plainly the settled rule of the Corpus Iuris.

The rule applied even though the master offered them or an outsider was willing to pay their price[15]. Ownership shewn as a fact, whatever its origin, barred the *quaestio*[16]. Nor could those who had formerly belonged to him be heard[17]. *Bonae fidei* possession equally barred the evidence[18]. It was not merely excluded: it was capitally punished, at least if volunteered[19], and it may be added that evidence without torture was equally inadmissible[20]. The exclusion applied also

---

[1] 48. 18. 10. 3.
[2] Mommsen, *op. cit.* 412: a slave witness is likely to become a defendant: the texts do not distinguish clearly.
[3] C. 4. 20. 8; C. 9. 41. 6, 7, 14.
[4] P. 1. 12. 3; 5. 13. 3; 5. 16. 4; C. 4. 20. 8; 9. 41. 6, 7; D. 1. 12. 1. 8; 48. 18. 1. 5, 9. 1, 15. 2, 18. 5, 6, 7.
[5] P. 5. 16. 6; C. 9. 41. 13; D. 48. 18. 3. In civil or criminal cases, P. 5. 16. 5.
[6] Ann. 2. 30.   [7] Dio Cass. 57. 19.
[8] Pro Milone, 22; Pro Rege Deiotaro, 1.
[9] Taciti Ann. 2. 30; 3. 67; Dio C. 55. 5.   [10] Dio C. 57. 19.
[11] Ann. 3. 14.   [12] 48. 18. 17. 2.
[13] P. 2. 17. 12. He seems to admit it in D. 29. 5. 6. 2. But it was allowed in the case there dealt with. *Post*, p. 95.
[14] C. 9. 41. 6.   [15] 48. 18. 1. 18, 18. 7.
[16] 48. 18. 18. 8; P. 5. 16. 8b. It was the first thing looked at. *Servus heredis* could not be tortured *in re hereditaria* though it was supposed he had been bought to bar his evidence, 48. 18. 1. 6.
[17] C. 9. 41. 14; *e.g.* a *servus poenae* formerly his, 48. 18. 17. 3, or one he had redhibited or sold (48. 18. 11, 18. 6; P. 5. 16. 8. Cp. 21. 1. 60; 47. 2. 17. 2; *ante*, p. 61).
[18] 48. 18. 1. 8. If ownership in litigation, he who gave security was owner for this purpose, *h. t.* 15. 2.
[19] Mommsen, *op. cit.* 415, citing C. Th. 9. 6. 3, 10. 10. 17 (C. 9. 1. 20; 10. 11. 6), C. 10. 11. 8. 2. Bruns, Fontes, i. 250.
[20] 48. 18. 1. 16, 9. 1.

to slaves owned by father, child, or ward, except, in the last case, in the *actio tutelae*[1].

On the other hand an ownership created after proceedings were begun was no bar, nor was apparent ownership under a transaction which was absolutely void[2]. The slave of a corporation could be heard against its members: they did not own him[3]. And *servi hereditarii* are not slaves of the claimants of the *hereditas*, at any rate in an action concerning it, involving an allegation that the will was forged[4]. The uncertainty of ownership is mentioned, but this might better have led to exclusion.

It was not only in relation to evidence on behalf of the *dominus* that the rules underwent change: it is clear that in many other points the rules of later law are the result of an evolution, the tendency being always in the direction of exclusion. Thus Paul allows torture of a slave, collusively purchased, the purchase being rescinded and the price returned[5]. The Digest appears to limit this to the case where the acquisition is after the case has begun[6]. So Paul says that a slave manumitted to avoid torture can still be tortured[7]. The Digest in an extract from a work of Ulpian lays down the same rule, attributing it to Pius, and adding, *dummodo in caput domini non torqueatur*[8]. If a slave under torture did incidentally reveal something against his master, it was laid down by Trajan that this was evidence[9], and Hadrian speaks, obscurely, in the same sense[10]. Elsewhere, however, Hadrian and Caracalla are credited with the contrary view[11], and we are told that the opinion of Trajan was departed from in many constitutions[12]. Severus and Caracalla say that such evidence is to be received only when there is no other proof[13]. Paul declares that it is not to be listened to at all[14]. In A.D. 240 this is declared to have been long settled[15], and, the enactment of Severus and Caracalla having been inserted in the Digest, in a somewhat altered form[16], this must be taken as the accepted view: the safety of owners is not to be in the hands of their slaves. What is demonstrated in these cases is highly probable in some others. Thus it is likely that the extensions from owner to *bonae fidei* possessors[17], and to slaves of near relatives and wards, are late[18]: the original rule having applied only to actual owners.

---

[1] *h. t.* 10. 2, even *castrensis peculii*, C. 9. 41. 2.
[3] 1. 8. 1; 48. 18. 1. 7.
[2] 48. 18. 1. 14. 15.
[4] C. 9. 41. 10. D. 48. 18. 2 lays it down more generally.
[5] P. 5. 16. 7.
[6] 48. 18. 1. 14.
[7] P. 5. 16. 9.
[8] 48. 18. 1. 13.
[9] 48. 18. 1. 19.
[10] *h. t.* 1. 22.
[11] *h. t.* 1. 5.
[12] *h. t.* 1. 19.
[13] C. 9. 41. 1. 1.
[14] 48. 18. 18. 5; P. 5. 16. 4.
[15] C. 9. 41. 6.
[16] 48. 18. 1. 16. Cf. C. 9. 41. 1. Wallon, *op. cit.* 3. App. 12 for some temporary cases.
[17] 48. 18. 1. 8.
[18] *Ante*, p. 88. So the rule that *servus damnati* can be tortured, *in caput eius*, may have been law always, but the assigned reason, *quia desierunt eius esse* (48. 18. 1. 12), squares ill with what has been said as to past ownership (p. 88) and suggests that the rule of exclusion was late.

There were some crimes to which the rule did not apply[1]. Cicero speaks of corruption of Vestal Virgins, and *coniuratio*[2] as exceptions. It is, however, remarked by Mommsen that these republican exceptions are political[3], and he thinks legal exceptions do not begin till Severus. It seems likely, however, that the exception, shortly to be mentioned, for the case of murder of a master was earlier. However this may be, Severus allowed the evidence in adultery, *maiestas* and fraud on the revenue[4]. These exceptions are constant (except for a short time under the Emperor Tacitus, who abolished them all[5]) and are repeatedly reaffirmed[6]. Other exceptions are mentioned. Several texts mention regrating, *i.e.* creating an artifical scarcity in food supplies[7]. Hermogenianus mentions coinage offences[8]. Constantine allowed the evidence where a woman cohabited with her slave[9], and also laid it down that a slave might be tortured, to discover if his *dominus* had prompted him to run away to a third person in order to involve him in the liability for receiving *fugitivi*[10]. The evidence was not admitted in ordinary crimes of violence[11]. Thus the texts of the Digest allowing the slave of common owners to be tortured in the case of murder of one of them, where the other is suspected[12], are the result of the *Sc.* Silanianum, and the complementary legislation[13].

Paul[14] tells us that if a slave, who has run away, says, on discovery, in the presence of trustworthy people, that he had previously run away from his master, this is evidence available in the *actio redhibitoria*. Elsewhere[15] he tells that in absence of proof of earlier flight, *servi responsioni credendum est: in se enim interrogari non pro domino aut in dominum videtur*. This text appears in the Digest with *quaestioni* instead of *responsioni*. The reason is bad and Paul is the only authority for the rule. In the Sententiae he expresses a rule that a slave's evidence in such a matter is admissible; the change of word in the Digest means little. But the other text, which may be the original statement, need mean no more than that the evidence of trustworthy people as to what the slave had been heard to say on such a matter, out of court and not under pressure, was admissible.

In relation to offences under the *Lex* Iulia *de adulteriis* elaborate provisions are laid down. Slaves could be examined against their

---

[1] 1. 12. 1. 8.   [2] Pro Milone, 22; Part. Orat. 34. 118.
[3] *op. cit.* 414.   [4] C. 9. 41. 1.   [5] Flav. Vop., Tacitus 9. 4.
[6] C. Th. 9. 6. 2; C. 5. 17. 8. 6; 9. 8. 6; D. 5. 1. 53; 48. 4. 7. 2; 48. 18. 10. 1. Some of the texts deal with delation and accusation, but if this was allowed evidence was.
[7] 5. 1. 53; 48. 12. 1. All dealing with accusation. Cp. 48. 2. 13.
[8] 5. 1. 53.   [9] C. Th. 9. 9. 1; C. 9. 11. 1.   [10] C. 6. 1. 4. 4.
[11] Milo's manumissions are a precaution not so much against law, as against an uncontrollable administration.
[12] 29. 5. 6. 2; 48. 18. 17. 2. Hadrian.
[13] *Post*, p. 95. Thus when owner is killed, *servi hereditarii* may be tortured though *heres* is a *suus*, and the evidence implicates him. 29. 5. 6. 1.
[14] 21. 1. 58. 2.   [15] P. 2. 17. 12; D. 22. 3. 7.

owners, whether the accuser were a relative or not[1]. It might be a slave of the accused or of the husband or wife of the accused[2]. The point seems to be not only that slaves may here be tortured against their master, but that this is the regular mode of procedure and that there need be no preliminary evidence, or any special reason to think this slave knows something about the matter. If a slave, liable to torture in such a case, is freed to avoid the torture, the manumission is null, a rule of Paul, somewhat stronger than that laid down by him in other cases[3]. The accuser and the accused must both be present[4]. After torture the slaves vest in the State, if and so far as the accused had any interest in them, in order that they may not fear to tell the truth[5]. Even if they deny, they still become public property, that they may not profit by any lie[6]. So also do slaves of the accuser, but not slaves of *extranei*, since in their case the reason does not exist[7]. If the accused is acquitted he or she can recover from the accuser, apart from *calumnia*, the estimated single value of the damage[8]. If he is condemned, the surviving slaves *publicantur*[9].

The general proposition that slaves were liable for crime needs no proof[10]. The master's right of punishment (which did not necessarily exclude the right of the public authority) was lost, as to serious crime, early in the Empire[11]. They must be tried where they had offended[12], and thus the *dominus*, (who could defend by himself or a procurator[13],) must defend there, and could not have the case removed to his own province[14]. The master's refusal to defend did not amount to a conviction, or to dereliction. He remained owner; the slave might be defended by anyone, and would in any case be tried, and if innocent acquitted[15]. Slaves might be tortured on suspicion, and there was an *actio ad exhibendum* for their production for this purpose[16]. They might

---

[1] 48. 18. 4, 5, 17. *pr.* not merely to give every protection, but because it could hardly have been done without knowledge of the slaves, Coll. 4. 12. 8. It was not allowed for *stuprum* (48. 18. 4, 17. 1) or incest unless adulterous 48. 5. 40. 8; 48. 18. 5. Val. Max. 6. 8.
[2] Coll. 4. 11. 1; 4. 12. 8; C. Th. 9. 7. 4; C. 5. 17. 8. 6; 9. 9. 3; D. 48. 18. 1. 11, or of ascendents or even strangers if employed by the accused, 48. 5. 28. 6, or one in whom he or she had a usufruct, or *b. f.* possession: it might be a *statuliber* or one to whom fideicommissary liberty was due, 48. 5. 28. 8—10. Macrobius, Sat. 1. 11. If the slave is declared by both parents to have been dear to the accused his evidence is to have little weight.
[3] P. 5. 16. 9; Coll. 4. 12. 8. [4] 48. 5. 28. 7.
[5] 48. 5. 28. 11, 12. [6] *h. l.* 13. [7] *h. l.* 14.
[8] 48. 5. 28. 15, 29, *Cond. ex lege.* If the slave is accused double his value may be payable, 48. 5. 28 *pr.*
[9] 48. 18. 6.
[10] From ante-Justinianian sources: *Plagium* (Coll. 14. 3; C. Th. 9. 18. 1); crimes of violence (P. 5. 18. 1; C. Th. 9. 10. 4; 9. 24. 2; 9. 45. 5). Fiscal offences and Delation (*ante*, p. 85). Coining (C. Th. 9. 21. 1). See also P. 5. 13. 3; Coll. 14. 2. 3; C. Th. 7. 18. 2; *h. t.* 9. 3; 9. 9. 1; 12. 1. 6, 50 etc. Cp. C. 1. 12. 4; 9. 24. 1; D. 2. 1. 7. 1; 47. 9. 1. *pr.*; 48. 8. 4. 2; 48. 10. 1. 13, etc.
[11] *Ante*, p. 36. [12] 48. 2. 7. 4.
[13] 48. 1. 11; C. 9. 2. 2; anyone in fact can defend, 48. 1. 9; 48. 19. 19.
[14] 48. 2. 7. 4.
[15] 48. 1. 9; 48. 19. 19. Though his ownership remained he could not free, *post*, Ch. xxv.
[16] 10. 4. 20.

not, however, be tortured till the accuser has signed the charge, and given the usual undertakings[1]. One to whom fideicommissary liberty was due was not to be tortured till the confession of someone else had raised suspicion against him[2]. *Servi hereditarii* left to a *heres* or *extraneus* might be tortured on suspicion of having made away with property, and need not be delivered till after this was done[3]. So a slave might be tortured on suspicion of adultery with the wife, she being tried first to avoid *praeiudicium*[4].

In capital charges whoever was defending must give security *iudicio sisti*, otherwise the slave would be kept in chains[5]. The rules of procedure and general principles are the same as when the accused is a free man[6], but it must be remembered that at no time was there a general criminal law. There was a mass of criminal laws, and principle is not easy to find.

It should be noticed that the rule that slaves cannot take part in judicial proceedings is applied even where they are the accused. We have seen that the master, or indeed anyone, may defend them, and that the defender is the real party is shewn by the fact that it is thought necessary to say that, after trial, it is the slave, not the defender, who is condemned[7]. If no one defends, the court will not sentence at once, but will try the issue[8], and in such a case the slave is allowed, *ex necessitate*, to plead his own cause—*ut ex vinculis causam dicat*[9]. In like manner slaves could not appeal though others could for them. Modestinus says that, if no one will, *ipsi servo auxilium sibi implorare non denegabimus*[10]. The meaning of this is not very clear: in any case it seems probable that in earlier law the slave who could get no one to appeal was helpless. The concession, whatever it amounts to, may be due to Justinian.

The conditions of liability are not always the same. Some crimes could be committed only by slaves. Thus none but slaves could incur the penalties falling on *fugitivi*[11]. It was capital for a slave knowingly

---

[1] C. Th. 9. 1. 14; C. 9. 2. 13. Undertakings, 48. 2. 7.
[2] 48. 18. 19. The following notes give many references to torture on suspicion.
[3] 30. 67. *pr.*; 10. 2. 18. *pr.*
[4] 1. 12. 1. 5; 48. 5. 34. *pr.* Pius. One claiming torture of slave on suspicion of adultery or other crime must at judge's direction pay double his value to the person interested, owner, pledgee or *bona fide* buyer from non-owner, division being made between common owners and owner and fructuary, 19. 5. 8; 48. 5. 28. *pr.* –4. This is by way of security as in case of single value where torture of slave as witness is claimed, 48. 5. 28. 16. In 12. 4. 15 a slave handed over for *quaestio* to be returned if innocent is handed to *Pr. vigilum* as if caught in act and at once killed. *Condictio* and, if ownership did not pass, *furti* and *ad exhibendum*.
[5] If *dominus* is away or has not at the moment the means, he can come in later without undue delay, 48. 2. 17; 48. 3. 2.
[6] 48. 2. 12. 3 (*Sc.* Cottianum, A.D. 20). Those barred from accusing a freeman of adultery cannot accuse a slave. But Domitian provided that general pardons on occasion of *feriae* did not apply to slaves who were undefended, 48. 3. 2; 48. 16. 16. Minor differences, *e.g.* C. 9. 4. 6. 2, 3.
[7] C. 9. 2. 2.   [8] 48. 19. 19.   [9] 48. 3. 2; 29. 5. 25. 1.
[10] 49. 1. 15, 18.   [11] *Post*, Ch. XII.

to offer himself for military service[1]. Slaves might be capitally punished for bringing claims at law against the Fisc, in certain cases[2]. Slaves or *liberti* were punishable for aspiring to the decurionate[3]. Slaves were capitally punished for cohabiting with their mistresses[4]. In some cases delation was punishable in a slave where it would not have been so in a free man[5]. Conversely there were crimes for which a slave could not be tried, owing to the punishment or to the definition. Here the heterogeneous nature of the criminal law is brought into strong relief. Venuleius tells us that slaves can be accused under any law except those imposing money penalties, or punishments, like *relegatio*[6], not applicable to slaves, such as the *lex* Iulia *de vi privata*, which fixes only money penalties[7], or the *lex* Cornelia *iniuriarum*, for the same reason. But in this last case he says: *durior ei poena extra ordinem immanebit.* He also tells us that the *lex* Pompeia *de parricidiis* does not, on its terms, apply to slaves since it speaks of relatives, but that, as *natura communis est*, it is extended to them[8]. On the other hand we are told by Callistratus that *terminum motum*, for which the old law imposed a fine, was capital in a slave unless the master paid the *multa*, a rule akin to that applied in delict, and one which might have been expected to be generalised[9]. For *sepulchri violatio* a freeman incurred a fine: a slave was punished, *extra ordinem*[10].

In relation to punishment there were numerous differences. In theft and similar cases the criminal liability was alternative with a noxal action[11]. There was prescription in adultery but not if the accused was a slave[12]. The punishment might be different in the case of slaves, and in most cases was more severe[13]. And though they had obtained freedom in the interval, they were to be punished as slaves[14]. *Vincula perpetua* though always unlawful seem to have been occasionally imposed on slaves[15]. A sturdy vagrant was given

---

[1] Pliny, Epist. Traj. 30, but the Digest while excluding *damnati* of many kinds does not lay down this rule.
[2] Nov. Theod. 17. 1.   Apparently temporary.   [3] C. 10. 33.
[4] C. Th. 9. 9. 1; C. 9. 11. 1.   Extended to *liberti*, Nov. Anthem. 1.   Elaborate rules as to punishment of woman.
[5] *Ante*, p. 85.   [6] But see *post*, p. 94.
[7] Forfeiture of ¼ of *bona*.   Though not personally liable they might be the *homines coacti*, 48. 7. 2. 3.
[8] 48. 2. 12. 4.   The *lex* Cornelia *de falsis* covered slaves who in a will wrote gifts of liberty to themselves and by interpretation those writing gifts to their *domini*, 48. 10. 10, 15. 1.
[9] 47. 21. 3. 1.   Hadrian substituted ordinary criminal punishments (*h. t.* 2).   The similar change in *Plagium* may be due to the same cause, *ante*, p. 33.
[10] 47. 12. 3. 11.   [11] 47. 2. 93; C. 3. 41. 3.
[12] C. 9. 9. 25.   Here it was not time, but condonation.   M. Aurelius ordered a husband to prosecute the guilty slave, though the wife was protected by time, 48. 2. 5.   The *vir*, even a *filius familias* could kill a slave adulterous with his wife, under circumstances which did not allow killing of other than base persons, 48. 5. 25.
[13] 47. 9. 4. 1; 48. 19. 16. 3, 28. 16.   For list of punishments for slaves, shewing greater severity, 48. 19. 10.   Wallon, *op. cit.* 2. 198; Rein, *op. cit.* 913; Mommsen, Strafrecht, 1032.
[14] 48. 19. 1.'   [15] C. 9. 47. 6, 10; D. 48. 19. 8. 13.

to anyone who denounced him, a right of action being reserved to his *dominus*[1]. *Furtum* ceased to be capital in slaves when the Edict made it a private delict in freemen[2]. Though condemnation as a *servus poenae* ended ownership, temporary punishment did not, and the *peculium* of any slave condemned was restored to his *dominus*[3].

A slave being bound to obey, the command of the *dominus*, or of his tutor or curator, might be a defence in matters *quae non habent atrocitatem facinoris vel sceleris*[4]. Where a slave wrote a gift of liberty to himself, at the order of his *dominus*, who did not subscribe it, but acknowledged it in letters, he was not free but was not liable under the *lex* Cornelia *de falsis*[5]. But command was no defence for murder, robbery, piracy, or any violent crime unless committed in the course of a *bona fide* claim of right[6]. It did not excuse for *occisio*, under the *lex* Cornelia *de sicariis*, though reasonable defence of the master would. Apparently it did not excuse for *iniuria*[7] or for *furtum*[8]. In some cases it reduced the penalty. Thus, for a slave who committed gross violence, death was the penalty, under the *lex* Iulia *de vi*, but if it were by his master's orders he was condemned *in metallum*[9]. So, for demolishing sepulchres the penalty was *metallum*, but, if it were done *iussu domini*, the penalty was *relegatio*[10]. We are told elsewhere that this punishment was not applicable to slaves[11]. Mommsen suggests[12] as the reason that their place of residence was not at their discretion. The reason is hardly conclusive, and we have here an exception. But these present enactments are somewhat haphazard: it is not clear that they express any real principle or policy.

The killing of masters by their slaves was the subject of special legislation. There was a tradition of an ancient usage for all the slaves in the house to be killed, if one had killed the master: Nero, in A.D. 56, obtained a *senatus* consult confirming this in general terms. The rule errs by excess and defect: it is needlessly cruel, and it requires prior proof that one of the slaves has actually killed. It does not appear in the later law[13].

---

[1] C. Th. 14. 18. 1; C. 11. 26. 1. For light offences, *flagellis verberati*, 48. 2. 6; plotting against life of *dominus*, burnt alive, 48. 19. 28. 11; *atrox iniuria*, condemned *in metallum*; ordinary cases, scourged and returned for temporary chains, P. 5. 4. 22; 47. 10. 45; similar rule for *abactores*, P. 5. 18. 1. As to return to *dominus*, Mommsen, *op. cit.* 898. If *dominus* would not receive them, sold if possible, if not, perpetual *opus publicum*, 48. 19. 10. *pr.*, *post*, Ch. XVII. For coining, killed, but no right of fisc arose: no forfeiture unless *dominus* knew. This rule was general, P. 5. 12. 12; C. 9. 12. 4.

[2] G. 3. 189. A slave who dug up a public way might be fustigated by anyone: a freeman would be fined, 43. 10. 2. Another case, 47. 9. 4. 1.·

[3] Schol. Bas. (Heimbach) 60. 52. 12; C. 9. 49. 1.

[4] 43. 24. 11. 7; 50. 17. 157. *pr.* *Factum vi aut clam*, 43. 24. 11. 7, undertaking tacit *fideicommissum*, 35. 2. 13.

[5] C. 9. 23. 6, *post*, Ch. xxv. Effect of *subscriptio*, 48. 10. 1. 8, 14, 15. 3, 22. 9.

[6] 44. 7. 20.   [7] 47. 10. 17. 8.   [8] 25. 2. 21. 1.

[9] C. Th. 9. 10. 4; C. 9. 12. 8.   [10] C. 9. 19. 2 (390).

[11] *Ante*, p. 93. But 40. 9. 2 also assumes its possibility.   [12] Mommsen, *op. cit.* 968.

[13] Tac. Ann. 13. 32, 14. 42.

A *Sc.* Silanianum, apparently of the time of Augustus, confirmed by a *Sc.* Claudianum and a *Sc.* Pisonianum, and again by an *Oratio* M. Aurelii[1], provided for the torture of slaves if there was reason to think the master had been killed by them. After the truth had been discovered by torture the guilty slave might be executed[2]. The slaves who might thus be tortured were those under the same roof or hard by—all who were near enough to help the master and failed to do so[3]; not, for instance, slaves who were in a remote part of the property, or on another estate[4]. If it occurred on a journey, those with him, or who had fled, might be tortured, but if none was with him the *Scc.* did not apply[5]. Those partly his might be tortured unless at the time protecting another owner[6]. Slaves freed by the will might be tortured, but with caution[7]. Trajan added even *inter vivos liberti* with *ius anuli aurei*[8].

The power extended to slaves of children not in *potestas*, to slaves *castrensis peculii*, and, by a *Sc.* of Nero, to those of wife or husband[9]. It applied also on the death of a child, actual or adopted, living with the *paterfamilias*, whether in *potestas* or not (though the latter case was doubted by Marcellus), even if the *paterfamilias* were at the moment *cum hostibus* or even dead, if his *hereditas* were not yet entered on[10]. But it did not apply to slaves of the mother where a child was killed[11], nor of *socer* where *vir* or *uxor* was killed[12]. Where a son, instituted by his father, was killed before entry, a slave legated or freed by the father's will might be tortured, the gift failing by the torture[13]. The difficulty is that he is not and never would be the heir's. Scaevola decides that the *Sc.* applies, probably because the slave is the property of the *hereditas*, which represents the deceased father[14]. If it were a disinherited son, Paul holds that the slaves of the father could not be tortured till it was seen if the *hereditas* was entered on: if not, they could be tortured, for they would be his; if it was, they were *alieni*[15].

---

[1] 29. 5; *h. t.* 8; C. 6. 35. 11. Exact relation of these laws uncertain.
[2] P. 3. 5. 6.
[3] P. 3. 5. 3; D. 29. 5. 1. 27, 28; C. 6. 35. 12. Hadrian laid down the restriction clearly, Spartian, Hadrian, 18. 11.
[4] Except suspects on other grounds, 29. 5. 1. 26, 30; P. 3. 5. 7.
[5] P. 3. 5. 3, 6, 8; D. 29. 5. 1. 31.
[6] 29. 5. 3. 4. So might those subject to pledge or usufruct, or *statuliberi*, or those conditionally legated. But no torture of those to whom *fc.* of liberty was due unless suspected, nor of those held in usufruct or *bonae fidei* possessed by deceased, 29. 5. 1. 2—5. The *Sc.* speaks of *domini*.
[7] 29. 5. 3. 16; C. 9. 41. 5.   [8] 29. 5. 10. 11.
[9] 29. 5. 1. 14, 15; P. 3. 5. 5.   [10] 29. 5. 1. 7—9, 12, not those given in adoption.
[11] 29. 5. 1. 11.
[12] And killing of foster-child did not bring the *Sc.* into operation, 29. 5. 1. 10, 16.
[13] 29. 5. 1. 13.
[14] The reason in the text cannot be right (*quia exstinctum legatum et libertas est*). The will might not fail: there might be other *heredes*.
[15] 29. 5. 10.

The basis of the liability was that they did not render help, *armis, manu, clamore et obiectu corporis*[1]. The torture was not punishment: it was a preliminary to the *supplicium* which awaited the guilty person. Not doing his best to save the *dominus* sufficed to justify torture: more than this would of course be needed to conviction of the murder. Though it were clear who killed, the *quaestio* must continue, to discover any prompters[2]. The *lex* Cornelia gave a money reward for revealing the guilty slave[3]. Though the heir was accused the slaves might still be tortured[4]. The *Sc.* applied only to open killing, not to poisoning and secret killing, which the slaves could not have prevented[7]: it must be certain that he was killed violently[5]. If the owner killed himself, only those might be tortured who were present, able to prevent, and failing to do so; in that case they were liable not merely to torture, but to punishment[6].

Fear of personal harm was no defence, if they took no steps in protection: they must prefer, says Hadrian, their master's safety to their own[7]. But as failure to help was the ground of liability there were several excuses. Thus, unless circumstances shewed them to be *doli capaces*[8], child slaves might not be tortured, though they might be threatened[9]. Nor could those be tortured who did their best though they failed to save[10]. If the master lived some time and did not complain of the slaves, or if, as Commodus ruled, he expressly absolved them, they were not to be tortured[11]. If the husband killed the wife in adultery, there was no torture, and if either killed the other, slaves were not to be tortured without proof that they heard the cries and did not respond[12]. It should be added that even the master's dying accusation was not proof entitling the authorities to proceed at once to *supplicium* without further evidence[13].

These provisions are merely ancillary to the main provisions of the *Sç.* Silanianum, the object of which was to secure that the death should be avenged, by preventing beneficiaries of the estate from taking it, and therefore freed slaves from getting freedom so that they could not be tortured, till steps had been taken to bring the slayer to justice. It

---

[1] *h. t.* 19.   [2] *h. t.* 6. *pr.*, 17; P. 3. 5. 12.
[3] 29. 5. 29. *pr.*, and conversely, punished one who concealed a slave liable under the *Sc.*, *h. t.* 3. 12.
[4] 29. 5. 6. 1; P. 3. 5. 9.
[5] 29. 5. 6. 3, 1. 17—21, 24; P. seems to hold that there might be torture in case of poisoning, P. 3. 5. 2. This refers to the other provisions of the *Sc.*, *i.e.* the exclusion of the *heres* who does not seek the murderer.
[6] P. 3. 5. 4; D. 29. 5. 1. 22, 23. The text observes that the *Sc.* does not apply.
[7] 29. 5. 1. 28, 29.   [8] *h. t.* 14.   [9] *h. t.* 1. 32, 33.
[10] *h. l.* 34, 35. Mere pretence at help was no defence, *h. l.* 36, 37. Other excuses were sickness, helpless age, blindness, lunacy, dumbness so that they could not call, deafness so that they could not hear, shut up or chained so that they could not help, at the time protecting wife or husband of the owner, *h. t.* 3. 5, 11.
[11] *h. t.* 1. 38, 2.   [12] *h. t.* 3. 2, 3.
[13] *h. t.* 3. 1. Slave so handed for *supplicium* was not in the *hereditas pro Falcidia*, 35. 2. 3. 39.

provided that the will should not be opened till the *quaestio* had been held (*i.e.* all necessary enquiry made), with a penalty of forfeiture to the Fisc, and a further fine[1]. The will was not to be opened, no *aditio* was to be made, or *bonorum possessio* demanded, till the *quaestio*[2], the time for claims of *bonorum possessio* being prolonged accordingly, except in case of poisoning, where as there would be no *quaestio* there need be no delay[3]. There was an *actio popularis* (half the penalty going to the informer) against any who opened the will before the *quaestio* had been held[4]. If some slaves ran away and the will was opened and they were freed by it they could still be tortured[5].

[1] P. 3. 5. 1; C. 6. 35. 3. Other enquiry may be needed besides torture of slaves, 29. 5. 1. 25. By *Sc.* Taurianum penalties not enforceable after five years, save in parricide, when they are perpetual, 29. 5. 13.
[2] 29. 5. 3. 18, 29; P. 3. 5. 1.
[3] 29. 5. 21. *pr.* It appears that in later law similar delays might be ordered where other offences were supposed to have been committed by slaves. Daroste, N. R. H. 18. 583.
[4] 29. 5. 25. 2.
[5] *h. t.* 3. 17, *h. t.* 25. 1. Justinian provided for a doubt left by this legislation as to the date at which, in such cases, the liberty took effect, C. 6. 35. 11. Many details of these matters are omitted, and see *post*, Ch. xxv.

CHAPTER V.

THE SLAVE AS MAN. NON-COMMERCIAL RELATIONS (CONT.).
DELICTS BY SLAVES.

WE have now to consider the rights and liabilities which may be created when a delict is committed by a slave. The general rule is that upon such a delict a noxal action lies against the *dominus*, under which he must either pay the damages ordinarily due for such a wrong, or hand over the slave to the injured person. We are not directly concerned with the historical origin of this liability: it is enough to say that it has been shewn[1] that the system originated in private vengeance: the money payment, originally an agreed composition, develops into a payment due as of right, with the alternative of surrender: the pecuniary aspect of the liability becomes more and more prominent, till the surrender of the slave loses all trace of its original vindictive purpose, and is regarded as mere emolument, and the money composition comes to be regarded by some of the jurists as the primary liability[2]. But the system as we know it was elaborated by the classical jurists, who give no sign of knowledge of the historical origin of the institution, and whose determinations do not depend thereon[3].

The XII Tables distinguish between *Furtum* and *Noxa*[4]. *Furtum* here means *furtum nec manifestum*, (the more serious case was capitally punishable,) and *Noxa* no doubt refers to the other wrongs—mainly forms of physical damage—for which the Tables gave a money penalty[5]. The provisions of the Tables as to most of these other matters were early superseded, but the verbal distinction between *furtum* and *noxa* was long retained in the transactions of everyday life. Varro, in

---

[1] Holmes, Common Law, 9 *sqq.*; Ihering, Geist. d. R. R. § 11 a; Girard, N. R. H. 12. 31 *sqq.* But see Cuq, Institutions Juridiques, 1. 368.

[2] G. 4. 75; In. 4. 8. *pr.*; 4. 17. 1; D. 5. 3. 20. 5; 9. 4. 1; 42. 1. 6. 1.

[3] The texts give the reason for the alternative mode of discharge as being the injustice of making the owner pay more than the value of the slave for his wrongdoing, the point apparently being that as he has not been guilty of *culpa*, there is no logical reason why he should suffer at all. See texts in last note and 47. 2. 62. 5.

[4] Bruns, Fontes, i. 38.

[5] Some said *Noxia* meant the harm done, *noxa* the slave, and that this was the origin of the name—noxal actions, 9. 3. 1. 8; 9. 4. 1. In. 4. 8. 1. On the verbal point, Roby, de usufructu, 132; Mommsen, Strafrecht, 7.

his forms of security on sale, uses the formula, *furtis noxisque*[1], and the same distinction is made in the contract notes of the second century of the Empire[2]. It is clear that the expression *noxa* covered *furtum* in the classical law[3], so that the distinction is not necessary. The Edict as recorded by Justinian speaks only of *noxa*[4], and though Pomponius speaks of a duty to promise *furtis noxisque solutum esse*[5], it is likely that he is merely reflecting persistent usage.

It may almost be said that there was no general theory of noxal actions. We are told that they originated for some cases in the XII Tables, for another case in the *lex* Aquilia, and for others (*rapina* and *iniuria*) in the Edict[6]. In *damnum* the special rules under the *lex* Aquilia seem to be of a very striking kind, and in the case of those interdicts which were really delictal, we shall see that there were yet other differences[7].

The system of noxal actions applies essentially to delict, *i.e.* to cases of civil injury, involving a liability to money damages: it does not apply to claims on contract or quasi-contract, or to criminal proceedings of any kind, or to proceedings for *multae*[8]. This limitation is laid down in many texts. In the case of *multae* the *dominus* was sometimes held directly liable for a penalty for the act of his slave[9]. It has been urged on the evidence of two texts, that, at least in those cases where a punishment was imposed on private suit (as opposed to *iudicia publica*), e.g. *furtum manifestum* under the XII Tables, noxal surrender was allowed. But it has been shewn[10] that while one of these texts[11] refers to the *actio doli*, which was certainly noxal in appropriate cases, the other[12] though it refers both to criminal proceedings and to noxal actions does not suggest that they are overlapping classes[13].

The system applies to the four chief delicts, and to the various wrongs which were assimilated to them by *actiones utiles*, etc.[14] But it applies also to a very wide class of wrongs independent of these. Where a slave, without his master's knowledge, carried off an *in ius vocatus*, there was a noxal action[15]. If my slave built a structure which caused rain to injure your property, my duty to remove it was noxal[16]. There

---

[1] Bruns, *op. cit.* ii. 65.   [2] *Id.* i. 288 *sqq.*
[3] 9. 4. *passim*, where most of the concrete cases handled are of *furtum*.
[4] 21. 1. 1. 1.   [5] 21. 1. 46.
[6] G. 4. 76; In. 4. 8. 4.
[7] *Post*, p. 128.
[8] G. 4. 75; In. 4. 8. *pr.*; D. 21. 1. 17. 18; 21. 2. 11. 1; 50. 16. 200, 238. 3.
[9] See *l.* Quinctia (Bruns, *op. cit.* i. 116), *Si servus fecerit dominus eius HS centum milia populo Romano dare damnas esto.*
[10] Sell, Noxalrecht, 112 *sqq.*   [11] 4. 4. 24. 3.   [12] 2. 9. 5.
[13] For *terminum motum* there was something analogous to noxal surrender: *dominus* must pay the *multa* or hand over the slave for capital punishment, 47. 21. 3. 1.
[14] G. and In. *locc. citt.*; P. 5. 20. 4; Coll. 12. 7. 6—9; D. 9. 4. 38. 3; 47. 8. 2. 16; 47. 10. 17. 4, but not for *damnum in turba factum*, 47. 8. 4. 15.
[15] 2. 7. 1; 2. 10. 2.
[16] 39. 3. 6. 7.   So generally for *opus novum*, 43. 1. 5; 43. 16. 1. 11—16; 43. 24. 14.

was a *popularis actio sepulchri violati*: if B.'s slave lived, or built, in A's sepulchre he was punished, *extra ordinem*: if he only resorted to it, A had the above action in a noxal form[1]. The action under the *lex* Plaetoria for overreaching minors appears to have been noxal[2]. We are told that the *actio doli* was noxal, if the matter in which the *dolus* occurred was of the kind which gives rise to noxal actions, but *de peculio*, if it was a matter which ordinarily gives rise to the *actio de peculio*[3]. Although *iniuria* was an ordinary delict, and thus gave rise to a noxal action, it does not seem that this was the usual course. Probably the damages in *iniuria* by a slave were ordinarily so small that there would be no question of noxal surrender[4], and another course commonly taken was to hand over the slave to receive a thrashing and be handed back again[5]. This alternative punishment depended on the common consent of the *dominus*, the *iudex* and the complainant[6]: once duly carried out it barred further action by the injured person[7].

Though in principle it is clear that noxal surrender is not applicable in cases of contract or crime, there are some cases that create difficulty. Delict may occur in connexion with contract, and the questions to which these cases give rise will require attention later[8]. As to crime there is no real difficulty, but it is observed by Cujas that in relation to a number of cases, mostly of *actiones populares*, it is difficult to find any principle. He remarks[9] that in some such cases there is noxal liability, *e.g.* for *deiecta et effusa*, where the slave is identified[10]: in others, such as *Albi corruptio*, there is no noxal surrender, but there is punishment of the slave[11], *extra ordinem*, apart from criminal liability[12]. This punishment, *extra ordinem*, is sometimes called action *in servum*: it arises also as we shall see in some cases of *deiecta et effusa*[13]. It arises in some private delicts, *e.g. damnum in turba, incendium, iniuria*[14]. The *actio popularis sepulchri violati* was ordinarily *in servum*, but, as we have

---

[1] 47. 12. 3. 11.
[2] Fr. ad form. Fabian. See Collectio librorum iuris anteiust. p. 300. D. 4. 4. 24. 3 puts the case on the level of *iniuria*—see below. Other cases are, *metus* (4. 2. 16. 1), *servi corruptio* (11. 3. 14. 3), *arborum furtim caesarum* (47. 7. 7. 5—7), wrongful measurement by slave of *mensor* (11. 6. 3. 6), refusal to allow entry of a *missus in possessionem* (39. 2. 17. *pr.*) and disobedience to certain interdicts. *Post*, p. 128.
[3] 4. 3. 9. 4; 4. 4. 24. 3. Thus if a slave *dolo malo* ceased to possess a thing the master was no longer liable to *ad exhibendum*, but he was noxally liable for *dolus* or *furtum* (10. 4. 16). In a matter arising out of contract the *actio doli* was *de peculio*, 47. 7. 49.
[4] Under the *lex* Plaetoria where there was a similar alternative, the harmful transaction was set aside so that there might be no damage.
[5] 2. 9. 5; 47. 10. 45. One text suggests that this was the proper course (47. 10. 9. 3), though we are told elsewhere (*h. t.* 17. 3) that what might be a light matter if done by a freeman might be serious if done by a slave: *crescit contumelia ex persona*.
[6] 47. 10. 17. 4. C. Th. 13. 3. 1 (321) provides that, if a slave insult a professor, his master must flog him in the presence of the professor or pay a fine. The slave might be held as a pledge but it is not said that surrender released. In the Const. as it appears in the Code (C. 10. 53. 6), these provisions are omitted.
[7] 47. 10. 17. 6.   [8] *Post*, pp. 122 sqq.   [9] Cujas, Observ. xxii. 40.
[10] 9. 3. 1. *pr.*; *h. t.* 5. 6.   [11] 2. 1. 7; P. 1. 13a. 3; Lenel, Ed. Perp. § 7.
[12] 48. 10. 32. *pr.*; P. 5. 25. 5.   [13] 9. 3. 1. 8.
[14] 47. 8. 4. 15; 47. 9. 1. *pr.*

seen, it might be noxal[1]. Under the *lex* Plaetoria there was, in the action developed by the Praetor, as in *iniuria*, the alternative[2]. Cujas discusses[3] some of these inconsistencies, and explains them on the ground that no action is noxal except by express enactment by *lex* or edict, and that all these inconsistencies occur in the edict, the Praetor deciding whether the proceeding shall be noxal or not by considerations, apparently rather arbitrary, of the kind and magnitude of the offence.

Noxal liability is only for the actual wrongdoing of the slave. If my slave occupies a house from which something is thrown, he is the occupier and, if he were a freeman, he would be liable. But I shall not be noxally liable: it is not his delict. Ulpian thinks that as the thing ought not to go unpunished, the only thing to do is to deal with the slave *extra ordinem*[4]. So where a slave is *exercitor* and goods are wilfully destroyed by an employee, the master's liability will not be noxal, if the employee is not his slave[5]. If he is, there will be a noxal action, and if he is a *vicarius* of the *exercitor* this action will be limited to the *peculium* of the *exercitor*[6].

The person primarily liable to be sued on the slave's delict is his *dominus*[7]. The proceedings might begin, if necessary, with an *actio ad exhibendum*, for the production of the slave, but since the action might proceed in his absence, this would be needed only where there was doubt as to the identity of the slave who had done the harm. In that case there might be *actio ad exhibendum* for production of the *familia*, and the plaintiff could then point out the one on account of whom he wished to proceed[8]. The liability depends not on the mere fact of ownership, but on *potestas*, which is defined as *praesentis corporis copiam facultatemque*[9] and again as *facultatem et potestatem exhibendi eius*[10]. These explanations are not too clear, but it seems most probable that the word refers to a physical state of things and has no relation to right[11]. A slave in flight, or even away on a journey, *peregre*, is not in *potestas*[12]. On the other hand a slave merely lent or deposited is still so[13]. The same rule is laid down for one pledged; it is remarked that the holder has not *potestas* in these cases, and the owner has, if he has the means to redeem the man[14]. But though we are

---

[1] 47. 12. 3. 11.   [2] 4. 4. 24. 3.   [3] *loc. cit.*
[4] 9. 3. 1. 8. So also a noxal action is denied for the case of things suspended over a public way, 44. 7. 5. 5.
[5] 47. 2. 42. *pr.*   [6] *Post*, Ch. x.
[7] Exceptional cases later.   [8] 10. 4. 3. 7.
[9] 50. 16. 215.   [10] 9. 4. 21. 3.
[11] Lenel, *op. cit.* § 58. This seems to follow from the structure of 50. 16. 215. The contrary opinion of Girard is due to his view as to the nature of the *interrogatio*, shortly to be considered.
[12] 9. 4. 21. 3; 47. 2. 17. 3.   [13] 9. 4. 22. *pr.*   [14] 9. 4. 22. 1, 2.

told that an owner has not *potestas* over a pledged slave whom he
has not the means to redeem, it hardly follows that the holder has, and,
even if he has, it must be remembered that the liability does not
depend on *potestas* alone.   A pledge creditor was not directly liable,
though, as we shall shortly see, he could in the long run be deprived of
the slave.

The parties being before the Praetor the proceedings begin, or
may begin, with an *interrogatio* of the defendant, as to his position
with regard to the slave.   Upon the exact content of the *interrogatio*
there has been much controversy[1].   Many texts speak of it as being,
an eius sit, i.e. on the question of ownership[2].   There are others which
assume it to be, *an in potestate habeat*[3].   And there is at least one
which may be read as implying that they mean the same thing[4].   The
most probable view seems to be that now adopted by Lenel[5].   He holds
that there were two interrogations, for different cases.   The procedure
was certainly different according as the slave was present or absent.
Only an owner could defend an absent slave, but anyone could defend
a present slave if the owner were away[6].   In Lenel's view the point is
that defence by the third party is in the interest of the owner, not of
the slave, but this interest exists only where the slave, since he is
present, is liable to *ductio*.   Many texts shew that the Edict, *Si negabit*,
giving alternative courses where *potestas* is denied, refers only to absent
slaves[7].   And Ulpian in a very important place, (probably the beginning
of his comment,) emphasises the importance of the question, whether
the slave is present or absent[8].   If the slave were there, the question as
to *potestas* would be absurd : the only question would be whether the
ownership was admitted or denied.   If it were denied there was a right
of *ductio*, but if the plaintiff thought he could prove ownership he
might do so, since he had then a right to a proper conveyance of the
slave : hence the question, *an eius sit*[9].   But if the slave were absent,
the defendant, who admitted ownership, might deny *potestas*.   There
would be an *interrogatio* as to this, and it is to this alone that the
edict refers which gives the plaintiff, in the case of denial, a choice
between the oath and a *iudicium sine deditione*.   This edict does not
deal with the case where it is admitted ; here, clearly, the defendant
must defend, or give security for noxal surrender.   In stating this view
of Lenel's, it has been necessary to anticipate some of the details which

---

[1] Girard, Nouv. Rev. Hist. 11. 429 ; Kipp, Z. S. S. 10. 399 ; Lenel, Z. S. S. 20. 9 ; *Id.*, Ed.
Perp. (French Edition) 1. 180.
[2] 9. 4. 26. 3, 27. 1, 39. 1 ; 11. 1. 13. 1, 14. *pr.*, 20. *pr.*
[3] 9. 4. 24. 11. 1. 5, 16. *pr.*   [4] 11. 1. 17.   [5] *loc. cit.*
[6] Or a *bonae fidei possessor.*
[7] 2. 9. 2. 1 ; 9. 4. 21. 1.
[8] 9. 4. 21. 1, 21. 4, 22. 3, 26. 5.   [9] See, however, *post*, p. 103.

will have to be stated in the systematic account of the action which must now be given[1].

The *dominus* who has admitted his title may "defend" the slave. This involves giving security that the slave shall be present at the hearing—*cautio iudicio sisti.* There were differences of opinion as to what was implied in this promise. Labeo held that the defendant must not do anything to lessen his right in the slave meanwhile, or use delays till the action was extinct: he must do nothing to make the plaintiff's position worse[2]. Any alienation of him to a person out of jurisdiction or to a *potentior* whom it might be difficult to bring before the court, was a breach of this undertaking[3]. Noxal surrender was not, (though Ofilius thought otherwise,) for the liability still attached to the man, on the principle, *noxa caput sequitur*[4]. (It must be noted that in all these cases the security is only *donec iudicium accipiatur*[5], so that there is no question of an intervening *litis contestatio* : the action can be simply transferred.) To produce, free, one who had been a *statuliber* before, satisfied the promise, since the possibility of his becoming free was to have been reckoned upon[6].

If, admitting his title, the *dominus* is not inclined to defend the slave, his proper course is to surrender him to the plaintiff, making according to the Digest a formal transfer of him[7]. If he does this he is absolutely released, though there exist minor rights in the man[8]. In the classical law it seems likely that simple abandonment, that the slave might be *ductus*, sufficed, since the master's mere presence would not impose a duty on him which he could have avoided by staying away; and in absence of the master *ductio* released[9]. Thus an outstanding usufruct is no bar, and the usufructuary cannot recover him without paying *litis aestimatio* to the surrenderee, provided the surrender was in good faith[10]. The effect of the transfer is to make the transferee owner[11]. Thus if it be to the usufructuary the usufruct is ended by *confusio*[12]. The fact that the slave dies after surrender is of course not material[13].

---

[1] The effect of silence of deft. on the enquiry is not stated. Lenel thinks an answer could be compelled, citing an analogous case (25. 4. 1. 3). But as the text shews, in the special case there handled the needs of the parties could not otherwise be met. This is not so in our case, and it has been suggested that here, as in some other cases, silence was treated as contumacy equivalent to denial. Naber, Mnemosyne, 30. 176. The person interrogated may ask for delay, since his answer may have serious results, 11. 1. 8.

[2] 2. 9. 1. 1.   [3] *Ibid.*   [4] 2. 9. 1. 2.   [5] 2. 9. 1. *pr.*

[6] 2. 9. 6. The same was true in other cases of freedom: he could still be sued. This did not hold in *iniuria* since the fact that he was free would prevent the corporal punishment which here ordinarily replaced damages or surrender, 2. 9. 5.   *Ante*, p. 100.

[7] 50. 16. 215; 9. 4. 21. *pr.*, 33. 29, which Eisele thinks interpolated (Z. S. S. 13. 124). *H. t.* 32 (which he also thinks interpolated) says that *dominus* handing him over must *de dolo promittere, i.e.* that he has not made his right in him worse in any way, 9. 4. 14. 1.

[8] 9. 4. 15; In. 4. 8. 3.   [9] Cp. 6. 2. 6; 9. 4. 29. See also *post*, pp. 104, 106.

[10] 7. 1. 17. 2; 9. 4. 27. *pr.* So where the slave was pledged, 4. 3. 9. 4. As to these texts, *post*, p. 117.

[11] In. 4. 8. 3.   [12] 7. 4. 27.

[13] The Institutes say (4. 8. 3) that the slave was entitled to freedom, *auxilio praetoris invito domino*, when he had wiped out by earnings the damage done—an extension to slaves of the rule applied to noxal surrender of sons, obsolete in Justinian's time. It is not in the Digest or Code.

If the *dominus* will neither surrender nor defend he is liable to an *actio in solidum* with no power of surrender[1].

If the defendant is present and the slave absent, and the defendant denies *potestas*, the plaintiff has alternative courses. He may offer an oath on the question of *potestas*[2]. If this is refused condemnation follows, with the alternative of surrender[3]. If it is taken, the action is lost[4], but this does not bar a future action based on a new *potestas*, beginning after the oath was taken[5]. The alternative course is to take an action, *sine noxae deditione*, there and then[6], which imposes obligation *in solidum*, but is lost unless actual present *potestas* be proved or loss of it, *dolo malo*[7]. This action on denial of *potestas* may of course be avoided by withdrawing the denial before *litis contestatio*[8], and as it has a certain penal character it is not available against the *heres* of the denier[9]. If the defendant did not deny *potestas*, Vindius held that he could be compelled either to appear with the slave to accept a *iudicium*, (*iudicio sisti promittere*,) or, if he would not defend, to give security to produce the man, whenever it should be possible[10]. But it appears that the action could not be brought and defended in the absence of the slave, if there was any doubt as to the defendant's being a person liable for him, *i.e.* owner or *bonae fidei possessor*. Where he has given such security he will be free from liability if, whenever it is possible, he conveys him to the plaintiff.

If the *dominus* is absent from the proceedings *in iure*, and the slave is present, he may be taken off (*ductus*) by the claimant, *iussu praetoris*[11]. This releases the defendant[12], and as in the case of an *indefensus*, gives the holder the *actio* Publiciana[13]. But on the return of the *dominus*, the Praetor may, for cause shewn, give him leave to defend[14]. The slave must then be produced by the plaintiff. A difficulty arose from the fact that the praetor's order had put the man in the *bona* of the plaintiff, and a man cannot have a noxal action on account of his own slave, but the Praetor made an order restoring the extinguished action[15]. Moreover, in the absence of the *dominus*, anyone interested, for instance a pledgee or.usufructuary[16], might defend the slave for him, and would have an *actio negotiorum gestorum* against him[17]. And such persons, like the owner, might, if they were absent in good faith, come in later and defend[18].

---

[1] 9. 4. 21. 4, 22. 3.   [2] 9. 4. 21. 2.   [3] *h. l.* 4.
[4] *h. l.* 6.   The oath might be taken on his behalf by tutor or curator, but not by procurator, *h. l.* 5.
[5] *h. l.* 6; *h. t.* 23.   Neratius points out that in the new *potestas* there might even be an action *sine deditione*, if the circumstances give rise to it, although on the existing *potestas* the oath was alternative to and thus exclusive of such an action.
[6] 2. 9. 2. 1; 9. 4. 21. 2.   [7] 2. 9. 2. 1; 9. 4. 22. 4.
[8] 9. 4. 26. 5, or later if deft. a minor.   [9] *Ibid.*   [10] 2. 9. 2. 1.
[11] *Ibid.*   [12] 9. 4. 39. 3, *exceptio doli.*   [13] 6. 2. 6.
[14] 2. 9. 2. 1.   So if *dominus* who refuses to defend is entitled to *restitutio in integrum.*
[15] 2. 9. 2. 1.   [16] 2. 9. 2. 1; 9. 4. 26. 6.
[17] 3. 5. 40.   [18] 9. 4. 26. 6, 30.

But the case of one who defends for an absent master must be distinguished from that of one who, not being *dominus*, has, upon *interrogatio*, admitted his responsibility as such. A person who has thus admitted *potestas*, is noxally liable, and if he is sued the *dominus* is released[1]. His liability is as great as that of the *dominus*[2], but he must give security *iudicatum solvi* as he is not the real principal[3]. Payment by him before *litis contestatio* would release the *dominus*, as well as payment under the judgment[4]. As the mere surrender by a person who is not owner does not pass *dominium*, the release is not *ipso iure*, but, in fact, it is effective. If the *dominus* sues for the slave he will be met by the *exceptio doli*, unless he tenders the damages[5]. The receiver by the surrender acquires the *actio Publiciana*, and if the *dominus* replies by an *exceptio iusti dominii*, he has a *replicatio doli*[6].

If the wrong is to two people, the damages will be divisible, and each must sue for his share. But if one sues the surrender will have to be *in solidum* to him, as it does not admit of division. He will be liable to the other by *iudicium communi dividundo*, i.e. if it is damage to some common thing. And if both sue together the judge may order surrender to both[7], in common.

The *intentio* of the formula in noxal actions states the duty as being either to pay or surrender, and these may be described, provisionally, as alternative obligations. The *condemnatio* leaves the same choice, but now the primary duty is to pay; surrender has become a merely "facultative" mode of release. Thus a judgment simply ordering surrender is null[8]. It follows that the *actio iudicati* is only for the money: if this is defended the right of surrender is lost[9]. But surrender after *condemnatio* does not release, if there are any outstanding rights in the man, such as usufruct[10], and the plaintiff can sue by *actio iudicati*, without waiting for actual eviction, unless the outstanding right is extinguished[11].

The typical defendant is the owner having *potestas*, but the Praetor extended the liability to one who would have had *potestas* but for his

---

[1] 11. 1. 8, 20 or the future *dominus* in case of *servus hereditarius*, *h.t.* 15. *pr.*
[2] 11. 1. 14. *pr.*, 15. 1, 16. 1, 20. *pr.*
[3] *causa cognita*, *i.e.* if it appears that he is not owner. A non-owner sued need not, as he did not assume the position, 9. 4. 39. 1.
[4] 9. 4. 26. 3. Such confessions bind only if they can conceivably be true, *e.g.* not in any case in which admitter could not possibly be owner. But the Roman juristic doctrines as to the nature and effect of impossibility are imperfectly worked out, 11. 1. 16. 1, 14. 1.
[5] 9. 4. 27. 1, 28. *pr.*   [6] 9. 4. 28.
[7] 9. 2. 27. 2; 9. 4. 19. *pr.* These rules apply only where there is such a common interest: if the damage was to distinct things of different owners, there were two distinct delicts.
[8] 42. 1. 6. 1.
[9] 5. 3. 20. 5. If before judgment he has promised to pay or surrender, the action on his promise of course allows him both alternatives.
[10] 42. 1. 4. 8.
[11] 46. 3. 69. Perhaps surrender of him as *statuliber* sufficed, but it is not clear that the text which says this (9. 4. 15) refers to surrender after condemnation.

fraud[1]. The rules are in the main as in ordinary noxal actions, but as he is treated as if he still had *potestas,* and he has, in the ordinary way, denied *potestas,* he is liable *in solidum*[2]. The action lies, whether some other person is liable or not, *e.g.* when the slave was simply told to run away[3]. But if there is a new owner ready to take the defence, or the slave, having been freed, presents himself to do so, with security, the old master has an *exceptio*[4] and the plaintiff who has elected to take one liability cannot fall back on the other[5]. In one text we are told that if after *litis contestatio* in this praetorian action based on *dolus,* the slave appears, and is then *ductus* for lack of defence, the *dominus* is entitled to absolution, *exceptione doli posita*[6]. The hypothesis seems to be that the plaintiff, having brought this praetorian action, elects on the appearance of the slave, to treat the refusal to admit *potestas,* as having been a refusal to defend. Though there has been *litis contestatio* in the action, he may do this, but the defendant will be absolved. This is an application of the principle, *omnia iudicia absolutoria esse*[7], since as we have seen this *ductio* of an *indefensus* would have released, had it been done before *litis contestatio*[8].

The principle, *Noxa caput sequitur,* which underlies these rules is simple. The owner with present *potestas* is liable, whether he was owner at the time of the wrong or not. Thus a buyer even about to redhibit is noxally liable, and, as he might have surrendered, he can recover from the vendor no more than the price[9]. This minimal cost of surrender he can recover, whether he actually defended the slave, or surrendered him on a clear case[10]. It is enough that he is present owner : the fact that the sale is voidable as being in fraud of creditors, or that he is liable to eviction by the vendor's pledgee, or that the vendor is entitled to *restitutio in integrum*—all these are immaterial[11]. As the master's liability depends on *potestas,* it is determined, (subject to what has been said as to *dolus,*) by death, alienation or manumission of the slave before *litis contestatio*[12] : a mere claim of liberty does not destroy the noxal action, but suspends it so that if the man proves a slave it will go on : if he proves free it is null[13]. A *bona fide*

---

[1] 9. 4. 12, 21; 47. 2. 42. 1. The action is often opposed to the "direct" noxal action, 9. 4. 24, 26. 2.

[2] 9. 4. 16, 22. 4, 39.   [3] 9. 4. 24.   [4] 9. 4. 24, 25, 39. 2.

[5] 9. 4. 26. *pr.*; 47. 2. 42. 1.   [6] 9. 4. 39. 3.   [7] In. 4. 12. 2.

[8] *Ante,* p. 103. As in this action the *intentio* said nothing about surrender, the *ductio* is not *ipso iure* a discharge. Hence the *exceptio doli.*

[9] 21. 1. 23. 8.   [10] 19. 1. 11. 12.

[11] 9. 4. 36. Where A's slave was stolen by B and stole from B we are told that A when he got the man back was noxally liable to B (47. 2. 68. 4). This absurd-looking rule is said to be based on public grounds: it conflicts with principle. One noxally liable for a man cannot have a noxal action for his act (C. 6. 2. 21. 1). A *malae fidei possessor* is noxally liable (9. 4. 13), and if the slave has been, since the act, in such a position that the action could not arise it cannot arise later (G. 4. 78; D. 9. 4. 37, *etc., post,* p. 107).

[12] 9. 4. 5. 1, 6, 7. *pr.,* 14. *pr.* Even after action begun, 47. 2. 41. 2, 42. 1.

[13] 9. 4. 42. *pr.*

abandonment releases the master, but the slave himself will be liable, if alive and free, (assuming the master not to have been sued,) and cannot surrender himself[1], and so will anyone who takes possession of him[2]. If a *servus noxius* is captured by the enemy, the right of action revives on his return[3]. If a *civis* becomes a slave after committing a wrong his *dominus* is liable[4].

There is an important rule, that there can be no noxal liability between master and slave, and thus, whatever changes of position take place, an act by the slave against his *dominus* having *potestas* can never create an action either against another owner or against the slave if freed[5]. Moreover, it is finally extinguished if the slave comes into the hands of one with whom the action could not have begun[6]: where the injured person acquires the slave the action will not revive on sale or manumission. This is the Sabinian view which clearly prevailed in later law[7]. It is immaterial how temporary or defeasible the *confusio* may be. A buyer redhibiting, either by agreement, or by the *actio redhibitoria*, has no noxal action for what the slave has stolen while his[8], though as we have seen there is a right of indemnification, with the alternative of leaving the slave with the buyer, *noxae nomine*[9]. Even though the sale be annulled, the slave being *inemptus*, there can be no *actio furti*[10].

The case of legacy of the slave gives rise to some distinctions. Gaius, dealing with *legatum per damnationem*, in which the property is for the time being in the *heres*, says that, if the slave has stolen from him either before or after *aditio*, he is entitled, not to a noxal action, but to an indemnity, before he need hand over the slave[11]. Julian, dealing no doubt with a *legatum per vindicationem*, says that in a case of theft before *aditio*, there is an ordinary noxal action[12]. What is said of *legatum per damnationem* is no doubt true of any case in which the ownership is for the time in the *heres*. He is noxally liable for such slaves: Africanus[13] tells us that if he is noxally defending such

---

[1] G. 4. 77; In. 4. 8. 5; 47. 8. 3; C. 4. 14. 4.

[2] *Ibid.*; 9. 4. 7. *pr.*; 13, 21. 1; 47. 2. 65; P. 2. 31. 8. It avails against *heres*, but *iure dominii*, 9. 4. 42. 2. This is all that the word *perpetua* seems to mean. *Donatio mortis causa* of a *servus noxius* was a gift only of what he was worth as such, 39. 6. 18. 3.

[3] 13. 6. 21. 1; 47. 2. 41. 3.   [4] In. 4. 8. 5; G. 4. 77; cp. P. 2. 31. 7, 8, 9.

[5] Unless he "contrect" afterwards, 47. 2. 17. *pr.*, 1; G. 4. 78; In. 4. 8. 6; C. 3. 41. 1; 4. 14. 6. For the restriction to the case in which he is actually in *potestas*, see 47. 2. 17. 3. The stolen property could be recovered from any holder, C. 4. 14. 1.

[6] 47. 2. 18.

[7] *Ib.*; 9. 4. 37; G. 4. 78; In. 4. 8. 6. Gaius tells us that the Proculians had held that the action revived when the confusion ceased—a rule which would have most inequitable results.

[8] 47. 2. 17. 2; *h. t.* 62. 2.   [9] *Ante*, p. 62; D. 21. 1. 31. 1, 52, 58; 47. 2. 62. 2.

[10] 47. 2. 68. 3.   [11] 30. 70. *pr.*, 3.

[12] 9. 4. 40, *a fortiori* if it was after *aditio*. In 47. 2. 65 Neratius gives the rule and the reason.

[13] 47. 2. 62. 9. A rule which Ulpian expresses with perhaps more regard for principle when he says there was, in such a case, absolution, *officio iudicis*, 9. 4. 14. 1. As to heir's duty of warranty as to *noxa*, *ante*, p. 16.

a slave who is a *statuliber*, and the condition is satisfied during the *iudicium*, he is entitled to absolution.

If the *confusio* arises only after *litis contestatio*, the vendor is not released, any more than he would be in the same case, by selling to a third person, or by freeing the slave, and here, as there, since he has deprived himself of the power of surrender, he must pay in full[1].

These rules give rise to a difficulty, at least apparent. If the event which divests the ownership of the defendant occurs before *litis contestatio*, a new action can of course be brought against the new owner. If it occurs after *litis contestatio* it might seem that any fresh action might be met by an *exceptio rei in iudicium deductae*. It is clear however that, at least in the case in which the slave became free, this was not the case: it was the duty of the Praetor to order the transfer of the *iudicium* to him[2]. This way of putting the matter shews that the action was one and the same: it was only the *iudicium* that was transferred—the intervention of the Praetor being needed to make the necessary changes in the formula[3]. In like manner the ordinary noxal action and that *sine noxae deditione* against *dominus sciens* were really one and the same, so that the plaintiff could pass freely, *pendente iudicio*, from either to the other[4]. The act was done by the slave; the obligation centred in him, and the action, in all its forms, is really one. Hence it seems that if the case were one of transfer of ownership the pending *iudicium* would simply be transferred to the new owner in the same way. It may be noticed that, in those cases in which the renewal of the action is declared to be impossible, the fact that the action is already decided is expressly emphasised. In one case it is because *res finita est*[5]. In another it is *quasi decisum sit*[6]. *Translatio iudicii* was a recognised incident of procedure, though there are few texts which deal with it expressly.

Leaving out of account the difficulties of this *translatio iudicii*[7], and the cases in which there is no release because the fact which divested the ownership was caused by the defendant, we must consider some of the cases of transfer. The texts which deal with the case of *statuliber* lay down clear rules but have been abridged, at least, by the compilers, and shew that there were disputes among the earlier lawyers[8]. It is laid down, on the authority of Sabinus, Cassius and Octavenus, that the *heres*, noxally sued, may surrender the *statuliber*, and is thereby released, as having transferred all his right[9], being required, however,

---

[1] 6. 1. 58; 9. 4. 14. 1, 15, 37, 38. *pr.* [2] 9. 4. 15.
[3] In 3. 2. 14 the slave made *heres* is noxally liable as *heres*, since there was a pending action. The text does not illustrate the present point.
[4] 9. 4. 4. 3. [5] 9. 4. 3. 3. [6] 47. 2. 42. 1; 47. 8. 3. Cp. 9. 4. 14, 15.
[7] Koschaker, Translatio Iudicii. See also Girard, Manuel, 1006, and *post*, App. II.
[8] Koschaker, *op. cit.* 199 *sqq.* [9] 9. 4. 15; 40. 7. 9. 2.

to give security against any act of his, whereby the man may become free[1]. The doubt which existed may have been due to the fact that as the man passes into the *potestas* of the injured person the remedy is for ever destroyed, while the condition may immediately supervene and release the offending slave[2]. On the Proculian view, which allowed revival of noxal claims when the *confusio* ceased[3], the difficulty would not have arisen, at least, if the surrender had been without judgment. If the condition arrived, pending the noxal action, the possibility of surrender was at an end and we are told that the defendant was released[4] (the *heres* having however to hand over to the injured person any moneys he had received under the condition, in so far as they were not paid out of the *peculium*, which belonged to him[5]). This rule has been remarked on as exceptional, as, in other cases in which the ownership passes, the defendant is not released from his obligation to pay the damages[6]. This seems to be the law in the case of death[7], and it is clearly laid down for the case in which the slave is evicted, while the noxal action is pending[8], and for that in which a slave is noxally surrendered while another noxal action is pending[9]. On the other hand, where a fideicommissary gift takes effect, or the condition on a legacy of the slave arrives, before judgment in the noxal action, Ulpian treats the case as on the same level with that which we are discussing, as he does also that of one declared free in an *adsertio libertatis* while a noxal action is pending: he says that the noxal *iudicium* becomes *inutile*[10].

The difference is rather formal than important. Though the owner of the dead slave is still liable he is released in classical law by handing over the corpse, or part of it[11]. And the evicted defendant need not hand over the man to the successful claimant till security is given for the damages in the noxal action[12]. And in the case in which he is noxally surrendered to A while B's noxal action is pending, though judgment will go for B, there is no *actio iudicati*[13]. It is probable that the original starting-point is that of continued liability, if the divesting fact occur after *litis contestatio*. The inequitable effect of this led to modification, arrived at, in a hesitating way, by the help of a gradually increasing freedom in the conception of *translatio iudicii*. In the case of the *statuliber*, the supposed slave declared free, the slave freed by *fideicommissum*, there was absolute release

---

1 9. 4. 14. 1.   2 40. 7. 9. *pr.*   Cp. 47. 2. 62. 9.
3 *Ante*, p. 107.   4 9. 4. 14. 1—16.
5 47. 2. 62. 9, *post*, Ch. xxi.   6 Koschaker, *loc. cit.*
7 *Post*, p. 111.   8 6. 1. 58.   9 9. 4. 14. *pr.*; cp. 9. 4. 28.
10 9. 4. 14. 1, 42. *pr.*; cf. 40. 12. 24. 4.   The *absolutio* is however *officio iudicis* in the case of satisfaction of the condition (9. 4. 14. 1).   In the other case eviction does not mean that he was never liable: a *b. f. possessor* is liable.   As to the case of *adsertio*, *post*, Ch. xxviii.
11 *Post*, p. 111.   12 6. 1. 58.   13 9. 4. 14. *pr.*

with *translatio iudicii.* In the case of death, where this was inconceivable, there was no release, but from early times surrender of the
corpse sufficed. In the case of eviction there was no release, but the
man need not be handed over without security for the damages in
the forthcoming noxal judgment. It is not clear why this case was
not grouped with those of *statuliber*, etc., since here *translatio* was
quite feasible. It is true that in case of eviction there has, in strictness, been no divesting fact; the legal ownership is unchanged, but this
is equally true of the case of the slave declared free in an *adsertio libertatis*. In the case of noxal surrender the solution was not release, but
refusal of *actio iudicati*. No doubt it is possible to find distinctions in
these cases, but it seems more rational to regard the rules as a gradual
development, in which the Sabinians took the progressive side, but
which was hardly complete even in the time of Ulpian.

Some details are necessary to complete the general account of the
action. It must be defended where the wrong was done[1]. *Compensatio*
is allowed, at least in Justinian's time[2]. Upon surrender the surrenderee normally becomes owner, but not if the surrenderer was not
owner, or the slave was *ductus* because the *dominus* was absent or
refused to defend or surrender. In such a case the surrenderee *iuste
possidet*, and has the Publician action[3], whether he knew, or not, that
the person sued was not the owner[4].

There is a curious text[5] dealing with the *exceptio doli*, in which
Ulpian, after observing that a vendee is not liable for his vendor's
dolus, and therefore, if he has need to vindicate the *res*, cannot be met
by an exception based on fraud of his vendor, adds that this is true of
other transactions such as *permutatio* which resemble sale, but quotes a
view of Pomponius that it is not true in case of noxal surrender. This
is hard to justify[6]. It is clear that the noxal claimant could have
recovered the slave from the person aggrieved by the *dolus*, if he had
still held him, and there seems no reason why the *dolus* of the intermediate possessor should affect the matter. The rule seems in conflict
with the general priority assigned to the noxal claim, which has already
been noted and is illustrated by the treatment of cases where the noxal
claim and a claim of ownership are competing. If the possessor is sued
by A for the slave, and by B on a *noxa*, and judgment on the *vindicatio*
comes first, the slave need not be handed over till security is given for
what may have to be paid on the noxal claim[7], while if judgment in the

---

[1] 9. 4. 43.   [2] 16. 2. 10. 2.   [3] 6. 2. 5. 6.
[4] *Ante*, p. 105, nn. 5, 6.   [5] 44. 4. 4. 31.
[6] The reason in the text, *i.e.* that it was a *lucrativa adquisitio* can hardly apply to this case,
which often had nothing *lucrativa* about it.
[7] 6. 1. 58.

noxal action comes first and the slave is surrendered the surrenderer is not liable for failure to deliver under the *arbitrium iudicis*[1].

It may be convenient to group together the rules as to the effect of death of the slave during the proceedings. If the slave died before the action was brought, or before *litis contestatio*, the *dominus* was released, even though he had *dolo malo* ceased to possess, at the time of the death, unless indeed he were already *in mora* in accepting the *iudicium*[2]. If the death occurred after *condemnatio*, the primary obligation is as we have seen for a sum of money: surrender is now only a facultative mode of discharge[3]. It appears therefore that death of the slave would not release. An imperfect text of Gaius seems to discuss this case, and the question whether the surrender of the slave dead would suffice[4]. The Autun commentary[5] on Gaius carries the matter further. It declares that, after condemnation, the death does not release, but the *dominus* may surrender the body or part of it, though in the case of animals this could not be done. The text mentions a doubt, whether hair and nails were a part for this purpose, perhaps because they could not be identified, and so, as Mommsen says, would be no check on a false statement that the slave was dead[6]. The text is very imperfect, but it apparently goes on to discuss, without determining, the question whether this right existed if the death was caused by *culpa* of the *dominus*, or in lawful exercise of his power of punishment. It must be noted that all this refers only to death after *condemnatio*, and that no trace of these rules survives into Justinian's law. The questions therefore remain : what was the rule in Justinian's time as to death after *condemnatio*, and what was the rule in case of death, *pendente iudicio* ? It seems to be universally assumed that death after *condemnatio* did not in any way release the defendant, in Justinian's law[7]. This solution, consistent with the subordinate position of surrender after condemnation[3], is probably correct. But it cannot be deduced with certainty from anything said in the sources, and it represents an increased burden on the *dominus*. As to death after *litis contestatio*, but before judgment, it may be assumed that the rule was no severer in classical law, and that thus a corpse might be

---

[1] 5. 3. 20. 5 ; 6. 1. 58. The complications of 9. 4. 38. 2 and 47. 2. 35. 1 do not concern us. The *dominus* is liable for any proceeds of the wrong which reach him, *e.g.* by *cond. furtiva*, 13. 1. 4. We are told that there is *condictio* to the extent of profit with a power of surrender, *in residuum*. This is an allusion to *a. furti*, a confusion of language not uncommon in the texts. Cp. C. 3. 41. 4; D. 4. 2. 16. 1; 47. 1. 2. 3.

[2] 9. 1. 1. 13; 9. 4. 5. 1, 7. *pr.*, 26. 4, 39. 4.   [3] *Ante*, p. 105.

[4] G. 4. 81.   [5] §§ 82—87.   See Ed. 4 of Krueger and Studemund's Gaius.

[6] Z. S. S. 20. 236. M. seems to hold that in case of animals, there was no liability at all. But it is clear on the text that the right to surrender the corpse was a privilege, not a further liability. He links the rule with expiatory surrender for breach of *foedus*, Liv. 8. 39.

[7] Girard, *loc. cit.*

surrendered, and the view is most widely held that in later law death did not release[1]. This view rests on the following considerations :

(i)   It is clear that death of the offending animal at this stage did not release the *dominus* in the *actio de pauperie*[2]. Analogy suggests the application of the same rule to the case of slaves, though the actions were not identical in all respects.

(ii)   In one text[3] it is said that one who has accepted a *iudicium*, on account of a slave already dead, ought to be absolved, *quia desiit verum esse propter eum dare oportere*. This would hardly be said if death after *litis contestatio* discharged the liability.

(iii)   Several texts dealing with one who has *dolo malo* ceased to possess, make it clear that, in that case, death after *litis contestatio* did not discharge[4], and one of them uses words which may be read to imply that the conditions of this action are, in this respect, the same as those of the ordinary noxal action[5]. But these texts lose much of their force in view of the well-known rule that *dolus pro possessione est*[6].

(iv)   The formula expresses payment and surrender as alternatives, and in alternative obligations the impossibility of one alternative did not release from the duty of performing the other[7]. But as we shall shortly see the obligation differed in certain ways from an ordinary alternative obligation[8].

There has been much discussion among commentators as to the essential character of noxal liability as contemplated by the classical lawyers[9]. Is the master's liability personal or is he merely defending, as representative of the slave, primarily liable ? That a slave is in theory civilly liable for his delicts is shewn by a text which says that he is liable, and *remanet obligatus* after manumission[10]. It is certain however that he could not himself be sued. This has led some writers to hold that the master's liability is as *defensor* of a person who cannot defend himself, an opinion which finds indirect support in the texts[11]. Thus there are texts which shew that the action against the slave after manumission is the same as the noxal action, merely transferred to him[12]. Other texts expressly describe the action as *defensio servi*[13].

---

[1] Girard, *loc. cit.*, and N. R. H. 11. 435.
[2] The owner can recover, *ex* Aquilia, the amount he will have to pay owing to inability to surrender and can cede his actions in lieu of surrender, 9. 2. 37. 1 ; 9. 1. 1. 16.   So we are told that *de pauperie* is extinct if the animal die before *litis contestatio*—which implies that it was not ended by death after, 9. 1. 1. 13.
[3] 9. 4. 42. 1.   [4] 9. 4. 16, 26. 4, 39. 4.   [5] 9. 4. 26. 4.
[6] 50. 17. 131, 150, 157.   Lenel, Ed. Perp. § 90.
[7] Windscheid, Lehrbuch, § 255.   [8] *Post*, p. 113.
[9] Girard, N. R. H. 12. 31 *sqq.*; Kipp, reviewing foregoing, Z. S. S. 10. 397 *sqq.*; Sell, Noxalrecht, 23—96 *etc.*
[10] 44. 7. 14.   [11] Sell, *loc. cit.*
[12] *Ante*, p. 108.   [13] 9. 4. 33; Sell, *op. cit.* 76.

The expression is of course also applied to defence of property against claims[1], but one text is cited to shew that this could not be its meaning here, since in the case of a son, failure to defend him noxally would not involve loss of him[2]. Similar inferences are drawn from the use of the expressions *pro servo, servi nomine,* and the like[3]. Moreover, it did not imply *culpa* in the *dominus*: such an idea is inconsistent with the rule, *noxa caput sequitur,* with the rule that an *impubes dominus* was liable[4], and perhaps with the power of surrender.

On the other hand the *defensio* cannot be understood in any procedural sense. It has none of the ordinary attributes of representation. The *vocatio in ius,* the formula, the judgment, the *actio iudicati* all deal with the *dominus,* and though he cannot be compelled to defend the slave, we have seen that he can be compelled to produce him as if he were being sued for a piece of property[5]. Nor can much stress be laid on the use of the word *defensor,* since, while the liability of a *defensor* was exactly the same as that of the person defended[6], the master's liability differed from that of the man himself, as the latter had no power of surrender. And though primitive law does admit guilt in animals, the owner's liability can hardly have been representative: Justinian indeed calls the owner the *reus*[7], and the actions are closely analogous. Moreover when noxal actions were introduced it is doubtful whether either son or slave could be civilly liable, and there was then no representation in lawsuits. If we refer the idea to classical times it is no longer true that a son could not defend himself. And the common use of such expressions as *rem defendere,* and *pro fundo*[8], destroys the force of such terms applied to slaves.

The fact seems to be that noxal liability is entirely *sui generis*: its form is due to its descent from ransom from vengeance. It has points of similarity with both direct and representative liability, and expressions are used implying one or the other according to the needs of the moment[9].

Another question which has divided commentators is that whether the right of surrender is alternative or facultative[10]. It is clear that, after *condemnatio,* which is primarily for a sum of money, the surrender is merely facultative, *in solutione*[11]. Apart from the state of things after condemnation, there are many texts which treat the payment as the primary, the surrender as a subsidiary, liability[12], and several which put

---

[1] 6. 1. 54; 44. 2. 9. 1. Sell, *loc. cit.*   [2] 9. 4. 33.
[3] 9. 4. 39. 1; 2. 9. 2. 1.   [4] 47. 8. 2. 19. Girard, *loc. cit.*
[5] *Ante,* p. 101.   [6] Roby, Roman Private Law, 2. 48.
[7] In. 4. 9. *pr.*   [8] 39. 2. 9. *pr.,* 9. 4. 38. 2, *etc.*; Girard, N. R. H. 12. 31 *sqq.*
[9] Nothing turned on the distinction: it may have been more readily regarded as representative as there was no logical ground for personal liability.
[10] Former view, Girard, N. R. H. 11. 440; latter, Sell, *op. cit.* 11 *sqq.* It is an old topic. Haenel, Dissensiones Dominorum, 188.
[11] 42. 1. 6. 1. *Ante,* p. 105.   [12] 9. 4. 1; 42. 1. 6. 1; 47. 2. 62. 5, *etc.*

surrender in the forefront, and treat payment as subordinate[1]. But the view that surrender is facultative, (*in solutione*,) cannot now be held, for Lenel has shewn that the *intentio* sets forth the payment and surrender as alternatives[2]. Girard infers that it is a case of alternative obligation and cites several texts as stating it so[3]. But since impossibility of one alternative did not release from the duty of satisfying the other[4], and death of the slave did release the *dominus*, he considers that it was only after *litis contestatio*, when death did not release, that it became alternative. To this it has been objected that the *intentio* cannot express any kind of obligation different from that which was due before, and that in a true alternative obligation the *iudex* would estimate the value of the creditor's right, and fix the *condemnatio* accordingly, so that the *ea res*, the money condemnation, would not exceed the value of the slave[5]. In our case it might do so: it was the *litis aestimatio* which a freeman would have to pay for the wrong[6].

In fact, here too, the character of the obligation is determined by its history: it is *sui generis*, and cannot be fitted into the normal moulds. In nothing is this more clearly shewn than in the retention of the power of surrender in the *condemnatio*. It has been said that this is *arbitrium*, and the *actio* an *actio arbitraria*. This view is based on a text of the Institutes[7], which, however, as Girard points out, says merely that an *actio arbitraria* may result in a noxal surrender[8]. The power of surrender is in fact very different from *arbitrium*: here the discretion is with the defendant; there it is with the *iudex*.

The master's freedom from personal liability depended on a total absence of complicity. If he was ignorant or forbade the act his liability was noxal[9]: if he took part, or aided, or connived, his liability was personal and *in solidum*[10]. There is a good deal of information as to the state of mind which entailed this liability *in solidum*. Of course, *iussum* sufficed[11]. But failure to prohibit, knowing, and having the power, is·enough, and this is implied in the word *sciens* in the Edict[12].

---

[1] 2. 10. 2; 9. 4. 2. *pr.*, *etc.*
[2] Ed. Perp. 155. He shews that the intention is set forth in 9. 1. 1. 11, in words which, seeming to be the end of a comment, are in fact the words commented on in the following text.
[3] *loc. cit.* *Lex Rubria*, 22; D. 9. 1. 1. *pr.*; G. 4. 75; In. 4. 8. *pr.*
[4] Dernburg, Pand., 2. 79; Savigny, Oblig, § 38; Van Wetter, Oblig. 1. 208.
[5] Kipp, Z. S. S. 10. 397 *sqq.*, reviewing Girard.
[6] 9. 4. 1, 2. *pr.*, *etc.*   [7] In. 4. 6. 31.
[8] *loc. cit.* He cites 5. 3. 40. 4. Other cases, *post*, p. 123. Sell, *op. cit.* 160. Accarias, Précis, § 886, thinks them *arbitrariae* in special sense, and cites two texts (9. 4. 14. 1, 19. *pr.*) which shew only that in some cases there was room for *officium iudicis*. *Ante*, p. 107.
[9] 9. 4. *pass.*; C. 3. 41. 2.
[10] P. 2. 31. 28; C. 3. 41. 4; 9. 4. 2, 3, 5, *etc.* As to *cond. furtiva*, C. 3. 41. 5. In *rapina*, fully liable for men *coacti* by him, 47. 8. 2. 4. So under L. Cornelia where slaves to his knowledge took up arms to seize a property by force, 48. 8. 3. 4. The rules penalising writing gifts to yourself covered dictating them to a slave, 48. 10. 15. *pr.* *Positum* to danger of passers is hardly an instance, 9. 3. 5. 10.
[11] 47. 10. 17. 7.   [12] 9. 4. 3; 47. 6. 1. 1; 47. 10. 9. 3.

If the slave refused to obey or was out of reach or was *proclamans in libertatem*[1], the master was not personally liable[2], nor was he where, whatever his state of mind, he was not *dominus* at the time of the delict[3]. Where the *dominus* was liable *in solidum*, death, sale or manumission of the slave did not release him[4], but, as in all delict, the *heres* was not liable[5]. The personal liability and the noxal liability were essentially one[6], and thus one liable *in solidum* could be sued noxally[7], and the plaintiff could at any time before judgment change from one to the other. And one action excluded the other and thus one sued *in solidum*, and absolved as not *sciens*, could not afterwards be sued noxally[8]. If the slave was alienated before action the buyer became noxally liable, while the vendor was still liable *in solidum*[9]. If the former was sued, Ulpian cites Pomponius as holding that the vendor was released[10]. Though the obligation is one the parties are different[11]. If the slave was freed there is some difficulty as to his liability. If he had obeyed his master's *iussum*, he was excused as being bound to obey[12], unless the thing was so serious that even a *dominus* ought not to be obeyed therein[13]. Celsus thought that if it were a case of personal liability, it could not be noxal, (a view clearly negatived above[14],) and that thus if the *dominus* was personally liable the slave was not (so that absence of prohibition would serve to excuse him), but that, as the XII Tables speak generally of delicts by a slave as noxal, the liability in the case of failure to prohibit would survive against the slave in that case, but not in the case of the later *leges, e.g.* the *lex* Aquilia. But Ulpian, who tells us these views of Celsus, remarks that mere absence of prohibition was no excuse in any case[15], and that the opinion generally held was that due to Julian, *i.e.* that the rule of the XII Tables, and the words *noxiam noxit*, applied to the later *leges* as well, and thus in all delicts, if the owner's participation was short of absolute *iussum*, the slave was liable and remained so after manumission. The *obligatio in solidum* burdens the *dominus*, but does not release the slave[16]. It must be noted that *iussum* here means command, not, as in many places, authorisation.

[1] In which case *dominus* has no power over him, *post*, Ch. xxviii.
[2] 9. 4. 4. *pr.*, 1. [3] 9. 4. 2. 1, 4. 1. [4] 9. 4. 2. 1, 2.
[5] 9. 4. 5. 1. So where the action was *in solidum* on any ground, 9. 4. 16.
[6] As in case of noxal liability of *dominus* and personal liability of slave, *ante*, p. 108.
[7] Sell, *op. cit.* 148—155; 9. 4. 4. 2. [8] 9. 2. 4. 3; *ante*, p. 108.
[9] 9. 4. 7. [10] 9. 4. 7. 1.
[11] The texts suggest that *litis contestatio* barred, but it is not clear, and analogy suggests that the bar only arose after judgment (Sell, *op. cit.* 169—172), while 9. 4. 17. *pr.* treats this as the civil law rule, relieved against by the Praetor.
[12] 9. 4. 2. 1.
[13] *Atrox iniuria* or killing not in defence of *dominus*, 47. 10. 17. 7, 8; 43. 24. 11. 7. Similar rule in criminal law, *ante*, p. 94.
[14] 9. 4. 4. 2, 3.
[15] 9. 4. 2. 1. The reasoning of Celsus does not distinguish clearly between command and non-prohibition.
[16] *Ib.*; 9. 4. 6. Marcellus and Julian: it was not a conflict of the Schools. As the damages would be the same and there could be no surrender it may be assumed that action against one left no action surviving against the other even in Justinian's time.

If a slave has committed several delicts against the same or different persons, the master is released by delivering him under the first judgment[1], *e.g.* where he stole a man and then killed him[2]. This seems to lead, from the rules already stated[3], to the conclusion that the last of several plaintiffs will keep the slave, for all the others in turn will be noxally liable. This squares well enough with the idea of vengeance[4], and though it looks odd in later law, it is not irrational[5].

The case of existence of minor rights in the slave has already been mentioned: it will be convenient to set forth the rules in a connected form. We are told that a *dominus* has *potestas* over a pledged slave, if he has the means to redeem him[6], and that in no case is the pledgee (or *precario tenens*) noxally liable[7]. The question arises: what is the state of the law where the debtor cannot redeem him? As we have seen, if the noxal claimant has brought the slave before the court, then, if the *dominus* is absent, or refuses to defend, the man can be *ductus*, unless the pledge creditor will take up the defence. But this does not meet the very possible case of the slave's being kept out of the way by the pledge creditor. It seems that there must have been some machinery for bringing him before the court. The same question arises in relation to usufruct, which is in general placed on the same level, in this connexion, with pledge[8].

Apart from this matter, the rules are in the main simple. Usufructuary is not noxally liable, and has therefore, in accordance with principle, a noxal action against the *dominus*[9], surrender by whom, even before condemnation, releases him, and ends the lesser right by *confusio*[10]. If an owner, sued noxally by a third person, is condemned, we have seen that he is released only by paying or handing over the unrestricted ownership. If there is an outstanding usufruct, he can apply to the Praetor, on the opening of proceedings in an *actio iudicati*, to compel the usufructuary to pay the value of the usufruct, or cede the right itself, *i.e.* to the *dominus*[11]. If on such facts the owner, instead of defending, hands over the slave, he is released from liability[12]. But lest his *dolus* or *culpa* should injure the fructuary the latter is allowed, there and then, if present, later, if absent, to undertake the defence of

---

[1] 9. 4. 14, 20. [2] 47. 1. 2. 3. [3] 2. 9. 1, 2.
[4] Girard, N. R. H. 12. 49.
[5] An owner holds subject to liability for delicts past and future: such surrender could hardly be a *dolo malo* ceasing to possess, even where it was for a minor delict.
[6] 9. 4. 22. 2.
[7] *h. l.* 1; any more than a *commodatarius* or depositee would be, *h. l. pr.*; 11. 3. 14. 4
[8] If *dominus* has hired the slave from fructuary, he is liable to action with noxal surrender. The fact that he is conductor does not alter the fact that he is owner: he is liable precisely because, being owner, he now has the *de facto* control of the slave. This agrees with the rule that the owner was not liable unless he had the means of getting the man from the holder of the lesser right, 9. 4. 18. See Naber, Mnemosyne, 30 (N. S.) 171. Cp. as to pledge, 9. 4. 36.
[9] 9. 4. 18; 11. 3. 14. 3; 47. 2. 43. 12; 47. 10. 17. 9.
[10] 7. 1. 17. 2; 7. 4. 27; 9. 4. 18. [11] 9. 4. 17. 1. [12] *Ante*, p. 103.

the slave[1]. If he will not, his right is barred, unless he is willing to pay the *litis aestimatio*[2]. If he hands him over he is not liable to the *dominus*[3]. These texts agree with the common sense view that, as the owner is released by the surrender, justice requires that the holders of outstanding rights should also be barred. The case is different where the action against the *dominus* has reached *condemnatio*. There is now a judgment standing against him for a sum of money in first instance : *deditio* is now merely facultative. This is a personal liability of his[4]. He can still be released by handing over the slave, but this is not a result of the rule *noxa caput sequitur* ; the judgment is against him personally and this rule has now no application: the release is the result of an express statement to that effect in the *condemnatio*, and it requires transfer of complete ownership. Since the injured person has his remedy against the old owner so long as unencumbered ownership is not given to him, justice requires that the holders of minor rights should not be barred, as there is now no question of undertaking the defence. They could therefore enforce their claim at once, and whether they did so or not, the plaintiff, as soon as he knew of the existence of their right, could bring *actio iudicati* against the old owner, at once, without waiting for actual eviction[5].

Three texts create difficulties in the application of this coherent scheme. One seems to give an action against the fructuary in the first instance[6]. The facts seem to be that an action has been brought against him as owner : he denies the fact. It then transpires that he is usufructuary, and he is invited to take up the defence. If he refuses his right is barred. Looked at in this way the text says nothing exceptional[7]. A second text[8] seems to subject the owner's right to surrender one, in whom there is a usufruct, to the condition that the surrender is *sine dolo malo*. This however is not what the text really means. The absence of *dolus* is not a condition on his right of surrender, but on his freedom from liability to the fructuary for any damage to his interests that the surrender may cause[9]. The third text is a more serious matter. It observes that if an owner hands over a pledged slave *per iudicem*, and so is *absolutus*, he is liable, *de dolo*, if it shall appear that the man was given in pledge, and this *actio doli* will be noxal[10]. This is a surrender between *litis contestatio* and *condemnatio*.

---

[1] 9. 4. 17. 1, 26. 6, 30.   [2] 9. 4. 17. 1, 27. *pr.*
[3] 9. 4. 17. 1. The text looks corrupt: in its original form it may have thrown light on the case in which there are several delicts.
[4] *Ante*, p. 105.
[5] 9. 4. 14. 1 ; 42. 1. 4. 8 ; 46. 3. 69. If outstanding right be extinguished, liberation of old owner follows. For different views, see Koschaker, Translatio Iudicii, 209, and Elvers, Servitutenlehre, 517.
[6] 2. 9. 3.   [7] Elvers, *op. cit.* 515.   [8] 7. 1. 17. 2.
[9] See 9. 4. 26. 6.   [10] 4. 3. 9. 4.

It seems clear that the liability is to the surrenderee. But he does not suffer since on such facts the pledgee could not claim the slave without paying the claim[1]. It is a possible conjecture that the surrender was after *condemnatio*; the word *absolutus* having been wrongly used for *officio iudicis liberatus*[2]. The hypothesis would be that, after condemnation, the man has been handed over, and the judge, thinking unencumbered ownership has been given, declares the defendant free from liability. But in all probability the text is corrupt or interpolated or both[3,4].

If a delict is committed by several persons, each is wholly liable: judgment and execution against one do not bar action on the delict against the others[5]. The rule was different, at least in some cases, where the wrong was done by several of a man's slaves. Here the Praetor limited the claim to as much as would be due, if the wrong had been done by a single freeman, with restitution in appropriate cases[6]. The rule did not apply to all delicts, and may have gradually extended from the case of *furtum*. The privilege seems to have applied to cases under the Edict as to *bona vi rapta* and to *damnum hominibus coactis*[7]. There was certainly a noxal action, expressly mentioned in the Edict where the wrong was done by the *familia*[8], and one text says that, in noxal cases, the amount that could be claimed was limited to fourfold[9]. The form of the text shews that this was not an express provision of the Edict. The adjoining text[10] observes that the noxal surrender will be only of those who are shewn *dolo fecisse*; not, that is, of slaves among the *homines coacti* who may have been acting innocently[11].

As to ordinary *damnum iniuria datum*, Paul thought the restriction had no application, since each piece of damage was a separate wrong: there were *plura facta* not *unum* as in *furtum*[12]. On the other hand Ulpian allowed it on equitable grounds, if the damage had been done merely *culpa*[13]. And Gaius allowed it generally, because it might be

---

[1] *Ante*, p. 117, n. 2.   [2] See 5. 3. 20. 5.
[3] The next part of the extract is corrupt: the preceding part is treated by Gradenwitz as interpolated (Interp. 144). Our text is incorrect in the Florentine. See also Pernice, Labeo, 2. 1. 202. As the fraud is that of *dominus* the noxal character of the *actio* needs explaining. The point is that the *actio doli* is merely indemnificatory (4. 3. 17) and that complete transfer of the slave, since it would have satisfied the original liability, is all that can be asked for. The words referring to noxal character are not in the Basilica.
[4] Several texts put pledgee on the same level as fructuary, giving him no liability but a right to defend. The only notable difference is that if he refuses and so is barred, his pledge is ended (*nullum enim est pignus cuius persecutio denegatur*), while usufruct, as a substantive *ius*, continues technically till it is destroyed by non-use, 9. 4. 22. 1, 26. 6, 27, 30.
[5] 9. 2. 11. 2.   [6] 9. 4. 31; 47. 6. 1, 2.   [7] 47. 8.
[8] Cicero, Pro Tullio, 3. 7; 13. 31; D. 47. 8. 2. 14; 50. 16. 40 (which is from that book of Ulpian's Commentary which deals with this matter), 50. 16. 195. 3. Lenel, Ed. Perp. § 187. Cp. P. 5. 6. 3.
[9] 47. 8. 2. 15.   [10] *h. l.* 16.
[11] For *damnum in turba factum*, the action lay, it is said, *in familiam*. But it was not noxal and there is no sign that the present rule applied, 47. 8. 4. 15.
[12] 2. 1. 9. No doubt he contemplates distinguishable traces of damage.
[13] 47. 6. 1. 2.

culpa, in any given case[1]. It is clear that there was no Edict as to this, and the varying voices suggest a late development. For *iniuria* it was never allowed: here there were as many delicts as there were slaves— *plura facta*[2]. There was no such provision in *albi corruptio*, partly it seems because of *contempta maiestas Praetoris*, partly as it contained *plura facta*. This seems to have been the operative reason, since Octavenus and Pomponius agreed that it might apply, if they procured an outsider to do it, for here there was only *unum factum*[3]. Whatever be thought of the reasoning it is clear that it ignores the argument drawn from the contempt of the Praetor involved in the act.

The rules are laid down in detail for *furtum*[4]. If the *dominus* is being sued noxally for one, the action as to the others is suspended, so long as the minimum amount is recoverable[5]: when that has been recovered, all actions cease against any owner or any slave manumitted[6], and it is immaterial, (so Sabinus and Cassius held, and Pomponius agreed,) whether the amount was made up in money or in the value of surrendered slaves[7]. Even if the *dominus* has *dolo malo* ceased to possess, and is condemned on that ground, he still has this protection[8]. And, since the value of all the slaves may be less than the fourfold penalty, he is entitled to absolution if he hand over all the slaves who were in the mischief, having pointed them out himself, not the whole *familia*[9]. But previous recovery from a *manumissus* does not protect the *dominus*, who still has the *familia*, as it cannot be said to have been paid *familiae nomine*[10]. The point is that the whole rule is rather an inroad on the rights of the injured person, and to protect the *dominus* in this case would be to exempt him from liability. For the converse reason, if the buyer of a slave has paid, action against the vendor is barred, for the vendee can recover the amount from him under the ordinary warranty, that he was *noxa solutus*[11]. And since legatee or donee of the slave could not so fall back on the old owner, action against them did not bar a claim from the owner of the others[12].

The fact that the rule is a great restriction on the common law liability of the *dominus* led apparently to a very literal interpretation of the Edict. It provides that the *actor* can recover only what would be due from a single offender[13]. If now the injured person had died leaving two *heredes*, Labeo held that each of these, suing, would be

---

[1] 9. 2. 32.   [2] 2. 1. 9; 47. 10. 34.   [3] 2. 1. 9.
[4] 47. 6.   [5] 47. 6. 1. 3; 47. 8. 2. 15.   [6] 47. 6. 3. *pr.*
[7] 9. 4. 31.
[8] 47. 6. 3. 2. In reckoning the amount due, the *condictio furtiva* would come into account, so that he must surrender, or permit to be *ducti*, enough slaves to cover the damages in this as well as in the penal action, 9. 4. 31.
[9] 47. 6. 1. *pr.*; 47. 8. 2. 16.   [10] 47. 6. 3. *pr.*   [11] *Ib.*
[12] *h. l.* 1. The liability did not of course apply to slaves acquired after the offence, 9. 4. 31.
[13] 9. 4. 31.

actor and could recover the whole of the limited amount, not being barred by action by the other, provided of course that the common law liability was not overstepped[1]. Cervidius Scaevola repudiates this, on the ground that it would be unfair, and a fraud on the Edict, to allow the *heredes* to recover more than their ancestor could[2]. In the same way if the deceased had recovered only part, each of the heirs could recover all that was still due. Scaevola confines them to their share[3].

There were special rules in the case of *Publicani*. Two separate Edicts dealt with their liability for acts of employees[4], but the compilers of the Digest have so confused them in statement, that it is not possible to make out, with certainty, the original content of each. As they appear, they overlap, but it is now generally agreed that one of them dealt with *ademptio vi* and *damnum*, done in the course of collecting the revenue, by the *publicanus*, or his employees, and the other with *furtum*, not necessarily in the actual course of collection[5]. Whatever differences there may have been between the two sets of provisions, the compilers seem to have designed to assimilate them, and they have carried over words from each Edict to the other, so that they are both made to refer both to *furtum* and *damnum*. As to the actual content of the liability, Karlowa[6] detects many differences between the actions, but the evidence for most of them is unconvincing. He is probably right in holding that the Edict dealing with *ademptio* did not apply to the provinces. He infers from a comparison of some texts, really inconclusive[7], that the *familia* in the Edict as to *furtum* included only slaves, or apparent slaves, of the *publicanus* sued, while it is clear that in the other case, it covered all persons employed on the business[8]. He thinks that the action under the Edict as to *ademptio* was not penal, but the whole content of it as recorded is opposed to this view. He thinks that, in the case of *furtum*, the action *sine noxae deditione* was only against the owner, while in the other it was certainly against any of the *publicani*[9].

The rules as to the case of *ademptio vi* are fairly fully recorded. To guard against forcible seizure by the *publicani* or their men, they were made liable for any such seizure or damage, by themselves or their staff[10], in the course of the collection, any *socius vectigalis* being

---

[1] *i.e.* his share of what the late owner could have recovered apart from this Edict.
[2] 47. 6. 6.
[3] *Ib.* It must be added that the whole rule applied only where the master was innocent: if he was *sciens*, he could be sued, *suo nomine*, and noxally for each of the slaves, 47. 6. 1. 1. No doubt the liabilities are alternative.
[4] 39. 4. 1. *pr.*; *h. t.* 12.
[5] Lenel, Ed. Perp. (French ed.) § 138; Karlowa, R. R. G. 2. 35.
[6] *loc. cit.*   [7] 39. 4. 1. 5; 39. 4. 13. 2; 50. 16. 195. 3.
[8] He points out that in the few words on the Edict as to theft, nothing is said as to free employees, 39. 4. 12. 2; cp. 39. 4. 1. 5.
[9] This rests merely on the use of *dominus* in the singular, 39. 4. 12. 1, Lenel, *loc. cit.*
[10] 39. 4. 1. Under colour of the abolished *pignoris capio*.

liable[1]. The action was for twofold within a year, *in simplum* after a year[2], and, as in the last case, the employer was released by payment of what would have been due if the wrong had been done by one freeman[3]. Though the term *familia* usually covers all slaves, it applied in this case only to persons employed in the collection[4]. There must be a demand for the production of the slave or slaves, or of all the slaves, so that the actual wrongdoer could be pointed out[5]. They might not be defended in their absence[6], but if they were produced there would be an ordinary noxal action[7]. If they were not produced there was a *iudicium sine noxae deditione*, whether the defendant could not or would not produce them, and though they were no longer in his *potestas*[8].

The action, though severe in some respects, was mild in others, since the penalty was only twofold, and this included the *res*, while by the ordinary action it would be in some cases fourfold. Accordingly the injured person, if he could prove the identity of the slave, might proceed by the ordinary action instead[9]. How far these rules may be extended to the Edict as to *furta* is uncertain. That it was an independent Edict is shewn by the fact that Gaius discusses it in his commentary on the Provincial edict, and Ulpian in the part of his commentary which dealt with theft : the other Edict was treated under the heading *de publicanis*[10]. It provides for an action *sine noxae deditione*, in the case of *furtum* by the *familia publicani*, if the wrongdoer is not produced, whether it was in the collection or not[11]. It is probable from the allusion to *publicanorum factiones*[12] that it applied whether they were slave or free. It can hardly fail to have been penal[13], and probably the penalties were those of *furtum*. The *publicanus* remained liable though he sold or freed the slave, and even if the slave ran away[14]. The text adds that if the slave is dead the *publicanus* is freed, since he has not the *facultas dedendi*, and has not been guilty of *dolus*[15].

Other cases of exceptional liability may be shortly stated. The special liabilities of *exercitor navis*, *caupo* and *stabularius* included a

---

[1] *h. t.* 3. 1.
[2] 39. 4. 1. *pr.* Restitution before *litis contestatio* ended the claim, 39. 4. 1. *pr.*, 5. *pr.* The text adds that it will discharge even after *litis contestatio*. This is not an application of the rule *omnia iudicia absolutoria*: restitution is less than the action would give. Probably Tribonian.
[3] 39. 4. 3. 3.   [4] 39. 4. 1. 5; 50. 16. 195. 3.   See 21. 1. 1. 1; *h. t.* 25. 2, *etc.*
[5] 39. 4. 3. 2.   [6] 39. 4. 2.   [7] 39. 4. 3. *pr.*
[8] 39. 4. 1. 6.   The action being penal lay against *heres* only to extent of his profit, 39. 4. 4. *pr.* If several *publicani*, liable only *pro parte*, and, so enacted Severus and Caracalla, for any deficit not recoverable from the others, 39. 4. 6.
[9] 39. 4. 1. 3—4.   [10] Lenel and Karlowa, *locc. citt.*
[11] 39. 4. 12. 1.   As to corruption and interpolation, Lenel, *loc. cit.*
[12] 39. 4. 12. *pr.*   Cp. *h. t.* 13. 2.
[13] Lenel, *loc. cit.*   Karlowa contra, *loc. cit.*   He cites the rule that it was perpetual (39. 4. 13. 4), but so were many penal actions. See *ante*, p. 34, and *post*, p. 122. And the rule here may be a Tribonianism. Gaius would hardly say : *hanc actionem dabimus.*
[14] 39. 4. 13. 2.
[15] *h. l.* 3.   The remark would apply equally to the case of a runaway: the rule seems to be the settlement of a dispute and may be due to Tribonian.

liability *in solidum* for what they had received, *salvum fore*, without
reference to such *dolus* or *culpa* as an ordinary contractual action would
have required[1]. Thus even if the thing were stolen by a *servus
exercitoris* there was no *actio furti noxalis*, since the *exercitor* was
liable personally in full, under this special Edict[2]. The action was not
delictal or penal: it was perpetual and available against the *heres*[3]. A
still more striking result of its character is that it was available though
the injured person were the owner of the slave, and thus would be
noxally liable for him[4]. But there was a further liability which more
nearly concerns us. There was an action *in factum* against such
persons, for any theft or[5] *damnum* committed by their employees in the
course of the business, beyond their liability for goods they had
insured[6]. The action was delictal: it involved proof of the theft or
damnum, and it was *in duplum*[7]. It was *perpetua* and availed to but
not against the *heres*[8]. Death of the wrongdoer did not release the
principal, if it was a *servus alienus*, for as he was definitely hired for the
work, the liability was *in solidum*[9]. If it was his own slave, the liability
was noxal, and thus it may be presumed that death released[10].

We have now to discuss the questions which arise where the facts
which raise a noxal claim occur in connexion with a *negotium* between
the parties, so that there is, or might conceivably be, an action
ex contractu. It will be convenient to consider two distinct cases:

(i) Where there is a contract between the parties, and the slave of
one of them commits a delict, in relation to its subject-matter.

(ii) Where the slave himself is the subject of the *negotium*.

(i) If in the carrying out of a contract between two persons, one of
the parties commits an act which is both a breach of the contract and a
delict, it is clear[11] that in the classical law the person injured could
proceed in either way. But the case was different if the person who
actually did the wrong was the slave of the party. Here the slave has

---

[1] 4. 9. 1. *pr.*, 3. 1—2; 47. 5. 1. 4.   [2] 4. 9. 3. 3.
[3] *h. l.* 4.   [4] 4. 9. 6. 1.
[5] As to theft there was a special Edict (47. 5): as to *damnum* the action followed the same
rule, but there may have been no Edict, Lenel, *op. cit.* § 78.
[6] 47. 5. 1. *pr.*, 4.   [7] 4. 9. 7. 1; 47. 5. 1. 2; In. 4. 5. 3.
[8] 4. 9. 7. 6; In. 4. 5. 3.
[9] 4. 9. 7. 4; 47. 5. 1. 5.   The reason of its being noxal is in one case said to be that one
using his own slaves must use such as he has, while one who hires must use care in selection
(4. 9. 7. 4). In the other it is said that some consideration is due to one afflicted with a bad
slave (47. 5. 1. 5). It is in fact an application of what seems to have been accepted as a first
principle, that a man cannot be liable for his slave's act beyond his value. Lenel however (Ed.
Perp. § 136) attributes the restriction to an express provision of the Edict, being led to his view
by the form of Ulpian's remarks.
[10] Theft severely dealt with because of the circumstances, *e.g.* theft from wreck, was still so
where the wrongdoer was a slave (47. 9. 1. *pr.*). Conversely the rule that *Vi bonorum raptorum*
was *annalis* applied where it was noxal, so that a freed slave could not be sued after the year,
though the master had not been: the actions were the same, 47. 8. 3. See *ante*, p. 115.
[11] Reff.: Accarias, Précis, § 856. We are not here concerned with the barring effect of one
action on the other. Girard, Manuel, 397.

committed a wrong for which a noxal action will lie. It was not the slave's *negotium* and there can be no question of *actio de peculio*[1]. On the other hand the master who made the contract has personally committed no breach of it. Hence there arose a difference of opinion, mainly expressed in relation to the case where slaves of *colonus* or *inquilinus* negligently burnt the property. Sabinus held that their *dominus* could not be sued *ex locato*, though he could, *ex* Aquilia, noxally. Proculus however, of the other school, held that he could be sued *ex locato*, subject to the provision, (due to the idea that a man ought not to be liable for a slave's act beyond the value of the slave[2],) that he would be free from liability on handing over the slave[3]. This is the view that prevailed[4]. If however there was any *culpa* in the actual party, *e.g.* in choosing, for the care of a fire, unsuitable persons, then he was personally liable *in solidum*[5]. The same principle no doubt applied in other cases, but there seems no authority even on the obvious case of a thing deposited, injured by a slave of the depositee. As he was not liable for his own *culpa* he can hardly have been for his slave's. As he was liable for *dolus*, it is likely that the rule in that case was as in *locatio*.

Where the delict was *furtum* a difference is created by the fact that the holder may be liable for *custodia*, and as he is liable for the thing, on the contract, the owner has, on a well-known principle, no *interesse* and thus no *actio furti*[6]. Thus where the slave of the *commodatarius* stole the thing the owner had no *actio furti*[7]. If the commodator's slave stole it, the *commodatarius* was liable *ex commodato*, and had therefore an *interesse*, giving him *actio furti* against the commodator[8]. Paul quotes this from Sabinus with a further remark to the effect that if the *actio commodati* is remitted or the damages are refunded the action on theft "*evanescit*[9]." The reason of this last rule is not obvious. Many facts, such as release and satisfaction, put an end to rights of action, but this is not one of them[10].

The explanation seems to be this. Persons who held a mere *ius in personam* in a thing might have an *actio furti* in respect of it, but only in virtue of their liability, not on account of the advantage they lost:

---

[1] *Post*, Ch. IX.   [2] 47. 2. 62. 5.   [3] Coll. 12. 7. 9; D. 47. 1. 2. 3.
[4] 9. 2. 27. 11; as to contractual liability, *post*, p. 162.
[5] Coll. 12. 7. 7; D. 9. 2. 27. 9, 11; 19. 2. 11. *pr.* Paul notes that where slaves let with a house commit a delict against the tenant the owner is liable noxally but not *ex contractu*. Their act is no breach of the contract, 19. 2. 45. *pr.*
[6] G. 3. 205—7.
[7] Apart from Justinian's changes of which the text takes no note, 47. 2. 54. 2. The text does not discuss insolvency of the *commodatarius*.
[8] 13. 6. 21. 1; 47. 2. 54. 1. If depositor was the thief there was no *actio furti*: as he could not enforce the duty of *custodia*, P. 2. 31. 21.
[9] 47. 2. 54. 1.
[10] Monro, De furtis, 75 assumes the claims to be equal. There seems no warranty for this.

their right was not considered[1]. The whole theory of this *interesse* of a person with no *ius in rem* is a juristic development. It is abnormal: it is not thoroughly worked out, and this is not the only point at which its logic breaks down. We know from Gaius, and the Digest[2], that an insolvent borrower had not the *actio furti*, (though Justinian speaks of ancient doubts[3],) yet he technically had the liability. His insolvency did not release the debt: he might be sued on it later. Moreover the texts excluding action by the insolvent refer to insolvency in the present, not at the time of the theft[4]. The abnormal right was allowed only if and in so far as its denial would operate unjustly, and it is clear that in the case of supervening insolvency, and in that with which we are directly concerned, the real interest of the borrower has substantially ceased[5].

(ii) The case is more complex where the slave is, himself, the subject of the *negotium*. We have seen that the existence of a contractual obligation is no bar to that of a delictal. A general view of the texts, dealing with our present topic, suggests that if a slave, the subject of a *negotium*, committed a delict against his holder, the latter had no delictal action against the *dominus*, but only the contractual action subject to that right of quasi-noxal surrender which we have just noted as appearing in such actions. But this is not the case, though the rules as given present a somewhat misleading approximation to that state of things. How this arises may perhaps best be shewn by dealing first with the case of the man who is now owner of the slave, but is entitled to hand him back, or is bound to hand him on. Such a person can have no noxal action for what occurred while he was owner[6] Justice however may require that he should have compensation, and the sources discuss several such cases. Thus the *vir*, being owner of dotal slaves, can have no noxal action, against his wife, for what they do[7]. But in any action for recovery of the *dos*, account is taken of the theft up to the value of the slave, and if the wife knew of his quality, *in solidum*[8]. So a redhibiting buyer is noxally liable for the man[9], and thus cannot bring a noxal action, but he has a claim to compensation

---

[1] 47. 2. 12. *pr.*, 14. 12—15. The holder *in precario* lost advantages by the theft but he had no *actio furti*, 47. 2. 14. 11.
[2] 47. 2. 54. 1; G. 3. 205.   [3] C. 6. 2. 22.
[4] *e.g.* 47. 2. 12. *pr. si solvendo non est ad dominum actio redit*; In. 4. 1. 15; D. 47. 2. 54. 1, *rem subripuerit et solvendo sit, sqq.* A positive *interesse* need exist only at the time of the theft, 47. 2. 46. *pr.*
[5] If the *negotium* did not impose a liability for *custodia* (*e.g.* deposit) the holder had no *actio furti*, G. 3. 207; In. 4. 1. 17. If it were stolen by slave of depositee an ordinary noxal action arose.
[6] *Ante*, p. 107; 21. 1. 52.
[7] The fact that no delictal actions lie directly between them is no bar to an action *servi nomine*.
[8] 25. 2. 21. 2.   [9] 19. 1. 11, 12; 21. 1. 23. 8; *ante*, p. 107.

subject to *pro noxae deditione*[1]. The right of indemnity covered any theft from him whenever committed and any thefts from third persons to whom the buyer had had to pay damages[2]. Legacies afford an instructive contrast. Where a *servus legatus* stole from the future heir, before entry, Julian allowed the *heres* an *actio furti noxalis* against the legatee, *qui legatum agnoverit*[3]. The case contemplated is one of a *legatum per vindicationem*. On the other hand Gaius tells us that the *heres* need not hand over a *servus legatus* unless an indemnity, (not a penalty,) not exceeding the value of the slave, is given to him, and this whether the theft was before or after entry[4]. It is clear·from the language and the context that Gaius is speaking of a *legatum per damnationem*, in which the *heres* was owner for a time. The compilers have extended it to all legacies, though, for Justinian's law, Julian's rule would seem the most logical. This is a transference of the kind which seems to lie at the bottom of most of the cases we shall have to discuss.

The texts dealing with theft by a pledged slave are few, all from the same section of the same book of Africanus. They lay down the rule that, in such a case, the creditor can recover, (by the *actio pigneratitia contraria*,) an indemnity, subject to a right of *pro noxae deditione*, where the owner was not aware of the quality of the slave: otherwise he is liable *in solidum*. There is no hint of *furti noxalis*[5]. Of the texts on which this rule is based one is claimed, by Lenel, as relating to the *actio fiduciae*[6]. As, of the others, one merely repeats this, and all are from the same place, it seems probable that all were written of *fiducia*, in which, as ownership passed to the creditor, there could be no noxal action, and that this is simply a hasty transfer to *pignus* of rules which developed in *fiducia*[7].

Mandate gives similar texts of more various origin. It is laid down that if A buys a slave under mandate from B, and the slave steals from A, and A is not *in culpa*, he need not hand over the slave till account is taken of the theft, in an *actio mandati*[8]. Nothing is said of an *actio furti*. If the mandator knew his quality the liability is *in solidum*: Africanus indeed suggests that it should be so in any case, since, reasonable as it is that·one should not be liable for a slave's act beyond the value of the slave, it is still more reasonable that a man's unpaid

---

[1] 21. 1. 58. *pr.* Though the fact that the man stole was not itself a ground for redhibition, 21. 1. 52.
[2] 30. 70. 2; 47. 2. 62. 2. His claim would not exceed the value of the man unless the vendor had warranted him not a thief, in which case he was entitled *in solidum* at least as to thefts from himself, 21. 1. 31. 1; 47. 2. 62. 4.
[3] 9. 4. 40.   [4] 30. 70. *pr.*, 3; cp. 47. 2. 65.
[5] 13. 7. 31; 47. 2. 62. 1.
[6] 13. 7. 31; Lenel, Palingen., 1. 30; Heck, Z. S. S. 10. 125.
[7] Other cases, Lenel, Z. S. S. 3. 104 *sqq.*; Girard, Manuel, 518.
[8] 17. 1. 26. 7; 30. 70. 2; 47. 2. 62. 5—7.

service should not be an expense to him[1]. If the *mandatarius* was careless in trusting him unduly, this was *culpa* and barred his remedy[2]. These are the views of Neratius, Africanus, Gaius and Paulus. Most of the texts are contexted with the case of the redhibiting buyer. A slave was a *res mancipi*, and *mancipatio*, which was at the time of these writers still the usual mode of conveyance of such things, necessarily left the *dominium* for the time being in the agent. Even by *traditio*, there could be, at that time, no question of a direct acquisition by the employer. Gaius and Paul are clear on the point[3]. Here too we have rules laid down for the case where the victim of the theft was for the moment owner, and applied to conditions in which this was no longer the case.

Similar rules are found in deposit, Africanus, citing Julian, being apparently the only authority. The rules are as in mandate, but Julian is not cited as holding the extreme view, that compensation should be *in solidum* because the service was gratuitous[4]. As in *pignus*, these texts are from the same part of the same work. One is referred by Lenel[5] to the *actio fiduciae*, the other set come from the group of texts already handled, dealing with ownership. It can hardly be doubted that the texts were originally written of *fiducia cum amico*, which seems to have lasted up to the third century, side by side with the later form of deposit[6].

In the case of *commodatum*, there is difficulty. Africanus lays down the rule that, for theft from the borrower by the commodated slave, the commodator is liable by the *contrarium iudicium commodati*, up to the slave's value, but if guilty of *dolus*, then *in solidum*. We have seen reason to think that this text[7] dealt originally with *fiducia cum amico*, in which the holder was owner. The same rule is also laid down by the same writer in a text which, as we have seen, Lenel attributes to *fiducia*[8]. But Paul, in another text[9], after remarking that it is doubted (*quaeritur*) whether, on such facts, the *contraria actio* suffices, and whether there ought not to be *actio furti noxalis*, adds that, *procul dubio*, the *commodatarius* has *furti noxalis*, and that the commodator is liable *in solidum* if he knew the character of the slave. Gradenwitz, discussing another point, has no difficulty in shewing that this text has been altered[10]. In Paul's time *fiducia cum amico*, if not gone, was rare, and Paul doubts whether the rule of *fiducia* ought to be applied to the

---

[1] 47. 2. 62. 5.
[2] *h. l.* 7. The liability could hardly be *in solidum* where it was a general mandate: to buy such a man under such a mandate was rather like *culpa*.
[3] They, and Neratius, admit acquisition of possession by a procurator, but that is a different matter, 41. 3. 41; G. 2. 95; P. 5. 2. 2.
[4] 13. 7. 31; 47. 2. 62. 5, 7.   [5] 13. 7. 31. Lenel, Paling., 1. 30.
[6] Girard, Manuel, 520.   [7] 47. 2. 62. 6.
[8] 13. 7. 31.   [9] 13. 6. 22.   [10] Gradenwitz, Interpolationen, 120.

newer method. The compilers put into his mouth a reasonable solution for their own times. It is not however clear why they did not deal in the same comparatively rational way, with mandate pledge and deposit. It may be, since their work was done hastily, because no jurist, writing after the decay of *fiducia cum amico*, hints a doubt, in the other cases. Paul, whose question led to the solution of the problem here, does not suggest a doubt in mandate[1], in which case indeed the double conveyance was still necessary in his day, and he is not cited as discussing the other cases[2].

In *locatio*, which had not the same historical associations with ownership in the temporary holder, there is no difficulty. The injured conductor has *actio furti noxalis*, and has no *actio conducti*. There has indeed been no breach of contract. If the locator was guilty of *dolus* there was no right of surrender[3].

Two texts only seem to deal with the case where the thieving slave had made the contract, as to himself. They relate to cases under the Edict as to *nautae, caupones, etc.*, and the special rules there applied destroy the significance of the texts in the present connexion. But they are noticeable on other grounds. In one of them[4] it is said that an ordinary noxal action lay for a delict, by the *vicarius* of a slave *exercitor*, to which the *exercitor* was privy. This only illustrates the rule that contractual relation did not exclude delictal. The other, also from Paul[5], deals with a slave, *exercitor sine voluntate domini*, on whose ship something perishes, the liability here being independent of *culpa* and thus not necessarily delictal. If the loss is caused by the slave *exercitor*, there is a right to noxal surrender, if the *actio exercitoria* is brought against the *dominus*. This is a normal application of the principle that a man ought not to be liable on a slave's act beyond his value[6]. But some cases arising out of the common case of a free *exercitor* do not seem quite logical. We have seen that an *exercitor* was liable for *furtum* or *damnum* by slaves employed in the ship[7], but that in the case of his own slave the liability was noxal[8]. This agrees with the foregoing principle but hardly with the basis of the whole liability expressed in the same text, *i.e.* that it was his own *culpa* for putting such slaves on such business[9].

---

[1] 17. 1. 26. 7.
[2] Analogous case of common ownership, *post*, Ch. xvi.
[3] 19. 2. 45. *pr.*, 47. 2. 62. 6. Not *actio furti* with no right of surrender, but *actio ex conducto*, for complete indemnity. The *dolus* is not privity, but knowledge that the man is a rascal.
[4] 9. 4. 19. 2. Discussion of this text and its difficulties, *post*, Ch. x.
[5] 47. 2. 42. *pr.*
[6] The text shews that as there was no authority, there would also be a limitation to the *peculium*.
[7] *Ante*, p. 122.
[8] 4. 9. 7. 4 ; 47. 5. 1. 1—5.
[9] 47. 5. 1. 5. The text notes the difficulty: the explanation it gives is not adequate: *ante*, p. 122.

Some interdicts have their interest from the point of view of noxal surrender. Possessory interdicts are not delictal. Those dealing with public rights are not noxal: for interference with public ways and the like, a slave, it is said, was to be flogged by any who detected him[1]. But there are two interdicts which are expressly described as *interdicta noxalia*. They are *Unde vi* and *Quod vi aut clam*[2]. They have peculiarities of detail, but no real departure from ordinary principles. The interdict *unde vi* speaks of *deiectio* by the defendant or the *familia*[3], which covers one or more slaves[4] or persons actually held as slaves[5]. If it were *ex voluntate domini*, or ratified by him, it was his *deiectio*[6]. Apart from this his liability for slaves is not *in solidum*, though the Edict specially mentions them: it is a case for noxal surrender, for though the facts are criminal under the *lex* Iulia, the interdict is merely penal[7]. If he will not surrender he must pay in full, and he must in any case refund what he has received[8].

In the case of *opus vi aut clam factum*, the rules are more complex. The interdict is to secure the undoing, with necessary compensation, of any *opus*, done *vi aut clam*, on ·the plaintiff's property: it does not expressly mention slaves[9]. If it were *iussu domini* it was his act[10], unless he ordered it not intending secrecy, and the slave, knowing the other party would object, did it secretly. Here it was noxal[11]. The liability is either (i) to put the matter right, or (ii) to let it be put right and surrender the slave, or (iii) to pay the cost of putting it right[12]. If the slave has been alienated or freed, or has died, the master is only bound to let it be put right, the freed slave being liable to pay the cost, and a buyer of the slave being similarly liable with a right of surrender[13]. If the master will not let it be undone he is as liable as if he had done it himself[14]. One important point remains. The noxal liability of the slave's owner arises only if the act was done in his name, or on his account, or *mero motu* by the slave. If it was done for a temporary employer it is against him that the interdict should go[15], and he has not the privilege of surrender. If the owner of the slave or any buyer has made full compensation there can be no proceedings against the *dominus operis*, but if only *noxae deditio* has been made, the interdict may still go against the *dominus operis*, for compensation, no doubt, less the value

---

[1] 43. 10. 1. 2.   If the *dominus* was privy, no doubt he also was liable.
[2] 43. 1. 5.   [3] 43. 16. 1. *pr.*, 11, 16.   [4] 43. 16. 1. 17.
[5] *h. l.* 18.   [6] 43. 16. 1. 12, 15 *h. t.* 3. 11.
[7] Thus not available against *heres* except to extent of profit, 43. 16. 1. 48.
[8] 43. 16. 1. 15, 19.   Similar rules in *De vi armata*, 43. 16. 3. 11.
[9] 43. 24. 1.   The word *opus* is used in a very wide sense.
[10] 43. 24. 5. 14.   It is in fact punishable in the slave, but not if under *iussum*: it is not an *atrox facinus* and he must obey, *h. t.* 11. 7.   *Iussum* by guardian of a *dominus incapax* left it noxal, 43. 24. 11. 6.
[11] *h. t.* 21. 1.   [12] 43. 1. 5; 43. 24. 7. 1.   [13] 43. 24. 7. 1, 14.
[14] 43. 1. 5.   [15] 43. 24. 5. 11.

of the slave[1]. The absence of liability for what the slave does at the behest or on account of a third person is due to a juristic inference from the fact that that other is liable, and this in turn is due, says Labeo[2], to the fact that the interdict says *quod factum est,* and not *quod feceris.*

We know that there were noxal provisions in the XII Tables, in the *lex* Aquilia and in the Edict[3]. As rules of law are constantly built up on the words of enactments we might expect differences. We have seen some differences in detail, but there remains at least one important distinction in principle between the rules in *furtum* and those in *damnum.* Celsus observes that the XII Tables declare the *dominus* liable *servi nomine* for the slave's wrong, whether privy or not[4]. Hence the liability is noxal, and follows the slave. But in the case of the *lex* Aquilia, if *sciente domino,* it is a direct liability of the master and the slave is not liable. But Julian, Marcellus and Ulpian are agreed that there is no difference: the words *noxiam noxit* and the rest, in the old law, apply to later *leges* as well, so that both master and slave are liable. The difference is thus overridden, but it is important to notice who the jurists are who observe the difference and see a way out of it[5].

Another difference is more striking and important, for it remained. Ulpian tells us that if a slave is *in fuga,* the *dominus* has *furti noxalis* against a *bonae fidei possessor,* for since he has not *potestas* he is not noxally liable for him[6]. He cites Julian in support, and Paul also holds the owner not liable[7]. And the liability of the *bonae fidei possessor* is laid down in many texts which seem conclusive[8], though one text of Justinian in his Code hints a doubt[9]. It so happens that an opposite rule is laid down for *damnum* on both points, by Julian, Marcellus and Ulpian[10]. If a slave *occidit,* the owner is liable and the *bonae fidei possessor* is not, and the *dominus* is liable for the slave *in fuga.* What is the cause of these distinctions? They are so sharp and rest on such circumstantially stated authority that it is difficult to dispute their genuineness, and they are so connected that it is *a priori* probable that they rest on a real distinction of principle. This impression is strengthened by the fact that the jurists who support these distinctions are those whom we saw considering another possible distinction of principle between the XII Tables and later legislation. Yet attempts to explain away the texts have been made persistently even so far back as in the Basilica. Most of these attempted explanations have been reviewed and shewn to

---

[1] 43. 24. 7. 1. Why does *dominus* surrender if the *dominus operis* is the person really liable? Perhaps A's slave, *mero motu,* secretly does, on B's land, work which injures C.
[2] 43. 24. 5. 13.
[3] G. 4. 76; In. 4. 8. 4; D. 9. 4. 2. 1; 47. 1. 1. 2. There were also the interdictal cases just discussed.
[4] 9. 4. 2. 1, 6.   [5] *Ante,* p. 115.   [6] 9. 4. 11, 21. 3; 47. 2. 17. 3.
[7] P. 2. 31. 37.   [8] 9. 4. 12, 13, 28; 47. 2. 54. 4.
[9] C. 6. 2. 21, *pr., post,* Ch. xv.   [10] 9. 2. 27. 3.

be unsatisfactory by Girard, and they need not be stated in detail here[1]. Among the older explanations are those of the Basilica, (shared as to the case of *fuga* by the *lex* Romana Burgundionum[2], and formerly by Lenel, who now admits its insufficiency[3],) the framers of which are plainly dissatisfied with them, Cujas (shared by Pothier as to the case of *fuga*) and Voet. Pernice[4] holds that the rule as to *fuga*, in *damnum*[5], is a mistake of Ulpian's, but Girard observes that Julian is in the mistake on both points, and the same may be said of Marcellus[6]. Grueber[7] thinks no satisfactory explanation of the difference between *damnum* and *furtum* has been given. He does not notice the difference, in the case of *fuga*, and seems to regard the rule that a *bonae fidei* holder is not liable[5], as the normal one, and the texts laying down the other rule for *furtum* as needing explanation. He ignores the whole theory of *Potestas*.

Girard considers that there is a difference of principle. He traces it to the wording of the formula, based no doubt on that of the *lex*. The whole theory of *potestas* is the work of the Jurists. It was readily applied to the fluid words of the Edict and to the not very precise language of the XII Tables, but no existing text applies it to cases under the *lex* Aquilia. Something in the *lex* made it impossible. This he conjectures to have been an energetic reference to the *dominus* as the person noxally liable, as in the converse rule : *ero, id est domino, competit*[8]. In support of his view he cites the words (applying them to the *lex*), *verba efficiunt ut cum noxae deditione damnetur*[9]. He points out that while several texts[10] say that one who, on *interrogatio in iure*, says that another's slave is his, is noxally liable, one which says the same for *damnum*[11] adds, *quasi dominus*, as if this needed emphasis here. It may be further noted that in one text[12] the difference between *furti aut damni* in one line, and *furti* alone later on seems to turn on this distinction, or at least to make it clear that, in Mela's opinion, the *actio noxalis* Aquilia did not lie against a mere possessor, while other noxal actions did. Moreover exactly the same point is made on the same verbal ground in connexion with the *Sc. Silanianum*[13].

Upon all the evidence Girard's theory seems to earn acceptance. It is not generally adopted, but it has not been refuted[14].

---

[1] Nouv. Rev. Hist. 11. 430 *sqq*. Those explanations which do not regard the divergence as simple error explain the two rules in *damnum* independently, though it seems obvious that they are connected. [2] Bas. (Heimb.) 5. 289 ; Lex Rom. Burg. 15. 1.
[3] Ed. Perp. (French Ed.) 1. 180. [4] Akad. d. Wissens. Berlin, Sitz. 1885, p. 454.
[5] 9. 2. 27. 3.
[6] Accarias (Précis 2. 1048) gives another explanation. The slave is the instrument. The *bona-fide* possessor has not handled. How can he be liable? The *dominus* is made liable in order that some one shall be. Apart from its speculative nature, this assumes the delict to be the employer's, which it is not, though the liability may be.
[7] *Lex* Aquilia, 82. [8] 9. 2. 11. 6.
[9] 9. 4. 19. 1. [10] 9. 4. 26. 3, 27. 1; 11. 1. 16. 1.
[11] 11. 1. 8. [12] 40. 12. 24. 4. [13] 29. 5. 1. 1, 2.
[14] Lenel declares it inacceptable (*loc. cit.* n. 3). Kipp rejects it for inherent improbability, Z. S. S. 10. 399 *sqq*. (a review of Girard's essay).

CHAPTER VI.

THE SLAVE AS MAN. COMMERCIAL RELATIONS, APART FROM
PECULIUM. ACQUISITIONS.

IT is hardly an exaggeration to say that, in the age of the classical lawyers, Roman commerce was mainly in the hands of slaves. The commercial importance of different slaves would of course vary greatly. The body-servant, the farm labourer, the coachman, have no importance in this connexion, and there were many degrees between their position, and that of a *dispensator* or steward, who seems often to have been allowed almost a free hand[1]. The Digest gives us several striking instances. A slave might carry on a bank, with or without orders, the master's rights varying according as it was or was not with the *peculium*[2]. A slave might be a member of a firm[3], and his master's notice to him, without notice to the other party, would not end the partnership[4]. Even sale of the slave would not, in fact, end the firm: the new master would acquire the rights from the date of transfer, though as a slave's faculty is purely derivative the firm would be technically a new one[5].

A *dominus* can acquire or continue possession through a *servus* or *ancilla*[6]. But possession differs from other rights in that it has an element of consciousness. A man may begin to own without knowing it, but he cannot ordinarily so acquire possession. Accordingly we learn that (apart from *peculium*) a man does not possess what his slave has received, unless and until he knows of it. When he learns the fact he possesses, and he is said to possess by his own *animus*[7] and the slave's *corpus*[8]. Hence it may be loosely said that the slave provides the physical, and the master the mental element in possession, but this is not quite exact. One simple limitation is that for the later classical

---

1 See for a doubtless exaggerated instance, Petronius, Sat. 53.
2 2. 13. 4. 3.　　　　　3 17. 2. 63. 2.　　　　　4 17. 2. 18.
5 17. 2. 58. 3.　More striking instances later in connexion with *peculium*, Ch. VIII.
6 G. 2. 89; In. 2. 9. 3; D. 41. 1. 10. 2; 41. 2. 1. 12, 48; 41. 3. 44. 7.
7 As to what is involved in *scientia*, *post*, p. 135.
8 41. 2. 1. 5, 3. 12, 8. 24, 44. 1, 44. 2; P. 5. 2. 1.

lawyers it was clear that previous *iussum* was as good as actual knowledge[1]. Another point is more important: the taking of possession is necessarily a conscious act, and the slave must be regarded as contributing to the mental part in that he must be a person capable of understanding the nature of his act. Thus a man cannot acquire possession through an insane slave[2], or through an *infans*[3]. What the *dominus* contributes, so far as we are here concerned, (for we need not consider difficulties as to the nature of the *animus* necessary to possession,) is intelligent consciousness of the act done. It follows that, if either slave or master is of defective capacity, there is no possession. It is clear that this would create great practical difficulties: the texts shew that these were felt, and that considerations of convenience triumphed over strict logic. Thus Paul tells us that an *infans* can acquire possession with the *auctoritas* of his *tutor, utilitatis causa*[4], and that an *infans* can possess through a slave *peculiari causa*. Pomponius had already, it seems, laid down a more sweeping rule, to the effect that if delivery was made to the slave of an *infans* or a *furiosus*, the *dominus* could usucapt[5]. But it is said elsewhere that an *infans* acquires possession only *tutore auctore*, while another *pupillus* does not need *auctoritas*[6]. This is plainly a departure from ordinary principles: according to these if an *infans* needs *auctoritas*, so does any other *pupillus*. But the fact is this is not a case for *auctoritas*: the pupil incurs no obligation. The requirement is added in the case of the *infans* to get rid of the difficulty arising from his lack of capacity. In other words, here, quite exceptionally, the *tutor* makes up not, as in ordinary cases, a defective *iudicium*, but a lacking *intellectus*[7].

It must be observed that we are concerned only with the acquisition of possession: a possession which has begun is not lost merely by the slave's becoming insane, any more than it would be by his going to sleep[8].

A text of Ulpian[9] lays down a general rule that a slave of ours can acquire possession for us without our knowledge. Ulpian bases this view on a statement of Celsus to the effect that a *servus alienus* in the possession of no one acquires possession for me if he takes the thing, *meo nomine*. As it stands, this remark is no authority for Ulpian's proposition. Celsus says nothing about ignorance, and is arguing from

---

1 41. 2. 1. 13, 19; 41. 3. 31. 3 (Paul); 41. 2. 34. 2 (Ulp.); 41. 2. 48 (Papin.).
2 41. 2. 1. 9, 10.
3 *Arg.* 41. 2. 1. 5. An older *impubes* may of course have the necessary *intellectus*, 41. 2. 1. 11.
4 41. 2. 32. 2: cp. C. 8. 53. 26.   5 41. 3. 28.
6 41. 2. 1. 13, 32. 2. Other texts seem to require *auctoritas tutoris* for the case of any *pupillus, h. t.* 1. 11, 13. As to a possible case of liability, *post*, p. 134.
7 An *infans* was not ordinarily capable of acting with *auctoritas*. Cp. the somewhat analogous case of captive slave or master, in which there was no possession, *post*, Ch. XIII.
8 41. 3. 31. 3.   9 41. 2. 34. 2.

the newly developed rule that possession can be acquired through a procurator. If so, why not through a *servus alienus*, provided he is not in the possession of anyone else, to whom he could acquire[1]? When we remember that *nominatio* and *iussum* were almost equiparated in later classical law, for the purpose of transactions by a slave possessed in good faith or held in usufruct[2], it seems likely that Ulpian is doing the same thing here, and holding that you acquire possession through your slave if you know it, or have authorised it, or the possession is taken in your name. But the cases are not on the same plane. In the case of *bonae fidei possessio* the equalisation of *iussum* and *nominatio* is to determine the destination of an acquisition, not its possibility. They equally exclude the *dominus*, but no text, applying the rule to the acquisition of possession, says that if there was *nominatio*, the requirement of *scientia* in the *bonae fidei possessor* did not exist.

Another remarkable text is credited to Paul. He holds that we do not acquire possession through our slaves unless they intend to acquire to us, and he takes the case of *iussum* by the owner A, the slave taking with the intention to benefit B. There is, he says, no possession[3] in A. It is generally agreed that this text, making the effect depend on the will of the slave, is not good law for the classical age[4].

The notion that one could not acquire possession through one he did not possess[5], though it was set aside, as an absolutely general rule, in the classical law, survived for some purposes up to the time of Justinian. It was still true that a *dominus* could not ordinarily acquire possession, through his slave whom he did not possess. But it must be remembered that such a case could not ordinarily arise, except where the slave was *in libertate*, or in the adverse possession of some other person, and in such cases it is hardly conceivable that a *dominus* could be supposed to acquire possession through him. If he was *in libertate* no one acquired possession through him[6]. Where any inconvenience did arise the rule was readily set aside[7]. It is of course clear that, the slave's power being purely derivative, he could acquire nothing for himself, and this principle has its corollary[8] in the rule, that a man in apparent slavery could acquire nothing for himself.

---

[1] See Salkowski, Sklavenerwerb, 166. In 41. 3. 31. 2 it is said, perhaps by Tribonian, that a slave *in libertate* can acquire possession for anyone in whose name he takes. In 41. 1. 53 it is said that we can acquire possession through anyone, if we intend to possess.
[2] *Post*, Ch. xv.   [3] 41. 2. 1. 19.
[4] Ihering, Besitzwille, 287; Gradenwitz, Interpolationen, 220; Salkowski, *op. cit.* 46. They disagree as to whether it is an error of Paul or an interpolation: the latter seems most probable. See Gradenwitz. Note also the plural *diximus*. In other parts of the text Paul says *puto*.
[5] G. 2. 94, 95.   [6] 41. 3. 31. 2.
[7] Where a *causa liberalis* is pending the man is *in libertate*; yet, if he is really a slave, what is given to him vests in his master, even, says Gaius, possession, though it is clear there had been doubt. He justifies the rule by the case of the *fugitivus*, but this is not sound. The *fugitivus* is still possessed and his case provides not the reason, but the excuse, 40. 12. 25. 2; *post*, Ch. xxviii.
[8] 50. 17. 18.

Where the possession has not yet, *e.g.* for lack of knowledge, vested in the *dominus*, it may nevertheless be legally important to him. If the act of taking was a delict, he will be liable to a noxal action: in some other cases he may be liable to an *actio de peculio*. When it has vested in him, the effect is in general as if he had himself received the thing. Thus, where a slave buys, the *dominus* has possession *pro empto* or *pro suo*[1]. If a slave is *deiectus*, the master, though he knew nothing of the expulsion, has the interdict *de vi*[2].

The mere possession may in some cases impose liability. Thus a master is liable to *hereditatis petitio* for things which a slave has taken, if he possesses them or their price, or has an action for their price[3]. So in general an action lies against the master for things detained by the slave[4]. But there are some difficulties. Any person sued must take care of the thing: what is the position of the *dominus*, whose slave, holding the thing, disappears between *litis contestatio* and judgment? What is the position of an *impubes* whose slave acquires possession of a thing in some way which creates liability? A *malae fidei possessor* is liable for the safety of the thing: what is the position of the *dominus* who knows of the possession, but not of the *mala fides*? We are told, in the case of the defendant whose slave has disappeared with the thing, at the time when judgment is to be given, that the judge must either postpone judgment, or allow the defendant to satisfy it by giving security for the restoration of the thing when he gets it[5]. But the case of actual litigation is on a different footing from the others. It may be permissible to argue from an analogous case. A husband is under a duty to take care of *dos*. If his slave receive a thing as *dos* it vests in him, but he is not under this duty until he has ratified the act[6]. A similar rule may well have applied here, and no doubt in the case of an *impubes* this ratification would not be valid without the *auctoritas* of the tutor. In all these cases there would be *actio de peculio* so far as the damage resulted from a *negotium* of the slave[7].

In close connexion with this topic comes, necessarily, that of acquisition of *dominium* by *usucapio*. In general the possession will lead to *usucapio*, subject to the ordinary rules. Some points must,

---

[1] 41. 10. 5. A slave cannot possess *pro herede* (41. 3. 4. 4). This does not mean that he cannot be the vehicle of such a possession, but that if a slave, thinking he is *heres* or that a thing belongs to a *hereditas* to which he has a claim, takes it while still a slave, he does not possess *pro herede*.
[2] 43. 16. 1. 22.
[3] 5. 3. 34, 35. If a slave fraudulently makes away with a thing to the knowledge of his master, the latter is liable to *A. ad exhibendum*: if he did not know of the wrongdoing, only noxally, 10. 4. 16. If the slave holds someone's will, the master is liable to the interdict *de tabulis exhibendis*, 43. 5. 3. 4.
[4] C. 3. 32. 20.   [5] 6. 1. 27. 4.   [6] 23. 3. 46.
[7] Another illustration 43. 26. 13. *Post*, p. 157, as to the question how far knowledge of the slave is imputed to the master.

however, be noted[1]. The slave's power, being purely derivative, cannot increase that of the *dominus*. Thus if the master is absolutely incapable of *usucapio* he cannot usucapt through his slave[2].

There is somewhat more difficulty in relation to *bona fides*. Apart from *peculium* the rule seems to have been, (Paul, quoting Celsus, is our authority, but the text is inconclusive,) that both master and slave must have been in good faith—the slave when he took the thing—the master when he knew of the taking. It is not clear whether the slave must be in good faith at that time, but this seems the more logical view, since that is the *initium possessionis*. Pomponius is quoted to the effect that if the acquisition is *domini nomine* the master's state of mind is the material one, but in view of the language quoted by Paul from Celsus in the same text this is commonly understood to mean, "is primarily considered[3]." The language of Pomponius, and the general drift of the text, however, appear to express the view that, if the acquisition was *domini nomine*, the state of mind of the slave was immaterial, but the other view is more in harmony with the rules arrived at in other cases[4]. It must be remembered that *usucapio* results from possession[5], and that in acquiring possession the master and the slave cooperate. It is difficult to say what the master's *scientia* involved. It was something that the slave could not contribute[6], and probably it included the *animus sibi habendi*, of which the slave, who could not *habere*, was clearly incapable. As we have seen that he also cooperated mentally, since he must have intelligence for taking[7], it is natural that the *bona fides* of both parties should have been necessary. And this is the rule that Papinian lays down for the analogous case of sons[8]. As will be seen later, the rules in acquisitions to the *peculium* are different: here it is enough to say that where the acquisition is *peculii causa*, and the slave was in bad faith, if the thing ceases to be *in peculio*, *e.g.* by ademption of the *peculium*, or by its being paid by the slave to the master, *e.g.* for his liberty, this is not a new possession in the master, and the thing cannot be usucapted: *causa possessionis durat*[9].

Apart from these considerations there is no great difficulty in the law of acquisition of property, *inter vivos*, by a slave for his master. The slave though he can have nothing of his own[10] acquires for him in nearly every way, and without his knowledge or consent[11]. Things

---

1 Among the cases in which "putative *causa*" was allowed by some jurists, was that in which your slave alleged that he had bought the thing: a man may reasonably be in error as to the act of another, 41. 4. 11; 41. 10. 5; cp. 23. 3. 67. But this controversy has little to do with slavery.
2 41. 3. 8. 1. *Eum qui suo nomine nihil usucapere potest ne per servum posse Pedius ait.*
3 41. 4. 2. 11, 12. Pothier, Pand. 17. 193.   4 6. 2. 7. 13; 41. 3. 43. 1.
5 G. 2. 89; In. 2. 9. 3; D. 41. 2. 3. 3.   6 See *ante*, pp. 131 *sq.*
7 41. 2. 1. 10, *etc.*   8 41. 3. 43.   9 41. 4. 2. 12, 14.
10 G. 2. 87; In. 2. 9. 3; D. 41. 1. 10. 1.
11 In. 2. 9. 3; D. 41. 1. 32. If a slave buys, his master has the Publician, 6. 2. 7. 10. If he finds treasure it is as if the master had found it, 41. 1. 63, *pr.*

delivered to him are acquired to his master unless the slave was
intended to act as a mere messenger: in that case the acquisition is
not complete till the thing reaches the master[1]. A slave can acquire
by formal means, *e.g.* by *mancipatio*, but not by *adiudicatio* or *cessio in
iure*[2], since he can take no part in a judicial process. If the ownership
of the slave is in suspense, the question in whom any acquisition takes
effect will also be in suspense; *e.g.* where a slave is given by husband to
wife, by way of *mortis causa donatio*[3], or where the slave is *legatus* and
the legatee has not yet accepted[4]. The slave acquires to his bonitary,
not his quiritary owner[5]. We are told by Paul that a slave, mancipated
metu, acquires for his old master[6]. The point is that, though *mancipatio*
transfers *dominium* even in this case, the former *dominus* still has the
slave *in bonis*[7].

Was it necessary that the slave should intend to acquire to the
master? We have seen[8] traces of a view that this was essential (at
least for late law) in the case of possession, but so was knowledge of
the *dominus*, and both these might seem material where the question
was whether the *dominus* had acquired the substance of control. But
in the present case it is clearly and repeatedly laid down in the Sources[9]
that knowledge of the *dominus* is not necessary. (The view that the
slave must consent seems to rest on a false definition of tradition, as
transfer of *dominium* by transfer of possession, itself based on texts
which speak of acquisition of possession and through it of ownership[10].)
A priori, one would not expect the *voluntas* of the slave to be considered in such a matter, and the law seems to have disregarded it[11].
But there is one text sometimes cited as proving the contrary[12]: the
case is, however, one of a common slave and of a *donatio*, both material
circumstances[13].

A case which might have created difficulty is that in which the
transferor hands over the thing, intending to transfer ownership, but
to transfer it to X, who is not, but whom he supposes to be, the slave's
master. If he said nothing of his intent the gift would take effect in
the slave's master, though, on general principle, the donor would have a
condictio. If he expressly said that he intended to convey the thing to

---

[1] 39. 5. 10; C. 4. 27. 1.   [2] G. 2. 87; 2. 96; 3. 167; U. 19. 18.
[3] 24. 1. 20.   [4] 30. 86. 2.
[5] G. 2. 88. What a *servus peculii castrensis* acquires is the son's, not the father's, 49. 17. 19. 1.
See also 18. 6. 16; 19. 1. 13. 18. *Ante*, pp. 42, 43.
[6] P. 1. 7. 6.
[7] 4. 2. 9. 6. See Huschke *ad* P. 1. 7. 6. As to the actual form used by the slave in
mancipatio, see *post*, App. III.
[8] *Ante*, p. 133.
[9] See the texts cited by Salkowski, Sklavenerwerb, 34—40.
[10] *e.g.* 41. 1. 20. 2.   [11] 39. 5. 13.   [12] 41. 1. 37. 6.
[13] *Post*, Ch. XVI. The inconveniences which might result from acquisition without consent
could be in part avoided by abandonment, but a more effective protection was found in a rule
that the liabilities which might result did not attach till ratification, *post*, p. 155.

X, it seems that ownership would not pass to anybody, though possession would as soon as the master knew of the receipt[1].

The law in the case of the institution of a slave is more complex. A man may institute his own slave or a *servus alienus*; in either case *pure* or conditionally[2]. But an institution of his own slave, *cum liber erit*, or *sine libertate*, is a mere nullity[3]. A *servus alienus* would, however, ordinarily be instituted without liberty, and the words *cum liber erit* may be added: the words *sine libertate* or *cum libertate* are mere surplusage[4]. The institution of a *servus proprius* remains valid though he be alienated or freed: in the former case he acquires to his new master[5], in the latter to himself.

Institution of a *servus alienus* is for most purposes institution of his master[6]. Thus the master must have *testamenti factio* with the testator[7], has the right to the *spatium deliberandi*[8], can get *bonorum possessio*[9], and may be burdened with *fideicommissa*[10]. These are due from him only if he acquires through the slave. If he frees before acceptance neither he nor the slave is strictly liable (for the latter was not *rogatus*), but this is met by a rule that an *actio utilis* lies against him who got the *emolumentum hereditatis*[11]. If the owner sell the slave before acceptance, he remains liable for the *fideicommissum* as having the value in the price, and the buyer is not liable unless the vendor is insolvent[12]. This rule is an equitable compromise: the buyer is strictly *heres* and liable. There seems no authority for the case of gift of the slave. Probably the donee is liable if he accepts the *hereditas*. There are many illustrations of this fact that a gift to a slave is essentially one to his master. If a slave is instituted, a legacy, *poenae causa*, to annoy his master is void[13]. If a man prevents the revocation of a will in which his slave is instituted, he can take nothing[14]. Writing a gift to your slave is penalised under the *lex* Cornelia *de falsis*, as writing a gift to yourself[15]. If a *libertinus* institutes his child's slave this bars the patron as if it had been the child himself[16].

---

[1] Not expressly discussed, except where on the facts there were other persons to whom the slave might possibly acquire, *post*, Ch. xv.

[2] 28. 5. 3, 31.

[3] U. 22. 7, 11, 12; D. 28. 7. 21, 22. It was treated as shewing no real intent to give.

[4] 28. 5. 3. *pr.*; P. 3. 4 b. 7. ,

[5] G. 2. 185, 188; Ulp. 22. 12. D. 31. 83 is a case of construction raising some of these points.

[6] As to the difference of personality, *post*, p. 140.

[7] Ulp. 22. 9; D. 28. 5. 31; *h. t.* 53; 36. 1. 67. *pr.*   [8] 28. 8. 1.

[9] 37. 11. 2. 9. If alienated while time is running the new *dominus* has only the rest of the time, 38. 15. 5. 2.

[10] Even in favour of the slave himself, *cum liber erit*, 36. 1. 26. 1. As to operation of *Sc.* Pegasianum, D. 30. 11.

[11] 31. 62.   [12] 30. 11, 94. 1.   [13] 34. 6. 1.

[14] 29. 6. 1. 1; 38. 13. 1. Nor can the slave if freed, or children, even not in *potestas*. They are "within the mischief" of the rule.

[15] Or striking out a gift of liberty to a slave left to you. But writing a gift to a slave *cum liber erit*, or one of liberty to your own slave was not enough, 48. 10. 15. 4, 22. *passim*.

[16] At any rate if the child acquires, 37. 14. 21. 3.

The gift is to the master whose the slave is at the time of entry: intervening alienations are immaterial[1]. Where a *servus alienus* was instituted, afterwards conveyed to a *servus hereditarius* and then usucapted by an *extraneus*, the institution was still good—*media tempora non nocent*[2]. Where a slave of one without *ius capiendi* was instituted and was freed, or sold, *sine fraude legis*, before any steps were taken, though after the death, the gift stood[3]. This was originally written when, and of a case in which, the man without *ius capiendi* was not *incapax*, but, though he had *testamenti factio*, was barred, by reason, *e.g.* of celibacy, from taking. The general rule was that we could institute the slave of one with *testamenti factio*, and no other[4]. But in Justinian's time a man without *ius capiendi* was an *incapax*. It may be, then, that in his day the institution of the slave of one without *testamenti factio* (*e.g. intestabilis*) was good if he was alienated. It cannot have been so for classical law.

The owner of the slave is the person to benefit, whatever the intent of the testator[5], even though he have to hand over the succession to some other person. Thus if a *heres* is under a *fideicommissum* to hand over the *hereditas*, and a *servus hereditarius* has an inheritance left to him, the *heres* can order him to enter. Like other acquisitions made after entry, this will not have to be handed over, unless there was an express provision, in the will, that even such things were to go[6].

As a *hereditas* may involve liabilities the slave cannot effectively enter without the authorisation (*iussum*) of the owner[7]. We have a good deal of detail about this *iussum*. It must precede the entry: ratification did not suffice[8]. This is due to the fact that *aditio* is an *actus legitimus*, and does not admit of what is in effect a suspensive condition[9]. The *iussum* must *durare*: the authorisation of the master must be still existing at the time of the entry. Thus if he become insane before the entry, there is no *iussum*: *furiosi nulla est voluntas*[10]. So, if the slave is alienated before the entry, the new master is not bound by the old *iussum*[11]. It may be in any form, *e.g.* by letter or messenger. It may even be *nutu*, in the case of a dumb, but not mentally defective, *dominus*[12].

---

[1] In. 2. 14. 1.   *Ambulat cum dominio*, 37. 11. 2. 9.
[2] 28. 5. 6. 2.   As to *h. t.* 50. *pr.*, see *post*, Ch. xx.
[3] 29. 2. 82.   [4] Ulp. 21. 9; D. 28. 5. 31.
[5] G. 2. 89; Ulp. 22. 13; C. 6. 27. 3.
[6] 36. 1 28. 1; *h. t.* 65. 4 (last clause Tribonian).
[7] Ulp. 19. 19; 22. 13; C. 6. 27. 3; D. 41. 1. 10. 1, *etc.*   [8] 29. 2. 25. 4; 36. 1. 67. *pr.*
[9] 29. 2. 51. 2; 50. 17. 77. No entry before *iussum*, but a condition on the institution can be so satisfied, *quia eo facto nemo fraudatur*. The satisfaction is no part of the entry, 35. 1. 5. 1.
[10] 29. 2. 47. Or an authorising *tutor* die before the entry, *h. t.* 50. If the *iussor* change his mind, or is adrogated, there can be no entry under the old *iussum*, *h. t.* 25. 14, 15.
[11] 29. 2. 62. 1.   [12] 29. 2. 25. 4, 93. 1.

The *iussum* must refer to that particular *hereditas*[1], and there can be no *iussum* to enter on the *hereditas* of one not yet dead, though it is not essential that the master be certain either that the man is dead or that the slave is *heres*. Paul, indeed, observes that the *paterfamilias* must know whether it is *ex asse* or *ex parte*, by institution or substitution, on intestacy or by will[2]. Ulpian says, more exactly, that if the *iussor* thinks it is *ex asse* and it is *ex parte*, or *ab intestato* and it is by will, the entry does not bind him because such entry would, or might, put him in a worse position than he contemplated. If the error is the other way, it is a good entry, and error as to whether it was institution or substitution is equally immaterial[3]. A *iussum* may be conditional or dependent on someone's consent[4], and this must be given before the entry. Where the *institutus* reported that he thought the inheritance good, the *paterfamilias* replied that he had heard rumours to the contrary, and that he authorised the *institutus* to enter, if after careful investigation he was satisfied that the estate was solvent. He entered at once, and Africanus held that this entry did not bind the *paterfamilias*[5]. The *iussum* might be more or less explicit, and after disputes it was settled that authorisation to take *bonorum possessio*, or *pro herede gerere*, justified entry by the slave[6].

Fideicommissariae hereditates and *bonorum possessio* are on the same level, so far as the substance of the right is concerned, but there are some differences of rule which need explanation. As the acceptance of *fideicommissa*, or of *bonorum possessio*, is not an *actus legitimus*, the necessary consent of the *dominus* may be by ratification[7]. We know that a *dominus* cannot enter for a slave, though he can depute a slave to enter for him[8]. We are told, indeed, not only that the slave must himself make *aditio*, but that he must give a real consent, and thus if an apparent consent is obtained under threats, and so is unreal, there is no sufficient *aditio*[9]. The line between this and a real consent obtained by command, which appears in some texts, must have been rather narrow[10]. It should be observed that the *dominus* can *pro herede gerere*, by consent of the slave[11], and that Pius enacted that if the

---

[1] 29. 2. 25. 5. If the slave is alienated before *bonorum possessio* is obtained, the buyer has only the residue of the time, 38. 15. 5. 2.
[2] 29. 2. 93. *pr.*
[3] 29. 2. 25. 11. Paul's dictum must be understood of pupillary substitution, involving possible liability for debts of the *pupillus*. Ulpian says (*h. l.* 12, 13) that *iussum* to enter under the will of X does not authorise entry as a substitute of an *impubes* unless the words of authorisation cover this, and shew that it was contemplated.
[4] 29. 2. 25. 10.   [5] 29. 2. 51. 1.
[6] 29. 2. 25. 7. See *h. l.* 8, 9 as to what is a sufficient *iussum*. Though a dumb slave cannot make formal *aditio* by speech he can of course *pro herede gerere* (29. 2. 93. 2). *Mutus heres* could not make a formal acceptance, but might depute a slave (29. 2. 5, 26). There seems no reason to doubt that a slave could make *cretio* for his master. It is somewhat on the same footing as *mancipatio*.
[7] 29. 2. 6. 1, 48; 36. 1. 31. 2, 42, 67. *pr.*   [8] 29. 2. 26, 36.
[9] 29. 2. 6. 7.   [10] 29. 4. 1. 3; C. 6. 24. 3. 2. *in fin.*
[11] C. 6. 30. 4.

dominus continued long in enjoyment, in any case, this should be a valid *gestio* : a somewhat untruthlike presumption of the consent of the slave[1]. The rule in *fideicommissa* is different: the *dominus* himself can accept[2]. *Bonorum possessio* may be applied for by anyone for anyone[3], and thus, no doubt by the *dominus*. But, we are told, the consent of the slave is needed as in *aditio*[4]. This may be because the words of the Edict, declaring that a grant will be made to him, imply his personal assent. It seems likely, though there is no conclusive text[5], that a *dominus* cannot himself repudiate the slave's institution : it is clear that he cannot repudiate a *fideicommissum*[6]. On the other hand he can repudiate a *bonorum possessio* to which the slave has a claim[7]. This is surprising in view of the rule that the slave's consent is necessary to *bonorum possessio* and of the maxim, *Is potest repudiare qui et acquirere potest*[8].

The slave and his master are distinct persons, and are so regarded for many purposes in this connexion. It is difficult, however, to lay down any general principle which will cover all the cases. They are not treated as independent persons where this would defeat the purpose of some rule of law[9]. Where A was instituted, and his slave, S, substituted, and A ordered S to enter, as substitute, in order to avoid legacies, all are due, subject to the Falcidian fourth[10]. But they are not lumped together: those charged on A are paid first, and then those charged on S, so far as the *lex* Falcidia allows[11]. This preference is applied in all such cases where a man obtains a *hereditas, omissa causa testamenti*[12]. But in our present case it is a recognition of duality, for a man cannot be simply substituted to himself[13].

Where A and his slave S are instituted, in unequal shares, and less than three-fourths are left away from the share of S, Paul tells us that the difference is added to the share of A, for the benefit of legatees claiming from him. This prevents the unfair treatment of legatees by a misapplication of the rule that the Falcidia is, in the case of distinct charges on different heirs, reckoned separately for each heir[14]. Here too duality is disregarded only so far as is necessary to prevent the evasion. If they were treated as two absolutely, no such account would be taken. If as one the Falcidian deduction would be spread over all. It will be observed that this is not the rule of *confusio* which causes so much discussion in the case of an *institutus* who acquires also as *substitutus*[15].

[1] 29. 2. 6. 3.   [2] 36. 1. 67. *pr.*   [3] 37. 4. 7.
[4] 36. 1. 67. *pr.*   [5] 29. 2. 13. 3, 18.   [6] 31. 34. 2.   [7] 38. 9. 1. 3.
[8] 29. 2. 18; 38. 9. 1. 1.   Lenel thinks the general provisions as to repudiation were in the Edict (Ed. Perp. § 165). The point of the present rule seems to be that, as the cooperation of both is needed to acquisition, the repudiation by the master is enough to shew that this is impossible.
[9] See *ante*, p. 137, for some illustrations of this.
[10] 29. 4. 25.   [11] 35. 2. 22. 2.   [12] 29. 4. 6. *pr.*
[13] 28. 6. 10. 7.   [14] 35. 2. 21. 1.
[15] See *e.g.* Vangerow, Pand. § 535; Windscheid, Lehrb. § 653, n. 8.

There, if *confusio* occurs at all, the legacies are grouped together and all suffer equally. Here there is no relief to the legatees from the *dominus* except so far as there is a surplus over the *quarta* Falcidia in the share of the slave. The same rule applies in the case of a father and son[1]. Paul's rule deals only with the case in which the legacies charged on the *dominus* are in excess, not with the case in which those charged on the slave are so. In the case of institution and substitution it seems clear on the authority of Paul[2] that there was no *confusio* in favour of legacies, charged on the *heres* who failed to take, in so far as they were chargeable on the substituted *coheres*. In our present text[3], Paul goes on to say something, which is commonly interpreted as meaning, that, here too, there was no relief in the case in which it was the legacies charged on the slave which were in excess. But the wording is so corrupt that it is impossible to be sure as to its meaning.

Where X whose slave was *heres* by will, and who was himself *heres ab intestato*, directed his slave to enter, and the slave did not do so, it was as if X had praetermitted. He should have made the man enter[4]. It is not easy to see the necessary *dolus malus* on these facts[5]. Where a slave is made heir there can be no legacies from the master, though there may be *fideicommissa*, and in such a case the legacies are first reckoned with any deduction for the *lex* Falcidia, and the *fideicommissum* is payable on the rest[6].

Where a slave is instituted *pure* for part and conditionally for another part, and there is a coheir, and the slave duly enters for the first part, Paul tell us he must enter again for the second, and it will pass with him if he is freed or alienated before entry[7]. This is one of a group of texts which have given rise to much controversy[8]. If X is instituted *pure* for one part, and conditionally for another, then, apart from controversy as to what happens if he dies, he is at once *heres ex asse*, if there is no substitute to the conditional part[9]. No fresh entry is needed even if there is a coheir[10]. In our case[11], where it is a slave, Paul justifies his different view on the ground that in order that all may be acquired by the one entry, it is necessary that all remain in the same state : the rule, that one entry suffices, does not, moreover, according to him, apply where the *hereditas* is acquired through another person[12]. That it should vest in the new owner seems consistent with principle. The conditional share is certainly not acquired till the

---

[1] 35. 2. 25. *pr.*   [2] 35. 2. 1. 13.   Vangerow, *loc. cit.*
[3] 35. 2. 21. 1.   [4] 29. 4. 1. 3.
[5] *h. l.* 4 adds that if *dominus* does not know, and himself enters *ab intestato*, he is not liable under the Edict, *nisi si fingit ignorantiam.*   This last remark is Tribonian, but it is clear that the master's liability depends on his *dolus*, not on that of the slave.
[6] Ulp. 24. 21; D. 35. 2. 22. 1.   [7] 29. 2. 80. 2.
[8] Salkowski, *op. cit.* 10.   [9] 28. 5. 33; 29. 2. 35. *pr.*, 53. *pr.*, 81.
[10] 28. 5. 60. 6.   [11] 29. 2. 80. 2.   [12] 29. 2. 80. 3.

condition is satisfied[1] and at that time the old owner is no longer owner. Since nothing remains even momentarily in the slave[2], another entry must be necessary. The view that, even if there is no change, fresh entry is necessary, is a natural result. But there is a text of Ulpian[3] which applies the rule that entry for one share is entry for all, and declares, as it is commonly understood[4], that if the slave has once entered, though he be sold, a substituted share which falls in will go to his old master, as being a mere appendix. The text is obscure : it may indeed be read as agreeing with Paul's view. Its form is, however, opposed to this, and elsewhere Ulpian and Modestinus decide a case in terms which suggest that the common interpretation is the right one. They say that if one substitutes to an *impubes* "Whoever shall be my heir," this means *heres scriptus*, and thus if a man has taken a share through a slave he cannot claim under this substitution, if the slave is no longer his, because he is not personally the *heres scriptus*[5]. They treat this as the fact which bars : if they had taken Paul's view the the question could not possibly have arisen[6].

According to the view almost universally held by the classical lawyers, an unconditional legacy to the slave of the *heres* was void *ab initio*, by the *regula* Catoniana. But the rule was different in the converse case of a legacy to the *dominus* of an instituted slave. Such a legacy was good *ab initio*, though it would " evanesce," if the *dominus* became *heres* through the slave[7]. The reason assigned in the texts is that it is not true that if the testator died at once the gift could have no force : the legacy would cede at once in the *dominus*, but he might transfer the slave before ordering entry.

There are other illustrations, of a different type, of this principle that the slave is a distinct person, and that his *persona* is considered rather than that of the *dominus*, except in relation to capacity to take[8]. If the terms refer expressly to the slave, it is he who must do any act rendered necessary. A slave, being in a manner an instrument of his master, can enter for him. But the master cannot so enter for the slave. Thus if X and his slave are instituted, the slave entering at X's order acquires all for him, but if X enters, he acquires only his share : the slave must still enter for the other[9]. Where knowledge is

---

[1] 29. 2. 13. *pr.*   [2] 29. 2. 79.   [3] 29. 2. 35. *pr.*
[4] Salkowski, *loc. cit.*   [5] 28. 6, 3, 8. 1.
[6] A patron's son has a right to *operae* promised, and to *iura in bonis*, if he is his father's *heres*, but not if having been emancipated or disinherited, he acquires his father's *hereditas* only through the institution of his slave, 38. 1. 22. 1; 38. 2. 13.
[7] G. 2. 245; In. 2. 20. 33; D. 35. 2. 20; 36. 2. 17. Cp. 30. 25, 91. *pr.* See Machelard, Dissertations, 500.
[8] See, *e.g.* 31. 82. 2.
[9] 29. 2. 26, 36. A *furiosus* could not accept a *hereditas* or direct his slave to enter, nor could his curator authorise his entry, 29. 2. 63, 90. *pr.* As to the ways in which this difficulty

material it is the knowledge of the *servus institutus* and not of his *dominus* which is considered. Thus where a slave is instituted, *vulgari cretione*, it is the state of his knowledge which determines the time allowed[1]. An *institutus* can enter if he is sure that an alleged posthumous child does not exist, but not otherwise. If he is a slave and he is sure, but the *dominus* has his doubts, the entry is valid[2].

We have also to consider the case of a slave instituted by one who thought he was free. This is really a case of a wider problem : what is the effect of error on an *institutio* ? Vangerow[3] thinks the rule to have been, that, if the error were such that the institution would not have been made in knowledge of the facts, it was absolutely void, and he treats any departures from this as exceptional. There is no doubt of the rule for legacies[4], but in view of the dislike of intestacy it would not be surprising if a different rule were applied here. Of the texts he cites, one[5] says that where a child instituted proved to be *suppositus*, the inheritance was taken away, *quasi indigno*. This really makes against Vangerow's view, for it implies that such an institution was *prima facie* valid. The same case is discussed in an enactment of Gordian[6], who on the authority of Severus and Caracalla, uses similar language—*auferendam ei successionem*. His other cases are of exheredations declared null on the ground of error. They are cases in which a false reason is expressly assigned for exheredation[7] and thus are mere illustrations of *falsa causa* treated as condition, and of little weight in the present connexion[8]. On the whole the view of Savigny[9] seems preferable, that these institutions under error were valid, the cases in which they were set aside being exceptional. The same conclusion can be drawn from two cases which directly concern us. One[10] is the well-known case of Tiberius' slave, Parthenius. A slave is instituted under the impression that he is a *paterfamilias*, and X is substituted to him *si heres non erit*. Tiberius decides that he and X shall divide. This is justified by Julian[11] on the ground that the words, *si heres non erit*, when spoken of a man supposed to be free, mean " if neither he, nor anyone to whom he shall *hereafter* become subject, becomes heir." This condition[12] is satisfied on the facts and the substitute is admitted. But there is nothing to exclude the *institutus*, and thus they share[13]. The reasoning requires

---

was met, see, *e.g.* Accarias, §§ 349, 465. But if the slave were instituted, he could enter, no doubt with consent of *curator*, 29. 2. 63. If a beneficiary has been directed to pay money to a slave *heres*, it may not be paid to his master, 35. 1. 44. *pr.*

1 G. 2. 190.   2 29. 2. 30. 7.   8 Lehrb. § 431.
4 32. 11. 16.   5 49. 14. 46. *pr.*   6 C. 6. 24. 4.
7 28. 2. 14. 2, 15.
8 35. 1. 72. 6.   In fact a contrary inference might be drawn from them.
9 System, 3. 377, *cit.* Vangerow, *loc. cit.*   10 In. 2. 15. 4.   11 28. 5. 41.
12 A substitution is essentially a conditional institution.
18 The decision is exactly similar to that given by Gaius (2. 177) in the case of *cretio imperfecta*.

that error shall not vitiate an institution, and is strictly logical, if the interpretation given to the words, *si heres non erit*, be accepted. It is a strong case of interpretation according to intent, the ordinary rule in testaments[1], but the decision does not deserve the severe language which is sometimes used of it[2].

The case may be compared with one considered by Severus[3]. A, a *miles*, institutes J, *ut libertum suum*, and adds, "if he will not or cannot enter from any cause, I substitute V." J proves to be a common slave of A and Z. Severus says that the result is a question of intent. If A thought J his own sole *libertus*, and did not mean any other person to acquire through him, the condition of the substitution has arisen, and V can take the inheritance. If, however, the words were used in the ordinary sense, and J entered at the command of Z, V has no claim[4]. There can be no question of sharing, for if J takes anything at all, he does *adire*, and the substitute V is excluded. Here the interpretation by intent resembles that in the last case, but it is more forced : the word *adire* has not the ambiguity which, with a little good will, can be seen in the expression *si heres non erit*, and J is here allowed to shew that the testator gave the words a meaning that they cannot possibly bear. The fact that the testator is a *miles* is emphasised, and it may be that this accounts for the liberal interpretation[5].

The main principles in the case of legacies and *fideicommissa singularum rerum* are much the same[6]. A legacy *sine libertate* to the testator's own slave is invalid[7]. A gift to A and one to his slave, though they are distinct legacies, are one for the purpose of the *lex Falcidia*[8]. Gifts to *servi alieni* depend on the *testamenti factio* of the master, and are in the main equivalent to gifts to him[9]. The rules as to the admissibility and construction of gifts *cum* or *sine libertate* are, in classical law, as in institutions[10]. A legacy to a *servus alienus* is void if the testator buys him, as it is now *in ea causa in qua incipere non poterat*[11]. A legacy without liberty to the testator's slave, not legated, is void, and ademption of the liberty is ademption of the legacy[12]. Acceptance of a legacy to his slave bars the *dominus*

---

[1] 50. 17. 12; see 28. 5. 2, 52. 1; 28. 6. 4. 2, 24; 50. 16. 116, 243; 50. 17. 17.
[2] *e.g.* Vangerow, *loc. cit.*; Girard, Manuel, 826.   [3] C. 6. 24. 3.
[4] The text is applying the rule that if one of co-owners institutes the slave, all goes to the others, *post*, Ch. xvi.
[5] As to error in legacies, *post*, p. 151.
[6] 28. 1. 16; 30. 53. 2.   [7] 30. 34. 9.
[8] 30. 53. 2; 35. 2. 56. 4. Compare the rule in the converse case, *ante*, p. 140.
[9] 28. 1. 16; 30. 12. 2; 41. 1. 19. 1. A *fideicommissum* (and *a fortiori* a legacy) to a slave of a *deportatus* went to the Fisc, 32. 7. The *dominus* might be burdened with *fideicommissa*, 30. 11.
[10] 34. 4. 20. See *ante*, p. 137.   [11] 34. 8. 3. 2.
[12] 30. 34. 9, 102; 34. 4. 32. 1. Money was left to X with a *fideicommissum* to a slave of testator. Both were void, 31. 88. 13.

from attacking the will[1], and, if he does attack it, he loses any benefit[2].

If a legacy is left to two of my slaves independently, or to me and one of my slaves, or to my slave in the will, and to me in a codicil, and I refuse on one gift, I can take all on the other[3]. This is the law of Justinian : in classical times it would have depended on the form of the gift. Thus in *legatum per damnationem*, apart from the *leges caducariae*, one of the shares would have gone, on this hypothesis, to the *heres*.

The ownership of the slave at the time of *dies cedens* determines the fate of the legacy[4], assuming initial validity, and thus if he is alienated or freed before that date, the right will pass to his new owner or himself as the case may be[5]. It must be noticed that, in legacies to a slave, the time of *dies cedens* is postponed. Thus if there is a legacy to a slave also freed, it does not cede till *aditio*, since otherwise it must fail as he is not qualified to take till the heir enters[6]. It is similarly postponed in the case of a slave who is himself *legatus*, so that the rule applies to all possible legacies to a slave of the testator[7]. The text adds that if the slave has been freed after the will is made he can take the legacy himself, the fact that he was a slave of the testator being no bar, since, even if the testator had died at the time of making the will, the benefit and burden of it would never have been on the same person. These rules are simple : they are applied in the texts to the solution of many complex cases.

Where A was legatee of an *optio servi*, and there was a legacy to a slave of the testator, without liberty, then, if before any heir entered he became the only slave of the testator, he was a *servus legatus* and the legacy to him was good. But if he did not become the sole slave, or in any case if there was a *heres necessarius*, the legacy to the *servus proprius* would fail[8]. The case does not conflict with the *regula Catoniana*. Since it is always possible for this diminution to occur, so that he becomes a *servus legatus*, whose gift does not cede till *aditio*, it is not true that if the testator had died at once the benefit and burden must have been in the same person. If the *heres* were a *necessarius* it would be bad, for though the diminution might occur before the death, it still remains true that, had the testator died at once, the gift must have failed. If the legacy to the slave was simple, and that of the slave was conditional, the former must fail unless the condition of the latter is satisfied before *dies cedit* for the former. This is the form in which

---

[1] 38. 2. 8. 2; cp. *h. t.* 45, 50. *pr.*; 37. 4. 3. 15.
[2] 34. 9. 5. 3, 4; P. 5. 12. 3.　　　　　　　[3] 30. 101; 31. 59.
[4] 30. 91. 6; 36. 2. 5. 7, 14. 3.　　　　　　[5] 30. 91. 2, 3, 114. 10.
[6] 35. 2. 1. 4, *post*, Ch. xx.
[7] 36. 2. 7. 6, 8, 17.　Otherwise it would fail, as the slave is the property of the *hereditas*. If the legacy of him takes effect, the gift to him goes to the legatee, 30. 69. *pr.*
[8] 33. 5. 13.

the foregoing case would, it seems, have presented itself to the jurists who held that *legatum optionis* was conditional[1]. Justinian's change did not affect the matter, since the ownership of the slave did not pass even now till a choice was made, so that if there were still several slaves, the ownership of the slave legated would still be in the *heres*, at the time when the legacy to him vested. It may be noticed further that as this choice could not be made till after *aditio*, the fact that the legatee did in fact choose the same slave would not save the legacy to him[2].

A simple legacy to a slave of the *heres* is bad *ab initio* by the *regula* Catoniana[3]. It is in substance a gift to the *heres*, and it is not saved by the considerations we have been discussing. The coming of *dies cedens* fixes the legacy on the *heres*, and benefit and burden must therefore be on the same person. If other heirs enter, then, whether he enter or not, the legacy will be good so far and so far only as it is chargeable on the other heirs[4]. There had been disagreement as to these rules. Servius declared all such gifts valid, perhaps ignoring altogether the *regula* Catoniana, but said that it would "evanesce," if at *dies cedens* he was still in *potestas*. This suggests that he is treating the *dies cedens*, rather than the making of the will, as the *initium*. The Proculians in general held that all such gifts were bad, because, says Gaius, we can no more owe conditionally, than we can simply, to one in our *potestas*, a reason which is little more than begging the question. The Sabinians took the view which Justinian ultimately adopted, limiting the rule to simple gifts, so that a conditional legacy would fail only if, at *dies cedens*, the legatee was still in *potestas* of the *heres*[5].

Another text raises new hypotheses[6]. A legacy adeemed under a condition is regarded as given under the contrary condition[7]. If it was originally given *pure*, this makes it a conditional gift. Does this exempt from the *regula* a legacy originally given *pure*? Florentinus tells us that it does not: ademption is to take away, not to confirm a legatee's right[8]. A testator who intended to remove the difficulty would hardly put the alteration in that form. The decision turns on that point: how will it stand if, in a codicil, he gives the legacy subject to a condition, clearly *corrigendi animo*? Here it is not so clear that he does not mean to benefit the legatee: it may be that the gift would be regarded

---

[1] *Ante*, p. 18; Machelard, Dissertations, 525.
[2] 33. 5. 15. A slave, S, is left to X, a legacy to S, and *optio servi* to Y. Y chooses S. X takes the gift to S as being his owner when *dies cedit*, 33. 5. 11.
[3] 34. 4. 14. *pr.*; G. 2. 244; In. 2. 20. 32.
[4] Machelard, *op. cit.* 504.
[5] *Dies incertus* is a condition in wills, 30. 30. 4, and, further, no security could be exacted by the slave for such a legacy. If however he became free *pendente conditione*, personal security, with a hypothec, could be taken as a compromise between the claims of *obsequium* and the rights of ordinary legatees, 36. 3. 7.
[6] Machelard, *op. cit.* 514.   [7] 34. 4. 10. *pr.*
[8] *h. t.* 14. *pr.*

as conditional *ab initio,* and so free from the rule. As a correction it would supersede the earlier gift and the legacy would be good[1]. How if a gift, originally conditional, becomes simple by satisfaction of the condition, *vivo testatore?* May we not say that the rule should not apply, and the legacy should stand, if the slave is not the property of the *heres* at *dies cedens?* For it would not have failed if the testator had died when he made the will, which is the test of Celsus[2].

The case of a legacy of A's property to A's slave has been supposed to create a difficulty. We are told that such a legacy is valid[3]. It has been said however that, as it would be null, if the testator died at once, it infringes the *regula* and might be expected to be void. Several attempts to explain the rule have been made on these assumptions[4]. But the text says not a word about the *regula* Catoniana, and it is clear, on an unbiassed reading of it, that Paul is talking of a legacy which he regards as absolutely valid[5], and in no way dependent on alienation or manumission of the slave. It is a strong expression of the slave's individuality : *cum enim,* says the text, *servo alieno aliquid testamento damus, domini persona ad hoc tantum inspicitur ut sit cum eo testamenti factio, ceterum ex persona servi constitit legatum.* The heir must give the *dominus* the value of the thing. The case is thus easily distinguished from that of legacy to a slave of the *heres,* which must be meaningless, if the testator die at once, since the *heres* would have to pay himself, and from that of a legacy to A of his own property, which would be valid only if there were a condition, *si vivo testatore id alienaveris,* or the like[6].

Doubtless this recognition of the slave's individuality is progressive, but here as in institutions, it may be said that the rule, in the later classical law, was that the full effect of duality was allowed, except where it amounted to an evasion of some restrictive law[7]. An interesting case somewhat analogous to that which we have been discussing is considered by Africanus. A legacy is left by X to A. B makes a *donatio* of the same thing to A's slave. The master can still sue *ex testamento,* notwithstanding the rule as to *duae lucrativae causae.* This is not covered by Paul's rule, since a *donatio* is not a testamentary gift, and Paul's general proposition applies only to these. But Africanus[8], writing earlier than Paul, though probably as late as Valens, does not rest his decision on this principle, but on a rather more subtle idea. He says that if the gift had been a discharge of the legacy, so would a similar gift from the *heres* of X. This he says is inadmissible, since a debt to

<hr />

[1] 35. 1. 89.
[2] 34. 7. 1. *pr. media tempora non nocent,* 28. 5. 6. 2. The principle if not the maxim applies to matters other than institutions. See, *e.g.* G. 2. 196.
[3] 31. 82. 2. Paul, quoting Valens.   [4] Machelard, *op. cit.* 506 *sqq.*
[5] Pellat, Revue Historique de Droit, 9. 224.   [6] 34. 7. 1. 2; In. 2. 20. 10.
[7] *Ante,* p. 140.   [8] 30. 108. 1.

the *dominus* is not discharged by a payment, *invito eo*, to the slave[1].
This is indeed a recognition of individuality, but of a very different
kind: it expresses the principle that a slave cannot bind his *dominus*[2].
A legacy to a slave, *post mortem domini*, is valid, says Gaius[3]. It
goes to the *heres* even though the slave is freed by his master's will,
since *dies cedit* on the death, and the liberty is not operative till later.
If however the *heres* is a *necessarius*, the text says doubtfully that
it will go to the slave, as both events occur at the same time. A
text which is a model of ambiguity seems to discuss a converse case[4].
If a slave is legated and the will contains a gift to him *cum morietur
ipse servus*, this is valid. It is not obvious why there was any doubt.
The text adds by way of reason: *propterea quod moriente servo, id quod
ipsi legatum erit ad eum cui ipse legatus fuerit perventurum sit*. There
may have been doubt as to whether this was not a conditional legacy,
which might fail because it did not vest in the life, of the legatee, but
Papinian and Ulpian[5] are clear that there is no condition.

Where a will was upset by *bonorum possessio contra tabulas*,
legacies to a slave were not saved though the *dominus* was one of those
persons, legacies to whom were still good: we are not to enquire who
benefits, but whom it was intended to honour[6].

One text, of Julian, gives an odd illustration of the duality we
are discussing. A slave is left, *generaliter*, to P the slave of T. After
dies cedens, T frees P. If T chooses a slave, *extinguitur Pamphili
legatum, quia non esset in hereditate qui optari possit*. But if T
repudiates P can choose. For though by the manumission two distinct
personae are established, yet there is an alternative legacy of one thing
between them, so that if T vindicates, the option is at an end, but if he
repudiates P can choose. The text[7] lays down strange doctrine. The
case is one of *legatum generis*, for *dies cedit* before choice, and T
"vindicates" the man he chooses. But, as we have seen, *dies cedens*
fixes the legacy on T, and P's manumission after that date can give
him no right: if T repudiates the *heres* should benefit[8]. The text may
have been altered[9], but, even so, it is difficult either to restore the

---

[1] C. 8. 42. 19.
[2] *Post*, p. 163. The text adds, after the statement that the legacy is still valid, the words, *et maxime si ignorem meam factam esse*. If this is limitative, it destroys the rule, for the *heres* will see that the legatee is informed. The grammar is doubtful, and there is corruption: the words are probably interpolated.
[3] 30. 68. 1. Conversely a legacy of a usufruct to a slave *post mortem suam* is bad. V. Fr. 57. Whether, in classical law, an ordinary legacy to him *post mortem suam* was bad is not stated. It is hardly 'within the mischief' of the rule.
[4] 30. 107. 1.		[5] 36. 2. 4; 35. 1. 79. *pr.*
[6] 37. 5. 3. 2. The existence of *fideicommissa tacita* involved forfeiture: Trajan provided that the beneficiary could keep half if he informed the Fisc, but he could not avail himself of this if the *fideicommissum* were to his slave, 49. 14. 13. 8.		[7] 33. 5. 10.
[8] *Ante*, p. 145. Even if we treat it as *l. optionis*, it is no better: the text makes T capable of making the legacy vest in his favour after he has freed P, a thing impossible.
[9] Note the expression *dies cesserit*, the absurd reason given for the fact that, if T chooses, P is barred, and the accumulation of hypotheses. See Eisele, Z. S. S. 7. 19 *sqq*.

original form, or to say what principle it expresses for Justinian's time.
As it stands it interprets the gift as if it were "to T and if T refuses
then to P." It is a sort of substitution, and the alternative legacy
to P does not cede till he is freed, so that he can take it. This
interpretation is suggested by the words *inter eas vertitur*[1] and by the
fact that T's vindication or repudiation is supposed to occur after the
manumission: if it occurred before, the case would be that discussed
elsewhere by Julian himself[2] of a gift to A and another gift of the
same thing to A's slave. If A refuses the gift to himself he can still
claim under the gift to the slave.

The law as to Ademption of legacies gives rise to several points of
interest. If a legacy is left to a slave, the inference is that, no matter
who ultimately benefits, the slave is the person the testator had in
mind, and thus it can be adeemed only from him and not from his
dominus[3]. There are more striking results. If a slave is legated and
there is a legacy to him, and he is sold or freed, this may be, and usually
is, ademption of the legacy of him[4]. But intent to deprive the donee of
the slave is not necessarily intent to revoke the gift to the slave, and
thus we are told, by Julian, that if on such facts the slave is sold or
freed, the legacy to the slave is due to his buyer or to himself[5]. So too
there may be a legacy to a freed slave, and alienation of the slave is an
ademption of the gift of liberty[6]. Express ademption of the gift of
liberty destroys the legacy to him[7], for the legacy has come into a
position in which it could not have begun[8]. But it does not seem that
sale of him would necessarily do so, at all events in late classical law.
Thus Paul[9] deals with a case in which there was a legacy with liberty
to a slave. The slave was sold and the liberty thereafter expressly
adeemed. The ademption he says is strictly ineffective, since as the
slave is now *alienus* the liberty is already gone. Yet as the slave might
be rebought the *ademptio* is not a mere nullity, and thus it has its
indirect effect of adeeming the legacy to him, which will not go to his
buyer[10]. If he had been freed, instead of sold, the ademption must be
an absolute nullity, and therefore says Paul, (though there had been
disputes,) it will not destroy any legacy, which the will gave him with
his liberty: *supervacua scriptura non nocet legato*[11]. The distinction
between the two cases is that while you can contemplate repurchase
you cannot contemplate reenslavement, *nec enim fas est eiusmodi casus
exspectari*[12]. If he is reenslaved, he is a new man. This distinction

---

[1] So also by the words *si T vindicaverit, extinguitur Pamphili legatum.*
[2] 30. 10. 1.　　　　　　　　　　　[3] 34. 4. 21; 37. 5. 3. 2.
[4] 34. 4. 18; In. 2. 20. 12.　　　　　[5] 30. 91. 2, 3, 5.
[6] *Post*, Ch. xx.　　　　　　　　　[7] 34. 4. 32. 1; *post*, Ch. xx.
[8] It is a simple legacy to a slave of the testator, 34. 8. 3. 2.　　　　　[9] 34. 4. 26. *pr.*
[10] 34. 4. 26. *pr.*　　　　[11] *h. l.* 1.　　　　[12] 18. 1. 6. *pr.*, 34. 2; 45. 1. 83. 5.

is overlooked by Salkowski, who regards the distinction drawn as sophistical[1]. He seems indeed to consider these cases as in some sort evasions of the *regula* Catoniana. But neither of them seems to conflict in any way with that rule. Even if we consider dates between the making and the death to come into account, which is far from certain, there is no moment in which a legacy to that slave would be necessarily bad[2].

In the adjoining text Paul deals with the analogous case of a slave legated with a legacy to him. One would expect the same decision, for if ademption of his liberty by alienation or freeing does not adeem a gift to him, neither certainly will ademption of a gift of him in the same ways. But the text presents some difficulty. It remarks that if a slave, *legatus* with a legacy to him, is sold and the legacy to him is adeemed the ademption is good. This is clear, but Paul adds the reason, *quia et legatum potest procedere si redimatur*[3]. This implies that *ademptio*, by sale, of the gift of him adeemed the gift to him, for, unless the allusion is to the revival of *both* gifts by the repurchase, it is not to the point. This part of the text is, so far as its reasoning goes, (but no further,) in conflict with accepted doctrine[4]. Cujas explains it by supposing the legacy given *contemplatione legatarii cui servus relictus est*[5], but he gives no authority germane to the matter, and the text is quite general. The simplest solution is to suppose it one of the not uncommon cases in which Paul gives a correct rule, with a wrong reason[6].

From the principle that the personality of the slave is considered in relation to every thing but *testamenti factio*, it follows that if the slave be dead at the time of *dies cedens*, the gift will fail[7]. A more striking application of the same principle is found in the rule laid down, by Julian, Papinian and Paul, that no legacy could be made to a *servus alienus* unless the gift would have been valid if left to him when free[8]. The only illustration we have is that of a legacy of a praedial servitude to a slave: such a gift is bad, though he could stipulate quite effectively for it, provided the *dominus* owned the land to which it was to attach[9]. A text of Maecianus says: *servitus servo praedium habenti recte legatur*[10], which seems to mean that the rule did not apply if the *fundus* were in

---

[1] Sklavenerwerb, 32, n. 59.

[2] A simple ademption, leaving the slave in the possession of the testator, would destroy the legacy (28. 5. 38. 4), not however by reason of the *regula* Catoniana. Gifts to a slave of the testator are bad whether simple or conditional (28. 5. 77; 30. 102; C. 6. 37. 4), and the *regula* does not affect conditional gifts, 34. 7. 3.

[3] 34. 4. 27. *pr.*

[4] The text then says that if a slave legated is freed *inter vivos*, an ademption of the legacy of him is a nullity, and *therefore* he will take any legacy to him. The reason is that he is if reenslaved a new man (34. 4. 27. 1). Here too is the idea that ademption of a gift of him adeems a gift to him, but this is clear: it is a case of direct ademption. It implies also that manumission though it adeems the legacy of him does not affect the gift to him.

[5] Cujas, cited Pothier *ad h. l.*   [6] See *post*, Ch. xx.

[7] 31. 59; 36. 2. 16. 1.   [8] 31. 82. 2; 33. 3. 5.

[9] 33. 3. 5; 45. 3. 17; V. Fr. 56.   [10] 32. 17. 1.

the slave's *peculium*. Mommsen[1] disbelieves the text and amends it so as to destroy its application to slaves. This may be because a slave cannot strictly be said *habere*. But the word was freely used in a loose sense in the case of slaves[2], and the text is in harmony with the whole tendency of the law, since it is no doubt from the notion of *peculium* that the recognition of the slave's individuality started[3]. A converse case is considered by Ulpian[4]. A legacy is made, to a slave, of a *militia*, i.e. an office of the kind which had become vendible. A slave could not hold such an office. The master was not the donee. But the slave could have held it if free. Accordingly the gift is good, the master getting the value of the office[5]. We learn incidentally, from this text, that, if the testator supposes a slave legatee to be free, the gift is not good, at any rate if the thing is one he would not knowingly have left to a slave[6].

It is stated by Paul[7] that the *dominus* can repudiate a legacy to his slave. It is equally clearly stated, by Modestinus, that he cannot so repudiate a *fideicommissum* to him[8]. The reason why legacy was put on this footing seems to be that *is repudiare potest qui et acquirere potest*[9], and a legacy to a slave, according to the doctrine which prevailed[10], vests in the legatee, with no act, immediately on *aditio*. As it cannot vest in the slave it is in the master, and it is therefore for him *agnoscere* or *repudiare*. In *fideicommissa*, there is no such transition of ownership: the property passes only on *restitutio*. The probable reason why, though the *dominus* can accept, he cannot repudiate is that the conception of repudiation is not applicable at all to *fideicommissa*, and indeed our text does not say that the *dominus* cannot repudiate, but that a *fideicommissum* cannot be repudiated. All that the beneficiary has is a sort of obligation, which can of course be released in certain formal ways, like other obligations. As the text goes on to say, an informal act could at most give rise to an *exceptio doli*.

If a gift be made to a slave, *mortis causa*, it is a question of intent whether it is his death or that of his master, *vivo donatore*, which gives rise to a *condictio* for recovery[11].

As to the acquisition of *iura in re aliena*, the only cases as to which we have any authority are those of *ususfructus* and the like. We have

---

[1] *ad h. l.*
[2] *e.g.* 45. 1. 38. 6, 9. *Post*, p. 156. There is a further difficulty since the gift would be of a *ius (eundi, etc.)*, which cannot attach to a slave. In its present form the rule is probably late.
[3] Pernice, Labeo, 1. 139, *post*, p. 187. See however, V. Fr. 56.   [4] 32. 11. 16.
[5] In legacy of *militia, aestimatio videtur legata*, 31. 49. 1. Vangerow, Pand. § 525.
[6] Gift to slave may be conditional, and the slave may fulfil the condition without *iussum*, 35. 1. 5. 1, cp. *ante*, p. 138.
[7] 30. 7. The allusion is no doubt to *l. per vindicationem.*
[8] 31. 34. 2. He can repudiate *bonorum possessio*, but perhaps not institution, *ante*, p. 140.
[9] 29. 2. 18.   [10] G. 2. 195.
[11] The right vests in the master immediately on the death (39. 6. 44) and thus if the slave is freed between death and entry of a *heres*, he does not take the gift with him. As to legacy of *cibaria, etc.*, to a slave see *post*, Chh. XIII, XX.

seen that, except in case of *peculium*, a slave cannot acquire a praedial servitude by will[1]. He can acquire it *inter vivos*, and *ususfructus*, *usus*, *habitatio*, and *operae servorum* can be acquired by him in all the ordinary ways[2]. As a slave's possession is his master's, so is his enjoyment of a servitude[3]. It is in connexion with these rights that we get the most striking illustrations of the principle that in gifts by will the personality of the slave is most considered, that of the master being material only so far as *testamenti factio* is concerned. A legacy of usufruct, whether to a slave or not, vests only when the heir enters[4]. The reason, credited by Ulpian to Julian, is: *tunc enim constituitur ususfructus cum quis iam frui potest*[5]. If the slave were dead at that time, the gift would of course fail[6]. But, in the classical law, the usufruct failed at once whenever the slave died, if it had been left *pure*, *per vindicationem*[7]. And since the right has taken effect in the master, but still attaches to the individuality of the slave, the same effect is produced if the slave be alienated or freed[8]. If it was created *inter vivos*, the slave's individuality is not considered, and thus it is not affected by these facts. Moreover though, as we have seen, a legacy to a slave, *post mortem suam*, must fail, he can validly stipulate for a usufruct in this form[9].

What is true of creation *inter vivos* is no doubt also true of creation by *legatum per damnationem*, or by *fideicommissum*, which have to be completed *inter vivos*. One text suggests the question whether, in the case of a conditional legacy, the usufruct is constituted *ex persona servi*. The text says that if two slaves are instituted and there is a simple legacy of land to X, *deducto usufructu*, the usufruct is based on the *persona* of the slave, but that if the legacy of the land was conditional, it is *ex persona domini*[10]. Here the usufruct is regarded not as a part of the *dominium*, but as a distinct thing, which does not exist till the condition occurs and the land passes[11]. The land then passes directly from the master, leaving the usufruct in him: the slaves do not appear in the matter. If the legacy of land had been simple, the usufruct would have sprung into existence at *aditio*, and would have been a normal acquisition *ex testamento*, through the slaves. But the same point would not arise in a direct legacy of usufruct. The

[1] *Ante*, p. 151.
[2] 7. 1. 6. 2, 3; 7. 8. 17; 36. 2. 9; V. Fr. 82. If a slave demands a *precarium, ratihabente aut auctore domino*, the *dominus* has it, and is liable to the interdict. If he did not consent there is only *de peculio*, or *de in rem verso*, 43. 26. 13. See *ante*, p. 134.
[3] 43. 19. 3. 4.   [4] 7. 3. 1. 2; V. Fr. 60.
[5] Labeo had held a different opinion, *i.e.* that they ceded like other legacies (V. Fr. 60). But the chief advantage, that of transmissibility, did not arise here.
[6] 36. 2. 16. 1.   [7] V. Fr. 57.   [8] *Ib.*; C. 3. 33. 17.
[9] V. Fr. 57. Creation of usufruct in a slave in whom you have a usufruct does not affect it, 7. 4. 5. 1.
[10] V. Fr. 82.
[11] 46. 4. 13. 2. It was looked at in both ways. Roby, de usufructu, 42.

usufruct, even where it is left conditionally, comes to the master directly through the slave. And the principal text is quite general[1].

Several texts discuss difficulties arising in the application of these principles, in cases, like the foregoing, where the gift is to two, the question being usually as to the existence of *ius accrescendi*. Justinian[2] tells us that if one of two slaves through whom, or part of the slave through whom, the usufruct was acquired, were alienated, there had been doubt as to the effect on the usufruct. Some held it wholly destroyed ; some *pro parte* lost; others, including Julian, held that it remained unaffected. This view Justinian adopted, before he passed the enactment sweeping away the importance of the continued ownership in all cases[3]. This is a case of *ius accrescendi* ; it is so explained by Julian and Pomponius, cited by Ulpian, in the analogous cases of death of one of the slaves, or repudiation of the gift so far as it was acquired through one of them[4]. These and similar matters were the subject of much discussion, the doctrines being ultimately settled by Julian.

In order to state them, as far as they are known, it is necessary to examine some questions of more general kind among the many to which the thorny topic of legacy of usufruct gives rise.

It is clear that there is *ius accrescendi* between fructuaries, if the thing is left *per vindicationem coniunctim,* or *disiunctim,* but not where it is left separately to two in parts[5]. And though there is *ius accrescendi* similarly in a legacy of property, there is the difference that in that case it occurs only if the gift never really takes effect in one of them: here it arises, even in case of subsequent failure[6]. Accordingly if it is left to two of a man's slaves, the owner has *ius accrescendi*, as we have just seen[7]. How if it is left to a common slave, and one master loses or repudiates it? Ulpian quotes an array of jurists on this point—himself adopting Julian's view that in such a case the other holder gets all. To the objection that there ought to be no more accrual here than there would be, *e.g.*, where the holder of a usufruct loses by nonuse the usufruct of a divided part of it, he replies that it is not a question of *ius accrescendi*, but that so long as the slave whose *persona* is considered is his, no part ought to perish. The objection thus met seems to rest on the notion that the acquisition to the common owners is *ab initio* in parts, and the reply emphasises the individuality of the slave and also expresses the idea of continuous acquisition[8]. In the legacy of a usufruct to a slave however owned the acquisition is a single one made by him. Thus if it

[1] V. Fr. 57.　　　[2] C. 3. 33. 15.　　　[3] *h. t.* 17.　　　[4] V. Fr. 82.
[5] V. Fr. 75. 1 (D. 7. 2. 1. *pr.*).　V. Fr. 77 (D. 7. 2. 1. 3).　Vindius differed on the last point.
[6] V. Fr. 77; D. 7. 2. 1. 3.　The idea at the bottom of this is that *ususfructus* is not acquired, like *dominium*, once for all, but *cotidie constituitur*.
[7] V. Fr. 82.　　　[8] V. Fr. 75; D. 7. 2. 1. *pr.*

were left to a common slave and T, then on lapse of the share of one common owner, all goes to the other, not to T[1]. The case is contrasted with that in which two heirs are instituted, and land is left to X, *deducto usufructu.* Here all are agreed that the heirs will have no *ius accrescendi.* Julian assigns as the reason : *videri usumfructum constitutum non per concursum divisum*—an obscure expression which must mean " originally created in *partes*[2]," since it is added that this agrees with the view of Celsus, that there is *ius accrescendi* only where it was divided *concursu, in duobus qui solidum habuerunt*[3]. Celsus and Neratius apply the same rule in the case of common owners who mancipate, *deducto usufructu*[4]. There is no accrual. Consistently with this it is said by Ulpian, on the authority of Julian, Pomponius and Neratius, that if two slaves are instituted and there is a legacy of land, *deducto usufructu*, there is no *ius accrescendi* on lapse of the part acquired by either slave, but the legatee of the land gets the benefit[5]. The case of a common slave instituted, with the same gift to an *extraneus*, is not considered : presumably in such a case the co-owner would benefit by a lapse, on the principle laid down by Ulpian in the case of legacy[6]: it is not exactly *ius accrescendi.* But this question is bound up with that whether the institution of a common slave was one institution or two—a matter which will call for discussion later[7].

A principle running through all these cases is, that where two persons receive a gift by institution, they are regarded as taking distinct parts *ab initio*, while in a case of joint legacy, each is *prima facie* entitled to the whole : it is the accident that there are two of them which compels division[8].

Justinian[9] provided that however a usufruct was acquired through a slave, it was not to be affected by death, alienation, or manumission of him. This enactment lessened the possible cases of lapse and so far simplified the law. But it does not involve any general alteration of the way in which gifts were affected by the fact that they were acquired through slaves. And thus most of these rules pass into the Digest[10].

In relation to *iura in personam*, the governing principle, that a slave can better our position but cannot deteriorate it[11], has many obvious illustrations. The slave has the power of stipulating *ex persona. domini*

---

[1] V. Fr. 76; D. 7. 2. 1. 2.   [2] Mommsen *ad h. l.*
[3] V. Fr. 78, 79; D. 7. 2. 1. 4; 7. 2. 3. *pr.*
[4] 7. 2. 3. 1; V. Fr. 80, 81.   [5] V. Fr. 82.
[6] V. Fr. 75. 5.   See above.   [7] *Post*, Ch. xvi.
[8] See for an illustration, 7. 2. 11. The distinction may be connected with the fact that in ordinary joint legacies nothing was said of shares, while in joint institutions they were usually mentioned: the right of one to take all in case of lapse being a result of the rule: *nemo pro parte testatus.*
[9] C. 3. 33. 17; A.D. 531.
[10] D. 7. 2.   [11] 50. 17. 133.

and the right vests in the *dominus*[1]. He acquires *invito*, even *vetante*, *domino*, even where it is an acquisition involving liabilities[2]. But here the risk is not with the *dominus* until he knows and assents, nor, till then, can he be guilty of *culpa* in relation to the matter. Thus, we are told, in a case of such a promise of *Dos*, that, as it is an unfair acquisition, the other party has a right to a *condictio* for repayment, or release, as the case may be[3]. As a stipulation derives its force *ex praesenti*, the *dominus* acquires the right even though its operation be postponed, by condition or otherwise, till after alienation or manumission[4]. It is indifferent whether the slave names himself or his master or a fellow-slave or no one[5]. His stipulation, *domino aut extraneo*, is valid : his master alone can sue, but the *extraneus* being regarded as *solutionis causa adjectus*, payment can be made to him[6]. On similar principles an *acceptilatio* taken by a slave on his transaction, or his master's, bars action against the latter[7]. A slave's capacity for stipulation being purely derivative, there are many limitations on it. Thus one who has no owner, a derelict, cannot stipulate[8], and a slave cannot make a stipulation which would not be good in substance if made by his master[9]. He cannot stipulate for a praedial servitude, unless the master has the *praedium* to which it is to attach[10]. As a slave derives his capacity from his master, it might be supposed that he could not have more than the master had. But this would have involved inconvenience, and it is clear that for a master incapable of contracting from mental or physical defect, the slave could stipulate[11]. The rule seems illogical, but its illogicality is concealed by the fact that a slave's stipulation, as we have seen, did not require the consent or knowledge of the master.

The difference of individuality has many marked effects in this connexion. A slave could not be *adstipulator*, this form of obligation being essentially personal[12]. A slave's contract is, for the purpose of jurisdiction, made at his domicile, rather than his master's[13]. There is a very important rule that *quae facti sunt non transeunt ad dominum*[14]. This means in effect that the terms of the stipulation are to be literally interpreted, and thus where the stipulation involves any act to be done

---

[1] 41. 1. 10. 1; 45. 1. 38. 17; In. 3. 17. *pr.*; G. 3. 114; 4. 134, 5. As to *filius miles*, 49. 17. 15. 3.
[2] 12. 1. 31. 1; 45. 1. 62.　　　[3] 23. 3. 46.　　　[4] 45. 3. 40.
[5] 45. 1. 45. *pr.*; 45. 3. 1. *pr.*—3, 15. Just as a *dominus* stipulating for his slave acquires to himself, 45. 1. 39, 40, 56. 3, 130; 45. 3. 28. 2; C. 8. 37. 2. Slave's stipulation for an *extraneus nominatim* is of course void, 45. 3. 1. 3, 30; C. 8. 38. 14.
[6] 45. 3. 13. His stipulation *domino et extraneo* gave rise no doubt to the same questions as did that of a freeman *sibi et Titio*. As to common slaves, *post*, Ch. xvi.
[7] 46. 4. 11. *pr.*
[8] 45. 3. 36. Or one in a derelict *hereditas*, 45. 1. 73. 1.
[9] Thus he cannot stipulate for a freeman or a *praedium litigiosum* (16. 1. 27. 1) or for what is his master's (45. 3. 9. *pr.*) or *post mortem domini*, In. 3. 19. 13.
[10] 45. 3. 7. 1; V. Fr. 56.　　　[11] *Arg.* 27. 8. 1. 15.
[12] G. 3. 114.　　　[13] 5. 1. 19. 3. At least if he was lawfully there.
[14] 35. 1. 44. *pr.*

by or to the slave, it cannot be done by or to the master, though it is he who will enforce the contract if need be. Thus if a slave stipulates that he may be allowed to cross a field it is he who may do so, not his master[1]. If he stipulates for this thing or that, as he shall choose, the choice is personal. But no question of *dies cedens* arises as in legacy, and if the slave dies before choosing, the right to choose passes to the master[2]. If A promises to pay to me " or to the slave of T," it is no discharge to pay the money to T: he is not the *solutionis causa adiectus*[3]. But the maxim, *quae facti sunt non transeunt*, does not adequately express the rule. It is wider: nothing which is expressed to be done to the slave, or had by him, *transit ad dominum*, whether it be expressed as a matter of fact, or as a legal right. This leads to difficulties. If he simply stipulates for a right the matter is clear. But if he stipulates that he is to have that right, there is the obstacle that a slave is incapable of a right. He cannot acquire the right to himself, and the mention of himself excludes the *dominus*. Julian thought that even such expressions as *sibi habere licere* and *possidere licere, prima facie* express a right, and so vitiate the stipulation. But Ulpian found a more reasonable way. Such words, he says, admit of being understood otherwise, as expressing merely detention, of which a slave is capable, and the accepted rule of the Digest is that where a slave so contracts, the words are to be so construed[4]. The result is that his master has a different right from that which would have been created if the word *mihi* had not been used[5]. There is no trace of the further step of ignoring that word. If the stipulation refer to something that does not admit of such an interpretation as excludes the question of right, it is void, even under Justinian. Thus if a slave of the patron stipulates with a *libertus* that *operae* shall be rendered to him this is void, though if he does not say *mihi* it is quite good. This is laid down by Pomponius and Celsus, and similar rules are expressed by Ulpian and Papinian[6]. This hidebound logic seems out of place in the law of Justinian. The recognition of the slave's individuality was due to considerations of convenience, and common sense, which might have led to its being disregarded in this case[7].

Justinian's enactments as to *cautiones* shew that the same principles were applied in the case of other unilateral contracts[8].

---

[1] In. 3. 17. 2.   [2] 45. 1. 76. *pr.*, 141 *pr.*
[3] 35. 1. 44. 1.   So in stipulation to pay to a slave, 46. 3. 95. 7.   A slave, to be free on paying to a *servus heres*, could not pay to the *dominus* except with consent of the *servus*, 35. 1. 44. *pr.*, 1, 2; 46. 3. 95.7.   Converse rules where the payment was to be to the *dominus*, though *versio in rem domini* sufficed, 35. 1. 44. 3, 46. 3. 9, 95. 7, *post*, Ch. xxi.
[4] 45. 1. 38. 3—9.   [5] *e.g.* 45. 1. 130.
[6] 38. 1. 10. *pr.*; 45. 3. 2, 18. 1, 38.
[7] The logical difficulty in this playing fast and loose may have seemed too great.
[8] C. 8. 37. 14.

In relation to bilateral contracts the matter is more complex. The general rule is that the slave binds the other party to his master, but not *vice versa*, apart from cases within the special praetorian remedies to be later discussed. But it is easy to state cases in which this rule would operate unjustly. Accordingly while the principle that the *dominus* could not be sued on his slave's contract remained intact, his enforcement of his rights thereunder was made subject to his satisfying the claim of the other party. If he sued on his slave's contract, *compensatio* would be *in solidum*, though he could have been sued only *de peculio*[1]. Where a slave bought, the master had an *actio ex empto* against the vendor[2], but to entitle himself to sue he must pay the whole price[3]. Where A buys B's slave S from a thief and S buys a man V, B acquires the *actio ex empto* against the seller of V, subject to his paying all that would have been due had V been bought by a free man[4].

But here too the individuality of the slave is material in many ways. It was penal to buy a *res litigiosa* knowingly. If a slave bought, knowingly, the penalty attached, unless it was under special mandate: in that case the master's knowledge, and his alone, was material[5]. In the *actio redhibitoria* the same principle applied : it was the slave's *scientia* which barred the action unless it was under special mandate, in which case the master's knowledge was material[6]. The text remarks that good faith requires that deception of the slave should not hurt the master, while deception by him should[7].

If the buyer from a slave is evicted he must give notice to the slave himself if he is alive[8]. If a slave is to be free on paying to the heir there was a rule that if alienated he must pay it to the buyer[9]. But if a slave were the buyer, the payment must be made, apart from *peculium*, not to him but to his *dominus*, notwithstanding this principle[10]. This provision is probably due to the wording of the original rule in the XII Tables, where the word used was *emptor*, which means not buyer but acquirer[11]. This is not the slave but his master.

There is less authority in relation to other contracts, but the principles are the same. The *dominus* can avail himself of a mandate by or to the slave even given against his will[12]. If my slave commodates

---

[1] 16. 2. 9. *pr.*   [2] 21. 2. 39. 1.
[3] 21. 1. 57. *pr.* Where a slave bought and his master brought the *actio redhibitoria*, the counter claim, if any, was *in solidum*, not confined to *peculium*, though, if the slave had sold, the *actio redhibitoria* against his *dominus* would have been so limited, 21. 1. 57.
[4] 12. 1. 31. 1.   [5] 44. 6. 2.   Julian.
[6] 21. 1. 51, Africanus; see also 18. 1. 12. 13.   In 21. 1. 51 he says, disagreeing with Julian, that even in special mandate the knowledge of the slave might bar action.   The text is from the Quaestiones.   It was no doubt disputed.
[7] For puzzling texts as to effect of *dolus* of a slave, see *post*, p. 163.   In general his *dolus* is imputable to his master, but only in relation to the transaction in which it occurred, 44. 4. 4. 17 *h. t.* 5. 3.
[8] 21. 2. 39. 1.   [9] *Post*, Ch. XXI.   [10] 40. 7. 6. 6.
[11] 40. 7. 29. 1. 6. 3   Ulp. 2. 4.   [12] 17. 1. 22. 8; C. 6. 2. 1.

against my will I can sue the *commodatarius*[1]. In the same way a *constitutum* may be made to a slave and he acquires the right to his master though the agreement be to pay the money to him[2].

Some contractual rights are acquired only as the result of an alienation. We shall see later that these require authorisation as the alienation does. Thus if a slave lends money without authority, there is no *actio ex mutuo*, but the money can be vindicated[3]. If he pay under a *fideiussio* duly authorised, the owner will have *actio mandati*[4]. But if there was no authority to alienate the money, there can be no such action[5].

If in order to benefit me, X paid under a *fideiussio* I had undertaken, I was entitled to recover the money from the principal debtor: it was as if I had paid[6]. If the *fideiussio* had been by my son or slave, and the intent was to benefit him and not me, I had, says Ulpian, quoting Marcellus[7], no *actio mandati* against the principal debtor, though he is released. It is presumably the expressed intent not to benefit the *dominus* which excludes him; but one would have expected the action to be allowed, the proceeds being *in peculio*[8].

Rights *ex delicto* are acquired in the same way. Thus the master has *actio furti* for what is stolen from his slave[9]. If it was a thing borrowed by the slave the master is entitled to *actio furti* so far as he is liable *de peculio*[10]. If my slaves are ejected I am entitled to the interdict *de vi*[11]. Work done against my slaves' opposition or concealed from them entitles me to the interdict *quod vi aut clam*[12]. It may be added that delictal actions and *condictio furtiva* acquired through the slave are not lost by alienation or manumission of him[13].

In general the recognition of the slave's individuality is the satisfaction of an obvious practical need, and the restrictions on it, though sometimes compelled by the words of an enactment, are for the most part inspired by considerations of the same kind. The texts provide a simple illustration of this. We are told that a master cannot get *restitutio in integrum* on the transaction of a minor slave. The point is that as no such transaction can bind the master unless he has in some way authorised it, he has himself to blame—*sibi debebit 'imputare, cur rem minori commisit*[14].

---

[1] 13. 6. 14. If the latter knew that the slave had no business to do it, there would be *furti* as well. Where on similar facts the *commodatarius* pledged the thing, the pledgee refused to restore it till he was paid. The text discusses the circumstances under which the money could be recovered, but assumes the validity of the *commodatum*, 12. 6. 36.
[2] 13. 5. 10. A master does not lose his action of deposit acquired through the slave by the alienation or manumission of the slave, 16. 3. 1. 17, 30.
[3] 12. 1. 11. 2. See p. 159.   [4] 17. 1. 12. 3.
[5] 46. 1. 19. As to difficulties where he has *administratio peculii, post,* Ch. VIII.
[6] 17. 1. 12. 1.   [7] *h. l.* 2.
[8] The allusion to the slave may be interpolated: it is not carried through the text. Under many circumstances the son might have *actio mandati*.
[9] P. 2. 31. 20.   [10] 47. 2. 52. 9.   [11] 43. 16. 1. 22.
[12] 43. 24. 3. *pr.*   [13] 44. 7. 56.   [14] 4. 4. 3. 11, 23.

CHAPTER VII.

THE SLAVE AS MAN. COMMERCIAL RELATIONS APART FROM *PECULIUM*. LIABILITIES.

To alienation of the master's property his consent was always necessary[1]. With that consent, which might be by ratification[2], or by a general authorisation if wide enough in its terms[3], the slave could alienate anything[4]. He could not of course make a *cessio in iure*, because this was in form litigation[5], but apart from that the form is immaterial. There is indeed little authority for *mancipatio* by a slave, but what little there is is in favour[6]. Julian[7] contemplates the transfer of *proprietas* in a slave, by a slave with authority, but it is possible that the text, which speaks of *traditio*, may have been originally so written, so that the reference would be only to Praetorian ownership. Of course the *dominus* could not authorise the slave to do what would have been unlawful had he done it himself. Thus a slave could not validly make a *donatio* to his owner's wife[8]. Without authority, the slave was powerless: he could not transfer *dominium*[9]. If he sold and delivered, possession passed but no more, and the taker, if he knew that there was no authority, could not prescribe, and was indeed a *fur*[10]. Money lent, *citra voluntatem*, could be vindicated[11], as could money paid by a fugitive slave for the concealment of himself or his theft[12].

Similar rules applied where, having authority, he exceeded it[13]. Where A owed B 10 *ex fideicommisso* and 10 on an independent *obligatio naturalis*, and a generally authorised slave paid 10 expressly towards the whole debt, 5 could be vindicated, as a general authority

---

[1] 21. 2. 39. 1. No requirement of form: an endorsement of the *cautio* sufficed, 45. 1. 126. 2.
[2] 43. 26. 19. 1.   [3] 15. 1. 46; 46. 3. 94. 3.
[4] 6. 1. 41. 1. He could pledge all his master's goods, himself included, or give himself in *precarium*, 12. 6. 13. *pr.*; 20. 1. 29. 3; 43. 26. 19. 1. Delivery with authority would give the buyer *accessio temporis*, 41. 2. 14. *pr.*; 44. 3. 15. 3.
[5] *Ante*, p. 83.   [6] Cic. Att. 13. 50. 2. See Roby, Roman Private Law, 1. 432.
[7] 21. 2. 39. 1.   [8] 24. 1. 3. 3.
[9] C. Th. 2. 30. 2; 2. 31. 1; D. 12. 6. 53; 21. 2. 39. 1.
[10] 13. 6. 14; C. 4. 26. 10. An *ancilla* without authority gave money purporting to be her *dos*: the master could vindicate, subject to a possibility of *usucapio*, 23. 3. 67, cp. C. 4. 26. 6.
[11] 12. 1. 11. 2; 46. 1. 19.   [12] 12. 5. 4. 4, 5. *Condicere, quasi furi*.
[13] If being authorised to pay 8 he paid 10, the owner could vindicate 2. D. 15. 1. 37. 1.

to pay is not held to apply to natural obligations[1]. There must be real authority : a mere *bona fide* belief, however reasonable, did not suffice[2]. There is some difficulty as to the loss of possession by the act of the slave. Before discussing the texts it must be pointed out that, from the present point of view, it is immaterial whether the possession was originally acquired by the slave or not : in either case he is now a *detentor* through whom the possession is realised. Moreover we are told that the rules are the same whether it is a slave, a *procurator* or a *colonus*[3]; the slave's lack of capacity does not enter into the question, and thus there is no room for the maxim that a slave cannot make his master's position worse. It is indeed mentioned in this connexion, but only in an enactment of Justinian's[4] in which he excels himself in obscurity. It is the fact that possession is on a very different level from other rights, that is at the bottom of the whole difficulty.

If a slave possessed by his master still held the thing, it might be supposed that, however he attempted to exclude the master, the latter would still possess, as the slave's possession is his. And so the rule is laid down by Africanus for the case where the slave of a pledgee turns his master out of pledged land[5]. But Paul lays down a different rule for moveables. If my slave takes my property I do not possess it till he restores it[6]. In the next text[7] he cites Labeo and Pomponius in support of the view that, for this purpose, adding it to his *peculium* is not restoration, unless it was in the *peculium* before, or the owner assents to its being there. The difference may turn on the fact that, the land being immoveable, no change has occurred in the relation of the *dominus* thereto, while this would not be the case in regard to the moveables. But the solution is more likely to be found in considering the case as one of a *fugitivus*. The view that his owner still possessed a fugitive was slowly accepted, and not all those who accepted it agreed that there could be possession through him[8].

If a slave is deprived of the thing of course the master loses possession. Thus if a slave occupying land is *deiectus*, the *dominus* has the

---

[1] 46. 3. 94. 3. Eisele suggests (Z. S. S. 26. 66 *sqq.*) that where acquisition depended on alienation, as in purchase, no authority was needed. This is inconsistent with 15. 1. 37. 1 and with the rules as to *mutuum* (*ante*, p. 159), and has no support in the texts. That in connexion with which Eisele applies this principle does not, on its face, express such a rule and admits of a different explanation. *Post*, Ch. xv, and App. iii.
[2] 12. 6. 53. So, it would seem, of an expired authority, whatever the belief of the receiver (*Arg.* 12. 1. 11. 2).
[3] 41. 2. 25. 1.　　　　　　　　　　[4] C. 7. 32. 12.
[5] 41. 2. 40. *pr.* Labeo remarks that, where the *heres* of a *colonus* takes possession thinking the *colonus* was owner, the true owner still possesses, 19. 2. 60. 1.
[6] 41. 3. 4. 8. Nor even then if I knew of the theft, till I know of the return.
[7] 41. 3. 4. 9.
[8] *Post*, Ch. xii. There are signs of a school controversy in which the Proculians, including Pomponius, took the view that it was impossible. The rule that a holder cannot *causam possessionis mutare* is sometimes used to explain the rule in the case of land. Ihering, Besitzwille, 347 *sqq.* He appears to hold that the rule applies to a *detentor* attempting to convert his holding into possession.

Interdict *unde vi*, whether he know of it or not[1]. Conversely, if his slaves are left in possession of the land, the owner has not been *deiectus*, even though he himself has been expelled, unless indeed they have passed into the possession of the *deiector*, as would result from their being bound or acting at his orders[2].

Mere momentary absence with no intention to abandon is of course immaterial[3]. The same appears to be true of death or insanity of the slave. It is true that he cannot any longer be holding consciously for the owner, but it is clear on the texts that the possession is not lost till a third person has taken the thing or the master has neglected to get actual control of it. The slave is a mere instrument: his death and, *a fortiori*, his insanity, do not of themselves affect the master's relation to the thing[4]. But in the case of intentional abandonment there was a conflict[5]. Pomponius and Africanus tell us that possession is lost[6]. Paul and Papinian hold that it is not lost till a third party has entered[7]. The dissidence cannot turn on anything peculiar to slaves, for both Paul and Papinian speak of slaves or *coloni*, though it chances that the texts which declare possession lost speak only of *coloni*. It seems to be no more than a difference of opinion as to what is substantial loss of control. Justinian decides, as it seems, that possession is not lost[8].

If the possession has passed to an adverse possessor the texts are agreed that possession is lost[9]. Justinian, however, in the enactment just mentioned, in which he appears to lay down the opposite rule for this case also, says that here too there had been dispute. It is sometimes said that this is a mere mistake of his[10]. But it is at least possible that the dispute was whether the entry of the third party ended the possession, till it was known to the person concerned[11]. Thus Papinian tells us that knowledge was not required[12], while he says that, of *saltus hiberni*, which are possessed only *animo*, the possession is not lost till knowledge, since, till then, the *animus* exists[13]. It may well be that some lawyers thought the same rule ought to apply where the slave had abandoned possession, for, if possession is retained, it can be only *animo*.

We shall have shortly to consider how far a slave's contract can bind his master. But there is a difficult topic, which must first be

[1] 43. 16. 1. 22.   [2] *h. l.* 45, 46.   [3] 41. 2. 3. 1.
[4] 41. 2. 3. 8, 25. 1, 40. 1. So if he lets the land to another—the possession is still in the master. The texts apply to land, but the principle should apply to moveables.
[5] See Windscheid, Lehrb. § 157; Dernburg, Pand. 1. § 183; Girard, Manuel, p. 274.
[6] 41. 2. 31, 40. 1.
[7] 41. 2. 3. 8, 44. 2. Proculus may be of this opinion, but he may mean only that the facts he gives do not amount to abandonment, 4. 3. 31.
[8] C. 7. 32. 12. His enactment is so obscure that a dispute as to its meaning, begun by the Glossators (Haenel, Diss. Domm. 5), still rages. See the reff. in n. 5. The Digest texts are not much guide towards his meaning. Ihering holds that the meaning is merely that he can recover possession by interdict—an extended *Unde vi*. Grund d. Besitzessch. 114. See also C. 7. 32. 5.
[9] 41. 2. 40. 1. 44. 2.   [10] Girard, *loc. cit.*   [11] Windscheid, *loc. cit.*
[12] 41. 2. 44. 2.   [13] 41. 2. 46.

considered. How far is a master bound by the unauthorised acts of his slave in transactions, essentially not the slave's, but the master's? It is obvious that, in a great number of transactions, the actual carrying out of the contract will be left to slaves, and it is of importance to note how far it is material that the performance, or the breach, is not the act of the contracting master himself. The story told by the texts is not consistent at all points, but in general the principle is that a man is not, apart from his own privity or neglect, liable for conduct of his slave in relation to a contract not made by the slave[1]. Where a slave, being directed by his master to point out the limits of a property sold points them out wrongly the land sold is that agreed by the master, not that pointed out[2]. A redhibiting buyer is indeed liable for damage done by his *familia*, but this is by virtue of an express rule of the Aedilician Edict[3].

The rule protecting the master is laid down in general terms by Ulpian, who says: *neque enim esse aequum servi dolum amplius domino nocere quam in quo opera eius esset usus*[4]. But this lacks precision: so far at least as *culpa* is concerned the employment contemplated is employment in making the contract. Alfenus, in the case of a house set on fire by the vendor's slaves[5], and Labeo in that of a mule killed by the negligence of a slave let on hire[6], lay down the same rule: a man is not liable, *ex contractu*, on his own contract for the *culpa* of his slave. A little later there appears a difference of opinion. Oddly enough it is Sabinus of the other school who lays down the rule as it was stated by Labeo (and his teacher Alfenus), and Proculus who holds that the master is liable on the contract, subject to a right of abandoning the slave instead of paying damages[7]. This text is in the Collatio[8]. As inserted in the Digest[9], it gives as law the view of Proculus and omits that of Sabinus. On the other hand Paul[10] dealing with the case of slaves, let with a property, who steal from the tenant, says that the *locator* is not liable *ex contractu*, but only *ex delicto*, noxally. Neratius, a Proculian[11], gives a view which, though in form intermediate, is in essence the view of Sabinus. He says the master is liable *ex contractu* on such facts, if he was negligent in employing such slaves. This of course is personal *culpa* in the master. Ulpian expresses the same rule in a text which is not above suspicion of interpolation[12]. Another text, by Paul and Ulpian[13], says that, where slaves are employed under a contract, damage done by them may create a claim *ex contractu*

---

[1] It is not necessarily enough to put a man in *mora* that notice was given to his slave, though circumstances may make it so: *mora* or not is a question of fact, 22. 1. 32. *pr.*
[2] 18. 1. 18. 1.   The slave might be liable if freed, cp. 4. 3. 7. *pr.*
[3] 21. 1. 25. 1.   [4] 44. 4. 4. 17.   [5] 18. 6. 12.
[6] 19. 2. 60. 7.   [7] *Ante*, p. 123.   [8] Coll. 12. 7. 9.
[9] 9. 2. 27. 11.   [10] 19. 2. 45. *pr.*   [11] Coll. 12. 7. 7; D. 9. 2. 27. 9.
[12] 9. 2. 11. *pr.*   [13] 13. 6. 10. 1—12.

against the master *qui non tam idoneum hominem elegerit.* And Julian says[1] that, if the man chosen to return a thing lent is one who might properly be trusted, the master is under no liability. On the whole, this rule that he is liable, if he has shewn *culpa in eligendo*[2], must be taken to be that of the classical lawyers. But some texts suggest that some jurists were inclined to hold that *res ipsa loquitur,* and a man who employs negligent slaves is himself negligent[3]. Such a theory is more likely to be of the sixth century than of the second. It appears in the Institutes[4] in connexion with the special liabilities of *caupo,* etc., and similar language is used in texts[5] in the Digest dealing with the same cases. But it may be doubted if the reasoning is that of the original text : the rules are a direct creation of the Edict[6] : they are rather cases of insurance and there is no need to resort to the hypothesis of *culpa*[7].

The principles that a slave has no authority to make his master's position worse, and that liability through him ought to be limited, are reflected in the texts dealing with his *dolus. Dolus* is a delict, and we are told that if a slave's *dolus* arises in connexion with an affair which gives an *actio de peculio,* the *actio doli* is *de peculio,* but otherwise it is noxal[8]. A master suing can be met by an *exceptio doli* for what his slave did, but only if the transaction, in which it was done, was that now sued on, and was one in which the slave was employed. If indeed it was a *peculiare negotium* then it is immaterial when or in what connexion the *dolus* was committed[9], and the same is true if the slave was his master's *actor,* i.e. one who had a general authority to act on his behalf[10]. We are also told that we may have an *exceptio doli* for the act of our own slave, (so far is he from binding us,) *et de eorum dolo quibus adquiritur*[11].

A few other illustrations may be given of the principle that the slave's intervention in a transaction, which was not his, does not bind his master. Money lent by a slave can be validly repaid to him[12], even though it was *dominica pecunia,* provided that in this case the loan was authorised[13], as otherwise there would have been no alienation of the money[14]. The same rule is laid down for the case of deposit by the slave, or of sale by him. But here it is observed, on the authority of Sabinus, that this is true only if the other party has no reason to think

---

[1] 13. 6. 20.
[2] As to this and the literature, Windscheid, Lehrb. § 401, n. 5.
[3] See especially 13. 6. 10. 1—11.   [4] In. 4. 5. 3.
[5] 4. 9. 7. 4; 47. 5. 1. 5.   [6] Lenel, Ed. Perp. §§ 49, 136.
[7] In *societas,* owing to its confidential nature (17. 2. 63. *pr.*; C. 4. 37. 3) a master who was a *socius* was fully liable for negligence of his slaves, authorised to act, 17. 2. 23. 1.
[8] 4. 3. 9. 4a.   [9] 44. 4. 4. 17.   [10] 44. 4. 5. 3.
[11] 44. 4. 4. 17. This is obscure : the *dolus* must proceed *ex parte actoris* (*h. t.* 2. 2), and the case must be that of a slave in whom other persons have such rights that they can acquire through him, and who is contracting for them with his master.
[12] 44. 7. 14.   [13] 46. 3. 35.   [14] *Ante,* p. 158.

the *dominus* would not assent to such redelivery[1], and doubtless this must be generalised. Payment to a slave is not satisfaction of a condition of payment to the master unless the latter consent[2]. A similar idea governs the rule that if A owes B a *res* under a will, and C gives B's slave the thing, the right under the will is unaffected. There is here, however, another point : *alioquin consequens erit ut etiam si tu ipse servo meo eam donaveris, invito me libereris. quod nullo modo recipiendum est, quando ne solutione quidem invito me facto libereris*[3]. There is no *solutio* without consent of the person entitled[4] : he may be in *mora* for refusing a proper tender, but till he has accepted it there is no *solutio*.

There is not much authority as to acknowledgements and receipts given by slaves apart from *peculium*. We learn that they can novate, by order or with ratification[5], but not without any authority : in that case they acquire a new right to the master, without, *ipso iure*, destroying the old[6]. This is so, whether it was the slave's or the master's contract : in the former case one might have thought that as *solutio* could be made to him, so might *novatio*. But *novatio* is not in fact *solutio* and it requires that the obligation should be in some way altered, and this would be to bind the master, and might prejudice him. Conversely we are told by Gaius that if a slave promises, *novandi animo*, this is a mere nullity : it is as if the stipulation had been a *nullo* and the old obligation is unaffected[7]. This is said quite generally and seems to exclude even the case of *iussum*, and the titles in the Digest and Code[8] dealing with novation do not mention a novatory promise by a slave. The explanation is to be found in the character attributed to promises by slaves, shortly to be considered[9]. In a similar way, though he can take an *acceptilatio*[10], he cannot give one, even *iussu domini*[11].

A slave can give a good receipt for money paid to him[12], at least if he lent the money under authority both to lend and to receive[13], and we may assume, in view of the texts above cited, that the first implies the second, unless the contrary appears.

Thus, apart from special authority, a slave cannot release or vary in any way an obligation he has acquired to his master : *a fortiori*, an obligation not acquired through him[14]. A gave B's slave a mandate to

[1] 16. 3. 11.
[2] 35. 1. 44. *pr.*—3. If a man undertakes to pay to A or the slave of T, the payment may not be to T. So a condition of payment to the *heres* is not satisfied by paying his master.
[3] 30. 108. 1.   [4] *Ibid.*; C. 8. 42. 19.   [5] P. 5. 8.
[6] 46. 2. 16.   [7] G. 3. 176, 9; In. 3. 29. 3.   [8] 46. 3; C. 8. 41.
[9] *Post*, p. 165.   [10] 46. 4. 11. 1.   [11] 46. 4. 22.
[12] 46. 3. 102. 2.   [13] C. 8. 42. 19.
[14] Where A's slave, B, made a contract of maritime loan with X, and X desired a release from some of the obligations, a release or variation agreed to by C, another slave of A, who was to be with X on the voyage, having certain duties, but no contractual powers, was a mere nullity, 45. 1. 122. 1.

pay money which A owed to B. He borrowed it from X. In B's accounts the slave put it down as received from A. X had not lent the money with any special reference to A. A was not released and B had not acquired an *actio mandati* against A through the slave. If it had been expressly lent for the purpose of paying A's debt A would have been released, but would have been liable *ex mandato*[1]. The point is that if the loan was not in pursuance of the mandate it can give no *actio mandati*. At the time the money was attributed to A's debt, it was already the property of the creditor, and though the transaction be, as this probably was, within the slave's general authority, this does not entitle him to give what is essentially a fictitious receipt.

Under what circumstances did a slave's contract bind his master, apart from *peculium*? Obligation was a personal matter. Agency in the modern sense was unknown to the civil law. We know that at civil and praetorian law a slave was *pro nullo*, but that *iure naturali* he was a man like another[2]. Hence the rule: *servi ex contractu civiliter non obligantur, naturaliter obligant et obligantur*[3]. Thus his promise creates a *naturalis obligatio*, but this *obligatio* which, as we shall see later, survives manumission, affects only himself, not his master[4]. Here we are concerned only with the master's liability to action.

Broadly the slave's contract did not bind the master apart from the *peculium* unless it came within certain categories for which the Praetor established actions, *i.e.* unless it was made under *iussum*, or as *magister navis*, or as *institor*, or the master profited. There were, however, some exceptions at least apparent.

(i) In all *bonae fidei* transactions, of the slave, the master was liable *in solidum* for his own personal *dolus*[5]. The rule in *stricti iuris* transactions is not easily made out, owing to the comparative rarity of references to promises by slaves: there is some obscurity as to the effect of *dolus* of the promisor, in general. It is sometimes said that a promise by a slave could not have any specifically civil law effects, and was thus in no way different, at least as far as civil law was concerned, from a mere pact[6]. Upon the texts it seems that, in classical law, the only remedy for *dolus* by the master in such a case was an *actio doli*, the point being that it was the slave's contract and another man's misconduct. In later law an *actio utilis* was, it seems, given against the master[7].

---

[1] 17. 1. 22. 8.
[2] *Ante*, p. 73. Their nullity at praetorian law is only as to their own capacity for right.
[3] 44. 7. 14.   [4] *Post*, Ch. XXIX.
[5] 15. 1. 36; 13. 6. 3. 5. Lenel shews that this did not need a special clause in ordinary *bonae fidei* actions, though it did in *actio fiduciae*. Ed. Perp. § 107.
[6] Accarias, Précis, § 506.
[7] 4. 3. 20. *pr.* (*hortatu tuo* is not *iussu tuo*); 45. 1. 49. *pr.* The present point is not noted by Lenel in his remarks on this *utilis actio*. Ed. Perp. § 102.

(ii) Ulpian tells us that if a slave *quasi tutor egerit*, Severus provided that a *iudicium utile* lay against the *dominus*[1], a variant of the *actio negotiorum gestorum contraria*. The text expresses no limit. But it does not say that the liability was *in solidum*, and it was probably limited, like the other actions on a slave's transactions, to the *peculium*, etc. It may be objected that, if so, it would not have been *utilis*: it would have been simply an *actio protutelae de peculio*, on the analogy of *negotiorum gestio*[2]. The explanation seems to be this. The *actio protutelae* was *fictitia*, though we do not know the exact form[3]. A slave, though capable of ordinary quasi-contractual relations, could not conceivably be a tutor. Thus the fiction which would suffice for a freeman would not serve for the case of a slave. Hence a double fiction and the designation of the action as *utilis*[4].

We pass now to the four actions above mentioned.

A.   *ACTIO QUOD IUSSU*.

By the Praetor's Edict[5] the *dominus* was liable *in solidum* on an undertaking of his slave of either sex[6], made *iussu eius*[7]. No special form of authorisation was needed: it might be general or special[8], by mandate[9] or by ratification[10]. There is indeed one text which seems to suggest that ratification was not enough[11], but it does not say so and another text shews that ratification sufficed[12]. Endorsing the slave's *chirographum* sufficed, and this looks like ratification[13]. The *iussum* is not a command but an authorisation[14], and the majority of the texts speak of it as an authorisation to the third party, not to the slave[15]. There are a few that do not make this presumption, but none expressly contradicts it. It is now almost universally held[16] that a communication to the slave can never suffice to create the liability, unless it involves

[1] 27. 5. 1. 2.   Called in the texts *actio protutelae*, *h. t.* 1. *pr.*, 6, 8.   Ulpian.
[2] 3. 5. 13.   [3] See, however, Lenel, Ed. Perp. § 126.
[4] Cp. Lenel on *A. institoria utilis*.   Ed. Perp. § 102.
[5] 15. 4; 16. 1. 25; C. 4. 26. 13; C. Th. 2. 31. 1.
[6] 15. 1. 27. *pr.*; 15. 4. 2. 1.
[7] G. 4. 70; P. 1. 4. 6; In. 4. 7. 1; D. 15. 3. 5. 2; 15. 4. *pass.*; 16. 1. 25; any contract, even *votum*, 50. 12. 2. 1.   See Sell, Noxalrecht 31. n. 2.
[8] 15. 4. 1. 1.   Thus *mutus* or *surdus* could authorise, 45. 1. 1. *pr.*
[9] 15. 4. 1. 3.
[10] 15. 4. 1. 6.   The language of the text is suspicious: *si quis ratum habuerit...in eos datur*.
[11] 15. 3. 5. 2.
[12] Drechsler (Actio quod iussu, 63 *sq.*) seeks to reconcile these texts, both from the same part of the same book of Ulpian.   He notes that it is not exactly said that ratification is insufficient. But it is clear that this is what the writer means.   It is more likely, in view of the *si quidem...sin vero...si quidem...si vero*, that the words are due to the compilers (see Eisele, Z. S. S. 7. 19 *sqq.*).
[13] 15. 4. 1. 4.
[14] No attempt is here made to fix on the word *iussum* a precise meaning which it shall bear in all its many applications.   See hereon Mandry, Familiengüterrecht, 2. 554 *sqq.*; Roby, Rom. Pr. Law, 2. 122; Drechsel, *op. cit.* 17 *sqq.*   It is not necessarily a mandate, for this implies a desire in *mandator*.
[15] 15. 4. *pass.* and others cited by Windscheid, Lehrb. § 482 n. 6.
[16] Windscheid, *loc. cit.*; Karlowa, R. R. G. 2. 1165.

an indirect communication to the other party. It may be remarked that this requirement of communication to the third party is nowhere expressly asserted[1]. Gaius indeed observes that the third party contracts with a view to the liability of the *dominus*[2]. But it has been pointed out that similar language is used in the case of the *actio de peculio* where knowledge that a *peculium* exists is not necessary[3]. Moreover this communication could not have occurred where the *actio quod iussu* was made possible only by ratification[4]. Such expressions as *iussu domini cum servo contractum est*[5] are common and imply that the authorisation is communicated to the third party. But elsewhere the action is given *si voluntate domini servus emit*[6], and this suggests the other view. The fact that communication occurs in most of the texts shews that this is the usual case but not that it is essential. As this additional liability would hardly be undertaken except as an inducement to the other party to contract, it seems obvious to communicate it to him, but not that this should be essential to liability. In some of the texts which speak of *iussum* to the slave, and are disposed of by Windscheid as implying indirect communication to the third party[7], there is no sign of any such step and their plain sense seems to exclude it.

It may be pointed out by way of analogy that where a *filius familias* or slave acted as a *nauta*, the *paterfamilias* was, by the Edict, liable in *solidum* for his *receptum*, if he received *voluntate eius*[8]. Nothing is said of communication to the *extraneus*. Thus there is nothing improbable in the idea that *quod iussu* was subject to the same rule. And the *deceptio* mentioned in one text was not likely if the *iussum* had been communicated to the third party[9].

The general result is that while the texts leave doubt as to the earlier law, they are clear that, under Justinian, the contractor has the right to *actio quod iussu* if a *iussum* exists whether he know it or not[10]. It would seem to follow that it is not essential that it be known even to the slave[11]. Whether the *iussum* might be a general authorisation to any one to contract, or must have reference to a specific person cannot be said from the texts.

---

[1] Windscheid, *loc. cit.*, cites many texts in the form *iussu domini contractum est*, but this impersonal form proves nothing. Honorius (C. Th. 2. 31. 1 = C. 4. 26. 13) declares, for the case of loans to slaves administering estates away from their master, that there must be express *iussum* to the lender. But this besides being a special case is understood by the *interpretatio* as laying down a new rule. And it is clear that what it is intended to exclude is pretended *iussum* based on words which do not amount to authorisation.

[2] G. 4. 70.   [3] Schlossmann, Kieler Festgabe für Ihering, 229; D. 15. 1. 19. 1, 32. *pr.*
[4] 15. 4. 1. 4, 6.   [5] 15. 4. 4.   [6] 15. 3. 5. 2.
[7] *e.g.* 15. 3. 5. 2; 46. 1. 10. 2; 18. 1. 63. *pr.*; see also 17. 1. 5. 4.
[8] 4. 9. 3. 3.   [9] 14. 5. 4. 5.
[10] The two main texts against the requirement (15. 4. 1. 6; 15. 3. 5. 2) are both suspicious, 15. 4. 1. 4 is not conclusive. The Glossators favoured on the whole the view that communication to the third party was not needed. Haenel, Diss. Domm. 523.
[11] Vangerow thinks (Pand. § 240) that the use of the word *iussum* shews that communication to the slave is what is meant. Drechsler thinks the *iussum* might be to the slave, but the third person must have heard of it. *Op. cit.* 56, 59, 110. *Post*, App. I.

The liability applies only to contracts of his own slave[1], and not of those acquired after the transaction[2], and it is to be supposed that as previous *iussum* is useless here, so is ratification: the reasoning in the text would certainly cover it. There must be express words of authorisation: mere words of confidence and the like do not suffice[3]. Thus becoming surety for the slave did not suffice: this was acting as a stranger, and if the *fideiussio* should be unenforceable, *quod iussu* would not lie[4]. A pupil requires his tutor's *auctoritas*. According to Paul the tutor himself can give a *iussum*, and the action will be given, *quod iussit tutor*, but only if the transaction was for the benefit of the *pupillus*[5]. The reason for the restriction is not clear, in view of the fact that, according to Labeo, the *iussum* of a *curator* of a *prodigus*, *furiosus* or *minor*, and even that of a *procurator*, suffices without this restriction[6]. In the case of *actio institoria*, curator and tutor are on the same level[7]. Paul's view may be an expression of the idea that the contract must have relation to the affairs of the person to be made liable. It is indeed held by some writers[8] that this is the case, but there is little support for this in the texts, this passage not being usually cited in support of it. On the whole it seems probable that it is merely a personal doctrine of Paul.

The *iussum* is revocable in all cases up to the time when the contract is actually made[9]. It does not exclude the *actio de peculio* though *quod iussu* is always better[10]. Like other contractual actions it is available against the *heres*[11], though the *iussum* itself is revoked by the death of *iussor*[12].

The *iussum* must be exactly followed. Thus if a slave, authorised to sell to A, sells to B, the master is not bound[13]. But an act in excess of instructions does not wholly vitiate the transaction: it is valid so far as the authority goes. If a slave, authorised to borrow at 6 %, borrowed at a higher rate, the master owed 6 %[14]. If a slave, authorised to sell for 10 sold for 8, the master could vindicate the thing and there was no *exceptio*, without indemnification[15]. These texts shew no trace of the dispute which existed on similar points in relation to mandate[16],

---

[1] 15. 3. 5. 2.   [2] 15. 4. 2. 2.   [3] C. Th. 2. 31. 1.
[4] 15. 4. 1. 5.   [5] 15. 4. 1. 7, 2. *pr.*
[6] 15. 4. 1. 9.   Not a *procurator voluntarius*.   [7] 14. 3. 5. 18.
[8] *e.g.* Dernburg, *op. cit.* 2. § 14.   See Windscheid, *op. cit.* § 482; Mandry, *op. cit.* 2. 553. Drechsler (*op. cit.* 70, 76, 84) holds that there must be a reference to the concerns of *dominus*; he relies on 15. 4. 1. 5, which however only means, as it says, that *fideiussio* is not *iussio*. He seems to regard the action as excluded *because* the *fideiussio* is void: the exclusion is *although* it is void. The objection is that the state of mind is different; there is no intent to adopt the contract as his own.
[9] 15. 4. 1. 2.   [10] G. 4. 74; In. 4. 7. 5.   [11] C. 4. 35. 8.
[12] 46. 3. 32. *in fin.*   We are not told the effect of insanity. Probably the analogy of mandate sufficed.
[13] 18. 1. 63. *pr.*   Nor by a pledge in an authorised contract, unless this too was authorised, 15. 4. 3.
[14] *Ibid.*   [15] 17. 1. 5. 4.   [16] G. 3. 161; In. 3. 26. 8.

though the reasoning which guided those, who there took the view that it was void, would apply equally here: *nam qui excessit aliud quid facere videtur*[1]. Here the dispute is between the principal and the third party, while in mandate it is between the principal and his agent: the matter is not mentioned in the few texts we have dealing with the action *ad exemplum institoriae*, brought by the third party against the principal[2]. This, however, scarcely seems material, and the difference, so far as it goes, supports the view that the *iussum* need not be known to the third party. His state of mind is not material: what matters is that the *dominus* has declared his willingness to accept a certain obligation[3].

The transaction must be by the slave: a *dominus* borrowing and directing the money to be paid to a slave is liable directly and not *quod iussu*[4]. In one text the separate individuality of the slave is very clearly brought out[5]. If he is in partnership, *iussu domini*, the latter's liability is *quod iussu* with no limitation to *quod facere potest*. He is not the partner, and this defence is not available to anyone else, even heirs or other successors. It is however indifferent[6] whether the transaction be in the master's affairs, or connected with the *peculium*[7].

B.   *ACTIO INSTITORIA*.

This action is given by the Edict[8] against a *dominus* or *domina* who appoints a person of either sex, slave or free[9], to manage a business[10]. It applies to all transactions of the business, and is *in solidum, quasi iussu*[11]. The *institor* may be a *servus alienus*[12], but, if he is, the liability is not accompanied, as in the case of *servus proprius*, by acquisition of all the rights also. These vest in the true *dominus* and the transfer of them, or their results, can be obtained by an *actio negotiorum gestorum contraria*[13]. Thus where A appoints B's slave, A will be liable to the present action and B will, or may, be liable to the *actio de peculio*[14]. The liability rests on the *voluntas* of the *dominus*[15], and thus if a son or slave appoints an *institor* without actual consent of the *paterfamilias*, the latter is liable only to an *actio institoria de peculio*[16]. The liability is perpetual and extends to the *heres*[17].

---

[1] 17. 1. 5. *pr.*
[2] *e.g.* 3. 5. 30. *pr.*; 14. 3. 5. 8, 16, 19. *pr.*; 17. 1. 10. 5; 19. 1. 13. 25.
[3] Cp. 4. 3. 20. *pr.* where there was no such declaration. Mandry, *op. cit.* 2. 565 *sqq.*, takes a different view.
[4] 15. 4. 5.   [5] 17. 2. 63. 2.
[6] *Ib.*; 15. 3. 5. 2; 15. 4. 1. 1, 5; 16. 1. 25, mostly cited Vangerow, Pand. § 240.
[7] As to formulation, *post*, App. II.   [8] 14. 3.   [9] 14. 3. 7. 1, 8.
[10] 14. 3. 1: as to different sorts of *institores*, 14. 3. 5, 16; P. 2. 8. 2. See also Mayer, Actions *Exercitoria* et *Institoria*, 25—32.
[11] 12. 1. 29; P. 2. 8. 1.   [12] P. 2. 8. 2.
[13] 14. 3. 1.   For a case in which he is the slave of the other party, see 14. 3. 11. 8.
[14] 14. 3. 7. 1, 17. 1.   [15] 14. 1. 1. 20; C. 4. 26. 1, 6.   [16] 14. 1. 1. 20.
[17] 14. 3. 15.   It is not affected by freeing the slave: if he continues to manage the business, no new appointment is needed, 14. 3. 19. 1.

A *pupillus dominus* is liable if he appointed *auctoritate tutoris*, or if *locupletior factus*, the liability in that case having an obvious limit. Apparently on such points the rules are as in the *actio quod iussu*[1]. On the death of the appointer, the *heres* is liable, and will be liable, if he allow him to continue his management, for future transactions[2]. As to transactions, *vacante hereditate*, the *heres*, even *impubes* or insane, is liable to any creditor who did not know of the death[3], and, according to one text, even if the creditor did know[4]; the reason assigned being *propter utilitatem promiscui usus*. The fact that *actio institoria* is available does not bar other actions to which the transaction may give a right, *e.g. redhibitoria*[5]. But if rightly brought it necessarily excludes the *actio tributoria* since, while that refers necessarily to *res peculiares*, this refers to *dominica merx*[6].

The liability is only on those transactions connected with the business to which the man was appointed[7]. This rule plainly leads to a number of distinctions. Thus one appointed to buy cannot so bind his master by selling, and *vice versa*[8]. But a loan, for the purpose, to one appointed to buy, was enough, and if the creditor knew that the loan was for the purpose of the business, he need not see that the money is so spent[9]. A loan of oil to one appointed to deal in oil is good[10], and, generally, if a transaction is within the scope of the employment a pledge or security in connexion with it is good and imposes on the master the liabilities of a pledgee[11]. Where A was appointed to two distinct functions, to trade in oil, and to borrow money, and X lent him money in view of the first business, but it was not received for that purpose, X sued on the assumption that it had been so received, but failed as being unable to prove this point[12]. Novation of the obligation destroys the *actio institoria*, the *obligatio* being no longer that contemplated by the appointment[13].

The liability may be limited in various ways. Thus a number of *institores* may be required to act together[14], or dealing with a particular person may be prohibited by notice to that person[15], or they may be required to contract only with security[16]. But the exception based on such prohibitions may be met by a *replicatio doli*, ·if the defendant do not offer what might have been recovered by the *actio de peculio et in rem verso*[17]. Any other conditions imposed on the power

[1] 14. 3. 5. 18, 6, 9, 10, 17. 2.   [2] 14. 3. 17. 2.
[3] 14. 3. 5. 17, 17. 2.   [4] *h. t.* 17. 3.   [5] *h. l. pr.*
[6] 14. 3. 11. 7.   *Post*, App. II.
[7] 14. 3. 5. 9—11; G. 4. 71; In. 4. 7. 2, not confined to operations in any one place, 14. 3. 18.
[8] 14. 3. 5. 12.   [9] 14. 1. 7. 2; 14. 3. 5. 13.   [10] 14. 3. 5. 14.
[11] If *arrha* was taken and not returned by an *institor* to sell, the master was liable, *h. t.* 5. 15, 16.   An *institor* appointed to lend does not necessarily bind his master by becoming surety, but if instead of lending money to A he promises it to A's creditor, this is good, *h. t.* 19. 3.
[12] 14. 3. 13. *pr.*   As to the point of *litis consumptio* raised by the text, see *post*, App. II.
[13] 14. 3. 13. 1.   [14] *h. t.* 11. 5.   [15] *Ib.*; *h. t.* 17. 1.
[16] *h. t.* 11. 5.   [17] *h. t.* 17. 4.

of contracting must be observed: just as they might be barred from contracting with a person or class, so their contracts might be limited to dealings with a person or class. If these restrictions are repeatedly changed, in such a way that contractors are deceived, they do not protect[1]. In like manner the liability may be limited, or barred, by notice over the shop door[2]. This must be plain and in a conspicuous place, and couched in a language locally known[3]. But if it is duly set up it is immaterial that a contracting person did not see it[4].

The liability of the *institor* does not concern us. Of the master's right against a third party it is enough to say that in late law the principal acquires rights of action against the other party to the contract, though the *institor* be not his own slave, or even not a slave at all, provided there is no other way of recovering[5]. But he always has an action of mandate, or *negotiorum gestorum*, against the *institor* for cession of his actions and against his master if he was a slave. In this case it may be only *de peculio* if the slave offered his own services. If he should be the slave of the other party, the *dominus* is not directly liable, since the contract is made with his own slave. But he can be sued *de peculio*, as on the mandate given to his slave, or *de in rem verso*, for the price which he owes to his own slave[6].

Lenel[7] holds that the action for the case where the *institor* is a slave is properly called *utilis*: the primary action being that for the contract of a *liber homo*. He accounts for the fact that it is not so called in the Digest on the ground that it was the commonest case, and he shews a text of Julian, in which the word *utilis* does survive[8]. This case is however exceptional on other grounds: the *institor* is the slave of the other party. Lenel sees in this not the original cause of the epithet *utilis*, but the cause of its retention in the Digest. The point is not very material in substantive law, but the fact that the *dominus* is acquiring by his contract with his own slave, a right against a third person, is, as Lenel himself notes, a reason for hesitating as to whether the action was the normal *actio institoria*. He observes however that Ulpian tells us that it is a sale[9], and thus would satisfy the Edict, which gave the action on actual legal transactions alone. But he does not note that this question was in dispute. Paul, and even Ulpian himself in the case of a son, say definitely that such a transaction was not a sale[10]. They are writing long after Julian. It is thus easy to see why

---

[1] *h. t.* 11. 5.   [2] 15. 1. 47. *pr.*; 14. 3. 11. 2.
[3] 14. 3. 11. 3. If illegible from any cause, or removed by principal or anyone so that it could not be seen, the action was not barred, *h. l.* 4.
[4] *h. l.* 3.   [5] 14. 3. 1, 2.
[6] 14. 3. 11. 8, 12. It is a *vicarius* who is appointed. As to the resulting questions see 14. 1. 5. *pr.* The matter is fully discussed, *post*, Ch. x.
[7] Ed. Perp. § 102.   [8] 14. 3. 12.   [9] 14. 3. 11. 8.
[10] 18. 1. 2; 18. 2. 14. 3.

he calls the action in this case *utilis*.   In the next text[1] another exceptional case is considered, and there too Julian is cited as holding that, though on the facts the *actio institoria* was excluded by consumption, an *actio utilis* lay.   Here too the *institor* was a slave.   This is hardly a likely form, if the action lost had also been an *actio utilis*, and the explanation which Lenel offers for the other text, (this one he does not note,) namely that Julian's language has been freely altered, seems hardly sufficient.   On general principles it seems unlikely that the action which was primary in importance, and in all probability first in time[2], would be called *utilis*.   Nor does the fact, probable in itself, that the *actio* was *fictitia* require that it should be called an *actio utilis*.

So far the rules of the action are fairly simple, but there is one point which has been the subject of much controversy.   It is the question whether, and if so, how far, the fact of the appointment, and the pertinence of the contract to the business, must be known to the other contracting party[3].   It is clear that if the fact of the appointment and the relevance of the contract are known, the action lies in the absence of special restrictions, proper steps to secure the publication of which must have been taken[4].   But no text anywhere hints that it is an essential of liability that the third party know of the appointment, and when it is remembered that the rules relate to continuous commercial enterprises, it seems far more probable that there was no such requirement, but that the setting up of a man in trade, and so inviting people to deal with him, imposed on the principal the Edictal liability. This is confirmed by the words of Ulpian upon the *actio exercitoria* which is governed by the same principles: *igitur praeposito certam legem dat contrahentibus*[5].   It is the appointment, not notice, which creates the situation contemplated by the Edict.   Moreover, unless the *praepositio* bound, without express notice, it is difficult to see how Ulpian should have thought it worth while to say: *Conditio autem praepositionis servanda est: quid enim si certa lege vel interventu cuiusdam personae vel sub pignore voluit cum eo contrahi vel ad certam rem? Aequissimum erit id servari in quo praepositus est*[6].   On the whole the better view seems to be that the agency need not be communicated.

But the attention of commentators has been mostly turned to the other part of the question: was it necessary to the liability that the

---

[1] 14. 3. 13. *pr.*   [2] See the opening words of 14. 3.   Mayer, *op. cit.* 36.
[3] See Karlowa, R. R. G. 2. 1128; Schlossmann, Kieler Festgabe für Ihering, 217 *sqq.*
[4] *Ante*, p. 171.   [5] 14. 1. 1. 12.   See also 4. 4. 4.
[6] 14. 3. 11. 5.   The same result follows from another remark of Ulpian's, that the *actio institoria* is less necessary than the *exercitoria*, since in the former case the customer has always time to make any enquiry he thinks fit as to the status of the other party, and contract accordingly, while in dealing with shipmasters he has often to act in haste without inquiry.   14. 1. 1. *pr.* See also 14. 3. 5. 13, C. 4. 25. 5.

third party should have known that the contract related to the business to which the *institor* was appointed ? The dominant view is that this too was necessary, that it was not enough that it had to do with the business, but the parties must have also contemplated this. Karlowa[1] supports this view, partly on the ground that the words, *si eius rei gratia cui praepositus fuerit contractum est*[2], must grammatically mean " with a view to," and not merely " within the scope of." He adds that any other view would make the principal liable if the *institor* contracted only on his own account. The intent of the *institor* to act for the business is thus necessary, and this could have no meaning unless it were communicated. All this is of doubtful force when it is a question of a piece of positive legislation. Mandry[3], taking the contrary view, denies that *eius rei gratia, nomine, causa*, need bear the meaning for which Karlowa contends, but rests his case mainly on the texts. Those that have played a part in the controversy are set forth by Schlossmann[4]. They are not conclusive either way. He observes of the texts[5], that one[6] has no relation to the action, that the force of another depends on taking *lex* to mean a condition of which notice is given, which it does not imply[7], that of another the force depends on understanding *permisit* to mean " expressly authorised," which it need not mean[8], that in another[9] there was in fact no existing authority, and that in the others the transaction is of an ambiguous nature[10]. Of the texts cited in reply[11] one shews that there was no communication of the agency, and that this of itself is plainly not regarded as fatal to the action[12].

It may be observed that the arguments, in favour of the view that the agency must be communicated, seem to confuse two things ; intent to contract in view of the agency and intent to contract in relation to the business to which the agent was appointed. Thus Karlowa[13] infers from *eius rei gratia* that the contract must have been made with the *institor*, as such. But the *res* is the *negotiatio*, not the *praepositio*, and even on his own narrow interpretation of the words, they can mean no more than that it was with a view to that trade and they need mean no more than that the matter must be connected with the business. Thus the text lends no support to Karlowa's thesis. It should also be noted that the two principal texts[14] relied on by the supporters of this view go no further. They both speak of dealing with express reference to the *negotiatio* : they say nothing of the *praepositio*. The right conclusion seems to be that it was necessary to shew that the transaction

---

[1] *Op. cit.* 2. 1128, 9.   [2] 14. 3. 5. 11.   [3] *loc. cit.*
[4] Kieler Festgabe für Ihering, 219 *sqq.*   [5] As to G. 4. 70, *ante*, p. 167.
[6] C. 5. 39. 3.   [7] 13. 1. 1. 12. It seems to mean the contrary.
[8] 14. 3. 5. 9. Nor is the impersonal form conclusive.   [9] *h. t.* 5. 17.
[10] 14. 1. 1. 9; 14. 1. 7. *pr.*   [11] 14. 1. 1. 7; 14. 3. 5. 16—7. *pr.*, 13. *pr.*, 19. *pr.*
[12] 14. 3. 13. *pr.*   [13] R. R. G. 2. 1128, 9.   [14] 14. 1. 1. 9; 14. 1. 7. *pr.*

was with reference to the business to which he was in fact *praepositus*.
In most cases this needed no proof—*res ipsa loquitur*. But some transactions were ambiguous : a loan of money to a shopkeeper may not be
meant for any purpose connected with the shop. For the lender to be
entitled to the *actio institoria* he must be able to shew that it was.
This he may do by shewing that it has been applied to shop purposes
or that its application thereto was expressly contemplated[1].

C. *ACTIO EXERCITORIA.*

On nearly all points of principle which concern us, this action is on
the same footing as that we have been discussing. It is a praetorian
remedy modelled on the *actio institoria*, and therefore later, though it is
described as even more necessary[2]. The general principle is that the
person who is receiving the profits of a ship, (whether the owner or not,)
called the *exercitor*[3], is liable *in solidum* on the contracts of the person
placed in command of the ship, (who is called the *magister navis*,)[4] if
the ship was to serve a commercial purpose and the contract was within
those purposes for which he was appointed[5]. The purposes covered
money lent for the purposes of the ship, even though not so used, if the
creditor took care to see that it was reasonably necessary, and proportionate to the needs[6]. Authority is the limit of liability. *Voluntas*
of the *exercitor* must be shewn, not merely *scientia*[7]. Thus if the ship
carried goods of an unauthorised class, or was otherwise used for an
unauthorised purpose, or was let, without authority, the action was not
available[8]. If the borrower of money did not say it was for the ship,
and meant fraud *ab initio*, there was no remedy against the *exercitor*[9].

A *magister* must be in command of the whole ship[10]. If, however,
there are several with undivided functions, the contract of any binds
the *exercitor*: if they are of divided functions, *e.g.* one to buy and one
to sell, each binds only within his scope[11]. Their power may be so
limited that all must act together[12]. A contract by one of the sailors
does not give rise to this action : they are not authorised to contract[13].
The liability covered, however, *ex utilitate navigantium*, the contracts of
a deputy appointed by the *magister*, even though the *exercitor* had

---

[1] 14. 3. 17. 3. So substantially Schlossmann, *loc. cit.* For similar case, *post*, p. 183. The
Edict as restored by Lenel says nothing of notice (Ed. Perp. § 102), but elsewhere L. argues in
favour of the existence of this requirement. See *post*, App. i.
[2] 14. 1. 1. *pr.*; C. 4. 25. 4. But the relative dates of introduction of the aedilician actions are
very uncertain. Mayer, *op. cit.* 18—25.
[3] 14. 1. 1. 15.   [4] 14. 1. 1. 1.
[5] 14. 1. 1. 3, 7. *Magister* might be male or female, slave or free, *proprius* or *alienus*, even an
impubes, D. 14. 1. 1. 4.
[6] 14. 1. 1. 7, 9. Or a loan to pay a debt incurred for such a purpose, *h. l.* 11.
[7] 14. 1. 1. 20, 6. *pr.*   [8] 14. 1. 1. 12.   [9] 14. 1. 1. 9—10.
[10] 14. 1. 1. 1.   [11] *h. l.* 13.   [12] *h. l.* 14.
[13] *h. l.* 2. In delict the rule was different. *Ib.*; 4. 9. 7. 3; *ante*, p. 122.

forbidden this, or any, deputy. In this point this action differs from the *actio institoria*[1], but the rule shews how little agency in the modern sense had to do with the matter.

The action is *perpetua*, is available to and against the *heres*, and is not lost by death or alienation of the slave[2]. The case of my slave who is your *magister* gave rise to questions as in the *actio institoria*. I have an action against you if he contracts with me. But the *exercitor* has no direct action against one who contracts with his *magister*, who is not his slave. We saw that in the *institoria* this was allowed only as a last resort[3]: here it exists only, *extra ordinem*, at the discretion of the *praeses*[4]. His remedy is to claim cession from his *magister*, by action *ex conducto*, or *ex mandato*, according as the man was paid or not, and in the case of a *servus alienus* this will be limited to the *peculium* unless the master was privy to the appointment[5].

The *exercitor* himself may be man or woman, *pater* or *filius*, slave or free[6]. If he be a slave or *filius familias* the *paterfamilias* is liable *in solidum*, if the *exercitio* is *voluntate eius*[7]. There is mention of a difference between this, and the rule in *institoria*, due to the greater importance of the present case. But in fact the text[8] lays down the same rule for both, *i.e.* that if it is *voluntate*, the liability is *in solidum*, but if only *sciente domino*, it is either *tributoria* or *de peculio et in rem verso*[9]. If such an *exercitor* is alienated or dies, the liability continues as in the case of a *magister*[10], and is not subject to an annual limit, as *de peculio* is[11], but this rule applies only where it is not in fact itself an *actio de peculio*, as we have seen it may be[12].

A further complication arises if my slave is *exercitor* and I contract with his *magister*. I can have no *actio exercitoria*, but if the *magister* is free I can sue him[13], and, if he is a *servus alienus*, his owner. In like manner if a *filius familias* appoints a *servus peculiaris*, or a slave a *vicarius*, as *exercitor*, the *paterfamilias* is liable only *de peculio* unless he approve, in which case he is liable *in solidum* whether the contract is with *exercitor* or *magister*, the *filius* who appointed being also liable[14]. The liability on contracts of the *exercitor* also in such a case is insisted on, though the Edict speaks only of the *magister*. What this action on the contract of the *exercitor* would be is not clear. It is not stated as an equitable extension of the *exercitoria*: it seems more probable that it

---

[1] 14. 1. 1. 5.   [2] 14. 1. 4. 4.
[3] *Ante*, p. 171.   [4] 14. 1. 1. 18.
[5] 14. 1. 5. *pr.*; *h. t.* 1. 18; 14. 3. 1, 11. 8, 12.
[6] If a free *pupillus*, enrichment or *auctoritas tutoris* is needed, 14. 1. 1. 16, 19, 21.
[7] *Ibid.*; 4. 9. 7. 6.   [8] 14. 1. 1. 20.
[9] 14. 1. 6. *pr.*; 14. 1. 1. 22; and see n. 6.   [10] 14. 1. 4. 3.
[11] 14. 1. 4. 4.   [12] 4. 9. 7. 6.
[13] 14. 1. 5. 1. The case of his being appointed *exercitor* by another is not considered.
[14] 14. 1. 1. 22, 23; 14. 1. 6. *pr.* *Tributoria* if *sciens* but not *volens*.

was an ordinary *actio quod iussu,* and that the text supports the view
that knowledge of the authority was not necessary in that action[1].

D. *ACTIO DE IN REM VERSO.*

This, as we know it, is not strictly an independent action. It is
always found combined with the limitation to the *peculium,* and is thus
a clause by way of *taxatio* inserted in the *condemnatio* of the action,
whatever it may be. It expresses the rule that, on a slave's transaction,
a master is liable, even beyond the *peculium,* to the extent to which he
has profited. But as the liability has its own rules it can be conveniently considered by itself.

The general principle is that a *dominus* is liable on the contract of a
servus so far as the proceeds have been applied to his purposes[2], irrespectively of consent or even knowledge[3]. The action is not subject to an
annual limit, on the death of the slave, and is available against the
heres[4] of the *dominus.* It is regarded as the owner's personal
liability, and it is considered in the action before the question of
peculium[5].

The main question is: what is *versio* ? We are told that a *versum* is
what is handed to the master or spent on purposes necessary or useful
to him or ratified by him[6], or disposed of at his orders however
wastefully[7], or, generally, used in such a way as would give a *procurator*
a right of action[8]. The texts give us many illustrations[9]. To spend
the money in a normal way on the master's property is a *versio,* but not
useless and unauthorised ornamentation of his house[10]. Money paid to
a creditor of the *dominus* is a *versum*[11], even, it seems, where the creditor
is the slave himself, since a debt due from the master to the *peculium*
is, in the developed law, a burden on the *peculium*[12]. An acquisition
may be in part *versum,* and so subject the *dominus* to this liability only
in part[13]. Thus, if unnecessary slaves are bought as necessary, they are

---

[1] Of several *exercitores,* each is liable *in solidum* (14. 1. 1. 25; *h. t.* 2, 3), whether one is
magister (*h. t.* 4. *pr.* 1) or they have appointed another, slave or free, 14. 1. 1. 25, 4. 2, 6. 1 (and
thus if one of them contracts as customer with the *magister,* he has *actio exercitoria* against the
others, 14. 1. 5. *pr.,* perhaps *utilis, arg.* 14. 3. 11. 8, 12). But if they are actually working the
ship together each is liable only *pro rata.* Where each is liable *in solidum,* there is adjustment
by *pro socio.*
[2] 15. 1. 1. 3, or *ancilla.* 15. 3. 1. *pr.,* 7. 4; C. 4. 25. 1, 2; In. 4. 7. 4; P. 2. 9. 1.
[3] 15. 3. 5. 1; C. 4. 26. 3; Greg. Wis. 9. 1.   [4] 15. 2. 1. 10; C. 4. 26. 7.
[5] 15. 3. 1. *pr.*; In. 4. 7. 4.   No liability for interest, apart from promise.
[6] 15. 3. 5. 2, 7. 1.   [7] *h. t.* 3. 6.   [8] *h. t.* 3. 2.
[9] 15. 3. *pass.*; In. 4. 7. 4; P. 2. 9.
[10] 15. 3. 3. 2, 4.   In the last case the creditor may take the things away so far as is possible
without damage. Money used about the household, perfumes used by the slave in a funeral in
which the *dominus* was interested, these are *versa*; *h. t.* 3. 1, 3, 7. 3, In. 4. 7. 4. If your slave
sells me an inheritance belonging to you and you take it away after I have paid a creditor, I can
recover the amount as a *versum,* 15. 3. 7. 4.
[11] *h. t.* 3. 1, 10. *pr.* In. 4. 7. 4, even a supposed creditor, if it is recoverable by *condictio
indebiti h. t.* 3. 1.
[12] *e.g., h. t.* 7. 1.   [13] *h. t.* 10. 4; In. 4. 7. 4.

versi for value, but not for price[1]. A let a farm to his slave, and gave
him oxen. These being unfit, he told him to sell them and buy others.
The slave sold and bought, but did not pay, having wasted the price
received. The new oxen being in the possession of the *dominus*, the
vendor had the *actio de in rem verso* for the difference between the
value of the new oxen and the price paid for the old[2]. A slave owing
his master money borrows and hands the money to his master: this is a
versum so far as it exceeds the debt. So far as it does not exceed the
debt it is not a *versum* whatever else it may be, even though borrowed
at the master's advice[3].

The money would usually be received under express contract[4], but
this is not essential: *negotii gestio* is enough[5], and even *condictio
furtiva* lies for what a slave has stolen, so far as it is *versum*[6]. The fact
that there is another remedy is no bar: money is lent to the slave
of a *pupillus* by the slave of one who. is absent *reipublicae causa*, the
tutor signs and makes himself personally responsible. Nevertheless if
the money has been devoted to *res pupillares*, this action lies[7].

It is essential that there actually have been a *versio*. The slave's
statement that he is going to apply the thing to his master's purposes
does not make the latter liable: the creditor should see that it is so
applied, or rather, not applied to anything else[8]. You gave silver to
my slave, and he was to make you a cup, not necessarily out of that
silver. He made a cup out of my silver, gave it to you and died.
Clearly I could vindicate the cup. Nor was there any *versio*. So far
as appears the silver you gave had been devoted to no purpose of mine.
Mela was of a different opinion, because, it seems, of the right to
vindicate the cup. But this could give only an *actio de peculio* on the
slave's contract[9].

It is essential that the property remain *versum*. All that this means
is that payment to the master may cease to be *versum*, if it be handed
back to the slave's *peculium*[10]. It has no relation to the actual preservation of the thing: though that be lost by accident, it is still *versum*[11].
A slave borrows money to buy clothes: the price being paid, the lender
has *de in rem verso* though the clothes perish. If the price is not paid,

---

[1] *h. t.* 5. *pr.* See also *h. t.* 12.
[2] *h. t.* 16. See also 14. 3. 12; 5. 3. 36. *pr.* If I buy a *hereditas* from your slave, the price to
be set off against his debt to me, whatever of the *hereditas* reaches you is *versum*, 15. 3. 7. 4;
see *post*, p. 183, and Mandry, *op. cit.* 2. 497. If my slave pays me money, borrowed, and so
induces me to free him any excess in the money over his value is *versum*, 15. 3. 2, 3. *pr.*
[3] 15. 3. 10. 7; 4. 3. 20. *pr.*
[4] *e.g.* 15. 1. 36.   [5] 3. 5. 5. 8.
[6] 13. 1. 4. If a slave cheated a minor, *domini causa*, and the minor obtained *restitutio in
int.*, there was *de i. r. v.* 4. 4. 24. 3.
[7] 15. 3. 20. 1.   [8] 15. 3. 3. 9.
[9] *h. t.* 7. 2.   [10] *h. t.* 10. 6.
[11] 15. 3. 3. 7, 8. A slave borrowed for his master, not for the *peculium*. The money was lost
in the slave's hands, it was still *versum*, 15. 3. 17. *pr.* See, however, Dernburg, Pand. § 14, n. 8.

and the money is lost, and the clothes are in use in the family, both creditors have the action, as also if both money and clothes have perished[1]. This is Ulpian's view, and in accord with principle: for the time being, both were *versa*, and the destruction of one or both makes no difference. But, in the next text, Gaius[2] says the *dominus* is not liable to both; the first person who sues gets the benefit, on some obscure principle of fairness. This application of the rule, "first come, first served," is isolated: it disturbs the principle that the loss should lie where it falls, and that destruction of the *versum* is immaterial[3].

The rule that the *versio* ceases if the thing return to the *peculium* is illustrated in several texts. If the master hand back the money to the slave it is no *versum*, even though the slave lose it, and do not pay the creditor, and even though the master knew this to be the likely result, though here there would be *actio doli*[4]. If the *dominus* pay the *versum* to a creditor it is still a *versum*, unless it were to a creditor of the *peculium*[5]. A slave who had borrowed on his master's account lent the money to X, also on his master's account: it was still *versum*. But the *dominus* can free himself by ceding his claim against X, since the *nomen* against X is the form the *versum* now has[6]. If the *versio* has once ceased by any form of merger in the slave's counter debt, it does not revive, if that debt is paid[7]. Conversely it must be noted that some forms of *versio* are in their nature indestructible[8].

It is usually said that *versio* is enrichment[9], but this needs some limitation or explanation. An addition to the *peculium* is an enrichment of the master, but it is not a *versio*[10]. The law regards the *peculium* as distinct from the master's property: that only is a *versio* which increases the latter fund[11]. The expression, *locupletior factus*, is commonly used to express the condition of liability resulting from enrichment[12]. It is not used in this case in the formal statement of the obligation[13], though it is incidentally[14]. Moreover the case differs from ordinary cases of liability resulting from enrichment, in that destruction or loss by accident does not destroy the right to recover[15], as it does in other cases[16]. When

---

[1] 15. 3. 3. 10.   [2] *h. t.* 4.

[3] It must be remembered that the whole theory starts from the single word *versum*. It is probable that the words from Gaius are misapplied by the compilers.

[4] 15. 3. 10. 6. The payment to the slave must have been to repay him: a casual gift even of the same amount would not destroy the *versio, h. l.* 7.

[5] 15. 3. 1. 2.

[6] *h. t.* 3. 5. If the master has a *versum* through a particular slave, who is or becomes indebted to him, the *versum* is reduced by the amount of the debt, though there be in the *peculium* enough to meet it, *h. t.* 10. 7, 8.

[7] *h. l.* 9.

[8] *e.g.* money paid to creditor, or in perishables which are consumed, *h. t.* 3. 1, 3. 6—10, 17. *pr. etc.*

[9] Windscheid, Lehrb. § 483; Dernburg, Pand. 2. § 14; Mandry, *op. cit.* 2. 467 *sqq., etc.*

[10] 14. 3. 17. 4; 15. 3. 2, 5. 3, 6.

[11] *h. t.* 3. 5, 11. Some texts confuse this distinction, but raise no real difficulty. See *h. t.* 1. 1, 19.

[12] 3. 5. 36. *pr.*; 12. 6. 14; 50. 17. 206.   [13] 15. 3. 1. *pr.*   [14] *e.g.* 14. 3. 17. 4.

[15] *Ante,* p. 177.   [16] 3. 5. 36. *pr.*; 5. 3. 36. 4, 40. *pr.*; 11. 5. 4. 1.

it is remembered that the principles of this action are developed by the jurists from the scanty words of the Edict[1], and are governed by those words, it will not seem strange that its rules should not exactly square with those of the *iure civili* remedy for causeless enrichment. So far the matter seems fairly plain. We have now to consider some controversial points.

We have seen that if a slave has expended money in a way which would give an *extraneus* an action on *negotia gesta*, this is a *versio*[2]. This may be read as expressing a limit : it is very widely held that it does, and that the principle governing the action is that it lies, then, and then only, when a free person would have an *actio* on the *negotium gestum*[3]. But this idea seems to have been struck out to explain one or two awkward texts, which can, however, be far better explained without this doctrine, which raises more difficulties than it settles, so that on the whole the modified theory of enrichment, which also has many supporters[4], is to be preferred. But strictly it is not possible to fit in the texts with the theory appropriate to any other remedy or claim. *Versio* is a conception by itself: in the hands of the jurists, it seems to have meant embodiment in the *patrimonium* as opposed to the *peculium*. The *gestio* theory fails in conciliating the texts : the enrichment theory nearly succeeds. The chief texts are the following. A slave makes a present to his master, out of the *peculium*. This is not a *versio*. So says Ulpian[5], and this text is taken as an authority for the *gestio* theory. But the context shews that the reason why it is not a *versio* is that, in the writer's opinion, the *dominus* is not enriched. It seems to mean that the thing is still a *res peculiaris*, and that the transaction is on the same footing as the case where the master sells a *res peculiaris* and keeps the price. This is a *dolo malo* removal from *peculium*, and so leaves its amount unaltered as against creditors[6]. In the immediately following text a slave borrows money from an *extraneus* and pays it to the master *donandi animo*, not intending him to be a debtor to the *peculium*. This is a *versio*. This is irreconcilable with the *gestio* theory, and also with the text just cited, if it is explained in terms of that theory. But the texts adjoin and are from the same pen. The point is that the present transaction is wholly independent of the *peculium*[7].

---

[1] Lenel, Ed. Perp. § 104.   [2] 15. 3. 3. 2, 5. 3, 17. *pr.*
   [3] See the literature cited by Windscheid, *loc. cit.* n. 5; Karlowa, R. R. G. 2. 1156; Von Tuhr, *Actio de in rem verso*, holds a variant of this view. *Post*, p. 185. Similar words in 47. 8. 2. 23 clearly do not express a limit, cp. *h. l.* 24.
   [4] *e.g.* Mandry, who cites (p. 454) the earlier literature; Dernburg, Windscheid, *locc. citt.*
   [5] 15. 3. 7. *pr.*
   [6] The text expresses the mutual independence of *peculium* and *patrimonium*. A slave, even with *administratio*, could not reduce his *peculium* by *donatio*. *Post*, p. 204. As an act of the slave the gift is null: as an act of the master it is a dolose withdrawal; in either view it is still in the *peculium* and so not *versum*.
   [7] 15. 3. 7. 1. Von Tuhr, *op. cit.* 198, explains it on the ground that the *animus donandi* supervenes after the acquisition, and holds that this does not affect the creditor's right.

A slave borrows money to procure his freedom. He pays it to his master and is freed. There is a *versio* as to any excess in the loan over his value. This is clear apart from the *gestio* theory, but cannot be reconciled with it[1]. A slave pays a master's debt with money he has borrowed, he himself being indebted to the master at the time. There is a *versio* of the difference. If he was not indebted to the master, and the latter reimburses him, the *versio* ceases, but if the master's payment to him were not by way of reimbursement, but independent gift, the *versio* is not affected[2]. The text is a long one and discusses the reasons: it speaks of nothing but enrichment.

One text raises a difficulty. A father owes money: the *son* promises it and is sued. This is a *versio*, so that if the son does not pay the father can still be sued, "unless the son in taking over the obligation intended a gift to the father." This is exactly in point, for it makes the right depend on the son's having a claim as *negotiorum gestor.* But the words are in a *nisi* clause, of suspicious form[3], and it must be remembered that in Justinian's time a son's finances constituted for practical purposes a distinct estate. If he gave *donandi animo,* it was as if a stranger had done so.

The fact that the jurists do repeatedly refer to the principle of *gestio* is explained when we note that, as Windscheid observes[4], the text which states it[5] most fully is considering what amounts to the necessary enrichment. From this point of view the use of the conception of *gestio* is clear. A man has the *actio de in rem verso* when there would have been an *actio mandati* or on *negotia gesta,* if it had been done by one acting with the intent needed for those actions: whether in the actual case it was done with that *animus* is immaterial. There, as here, the action lies, though the benefit conferred is destroyed by accident. There, as here, the action does not lie if the expenditure is of a useless nature, with whatever intent it was made[6].

Mandry[7] distinguishes between "direct" *versio,* where the thing was never *in peculio,* and "indirect" *versio,* where the thing, having been *in peculio,* is transferred in some way to the *patrimonium.* He observes that in several cases of such transfer there is no *versio*[8], and holds that here, (though not in direct *versio,*) there is no claim unless the transfer would have given rise to an action on *negotium gestum,* or the like.

---

[1] 15. 3. 2, 3. *pr.* (considered by Von Tuhr, *op. cit.* 78 *sqq.*). Your slave lets to me a *vicarius*: I make him *institor,* and in that capacity he sells to you. There is a *versio.* But there has been no *gestio* on your behalf, 14. 3. 11. 8, 12. If I give notice to you not to give credit to a certain slave, my *institor,* and you do so, your *actio institoria* against me is barred. But if I have received the thing and do not return it there is a *replicatio doli, i.e.* I am liable for the *versio,* though there is no real *gestio,* 14. 3. 17. 4 ; cp. 3. 5. 7. 3./   [2] 15. 3. 10. 7.

[3] 15. 3. 10. 2. *nisi si donare patri filius voluit dum se obligat.* In this and the adjoining texts some cases of *versio* are discussed which could not arise in the case of a slave. See Mandry, *op. cit.* 2. 502.

[4] *loc. cit.*   [5] 15. 3. 3. 2.   [6] 3. 5. 9 *etc. Ante,* pp. 176, 7.

[7] *op. cit.* 2. 522 *sqq.*   [8] 15. 3. 5. 3, 6, 7. *pr. etc.*

His reasoning seems to be that the right results from the act of the slave—the slave himself would have no claim except in such a case—and the relation of the master to the third party must be governed by the same principle as that with his slave, on pain of "inner contradiction." Apart from this rather doubtful principle, the author finds support in those texts which speak of *gestio* as a basis[1]. But these apply equally to direct *versio*, and there the author admits that they do not set a limit. He relies also on a text[2] which says that if the master adeem the *peculium* or sell it or part of it and keep the price, there is no *actio de in rem verso*. This text is one of those which must be considered later[3], in connexion with difficult questions as to the effect, on the liability *de peculio*, of ademption and sale of the *peculium*. The text following it in the Digest[4] rests the exclusion on the ground that there has been no enrichment. From this and some other texts, it seems likely that all these facts are viewed as not affecting the liability *de peculio* at all : the things are still regarded as in the *peculium*, and the *dominus* is in no way enriched. Thus the text which Mandry cites shews merely that it is difficult to frame a case of indirect *versio* in which there was no debt to the *peculium*.

We have seen that there must be a *negotium* and a *versio*. What is the connexion between the two ? It is sometimes said on the authority of the *gestio* texts, that the *versio* must be an act of the slave's, and it is clear that in the majority of cases it was so, for direct *versio* by the third party, under a contract with the slave, is substantially the same thing. But there is nothing in the form of the edict or the formula so far as we know them[5], requiring or stating any such limitation. And there is one text[6] which gives the action where the master himself applies the thing, and the circumstances shew that it was impossible for the actual acquirer of it, (in the case, a son,) to have been privy[7]. Not a few writers require however a great deal more than this. They hold that there must have been, between the original *negotium* and the ultimate *versio*, what may be called a causal *nexus*. There seems a close connexion between this and what has been called above the *gestio* theory. But in fact it is held by some who reject that theory, and rejected by some who accept it. Karlowa[8], who adopts the *gestio* theory, thinks there was a difference of opinion on the present point.

---

[1] 15. 3. 3. 2, 5. 3, 17. *pr.*   [2] 15. 3. 5. 3.   [3] *Post*, p. 219.
[4] 15. 3. 3. 6.   But the course of thought may not be that of the original writers.
[5] Lenel, Ed. Perp. § 104.   [6] 15. 3. 19.
[7] He was dead. But the text is compatible with the view that the claim rested on right to compensation.
[8] In favour of the requirement, P. 2. 9. 1.   Against, 15. 3. 3. 1, 5. 3, 10. 10.   Dernburg, *op. cit.* 2. § 14, rejects *gestio* as a requirement but requires causal *nexus*.   Windscheid (*gestio*), *op. cit.* § 403, thinks causal connexion not necessary in general.   Von Tuhr, *op. cit.* 193, holding a special form of the *gestio* theory, thinks causal *nexus* needed, but the texts inconclusive.

If the *versio* is direct there is no difficulty[1]. It is only where the thing has been for a time in the *peculium* that the question arises. In relation to this the idea that the creditor must have contemplated the *versio, ab initio,* has little, *a priori,* to recommend it. The claim is a remedy for unfair enrichment and the intent of the third party seems rather immaterial. The Roman law was, perhaps, not liberal in remedies in cases of this kind[2], but here the remedy does exist and there is no obvious reason why it should be so limited.

On the texts however the question is not without difficulty. The majority of them are opposed to the requirement, though it is nowhere expressly denied. In one text Paul quotes from Neratius[3] (in a passage which can hardly be interpolated) the case of a son who bought a *toga*. The son died, and his father applied the *toga*, thinking it was his own, to the purposes of the funeral. The text adds that if the circumstances were such that the *pater* was under a duty to buy a *toga* for the son, the *versio* dates from the purchase; if not, from the funeral. It is clear that this was in the beginning a " peculiar " transaction, and the intent of the creditor was not material. In another group of texts Paul and Ulpian[4], citing and limiting the views of Mela and Pomponius, discuss the case of a son who, having borrowed money, applies it to the *dos* of his daughter or sister. This is a *versio in rem patris,* so far as the father was going to give a *dos,* provided the application was with a view to carrying out a *negotium* of the father but not otherwise. Nothing is said of the intent with which the money was lent: the point of the text is that it might equally well on such facts be a *negotium* of the son's. The text then lays down the same rule for the case of a slave. The form of the addition is against any causal connexion, but the remark may be compilers' work. In many texts, Ulpian in discussing the nature of a *versio,* uses language which seems to exclude the materiality of the creditor's intent[5]. It may be added that the Institutes, which explain the action at some length, say nothing of any such requirement[6]. Less direct evidence is afforded against the need of causal connexion in the texts which make the *versio* déstructible, by the fact that the slave becomes indebted to the *dominus*[7]. Such a rule makes the intent of the creditor a very unsafe protection.

But there are texts the other way. In his Sentences, Paul definitely[8] subjects the right to bring the action to the condition that the money

---

[1] See *e.g.* 15. 3. 7. 4.
[2] Notwithstanding the well-known text: *iure naturae aequum est neminem cum alterius detrimento et iniuria fieri locupletiorem,* 50. 17. 206.
[3] 15. 3. 19.   [4] *h. t.* 7. 5—9.
[5] 15. 3. 3. *pr.,* 3. 1, 5. 2, 5. 3, 7. 3, and especially *h. t.* 10. 10. See also C. 4. 26. 3, 7, 12.
[6] In. 4. 7. 3, 5. See also Greg. Wis. 3. 7. 1, which, like the text in the Institutes, implies that if the facts would give *de peculio,* any later *versio* would give *de in rem verso.*
[7] *e.g.* 15. 3. 10. 6 *sqq.*   [8] P. 2. 9. 1.

was given for the purpose of the *versio*. In the Digest[1] he gives it in a case in which he speaks of the contract as made with this object, as if that were a material factor. These might pass as mere expressions of Paul's preference for subjective tests[2], but there are texts independent of Paul. Ulpian[3], in a case of loan of money, says that there is an *actio de in rem verso* if the money was lent for the purpose. In the immediately preceding text[4] he seems to lay down a similar rule in a case of acquisition of goods. But all that he is there discussing is the question whether, if it is not applied to the master's purposes, the fact that it was given for that purpose suffices to give the action, and he decides that it does not. In another text[5] Africanus seems, though not very clearly, to require it in a case of loan of money. In the next text[6] Neratius discusses a case in which goods have been bought expressly for the *dominus*, and A has become surety for the price. He holds that A has no *actio de in rem verso*, though he pay the price. The actual decision does not here concern us : the point for us is that the intent of A is clearly regarded as material. If now we examine the texts which really treat the intent of the third party as material[7], we shall see that they are, as it seems without exception, cases in which the claimant of the action has paid money. This circumstance seems significant and enough to explain them. What is needed in this action is, as Neratius says[6], identity of what was received with what was *versum*. A payment of money was in itself a colourless thing. It was no easy matter to follow and prove the application of the actual coins, and accordingly some lawyers lay down the rule, (and none deny it,) that if money is lent for the purpose of a *versio*, and the *versio* follows, the identity of the money received with that *versa* is assumed. This view is confirmed by the fact that in the case[8] where the question is whether the lender of money to buy goods, and the supplier of the goods, have both in certain events the *actio de in rem verso*, the text emphasises the need of privity in the case of the lender, but does not mention it in the case of the vendor.

The question of the relation of this action to the *actio de peculio* is one of some difficulty. As described to us, it is not so much an independent action as a clause in the formula of the *actio de peculio*[9], and the question arises whether it had an independent existence; whether

---

[1] 14. 6. 17.
[2] As where he says that if a slave borrows, *ut creditori suo solveret*, this is no *versio* though the *dominus* is released from an *actio de peculio*. The objective fact that it is not applied to any patrimonial purpose is enough to exclude *de in rem verso*, 15. 3. 11.
[3] 15. 3. 3. 10. [4] 15. 3. 3. 9.
[5] *h. t.* 17. *pr.* [6] *h. t.* 18.
[7] P. 2. 9. 1; D. 14. 6. 17; 15. 3. 3. 10; *h. t.* 17. *pr.*; *h. t.* 18. Doubtful: 12. 1. 12; 14. 3. 17. 4. See also 15. 3. 7. 4.
[8] 15. 3. 3. 10. [9] *e.g.*, In. 4. 7. 4 b.

there was such an action which contained in its formula no reference to a *peculium*, and, in any case, whether it could be brought if there were no *peculium*. Von Tuhr[1] holds, as an outcome of his special theory as to the basis of our action, that there could be no *de in rem verso* if there were no *peculium*. He considers its purpose to be to provide for the case where the liability of the *dominus* to the slave is to release him from an obligation, not to pay money. This duty does not admit of exact estimation and so cannot be treated in the ordinary way as an addition to the *peculium*. As there can be no natural obligation to the slave, unless there is a *peculium*, it follows that there can be no *actio de in rem verso*. We shall shortly consider his general theory: here it is enough to say that he has to treat the texts with some violence in order to support this minor part of it[2]. He explains[3] the perpetuity of the action, notwithstanding the ending of "peculiar" liability, apparently by the principle that the liability to the creditor is the primary liability and that subsists: the liability to the slave was little more than a *facultas solvendi*, and that is ended. But it cannot be both an obligation and a *facultas solvendi*, and the rule is in fact in conflict with his general theory[4]. On the whole evidence it seems likely that this action could be brought independently. It is clear that it lay when there was nothing in the *peculium*, for even the *actio de peculio* did[5]. It is also clear that it could be brought when *de peculio* no longer existed, because either the *peculium* had been adeemed without *dolus*, or the slave had ceased to be the defendant's and the year had passed[6]. There are of course many texts which give it without mention of *peculium*, but there is none which unequivocally gives it where there has never been a *peculium*. But all that this shews is that an *extraneus* would not ordinarily trust a slave who had neither a *peculium* nor authority from his master. It may also be remarked that the use of the formula referring to the *peculium*, as well as to the *versio*, no more shews that an actual *peculium* was necessary than it shews that *de peculio* would not lie unless there was also a *versio*. It must not be forgotten that *de in·rem verso* appears as the primary liability.

The *peculium*, as described in the Digest, includes not only

---

[1] *op. cit.* 238 *sqq.*
[2] He cites Baron as holding the same view. See Bekker, Z. S. S. 4. 101.
[3] *op. cit.* 236.
[4] Karlowa thinks there was an independent *de in rem verso*, introduced later than *de peculio*, arguing from the introductory words of D. 15. 1 and 15. 3 (R. R. G. 2. 1154). Mandry takes the same view, *de in rem verso* having a separate basis in enrichment (*op. cit.* 2. 456). Lenel dealing with the question shews that the Edict gave only the one formula (Ed. Perp. § 104). See also Windscheid, *op. cit.* § 483.
[5] 15. 1. 30. *pr.*   But this is not to say that it lay when there was no *peculium*.
[6] 15. 3. 1. 1, 2, 14, as to which last, *post*, Ch. XVI.

corporeal things, but also debts due to the *peculium* from the master. As the subject of an *actio de in rem verso* is also usually the subject of such a claim from the master, and is thus already covered by the *actio de peculio*[1], the question arises: what purpose is served by the *actio de in rem verso*? The point is raised in the title, and it is answered by reference to certain circumstances under which it gives a remedy where there is no *actio de peculio*. Thus it is said that our action is available, though that *de peculio* is extinct, owing to ademption of the *peculium sine dolo*, or death or alienation of the slave, and expiration of the *annus utilis*[2]. But it cannot be supposed that these exceptional cases were the cause of introduction of the action, and indeed the texts shew clearly that this was not so. It is contemplated that, in the normal case, the actions are brought together—the question of *versio* being first considered[3], and it is clear that the *actio de in rem verso* is regarded as giving the plaintiff more than he could have recovered by *de peculio* alone—*proficere ei cuius pecunia in rem versa est debet, ut ipse uberiorem actionem habeat*[4].

The elements of a solution may be found in the answer to certain historical questions. The natural obligation between slave and master is of later introduction than the *actio de peculio*[5], and the *actio de peculio* did not at first cover anything but the corporeal things in the *peculium*. At that stage the *actio de in rem verso* would have the obvious advantage of giving the particular creditor a better claim[6]. When the *peculium* is extended to cover debts to it, this utility is lost, and[7] the subsidiary advantage of perpetuity alone remains. This view is confirmed by the fact that the classical jurists see little use in this action, and, in explaining it, fall back on these subsidiary cases. Von Tuhr, however, while he notes these changes[8], is not satisfied with this explanation. He holds that when debts were included in the *peculium*, the *actio de in rem verso* changed its basis. Instead of resting on enrichment, it came to rest on a liability of the master to the slave, of a kind which could not be added to the *peculium*, because it could not be exactly assessed in money[9]. The case he has in mind is that in which the master's obligation is, not to pay money, but to release the slave from some obligation he has undertaken. This may be done by other means than payment, and at less expense. It cannot be added to the *peculium*, and thus becomes the special subject of the *actio de in rem verso*, available only to the creditor whose property has been *versum*. The application of this theory to the texts, in which it is nowhere

---

[1] *e.g.* 15. 3. 19 *in fin.*   [2] *Ib.*; 15. 3. 1. 1, 2. See *post*, p. 227.
[3] In. 4. 7. 4.   [4] 15. 3. 1. 2.
[5] Pernice, Labeo, 1. 152 *sqq.* *Post*, Ch. xxix.   [6] 15. 3. 1. 2.
[7] For expression and citation of contrary views, Mandry, *op. cit.* 2. 31, 32.
[8] *op. cit.* 259 *sqq.*   [9] *op. cit.* 82.

indicated, and with a number of which it is irreconcilable, involves a great number of emendations and insertions.

The foregoing pages are an attempt to explain the rules of the *actio de in rem verso*, as set forth in the Digest. But even if they be regarded as doing this, it must be admitted that they do not account for all the language of the texts. Thus, to take a single instance, though we have not accepted the *gestio* theory, it is clear that the language of many texts is coloured by it. It is easy to account for this. The task of the lawyers was to define the meaning of the expression *versio in rem* of the Edict. To this end the existing institutions of the civil law, while they gave no sure guide, provided many analogies. These different analogies have coloured the language of the lawyers. The title shews indeed that there were differences of opinion as to the actual rules. How far these differences went, in particular, how far specific views can be associated with individual jurists, is a question too speculative to be here considered. Attempts to answer it have not been lacking, the writer in some cases going into very exact detail[1].

A text in the Institutes[2] tells us that what could be recovered by any of these four actions could also be recovered by direct condiction. This proposition, which has no equivalent in Gaius, has a little support from two texts in the Digest[3], one at least of which has a *prima facie* look of genuineness[4]. As the substantive rights of the parties are not affected, the topic is of small importance to us, though it is of great interest in connexion with the general theory of *condictio*. The text has been the starting-point of a great mass of controversy[5]. Here it is enough to express a doubt as to the classical character of the rule, notwithstanding the reference in one of the texts to Julian[6].

---

[1] See, *e.g.* Von Tuhr, *op. cit.* 287, n. 47.   [2] In. 4. 7. 8.
[3] 12. 1. 29; 14. 3. 17. 4, 5.   [4] 12. 1. 29.
[5] See Mandry, *op. cit.* 2. 326. He cites the earlier literature. See also Girard, Manuel, 668.
[6] 12. 1. 29.

CHAPTER VIII.

THE SLAVE AS MAN. COMMERCIAL RELATIONS. *PECULIUM.*
ACQUISITIONS, ALIENATIONS, ETC.

THE foregoing statement of the slave's various activities, apart from *peculium*, would be very misleading unless it were borne in mind that a slave, in any way engaged in commerce, had, as a matter almost of course, a *peculium*: it was the existence of this which made it more or less safe to deal with him[1]. In essence the *peculium* was a fund which masters allowed slaves to hold and, within limits, to deal with as owners. It was distinct from the master's ordinary property—the *patrimonium*, and though in law the property of the master, it is constantly spoken of as, *de facto*, the property of the slave[2]. It is an aggregate of *res peculiares*[3], which belong to the master[4], and of which the slave is administrator. It is described as *pusillum patrimonium*, and *velut patrimonium proprium*[5]. We are concerned with it as it was in classical and later law, but it may be well to premise a few remarks as to its earlier history[6].

(1) At first it seems to have been unimportant and to have consisted merely of small savings on allowances, and unexpended balances on authorised transactions. But by the beginning of the Empire, it might be of great value, and of any form. It might include other slaves, (one in the *peculium* of another slave being called a *vicarius*,) and the *peculia* of *vicarii* (even *vicarii vicariorum*), land, inheritances, obligations and so forth[7]. The *vicarius* might indeed be more valuable than the principal slave[8]. It might thus reach a very large amount[9].

---

[1] As early as Plautus it seems to have been a mark of bad character not to be so far trusted. Pernice, Labeo, 1. 123.

[2] *Rem peculiarem tenere possunt, habere possidere non possunt, quia possessio non tantum corporis sed iuris est*, 41. 2. 49. 1; 41. 1. 10. *pr.*, 1; G. 2. 86; In. 2. 9. *pr.*   For Talmudic Law, Winter, *op. cit.* p. 51.

[3] 6. 1. 56; *peculiaris* ordinarily means belonging to the *peculium*. In 33. 6. 9. 3 it means "for the use of slaves."

[4] 18. 1. 40. 5.   [5] 15. 1. 5. 3, 39; In. 4. 6. 10.

[6] The following observations on this matter are from Pernice, Labeo, 1. 123 *sqq.*; Mandry, *op. cit.* 2. 22 *sqq.*

[7] 15. 1. 7. 1—5, 57; 33. 8. 6, 25.   [8] 21. 1. 44. *pr.*

[9] As to the origin of the word, Festus, *s. v. Peculium*, Bruns, Fontes, ii. 23.

(2)   Even after it had become possible for the *peculium* to be of great value, it was still employed under the eye of the master: the slave pursued his craft as a journeyman, the master supervising all. But, here too, the manners of the Empire produced a change: slaves are set up in business for themselves. A *peculium* may consist of a stock in trade, *e.g.* of slaves. Commercially the slave appears as quite distinct from his master, with whom he frequently enters into legal relations. We hear of a slave owning a slave in common with his master[1], cultivating a farm of his, *non fide dominica, sed mercede ut extranei coloni solent*[2]. A master leaves to his slave "the money I owe him," and this is valid, being construed *naturaliter*[3].

(3)   There remained another development. If a slave contracted, the right of action was in the master, and was not at first regarded as part of the *peculium*. Gradually however such rights, *in re peculiari*, were regarded as part of the *peculium* for certain purposes, though their realisation would require the cooperation of the master. On the other hand, the slave's debts to third parties were not treated as deductions from the *peculium*, but this turned on considerations connected with the *actio de peculio*, to be considered later. In the same way debts due from the master himself were included, though it is clear that this was a later development[4]. On the other hand, debts due to the master were deducted as against other creditors, for reasons also to be considered later. These debts from slave to master, and from master to slave[5], constituted, when they were recognised, a very important factor in the *peculium*[6]. To say money is owed to or by a slave is in strictness an inaccurate mode of expression: it is the master who can sue, and with certain limitations, be sued. But the usual form of words expresses the fact, with its legal consequences, that the obligation is contracted *servi nomine*[7].

As we shall see later, *peculium* is a collective term: it covers physical things and obligations, and is liable to deductions on account of claims due from it. Thus it has a significance other than that of the specific things which make it up. Moreover it is the whole "property" (*de facto*) of the slave, and thus has at least in form the character of a *universitas*, even, as Mandry says[8], of a *universitas iuris*. But, as he

---

[1] 33. 8. 22. 1.   [2] 33. 7. 20. 1.   [3] 35. 1. 40. 3.
[4] Pernice, *loc. cit.*; Von Tuhr, Actio de in rem verso, 260 *sqq.*
[5] 12. 6. 64; D. 15. 1 has many illustrations. The slave might pay a dominical debt: the master might receive payment of a debt due to the *peculium*, 15. 1. 7. 6.
[6] 15. 1. 7. 7.   Debt between slave and fellow slave, 14. 4. 5. 1.   Debt between slave and *vicarius*, 33. 8. 9. *pr.*
[7] So far as the slave is contemplated as the party, such debts can be only *obligationes naturales.*   G. 3. 119a; D. 35. 1. 40. 3.   *Post*, Ch. xxix.
[8] *op. cit.* p. 18   15. 1. 39, 40; 31. 65. *pr.*

remarks, this conception serves little purpose in this connexion. It is not necessary to the explanation of any of the rules, and indeed the various *universitates* differ so much, *inter se*, that few principles can be drawn from the identification. Nevertheless, in discussing the rules, we shall come upon several cases in which the possibility of a *peculium*, in what may be called an ideal, or potential, form, is material.

The detachment of the fund from the master and establishment of it as a sort of property of the slave, is expressed in a host of rules, some of which may be mentioned here by way of illustration.

Slaves might have procurators to manage affairs of the *peculium*[1]. In the case of claim of a slave, if the slave died, the action must continue, to determine whose was the *peculium*[2]. A stolen *res peculiaris* ceased to be *furtiva* on getting back to the *peculium*, and conversely, if a slave handled his *res peculiares* with fraudulent intent, they did not become *furtivae* till they reached a third person[3]. Upon manumission of a slave, *inter vivos*, whether *vindicta* or informally, he took his *peculium*, unless it was expressly reserved[4]. What passed on such a manumission was merely the physical things: there was no question of universal succession, and thus rights of action did not pass, *nisi mandatis...actionibus*[5]. It does not appear that cession could be claimed as of right, for in one text, in which the point arose, an express but informal gift of the rights of action was ineffective[6]. The principle seems to have been that the presumption applied only to those things of which the slave was in actual enjoyment. As to these it was apparently treated as a case of *donatio inter vivos*, completed by the slave's possession after freedom. In other cases of transfer, however, the *peculium* did not pass except expressly[7]. Even in manumission on death, it did not pass unless it was expressly given; whether it was so, or not, being a question of construction[8]. Thus a gift of liberty with an exemption from rendering accounts was not a gift of the *peculium*. The slave had still to return what he held : he was merely excused from very careful enquiry as to waste, though not as to fraud[9], and he was not

---

[1] 3. 3. 33.　　　　　[2] C. 7. 66. 5.　　　　　[3] 47. 2. 57. 2, 3.
[4] 15. 1. 53; 23. 3. 39. *pr.*; In. 2. 20. 20; C. 7. 23; V. Fr. 261. Very little sufficed for a reservation. Where a slave on manumission was ordered to give in a list of properties in his possession nothing was tacitly given, 23. 8. 19. *pr.* In 10. 2. 39. 4 the *peculium* must have been expressly reserved. The general rule is attributed to Severus and Caracalla, but they were probably confirming a long-standing practice. Pernice, Labeo, 1. 148.
[5] 15. 1. 53.
[6] 39. 5. 35. *pr.* See Schirmer, Z. S. S. 12. 24. As to actions the manumission could be no more than a pact to give. According to the Syro-Roman Law-book (Bruns and Sachau, 196) the presumptive gift was good only against the manumitter: the *peculium* could be claimed by the *heres*. This rule seems to be credited to Theodosius (*ibid.* 89): it does not seem to have been a law of the Empire as a whole. It is connected with Greek law (Mitteis, Reichsrecht und Volksrecht 372—4; 382—4). Diocletian had found it necessary to declare that for no purpose was it necessary that a son of the manumitter should sign the *instrumenta*, C. 7. 16. 32.
[7] As to sale and legacy, 18. 1. 29; 21. 2. 3; 33. 8. 24.
[8] 33. 8. 8. 7; 34. 3. 28. 7; C. 4. 14. 2; 7. 23.　　　　　[9] 30. 119; 34. 3. 31. 1.

released from debts due to the *dominus*[1]. But if he were to be free on rendering accounts, and paying the heir 10, this was a gift of the *peculium*, less that sum[2]. A sum so ordered to be paid as a condition on a gift of freedom, could be paid out of the *peculium* without any direction to that effect, even though the heir had in the meantime sold the man *sine peculio*[3].

The reason for the distinction between the two cases, a distinction of old standing[4], is not stated. The *peculium* is *res hereditaria*[5], and perhaps the governing idea is that the *heres* is not to be deprived by a too easy presumption. In accordance with this is the above rule of the Syro-Roman[6] Law-book: in the place and time at which that rule was law, the presumption, even in manumission *inter vivos*, was only of intent to deprive himself.

It is noticeable that if on such a manumission there was a gift of the *peculium*, the *libertus* had a right to claim transfer of actions, as debts due to the *peculium* were a part of it[7].

There are a number of special rules to consider in the case of a legacy of the *peculium*, either to the slave or to an *extraneus*[8]. *Peculium* is a word with a recognised denotation, and in general means the same whether it is being defined in view of a slave legatee or an *extraneus* legatee or a creditor having claims on it[9]. But as a gift of the *peculium* is a voluntary benefit, the donor can vary, enlarge or restrict it, as he pleases, whereas, when he is being sued on it, there is need of an exact definition of the *peculium*, so that neither party can vary it as against the other[10]. As we have seen, the *peculium* is to a certain extent regarded as a *universitas*: it is conceived of as a whole. Thus a legatee of it might not accept part and reject part[11]. On the other hand, in his action to recover it, he must vindicate the specific things: there was no general action like *hereditatis petitio*, nor indeed a *vindicatio* of the *peculium* as such, as there was in a *legatum gregis*[12]. Again, as in all legacies, its extent is, in part, a matter of construction. Some rules are stated as expressing what is presumed to be the testator's intention. On the other hand, some appear as resulting from the legal conception

---

[1] 33. 8. 23. 2, 3.   [2] 33. 8. 8. 3, 7; In. 2. 20. 20.
[3] 35. 1. 57; 40. 7. 3. 1, 3. 7, 31. 1, 39; C. 4. 6. 9. As to difficulties in connexion with these payments, *post*, Ch. XXI.
[4] C. 7. 23.   [5] 5. 3. 13. 6.   [6] See p. 189, n. 6.
[7] 33. 8. 19. 1. The legacy is a completed gift. If ordered to restore *peculium* he must give everything, not deducting anything for debts due to the master though these *ipso facto* reduce the *peculium*, 40. 5. 41. 8.
[8] Mandry, *op. cit.* 2. 182 *sqq.*; Karlowa, *op. cit.* 2. 1137 *sqq.*
[9] Whether a legatee is claiming or a creditor is suing in respect of it, debts to *dominus* are deducted from the apparent mass, 33. 8. 6. *pr.*
[10] Karlowa observes (*loc. cit.*) that the frequency and form of references to legacy of *peculium* shew that it was common and of scientific interest. In fact the rules in the Digest are a compromise among conflicting tendencies.
[11] 31. 2, 6.   [12] 6. 1. 56; cp. In. 2. 20. 18.

of a *peculium*, even where the result is in conflict with expressed intention.

A legacy of the *peculium* to the slave himself includes all acquisitions up to the time of *dies cedens*, while, if it is left to an *extraneus*, nothing goes to the legatee which has accrued since the death, except ordinary accretions to the *peculiares res*[1]. This distinction is repeatedly credited to Julian, whose influence may be supposed to have converted a common rule of construction into one of law. He regards it as carrying into effect the presumed intention of the testator[2], and thus as liable to be set aside on proof of contrary intent. It does not seem at first sight necessary to appeal to intent, or to the authority of Julian, since in each case the content of the legacy seems to be fixed as it is on *dies cedens*, (which in the case of the slave is the entry of the heir,) and this is the ordinary rule[3]. The text of the Institutes above cited[4] gives this as the reason in the case of the slave. But the case is exceptional. The general rule is designed for specific things, while the *peculium* is a collection, subject to constant variations, of diverse things[5]. Julian's decision amounts to the view that the testator must be regarded as contemplating the *peculium* as a whole, and not the specific things which made it up, at the time when the will was made. The rule he gives then follows, except that it may still be asked: what was the rule when the legacy was subject to a condition so that *dies cedens* was still later? Was the heir, or was the legatee, entitled to additions other than accretions after the death, or entry of the heir, as the case might be? No answer is given, but consistency seems to require that they should go to the legatee, at least in the case of the slave. At the time when Julian wrote, *dies cedit*, in the other case, not at death, but at the opening of the will. If his text has not been altered, the content of the legacy does not depend so far as the *extraneus* is concerned on *dies cedens* at all, and, even though that be postponed, the legatee will not get later additions.

The question arises whether a legacy of *peculium* can be made, by anticipation, at a time when no *peculium* yet exists. The single text[6] says that it is immaterial that there be at the moment *nihil in peculio*. This implies an existing *peculium*, but one either overburdened with debts, or such that at the moment it is without assets, but the text continues *non enim tantum praesens sed etiam futurum peculium legari potest*. This may mean that it is immaterial whether there is any

---

[1] Not, *e.g.*, acquisitions *ex operis*, or *ex aliena re*, gifts, *etc.* 15. 1. 57. 1, 2; 33. 8. 8. 8; In. 2. 20. 20.
[2] *Ibid.* Mandry seems to treat this as Ulpian's gloss, but both Tryphoninus and Ulpian speak of Julian as so accounting for the rule.
[3] 36. 2. 8; In. 2. 20. 17, 20.   [4] In. 2. 20. 20.
[5] Even a *grex*, to which the general rule applied, has a unity very different from that of a *peculium*, In. 2. 20. 18.   [6] 33. 8. 11; cp. 32. 17. *pr.*

peculium at the time, and it is probable that this was the case. We hear of legacies of "all my slaves with their *peculia*[1]," and it is unlikely that a distinction would be drawn excluding those *peculia* which had been created after the will was made. But here another question arises. Legacies of *peculium* seem usually to have been made *per vindicationem*[2], though there are cases recorded of gifts by *fideicommissum*[3]. Principle requires that what is left, *per vindicationem*, shall belong to the testator at the time of testation, and so far as we are expressly told this was departed from only in the case of "fungibles[4]." Accordingly Karlowa[5] holds that a legacy *per vindicationem* of a *peculium* would have failed, before the *Sc.* Neronianum, as to after acquired things, since the texts give no hint of any relaxation in the case of *peculium*. Thus the testator if he wished to ensure the full efficacy of his gift would have to fall back on the form *per damnationem*[6]. Mandry[7], on the other hand, holds that the restriction did not apply, that the *peculium* was considered as a unity, distinct from its content, and that this view, settled in early times, was adhered to in later ages, on grounds of convenience, whatever logical objections might be made to it[8].

In all these rules the conception of the *peculium* as a unity has played a part; but this conception is entirely disregarded when the legatee sues for the property. He cannot bring a general action, but must sue for the specific things[9]. This is easily understood. The unity of the *peculium* is not intrinsic: it depends on its existence as a separate fund in the hands of the slave. When that separation has ceased, as it has in the typical case where the slave is the legatee, it differs in no way from other possessions of the person who has it. This excludes such an action as the *vindicatio gregis*[10], but not an action analogous to *hereditatis petitio*. Such an action would however be an express creation, and apart from the less importance of the case, the analogy is defective. The *hereditatis petitio* was primarily aimed at adverse assertors of the same title[11], a restriction which would make the action meaningless here. And whereas the *heres*, by *aditio*, has become seised of all the rights in the *hereditas*, we know that the legatee of *peculium* has not acquired the rights of action: he cannot "intend"

---

[1] See *e.g.* 30. 52. *pr.* As to contemplation of a future *peculium*, 15. 1. 7. 7.
[2] Mandry and Karlowa, *locc. citt.* [3] 33. 8. 23. *pr.*
[4] G. 2. 196. [5] *loc. cit.*
[6] This is the form Karlowa supposes to be presumed in the texts which make the *heres* and not the legatee liable *de peculio, loc. cit. Post*, p. 231.
[7] *loc. cit.*
[8] The principle itself is no obstacle to a legacy *per vindicationem* of a *peculium*, not yet existing, since its content may have been the property of the testator. But if the strict rule applied, we should have expected the resulting difficulties to have left some mark on the texts, notwithstanding the *Sc.* Neronianum.
[9] 6. 1. 56. [10] 6. 1. 1. 3. [11] 5. 3. 9.

that the *peculium* is his as the heir can say the *hereditas* is his, and the possibility of this assertion is the theoretical basis of the *hereditatis petitio*[1].

We have now to consider how debts due to the *peculium*, and from it, are dealt with. Such debts are of several kinds. There may be debts due from the master, as the result of *negotia* between him and the slave; there may be debts due from him as having recovered from third persons debts due to the *peculium*; there may be debts due from outsiders, not yet recovered. On the other hand there may be debts due to the *dominus* and to other persons in the family, and there may also be debts to outsiders. On each of these cases there are some remarks to be made.

Apart from special questions of construction resulting from exceptional facts, or from the use of exceptional words, a gift of *peculium* means, in general, a gift of the nett *peculium*, *i.e.* the fund which would be available to a creditor *de peculio*. The extent of this will be considered in the next chapter: here it is enough to state the general principle. Debts due to the *dominus* are deducted[2], as also are those due to the *heres*[3], even though, owing to the fact that the gift of liberty was unconditional, he was never *dominus*[4]. In like manner debts to fellow slaves are deducted[5], but not, for obvious reasons, those due to a *vicarius* of the slave[6]. Debts will ordinarily result from *negotia*, but they may not. Thus if a slave has stolen or damaged property of his master, *e.g.* a fellow slave, the damage may be deducted, but only *in simplum*[7].

As the vindication is only of specific things, and the debts are chargeable *pro rata*, the legatee, where there are debts, will be entitled only to a part of the thing sued for. Accordingly we are told that he has a *vindicatio incertae partis*[8], since it cannot be known with certainty, beforehand, how much must be deducted[9]. It follows that before any judgment can be given in this *vindicatio* it must be made clear what the total fund and burdens are, and this difficulty has led to the view that all can be vindicated at once, *i.e.* in one *formula*. But, as Mandry observes[10], trial of all by one *iudex* would serve the same purpose[11].

As in the *actio de peculio*, debts to third persons are not deducted[12]. But inasmuch as the legatee is not always liable as such, the *heres* is not bound to hand over the *peculiares res* till security is given for

1 Mandry and Karlowa, *locc. citt.*   2 33. 8. 6. 1, 5.   3 33. 8. 6. 5.
4 33. 8. 8. 1.   Even money lent after the death but before the liberty took effect, *h. t.* 8. *pr.*
5 15. 1. 9. 3; 33. 8. 8. 2.   6 33. 8. 9. *pr.*
7 33. 8. 9. 1.   No deduction if he damaged himself or diminished his own value, 15. 1. 9. 7; 33. 8. 9. 2, *post*, p. 223.
8 10. 3. 8. 1.   9 33. 8. 6. *pr.*   10 *loc. cit.*
11 33. 8. 6. *pr.*   If the debts were paid the *vindicatio* would be *in solidum*, 33. 8. 22. *pr.*
12 33. 8. 6. *pr.*, 1, 5, 8. 1, 22. *pr.*

debts to *extranei* on contract, or the like, and even on *noxae* which are already *in iudicio*[1].

No right to sue debtors to the *peculium* passes *ipso facto* by the legacy: obligations cannot pass without express cession of actions. It is clear that the legatee can require the *heres* to cede to him the right of action against debtors to the *peculium*, and to pay over to him anything recovered in any such action, and anything he himself owes[2], though the debt accrued after the death of the testator[3]. The texts say nothing of the possible case of natural obligations to the *peculium*, but it must be assumed that if they are in any way paid to the *heres*, he must hand over the money received.

As to debts due from the master there is some difficulty. It is clear that a mere acknowledgment of indebtedness does not create a debt, and gives no right to claim[4]. Severus and Caracalla go further and lay it down that a legacy of *peculium* does not of itself entitle the legatee to claim to have money returned to him which he has expended out of the *peculium* on the master's affairs[5]. This appears to be a rule of construction, resting on no general principle. Accordingly Ulpian observes[4] that there is no reason why he should not have it, if the testator so intended, and he adds that, in any case, he is entitled to set off such a claim against debts due to the *dominus*. And Scaevola appears as holding, in a case in which a slave set up such a claim, and it was proved that it was the settled practice of the testator to refund such payments, that the slave was entitled to recover the money[6]. Here too the decision seems to be one of construction, resting on the proved custom. But Scaevola was writing before the date of the rescript, and it is possible to doubt whether the text is a mere survival, or is preserved by the compilers as expressing a limitation of the rescript on the lines suggested by Ulpian.

In any case, the concluding words of this text, coupled with the fa⌣⌣ that the *heres* must pay over what he owes, and what he has received from debtors to the *peculium*[7], shew that other debts due from the *dominus, e.g.* those resulting from receipt of debts to the *peculium*, can be claimed. The same inference can be drawn from the rule laid down in the above cited case of father and daughter, but it is remarkable that it should not be more clearly expressed[8]. The rule cannot safely be inferred from the general principle that *peculium* is the same, whether

---

[1] 33. 8. 17, 18, *post*, p. 222.   Not on delict not yet before the court: *noxa caput sequitur.*
[2] 33. 8. 5, 19. 1, 23. *pr.*
[3] If a thing *in peculio* were sold to the *heres* the price would presumably be *in peculio.*
[4] Where a father had been in the habit of allowing his daughter money, and had not paid it on a certain occasion, the fact that he had entered it as due did not give the daughter, legatee of her *peculium*, the right to claim it, 33. 8. 6. 4.
[5] *Ib.*; In. 2. 20. 20. *in fin.*			[6] 33. 8. 23. 1.			[7] See n. 2.
[8] n. 6. See Mandry, *op. cit.* 2. 188 *sqq.*

it be the subject of a legacy or of an action, for it is precisely in relation
to these additions to the "peculiar" fund that the resemblance is not
complete[1]. There were many circumstances, under which the removal
of a thing, from the *peculium* to the *patrimonium*, was a dead loss to
the legatee, merely because on the facts there could be no suggestion
of a debt[2]. As it is said by Papinian: *id peculium ad legatarium
pertinet quod in ea causa moriente patre inveniatur*[3].

The conception of *peculium*, as meaning, not exactly the *peculiares
res*, but the nett *peculium*; *i.e.* that proportion of each thing which is
left when deductible debts are allowed for, finds expression in a text
of Ulpian[4]. He considers the effect of a legacy of *peculium non deducto
aere alieno*. He says that such an addition is contrary to the nature of
the legacy, and might almost be supposed to nullify it, but that the
better view is that the gift is good, the addition adding nothing to it:
nec enim potest crescere vindicatio peculii per hanc adiectionem. The
point is that as the legacy is a gift of the *peculium*, which is in fact a
certain proportion of each *peculiaris res*, *i.e.* that left when debts are
allowed for, it can give no more. The addition is meaningless, for there
are no debts to deduct from this, and it might be treated as contradictory, since, if the *adiectio* is given any meaning at all, the gift is to
be one both with and without deductions. It is observed by Mandry[5]
that this shews the conception of *peculium* as nett *peculium* to be not a
mere interpretation of the testator's wish, otherwise the obvious will of
the testator would be allowed effect. And this also appears from
Ulpian's further observation[6], that if the legatee happens to get possession of the whole of a thing, he can meet the heir's *vindicatio* with an
exceptio doli, since his holding is in accord with the testator's wish[7].
The case will be different, as Ulpian notes, if instead of adding those
words, the testator has expressly remitted all debts or has released the
debt, as he could, by a mere admission that there were no debts. Here
there will be no debts to deduct and the legacy will take effect on
the gross *peculium*. The same result would be attained by a legacy of
all the *peculiares res*[8]. Conversely, notwithstanding this rigid interpretation of the word *peculium*, if the *heres* is forbidden to sue a
particular debtor thereto, he will have no right of action to cede and
the *peculium* will be so much the less[9].

---

[1] In legacy there could be no imputations for *dolus*.
[2] A slave was to be free on paying 10 and to have his *peculium*. The 10 were not *in peculio*.
A man agreed with a slave to free him for 10. 8 having been paid he freed him by will, *cum
peculio*. The 8 were not *in peculio*, 33. 88. 5.
[3] 33. 8. 19. 2.   [4] 33. 8. 6. 1.   [5] *op. cit.* 2. 193.   [6] 33. 8. 6. 1.
[7] He does not discuss the case in which the legatee, having received so many things as
amount in value to the nett *peculium*, sues the *heres* for the *incerta pars* of another thing.
Apparently, as there is a legacy of that, he can recover, subject to *exceptio doli*.
[8] 33. 8. 10.
[9] 33. 8. 8. 6. Where the *peculium* was left to the slave, and there was a gift to wife of "all
my *ancillae*," one in the *peculium* went to the slave, 33. 8. 15. Cp. *h. t.* 21; 32. 73. 5. As to

It may be added that, as a matter of construction, a legacy of *servum cum peculio* failed if the slave died, or was freed or alienated before it took effect: the *peculium* being a mere accessory, the gift of it depends on the principal gift, and fails if that does. The case is contrasted with that of a gift of *servos cum vicariis*, or of *ancillas cum natis*. Here the death, etc., of the principal thing will not bar the gift of the others, as they are more than mere accessories. The rule could be evaded by the use of apt words: all that the text says is that the expression *servum cum peculio* is not enough[1].

Any slave may conceivably have a *peculium*, even an *impubes* or a *furiosus*[2]. But on a well-known principle, no liabilities arise on the transactions of *impubes*, save so far as the *peculium* is enriched, and the same is no doubt true in the case of a *furiosus*[3].

It is essential that the *peculium* have been assented to by the *dominus*[4], and thus, though the slave of a pupil or of a madman may have a *peculium*[5], it must be in the first case the result of a concession by the father, and in the second of a grant during sanity[6]; neither the death nor the insanity of the master suffices of itself to destroy the *peculium* if it remains in the hand of the slave. A tutor cannot authorise the grant of a *peculium*[7], or grant one himself by way of *administratio* (the second rule not being expressly stated, but seeming to follow from the language of the texts[8]). This is surprising since the tutor can give *administratio peculii, iussum*, and such authorisation as will give the *actio institoria*, while his knowledge suffices for the *actio tributoria*[9]. Mandry[10] is inclined, doubtfully, to rest the rule on the fact that the concession is in the nature of a gift, and a tutor cannot make or authorise this. He notes that this does not harmonise with the rule that a slave even without *administratio* can give his *vicarius* a *peculium*[11], but adds that the Romans may not have felt this difficulty since they rest the right on a circuitous grant by the *dominus*. The cases of *iussum* and so forth may be distinguished on the ground that they are all interpretations simply of the Edict, while the question whether there is a *peculium* is one of civil law, which, in view of legacies of *peculium*, had its importance apart from the *actio de peculio*, and

---

these and connected texts, *post*, Ch. x. In. 33. 8. 14. Alfenus considers a gift: *servus meus peculium suum cum moriar sibi habeto liberque esto*. He is asked whether the legacy is good since the slave is to have it before he is free. His answer, that the order is immaterial and the legacy good, seems, at least in form, to miss the point. The words *cum moriar*, which can apply only to the legacy, must be ignored to make the gift good. *Post*, Ch. xx.

[1] 10. 2. 39. 4; 33. 8. 1, 2, 3. 4; In. 2. 20. 17.
[2] 13. 6. 3. 4; 15. 1. 1. 3, 7. 3, 27. *pr.*
[3] 15. 1. 1. 4. Immaterial whether owner male or female, *h. t.* 3. 2.
[4] 15. 1. 5. 4.   [5] 15. 1. 3. 4.   [6] *h. l.* 4; *h. t.* 7. 1.
[7] 15. 1. 3. 3, 7. 1.   [8] Mandry, *op. cit.* 2. 73.
[9] *e.g.* 14. 3. 5. 18, 9; 15. 4. 1. 7, 2.   [10] *loc. cit.*; Pothier *ad* 15. 1. 1. 3.
[11] 15. 1. 6.

even before that existed. There still remains a difficulty in regarding the *concessio peculii* as a gift, in view of the restrictions which existed on the slave's power of binding the *peculium* gratuitously[1]. The origin of the rule may perhaps be looked for at a time when such a *concessio* created no obligation, so that there would be no case for *tutoris auctoritas*, when such a thing could not enter into the narrow field of *administratio*, as yet non-obligatory[2], and when the *impubes* as an *incapax* could not be supposed to know whether a slave did or did not deserve the favour.

The concession may be tacit[3]. But there must be more than intent to create a *peculium*: there must be an actual placing of the thing at the disposal of the slave in some way: *desiderat enim res naturalem dationem*[4]. Most of the texts dealing with this matter are concerned with increase of the *peculium* rather than with its establishment, but they may safely, so far, be applied to this. So far as *res corporales* are concerned there is little difficulty. There must be something in the nature of an act of dedication[5], though it may be tacit, as by leaving the things in the hands of a slave, in an inheritance to which one has succeeded[6], the point being that the slave must have control: it must be *re non verbis*[7]. Naturally, not every case in which things are left with a slave amounts to *peculii concessio*. But general knowledge and assent to the *peculium* is enough: if it is the sort of thing the *dominus* commonly allows to be in the *peculium* it is so without his express knowledge in each case[8].

The *peculium* will thus cover not only what the master has given expressly, but also savings out of allowances, trading acquisitions, and gifts by outsiders intended to benefit the *peculium*[9]. It will include the *peculium* of a *vicarius*, which itself may come from many sources[10]. On the other hand, nothing acquired by a *maleficium*, committed against the *dominus* or another, can possibly found, or be in, a *peculium*[11]. And it is important to note that a slave is not, for any purpose, in his own *peculium*[12]. Obviously it may often be a difficult question of fact whether a *res* is or is not in the *peculium*, and whether there is a *peculium* or not[13]. Thus a gift of necessary clothing to a slave does not amount to a grant of a *peculium*, though apparently a gift of clothing, in excess of needs, might be so interpreted. On the other hand, when a slave has a *peculium* his ordinary clothing will be a part of it, but

---

[1] *Post*, pp. 204, 214.   [2] See Cuq, Institutions, 1. 325.
[3] 15. 1. 6, 7. 1.   Karlowa, *op. cit.* 2. 1133.   Mandry shews (*op. cit.* 2. 82) that the slave's consent was not needed.
[4] 15. 1. 8.   [5] 15. 1. 4.   [6] 15. 1. 7. 1.
[7] 15. 1. 4. 1.   It must be clear that the slave is to hold it on his own account, not as caretaker or as managing his master's business, *h. t.* 5. 4.   It would not cover things deposited with him and vindicable by their owners, or things pledged with him even on a debt to the *peculium*, 13. 7. 28. 1; 14. 4. 5. 18.
[8] 15. 1. 49. *pr.*; *h. t.* 7. 2.   [9] 15. 1. 39.   [10] 15. 1. 4. 6; *h. t.* 17.
[11] 15. 1. 4. 2; 41. 2. 24; cp. 41. 3. 4. 7.   [12] 15. 1. 11. *pr.*, 38. 2.
[13] *e.g.* 15. 3. 16.

not such clothing as is merely handed to him to be worn on state occasions or when attending on his master[1].

But a *peculium* may consist of claims as well as of *res corporales*, and it may be created by a gift of *nomina* and nothing more[2]. That these can be only claims from third parties is not absolutely certain on the texts, but Mandry[3] supposes this limitation. Assuming it confined to debts from third persons, the question remains: what is the act of dedication? How do they become so transferred as to be in the *peculium*? Mandry gives the answer, that it is as soon as facts have occurred which would make a payment of the debt or interest to the slave a valid *solutio*[4]. He cites a text shewing that the fact that the transaction was in the slave's name suffices[5].

We have now to consider the conditions under which a thing acquired vests in the *peculium*. From many texts we learn that things are acquired to it, if the acquisition is *ex peculio*, or *ex* (or *in*) *peculiari re* or *peculiari causa*, or if it is *peculii nomine*[6]. These terms seem all to mean much the same thing, but we nowhere have any explanation of their significance. We have therefore to find on the evidence of the texts what the conditions are under which a thing acquired vests in the *peculium*. It may be assumed that the expressed intent of the *dominus* is overruling: if he says it is to be *in peculio*, it is: if he says the contrary, it is not[7]. But apart from this there has been much discussion as to what are the decisive considerations[8]. It is desirable to consider two distinct cases.

(i) Cases of acquisition through a transaction creative of obligation— an "onerous transaction." Here if the thing is acquired through the application of a *res peculii*[9], or earned by labour, and the slave's earnings are to be in his *peculium*, there can be no doubt that the *peculium* is increased by it[10], *i.e.* by the debt so long as it is unpaid, the thing when it is delivered. The same rule applies to acquisitions from actions on delict affecting *res peculiares*[11]. It is held by some writers[12] that the intention of the slave is material. This view seems to rest mainly on the use of the expression, *peculii nomine*, which occurs frequently[13]. Both Mandry and Karlowa are clear that though this intent is necessary it need not be expressed to the third party, though the latter holds

---

[1] 15. 1. 25, 40.   [2] 15. 1. 16. *in fin.*
[3] *op. cit.* 2. 65 *sqq.* He remarks that obligation between slave and master implies *peculium*, that, apart from existing *obligatio* the debt would be unreal, and would consist in mere *verba*, not as principle requires, in *res*, and that this would certainly not suffice to increase an existing *peculium*, 15. 1. 4. 1, 49. 2.
[4] If a slave *expromisit* for a debtor to *dominus*, and the master deducts this in *de peculio*, the debt becomes a *nomen peculiare*, 15. 1. 56.
[5] 33. 8. 26, *post*, p. 199.
[6] For illustrative texts, Mandry, *op. cit.* 2. 118.   [7] 15. 1. 8.
[8] Mandry, *loc. cit.*; Karlowa, *op. cit.* 2. 1134, 5; Pernice, Labeo, 1. 139 *sqq.*
[9] *e.g.* by sale or hire of it, or if it has provided the capital of a *societas*.
[10] *e.g.* 41. 3. 44. 7.   [11] 15. 1. 7. 4, 5.
[12] Mandry, Karlowa, *locc. citt.*   [13] *e.g.* 21. 1. 51; 41. 3. 31. 3; 41. 4. 2. 12.

that it must have been possible for him to know it. Both hold that objective connexion will cause the intent to be presumed. As the *dominus* need know nothing of the matter, the only meaning that the rule can have, is that if the slave selling a thing, for example, in any way announced his intent that the price should be patrimonial, it would not be in the *peculium*. But for this there is no authority, and it is hard to reconcile it with the rule, laid down by Mandry himself[1], that a thing was in *peculio*, if it was so intended to be by the *dominus*, and it was in fact at the slave's disposal whatever his intent. The true result of such a state of things is that the property is still in the *peculium*, but the slave has declared his intent to make a *donatio* of it to his master[2].

(ii) Cases of "lucrative" acquisition. Under what circumstances is a *donatio* or a legacy or a *hereditas* given by another person to the slave, in his *peculium*[3]? It is certain that such a thing might be in the *peculium*[4], and it is a fair inference from some of the texts that in the ordinary case it would be so. Thus we are told that legacies and inheritances are in the *peculium*[5], and that what *officio meruit a quolibet sibi donari* is in *peculio*[6]. A similar inference may be drawn from the texts dealing with gifts by one of common owners to the slave, where it seems to go as of course, though this is not expressly stated[7]. Where a slave receives from an *ancilla* a quàsi *dos* this seems to be an effective transfer from one *peculium* to the other[8]. Again we are told that a dotal slave may have a *peculium, duplici iuris,* and the illustration given is of a *hereditas* left to him, *respectu mariti*[9]. The rule may be brought into harmony with principle by a text which observes that the *peculium* includes not only that to which the *dominus* has assented, but that to which he would assent if he knew of it[10]. But we are also told that, if a *legatum purum* is left to a slave, and he is freed after *dies cedens* he leaves the legacy with the *dominus*[11]. In view of this text, and since a slave freed *inter vivos* takes his *peculium* with him unless it is expressly reserved, Mandry[12] holds that such things are not normally *in peculio* though they may be. But this text is not conclusive, since this tacit passing of the *peculium* is not a rule of law, but only a presumption of intent of the master to disseise himself. And though the

---

[1] See *ante,* p. 197.   15. 1. 4. *pr.*   Cp. 15. 3. 3. 1. *in fin.*
[2] Mandry thinks (*loc. cit.*) that the fact that the thing was acquired by a transaction out of which an *actio de peculio* arose, satisfied the requirement of objective connexion. As he says, in view of the wide range of that obligation, this covers any case of non-lucrative acquisition. The proposition seems to have little real content, since if the master knew nothing of it, his consent would not exist, unless the case were within *peculiaris causa* in the narrower sense. If he did consent it would be within the *peculium,* whatever its origin.
[3] Mandry, *op. cit.* 2. 123 *sqq.*; Karlowa, *op. cit.* 2. 1135 ; Pernice, *op. cit.* 1. 149 *sqq.*
[4] 15. 1. 7. 5, 19. 1, 39 ; 23. 3. 39. *pr.*   [5] 15. 1. 7. 5.
[6] 15. 1. 39.   [7] 15. 1. 16 ; 41. 1. 37. 1, 2, 49.   [8] 23. 3. 39. *pr.*
[9] 15. 1. 19. 1. *Dos* given to a *filius familias* by an *extraneus* is *in peculio,* 24. 3. 22. 12, 25. *pr.*
[10] 15. 1. 49.   [11] 36. 2. 5. 7.   [12] *loc. cit.*

expression, *apud dominum…relinquet,* points to *inter vivos* manumission, the writer no doubt has all cases of manumission in his mind, and in manumission on death the *peculium* does not pass except expressly. On the whole the true view seems to be that such things are in the *peculium* unless the contrary appears.

Apart from these questions as to the nature of the *peculium,* it is necessary to consider some points relative to acquisition and alienation of *peculiares res.* In relation to the *peculium* a slave is allowed, *iure singulari, utilitatis causa,* to acquire possession for the *dominus* without the latter's knowledge[1]. Possession so acquired gives the same right to the master as if it had been acquired by him, at least so far as *usucapio* is concerned: there is no authority as to Interdict. Thus the master has the Publician[2], and, conversely, any *vitium* in the slave's possession affects the master, even ignorant of the possession, and even though the *peculium* have been adeemed[3]. Thus a man cannot usucapt a thing his slave has taken in bad faith[4]. But as the slave's power is purely derivative, it is essential that the *dominus* have the power to acquire; if this is present the *usucapio* is complete without his knowledge[5]. If a *res peculiaris* is stolen from my slave, I reacquire possession as soon as he gets it back, though I do not know it, unless I had in the meantime determined that it was not to be in the *peculium* : in that case as it is not in *peculium,* I do not reacquire possession till I know[6]. The text adds that if my slave lose a (non-peculiar) thing and regain it, I do not repossess till I know. If my slave steal a thing from me and keep it *in peculio,* it is not really a part of the *peculium* : it is a *res furtiva,* and I do not possess it till I begin to hold it as I did before, or, knowing the facts, allow him to keep it in the *peculium*[7].

As to *iura in re aliena,* there is a slight difficulty. We have seen[8] that a legacy to a slave is valid only if it is such that it could take effect if he were free. But we are told that, if a slave had a *fundus* in his

[1] 41. 2. 1. 5, 24, 34. 2, 44. 1. D. 41. 2. 34. 2 does not mention *peculium,* but the restriction is implied. 41. 3. 31. 3 implies that there might be cases in which he might possess *meo nomine ignorante me.* This merely means that *iussum* is as good as knowledge, *ante,* p. 132. (The *peculium* did not include acquisitions from delict so that the rule did not cover these, 41. 2. 24.) The rule is one of mere convenience, though Paul rests it on the idea that previous authorisation (*i.e.* to have a *peculium*) is as good as knowledge (*i.e.* that he has that thing), 41. 2. 1. 5. But that principle applies only where the authority and knowledge apply to the same thing. *Ante,* p. 132.
[2] 6. 2. 7. 10.
[3] 41. 4. 2. 11, 12. Paul, resting on Celsus, says that even *in re peculiari,* if the *dominus* knows that the thing is *aliena* when the slave takes possession, there is no *usucapio* (h. l. 13). Thus *dominus* need not know, but if he does his bad faith is material. The rule may not have been accepted by the Sabinians who first admitted possession of *res peculiares* without knowledge by *dominus* (41. 2. 1. 5). See *ante,* p. 132.
[4] 41. 4. 2. 10. Though it had been conveyed to the master in a transaction with the slave: *causa durat,* 41. 4. 2. 14.
[5] 41. 3. 8. *pr.* So a buyer from a slave can add the vendor's time to his own, for *usucapio, in re peculiari,* 44. 3. 15. 3.
[6] 41. 3. 4. 7; 47. 2. 57. 2.   [7] 41. 3. 4. 9.   [8] *Ante,* p. 150.

peculium, he could acquire a right of way to it even by legacy[1]. The case has already been discussed[2]: it is enough to say that this is only one of a large number of exceptional rules applied *utilitatis causa*[3].

We pass to the law as to alienation of things in the *peculium*. The mere possession of a *peculium* did not in itself increase the slave's power of alienation: the *voluntas* of the *dominus* was still necessary[4]. But the expression of this *voluntas* might take the form of a grant of *plena* or *libera administratio*, which did away with the need of special authorisation in each case[5]. The gift of *administratio* might be expressly enlarged beyond its ordinary limits, or it might be expressly limited, and its extent, in any case, was a question of fact[6]. Apart from such variations the general rule was that *administratio* was necessary for any alienation or pledge[7] of property, and that of itself it did not validate alienations by way of gift[8]. It authorised payment of a debt of the *peculium*, with the effect of transferring the property, discharging the debt and so releasing any surety[9]. Any alienation without, or in excess of, authority was void: it did not give *iusta possessio*, to one who knew of the defect[10]: such a person might indeed be liable for theft[11]. Even a receiver in good faith, though he could usucapt, had no *accessio temporis*[12].

Similar principles apply to matters other than alienation and pledge. A slave's pact that he would not sue was null for obvious reasons. But he could effectively make such a *pactum in rem*, if it were *in re peculiari*, and he had *administratio*, but not *donandi animo*[13]. He could make a valid compromise with a thief, *bona fide*, in the interest of the *dominus*[14]. He could "delegate" his debtor[15], while, as we have seen, without this power he could neither delegate nor novate[16]. He could offer an extra-judicial oath, the taking of which would give the other party an *actio de peculio*[17]. He could himself take the contrary oath, originally offered, or offered back, to him[18].

Some cases need special discussion.

---

[1] 32. 17. 1.   [2] *Ante*, p. 156.

[3] As to contract, it may be added that the rights of action enure to his master, and that, as he does not cease to be a slave by having a *peculium*, he cannot adstipulate, even *in re peculiari*, 15. 1. 41; G. 3. 114. As to *dolus* by slave *in re peculiari* see *ante*, p. 163.

[4] 6. 1. 41. 1; Lex Rom. Burg. 14. 6 (C. Herm. 16. 1).

[5] 15. 1. 46. The expression *libera* adds nothing to the meaning, Mandry, *op. cit.* 2. 103 *sqq.*

[6] 20. 3. 1. 1.   [7] 12. 6. 13. *pr.*; 13. 7. 18. 4.

[8] Even with *administratio* he could not gratuitously pledge a thing for a third person, or release a pledge, or give away anything of the *peculium*, or acceptilate, 20. 3. 1. 1; 20. 6. 8. 5; 46. 4. 22. Of course he could not manumit. C. 7. 11. 2.

[9] 12. 6. 13; 46. 3. 84.

[10] C. 4. 26. 10. The *dominus* could vindicate, 12. 6. 53.   [11] See n. 4.

[12] 41. 2. 14; 41. 3. 34; 44. 3. 15. 3.   [13] 2. 14. 28. 2.

[14] 47. 2. 52. 26.   [15] 15. 1. 48. 1.   [16] 46. 3. 19.

[17] 12. 2. 20, 22, 23.   [18] 12. 2. 25, *ante*, p. 84.

(*a*) Payment of debt. It is clear that this needs authority[1], though, as Mandry points out[2], many texts say nothing of the requirement. But there is a difficulty on one point. In general, if the alienation is not within authority, it is void, and the property, even money, can be vindicated[3]. But in the case of payment of a putative debt by a slave who has *administratio*, but not a power of making gifts, the texts are in conflict. Ulpian, in two texts, discusses the case of a *filiusfamilias* who has repaid money borrowed in contravention of the *Sc.* Macedonianum. In one case the money is vindicable[4]: in the other there is a *condictio*. But the argument leads plainly to a *vindicatio*[5], and the *condictio*, contradicting what the text said, is probably an interpolation. Another case is more difficult. A slave pays *ex peculio* on a surety, in a matter which was no concern of the *peculium*. Papinian, whose hypothesis shews that the slave had some authority to alienate, gives the master a *vindicatio*[6]. Julian gives *condictio*[7]. He does not speak of authority, but other parts of the passage shew that this is assumed. Julian held that alienation needed *administratio*[8], and that *administratio* did not give an unlimited right: he adverts elsewhere to the well-known limit[9]. Mandry[10] distinguishes the texts by the view that *administratio* gave an unlimited right of *solutio ex peculio*. There was a *naturalis obligatio* on the slave[11], and we know, further, that *usucapio pro soluto* did not require a real debt[12]. But this still leaves it an individual view of Julian's since the case in Papinian's text is the same. Moreover Julian arrives at the same conclusion where a slave bribes a man not to inform of a theft by him. On the authority of Proculus he gives no *vindicatio* to the *dominus* but a *condictio*[13]. This is not a *solutio*. Pernice, accepting Mandry's view[14], but observing that the opinion is special to Julian, thinks it is a survival of an old rule that a slave could alienate *res peculiares* without *administratio*, a rule which he thinks may have been cut down by Proculus[15]. He does not advert to the text just cited[13] in which Proculus is playing the opposite part, or to the fact that in the texts of Papinian and Julian there was authority, the only question being as to its extent. The better view seems to be that Julian while excluding *donatio*, contemplates *animus donandi*. This was not necessarily present in either of his two texts[16]. And though he gives a *vindicatio* where a son has lent money, contrary to the *Sc.* Macedonianum[17], it is likely that here there was such an *animus*.

---

[1] *Ante*, p. 201.   [2] *op. cit.* p. 95.
[3] *e.g.* 12. 1. 11. 2; 14. 6. 3. 2; 42. 8. 12; C. 4..26. 10.   [4] 12. 1. 14.
[5] 14. 6. 9. 1.   [6] 46. 3. 94. 3.
[7] 46. 1. 19. The recovery is from the payee, *h. t.* 20. Even if *dominus* had paid, it could have been recovered as an *indebitum*.
[8] *e.g.* 14. 6. 3. 2.   [9] 14. 6. 3. 2.   [10] *op. cit.* 2. 114.   [11] *Post*, Ch. xxix.
[12] See Esmein, Mélanges, 204.   [13] 12. 5. 5.   [14] Labeo, 1. 135.
[15] He cites 46. 3. 84.   [16] 12. 5. 5; 46. 1. 19; cp. 46. 2. 34. *pr.*   [17] 14. 6. 3. 2.

(*b*) Receipt of payment. The receipt of payment has the effect of discharging the debtor, and so of destroying a right of action. It is accordingly held, by some writers[1], that such a receipt requires *administratio*. Logically there is much to be said for this view, but the texts are adverse to it. It is true that Gaius, in a short phrase[2] inserted between two texts of Paul, dealing with an analogous topic, observes that debts may be paid to one who has *administratio*. But this is far from shewing that that is the only condition on which payment can be made to him. Other texts shew that it is not. Where the contract was one which the slave could not have made without *administratio*, texts, referring to *solutio*, refer also to *administratio*[3]. But even here and in the text of Gaius (taken with its context) the point made is that the loan must have been with due authority, not the *solutio*[4]. On the other hand it is clear on several texts that any contract which has been validly made with a slave can be validly performed to him, and not one of these texts speaks of *administratio*. Ulpian says that any "peculiar" debtor can pay to the slave[5], and, elsewhere[6], that a slave's deposit can be returned to him[7]. Thus the true rule is that any contract which the slave could validly make can be performed to him[8]. Some of these contracts need authority, while others do not, but this is material only on the question whether the contract is valid or not. The rule is stated as one of good faith[9], and thus, on the one hand, it does not apply where the person bound has reason to think the *dominus* does not wish the payment to be so made, and, on the other, it does apply in the absence of such knowledge, even though, by manumission of the slave, or otherwise, the whole situation has in fact changed[10].

(*c*) Novation. It is clear on the general tendency of the texts that a slave with *administratio* can novate debts, but not without it[11]. He cannot of his own authority destroy an obligation, and therefore, if he has no *administratio*, his stipulation, while it will on ordinary principles create a new obligation, will leave the old one unaffected[12]. But though the rule is clear, the texts call for some remarks. A novation may be effected in various ways. The texts consider the cases of a stipulation by the slave himself and of *delegatio crediti*. If the

---

[1] Mandry, *op. cit.* 2. 93; Karlowa, *op. cit.* 2. 1132.   [2] 12. 2. 21.
[3] 23. 3. 24; C. 8. 42. 3, *mutuum*.   [4] Cp. 2. 14. 27. *pr.*; 44. 7. 14; 46. 3. 32.
[5] 12. 6. 26. 8.   [6] 16. 3. 11.
[7] So Alfenus (46. 3. 35) and Pomponius (23. 3. 24).
[8] This does not mean that the slave's receipt was good, though the debt was not fully paid, but that the payment was a *solutio*, though made to the slave.
[9] 16. 3. 11.
[10] 12. 6. 26. 8; 16. 3. 11; 46. 3. 32, 35; C. 8. 42. 3. *Post*, p. 205. Mandry recognises the rule (*loc. cit.*) but remarks that it rests on principles independent of the *peculium*. This is true, but it leaves no room for his contrary rule. See above, n. 1. One to whom payment can be made can novate (2. 14. 27. *pr.*; 46. 2. 10). Among exceptions Celsus, Paul and Pomponius mention contracting slaves (2. 14. 27. *pr.*; 46. 2. 25; 46. 3. 19). Since if they have *administratio* they can novate, it is clear that *administratio* is not needed to acceptance of *solutio*.
[11] 12. 2. 21; 46. 2. 25 (*per se*), P. 5. 8, *etc.* Cp. 46. 2. 20.   [12] 46. 2. 16.

"peculiar" debtor promises to a third party, to whom the *peculium* is indebted, the effect is no doubt a *novatio* of the debt to the *peculium*[1]. But if the person to whom he promises is not a creditor of the *peculium*, Gaius tells us that there is no novation, if it was done *donandi animo*, but only if the slave authorised the stipulation as an act of *gestio* for him, so that the *peculium* acquires an *actio mandati*[2]. In the case of a new *stipulatio* by the slave himself, he says that there is a *novatio*, *maxime si etiam meliorem suam condicionem eo modo faciunt*. The use of the word *maxime* makes it uncertain what is the rule the text is intended to state. But it can hardly be that the novatory effect depended on the goodness of the bargain driven by the slave, and the grammar of the clause suggests interpolation[3].

It is clear that *administratio* did not allow *donatio*[4]. Many things are in effect gifts which are not so expressed, and it is not quite easy to tell what was the real principle. There is no reason to think an alienation was bad merely because it was an unwise bargain, or because it became in effect a total loss. But where the transaction was foredoomed to be a loss, because the law forbad recovery, it seems clear from texts already considered[5] that the intent of the slave was not material[6]. As the extent of *administratio* was a question of fact, it might be so wide as to cover *donatio*, and we are told that such an extension did not authorise *mortis causa donatio*[7]. It must also be remarked that *administratio* did not authorise alienation in fraud of creditors[8]. The text, which refers to *filiifamilias* but must apply equally to slaves, is solitary and has some obscurity. The reference is certainly to creditors of the son: we learn that if authority has been given, to do even this, it is as if the father had done it, and action against him is enough, as the creditors of the son are his creditors *de peculio*. The point of the text seems to be that any such alienation (*i.e.* detrimental and fraudulent in intent) was not merely voidable under the Paulian edict, but was void as not within the limits of *administratio*.

The power of alienation does not depend on solvency of the *peculium*. Even though its debts exceed its assets, so that there is *nihil in peculio*, its property is still *res peculiares*, and the foregoing rules apply[9].

---

[1] 15. 1. 48. 1.   [2] 46. 2. 34. *pr.*
[3] The rule presumably is that there was no novation if the terms of the new stipulation clearly involved loss to the *peculium*.
[4] The rule in 39. 5. 7. 3 can hardly have applied to slaves.
[5] *Ante*, p. 202.   [6] See however, Mandry, *op. cit.* 2. 109.
[7] 39. 5. 7. 2, 5; 42. 8. 12. See Mandry, *op. cit.* 2. 110. The rule as to *m. c. donatio* can hardly apply to slaves.
[8] 42. 8. 12.
[9] 15. 1. 4. 5. Alienation under contract may give rise to counter obligations: so far as these are enforceable by action this will be *de peculio*, 21. 1. 23. 4, 57. 1.

The rules as to gift and ademption of *administratio* are not fully stated: it seems that the statement would be but a repetition of the rules in *iussum*. Thus we are told that *tutor* and *curator furiosi* could give or deny (and therefore adeem) it to a slave[1]. From the texts dealing with payment to a slave who has lent, with *administratio*[2], it may perhaps be inferred that death ended the power. Probably the rules of mandate applied.

As we have already seen, a transaction duly entered on by a slave was essentially the slave's transaction whether it was *in re peculiari*, or *in re dominica, iussu domini*. The rules of *administratio* illustrate this, but add no new principle. Thus if a slave had acquired a right, payment, *ex contractu*, to him discharged, whether he had *administratio* or not[3]. Such a repayment could be validly made to him till the *peculium* was adeemed and the payer knew this[4]. It might be done though the master were dead, or the slave sold or freed, unless, in the case of death of the master, his death was known to the payer (the case being similar to mandate), or, in the other case, there were circumstances known to the payer shewing that such payment would be contrary to intent. Such circumstances would be that the slave had been freed *sine peculio*, or that his new master did not wish it[5]. We are however told that if a debtor to the *peculium* paid the slave *fraudulenter*, he was not released. From the context this seems to mean "if he knew the slave was going to commit malversation[6]." It should be added that a stolen or fugitive slave, or one as to whom it is uncertain whether he is alive or dead, did not retain administration[7]. It may be presumed that knowledge of either of these states of fact would invalidate a payment to the credit of the slave.

It remains to consider how a *peculium* may cease to exist. To the existence of it, both intent of the master, and *de facto* control of the slave are necessary[8]. If the one or the other do not exist, there can be no *peculium*. Thus if the master takes a thing away, or expresses his determination that it is not to be *in peculio*, it ceases to be so[9]. And a similar mere expression of intent will suffice to adeem the *peculium* as a whole[10]. It should be noted that ademption does not require that the thing be removed from the custody of the slave.

---

[1] 15. 1. 7. 1, 24.   [2] 46. 3. 32, 35.   [3] *Ante*, p. 203.   Cp. 40. 7. 6. 6.
[4] C. 8. 42. 3.   [5] 46. 3. 32, 35.   As in case of *iussum*.
[6] 15. 3. 10. 6.   *Actio doli* seems more applicable.   [7] 15. 1. 48. *pr.*
[8] *Ante*, p. 196.   [9] 15. 1. 7. 6; 41. 3. 4. 7.
[10] 15. 1. 8.   We shall see (*post*, p. 218) that in the *actio de peculio* this is less important than it seems.

If a thing ceases to exist it is, of course, no longer in the *peculium*. If its destruction gave a right of action, this right is. But if it was by accident, the *peculium* is simply by so much the poorer. Mandry[1] discusses a question which arises from this. If everything in the *peculium* ceases to exist in such a way, has the *peculium* ceased? Many texts speak of a state of things in which *nihil est in peculio*, but, as Mandry shews, this means no more than that the debts exceed the value of the property. If a *peculium* is no more than a mass of *res peculiares*, it can have no real existence, in the absence of any *res*. The correct analysis of the situation would seem to be (and this is substantially Mandry's view), that there is no more than a *concessio* which will be realised as soon as the slave has possession of anything within its terms. Thus, if I tell my slave he may keep his future earnings as *peculium*, he has no *peculium* until, and unless, he has some earnings. The rules of the *actio de peculio* deprive the question of any practical importance in that connexion: it may however have some significance in relation to *legatum peculii*[2].

It may be remarked, then, by way of conclusion, that the *peculium* does not alter the slave's legal character: it implies certain authorities and makes others possible. But he is still a slave, and his faculties are still derivative. No legal process which is closed to the slave with no *peculium* is open to him if he has one, for it must be remembered that novation and delegation are not special processes, but processes devoted to a special purpose. So far as he can take part in a *mancipatio* with a *peculium*, he can without it: it is merely a question of authority[3].

---

[1] *op. cit.* 2. 9 *sqq.*; 163 *sqq.*

[2] *Ante*, p. 191. That a potential future *peculium* could be regarded as existing is clear from 15. 1. 7. 7, at least for later law.

[3] *Ante*, pp. 136, 159. The effect on *peculium* of death of either party or sale or manumission of the slave, is considered in connexion with the *actio de peculio, post*, pp. 227 *sqq.*

CHAPTER IX.

THE SLAVE AS MAN. IN COMMERCE. *ACTIO DE PECULIO. ACTIO TRIBUTORIA.*

A. *ACTIO DE PECULIO.*

WE have seen that the *actio de in rem verso* was one with the *actio de peculio*; *i.e.* that a creditor suing on a slave's contract could claim to be paid out of what had been devoted to the purposes of the master, and, if that did not suffice, out of the *peculium* of the slave in question[1]. The *actio de peculio* can, however, be treated as an independent action of which we can now state, by way of preliminary, the general principles. We know that the *dominus* is liable so far as the *peculium* will go, upon the slave's *negotia*[2], that the action is based on the Edict[3], and that, in point of form, an important characteristic is that the *formula* contains, probably in the *condemnatio*, a limitation or *taxatio*, in the words *dumtaxat de peculio*, or the like.

The liability is in a sense not of the master but of the *peculium*[4]. Though, in view of legacies of it, the term *peculium* must have already had a legal meaning, there can be no doubt that the introduction of this action gave precision to the conception, since the liability is based on the existence and independence of the *peculium*. The practical meaning of this proposition is that it is essential to the claim that there be a *peculium*: if there be none there is no action[5]. It does not depend on *voluntas domini*, and thus it is not barred by the master's prohibition to trade[6], or by the fact that he is a *pupillus*[7]. On the other hand, if there is a *peculium*, the fact that, at the moment, *nihil est in peculio*, does not bar the action: all that is necessary is that there be something at the time of judgment[8]. Other results of the view that it is a liability dependent on the *peculium* may be noted. A *fideiussor* for a *dominus*

---

[1] 15. 3. 5. 2.   [2] In. 4. 6. 10; 4. 6. 36; 4. 7. 4; G. 4. 73; C. 4. 26. 12; C. Th. 2. 32. 1.
[3] C. 4. 26. 12.
[4] Or rather of the *dominus* as holder of the *peculium*. *Ib.*; Greg. Wis. 9. 1. Pernice has shewn (Labeo, 1. 125 *sqq.*) that the development of the action shews that it is not a case of representation: the slave is dealing on his own account.
[5] 21. 1. 57. 1. Apart from *dolus*.   [6] 15. 1. 29. 1, 15. 1. 47. *pr.*
[7] 42. 4. 3. 1. It does not depend on *potestas*, in the sense in which noxal actions do: the only *interrogatio* is, if any, *an peculium apud eum sit*, 11. 1. 9. 8.
[8] 15. 1. 30. *pr.*; 34. 3. 5. 2.

on a liability *de peculio* was liable only *de peculio*[1]. A *dominus* who handed over the *peculium*, without fraud or delay, was entitled to release from a pending *actio de peculio*[2]. But this view of the liability was attained, like most juristic developments, only gradually. Thus a text on *interrogatio*[3] has evidently been handled by the compilers, and that on the liability, though there be nothing in the *peculium*[4], records a doubt. We are told[5] that a creditor *de peculio* cannot get *missio in possessionem rei servandae causa*, if there is nothing in the *peculium*, where a *dominus latitat*, since he cannot be doing so fraudulently as, if the action were tried, he would be entitled to absolution. The case is compared with that of a debtor *sub conditione*, as to whom the same rule is laid down, though he may be afterwards condemned, *iniuria iudicis*. This parallel of Papinian's seems to ignore the rule that the *actio de peculio* lies though there is nothing *in peculio*: it puts on the same level two cases, in one of which the condemnation is lawful, while in the other it is not. The true rule, at least for later law, is that laid down by Ulpian[6], which allows *missio* in such a case, precisely because the question whether there is anything *in peculio* is material only at judgment.

The liability of the master is distinct from the *obligatio naturalis* of the slave himself[7]. Hence arises an important distinction. Apart from questions of fraud, and the like, any transaction of the slave might impose an *obligatio naturalis* on him[8], but it was not every transaction, by which a slave purported to bind himself, that imposed an *obligatio de peculio* on his master. This fact leads some writers to hold that the whole theory of the liability of the master rests on representation of him by the slave. But the texts do not justify this view. A liability which arises, as we have seen, even though this transaction or all transactions were prohibited, can hardly be regarded as representative[9]. No doubt the limits on the master's liability were gradually defined by the jurists, who, reasoning from the scanty words of the Edict, interpreted them in the light of current theories as to the basis of the obligation. The notion of representation had its share in settling the rule that the master was not to be liable on transactions in which neither he nor the slave had any economic interest, but it is not possible to be more precise than this, and there is danger in pressing, beyond the texts, the operation of any one theory, to the exclusion of potential rivals. The needs of trade were more important than any theory[10].

---

[1] 46. 1. 35.   [2] 10. 3. 9.   [3] 11. 1. 9. 8.   See p. 207, n. 7.
[4] 15. 1. 30. *pr.*; cp. 34. 3. 5. 2.   [5] 15. 1. 50. *pr.*
[6] 42. 4. 7. 15; cp. 15. 1. 30. *pr.*; 34. 3. 5. 2.   Similar questions arise as to the *consumptio* of the *naturalis obligatio* by *litis contestatio* in this action.   *Post*, Ch. XXIX.
[7] 15. 1. 50. 2.   [8] *Post*, Ch. XXIX.   [9] See Pernice, Labeo, 1. 125, 129.
[10] Papinian reflects this way of thought: *verius et utilius videtur Praetorem de huiusmodi contractibus non cogitasse*, 17. 1. 54. *pr.*

The transaction giving rise to the *actio de peculio* must be a *negotium*[1]: this action is not the proper remedy for a delict. If a slave inhabits a house from which something is thrown, there is no *actio de peculio*, though, unless the throwing is by the slave himself, there is no noxal action either[2]. But this must be looked at carefully. A delict may give rise to a liability apart from that *ex delicto*, and this, if it is contractual or quasi-contractual[3], gives an *actio de peculio*[4]. It is held by Mandry[5] that the contractual or quasi-contractual character of the obligation constitutes the test of the possibility of the *actio de peculio*. He discusses several apparent exceptions and shews that they have no bearing on the law of this action[6]. But there are some cases which raise difficulty. In one text we are told[7] that where a slave received property in fraud of the payer's creditors without his master's knowledge: *ait Labeo hactenus eum teneri ut restituat quod ad se pervenit aut dumtaxat de peculio damnetur vel si quid in rem eius versum est.* This is delictal: the words *quod ad se pervenit* make the allusion to *de peculio et in rem verso* look like an interpolation[8]. Another text[9], raising the same question, where a slave has received from a *libertus, in fraudem patroni*, remarks: *et mihi videtur sufficere adversus me patremque arbitrioque iudicis contineri tam id quod in rem versum est condemnandi quam id quod in peculio.* Here too the text is corrupt, and contains, in all probability, a new rule of the compilers.

In these cases, where this action is given, but there is no contract, or the like, between the parties, there is a further limitation to the extent to which the defendant *dominus* has benefited[10]. This is, as Mandry shews[11], a mere application of a general rule applicable to all cases in which A is liable to make restitution on what is, in essence, a delict, not his own. It is however immaterial whether the enrichment be to the patrimony or to the *peculium*[12].

If the liability arises out of a *negotium*, the fact that it involves a delict does not of itself exclude the *actio de peculio*, and thus similar facts may give rise to *actio noxalis*, or *de peculio*, according to circumstances. Thus an *actio doli, servi nomine*, will be *de peculio* if the relation in which it arises is one which gives rise to that action, while if the transaction is such as gives rise to a noxal action, the *actio doli* will itself be noxal[13].

1 15. 1. 1. 2.   2 9. 3. 1. 8, *ante*, p. 100.   3 Mandry, *op. cit.* 2. 234 *sqq.*
4 For slaves the chief case is *condictio furtiva*, 13. 1. 4, 19; 15. 1. 3. 12; 19. 1. 30. *pr.* As to its quasi-contractual nature, Monro, De furtis, App. 1. There was *de peculio* on a judgment for a son's delict, based on the contractual view of *litis contestatio*, 9. 4. 35; 15. 3. 11. For this and another case, Koschaker, Translatio Iudicii, pp. 189, 194.
5 *loc. cit.*   6 4. 2. 16. 1; 43. 16. 16.   7 42. 8. 6. 12.
8 Mandry, *loc. cit.*, gives another explanation.
9 38. 5. 1. 22. Mandry does not discuss this text in this connexion.
10 See n. 4.   11 *op. cit.* 2. 239 *sqq.*   12 15. 1. 3. 12; 19. 1. 30. *pr.*
13 4. 3. 9. 4. As to this text see *ante*, p. 118. Further illustration, 4. 9. 3. 3; 47. 2. 42. *pr. Ante*, p. 100.

Some cases give rise to an alternative between our action and noxal surrender, on principles which are not altogether clear. Ulpian[1] cites Pomponius as saying that the action *in factum* against a *mensor* is, in the case of his slave, *magis noxalis*, although the *actio de peculio* is also available. This seems to be a compromise due to the doubtful nature of the relation between the *mensor* and other party, the former being an official, at least in later law, and the relation being not strictly contractual, since the *mensor* is not civilly liable, and there is no *locatio*[2]. Misconduct is in essence delictal, since the action lies only for fraud[3]. It is to be noted that the text gives the choice to the injured party. In another case in which a slave *circumscripsit* a minor and Praetorian *restitutio in integrum* is claimed, Pomponius says[4] that the *dominus* must give back what he received and, *ex peculio*, anything more. If this does not satisfy the claim and the slave was guilty of *dolus* he must be flogged or surrendered. This last clause has rather the look of an addition by the compilers. The case is one of a *negotium* and thus would give an *actio de peculio* but for the fact that the remedy is not an *actio* at all, but a praetorian *cognitio*[5]. The essence of *restitutio* is that each party is to be restored to his original position[6], and the jurist's rule arrives at this, so far as it is consistent with the overriding principle that a slave is not to make his master's position worse[7].

Pomponius mentions a case[8] in which a slave of the *heres* steals a *res legata*, and sells it, and he gives the opinion of Atilicinus that there is an *actio in factum* against the master, claiming either noxal surrender or payment, *ex peculio*, of what has been received on the sale. Here the theft was before entry, otherwise the legatee would have had *actio furti noxalis* and *condictio furtiva de peculio*. The mention of sale is made to exclude the possibility of any contrectation after entry[9]. There is thus no *actio furti* or *condictio furtiva*, since the legatee is not owner, and it is a *res hereditaria*[10]. At the time of the theft there is no contractual or quasi-contractual relation between the legatee and the heir or the slave, so that there is no *actio de peculio*. There is no *crimen expilatae hereditatis*, since the injured person is not the *heres*[11]. The decision is thus a juristic expedient, not very logical, to provide for a *casus omissus* in the law of *expilatio* : it gives the legatee the same compensation, apart from *delict*, as he would have had had he been owner, subject to the further restriction, due to the delictal air of the facts, that the master is not to be liable beyond the value of the slave[12].

---

[1] 11. 6. 3. 6. [2] Though a wage be paid, 11. 6. 1.
[3] *Ib.* [4] 4. 4. 24. 3. [5] *h. l.* 5. [6] *h. l.* 4.
[7] C. 2. 3. 3 *etc.* There is not necessarily any delict in the matter, 4. 4. 16. *pr.*, 24. 1.
[8] 30. 48. *pr.* [9] Cp. 47. 2. 57. *pr.* [10] 47. 2. 69; 47. 19. 3. [11] 47. 19. 3.
[12] Cp. the case of *iniuria, ante*, p. 100. The option is with the owner of the slave: the writer has present to his mind the analogy of a delict by a slave acting under his master's contract. (*Ante*, p. 114.) But here there is no contract by the master, but only a subsequently

As a slave of an *impubes* may have a *peculium*, and the *actio de peculio* does not depend on authority, it may lie against an *impubes*. On the other hand, if the slave is an *impubes*, the action is limited to the extent of enrichment[1], as it would be in the case of contract without *auctoritas* by an *impubes paterfamilias*, and the same rule seems to have applied in the case of an *ancilla* so long as *tutela* of women survived[2]. The ordinary quasi-contractual relations give rise to this action[3]. A man gave his daughter in marriage to a slave, with a *dos* and agreement for its return, as if it had been a deposit, on the death of the slave, the point being that he knew there could be no real *dos*. The money was recoverable by *actio depositi de peculio*, by the daughter, who was her father's heir[4]. This is pure contract, but where a freewoman married a slave thinking him free she could condict the *dos*, *de peculio*[5]. The *dominus* is liable to refund, *de peculio*, what the slave has won in a gambling house: it is not noxal, *quia ex negotio gesto agitur*[6].

Any ordinary *negotium* gives the action[7], but it must be a *negotium* of the slave. This is illustrated in many texts[8] and expressly laid down in the Edict, in the words: *quod cum eo qui in alterius potestate esset negotium gestum erit*[9].

In general the obligation is what that of the slave would be, if he were a freeman[10], and thus[11] it is affected by his acts after the making of the bargain. This would follow from the ordinarily accepted *formula* of the action, which expresses the obligation as that of the subordinate[12], and this seems a sufficient basis, itself resting on the Edict. But Mandry, observing that the same character recurs in other accessory obligations where the *formula* is not so expressed, prefers to rest it on the accessory nature of the obligation[13], the *dominus* being in fact a *defensor*, whose obligation is necessarily the same as that of the principal debtor. As, however, the slave cannot be attacked in any way it is difficult to see *defensio*, and Mandry[14] finds *defensio* not of the slave, but of the *negotium*. But this is fanciful[15]. The obligation starts from the

arising quasi-contractual relation: hence a further limitation to the *peculium*, as a slave may not make his master's position worse.

[1] 15. 1. 1. 4.   [2] C. 4. 26. 11.   Cp. 15. 1. 1. 3, 27. *pr.*; Mandry, *op. cit.* 1. 346 *sqq.*
[3] *Negotiorum gestio* by a slave, or, *in re peculiari*, for a slave, 3. 5. 5. 8; P. 1. 4. 5. A slave acting as tutor, 27. 5. 1. 2; 15. 1. 52. *pr.*, as to which case, *post*, p. 217.
[4] 16. 3. 27.   [5] C. 5. 18. 3.   [6] 11. 5. 4. 1.
[7] Sale, 21. 1. 23. 4, 57. 1; 21. 2. 39. 1; 42. 8. 6. 12. *Locatio*, 14. 3. 12; 19. 2. 60. 7. Deposit, 15. 1. 5. *pr.*; 16. 3. 1. 17, 42. *Commodatum*, 13. 6. 3. 4. *Mutuum*, 4. 3. 20; 15. 1. 50. 3; In. 4. 7. 4. (C. 4. 26. 13 negatives only *quod iussu*, on the facts. Haenel, Dissens. Dom. 198.) *Constitutum* by slave, 13. 5. 1. 3 (as to *constitutum* by master, 13. 5. 19. 2). Pledge or *precarium* to him, 15. 1. 5. 1, 36; 43. 26. 13. *Societas*, 16. 2. 9. *pr.* Contract by slave *exercitor*, 4. 9. 7. 6; 14. 1. 1. 20.
[8] 13. 6. 21. 1; 47. 2. 54. 1, where there would be no difficulty if *de peculio* were available. See also *ante*, p. 207.
[9] 15. 1. 1. 2; In. 4. 7, Rub.   [10] 15. 1. 1. 4; 19. 1. 24. 2.
[11] *op. cit.* 2. 303 *sqq.* He illustrates by cases of *dolus* (4. 3. 9. 4; 13. 6. 3. 5; 16. 3. 1. 42), *culpa* (47. 2. 14. 10, 52. 9), *mora* (22. 1. 32. 3; 45. 1. 49), and destruction of the thing (45. 1. 91. 5). [12] *Post*, App. II.   [13] 45. 1. 91. 4, 5.   [14] *op. cit.* 2. 277.
[15] And it cannot be reconciled with the limitation to the *peculium*.

14—2

words of the Edict and its nature is determined thereby. That the Praetor was guided by the idea of *defensio* is unlikely: he saw that the better class of men honoured the contracts of their slaves by allowing them to fulfil them *ex peculio*, and he voiced popular morality by enforcing this as a legal duty[1].

Logically, acts of the *dominus* ought to be immaterial to the obligation *de peculio*. There is no authority in the case of slaves. In the case of sons the rule is so expressed, and there are evidences of an attempt to get rid of the injustice which must result, if the act of the *dominus* was in any way wrongful[2]. But as the son is liable to an action, the conditions are different from those in the case of a slave. No doubt in an appropriate case there would be an *actio doli*[3]. For *mora*, causing discharge of the obligation, the *actio utilis* would suffice[4], and there seems no reason for imposing any liability at all in respect of *culpa*[5]. The case of father and son is one of solidary obligation: two are liable for the same debt. As it is primarily the debt of the son, the father's liability is accessory, akin to surety[6]. But the slave is not liable to action: the master is not answerable for another's debt: there is no solidarity. No doubt the principles in one case may react on the other, but it is doubtful if the conception of solidarity is of any help in this connexion[7].

The action lies, generally speaking, on any contract of the slave: it need not have been in any close relation to the *peculium*, and on the other hand it need not have had any reference to the *dominus*[8]. This follows indeed from the usually adopted formulation of the action, according to which the master is liable, so far as the *peculium* will go, to the extent to which the slave would have been liable, if he had been free. With this agree the rule that prohibition of this, or all contract, by the *dominus* does not bar the action[9], and the rules as to liability of the alienee, *ex ante gestis*[10]. It would seem also to lead to a liability *de peculio* on contracts made before there was a *peculium*, since in that case too the slave if free would have been liable. On the other hand the conception of the liability, as based on the creation of a *peculium*, is

---

[1] Cp. the discussion in connexion with noxal actions, *ante*, p. 113. No doubt *defensio* is one of the analogies present to the minds of the Jurists who interpret the Edict.

[2] An *actio utilis* is given against him where his *mora* has allowed the obligation to be discharged, *e.g.* by destruction of the thing due (45. 1. 49. *pr.*), and there is analogy for *restitutio actionis*, 46. 3. 38. 4. Fully discussed by Mandry, *op. cit.* 2. 305 *sqq.*

[3] *Arg.* 4. 3. 18. 5—20. [4] See n. 2; 45. 1. 49. *pr.*

[5] M. holds that there was a remedy here too but the texts do not bear this out, *op. cit.* 2. 309 *sq.* As to *dolus* in relation to the fund available, *post*, p. 218, and as to another special case, *post*, p. 219.

[6] Machelard, Obl. Solid. 416; Van Wetter, Obligations, 1. 260 *sqq.*; Mandry, *op. cit.* 2. 288 *sqq.* The point is important in relation to release of one by act of the other.

[7] A slave with authority, but not without, could discharge a debt by payment (*ante*, p. 159) and a slave could take an *acceptilatio* (*ante*, p. 155). His pact, *ne peteretur*, whether *in rem* or in the name of *dominus* was a good defence to an *actio de peculio* (2. 14. 17. 7, 18, 21. 5). And with authority he could *delegare debitorem*, 15. 1. 48. 1. As to novation of his liability, see *post*, p. 216.

[8] 3. 5. 5. 8, 13; 15. 1. 27. 8. [9] 15. 1. 29. 1, 47. *pr.* [10] *Post*, p. 229.

somewhat opposed to this. Only three texts[1] seem to raise the point. One says[2] that an adrogator is liable *de peculio quamvis Sabinus et Cassius ex ante gesto de peculio actionem dandam non esse existimant.* If this refers to contracts by the *adrogatus* it is conclusive for later law, since a *civis sui iuris* cannot have a *peculium.* But it is in direct conflict with the Edict on the matter, which runs: *Quod cum eo qui in alterius potestate esset negotium gestum erit*[3]. This would not cover the case of the *adrogatus,* and the opposition of Sabinus would have rested on more definite grounds. Moreover, one would have expected an analogous rule in the case of a freeman enslaved, *i.e.* that there was a general liability *de peculio.* But what we do find, and we find it in the case of *adrogatus* too, is that the new *dominus* or *pater* is liable to the extent of the *bona* he receives, and there is no word of *actio de peculio*[4]. It appears then that the rule laid down and opposed by Sabinus and Cassius is that if the *adrogatus* had a slave the *adrogator* is liable *de peculio* on his contracts made before the adrogation. This is the rule of the Digest for all cases of alienation, but understood in this sense the text says nothing as to the need of a *peculium* at the time the contract was made. In another text a slave living as a freeman acts as tutor[5]: there is no *actio de peculio.* But this text is so obscure as to be quite inconclusive[6]. The third[7] contemplates a debt from a fellow-slave who acquires a *peculium* only after the *negotium.* But the words *vel prout habebit* are probably an addition by the compilers. On the whole it seems probable, though far from certain, that in view of the form of the Edict, coupled with the fact that there is no text throwing doubt on the inference from it, there need not have been any *peculium* at the time of the *negotium*[8]. If this is so, it must follow that there need be no knowledge that there is a *peculium.* This is indeed clear on other grounds. For though there are several texts which speak of the creditor as contracting in view of the *peculium*[9], there are others the facts of which are such as to exclude this knowledge, and this is not made an objection[10]. And it is impossible to apply the notion of reliance on the *peculium* to the case of *condictio furtiva*[11].

There remains another difficulty to be met in deducing the rules of this action from the words of the Edict. These would lead to the

---

[1] In 15. 1. 47. *pr.*, sometimes cited, there is nothing to shew that the slave had no *peculium.*
[2] 15. 1. 42.   [3] 15. 1. 1. 2.
[4] *Post,* Ch. xviii.   But Mandry understands the text in this sense. *Op. cit.* 2. 133.
[5] 15. 1. 52. *pr.*   [6] See *post,* p. 217, and for a different view, Pothier *ad h. l.*
[7] 15. 1. 7. 7.
[8] See also 15. 1. 27. 2, *cit.* Mandry, *loc. cit.* In 15. 1. 27. 8 Julian may seem to contradict this. But his meaning, as appears from 34. 3. 5. 2, is merely that even if a man cannot recover what he has paid in excess of *peculium,* it does not follow that a co-owner can so pay and charge it against him. See p. 217.
[9] 15. 1. 19. 1, 32. *pr.*   [10] 15. 1. 3. 8, 38. *pr.*
[11] Or where the action is given, *nomine filii,* on *iudicatum* on a claim not enforceable by *actio de peculio,* 15. 1. 3. 11. As to 2. 14. 30. 1, *post,* p. 216.

allowance of the action in every case which satisfied the foregoing conditions, but it is clear that in many cases, in most of which the slave's intervention is essentially *donandi animo,* the action is refused, the cases closely approximating to those which were not covered by a grant of *administratio.* The exclusion is a piece of juristic work, resting for the most part on grounds of equity, not in all cases the same. It was reasonable to protect the master from liability for what were in effect gifts, but it was clear to the lawyers that the Edict did not always protect where protection was needed and a way out was found in such phrases as *verius...videtur praetorem de huiusmodi contractibus servorum non cogitasse*[1]. Other exclusions may be explained as turning on the point that there must be an actual *negotium,* and thus if what is done is a nullity, if done by a slave, there is no *actio de peculio,* even though it would have been valid if done by a freeman. The chief cases are the following:

(a) Transactions involving alienation. The slave's act is void unless it was in some way authorised, and thus the subsidiary rights, such as the *actio de peculio,* will not arise. Thus the action does not lie on unauthorised pledge or *precarium* by a slave[2].

(b) Judicial and quasi-judicial proceedings. As a slave cannot take part in such matters[3], he cannot consent to a reference; any decision on it is null and gives no *actio de peculio.* That this is due to the procedural aspect of the matter appears from the fact that, even though the decision is the other way, the master acquires no right[4]. A similar point arises in connexion with the offer of an oath to the adversary. Either party may, during the procedure, with certain preliminaries, offer an oath to the other party, who will lose the action unless he either takes the oath or offers it back,—*relatio iurisiurandi.* This is called *iusiurandum necessarium* and a slave can have no part in it[5]. But, before litigation, either party can offer an oath to the other, who may take it or leave it, but cannot offer it back in any binding way. If taken, it gives either *exceptio iurisiurandi,* or as the case may be, an action in which the issue is only the taking of the oath. This is *iusiurandum voluntarium.* As it is extra-judicial, there is no clear reason why it cannot be taken or offered by a slave. But it is similar to the other in effect: it is described as being almost equivalent to *res iudicata*[6], and there may therefore be doubt as to whether a slave can take any part in it. It is clear, however, that if a slave takes such an oath, the master has the benefit, so that no procedural objection is felt[7]. Ulpian however holds that if he offer

---

[1] 17. 1. 54. *pr.*
[2] 13. 7. 18. 4; 16. 3. 33. See *ante,* p. 160 and *post,* App. III.
[3] *Ante,* p. 83.
[4] 4. 8. 32. 8; 15. 1. 3. 8.
[5] *Ante,* p. 84.
[6] 44. 5. 1. *pr.*; C. 4. 1. 8.
[7] 12. 2. 20, 23, 25.

an oath and it is sworn there is no *actio de peculio*, as there would be in the case of a son[1]. If the money is not due it is in effect a gift. Paul hints doubtfully at a contrary view. *Quidam et de peculio actionem dandam in dominum si actori detulerat servus iusiurandum. eadem de filiofamilias dicenda erunt*[2]. This, being merely obligatory, would not depend on *administratio*. Again he says: *Servus quod detulit vel iuravit servetur, si peculii administrationem habuit*[3]. The way in which the text is continued from Gaius suggests that Paul did not write it as it stands. There can be no doubt that Ulpian's is the rational view[4].

(c) Promises by slaves. There is difficulty in this case, since texts dealing with such *promissiones* are few. But so far as primary obligations are concerned (*i.e.* apart from surety and *expromissio*) there are several texts which shew that they can be made by slaves, so as to give an *actio de peculio*[5], subject to the ordinary restrictions on stipulation[6]. As they have a power derived from the *dominus* they can even promise in the form: *Spondeo*[7], but as their *sponsis* is void at civil law and gives only a praetorian right of action it is doubted by Gaius[8] whether it can be guaranteed by *sponsor* or *fidepromissor*. But from what has been seen in the case of alienations, and will shortly be seen in the case of surety, it is likely that a promise by a slave made gratuitously, or *donandi animo*, is simply void[9], though this is not expressly stated.

(d) Surety and the like. In the case of *fideiussio*, by the slave, the rule is simple: the transaction creates liability *de peculio*, only if it is *in re domini* or *peculiari*[10], not if it is given in a matter in which neither he nor *dominus* has any interest. There must be a *iusta causa interveniendi*[11]. So also in the case of mandate operating as surety. Any ordinary mandate gives *actio de peculio*[12]. But, in *mandatum qualificatum*, there will be *actio mandati de peculio* if the transaction affects the *peculium*[13], but not for an independent voluntary act of surety[14].

The same principle applies to *expromissio*—à promise by the slave to pay the debt of a third person. This is valid and gives *actio de peculio*, if there is a *iusta causa interveniendi*[15]—otherwise it is a mere

---

[1] 15. 1. 5. 2.   [2] 12. 2. 22.   [3] 12. 2. 20.
[4] In 2. 8. 8. 2 a slave, thought free, gave security *iudicatum solvi*. This was *ante litem acceptam*. If he had been a party to the suit the whole thing would be null: here it is clearly regarded as capable of giving rise to *de peculio*.
[5] 2. 14. 30. 1; 45. 1. 118; 45. 2. 12. 1; 46. 1. 56. 1; 46. 4. 8. 4.
[6] Thus in the case in 12. 5. 5, they would be void.   [7] 45. 2. 12. 1.
[8] G. 3. 119.   [9] 2. 14. 30. 1; 20. 6. 8. 5.
[10] 2. 14. 30. 1; 15. 1. 3. 5, 3. 6, 47. 1; 46. 1. 19—21. 2.
[11] Not so in case of son: his *fideiussio* always bound his *paterfamilias, de peculio*, 15. 1. 3. 9. The slave, says Ulpian, has no power of contract independent of his master: the son has. Thus we do not look behind his contract; we do in case of slave, to see whether it was within his power, 15. 1. 3. 10.
[12] *e.g.* 14. 3. 12. As to mandate to buy himself, *post*, p. 216.
[13] *e.g.* where he gives X a mandate to pay on behalf of a creditor of the *peculium*.
[14] 15. 1. 3. 5—7.   [15] 2. 14. 30. 1.

nullity. But in no case can it produce the usual effect of *expromissio*: it can never novate the existing debt[1]. This is because the slave's promise is at civil law no more than a mere pact: it is not a contract *verbis*, such as novation requires[2], and though it gives an *actio de peculio*, this is because it would have been a contract *verbis* if he had been free[3]. Sabinus[4] seems to have held that the form of words was the material point, and that if they were gone through with a slave, *novandi animo*, the old obligation was ended, whether a new one was created or not. But the other is clearly the better view. However, though it does not novate, it is at least a pact, giving an *exceptio pacti conventi*, if the circumstances are such that an *actio de peculio* is available, since the creditor evidently means to accept this liability instead of that of the debtor[5]. The text adds that the plea is not allowed if he thought the slave free, but this is not because there is no *actio de peculio*, for there may be[6], but because his agreement contemplated a liability in full and this he has not got.

(e) *Slave's mandate to third person to buy him.* Papinian[7] tells us that a slave's unauthorised mandate, for this purpose, is null, and gives no *actio de peculio*. The reason is that the Praetor cannot be supposed to have contemplated contracts of this kind *quo se ipsi mala ratione dominis auferrent*. Diocletian[8] gives a different reason for the rule. He says that it cannot be good *ex persona servi*, since, if he were free, his mandate to buy him would be null, nor *ex persona domini*, since a man's mandate to buy what is his already is bad. Nevertheless, he observes, the resulting sale will be good, and will give the master a right of action, thus presumably subjecting him to *de peculio*. But he is clearly contemplating an underlying purpose of manumission, in connexion with which topic, these texts belong to a group which give great trouble[9]. Ulpian cites Pomponius[10] as discussing the effect of a mandate to buy himself on the understanding that· he· is to be re-purchased. He lays it down that the sale is good if it takes place, but that no action will lie on the mandate to secure either the sale or the repurchase: as to the last case he says: *esse iniquissimum ex facto servi mei cogi me servum recipere quem in perpetuum alienari volueram*.

There are a few texts which suggest that a master is not liable *de peculio* on the contracts of a fugitive who is acting as a free man. The rule would presumably be juristic—based on such considerations

---

[1] G. 3. 176, 179; In. 3. 29. 3; D. 15. 1. 56.
[2] See Machelard, Oblig. Naturelles, 165 *sqq*.
[3] Gaius, in saying that his promise no more novates than if it had been stipulated *a nullo* (G. 3. 179), or by *sponsio* from a peregrine, does not mean that it is a nullity but that it is a nullity for this purpose.
[4] G. 3. 179.   [5] 2. 14. 30. 1.   [6] See below.   [7] 17. 1. 54. *pr.*
[8] C. 4. 36. 1.   [9] *Post*, Ch. xxvii.   [10] 17. 1. 19.

as exclude the action in the class of cases last discussed[1]. But in fact the rule can hardly be so. It is clear that the owner acquires through such slaves[2], and the observation, *aequum Praetori visum est sicut commoda sentimus....ita etiam obligari*, seems to require the liability. In one text liability *de peculio* is clearly contemplated on such facts[3]. The unfavourable texts can be otherwise explained. One has just been considered[4]. In another the action would have been refused in any case: the apparent freedom is mentioned only to explain the events[5]. In the third the action is not refused, but declared useless because on the facts there is *nihil in peculio*[6].

. It must be borne in mind that the Edictal liability of the master is distinct from the "natural" liability of the slave. Many circumstances might end the one without affecting the other[7]. Thus we are told that a surety may be validly taken for the slave's obligation, after an *actio de peculio* has been begun against the master, since the *naturalis obligatio* has not been put in issue[8]. These points will recur later[9]. Here it must be noted that, though distinct, they have the same object, and that thus, as in solidary obligations, discharge of one will destroy the other, if it amount to real or fictitious satisfaction. Thus *acceptilatio* to a slave bars the *actio de peculio*[10]. We are told by Ulpian that payment by the master in excess of the *peculium* cannot be recovered[11]. The reason of this is not clear[12]. It may be said that, as the limitation, *de peculio*, is placed, as is commonly held[13], not in the *intentio* but in the *condemnatio*, the master's obligation covers the whole debt, and thus it cannot be said that the money was not due. But the Edict expresses the limitation to the *peculium*. The point may be that there is an actual pending action, in which the obligation is stated generally, as we have said, and thus it cannot be said not to be due[14]. Although the action is essentially one in which the liability is limited to the *peculium*, the actual loss may in fact exceed this. Thus if the *dominus* sues on the transaction the defendant may set off a claim in full, though any action by him would have been limited to the *peculium*[15]. So, if a slave has bought, the *dominus*, if he wishes to redhibit, must give back all

---

[1] The fact that the *peculium* is not relied on is immaterial.   [2] 46. 3. 19, 34. 5.
[3] 14. 3. 1. *pr.*; 2. 8. 8. 2.   [4] 2. 14. 30. 1.   [5] 15. 1. 3. 8. *Ante*, p. 214.
[6] 15. 1. 52. *pr.*   *Ante*, pp. 211, 213.   Cp. 27. 5. 1. 2.   [7] *Post*, Ch. xxix.
[8] 15. 1. 50. 2.   [9] *Post*, Ch. xxix.   [10] 46. 4. 11. 1.   [11] 12. 6. 11.
[12] Machelard, *op. cit.* 286, sets it down to the natural obligation of a father to pay his son's debts. But it is not confined to sons, and there is no obvious natural obligation to pay a debt the contracting of which may have been prohibited.
[13] *Post*, App. ii.
[14] 15. 1. 47. 2 marks off *de peculio* from another case, precisely because in the latter, the debtor *universum debet*, though it speaks of all as due even here. Vangerow, Pand. § 625, treats the rule of 12. 6. 11 as an application of the rule that if the money is due, it cannot be recovered, though it be paid by the wrong person (12. 6. 44) if it is paid in satisfaction of that debt. He assumes that it was paid on account of the slave's liability, which is inconsistent with the words *per imprudentiam*. In 34. 3. 5. 2 where Julian forbids recovery, Ulpian and Marcellus allow it, the money not being due. Here there is no pending action. See p. 213.
[15] 16. 2. 9. *pr.*

accessories *in solidum*, and he cannot sue *ex empto* without having paid the price[1]. Thus the *dominus* cannot benefit by bringing his action when there is nothing in the *peculium*.

More important are the imputations to the *peculium* on account of *dolus*. The Edict contains an express provision[2] that the liability is to cover not only the actual *peculium*, but also anything which would have been in the *peculium* but for the *dolus* of the defendant. Such *dolus* may take various forms[3]. But payment to another creditor is not *dolus*, as the principle of the action is that there are no priorities[4]. It need not be the master's own fraud: it is enough if it be that of his *tutor*, *curator* or *procurator*, but here the liability is limited to what he has received, and is made dependent on the solvency of the tutor[5]. The rule is Ulpian's. Elsewhere he lays down a similar rule without special reference to this action, but there he does not require solvency of the tutor, and does require actual enrichment of the pupil[6]. Thus the rule is that he is liable so far as he is enriched, and, even though what he has received has not enriched him[7], if the tutor is solvent so that he can recover from him. The act must have been done fraudulently, *i.e.* with knowledge that it was detrimental to persons who were likely to claim: for this purpose, knowledge that there is a debt is enough[8].

The effect is not to make the act done void: the thing is not *in peculio*, but its value *peculio imputatur*[9]. As such an imputation is made only if the creditor's claim cannot otherwise be met, the same money cannot be imputed twice, having been in fact paid away[10].

As *dolus* is a delict, this imputation has a delictal character, and is therefore subject to the limit that it cannot be made more than an *annus utilis* after the right arose[11]. It is curious to find this rule in what is essentially a contractual action[12]. But in fact the *dolus* has nothing to do with the obligation. It is not mentioned or involved in the *intentio*, which expresses a liability to pay a certain debt. There are subsidiary instructions to the *iudex* as to the fund available, and this includes property obtained by *dolus*. It is a natural analogy, and no more, to limit the claim in the way in which it would be limited, if this money were the direct object of the action[13].

---

[1] 21. 1. 57. *pr.* 　　　　[2] 15. 2. 1. *pr.* Lenel, Ed. Perp. § 104. 1.

[3] *e.g.* adeeming the *peculium* or part, conniving at the slave's so dealing with the *peculium* as to damage the prospects of creditors, destroying the property or putting it to non-peculiar uses, or any similar act by which the fund is lessened, 15. 1. 9. 4, 21. *pr.*; 15. 3. 19.

[4] 15. 1. 21. *pr.*

[5] 15. 1. 21. 1, 2. The same rule is applied to the *dolus* of anyone under whom he holds.

[6] 4. 3. 15 ; 44. 4. 4. 23. 　　　　[7] *Ante*, p. 178.

[8] 15. 1. 21. *pr.* 　　　　[9] 15. 1. 21. *pr.* See Mandry, *op. cit.* 2. 403.

[10] 15. 1. 26. So if instead of being paid to a creditor, it is set off against claims from the slave.

[11] 15. 1. 30. 6. 　　　　[12] Mandry, *op. cit.* 2. 404.

[13] As the amount of the *peculium* is not in issue, *litis contestatio* in no way fixes it: the *iudex* must take into account *dolus* after that date, 15. 1. 21. 2.

These rules raise the question what is to happen if the *dominus* convert property *ex peculio* to his own use, *sine dolo malo*. The answer to this question takes us back to the *actio de in rem verso*. In the later state of the law there can be no doubt that, in such a case, the *actio perpetua de in rem verso* was available. We are so told in one text[1], and the case in which there had been such a conversion of *res* from the *peculium* is that discussed in the text immediately following[2]: *Si plures agant de peculio, proficere hoc ei cuius pecunia in rem versa est debet, ut ipse uberiorem actionem habeat.* This is consistent with the conception of the *actio de in rem verso* which we have adopted, though not with others discussed. We are told indeed in one text that *ademptio* is not a *versio*[3]. But on the broad meaning given to the notion of *dolus*, it is clear that dolose ademption was the normal case. It is dolose ademption which is here in view, as in another text which says: *dolum malum accipere debemus si ademit peculium*[4]. There is involved in this matter a historical development[5]. At one time, before the imputation for *dolus* was introduced, and before debts to· the slave were included in the *peculium*, the *actio de in rem verso* lay in all cases of *ademptio* and the like, being indeed a very necessary supplement to the rather ineffective *actio de peculio*. The successive introduction of these two extensions of the "peculiar" claim improved the position of the ordinary creditor *de peculio*, at the possible cost of the creditor *de in rem verso*, from whom specific things had been received. At that stage the utility of *de in rem verso* is confined to the rare case of *ademptio sine dolo malo*[6], and that of expiration of the *actio de peculio*, so that it became possible to doubt, as it was doubted, according to Ulpian, whether the *actio de in rem verso* was of much use[7].

There exists, in certain cases, a still further liability for *dolus* of the *dominus*. Ulpian tells us[8] that where *dos* has been paid to a son, and *actio de peculio* is brought there is a liability, *si quid dolo malo patris capta fraudataque est mulier*, as when, having the property, he will not restore it. He cites Pomponius as saying that this was expressed in the case of pledge, and applies equally to all *bonae fidei iudicia*[9]. So stated this looks like a sweeping exception to the rule that *dolus* of the *dominus* (apart from dolose withdrawal) is immaterial[10]. But it is shewn by

---

[1] 15. 3. 1. 1.   [2] 15. 3. 1. 2.   [3] 15. 3. 5. 3.
[4] 15. 1. 21. *pr.* Mandry, *op. cit.* 2. 402.
[5] *Ante*, p. 185.   [6] See 15. 3. 14.
[7] 15. 3. 1. 1. As to date of introduction of these two factors, there is no certainty. The *dolus* clause is likely to be the older, as involving a less abstract conception, as not involving natural right or obligation in the slave, as being expressed in the Edict, and as having been known to the Augustan jurists. The inclusion of debts cannot be traced earlier than Pomponius, 15. 1. 4. 1, 21. *pr.*, 49. 2; 15. 3. 1. 1. See Von Tuhr, Actio de in rem verso, 275.
[8] 15. 1. 36.
[9] Other texts: deposit, 15. 1. 5. *pr.*; 16. 3. 1. 42; 2. 13. 4. 3; *Commodatum*, Pledge, 13. 6. 3. 5; *Dos*, 15. 1. 36. See *post*, p. 224.
[10] *Ante*, p. 212.

Lenel that the citation from Pomponius referred originally to *fiducia,* in the formula of which action he finds other evidence of the existence of such a clause[1]. Its utility here was plain, since the *dominus* would be owner of the thing. It was carried over, naturally, to *pignus,* and thence by juristic interpretation to other *bonae fidei* actions in which restitution was desired. Here it was not so necessary since the injured party could vindicate the thing, or bring the *actio ad exhibendum.* This indeed is what Africanus tells him to do[2]. Apart from *fiducia* the liability is not expressed in the *formula*: it results from juristic interpretation[3]. Thus, notwithstanding the general words of the main text[4], it applies only to *dolus* taking the form of non-restitution, and only to the actions in which that point arises[5].

We have seen that the *peculium* may consist not only of *peculiares res,* but also of debts to it[6]. It must be noted that these are not merely imputed to the *peculium* for the purpose of the *actio de peculio,* but are an integral part of it[7], and thus are, *e.g.,* included in a legacy of it[8]. Such debts may be either from outsiders or from the *dominus* himself. Claims against outsiders, on delict, contract or any other *causa,* are in the *peculium*[9], but not necessarily at their face value: allowance is to be made for cost of recovery and risk[10]. Debts from the master, on contract and quasi-contract, are in the *peculium* unless the master has decided that they shall not be. For, as we have seen that the whole *peculium* can be destroyed by his mere wish, so we learn that he can release himself from any debts[11], though he cannot thus make himself a debtor. For this result there must be what would be a debt *in causa civili*: a mere acknowledgment *sine causa* will not suffice[12]. This does not mean that they must be such as would be actionable if the parties were independent, but that they must be such as would in that case create some legal obligation[13].

Such debts must be connected with the *peculium*[14], but they may be from the *dominus* himself, or from any fellow-slave who has a *peculium*[15], and, in ·the last case, it is immaterial whether they are from delict or

1 Ed. Perp. § 107; Cicero, de Off. 3. 17; D. 13. 6. 3. 5.
2 15. 1. 38.   This may give an indication of date. Julian gives it in *pignus,* in an un-interpolated text (13. 6. 3. 5; Lenel, *loc. cit.*). Africanus ignores it in deposit. Ulpian allows it in all this group of actions, 15. 1. 5. *pr.,* 36; 16. 3. 1. 42 (where the reference to Julian hardly justifies the view that he allowed it in deposit); 13. 6. 3. 5; 2. 13. 4. 3; 24. 3. 22. 12.   He is following Pomponius who is of the same date as Africanus.
3 13. 6. 3. 5.   4 15. 1. 36.
5 See as to this Lenel, *loc. cit.*; Karlowa, *op. cit.* 2. 1146, 7; Mandry, *op. cit.* 2. 407.
6 *Ante,* pp. 193, *sqq.*   7 15. 1. 7. 6.
8 *Ante,* p. 194.   9 15. 1. 7. 4, 5.
10 15. 1. 51. If creditor claims to reckon them in full he must accept cession of actions as payment.
11 15. 1. 7. 6.   12 15. 1. 4. 1.
13 15. 1. 49. 2.   *Post,* Ch. xxix. It may be doubted if Justinian's validation of *pactum donationis* (C. 8. 53. 35. 5) made such pacts create a debt to the *peculium.*
14 *Post,* Ch. xxix.   15 15. 1. 7. 7.

contract¹. The adjoining text², however, says: *Si damnum servo dominus dederit, in peculium hoc non imputabitur, non magis quam si subripuerit.* The context suggests that what is contemplated is damage to or theft from the *peculium.* But such acts would amount to dolose removal, except in case of negligent damage : the text must be understood of acts affecting the slave himself, who is not in his own *peculium.* Presumably there is no liability for mere negligent damage to a *res peculiaris*³.

In arriving at the nett *peculium* there is another important step to be taken. The *dominus* may deduct all debts due to him⁴. No such deduction is made for debts due to third persons: the principle of the action is, *occupantis melior solet esse condicio*⁵. But he may deduct debts due to persons in his *potestas*, since such debts are, on ordinary principles, acquired to him⁶. He may deduct also debts due to persons whose *tutor, curator* or *procurator* he is. This is subject to the provision that he may not do it fraudulently, which seems to mean that he may not so deduct if there is a sufficient remedy for his *pupillus* otherwise⁷.

Debts so deductible may have the most various origins. Any form of contract which was open to slaves might base such a deduction⁸. A case which recurs in several texts is that of money promised for manumission, which is deductible, as soon as the manumission has taken place⁹. One text is considered by Mandry¹⁰ to raise a difficulty in this connexion. A slave agrees by pact for a sum to be paid for manumission, and then finds a *reus* to promise it to the *dominus*¹¹. Mandry regards this as a case of *expromissio* novating the natural obligation of the slave. This would make a pact capable in itself of creating a natural obligation. But the contract of the *reus* is not contemplated as secondary: it is primary, and the *pacisci* of the slave is no more than an understanding with the master as to the terms which he will accept. It is not in the least obligatory. As to quasi-contract (apart from matters connected with delict), there are some points of interest. There may be a claim on *negotiorum gestio* by the slave, or, conversely, on account of *gestio* by the *dominus*¹². Payments made on behalf of

---

¹ 15. 1. 9. 1.   ² 15. 1. 9. *pr.*
³ He is liable, like any third person, for such proceeds of a theft by one of the slaves as he may have received, 15. 1. 9. 1. As to debts between slave and *vicarius, post,* pp. 244 *sqq.*
⁴ 15. 1. 5. 4; G. 4. 73; etc.   ⁵ 15. 1. 52. *pr.*
⁶ 15. 1. 9. 3; 33. 8. 6. *pr.*; G. 4. 73; In. 4. 7. 4. Not debts to their *vicarii.* Nor of course debts due to *servi castrensis peculii* of a son, 49. 17. 10.
⁷ 15. 1. 9. 4. See *post,* p. 224. Machelard has observed (*op. cit.* 174) that this may operate detrimentally to himself. For while the privilege of *dominus* takes priority (15. 1. 52. *pr.*) the debts it covers take priority by date. If there is a debt to the pupil older than that to *dominus* and there is not enough to pay both, the pupil has first claim.
⁸ 15. 1. 9. 6, 56.   ⁹ 15. 1. 11. 1.   ¹⁰ *op. cit.* 1. 378.
¹¹ 45. 1. 104.   ¹² 15. 1. 9. 7, 8, 49. 1.

the slave are deductible if they would have created obligation apart
from the slavery[1]. There are, however, some difficulties, if he has
bound himself for the slave, *e.g.* by becoming surety for him, or by
giving a mandate for a loan of money to him[2]. It was thought by
some jurists that the sum could be deducted before payment, but the
view which prevailed was that no such deduction should be made, but
that security should be taken from the creditor suing, to refund if the
dominus were ultimately called on to pay. The chief practical difference
is that the creditor has the use of the money in the meantime.
What is true of his own liability is true of obligations *de peculio*. If
he has rightly paid under such an obligation, he can deduct. If he has
been condemned he can deduct before payment. But he cannot deduct
for a claim which is pending or threatened, since *melior est condicio
occupantis,* and it is only the judgment which definitely gives priority[3].

We are told that the *dominus* is not entitled to deduct the cost of
curing the slave, in illness, because *rem suam potius egit*[4]. This hardly
seems a sufficient reason, since the slave certainly has an interest in his
own health, and the presence of personal interest in the *gestor* does not
bar the action[5]. The fact that the slave is not in his own *peculium* is
not material, for it is clear that the debts on account of which a
deduction may be made have no necessary connexion with the *peculium,*
as is shewn by the rules as to compensation for wrongs done by the
slave, shortly to be considered[6].

For delictal penalties in respect of wrongs to the *dominus* no
deductions can be made[7]: we know that no action can ever lie on
account of such wrongs, and the master's power of correction does away
with the need of such penalties[8]. On the other hand, if the slave or his
vicarius commits a delict against a third person, and the master pays
damages in lieu of surrender, these may be deducted[9]. It is the
more surprising to find that if he surrenders the slave he may not,
in any *actio de peculio,* deduct the value of the slave[10]. If it were a
vicarius this is obvious, since the man is no longer in the *peculium,*
and such a surrender is not *dolus,* and thus, assuming the values
equal, the fund for the creditor will be the same as if he had paid
and deducted the damages. But, in the case of the principal slave, as

---

[1] 15. 1. 9. 8, 11. 1.   [2] 15. 1. 11. 1.
[3] 15. 1. 9. 8, 10. Money received by *servus* on behalf of *dominus* may be deducted if *dominus*
ratify: if not it is an *indebitum* and the debtor may condict, 15. 1. 11. 2.
[4] 15. 1. 9. 7.
[5] 3. 5. 5. 5. See however, Windscheid, Pand. § 431; Van Wetter, Oblig. 3. 305.
[6] If the sick slave were a *vicarius* of the slave whose contract is the subject of suit, the cost
would probably be deductible, not because he is in the *peculium,* but because it is *potius res servi.*
[7] Mandry, *op. cit.* 1. 355.   [8] *Ibid.*; Karlowa, *op. cit.* 2. 1144.
[9] 15. 1. 11. *pr.,* 23; 33. 8. 16. So could payments to avoid *missio in possessionem* of *aedes
peculiares* which threatened adjoining property—a matter closely akin to noxal liability, 15. 1.
22, 23.
[10] 15. 1. 11. *pr.*

he is not in his own *peculium*, the creditor will have a less fund, if the master pay and deduct, than if he surrender. The theoretical justification is that surrender of the slave cannot by any process be brought within the notion of *negotiorum gestio* on his behalf, or any other form of quasi-contractual obligation.

Though there is no claim for penalties in respect of theft of, or damage to, the master's property[1], there is a claim, *in simplum*, in the nature of *condictio furtiva*[2], and also for the damage[3]. An illustration given of this is damage to a fellow-slave[4], but we are told that if a slave kill or injure himself, there is no deduction[5]. The text gives the grotesque reason that a slave has a perfect right to knock himself about. The truth underlying this curious statement is that the whole conception of debts between master and slave assumes their independence *pro tanto* from an economic point of view. From this standpoint an act of the slave, taking effect entirely in himself, cannot be regarded as creating an obligation to the *dominus*. If the master spends money in treatment of a slave who has so injured himself, we are told that this can be deducted[6]. Like medical treatment of a sick slave, it is the master's own affair, but it is an expense to him caused by the slave's act[7].

Just as the *actio de peculio* will lie *ex ante gestis*, so, too, debts may be deducted, though they arose before ownership of the slave began[8]. Thus the *heres* may deduct for debts due to himself before he became owner of the slave[9]. Mandry remarks that these texts shew that the jurists, before Julian, doubted whether this rule would apply where, owing to the slave's being *pure legatus*, the *heres* never was actually *dominus*. He suggests that this is due to the standing expression, *deducto eo quod domino debetur*[10]. It was agreed, however, that if the *heres* did become owner he could deduct for damage done, by the slave, to the *hereditas iacens*[11].

The owner of a slave may become *heres* to a creditor *de peculio*. No doubt, in such a case, he may deduct the amount of that debt as against his own creditors *de peculio*. But if he sells the inheritance he must account for that debt, *i.e.* the vendee can claim what he would have had if the *hereditas* had been in other hands[12], just as he could if the master himself had been the debtor[13]. On the same facts it was settled after some doubts that the *peculium* was to be taken as it was at the death, for the purpose of determining the amount of the *hereditas*,

---

[1] *Ante*, p. 222.   [2] 15. 1. 4. 3, 4, 9. 6; 19. 1. 30. *pr.*   [3] 15. 1. 4. 3.
[4] 33. 8. 9. 1.   [5] 15. 1. 9. 7.   [6] *Ibid.*
[7] Delict to ward of *dominus* is not discussed: the tutor being noxally liable, the case is presumably on the level of delict to third person.
[8] 15. 1. 11. 8, 52. *pr.*   [9] 15. 1. 9. 5; 33. 8. 6. 5—8. 1.   [11] 15. 1. 27. 1.
[10] *op. cit.* 2. 385; 15. 1. 5. 4, 9. 2.
[12] 18. 4. 2. 6.   [13] 18. 4. 20.

in view of the *lex* Falcidia[1]. But this is only a minimum, as in other cases, and thus if the *peculium* increases, so that a greater part of the debt can be paid, the *hereditas* is increased, *ex post facto*[2]. Ulpian tells us that the right of deduction is to be applied only, *si non hoc aliunde consequi potuit*[3]. Mandry[4] shews that this must not be taken as putting the right of deduction in a subordinate position. He cites several cases in which the rule was not applied[5], and concludes that it operated only where deduction would be a fraud on the "peculiar" creditor. He illustrates this by the remark of Ulpian, that the *dominus* may deduct for debts due to his ward, *dummodo dolo careat*[6]. It may also be pointed out that the word *potuit*[3] limits the rule to the case in which he has in the past had an opportunity of getting in the money and has neglected to do so, and that this was precisely the case in the only hypothesis of fact to which the rule is applied[7]. The other texts shew that the mere fact that he might have brought an action is not such an opportunity[5].

It is important to notice that the effect of a deduction is merely to determine what is the fund available for the creditor. If the *peculium* is solvent there is no question of deduction, and where a deduction has to be made its effect is merely the striking of an authoritative balance. It is not in any sense payment to the *dominus*[8]. Hence it follows that if nothing is actually taken from the *peculium*, by the *dominus*, the debt to him still exists, and consequently the deduction can be made again if an action is brought[9].

We have seen that debts to the *dominus* take precedence of all others, that, in fact, debts to him are deducted as a preliminary in determining what the *peculium* is. Hence *nullum privilegium domino praeponi potest*. This does not affect the existence of privileges *inter se* among other creditors[10], and we have an illustration of privilege in the claim of *dos*[11]. But there is a text[12] which seems to put the claimant of *dos* in a better position. It observes that the wife has a privilege in an action for recovery of *dos*, over other creditors, and adds, *et si forte domino aliquid debeat servus, non praeferatur mulier, nisi in his tantum rebus, quae vel in dotem datae sunt vel ex dote comparatae, quasi et hae*

---

[1] 15. 1. 50. 1; 35. 2. 56. *pr.*
[2] 35. 2. 56. 1. If there are two debts of 10, one to the deceased and one to X, and the *peculiares res* are 10, the whole 10 are in the *hereditas*. For the debt to *dominus* removes the 10 from the *peculium*, and, as it is acquired by *hereditas*, it is included therein. This may operate adversely to *heres*, for it increases the *hereditas* for the benefit of legatees, and he may yet have to pay the debt to X, 35. 2. 56. 2.
[3] 15. 1. 11. 6.   [4] *op. cit.* 2. 387.   [5] 15. 1. 11. 8, 47. 4, 56 *etc.*
[6] 15. 1. 9. 4.   [7] 15. 1. 11. 7, on authority or Julian.   [8] *Post*, Ch. xxxx.
[9] 15. 1. 11. 3. Where a sum was due to *dominus*, he "deducted" a *vicarius* of that value, but left him in the apparent *peculium*. The *vicarius* died. Another creditor sues *de peculio*. The sum can still be deducted. Mere deduction without removal did not alter the fact that he was a *peculiaris res*. What was due to *dominus* was a debt, 15. 1. 11. 4.
[10] 15. 1. 52. *pr.*   [11] *h. l.* 1.   [12] 24. 3. 22. 13.

dotales sint. This text has been supposed to raise a difficulty[1], since a privilege in any person is inconsistent with the principle on which rests the deduction of the debts of the slave to *dominus, i.e.,* that the available fund does not include them. But the language of the text shews that it contemplates something narrower than the ordinary privilege. It confines the claim to specific *res dotales,* and is thus merely an application of the rule, as to plaintiffs *capti et fraudati* by refusal to return specific extant things, which we have discussed and seen to apply to the case of *dos*[2].

What is the juristic basis on which the right of deduction rests? Why is it that debts to the *dominus* are regarded as standing subtractions from the apparent *peculium*[3]? It must be noted first, that it is independent of the Edict and *formula,* neither of which contains any words so limiting the idea of *peculium.* It is involved in the very definition of the fund[4]. This conception is the result of practice, and, probably, apart from the *actio de peculio,* and before its introduction, masters who were in the habit of honouring their slave's transactions had refused to consider as *peculium* any more than the nett fund left after their claims were deducted[5]. This might be merely a juristic construction, but it is probably the true explanation: the jurists adopt the definition accepted in practice. A somewhat different point is mentioned by Ulpian[6] (as if it were the same), as the reason why he can also deduct for debts to his ward : since he is treated as having first sued on his own account, he ought to do the same for his ward. This gives a similar result, since as we shall see[7], it is the giving of judgment which determines priority among creditors, though the judgment be still unsatisfied. But it is, in fact, no explanation, for it does not shew why he is supposed *praevenisse.* The same explanation occurs in the same text in a still more questionable form. It is supposed that the *dominus* not only *egit* but *exegit.* Of itself this might mean no more, but the words which follow are quite inadmissible : *defendendum igitur erit quasi sibi eum solvere cum quis de peculio agere conabitur*[8]. We have, however, seen that *deductio* is in no sense a *solutio,* and the words have rather a Byzantine look about them. The

---

[1] Mandry, *op. cit.* 2. 393, and the literature there cited.
[2] *Ante,* p. 219 ; Demangeat, Fonds Dotal, 147 ; Bechmann, Dotalrecht, 2. 464.
[3] Mandry, *op. cit.* 2. 394 *sqq.*; Pernice, *op. cit.* 1. 129 *sqq.*
[4] 15. 1. 5. 4 ; G. 4. 73 etc.
[5] 15. 1. 9. 4.   This does not imply any legal force in such debts. It is the view of Pedius, described by Ulpian as *elegans : ideo hoc minus in peculio est quod...domino debetur, quoniam non est verisimile dominum id concedere servo in peculium habere quod sibi debetur.* The deduction is no doubt as old as the action.
[6] 15. 1. 9. 4.   See also *h. t.* 9. 2, 5.   [7] *Post,* p. 226.
[8] B. 1. 9. 4.

real origin was forgotten in the later classical time: these are mere constructions.

The *actio de peculio* is always *in personam*[1], and therefore[2] the *dominus* is bound *litem defendere*, with all that that implies. If the plaintiff has a right *in rem*, or a possessory right, he can of course proceed by *vindicatio* or other appropriate remedy, and has no need to appeal to any fund[3]. The action *meliorem facit causam occupantis*[4], priority being determined not by date of *litis contestatio*, but by that of judgment. Thus if two actions are pending at once, the amount of the first *condemnatio* is deducted from the fund available for what may be due under the second[5]. On the other hand, the priority so gained yields to any legal privilege, attaching to any other debt, as to which there seem to be no rules peculiar to this action[6]. The *intentio* of the action brings into issue the whole obligation, but the terms of the *condemnatio* limit the liability to the present amount of the *peculium*, which is considered as it is at *condemnatio*, the action being regarded as exhausting the creditor's right to its then content[7]. But judgment or payment releases, in effect, only *pro tanto*: the creditor may renew his action till complete satisfaction[8]. If the debt is not fully paid under the action no security can be exacted for the remainder. The text contrasts this case with that of *pro socio*. In that case we are told that such security can be required, *quia socius universum debet*[9].

A few rather complex cases may be taken from the texts as illustrations of these rules. A, in good faith, buys B's slave from C, who has stolen him. The slave, with *peculium* which belongs to B, buys, from D, a man who is conveyed to A[10]. B can condict the man from A, while A can sue B for any loss he incurs on the transaction by the slave, *ex negotio gesto*[11]. On the other hand, B, as owner of the slave, may, as an alternative, bring *actio ex empto* on the contract made by his slave, provided he pay the price *in solidum*, and C can condict the man from A. Or the *peculium*, being still B's, can be vindicated by him, and if he does this he is liable *de peculio* for the price of the man bought by his slave. If, however, the *res peculiares* have been consumed in the hands of the vendor, D, they cannot be vindicated, and there is no *actio de*

---

[1] In. 4. 6. 8.   [2] 15. 1. 21. 3.   [3] 15. 1. 23, 52. *pr.*
[4] 14. 4. 6; 15. 1. 52. *pr.*   [5] 15. 1. 10.   [6] 15. 1. 36.
[7] 15. 1. 32. 1. Hence a difficulty in the law of legacy. A creditor left a legacy of *liberatio* to a debtor *de peculio*, and there was then nothing *in peculio*. Is the gift null? Tryphoninus suggests diffidently (34. 3. 27) that it is in suspense till there is something *in peculio* on the analogy of *legatum spei*. Julian treats the state of the fund as immaterial: *securitatem enim pater per hoc legatum consequitur*, 34. 3. 5. 2.
[8] If he paid more than was in the fund, *per imprudentiam*, it could not be recovered as an *indebitum*, 12. 1. 11, *ante*, p. 217, and *post*, App. II.
[9] 15. 1. 47. 2. Cp. 17. 2. 63. 4. As to renewal of *de peculio*, *post*, App. II.
[10] 12. 1. 31. 1. The text is obscure.
[11] Presumably *de peculio*.

peculio for the price against B, since it has been paid. And if the vendor, D, has paid them away to a *bonae fidei possessor* he is entitled to absolution in the vindication, on ceding any actions he may have against him, and in that case there is no *actio de peculio.*

Hereditatis petitio is brought against A, who possesses, *inter alia,* the price of goods belonging to the inheritance, which have been sold by slaves who still hold the money[1]. The action will not be *de peculio,* since *hereditatis petitio* is an *actio in rem.* If however the ground of claim is not sale of any goods, but the fact that one of the slaves is a debtor to the *hereditas* (and the defendant claims to be *heres*)[2], the action will be limited as if it were *de peculio*[3].

If a slave sells, the *actio redhibitoria* is *de peculio.* The text adds: *in peculio autem et causa redhibitionis continebitur*[4], and goes on to explain this obscure expression in terms which shew that *causa redhibitionis* means either the difference between the value and the price, or the actual value of the man sold. As the former meaning is insignificant, since the whole price is in the *peculium,* the latter is to be preferred, so that the *peculium* will contain not only the apparent *res peculiares,* but also the value of the man whom the vendor will receive back, if steps are taken by the buyer[5]. It follows that the limitation to the *peculium* is not likely to be detrimental to the buyer, though the text goes on to observe that it is possible even then for the *peculium* to be so overburdened with debt to the *dominus* that the buyer may not get back his price.

We have hitherto assumed that the relation between the various parties has not altered since the date of the *negotium*: we must now consider the effect of death of the *dominus* and death, manumission or alienation of the slave.

The *peculium,* in strictness, ceases to exist if from any cause the *dominus* ceases to have the slave[6]. It is plain that this might lead to injustice, and accordingly a rule was introduced, by a special Edict, that an owner liable *de peculio* remained so liable for one *annus utilis* from the death, alienation or manumission of the slave[7]. It is not a juristic extension but a separate provision[8]. This is not without importance. A creditor *de peculio,* who thinks the contracting son dead, brings this *actio annalis.* He is repelled by evidence that the son has been dead

---

[1] 5. 3. 36. *pr.*   [2] 5. 3. 9.
[3] So if in the case of sale the slave who held the money has consumed it.
[4] 21. 1. 57. 1.
[5] So Pothier, *ad h. l.*   But see Otto and Schilling *ad h. l.*
[6] 15. 1. 3; 15. 2. 3.
[7] 4. 9. 7. 6; 14. 1. 4. 4; 15. 1. 14. 1, 32. *pr.,* 15. 2. 1. *pr.,* 15. 3. 1. 1; C. 4. 26. 7, 11.
[8] 15. 2. 1. *pr.*   Itself juristically extended to, *e.g.,* the cesser of a usufruct, 15. 2. 1. 9.

more than a year. The son is not really dead at all. There is nothing to prevent him from bringing the ordinary *actio de peculio*, for his right under this edict has not been in issue, and is not consumed[1].

The year runs, according to the Edict, from the time *quo primum de ea re experiundi potestas erit*[2]. On its terms this seems to cut down the action to what might be less than one year from the death, but it is explained as running only from the death[3], and then only if the claim is already actionable[4]. The liability is essentially *de peculio*[5], and thus there must have been an unadeemed *peculium* at the time of the death[6], etc., and it must have remained with the former owner[7]. It covers this, and what has been fraudulently removed therefrom[8]. It is subject to the ordinary additions and deductions for debt, except that the defendant cannot deduct for debts incurred since the alienation[9]. So long as the liability exists the fund is regarded as capable of increase by accretion, and of loss by any diminution in value, or destruction[10], but as it has lost its objective separateness, it is probable that there can be no dolose removal after the slave is gone[11]. The condemnation is, as in all cases, limited to the content of the fund at judgment[12]. The liability applies only to obligations entered into before the sale[13], etc., but with that restriction it covers all cases of "peculiar" liability[14].

Though it is brought under a different Edict the action is in general the same in form and in essence as the ordinary *actio de peculio*[15]. Thus the *intentio* says nothing as to the limit of a year: this point is raised by *exceptio*[16]. As the defendant may not have the *peculium* it has been thought that the *formula* contained words expressing this requirement[17]. But this is nowhere stated, and it may have been regarded as *officio iudicis*. Indeed if they are wanted here they are wanted in every action, since even where a sole owner is sued, there may be a *peculium* in the hands of a *bonae fidei possessor* or usufructuary[18].

So far the matter is clear, but there are difficulties which can best be considered by taking the various cases of transfer one by one.

---

[1] 15. 2. 1. 10.   *Post*, App. II.   [2] 15. 2. 1. *pr.*   [3] *h. t.* 1. 1.
[4] Thus in conditional obligations, the year ran from satisfaction. As it was a limit and not an extension, some actions might be barred earlier, *e.g.*, *redhibitoria*, 15. 2. 1. 2; 15. 2. 2. *pr.*
[5] 15. 2. 1. 3, *obligationem produci*.   [6] 15. 3. 1. 1.
[7] 15. 1. 33—35, 37. 2; 15. 2. 1. 7. As to this, *post*, p. 232.
[8] 15. 1. 26; 15. 2. 1. *pr.*   [9] 15. 1. 38. 3.   [10] 15. 2. 3.
[11] Hence Karlowa (*op. cit.* 2. 1153) prefers the *est* of the vulgate to the *fuerit* of Lenel and Mommsen. Cp. 15. 1. 47. 5.
[12] 15. 2. 3.   [13] *Post*, p. 229.
[14] *e.g. condictio furtiva* (47. 2. 42), and alienation in fraud of patron (38. 5. 1. 25). The allusion, in Frag. Fab. 5, to perpetuity, probably means only that there was a remedy independent of *de peculio*. The Edict covers all modes of alienation (15. 2. 1. 5, 6), but only alienation before the action. If the deft. alienates *pendente lite*, he will be liable to extent of all *peculium* in his or the buyer's possession, since it is his fault that he has it not, 15. 1. 43.
[15] 15. 2. 1. 3.   [16] 15. 2. 1. 10.
[17] *e.g.* Karlowa, *loc. cit.*; Lenel, *op. cit.* § 104.
[18] See, however, Lenel, Ed. Perp. § 104.

(a)   Transfer of the slave, *inter vivos*, by sale or gift. All alienations are on the same footing[1]: both alienor and alienee are liable, the former for a year, the latter, like any other owner, *in perpetuum.* Each is liable to the extent of the *peculium* he holds[2]. The liabilities are distinct. Thus the alienee is not accountable for *dolus* by the alienor[3], while, on the other hand, he is liable to the extent of all the *peculium* in his hands, whether it came from the alienor or not[4]. There can, however, be no *actio de peculio* against him, unless the fund in his hand is really a *peculium, i.e.* unless he has made a tacit or express *concessio*[5]. Neither, if sued, can deduct any debt due to the other[6], though the alienee can deduct debts due to himself, even before the acquisition, on which he has *de peculio* against the old owner[7]. He is in fact choosing deduction instead of action. If he prefers to sue the old owner *intra annum* he may do so, but in such a case he must allow for any *peculium* the slave has with him[8]. On the other hand, the vendor may have the *actio de peculio* against the vendee, for claims accruing after the sale, even within the year, and he need not allow for *peculium* in his possession[9]. But he has no *actio de peculio* in respect of a contract before the sale, either with himself or with another slave, even though it were before he (the vendor) became owner[10].

Action against one does not, in practice, bar action against the other for any balance due, no matter who was sued first[11]. According to Proculus, Ulpian and Paul, the plaintiff may choose which he will sue, but cannot sue both at once: he must rest on his right to sue again for any balance[12], there being moreover a rule, that, if he was met in his first action (*i.e.* against the vendor) by any *exceptio* except the *annua exceptio*, he cannot sue for what, but for the defence raised, he might have received from that *peculium*[13]. But a text of Gaius says: *Illud quoque placuit, quod et Iulianus probat, omnimodo permittendum creditoribus vel in partes cum singulis agere, vel cum uno in solidum*[14]. As the adjoining texts both deal with sale, this is sometimes held[15] to be a conflicting view. If so, it is an extremely direct conflict, for the opposite rule is expressed in equally strong terms: *potest eligere*[16], *non*

---

[1] 15. 1. 47. 6; 15. 2. 1. 6.   [2] 15. 1. 11. 8.
[3] 15. 1. 21. 2.   [4] 15. 1. 27. 2, 32. 1.
[5] 15. 1. 27. 2.   If knowing of the debt he has taken the fund away, this is dolose ademption: without knowledge—a *versio*, at any rate as to traceable property. *Ante*, p. 219.
[6] 15. 1. 13.   [7] 15. 1. 11. 8.
[8] 15. 1. 27. 6, 47. 4.   [9] 15. 1. 38. 3.
[10] 15. 1. 27. 4—7. The restriction, due to Julian, rests on good faith. They could have been deducted and can be recovered, 15. 1. 11. 7, *post*, p. 230. If the *peculium* has not passed there is no reason why the late master should acquire rights against the new fund. The end of 15. 1. 11. 7 seems to mean (it is obscure), that if there was a debt conditionally due to the *peculium*, at time of sale, and the condition arrives, the old owner can claim out of this, though it is in fact added to the *peculium* after the sale.
[11] *Restitutio actionis*, 15. 1. 11. 8, 32. 1, 37. 2, 47. 3.   *Post*, App. II.
[12] 15. 1. 11. 8, 30. 5, 47. 3.   [13] 15. 1. 30. 5.
[14] 15. 1. 27. 3; cp. *h. t.* 37. 2.   [15] Karlowa, *op. cit.* 1. 1150.   [16] 15. 1. 11. 8.

esse permittendum actori dividere actionem[1]. But the text seems to refer to another matter. Its language is inappropriate to the present case. *Cum singulis, cum uno,* are not appropriate words for persons standing in the relation of vendor and purchaser. They denote a group in the same position. And what *partes* can be meant? It seems most likely that, as Mommsen assumes, this text deals with a case in which there are several heirs[2].

We have seen that the vendor is liable so far as he retains the *peculium.* But what is retention of the *peculium?* If the man is sold, *sine peculio,* there is no difficulty. If a price is fixed for the *peculium,* that and not the *peculiares res* is the *peculium*[3]. But if no separate price is reserved for it, Ulpian tells us that the vendor is not regarded as retaining it: the price of the slave is not *peculium*[4]. This is a rather unguarded statement, since some of it is clearly the price of the *peculium.* No doubt, what the rule means, in practice, is, that if the *peculium* were of any importance, and went with the man, it was not allowed to pass as a mere accessory, but an express price was put on it. If the vendor is liable *de peculio,* because he has transferred the man *cum peculio,* with a special price for the latter, he cannot deduct for debts due to him[5]. If the vendor is liable *de peculio,* because the man was sold without it, he can deduct only for debts which accrued before the sale: those subsequent have no relation to his position as owner: his remedy is *de peculio*[6].

(*b*) Manumission *inter vivos.* If the *peculium* is retained, the old owner is liable to the *actio annalis*[7]. If it passes, the question whether the new *libertus* can be sued is perhaps to be answered as in the case of manumission by will *cum peculio*[8]. But the cases are not quite the same: there is *dolus* in the *dominus* who hands over the *peculium,* and he may be liable on that account. The case is not discussed[9].

(*c*) Transfer on death[10]. Under this head there is some difficulty, and, as it seems, some historical development. There are several cases, which must be taken separately.

If the heirs succeed to both the slave and the *peculium,* the liability *de peculio* is, as in the case of other hereditary debts, divided, *ipso iure,*

---

[1] 15. 1. 47. 3. [2] Of the vendor? *Post,* p. 231.
[3] 15. 1. 33, 34. [4] 15. 1. 32. 2.
[5] He could have deducted before delivery, and can recover by *cond. indeb.* and *ex vendito* so far as *peculium* will go. If now allowed to deduct he would unduly profit, as he has received the full value of the *res peculiares,* and the creditor cannot proceed against the buyer at least on account of the old *peculium.*
[6] 15. 1. 38. 3, 47. 5. A gift of the slave, *cum peculio,* creates the same liability as sale without a price for it, the new owner is liable to the ordinary *a. de peculio;* the old owner is not liable at all, 15. 2. 1. 6, 7. If it were *sine peculio,* the new owner is not liable, the old one is liable to the *actio annalis.*
[7] 15. 2. 1. 7. [8] *Post,* p. 231.
[9] See, however, C. Th. 2. 32. 1 (C. 4. 26. 13. 4).
[10] Death of the slave leaves the *actio annalis* and nothing more, 15. 2. 1. *pr.* As to the special edict for emancipated sons *etc.,* see Lenel, Ed. Perp. § 104.

quite apart from any division of res hereditariae[1]. But though as heirs they are liable pro parte, they are also common owners, and thus, like other common owners, they are liable in solidum[2]. Accordingly a creditor may choose in which way he will proceed. He may sue the heirs, as such, pro parte, in which case the right of deduction will also be divided, or he may sue any one as being one of common owners, in solidum. This seems to be the true meaning of a citation from Julian, which has already been mentioned as being misplaced and maltreated by Ulpian or Tribonian[3]. Illud quoque placuit, quod et Iulianus probat, omnimodo permittendum creditoribus vel in partes cum singulis agere, vel cum uno in solidum. Mommsen refers the text to heirs of a vendor, liable to the actio annalis. But Julian himself elsewhere denies the right to sue one of the heirs by the actio annalis in solidum[4].

If the heirs succeed to the peculium without the slave, because he died, or was freed inter vivos, or sold, by the deceased, or freed or legated by the will, they are liable to the actio annalis for the year or the unexpired part of it[5]. Each heir is liable only pro parte[6] and can deduct only what is due to him[7]. Each is liable for dolus so far as he has profited, and absolutely for his own[8]. Action against one releases all, but, as this would operate unjustly in view of the limitation just mentioned, the creditor can get restitutio actionis on equitable grounds[9]. Here, too, any of the heirs may be creditors, but, as they are not common owners they may have de peculio inter se[10]. Such a creditor must, presumably, allow for the peculium which has come to him[11]. It may be added that the slave himself, if he is a heres, is liable de peculio[12]. There can be no personal liability in the freedman: his contracts do not become actionable against him by his manumission[13]. The legatee of the slave will be his owner and liable as such.

But difficulties arise where the slave is freed or legated, with the peculium. Here it is clear that views changed, and conflicting opinions are retained by Justinian[14]. In the case of manumissus it might be supposed that the actio de peculio was inapplicable to him, since it presupposes

---

[1] C. 3. 36. 6; D. 11. 1. 18. [2] 10. 3. 8. 4 etc., post, Ch. XVI.
[3] 15. 1. 27. 3. Ante, p. 230.
[4] 15. 1. 14 (where they are not common owners). If one of the heirs is a creditor, it is no doubt treated as a case of common ownership: there is no question of de peculio, the matter being adjusted by familiae erciscundae (arg. 15. 1. 14). Where one of the heredes was praelegatee of a slave cum peculio, the other heredes had no de peculio against him for what the slave owed to dominus, says Scaevola (15. 1. 54, 58). What he owed need not have been handed over and must be allowed for in familiae erciscundae.
[5] 15. 1. 14; 15. 2. 1. 4, 7. Though penalties for delicts to dominus could not be deducted (ante, p. 222) the heir might claim to deduct for damage to the hereditas before aditio, 15. 1. 27. 1.
[6] 14. 3. 14; 15. 1. 14, 30. 1, 32. pr. Paul (14. 3. 14) gives the unnecessary reason that there is no communi dividundo.
[7] 15. 1. 14. [8] 15. 1. 30. 7, 31. [9] 15. 1. 32. pr.
[10] 15. 1. 29. pr. [11] Arg. 15. 1. 27. 6, 47. 4. [12] 15. 1. 30. 2. [13] Post, Ch. XXIX.
[14] Pernice, Labeo, 1. 151 sqq.; Mandry, op. cit. 2. 194 sqq.; Karlowa, R. R. G. 2. 1159.

potestas[1], but Labeo, Julian, Javolenus[2], and Caracalla in the Code[3] all make him liable, and the *heres* exempt. On the other hand, Pomponius, Caecilius, Ulpian (remarking that there had been doubts), and Marcian (very decidedly), take the view that the *heres* is liable, the action not lying against the *manumissus*[4]. There is a similar conflict in the analogous case of legacy to a third person *cum peculio* : the cases are grouped together and are, no doubt, governed by the same principle. It seems clear that the older view was that of Labeo, that the *heres* was not liable, and that while this view is held by some as late as Paul, the view that has by this time really triumphed is that the *heres* is liable and that he must protect himself by taking security from the legatee, before handing over the *peculium*. If he has so guarded himself he is not liable[5]. This way of looking at the matter, coupled with the fact that Julian[6] is clearly talking of a legacy *per damnationem*, leads Karlowa[7] to think that the dispute applied only to this form of legacy, that the legatee was always liable in legacy *per vindicationem*, and that, after doubts, it was settled that, in legacy *per damnationem*, the *heres* was liable, even after transfer. This conjecture is more or less confirmed by the fact that the texts in question speak of a duty on the heir to hand over the *peculium*. But the language of Ulpian in discussing the doubt seems inconsistent with this limitation[8]. Moreover the duty to transfer the *peculium* does not imply a duty to transfer ownership : such language is used where it is clearly a legacy, *per vindicationem*. Thus Ulpian cites Labeo as exempting the *heres*, *quia neque ad eum pervenerit*, which must refer to *vindicatio*, and Pomponius says that in this very case he must take security before handing over[9].

What is the difference of principle underlying these doubts[10] ? All are agreed that possession of the *peculium* is essential to the liability : indeed Javolenus seems to hold that of itself enough, for in a case in which the *peculium* alone is left, he regards the liability as passing in all except pending actions[11]. There is, however, the difficulty, that the *actio annalis* is, as the form of the Edict shews[12], intended for use against the former master[13]. Accordingly the jurists seek to make the

---

[1] Lenel, Ed. Perp. § 104. But that is not really material.
[2] 14. 4. 9. 2 ; 15. 1. 35 ; 15. 2. 1. 8 ; 33. 4. 1. 10. In 3. 5. 17 Proculus, Pegasus, Neratius and Paul may be expressing the same view, but they are probably considering only the case of a *gestio* begun before manumission and continued after.
[3] C. 4. 14. 2.   [4] 14. 4. 9. 2 ; 15. 2. 1. 7 ; 33. 8. 18.
[5] 15. 1. 35 ; 15. 2. 1. 7. *I.e.* he can avoid liability by ceding his rights against donee of *peculium*. *Arg.* 15. 1. 51.
[6] 33. 4. 1. 10.   [7] *loc. cit.*
[8] 15. 2. 1. 7. *Si cum peculio...liberum esse iussit.*
[9] 14. 4. 9. 2. A gift of *peculium* is not always a gift of the *peculiares res* but only of a *pars incerta* (*ante*, p. 193), so that the question might arise in *leg. per vindicationem*.
[10] The question is of the *annalis actio*: if legatee makes a *concessio* of the same fund as *peculium*, he is liable on old debts on ordinary principles.
[11] 15. 1. 35 ; 33. 8. 17.   [12] 15. 2. 1. *pr.*
[13] Or his heirs, Mandry, *op. cit.* 2. 376.

heir liable, by an artificial view as to what is retention of the *peculium*, analogous to that taken in the case of sale, with which Paul associates this case[1]. Caecilius holds that he retains it by handing it over, since he is thereby released from his obligation to do so, and is thus so much the better off[2]. This is subterfuge: if the economic or "beneficial" state of things is to be decisive, the *peculium* was never his at all[3].

B.   *ACTIO TRIBUTORIA*[4].

The general principle of the liability enforced by this action, (which, like the others, is Edictal,) is that if a slave trades with the *peculium* or part of it to the knowledge of his *dominus*, (though not necessarily with his consent,) the *dominus* is liable so far as that part of the *peculium* will go, its proceeds and profits being included, the master having no right to deduct what is due to himself, but ranking as an ordinary creditor, the fund being distributed among the creditors *pro rata*[5]. The actual *actio tributoria* is only the last stage in a rather elaborate procedure, set forth in the Edict. It contains a rule that any creditor of the class stated, can call on the *dominus* to distribute the *merces*, according to the above-mentioned principle—*vocatio in tributum*[6]. The distribution is done by the master unless he prefers to hand over the fund as a whole, in which case the Praetor will appoint an *arbiter* to carry out the distribution[7]. The Edict then lays down the rule that if the *dominus* fails to make proper *tributio*, then, and then only, the actual *actio tributoria* can be brought[8]. Of the procedure in the *vocatio*, the texts tell us little or nothing. The *vocatio* is generally held to proceed from the Praetor; mainly, it seems, on the grounds that the word *vocatio* is used so often that it must be Edictal[9], and that, as the *dominus* and the other creditors are *vocati*[10], the summoner must be the Praetor[11]. The acceptance of this view raises another question. If the *vocatio* is by the Praetor, is it contained in the Edict (set in operation by a creditor), as Lenel seems to hold in his conjectural restoration[12], or does it require a subsequent act, a *decretum* of the Praetor, as is held by some writers[13]? The *Corpus Iuris* contains no evidence of any such *decretum*[14], but it is very faintly suggested by the language of Theophilus,

---

[1] 15. 1. 47. 6.   [2] 15. 2. 1. 7.
[3] Other jurists hold that to hand it over without taking security is *dolus*, so that the amount is still imputable, 14. 4. 9. 2; 15. 2. 1. 7.
[4] Mandry, *op. cit.* 2. 424 *sqq.*; Karlowa, *op. cit.* 2. 1159.
[5] 14. 4. 1. *pr.*—3, 5. *pr.*, 5. 6, 5. 11; G. 4. 72; In. 4. 7. 3.
[6] 14. 4. 1. *pr.*, 5. 6.   [7] 14. 4. 7. 1.   [8] 14. 4. 7, 8, 12.
[9] 14. 4. 1. *pr.*, 5. 6, 5. 15, 5. 18, 7. 1.   Lenel, Ed. Perp. § 103.   [10] 14. 4. 5. 15, 18.
[11] Karlowa, *op. cit.* 2. 1159.
[12] Lenel, *loc. cit.* The *vocatio* is however not *edicto*, but *ex edicto*, 14. 4. 1. *pr.* Karlowa, *loc. cit.*
[13] Karlowa, *loc. cit.* For others see Mandry, *op. cit.* 2. 439, himself disagreeing.
[14] It is not to be inferred from occasional use of the expression *actio tributoria* to cover the whole procedure, 14. 4. 5. 5.

commenting on the text of the Institutes[1] in which this action is treated, and still more faintly by the corresponding *scholia* in the Basilica[2]. But, in fact, the assumption that the *vocatio* issues from the Praetor is somewhat hasty. It is nowhere said that the Praetor *vocat*: the impersonal form is always used. It does not follow from acceptance of the view that the word stood in the Edict. It does not follow from the fact that creditors are *vocati*. The simplest and most obvious view, entirely consistent with the texts, is that the creditor or creditors, who *desiderant tribui*, by that act *vocant ad tributum* the *dominus* and the other creditors[3]. In any case a creditor applies, and the Edict authorises the *dominus* to conduct the distribution[4].

It is essential that the slave have been engaged in trade. Though the word *merx* is used, the Edict covers all kinds of business[5], handicrafts as well as dealing[6]. But it must be a *negotiatio, i.e.* a continuous course of trading, something more than an isolated *negotium*[7]. The trading must have been with the *peculium* or part of it[8], and the master must have known of the matter, though not necessarily of the individual transaction[9]. The texts make it clear that mere knowledge suffices: it is not necessary that he approve. He need not *velle*; *non nolle* is enough, *patientia*, not *voluntas*. An attitude of indifference, *non protestari et contradicere*, satisfies the Edict[10]. Nothing could be more explicit, and this same distinction is also brought out in other connexions[11]. Yet Mandry[12] regards *scientia* as involving *voluntas*, on account of the rule that *scientia pupilli domini* does not suffice[13], a rule that he considers to depend on the fact that such a person is not *willensfähig*, which implies in turn that *scire* is, in this connexion, an act of the will, *i.e. voluntas*. But apart from other objections, the real point of this text is that the effect of the state of mind, whatever it be, is to impose an obligation, and a *pupillus* cannot bind himself[14]. The *scientia* of a *pupillus* does not suffice[15]: that of his tutor, or of the curator of a *furiosus*[16], or of a general procurator does[17].

The right to demand *tributio*, and, therefore, to share in it, applies only to creditors of the trade, and in respect of debts due in connexion

---

[1] In. 4. 7. 3 "ἀναγκάζει τὸν δεσπότην."
[2] Bas. XVIII. 2. 1. n. f.   The *ita ius dicit* of G. 4. 72 in no way implies that the *vocatio* is by the Praetor.
[3] Cp. the similar language where there is a composition with creditors and they are *vocati* by the tutor who made the agreement, 2. 14. 44 (= 26. 7. 59).
[4] 14. 4. 5. 19, 7. 1.   If he prefers to leave it to an arbitrator, there is no reason to think he loses his right to share, as is sometimes said on the authority of a dissidence among the Byzantine scholiasts, 14. 4. 7. 4.   Cp. Mandry, *op. cit.* 2. 437.
[5] Including slave trading though slaves are not *merces, ante,* p. 39.   [6] 14. 4. 1. 1.
[7] See 14. 1. 1. 20, and the constant use of the word *negotiatio*.   [8] 14. 4. 1. *pr.*, 5. 11.
[9] *Si scierit servum peculiari merce negotiari*, 14. 4. 1. *pr.*   [10] 14. 4. 1. 3.
[11] 14. 1. 1. 20; 9. 4. 2. 1; 50. 16. 209.   [12] *op. cit.* 2. 427, 8.   [13] 14. 4. 3. 2.
[14] Effect of death or supervening insanity of *dominus* on later transactions is not discussed, and analogy does not help; there is similar lack of authority in other cases under these edicts. *Ante,* pp. 168, 170; Mandry, *op. cit.* 2. 428.
[15] 14. 4. 3. 2; 50. 17. 110. 2.   [16] 14. 4. 3. 1.   [17] 14. 4. 5. *pr.*

with it[1]. It is possible on the words *eius rei causa,* and *nomine,* that the creditor must, as he naturally would, be aware of the connexion of his contract with the trade[2]. This is denied by Mandry, who thinks objective connexion enough[3], but he hardly seems to distinguish between knowledge of the business, and knowledge of the master's *scientia.* Nothing in any text justifies the view that any knowledge of this last kind was needed[4]. The contract need not have been made with the slave himself: it might be with his *institor,* or if he were an *exercitor,* with his *magister navis,* provided that the *exercitio* were to the master's knowledge[5]. We are told that the *dominus* comes in *velut extraneus creditor*[6], and that debts due to him, or to a person in his *potestas*[7], or to any master if there are several[8], are brought into account. But there is one important distinction : these persons are not, like other creditors, confined to debts connected with the business. All debts due to them can be proved, of any kind, and even if they accrued before the trade existed. The rule is somewhat illogical, and seems to have been developed by the jurists on some ground of justice. Labeo accounts for it by saying, *sufficere enim quod privilegium deductionis perdidit*[9].

If a slave has several businesses of the same or different kinds, the *tributio* is made separately for each one, and thus a creditor will be confined to the trade or trades, in connexion with which his contract was made[10]. The rule, no doubt juristic, is explained by Ulpian as based on the fact that credit was given to that particular business, which, if the slave had two businesses of the same kind, is not certainly true. He adds that the other rule might cause loss to one who dealt with a solvent business, for the benefit of those who had trusted an insolvent one[11]. The fund available for distribution covers not only stock and its proceeds, but tools of trade, *vicarii* employed in the business, and debts due to it[12]. Obviously it does not cover goods entrusted to the slave for sale : these and goods deposited for custody and the like can be vindicated by their owner[13]. In the same way a creditor with a pledge can enforce it against the other creditors[14]. The division of the fund is *pro rata* among the creditors who have proved their claim, and so far as the texts go, there is no indication of any

---

[1] 14. 4. 5. 4, 15, 18; G. 4. 72; In. 4. 7. 3.
[2] On this view a casual transaction with one who afterwards turned out to be managing such a business would not suffice.
[3] *op. cit.* 2. 429. See *post,* App. I.
[4] Ulpian speaks of creditors giving credit to the *merx*: he does not speak of the *dominus,* 14. 4. 5. 15.
[5] 14. 4. 5. 3; 14. 1. 1. 20, 6. *pr.* It is called *quasi tributoria, exemplo tributoriae.* This is because the contract is not the slave's.
[6] 14. 4. 1. *pr.*   [7] *h. t.* 5. 9.   [8] *h. t.* 5. 10.   [9] *h. t.* 5. 7.   [10] *h. t.* 5. 15, 16.
[11] How in such a case debts due to the master not attaching to any business were dealt with does not appear: perhaps charged *pro rata.* Mandry, *op. cit.* 2. 433.
[12] 14. 4. 5. 12—14.   [13] *h. t.* 5. 18.
[14] There must be an actual pledge: the mere fact that all the stock had been bought from one creditor and he was unpaid gave him no priority, *h. t.* 5. 8, 17.

privilege for particular debts. It does not appear whether the *merx* is sold or distributed in kind. Two texts do, indeed, suggest sale of it[1], and no doubt this would usually be the most convenient course, but there is no indication that this was necessary, nor are we told of any rules as to the conduct of the sale. But there is not here, as there is in the *actio de peculio*, any preference for first comers[2]. The demand of one creditor does not compel others to come in[3]: it merely authorises them to do so, and thus, if less than the whole number appear and divide the fund, they must give security for a refund on account of other claims by outstanding creditors, and for any debts, due to the *dominus*, which may not then be reckonable[4]. It may be presumed that if the *dominus* or a creditor who has come in has deliberately refrained from proving any liquid debt, he cannot avail himself of the security[5].

It is in carrying out the distribution that the *dominus* may incur liability to the actual *actio tributoria*[6]. Mere failure to carry out his duty properly is not enough: there must have been *dolus*[7]. Liability does not arise if the act were done by mistake and not persisted in after discovery of the error[8]. Of course *dolus* may take many forms[9]. One text on the nature of the necessary *dolus* raises a curious point. Labeo, deciding a doubtful point[10], observes that if the *dominus* denies, *cuiquam deberi*, this is such *dolus* as justifies the action, for which view he, or Ulpian, gives the reason *alioquin expediet domino negare*. No one can have doubted that refusal to satisfy a liquid and known claim was *dolus*: this cannot have been the doubtful point. The real question is: if a creditor claims *tributio*, and the master says there are no debts, and there is therefore no *tributio*, can this be said to be *dolus in tribuendo*? Yes! says Labeo, otherwise a master need never be liable to the action.

Dolus must on general principle be proved by the plaintiff, and in its absence the defendant is entitled to absolution[11].

If the slave of an *impubes* or *furiosus* trades, *sciente tutore vel curatore*, we have seen that there may be *tributio*. But he is not to profit or lose by his guardian's *dolus*, and we are told that he is liable only so far as he has profited. Pomponius thinks he is liable, but

---

[1] *h. t.* 7. 3, 12. The language negatives the hypothesis that the method was similar to that in *bonorum venditio*.
[2] *h. t.* 6.   [3] Mandry, *op. cit.* 2. 437.
[4] See, *e.g.*, *h. t.* 5. 19, 7. *pr.* Probably security for possible refund was always taken.
[5] The case was not likely to arise. Though the *tributio* exhausted the claim to that particular fund, it had, so far, no novatory effect: the creditor might still sue *de peculio* for any unpaid balance.
[6] *h. t.* 7. 2.   [7] *h. t.* 12.   [8] *h. t.* 7. 3.
[9] Paying himself too much, paying another too little, not paying the right amount into the fund, wasting the assets, not enforcing debts *etc.*, *h. t.* 7. 2—4.
[10] *h. t.* 7. 4.
[11] Hence a difficulty. If the action was brought, *e.g.* on account of denial of the debt, and it appeared that the money was due but the *dominus* had acted in good faith, what was the result? If it was made clear before the action, to persist in the refusal was *dolus* (*h. t.* 7. 2), but what if the explanation were after *litis contestatio*?

will be discharged by cession of the actions which the facts have given him against his guardian. Ulpian agrees that at any rate he must cede those actions[1]. But if the *incapax*, during or after the incapacity, but while he is *doli capax*, is himself guilty of *dolus*, he is liable : the guardian's *scientia* is needed to bring the Edict into operation, but the ward's *dolus* suffices[2].

The action is *perpetua* though the slave be dead[3], and it lies against the *heres*, or other successor, only in so far as he has received anything. Hence if the slave is freed by will, and his *peculium* is left to him, Labeo says the *heres* is not liable, since he has not received the *peculium*, and has committed no fraud. But we have seen that it is his right and duty to take security for *peculiares actiones*[4], at least according to the view which prevailed, and, accordingly, Pomponius here observes that if he has failed to do this or to deduct, he is liable, since this is practically *dolus* in him[5].

It is clear that these last rules have a very delictal look, and it is commonly held that the action is essentially delictal[6], partly on the evidence of these rules, and partly on that of the use of the expression, *dolum malum coercet domini*[7]. But we are told by Julian[8] that the action, *non de dolo est, sed rei persecutionem continet*, from which fact he deduces the further rule that it is *perpetua* against the *heres*, though the slave be dead, *quamvis non aliter quam dolo interveniente competat*. This language seems to negative delictal character, and Mandry[9] holds that the action is contractual, and grouped with the other *actiones adiectitiae qualitatis*. He observes that there were other *actiones* based on *dolus*, but contractual, *e.g., depositi*, and it may be added that the rule that *heres* was liable only so far as he profited applied there too[10]. He points out that if a *vicarius* traded *sciente ordinario*, the master was liable *de peculio ordinarii*, and the debts due to *ordinarius* were not deducted[11] : this he regards as an *actio tributoria de peculio*, and as negativing the delictal character of our action, since *de peculio* does not lie on delict. Karlowa[12] contends that this action is not *tributoria* at all, but an ordinary *actio de peculio*, given on the *peculium* of the *ordi-narius* for contract by *vicarius* made with his knowledge. But such an *actio de peculio* is inadmissible : there is no way of harmonising this text with ordinary principle except by treating it as a *tributoria de peculio*[13]. It may be said, further, that the place of our action in the Edict[14], and its treatment in the Institutes[15] indicate that it is an

---

[1] 14. 4. 3. 1.   The rule differs in form, though perhaps no more, from that laid down in *de peculio, ante*, p. 218.
[2] 14. 4. 3. 2, 4.   [3] *h. t.* 7. 5, 8.   [4] 33. 8. 18 ; *ante*, p. 232.   [5] 14. 4. 9. 2.
[6] See the literature cited, Mandry, *op. cit.* 2. 450.
[7] 14. 4. 7. 2.   Karlowa, *op. cit.* 2. 1162.   [8] *h. t.* 8.   [9] *op. cit.* 2. 450.
[10] 16. 3. 1. 47.   [11] 14. 4. 5. 1.   [12] *op. cit.* 2. 1163.   [13] *Post*, pp. 243 *sq.*
[14] Lenel, Ed. Perp. § 103.   [15] In. 4. 7. 3.

ordinary *actio adiectitiae qualitatis*, of like nature with the rest, and this seems the better view[1].

Between this action and that *de peculio* the creditor must choose, for having sued by one, he cannot fall back on the other[2]. Mere *vocatio in tributum* will not bar *actio de peculio*: the facts thus ascertained will determine his choice, since, in the absence of the actions by which he can recover *in solidum*, the *actio de peculio* may be, on the facts, the best. There is no need to prove *dolus,* and though the *dominus* can deduct, the fund may be so much increased as will more than counterbalance this[3]. On the assumption that the action is contractual, there is no reason to see, in this rule of choice, anything more than the ordinary consumptive effect of *litis contestatio.* But those who think the action delictal cannot accept this view, for it would then seem that, on the analogy of the concurrence of *actio* Aquilia and a contractual action, the one does not necessarily bar the other, as to any excess recoverable by it[4].

Presumably the action exhausts the claim to the then existing *merx,* and presumably also, there may be a renewed *vocatio* for later additions, to the same extent as there might be renewal of the *actio de peculio.*

There is little authority as to the relation of this action with the other Edictal actions. We are told that, as the facts which would base *institoria* (or *exercitoria*) cannot base *tributoria,* the bringing of the former has no effect on the right to bring the latter, and probably the converse is true[5].

---

[1] Nothing important turns on the point, as it does not help us to reconstruct the formula of which we know nothing. Lenel, Ed. Perp. § 103. The action has a certain penal character. The defendant must account for all that he would have handed over apart from *dolus*, 14. 4. 7. 2. He may thus have to pay more than the *peculium* now contains, since it may have been diminished by accident.

[2] 14. 4. 9. 1.

[3] *h. t.* 11; G. 4. 74 a; In. 4. 7. 5. Where one creditor had brought *de peculio* and another *tributoria*, the owner could deduct, in *de peculio,* any sum he had unduly paid to himself, in the distribution, in payment of debt due from the slave, since, as he would have to refund it, it was still due from the slave, *h. t.* 12.

[4] Thus Karlowa holds (*op. cit.* 2. 1164) that he is compelled to choose on grounds of fairness, as against other creditors and the *dominus.* Choice of this action did not of course bar *de peculio* for any other debt, *h. t.* 9. 1.

[5] As to these points see App. II. As to the procedural relations of the various actions see G. 4. 74; In. 4. 7. 5; D. 14. 5. 4. 5 etc.

CHAPTER X.

WE are told in the Sources that *servorum una est condicio*[1]. This proposition expresses, in an inaccurate way, a fact; *i.e.* that in general all slaves are in the same position, in that their faculties are derivative. The slave, as such, has scarcely anything that can be called a right, and the liabilities of most slaves are much alike. But whatever Justinian and his authorities may mean, there is no evident sense of the phrase in which it is exact. In social standing there is the widest difference between different slaves. In legal capacity they differ, if not so widely, at least considerably. These differences are however for the most part not due to any peculiarities in the slave, but result from something affecting the holder, or his title, or from something in the authorisation conferred on the slave. A slave with *peculium* is the same kind of slave as one without. So in the case of a derelict slave, or one *pendente usufructu manumissus*. But there are some cases which cannot be so explained away. Such are that of the *statuliber*, who has a sort of incapacity to be jurally injured, though he is still a slave, and those of *servi publici populi Romani, servi fiscales*, and, possibly, *servi municipii*, who have privileges not distinguishable from property rights[2].

Real or apparent, inherent or resulting from their special relations with other persons, these distinctions need discussion: accordingly we shall consider the special cases in which the position of the slave causes exceptional results to flow from his acts, or from acts affecting him. As the cases are for the most part quite distinct, no attempt is made at anything more than rough grouping.

I. *SERVUS VICARIUS.*

The *servus vicarius,* in the sense in which the expression is here used, is one who forms part of another slave's *peculium.* Erman[3] traces

---

[1] 1. 5. 5. *pr.*; In. 1. 3. 4; Theoph. 1. 5.

[2] The slave informally freed before the *lex* Iunia, and the *servus poenae*. And see C. Th. 4. 12. 5.

[3] Erman, Servus Vicarius, ch. 1, § 4. This valuable monograph has been much used in the preparation of the following remarks. It has a good list of texts and inscriptions. The author deals largely with the "Family Law" of the matter.

the name to the practice of allowing slaves to procure others to serve as deputies for them, in their special services to the master, but, as we know him in the Sources, the *vicarius* is not an agent or deputy for the principal slave, except in the same degree and way in which a *servus ordinarius* may be said to be a deputy for his master. Legal texts dealing with *vicarii* are few, a circumstance which proves not that they were few, but that they were not legally important. Thus of the existing texts a large proportion deal with them only as chattels, and there seems to be only one[1] which refers to the acquisition of property by a *vicarius*, though others mention *vicarii vicarii*[2]. On the other hand there are several which deal with contractual liabilities incurred *nomine vicarii*, a fact which suggests that they usually belong to persons like *dispensatores* and *institores*, acting indeed as clerks to these[3]. The value of the principal slave bears no necessary relation to that of his *vicarius*, which may be much greater, especially in the case of an old slave who has amassed a large *peculium*[4].

As the *peculium* is *de facto* the property of the slave, so, necessarily, is his *vicarius*. This conception is allowed to determine points of construction in wills in a striking way. Ulpian quotes Pomponius as saying that a gift of *servi mei* will not include *vicarii*[5]. But it is clear that this could not always be so: there must have been some circumstance raising a presumption that all slaves were not included. Other texts go in the same direction, but there is always something to raise a presumption. Alfenus says that if his *peculium* is left to a freed slave, and the will also contains a gift to X of *omnes ancillas meas*, this last does not cover *ancillae* in the *peculium*[6]. Here the rule really is that the specific gift takes precedence of the more general[7]. Where a slave and his *vicarius* were freed and given their *peculia*, a *vicarius vicarii* did not become common, a rule expressly based on *voluntas testatoris*, which would hardly have been necessary if, as a matter of law, a *vicarius* was not regarded as the property of his master's owner[8]. All these, being constructions of wills, shew only what was the common mode of speech which the testator was likely to have used, and the rule goes no further. Erman[9] indeed seems inclined to consider it as more

---

[1] 15. 1. 31.   [2] *e.g.* 33. 8. 6. 3; 33. 8. 25.

[3] Erman, *op. cit.* §§ 4, 5. He comes to this conclusion largely on the evidence of inscriptions.

[4] 21. 1. 44. *pr.* It must not be inferred from the word *accedit* that *vicarius* was an accessory. In a legacy of *servus cum vicariis*, the legacy of *vicarii* is good, though *servus* be dead. In. 2. 20. 17; D. 33. 8. 4. If the slaves on a farm are pledged, *vicarii* not employed there are not included, 20. 1. 32.

[5] 32. 73. 5.   [6] 33. 8. 15.

[7] 50. 17. 80. A *peculium* including a *vicarius* was left; there was a gift of liberty to the *vicarius*: it took effect on that ground, 40. 4. 10. *pr.*

[8] 33. 8. 6. 3. Where "all the slaves dwelling on a farm" were left, Ulpian quotes Celsus as holding that this did not cover *vicarii eorum* (33. 7. 12. 44; cp. 20. 1. 32), a rule which is somewhat obscure.

[9] *op. cit.* 450.

important, and cites a text dealing with construction of an agreement, as laying down the same rule. But it does not : the construction there applied excludes all slaves only momentarily on the farm, whether *vicarii* or not[1]. In one text[2], *dominus* (D) and slave (S) have a common slave, V. D, by will, frees S, *cum peculio*, and also leaves V to S and L. Labeo and Trebatius agree that L gets only a quarter. That is, the special gift is not contemplated as destroying the general gift : each covers half. Pothier[3] considers this to be due to the fact that, as the special gift covers something not in the general gift, it can be given a meaning without infringing on the latter, and is therefore so interpreted. But it is at least equally likely, since the authors are early, that it expresses a logical rule on which the principle of construction by *voluntas* has not made, as yet, much inroad.

Two texts are difficult. A slave, S, is freed, *cum peculio*, and his *vicarius*, V, is left to T. Julian says, *teste* Scaevola, that what is *ipso iure* deducted from the legacy of *peculium* on account of debt to *dominus*, goes to T, the legatee of the *vicarius*[4]. This obscure text may perhaps mean that Julian does not here apply the rule that a specific supersedes a general legacy. There are thus two legacies of V. But that to S is only of a part of V, since part of him is not *in peculio*, by reason of debts[5]. That part of V which S does not take goes to T, who thus will take more than half. They are in fact *re coniuncti* as to a certain part of V. This they divide. T takes the rest[6].

Another text says that a legacy of *vicarius* includes one of his *peculium*[7]. This is so contrary to principle, and to express texts[8], that it gives rise to doubts. The opening and concluding clauses are regarded by Gradenwitz as interpolated[9]. This of itself would throw doubt on the rest which though short is the most important part. But this looks as doubtful as the other parts : Ulpian is as little likely to have said *putamus* as to have described himself as a slave[10].

Except for one unimportant chance allusion[11], the texts seem to be silent as to acquisition and alienation by *vicarii*. This is probably due to absence, or rarity, of practice. The *vicarius* is the lowest class of slave and probably rarely acts independently. As a clerk he contracts, and there are difficult questions to answer, as to the effect of his contracts. It is easy to see that similar difficulties might arise in connexion with *iura in rem*, and rarity seems the only explanation of the silence of the

---

[1] 20. 1. 32.   It implies that if definitely employed on the farm *vicarii* were included.
[2] 33. 8. 22. 1.   [3] *ad h. l.*   [4] 33. 8. 21.   [5] *Ante*, p. 225.
[6] Other explanations: Pernice, Labeo, 1. 383 (somewhat similar) ; Mandry, Familiengüterrecht, 1. 193 ; Pothier, *ad h. l.*
[7] 33. 8. 6. 2.   [8] *e.g.* 33. 8. 24.   [9] Gradenwitz, Interpol. 215.
[10] To complete the account of him as a chattel it should be said that the ordinary warranty of soundness exists on sale of *vicarius*. But, apart from express warranty, *vicarii*, included in a *peculium* sold, are sold *tales quales*, 21. 1. 33. *pr.*
[11] 18. 1. 31.

texts. It is not desirable to occupy much space with speculation: it must suffice to suggest a few of the questions which arise. In general it is clear that he acquires to the *servus ordinarius*, his acquisitions forming part of the *peculium*; but it is also not to be doubted that he can acquire, directly, to the *dominus*[1]. This would result from *iussum*, and perhaps, though this is not so clear, from acquisition *nominatim* to him. The ordinary results of his *operae* will go to *servus ordinarius*[2]. But will acquisitions *ex re domini* go to the *dominus* directly or into the *peculium*? At first the former seems obvious, but it cannot be called certain. There is more. or less of a relation of joint ownership between *dominus* and *ordinarius*, but we cannot apply the rules of common ownership: these would make such acquisitions common[3], but so they would acquisitions *ex operis*. The relation is more like that of usufructuary and owner, but even this analogy is imperfect since a legacy to the *vicarius* would probably go to the *ordinarius*. On the other hand it is not like the case of a *servus peculii castrensis*[4], since the *dominus* certainly has a real right in the slave. We know that for acquisition of possession *in re peculiari*[5], the knowledge of *dominus* is not needed, and no doubt an analogous rule applies here. The difficulties which arise in connexion with *bona fides*, and similar matters, in relation hereto, can be judged from those which arise in the case of an ordinary slave[6]. In relation to the acquisition of a usufruct by will, it is not possible to say how far the life of *vicarius* or *ordinarius* set a limit of duration[7].

It is surprising that there is not a single text dealing with a claim by the master on a contract by *vicarius*, though there are many texts dealing with liability on his contracts. Of course the right must vest in the master; the distribution of any proceeds of action being determined by the rules of acquisition as between the master and the *ordinarius*, of which we have had to admit ignorance.

It is not ·possible to consider the further complications which result in all these cases if the *vicarius* has himself a *peculium*. But since we shall have to deal with the liabilities resulting from his acts, and are not in this case left so much in the dark by the texts, it is important to say a word or two about his *peculium*. We are told that gift of a *peculium* to a slave is a gift of one to his *vicarius*[8], which no doubt means that *ordinarius* can give him one without further authorisation from · the *dominus*. As the *peculium* of *vicarius* is part of that of

[1] Erman, *op. cit.* 452—455.   [2] 18. 1. 31.   [3] *Post*, Ch. xvi.; cp. 33. 8. 22. 1.
[4] 49. 17. *pass.*   [5] *Ante*, p. 200.   [6] *Ante*, p. 135.
[7] *Ante*, p. 152. So, in institutions, the question for whom he acquired was probably decided on principles similar to those applied between owner and fructuary (*post*, Ch. xv.). No doubt owner must assent, and it was the knowledge of *vicarius* which was material for *cretio*, *ante*, p. 143.
[8] 15. 1. 6.

ordinarius this is enabling another person to pledge the owner's credit, to the extent at least of part of the *peculium*. It does not follow from this that a slave with *libera administratio* can confer a similar right on his *vicarius*: indeed the absence of texts dealing with alienations by *vicarius* suggests that this is not so[1]. The principles of *concessio peculii* were fixed, as we have seen[2], early, and not in view of any resulting obligation. But a gift of *administratio* is a later idea and definitely authorises alienation. It is by no means obvious that a delegation of this power should proceed as a matter of course. It is to be remembered also that, so long as a *peculium* exists, contracts, even if prohibited, bind the master[3], but this is not true of specific alienations under an existing *administratio*[4].

The *peculium* may consist wholly or in part of property given by the owner of the *ordinarius*[5]. In arriving at the actual content of the *peculium*, complications result from the existence of debts between *ordinarius* and *vicarius*. Thus a debt of *ordinarius* to *vicarius* is not deducted in a legacy of *peculium ordinarii*[6], for obvious reasons, though it is in strictness a debt to a *conservus*, while conversely a debt of *vicarii* to *ordinarius* will be deducted from a legacy of *peculium vicarii*.

Upon the liabilities created by the contracts of *vicarius*, there is a good deal of authority, not all of a very intelligible kind. The chief difficulty is due to the fact that, besides the liability of the master to the extent of the *peculium vicarii*, which certainly exists, however it may be enforced, there is, or may be, also, a secondary liability limited to the *peculium* of the *ordinarius*, for acts done under his authority, or with his knowledge, such that, if done by the *ordinarius*, under the authority, or with the knowledge, of the *dominus*, they would impose a special liability on the latter.

Before entering on the difficulties of the texts, it is necessary to face an important question. We have seen that the *vicarius* is the slave of the *ordinarius*, and only secondarily the slave of the *dominus*. But this notion can be pushed too far. One critic[7] goes so far as to say that as *vicarius* was not directly the slave of the *dominus*, no direct *actio de peculio, etc.*, could be brought against the *dominus* on his account, but that all such actions took the form of an *actio de peculio ordinarii*, *vicarii nomine*, a view which leads Affolter to such awkward forms as *actio de peculio ordinarii de in rem verso vicarii nomine*, and *actio de*

---

[1] See, however, Erman, *op. cit.* 477.   [2] *Ante*, pp. 187, 196.
[3] *Ante*, p. 212.   [4] *Ante*, p. 204.
[5] 15. 1. 4. 6. As to what was in his *peculium*, no doubt rules analogous to those as between owner and *ordinarius* were applied. He and his *peculium* were in that of *ordinarius*, but of course he was not in his own *peculium*, 15. 1. 7. 4, 38. 2; 33. 8. 16. 1.
[6] 33. 8. 9. *pr.*
[7] Affolter, Kr. Viert. 42, p. 351; Z. S. S. 23, p. 61.

peculio ordinarii quod iussu vicarii nomine. This view is rested mainly on principle, reinforced by the consideration that the direct action cannot be made out from the texts, while this indirect form is often mentioned. But the facts are otherwise. An *actio de peculio vicarii* is mentioned at least three times[1], and, for Affolter's form, he gives no reference, and search has not revealed any instance. We have seen the *dominus* giving money to *vicarius* for his *peculium*[2], authorising *exercitio* by the *vicarius*[3], having knowledge of his trading[4], and benefiting by *versio in rem eius* of his acquisitions[5]. The evidence is overwhelming in favour of a direct *actio de peculio* on contracts by *vicarius*.

The rules as to deductions from the *peculium vicarii* present little difficulty. In an action *de peculio ordinarii*, debts due from *vicarius* to *dominus* or a *conservus* can be deducted, but only from the *peculium* of *vicarius*, since outside that they have no existence[6]. The next text[7] applies this principle to legacy of *peculium ordinarii*, and elsewhere[8] Africanus points out that they cannot be deducted, even to the value of the *vicarius* himself, since he is not a part of his own *peculium*. Debts due from the *ordinarius* to him are not deducted though he is a *conservus*, since this would only mean removal of the sum from one part of the available *peculium* to another[9]. Conversely debts due from *dominus* to *vicarius* would be *in peculio ordinarii*, while debts due from *vicarius* to *ordinarius* would be neglected. In an *actio de peculio vicarii*, debts due to the *dominus* or *ordinarius* are deducted[10], and, conversely, debts from them are added so far, in the case of *ordinarius*, as his *peculium* will go. Erman points out[11] that this may practically have much the same effect as if *vicarius* were in his own *peculium*. A creditor of *peculium vicarii*, enforcing a claim against *ordinarius*, might have the right to claim *vicarius*, or his value, as a part of *peculium ordinarii*[12].

It is also held by Erman[13] that debts due to *dominus* from *ordinarius* can be deducted in an *actio de peculio vicarii*, since he is entitled to pay himself out of any part of the *peculium* of *ordinarius* at any time. He regards the right as subject to the limitation that such a payment might be dolose removal from the *peculium*, if the rest of the *peculium ordinarii* would suffice to pay it. The same result would be reached by the rule that deduction can be made only, *si non hoc aliunde consequi potuit*[14]. It may be doubted indeed whether it could be *dolus* to pay

---

1 14. 3. 12 ; 15. 1. 19. *pr.*; 15. 3. 17. 1.
2 Pomponius treats it as the normal case, 15. 1. 4. 6.   3 14. 1. 1. 22.
4 14. 4. 5. 1.   5 15. 3. 17. 1.   6 15. 1. 17, 38. 2.
7 15. 1. 18, 38. 2.   8 33. 8. 16. 1.
9 In. 4. 7. 4; G. 4. 73; D. 15. 1. 17.   In 33. 8. 9 the same principle is applied to legacies.
10 15. 1. 17.   11 *op. cit.* 475, 6.
12 15. 1. 38. 2. This is all Erman means, though he once speaks of *vicarius* as actually in his own *peculium* (p. 475). Affolter seems to treat this as Erman's real view, Z. S. S. *loc. cit.*
13 *op. cit.* 475, 479.   14 15. 1. 11. 6.

yourself with your own money, and, moreover, any debt deductible at all is, *ipso facto*, not in the *peculium*: there can be no question of removal[1]. This circumstance destroys the force of the analogy set up by Erman between this case and that of a man who pays his own debts with the *peculium* of a slave, to the prejudice of the creditors of the latter[2]. But it is not clear that the right of deduction for such debts exists at all, even so limited. It seems to be asserted in one text[3], but, as Affolter remarks[4], the allusion is, on the face of it, to an *actio de peculio ordinarii*. And there is a text which throws doubt on it. Africanus tells us[5] that if under a contract by *vicarius*, something is *versum in peculium ordinarii*, the creditor has an *actio de in rem verso, de peculio ordinarii*, and therefore subject to deductions for debts due to the *dominus* from that *peculium*. But if it is *versum in rem domini* there is no deduction for debts of the *ordinarius*. There will certainly be a deduction for debts due to the *dominus* from the *vicarius*[6], since such debt, on general principle, destroys a *versum*[7]. But if Erman's view is correct, debts due from *ordinarius* ought to be deducted too, for they would be covered by the rule that a *dominus* can set off against a *versum* what he may claim from the *peculium* of the slave who made the *versio*.

One text dealing with *actio de peculio* is difficult. We are told that if an *actio de peculio ordinarii* has been brought there can be no further *actio de peculio vicarii*, but that if an *actio de peculio vicarii* has been brought, there may be an *actio de peculio ordinarii*[8]. Leaving out of consideration the question of *consumptio litis*[9], the difficulty remains that, as it is a transaction of the *ordinarius* which gives *de peculio ordinarii*, and one of the *vicarius* which gives *de peculio vicarii*, it is not easy to see what this transaction is, which may give rise to either. We might of course suppose a transaction in which they both took part, but it is more likely that the case is one in which the *vicarius* made the contract with such privity of *ordinarius* as, if it had been of *dominus*, would have given an *actio in solidum*. We shall have shortly to consider such cases.

There is little authority as to the *actio de in rem verso*. So far as the *versio* is *in rem domini* the ordinary principles apply: the *versio* is liable to cancellation for debts of the *vicarius*, but, as the text says, not for those of *ordinarius*[10]. But, if it is *in peculium ordinarii*, the action is subject to another limit. It is practically *de peculio ordinarii*, and like any other such action is temporary, (not, as an ordinary *actio de in rem verso* is, perpetual,) and liable to be limited, by the death of the

[1] It is in no sense *solutio*. This is brought out in two texts dealing with *vicarii*. 15. 1. 11. 4, 5 has already been considered (*ante*, p. 224). See also 10. 3. 25. This principle is not affected by the rule that in some cases deduction is allowed only *si dolo careat*, 15. 1. 9. 4. This has no connexion with the rules as to dolose removal.
[2] *op. cit.* p. 479.   [3] 15. 1. 17.   [4] Krit. Viertel., *loc. cit.*
[5] 15. 3. 17. 1.   [6] Affolter, *loc. cit.*, denies this.   [7] 15. 3. 10. 7, 8.
[8] 15. 1. 19. *pr.*   [9] *Post*, App. II.   [10] 15. 3. 17. 1. It does not mention debt of *vicarius*.

ordinarius, to an *annus utilis*, and to be cancelled by his debt to the *dominus*. Africanus observes that the *actio de peculio et in rem verso* is here brought on the *peculium vicarii*, and that it may seem odd that it should be affected by the death of the *ordinarius*. But, he adds, *ea res* cannot be in the *peculium vicarii*, except so long as the *peculium ordinarii* exists. The *ea res* is the *versum*, the reason being, as is said above, that the liability only arises by the intervention of the *ordinarius*, and is therefore subject to the limitation attaching to other obligations established by him. It does not mean, as the glossators supposed[1], that the *peculium vicarii*, and therefore all liability on his contract, ended with the *peculium ordinarii*. Whether that endured after the death of the *ordinarius* depended on the action of *dominus*: if he left it, it was still *peculium*. All that is needed is that he does not take it away[2]. There seems no reason to think Africanus adopted the form *ea res non est in peculio vicarii* when he meant "there is no *peculium vicarii*[3]."

The meagreness of the textual authority[4] strongly suggests that these cases were rare, and it may be that the discussion is mainly academic. An impression of the same sort is left by the one text[5] which deals with *actio tributoria*. It leaves so many practical points undecided that the general result is not very informing. If the trading was with the knowledge of *dominus* but not of *ordinarius*, there is a direct *actio tributoria*[6]. The effect is that debts due to the master come into *tributio*, but those to *ordinarius* do not, but are deducted in full, notwithstanding the rule that debts due to *conservi* come into *tributio*[7]. If the *ordinarius* alone knew, the text says there is an *actio de peculio ordinarii*, such that what is due from *vicarius* to *dominus* is deducted, but not what is due to the *ordinarius*. The text expressly contrasts this with *actio tributoria*, and this seems to imply that it is not itself such an action. But, as Erman remarks[8], it is incredible that the whole *peculium* of *ordinarius* should be liable on such a contract, not of his making or authorisation. It would be to put the case on the same level as that in which the *ordinarius* has given *iussum* for the contract. The "*inelegantia*" of this is obvious. If it is *tributoria*, the fund available is the *merx peculiaris vicarii*, as in the direct *actio tributoria*, but the present one has the disadvantage of being liable to extinction by the cesser of *peculium ordinarii* from any cause, and, further, that debts due to *dominus* are deducted *in solidum*, while in the other they come

---

[1] Erman, *op. cit.* 481 *sq.*   [2] 15. 1. 7. 1.
[3] 15. 3. 17. 1. This text contains the only allusion to *quod iussu, nomine vicarii*. Apparently the rules were the same.
[4] 14. 3. 12 also contains a reference to *de in rem verso*, *post*, p. 248.
[5] 14. 4. 5. 1.
[6] Affolter, Krit. Viertel., 1900, who denies any such direct action, does not deal with this text.
[7] 14. 4. 5. 9.   [8] *op. cit.* 488.

into *tributio*. But as debts to *ordinarius* are probably commoner, and as to these the rule is reversed, this may be rather an advantage. The general result is more rational, and is not wholly excluded by the fact that the action is expressly contrasted with *actio tributoria*. Such an action cannot be, properly speaking, *tributoria*, since the *negotium* is not *sciente eo cuius in potestate est*, as the Edict requires[1]. It can be only an *actio utilis* or *ad exemplum tributoriae*.

There is a still further difficulty. If both knew, we are told that the creditor has the choice of these two actions, *sic tamen ut utrumque tribuatur*. If this applies to both actions, it is difficult to see the meaning of the option, so long as there is any choice, (*i.e.* so long as *peculium ordinarii* subsists,) since the *merx* available is the same, the claims are the same, and the same debts are brought into *tributio*. If the words quoted apply only to the direct *actio tributoria*, as Erman seems to hold[2], then this must always be the best, since the debts due to *dominus* would be deducted *in solidum* in the other. It is difficult to suppose, as Erman does, that the option is mentioned only with a view to symmetry. The option indeed suggests that the action which is not *tributoria* is the ordinary *de peculio ordinarii*, in which the fund would be different. We have seen above that this leads to an inadmissible result. It is difficult to avoid the impression that the whole thing is an unconsidered dealing, either by Ulpian or by Tribonian, with a topic which did not arise in practice, and that impression is strengthened by the omissions[3].

If a *vicarius* acts as *magister navis* or *institor* for the *dominus*, the ordinary rules apply[4], these actions having indeed no necessary connexion with the household relation. In relation to *actio exercitoria*, we are told that if *vicarius exercet* by authority of *ordinarius*, the *dominus* is liable *de peculio ordinarii*, a plain application of principle, and if *ordinarius* himself is *exercitor* without authority, and *vicarius* is his *magister navis*, the same result of course follows[5]. The only text dealing with the *actio institoria* in this connexion[6] deals with a *vicarius* who is hired from the *ordinarius* and made *institor* by the third-party, in which capacity he sells to his own *dominus*. The text observes that this is a sale, for, though the master is not liable to his slave, yet he can possess *pro emptore*, and usucapt. The owner has *institoria utilis* against the hirer. Its *utilis* character may be due to the fact that the transaction was between a man and his own slave[7]. The remedy the

---

[1] Lenel, Ed. Perp. § 103.   [2] *op. cit.* pp. 489, 490.
[3] Did *ordinarius* carry out the *tributio*? He could not unless he had *administratio peculii*, since it involved alienation (*ante*, p. 201). If he did not, did the *dominus*? If so, it is, or may be, his *dolus* which bases the action, and the distinction between the two cases becomes unreal.
[4] 14. 1. 1. 22, *in fin.*   [5] 14. 1. 1. 22, 23.   [6] 14. 3. 11. 8, 12.
[7] In 14. 1. 5, where D contracts with his own slave acting as *magister navis* for X, Paul avoids giving the action a name.

other way is, for analogous reasons, a little indirect[1]. The *vicarius* has
no right of action to cede to his principal. Accordingly the text gives
the employer an *actio de peculio ordinarii* on the contract of hire of
vicarius, and *de peculio vicarii* on the mandate to him to sell. It then
adds : *pretiumque quo emisti in rem tuam versum videri poterit eo quod
debitor servi tui factus esses.* Apparently Julian's point is that as the
contract was with his own slave it is not directly enforceable, so that in
a sense the rights acquired by him under it are clear profit[2].

The law as to noxal liability for a *vicarius* is not quite clear. Africanus tells us[3] that if a *dominus* has defended a *vicarius* noxally, and has
paid the damages, and afterwards freed the *ordinarius, cum peculio,* he may
deduct from the *peculium* of the *vicarius* what he paid, since it was *pro
capite vicarii,* and so made him a debtor. If there is not enough in that
peculium, he can deduct from the rest of the *peculium* of the *ordinarius,*
but, in that case, only up to the value of the *vicarius,* this being all for
which *ordinarius* could have been liable. This text leaves open the
question whether the liability is limited to the *peculium ordinarii.*
Any such limitation seems unfair to the injured person, and, on the
view of them which we have taken, is in no way compelled by the
relations between *vicarius* and *dominus.* Pomponius lays down the rule
in accordance with this view of the matter. He says[4] the *dominus* is
liable either to pay *in solidum* or to surrender. It is the more surprising to find that Paul takes, or seems to take, a contrary view. He is
dealing with the case of a *servus exercitor* whose *vicarius* does damage,
and he says[5] that *dominus* is liable, *ac si is exercitor liber et hic vicarius
servus eius esset ut de peculio servi tui ad noxam dedere vicarium dam-
neris,* with a further remark that if your *ordinarius* was privy to the
damnum, you are noxally liable on his account. The words, *de peculio
...ad noxam dedere,* look doubtful, since they set up no alternative such
as is usually found in noxal actions, and, instead, limit even the surrender to what may be less than the value of the *vicarius.* Accordingly
it has been proposed[6] to read *aut noxae dedere,* which avoids that
difficulty explains the language of our text, and has some authority.
But this leaves the contradiction absolute. If the text was written as
it stands, by Paul, which is not certain[7], it is not clear that there is a
contradiction. The text is dealing with the *actio in factum* against
exercitor for damage by persons employed on the ship[8], which, as Lenel

---

[1] Lenel. who holds that the *actio institoria* was always *utilis* where *institor* was a slave (Ed.
Perp. § 102), thinks the exceptional circumstances account not for the use of the word, but for its
retention by the compilers.
[2] For other explanations see von Tuhr, De in rem verso, 260 *sqq.* It may be noted that the
text is another authority for direct actions on account of *vicarius.*
[3] 33. 8. 16. *pr.*   [4] 15. 1. 23.   [5] 9. 4. 19. 2.   [6] See Mommsen's text.
[7] The part we have considered is oddly expressed, and the final clause besides being corrupt
mere repetition.
[8] *Ante,* p. 122.

says[1], may not have had any special edict, but, in any case, makes the *exercitor* personally liable, and not merely indirectly and vicariously, as in the case of ordinary liability for slaves. That this distinction is real appears from the fact that though, if the wrong-doer is his own slave, he is released by noxal surrender, the jurist finds it necessary to justify this by special reasons[2], instead of letting it go as a matter of course. As the liability is personal to the *exercitor*, it is, of necessity, *de peculio*, if he is an unauthorised slave, for it is not a delict of his. And the power of noxal surrender, being a special privilege, could not increase his liability. Hence the duty of *dominus* is to pay *de peculio* or surrender.

II. SERVUS FILIIFAMILIAS.

Of this slave there is little to be said. So far as we are here concerned the *servus castrensis peculii* is the slave of his immediate master[3]. No doubt the same is true for *servus quasi castrensis*, but authority is lacking.

On the other hand, slaves of a *peculium profectitium* are in much the same position as *vicarii*. The few differences are indicated by Erman[4], the most important one being that the various actions *adiectitiae qualitatis* may be brought against the *filiusfamilias*. But here some difficulties arise. It is a matter on which the texts are absolutely silent, and the commentators have made it their own. There is a controversy, on which we will not enter, as to what actions could be brought against a *filiusfamilias*: it is clear that the solution affects the present question. Thus it is said that no action attributing property could be brought against a *filiusfamilias*. Hence the actions which rest on command or authorisation, such as *quod iussu, exercitoria, institoria*, would be available, while *de peculio* and *tributoria* were not, and must be brought against the *pater*. This leads to the odd result[5], that a *filiusfamilias* might be sued *de peculio* for what he had fraudulently removed from the *peculium*, but though the action was the same, the *iudex* must ignore what is still in the *peculium*. This seems most unlikely, and indeed there is nothing in these edicts, so far as they are known, requiring *dominium* of the *peculium* in the defendant. On the other hand there is in the *actiones quod iussu, de peculio, de in rem verso*, and *tributoria* a requirement that defendant have *potestas* over the slave[6].

---

[1] *op. cit.* § 78.
[2] 4. 9. 7. 4. And it explains the language of our text. Cp. 47. 5. 1. 5. In simple delict the personality of the *ordinarius* would not appear at all.
[3] For the texts, Erman, *op. cit.* 518 *sqq.*   [4] *loc. cit.*
[5] Erman accepts it, *op. cit.* 521.
[6] Lenel, Ed. Perp. *ad haec.* The difficulties would be readily met by *actiones utiles*, but we have no information. Whether, on condemnation, he could pay *ex peculio* without *administratio* is disputed. See the authors cited, Erman, *op. cit.* 522. There is no evidence.

There is another case in which texts are equally lacking, and are much to be desired, since it is one which calls for clear distinctions. It is that of *servus bonorum adventitiorum*, of *materna bona* and the like. We are left in the dark. The fact is not surprising since the whole institution is post-classical. According to the main statutes which governed the matter up to the time of Justinian[1], the father had for the time being, a usufruct, but such that he could neither alienate nor pledge[2] the property, but must, on the other hand, bring and defend all actions, and, generally, administer as if he were full *dominus*. This state of things is very anomalous[3], and we cannot tell what it may have meant in our subject. Justinian legislates on the matter with amazing verbosity[4], but he does not help us much. He gives the father certain powers of alienation, in case of need, and emphasises his independence in his administration: he is not to be interfered with in any way by the son. It is clear that he is in a very different position from that of an ordinary usufructuary: it seems likely that he is for all legal purposes owner, subject to such express restrictions as are placed on his powers, and to a general duty to account to the son.

III. *Servus in Bonis.*

This case could not occur under Justinian, and accordingly is not discussed in his compilations, our chief source of information. We have therefore no details as to these slaves. Broadly, the *nudum ius quiritium* counted for nothing, except for *tutela*. The *lex* Iunia[5] expressly enacts that the *tutor* of a *latinus impubes manumissus* shall be he who had *ius quiritium* before the *manumissio*, so that *tutela legitima* and right to *bona* would be separated. All that a slave so held acquired he acquired to his owner *in bonis*[6]. The quiritary owner could not free him[7]. On the other hand the bonitary owner could not make him a *necessarius heres*, because the manumission would make him only a Latin, and Latins could not take inheritances[8]. Perhaps he could be instituted as a *servus alienus* could, and then if the ownership had ripened, he would be *necessarius heres*. If he were instituted with other heirs it seems that he would become a Latin, if, and when, some other heir entered[9].

---

[1] C. Th. 8. 18; C. 6. 60.
[2] C. Th. 8. 18. 7; C. 6. 60. 2.
[3] See Gothofredus *ad* C. Th. 8. 18. 3.   He points out a conflict with 28. 8. 7. 2 *in fin.*
[4] C. 6. 61. 6, 8.   [5] Ulp. 1. 19; G. 1. 167.
[6] Ulp. 19. 20; G. 1. 54; 2. 88; 3. 166.   Even, so some taught, though he stipulated or received by mancipation in the name of the Quiritary owner, but Gaius declares this a nullity.
[7] C. 4. 49. 11; 7. 10. 5.   [8] Ulp. 22. 8.
[9] If the object were merely to benefit the Latin, this could be done by directing the *heres* to free and hand over the property when the ownership had ripened.

IV. *SERVUS LATINI.*

This case could not occur under Justinian, and we have little information. Latins of all kinds had *commercium*, so that over a large field the ordinary law applies. Colonary Latins could make wills, and thus what was said of the last case applies to a certain extent here. Junian Latins could not make wills, and thus that class of question could not arise in connexion with them. The slave of a colonary Latin could acquire legacies and inheritances for his master: those of a Junian Latin could not, though the legacy or institution was not void but depended on the acquisition of citizenship by the Latin, before it was too late to claim[1]. This at least seems the natural inference from the texts dealing with gifts to the Latin himself[2].

V. *SERVUS PEREGRINI.*

Though foreigners were still peregrines, it is practically true to say that, for legal purposes, the class of peregrines had ceased to exist under the law of Justinian. Here too we know but little. A peregrine had no *commercium*. Thus a slave could not acquire for him by *mancipatio*, or by direct testamentary gift[3]. Manumission could make him no more than a peregrine. Subject to such absolute restrictions as that a slave could not take part in any judicial proceeding, or in witnessing a will, he could do by derivation from the peregrine any commercial act that the peregrine could himself do. As a peregrine could himself sue or be sued[4], on the fiction that he was a *civis*, it may be assumed that noxal actions were possible by means of analogous contrivances. *Mutatis mutandis* the same may be said of the actions *de peculio etc.*

---

[1] G. 1. 23, 24; 2. 110; 2. 275.
[3] G. 1. 25; 2. 218 *etc.*

[2] Arg. Ulp. 17. 1; 20. 8; 22. 3 *etc.*
[4] G. 4. 37.

CHAPTER XI.

SPECIAL CASES (*cont.*). S. HEREDITARIUS. S. DOTALIS. S. DEPOSITUS, COMMODATUS, LOCATUS, IN PRECARIO.

VI. *SERVUS HEREDITARIUS.*

THE slave who forms part of an inheritance on which an *extraneus heres* has not yet entered, owes his prominence in the texts to the importance of the *hereditas iacens* whose mouthpiece or agent he is. The *hereditas iacens* cannot exist where there is no interval between the death and the succession, for instance in the case of institution of a *suus heres*. Even the development of *ius abstinendi* does not affect this, and the rules as to the acts of slaves, where there is a *suus heres* whose taking is still doubtful, are nowhere fully dealt with[1].

Most of the doubts and difficulties in connexion with *servus hereditarius* are the outcome of differences of opinion as to the nature of the *hereditas iacens*. We cannot deal with this in detail, but a few points may be noted. The *hereditas* is, not exactly a *persona ficta*, for the Romans never use this conception, but a sort of representation or symbol of the *dominus*. It is pointed out in several texts that it is not strictly a *dominus*[2], but *domini loco habetur*[3]; *sustinet personam domini*[4]. In three texts it is actually described as *dominus*. But of these one says, *dominus ergo hereditas habebitur*[5], after having said, *cum dominus nullus sit huius servi*; in the second[6] the words, *hoc est dominae*, are, evidently, an insertion; the third[7], which contains the words *hereditatem dominam esse*, is as it stands unintelligible: it is clear that they are all interpolated. The *hereditas* does not however represent the *dominus* for all purposes: *in multis partibus iuris pro domino habetur; in plerisque personam domini sustinet*[8]. These expressions are sufficiently accounted for by the restrictions, soon to be discussed, on the powers of *servus hereditarius*, and by the obvious fact that many rights and duties failed at death. But they may be connected with another question: if

---

[1] The cases of conditional *institutio* of a slave of the testator, of the existence of a *suus captivus*, and of a *postumus omissus* may have been similarly dealt with, but there is no authority for applying the theory of the *hereditas iacens* to them. See Pernice, Labeo, 1. 358 *sqq.* As to *peculium castrense, post,* p. 258.

[2] 47. 19. 6; 48. 18. 2.   [3] 11. 1. 15. *pr.*   [4] C. 4. 34. 9.   [5] 9. 2. 13. 2.

[6] 47. 4. 1. 1.   [7] 28. 5. 31. 1.   [8] 41. 1. 61. *pr.*; In. 3. 17. *pr.*

hereditas sustinet personam domini, who is this *dominus*? The heir or the deceased? There was an old opinion that it was the heir: *transit ad heredem, cuius personam interim hereditas sustinet*[1]; *heres et hereditas unius personae vice funguntur*[2]. This view is supported by a number of texts, which make the entry of the *heres* date back to the death[3]. But, notwithstanding traces of dispute in the Digest[4], there can be no doubt that the general rule of later law is that it represents the deceased and not the heir[5]. Thus it is said that where a *servus hereditarius* stipulates or acquires by *traditio*, the act *ex persona defuncti vires accipit*[6].

The *servus hereditarius* is a part of the *hereditas*. As, in strictness, the *hereditas* is not his master[7], we should expect that he might be tortured *in re hereditaria*. And so Ulpian says, holding that so long as it is uncertain to whom the *bona* belong, he cannot be said to be tortured *in re domini*[8]. Several other texts discuss the matter, but do not distinguish clearly between the case where the *hereditas* is still *iacens*, and that in which it is not, or may not be, so. Thus Papinian allows torture of such slaves where it is a question of a supposititious child, or where one claimant is alleged not to be really a member of the family. He allows it because it is not *contra dominos ceteros filios*, but *pro successione*[9]. Clearly he is laying down a limitation to the rule that a slave cannot be tortured *in re domini*. So Paul says[10] that a judge who cannot decide *de fide generis* may torture *servi hereditarii*, the allusion appearing to be to a claim of relationship, irrespective of the question whether there has been *aditio* or not. In fact, where there has been an *aditio*, and the question is whether it is valid or not, it cannot be told till after the event, whether the *hereditas* was actually *iacens* or not.

There was a good deal of legislation on this matter, after classical times. Diocletian declared it settled law[11] that *servi hereditarii* could be tortured, where the allegation was that a will was forged, even though the slaves were freed by it, and also[12] that it was allowed in any claim of the *hereditas*, the reason here assigned being that ownership is doubtful. There was evidently other legislation, for Justinian alludes to past legislation and distinctions, which he abrogates, and he enacts that slaves of the *hereditas*, including those freed by the will, may be tortured, but only if the question is as to specific things and not claims of the *hereditas*, and only if they have the care of these things, and the applicant for

---

[1] 46. 2. 24. *Eius* may have dropped out before *cuius*.   [2] 41. 3. 22.
[3] 29. 2. 54; 45. 3. 28. 4; 50. 17. 138. See Accarias (Précis § 347) as to a possible non-juristic origin of this view. Cicero, de legg. 2. 22. D. 45. 3. 28. 4.
[4] *e.g.* as to stipulation by slave in name of future *heres*. *Post*, p. 260.
[5] 28. 5. 31; 30. 116. 3; 31. 55. 1; 41. 1. 34; C. 4. 34. 9; In. 2. 14. 2; Theoph. *ad h. l.*
[6] This view, and that *testantis personam spectandam esse*, Ulpian in his Disputationes credits to Julian. Such a work was mainly occupied with old *cruces*, 41. 1. 33. 2.
[7] 9. 2. 13. 2; 1. 8. 1. *pr.*   [8] 48. 18. 2, *ante*, p. 86.
[9] 48. 18. 17. 2.   [10] *h. t.* 18. 4.
[11] C. 9. 41. 10.   [12] C. 9. 41. 13.

their torture has taken an oath of good faith[1]. But they cannot be tortured against one who, having given security, has obtained possession of the *hereditas* : *domini loco habetur*[2].

The rules applied in case of damage to a *servus hereditarius* seem, rather illogically, to treat the *heres* as if he was the owner, *i.e.*, to apply the notion that the *hereditas* represents the *heres*, so far, at least, as is necessary to do justice. Thus, though the *actio* Aquilia is available only to the *dominus*[3], and does not pass to a new *dominus*, except by cession[4], we are told that if a *servus hereditarius* is killed or injured, the *heres* has the action on *aditio*, for though no one was owner, *hereditas dominus habebitur*[5]. Unless it can be said to be inherited[6], this seems to make the *hereditas* represent the *heres*. This inadequate justification is eked out by another. We are told[7] that the *lex* does not mean, by the word *dominus*, him who was owner at the time of the injury. There is little doubt, however, that that is what it does mean[8], and in fact the explanation will do only for damage, not for destruction, unless the *lex* means by " owner," one who never was owner[9]. If the slave be the subject of a legacy or *fideicommissum*, and the *heres* kill him before *aditio*, there is no *actio* Aquilia, or *de dolo*, as the *dolus* would give a claim *ex testamento*[10]. If he is killed by another person, similarly, we are told, the legatee can have no action, though the heir has. But if it was merely damage, the legatee on acquiring the slave can call on the heir to cede the action[11]. For theft of the slave no doubt the ordinary rules of *expilatio hereditatis* are applied[12]. For *iniuria* to the slave the *heres* has the *actio iniuriarum*, and in the case of *verberatio* it remains with him, even though the slave be freed by the will[13]. The same rule would apply, *a fortiori*, to other forms of *iniuria*, for *verberatio* was precisely the one in which the feelings of the slave were considered[14]. But that belongs to later law : the present text is from Labeo.

As to wrongs done by the slave to outsiders, the ordinary rules apply, except that, for the moment, there is no one who can be sued. If,

---

[1] C. 2. 58. 1. 1; 9. 41. 18.   [2] 48. 18. 15. 2.
[3] 9. 2. 11. 6.   [4] 9. 2. 11. 7.
[5] 9. 2. 13. 2.   In 5. 3. 36. 2 the point is the same : has the possessor validly entered?
[6] See 36. 1. 68. 2, and 47. 10. 1. 6.   [7] 9. 2. 43.
[8] Monro, Lex Aquilia, *ad h. l.*
[9] The text observes that any other rule would cause intolerable injustice. But an *actio in factum* might have sufficed.
[10] 4. 3. 7. 5; 30. 47. 4, 5. *Ante*, p. 18. If it were after entry, he might be liable to legatee *ex* Aquilia, 9. 2. 14.
[11] 9. 2. 15. *pr.* The case seems to be treated *pro tanto* as one of principal and accessory, 33. 8. 2. Paul says (36. 1. 68. 2) that if there were a *fc. hereditatis*, and a slave was damaged, the action did not pass to *fideicommissarius*, as it was not *in bonis defuncti*. As Pernice remarks (Sachbeschäd. 189) this denies merely the *ipso facto* passing of the action. He thinks the text refers to damage after *aditio*, but this is far from clear and does not seem material. So far as the heir's right is concerned, the same rule applied to *servi corruptio*, 11. 3. 13. 1. For an analogous case see 36. 1. 75. *pr.*
[12] 47. 19. The exceptional cases in which *furti* lay have no special relation to slaves, 47. 2. 69—71.
[13] 47. 10. 1. 6, 7.   [14] *Ante*, pp. 79, 80.

being *pure legatus*, he steals from the legatee, no question arises. If he steals, or damages, property of the future heir, then, in the same case, the legatee will be liable to noxal action, since the man never belonged to the heir[1]. Analogous rules apply if the slave, freed *pure*, does the act before the entry of any heir[2]. If he is freed conditionally, special rules apply which will be considered later[3]. If he is left conditionally *per vindicationem*, there will be no action on the Sabinian view that in the meantime he belongs to the heir: on the other view the heir will have his remedy. The Sabinian view appears to have prevailed, though the matter is not absolutely clear[4]. If such a slave steals from one of coheirs before *aditio*, there can be no *actio furti*, but the matter is adjusted in the *iudicium familiae erciscundae*, the simple value, or in the alternative the slave, being allowed[5]. If he is left *per damnationem*, he belongs for a time to the heir, who can thus have no *actio furti*[6].

If a *servus hereditarius* takes *res hereditatis*, since these cannot be stolen, there can be no noxal *actio furti*, though there may be *actio ad exhibendum*[7]. If he is *legatus* in such a way that for a time he is the heir's, there can be no such remedy, any more than if he were to stay in the *hereditas*. If he is freed there is no civil remedy, but there is a special edictal procedure. It is provided that if a slave, freed by the will, damages the interest of the *heres* in any way, *dolo malo*, before *aditio*, he is liable to an action for double damages within an *annus utilis*[8]. The reason assigned for the creation of this action is that there can be no civil remedy, and he knows he is in no danger of being punished as a slave. Provided his act was dolose, for negligence is not enough, the nature of the wrong is immaterial[9]. The action is available to other successors as well as the heir, and if a *pupillus* is heir, and dies, the right arises in the interval, before the entry of the substitute, if the slave is to be free only in that event[10]. Even if the liberty is fideicommissary, and unconditional, this action lies, as the man cannot be treated as a slave[11]. But it does not lie if there is any other delictal remedy, though it may coexist with a *vindicatio*, or other action *ad rem persequendam*[12]. If the slave is freed only conditionally, since he can in the meantime be punished as a slave,

---

[1] 9. 4. 40; 47. 2. 65.   [2] 9. 2. 48; 47. 2. 44. 2.   [3] *Post*, Ch. XXI.
[4] See texts cited by Huschke, *ad* G. 2. 195, 200. Cp. Girard, Manuel, 922, and C. 6. 43. 3. 3.
[5] 10. 2. 16. 6.   [6] 30. 70. *pr.*, 2; *ante*, p. 125.   [7] 9. 4. 40.
[8] 47. 4. 1. *pr.* Several concerned could be sued together: payment by one did not release the others, *h. l.* 19.
[9] 47. 4. 1. 1, 2, 14. If it was theft the *res* need not have been the property of the testator, if its safety concerned the *hereditas, e.g.* things lent or pledged to the deceased, or held in good faith by him, and *fructus, fetus* and *partus* born after death, *h. l.* 10, 11, 13.
[10] *h. l.* 9. In this case it covered acquisitions by *impubes, h. l.* 12. These rules as to *impubes* are possibly due to Tribonian. Cp. Eisele, Z. S. S. 7. 18.
[11] *h. l.* 7. A juristic extension.   [12] *h. l.* 16, 17.

the action does not lie[1], even though the *heres* does not know of the wrong till he is free[2], though Ulpian is cited as quoting Labeo to the effect that if the condition supervenes suddenly on the act, the action lies, since there was no practical chance of punishing him[3]. The absence of any civil remedy, as we are told, caused the introduction of the action, and this absence was due to the conception of the *hereditas* as at least representing the *dominus*[4], so that the *crimen expilatae hereditatis* is barred.

All this would apply equally well to the case of a slave *pure legatus*, but the Edict[5] deals only with the freed slave. There is, however, a text which says that the action is available if the slave is *pure legatus*, and adds that it lies if the ownership in him is changed[6]. This is obscure, but it is clear that the case is not within the actual words of the Edict—*hanc actionem indulgendam*. As extant, the text says the action is to lie if ownership is changed or lost, or liberty is gained *post intervallum modicum aditae hereditatis*. The form and content of this text suggest that it may be a pure insertion of the compilers. However this may be, it is certain that its sweeping generality cannot represent the law, for it gives the action where liberty is not attained. Mommsen[7] corrects by omitting *vel libertas competit*, so that the acquisition of liberty is implied in all the cases it deals with, but this alteration makes the words *post intervallum modicum, etc.*, apply to the transfer of ownership. This is inconsistent with what has been said, and moreover would make the rule apply where the *heres* himself sold the slave[8]. The alteration of *vel* into *et* before *libertas competit* brings the new rule into exact line with the principle of the Edict, and the scribe's error would be a very likely one in view of the two preceding expressions with *vel*.

The *hereditas* being *pro domino*, the slave can acquire for it[9]: his acquisitions of whatever kind belong to it, and therefore go to the *heres postea factus*[10], even though the slave is *legatus*[11]. What he acquires is reckoned in *iudicium familiae erciscundae*, and can be recovered by *hereditatis petitio*[12]. As to his acquisition of possession, there were disputes. In one text it is said[13] that if such a slave buys, and acquires possession, and then loses it again, the *heres* on entry has the Publician, *quasi ipse possedisset*, whether the dealing was *peculiari*

---

[1] *h. l.* 3. [2] 47. 4. 2. [3] 47. 4. 1. 4, 3.
[4] 47. 4. 1. 1, 15. [5] 47. 4. 1. *pr.*; Lenel, Ed. Perp. § 135.
[6] 47. 4. 1. 5, 6. [7] *ad h. l.*
[8] The action cannot lie against legatee, for if it is a debt purely due from *peculium* (15. 1. 27. 1), *heres* should have deducted and can now condict (*ante*, p. 229). If it be regarded as noxal it is excluded as the *crimen expilatae hereditatis* is.
[9] 41. 1. 61. *pr.*; 45. 3. 16; 49. 15. 29.
[10] In. 2. 22. 2; 3. 17. *pr.* [11] 31. 38.
[12] 10. 2. 12. 1. [13] 6. 2. 9. 6, 10.

nomine or not. In view of the controversy as to whether legal possession was needed for the Publician or not, the text does not prove that his possession is the heir's : it rather suggests that it is not, except *in re peculiari*. It is clear that such a slave can continue and complete *usucapio* already begun, but this is of little importance, since all that is needed for that, in the case of a *hereditas*, is that there be no adverse possession[1]. Apart from this, even *in re peculiari*, the matter is not clear. In two texts of Paul and Julian in which the power is asserted the language is obscure and the remark may be compilers' work[2]. Papinian tells us, in one text[3], that if such a slave begins *tenere peculiari causa*, *usucapio* does not begin till *aditio*, for how, he asks, can that be usucapted, which the deceased never possessed ? In another text[4] he tells us that if such a slave *comparat*, *usucapio* begins to run, but this is *singulari iure*. This is so like Papinian's own way of looking at acquisition of possession *peculii causa*, as allowed on utilitarian grounds, and not based on principle[5], that it seems necessary to understand this text only of "peculiar" acquisition. It then contradicts the other. Mommsen suggests that a *nisi* has dropped out of the text first mentioned[6], so that the denial would apply only to extra-peculiar acquisition[7].

Legacies and *institutiones* can be made to a *servus hereditarius*, owing to the rule that *servi persona inspicienda est et in testamentis*[8]. But though he can be instituted, he cannot enter[9]. *In quibus factum personae operaeve substantia desideratur nihil hereditati adquiri potest*, and therefore, *quia adire jubentis domini persona desideratur, heres exspectandus est*[10]. It follows that he never really acquires a *hereditas* to the *hereditas*, but only to the *heres*. Thus it does not form part of the *hereditas*[11]. The *institutio* depends for its validity on the *testamenti factio* of the deceased, whom the *hereditas* represents, not on that of the *heres*, though, of course, the *heres* will not get it unless qualified to take, or beyond the proportion he is qualified to take[12].

A *miles filiusfamilias* can make a will. This creates a sort of quasi-inheritance, the existence of which depends on entry. If no one enters it is *peculium* and belongs to the *paterfamilias*[13]. Hence arise some difficult cases. Acquisitions by legacy or stipulation, by a

---

[1] 41. 3. 20, 31. 5, 40. [2] 41. 2. 1. 5; 44. 7. 16. [3] 41. 3. 45. 1.
[4] 41. 3. 44. 3. [5] 41. 2. 44. 1. [6] *ad* 41. 3. 35. 1.
[7] It is surprising that the titles dealing with possessory interdicts do not discuss dispossession of *servi hereditarii.*
[8] 28. 5. 31. 1, 65; 30. 116. 3; 31. 82. 2.
[9] 28. 5. 6. 2, 21. 1, 53. [10] 41. 1. 61. *pr.*
[11] Where a *heres coactus*, on entry, ordered a *servus hereditarius* to enter on a *hereditas* left to the slave, he acquired and need not hand it on to the *fideicommissarius*, 36. 1. 28. 1.
[12] 28. 5. 53; 31. 55. 1. [13] 49. 17. 14. *pr.*

17

servus castrensis where there is a will, but no one has yet accepted, go like those of *servus hereditarius*, if an heir enters, but if not, they go to the *pater*. Thus if a usufruct is left to him it takes effect for *heres* or father. The event does not transfer it from one to the other[1]: it vests in one or the other[2] according to the event. So if a thing is stolen from the slave the *heres* if he enters has no *actio furti*, for *furtum hereditati non fit*, but if he does not enter the father has the action[3]. There were clearly some doubts, but the result of this way of looking at the matter is that the father has no interest in the meantime. Thus where a slave, common to X and a *peculium castrense*, stipulates after the death of the *miles*, and before the heir has accepted, X acquires the whole. For, the text says, there is no real *hereditas*, but only, by imperial constitutions, a right of testation, which becomes a *hereditas*, then and then only when the *heres* has accepted. Accordingly it cannot be acquired to the *hereditas* : the fact that no right is allowed to the father, to take half, expresses the view that in the meantime he has nothing in the property[4]. But this reasoning would lead to the view that all transactions of a *servus castrensis peculii* in the interval are void, if the devise is not accepted. Papinian, in fact, raises this question, in relation to stipulation and *traditio*, and decides that notwithstanding the father's interim lack of interest *paterna verecundia* compels the view that such things are acquired to him[5]. The text adds that if a legacy is left to such a slave, though, *propter incertum*, it is for the time being acquired to no one, it vests in the father if the will does not operate[6]. Another text, of Tryphoninus[7], discusses the case of a legacy to a *servus castrensis peculii* vesting during the heir's deliberation, the legacy being under the will of a person in relation to whom the father was an *incapax*. Certainly, says the writer, it will go to the *heres*, the point of the observation being, apparently, that here there can be no question of its having vested in the father in the meantime, and only shifting at entry of the heir. He has already remarked that the *imago successionis* has prevented the father's ownership of the slave from existing in the interval. He uses the same case to exclude the notion of a pendency of *dominium*, but it only proves that the gift to the *heres* can take effect though there be no pendency : the real objection to the notion is that the very idea of *hereditas* implies

---

[1] *h. t.* 19. 5.
[2] 41. 1. 33. *pr.*   Ulpian, adopting views of Scaevola and Marcellus.
[3] 41. 1. 33. 1.   [4] 45. 3. 18. *pr.*
[5] 49. 17. 14. 1.   The text does not expressly connect the rule with the principle that stipulation *ex praesenti vires accipit.*
[6] 49. 17. 14. 2.   The text adds—*cum si fuisset exemplo hereditatis peculio adquisitum, ius patris hodie non consideraretur.*   The words are as they stand unintelligible.   See the notes in Otto and Schilling's translation.   See also Pothier, *ad h. l.*
[7] 49. 17. 19. 5.

that in the meantime the property does not belong to anyone, which is inconsistent with the notion of pendency, as applied elsewhere[1].

Gifts of usufruct to *servus hereditarius* create difficulties. They cannot be completely acquired because *ususfructus sine persona constitui non potest*[2]. For the same reason, such a slave cannot stipulate for one, even conditionally[3]. But there may be a legacy of usufruct to him, and as the *persona* is necessary, *heres exspectandus est*: it does not cede till entry of the heir, so that there can be no question of its failing then, *quasi mutato dominio*[4]. The *aditio* here mentioned is that on the *hereditas* to which the slave belongs: the rule is independent of the fact that legacy of usufruct never cedes till entry under the will by which it is created. In a certain will a slave is legated. Before *aditio*, another inheritance, under which a legacy of usufruct is left to this slave, is entered on. The legacy does not . cede until the inheritance, in which he is, is entered on, and will fail if he dies in the meantime. On entry it will go to the then owner of the slave[5].

Before leaving this branch of the subject, it is necessary to consider a group of texts, the gist of which is that the *heres* cannot acquire, by a *servus hereditarius*, what is part of the *hereditas*. At first sight these texts seem merely to lay down the truism that as *heres* is not owner till entry, the acquisition of things by *servi hereditarii* cannot be acquisition to him. And this is the only obvious meaning which can be given to the texts which apply the rule to acquisition of the *hereditas* or part of it[6]. But another text[7], dealing purely with possession, speaks of the rule as having been laid down by the ancients (*veteres putaverunt*), an expression not likely to have been used about so obvious a rule. And the text is followed by remarks which shew the case contemplated to be that of acquisition of *res hereditariae* after entry, *i.e.* solely a question of possession, since ownership in such things is acquired by the fact of entry ; the slave having of course ceased to be a *servus hereditarius* in the technical sense. Other texts, which shew that the rule is applied only to slaves acquired by the strictly hereditary title, deal also expressly with possession. Thus of slaves legated to us we can acquire the possession of all by one, as well as if they had been given or sold

---

[1] See Otto and Schilling, *ad h. l.* See also *post*, Ch. XVI.   [2] 41. 1. 61. 1.
[3] Vat. Fr. 55, 60; D. 45. 3. 26, *ex praesenti vires accipit stipulatio quamvis petitio ex ea suspensa sit.*
[4] *Ib.*; 7. 3. 1. 2; 7. 4. 18, *i.e.* in the slave: the remark is belated in the Digest. *Ante*, p. 152.
[5] *i.e.* the legatee. If the slave had not been legated it would have belonged to the *heres.* Text doubtful, but this seems to be the sense. There was another difficulty. Acquisitions by *servi hereditarii* were divided among coheirs (*post*, Ch. XVI.). But no part of this, a usufruct, could be separated from the person to whom it was given,—*nec a personis discedere potest.* It could not be divided by the *iudex* in *familiae erciscundae*: if the heirs would not hold it in common, he must arrange for enjoyment and compensation with security, 10. 2. 15, 16. *pr.* Text doubtful.
[6] 29. 2. 43; 41. 1. 18. As to common slaves, *post*, Ch. XVI.   [7] 41. 2. 1. 16.

to us[1]. And where A is *heres pro parte* and a slave is legated to him, he can, on *aditio*, acquire by that slave possession of a *fundus hereditarius*[2]. And where A has sold a slave to B, or owes him a slave in any way, and delivers him after B's death to B's heir, the heir can acquire possession of *res hereditariae* through him, precisely because he was not acquired *iure hereditario*[3]. When it is remembered first, that the rule is an ancient one[4], so ancient indeed that the classical jurists give no reason for it and treat it as a technicality to be confined within as narrow limits as possible, secondly, that every text which does not apply it to the *hereditas* or part of it applies it expressly to possession, and, thirdly, that *hereditas* was susceptible of possession and usucapion in early law[5], it seems safe to regard the rule as applying properly to acquisition of possession alone[6].

Even so limited, what is the *rationale* of the rule? No doubt difficult questions might arise in the absence of such a rule[7], but the same difficulties would arise in the case, for instance, of the slave *legatus* to the heir. Moreover, the rule has a technical look about it, and is hardly likely to rest on a purely utilitarian basis. The rule contemplates things possessed by the deceased, which, as we know, are not possessed by the *heres* till he has actually taken them[8]. It appears to rest on the unity of the inheritance : a taking by one of the slaves (whether authorised or not) of a thing in the possession of the *dominus* or of another slave would have effected no change in possession during the life of the ancestor, or while the *hereditas* was *iacens*. The same act is not allowed to produce a different effect merely because the ownership of the *hereditas* has changed.

We have anticipated some of the rules as to contract by a *servus hereditarius*. It is laid down that he cannot contract in the name of his late owner : there is no such person[9]. The question whether he can stipulate in the name of the future heir is much debated, the decision really turning on the question already considered whether, and how far, the *hereditas* can be said to represent the future heir[10]. Cassius, Gaius and Modestinus are reported as holding that he can do so, on the ground, in the case of the first two, that *aditio* relates back[11] But the weight of authority is the other way : we may take the rule

---

[1] 41. 2. 1. 16.   [2] 41. 2. 1. 17.   [3] 41. 2. 38. 2.
[4] 41. 2. 1. 16.   [5] G. 2. 54.
[6] The texts are concerned only with acts of acquisition by the slave: they do not for instance mean that if I acquire possession of one of the slaves I do not thereby acquire possession of his *peculium* which he possesses. It would perhaps, but this is less probable, not require an independent act of acquisition of even *res non peculiares*, which the slave now possessed by me had acquired to his late owner and held through the interval.
[7] *e.g.* if *heres* gave a general *iussum* to all the slaves to take possession.
[8] 41. 2. 23. *pr.*
[9] 12. 1. 41; 45. 3. 18. 2; In. 3. 17. 1.   [10] *Ante*, pp. 252, 3.
[11] 45. 3. 28. 4, 35.

as being that he cannot[1]. Of course he can make a stipulation or pact *in rem*[2], or in the name of a fellow slave, or of the *hereditas*, or with no name at all[3]. So in bilateral transactions. If he grants a *commodatum* or a *depositum*, the *heres* can recover the thing, and has the ordinary rights of action[4].

The *hereditas* is released by an *acceptilatio* to such a slave on a promise by his deceased master[5].

Promises in certain forms by way of surety are subject to special time limits. If a promise is made to a *servus hereditarius* and security taken by way of *fideiussio*, it is not clear when time begins to run. Javolenus holds[6] that it ought to begin at once, since a plaintiff's incapacity to sue, for which the surety is in no way responsible, ought not to increase the latter's liability. Venuleius[7] records a doubt, and cites the contrary view of Cassius that in such a case, time runs only from the day when action became possible. The form of the hypothesis suggests that the texts were originally written of *fidepromissores*, who were released in two years, by the *lex* Furia. This is an express release by statute for a particular case. It is not necessarily governed by the general rules of prescription of actions: hence the doubt.

The *heres* is liable *de peculio* on transactions by *servus hereditarius*, *e.g.* sale[8], though he may deduct, as a debt due to the *dominus*, any damage done to the *hereditas*[9]. In *quod iussu*, analogy suggests that a contract made after the death of a *dominus* on his *iussum*, does not bind the *heres in solidum*, as *iussum*, like mandate, is in most cases revoked by death, at least as against one who knew[10]. The same question arises in connexion with *actio institoria*. Ulpian says[11] that if a man has appointed his slave *institor*, and died, the *heres* is liable on contracts made with him after the death, by one who did not know of it. This expresses the same rule, but Paul says[12], very explicitly, that the action lies, even though the other party knew of the death, and the *heres* was mad, so that there could be no question of his having authorised it. He cites Pomponius, who says that a creditor who contracted with a going concern ought not to be defeated by knowledge that the *dominus* was dead. This way of looking at the matter makes the *hereditas* represent

---

[1] 2. 14. 27. 10; 45. 3. 16, 18. 2, 28. 4.   [2] 2. 14. 27. 10.
[3] In. 3. 17. *pr.*; D. 45. 3. 18. 2; 45. 3. 35.
[4] 16. 3. 1. 29; C. 4. 34. 9.   *S. hereditarius* lent money and took a pledge and handed the pledge back to the debtor in *precarium*. The *precarium* was valid, *i.e.* the thing could not be usucapted by the debtor, 44. 7. 16. This has a meaning as it stands, as the thing might not have been his own, (see however Gradenwitz, Interp. 38,) but it was originally written of *fiducia*, in which the ownership passed. He could not reacquire it by *usureceptio*. As it stands in the Digest the rule is confined to *res peculiares*, of which alone the slave could have acquired possession. The limitation is added presumably by the compilers: it would not be needed in the other case.
[5] 46. 4. 11. 2.   [6] 44. 3. 4.   [7] 45. 3. 25.
[8] 15. 1. 3. *pr.*; 18. 5. 8.   [9] 15. 1. 27. 1. Also in *de in rem verso*. See 15. 1. 3. 1.
[10] See Roby, Rom. Priv. Law, 2. 122.
[11] 14. 3. 5. 17.   [12] 14. 3. 17. 3.

the deceased, but emphasises the fact that credit is given to the business rather than to the owner, and avoids the paralysis of business which would result from adoption of the view that death ended the liability.

Africanus discusses the case[1] of a man freed and *ex parte heres* who, not knowing his status, goes on with his dealings. He is not a *servus hereditarius*, but on the facts he is a *bona fide serviens* of the other heirs, and the case is dealt with on those lines. What would have been the result if the heirs had known? So far as contractual rights and liabilities are concerned, it seems that the *heredes* could not be liable except so far as the facts could be brought within the field of *actio institoria*. And they would have the *actio negotiorum gestorum contraria* against him, since there is nothing on the facts involving any disqualifying fraud. But, directly, they would acquire nothing through him[2].

All rights resulting from transactions of *servus hereditarius* depend on the entry of the heir. They are in a sense conditional, and fall to the ground if there be no *heres*[3]. But any *heres* suffices. A slave who was *heres* under a substitution which took effect was liable *de peculio et in rem verso* on his contracts made in the interim[4].

As to the actual result where no heir enters, we have no information. The property will pass to the fisc, subject to the rights of creditors. The fisc can vindicate what the man has purported to convey, and must give back what has been given to him. But this will not do justice in all cases. The slave may have done damage, for which a noxal action would have lain against the heir. Goods handed over, under one of his contracts, may have been consumed. Is the fisc liable in this and similar cases[5]? We are not told, and, indeed, except in regard to freedom of slaves, we are told very little as to the obligations of the fisc in such cases, though there is some detail about its rights. Of course if no heir enters, it is usually because there is no profit in it, and nothing will go to the fisc, but this would not always be so—there must be cases in which no heir is discoverable[6].

VII. SERVUS DOTALIS.

The special rules relative to *servi dotales* are due mainly to the peculiar double ownership in *dos*[7]. We know that the *vir* is owner,

---

[1] 12. 1. 41. See *post*, p. 332.
[2] In any case payment to him in good faith on previous transactions discharged the debtors, and gave the other heirs a claim on *negotia gesta*. The man not having received the money as *heres, familiae erciscundae* was not available. If in the meantime the man had purported to lend money, the property did not pass and it could be vindicated.
[3] 45. 1. 73. 1.   [4] 15. 1. 3. 1.
[5] Probably not on the contract, but on the delict: *noxa caput sequitur*.
[6] Forfeiture (34. 9) might bring the rules into operation.
[7] The wife's interest is a statutory limitation, not based on principle. See Windscheid, Lehrb. §§ 492, 496. 3.

subject to a duty of return, in certain events, at the end of the marriage. Thus a slave given in *dos* is alienated, for the purpose of making *annalis* the *actio de peculio*[1]. On the other hand, the wife has a definite though postponed interest in the *dos*: *quamvis in bonis mariti dos sit, tamen mulieris est*[2]. But this does not exactly state the case: in fact it cannot be stated in terms of any other situation. The rules are, to a great extent, the product of compromises. The *vir* has more than bonitary right: he has *vindicatio*, even from the wife[3], and thus, though he somewhat resembles a usufructuary, his rights are really much greater. But the wife's interest is not absolutely postponed: there are several texts which shew that she can take steps to protect it.

The law of noxal liability might be expected to provide problems arising from this state of things. Yet the Sources yield apparently only one text dealing with the matter: it tells us[4] that if a dotal slave steals from the husband, the wife is liable to compensate, with a right, if she did not know his quality, to surrender the slave. We have already seen[5] that this is not really noxal liability, and we must not infer that the *vir*, having this claim, is not noxally liable. Certainly the slave is not *in potestate uxoris*. The *vir* has the ordinary powers of owner, and thus can manumit, and becomes the patron of the *libertus*[6]. The *lex* Julia, prohibiting alienation of land, says nothing of slaves; they may thus be alienated, their price being part of the *dos*, and the *vir* being accountable for wasteful dealing. In the same way the wife's interest in the slave leads to the rule that the *vir* is liable for illtreatment of him, even though he habitually illtreats his own slaves[7].

As to acquisitions the general rule is that the *vir* is entitled to fruits without accounting and to what is acquired *ex operis*, or *ex re mariti*, but other acquisitions are part of the *dos*[8]. *Partus ancillarum* are not fruits[9], and thus are dotal and do not belong absolutely to the *vir*[10]. But if, as is often the case, the slaves have been received at a valuation, and their value is to be returned, this is looked at as a sort of sale, and as the risk is with the *vir*, he may keep *partus* and other accidental accretions[11], the rule applying equally if the wife has the choice between the slaves and their value[12]. If the *vir* manumits a slave the *iura in bonis*

1 15. 2. 1. 6.   2 23. 3. 75 ; 24. 3. 24. 5, *alienos*.   See Windscheid, *op. cit.* § 496. 3.
3 25. 2. 24.   She has no such right, C. 3. 32. 9 ; 7. 8. 7.
4 25. 2. 21. 2.   5 *Ante*, p. 124.
6 C. 7. 8. 7 ; D. 38. 16. 3. 2.   There is a duty to account.   *Post*, Ch. xxv.
7 24. 3. 24. 5.   His liability for this wrongful conduct is not affected by the rule that he need shew in relation to *res dotales* only *diligentia quam suis*.
8 15. 1. 19. 1 ; 24. 3. 67.   As to what is *ex operis*, *post*, p. 342.
9 *Ante*, p. 21.
10 23. 3. 10. 2 ; *h. t.* 69. 9, which remarks that a pact varying this and making them common, would be void as a gift between *vir* and *uxor*.
11 23. 3. 18, 10. 4 ; 24. 3. 66. 3.   As to the history of this notion of sale, Bechmann, Dotalrecht, 2. 188.   12 Vat. Fr. 114.

will normally form part of the *dos*[1]. This is inevitably so, if the manumission is without consent of the wife[2]: but there are other possibilities. If the wife assents, and intends a gift to her husband, then, since gifts between them are allowed *manumittendi causa*[3], the slave is in fact the husband's and the *dos* has no claim on the *iura patronatus*[4].

The husband's right to fruits depends on the existence of the marriage, and thus everything which is acquired by a slave, given in *dos*, before the marriage takes place, or after its end, is part of the *dos*[5]. As to legacy, *hereditas*, and, probably, other gifts, acquired during the marriage, there is an apparent divergence of opinion. We are told by Julian[6] that as *aditio hereditatis* is not *in opera servili*, any *hereditas* on which a dotal slave enters belongs to the *dos*. Modestinus seems to agree[7]. And Paul[8] seems to say that any land left to a dotal slave is dotal. On the other hand, Pomponius[9] holds that such things are dotal, *si testator noluit ad maritum pertinere*. And Ulpian[10] says that the gift is not dotal, *si respectu mariti heres sit institutus vel ei legatum datum*. And Julian himself says[11] that they go back if they are acquired before the marriage or after its end, which seems to imply that they would not necessarily do so, if acquired during the marriage. It must also be remembered that Julian[12] in another connexion tells us that an institution of a slave, *propter me*, is an acquisition *ex re mea*, which, if applied to dotal slaves, gives the same result. It is likely that Julian's remarks as to acquisitions not actually during the marriage do not concern our case, but that he is laying down the rule that even though, strictly, *dos* exists only during the marriage, the husband's duty to account is the same at any time when he is holding it as *dos*[13]. The true view of the texts seems to be that such things are as a general presumption, in the *dos*[14], but that if the gift is expressly with a view of benefiting the *vir*, then it is *ex re eius* and he acquires it absolutely[15]. But it is still possible that this application of the conception of acquisition *ex re* was a novelty in Julian's time.

We are told[16], but the remark must be confined to cases in which the acquisition is dotal, that though *aditio* is always at the command of the *vir*, the wife must be examined before witnesses, lest she be prejudiced. If they both wish to refuse, the *vir* can safely do so. If she wishes to

---

[1] 48. 10. 14. 2.   [2] 24. 3. 61.
[3] 24. 3. 24. 4, 62, 63.   [4] For details and other cases, *post*, Ch. xx.
[5] 23. 3. 47; 24. 3. 31. 4.   Bechmann, *op. cit.* 2. 187, thinks, with the Basilica, that in 47 it is a *servus aestimatus*.
[6] 29. 2. 45. *pr.*, 1.   [7] 24. 3. 58.   [8] 23. 5. 3.
[9] 23. 3. 65.   [10] 15. 1. 19. 1.   [11] 23. 3. 47; 24. 3. 31. 4.
[12] 29. 2. 45. 4.   [13] Demangeat, Fonds dotal, 180 *sqq.*
[14] 29. 2. 45. *pr.*, 1; 24. 3. 58; 23. 5. 3.   [15] 15. 1. 19. 1; 23. 3. 65; 29. 2. 45. 4.
[16] 24. 3. 58.

accept but he does not, he may convey the slave to her to be reconveyed to him after entry; in this way he runs no risk[1].

A single text[2] seems to be all the existing authority as to the *actio de peculio, etc.* in the case of a dotal slave. Its decision starts evidently from the fact that *vir* is owner of the slave. There may be two *peculia*, but, for the purpose of the *actio de peculio*, it is immaterial whether the contract was in connexion with the dotal part of the *peculium* or the other: all alike is liable, as belonging to the *vir*. It follows that all debts due to him, or to his household, may be deducted. But when the time comes for settlement of accounts, he must charge himself with what, on principles already laid down, concerned him, and charge to *dos* what was paid on dotal account[3]. Similar rules would apply to *quod iussu* and *de in rem verso*. But as to *tributoria* and *exercitoria* or *institoria* it may be doubtful. For all the profit of any transaction of the slave results from his *operae*, and goes to the *dominus*, who should therefore bear any loss. The title[4] dealing with his right to deduct says nothing about damages in such actions. He cannot charge for the maintenance of the thing, even though the money expended was not directly with the aim of turning it into profit, but for the general preservation of it[5]. Moreover so far as fungibles in the *peculium* are concerned[6], they are at his risk: he must give them back to the same amount, whatever has happened in the meantime.

VIII.   *Servus Commodatus, Locatus, Depositus.*

As such a relation gave the holder no right in the slave, but only a right, *ex contractu*, against the *dominus*, there is not much to be said about the case. The holder was not noxally liable for what the slave did[7]. We have already discussed the historical development of the law as to his rights on delicts committed by the slave, in respect of him or his property, and of damage, by a slave of the borrower, to a thing lent[8]. If such a slave did harm to a third party, and the owner was sued, he had no regress, *ex locato, etc.* The liability of the borrower for damage to the slave is governed by the ordinary law of contract: the contractual relation would not in any case bar the *actio servi corrupti*. There are, however, special cases in which a man might be liable for the wrongs of

---

[1] If she wished to refuse but he ordered *aditio*, he was no doubt responsible for any resulting loss.
[2] 15. 1. 19. 1.
[3] The rule is simple and consistent, but there had been doubts. Ulpian brings the analogous cases of usufruct and *bonae fidei possessio* into discussion.
[4] 25. 1.   [5] *e.g.* 25. 1. 16.   [6] 23. 3. 42.
[7] 9. 4. 22. *pr.*; 13. 6. 5. 13.   [8] *Ante*, pp. 124 *sqq.*

slaves in his employ, even though his right in them were only a *ius in personam*. All these cases seem to be of praetorian origin[1].

Such holders were liable on the contracts of such slaves whom they had appointed *institores* or *magistri navium*, and though they did not acquire contractual rights through them, they could sue the *dominus*, *ex commodato* or *ex conducto*, for cession of the actions which had been acquired through them[2]. It is sometimes held[3], not on textual authority, but by reason of the inconveniences which would be caused by the contrary rule, that a slave hired to serve as *institor* or *magister navis* acquired *dominium* to his employer. The difficulty undoubtedly exists. Yet the refusal to allow acquisition of actions through his contracts, the fact that the only known legal results of the relation are praetorian, the absence of any reference to this case in the passages and titles which deal with acquisition through others, and the fact that one held *in precario* acquired nothing to his holder[4], make it difficult to accept this opinion. The case of *servus fructuarius* so appointed is no authority: the text means that this is an acquisition *ex re*. There is however no reason to think a *servus alienus* was often so appointed[5].

IX.   Slaves held *in Precario*.

As a holder *in precario* is commonly assimilated to a *commodatarius* it is not surprising that we find little mention of the rights and liabilities of *precario tenens* on acts of the slave. A few remarks are all that is possible. *Precarium ancillae* is, by a presumption of intent, *precarium partus*[6]. The *tenens* is not noxally liable[7], and has no *actio furti* if the slave be stolen, at any rate until the interdict *de precario* has been issued, when he becomes liable for *culpa* (*custodia*), and so has the same interest as *commodatarius*[8]. Presumably the *dominus* is liable on delicts done by the slave to the *tenens*[9]. The *tenens* can acquire nothing through the slave[10] and, probably, is liable on his contracts only when any other *extraneus* would be.

---

[1] *e.g.* the edicts as to extortion by *familia publicani*, and as to liability of *nautae, caupones, etc. Ante*, pp. 120 *sqq.*
[2] 14. 3. 12; 14. 1. 5. *pr.*
[3] Salkowski, Sklavenerwerb, 50. He gives a striking picture of the inconveniences.
[4] 41. 1. 22.   [5] 7. 8. 20. It did, however, happen. See *e.g.* 14. 3. 11. 8.
[6] 43. 26. 10.   [7] 9. 4. 22. 1.   [8] 47. 2. 14. 11.
[9] Unless such liability was barred by something in the origin of *precarium*, which some writers connect with *clientela*, 47. 2. 90. See Ihering, Geist, § 19.
[10] 41. 1. 22.

CHAPTER XII.

SPECIAL CASES (*cont.*). SERVUS FUGITIVUS. S. PRO DERELICTO. S. POENAE. S. PENDENTE USUFRUCTU MANUMISSUS. S. PIG- NERATUS MANUMISSUS.

X. *SERVUS FUGITIVUS.*

BROADLY speaking a *fugitivus* is one who has run away from his *dominus*. The word is used, however, in two senses which must be kept distinct. One of the regular warranties exacted on the sale of a slave is that he is not *fugitivus*[1]. This means that he has never been a *fugitivus* in the above sense. It is a breach of this warranty, if he be *fugax*, given to running away—which is itself a punishable offence[2]. For the purpose of the peculiar incapacities and penalties we have to consider, it is necessary that he be in flight at the present moment, and this is what is ordinarily implied in the expression *servus fugitivus*. It is in connexion with sale that the private law deals most fully with these slaves, and it is there we must look for an exact answer to the question: what is a *fugitivus*? He is one who has run away from his master, intending not to return. His intent is the material point, a fact illustrated by two common cases. He runs away, but after-wards repents and returns: he has none the less been a *fugitivus*[3]. He runs away and takes his *vicarius* with him: the *vicarius* is not a *fugi-tivus*, unless he assented, in full understanding, and did not return when he could[4]. It is not essential that he be off the property of his master[5], if he be beyond control[6], and thus one who hides in order to run away when he can is a *fugitivus*[7]. He does not cease to have been a *fugitivus* by renouncing his intention, *e.g.* by attempting suicide[8]. It is not essential that the flight be from the *dominus* in physical possession: it may be for instance from a pledge creditor[9], or from a *commodatarius*, or a teacher, if he do not run to the master[10]. Flight

---

[1] *Ante*, p. 55.   [2] C. Th. 2. 1. 8.   [3] 21. 1. 17. *pr.*, 1.
[4] 21. 1. 17. 7.   [5] 21. 1. 17. 8, 15.   [6] *h. l.* 9, 13.
[7] 21. 1. 17. 7. The fact that the flight was the result of bad advice is no defence, *h. t.* 43. 2.
[8] 21. 1. 17. 5, or by going to the statue of the Emperor or to the sale yard, *h. l.* 12. Conversely it was in itself no *fuga* to run to these places or to hide from punishment, or to attempt suicide. *Ib.*, *h. l.* 4.
[9] *h. l.* 11.   [10] *h. l. pr.*, 4.

from a *bonae fidei possessor* may be *fuga* whatever be the slave's state
of knowledge, unless it be with the intent of returning to the real owner[1].
On the other hand he must have done more than form and express
an intention: he must have actually started[2], with intent to get away
from his master. It is not *fuga* to run from enemies, or fire, or to
escape punishment by teacher or *commodatarius*, if he run to the
master[3], a way of putting the matter which seems to imply that there
would be a presumption of *fuga*. It is not *fuga* to run to a friend of
the master to secure intercession, and in this case mere failing to return
is not *fuga* : there must be some definite act of flight[4].

Fugitivi were a great administrative difficulty, and no doubt a public
danger. There was much legislation dealing with the capture and
return of such people. Much of it was no doubt temporary and local :
the most important permanent part having for its starting-point the
edict, *de fugitivis*[5]. This provided that the municipal magistrates must
guard *fugitivi* brought to them, binding them if necessary, till they
could be brought before the *Praeses* or *Praefectus vigilum*. They were
to make full note of physical characteristics, scars, etc., and hand this on
to the higher authority[6]. The edict was supplemented by *senatus consulta*, and constitutions, so that it is not clear what was done by each
agency. There was a penalty for failing to report *fugitivi* to the local
authority within twenty days of discovering them on your land[7]. The
senatus consultum which seems to have provided this, on the motion of
Antoninus Pius[8], gave a right of entry, on warrant, to search for *fugitivi*,
with a fine for refusing assistance or in any way hindering the search.
The *Praeses* and local authorities, including *limenarchae* and *stationarii*,
were required by Commodus, Marcus Aurelius and later emperors[9], to
help in such matters, to restore the .fugitives and to punish offenders.
Any such official who, on such enquiry, found a *fugitivus*, must hand
him over to the municipal authority[10]. Simple *fugitivi* were, it seems,
merely to be handed back to their owners, but those pretending to be
free were more severely dealt with[11]. Even one who had given himself

---

[1] 21. 1. 43. 3.   [2] 50. 16. 225.   [3] 21. 1. 17. 1—3.
[4] 21. 1. 17. 5; *h. t.* 43. 1.   A slave sent to a province hears that his master is dead and has
freed him. He lives as though free: he is not a fugitive, though his master is not dead.
Though he know he is not free, his so acting is not *fuga* whatever else it may be, if he stays
where he is and carries on the business, 21. 1. 17. 16.   The text is corrupt.
[5] Lenel, Ed. Perp. § 4.
[6] 11. 4. 1. 6—8; P. 1. 6a. 4.   A text which says that posting up such marks was enough is
commonly regarded as a meaningless interpolation, on its merits and on grammatical grounds,
11. 4. 1. 8a.   Lenel, *loc. cit.*; Pernice, Labeo, 2. 1. 107.
[7] 11. 4. 1. 1 ; Apuleius, Met. 6. 4.   [8] 11. 4. 1. 2.
[9] *Ib.*; 11. 4. 4; P. 1. 6a. 5.   Marcus Aurelius declared land of Caesar and the fisc liable to
the search, 11. 4. 3; P. *loc. cit.*; special rules of later law as to fugitive slaves of the Emperor,
C. Th. 10. 20. 2.   [10] 11. 4. 1. 3, 6.
[11] 11. 4. 2.   There was a temporary enactment of Macrinus requiring all *fugitivi* to fight in
the arena. Iul. Cap., Macrinus 12.   No doubt there were many cases of special punishment.
Those attempting to escape to *barbaricos* were to have a foot amputated or were condemned to
penal slavery, C. 6. 1. 3 (Constantine).

to fight in the arena must be returned[1]. Any fugitive whom his owner did not claim was sold by the fisc, and the buyer, if evicted, could claim the price from the fisc within three years[2]. Labeo held that an *erro* was a fugitive for this purpose, but the child of a *fugitiva* was not[3].

It was theft to conceal a *fugitivus* or aid him to escape[4]. There was a punishment for *mala fide* maintaining *fugitivi* in claims of liberty[5]. Heavy damages were payable, under legislation of Constantine, for retaining a fugitive without his master's knowledge except in *bona fide* belief that he was a free man. These damages were increased on repetition of the offence, and punishment might be awarded if the damages were not recoverable. There seems also to have been a fear that the rules would lead to blackmailing, for the enactment provided that if the master had fraudulently sent the slave with a view to profit, a question which was to be determined by torture of the slave if necessary, the slave was to be forfeited to the fisc[6]. Though it was the duty, and interest, of persons to point out the whereabouts of *fugitivi* they had discovered, so as to avoid suspicion of theft, humanity or corruption might make them reluctant to give the information. Hence it was permitted to offer rewards, and these could be sued for: it was not a *turpis causa*[7].

A slave in *fuga* could not be bought or sold or given away, and there was a penalty due from each party to such a transaction[8], these rules being partly contained in, and partly based on, the *lex* Fabia[4]. There were of course some necessary relaxations of these rules. Thus *coheredes* and common owners might reckon such slaves in the division[9], and it was not uncommon to agree for the sale of a *fugitivus*, the agreement not to take effect till capture. Instructions to a *fugitivarius* (a person who catches slaves for reward[10]), to catch and sell him, were valid[11].

A *fugitivus* is still possessed by his owner: he is the only *res se movens*, possession of which is not limited by control[12]. Various reasons

---

[1] 11. 4. 5.
[2] P. 1. 6a. 6, 7.   Huschke *ad h. l.* thinks it should be four, referring to C. 7. 37. 1. A soldier who had charge of a fugitive to return him to his master and lost him was liable to pay his value, 48. 3. 14. 7.   [3] 11. 4. 1. 5.
[4] *Ante*, p. 33.   T by alleging himself to be owner obtained release of a fugitive who was in custody: this was *furtum*, 47. 2. 52. 12.   It was not theft to point out the way to a fugitive who asked it, *h. t.* 63.   For a case on the border line, see Aul. Gell. Noct. Att. 11. 18. 14.
[5] C. 6. 1. 6.
[6] C. 6. 1. 4. 4.   In Asia the rule developed that a man might be enslaved for concealing a slave.   Syro-Roman Lawbook, Bruns-Sachau, 215.
[7] 19. 5. 15.   For illustrations see Bruns, Fontes, 1. 320; Blair, Slavery among the Romans, 249.
[8] 48. 15. 2, 4, 6. 2; P. 1. 6a. 2; Fr. d. i. Fisci, 9; Coll. 14. 2. 1, 3; C. 9. 20. 6.
[9] 10. 3. 19. 3.
[10] 19. 5. 18; P. 1. 6a. 1.   Either in an individual case or as a business.   They were punished if they concealed the fugitives, C. Th. 10. 12. 1, 2.
[11] 48. 15. 2. 2; C. 9. 20. 6.
[12] 41. 2. 1. 14, 3. 13, 13. *pr.*; 47. 2. 17. 3; P. 2. 31. 37.   Modestinus does not contradict this (41. 1. 54. 4); he says there are cases in which we do not possess a fugitive.

are assigned in the texts for this odd-looking rule : *ne ipse nos privet possessione*[1]*; alioquin per momenta servorum quos non viderimus interire possessionem*[2], or because he may have the intention of returning, which other *res se moventes* have not[3], or, *utilitatis causa ut impleatur usucapio*[4]. The doctrine seems to have been definitely laid down by Nerva *filius*, though he appears to allude to earlier authority[5]. Girard[6] considers it to be a merely empirical rule of classical law. But though the above-cited texts shew that when they were written, there was no certainty about the principle of the rule, it seems probable that it does not rest purely on empirical (if this means utilitarian) considerations, but on some view as to the nature of possession. For it is noticeable that the rule itself was settled before (and thus without reference to) an important economic result, *i.e.* acquisition of possession through the slave[7]. And a slave who has run away differs in no external respect from one who is away about his owner's affairs. The owner still has the external appearance of ownership. But the doubts which existed as to the limits of the rule shew an uncertainly conceived principle. The jurists were not agreed on the question, how long we possessed such a slave. It was clear that if a third person took possession of him, the owner's possession was ended[8]. If the unchanged external appearances are the basis of the continued possession by the owner, the possession ought to cease as soon as he begins to act as a free man : *pro libero se gerere.* There seems to be no extant text asserting this, though it may seem to be implied in certain texts which deny that we can acquire possession through such a slave. These will shortly be considered[9]. Probably the later law is that laid down by Paul[10], that we do not cease to possess him by his acting as a free man. Yet Paul himself lays down a rule[11] that a slave *in libertate* can acquire possession for one in whose name he acts. This either implies that a slave in that position is no longer possessed, apparently contrary to Paul's own view, or it conflicts with a rule, also laid down by Paul[12], that we cannot acquire possession through one who is possessed by another. A text of Ulpian and Celsus[13] to the effect that a slave possessed by no one can acquire possession for one whom he names, may mean the same thing, but it is not explicit as to the circumstances under which the man is not possessed. It may be that the case is one in which he has begun, or is prepared[14] to begin, a *causa liberalis*, which might quite change the situation. It might be possible to harmonise some of these

---

[1] 41. 2. 13. *pr.*   [2] *h. t.* 44. *pr.*   [3] *h. t.* 47.
[4] *h. t.* 1. 14, the only text which extends the continuance of possession to anyone but *dominus.*
See also 41. 2. 15.
[5] 41. 2. 1. 14, 3. 13, 47.   [6] Manuel, 273.   [7] *Post,* p. 272.
[8] 41. 2. 1. 14, 50. 1.   [9] *Post,* p. 272.   [10] 41. 3. 15. 1.
[11] 41. 3. 31. 2.   [12] 41. 2. 1. 6; 41. 1. 54. 4.   [13] 41. 2. 34. 2.
[14] 41. 3. 15. 1.

texts on the view that a man *pro libero se gerens* is not necessarily *in libertate*, this state of things arising only on cesser of the owner's possession[1]. On this hypothesis the law may be thus stated : the owner possesses until a third person possesses, or the slave begins a *causa liberalis*, or *pro libero se gerit* in such a way as to shew that he is prepared to defend his claim of liberty against the master, or has been so long left to himself that tolerance by the master may be inferred[2] : in these latter cases he is said to be *in libertate*. But the evidence of the texts is more correctly represented by the proposition that they shew a tendency to the acceptance of these distinctions rather than an actual expression of them[3].

A *fugitivus* is a *fur sui*, and thus cannot be usucapted, even by a *bonae fidei possessor*[4]. We have already considered the rule in the case of *partus ancillae furtivae*[5].

Where a *fugitivus* is left as a legacy, questions arise as to the resulting rights. The principle arrived at is that the recovery of the slave is at the cost and risk of the legatee, unless his non-production is in some way due to the negligence of the *heres*[6]. In that case the *heres* must pay his value. In the other, it is sufficient if he give security to hand him over if and when he is recovered. The same rule applies if the *servus fugitivus legatus* is *alienus*[7]. If "A or B" be left, and either be a *fugitivus*, the heir, not in *mora*, may give either the present one or the value of the absent one, the reason assigned by · Ulpian for thus increasing the liability of the *heres* being *totiens enim electio est heredi committenda quotiens moram non est facturus legatario*[8]. The point seems to be that the legatee is delayed in getting his slave by the choice of the *heres*, a rather doubtful piece of logic. If both are *in fuga* the security must be that, if either return, the *heres* will give the value either of him or the other. This expresses the same principle[9].

A *fugitivus* is none the less the property of his master, and thus acquires for him, apart from questions of possession. Thus we are told that where a *fugitivus* buys goods, and they are violently taken from him, his owner can bring the *actio vi bonorum raptorum*, because the goods were in his *bona*[10]—quite independently of the question whether he has ever possessed them. Again, if my slave in flight buys a thing from a non-owner, Pomponius says I have the Publician, even though I have not acquired possession through him[11]. The difficulties of this

---

1 As to the special rules in a pending *causa liberalis, post*, Ch. xxviii.
2 41. 2. 3. 10.   3 *Post*, p. 338.
4 47. 2. 61; C. 6. 1. 1; In. 2. 6. 1, *etc.* A protection to *domini*.
5 *Ante*, p. 24. Where such persons cannot be usucapted, the holder has no Publiciana, 6. 2. 9. 5.
6 30. 108 *pr.*   7 30. 47. 2.   8 *h. l.* 3.
9 *Ante*, p. 16.   10 47. 8. 2. 25.   11 6. 2. 15.

text, which has been much discussed, do not here concern us[1] : in any case, it shews that acquisition is not barred by the fact that the slave is a *fugitivus*[2].

Of acceptance of an inheritance there can be no question. No texts discuss legacies to *fugitivi*, but no doubt ordinary rules apply. There remains the case of possession. We have seen that a slave cannot acquire possession for his *dominus*, unless the latter knows of it, or has authorised it, or it is *in re peculiari*[3]. We have seen, or been told, for the authority is doubtful[4], that the slave does not acquire possession to his master, if he does not intend to do so. Such rules and the fact that a *fugitivus* is not likely to have a *peculium*, since the owner can adeem it *nutu*[5], would seem to preclude any question of acquisition of possession by a *fugitivus*. For though the ancients had held that we could not possess except through one whom we possessed, the converse was far from necessarily true. Yet, as in the case of *res peculiares*, there seems to have been a gradual recognition, *utilitatis causa*, of possession by the master through the *fugitivus*. Nerva *filius*, who seems to have accepted, with some reluctance, the view that we possess a fugitive, denies that we can possess through him[6], and Pomponius appears to hold the same view[7]. But Ulpian tells us that possession can be continued through such a slave[8], and Paul accepts the view, which he credits to Cassius and Julian, that a *dominus* can acquire possession through a fugitive, *sicut per eos quos in provincia habemus*[9]. These names suggest a school controversy. Hermogenianus adopts the same view with the characteristic limitation, " unless he thinks he is free[10]." All are agreed, on the other hand, that we cannot possess through him, if another person possesses him[11]. But what is the exact force of Julian's parallel, *sicut per eos quos in provincia habemus*? Cassius and Julian cannot have supposed acquisition of possession by a slave *in provincia* to be independent of the knowledge of the *dominus* : they are the very writers cited to shew that this was a special rule, *in re peculiari*[12]. But if we are to suppose the acquisition of possession by a *fugitivus* to the *dominus* to require knowledge or *iussum* of the latter, this is almost to deny its possibility, for all practical purposes, since ratification does not seem to have been retrospectively effective in such matters. And this is in accordance with principle, and could have caused little in-

---

[1] See Appleton, Propriété Prétorienne, § 82.
[2] Where my slave, a fugitive *apud furem*, and so not in my possession, acquired money and bought slaves with it, and T received them from the vendor with the slave's consent, I had *actio mandati* against T on my slave's mandate. If it was not with the slave's consent, I had *ex empto* against the vendor. The obligation was acquired though he was a fugitive, 17. 1. 22. 9.
[3] *Ante*, pp. 131, 2.   [4] 41. 2. 1. 19, *ante*, p. 133.
[5] *Ante*, p. 205.   [6] 41. 2. 1. 14.   [7] 6. 2. 15.
[8] 44. 3. 8.   [9] 41. 2. 1. 14, *in fin.*   [10] *h. t.* 50. 1.
[11] *Ib.*; *h. t.* 1. 14.   [12] *h. t.* 1. 5.

convenience : it is only the language attributed to Cassius and Julian[1] which raises difficulty.

If the fugitive *in libertate moretur*, we are told by Paul that we do not acquire possession through him[2]. This may mean one who is in such a state of apparent freedom, as exceeds what is implied in *pro libero se gerere*[3], but we are told the same thing by Hermogenianus[4] of the slave *in fuga* who thinks himself free, a phrase which for this purpose means no more than *pro libero se gerere*. Julian says[5] that if a fugitive *pro libero se gerens* sells a thing, a valid obligation (as it seems, *ex empto*) is created, from which the buyers are not released by paying the fugitive. If this is not a *solutio*, that must be, assuming good faith[6], because the possession does not vest in the *dominus*, for it is clear that the *dominium* does. Pomponius cites Labeo as holding a different view. Such a *fugitivus* lent money which he had stolen from his master (*i.e.* not *ex peculio*). Labeo says an obligation is created from which the debtor is released by payment to the *fugitivus* thinking him free : the money is made the master's, and there is a *quasi-solutum* to him[7]. This implies that the *dominus* gets possession of the money. The contradiction is exact. No doubt here, as in the cases of a similar type we have just considered, harmony might be reached by conjectural additions to the hypothesis. But it is better to treat it as another instance of the constant flux of opinion in these matters in minds swayed alternately by considerations of logic and of convenience. It would be a mistake to suppose even that there was a steady unbroken tendency in one direction, or that the views of any one jurist represent necessarily any coherent scheme.

The power of the *fugitivus* to bind his *dominus* is necessarily limited. Though he have a *peculium*, he loses any power of *administratio*[8]. In the two texts last discussed, he appears as selling and lending money, both transactions involving transfer of property. But the text on sale speaks[9] only of the contract : so far as we are told, the owner might have vindicated the property if he liked. And in the other case[10], we are told only that an obligation is created. It need not have been *mutuum* : it may well have been a *condictio* based on consumption. Ulpian[11] deals with an exactly similar state of facts, and says that there is no *mutuum*, since the property does not pass. The money can be vindicated if traceable ; if it is not, there is *ad exhibendum* or *condictio sine causa*, according as it has been made away with in bad or in good faith[12].

1 41. 2. 1. 14.   2 41. 3. 31. 2.   3 *Ante*, p. 270.
4 41. 2. 50. 1.   5 46. 3. 34. 5.   6 *Ante*, pp. 163, 4.
7 46. 3. 19.   8 15. 1. 48.   9 46. 3. 34. 5.
10 46. 3. 19.   11 12. 1. 11. 2.   See also 12. 1. 13.
12 Presumably all authority is revoked *ipso facto* by the flight, without express withdrawal. It may also be assumed that there is no *actio institoria*, or *quod iussu* on transactions by a

It has been remarked above that a slave may be a *fugitivus* without being *in libertate* or even *pro libero se gerens*. The converse is equally true: a slave may be *in libertate* without being a fugitive[1]. It does not appear that this would make any difference in the rights or liabilities of the *dominus*: the texts at least draw no distinction[2]. Such a man may be in the apparent *potestas* of another acting in good faith. This is not a case of *bonae fidei possessio*. It is clearly laid down that the apparent father can acquire nothing through the apparent son, even though he is in good faith[3]. In all such cases it may be presumed that he acquires property for his *dominus*, but not possession. The liability *de peculio* can hardly arise, and the rule as to noxal liability would be as in the case of *fugitivus*.

XI. SERVUS PRO DERELICTO.

The expression *servus derelictus* is very rare: the usual form is *servus quem dominus pro derelicto habet*[4]. This is so not only in connexion with *usucapio*, or where the abandonment may not have been by the owner, where the usage would explain itself, but in all contexts. The explanation is historical. There was an old dispute as to whether *derelictio* was at once complete, or whether ownership was divested only when a third person took possession. The former view prevailed in relation to slaves as well as other things[5].

We shall see that under imperial legislation abandonment of a sick slave might under certain circumstances make him free, and that in Justinian's latest law any abandonment might have that effect[6]. Here, however, we are concerned with the normal case, in which a slave abandoned by his owner remained a slave[7].

The developed Roman law permitted complete abandonment of ownership in slaves, at any rate so far as the advantages of ownership were concerned[8]. As to what amounted to a *derelictio*, this was a question of fact, which had few rules peculiar to the case of a slave. There must be intention to abandon[9], coupled with an actual casting

fugitivus: the case is not mentioned. There may be *de peculio* (15. 1. 3. 8, 52. *pr.*), and, though it would need rather improbable facts, *de in rem verso*. *Tributoria* is probably barred. Noxal liability, *ante*, p. 129.

  [1] As to rules in a *causa liberalis*, *post*, Ch. xxviii.
  [2] *e.g.* 15. 1. 3. 8, 52. *pr.*; 41. 2. 3. 10; 41. 3. 31. 2.
  [3] 41. 2. 50. *pr.*; 41. 3. 44. *pr.* The case might arise where, *e.g.*, a child abandoned by its slave mother was reared and given in adoption, or gave himself in adrogation.
  [4] In 45. 3. 36 both forms appear.
  [5] 41. 7. 2. 1; 9. 4. 38. 1. In relation to slaves the other view is not mentioned. Both these texts credit the rule to Julian.
  [6] *Post*, Ch. xxvi.
  [7] Jewish slavery did not admit of the existence of this class. Slavery being relative, liberty was only hidden by the power of the master. Winter, Stellung der Sklaven, 30.
  [8] 41. 7. 1 and *pass.*; 45. 3. 36. C. Th. 5. 9. 1 seems to hint at a right of preemption in an abandoning owner of an *infans*.
  [9] C. 8. 51. 1.

off of possession[1], and thus mere refusal to defend on a capital charge did not amount to a dereliction[2]. The main effect of abandonment was to make the slave a *servus sine domino*, on whom his late master had now no claim. Thus he could not acquire through the slave, who had indeed no capacities, his derivative capacity having ceased to exist. Thus any stipulations or other transactions of his were merely null[3]. As he had no derivative capacity, and the institution of slaves depended on the *testamenti factio* of their *domini*[4], it would seem that any institution of such a person would be void, though absence of *ius capiendi* in the *dominus* did not prevent the institution, but allowed the slave to enter if alienated[5]. But our case is not discussed. And while we are told that corporations could not be instituted[6], we are told that if the slave of a municipality was instituted, and was alienated or freed, the institution could take effect[7]. For Justinian's own law this would hardly seem worth stating, since municipalities could then be instituted[8]. If it be accepted as a classical rule, it creates a doubt for our present case. But as it purports to be from Ulpian, and is opposed to his very general statement[9] on the matter, it seems likely that it has been altered, perhaps by the omission of a negative. Whether this be so or not, the case of a *dominus incapax* is different from that of no *dominus* at all. The texts which bear on that state of facts are against admitting any possible validity in such an institution. Thus we are told that Antoninus Pius declared in a rescript that the institution of a *servus poenae* was absolutely null[10]. And Javolenus says *servus hereditarius* can be instituted *quamvis nullius sit*; an implication that an ordinary *servus nullius* could not be instituted[11].

The rule, *noxa caput sequitur*[12], protected the former master against liability for past or future delicts. On the other hand, dereliction did not destroy any rights of action the master might have acquired on account of delict committed in respect of the slave[13], any more than it would rights of action, on contract, already acquired through him. As to liability on past contracts, on *derelictio* the *actio de peculio* would become *annalis*, but any other existing edictal actions of this class would not be affected, as they are *perpetuae*. It must be supposed that the former *dominus* would not be liable on any contract made after the dereliction, except, indeed, in the improbable case of an owner who abandoned his slave, but retained his services as *institor* or the like.

---

1 41. 2. 17. 1.   2 48. 1. 9.
3 41. 7. 8; 45. 3. 36. After *occupatio* by a new *dominus* he acquires for him under ordinary rules.
4 28. 5. 31. *pr.*; U. 22. 9.   5 29. 2. 82.   6 U. 22. 5.
7 29. 2. 25. 1.   8 C. 6. 24. 12.   9 U. 22. 1, 5, 9.
10 29. 2. 25. 3.
11 28. 5. 65; cp. *h. t.* 31. 1. No doubt the fact that the slave became *nullius* after the will was made would be no bar if he were now in the hand of a *capax*. See 28. 5. 6. 2.
12 *Ante*, p. 106; D. 9. 4. 38. 1.   13 47. 2. 46. *pr. in fin.*

Difficulties might arise from contracts made, in ignorance, with a derelict slave, but they are more apparent than real. Any property handed over on the faith of such a contract could be vindicated. This would not indeed apply to consumables, or to services rendered at cost of time or money, and it does not seem that the law would give any remedy[1].

Curious questions arise where the slave abandoned is, at the time, the subject of lesser rights than *dominium*, vested in some third person. So far as these are mere contractual rights arising from *commodatum* or the like, the case is simple though the texts give us no help. The only right of the *commodatarius* is one on the contract. So long as he is undisturbed, no question arises. If a third party seizes the slave, his remedy is an *actio commodati contraria* against the lender. But there are greater difficulties if the right created was a *ius in rem*. Two typical cases alone need be considered.

1. The case of a slave abandoned by his *dominus* when some third person has a usufruct in him. We are nowhere told what happens. We know that usufruct is not affected by death of the *dominus*. If this be understood as perfectly general, and as applying in the case of a man who dies without representatives, and whose estate the fisc will have nothing to do with, it is an authority for the view that usufruct is absolutely independent of the fate of the *dominium*. This brings us in face of a wider question, *i.e.* that of the possibility of the existence of servitudes without *dominium*. Our case is discussed by Kuntze[2], who considers the usufruct as unaffected. There seems no reason to doubt his conclusion, which rests mainly on the analogy of the classical law in the cases of *servus pendente usufructu manumissus*, and that in which a man is a party to a fraudulent sale, to a *bona fide* buyer, of a usufruct in himself[3]. Two remarks may however be made. In Justinian's latest law, every abandonment seems to have been a manumission[4]. It follows that the present case would then be only an instance of a *servus sub usufructu manumissus*, who, under his law, is no longer a *servus sine domino*. The other remark is that no conclusion can be drawn from this case to that of praedial servitudes, *sine dominio*, partly because slaves may very well have been exceptionally treated in such a matter[5], but also because the classical texts give us no warrant for applying to usufruct in the classical law that dependence on *dominium* which is involved in the name *servitus*.

---

[1] Cases may readily be conceived in which the late owner was liable on account of *dolus*, but dereliction of slaves with whom anyone was likely to have commercial dealings must have been rare.

[2] Servus Fructuarius, 60 *sqq.*

[3] *Post*, p. 278 and Ch. XVI. *in fin.* In both cases there was usufruct without *dominium.*

[4] *Post*, Ch. XXVI.   [5] Kuntze, *loc. cit.*

There seems to be no text in the surviving ante-Justinian legal literature, which applies the name *servitus* to usufruct or the like, and there are obvious signs of a usage confining it to praedial servitudes¹.

2. The case of a slave abandoned by his owner while he is pledged. Pledge is not servitude. The creditor's right is a right to possess, in a limited sense of that word, and no more. We have not the logical difficulty involved in the conception of *servitus* without *dominium*: *pignus* being only a praetorian right to hold, is never contemplated as a part of *dominium*. The title dealing with release of pledge² makes it clear that no act of the debtor's can affect the creditor's right of possession without his consent³. There can be no doubt that *derelictio*, whether followed by *occupatio* or not, leaves the creditor's right intact.

XII.   *SERVUS POENAE.*

There is little to be said here of these persons: most of the points of interest will arise in connexion with the law of enslavement and manumission⁴. A few points may, however, be discussed. A *servus poenae* may have been, before his condemnation, either a slave or a freeman. In the latter case he was destroyed by the enslavement, and if freed, was not the same person: slavery was akin to death⁵. If he had been a slave, the condemnation destroyed the ownership⁶, and it did not revive on pardon⁷. What then was his position? The matter seems to have been obscure till, under Caracalla or a little later, it was accepted that he vested in the fisc⁸. *Servi poenae* themselves were not the property of anyone: they were slaves of punishment, not belonging to Caesar or the fisc⁹. Having no owner, they could have no derivative faculty or *peculium*, and, as slaves, they could have no faculty or property of their own. It seems obvious that they could not contract, though this is not stated. Their earlier made will was *irritum*¹⁰. Institutions of them or legacies to them were *pro non scriptis*, whether they were condemned before or after the will was made; the

---

¹ *e.g.* Vat. Fr. 54; G. 2. 14. Other texts shew that the relation of usufruct to *dominium* was disputed among the classical lawyers, Roby, de usufructu, 42.
² 20. 6.   ³ See for a strong case, 20. 6. 4. *pr.*   ⁴ *Post*, Ch. XVII.
⁵ 50. 17. 209; Nov. Just. 22. 9. For some effects see 36. 1. 18. 6.
⁶ 48. 19. 8. 12. The *peculium* remained with the former owner, C. 9. 49. 1.
⁷ 48. 19. 8. 12. If in temporary *vincula*, expiration of sentence freed them from all results, so that, as Divi Fratres laid down, they could take any form of gift if released when the *hereditas* under which the gift arose was entered on, 48. 19. 33. Papinian says that this limitation results not only from the constitution but from the reason of the thing. The point is that otherwise the gift cannot operate at once and there is no reason for postponement. The case is not one of *servitus poenae*: temporary or even permanent chains (*h. t.* 8. 13) or whipping (*h. t.* 28. 4) does not affect ownership. On release the slave reverts. If his master refuses him he is offered for sale. If this fails he is a *servus poenae*, 48. 19. 10. *pr.* See C. 9. 47. 13.
⁸ 40. 5. 24. 5. Details, *post*, Ch. XVII.
⁹ 34. 8. 3; 48. 19. 17. *pr.*; 49. 14. 12.   ¹⁰ 28. 3. 6. 6.

practical result being that the gift was not *caducum*, and did not go to the fisc[1]. The texts refer to Pius as having resolved these points; it may have been doubtful before whether such people were not the property of the fisc. Gifts of liberty to them were void, though if, and when, they vested in the fisc, on pardon, effect would be given to any such fideicommissary gift to them[2].

Tutela on either side was destroyed by condemnation[3]. Children of any condemned woman would be slaves[4], subject to some exceptions, *favore libertatis*, to be later considered[5]. They would not however be *servi poenae*, but ordinary slaves, capable of receiving fideicommissary gifts of liberty[6]. There must have been some doubt as to the ownership of them. Antoninus Pius seems to have settled it, perhaps by the same enactment as that mentioned above[7], by providing that they might be sold by the public authority[8]. We are told that *servi poenae* could not delate, *i.e.* were not allowed to report cases of fraud on the treasury, *e.g.* by way of unlawful *fideicommissum* or the like, in the hope of reward. But this was not a result of their position: it was a precautionary measure, *ne desperati ad delationem facile possint sine causa confugere*[9].

XIII. Servus pendente Usufructu Manumissus.

In Justinian's time such a slave became free, and there is no question for us. The only points to consider arise in connexion with his relation to his former owner, in earlier times, when he became a *servus sine domino* as the immediate result of the manumission[10]. We have little authority, but, in general, there is no great difficulty. The fructuary's rights were unaffected. The master necessarily ceased to be noxally liable for the man as to future acts, and as he had ceased to have *potestas* or *dominium*, he was free from liability for acts already done[11]. Similarly he could have no action for damage to the slave or for theft of him. He would seem to have the same noxal rights against the fructuary or any *bonae fidei possessor* as any third person would have. He would not be liable on any future contracts, except, indeed, by the *actio institoria*, if the man still acted in that capacity, as any freeman or *servus alienus* might do. His liability on past contracts would not be affected so far as the *actiones quod iussu*, and *de in rem verso* were

[1] 29. 2. 25. 3; 34. 8. 3; 48. 19. 17. *pr.*; 49. 14. 12.
[2] 40. 5. 24. 5. But this is administration, not law. As to the general attitude of the fisc in such cases, *post*, Ch. xxvii.
[3] In. 1. 22. 4.   [4] 40. 5. 24. 6.   [5] *Post*, Ch. xvii.
[6] 40. 5. 24. 6.   [7] See n. 1.   [8] 40. 5. 24. 6.
[9] 49. 14. 18. They shared the disability with women, *clarissimi*, *veterani* and others barred on different grounds.
[10] Fr. Dos. 11; U. 1. 19; C. 7. 15. 1.
[11] Subject to liability for *dolus*, *ante*, p. 106.

concerned. The *actio de peculio* would presumably become *annalis*, subject to the rules already stated[1]. To the *actio tributoria* he no doubt remained liable, if he retained the *peculium*[2]. But if he gave the man his *peculium*, it is not quite clear what would be the result. It would pass to the fructuary only if this intent were declared, and in that case the rules as to the liability of the fructuary in the *actio de peculio* would apply[3]. If it did not go to the fructuary, it could not go to the slave himself. It must either remain with the master or become derelict: the effect would be the same in most cases so far as liability *de peculio* is concerned, since this would ordinarily be such *dolus* as is contemplated by the Edict[4]. It would seem from the wording of Justinian's enactment that the master could acquire nothing through him, and the same result follows from general principle, since he was not now the slave's *dominus*[5].

XIV. SLAVE INFORMALLY FREED BEFORE THE *LEX IUNIA*.

The state of facts here referred to will be considered later[6]. The class was so early obsolete that it is idle to try to lay down rules about them. It is enough to say that though the Praetor protected them in *de facto* liberty, so that their master could not make them work, they were still his slaves and he still acquired through them[7]. He would still be liable, *de peculio et in rem verso*: indeed in all respects he would still be liable for them as for ordinary slaves, though the point would presumably not often arise. Whether he was noxally liable or not depends on the unanswerable question, whether the theory of *potestas* in this matter had developed so early. As this theory does not apply to *damnum*[8], it seems that he would be liable *e lege* Aquilia. Conversely he could have no noxal action for anything done by such a man, so far as the *lex* Aquilia was concerned, but he might conceivably have had an action against a *bonae fidei possessor* for other delicts. Presumably he would have an action for damage to such people, as this would lessen their power of acquisition, and no doubt he had the *actio furti*. As they were still slaves it may be assumed that the child of an *ancilla* in such a position was an ordinary slave.

XV. PLEDGED SLAVE FREED BY THE DEBTOR.

We are told in many texts, of Justinian's time, that such a manumission was absolutely null[9]. It follows that the relations of master

1 *Ante*, pp. 227 *sqq.*   2 *Ante*, p. 237.   3 *Post*, p. 359.
4 Arg. 14. 4. 7. 2, 3.   5 C. 7. 15. 1; G. 2. 95; In. 2. 9. 5.
6 *Post*, Ch. XIX.   7 Fr. Dos. 5.   8 *Ante*, p. 130.
9 *e.g.* C. 7. 8, *pass.*; D. 40. 1. 3; 40. 5. 24. 10. *Post*, Ch. XXV.

and slave were absolutely unaffected by it. Two points may be noted. The case cannot be regarded as equivalent to a *derelictio*, for one who frees a slave acquires a *libertus*, a potential asset of some value[1]. Thus to treat an attempted manumission as abandonment would be to go far beyond the manumitter's intention. Whether it can be treated as a case of informal manumission, for the earlier law, depends on the view that is taken of the only text[2]. It is defective but appears to mean that the slave became a Latin when the pledge ceased to be operative. This interpretation suggests that before the *lex* Iunia, the praetor would have intervened and treated the case as one of informal manumission, so soon as, but not before, the pledge was in some way released, *i.e.* so soon as capacity was restored—overlooking the fact that there was no capacity at the time the act was done. Till then its effects were null. If Huschke's view is accepted, that the slave became a Latin at once, this will imply that in the Republic the Praetor's protection is given at once, and the case will come under the class last mentioned[3].

---

[1] In 50. 17. 126. 1 we are told: *locupletior non est factus qui libertum adquisierit.* A *libertus* is not necessarily a source of profit, even by way of succession.
[2] Fr. Dos. 16.   [3] *Post*, Ch. xxv.

CHAPTER XIII.

SPECIAL CASES (*cont.*). SERVUS PIGNERATICIUS, FIDUCIAE
DATUS, STATULIBER, CAPTIVUS.

XVI. *SERVUS PIGNERATICIUS.*

THE law concerning a pledged slave derives some peculiarities from
the fact that, while on the one hand the rights acquired by the pledge
creditor are slight (being essentially no more than the right to hold the
slave without deriving profit from him), on the other hand the institution is only a praetorian modification of the old fiduciary mancipation,
under which the creditor became owner. Many of the texts in the
Digest which now speak of *pignus* were originally written of *fiducia*, and
the compilers have not always succeeded in making the changes so as
to produce a neat result.

A pledged slave is still *in bonis debitoris*[1], and thus a legacy of my
slaves includes those I have pledged, but not those pledged to me[2]. The
debtor retains the *actio servi corrupti*[3]. The pledged slave is treated
for the purpose of the *Sc.* Silanianum in all respects as if he had not
been pledged[4] But there are many respects in which the creditor's
interest comes effectively into play.

If[5] the pledge creditor kills the slave, the debtor has the *actio*
Aquilia against him, or, if he prefers, he may bring the action on the
contract[6]. If on the other hand the debtor kills the slave, the creditor
has not the *actio* Aquilia, even *utilis*, but is given an *actio in factum*[7].
If the slave is killed by a third party, the pledger has the *actio* Aquilia,
and the creditor is allowed an *actio utilis*, because in view of possible
insolvency of the debtor he has an *interesse*. A text[8] credited to Paul,
hints, in a rambling manner, that the creditor's action is given only in
the case in which the debtor is insolvent, or the creditor's remedy, apart
from the pledge, is time-barred, and says that, in that case, the debtor

---

[1] C. 4. 24. 9.   [2] 32. 73. 2.   [3] 11. 3. 14. 4.
[4] 29. 5. 1. 3; *ante*, p. 95.
[5] Theft and damage in relation to pledged property, Hellwig, Verpfändung von Forderungen,
43—50.
[6] 9. 2. 18.   [7] *h. t.* 17.   [8] 9. 2. 30. 1.

has it only if the debt is less than the value of the slave. Gradenwitz shews conclusively that these later propositions are from the compilers[1].

The case of theft of a pledged slave presents difficulties: they have nothing to do especially with slaves but cannot well be left undiscussed, as one or two of the most difficult texts deal with slaves. Many texts shew clearly that the pledge creditor has *actio furti* if the thing is stolen[2], even by the debtor[3], and that he will himself be liable to the action if he exceeds his right[4]. Beyond this it is difficult to get a clear doctrine: there are divergences on all material points. In seeking the basis of the pledge creditor's *interesse*, it is natural to think of his obligation *custodiam praestare*, either absolute, except for *vis maior*[5], or only *diligentiam exactam praestare*[6]. And two texts of Ulpian[7], in one of which there is an appeal to older authority, seem to start from this point of view, but the first shews that there is an *interesse* independent of *obligatio*[8], and the words from *hoc ita* to *competit* are probably from Tribonian. The responsibility is limited to the case of *culpa*, and there is some reason to think that at least in the case of *pignus*, this limitation dates from the later Empire[9]. What Pomponius approves is the earlier part of the text. In the other[10], the words *item locati pignorisve accepti* may be interpolated, but, indeed, the whole text looks corrupt[11].

It is clear on other grounds that the obligation whatever its extent cannot have been the sole basis of the *interesse*. Had it been so, there would have been, at least, doubts as to the right of action where the debtor stole the thing, since in that case the obligation did not exist[12].

---

[1] Interpolationen, 89 *sqq.* Do they represent even later law? G. points out that where, as here, two can sue, though substantially only one sum is due, the normal course is for the first plaintiff to give security for defence of the person liable against the other.

[2] 13. 7. 22. *pr.*; 47. 2. 14. 16, 15. *pr.*; In. 4. 1. 14; 4. 2. 2; *etc.*

[3] 13. 7. 3; 41. 4. 5; 47. 2. 12. 2, 67. *pr.*; C. 7. 26. 6; G. 3. 200, 203; P. 2. 31. 19; *etc.*

[4] 13. 7. 4, 5; 47. 2. 52. 7, 55. *pr.*, 56, 74; C. 9. 33. 3; *etc.*

[5] 13. 7. 13. 1, 14; C. 8. 13. 19.   [6] C. 4. 24. 5, 8; In. 3. 14. 4.

[7] 47. 2. 14. 6, 16.   [8] 47. 2. 14. 6.

[9] As to the nature of *custodia* the most acceptable opinion seems to be that which may still be called the orthodox view. (See for this, with variations, Pernice, Labeo, 2. 1. 345; Lehmann, Z. Sav. Stift. 9. 110; Biermann, same review, 12. 33; Girard, Manuel, 655. *Contra*, Ferrini, Archivio Giuridico, 53. 260.) According to this doctrine, *custodia* meant originally the obligation to keep the thing as against thieves, but not as against robbers. This was gradually modified, till except in a few cases, it was no longer to be distinguished from the obligation *diligentiam maximam praestare*. This development explains such texts as speak of *custodiam diligentem* (*e.g.* 13. 6. 5. 5) and the like. But there is room for difference of opinion as to the date of this change. Pernice attributes it to the influence of Julian. Biermann is, in general, of the same opinion, but considers that in regard to *pignus*, the change is of the later Empire, since Diocletian still distinguishes in this connexion between *culpa* and *custodia*. Paul and Ulpian make the same distinction in other connexions (P. 2. 4. 3; D. 19. 1. 36; 47. 2. 14. 6, *etc.*), but this Biermann regards as mere *historische Reminiscenz*. But that kind of reminiscence is more characteristic of Tribonian than of Ulpian or Paul, and as they state the distinction clearly it is likely that the law of their time admitted it. It seems highly probable that the assimilation in most cases of the liability *custodiam praestare* to that *diligentiam praestare* was a development of the later Empire, except in the case of *commodatum*, which had special rules. It is to be observed that nearly all the texts which state the newer doctrine are confused in form (*e.g.* 18. 6. 2. 1; 18. 6. 3; 13. 6. 10; 47. 2. 14. 12; 47. 8. 2. 22, 23).

[10] 47. 2. 14. 6.

[11] Doubts in the case of *commodatum* are plentiful: 13. 6. 5. 6; 47. 2. 14. 16, and many in C. 6. 2. 22.

[12] 13. 6. 21. *pr.*

But many texts give the action in that case and none denies or doubts its existence[1]. Again, in all cases except where the thief is the debtor, the creditor must set off what he recovers against the debt[2], while in the other cases of *interesse* based on obligation, the plaintiff keeps what he recovers[3]. Again, if the right were based on obligation, the creditor's action would exclude that of the debtor[4], but, here, both parties have the action[5]. Ulpian tells us indeed[6], that there had been doubts as to the creditor's action if the debtor were solvent, but himself holds, with Julian, Pomponius and Papinian, that he has an interest in all cases, a rule for which the Institutes give the reason, *quia expedit ei pignori potius incumbere quam in personam agere*[7]. The text says nothing about obligation. Again, if the right were based on obligation it would not exist, as it does, where there is a mere hypothec, since here the obligation does not exist[8]. It seems clear, then, that, at least on the dominant view, the creditor's right does not depend on his liability. There is, however, one difficulty. Two texts of Paul[9] allow the creditor to recover the value of the *res*. This is consistent with the view that his right rests on obligation, and not easy to reconcile with any other view. But one of them definitely gives the action against the debtor, which is inconsistent with that view[10], and though Paul here notes that in that case the recovery is limited to the amount of the claim, this itself shews that there is another basis of *interesse*. There are, however, a number of texts, mainly from Ulpian[11], which limit the creditor's right in all cases to the amount of his claim.

What is this other basis of interest? The mere fact of possession would not suffice, if indeed the pledge creditor can be said strictly to have possession[12]. But his right, narrow as it is, exceeds mere possession. It has an economic content. He has a right to keep the thing until his claim is satisfied, and thus he will win, not only in possessory proceedings, but also even if the owner vindicates the thing. It is this *ius retentionis* which bases his *actio furti*[13]. This is why his interest is limited to the amount of the debt, and why, if there are several things pledged together for one debt, the action, if any one of them is stolen, is limited only by the total amount of the debt[14]. Paul's texts giving a right to recover the whole value[15] do not seem to have been retouched: they may perhaps be based on a recognition of the right resting on

---

[1] See *ante*, p. 282, n. 4, and 41. 3. 49; 47. 2. 19. 6, 88; In. 4. 1. 10, 14.
[2] 13. 7. 22. *pr.*; 47. 2. 14. 6, 14. 7, 15. *pr.*
[3] 13. 6. 7; 19. 2. 6; C. 6. 2. 22. 3.   [4] G. 3. 203, 6; D. 47. 2. 12. *pr. etc.*
[5] 47. 2. 12. 2, 46. 4, 52. 7, 55. *pr.*, 74.   [6] 47. 2. 12. 2.
[7] In. 4. 1. 14.   [8] 47. 2. 19. 6, 62. 8.
[9] *h. t.* 15. *pr.*, 88.   [10] *h. t.* 88.
[11] 47. 2. 14. 5—7, 46. 4, 5; 47. 8. 2. 22, 23; In. 4. 2. 2.   [12] 2. 8. 15. 2.
[13] 47. 2. 46. 5.   Obscure, but bringing out the fact that his *interesse* is distinct from that of owner.
[14] 47. 2. 14. 5—7.   [15] *h. t.* 15. *pr.*, 88.

liability, but their explanation is more likely to be found in the known genealogy of *pignus*. The rule of *fiducia*, by which the creditor, being owner, recovered the whole value, simply passes over to *pignus*. Perhaps as early as Pomponius[1], the more logical view appears which limits his action to the amount of his claim. Later on, the pledgee is so far assimilated to other holders who *custodiam praestant*, that his right based on liability is recognised, without excluding the other. But this is of late law, and, even in the Digest, the dominant doctrine ignores it. It may be noted that in several other cases, in some of which there would not be a possessory right, the *ius retinendi* gives an *actio furti*[2], on the analogy of pledge[3].

In one text already mentioned[4], Ulpian seems to give the debtor (the owner) an action only if the thing is worth more than the debt. There is no obvious reason for this limitation, and he elsewhere ignores it[5]. The interjected form of the limitation in the text suggests interpolation. On the other hand it may be a survival from the system of *fiducia*, in which the debtor, having neither ownership nor possession, has no clear basis of action. The text certainly treats the debtor's right to sue as of an exceptional nature.

The rules as to noxal liability for the slave have already been discussed[6]. It may be added that the *actio ad exhibendum* lies against the creditor and not against the debtor: he has no power of producing the man[7].

As to acquisitions, the rule is simple. The slave cannot acquire for the pledge creditor in any way, by *traditio*, *stipulatio*, or otherwise, not even possession, though the creditor possesses him for interdictal purposes[8]. All fruits and acquisitions *ex operis* are the debtor's, and go to reduce the debt, any balance over the amount of the debt being recoverable by the debtor[9]. All ·other acquisitions, *e.g. hereditas* or *donatio*, go of course to the debtor. And the rules as to the effect of acquiring or purporting to acquire expressly for any person other than the owner are ·in no way exceptional in this case. The debtor cannot acquire possession through the slave since he is possessed by another, except so far as bars *usucapio* by the creditor, and allows the debtor to usucapt things of which possession had already begun[10].

The creditor must not misuse the thing pledged and thus if he prostitute a pledged *ancilla*, the pledge is destroyed[11]. Unusual expenses may be added to the charge, and thus, if a pledged slave is

---

[1] 47. 2. 14. 6, 7.   [2] *h. t.* 14. 1, 15. 2, 54. 4, 60; In. 4. 1. 14.
[3] Modestinus (Coll. 10. 2. 6) denies *actio furti* to depositee even with *ius retentionis*. The reason is not clear and the rule is not in the Digest. The rule probably began with *pignus*.
[4] 47. 2. 46. 4.   [5] *h. t.* 12. 2.   [6] *Ante*, pp. 116, 125.
[7] 41. 3. 16.   [8] 41. 1. 37. *pr.*; 41. 2. 1. 15.   [9] C. 4. 24. 1, 2.
[10] 41. 2. 1. 15. Or the slave himself. The rule does not oı course apply to hypothec.
[11] 13. 7. 24. 3.

captured and redeemed, the creditor's right revives when he has paid off the lien of the redeemer, and he may add the amount paid to his charge[1]. In the same way he may add to the charge any reasonable expenses incurred in training the slave in either necessary arts, or those in which the debtor had already begun to train him, or those to his training in which the debtor has assented[2]. Expenses incurred in paying damages for a delict by him can also presumably be added, for we know that the creditor is compellable to pay them or abandon his pledge[3].

XVII. SLAVE HELD IN *FIDUCIA*.

Upon this case the texts give us little information: the institution was obsolete in Justinian's time, and, as we have learnt from Lenel, many of the texts which really dealt with *fiducia cum creditore* have been applied by the compilers to *pignus*, with or without alteration. But of these there are very few which have any special importance in regard to slaves as opposed to other chattels. Such slaves were technically the property of the *fiduciarius*. Thus a legacy of "my slaves," by the debtor, did not cover those he had so conveyed[4]. And what such slaves acquired in any way was the property of the *fiduciarius*. But this ownership was little more than nominal, for he must account for all such receipts, setting them off against the debt, and being liable for any balance[5], having however the same right of charging expenses as the creditor in a *pignus*[6]. Moreover, a thing given in *fiducia* could be left *per preceptionem*, at least according to the Sabinians, the heirs being bound to free it, though in general such legacies were confined to the property of the testator[7]. The Sabinians did not consider this form to be confined, as legacy *per vindicationem* was, to the quiritary property of the testator, but applied it to anything in his *bona*[8]. But this is, as Gaius observes, a still further extension, for technically such a slave is not *in bonis debitoris*. As we have seen, however, the rules of account make this formal rather than real; Gaius, in fact, treats the transaction as essentially a pledge, the heirs being under a duty to reduce the thing into possession[9].

---

[1] 49. 15. 12. 12.

[2] 13. 7. 25. Paul, wrongly attributed to Ulpian. See Lenel, Paling. *ad h. l.* Originally written of *fiducia*.

[3] *Ante*, p. 116. Apart from agreement the pledge did not cover *peculium* wherever acquired, 20. 1. 1. 1. The case of *partus* of pledged *ancilla* has already been considered. *Ante*, p. 23.

[4] P. 3. 6. 69.   [5] P. 2. 13. 2.   [6] Cp. 13. 7. 25.

[7] G. 2. 220. This does not conflict with P. 3. 6. 69. That is a rule of construction as to what certain words mean: here the only question is whether a certain gift is good.

[8] G. 2. 219—222.

[9] Cp. P. 3. 6. 16; In. 2. 20. 12, *etc.* Another relaxation, P. 3. 6. 1. If the creditor held the slave, the debtor could not acquire possession through him. If he was with the debtor, this resulted from a *precarium* or *locatio* or *commodatum*: the position of the debtor was governed by the rules of these relations independent of their origin.

As the creditor was owner he could have no noxal action for any-thing done by the slave, but it may be inferred from some texts discussed in the chapter on noxal liability that he had a right to an indemnity[1], the amount of which could be added to the debt. The debtor could, however, abandon the slave instead of paying, leaving the original debt intact, but only if he was unaware of the character of the slave he was mancipating[2]. Conversely it seems to follow that the creditor was noxally liable for anything the slave did, but of course this surrender while it ended the security did not destroy the debt, and did not impose on the creditor any liability for the value of the slave[3]. If the slave stole from the debtor there ought to be a noxal action against the creditor, but such an action would be of little use. For if the creditor surrendered the slave the debt remained, and he was usually in a position to require fresh security. If he paid the debt, because it was less than the value of the slave, it would seem that he could add the money so paid to the debt. But direct authority is lacking.

XVIII. *STATULIBERI.*

The most important points in relation to these will arise for dis-cussion under the law of manumission, but something must be said here as to their position while still slaves. It is not necessary to define them with any exactness. Broadly, they are persons to whom liberty has been given by will under a condition, or from a day, which has not yet arrived[4].

The main principle as to their position is that till the gift of liberty takes effect in some way[5], they are still slaves of the heir[6], for all purposes. Thus they may be examined under the *Scc.* Silanianum and Claudianum, if the heir is killed[7]. Children of an *ancilla statulibera* are slaves of the heir[8]. *Statuliberi* are subject to the ordinary incidents of slavery, with the restriction that no act of the heir can deprive them of their prospect of liberty, on the occurrence of a certain event, and some other restrictions shortly to be stated. Thus they may be sold, legated, delivered by *traditio*, adjudicated, and even usucapted, but always carrying with them their conditional right to liberty[9]. They may be pledged, but arrival of the condition destroys the creditor's lien[10]. A usufruct may be created in them[11]. They may be noxally

---

[1] *Ante,* p. 125.   [2] *Arg.* 47. 2. 62. 3.   [3] *Arg.* 9. 4. 17. 1. *Ante,* p. 116.
[4] 40. 7. 1. One as to whom it is doubtful if his freedom is in fraud of creditors is a *statuliber. Ibid.* See Festus, s.v. *Statuliber.* And see *post,* Ch. xxi.
[5] As to cases in which the gift took effect without satisfaction of the condition, *post,* Ch. xxi.
[6] U. 2. 2; D. 40. 7. 16, 29. *pr.*   [7] 29. 5. 1. 4.   [8] 40. 7. 16; C. 7. 4. 3.
[9] 30. 81. 9; 40. 7. 6. 3, 9. 1; U. 2. 3; C. 7. 2. 13; *etc.* The condition may be such that alienation destroys the *spes, e.g.* "to be free if my *heres* do not sell him," 40. 7. 30. A sale may be with or without *peculium,* 40. 7. 3. 7, 6. 6, 27, 35.
[10] 20. 1. 13. 1.   [11] 33. 2. 20.

surrendered, and this will discharge the *dominus*, without affecting their hope of liberty, and if the condition be satisfied during the litigation, the *dominus* is entitled to absolution[1]. As they belong to the heir, they cannot receive a legacy under his will, unless the condition is satisfied at his death, or the legacy is under the same condition as that under which they are to be free[2]. So, too, a *statuliber* can acquire for the *hereditas*[3].

But there are respects in which their position differs from that of an ordinary slave. Though they can be sold, the sale may not be under harsh conditions[4]: the *heres* may do nothing to make their position worse[5]. He may be validly directed to maintain them till the condition arrives, *cibaria dare*, a special enactment of Severus and Caracalla forming an exception to the rule that a legacy cannot be made to your own slave *sine libertate*[6]. It would seem to be aimed at preventing the *heres* from abandoning a slave from whom, as he is about to be free, no great profit can be expected[7]. A legacy of *optio servi* or *legatum generis* does not give the legatee a right to choose a *statuliber*, so long as the condition is possible[8]. Such a choice is hardly likely since he takes his *spes* with him. But in any case, the rule is merely one of construction : a testator who has made both gifts cannot be supposed to have meant the choice to cover the man freed, and the rule that if the condition fails, he may be chosen, rests on the view, of Q. M. Scaevola, that a gift of which the condition has failed is to be regarded as completely non-existent.

Slaves can ordinarily be tortured as witnesses but *statuliberi* may not, at least from the time of Antoninus Pius, in ordinary pecuniary cases, though they may in a case of adultery without prejudice to their ultimate right to liberty[9].

Where his value is material a *statuliber* is reckoned at his value as such, *e.g.*, in *actio furti* and *condictio furtiva*[10], and for the purpose of the *lex* Falcidia. If the slave so freed dies, he is reckoned as part of the *hereditas* at his value as a *statuliber*, if, as the event turns out, the condition fails, but if the condition arrives after he is dead, he is not reckoned at all[11]. A text of Julian deals with a similar question in relation to *condictio furtiva*. If a thief, or his heir, is sued by *condictio furtiva*, and the thing stolen ceases to exist, *e.g.* a stolen slave dies, the plaintiff is still entitled to judgment[12]. But Julian says[13] that if a slave,

---

[1] 40. 7. 9. *pr.*, 2; 47. 2. 62. 9. In this case liberty was attained by paying 10 to *heres*. He must give this to plaintiff unless it comes out of *peculium*. This is because the *heres* might in that case have forbidden the payment without barring the liberty. *Post*, Ch. XXI.
[2] 31. 11. *pr.*   [3] 40. 7. 28. 1.
[4] *h. t.* 25.   Such as, *ne intra loca serviant, ne unquam manumittantur.*
[5] *h. t.* 33 ; C. 7. 2. 13.   [6] 30. 113. 1.
[7] No mode of enforcement is stated.   Probably failure would ground appeal to the Emperor under the rule then newly laid down by Antoninus Pius, *ante*, p. 37.   See *post*, Ch. XX.
[8] 33. 5. 9. 1.   [9] 48. 18. 8. 1, 9. 3.
[10] 13. 1. 14. *pr.*; 47. 2. 52. 29, 81. 1.   [11] 35. 2. 11. 1.
[12] 13. 1. 8. 1, 20.   The thief is always *in mora*.   [13] 13. 1. 14. *pr.*

left conditionally, is stolen, the *heres* has *condictio furtiva* so long as the condition is unfulfilled, but if, pending the action, the condition arrives, there must be absolution. He adds that the same is true if the gift is one of liberty, since the plaintiff has now no *interesse* and the thing has ceased to belong to the thief, without *dolus* of his. The second reason is none, for it is indifferent in this action whether the thief is still owner or not[1]. The first reason is hardly satisfactory. If a stolen slave is dead, we are told that the action must still proceed, because there may be other interests than the personal value of the slave, *e.g.* the loss of an inheritance to which he was instituted, on which his master has been prevented from making him enter[2]. The same reasoning might have applied here. In another text Ulpian says the same thing[3] about *actio furti* for a *statuliber*. But he confines the rule to the case in which the condition is satisfied before *aditio*, so that the slave never was the heir's. In the case of *condictio*, Julian allows release if the condition is satisfied at any time before judgment. This requires altogether different reasoning. It is no doubt, as Windscheid says[4], an application of the rule *soli domino condictio competit*. There is nothing remarkable in allowing the cesser of ownership after *litis contestatio* to affect the matter, in view of the tendencies of classical law, but it seems somewhat unfair in *condictio furtiva*. It is in fact an application to this action of the principle applied to real actions (though ill evidenced in the texts[5]), that the plaintiff cannot recover unless his interest continues to the time of judgment.

As to criminal liability there is some difficulty. In one passage we are told, by Pomponius, that *statuliberi* are liable to the same criminal penalties as other slaves[6]. But Modestinus and Ulpian say[7] that, on account of their prospect of liberty, they are to be punished as freemen would be, in the like case. The contradiction is absolute. Ulpian attributes the rule to a rescript of Antoninus Pius[8], and as Pomponius is much the earliest of these jurists and wrote some work under Hadrian, it may be that this text states the older law, before the rescript, and that its insertion in the Digest is an oversight of the compilers.

We have seen that *statuliberi* may be bought and sold, but it is clear that one who wishes to buy a slave will not be satisfied with a *statuliber*. We are told in one text that if Titius owes Stichus *ex stipulatu*, and hands him over, the promise is satisfied though he is a *statuliber*. This view is credited by Ulpian to Octavenus[9]. It deals

---

[1] See *ante*, p. 287, n. 12.   [2] 13. 1. 3.   [3] 47. 2. 52. 29.
[4] Lehrbuch, § 361.   [5] 10. 4. 7. 7. See Pellat, De rei vind. 226.
[6] 40. 7. 29. *pr.* Gaius and Ulpian say that a *statuliber* may *ut servus coerceri*. They mean only that as he is a slave and can be punished by his master he cannot be treated as free and sued after his liberty is complete, under the Edict as to damage to the *hereditas* by freed slaves. See 47. 4. 1. 3, 2, 3; *ante*, p. 255; *post*, Ch. xxix.
[7] 48. 18. 14; 48. 19. 9. 16.   [8] See Pothier *ad h. l.*   [9] 40. 7. 9. 2.

of course only with the case of a promise of a particular man, who must be taken *talis qualis*. Thus Africanus tells us[1] that if a man *hominem promisit*, and delivers a *statuliber*, this is not performance. The receiver can sue on the stipulation, without waiting till the condition is satisfied. Africanus adds that if in the meantime the condition fails, there is no loss and therefore no right of action. It is in relation to sale that this matter is most fully discussed. There are several possible cases.

(*a*) The slave is sold with no mention of the fact that he is entitled to liberty on a condition. Ulpian says there is weighty authority for regarding this as *stellionatus*, but whether this be so or not, there is an *actio ex empto*[2]. But subject to the ordinary rules as to notice, there is also the ordinary remedy *evictionis nomine, i.e.* the express or implied *stipulatio duplae*[3]. This of course depends on the buyer's ignorance, and is subject to one deduction which may be important. The condition may be *si decem dederit*, or the like. In that case if the money has been paid to the buyer, as it would ordinarily be, he must allow for it, unless it has been paid out of the buyer's property, for instance out of the slave's *peculium*[4].

(*b*) The vendor says that the man is a *statuliber*, but does not say what the condition is. Here if he knew what the condition was, but the buyer did not, he is liable, not *evictionis nomine*, but *ex empto*[5]. The text repeats itself. The first statement looks like Scaevola's own, which the compilers proceed to amplify, and justify, which Scaevola very rarely does. It is not obvious why the buyer should have any action at all, and this is perhaps what struck the compilers. The rule seems to be that if the vendor gives the buyer to understand that he is buying a *statuliber*, he saves himself from liability on the warranty but if he does so loosely, *perfusorie*, laying no stress on it, knowing all the time that it is a likely contingency, he may very well have deceived the buyer, who may bring the *actio ex empto*. As this is a *bonae fidei iudicium*, the *iudex* will ascertain, without any *exceptio*, whether there was *dolus* and the buyer was deceived.

(*c*) The vendor states a condition, but states one entirely different from the actual one. Here the liability is *evictionis nomine*[6]. Thus where a slave was to be free on accounting, and there was in fact nothing due on his accounts, and the vendor said the liberty was conditional on payment of so much money, he was liable as for eviction, the man sold not being a *statuliber* at all, but already entitled to his liberty[7].

---

[1] 46. 3. 38. 3.   [2] 40. 7. 9. 1.   [3] 21. 2. 39. 4, 46. 2, 51. 1.
[4] 44. 4. 2. 7.   If the man has already paid the vendor the money or part, this can be recovered by the vendee, but only if he releases the liability *ex evictione*, 44. 4. 3.
[5] 21. 2. 69. 5.   [6] 21. 2. 69. 2.
[7] *h. l.* 4.   Same rule where one whose liberty was unconditional was sold as a *statuliber*, *h. l.* 1.

(*d*) The vendor states the condition but states it inaccurately so that the buyer is prejudiced. There were evidently different opinions here, the dispute being not exactly as to what the remedy was in this case, but as to what cases ought to come under this head, rather than the last. The case discussed is that in which the vendor says there is a condition of payment, but overstates the amount. · Here, on the authority of Servius, the view prevailed that this was not a case for the eviction penalty, but only for *actio ex empto*[1]. In a text of Paul the same rule is laid down, but the remark is added that, if there has been an express *stipulatio duplae*, the action on this arises. This seems contradictory and the grammatical form of the sentence suggests that it is compilers' work[2]. A similar case arises where the slave is to be free on accounting, and there is money due on his accounts, and he is sold as *decem dare iussus*. Here if what is due is less than ten, an *actio ex empto* arises. If it is the same or more, there is no prejudice, and thus no action[3]. On the other hand, if the sum is stated correctly, but it is payable to a third person, so that it does not pass to the buyer, this is essentially a different condition, and the facts come under· case (*c*), giving rise to the eviction penalty[4].

(*e*) The vendor excepts generally the case of his freedom : here if he is already free or is now entitled to liberty, there is no liability at all. It may be presumed that if he has led the buyer to believe that the liberty is not yet due, there will be an *actio ex empto*[5].

All these liabilities depend on prejudice to the vendee. We have already seen this, in the case of the liability *ex empto*[6]: the same rule is laid down for the liability *evictionis nomine*. Thus where the condition was *si Titius consul factus fuerit*, but on the sale the condition declared was *si navis ex Asia venerit*, and this latter event occurred first, there was no liability at all[7]. Africanus seems to add that the same rule applies where, though the slave was entitled to liberty on the easier condition, he actually does satisfy the condition stated in the sale. He takes the case of a gift of freedom in one year, the condition stated in the sale having been of freedom in two years. Here, if the slave does not claim the liberty for two years, there is no liability. So also if there was a condition to pay 10 and the vendor says 5, and he pays the 10[8]. Neither of these cases is clear. The second is, as stated, no illustration of the proposition, for the condition named is less onerous than that which actually exists. The case is rendered a little confusing by the fact that if the money is not payable out of the *peculium,* the larger payment, while more onerous to the slave is also more beneficial to the

---

[1] 21. 2. 54. 1, 69. 3.
[2] 40. 7. 10.
[3] 21. 2. 69. 4.
[4] *h. t.* 54. 1.
[5] *h. t.* 69. *pr.*
[6] *h. t.* 69. 4.
[7] 21. 2. 46. 2.
[8] *h. l.* 3.

buyer, who will receive the money. But that does not affect the matter. In the first illustration, the decision is unfair, since the slave is free from the year, and this makes a great difference as to the destination of his acquisitions, during the second year, even though he be in that year a *bona fide serviens*. There is some authority for reading the text differently[1], and making the real condition two years, and that stated, one. This brings the two illustrations into line, but makes them illustrate only the obvious proposition that if there is no possibility of prejudice to the buyer there is no liability.

The various rules as to immutability of *status* apply only if the man actually is a *statuliber*. But he is not a *statuliber* till an heir has entered under the will. Thus the rule is laid down by Ulpian that, if, before entry, he is delivered by *traditio*, or usucapted or manumitted, his hope of liberty is lost[2]. But elsewhere he tells us that on such facts, if a *heres* does ultimately enter under the will, the man's position as a *statuliber* is restored *favore sui*[3]. He says this only in relation to *usucapio*, but it is presumably general[4]. Marcellus is quoted by Marcian[5] as laying down the same rule for *usucapio*[6]. Indeed this, and manumission by the usucaptor, are the only cases which are likely to happen, for it is not easy to see how a slave in such a position can be effectively transferred by anyone before *aditio*[7].

XIX. *CAPTIVI.*

The circumstances under which a man became a *captivus* should properly be discussed later in connexion with modes of enslavement, and those under which he regained his liberty with the modes of release from slavery. But as the matter stands somewhat apart from the general law of slavery, it seems best to take it all together. The sources deal almost exclusively with the case of a Roman subject captured by the enemy.

The principle governing the matter is that persons captured become slaves[8]. In general the capture will be in a war, and those captured will be part of a force. But they may be persons taken in the hostile country when the war breaks out[9], and it is not always

---

[1] Mommsen, *ad h. l.*
[2] 40. 7. 2. *pr.* He loses by manumission the position of *libertus orcinus*.
[3] 40. 7. 9. 3.   [4] *Post*, Ch. xxi.
[5] 40. 5. 55. 1. He says it might be regarded as due to their *culpa* that they were so dealt with; except in the case of children: he does not seem to mean that such *culpa* would bar.
[6] The favourable rule is clearly late and is not in the Edict. It seems that the point was decided by *cognitio* of the Praetor, 40. 5. 55. 1. As to whether persons so relieved were *cives* or Latins, *post*, Ch. xxiii.
[7] Probably the words *sive tradetur* are incautiously adopted from the earlier part of the text where they are rightly used.
[8] In. 1. 3. 4. They must be actually removed to the foreign territory, 49. 15. 5. 1.
[9] 49. 15. 12. *pr.*

the case that there is a war: persons who are found in a State with which Rome has no agreed friendly relations are liable to be made captives, though there is no declared war[1]. But if it is a war it must be one with a foreign people[2]. Those taken by pirates or robbers, or in civil war, remain free[3].

If captured by the forces they become, it is clear, the property of the State[4]. Whether under any circumstances they belong to an individual captor is not clear[5]. Where they become the property of the State, they do not necessarily become *servi publici populi Romani*. In many cases they are given freedom[6]. Often they are sold, *sub hasta*, or *sub corona*[7]. Some are made *servi populi*, with or without a view to their manumission if they properly carry out the duties entrusted to them. Some remain the property of the State but without the status of *servi publici*, being set to meaner labours, and often, no doubt, intended to be sold in course of time[8].

The person captured may have been before his capture a slave or a freeman: if he return he is restored to his old position by *postliminium*[9], subject to some important restrictions, and in some cases to a redeemer's lien, both of which will require detailed discussion. While in captivity he is a slave: if he die captive he is regarded as having died at the moment of capture, though there were doubts as to this in classical law[10].

So far as the doings of the *captivus* during his captivity are concerned there is nothing to be said: he is a slave and the ordinary rules of slavery apply to him[11]: the possibility of *postliminium* does not affect the matter, any more than the possibility of manumission does in other cases[12]. But the case is different with his property and family left behind. Here the provisional nature of his status is freely expressed in the rules, which can hardly be stated so as to present a logical appearance. It is necessary to consider the state of things during his life in captivity, the effect of his death in captivity, and the conditions and effect of *postliminium*.

The general principle governing the rules as to transactions and events during the captivity is that the status of the captive is in suspense and the destination of the acquisition, etc., will be determined by the event of death or return. But it is clear that this rule is

---

[1] *h. t.* 5. 2. See Sueton. Tiberius, 37. So captures might be made by unauthorised raids on such territories.
[2] 49. 15. 24.   [3] *h. t.* 19. 2, 21. 1, 24; C. 7. 14. 4.
[4] 48. 13. 15; Livy, 26. 47.
[5] Girard, Manuel, 281. The rule of the foreign capturing State would not necessarily be the same.
[6] Livy, 6. 13; 26. 47; 32. 26; Halkin, Esclaves publics, 17.
[7] Marquardt, Vie Privée, 1. 196.
[8] See Mommsen, Droit public, 1. 275; Staatsrecht (3) 1. 241, as to the rights of the general in command. See also Blair, Slavery among the Romans, 17.
[9] C. Th. 5. 7. 1.   [10] G. 1. 129.
[11] See the emphatic language of In. 1. 3. 4.
[12] An exception in case of wills to be considered shortly.

a gradual development, which in some parts of the law is far from complete : in some, indeed, there is no trace of the rule of suspense; the captivity ends the right.

The son or slave of a *captivus* can acquire and the effect of an acquisition is in suspense[1]. There is no conflict of opinion, and the rules are assimilated to those applied in the case of transactions by a *servus hereditarius*[2]. No doubt the rule applies to all cases of direct acquisition[3]. This condition of suspense raises difficulties both theoretical and practical as to the interim ownership. There is here no such conception as the *hereditas* in which acquisitions can vest, and thus it is not easy to say to whom any acquisition is made in the meanwhile. Paul and Pomponius are clear that the property is not in the *captivus*[4]. On the other hand Javolenus says that *in retinendo iura... singulare ius est*[5]. And Diocletian[6] and Justinian[7], speaking of protection of the property, use language which attributes interim ownership to the captive. This is in fact a mere question of language: the real difficulty is that, whether he is owner or not, he is not there to protect his own interests. Some protection must be devised. Certain forms of pillage can no doubt be dealt with criminally, and the fact that no seizer can make a title is *pro tanto* a protection. But these cannot suffice. The earliest protection of which we know anything is provided by a *lex* Hostilia, certainly early but not mentioned in any extant text earlier than Justinian, a fact which has led some writers to doubt its authenticity[8]. It authorises action on behalf of those *apud hostes*, perhaps a *popularis actio*[9], for the case of spoliation. But it probably plays but a small part, and in later times we find a more effective remedy in the power, of those who would succeed to the property, to apply to have a *curator bonorum* appointed in their interests, who gives security to a public slave[10]. This *curatio* does not seem to have been an ancient institution. It is mentioned only by Diocletian and Ulpian[11], the latter speaking of it as a well recognised institution[12]. There is no trace of it in the Edict. Moreover, while it is clear that such a *curator* can sue, and be sued, as *defensor*[13], Papinian says that if a *heres* has given security for a legacy and is then captured, his sureties cannot be sued as there is no person primarily liable under the

---

[1] Stipulation (45. 1. 73. 1; 45. 3. 18. 2; 49. 15. 1, 22. 1. 2); legacy (49. 15. 22. 1); *constitutum* and *acceptilatio* (13. 5. 11. *pr.*; 46. 4. 11. 3); *negotiorum gestio* (3. 5. 18. 5); *institutio* (28. 5. 32. 1), though there could be no entry on such an *institutio* in the meantime, 49. 15. 12. 1.
[2] 9. 2. 43; 45. 1. 73. 1; 45. 3. 25; 49. 15. 29.
[3] 49. 15. 12. 1, 22. 1—2.   [4] 3. 5. 18. 5; 9. 2. 43.
[5] 41. 2. 23. 1.   [6] C. 8. 50. 3.   [7] In. 4. 10. *pr.*
[8] *Ib.*; Theoph. *ad h. l.* See Pernice, Labeo, 1. 378, and the literature there cited.
[9] Pernice, *loc. cit.*   [10] C. 8. 50. 3.
[11] C. 8. 50. 3; D. 4. 6. 15. *pr.*; 26. 1. 6. 4; 27. 3. 7. 1; 38. 17. 2. 30. See Cuq, Institutions, 2. 172.
[12] 4. 6. 15. *pr.*   [13] C. 8. 50. 3; D. 27. 3. 7. 1.

stipulation[1]. Ulpian sees no such difficulty in an analogous case[2]. The reasonable inference is that Papinian did not know of this application of *curatio*. It seems to have been a development from the better known case of *curatio bonis* in the interest of creditors. There could be no *bonorum venditio* in the case of a captive debtor[3], but the creditors could apply, under the general edict[4], for the appointment of a *curator bonis*[5]. Such a *curator* has no functions except to protect the property: his powers and duties are in the field of procedure, and it does not appear that he could, by contract or the like, create rights or duties for the estate[6].

As a *captivus* is himself possessed he cannot possess. It follows that capture definitely ends possession by the captive himself, and thus interrupts *usucapio* by him. Nor is there any question of suspense: if he return he does not reacquire possession except by retaking, and his retaking has no retro-active effect, even though no one has possessed in the meantime[7]. Thus his possession is a new one, a fact which may be material, if for instance he has learnt in the meantime that he is not entitled: this will prevent him from usucapting, and bar the *actio* Publiciana. If the possession was not by himself, but by a son or slave, the rule is the same[8], unless the matter was one of the *peculium*. But there is a difference of opinion if the *res* is *peculiaris*, held at the time of the capture, or subsequently received. According to Labeo's view[9], the rule is the same in this case. This may be the logical view, at least in the case of a slave, since his capacity is purely derivative, and the captive, himself now a slave, has none. But the view which prevails is that of Julian, justified by obvious considerations of convenience, that in this case the possession continues, if the slave still holds, and ripens to ownership by usucapion at its proper time[10]. Julian, it may be remarked, says that the *usucapio* is in suspense so that it will be effective, if the captive returns, but he doubts for the case of his death[11]. This turns on difficulties as to the *fictio legis* Corneliae, to be considered later. Marcellus thinks[12] on the other hand that, if he dies, since his death is then supposed to have occurred at the moment of capture, it ought to make no difference whether he or the slave possessed, since from the moment of capture there was a *hereditas*, and the *hereditas iacens* was by his time capable of possession[13]. But this view is not

---

[1] 36. 3. 5. *pr.*   [2] 46. 6. 4. 5.   [3] 42. 4. 6. 2.
[4] 42. 7.   [5] 42. 5. 39. 1.
[6] This would be to be a procurator: a captive as a slave could have none, 4. 6. 15. *pr.*
[7] 41. 2. 23. 1; 41. 3. 11, 15. *pr.*, 44. 7; 49. 15. 12. 2, 29.
[8] 41. 3. 11.   [9] 49. 15. 29.   •
[10] 41. 3. 15. *pr.*, 44. 7; 49. 15. 12. 2, 22. 3, 29. Papinian and Paul justify the rule on the ground that even if he were present his knowledge and cooperation would not be needed, 41. 3. 44. 7; 49. 15. 29. But we have seen (*ante*, p. 200) that this rule rests merely on convenience, and cannot be argued from. Here he is *incapax*.
[11] 49. 15. 22. 3; 41. 3. 15. *pr.*   [12] 41. 3. 15. *pr.*   [13] *Ante*, p. 257.

accepted. Marcellus goes indeed so far as to hold[1] that whether he dies or not there ought to be usucapion of what he has possessed, presumably on the ground that the fiction of *postliminium* was that he had never been away. But this ignores the real point, namely, that the fiction of presence and the fiction of possession are not the same thing : we shall see that there are many things that the *postliminium* does not *ipso iure* undo. From the fact that a *captivus* has *restitutio in integrum*, within an *annus utilis* of his return, or even before his return, if a *curator* has been appointed to his property[2], we know that *usucapio* runs against him *ipso iure*, that actions by or against him may be barred by time, and so forth. If, as we are told, he does not lose his right as *suus* or *legitimus heres* or his right to *bonorum possessio contra tabulas*, this is precisely because these claims are not subject to any statutory limit[3]. The case in which a slave of a *captivus* stipulates and takes a surety, is on the same footing as that of such a contract by *servus hereditarius*[4]. This branch of the matter may be left with the remark that if a man has given security for his appearance in court (*iudicio sisti*), supervening captivity is an excuse and his sureties are not liable[5].

The law of family relations is governed by the same principle. Paul indeed says[6] that a captive ceases to have his children in *potestas*. But this means only that their status is in suspense, just as is that of a *captus filius familias*[7]. Thus no tutor can be given to one whose *pater* is captive, and (though there were doubts) Ulpian holds that such an appointment is not merely suspended in operation, but absolutely null[8]. On the other hand the *tutela* is ended by captivity of the tutor or of the ward, so completely that, though it is possible for the tutor to regain his position, his sureties may be sued[9]. Consideration of the purposes for which a tutor is appointed will shew that any rule of suspense would cause intolerable inconvenience. But if a person otherwise entitled to *legitima tutela* is a captive the person next entitled is not let in ; a praetorian tutor is appointed[10], and thus though we learn that the old *tutela* is recoverable by *postliminium*, this cannot be retrospective[11].

As we have seen, a captive does not lose his rights of succession[12], and there are many texts laying down the rule, for various cases, that if, upon a death, there exists a *heres* who is a captive, though he cannot himself make a present claim, he excludes from claiming those who would be entitled if he did not exist[13]. In many other ways his existence

---

[1] 49. 15. 12. 2. [2] 4. 6. 1. 1, 15. *pr.*
[3] P. 4. 8. 22; D. 37. 4. 1. 4. As to *bonorum possessio* see 38. 15. 2. 5.
[4] *Ante*, p. 261. [5] 2. 11. 4. 3. [6] P. 2. 25. 1.
[7] 38. 16. 15; 49. 15. 12. 1, 22. 2; In. 1. 12. 5; G. 1. 129.
[8] 26. 1. 6. 4. [9] 26. 1. 14. 2; 27. 3. 7. 1; 46. 6. 4. 5.
[10] 26. 4. 1. 2. [11] G. 1. 187. [12] 37. 4. 1. 4; P. 4. 8. 22.
[13] 38. 16. 1. 4, 2. *pr.*; 38. 17. 2. 7.

is recognised. Thus his mother must apply for a *curator bonorum* to be appointed to him, if she wishes to preserve her rights under the *Sc.* Tertullianum, just as she would have had to get a tutor appointed to an *impubes,* not captive[1]. A captive, or his slave, may be validly instituted[2], though there can be no question of entry. Similarly, since he is not dead, there can be no entry on his *hereditas*[3]. But a child born in captivity to a *captivus* is no relative to him apart from *postliminium*[4].

It is clear that capture of either party dissolves a marriage, and that it is not restored by *postliminium,* but only by renewed consent[5]. Paul is reported as saying that, if the wife refuses this renewal of consent without just cause, she is liable to the penalties resulting from causeless divorce[6]. It may be doubted whether this remark is really from Paul. The evidence for the existence of definite money penalties for causeless divorce in classical law is very doubtful[7]. The cesser of the marriage might seem to be explained by the fact that there can be no *connubium* with a slave[8], but this would not of itself account for the refusal to treat the matter as in suspense. And its insufficiency is also shewn by the fact that if the wife is a *libertina,* freed for the purpose of marriage, the marriage still subsists though the patron be captured, according to a rule laid down by Julian and reported by Ulpian[9]. The real reason is one of convenience, and the rule brings into strong relief the *de facto* nature of marriage as conceived by the Roman Law.

But though the marriage has ceased it does not follow that there. is complete liberty to marry again, and the texts create some difficulty[10]. Justinian in a Novel[11] observes that captivity is such a dissolution of marriage as had involved no penalties. But he adds that he takes a humaner view, and lays it down that the marriage is to subsist so long as it is certain that the captive, male or female, is alive; and the other party cannot contract another marriage without incurring the penalties for causeless divorce. But if it is uncertain whether the captive is alive or dead, there must be five years' delay, after which, if the uncertainty still exists, or the captive is dead, the party at home may remarry, without fear of any penalties, as if there had been a perfectly valid *repudium.* If this stood alone there would be no difficulty: it is a typical piece of Byzantine legislation. But though it looks like new legislation, and probably is so, as to the continuance of the marriage, it certainly is not absolutely new as to the bar to remarriage. For it is later than the Digest, which contains two texts which speak of a similar rule. Paul is reported as saying[12] that the wife is free to marry *post*

---

1 38. 17. 2. 23, 30. 2 28. 5. 32. 1. 3 C. 8. 50. 4.
4 38. 17. 1. 3; 49. 15. 25; C. 8. 50. 1. See *post,* p. 308.
5 24. 2. 1; 49. 15. 8, 12. 4, 14. 1. 6 49. 15. 8.
7 See especially the tenor of C. 8. 38. 2. 8 Nov. 22. 7; D. 23. 2. 45. 6.
9 23. 2. 45. 6. 10 Karlowa, R. R. G., 2. 120.
11 Nov. 22. 7. 12 49. 15. 8.

constitutum tempus, and Julian as laying down a rule[1] which is substantially that of the Novel except in two respects. He does not say that the marriage continues, but only that it may seem to continue from the fact that remarriage is barred. And he is more explicit as to the date 'from which the five years are to run: it is the commencement of the captivity. Karlowa is of opinion that the five year rule was contained in the *lex* Papia, or in connected legislation, since the text of Paul in which he mentions the rule[2], is in his commentary on that law, and thus, that the text of Julian, notwithstanding its florid style, is genuine so far as that rule is concerned[3]. But it is generally thought that the allusion in the text of Paul is interpolated, and Lenel[4] treats it, and nearly the whole text of Julian, as compilers' work. And this seems the more probable view. The Novel[5] refers to earlier legislation dealing with the matter, and we have some of this in the Code. Theodosius provides that on divorce by a wife without cause, she may not remarry at all within five years[6]. Julian's opening remark is probably no more than an allusion to the fact that those whose husbands were captured were forbidden, though not absolutely prevented, from marrying for a certain time for reasons sufficiently obvious; the rule applied primarily to widows and divorced women[7]. The compilers build on it an extension of the limit of five years, if it is uncertain whether the husband is alive or dead, to this case of captivity, the rule being a prohibition; but not a bar. The Novel declares the marriage still on foot and applies the five year rule to both sexes equally.

A captive father cannot assent to his son's marriage, and public convenience makes it necessary to dispense with his approval though in the event this may cause children to be added to his *familia* without his consent[8]. If he does not assent, says Tryphoninus, at least he does not dissent. This text imposes no delay. But Ulpian appears[9] as holding that a son can marry only after three years. Paul lays down a similar rule[10] for son or daughter where the whereabouts of the father is not known, and Julian observes[11] that if a son or daughter of a captive, or *absens*, marries before the three years are over, the marriage is good if the spouse is one to whom the father could not have objected. These texts do not tell a consistent story, and it is perhaps impossible to extract the development of the law from them. There is no trace of any earlier legislation on the matter, and the jurists could hardly have established the positive term of three years. The texts contain many errors of grammar and peculiarities of diction, which suggest Tribonian, and

---

[1] 24. 2. 6.   [2] 49. 15. 8.
[3] *loc. cit.* He thinks that the distinction between certainty and doubt is an interpolation.
[4] Paling. *ad hh. ll.*   [5] Nov. 22. 7.   [6] C. 5. 17. 8, 9.
[7] Girard, Manuel, 162.   [8] 49. 15. 12. 3.   [9] 23. 2. 9. 1.
[10] *h. t.* 10.   [11] *h. t.* 11.

perhaps the right solution is that classical law allowed marriage without consent, and Justinian allowed it only after three years of captivity, unless the person was one to whom no exception could be taken by the father[1].

If the person captured was a slave, old rights in him cease to exist, subject, of course, to *postliminium*[2]. Thus if he has been pledged, the pledge does not exist for the time[3]. Ownership is gone: he is for the time a *servus hostium*[4]. Usufruct in him is gone, though it may be restored by *postliminium*[5]. If in the meantime the period of nonuser has passed, it would seem that some form of *restitutio in integrum* may be necessary since usufruct needs positive enjoyment to its retention, not, like *dominium*, mere absence of adverse possession. But the text seems to negative this requirement, and the Edict does not mention this case. The slave loses for the time his old characteristics. He becomes incapable of possessing[6]. He ceases to be a *servus poenae*, if he was one before[7], and if he has been from any cause incapable of manumission, the defect does not apply to him till *postliminium*[7]. But several texts bring out the suspensive and provisional character of these rules. The slave still exists. Thus an *actio de peculio* on his account does not become *annalis*, so long as he can possibly return with *postliminium*. A legacy of him, made before or after he was captured is good, and the heir must give security, not for his value, but for his delivery on his return[8].

The situation is of course completely changed if the captive dies *apud hostes*. The matters in suspense are now decided, and the nature of the settlement calls for a good deal of discussion. Matters are in general adjusted as if there had been no captivity[9]. The captive's children become *sui iuris*, and though for Gaius it is doubtful from what date their independence is regarded as beginning[10], he stands alone in this doubt. Ulpian indeed says merely that they become *sui iuris*[11]. But the Digest is quite explicit, and the texts do not seem to be interpolated. Tryphoninus says that on the death of a *captivus* his children are *sui iuris* as from the day of capture[12]. Julian lays it down

---

[1] See Accarias, Précis, § 84. Karlowa thinks (R. R. G. 2. 121, following Bruns) that in the text of Julian a "*non*" has dropped out. The three years rule is classical for captives (hence Paul's doubt as to absence); the compilers extended it to *absentes* and Julian's allusion to these is an interpolation. He remarks however that Bechmann reverses this. It may be noticed that if a *non* is inserted in Julian's text, the resulting rule is so severe as to give little relief, and that all Karlowa's argument is equally in favour of the more complete interpolation.

[2] 35. 2. 43; C. 8. 50. 10. 12, *etc.*　　　　　[3] 49. 15. 12. 12.

[4] 40. 7. 6. 1; 49. 15. 5. 2.　　　　　[5] 7. 4. 26.

[6] 41. 3. 11.　　　　　[7] 49. 15. 12. 16.

[8] 30. 47. 2. A legacy of A or B where B is a *captivus* is treated like one in which he is a *fugitivus*, *ante*, p. 271.

[9] 24. 1. 32. 14 *in fin.*; 24. 3. 10. *pr.*; 38. 16. 1. 4, 2. *pr.*; 38. 17. 2. 7; C. 8. 50. 4.

[10] G. 1. 129.　　　　　[11] U. 10. 4.

[12] 49. 15. 12. 1, and thus can have a *hereditas*, 38. 16. 15.

that what a son of a captive stipulates for, or otherwise acquires, is his own if his father dies still a captive[1]. And it is repeatedly laid down generally that in all parts of the law the effect of the death is the same as if it had occurred at the moment of capture[2]. So, on his death, since (as we shall shortly see) his will operates, he is restored to his place in his father's succession, and thus the other representatives, even his own children, may be excluded[3]. Papinian discusses the case of a son or slave, of a captive, who stipulates in the name of the father or master, and considers the effect if the captive die in captivity[4]. He observes that though, in a simple stipulation, the effect would be different in each case, since the slave would benefit the heir of the *dominus*, and the son would benefit himself alone, yet here they are on the same level. Both are bad. In the case of the son this is because he stipulates *alii*, *non sibi*: it is in fact for a non-existent person. In the case of the slave it is a stipulation for his dead master, which, as we have seen, is void[5]. One case is peculiar. We are told by implication, by Paul[6], that where a slave is *captus*, the *actio de peculio* on his account becomes *annalis* on his death, but it is evident that the year is not counted from the capture.

It is in connexion with the succession to the dead captive that the most difficult questions arise. The man dies a slave and cannot in strictness have any will or indeed any inheritance[7]. We are told explicitly by Ulpian that his will becomes *irritum* on his capture[8]. As he is a slave he cannot make a will in captivity[9], and though as we shall see there is relief against the destruction of a previously made will, codicils made during captivity are not confirmed by it: they are not valid even for the purpose of creating *fideicommissa*, since at the time of making them he had not *testamenti factio*[9]. Whether, in very early law, succession to such a person did not exist at all cannot be said. Perhaps the relief developed *pari passu* with the notion that a captive suffered *capitis deminutio maxima*[10]. However that may be, it was provided, directly or indirectly, by a certain *lex* Cornelia[11], that the succession to such a person should be regulated as if he had died *in civitate*[12]. The exact nature and scope of this provision cannot be clearly made out from the texts. The rule is sometimes stated as a direct

---

[1] 49. 15. 22. 2, 2a.
[2] 49. 15. 18, 22; C. 8. 50. 1, *etc.* A legacy to a captive is null if he dies still a captive (30. 101. 1), but if his slave is instituted the gift is good, and goes, if the captive dies *apud hostes*, to the person who takes his inheritance, 28. 5. 32. 1; 49. 15. 22. 1.
[3] 38. 16. 1. 4. The text is rather obscure. As to the case of *postumi*, 28. 2. 29. 6. So if my son is captured while my father is alive, and dies *apud hostes* after I am a *paterfamilias*, his children take his place in succession to me, 38. 16. 1. 5, and see *post*, p. 301.
[4] 45. 3. 18. 2.   [5] *Ante*, p. 260.   [6] 15. 2. 2. 1.
[7] 50. 16. 3. 1.   [8] 28. 3. 6. 5.
[9] P. 3. 4a. 8; In. 2. 12. 5; D. 49. 15. 12. 5.   [10] Cuq, Institutions, 1. 573.
[11] Sulla? Karlowa, R. R. G., 2. 124.   [12] U. 23. 5, *etc.*

provision of the *lex*[1]. Sometimes it is called the *beneficium legis Corneliae*[2], sometimes the *fictio legis Corneliae*[3]. While many texts speak of the rule as creating a *hereditas*[4], others do not use this expression, and Ulpian, in two texts, declares that it is not, strictly speaking, a *hereditas*, giving, as his reason, that a man who dies a slave cannot have a *hereditas*, and that one who could not make a will cannot properly be said to have died intestate. He adds that as succession is given to those to whom it would have been given, if he had died in the State, it is treated as if it were a *hereditas*[5]. It is widely held that the rule is not a direct provision of the *lex*[6], but a juristic interpretation of something therein, and conjecture has gone so far as to assume that this *lex* Cornelia is identical with the *lex* Cornelia *de falsis*, and that it contained a rule punishing the forgery of the will of one who was *apud hostes*, from which the jurists inferred that the will of such a person would be valid[7]. For this opinion there seems to be no evidence whatsoever[8], and it is difficult to hold it in face of the texts which say that the *lex* did contain a direct and express provision on the matter[9].

It is not easy to say what this provision was. It is fairly certain that it was in a form which left room for doubts, since it is observable that a large proportion of the texts dealing with the matter are from collections of *Quaestiones* and *Disputationes*[10]. It is also most probable that it was in the form of a fiction[11], and, from Ulpian's language[12], that it did not speak of *heres* or *hereditas*. Thus Paul tells us not that the *lex* but that the *fictio legis* Corneliae *et heredem et hereditatem facit*[13], though elsewhere both he and Papinian use more unguarded language[14]. One or two of the texts give us what purport to be explicit statements as to the content of the *lex*. Ulpian says that the *lex* confirms the will as if he had died *in civitate*[15]. Julian says that by the *lex* Cornelia the state of things is to be that...*quae futura esset si hi de quorum hereditatibus et tutelis constituebatur in hostium potestatem non pervenissent*[16]. Paul says it confirms wills, *legitimae tutelae* and *legitimae hereditates*[17]. On all this evidence it seems clear that the *lex* itself, without speaking of *heres* or *hereditas*, confirmed the succession to him as if he had not been captured, a provision which exactly accounts for Ulpian's purist

---

[1] *e.g.* 28. 6. 28; 49. 15. 10. 11. 1, 22. 3; U. 23. 5, *etc.*   [2] *e.g.* P. 3. 4a. 8; C. 2. 53. 5.
[3] *e.g.* 35. 2. 18. *pr.*; 41. 3. 15. *pr.*; C. 8. 50. 1. 1.   Confusion in C. 8. 50. 9.
[4] 28. 1. 12; 28. 6. 28; 35. 2. 18. *pr.*; 49. 15. 22. 1; C. 8. 50. 1, *etc.*
[5] 38. 16. 1. *pr.*; 50. 16. 3. 1.   [6] See Pernice, Labeo, 1. 375.
[7] Accarias, *op cit.* § 531.   [8] Girard, Manuel, 191.
[9] *Lex* Cornelia *quae...testamenta confirmat* (28. 6. 28. Julian); *qua lege etiam legitimae tutelae hereditatesque confirmantur* (P. 3. 4a. 8); *lege Cornelia...quae successionem eius confirmat* (U. 23. 5).   See also 28. 1. 12; 49. 15. 22. *pr.* and many others.   See Karlowa, *loc. cit.*, who sees in 49. 15. 22. *pr.* a verbal reminiscence of the *lex.*
[10] 28. 6. 29; 29. 1. 39; 35. 2. 18. *pr.*; 38. 16. 15; 49. 15. 10—12, *etc.*
[11] See n. 3.   [12] See n. 5.   [13] 35. 2. 18. *pr.*
[14] P. 3. 4a. 8; 49. 15. 10. 1.   [15] U. 23. 5.
[16] 49. 15. 22. *pr.* (see n. 9).   He makes a similar remark in 28. 1. 12.
[17] P. 3. 4a. 8.

objections, which do not in the least require that the whole rule be one of juristic inference[1]. The *lex* also dealt with *tutela*, as to which provision there is some difficulty. It had nothing to do with provision for *tutelae* in his will : it is expressly distinguished from the provision affecting wills[2]. It cannot have referred to a *tutela* held by or over the captive: he was dead, and in any case such *tutelae* were ended by the capture[3]. The *tutela*[4] is *legitima*. Karlowa[5] suggests that the provision referred to *tutela* of his children left behind. But it is difficult to see any need for this : it could not be retrospective, and these children and their agnates had suffered no *capitis deminutio*. More probably it was *tutela* over *liberti*. The *lex* enabled the children to claim *tutela* as *liberi patroni*, the *captus* not having really been patron at the time of his death, apart from the fiction.

The *lex* left open the question at what date the will was supposed to operate, and the lawyers developed the principle, which as we have seen, came ultimately to be applied generally[6], that the case was to be treated as if he had died at the moment of capture[7]. The texts do not state this refinement as part of the *lex*, which also left open the question of the application of the rule to pupillary substitutions— *secundae tabulae*—a matter which gave rise to much discussion. Apart from these substitutions the working of the rule is fairly simple, and can be illustrated very briefly.

Its general effect is that the succession is to go to those who would have had it if the deceased had never been captured[8], there being a right to enter as soon as it is known that he is dead[9], and if there are no *heredes* under the *lex*, the property goes to the State[10]. It is only wills made before capture which are thus validated[11]. The will can produce no more effect than it would if he were in the State. Thus where a man was captured while his wife was pregnant, and a child was born and died, the will was null, as it would have been had he not been a captive[12]. The validation of the will does not amount to *post-liminium*, and thus if a child is born *apud hostes*, and returns, but the father dies there, the child can have no claim under the *lex* Cornelia: he is a *spurius*, the father being regarded as having died at the moment of capture[13]. If a *filius familias miles* dies *apud hostes*, the rule applies,

[1] See also Julian in 28. 1. 12.
[2] P. 3. 4a. 8; 49. 15. 22. *pr.*
[3] Karlowa, *loc. cit.*
[4] P. 3. 4a. 8.
[5] *loc. cit.*
[6] *Ante*, p. 298.
[7] 29. 1. 39; 38. 16. 15; 49. 15. 10. *pr.*; *h. t.* 11. *pr.*; an enactment of Severus and Caracalla almost states this refinement as a part of the *lex*, C. 8. 50. 1. 1.
[8] 49. 15. 22. *pr.*
[9] C. 8. 50. 4.
[10] 49. 15. 22. 1.
[11] In. 2. 12. 5, *etc.* Codicils made during captivity could not be confirmed by anticipation in a previously made will, and as having been made by one without *testamenti factio*, they were invalid to create *fideicommissa*, 49. 15. 12. 5.
[12] 49. 15. 22. 4.
[13] 38. 17. 1. 3; 49. 15. 9, 25; C. 8. 50. 1. 1. A slave made *heres* will be free and *heres* whether he wishes to be or not, and a son will be *heres* at civil law, though as Julian observes, the expressions *necessarius* and *suus* are not strictly applicable, 28. 1. 12.

and if before his death his father has died, leaving a grandson (by the *miles*), and the grandfather has omitted the *nepos*, his will fails, but that of the soldier does not, if he has omitted his son, both rules being due to the fact that he is supposed to have died at capture while still a *filius familias*[1]. If a child, captured with his parents, returns, but they die in captivity, he has a right to succession by the *lex* Cornelia[2].

The effect of the rule, on pupillary substitutions, is discussed in several texts some of which give rise to difficulty[3]. If the father is *captus* and dies, and then the *impubes* dies, the pupillary substitution takes effect, as the *lex* covers all inheritances passing by the will of the captive[4]. To the objection that in fact the child was *sui iuris* before his father's death, Papinian answers that the accepted principle is that on his death the captive is regarded as having died at the moment of capture[5]. It is likely that the rule was not so settled till the classical law. In the following text Papinian seems to adopt the view that he has here rejected[6], but it is probable that, as Cujas suggested, the words *nihil est quod tractari possit* do not mean that there can be no question, *i.e.* of pupillary substitution, but that the case can give rise to no difficulty. Probably there has been abridgement.

If the son alone is captured after the father's death and dies *impubes* the *lex* applies and a substitution will be good, but this is really an extension of the *lex*, since the person who dies is not the actual testator, and the *lex* says only that the will of the dead captive is to be confirmed. Accordingly Papinian says the Praetor must give *utiles actiones*[7]. If the father die after the son's capture the *lex* has no application, for this would be to give the provision more effect than it would have had if he had died at the moment of capture, when he would have had no *bona*[8] : he has, in law, predeceased his father, and that destroys pupillary substitutions[9].

There is difficulty in the case where both are captured. There are two texts, both obscure. Papinian says[10] :

Sed si ambo apud hostes et prior pater dece'dat, sufficiat lex Cornelia *substituto non alias quam si apud hostes patre defuncto, postea filius in civitate decessisset.*

The only rule stated in this text is that if both die in captivity the substitution fails while if the son returns and dies *impubes* it takes

---

[1] 29. 1. 39. The traditional explanation of an obscure text. See Pothier *ad h. l.*
[2] C. 2. 53. 5. The text adds (it is an application of a rule already stated), that he has *restitutio in integrum*, like any other captive, against *usucapio, etc.*, within an *annus utilis*. In such a case it is an extension of the *restitutio*, since it is not he against whom time was running and he is not an ordinary successor. The rule is not confined to *milites*, 4. 6. 15. *pr.*
[3] Mühlenbruch-Glück, 40, 449 *sqq.*; Buhl, Salvius Iulianus, 1. 267 *sqq.*
[4] 28. 6. 28.   [5] 49. 15. 10. *pr.*   [6] *h. t.*.11. *pr.*
[7] 28. 6. 28; 49. 15. 10. 1.   [8] 28. 6. 28.
[9] So, if he had been a *pubes*, captured while his father was alive, the *lex* has no application, though the father ultimately die first.
[10] 49. 15. 11. 1.

effect, a decision which agrees, as Mühlenbruch observes, with the presumption, where an *impubes* and a *pubes* have died at unknown dates, that the *impubes* died first. But its opening words seem to foreshadow treatment of a case in which both die *apud hostes*, and as it stands the word *prior* serves no purpose. Among the proposed explanations[1] is that of taking *non alias* to mean *similiter*, and taking the text to mean that though both die in captivity, the substitution can take effect, if it be shewn that the father died first. But this is arbitrarily to change the meaning of words, though the rule itself would not be unreasonable. The earlier commentators, cited by Mühlenbruch, are not quite satisfied with it, and suppose that the father was captured first and the words *et prior pater decedat* are a gloss. This is very conjectural. Perhaps the suggestion of the insertion of the word *sint* after the first occurrence of *hostes* is best[2], though that does not account for the word *prior*. Better still is it to admit that we cannot reconstruct the original text : it is impossible to be satisfied with it as it stands.

The other text is from Scaevola[3] :

Si pater captus sit ab hostibus, mox filius, et ibi ambo decedant, quamvis prior pater decedat, lex Cornelia ad pupilli substitutionem non pertinebit nisi reversus in civitate impubes decedat, quoniam et si ambo in civitate decessissent veniret substitutus.

Here one would expect the substitution to be effective, since if each had died at the moment of capture, the father would have died first. Mühlenbruch[4] considers however that the rule is correctly stated in the text. He remarks that the *hereditas* is not *delata* till the actual death, that the *impubes* could have had no property, and that thus no one could inherit from him. The point as to *delatio* is hardly material, but this seems the right explanation of these texts. The child is a captive who had nothing at capture, and, not having returned, he has no *postliminium*. He can thus have acquired nothing by *hereditas* or otherwise. Thus there is nothing on which the *substitutio*[5] can operate[6]. The allusions to the date of the father's death suggest doubts as to the reference back to the date of capture. But as it is plain that the text now under discussion is not as it was originally written[7], it is also possible that these allusions here and in the other text are hasty interpolations. Many emendations have been suggested, starting from different points of view, but none of them is satisfactory[8]. The only thing certain is that Scaevola did not write it as it stands[9].

---

[1] Faber, *cit.* Mühlenbruch, *loc. cit.*   [2] Haloander, *cit.* Mommsen, *ad h. l.*
[3] 28. 6. 29.   [4] *loc. cit.*
[5] Treated as his will. A *substitutio vulgaris* would operate.
[6] 28. 6. 28.   [7] Lenel, Paling. *ad h. l.*
[8] Earlier views, Mühlenbruch, *loc. cit.* See also, Lenel, *loc. cit.*; Mommsen, *ad h.*
[9] But Mühlenbruch accepts both texts.

The next topic for discussion is *postliminium*. The prisoner of war who, under certain conditions, returns to Roman territory, is restored to his old legal position, with some limitations, this right of *postliminium* being suspended, if the captive was redeemed for money, till the redeemer's lien is paid off. There are thus three topics: the conditions of *postliminium*, its effects, and the law as to a redeemer's rights.

As we are concerned only with *captivi*, we shall not consider a voluntary change of State in time of peace. Most of the requirements for *postliminium* can be shortly stated. Not every captive who escapes is said *postliminio redire*[1]. He must actually have returned to the territory or to that of a friendly State[2], though it matters not how he effects his escape, whether by evasion, *vi aut fallacia*, by dismissal, exchange or recapture[3]. He must have returned as soon as it was possible for him to do so[4]. He must come to stay, not having any intention of returning to the enemy[5]. It may be that this requirement is of classical law though it is expressed by the traditions of republican Rome, which however are not contemporary. Regulus was declared not to have *postliminium*, not because he had sworn to the Carthaginians that he would return, but because he meant to keep his oath, *non habuerat animum Romae remanendi*[6]. The captives who were sent by Hannibal to Rome, on the same mission, and who stayed there, and shewed that they had never meant to go back, notwithstanding their oath, had *postliminium*, though they were declared *ignominiosi* and *intestabiles* for not keeping their promise[7].

Discreditable circumstances might bar *postliminium*. Thus, one who had surrendered when armed had no *postliminium*[8]. One who had been *deditus* by the *pater patratus* had no such right, though apparently this had been doubted[9]. There was a tradition of a difficulty in the case of Mancinus, who had been so surrendered to the Numantines, but they had refused to receive him. It was held, on his return to Rome, says Cicero[10], that he had no *postliminium*. Elsewhere the same authority throws doubt on the decision, or, rather, holds that the man had never ceased to be a *civis*[11], since there could be

---

[1] Festus, *s.v. Postliminium.* Or *postliminium redire*, a form expressing the result rather than the rule.
[2] 49. 15. 5. 1, 19. 3.   [3] 49. 15. 26; C. 8. 50. 5, 12.
[4] 49. 15. 12. *pr.*   [5] *h. t.* 5. 3, 12. 9, 26.   [6] *h. t.* 5. 3.
[7] Aul. Gell., Noct. Att. 7. 18. In the case of Menander, a Greek slave, who had been freed and made a Roman *civis*, and was employed as interpreter to an embassy to Greece, a law was passed that if he returned to Rome, he should again be a Roman *civis*. Cicero (Pro Balbo, 28) thought this law had some significance, though Pomponius says (49. 15. 5. 3) that it was thought needless, since if he returned he would be a *civis* and if he did not he would not be one, apart from this law. Perhaps for Cicero the requirement of intent to stay was not certain, but it is likely that the law was a precaution due to the fact that *postliminium* from captivity and *postliminium* from reversion to original *civitas* are not the same thing. See however Daremberg et Saglio, Dict. des Antiq. *s.v. Postliminium.*
[8] 49. 15. 17.   [9] 49. 15. 4.   [10] de Orat. 1. 181.
[11] Top. 37; Pro Caec. 98.

no such thing as *deditio*, any more than there could be *donatio*, without an acceptance. There is no *postliminium* for a *transfuga*, i.e. one who treacherously goes over to the enemy, or to a people with whom we have only an armistice, or one with whom we have no friendly relations[1]. As we shall see shortly, this rule is not applied in the case of slaves. But this exception is strictly construed: the rule applies in all its severity to the case of a *filiusfamilias*, notwithstanding his father's rights[2]. In strictness of course a person who never was a Roman *civis* cannot have *postliminium*. Even in the case of children born to *captivi*, this rule is so far applied that if the child reaches Rome, but neither parent does, he has no *civitas*: if he and his mother come he is a *civis* and her *spurius*: if he and both parents come, he is a *filiusfamilias*[3].

A further suggested requirement of *postliminium* has given rise to some discussion. It is laid down by some writers that to obtain *postliminium* the captive must return *eodem bello*, i.e. before the conclusion of peace[4]. This view seems to rest mainly on three texts. Pomponius tells us that a captive *si eodem bello reversus fuerit postliminium habet*[5]. Paul says that if a man returns during *indutiarum tempus*, i.e. during an armistice, he has no *postliminium*[6]. Finally he tells us[7] that if a captive returns after peace has been declared, and on a fresh outbreak of war is recaptured, he reverts to his old owner, by *postliminium*. The first text of Paul is of no weight: an agreement for an armistice involves, as he says, the maintenance of the *status quo* so long as it exists: *indutiae* and peace are not the same thing. The other text of Paul looks more weighty, since, as Accarias says, if he is still a slave of the old master, he has not been freed. But he was not freed by his old master, and the more reasonable inference is that *postliminium* gives him restitution only against his own State, apart from some special agreement. It is the allusion to the peace that is regarded as making the text important in the present connexion. But it may be noted that if the war is still continuing, my slave escaping to the enemy is a *transfuga*, and by virtue of the special rule in such cases will revert to me if recaptured[8]. Paul purposely takes a case to which this special rule would not apply. Neither of these texts is conclusive. That of Pomponius remains. Against it may be set a text of Tryphoninus[9], which says that there is *postliminium* on return after peace is made, if there is nothing in the treaty of peace to exclude it, and

---

[1] 49. 15. 19. 4, 19. 8; 4. 6. 14.
[2] 49. 15. 19. 7.   The Romans, says Paul, set *disciplina castrorum* before *caritas filiorum*.
[3] 38. 17. 1. 3; 49. 15. 25; C. 8. 50. 1.
[4] Karlowa, *op. cit.* 2. 118; Accarias, Précis, § 43.   [5] 49. 15. 5. 1.
[6] *h. t.* 19. 1.   [7] 49. 15. 28.
[8] 49. 15. 19. 5; 41. 1. 51. *pr.* This text is sometimes understood to mean that we acquire *transfugae* who come from the enemy.
[9] 49. 15. 12. *pr.*

goes on to make the same remark about those who were caught in the foreign country at the outbreak of war. There are other considerations. Returns after peace must have been not uncommon, and one would have expected discussion of the case of those who had not *postliminium*. Yet the texts, though they tell us that not every escaped prisoner has *postliminium*, say nothing about the state of things where it does not arise. And that *postliminium* is the common case appears from the fact that many texts speak of return of captives as giving *postliminium*, without more[1]. It may be added that while we have reference to agreements that there shall be no *postliminium*, after the peace[2], we have none the other way: what we have are agreements that prisoners shall be allowed to return[3], which is a different matter. As Karlowa says[4], a war ends either by surrender of the enemy—*deditio*—or by a treaty of *amicitia*, and he points out that we are told that between states in friendship there is no *postliminium*, since the subjects of each state retain their rights in the other[5]. But the reason shews that the writer is dealing with cases arising after the *foedus*, not with persons who were captives at the time of the treaty.

It may also be observed that the principal text[6] is not conclusive: it lays down a right of *postliminium* if the captive return *eodem bello*, and it is only in that case that a general proposition is justified: the fact that the treaty might exclude the right compels the limitation. Nevertheless the text is regarded as so conclusive as to require an emendation of the above cited text of Tryphoninus which is even more conclusive the other way[7]. For *his* it is proposed to read *non iis*. This drastic measure is defended as being necessary to account for the words: *quod ideo placuisse Servius scribit, quia spem revertendi civibus in virtute bellica ·magis quam in pace Romani esse voluerunt*, and for the contrast established later on in the text. But the remark of Servius is quite plain as the text stands. It is the practice of exclusion by treaty that he is justifying. And the contrast is between those who left Roman territory in time of peace and those who did so during the war, and no more[8]. If the contrast had been that supposed by Karlowa, the jurist would have said *tam in pace quam in bello* and not *tam in bello quam in pace.* The other contrast is an unreasonable one: a person who is in the other country at the outbreak of war is to be allowed an unlimited time for return, but one captured in the war is not. And the absurdity is emphasised by the jurist, who notes that these persons are there, *suo facto*[9]. There is no justification for so altering texts as to create this

---

[1] *e.g.* In. 1. 12. 5; U. 10. 4; G. 1. 129, all seeming to use a common form. See also Festus, *s.v. Postliminium.*
[2] 49. 15. 12. *pr.*   [3] *h. t.* 20. *pr.*, 28.   [4] *loc. cit.*
[5] 49. 15. 7.   [6] *h. t.* 5. 1.   [7] *h. t.* 12. *pr.*
[8] So the Gloss.   [9] 49. 15. 5. 2.

distinction, especially as those captured without war by a State with which there are no friendly relations are clearly under no such restriction. Altogether the requirement that, to obtain *postliminium* the captive must have returned before the peace, is not made out. It is impossible to be certain on the point, but the most probable view seems to be that there is no such rule, but that treaties of peace sometimes exclude *postliminium* for later returns.

What is the position of one who returns without *postliminium*? There is but little authority. *Transfugam*, we are told, *iure belli recipimus*[1]. This seems to mean that a slave *transfuga* reverts to his master. If he is not a slave he is at best a prisoner of war ; but he is ordinarily capitally punishable[2]. Apart from this case we know really nothing. Most probably their previous Roman condition is simply ignored, and they take the position, whatever it is, which they would have taken had they belonged originally (either as slaves or freemen) to the State from which they came.

We have now to consider the effect of *postliminium*. The general effect is to put the *civis* in the same position as if he had never been captured[3]. The captives, according to the traditional formula, *recipiunt omnia pristina iura*[4], and, it may be added, obligations too[5]. Moreover the effect is retrospective[6]: *fingitur*, says Justinian, *semper in civitate fuisse*[7], and this expression clearly represents the classical law. It is, says Paul, *ac si nunquam ab hostibus captus sit*, and the same conception is involved in the notion of pendency of rights, already considered[8]. It is not necessary to repeat, by way of illustration of the general rule, what has already been said. It may be observed in addition that he has *actio furti* for what has been stolen in the meantime[9], and probably the same is true of *actio* Aquilia. It may also be presumed, though the texts are silent, that he is noxally liable for what has happened in the meantime. An *actio de peculio* and the like will probably lie against him, though the texts are silent, and those dealing with restitution of actions, to and against him, where time has run, are not specific as to the date of the transaction[10]. But there can really be no doubt. A person who manages any affair for the *captivus* has an action on *negotia gesta* on his return[11]. The captive can sue, on his return, on contracts

---

[1] 41. 1. 51.　　　　　[2] 48. 19. 38. 1; 49. 15. 12. 17.
[3] P. 2. 25. 1.　　　　　[4] G. 1. 129; U. 10. 4, *etc.*
[5] If a *deportatus* before capture he is one on return, 49. 15. 12. 15.
[6] *h. t.* 12. 6, 16.　　　[7] In. 1. 12. 5.
[8] *Ante*, p. 293.　On the question whether the retrospective effect is republican see Karlowa, *loc. cit.*, and Pernice, Labeo, 1. 375, who thinks it an expression of the Ciceronian doctrine that a man cannot lose *civitas* without his own consent.
[9] 47. 2. 41. *pr.*　The text shews that there had been doubts.
[10] 4. 6. 1, 14, 15.　　　[11] 3. 5. 18. 5.

made, and securities taken, by his son or slave[1], and, in general, he is in the position of one succeeding to a *hereditas iacens*[2].

The questions as to the effect of *postliminium*, on the marriage of the *captivus* or of his child, and on *tutela*, have already been discussed[2]. There remain however some topics to consider. The rules as to the effect of *postliminium* on *patria potestas* are in the main fairly simple. The father, returning, regains *potestas* over his children, and acquires it over those of whom his wife was pregnant at the time of the capture, and even over the issue of any lawful marriage contracted by a son so born[4]. In the case of a child born to a captive there was evidently some difficulty. There could be no *postliminium* for one who was never *captus*. The law seems to have been settled by a comprehensive rescript of Severus and Caracalla, part of which is preserved in the Code. The practical result is that *postliminium* is given to those born in captivity, in right of their parents, but not otherwise, so that if both parents return the child is in *potestas*, with its parent's status, and with rights of succession[5]. But if the mother alone returns, with the child, the father dying captive, the child has no succession to the father, since the *lex* Cornelia, as it assumes the father to have died at capture, cannot give rights to those born in the captivity[6]. It is thus connected only with the mother, to whom it stands in the relation of any other child *sine patre*[7]. It is noticeable that no text mentions the case of the father returning with a child born in captivity, the mother having died *apud hostes* : the chief texts especially require the return of both parents[8]. Indeed since the marriage ended at capture, and the mother is supposed to have died then, it is difficult to see how the child can be regarded as having been born in wedlock.

His will made before he was captured is valid[9]. *Postliminium* does not validate what he has done as a captive, and thus a will made during captivity is void. The same is true of codicils even though an earlier will has confirmed them, since when they were made he had not *testamenti factio*. But Justinian alters a text of Tryphoninus, in a dubious way, so as to make him say that on grounds of humanity, they are to be enforced, if he returns with *postliminium*[10]. On the other hand, he or his slave may be instituted, and if he return he may make or order the necessary entry[11].

---

[1] 44. 3. 4; 45. 1. 73. 1; 45. 3. 18. 2, 25; 46. 4. 11. 3; 49. 15. 22. 2.
[2] 9. 2. 43; 45. 1. 73. 1.   [3] *Ante*, pp. 295, 296.
[4] 49. 15. 8, 23. Analogous restitution if the mother alone was *capta* and returned, Arg. C. 8. 50. 14. So if a child was *captus* alone and returned he regained his rights of succession, C. 8. 50. 9.
[5] C. 8. 50. 1; cp. 38. 17. 1. 3; 49. 15. 9, 25. In 49. 15. 9 the words mean that the parents have returned. See also 38. 16. 1. 1.
[6] C. 8. 50. 1.   [7] C. 8. 50. 16; D. 38. 17. 1. 3.
[8] C. 8. 50. 1; D. 49. 15. 25.   [9] U. 23. 5; In. 2. 12. 5.
[10] 49. 15. 12. 5.   [11] 28. 5. 32. 1.

As to ownership, a returned captive acquires at once all that is *in eodem statu*; and as to those rights which have been lost by *usucapio* or by non-use, he has, as we have seen, an *annus utilis* within which to recover them by *utiles actiones*. This is provided for in the edict as to *restitutio in integrum* for those over 25[1]. If a son has died in the meantime, his acquisitions vest in the returned captive[2].

He has ceased to possess and thus, subject to what has been said as to possession by sons and slaves *peculiari causa*[3], he has no possession till he has actually retaken it, even though no other person has possessed the thing in the meantime[4]. *Postliminium* has no application here[5]. This may have the result of barring his usucapion altogether. For it is a new possession, and if, since the purchase, he has learnt that there was no title, there can be, on well known principles, no usucapion[6]. It is immaterial whether he was already usucapting or a slave has received the things not *ex peculiari causa* during the captivity. If however he is still in good faith he will usucapt. The question whether he can add his former possession or must begin afresh is not resolved by the texts. Most writers hold[7] that the earlier time is quite lost. But the texts are far from conclusive[8]. They make it clear that possession is interrupted, and that it is not restored by usucapion. But they do not clearly deny that in such a case the two possessions can be added together, if both were begun in good faith, as in the case of a buyer, whose possession is equally a new one. They speak of *nova possessio*[9], *secunda possessio*[10], which it no doubt is, but they also speak of *reciperata possessio*[11]. They say that there can be no *usucapio*, if the second possession was begun in bad faith[12], and that, in any case, *postliminium ei non prodest*. But the words are added *ut videatur usucepisse*[13], which are limitative in form and are not inconsistent with allowance of *accessio temporum*. But the accepted view is that of most modern systems of law in analogous cases, and the silence of the texts as to *accessio* is in favour of it[14].

In the case of slaves, *postliminium* does not operate quite in the same way as in the case of freemen. It is a case of *postliminium rerum*, the principle of which is that ownership reverts only in those things which are useful in war, except arms and clothing, which, it is said, cannot have been lost without disgrace[15], a slave, of any sex or age, being regarded as

---

[1] 4. 6. 1. 1, 14, 15.   Gratian declares this effective against the fisc, C. 8. 50. 19.
[2] 38. 16. 15.   [3] *Ante*, p. 294.
[4] 41. 2. 23. 1; 49. 15. 12. 2.   If a slave bought, not *in re peculiari*, *usucapio* could not begin till *dominus* returned and took actual possession.
[5] 41. 3. 44. 7; 49. 15. 12. 2, 29.   [6] 41. 3. 15. 2; 41. 4. 7. 4.
[7] *e.g.* Windscheid, Lehrb. § 180; Pernice, Labeo, 1. 401; Accarias, Précis, § 237.
[8] 4. 6. 19; 41. 2. 23. 1; 41. 3. 5, 15. *pr.*, 15. 2; 41. 4. 7. 4; 41. 6. 5; 49. 15. 12. 2, *etc.*
[9] 41. 2. 23. 1.   [10] 41. 3. 15. 2; 41. 4. 7. 4.
[11] 41. 4. 7. 4.   [12] *Ibid.*; 41. 3. 15. 2.   [13] 41. 3. 15. *pr.*
[14] They speak of it only where there is in law no interruption.   [15] 49. 15. 2, 3.

a thing useful in war, since he can be employed in carrying messages or advising, and in many ways other than actual fighting[1]. No reason is assigned for this limitation[2]. In any case the rule has the odd result of discouraging the private recapture of such things, since the actual captor gets nothing out of it. A slave, though a thing, has a will of his own, and hence it is easy to see possible conflict between the traditional principles of *postliminium* and regard for the interests of the master. In three points the latter prevailed.

(*a*) A *transfuga* has no right to *postliminium*[3], but a slave *transfuga* does revert to his master. This is only in the latter's interest. If he has been a *statuliber*, and the condition has arrived during his absence, he loses the benefit of it[4], but the text is not very clear as to what does happen. Presumably he is punished as an ordinary *transfuga*: at any rate he does not revert, as his owner would not have had him after the arrival of the condition in any case.

(*b*) A freeman does not recover his rights by *postliminium*, unless his return is with intention to remain: a slave reverts by *postliminium* in any case[5].

(*c*) A freeman has returned as soon as he is in Roman territory, but as it is not on his own account that a slave has *postliminium*, he does not revert till he is in his master's possession, or in that of someone, as a slave[6].

Apart from those points the case is simple. If other conditions are unchanged, not only does his owner's right revive[7], but so do minor rights, such as usufruct[8]. If he was a *servus poenae* before, he is one still[9]. A *servus furtivus*, captured, recaptured and sold, remains a *res furtiva*, incapable of *usucapio* by the buyer[10]. If he was a *statuliber*, he is a *statuliber* still, but if the condition has arrived during his captivity he gets the benefit of it[11]. A legacy of him or to him or an institution of him before or during the captivity is effective on his return[12]. Moreover the captivity has operated no *capitis deminutio*: he is *eadem res*, and thus an *exceptio rei iudicatae*, which applied to him before the capture, applies to him still[13]. If he has been pledged before capture the creditor's right revives[14].

---

[1] 49. 15. 19. 10.
[2] Karlowa, *op. cit.* 2. 125, associates it with the alleged rule that there was *postliminium* only in the same war: he treats it as an inference from that rule. There is no obvious connexion: it is not here confined to the same war.
[3] 49. 15. 19. 4.   [4] *h. l.* 5, 6.   [5] *h. t.* 12. 9.   [6] *h. t.* 30.
[7] C. 8. 50. 10, 12; Festus, *s.v. Postliminium*; 49. 15. 28, *etc.*
[8] 7. 4. 26. If he returns after his owner's death he is in the *hereditas* for Falcidian purposes, 35. 2. 43.
[9] 49. 15. 6.   [10] *h. t.* 27.
[11] *h. t.* 12. 10. And thus the child of a *statulibera captiva* whenever conceived is *ingenua* if the mother returns with *postliminium*, 40. 7. 6. 1, 2. The application of the rule to one conceived in captivity is a humane extension. Cp. C. 8. 50. 16.
[12] 30. 98.   [13] 44. 2. 11. 4.
[14] 49. 15. 12. 12. If before the captivity he had been sold on the terms that he was not to be freed, or was subject to another impediment to manumission, the prohibition still applied if the conditions were unchanged in other ways, 49. 15. 12. 16. *Ante*, p. 72. *Post*, Ch. xxv.

It remains to consider how far these rights are suspended in the case of redemption for a price, by a third party. In the Christian Empire the provision of a fund for the redemption of captives seems to have been a usual form of charity. There is no trace of anything like organisation of such funds till the time of Justinian, who provided that if a man left all his property for this purpose, by making *captivos*, generally, his heirs, the institution was to be valid, the estate being kept in perpetuity for this purpose, the annual profits of all kinds, from rents and sales of produce, being applied without any reduction for the cost of administration. This was to be managed by the Bishop and the *Oeconomus* of the testator's place of residence, who were to have all the rights and liabilities of the *heres*[1]. Somewhat later he authorised the local churches to alienate any land, which had been given to them without any prohibition of alienation, for the purpose of redemption of captives[2]. Again, he provided that if any provision was made by will for the redemption of captives, and the will did not say who was to carry out the redemption, the Bishop and *Oeconomus* were to see to it. If someone were appointed, and neglected, after two warnings from the Bishop, to carry it out, his benefit was forfeited to the Bishop, who was to administer the whole for charitable purposes[3]. A provision inspired by the same spirit is that which makes neglect to redeem any ascendant a just cause of *exheredatio*, while if the ascendant dies in captivity, the neglectful descendant's share is forfeited to the Bishop and goes to redeem captives. And, generally, where any person is entitled on intestacy (whether a will has also been made in his favour or not) to succeed to any *extraneus* who is a captive, or, not being a relative, knows that he has been instituted heir, neglect to ransom is punished by similar forfeiture of benefits to the purpose of redemptions, the rest of the will standing good[4]. Justinian had also provided that donations for the redemption of captives were to be exempt from the rules as to registration[5]. It may be presumed that all these provisions as to the duties of relatives, etc., apply equally to the payment of money due to an actual *redemptor*, under the rules now to be considered.

A complex situation arises where a man has redeemed a captive, by paying a ransom. The general rule applied here is that the ransomer has a lien on the redeemed captive, and *postliminium*, with its various results, is postponed till the lien is ended[6]. There is no lien except for actual redemption money. Thus there is no lien if he is simply

---

[1] C. 1. 3. 48.   Neither they nor anyone else having Falcidian rights.
[2] Nov. 120. 9.   [3] Nov. 131. 11.
[4] Nov. 115. 3, 13.   The rule applies only if the *heres* is over 18. To prevent the excuse of lack of means, it is provided that such persons can pledge the property of the captive.
[5] C. 8. 53. 36.   [6] 38. 16. 1. 4 ; 49. 15. 12. 14, 20. 2.

captured from the enemy[1], though at a certain cost[2]. Nor is there any lien if the redemption is of relatives, *pietatis causa,* even though redemption is for a price, and the payer afterwards seeks to recover it[3].

The state of things so long as the money remains unpaid cannot easily be expressed in terms of any other institutions. It is apparently rather illogical. We are told that it is a state of pledge, not slavery[4], and yet we know that the captive has not yet *postliminium* from his captivity in which he was a slave. The practical meaning seems to be that the lien in itself has no enslaving effect, no reference being intended to the provisional slavery involved in capture. The significance of the proposition is shewn in the rule that when the lien is ended the old status is restored : the man is not a *libertus* and owes no *obsequium* to the *redemptor*[5]. The disabilities under which he suffers are not the result of the lien, but of the fact that he has not yet *postliminium.* He can serve no *militia*[6]. Apparently he cannot validly marry[7] He cannot in strictness enter on a *hereditas,* but, *favore ingenuitatis,* he is allowed to do so, or to receive a legacy, so that the money may be applied to the release from the lien[8]. A child redeemed with the mother is under the lien[9]. An enactment of Diocletian lays it down as undisputed law that a child born to a woman under such a lien is not itself subject thereto[10]. But Ulpian seems to imply that the pledge covers such issue[11], and Tryphoninus must have been of the same opinion, at least where the person redeemed was originally a slave[12]. But this is only a case of the dispute already considered as to whether *partus* is covered by pledge[13]. Pledge is not the only close analogy. The transaction is, from the captors' point of view, a sale: the *redemptor* is constantly spoken of as buying the captive, and it is part of the argument of Tryphoninus in the text just mentioned that the *partus* is to be treated as sold with her. Here too the same point has already been considered, with special reference to eviction and usucapion[14]. The better view is that in later law the pledge covers the *partus,* though the classics are not agreed[15].

The texts are not clear as to what advantage the *redemptor* can claim from a redeemed *ingenuus.* He can assign the lien, but not so as to increase the amount payable by the *redemptus,* the person who takes

[1] 49. 15. 21. *pr.*; C. 8. 50. 12.
[2] Or where he was handed over without a price (C. 8. 50. 5) or where help was rendered on the way home, *h. t.* 20. 1.

[3] *h. t.* 17.	[4] 28. 1. 20. 1 ; C. 8. 50. 2.	[5] C. 8. 50. 11.
[6] 49. 16. 8.	[7] C. 8. 50. 2.	[8] C. 8. 50. 15 ; D. 38. 16. 1. 4.
[9] 49. 15. 12. 18.	[10] C. 8. 50. 8.	[11] 49. 15. 21. 1.
[12] *h. t.* 12. 18.	[13] *Ante,* p. 23.	[14] *Ante,* p. 51.

[15] The lien has priority over other charges over the *redemptus,* and over any right of punishment: the fisc does not claim one *in metallum datus* without paying off the lien, 49. 15. 6, 12. 16, 17.

it over having an action against the *redemptor* for any excess[1]. We must assume that the *redemptor* is bound to maintain the man, and we have seen that his lien covers only what he has actually paid to the captors[2]. Unless we assume the *redemptor* to be a philanthropist of a most unselfish kind, and therefore the case of redemption kept by the law within very narrow limits, we must suppose that he may employ the man. We shall see that in later law, the captive may pay off the lien by labour[3], but this of itself does not prove that he can be made to work. As to acquisitions through an *ingenuus* so held we have no information. A pledgee does not take acquisitions, and the language of pledge is constantly used in this connexion[4], with the implied warning that it cannot be a true pledge, since the man is not a thing[5]. Thus he is so far in the holder's *potestas* that he cannot witness his will, and this, not slavery, is given as the reason[6]; and the reason why the interdict *quem liberum* does not apply to him is only that the holder *non dolo facit*[7]. The discharge of the lien is called *luitio*, the primary meaning of which is discharge of a pledge[8]. On the other hand, his purchase is regarded as an *emptio*[9], and where the *redemptus* was originally a slave the redeemer becomes, as we shall see later, his owner, in a limited sense[10]. Tryphoninus discusses the case of a *statuliber* under a condition of payment, and decides that the money can be paid by the *redemptus* out of any part of his *peculium* except what is acquired *ex operis suis* or *ex re redemptoris*[11]. This does not however imply that the holder acquires, like a *bonae fidei possessor*[12], only *ex re sua* and *ex operis servi*, at any rate where the person actually was a slave: a special constitution created logical difficulties in that case[13]. We shall see that the *redemptus* may free himself by labour, but we hear nothing of his freeing himself by means of his acquisitions. This may mean no more than that such a dealing would come within the general rule[11] as to repayment of the money. The texts clearly contemplate his paying the money himself[14], and it may be that his acquisitions *ex re redemptoris* and *ex operis suis* go to his holder, while other things go to himself.

The lien may be ended in various ways. Actual payment of course suffices[15]. Children redeemed with a man or woman may be freed from the lien by independent payments; either the sum specifically paid for them, or if there was no allotment, then a proper proportion[16].

[1] 49. 15. 19. 9.   [2] C. Th. 5. 7. 2; C. 8. 50. 20.   [3] *Post*, p. 314.
[4] See, *e.g.* 30. 43. 3; 49. 15. 15, 19. 9, 21. *pr.*; C. 8. 50. 8, 11, 13.
[5] Hence such expressions as: *naturalis pignoris vinculum, vinculo quodam*, C. 8. 50. 2; D. 28. 1. 20. 1.
[6] 28. 1. 20. 1.   [7] 43. 29. 3. 3.   Karlowa, *loc. cit.*
[8] 38. 16. 1. 4; 49. 15. 15; 49. 16. 8; G. 4. 32; Dirksen, Manuale, *s.v. luitio*.
[9] 49. 15. 12. 18, 19. 9; C. 8. 50. 17, 20. 2, *etc.*
[10] 49. 15. 12. 7.   [11] *h. t.* 12. 11.   [12] *Post*, p. 341.
[13] *Post*, p. 315.   [14] 49. 15. 19. 9; C. 8. 50. 17, 20. 2.
[15] C. 8. 50. 2, *etc.*   [16] So as to children born *apud redemptorem*, 49. 15. 12. 18.

It may be ended also by tender and refusal of the redemption money[1], or by any remission of the debt, which, however informal, cannot be revoked[2]. It is no doubt on this principle of remission that it is ended by the redeemer's marrying the *captiva*[3], indeed we are told that remission results from cohabitation with her[4]. The same result follows from his instituting the captive as his heir[5]. The pledge is ended, and the right to the money forfeited, if the *redemptor* prostitutes, knowingly, the woman redeemed[6]. It seems further that, at least in later law by a constitution of A.D. 408[7], five years' service ends the lien, at least in the case of a *civis* captured. It is clear from some of the rules just laid down that the lien is not affected by the death of the holder. In earlier law the death of the captive, though it of necessity destroyed any practical lien, left the debt standing and prevented the heirs from succeeding till they had cleared it off[8], the result being that they were worse off than if he had died still a captive. But Ulpian here mentions, and elsewhere accepts without comment[9], so that it is clearly the later law, a doctrine more favourable to the successors. The death ends the pledge: the *redemptus* gets *postliminium* and is restored to his old *status* so that the whole obligation is blotted out.

The effect of *luitio* is to bring into operation the ordinary *postliminium*[10]. Heavy penalties are imposed by Honorius, by the enactment of 408, on those who detain captives on whom there is no lien, or the lien on whom is from any cause ended. If the undue detention is caused by an agent, the principal being away, he is to be liable to *deportatio*, or even to *condemnatio in metallum*: if it is by the principal himself, he is liable to *deportatio* and forfeiture. To assist in enforcing this law the local clergy are to watch over such cases, and the *curiales* of the neighbouring localities are liable to penalties of 10 *aurei*, they and their *apparitores*, if they fail to see to the carrying out of the law[11].

Where the redeemed captive is a slave, there are special rules of some difficulty. Here too, though the slave is property, there is no lien except for money paid for redemption[12]: recapturers must give him up at once and have no right in him[13]. On repayment of the money he goes back to the *dominus*[14], and any old rights in him, *e.g.* pledge, revive.

---

[1] C. 8. 50. 6.　　　　　　　　[2] 43. 29. 3. 3 ; C. 8. 50. 17.
[3] C. 8. 50. 13.　　　　　　　[4] 49. 15. 21. *pr.*
[5] 29. 2. 71. *pr.*, and presumably from a legacy of him to himself: such a legacy from an outsider was equivalent to one of the money, 30. 43. 3.
[6] C. 8. 50. 7.
[7] C. Th. 5. 7. 2 (C. Sirm. 16) = C. 8. 50. 20.　On the occasion of Alaric's sack of Rome.
[8] 49. 15. 15.　　　　　[9] 38. 16. 1. 4.　　　　　[10] *Ante*, p. 307.
[11] Const. Sirm. 16.　It is abridged in C. Th. 5. 5. 2 and in C. 8. 50. 20.　But here it is not the clergy, but *christiani*: probably the meaning is the same.　In addition to these special penalties the *dominus* would have ordinary actions for recovery of him if he were a slave and, for a free man, there would be the interdict *Quem liberum*, 43. 29. 3. 3.
[12] C. 8. 50. 10.　　　　　　[13] *h. t.* 2.　　　　　　[14] 49. 15. 12. 7.

In fact a pledgee can pay off the lien, and add the sum to his charge, just as a creditor with a subsequent charge can confirm it by paying off a prior incumbrancer[1]. Apparently the lien cannot be paid off *pro parte* by one of common owners, but if all pay their share, or one pay the whole in the name of all, the lien is at an end; in the latter case the payment will come into account in the *actio communi dividundo*. If he is acting for himself or for some of the others, then, as to their shares, the lien is at an end, and the common ownership restored : as to the others it is an assignment of the lien, and the payers are in the place of the *redemptor*[2].

For convenience the right of the *redemptor* has been called a lien. In fact it is a great deal more. Tryphoninus tells us that a certain constitution *protinus redimentis servum captum facit*[3]. We have no information as to what this constitution was. Karlowa[4], in view of the form of the allusions to it, thinks it to have been a general provision, and he considers it identical with the *constitutio* Rutiliana, which Julian applies to the alienation of a woman's property without *tutoris auctoritas*[5]; the form of the allusion, here too, being such as to suggest that it had no special application to that case[6]. But it may be noted that the Rutilian constitution is cited as making *usucapio* possible. The present constitution is cited as causing *dominium* to pass and so making *usucapio* impossible. Moreover in that case the thing is the property of the alienor, the mode of conveyance being defective : here the defect is of a different kind, consisting in the overriding right of the old owner. All that they have in common is that the effect of the transaction can be set aside on the repayment of certain money. One of the allusions (not cited by Karlowa) looks as if the enactment dealt specially with this case : *at is de quo quaeritur lege nostra quam constitutio fecit civem Romanum dominum habuit*[7].

Whatever its nature, the effect of the constitution is to set up an exceptional state of things. There is an ownership in the *redemptor*, and another ownership in the old *dominus*, liable to come into operation at any moment. Cases of ownership which are to come to an end on failure of some condition, etc., are not uncommon, especially in relation to sale and *donatio*. But, in such cases, there is, in classical law, a need of reconveyance. In our case *postliminium* operates with no such need[8].

---

[1] *h. l.* 12. The text notes that as the pledgee is really the earlier incumbrancer it is only an artificial priority given to the lien which postpones him.
[2] 49. 15. 12. 13.   [3] *h. l.* 7, 8.
[4] *op. cit.* 2. 404.   [5] Vat. Fr. 1.
[6] Bechmann, *cit.* Karlowa, *loc. cit.* K. gives reasons for thinking it may have been a senatusconsult.
[7] 49. 15. 12. 9, *med.*   [8] 49. 15. 12. 7.

The *redemptor* is set in the position which the *hostis* held : if he does acts in relation to the man, which if done by the *hostis* would not be effective, as against the rights of the old owner, by the Roman law, how are these to be looked at, seeing that he is not actually a *hostis*, but a Roman *civis*? The question is considered in relation to several states of fact.

A *statuliber*, to be free on paying a certain sum, can pay it out of *peculium* to his master for the time being[1]. Such a master ordinarily derives title directly or indirectly from the donor of the freedom, and, at least, if he gave value, has a remedy, if he was not informed of the prospect of liberty[2]. How if he is a *redemptor*, as to whom none of this is true? Tryphoninus says[3] the man is free on payment to the *redemptor*. But in ordinary cases he cannot pay it out of any *peculium* but that which passed with him[1]. There is no such *peculium* here. Whether the *redemptor* bought him *cum peculio* so that his *peculium* represents that *apud hostes*, or did not, at any rate it does not represent that which belonged to the donor of liberty. Nevertheless, says Tryphoninus, he is allowed, *favore libertatis*, to pay it out of any part of his *peculium*, except what is acquired *ex operis* or *ex re redemptoris*. This is a sort of rough justice : it must not be understood to imply that the *redemptor* (and owner) acquired only what a *bonae fidei possessor* would have acquired.

The constitution applies to a purchase in the ordinary way of business : it does not require that the buyer shall know that he is redeeming a captive. If the purchase was made without that knowledge, can the buyer, since he is a *bonae fidei emptor*, usucapt the slave to the exclusion of the old *dominus*? The difficulty is that by the constitution he is owner and a man cannot usucapt his own. Tryphoninus, arguing from the view that the constitution is not designed, by making him owner, to make his position worse, concludes that on such facts, though the conception of *usucapio* is not applicable, the old owner's right to pay off the charge will be barred by the period of *usucapio*[4].

This topic leads the jurist to another. If the redeemer can usucapt, can he manumit? Tryphoninus remarks that, of course, manumission by the *hostis*, whose place he has taken, would not bar the old owner, and asks whether a manumission by *redemptor* will free, or will merely release his right, and cause the man to revert to his original *dominus*. Clearly the *redemptor*, in the case in which time has barred the old owner's claim, can free, and Tryphoninus observes[5] that even under the old law, if the redeemer had bought him knowing that he was (a captive and) *alienus*, and had sold him to a *bona fide* buyer, the

<hr>

1 *Post*, Ch. xxi.   2 *Ante*, p. 289.   3 49. 15. 12. 11.
4 49. 15. 12. 8.   5 49. 15. 12. 9.

buyer could usucapt and manumit, and thus the right of the original owner would be destroyed. Therefore he holds that the redeemer himself can manumit. He does not rest his view on the technical ownership created by the constitution, but rather on the fact that if the old owner never pays the *redemptor* the slave will be in the position of being incapable of manumission through no fault of his own. The argument is not convincing: the same thing is true of ordinary pledged slaves[1] and of many others. No doubt the ownership created by the constitution is really the deciding factor. The result, for which the strange provision of the constitution is to blame, is at any rate in appearance unfair, and Tryphoninus tries, with little success, to put a better moral face on it. Indeed his view as expressed would lead logically to a requirement of notice to the old owner.

Ulpian discusses the same case more shortly and without much reasoning[2]. He holds, somewhat doubtfully, *favore libertatis*, that the manumission frees him and that *postliminium* operates, not so as to restore him to his old master (*hoc enim satis impium est*), but to cause the *libertus* to be indebted to his old owner to the amount of his own value as a slave. Ulpian makes no reference to the constitution, and indeed, while Tryphoninus seems to be struggling with a logical necessity, leading to a power of manumission which he thinks inequitable, Ulpian thinks the logic the other way, and frees the man only *favore libertatis*. The language of Tryphoninus throughout the discussion does not suggest that the constitution he is discussing is an ancient one, a republican *senatusconsult*, as Karlowa thinks[3], but rather a new one the working of which is not yet clear. Nothing that is known of the dates of the two jurists makes it impossible for the text of Tryphoninus to have been written after that of Ulpian. It seems not impossible that Ulpian is writing under, or with reference to, a *régime* under which the *redemptor* is in an anomalous position, since he has acquired what Roman law recognises as the subject of ownership, from one whom Roman law recognises as its owner (*quod ex nostro ad eos pervenit illorum fit*[4]), and yet is not himself recognised as owner[5].

---

[1] *Post*, Ch. xxv.   [2] 29. 2. 71. *pr.*
[3] *loc. cit.*   [4] 49. 15. 5. 2.
[5] If the slave was incapable of being freed before capture he is so still in the hands of the *redemptor*, 49. 15. 12. 16.

CHAPTER XIV.

SPECIAL CASES (*cont.*). S. PUBLICUS POPULI ROMANI, FISCI, ETC.
S. UNIVERSITATIS.

XX. *Servus Publicus Populi Romani, Fisci, Caesaris.*

THE evidence as to the position of these slaves is so imperfect, that
nothing more than an outline is possible. But their interest is mainly
political and public: so far as private law is concerned there is little
to be said, and thus a short account of them will suffice.

It is impossible to make a clear statement on our topic, without
some remarks on the history of the relations of the popular treasury
(*Aerarium*), with the Imperial treasury (*Fiscus*) and with the *Privata
Res Caesaris*[1].

In the earlier part of the Imperial period the *Aerarium* is quite
distinct from the *Fiscus*, and so long as this distinction is real, the
expression *servi publici populi Romani* applies in strictness only to those
belonging to the people, and not to *servi fiscales*. The *Fiscus* is not
only distinct from the *Aerarium*: it is regarded as the private property
of the Emperor. In strict law it does not differ from the *res familiares*
and other *privatae res Caesaris*. It is however distinctly administered,
and it is the duty of the Emperor to devote it to public purposes[2]. It
passes as a matter of course to his successor on the throne. There is
another form of property of the Emperor, which is distinguished under
the name *patrimonium*. This too is more or less public in character:
the revenues of Egypt come under this head. While it is not strictly
fiscal it is administered on similar lines. There is no trace of any
attempt to devise it away from the throne. Much of it, perhaps all,
is public in everything except form. Besides this, there is the ordinary
private property of the Emperor, which he deals with exactly as a
private *civis* may, but which in the early Empire is not formally distinguishable from fiscal and patrimonial property, and in the Byzantine
Empire has again become, for practical purposes, confused with it.

---

[1] Mommsen, Droit Pub. Rom. 5. 290 *sqq.* Marquardt, Organ. Financ. 394 *sqq.*
[2] The separation of this property from the *privata res Caesaris* is said to date from
Severus: Marquardt, *loc. cit.*

In the course of the Empire great changes occur in the relations of these different funds. The *Fiscus* steadily grows to be regarded more and more as public property. Ulpian speaks of it as still the property of the Emperor[1], but Caracalla, and, later, Pertinax, both treat it as essentially public, and in the Monarchy, after Diocletian, all substantial difference between public property and fiscal property has disappeared. This change' in the position of the Fisc necessitates a more clear distinction between it and the private property of the Emperor, and accordingly from the time of Septimius Severus there appears a separate machinery for the administration of the true *res privatae* and *familiares* of the Emperor. Yet another change must be noted. Justinian, and, perhaps, earlier Emperors, shew a tendency to extend to their private property, while still retaining the advantages of private ownership, the same privileges as exist for the Fisc[2].

These gradual changes of attitude make it impossible to say with certainty whether a particular rule which is applied by classical law to *servi publici populi Romani* is or is not in later law extended to *servi fiscales* or to *servi privatae rei*. Existing texts give little but negative results.

The name *servus publicus populi Romani* implies something more than that the slave in question is the property of the people: it imports that he is in some way employed on public affairs, and on that part of public affairs which belongs to the Senatorian department rather than to the Imperial. As we shall see, captives do not become *servi publici* by the mere fact of capture, but only by their being devoted to the permanent service of the public[3]. It is this limitation of the name which accounts for the fact, noted by Mommsen, that there is no trace of female *servi publici*[4].

The true *servus publicus* is completely obsolete in Justinian's time, and is nearly so in the classical law, so that it is not surprising to find little mention of him in the juristic texts. Most of our information is from inscriptions, and a short statement is necessary as to the chief conclusions which have been drawn as to the position of these slaves.

Servi publici seem from the evidence of the inscriptions to have usually married, or cohabited with (for it is difficult to give a name to their connexion), freewomen, *ingenuae* or *libertinae*. Mommsen holds[5] that they never cohabited with *ancillae*. But though such connexions might not be usual or creditable, it is unlikely that they did not occur. Indeed there are at least three inscriptions which seem to shew that

---

[1] 43. 8. 2. 4.   [2] 49. 14. 6. 1; In. 2. 6. 14.   [3] Livy, 26. 47.
[4] Mommsen, *op. cit.* 1. 367; Staatsrecht (3) 1. 324; Halkin, Esclaves Publics, 117 *sqq.* M.'s remark that the State possessed no female slaves is too strong. A proscription or capture might vest such women in the State, but they would be sold: they never entered the class to which the name and privileges of *servi publici* applied.   [5] *loc. cit.*

such connexions did occur and were avowed, though clearly they were
open to objection on many grounds[1]. In one inscription we have a
memorial set up to a *libertinus*, by, *inter alios*, his patron, and his father
who is a *servus publicus*[2]. In another we have a man called Primitivos,
apparently therefore a slave, setting up a memorial to his father who
was a *servus publicus*[3]. In another we have a *servus publicus* setting up
a memorial to his son Neptunalis, apparently a slave[4]. Halkin cites
other inscriptions of the same type[5]. It is notable that in them, as in
those cited above, the mother is always free. Mommsen does not advert
to these cases, but Halkin disposes of them by assuming that the
connexion existed and the child was born before the man became a
public slave. It seems at least equally consistent with the evidence to
suppose that such connexions did occur, but that the public slave
commonly secured the manumission of the woman and her children.

In any case however the child of a *servus publicus* would not be a
servus publicus: no one was born into that position. They were thus
ordinarily acquired, a circumstance which is expressed in the second
name which most of them bore, commonly terminating in *ianus*, and
recording the name of their former owner[6]. In many cases however they
appear with only one name[7], a circumstance which may indicate that
they vested in the State otherwise than by purchase[8].

Public slaves, while forbidden to wear the toga, seem to have had a
special costume[9]. The *lex* Julia Municipalis alludes to assignments by
the Censor of sites for dwellings for the *servi publici*[10], but it is not clear
that this refers to slaves of the people, or even that, if it does, it expresses
any general rule.

During the Republic *servi publici* were employed on a great variety
of works: as in private life, the greater part of the business of Rome
seems to have been conducted through slaves. Most of their work was
subordinate, though not all[11]. It is not possible to go into their various
employments[12]. In connexion with some of these employments, though
not it seems with all, the slave received an annual stipend, or rather

<hr>

1 See C. 6. 1. 8.   2 C. I. L. 6. 2334.   3 C. I. L. 6. 2340.
4 C. I. L. 6. 2357.   5 *op. cit.* 119; C. I. L. 6. 2343, 2361.
6 Mommsen, *loc. cit.*, and for illustrations, C. I. L. 6. 2307 *sqq.*
7 C. I. L. 6. 2313, 2331, 2343—5, 2365, 2366, 2369—71, 2374, 4847, 11784, *etc.*
8 Capture, proscription, forfeiture. See Halkin, *op. cit.*, 17 *sqq.* He says that *dediticii*,
freed after they had been sold into perpetual slavery, came into this class. But we are told only
that they become the property of the Roman people, not that they enter this privileged
class, G. 1. 27.
9 Mommsen, *loc. cit.*   10 Bruns, Fontes, 1. 109.
11 They served as priests of Hercules, Halkin, *op. cit.* 49 *sqq.*
12 They were employed as messengers in all departments, as attendants on the magistrates,
as servants in the temples, some being attached as a *familia* to certain priesthoods. Not to
magistracies, on account, so Mommsen thinks, of the temporary nature of the office. They were
employed in collecting unfarmed revenue, in libraries, in administration of justice, in fire and
water services, and generally in public works. See as to this Mommsen, D. P. Rom. 1. 362 *sqq.*;
Staatsrecht (3) 1. 325 *sqq.*; Halkin, *op. cit.* 40—106; Wallon, Hist. de l'esclavage, 2. 86 *sqq.*, 3.
ch. 4. As to employment as soldiers, see *ante*, p. 73.

maintenance allowance—*cibaria annua*—paid annually from the *aerarium*[1]. Savings on this were doubtless among the sources of their *peculia*[2]. But mere temporary employment on public work did not entitle them to rank as *servi publici*. Thus Livy tells us[3] that of the prisoners taken by Scipio, some were declared to be public slaves, and these were set to various handicrafts with a prospect of liberty if they deserved it. Others were set to work as oarsmen in the naval galleys, and these were not regarded as public slaves at all[4].

So far as private law is concerned we hear little of *servi publici*. In a text which as it stands is very corrupt, we are told that they had a power of devise of half their *peculium*[5], the other half, and all if they were intestate, reverting no doubt to the State. As to acquisitions by the *publicus*, rights and liabilities on his contracts, and noxal liability for him, the texts tell us not a word. This does not mean that this sort of question did not arise, but that at the times when our texts were written the *servus publicus populi Romani* was obsolescent[6]. There can be no reasonable doubt that their acquisitions vested in the State, and little more that their free superior would be liable under a contract authorised by him. So much can be inferred from the rule in the case of slaves of municipalities. But beyond this there is no certainty : it is not to be taken for granted that they had an unrestricted right to bind their *peculia*. It seems that debt to the State could be paid to a public slave only with consent of the person entitled to receive it. If so paid without that consent the debt was still due, subject to a deduction for what was still in the *peculium*[7]. In relation to obligations incurred by them the rule may have been the same[8].

It is obvious that they took a social rank very different from that of ordinary slaves. Thus in one inscription, as Mommsen notes, they take precedence of their father who is a freeman[9]. In inscriptions relating to them it is not unusual to omit the word *servus*, and to call the person in question *publicus*, with, sometimes, a further description shewing his function, *e.g.* "Hermes Caesennianus *publicus Pontificum*[10]," "Glaucus *publicus a sacris*[11]." Of course most of the inscriptions relating to them are sepulchral, and it is easy to understand the omission of the unpleasant word. There are however many cases in which they are described as *servi*[12].

In the Empire the field of employment of *servi publici* rapidly

---

[1] Pliny, Litt. Traj. 31; Halkin, *op. cit.* 115.   [2] 16. 2. 19 ; C. Th. 8. 5. 58.
[3] Livy, 26. 47; Polybius, 10. 17.
[4] Gladiators were not public slaves, but often those of private owners, aspirants to office, or of Caesar.   [5] Ulp. 20. 16 ; C. I. L. 6. 2354.
[6] The surviving praejustinianian juristic texts contain no allusion to *servi publici populi Romani*.
[7] 16. 2. 19.   [8] *Ante*, pp. 163, 4, and, as to certain contracts by them, *post*, p. 322.
[9] C. I. L. 6. 2318.   [10] C. I. L. 6. 2308.   [11] C. I. L. 6. 2331.
[12] *e.g.*, C. I. L. 6. 2338, 9 (monuments erected by public slaves); 6. 3883 (monument to public slave); 3. 7906 (not sepulchral).

diminished. Mommsen could find no trace of any such persons outside the capital, after the founding of the Empire[1]. The low standard of morality with which slaves were credited naturally led to restrictions on the financial side. Alexander enacts that *cautiones, i.e.* receipts, by public slaves of municipalities are not to be valid unless countersigned by the person to whom the money was payable[2]. This is not strictly relevant to our topic, but it indicates a tendency. From Diocletian onwards all important public service is done by freemen, though in the various forms of labour slaves are still employed. In the time of Alexander *administratio* is essentially servile. Arcadius absolutely forbids the employment of slaves therein[3]. But as will shortly appear, all this later legislation has no direct bearing on *servi populi Romani*.

We have seen that in all probability the *servus publicus* was superseded outside the city under Augustus, and indeed the method of farming the republican revenues prevented his appearance in a field of activity in which the slaves of the Fisc are prominent in later times. But apart from this, the gradual absorption of the Senatorial power by the Emperor and of the *Aerarium* by the Fisc, seems to have involved the disappearance of the old *servus publicus populi Romani*. This absorption is said to have been completed early in the third century[4], at about which time the affairs of the Fisc come to be regarded as public[5]. There are however a few texts in Justinian's compilations in which the *servus publicus* seems to be referred to[6]. We are told of three cases in which security may be taken by a public slave in what is essentially private business. On adrogation of an *impubes*, the adrogator may give the necessary security to a public slave[7], since the obligation, as civil, would be destroyed by the *confusio* resulting from the *adrogatio*, if it was given to the *impubes* himself or to one of his slaves. So the goods of a person in captivity with the enemy may be placed in the custody of one who gives security to a public slave[8]. And, where a *pupillus* has no slave, an intended tutor, in the case in which security is needed, can give security *rem salvam fore pupillo* to a public slave[9]. Of course· the lawyers were aware that a *servus populi* was not the property of individual citizens[10], and indeed the texts nowhere rest the rule on any community in the slave. But it is difficult to resist the opinion that it is on this ground that a public slave is chosen: his stipulation, that the goods shall be given to the person entitled[11], would be void except for this fictitious ownership as a stipulation for a third person[12]. But the rule has convenience on its side, and that it is recog-

1 *loc. cit.*   2 C. 11. 40.
3 C. 10. 71. 3 ; 11. 37. 1. As to progress and causes of the change, see Halkin, *op. cit.* 224 *sqq.*
4 Marquardt, Org. Financ. 386.   5 Mommsen, D. P. Rom. 5. 293 *sqq.*
6 Wallon, *op. cit.* 3. 135 *sqq.*, cites several from the Codes but they all refer to slaves of *municipia*, or the Fisc.
7 1. 7. 18; C. 8. 47. 2.   8 C. 8. 50. 3.   9 27. 8. 1. 15; 46. 6. 2.
10 48. 18. 1. 7.   11 C. 8. 47. 2.   12 In. 3. 19. 4.

nised as having no more appears from the fact that in the case last stated, *i.e.* of the tutor, we are expressly told that the pupil acquires only an *actio utilis*[1]. All these texts give an intelligible sense, if they are understood of municipal slaves, and in none of them is the slave called a *servus publicus populi Romani*[2]. Nevertheless they cannot well be understood as representing the law of Justinian's time. In the case of the adrogator the Institutes say that the security is given *publicae personae hoc est tabulario*[3]. It is certain that public *tabularii* were not slaves in Justinian's time[4]. In the case of the tutor, one of the texts allows the magistrate to nominate a person to take the promise with the same resulting *actio utilis* to the *pupillus*, and the other text dealing with the same matter gives him the right to take the promise himself[5]. The fact seems to be that the fictitious part ownership which was the excuse for allowing the security to be given to a *servus publicus* was lost sight of in the later law, and his public character illogically regarded as the essential, so that in later law the security is given to a public person whether he is a slave or not. It may then fairly be assumed that the true *servus publicus populi Romani* has long ceased to exist in the law of Justinian.

Of slaves the property of the Emperor it is possible to make three classes : *servi* (*patrimoniales*) Caesaris or Augusti[6]; *servi fiscales*; *servi privatae rei* Caesaris. All of them are Caesar's, and most of the rules which are stated of *servi* Caesaris may be applied to all three.

Servi Caesaris present close analogies with the public slaves just discussed. The name however does not seem to be confined to those who exercise some function in Caesar's name, though neither *servi privatae rei* nor *vicarii* of *servi* Caesaris are commonly called *servi* Caesaris[7]. Like *servi publici* they wear a special dress[8], and it is common for them to have two names. Sometimes the second name has the termination *ianus* indicative of acquisition from a private owner[9], but more often it is not in this form[10]. In the majority of the inscriptions and in all the later ones, only one name appears[11] There are many references to *ancillae* Caesaris[12], some unmarried[13], some having

---

[1] 27. 8. 1. 15, 16; 46. 6. 4. *pr.*   [2] But their general form is opposed to this limitation.
[3] In. 1. 11. 3.   [4] C. 10. 71. 3.
[5] 27. 8. 1. 15; 46. 6. 4. Interpolation is immaterial here. In the same sequence of ideas comes the rule that the stipulation need not be made if the sureties are present and assent to the entry of their liability on the *acta*, 27. 7. 4. 3.
[6] C. I. L. 6. 586.
[7] Orelli, 2825, 2920, cited Erman, S. Vicarius, 417; C. I. L. 3. 556; 8. 8488, *etc.*
[8] Lampridius (Alexander, 23. 3) and Flavius Vopiscus (Aurelianus, 50. 3) cite these emperors as not giving a special dress.
[9] *e.g.*, C. I. L. 6. 239.   [10] *e.g.*, C. I. L. 6. 74, 8. 6974, 8488, *etc.*
[11] *e.g.*, C. I. L. 2. 4187; 6. 5349—52, 138, 614. Mommsen (*ad* C. I. L. 8. 12600 *sqq.*) thinks Hadrian suppressed the use of two names.
[12] Fr. de iure Fisci, 13; C. I. L. 5. 369; 8. 1129, 1898, 10628, *etc.*
[13] C. I. L. 8. 1129.

two names[1], and one who is described as a *vilica*, which, as her husband is not named, may mean, not the wife of a *vilicus*, but one herself exercising that function[2]. *Servi* Caesaris sometimes married freewomen[3], but more usually *ancillae*, often, it is likely, *ancillae* Caesaris[4]. Thus many *servi* Caesaris are so by birth : *vernae* Caesaris are common in inscriptions[5]. Persons so described are no doubt, usually, the offspring of a *servus* Caesaris and an *ancilla* Caesaris not in his *peculium*. If she were *in peculio*, the child would not be technically a *servus* Caesaris, but a *verna servi* Caesaris[6]: a *vicarius* of a *servus* Caesaris is not a *servus* Caesaris. Probably many of the slaves described as *vicarii servi* Caesaris are children of the *servi* concerned. In some cases we are expressly told that this is so[7], and this may be the reason for stating the obvious rule that they may not manumit their *vicarii*[8]. If the *ancilla* is not a *vicaria*, but a *serva* Caesaris, the child is a *servus* Caesaris[9] and may be a *verna*[10].

Of the various employments of *servi* Caesaris it is not necessary to say much[11]. There is the same history of a gradual transference of the higher posts held by them, to freemen, which has already been noticed in connexion with *servi publici*[12]. In general their range of employments is similar. Two points of difference must however be observed. The financial administration of the Imperial property was largely in their hands. The system of farming taxes, applied in a great many branches during the Republic, almost ceased under the Flavian emperors. It was never so freely used in Imperial matters, and even where it had been adopted it was almost completely abandoned[13]. Moreover the slaves of Caesar were largely employed in weaving and similar factory work, and there was legislation imposing heavy money penalties on those who concealed or abducted slaves belonging to these *gynecaea* or *textrina*[14].

Servi fisci or *fiscales* are those employed on the business of the *Fiscus*. This term excludes on the one hand slaves who have merely

---

[1] C. I. L. 6. 74.   [2] C. I. L. 8. 5384; D. 33. 7. 15. 2.
[3] C. I. L. 10. 529, *cit.* Mommsen, D. P. Rom. 5. 107.
[4] C. I. L. 5. 170; 369—71; 6. 4353; 8. 1844, *etc.*
[5] C. I. L. 3. 333, 349, 556, 1085, 2082, *etc.*
[6] Orelli, 2920; C. I. L. 6. 878; 14. 202, cited by Erman, *op. cit.* 416. He points out the difficulties of 3. 4828.
[7] C. I. L. 3. 4828.
[8] C. 7. 11. 2; cp. C. I. L. 6. 8495, *libertis eius et vicariis suis.*
[9] C. I. L. 3. 1470, 1994; 8. 4372, 3.   [10] C. I. L. 5. 371.
[11] Mommsen gives (C. I. L. 8. Supp. I. p. 1335 *sqq.*) an account of them from Carthaginian inscriptions.
[12] Wallon, *op. cit.* 3, chh. 3, 4.
[13] Mommsen, *op. cit.* 5. 110; Marquardt, *op. cit.* 396. It is difficult to trace any practical difference between fiscal slaves and those dealing with the public part of the *patrimonium.*
[14] C. Th. 10. 20. 2, 6—9; C. 11. 8. 5, 6; cp. C. 6. 1. 8. Even in the Byzantine Empire some of these workers were slaves.

become the property of the *Fiscus* by forfeiture or condemnation[1], those which belonged to estates forfeited for secret *fideicommissa*, those whose masters have died without heirs—*mancipia vaga*[2]—and those belonging to estates on which the heirs have refused to enter[3], and on the other hand those belonging to the *patrimonium* or to the *privata res* Caesaris. But there are many texts which shew the close similarity which existed between these classes. Some have already been noticed[4]. The Fragmentum de iure Fisci hardly seems to distinguish between them[5].

It is nowhere expressly said that either of these classes of slaves had any right of devise of the *peculium*. But a mutilated text tells us that certain persons, who may be either *servi* Caesaris or his *liberti*, may deal freely with their *res*, so long as their transactions are not *in fraudem portionis* Caesaris[6]. As the whole passage is dealing with slaves, it seems probable that this refers to the *peculium* of *servi* Caesaris, and that it implies an extension to them of a power of devise of a half. Huschke[7] remarks that their right was much the same as that of *filii familias* in their *peculium castrense*. But they had no power of manumission[8]. Nothing is known as to the mode of reckoning of this half[9].

Some Emperors reserved to themselves a power of punishment in excess of what was allowed to private owners[10], but in general the capacity and position of *servi* Caesaris were apparently normal in most respects. They could enter on inheritances on the order of the person concerned[11]. They could presumably acquire in other ways and contract like slaves in general. Clearly however there were some restrictions. Thus we are told that it was forbidden to lend money to a *dispensator* Caesaris, or to his *vicarius*, which here means, no doubt, any slave representing him[12]. The ordinary *servus* Caesaris must have had many occasions to contract, and it is not unlikely that on his private dealings his half of his *peculium* alone was liable, that of Caesar being in no way affected by his dealings, while on the other hand, on his contracts made on Caesar's business, probably the head of the department was liable, at any rate to the same extent as in the case of slaves of a municipality[13]. Trajan indeed provided that with slaves of the Fisc,

---

[1] They are called *fisci mancipia*, C. 9. 51. 8.
[2] C. Th. 10. 10. 20 ; 10. 12. 1, 2 ; 11. 1. 12.
[3] Any of these might become a *servus fiscalis*.
[4] *e.g.* 49. 14. 6. 1 ; In. 2. 6. 14.
[5] Fr. de i. Fisci, 12, 13. Property of deceased *liberti* Caesaris goes to the Fisc so far as it is not validly devised. So too of treasure found on land of the *fiscus* or of Caesar, the owner's part goes to the Fisc, 49. 14. 3. 10.
[6] Fr. de i. Fisci, 6 a. 　　　　　　　[7] *ad h. l.*, citing Ulp. 20. 16.
[8] C. 7. 11. 2, *post*, Ch. xxv.
[9] Many inscriptions shew *servi* Caesaris erecting monuments *de suo*, an expression used probably to make it clear that the *pars* Caesaris has not been encroached on. Dessau, 1654 ; 1821, cited Erman, *op. cit.* 413, 417 ; cp. C. I. L. 6. 479, 744.
[10] Flav. Vopisc. Aurelian, 49. 　　　　[11] 29. 2. 25. 2.
[12] Fr. de i. Fisci, 7. 　　　　　　　[13] Cp. 16. 2. 19.

the provincials should not contract at all under a penalty of, apparently, twice any resulting loss[1]. This refers of course to slaves engaged in the collection of revenue, the only ones to which the name *servus fiscalis* seems to be properly applicable. The language of this text and that just mentioned as to loans to *dispensatores* suggests that such a transaction though prohibited was not void. If so, the liability must have been *de peculio et in rem verso*.

Prohibitions of *delatio* did not prevent *servi fiscales* from reporting to the treasury in money matters: it was in fact their master's business[2,3].

We have already observed that the *fiscus* though technically the private property of the Emperor is practically, and in the later law admittedly, public property. We have also seen that the *privata res* follows somewhat the same course, or rather, to put the matter more accurately, that the Emperors claim for it the same privileges as those possessed by the *fiscus* and the public part of the *patrimonium,* while not in any way loosening their hold or power of disposition of it. Accordingly *servi privatae rei* are in most respects on a level, in later law, with those just discussed. They enter on inheritances for Caesar at the command of him or his procurator[4].

There are extant several enactments as to the tribunal which may try them. In A.D. 349 it was provided that crimes of slaves of the *res privata* might be tried in the provinces by the regular *iudices*, and the *interpretatio* perhaps makes this apply to patrimonial and fiscal slaves, while it seems to give the *procurator* Caesaris a right of intervention[5]. There was legislation about the same time requiring the presence of the *rationalis* both in civil and in criminal cases[6], but so far as criminal cases were concerned this was dispensed with in A.D. 398[7]. For the capital, at least, Theodosius and Valentinian laid down, in A.D. 442[8], a different rule. Any litigation civil or criminal in which the slaves of the household were concerned was to go before the *Praepositus sacri cubiculi* or *Comes Domorum*. This rule clearly does not apply to Fiscal slaves, though the rubric of the title groups together such slaves and those of the *privata res*[9].

---

[1] Fr. de i. F. 6.   [2] P. 5. 13. 2; *ante*, p. 85.
[3] We shall see (*post*, p. 417) that the rules as to freewomen cohabiting with *servi alieni* were specially severe in the case of *servi fiscales*.
[4] 1. 19. 1. 2; 49. 14. 46. 8.   [5] C. Th. 2. 1. 1.
[6] C. Th. 2. 1. 3; C. 3. 26. 8.   [7] C. Th. 2. 1. 11.   [8] C. 3. 26. 11.
[9] As to the relation in the later Empire between these different funds, see Marquardt, Org. Finan. 393 *sqq*.

XXI. *SERVI PUBLICI* OF *MUNICIPIA*.

These are really only an instance of the wider class of *servi univer-sitatis*. But as practically nothing is known of special rules affecting *servi* of other forms of corporate bodies, *servi collegiorum*, and the like, and as the slaves of municipalities played a very important part, closely analogous to that of the *servi populi Romani*, it seems convenient to treat them separately. Such slaves are the property of the community, not of the individual citizens or corporators[1]. Thus they can be tortured for or against such persons[2], and, after manumission, they are not *liberti* of individuals, and thus can bring legal proceedings against them without *venia*, though they cannot proceed against the corporation without it[3]. Heavy penalties are imposed on those who use slaves of the municipality for their own purposes[4]. The illogical exceptions recently discussed are not such as to create any real difficulty : they are recognised as mere subterfuges[5]. The texts may not refer to the slaves of towns at all, but there seems no reason why these should not be covered by them. Certainly such slaves are called public[6]. Ulpian and Gaius indeed tell us that the application of the epithet "public" to the property of anything but the State is incorrect[7], but the practice is perfectly clear though it may have begun in a false analogy. The municipality has in general the same rights of ownership as ordinary owners[8]. The slaves usually bear only one name, but some are found with two, of which one is sometimes that of the person from whom they were acquired[9]. It is clear on the evidence of juristic texts and inscriptions brought together by Halkin[10], that there are female slaves of towns, that these intermarry with the male slaves, and that the class of *servi publici* (*civitatis*) is recruited by birth. Children born into the class are themselves described as *publici*[11], so that, as here used, the name has no relation to their service.

They are employed in much the same ways as *servi publici populi*, but even more freely, since they serve in some cases as military guards[12]. They are employed in financial administration : even the responsible position of *actor* is ordinarily filled by a slave[13]. There is the same

---

[1] G. 2. 11.
[2] 1. 8. 6. 1; 48. 18. 1. 7.
[3] 1. 8. 6. 1; 2. 4. 10. 4.
[4] C. 6. 1. 5.
[5] *Ante*, p. 322,; 1. 7. 18; 27. 8. 1; 15, 16; 28. 6. 40; 46. 6. 2, 4. *pr.*
[6] G. 2. 11. See also many inscriptions cited by Halkin, *op. cit.* 160 *sqq.*
[7] 50. 16. 15, 16.
[8] Subject only to such restrictions in the matter of sale as were applied to them in late law in their dealings with all important property, C. 11. 32. 3.
[9] Halkin, *op. cit.* 145 *sqq.* As in the case of *servi populi* inscriptions often omit the word *servus*, Halkin, *op. cit.* 193. Most of what follows so far as it refers to the public law in this matter is due to Halkin, *op. cit.* 126—end.
[10] 38. 16. 3. 6; 38. 3. 1; Halkin, *op. cit.* 198 *sqq.*
[11] C. I. L. 11. 2656.
[12] Pliny, Litt. Traj. 19, 20.
[13] C. 11. 40. Inscriptions, Halkin, *loc. cit.*

tendency as in the case of slaves of the State, in the later Empire, to exclusion from responsible duties such as those of a *tabularius*[1]. They receive pay, or rather maintenance allowance[2]. They have *peculium*[3], which is the property of the municipality[4]. Halkin is of opinion[5] that they have the same right of devise of their *peculium* as have slaves of the Roman people. He cites in support of this an inscription from Calais in which a monument is set up to a public slave of the town by his two *heredes*[6]. But this is not conclusive. Such persons are frequently members of *collegia*[7], and, even though slaves, are allowed to leave their *funeraticia* to persons, who are called their *heredes*, precisely that they may put up memorial tablets[8]. On the other hand, the fact that their *peculium* belongs to the community is emphasised[9], and Ulpian, if his text is properly read, which is far from certain, imposes a limitation which, if Halkin's view is correct, is quite unnecessary, since he speaks only of slaves of the people[10]. It is noticeable that in the case of *servi* Caesaris to whom there is some evidence that the privilege extends[11] we are clearly told that half of their *peculium* is their own[12].

They can acquire for the municipality with all the ordinary results. Thus a *traditio* to a *servus publicus* entitles the *municipes* to the *actio Publiciana*[13]. According to the old view, municipalities cannot possess, *quia universi consentire non possunt*[14]. The reason is Paul's, and, as his language shews, is a confusion between common and corporate ownership. The true reason is that the corporation is incapable of either *animus* or the physical act of apprehension. It cannot authorise another to do what it cannot do itself; moreover, as the text adds, it does not possess its slave, and so cannot possess through him. Nerva *filius* however holds that the corporation can possess and usucapt what the slave receives, *peculiariter*[15]. This recalls the exception to the rule that a man cannot possess through his slave without his own knowledge[16]. But it clearly carries the exception further, as in the case of *captivi*[17]. Even the implied authorisation involved in the gift of a *peculium*[18] cannot arise here, for the corporation, unlike the captive, never was capable of authorising. The general rule that we cannot acquire possession through one whom we do not possess, early breaks down, but so far as our own slaves are concerned this case seems the only

---

[1] 50. 4. 18. 10; C. 7. 9. 3; Halkin, *op. cit.* 179. At pp. 153—192 he gives a full account of what is known of their employments.

[2] Pliny, Litt. Traj. 31.   [3] 16. 2. 19; 40. 3. 3.
[4] 50. 16. 17. *pr.*   [5] *op. cit.* 197.
[6] C. I. L. 10. 4687.   [7] Halkin, *op. cit.* 202.
[8] *Ante*, p. 75.   [9] *Procul dubio*, 50. 16. 17. *pr.*
[10] Ulp. 20. 16.   [11] *Ante*, p. 325.
[12] Fr. de i. Fisci, 6a.   [13] 6. 2. 9. 6.
[14] 41. 2. 1. 22.   [15] *Ibid.*
[16] *Ante*, p. 200.
[17] *Ante*, p. 294. There also capacity and possession in the principal are both ignored.
[18] 15. 1. 46; 41. 2. 1. 5.

exception, even in late law[1]. But convenience, which dictated the whole institution, needed a further step. Ulpian lays down the rule in general terms, that *municipes* can possess and usucapt through slaves[2]. No doubt, in non-peculiar cases, the *animus* was provided by *praepositi administrationi*.

The corporation acquires through its slave's stipulation[3], and thus he can take the various *cautiones* on its behalf[4]. There is not much authority on the liability of the corporation on its slave's contracts. We are told that a *praepositus administrationi* on whose *iussum* a contract was made with a slave of the corporation is liable to the *actio quod iussu*[5]. It may be supposed, though not confidently asserted, that similar rules apply to other actions of this class. The same conclusion may be reached with a little more confidence as to noxal liability for the slave, just as it is fairly clear that the *praepositus* was entitled to sue if the slave, or any other property, was injured[6].

Nerva provides that legacies may be made to *civitates*[7]. In the classical law towns and other corporations cannot be instituted heirs, for two reasons. They are regarded as *incertae personae*, says Ulpian, and moreover whether the gift is to the *municipium* or to *municipes* (of both which expressions the legal result is the same), the donee is incapable of the acts involved in *cretio* or *pro herede gestio*[8]. As we cannot institute the *civitas*, neither can we its slave, for we can never institute the slave of one with whom we have not *testamenti factio*[9]. To this rule the classical law admits few exceptions. A senatusconsult allows them (and thus their slaves) to be instituted by their *liberti*[10], and *bonorum possessio* can be claimed under such a gift or on intestacy[11]. The entry will be at the order of a *praepositus*. Again, though Hadrian forbids *fideicommissa* in favour of *incertae personae*, Ulpian records a senatusconsult allowing them in favour of municipalities[12]. He tells us also that certain deities can be instituted[13]. Classical law seems to have gone no further, so far as general rules are concerned, though there are traces of special concessions of *testamenti factio* to certain *coloniae*[14]. In one text it is said that slaves of a *municipium* or *collegium* or *decuria* instituted and either alienated or freed, can enter[15]. In Justinian's time this is obvious, but for Ulpian's it seems to imply that the institution may have this modified validity, that if the slave passes into such a

---

[1] 41. 2. 1. 15.   As to possession by *municipia*, *per alium*, 10. 4. 7. 3; 50. 12. 13. 1; Mommsen, Z. S. S. 25. 41.
[2] 41. 2. 2.   [3] 45. 3. 3; 22. 1. 11. 1.   [4] 3. 4. 10.
[5] 15. 4. 4.   [6] Vat. Fr. 335.
[7] Confirmed by Hadrian, Ulp. 24. 28; cp. D. 34. 5. 20.   Mommsen (Z. S. S. 25. 40) cites an earlier instance, C. I. L. 10. 5056.
[8] Ulp. 22. 5.   See however *ante*, p. 328, and Mommsen, Z. S. S. 25. 37.
[9] Ulp. 22. 9; D. 28. 5. 31. *pr.*; 30. 12. 2.   [10] Ulp. 22. 5.   [11] 38. 3. 1.
[12] Ulp. 22. 5; D. 36. 1. 27, Paul.   [13] Ulp. 22. 6.
[14] G. 2. 195; D. 28. 6. 30.   See Accarias, Précis, § 332.   [15] 29. 2. 25. 1.

position that a gift then made to him would be good, it may take effect.
But this is entirely contrary to general principle[1]. We know that
where the slave of one without *ius capiendi* is instituted the gift may
take effect if he is alienated[2], but that is a different matter : here it is
a case of lack of *testamenti factio*.

Leo allows all forms of gift by will to be made to municipalities[3].
As to other corporate bodies, we gather from an enactment of Diocletian[4]
that some *collegia* could be instituted by special privilege. Several
enactments authorised gifts to churches and charities[5], and finally
Justinian abolished the rule forbidding institution of *incertae personae*
altogether[6]. Wherever a body can be instituted, no doubt its slaves can[7].

---

[1] *Ante*, p. 137.   [2] 29. 2. 82.   [3] C. 6. 24. 12.
[4] C. 6. 24. 8.   [5] Girard, Manuel, 818.
[6] In. 2. 20. 25; C. 6. 48. 1.
[7] The difficulty that the body is not capable of the necessary *aditio* is not mentioned: it does
not seem to have been felt by the later lawyers. We know that in case of mere physical defect
or where there was no defect, there might be delegation, 29. 2. 26; 36. 1. 67. 3.

CHAPTER XV.

SPECIAL CASES (*cont.*). BONA FIDE SERVIENS. SERVUS MALA
FIDE POSSESSUS. SERVUS FRUCTUARIUS, USUARIUS.

XXII. *BONA FIDE SERVIENS.*

THE expressions *qui bona fide servit,* and *bona fide serviens* are
rather misleading. The *bona fides* really in question is that of the
holder. This would be *a priori* almost certain (for it is scarcely conceivable that the classical lawyers should have made the *animus* of the
slave decisive) and the texts leave no doubt. They are cited by
Salkowski, who shews that *bona fide possidere* and *bona fide servire* are
used interchangeably[1], and that there are texts which expressly make
the *bona fides* attach to the possessor[2].

As to what is involved in *bona fides* a few words are necessary.
Gaius tells us there must be a *iusta possessio*[3]. This appears to mean that
iusta causa is required. On the other hand it is immaterial that the
slave is *furtivus*[4]. So far as the *bona fides* itself is concerned, the texts
give no indication that the words have any meaning other than that
they bear in the law of *usucapio*. But just as a man may have *bona
fides* and yet be unable to usucapt, because the thing is *furtiva*, so it is
conceivable that one who cannot usucapt because his possession began
in bad faith, may become a *bonae fidei possessor* for our purpose in the
course of events. Broadly speaking a *bonae fidei possessor* is one who
supposes himself to have the rights of owner, and whose acts will be
regulated on that assumption. No man regards himself at the moment
as a *bonae fidei possessor*[5]. The holder may know of the defect in his
title before he is actually evicted: in that case he becomes a *malae fidei*

---

[1] Salkowski, Sklavenerwerb, 155. This work contains an exhaustive discussion of acquisition
in this case and in some others. The texts cited on the present point are 7. 1. 25. 6; 11. 3. 1.
1; 24. 1. 19. *pr.*; 41. 1. 23. 3, 54, 57; 45. 3. 19.
[2] 21. 1. 43. 3; 39. 4. 12. 2; 41. 1. 23. 1, 54. *pr.* See also G. 2. 94. A crucial case is that of
the *fugitivus*: it must have happened not infrequently that a slave ran away from a bad master
and became incorporated into the *familia* of one he thought better. There can be no doubt
that he acquired to his holder, notwithstanding his own bad faith.
[3] G. 2. 95.   [4] 19. 1. 24. 1 and *passim*.
[5] This fact must be borne in mind, since some of the rules cannot be intelligibly applied till
the *bonae fidei possessio* has ceased.

possessor from the moment when he learns that he is not entitled. It is easy to see that difficulties might arise as to bringing that knowledge home to him. Judgment, or admission on his part, will settle the matter, and many facts equally decisive may readily be imagined. But since *bona fides* is always presumed[1], it must often have been hard to recover profits already received by a *possessor*. This fact may have led some jurists to the view, represented in the Digest, that acquisition continues till eviction,—a view which certainly did not prevail[2].

It is a *bonae fidei possessor* who acquires: possession is necessary. To this general rule circumstances induced the admission of an exception. In discussing *servi hereditarii*[3] we saw that the ordinary rules as to acquisition through slaves were relaxed on considerations of convenience. We have here a somewhat similar case. In a text of Africanus[4] the case is put of a slave employed in commercial matters at a distance. His owner dies, having, by his will, freed him and instituted him *heres pro parte*. He, in ignorance of these events, continues his trading. Are the results of his dealings acquired to his coheirs? The answer given in the text is that if the other heirs have entered and know of the facts they cannot acquire, for they no longer have *bona fides*. But if they have not yet entered or have entered without knowledge of the facts affecting him, or were, like him, *necessarii*, and ignorant of the facts, then the text does allow acquisition through him, but in an inconsequent and incomplete manner. If debtors have paid him in good faith, they are discharged (on a principle already considered[5]). But the money they pay is not acquired to the *hereditas*, but to him alone, and he is liable to *actio negotiorum gestorum* on account of it, but not to *familiae erciscundae*. In view of the rule that, if money due to the testator is paid to one of the *heredes*, the others have *familiae erciscundae*[6], this must be due to the fact that he does not take it as heir, but as acting for his supposed master[7]. If he purports to lend money, there is no *mutuum* except as to his share and the money can be vindicated. But if he stipulates for the money lent, the *heredes* do acquire the action *ex stipulatu*: *hereditati ex re hereditaria adquiri*. To this extent he is a *bona fide serviens*, and the text adds that if there were two such persons they might be regarded as *bona fide servientes* to each other. All this is very unsatisfactory. Salkowski[8] points out that it dispenses with possession altogether as a

---

[1] C. 8. 45. 30.
[2] Julian (22. 1. 25. 2) allows a man to acquire for his holder, notwithstanding supervening bad faith, and Ulpian (41. 1. 23. 1) contradicts this in terms which shew that there had been dispute. See Salkowski, *op. cit.* 162—4 and the texts he cites.
[3] *Ante*, p. 256.
[4] 12. 1. 41. As to this difficult text, see Salkowski, *loc. cit.* and his references.
[5] *Ante*, p. 163.   [6] 10. 2. 9.   [7] Cp. C. 3. 36. 18, 20.
[8] *op. cit.* 159.

requirement for acquisition; substituting for it a rather obscure relation of *bona fide* service, which does not involve putative ownership, since at least in the last case neither of the two persons can possibly suppose himself owner. He seems prepared to accept the text as an authority for the view that *bona fide* service was recognised in the exceptional case of a *necessarius* acting without knowledge of the will, where possession was impossible, a rule which is clearly convenient, and for which there is, as Salkowski observes, the authority of another text of Africanus and one of Javolenus[1]. But apart from this particular rule the text has difficulties to which Salkowski does not advert. It gives no explanation of the fact that while the money paid to Stichus *ex re hereditaria* is not acquired to the estate, the stipulation is. It does not explain why if the *mutuum* was void except as to his share, the stipulation for repayment, which no doubt replaced, so far as his share went, the *mutuum*, was not *sine causa*, or at least capable of being met by an *exceptio doli*. The stipulation seems in some mysterious way to validate the *mutuum*. Down to the words *ut credendo nummos alienaret* the text is consistent with principle. Stichus acquires to himself, subject to a duty to account for what he receives. Then comes the reference to a *stipulatio*, leading to the odd doctrines just stated. This part of the text may well have been written or at least modified by a later hand. It is noticeable that at the point at which the stipulation appears the construction of the sentence changes—*referret* and *esset stipulatus* are used instead of the infinitives.

The person *bona fide* possessed may be either a *servus alienus* or a *liber homo*: the rules are in general the same, *mutatis mutandis*. We are concerned with the *servus alienus*, and shall consider the *liber homo bona fide serviens* only where some difference of rule calls for examination[2].

Though the *bonae fidei possessor* is not *dominus*, he is *de facto* in much the same position, and necessarily regards the slave as his. This fact is reflected in the law of legacy. Thus a legacy of "my slaves" may be construed to include those possessed in good faith by the testator, if this appears to be his intention[3]. Gifts to *liberti* are not within the restrictions of the *lex* Cincia, and we are told that gifts to one who, having been a *bona fide serviens*, has been declared free, are on the same level: he is *pro liberto*[4].

---

[1] 41. 1. 40; 45. 3. 34. But in both these there is the assumption that the *heredes* still possess.
[2] Thus though the holder may possibly usucapt a *servus alienus* (41. 1. 10. 5), he cannot a freeman. *Post*, Ch. XXVIII. For legislation as to disposition of his apparent *peculium* when he is found to be free, see C. Th. 4. 8. 6=C. 7. 18. 3.
[3] 32. 73. 1.
[4] Vat. Fr. 307. No doubt the rule will not apply to a gift to a *servus alienus* who has been in the donor's possession, nor for obvious reasons is such a slave owned for the purpose of the *Scc*. Silanianum and Claudianum, 29. 5. 1. 2.

Like other things *bona fide* possessed, slaves may have *fructus*. The law as to restitution of these received during the action if the slave is vindicated, has already been discussed[1]. The *fructus* of a slave are *fructus civiles*, earnings and the like, differing in character from *fructus naturales*[2]. There is however no reason to suppose that there was any difference in legal rule. It is now generally held that the rule requiring restitution of *fructus exstantes* is due to Justinian[3], and in fact it is not applied at all clearly to *fructus* of this sort. The texts which speak of restitution refer to *fructus* received during the action[4], and one of them gives, as the reason for the restitution, that he is not to make a profit out of a man who is already the subject of litigation[5]. Paul's remark that it is unfair to ask for fruits of an art acquired at the cost of the possessor does not seem to refer to earlier earnings[6].

The principles of the law as to delicts in respect of such slaves are in some respects difficult to gather. The *bonae fidei possessor* is not liable for *servi corruptio*, or for *furtum*, since he cannot be guilty of the *dolus* which these delicts require[7]: the case of *iniuria* is not discussed, but it is difficult to imagine a case in which he could be liable, even *servi nomine*. He may be liable to the *actio* Aquilia: Javolenus tells us that he is so liable, at least noxally[8].

On the other hand, he is not entitled to the *actio servi corrupti*[9], probably because the words *servum alienum* in the Edict[10] are regarded as imposing on the plaintiff proof of ownership, though Ulpian gives two other reasons, namely, that *nihil eius interest servum non corrumpi*, and that if he had the right the wrongdoer would be liable to two, which he thinks absurd. Neither of these reasons is worth much, in view of the rules in the other delicts. He may have an *actio iniuriarum* if the wrong is plainly *in contumeliam eius*, though an *iniuria* is primarily regarded as against the *dominus*[11].

It is clearly laid down that a *bonae fidei possessor* has an *actio furti* in respect of the slave[12], but the basis of his *interesse* is not clearly defined, though the rule is at any rate classical, and may be republican[13]. The right does not turn on the interruption of usucapion, since it is immaterial that the *res* is *vitiosa*[14]. His interest is not regarded as a

---

[1] *Ante*, p. 12.
[2] As to their relation to acquisitions *ex operis*, *post*, p. 342.   [3] Girard, Manuel, 322.
[4] 6. 1. 16, 17. 1, 20.   [5] 6. 1. 17. 1.   [6] *Ante*, p. 12.
[7] 11. 3. 3. *pr.*, 1.
[8] 9. 2. 38. There seems no difficulty in regarding a *bonae fidei possessor* as capable of the necessary *culpa*, but Pernice thinks otherwise, Sachbeschäd. 194. See also Pernice, Labeo, 2. 2. 1. 86; Monro, Lex Aquilia, *ad h. l.*; Willems, La loi Aquilienne, 80.
[9] 11. 3. 1. *pr.*, 1.   [10] *Ibid.*; Lenel, Ed. Perp. § 62.
[11] ln. 4. 4. 6; 47. 10. 15. 36, 37, 47, 48. The first clause of the Edict refers to *servus alienus*, which might exclude the *bonae fidei possessor*, as in *servi corruptio*, but there is a general clause: *si quid aliud factum esse dicetur, causa cognita iudicium dabo*, 47. 10. 15. 34.
[12] 47. 2. 12. 1; 47. 8. 2. 23, etc.   [13] 47. 2. 77. 1; G. 3. 200.
[14] 47. 2. 75; cp. *h. t.* 72. 1, 77. 1.

part of ownership, since what he recovers is not deducted from what the owner can get, as is that which the usufructuary recovers[1]. The Institutes tell us that the *bonae fidei possessor* has the action "like a pledge creditor[2]," and Javolenus tells us that the *interesse* depends on his possession[3]. But, as we have seen[4], the *interesse* of the pledge creditor is not easy to define and was differently conceived at different times. But whether it rest on his right of retention against the owner, or on his liability for *custodia*, neither of these applies generally to the *bonae fidei possessor*: in fact, however, the language of the Institutes hardly shews that the bases of the *interesse* were identical in the two cases. His right being not merely a part of the owner's right, it is not surprising that he has the action against the *dominus*. But here too the texts are not clear as to the basis of his right, or even as to its extent. Gaius says simply that he has the action[5], but in the corresponding passage of the Institutes, the words referring to *bonae fidei possessor* are omitted[6], as it seems from the form of the text, intentionally. In the Digest Paul gives the action against the *dominus* in general terms, to a *bonae fidei emptor*[7], and citing Julian, allows it to a donee from a non-owner only if he has a right of detention, *propter impensas*[8]. This is tantamount to refusing it to a donee as such, for even a *commodatarius* has it against the *dominus* on such facts[9]. This distinction in favour of the *emptor* can hardly be due to the fact that he loses his remedy against his vendor on eviction, for he secures this remedy by failing as plaintiff as well as if he fails in defence[10]. The fact that he has paid a price is relevant, for it is mentioned in a case where the action is against a third party, where it seems to serve no purpose except to shew loss[11]. The fact that this is recoverable from the vendor is presumably immaterial: he is for the time deprived of the advantage he paid for, and, as in the case of ownership, later recovery is immaterial[12]. As the limitation to the *emptor* is not found in the texts dealing with the case of theft by a third party, it seems that in that case the price is merely a guide for estimating damages, the *interesse* really consisting in the right to fruits and acquisitions. In the case of taking by the owner he loses only what he was not entitled to, as against the owner, and thus there is no *interesse* unless he paid a price. The possible case of a right to retention does not come into consideration: even one without *possessio* at all might have this right and would have the resulting *interesse*. This seems to be the later law, but it is likely that there were differences of opinion as to the *interesse* in classical law.

---

[1] 47. 2. 46. 1, 75. [2] In. 4. 1. 15. [3] 47. 2. 75.
[4] *Ante*, p. 282. [5] G. 3. 200. [6] In. 4. 1. 10.
[7] 47. 2. 20. 1. [8] 47. 2. 54. 4.
[9] 47. 2. 60. Probably in Justinian's law a depositee had it if he had a *ius retentionis* on any account, though this is denied in the Collatio, 10. 2. 6.
[10] 21. 2. 16. 1. [11] 47. 2. 75. [12] *h. t.* 46. *pr.*

For *damnum* to the slave the *bonae fidei possessor* has an *actio
in factum*, based on the *lex* Aquilia, even against the *dominus*[1]. As
against third persons this is intelligible, though it is our informant,
Ulpian, who tells us elsewhere that he has no *actio servi corrupti* as
nihil eius interest servum non corrumpi[2]. But it is surprising to find
that he has the action against the *dominus*. The deprivation of enjoyment can hardly be a wrong if done by the owner entitled to possession,
and accordingly it is generally held that the damage is the loss of his
eviction remedy against his vendor, since it is now impossible for him
to be evicted[3]. It is consistent with this that the text speaks only
of *occisio*[4], not of lesser damage. But another limitation, generally
received[5], does not seem so well founded. It is said that the action
must be confined to the case in which the owner knew of the other's
possession and so acted in a sense *mala fide*. The principle on which
this rests can demand no more than that he shall not know that he is
owner, which must have been the usual case. But even so limited it
does not seem to be justified. The *lex* Aquilia did not need *mala fides*.
This idea is in fact due to the opinion that an owner cannot be guilty
of *culpa*, and is an attempt to find another basis of liability. The other
branch of the alternative seems preferable. But the limitation which
has been accepted above, compels another, not indicated in the texts:
it excludes the action against the *dominus* where the *bonae fidei* holder
is a donee.

There remains another difficulty. It is said that a *bonae fidei
possessor*, against whom a real action is brought is required to hand to
the owner all profits he has received in respect of the thing, even
Aquilian damages[6]. If this is so, his action against the *dominus* means
little. But in point of fact this is said only for *hereditatis petitio*,
against a person claiming to be *heres*, who was very differently dealt
with from an ordinary *bonae fidei possessor*[7]. Moreover our *actio*
Aquilia lies in favour of the *bonae fidei possessor* only if the slave is
killed, and there can then be no question of a *vindicatio* of him. It
may be added that a duty to account to the owner for such profits
would not necessarily cover damages recovered from the *dominus*
himself: we have already seen that a pledge creditor must account to
the owner for damages for theft (probably also *ex* Aquilia), except
where the owner was the wrongdoer[8].

---

[1] 9. 2. 11. 8, 17. A *liber homo bona fide serviens* has it in his own name when the subjection
has ceased, 9. 2. 13. *pr*.
[2] 11. 3. 1. 1.
[3] Pernice, Sachbeschäd. 196, and literature there cited.
[4] 9. 2. 17.
[5] Pernice, *loc. cit.*
[6] 5. 3. 55. The rule in 6. 1. 17 is differently explained. See *ante*, p. 12.
[7] Girard, Manuel, 901 *sqq.*
[8] *Ante*, p. 283.

The *bonae fidei possessor* is *ipso iure* liable to noxal actions for the acts of the slave. He is released by handing over the man, since the owner, if he attempts to vindicate him, is met by *doli mali exceptio*, unless he pays the damages[1], and, if he gets possession, can be sued by the Publician action, the *exceptio iusti dominii* being met by *replicatio doli mali*[2]. A *bonae fidei possessor* when sued by the *dominus*, can set off the cost of noxal defence[3]. Where the *bonae fidei possessor* is liable the *dominus* is not[4], subject to questions of *dolus*[5]. The reason for the owner's non-liability is that he has not *potestas*, and thus if a *fugitivus* steals from his *dominus*, a later *bonae fidei possessor* will be liable noxally[6], if the man has not since been in the *potestas* of his owner. The owner can arrive at a similar result by bringing *vindicatio* for the slave, but in the noxal action he has not to prove *dominium*, and the holder cannot set off expenses. It should be added that a *bonae fidei possessor*, who *dolo malo* ceases to possess, does not cease to be liable, any more than an owner would[7].

These rules are set forth in the texts with some indications of doubt, but no conflict of opinion is expressed. But that there were such differences is stated by Justinian, and, in view of the technical nature of the distinctions drawn, was inevitable. Justinian observes[8] that if a slave in my *bonae fidei* possession stole from X or from me, it had been doubted whether I was liable to X, or could sue the *dominus*, and he refers to the rule which denies noxal right and liability in the same person. Some, in view of this rule, had held that the *bonae fidei possessor* was not liable, and could sue the *dominus* when the slave got back to him, for what he took while with the *bonae fidei possessor*, or before he got back to his owner. Justinian enacted that as he thought himself owner, he was to be liable for thefts committed by the thief while with him, and could have no claim against the *dominus* for thefts committed during that time. But when he ceases to possess the slave, and the slave gets back to his true owner, the former *bonae fidei possessor* ceases to be liable and has an action for things stolen by the slave from him at any time after the "retention" ceased. He adds that this lays down a general rule consistent with principle, making the possessor liable and not entitled for a certain time, and the owner liable and not entitled for another time. If really free, he is, after his freedom is shewn, personally liable, even to the *bonae fidei possessor*, and his late holder is not liable, this being not in any way inconsistent with the general principle excluding action by a person noxally liable for acts done while he was liable, even though the relation has ceased.

---

1 *Ante*, p. 116.
2 9. 4. 11, 28.
3 47. 2. 54. 4.
4 9. 4. 11.
5 *Ante*, pp. 104, 114.
6 47. 2. 17. 3.
7 9. 4. 12.
8 C. 6. 2. 21.

His point is that the action against the freeman is not a noxal action. It will be remembered that a former master has no action for delict against one he has freed[1], nor does Justinian allow it against an owner by a former *bonae fidei possessor*, for what was done during the possession[2]. But in the present case the man having been actually free all through there can never have been any real question of noxal liability.

Two or three remarks on this enactment are necessary :

(i) It is clear from it that the unanimity in the Digest is due to the compilers, but the doctrine Justinian lays down is not new : there is no reason to doubt that it was held by the jurists to whom the Digest credits it[3].

(ii) The spaces of time are not exhaustive. A *bonae fidei possessor* is liable so long as "retention" lasts, the owner as soon as the slave gets back to him. Is either liable for what the slave may steal in the interim, if he never in fact returns to either? Apparently, not. The word *retentio*[4] shews that the rule applies only while actual *potestas* lasts. The question is suggested, by way of digression, whether the rule that a *fugitivus* is still possessed, applies to a *fugitivus* from a *bonae fidei possessor*. Apparently it does. The owner possesses only till another possesses[5], and Paul says that the continuation of possession in a *fugitivus* is *ut impleatur usucapio*[6]. The context shews that this must mean *usucapio* in the slave himself and not in what he possesses. On the other hand we are told, by Paul[7], that to run away from a *bonae fidei possessor* is a case of *fuga*, unless the slave was intending to return to the owner. Paul says that the man's state of knowledge is indifferent, which suggests that the interest of the master alone is in question. No doubt the conception of *fuga* is here considered from an entirely different point of view, but, even so, these texts confirm the view already expressed that the principles governing possession of a *fugitivus* were never a coherent whole[8].

(iii) Justinian's enactment says nothing about *damnum*. ·We have already seen that here the texts lay down[9] an entirely different rule. The rules and the cause for the difference have already been considered:

---

1 47. 2. 17. 1.   2 C. 6. 2. 21. *in fin.*   3 *Ante*, pp. 101, 129.
4 C. 6. 2. 21.   5 *Ante*, p. 270.
6 41. 2. 1. 14.   7 21. 1. 43. 3.
8 *Ante*, p. 271. Salkowski (*op. cit.* p. 150) observes that logic requires that one who has run away from a *bonae fidei possessor* should be still possessed by him and acquire to him, but that the rule as to possession of a fugitive is a mere rule of convenience not to be extended. There are no texts, but he thinks that the fate of acquisition by such a man depends on events. If he returns to *bonae fidei possessor*, all acquisitions *intra causas* go to him: others to *dominus*. If he goes to *dominus* all is acquired to him. It may be remarked that while it is difficult to pursue the possible development of Roman rules on logical lines, it is practically impossible to say, without texts, what rules the jurists may have laid down on grounds of expediency.
9 9. 2. 13. 1, 27. 3 ; 41. 1. 54. 2.

here it is enough to say that the limitation of Justinian's enactment is an important confirmation of the views held by Girard[1].

The law as to the liability of the *bonae fidei possessor*, on the dealings of the slave is not easily to be made out. Of usufructuary, we are told by Pomponius, in general terms, that the various edictal actions are available against him only so far as the transaction was one out of which he would acquire, *i.e. ex re eius* or *ex operis servi*[2]. The fructuary is so constantly assimilated to the *bonae fidei possessor* for such purposes that it is safe to treat the statement as applying to both. This is confirmed by Paul for the *actio tributoria*: he is liable so far as the *merx* is his property[3]. Of *quod iussu* we are merely told by Marcellus and Ulpian[4] that the action is available against a *bonae fidei possessor*. It is doubtful whether the limitation above given applies to this action : on a transaction authorised by him, he might be expected to be fully liable. But if so, and if, as may well be the case, the transaction concerns what is not really his property at all, but the *peculium* which belongs to the real owner, what is his position ? No doubt his right of retention for *impensae* may be made effective in some cases, but many circumstances may bar this. He cannot proceed on *negotia gesta*, since he was acting purely on his own account[5], and for like reasons he does not seem to have a *condictio*. It might indeed be contended that the *iussum* was void if it was not in connexion with a matter out of which he acquired, like a *iussum* for a contract by *servus alienus*[6]. But there is no real reason for this : if I authorise a contract with my slave, the effect of performance of which is to vest property in a third person, I am none the less liable *quod iussu*. Of course, in the absence of some other determining factor, the fact that the contract was at my *iussum* would suffice to determine that it was *ex re mea*.

On the *actio de peculio* we have a good deal of information, but it is not satisfactory[7]. The action is available against the *bonae fidei possessor*, and he can deduct only what is due to him, not what is due to *dominus* or another *possessor*[8]. But here disagreement begins. Pomponius, speaking indeed expressly only of *servus fructuarius* (but there is no reason to doubt the applicability of the remark to a *bonae fidei possessor*), says that this action, like the other edictal actions, is available against the fructuary only so far as he can acquire, *i.e. ex re eius* and *ex operis*[9].

---

[1] *Ante*, p. 129. [2] 15. 1. 2.
[3] 14. 4. 1. 5, 2. *Institoria* and *exercitoria* raise no difficulty. [4] 15. 4. 1. 8.
[5] 10. 3. 14. 1. There were exceptions in favour of *bonae fidei possessor*, but they do not touch this point, 3. 5. 48; 5. 3. 50. 1. See Accarias, *op. cit.* § 656.
[6] 15. 4. 2. 2.
[7] *De in rem verso* does not seem to be mentioned in this connexion. Presumably it was available so far as the *versum* vested beneficially in the possessor.
[8] 15. 1. 1. 6, 13, 15; 21. 1. 23. 6. [9] 15. 1. 2.

But as the creditor contracts in view of the whole *peculium,* and has no means of determining the different *causae,* there is room for the view that the *possessor* is liable *de peculio* on all contracts, though of course he cannot be condemned beyond the amount of the *peculium* which belongs to him[1]. This view seems to have prevailed. Marcellus is of opinion that his liability ought to be perfectly general, but says that, at any rate, if the action is brought against the owner or fructuary, and full satisfaction is not obtained, the other can be sued for the balance. In this Ulpian and Papinian agree[2]. Elsewhere Ulpian perhaps holds for complete liability as between two *bonae fidei possessores,* and Papinian lays down this rule as between owner and *possessor*[3]. Julian inclines to the intermediate view, that the person directly concerned is primarily liable, the other only for what the *peculium* of the first cannot pay. He does not however, so far as a rather obscure *lex* can be made out[4], require action to be brought first against the principal really concerned, but only that, if the other is first sued, an allowance be made for what can be recovered from the *peculium* belonging to the person primarily liable. The extreme view that either might be sued, looking at the matter from the creditor's point of view, is quite in accordance with what is supposed to be the tenor of the Edict[5]. The intermediate views are equitable compromises. It is clear that Julian's text has been corrupted in some way: it is not impossible that, as originally written, it expressed the view that the person primarily interested must be sued first[6].

There remains a puzzling text which confines liability *de peculio* to the *dominus,* in a certain case. Money is lent to a slave, and he pays it to his *bonae fidei possessor,* on an agreement for manumission. The *bonae fidei possessor* goes through the form of manumission[7]. The lender asks against whom he may bring the *actio de peculio.* Papinian answers that though in general the creditor has a choice, here he may sue only the *dominus.* The money, he says, was acquired to him, and the payment by the slave to the *bonae fidei possessor* did not transfer the property, such a transaction, *pro capite servi facta,* being beyond the slave's power of alienation: and he adds that even if the manumission is gone through it is not acquired thereby to the *possessor,* as not being really *ex re eius,* but only *propter rem eius.* The point for us is that the *actio de peculio* is against *dominus* only, and that Julian emphasises the fact that he acquired on the loan. Salkowski[8] lays down the rule

---

[1] 15. 1. 32. *pr.* [2] 15. 1. 19. 1. *Restitutio, post,* App. II.
[3] 15. 1. 32. *pr.*, 50. 3. See *post,* App. II.
[4] 15. 1. 37. 3. Salkowski, *op. cit.* 229, discusses this text, but treats it as dealing in part with transaction between *serviens* and *possessor.*
[5] Lenel, Ed. Perp. § 104. [6] See also *post,* p. 359. [7] 15. 1. 50. 3.
[8] *op. cit.* pp. 125 *sqq.*

that *mutuum* was an exception to the general principle, and that only he in whom the money had vested could be sued *de peculio* on a *mutuum*. And the *bonae fidei possessor* would not acquire it unless it was received on his behalf, or applied to his concerns. The explanation is consistent with the text itself, but there is no other evidence of any such general rule as Salkowski seeks: the writer or writers of this text may well be laying down what is clearly a reasonable rule for an exceptional case[1].

We now pass to acquisitions through *bona fide serviens*. This topic has been thoroughly worked out by Salkowski[2], whose excellent book has suggested most of what follows on this matter. The well-known general rule is that what he acquires *ex re possessoris*, or *ex operis suis*, is acquired to the *bonae fidei possessor*, everything else to his owner, or to himself if he be really free, the rule applying equally to *dominium*, *iura in re, possessio* and *iura in personam*[3]. The right of the *possessor* is in no way derived from that of the owner; in fact it is adverse, a point of some importance. Thus if a *bonae fidei possessor* has acquired possession through the *serviens*, his master, or he himself, if free, can never claim *accessio temporum*[4].

There is one case in which one who is really a *bonae fidei possessor* acquires only *ex re*. This is the case of one who enters on an inheritance believing himself heir, but really not entitled. Such a person must restore to the *heres* all acquisitions through a slave except those *ex re*[5]. Thus the better way to put the rule in the text is that he acquires like any other *bonae fidei possessor*, but though he can, *e.g.*, vindicate an acquisition *ex operis*, he must account for it[6]. Another text lays down an exceptional rule. Pomponius quotes Proculus as holding that where a thing is sold and delivered to a *bona fide serviens*, not within the *causae*, it is not acquired to the *dominus* because he does not possess the slave[7]. This is an isolated text depending on the notion that acquisition by *traditio* depended on the passing of possession, and it is universally agreed that such a slave could not acquire possession for his owner[8]. The text is illogical in that it allows a *liber homo bona fide serviens* to acquire in such a case, though he was incapable of possession. But, in fact, acquisition by *traditio* does not involve acquisition of possession[9].

---

[1] Papinian's language does not look like application of a general rule: *quamquam creditor electionem aliter haberet tamen in proposito dominum esse conveniendum.* In 3. 5. 5. 3, which Salkowski cites in support, there is no *mutuum* at all: that text illustrates only the rule that in *mutuum* property must pass, 46. 1. 56. 2. Salkowski rightly rejects the view that our text extends to the *possessor* the rule that mandate by the slave to a third party for his own manumission gives no *de peculio* (*ante*, p. 216): here there is *de peculio*, but on the loan.

[2] Sklavenerwerb, Ch. II.

[3] G. 2. 86, 91, 92; In. 2. 9. *pr.*, 4; C. 3. 32. 1; D. 41. 1. 10. 4, 19, 23. *pr.*, 43. *pr.*; 41. 2. 1. 6, 34. 2; 41. 4. 7. 8.

[4] 41. 2. 13. 3.   [5] 5. 3. 33.

[6] Girard, Manuel, 902; Accarias, Précis, § 816.   [7] 41. 1. 21. *pr.*

[8] *Post*, p. 347.

[9] Salkowski, *op. cit.* 36; Appleton, Propriété Prétorienne, §§ 81 *sqq.*

The two conceptions, *ex operis* and *ex re*, are not easy to define.

I. *Ex operis.* This means "by virtue of" or "in course of" his labours, rather than "by active proceeding on his part." It does not however mean the immediate result of his labour. If I employ a slave to make a thing for me, I am using him but I am not acquiring through him. A *conductor*, who can acquire nothing through a slave, a usuary who cannot acquire *ex operis*, both of these will have the result of his labour[1]. It involves essentially the acquisition of a right *ex operis servi*. Its field is therefore narrow. According to Salkowski it covers only the case of the slave hiring out himself or his service, being in some way active for a third person for hire[2]. In two well-known cases the jurists discuss the limits of acquisition *ex operis*.

(*a*) Institution of, or legacy to, the slave. Here the view undoubtedly dominant is that the *bonae fidei possessor* cannot acquire such things, as they are neither *ex re possessoris* nor *ex operis servi*. This is said by Gaius, Pomponius (quoting Aristo), Celsus, Paul, Ulpian, Modestinus[3]. But there are traces of a conflicting view. In legacy there could be no question of *operae*, but in inheritance there is an act of entry. If this is done *iussu possessoris*, cannot this be regarded as *ex operis*? This doubt is suggested by Aristo (through Pomponius)[4], and is by him recorded as having agitated one Varius Lucullus. This view may be understood in two ways. It may mean that its supporters hold that such an act of entry is a piece of labour, and the right to the inheritance is a direct result of it: a sort of *uti*, as if the man had been told to make some article. On this view there would be no question of acquisition *ex operis*. It is more probable that the supporters of this view treat the case as one of acquisition *ex opera*. But this could not be admitted. The *opera* involved in acquisition *ex operis* is not that expended in making the acquisition, but that which is the consideration for the acquisition. Both these ways of looking at it are open to the fatal objection that they would require acquisition of all *hereditates*, not merely those in which the testator intended to benefit the apparent master, and not only all inheritances, but under any transaction effected *iussu possessoris*, a *reductio ad absurdum* of the view. Accordingly Julian, the only weighty authority who thinks a *bonae fidei possessor* can acquire such things in any case, suggests that if the intent were to benefit the *possessor*, the entry of the slave, *iussu possessoris*, might be regarded as an acquisition *ex re*

---

[1] 7. 8. 12. 6, 14. *pr.*; 18. 6. 17. They are fruits, *deductis impensis*. See Salkowski, *op. cit.* 118. He notes one text in which acquisition *ex operis* is referred to the immediate *operari*, 7. 1. 23. 1.

[2] Mandate for an *honorarium*; acquisition from a *societas* to which the slave has contributed labour; acceptance of a contract for work, by the slave.

[3] G. 2. 92; In. 2. 9. 4; D. 6. 1. 20; 28. 5. 60. *pr.*; 29. 2. 25. *pr.*; 41. 1. 10. 3, 4, 19, 54. *pr.*; 48. 10. 22. 4. See also C. Th. 4. 8. 6. See Salkowski, *op. cit.* 175 *sqq.*   [4] 41. 1. 19.

possessoris. He is clear that it cannot be *ex opera*[1]. There is something to be said for this view, but that which prevails is clearly that the *possessor* cannot acquire such things at all.

(b) Treasure trove[2]. If such a slave find. reasure trove, to whom does the finder's half go ? Tryphoninus states[3], and rejects, a suggestion that it may go to fructuary or *possessor*, as being *ex opera*. But of course it is not. The event may happen while he is labouring, but the very existence of a finder's half at all requires that the discovery shall not have been the object of his labour[4], and if it were possible to acquire it on intentional search, it would not be an acquisition *ex operis* but *fructus* or product.

II. *Ex re.* This is acquisition through or relating to the property of the *bonae fidei possessor*, not necessarily through any physical thing belonging to him. It would be perhaps more exact to say that acquisition *ex re* is acquisition by a transaction connected with his affairs[5]. Commercial dealings are so various that it is not possible to state the different forms, and a few illustrations, mostly from Salkowski, must suffice. Purchase with *peculium* belonging to the *possessor*[6], sale *ex peculio eius*, taking *traditio* of a thing bought by the *possessor*, stipulating for the price of a thing sold by the *possessor*, loan of money for purposes connected with his property, or the *peculium* which belongs to him[7], etc. Three cases appear to create a certain difficulty.

(a) Release of a debt. It is clear that if the *possessor* owes money, and the *bona fide serviens* takes an *acceptilatio*, or a *pactum de non petendo*, or any other pact which will base an *exceptio*, the benefit is acquired to the *possessor*. We are told that this is *ex re*[8]. Salkowski[9] finds some difficulty in accepting this. He attributes the view that it was *ex re* to the practical needs of life which made it inconvenient to make the effect of a release depend on its *causa*. He holds that for this reason a release by way of gift was put on the same level as one given in discharge of some obligation, and was thus called *ex re*. The explanation seems unnecessary : the discharge is *in re possessoris*, it is in his affairs. If the *possessor* has lent money to A and borrowed money from B, and the *bona fide serviens* has received the money from A and a release from B, both these transactions are equally *ex re possessoris*.

(b) *Donationes.* In one text Gaius denies that a gift can go to the *bonae fidei possessor*, as it is not within the *causae*. This is from the

---

[1] 29. 2. 45. *pr.*, *aditio hereditatis non est in opera servili*; 29. 2. 45. 4, *ut intelligatur non opera sua mihi adquirere sed ex re mea.*
[2] Salkowski, *op. cit.* 120.
[3] 41. 1. 63. 3 deals with fructuary, but doubtless applies equally here.
[4] In. 2. 1. 39.   [5] It is always *ex re*, never in the plural.
[6] 41. 1. 23. 3.   [7] This case is rare.
[8] 2. 14. 19. *pr.*, 59; 46. 4. 11. *pr.*   [9] *op. cit.* 122 *sqq.*

Institutes[1], and thus is a mere general statement which might admit of exceptions. It is confirmed in the same general form by Pomponius, quoting Aristo[2]. But Paul remarks that a gift given *indistincte* to a *bona fide serviens* goes to the *dominus*[3], which implies that expression of intent might divert it to the *possessor*. And Ulpian, in a text which has been retouched, after expressing some doubt, appears as saying that *donationes, mortis causa* and *inter vivos*, are acquired to the *possessor* if intent to benefit him was shewn[4]. It is not clear that this is Ulpian's. It is however an application to *donatio* of the extension of the notion *ex re* which Julian tentatively suggested for *hereditas*[5]. The intention to benefit the *possessor* may reasonably be regarded as making the transaction his affair, one in which his patrimony is concerned in a more definite way than by the mere fact that it would be better off for the acquisition. Ulpian says the same thing of a payment of money made to satisfy a condition on liberty. This is, if the money is payable, as it usually is, out of *peculium*, an authorisation to give, if he likes. It is not a *donatio* by the owner of the slave. The intended receiver would have no sort of claim against the *heres* for it. It is however a gift so far as the receiver is concerned. If it is *contemplatione fructuarii*, it goes to him[6].

(c) Gift by the *bonae fidei possessor* to the slave[7]. Such a transaction is clearly *ex re*. Its only legal effect is to transfer the thing into *peculium*. This is equally true though less obvious where the *possessor* gives the *servus* his *operae*. The only result is that the various acquisitions *ex operis* are *in peculio*[8].

Salkowski discusses[9] at some length the origin of this principle of the two *causae*. *Ex operis* presents no difficulty : such acquisitions are in essence *fructus*. *Ex re*, says the author, is a growth due to trade exigencies, to avoid roundabout adjustments which would otherwise have been necessary. The jurists recognise the anomalous nature of the rule. They do not apply it to the case of the apparent *filiusfamilias*[10], where the need is not so great, or to pledge creditor or to *precario tenens*[11]. He thinks that in usufruct acquisitions were at first limited to *operae*. Acquisition of rights through *servus fructuarius* was first allowed in the normal case—usufruct created by will[12]. According to Ulpian the rule was extended to all usufructs by Pegasus. *Ex re*

---

[1] G. 2. 92; In. 2. 9. 4; D. 41. 1. 10. 3, 4.   [2] 41. 1. 19.
[3] 41. 1. 19.　　　[4] 7. 1. 22.　　　[5] 29. 2. 45.
[6] This principle would cover the case of *acceptilatio* if it were really a gift; otherwise, *i.e.* if it were one of a series of transactions affecting the possessor's affairs, it was certainly *ex re*.
[7] Salkowski, *op. cit.* 130.
[8] 7. 1. 31; 7. 8. 16. 2; 41. 1. 49, all dealing with *s. fructuarius*, but equally applicable here.
[9] *op. cit.* 132 *sqq*.　　　[10] 41. 3. 44. *pr.*
[11] 41. 1. 22.　　　[12] 7. 1. 25. 7.

grows out of *ex operis*: traces of connexion appear[1]. And it is not, he says, fully developed till after Sabinus. In *hereditas* and treasure trove, Julian and Tryphoninus find it necessary to negative current wide views as to the nature of *ex operis*[2]. Then acquisition *ex operis* gets narrowed down to cases of employment[3] in trading, and it is recognised that *ex re* is *uti* not *frui*[4]. Salkowski remarks that there is little indication of development of an *a posteriori* juristic basis for these acquisitions[5]. The process of definition may have followed these lines, though in the state of the texts there is a good deal of speculation about any such conclusions. Salkowski is not very clear as to the reason for regarding acquisition through such slaves as anomalous. It seems the inevitable result of recognition of *bonae fidei* possession and usufruct as independent rights *in rem*, involving the right of employing the slave. To exclude his employment in the field of contract making, the most characteristic and important feature of slave labour in the absence of any theory of agency, would have been absurd, and illogical. That it was not allowed to pledge creditor or *precario tenens* is natural: the mere fact of possession, *ad interdicta*, was never recognised by the Romans as what is nowadays called a *ius in rem*: this has been achieved by more recent jurisprudence. And as the right of the *bonae fidei possessor* of a slave is a development from *bonae fidei possessio* in general, it is not surprising that it is not applied to putative *patria potestas*, where there is no possession at all. There seems no reason to regard *ex re* as the later of the two to develop: it may be remembered that in the case in which it was necessary to cut down the right of the *bonae fidei possessor*, i.e. in the case of *hereditatis petitio*[6], it was acquisition *ex operis* which was cut off, not that *ex re*: this was regarded as a matter of course.

We can now consider the effect of some transactions in cases in which there is not acquisition to the *bonae fidei possessor*.

(i) *Hereditas.* The *bonae fidei possessor* did not acquire, but the texts are not clear as to what did become of the *hereditas*. No entry of the *serviens* could bind his *dominus*, and if his circumstances became known in time, his *dominus* could make him enter[7]. But if he was a *liber homo*, Trebatius was of opinion that his entry, even *iussu*, made him liable as heir, since whatever his intent was he had gone through the act of entry. Labeo held that he was not bound by his entry unless he was willing to enter of his own account apart from *iussum*[8], and the texts shew that this view prevailed. *Velle non creditur qui*

---

[1] 7. 8. 14. *pr.*
[3] 7. 8. 16. 2, 20.
[5] See also Pernice, Labeo, 2. 1. 370.
[7] 41. 1. 10. 4.

[2] 41. 1. 19, 63. 3; 29. 2. 45.
[4] 7. 1. 12. 3; 45. 3. 36.
[6] *Ante*, p. 341.
[8] 28. 5. 60. *pr.*; 41. 1. 19.

obsequitur imperio patris vel domini[1]. Thus entry, merely *iussu*, does not bind him, but entry *sine iussu*, or where he was willing to enter apart from *iussum*, does[2]. One of the texts, speaking of the case in which the intent is to benefit the *possessor*, contains a very puzzling remark : *sed licet ei (sc. possessori) minime adquirit, attamen si voluntas testatoris evidens appareat restituendam eam hereditatem*[3]. The words, which are interpolated[4], seem to mean that if intent to benefit the *possessor* was clear then whether the *liber homo* entered *sponte* or *iussu*, or the *servus alienus* entered *iussu domini*, the person who acquired the *hereditas* would be under a *fideicommissum* to hand it back to the *bonae fidei possessor*. It would have been simpler, as Salkowski remarks[5], to allow the *possessor* to acquire where intent to benefit him was clear[6]. Salkowski doubts if the text be interpolated[7], since it disagrees with a rule laid down by Justinian for an analogous case. It is clear that a person who doubted whether he was a *filius* or *paterfamilias*, or free, or *statuliber*, was personally bound if he entered even *iussu*[8]. This might make one engaged in a *causa liberalis* hesitate to enter even *iussu*. Justinian accordingly provides[9] that if in the will he is described as *servus* Titii, he must enter on *iussum*, and if he refuses is to have no claim, even if really free. If however he is simply instituted, *ut liber*, in his own name, the *hereditas* will await the issue of the *causa liberalis*, which will decide its destination. Thus the mere mention of the name of the *possessor* is to be conclusive evidence of intention to benefit him, and entitles him to claim the *hereditas*, and not merely a *fideicommissum*. But this rule is on the face of it a departure from ordinary rules, for a particular case, and in no way bars Tribonian's authorship of the rule just discussed. The word *fideicommissum* is not used in our text[10], and there is some difficulty as to the event in which the trust takes effect. All that is clear is that, if he enters so as to bind himself, the direction takes effect. But if he enters only *iussu*, so that the entry is null, according to the rules already stated, or does not enter, so that the gift goes to substitutes, it is not certain that the direction is binding. Salkowski thinks that in that case the direction is null[11]. He holds also[12] that if *bona fide serviens liber* enters after his freedom is clear, there can be no question of restitution, for this would give *bonae fidei possessor* greater rights than those of a real owner, who can claim

[1] 50. 17. 4.
[2] 29. 2. 6. 4, 74. 2; 41. 1. 19, 54. *pr.*; cp. 29. 2. 25. 9. This would involve difficulties of proof, but these are held lightly by Roman lawyers. They lead Salkowski to think (*op. cit.* 184, 5) that the choice is made and intent shewn later, when the facts are known, but the texts are against this. 41. 1. 54. 4 speaks of intent to acquire to himself, which is difficult to understand in the case of one in apparent slavery. This leads S. to the view mentioned.
[3] 41. 1. 19.   [4] Lenel, Palingen., *ad h. l.*   [5] *op. cit.* 178.
[6] We have seen that Julian suggested this and that it was adopted in the case of *donatio*. *Ante*, p. 343.
[7] *op. cit.* 177.   [8] 29. 2. 6. 4, 34. *pr.*, 74. 4. Salkowski, *op. cit.* 182—4.
[9] C. 6. 30. 21.   [10] 41. 1. 19.   [11] *op. cit.* 185.   [12] *op. cit.* 178.

nothing if the slave enters after manumission. The analogy is not very close, for manumission is a voluntary surrender of all rights in the slave. And it is hardly possible to apply strict logic to the interpretation of interpolations of this sort.

(ii) Gift and legacy. In the cases in which these did not go to the *possessor*, they went to the *liber homo* or the *dominus*[1]. We do not learn that any rule was laid down as to restitution in case of intent to benefit the *possessor* in legacy. In *donatio mortis causa* the life of the actual beneficiary would be the material one from the point of view of survival[2]. The difficulties which might arise as to *usucapio* and consumption of such things do not here concern us.

(iii) *Possessio*[3]. Possession can be acquired for us by persons *bona fide* possessed by us, within the *causae*, and, if it is *in re peculiari*, without our knowledge[4]. But where these conditions are not satisfied we find a new principle. They do not acquire the possession for themselves or for the *dominus*. It is acquired to no one. One who is himself possessed cannot possess or usucapt[5]. An owner cannot possess through one who is possessed by another[6]. It is odd that Ulpian in one text[7] declares that what is possessed by a *filiusfamilias bona fide serviens, peculiari causa*, and thus not acquired to the holder, is possessed by the *paterfamilias*. This text conflicts with the rules already pointed out, and makes one capable of possessing through one possessed by another. It must be an error[8].

(iv) Contract. Here too the general principle applies: he acquires to the *bonae fidei possessor ex re eius* and *ex operis*[9]. The nature of the contract is in general immaterial[10], *mutuum* being not often recorded. The only topic for discussion is the rule that even within the *causae* what cannot be acquired to the *possessor* goes to the *dominus* or to the man himself[11]. The rule appears to be an extension by Julian of an analogous rule in the case of *servus communis*[12]. The case contemplated is that of a stipulation for what is already the property of the *bonae fidei possessor*. This is sound, since the owner can acquire anything, and the right of the *possessor* is merely cut out of his right. Conversely Paul

---

[1] 41. 1. 10. 3, 19.
[2] Salkowski, *op. cit.* 170, 1.
[3] Salkowski, *op. cit.* 164 *sqq*.
[4] G. 2. 94; In. 2. 9. 4; D. 41. 2. 1. 5; 41. 4. 7. 8.
[5] 41. 2. 1. 6; 50. 17. 118; and thus a captive is not restored retrospectively to possession by *postliminium*, 41. 2. 23. 1.
[6] 41. 2. 1. 6. Thus a pledge debtor cannot acquire possession through a pledged slave, though the creditor cannot, *h. t.* 1. 15. Salkowski, *op. cit.* 166, 7, finds traces of an older view, according to which any *possessio* gave the holder possession of what was held by the person possessed. But this is not classical or later law.
[7] 41. 2. 4.
[8] For some texts creating difficulties in the rules as to *servi ab aliis possessi*, see *ante*, p. 270.
[9] G. 3. 164; In. 3. 28. 1; Ulp. 19. 21; C. 3. 32. 1; D. 12. 1. 41.
[10] Stipulation, *constitutum*, deposit, *etc.* P. 2. 2. 2; D. 12. 1. 41; 13. 5. 6; 16. 3. 1. 27.
[11] 41. 1. 23. 2; 45. 3. 20. *pr.* The texts do not speak of *servus alienus*, but the rule may be assumed to cover his case, as 7. 1. 25. 3 lays down the same rule for *servus fructuarius*.
[12] *Post*, p. 389.

tells us[1] that if a *bona fide serviens* stipulates for something that is his, within the *duae causae*, it goes to his holder, the doubt in the text being due to the fact that it is his own thing, and one cannot stipulate for that. Paul meets that by the reply that within the *causae* he is to be regarded as the holder's slave, and to have no property beyond his *peculium*, of which the thing in question is not a part. But Ulpian says[2] that even if it is *extra causas* the *possessor* will acquire on such facts. This contradicts the general rule and makes the *possessor* capable of acquiring beyond the *causae*. It has been proposed to omit a *non*, which would make the text orthodox[3], but entirely empty. More acceptable is Salkowski's view[4], that it is a mistake of Ulpian's due to the appearance of logical sequence and symmetry, coupled with the fact that otherwise the transaction would be void. The impossibility of acquisition beyond the *causae*, Ulpian himself emphasises[5].

Most of the slave's dealings are in connexion with his *peculium* in ordinary cases. This *peculium* may be twofold, part belonging to the *possessor*, part to the owner, and the effect of his transaction will vary according to the part of the *peculium* with which it is concerned. His contract is often a part of a dealing entered on by his *dominus* or *possessor*. The *possessor* may sell and the slave stipulate for the price. In one case the *possessor* hands over money, by way of *mutuum*, out of that part of the *peculium* which belongs to the owner, and the slave stipulates in the name of the *possessor* for its return. If this *mutuum* were a contract, it would be acquired to the *possessor*, for it is made by him, and the stipulation would be *ex re*, and so acquired to him. A *mutuum*, however, needs conveyance of the money, and this, on the facts, never occurred: there was no *mutuum* and so far no liability, and thus it is not *ex re*[6]. If the stipulation was not *nominatim* to the *possessor* no doubt, as Salkowski says, Julian would treat it as acquired to the owner : unless this is so, it is not clear why the *mihi* is inserted.

Where A bought B's slave S from a thief, and S with the *peculium* which belonged to B bought a *res* and it was delivered to A, B could condict the thing from A[7]. The text adds that if A has incurred any expense in the matter, he has *de peculio* against B. This involves a quasi-contract of the slave with A[8].

---

[1] 45. 3. 20. *pr.*   [2] 41. 1. 23. 2.
[3] See for references, Salkowski, *op. cit.* 194, 5.   [4] *loc. cit.*   [5] 7. 1. 25. 3.
[6] 45. 3. 1. 1. Salkowski thinks (*op. cit.* p. 124) that if the coins are consumed the *possessor* acquires the stipulation. This is hardly consistent with the energetic language of the jurist (*nihil agit*), or with the nature of stipulation : *ex praesenti vires accipit*, V. Fr. 55. Subsequent events may determine to whom it is acquired, but hardly whether it exists or not. Nor is it needed : there is a *condictio* in any case if the money is consumed, 12. 1. 11. 2, 13. *pr.*
[7] 19. 1. 24. 1.
[8] S, with B's money, bought a thing for A. A's action is *negotiorum gestorum de peculio*. In 12. 1. 31. 1 the same case is discussed and alternative remedies are considered. *Ante*, p. 226.

Purchase of freedom with *peculium* is a common case. A *bonae fidei possessor* cannot manumit, and any payment to him for this object is not acquired to him, on its receipt by the slave. Thus money borrowed from an *extraneus* and paid to the *possessor* for manumission, vests in the *dominus*[1], or, if the man was really free, can be condicted by the payer[2]. If a *liber homo bona fide serviens* gives an *extraneus* a mandate to buy him, in order to free him, and gives him money out of his own *peculium*, the *extraneus* paying the price and then manumitting him, what is the result when he is declared *ingenuus*[3]? He has, say Ulpian and Julian, an *actio mandati* against the *extraneus* to claim from him cession of his actions. There is an *actio ex empto*, for the sale is valid[4]. The money has become the property of the *bonae fidei possessor*, as it became that of the *extraneus*: it cannot therefore be vindicated, nor, the transaction being a valid sale, is it a case for *condictio*[5]. If the money was *ex peculio possessoris*, he has simply received his own, and there are no actions to cede, for the *extraneus* cannot recover *ex empto*, not having really paid any price.

In some cases the answer to the question out of which *peculium* the consideration proceeds will determine who acquires, which is, till that is settled, in suspense[6].

The effect of a transaction is often modified by *iussum* or *nominatio*, *i.e.* the slave enters on it at the command of, or in the name of, X. The effect of this can be shortly stated. If the *serviens* contracts *nominatim* to the *possessor, ex re domini* (or rather not *ex re possessoris* or *ex opera*), the contract is null: the *possessor* cannot acquire *extra causas*, and the fact that the agreement names him prevents the *dominus* from acquiring[7]. If on the other hand he stipulates *nominatim* for his owner, *ex re possessoris*, the acquisition is to the *dominus*, as it is only the fact that the *possessor* acquires which prevents him from acquiring on any contract of the slave, and as the *possessor* cannot here take, the owner does[8]. If he stipulates *iussu possessoris* but *ex re alterius*, he acquires to his *dominus, quia iussum domino cohaeret*. It has not the same privative or negative effect as *nominatio*[9]. If he stipulates *ex re possessoris, iussu domini* he acquires for the *dominus*[10]. It is not clear why *iussum domini* excludes acquisition to the fructuary or *possessor ex re eius*, since *iussum* has not in other cases any privative effect[11]. Logic would seem to require division. The text is clear and does not seem to be interpolated: the result is more symmetrical than

1 15. 1. 50. 3.   2 12. 4. 3. 5.   3 17. 1. 8. 5.
4 18. 1. 4.   5 12. 4. 16.
6 *Post*, p. 363, in connexion with fructuary.
7 7. 1. 25. 1 ; 45. 3. 1. 1, 22, 23, 30, 31.
8 7. 1. 25. 1 ; 41. 1. 37. 5 ; 45. 3. 39.   Salkowski cites also 45. 3. 1. 5, 28. *pr.*; 46. 3. 98. 7.
9 45. 3. 31, 33. *pr.*   10 7. 1. 25. 3.   11 Salkowski, *op. cit.* 193.

logical. To give the *iussum* no effect at all would be to confine acquisition by owner to transactions *ex re sua*. To divide would be clumsy. The matter is the less important in that the acquisition *domino, ex re fructuarii vel possessoris*, is not definitive: we learn that there was doubt as to the remedy of fructuary or *possessor*, but on the authority of Cassius it is laid down that there is a *condictio*[1].

Transactions between the *possessor* and the *serviens* in which no other person is concerned (*i.e.* within the *causae*) can have no legal effect except so far as they may affect the amount of the slave's *peculium*[2] (and subject to a question as to the liability of a *liber homo bona fide serviens* on his promise). In the same way dealings between *serviens* and *dominus* (which are quite conceivable) will produce no other result so far as they are not within the *causae*. But if the contract with *possessor* be *iussu domini* or *nominatim domino* (and even this is conceivable though improbable), the *dominus* will acquire, and if, for example, the thing bought is paid for out of *peculium* which does not belong to the *possessor*, the owner acquires a right on the contract, (not *de peculio*, but absolute, for it is a contract made by his slave,) against the *possessor*. This needs no further authority[3]. In any case in which the owner acquires a right of action on the contract, the *possessor* must acquire, if it is a bilateral transaction, an *actio de peculio*, and conversely in any bilateral transaction in which the *possessor* acquires a direct action against the owner, the latter will have an *actio de peculio*[4]. In unilateral transactions the same rule holds. If the slave promises to *possessor, ex re eius*, the *possessor* acquires no *actio*. If it is *extra causas* he does[5]. What is and what is not *ex re* is to be determined on lines already laid down. The difficulty found by Salkowski on this point seems to be due to his regarding *ex re* as meaning "originating in the property of," instead of "connected with the concerns of" the *possessor*[6].

In the case of *liber homo bona fide serviens* we get new conditions. The jurists agree, apparently, that as he is a free man, capable of contracting, he must be liable to his holder on contracts with him. One case which attracts great attention is that in which the *serviens* manages the affairs of the *possessor*. Here, whether he acts *iussu* or

---

[1] 45. 3. 39; cp. 12. 7. 1—3. Pomponius expresses a present doubt and solves it on the authority of Cassius, who must have died fifty years before. He calls him Gaius *noster*. The remark may be from the compilers and refer to Gaius.
[2] 7. 1. 25. 5; 45. 1. 118. *pr.*
[3] See 7. 1. 25. 5. As to acquisition in suspense, *post*, p. 363.
[4] Thus where S bought from P a *res* and paid for it with money of his *peculium* which belonged to D, D acquired an *actio ex empto*, and P an *actio de peculio ex vendito*. If he bought the thing from D, no action would arise unless he paid with *peculium* of P, in which case it was as if D were an *extraneus*.
[5] 45. 1. 118. *pr.*
[6] *op. cit.* 225.

not, he is liable to the *possessor*. There were doubts in early law, but apparently only as to the right remedy. Labeo doubted whether *actio mandati* would lie, because the special liabilities of that case are hardly applicable where he acted *servili necessitate*[1]. But the view which prevailed was that if there was authorisation there was *actio mandati*, and otherwise there was *negotiorum gestorum*[2]. Thus Pomponius says he is liable to me *omnimodo*, if he promises to me, *quamvis in re mea*, *i.e.* even in cases which would not have given me an *actio de peculio* against his *dominus* had he been a *servus alienus*[3]. Elsewhere Pomponius lays down the same rule for *commodatum*, saying nothing expressly of the connexion with *res possessoris*[4]. In another text Pomponius says that the *liber homo* may be liable to us by promise, sale, purchase, letting or hiring. The expression *poterit obligari*[5] suggests some limitation, which at first sight seems to be called for, since it is obviously unfair that the *liber homo* should be liable on contracts the whole benefit of which has enured to the *possessor*. But the inclusive language of Papinian[6] is strongly opposed to such a limitation.

The injustice is in fact only apparent, as will appear on examination of three typical cases. The *possessor* expends money on *res peculiares* of his own, and stipulates with the *liber homo* for reimbursement. When the man's freedom is declared the former *possessor* can sue on the stipulation. But on the facts there is an *exceptio doli*. It is true that there was nothing fraudulent, but *ipsa res in se dolum habet*[7]. The *serviens* borrows from the *possessor* and buys things which are devoted to the *peculium* which belongs to the latter. There is no *mutuum*, as there was no intention to pass property to the *serviens*: the money is merely added to his *peculium*[8]. His alienation within his powers is indeed a transfer, but it is no *mutuum*, and it is noticeable that *mutuum* is not mentioned as one of the ways in which a *bona fide serviens* can become liable. The *serviens* contracts with the *possessor* to buy a *res* of him. If he has paid for the thing out of his own property there is no question[9]. If he has not paid at all or has paid out of *peculium possessoris*, he is liable. But he is entitled to the thing and the former *possessor* cannot bring *ex empto* without satisfying the ordinary requirements of this action. These cases shew that, except where he had a real economic interest, the liability of the *serviens* was only nominal. Not much is left of Papinian's *quamvis ex re mea*, for if it really is *ex re mea*, the obligation is nominal. Papinian's language shews that he is dealing

---

1 3. 5. 18. 2.   2 3. 5. 5. 7, 18. 2; 13. 6. 13. 2; 41. 1. 54. 3.
3 45. 1. 118. *pr.*   4 13. 6. 13. 2.
5 41. 1. 54. 1.   6 45. 1. 118. *pr.*
7 See 45. 1. 36.
8 See the texts as to *donatio, ante*, p. 343.
9 He is entitled to claim the thing.

with a conclusion forced on him by logic: *quid aliud dici potest quominus liber homo teneatur*. The equitable defence, the *exceptio doli*, where the benefit has gone to the *possessor*, is in no way opposed to his way of looking at the matter.

As to the rights of *serviens* on his contracts we have little information. We know that if the transaction was *ex re possessoris*, the *serviens* has no rights: from this point of view the transaction is one between a master and his slave[1]. Whether he necessarily had an action if it were *extra causas* is not clearly stated. In one case where he borrowed from an outsider and applied the proceeds to the concerns of the *possessor*, Paul allows him *actio negotiorum gestorum contraria*[2]. He has some doubts which turn on the fact that, as he was apparently acting for his master, his act can hardly be regarded as intervention by a friend. His right is due to the fact that he has made himself liable to an outsider, and throws no light on the matter. But as the *possessor* would undoubtedly have been liable to the owner had he been a *servus alienus*, it may be assumed that he was liable to *liber homo*[3].

In these matters the expression, *ex re possessoris*, is used in a way which may cause confusion. When we say that a *possessor* acquires on a slave's contract *ex re possessoris*, we are speaking of a right acquired *prima facie* by the slave, and enuring to the *possessor*. But here we have been dealing with a totally different state of things: it is not a case where the *possessor* is in the background acquiring by the slave; the *possessor* and the slave appear as two opposing contracting parties, and what the *possessor* acquires is not what is undertaken *to* the slave, but what is undertaken *by* him. This does not however require any modification of the conception, *ex re*[4]. In the case of *liber homo* the point is unimportant, since the liability is not affected by the distinction, but the *servus alienus* does not bind his owner by a promise to the *possessor ex re possessoris*. If the transaction is essentially in the concerns of *possessor* there will be no action against the owner: if it is not there will be *de peculio*. Thus if the slave sells and delivers to the *possessor* a *res* from the *peculium* which belongs to the *dominus*, the *possessor* will have *de peculio ex empto* against the *dominus*: not if it was in the *possessor's* part of the *peculium*. If he buy a thing from the *possessor* there will be the same distinction according to the fund which pays for it[5]. If he undertake a job, the question is, for which estate is it? There does not seem to be a difficulty of principle, though the line may sometimes be difficult to draw.

[1] 45. 1. 118. *pr.*   [2] 3. 5. 35.   [3] *Ante*, p. 351.
[4] *Ante*, p. 343.   [5] *Post*, p. 363.

XXIII. THE SLAVE *MALA FIDE* POSSESSED.

We are not concerned with a *liber homo mala fide* possessed : it is clear that mere forcible detaining of a freeman without pretence of right is not possession at all[1]. There are texts which equally deny possession to any *mala fide* holder of a *liber homo*[2]. Their logic is not very clear. Javolenus attributes the rule in the case of forcible detainer to the fact that *civiliter eum in mea potestate non habeo*[3]. Africanus says we do not possess him because we have not *animus possidendi*[4], which is not necessarily true : in fact he has in his mind the case of knowledge, not merely that we are not entitled, but also that he is really free[5]. Paul appears to hold that what is incapable of being commercially dealt with cannot be possessed[6], which would cover *bona fide* possession[7]. In fact it is probably a hesitation to admit that a freeman could be possessed that led to the preference for the expression *liber homo bona fide serviens*, though there is no doubt that he was possessed according to many texts[8]. There could be no noxal liability for such a person, and no acquisition through him. We are not told whether there was any liability on his contracts, but analogy suggests *actio doli*. The detainer would be liable to the interdict *Quem liberum*[9], and might come within the provisions of the *lex* Fabia[10].

There are some cases of possession which are neither *bonae fidei* nor *malae fidei*. Such are those of *precario tenens* and pledge creditor. There are others which are more like *malae fidei* possession. Such are those of a slave given by a woman *sine tutoris auctoritate*, or given by wife to husband and *vice versa*. Here the consent of the owner is given but the law prevents ownership from passing. Salkowski shews that all these, so far at least as acquisition is concerned, are treated as *malae fidei possessio*[11]. There is no authority upon other points, but from the reluctance with which it was admitted that in the case of gift to a wife even possession passed[12], it seems most probable that the law ignored the transaction and treated the slave for all purposes, as far as possible, as still held by the owner.

The case with which we are concerned is that of one who holds a *servus alienus* as his own, with knowledge that he is not entitled, and adversely to the owner. The great breadth of the definition of *furtum*

---

[1] 41. 2. 23. 2.   The title dealing with wrongful detention of freemen (43. 29) does not speak of possession.
[2] 45. 3. 34.   [3] 41. 2. 23. 2.   [4] 12. 1. 41.
[5] So has Javolenus in 45. 3. 34.   [6] 41. 2. 30. 1.
[7] See also 22. 3. 20; 4. 6. 11.   [8] 41. 2. 1. 6; 50. 17. 118, *etc.*
[9] 43. 29.   [10] 48. 15; *ante*, p. 32.
[11] *op. cit.* 146 *sqq.*   The chief texts are 41. 1. 57; 24. 1. 17—20.
[12] Salkowski, *loc. cit.* in note.

makes a *malae fidei possessor* usually a *fur*, though not always. But for our purpose this is immaterial.

A *malae fidei possessor* has no *actio furti* if the slave be stolen, his *interesse* not being *honestum*[1]: it may be inferred that he has no *actio* Aquilia *utilis*[2], or *servi corrupti*[3], though no doubt he is liable on both these.

He is liable noxally for wrongs by the slave[4]. The reason given by Gaius is that it would be absurd that a *bonae fidei emptor* should incur this liability and the mere *praedo* escape. A sufficient reason seems to be that the *malae fidei possessor* has the *potestas* on which in classical law the liability depends[5]. As he appears to be owner the action will be brought against him: if the fact that he knew that he was not entitled were a defence he must raise it himself, and the result would be abandonment of the slave, which would release him even if he were liable[6]. It is nowhere stated whether he is noxally liable for *damnum*, but in all probability he is not, in this case, since the theory of *potestas* is not applied to it, and the liability always rests on *dominium*[7]. On the other hand, it is surprising to find that a *malae fidei possessor* has *furti noxalis* against the owner[8]. This is in direct conflict with the rule that one who is noxally liable for a slave cannot have a noxal action for what he does[9]. Celsus, who so states the rule, appears to see that it needs special justification, and he defends it on the grounds that otherwise misdeeds would go unpunished and that *domini* would profit by them: *plerumque enim eius generis servorum furtis peculia eorundem augentur.* This is a poor reason: it gives a *malae fidei possessor* a profit which is at least as undesirable[10].

It is surprising also to find that there is no authority as to the liability of *malae fidei possessor* on the slave's *negotia*. *Malae fidei possessio* occurs in many texts and cannot have been very rare. For it to endure, the holder must find it necessary to act in all respects as if he were owner. There will be buying and selling, and all ordinary transactions, as appears indeed from the texts we shall have to discuss. But of contracts by the slave purporting to bind himself or his holder there is not a word. The holder will, like any *extraneus*, be liable to the actions *exercitoria* and *institoria*. Apparently he will not be liable to the *actio quod iussu*[11]. There will of course be *de peculio* against the *dominus*, and if the *peculium* is insufficient, it may be that there is *de dolo* against the *possessor*[12]. Such a slave may well have a *peculium, de facto*, belonging to the holder. There seems to be no *tributoria*[13], and

---

[1] 47. 2. 12. 1.   [2] 9. 2. 17.   [3] 11. 3. 1. 1.
[4] 9. 4. 13.   [5] *Ante*, p. 101.   [6] *Ante*, p. 103.
[7] *Ante*, p. 130.   [8] 47. 2. 68. *x.*   [9] *Ante*, p. 106.
[10] Other parts of this *lex* are suspected of interpolation on grammatical grounds. See Eisele, Z. S. S. 7. It may be a Tribonianism. See *ante*, p. 106.
[11] *Arg.* 15. 4. 2. 2.   [12] 4. 3. 6.   [13] *Arg.* 14. 4. 1. 5.

indeed there is no trace of any edictal action. No doubt *de dolo* is available if there is no other remedy, and there is no reason for creating a limited liability[1].

Besides this apparent *peculium* of the *possessor* there may be a real *peculium* belonging to the owner. In such case questions may arise as to rights and liabilities as between himself and his owner. As there can be no question of the two *causae*, it seems that every bilateral contract between the slave and the *possessor*, will give the owner a direct right of action on the contract against the *possessor*, and the possessor an *actio de peculio* against the owner[2].

The law as to acquisitions is simple and is fully stated. The *possessor* can acquire nothing[3], whether he is a thief, one who holds *vi clam aut precario*, or one whose possession began in good faith so that he is usucapting[4]. In like manner an heir who knows the man is *alienus* can usucapt him, but cannot acquire through him[5]. Acquisitions therefore go to the *dominus*, and on his claiming the slave all must be restored to him. Three remarks are necessary to complete this statement.

(*a*) Though a wife or husband, who has received a gift of a slave from the other, is so far in the position of a *malae fidei possessor*, that she (or he) can acquire nothing and must restore everything obtained through the slave, legacies, *hereditates, partus, etc.*[6], there is one relaxation. If a thing acquired by the slave is bought with money of the donee, he can claim to be allowed the price[7]. It seems that a *malae fidei possessor* cannot.

(*b*) Things indirectly acquired through the slave must be restored. Thus where a *malae fidei possessor* has let out the slave's *operae*, he acquires on his own contract, but is bound to pay the proceeds to the *dominus*: if the slave makes the contract, the money never vests in the *possessor*[8].

(*c*) There are some cases in which the *dominus* cannot acquire, and in that case no one does. Thus he cannot acquire possession through the slave[9], and a contract, *nominatim furi*, cannot be acquired to the *dominus* and so is simply void[10].

---

[1] There can hardly be *de in rem verso*: delivery to the slave vests the thing in *dominus*, and its application to a purpose of the holder's still leaves the owner a *vindicatio* or a *condictio*, according to circumstances.

[2] There must be limitations. If it is wholly *ex re possessoris* (*e.g. possessor* sells to slave a thing for his apparent *peculium*), the *dominus* must at least have had an *exceptio doli*.

[3] C. 3. 32. 1. 1. See Pernice, Labeo, 2. 1. 376, as to the possibility of a different view as to possession among the earlier lawyers.

[4] 41. 1. 22, 23. 1; 45. 3. 14.

[5] 41. 1. 40. The fact that in general the liability of *m. f. possessor* in *vindicatio* is greater than that of *b. f. possessor* has nothing specially to do with slaves. See *ante*, pp. 12 *sqq.*

[6] 24. 1. 28. 5.   [7] 24. 1. 19. 1.   [8] 12. 6. 55.   [9] 41. 2. 1. 6.

[10] 45. 3. 14. No doubt a stipulation by the slave for a servitude to attach to a *praedium* of the *possessor* would be equally void, 8. 1. 11; 45. 1. 140. 2, *etc.*

XXIV. *SERVUS FRUCTUARIUS*[1].

The prominence of Usufruct in Roman settlements of property makes this an important subject. No doubt the rules originated in relation to usufructs created by will: it is clear that this was always the normal case. The early history and development of the institution do not concern us: it is probable, as Kuntze says[2], that the principles of the matter were only settled by the classical lawyers: indeed this is probably true of nearly every institution, with elaborate rules, known to the classical law. It is unlikely that usufruct in individual slaves was a common case; most usually it would arise in connexion with usufruct of a *fundus instructus*, or of the whole content of an inheritance[3]. But though usually so created it might be set up *inter vivos*, and, at least in the developed law, its mode of origin was so far as we are concerned immaterial, the rights and liabilities of the fructuary being the same in both cases[4].

The usufructuary is not owner, and thus a legacy of "my slaves" does not cover those in which I have a usufruct, and does cover those in which I have granted a usufruct to someone else[5]. The rules under the *Scc.* Silanianum and Claudianum as to the torture of slaves whose master has been killed do not apply to the case of one living on an estate, of which, with its slaves, the deceased had the usufruct[6]. The danger must have been equally great, but the senatusconsult speaks of *domini*[7], and fructuary is not *dominus*. It is of course the interest of the *extraneus dominus* which compels this literal construction—not any feeling of hesitation in construing widely a penal provision. For the slaves of a son not *in potestate* could be tortured if under the roof of the murdered man[8]. Most of the rules affecting the *servus fructuarius* regarded as a chattel are familiar and obvious. A legacy in the terms "I wish my slave S to serve Titius" is, as a matter of construction, a legacy of the usufruct to Titius[9]. A usufruct may be validly created in a slave conditionally freed[10], or in mad, infirm or infant slaves[11]: their defects will be material in estimating the value of the gift for the purpose of the *lex* Falcidia, but not otherwise. We get little information as to the mode of reckoning of the value of usufruct of a slave. No doubt the cost of maintenance must be deducted

---

1 Salkowski, Sklavenerwerb; Kuntze, Servus Fructuarius.
2 *op. cit.* 12, 13.   3 7. 5. 1, 3.
4 7. 1. 25. 7. See Salkowski, *op. cit.* 138.   5 32. 73, 74.
6 29. 5. 1. 2.   *Ante*, p. 95.   7 29. 5. 1. *passim.*
8 29. 5. 1. 14.   So far as this text refers to *peculium castrense* it seems classical, but the words referring to a son not in *potestas* may be interpolated. If a husband or wife be killed the slaves of each may be tortured, but this seems to be an express provision, *h. t.* 1. 15.
9 33. 2. 24. 1.   10 33. 2. 20.   11 P. 3. 6. 18.

from the annual value of his *fructus, etc.*[1], but as the usufruct ends with the life of either party, and might end, in classical law, in some cases, by the death of a son or slave through whom it had been acquired, there is evidently a complex actuarial question turning on the multiple expectation, which the Romans give no sign of having faced[2]. An owner cannot of course be fructuary also, and thus if the fructuary becomes owner the usufruct ceases. We are told that if the owner of a slave make the fructuary his heir and leave the slave to another person, the slave is wholly due to the legatee, the usufruct being ended by *confusio*[3]. This *confusio* is rather remarkable, as the slave never belonged to the *heres*[4], who, in analogous cases, is treated as never having been owner[5]. It may be that our text really lays down a mere rule of construction, a view more or less strengthened by the fact that the text goes on to say that this would be avoided by a legacy of the usufruct to the *heres*[3]. But it is more likely, notwithstanding that the text in its present form gives the legatee a *vindicatio*, that Marcellus is considering a legacy *per damnationem*, which leaves ownership in the *heres*.

But though an owner cannot be usufructuary, one of common owners may be, *i.e.* in that part of which he is not owner. In such a case he must give the ordinary securities of a fructuary, since his rights in that capacity could not come into discussion in *communi dividundo*[6]. Of course a usufructuary cannot become owner by *usucapio*, not because he has not the necessary *animus*, for he might have it, but because he has not possession but only quasi-possession[7]. But here a curious question arises. T is in process of usucapting a slave who belongs to X. X dies leaving a usufruct of all his property to T, and making Y his *heres*. At the death of T, when all the facts are known, Y claims the slave on the ground that *usucapio* could not have continued after T had become usufructuary of the slave. The result is nowhere stated. It seems clear however that if T accepted the usufruct, knowing that the slave was included, he at once ceased to possess. So much may be inferred from the texts dealing with *conductio* by one in course of usucapting[8], and one of them is so general[9] as to suggest that whether T knew or not that the slave was included his possession would cease[10].

Usufruct, though usually for life, is not always so. It may be

---

[1] 7. 7. 4.   [2] Roby, de Usuf., 188.
[3] 31. 26.   [4] 31. 80.
[5] Thus he has a noxal action if a slave *pure legatus* steals from him before the legacy is accepted, 47. 2. 65.
[6] 7. 9. 10.   [7] G. 2. 92; In. 2. 9. 4.
[8] 41. 2. 19, 28.   [9] 41. 2. 19.
[10] It seems a case for the principle: *plus est in re quam in existimatione*, rather than for its opposite, 29. 2. 15; 40. 2. 4. 1.

for a fixed time: in the case of a slave, it may be till manumission[1], and there is no difficulty in creating a usufruct of a *statuliber*[2]. The usufructuary has a right to the services of the slave, and may hire them out. They are indeed the normal *fructus* of the man[3]. The fructuary can compel the man to work, can teach him an industry, and can employ him in it[4]. But he must not set him to inappropriate services, such as may lessen his fitness for the work for which he has been trained[5], a rule laid down in the interest of the owner. Similarly he must not put him to dangerous work, in particular he must not make him fight as a gladiator, though if the slave do so fight, the reward goes to the fructuary[6]. He may not torture the slave or beat him in such a way as to lessen his value, though he may correct him by reasonable castigation[7]. If he torture the slave, he is liable to the *actiones* Aquilia, *servi corrupti* and *iniuriarum*[8]. In the same way the owner may not so punish the slave as to make him worth less to the fructuary, though, subject to this, he has *plenissima coercitio* so long as there is no *dolus*[9]. Neither has *actio iniuriarum* against the other for mere castigation of the slave, though *dominus* may have the action against the fructuary, and the converse is apparently true[10]. In general an insult to the slave is regarded as against the owner unless it is plainly *in contumeliam fructuarii*[11]. If the slave be stolen, both have *actio furti*, based on their *interesse*[12]: the owner may have it against the fructuary and *vice versa*[13]. In the same way each may be liable to the other for *servi corruptio*, the fructuary's action being *utilis*[14]. The same rules apply under the *lex* Aquilia[15].

Though there had been doubts, it was early settled that fructuary did not acquire *partus ancillarum*. He had not even a usufruct in them, though of course special agreements could be made[16].

The usufructuary has noxal actions for *furtum, servi corruptio* and *iniuria*, and presumably by an *actio utilis* for *damnum*[17]. Surrender frees the *dominus* and ends the usufruct by *confusio*[18]. The *dominus*

---

[1] 7. 4. 15.   No doubt acceptance of such a usufruct avoided question as to assent to the manumission. *Post*, Ch. xxv.
[2] 33. 2. 20.   If a usufruct was created as the result of an ordinary sale, there would be a remedy for eviction if the man proved to be a *statuliber, ante*, p. 50.
[3] 7. 7. 3.   The wage received by the master who hires him out is not an acquisition *ex operis, ante*, p. 342.
[4] 7. 1. 23. 1, 27. 2.
[5] 7. 1. 15. 1, 2; *e.g.* set a *librarius* to work as a mason, a musician as porter, *etc.* V. Fr. 72.
[6] V. Fr. 72 as read by Huschke.   See however Mommsen, *ad h. l.*   The rule is not in the Digest, such fights being obsolete. *Post*, p. 405.
[7] 7. 1. 23. 1; P. 3. 6. 23.   [8] 7. 1. 66.   [9] 7. 1. 17. 1.
[10] 47. 10. 15. 37, 38.   [11] 47. 10. 15. 45—48; In. 4. 4. 5.
[12] 41. 3. 35; 47. 2. 46. 1.   [13] 47. 2. 15. 1, 46. 6.   [14] 7. 1. 66; 11. 3. 9. 1.
[15] 7. 1. 17. 3, 66; 9. 2. 11. 10, 12.   It has been suggested that if the slave is killed the usufructuary receives the whole value, having a quasi usufruct in it.   Grüber, Lex Aquilia, 45.
[16] G. 2. 50; P. 3. 6. 19; In. 2. 1. 37; 2. 6. 5; D. 7. 1. 68. *pr.*; 22. 1. 28. 1, *ante*, p. 21.
[17] 9. 4. 18; 11. 3. 14. 3; 47. 2. 43. 12; 47. 10. 17. 9.
[18] 7. 4. 27; 9. 4. 18.

being noxally liable to third persons may surrender to them without incurring any liability to the fructuary[1]. On the other hand, the fructuary is in strictness not liable for the slave's delict. This however means little, since as we have seen he can be indirectly compelled to pay or surrender the man[2]. It is remarkable that no text deals with the case of *damnum*. On principle it would seem that notwithstanding the special rules affecting noxal actions for this delict[3], it was on this matter on the same footing as the others: the *dominus* being liable, by *actio utilis*, to the fructuary, and the latter having the indirect liability already mentioned[4].

As to contractual liability the rules are in general simple. The fructuary is liable to the *actio quod iussu*, to the *actio tributoria*, and generally in the edictal actions, on matters through which he acquires to the slave—in others the *dominus* alone is liable[5]. But in *de peculio* he is liable on all contracts, since the other party relies on the whole of the *peculium*[6]. It is remarked by Salkowski[7] that any other rule would be unfair to the creditor since it might be impossible, and would often be difficult for him to say to whom the right was acquired. But, as he shews, other views are represented: they have been discussed in connexion with the parallel case of *bona fide serviens*[8]. The rule of later law seems to have been, so far as an obscure text of Julian can be made out[9], that the creditor is not bound to sue either party first on contracts specially affecting him, but that if the *dominus* is sued first on a contract affecting the fructuary, he may deduct what could be recovered from the *peculium* of the fructuary[10], so that the ultimate adjustment will be exactly as if the fructuary had been sued first. The rule is on the face of it anomalous, since the liability of *dominus* is unlimited: the reason of it may be that otherwise there would be no means of adjustment, since there is no *iudicium communi dividundo* or the like between them[11], and the obligations of a usufructuary do not clearly cover any reimbursement in such a case. If the case be reversed, and the usufructuary be sued first on a contract not affecting him, the same rule ought to apply, and with more logical justification, but the point is not raised in the texts. If there are two usufructuaries,

---

[1] 42. 1. 4. 8.
[2] 7. 1. 17. 2; 9. 4. 17. 1, 27. *pr.* See *ante*, p. 116 *sq.*   [3] *Ante*, p. 130.
[4] See 9. 4. 19. 1.   Kuntze thinks (*op. cit.* 41) that this text deals with *furtum* and gives fructuary a noxal action against *dominus*. That rule is clear, but this text deals with *damnum*: it is one of a group all from the same book, dealing with *damnum*. The words "*verba efficiunt,*" etc., which are meaningless as to *furtum*, are intelligible under the *lex* Aquilia. It has nothing to do with owner's liability to fructuary. It merely says that the existence of usufruct does not bar owner's liability *ex* Aquilia, where he has hired the slave. For whatever question might arise as to *potestas*, this does not affect *damnum*. *Ante*, p. 130.
[5] 14. 4. 1. 5, 2; 15. 1. 2; 15. 4. 1. 8.   [6] 15. 1. 19. 1.   See Erman, Z. S. S. 20. 247.
[7] *op. cit.* 204.
[8] *Ante*, p. 339.   Salkowski (*loc. cit.*) credits the wider view to Julian.   Chief texts, 15. 1. 2, 13, 19. 1, 37. 3, 50. 3.
[9] 15. 1. 37. 3.   [10] Salkowski, *op. cit.* 229.   [11] Cp. 10. 3. 8. 4.

and one has been sued, the plaintiff may proceed against the other or others till satisfaction[1]. Nothing is said here as to deduction of what is in the *peculium* of the fructuary really concerned, as there is *communi dividundo* between fructuaries[2].

It may be added that the liability *de peculio* lasted as in other cases for one year from the expiration of the interest[3].

Usufruct of a slave, as of anything else, may be lost by non-use, and there is a rather puzzling text[4] in which the question is raised whether if the slave runs away, this involves non-use, so that by lapse of *constitutum tempus* the usufruct will be lost[5]. Clearly mere adverse possession of the subject of the usufruct does not end it: the fructuary's right is independent and does not depend on possession[6]. Ulpian reports Pomponius[5] as thinking that if the slave transacts business *ex re mea*, this is enough to prevent time from running against me, the usufructuary. He adds that the mere fact that no effective use is made of him is immaterial, since no such use is made of sick or infant slaves, and yet our usufruct in them is unaffected. He cites Julian as holding that so long as the man is not possessed by a third person, the fructuary's right is in no way affected: his quasi-possession continues as does possession by an owner in the like case.

The argument as a whole is not very satisfactory. The analogy between these and infant and sick slaves is worthless: of them all the use is being made of which they are capable, which is not the case with the fugitive. It may further be questioned whether the exceptional rule that a *fugitivus* is still possessed should be extended by analogy[7], but if that step is taken, the further step is natural, *i.e.* to regard the continued quasi-possession as amounting to *uti*, since in technical language possession is often treated as equivalent to use[8]. And *uti* without *frui* is enough to preserve usufruct[9]. The analogy with loss of ownership by lapse of time is halting, since ownership is ended by adverse enjoyment, while mere non-enjoyment ends usufruct[10], with no requirement of adverse possession. Justinian in one text seems to lay down a rule that usufruct is to be barred only by such facts as would bar *vindicatio*, but another later text of his shews that he still regarded it as lost by non-use[11]. But all this affects Julian's analogy rather than any rule laid down. His curious parallel of usufruct[12] (instead of quasi-possession) with possession, which Salkowski thinks[13] to indicate a hazy view of the matter, seems rather to be due to the fact that there is no

---

[1] 15. 1. 32. *pr.* See App. II.   [2] 10. 3. 7. 7.   [3] 15. 2. 1. 9.
[4] Salkowski, *op. cit.* 152, 3; Kuntze, *op. cit.* 59.
[5] V. Fr. 89 = D. 7. 1. 12. 3, 4.   [6] 7. 6. 5. 1; 41. 2. 52. *pr.*
[7] Cp. 50. 17. 141. *pr.*   [8] Acquisition by long possession is called *usucapio.*
[9] 7. 4. 20; 50. 16. 115.   [10] 7. 1. 38.
[11] C. 3. 33. 16. 1; C. 3. 34. 13; Accarias, Précis, § 279.
[12] V. Fr. 89 *in fin.*   [13] *loc. cit.*

substantive to express "quasi-possession": his meaning is clear, that just as possession is not interrupted, so time is not running against the fructuary because his quasi-possession (*uti*) remains. In the next text, as it appears in the Digest[1] (but it is not in the Vatican Fragments), Julian (or Pomponius) considers the case of a slave who has passed into the possession of a third person. Quasi-possession has ceased, so that this form of *uti* has ceased. Time begins to run against the fructuary. But if the slave contracts *ex re fructuarii*, this is use, and keeps the usufruct alive, the acquisition being to the fructuary. There seems no objection to this view or any contradiction of what the jurist has already said[2].

Such infant slaves as are mentioned above can hardly be lost by non-use, other than adverse possession[3]. There is no profit in them, and till they are of such an age as to be able to work, they are regarded as valueless[4].

Before entering on the subject of acquisition it may be remarked that slaves held in usufruct have the same power of alienation as other slaves: they cannot, for instance, even with *administratio*, alienate by way of *donatio*[5].

In relation to acquisition through *servi fructuarii*, which is the most important topic, most of the questions of principle have been dealt with by anticipation in connexion with *bona fide serviens*. The general principles being the same in the two cases it is not necessary to repeat the discussions, and the rules, so far as they are identical, will therefore be dealt with mainly by way of reference. The general rule is that the fructuary acquires *ex re* and *ex operis servi*: all else goes to the *dominus*[6], the fructuary having no interest in it[7]. A few remarks are needed on cases of special interest.

(*a*) Inheritance and legacy. We have seen that after some doubts it was settled that *bonae fidei possessor* could not acquire such things through the slave. The same principle was generally held in case of *servus fructuarius*[8]. Most of the doubters speak only of *bonae fidei possessor*, but Labeo[9] thinks that usufructuary would acquire if testator intended to benefit him. Salkowski thinks[10] this must be accepted as

---

[1] 7. 1. 12. 4.
[2] Salkowski, *op. cit.* 153, seems to hold that one who says that quasi-possession is use cannot hold that there can be use without it, but this hardly follows. It may well be that from Tribonian's point of view a mere stipulation, *nomine fructuarii*, kept the usufruct alive, whether it was acquired to the fructuary or not. These texts do not say that the fructuary is acquiring *ex operis*.
[3] V. Fr. 89; 7. 1. 12. 3.   [4] 7. 1. 55, 68. *pr.*; 7. 7. 6. 1.   [5] 24. 1. 3. 8.
[6] G. 2. 86, 90, 92; 3. 165; Ulp. 19. 21; P. 5. 7. 3; V. Fr. 71 b; In. 2. 9. 4; 3. 28. 2; D. 2. 14. 59; 7. 1. 21; 41. 1. 10. *pr.*, 3, 37. 2; 45. 3. 27.
[7] 41. 1. 37. 2.   [8] 29. 2. 45. 3; *ante*, p. 342.
[9] 7. 1. 21. He puts legacy in the same position.   [10] *op. cit.* 174.

the law of Justinian's time, as the texts shew that they have been handled by the compilers. But this seems very doubtful in view of the large number of texts which contradict it[1]. It is more reasonable to suppose that the compilers fell here into a plausible error, than to read limitations into all the other texts.

(b) *Donatio*[2]. Here it is perfectly clear that in the later law the fructuary would acquire if the intent of the donor was to benefit him[3]. Releases to the slave for the fructuary are valid as being *ex re*[4]. Gifts by fructuary to the slave are dealt with as in the case of the *bonae fidei possessor*[5]. We are told by Paul, however, that, if the intent was to benefit the *dominus*, the gift may take effect in his favour. This is no doubt a late development and may be an interpolation[6].

(c) Possession[7]. Possession can be acquired, within the two *causae*, for the *fructuarius*[8], and through this possession *usucapio* may operate, subject to the ordinary rules as to knowledge of the principal in matters not within the *peculium*[9]. In relation to *usucapio* there seems no reason to distinguish, as Kuntze seems inclined to do[10], between *servus fructuarius* and *bona fide serviens*. There had been some doubt, mentioned by Gaius and rejected by Paul[11] (who refers to the analogous case of the *filiusfamilias*), as to whether there could be possession through such slaves, since they were not possessed. Papinian gives, as a reason for allowing it: *cum et naturaliter a fructuario teneatur et plurimum ex iure possessio mutuetur*[12]. Kuntze[13] remarks that the reason is not a good one since detention is not possession, and doubts whether these words be Papinian's. But though possession of the man is unnecessary to the acquisition of possession through him, the fact that he is not possessed is not without importance. We have seen[14] that if the *serviens* does not acquire possession for his *bonae fidei* holder, he does not acquire it at all, for the owner cannot acquire possession through one who is in fact possessed by another. This difficulty does not arise in the case of a *servus fructuarius:*

(d) Contract. Any contract which the slave can make at all he can make, within the *causae*, for the fructuary. Here, as in the case of the *bona fide serviens*, we get the rule that what he cannot acquire to the fructuary the slave acquires to the owner, even within the *causae*[15]. The rule is illustrated by the case of a *servus fructuarius* who stipulates for the usufruct in himself. This is a *res sua* so far as the fructuary is

---

[1] *e.g.* 29. 2. 45. 3 (Julian); *h. t.* 25. *pr.* (Ulpian); 41. 1. 47 (Paul); 41. 1. 10. 3 (Gaius); G. 2. 92; In. 2. 9. 4.   None of these texts speaks of intent.
[2] *Ante*, p. 343.   [3] 7. 1. 22, 24, 25. *pr.*; 41. 1. 49.
[4] *Ante*, p. 343; 7. 1. 23. *pr.*; 46. 3. 63; 46. 4. 11. *pr.*; V. Fr. 72.
[5] *Ante*, p. 343; 7. 1. 31; 7. 8. 16. 2.   [6] 41. 1. 49.
[7] *Ante*, p. 347; Salkowski, *op. cit.* 164 *sqq.*   [8] 7. 1. 21; 41. 2. 1. 8, 49. *pr.*; G. 2. 94.
[9] 41. 4. 7. 8; G. 2. 94.   [10] *op. cit.* 34.   [11] 41. 2. 1. 8; In. 2. 9. 4; G. 2. 94.
[12] 41. 2. 49. *pr.*   [13] *op. cit.* 34.   [14] *Ante*, p. 347.
[15] *Ante*, p. 347; D. 7. 1. 25. 3.

concerned and thus cannot be acquired to him : it goes therefore to the owner[1]. The doubt in the case of the *liber homo bona fide serviens* cannot arise here.

The rules as to the effect of *iussum* and *nominatio* are the same as in the case of *bona fide serviens*[2]. If the stipulation is *nominatim domino* or *iussu domini*, even *ex operis* or *ex re fructuarii*, it is the owner who acquires[3]. If, on the other hand, he stipulates *nominatim fructuario*, not within the *causae*, the agreement is null[4] : the *dominus* cannot acquire in contradiction of its terms. If it is at the *iussum* of the fructuary, the *dominus* can acquire[5]. The same principle is illustrated by the rule that if the stipulation is *domino aut fructuario*, not within the *causae*, the agreement is valid : all is acquired to the *dominus*, though payment may be made to the fructuary, who is regarded as *solutionis causa adiectus*[6]. On the other hand if he stipulates *domino aut fructuario, ex re fructuarii*, the agreement is void for uncertainty, since he can acquire in such a way for either, and we cannot say which has acquired and which is *solutionis causa adiectus*[7].

Many of a slave's transactions would relate to his *peculium*, and in the present case he may have two *peculia*. A transaction will be *ex re domini* or *ex re fructuarii* according to the *peculium* to which it belongs. Thus in bilateral transactions it may happen that till payment is made it may be impossible to say to whom the thing is acquired. Under this head three cases may be discussed[8].

(i) The slave, about to lend money, stipulates for its return from the intending borrower. Here, till the money is lent, any action by either can be met by *exceptio doli*. When it is lent the payment declares for whom the stipulation was acquired *ab initio*[9]. No doubt, as Salkowski says[10], it will be for fructuary to prove that it was *ex re eius*, the *dominus* being able to recover unless the borrower proves that it was *ex re fructuarii*. In another case the stipulation was for "whatever money I shall lend you[11]." The case seems exactly the same, though Salkowski holds[12] that here there is no obligation till the money is lent, and that it is in no way retrospective. But if the money is lent, and the stipulation is sued on, it must be that stipulation, and it must have

---

[1] 7. 1. 25. 4. Salkowski, *op. cit.* 193, accepts the view of the Gloss that the *stipulatio* is made with the fructuary himself.
[2] *Ante*, p. 349.
[3] 7. 1. 25. 3, 4; 41. 1. 37. 5; 45. 3. 22, 23, 39. The expression *ex re* is used inclusively : the slave's *operae* are *res fructuarii*.
[4] 45. 3. 22, 23, 31; 7. 1. 25. 3.
[5] 45. 3. 31. As to *condictio* for adjustment (45. 3. 39) see *ante*, p. 350.
[6] 45. 3. 1. 5, 28. *pr.*; 46. 3. 98. 7. Cp. In. 3. 19. 4.
[7] 45. 3. 1. 5; 46. 3. 98. 7.
[8] For full discussion see Salkowski, *op. cit.* 197—220, from which much of what follows is drawn.
[9] 7. 1. 25. 1.   [10] *op. cit.* 202.   [11] 45. 3. 18. 3.   [12] *loc. cit.*

been acquired when it was made. Fitting's view[1] that it is conditional and retrospective seems preferable.

(ii) The slave buys, and takes delivery with a credit term, so that ownership passes though the price is not yet paid. The ownership is in suspense till the price is paid. There are three distinct points :

(*a*) The rights of the parties during the suspense[2]. Neither fructuary or *dominus* can redhibit, for this would be to abandon rights which may not be his[3]. There can be no *actio ex empto*[4]. There can hardly be an *actio* Publiciana, since, the price not being paid, the slave knows that ownership has not passed, and it is his knowledge which is decisive[5]. There can be no *condictio furtiva*[6]. There is no *actio* Aquilia[7], at any rate unless there is some mistake of fact as to whether the price has or has not been paid[8]. On the other hand, on the principles already laid down the vendor can bring an *actio ex vendito de peculio* against either[9], and *condemnatio*, if for the full price, will end the suspense. Salkowski thinks it will end it in any case if there is no *peculium, apud alterum*[10]. But if the owner has paid half *de peculio*, and the fructuary then pays the other half, they will own *pro rata*[11].

(*b*) Termination of the suspense by payment. The thing vests in the owner of the money[12]. Only one text deals with this matter in detail[13]. If it is paid out of the *peculium* of one no question arises. If it is paid out of both, Ulpian reports Julian as holding, reasonably, that they acquire *pro rata*. Ulpian then goes on to consider other possibilities. If the slave pays the whole price out of each *peculium* the thing belongs to him out of whose *peculium* it was first paid for, the other being entitled to vindicate the coins since the slave has no power of gratuitous alienation. If it was all paid together, Ulpian holds that there is no alienation at all, and no payment[14]. All the money is vindicable.

(*c*) Effect of termination of the usufruct before the price is paid. Here, if the usufruct ends before the thing is handed over, the jurists are

---

[1] Cited by Salkowski, *op. cit.* 199.   [2] Salkowski, *op. cit.* 200 *sqq*.
[3] 21. 1. 43. 10.   [4] 19. 1. 24. *pr.*
[5] Salkowski, *loc. cit.* There is the possibility of mistake as to whether the money was paid or not.
[6] 7. 1. 12. 5.   [7] Salkowski, *op. cit.* 202.
[8] No text deals with *furti* or *servi corrupti*. A buyer who has not paid is liable for *culpa levis*, and therefore may have *actio furti*. *Servi corrupti* is specially for the owner (*ante*, p. 33): he has not this action, but can no doubt claim cession of actions.
[9] *Ante*, p. 359.   [10] *loc. cit.*
[11] Salkowski considers further complications where vendor delivers the thing not to slave but to owner or fructuary before or after payment.
[12] 19. 1. 24. *pr.*; 41. 1. 43. 2.   [13] 7. 1. 25. 1.
[14] It is not obvious why the thing did not become common, each being entitled to claim half his money back. Salkowski observes that Ulpian treats the coins as *corpora certa* and not as a quantity, contrary to Papinian and Pomponius (46. 3. 94. 1; 12. 6. 19. 2), and refers to Julian (45. 1. 54) and Ulpian himself (12. 1. 13. 2; 46. 3. 29). The result in the text would follow if he bought "*domino aut fructuario*," since here he can acquire only to one, and it is impossible on the facts to say which one. See *ante*, p. 363, and *post*, App. III.

agreed that payment by the fructuary cannot make the thing vest in him. He is now a mere third person, and cannot, by paying the price, acquire an *actio ex empto* on the slave's contract[1], and no delivery to the slave can make the thing vest in him. He ceases to be liable to the *actio de peculio* even *utilis* and *annalis*[2], not merely because the usufruct is ended, since liability *de peculio* is not bound up with acquisition, but because the vendor has not completed the requirements for an *actio ex vendito* before the fructuary's connexion with the slave ceased. If now the fructuary pays the price, after the usufruct is ended by *capitis deminutio*, Julian says[3] that he can have no *actio ex empto*, but has *condictio indebiti* against the vendor. There is the difficulty that the error must be one of law. But though it is generally held that the *condictio indebiti* would not lie on error of this kind, the opinion is not very securely based: this is not the only text which gives it on error of law[4].

If the thing has been handed over before the usufruct ends, and payment is made after its close, the view of Marcellus and Mauricianus is that no such payment can vest the thing in the fructuary. But Julian lays it down and Ulpian accepts it as the equitable view, that payment even then will determine the thing to the fructuary[5]. As Salkowski says[6], this equitableness seems to rest on the ground that the rule gives him rights correlative to his liability *de peculio*, which would logically require him to make the payment within one year, since his liability *de peculio* lasts no longer. But the texts give us no further assistance. Salkowski goes on to remark that the rule of pendency seems to have been settled by Julian. He infers an original doctrine, that the delivery vested the thing in the *dominus*, with a liability to divest on payment by the fructuary, and compares the case with that of *legatum per vindicationem*, according to the Sabinians[7].

It should be observed that this pendency is not a necessary accompaniment of a sale on credit to such a slave. Payment is only one way of determining with whose affairs the thing is connected, decisive only in absence of other evidence. If, for instance, the slave was managing a shop for the fructuary, and bought on credit stock-in-trade which was delivered to that shop, there can be no doubt that this is *in re fructuarii*, and payment by the owner will not affect the matter[8].

(iii) The slave lets out his *operae* for a term at so much a week or for a lump sum: during the term the fructuary dies. Here all the texts

---

[1] 19. 1. 24. *pr.*   [2] Salkowski, *op. cit.* p. 212; G. 3. 84; D. 4. 5. 2. 1.
[3] 19. 1. 24. *pr.*
[4] See also 36. 4. 1. *pr.*; 22. 6. 7, cited by Girard, Manuel, 617. Another difficulty, that of regarding the action as vesting in him personally after adrogation, is not great. See 7. 4. 2. 1, 3. 1.
[5] 7. 1. 25. 1.   [6] *op. cit.* 211.   [7] 30. 38. 1; G. 2. 185.
[8] For similar cases and resulting remedies, see Salkowski, *op. cit.* 203.

agree as to the law. The fructuary is entitled to the hire for the time for which the usufruct lasted, and the owner to the rest[1]. Salkowski thinks[2] that if it was for a lump sum the usufructuary acquires the whole, and *dominus* must condict his share. The text he cites[3] does indeed refer only to *annos singulos*, but it does not exclude the other case. Paul definitely includes it[4]. Nor is there any reason for the distinction: as Salkowski remarks, whether the payment is *in annos singulos* or not, it is equally one stipulation. But the jurists disagree as to the basis of the rule. Ulpian says[5] that for the years during which the usufruct lasts, the fructuary acquires, but for the later years *transit ad proprietarium stipulatio semel adquisita fructuario*. His language is confused, but he seems to mean that the whole is in the fructuary (it is indeed one stipulation), and part is divested. He remarks that this is unusual, since the owner is not a universal successor. He adds that there will be a repeated transition if the usufruct is lost by *capitis deminutio* and restored by virtue of *repetitio*. This is to state the rule, not to explain it. Kuntze[6] thinks it involves the notion that the obligation is really rooted in the slave, and passes with him. But as Salkowski observes[7] the language gives no hint of this, and one would expect so remarkable a principle to be mentioned, and the same result ought to arise in all cases of transfer of a slave who had made such a contract.

Papinian[8], quoting the rule from Julian, takes a different view. He treats it as a case of suspense. At the beginning of each year it is acquired to the fructuary for that year if the usufruct is still on foot. When this expires it is definitively acquired to the owner. Papinian's language is applicable only to the case of agreement for yearly payments, but the reasoning is equally applicable to the other case: it is as easy to divide a mass *pro rata* as a number of sums. This view differs in practical result: if the whole were regarded as vesting, as Ulpian holds, in the fructuary, it would be possible for him to destroy the owner's right by giving a release[9]. In other respects also Papinian's explanation is to be preferred. There is nothing exceptional in regarding a slave's stipulation as conferring independent rights on two people: this is the ordinary rule in contracts by a common slave[10]. And it is only in so far as the *operae* are within the usufruct that the fructuary acquires a promise in respect of them. If a slave stipulated for so much a year for *operae* during the usufruct, and then stipulated for the same rate afterwards the first would be acquired to the fructuary, the second to the *dominus*. Here the same result is attained by treating the one

---

[1] 7. 1. 25. 2, 26; 45. 3. 18. 3.   [2] *op. cit.* 217.   [3] 7. 1. 25. 2.
[4] *h. t.* 26.   [5] *h. t.* 25. 2.   [6] *op. cit.* 67.
[7] *loc. cit.*   [8] 45. 3. 18. 3.   [9] Salkowski, *loc. cit.*
[10] *Post*, p. 379.

stipulation as divided. This does not meet Ulpian's language, but that is very confused, and as Papinian shews[1] that the rule was Julian's and was not explained by him, it does not appear too much to regard Ulpian's words as an erroneous explanation by him or the compilers.

The case of transactions between the slave and his holder has already been considered in connexion with the *bona fide serviens*[2]. The same principles apply here. So far as they are *ex causis* they can only affect the *peculium*. This is expressed in several texts which mention letting of his *operae* to the slave, stipulation by the slave *ex re*, promise to the fructuary *ex re*, and hiring a thing from fructuary[3]. In such things fructuary is treated as *dominus*[4], and a general rule is laid down that a contract, which if made with a third person is acquired to fructuary, is legally null if made with him[5]. One case looks exceptional. If the slave stipulates for the usufruct in himself, he acquires this to the *dominus*[6]. The Gloss regards this as made with the fructuary, and Salkowski[7] explains the rule on the ground that as what is stipulated is a right which can be created only by *cessio in iure*, it would be null if the stipulation had been *sibi dari*, so that to make it valid it must be construed as if it had been *nominatim domino*. This artificial view is open to objections. It contradicts the general rule just cited[8], which says that all such things are void *nisi nominatim domino*. To say that because it would be invalid in any other form it is to be construed as if it were *nominatim domino* is to reduce these words to an absurdity, and they are stated in the adjoining paragraph[9]. If the view is sound the same rule must apply to a stipulation for a usufruct in any subject-matter of the usufruct. Indeed the restriction to usufruct is misleading, for the same rule must apply to any stipulation for a right, since it must be bad if the slave stipulated *sibi*[10]. But in fact there is no reason to treat the stipulation in our text as made with the fructuary: on the contrary, the case is paralleled with another in which it is clear that the stipulation was with a third person[11]. It is thus covered by the rule that what cannot be acquired by the fructuary goes to the *dominus*, even within the *causae*[12].

If the slave's contract with the fructuary be *iussu domini*, or *nominatim domino*, or if it be *extra causas*, it is acquired to the *dominus*, and he has an action on it against the fructuary, while, if it is bilateral, the latter has an *actio de peculio* against him[13]. If the slave deals with *dominus*, the agreement is null if *extra causas*, even though in the name or at

---

[1] 45. 3. 18. 3.
[4] 45. 1. 118. *pr.*
[7] *op. cit.* 223.
[10] *Ante*, p. 156.
[13] 45. 1. 118. *pr.*; 7. 1. 25. 4.

[2] *Ante*, p. 350.
[5] 7. 1. 25. 5.
[8] 7. 1. 25. 5.
[11] 7. 1. 25. 4.

[3] 7. 1. 25. 5; 45. 1. 118. *pr.*
[6] *h. l.* 4.
[9] *h. l.* 4.
[12] *Ante*, p. 362.

command of the fructuary. If it be within the *causae* the fructuary acquires on a promise to the slave, and the owner has an *actio de peculio* against him on bilateral transactions. These propositions do not need further authority, but one text raises a difficulty. Ulpian says[1] that the fructuary has sometimes an *actio de peculio* against *dominus*, as, e.g., if the slave has a *peculium* with *dominus*, and none, or less than he owes the fructuary, with the latter. The same is true, he says, conversely, though between common owners *pro socio* or *communi dividundo* suffices. If the text refers to contracts within the *causae*, it breaks the rule that promises to the fructuary in such matters are null[2]. If it refers to matters not within the *causae*, the limitation that he cannot sue if there is the means of satisfaction within his own *peculium* conflicts with what is implied in the text last cited. Salkowski[3] assumes it to refer to the latter, and justifies it on the ground that he can in fact treat the debt as 'peculiar,' and so make it effective against creditors *de peculio*. This is hardly satisfactory. It is not absolutely certain that he can deduct such a debt, since in such a matter the slave is a *servus alienus*. The rule that there could be no deduction if there were other means of recovery[4], and the present rule that it can be recovered by action if there is no means of deduction are a vicious circle, but the first of these rules is not so well established as to justify us in laying stress on this point.

But even admitting the right to deduct we are little better off. There may be no 'peculiar' creditors, and it is unfair to make him pay himself out of his own money, when the *dominus* has benefited under the transaction. Suppose the slave hires a house from the fructuary, *nominatim domino*, and *dominus* has lived or stored property in it. It is absurd that the fructuary should be compelled to recoup himself at his own expense or at that of creditors. Even if there are creditors the unfairness may be the same, for if the *peculium* is solvent the right of deduction is worthless, and *dominus* gets the house for nothing. Only if the *peculium* is insolvent is anything like justice done, for the disappointed creditors can proceed against the *dominus* under his subsidiary liability[5]. Only if it is penniless, and there are other creditors to the amount of the debt of *dominus*, is full justice done. The texts cited by Salkowski in support are not convincing. A person who has *de peculio* against the owner of a slave buys the slave. He has *de peculio* still against the vendor for a year, but, says Ulpian, he can, *if he prefers*, deduct the amount from the *peculium* if he is sued *de peculio*[6]. Gaius and Paul and Julian say that he must allow for what

---

[1] 15. 1. 19. 2. [2] 45. 1. 118. *pr.* [3] *op. cit.* 228.
[4] *Ante*, p. 224.
[5] 15. 1. 13; *h. t.* 19. 1. In the first illustration there might be *de in rem verso*, not in the second.
[6] 15. 1. 11. 8.

he has *in peculio* if he sues the vendor[1]. But here there is a voluntary acquisition of the slave after the debt was contracted, which quite differentiates the case. And his right to deduct, which gives an air of similarity to the cases, is due to the fact that the slave is now his slave. In our case he is still *servus alienus* so far as *res extra causas* are concerned. It may be added that the text, in declaring the rule to apply both ways, ignores the fact that while the *dominus* can conceivably acquire on all contracts of the slave, the fructuary cannot on those *extra causas*. This rather suggests that the text is to apply to those within the *causae*, as to which either can theoretically acquire, and that Ulpian is limiting the general rule laid down by Papinian[2], that there can in no ·ase be *actio de peculio* against *dominus* on such a contract.

XXV. *SERVUS USUARIUS. OPERAE SERVI.*

The difference between *ususfructus* and *usus* is expressed in their names, but it is not easy to say exactly what is involved in use as opposed to *fructus*. In the case of land there was a gradual improvement in the rights of usuary, till it was settled that he was even entitled to some of the fruits[3]. The case of the slave shews the same tendency, as we shall see in the matter of acquisitions. Apart from acquisition the rules were much the same as in usufruct, and the texts say little of *usus*.

Usus is indivisible : the only result which the texts draw from this we shall deal with under *operae servi*[4]. The usuary is entitled to *opera* and *ministerium*, he may employ the slave for the purposes of his family, not merely personal to him, and in his business. He may take his whole time, but he may not hand him over to anyone else[5]. He has an *interesse* for *actio furti*[6]. He is never mentioned in connexion with noxal rights and liabilities, so that the rules are no doubt the same as in *ususfructus*. Subject to the fact that his field of acquisition is less, the rules in the *actiones honorariae* are as in usufruct[7]. He can acquire a release by *acceptilatio* in the same way[8].

As to acquisitions there is a marked difference. The usuary is entitled *uti* and not *frui*. Hence he can acquire *ex re* and not *ex operis*, acquisition *ex re* being a form of *uti*[9]. It is possible for the slave to have a *peculium* in relation to usuary, and acquisition in connexion with this is *ex re*[10]. We have seen that employing a slave in business is *uti*, not

---

[1] 15. 1. 27. 6, 47. 4.   [2] 45. 1. 118. *pr.*
[3] See Accarias, Précis, § 281.   [4] *Post*, p. 370.
[5] 7. 8. 12. 5, 6, 15. *pr.*; In. 2. 5. 3.   [6] 47. 2. 46. 3.   [7] 15. 1. 2.
[8] 46. 4. 11. *pr.* No doubt the rules as to his liabilities and rights in case of damage to the slave are the same, *ante*, p. 358.
[9] 7. 8. 14. *pr.*; 45. 3. 23.   [10] 7. 8. 16. 2.

frui[1]; hence he can be employed as *institor* and his contracts in that capacity will enure to the usuary[2]. The text adds that usuary can acquire *iussu*; this does not mean that every *traditio* at *iussum* of usuary will be acquired to him, but only that *iussum* is an indication, not necessarily conclusive, that the acquisition is *ex re usuarii*. But hire for services is the slave's typical *fructus*, and therefore the usuary cannot locate his services, or rather cannot definitively acquire what is paid for the hire[3]. But Gaius tells us that he may take money from the slave in lieu of services[4]. This evasion is somewhat doubtfully put and is attributed to Labeo. The resulting situation is not explained. It can hardly mean that he lets the slave work for other people, the proceeds going into the slave's *peculium*, belonging to the usuary. This would be allowing the slave to locate his services. The reward for such services would unquestionably belong to the *dominus*. It may be that he allows the slave, in return for a sum, paid *ex peculio*, to dispose of the produce, *e.g.* of a farm he is allowed to till, the proceeds forming part of the *peculium*. It may mean that the money comes from the *dominus*, *i.e.* from the *peculium* which belongs to him, so that usuary can now get nothing out of his service though he can still acquire *ex re*. His service then belongs to the *peculium* attaching to his *dominus*.

Operae servorum may be called a kind of *usus*[5]. They are indivisible. Thus a legacy of *operae servorum* must be given in full, and money allowed if necessary for the Falcidian deduction, while in usufruct, though the valuation, to arrive at the amount to be deducted, has to be made in the same way, yet, when it is made, the *heres* can retain the proper proportion of the thing itself[6]. The rights of personal enjoyment in this case are as in *usus*[7], but it differs in several ways:

(i) No text refers to it, except as created by legacy, and it is commonly held that it can arise in no other way.

(ii) The beneficiary can let the *operae* or allow the slave to do so[8].

(iii) It is not lost by *capitis deminutio*, or by non-use[9].

(iv) It is not lost by death of the beneficiary, but passes to the heir[10]. Apparently it is commonly for the life of the slave, but it may be only for a fixed time.

(v) It is lost, as usufruct and *usus* are not, if a third person usucapts the man[11].

---

[1] *Ante*, p. 342. [2] 7. 8. 20.
[3] In. 2. 5. 3; D. 7. 8. 12. 6, 14. *pr.* See Salkowski, *op. cit.* 118.
[4] 7. 8. 13. [5] 7. 7. 5.
[6] 35. 2. 1. 9. In estimating its value, cost of maintenance must be deducted and nothing allowed for service of incapables or *pretium affectionis*.
[7] 7. 7. 5. [8] 7. 7. 3; 33. 2. 2.
[9] 7. 7. 1; 33. 2. 2. [10] 33. 2. 2.
[11] 7. 1. 17. 2; 33. 2. 2.

(vi) We are told that *in actu consistit*, and so it does not exist at all, until *dies venit*—until it is actually due[1]. The practical meaning of this seems to be that it cannot be lost, *e.g.* by surrender before that time[2]. The idea has one other remarkable result. The legacy of *usus* or usufruct "cedes" only on *aditio*[3]. This postponement is partly due to the intransmissibility of the right, and partly to the fact that earlier "ceding" might increase the risk of loss by *capitis deminutio*. Neither of these affects the present case, and yet, here, *dies cedens* is postponed still further. Ulpian settles a doubt by saying that it cedes only when it is actually claimed[4]. It is clear that Ulpian has in mind a legacy for a certain time, and his rule means that the days do not begin to run till the *operae* are claimed[5]. If the slave is unwell, the person entitled can wait till he is well again, but as Ulpian says, if the man falls ill after the claim is set up, the days count as against the legatee.

It may be noted that a gift of *operae servi* is necessarily a specific gift of the slave or slaves, alone, while one of *usus* might be, and probably usually was, part of a wider gift, *e.g.* of *usus fundi instructi*. As a specific institution it is a late juristic development. For Terentius Clemens and Julian it is another word for *usus*[6]. Papinian, Paul and Ulpian are the only jurists who treat it as having distinct rules, and Paul shews[7] that its rules were doubtful in his time. What was happening was the assignment of a strict legal meaning to an untechnical word of the lay vocabulary.

---

[1] 7. 7. 1.
[2] *Arg.* 46. 4. 12, 13. 9. It could be let or sold as *res futura*.
[3] 36. 2. 2, 3, 5. 1.   [4] 33. 2. 7.
[5] Cp. 45. 1. 73. *pr.*, *in fin.*   [6] 7. 7. 5.
[7] 35. 2. 1. 9. He cites Aristo as discussing the matter.

CHAPTER XVI.

SPECIAL CASES (*cont.*). S. COMMUNIS. COMBINATIONS OF DIFFERENT INTERESTS.

XXVI. *SERVUS COMMUNIS*[1].

REGARDED purely as a chattel, there is little to be said of the *servus communis*. The general principles of common ownership apply, and a few remarks will therefore suffice. He is the property of the owners in undivided shares[2], and possession of him by one of his owners, *omnium nomine*, is possession by all[3]. A legacy of "my slaves" includes those in whom I own a share[4]. They are reckoned, *pro* Falcidia, in the estate of each owner[5]. The rights of ownership are necessarily somewhat cut down in view of the rights of other owners. Thus one of common owners cannot put the slave to torture, save in a matter of common interest[6]. On the same principle, the *actio servi corrupti* is available to one master against another[7]. The text appears corrupt, and there are signs of doubt, which may be due to the fact that the slave is the wrongdoer's own in a sense—a fact which is allowed to bar any action on *servi corruptio*, for *receptio*, *i.e.* of a *fugitivus*, against a co-owner[8]. But even here Ulpian inclines to allow the action if the reception was *celandi animo*, though he quotes Julian as refusing it in any case. It is not easy to see why the relation makes any difference, since the act is presumably a *furtum*, for which Paul and Ulpian are clear that *actio furti* will lie against a co-owner[9]. In all these cases an indemnity can be claimed by *communi dividundo*, or, if they are *socii*, by *pro socio*[10].

---

[1] For an account of various modern theories as to the conception of common ownership, see Zur Nieden, Miteigentumsverhältniss, 13—26.
[2] 45. 3. 5.
[3] 41. 2. 42. *pr. Post*, p. 386. We shall see that these rules are important in relation to acquisition through such slaves.
[4] 32. 74. The legacy is valid only to the extent of the share.
[5] 35. 2. 38. 1.
[6] An application of a wider rule applicable to all common ownership, 10. 2. 27, 28.
[7] 11. 3. 9. *pr.*
[8] 11. 3. 9. *pr.* As to this reception, *ante*, p. 269.
[9] 47. 2. 45; P. 2. 31. 26. Probably the rule is a late development, which Julian would have rejected.
[10] 17. 2. 45; 11. 3. 9. *pr.*; see also 9. 4. 10 and *post*, p. 375.

For *damnum* to the slave by one of the owners the others have the *actio* Aquilia, *pro parte*[1]. For *iniuria* by one of the masters an action lies as if it had been by an outsider, except that no such action lies under the edict as to *verberatio*, because it uses the expression *servum alienum*, and the *verberatio* is done *iure dominii*[2]. For theft or *corruptio* or *damnum* by a third person, the common owners have their action. We are told that this is *pro parte* in the case of *damnum*[3], and from the fact that, in *furtum*, action by one owner did not bar action by the other, we may infer that the rule was the same[4]. In the case of *iniuria* the rule is laid down that, for striking by a third person, each owner has the action[5]. But if the person who did the beating did it by consent of one owner whom he thought sole owner, there is no *actio iniuriarum* to anyone: if he knew there were other owners he is liable to all except the one who consented[6]. There is an at least apparent conflict in the texts as to the distribution of damages. In the Institutes[7] we are told that the damages need not be strictly *pro parte*, but that regard is to be had to the position of the different masters. But Paul holds, citing Pedius[8], that the *iudex* must apportion the damages according to the shares in the slave. It is clear that the Institutes deal only with the case in which there is intention to insult the *dominus*, and the action is therefore *suo nomine*[9]. It cannot be said with equal certainty that the other text is confined to cases in which there was no intent to insult the owner, and the action is therefore *servi nomine*, but this is a plausible distinction[10].

The cases of redemption of a common slave who has been captured and of the Aedilician actions on sale of a common slave have already been considered[11].

For any injuries to the slave each owner can of course sue: the right to compensation is, as we have seen, divided. But noxal surrender must be *in solidum* to any plaintiff: *haec res divisionem non recipit*[12]. It is, however, in the discretion of the *iudex* to order a surrender to the owners jointly[13]. In these cases, if he has been surrendered to one, the matter can be adjusted in the *actio communi dividundo*[14].

For delict by a common slave[15] all his owners are responsible, and, on a principle somewhat like that applied in case of delict by several persons, the liability of each is *in solidum*. It is as if, says Gaius,

---

[1] 9. 2. 19.
[2] 47. 10. 15. 36.
[3] 9. 2. 19, 27. 2.
[4] 47. 2. 46. 5.
[5] 47. 10. 15. 49.
[6] 47. 10. 17. *pr.*
[7] In. 4. 4. 4.
[8] 47. 10. 16.
[9] *Ante*, p. 80.
[10] The text confines its statement to a case in which an action *servi nomine* would certainly lie.
[11] As to redemption of captives, *ante*, p. 315. As to redhibition, *ante*, p. 68. As to special rules where the vendors were slave dealers, *ante*, p. 39.
[12] 9. 2. 27. 2.
[13] 9. 4. 19. *pr.*
[14] *Ib.*
[15] See Sell, Aus dem Noxalrechte, 194 *sqq.*

quoting Sabinus, he was defending *totum suum hominem,* and he cannot be allowed to defend in part[1] : this is not *defensio* at all[2]. But while joint tort feasors are not released by proceedings against one[3], a different rule applies here: since it is essentially one delict by one man[4]. Satisfaction by one of the owners discharges them all, *e.g.* if with the consent of the others he surrenders the man[5] or if he pays the claim[6]. Action against one releases all the others on *litis contestatio*[7]. If the action proceeds to judgment he can free himself by surrender, and for this purpose he can call on the other owners to hand over their shares to him, for surrender, giving security for return if he does not surrender, the demand being made by *actio communi dividundo*[8]. If, instead of surrendering, he prefers to pay, he can sue his co-owners for their share, by *communi dividundo,* but can only recover their quota of the value of the slave, if on the facts the *condemnatio* was for more than the value, so that it would have been better to surrender[9]. If the other owners enable him to surrender, and he does so, but on the facts it would have been wiser to pay, it seems that the other owners will have a claim in *communi dividundo* against him[10].

Although if the action is once brought surrender of part is ineffective, an owner can always free himself before action brought by surrendering his part[11]. It hardly seems likely that the injured party can be compelled to accept this partial surrender, since it has the effect of making him part owner and thus bars any noxal action against the other owners[12]. It is even doubted whether he has the lesser right of compensation for the damage from his (now) co-owners by *communi dividundo,* since the wrong was before the community began. And though this is allowed, it is a much less valuable right than that of delictal damages[13]. If the one owner, before action brought, abandons his share, he will presumably be free from liability, and the share of the other owners will be increased. It may be added that if one owner refuses to defend any other can do so[14].

We have anticipated the rule, based on the principle that one who is noxally liable for a man cannot have a noxal action for his act[15], that one co-owner cannot have a noxal action against another[16]. The case is not without a remedy: the wrong must be allowed for by the other

---

[1] 2. 9. 4; 9. 4. 5. *pr.,* 8; 10. 3. 15; 11. 3. 14. 2.   [2] 46. 7. 17.
[3] 9. 2. 11. 2.   [4] As to this unity, Sell, *op. cit.* 198.
[5] 9. 4. 8.   [6] 11. 3. 14. 2.   [7] 11. 1. 20. *pr.*
[8] 9. 4. 8; 10. 3. 15.   [9] *Ib.*; 10. 3. 8. 3.
[10] The transfer is to enable him to surrender if and when it shall be reasonable: this appears from the fact that security is taken for return if there is no surrender.
[11] 9. 4. 8.   [12] See n. 16.   [13] 9. 4. 8.
[14] 9. 4. 26. 2, 6.   [15] *Ante,* p. 107.
[16] 9. 4. 41; 9. 2. 27. 1; 11. 3. 14. 2; 47. 2. 62. *pr.*; 47. 10. 17. 9.   Ulpian suggests, perhaps from Proculus, the reason that otherwise the slave might determine which he would serve (9. 2. 27. 1), but this would bar a noxal action in any case.

owner in the *actio communi dividundo*[1], and the *iudex* has discretion to allow surrender of the part in lieu of damages: the liability passes to a buyer from the co-owner exactly as noxal liability would. If the slave dies the remedy ceases, except as to any profit which has been received from the wrong[2].

The case is different where one of the owners was *sciens*. Such a person is liable in full with no power of surrender[3]. Some complications arise from the fact that while he is so liable, the other owner is none the less noxally liable. If the *sciens* is sued there can be no surrender, but the *ignorans* is freed[4]. If the *ignorans* is sued and surrenders, then notwithstanding the general law as to consumption of actions, the *sciens* can still be sued for any difference between the value of the slave and the *damni persecutio*, which presumably means the damages for the delict, and not the damage done[5]. The rules as to contribution are in the main simple. If the *ignorans*, being noxally liable, has been condemned to pay, he can recover half from the other[6]. It seems also that he has a claim against him for deterioration of the slave whichever of them has been sued, though one would have expected this rather in case of *iussum* than of mere *scientia*[7]. If the *ignorans* has surrendered he has no claim except in respect of deterioration[8]. These claims can be made effective by *iudicium communi dividundo*, if the community still exists, but as that is essential for the action, the right can be enforced in the contrary case, if they are *socii*, by the *actio pro socio*, if not, by an *actio in factum*[9]. If the *sciens* has been condemned *in solidum*, Paul tells us that he can recover the half, not of what he has paid, but of the value of the slave, *i.e.* that part of the ordinary noxal liability which would fall on *ignorans*[10]. But in another text Paul says that on such facts he can recover nothing: *sui enim facti poenam meruit*[11]. This is the unquestioned rule in the case of actual *iussum* in which Paul himself uses very similar language: he can recover nothing, *cum ex suo delicto damnum patiatur*[12]. In case of *iussum* the innocent owner is entitled to complete indemnity, and if sued can claim a complete refund from the *iubens*[13]. Thus Paul applies the rule for *iussum* to mere *scientia*, in conflict with himself. The usual explanation is that in the text in which he denies any claim in a case of *scientia* he really means *iussum*. Sell objects to this that it is purely arbitrary, and himself holds[14], from the use of the word *poena*[15], that when Paul says he can recover nothing, he means nothing but half the value of the slave, the

[1] 9. 4. 41; 47. 2. 62. *pr.*   [2] 47. 2. 62. *pr.*   [3] *Ante*, pp. 114 *sqq.*
[4] 9. 4. 9.   [5] 9. 4. 17. *pr.*   [6] 9. 4. 9; 9. 4. 17. *pr.*
[7] 9. 4. 10.   [8] The *sciens* must have given him half.
[9] 9. 4. 10.   [10] *h. t.* 17. *pr.* So says also Marcellus in a different connexion, 47. 6. 5.
[11] 9. 4. 9.   [12] *h. t.* 17. *pr.*   [13] 47. 6. 5.
[14] *op. cit.* 204, 5.   [15] 9. 4. 9.

rest being *poena*. In respect of arbitrariness this explanation has no right to reproach the other: the text says very clearly that he can recover nothing at all. The older explanation is preferable[1]: the matter is of little importance, the contradiction is sharp, and there can be no doubt as to which view represents the law.

There is a further complication : where several of a man's slaves are concerned in a delict, the Edict[2] limits noxal liability, and provides that the owner, while he can free himself by surrendering all the slaves concerned, cannot be sued noxally for each, but can only be made to pay what could be recovered from a single freeman who had done the act. The limitation is conditional on his innocence. If he was *sciens* he is liable *suo nomine* and noxally for each of the slaves. If he was a co-owner the innocent owner has the benefit of the Edictal limit, though he has not, but may be sued on account of all. He can recover from his co-owner only his share of the edictal liability, or if there were actual *iussum*, presumably nothing at all. If the *ignorans* has been sued he can recover half of what he has paid, and here, as in the case just discussed (though Marcellus speaks hesitatingly), the *sciens* may be sued for the rest of the damages[3].

If, of two *domini*, one *dolo malo* ceases to possess his part of a *servus noxius*, the injured person can choose whether he will sue the other holder by the ordinary noxal action, or bring the special praetorian action against the dolose owner, *in solidum*[4]. The text is clear that it is an *electio*, yet there seems as much reason for allowing an action against the wrongdoer to survive as in the other case[5].

If one of common owners sued *ex noxa* falsely denies possession the liability is *in solidum* against him but not against the other: no doubt here too the detailed rules are the same[6].

If all the *domini* were *scientes*, we learn that each of them is liable *in solidum, quemadmodum si plures deliquissent*, and action against one does not release the others[7]. We are told no more. The natural inference from this language is that the damages are recoverable from each, and that there is no right of regress[8]. The language used is precisely that employed where the liability of one is independent of what is paid by the other[9]. This implies the notion that they are separate delicts, which as our text shews is not exactly the case. Where there was absolute *iussum*, there is no reason to doubt that the law was so, and this has as a corollary the denial of any right of regress, which

---

[1] Both this and the adjoining 10 shew some confusion between *scientia* and *iussum*.
[2] *Ante*, p. 118.   [3] 47. 6. 5.   [4] 9. 4. 26. 2.
[5] Probably the text must not be understood to deny this: we may suppose the rules as to contribution to have been as in the last case. The case is not very practical. If all have *dolo malo* ceased to possess there is the same *electio*, 9. 4. 39. *pr.*
[6] 11. 1. 17.   [7] 9. 4. 5. *pr.*   [8] 9. 2. 11. 2; C. 4. 8. 1.
[9] 9. 2. 11. 2.

would be meaningless. Sell[1] thinks that payment by one discharges all, but that there is no right of regress[2], a refusal which he shews not to be inconsistent with discharge by one payment, by citing the case of *dolus* by two tutors[3]. But this release is a rule special to *dolus*[4] and other cases where the claim is for indemnification merely[5]. The rule is probably the same in case of mere *scientia*, but if it be held that payment by one releases, it is inevitable that there be regress at least to the same extent as against one who was *ignorans*—perhaps to the extent of half the damages[6].

We have seen that noxal actions do not lie for delicts by the slave against one of his masters[7]. Here too the law is somewhat affected by *scientia* on the part of one of the masters. In such a case there is a delictal action against the master personally[8]. This circumstance confirms the view taken above as against that of Sell, since the *scientia* is treated as amounting to a separate delict[9].

Where a common slave acts as *exercitor*, all the owners who consent are liable *in solidum*[10], and one owner may be liable to the other. So if he is *magister navis* for one *dominus*, another may have an action on that account[11]. The same rule applies to *institoria*, and where several owners appoint, as the obligation is *in solidum*, it is immaterial that their shares are unequal: adjustment is arrived at by the *actio communi dividundo* or *pro socio*[12]. In the *actio quod iussu* none are liable but those who command, but they are liable *in solidum*[13]. So also none is ordinarily liable to the *actio de in rem verso* except for what is *versum*[14] to him. It is said however in the next text that there is an exception to this[15]. Marcellus, commenting on the foregoing rule, laid down by Julian, observes that sometimes one co-owner may be liable to this action for what has been *versum* to the other, being able to recoup himself by action against the other[16]: *quid enim dicemus si peculium servo ab altero ademptum fuerit.* And Paul adds, *ergo haec quaestio ita procedit si de peculio agi non potest.* The rule is remarkable: the explanatory comment is obscure. Marcellus seems to mean that the *actio de peculio*

---

[1] *op. cit.* 207.   [2] *Arg.* 9. 4. 17. *pr.*   [3] 27. 3. 1. 14; *h. t.* 15.
[4] Girard, Manuel, p. 745.   [5] 4. 3. 1. *pr.* See also *ante*, p. 376, n. 5.
[6] So Sell, *loc. cit.*   [7] *Ante*, p. 374.
[8] 9. 2. 27. 1. The word used is *voluntas*. But in this connexion knowledge with failure to prohibit is said to be *voluntas*, 47. 6. 1. 1.
[9] If one owner is a *caupo* and uses the slave his absolute liability for theft, *etc.*, by the slave exists as against co-owners as well as *extranei*: it has no relation to ownership. But there is no personal delict and the liability is rather unreal, as he can claim compensation in *communi dividundo*, 4. 9. 6. 1. *Ante*, p. 122. There might of course be no claim in *communi dividundo*, *e.g.*, where the slave was hired *talis qualis*.
[10] 14. 1. 4. 2, 6. 1.   [11] *h. t.* 5. *pr.*
[12] 14. 3. 13. 2, 14.   [13] 15. 3. 13; 15. 4. 5. 1.
[14] 15. 3. 13. Though as we shall see each owner is liable *de peculio* for the whole fund. *Post*, p. 378.
[15] 15. 3. 14.   [16] Presumably *communi dividundo*.

is barred against one and not against the other. Paul seems to say it is barred altogether. The most commonly accepted view is that this is an analogous extension of the rule in the *actio de peculio* to that *de in rem verso*, in the case in which *de peculio* is no longer available against the owner who benefited by the *versio*[1], since this enables the creditor to recover by one action instead of compelling him to bring two[2]. This explanation requires, what is not impossible, that Paul and Marcellus ignore the rule that as between common owners, in view of the fact that all the *peculium* comes into account, an owner can be sued *de peculio* even though there is no *peculium* in respect of him[3].

In the case of the *actio tributoria*, all the *domini* who knew of the trading must bring their debts into *tributio*: what is due to one who did not know is to be deducted *in solidum*[4].

In the *actio de peculio* the matter is complicated by the fact that a slave may have *peculium* with one owner and not with the other[5], and the *peculium* may be either a joint fund or in distinct funds[6]. The general rule is that the *actio de peculio* may be brought against any one of the owners on the basis of the whole of the *peculium*[7]. As the owner sued is liable over the whole fund, he is entitled to deduct debts due to other *domini*[8], and the liabilities may be finally adjusted by *communi dividundo*[9]. The enlarged liability depends on the existence of this right[10]. But an owner in respect of whom there is no *peculium*, though he can be sued *de peculio*[11], cannot be made to bear any part of the burden in the ultimate distribution[12]. The action for contribution can be brought immediately on condemnation *de peculio*: it is not necessary to have actually paid[13]. We are not told expressly the basis of adjustment, but several texts[14] shew that it was not determined by the fate of the acquisition, but that the liability was borne in proportion to the shares in the *peculium*, the reason assigned being that the payment has released the non-payer from an obligation[15]. If the *peculium* does not suffice to pay all, the action can be brought again[16], and as in the case of

---

[1] Von Tuhr, De in rem verso, 240 *sqq.* He cites other explanations.
[2] *i.e. de peculio* against one owner followed by *de in rem verso* against the other.
[3] 15. 1. 12.   This text is Julian's, and shews that the present rule as thus explained, cannot be due, as Von Tuhr supposes, to him. It is possible that some part of the hypothesis of Marcellus has dropped out. See Von Tuhr, *loc. cit.*
[4] 14. 4. 3. *pr.*, 5. 10.
[5] 15. 1. 7. 1; 45. 3. 1. 2; and for several cases, 15. 1. 16.   [6] 15. 1. 15.
[7] 10. 3. 8. 4, 9, 15, 25; 14. 4. 3. *pr.*; 15. 1. 11. 9, 27. 8, 51.
[8] 14. 4. 3. *pr.*; 15. 1. 11. 9, 15.   [9] 10. 3. 8. 4, 15; 15. 1. 27. 8.
[10] 15. 1. 51. A and B have common property including a slave. A sells his share of the slave to C. A creditor sues C *de peculio*. C is not liable to the extent of A's *peculium*, as he has no means of redressing the balance. If the creditor sues B within the *annus utilis*, B is liable to the extent of A's *peculium*, since A is liable *de peculio* and, as they have common property, the matter can be adjusted. If the year is up, A's *peculium* is not reckoned in any case, *h. t.* 37. 2.
[11] 15. 1. 12.   [12] 15. 1. 27. 8.
[13] 10. 3. 15.   [14] 10. 3. 8. 4, 25; 15. 1. 27. 8.
[15] It must be remembered that acquisitions were common: there might however be a further adjustment, *post*, p. 386.   [16] *Post*, App. II.

vendor and buyer, no doubt the creditor having sued one owner is not in practice barred from suing another. As the comprehensive liability is due to the right of regress against the others, the *peculium* in their hands is not valued at its full amount, but deduction is made for cost and delay involved in recovering it, and as in similar cases, cession of the action against the other owner will discharge[1].

If the co-owner dies without representatives there is in strictness no longer any *peculium* of his, and accordingly, Julian tells us that in that case, the owner sued should be condemned only in the amount of actual *peculium*, and what can be recovered out of the *bona* of the deceased[2].

The right to claim contribution being completed by the condemnation to the "peculiar" creditor, it is not affected by subsequent loss or destruction of the *peculium* in the hands of the other owner, since, the *peculium* being a common fund, it is not fair that the loss should fall wholly on him who has to pay in the *actio de peculio*[3].

The liability may be complicated by the existence of a right to the *actio tributoria*. If the owner who knew of the trading is sued thus, all that is due to the other owner may be deducted, and if that other is sued *de peculio*, what is due to either is deducted[4].

The common liability extending over the whole, with the right of contribution, rests on the fact that it is a common fund, all the destinies of which ought to be common[5]: if therefore the *peculia* are not held as common but are kept distinct by the respective owners, then no owner can be sued for more than his own share, he can deduct only debts due to himself, and there is no occasion for contribution[6].

It remains to be said that if the creditor is himself a co-owner there is no *actio de peculio*: the rights are adjusted by means of *iudicium communi dividundo*[7].

The law as to acquisition through common slaves is rather complex[8]: the general rule is that acquisitions are common, *pro parte*, whether *inter vivos* or on death[9], and even where they are *ex re unius ex dominis*, though here they have to be accounted for[10]. So if I promise two things to a common slave, each owner is entitled to half of each, unless they are "fungibles[11]." This community of acquisitions could be avoided by the

---

[1] 15. 1. 51.   *Ante*, p. 220.   [2] 15. 1. 28.
[3] 10. 3. 9.   [4] 14. 4. 3. *pr.*   [5] 10. 3. 9.
[6] 15. 1. 15.   [7] *h. t.* 19. 2, 20.
[8] Elaborately worked out by Salkowski, *op. cit.* Ch. i.   Most of the following remarks are based on this book.
[9] G. 3. 59, 167; In. 3. 28. 3; D. 16. 3. 1. 31; 30. 50. *pr.*; 41. 1. 45; 45. 3. 5, 27.   In 12. 1. 13. 2 the money must be common.
[10] In *communi dividundo*, 10. 3. 24; 41. 1. 45.
[11] 46. 3. 29.   A common slave could stipulate for what none of the owners could, *e.g.* a right of way to a common farm, 8. 3. 19.   See Zur Nieden, Miteigentumsverhältniss, 33.

use of apt words.   Thus if the acquisition was *nominatim* for one or more
that one or more acquired the whole[1].   So if the acquisition was at the
iussum of one, though the matter is disputed, the rule is laid down that
he alone acquires: *iussum* is equivalent to *nominatio* for this purpose[2].
Further there are cases, in which one acquires alone apart from *iussum*
or *nominatio*, mainly dependent on the principle that what cannot from
any cause be acquired to one goes to the others *pro rata*[3].   But the
application of all these principles is full of difficulties.

The effect of *nominatio* must be carefully analysed.   It is a well
recognised rule that if a slave makes a stipulation, *nominatim*, in favour
of one who is not his master, the effect is merely null: the stipulation
is void.   The *nominatio* excludes his master, who is not named, but it
does not avail to give a right to the *extraneus*.   In other words its effect
is simply negative or exclusive.   The intent of the slave is not a
material point.   It cannot make an owner acquire what he would not,
apart from this intent.   The same principle governs the case of a
common slave.   The *nominatio* of one master necessarily excludes the
others.   The fact that the named one acquires the whole is due to the
principle that what cannot be acquired to one goes to the other[4].   Each
of his owners is his owner and can thus acquire all his acquisitions[5].   If
he stipulates *nominatim* for the owner to whom the thing belongs already
the stipulation is a mere nullity[6].   In one text we are told by Papinian[7],
that if a common slave of A and B stipulates from a third party for the
part of him which belongs to A, *nominatim* for B, this is valid and B
acquires, and that if no name is mentioned all goes to B in the same
way[8].   The text adds that if he stipulates for the same part *sibi dari*,
this is void, presumably as being an absurdity[9].   Elsewhere Ulpian
says[10] that he cannot stipulate for himself *sibi dari*, though he can
domino dari.   This is not quite the same case, for he stipulates for the
whole of himself.   It can be valid only for that part which the owner
has not already.   If it were, or could be read, *dominis dari*, each would
presumably acquire against the outsider an obligation for the part which
belonged to the other.   This is perhaps what Ulpian means by the
closing words: *non enim se domino adquirit, sed de se obligationem*.

The rule as to the effect of *nominatio* applies to all kinds of transaction, to stipulation[11], mancipation[12], *traditio*[13], *emptio, mutuum*[14], and

[1] Taking in proportion to their share in him.   G. 3. 167; In. 3. 28. 3; D. 41. 1. 37; 45. 3. 5,
7. *pr.*, 28. 3.
[2] 45. 3. 5, 6.   [3] 41. 1. 23. 3.
[4] 7. 1. 25. 4; 41. 1. 23. 3.
[5] Thus he can acquire correal obligations for both, 45. 3. 28. 2, 29.
[6] 7. 1. 25. 4.   [7] 45. 3. 18. 1.   [8] *Post*, p. 389.
[9] Salkowski, *op. cit.* 86.   [10] 45. 3. 2.
[11] G. 3. 167; In. 3. 28. 3; D. 41. 1. 37. 3.   [12] G. 3. 167.
[13] 41. 1. 37. 3.   This may have been written of *mancipatio*.
[14] 45. 3. 28. 3.

even *acceptilatio*[1], which, as being a release from debt, is a form of acquisition[2]. Gaius applies it to *quodlibet negotium*[3].

If a slave takes a promise to himself and one owner, *nominatim*, ordinary principles apply—the named *dominus* takes half, and all the *domini*, including the one named, take the other half *pro parte dominica*[4]. If he stipulates in the name of some or all of his *domini*, the principle above laid down would lead to the view that the *nominatio* will have no effect except to exclude those not named : the *nominatio* confers no right on any *dominus* which he had not apart from it. Thus the named masters ought to take *pro parte*, and if all are named the *nominatio* will have no legal effect. So Ulpian decides[5]. But Pomponius holds that if two *domini* are named, they take equally, though if it had been *dominis meis* they would take *pro parte*. If the words were to A and B, *dominis meis*, the order is material, the earlier being the material party, the later mere *demonstratio*[6]. As Salkowski shews[7], the origin of Pomponius' view is in the rules of interpretation applied to wills imposing burdens on the *heres*. If they are mentioned by name, and especially if some only are named, it is presumed that the testator intended them in their personal capacity, and the liability is equal. If they are called *heredes*, the liability is *pro parte*[8]. Salkowski holds the analogy applicable, but it seems out of place. In the case of a will we have to do with the intent of the testator, with words used by one who could make what disposition he liked, and whose intent governs the whole matter. In our case we have to do with a slave whose intent is not material, and whose *nominatio* has only a privative effect, a point which Salkowski seems here to overlook[9].

If the stipulation be to A or B (*domini*) it is void, as neither can be regarded as *solutionis causa adiectus*, for both can acquire on the stipulation, which is thus void for uncertainty[10]. If the same stipulation is made with a condition, "whichever be alive" on a day fixed in the stipulation for payment, Venuleius and Julian hold it still void. It is not saved by the condition, though on the day one be dead, so that there is no uncertainty[11]. Julian seems to hold that, as a stipulation *ex praesenti vires accipit*, there must be no uncertainty in the original

---

[1] 46. 4. 8. 1.   [2] 46. 3. 63.

[3] 45. 3. 28. 3.   Salkowski thinks, on the evidence of the language of the texts, that the rule applied originally only to cases in which the restriction appeared in the formula of the transaction and so not to informal transactions. *Mutuum* he thinks an early extension. *Op. cit.* 75.

[4] 45. 3. 4.   [5] 45. 3. 7. *pr.*

[6] 45. 3. 37.   [7] *loc. cit.*

[8] The rule being one of pure construction there were differences of opinion. See 30. 54. 3; *h. t.* 124; 45. 2. 17, cited by Salkowski.

[9] He urges a further argument *ab inconvenienti.*

[10] 45. 3. 9. 1, 10, 11 unless some other circumstance shews that one is only *solutionis causa adiectus*, 46. 1. 16. *pr.*   Cassius and Julian are cited in support: there is no sign of dispute.

[11] 45. 3. 21.

formulation.   Salkowski observes[1] that Julian's argument proves too much : it would, he says, invalidate any conditional stipulation. But this is hardly the case : the argument deals only with stipulations in which it is uncertain which acquires, not with those as to which it is uncertain whether there will be any acquisition at all. But the decision is not dependent on the rather ill-expressed argument. The stipulation is defective in that it leaves it quite uncertain what is to happen if they both survive. There seems little authority for the effect of conditions in saving stipulations which as drawn are subject to an ambiguity or doubt which may be cured by time[2]. Julian elsewhere discusses a somewhat similar case. The common slave stipulates for 10 to T, on a certain date, with a further clause : " if you do not then give it, do you promise to give M (the other owner) 20 ? " These, he says, are two stipulations, but if T sue after the day is past, he can be met by an *exceptio doli*[3]. In the foregoing case there cannot be two stipulations even with the help of the principle that a stipulation by a common slave is as many stipulations as he has masters[4].

Another case may be noted. A common slave stipulates, *sibi aut P aut S, dominis.* Ulpian holds that the word *sibi* acquires to all the masters and that the stipulation so far as it names P and S is void, on which account they are validly put in as *solutionis causa adiecti*[5]. This seems quite in accordance with principle. The word *sibi* confers the right on all *domini* : the names which follow could not in any case confer rights on anyone, and the word *sibi* prevents their privative effect. It is this word *sibi* which distinguishes this case from that of a stipulation : *Titio aut Seio, dominis*[6].

The principles are well illustrated in another text of Julian's. A common slave stipulates to one *dominus,* A, by name. Then from a *fideiussor* he stipulates for the same payment " to A or B, *domini.*" This is valid, B is only *solutionis causa adiectus*[7] ; the point is that as a *fideiussor* cannot be liable to one to whom his principal is not, there can be no question of B's being entitled.

To complete the statement as to *nominatio,* it must be said that the origin of the acquisition is immaterial : if a stipulation is *nominatim Titio ex re Maevii,* Titius alone acquires[8], and where on these rules one acquires or is excluded unfairly, the matter is adjusted by *communi dividundo* or *pro socio*[9].

---

[1] *op. cit.* 83.
[2] As to those which were impossible, see Accarias, Précis, § 508.
[3] 45. 3. 1. 6.   [4] *h. t.* 1. 4.
[5] 45. 3. 11.   It may also be Julian's view.
[6] Salkowski, *op. cit.* 84, objects to Ulpian's reasoning, but hardly takes enough account of this point and of the fact that *nominatio* is privative merely: it simply bars those owners who are not named.
[7] 46. 1. 16. *pr.*   [8] 41. 1. 23. 3.   [9] 45. 3. 28. 1.

As we have seen, *iussum* by one master is put by later law on the same footing as *nominatio*[1]. The rule in *nominatio* is a direct result of the fact that *nominatio* of a third party in any transaction prevented acquisition to the owner. This was not the case with *iussum* by a third party, and thus it is not surprising that the recognition of the effect of *iussum* was later. For the time of Justinian, the texts are explicit and general: *iussum pro nomine accipimus*[2]. But they are few and some are interpolated. Gaius tells us that the Sabinian school put *iussum* on a level with *nominatio*, while the Proculians treated it as having no effect at all[3]. The Institutes speak of the question as only finally settled by a constitution of Justinian[4]. On the other hand, texts of Ulpian which have no sign of interpolation treat the matter as quite settled[5], and the only rule laid down in Justinian's constitution is that if a stipulation is made on the *iussum* of one master, *nominatim* to another, the former will acquire[6]. The law speaks of this matter as having been much debated, but, apart from concurrence of the two, treats the recognition of *iussum* as settled. The only text in the Digest referring to the matter, and earlier than Ulpian, is one by Pomponius, the curious language of which suggests, first, that not all Sabinians, but only some named Sabinians, allowed force to *iussum*, and, secondly, that they were not sure of it: they say: *posse ei soli adquiri*[7]. The text has certainly been handled by the compilers. It is tempting to treat this text of Pomponius as shewing adoption by some Sabinians of the view that *iussum* was effective, that of Gaius as shewing the adoption of this view by all Sabinians, and those of Ulpian as shewing acceptance by all jurists. But such exactitude the texts are not strong enough to permit.

If *iussum* concurs with *nominatio*, *i.e.* a master orders a contract[8], and the slave contracts in the name of another, all we know of ante-justinianian law is that there were disputes. Justinian settles the matter, but his enactment contradicts itself, and commentators from the Glossators on have disagreed as to which line he takes. The most generally accepted view, *i.e.* that if the direction was to contract in the name of the *iussor* this prevails, but if it were a mere direction to contract, the *nominatio* does, is a mere plausible guess. It has no logical basis, but it may have approved itself to Tribonian[9].

It must be supposed that *iussum* could not be by ratification: the common acquisition once completed could not be varied by one master.

---

[1] *Iussum* here means direction to the slave: it has no close connexion with such *iussum* as bases an *actio quod iussu*.
[2] In. 3. 28. 3 ; D. 7. 1. 25. 6; 45. 3. 5—7. *pr.*
[3] G. 3. 167 a.   [4] In. 3. 28. 3.
[5] 7. 1. 25. 6; 45. 3. 5, 7. *pr.*   See Salkowski, *op. cit.* 93, 98.   [6] C. 4. 27. 3.
[7] 45. 3. 6.   See for discussion of this text, Salkowski, *op. cit.* 91 *sq.*
[8] Either in his name or without this instruction.
[9] See Salkowski, *op. cit.* 96, 98, for this and his own different hypothesis.

We can now return to the general principle. There are several special cases to consider[1].

(i)   Treasure trove. Here the rule is that if a common slave finds treasure in a third person's land, the finder's half is divided amongst his owners, *pro portione*[2]. This is clear, but the following text says that if it is found on land of one owner, both the owner's half and the finder's half go to the owner of the land[3]. Principle seems to require that he should take only his share of the finder's half. Salkowski holds that the rule stated is to be confined to the case in which the treasure is found during work ordered by the owner, which would put it on a level with acquisition *iussu unius domini*, with which the text expressly compares it[4].

(ii)   *Hereditas.* If a common slave is instituted his masters are entitled *pro portione*[5]. In strictness as there is only one institution there should be only one entry. But the slave can enter either at once for all or separately for each owner who authorises entry. We are told by Paul that the right of entering separately is not based on any theory of testator's intention but is in the interest of the masters, *utilitatis causa*, lest delay by one injure the others[6]. The effect of entry at the command of one is to acquire to that one only to the extent of his share, with ultimate accrual if the other *domini* do not order entry within the period allotted[7]. Each owner has a separate *tempus deliberandi*, which of course may not be the same in all cases[8]. If the slave has entered under the orders of one master and is afterwards freed, he can himself enter on his own account for the other half[9]. This must be true only if the time allowed to the other master for deliberation has not expired: whether he had a new time or only the residue of the old is not told us.

All this looks very like treating them as distinct institutions. But this is negatived partly by the rule that he could enter once for all, but more obviously by the fact that, if the slave has once entered, the death of another master without ordering entry will not make a *caducum*. But there are traces of the view that they are distinct *institutiones*, in a certain conflict as to substitution. If one is instituted for several parts, he cannot take one and refuse the other, whether anyone is substituted to the other part or not[10]. In like manner Paul, the author of this text, says, elsewhere, that if the common slave has a substitute, entry at the order of one master bars the substitute, *i.e.* it is one institution[11]. But Scaevola says that the substitute will take the share of any owner who

---

1   In the following remarks Salkowski's exposition is in the main followed.
2   41. 1. 63. 1.   3   *h. l.* 2.
4   *op. cit.* 3 *sqq.* He thinks the limiting words are purposely omitted as they occur in the next case.
5   In. 2. 14. 3.   6   29. 2. 68.   7   *h. t.* 67.   8   28. 8. 1. *pr.*
9   29. 2. 64.   10   29. 2. 80. *pr.*   11   *h. t.* 65.

does not authorise entry[1]. This must rest on the view that they are distinct institutions, and not in any way joint, *i.e.* the substitutions must be regarded as distinct substitutions in each case[2].

(iii) Legacies, *etc.*[3] The general rule is simple : a legacy to a common slave goes to his owners *pro portione*[4]. But when we get beyond this there are disputes due to differences of opinion analogous to those mentioned in connexion with institutions, *i.e.*, as to whether it is to be regarded as one legacy or several, whether the individuality of the slave is to be considered or those only of his *domini*. Thus if a legacy is left to a common slave under a condition of paying money, some jurists think the condition cannot be satisfied *per partes*, but only by paying all. The rule of the Digest given by Paul is that each owner can satisfy *pro parte* and so acquire[5]. This is the rule in cases where a legacy is left to two persons on such a condition—*enumeratione personarum videri esse divisa*[6], but not, says Javolenus, where it is left to one, even though circumstances divide it so that two stand in the place of the original legatee[7]. It is clear that the legacy to a common slave is for this purpose regarded as two. So Julian says, if a thing is left to a common slave, one can accept and the other refuse, *nam in hanc causam servus communis quasi duo servi sunt*[8]. On the other hand, a senatusconsult under the *lex* Cornelia *de falsis*, penalising the writing of legacies, *etc.*, to oneself, applies to legacies to a common slave : the name being a *falsum* must be struck out, and the whole gift is void[9]. A word cannot be *pro parte pro non scripto*[10]. Upon the question of accrual, the dispute is clearly brought out. In a *legatum per vindicationem* to two persons *coniunctim* or *disiunctim* if one refuses the other takes all, each being entitled *in solidum*—*partes concursu fiunt*. How if the legacy was to a common slave ? Here on the Proculian view reported by Celsus, there is no accrual, *non enim coniunctim sed partes legatas,—nam si ambo vindicarent*, each will have the part he had in the slave[11]. That is to say that each is not entitled *in solidum*, and limited to a share only by concurrence[12]. This construction of the gift does not seem inevitable, but it is accepted even by those who come to an opposite decision on the actual question, and hold that there is accrual. Julian holds, as reported by Ulpian[13], that if one of the common owners refuses, the other gets it all, notwithstanding that they take *pro parte dominica*, and not

---

[1] 28. 6. 48. *pr.*
[2] Salkowski, *op. cit.* 15.   But the last clause may be a hasty interpolation.
[3] Salkowski, *op. cit.* 19 *sqq.*   [4] 30. 50. *pr.*   [5] 35. 1. 44. 8.
[6] 35. 1. 54. 1, 56.   [7] *h. t.* 56.   [8] 30. 81. 1.
[9] 48. 10. 14. *pr.   Post*, p. 390.
[10] This is in fact the decisive point, which deprives the text of much force in this connexion.
[11] 31. 20.   The reasoning is defective : this would be equally true in a *legatum coniunctim.*
[12] Cp. 32. 80; D. 35. 1. 54. 1; 7. 2. 1. *pr.*, 3; Vat. F. 75, 76, 79.
[13] Vat. Fr. 75. 2; D. 7. 2. 1. 1.

equally. This, says Julian, is because the *persona* of the slave is looked at. That is not very lucid. But the next text in the Vatican Fragments, laying down the rule that if it be left to a *servus communis* and Titius, and one master refuses, his share lapses to the other, remarks that this had been disputed, but the author, Ulpian, approves Julian's view, not on the ground of *ius accrescendi*, but because *quamdiu servus est cuius persona in legato spectatur, non debet perire portio*[1]. It is curious to find Julian, who holds that a *servus communis* in case of legacy *quasi duo servi sunt*[2], cited as authority for this view which seems to contradict him.

(iv) Possession[3]. There is little to be said here. Possession by one of common owners is possession by all. This must be *nomine omnium*[4], and applies to retaining, not to taking, possession. There is no reason to suppose that apart from *peculium* one of common owners who had not given *iussum* possessed a thing held by a common slave till he knew the slave had it[5]. In general we acquire possession through a common slave, *sicut in dominio adquirendo*[6], which does not mean that when we acquire the one we acquire the other, but only that the rules as to the effect of *iussum* and *nominatio*, and as to acquisition *pro rata* in ordinary cases apply here too.

(v) Acquisition *ex re unius*. It is a general rule that the source of the money with which any acquisition was made is immaterial: the acquisition is common *pro rata*. A thing acquired by a common slave with stolen money is common[7]. So, obviously, if the thing with which it is acquired is the property of one owner: still the acquisition is to all, subject to adjustment by *iudicium communi dividundo*. This is laid down in general terms in many texts[8]. It is immaterial whether it is *ex peculio unius* or with his independent property, not held by the slave[9]. Where an owner hands over property to a common slave on the terms that it is to remain his, and the slave buys land with it, the land is common[10]. Adjustment by *communi dividundo* is of course a remedy for any injustice[11]: the rule is clear. A striking instance apart from *peculium* is that of *damnum infectum*. Where a common slave stipulates *damni infecti*, it is as if all the owners had stipulated, *pro partibus*. There is no hint that the menaced property was itself

---

[1] Vat. Fr. 75. 3—5; cp. 7. 2. 1. 2 and 31. 40 which Salkowski regards as possibly illustrating the same view.
[2] 30. 81. 1. He limits it: *in hanc causam*. The text refers only to usufruct, but the reasoning and the rule that the gift is only *pro parte* are not so limited.
[3] Salkowski, *op. cit.* 33—44.   [4] 41. 2. 42. *pr.*
[5] 41. 2. 1. 7.   [6] *Ib.* See also *post*, p. 387.
[7] 41. 1. 37. 2. But the text is not without difficulty. It raises the question what kind of payment suffices to cause the ownership to pass on delivery on a sale.
[8] 10. 3. 24. *pr.*; 41. 1. 37. 2, 45; 45. 3. 28. 1.
[9] 45. 3. 27.   [10] 41. 3. 37. 2.
[11] There must be difficulties as to this adjustment, where the slave has *peculia* of all his owners and is actively dealing with all of them. See Salkowski, *op. cit.* 70—73.

common[1]. One text raises an apparent difficulty. Julian says that if a common slave lends money out of the *peculium* of one owner, he alone acquires the action *ex mutuo*[2]. But as no person can acquire *ex mutuo* unless he was the owner of the money lent, this is a mere application of the principle that what cannot be acquired to one goes to the other[3].

(vi) Bilateral contracts. To say that each acquires the rights *pro portione* and is liable *in solidum, de peculio*, subject to adjustment by *communi dividundo*, does not sufficiently explain the situation. There is at least one case in which such a subdivision of the resulting rights is not possible. If a common slave buys, one of the owners cannot by paying his quota acquire an *actio ex empto* for delivery of his part[4], nor can he, on paying all, claim delivery of all: he has a right under the contract only to a part. If the thing bought has been delivered, there can be no redhibition unless all consent[5]. Other similar cases may arise, *e.g.*, under a sale in which the buyer has a right of withdrawal within a certain time[6], and under the other well known *pacta adiecta*. The texts do not discuss these cases. Can one owner claim relief for *laesio enormis*? If a common slave lets a house, can one owner forfeit for non-payment of rent, *pro parte*, or absolutely, if the others do not wish to do so? Probably, in all these cases, all must consent, but there is no authoritative answer to the questions.

(vii) Intent of the Slave[7]. We have already considered the question whether the intent of a slave can vary the effect of a transaction. One text, dealing with a slave of one owner, and saying that the master acquires possession through the slave only if the slave intends to acquire it to him, we have rejected as a statement of the classical law[8]. The same point arises in certain texts dealing with common slaves. In one text we are told by Paul that we can acquire by a common slave possession for ourself alone, *si-hoc agat servus ut uni adquirat, sicut in dominio adquirendo*[9]. Here too it seems likely that the words *si... adquirat* are a hasty and wrong explanation by the compilers, the cases in the mind of the jurist having been *nominatio* and *iussum*. But there is one pair of texts in sharp contradiction with each other which need careful examination. Ulpian says[10] that if one intending to benefit me delivers a thing to a common slave of me and Titius, and the slave takes it either for Titius or for both, then, notwithstanding the intention of the slave, I alone acquire, just as, if a thing were delivered to my procurator, with the intent that I should acquire, and he took it for

---

[1] 39. 2. 42.   [2] 45. 3. 1. 2.
[3] 12. 1. 2. 4, Salkowski, *op. cit.* 68—70.   [4] 21. 1. 31. 8.
[5] *h. l.* 7.   If a common slave is sold there is redhibition *pro parte*: the effect would not here be to force part ownership on one who was not common owner before, *h. l.* 10.
[6] 41. 4. 2. 5.   [7] Salkowski, *op. cit.* 45—64.   [10] 39. 5. 13.
[8] *Ante*, p. 133.   [9] 41. 2. 1. 7.

himself, he would acquire for me not for himself. On the other hand, Julian[1], dealing with a hypothesis which differs only in that the common owner has certainly given previous authorisation to the intending donor to deliver the thing to the common slave, says that if the slave takes it intending it to be for Titius, nobody acquires, and if the slave intended it to be common the transfer would be void as to half. And he says that in like case, if a procurator took it for himself there would be no transfer of ownership. It is clear on these texts that the deliverer names his intended beneficiary. But this has no relation to acquisition *nominatim*, for it is perfectly clear on the texts that in that case the *nominatio* proceeds from the slave. All the texts assume this and one expresses it very strongly[2].

Our two texts have been discussed and explained from time immemorial. None of the explanations has been accepted as solving the problem[3]. Only a few remarks will be made here, and those with little confidence. There are two questions: (1) Why was the acquisition, apart from the intent of the slave, not common? (2) Why was the slave's intent material? The intervention of a slave in a transaction may occur in three ways. He may be employed merely as a messenger to take the thing to his owner. In this case the delivery is not complete till the master has it: there can be no question of the personality of the slave[4]. He may be the party to the whole transaction or to the conveyance which completes it. In that case acquisition is through him, and in the circumstances of these texts the acquisition would on the face of it be common. For there is no *iussum* or *nominatio* and it is clear, from the earlier law as to *donatio* to a *bona fide serviens*, that the express intention of the donor to benefit the holder does not prevent acquisition to the owner[5]. But the slave's intervention may take a third form. If I direct my vendor to throw the thing in the sea, or in any way to dispose of it, and he does so, that is a valid *traditio* to me. The same is true if he delivers it to some other person for me, and it is immaterial who that person is: the acquisition is to me, if, for instance, the thing is delivered to a slave I have hired, who is to work on it. The slave is a mere receiver: there is no real question of acquisition through him[6]. This seems to be the present hypothesis and the acquisition is direct to the master who directed delivery to the slave. This makes Julian's text orthodox, as to the first point[7].

---

[1] 41. 1. 37. 6.
[2] 45. 3. 28. 3. So also it is not *iussu*, for the slave does not receive any *iussum*.
[3] See Salkowski, *op. cit.* 56 *sqq.* for explanation and references to literature.
[4] Salkowski, *loc. cit.*   [5] *Ante*, p. 344.
[6] See, *e.g.*, 15. 4. 5. *pr.*; C. 4. 26. 4.
[7] Ulpian says nothing of authority to deliver to the slave, but as S. shews (*op. cit.* 57) the structure of his argument requires it.

Is the slave's intent material? No, says Ulpian, but, according to Julian, the transfer is effective only in so far as the slave takes with the intent of receiving for the intended donee. It may be that Julian is guided by precisely the consideration that the slave is not the agent who acquires, but a mere receiver who cannot be such in so far as he refuses to act as such[1].

Both texts treat of *donatio*, and Salkowski holds[2] that the rule applies only to that case. If the above account is correct, it must apply equally to any case in which the transaction is essentially the master's altogether. But if a sale had been chosen, it would have been necessary to distinguish according to the circumstances of the previous contract. In *donatio* this is not the case. The declaration of intent to give is not itself a transaction and has no legal force. Whether it be made to the slave or direct to the master it is at once the master's transaction when it is communicated to him and he directs delivery to the slave.

There are cases in which, independently of *nominatio* or *iussum*, one of the common owners acquires to the exclusion of the other. They all turn on the general rule, adopted on practical grounds of convenience, that what cannot be acquired to one of the common owners goes to the other[3]. The rule is consistent with the principle that each owner, being owner, is potentially capable of acquiring *in solidum*. The cases discussed in the texts are the following.

(*a*) If a common slave stipulates for a servitude, it will be acquired only to such of his owners as have tenements to which it can attach. Those who have such tenements will acquire, each *in solidum*[4]. If he mentions the land to which it is to belong, then it attaches to the owner of that land, wholly and alone[5].

(*b*) Where one owner is about to marry and *dos* is promised to the common slave. Here the rule can apply only if the words used, or the circumstances, shew what marriage was in view[6].

(*c*) A thing promised to a common slave by a third party belongs already to one master. Whether the stipulation was *sine nomine*, or to all by name, the whole will go to those of his masters to whom it did not belong[7].

(*d*) A slave of A stipulates with C for a performance to a common slave of A and B. Here so far as the common slave belongs to B, he is *servus alienus*. But, says Julian, the rule applies that what one owner

---

[1] This may be the explanation of Paul's anomalous view in 41. 2. 1. 19, *ante*, p. 133.
[2] *op. cit.* 61.
[3] Salkowski shews (*op. cit.* 99) that the rule is one of great antiquity (26. 8. 12). It is stated many times (In. 3. 17. 3; D. 41. 1. 23. 3; 45. 3. 7. 1, 19, *etc.*). The following remarks are mainly from Salkowski.
[4] 45. 3. 17.   [5] 45. 3. 7. 1.   [6] 45. 3. 8.
[7] Though it be a part of himself, 45. 3. 18. 1.

cannot acquire the other does. To bring this rule into operation we have, he says, to treat the stipulation as two distinct stipulations, one valid, the other void, each for the full amount[1]. This is straightforward, but it has the difficulty that the transaction is not by the common slave at all. The acquisition is made by the slave of A. It is a bold rule of construction to avoid the inconveniences which would have resulted if the claim had been limited to one half[2]. It is in fact the Sabinian view of the effect of a stipulation "to me and a third person." The survival of this view into the Digest seems to be due to the fact that the words are here construed as two stipulations, and not as one, in which case A would acquire, in the Proculian and later view, only one half. The Sabinians treat such a stipulation as one, with a name uselessly added[3].

(e) Where a legal rule bars acquisition to one owner, the other takes all. Thus if a *pupillus* alienates to a common slave one of whose owners is his tutor, the conveyance to the tutor cannot take effect, as he cannot authorise a transaction for his own benefit[4]. Here too we have Julian to deal with, and it is probable that he regarded it as two transactions, otherwise, as Salkowski says[5], the authorisation being *pro parte* null, the gift ought to have been valid only *pro parte*. This seems the only case mentioned[6].

Many difficult questions arise where the transaction brings one or more of the common owners into play on both sides; *e.g.* on purchase by a common slave from one of his owners. The general principle is that such a transaction is void, so far as concerns the proportion of the slave which is vested in the other party. If he stipulates *nominatim* or *iussu* for one master, from another, the transaction is good, but if he stipulates simply, the contract is void as to that part of him which the promisor owns, since a man cannot stipulate with himself or his own slave. The rest goes to the others[7]. It is not a case for the rule that what cannot be acquired to one goes to the other: the transaction is *pro parte* wholly void. In one case the slave appears on both sides. Having stipulated for his master A from his master B, he takes an *acceptilatio* for B from A. This is quite valid[8]. If a common owner

---

[1] 45. 3. 1. 4.

[2] Salkowski discusses (*op. cit.* 106 *sqq.*) the inconveniences which would result from the other view, since we must assume that the form was not adopted for no reason, but because the other slave was concerned. He takes a somewhat different view of the meaning of Julian's reasoning.

[3] G. 3. 103.   [4] 26. 8. 12.   [5] *op. cit.* 112.

[6] S. (*op. cit.* 114) discusses the case of a man who writes a legacy to a man of whom he is part owner: the name being a *falsum* the whole thing is void, 48. 10. 14. 1. The text has traces of an earlier view that it may have been valid for the other owner. Julian appears obscurely. If he held it valid at all he must, it seems, have held it wholly valid as two distinct gifts one of which had failed. S. discusses other possible cases.

[7] 45. 3. 7. 1. He may stipulate for himself *nominatim* to one of his masters though not to himself, 45. 3. 2, 18. 1. See Salkowski, *op. cit.* 85.

[8] 46. 4. 8. 2. No authority on other contracts.

pledges his part of the slave to the other this is valid, and will have to be reckoned with in *communi dividundo*[1]. No doubt the slave can do it himself.

There are few texts dealing with conveyance *inter vivos*. Where an owner gives money to a common slave, if his intent is merely to add to his *peculium*, held on his account, there is no change of ownership. But if he gives it as he would have given it to a *servus alienus*, the others take that share of the gift which they have in the slave[2]: his own proportion remains with the donor. Another text, obscure and corrupt, seems to lay down the same rule[3]. It will be observed that the rule brings about the same result as if the conveyance had been wholly valid: the owner of the slave has his right share of the thing conveyed, but by retention, not on conveyance. There is another case in the same range of ideas, but turning on a different principle. A common slave gives from his common *peculium* to the wife of one of his owners: the gift is void in proportion to the husband's share in the slave[4].

In relation to *hereditas* there are some complications, but as most of these arise where the gift is accompanied by a manumission, they will be considered later[5]. If the slave is instituted without liberty, this is *ut alienus*[6], and he will take, on general principle, at the command of, and for the benefit of, his other master. If he is sole heir he takes all, and his other masters divide in proportion to their share in him[7]. If he is one of several *heredes*, we are not told exactly what share he will take. Salkowski[8] thinks that as he is *sine libertate institutus*, the gift being void as to that part of him which belonged to the testator, the other heirs can claim nothing, as his owners, through him, for they acquire him only on entry, and can claim nothing in the inheritance through him, as he is a *servus hereditarius*[9]. Thus his other owner will acquire through him the whole part of the *hereditas* which was left to the slave. It might be said, simply, that the gift ought to be void as to the share which belonged to the deceased, so that this part would go by accrual. But this is not to give sufficient force to Ulpian's energetic language[10]: the institution is to be regarded as if he were a *servus alienus*. Paul uses the same expression—*ut alienus*—in laying down the rule that if I institute my co-owner and a common slave, *sine libertate*, this is valid[11]. The rule seems to be that it is construed as *institutio* of a *servus alienus* for all purposes[12].

[1] 10. 3. 6. 9. [2] 41. 1. 37. 1. [3] *h. t.* 17.
[4] 24. 1. 38. *pr.* [5] *Post,* Ch. xxv. [6] Ulp. 22. 7, 10.
[7] In. 2. 14. 3. [8] *op. cit.* 16.
[9] 29. 2. 43. See however, *ante,* p. 259.
[10] Ulp. 22. 7, 10. [11] 28. 5. 90.
[12] And thus there is no reason to appeal to the obscure rule as to *servi hereditarii.* A *hereditas* is left to me. I direct a *servus communis* of me and the *hereditas* to enter. I acquire the *hereditas,* but here he is doing only a ministerial act, 41. 2. 1. 18.

In legacy the rule is clear that where a legacy is left by one of his owners to a common slave, the other owners take the whole gift, not merely the proportion corresponding to their shares, dividing it in proportion to their shares in him[1]. The reason for this is differently given by different jurists. Julian says it is because the other owner is the only one who can acquire at the time of *dies cedens*[2]. But this does not explain why it is not void *pro parte* as a gift *inter vivos* would be. In another text the same point arises, and Cassius is cited and approved, by Paul, as saying much the same thing, *i.e.* that it is to be treated as a case where all goes to one owner because the other cannot acquire[3]. This, as Salkowski says[4], is simply giving the rule as a reason for itself. Why is it construed not as gifts *inter vivos* from one master are, but as gifts from third parties are, where from some cause one owner cannot acquire? We know that the reason for this last distinction is, that in the case of gifts from an outsider there is no fundamental invalidity in the gift, but only in the receiver, so that the whole thing may conceivably be good, while, where the donor is one owner, the part of the transaction which is with himself is necessarily void, so that the gift fails *pro parte*[5]. Why is not this rule applied here? The answer may be that we have here an instance, not isolated, of the extension to legacies of a rule laid down for institutions. The common slave is *ut alienus* for this purpose[6], and is regarded as belonging to the other owners. This is expressed in a well-known text by Sabinus, Julian, Pomponius and Ulpian: it is acquired not *propter communionem sed ob suam partem*[7]. There is not the same theoretical difficulty that would have arisen in institutions, on the other construction, but here as elsewhere the same rule of construction is applied to all parts of the same document. The same thing is done in relation to the effect of impossible conditions[8]. The result is reasonable: it is unlikely that a testator who left money to a slave held in common with X meant his heir to share it[9].

Co-heirs of an owner are co-owners of a special kind, but the most important and special rules arise where they do not succeed to the slave himself.

In regard to the Aedilician actions, as in the case of co-vendors, there can be redhibition to the heirs of a vendor *pro parte*, singly[10], and,

---

[1] 33. 5. 11; P. 3. 6. 4.   [2] 33. 5. 11.   [3] 35. 2. 49. *pr.*
[4] *op. cit.* 29.   [5] *Ante*, pp. 390, 391.   [6] Ulp. 22. 10.
[7] 17. 2. 63. 9. Salkowski's explanation is rather abstract: he regards it as material that it is not acquired till entry (*op. cit.* 28—31). It may be noted that Paul tells us that if a co-owner makes his *socius* sole *heres* and gives a legacy to a common slave this is void: he is a slave of the *heres*, 28. 5. 90.
[8] In. 2. 14. 10; D. 28. 7. 14; cp. G. 3. 98 as to the dispute between the schools.
[9] So in *fideicommissa*, 35. 2. 49. *pr.*
[10] 21. 1. 31. 10.

conversely, if there are several heirs to a vendee, they cannot redhibit unless all consent[1], lest, as Pomponius says, the vendor be put in the awkward position of having the thing returned *pro parte*, while another heir claims damages. On the other hand if the slave be dead or redhibited, they may sue singly for any damage done to them[2]. As they must sue together in the *actio redhibitoria*, Pomponius thinks it best for them to appoint a common *procurator ad agendum*[3]. If one co-heir or a person for whom he is responsible has made the slave worse, *culpa* or *dolo*, since this bars redhibition unless satisfaction is made[4], the others can claim for the damages in the *iudicium familiae erciscundae*[5].

There can be no noxal action between them, and thus if a slave of the *hereditas* steals from an heir he has no *actio furti*, his remedy being *iudicium familiae erciscundae* for simple damages, or surrender[6]. Each heir is liable noxally, and if he has defended, and rightly paid, he can recover *pro parte* in the same way[7].

In relation to contractual liability, the point of interest is that if the slave is freed or dead or legated, *sine peculio*, they are not common owners, but they succeed, together, to the liabilities of the owner. As the slave is not common, and they may have nothing in common, they may have no *iudicium communi dividundo*, and as the *iudicium familiae erciscundae* can be brought only once, this may not be available for distribution of loss[8]. Moreover on general principle, debts are divided *pro rata* among the heirs. Thus, while common owners may be liable *in solidum, ex institoria*, the heirs not holding the slave are liable only *pro parte*[9]. So in the *actio de peculio*, where the liability is only *annua* owing to the death or freeing of the slave, the heirs may be sued all together or singly, but in this case each is liable only so far as his share of the *peculium* goes, and cannot deduct what is due to other heirs[10]. If the slave himself is one of the heirs[11], he is liable to be sued as such, *de peculio*, but he cannot be liable personally as a son would be[12]. *Coheredes* can sue each other *de peculio* (though common owners cannot), but, apart from ownership of the slave, only like other creditors, *pro parte*[13]. This applies only to debts due to them personally: even if the slave is left to one of the heirs, there is no *actio de peculio* for debts to the estate : these might have been deducted in handing over the *peculium*[14]. So in the *actio de in rem verso* a *heres* is liable only *pro parte* for what was *versum* to the deceased, though he is of course absolutely liable as to what he himself has received[15].

[1] *h. l.* 5, 7. [2] *h. l.* 6. [3] *h. l.* 5, 9. [4] *Ante*, p. 61.
[5] 21. 1. 31. 9. [6] 10. 2. 16. 6. [7] *h. t.* 25. 15.
[8] *h. t.* 20. 4; 14. 3. 14. [9] 14. 3. 14. [10] 15. 1. 14, 27. 3, 30. 1. [11] 15. 1. 30. 2.
[12] P. 2. 13. 9; C. 4. 14. 1, 2; D. 15. 1. 30. 2, 3; 16. 3. 1. 18. [13] 15. 1. 29.
[14] 15. 1. 54, 58. See as to the difficulties, *ante*, pp. 230 *sqq.*, and *post*, App. II.
[15] 15. 1. 30. 1.

XXVII. COMBINATIONS OF THE FOREGOING INTERESTS.

The texts deal mainly with questions of acquisition, and they are fully discussed by Salkowski[1] : a few remarks will suffice.

(I) Joint usufructuaries and *bonae fidei possessores*. In the range of contractual liabilities complicated questions might arise, but they would be matters of account rather than of law, e.g. in the *actio tributoria*, where, the slave having a common *peculium*, one alone of the holders or fructuaries knew of the trading. But there is no authority on this or on noxal rights or liabilities. As to acquisition it is to be remembered that neither *nominatio* nor *iussum* can make a fructuary or a *bonae fidei possessor* acquire beyond the two *causae*[2]. So, one cannot acquire *ex re* of the other holder, or *ex operis* beyond his share. If then he stipulates *ex operis* simply, they acquire *pro rata*. If he does it *nominatim* for one, that one acquires *pro parte* : the rest is void, for the *nominatio* excludes both the owner and the other holder[3]. There is no logical reason why *iussum* should have had the same effect, but the rule of later law may have been so—*iussum pro nomine accipimus*[4]. As to acquisition *ex re*, there is some difficulty. What the slave acquires *ex re utriusque* they take *pro parte*, unless he expressly names one, or it is *iussu unius*, in which case all goes to that one, subject to adjustment by *iudicium communi dividundo* (*utilis*)[5]. This at first sight seems as if one was acquiring *ex re alterius*. But it is impossible to say to what part of the affair the particular acquisition referred : the whole *res* concerns him[6]. But apart from *iussum* or *nominatio*, what exactly is meant by *pro parte*? In proportion to their interest in the slave, or, as Salkowski thinks[7], in the business ? This would be convenient, but it rests on an assumption which would be fatal to the rule just laid down as to the effect of *nominatio*, for it requires, since *nominatio* is privative only, that the named person shall acquire only to the extent of his interest in the concern. More probably his interest in the slave is the decisive point, subject to adjustment. No doubt they were often the same. There is another question. If it is *ex re unius*, and there is no *iussum* or *nominatio*, the other can acquire nothing. But does all go to the other fructuary, or does he acquire only to the extent of his interest in the usufruct, the rest going to the *dominus* ? In later law it is clear that all goes to the fructuary[8]. An earlier view limits it in the way suggested. Scaevola is cited as holding both views[9]. The doctrine which

---

1 *op. cit.* 237 *sqq.*
3 45. 3. 24.
5 45. 3. 32, 33. 1.   Salkowski, *loc. cit.* takes a different view of the effect of this text.
6 *Ante*, p. 343.
8 7. 1. 25. 6; 45. 3. 19.

2 *Ante*, pp. 349, 363.
4 *Ante*, p. 349.

7 *op. cit.* 244, 5.
9 *Ibid.*; 41. 1. 23. 3.

prevailed is rested on the view that the *dominus* cannot be concerned, as it is *ex re fructuarii*, and that what one fructuary cannot acquire must go to the other. The argument is rather ill put, but the result is convenient and may be supported in another way. An acquisition *ex re* is not like one *ex operis, i.e.* it is not from a *causa* to which the other party is in part entitled, and thus there is no reason for applying the same rule[1], and making it in any way dependent on the division of the usufruct. The other view fails to take account of this distinction[2]. There was never any doubt that if it was *iussu* or *nominatim* to the one whose *res* it was, he acquired the whole[3].

(II) A person not entitled holds the man in good faith, as usufructuary. The guiding principle is that he cannot acquire more than if he were a real fructuary, nor than any *bonae fidei possessor* can acquire[4]. As their acquisitions are the same, there is nothing to be said.

(III) A person not entitled is in possession in good faith as a common owner. The rule is the same[5], but here it is a real limit. Though the acquisition is wholly *ex re eius*, he can by the rule acquire only *pro parte*, as that is the rule between common owners. No doubt adjustment is made by *communi dividundo* (*utilis*).

(IV) There is an existing usufruct, but there is an adverse *bonae fidei possessor*[6]. It would seem from what has been said[7] that the fructuary can acquire only *ex re*, at any rate we are not told that acquisition *ex operis* will avail to keep the usufruct on foot. The *bonae fidei possessor* will acquire *ex re* and *ex operis*. The fructuary can hardly acquire possession *ex re*, for the slave is in the adverse possession of someone else[8]. If the slave stipulates, *ex operis, nominatim* for the fructuary, this will exclude the possessor. But it does not seem that it ought to entitle the fructuary, for that he should acquire the whole of it as the result of *nominatio* implies that he would have acquired some of it, apart from *nominatio*. Salkowski, however[9], takes an opposite view on this last point, on the ground that the fructuary could have acquired *ex operis* but for the concurrence of the *bona fidei possessor*, which is excluded by the *nominatio*. This gives *nominatio* more than a privative effect.

(V) One of common owners has a usufruct or *bona fide* possession. The matter is discussed in only one text[10] in which Paul says, sub-

---

[1] *i.e.*, that in 45. 3. 24.
[2] Salkowski rests the same view on another basis. He gives a necessarily somewhat hypothetical account of the causes and histories of the two views, *op. cit.* 247—252.
[3] 7. 1. 25. 6; 41. 1. 23. 3. See also Kuntze, Servus Fructuarius, 55 *sqq.* Each of joint fructuaries or possessors may be sued *de peculio*, being liable only to the extent of the *peculium* in his hands. Suing one releases the others, subject to a right of *restitutio actionis*, 15. 1. 32. *pr. Post*, App. II.
[4] 41. 1. 54. 3 a.   [5] *Ibid.*   [6] Salkowski, *op. cit.* 243.
[7] *Ante*, p. 360.   [8] Arg. 41. 2. 1. 6.   [9] *op. cit.* 244.
[10] 45. 3. 20. 1; cp. 7. 9. 10. Fully discussed by Salkowski, *op. cit.* 237 *sqq.*

stantially, that if a slave who belongs to two, and is in the *bona fide* possession of one of them, stipulates at the order of the possessor, *in re utriusque,* they both acquire. This cannot be right: a common owner, *jubens ex re utriusque,* acquires *in solidum*[1]: he cannot have acquired less because he was also a *bonae fidei possessor*[2]. Paul ignores either the common ownership or the *iussum.* The common owner must have acquired *in solidum,* subject to adjustment[3]. With *nominatio* the result would be the same, as also in the unlikely case of *iussum* or *nominatio* of the non-possessing owner. Apart from *nominatio* or *iussum,* if it is *ex operis,* or *ex re possessoris* he alone acquires. Otherwise it is divided. The fact that the *res* is also common does not affect the matter, at this stage, though it is material in the ultimate settlement[4].

[1] *Ante,* p. 383.
[2] The matter of the stipulation is doubtful on the text: the obscurity does not affect the present point.
[3] *Familiae erciscundae* or *hereditatis petitio.* See Salkowski, *loc. cit.*
[4] Salkowski enters on conjectural calculations which seem to imply (1) that a part fructuary acquired *ex re sua* only in the proportion to which he was fructuary, which was not the rule of later law, and (2) that the shares in the *res communis* would affect the matter, for which there is no evidence, *ante,* p. 394.

PART II.

ENSLAVEMENT AND RELEASE FROM SLAVERY.

CHAPTER XVII.

ENSLAVEMENT.

JUSTINIAN[1] classifies the Modes of Enslavement as being either *Iure Gentium* or *Iure Civili*, the former being those conceived of as common to all States, the latter as peculiar to Rome. According to the Institutes, birth is not strictly under either of these heads: the classification is applied only to those ways in which a living person becomes a slave. In the Digest it covers birth as well[2]. Gaius speaks of the rule as to birth as being *iure gentium*[3]: the distinction is clearly classical. It should be noted that it is only as to their general principle that any of these rules can be said to be *iuris gentium*. In relation both to birth and to capture, the Roman law had many special rules. The distinction is of no great practical importance, but it is authoritative and convenient.

MODES OF ENSLAVEMENT, *IURE GENTIUM*.

These are two in number:

(1) Capture in war. This has already been discussed[4]. It was found convenient in considering the legal position of a *captivus* to treat, in anticipation, all the law of the topic.

(2) Birth. This is, in historic times, by far the most important of the causes of slavery. The general principle is simple. The child born

---

[1] In. 1. 3. 4.   [2] 1. 5. 5. 1.   Marcian.
[3] G. 1. 82 *sqq.*   [4] *Ante*, pp. 291 *sqq.*

of a female slave is a slave, whatever be the *status* of the father, and
conversely, if the mother is free the child is free, whatever the *status* of
the father. This, says Gaius, is the rule of the *ius gentium*[1]—the
general rule that where there is no *conubium* the child takes the *status*
of the mother, *i.e.* her *status* at the time of the birth[2]. It may be
added that the slave issue belongs to the owner of the mother at the
time of birth, not at the time of conception[3].

This, however, is only the general rule. Cases may present themselves in which a freewoman has a slave child, and conversely, in which
a slave woman gives birth to an *ingenuus*. In relation to them there
arise questions of some difficulty.

Cases in which the child of a freewoman is a slave. There appear
to be only three.

(a) By the *Sc.* Claudianum (A.D. 53) it was provided that if a freewoman cohabited with a slave to the knowledge of his *dominus* the
child might, by agreement between her and the *dominus*, be a slave.
This rule, which was abolished by Hadrian, will be discussed later in
connexion with other provisions of this enactment and of legislation
which arose out of it. It is hardly possible to isolate this provision for
the purpose of discussion[4].

(b) Gaius observes that if a freewoman cohabited with a slave,
whom she knew to be one, the issue was a slave. This rule, operative
in the time of Gaius, but of earlier origin[5], is credited by him to a
certain *lex*, the name of which is lost. It is difficult to see why Hadrian
abolished the rule last mentioned without destroying this similar
inelegantia. Accordingly Huschke[6] suggests that a hiatus in the
manuscript should be filled by the words *e lege* Latina. His conjecture
starts from the idea that the law was not a Roman law, but local, a
view which gets some support from Gaius' allusion to those *apud quos
talis lex non est*[7]. Huschke adds that any such general rule as this
would render meaningless the above provision of the *Sc.* Claudianum.
The suggestion Latina, as opposed to any other people, is due to the
fact that Vespasian, who, as Gaius says, abolished one provision of this
law, is known to have innovated largely in the law of Latinity[8]. There
is little trace of the rule in later times, a circumstance which further

---

[1] G. 1. 32; cp. In. 1. 3. 4; D. 50. 2. 9. *pr.*; C. 7. 14. 9.
[2] Ulp. 5. 9—10; Greg. Wis. 6. 3; C. 3. 32. 7; D. 1. 5. 24. A *statulibera* was to be free on
having three children. She had one and then three at a birth. It is a question of fact which of
these was born last and so is *ingenuus*, 1. 5. 15, 16.
[3] 13. 7. 18. 2; 41. 1. 66; C. 3. 32. 12.   [4] *Post*, p. 412.
[5] G. 1. 85, 86. Older than Vespasian.
[6] The hiatus is very small and the words are clearly an insertion, as H. says. Most editors
insert something. Böcking, "*e lege Aelia Sentia.*"
[7] G. 1. 86.   [8] Reff., Huschke, *loc. cit.*

supports the view that it was not a general law. What may be traces of it are found in two or three texts. Thus it is said by Papinian that an enquiry into the *status* of a child may prejudice that of his deceased father[1]. So in A.D. 215 a woman who has married a slave thinking him free is informed that her child is *ingenuus*[2]. There must have been some reason for the enquiry, and both these texts are after Hadrian's repeal of the rule in the case last discussed. But, as we shall see shortly, there survived other rules under the *Sc.* which would account for the remarks[3].

(c) In A.D. 468 Anthemius[4] enacted that any woman marrying her own *libertus* was liable to deportation, the issue to be slaves, and to belong to the Fisc.

Cases in which the child of an *ancilla* is free. There are several.

(a) Among the many rules introduced, we are told, *favore libertatis*[5], was one that if the mother were free at any moment between conception and birth, the child is free[6]. The rule seems to have begun in an isolated humane decision of Hadrian[7], adopted in practice as a general rule. So far as the rule is concerned that the child is free if the mother is free at the time of the birth, there is no *favor libertatis*: it is common law[8]. It may not indeed be necessary to appeal to *favor libertatis* in any case. There is a rule of much wider application that a child in the womb is to be regarded as already born so far as this makes to his own advantage, but not for the advantage of other people or to his own detriment[9]. But the present may well be its earliest application, as it is assuredly its most important, so that this wider rule may be only a further generalisation. It is repeatedly laid down in relation to the case we are discussing. *Media tempora libertati prodesse, non nocere possunt*[10]. *Non debet calamitas matris nocere ei qui in ventre est*[11]. It must be noted that Gaius[12] cites a current opinion which would in part except from this rule the case of a *civis* Romana who was enslaved *ex Sc.* Claudiano. A child of which she was already pregnant was on this view a slave if *volgo conceptus*, free if *ex iustis nuptiis*.

(b) The principle was carried still further in the interest of the child. If the mother was a *statulibera* and the child is born after

---

[1] 40. 15. 2. *pr.* This was a puzzle to the Glossators, Haenel, Diss. Domm. 185.
[2] C. 5. 18. 3.   [3] *Post*, pp. 412 *sqq.*
[4] Nov. Anthem., 1. No trace of this rule in Justinian's law.
[5] P. 2. 24. 2.   [6] In. 1. 4. *pr.*; C. 9. 47. 4.
[7] 1. 5. 18; Girard, Manuel, p. 99.   [8] G. 1. 39.
[9] 1. 5. 7, 26; 38. 17. 2. 3; 50. 16. 231.   [10] P. 2. 24. 3.
[11] 1. 5. 5. 2, 3. Specially illustrated in the case of *captiva* and *serva poenae*, 1. 5. 18; 38. 17. 2. 3; 48. 23. 4. A *condemnata* is kept till her child is born: he is then *ingenuus*, C. 9. 47. 4. She may not even be tortured, 48. 19. 3; P. 1. 12. 5.
[12] G. 1. 91. The epitomator of Gaius states it as law, G. Ep. 1. 4. 9. See *post*, p. 414. For another exception in the case of *libertae ingratae*, *post*, p. 427.

the condition is satisfied, it is free even if the mother never actually became free, owing to captivity[1] or *condemnatio*[2]. The supervening slavery which bars the mother's liberty is not allowed to prejudice the child. In the first case the liberty will take effect by *postliminium,* even though the child was not conceived till the captivity had begun[3]. It is unlikely that this is also the case where the mother has been condemned: there is in that case no principle of *postliminium* to help it out. There never was a time during gestation in which there was a *spes libertatis.*

(*c*) Gaius[4] tells us that, by the doubtful *lex* Latina already mentioned, male issue of a freeman and an *ancilla* whom he thought free was *ingenuus.* Vespasian repealed this rule, though he left the other.

(*d*) By a *Sc.* Silanianum[5] the inheritance of a man who is supposed to have been killed by someone of his household may not be entered on, or his will opened, till an enquiry has been held[6]. If, during the delay thus caused, an *ancilla,* freed by the will, has a child, Justinian decides, settling certain doubts, that if the will ultimately takes effect the child so born is an *ingenuus*[7].

(*e*) If the mother is a slave at the time of the birth, but already entitled to her freedom under a *fideicommissum* the child is an *ingenuus* if the delay is due to the fault of the *fiduciarius*[8], the mother having demanded the manumission[9], but not if it is an unavoidable or purely accidental delay[10]. If, in case of fault, the mother has not demanded it, the child is a slave, but the mother is entitled to have it handed over to her for manumission[11], and the same rule applies where the liberty is not strictly due, because the heir had delayed entry so that the child shall be born his slave. Here too she is entitled to have the child handed over for manumission[12]. These cases will arise again for discussion[13].

(*f*) If there is a direct gift of liberty by will to a woman, and the heir delays entry, a child born to her during the delay will be declared free on application to the Praetor, on the same principles as in the case of *fideicommissum*[14].

(*g*) If there is a direction that freedom is to be given to an unborn person, Justinian decides, settling doubts, that the child shall be free, whether the mother is still a slave or not[15].

---

[1] 40. 7. 6. 1.　　　　　[2] *h. l. pr.*　　　　　[3] *h. l.* 2.
[4] G. 1. 85.　　　　　[5] *Ante,* p. 94.　　　　　[6] P. 3. 5; D. 29. 5.
[7] C. 6. 35. 11.　He did not here deal with the case of an *ancilla* entitled to immediate freedom under a *fideicommissum.*
[8] 1. 5. 22; 38. 16. 1. 1; 38. 17. 2. 3; 40. 5. 53; C. 7. 4. 3; P. 2. 24. 4.
[9] 40. 5. 26. 1; C. 7. 4. 4.　　　　　[10] The texts cited base the rule on *mora.*
[11] 40. 5. 26. 1.　　　　　[12] 40. 5. 53.
[13] *Post,* Ch. xxvii.　　　　　[14] Perhaps due to Marcellus, 40. 5. 55. 1.
[15] C. 7. 4. 14; *post,* Ch. xxiv.

(h) If a manumission is of a sort that is valid only on cause shewn before the *consilium*, and a child is born while the enquiry is in progress, the child is *ingenuus* if the manumission is ultimately allowed[1].

(i) Another possible case is suggested by a constitution of Justinian. He enacts that an *ancilla* whom her owner has treated as a concubine till his death is free, and her children are *ingenui*. The enactment is obscure: it may be that the gift is retrospective, in which case the *ingenuitas* of the children is not exceptional[2].

We pass now to the *iure civili* causes of enslavement. Several of these belong to early law, and do not really concern us. Such are:

(a) *Furtum manifestum*. By the XII Tables, while a slave who was caught in manifest theft was scourged and thrown over the Tarpeian Rock, a freeman was scourged and *addictus* to him from whom he had stolen[3]. Gaius, speaking of the *addictio*, says that the *Veteres* were not agreed as to the exact effect of this, whether he became at once a slave, or was in the position of an *adiudicatus*[4], who would not become a slave till after some delay, and then was sold *trans Tiberim*. It is idle to attempt to settle what was controverted among the early lawyers themselves, but it is not easy to see what the delay could mean here. Aulus Gellius, quoting Sextus Caecilius, speaks of it as *in servitutem traditio*, and seems to imply that the man remained as the slave of the injured person[5]. In any case the punishment was *capitalis*, and reduced him ultimately to slavery. But the whole rule fell into disuse when the Praetor introduced the fourfold penalty[6].

(b) Evasion of the census. Persons who were *incensi* were liable to be sold by the public authority[7]. The object of this was to punish avoidance of taxation. It became unimportant when the State ceased to tax *cives*, about 166 B.C., and passed into oblivion with the census itself[8].

(c) Evasion of military service. Gaius, whose text is imperfect, and Ulpian, do not mention this. It might be by evasion of the census, or by desertion, or by self-mutilation[9]. Offenders were sold, presumably *trans Tiberim*[10].

---

[1] 40. 2. 19. A minor under 20 could free *matrimonii causa*. He must marry the woman within six months. If she is pregnant when freed, and a child is born before the marriage, its status will depend on the event, marriage or not. *Post*, Ch. xxiii.
[2] C. 6. 4. 4. 3. Apparently part of a comprehensive enactment, mainly declaratory.
[3] Aul. Gell. 11. 18. 8.   [4] G. 3. 189.
[5] Aul. Gell. 20. 1. 7. It is possible that a practice of redemption on payment of fourfold may have existed.   [6] G. 3. 189; In. 4. 1. 5.
[7] G. 160; Ulp. 11. 11. See Cicero, Pro Caec. 34. 99 and Dion. Hal. 4. 15.
[8] Cuq, Instit. Jurid. (Ed. 1) 1. 542. Gaius says, *pridem desuetudine abolitum est*. See Livy 1. 44. Cicero holds (Pro Caec. 34. 99) that the state is not depriving him of his liberty (no *lex* can do this), but that by not putting his name on the roll he has abdicated his rights. As to this see Mommsen, Strafrecht, 945.   [9] See references in Willems, Droit P. R. 117.
[10] The Digest shews it to have been long obsolete: there is no trace of it in the Empire, 49. 16. 4. 10.

(*d*) A judgment debtor might ultimately find himself sold into slavery[1]. The position of the *iudicatus* in early law is in some points obscure, and as, so far as these provisions are concerned, the system was very early obsolete and belongs to quite another branch of the law it is unnecessary to discuss it[2].

There were other causes of enslavement which continued to exist in law (though some were obsolete in practice), till Justinian's time, and were abolished by him.

(*a*) By the *lex* Aelia Sentia certain degraded slaves were ranked, on manumission, not as *cives*, but with the *dediticii*. Among their disabilities was the rule that they might not inhabit (*morari, habere domicilium*) within 100 miles of Rome. If they did so, they and their goods were to be sold by the public authority, on the condition that they were to be kept beyond that limit, and never freed: if they were manumitted they were to become *servi populi* Romani[3]. We are not told how they were to be dealt with if brought by their purchaser within the forbidden area. In the later law *dediticii* altogether disappear, and Justinian, remarking that no trace of the class is left and that it has become *vanum nomen*, definitely abolishes it[4].

(*b*) *Liberi expositi*[5]. Children exposed did not become slaves in classical law[6]. But there was a time, during the later Empire, in which a harsher rule prevailed[7]. Constantine enacted that one who charitably reared a boy (or girl) who had been exposed in early infancy by the father (or owner), or to his knowledge, might bring him up either as his child or as a slave, and the real father (or owner) should have no right in him[8]. We are here concerned only with those who were actually free-born. This rule is perhaps that referred to allusively in an enactment of 366, which speaks of persons who become slaves *bello*, praemio, *coniunctione*[9]. It is a reward to the charitable fosterer. In 374 the practice of exposing children was forbidden in very general terms. But though the statute speaks of an existing punishment, apparently severe, the rule must have been disregarded[10]. Justinian provided that no one who reared a child so exposed should have any right to claim him as a

---

[1] Aul. Gell. 20. 1. 47.
[2] Other cases mentioned by Cicero (de oratore, 1. 40; Pro Caec. 34. 98) do not concern us. Mere arbitrary condemnations by Emperors in specific cases are omitted. Mommsen, Strafrecht, 858. The rule that seems to have developed in Asia of enslaving those who conceal *fugitivi* is not Roman. Syro-Roman Law Book, Bruns-Sachau, 215.
[3] G. 1. 27, 160.   [4] C. 7. 5.
[5] See as to the sale of children so found, Mitteis, Reichsrecht und Volksrecht, 361.
[6] See the two cases in Suetonius, de Grammaticis, 7, 21, especially the later. When freed (and before), they were *ingenui*. See also, Pliny, Litt. Trai. 65, 66. Blair says (*op. cit.* 44) that in earlier law they were enslaved, but the authorities amount to little.
[7] Roby, Rom. Priv. Law, 1. 46; Wallon, *op. cit.* 2. 19 and 3. Ch. 10.
[8] C. Th. 5. 9. 1, 2. Cp. C. 8. 51. 1. It seems from C. 5. 4. 16 that under Diocletian they were free.
[9] C. Th. 4. 12. 6.   [10] C. 8. 51. 2. *Animadversio.*

slave or *adscriptitius*, but that such a child should retain his status as an *ingenuus*[1].

(*c*) *Coloni fugitivi.* These were an administrative difficulty: there is much legislation as to the penalties they incur. A constitution of Constantine says, of such fugitives, that *in servilem conditionem ferro ligari conveniet...ut officio quae liberis congruunt merito servilis condemnationis compellantur implere*[2]. This is not very clear: the *interpretatio* treats it as meaning actual slavery. It is not found in Justinian's legislation.

(*d*) The case of sale of *sanguinolenti* who were issue of a forbidden union with a barbarian, which was obsolete under Justinian, must be mentioned here, but will be treated in connexion with the general case of *sanguinolenti*[3].

Two cases of greater importance remain.

(*e*) *Servi poenae.* The general rule may be shortly stated thus: a person convicted of crime and sentenced in one of certain ways suffered *capitis deminutio maxima*, and became a slave. It was essentially capital punishment[4], and the *capitis deminutio* had all its ordinary results. It occurred at once on the final *condemnatio*[5], when there had been no appeal, or when an appeal had been decided against the accused[6], or in some cases when the Emperor had confirmed the rejection of the appeal[7]. The sentence must be one legal in relation to both the person and the crime. Thus the man was not a *servus poenae* if the magistrate had no jurisdiction or if he, being a *decurio*, was sentenced to a punishment not legal in regard to that class[8].

It was not every capital punishment which reduced the criminal to penal slavery. Anything which deprived him of *civitas* was capital[9]: many cases were punishable by *publicatio* and loss of *civitas*, and nothing more. A man so punished was not a *servus poenae*: he lost *quae iuris civilis sunt* but not *quae iuris gentium*[10]. Such a punishment was *deportatio*[11]. *Opus publicum perpetuum*, which meant road making and the like, was on the same level[12]. It was an ordinary way of punishing the lower class of freemen, but it could not legally be applied to *decuriones* on the one hand or to slaves on the other[13]. Such also

---

[1] C. 8. 51. 3 = C. 1. 4. 24. The text says nothing of any claim of the true father: its language strongly suggests that there was no *patria potestas* in anyone.
[2] C. Th. 5. 17. 1. 1. A good ms. reads *non congruent*. Mommsen *ad h. l.*　　[3] *Post*, p. 420.
[4] 48. 19. 2. *pr.*　　　　　[5] 28. 3. 6. 7, 8.　　　　　[6] *Ib.*; 48. 19. 2. 2.
[7] 28. 3. 6. 9. As to time limit and other restrictions on appeal see 49. 1. 1—13; P. 5. 33.
[8] 28. 3. 6. 10. *Post*, p. 405. Accused is not to be condemned in absence: notice must be given by the magistrate in his district. If he does not appear in one year from the publication of this notice his goods are forfeited to the Fisc, and in the meantime living things and other perishables may be sold. But he does not become a *servus poenae*, 48. 17.
[9] 48. 1. 2; 48. 19. 2. *pr.* Mommsen, Strafrecht, 907.　　　　　[10] 48. 19. 17.
[11] *Ib.*; C. 9. 47. 1; P. 5. 17. 2.　　　　　　　　　　　　　[12] C. 9. 47. 1.
[13] 48. 19. 34. *pr.*; C. 9. 47. 3. *Opus publicum* was usually temporary, and thus not capital and not involving loss of *testamenti factio*, 48. 19. 10. *pr.*, 28. 1, 34. *pr.*; P. 3. 4a. 9. In 48. 1.

were *proscriptio*[1] and *aquae et ignis interdictio*[2]. It was essential to *servitus poenae* to be lifelong, and thus it did not result from condemnation to *castigatio* or *vincula*[3]. Even condemnation to perpetual chains did not involve it, for though such punishments were not unheard of, they were always unlawful[4]. Imprisonment was not a recognised mode of punishment: *carcer ad continendos homines non ad puniendos haberi debet*[5]. Its essential purpose was the detention of persons accused of crime[6]. And though condemnation to work in the mines was a typical case of penal slavery, condemnation to help the miners (*ad ministerium metallicorum*), or even *ad metallum*, for a term, was not *servitus poenae*, and thus children born to women so condemned were free[7]. The most usual form of penal slavery was that resulting from condemnation *in metallum* or *ad opus metalli*[8], the latter being a little lighter in the matter of chains[9]. These were essentially perpetual, and if the sentence were expressed in terms which made the punishment temporary, it was construed as *ministerium metalli*[10], and thus was not slavery. There was no system of ticket-of-leave, but Antoninus Pius provided that old and infirm prisoners might be released, after 10 years' service, if they had relatives to look after them[11]. Another form of penal slavery mentioned in the Digest is *ludum venatorium*. This was a lighter punishment, involving hunting, with arms, wild beasts in the arena, applied to young offenders who had incurred capital liability. It involved some training and skill, and little danger, and on this account some jurists doubted whether it were really penal slavery. But it was perpetual, and the Digest is clear[12].

A death sentence also involved penal slavery for the interval between sentence and death[13]. This is not quite so empty a statement as it seems. The Roman law had a number of forms of execution, *e.g.* beheading, *ad gladium* (or *ad ferrum*) *traditio*, crucifixion, burning (of late introduction), *etc.*[14] Even in these cases there might be an appreciable interval, for it was not unusual to keep condemned men in order to extract from them, by torture, evidence against other men[15].

9. 10. *pr.* a slave refused by his master after punishment is sent to *opus publicum in perpetuum*, but this is not exactly punishment.
   [1] C. Th. 9. 42. 24.
   [2] P. 5. 17. 3, 26. 3, 29. 1; G. 1. 90 *etc.* *Aquae et ignis interdictio* though mentioned in the Digest (1. 5. 18; 48. 1. 2) and Code (C. 5. 16. 24) is superseded by other punishments in later law, 48. 19. 2. 1.
   [3] 48. 19. 10. *pr.*, 28. 4, 33, 34.
   [4] P. 5. 4. 22; 5. 18. 1; C. 9. 47. 6, 10; D. 48. 19. 8. 13, 35.   [5] 48. 19. 8. 9.
   [6] C. Th. 11. 7. 3. As to its use in *coercitio*, Mommsen, *op. cit.* 48.
   [7] 48. 19. 8. 8, 28. 6. If no term was stated, temporary condemnation was for ten years.
   [8] 48. 19. 8. 6, 36. Work *in calcaria vel sulpuraria* was *in metallo, h. t.* 8. 11.
   [9] *h. t.* 8. 6.   [10] *h. t.* 28. 6.   [11] *h. t.* 22.
   [12] *h. t.* 8. 11, 12. For a full account of penalties, Mommsen, Strafrecht, 949 *sqq.*
   [13] 28. 3. 6. 6; 48. 19. 29. As to the use of the word *animadvertere* in connexion with death sentences, Mommsen, Strafrecht, 911.
   [14] P. 5. 17. 2; Coll. 11. 6, 7, 8; C. Th. 9. 7. 6; D. 28. 1. 8. 4; 48. 19. 28. *pr.* Mommsen, *op. cit.* 911 *sqq.*
   [15] 48. 19. 29. Statutory rules fixing minimum delays, Mommsen, *op. cit.* 912.

But the classical law required those condemned *ad gladium* to be destroyed within the year, a rule which no doubt applied to other modes of direct execution and existed in the later law as well[1]. There are however two cases which are on a different footing. These are condemnation to the arena, to fight either as a gladiator or with wild beasts. The former punishment was abolished by Constantine for the Eastern Empire in A.D. 325[2]. In the West it continued till 404, when Honorius put a stop to such shows on the advice of Prudentius, on the occasion of the death of Telemachus, a monk who was stoned to death in the arena while exhorting the gladiators to peace[3]. But condemnation *ad bestias*, a very common punishment in classical times[4] and later[5], is repeatedly mentioned in Justinian's laws[6], and perhaps was never abolished. In these cases much time might elapse between the condemnation and the death. Thus Ulpian tells us that after three years in the arena they might be released from further service, and if having earned this they continued for two years more, they might get a complete pardon[7].

Freemen and slaves alike might be *servi poenae*[8], but the law was not alike for all. Slaves were in general more severely punished than freemen[9], and, apart from this, there were many special rules on this matter, which varied no doubt from time to time. Thus though death and other capital punishments might be inflicted on *decuriones*[10] it was essential that the matter be referred to the Emperor before it was carried out[11], and the same rule seems to have applied to *relegatio*[12]. But to degrading punishments they could not be condemned at all[13]. Their ascendants and issue were similarly protected[14], and the protection covered children born before the *decurionate* began, or after it ceased, provided they were conceived before its end[15]. The practical result is that a *decurio* could rarely become a *servus poenae*. The only possible case left is that of death *per gladium*. But there is a sweeping rule laid

---

[1] P. 5. 17. 2 ; Coll. 11. 7. 4.

[2] C. Th. 15. 12. 1 = C. 11. 44. 1. J. Gothofredus thinks he forbade gladiatorial shows altogether, arguing from the word *omnino*, but the next *lex* treats such shows as still in existence, and G. quotes from Libanus an account of them at Antioch, in 328. Probably as a punishment this was never common.

[3] Theodoretus, Hist. Ecc., cited Gothofredus, *loc. cit.*

[4] P. 5 *pass.* ; Coll. 11 *pass.*   [5] C. Th. 9. 18. 1 (= C. 9. 20. 16), *etc.*

[6] In. 1. 12. 3 ; C. 9. 47: 12 ; D. 28. 1. 8. 4 ; 48. 19. 11. 3, 12, 29, 31 ; 49. 16. 3. 10, 4. 1 ; 49. 18. 1, 3.

[7] Coll. 11. 7. 4.   Constantine's enactment (C. Th. 9. 18. 1) that, for offences under the *lex* Fabia, a freeman should be made to fight as a gladiator on the terms that before he could defend himself he should be *gladio consumptus*, is really a direction to execute *per gladium*.

[8] C. 9. 47. 11 ; 14. 2. 3.   See *ante*, p. 277.   [9] 48. 19. 16, 3 ; *ante*, p. 93.

[10] C. Th. 9. 42. 24 = C. 9. 49. 10.

[11] 48. 8. 16, which exempts persons holding any *honor*. See also 48. 19. 27. 1, 2.   [12] *Ibid.*

[13] *Fustibus caedi, metallum, opus metalli* or *ministerium metalli, furca*, burning, fighting with beasts, *etc.*: such penalties were altered or discharged by the Emperor. Even *opus publicum* was forbidden, C. Th. 12. 1. 47, 80 ; C. 9. 47. 3, 9, 12 ; D. 48. 19. 9. 11.

[14] 48. 19. 9. 12, 13 ; C. 9. 47. 9, 12.

[15] 48. 19. 9. 14, 15 ; 50. 2. 2. 2, 3, 6.   A child conceived and born during temporary removal from the *ordo* was protected, though his father died before the time expired, 50. 2. 2. 5.

down by Hadrian that a death penalty was not to apply to a *decurio* except for parricide[1]. It may be that this, like those already noted, is only a requirement that the Emperor must intervene before it could be carried out. Certainly another text contemplates a death penalty under this condition[2]. In any case it is clear that these persons could not be ordinary *servi poenae*.

Milites and *veterani* and their children were in much the same position: they were not punishable by *metallum, opus metalli*, fighting with beasts, *furca, fustigatio*, or, generally, any penalty from which a *decurio* was protected[3]. Nothing is said of *parentes*, and the privilege may not have applied to remoter issue[4].

Other privileged classes are mentioned who could hardly become *servi poenae*, but we have no details[5]. There is, however, at least in later law, a general rule. We learn that, by various Imperial enactments, *honestiores* were not liable to *fustigatio*[6], and also that those who were not liable to *fustigatio* were to have the same *reverentia* as *decuriones* had[7], and so could not be condemned *in metallum*[8]. This is in the Digest, but rules of this kind are laid down in relation to a number of different crimes, by a large number of earlier texts. There are, of course, many texts in which a capital punishment is declared without distinctions[9]. But there are many cases in which, while *humiliores* are killed, or condemned *in metallum*, *honestiores* are deported[10] or even merely *relegati*[11], which involves no *capitis deminutio*. There are others in which *honestiores* appear as liable to capital punishment, but in less degrading forms than those which apply to *humiliores*[12]. In one text a similar distinction is drawn between *ingenui* and others[13], and in another it is between slaves and free[14].

The goods of a person capitally condemned were forfeited to the

---

[1] 48. 19. 15; cp. 48. 22. 6. 2. Mommsen (*op. cit.* 1036) adds *maiestas*.
[2] 48. 8. 16.
[3] 49. 16. 3. 1; 49. 18. 1, 3. A *miles condemnatus* for a military offence, though to death, is not a *servus poenae*. He can make a will, 28. 3. 6. 6.
[4] C. 9. 47. 5. A *miles* loses his protection if he becomes a *transfuga*, 49. 16. 3. 10. Special liabilities of *milites*, 48. 19. 14, 38. 11, 12; 49. 16 *passim*.
[5] Bishops, C. Th. 16. 2. 12; *Senatorii*, C. Th. 9. 40. 10. As to *Clarissimi* and *Illustres*, C. Th. 9. 1. 1; C. 3. 24. 1; and D. 48. 8. 16.
[6] 48. 19. 28. 2.
[7] Mommsen observes (Strafrecht, 1036) that though the rules are expressly laid down merely for *decuriones*, this is because they are the lowest of the privileged classes: what holds for them holds *a fortiori* for the higher classes. It should be noted, however, that some of the exemptions are introduced to make the decurionate less unpopular: other applications are secondary.
[8] 48. 19. 28. 5.
[9] *e.g.* P. 5. 20. 1; 5. 21. 1, 3, *etc.*
[10] P. 1. 21. 4, 5; 5. 19. 1; 5. 21. 2; 5. 25. 1, 2, 7 (=D. 48. 19. 38. 7); 5. 26. 1; Coll. 8. 5. 1; 12. 5. 1.
[11] P. 5. 20. 2; 5. 23. 14 (=D. 48. 19. 38. 5); 5. 23. 19; 5. 25. 8, 9; 5. 26. 3; Coll. 1. 7. 2; 11. 8. 3; 14. 2. 2; cp. C. Th. 7. 18. 1; D. 48. 19. 38. 3.
[12] P. 5. 23. 1, 16; Coll. 8. 4. 2. *Plebei, tenuiores*, Mommsen, Strafrecht, 1035.
[13] C. Th. 9. 18. 1 (= C. 9. 20. 16).
[14] P. 5. 22. 2. As to the line between *honestiores* and *humiles* see Mommsen, *loc. cit.*

Fisc[1], but this *publicatio* occurred only on final *condemnatio,* not on death pending appeal[2], unless the prisoner committed suicide in order to avoid liability for crime[3] such as would involve forfeiture[4]. From the forfeitable fund were excluded certain things in which the criminal had only a limited interest, and also gifts to emancipated children made before the accusation, although the *hereditas* would practically include this in consequence of the rules as to *collatio*[5]. A *dos* given by him to his daughter was not forfeited by his condemnation, even though she died, unless it was given in expectation of condemnation[6], and thus a *dos* which he had promised to give might be recovered from the Fisc by the husband. If her marriage was dissolved before the father's condemnation and she had assented to the father's receiving the *dos,* the Fisc could claim it: if she had not, it was her property[7]. All this shews that what was forfeited was what was his own, including, however, what had fallen to him after the condemnation[8]. It must further be noted that collusive or gratuitous alienation after the accusation would not save the property so dealt with[9], and that the Fisc here, as in other cases, took the estate subject to all debts. If it was solvent the Fisc paid the creditors and took the surplus: if insolvent the goods were sold and the Fisc took nothing[10].

This rule of forfeiture was subject to restrictions, dating from the classical law, in favour of the criminal's natural heirs. From the title of, and some citations from, a book of Paul's on the matter, it can be inferred that no relatives but *liberi iusti* had a claim, and that their claim was only to a part of the goods, though Hadrian, by way of grace, allowed the whole to be divided where there were several sons[11]. Any children conceived before the condemnation were entitled to share[12], and even children adopted in good faith before the accusation[13].

The rules as to the persons who were entitled to share, and as to the proportion of the estate to be so restored, were the subject of

---

[1] C. 9. 49. 4; P. 5. 12. 12; D. 48. 20. 1. *pr.* Apparently the clothing of the criminal was disposed of by the executive in its service, 48. 20. 6. *Publicatio* is part of the deterrent punishment. It does not result from the man's vesting in the Fisc: he does not. See *ante,* p. 277.
[2] 48. 20. 11. *pr.*   [3] P. 5. 12. 1; C. 9. 50. 1, 2.   [4] 48. 21. 3. 1.
[5] The *dos* and *donatio propter nuptias* of the criminal were not forfeited. See on these rules, C. Th. 9. 42. 1; *h. t.* 15; C. 5. 16. 24; 9. 49. 9.
[6] 48. 20. 8. 4, 9.   [7] 48. 20. 10. 1.
[8] 48. 20. 7. 5, 10. This could not occur in case of a *servus poenae* as his enslavement destroyed his power of acquisition, 49. 14. 12.
[9] 39. 5. 15; 48. 20. 11. 1.
[10] 49. 14. 1. 1, 11, 17, 37. It is liable to creditors of the estate (48. 20. 4, 10. *pr.*; C. 9. 49. 5) and conversely it can claim from debtors thereto, 49. 14. 3. 8, 6, 21.
[11] 48. 20. 7. *pr.*, 3.   [12] *h. t.* 1. 1.
[13] *h. t.* 7. 2. Of course nothing acquired through the crime was included, *h. t.* 7. 4. A woman entered *iussu patris* on the *hereditas* of one she had poisoned. Antoninus Pius declared this forfeited, though it was never hers, *Ib.* These rules seem to be all imperial. They can hardly be juristic and there is no reference to any *lex* or *Sc.* or Edict.

much legislation, of which, though the record is not complete, a general account can be given. Some constitutions refer only to *deportati*, but in most cases it seems clear that they cover *damnati* also. The general principle that children are to be entitled to a share is laid down by Callistratus in terms which suggest that part only went to them[1], though it may be that by A.D. 241 the whole was available[2]. All details must be looked for in the Codes. In 356 it was enacted that all relatives to the third degree were to have a claim, before the Fisc, to all the goods, except in cases of *maiestas* and magic in which even *liberi* were to get nothing[3]. Two years later this was repealed: all was to go to the Fisc in all cases[4]. In 366 it was enacted that children were to have all the goods except in case of *maiestas*[5]. In 380 Theodosius I legislated comprehensively on the matter. His enactment dealt, in terms, only with *damnatus interfectus*, but it no doubt covered the *servus poenae*. He gave children and grandchildren all the estate, while if there were only remoter issue, through males, they shared half. He added provisions giving a constantly lessening share to father, mother, with or without *ius liberorum*, paternal grandparents, and brothers and sisters, agnatic, emancipated and uterine[6]. No one else was to exclude the Fisc. In 383 he included *postumi*, probably to settle doubts[7]. In 421 all claims were suppressed except those of parents and children[8]. In 426 Theodosius II seems to have suppressed all claims but those of *filii*, who were to have half[9]. Justinian accepted this enactment, changing *filii* to *liberi* and giving the language a more general form[10]: as Theodosius wrote it, it might have referred only to a special case. He also accepted the rule admitting *emancipati* and *postumi*[11]. This represents the law of his time[12] till 535 when he gave all the property to successors, suppressing any claim of the Fisc[13]. Three special cases need mention.

(*a*) Women. If a woman was condemned her children could claim nothing[14]. The rule is expressed as one of undoubted and, apparently, ancient law. This exclusion is shewn by Paul's language to have been

---

[1] 48. 20. 1.
[2] C. 6. 6. 5. They are to have *obsequium* of (all) the *liberti* of the *damnatus*. But the rights of *liberi patroni* are independent of those of patron, G. 3. 45; Ulp. 29. 5. This rule existed at a time (37. 14. 4) when it is fairly clear that they had only a share of the *bona*. In the earlier empire it was usual to give part to the children in individual cases though there was no general rule. Tac. Ann. 3. 17; 4. 20; 13. 43; Plin. Epist. 3, 9, 27 cited Mommsen, Strafrecht, 1006. The rule, *nullam esse divisionem libertorum*, does not affect this matter, 10. 2. 41; 37. 14. 24.
[3] C. Th. 9. 42. 2.
[4] *h. t.* 4.   Constantius may have meant only to restore the old law.
[5] *h. t.* 6.   The *interpretatio* says, *ad filios vel ad heredes legitimos.*
[6] *h. t.* 9.   [7] *h. t.* 10.
[8] *h. t.* 23.   No claim is allowed in *maiestas*.   [9] *h. t.* 24. *pr.*
[10] C. 9. 49. 10.   [11] C. 9. 49. 8, 10.
[12] Fines short of *publicatio*, P. 5. 23. 14, 19; D. 48. 20. 1, *etc.*
[13] Nov. 17. 12.
[14] C. 9. 49. 6.   The text speaks of *deportatio* but no doubt the rule is general.

due to the fact that the real basis of the claim of the children in such cases was their civil law position as *sui heredes*[1]. He remarks that as parents could not arbitrarily exclude them by an expression of will, so they ought not to be able to do so by crime. None of this language applies to children of women: it is a late expression of the old civil law view of succession.

(*b*) *Decuriones.* The enactment of 426 provided that on *condemnatio* of a *decurio* his property should go to the *Curia*, which might keep it, or allot it to anyone who would take over his responsibilities. If, however, there were male issue alone they took the property and the responsibilities. If there were daughters alone they took half. If there were both the males took half on account of their curial responsibility, and divided the other half with the females. Justinian adopted this, adding that *postumi* were to be entitled, and excluding any claim in *maiestas*[2].

(*c*) *Liberti.* The only statement we have of the rules in this case is in the Digest, and it may not represent classical law. A patron is to have the share he would have had in an ordinary case of death, the Fisc taking the rest[3]. This purports to be from Paul's book on the matter. Another text, from Macer, applies a similar rule to *liberi patroni*[4] and adds that if there are children of the *libertus* they exclude the children of the patron, and as these exclude the Fisc, the latter has no claim[5]. This is rather obscure: on the face of it, it gives them all, while, both in Paul's time and in Justinian's, the children of *ingenui* took only half: the reasoning shews that the exclusion was only from the part the patron would have taken[6].

A person condemned to penal slavery was ordinarily in that position for life, which, in the case of death sentences, would be short. But we have already seen that even persons condemned *ad bestias* had a hope of pardon[7], and of course in the case of a *damnatus in metallum* the chance of pardon was greater: it is clear on the texts that the case was not uncommon. We hear of *restitutio in integrum ius*, and of simple pardon. Each such release was an express act of authority, and the warrant would state the terms of it, which might, and as we shall see, often did, give rights more than mere pardon and less in various ways than complete restoration. A striking point is that in this connexion

---

[1] 48. 20. 7. *pr.* Her *dos* is subject to special rules. In some important crimes it is forfeited subject to claims of *vir*: in others it passes as if she were dead, 48. 20. 3—5.
[2] C. Th. 9. 42. 24; C. 9. 49. 10.　　　　　　　　　　　　　　　　[3] 48. 20. 7. 1.
[4] 48. 20. 8. *pr.* Though they do not claim *bonorum possessio* they exclude the Fisc as to their part, *h. l.* 2.
[5] 40. 20. 8. 1.
[6] The texts were written under the regime of the *lex* Papia, obsolete under Justinian. Complex questions arise but do not concern us.
[7] *Ante*, p. 405.

we hear nothing of manumission. A *servus poenae* was not the property of anyone, and could not well be released from anyone's *manus*: he regained his liberty by the Emperor's decree[1].

A pardon was commonly by *indulgentia generalis* or *communis*, no doubt on occasions of public rejoicing[2]. It released from the labour and made a man, who had been free, once more a freeman[3]. But it did not restore his former private rights. His property remained with the Fisc[4]. He did not recover old rights of action[5]. He did not recover *potestas*, and thus he could not acquire through his children[6]. He was not liable to old actions[7]. In one remarkable text, Ulpian is reported as saying that a person merely pardoned, and not *restitutus*, could not have succeeded under the *Sc.* Orphitianum, but, *humana interpretatione*, he was allowed to do so[8]. This last rule is no doubt Tribonian's: it jars with the others. The question whether it expresses a rule applicable in late law to other cases of succession must, on the texts, be answered in the negative[9]. One who had been a slave did not on pardon revert to his old *dominus*[10]. That ownership was gone, and though, up to the time of Caracalla, there seems to have been some doubt as to whether he vested in the Fisc, Ulpian, recording Caracalla's doubt, declares this to be the law[11], as also does a rescript of Valerian[12]. He was now an ordinary slave, capable of receiving fideicommissary gifts of liberty[13], and presumably of being sold[14]. Such a state of things is hardly applicable to a case where the slave was ultimately proved to have been innocent : it involves an unjustified injury to the *dominus*. Nor was *restitutio in integrum ius* applicable to a slave. For such cases the proper provision was the *revocatio* of the sentence, the effect of which was to restore the slave to his former position. The effect of the condemnation being completely undone, the old ownership revived. In a case recorded he had been instituted by his *dominus*, and he became again a *heres necessarius*. So too, a *statuliber revocatus* would still be free on the occurrence of the condition[15].

The release or pardon might be accompanied by a more or less complete restoration to his original position. The effect of complete restitution is illustrated in many texts. The man regained all rights of

---

[1] *Servi poenae* were released by local authority and put to work appropriate to *servi publici*. Trajan ordered them back to slavery, except old men who had been so released 10 years: these were put to inferior work. Pliny, Litt. Trai. 31, 32. In the early empire the Senate usually gave the pardon. Mommsen, Strafrecht, 484.
[2] C. 9. 51. 5, 9.
[3] Presumably to citizenship, though in a case in C. 9. 51. 3 this is expressly given.
[4] C. 9. 49. 4; 9. 51. 2.   [5] C. 9. 51. 5.   [6] *h. t.* 9.
[7] *h. t.* 4; D. 44. 7. 30.   [8] 38. 17. 1. 6.
[9] *h. l.* 4. See *post*, as to *restitutio*.   [10] 48. 19. 8. 12.
[11] 40. 5. 24. 5.   [12] C. 9. 51. 8.
[13] 40. 5. 24. 5.   [14] *Arg. h. l.* 6.
[15] 40. 4. 46. Restitution is not spoken of in connexion with those who had been slaves.

succession[1]; his will was revalidated[2]; he recovered his *potestas*[3], his property[4], *honores, ordo, munera* and so forth[5]. He became a good witness[6]. He regained all rights of action, and conversely became liable to old debts[7]. The actions were not *utiles* but *directae*[8]: in short, the effect of the enslavement was completely annulled[9].

This complete restitution was expressed by the words *per omnia in integrum*[10]; *in statum pristinum cum bonis*[11]; or the like, or by the mere word *restitutus*[12]. But less comprehensive forms are found giving a limited restoration. These naturally gave rise to questions of construction, some of which are recorded in the texts. If part of his property was restored, old debts revived against him *pro parte*[13], and presumably his old rights of action revived to the same extent[14]. If his pardon was accompanied by a regrant of *potestas*, he again acquired through his children[15]. Restitution to *praecedens dignitas*, with no reference to *bona*, did not restore any property or rights of action or any liabilities[16]. It did not replace him in his old *potestas*[17], for this involves property rights: it dealt only with public rights.

It is obvious that a restoration of *bona* may create complications where part of the property has passed to heirs. We do not know how these were dealt with at the time when even collateral heirs took some of the property: the rules we have are embodied in legislation of Constantine at a time when, so far as we know, the claim was confined to children. It is laid down on Papinian's authority, that acts done by a son of full age are confirmed, and not affected by his reentry into *potestas*—even any will he may have made. As to any acts done by a *pupillus, auctore tutore*, the law is obscure. The *tutela* of course ends unless, in the bad character of the father, there is a special reason for retaining it. The law is confirmed by insertion in Justinian's Code[18]. It will be remembered that by his time the rule confining claims to children was restored[19]. Justinian adopts the constitution with none

---

[1] P. 4. 8. 22; In. 1. 12. 1; 37. 1. 13; 37. 4. 1. 9, 2; 38. 17. 1. 4. The right of succession covered succession to those conceived before slavery, or if conceived during slavery, born after the restitution, 38. 17. 2. 3. In 48. 23. 4 it is said that if the child is conceived and born during slavery, the right of succession exists on grounds of humanity. This may be Tribonian.
[2] 28. 3. 6. 12.   [3] C. Th. 9. 43. 1; C. 9. 51. 13.
[4] Even payments due in the meantime, 34. 1. 11.
[5] 50. 4. 3. 2; C. 9. 51. 1.   [6] 22. 5. 3. 5.
[7] C. 9. 51. 11, 12; D. 48. 23. 2, 3.   [8] 48. 23. 2. 3.
[9] His *iura patronatus* are revived, a rule admitted with hesitation, of which there are signs in other of these rules, 48. 23. 1. 1; 37. 14. 21. *pr.* Conversely if he is a *libertus*, 38. 2. 3. 7. See 48. 23. 4; *h. t.* 1. 1. The doubts seem to turn on the point that slavery being akin to death must have extinguished these rights. They are not raised in other cases, *e.g. deportatio*.
[10] P. 4. 8. 22.   [11] C. 9. 51. 4.   [12] 38. 17. 1. 4.
[13] C. 9. 51. 3. A mere gift of money by the Emperor on his pardon produced no such effect. *Ib.*
[14] It does not follow. That he should receive his goods without liabilities is unjust to his creditors. No such point arises in the converse case.
[15] C. 9. 51. 9.   [16] 48. 23. 2, 3.   [17] C. 9. 51. 6.
[18] C. Th. 9. 43. 1 = C. 9. 51. 13, *remotis Ulpiani atque Pauli notis*.   [19] *Ante*, p. 408.

but very slight verbal changes, a circumstance which is unfortunate in view of its rambling and obscure character[1].

In 536 Justinian by a Novel[2], adverting to *condemnatio in metallum* as the typical form, definitely abolishes the rule that a convict becomes a *servus poenae*. His primary object is to prevent dissolution of marriage, and he lays down this rule, very characteristically in the middle of a long and comprehensive set of provisions on the subject of marriage[3].

(*f*)   Cases under the *Sc.* Claudianum and connected legislation.

By this enactment, of A.D. 52, it was provided (no doubt, *inter alia*), (1) that, if a freewoman[4] lived with the slave of another person after notice (*denuntiatio*) by the owner that he forbade it, she, and the issue, became his slaves[5]; (2) that, if the owner consented, she could remain free *ex pacto*, the issue being slaves[6]. This second rule Gaius tells us was abolished by Hadrian as being harsh and *inelegans*. For the future if the owner consented so that the mother remained free, the child was also to be free[7]. The text of Tacitus cited above says that there might be an agreement that she should be a *liberta*[8]. A point of status seems to be left to private agreement notwithstanding the maxim : *Conventio privata neque servum quemque neque libertum facere potest*[9]. The fact is that these are not mere private agreements : they are confirmed by the Senatusconsult[10].

The woman became the slave of the owner of the man if she persevered in the cohabitation after *denuntiatio* by him. It appears that one denunciation did not suffice : it must be three times repeated[11], and the third denunciation had, by an enactment of A.D. 317, to be in the presence of seven Roman witnesses[12]. One constitution speaks of the three denunciations as expressly provided for by the *Sc.* Claudianum[13], but it is at least equally probable that it was a juristic interpretation of

---

[1] It is not certain that as it appears in the Code of Theodosius it represents the original text.
[2] Nov. 22. 8.
[3] Nov. 134. 13 enacts that in case of *maiestas* the Fisc shall take *dos* and *donatio*, but lays down an order of preferential claims in other cases.
[4] Knowing she was free, P. 2. 21 a. 12.
[5] Taciti Annales, 12. 53; G. 1. 91, 160; P. 2. 21a. 1; Ulp. 11. 11; Tertullian, ad uxorem, 2. 8. Suetonius attributes the rule to Vespasian (Vesp. 11) but he only modified existing legislation, G. 1. 85.
[6] G. 1. 84; P. 4. 10. 2. As to the distinction between cohabitation in the owner's house and elsewhere, made in the Syro-Roman Law book, see Mitteis, Reichsr. und Volksrecht, 366; Mommsen, Strafrecht, 855.
[7] G. 1. 84.
[8] See Huschke, ad P. 4. 10. 2. One text, at least, suggests agreements affecting the children. Thus Ulpian speaks of *filius* and *filia* becoming *liberti*, and his language shews that it is a case which might have occurred both in Julian's and in Ulpian's time, 38. 17. 2. 2. See also P. 4. 10. 2.
[9] 40. 12. 37 ; C. 7. 16. 10.
[10] G. 1. 84. The latest reference to such agreements seems to be Cons. 9. 7, where some obscure words are understood by Huschke to refer to them.
[11] P. 2. 21a. 1; C. Th. 4. 12. 2, 3, 5, 7.
[12] *h. t.* 2.   [13] *h. t.* 5.

the word *perseveratio*, which is used in comments on the Sc.[1], and may have been contained in it. The enslavement was completed by a magisterial decree, following the third denunciation[2]. Neither Ulpian nor Gaius refers to the need for three denunciations, or to the decree, and Justinian in abolishing the whole rule speaks of Claudianum *senatus-consultum et omnem eius observationem circa denuntiationes et iudicum sententias*[3], language which suggests a construction of the lawyers[4].

In A.D. 314 Constantine seems to have enacted that no denunciations were needed, but, if this is really the effect of his enactment, it must have been repealed almost at once, for three years later we find the three denunciations assumed to be necessary[5]. In 331 he reverts to the rule of 314, declaring that no denunciations shall be needed[6]. In 362 Julian confirms the Sc. Claudianum, repealing all contrary laws, so that a freewoman cohabiting with a *procurator* or *actor* or any other slave, is not to be enslaved till after three denunciations[7]. The language suggests that in another law it was provided that the harsher rule should apply only where the slave was in a position of trust[8]. A law of 365 seems to shew that the three denunciations had gone out of use again[9]. In 398 Honorius and Arcadius again assert the need of them[10].

We are nowhere told expressly what becomes of her property. The Institutes say that she loses liberty *et cum libertate substantiam*[11], which does not prove that her *dominus* gets it. Another text says that if liberty is lost with *capitis minutio* there is *actio utilis* against the *dominus* for the debts[12]. This implies that he gets the property, but it does not expressly mention this case, and it would not strictly be true for all cases, *e.g. captivitas*. The only other view possible is that it goes to the natural heirs as on death: *servitutem mortalitati comparamus*[13]. But though this gets a certain support from the expression *successio misera-bilis*[14], it is most improbable in view of the general language of the texts above cited. Assuming that the *dominus* gets the property he is liable to *actiones utiles* already mentioned, and also to noxal actions[15].

Many of the texts speak of the woman to whom these rules applied as *civis* Romana, and Gaius seems expressly to limit the rule to this case[16]. It is clear that it applied also to Latinae: Paul puts them on

---

[1] P. 2. 21 a. 13, 18; Tertullian, ad uxorem, 2. 8. [2] P. 2. 21 a. 17.
[3] C. 7. 24. P. 2. 21 a. 17 shews that the Sc. did not provide for the *decretum*. Cp. C. 7. 15. 1. *pr.*
[4] *Denuntiatio* might be by *procurator* or duly authorised son or slave, P. 2. 21 a. 4.
[5] C. Th. 4. 12. 1, 2. [6] *h. t.* 4. [7] *h. t.* 5.
[8] Gothofredus thinks a special rule as to these was contained in *h. t.* 2.
[9] Consult. 9. 7. Gothofredus inserts this in C. Th. 4. 12.
[10] C. Th. 4. 12. 7. If the *denuntiationes* were a juristic creation these variations are intelligible.
[11] In. 3. 12. 1. [12] 4. 5. 7. 2; cp. G. 4. 77.
[13] 50. 17. 209. [14] In. 3. 12. 1; cp. In. 3. 3. 2.
[15] As in *adrogatio*. It may be therefore that rights of action passed absolutely as they did there, but the texts do not say so.
[16] G. 1. 84, 91, 160; Ulp. 11. 11.

the same level[1]. The later law seems to have been still more severe, and the enactments in the Codex Theodosianus speak simply of *mulieres liberae*[2]. The text of Tertullian already cited[3] seems to hint of a possible application of the rule to freemen cohabiting with *ancillae alienae*. Whether his words really mean this or not, it is clear that some such view was propounded, for it is categorically denied by an enactment of 226[4], while another, of 294, denies that such cohabitation could give the owner of the *ancilla* any right of succession[5]. This seems to mean that someone had an idea that the man might become a *libertus, i.e.* by the owner's assent to the union. Justinian's enactment abolishing the whole system makes it clear that it applied only to women[6].

The state of the authorities makes it difficult to say what was the effect of the enactment on the woman's children in case of prohibition. Most of our earliest authorities say nothing about children. Paul, dealing, *ex professo*, with the whole matter, does not mention them[7]. Nor does Ulpian, in his Regulae[8]. Nor do Suetonius and Tertullian[9]. Justinian's general repealing enactment mentions no special rule about children[10]. The allusion in the text of Tacitus deals only with agreements as to the mother's status[11]. Gaius says that some thought that, apart from agreement, children already conceived were free if *ex iustis nuptiis*, slaves if *volgo concepti*[12]. The language of the much later Epitomator of Gaius suggests that he thought this was the law[13]. But rules as to children were certainly laid down in the later law. Apart from any possible effect of agreement, the course of things may have been as follows. The Senatusconsult said nothing of children. As the rule making the child free, if the mother were free at any time between conception and birth, had not yet developed[14], the effect would be that all children born after the enslavement were slaves. In time the rule was accepted that freedom of the mother at any intermediate time saved the child. This was a juristic development, and it was doubted how far it ought to apply to a case like this, where the child might well be the fruit of the forbidden intercourse[15]. This doubt ultimately led to legislation, in an enactment of 314, which provided that the *filii* should be slaves. This was confirmed in 366[16]. An enactment of 320 provides that if it were a fiscal slave the child would be a Latin[17].

There remain for discussion several cases in which complications might arise owing to the position of one or other of the parties.

[1] P. 2. 21a. 1.   [2] C. Th. 4. 12. 1, 5, 7; In. 3. 12. 1; C. 7. 24.
[3] Tertullian, ad uxorem, 2. 8.   [4] C. 7. 16. 3.   [5] C. 6. 59. 9.
[6] C. 7. 24.   [7] P. 2. 21a.   [8] Ulp. 11. 11.   [9] *locc. citt.*
[10] C. 7. 24.   [11] Taciti Ann. 12. 53; *ante*, p. 412.   [12] G. 1. 91.
[13] G. Ep. 1. 4. 9.   [14] *Ante*, p. 399.   [15] See G. 1. 91.
[16] C. Th. 4. 12. 1, 6.   Mitteis, Reichsrecht und Volksr., 370, following Zimmern, holds that it applied to children already born.
[17] C. Th. 4. 12. 3.

(*a*) Cases of *tutela*[1]. If the slave was the property of a *pupillus* the *tutor* could denounce[2], while if he was the slave of a woman in *tutela* she herself could do so[3]. The latter part of this text is imperfect, but the form of it seems to imply that the *pupillus* himself could not denounce[4].

(*b*) Common ownership of the slave. The only text dealing with this case says that, if all the owners denounced, the *ancilla* was common, but that in other cases she became the property of the owner who first denounces[5]. This was not a case of acquiring through the slave: it was acquisition by denunciation. The slave was no more than one of the facts basing the denunciation. But the rule as it stands hardly looks practical: probably it means that if any owners had, with knowledge, refused to denounce, they could not afterwards claim any share in the *ancilla*.

(*c*) Cases of *patria potestas*. If the slave was in the *peculium* of a son, it was the son who denounced and the father acquired without his knowledge, and even against his will[6]. If the slave was in a *castrense peculium* the *ancilla* acquired on the son's *denuntiatio* was also therein[7]. This text was written before the introduction of *peculium quasi castrense*: no doubt the rule must be extended to this and also to *bona adventitia*.

If the woman was a *filiafamilias* she did not lose her status on *denuntiatio*, since this would involve her having the power to impoverish her father in a certain sense, by depriving him of a daughter[8]. But if she continued the cohabitation after she was *sui iuris* the ordinary rule applied[9]. If, however, she was acting under the *iussum* of her father she became a slave on *denuntiatio*, since, says Paul, fathers can make their children's position worse[10]. The word *iubere* here cannot mean command but authorise: it is incredible that the father could have power to order such a connexion[11]. But this makes the reasoning unmeaning: the father does not make the child's position worse, but only enables her to do so. By assenting he waives his right.

If the slave was the property of the freewoman's own son, respect

---

[1] Not including cases in which *iura patronatus* also arise.
[2] P. 2. 21 a. 2.   [3] *h. t.* 3.
[4] So usually understood, but as the act is so far as the pupil is concerned purely acquisitive, this seems an unnecessary precaution. But any other interpretation seems to need bold emendation.
[5] P. 2. 21 a. 15.
[6] *h. t.* 5. The rule as to denunciation is no doubt the same where the slave is in the *peculium* of another slave, since the denunciation is in no way judicial, but the final decree seems to require the intervention of the *dominus*.
[7] P. 2. 21 a. 8.   [8] *h. t.* 9.   [9] *h. t.* 18.
[10] *h. t.* 10.
[11] It would be an indirect way of enslaving her, which he could not do directly. C. Th. 4. 8. 6 = C. 8. 46. 10.

for the maternal relation prevented the right of denunciation from arising[1].

(*d*) Cases of *iura patronatus*. If the woman was a *liberta* her patron's rights came into play. If he was aware of the transaction and assented, the owner of the slave acquired the woman as an *ancilla* by denouncing[2]. But a *patrona*, so long as perpetual *tutela* lasted, could not lose her rights by assenting without the *auctoritas* of her *tutor*[3]. If the woman's patron did not know, she became his slave and she could never be made a *civis* by manumission by him[4]. From the wording it seems that he could make her a Latin[5], and that if she were sold the buyer had a complete power of manumission. The rule was no doubt the same in the case of a *patrona*, *i.e.* that though her assent was ineffective to give the owner the right to denounce, it was effective to bar her from exercising the analogous right. If the slave belonged to the woman's patron the union produced no such legal effects[6]. If the owner of the slave was the *libertus* of the woman, he could not denounce for reasons analogous to those in the case in which he was her son[7]. These rules present no difficulty, but their origin is obscure. Some of them may be juristic, but some must have been express legislation, *e.g.* the rule making her the *ancilla* of her patron with limited power of manumission. This is probably part of the legislation of Vespasian referred to by Suetonius[8].

(*e*) Municipal slaves. The few texts shew that special rules were applied to this case, but they are not complete enough to enable us to state the development of the law with certainty. We learn that in the classical law an *ingenua* who cohabited with a slave of a municipality, knowingly, became a slave without *denuntiatio*, but not if she was unaware that he was a municipal slave, and ceased from cohabitation as soon as she knew. Presumably a *liberta* was subject to the ordinary law. Nothing is said as to assent of the municipality: apparently the possibility of this was not considered[9]. The concluding words of a law in the Codex Theodosianus shew that *improvidus error, vel simplex ignorantia, vel aetatis infirmae lapsus* were to exclude this special rule, but it is not clear whether this is a new rule or a recital of the old[10]. The enactment of 362 confirming the need for three denunciations was not to apply to slaves of municipalities[11].

---

[1] P. 2. 21a. 16.   [2] P. 2. 21a. 6.   [3] Ulp. 11. 27.
[4] P. 2. 21a. 7.   [5] Huschke, *ad h. l.*
[6] P. 2. 21a. 11, *quia domum patroni videtur deserere noluisse.*
[7] *h. t.* 13.   See *h. t.* 16.   [8] Suetonius, *loc. cit.*
[9] P. 2. 21a. 14, *Universi consentire non possunt, ante,* p. 328.
[10] C. Th. 4. 12. 3.   *Error* here means probably mistake of law, and *ignorantia*, mistake of fact: the terms are occasionally so distinguished, *e.g.* 22. 6. 2.   But this is far from uniform: *error facti* and *ignorantia iuris* are common, 22. 6. 7, 9.   Error of law was allowed to a woman as a defence in some cases *propter sexus infirmitatem*, 22. 6. 9. *pr.*
[11] C. Th. 4. 12. 5.

(*f*) Fiscal slaves. There were special rules of a somewhat similar character for *servi fiscales*. We learn that *ingenuae* who cohabited with fiscal slaves were, in classical law, deprived of their *natalia*, without regard to ignorance or youth. This is stated in the Codex Theodosianus[1], and confirmed by the fragment, *de iure fisci*, which speaks of *libertae Caesaris coniunctione effectae*[2]. It is added that the rights of fathers or patrons not assenting are not to be affected. This differs from the rule in the last case, in that they became *libertae* and not slaves, and in that error was not material. The rule that they were to be *libertae* is no doubt due to the superior dignity of fiscal slaves: these frequently, if not usually, "married" freewomen[3], so that the degradation was less, and the lesser effect of the union will account for the harsh looking rule that ignorance was not considered. The provision as to rights of fathers and patrons presumably means that if the father did not assent the general rule applied and the woman did not lose her status[4]. If the woman was a *liberta* already she had no *natalia*: here the proviso means that she remained the *liberta* of the patron, who could himself denounce her and claim her as a slave. It may be noted, that the rule as cited in the Codex Theodosianus deals only with *ingenuae*. If the patron assented the woman no doubt became a *liberta* Caesaris[5]. The law of 320[6], reciting the old rule, lays down a new one. If an *ingenua* knowingly or in ignorance cohabits with a fiscal slave or with one belonging to the *patrimonium* or to the *privata res* Caesaris, her status is not affected, but the children are latins subject to rights of patronage in Caesar. Nothing is said about *libertae*, and it may be that the old rule still applies to them. It is probable that the declaration that the rule is to cover all kinds of slaves of Caesar is not new. The enactment of 362[7], confirming the need of three *denuntiationes* does not apply to the case of fiscal slaves.

(*g*) An obscure enactment of 415[8] refers to the *Sc.* Claudianum and seems to provide that if the woman was descended from a *decurio* any child of which she was pregnant at the time of condemnation was not only free, which is contrary to the rules already stated, but was also liable to serve on the *Curia*. The point is that descent on the mother's side did not ordinarily create that liability[9]. At the end of the constitution it is said that *servus actor sive procurator* is to be burnt. Another enactment had provided that any *servus actor* of a municipality who connived at connexion between a *decurio* and an *ancilla aliena* was to be severely dealt with[10]. The aim of this is to secure successors to

---

[1] *h. t.* 3, *ius vetus.* 　　　　　　[2] Fr. de i. Fisci, 12. Text corrupt.
[3] *Ante*, p. 324. The Fr. de i. Fisci does not distinguish between fiscal slaves and others of Caesar.
[4] P. 2. 21a. 9. 　　　　[5] *h. t.* 7. 　　　　[6] C. Th. 4. 12. 3.
[7] *h. t.* 5. 　　　　[8] C. Th. 12. 1. 179. *pr.*
[9] See references cited Gothofredus, *ad h. l.* 　　　[10] *h. t.* 6 = C. 5. 5. 3.

decuriones and so to keep the lists full. The purpose of the law with which we are more directly concerned is much the same. It may therefore be assumed that the slave so to be dealt with was not the slave with whom she cohabited[1], but any slave of the *civitas* in a position of trust who connived at this or any other matters forbidden in the constitution.

The whole of the law of the *Sc.* Claudianum disappeared under Justinian. We are told in the Institutes[2] that it was not to be inserted in the Digest at all. The abolishing enactment[3] says nothing about that, and in point of fact the Digest does contain by oversight at least one reference to the abolished[4] rule. The enactment in the Code retains a punishment for the slave concerned[5].

---

[1] It may be remembered that slaves cohabiting with their own mistresses were burnt, C. Th. 9. 9. 1 = C. 9. 11. 1.   *Ante*, p. 93.

[2] In. 3. 12. 1.   [3] C. 7. 24.

[4] 16. 3. 27.   The words *nulla...facta* should have been struck out.

[5] Several laws reduce to the rank of their husbands women who cohabit with the semi-servile labourers, C. Th. 10. 20. 3 (= C. 11. 8. 3); C. Th. 10. 20. 10.   For another possible case, *post*, p. 433.

CHAPTER XVIII.

ENSLAVEMENT (cont.).

WE have now to consider those cases of enslavement *iure civili* which Justinian introduced or retained. Several are recorded, but few are important in the general law. The less important will be treated first.

(a) Defaulting claimants of liberty. As we shall see later, Justinian abolished the need of *adsertores* (free persons acting on behalf of the claimant of liberty), in *causae liberales*, and allowed the claimants to conduct their own cases. He required them to give personal security, but if this were impossible, they were to give a sworn undertaking—*cautio iuratoria*. If after these preliminaries they failed to appear, and, being duly cited, remained absent for a year, they were adjudged slaves of the other party, whatever the real merits of the case may have been[1].

(b) False pretence and collusion of *dominus*. If an owner by his fraud and collusion passed his slave off as a freeman and obtained a judgment to that effect, Domitian provided that the person so adjudicated free should be decreed a slave of anyone who denounced him[2]. But as he can hardly be said to have been free before, this case will be more appropriately discussed later, in connexion with the general law as to the effect of such adjudication[3].

(c) Slaves sold for export and freed. The Vatican Fragments[4] contain a text, in part corrupt, to the effect that if a slave is sold with a condition that he is to be kept away from a certain place[5], with a power of seizure on return, and he does return, still a slave, the vendor may seize him and keep him as his slave. If he is freed by the buyer and then returns, he is sold by the Fisc into perpetual slavery on the same condition. This amounts to re-enslavement, for the manumission by the buyer before he had broken the condition was perfectly valid[6].

---

[1] C. 7. 17. 1. 2. *Post*, Ch. xxviii.
[3] *Post*, Ch. xxviii.
[5] As to this see *ante*, p. 69.

[2] A senatusconsult, 40. 16. 1.
[4] Vat. Fr. 6.
[6] C. 4. 55. 1.

The same rule is laid down by Severus and Caracalla[1]. Some details are necessary to complete the statement. The power of seizure (*manus iniectio*) is merely a right to take the slave : it has nothing to do with *legis actio*. If the vendor has agreed not for a right of seizure, but for a money penalty, the Fisc seizes the man, though he is still a slave, and sells him as in the case of return after manumission[2]. If the slave returns without the buyer's consent, there is no right of seizure, for the slave cannot be allowed to deprive his owner of himself[3]. If the buyer instead of exporting him, frees him in the State, the manumission is void and the vendor has the right of seizure[4]. If the buyer resells him under the same condition and he comes to the forbidden place with assent of the second buyer, the original vendor has the right of seizure, not the first vendee, whose imposition of the same condition is merely regarded as notice to his vendee, to protect himself from liability[3]. As the vendor imposed the condition for his own protection, he can remit it at any time while the man is still a slave, and so either seize the slave and keep him at Rome, or free him, or, waiving the right of seizure, allow the buyer to keep him at Rome[5]. But the case is different if the slave returns to the place as a freeman. The vendor has now no means of control over him, and might be terrorised into remitting the prohibition. Accordingly the Fisc takes the matter in hand and sells the man as above[6].

(*d*) Young children sold under pressure of poverty[7]. It was a rule of the developed Roman law that a father though he had, at least in theory, a *ius vitae necisque* over his issue, could not sell them into slavery. Paul lays down the rule of classical law that such a sale cannot prejudice their *ingenuitas,* since a freeman *nullo pretio aestimatur*[8]. He adds that therefore the father cannot pledge them, or give them in *fiducia,* and that a creditor who knowingly receives them as security is punishable[9]. Caracalla says much the same as to sale, describing it as illicit and shameful and in no way prejudicing the child[10]. Diocletian speaks of the rule utterly forbidding sale as settled law[11]. Such a pledge is void[12] and such a sale in some way punishable[13]. Even later the rule is laid down in quite general terms by Constantine in 315 and 323[14].

---

[1] *Ibid.*
[2] C. 4. 55. 2. So, probably, if the conditions were imposed without expressed penalty.
[3] 18. 7. 9.   [4] C. 4. 55. 3.
[5] 18. 7. 1; Vat. Fr. 6.
[6] This seems to be the meaning of Vat. Fr. 6 *fin.,* read in connexion with C. 4. 55. 1.
[7] As to the practice of sale of self and children in eastern provinces, see Mitteis, Reichsrecht und Volksrecht, 358.
[8] P. 5. 1. 1.   [9] *Ib.*; D. 20. 3. 5.   [10] C. 7. 16. 1.
[11] C. 4. 43. 1.   [12] C. 8. 16. 6; cp. *h. t.* 1.
[13] C. 7. 16. 37.   Huschke makes Vat. Fr. 27 lay down the general rule, but this is doubtful.
[14] Vat. Fr. 33; C. Th. 4. 8. 6.   An enactment of 322 records the fact that provincials had been in the habit of selling their children under pressure of poverty, and orders that, to prevent this, such people are to be relieved from the treasury, C. Th. 11. 27. 2. It does not appear that the sales were lawful.

But a constitution, earlier than the first of these dates, introduces or mentions an exception. As early as 313, Constantine treats as valid the sale of a new-born child (*sanguinolentus*)[1], and in 329 he says that this is law established by earlier Emperors[2]. His own contribution to the matter seems to have been to regulate it by laying down several rules to which such sales must conform. The transaction must be evidenced by written documents. A proper price must have been paid[3]. If these are not attended to the sale is void. The buyer may lawfully possess him and may even sell him, but only for the payment of debts: any sale in contravention of this law is penalised and presumably void. The vendor, or the person sold, or anyone else, may redeem him on payment of what he may be worth, or by giving a slave of equal value in his place, but there is no right of redemption if the child is the issue of union with a barbarian[4].

The rules as to evidentiary documents, as to issue of marriage with barbarians, and as to restrictions on sale of the person bought, seem to have disappeared, but the main principles are retained in a constitution of Constantine which is inserted in Justinian's Code and represents the law of his time[5]. But traces remain in the Codex Theodosianus which shew that between the ages of Constantine and Justinian there had been variations of practice if not of law. In 391 it was provided that those who had been sold into slavery by their parents should be restored to *ingenuitas* and that a holder whom they had served, for *non minimi temporis spatium*, should have no claim to remuneration. This is not in terms confined to *sanguinolenti* and may indicate a practice of selling older children[6]. It is not in Justinian's Code. Again a Novel of Valentinian says that the prevalent distress throughout Italy had caused parents to sell their children, and that thus life had been saved at the expense of liberty. Where this had happened their *ingenuitas* was not to be affected and, in accordance with *statuta maiorum*, the sale was to be set aside, but so that the buyer received back the price he paid, plus 20 %[7]. Any real price for them seems absurd if they were new-born infants, and in any case it must have been so small that 20 % added could have been no return for the cost of rearing. Thus it seems that a practice had grown up of selling older persons

---

[1] Vat. Fr. 34.   [2] C. Th. 5. 10. 1.
[3] Vat. Fr. 34; C. Th. 5. 10. 1.
[4] *Ibid.* Unions with *barbari* were forbidden a little later, and capitally punished, C. Th. 3. 14. 1. A rule laid down much later by Valentinian may have been due to Constantine, viz. that any such sale for export to barbarians was heavily penalised, Nov. Val. 33. He speaks of such sales as already forbidden.
[5] C. 4. 43. 2. Probably identical with C. Th. 5. 10. 1.
[6] C. Th. 3. 3. 1. The *interpretatio* says, *si servitio suo satisfecerit*, which suggests sale for a definite time. Gothofredus, *ad h. l.*, suggests five years, on the analogy of *captivi* redeemed. See *ante*, p. 314, and *post*, Ch. XXVIII. But this would exclude limitation to *sanguinolenti*.
[7] Nov. Val. 33.

and had been recognised as legal[1]. There is no such right under Justinian.

The language of these last two laws shews that the status was one of true slavery. But this is not so certain of the more permanent institution regulated by Constantine. The expression, reversion to *ingenuitas,* used by Constantine[2] seems inconsistent with his being a slave, but as the law also speaks of the buyer as *dominus* and *possessor*[3], it is generally held that it was genuine slavery. It is indeed conceivable that this was no longer so in Justinian's day, for one of Constantine's laws as reproduced by Justinian in his Code speaks of the buyer as entitled to use the man's services[4]. Justinian's own enactment as to *liberi expositi*[5] jars rather with the rule now under discussion, but, slavery or not slavery, it is clear from the insertion of Constantine's enactment in Justinian's Code that the institution continued to exist[6].

There remain two cases[7] of much greater importance.

(e) The *libertus ingratus.* The general principle of this matter is set forth in the Institutes[8] in four words: *liberti ut ingrati condemnati.* The rule referred to is that *liberti* might on complaint of their patron be re-enslaved on the ground of ingratitude. The history of the matter is somewhat obscure. Neglecting *dediticii,* there were up to the time of Justinian two kinds of freedmen, *cives* and latins; the liability applied more or less to the freedmen and to their issue; not only the patron but also some of his heirs had the right of complaint, and ingratitude did not always lead to re-enslavement to the old master, but was sometimes met by other punishments, ranging from reprimand to penal slavery. It is not easy to tell from the sources how all these factors were combined.

No legal text refers to the rules as to this matter during the Republic. It must not be assumed from this that ingratitude on the part of a *libertus* was not repressed, but only that the powers of domestic

---

[1] It became the rule of West-Gothic law, Z. S. S. Germ. Abth. 7. 238; 9. 45. Traces of the practice are in the Code and Novels, Mitteis, *op. cit.* 363.
[2] C. Th. 3. 3. 1; C. Th. 5. 10. 1 = C. 4. 43. 2.
[3] C. Th. 5. 10. 1; Vat. Fr. 34.
[4] C. 4. 43. 2. [5] C. 8. 51. 3; *ante,* p. 402.
[6] The importance of the question whether the child was slave or free in the meantime is plain, but the texts do not consider it. See as to the analogous case of *liberi expositi,* C. 8. 51. 3, and *ante,* p. 402. It should be noted that Constantine gave the same right of repurchase or substitution where the *sanguinolentus* was a slave, C. Th. 5. 10. 1. But in 419 it was provided that, as such a reclaim was unfair to the rearer, this right should be conditional on payment of double value and all charges (Const. Sirm: 5). This made the right worthless except for natural children. The Code of Justinian does not refer to this right, even in the enactment of Constantine which provides for freeborn children.
[7] For another exceptional mode of enslavement under Justinian see *post,* Ch. xxvi at beginning.
[8] In. 1. 16. 1.

authority sufficed[1]. With the imperial system came a change: the old methods no longer served and legislation began. The *lex* Aelia Sentia (A.D. 4) allowed a formal accusation. We do not know by legal texts what were the penalties it authorised, but there is no reason to think they amounted to re-enslavement[2], and a non-legal writer seems to say that they did not go so far[3]. The Digest contains many references to these minor punishments. The matter seems to have been the subject of repeated imperial regulation, and no doubt a wide discretion was left to the magistrate as to the degree of punishment in each case. Thus one text tells us that the magistrate was to sentence to fine, forfeiture of part of his property to the patron, or whipping, according to the nature of the offence[4]. Others are more specific. They tell us that for defect in *obsequium*, *liberti* were to be punished by whipping, reprimand and warning as to severer punishment if the offence was repeated[5]. For *convicium* or *contumelia* the same punishments are suggested together with temporary exile[6]. For assault or *calumnia* or conspiracy or subornation of delators they were to be condemned *in metallum*[7]. It is noticeable that though the list has an air of completeness no case is given in which the punishment is re-enslavement to the patron. It may be that the patron might choose whether the man should go *in metallum* or revert to his *dominium*[8]. One punishment is of special interest. Salvianus, who was Bishop of Marseilles about 440, uses language which seems to mean that patrons had the right to reduce their *liberti* to the position of latini for ingratitude[9]. Constantine, in 326, refers to a *libertus* reduced from citizenship to latinity[10], and Suetonius, writing of the time of Nero, and speaking of ingratitude as involving loss of right of testation[11], seems to have the same rule in mind.

The history of re-enslavement as a punishment for ingratitude, can be shortly stated, so far as it is known. Claudius provided that any *libertinus* who suborned delators, to dispute his patron's status, might be re-enslaved by him[12]. In the next reign the Senate seems to have tried to lay down some general rule of re-enslavement, but Nero refused his assent to this, requiring each case to be considered on its merits, but clearly contemplating re-enslavement as a possibility[13]. It was

---

[1] For traces of this see 47. 2. 90.   [2] 50. 16. 70; 40. 9. 30, and rubric.
[3] Dositheus, Sent. Had. 3, cited by Gothofredus *ad* C. Th. 2. 22. 1.
[4] 37. 14. 7. 1.   [5] 1. 16. 9. 3; 37. 14. 1.
[6] 1. 12. 1. 10; 37. 14. 1; cp. Tacit. Ann. 13. 26.   [7] *Ibid.*
[8] In C. 6. 7. 2 we are told that the penalty could be rescinded on application of the patron.
[9] Ad Eccles. 3. 33.   [10] C. Th. 2. 22. 1.
[11] Suetonius, Nero, 32. Gothofredus *ad* C. Th. 2. 22. 1, suggests that *cives* were made latins, the penalty of enslavement being usually confined to latins. This is highly probable, though the case put in C. 6. 7. 2 shews that enslavement of *cives liberti* for ingratitude could occur. Cp. Tacit. *loc. cit.*
[12] 37. 14. 5. Suetonius says, too generally: *ingratos et de quibus patroni quererentur revocavit in servitutem*, Claud. 5.
[13] A.D. 56. Tacit. Ann. 13. 26.

reserved for that accomplished *censor morum*, Commodus, to lay down the general rule[1]. He is said by Modestinus to have enacted that on proof that *liberti* had treated their patrons with contumely, or struck them, or neglected them in illness or distress, they were to be restored to the *potestas* of their patrons, and, if that did not suffice, they were to be sold by the *praeses* and the price given to the patron[2]. In 205 the power of re-enslavement is treated by Severus as existing[3]. An enactment of Diocletian seems to refer to a general rule of re-enslavement for ingratitude[4], but another notes[5] that there is no re-enslavement for mere lack of *obsequium*[6]. Constantine speaks more severely, and declares that *liberti* may be re-enslaved, if *iactancia vel contumelia cervices erexerunt* or even if *levis offensae contraxerunt culpam*[7]. Later enactments, of 423[8] and 426[9], speak of re-enslavement without stating the limits on the power. It can hardly be doubted, however, that it was rare in the later Empire. The only texts mentioning it in the Digest are those giving the rule of Claudius and that of Commodus, together with one to the effect that if a woman, having offended her patron and thereby endangered her status, agrees to pay him something to avoid reduction to slavery, the agreement is valid and not a case of *metus*[10]. The texts from the Code and the words of the Institutes shew that the rule was still in operation, and in the Novels it is again laid down very generally[11]. Upon the whole record it seems that there could not at any time be re-enslavement for mere lack of *obsequium* (though Constantine's rule goes very near to it), but that it might be incurred for any worse form of ingratitude. Other punishments might be chosen and usually were, so that the *libertus ingratus* re-enslaved to his patron was at no time common.

Such accusations are deemed to require careful trial. They are tried as *iudicia extraordinaria*[12] and must go before the chief magistrate of the province in which they arose[13], the Proconsul[14] or other *praeses*[15], or, in the city, the *praefectus urbi*[16]. Constantine speaks of them as going before *iudices pedaneos*[17]. They are capital, and ought therefore

---

[1] For statement and criticism of Leist's view that it is much older, see Pernice, Labeo, 3. 81.
[2] 25. 3. 6. 1. Similar rule to this last was laid down for a different reason by Antoninus Pius for slaves illtreated, see *ante*, p. 37.
[3] C. 6. 3. 2.
[4] C. 6. 3. 12. But the words, *nisi ingrati probentur*, may be interpolated.
[5] C. 7. 16. 30.   [6] C. 7. 16. 30.
[7] C. Th. 4. 10. 1 = C. 6. 7. 2.   [8] *h. t.* 2 = C. *h. t.* 3.
[9] *h. t.* 3 = C. *h. t.* 4.   [10] 4. 2. 21. *pr.*
[11] Nov. 78. 2. This wordy law does not suggest that there was liability to enslavement for mere lack of *obsequium*, but it brings in a new point. Intolerable waste is mentioned (ζημίαν), which presumably means waste of property he is administering, not of his own property to the prejudice of the patron's potential succession.
[12] C. 6. 7. 1; Tacit. Ann. 13. 26.   [13] Tacit. *loc. cit.*
[14] 1. 16. 9. 3.   [15] 37. 14. 1; *h. t.* 7. 1.   [16] 1. 12. 1. 10.
[17] C. Th. 4. 10. 1 = C. 6. 7. 2. These were the newly introduced deputies to the magistrates.

to involve personal intervention of, at least, the accused—the general
rule of capital charges[1]. But the very enactment of Severus and
Caracalla on which this obvious precaution is based[2] allows a procurator
to appear on either side, by way of exception[3]. This, too, indicates
that it was not often capital. The whole rule here excepted from does
not, it may be supposed, apply to failure in *obsequium*, for though this
is ingratitude[4], it cannot lead to enslavement[5], and we are further told[6]
that a case of this sort may be disposed of *de plano*.

If there are several patrons they may all accuse (in which case they
will reacquire the slave *pro parte*) or, if the ingratitude were clearly to
one of the patrons alone, he can accuse (and so acquire the slave), but
only with the consent of all[7]. Of a *servus castrensis* freed by the son
he is patron and he can therefore accuse[8], but of any slave freed by
him, *iussu patris*[9], the father has the right of accusation as if he had
manumitted[10]. All this merely illustrates the rule that it is the person
who is substantially patron who can accuse. But there are several
cases in which the patron has not the right of accusation. The principle
is laid down by Caracalla that he has it only when the manumission is
gratuitous and voluntary, and not when it is in pursuance of an obligation[11]. Hence he cannot accuse one whom he was bound by *fideicommissum* to free[12], or whom he had bought with the "slave's own
money" and freed[13], or one conveyed to him on a condition that he
would free him[14], and this whether he actually did free him or the slave
acquired his freedom under the Constitutio Marci[15]. All these cases
turn on the fact that though the manumitter is technically patron[16], he
has conferred no favour: he has done no more than he was legally
bound to do and there is no occasion for gratitude. One case looks
indeed at first sight exceptional. If a master has taken money from
his own slave, or a friend, as the price of freedom and has freed
accordingly, he has the right of accusation; for, says the text, though
it was not done for nothing he did in fact confer a benefit: he was not
like a mere fiduciary manumitter who simply *operam accommodat*[17].
But his position is exactly that of one who has taken a legacy with a
fideicommissum to free a slave of his own. Such a manumitter cannot
accuse, though he shares with the case now under discussion the one
characteristic which marks it off from the other cases mentioned;
i.e., the fact that the ownership of the slave was not created merely

[1] 48. 19. 5. *pr.*   P. 5. 5a. 9.
[2] 48. 17. 1. *pr.*; also expressed by Trajan, 48. 19. 5. *pr.*, and Gordian, C. 9. 2. 6.
[3] P. 5. 16. 11; D. 37. 15. 4.   [4] 37. 14. 1, 19.   [5] C. 7. 16. 30.
[6] 1. 16. 9. 3.   [7] 40. 9. 30. 4.   [8] *h. t.* 30. 2; 37. 14. 8. *pr.*
[9] *Post*, p. 458.   [10] 40. 9. 30. 1.   [11] C. 6. 7. 1.
[12] *Ibid.*   [13] C. 6. 3. 8; *post*, Ch. xxvii.   [14] C. 6. 3. 2.
[15] 37. 14. 8. 1; 40. 9. 30. *pr.*; *post*, Ch. xxvii.   [16] See nn. 11—15.
[17] 37. 15. 3.

with a view to the manumission.   And in later law the distinction is
very unreal.   In this case there is a right *extorquere libertatem*, as in the
case of *servus suis nummis redemptus*, or one bought *ut manumittatur*[1].
But as it does not exactly come under the words of the Constitutio,
and is clearly an extension, *favore libertatis*[2], and Marcellus, the author
of our text, lived at the time of the promulgation of the original decree,
the text was probably written long before the principle was extended
to this case, and its retention by Justinian is thus an oversight[3].

It hardly needs statement that the act basing the accusation may
be one done only indirectly to the patron, *e.g.* refusing to undertake the
tutela of a son of his[4].   But the rule goes further and allows the
heres of the patron to accuse.   The *lex* Aelia Sentia allows a *filius
heres patroni* to accuse[5], and Diocletian provides that as freedmen owe
reverentia to the *filii patroni* these can accuse them for ingratitude[6].
Marcellus lays down a similar rule for *filius et heres*[7].   In 423 a wider
rule seems to have been laid down, giving the right of accusation to
any *heres* of the patron[8], and this for ingratitude not to the late patron
but to them.   In 447 Valentinian seems to have utterly destroyed this
right in sons or other heirs: he provides[9] that they cannot accuse,
but have ordinary actions (*iniuriarum, etc.*).   This prohibition is not
found in Justinian's law.   He adopts the law of 423 and there are
texts in the Digest which give the right of accusation to *filii heredes*[10],
and again to *liberi patroni*[11].   In spite of the generality of the words in
the Code[8], it is doubtful whether any right exists in later law for *heredes*
other than children, and it may be taken for granted that the right is
so far connected with the right of succession to the *libertus* that one
who is from any cause excluded from that succession cannot accuse.
Thus Ulpian tells us that if the *libertus* is *assignatus*, only the assignee
can accuse[12].   It must also be noted that none of these texts dealing
with accusation by a *heres* says anything about a right of re-enslavement
to them, though there is one which may mean that condemnation *in
metallum* is possible[13].

Authority on the converse case, that of the *filius liberti*, is scanty.
On the one hand we are told in the Digest that the *heres liberti* has all
the rights of an *extraneus* against the patron[14], a statement which, in

---

[1] Probably not, however, till the time of Justinian, *post*, Ch. xxvii.
[2] Note the language of 40. 12. 38. 1 and 40. 1. 19.
[3] The right of accusation is perpetual, but it is lost if the intending accuser ceases to be
patron, 40. 9. 30. 3.
[4] 1. 12. 1. 10 ; 37. 14. 19.   [5] 50. 16. 70.   Not *heres heredis*.
[6] C. 6. 3. 12.   [7] 37. 15. 3.   [8] C. Th. 4. 10. 2 = C. 6. 7. 3.
[9] Nov. Valent. 25. 1.   [10] 37. 15. 3 ; 40. 9. 30. 5.
[11] 1. 16. 9. 3 ; 37. 14. 1.   But these texts are not clear.   They may be read as merely giving
the patron rights in respect of acts done to *liberi*.   This is clearly the meaning of Nov. 78. 2
(*filius*).
[12] 40. 9. 30. 5.   [13] 37. 14. 1.   [14] 37. 15. 8.

view of its context, seems to mean that he owes him no *reverentia* or *obsequium*, and, as there is also no right of succession in the patron, it would seem to follow that there can be no accusation. But elsewhere we learn that in 426 it was enacted that children of a freedman even holding an office within the class of *militiae* can be re-enslaved for ingratitude. The enactment is, even in the Codex Theodosianus, in a mutilated form, and Justinian abridges it still more[1]. In the earlier form it speaks of *reverentia* as due from the *filius liberti*, and Justinian, striking out this duty, on which the right to accuse logically rests, reserves, nevertheless, the right of accusation. In the earlier form the right extends to children of the patron, but Justinian omits this. The rule is again mentioned, but not so as to explain anything, in the Novels[2]. It may be conjectured that the duty of *reverentia* is newly imposed on *liberi*, by the enactment of 426.

An enactment of Constantine in the Codex Theodosianus dealing with these accusations, and dated 332, reappears in Justinian's Code as of a slightly earlier date[3]. It contains here much that is not in the earlier form, and, no doubt, two constitutions have been run together. As given by Justinian it contains two rather strange rules. It provides that re-enslavement of a *manumissus* to his patron shall affect afterborn children, *filiis etiam qui postea nati fuerint servituris, quoniam illis delicta parentum non nocent quos tunc esse ortos constiterit dum libertate illi potirentur.* The only way in which this can be made intelligible is to refer this provision to *manumissae*[4]. The other curious rule is that the person enslaved for ingratitude after having been freed, *vindicta, in consilio*, will not be restored to liberty on petition except at the patron's request. This, since it does not speak of manumission, seems to refer to *servitus poenae*, which suggests that the other constitution of Constantine, which is lacking in the Codex Theodosianus, but appears in Justinian's Code in the form of a clause added to the one which is in the earlier Code, dealt with *servitus poenae* as a punishment for ingratitude[5].

(*f*) A freeman allowing fraudulent sale of himself. This is one of the many legal institutions which resulted from the fact that slave and free cannot be distinguished by inspection[6].

The general rule is that any *liber homo* over twenty years of age who knowingly allows himself to be sold as a slave, in order to share

---

[1] C. Th. 4. 10. 3 = C. 6. 7. 4.   [2] Nov. 22. 9.
[3] C. Th. 4. 10. 1; C. 6. 7. 2.
[4] C. 6. 7. 2. 1. They are not to have the benefit of their mother's freedom between conception and birth. *Ante*, p. 399.
[5] The allusion to the *consilium* seems to shew that this was originally a rescript dealing with a special case.
[6] 18. 1. 5; *ante*, pp. 5, 6.

the price, is enslaved, or, as it is more usually expressed, is forbidden *proclamare in libertatem, i.e.* to claim his liberty[1]. It is a *capitis deminutio maxima*[2]. The rules are stated in the Digest with a good deal of detail, most of which is fairly clear. It is essential that the object was to share the price[3]. If it was not, then, whatever other fraud was contemplated, liberty can still be claimed[4]. Even though the man had this object he is not barred unless he has actually received a part of the price[5]. It is essential also that the buyer have been deceived: if he knew, then there is no bar to the claim of liberty[6]. But if he in turn sell to an innocent buyer, the subject of the sale is barred from claiming if he has received part of the price, it would seem, on either sale[7]. If there were two buyers, and one knew of the fraud while the other did not, there is a conflict in the texts. The man cannot be partly free. To allow him to be wholly free would make it easy to defeat the whole rule. Accordingly Paul says that as the wrongdoer can claim nothing the man must go wholly to the other: a rational rule, but one in which Ulpian sees a difficulty. He holds that the buyer bought only a share and can therefore be entitled to no more: the rest must therefore go to the buyer who knew the facts, who thus profits· by the ignorance of the other buyer[8]. But this rule that he cannot be entitled to more than the share he bought is not inevitable. The case is closely analogous to that of manumission by one of common owners in the classical law, in which case all vested in the other[9]. In fact, the beginning of Ulpian's text looks as if he was about to lay down the rule adopted by Paul: it is probable that the actual solution in the latter part of the text is not his but Justinian's[10].

A person under the age of 25 has in most cases a right of *restitutio in integrum*, but not in this case. The reason given by Ulpian, following Papinian, is that there can be no *restitutio in integrum* from *status mutatio*[11]. This is sufficient: the texts which say that there is *restitutio* in cases of *status mutatio*[12] merely mean that actions that have been lost by the change can be restored by the help of a Praetorian fiction, not that the status can be restored[13]. They have no bearing on the present case[14]. If, however, he was a minor under 20, he is not barred even though he refrains from taking steps till he is over that age. But

---

[1] In. 1. 3. 4; D. 1. 5. 5. 1; 4. 4. 9. 4; 40. 14. 2. *pr.*; C. Th. 4. 8. 6; C. 7. 18. 1. Male or female, D. 40. 13. 3; C. 7. 16. 16.
[2] In. 1. 16. 1.   [3] C. 7. 18. 1; 7. 16. 5. 1.   [4] 40. 12. 7. *pr.*
[5] 40. 13. 1. *pr.*; C. 7. 18. 1.   [6] 40. 12. 7. 2, 33.
[7] *Ibid.*   [8] 40. 13. 5; 40. 12. 7. 3.   [9] *Post*, Ch. xxv.
[10] Other parts of the text are interpolated, Gradenwitz, Interp. 101.
[11] 4. 4. 9. 4.   [12] 4. 1. 2; P. 1. 7. 2.
[13] *e.g.*, against an *adrogatus* in the matter of debts.
[14] The fact that he was a wrongdoer might have barred restitution in any case, in the absence of *metus*, 4. 4. 9. 2; 4. 1. 7. 1.

if, having been sold under 20, he shares the price after he has reached that age, then the rule barring claim applies to him[1].

The texts speak usually of sale, but it is obvious that many other transactions might have substantially the same result, and accordingly we are told that pledge, gift and giving in *dos* are all on the same level as sale[2], though it is difficult to apply the notion of sharing price to these transactions[3]. So, again, what is sold need not be the *dominium*. Thus Paul discusses the sale of the usufruct of a freeman as a slave, and says, on the authority of Quintus Mucius, that *cessio in iure* under such an agreement makes a slave of him: the buyer will have the usufruct of him, and, the vendor being fraudulent, he is a *servus sine domino*. If, however, the vendor was in good faith he acquires the *nuda proprietas*[4].

Questions of difficulty arise, and are not very clearly dealt with, where the person sold was not actually free, but was entitled to be freed. Where a person to whom fideicommissary liberty was due allowed himself to be so sold, a consultant of Paul remarks that while one feels he ought not to be better off than a freeman in the same case, there is the difficulty that there was a valid sale and a vendible thing sold. Paul's answer is that the contract is valid in each case (which is hardly to the point), that if the buyer knew, no question arises, and that if he was innocent, then the slave who could have demanded liberty and preferred to be sold is barred from claiming his liberty as unworthy of the aid of the Praetor *fideicommissarius*. The fact that he was still a slave and could thus be sold against his will is no defence to him, since he had but to disclose his position to end the whole matter. The case is different, he says, with a *statuliber*. Here a condition has yet to be satisfied, and when it arrives he will, notwithstanding his knowledge and fraud, be allowed to claim his liberty, even though the condition was one within his own power[5]. The point of this last remark is that though it be in his own power, it may be something substantial, and thus differs widely from merely having to state the facts. All this cannot be called satisfactory, though it seems to represent both classical and later law.

The texts throughout speak of the rule as applying to *liberi homines* without any restriction to *cives*, and though it is not expressly so stated, it is clear that no such restriction existed. Thus in the chief enactment

---

[1] 40. 12. 7. 1; 40. 13. 1. 1; cp. C. Th. 4. 8. 6.
[2] 40. 12. 23. 1. See also the Syro-Roman Law-book, Bruns and Sachau. pp. 22, 55, 88, 102, 124, and Syrische Rechtsbücher, Sachau, pp. 13, 67, 99, 165. These speak only of *ancillae* as given in *dos*.
[3] *Post*, p. 432.
[4] 40. 12. 23. *pr.* Kuntze, Servus Fructuarius, 64, remarks that where he is *servus sine domino* he will reacquire his liberty at the end of the usufruct, *post*, Ch. xxv.
[5] 40. 13. 4; C. 7. 18. 1.

in the Code on the matter, the rule is applied, even though he be a *civis*[1]. In fact the rule that a man cannot validly sell himself into slavery is based on the sanctity of liberty, not on that of citizenship[2]. We have seen that private agreements could not make a man a slave or a *libertus*[3] and we know that in the theory of the Republic, at least as expressed by Cicero, the State could not deprive a man of *civitas* or *libertas*: he was always regarded as abdicating his rights[4]. Exile was voluntary. In like manner in this case the man enslaved is regarded as having abdicated his liberty, and similar language is used in relation to other causes of enslavement *iure civili*[5].

In most of the texts, though not in all, the offender is not described as re-enslaved but as forbidden *proclamare in libertatem*[6]. This rather suggests that he is not exactly enslaved, but is, so to speak, estopped from claiming his liberty. This way of looking at the matter receives some slight support from the words of a text which says that Hadrian, while laying down the general rule, nevertheless, *interdum*, allowed him to proclaim his liberty if he restored the price, *i.e.* he became free again without manumission[7]. From the fact that this is in the Digest it is likely that it was a general rule for later law[8]. But though it suggests that the bar was only procedural, it is really only a case of restitution analogous to that mentioned in the case of *servi poenae*[9] and *liberti ingrati*[10], where there is no suggestion that the slavery was not real. The evidence that it was not mere estoppel but actual slavery is overwhelming. It is so described in many texts[11]. It is called a *status mutatio*, and *restitutio in integrum* is refused on that account[12]. It is a *capitis deminutio maxima*[13]. Manumission is the normal mode of release, and on manumission the man is a *libertinus*, not an *ingenuus*[14], and this is noteworthy, as one might have thought that manumission ended the punishment. But he is barred from claiming *ingenuitas* even after manumission[15]. Again if a woman is so sold her children born during her slavery are slaves[16]. Such a man is the subjèct of *dominium*[17]. It

---

[1] C. 7. 18. 1; C. 7. 16. 5. 1 and In. 1. 16. 1 are dealing only with *cives*.
[2] The class of slaves was recruited by purchase from *barbaros* outside the protection of the Empire (Mitteis, *op. cit.* 360 *sqq.*), but this is hardly material.
[3] 40. 12. 37; C. 7. 16. 10. See also C. Th. 4. 8. 6 = C. 8. 46. 10. Apparent exception under *Sc.* Claudianum, *ante*, p. 412.
[4] Cicero, Pro Caec. 33 and Pro Domo 29, *etc.* As to some exceptional cases, C. Th. 3. 4. 1; 5. 8. 1; Vat. Fr. 34.
[5] *e.g.* 1. 5. 21; C. Th. 4. 12. 6. This language does not seem to be used about *libertus ingratus*.
[6] *e.g.* 40. 12. 14, 40; 40. 13. 3, *etc. Post*, Ch. xxviii.
[7] 40. 14. 2. *pr.*
[8] It accords with *favor libertatis* and seems to involve a penalty of part of the price.
[9] *Ante*, p. 411.   [10] *Ante*, p. 427.
[11] *e.g.* C. 7. 18. 1; In. 1. 3. 4; 1. 16. 1.
[12] 4. 4. 9. 4.
[14] 1. 5. 21; 40. 12. 40.
[16] 40. 13. 3.
[13] In. 1. 16. 1.
[15] 40. 12. 40.
[17] 40. 12. 23. *pr.*

is clear that it is true slavery, and the point could be raised without *exceptio* as a reply to an *adsertio libertatis*[1].

The rules set forth in the foregoing pages give an account of the institution as it appears in Justinian's law. But the state of the sources raises a curious question as to the origin of the rules. Every legal text which mentions the matter, with two exceptions (a provision of Constantine which is in the Codex Theodosianus but not in Justinian's[2], and one in the Syro-Roman Law-book[3]), is from Justinian's compilations. The institution is of so remarkable a nature that one would have expected to find it frequently mentioned. Yet it appears also, though such a statement must be open to correction, that the historians, poets, grammarians, antiquaries, Christian fathers, and in fact all literature, are equally silent. Plautus handles such a fraud[4], but he does not mention the rule. In view of this conspiracy of silence, we are driven to Justinian to find the origin of the rule. The result is not very informing. From one text we learn that Quintus Mucius was acquainted with it[5]. Another tells us that Hadrian laid down such a rule[6]. In the Code, legislation on the matter is referred to by Gordian, who treats it as an existing institution[7]. Paul treats the matter in a work on the *Sc.* Claudianum[8], and Pomponius speaks of it as to be looked for in *Senatusconsulta*[9]. All this tempts us to think of the Edict, confirmed and extended by *Senatusconsulta* and constitutions, after the Edict had lost its vitality. Some commentators definitely treat it as Edictal[10], but there is no direct evidence for this, except that the Edict did provide for an *actio in factum*, where there had been such a fraud, but the circumstances were not such as to bar claim of liberty. It seems hardly likely that this alone would be stated if both belonged to the Edict. Indeed the words in which Ulpian refers to the *actio in factum* are such as strongly suggest that this was the only Praetorian remedy, and that it first existed at a time when there was no other[11]. There is no trace in the remaining fragments of the Edict of anything remotely resembling a penalty of re-enslavement. And the fact that Marcian speaks of it as *iure civili* is strong evidence that it was not of

---

[1] From the fact that Gaius does not mention it in his list of *cap. dem. max.* (G. 1. 160), Karlowa infers (R. R. G. 2. 1116) that the effect was then only procedural, becoming substantive later. But G. also omits *libertus ingratus* and *servus poenae.*

[2] C. Th. 4. 8. 6. See the *interpretatio.* As this law appears in Justinian's Code this point is omitted, C. 7. 18. 3; 8. 46. 10.

[3] Syro-Roman Law book, Bruns and Sachau, § 73; Syrische Rechtsbücher, *locc. citt.*

[4] Pers. 1. 3.

[5] 40. 12. 23. *pr.* But it may be Quintus Cervidius Scaevola (Mommsen, Strafrecht, 854). The original Florentine reading was *meus.* Mucius is a generally accepted correction in the MS., but it is late (Mommsen, Digest, Ed. mai. *ad h. l.*). Under the circumstances Quintus *meus* seems rather less likely than Scaevola *noster* which M. cites in support of it.

[6] 40. 14. 2.   [7] C. 7. 18. 1.   [8] 40. 13. 5.

[9] *h. t.* 3.   [10] *e.g.* Karlowa, *loc. cit.*; Girard, Manuel, 100.

[11] 40. 12. 14. *pr.*, 1.

Edictal origin[1]. It is true that among the books in which it is treated are Paul's and Ulpian's commentaries on the Edict. But Ulpian's Book 11[2] is on *restitutio in integrum*, and this matter comes in incidentally. Paul's Book 50 and Ulpian's Book 54[3] are on a topic in which this matter would naturally come if it were in the Edict, *i.e.* *de liberali causa*[4], and they are in those books of the commentary which according to Blume belonged to the Edictal group. But they are books which, it has been supposed[5], were transferred to the Edictal group from the Sabinian to save time[6].

Examination of the texts raises another question. It is clear that in Justinian's time, sharing the price was essential[7]. It is made the test as early as Gordian[8], and even Hadrian is cited as regarding it as necessary[9]. Yet many of the texts do not mention this requirement[10]. This of itself would mean little, as they may be expressed too generally, but the omissions are noteworthy in kind. In none of the texts from Paul is the requirement mentioned[11], and it is he who cites Quintus Mucius[12], and in the same *lex* tells us that *dos, donatio* and pledge are on the same footing as sale[13]. It is difficult to square the notion of sharing price with this, and still more difficult to understand how he could have discussed the matter without adverting to this difficulty if the requirement had existed. The only Roman text independent of Justinian says nothing of this requirement[14]. The texts dealing with the *actio in factum* for cases of fraud where *proclamatio* was not barred do not speak of this as a distinguishing mark[15]. A text which says that a *miles* allowing himself to be sold as a slave is capitally punishable says nothing of this requirement[16]. It may be added that, while some texts speak of sharing the price[17], others speak simply of receiving it[18] On the other hand it is perplexing to find price sharing mentioned in every one of Ulpian's texts[19]. So too the age rule is not treated uniformly. Some texts do not mention it[20]. Others speak merely of *maior* and *minor*[21]. All this suggests that the rule as we have it in the

---

[1] 1. 5. 5. 1. Explained away by Girard (*loc. cit.*) as a reference to confirmation by *Scc. etc.*, and by Karlowa (*loc. cit.*), who observes that the contrast is with *ius gentium*.

[2] 4. 4. 9. 4; Lenel, Ed. Perp. (2) xxii.   [3] 40. 12. 7; *h. t.* 23.

[4] Lenel, Ed. Perp. (2) xxii.   [5] Roby, Introd. to Digest, liv'.

[6] Lenel does not treat it as Edictal.   [7] 4. 4. 9. 4; 40. 12. 7. *pr.*; 40. 13. 1.

[8] C. 7. 18. 1.   [9] 40. 14. 2. *pr.*

[10] 1. 5. 21; 40. 12. 23, 33; 40. 13. 3, 4, 5; C. 7. 14. 14; 7. 16. 16; C. Th. 4. 8. 6, *etc.*

[11] 40. 12. 23. *pr.*, 1, 33; 40. 13. 4 (a long and argumentative text).

[12] 40. 12. 23. *pr.*

[13] See also C. 7. 16. 16, and Syrische Rechtsbücher, *locc. citt.*

[14] C. Th. 4. 8. 6.   [15] 40. 12. 14—22.   [16] 48. 19. 14.

[17] 4. 4. 9. 4; 28. 3. 6. 5; 40. 12. 7. *pr.*, 1, 40; 40. 13. 1. 1; C. 7. 18. 1.

[18] 40. 13. 1. *pr.*; 40. 14. 2. *pr.*

[19] 4. 4. 9. 4; 28. 3. 6. 5; 40. 12. 7; 40. 13. 1. 1. Of these some are corrupt. 28. 3. 6. 5 and 40. 12. 7 shew that price-sharing was not the only case. The different MSS. of the Syro-Roman Law-book deal capriciously with this point. In one, and that, it seems, an early one (Syrische Rechtsbücher, 67), the rule is applied though he gets none of the price.

[20] 1. 5. 21; 40. 12. 23, 33; C. 7. 18. 1.   [21] 40. 14. 2. *pr.*; C. Th. 4. 8. 6.

Digest is the result of an evolution[1]. But the stages in that evolution cannot be stated with any confidence. It is probable that the rule of enslavement is as old as Q. M. Scaevola, but even this is not certain, as the Quintus mentioned may be Q. Cerv. Scaevola[2]. The rule of price sharing is probably not nearly so old. No text takes it further back than Hadrian, and in the text which treats the requirement as known in his time, the words referring to price are in a parenthesis. The course of events may have been as follows: A praetorian *actio in factum* was given covering all cases. Then, perhaps still under the Republic, but probably later[3], the more drastic remedy was introduced apparently by *Senatusconsulta*[4], which specified the cases in which *proclamatio* was refused. They were at least two, price sharing, and desire to exercise the function of *actor*[5]. As time went on this last died out. In private life, as in public affairs, there was a great development of free labour, and the increased power of representation in the field of contract made it possible and usual to employ free *actores*[6]. By the time of Justinian price sharing was the only case of importance left, and thus it appears as a general condition on the bar. The allusion to it appears in most cases in a parenthetical form[7], and may well be, at least in some cases, an interpolation.

The *actio in factum* above mentioned has, in strictness, nothing to do with enslavement, and thus it is not necessary to state its rules in detail[8]. It covered any possible case in which a freeman *dolo malo* allowed himself to be sold as a slave, not covered by the other rule. Ulpian so expresses its scope[9], a fact which indicates that its field varied with changes in the scope of the more severe rule. It required *dolus*, beyond mere silence, and thus capacity for *dolus*, on the part of the man; but, apart from that, his age was not material[10]. The nature of the fraud was not material, and he need not have profited. The action was for double any loss or liability: it was independent of any contractual remedies against the actual vendor, and the buyer must have been ignorant of the facts[11].

---

[1] As to interpolation of some of these texts, see Gradenwitz, Interp. 100 *sqq.*
[2] 40. 12. 23. *pr.* See *ante*, p. 432. Karlowa, R. R. G. 2. 1117, thinks this text has nothing to do with our rule.
[3] Karlowa, *loc. cit.*, supposes our rule republican, on account of 40. 12. 22. 5. But that assumes that it antedated the *actio in factum*, which does not seem likely.
[4] 40. 13. 3.
[5] Karlowa, *loc. cit.*; 28. 3. 6. 5; C. Th. 4. 8. 6. 1. Allowing themselves to be included in a *dos* is another probable case. See Syro-Roman Law-book and Syrische Rechtsbücher, *locc. citt.* Not much can be safely inferred for Roman law from these sources. See Mitteis, Z. S. S. 25. 286 *sqq.* But Paul, too, refers to this case as also to that of allowing himself to be included in a pledge or a gift, 40. 12. 23. *pr.* It is possible that the actual limitation of the rule to price sharing is due to Ulpian.
[6] Wallon, *op. cit.* 3. 107 *sqq.*
[7] *e.g.* 4. 4. 9. 4; 40. 14. 2. *pr.*
[8] They are fully set out in 40. 12. 14—22.
[9] 40. 12. 14. 1.
[10] 40. 12. 14. 2, 15.
[11] *h. t.* 18, 16. 2, 20. 4.

B. R. L.

28

It remains to consider shortly the general effect of enslavement on the man's preexisting rights and duties. It must be borne in mind that the vast majority of slaves were so by birth, and that as to them no such question can arise, while of the rest, a number, which must have varied greatly from time to time, were so by capture. Their position, which was abnormal, has already been considered[1]. The remainder, whom alone we have to discuss, must have been relatively very few.

A number of general propositions on the matter are familiar. Every enslavement is a *capitis deminutio maxima,* for this is declared to result wherever liberty and citizenship are lost[2], and it is mentioned expressly in several cases, *e.g.* those of *servus poenae, libertus ingratus* and fraudulent sale[3]. These are, of course, the most important cases in later law. For earlier law it is stated for *incensi, dediticii* reenslaved, and cases under the Sc. Claudianum[4]; this list also being representative rather than complete.

A slave is a mere nullity at civil and praetorian law[5]. He has no *caput,* or what seems to be the same thing, his *caput* has no *ius*[6]. The principle is summed up in the remark that supervening slavery is akin to death[7]. Yet this does not adequately express the matter: the event is in some ways more destructive than death. Like death it destroys usufructs and similar rights[8]. There needs no authority for the statement that it ends all those relations of private and public life which imply that the persons concerned are *cives.* It ends any office, private or public, such as *tutela.* It ends marriage. It ends partnership, precisely as we are told, because the man is regarded as dead[9]. It produces all the effects of other *capitis deminutiones,* which need not be particularised. But it does much more. A will, which death brings into operation, is rendered *irritum* by enslavement[10]. Death avoids any gift, to the person who dies, by a will not yet operative (subject to some exceptions), and so does enslavement, *quia servitus morti adsimilatur*[11]. But even if it was after *dies cedens* he could not claim, nor do we learn that his heirs could, as they could in case of death[12]. It destroys all rights resulting from cognation or affinity[13]. We are told that *iura*

---

[1] *Ante,* pp. 291 *sqq.*   [2] 4. 5. 11.   [3] In. 1. 16. 1.
[4] G. 1. 160; Ulp. 11. 11. *Captivitas* is not in these lists. The case is a special one. The law of *postliminium,* and the effect allowed to the will of one who dies a captive, make this a rather abnormal case. See *ante,* pp. 291 *sqq.*
[5] 28. 8. 1. *pr.*; 50. 17. 32. The text adds that they are equal to other people by natural law. This justifies the natural obligation of the slave (*post,* Ch. XXIX.) and counts for something in the gradual recognition of *cognatio servilis. Ante,* p. 76.
[6] 4. 5. 3. 1; In. 1. 16. 4.   [7] 50. 17. 209; Nov. 22. 9; G. 3. 101.
[8] 7. 4. 14; In. 2. 4. 3; C. 3. 33. 16. 2; P. 3. 6. 29.
[9] 17. 2. 63. 10; In. 3. 25. 7. If entitled under *fideicommissum* to appoint property among his issue he cannot do it when enslaved: it is as if he had died without doing it, 36. 1. 18. 6.
[10] 28. 3. 6. 5, 6, 8—12; In. 2. 17. 4, 6; G. 2. 147.
[11] 35. 1. 59. 2; 49. 14. 12.   [12] 38. 17. 1. 4.   [13] 38. 8. 7; 38. 10. 4. 11; In. 1. 16. 6.

sanguinis cannot be destroyed by any civil law[1], but slavery is *iuris gentium.*

In dealing with the effects on debts due to and by him we have to remember that persons made slaves fall into two classes: they pass either into private ownership or into none. For it is a noticeable fact that there is no case (with the exception, if it be an exception, of the *captivus*) in which he vests in the Fisc. In some cases the Fisc sells him, but it does not appear that the State has the *dominium*, even where the price vests in it.

For delicts committed by such persons we know that the new owner is noxally liable: *noxa caput sequitur*[2]. But where the man was free before, there is in addition to this noxal liability the personal liability of the man. This is a burden on his estate, and need not be distinguished from other debts, except that like all debts *ex delicto*, it falls on successors only to the extent of their benefit, if any. In the case of *servi poenae* there can be no noxal action. There is no owner; moreover they cannot be allowed to pass from their terrible position into that of ordinary slaves because they have committed a wrong.

As to contractual and quasi-contractual debts, direct authority is very scanty. It is fairly certain that the liabilities and rights, so far as they survive, go with the *bona*. We are told that this is so as to liabilities[3], the man's own liability being extinct[4]. Another text tells us that there is an *actio utilis* against the *dominus* and if it is not defended *in solidum*, there is *missio in possessionem* of the goods of the former freeman[5], a rule analogous to that in the case of *adrogati*[6]. This implies that the property goes to the *dominus*, which is no doubt the case under the Sc. Claudianum[7], and in fraudulent sale.

As to the converse case, that of debts due to the enslaved man, there seems to be no textual authority at all. It seems likely that the analogy with *adrogatio* governs this· case also. If that be so the *dominus* acquires rights of action *ipso iure*[8]. The case is differentiated from that of *bonorum emptor* in that there he has no civil law right; his succession is edictal, and thus his actions are indirect[9]. None of our cases is edictal, subject to what has been said above[10] as to the case of reenslavement for ingratitude.

Altogether different considerations arise in relation to *servus poenae*. Here, in general, the Fisc acquires, though it does not own the man.

---

[1] 50. 17. 8.   [2] In. 4. 8. 5; G. 4. 77.   [3] 4. 5. 2. *pr.*
[4] *Novus homo videtur esse,* 34. 4. 27. 1; 44. 7. 30.
[5] 4. 5. 7. 2.   [6] In. 3. 10. 3.
[7] *Ante,* p. 413. In Justinian's latest legislation the rule may have been different in the case of *libertus ingratus.* Nov. 22. 9, of which the rubric seems hardly consistent with the text, may mean that the children took some of the goods. If so they no doubt incurred proportionate liability, but the text is extremely obscure.
[8] In. 3. 10. 1, 3.   [9] G. 3. 80, 81.   [10] *Ante,* p. 431.

There seems no reason to distinguish this from other cases in which the
Fisc takes a succession[1]. On this view all that need be said is that the
Fisc takes the estate subject to its debts[2]. The creditors can make
their right effective by *bonorum venditio*[3]. The Fisc can prevent the
forced sale of a clearly solvent estate by paying off the creditors. On
the other hand if the property has definitely vested in the Fisc, it can
sue for debts due to the estate, having in such cases only such privileges
as the private creditor would have had[4]. We must remember however
that a share of the property goes to the children (and at some dates to
other successors[5]). Where the Fisc takes no share at all, it seems clear
from the language used in the different texts, that it is an ordinary case
of succession[6]. So also where the man was a *decurio*, and part goes to
the children (in some cases) and part to the *curia*[7]: both the children
and the *curia* appear to inherit. So too where he was a *libertus* ; the
rights of *patroni* and *filii patroni* are not affected : they inherit as to
their share[8]. But, at least in the time of Justinian, where the children,
and they alone, get a share, they do not appear to inherit, but to receive
a grant from the Fisc[9]. As the Fisc takes only subject to debts and
has a right of action, we must assume that the children have none,
and are not liable. But we cannot be sure that this is the right interpretation, and, if it is, we cannot be sure that the classical rule was
the same. Hadrian's rule is expressed in the same language[10]. But
that of the law of 380 is obscure and may mean that they are heirs
pro parte, though the expression, *fiscus concedit*, appears therein, as in
the abridged edition in the Code[11].

1 The omission of this case in 49. 14. 1 is due to the fact that here no *nuntiatio* was in question.
2 49. 14. 1. 1, 11, 12, 17, 37 ; Lenel, Ed. Perp. § 212.
3 48. 20. 4, 10. *pr.*; C. 9. 49. 5.
4 49. 14. 3. 8, 6. *pr.*, 21.   5 *Ante*, p. 407.
6 C. Th. 9. 42. 2, 6, 9, 10, 23.   7 C. 9. 49. 10 = C. Th. 9. 42. 24.
8 48. 20. 7. 1, 8.   9 *h. t.* 1, 7. *pr. etc.*   10 *h. t.* 7. 3.
11 C. Th. 9. 42. 8 = C. 9. 49. 8 ; C. Th. 9. 42. 9. As to *postliminium, ante*, pp. 304 *sqq.* ; *restitutio servi poenae, ante*, p. 411 ; *sanguinolentus*, reverting to *ingenuitas, ante*, p. 422 ; redemption of person who fraudulently sells himself by return of price, *ante*, p. 430.

CHAPTER XIX.

IT is not necessary to attempt the hopeless task of defining liberty.
Justinian adopts from Florentinus[1] the definition : Liberty is the natural
capacity (*facultas*) of doing what we like, except what, by force or law,
we are prevented from doing. This definition no doubt expresses certain
truths. Liberty is "natural": slavery is *iuris gentium*. It is presumed
that a freeman can do any act in the law : his incapacity must be proved.
The reverse is the case with a slave. But, literally understood, it would
make everybody free. As a matter of fact all persons not slaves are
free, and as we have arrived at a more or less exact notion of Roman
slavery we may leave the matter there.

The conception of manumission needs some examination. It is not
in strictness transfer of *dominium*. A man has no *dominium* in himself
or his members[2]. Nor is it an alienation of liberty. The right received
is not that of the master, and the rule that a man cannot give a better
liberty than he has is intelligible without reference to such an idea.
Nor is it a mere release from the owner's *dominium* : that is *derelictio*,
from which manumission differs in several ways. Dereliction does not
make the man free, it merely makes him a *res nullius*[3]. Moreover
manumission leaves many rights in the master, and there is no such
thing as partial dereliction[4]. If it had contained a dereliction, then,
since *derelictio* is purely informal, a manumission which failed for
lack of form would have been a dereliction. But this was not the case.
At civil law such a defective manumission produced no effect at all, and
even under the Praetorian law and the *lex* Iunia it left large rights in
the master, and entitled no third person to seize[5]. We have seen[6] that
the Roman conception of slavery was subjection to ownership, actual or
potential : a slave was a human *res*. Manumission is an act emanating

---

[1] 1. 5. 4; In. 1. 3. 1.   [2] 9. 2. 13.   [3] 41. 7. 2.
[4] *h. t.* 3.   [5] *Post*, p. 445.
[6] *Ante*, p. 2. As to the nature of manumission, see further, *post*, App. IV.

from the holder of ownership removing the man (by the authority of
the State, which is present in all formal manumission) from that class.
It is essentially a release not merely from the owner's control, but from
all possibility of being owned.   It does indeed confer rights and
capacities on him[1], but it is from the notion of destroying capacities
for rights over him that the conception starts.

There are some general rules which may be shortly stated here,
though some of them will need more detailed treatment later.

An *ingenuus* is a freeborn person who has never been in lawful
slavery[2].   One who has been a slave is, on release from that position,
a *libertinus*[3].   The law favours freedom on the one hand but guards the
purity of *ingenuitas* on the other.   An *ingenuus* does not cease to be
one by being sold by his father[4], or by manumission from apparent
slavery[5], or by being treated in any way as a slave, wrongly[6].   Even
a declaration by the man himself under pressure that he is not an
ingenuus does not deprive him of that position[7].   Adverse decision does
not prevent repeated assertion of liberty, though a decision in favour of
liberty may prevent its being again disputed[8].   In the same way a man
cannot become a slave by lapse of time spent in apparent slavery[9],
though he may be free by prescription[10].   All these are evidences of the
favour shewn to liberty: *infinita est aestimatio libertatis*[11].   On the other
hand, though a *libertinus* may be adopted, at any rate by his patron, he
does not thereby become an *ingenuus*[12], so far, at least, as rights in
relation to third persons are concerned[13].

To these general rules there are some exceptions, little more than
apparent, which need only mention.   They can be grouped under three
heads.

(i)   A *libertinus* may by special grace acquire the rights of an
ingenuus.   With this case we shall not deal[14].

(ii)   It is possible in certain cases, already discussed, for a person
to be a *libertus* without having been a slave[15].

(iii)   It is possible for one who has been validly enslaved to become
an *ingenuus* on again becoming free[16].

There is a general tendency, doubtless accentuated in later law, to
interpret rules and facts as far as possible in favour of liberty.   It is a

---

[1] *Post*, p. 439.   [2] G. 1. 11.   [3] 1. 5. 6; In. 1. 5. *pr.*; G. 1. 11.
[4] P. 5. 1. 1; C. 7. 16. 1, *ante*, p. 420.   [5] P. 5. 1. 2; In. 1. 4. 1.
[6] P. 5. 1. 3.   [7] *h. t.* 4.   [8] C. 7. 16. 2, 4.
[9] C. 7. 22. 3.   [10] C. 7. 21. 7; 7. 22. 1, 2; *post*, Ch. xxviii.
[11] 50. 17. 176. 1.   [12] 1. 5. 27; 1. 7. 46; Aul. Gell. 5. 19. 12.
[13] 1. 7. 15. 3, 46; 2. 4. 10. 2; 37. 12. 1. 2; 38. 2. 49.   An *ingenuus* adopted by a *libertinus*
was still of course *ingenuus*, 1. 7. 35.   From the texts cited in this and the last note, with
others, it appears that adrogation of *libertini*, by any but the *patronus*, was one of the things
which *non debent fieri, sed facta valent.*
[14] See, *e.g.*, Moyle, ad In. 1. 5. 3.   [15] *Ante*, p. 412.
[16] Thus *captivus* is a slave but reverts to *ingenuitas* by *postliminium* (*ante*, p. 304).   See also
the case of children sold, *ante*, p. 420, and see p. 410.

general principle that in doubtful or ambiguous cases it is best to follow the more liberal view[1]. Liberty being of immeasurable value and *omnibus rebus favorabilior*[2], the principle is naturally laid down that in doubtful questions affecting liberty, *secundum libertatem respondendum erit*[3]. Countless illustrations of this tendency will be found in the following chapters.

A slave may become free either as the result of manumission by his *dominus*, or without the latter's consent. It is convenient to begin with manumission, and, as the topic is somewhat complicated, to deal first with the simplest case. This is manumission, by a sole and unencumbered owner who is a *civis* not under any disqualification, of a slave, himself under no disqualification, and in whom no other person has any right. And this must be treated historically.

With the very early law we are not concerned, and indeed little but guesswork is possible in relation to it. The origin of manumissions is unknown. Dionysius of Halicarnassus credits the foundation of the law on the point to Servius Tullius[4], but as he refers nearly everything else to that king no particular weight attaches to his testimony. The XII Tables shew that at their time it was an established institution[5]. All manumission is regarded as an institution of the *ius gentium*[6]. It is a *datio libertatis*: *liberatur (servus) potestate*[7]. But it is more than that: it is, at any rate during the Republic, the making of a *civis*. Ulpian tells us that *legitime manumissi, nullo iure impediente*[8], become *cives*. In the Digest he speaks of the patron's rights as a return for having made *cives* of the slaves[9]. Thus citizenship is always the ordinary result of a typical manumission. From this characteristic of manumission it follows that all the modes of manumission are public, *i.e.* are in some way under public control. The State is interested in seeing that *civitas* is not bestowed on unworthy persons[10].

Of these modes of manumission there are three.

I. *Censu.* Although the Census survived into the Empire, it is so essentially a republican institution that it seems best to say here the little that is to be said about it.

It is not necessary to discuss the Census in general : we are concerned with it only as a mode of manumission. It is probable that this form of manumission is extremely old, but it hardly survives into the classical

---

[1] *Benigniora praeferenda ; benigniorem sententiam sequi non minus iustius quam tutius est ; humaniorem sententiam sequi oportet*, 28. 4. 3 ; 34. 5. 10. 1 ; 35. 2. 32. 5 ; 50. 17. 56, 192. 1.
[2] 50. 17. 122.
[3] 50. 17. 20.   The language, though not the decision, of C. 2. 4. 43 is in the same vein.
[4] Dion. Hal. 4. 22.   [5] Bruns, Fontes, 1. 24, 28.   [6] In. 1. 5. *pr.*
[7] *Ib.*; D. 1. 1. 4.   [8] Ulp. 1. 6.
[9] 38. 2. 1. *pr.*; 38. 16. 3. 1.   [10] Boethius in Cic. Top. 2. 10.

law with which we are really concerned. There was a census in A.D. 74, and there was at least the name of one in 243. But this form of manumission was really extinct. Paul does not mention it. Ulpian says, *olim manumittebantur censu*[1]. Gaius, however, writing somewhat earlier, speaks of it in several texts as if it still existed[2]. The Fragmentum Dositheum of about the same date as Gaius discusses it as a living institution[3]. But in several other texts in the Fragment, where we should have expected to see it side by side with *vindicta*, it is not mentioned[4]. This circumstance and the known facts of history[5] make it clear that the texts are discussing an unreality. The institution is obsolete. Such counting of the population as occurs under the Emperors may be called by the same name, but it has little or no relation to the republican Census.

The Census, taken every five years[6], is in essence a list of *cives* made for fiscal purposes and for the regulation of military service. The form of manumission is the inscription of the name of the man on the list of citizens. It involves three steps. The slave presents himself and claims to be a citizen: *censu profitebantur*[7]. The assent of the owner is shewn: *iussu* or *consensu domini*[8]. The Censor inscribes the name on the list of *cives*. On each of these three requirements there is something to be said[9]. The *professio* mentioned is the formal presentation of himself which each *civis* was bound to make to avoid the penalties falling on an *incensus*[10]. The *iussum* of the master does not seem to have been a formal part of the ceremony, though of course the Censor would not enrol the name without it[11]. It is an authorisation to the slave, not to the Censor, and its informal nature is expressed in Cicero's description of it as *consensus*[12]. We are not expressly told that the master had to be present, but this was probably the case, especially in view of the fact that in 176 B.C. a temporary rule was laid down that in certain cases of ·manumission before the Censor or other magistrate the owner was required to take a certain oath[13]. No juristic text actually mentions the entry on the roll as an essential, but Cicero does[14], and the very name of the institution and the language of the other texts obviously take it for granted[15]. The Censor could no doubt refuse to enrol the man.

---

[1] Ulp. 1. 8. [2] G. 1. 17, 44, 138, 140. [3] Fr. Dos. 5, 17.
[4] Fr. Dos. 11, 13, 15. [5] Mommsen, Röm. Staatsr. (3) 2. 1. 415; D. P. R. 4. 98.
[6] Fr. Dos. 17. In early times it was frequently less. [7] Ulp. 1. 8.
[8] *Ibid.*; Cicero, De Orat. 1. 183.
[9] Fully discussed by Degenkolb, Befreiung durch Census, 3—14, of which work much use has been made.
[10] *Ante*, p. 401.
[11] Degenkolb treats it as essential but not as part of the form. It is in this way that he explains release from *mancipium* without consent of the holder.
[12] Cicero, *loc. cit.* [13] Livy, 41. 9.
[14] Cicero, de Orat. 1. 183.
[15] Fr. Dos. 17; Theophil. 1. 5. 4. He describes the process inexactly.

The process could take place only at Rome, for it was only at Rome that the true Roman Census was held[1]. The slave must be the property *ex iure quiritium* of the manumitter[2], and it is plain that no modality of any kind could be attached to manumission in this form. But it must be borne in mind that the freedman's oath was not a condition, and, no doubt, by means of it many conditions could practically be imposed, breach of the undertaking being a punishable case of ingratitude.

The procedure of the Census is a long business: the new lists cannot be prepared in a day. Apparently it was not usually till towards the end of their eighteen months of office that the lists were completed and the Censors proceeded to the formal act, *lustrum condere*, which brought the new lists into operation. It was not clear whether the slave was free from the moment of enrolment, or only when the new lists came into operation. The doubt is referred to by Cicero, and again in the much later Fragmentum Dositheum[3]. It was not confined to this question, but extended to all acts of the Censor taking effect in the Census Roll, *e.g. notae censoriae* and the like. It would seem that the question must have been of great practical importance, and yet that it was never determined. It may be that these various acts, which were more than mere records of fact, were postponed till the last moment. Logic seems to require that, at least in our case, the later date should apply. It seems that it must have been so, so far as concerns public law. But it may well be that for private law the practice was otherwise. The entry does not purport to make him a *civis*: it is a fictitious renewal of an entry, and the Censor is recording the fact that the man is a *civis*, not making him one. Strictly indeed he is only recording the fact that the man has claimed to be a *civis*, and if such an entry is made in error it is null[4], and cannot operate by lapse of time, for it is not till much later that we find rules as to liberty by prescription[5].

Some of the early Emperors were Censors, and Domitian was Censor for life. It does not seem that he proceeded to any census, or *lustrum condidit* in the old sense. There are no signs of manumission before him as Censor: the whole institution is at an end.

II. *Vindicta.* This is a "fictitious" application of the procedure in a *causa liberalis.* If a claim of liberty was made on behalf of a man

---

[1] Fr. Dos. 17.   [2] *Ibid.*   [3] Fr. Dos. 17; Cicero, *loc. cit.*
[4] Mommsen, Röm. Staatsr. (3) 2. 1. 374, Dr. Pub. Rom. 4. 521. Degenkolb remarks that the doubt shews that enrolment was needed.
[5] *Post*, Ch. xxviii. Late in the Republic the rules were so far relaxed that the collection of statistics was made in some cases in the various *municipia*. But this was not the actual Census, and it does not seem that the Censors were present. See Mommsen, Röm. Staatsr. 2. 1. 368; Dr. P. R. 4. 45.

alleged to be wrongully detained as a slave, the claim took the form of an action brought by an *adsertor libertatis*, claiming him as a free man, the form being, at this time, that of *sacramentum*[1]. Used as a mode of manumission it was essentially a case of *cessio in iure*[2]. The *adsertor libertatis* who, at least in later times, was often a *lictor*, claimed him before a magistrate as free, touching him with the wand which appears in *sacramentum*, and which gave its name to this mode of manumission. The *dominus* made no defence and the magistrate declared the man free[3]. As it was an *actus legitimus*, no condition or suspension was possible: by addition of *dies*, or condition, *actus legitimi in totum vitiantur*[4].

From the form and nature of the process it is clear that the presence and assent of the magistrate were necessary. From the text of Livy already cited[5] it may be assumed that the actual presence of the *dominus* was needed, though the oath there referred to was a temporary matter[6]. As it was in form a *vindicatio*, the slave must be on the spot.

We are not concerned with the position of a *libertinus*, but it may be as well to observe that it was not unusual to exact an oath, before manumission, that the man would render certain services. The oath was not in itself binding, but was regarded as putting the slave under the duty of swearing again, or promising, immediately after the manumission[7]. Breach of the undertaking would expose the freedman to the ordinary liabilities for ingratitude[8]. Even though the *libertus* were *impubes*, if he were old enough to take an oath, an *actio utilis* would lie to enforce the duties after puberty, and there were some duties which he could render even *impubes*; for instance, he could act as *histrio* or *nomenculator*[9].

III. *Testamento.* Gratuitous benefits are, naturally, given most readily at death. This mode of manumission was therefore by far the most important in the law. It will be necessary to deal with it at some length when we are discussing the classical law[10]: here it will suffice to describe its general nature, and to lay down a few main rules.

The origin of the institution is not certainly known[11]. It is clearly as old as the XII Tables. Pomponius tells us that they gave a very wide power of, *inter alia*, manumission, by the *uti legassit* clause, a power afterwards restricted in divers ways[12]. So Ulpian, in an imperfect

---

[1] As to its working in an actual claim, *post*, Ch. xxviii.   [2] *Post*, p. 451.
[3] Ulp. 1. 7; G. 1. 17; Roby, Rom. Priv. Law, 1. 26.
[4] 50. 17. 77. As to tacit conditions and suspensions, *post*, p. 455.   [5] Livy, 41. 9.
[6] Some remarks of Diodorus Siculus (36. 4. 8) suggest that in time of crisis the Praetor could free without consent of *dominus*.
[7] 40. 12. 44. *pr.* The name of the patron's wife might be used in the stipulation, *h. l.* 1.
[8] *Ante*, p. 422.   [9] 40. 12. 44. 2.   [10] *Post*, p. 460.
[11] Fully discussed, Appleton, Le testament Romain, 86 *sqq.*
[12] 50. 16. 120.

text, seems to base the law on the XII Tables[1]. But there is reason to think it older. The incomplete text of Ulpian ends with the word *confirmat*, and may mean that the *lex* confirmed an existing practice, or that it confirmed the testator's declarations. But the most important point is that the *lex* contained detailed rules as to succession to freedmen, as to conditional gifts of liberty, as to the person to whom a man might make a payment on which his liberty was conditioned, and so forth[2], a state of things which is most unlikely if the whole institution was new. We will not enter on the still more speculative question as to the relative antiquity of this and the other two modes, but will merely remark in passing that it is the only one of the three which is direct, *i.e.* is not based on a fiction. From this it has been inferred[3] that it was the oldest: the contrary conclusion seems more reasonable.

The will of this age was, of course, the *testamentum in comitiis calatis*. The disappearance of public control is shewn by the extension of the rules to the mancipatory will of the later Republic: in that will the public aspect of the transaction has become a mere tradition.

Liberty could be given directly only to slaves of the testator, the model followed being plainly that of a *legatum per vindicationem*[4]. In conformity with the same principle Servius established the rule that the slave must have been the property of the testator both at the time of the will and at the time of death[5]. This is the rule in such legacies[6], apart from the *lex* Papia which postponed *dies cedens* to the opening of the will. We are not indeed told that our rule has anything to do with *dies cedens*, but it seems probable that it had, and this may serve to explain an apparent conflict. As in the case of legacy, *media tempora non nocent*. Sale and reacquisition after the will was made left the gift valid[7]. Maecianus tells us that if liberty was given to a slave, and he was sold, but became again the property of the *hereditas*, before *aditio*, the gift was valid[8]. Gifts to slaves ceded only on *aditio*[9], a fact which brings the present rule into connexion with the theory of *dies cedens*[10].

Of the form of the gift little need be said here: it will be considered later. There must be a clear expression of intent that the man should be free. Thus it might be *liber sit, liber esto, liberum esse iubeo,* and the like[11]. Implied gifts are not readily admitted even in later times[12]. It will be seen that the above forms follow closely that of *legatum per*

---

[1] Ulp. 1. 9.	[2] Ulp. 2. 4; D. 40. 7. 25, 29. 1.	[3] Appleton, *loc. cit.*
[4] C. 7. 2. 9.	So, if a *servus alienus* is freed directly and *legatus* in the same will, the legacy is good, for he can be legated, though not *per vindicationem*, 30. 108. 9.
[5] 40. 4. 35.	[6] G. 2. 196.	[7] *Ibid.*
[8] 40. 4. 58.	[9] In. 2. 20. 20.
[10] The position of *statuliber* is in strictness acquired only on *aditio*, though this is relieved against in later law, 40. 7. 2. *pr.*, 9. 3, *ante*, p. 291.
[11] Ulp. 2. 7; P. 4. 14.	[12] *Post*, p. 461.

vindicationem. The question may be asked : what would be the effect
of such a gift as *heres meus damnas esto Stichum liberum esse sinere*?
Such a gift must, it seems, have been null. A legacy in that form gave
only a *ius in personam* and this could not have given more. But it
could not have given a right of action to the man, and fideicommissary
gifts were not yet invented. The same would no doubt be true of a
gift *heres meus damnas esto Stichum manumittere*[1]. The same reasoning
applies. No doubt the institution might be made conditional on the
manumission by the *heres* of his or a third person's slave. But this is a
wholly different matter : it is in no way enforceable by the slave. It is
another question how far a person who disregarded such an injunction
to free one of the slaves might incur the disapproval of the Censor.

The gift takes effect only upon the actual operation of a valid will,
but if the *heres* has accepted, the gift remains effective even though he
afterwards gets *restitutio in integrum*[2]. If, however, the will is *ruptum*,
it was never valid at all, and, apart from collusion, a liberty which may
have apparently taken effect by entry is void[3]. So also it fails in an
ordinary case of *testamentum destitutum*, where, apart from collusion, no
heir enters[4]. There are, however, exceptional cases in which the gift
will be effective, though the will does not operate, for instance, where a
heres, entitled both by the will and on intestacy, takes on intestacy—
omissa causa testamenti. Other cases of this type will be considered
later[5].

Such gifts might, like legacies, be adeemed, and though they were
not subject to the *lex* Falcidia, passed just at the close of the Republic,
their existence in a will gave rise to some difficult questions when that
lex operated. Both these topics will be more conveniently considered
in connexion with the classical law[6].

These three were the only forms of manumission which were
recognised during the Republic. They all, whenever they were valid
at all, made the freedman a *civis*, if we leave out of account for the
present the slave freed by a Latin owner. But it is obvious that
occasions must have arisen under which the intention to free a man,
there and then, was expressed in less formal ways. Two such are in
fact recorded. They are the declaration, *inter amicos*, that the man is
free, and writing him a letter of enfranchisement[7]. Such declarations
were void in early law. But, towards the close of the Republic, the

---

[1] Accarias, Précis, § 56, thinks such a gift valid. He does not advert to the question of the
remedy.
[2] C. 7. 2. 3. As to case of *heres necessarius, post*, pp. 505 *sqq.*
[3] *h. t.* 12. 2; D. 40. 5. 24. 11.   [4] C. 7. 2. 12.
[5] 40. 4. 23. *pr. Post*, Ch. xxvii.   [6] *Post*, pp. 473 *sqq.*
[7] See *e.g.* G. 1. 44. *Amici* are *testes*. See G. 2. 25, and Bruns, Syro-Roman Law-book, 195.
See also Suetonius, de Rhet. 1. As to manumission *in convivio, post*, p. 446.

Praetor interfered to protect persons who had been so declared free and gave them *de facto* enjoyment of liberty. Hence they were said *in libertate servari auxilio Praetoris*[1], *in libertate tuitione Praetoris esse*[2], *in libertate domini voluntate morari*[3] (or *esse*). The texts are explicit that, notwithstanding the declaration, they were still slaves (*manebant servi, non esse liberos, ex iure quiritium servi*), and in accordance with this we learn that their *peculia* and all that they acquired belonged to their (former) master. It is clear that it was not revocable, and there is no reason to doubt that it was binding on successors in title of all kinds. It is also fairly clear on our few authorities that the status was not heritable: such persons were slaves and the child of a woman in such a position would be an ordinary slave. The main, indeed, as far as can be seen, the only, effect was to free them from any duty of working, so that if the owner tried, by force, to make them work for him, the Praetor intervened to prevent it[4]. They were evidently not *derelicti*: the informal declaration that they were to be free was very far from an abandonment of all rights.

Doubt may be thrown on some of these conclusions by other language of these texts. Thus Gaius speaks of them as *ex iure quiritium servi*, and goes on to speak of the master as *patronus*[5]. And the Frag. Dositheum speaks of him as *manumissor* and *patronus*, and says that the person so dealt with, *omnia quasi servus acquirebat manumissori*[6]. But it must be remembered that these texts were written a century and a half after the *lex* Iunia had turned these processes into real manumissions, and this part of the language is coloured by that fact. More weight must be given to the words which express what was certainly not the law of the age in which they were written.

The Fragment gives some further details. The protection of the Praetor did not proceed as a matter of course, but only if the Praetor thought the slave a fit person to have this *de facto* liberty[7]. Moreover *voluntas domini spectatur*, and thus his consent must be real. The Praetor would not intervene if the master's declaration that he wished the slave to be free was made under pressure[8]. He would not intervene if the owner was a woman who had not her tutor's *auctoritas*, or, presumably if it was an *impubes* in the same case. The text remarks that the Praetor would not intervene if the owner were under twenty. As it stands this may be a result of the *lex* Aelia Sentia, but it is equally probable that that enactment only followed in this respect what had

---

[1] G. 3. 56.　　　　[2] *Ibid.*　　　　[3] Fr. Dos. 4, 5.
[4] Fr. Dos. *loc. cit.*; G. *loc. cit.*　　　　[5] G. 3. 56.
[6] Fr. Dos. *loc. cit.* Conversely Tacitus (Ann. 13. 27) seems to speak of a *locus poenitentiae*. But he probably means no more than that the donor may decline to make a more formal manumission.
[7] Fr. Dos. 8.　　　　[8] Fr. Dos. 7; cp. D. 40. 9. 17. 1.

been the practice of the Praetor. The age of the slave was immaterial[1]. The master must be one who held the slave *in bonis*, but he need not be the quiritary owner[2]. If the slave were common, the declaration by one of the owners that the slave was to be free produced no effect at all[3]. These texts are mainly concerned with latinity under the *lex Iunia*, but are made relevant to our case by some words which indicate that that latinity was granted on informal manumission under such circumstances as would have led the Praetor to protect *de facto* liberty[4]. This entitles us to say that this partial relief might be given when a master, incapacitated from formal acts by physical defect, yet wished to free his slave. Thus Paul tells us that a *mutus surdus*, though he could not manumit *vindicta*, could do so *inter amicos*[5]. Wlassak, in the course of an exhaustive article[6], in which he shews that Praetorian rights were not exempt from rules of form, establishes certain conclusions in relation to these manumissions. He shews that in such manumission there was needed express declaration of intention to free, not merely to allow to be *in libertate*. He shews further that the evidence on which it has been generally held[7] that there were many of these modes of manumission shews only that there were many ways of obtaining latinity, and that of the well-known three, that *in convivio* is not mentioned till the later Empire[8]. He objects to the expression "informal," since in fact each has its form. It seems, however, justifiable to call them informal, since the presence of witnesses is rather a substantial guarantee than a formal one[9]. He discusses[10] certain texts which suggest that it was enough that the master had expressed a willingness for the slaves to be *in libertate*, *i.e.* that *animus manumittendi* was not needed. The non-juristic texts[11] he holds to be mere inaccuracies of expression. This is probably correct, but such allusions shew that manumissions which required only declaration before an unspecified number of witnesses must have taken place under such varying conditions as to have given an impression of formlessness. Two juristic texts[12] which raise the same suggestion are referred by Wlassak to another matter[13].

---

[1] Fr. Dos. 13—15.
[2] Fr. Dos. 9.
[3] Fr. Dos. 10.
[4] Fr. Dos. 5—7; G. 3. 56.
[5] P. 4. 12. 2.
[6] Z. S. S. 26. 367 *sqq.*
[7] In. 1. 5. 1; 1. 5. 3; 3. 7. 4; C. 7. 6. 1.
[8] He cites (*op. cit.* p. 404) as mentioning it Pseudo-Dion., *ad* Paul. Sam.; G. Ep. 1. 1. 2; Lex Rom. Burg. c. 44; Theoph. *ad* Inst. 1. 5. 4. It is not in the Digest or in the comprehensive C. 7. 6.
[9] It may be noted that in the record of manumission *inter amicos* which we possess (Girard, Textes (3), Appendice) the witnesses are not named and do not sign as in the recorded mancipations (Girard, *op. cit.* 785, 806 *sqq.*).
[10] p. 391.   [11] Pseudo-Quintil. Declam. 340, 342.   [12] 40. 12. 24. 3, 28.
[13] *Post*, Ch. XXVIII. That such transactions as those recorded in Suetonius and the Declamationes, *locc. citt.* should have been thought valid by anyone shews how little any notion of form enters into the matter. In dealing with Latini Iuniani we shall see that either the conception, *inter amicos*, was very widely construed or before Justinian a number of informal modes had come to be recognised.

The texts do not touch the question whether a manumission in a Praetorian will could be enforced in this way. It seems very unlikely for many reasons. It seems almost certain that if it had been so we should have heard of it, for we hear in various places a good deal about these wills, and about the ways in which Junian latinity could be obtained, and it is nowhere mentioned in either of these connexions. All informal, manumission seems to be contemplated as *inter vivos*. Moreover the expression Praetorian will is a little misleading. It is far less than a will. It operates under certain edicts, to the effect that if the document is in a certain form claimants under it will be given possession of the *bona*. All that can be got under it is *bonorum possessio*, and this *de facto* liberty cannot be brought under that conception. The enactment of Justinian abolishing latinity deals with two cases closely akin to this. Liberty given by codicils is mentioned allusively[1], and the case is discussed of a direction by the testator that certain slaves should share in his funeral, wearing the pileus which was the sign of liberation. This last he adds to his list of informal manumissions, remarking that as such a gift it had been of no effect before his time[2]. It seems that so verbose a draftsman must have adverted to the case we are concerned with, if it had existed.

The same question calls for the same answer, in the case of gifts made in indirect forms before the introduction of *fideicommissa*[3].

Some peculiar cases of manumission, perhaps exceptional in form, are mentioned by other than legal writers. Festus, in two passages[4], refers to *manumissio sacrorum causa*, to which we have no other reference. It is manumission by a solemn declaration that the man is to be free, the master holding him by a limb and undertaking to pay a sum of money if the man so freed departs afterwards from the *sacra*. Then he turns him round and releases him and he is free. This may be a case of *manumissio vindicta*. If this is so, either it is very incompletely stated (which, in view of the author's purpose, is likely enough), or the breakdown in formality of manumission *vindicta* is much earlier than is commonly supposed. Mommsen[5] treats it as no manumission at all, but only a sale to the temple with an agreed penalty for taking him away. It is connected with a similar Greek practice[6]. In Greece it was common to sell slaves to the service of a deity, in which case they became sacred and free, at least from the secular law. Gradually the process came to be applied, as a fiction, for what was plainly manu-

---

[1] C. 7. 6. 1 c, 2.
[2] C. 7. 6. 5; *post*, Ch. xxiv. His language may mean that this had given latinity.
[3] Praetorian protection in case of other defects, *post*, Ch. xxiii.
[4] Festus, *vv.* manumitti, purum.
[5] Mommsen, Röm. Staatsr. 3. 1. 421; D. P. R. 6. 2. 2.   [6] See Wlassak, Z. S. S. 28, pp. 22 *sqq.*

mission[1]. But the process recorded by Festus never seems to have got further than the devotion of the man to the service of the deity. Festus is however very clear that it was a manumission, though his authority cannot be ranked as very high in view of the antiquity of the institution.

Aulus Gellius observes[2] that many jurists had laid it down (though he treats the matter as of purely antiquarian interest) that a master could give his slave in adoption. This too seems to be ordinarily regarded[3] as a case of manumission *vindicta*, with some special formalities, and it seems to be sometimes treated as the same rule as that which Justinian attributes to Cato[4], that is, that a master could adopt his own slave and so free him. But the two cases are not the same. The language of Aulus Gellius shews that he is contemplating an adoption by *vindicta* or an analogous process, and by a person who is not the *dominus*: *servus a domino per praetorem in adoptionem dari potest*. On the other hand the case in the Institutes is plainly one of adoption by the *dominus* himself. It is hard to see how this could be done directly by *vindicta*, and we have no right to suppose a transfer to a third person, followed by adoption. On the whole it seems more likely that it was a case of adrogation, in effect a shortening, by leave of the Comitia, of the form of manumission followed by adrogation of the freedman by his patron. This last we know to have been a familiar case[5]. Wlassak[6] objects to the view that it is an adrogation on the ground that a slave could not have appeared *in comitiis*. If a woman could not be adrogated a slave could not. He supposes a fiduciary sale followed by adoption. There is no logical answer to this objection, but it may be doubted whether so severe a logic can be safely applied in such a case[7]. In any case the institution is not important to us for it leaves no trace in the classical law[8].

---

[1] See the literature cited by Girard, Manuel, 116. See also Dareste, Recueil des Inscriptions Grecques, Série 2, pp. 234 *sqq.* For various opinions as to the nature of the Roman institution, see Vangerow, Latini Iuniani, 59.
[2] Aul. Gell. Noct. Att. 5. 19. 13—14.
[3] Moyle, *ad* Inst. 1. 11. 12; Vangerow, *op. cit.* 62.
[4] In. 1. 11. 12.   [5] 1. 5. 27; 1. 7. 46 *etc.*   [6] Z. S. S. 26, 387.
[7] The effect of the transaction is to make him *capax*; it is not so in the case of a woman.
[8] The declaration *apud acta* that the slave is your son which seems to have given latinity before Justinian (*post*, Ch. xxiii.), is a similar institution, but it is an innovation rather than a survival.

CHAPTER XX.

THE period covered by this heading extends over nearly 600 years, if we regard Justinian's reign as the end of things. It ought in strictness to be treated as at least three distinct periods, but as nearly the whole of our information is derived from Justinian's compilations, it is not easy so to divide it. But it is plain that he made many changes, and it is possible thus to treat the matter as having a history in two periods, of which the first ends with the accession of Justinian. It must, however, be remembered that changes are going on rapidly throughout this period, and thus it is important to keep perspective in view. Moreover, of a great mass of detail, it is not easy to tell how much of it is classical and how much is of a later age. This will be treated, for the most part, in the discussion of the first period, so that the law under Justinian will be dealt with more shortly.

It was no longer true in the Empire that all manumission made the slave a *civis*, but, for the present, we shall discuss the normal case, leaving the special statutory rules and restrictions for a later chapter.

The formal modes of manumission are (1) *Censu*, (2) *In sacrosanctis Ecclesiis*, (3) *Vindicta*, (4) *Testamento*.

1. CENSU. This is practically obsolete[1].

2. IN SACROSANCTIS ECCLESIIS. This is a method which it seems somewhat out of place to consider so early, for, as we know it, it dates only from the time of Constantine. It is of little importance in the general development of the law, and therefore may be disposed of at once, and there is this further justification for treating it here, that it retains a trace of that element of public control which is dying out in the other forms, and which makes it more or less a successor of the method by *Census*.

A constitution of Constantine, addressed in A.D 316 to a certain bishop, and plainly reciting only earlier law, remarks that it has long been allowed for masters to give liberty to their slaves *in ecclesia*

---

[1] *Ante*, p. 440.

catholica. It must be done before the people in the presence of the priests, and there must be a writing signed by the *dominus, vice testium*[1]. The next constitution, five years later, also addressed to a bishop, provides that such a gift of liberty before the priests shall give citizenship[2]. The rule is mentioned in the Institutes, and in the paraphrase of Theophilus[3], but it does not seem to be mentioned in the Digest, though it gives rise to some questions which the bare provisions of the Code do not determine. The following remarks may be made on it.

(*a*) Constantine in stating the rule says *dudum placuit*. What degree of antiquity this imports is uncertain. There is evidence that he published a third constitution on the matter[4], which has been lost, and which may be earlier than those we possess: this may be the origin of the rule, since Justinian treats it as *ex sacris constitutionibus*[5]. The use of the word *dudum* does not exclude a recent origin[6]. In the Syro-Roman Law-book are traces of what may be this other enactment: there is a rule requiring bishop and priests to be present[7].

(*b*) It would seem that under the original rule *civitas* was not conferred. The enactment of 321 first speaks of this and calls it *civitas romana*, which suggests that till then the process had given only *latinitas*, that in fact it began as an " informal " mode before Constantine legislated at all. For what one might do *inter amicos* without other formality, one might surely do in full congregation. The expression, *vice testium*, imports the same suggestion[8].

(*c*) The requirement of signed writing is mentioned in the enactment of 316, of which we have only Justinian's edition, but not in that of 321 which gives the larger right and which we have in the earlier form of the Codex Theodosianus. It seems likely that the provision is added by him. The signature is to be *vice testium*, and the express requirement of witnesses in certain cases of informal manumission seems to be due to him[9].

(*d*) The presence of the slave is not indicated as necessary.

(*e*) It is supposed that the institution descends from or is suggested by the manumission by offer to the temple of a deity[10].

(*f*) Such manumissions are not subject to the rule as to the age of the slave[11] which is laid down by the *lex* Aelia Sentia[12]. This again suggests its origin as an informal mode : latinity in no case requires a slave to be over 30. It may be presumed that they are subject to the other restrictive rules.

[1] C. 1. 13. 1.   [2] C. 1. 13. 2 = C. Th. 4. 7. 1.
[3] In. 1. 5. 1; Theoph. *ad h. l.*; Gai. Ep. 1. 1. 2.   [4] Gothofredus, *ad* C. Th. 4. 7. 1.
[5] In. 1. 5. 1.   [6] Brissonius, De Verb. Sign. *s.v. dudum*.
[7] Ed. Bruns-Sachau, 196.   [8] *Ante*, p. 446.   [9] *Post*, p. 554.
[10] *Ante*, p. 447. See especially Mitteis, Reichsrecht und Volksr. 100, 376.
[11] C. 7. 15. 2. But the reference may possibly be to the institution mentioned *post*, p. 451.
[12] *Post*, Ch. XXIII.

(*g*) These enactments contain a further rule giving exceptional privileges to priests who own slaves. That of 316 tells the bishop to whom it is addressed that he may free his slaves in what manner he pleases, provided his intention is clear. That of 321, also addressed to a bishop, lays down a similar rule for all priests, expressly dispensing with witnesses, and declaring that the gift shall take effect from the moment of the declaration, even if it is *postremo iudicio*. The text seems to contemplate his making a will and declaring its effect at once[1]. No doubt the effect would be to give the slave citizenship. These provisions seem to have left no other mark on the sources.

3. VINDICTA. The general character of this process has already been described[2]. It is in form a *legis actio* : a claim of liberty on the lines of *sacramentum*, stopped by a tacit admission that the claim is well founded. The *adsertor libertatis* claims in formal words that the slave is free: the master, on enquiry by the Praetor, makes no counter-claim in express words, but it is clear that, at some point, he, like the *adsertor*, touches the slave with a *festuca*, exactly as is done in a real *adsertio libertatis*[3]. This counter-vindication, if such it is, does not occur in ordinary *cessio in iure*, and Karlowa[4] regards it not as a claim of ownership against the *adsertor*, but as an assertion of *potestas*, material as a preliminary to the manumission. He remarks that the name of the process and the repeated reference to the *impositio vindictae* shew that in the eyes of the jurists this is the kernel of the process. In conformity with this he holds that the process is, formally, a declaration of intention to free, and he refers to language of Festus[5] in relation to manumission *sacrorum causa* as shewing that there was an express declaration of intent to free. But the relevance of the words of Festus to an ordinary manumission *vindicta* is very doubtful[6]. Karlowa regards the magistrate's *addictio* not as a judgment, even in form, but as a magisterial recognition of what has been done. Some non-juristic texts speak of the master as taking the slave by a limb, slapping his cheek[7] and then turning him round. This also Karlowa regards as a part of the legal formality, the slap being a last indication of slavery, the turning round a sign of his changed position[8]. He remarks that in later times the whole appears fused as one act, striking with a rod, *festuca ferire*. On these views two remarks may be made.

---

[1] The allusion may be only to deathbed gifts.   [2] *Ante*, p. 441.
[3] 40. 12. 12. 2; 40. 1. 14. 1; 49. 17. 19. 4; C. 2. 30. 2. All cited by Karlowa, R. R. G. 2. 133.
[4] G. 2. 24; Karlowa, *loc. cit.* As to the significance of the various steps see *post*, App. IV.
[5] Festus, *s.v. manumitti*.   [6] *Ante*, p. 441.   [7] Isod. Sev. 9. 48.
[8] See the references in Karlowa, *loc. cit.*; Willems, Droit Publ. Rom. 144, 145; Roby, Rom. Priv. Law, 1. 26.

(i)   The process is so plainly a modification of a true *adsertio liber-tatis* that the originally quasi-judicial nature of the magistrate's act can hardly be doubted. Doubtless the real nature of the act would tend to appear through the form, but it is most unlikely that the *vindictae impositio* by the master contained originally any idea other than that of counter-claim. The fact that the master does actually vindicate the slave and so carries the form a little further than it goes in ordinary *cessio in iure* is explained by the fact that the judgment is in favour of the slave, not, as in other cases, in favour of the opposing party : the master's *vindictae impositio* brings out the fact that the matter is between him and the slave[1].

(ii)   The slap and turning round as part of a legal process are unexampled : they are simple enough regarded as conventional practices. They are mentioned in no juristic text[2]. Moreover we are told that a *mutus* cannot manumit *vindicta*. As he need not speak, this is explained by the fact that the law requires as evidence of renunciation nothing but silence, which, in the case of a mute, can have no such significance. If the definite act of turning round was required by the rules of form, there would be no reason for excluding mutes[3].

The judicial character of the process, always somewhat unreal, is freely disregarded in the imperial law. The forms are much relaxed in all ways. It is impossible to fix a date for these relaxations, which are progressive, but it is clear that they are not complete till late in the classical age. Ulpian notes, as apparently a new relaxation, that he has seen such a manumission done in the country by the Praetor without the presence of a lictor[4]. It is no longer necessarily done *pro tribunali*: the Praetor may do it *in transitu* on his way to the baths or theatre, or his business, or anywhere[5]. Hermogenianus says the whole thing may be done by lictors, *tacente domino*[6]. This is obscure, since there is no other indication that the *dominus* has to speak[7]: it is probable that he means that no sacramental words need be spoken at all and that the *vindictae impositio* by the master may be dispensed with. The lictors can act as assertors, but it must not be inferred that the presence of the magistrate is unnecessary. Macrobius quotes from Trebatius[8] the rule that this process, like all *iudicia*, can be gone through on *nundinae*. But it can be done on days not open to true

---

[1] See however Wlassak (Z. S. S. 25. 102 *sqq.*) as to the nature of *cessio in iure*. He considers it not as a piece of fictitious litigation but as an avowed act of conveyance, the magisterial intervention being an act of sanction, not a decision.   But it is difficult to see an act of con-veyance in the last step in *adoptio*. See *post*, App. iv.
[2] But often in non-juristic. See *ante*, p. 451, n. 8.
[3] *i.e.* for maintaining the rule, which applied generally in *legis actio*.   [4] 40. 2. 8.
[5] G. 1. 20; In. 1. 5. 2; D. 40. 2. 7.   Karlowa (*loc. cit.*) thinks this not a relaxation but an original rule, shewing the difference between this and a real process.
[6] 40. 2. 23.   [7] Manumission *sacrorum causa* (*ante*, p. 447) is here disregarded.
[8] Sat. 1. 16. 23.

litigation. Constantine allows it to be done on Sundays[1], and the 14 days round Easter, while excluding lawsuits. Later legislation follows apparently the same lines, though manumission is not mentioned[2]. An enactment of 392 forbids *actus publici vel privati* in the fortnight around Easter. Justinian adopts the same law so altered as to allow manumissions[3].

It is the practice in all manumissions to give *instrumenta manumissionis*[4], which it is not necessary for the son of the manumitter to sign[5]. It is hardly necessary to say that several can be freed together if present[6].

As it is in essence a *legis actio*, Ulpian lays down the rule that the person before whom it is done must be a magistrate of the Roman people (*i.e.* one who has the *legis actio*[7]), and he mentions Consul, Praetor or Proconsul[8], these being the magistrates most commonly mentioned in connexion with it[9]. But this must be understood to include *legati* Caesaris[10], who govern imperial provinces, and are in fact propraetors[11]: thus a number of texts speak merely of Praesides[12]. Paul tells us, and a constitution of 319 (?) repeats, that a manumission may take place before a municipal magistrate, if he has the *legis actio*[13]. The Proconsul has "voluntary jurisdiction," *i.e.* for such acts as manumission or adoption, so soon as he has left the City, though he does not acquire contentious jurisdiction till he has reached his province[14]. As to the power of his *legatus*, there is some difficulty. Paul definitely says that there can be manumission before him[15]. Marcian says that there cannot, because he has not *talem jurisdictionem*. Ulpian agrees, *quia non est apud eum legis actio*[16]. It seems clear however that the legate may have the *legis actio*[17], but only by virtue of a *mandatum jurisdictionis* to him by the Consul. Such a mandate cannot be made so as to take effect till the Proconsul has actually entered his province[18], but as the reason assigned is that he cannot delegate a jurisdiction he has not acquired the restriction may not apply to this case[19].

Even as early as Augustus, the right to preside at such a manumission is conferred on the *Praefectus* Aegypto, the *Procurator* Caesaris in what is regarded as patrimonial property of the Emperor, an officer therefore who cannot at this time be regarded as a magistrate of the

---

[1] C. Th. 2. 8. 1. [2] C. Th. 2. 8. 18, 19; C. 3. 12. 6.
[3] C. Th. 2. 8. 21; C. 3. 12. 7.
[4] 4. 2. 8. 1; C. 7. 16. 25, 26. In view of their importance in case of later dispute the manumitter was compelled to give them, but their absence did not vitiate the manumission.
[5] C. 7. 16. 32. *Ante*, p. 189. The practice in Greek law was for the heir to sign the documents. See Dareste, Recueil des Inscript. Grecq. Série 2, 253.
[6] 40. 2. 15. 2. [7] 1. 7. 4; P. 2. 25. 4.
[8] Ulp. 1. 7. [9] G. 1. 20; In. 1. 5. 2; D. 40. 2. 5, 7, 8, 20. 4; C. 7. 1. 4.
[10] 40. 2. 7. [11] Mommsen, Droit Publ. Rom. 3. 280; Staatsrecht (3) 2. 1. 244.
[12] C. 7. 1. 4; D. 1. 18. 2; 40. 2. 15. 5; 40. 5. 51. 7. [13] C. 7. 1. 4; P. 2. 25. 4.
[14] 1. 16. 2. *pr.*; 40. 2. 17. [15] 40. 2. 17. [16] 1. 16. 2. 1, 3.
[17] Girard, Manuel, 972. [18] 1. 16. 4. 6.
[19] Paul's words seem to contemplate a legate's action apart from entry, 40. 2. 17.

Roman people[1]. Constantine lays it down that there may be manumission *apud consilium nostrum* [2]: this is a form of the judicial activity
of the Emperor in council[3].

Just as a magistrate has jurisdiction for this purpose before entry,
so conversely, he retains it on expiration of his office till he has notice
of his successor's arrival[4]. The Praeses may act even though the
parties are not domiciled in his province[5], a rule laid down by the
sc. Articuleianum. Either consul or both can conduct the manumission[6]. But what one begins he must finish, except, by virtue of a
Senatusconsult of unknown date, where he is prevented by infirmity
or other sufficient cause[7].

It is immaterial that the magistrate is a *filiusfamilias,* even a
filius of the owner of the slave, though *filiusfamilias* has himself no
power of manumission[8]. This is a mere illustration of the separation
of public from private capacities.

It is settled law that a magistrate can free his own slave before
himself[9], either by himself or by authorising his *filiusfamilias* to free
on his behalf[10]. Thus he is at least in point of form judge in his own
cause[11]. In the same spirit we are told that he may be tutor and autho-
riser of a pupil who frees before him[12]. On the other hand we are told
by Paul that he cannot free before his *collega, i.e.* one with *par imperium,*
though a praetor can, before a consul[13]. This is the more surprising in
that, though he cannot be *in ius vocatus* before his equal colleague, a
man can voluntarily submit himself to an equal or even to a minor
jurisdiction[14]. Moreover, whereas in one text we are told that a consul
can free his own slave before himself, even though he be under 20,
the same writer, Ulpian, in the same section of the same book, says
that a consul under 20 cannot free his own slave before himself, as he
would have to enquire into the *causa,* and he must therefore do it
before his colleague[15]. Here Ulpian appears in conflict with himself
on one point and with Paul on another. Probably Paul is expressing
a rule already obsolete in saying that there can be no manumission
before an equal colleague: the *dominus,* in the later classical law, may

---

[1] 40. 2. 21.   [2] C. 7. 1. 4.   [3] Cp. C. 7. 10. 7.
[4] 1. 16. 10; 1. 18. 17.   [5] 40. 5. 51. 7.
[6] The rule applies no doubt to other duplicated magistracies.
[7] 1. 10. 1. 1. In the later Empire difficulties arose through the quasi magistracies of
usurpers. Enactments dealing with acts of Magnentius, Maximus and Eugenius annulled their
acts in general, but allowed manumissions before them to be good, *favore libertatis.* In the case
of Heraclianus they were void, but the manumitter was required to repeat them, C. Th. 15. 14.
5, 8, 9, 13.   [8] 1. 14. 1; 40. 2. 18. *pr.*
[9] 1. 10. 1. 2; 1. 18. 2; 40. 2. 5, 20. 4. Probably as old as Cicero (Ad Att. 7. 2. 8), see
Wlassak, Z. S. S. 28. 42 *sqq.,* who shews that the difficulty felt in 40. 2. 5, surmounted on the
authority of Javolenus, was as to manumission of a slave under 30, where the magistrate
presided in the *consilium.*
[10] 40. 2. 18. 2. *Post,* App. v.   [11] Cp. 2. 1. 10.
[12] 40. 2. 1.   [13] 40. 1. 14; 40. 2. 18. 1.
[14] 2. 1. 14.   [15] 1. 10. 1. 2; 40. 2. 20. 4.

do it before himself or before a colleague. If however he is under 20 he can do it only before a colleague: the text in which Ulpian seems to allow him to do it, *apud se*, is probably the work of the compilers.

Manumission *vindicta* is a *legis actio*: it is an *actus legitimus*. Accordingly, if it be formally gone through, there is a manumission, if the parties were in the proper relation, whatever their state of mind, *i.e.*, even though one or both parties wrongly thought they did not so stand[1]. But there is another more practically important result. An *actus legitimus* is vitiated by any express *dies* or condition[2]. The point of such a manumission is an official declaration that the slave is free, and thus the freedom cannot be, expressly, in the future or conditional. But the text which lays down the general rule adds the proviso: *nonnunquam tamen actus (legitimi) tacite recipiunt quae aperte comprehensa vitia adferunt*. This proposition the text proceeds to illustrate, and thereby raises obscurely the question whether manumission *vindicta* can be subject to a tacit *dies* or condition. It is sometimes said[3] that the text just cited implies that there may be tacit condition. But no such general proposition can be justified. The text illustrates its statement by the case of an *acceptilatio* of a conditional debt. It remarks that there is no *acceptilatio* till the condition occurs. But this is not a condition voluntarily created: it is one which *inest* in the transaction. The act is meaningless unless there is a debt. Analogous cases can readily be found in manumission *vindicta*. If a slave is legated the ownership is, in the Sabinian view, which clearly prevailed, determined retroactively by the acceptance or repudiation of the legacy. If, now, the *heres* has freed a *servus legatus*, the act is a nullity if the legatee accepts, but, if he refuses, the gift is perfectly good[4]. This is not a conditional manumission. In the events which have happened the slave was the manumitter's at the time of the manumission, and it is an absolute manumission. The words of the text shew clearly that this is the proper view to take: *retro competit libertas*. It cannot be said that this text goes far towards authorising tacit conditions in manumission *vindicta*. Nothing in this or in the above general text suggests that a manumission *vindicta* can be so made, at the will of the parties, that the slave freed is in a certain event to remain the property of the manumitter. No text carries the matter further[5], except in relation to manumission *mortis causa*, as to which there is one text which requires careful examination. This text remarks[6] that a slave can be freed *mortis causa*, in such sense that *quemadmodum si vindicta eum liberaret absolute, scilicet quia moriturum se putet mors eius expectabitur,*

[1] 40. 2. 4. 1. [2] 50. 17. 77. [3] *e.g.* Accarias, Précis, § 56.
[4] 40. 2. 3. [5] As to pledged slaves, *post*, Ch. xxv.
[6] 40. 1. 15. See also In. 3. 11. 6.

so too in this case the gift takes effect at death, provided the donor does not change his mind. However this rather obscure text is understood, it implies as it stands that if a slave is freed *vindicta, mortis causa*, the gift takes effect only on the death. This is hardly a conditional gift, for *dies incertus* is not a condition except in wills[1]. But whether it is strictly a condition or not is less important than the determination of the exact scope of the rule. On that point the following may be said.

(1) That part of the text which refers expressly to manumission *vindicta* has not been unchallenged. Mommsen, led presumably by the word *absolute*, would cut out the words *mors eius expectabitur*, in which case the text would say for our purpose no more than that it is possible for a man to free his slave when he thought he was dying. One other text is, however, understood by Huschke to assert the rule that in manumission *mortis causa* by *vindicta*, the gift does not take effect till the death. But the restoration is so hazardous that no great weight can be attached to it[2]. If Mommsen's emendation be accepted, we may infer that suspension in such cases till the death is an innovation of Justinian's.

(2) The text does not, even accepted as it stands, shew that the power of revocation applies. On principle it is hardly possible that it should apply. The last part of the text, which alone speaks of revocation, is dealing with other manumission, contrasted with that *vindicta*[3], and this may have been informal manumission, at least in Justinian's time. The whole text looks corrupt and rehandled. It is worth noting that none of the ante-Justinian texts which deal with revocable *donationes mortis causa* speak of any which result from an *actus legitimus*, such as *cessio in iure* or *mancipatio*, and those which deal with land speak of *traditio*[4]. It is a fair inference that manumission *vindicta, mortis causa*, is not revocable as other *donatio mortis causa* is.

(3) *Dies certus* is nowhere mentioned in this connexion: there is no reason to think such a modality can occur.

(4) Within the very narrow limits in which this suspended effect can be shewn to occur, there is a question to which we have no answer, as to the actual condition of the man in the meanwhile. In the case of the legated slave[5], no doubt the effect of transactions by him, *e.g.* alienations and acquisitions, or affecting him, *e.g. usucapio*, will be determined retrospectively by the event. But in the case of the *mortis causa*

---

[1] 35. 1. 75, *post*, p. 480. There is no authority for applying the same conception to *dies incertus* outside wills.
[2] Valer. Prob., Notae, 46—50. The text is differently understood by Krüger.
[3] It may conceivably be a contrast between manumission *vindicta, absolute* and *mortis causa*.
[4] See Fr. Vat. 249. 6, 258.   [5] 40. 2. 3.

vindicta manumissus we have no information and no good analogy to guide us[1].

A question involving some difficulties may conveniently be taken here : how far and in what forms can manumission be carried out by a representative? We need consider only two cases, manumission *vindicta* and informal manumission[2]. It is far from certain that the same rule applies to both cases, at any rate before Justinian. Leaving representation of a *pater* by a *filiusfamilias* out of account for the moment, the texts are not numerous. It must be remembered that manumission *vindicta* is in point of form a *legis actio*, however degenerate. There can be no *legis actio* on behalf of another person except in certain cases of extreme urgency, and accordingly we are told that it is undoubted law that a wife cannot free *vindicta, per maritum*, or anyone, *per procuratorem*[3]. Other texts lay down similar prohibitions, not confining them to the case of *vindicta*. Thus a tutor cannot give the liberty due from his *pupillus* under a *fideicommissum*[4], and a *curator furiosi* cannot free slaves[5]. The reason assigned is that such an act is not included in *administratio*[6]. Octavenus is reported[7] as suggesting a way out of the difficulty, where the manumission is due under a *fideicommissum* : the curator can convey the man to another person to free. This however gives the odd result that while manumission is not an act of administration, conveyance to another person, in order that he may free, is, for we are told that a transfer by a *curator furiosi* is void unless it concerns the *administratio*[8]. Whether a *curator furiosi* may " *lege agere*," on behalf of his charge, we are not told, but if he can, as seems most probable, and as is generally held, the prohibition seems an unnecessary inconvenience, resulting from a too rigid conception of *administratio*. In any case the texts do not help us.

There are one or two texts which seem to imply that consent of *dominus* will validate a manumission by a third party. Thus we are told that manumission without consent of *dominus* is not valid, even though the manumitter become *heres* to the *dominus*[9]. Again, we are told that if a father frees his son's slave, by his consent, the son being under 20, the manumission is invalid[10], which seems to imply

---

[1] Shortly considered by Bufnoir, Conditions, 58. See also Haymann, Freilassungspflicht, 30. As to a somewhat analogous case, *post*, Ch. XXVII, where it is a question of mancipation.
[2] The point could not arise in wills. *Census* was obsolete, and manumission *in ecclesiis* is too little known to be worth discussing here. It is an ancient difficulty, Haenel, Diss. Domm. 108.
[3] C. 7. 1. 3. A procurator could prove the necessary *causa*, 40. 2. 15. 3. The rule that one may " *lege agere* " *pro libertate* for another, refers only to the *adsertor*, G. 4. 82.
[4] C. 7. 11. 6.   [5] 40. 9. 22.   [6] 27. 10. 17 ; 40. 1. 13.
[7] 40. 1. 13. *Traditio* has been substituted for *mancipatio*.
[8] 27. 10. 17.   [9] 40. 9. 20.
[10] C. 7. 10. 6. Texts as to dotal slaves, sometimes cited, do not seem in point.

that if the son were over 20 the manumission would not be necessarily void. As there is nothing contrary to general principle in the idea that a man can authorise another to complete a formless manumission for him, it seems probable that the true rule deducible from these texts is that a man cannot manumit *vindicta* for another, that he cannot free informally without express authority, from one fully *capax*, but that there is nothing to prevent the appointing of a third person to make the necessary communication or declaration, a person so employed being in fact a mere *nuntius*[1].

Within the family there are powers of delegation which belong to the classical age. A *filiusfamilias*, not being owner, cannot free on his own account, but in classical law he can free by the authority of his *paterfamilias*, though not of his mother[2]. The effect is to make the former slave the *libertus* of the *paterfamilias*[3]. The authorisation may be such as to give him a choice among the slaves[4]. But though carried out by the son it is essentially the father's manumission[5], and thus though the son be under 20, no cause need be shewn: the father's consent suffices[6]. On one point two opposing views are set down to Julian. In one text he says that if the father authorises the manumission, and dies, and the son, not knowing of the death, carries out the manumission, the act is void, as it is if the father changes his mind[7]. In another text he lays down the same rule as to change of mind, but in the case of death says that the slave is free, *favore libertatis*, since there is no evidence of a change of mind[8]. This is no doubt a Tribonianism.

This statement of the rules as to authorisation by the *paterfamilias* leaves open a point of some difficulty for the law of the classical age. Some of the texts do not specify any mode of manumission: others speak of manumission *vindicta*. When it is remembered that so to manumit is *lege agere*, and that this cannot be by agent, and also that, according to the view generally held, and confirmed by a statement in one of the Sinaitic Scholia (on Ulpian[9]), a *filiusfamilias* is not capable of *legis actio*, it is clear that there may be doubt. Such a doubt has recently been raised by Mitteis[10]. The present writer has discussed the matter elsewhere[11]: as a treatment of it is necessarily somewhat

---

[1] The grammar of 40. 9. 20 is defective: the rule may possibly be of Justinian's age.
[2] P. 1. 13 a. 2.   [3] 37. 14. 13; 40. 1. 16, 22. It might be a grandson *ex filio*.
[4] 40. 2. 22.   [5] 23. 2. 51. 1; 40. 2. 22.
[6] 40. 1. 16. The father can accuse for ingratitude: though he did not free the case is to be treated as if he had, 40. 9. 30. 1. A deaf and dumb father can authorise, while a *furiosus*, being *incapax*, cannot, 40. 2. 10. If the son frees *iussu patris matrimonii causa*, no other person can marry the woman without the father's consent, 23. 2. 51. 1 (Mommsen).
[7] 40. 9. 15. 1.   [8] 40. 2. 4. *pr.*
[9] Schol. Sin. 49 (Krüger's Edit.).   [10] Mitteis, Z. S. S. 21. 199.
[11] Buckland, N. R. H. 27. 737. Reply by Mitteis, Z. S. S. 25. 379.

lengthy, he has placed in an appendix a statement of the reasons which lead him to accept the numerous and unanimous texts and to hold that even in the classical law a *filiusfamilias* could free, *vindicta*, under the authorisation of his *pater*[1].

Though manumission by a *filius* without authority is null, it may have some legal importance, in relation to questions of construction, *e.g.* in legacies. A son has a *servus peculiaris*, and purports to free him, but without authority. The father in his will leaves the son his *peculium*. The gift does not include this slave, who therefore is common to all the heirs, for the *peculium* must be taken as it is at *dies cedens*, and the son's manumission was an abandonment of him, as a part of the *peculium*, whether it was before the will was made or after[2]. In another text a similar case is discussed by Alfenus Varus[3], but he decides as a matter of construction, that if the will was before the manumission, the testator must have intended to include him in the legacy, but not if the manumission came first. This view may seem to ignore the decisive fact that the slave is not in the *peculium* at *dies cedens*, and thus by a well-known rule is not covered by the legacy. But in fact all it shews is that the testator does not contemplate him as part of the *peculium*.

The rules are altogether different where the *filiusfamilias* is a *miles*. A slave in his *peculium castrense* he can free without authority, and from Hadrian's time onward, he becomes patron for all purposes[4]. Before that time it seems that the *pater* would have been patron, the son having preference in the *bona*[5]. Similar rules apply, by a rescript of Hadrian, to any *servus castrensis peculii*. The *filius* who manumits is patron[6], having *iura in bonis*[7], and the right of accusing for ingratitude[8]. The *pater* has no such right, such slaves not being reckoned in his *familia*[9], at least *inter vivos*[10]. On the same principle if the *pater* institutes a *servus castrensis peculii*, the son is *heres necessarius*[11]. The manumission of such slaves gives rise however to one knotty question, but this will be considered in connexion with manumission by will[12].

We have already discussed the rule that on manumission *inter vivos*, the *peculium* goes with the man unless expressly reserved[13].

---

[1] *Post*, App. v.   [2] 33. 8. 19. 2, 20.
[3] 40. 1. 7. Very confused and so badly corrupted as to be of little value.
[4] 37. 14. 8. *pr.*; 38. 16. 3. 7.
[5] 38. 2. 3. 8; 38. 2. 22. This applies only to the *peculium castrense*. Where a soldier's wife made him *heres* while on service, a slave so acquired was in his *peculium* and could be freed by him, 49. 17. 13. So where the wife gave him a slave to free for service in the legions. If he was given merely to be freed with no remoter aim, he is not *castrensis*: the *paterfamilias* must consent and will be patron, 49. 17. 6.
[6] 38. 4. 3. 3.   [7] 38. 2. 3. 8.   [8] 40. 9. 30. 2.
[9] 40. 1. 17.   [10] *Post*, p. 465.   [11] 49. 17. 18. *pr.*   [12] *Post*, p. 465.
[13] *Ante*, p. 189. As to taxes on manumission see Marquardt, Organisation Financière, 355.

4. TESTAMENTO. It is evident from the texts that, as was naturally to be expected, this form of manumission always remained by far the most important. Apart from statutory rules and restrictions, to be considered later, a great change had occurred which revolutionised the law. This was the authorisation of *codicilli*, and therewith, and more important, of *fideicommissa*. These introduced a wholly new set of rules which will have to be separately considered[1], since fideicommissary gifts require completion by an act of manumission *inter vivos*. Direct gifts alone can be properly regarded as manumission by will, and we shall deal with these alone for the present.

Some points in relation to the form of such gifts have already been touched on[2]. It must be an express gift, and the *legitima verba, liber esto, liberum esse iubeo*[3], and the like, are analogous to those used in *legatum per vindicationem*, though Greek words would do as well, at least in the later law[4]. Not only must the gift be express, it must be peremptory—words expressing mere desire, such as *volo*, do not suffice[5]. It must also be *nominatim*, a rule which Gaius attributes to the provisions of the *lex* Fufia Caninia[6], to be considered later[7]. But a correct description is enough. Thus Paul tells us that *qui ex illa ancilla nascetur*, or a description of the office he fills, is enough[8]. He adds that this is a regulative provision of the *sc.* Orphitianum, and that if there are two, of the same office, it must be shewn which is meant. Thus a gift of liberty to Stichus, by one who has several slaves of that name, is void[9], but a mere error in name will not bar the gift if it is clear who is meant: *falsa demonstratio non nocet*[10]. The rule that such a gift cannot be made to an *incerta persona* has probably nothing to do with the rule of *nominatio*, for an *incerta persona* can be exactly described: it is a mere application of the general rule forbidding gifts by will to *incertae personae*, though Gaius connects it with the same *lex*[11].

There seems to have been some doubt as to the effect of a gift of liberty "to A or B." All that we are told of the earlier law is that it was disputed whether it was simply void, or whether both were free, or whether only one, and if so, which one; either the first, and if he die the second, a sort of *substitutio*, or the second as representing the last will, and so adeeming the first. As the gift is direct there can be no question of any choice in the *heres*. Justinian decides that both are

---

[1] *Post*, pp. 513 *sqq.*
[2] *Ante*, p. 442.
[3] G. 2. 267; Ulp. 2. 7; P. 4. 14. 1.
[4] C. 7. 2. 14.
[5] 40. 5. 41. *pr.*
[6] G. 2. 239.
[7] *Post*, Ch. XXIII.
[8] P. 4. 14. 1.   Unborn persons, *post*, p. 476.
[9] 34. 5. 10. *pr.*
[10] 40. 4. 54. *pr.*
[11] In. 2. 20. 25.   Justinian says that even under the old law a legacy to an uncertain member of a certain class was good. If this is true of liberties the rule is of little importance as to direct gifts, and will not bar, *e.g.*, a gift to "that one of my existing slaves who shall first do" such and such a thing. As to these gifts to *incertae personae*, see *post*, p. 477.

free[1]: the principle of later law is that *in obscura voluntate manumittentis favendum est libertati*[2].

Like legacies, such gifts are invalid if given before the institutions, except in the case of a *miles*. If they are in the middle of the institutions, *e.g.* between that of A and that of B, and both enter, they are void, there being an heir instituted after them : *a fortiori*, if B alone enters. If A alone enters they will be good, by early law. But the *lex* Papia makes a change. If B refuses to enter, the gift becomes a *caducum*[3]. If A has either the *ius antiquum* or the *ius liberorum* this will make no difference, since he will take the lapsed gift. But in other cases the share will pass to other persons entitled under the *lex* Papia, and so the liberty will fail. Ulpian adds that there were some who thought it would take effect even in this case[4]. The reason of this divergent view is no doubt that the devolution under the *lex* is not an institution, whatever it is, and thus the technical rule ought not to apply. It has no connexion with the rule that *caduca* go with their *onera*[5]. On all these points the classical law seems to have treated legacies and manumissions alike.

Manumissions might be made either in the will or in a codicil confirmed by a will either afterwards or by anticipation[6].

The rule that the gift must be express cuts out implied gifts, but there may be cases in which it is doubtful whether there is or is not an express gift. Some texts shew by their language that in such matters the earlier tendency was to strictness. In one case the words of the will were Titius *heres esto, si* Titius *heres non erit,* Stichus *heres esto,* Stichus *liber esto.* Titius took the inheritance. Aristo held that Stichus was not free : his reason seems to be that the liberty was given only in connexion with the institution which did not take effect. Ulpian allows him to be free, as having received liberty not in one grade only but *dupliciter, i.e.* as if it had been written out twice[7]. It might be supposed that *favor libertatis* would lead to ready acceptance of implied gifts. But it is one thing to accept informal words, and in this direction a good deal was done[8]: it is another to accept as gifts of

---

[1] C. 6. 38. 4 deals also with other alternatives but they refer to other forms of gift.
[2] 50. 17. 179. See, as to these gifts, *post*, p. 556.
[3] G. 2. 230 ; Ulp. 1. 20, except in a soldier's will, *post*, p. 477.   [4] Ulp. 1. 21.
[5] Ulp. 17. 3. See, *e.g.*, Accarias, Précis, § 374.
[6] 40. 4. 43. They are read into the will, 29. 7. 2. 2 ; P. 4. 14. 2. As to this, *post*, p. 515. An enactment of Diocletian (C. 7. 2. 11) seems to say that they may be given by a will which is good only as a codicil by virtue of the *clausula codicillaris*. As this contradicts a considerable mass of evidence (*e.g.*, Ulp. 2. 12 ; 24. 29 ; C. 7. 2. 1 ; D. 40. 4. 43) it implies the existence of another will or is confined to *fideicommissa*.
[7] 40. 4. 2. So where a slave was substituted with liberty and a legacy was made to him without liberty, Pius and Divi Fratres decided *favorabiliter* that it was to be held as if *libertas adscripta esset*, 40. 4. 26.
[8] 50. 17. 179.

liberty what may not have been so intended, and this is the meaning of the refusal to recognise implied gifts. Several texts shew this. "Let X not be free unless he renders accounts" is not a gift of freedom even if he does[1]. "I leave Stichus 10 because he was born after his mother was free," is not a gift of liberty if he was not so born[2].

On the other hand, where the intent to free is clear, but it may be doubtful whether the gift is direct or fideicommissary, the tendency is to treat it as direct, if possible. If a man is freed twice it is in general the first effective one which operates[3]. But if one gift is direct and the other by *fideicommissum*, Marcus Aurelius enacts that he may choose in which way he will have it[4]. One type of case seems to have given rise to doubts, though the texts as they stand give a coherent rule. It is the case of gift of a slave by will with a direction that, if the donee does not free him, he is to be free. Here if there is a simple direction to the *heres*, or legatee, to free, followed by a gift of freedom in default, the rule is clear that the slave is free *directo*, the gift of him being a nullity[5]. In some of the texts there is also a legacy to the slave and the rule has the incidental effect of making this valid. The decision rests no doubt on the fact that a mere gift, *ut manumittatur*, shews no intent to benefit the donee. But where there is no *fideicommissum* of liberty, but only a gift of liberty if the donee does not free, it is not clear that there is no intent to benefit the donee. Thus if the direction is that if he is not freed within a certain time or by the donee's will, he is to be free, this is a direct gift of liberty, conditional on his not being freed by the donee[6]. If no limit of time is set down, it might be supposed that the donee had all his life within which to free. But Paul lays down the rule that he must do it so soon as he reasonably can without seriously deranging his own affairs, otherwise the man is free *directo*. This seems to be a somewhat unwarranted interpretation of the testator's words, no doubt, *favore libertatis*.

Two cases of implied gift gave rise to some dispute. Gaius tells us positively that a mere gift of the inheritance without a gift of liberty did not imply such a gift and was therefore void. And as the heir must have had *testamenti factio* at the time when the will was made, the

---

[1] 40. 4. 59. 2.
[2] 40. 4. 60 (the text is obscure). Stichus, *imo* Pamphilus *liber esto*. P. alone is free, 40. 4. 21. Sticho *liberto do lego*, is not a gift of liberty, C. 6. 21. 7. Cp. Plin. Epist. 4. 10. Otherwise had the gift been of the *hereditas*: dislike of intestacy reinforces *favor libertatis*, C. 6. 27. 2.
[3] 40. 4. 1.   [4] 40. 4. 56.
[5] 40. 4. 9. *pr.* (*saepe responsum*); 40. 4. 19; 40. 5. 34. 2; 40. 7. 37. See the case of a gift *inter vivos, ut manumittatur, post*, Ch. XXVII.
[6] 40. 4. 15; 40. 5. 34. 2, both by Julian who is the author of one of the other set (40. 4. 19). See also Paul, 40. 7. 20. 6, *in fine*.

matter is not mended by a manumission of the slave *inter vivos*[1]. No
other surviving classical text states the rule[2], and Justinian altered the
law. But the Constitution by which this was done[3] declares that the
old lawyers had had many disputes about the matter, and in the
Institutes[4] it is said that Paul quotes Atilicinus as holding that the
institution implies the liberty. A similar question arises in connexion
with the appointment of a slave by his master as testamentary tutor.
Did this imply manumission? It is clear that such an appointment
implied some sort of gift of liberty even before Justinian[5]. But the
language of the texts which justify this statement do not make it clear
whether the gift was direct or fideicommissary, and they suggest that
the whole rule was rather late. A text attributed to Paul shews that
in Justinian's time it implies a direct gift. The slave is free from
aditio[6]. But the difficulty discussed in the text, *i.e.* that the slave
being under 25 could not be tutor, was one created by Justinian's
new rule, and so cannot have been discussed by Paul. In his
time the difficulty would have been that the man was a latin, and
this was a permanent disability. This would suggest that Paul treated
it as implying a fideicommissary gift, as, in the resulting manumission
inter vivos, the difficulty would be met by shewing cause *apud consilium*.
But that would apply only to cases of this type. In general there is no
reason why it should be construed as fideicommissary rather than direct
if it is recognised at all, though it would not be the only case in which
a defective direct gift was construed as a *fideicommissum, i.e.* as imposing
a pious duty[7]. That treatment however would create difficulties, since
the man could not be tutor there and then, but only when freed, a
difficulty which is noted by Papinian and Paul in respect of fideicommissary gifts in general[8] On the other hand an enactment of
A.D. 260[9] declares that it does take effect as a *fideicommissum*, and a
text of Ulpian naturally understood says the same thing[10]. But it has
been pointed out[11] that this text may mean merely that just as an
appointment of your own slave as tutor implies a direct gift, so the
appointment of a *servus alienus* implies one by *fideicommissum*[12]. It
has also been noted that the enactment of 260[13] uses the odd expression
per fideicommissum manumisisse, which leads to the view that the
words *per fideicommissum* are a hasty insertion by the compilers[14],

[1] G. 1. 21; 2. 186—8. The provisions as to *addictio bonorum libertatis causa* are an
exception, *post*, Ch. XXVII.
[2] Ulp. 22. 12 implies it.   [3] C. 6. 27. 5. 1.   [4] In. 2. 14. *pr.*
[5] C. 6. 27. 5. 1 d. See also D. 26. 2. 10. 4, cited Syro-Roman Law-book, Bruns-Sachau, 203.
[6] 26. 2. 32. 2. Bodemeyer, de manumissione testamentaria, 38—42.
[7] *Post*, p. 514.   [8] P. 4. 13. 3; D. 26. 2. 28. 1. See *post*, p. 515.
[9] C. 7. 4. 10.   [10] 26. 2. 10. 4.
[11] Bodemeyer, *loc. cit.* The end of the text is probably Byzantine.
[12] But see *post*, p. 514.   [13] C. 7. 4. 10.
[14] A. Faber, Coniec. 6. 16, cited Wlassak, Z. S. S. 26. 409.

misled by the case in the immediate context. But similar language
is found elsewhere. Marcian uses the same form in a text which looks
genuine[1], and Paul uses similar language[2], though the exact meaning
of his words may be doubted. On the whole it seems most probable
that the rule of later classical law is that appointment as tutor implied
a *fideicommissum* of liberty, the appointment being magisterially confirmed after the man is freed[3].

For the gift to take effect the slave must have been the property of
the testator[4], both at the death and at the date of the will[5]. This is a
result of the analogy between this case and that of legacy *per vindicationem*[6]. We have already considered a text which treats *aditio* and
not death as the critical date[7]. The rule led to one apparently harsh
result. The codicil is read into the will. If therefore the slave belonged
to the testator at the time of the codicil, but was *alienus* at the time of
the will, there was no valid direct gift, though, at least in later law, it
was a good *fideicommissum*[8].

From the same analogy results the rule that he must be the quiritary
property of the testator, not merely bonitary[9]. The testator must also
be bonitary owner: the bare *nudum ius Quiritium* gives no right to
free[10]. A buyer cannot free even if the slave has been delivered, unless
he has paid the price or given security[11]. As it must be the testator's
own slave, a gift of freedom "if my heir sell him," or "if he cease to
belong to my heir" is regarded as bad, since it is to operate only at a
time when the slave is *alienus*, and its operation is therefore impossible.
The text notes that this is different from the case of sale of a *statuliber*
by the *heres*: in that case there is a valid gift which the *heres* cannot
destroy[12]. With this rule can be compared another[13], to the effect that if
a slave is given in usufruct to T, and to be free if that interest ceases,
this is a valid conditional gift: he is not by the usufruct rendered
alienus[14]. It should be observed that the gift cannot be treated as good
on the analogy of such rules as that a slave can acquire *hereditas* and
liberty at the same moment or that a contract for performance at death is

---

[1] 40. 5. 50. [2] 40. 5. 38. [3] P. 4. 13. 3; D. 26. 2. 28. 1.
[4] G. 2. 267, 272; D. 30. 108. 9; cp. C. 7. 10. 4.
[5] G. 2. 267; Ulp. 1. 23; In. 2. 24. 2. D. 40. 4. 35 shews that there had been doubts, but no
grounds appear.
[6] Where a man instituted a *servus alienus* with a gift of freedom and afterwards acquired the
slave this did not save the disposition, 28. 5. 50. *pr.*
[7] *Ante*, p. 443, where other points under this rule are considered.
[8] 29. 7. 2. 2; *post*, p. 515; cp. P. 4. 14. 2; it is thought that the *non* in the passage which
deals with the converse case should be omitted, Pothier, *ad h. l.*
[9] G. 2. 267; Ulp. 1. 16, 1. 23. As to the power of bonitary owner to give latinity, *post*, p. 549.
[10] Fr. Dos. 9. Where slaves given away had been *traditi*, the *donator* could not free, C. 7.
10. 5. As to concurrence with bonitary owner, and *iteratio*, *post*, App. IV.
[11] 40. 12. 38. 2. [12] 40. 4. 39. [13] 35. 1. 96. *pr.*
[14] Possibly under Justinian a gift of this sort which failed as a direct gift might be treated as
a *fideicommissum*. *Post*, p. 515.

valid: in the present case the wording of the gift definitely postpones it to the event which renders the gift impossible. This rule that associates power of manumission and ownership has many illustrations, some of a striking kind. A vendor or promisor of the slave can free him before delivery[1]. A manumission is good even though at the date of the will and of the death the slave is *apud hostes*: an application of the principle of *postliminium*[2]. A *heres, damnatus* to hand over a slave of his own, can free him, though he will be liable for his value[3]. A text of Paul is in direct contradiction with this[4], but it seems probable that the case originally contemplated was one of a slave of the testator conditionally freed[5]. After Justinian fused the different forms of legacy, and gave a *ius in rem* in all cases, the only way to give any point to the word *damnatus* was to apply it to a slave of the *heres*, in whom, as he was not the property of the testator, the ownership could not pass. We are told that a *heres* under a trust to hand over the *hereditas*, can free before doing so, being liable for the value of the slave whether he knew of the trust or not[6]. Though he is owner, we are told that this was only *favore libertatis*[7].

The fact, that if a son with a *peculium castrense* dies intestate it reverts to the father, leads to a difficult situation discussed in two texts. If the father by his will frees a *servus peculii castrensis*, what is the result if the son dies intestate? Tryphoninus observes that he cannot be the separate property of both the son and the father and that after Hadrian's enactment he certainly would be the son's *libertus* if he freed him. However he concludes that if the son dies intestate the manumission by the father is validated by a sort of *postliminium*—the father having retrospectively reacquired ownership over the man. The father's right is excluded only so far as the son uses his. How if the son does free him by will but his inheritance is not entered on? Here he decides that it is in suspense according to the event: he feels some logical difficulty, but concludes in favour of the manumission[8]. Ulpian[9] discusses only the simpler case of the son's death intestate, and states the same result. There can hardly be said to be a principle under this: the institution itself is illogical[10].

Of a rule stated above it is said: *inter libertatem et legatum quantum ad hanc causam nihil distat*[11]. Gifts of liberty resemble

---

[1] 40. 1. 18; C. 7. 10. 3. He is liable on the sale and must give security for patronal rights, and for all the buyer would have been entitled to if there had been no manumission. See *ante*, p. 40. A *mandatarius* to buy, in the days of double conveyance, could free the slave, C. 7. 10. 2.
[2] 40. 4. 30. [3] 30. 112. 1. [4] 40. 9. 28.
[5] Pothier, *ad h. l.* [6] 36. 1. 26. 2. [7] *Post*, pp. 558 *sq.*
[8] 49. 17. 19. 3—5. [9] 49. 17. 9.
[10] A less liberal view was held where liberty was not in question, *ante*, p. 258.
[11] 40. 4. 39; cp. 34. 4. 32. 1.

30

legacies in many ways, and they have a close affinity to *legata per vindicationem*. Thus gifts of liberty *post mortem heredis*, or *pridie mortis*, and the like were void, as such legacies were[1]. A slave attempting to upset a will loses a gift of liberty under it[2]. Such a gift may be subject to *dies* and *conditio*[3], and we have already noted many rules of form, *etc.*, which apply equally to both. But it is not a legacy and is carefully distinguished from one in the texts[4]. Accarias points out[5] that it differs in some essentials, *e.g.* it is incapable of estimation in money; it cannot be refused; it can be given to a sole *heres*. There are a number of differences in detail, turning for the most part on the fact that it is indivisible and incapable of estimation in money, and on *favor libertatis*[6]. Although a legacy given *poenae nomine* was void, there was doubt in the case of a gift of liberty, though Gaius treats the doubt as obsolete and puts them on the same level[7]. Justinian allows such penal gifts, striking out the condition, if it is in any way improper[8]. Thus a legacy to a woman provided she did not marry was good and the condition was struck out[9]. But if a slave was left to a widow to be free if she married, the whole disposition was good[10]. At first this seems rather *contra libertatem*: it might be thought that the condition, being *contra bonos mores*, would be struck out and the man be free at once. There are in fact however two gifts—one to the woman on the condition that she does not marry. This the law treats as an absolute gift. Then there is a gift of liberty to the slave if X marries. There is nothing objectionable in that. When she marries there are thus two conflicting gifts, and Paul tells us in accordance with principle that *libertas potior est legato*[11]. The *sc.* Neronianum had no relation to gifts of liberty: it hardly could have[12].

Like legacies, gifts of liberty may be adeemed, though there may at one time have been doubts of this[13]. In general the same principles are applied as in case of legacy[14]. Ademption of liberty is of course ademption of any gift to the slave, for a legacy without liberty to a *servus proprius* is a nullity[15]. If several slaves of the same name, *e.g.* Stichus, are freed, *ademptio* of liberty to Stichus adeems all the gifts as in

---

[1] G. 2. 233; Ulp. 1. 20.   [2] 34. 9. 5. 15.
[3] G. 2. 200; Ulp. 2. 1; *post*, pp. 479 *sqq*.   [4] 30. 94. 3; G. 2. 229, 230, *etc.*
[5] Précis, § 56, citing 50. 17. 106.
[6] A gift of liberty could not be adeemed *pro parte*, 34. 4. 14. 1. One who had liberty alone could not be burdened with *fideicommissa*, though set down in the will as in lieu of *operae*, 30. 94. 3, 95. As to freedom on condition of payment of money, *post*, p. 496.
[7] G. 2. 236.   [8] In. 2. 20. 36; C. 6. 41. 1.
[9] 35. 1. 62. 3, 63. *pr.*   [10] 35. 1. 96. 1; 40. 7. 42.
[11] 35. 1. 96. 1; *post*, p. 468. If the gift over had been a legacy, *e.g.*, the man himself was to go to another person, the logical result would be that each gift being good, the widow and the second donee would share.
[12] G. 2. 197, 212, 218; Ulp. 24. 11; Vat. Fr. 85. Other differences between legacies and *libertates, post*, pp. 485, 491, 493.   [13] 28. 5. 6. 4; 40. 4. 10; 40. 5. 50; 40. 6. 1.
[14] *e.g.*, 28. 5. 38. 4; 34. 4. 26.   [15] 34. 4. 32. 1.

legacy[1]. A gift of liberty or a legacy left so uncertainly, is void: an *ademptio* is handled the other way, presumably because it introduces uncertainty into the gift. A curious difficulty is raised as to adeeming a condition. If a gift of liberty is conditional, can the condition be adeemed? Julian thinks it cannot be done so as to make the gift simple, for which opinion Papinian gives the rather pedantic reason that *adimere* means to take away, and can apply only to what is *datum*, conditions being not *datae* but *adscriptae*. Ulpian thinks it best to ignore this verbal distinction, and to treat them as adeemable[2].

Ademption is not necessarily by declaration in express words: it may be implied from certain dealings with the slave. An express ademption must no doubt be in the form required for ademption of legacies, and, in general, the tacit ademptions are of the same kind[3]. The chief are the cases of alienation and legacy of the slave.

Alienation of the slave is ademption of a gift of liberty to him, with a possibility of revival[4], and ademption of the gift of liberty is ademption of a legacy to him[5]. There is however a distinction to be drawn. S was given freedom and a legacy. He was sold and then the liberty was adeemed. Paul says that though the ademption was unnecessary, since the sale had adeemed the gift, it is not a mere nullity: it can be given a meaning, as the slave might be repurchased, and apart from the express ademption this would revive the gift. Thus the vendee will not get the legacy[6]. This implies that the mere sale, though an ademption of the liberty, would not necessarily have adeemed the legacy, the rule just stated being confined to express ademptions which have the effect of making the legacy a gift to *servus proprius* without liberty, and thus void. The sale of the slave might be regarded as mere *translatio* of the legacy[7]. Paul's text[8] continues with the case of a man freed by will, then freed *inter vivos*, and the liberty given to him by the will adeemed by codicil. This *ademptio* is an absolute nullity, for though you may contemplate repurchase, you may not contemplate reenslavement, and therefore it will not destroy a legacy given to him by the will. So we are told that if a slave is legated, with a legacy to him, and is freed *inter vivos*, and then the legacy of him is adeemed, this *ademptio* is a mere nullity and does not prevent him from taking what is left to him by the will. The mere freeing has not

---

[1] 34. 5. 10. *pr.*   [2] 34. 4. 3. 9; 35. 1. 53.
[3] Girard, Manuel, 916. Testator directed a slave to be free if he paid testator's debt to X. There was no debt: this was a gift *pure*. If testator paid the debt after the will was made, this was an ademption, 35. 1. 72. 7. Supervening impossibility was not treated as voiding the condition, *post*, p. 489.
[4] *Ante*, pp. 443, 464.   [5] 34. 4. 32. 1.   [6] *h. t.* 26. *pr.*
[7] Marcellus discusses the form, *S liber esto si meus erit*, followed by an unconditional legacy to him. S is sold. The buyer will take the gift: the words *si meus erit*, expressing what would be law in any case, imply that the legacy is to be good even though *meus non erit*, 35. 1. 47.
[8] 34. 4. 26. 1.

of itself adeemed that gift. But an effective express ademption of the legacy of him would have done so. If instead of being freed he had been sold, an express ademption of the legacy to him would not be a nullity: the gift might otherwise take effect in the alienee[1].

An obvious mode of ademption is by making a legacy or *fidei-commissum* of the slave, but as a gift of liberty may be an ademption of a gift of him, rules are necessary as to which is to prevail, where both occur in the same will or one is in the will and the other in a codicil construed with it. The general rule where there is no further complication is that the later direction is the effective one, as representing the last will, whether they are in one document, or not. If however the form of words raises a doubt, there is a general presumption in favour of the manumission, *favore libertatis*[2]. Whatever the order, a specific gift of liberty takes precedence of a general legacy, and thus where there is a legacy of his *peculium* to a slave and a gift of liberty to a particular *vicarius* in that *peculium*, the gift of liberty takes effect[3]. We are told that it is only effective manumission which bars a legacy of the slave, not the mere form of words, and thus, if the liberty cannot take effect, as being fraudulent, or of a pledged slave, or of one incapable of manumission, the legacy is still good[4]. It might have been thought that the attempt to free shewed intention to revoke the gift, but, of itself, it does not satisfy the requirements of ademption: the testator might still wish him to go to the legatee rather than to the *heres*. But there may be other complications. Though there is in general a presumption in favour of the liberty against the legacy, it must be noticed that they need not be inconsistent. Thus a gift of the slave or a gift of liberty to him, according to a certain event, *i.e.* on mutually exclusive conditions, can create no difficulty. It is also laid down that if he is *pure legatus*, and conditionally freed, the legacy is subject to the contrary condition. If the condition occurs the legacy fails: if it does not occur the manumission fails. The text notes one important result of the treatment of the legacy as conditional: if the legatee dies before the condition is satisfied, as the legacy has not vested, it fails. This does not make the gift of liberty independent of the condition but only makes the *heres* under the will benefit instead of the *heres* of the legatee[5]. On the other hand if the slave is legated, and freed *ex die*, the legacy of him

---

[1] 34. 4. 27. *pr.*, 1. Paul's reasoning creates difficulty in interpreting the text, which has already been considered, *ante*, p. 150.

[2] 40. 5. 50; 28. 6. 16. *pr.* Paul seems to think that, even if the legacy was last, the liberty is still good unless intent to adeem is clear, but probably no difference of rule is meant, 31. 14. *pr.*; 40. 4. 10. 1. The remark as to proof of intent may be interpolated.

[3] 40. 4. 10. *pr.*

[4] 30. 44. 7; 31. 37. A legacy of the slave with an institution of him, *sine libertate*, could have no more effect than to benefit the legatee. Even for it to do this the institution must be in some way suspended, 28. 5. 38. *pr.*; cp. G. 2. 187. [5] 30. 68. 2; 40. 7. 42.

is void, *quia diem venturam certum est.* This inevitable definite determination is inconsistent with a gift of ownership of the slave[1]. In a case in which the slave is left to T, with liberty after the death of T, Papinian tells us that both gifts are good, whether it is a legacy to an outsider, or a *praelegatum* to one of the *heredes*, and in the last case, whether the praelegatee enters on the inheritance or not, the liberty taking effect on the death of T[2]. On the other hand Gaius cites Julian as thinking that if a slave is left to T to be free after T's death, the legacy is void, *quia moriturum Titium certum est*[3]. The explanation seems to be that Papinian applies the rule, and Julian does not, that *dies incertus in testamento facit conditionem*[4]. Julian regards the gift as *ex die* merely, and so annulling the legacy[5].

In another text we are told that there was a dispute as to the effect of the words: *Stichum Attio do lego, et, si is ei centum nummos dederit, liber esto.* Servius and Ofilius held that he was not a *statuliber*: Quintus Mucius, Gallus and Labeo held that he was, and Javolenus accepts this view[6]. The point is that a *statuliber* is in general a slave of the *heres*, and if effectively legated, this he cannot be. All the jurists are early: the reason which leads Quintus Mucius and the others to disregard the difficulty does not appear. That which is given, apparently the view of Javolenus, is that he is the slave of the *heres* and not of the legatee. This expresses the classical lawyers' way of surmounting the difficulty, just stated: the legacy is treated as under the contrary condition[7].

In a long and obscure text, of Scaevola, the effect of the following words is discussed[8]: *Titius heres esto. Stichum Maevio do lego: Stichus heres esto. Si Stichus heres non erit, Stichus liber heresque esto.* If T had entered no question would have arisen[9]. But in the present case, T did not enter, and Scaevola construes the words ignoring the institution of T. His view seems to be this: the two institutions of S are not a substitution, the second having no new condition. It is as if the words were "let S be heir, if not, let him be heir." It is thus *in uno gradu.* The gift of liberty, coming after, destroys the legacy of S,

---

[1] 30. 68. 3. A legacy of usufruct in him, till then, is good, 35. 2. 56. 3.
[2] 31. 65. 2, 3.
[3] 30. 68. 3 *in fin.* This view of Julian's is not contradicted by him in 28. 5. 38. *pr.*, where he says that a slave can be validly instituted after the death of a person to whom he is legated, even if the legatee is a *filius impubes exheredatus.* As there is no liberty in question there is no conflict of claim.
[4] 35. 1. 75, *post*, p. 480.   [5] *Post*, p. 481.   [6] 40. 7. 39. *pr.*
[7] 30. 68. 2. The words which follow in 40. 7. 39. *pr.* (*utpote cum legatum statulibertate tollitur*) are not clear. Mommsen omits *statu*, thus making the text say that even a conditional liberty annuls the legacy. This must be the meaning, but the words are probably due to the compilers: they go beyond what is needed and what is the rule of other texts.
[8] 28. 6. 48. 1. *Post*, p. 510.
[9] Thus where *filius impubes* was instituted and a slave was *legatus*, and under the pupillary substitution he was to be free, here if the *filius* took definitively, the legacy was good, the liberty null: if the substitute took things were reversed, 28. 6. 18. 1; 30. 81. 10.

and thus Maevius takes nothing and Stichus is free and *heres*. Scaevola quotes Julian as holding the same view[1].

We are told that if a gift of liberty is adeemed *lege*, it is to be taken *aut pro non data aut certe observari ac si a testatore adempta esset*[2]. We have no comments on this proposition, which is the only *lex* in the title *de ademptione libertatis*. It is from a treatise by Terentius Clemens on the *lex* Iulia *et* Papia. The case in view is no doubt that of a disability under the *lex* Iulia *de adulteriis*, and the expression *ademptio* implies that it is a supervening disability. The point is probably that it is not to be treated as a *caducum*[3]. The jurist's correction of his language may be no more than an effort at greater accuracy, since the gift had once certainly been valid, but it seems to involve a distinction in effect. If the gift is *pro non scripto* there can be no question of revival, but, regarded as one adeemed, then, as the ademption is not express, it may presumably revive by the disappearance of the prohibition, with no act of revival, just as such a gift adeemed by sale revived on repurchase[4].

The ademption of liberty may be conditional, the effect of which is to subject the liberty to the contrary condition[5]. It is laid down by Florentinus that ademption being a privative act cannot validate a gift. A legacy is made to a slave of the *heres*: it is conditionally adeemed. Although this makes it a conditional gift, and therefore *prima facie* valid, Florentinus denies it any such effect in this case[6]. The ademption of a condition may of course make the gift valid. Thus a manumission *poenae causa* is void, but if the condition is adeemed it may presumably take effect.

In general, manumissions stand or fall with the will[7]. One text however seems in its present form to contemplate validity in a gift of liberty though the will has failed. The difficulties of the text will be considered later: here it is enough to say that the text must probably be read, as Krüger suggests[8], as of a dispute affecting the inheritance not of the donor of the liberty, but of his heir, so that the present difficulty is only apparent.

Legacies to freed slaves give rise to several points for discussion. Such legacies vest only on entry of the *heres*, a rule said to be due to the fact that if they were construed as vesting before they must necessarily fail, as he has not capacity to take till he is free. Till then it

---

[1] Mommsen refers to *h. t.* 10. 7 (Julian). The point is the same: of two institutions of the same person one is not necessarily in substitution.
[2] 40. 6. 1.   [3] Pothier, *ad h. l.*   [4] *Ante*, pp. 443, 464, 467.
[5] 40. 7. 13. 5.   [6] 34. 4. 14. *pr.*
[7] *e.g.*, where *bonorum possessio contra tabulas* is given, 37. 5. 23. Exceptions, *post*, Ch. xxvii.
[8] 40. 7. 29. 1. Krüger, Z. S. S. 24. 193. *Post*, p. 502.

is a legacy to the testator's own slave[1]. This rule leads to another affecting the construction of such a gift. If the *peculium* is left to an *extraneus* he takes it as it was at the time of death, having no right to later accessions, except pure increment of existing *res peculiares*. If it is left to the slave he takes it as it is at the time of *aditio*. This rule Julian bases on an assumption as to the intent of the testator and thus it might be varied by evidence of contrary intent[2]. It is essential that the legacy be accompanied by a gift of liberty : if it is not it is void and it is not validated by the man's getting liberty in any other way *post mortem* and before *aditio*[3]. The rule has no connexion with the *regula* Catoniana, which does not apply to legacies which vest only on *aditio*[4].

So far as both gifts are unconditional and unrestricted the rules are simple and the texts deal only with questions of construction. Where the words were " let S be free and I desire my heir to teach him a trade by which he may live," Pegasus held the *fideicommissum* void for uncertainty, the kind of trade not being mentioned. But the rule stated by Valens is that it is valid, and the Praetor or *arbiter* will direct the teaching of a suitable trade[5]. Where liberty was given to A and B, and certain land was left to them, the will elsewhere praelegated to one of the *heredes*, T, " all that X left me." This included the land. The question was: did A and B have it, or T, or all three ? As a matter of construction Scaevola holds that the specific gift to A and B is to be preferred to the general gift to T[6].

More difficult questions arise where one gift is simple and the other conditional. If the gift of liberty is simple, the legacy may be either conditional or simple[7]. But if the legacy is simple and the liberty conditional, the general rule is that if the condition both can be and is satisfied before *aditio*, the legacy is good, but in other cases bad. Thus the legacy is necessarily bad if there is any condition on the liberty and the *heres* is a *necessarius*, or if the condition cannot be satisfied till after *aditio*[8], or if in fact it is still unfulfilled at the *aditio*, though it need not have been[9]. It is observable that if there is a *heres necessarius* the simple legacy is declared null in any case, *i.e.* even if the condition on the liberty be satisfied *vivo testatore*. This harsh rule is a result of the *regula* Catoniana[10]. As the legacy in this case vests at

---

[1] 36. 2. 7. 6, 8 ; 35. 2. 1. 4 ; In. 2. 20. 20.   [2] 33. 8. 8. 8 ; In. 2. 20. 20.
[3] 28. 5. 77 ; C. 6. 37. 4. Or before the death, 30. 102. Codicils being read into the will a gift therein suffices, 29. 7. 2. 2, 8. 5.   [4] 34. 7. 3 ; 35. 1. 86. 1.   [5] 32. 12.
[6] 32. 41. 3. Where the words were *Pamphilus peculium suum cum moriar sibi habeto liberque esto*, some seem to have thought this might be bad, as the gift of *peculium* comes first before he is free. Alfenus remarks (33. 8. 14) that as they take effect at the same time the order is not material. In the Syro-Roman Law-book the right to make such legacies seems to be confined to the case of slaves who are natural children of the testator. Ed. Bruns-Sachau, 199.
[7] 30. 91. 1.   [8] *e.g.*, " if he give the *heres* 10 " or " if he go to Rome after the *aditio*."
[9] 30. 91. 1 ; 35. 1. 86. 1 ; 36. 2. 7. 6, 8.
[10] Machelard, Règle Catonienne, § 59 ; Dissertations, 517.

death it is not protected by the rule which excludes the *regula* in legacies which vest only on *aditio*[1], and it would certainly have failed if the testator had died at the time of making the will[2].

In applying these principles there is however a general tendency to save the legacy if possible by treating the condition as applying also to it, if this is possible on the wording of the will. Where a slave is to be free on rendering accounts, and the heir is to give him some land, Callistratus holds the legacy good, if the condition applies to it also, but not otherwise[3]. Where a slave is directed to give 10 to the *heres* and so be free, and to have a legacy, Maecianus, quoting Julian, says the legacy is bad unless the condition applies to both, which it may, by construction, though not expressly stated to be so applicable. It follows that if he is freed *inter vivos*, he cannot claim the legacy unless he pays the 10[4]. Where a slave is freed conditionally and receives a legacy *pure*, and the testator frees him *inter vivos, pendente conditione*, he takes the legacy whatever happens to the condition, but if the condition fails before he is freed, the legacy is void, as not accompanied by a gift of freedom: the subsequent manumission *inter vivos* being ineffective to save it, it is *irritum*[5]. This is also from Julian: the difference between this case and the last is that here the condition is not one incapable of fulfilment before *aditio*, and thus it is not necessary to the saving of the legacy that the condition be read into it. Where the words were " let my *heres* give S my slave 10, and if he serve my *heres* for two years, let him be free," jurists so early as Labeo and Trebatius were agreed that even here the condition could be read into the legacy, which is thus saved[6]. But of course the terms of the legacy might exclude this resource[7].

Other texts shewing rules of construction favourable to such gifts can be cited. A slave was to be free in 10 years and to have an annual allowance from the testator's death. He will get the annuity from the liberty, and *alimenta* meanwhile[8]. This does not mean that he can enforce the payment of *alimenta*, but that the *heres* who has

---

[1] 34. 7. 3 ; 35. 1. 86. 1.

[2] The same rules apply if the manumission though simple in form is delayed by some rule of law, *e.g.* that under the *lex Iulia de adulteriis*, till after the *aditio*, 31. 76. 4, *post*, Ch. xxv.

[3] 35. 1. 82.

[4] *h. t.* 86. *pr.* So if there is a *fideicommissum* subject to the same condition as the liberty, and the *heres* frees the man *pendente conditione*, he is entitled to the *fideicommissum* when the condition occurs, 35. 1. 66.

[5] 28. 5. 38. 4.   [6] 32. 30. 2.

[7] 35. 1. 86. *pr.* In 40. 7. 28. 1 Javolenus quotes Cassius, as saying that if there is a legacy of *peculium* and conditional liberty, acquisitions to the *peculium* will not go to the man unless the legacy *in tempus libertatis collatum esset*. He corrects by saying that mere accessions go unless taken away by the *heres*. The legacy ought however to be wholly bad. Pothier (*ad h. l.*) supposes the legacy conditional and explains these words as meaning, unless it is expressly given as it is at the time of liberty. This may be the solution of a question already raised, *ante*, p. 191. It should be noted that if the *heres* adeems the *peculium* he does not destroy the legacy but only prevents additions to it.

[8] 33. 1. 16.

paid them can charge them against his *coheredes*, and they can be claimed by the person interested in the slave in the meantime[1]. Thus, if the slave dies before the time is up, though the legacy is not due to him, and therefore the *alimenta* cannot be due either, the *alimenta* paid, if consumed, cannot be recovered, by the *heres* who paid them, from him who had the slave at the time of payment[2]. The last point is an ordinary result of the rules of *bonae fidei possessio*. The main provision is not exactly reading the condition into the legacy in defiance of the words of the will: it is treating the testator as having in one form, made two gifts, perfectly valid. The legacy of annual payments is to run from the liberty. There is also a direction to the *heres* to give a maintenance allowance at once. This is equivalent to a gift of *cibaria*, and it is expressly enacted by Severus and Caracalla that such a direction is binding on the *heres*[3].

Where the will said, "let S be free and let my *heres* give him 5," he gets the legacy though he is freed *inter vivos*[4]. This is in accord with what has been said[5]. The result is the same if the words were "let S be free," either now or at a future time, "and, when he is free, let my heir give him 5[6]." The text adds that if the words were "let S be free and if I free him *vindicta*, let my heir give him 5," here even if he is not so freed but the gift by will takes effect, the gift of money is still good, on grounds of humanity, says the text, though the condition did not strictly occur. *Humanitas* is a bad reason for de-spoiling the *heres*—the decision really is that the testator meant this.

There is no special difficulty in the application of the *lex* Falcidia to legacies to freed slaves[7], but the relation of that *lex* to gifts of liberty does call for discussion. If the man is absolutely freed, and survives *aditio*, there is no difficulty. He does not count in the *hereditas*[8]. If however he dies before *aditio*, then he never was actually free, and he must be treated as a slave and counted in the *hereditas*, a rule expressed in the form: *heredi perit*. But as he could never have belonged to the heir his value is merely nominal: Papinian tells us that he is to be valued as a dying slave[9].

If the gift of liberty was conditional or *ex die*, there are some difficulties. Some of them are caused by the fact that practice was not

---

[1] 34. 1. 15. 1.   [2] 10. 2. 39. 2.
[3] 30. 113. 1; cp. 34. 1. 11. This gives no right to the slave: it makes money so paid irrecoverable and entitles any *heres* who has paid it to charge it against his *coheredes*. It does not appear that the slave after he was free could claim arrears. Presumably the person on whom the maintenance of the slave had fallen could claim.
[4] 40. 4. 4. *pr.*   [5] Cp. 28. 5. 38. 4.
[6] 40. 4. 4. 1.   [7] 35. 2. 1. 4.
[8] In. 2. 22. 2, 3; *etc.* The same rule applied in the *Querela*, 5. 2. 8. 9. There were of course other ways in which he might cease to be in the *hereditas*, 35. 2. 39.
[9] 35. 2. 11. 4.

settled in classical law, as to what was to be done in the matter of
charging conditional legacies. According to one view the parties had
their choice either to treat the conditional legacy as a legacy, valuing
it at what it would sell for as a conditional right[1], or to treat it as no
legacy, so that it would not count to make up the three-fourths allowed.
In both cases it is estimated in the *hereditas* at its full amount, but
in the last the other legatees are called on to give security to refund,
in the event of the total sum of legacies being made to exceed three-
fourths by the arrival of the condition on this, so that it takes effect.
It is clear that this is the simplest course: it is certainly the practice
in later law[2]. When the condition arrives it becomes clear what is
due to the *heres, ex* Falcidia. To it is added interest for the time
during which it has been unpaid. From it is deducted what the *heres*
has received in the way of fruits from what was conditionally legated[3].
In arriving at the sum due to the *heres*, the legacies are taken at their
nominal value. But in distributing the burden among the legatees,
account is taken of the fact that the conditional legacy was really
lessened in actual value by what had been received by the *heres*, and
thus, in apportioning the payment to the *heres*, but for that purpose
only, the legacy is reckoned at the smaller amount[4].

If the legacy is simply *in diem*, then, as it is certain to be due, it
is reckoned at once towards the three-quarters, but only at its present
value[5]. This is simple in the case in which the legacy is money, but
if it is a thing producing irregular and uncertain fruits, such as a slave,
it seems likely that it is treated as conditional gifts are[6].

Similar questions present themselves in the case of a man freed
conditionally or *ex die*, and are further complicated by the fact that he
may be also the subject of a legacy. Where he is not legated, the
question is how far he is to be reckoned as part of the estate, so
as to increase the amount going to the *heres*, of which not more than
three-quarters can be legated. Here, apart from the death of the
slave, the rule is that if the condition fails he is a part of the *hereditas*,
and if it does not fail he is not: the *lex* Falcidia does not of course
affect the gift of liberty itself[7]. In the meantime the practice is to
treat him as a part of the *hereditas*, the legatees giving security to
refund if the condition arrives[8]. We are told by Hermogenianus[9] that

---

[1] 35. 2. 45. 1.
[2] 35. 2. 73. 2.   Paul speaks of it as the only possible course, *h. t.* 45. 1.
[3] *h. t.* 24. 1, 88. 3.
[4] *h. t.* 88. 3, Africanus, to the benefit of that legatee as against others. Ulpian is probably
dealing with the same aspect of the matter in *h. t.* 66. *pr.*
[5] *h. t.* 45. *pr.*, 73. 4.
[6] In this case the fruits received by the *heres* will be charged against the quarter and the slave
reckoned temporarily at his full value, *h. t.* 56. 3, 66. *pr.*
[7] In. 2. 22. 3.   [8] 35. 2. 73. 3.   [9] *h. t.* 38. *pr.*

statuliber heredis non auget familiam, which seems to mean that if a *heres* has succeeded to an estate including a man given conditional liberty under the will, and he himself dies before the condition occurs, the man is not counted in his inheritance against his *heres.* It is not easy to see why this is so. The man was imputed against him as *heres* and might have been expected to be imputed against his *heres.* The fact that the deceased *heres* did not himself impose the condition does not seem to be material. It seems an avoidance of complication at some sacrifice of consistency.

If the manumission is *ex die,* it seems, though there is little evidence, that the man is treated as part of the *hereditas* till the time comes[1]. He is then deducted, and if this makes the legacies exceed three-quarters, the legatees must refund, less any profits the heir has made by the man.

If the man dies after the death of the testator, Papinian tells us that if the condition is satisfied (*i.e.* at any time), he does not perish to the *heres, i.e.* he is not charged as a part of the inheritance, but if the condition fails he is then to be included, *sed quanti statuliber moriens fuisse videbitur*[2]. Two remarks suggest themselves. If he is absolutely freed and dies before entry of the *heres,* it is Papinian who tells us[3] that he is imputed, though only at a nominal value. In the present case where he dies after the condition is satisfied we should have expected the same result. But here he says the slave is not imputed at all. The difference is very slight : it may be that the meaning is the same. If the condition fails we should have expected it to be as if he had never been freed at all : in that case we are told that the death of a slave between death and entry of the *heres* leaves him imputable at his full value[4]. But here we are told he is to be valued as a dying *statuliber, i.e.,* at a mere nominal sum. This may however conceivably mean the same thing, since we know that in the settled practice a *statuliber* is taken at his full value subject to readjustment if the condition occur[5]. But it is plain that the clause *sed quanti... videbitur* implies something different from *heredi periisse,* since it is stated as a modification of that proposition. It may be a representation of a view analogous to, but not identical with, that held by some early jurists in the case of legacy, that he was valued *ab initio* as a *statuliber,* and that failure of the condition was not to disturb that estimate[6]. But as the writer has just told us that arrival of the condition causes him to be valued at nothing, this is hardly probable. It may be an addition of the compilers[7].

---

[1] Arg. 35. 2. 56. 3. But see *post*, p. 522. [2] 35. 2. 11. 1.
[3] *h. t.* 11. 4. [4] *h. t.* 30. *pr.*
[5] *h. t.* 73. 3. [6] Cp. *h. t.* 73. 1.
[7] The same may be said of *h. t.* 37. *pr., post*, p. 522, in connexion with *fideicommissa.*

Further questions arise, and there is really no textual authority, where the freed slave is also the subject of a legacy. Here there are to be considered two questions. How far is he a legacy counting towards the three-quarters? How far is he counted in the *hereditas* towards the heir's quarter? Such a legacy is, as we have seen[1], regarded as subject to the contrary condition. As it is a conditional legacy, it is treated as no legacy, in the meanwhile[2], and if the condition determines in favour of the legacy, the rule applied must be that already stated for conditional legacies: the legatees may have to refund something on account of the extra legacy, which may have brought the total above three-quarters, and they have a right to allowance, in that case, for anything the *heres* has received. If it is decided in favour of the liberty[3], the legatees will have to refund whatever may be due by reason of the reduction in the total inheritance with the same right to allowance[4].

If the slave legated is also freed *ex die*, we have seen that the rule of later law is that the legacy is void[5]. But a legacy of the use of him till the day is valid, and in that case the interim receipts are a legacy and subject to a Falcidian deduction[6].

The texts do not discuss the case of a slave conditionally freed and legated and dying before the condition is satisfied. Presumably, as in the case just discussed, the event of the condition determined the solution, which was as if there had been no liberty or no legacy as the case might be.

A question of some interest is: could liberty be given to unborn persons, directly? Justinian, determining a long-standing doubt, declares such gifts lawful. The enactment[7] was published three years before the Digest, so that we have little authority for the earlier law. But he expresses the doubt as relating only to *fideicommissa*: as to direct gifts he seems to be making new law. Paul admits the validity of a gift in the form *qui ex ea ancilla nascetur liberum esse volo*[8], which must be a *fideicommissum*. We have seen that direct gifts of liberty, though not legacies, are closely analogous thereto[9], and the same principles may probably be applied. It might conceivably be doubted whether the validity of the gift is to be judged by the quality of the slave regarded as the thing given or as the donee. Legacies of an

---

[1] *Ante*, p. 472.   [2] *Ante*, p. 474.   [3] *Ante*, p. 474.
[4] Thus if the estate is 400 of which the slave is 100 and there are legacies of 300, legacies will be paid in full. After three months, in which S has earned 25 for *heres*, the condition arrives in favour of the legacy. 100 must be refunded, with, say, 5 for interest, and less 25. If the condition is decided in favour of liberty, the estate is reduced to 300 of which 75 must be refunded, with interest and less the earnings.
[5] *Ante*, p. 468.   [6] 35. 2. 56. 3.   [7] C. 7. 4. 14.
[8] P. 4. 14. 1.   [9] *Ante*, p. 466.

unborn slave or of a usufruct in one are allowed[1]. But in earlier law this could be only by *damnatio* (or perhaps *sinendi modo* if the slave were alive at the death[2]), not by *vindicatio*[3]. But gifts of liberty in the form of *damnatio* could not have been valid except as *fideicommissa*[4]. It is on the whole more likely that such gifts would be regarded as gifts to the slave. They vest only on *aditio*[5], and the language of the texts in other respects favours this view[6]. The result is the same. Gaius tells us that gifts of liberty to *incertae personae* are bad[7]. But he bases this on the *lex* Fufia Caninia, and not on anything which applies, as the rule does, to legacies. But, as the above text of Paul shews[8], they are not *incertae personae*, but *postumi alieni*, a class usually kept distinct[9]. Legacies to such persons are void[10], and it is likely that liberties are equally so[11].

The gift takes effect at the moment when any heir enters under the will[12], *in eodem gradu* ; not, for instance, if it follows the institutions, and all the heirs primarily instituted refuse, so that a substitution later in the will takes effect[13]. The fact that some of the institutions fail is in general immaterial. Where A and B were instituted *pure* to one quarter each, and B was given one half conditionally, liberties were good even though the condition failed, since in any case A and B would take the whole *hereditas*[14]. Assuming a valid entry the liberty is not affected by subsequent happenings. Thus it is not delayed by an accusation of theft brought by the *heres* against the *libertus*: there are other remedies[15]. And where a *heres* refuses to give the necessary security to legatees who are on that account put into possession, liberty is not affected or delayed[16]. More striking is the fact that it is not affected though the *heres* gets *restitutio in integrum*[17].

Many of the rules laid down in this chapter are departed from in the case of the will of a *miles*. A few of these relaxations may be given, but it is unnecessary to attempt an exhaustive list or to set out those relaxations in rules of form which apply to gifts of liberty as to all other kinds of gift. Nor are we concerned with the principle on which they depend[18]. The following may be noted.

---

[1] 7. 1. 68; 30. 24. *pr.*; 31. 73; 35. 1. 1. 3.   [2] G. 2. 203, 211.
[3] G. 2. 196.   [4] *Post*, p. 513.   [5] 31. 65. 2; 40. 4. 58.
[6] *e.g.* 40. 5. 24. 3.   [7] G. 2. 239.   [8] P. 4. 14. 1.
[9] G. 2. 287.   [10] *Ibid.* But see 34. 5. 5. 1, 6, 7.
[11] As to later law, Haenel, Diss. Domm. 463, and *post*, p. 557.
[12] 40. 4. 11. 2; C. 6. 51. 1. 6.   [13] 40. 4. 25.   [14] 35. 2. 87. 3.
[15] 40. 4. 11. 2.   [16] 36. 4. 59. 1.
[17] C. 7. 2. 3. Exceptional cases in which the gift operates though there is no *aditio*, *post*, Ch. xxvii. *init.*
[18] See Roby, Roman Priv. Law, 1. 216; Girard, Manuel, 811, *etc.*; C. 6. 21. 3.

(*a*) The institution of a slave implies a gift of liberty[1] : indeed even a legacy to him does[2], and this though the legacy be conditional[3].

(*b*) Words implying that the slave has already been freed constitute a gift of liberty if there is no error; *e.g. Fortunato liberto meo do lego*[4], *Samiam in libertate esse iussi*[5].

(*c*) Liberty may be given before the *institutio*, and *post mortem heredis*[6].

(*d*) There is a difference in treatment where the *institutus* and *substitutus* died before entry[7].

---

[1] 29. 1. 13. 3.   *Ante*, p. 463.   [2] See Nov. 78. 4.   [3] 29. 1. 40. 1.
[4] C. 6. 21. 7.   Cp. *ante*, p. 462.   [5] 40. 4. 49.   [6] Ulp. 1. 20; *ante*, pp. 461, 466.
   [7] 29. 1. 13. 4; 40. 5. 42.   In 29. 1. 13. 3 it is said that if a *miles* institutes a *servus proprius*, whom he thought *alienus*, without a gift of liberty, this is null. The point is that since the whole thing would be null at common law there is no point in applying the privilege where the effect would not be to carry out the intention of the *miles*. See *ante*, p. 143.

CHAPTER XXI.

MANUMISSION DURING THE EMPIRE (*cont.*). MANUMISSION BY WILL. DIES, CONDITIO, INSTITUTION.

A GIFT of liberty by will is not necessarily absolute and immediate: it may be subject to a condition or deferred to a future day. Pending the event the man is a *statuliber*: we have already considered his position[1] and have now to discuss the other questions affecting these modalities.

Where the liberty is deferred to a certain future time, it is said to be subject to *dies certus*. If the words *ad annum* are added, *e.g. ad annum liber esto*, they are construed as meaning " at the end of a year[2]." If the words are *ad annos decem*, they are treated as *supervacua*[3]. A gift of freedom *intra annum post mortem* entitles the donee to liberty at once. The rule is attributed to Labeo, and is declared to be justified by him as an inference from the rule that where the gift is : Let him be free *si heredi intra decimum annum decem dederit*, the man is free if he pays at once[4]. It is plain that this does not justify the rule. The one rule says merely that to impose a time within which the condition must be satisfied is not to impose *dies* in addition to the condition : it leaves the choice of time within a certain limit to the slave himself. The other does not : it does not say who is to have the choice of time, and the actual rule is a case of *favor libertatis*. We saw that *ad annum* meant at the end of the year. The text adds that this is to be reckoned from the death, but that if the words are such as to require the time to run from the date of the will, and the testator dies within the time the gift is not void[5], but the time must be waited for. The same rule applies no doubt to all cases in which that construction is given. It is not too plain why anyone should have thought

---

[1] *Ante*, pp. 286 *sqq.*   [2] 40. 4. 18. 2.   It cannot be *in diem*, 40. 4. 33.
[3] 40. 4. 34.   If it is *in annos decem*, he is free at the end of ten years, 35. 1. 49; 40. 4. 41. To be free *post annos*, means, *favore libertatis*, at the end of two years, 40. 4. 17. 2 (Tribonian discusses evidence of contrary intent). To be free *anno duodecimo post mortem* means at the beginning of the twelfth year ; *post duodecim annos* means at its end, 40. 4. 41. *pr.*
[4] 40. 4. 41. 2.   [5] 40. 4. 18. 2.

it void. The context suggests that Julian is simply emphasising the fact that it differs from a case in which the testator does not die within the year. Such a gift would perhaps be in strictness void in that event, as was one which gave liberty if a condition to be satisfied to the heir was satisfied within 30 days from the death, and there was no *aditio* till after that date. But here, and perhaps in the other case, the gift was allowed to be valid, *favore libertatis*[1]. It may be said in conclusion that *certum est quod certum reddi potest:* there may be *dies certus* where it is not so expressed. Thus a gift *cum per leges licebit* is valid and *ex die*[2].

Dies incertus is on a different footing. *Dies incertus* both *an* and *quando* is a condition and will be considered later[3]. As to *dies certus an, incertus quando,* of which *cum T moreretur* is the type usually cited, we are told by Papinian in a famous text[4], that *dies incertus conditionem in testamento facit,* and the proposition is confirmed in many texts[5]. It has, however, been the subject of much discussion in recent times. The existence of the rule itself has been doubted; the view being held that the *dies* referred to by Papinian is a *dies incertus an et quando.* But in view of the emptiness of the remark in that sense, the generality of his text and the content of the other texts cited, it is not necessary to do more than advert to this view[6]. But the admission of the rule leaves, still, a number of doubts, which the texts do not clear up. The main effect of the rule is to prevent transmissibility of the legacy to which the modality is attached, and that this is probably due to *intuitus personae, i.e.* a recognition of the testator's presumed intention to benefit a particular person who may not be alive at the time of the event, appears from the language of at least one of the texts[7], and from the fact that the rule was not applied to a gift *cum legatarius morietur,* since here the point could not arise: the testator's intent was clear[8]. It is not easy to see why the rule was not applied to *dies certus,* in which the same uncertainty would arise. There have been attempts to give the rule a rational basis, but none are satisfactory[9], and it is precisely this difficulty which has led some writers to try to explain the rule out of existence, notwithstanding the texts. The adoption of the view, for which some evidence will shortly be stated, that the rule as laid down by Papinian is a generalisation from the case of insti-

---

[1] 40. 7. 28. *pr.* [2] 40. 4. 38.
[3] *Post,* pp. 483 *sqq.* [4] 35. 1. 75.
[5] Ulp. 24. 31; D. 30. 30. 4, 104. 6; 31. 12. 1, 65. 2, 3; 35. 1. 1. 2, 79. 1; 36. 2. 4, 13; cp. C. 6. 51. 1. 7.
[6] Brunetti, Dies Incertus, c. 3, states and refutes this view. As to attempts to confine the rule to gifts *cum heres morietur,* see *op. cit.* p. 41.
[7] 35. 1. 79. 1. [8] *Ib.*; 36. 2. 4. Brunetti, c. 5.
[9] The latest seems to be that of Brunetti, *op. cit.* Pt. 2, as to which see Audibert, N. R. H. 21. 96.

tution, results in reducing the problem to the familiar one : why was *dies certus* struck out in institutions while *dies incertus* was treated as a condition? This obscure question is too far from our topic for discussion. All attempts to explain it on logical lines seem to have failed[1], and perhaps it is a mistake to assume that it must have had a logical basis. The rule may very well shew no more than that the notion of direct continuity which is certainly involved in *hereditas* is inadmissibly offended by a direct postponement of *aditio*, though it may be practically no less interfered with by postponement in disguised form[2]. In these cases there is always the possibility that the succession may be immediate.

That the rule of Papinian which is our immediate concern was in fact extended from institutions to other gifts appears from the fact that all the jurists who lay it down in general terms or apply it to gifts other than institutions seem to be rather late : Pomponius is, it appears, the earliest[3]. Others are Papinian[4], Ulpian[5] and Paul[6]. On the other hand, Julian, while he admits the rule in the case of institutions[7], denies its applicability to a gift of liberty[8]. He is discussing the coexistence of a simple legacy of the slave and a gift of liberty to the slave at the death of the legatee, and he is reported by Gaius as considering the legacy void, on a principle already discussed[9], by reason of the existence of a gift of liberty subject only to *dies*. Papinian on the other hand, who discusses the same case, considers both gifts good, the *dies incertus* having clearly, for him, the effect of a condition[10].

This view, that the idea is carried over from the case of institution, though it is strongly suggested by the foregoing case, and is supported by the existence of analogous extensions, *e.g.* the treatment of unlawful and impossible conditions[11], has, however, to face some difficulties. It may be said that if this rule was carried over, the rule excluding *dies certus* ought to have come over too. The answer seems to be that this last rule is not one of interpretation : there is not the logical reason which exists in our case. The question whether certain words are to operate as a condition or not cannot depend on the kind of gift to which they are attached even though they may have been declared conditions for ulterior reasons which apply only to institutions.

It may also be objected that Labeo is found applying the rule to legacies[12]. But Labeo is speaking of a gift *si moritur*, and though the difference between *cum* and *si* would not be conclusive to a classical

---

[1] See Dernburg, Pandekten, 3. § 82, n. 1, and literature there cited; Bufnoir, Conditions, 12.
[2] Karlowa, R. R. G. 2. 871.   [3] 35. 1. 1. 2; 36. 2. 13.
[4] 31. 65. 2, 3; 35. 1. 75, 79. 1.   [5] Ulp. 24. 31; D. 30. 30. 4; 36. 2. 4.
[6] 31. 12. 1.   [7] 30. 104. 6.
[8] 30. 68. 3.   [9] *Ante*, p. 468.
[10] 31. 65. 3.   [11] Girard, Manuel, 912.
[12] 35. 1. 40. 2.

jurist[1], it is by no means clear that it would not have been so to Labeo. It may be noticed that he speaks of it simply as a conditional gift, and not as one which has for this purpose the effect of a condition, as Papinian says for our case[2].

It may also be said that the Code contains an enactment of Diocletian, *extraneum quum morietur heredem scribi placuit*[3], which seems to shew that the rule in this case differs from that in legacy, which thus cannot have been simply borrowed. For the text treats the gift at death of the beneficiary as conditional, since if it were mere *dies* it would be struck out, while in legacy we have seen that in that case the modality was treated as *dies*[4]. But, as it stands, the text can have but little meaning: such an institution could have no force, since it could not be entered on and thus was not transmitted in classical law. Two possible ways of dealing with it have been suggested. It may be that in such a case the words *cum (heres) morietur* were struck out as being *dies*, which would get rid of the difficulty[5]. This view does not however account for the limitation to an *extraneus*, since the same rule would apply to an institution of a *suus*. It is difficult to suppose, as Accarias does[6], that the text really means that the rule applied to both cases: the word *extraneus* must have been put in for some reason. Another view adopted by the older editors is that the text refers to a gift on the death of a third person, and they accordingly insert *quis* (*cum quis morietur*). This would make the text an ordinary illustration of our rule, but it has no MS. authority. The text may be left with the remark that its extremely terse and truncated form does not inspire confidence.

It has been pointed out that the chief text, one of Papinian, does not say that *dies incertus quando, certus an*, is a condition, but only that it *facit conditionem, i.e.* has the effect of a condition[7]. The distinction is exact as a matter of words, and Ulpian has no doubt the same point in mind when he says that such a modality *appellatur conditio*[8]. A condition is essentially *incertus an*. Elsewhere, Papinian, Ulpian and Julian ignore this distinction[9], though it recurs as late as Justinian, who carefully distinguishes the cases of *dies incertus* and *conditio*, though he gives both of them the effect of postponing *dies cedens*[10]. It does not seem indeed that the distinction involves any difference of effect[11].

Condition is a somewhat complex matter. A condition is a future

---

[1] See 45. 1. 45. 3.   [2] 35. 2. 75.   [3] C. 6. 24. 9.
[4] *Ante*, p. 480.   [5] So Accarias, Précis, § 324 (cp. § 384) following Machelard.
[6] *loc. cit.*   [7] 35. 1. 75.   Brunetti, *op. cit.* 22, 37.
[8] 30. 30. 4.   [9] 30. 104. 6; Ulp. 24. 31; D. 35. 1. 79. 1.   [10] C. 6. 51. 1. 7.
[11] Brunetti, *op. cit.* 37, explains by it the view taken by Julian in a text already discussed

and uncertain event. It seems that every restriction which makes the event depend on an occurrence which may not happen is a condition even though it be such that if it occur it must occur at a certain time —*incertus an, certus quando.*

A gift of liberty is not conditional, and therefore delayed, unless it is clear that this was the intent. Some provisions which look at first like conditions may be only directory: it is a matter of construction, to be decided for each case. Thus where a man is to be free *ita ut rationes reddat,* this is not a condition: it is a direction. He must carry it out; indeed every slave who has administered has to render his accounts whether such a direction is given or not[1]. Where slaves are to be free if they attend in alternate months to the *sollennia* of the testator's tomb, this is a direction: it is to be carried out after liberty is attained, and they can be compelled *officio iudicis,* to do the duty. But the liberty is not conditional[2]. Where one is to be free "*sic tamen ut*" he stays with the heir so long as the latter is a *iuvenis,* and, if he does not, *iure servitutis teneatur,* this too is only a direction to be carried out after the man is free[3]. On the construction of the whole gift, even the strong words at the end are not allowed to limit what the jurist thinks to be meant as an immediate gift of liberty.

· Another type of case is represented by such gifts as *Sticha cum liberis libera esto.* This is not a condition: she is free, apart from evidence of intention, though she have no children or they cannot from any cause be freed[4]. So where the gift was "Let S and P be free if they are mine when I die," either may take though the other has been alienated: there is no condition[5].

A condition involves future uncertainty, and thus a gift which is expressed in conditional form, but the event is one which must necessarily be determined by the time the gift operates, is not really conditional. The donee can never be a *statuliber* under it. Thus, "to be free when I die[6]," or "to be free if I do not veto it by codicil[7]" or the like: these are not conditional[8]. "To be free if he pays what I owe

---

(30. 68. 3) as to legacy of a slave with a gift of liberty on the death of the legatee. But we have seen (*ante,* p. 469) by comparing the text of Papinian (31. 65. 3) that the true explanation is historical. And this latter text makes it clear that the treatment of *dies incertus* as a condition produced other effects than the postponement of the vesting of a transmissible right. Such an effect would have no meaning in the case of gift of liberty discussed in the texts.

[1] 40. 4. 17. 1; 40. 5. 37.   [2] 40. 4. 44.

[3] 40. 4. 52. See the Testamentum Dasumii (Girard, Textes, 767) where testator directs a slave to be free *cum contubernali sua ita ut eam in matrimonium habeat fidele.*

[4] 40. 4. 13. 3. The jurist is helped to the conclusion by the construction put on the Edict: *ventrem cum liberis in possessione esse iubebo,* 37. 9. 1. *pr.*; cp. 35. 1. 81; 40. 7. 31.

[5] 28. 7. 2. 1.   [6] 40. 4. 18. 1.   [7] *h. t.* 28.

[8] "To be free if he has managed my affairs well" is not conditional, he is free if the testator having long survived the making of the will has made no complaint, 40. 5. 18; "if I have no son when I die" is no condition: the gift is good or bad according to the event, 40. 4. 7: *cum moriar* being understood to include *postumi,* there might be a lapse of time.

to T " is no condition if there was no debt to T[1]. If there was a debt and the testator has paid it, the condition is treated as having failed: it was in fact an ademption[2]. It is clear that in all these cases where there is an express hypothesis on which the gift is made to depend, there may be need for enquiry on the result of which the fate of the gift will hang. In common speech they would be called conditional, and they are in fact sometimes so called in the texts. This is the case with the gift "if mine when I die[3]," and *qui sine offensa fuerunt liberi sunto*[4]. Although, as the rest of this text shews, the words refer entirely to the past, the gift is called conditional, but the man is not a *statuliber* even though there be some delay, before it is clear whether he is free or not[5]. The description of such gifts as conditional is not correct: the practical point is that when the matter is settled they are free and have been so from the time of *aditio*[6]. Thus, for instance, their interim acquisitions are their own.

Just as a gift, on the face of it conditional, may be *pura*, so, conversely, a gift on the face of it *pura* may be in fact conditional. There may be tacit conditions. Thus in the case of divorce a woman who frees within the 60 days of the *lex* Iulia makes the man a *statuliber*[7]. A slave freed in fraud of creditors is a *statuliber* till it is certain whether they will avoid the gift or not[8].

Impossible conditions are struck out—a Sabinian extension of the rules as to institutions, accepted in later law[9], and it may be assumed that the same was true as to illegal or immoral conditions, though texts seem silent[10]. Impossible conditions are those impossible in the nature of things[11]. These cases, where impossibility is patent on the gift, create no difficulty, but there are other types. Impossibility to the person concerned is no objection to the condition, and the texts put on the same level gifts on which a condition or *dies* is imposed such that, though it is not contrary to the nature of things, it is practically certain not to occur. Such for instance is a condition of paying a vast sum of money or living a hundred years[12]. Such a gift is on a level with one *cum morietur*[13], and is treated as illusory and void. It is clear that the line between these two is shifting, and probably the matter is not thoroughly thought out by the Romans[14]. Some conditions so treated

---

[1] 35. 1. 72. 7. It is a *falsa conditio*, treated as impossible. So where one who had never administered was to be free on rendering his accounts, 40. 5. 41. 16; 40. 7. 26. 1; cp. for legacies, 30. 104. 1.
[2] 35. 1. 72. 7.   [3] 28. 7. 2. 1.   [4] 40. 4. 51. 1.
[5] In the preceding text, *prout quisque meruisset* is not treated as conditional, 40. 4. 51. *pr.* Cp. *h. t.* 8; 40. 5. 41. 4; 40. 7. 21. *pr.*
[6] 40. 4. 7.   [7] 40. 9. 13; *post*, Ch. xxv.   [8] 40. 7. 1. 1.
[9] In. 2. 14. 10; G. 3. 98.   [10] Cp. 28. 7. 9, 14; 38. 16. 3. 5; 40. 9. 31.
[11] In. 3. 19. 11. To which *natura est impedimento, ut si caelum digito tetigerit*.
[12] 40. 7. 4. 1.   [13] 40. 4. 17. *pr.*; cp. *h. t.* 61.
[14] Bufnoir, *op. cit.* 21 *sqq.*; Accarias, Précis, § 325.

seem out of place. Thus where a slave is to be free, "if my heir alienate him," this is held illusory, since it cannot operate till the slave is *alienus*. There must, one would think, have been some other evidence of intention here; if not, the interpretation seems not very consistent with *favor libertatis*[1]. The view is Paul's, who comes to the same unfavourable conclusion, rather more rationally, on the words, *liber esto, si heredis esse desierit*[2]. Another case is that of a condition, possible on the face of it, but already impossible at the death owing to circumstances. This case, and the analogous one of supervening impossibility, will be discussed later in connexion with the topic of satisfaction of the condition[3].

Some conditions would doubtless avoid the gift: in general they are those which would avoid an institution[4]. There are, however, cases in which a condition is allowed in manumissions which would be differently treated in legacies. Ulpian tells us that a manumission at the discretion of a third party is valid[5], while we learn elsewhere that gifts by will in such a form are void[6], though they can be effectively made in a disguised form, *e.g. si Maevius Capitolium ascenderit*[7]. But there is perhaps no distinction here, since Ulpian seems to have rejected this rather absurd differentiation, and to have considered all such gifts valid whether disguised or not[8]. As in' case of legacy the gift might be at the discretion of the donee himself[9].

A case of more importance is that of negative conditions. Liberty on such a condition, if taken literally, is nugatory, for till the death of the man it cannot be said that he will not do the thing, and the *cautio Muciana*, by which this difficulty is avoided in ordinary legacies, has no application here. Liberty once effective is irrevocable: it is inconceivable that the man should become a slave again on failing to observe the condition. Moreover, as liberty is inestimable it is impossible to give security for it. Thus such gifts seem to have been made in a derisive way, and Pomponius, taking the case, *si Capitolium non ascenderit*, says that Julian holds that if it appears that the testator meant the gift not to take effect till death it is a nullity, as a gift *cum moreretur* would be[10]. On the other hand if there was no such intent, the words

---

[1] 40. 4. 39. An analogous *institutio* was better treated. Where a man was to be *heres* if he freed a *servus hereditarius*, the mere act of manumission was held by Labeo to be a satisfaction of the condition though it was void: *verum est eum manumisisse*, 28. 7. 20. 1.
[2] 40. 4. 39. *in fin.*
[3] *Post*, p. 489. See De Ruggiero, Dies Impossibilis, 29 *sqq.*; Rabel, Aus Röm. und Bürg. Recht, 193 *sqq.*
[4] Accarias, *loc. cit.*
[5] 40. 5. 46. 2. The text deals with a *fideicommissum*, but its reasoning applies to direct gifts.
[6] 28. 5. 32. *pr.*; 35. 1. 52.   [7] 28. 5. 69; 35. 1. 52.
[8] 30. 43. 2; 31. 1. *pr.*; 40. 5. 46. 2. Bufnoir, *op. cit.* 195 *sqq.* As to such discretion in *fideicommissa, post*, pp. 516 *sq.*
[9] 40. 5. 46. 1. This may be true only of *fideicommissa*. Apart from condition he could not refuse.
[10] 40. 4. 61. *pr.*; 40. 7. 4. 1.

were construed also by Julian *favore libertatis*, as if they were "if he does not do it at the first opportunity[1]," so that if at any time he was able to do the thing and abstained, he was free. It is plain that in one of these cases the gift is treated as puerile and empty, while in the other the condition is put on that level.

But there are traces of another way of looking at the matter. It is obvious that a patron may have reasons for wishing a thing not to be done by the freedman, and it is not unreasonable that he should have his way here, as in legacies. The way seems to have been found by allowing *conditiones iurisiurandi*. We are told that where liberty is given on the condition of taking an oath, this cannot be remitted by the Praetor, since to remit the condition is to bar the gift, as the liberty cannot be attained *aliter quam si paritum fuerit condicioni*[2]. Such conditions are invalid in institutions and legacies[3], and our text adds that if the liberty is coupled with a legacy, and the same condition is applied to both, he does not get the legacy unless he swears[4]. Clearly not, for he is not free, and if it were struck out from the legacy alone, the legacy would be void[5]. If the legacy is under a condition of swearing, and the liberty simple, there is no difficulty: the condition is remitted[6]. The validity of such conditions in manumission applies to any act[7], but its importance is most obvious in reference to negative conditions, and it seems possible that it is on their account that the condition is allowed. Where a condition of swearing is remitted and the thing sworn is not improper, the beneficiary is not entitled to the gift until he does the thing[8], or, no doubt, in negative conditions, gives the *cautio* Muciana. Now, in manumission, if the condition of swearing not to do were remitted, it would be quite impossible to give the *cautio*: it is inapplicable. Accordingly, as the text says, to remit the oath is to bar the gift[9]. The oath is no great security since at least in later law it is not binding[10], though Venuleius[11] records an earlier doubt, but he speaks of those who have taken such an oath as *religione adstricti*[12].

We have already seen that a condition imposed may be adeemed, even in the same will, notwithstanding the technical point that it is, in strictness, not *datum* but *adscriptum*[13]. Apart from this, the slave is,

---

[1] 40. 4. 17. *pr.*; cp. 35. 1. 29.   [2] 40. 4. 12. *pr.*   [3] 28. 7. 8.
[4] 40. 4. 12. 1.   [5] *Ante*, p. 471.   [6] 40. 4. 12. 2.
[7] 40. 4. 36; 40. 7. 13. 3.   [8] 28. 7. 8. 6, 7.   [9] 40. 4. 12. *pr.*
[10] 38. 1. 7. *pr.*, 2; 40. 4. 36.   [11] 40. 12. 44. *pr.*
[12] Bodemeyer, *op. cit.* 54, cites many attempts at explaining the allowance of *conditiones iurisiurandi*. His own requires *impedire* to mean "make more difficult." Bufnoir, *op. cit.* 47, following Vangerow, Pand. § 434, thinks the right conferred by the Praetor in remitting the penalty is only praetorian, and as there is no true praetorian liberty, the freedom could be acquired only by doing the thing. Here too *impedire* is given the above sense. See also Karlowa, R. R. G. 2. 137. But Pernice has shewn (Labeo, 3. 54) that the effect of release of the condition is not to give a merely praetorian title.
[13] 34. 4. 3. 9; 35. 1. 53.

till the condition is wholly satisfied, the slave of the heir[1]. He may not know at once when it is satisfied, and it is provided that if, in ignorance of the arrival of the condition, he enters on an inheritance at the order of the *heres* who holds him, he is not personally bound[2]. But if he is in doubt as to whether it is satisfied or not, Paul cites Julian as holding that he is, so to speak, " put upon enquiry," and so is bound[3].

There remains for discussion, in relation to conditions in general, the question, what amounts to fulfilment of the condition ? The rule is that it must be actually and completely fulfilled[4], though *in obscura voluntate manumittentis favendum est libertati*[5].

The meaning of a condition " to serve my *heres* (or Titius) for a certain time " is the subject of discussion. *Servire* and *operas dare* are equivalent, neither need involve slavery and thus they may be done to a third person[6]. The service must be personally rendered[7], and 100 *operae* means 100 days' work[8]. They should be rendered continuously, but days during which the man is prevented from working by illness or other good cause are credited to him as days of work[9].

Satisfaction of the condition is all that is needed[10]. If the condition is a promise or oath to do something, the promise or oath fulfils the condition and the freedom is gained, though, as we have seen, the promise is void as having been made by a slave[11]. Where the condition was " to be free on handing over the *peculium*," and the man gave up everything, he was free though he owed debts to his owner[12]. In answering the question whether the condition is satisfied or not there is a general *favor libertatis*. Thus where the condition of liberty given to a woman was " if her first child be a male," and she has twins, one of each sex, there is a presumption, apart from actual knowledge, that the male is the elder, and thus the daughter is *ingenua*[13]. If two are made free on the same condition, it is applied separately to each, if this is possible and will save the gift, *e.g.* " if they are mine at my death[14]."

---

1 Ulp. 2. 2; D. 40. 7. 9. *pr. Ante*, p. 286.
2 29. 2. 74. 3. As to any right of *bonae fidei possessor, ante*, p. 346.
3 29. 2. 74. 4.   4 40. 7. 3. 12.
5 50. 17. 179. "To be free when my debts are paid." They must be paid : it is immaterial that the *heres* is rich, 40. 7. 39. 1. If the *heres* wilfully delays, the rules as to prevention may come into operation, 40. 5. 41. 1. "To be free if he goes to Capua." He must go though the journey be otherwise aimless, 40. 4. 61. 1. The element of time may be material here. See also 35. 1. 44. 10.
6 40. 7. 4. 4, 41. *pr.* The text (4. 4)⁻adds that the will may shew that the testator meant " be a slave to." See *post*, p. 493.
7 40. 4. 13. *pr.*; 40. 7. 20. 5, 39. 5.   8 40. 7. 20. 5.
9 40. 7. 4. 5. This does not turn on impossibility, but on the notion that such a prevention is an ordinary incident of continuous service. Days in which the man is *in fuga*, or raising a claim of liberty, or suffering punishment for crime, do not count, and other days must be served in their stead, 40. 7. 4. 8, 14. 1, 39. 3.
10 But *cum dare poterit* means when he does pay, 40. 7. 4. 12.
11 40. 7. 13. 3, 24, 41. 1.   12 40. 7. 40. 1.   13 34. 5. 10. 1.
14 32. 29. 4. The rule is the same in legacy. Where two were to be free on paying 10, either was free on paying 5. As to legacies, cp. 35. 1. 112. 1.

So where the condition was *si rationes reddiderint*, unless it had been a joint administration, in which case neither was free till the whole was adjusted[1]. If the act is indivisible, both are free if one has done it[2]. If there are two different gifts the *statuliber* may choose the easier[3] (which he may not in legacy), or, as it is put in other texts, the *levissima scriptura* applies, and that is *levissima* through which liberty is attained[4], *i.e.* he has not to make a choice, but may take the benefit of that which occurs first. This applies only if the two gifts are distinct; if they are *coniunctim*, *i.e.* "if he do this and that," he must satisfy both[5].

If a *statuliber* is alienated, and the condition is an act to be done by him in relation to someone else, the question arises: to whom must he satisfy the condition? This will be discussed in relation to two specially important conditions, *pecuniam dare* and *rationes reddere*, which will need separate discussion. Here it is enough to lay down the general rule. Any condition which admits of it may be done to the acquirer[6], but personal service, such as to teach his child, remains with the *heres* though the man be assigned[7]. But it must be an alienation of the *dominium*: to give a usufruct to a third person does not enable the payment or other act to be rendered to the usufructuary[8]. It should be added that if the condition is doing work for anyone, the slave himself must do it, but money may be paid by anyone[9].

There were, however, circumstances under which the liberty took effect though the condition was not in fact satisfied. Before entering on these it is desirable to point out that *dies* and *conditio* are sometimes intermingled in a way which makes two observations necessary.

(i) The same modality may be construed as *dies* in one case and as *conditio* in another, the decision turning sometimes on construction of the testator's language and in others on extraneous considerations such as *favor libertatis*. This is most commonly illustrated by cases in which a gift is to take effect "when X is 20," and the like. Here if X dies under 20 it may be said that the condition has failed, or it may be said that the words were a mere way of describing a certain date which has in fact arrived. Both views are found[10].

---

[1] 40. 4. 13. 2.   [2] *h. l. pr.*
[3] 35. 1. 51. *pr.*, 87—89.   [4] 35. 1. 35; 40. 4. 5.
[5] 40. 4. 45. In one case the words were "Let S be free when he is 30. Let S be not free if he does not give 10." These are not alternative gifts, one *ex die* and the other conditional. The second is in form an ademption, which puts the gift under a contrary condition, so that he is to be free at 30 if he pays 10, D. 40. 7. 13. 5. Cp. 34. 4. 14. *pr.*; 40. 4. 59. 2.
[6] 40. 7. 6. 3. The rule is as old as the XII Tables, *h. t.* 29. 1. See Appleton, Le Testament Romain, 86.
[7] 40. 7. 6. 7, which shews a more complex rule in relation to the condition of rendering accounts.
[8] 40. 7. 7.   [9] *h. t.* 39. 5.
[10] *e.g.* 36. 2. 22. *pr.*; C. 6. 53. 5; 7. 2. 8. Brunetti, Dies Incertus, 160; *post*, p. 491.

(ii) A condition may, indeed it usually will, include *dies*. Here, though from any cause the donee be released from the condition, the gift will not take effect till the time has elapsed. This is illustrated in a number of texts[1] and must be borne in mind when these cases of release are under discussion. The plain reason is given, by Paul, that it is absurd that the gift should take effect before it would have done so had the condition been satisfied in the ordinary way[2], the testator having imposed both condition and *dies*, and the former alone having been released. If, however, there is no express *dies* and the condition is invalid *ab initio*, the *dies* is not considered[3].

In discussing the circumstances under which a condition is released it is necessary to look somewhat closely at the Roman conception of Impossibility. We know that where a condition is impossible in the nature of things[4] it is struck out in all gifts by will. But it is not easy to say what is impossible in the nature of things. What seemed inconceivable to a Roman might be an everyday event now[5]. But the exact position of the line is not important: the point to note is that it commonly means a condition which is on the face of it inconceivable[6]. This opens up the question how the jurists looked at impossibility on the facts—latent impossibility, either existing at the time of the will or supervening. It may be said at once that, at least in the case of wills, they do not seem in general to have applied the notion of impossibility to cases of supervening impossibility—it is indeed difficult to treat a provision as *non scriptum* by reason of an event subsequent to the making of the document. It is in fact *casus* rather than impossibility[7]. There are evidences of doubt as to the treatment of cases in which the condition becomes, or is, impossible in fact, before the *aditio*: with these we shall shortly deal. Another point of interest is that the illustrations of patent impossibility always seem to be cases in which there was something to be done or left undone by the donee. Such a condition as "if there shall be 370 days in the year" is never taken as an illustration. In one text which contains some dispute, and traces of more, the condition is *si filia et mater mea vivent* and one of these is dead at the time of the will[8]. This is a case of latent impossibility existing at the time of the will, and the condition does not contemplate action by the donee. It is clear that it gives difficulty and Pomponius, or perhaps Tribonian, describes it as a case of "quasi-impossibility."

1 *e.g.* 40. 4. 41. 1 (corrupt); 40. 5. 41. *pr.*; 40. 7. 3. 15, 4. 2, 20. 5.   Cp. 34. 1. 18. 2; 45. 1. 8.
2 40. 7. 4. 2.   The final words in 40. 4. 41. 1 are an interpolation.
3 Cp. 45. 1. 8.   An analogous rule in case of prevention, *post*, p. 493.
4 P. 3. 4 b. 1.   See *ante*, p. 484.
5 A man was instituted "if he build a monument in three days." Even this the lawyers, after hesitation, decide to be quasi impossible, 28. 7. 6.
6 There were forms of such impossibility in institutions which could not have arisen in gifts of liberty, 28. 7. 4. *pr.*, 10, 20. *pr.*
7 Cp. C. 6. 46. 6.   8 35. 1. 6. 1, *in fin.*

We can now consider the different cases which present themselves in the texts.

There is a well marked type of case in which the gift is made to depend on the attainment of a certain age by X—the man is to be free if (or when) X is 20. This is a case of *dies incertus an, certus quando*. Here, in the texts which speak of gifts of liberty either fiduciary or direct, the death of X under 20 is treated as immaterial[1]. On the other hand some of the texts make it clear, by way of contrast, that in the case of legacy on the same condition, the death under the age would be regarded as amounting to failure of a condition[2]. This of itself would shew that the rule has nothing to do with impossibility, since, if it were treated as impossible both sorts of gift would be valid. We are, however, left in no doubt: we are told that it is an exceptional rule laid down *favore libertatis*, the modality being treated as *dies* in this case[3].

The case of ordinary condition to be performed by the donee is treated in the same way, where impossibility supervenes after *aditio*. In the case of legacy, the condition is regarded as having failed[4]: in gifts of liberty the other view is taken, *favore libertatis*, and the gift takes effect[5]. In the case in which the condition is the payment of money to X and X dies before it is paid, there may be the further complication that the man was not ready to pay the money at the time of the death. But Julian observes that the whole favourable rule is a matter of *constitutum ius* resulting from *favor libertatis* and not resting on any logical principle of interpretation, and that thus the man will be free if at any time he has the money[6].

In the case of latent impossibility arising before the *aditio* there is more difficulty. Where the thing not only is impossible, but always was, *i.e.* where it assumes a state of facts which never existed, it is a *falsa conditio* and the gift whether of property or liberty is good[7]. The same seems to be the case where part of the condition is on that footing, the rest being separable, e.ʹ. a gift of *hereditas* "if my wife and my daughter X survive," and the testator never had a daughter: the

---

[1] 40. 4. 16; 40. 5. 23. 3, 41. 10; 40. 7. 19; C. 7. 4. 9.   [2] 40. 4. 16; 40. 5. 23. 3.

[3] *Ibid.*; 40. 7. 19. The case of death of X under the required age before *dies cedens* is not considered. Probably the gift is good, arg. 40. 7. 28. *pr.*

[4] 35. 1. 31. *fin.*; *h. t.* 94. *pr.*; 40. 7. 20. 3; C. 6. 46. 4.

[5] 35. 1. 94. *pr.*; 40. 7. 4. 2, 20. 3; Ulp. 2. 6.   The decision in 35. 1. 112. 1 is a forced separation of the conditions, *benigna interpretatione*.

[6] 40. 7. 20. 3. Where the gift was *S si rationes reddiderit cum contubernali sua liber esto*, and S died after the *aditio* without rendering accounts, Paul appears to doubt if there is any real *coniunctio*, and suggests that the condition does not apply to the gift to the woman. But he holds that if it does and if there are accounts to render, the whole thing fails, 35. 1. 81. Julian quoted by Gaius in a very ambiguous passage thinks the gifts are distinct but under the same condition, so that the woman can satisfy it, 40. 7. 31. 1.

[7] 30. 104. 1; 35. 1. 72. 7, 8; 40. 5. 41. 16; 40. 7. 26. 1; *ante*, p. 484. In some of these cases it is an act to be done.

gift is good, the reference to the daughter being ignored[1]. Where the impossibility is one which arises before the will is opened, whether before or after it is made, the matter is complicated by questions of interpretation, themselves affected by the existence of provisions independent of the purpose of the gift. But, so far as can be made out, the view of the later classics, accepted in the Digest, seems to be that in case of liberty the gift takes effect, though it is clear that this is *favore libertatis,* and independent of logic[2]. In case of legacy the gift fails[3], so that it is no question of impossibility. But there are some texts which seem at least to contradict these conclusions and which need to be carefully looked at.

In one text Paul makes the liberty fail[4]. The man is to be free if a usufruct in him given to X by the will ceases to exist. In point of fact it never arose, the fructuary not having survived to take it. On such facts the gift fails, says Paul. The condition fails, since that which never began cannot have ended. The rule, which is from Neratius, ignores *favor libertatis,* and is moreover a piece of literal interpretation, which quite disregards the plain intent of the testator. The gift is in effect one at the death of X.

Where a woman is to have a legacy if she marries *arbitratu Seii* she will take the legacy though she marry without his consent, and even though he be dead, *vivo testatore*[5]. This is due to the fact that such a condition is in practice one that she shall not marry without his consent, which is void[6]. The reason assigned for allowing the gift to be good though S be dead is given by Papinian in the words *quia suspensa quoque pro nihilo foret,* words which shew that some special reason was needed and that in ordinary cases the gift would have failed. Pomponius, however, while dealing with this case[7] applies the same rule to a legacy, *si eum manumisisses,* where the man died *vivo testatore.* His reasoning uses language appropriate to prevention, *quia per te non stetit quominus perveniat ad libertatem,* a principle which, as we shall shortly see, ought not to be applied with this breadth to legacies. Javolenus applies it to a case of impossibility arising before *aditio* in a case of liberty, but expressly observes that it is *favore libertatis*[8].

---

[1] 28. 5. 46.   [2] 40. 7. 28. *pr.*, 39. 4.   [3] 35. 1. 31.
[4] *h. t.* 96. *pr.*   [5] 30. 54. 1, 2; 35. 1. 72. 4, 28. *pr.*
[6] Other texts, Pothier ad D. 35. 1, § xxxviii.
[7] 30. 54. 2. Pothier (*ad h. l.*) supposes this rule to apply where it is a condition not involving cooperation of another person.
[8] 40. 7. 28. *pr.* Bufnoir, *op. cit.* 91, shews that Ulpian in 9. 2. 23. 2 holds that the condition has failed in such a case. He cites and refutes reconciliations by Vangerow and others. B. himself holds that 30. 54. 2 deals with *modus.* But on its terms it does not. But, where one is to be *heres* if he swears to free S, and S dies *vivo testatore,* the gift is good, though in such cases the condition is remitted and actual freeing substituted. This confirms our rule, since the substituted act is to be done after the acquisition. It is *modus,* not condition: this, as appears from the hypotheses cited in support, is why the gift is good, 28. 7. 8. 7. *Ante,* p. 483. Bufnoir, *op. cit.* 90.

The view stated above as that of the later classics was not accepted without dispute, of which the texts shew traces. Thus we are told that Labeo and Ofilius declared a gift of liberty to fail, if the person to whom money was to be paid as a condition died, *vivo testatore*, and that Trebatius held the same view if the death was before the will was made[1]. This last view may, of course, possibly mean merely that Trebatius has a derisory gift in mind[2]. Pomponius[3] discusses a case of gift of *hereditas* on condition of freeing certain slaves, some of whom were in fact dead when the will was made. He cites Neratius, (whom we have just seen holding a severe view[4],) as thinking that the condition has failed, and that the notion of impossibility is not applicable. But he cites Labeo and Servius as holding that in a similar case, where however the condition was not something to be done[5] but the survival of two persons of whom one was dead at the time the will was made, the condition has not failed, and Sabinus and Cassius as holding that this is a case of quasi-impossibility[6]. This text involves two points, *i.e.* that the distinction between legacy and liberty where the impossibility occurs *vivo testatore* must be limited to the case *post testamentum factum*, and that where a condition has separable parts, each part has to be considered by itself for the purpose of these rules. But this can hardly be an adequate account of the law where impossibility had arisen before the will was made. The text tells us too little. Probably the state of the testator's knowledge was material, and no doubt this text is an indication of far-reaching differences of opinion[7].

Prevention of fulfilment brings other distinctions into prominence. Just as it was difficult to set exact limits to the notion "impossible," so it is not quite easy to say exactly what is meant by " prevention," but for the purpose of the rules now to be stated, two points must be made clear. Prevention is essentially an interference with the action of the donee. Hence the rules do not apply to conditions which have to be satisfied without the cooperation of the donee. This appears, apart from the specific rules which express the distinction, in the language commonly used in expressing the principle generally. The texts usually speak of *his* satisfaction of the condition being prevented[8]. Further, the thing done does not amount to prevention, unless it was

---

[1] 40. 7. 39. 4.   Javolenus considers Labeo right in principle but says that a more liberal view is accepted.
[2] *Ante*, p. 485.   [3] 35. 1. 6. 1.
[4] 35. 1. 96. *pr.*   [5] *Ante*, p. 489.
[6] The rule as to the effect of impossibility in wills is Sabinian, G. 3. 98.
[7] Cp. Pothier, ad 35. 1, § xx; Bufnoir, *op. cit.* 23; Vangerow, Pand. § 435.
[8] *Quominus statuliber conditioni pareat*, Ulp. 2. 5; *quominus statuliber conditionem praestare possit*, Festus, *s.v. statuliber; si nemo eos impediat*, 40. 7. 3. *pr.*, and the like, 40. 4. 55; 40. 7. 3. 1.

done with a view to prevention[1]; at least where the prevention takes the form of prohibition and not of rendering the thing impossible. On the other hand if it is a definite act of prevention it is presumed to have been so intended rather than as a normal exercise of right[2].

The general rule on the matter is that, where the *statuliber* is prevented from doing the act which[3] is a fulfilment of the condition, he is placed in the same position as if the act had been done. It is immaterial for this purpose whether the person who prevents is one like the *heres*, interested in its non-performance[4], or one to whom or with whose cooperation it is to be done[5], or any third person: it is enough that someone prevented fulfilment[6]. It may be noted that the rule in *hereditas* and legacy is not so wide: it releases only in the first two cases[7]. On the other hand where the condition is to be fulfilled without the cooperation of the slave and the person to do it refuses, or fails to do it, there is no relief, any more than there would be in any other form of gift[8].

Prevention has the effect of putting the man in the same position as if he had not been prevented. If even apart from the prevention he could not have satisfied the condition, the prevention does not make him free: it is not true that *non per eum stat*. Thus where the *heres* refuses to receive the accounts but the *statuliber* is in arrear and has not the means to pay up the balance due from him he is not free[9]. In the same way, if the act would necessarily take time, *e.g.* to do so many days' work for the *heres* or another[10], to go to Capua, to go to Spain and gather in the crops[11], or to make a series of periodical payments[12], the man is not freed by refusal to let him begin work, or start on the journey, or make the first payment. These rules, however, seem to apply only to such prevention as takes the form of prohibition or refusal: if it takes the form of making the thing impossible, the man seems to be free at once. Thus where he was directed *servire heredi* for a time and was manumitted or sold by the *heres*, he was free *ex testamento*[13] at once[14]. The word *servire* here means " be slave to ": in the one case this is made impossible: in the other it is made impossible for the *statuliber* to do it. It is not clear why the time was not required

---

[1] 40. 7. 38.   [2] *h. t.* 3. 3.
[3] With or without the cooperation of another person.
[4] Ulp. 2. 5; Festus, *loc. cit.*; D. 35. 1. 24, 57, 78; 40. 7. 3. 13, 4. 16, 17, 23. 1; 50. 17. 161.
[5] Or his guardian, Ulp. 2. 6; D. 35. 1. 78; 40. 7. 3. 10, *etc.*
[6] 40. 5. 55; 40. 7. 3. *pr.*
[7] 28. 7. 3, 11; 30. 92. 1; 35. 1. 14, 21, 31; 36. 2. 5. 5; 50. 17. 161.
[8] Consistently with all this, if one *heres* prevents a payment on which liberty is conditioned, the *statuliber* is free, 40. 7. 3. 4, while if he was to pay to two and one refuses he is released only *pro parte*, but can tender the same money to the other, 40. 7. 4. 3. See *post*, p. 503.
[9] 40. 7. 34. 1.   [10] 34. 1. 57; 40. 7. 3. 15, 4. 4, 20. 5.
[11] *Ibid.*; 40. 7. 34. 1.   [12] As to a difficulty in 40. 4. 41. 1, *post*, p. 499.
[13] 40. 7. 3. 15, 17.
[14] In classical law the manumission would commonly make him only a latin: in no case would it make him *libertus orcinus*.

to elapse.   One text purports to give the reason[1], but all this amounts to is that refusal is only prevention of a part: the logical result would be that in the case where it was made impossible the man is free at the expiry of the time with no further tender, not that he is free at once.

An enactment of Justinian's[2] deals with a case which he declares to have divided the jurists.   A slave was to be free on paying money to the heir.   He started to travel with it to the heir, but was robbed of the money on the way.   The question was, did this suffice under the condition ?   Clearly there was no impossibility, though on the facts it had become impossible to the man.   The question seems to mean : was this prevention, *i.e.*, could it be said *per eum non stare*, since it was his going on the journey which made it possible to rob him ?   Justinian settles it by deciding that in such cases *per eum stat* only when he intentionally does not fulfil the condition : in all other cases of prevention by persons or *casus* he is to be free, but to remain liable for the value of the render, except in so far as it has been repudiated by the person to whom it was to have been made.

There remain for consideration two conditions of exceptional importance.

(*a*)   *Rationes reddere.*   The importance of this condition is shewn by the frequency of its appearance in the Digest.   It is found also in a surviving roman will[3].   Though, as we have seen, all freed slaves may be called on to render an account[4] of what they hold, the importance of making it a condition is that less risk is run, since he must make the statement and render before he is free.   Moreover all that can be required of him after the freedom, apart from the condition, is that he hand over the accounts and the property of the testator which he holds.   No personal action will lie against him for anything done while he was a slave[5].

The condition practically means that he must state and account for all moneys that he has had to administer[6].   He must make his account in good faith and with due care, though a mere mistake, even negligent, is not a breach of the condition[7].   His account must shew his *gestio* to have been in good faith, at least to the extent that he must debit himself with anything he has wrongfully taken away, and of course there must be no false credits[8].   He must state all needful details, going over his account books, and giving a proper account of matters not in writing[9].   The condition covers the whole field of administration,

---

[1] 40. 7. 3. 15.   [2] C. 6. 46. 6.
[3] Testamentum Dasumii, Girard, Textes, 767.
[4] 40. 4. 17. 1; 40. 5. 37.   [5] *Ibid.*; C. 7. 2. 4.   *Post*, ch. xxix.
[6] If he has never administered it is a void condition, 40. 7. 26. 1.
[7] 35. 1. 32, 112. 3; 40. 4. 22.   [8] 35. 1. 111; C. 7. 2. 4.
[9] 40. 7. 26. *pr.*

not merely trading[1]. If he has given credit, he must shew, not indeed that the debtor is solvent, but that at the time of the transaction he was such that a *bonus paterfamilias* might reasonably have such dealings with him[2]. He has not merely to render an account: he must hand over the *reliqua*, *i.e.* all property of the estate in his possession[3]. This implies that he must get in all debts now recoverable, rents due and so forth, and must make good anything he has made away with and bad debts incurred through his negligence[4], but not losses resulting from *casus*[5]. What is required is a true and just account and render: the law prescribes no exact steps[6]. He must account for receipts since the death, and, if this seems to be intended, give the same detailed account of his administration since, as before[7]. The account must be rendered where the person is, to whom it is to be rendered, at least if that person is away on public business, but in other cases reasonable arrangements may be made to suit the case[8], and a deputy appointed to receive the account[9]. Each heir is entitled to his share of the *reliqua*, and though this may be excluded by apt words, it will not be by the naming of some of the heirs in the condition[10].

The condition adds, as we have seen, to the obligation on the slave[11], but a good deal turns on the wording of it. If it was merely *reliqua reddere*[12], this is satisfied by paying over the balance without giving the full means of examining the accounts which was needed under the condition *rationes reddere*[13]. If the condition is that he is so to render accounts as to satisfy X, he must do this: even satisfaction of the curator of X *apud iudicem* will not suffice, unless X is present and assenting[14] If the condition is *si rationes diligenter tractasset*, this involves *rationes reddere*, and proof that his diligence has been exercised in the interest of the master, and not in his own[15]. Where it is *si rationes diligenter tractasse videbitur* this means *videri poterit*[16]. If a time is set within which the account is to be rendered, and by his fault it is not done at the expiry of the time, he has not satisfied the condition[17]. As we have seen, if the condition is to account within

---

[1] 35. 1. 111; 40. 5. 41. 11 *omne quod quoquo genere actum fidemque servi respiceret.*
[2] 35. 1. 111; 40. 5. 41. 17.
[3] 35. 1. 111; 40. 7. 31; C. 7. 2. 4.   Liquid assets must be given at once and security for the rest, 40. 7. 5. *pr.*   [4] 40. 7. 40. 4—8.
[5] 40. 4. 22; 40. 5. 41. 7. He is responsible for *adiutores* if their malversation is in any way due to his negligence, 40. 7. 40. 4.
[6] Thus the fact that where *peculium* is left to him he takes it away before he has rendered his account does not bar liberty, *h. l.* 6. Nor does the fact that the testator, having been ill, has not signed the accounts for a long time, *h. l.* 3.
[7] *h. l. pr.*; 40. 5. 41. 10. If needed an *arbiter* will be appointed to settle disputed points, 35. 1. 50; 40. 1. 5. 1; 40. 7. 21. *pr.*
[8] 35. 1. 112. 3.   [9] 40. 7. 4. *pr.*   [10] *h. t.* 12; *post*, p. 500.
[11] 3. 5. 16—18. 1, 44. 1.   [12] 35. 1. 82.
[13] *Ibid.* A condition *ne rationes reddat* is not a gift of *peculium*, but an absolution from the duty of rendering strict account, the liberty being unconditional. He must hand over any balance and account for *dolus* but there will be no enquiry into negligence, 30. 119.
[14] 40. 4. 53.   [15] *h. t.* 8; 40. 7. 21. *pr.*
[16] *i.e.* to an *arbiter*, 40. 7. 21. *pr.*   [17] 40. 5. 41. 12.

30 days from the death, and the *aditio* is not till later, the liberty
does not fail, as it is not his fault[1]. Titius by his will[2] left certain
servi actores to different persons, *si rationes heredi reddiderint*, and in
another place said, " All the slaves whom I have legated or freed, I
wish to render their accounts within four months, and to be handed
over to those to whom I have left them." Later in the will he freed
other *actores*, with the condition *si rationes heredi reddiderint*. The
time passed and without any fault of the heir[3], the accounts were not
rendered. Were the men barred or could they still claim their liberty
by satisfying the condition later? The answer given by Scaevola is
that it is for the person before whom the case comes to consider
whether this is intended as a condition limiting the time given to the
slaves or whether it is really intended to impose speediness on the
heirs, by preventing them from dawdling in the matter. In the former
case the claim is barred : in the latter it is not[4].

The ordinary rules apply as to prevention. If the slave is prevented
by the *heres* from paying over the *reliqua* after the account has been
adjusted and the *res peculiares* have been sold, he is free as if he had
paid[5]. So if the *heres* is *in mora* in receiving the accounts, the slave
is free if he tenders them and the balance[6]. The text adds that it is
for the *arbiter* to decide which party is *in mora*, and to determine
accordingly, and further that declaration of waiver of right to the
balance, by the heir, satisfies the condition.

Some cases in which the difficulties are really of construction are
discussed[7]. In one of these the *heres* is *impubes*. S is freed *ratione
reddita*, and he agrees with the *tutor* to take some of the money due
and divide it. The *tutor* certifies the account as correct. The man
is not free, for though the rule is that the *reliqua* may be paid to
the *tutor* of the *heres*, and his prevention of payment has the same
effect as the heir's, this applies only where the *statuliber* and the *tutor*
are not fraudulent. Here, the text says, as in alienation of property, the
tutor can deprive the *pupillus* only where there is no collusive fraud[8].

(*b*)   *Pecuniam dare.* If we may judge from its frequent recurrence
in the sources, this was the most common and economically important
of all the conditions. Its typical form is, *si* 10 *det heredi*, but *cum
decem dabit* or *cum decem dare poterit* are equivalent forms[9].

---

[1] 40. 7. 28. *pr.*   [2] 40. 7. 40. 7.   [3] Mommsen, *ad h. l.*
[4] The text adds, but the words look like Tribonian, that there is a general presumption in
favour of the *statuliber*.
[5] 40. 7. 23. 1.   [6] *h. t.* 34. 1.
[7] As to *S si rationes reddiderit cum contubernali sua liber esto*, *ante*, p. 490. The words are
clearly capable of many interpretations.   [8] 40. 4. 22.
[9] 40. 7. 3. 12. Money was sometimes borrowed by the slave for the purpose. It is in such
cases and where the *peculium* has been left to him that the rule is important that what is paid
wrongly or in excess can be recovered, 12. 4. 3. 6 ; 40. 7. 3. 6.

Money paid under such a condition is a *mortis causa capio*, though it is not a *donatio*, no matter by whom or to whom it is paid[1]. A question of some difficulty arises where the *lex* Falcidia and similar legislation comes into operation. The point of importance seems to be that though it is a *mortis causa capio*, it is not necessarily acquired *hereditario iure*[2]. If, however, it is *ex bonis mortui* (which certainly covers the *peculium* which the *statuliber* had at the time of the death) and is paid to the heir, it is acquired *iure hereditario* and must be debited to him, when his quarter is being made up for the purpose of the Falcidia[3]. So too it counts towards the half that an *orbus* may take[4]. If there are two or more heirs, and the payment is to be made to one, only that part of it which corresponds to his share in the *hereditas* is acquired *hereditario iure*, and counts towards making up his quarter: the rest is an independent *mortis causa capio*[5]. If it is paid from outside—not *ex bonis mortui*, the *lex* Falcidia has no application to it[6]. There are, however, cases in which it seems to be doubtful whether it is *ex bonis mortui* or not. According to Ulpian, if the slave acquires the money only after the death, it cannot be said to be *ex bonis mortui*, and so will not be imputable[7]. Papinian, however, holds that even though it were given to the *statuliber* to be paid to the *heres* it becomes part of the *peculium*, and even if it were handed direct by the *extraneus* in the presence of the *libertus*. It is only if it is handed over by a third person without the presence of the *libertus* that the taker holds it really *aliunde*, so that it is not acquired *hereditario iure*[8]. Apparently Ulpian's view would exclude all acquisitions to the estate after the death—which certainly was not the law for his time[9].

Money validly paid under the condition is of course irrecoverable. But if it was not due it can be recovered, like an *indebitum*[10]. The remedy will be *condictio* or *vindicatio* according as the transaction has or has not vested ownership in the *heres*. This is illustrated by many texts. There can be no recovery if it was paid in full knowledge of the facts[11]. It is not strictly an *indebitum* in any case, and it is treated mainly under the head, possibly a creation of the compilers, of *condictio causa data causa non secuta*[12]. If there is no condition and he is really

---

[1] 39. 6. 8. *pr.*, 31. 2, 38. See *post*, p. 501.   [2] 35. 2. 76. *pr.*
[8] 39. 6. 41; 35. 2. 76. *pr.*
[4] 39. 6. 36. It must be accounted for in *hereditatis petitio*, and in *restitutio hereditatis* under a *fideicommissum*, 39. 6. 41.
[5] 35. 2. 76. *pr.* It is in no way common and need not be accounted for in *familiae erciscundae*, 10. 2. 20. 9.
[6] 35. 2. 44, 76. *pr.*   [7] 39. 6. 36.   [8] 39. 6. 41.
[9] *Ante*, pp. 256 *sqq.* The rule interpreted in these texts is that what a *heres* acquires *hereditario iure ex bonis mortui* counts towards the Falcidian quarter.
[10] In that case it is not imputable under the *lex* Falcidia, 35. 1. 44.
[11] *e.g.* by way of ingratiation or to gain some indirect advantage, 12. 4. 3. 7.
[12] 12. 4. As to this and its relation to *condictio ob rem dati*, Roby, Rom. Priv. Law, 2. 77. The matter is discussed in two texts in the title on *condictio indebiti*, 12. 6. 34, 53.

free, and he has paid it out of his own money he can condict it[1]. But
if he has given it out of *peculium* to the *heres*, thinking, as he would,
that the money already belonged to the *heres*, there has been no
transfer of *dominium*, and if it came, for instance, from a part of the
peculium which he has acquired after he is free, the ownership remains
with him and he can vindicate[2]. And supposing the payment was not
to the *heres* but to an *extraneus*, here too if it was a *res peculiaris*, as
he was not authorised so to deal with it, the ownership will not pass
and the *heres* can vindicate. But if a third person has paid it to the
extraneus, or the man has paid it himself, after he is really free, out
of his property, the *dominium* will pass and the proper remedy is
condictio[3].

Proculus lays down the same rule for the case where the will is
not valid : money paid *ex peculio* to an outsider can be vindicated[4].
Scaevola discusses another case. A man really free but supposed to
be a slave, receives a gift of liberty from his supposed *dominus* on a
condition of 10 annual payments to the *heres*. After paying 8 he
discovers that he is an *ingenuus*. He can recover by *condictio* if he
has paid out of what he has acquired otherwise than *ex operis* or *ex re
possessoris*. If it did come from that, he was merely giving the *heres*
what was his already[5]. In all these cases there is no real divergence
of opinion, but in another case there is. In a will a slave receives
liberty on condition of payment to the *heres*. By a codicil he receives
an unconditional gift. Before he hears of the codicil he pays the
money. Can he recover it ? Celsus *pater* thinks he cannot. Celsus
filius, on grounds of equity, says that he can, and Ulpian adopts this
view[6]. Nothing is said as to the reason for the view of the elder
Celsus, or as to the source from which the money came, and each
omission increases the difficulty of repairing the other. For the question
to arise at all the money must have been paid from something which
was not at the time of payment the property of the *heres*. The point
is perhaps that the condition not having been adeemed, perhaps not
having been adeemable[7], exists, and he has acted under the wrong gift[8].

As to what amounts to fulfilment of the condition, the ordinary
principles apply, but some special rules need mention. A condition
to give is satisfied by payment by a third person either with or without

---

[1] 12. 4. 3. 6.   [2] *h. l.* 8.
[3] *Ibid.* We do not discuss the point that here he is handing over his own property thinking
it another's and yet Ulpian allows property to pass. He denies this elsewhere (41. 1. 35), but
Marcellus asserts it (17. 1. 49). See Monro, De Adquirendo Dominio, *ad* 41. 1. 35, and the
references.
[4] 12. 6. 53. He adds that where it is paid to *extraneus* by a third person the master of the
slave is strictly the proper person to condict it but that it is *benignius* and *utilius* to let the
actual loser sue directly.
[5] 12. 6. 67. *pr.*   [6] 12. 4. 3. 7.   [7] *Ante*, p. 467.
[8] See *ante*, p. 488. Pomponius may have introduced the rule there stated.

the presence of the actual slave[1]. The whole must be paid[2]. Further, as the payment is in satisfaction and not under an obligation, there is no alienation at all, till all is paid: up to that time the owner of it can vindicate it, and the alienation does not relate back for any purpose[3]. If a time is fixed, the payment must be within the time[4], which runs from _aditio_ if the will is not explicit[5], and even "thirty days from the death" is reckoned from the _aditio_, at least if it is necessary so to do to save the gift[6]. Where a man was to be free on paying 10 a month for 5 years, he is not free unless he pays it every month[7]. The heir's refusal of one payment does not release the _statu-liber_ from the others, though, as it does from that one, and the _heres_ may not change his mind, the same money may be offered when the next pay-day comes[8]. These texts point out, as we have already seen, that such directions involve _dies_ as well as _conditio_. It is, therefore, surprising to find two texts which say that if he offers all future payments at the date fixed for the first he will be free. In one of these texts the rule is justified by the consideration that the earlier loss of the slave is compensated by the earlier receipt of the money[9]. As the interest of the money bears no necessary relation to the value of the slave's services, the argument is not strong, and the form of the remarks strongly suggests Tribonian. In the other[10] it is given as a _benignior_ rule, and we are told that both benefit, the one by earlier freedom, the other by earlier payment. The point is the same, with the added suggestive fact that this line of argument is one which Justinian employs elsewhere[11]. Altogether it is difficult to credit this view to the classical law.

The giving must make the alienee owner of the money: thus it may not be stolen money[12]. The transfer must not be merely illusory. Where the _heres_ gave the man the money, "to pay me with," and he returned it, he was not free, though he would have been if the gift to him had been absolute[13]. It need not take the form of an actual _traditio_ to the _heres_. We have just seen that release of the payment sufficed[14]. If at the death of the _heres_ the man is found to have enriched the _hereditas_ to the required amount, _e.g._ by payment to creditors, provision of stores or the like, he is free[15].

If it is payable to the _heres_, the commonest case, since it is payable

---

1 39. 6. 41; 40. 7. 39. 5.
2 It may be by instalments but security does not suffice, 40. 7. 4. 6, 5. 1.
3 40. 7. 3. 5.   4 _h. t._ 23. _pr._   5 35. 1. 46.
6 40. 7. 3. 11.   7 _h. t._ 40. 2.
8 40. 7. 3. 13, _h. t._ 18. The _heres_ can release the payment, and manumission by him without payment does so, so as to bar his _heres_ from claiming, _h. t._ 34. _pr._
9 40. 4. 41. 1.   10 40. 7. 3. 14.   11 _e.g._ In. 2. 9. 2.
12 Unless _bona fide_ consumed by _heres_. But it may be proceeds of theft, 40. 7. 3. 9.
13 40. 7. 11.   14 _h. t._ 34. 1.   15 40. 7. 15. _pr._

to him if the will does not say to whom it is payable[1], we are told in several texts that it may be paid to *heres heredis*, the rule being due to Hadrian[2]. The point is that the personality of the payee is not imported into the condition, *favore libertatis*, for in legacy it is[3]. If the *heres* has died leaving no successor, we are told by Hermogenianus, that, *constituto iure*, the man is free, without paying at all. It is not clear whether he must have the money at the time of failure of heirs: this is suggested by the earlier part of the text[4], though the contrary suggestion is found in a remark of Julian reported by Ulpian, already considered[5]. The rule is the same even if the *heres* is mentioned by name[6]. He cannot pay it to a *pupillus heres* without the *auctoritas* of the *tutor*[7], a rule laid down rather on grounds of analogy than on strict principle, for it is not the payment of a debt[8]. If the words are *heredibus dato*, they take *pro rata*, but if they are mentioned by name they take *partes viriles*[9]. The text seems to indicate that if they are called *heredes* and also named they take *pro rata*[10]. If one *heres* renounces the institution the payment is to be made wholly to the other[11], though if having actually entered he refuses the money, there is no accrual to the other, who is only entitled to his share, which may be satisfied with the same money[12].

If it is to be paid to an *extraneus* the rules are much the same. If the payee is dead, the money can be paid to his heir, or if there be none, the man is free without paying, if at any time he has the means to pay[13]. If, however, there are several *extranei*, they take *partes viriles* unless some other division is prescribed, and thus where there are both *heredes* and *extranei*, the *heredes* will take *partes hereditariae*, and the *extranei, partes viriles*[14].

It may be added that a payment to the heir is retained by him even though he hands over the inheritance under a *fideicommissum* and even though he entered only under compulsion[15]. Ulpian tells us that if the payment was ordered to be to an *extraneus*, and he became *heres* to the *heres*, the payment would be made to him *non quasi in extranei*

---

[1] *h. t.* 8. *pr.*, 21. *pr.*
[2] 35. 1. 51. 1, 94. 1; 40. 7. 6. 4, 20. 3, 4.   All the writers are late.
[3] 35. 1. 51. 1, 94. *pr.*   It may even be paid to a legatee of the *heres* if the *heres* so directs in his will, 40. 7. 20. 4, where *testator* must be read *heres*.
[4] 35. 1. 94.   [5] 40. 7. 20. 3, *ante*, p. 490.
[6] 35. 1. 94. 1.   The rule does not apply to legacies.   [7] 46. 3. 68.
[8] But he could pay it to the *tutor*, though he could not safely so pay a debt, 40. 4. 22; In. 2. 8. 2.   If the *heres* were away *reipublicae causa*, he was free on paying into court, 40. 7. 4. *pr.*
[9] 40. 7. 8. 1.
[10] *h. t.* 22. 1 obscurely says *Si quidam ex heredibus quibus dare debeat nominati sint dabit his pro hereditariis portionibus*, which seems to mean that if some of the payees (*heredes*) are named the division as among them is *pro rata*.
[11] 40. 5. 41. 14.   [12] 40. 7. 4. 3.
[13] Ulp. 2. 6; D. 35. 1. 94. *pr.*; 40. 7. 20. 3, *ante*, p. 490.   The rule as to payment to *tutor* was the same in this case, 46. 3. 68.
[14] 40. 7. 22. 2.   [15] 35. 1. 44. 4, 5.

persona, sed quasi in heredis[1]. The point appears to be that it might be imputable from the point of view of the *lex* Falcidia[2].

We have seen that, on alienation, conditions *dando* go to the alienee, while services remain with the *heres*[3]. Thus, if the condition is *rationes reddere*, the account is made and the books are produced to the *heres*, but the money is paid to the alienee[4]. The rule applies not only to sale but to all transfers of *dominium*, *e.g.* under sale, gift or legacy[5]. And the heir of the acquirer succeeds to the right as *heres heredis* does[6]. But it must be an alienation of *dominium*: conferring a usufruct on a third person does not entitle him to receive the payment[7]. On successive alienations the right passes to the last alienee[8]. If the purchase was by a slave, payment may be to the master or to the slave, if the purchase was on account of *peculium*, and this is not adeemed[9]. A buyer of a part must be paid a proportionate part of the money[10]. If the alienation is after payment of a part, the rest must be paid to the alienee[11]. We are told that on sale the *heres* may reserve the payment to himself, and this will have the effect, not merely of a covenant between buyer and seller, but of compelling the man to pay to the *heres*, in order to satisfy the condition. So in the same case he may nominate some other person to receive the money, with a similar effect[12]. It may be presumed that an alienee has the same right, and that a testator may by express words limit and vary the rules expressed in this paragraph. But whether an *extraneus* not an alienee can nominate a person to receive the payment cannot be confidently stated, though it is suggested by the last words of this *lex*.

We are told[13], as we should expect, that one *dare iussus* to a slave (*heres* or not) may not pay his master except with the slave's consent, or *vice versa*, unless the money is *versa in rem domini*. The texts are general[14], but do not expressly refer to gifts of liberty, and though these are probably the commonest case, there are others. And two texts create doubt. In one we are told[15]: *certe statuliber quin domino dare debeat non est dubium*. The use of the word *debeat* shews, when the adjoining texts are looked at, that there is no concession here. The text, which has been shortened, may be merely emphasising the rule, but it may refer to the case of one directed to pay to a fellow-slave. Here as they are in the same *hereditas*, and the money is *res heredi-*

---

[1] 40. 7. 6. 4. [2] *Ante*, p. 497. [3] 40. 7. 6. 7; Ulp. 2. 4, *ante*, p. 488.
[4] 40. 7. 6. 7. [5] *h. t.* 6. 3. [6] *Ibid.*
[7] 40. 7. 7. [8] *h. t.* 27.
[9] *h. t.* 6. 6. The word in the XII Tables was no doubt *emptor*. This means acquirer, and it is the master who acquires. As the slave is the actual contracting party, the payment may be made to him.
[10] *h. t.* 8. 1, 32. [11] *h. t.* 6. 5. [12] *h. t.* 15. 1.
[13] *Ante*, p. 156. [14] 35. 1. 44. *pr.*, 3; 46. 3. 95. 7.
[15] 35. 1. 44. 2.

taria, payment to a fellow-slave would effect no change in possession, and it may have been thought that for this reason it must be to the *dominus*. In either case it does not affect the rule. Another text is more serious. We learn[1] that where the condition of liberty is payment to a *filiusfamilias heres*, it may be done to the father, since he gets the profit of the *hereditas*, which applies equally to a slave. It is observable that nothing is said of *favor libertatis*, and the reason would equally apply to other cases in which the rule was as wę have seen otherwise. Thus though the text may mean that the rule was relaxed in gifts of liberty, it is more likely that it is an individual view of Ulpian's.

There is difficulty where the inheritance is disputed: there is only one text and that as it stands is unintelligible[2]. It seems to begin by assuming that though the will be upset by a judgment, the gift of liberty on paying 10 to the *heres* may still be good. Part of its incomprehensibility is swept away if we adopt Krüger's emendation and read *heredis* for *his* early in the text[3]. On that view the text raises no difficulty as to the date of introduction of the principle that the setting aside the will by judgment in favour of a *heres ab intestato* is a bar to all claims under it[4]. The question it would raise is this: S is to be free on paying 10 to the *heres*. The *heres* enters and dies, and there is a dispute as to his succession. It is between one claiming under a will and one claiming on intestacy. The latter wins[5] and the man asks if he can pay the winner. Quintus Mucius says yes, and, further, that whatever be the truth of the matter he cannot pay the one who has been beaten. Labeo thinks that, as he is in no way claiming under this succession, he is free if he pays to the party really entitled. Aristo gives Celsus an opinion to the effect that only the winner is capable of being paid the money: if he is the true *heres* well and good, if not it is a case of alienation and he is entitled in that way. If the money were paid to the loser, it would be his duty to hand it over, like other acquisitions, to the winner, and when that was done no doubt the man would be free[6].

Whether the money is to be paid to the *heres* or to an *extraneus*, it can always be paid out of *peculium*[7]. The *statuliber* can of course pay it, if he prefers, from other sources[8], but not out of moneys entrusted to

---

[1] 40. 7. 6. 4.   [2] 40. 7. 29. 1.   It has been discussed from the Gloss onwards.
[3] Krüger, Z. S. S. 24. 193 *sqq.   Paterfamilias in testamento scripserat "si A, servus meus, heredi meo dederit decem, liber esto."   deinde de his bonis coeperat controversia esse.* K. reads *de heredis bonis.*
[4] See Appleton, Le Testament Romain, 87, cited Krüger, *loc. cit.*
[5] The text makes it the former, but it is universally admitted that the rest of the text requires an emendation here. Krüger, *loc. cit.*
[6] Presumably the slave paid not knowing of the dispute.
[7] 40. 7. 3. 1; 35. 1. 57.   As to the effect of prohibition by *heres, post*, pp. 503 *sq.*
[8] 40. 7. 3. 8.

him and not forming part of the *peculium*[1]. He may pay it out of subsequent earnings, but may not count towards it money paid to the *heres* in lieu of services due to him, any more than· he could the rent of a farm he hired of the *heres*[2]. Even though he is alienated *sine peculio*, he can still pay it *ex peculio*[3]. But he may not pay it out of the *peculium* belonging to his new master, for the testator's intention could not be extended to that, not even though he had been sold *cum peculio* and the vendor had failed to hand it over[4]. If he is ordered to pay it *ex peculio*, and has none, or owes all that is in it to his *dominus*, he cannot at that time satisfy the condition at all[5].

If a person to whom liberty has been given on such a condition is captured in war, and is redeemed, he may satisfy the condition out of his *peculium coram redemptore*, provided it is not *ex operis* or *ex re redemptoris*[6], but he will still be subject to the lien of the *redemptor*[7].

In this case as in others prohibition makes the man free. If the *heres* refuses the payment or refuses to let it be made to the *extraneus*, the man is *ipso facto* free[8]. If it is to be paid to a coheir and one heir refuses to allow the payment, the man is free[9]. There are other things besides direct refusal which have this effect. If there is a debt due to the *peculium*, and the *heres* refuses to sue for it so as to provide means to fulfil the condition, or money is due from the *heres* to the *peculium*, and he will not pay it, the slave is free from the *mora*. Servius was inclined to limit this to the case where the *peculium* was left to the slave, but the wider view prevailed, and seems the more logical[10]. If the *heres* delays *aditio* intentionally, the slave is free if he had the money at the right time, even though he has ceased to have it at the time of the *aditio*[11]. If, having been *dare iussus*, he is alienated *sine peculio*, there is no prohibition, until he actually is prevented from taking the money[12].

These texts create one serious difficulty. It is obvious that if a testator says: " if S pays 10 to T, let him be free," there is nothing in these words to give T any right. There is no duty in anyone to pay the money—there is no pact, no juristic relation between the *heres* (or

---

[1] 40. 7. 39. 2.

[2] Unless testator has expressly directed that *operae* may be counted towards it, *h. t.* 3. 8, 14. *pr.*

[3] *h. t.* 3. 7, 40. 7.

[4] *h. t.* 35. See also Pap. Resp. Fr. 9. 17 (Krüger).

[5] 40. 7. 17.   [6] 49. 15. 12. 11.

[7] *Ante*, p. 312.   [8] 12. 4. 3. 9 ; 35. 1. 110 ; 40. 7. 3. 1, 20. 3.

[9] 40. 7. 3. 4. Refusal or its equivalent by guardian of *heres* has the same result, *h. l.* 10.

[10] *h. l.* 2. In *h. t.* 20. 2 it is said that the slave can set off the debt and so be free: this would mean that no demand was required.

[11] 40. 7. 3. 11. It must be prevention of the whole: refusal of the first of a series of payments does not free, though it releases from that payment and *heres* may not change his mind, *h. l.* 13.

[12] *h. l.* 7. To bar him from working to earn money wherewith to pay is not prevention (for the services belong to *dominus*), unless the testator provided that the money was to be payable out of *operae*, *h. l.* 8.

the slave) and the man who is to receive it. The payment if made is a *mortis causa capio*, but as Gaius and Marcellus tell us it is not a *donatio*[1]. Accordingly several texts tell us that the *heres* will do wisely to forbid the payment of the money, for thereby he will save it, and the slave will not lose his liberty[2]. Some others use argument which involves the same conclusion[3]. But these texts do not stand alone and there are puzzling conflicts. Pomponius tells us that if the slave pays it notwithstanding the heir's prohibition, the receiver holds it only *pro possessore* and is bound to restore it[4]. On the other hand Paul gives us Julian's opinion that even in this case he makes the receiver owner[5]. Both these texts appear to be genuine: they shew a quite intelligible difference of opinion. The view of Pomponius rests on the rule that a slave cannot alienate *peculium* unless he is authorised to do so[6]. That of Julian and Javolenus rests on the fact that the payment is authorised by the will under which the *heres* holds. But other texts go further. Where it is payable to one of *coheredes*, and another forbids the payment, Ulpian appears to tell us that the *coheres* will recover (in the *actio familiae erciscundae*), *quod sua intererat prohibitum statuliberum non esse*[7], which is less than the whole amount, since some of it will come to him as *heres* if it·is not paid under the condition. This text may be genuine: there may have been provisions under the will which would have made the payment essential to the carrying out of the testator's whole intention[8]. Nevertheless the remark has rather the air of an afterthought, and may be Tribonian's. One text goes further still: we are told, nominally by Ulpian[9], that if the *heres* forbids the payment, the *extraneus* to whom it was to have been made, *adversus heredem in factum actione agere potest, ut testatori pareatur*. It is certain that this is from Tribonian. The expression *in factum actione agere* is no more than suspicious[10], as is the remark that the payment would be *testatori parere*. But the conclusive fact is that the very same fragment in the immediately preceding sentence lays down the opposite rule, *si tamen vult heres nummos salvos facere, potest eum vetare dare: sic enim fiet ut...nummi non peribunt*. The fragment is

---

[1] 39. 6. 31. 2, 38.
[2] 12. 4. 3. 9; 35. 1. 57; 40. 7. 3. 1.
[3] The *peculium* was left to S, who was freed on giving 10 to an *extraneus*. The *heres* forbade the payment. The slave became free and sued for the *peculium*. The *heres* might deduct the 10: if he had not forbidden the payment the slave would not have had it, 40. 7. 20. *pr.* S, *decem dare iussus*, was noxally defended by the *heres*. During the action he gave the *heres* 10 and was free. Is *heres* entitled to absolution only on handing over the 10? Africanus says that if it was not from the *peculium* he must hand it over, since the plaintiff would have had it had the man been handed over at *litis contestatio*. Not if *ex peculio* since he need not have allowed the payment, 47. 2. 62. 9.
[4] 35. 1. 110.   [5] 40. 7. 20. 1; see Javolenus, *h. t.* 39. *pr.*
[6] *Ante*, p. 201.   [7] 40. 7. 3. 4.
[8] *e.g.* if the slave was *praelegatus* to the *heres* to whom the payment was to have been made.
[9] 12. 4. 3. 9.   [10] Kalb, Juristenlatein, 36.

part of an extract many other parts of which have been convicted of interpolation[1].

The fact that a slave is instituted as well as freed is not a modality, but the treatment of the matter in the same chapter is perhaps justified by the fact that the one gift depends very much on the other, and questions arise as to how far modalities affecting one are to be applied to the other.

The general principle is that a slave so freed and instituted is a *necessarius heres*, *i.e.* he is *heres* without entry, and has no *ius abstinendi*[2]. We have already seen that in classical times, a gift of *hereditas* did not imply a gift of liberty. So strictly were such implications excluded that if a slave was freed, whether instituted or not, and was elsewhere substituted, it was necessary, in the opinion of some jurists, to repeat the gift of freedom, the first gift being bound up with the institution and failing if it failed[3]. It is essential that the man belong to the testator[4]. He must be the testator's at the time of the death, so that if he is freed or sold *inter vivos*, he is not a *necessarius*, but enters for himself or his master as the case may be[5], the gift of liberty in such a case being a mere nullity, just as an institution of your own slave without a gift of liberty is[6]. If at the time of the death the owner is without *testamenti factio*, the whole thing is of course void[7]. But a slave given to the wife *mortis causa* is still the husband's and if instituted with a gift of liberty in the will, he is a *necessarius heres*[8]. He must have been the testator's at the time of the will[9], though part ownership at that time is enough[10]. Where a man gives liberty and *hereditas* to a *servus alienus*, and then buys him, both gifts are bad, for the liberty to *servus extraneus* is a nullity, and the institution cannot stand without it[11]. On the other hand, if he was the property of the testator at the time when the will was made and at the death, he is a *necessarius*: the fact that he has been sold and rebought in the interval is not material[12]. The common form of his institution is *Stichus liber et heres esto*, but any imperative form suffices: equivalents are *S. liber esto : si liber erit, heres esto*, and *S. liber esto, et postea quam liber erit heres esto*[13].

---

[1] See, *e.g.*, Gradenwitz, Interpolationen, 148 *sqq.*
[2] 29. 2. 15; Ulp. 22. 24; In. 2. 19. 1.
[3] 28. 6. 10. 7; C. 6. 27. 4. 1. The Syro-Roman Law-book still expresses this rule. It has also a rule that a man who has children cannot institute a slave. Bruns-Sachau, 202.
[4] As to institution by pledgor, see C. 6. 27. 1; D. 28. 5. 30; 40. 1. 3; *post*, Ch. xxv.
[5] G. 2. 188; In. 2. 19. 3; D. 28. 5. 7. 1, 9. 16.   [6] G. 2. 187.
[7] 28. 5. 51. *pr.*   [8] 28. 5. 77.   [9] 40. 4. 35.
[10] 28. 5. 6. 3; *post*, Ch. xxv.   [11] *h. t.* 50. *pr.*
[12] *h. t.* 9. 16, 51. *pr. Media tempora non nocent.*
[13] *h. t.* 9. 14, 52. Both these forms assume liberty before inheritance, which is impossible where he is sole *heres*. But Labeo, Neratius and Aristo agree, no doubt *favore libertatis*, to ignore the word *postea*, and the other form is declared admissible by Marcus Aurelius.

Cases of error in this matter are scantily dealt with. If I institute and free a *servus alienus*, supposing him mine, his owner takes[1]. If a *miles* institutes his slave, thinking him free, the institution is void as there is no gift of liberty, and no doubt the rule is the same in the case of a *paganus*[2]. If it was a *servus alienus*, it would seem from the compromise laid down in the case of Parthenius, that the institution stands good if there is no substitution. If there is a substitution then, on a reasonable though hardly logical compromise, the substitute takes half in any case[3].

Where a slave is freed and instituted *ex parte*, he is free and *necessarius heres* before the other *heres* enters : he is said to derive his liberty from himself and not from his *coheres*, on whose entry indeed it does not in the least depend[4]. This has noticeable results. Thus, according to Julian, if a slave is a *necessarius heres* it is not possible to adeem the gift of liberty in a codicil, for just as a legacy to the *heres* is void, so is the ademption of a gift[5]. The point of the argument is that a gift taken from any beneficiary vests in the *heres*, and as he is the *heres* it is in this case a nullity. It may be said that for all purposes but *fideicommissa* the codicil requires the existence of a will, and the will would fail if effect were given to this codicil[6].

Necessarii heredes are *heredes* without their own consent : there is no question either of entry or abstention. In case of insolvency the goods are sold in their name, and the resulting *infamia* attaches, on the view which prevailed, to the slave personally, though Sabinus was of a different opinion[7]. Such a *heres* has the *beneficium separationis*, *i.e.*, if he is careful not to deal with the goods of the testator, his own after-acquired property will not be liable to seizure by the creditors. If, therefore, the goods have been sold up once, there is no danger of any further proceedings unless the *heres* makes some further acquisition *ex hereditate*[8].

The *necessarius* is not necessarily the *institutus* in first instance : he may be a substitute, or substituted to a substitute, or even a pupillary substitute, in which case he is *necessarius heres* to the *pupillus*[9]. This rule is accepted *utilitatis causa*[10], at least as to pupillary substitution. The point is that the testator is making him *necessarius heres* to someone

---

[1] 46. 1. 33.   [2] 29. 1. 13. 3.   [3] 28. 5. 41, 42; In. 2. 15. 4.
[4] 29. 2. 58; 40. 7. 2. 3.   Paul points out that where the gift to him is made to be dependent on entry of another *heres* (*cum mihi quis heres erit S liber et heres esto*) this independence does not exist, 29. 2. 58.
[5] 28. 5. 6. 4.   [6] In. 2. 25. 2.
[7] G. 2. 152—4; In. 2. 14. *pr.*, 1.   C. Th. 2. 19. 3 (332) observes that they are instituted quite as much to get the *infamia* as to get the *hereditas*.
[8] 42. 6. 1. 18; G. 2. 155; In. 2. 19. 1.   A minor slave so instituted and meddling with the property, can get *restitutio in integrum*, 4. 4. 7. 5.   This title gives details as to the *separatio*.
[9] 28. 6. 10. 1, 36. *pr.*; 40. 7. 2. 4.
[10] 40. 7. 2. 4, 36.   Pius and Severus may have dealt with the matter, 4. 4. 7. 10.

to whom he certainly did not belong at the time when the will was made. On the same notion of utility depend also the rules that if a·man institutes a young slave as *necessarius*, and substitutes another to him, this second slave, even a *postumus*, will be *necessarius heres* to the first[1], and also that a slave made a pupillary substitute is in effect a *statuliber*; a rule laid down by Celsus, and justified by Papinian, on the ground that the rule has the effect that if the heir sells him he is sold *cum sua causa*, while any other rule would have enabled the *filius*, or rather his *tutor*, to upset the father's intentions[2]. Strictly he cannot be a *statuliber* as he acquires his liberty from himself[3]. Where a man made his *impubes* son his *heres*, and gave his slave liberty and then made the slave pupillary substitute without a fresh gift of liberty it was doubtful whether this could make him a *necessarius*, as the liberty and the institution were in different grades. Justinian of course provides that the gifts are valid and make him a *necessarius heres*[4]. If the substitution of a slave takes effect, and the slave becomes free, his liberty being irrevocable, he remains free even though the *heres* is *restitutus in integrum*[5]. In like manner it seems from some obscure provisions that as a slave is instituted in order that he shall bear any resulting *infamia*, he is an *infamis*, and thus brothers or sisters can bring the *querela* against him. The will may thus be upset, but the slave retains his liberty[6].

A *servus proprius* instituted with liberty is thus always a *necessarius heres*, but it is only in case of insolvency that the most important point arises. The *lex* Aelia Sentia allows institution of *necessarii heredes* even in fraud of creditors, partly no doubt on account of the extreme dislike of intestacy, but more in order that the *infamia* attaching to insolvency shall fall on the slave and not on the memory of the dead man. But as one is enough for this purpose, only one is allowed, and thus if two are named, only the first is free[7]. Where A was instituted and two slaves with direct liberty were given a *fideicommissum* of the *hereditas*, the testator proved insolvent. The *heres* refused the inheritance and was compelled to enter on the principle of the *sc.* Pegasianum. He handed over the whole *hereditas*, but only the first of the two slaves was entitled[8]. So if a slave was instituted, and another substituted to whom the testator owed fideicommissary liberty, Neratius held that if the testator was insolvent, the second was *heres*, since his manumission

---

[1] 28. 6. 10. 1.   [2] 40. 7. 2. 4, 36.   [3] 40. 7. 2. 3.
[4] C. 6. 27. 4.   [5] 4. 4. 7. 10; cp. In. 3. 11. 5.
[6] If the goods were not sold he ought not to be *infamis*: if they were, the brother gains nothing. The case is no doubt that of a testator who has mistaken his own financial position. Justinian abolished the rule, C. Th. 2. 19. 3; C. 3. 28. 7.
[7] Ulp. 1. 14.
[8] 28. 5. 84. 1, *post*, p. 509. An insolvent instituted "the two Apollonii." If one died the survivor took: if both lived the gift was void, for only one could take, as the testator was insolvent, 28. 5. 43, 44.

would not be *in fraudem creditorum*[1]. This is carried still further. If the substitute to the slave was a free man or one entitled to freedom, he must be asked first, for it is a fraud on creditors to allow the slave to be free if there is a free man willing to accept the inheritance[2]. A curious case is given in which there may be two *heredes* in such a case. A slave is instituted and the testator then says: *T heres esto si S heres fuerit*. The testator is insolvent. S is *heres necessarius*. T can now take, S is *heres* still, because *semel heres semper heres*, and of course T's claim does not in any way prejudice the creditors[3].

It may be noted that one who is barred from liberty by any enactment other than the *lex* Aelia Sentia cannot be a *heres necessarius*. The provision of this *lex* frees him from the restrictions created by the *lex* itself, but not from any other[4]. Also, the institution of a *heres necessarius* frees from the creditors none of the property except himself. Where, not knowing that the estate is insolvent, he pays certain legacies, these are recoverable by *utilis actio* under the edict for revocation of acts done in fraud of creditors[5].

On the other hand he is not a *necessarius* unless he actually gets his liberty by the will. Thus where a slave is freed under conditions, and before these are satisfied, is given liberty by the Praetor for detecting his master's murder, he is not a *heres necessarius*, but on satisfying the condition he can take the inheritance if he wishes[6].

It is enough that he belong to the testator. A slave is given liberty by *fideicommissum* under a condition. The *heres* institutes him and dies before the condition is satisfied. He becomes *heres necessarius* to this testator. But if the condition on the other gift occurs, he will cease to be *necessarius*, not, we are told, that he will cease to be *heres, sed ut ius in eo mutetur successionis*[7]. A person to whom fideicommissary liberty is due is a quasi *statuliber*[8], and the *heres* cannot make his position worse. Thus his position as a *necessarius heres* must depend on the non-arrival of the condition[9]. Where a slave, S, is instituted and freed, *si meus erit cum morior*, the words are not mere surplusage, though the gift of liberty would fail in any case if S were alienated *vivo testatore*, since it requires ownership at the time when the will operates.

---

[1] 28. 5. 56.
[2] *Ibid.* This is no breach of the rule *semel heres semper heres*. In insolvent estates the *necessarius* is a *statuliber* till it is clear whether the creditors will attack the gift on the ground of fraud, *ante*, p. 484, *post*, p. 562.
[3] 28. 5. 89.   [4] *h. t.* 84. *pr.*
[5] *Utilis* because there is no actual fraud, 42. 8. 6. 13; *h. t.* 10. 10. There could be no *condictio indebiti*, if the legacy were *per damnationem*, but there might in other cases: the legacies were not due, 42. 8. 23.
[6] 28. 5. 91; so if freed *vivo testatore, h. t.* 7. *pr.*
[7] *h. t.* 3. 3.   [8] *Post*, p. 524.
[9] What is the effect of ceasing to be *necessarius* without ceasing to be *heres*? If the goods have been sold he will cease to be *infamis*. Unless on the occurrence he is a voluntary *heres* who has not yet accepted, his position is bad as he loses the *beneficium separationis*.

But apart from them he would acquire the *hereditas* to the alienee[1]. They operate as a sort of condition. The text goes on to consider what will happen if he has been freed *inter vivos*. He cannot be a *necessarius*, but he can take the *hereditas*, since he satisfies the terms of the gift: he is *meus*, not *servus*, but *libertus*[2]. If he was freed *si meus erit* and instituted *pure*, he can, if alienated, take *iussu domini*. Here too the text points out that words which so far as their primary purpose goes lay down only what the law enacts may nevertheless incidentally change the effect of the gift[3].

It is in general essential that institution and liberty be *in eodem gradu*, and, *a fortiori*, that both be direct gifts. But there are relaxations of which the limits are not clear: perhaps it is useless to seek for a principle. The relief is greatest in the case of a *miles*. A soldier institutes X and gives S liberty and a *fideicommissum hereditatis*. X dies without making *aditio*. Ulpian tells us that Severus and Caracalla construed this as a direct gift to S[4]. Maecianus considers whether this applies to *pagani*, and decides, or is made by the compilers to decide, that it applies only if the testator did not know of the death[5]. Where the *heres* does not die but refuses, the risk of *infamia* makes the need of relief more urgent. Accordingly Gaius holds that the same relief is given here: he treats it as a direct gift to S, *ex sententia legis* (Aeliae Sentiae), *i.e.* of the clauses as to fraud of creditors and *necessarii heredes*. He remarks[6] that, on the facts, the estate being insolvent, and S not a *necessarius heres*, X cannot be made to enter, and if he does enter S cannot be free or take a transfer. But in another case in which the facts are the same so far as the present point is concerned, Scaevola says[7] that a *senatusconsultum* of Hadrian's time provides that S can compel X to enter, whether the gift of liberty is direct or only fideicommissary[8]. In the actual case there are two such slaves, of whom only one can take, but that does not seem material. The solution of Gaius evades the difficulty by a forced construction: that of Scaevola involves a new definition of *necessarius heres*. Another text goes further. Even where the *fideicommissum* is conditional, the slave, freed *pure*, compels the *heres* to enter, says Marcian, and if the condition fails, his freedom will stand good[9].

In one case the slave has a gift of liberty, and a *fideicommissum* of the *hereditas*. He compels the *heres* to enter. Then the slave, now free, dies before he has in any way delayed to take over the *hereditas*, leaving T his *heres*. T refuses to take the *hereditas*. Marcellus observes that the *senatusconsultum* (Trebellianum) deals only with the *manumissus*

---

[1] *Ante*, p. 137.	[2] 28. 5. 52. 1.	[3] Cp. 35. 1. 47.
[4] 29. 1. 13. 4.	[5] *h. t.* 14. The language is that of a legislator.	
[6] 36. 1. 65. 15.	[7] 28. 5. 84. 1. Or Tribonian as to *fideicommissum*.	
[8] *Post*, p. 523.	[9] 36. 1. 32. *pr.*	

and not with his *heres*, but concludes on the whole that the *heres* cannot refuse what the *manumissus* would have been bound to take. He adds that if the slave had died without successor before the estate was handed over, the creditors would have had the right to seize the goods as if there had been *restitutio hereditatis*[1].

Substitutions gave rise to some rather complex questions. It is hardly possible to deal with them systematically, for they represent a series of " hard cases," in which *favor libertatis* and the desire to save a will, and to secure a successor to an insolvent, led to distorted views of principle.

A father substitutes to his *impubes* son the slave S, with liberty. The *impubes* sells him to T. T, having already made a will, makes another in which S is made free and *heres*. This will upsets his first, since it is validly made and there may be a *heres* under it. But so long as S can be *heres* to the *impubes*, he cannot be *liber* and *heres* under the will of T. If the *impubes* matures, S will be *heres necessarius* to T. If the *impubes* dies under age, he will be *heres necessarius* to the *impubes*, though of course there is nothing in that to prevent his being *heres voluntarius* to T[2]. The object is, as the texts say, to save the *necessarius* to the father's will, and the principle applied is that the slave is a kind of *statuliber*, and is thus alienated *cum sua causa, i.e.* subject to his becoming *necessarius heres* of the *impubes*, though at the time of the death of the latter the slave is in other ownership[3].

In a very long, very obscure, and in some parts, corrupt text, a will is considered which ran : T *heres esto*; S Maevio *do lego*; S *heres esto*; *si* S *heres non erit*, S *liber heresque esto*. It is impossible to be sure of the meaning of the words, which have already been considered from another point of view[4]. The first point is : under what circumstances can a man be substituted to himself ? It is held that there is no substitution here : there is one institution with a gift of freedom, the whole dependent on the failure of T. The legacy to Maevius is void[5]. It is an attempt to interpret hopelessly obscure words[6].

In the cases in which the institution or the liberty, or both, are subjected to modalities of various kinds, there is a strongly marked tendency to such a construction as will preserve the status, if it may be so called, of the *necessarius heres* and to secure that he shall not get the liberty without the *hereditas*.

If a slave is instituted *pure*, and freed *ex die*, the institution is valid,

---

[1] 36. 1. 46. *pr.* The text is obscure and seems to contain a truncated discussion of the possible effect of delay on the part of the *heres*.
[2] 28. 5. 55; 28. 6. 48. 2.   [3] Cp. 40. 7. 2. 3.   [4] *Ante*, p. 449.
[5] 28. 6. 48. 1.   [6] Cp. 40. 4. 10. 1; 40. 5. 50.

being deferred until the day named. When that day comes, if there has been no alienation, he will become free and *heres necessarius*, and if he has been alienated or freed, he can at once take the *hereditas* for his master or himself[1]. The difficulty thus avoided by reading the *dies* into the institution is that if this is not done, the institution must necessarily fail, since at the time the will is opened he cannot take the *hereditas*, as he cannot be free. In the next following text the matter is carried still further. If the slave himself is not alienated, but the usufruct of him is, he is still the property of the testator. But he cannot be free, during the usufruct, at least in classical law, and accordingly the institution is postponed to the expiration of the usufruct, when he will be *necessarius*[2].

Where a *servus proprius* is instituted *pure*, and given liberty conditionally, the same difficulty is evaded in the same way; the institution is deferred till he is entitled to freedom, when he becomes *heres necessarius*[3]. If while the condition is still pending, the testator sells him, the effect is to destroy the gift of liberty, and he can therefore enter at the command of his new master[4]. But if the testator alienates him after the condition has failed, he cannot enter at the command of the buyer, *quia eo tempore ad eum pervenisset quo iam exstincta institutio inutilis fuerat*[5]. All this is an artificial construction. In order to save the institution the condition on the liberty is read into it, and as it is read in for one purpose on the assumption that the testator meant it to be there, there is nothing to be done, but to read it in for all purposes.

If the man is freed *pure* and instituted conditionally, there is also reason for reading the condition into both gifts. Unless it is satisfied when the will operates, the man will not be a *heres necessarius*. Both gifts therefore await the condition, and if it occurs he will be *liber* and *heres necessarius*. But what if the condition does not occur? Here, *favore libertatis*, logic is disregarded and he gets his liberty. Ulpian states this generally, but Julian is more guarded—*habetur ac si libertas sine hereditate data fuerit*: unless there is another heir, the gift must fail[6]. If a slave is freed *pure* and instituted under a condition, and to have a legacy if he is not *heres*, Marcian cites Pius as saying that the legacy is subject to the same condition[7]. This is puzzling, but Marcian's source is Papinian, whose text[8] shews that Pius meant the condition of liberty, not the other.

---

[1] 28. 5. 9. 17—19. This is very like *dies* in an *institutio*.
[2] 28. 5. 9. 20. Quite apart from this point a condition on one gift might be read into another as a matter of construction. Where a *fideicommissum* of liberty was given to a *servus alienus* and he was also substituted, the condition of liberty was read into the substitution, 31. 83.   [3] 28. 5. 3. 1.
[4] *h. t.* 38. 2. So if he were a common slave, *h. t.* 7 (Mommsen).   [5] *h. t.* 38. 3.
[6] 40. 4. 14; 28. 5. 21, 22. It might be effective as a *fideicommissum* on the *heres ab intestato*, but the texts treat it as a direct gift.
[7] 28. 7. 18. *pr.*   [8] 35. 1. 77. *pr.*

If the slave is freed *ex die* and instituted conditionally, it follows from what has been said that if the condition is satisfied before the day, the institution will take effect on the day, being also subject to *dies*. If the condition is fulfilled only after the day, we are expressly told that he is free and *heres* only from the day when the condition arrives[1].

Of the possible case of liberty under one condition and institution under another we hear little. We can, however, infer from one text that though logic requires, on the principles we have stated, that each gift should be subject to both conditions, the view of Julian was accepted, that if the condition on the institution fails he may still get his liberty, being regarded as an ordinary *statuliber*, the gift of *hereditas* being ignored[2]. This is a simple case of *favor libertatis*[3].

One case is rather puzzling. S is instituted *pure* and given freedom if he pays 10 before a certain date. In a codicil there is an unconditional gift of liberty. He will not be free or heir before the date, unless he pays the 10, but if at that date he has not given the 10 he will be free by the codicil[4]. The principle appears to be this: as the testator has given liberty and inheritance by the will, S cannot have the latter without the former, so far as the will is concerned, and therefore the condition is read into the institution. The codicil cannot alter that: an institution cannot be varied by codicil. But the institution being thus conditional, the gift of liberty must also, even in the codicil, have the condition read into it: the codicil is treated as if it were in the will[5]. Thus he cannot get his liberty without satisfying the condition. But, when it is no longer possible to give effect to the institution, Julian allows *favor libertatis* to have play, and the gift of liberty has its effect as if there had been no condition on it.

Where liberty is given to S directly but *ex die*, and there is a *fideicommissum hereditatis* in his favour, as he is not *ipso facto* free by the entry he has no *locus standi* to make the *heres* enter and hand over the *hereditas*, nor is there any evidence of the testator's wishing him to be *necessarius heres*[6].

It should be added that if the inheritance is conditional, *e.g.* on the payment of money, and no time is fixed for satisfaction of the condition, the creditors may apply to have one fixed, and if he does not pay the money within this time, they may proceed as if he was not instituted. But this affects only his right to any *bona*, not probably a very serious matter in such a case. It in no way affects his right to be free whenever he satisfies the condition. Strictly he would still be *heres*: the rule is a purely praetorian one, affecting nothing but the *bona*[7].

1 28. 5. 9. 18.   2 40. 7. 2. 3.
3 28. 5. 21. *pr.* gives another case of favourable construction. A testator says: *quisquis mihi heres erit, S liber et heres esto.* Strictly this is a condition, and S ought to take nothing until there is another *heres*. It is allowed effect as if unconditional.   4 28. 5. 38. 1.
5 Machelard, Règle Catonienne, 40.   6 36. 1. 32. 1, 57. 1.   7 42. 5. 4.

CHAPTER XXII.

MANUMISSION DURING THE EMPIRE (cont.).
FIDEICOMMISSARY GIFTS.

LEGACIES and *fideicommissa* in general underwent a process of assimilation at the hands of Justinian, but there never was much real assimilation of direct and fideicommissary gifts of liberty. The former were a good deal relaxed in form, and this is so far an assimilation. But the fact that direct gifts could be made only to the testator's slaves and made them *liberti orcini*, while the others could be made to *servi alieni* and made them *liberti* of the *fiduciarius*[1], formed an unbridgeable gap between them. It must also be noted that a gift by *fideicommissum* is not in strictness manumission by will at all: it has to be completed by an act of manumission by the *fiduciarius*[2], and this will often be *inter vivos*. But as the direction is contained in a will or codicil, and, apart from condition, operates on entry, it is convenient to treat it here. Indeed more than convenience is involved: as we shall see later, a gift by *fideicommissum* is subject to the rules of the *lex* Fufia Caninia[3] and to others specially applicable to testamentary provisions[4]. On the other hand there is room in such gifts for *causa*, to complete a gift in some way defective, and this applies essentially to gifts *inter vivos*[5].

A *fideicommissum* of liberty is in effect a direction contained in a will or codicil, addressed to some person and requiring him to free a slave. It may even be in an unconfirmed codicil, and so bind the *heres ab intestato*[6]. It may be given by word of mouth before witnesses, where the giver is *in articulo mortis*, and will then bind any *heres*[7]. We have surviving instances of such gifts by will and codicil[8]. No particular words are needed, but the intent must be clear[9], and the recorded

---

[1] C. 7. 4. 7; G. 2. 266—7; In. 2. 24. 2.
[2] C. 7. 4. 11; In. 2. 24. 2, *etc.*   [3] *Post*, p. 547.
[4] They are equal to direct gifts for Falcidian purposes (35. 2. 36. 2, 37, *etc.*). A legacy of *alimenta* to freedmen covered those freed by *fc.* (34. 1. 2). It is the age of the testator which is material in such manumissions, *post*, p. 541. See also the rules as to *addictio bonorum*, *post*, Ch. xxvii.
[5] *Post*, p. 538.
[6] 40. 4. 43. Or in a will operating as a codicil, 40. 5. 24. 11. Vangerow, Pand. § 527.
[7] 40. 5. 47. 4.
[8] Bruns, Fontes, 1. 273, 279. On p. 273 there is a legacy of a slave with a *fideicommissum* not to free.
[9] 40. 5. 16. The word *commendo* was not enough, P. 4. 1. 6; C. 7. 4. 12.

instances seem to shew some variation of practice as to what is enough.
In general the construction is favourable. Thus where X was made,
by the will, *tutor* to the *heres* and a *fideicommissum* was imposed on X
to free a certain slave of his own, X was excused from the *tutela*. Other
tutores were appointed and it was held that the trust was essentially
imposed on the *heres*, and therefore the new *tutores* were obliged to buy
the slave with money of the estate and free him[1]. But though one who
has liberty by *fideicommissum* under a will can take gifts under the
same will[2], yet a *fideicommissum* of money, *sub conditione*, with no gift
of liberty, is not held to imply such a gift[3]. Such words indeed do
not clearly shew that any gift is intended. But even where it is clear
that a gift is meant, there is no rule, at least in classical law, that an
intended direct gift, in some way defective, can be construed as a fideicommissary gift to save it. This is indeed often done, but usually
because the circumstances seem to impose a pious duty on someone to
carry out the wishes of the deceased. Where a will gave a foster-child
liberty and a *fideicommissum* and the will was imperfect, and the estate
was administered as on intestacy, Paul tells us that the Emperor decided
that the *alumnus* was entitled to be freed by the *heres ab intestato*,
though the will contained no *clausula codicillaris*[4]. But he lays great
stress on the duty of children to do what their father would have wished.
A will said: *cum Thais heredi servierit* 10 *annos volo sit mea liberta*.
The word *volo* is not enough for a direct gift, and the heir by freeing
could not make her the testator's *liberta*. Scaevola holds that this is a
fideicommissary gift, but ignores the words *mea liberta*[5]. Where the
object is to appoint a *tutor*, a good many difficulties are evaded.
To make a *servus alienus tutor* to your son is held to imply the
condition *cum liber erit*, at least in later law[6]. It is true that the
Institutes deny this[7], but the evidence is strong. The text cited[6] goes
on indeed to say that unless this is plainly contrary to the wish of the
testator such an appointment implies a *fideicommissum* of liberty. The
reason assigned is that it is favourable to the pupil, to liberty and to
the public interest, and a text in the Code also declares that the effect
is a *fideicommissum* of liberty. But the mode of expression in both
cases is a little Byzantine[8], and it seems likely that while the insertion
of the condition is classical, the further extension dates only from
Justinian. Paul[9] discusses the case of a slave of the testator given
freedom by *fideicommissum*, and appointed *tutor*, and observes that

---

[1] 40. 5. 41. 2.
[2] See 32. 8. 1, and *ante*, p. 146, for gifts to *servus heredis*.
[3] C. 6. 42. 28.   [4] 40. 5. 38.
[5] *h. t.* 41. *pr.* The case in 40. 4. 42 is construed as a legacy of the slave with a *fideicommissum* of liberty.
[6] 26. 2. 10. 4.   [7] In. 1. 14. 1.
[8] C. 7. 4. 10. But it attributes the opinion to *prudentes*.   [9] P. 4. 13. 3.

there is a difficulty, since he cannot be tutor till he is free, or free till there is a *tutor*[1], since an *impubes* cannot free *sine auctoritate*[2]. But, he adds, it will be treated as a case of absent *tutores*, so that under the *decretum amplissimi ordinis* he will be free and *tutor*. The reference is presumably to the *sc.* Dasumianum and connected legislation[3].

In one text[4] a direct gift which fails is, apparently for that reason alone, treated as fideicommissary. The rule laid down is that what is in a codicil is treated as if it were in the will, and thus if liberty is given in a codicil to one who was not the testator's property at the time of the will, but is at the time of the codicil, the gift fails as being to a *servus alienus*. The text adds : *et ideo licet directae libertates deficiunt attamen ad fideicommissarias eundum est*. The grammar and form generally of this remark, coupled with the fact that no reason is given, strongly suggest that this comes from Tribonian[5].

Implied gifts inferred from the words of the testator are a good deal discussed in the texts, and were freely admitted.

A direction not to alienate is, we are told, a *fideicommissum* of liberty, *si modo hoc animo fuerit adscriptum quod voluerit eum testator ad libertatem perduci*[6]. But if this means an immediate gift, the text must be interpolated, as indeed its language suggests[7]. A direction *ne postea serviat* is certainly an immediate *fideicommissum* of liberty[8]. Directions that he is not to serve anyone else or not to be alienated or the like, are *fideicommissa* of liberty to take effect at the death of the *fiduciarius*, or, if the man is alienated, at once[9]. An alienation not voluntary, but resulting inevitably from what the testator has ordered, is, not an alienation for this purpose, the testator not being supposed to have meant to include this. The text seems to add that on such facts if the direction is that he is to serve no other, freedom is due at death of fiduciary[10]. If on the other hand it is neither due to the testator, nor voluntary, *e.g.* where the fiduciary is *publicatus*, the condition is declared to be satisfied, and the slave is to be freed, if necessary by the public

---

[1] C. 5. 28. 5.   [2] 40. 5. 11.
[3] *Post*, Ch. xxvii. One given freedom by *fideicommissum* cannot properly be made *tutor*, but, says Papinian, after he is free the appointment will be confirmed, 26. 2. 28. 1.
[4] 29. 7. 2. 2, *ante*, p. 463. Fein-Glück, 1511 c, p. 237 *sqq.* treats it as the general rule, but of the texts he cites the only one in point (40. 5. 24. 10) is considered *post*, p. 573.
[5] So A. Faber and apparently Mommsen. Fein-Glück, *loc. cit.*, treats it as an expression of Julian's equitable tendency. The text gives the same rule where the slave belonged to the testator when the will was made but not at time of codicil. The view of Cujas (Ad Afr. Tract. 2) has been generally accepted, *i.e.* that a *non* should be omitted, since time between will and death is immaterial, assuming that he was in the estate at the time of death. See Fein-Glück, *loc. cit.* and Lenel, Paling., *ad h. l.* Cujas notes that Paul holds such a gift good, 34. 4. 26. Mommsen, Ed. mai. *ad h. l.*, thinks that as the concluding words of the text put the cases on one footing, the *non* is due to the compilers. Fein-Glück, *loc. cit.*, gives an account of the many points which arise in this text. One other case may be mentioned here. A gift written in favour of oneself is void : where a slave wrote a gift of liberty to himself *iussu domini*, this was in strictness void, but the Senate decided that it should impose a duty on the *heres* to free. Pius decided that it was to be as if written by his *dominus*, whom he was bound to obey, 48. 10. 15. 2, 3.
[6] 40. 5. 24. 8.   [7] Gradenwitz, Interpol. 212.   [8] 40. 5. 24. 7.
[9] 40. 5. 9, 10. *pr.*, 21.   [10] *Ibid.*

authority[1]. If the fiduciary having sold him buys him back this does not mend matters: the condition is already satisfied[2]. All this suggests, as Gradenwitz points out[3], that the proposition at the beginning of this paragraph is interpolated, and, as he further observes, the same thing is probably true of the remark in the same text[4] that the favourable effect of such a direction as *ne alienes,* however far it goes, does not apply if there was some other object, as that the *heres* should keep him and beat him severely, the burden of proof of this contrary intent being on the *heres.*

A gift *si heres voluerit* is void: the *heres* can of course free if he likes, but is under no duty[5]. Very little more, however, will turn it into a duty. The words *si volueris fidei tuae committo, si tibi videbitur peto manumittas, si tibi videbitur manumittas, si voluntatem probaveris*[6], these, or any Greek equivalent, compel the *heres* to use the discretion of a *bonus vir* about the matter, and to free the man if he deserves it[7]. This may be a case of *favor libertatis,* since we are told that the words, *si volueris fidei tuae committo,* have no effect in other testamentary matters[8]. So also " if you find them worthy," or *si te promeruerint dignos eos libertate existimes* are good fideicommissary gifts[9]. These forms seem to mean much the same thing: the man is entitled to be freed if he is reasonably worthy, *i.e.* if he has done nothing making him clearly unworthy. His right is not to depend on his having rendered such services to the fiduciary as to have deserved liberty of him[10]. But it may be left to the *fiduciarius* to choose when he will free[11], and in the cases we have been discussing he might do it at any time during his life, and if he died without having done it, his *heres* was bound to free at once[12].

The words *si placeat* seem to be of the same class, and to impose a duty on the *heres* if the man be fit. But two texts in which this word is used create some difficulty. A slave is directed to be freed, *si uxori meae placeat,* the wife being one of the instituted *heredes.* She refuses her share, so that all falls to the other *heres.* Alexander decides that the man is entitled to his freedom if the wife does not object[13]. Elsewhere, Modestinus holds that her ceasing to be *heres* must not prejudice the man, and moreover that her dissent is immaterial[14]. As fideicommissary gifts are binding on substitutes and *coheredes*[15], and a gift

[1] *h. t.* 12. *pr.*   [2] *h. t.* 21.   [3] *loc. cit.* and *op. cit.* 38.
[4] 40. 5. 24. 8.   [5] *h. t.* 46. 3.   [6] *Ibid.*
[7] 40. 5. 46. *pr.*, 3.
[8] *Ib.* But even in other cases anything shewing that he was to exercise discretion would validate the gift, 32. 11. 7. See Bufnoir, Conditions, 193.
[9] 40. 5. 46. 3.
[10] 40. 4. 20, 51. 1; 40. 5. 41. 4, 46. 3. Where such a word as *iudicium* was used it is clear that the testator meant the *heres* to have a discretion: there was no absolute *fideicommissum,* 40. 5. 41. 6.
[11] 40. 5. 17, 46. 4.   [12] 40. 4. 20.   [13] C. 7. 4. 8.
[14] 40. 5. 14.   [15] 31. 61. 1, *etc., post,* p. 523.

of liberty may be at the discretion of a third party[1], it is not clear why anyone should have thought the gift must fail on the above facts, as it appears that someone did. It must be assumed, as is suggested above, that the words give not a mere power of veto, but impose a duty to free if the man is worthy. This might create a difficulty where the person on whom the duty is imposed cannot free, as not being *heres*, but both texts agree that this is not fatal. But Alexander[2] lays it down that she can still exercise her discretion, though he does not commit himself on the question whether it is now an absolute discretion or not. Modestinus, on the other hand[3], thinks that the discretion is vested in her as *heres*, and is now therefore not exercisable at all— apparently he regards it as struck out, as being quasi-impossible[4].

As the gift may be at the discretion of a third person[1], so it may be at that of the slave himself[5]. Even if it is not so expressed, the gift will not take effect, *invito servo*, as it is for his benefit, unless it is clear that there was an intention to benefit his master, *e.g.* if a *heres* is ordered to buy a slave at a very high price, and free him. In such a case the *heres* is compellable by the owner to buy him[6].

Where the *heres* is directed to free one of several slaves, but there is no evidence as to which the testator meant, the gift is void[7]. The case contemplated seems to be where the words are "Let my *heres* free two of my *familia rustica*" or the like, and where there is no direction to the *heres* to choose, the analogy of a *legatum generis* is not applied: in fact the analogy would be rather with a gift to one of two persons. And here the rule of legacy is followed. But where a man who has three slaves directs the *heres* to choose two and free them, this is a valid gift and the *heres* may choose as against a legatee of the slave[8]. This last point is noticeable as a case in which a more or less general gift takes precedence of a specific gift, *favore libertatis*. The case gave rise to difficulties where the *heres* failed to free any of them[9]. It may be added that in the case of *fideicommissa* in varying terms, Pius enacted that the last was to be preferred, as expressing the last will of the testator[10]. In direct gifts, as we have seen, that operates which is most favourable to liberty[11]. The difference seems to result merely from over general language of the Emperor, since in legacies also, apart from liberty, the later gift is preferred[12].

The principles to be applied as to condition and the like are much

[1] 49. 5. 46. 2. [2] C. 7. 4. 8. [3] 40. 5. 14.
[4] *Ante*, p. 489. [5] 40. 5. 46. 1.
[6] *h. t.* 32. 1; cp. 28. 5. 84. 1, *post*, p. 530. [7] 34. 5. 27.
[8] 40. 5. 46. 5. If one died the others were entitled to be freed.
[9] *Post*, p. 556. [10] 35. 1. 90; 40. 4. 5; C. 6. 38. 4. *pr.*
[11] *Ante*, p. 488. [12] 35. 1. 51. *pr.* As to gifts "to A or B," *ante*, p. 461, *post*, p. 556.

the same as in direct gifts[1]: a few illustrations may be given. A slave to be freed when a certain person reaches 16 is entitled to freedom at that date though the person be dead[2]. A slave to be freed on rendering accounts is not responsible for losses not imputable to his negligence[3], nor, when the *dominus* had approved and signed his accounts, for the insolvency of any debtors therein set out[4]. On the other hand if the freedom is not due at once, he must render account of his administration since the death, it being enough that he pay over all that is due. Thus where *tutores* have approved his accounts since the death he need not get them approved again, even though the *tutores* are themselves condemned in the *actio tutelae*[5]. To be freed *in 8 annos* means after 8 years, and it is a matter of construction whether they run from the death or the date of the will[6]. Where a son is to free a slave after 5 years, if he pays so much a day, and he omits the payment for 2 years, he is not free unless the *heres* has taken his services instead; in that case the condition is so far satisfied, since *non per eum stat* that it is not carried out[7]. If the slave given liberty conditionally by *fideicommissum* is also legated, the legatee is entitled to take him but must give security for his restoration if the condition occur. Ofilius, however, was of opinion that this was so only if the liberty was intended to adeem the legacy *pro tanto*, the legatee being entitled to shew, if he could, that the testator meant to burden the *heres* with the cost of repurchase[8]. The text remarks that the rule is the same in direct gifts[9].

The gift may be accompanied by one of the *hereditas*. In such a case the man can compel the *heres* to enter, free him, and hand over the *hereditas*[10]. A Senatusconsult provides that if he is *impubes*, the *heres* shall be bound to enter, and a *tutor* will be appointed to take the *hereditas*, and see that all proper securities are given[11]. Where several are freed by *fideicommissum*, and the *heres* is directed to hand over the inheritance to them, and he doubts its solvency, he can be compelled to enter, and hand it over to the first, who will be free and

---

[1] The rules as to the effect of prevention are as in direct gifts, 40. 5. 33. 1, 47. 2; *ante*, p. 492. For a case of *modus* see Testamentum Dasumii, 1. 44.
[2] C. 7. 4. 9; D. 40. 5. 41. 10; *ante*, p. 490.
[3] 40. 5. 41. 7; *ante*, p. 494.   [4] 40. 5. 41. 7.
[5] *h. l.* 10. Where he is to return the *peculium* he must give also anything he has received on account of *dominus* and added to the *peculium*, and he may not deduct anything on account of debts due from the master to the *peculium, h. l.* 9; *h. l.* 8 (obscure).
[6] *h. l.* 15; *ante*, p. 479. The concluding words suggesting a presumption that they run from the date of the will are apparently an inept interpolation. Gradenwitz, Interp. 182.
[7] 40. 5. 23. 4. Where a slave was to pay, *filiae et uxori meae*, so much, and then be freed, and the wife abstained, all was payable to the daughter, *h. t.* 41. 14. Where he was to be freed when debts were paid, they must be paid unless the *heres* wilfully delayed so as to keep him, *h. l.* 1.
[8] 40. 4. 40. 1; 40. 5. 47. 3.
[9] For a strained construction, *favore libertatis*, to exclude a certain condition, 40. 5. 56.
[10] 36. 1. 23. 1.
[11] 26. 5. 13. The text adds that Hadrian laid down the same rule where the gift was direct.

take the *hereditas*[1]. If a *servus alienus* is appointed *heres,* there may be a *fideicommissum* of liberty to him, *post mortem domini,* which will leave his *dominus heres*[2].

Like other gifts they are liable to revocation and destruction. We are told that they may be adeemed in the form in which they were made. This does not mean, as the text seems to suggest, that if given by will they cannot be adeemed by codicil, or *vice versa,* but that the form of words used must be the same in the ademption as it was in the gift[3]. There are many forms of implied *ademptio.* Thus if the gift is prevented from taking effect by the operation of some restrictive statute, *e.g.* the *lex* Iulia, this is a practical ademption[4]. Punishing by chaining by the testator is an implied ademption[5], and it may be presumed that, in general, what would adeem any direct gift would adeem a *fideicommissum.* A legacy of the slave will ordinarily have the same effect upon the gift of liberty as it would have on a direct gift[6]. In general the latest written is preferred, whether it is the legacy or the liberty, but there is a presumption, in case of doubt, in favour of the liberty[7].

If the will completely fails from any cause, the gift fails unless it is also imposed on the *heres ab intestato,* a construction readily adopted[8]. So if the codicil in which they are given becomes *irritus* they fail, but if the *heres* confirms them and lets the slaves *in libertate morari,* it is laid down by Severus and Caracalla that the liberty is complete[9]. As it stands this is a puzzling statement. There has been no formal act of manumission, and at this time the informal permission of the heir could have given no more than latinity. If in its present form it is to be put down to the Emperors at all, it must be regarded as a *privilegium.*

The results of lapse can be shortly stated so far as they are known. If the will fails, the gift fails, unless it is charged also on the *heres ab intestato*[10], subject to the rule that if the *hereditas,* or indeed the gift on which the *fideicommissum* is charged, goes to the fisc, that authority must carry out the gift so far as possible[11]. If the gift lapses to an heir, the rule of earlier classical law is that he takes it free of the burden, so far as it is a case of lapse under the *ius antiquum*[12], but *caduca* and the like take their burdens with them[13]. Severus provided that burdens should bind substitutes, and Ulpian cites Julian as in-

---

[1] If the estate is insolvent this ends the matter : one alone can be free. If the others claim to be freed and have their share, this will be gone into when they claim before the Praetor, 28. 5. 84. 1.　So also in case of direct gift. *Ante,* p. 507.
[2] 31. 14. 1.　　　　　　　[3] Ulp. 2. 12; D. 46. 4. 14.　　　[4] 40. 6. 1.
[5] 40. 5. 43.　　　　　　　[6] *Ante,* p. 468.　　　　[7] 40. 5. 50; cp. *h. t.* 47. 4.
[8] 40. 5. 24. 11, 47. 4; C. 7. 2. 12.　　　　　　　　　[9] 40. 5. 30. 17.
[10] 40. 5. 24. 11, 47. *pr.*
[11] 30. 96. 1; 35. 1. 60. 1; 34. 9. 5. 4; 40. 5. 5, 12. *pr.,* 2, 51. *pr.*　As to the case of the fisc, see also *post,* Ch. xxvii.
[12] 31. 29. 2, Celsus.　　　　　　[13] Ulp. 17. 3.

ferring that if a *legitimus heres* refused, a *fideicommissum* charged on him would bind his coheir[1]. This is a doubtful inference, and in any case it is no authority for the case of lapse of a legacy to a *heres* or co-legatee. It is not clear whether the distinctions which applied to other burdens in case of lapse applied to gifts of liberty. We are told nothing as to manumissions charged on joint legacies, but there is reason to think they were more favourably treated than other trusts in later classical times. Where a legacy burdened with such a gift is *pro non scripto*, Papinian says, on grounds of equity, that the *heres* must carry out the trust[2]. And Ulpian lays down a similar rule, precisely because such gifts are to be favoured[3]. Paul deals in the same spirit with the case in which the legatee refuses the gift of the slave[4].

The rules under the *sc.* Pegasianum, as to compulsion to enter, have no application in the case of a mere gift of liberty without *hereditas*, but there are nevertheless some exceptions to the rule that failure of the *heres* to enter avoids the gift. Thus a collusive repudiation in order to avoid the gift leaves it still binding[5]. So where the *heres* "omits" the will and takes on intestacy, he must free those whom either he or a substitute was under a *fideicommissum* to free[6], even though they be slaves of third persons[7]. And though the gift is not binding on the *heres ab intestato*, still if the heir under the will took money not to enter he must free the slaves[8]. It should be remarked that the gift is binding on all successors of the fiduciary, of any kind[9].

If the fiduciary has charges against the slave, of malversation, or the like, this is not a ground for delaying the liberty. This is declared to have been repeatedly laid down by Marcus Aurelius, Severus and Caracalla[10]. But the Praetor, in adjudicating, will take into consideration what is due on these accounts, by means of an *arbiter* if necessary, and order securities accordingly[11]. Moreover in an appropriate case the *actio expilatae hereditatis* will lie[12], since manumission does not destroy liability for delict[13]. In the same way, the personal need of the fiduciary or the badness of the slave affords no reason why the manumission should not be carried out[14]: Cassius was of a different opinion, but was overruled on the ground that there was no compulsion to take the correlative benefit, but he might not have one without the other.

---

[1] 31. 61. 1.   [2] 36. 1. 55.   [3] 40. 5. 26. 6.   [4] 40. 5. 33. 2. See *post*, p. 528.
[5] C. 7. 2. 12.   [6] 29. 4. 12, 22. *pr.*, 29.   [7] *h. t.* 28. 1. See also 25. 6. 1. 9—11.
[8] C. 7. 4. 1. Pius enacted that if the *heres* and substitute died suddenly without entry and there was a *fideicommissum* of *hereditas* and liberty, the liberty should take effect but not, except in soldiers' wills, the gift of *hereditas*, 40. 5. 42. This expresses only *favor libertatis.* Analogous cases, 34. 9. 5. 4; 36. 1. 55 ; C. 3. 31. 12.
[9] 40. 5. 12. 1, 51. *pr.*; P. 4. 13. 2. But not one taking adversely, 40. 5. 31. 3.
[10] 40. 5. 23. *pr.*; 47. 4. 1. 7.   [11] 40. 12. 41, 43; 47. 4. 1. 7.
[12] 47. 4. 1. 7.   [13] *Ante*, p. 106; *post*, Ch. xxix.   [14] 40. 5. 35.

The *lex* Falcidia and the *sc.* Pegasianum have obvious applications in this matter. A legacy of a slave to be freed is not liable to the Falcidian deduction, nor is the man counted in the *hereditas*, but anything left with him is of course subject to the deduction[1], as is money left to a man in order that he may free a slave[2]. Indeed the rule goes further, for if. a slave and money are left to X and there is a *fideicommissum* to free the slave, the Falcidian quarter is reckoned, it seems, on the whole of the gift, including the slave. But it can be taken only óut of the money, so that in effect the gift of the slave stands good in its entirety, and the man is entitled to his freedom[3]. The same rule is applied where the legacy is to the slave himself who is to be freed[4]. According to the rules laid down by Ulpian, the fideicommissary gift must be carried out by the fiduciary, if he has accepted the gift, however small this is (but not if it proves to be nothing at all), if the slave affected is his own. But if the slave is to be purchased he is not required to spend more than the gift in buying him. If, however, the gift increases in value, so as to amount to the price of the slave, the donee must buy him, and, conversely, if it was enough when it was received the fact that it has diminished in value does not release him. On the other hand if he has accepted the gift under a mistake as to its value, he is allowed to restore it. There are evidences of dispute, but all this is clearly the rule of later law[5], and there seems no reason to doubt that it is classical.

Paul considers the case in which the gift is in itself enough but is cut down by the *lex* Falcidia, so that it is too small. He mentions diverse views, *e.g.* that the donee may keep the gift and not free even in the case of his own slave (a view in conflict with that just stated, and with settled law[6], at least as to this last point), and that if he has accepted the three-quarters he must buy and free[7]. The view finally accepted is, it seems, that in this case, too, if it is his own slave he must free, but he need not buy for more than the gift: in fact the case of reduction by the *lex* Falcidia is put on the same level as original insufficiency[8]. The text of Paul ends with the solution, which must be due to the compilers, that in such a case the *heres* must pay the legacy in full as if the testator had so directed. Before the time of Justinian such a direction would have had no force[9].

Just as a slave freed is deducted in arriving at the amount of the *hereditas*, so if the *heres* is directed to free his own slave, or a *servus alienus*, he is entitled to deduct the value of this slave from the *hereditas* as a debt[10].

[1] 35. 2. 33, 34, 36. 3.   [2] 35. 2. 34.
[3] *h. t.* 36. 3.   The legacy of the slave may have value if the man is not to be freed at once.
[4] *h. t.* 35.   [5] 40. 5. 24. 12—16, 45. 1; 35. 2. 36. 1; C. 6. 50. 13.
[6] *Post,* p. 529.   [7] 40. 5. 6.   [8] 40. 5. 22. *pr.*; 35. 2. 36. *pr.*, 1.
[9] Nov. 1. 2.   [10] 35. 2. 36. 2, 37. 1.

Where the *fideicommissum* is not immediate, but is subject to *dies* or condition, there is, as in the case of direct gifts, some difficulty. The few texts dealing with the matter suggest that it is immaterial whether the gift is direct or fideicommissary[1]. We have seen[2] that the rule is not easy to make out in the case of direct gifts, and there certainly is the difference that, at least in later law, a legacy of a slave to whom a direct gift of liberty *post tempus* was made, was void[3], which could not be the case where the legatee was directed to free him. We are told that if a slave, the only property of the testator, is left to be freed after three years, this is in effect a legacy of three years' enjoyment of him and one fourth of the acquisitions *ex operis* will belong to the *heres*[4]. This is simple, but not very logical, since this would certainly not represent one fourth of the benefit to the *legatarius*, nor would it be what would come to the *heres* if the slave were regarded as his, as to one quarter, in the meantime. In fact the conveyance of the slave is not treated as a benefit at all: what is regarded as left is the right of acquisition *ex operis*. It is clear that no really cogent solution was reached. Another text which may be regarded as dealing with the case where the slave is legated *pure*, with a conditional *fideicommissum*[5] of liberty, reflects still more the obscurity of the matter. It is the work of Paul, citing Caecilius, and while it is not clear that Paul adopts the views of Caecilius, it is still more uncertain what those views were. The problem is whether the gift of the slave is to be regarded as a legacy, subject to a Falcidian deduction. The answer of Caecilius seems to be that the gift of the slave is a legacy and that thus a certain part of him may remain with the heir, under the *lex* Falcidia[6]. When the condition happens he vests wholly in the legatee. Caecilius adds: *si quid ex operis eius medio tempore consecutus fuerit heres, id in pretium eius erogare eum debere, propter legis Falcidiae rationem*. And Valens adds that the man is to be valued as a *statuliber*. The plain meaning of these words is that he is not in the *hereditas* at his full value, since, unlike a thing legated, which, as we have seen, was imputed at its full value[7], he, if freed simply, was not imputed at all: a legacy given absolutely was of course counted in the inheritance. The words of Caecilius seem to mean that what comes to the *heres* as part owner, must be set off by him against the value of the slave as a *statuliber*, so that, so soon as he has received what equals the quarter of the man's value, he vests wholly in the legatee[8]. This agrees in principle with the other text[9], but is not wholly satisfactory[10].

[1] *h. t.* 36. 4, 56. 3.   [2] *Ante,* pp. 474 *sqq.*   [3] *Ante,* p. 469.   [4] 35. 2. 56. 3.
[5] 35. 2. 36. 4, 37. *pr.*   The argument turns on uncertainty though *dies* is mentioned.
[6] Cp. 35. 2. 49. *pr.*   [7] *Ante,* p. 474.
[8] So in principle, Pothier, *ad h. l.* (*in tit.* de legatis, LXXVI).   [9] 35. 2. 56. 3.
[10] Mommsen (perhaps also Lenel) expunges the word *heres* and presumably understands the text differently. See *ante,* p. 475, n. 7.

The Trebellian (or Pegasian) principles are the same, but other and more important questions arise in connexion with them. The main point to note is that the power of compelling the *heres* to enter to save the *fideicommissum* does not apply to *fideicommissa* of liberty alone[1]: it is allowed only for the benefit of *fideicommissariae heredi-tates*. The rule is illustrated by many "hard cases." A man who is given a *fideicommissum* subject to a further *fideicommissum* of the whole cannot, it seems, compel the *heres* to enter, as he is to get nothing. Accordingly where A is *heres* with a *fideicommissum* of liberty and *hereditas* in favour of S, and S is subject to a *fideicommissum hereditatis* in favour of B, S cannot compel the *heres* to enter, as liberty, which is all he will get, is not enough. But it will not greatly matter, if the estate is solvent, for B is allowed to compel the *heres* to enter, and will then be bound to free S[2]. Where A and B are *heredes*, S has a *fideicommissum* of liberty from A and of *hereditas* from B. Both refuse to enter. S cannot compel them. There is no compulsion for liberty alone, and B not being bound to the liberty cannot be bound to one who has no right to be free. But though in the facts as stated the liberty will fail, still, if A alone refuses, B. takes all, and can be compelled to enter, as S now has a claim against him for both liberty and *hereditas*[3]. On the same facts if A enters and frees S, then as there can be no question of intestacy, and S is free, he can compel B to enter and hand over the *hereditas*[4]. This is a provision of Antoninus Pius, whom we shall find legislating freely in cases of hardship in this connexion. It must be remembered that, in his time, the gift specially charged on B would not have bound A if, B having failed to take, A had acquired the whole by *ius accrescendi*. Later, as the result of a rescript of Severus and Caracalla, the provision would have been unnecessary, as A would have been bound by the *fideicommissum hereditatis*[5].

Where a *heres* is required to give liberty and the *hereditas* to his own slave, he cannot be compelled to enter, though, if he does, he must carry out the *fideicommissa*[6]. On the other hand there are many cir-cumstances under which the slave can compel the *heres* to enter. Thus where the testator's slave is freed *directo*, or by *fideicommissum*, with a *fideicommissum* of the *hereditas*, he can compel the *heres* to enter[7]. Where T was *heres*, and there was a direct gift of liberty to S, S's child Z was left to S with a *fideicommissum* to free it, and there was a *fideicommissum hereditatis* in favour of Z. T refused to enter. On

---

[1] 36. 1. 54. 1, 57. 2.   As to *bonorum addictio, post*, Ch. xxvii.
[2] 36. 1. 57. 2.   [3] 36. 1. 54. 1.   [4] *h. t.* 17. 17.
[5] See *e.g.* 31. 29. 1.   As to lapse in general, *ante*, p. 470.   Where S had a *fideicommissum hereditatis* from A the *heres* and of liberty from B a legatee, he could not make A enter, as his right was dependent on B's and B could not.   B was in fact dead and the case was decided as one of lapse, 36. 1. 55, *ante*, p. 519.   [6] 36. 1. 57. 13.
[7] *h. t.* 23. 1.   Where a *heres* is *rogatus* to free S and there is a *fideicommissum hereditatis* in favour of T, and T is directed to hand the *hereditas* to S, S can make the *heres* enter, *h. t.* 17. 16.   It must be presumed that the slave belonged to the testator.

application to the Emperor (Pius), it was ordered that T should enter. This made S free. Her child was then to be handed to her, and to be then freed by her, and a *tutor* appointed, by whose *auctoritas* Z could accept transfer of the *hereditas*. The will directed the inheritance to be handed to Z only when she was of marriageable age. To prevent evil results from this, as the child might die under age and the *heres* have the estate on his hands, it was ordered that if the child did so die, the estate should be sold as if there were no *heres*. The text adds that this constitutes a precedent[1]. Much in this case turns on matters which do not concern us. It seems, however, difficult to reconcile it with some of the cases already discussed: one might have thought that neither S nor Z could compel entry, for S is to get nothing but liberty[2], and Z's right is subordinate to that of S[3]. It does not appear that it is in this connexion that the text treats itself as creating a precedent, but it is clear that when the substantial intent was to give to a slave of the testator liberty and the *hereditas*, Antoninus thought it should not be hampered by too great regard for legal principle. We know that if the *heres* was to free his own slave and hand him the *hereditas*, the value of the slave so freed might be deducted from it as a debt[4].

We have seen that these gifts need for completion an act of manumission. Till that has been done, or there has been *mora*[5], they are still slaves for all purposes[6]. Their children born in the meantime are slaves and belong to their owner[7]. But the beneficiaries themselves are quasi *statuliberi*, which much improves their position. Thus their status is not affected by alienation or usucapion even though the liberty was conditional at the time when the alienation occurred, and the alienation was *inter vivos* or *mortis causa*[8]. The *fiduciarius* cannot in any way make their position worse[9]. Marcus Aurelius lays it down that no act or defect of his is in any way to affect the slave[10]. Of these acts and defects we shall have illustrations, when we come to deal with statutory restrictions[11]. Others can be taken here. If the slave is instituted by the *fiduciarius* with a gift of liberty, he is not a *heres necessarius*[12]. If the *fiduciarius* chains the slave, this is no bar to his liberty[13]. The *fiduciarius* may not hand him to another to free[14]: if, however, he does in any way alienate him, we have seen that the holder is bound to free him[15]. But he may choose, if he prefers, to be freed by the original *rogatus*—so it was provided by Hadrian and by Antoninus Pius[16]—and the *fiduciarius*

---

[1] *h. t.* 11. 2.   [2] 36. 1. 57. 2, *fin.*   [3] *h. t.* 55.
[4] *h. t.* 28. 17.   *Ante*, p. 521. The rule that in estimating the value of a *hereditas*, the value of slaves to be freed is deducted, is confined to these cases of deduction of a quarter. Thus in reckoning the burden of funeral expenses of a woman, *heres* and *vir* are liable in the proportion of the *hereditas* and of that part of the *dos* which remains with the *vir*. But there is no deduction in respect of freed slaves, 11. 7. 20—25.
[5] *Post*, Ch. xxvii.   [6] 40. 5. 45. 2.   [7] C. 7. 4. 3; D. 35. 2. 24. 1.
[8] 40. 5. 24. 21, 45. 2, 51. 3.   [9] 40. 5. 15.   [10] *h. t.* 30. 16.
[11] *e.g. post*, pp. 537 *sqq.*   [12] 28. 5. 85. *pr.*   [13] P. 4. 12. 4.
[14] 40. 5. 34. *pr.*   [15] *h. t.* 24. 21; 19. 1. 43.   [16] 40. 5. 10. 1, 24. 21.

will then be bound to buy him back and manumit him[1]. So where the *heres* dies without having done it, and his *heres* hands on the *hereditas*, *ex Trebelliano*, the slave may choose by whom he will be freed[2]. Even if he has actually been freed by the wrong one, Pius decides that he can, on claiming, become a *libertus* of the original *rogatus*, the rule being perfectly general, and applying whether the alienation was voluntary or not[3]. All this is a rough and ready way of securing adherence to the testator's intention, and thus the rule is not applied if the will shews that the testator meant any holder to free[4]. Moreover if the *fiduciarius* should have died without successors, the man will be the buyer's *libertus*, since otherwise, the buyer, having no one from whom to claim, will lose both the price and the *libertus*[5]. As to those texts which say that if the *heres* dies without freeing the man, his *heres* must[6], it should be noted that under Antoninus Pius the rules of *mora* were applied in this case and he was treated as if he had been duly freed[7].

The fiduciary, as he may not make the man's position worse, may not exact services from him, even though the will authorise this: *iure publico derogare non potuit fiduciarius*[8]. Even if the *manumissus* promise them, his promise is null, for it must be *libertatis causa*, and he is entitled to his liberty[9]. But if he promise, after freedom, knowing he need not, this is a valid *donatio*[10]; if the will shews that the testator meant the fiduciary to have the full rights of patronage, then, perhaps, it is said, he may impose services[11]. Where a son was told to free his father's slave, Paul is made to say[12]: *dicendum est posse eum etiam contra tabulas habere et operas imponere: hoc enim potuisset etiamsi directam libertatem accepisset, quasi patroni filius.* This is unintelligible; a son cannot ignore his father's manumission. But for the last three words it might perhaps be understood of a son who has obtained *bonorum possessio contra tabulas* and can wholly ignore the manumission[13]. But *patroni filius* cannot impose *operae*. It seems idle to guess at what Paul may originally have written.

We have hitherto assumed the general validity of the gift: we have now to consider by whom, in favour of whom, and on whom they may be created and charged.

Any person who can make a *fideicommissum*, may make one of liberty[14], subject to the requirement of age under the *lex* Aelia Sentia[15].

---

1 40. 5. 15.   2 *h. t.* 23. 1. He might thus get an older patron, *h. t.* 15, 51. 3.
8 *h. t.* 24. 21, 26. *pr.* Of course in this case there was no handing back.
4 49. 5. 24. 21. *fin.*   5 *h. t.* 25.   6 *h. t.* 12. 1; 40. 4. 20; P. 4. 13. 2.
7 40. 5. 26. *pr.*; *post*, Ch. xxvii. He is in some ways better off than a *statuliber*, *e.g.* in relation to the *sc.* Silanianum, *ante*, p. 95.
8 38. 1. 13. 1, 42; 38. 2. 29. *pr.*; cp. Vat. Fr. 225.
9 38. 1. 7. *pr.*, 7. 4, 13. 1.   10 *h. t.* 47.   11 38. 2. 29. 1.
12 40. 5. 33. *pr.*   13 So Otto and Schilling.   14 40. 5. 24. *pr.*
15 C. 7. 4. 5; *post*, p. 537.

More detail is needed as to the person in favour of whom it may be made. It may be a slave of the testator or of the *heres* or of a legatee or of a *fideicommissarius* or even of a person taking nothing under the will[1], provided, according to one text, that there was *testamenti factio* with his owner[2]. The reason for this last rule is obscure: the outsider is no party to the will. There was nothing to prevent a man's buying a slave from a *peregrinus* and then freeing him, and it is not easy to see any reason why he should not be able to direct his *heres* to do so. It seems most probable that the jurist had in mind the case of an *extraneus* who was also the *fiduciarius*. One could not require a man to free his slave without giving him something by the will and one could not give him anything at least by direct gift unless there was *testamenti factio*. Indeed whatever the origin of the rule it must have been narrower than it seems or have had exceptions. Thus in one text it is doubted whether a *fideicommissum* of liberty could be given to a *servus hostium*. The objection is not, as might have been expected, that there is no *testamenti factio* with his *dominus*, but that such a person is unworthy to become a Roman citizen. The objection is overruled so far as to allow such a gift to be valid, if it were given for the event of his passing to Roman ownership[3]. It may even be given to a *servus poenae*, and will take effect if he is pardoned, though there is, in such cases, no *postliminium*[4].

It may be made in favour of a person actually free, and if at the time of the death, or, if it is conditional, at the time when the condition is fulfilled, he has become a slave, the gift will take effect[5]. It will be noticed that this is an exception, *favore libertatis*, to the rule that one cannot make provisions contemplating the enslavement of a free man[6]. It is perhaps for this reason that it is valid only if he is a slave at the time when the gift can first operate, a restriction which finds no analogy in the cases we have just discussed.

Such a gift may be made in favour of 'an unborn person. Paul's text is not free from difficulty[7], and Justinian speaks of a division of opinion among the jurists on the matter[8]. Against the validity of such gifts there is the rule that *fideicommissa* in favour of *incertae personae* and *postumi alieni* are void[9]. On the other hand, it is a very reasonable application of *favor libertatis*, and there are texts which make it uncertain whether such a *postumus* could be an *incerta persona*, at any rate if born before the testator died[10]. There are other texts which

---

1 G. 2. 264; Ulp. 2. 11; C. 7. 4. 6; D. 32. 8. 1; 40. 5. 16; 40. 7. 13. 4.
2 40. 5. 31. *pr.*   3 40. 5. 24. 2.
4 *h. l.* 5, *ante*, p. 410. It may be given to one conceived and born *ex damnata*, since he is an ordinary slave, or to the slave of an unborn person, *h. l.* 4, 6.
5 *h. l.* 3.   6 18. 1. 34. 2.   7 P. 4. 14. 1. The MS. reads *nascitur*.
8 C. 7. 4. 14.   9 *e.g.* G. 2. 287.
10 *e.g.* 34. 5. 5 *sqq.* The classes of *incertae personae* and *postumi* are usually kept distinct.

speak of *fideicommissa* in favour of the children of a certain person, with no indication that the gift was confined to those which were born at the time the will was made[1].

If the testator thought the slave to whom fideicommissary liberty was given was his own, but he was really *alienus*, the gift is nevertheless good[2]. As the text notes, this would not be true of a *fideicommissum* of property[3]: it is a case of *favor libertatis*.

We pass to the question: on whom may such gifts be charged? The general rule is that they may be imposed on anyone who can be charged with any *fideicommissum*[4], *i.e.* substantially, on any person who takes a pecuniary benefit under the will, or the *paterfamilias* of any such person[5]. It is noticeable that Gaius does not speak of *fideicommissarii* as being liable to such charges, but we have already seen such cases[6]. If he takes anything under the will, it is enough, even though he renounces, or is excused from, some of its provisions[7]. On the other hand, if it appears as a matter of construction that the direction to free was with special reference to a particular gift, and that gift was not made or did not take effect, then even though he is entitled to benefits under other parts of the will, he may not be bound to this *fideicommissum*[8]. It must be a gift having a pecuniary value, and thus one who has received nothing by the will except the release of a lien over property for the security of a debt, which, however, remains still due, cannot be burdened with a *fideicommissum*[9]. This general statement may be ended with the remark that as the freeing is not voluntary and is not exactly an alienation, one who is bound to free under a *fideicommissum* may do so even at a time when he is forbidden to alienate[10], though a *pupillus* may not do it without the *auctoritas* of his *tutor*[11].

The cases are, however, of such different types that they must be treated under distinct heads.

A.   Where the *fideicommissum* is charged either on the *heres*, the slave being an unlegated slave of the testator, or on a person to whom the slave is given either by legacy or *fideicommissum*. It may of course be charged on one or more or on all the *heredes*, and it is sometimes difficult to say which the testator meant. The *heres* charged may have only a part of the slave, in which case he must procure the other parts from his *coheredes*[12]. A difficulty arises where one of the *heredes* not

---

[1] *e.g.* C. 7. 4. 16. *pr.*, *ante*, p. 476.
[2] 40. 5. 39. *pr.*   [3] P. 4. 1. 8; Ulp. 25. 5.   [4] Ulp. 2. 9.
[5] G. 2. 263 *sqq.*; Ulp. 25. 10 (cp. 24. 21); In. 2. 24. 2; D. 29. 7. 8. 1; 36. 1. 80. 2; *etc.*
[6] 36. 1. 17. 16; G. Ep. 2. 7. 2.   [7] 40. 5. 41. 3.   [8] 31. 34. *pr.*
[9] 32. 3, 4. The further *fideicommissum* must it seems be of liberty or something of pecuniary value. Where one was directed to free a slave in order to marry her he must free but need not marry, 40. 5. 51. 12.
[10] 40. 5. 31. 2.   [11] *h. t.* 11.   [12] 29. 7. 11—13.

charged is an *infans*, and is thus incapable of selling. It is settled by a *sc.* Vitrasianum, and a decree of Antoninus Pius, that the persons charged shall in that case be able to free him, a valuation being taken of the part belonging to the *infans*, and they being liable to him as if there were a judgment for that amount[1]. If the *fiduciarius* frees the slave by will and leaves his *hereditas* to him, he is not a *heres necessarius*, as he was already entitled to liberty, but if the original liberty was conditional he will be *necessarius*, unless and until the condition occurs, and then *voluntarius*[2].

The gift need not have been by actual legacy. If a slave is given to a man by *donatio mortis causa*, and there is a *fideicommissum* of liberty, and he gets nothing else he is bound to free[3], but not if it is a simple gift *inter vivos*[4]. And of course there is no *fideicommissum* on one who gets neither the slave nor anything else[5]. Where a legatee is under a *fideicommissum* to free we are told that the *heres* can refuse delivery of the slave unless the legatee will give security to carry out the manumission[6]. This rule of Julian's seems an excess of caution, in view of the machinery for compelling completion which we shall have to consider later[7], and which was certainly in existence in Julian's day. The additional precaution is rendered possible by the fact that the words used by the testator make the legacy one *sub modo*, and in the case of such gifts the *heres* has in general the right to require security for the completion of the intended purpose[8]. If on the other hand the legatee refuses to receive the slave, he may be compelled to cede his actions to some nominee of the slave, so that the liberty may not fail[9].

If a slave is left to X to free, the terms may be such as to give some profit to him (X), *e.g.* the manumission may be conditional or *ex die*. In that case a *fideicommissum* beyond that of liberty may be imposed on X in favour of the slave or any third person[10].

Where a slave was legated to be freed, and the *heres* refused to give him and was condemned to give his value, the jurists doubted whether he was entitled to be freed and if so by whom, and if by the *heres* whether the legatee was entitled to keep his legacy. Justinian is our sole authority for the dispute. After adverting to the stupidity of the judge, who had power to order delivery and not damages, he goes on to settle the point in a way we shall have to consider later[11].

---

1 40. 5. 30. 6.   2 28. 5. 3. 3, 85. *pr.*   3 32. 37. 3.
4 40. 5. 40. *pr.*   5 40. 5. 26. 6.   6 40. 5. 48.
7 *Post*, Ch. xxvii.   8 32. 19, *etc.* See Pernice, Labeo, 3. 1. 37.
9 40. 5. 33. 2. It is not a case of failure of the gift.   10 32. 3. 1.
11 C. 7. 4. 17. If the fiduciary is a *fideicommissarius* of the *hereditas*, and it is only informally handed over, it is likely that, before Justinian, the manumission could not be completed so as to make the man a *civis* till he was acquired by *usucapio*. See Pap. Resp. 9. 2; Esmein, Mélanges, 352.

B. Where a *heres*, legatee or *fideicommissarius* is charged to free his own slave. The general rule is that if he accepts the benefit he must free the slave, even though the man is worth more than the gift[1]. Where X was left land and money with a direction to free a slave, he was bound to free even though, owing to the *lex* Falcidia, he did not get the money[2]. But he must get a real benefit. Thus, accepting a *legatum dotis* does not bind the wife to free a slave of hers[3]. Upon one point there seems to have been a difference of opinion. If a man accepted a legacy burdened with such a *fideicommissum*, but the legacy reached him lessened in value, either as having been cut down by the *lex* Falcidia, or from some other cause *imminutum*, there were some jurists who thought that he was entitled to rescind his acceptance[4].

Ulpian[5] goes on to lay down the rule for the case where the instruction is to free several slaves, and the gift is not enough for all. The donee must free so many as the money will serve for. They are to be taken in the order of the will, or if this is not possible, the matter must be decided by lot or by the decision of an *arbiter*. We should be inclined to apply this text to the case of instructions to purchase and free, but for the fact that the writer immediately proceeds to discuss that as a distinct case. The rule is perhaps to be justified on the ground that while a single liberty cannot be divided, several can. But the text is corrupt and such a set of positive provisions have a Byzantine look.

Some exceptional cases may be noted[6]. Where the legatee attacks the will and thus loses his legacy, the *fideicommissum* must fail. Paul says that in such a case it is the business of the Fisc to buy and free the slave, if the *fiduciarius* will sell, which he cannot be compelled to do[7].

A *libertus* institutes his patron for his *legitima pars* and gives him a further legacy, directing him to free one of his slaves. If he takes the legacy he must free, but he may refuse it and keep the *legitima pars*. If he is made sole *heres* and accepts, he must free. But, if there is a substitute, he may by Praetorian decree take the *legitima pars*, leaving the rest to the substitute, who must free if he can buy the slave[8]. There can be little doubt that this text is interpolated[9], but

---

[1] 40. 5. 8, 24. 12, 24. 13, 45. 1; C. 6. 50. 13. *Restitutio* if donee is a minor: he can restore the gift before the liberty is given, 4. 4. 33.
[2] 40. 5. 22. *pr.*   [3] *h. t.* 19. 1.
[4] *h. t.* 6. Another text credits this view to Ulpian (*h. t.* 24. 16), but it may be that Tribonian is speaking, as he certainly is in the concluding words of both these texts.
[5] *h. t.* 24. 17.
[6] Where a *paterfamilias* desired his sons to free a slave, in fact, but not to the father's knowledge, in the *peculium castrense* of one of them, that one must free: the error coupled with the fact that the father provided the *peculium castrense* makes it unfair to make the other son buy half and then free. This is a mere matter of construction involving no principle, 40. 5. 23. 2.
[7] 34. 9. 5. 4. In such a case the gift went to the fisc.
[8] 38. 2. 41.
[9] Gradenwitz, Z. S. S. 23. 342; Kalb, Juristenlatein, 75.

it is hard to say how far. The jurist's difficulty is to reconcile the rule, that one who receives a benefit may be burdened with a *fideicommissum*, with the duty to the patron not to impose on him a distasteful manumission. The point is not merely financial, and the rules cited by Gradenwitz[1] as to the extent to which manumissions are binding on the patron are hardly material: the point is that it is one of his own slaves, not the testator's. It seems clear that the mere gift to the patron of what he is entitled to, does not enable the testator to impose a *fideicommissum*[2], but this text, though it raises this point, does not decide it. The actual solution given is in itself rational, but it conflicts with the principle that one entitled to the whole cannot enter for half[3]. It is however probably not from Tribonian, but an abridgement of what Papinian said. The text contemplates some other application of the *decretum* than that mentioned above: it may be that, as Gradenwitz[4] supposes, Papinian suggested some solution for the case of legacy to the patron, which Tribonian has suppressed[5].

A legacy is left to A with a *fideicommissum* to free S, and a further *fideicommissum* of the legacy in S's favour. Here neither *fideicommissum* is binding. For A cannot be bound unless he gets something, which on the facts he does not, as, if he freed S, he would have to give him the money. It is as if he was under a *fideicommissum* of the money in favour of a third person. Of course he is bound if the *fideicommissum* of the money is *ex die* or *sub conditione*, so that he gets something from it[6].

C. Where a beneficiary is directed to buy and free a slave. Here the general rule is that if he takes the gift he is bound to carry out the *fideicommissum*, if he can with the money, but he need not give more than he has received, and if the owner will not sell the slave at that price the fiduciary may keep the legacy *ex voluntate testatoris*[7]. But there are complications and difficulties. If the owner has himself taken a benefit under the will, he is of course bound to sell him to the *fiduciarius* at a reasonable price and then no difficulty arises[8]. If there are several slaves and the money is not enough for all, they must be bought and freed so far as the money will go, in the order of the will if that is discoverable, if not either by lot or on the decision of an *arbiter*, as in the analogous case of a person directed to free a number

---

[1] *loc. cit.* He refers to C. 6. 4. 6. 16 b.   [2] 30. 114. 1; cp. 40. 5. 31. 3.
[3] 29. 2. 1—3.   [4] *op. cit.* 343.
[5] It may be that Papinian allowed the patron to keep the legacy without freeing. This is consistent with Papinian's known characteristics. See Roby, Introduction to Dig. cxciv.
[6] 40. 5. 19.   But there was disagreement on the point.
[7] 35. 2. 36. 1; 40. 5. 24. 12, 51. 2. An application of the principle that a *fideicommissum* may not exceed the gift on which it is charged. The rule applies only where, as here, the two are strictly commensurable, not, *e.g.*, where the *fideicommissum* is to free the fiduciary's own slave.
[8] C. 7. 4. 6, 13.

of his own slaves[1]. If the owner will not sell, or will not sell at a reasonable price (for it does not seem that the fiduciary is bound to give more, however large the benefits he has received), nothing can be done[2]. If the price asked is not obviously unreasonable, the difficulty being merely that they cannot quite come to terms, the Praetor will on application fix a price which the owner may accept if he likes[3]. If the gift of liberty is conditional and the condition is not yet satisfied, the *fiduciarius* is not bound to buy and free, even though the owner has prevented the fulfilment, and so *non per servum stat* that the condition is not satisfied. This is a common sense rule: the condition might be one benefiting the *heres*, and costing the owner something[4]. If both the owner and the slave are willing, the owner can compel the fiduciary to buy and free, or, in the alternative, he may, by a provision of Caracalla, free the slave himself and sue the fiduciary for his value[5]. In any case, the owner cannot be compelled to free or hand the man over, till he has received security for the price[6].

If the owner refuses to sell at a fair price what is the effect? Gaius and Ulpian say the gift is annulled, as does the much later Epitome of Gaius[7]. But Justinian says the gift *differtur* till the opportunity arises[8], and he inserts in his Code an enactment of about A.D. 220 which lays down the same rule[9]. It is possible that this is interpolated, though that seems unlikely. The texts in the Digest hardly touch this point, but those that approach it shew no sign of much handling[10]. On the whole it seems likely that the constitution attributed to Alexander is genuine, and that while the classics allowed pendency of the gift for the case where by any change of value it might come within the value of the legacy, Alexander allowed it also for the possibility of change of mind in the vendor. Whether these rules are of Justinian's time or earlier, they are as follows. If the owner does not sell now, the gift will be in suspense till he will[11]. The fiduciary on taking his gift may be required to give security (*cautio*), to carry out the purchase and manumission, if the owner should lower his demand, or the slave diminish in value, or the legacy increase in amount or value, though it be only by fruits or interest, provided it reach the necessary sum[12]. If he refuses to give this security, his action for the legacy will be met by an *exceptio doli*[13].

---

[1] 40. 5. 24. 18; cp. *h. l.* 17.   [2] *h. t.* 31. 4.   [3] *Ibid.*   [4] 40. 4. 55. 2.
[5] 40. 5. 31. 4; C. 6. 50. 13; *post*, Ch. XXVII.   [6] 40. 5. 32. *pr.*
[7] G. 2. 265; Ulp. 2. 11; G. Ep. 2. 7. 7.   [8] In. 2. 24. 2.
[9] C. 7. 4. 6.
[10] Most of them are in 40. 5. 24. Gradenwitz shews (Interpolationen, 41) that parts of this *lex* are interpolated, but he does not refer to any passage touching this point.
[11] C. 7. 4. 6.
[12] 40. 5. 7, 24. 14—16, 31. 4. In 40. 5. 24. 16 pendency may be contemplated in that part of the text of which the grammar is normal, but there is an appended clause which can hardly be by the hand which wrote the beginning.
[13] As to the case of diminution of the legacy, *ante*, p. 521.

It is likely that this *fideicommissum* to buy and free was never a common case, and it is also probable that the difficulty which certainly exists in reconstructing the classical rules is in part due to the fact that, on a considerable number of points, there were doubts among the jurists. It is noticeable that even in A.D. 220 Alexander feels it necessary to declare that such a gift is possible[1].

[1] C. 7. 4. 6.

CHAPTER XXIII.

MANUMISSION DURING THE EMPIRE (cont.). STATUTORY CHANGES.
Ll. IUNIA, AELIA SENTIA, FUFIA CANINIA.

OF these three statutes the first mentioned, perhaps the last in date, was essentially different in object from the others. It enlarged existing rights: they were restrictive. For this reason, and because some of the provisions of the *lex* Aelia Sentia seem to presuppose the *lex* Iunia, it is well to deal with this law first.

LEX IUNIA.

This statute defined the position of those who had been *in libertate tuitione praetoris* by the earlier law[1]. It made them *latins,* giving them broadly the position of colonary latins, subject to certain disabilities of a very serious kind. Because of these restrictions they were called Latini Iuniani to mark them off from the others[2]. The cases with which it dealt were, apparently, the slave freed by his bonitary owner[3], the slave informally freed[4], and the slave freed under 30[5], though as to this case we shall see that there is doubt as to what is due to this *lex* and what to the *lex* Aelia Sentia[6]. Most of the points of difficulty under this *lex* will be more conveniently discussed later: here it is enough to mention a few points.

Notwithstanding the language of Gaius[7] it is clear that a bonitary owner could give freedom by will[8]. It is hardly so clear whether he could do it *vindicta*[9]. And it seems that manumission *censu* must have given *civitas* or nothing[10]. Apparently the entry of the man's name must have been a nullity, of no more force than any other mistake of the Censor's[11]. And it does not seem that it amounted in itself to a manumission *inter amicos* or *per epistolam*[12].

[1] *Ante*, p. 444.   [2] G. 1. 22; 3. 56.
[3] G. 1. 167; Ulp. 1. 16; 11. 19; 22. 8; Fr. D. 9.
[4] G. 1. 17, 22; 3. 56; Ulp. 1. 10; Fr. Dos. 4, 6—9, 14; C. 7. 6. 1. *Ante*, p. 444. Consent of *consilium* if *dominus* under 20, G. 1. 41; *post*, p. 538.
[5] G. 1. 17, 18; Ulp. 1. 12.   [6] *Post*, p. 542.   [7] G. 2. 267.
[8] Ulp. 1. 23; 22. 8.   [9] *Post*, p. 543.
[10] See however Vangerow, Latini Iuniani, 20.
[11] Mommsen, Röm. Staatsrecht (3) 2. 1. 374; Dr. P. R. 4. 52.
[12] *Ante*, p. 446.

Only such a slave was protected and thus became a latin as was *talis ut praetor libertatem tueatur*[1]. The language seems to contemplate defects in the slave[2], and though, as we have seen[3], the limitation is mainly referred to in connexion with the accompaniments of the manumission, it is important to remember that the words imply that protection could be refused to unworthy slaves.

Most, probably all, of the other cases of latinity we shall have to consider are of later origin. This type of status, having once been invented, had new groups added to it from time to time, by an economy of invention to which the Romans were prone. Just as the rules as to *dediticii* were made to apply to cases quite different from that for which they were invented, and Junian latins themselves are an extension of the idea of latinity, so there come to be latins under like rules who have nothing to do with the *lex* Iunia.

There are cases of inferiority in manumission which it does not in any way affect. Thus a peregrine owner could not give the slave in any case a better status than that he had himself[4]. He could it seems use only informal methods. And it may be supposed that any latin owner might use the method *per vindictam*, and any colonary latin that by will. But we are without information[5].

The only other topic to consider in connexion with this *lex* is its date. It is always called *lex* Iunia by the classical writers[6], and usually even in Justinian's time[7], but in one passage of the Institutes it is called *lex* Iunia Norbana[8]. No direct evidence as to date exists, but as the *Fasti* give consuls bearing the names Iunius and Norbanus for A.D. 19, this has been commonly accepted as the correct date. The matter has been the subject of much controversy[9], of which some statement is necessary, though the point is not important enough to justify a long account. The same names are not found again in any one year, but in 82 B.C. one of the consuls is called Norbanus. This date is impossible: Cicero, writing later[10], enumerates the modes of manumission, and could hardly have failed to mention so important a law had it existed. The date A.D. 19 is supported by the fact that the *lex* clearly belongs to a time near that of the *lex* Aelia. And Gaius, by his expression *per legem* Aeliam Sentiam *et* Iuniam[11], seems to treat it as the later of the two. But the absence of early authority for the name Norbana makes the evidence for the actual year 19 very slight,

---

[1] Fr. Dos. 8.   [2] Vangerow, *op. cit.* 13.
[3] *Ante*, p. 445.   [4] Fr. Dos. 12; *post*, p. 594.
[5] As to certain questions concerning the position of Junian latins, *post*, App. IV.
[6] *e.g.* G. 1. 22, 80, 167; 2. 110, 275; 3. 56, 57, 70; Ulp. 1. 10; 3. 3; 11. 16; 20. 14; Fr. Dos. 6, 7, 8, *etc.*
[7] In. 3. 7. 4; C. 7. 6. 1.   [8] In. 1. 5. 3; Theoph. *ad h. l.*
[9] See especially Vangerow, Latini Iuniani, 4 *sqq.*; Voigt, R. R. G. 2. 160; Karlowa, R. R. G. 1. 621; Cuq, Inst. Jurid. 2. 148.
[10] Topica, 2.   [11] G. 1. 80.

and there are serious difficulties. The *lex* Aelia Sentia, A.D. 4, creates
and deals with a case of Junian latinity, *i.e.* that of the person freed
under 30[1], and thus assumes the existence of the status. No other
enactment of Tiberius extends or improves the rights of *libertini*: from
the *lex* Visellia[2] it would seem that the tendency was the other way.
Suetonius tells us that Augustus dealt with the different conditions of
libertini as well as with *dediticii*[3]. This may refer either to the *lex*
Aelia, as to persons under 30, or to the *lex* Iunia, but in either case it
seems to assume the existence of Junian latins under Augustus, and
thus to negative the date 19. But it is a mere general statement of
no great weight. It is plain that the *lex* Iunia invented the status.
The name shews it: we are frequently so told, and nearly every rule
relating to them is repeatedly referred to that law[4]. Gaius tells us[5]
that those who are Latini Iuniani were slaves before the *lex* Iunia,
which would not be true, for those freed under 30, if it were later than
the *lex* Aelia. No inference for the view that the *lex* Aelia was the
earlier can be drawn from the fact that it gives the right of *anniculi
probatio* only to latins manumitted under 30. This is not because at
that time there were no others, in which case the language of Gaius
in his account of the matter would be pleonastic, but because it is dealing
only with persons who would have been *cives* if it had not passed, and
so does not add a new class of *cives* as a wider provision would. On
the other hand, the *lex* Aelia may have put those freed under 30 merely
in libertate, and the *lex* Iunia have conferred latinity on them[6]. It
must not be forgotten that one text refers the rules of *anniculi probatio*
to the *lex* Iunia[7]. If this is correct one great difficulty in accepting
the later date is removed, since if it was not till later that a man
manumitted under 30 became a latin, it is not easy to see how the
lex Aelia can have contemplated his marriage with a latin or a *civis*.
But the earlier and repeated testimony of Gaius[8] is more weighty than
an isolated text of Ulpian, especially as Gaius is more or less confirmed
by another text of Ulpian, unfortunately rather corrupt[9]. It must also
be noted that some texts suggest that the *lex* Iunia dealt only with
informal manumission[10], though the weight of evidence is in favour of
a wider scope[11]. Again Ulpian[12] tells us that slaves who had been guilty
of misconduct became, on manumission, *dediticii, quoquo modo manumissi
sunt*, and adds that this was enacted by the *lex* Aelia Sentia. The

---

[1] *Post*, p. 542.
[3] Aug. 40.
[5] G. 3. 56.
[7] Ulp. 3. 3.
[2] Date however doubtful, see Willems, Droit Pub. Rom. 113.
[4] See the texts cited in nn. 6, 7, 8 on p. 534.
[6] So Vangerow, Lat. Iun., 4 *sqq.*
[8] G. 1. 29, 31, 66.
[9] Ulp. 7. 4.   Ulp. 1. 12, sometimes cited on this side, seems rather to support the other view.
See *post*, p. 536, n. 3.
[10] Fr. Dos. 7; Ulp. 1. 10. So G. 1. 167 and Ulp. 11. 19, dealing with *tutela* of latins, seem
to treat the *lex* as dealing only with slaves freed by bonitary owners.
[11] *e.g.* G. 1. 22 ; 3. 56, *etc.*   [12] Ulp. 1. 11.

words quoted have little point unless they are an allusion to informal manumission. But this means that if the *lex* Aelia is earlier than the *lex* Iunia, either Ulpian is wrong or a man freed informally would be a slave if he had done no wrong—free if he were a rascal[1]. Moreover Gaius[2] in dealing with the law as to the distribution of the goods of *dediticii* uses language which implies that *latini* (*iuniani*) existed at the date of the *lex* Aelia. On the other hand in one text of Ulpian in which he is speaking of the *lex* Aelia, his language is not that which would have been expected if the *lex* Iunia had been the earlier: the *ideoque latinus fit* is certainly an inference for the present: the *lex* is cited as putting the man *in libertate*[3]. Most of these and many other considerations (*e.g.* the general character of the policy of Augustus as opposed to that of Tiberius) are weighed by Schneider in his full discussion of the question[4], and he concludes that the *lex* Iunia is the earlier. He thinks the name Norbana is a mere error, a view which leads him to disregard, as evidence for any date, the occurrence in any year of a magistrate called Norbanus. Indeed the real question is: was the *lex* Iunia earlier or later than the *lex* Aelia? The actual year matters little. There were a consul Iunius in B.C. 24 and a consul Norbanus in B.C. 23. This has led to the view[5] that the law was passed in the earlier year during the absence of Augustus in Spain, approved by him on his return in the next year, and re-enacted perhaps with some alteration. But this is an improbable suggestion: no other instance exists of such a nomenclature resulting from such facts.

So far as the general question goes, opinion seems on the whole to favour the view that the *lex* Iunia is the older[6]. But the contrary view has many supporters[7]. Karlowa[8], following Brinz, argues strongly for it. He points out that though Gaius says the *lex* Aelia deals with latins under 30, he nowhere says that they got latinity by that law, which must have been the case if the *lex* Iunia had already been passed. Indeed in one text he implies that they got it through the *lex* Iunia[9].

---

[1] Vangerow thinks (*op. cit.* 13) that a criminal slave freed informally was not protected by the Praetor. Fr. Dos. 10. This would avoid the absurdity. He notes that the *lex* Iunia gives latinity to all persons protected. G. 3. 56. He holds it to be only by a *Sc.* that these became *dediticii*. The remarks of Ulp. 1. 11 and G. 3. 74 that on this point the *lex* Aelia makes no difference between formal and informal manumission he treats as reading later rules into the *lex*. See Wlassak, Z. S. S. 28. 54 *sqq.*

[2] G. 3. 56, *latini essent*.   [3] Ulp. 1. 12. So Vangerow, *loc. cit.*

[4] Schneider, Z. S. S. 5. 225 *sqq.*, 6. 186 *sqq.*, 7. 31 *sqq.*

[5] Du Caillaud, *cit.* Schneider, Z. S. S. 5. 241.

[6] See, *e.g.*, Girard, Manuel, 124; Mommsen, Staatsr. (3) 3. 1. 626; Dr. Pub. Rom. 6. 2. 248; Roby, Rom. Priv. Law, 1. 38, *etc.*

[7] *e.g.* Cuq, Inst. Jurid. 2. 148; Karlowa, R. R. G. 1. 621 *sqq.*; Hölder, Z. S. S. 6. 205 *sqq.*, 7. 44 *sq.*   [8] *loc. cit.*

[9] G. 3. 56. The fact that it is not called Norbana by early writers he thinks proves nothing: many consular laws are cited under one name. The point is, however, not that the absence of the name Norbana shews that the *lex* is not of A.D. 19 but that the fact that it is once so called 500 years after the assumed date proves little in favour of that date, especially as the MSS. differ and the Greek paraphrase is equivalent to *Urbana*. Schneider, Z. S. S. 5. 225. Vangerow, *op. cit.* 9, points out, however, that Norbanus was also called Iunius.

It is true that the *lex* Aelia Sentia seems to speak of marriage[1] of those freed under 30, which implies latinity. Vangerow holds that the *lex* Aelia Sentia spoke only of *contubernium* and that Gaius is antedating the expression *uxorem ducere*[2].

On the whole, as Mommsen says[3], while the priority of the *lex* Iunia is the solution which creates least difficulty, certainty is unattainable. But it is only certainty on this point that can give certainty as to the meaning of some of the obscure texts in which the classical jurists seem to be at odds on points connected with this legislation.

LEX AELIA SENTIA, A.D. 4.

This is a comprehensive enactment dealing with the relations between *libertini* and their patrons, and also imposing restrictions on manumission. It is only with these last provisions that we are concerned. There are four rules, which do not all start from the same point of view or protect the same interests, but have the common quality that between them they constitute the first inroad on the principle that a formal manumission by a quiritary owner makes the man a *civis*. The rules need separate consideration.

I. The manumitter must not be under 20, otherwise the manumission is void *ipso iure*, the rule being prohibitory and nullifying[4]. It applies to all cases *inter vivos* or on death, and even soldiers' wills are not exempt[5]. As the law does not divide days it is enough if he has completed the day before the 20th anniversary of his birthday. He cannot then be said to be less than 20 and the *lex* does not require him to be more than 20[6]. The rule is in one respect very favourably construed. If the manumitter was 20 when he made a codicil in which he made a direct gift of liberty, it is immaterial that the will, confirmation by which is needed, was made before he reached that age[7]. Usually the codicil is read into the will, the effect of which is in some cases to destroy the gift[8]. The text in the Code gives as the reason for laying down the more favourable rule, *nec enim potestas iuris sed iudicii consideratur*. This, which is not literally correct, since it is a question of *potestas iuris*, must mean that as the case is clearly not within the mischief attacked by the rule, and the rule itself is restrictive of a civil right, it is to be construed narrowly. The rule applies only to a manumission : thus a minor pledgee of a slave can give the assent without which the manumission is void[9].

---

[1] G. 1. 31.   [2] *op. cit.* 8.   [3] *loc. cit.*
[4] G. 1. 38—40; Ulp. 1. 13; In. 1. 6. 4—7; C. 2. 30. 3. *pr.*
[5] 29. 1. 29. 1; 40. 4. 3; C. 6. 21. 4. 1.   [6] 40. 1. 1.
[7] C. 7. 2. 1.   [8] *Ante*, pp. 461, 464.
[9] 40. 2. 4. 2; *post*, p. 573.

As might be expected attempts were made to evade the *lex*. One
at least of these was checked by a Senatusconsult which provided that
a gift by a minor to a man of full age, in order that he might free, was
void[1]. In the same way he could not, in his will, validly direct liberty
to be given[2]. Where a minor sold a slave *ut manumittatur*, the sale
was void, even though the slave was delivered, and even though the
intent of the minor vendor was that the manumission was not to take
place till he was of age[3]. The point is that his judgment was not
regarded as yet sound enough, and if the transaction was allowed to
stand, he would be unable to change his mind. Where a common
owner, a minor, abandoned his share to a common owner *animo
manumittendi*, the receiver could not free—the transaction being null:
nihil aget[4]. Where a minor released a debtor on his promising to free a
slave, the stipulation was void, and there was thus no novation of the
old debt[5]. It is evident that the Senatusconsult[6] was somewhat general
in its terms. Probably it prohibited what Proculus calls *fraus legi*[7], and
left a good deal of room for juristic interpretation[8]. The fact that there
was a gradual development may perhaps account for the view attributed
to the early Campanus, that if a minor requested his *heres* to free a
slave of his (*i.e.* of the *heres*), this was valid and not affected by the
lex[9]. It is not easy to distinguish this from the last case: presumably
the *lex* and the Senatusconsult were at first regarded as applying only
to freedom given to the minor's own slave[10].

But where a *filiusfamilias* freed under the authorisation of his
paterfamilias, this was valid whatever the age of the minor, for here the
father was the true manumitter[11].

All this is subject to the very important exception that if *causa* was
shewn to a body called the *Consilium*, the minor might with its approval
manumit *per vindictam*, and as proof of the *causa* did away with the
statutory bar, he might even free informally, with the effect of making
the slave a latin[12]. But, ordinarily, the manumission was done at once,
on approval of the *causa*, by *vindicta*, before the magistrate whose
consilium had approved: hence the manumission is sometimes said to
be done *apud consilium*[13]. This *consilium* was a council chosen by the

---

[1] 40. 9. 7. 1; 18. 7. 4; C. 7. 11. 4. The *Sc.* seems only to have confirmed a juristic rule.
[2] C. 7. 4. 5. See below, n. 9.   [3] 18. 7. 4.
[4] 40. 9. 16. 1.   [5] 45. 1. 66.   [6] C. 7. 11. 4.
[7] 40. 9. 7. 1.   [8] *i.e.* apart from *Scc.*
[9] 40. 5. 34. 1. As to the date of Campanus, see Roby, Intr. to Dig. clv.
[10] See n. 1. A minor freed a slave *inter vivos*, and in his will gave him a legacy. After he
made the will he sold the man, the buyer freed him before the minor died. The legacy was
void: it was in effect a gift to his own slave *sine libertate*, 30. 102, *ante*, p. 144. A minor freed
a slave *inter vivos*, having by will made a *fideicommissum* of the estate to which the slave was
attached with its slaves. The man was not included: the manumission, though void, shewed
that he did not mean him to be included, 33. 7. 3. 1.
[11] 40. 1. 16. *Ante*, pp. 457 *sqq.*   [12] G. 1. 37, 1.
[13] G. 1. 38; D. 40. 2. 24, 25; Fr. Dos. 13. As to the unity of the whole transaction see
Wlassak, Z. S. S. 28. 37 *sqq.*

magistrate who presided in it. It consisted, at Rome, of five Senators and five Equites, and it sat to enquire into *causae* on certain specified days. In the provinces it consisted of 20 Recuperatores, Roman citizens, and this class of business was attended to on the last day of the *Conventus,* the judicial Assize or Session[1]. This particular business however hardly seems to have been looked on as judicial, since we learn that a person domiciled in one province could shew cause in this way, and manumit, in any other province in which he chanced to be[2]. It was immaterial that the Praetor who presided was his tutor[3]. The magistrate himself might be under 20: this would not prevent him from presiding, unless it were his own slave: in that case he could not do so in earlier classical law, as he would have to nominate the *consilium*[4].

As to what was a sufficient *causa,* we have a considerable list, and we are told moreover that there was no hard and fast rule: the sufficiency of the *causa* would be determined in each case[5]. A cause duly approved, whatever it was, sufficed, and after the manumission it could not be called into question. Thus an enactment of Valerian lays it down that while a manumission by one under 20 without cause shewn was a mere nullity, one after cause shewn did not admit even of *restitutio in integrum*: liberty is irrevocable[6]. This is only an application of a well-known principle. But a text of Marcian goes a little further. He tells us that Antoninus Pius laid it down, that when once the *causa* had been accepted, then, however defective it really was, the liberty must proceed: *causas probatas revocari non oportere...nam causae probationi contradicendum, non etiam causa iam probata retractanda est*[7]. This means presumably that there was no appeal: it would not prevent a magistrate from vetoing any further steps, where a fraud was proved[8].

Apparently the only fixed requirement for a *causa* (and this was a creation of practice) was that it must be *honesta causa, non ex luxuria sed ex affectu, non deliciis sed iustis affectionibus*[9]. Among the more obvious *causae* were blood-relationship of any kind or degree, the relation of nurse or *paedagogus,* foster parent or child, foster brother or sister[10]. The *causa* might be notable services in the past, *e.g.* the protection of life or honour[11].

---

[1] G. 1. 20; Ulp. 1. 13 a.   [2] 40. 2. 15. 5; cp. 40. 5. 51. 7.
[3] 40. 2. 1.   [4] D. 1. 10. 2; but see *ante,* p. 454.
[5] 40. 2. 15. 1; G. 1. 19.   [6] C. 2. 30. 3. *pr.*; D. 4. 3. 7. *pr.*
[7] 40. 2. 9. 1. This may mean no more, but it seems to imply that, *causae probatio* having annulled his incapacity, he can now free.
[8] These texts deal only with insufficiency of *causa*; others shew the rule to be the same in case of *falsa causa,* In. 1. 6. 6; C. 7. 1. 1. See Haenel, Diss. Domm. 166. If approval was obtained through *culpa* or fraud of the *libertus* there was a remedy, even in extreme cases a criminal remedy, C. 2. 30. 3. *pr.* This seems to imply more than mere insufficiency.
[9] 40. 2. 16. *pr.*
[10] G. 1. 19, 39; In. 1. 6. 5; D. 40. 2. 11—14. *pr.* The case of foster child applied especially to women freeing, but it was allowed in case of men who had provided for nurture of the child.
[11] 40. 2. 9. *pr.,* 15. 1.

There is more complication as to those *causae* which contemplated the future. If the slave was over 18, desire to have him as a procurator was enough[1], provided that the manumitter had more than one slave[2]. It is laid down, though not without some doubts, that the desire to have the man as *tutor* was not enough: the reason assigned being that he who needs a *tutor* is not fit to choose one[3]. The reason seems hardly satisfactory. The enquiry into the sufficiency of the *causa* would include an enquiry into the fitness of the man. The argument of the text seems indeed to suppose that the cases in which manumission by a minor was allowed were those in which even an immature mind was able to decide, but it is obvious that this was not the principle at all. The truth is that for *pupilli* without testamentary or statutory *tutores* the law provided another well-known method of appointment.

A common and much discussed *causa* was intention to marry. To make such a *causa* admissible it was required by a Senatusconsult (perhaps the one which dealt with *fraus legi*) that the minor should swear to marry the woman within six months. If he did not so marry, the manumission was null[4], so that if she had a child in the meantime, its status was in suspense till the marriage or the expiration of the six months[5]. There were obvious limitations on this *causa*. Not more than one could be freed for this purpose, and the manumitter must be of a class a member of which might reasonably marry a *libertina*[6]. That the woman might marry a third person was no *causa*, and if no other was shewn, then, even though, *e.g.* on divorce by the third party, the minor married her within the six months, this did not save the manumission: it was simply void, and could not be saved by an *ex post facto causa*[7].

A woman freed *matrimonii causa* could not refuse[8] or marry any other without the manumitter's renunciation of his right[9]. It is said that she could not divorce, but this is contrary to the Roman conception of marriage, and the rule, as Julian says, really means that if she did divorce, she could not marry anyone else. No doubt the patron could divorce her[10].

---

[1] 40. 2. 13. The Institutes make it 17, the minimum age for *postulatio in iure*: our text may mean, having entered on his 18th year.

[2] *Ibid.* The language of this text does not shew whether this rule was confined to this case or not. It is a juristic rule probably more accurately expressed as being that if he was the only slave a specially strong *causa* would be needed.

[3] 40. 2. 25.   [4] 40. 2. 13.

[5] 40. 2. 19.

[6] 40. 2. 20. 2. *Spado* could free *matrimonii causa* as he could marry: *castratus* could not, 23. 3. 39. 1; 40. 2. 14. 1.

[7] 40. 9. 21. Common owners could not free *matrimonii causa*: as to the share of one this was for marriage to a third person which was not enough, 40. 2. 15. 4. The technical difficulty was easily overcome.

[8] 23. 2. 29.   [9] 23. 2. 51.

[10] 24. 2. 10, 11. It must be remembered that there was no manumission at all unless the minor married her within six months. She was of course not so bound if he was under a *fc.* to free her, 23. 2. 50. As to the rule in case of acquisition *ut manumittatur* or purchase *suis nummis*, see 23. 2. 45, and *post*, Ch. xxvii.

A woman could free on most of these *causae*, but not, it seems, *matrimonii causa*, unless she was a *liberta*, and a slave, *e.g.* a fellow-slave, had been left to her for this purpose[1].
There are other *causae* of a totally different nature which need separate treatment. If a minor was instituted *heres* on condition of freeing a certain slave, this was a sufficient *causa*: his *iudicium* was not in question[2]. If a slave was conveyed to a man *ut manumittatur*, whether gratuitously or for a price, it was provided by Marcus Aurelius, about A.D. 178, that the man should become free, though nothing was done, by the effect of the disposition[3]. It is clear therefore that if he was so delivered to a minor, there was no need for the minor to shew *causa*, since he could not help the freedom. Accordingly we are told in two texts by Papinian and Ulpian dealing with *donatio ut manumittatur*, that there was no reason to shew cause[4]. But another text of Ulpian says[5] that where the slave was so given, either for nothing or for a price, the minor might prove by way of *causa*, either the *lex donationis*, or the intent of the transferor, otherwise shewn. If there was a price, there was obvious reason for shewing the *causa*, since it might involve a loss, but the text expressly covers also the case of *donatio*. The texts may perhaps be harmonised on the supposition that the expression *causae probatio* is here used untechnically, and the meaning is that where the manumitter is under 20, the Praetor presiding will require to be satisfied of the circumstances, and the matter can be referred over to the *consilium*, if need be, as in the case of sale for a price[6]. In the analogous case of a slave *suis nummis emptus*, there was a rule, a little earlier in origin, that if not freed he could apply to the Court and get an order directing the holder to free him[7]. We are told that this constitution applied even though the owner were a minor[8]. We are not told whether if the minor proceeded to free he must prove the *causa*, but from the argument of Papinian in the case last discussed[9] it is to be presumed that he must, since the liberty would not take effect of itself.
Another analogous case is that of *fideicommissum*. Here there are distinct cases. We are told that a minor could not free by direct gift by will, but that he could do so by *fideicommissum*, and that the gift would be valid, if the man was one as to whom the minor could have shewn cause, if he had freed *inter vivos*[10]. We are not told that the adult *fiduciarius* must shew cause, and, indeed, the form of the texts is opposed to this. He had a perfect right to free, and the transfer to

---

[1] 40. 2. 14. 1, 20. 3.   [2] 40. 2. 15. *pr.*   [3] *Post*, Ch. xxvii.
[4] 40. 1. 20. *pr.*; 40. 2. 20. 1.   [5] 40. 2. 16. 1.
[6] So apparently A. Faber, Jurispr. Scient. 267 *sq.*   [7] *Post*, Ch. xxvii.
[8] 40. 1. 4. 8.   [9] 40. 1. 20. *pr.*
[10] 40. 5. 4. 18; C. 6. 21. 4. 2; 7. 4. 5. It is possible on the form of the texts that the authorisation to free, if cause could have been shewn, is due to Justinian.

him could not be regarded as null as it could *inter vivos*[1]. If, however, the slave attempted to put in operation the compulsory machinery, he would have to satisfy the court that a *causa* existed. Another case is that of a *fideicommissum* of liberty imposed on a minor. Here we are told by Papinian[2], consistently with his view in the case of a slave *donatus ut manumittatur*, that the minor must prove the *causa*. In this case the man would not become free *ipso facto* without the intervention of a magisterial decree.

It has already been noted that the presence of *causa* nullified the statutory defect. Accordingly it justified some of those acts, by a minor, *manumittendi causa*, which without it were void. Thus a minor with *causa* could convey his part to the co-owner for manumission, though he could not without[3]. But the existence of *causa* did not do away with restrictions independent of the *lex* Aelia Sentia. Thus an *infans* could not free, whatever his *causa* was, for he could not be authorised and his tutor could not free. A *pupillus* not *infans* could however free, *tutore auctore*, but not, says Paul, so that the *peculium* passed[4].

II. The slave must be over 30 or he does not become a *civis*[5]. There can be no doubt that the *lex* Aelia Sentia went as far as this: whether it went further and defined a slave freed under 30 as a latin is uncertain. The answer depends on the relative dates of the two *leges*. If the *lex* Iunia was the later, the *lex* Aelia probably placed such persons in the same position as those informally freed[6]. The effect of *causa* is exactly as in the last case, *i.e.* if the man were freed *vindicta*, after cause approved, he became a *civis*[7]. There is however some difficulty as to what happened if there were no *causa*. If he was manumitted by will directly, he became a latin: there could be no question of *causa*[8]. So too there is no sign of *causa* in relation to manumission *censu*. If the man was over 30 he became a *civis*: if he was not it was presumably void[9]. But the point is unimportant, for when these texts were written, the *census* was long obsolete in practice. If the manumission was informal, the man could not be a *civis* in any case, so that proof of *causa* would serve no purpose. We have seen that a man under 20

---

[1] *Ante*, p. 538.
[2] 40. 1. 20. 1; Pap. Resp. 9. 5 (Krüger) may refer to this case or to the slave under 30. 40. 2. 20. *pr.* (where the 20 is correct, as the text is dealing with *restitutio in integrum*) is not in conflict. Ulpian means that the proof of the *fc.* is a simple matter, and that is all that the *consilium* has to consider.
[3] 40. 9. 16. 1, immaterially altered. A minor who has bought *ut manumittatur* or is under a *fc.* to free can alienate to another with a direction to free, 40. 9. 16. *pr.*, see *ante*, pp. 524, 538.
[4] 40. 2. 24. The tutor could not in general authorise a *donatio*. Accarias, Précis, § 148.
[5] G. 1. 18; Ulp. 1. 12. Vangerow (*op. cit.* 17 *sqq.*) shews (citing G. 1. 17, 18, 29, 31; Ulp. 1. 12; Fr. Dos. 17; Theophil. 1. 5; C. 7. 15. 2) that the rule of the texts is that the man does not become a *civis*, not that the manumission is void.
[6] *i.e. in libertate*, *ante*, p. 446.
[7] G. 1. 18; Ulp. 1. 12; Fr. Dos. 17.
[8] *Ibid.*; G. 1. 17.
[9] Fr. Dos. 17.

could not give liberty even by way of postponed *fideicommissum*[1]. The same reason does not apply here, and we are told[2] that a direct or fideicommissary gift of liberty to take effect when the man reached 30 was valid. The distinction shews that the reason for refusing *civitas* to slaves freed under 30 was not that till that age it was not possible to be sure of their fitness, but that till that age they were not fit to be entrusted with the responsibilities of citizenship.

The effect of manumission *vindicta sine consilio* is not clear: the only text on the matter is corrupt. As it stands it tells us that (*lex?*) *sine consilio manumissum Caesaris servum manere putat*[3]. This is absurd. He cannot *manere* what he has not been. Nor is there any reason why he should become the property of Caesar: a *derelictio* would not have this effect, but would leave him *res nullius*, and manumission, which leaves the manumitter *patronus*, is much less than that[4]. The text does not say who *putat*: it must presumably be the *lex* which is the subject of the preceding and the following sentences. To say that a *lex putat* in a text which is setting forth its provisions is perhaps unexampled[5]. Of the many suggestions for emendation[6], the old one that the word was originally the name of some jurist is the most plausible. To make this sort of emendation rational it must be assumed that in early law, at least in the opinion of some jurists, manumission *vindicta* could not make a man a latin: it must be *civitas* or nothing. There are some circumstances which tend to make this possible. No specific case of manumission *vindicta* giving latinity can be found in classical texts, and though some are mentioned in Justinian's constitution[7] abolishing latinity, they all seem to be instances of that mass of legislation and practice, creative of latinity, which he tells us overlay the ancient law, and of which, as he also tells us, he was at pains to remove the traces[8]. Moreover manumission *vindicta* is an *actus legitimus* of extreme antiquity, and for this reason may have been regarded as a nullity if not completely operative[9]. However this may be, it is probable that practice early

[1] C. 7. 4. 5.
[2] G. 2. 276; 10. 2. 39. 2; 40. 4. 38. 1; 40. 7. 13. 5; 34. 5. 29; cited by Vangerow, *op. cit.* 38.
[3] Ulp. 1. 12.
[4] It may make him *servus sine domino* (Fr. Dos. 11), but that is not quite the same thing.
[5] The expression does occur, but not apparently as a reference to an explicit provision. See 40. 7. 25 and Cicero, de Rep. 4, cited Vangerow, *op. cit.* 25.
[6] Among them are: to omit *Caesaris*, to substitute *Senatus* (suggesting regulation by *Sc.*), to substitute the name of a *lex*. These Vangerow cites and rejects on what seem adequate grounds (*op. cit.* 25 *sq.*). He also rejects the suggestion of the name of a jurist (Cassius; Caelius Sabinus) on less convincing grounds. He treats the whole clause as a gloss. He considers that the act, as it shews intention to free, is an informal manumission. This ignores the probable view that not every declaration makes the man free, but only one which comes within the conceptions *inter amicos* or *per epistolam*. *Ante*, p. 446. He also urges that the statutory bar to its giving *civitas* ought not to have prevented it from producing other effects. See also Krüger, *ad h. l.* Schneider thinks the text rational as it stands (Z. S. S. 6. 189; 7. 31 *sqq.*), but see Hölder, Z. S. S. 6. 205 *sqq.*; 7. 44 *sq.* Justinian deals with this case apart from the other cases of latinity, C. 7. 15. 2.   [7] C. 7. 6. 6, 7.
[8] The hypothesis of later legislation might account for the obscure texts as to *servus pigneraticius* and *fructuarius*, *post*, pp. 574, 579.
[9] Cp. 50. 17. 77; see App. IV.

developed disregarding these considerations, and from the generality
of Gaius' language in connexion with *anniculi probatio*[1], it seems
possible that for him both formal and informal modes were on the
same level, as to the present point.

III.   Manumission in fraud of creditors or patron is void.
This will be dealt with fully in the law of Justinian's time.   Here it
is enough to state a few general rules.   The rule applied to peregrine
manumitters though the other parts of the *lex* did not[2].   The manumission was absolutely void[3].

A manumission was fraudulent if the manumitter was, and knew
himself to be, insolvent either before or as a result of the manumission,
and it must be shewn that the creditors actually were injured[4].   Thus
a manumission was not in fraud of creditors if the manumitter had a
maritime venture under way, which at the time had become a total loss,
though he did not know it[5].

Fraud on the patron would occur for instance if a *libertus* made it
impossible for himself to render the due aids and services, or if a dying
latin freed his slaves, or if a *civis libertus* did so when he had no
children.   We are, however, without any direct information as to this
rule, and can only argue by analogy from the rules as to alienations in
fraud of patron[6].   The rule as to the patron does not recur under-
Justinian's law and even traces of it are hardly discoverable[7].   There
are very few references to it even in the classical law.

IV.   Certain slaves become on manumission *dediticii*.
These were slaves who had been punished by their master with
chains or branding or imprisonment, or had been tortured for wrongdoing, and convicted or made to fight with wild beasts.   On manumission they were *in numero dediticiorum*, no matter how formal the
manumission, or how complete the capacity of all parties in other
respects[8].   This type was a mere addition to a pre-existing class, the
dediticii, with whose origin we are not concerned.

The different possibilities as to form of manumission make some
difficulty in this connexion.   In the case of will the matter is plain, but
it is clear that the manumission might be *inter vivos*[9].   If it was formal
and subject to no defect but the badness of the slave, he became a

---

[1] G. 1. 29—31, see also G. 1. 18.   [2] G. 1. 47.
[3] *Prohibet lex*, Ulp. 1. 15; *obstat libertati, vetat*, Fr. Dos. 16; *nil agit, liberi non fiunt*, G. 1.
37, 47.   See further, *post*, p. 563.
[4] In. 1. 6. 3; C. 7. 11. 1.   No merit of the slave would save the gift if creditors suffered,
40. 9. 23.
[5] 40. 9. 10.   [6] P. 3. 3; D. 38. 5.
[7] 40. 12. 9. 2.   See Bodemeyer, *op. cit.*, 22.   [8] G. 1. 13; Ulp. 1. 5, 11.
[9] G. 1. 15; Ulp. 1. 11.

dediticius. But the manumission might be such as to have made the man a latin apart from his defect. If and when the view was adopted, that manumission *vindicta* need not make the man a *civis*[1], there was no difficulty in the case of manumission *vindicta* of one under 30, *sine causa.* But informal manumission creates a dilemma. If the *lex* Aelia makes him a *dediticius* and the *lex* Iunia is later, it follows that the rascal would be free, though a *dediticius*, while the honest man would be still a slave, though *in libertate.* The difficulty does not exist if the *lex* Iunia is the earlier. On the other view, the solution of Vangerow[2] may be stated, that the *lex* Aelia Sentia applied its rule as to *dediticii* only to formal manumissions, and that its extension to all forms was due to a later Senatusconsult. But this is rather heroic in view of the texts which say that for this purpose the *lex* Aelia did not distinguish between the forms[3]. It involves the further corollary that after the *lex* Aelia the informal manumission of such a degraded slave was a nullity, since it is clear that the *lex* Iunia gave latinity to all[4] who were protected by the Praetor. This is in itself not improbable, for, as Vangerow remarks, they would be just the persons to whom the Praetor might refuse his protection. But the texts give no hint of all this and much of it is, as we have seen, in contradiction with them. On the whole evidence the view that the *lex* Iunia was the earliest seems to be the most probable.

Their position was carefully defined. They were incapable of *civitas*, and thus, for instance, if they satisfied all the rules of *erroris causae probatio*, though the other effects of the rule were produced, the deditician member of the union remained a *dediticius*[5]. They had no *testamenti factio* of any kind. They could neither make wills nor take under them[6]. Their property reverted to their patron on their death under rules which hardly concern us, but which seem to have been obscurely stated in the *lex*[7]. It appears to have provided that the *bona* were to go as if they had not been *dediticii*[8]. This might mean "as if they were still slaves." But it was construed as meaning "as if they had not suffered from the defect which made them *dediticii.*" This interpretation, however, itself needed limitation. As it stands it would make the goods go as those of a latin in some cases and as those of a *civis* in the others. But this would be to give a right to the children, as well as a right of testation. Neither of these existed, and the rule of the classical jurists was that the goods were to go to the patron in any case, as those of a latin, if the man would have been a latin but for his offence,

---

[1] *Ante*, p. 543.
[2] *op. cit.* 13; Wlassak, Z. S. S. 28. 57 *sqq.*
[3] G. 1. 15; 3. 76; Ulp. 1. 11.
[4] G. 3. 56, *cit.* Vangerow, *loc. cit.*
[5] G. 1. 15, 26, 67, 68.
[6] G. 1. 25; Ulp. 20. 14; 22. 2.
[7] G. 3. 74—76. See as to these Schneider, Z. S. S. 6. 198 *sqq.*
[8] As to this form see the Berlin Fragment, printed in Collectio lib. iuris anteiust., 3. 299.

otherwise as those of a *civis*. In the first case this would be a reversion of *peculium*, in the other it would be a succession, the distinction being important in many ways[1].

If they stayed, or dwelt, within 100 miles of Rome, they were sold into perpetual slavery beyond that limit, and if then freed they became, so Gaius tells us, *servi populi Romani*. Though Gaius seems to say that these detailed provisions are in the *lex* Aelia Sentia, this is not the necessary meaning of his words, and there may have been *senatusconsulta*[2].

The disabilities resulting from this degradation are very grave, and Paul shews that very definite rules were laid down as to the cases in which it took effect. Thus torture without confession was no bar to complete liberty, nor was punishment by one under a *fideicommissum* to free, since he could not make the position of the slave worse. Nor, for the same reason, was punishment by one of two owners, or by pledgee or pledgor of the slave, or by a master who was insane or a *pupillus*. But punishment by a subordinate whose act was authorised or ratified was enough. Here, however, if the master knew that the man was innocent, at any time before the punishment was actually inflicted, the facts would not be a bar to future complete liberty[3].

None of these four restrictions applied, not even the last, in a case of manumission by will to provide a *necessarius heres* to an insolvent[4], in order to avoid intestacy resulting from refusal of the *heres* to enter. We have already discussed the general principles of the law as to these *heredes necessarii*[5], and a word or two here will suffice. The privilege was strictly and narrowly construed. If any other *heres* entered, the gift to the slave was not saved[6], and it was only against the restrictions of the *lex* Aelia Sentia that the exception held good[7].

LEX FUFIA CANINIA (B.C. 2)[8].

Slaves were very numerous in the Augustan age—an individual *civis* sometimes owned thousands—a state of things very different from that existing in earlier days, if tradition is to be believed[9]. It was a natural consequence that manumission became frequent. It appears indeed that the number of *libertini* became a public danger. Manumission by will was the most common, as it cost the owner nothing, and ensured the attendance of a number of grateful *liberti* at his funeral. The result was an undesirable increase in the number of *libertini*, and

---

[1] G. 3. 64—70.   [2] G. 1. 27; 1. 160.
[3] P. 4. 12. 3—8. That children of *dediticii* could become *cives* appears from the rules of *erroris causae probatio*, G. 1. 26, 67, 68. As not subject to the special disabilities of their mother they were presumably on the same level as ordinary *peregrini* of the region. See Ulp. 22. 2.
[4] G. 1. 21; Ulp. 1. 14; In. 1. 6. 1; C. 6. 27. 1; D. 40. 4. 27.   [5] *Ante*, pp. 505 *sqq*.
[6] Ulp. 1. 14.   [7] 28. 5. 84. *pr*.   [8] See Mitteis, Z. S. S. 27. 357.
[9] See the cases mentioned in Apuleius, Apol. 17. See also Wallon, *op. cit.* 2. Ch. III.

occasional ruin to *heredes*. The *lex* Fufia Caninia was passed to check the evil. It provided that a man with 2 slaves could free both by his will, with 2 to 10, one half, with 10 to 30, one third, with 30 to 100, one fourth, with 100 to 500, one fifth, and never more than a hundred[1]. The maximum in each case is called the *legitimus numerus*[2]. The *lex* further provided that the power of manumission was never to be diminished by an increase in the number of slaves[3]. If more than the right number were freed, only the earlier, up to the *legitimus numerus* were free[4]. To prevent evasion the *lex* required that they should be freed *nominatim*[5]: the *sc.* Orphitianum provided that a clear description would do as well, if there were no ambiguity, for instance, "my cook," if there were only one, or "whoever shall be born of such and such an *ancilla*[6]." If the gift broke this rule, *e.g.* a gift of freedom to "all my slaves," the whole gift was void[7]. So also if the names were written in a circle in such a way that it was impossible to say which came first, the whole was declared void under a provision of the *lex* annulling *quae in fraudem eius facta sint*. Other similar attempts to evade the *lex* were met by *senatusconsulta*[8], which have, however, left little trace. There may be, indeed, one case. The *lex* applied only to manumission by will or codicil[9], and Gaius tells us that it left manumission *vindicta, censu,* and *inter amicos* quite free[10]. His epitomator makes a similar remark, substituting *in ecclesiis aut ante consulem aut per epistolam aut inter amicos*, but he adds that if a man on the point of death freed a number of slaves *inter vivos, in fraudem legis*, the manumissions were valid only up to the *legitimus numerus*[11]. Perhaps this is the effect of a Senatusconsult[12].

In calculating the number of slaves, fugitive slaves were taken into account, a rule for which Paul finds it necessary to give the reason that such slaves are still possessed by their owner[13]. We are nowhere told how common slaves were reckoned. As the common owners' rights in the slave were in nearly every case *pro parte*[14], it is probable that the slave counted only as a fraction.

None of these texts applies the rule in express terms to fideicommissary gifts, and the enactment by which Justinian repeals the *lex* Fufia Caninia[15] is rather ambiguous. It is plain, however, that unless it did apply to them it must have been nearly nugatory, and Paul, dealing

---

[1] G. 1. 43; P. 4. 14. 4; Ulp. 1. 24.   [2] P. 4. 1. 16.
[3] *e.g.* a man with 30 to 43 could free 10. With 44 he could free 11. G. 1. 45; Ulp. 1. 24.
[4] G. 1. 46; G. Ep. 1. 2. 2. Liberties in a codicil were treated as subsequent to those in a will, though the will were later, since they owed their validity to the will, P. 4. 14. 2.
[5] Ulp. 1. 25; P. 4. 14. 1.   [6] P. 4. 14. 1.
[7] G. Ep. 1. 2. 2.   [8] G. 1. 46.
[9] G. 1. 44; P. 4. 14. 1.   [10] G. 1. 44.   [11] G. Ep. 1. 2. 1.
[12] Probably later than Gaius. The text limits the rule to the case in which the master is already ill (of the malady of which he dies): probably no other evidence was needed to prove *fraus legi*, G. Ep. 1. 2. 3, 4.
[13] P. 4. 14. 3. Huschke (*ad h. l.*) points out that the *lex* says *habet*.
[14] *Ante*, p. 379.   [15] C. 7. 3. 1.

with this *lex,* gives, as an illustrative case, *qui ex ea ancilla nascetur*[1], which could have been effective only as a *fideicommissum.* It has been suggested[2] that as at the time of the enactment *fideicommissa* were novelties, it probably did not apply to them at first, but was made to do so by one of the *senatusconsulta* to which Gaius refers. The writer notes that the various *senatusconsulta* affecting fideicommissary gifts of liberty do not begin till the time of Hadrian. He thinks that Justinian's enactment[3], abolishing the rule, is clear for its application to *fideicommissa* in later law, and he cites a text of Paul[4] in the Digest which seems to shew that it applied in the time of Neratius. There seems little reason to suppose a Senatusconsult: such a case would be well within a possible juristic interpretation of the prohibition of fraud contained in the *lex.* And the language of Paul's text is much in favour of this view[5].

Before passing to the law of Justinian, it may be well to discuss shortly the circumstances under which the status of latinity could arise[6]. The following list has no claim to completeness.

1. The slave informally freed by a competent *dominus*[7]. It has been shewn by Wlassak that the classical law knew of but two of these modes, *per epistolam* and *inter amicos,* and that manumission *in convivio* is of much later introduction[8]. He remarks also that there is nothing, in the form of the rule in the *lex* Iunia to prevent its application to methods of later introduction[9]. The form of manumission *inter amicos* is not very precise. In one, the record of which has come down to us[10], the witnesses do not sign and are not named. The transaction was in Egypt and some of its provisions are coloured by Greek law[11], but there is no reason to doubt that this was in conformity with Roman practice. Hence the idea would naturally appear that any public manifestation of intent sufficed. This accounts for the acceptance of manumission *in convivio*[12], and the enactment of Justinian abolishing latinity gives other instances of the same thing, such as declaring *apud acta* that he is a son[13], giving him or destroying the papers evidencing his slavery[14], and

---

[1] P. 4. 14. 1.   [2] Bodemeyer, *op. cit.* 34.   [3] C. 7. 3. 1.   [4] 35. 1. 37.
[5] Bodemeyer (*op. cit.* 33) considers whether the rule applied to soldiers' wills. He thinks the rule as to naming did, as even a *miles* might not institute an *incerta persona,* In. 2. 20. 25. From 40. 4. 51 he thinks the main rule did not. It is not, however, clear that the *centurio* is freeing all his slaves. He remarks that 29. 1. 29. 1 shews only that some restrictions applied, not that this one did. The text looks altered, and it is possible that it is precisely this *lex* which has been struck out, as repealed.
[6] As to other legislative restrictions, see *post,* Ch. xxv., and as to *iteratio, post,* App. IV. For most of the following cases see Vangerow, Latini Iuniani, Capp. I, v.
[7] G. 1. 17; Fr. Dos. 4.   [8] Z. S. S. 26. 374, 404; *ante,* p. 446.
[9] *op. cit.* 420.   [10] Girard, Textes, Appendice.
[11] Mitteis, Reichsr. und Volksr. 8 *sqq.* There was a money payment and the person who provided it undertook not to claim the freedwoman as a slave. A right to keep her till reimbursement is common in Greek documents. See, *e.g.,* Dareste, Recueil des Inscr. Jurid. Grecq. II. 263, 267, 274.
[12] G. Ep. 1. 2.   [13] C. 7. 6. 10.   [14] C. 7. 6. 11.

perhaps also the direction in the will that he is to stand, *pileatus*, at the grave of the deceased[1]. It is observable that here it is indifferent whether the direction is by the deceased or the *heres*. Justinian provides that even if there was no intention to free but only to make a false shew of humanity, the men are to be *cives*, but in this case they would not have been latins in earlier law. It may be added that the *lex* Iunia required the manumission to be *nominatim*[2], but all this means is that the slaves must be *evidenter denotati*[3].

2. A slave informally freed by a master under 20, with the approval of the Consilium[4].

3. A slave manumitted under 30[5].

4. A slave manumitted by his merely bonitary owner[6]. Neither Gaius nor Ulpian enumerates the relevant cases of bonitary ownership: the latter mentions, as an illustration, the typical case of a slave acquired by mere *traditio*. But the rule must have applied equally to other cases of Praetorian ownership. Such would be the case of one held by praetorian succession (*bonorum possessio cum re*), the case of a slave *ductus* under a noxal action, that of one received under a decree of *missio in possessionem*, or a *bonorum venditio*. The case of a slave handed over under a *fideicommissum* is no doubt on the same footing, unless he was formally conveyed. The case of an owner *in integrum restitutus*, in respect of a slave, might seem to be on the same level, since it is a praetorian remedy, contradictory of the civil law, and giving rise to *actiones fictitiae* and the like. But it is clear that the Praetor restored the old state of things so far as possible, so that in this case such a reconveyance would be compelled (either *officio iudicis* or by the Praetor himself in those cases in which he carried out the *restitutio*) as would restore the quiritary ownership[7].

5. By an edict of Claudius a slave cast out because of sickness became free and a latin, provided the master *publice* ejected him and, having the means, took no steps to have him looked after or sent to a hospital[8].

6. If a slave had brought a *causa liberalis* against his master and lost, and the price of the slave was paid to his master by an outsider to secure his manumission[9], the slave, on manumission, became only a latin, as a sort of punishment[10]. The date of this is not known: Justinian credits it to *antiquitas*. It must have been express enactment.

7. If an *ancilla* was married by her *dominus* to a freeman, with a *dos*, she became a latin. This may be no more than a case of informal

---

[1] C. 7. 6. 5.
[3] See *ante*, p. 460, and *post*, p. 556.
[5] G. 1. 17; Ulp. 1. 12.
[7] 4. 2. 9. 7, 10. 1; 4. 4. 24. 4.
[9] *Post*, p. 640.

[2] Ulp. 1. 10; Wlassak, *loc. cit.*
[4] G. 1. 41.
[6] G. 1. 35, 167; Ulp. 1. 16; 22. 8.
[8] C. 7. 6. 3; *ante*, p. 36.
[10] C. 7. 6. 8.

manumission. Justinian made it give citizenship[1], as such manumission did. But the rule may have also covered the case of fraud.

8. Where an *ancilla* was sold with a condition against prostitution, but was nevertheless prostituted by the buyer, or where there was a condition for re-seizure in the event of prostitution, and her old owner did so seize her, and himself prostituted her, she became free and a latin[2].

9. A *libertus ingratus* under the conditions already discussed[3].

10. If a testator has given a slave liberty, conditionally, and while the condition is still pendent the *extraneus heres* frees him, he becomes only a latin[4]. The text refers only to *extraneus heres*: probably a *suus heres*, whose the slave was apart from the will, might ignore the restrictive effect of the condition[5]. The date of our rule is not known: Pomponius[6] quotes Octavenus as holding that if one freed a slave by will conditionally, and expressed the desire that the *heres* should not free the slave pending the condition, this direction was of no force. From this it has been inferred that our rule is as old as the first century of the Empire.

11. A *liberta* who cohabited with a *servus alienus* without her patron's knowledge was enslaved, and became only a latin if freed by him[7].

12. Slaves who detected rape were under certain circumstances made latins by Constantine. Justinian gave them *civitas*[8].

13. A freewoman, *sciens vel ignara*, cohabiting with a slave of the Fisc, remained free under a provision of Constantine, but the children of the union were latins[9].

There remain several cases of a doubtful kind.

14. Where a person was freed formally with an expression of intent that he should be only a latin, the effect seems to have been doubtful. Justinian enacts that such expressions are to have no effect[10].

15. The *sc.* Silanianum may have contained a case, to be discussed later[11].

16. A pledged slave could not be freed[12]. But, on a text, which is imperfect, most editors seem agreed that he became a latin if so freed, at least when the debt was paid[13]. But Justinian does not mention this case in his general enactment[14].

---

[1] C. 7. 6. 9. [2] C. 7. 6. 4; *ante*, p. 70; *post*, p. 603.
[3] C. Th. 2. 22. 1; *ante*, p. 423.
[4] C. 7. 6. 7. Other texts imply a power in the *heres* to free, *e.g.* 28. 5. 3. 3; 40. 4. 61; 40. 7. 3. 15, *etc.* See *post*, p. 586. [5] 4. 3. 32.
[6] 40. 4. 61. 2 ; *post*, p. 586. [7] *Ante*, p. 416; *post*, p. 552.
[8] C. Th. 9. 24. 1. There were probably other cases of the same type, *post*, p. 598; C. 7. 13. 3.
[9] C. Th. 4. 12. 3; *ante*, p. 417. [10] C. 7. 6. 6.
[11] *Post*, p. 602. [12] *Post*, p. 573.
[13] Fr. Dos. 16. See Krüger and Huschke, *ad loc.* [14] C. 7. 6.

17. If a woman freed a slave without her tutor's *auctoritas*, this was not valid. But if *auctoritas* was given at the time an informal letter of manumission was written, it was held and finally decreed that this should suffice[1]. The text is obscure and may refer only to formal manumission, in which the tutor, though not present at the formal act of manumission, had been present and assenting when the mistress wrote a letter to the slave declaring her intention, but it is usually taken to mean that an informal manumission was good, and made the slave a latin, even though the tutor gave *auctoritas* only when the letter was written, and had altered his mind when it was received[2]. The latter view better fits the words of the text.

18. If a slave was under usufruct he could not be freed. A certain truncated text on the matter is commonly taken to mean that though the owner could not free the man *vindicta*, still, if he did go through the form, the man became a latin when the usufruct ended[3].

19. It was a standing rule of manumissions that a manumissor could not give the slave he freed a better status than his own: it may be presumed therefore that a man freed by a Junian latin was himself a Junian latin[4].

20. If a slave was freed conditionally by will, he did not become a *statuliber* till the heir entered. We are told, however, that if he was usucapted, in the meantime, the Praetor would protect his liberty[5]. In another text it is said that his *spes libertatis* is restored *favore sui*[6]. The language of the first text has led to the suggestion that the slave, on the satisfaction, became a latin[7]. This seems improbable: it is hardly consistent with the language of the other text. The help of the Praetor is referred to in other cases where the slave became a *civis*[8], and the difficulty resulting from the fact that when the *heres* entered the man was the property of another would suggest rather a *fideicommissum* than resulting latinity. But in fact the difficulty was disregarded *favore libertatis*.

[1] Fr. Dos. 15.   [2] Böcking, Huschke, Krüger, *ad loc.*
[3] Fr. Dos. 11.   See Ulp. 1. 19; C. 6. 61. 8. 7; C. 7. 15. 1, and *post*, p. 579.
[4] Girard, Manuel, 123, and *post*, p. 594.   [5] 40. 5. 55. 1.
[6] 40. 7. 9. 3.   [7] A. Faber, Coniect. 16. 10, *cit.* Bodemeyer, *op. cit.* 49.
[8] Thus in the two texts last cited it is said that the Praetor will protect in other cases where there can be no suggestion of latinity.

CHAPTER XXIV.

MANUMISSION UNDER JUSTINIAN[1].

MANY of Justinian's changes, not directly concerned with the law of manumission, had, indirectly, great effect upon it. It may be as well to enumerate the chief of these changes before stating the law systematically. He abolished the distinction between quiritary and bonitary ownership[2]. He repealed the *sc.* Claudianum, with its connected legislation[3]. He abolished the classes of *latini* and *dediticii*[4] (thereby doing away with the rule that the slave must be 30[5], and with the restrictions as to criminal slaves who were freed), and he repealed the *lex* Fufia Caninia[6].

The rules in his time may be stated thus.

A. FORM. *Census* is gone. *Vindicta* remains, having long since ceased to be, if it ever was in any reasonable sense, a judicial process. Manumission *in ecclesiis* still continues[7]. Manumission by will of course still remains. The general effect of legislation of the later Empire having been to abolish the praetorian will, the question whether freedom can be given by it is obsolete. The place in the will is now immaterial[8]. Implied gifts are more freely recognised. Whatever may have been the earlier law it is now clear that appointment of *servus proprius*, as tutor, implies a direct gift of liberty[9]. The rule is subject to some obvious restrictions. Thus, as it turns on an implication of intent, the rule does not apply where the facts negative this intent, *e.g.* where the testator thought the slave free[10]. And where the slave is appointed *cum liber erit*, the appointment is a mere nullity. Conversely the appointment of *servus alienus* without such words is a mere nullity[11], though there is one text which seems to say that the condition will be implied and even that such a gift amounts ·to a fideicommissary gift of liberty[12].

---

[1] Many rules being common to Justinian and the classical law, convenience has decided the question which should be discussed here and in earlier chapters. The same consideration accounts for some repetition.
[2] C. 7. 25. [3] In. 3. 12.
[4] C. 7. 5, 6; In. 1. 5. 3. He remarks that *dediticii* have disappeared already in practice.
[5] C. 7. 15. 2. [6] C. 7. 3; In. 1. 7. [7] C. 7. 15. 2.
[8] In. 2. 20. 34.
[9] *Ante*, p. 463. The chief text (26. 2. 32. 2) gives liberty at once but delays the *tutela* till the *libertus* is 25. This is due to Justinian, but how far the alteration goes is uncertain.
[10] 26. 2. 22. [11] In. 1. 14. 1. [12] 26. 2. 10. 4; *ante*, p. 463.

In the same way a gift of the *hereditas* to *servus proprius* implies, in Justinian's time, a gift of liberty[1]. Thus where a slave is instituted with a gift of liberty, and, in the same will, the gift of liberty is adeemed, this cannot be construed as taking away the institution, for it is a rule of law that a *hereditas* cannot be adeemed. The institution stands good, and this implies a gift of liberty, so that the slave takes the inheritance, with liberty[2]. Justinian bases his rules on a presumption of intention, but he is hardly logical, for although a legacy to a man cannot take effect unless he is free, he does not allow a gift of liberty to be inferred from a legacy[3]. The fact is that the inference from another gift is not accepted unless in addition to the benefit to the slave, and *favor libertatis*, there is also some other public interest to be protected. In the case of institution, there is intestacy to be avoided: in the case of *tutela* there is the interest of the ward.

An inference from a form of words not amounting to a formal express gift is on another footing. Here the intent must be absolutely clear. Thus the words, *in libertatè esse iussi*, do not suffice[4]. And mere intent to free is not manumission. Thus where it was clear that certain slaves were destined to look after a temple about to be built, if they were not actually freed they were the property of the *heres*[5].

The refusal of classical law to make implications left room for many doubts, nor were these removed as a matter of course by the mere admission of such implications. Accordingly Justinian finds it necessary to settle a number of doubts by express provision. It is not to be expected that any clear principle shall be discovered in relation to these numerous specific decisions on points of detail and construction, but they must be set forth as illustrative of the manner and tendency of his changes. Where the institution was in a will and the liberty in a codicil, the ancients had doubted, since the institution would not have been good without the gift of liberty, and as this was in a codicil there was in effect a gift of the *hereditas* by codicil. Both are now to be good[6]. Where A made his child *heres* and freed a slave, and then made a pupillary substitution in favour of the slave without any gift of liberty, the ancients had doubted, as the institution and the liberty were in different grades. Justinian declares that the slave is *heres necessarius*[7]. A made two *heredes*: one was his slave, but had no gift of liberty. He then left the slave to a third party. The ancients doubted as to the result, whatever the order of the gifts. Justinian

---

[1] In. 1. 6. 2; C. 6. 27. 5. 1.　　　　[2] 28. 2. 13. 1.
[3] 34. 4. 20, except in a soldier's will, in which even a conditional legacy suffices, 29. 1. 40. 1, 2. Justinian provides that though the legacy does not imply liberty the *heres* must give the thing to the slave: apparently it is to go to the *peculium*, C. 6. 27. 5. 2.
[4] Except in a soldier's will, 40. 4. 49.　　　　[5] 40. 12. 35.
[6] C. 6. 27. 5. 1 d.　　　　[7] C. 6. 27. 4; *ante*, p. 509.

directs that the institution is to take effect notwithstanding the legacy[1]. If a slave was left as a legacy, and, later in the will, there was a pupillary substitution in his favour without a gift of liberty, the effect was doubtful. Justinian decides that the legacy is in suspense, till it is clear whether the substitution takes effect or not, which is the view that had formerly been held where the substitution had been accompanied by a gift of liberty[2]. A *servus proprius* is instituted *pure* and given liberty under a condition. If it is in his power and he fails to satisfy it, he loses both: if it is not in his power and is not satisfied, he is to be free nevertheless, but not to have the *hereditas* unless the estate is insolvent, in which case he is *heres necessarius*[3]. The reading of the condition into both gifts presents no difficulty: it was the settled rule[4]. But the reading it out again from the gift of liberty, in connexion with which it is expressed, is an illogical piece of *favor libertatis*, due to Justinian.

Fideicommissary and direct gifts can now be made to unborn persons, so that they shall be born free, and, if there are twins or more, all will be free[5]. The latter part of the rule does not look very rational: we should have expected the first born to be free[6].

As to the informal modes, Justinian legislates elaborately. He enacts that some shall be valid with witnesses, others without, and the rest shall be void[7]. Those valid are to have the same effect as manumission *vindicta* and are *legitimi* modes. Those allowed with witnesses are:

1. *Per epistolam*, five witnesses writing their names on the letter, *quasi ex imitatione codicillorum*. If the slave is absent the letter makes him free only when he receives it[8].

2. *Inter amicos*, also with five witnesses in imitation of a codicil. The act must be formally recorded by the master, and the slave must get the testimony signed by the five witnesses, and also by *publica persona, i.e.* a *tabellio*[9].

3. Formally recording the slave as a son, *apud acta*, involving of course an official witness[10]. We have seen that in this and the other case now to be stated, latinity had resulted, though probably not in classical law[11].

4. Giving to the slave, or destroying, in the presence of five witnesses, the papers evidencing his slavery[12].

---

[1] C. 6. 27. 5. *pr.*   [2] C. 6. 27. 5. 3; *ante*, p. 468.
[3] C. 6. 27. 6.   [4] *Ante*, p. 468.
[5] C. 7. 4. 14; *ante*, p. 476. As to direction to *heres* to choose and free slaves and his neglect do so, *post*, p. 610.
[6] The exact meaning of Justinian's rule is discussed later. See *post*, p. 557.
[7] C. 7. 6.   [8] 41. 2. 38. *pr.*; C. 7. 6. 1.   [9] C. 7. 6. 2.
[10] C. 7. 6. 10; In. 1. 11. 12.   [11] *Ante*, p. 548.   [12] C. 7. 6. 11.

Other informal modes allowed were[1]:

5. If by order of the deceased or of the *heres* they stand around the funeral couch, or walk in the funeral procession, *pileati, i.e.*, wearing the cap of liberty[2].

6. If a slave woman is given in marriage to a freeman with a *dos*[3].

In the other cases, apart from informal manumission, in which latinity had been conferred[4], *civitas* was now to result.

B. EFFECT AND REQUIREMENTS.

I. All valid manumission makes the slave a *civis*, and a declaration that a slave freed is to be a latin is to have no effect[5].

II. The master must be 20 years of age. To this rule there are, however, some exceptions.

(*a*) A slave may be made *necessarius heres* if the master is 14[6].

(*b*) A minor may free *vindicta* before the *consilium* for a cause approved by that body. An *impubes* needs *auctoritas tutoris*[7].

(*c*) Justinian allows it to be done by will at 17, as a man could make a will for all other purposes at 14. This *via media* seems to be adopted rather hastily. It is not mentioned in the Digest or in the Code, and it is not long preserved, since in 549 it is provided that a man may free by will at 14[8].

(*d*) The rule does not apply if the slave has been received *inter vivos*, from a competent person, on a condition to manumit[9].

It will be observed that there is in Justinian's law no limit of age in the case of the slave: he may be an infant, just as a mad slave may be freed, though a mad *dominus* cannot free[10].

III. The consent of the slave is not needed. The principle is expressed in the rule that an *infans* or a *furiosus* can be freed, and Justinian lays down the general rule that a slave is not allowed to refuse[11]. This seems to conflict with the principle that *invito beneficium non datur*[12]. It has been explained on the ground that it is a mere release of a right over a thing, and analogous to releasing a bird, and as being no more than the restoration of a "natural" state of things[13]. But manumission is not dereliction, and to be a Roman citizen is hardly

---

[1] The absence of the requirement of witnesses in these cases shews that they cover cases where there was no intent to free: they are constructive manumissions.

[2] C. 7. 6. 5.	[3] *h. t.* 9.

[4] *Statuliber* freed by *heres extraneus pendente conditione* (*h. t.* 7); loser in a *causa liberalis* afterwards freed (*h. t.* 8), sick slave abandoned (*h. t.* 3), slave freed under 30 (C. 7. 15. 2), *ancilla* prostituted contrary to condition (C. 7. 6. 4), slave detecting rape (C. 7. 13. 3).

[5] C. 7. 6. 6.	[6] *Ante*, p. 546.

[7] *Ante*, p. 538; 40. 9. 27. 1.

[8] In. 1. 6. 7; Nov. 119. 2. At 17 a boy could *postulare in iure.*

[9] As to this and the analogous case of a *fc.* imposed on a minor, *ante*, pp. 538, 541.

[10] 40. 1. 25, 26.	[11] C. 7. 2. 15. 2 a.

[12] 50. 17. 69.	[13] A. Faber, Jurisp. Pap. Scientia, 95, 188.

"natural." It seems more in the Roman way and more in keeping with Justinian's language to say that so mean a creature was not to be allowed to spurn Roman citizenship. The rule is not prominent in the texts and in the one in which it is clearly laid down, Justinian proceeds to state an important exception: in an *addictio bonorum libertatis causa* a slave may sometimes refuse the liberty[1].

IV. The manumission must be *nominatim*[2]. The rule remains, though the chief point of it is destroyed by the repeal of the *lex* Fufia Caninia. The survival of the rule is the more remarkable, in that its existence is expressly set down by the classical writers to that *lex*[3]. It is somewhat confused with the rule that liberty cannot be given to an *incerta persona*, which is itself based on the *lex* Fufia[4]. But this wider rule has clearly disappeared in Justinian's law, at least in analogous applications[5]. Error in name is immaterial if there is no ambiguity[6]. Thus the gift is void if there are several of the same name and there is nothing to shew which it is[7], and, in general, the gift is void for uncertainty if it is not clear who is meant[8]. It must be noted that the case contemplated is one in which the testator appears to wish that a particular one shall be free, but has not made it clear which he meant. The case is different where the language is such as to cover either of two, but it is clear that the testator was indifferent as to which was free. Such a case is that of a direction that either A or B is to be free. Justinian tells us that the effect of this was much disputed among the classical lawyers. Some held the gift null: some said both were free: some said the first named was free, in any event. Others held that if it failed, as to the first, it might take effect in favour of the second. Justinian decides that both shall be free[9], a decision which seems to deserve the contempt which commentators have thrown on it. It has been pointed out[10], however, that Justinian is only applying a rule which had already developed—as a theory at least—among the jurists, not only for this case, but also for the case in which the *heres* has a choice as to which he will free and dies without freeing either[11]. A similar case but avoiding the doubt is that in which the heir is directed to choose among certain slaves. Here the heir has the choice[12]. The only point of interest is the question what fact is sufficient to determine the

---

[1] C. 7. 2. 15. 2 a; *post*, p. 625.   [2] 40. 4. 24.
[3] G. 2. 239; Ulp. 1. 25; P. 4. 14. 1.   [4] G. 2. 239; In. 2. 20. 25.
[5] In. 2. 20. 25; C. 6. 48. 1. According to the *Sc.* Orphitianum, it is enough that he is so described that his identity is clear, 40. 4. 24, *ante*, p. 460.
[6] 40. 4. 21, 54. *pr.*   [7] 34. 5. 28—30; 40. 4. 37.
[8] Fr. Vat. 227. The manumission may be in the will and the description in a codicil or *vice versa*, 40. 4. 37.
[9] C. 6. 38. 4.
[10] Bernstein, Z. S. S. 4. 177 *sqq.* He is discussing, generally, various types of alternative gift and obligation.
[11] C. 7. 4. 16; *post*, p. 610.   [12] 40. 5. 22. 1, 46. 5.

choice, and entitle a particular man to his freedom[1]. An analogous case is that of a *fideicommissum*, charged on a beneficiary, to free a certain number of slaves. What is the effect where the gift is less than the value of all the slaves? Ulpian[2] appears to decide that as many of them must be freed as the amount will cover and then asks the question —which? The answer is rather in the manner of Tribonian. There is nothing to indicate any right of choice in anyone. But the text says that the order in the will should determine. If this will not serve, the matter is to be determined by lot, or by an *arbitrium*, on their merits. It is not to be left to the Praetor, lest suspicion rest on him, of *ambitio vel gratia*. It is difficult to believe that this is Ulpian. Indeed it would seem that in classical law the principles which we have already discussed would require that he should be compelled to free them all, even though they are worth more than the gift[3].

Such a gift may be made in favour of an unborn person[4]. Here too Justinian changed the law. The earlier law is not absolutely clear, but on the whole, Paul's text is very strongly in favour of the possibility of such gifts, by way of *fideicommissum*[5], and Justinian elsewhere[6] states a rule in terms which assume, as a matter of course, that such gifts were possible in early law. The doubt which Justinian suggests in his enactment[7] dealing with the matter is perhaps not as to whether such a gift could be made, but whether, if it were made, the child was born free. He enacts that both direct and fideicommissary gifts may be made in favour of unborn persons, at least if conceived, and this whether the mother be given freedom or not. The effect will be, he says, that they will be born free. It is difficult to apply this to fideicommissary gifts, since these require an act of manumission, but Justinian is not so logical that we can be quite sure that he troubled about this: it may be that he meant them to be free *ipso facto* in such a case, but to be *liberti* of ~~the~~ *heres*. Whether "born free" is to be taken as meaning *ingenui* is not clear: it seems hardly probable. What he says is that *cum libertate solem respiciat*. The logical difficulties are obvious: they are discussed elaborately but not to much purpose by the early commentators[8]. It is in no way inevitable that Justinian should have considered these words as meaning *ingenuitas*, though they cannot in strictness mean anything else.

---

[1] Bernstein, *loc. cit.*   [2] 40. 5. 24. 17.
[3] *Ante*, p. 529. As to the question how far *optio* constitutes a condition, see *ante*, p. 18, and *post*, p. 583.
[4] As to the general question of gifts to *incertae personae*, see the Gloss on 34. 5. 5. See also Girard, Manuel, 817.
[5] *Ante*, p. 526.   [6] C. 7. 4. 16. *pr.*   [7] C. 7. 4. 14.
[8] Haenel, Diss. Domm. 463. The case is linked with the rule just discussed by the provision that if after such a gift two are born, or more, all are free though the gift was in the singular, C. 7. 4. 14. 1.

V. Manumission must be by the owner. We have already[1] considered this rule. No great change of principle seems to have occurred under Justinian, but the rules require some further discussion and illustration.

We have seen that an ownership liable to determine still entitles its holder to free. Thus a *heres* under a trust to hand over the *hereditas* can free before doing so, being liable for the value of the slave whether he knew of the trust or not[2]. The rule is no doubt classical, but the text has been mutilated by the compilers, who speak of the validity of the liberty as a case of *favor libertatis*. There could be no meaning in this for classical law: the case is on all fours with that of one who has agreed to sell the *hereditas* and who frees a slave before handing it over. He is owner and the gift is good, but nothing is said about *favor libertatis*[3]. But Justinian's fusion of legacy and *fideicommissum*, and his provision that a real action was always available, led to a good deal of confusion[4].

There must, however, be real ownership. To free another man's slave is a nullity: in some cases it is penalised[5]. We are told, however, that where A manumit B's slave, B can have, if he likes, the value of the slave instead of the man, and this is said to have been *saepe rescriptum*[6]. So far as this represents classical law it presumably means no more than that the old owner could, if he preferred, treat the matter as a sale: it does not imply that the manumission was good or would be validated by the quasi-purchase. But it is not unlikely, judging by other texts, that this is what it means for Justinian. Thus while we are told that manumission of a *servus alienus* was not confirmed by subsequent inheritance of the slave[7], we are told elsewhere that if X is directed to free a *servus hereditarius* and so be *heres*, and he does manumit, *nihil agit*, so far as freeing is concerned, yet he has manumitted and thus satisfied the condition. And the text adds: *post aditionem manumissio ...convalescit*[8]. This last clause must be an addition by Tribonian.

If a man freed a slave of his own by *vindicta* thinking he was *alienus*, or if the slave or both were under the mistake, the manumission was good[9]. The text gives as one of the reasons that, after all, he is free *voluntate domini*, which is hardly the case if the master thought his act was a nullity.

---

[1] *Ante*, pp. 464 *sq.*   [2] 36. 1. 26. 2.   [3] C. 7. 10. 3.
[4] As to this and the case of *servus legatus, post,* p. 580.
[5] A man tricked the Emperor into approving his manumission of a *servus,* in fact *alienus.* The approval was annulled; the slave was to be restored with two similar slaves and three were to be given to the Fisc. Penalties not to be enforced if the slave had by lapse of time acquired a prescriptive right to liberty, C. 7. 10. 7 = C. Th. 4. 9. 1. The *interpretatio* puts manumission *in ecclesia* on the same level: the actual case is one of manumission *vindicta* before the Emperor.
[6] C. 7. 10. 1.   [7] 40. 9. 20.   [8] 28. 7. 20. 1.
[9] 40. 2. 4. 1. This text has been much discussed. See Appendix v.

In one text we are told that a *coheres rogatus manumittere*, can, by a rescript of Pius, free the slave even before partition, (when he cannot be sole owner,) where the other *heres* is an *impubes non rogatus*. But this is part of the law as to the enforcement of *fideicommissa* not carried out[1]. Other exceptional cases may be noted. If a man is free at the time when a will is made, a fideicommissary gift of liberty to him is good, if he is a slave at the time of the death or of the satisfaction of any condition[2]. But this is not a real exception to any rule laid down, for he will be the property of the person who actually frees him. It is only noticeable in that it is a case in which it is permissible, *favore libertatis*, as it seems, to contemplate supervening slavery[3].

Where A gave a slave to his wife *mortis causa*, (which was valid,) and instituted the same slave with liberty, if the institution came last and was intended as a revocation of the gift, the slave was a *necessarius heres*. If it was not so intended, or the gift came last, the gift prevailed, and the wife got the *hereditas* through the slave[4].

The exceptional cases in which Justinian allows effective manumission by a person not *dominus* do not represent any change of principle. They are no more than attempts to do equity, in a particular case, without any thought of the relation of the decision to ordinary legal rule. It still remains true that manumission cannot be by agent. But, whatever may have been the law before, it is now clear that manumission can be carried out by a *filiusfamilias* on behalf of his *paterfamilias* by any method *inter vivos*[5]. An extension of this principle is due to Justinian. In 530 he provides[6] that ascendants of either sex might authorise their descendant of either sex, whether in *potestas* or not, to free on their behalf—a rule which follows, as he says, the general breakdown of the old narrow conception of the family. It is noticeable that, notwithstanding its date, there is no trace of this extension in the Digest, published three years later.

As a part of his rearrangement of the rights of the father in acquisitions of the son he provides[7] that if a slave is given *ab extraneo* to a *filiusfamilias* to free, he may do so, the father's usufruct established by Justinian being disregarded, as unreal, in such a case, where the whole ownership is merely formal, since there is a duty to free at once[8].

VI. Manumission in fraud of creditors is void. Nothing is said by Justinian in this connexion about fraud on the patron[9]. The reason

---

[1] 40. 5. 30. 6; *post*, pp. 611 *sqq.*   [2] 40. 5. 24. 3.   [3] Cp. 18. 1. 34. 2.
[4] 24. 2. 22.   [5] *Ante*, pp. 457 *sqq.*; App. v.
[6] C. 7. 15. 1. 3.   [7] C. 6. 61. 8. 7.
[8] In earlier times the gift would have vested in the father.
[9] It is casually mentioned, 40. 12. 9. 2; Accarias, Précis, § 69. See also 38. 5. 11. Bodemeyer, *op. cit.*, 20.

for the disappearance of this from the rule is not clear. No doubt Junian latins were abolished, and it was in their case that the rule was most important, since all their property went to their patron when they died. But this does not account for the omission : it would require all the rules as to fraud of patron to disappear, which they do not[1]. It has been suggested that the omission is linked with the general rearrangement of patronal rights[2]. But if Justinian had intended a definite change in the law he would probably have said something about it. It has also been suggested that the matter is sufficiently provided for by the rules as to revocation of acts done *in fraudem patroni*[3]: we are told that *omne in fraudem patroni gestum revocatur*[4]. And elsewhere Justinian tells us that when alienation is inhibited by a *lex* or other agency the words cover manumission[5]. But the title in the Digest[3], though of some length, never mentions manumission, and the application of the above text to it conflicts with the important rule, shortly to be considered, that liberty was irrevocable. The *lex* Aelia Sentia makes the manumission void *ab initio*, and the distinction is clearly recognised in matter of alienation[6]. Some modern commentators appear to ignore the reference to the patron in connexion with this provision of the *lex*. But Gaius and Ulpian are quite explicit[7].

The general principle is that the manumission, to be void, must have been intentionally fraudulent[8]. Thus where an insolvent gave liberties "if my debts are paid" there was a general agreement among jurists, though Julian doubted, that this could not be fraudulent[9]. In another text in which the same rule is laid down, Julian seems to have no doubt[10], but probably his conformity is due to Tribonian. It has been suggested[11] that Julian was inclined to hold the gift void on grounds independent of the *lex* Aelia Sentia, as not having been seriously meant. But the gift obviously was seriously meant, and the whole structure of the text brings Julian's view into connexion with the *lex*. It is true that the latter part of the text expressly negatives fraud, but this, again, does not look like a part of the original text[12].

According to the Institutes the gift is fraudulent if the owner is insolvent and knows it, or knows that he will become so by the manumission, though the text hints at an abandoned view that the fact was

---

[1] The *lex* Aelia, which introduced the rule, is not much concerned with latins.
[2] Demangeat, Droit Rom. 1. 202.   [3] 38. 5.
[4] *h. t.* 1. 3.   [5] C. 4. 51. 7.   [6] 37. 14. 16.
[7] G. 1. 37; Ulp. 1. 15.   Girard, Manuel, 120; Sohm, Instit. § 32; Muirhead, Rom. Law, 337.
[8] G. 1. 37, 47; Ulp. 1. 15; Fr. Dos. 16; In. 1. 6. *pr.*; D. 40. 9. 16. 2; 42. 8. 6. 5; C. 7. 11. 1.
[9] 40. 4. 57.   [10] 40. 9. 5. 1.
[11] A. Faber, Jurisp. Pap. Sci., 209 *sq.*
[12] There is reason for the doubt. If the gift is valid these slaves could have only the value of *statuliberi*, however insolvent the estate was. If an insolvent *heres* entered the loss to creditors might be serious. See *post*, p. 562.

enough without knowledge of it[1]. The source ot the text is a passage from Gaius, which is cited in the Digest, where, however, nothing is said about knowledge[2]. It has been suggested that Gaius did not require this, but it is at least possible that he is citing an older view only to reject it, the doctrine of the Institutes being his own[3] as it certainly was the Sabinian[4]. However this may be, it is clear for later law that *consilium fraudis* was needed. Thus we are told that if a son frees *volente patre*, the gift is void if either knows of the insolvency[5]. The rule applies only to an ordinary voluntary manumission. Thus it has no application where the manumission is of a slave received *ut manumittatur*[6]: such a person would be free without manumission if the direction were not carried out[7]. So also where the manumission is under a *fideicommissum*[8], or is in return for money[9].

If it is given *fraudandi animo* in a codicil, it is bad though at the date of a previous confirmatory will the testator was solvent[10], but if he was solvent when he made the codicil, the fact that he had been insolvent at the date of the will was immaterial.

Besides intent, there must be actual *damnum* to the creditor— *eventus* as well as *consilium*[11]. Thus insolvency at *aditio* might destroy a gift designed in fraud, but solvency at *aditio* would always save it[12]. Two cases raise some difficulty here. It was possible for a *heres* who doubted the solvency of an estate, and yet wished to save the fame of the deceased, to agree with the creditors, before entering, that they should accept a composition, and it was provided, apparently by Marcus Aurelius and Antoninus Pius, that if a majority of the creditors agreed, the composition could be confirmed by magisterial decree, and thus forced on the other creditors[13]. Scaevola in two texts[14] discusses the question whether under such circumstances manumissions in the will are valid. It is clear that legacies are not unless the estate shews a profit to the *heres*. But he lays it down that liberties are valid unless they were given *in fraudem creditorum*. It is not clear that there was any *eventus damni*, since the creditors when they made their agreement knew of these liberties. The point is, however, that the *heres* could offer more if these slaves were assets.

Another noteworthy case is that of solvency of the *heres*. Some jurists held that this would save the liberties, but the view which pre-

---

[1] In. 1. 6. 23. If more than one were freed the gift might be void only to the extent of the excess, taken in order unless differences of value made it more favourable to liberty to alter the order, 40. 9. 25.
[2] 40. 9. 10.   [3] A. Faber, Jurisp. Pap. Sci. 199.
[4] 40. 4. 57.   [5] 40. 9. 16. 5.
[6] 40. 1. 10; 49. 14. 45. 3; Fr. de i. Fisci, 19.
[7] *Post*, p. 628.   [8] 28. 5. 56; Fr. de i. Fisci, 19.
[9] C. 7. 11. 5. As to fideicommissary gifts, *post*, p. 565. The texts say nothing of collusion.
[10] 40. 9. 7. *pr.*   [11] C. 7. 11. 1.
[12] 40. 9. 18. *pr.*   [13] 2. 14. 7. 17—10. The texts give further details.
[14] 40. 4. 54. 1; 42. 8. 23.

vailed was that it was immaterial[1]. In a text which seems to say the contrary it is clear from the context that a *non* has dropped out[2]. Another text declares to be governed by the same principle the case in which the liberty is conditional on the payment of money, and a third party is willing to pay it, so that the estate suffers no loss[3]. It has been suggested that the reason for this rule is to induce the *heres* to enter[4]. This is open to the objection that as the estate is rendered solvent by the entry, the creditors have no interest in getting the gift declared void, and the *heres* has, as we shall see shortly, no power to do so. Moreover the principle would not apply to the second case, in which the *heres* would not lose, as he gets an equivalent, and yet the principle to be applied, whatever it is, is common to both cases. It seems more probable that it merely represents a close adherence to the idea that the state of the actual *hereditas* and the intent of the testator are the only material things. But this makes the rule applied in the case of a gift, "if my debts are paid," all the more remarkable. It can only be justified on the ground that the use of this formula negatives fraudulent intent. But as we have just seen it might have been used as rather an ingenious way of injuring the creditors, and Julian's doubt seems to be fully justified.

The rule applies to soldiers' wills[5] and, unlike other provisions of the *lex*, it applies to manumissions by peregrines[6]. Most of the texts apply to direct gifts by will, obviously the commonest case, but the rule applied equally to gifts *inter vivos*[7], and to those by way of *fideicommissum*[8].

A creditor for the purpose of these rules is anyone who has an action, or an inchoate right to sue, even though the debt be *ex die* or conditional, so that there is no present liability[9]. There is, however, one distinction to be noted: a claim on account of legacy or *fideicommissum* is a sufficient debt[10]. But if the debt is merely a conditional legacy or *fideicommissum* due from the manumitter, this is not enough[11], probably because, as there has been no *negotium* or other legal act between them, the legatee or *fideicommissarius* is not a creditor till the condition arises[12]. If the debt which makes the man insolvent is conditional, we are told that the slave is a quasi *statuliber*, pending the arrival or failure of the condition[13]. Elsewhere we are told that in the case of an absolute debt the slave is a *statuliber* till it is certain whether the creditor will

---

[1] 40. 4. 57; C. 7. 2. 5. [2] 40. 9. 5. *pr.*
[3] 40. 9. 18. 1. *Sed si heres locuples non proficit ad libertates nec qui dat pecuniam prodesse potest.* The case in C. 7. 11. 5 is different: there is there no *damnum* and no *animus*.
[4] Accarias, Précis, § 71. [5] 40. 9. 8. 1.
[6] G. 1. 47. A *sc.* under Hadrian. [7] 40. 9. 5. 2.
[8] C. 7. 11. 7. Roby considers on the authority of 28. 5. 84. 1 that this rests on a *sc.* under Hadrian.
[9] 40. 9. 8. *pr.*, 16. 2, 27. *pr.* [10] 40. 9. 27. *pr.*; C. 7. 11. 1; *i.e.* due from the testator.
[11] 40. 9. 27. *pr.* [12] Cp. 44. 7. 5. 2. [13] 40. 9. 16. 4.

use his right[1]. This suggests that the more accurate way in which to state the law is that the gift is bad if there is *animus*, if there is damage to the creditor, and if the latter takes steps[2].

The creditor may be an individual *civis*, a corporation, or the Fisc, *animus fraudandi* being as necessary here as elsewhere[3]. The Fisc does not seem to have had any privilege in the matter in classical law[4], and as *civitates* and the Fisc are not creditors in the strict sense of the *lex*, it seems that special enactments were necessary to bring them within the *lex*[5].

If the master was insolvent at the time of manumission, and afterwards pays off all his creditors, new creditors cannot attack the gift, since there was no intention to defraud them. Julian is quite clear that the *animus* and the *eventus* must apply to the same creditor[6]. The following text adds as a note of Paul on Papinian that this does not apply if there is proof that the money to pay off the old creditors was derived from the new[7]. In another text however, from Papinian, and apparently from the same book[8], a general rule is laid down that new creditors can attack the gift. It is possible that this was Papinian's view, corrected elsewhere by Paul. In any case it is clear that the rule of later law is otherwise : proof must be forthcoming that money of the second creditor has been used to pay the first. It has been suggested[9] that the texts may be harmonised by supposing that Papinian is dealing with a case in which there is intent to defraud future creditors as well, while in Julian's case the intent is to defraud the present creditor. The texts shew no trace of any such distinction. And when we remember that Julian, in speaking of fraudulent intent[10], speaks of it merely as knowledge of insolvency, it is difficult to resist the impression that the determination of the *animus* to the one creditor is considered by him to result from the fact that he is the only creditor, and not from any mental act of the manumitter. It is difficult to see indeed how his intent could be made out. On the whole it seems more probable that Papinian's text is a little too widely expressed[11].

We have seen that the *lex* makes the manumission absolutely null[12]. If it is set aside the man never was free and thus he is fairly called a *statuliber* in the intervening period[13]. There are, however, some texts

[1] 40. 7. 1. 1.
[2] As this will occur if at all after *aditio*, the gift is in effect conditional. See A. Faber, *op. cit.* 218.
[3] 40. 9. 11; 49. 14. 45. 3; C. 7. 11. 5.   [4] As to 40. 9. 16. 3; see *post*, p. 564.
[5] 40. 9. 11. The nullity was dependent on certain steps being taken: the Fisc itself could not take these steps.
[6] 42. 8. 15.   [7] *h. t.* 16; cp. *h. t.* 10. 2.   [8] 40. 9. 25.
[9] A. Faber, *op. cit.* 202. Bodemeyer, *op. cit.* 23, 24.   [10] 42. 8. 15.
[11] A having two slaves, S and P, and no other property, promises " S *aut* P." Julian says the *lex* prevents his freeing either. If he frees one the other may die. Scaevola confines this to the case of his having no other property, as otherwise anyone who had promised "a slave of mine " could free none at all, 40. 9. 5. 2, 6.
[12] See the references on p. 544, *ante*.   [13] 40. 7. 1. 1.

which look as if the gift were only revocable. Thus we are told that the Fisc can *revocare in servitutem*[1]. But this is correct, for in the meantime the man has been or may have been *in libertate*. Other texts in which the creditor is the Fisc say *retrahi placuit*[2]. Others having nothing to do with the Fisc use similar language[3]. These can hardly be more than mere loosenesses of language. The view that the case of the Fisc is on a special footing in this matter[4] is negatived by the fact that many of these texts do not refer to the Fisc, and on the other hand there are texts dealing with the Fisc which declare the gift absolutely void[5]. The view that the case of the Fisc and of *civitates* was regulated on this point by special enactments rests on little evidence : there is no reason to suppose that the constitutions[6] and *senatusconsulta* did more than declare the *lex* to apply. It is highly improbable that the Fisc would be placed in an inferior position, or that a revocable liberty would be casually introduced in this way. On the whole we must assume that in all these cases the manumission is either void or valid.

Apart from some special provision it would seem that the nullity of such a gift ought to be capable of being pointed out at any time. There were such provisions. Liberty begun in good faith was protected after a lapse of time which varied from time to time and will be considered later[7], while if it began in bad faith it was not protected at all[8]. Similarly the status of one apparently free was not to be disputed five years after his death, though it might be up to that time[9]. These rules seem to account sufficiently for the text which tells us that the slaves we are dealing with were *statuliberi dum incertum est an creditor iure suo utatur*[10]. However other explanations have been suggested. According to one view it must be within one year from the sale of the goods, this being the time within which fraudulent alienations must be revoked[11]. But there seems no ground for assimilating the void to the voidable in this way, and there would be difficulty in applying the rule to the case, which might occur, of nullity on this ground where the goods were never sold at all[12]. Others take the view that he had ten years, arguing from a text of Paul which says that a slave freed *in fraudem fisci* is not to be recalled into slavery *si diu in libertate fuisset, id est non minus decennio*[13]. But neither Paul nor Aristo whom

---

[1] 40. 9. 16. 3 ; 49. 14. 30.　　　　　[2] 49. 14. 45. 3 ; Fr. de i. Fisci, 19.
[3] "*Revocabitur quemadmodum si in fraudem manumisisset*" (42. 8. 6. 5 ; 5. 2. 8. 17) ; "*per legem Aeliam rescinditur*" (42. 8. 15 ; 40. 9. 5. 2) ; "*libertates in fraudem creditorum revocari*" (C. 7. 11. 1) ; "*si fraudem se fecisse creditoribus ut revocet libertates*" (C. 7. 8. 5). *Rescindi* is less significant than the others. See A. Faber, *op. cit.* 204.
[4] *Ante*, p. 563.　　　　　[5] 40. 9. 11. 1 ; C. 7. 11. 5.
[6] 40. 9. 11.　　　　　[7] *Post*, p. 648.　　　　　[8] C. 7. 22. 1.
[9] C. 7. 21. *pass.*; *post*, p. 651. The protection did not apply to those *in fuga* or *latitantes*, C. 7. 21. 8.
[10] 40. 7. 1. 1.
[11] 42. 8. 6. 14 ; see Accarias, Précis, § 71.
[12] 40. 4. 57.　　　　　[13] 40. 9. 16. 3.

he is quoting could have laid down this positive rule of time: it is clear that it is the work of the compilers, or at any rate of some later hand. If that is so it seems to establish a privilege of the Fisc, for there is strong reason to think that a private person could not attack the status of a person apparently free, after the lapse of five years from a traceable *prima facie* valid manumission by his *dominus*[1].

There remains one point: the manumission being void, who is entitled to have the nullity declared? Clearly the creditors can, and the language of one text seems to shew that they alone can[2]. There is no question of a *popularis actio*. As the slave was in possession of liberty, the proceeding would take the form of some sort of claim to him. If no *heres* enters, so that the *bona* are sold, the creditors can of course make a claim. If the *heres* enters he will clearly have a sufficient interest. But though as we have seen the question may be raised although there is no sale[3], it is clearly laid down in three texts that the *heres* of the manumitter is barred from bringing proceedings[4]. Thus it is difficult to say what happens if a solvent *heres* enters on an insolvent estate. The *heres*, the only person interested, has no *locus standi*. The creditors, secure of payment, will hardly move. It has been suggested[5] that the *heres* himself can proceed directly in this case but the contrary texts seem too strong. If the creditors have a claim it is possible that they may transfer their right to the *heres*, e.g., by authorising him to proceed as *procurator in rem suam*, but even this seems barred by the wide language of the text. Probably the proceeding is a special one organised under the *lex*, and not an ordinary *vindicatio in servitutem*, so that the creditor's right does not depend on any claim to the slave but on the mere fact that he is a creditor. If that is so, he need not wait for a decree of *missio in possessionem*, and he would not be barred by the mere fact of entry of a *heres*, so that the *heres* might enter only on the undertaking of the creditor to proceed. The texts seem to mean that if he did not take this precaution he would have no remedy.

It may be added that there is no reason to suppose all creditors need join, and that the manumitter could not himself impeach his own manumission *inter vivos*[6].

There is some difficulty as to the application of the rule about fraudulent manumission in the case of fideicommissary gifts. The texts make it clear that, after some dispute, the rule was settled that in the case of such gifts the *animus* was not considered—the *eventus* alone determined whether the gift was valid or not[7]. What is the reason of this? It must be remembered that it was only by adoption of the Sabinian view[8] that the rule was reached which made *animus*

---

[1] *Post*, p. 650. [2] 40. 7. 1. 1. [3] 40. 4. 57.
[4] 40. 12. 31; C. 7. 8. 5; 7. 16. 7. [5] Accarias, Précis, § 71. [6] C. 7. 8. 5.
[7] 40. 5. 4. 19; C. 7. 11. 1, 7. [8] 40. 4. 57.

material in direct gifts. The texts shew that the non-application of
this to fideicommissary gifts was not a mere oversight, but was a positive
decision. It is perhaps idle to speculate as to the unrecorded reasons
which led to this view. It may perhaps be due to the notion that the
testator in abstaining from completing the gift may be regarded as
having tacitly subjected his direction to the condition of solvency of the
estate. If that is the explanation the rule does not depend on the *lex*
Aelia at all, and any such dependence cannot be made out on the texts.

VII. Manumission must be in perpetuity. Any limit of time which
it was sought to fix was simply struck out[1]. This idea of irrevocability,
already mentioned, can be illustrated by many texts. *Civitas* once
obtained cannot be added to or subtracted from by any subsequent
manumission[2]. If a man frees a slave under a *fideicommissum* contained
in a codicil which is afterwards shewn to be a *falsum*, or by way of
fulfilling a condition which is afterwards shewn to be, from any cause,
not binding, the manumission is still valid[3]. A slave is given to a
legatee under a codicil which is declared false. There has been actual
conveyance so that the legatee is certainly owner. If he has freed the
slave the gift is good[4]. Even where the gift is such as to work a fraud
on a third party, if validly given it is irrevocable. Thus where a son
was under a *fideicommissum* to free a slave praelegated to him, when
accounts had been rendered to the *heredes*, and he freed him before this
·was done the manumission was valid[5]. So when a *heres* under a *fideicommissum* to hand over the *hereditas* frees a slave, the gift is valid[6].

The case of *restitutio in integrum* is discussed in many texts. The
general principle is that there is no help to a minor *adversus libertatem*[7].
The following text says, "except *ex magna causa* on appeal to the
Emperor." What would be a sufficient *magna causa* does not appear,
and it is likely that the words, which purport to be Paul's, are misapplied
by Tribonian[8]. Thus liberties which have taken effect, by the *aditio* of
the minor, are not undone by his obtaining *restitutio in integrum*[9]. If
the minor is under a *fideicommissum* to free and does so, and afterwards
gets *restitutio*, the liberty is unaffected[10]. A slightly more complex case
is that in which a slave is substituted to a minor. Here if the minor
repudiates, the slave is *necessarius heres* and free. If now the minor is
restitutus, the liberty, having taken effect, is not affected. But if the

[1] 40. 4. 33, 34; the rule was the same in Jewish law. Winter, Stellung der Sklaven, 35, 36.
[2] C. 7. 1. 2.   [3] 40. 4. 47. *pr.*, 1; 5. 2. 26.
[4] 37. 14. 23. 1.   [5] 4. 3. 32.
[6] 36. 1. 72. 1. A gave a slave to B to free on the terms that he was to receive one in return.
The man was freed but the other slave was not given: the manumission stands, 19. 5. 5. 5.
[7] 4. 4. 9. 6; In. 3. 11. 5.   [8] 4. 4. 10.   [9] C. 7. 2. 3.
[10] 4. 4. 31. Where the Praetor had declared fideicommissary manumissions due and the
minor gave them, but they were not due, there was no *restitutio*, C. 2. 30. 1.

minor has accepted in the first instance and then obtained a decree of *restitutio*, Papinian thinks the slave will be neither *heres* nor free. But Ulpian disagrees, remarking that a rescript of Pius and one of Caracalla (?) have decided that on such facts the substitute is free and *necessarius*[1]. The reason for Papinian's difficulty is no doubt the rule *semel heres semper heres* : praetorian relief cannot alter that. No doubt the rescripts were necessary. It will be seen that at the end of the text Ulpian uses this principle to shew that in the first case the slave is still technically *heres*.

The principles are the same if the matter is wholly *inter vivos*. If a minor is led by the fraud of his slave, or of anyone else, to free him *vindicta*, with cause shewn, the manumission is good[2]. If a minor sells a slave and the buyer frees him, and the minor is *restitutus*, the liberty holds[3], even though the slave managed the affair in fraud[4]. If a minor over 20 sells *ut manumittatur* and the man has been freed, it cannot be undone, and if a minor acquires under this condition, he cannot be *restitutus* after he has freed[5]. We are further told that if in proceedings between the minor and a slave the latter has been declared free, there can be no *restitutio in integrum*, but only an appeal[6]. As between the parties the man must be presumed free.

The *Querela inofficiosi testamenti* raises similar points. In estimating the estate, for the purpose of the *pars legitima*, the value of freed slaves is first deducted[7]. If a will is void direct liberties are null[8]. As to fideicommissary gifts, if the slave belonged to the fiduciary, the gift, when once carried out, is good, as we have seen. If the slaves were in the *hereditas* direct gifts are good in the same way, if the testamentary *heres* enters for his share, though the will is upset by *bonorum possessio contra tabulas*, but not otherwise[9]. A will upset by the *querela* is not void, but voidable, a distinction which might have been thought material, but, as in other respects, the point is not logically treated, and the result is much as if the will were void. In a case of simple successful *querela* in which the will fails, the direct liberties fail[10]. But we are told that fideicommissary gifts must be carried out[11]. The statement is directly quoted by Modestinus from Paul, and is thus probably genuine, but it is odd to find fideicommissary gifts treated as more binding than direct. The rule looks as if the will were *pro tanto* treated as a codicil binding on the successful litigant, since fideicommissary gifts might be in a

---

[1] 4. 4. 7. 10.
[2] If no cause were shewn it was simply void, C. 2. 30. 2, 3.
[3] 4. 4. 48. [4] 4. 3. 7. *pr.*
[5] 4. 4. 11. 1. This has been retouched though it may represent classical law. Gradenwitz, Z. S. S. 23. 346.
[6] C. 2. 30. 4. [7] 5. 2. 8. 9. As for the *Quarta* Falcidia.
[8] 40. 4. 25. But see *post*, p. 609. [9] 37. 5. 8. 2.
[10] 5. 2. 8. 16, 9, 28; unless the *institutus* also takes on intestacy, C. 6. 4. 26 b.
[11] 5. 2. 9.

codicil while direct could not. But it is not easy to see why in that view other *fideicommissa* were not binding, and perhaps the text really means only that, if they have been carried out, they are good. This is confirmed by the further rule it contains, shortly to be considered, as to compensation, but it is not what the text says. If, as may, *ex magna causa*, be the case, the *querela* is allowed after five years, the manumissions are good[1]. This is in accordance with a principle of which we have seen and shall see other traces, *i.e.* that apparent liberty cannot ordinarily be disputed after five years from a traceable *prima facie* valid manumission by the *dominus*[2]. A constitution of Severus and Caracalla says that where a will has given fideicommissary liberty to slaves of the *hereditas*, and, there having been delay, a decree of the Praetor has ordered them to be carried out, and this has been done, the liberties are to remain good even though the will is upset by the *querela* brought by a son[3]. This is in accord with what has already been said, but there is a point in which it takes the rule a little further. It enacts that the validity of the fideicommissary gifts carried out shall not depend on their having been given by an undisputed owner: it is equally so if they were slaves of the *hereditas*. It might have been thought that these would be treated like direct gifts[4].

If, as may happen, the will stands partly good, after the *querela*, all the liberties both direct and fideicommissary stand good[5].

In many of these cases in which the principle of irrevocability causes liberties to be good, under circumstances which create injustice, there is an obligation to give compensation, but any general rule is not easily made out. In the case of liberty given under a false codicil Hadrian provided that the *libertus* must pay 20 *solidi* to the owner who lost him by the manumission[6]. In one text it is said, apparently in error, that the slave's value is to be paid[7]. How far the rule could be extended to analogous cases was, it seems, disputed. Papinian says, in his Quaestiones, that *constitutum est* that the same rule must be applied where one frees under a condition in an institution, and the

---

[1] 5. 2. 8. 17.　　　　　[2] *Post*, p. 650.　　　　　[3] C. 3. 28. 4.
[4] An imperfect admission of the principle that the ownership of the *heres* was good for the time being. Cp. 4. 4. 31; 37. 5. 8. 2. It may be that in C. 3. 28. 4 the *institutus* was also a *filius*.
[5] 31. 76. *pr.*; 37. 7. 6; 44. 2. 29. *pr.*; C. 3. 28. 13. A mother thinking her soldier son dead, instituted X and gave liberties. The son returned. Hadrian gave him the *hereditas*, but required him to carry out liberties and legacies. This is not *querela*: the will is void. The liberties are not valid: the direction to the *heres* is an exceptional rule: it is perhaps to be erected into a general rule for mistakes of this kind. But the text expressly says that it is not to be treated as making further inroad on the principle that if the will is void or avoided by *querela*, the liberties fail, 5. 2. 28. In another similar case the gifts are simply void, 40. 4. 29.
[6] 40. 4. 47. *pr.*; C. 7. 4. 2. As a medium value, Cujas, Papiniani Quaestiones, *ad* 40. 4. 47. Cp. 30. 81. 4; C. 6. 1. 4.
[7] 37. 14. 23. 1.

institution is void[1]. His language shews that this is an extension of Hadrian's rule. Ulpian, in his Disputationes, says that the slave's value must be given, which Cujas regards as meaning the same thing. But his language treats it as a juristic extension, *aequum est*[2]. The same rule is applied where the *querela* is successfully brought after five years, *ex magna causa*[3], but here the remark as to compensation may be due to Tribonian. Where the *querela* is successfully brought within the five years direct liberties are void. But as we have seen[4] Modestinus quotes Paul as holding that fideicommissary gifts must still be carried out, 20 *aurei* being paid for each[5]. This seems absurd. Hadrian's rule is meant to deal with cases in which a manumission, having taken effect, cannot be undone, but an injustice results which this payment partly remedies. To treat them as binding on the *heres ab intestato* is inconsistent with the theory on which the *querela* rests[6], and in any case, if there is an injustice not yet complete, there is no reason in an order to carry it out, subject to compensation for the injustice done. To treat it as a case of *favor libertatis* is impossible, for direct gifts are left void. It is difficult to resist the impression that the words are corrupt[7]. In the case of a partly successful *querela* where all the liberties stand good, we are told that it is the duty of the *judex* to see that an indemnity is paid to the "victor and future manumitter[8]." That is to say, as the sense requires and the context suggests, the successful claimant is to receive compensation from the freedmen concerned in respect of those gifts of liberty which were charged on the shares which failed[9]. Whether this was to be calculated on the basis of 20 *solidi* per head we do not learn[10].

As a minor is entitled to *restitutio in integrum* where his interests are damaged, and actual restitution is not possible in this case, he has a claim for his *interesse*[11]. But, apart from wrong done, if the minor does not suffer there is no compensation to anyone who does. A woman enters and frees *ex fideicommisso*. She is then *restituta* for minority. The liberties are good, having been given *optimo iure*, and the *heres ab intestato* has no claim for compensation. The minor has not suffered in any way and her restitution can give no other person a claim for compensation[12]. As the text puts it, the *manumissi* have

---

[1] 40. 4. 47. 1.   [2] 5. 2. 26. Cujas, *loc. cit.*   [3] 5. 2. 8. 17.
[4] *Ante*, p. 567.   [5] 5. 2. 9.   [6] 5. 2. 13.
[7] The use of the word *aureus* suggests interpolation, Kalb, Juristenlatein, 77.
[8] 40. 4. 29.
[9] And in respect of that part of other liberties which would fall on them?
[10] A will was upset by a son whose existence was unknown; the liberties were void. But where the man had been *in libertate* for five years, the liberty stood. Nothing is said of compensation. This last rule is probably Tribonian's, 40. 4. 29. *Ante*, p. 568, and *post*, p. 650.
[11] 4. 4. 11. *pr.*, 31, 48. 1.
[12] 4. 4. 31. She is still *heres* and her manumission is good. Cujas, *loc. cit.*

not to pay the 10 *aurei*, which shews that some had thought of extending Hadrian's rule to this case.

In all these cases there is no suggestion of fraud, and the compensation comes from the freedman, but if the manumission had been induced by fraud, or carelessness in one under a duty, there may be a claim, on the part of him who suffers, for full indemnity against the wrong-doer[1]. The manumitter is not necessarily the injured person, and where the manumitter is guilty of *dolus* the *actio doli* is always available to any injured person. Thus a *heres*, under a trust to hand over, who frees a slave is liable *ex fideicommisso*, and this, at least in later law, whether he knew of the *fideicommissum* or not[2]. So a *heres*, under a *fideicommissum* to free on accounting, is liable *ex dolo* to the other *heredes* if he frees at once to prevent accounting[3]. A more complex case is that in which A, entitled in any case to a *pars virilis*, enters under a will which is liable to be set aside. The liberties take effect. He is liable *de dolo* to the persons entitled to *bonorum possessio contra tabulas*, if they have given him notice and promised him his *pars virilis* (but not otherwise, though there had been disputes[4]). The view that a *heres* was liable who did not know of the *fideicommissum* seems to rest on the notion that he was under a duty to enquire on such matters before taking steps which might injure other people. But it is pushing that notion rather far, since it is said to apply even though the codicil was not to be opened till after his death, and he did not know that it had been made[5]. In fact the text (of which this clause is certainly compilers' work) seems to rest the claim not on *dolus*, but on the resulting damage. But compensation on this score ought to have come from the *manumissus* if from anyone.

To the rule that manumission is perpetual and irrevocable the case of fraudulent manumission is only an apparent exception: the manumission is null. He who had been *in libertate*, is *in servitutem revocatus*. He is assimilated to a *statuliber*[6], but there is the *de facto* difference, that while he is *in libertate*, the *statuliber* is *in servitute, pendente conditione*[7]. Similarly unreal is the case of a manumission void because the manumitter was *vi coactus*[8]. So, too, new enslavement for ingratitude is not an exception[9]: freedom does not involve incapacity ever to become a slave.

---

[1] C. 2. 30. 1; D. 4. 4. 11. *pr.*, even *manumissus*, 4. 3. 7. *pr.* But see *post*, Ch. xxix. The right to damages seems to exist in such cases, where the manumitter is the injured person, only if he is a minor. In 4. 4. 48. 1 the minor has a remedy, based on *dolus* not apparent on the statement.

[2] 36. 1. 26. 2, 72. 1.   [3] 4. 3. 32.

[4] 37. 5. 8. 2.   [5] 36. 1. 26. 2, 72. 1.

[6] 40. 7. 1.   [7] Cp. 40. 9. 16. 4.

[8] 4. 2. 9. 2. Cp. Fr. Dos. 7.

[9] *Ante*, p. 424. So too the case of one sold *ne manumittatur* and freed is only an apparent exception, *ante*, p. 72; *post*, p. 585. A real exception, *post*, p. 600.

But though manumission could not be *in diem*, it might, as we have seen, be conditional or *ex die*[1]. The authority on conditions is confined almost entirely to conditions on direct manumissions. In strictn. is it appears that only in such a case did the status of *statuliber* arise[2], b t, from the very few texts that mention the matter, it may be inferred that similar principles applied to fideicommissary gifts of liberty subject to conditions[3]. We must remember that even if there is no condition, a slave in whose favour such a gift has been made is *in loco statuliberi*[4], and this is not altered by the presence of a condition: in such a case, *cum sua causa alienetur*[5]. Thus where there is a conditional *fideicommissum* of liberty, anyone to whom the man is conveyed must give security to restore him for the purpose of the manumission when it becomes due, *nam in omnibus fere causis fideicommissas libertates pro directo datis habendas*[6]. Thus there is nothing to add as to them in the matter of conditions. With regard to manumissions *inter vivos* there is more difficulty. We have already considered whether and if so how far conditions could be imposed on manumission *per vindictam*[7]. As to informal manumissions there is nothing in their nature to exclude either tacit or express conditions, and the later part of a text already considered[8] seems to say that they might be made *mortis causa*, and revocably, in the sense that they were not to take effect unless the expected death occurred. In such a case no doubt alienation would revoke the gift as it did a *donatio mortis causa*, and the slave could in all probability be usucapted. It is not easy to say what the law was as to an ordinary *dies* or condition. One text vaguely suggests that a slave freed *ex die* was at any rate to a certain extent in the position of a *statuliber*[9]. But it is not dealing exactly with such a case, but with one transferred, *ut post tempus manumittatur*, which is a different thing, and it expressly adds that these persons are not, in all respects, like *statuliberi*. In one text it is said that if the father of a woman accused of adultery manumits, by will, a slave in her service, before the 60 days have expired, the man is a *statuliber*, *i.e.* the gift will fail if the testator dies before the days are up[10]. In a neighbouring text we are told that if the woman manumits *inter vivos*, within the time, the gift is void—which seems to imply that there is no power of suspension[11]. But this was probably written of manumission *vindicta*. It is true that the most authoritative definition of *statuliberi* is in terms which cover a *manumissus sub conditione*

---

[1] *Ante*, Ch. XXI.
[2] 39. 6. 8; 40. 7. 2.   Expressly stated, 21. 2. 69. 1.   See Festus, *s. v. Statuliberi*.
[3] *Ante*, p. 518.   [4] 40. 5. 51. 3.   [5] *h. t.* 24. 21.
[6] 40. 4. 40. 1.   The laxly expressed reason may be Tribonian's.   See also 40. 5. 47. 3.
[7] *Ante*, p. 455.   [8] 40. 1. 15; *ante*, p. 455.   [9] 40. 1. 20. 3.
[10] 40. 9. 13; *post*, p. 585.   [11] 40. 9. 14. 2.

inter vivos[1], but, on the other hand, the language of Festus[2] and the whole drift of the title on *statuliberi* seem to ignore this case. The absence of texts makes it impossible to say what the law really was. If such things occurred, no doubt the slave was still a slave, but he was probably not a *statuliber*, and would not carry his status with him. It is likely that an alienation would be regarded as annulling the intent to free, which had not yet operated, and probably also the slave could be usucapted. But all this is obscure, and perhaps the right inference from the silence of the texts is that such things did not occur. There could be little use in them. On the other hand there were obvious advantages about manumissions *mortis causa*, and conditions on such gifts were reasonable enough.

---

[1] 40. 7. 1. *pr.*   [2] Festus, *s. v. Statuliberi.*

CHAPTER XXV.

MANUMISSION. SPECIAL CASES AND MINOR RESTRICTIONS.

I. THE Pledged Slave. The main rules can be shortly stated. A slave who is the subject of a specific pledge, express or tacit, cannot be freed however solvent the owner may be[1], unless the creditor assents[2], or security in lieu of the slave is given[3]. The rule does not apply to a general hypothec, tacit or express, unless the slave has actually been seized under it, but of course the manumission must not infringe the rule of the *lex* Aelia Sentia[4] as to manumission in fraud of creditors. One text seems to imply that an express general hypothec is a bar, but this is clearly negatived by the other texts, and as the text is corrupt[5] it probably means no more than that even though the manumitter is insolvent, a manumission of a slave received for the purpose cannot be impeached on the ground of fraud, though, in general, manumission by an insolvent who had given such a pledge would be at least suspicious[6]. It is immaterial whether the manumission be *inter vivos* or by will, though as the latter operates only on *aditio* the gift will be good if the pledge is at an end at that date[7]. If the pledge still exists the gift, as a direct gift, is void. But, at least in later law, there is a more favourable construction: such a gift implies a fideicommissary gift, so that when the pledge ceases to exist the slave can claim to be freed[8]. It may be added that Severus provided by rescript that a pledged slave could be made *necessarius heres*[9].

Here, however, some difficulty arises on the texts. Most texts treat the manumission of a pledged slave as a mere nullity, but there is

---

[1] 40. 1. 3; 40. 8. 6; 20. 2. 9; C. 7. 8. 1, 3, 6. Even though the pledge covers other things of greater value than the debt, 40. 9. 5. 2.

[2] C. 7. 8. 4. A *pupillus* creditor needs *auctoritas*, 40. 9. 27. 1. A creditor over 14 can assent: he is not freeing, but assenting, so that the age rule of the *lex* Aelia Sentia does not apply, 40. 2. 4. 2.

[3] 40. 9. 27. 1; C. 7. 8. 5.   [4] 20. 2. 9; 40. 9. 29; 49. 14. 45. 3; C. 7. 8. 2, 3.

[5] 40. 8. 6. Mommsen omits *obligatum*: others insert *non*, cp. 40. 1. 10.

[6] Cp. 40. 1. 10; 49. 14. 45. 3.   [7] 48. 19. 33.

[8] 40. 5. 24. 10. In the creditor's will the debtor was asked to free the pledged slave. This was a valid *fideicommissum* and he could be compelled to carry it out whatever the value of the slave if he accepted the will in any way, *e.g.*, by pleading the direction when sued by the *heres*. It was apparently treated as a gift of the value of the slave.

[9] 28. 5. 30. The case is not within the rule of the *lex* Aelia Sentia. The text adds *ita tamen si paratus sit prius creditori satisfacere*, an addition which destroys the point of the text and as it contains a sudden change of subject is probably due to Tribonian, 40. 9. 27. 1.

some doubt. The favourable construction just mentioned is no doubt a late development. In any case it negatives what might otherwise have been likely, the recognition of release of the pledge as a tacit condition. But if this was not admitted in wills, it can hardly have been so *inter vivos*. So Scaevola remarks that if the debtor manumits while the charge exists the slave is not freed. But Paul adds a note by way of inference : *soluta ergo pecunia illa voluntate liber fit*[1]. It seems clear that he is speaking of payment after the act of manumission. So an enactment of 223[2] says that if the creditors are paid, pledged *ancillae* who had been manumitted become free. It is clear that the manumission was *inter vivos*, though the manumitter is now dead. This text is, however, of less significance. The question is one of fraud of creditors :. so far as appears the pledge may have been a general one. One earlier text which deals with the matter is imperfect and corrupt[3]. It seems to say that a pledged slave cannot be freed, by reason of the *lex* Aelia Sentia, unless the debtor is solvent. As solvency is not material[4] and the rule does not rest on the *lex*[5], it seems likely that here too the main subject of the text is a case of general pledge and fraud on creditors. But it ends with the words *sed latinum*, as the beginning of a sentence. It is commonly treated therefore[6] as laying down the rule that after manumission *inter vivos* the slave becomes a latin if and when the debt is paid. Such a view might well have developed : whether it was *vindicta* or *inter amicos* it would have only the effect of an informal manumission[7], so that we have not to do with tacit conditions on a manumission *vindicta*[8]. Justinian does not indeed specifically mention this case in his list of causes of latinity, but he observes that in all cases in which a constitution speaks of *libertas* without expressly mentioning latinity, this is to be read for the future as *civitas*[9]. It is noticeable that both in the enactment of 223 and in Paul's text[10], the slave is spoken of as becoming *liber*.

We are not told the origin of the rule. Though one or two texts suggest the *lex* Aelia Sentia[11], others shew that the two rules are independent. A general hypothec is no bar unless it conflicts with the *lex*[12]. Solvency is immaterial[13]. It was not the *lex* but a provision of Severus which made it possible to institute a pledged slave as a *necessarius heres*[14]. One at least of the texts referring to the rule was written of *fiducia*[15], and the institution may have been carried over from it. Some of the rules are, however, opposed to this view. A gift to a slave in *fiducia*

---

[1] 40. 9. 26.   [2] C. 7. 8. 5.   [3] Fr. Dos. 16.
[4] 40. 1. 3.   See on these matters, Vangerow, Latini Iuniani, 53.
[5] 40. 9. 29; C. 7. 8. 2.   [6] See, *e.g.*, Krüger, *ad h. l.*
[7] See *ante*, p. 550.   [8] *Ante*, p. 455.   [9] C. 7. 6. 12 a.
[10] C. 7. 8. 5; C. 40. 9. 26.   [11] 40. 9. 5. 2, 6; Fr. Dos. 16.
[12] 40. 9. 29. *pr.*; C. 7. 8. 2.   [13] 40. 1. 3.
[14] 28. 5. 30.   [15] 40. 1. 3; Lenel, Ed. Perp. xix.

could not have been saved by release before *aditio*: he must have been the testator's when the will was made[1]. Assent of the creditor, the owner[2], would not have enabled the debtor to free. But these modifications in favour of liberty were consistent with the interests of the creditor, and were possible now that the debtor was owner. Indeed the whole rule had now no logical basis and was maintained on grounds of equity only, by juristic authority. It was not easy to give a basis to it, in view of the difficulty of finding a place for the creditor's right in such a scheme of property law as that of the Romans[3]. Hence the tendency to rest the rule on the *lex* Aelia Sentia. Hence the fact that general statements of the rule are found in Ulpian's Disputationes[4], and Papinian's Quaestiones[5]. Hence the enquiry addressed to Scaevola as to whether the rule bound the *heres* of the debtor[6], and Ulpian's treatment of it as a legal subtlety[7].

II. *Servus Communis.* A man cannot be partly free, partly a slave. On the other hand the owner of half cannot free the other half. Hence the classical jurists held that if one of co-owners purported to free the slave, the manumission did not take effect. The act was not, however, necessarily a mere nullity. If the manumission was formal, *i.e.* done *vindicta, censu* or *testamento*, the effect was to vest the share of the freeing owner in the other owner by accrual. So far all were agreed. Proculus indeed held that the same effect was produced even by an informal manumission[8], but it does not appear that any later jurist took this view: in this case the act of manumission was regarded as a mere nullity[9]. The texts express this by confining the accrual to cases in which he would have become a *civis* if the manumitter had been sole owner[10]. Accrual is a quiritary mode of transfer, and thus does not take effect unless the part owner has divested himself of his quiritary rights in the man. Notwithstanding the *lex* Iunia the old owner retained large rights in the man informally freed, though, in the main, they became effective only on his death. The same principle is expressed by Julian's rule that if a minor common owner frees, he must shew *causa, i.e.* the act cannot produce its effect of accrual (as a manumission it is void in any case) unless all the rules of valid manumission at civil law are complied with[11]. The rule barring manu-

---

[1] 48. 19. 33; *ante*, p. 464.
[2] 40. 9. 27. 1; C. 7. 8. 4.
[3] *Possessio* as being without economic content is hardly, it would seem, a *res*. See significant C. 8. 13. 18.
[4] 40. 9. 4.   [5] 48. 19. 33.   [6] 40. 9. 26.
[7] 40. 5. 24. 10.   [8] Fr. Dos. 10.
[9] Ulp. 1. 18; P. 4. 12. 1; Fr. Dos. 10.   [10] P. 4. 12. 1; Ulp. 1. 18.
[11] 40. 2. 4. 2. The text may, however, mean merely that he cannot concur unless he has a *causa*. But this seems difficult to reconcile with 40. 2. 6.

mission by one owner did not of course prevent the man from becoming free by other causes[1].

If all joined the slave was free, and they were joint patrons[2]. If they were under 20 it was enough if one shewed cause[3]. We are told that a minor common owner freeing[4] must always shew cause: it is to be presumed that in this case, the fact that the other has a *causa* is sufficient[5]. If one owner is a minor, we are not told that the fact that the other desires to free is sufficient, but this seems to follow from this last rule. In general such manumission will be *inter vivos*, since, if the two gifts do not operate simultaneously, there will be accrual. But the case of manumission by will might occur. Thus, where one of common owners frees by will " if my partner does," and the partner afterwards frees *inter vivos*, the man is free, holding his liberty by two titles[6]. Indeed both manumissions might be by will, though the necessary hypotheses are rather artificial. Two cases are mentioned in the same text. In one two owners have freed and instituted the slave in their wills, and they die together in a catastrophe[7]. Here the first gift might have failed had he not been instituted, for entry under the wills might have been made at different times. In the other case both had freed him under the same condition[8]. Where a slave was left unconditionally to two, and one freed him and the other afterwards repudiated the gift, the manumission was good[9], on principles already considered. The repudiation made the other legatee sole owner, retrospectively[10].

Some points of interest and difficulty arise where the manumission is accompanied by an institution of the slave[11]. If one of two owners institutes the man, he may do so either *cum* or *sine libertate.* In the latter case, the slave is *quasi alienus*. In the former he is *quasi proprius*[12]. We know that if both free and institute him and the gifts chance to operate at the same moment, he is free and *heres necessarius* to both[13]. It is presumably to cases of this kind that reference is made in a text which says that if a common slave is *heres necessarius* to one or two or all of his owners, he cannot abstain from any of them[14].

If the instituting and freeing owner acquired the whole of the slave, the man, having ceased to be a *servus communis,* was free and *heres*

---

[1] A common slave who detected the murderer of one master was freed: the other being entitled to compensation, 29. 5. 16.

[2] 38. 1. 4; 2. 4. 23.   [3] 40. 2. 6, '*non*.' A. Faber, Jur. Pap. Sci. 265.
[4] 40. 2. 4. 2.   [5] A. Faber, *loc. cit.*
[6] 40. 4. 48.   [7] 28. 5. 8. *pr.*
[8] *h. l.* 1.   [9] 40. 2. 3.
[10] 29. 1. 31; 40. 1. 2; 33. 5. 14. Fr. Vat. 84. This does not apply if the repudiated gift becomes a *caducum*: in that case the lapsed gift may vest in another so that the manumitter is not sole owner. Fr. Vat. *cit.*
[11] As to institution without liberty, see *ante*, p. 391. There is no reason to think that Justinian's rule that institution implied a gift of liberty covered this case: he is thinking of a sole owner. *Ante*, p. 553. In. 1. 6. 2; C. 6. 27. 5. 1.
[12] 28. 5. 90; Ulp. 22. 7, 10.   [13] 28. 5. 8.
[14] 29. 2. 66.

necessarius[1], the testator having been part owner at the time the will was made[2]. So, if a common slave was substituted to a *pupillus* by one owner, who afterwards bought the rest of him, he became a *necessarius heres* to the *pupillus*[3]. If, however, he was bought by the *pupillus*, Julian thought he would not be *heres necessarius* to him: he could not in any sense be said to have been the property of the testator at the time when the will was made[4]. Ulpian appears to add[5] that, on grounds of equity, the man may be allowed to buy the share of himself from the other owner, and so acquire freedom and the *hereditas*. But it may be that this is an addition by the compilers, expressing Justinian's rule shortly to be stated.

If the slave is simply freed and instituted, by one of his owners, and no change occurs till his testator's death, the texts do not say what happens. It is generally held that he enters at command of and for the benefit of the other owners. It is likely that this was the case, though Salkowski observes[6] that it is difficult to account for it logically. His difficulty is that the slave can get liberty only on acquiring the *hereditas*. That he cannot acquire till *iussum*, and that implies that accrual has already taken place. And accrual can result only from the manumission. Both ought, he thinks, to fail. The solution he suggests as most probable is, that, contrary to the rule in a case of *servus proprius*, the institution was allowed to stand good though the manumission failed. The same result may be arrived at on the view that if the manumission of a *servus communis* failed, where there was also an institution, the manumission was simply ignored, exactly as it was in the case of a *servus proprius*[7].

The effect of manumission by one of common owners is completely changed by Justinian[8]. The rules he lays down are these:

1. If one owner desires to free *inter vivos* or by will the others shall sell their shares to him or his *heres* who shall then free[9]. If the price of the share is refused, it may be deposited with a public authority and the manumission can proceed. His accounts are to be gone into if necessary, and made up on a day fixed by a *iudex*.

2. The price is to be fixed judicially. A maximum tariff is settled ranging from 10 to 60 *solidi*, according to age, sex, function, training, education, *etc.*, with an increase in each case if he is a eunuch, but a maximum of 70 *solidi*.

3. The *peculium* will go *pro rata*; the manumitter is sole patron, and can give his share to the *libertus*.

---

[1] 28. 5. 6. 3.   [2] *Ante*, p. 443.   [3] 28. 6. 18. *pr.* See *ante*, p. 510.
[4] 28. 5. 6. 3; 28. 6. 18. *pr.*; cp. 28. 6. 10. 1, 36. *pr.*; 40. 7. 2. 4.
[5] 28. 6. 18. *pr.*   [6] Sklavenerwerb, 18.   [7] *Ante*, p. 462.
[8] C. 7. 7. 1.   [9] C. 7. 7. 1. 1. The form is immaterial.

4. If several wish to free, the first is to be preferred. If all at once, there will be no question of price: *peculium* and *iura patronatus* are divided *pro rata*.

5. The *ius accrescendi* is wholly swept away.

6. If a part owner left to a slave his part in him it had been doubted what the result was, as the intent might have been to free in part or to benefit the *socius*. Whatever the testator's intent may have been, it is now, *favore libertatis*, to be treated as a gift of liberty[1].

Hitherto nothing has been said of fideicommissary gifts. There seems no difficulty in such a gift, but there is the point that the other owner might decline to sell[2]. Most of our information is contained in the obscure preamble to the foregoing constitution of Justinian. It is impossible to be certain of his meaning, but the following is a possible interpretation. Africanus had held not only that such gifts were valid, but that the co-owner could be compelled by the Praetor to sell his share, a view reported and apparently adopted by Julian, Marcellus, Ulpian and Paul[3]. Further Marcian reports a decision of Severus that in a certain case, where a soldier had made a direct gift to a common slave, his *heres* was bound to buy and free the man, and, a little later, Severus and Caracalla lay down a general rule to this effect, the co-owner being bound to sell. This forms the model for Justinian: his language seems to imply that it had dealt only with *milites*, but was not confined to a specific case as the earlier one had been[4].

III. *Servus Fructuarius.* The fructuary or usuary, not being owner, could not free. His manumission *vindicta* was in form a *cessio in iure*, involving an acknowledgment that he had no right in the slave. We may infer that some jurists held that his usufruct reverted to the *dominus*, but that the view prevailed that the act was a nullity[5]. Justinian regulated this matter in a way to be stated shortly[6].

If the owner freed by will, it seems clear that the gift was good, but conditional on the expiration of the usufruct. Thus where a slave was instituted *cum libertate*, and afterwards a usufruct was created in him, the institution and manumission were both good, but took effect

---

[1] C. 7. 7. 1, 2. A text which says (40. 7. 13. 1) that a common slave freed under a condition of payment can take the money from which *peculium* he will, as being an ordinary *statuliber*, subject to ordinary rules, expresses the law of Justinian's time, when the liberty would take effect. For classical law it would seem to apply only where all join.

[2] 40. 5. 47. 1 seems to assume the validity of the gift, but it may be the case of a slave common to the *heres* and another.

[3] Cp. 28. 6. 18. *pr.* where it is, however, a direct gift, but nothing is said of compulsion, Mitteis, Archiv für Papyrusf. 3. 252.

[4] Roby, R. P. L. 1. 28 and Mitteis, *loc. cit.* think the rescripts applied only to fideicommissary gifts, as the opinions of the jurists did. This makes it difficult to see what is the difference, between *milites* and other people, which Justinian is ending. Mitteis also holds that the second rescript, described as 'general,' applied also to *pagani*.

[5] Cp. G. 2. 30; P. 3. 6. 32; D. 23. 3. 66.　　　　[6] C. 7. 15. 2.

only on the expiration of the usufruct[1]. Where the usufruct of a slave was given as a legacy, and he was to be free at its expiry, this was valid: the expiry of the usufruct was a condition on the·gift, so that though the beneficiary compromised for a sum of money, the slave was not free till death or *capitis deminutio* of the donee[2]. Where an owner instituted the fructuary, and gave the slave freedom on a condition, the *confusio* destroyed the usufruct, and the slave became free at once on the occurrence of the condition[3]. The act of the owner shews that he did not contemplate the natural expiry of the usufruct as a condition[4]. These texts are all from the Digest, but there is no reason to doubt that they represent classical law.

The case is different with manumission *inter vivos*: a manumission by will can be conditional, while one *vindicta* cannot[5]. Such a manumission was good if the fructuary assented (even though he was under 20[6], for he was not freeing), with the *auctoritas* of his tutor if he was a *pupillus*[7]. But beyond this there is some uncertainty as to what the classical law was. Ulpian tells us that a *servus fructuarius* freed by his owner becomes a *servus sine domino*[8]. This is a perfectly logical effect to be produced by the *cessio in iure*. The same thing is said elsewhere[9], with the addition: *sed latinum*.... This text observes that the existence of the usufruct prevents the manumission *vindicta* of the slave. This leaves open several questions. Does the restriction apply only to formal manumission? Does it nullify the act or merely suspend it till the end of the usufruct? If the latter view be taken, does the slave become a latin or a *civis* at the expiration of the usufruct? Various answers have been given to each of these questions[10]. Justinian's remarks in his reorganising enactment give us little help. It may be noted, however, that whatever the law was, it seems to have been clear: he does not refer to any disputes, but merely declares that he is modifying the law. He seems to imply in the same text that the manumission was merely void—*libertatem cadere*[11], but, on the other hand, it appears from another enactment of his that the existence of the usufruct had been only an obstacle to the slave's being free *statim*[12]. There is no reason why informal manumission should not have made

---

1 28. 5. 9. 20. He need not be sole *heres*.
2 7. 1. 35. 1.   3 40. 4. 6.
4 If a usufruct is given "till he is freed," the *dominus* can free at any time, 7. 4. 15.
5 *Ante*, p. 455.   6 40. 2. 2.   7 40. 9. 27. 1.
8 Ulp. 1. 19.   9 Fr. Dos. 11, confined expressly to manumission *vindicta*.
10 Vangerow, Latini Iuniani, 44 *sqq*., who cites some earlier writers, thinks that when the usufruct ended he became a latin or *civis* according to the circumstances, the manumission *vindicta*, but only that, operating at once to make him a *servus sine domino*, by destroying the quiritary ownership. Kuntze, Servus Fructuarius, 62, also thinks the rule merely suspensive, but rests his view mainly on the texts dealing with manumission by will, of small force in this connexion. Huschke, *ad Fr. Dos.* 11, thinks *vindicta* was null, and informal suspended. Krüger,;*ad h. l.*, thinks he became a latin in both cases at expiry of the usufruct.
11 C. 7. 15. 1. *pr.*   12 C. 6. 61. 8. 7.

the man a latin at the end of the usufruct, and probably the Dosithean fragment was about to lay down some such rule. A manumission *vindicta*, regarded as such, could hardly have had such a suspended operation[1]. But the process was at least a declaration of intent to free, even though void as a formal act, and thus might possibly operate, as a declaration *inter amicos*, to make the man a latin, when the obstacle was removed[2]. It may be noted that, regarded as a *cessio in iure*, it was in no way defective: there was no condition to vitiate it: it was only the existence of the usufruct which prevented it from producing all the effect which was desired. Thus it makes the man, in the meantime, a *servus sine domino*[3].

Of the origin of the rule it is hardly possible to say more than that it appears to be a civil law rule independent of statute. Justinian declares it to be a rule of *observatio*[4], which seems to mean " of juristic origin."

Justinian reorganised the system, laying down the following rules:

1. If owner and fructuary concur, the manumission is valid in all respects.

2. If the owner frees without consent of the fructuary, the slave is free, and his *libertus*, though acquiring thereafter for himself, must serve the fructuary, *quasi servus*, till the usufruct ends. If he dies before that event the property goes to his *heredes*.

3. If the fructuary alone frees, intending a benefit to the slave, the ownership is not affected, but, till what would have been the end of the usufruct, the *judices* will protect him from interference by his *dominus*. At that time he reverts and his mesne acquisitions go to his *dominus*. If the fructuary frees him by way of ceding to the *dóminus*, full *dominium* is at once reintegrated[5].

IV. *Servus Legatus.* If the slave has passed into the ownership of the legatee, he can free, even in the extreme case in which the slave has been conveyed by the *heres* under a legacy contained in a codicil afterwards shewn to be a *falsum*[6]. Where a legacy was left to two, and one of them, having accepted the gift, freed the slave, and the other legatee afterwards repudiated the gift, the manumission was good[7]. These texts, of Marcellus, Paul and Ulpian, accept the Sabinian view that in the case of a legacy *per vindicationem* refusal by the legatee acts

---

[1] *Ante*, p. 455.
[2] That Justinian does not mention it among the causes of latinity (C. 7. 6) is explained by the fact that his reorganising enactment (C. 7. 15. 1) was of a little earlier date. See, however, *ante*, p. 543 and App. IV.
[3] It must be presumed that as to such acquisitions as did not go to the fructuary, he was in the position of a derelict slave, *ante*, p. 274.
[4] C. 7. 15. 1. *pr.*
[5] C. 7. 15. 1. The form of manumission is immaterial.
[6] Subject to compensation, C. 7. 4. 2; cp. D. 39. 6. 39; *ante*, p. 568.
[7] Fr. Vat. 84; D. 29. 1. 31; 40. 2. 3.

retrospectively, to vest the thing in him to whom it would have belonged apart from the legacy[1] : in this case the other legatee. The two were at no time joint owners of the slave. The liberty dates from the manumission[2].

No authority is necessary for the proposition that if the *heres* has ceased to be owner he cannot free. But as to his position while the slave has not yet become the property of the legatee, it is difficult to say what the law was at different dates, in the various possible cases.

If the legacy was of a slave of the *heres*, it is clear that in classical law, at any rate, he was the slave of the *heres* till delivery. According to the view generally held this was also the case under Justinian[3]. Ulpian quotes Marcellus as saying that if, where there was such a gift, the *heres* freed the slave, the manumission was good[4], and this text which is in the Vatican Fragments, no doubt expresses classical law. The Institutes express the same rule, crediting it to Julian, and remarking that the state of knowledge of the *heres* is immaterial[5]. The Digest quotes the same doctrine from Marcian[6]. But elsewhere the rule is laid down and attributed to Paul, that the manumission is void whether the *heres* knew of the legacy or not[7]. The reasoning of the text is ill-fitted to the rule it states, and it seems likely that the decision is of the compilers, and is a misapplication of the enactment of Justinian[8], as to manumission and alienation of legated property, shortly to be considered.

The case of the slave of the testator left *pure per damnationem* should, it seems, be dealt with in the same way, but there are no texts : the case was obsolete under Justinian. Where he was left *pure per vindicationem* the case was complicated, for classical law, by the controversy which existed as to the state of the ownership pending acceptance by the legatee. It is generally held, notwithstanding the language of Gaius[9], that the view which prevailed was that of the Sabinians, that the ownership was in suspense till the legatee made up his mind, and that, if he refused, the thing was treated as having been the property of the *heres* from the date of operation of the will. This view is confirmed by the surviving texts dealing with the matter, which declare that the manumission by the *heres* is void if the legatee accepts, valid if he refuses : *retro competit libertas*[10]. Upon the same principle, if a slave is left *pure* to two, and one, having accepted, frees the man, the manumission is good if the other refuses, unless, before Justinian, the effect of the refusal was to make the gift a *caducum*, in which case the lapse

---

[1] Girard, Manuel, 922.
[2] 40. 2. 3; D. 29. 1. 31 is not really in contradiction.
[3] But it is not possible to be certain as to the exact meaning of his enactment, C. 6. 43. 1.
[4] Fr. Vat. 84.   [5] In. 2. 20. 16.   [6] 30. 112. 1.
[7] 40. 9. 28.   [8] C. 6. 43. 3.
[9] G. 2. 195 ; see, *e.g.*, Girard, Manuel, 922.
[10] 29. 1. 31; 40. 1. 2; 40. 2. 3.

might not benefit the other legatee[1]. In an enactment of A.D. 531[2], Justinian lays down a rule that where a slave is left *pure* or *ex die*, the *heres* is to have in no case any power to free. It is plain from the context that this is intended to clear up doubts as to the effect of his general enactment assimilating all kinds of legacy[3]: there is no reason to suppose it was intended to alter in any way the rule which made the effect of a manumission by the *heres*, of a *servus legatus*, depend on the fate of the legacy.

Where the legacy was conditional, the Proculians held that, *pendente conditione*, the slave was a *res nullius*, and there could be no question of manumission by the *heres*. But the view prevailed that the *res* was in the interim the property of the *heres*[4]. On this view he ought to have been able to free, but two texts in the Digest make it clear that he cannot do so[5]. As Gaius seems to express a view which he rejects in his Institutes[4], it is not unlikely that the rule is new in Justinian's law, and that the old rule was that the *heres* could free, subject to compensation. It is noticeable that Justinian in his enactment, just cited[2], in which he prohibits dealings with things legated, assumes a *prima facie* right to alienate things conditionally legated, but declares any such alienation *irritum* if the condition arrives. He says nothing about manumission in this part of the *lex*, and it is clear that such things could not be voidable. It seems that the texts in the Digest[5] have been altered so as to state an arbitrary rule placing manumissions on the same level as other gifts, so far as is consistent with their irrevocable nature[6]. It is hardly possible to apply the rule that the effect of the manumission in classical law was in suspense, so that it failed if the condition arrived, for this would imply that acquisition to the legatee was retrospective, and this does not seem to have been the case[7]. There are, however, two texts which deal with legacy of *optio servi*, which raise a difficulty. In one we are told[8] that the legatee cannot by freeing lessen the right of the legatee, since each slave is regarded as conditionally legated. The other says that the man is not made free in the meantime, but that he will be free if the legatee chooses another slave[9]. These texts are not in conflict with each other, but they may seem difficult to reconcile with what has just been said. It is clear, however, that in Justinian's law a *legatum optionis* was not

---

[1] Fr. Vat. 84; D. 29. 1. 31; 40. 2. 3. If the other legatee accepted, the manumission would be void before Justinian, as having been made by one of co-owners. Presumably under his legislation the freeing owner would have to compensate the other, *ante*, p. 568.
[2] C. 6. 43. 3. 2 a, 3.   [3] *h. t.* 1.
[4] 40. 9. 29. 1; G. 2. 200.   [5] 40. 1. 11; 40. 9. 29. 1.
[6] This is more or less confirmed by the fact that there survives into the Digest a text which tells us that when there was a *fideicommissum* of a slave under a condition and the *heres* freed the man the manumission was good, but the *heres* had to pay compensation whatever his state of mind, 36. 1. 26. 2.
[7] See the texts cited by Accarias, Précis, § 379, n. 3.   [8] 40. 9. 3.
[9] 33. 5. 14.

conditional. Our text only speaks of each slave as *quodammodo*[1] conditionally legated, and in the Institutes[2] Justinian says that formerly such a gift *conditionem in se habebat.* But he took away the intransmissibility of right of choice, which gave such a gift its apparently conditional character, and we have seen[3] that the passage in the Institutes is very doubtful history. It may well be that those jurists who thought the gift ought to fail if the legatee failed to choose, thought so, not because there was an unsatisfied condition, but because there was no slave who answered the definition in the will. In fact the expression *optio servi* covers two forms of gift—*utrum elegerit habeto,* and *optionem do.* In the former case if he chooses none there is none which satisfies the definition, in the latter there is no sort of reason why the *heres* of the legatee might not choose. It is idle to attempt to reconstruct the debates[4], but enough has been said to shew that we are not entitled to construe such gifts as conditional in all respects. For Justinian they are *pure legata,* and the rule laid down is the normal rule in such cases.

V. *Servus Dotalis.* All the texts which deal with this case are from the Corpus Iuris, with the exception of one which has not been deciphered[5]. It does not appear, however, that Justinian's changes in the law of *dos* affected the right of the husband to manumit during the marriage, so that these texts probably represent classical law. The *vir* is owner and can therefore free[6], with the effect of becoming patron and *heres legitimus*[7]. But though the *vir* could free it does not follow that he would not have to account for the resulting loss to the *dos.* On this matter elaborate rules are laid down[8]. If the wife assented to the manumission, and did so with the intention of a gift to her husband, he will not have to account for any of the rights he has over the *libertus,* either *ipso iure* or expressly imposed, or even for the slave himself[9]. The gift is valid, notwithstanding that it is a gift from wife to husband, just as a gift to him, *ut manumittat,* would be[10]. If the wife assented or did not oppose, but it was *ex negotio,* as a matter of business, the *vir* must account for all he gets *ex bonis,* or *ex obligatione,* including anything specially imposed[11], even though after the manumission[12]. Thus if he accepts the man as debtor or surety *iure patroni,* the

---

[1] 40. 9. 3.   [2] In. 2. 20. 23.   [3] *Ante,* p. 19.
[4] In 33. 5. 9. *pr.* Julian evidently adverts to an analogous difficulty of construction, and refuses on common sense grounds to accept the logical interpretation of the words of the gift, under which the legatee would be entitled to both slaves if he chose neither.
[5] Responsa Papiniani, 9. 9.   [6] C. 7. 8. 7.
[7] 38. 16. 3. 2; 48. 10. 14. 2; but he has no more right than any other owner, so that he cannot free if the slave is pledged to the wife or if he is insolvent, though the only creditor be the wife for the *dos,* C. 7. 8. 1; D. 40. 1. 21.
[8] See Demangeat, Fonds Dotal, 18 *sqq.*   [9] 24. 3. 24. 4, 62, 63.
[10] 24. 3. 63; P. 2. 23. 2.   [11] 24. 3. 24. 4, 64. *pr.* 1.
[12] *h. t.* 64. 3.

obligation so acquired must be accounted for[1]. And by the *lex* Iulia
the obligation covers not only what was received, but what would have
been received but for *dolus* of the patron[2]. On the other hand, two
limits are expressed on this duty of accounting. He is liable for *operae*,
if he receives their value, but not if they are actually rendered to him[3].
And while he is accountable for everything he has received *iure patroni*,
he need not account for extraneous benefactions from the *libertus*, and
thus not for any share of the estate of the *libertus*, to which he was
instituted, beyond his share as patron[4]. If, however, the manumission
was against the will of the wife it appears that he must account for
everything he receives through the *libertus*, as well as for the value
of the man himself[5].

There is some difficulty as to the law in the case of manumission by
will. In the classical law the remedy of the wife or other claimant for
return of the *dos* was a personal action[6]: the slave was still the
property of the husband or his estate, and thus he could free by will[7].
Though the slave could be claimed before the manumission was completed, it was impossible to set it aside when it had been carried out.
On the other hand Scaevola tells us[8] that where the woman died *in
matrimonio* she could free slaves by·her will, at least if there had been
a pact to restore the *dos* to her brother, under which pact he had
stipulated for this return—a point which does not seem material. Some
of the language suggests a direct gift, and a woman could certainly not
free directly by will a slave who did not belong to her when she made
the will[9]. But the concluding words of the text look as if the gift was
fideicommissary, since the *heredes* are spoken of as bound to carry out
the manumissions, and in that case there is no difficulty[10].

VI. Divorce. A woman who divorces or is divorced[11], whose marriage ends, indeed, in any way but *bona gratia*, or death, or civil death
of a party, cannot free or alienate any of her slaves for 60 days from
the end of the marriage[12], whether they had been hers during the
marriage or not. The object is to prevent her from evading the
quaestio for them, in the matter of adultery. The rule is laid down in

---

[1] *h. t.* 64. 4.   [2] *h. l.* 6, 7.   [3] *h. l.* 2.   [4] *h. l.* 5.
[5] 24. 3. 61. It does not seem that any deduction from this was made for his value as a
libertus. This seems to have been regarded as too problematical to be estimated ; see 50. 17.
126. 1.
[6] Girard, Manuel, 950.   [7] C. 5. 12. 3.
[8] 23. 4. 29. 2.   [9] *Ante*, pp. 264, 464.
[10] There is no reason to suppose a direct gift construed as fideicommissary, *favore libertatis.*
We have seen that this is not commonly done (*ante*, p. 514). In a reforming enactment of 529
Justinian uses language which suggests that the husband's right was reduced to a usufruct, the
wife being *dominus.* This is inconsistent with the foregoing texts and with an enactment of the
following year imposing restrictions on his power of alienation (C. 5. 12. 30; C. 5. 13. 1). See
Girard, Manuel, 960.
[11] 40. 9. 12. 1, 14. 2.   [12] 40. 9. 14.

the *lex* Iulia de adulteriis, *quod quidem perquam durum est, sed ita lex scripta est*[1]. Whenever under these rules they cannot be freed, they can be tortured[2]. The *paterfamilias*, the mother, the *avus* or *avia* cannot free or alienate, for the same time, any slaves who had been employed on the wife's service, nor can any person whose slaves would be liable to the *quaestio* in the matter[3]. If such persons, dying within the 60 days, manumit by will, the slave is a *statuliber*; the condition being that there is no accusation within the 60 days[4]. Though the husband dies within the 60 days the bar still continues, as the father can still accuse[5]. Africanus thought the time fixed by the *lex* was too short, since the trial would not be over in that time. Accordingly the rule develops that if a charge is actually begun, manumission is barred till it is over[6]. Similar rules are applied if the manumission is *in fraudem legis, i.e.* in contemplation of a divorce[7]. Justinian provides that death of the wife shall not end the prohibition, but that it shall go on for other two months, as it may still be important on the question of disposition of *dos*. After that time the *heres* may free, unless his *culpa* has delayed the husband in bringing the charge[8].

With this matter may be stated the connected rule that, if a woman is accused of adultery with her slave, she cannot free the alleged accomplice pending the accusation[9]. Under the juristic extension of the more general rule above stated this ceases to be important. Justinian preserves it only in connexion with, and for its bearing on, the law of *institutio*.

VII. Slave transferred with a condition against manumission[10]. If a slave is alienated *inter vivos* with a condition against manumission, any manumission is void[11]. It is laid down by Justinian, though the form of the text shews that the rule is older, that a prohibition of sale includes a prohibition to free. This whole rule is noticeable as a case where an agreement between two persons has an effect *in rem*: the covenant "runs with" the slave[12].

In the case of a slave left by will under a similar condition, there is more to be said. The general rule is the same: the manumission is void[13], and a direction not to sell includes a direction not to free[14]. The restriction may be temporary. We are told that where that is the case, the validity of any manumission, *e.g.* by will, depends on the time

---

[1] 40. 9. 12.   [2] C. 9. 9. 3.
[3] 40. 9. 12. 3—5; including the husband, C. 9. 9. 25; *ante*, p. 91.   [4] 40. 9. 13.
[5] *h. t.* 14. *pr.*   [6] *h. t.* 12. 6.   [7] *h. t.* 14. 5.   [8] C. 9. 9. 35. 3.
[9] In. 2. 14. *pr.*, Severus and Caracalla; 28. 5. 49. 2.   [10] *Ante*, p. 72.
[11] 18. 7. 6; 40. 1. 9; 40. 9. 9. 2. Perhaps originally applied in sale of *captivi*, Sueton. Augustus, 21; Blair, Slavery among the Romans, 18.
[12] C. 4. 51. 7. *Conditio personae eius cohaesit*, C. 4. 57. 5. *pr.*
[13] 40. 1. 9; 40. 9. 9. 2; C. 7. 12. 2. *pr.*
[14] C. 4. 51. 7. The converse is not true: a direction not to free is not a direction not to sell.

when the gift would take effect, not on the date of the will[1]. The
inference that it is to be only temporary may be drawn from the facts.
If the restriction is not imposed as a penalty, but, *e.g.*, in order to have
some person to look after the *heres* or his estate, it will be impliedly
temporary and the bar will cease if the *heres* dies[2]. In some cases the
reason is stated, perhaps to avoid implications. Thus in the will of
Dasumius the *heres* is requested not to free certain slaves, so long as
they live, because they have neglected their duty[3]. It is not anywhere
expressly said that the condition runs with the slave, and in some cases
words are used which seem rather to negative this. Thus in the text
just mentioned the direction was that neither donee nor his *heres* was to
free. In the will of Dasumius[3] the direction is that the *heres* is not to
free. But from the way in which this case is grouped with that last
discussed it seems likely that, apart from expressed intention, the
restriction is quite general[4]. It may be applied to a slave of the
testator or of the *heres*, but not it seems to one of a third person[5].

One point is somewhat difficult. How far, in classical or later law,
is a conditional manumission by will a direction to the *heres* not to free
till the condition is satisfied? Justinian tells us, as we have seen[6], that
in earlier law the effect was, where the *heres* was *extraneus*, to prevent
him from making the slave more than a latin, and that he provides
that the *heres* can make the man a *civis*, but that if the condition
arrives, the man shall be *libertus orcinus*. Antoninus Pius is quoted
by Marcian[7] as laying down or mentioning the rule in most general
terms, not confining it to *heredes extranei*, but it is quite clear that
there were possibilities of making the slave a *civis* in some cases[8].
Pomponius observes[9] that some masters, desiring that their slaves
should never be free, wrote gifts of liberty to them to take effect on
their death, and quotes Julian as holding that such derisory gifts were
mere nullities—*nullius momenti*. This appears to mean only that they
were invalid as gifts, but, as expressed, it also means that they were of
no force as restrictions, the idea perhaps being that, as there was no
express restriction, one could not be implied from a gift which did not
take effect. Pomponius goes on, however, to quote Octavenus[10] as holding
that if a testator, having given a conditional freedom, adds the words:
nolo ante conditionem eum ab herede liberum fieri, the addition is of no
effect, *nihil valere*. In the law as we know it, it is clear that such a

---

[1] 40. 9. 17. 2.   [2] C. 7. 12. 2.
[3] Bruns, Fontes, i. 273. It does not of course bar the testator himself from freeing *inter
vivos*, or even by will, 40. 5. 40. 1.
[4] Cp. 31. 31; 35. 1. 37, where a legal prohibition (*e.g. lex Iulia*) seems to be in question.
[5] A gift of land to a third person if he do not free Stichus does not bar: it is a condition on
the gift giving rise to *cautio Muciana*, but nothing more, 35. 1. 67.
[6] C. 7. 6. 7; *ante*, p. 550.   [7] 36. 1. 32. 1.
[8] 28. 5. 3. 3; 4. 3. 32. See also 40. 7. 3. 15. *Ante*, p. 550.   [9] 40. 4. 61. *pr*.
[10] 40. 4. 61. 2.

restriction could be imposed. Pothier[1] adopts the view suggested, with others, by the Gloss, that the words mean merely "I do not desire my *heres* to free before the time," and not "I desire him not to free." But the words do not mean this, and if they did their emptiness would be so obvious that Octavenus would hardly have made the remark, or Pomponius thought it worth citing. On the other hand if they are understood, as the Gloss also suggests, as useless, since they do no more than the very existence of the condition does, this is not true for the case of a *suus heres*, even if we ignore the fact that any *heres* could make the man a latin, and they are anachronistic in the time of Justinian. In any case the remark of Octavenus seems to be out of date. It must be remembered that the right to impose such a restriction is not a matter of course: we are told in two texts[2] (also cited by the Gloss) that a testator could not impose a general permanent restriction on alienation, apart from *fideicommissum*. Octavenus was an early writer, and it is possible that in his time the power had not developed. The implied restriction contained in a conditional gift is probably later still, and may not be earlier than Antoninus Pius, who seems to have legislated on these matters[3]. If that is so it is probable that the rule that in such a case the manumission, though void as such, was at least a declaration of wish that the man should be free, and thus made him a latin, was later still[4].

VIII. The slave of a person under guardianship. Manumission by an *infans* is impossible, and thus if such a person is under a *fideicommissum* to free, the beneficiary will be declared free on application : it is in fact an ordinary *fideicommissum* which the fiduciary, without personal *culpa*[5], has failed to carry out. Other *pupilli* and women under *tutela* cannot free without the *auctoritas* of the *tutor*, and, even if that is given, the manumission will not include a gift of the *peculium*[6], as it ordinarily does in manumission *inter vivos*[7]. The reason is that a *tutor* has, in general, no power to authorise gifts[8]. It should also be noted that in any manumission, by a *pupillus*, or a *pupilla* under 20, *causa* must be shewn[9]. If the *tutor* refuses to authorise a manumission due under a *fideicommissum* the same rule applies as in the case of *infans*[10].

---

1 *Ad h. l.*   2 30. 114. 14; 32. 93. *pr.*   3 30. 114. 14; 36. 1. 32. 1.
4 See *ante*, p. 543, and App. IV.   5 40. 5. 30. 1—4; *post*, p. 611.
6 40. 2. 24; Ulp. 1. 17.   7 *Ante*, p. 189.
8 27. 3. 1. 2.   9 26. 8. 3. 1.
10 40. 5. 11, 30. 3. In general manumission *per epistolam* operates only when it becomes known to the man, 41. 2. 38. *pr.* Thus Julian holds that the *auctoritas* must be given (and the *tutor* be present?) when the slave receives the letter (Fr. Dos. 15). But an older view, of Neratius Priscus, at least in the case of *domina*, that it is enough if the *tutor* authorises at the time of writing, is confirmed by imperial enactment (*ib.*). No doubt a part of the breakdown of *tutela* of women. Perhaps not to be applied to other cases.

A minor under 20 must of course shew cause whether he has a *curator* or not, and we are told repeatedly that a minor over 20 who frees cannot get *restitutio in integrum*[1]. These texts do not in any way distinguish between the case in which there was a *curator* and that in which there was none, a fact which is somewhat opposed to the opinion now generally held, that a minor who has a *curator* is incapable of making his position worse[2].

A *furiosus* is incapable of freeing, and his *curator* cannot free for him, as manumission is not administration[3]. The imposition of a *fideicommissum* on a *furiosus* creates an obvious difficulty. He cannot authorise his *filius*, if he has one[4]: his personal *iussum* is impossible. Octavenus[5] suggests as a way out of the difficulty that the *curator* can convey him to someone else to free. That this should have been regarded as administrative while the direct act was not is rather surprising. Antoninus Pius settled the matter by providing that the rule above stated for *infantia* was to apply[6].

IX. Slaves of corporate bodies[7]. Marcus Aurelius gave a general power of manumission *omnibus collegiis quibus coeundi ius est*[8], and they, and municipalities whose slaves are freed, have rights of succession and the other patronal rights[9]. It has been said[10] that before these enactments such a slave if freed could not become a *civis*. But in fact Varro, the contemporary of Cicero, speaks[11] of *libertini* of towns, and of their names, in terms which shew that they were not merely *in libertate morantes*, but *cives*, and he makes allusion to slaves of other corporations, obscurely indeed, but in such a way as to suggest that they were on the same footing. An enactment of Diocletian[12] refers to an ancient law authorising municipalities in Italy to free, and speaks of the right as extended to towns in the provinces by a Senatusconsult of A.D. 129. Probably many corporations other than towns had the right, but there was no general right in *collegia* till the enactment of Marcus Aurelius.

As such manumissions were *inter vivos*, the *libertus* of a town, (and presumably of any corporation,) kept his *peculium* unless it was expressly taken away, so that debts to the *peculium* were validly paid to him[13]. The form of manumission by a *collegium* is not known[14]. Slaves of

---

[1] *Ante*, p. 566. [2] But this opinion rests on little evidence. See Girard, Manuel, 231.
[3] 40. 1. 13; 40. 9. 22. [4] 40. 2. 10. [5] 40. 1. 13; *ante*, p. 457. [6] 40. 5. 30. 7.
[7] Mommsen, Z. S. S. 25. 39, 49; Mitteis, Röm. Privatr. 1. 385, 399; Halkin, Esclaves Publics, 142.
[8] 40. 3. 1. [9] 40. 3. 2, 3; 38. 16. 3. 6.
[10] Halkin, *loc. cit.*; Rauter, Société, 37. [11] Varro, de ling. lat. 8. 83.
[12] C. 7. 9. 3. The text calls it *lex* Vetti Libici. Of the suggested emendations, that of Mommsen (*ad h. l.*), *lex veteris reipublicae*, seems the most probable. See Mommsen, Z. S. S. 25. 49. [13] 40. 3. 3; *ante*, p. 205.
[14] As the Senate freed slaves of the State and the *Ordo* freed slaves of towns, it seems likely that a vote of the *collegium* or its governing body, if it had one, sufficed. Probably, as Mommsen says (*op. cit.* 39), recognition of a given corporation would be accompanied by regulations hereon. He suggests authorisation to a delegate (*actor*?) to free *vindicta*, but this seems unlikely.

towns were freed by a *decretum* of the local senate (*ordo, curia*) with the consent of the *Praeses* or *Rector*[1]. They took the name either of the town or of the magistrate who freed them[2]. Bruns[3] gives a case of wholesale manumission of slaves of a municipality, probably for services rendered, in B.C. 188, but this is an overriding decree of the Proconsul[4]. It seems to have been a common thing for them to give a *mancipium* in the place of themselves[5], but there is no reason to think this was a legal requirement[6]: it occurred commonly in other manumissions[7]. Such a substitute was called in some cases *vicarius*, which, in this connexion, no doubt implies that he was qualified for the same function[8].

Any person could give a *fideicommissum* of freedom to the slave of a municipality[9]. And conversely where any townsman suffered forfeiture of his goods, any slave he was bound to free was declared free by the municipal authority[10].

It is a vexed question whether *societates vectigales* were, or might be, corporate bodies. The evidence is mainly one obscure text[11]. Into the various solutions which have been offered of the problem it presents we will not enter[12]. If (or when) it was a corporation it would be governed by the rules just stated. Varro seems to refer to freedmen of *societates*[13], and may be thinking of this case, but the text is not strong evidence, and no surviving juristic text mentions the matter.

X. *Servi Publici Populi Romani, Caesaris, Fisci.* Of the manumission of ordinary *servi publici* there is little trace[14]. Mommsen can find one case only under the Empire. No real case is recorded, it seems, in Republican times. The nearest approach to a case is that in which Scipio promised liberty, on conditions, to some captives whom he had declared *servi publici*[15]. But there are many instances of gifts of liberty as a reward for services to slaves who vested in the State. In some cases they are slaves of private owners, bought and freed as a reward for revealing crime, or betraying the enemy[16], or for service in

---

[1] C. 7. 9. 1, 2, 3; 11. 37. 1.   [2] Varro, *loc. cit.*   [3] Fontes, i. 231.
[4] Acting apparently under the authority of the Senate. It is not, however, quite clear who these slaves were.
[5] C. 7. 9. 1.
[6] See, however, Wallon, Histoire de l'Esclavage, 2. 500; Erman, Servus Vicarius, 432.
[7] *E.g.* C. 6. 46. 6. *pr.*; C. Th. 4. 8. 7; D. 38. 1. 44; 41. 3. 4. 16, 17; 41. 4. 9.
[8] Erman, *loc. cit.*   [9] 40. 5. 24. 1.   [10] *h. t.* 12. *pr.*   [11] 3. 4. 1. *pr.*
[12] See Mitteis, Röm. Privatr. 1. 403 *sqq.* He gives references to earlier literature.
[13] Varro, de l. l., 8. 83.
[14] Mommsen, Staatsr. (3) 1. 322; D. P. R. 1. 369; Willems, Sénat, 2. 354; Halkin, Esclaves Publics, 22 *sqq.* The following references are mainly due to this writer who collects and discusses the texts. It is clear from Varro, de l. l., 8. 83, that they were sometimes freed. He notes that anyone so freed had been called *Romanus* (cp. Livy, 4. 61), but was now called after the magistrate concerned.
[15] Livy, 22. 57, 26. 47.
[16] Livy, 2. 5, 4. 45, 4. 61, 22. 33, 26. 27, 27. 4, 32. 26; Cicero, pro Rab. 11. 3, pro Balbo, 9. 24; Val. Max. 5. 6. 8, 6. 5. 7; Dion. Hal. 5. 13; Sallust, Catil. 30; Plutarch, Popl. 7; Macrob. Sat. 1. 11. 40. But see, as to their ownership, *post*, p. 598.

war[1] : in others they are captives freed for betraying the enemy or for services after capture[2]. It may be assumed that the mode of manumission would be the same for all slaves of the people, and it is clear that the ordinary course is for the Senate to authorise the liberty and for the magistrate to declare it. In some cases this is stated[3] : in others we are merely told that liberty was given—an impersonal form, better suited to describe an act of the Senate than an independent act of the magistrate[4]. Sulla certainly freed on his own authority, but this was when he was dictator with almost absolute power[5]. Scipio perhaps freed captives on his own authority; it may be, as Mommsen says, he did this by virtue of the commander's power to dispose of booty[6]. In many cases the *libertus* receives money as well : this and indeed the abandonment of property rights in the man seem to be essentially the business of the Senate[7]. For the act of the magistrate no form is necessary. Only in a very early and doubtful case is the use of the form of *vindicta* recorded[8]. The magistrate is usually a Consul or Proconsul, but this is not essential : in one case it was the Praetors[9].

In most cases the freedman is declared to have *libertas* and *civitas*. In one case Cicero says : *libertate, id est civitate, donari*[10]. But in some cases liberty only is mentioned[11], and it is quite possible that in earlier days where the event occurred in a latin region the freedman may have received the status of the ordinary inhabitants of the district.

In many cases the slave to be freed has to be first acquired from his owner. We are not expressly told that he could be compelled to transfer. But resistance to the decree of the Senate was improbable, and a power of compelling sale was not without analogies[12].

The only known case in post-republican times appears to have been carried out by the Emperor[13]. Whether the Senate concurred or not cannot be said, but such a concurrence must have soon become merely a form.

There is a good deal of evidence as to the existence of *liberti* Caesaris but it is hardly possible to distinguish between the different grades[14]. No doubt the Emperor could free by will those slaves who

---

[1] Livy, 22. 57, 26. 47; Val. Max. 7. 6. 15; Florus, 1. 22. 30.
[2] Cicero, Philipp. 8. 11; Polyb. 10. 7. 9; Servius in Aen. 9. 547; Macrob. Sat. 1. 11; Plutarch, Sulla, 10; Dio Cass. 39. 23.
[3] Livy, 2. 5, 24. 14, 32. 26 (cp. 39. 19); Sallust, Catil. 30; Macrob. Sat. 1. 11. 40; Plutarch, Cato Min. 39.
[4] Livy, 4. 45, 4. 61, 22. 33, 26. 27, 26. 47, 27. 4; Cicero, pro Rab. 11. 3, pro Balb. 9. 24; Florus, 1. 22. 30; Plutarch, Sulla, 10; Dion. Hal. 5. 13.
[5] Appian, B. C. 1. 100; Val. Max. 6. 5. 7.   [6] Livy, 26, 47; Polyb. 10. 17. 9.
[7] Livy, 2. 5, 4. 45, 4. 61, 22. 33, 26. 27, 27. 4, 32. 26; cp. Livy, 39. 19; Eutrop. 2. 27.
[8] Livy, 2, 5; Plut. Popl. 7.   [9] Sall. Catil. 30.
[10] Cicero, pro Balbo, 9. 24.   [11] *E.g.* Livy, 4. 45, 22. 33, 26. 47, *etc.*
[12] Caesar, de Bell. G. 3. 32; Willems, Senat, 2. 354; Halkin, Esclaves Publics, 25.
[13] C. I. L. 6. 2340; Mommsen, *loc. cit.* The *liberti* Romanae *nationis a principe manumissi* of the *lex* Rom. Burg. (3. 2) are no doubt *liberti* Caesaris. See also C. Th. 8. 5. 58.
[14] C. 3. 22. 5. See the information collected by Wallon, *op. cit.* 2, pp. 506 *sqq.*

were his own private property[1], but there is no sign of an attempt to do so in the case of those in any sense State property. *Inter vivos* the manumission was done by the Emperor himself, and there exists a constitution warning magistrates that it is unlawful for them to do it[2]. He did not manumit *vindicta*, since he was subject to no jurisdiction. But we are told that *ex lege* Augusti, at his mere expression of desire, the slaves are free[3], and the Emperor has full patronal rights[4]. Whether they were always *cives*, or the *Princeps* could make them latins, or did so if they were under 30, is not clear. It may be noted that slaves in the *peculium* of *servi* Caesaris could not be freed by them, even *per interpositam personam*, *i.e.* slaves could not be validly transferred *ut manumittantur*[5]. For this rule to be effective the conveyance for this purpose must have been *ab initio* void. Naturally, fideicommissary gifts of liberty could be made in favour of such persons.

XI. Guilty Owners and Slaves. It was provided by Antoninus Pius that a *deportatus* could not free[6]. The rule refers to slaves acquired since the deportation, for of the others he has ceased to be owner. As he is not a *civis* he cannot of course give *civitas*. But as he has all *iure gentium* rights, he could no doubt, apart from this express enactment, have given them the same rights as he had, just as a *relegatus* could free so as to give the man the rights he had but not so as to enable him to go to Rome[7]. A person condemned, even after his death, for *maiestas*, could not free, and thus gifts of liberty in his will were nullified by subsequent condemnation[8]. The same was true of other capital crimes, and the rule, though it is vaguely expressed, seems to have been, as laid down by Antoninus Pius, that any person actually accused lost his power of manumission for the case of his ultimate condemnation[9].

Servi poenae could not be freed[10]. Even where the sentence was not capital, there were cases in which the magistrate might impose as part of the sentence on a guilty slave, an incapacity for manumission[11]. In some cases there was a permanent rule that the slave could not be freed[12]. A slave who had been guilty of some offence under the *lex*

---

[1] Marquardt, Org. financ. 394.
[2] C. Th. 8. 5. 58. There was now no practical difference between *publici* and *Caesaris*. As to freeing by the fisc, *post*, p. 626.
[3] 40. 1. 14. 1. There may have been a *Sc.* authorising the Emperor generally.
[4] 38. 16. 3. 8.   [5] C. 7. 11. 2; *post*, p. 595.   [6] 48. 22. 2.
[7] 48. 22. 13.   [8] C. 9. 8. 6; cp. D. 48. 2. 20.
[9] 40. 1. 8. 1, 2; 40. 9. 15. *pr.* This is not a condition: there is nothing future and uncertain. The incapacity depends on the guilt and the accusation: the conviction only brings it to light. No capitally convicted person can free (40. 1. 8. *pr.*), but manumission before accusation is good, 40. 1. 8. *pr.*; C. 4. 61. 1.
[10] *Ante*, p. 410.   [11] 40. 1. 9.
[12] Slaves who had been part of a band of robbers and had by decree become private property could not be freed, C. 7. 18. 2. A *servus relegatus* who stayed in Rome could not be freed, 40. 9. 2, *ante*, p. 94.

Fabia, for which his master had paid the fine, could not be freed for 10 years. The text adds that in the case of a will the date of the death, not that of the will, is the date taken as that of the gift[1]. Severus appears to have provided that persons condemned to perpetual *vincula* could not be freed. But as this punishment was always illegal[2], and the enactment which recites this provision goes on to treat the case as one of temporary bonds, it is probable that the original enactment dealt with that case. The reciting enactment, which is so rubricated and described[3] as to make its origin uncertain, but which is probably by Caracalla alone, or with Geta, provides that a gift of liberty which takes effect while the slave is undergoing the penalty of *vincula* is void. Expiry of the sentence would enable him to be freed, but would not revive the gift. Here, too, it is the date of the *aditio*, not of the will, which is determining. There was a still severer rule: Hadrian provided that a gift of liberty would be null if it were made only to prevent a magistrate from punishing the slave in the way appropriate to slaves[4], who, for many offences, were more severely punished than were *cives* or any freemen[5].

XII. Cases connected in other ways with criminal offences. If any person wrote a gift to himself in any will, an edict of Claudius, based on the *lex* Cornelia *de falsis*, voided and penalised the transaction. If, however, the testator noted specially that he dictated the gift in question, it was valid, and even a general *subscriptio* prevented the penalty from applying[6]. Similar rules were applied to gifts of liberty. If a slave wrote a gift of liberty to himself, it was in strictness void, but the penalty was remitted if it was shewn that the writing was at the dictation of the master, whom the slave was bound to obey[7]. If, moreover, the testator subscribed the will, the gift though not valid was declared by the Senate to impose on the *heres* a duty to free[8]—the words of the *lex* being presumably too general and peremptory to be disregarded even in this case. Antoninus Pius had a freer hand and declared that the gift should be absolutely valid if the testator acknowledged in the will that the gift was written at his dictation[9].

A master could not free his slaves so as to save them from the *quaestio* in any case in which they were liable to it, *e.g.* for adultery, which need not be adultery of the slave or his owner[10].

---

[1] 40. 1. 12. If the *dominus* died before the 10 years were up, it was probably *ex die*.
[2] *Ante*, p. 93.   [3] 48. 19. 33; C. 7. 12. 1.
[4] 40. 1. 8. 3; 40. 9. 17. 1.   [5] *Ante*, p. 93.
[6] In case of ignorance or the like the penalty was readily remitted on express renunciation of the gift, 48. 10. 15. *pr.*; C. 9. 23.
[7] C. 9. 23. 6.   [8] 48. 10. 15. 2.   [9] *h. t.* 15. 3.
[10] The rule is mentioned in connexion with adultery but is no doubt wider, 40. 9. 12. *pr.*; P. 5. 16. 9; Coll. 4. 12. 8. *Ante*, p. 90.

The case of the *senatusconsultum* Silanianum has already been dealt with[1]. Here it is enough to say that where, under this senatusconsult the will has not been opened, owing to the killing of the *paterfamilias*, and there is ultimately an entry under it, the gifts of liberty which take effect do so retrospectively, so that the slaves have, as their own, their interim acquisitions, and the child of a woman in such a case is born free. This is settled by Justinian, putting an end to doubts[2]. If, however, some slaves had run away, and the enquiry had been held, and the will opened, a gift of liberty to them would not prevent their being put to the *quaestio* in the matter if there was any further enquiry[3]. But the language of the texts implies that the gifts were not void, but were only ignored so far as was necessary for the purposes of the enquiry and resulting steps. We are told that if any slave brings a claim of liberty under the will of one whose death has given cause to an enquiry under the senatusconsult, judgment on the claim may not be given till the enquiry is ended[4].

XIII. Cases of *Vis* and *Metus*. A manumission is null if the slave compelled his master to do it by threats or force[5]. The same is true if the fear is inspired by a third person or by popular clamour[6]. On the same principle Marcus Aurelius nullifies any manumission *ex acclamatione populi*[7]. By what may have been the same enactment—in form a senatusconsult—he nullified all manumissions, by anyone, of his own or anyone's slaves at the public games[8], and Dio Cassius credits similar legislation to Hadrian[9]. The reference to others is probably an allusion to a direction by some prominent person to free[10]. Conversely where a man compelled conveyance of a slave to him, and freed him by will, the manumission was null, the reason being that had it been allowed to take effect there would have been no remedy against the *heres*, as he had not benefited[11].

XIV. Slave in bonitary ownership. It has already been noted that a bonitary owner could make the slave no more than a latin[12]. The only thing that need be said here is that mere *traditio* instead of *mancipatio* is not the only source of this inferior ownership[13].

XV. *Servus Incensi*[14]. The only real authority is a very defective fragment of the Responsa Papiniani[15], too imperfect to admit of certain

1 *Ante*, pp. 94 *sqq.*   2 C. 6. 35. 11.   3 29. 5. 3. 17, 25. 1.
4 40. 12. 7. 4.   5 40. 9. 9. *pr.*   6 Fr. Dos. 7; D. 40. 9. 17. *pr.*
7 40. 9. 17. *pr.*   8 C. 7. 11. 3.   9 Dio Cass. 69. 16.
10 See Sintenis, *ad h. l.*, in Otto and Schilling's translation.   11 40. 13. 2.
12 Ulp. 1. 16; *ante*, p. 533.   13 *Ante*, p. 549, and Esmein, Mélanges, 352.
14 The following remarks are from Esmein, *op. cit.* 354–8.
15 Pap. Res. 9. 6.

interpretation. Esmein treats the text as meaning that an *incensus*, though liable to *capitis deminutio maxima*, was not barred from manumitting merely by the fact that he was *incensus*, but only by actually being adjudged so. The persons so manumitted would be free, but if the manumission took place before the *census* was closed, they themselves would be *incensi*, and subject to the same penalty. If, however, the manumission was after the *census* closed, they were in no way wrongdoers, and thus were not liable.

XVI. *Servus Latini.* The slaves of latins could possibly be freed *vindicta*, as latins had *commercium*, but not, it would seem, *censu*. A Junian latin could not, of course, free by will. The *manumissus* could never be more than a latin, though, apparently, he would always be that, if the manumission conformed to local rules, unless the rule of the *lex* Aelia Sentia as to *dediticii* applied to latins manumitting[1]. The *lex municipalis* Salpensana provides for manumission *apud IIviros* in a latin colony: the *libertini* are to be latins: *causa*, in the case of an owner under 20, is to be shewn before a committee of *decuriones*[2]. Elsewhere language is used which confirms the view that the freedman of a latin was a latin[3]. The rights of succession to such *libertini* were governed by the *lex municipalis*, and clearly differed from, and were more favourable to, patrons than those which applied to *cives*[4].

XVII. *Servus Peregrini.* Such slaves could not be freed *censu* or *vindicta* or by will, except under the local law. They could be no more than peregrines, indeed so far as the Roman law was concerned, they were only *in libertate*, as having been informally freed, subject, however, to the provisions of the relative *lex peregrina*[5]. In later law, the rule is clear that the manumitted slave of a provincial belonged to the community of his manumitter[6], even fiduciary, though the slave had been an inhabitant of another region[7]. The rules as to manumission in fraud of creditors applied to this case, by a senatusconsult of Hadrian, though the other provisions of the *lex* Aelia Sentia did not[8].

XVIII. *Servus Fugitivus.* A senatusconsult, based on the *lex* Fabia, forbade the sale of slaves *in fuga*[9]. It was allowed, however, to

---

[1] G. 1. 47. If the forms were not observed he would be presumably *in libertate* and after the *lex* Iunia a Junian latin.
[2] Bruns, Fontes, i. 146.   [3] Fr. Dos. 12.
[4] *Lex munic.* Salpensana, xxiii; Bruns, Fontes, i. 143.
[5] Fr. Dos. 12; Plin., Litt. Trai. 5.   [6] C. 10. 40. 7.
[7] C. 10. 39. 2.   [8] G. 1. 47.
[9] *Ante*, p. 268.

authorise *fugitivarii*, persons who made it their business to capture such fugitives, to sell one when caught[1]. Moreover any *fugitivus* whom his master did not claim would be sold by order of the *praefectus vigilum*. The buyer could recover the price from the Fisc at any time within three years, and the slave could in no case be manumitted for 10 years without consent of the former owner[2]. The rule as to recovery of price is obscure: it probably implies that the former owner was entitled to claim the slave at any time within three years[3].

XIX. Deaf and dumb owners. A deaf mute could free informally but, before Justinian, not by *vindicta*. The distinction was important, since informal manumission gave only latinity. One way of evading the difficulty was no doubt to authorise a son to free: the defect was purely physical, and did not prevent *iussum*. It was also possible to convey the slave to a competent person with a condition that he should be freed[4]. A person born deaf was allowed to free, *utilitatis causa*[5]. This must refer to manumission *vindicta*, since such a person could not be worse off than a deaf mute, and it is clear that a deaf mute could free informally.

XX. *Servus Indefensus.* Where a slave is accused of a capital crime and his master does not defend him, and he is, in the event, acquitted, it is laid down that the *dominus* cannot free him[6]. This looks like a penalty on the slave for the master's cruelty. The text may mean no more than that he cannot do so, so as to acquire the rights of a patron, but neither its language nor its position in the Digest suggests this meaning. It is more probable that it is an arbitrary rule, based on the idea that manumission is a reward and ought not to be used as a means of getting rid of a slave of whom one has a very bad opinion. It is clear that the refusal to defend does not amount to manumission or to *derelictio*: he is still the property of the old owner[7].

XXI. Manumission by *persona interposita*. There was a general rule that if a person was incapable of manumission and he left the slave to someone *ut manumittatur* the direction was void and liberty given would be null. The texts differ as to whether the legacy itself was valid[8]. The rule must clearly be limited to cases in which the prohibition was perpetual and not due to a merely physical defect, but with

---

[1] 48. 15. 2; C. 9. 20. 6.   [2] P. 1. 6a. 1, 6, 7; *ante*, p. 269.
[3] The text is not of the highest authority: it is one of those restored by Cujas from the Vesontine MS. now lost.
[4] P. 1. 13a. 2; 4. 12. 2; D. 40. 2. 10. Could he mancipate? Cp. Ulp. 20. 7, 13.
[5] 40. 9. 1.   [6] 40. 9. 9. 1.
[7] 1. 5. 13; 48. 1. 9.   [8] 31. 31; 35. 1. 37.

that limitation it seems probable that the rule was absolutely universal, and not confined to gift by will[1].

Similarly a slave could not free a slave in his *peculium*, even though he were a *servus* Caesaris and so had real rights in the fund[2]. This applied even to a manumitter who was not found to be a slave till after the manumission[3], and to *servi poenae*[4], who had been *cives*. And we are expressly told that a slave could not do it indirectly by *interposita persona*[2].

XXII. A *dediticius* enslaved for living within the prohibited area was sold into perpetual slavery beyond it[5]. If he was then freed, the manumission was not a mere nullity, but had a peculiar statutory effect. It made him a slave of the Roman people[6]. This does not mean that he became *servus publicus populi Romani*: this was a slave the property of the State, and devoted to the public service[7]. These were always men and a privileged class[8]. The person we are now dealing with, who might be man or woman, was in no way privileged, but at the disposal of the State. The rule is obsolete in later law[9].

XXIII. Manumission in a will *post mortem heredis* was void—a rule based on the similar rule in legacies[9]. Justinian abolishes the rule in general terms[10].

XXIV. A *liberta* cohabiting with a *servus alienus* without the patron's knowledge was reenslaved without possibility of citizenship[11]. This rule disappears with the rest of the provisions dependent on the *sc.* Claudianum, under Justinian's legislation[12].

XXV. Manumission *poenae nomine*. Such manumissions were void in classical law. It is not always easy to say what are *poenae nomine* : it is a question of the intention of the testator, *i.e.* whether his real object was rather to penalise the *heres* than to benefit the donee[13]. Justinian abolishes the rule which forbade such gifts[14].

XXVI. An enactment of Alexander provides that a man may not free one whom he had been forbidden by his mother to free, *ne videaris iura pietatis violare*[15]. The words and the general character of the whole text shew that there is here no case of application of a legal principle.

XXVII. If an estate devolved on the Fisc, Severus and Caracalla enacted that the *procuratores* Caesaris were not to alienate *servi*

---

[1] *e.g. ante*, p. 538.
[4] 40. 1. 8. *pr.*
[7] *Ante*, p. 319.
[9] *Ante*, p. 552.
[11] P. 2. 21 a. 7.
[13] 34. 6. 2. Severus and Caracalla.
[15] C. 7. 2. 7.

[2] C. 7. 11. 2.
[5] G. 1. 27.
[8] Ulp. 1. 20; G. 2. 233.
[10] In. 2. 20. 35; C. 4. 11. 1; 8. 37. 11.
[12] *Ante*, pp. 418, 552.
[14] C. 6. 41. 1; In. 2. 20. 36.

[3] 40. 9. 19.
[6] G. 1. 27.

actores of the estate, and that if they were manumitted the manumission should be void. The rule is one of obvious prudence: it is not safe, however, to infer from it that the *procurator* Caesaris ever had the power of manumission [1].

XXVIII. The case of slaves sold for export has already been considered [2].

XXIX. It may be doubted whether alien captives could be freed by a private owner. There seems to be no real authority. Of course so long as they were the property of the State they could be freed by the public authority [3]. But as to private owners, texts are wanting.

It remains to remark that there was a general rule applicable to each of these cases, that prohibition meant nullification [4]: it was not one of those transactions which *non debent fieri sed facta valent*.

---

[1] 49. 14. 30. As to the word *revocantur, ante*, p. 564.   [2] *Ante*, p. 69.
[3] *Ante*, p. 589.   [4] 40. 6. 1.

CHAPTER XXVI.

FREEDOM INDEPENDENT OF MANUMISSION.

THESE cases may be most conveniently discussed under three heads. (i) Cases of reward to slaves. In relation to this matter it should be observed that these are cases in which the State intervenes to give liberty to the slaves of private persons, usually, as a matter of course, compensating the former owners. We have already considered some such cases[1], and assumed that the effect of the transaction with the owner was to vest the ownership in the State so that the act may be regarded as a manumission. It is not, however, clear that this is in all cases a correct analysis of the transaction. It is possible for the State by an overriding decree to give liberty to a slave who does not belong to it. We have seen such a case in connexion with *servi poenae*[2]. The cases shortly to be considered in which liberty is given in excess of any possible interpretation of the testator's intent, are not essentially different. The cases in which freedom is given as a punishment to the master can be explained only in the same way[3]. These are of course legislative acts, but it is not clear that such things would have been beyond the administrative powers of the republican Senate and the magistrate[4] even though the slave was not the property of the State. It is true that the Senate cannot make grants of *civitas*[5], but this is an equal difficulty if the transaction be regarded as a manumission.

In some of the cases which follow either interpretation is possible on the recorded facts.

(*a*) A senatusconsult, elaborating the provisions of the *lex* Cornelia *de iniuriis*, punished those who wrote, or trafficked in, libellous writings. A reward was payable to the informer, fixed by the *iudex*, and varying with the wealth of the accused. Where the informer was a slave the reward might even be a gift of liberty, but only in a case in which the discovery was of public importance[6]. The reward seems

---

[1] *Ante*, pp. 589 *sqq.*   [2] *Ante*, p. 410.   [3] *Post*, pp. 602 *sqq.*
[4] Willems, Sénat, 2. 270.   [5] Willems, Sénat, 2. 683.
[6] 47. 10. 5. 10, 11.

to have been payable out of the means of the accused, and it is possible that the text means that the master was compelled to manumit, being compensated from the accused's estate. There is no suggestion that the public authority was to buy and free the man. But the whole allusion to liberty in this connexion is Byzantine in form[1] : and it is almost certain that this part of the rule is the work of the compilers. It is therefore most probable that the method of application of the rule was not in fact worked out.

(*b*) A slave who denounced the commission of rape on a virgin or widow, which had been either concealed or compromised, was given latinity by Constantine, the parents, if parties to the concealment, being deported. Justinian adopts the enactment, declaring that the man is to get liberty, which in his time means *civitas*[2]. Nothing is said of compensation to the owner, but on the analogy of the next case to be stated, it seems likely that where the owner was not the wrongdoer the Fisc paid compensation.

(*c*) Slaves who denounced coiners, were given *civitas* by Constantine, their owner being compensated from the Fisc[3].

(*d*) In A.D. 380 it was provided that slaves who denounced deserters should get liberty. Justinian adopts the enactment, and with him liberty means *civitas* : it may be doubted whether this was its meaning in the original enactment. The texts say nothing about compensation[4].

(*e*) If a freewoman cohabited secretly with her slave this was capital in both. Constantine provided that a slave might inform of this with the reward of liberty on proof, and punishment if the information were false. Justinian adopts the law and speaks of liberty. Nothing is said about compensation, and it is clear that the case directly contemplated by the law is that of information given by another slave of the woman[5].

(*f*) Leo gave freedom and *ingenuitas*[6] to all persons given to the *sacrum cubiculum,* it being unseemly, in his view, that the Emperor should be served by any but freemen. But this was only where the man was voluntarily given to the *cubiculum* : an owner who alleged that this was not so could get the slave back with his *peculium* within five years. This is rather like manumission, but it is a general rule laid down once for all : nothing is done in the individual case, and it is not essential that the master have intended to make the man free[7].

---

[1] Kalb, Juristenlatein, 71.
[2] C. 7. 13. 3; C. Th. 9. 24. 1.   If a latin he became a *civis*.
[3] C. 7. 13. 2; C. Th. 9. 21. 2.   [4] C. 7. 13. 4; C. Th. 7. 18. 4. 1.
[5] C. 9. 11. 1; C. Th. 9. 9. 1.
[6] So that there were no patronal rights, cp. Nov. 22. 11.
[7] C. 12. 5. 4.   Not a case of revocable freedom : if there had been no real gift there was no real freedom.   If the owner lets the slave stay for five years it is conclusively presumed against him that there was a gift.

(*g*) There are traces of a custom of giving *ancillae* liberty if they have a certain number of children, but it is not clear that this is more than a conventional title to manumission[1].

(*h*) As part of the encouragement of monasticism by the Christian Emperors, Leo and Anthemius provided that a slave becoming a monk, *volente domino*, was free, but reverted if he left the monastery. In view of the civil incapacities of a monk, and of the revocable nature of the change of status, it is not quite clear that this amounted to freedom. All that the text says is that he escapes *servitutis iugum, donec in eodem monachorum habitu duraverit*[2]. But Justinian went further. By a Novel[3] he provided that any slave might, by entering a religious house and serving a novitiate of three years, become a monk and a freeman without his master's consent. The only way in which the master can get him back is by shewing that he entered the monastery to avoid liability for theft or other misconduct. But even this claim must be made within three years : after that lapse of time the man is definitely a monk, and the master can reclaim only any property he brought with him. So far, the rule, though it favours the religious life at the expense of the *dominus*, is plain enough, but the text proceeds to say that if at any time the man leaves the monastery he reverts to his old slavery. This looks very like a revocable liberty, since in the earlier part of the text it is said that by his three years' novitiate *arripiatur in libertatem*, and the case is compared with others in which liberty is given *ex lege*. It is perhaps not necessary to scrutinise too closely the consistency of a Novel with legal principle, especially as in view of the disabilities of a monk the liberty so given is hardly more than an honorific title. In a later Novel Justinian departs, so far as language goes, even further from the old principles. He provides that if a slave is ordained with the knowledge of his master, he becomes free and *ingenuus*, and even if the master did not know, he has only one year from the ordination in which to reclaim the man[4]. That past, he is on the same footing as if the master had known. But here too if he abandons clerical life he reverts to his master. Here the breach with principle is quite definite : the liberty and *ingenuitas* in the case of the priest are very real things, his incapacities being few, and the liberty is revoked by his resigning clerical life.

(*i*) Slaves denouncing the murderer of their master. There is a general rule, stated many times in the Digest, that a slave who has discovered and denounced the murderer of his *dominus* is entitled to liberty. The history of the matter is obscure, but the rule seems to

---

[1] Columella, de re rust. 1. 8. *fin.*; Fr. de i. Fisci, 13.
[2] C. 1. 3. 37.   [3] Nov. 5. 2. *pr.*—3.
[4] Nov. 123. 17. Consent immaterial, so long as he does not forbid. Cp. Nov. 123. 4.

have been introduced by the *senatusconsultum* Silanianum and thus to have applied at first only where the murderer was supposed to be one of the slaves, (perhaps only where this was proved,) and to have been made a general rule[1] by later legislation. The rule itself is simple: the slave is entitled to his freedom and will be declared free by the Praetor[2]. But its working gives rise to many questions. What is the effect of a bar upon manumission ? Here, at any rate in cases under the Silanianum, the reward prevails: the slave is free even though he has been *legatus* by the testator[3], and even though he was acquired by the owner with a proviso against manumission[4]. What is the rule where there are other interests in the slave ? For the case of common ownership the rule is laid down that the man is free, the other owner being compensated[5]. Nothing is said about slaves in whom another person has an interest such as usufruct, but it seems likely that analogous rules applied. The obstacle in this case being of merely juristic creation there would be even less difficulty in applying the statutory rule. It is difficult to say what is done in the case of a pledge creditor—possibly a slave of equal value is given as a substitute. Conversely it may be assumed that denouncing the killer of a usufructuary or of any person other than the actual owner gives no claim to liberty.

The slave may or may not have been *sub eodem tecto*, and so may or may not have been himself liable to torture *ex* Silaniano[6]. If he was, he has no claim to liberty unless he has declared the murderer voluntarily, *i.e.* before he himself is denounced or tortured[7]. Here, however, a distinction arises. If the slave is due to an *extraneus, ex stipulatu*, and is freed in this way, the *stipulator* has an action *ex stipulatu* if the slave was not under the same roof, but if he was, then the *stipulator* has no remedy, since he loses no more than he would have lost if the slave had been put to torture, which might lawfully have been done[8].

A question on which the texts are not quite clear is that as to whose *libertus* the freedman is. According to Ulpian, who gives the fullest statement, the Praetor may declare whose *libertus* he shall be. If no such declaration is made he is the *libertus* of him whose slave he would have been, and that person would claim succession to him[9]. But Marcian tells us that one who so gains his liberty is a *libertus orcinus*[10], and Paul remarks[11] that as he is free *quasi ex senatusconsulto*, it is clear law that he is the *libertus* of no one. It is impossible to be sure that there

---

[1] C. 7. 13. 1; D. 38. 2. 4. *pr.*
[2] 38. 2. 4. *pr.* He is not in the *hereditas, pro Falcidia*, 35. 2. 39.   [3] 29. 5. 12.
[4] 29. 5. 3. 15, on grounds of general utility. *Ante*, p. 585.   [5] 29. 5. 16.
[6] *Ante*, p. 94.   [7] 29. 5. 3. 14.   [8] *h. l.* 13.
[9] Unless the right is taken away for *indignitas*, 38. 16. 3. 4.   Tryphoninus shews what this means by the remark that if a son leaves unavenged the father's death, he will not be the patron of the denouncer, *quia indignus est*, 37. 14. 23. *pr.*
[10] 40. 8. 5.   [11] 38. 2. 4. *pr.*

is here no conflict. The last two texts agree—all that Paul means is that the man has no living patron. But that does not account for the other texts. Probably the texts of Ulpian and Tryphoninus, notwithstanding their general language, are dealing only with rights of succession. A *filius patroni* is not patron though he may have rights of succession.

In Justinian's time the slave necessarily becomes a *civis*, and we have no earlier texts. One of the texts speaks of him as *civis Romanus*[1], but this may well have been *Latinus* in the original. It may be that the Praetor could declare which the man was to be[2].

(ii)   Cases of punishment or penalty imposed on *dominus*.

(*a*)   Slaves exposed on account of sickness. By an Edict of Claudius it was provided that if a master abandoned a slave who was seriously ill without making any provision for his care or cure, the slave became a latin[3]. Justinian provided that the slave should become a *civis*, and the former *dominus* be barred from any rights of patronage, including that of succession. It is not clear whether his children were equally barred from succession[4].

(*b*)   An *ancilla* whom her master had given in marriage to a freeman with a written contract of dowry became under earlier law a latin[5]. Justinian, as we have seen, turned this into citizenship[6]. There may be no fraud in this. But in the Novels Justinian lays down a general rule that if a *dominus* procures, or assents to, or connives by silence at, the procuring of, a marriage between a *servus* or *ancilla* of his, and a free person who supposes the other party free, the slave shall be free and *ingenuus* so that there are no patronal rights[7].

(*c*)   By Justinian's final legislation it appears that a slave treated *pro derelicto* by his master became free[8]. If this is to be understood literally[9] it destroys the law of manumission *inter vivos* as to form, and also the significance of the texts which consider the position of a *servus derelictus*. As the case is dealt with in connexion with that of sick slaves, it is probable that the *dominus* in this case has no patronal rights.

(*d*)   We have seen that eunuchs commanded a high price[10]. Thus there was a great inducement to owners to castrate slaves. By legislation of Constantine and Leo this was made severely punishable, at least among Romans, though the purchase of eunuchs from *barbarae gentes* was not forbidden[11]. The practice, however, continued, and Justinian found

---

[1] 38. 16. 3. 4.
[2] *Ante*, pp. 422 *sqq.* for a possible analogous discretion. One text suggests a possible wider discretion in later times. C. 7. 13. 1 may mean that the *Praeses* could decree liberty to one who had been active, though not the actual denouncer. But the *lex* is obscure and may be expressing only the general rule.
[3] *Ante*, p. 36.   [4] 40. 8. 2 ; C. 7. 6. 1. 3.   Similar rule, Nov. 22. 12.
[5] *Ante*, p. 550.   [6] C. 7. 6. 1. 9.   [7] Nov. 22. 11.
[8] Nov. 22. 12.   [9] The text may refer only to sick slaves.
[10] *Ante*, p. 8.   [11] C. 4. 42. 1, 2.

it necessary to confirm the rule in a Novel[1], punishing everybody knowingly concerned in such a thing. It appears from the language of the Novel that even in earlier law the rule went further and that the slave was free[2]. However this may be, the Novel itself provides that all persons castrated by anyone after a certain date shall be free, and that no validity shall attach to any consent of the victim however formally given. The same result is to apply, even if the castration is imposed for a reasonable medical purpose. The Novel says nothing about the rights of patronage.

(e) Slaves prostituted. In the Empire there is a considerable history of provisions against the prostitution of slaves. The rules have already been discussed[3], but not completely as to their liberating effect.

If any owner compelled an *ancilla* to prostitution against her will it was provided by Theodosius that on appeal by the slave to the Bishop or Magistrate the master should lose his slave and also be severely punished[4]. The *lex* is not clear as to whether the slave was free or not, but a little later it was provided by Leo that the slave could be claimed as free by anyone[5]. Nothing is said here as to consent of the *ancilla*, and the wording of the *lex* seems rather to suggest that her consent did not affect the matter.

There is earlier and more elaborate provision for the case of sale with a proviso against prostitution. Three cases are to be distinguished.

(1) Where the sale merely contains a provision *ne prostituatur*. Here it is provided that upon prostitution the woman is free, even though all the owner's goods are under such a pledge that he could not have manumitted her in an ordinary way[6].

(2) Where it is provided that if prostituted the woman is to be free. If such an agreement accompanies the sale, even though only by verbal pact, the woman is free *ipso facto* if the buyer prostitutes her, and will be the *liberta* of her vendor[7]. Modestinus tells us that Vespasian decreed that if a buyer on such terms resold her, without notice of the terms, she would, on prostitution, nevertheless be free, and would be the *liberta* of the first vendor, *i.e.* the one who imposed the condition[8].

The origin of the rule is uncertain. For Vespasian, it was clearly an existing institution. It was probably due to an Emperor. As we

---

[1] Nov. 142.   [2] Perhaps by another enactment of Leo. Cp. Krüger, *ad* C. 4. 42.
[3] *Ante*, p. 70.   [4] C. 1. 4. 12 = C. 11. 41. 6 = C. Th. 15. 8. 2.
[5] C. 1. 4. 14 = C. 11. 41. 7. No fees are to be paid in such a case.
[6] 40. 8. 6. Alexander provides that such provisions are to be liberally construed. The words *ne corporis quaestum faceret* covered a case in which she was employed at an inn and committed fornication. In the existing social conditions this was a mere evasion, C. 4. 56. 3.
[7] 2. 4. 10. 1 ; C. 4. 56. 2. In 21. 2. 34. *pr.* Pomponius says that if the buyer does prostitute her and she becomes free he has no claim against the vendor. This seems to mean that the ordinary Aedilician actions are not now available. *Ante*, pp. 52 *sqq.*
[8] 37. 14. 7. *pr.* This does not negative a right of action against his vendor by the second purchaser.

shall see in the next case, Hadrian legislated on the matter, but the reference to Vespasian is very clear. There is nothing to connect the rule with the Edict.

(3) Where there was a condition *ne prostituatur*, with a right of seizure (*manus iniectio*) in the event of breach. The existence of such a condition negatives the liberty which would otherwise have resulted from prostitution and the condition is effective against ulterior buyers, even without either similar conditions, or notice of the condition[1]. But even where such a condition exists, freedom may result. Hadrian seems to have provided that if the person, who has the right to seize, waives it and permits the prostitution, the woman will be free, and will be so declared on application to the Praetor[2]. This is stated in an enactment of Alexander, which appears to be purely declaratory. Ulpian says that if the vendor, who has reserved the right of seizure, prostitutes the slave himself, she becomes free in the same way[3], and Paul says that *Imperator et pater* (probably Caracalla and Severus) lay it down that if he gives up his right of seizure, for a price, she becomes free, since to allow the prostitution is the same thing as to prostitute her himself[4]. All these remarks seem to be glosses on Hadrian's enactment, which we do not possess[5].

A case is discussed which might have created difficulties. A woman was sold to be free if prostituted, and resold with a right of *manus iniectio* in the same event. Here, the subsequent transaction cannot lessen the right created by the first, and it is clear that on prostitution she will be free. But what if the order of conditions were reversed? Logically she ought not to have been free, but it is held, *favorabilius*, that here too she is free[6].

(*f*) Religious Grounds[7]. Under the Christian *régime* from Constantine onwards, similar rules were laid down in the interest of Christian orthodoxy. The rules we are concerned with were merely ancillary to the general purposes of the legislation, which were to crush heresy, and to prevent proselytising to the tolerated non-Christian faiths. Even before Christianity became the official faith, there was legislation on this matter against Judaism. Paul tells us that *cives* who allowed themselves or their slaves to be circumcised suffered forfeiture and *relegatio*, the operator being capitally punished[8]. And Jews who

[1] 18. 1. 56; C. 4. 56. 1.   [2] C. 4. 56. 1.
[3] 2. 4. 10. 1.   [4] 40. 8. 7.
[5] Although the vendor is technically patron, and preserves his rights of succession, the texts shew that his misconduct deprives him of the honour due to a patron, so that he can, *e.g.*, be *in ius vocatus* by the woman.
[6] 18. 7. 9. The reason given is that both provisions are for her benefit, and the liberty releases her from her shame as much as the seizure would. But this is no reason: the true reason is *favor libertatis* and that in the text is probably an interpolation.
[7] For analogous rules among the Jews, Winter, Stellung d. Sklaven, 37—40.
[8] P. 5. 22. 3.

circumcised non-Jewish slaves, however acquired, were deported or otherwise *capite puniti*[1]. Our other authorities are all from the Christian Empire. The earliest legislation of known date on the matter was of A.D. 335. It provided that if a Jew acquired a non-Jewish slave, and circumcised him, the slave was entitled to freedom[2]. It appears also that Constantine provided that a Jew might not have Christian slaves, and that any such slaves could be claimed by the *ecclesia*. This does not seem to give liberty[3]: its exact meaning will be considered shortly[4]. In 339 the sons of Constantine laid down a rule that if a Jew acquired any non-Jewish slave, the slave would go to the Fisc: if he acquired a Christian slave, all his goods should be forfeited, and it was declared capital to circumcise any non-Jewish slave[5]. In A.D. 384 it was provided that no Jew should acquire any Christian slave or attempt to Judaise any that he had, on pain of forfeiture of the slave, and, further, that if any Jew had any Christian or Judaised Christian slave, the slave was to be redeemed from that servitude at a fair price, to be paid by *Christiani*[6], which Gothofredus takes to mean the local church[7]. Here too it is not clear what this means; *i.e.* whether the man belonged thenceforward to the Bishop or whether he was free. The more probable view is that he did not become free.

At this point a new factor came in: various heresies needed to be checked. In A.D. 407 it was provided that Manichaeans and some other heretics were to be outlawed and *publicati*, but slaves were to be free from liability if they avoided their master's heresy and *ad ecclesiam catholicam servitio fideliore transierunt*[8]. The meaning of this is not clear. Gothofredus thinks it means not that they belonged to the church (which indeed the text hardly suggests), but that they became free[9]. He bases this on the fact that by an enactment of A.D. 405 it had just been provided that slaves who had been compelled to be rebaptised under the Donatist heresy should acquire freedom by fleeing to the Catholic church[10]. But the argument is not convincing; the language of the texts is very different, as are the facts. The slave who has been compulsorily rebaptised has suffered a serious wrong, for which he gets compensation in the form of liberty. The other has not, and is merely allowed to escape punishment by recantation. The text does not touch, at this point, on the question of the ownership of the

---

[1] P. 5. 22. 4. [2] C. Th. 16. 9. 1.
[3] C. Th. 16. 8. 22. The author of the Vita Constantini says, wrongly, that the slave was free. See Gothofredus, *ad* C. Th. 16. 9. 1.
[4] *Post*, p. 606.
[5] C. Th. 16. 9. 2; cp. C. 1. 10. 1. Non-juristic texts, Gothofredus, *ad* C. Th. 16. 9. 1, and Haenel, Corpus Legum, 209.
[6] C. Th. 3. 1. 5. [7] *Ad* C. Th. 3. 1. 5.
[8] C. Th. 16. 5. 40. 6 = C. 1. 5. 4. 8. [9] Gothofredus, *ad h. l.*
[10] C. Th. 16. 6. 4. 2.

slave: that was already settled by the statement that the late master was *publicatus*. In A.D. 412 and 414 there was further legislation punishing Donatists, slave or free, and even orthodox owners of Donatist slaves, if they did not compel the slaves to abandon their heresy[1]. In A.D. 415 an enactment[2] aimed at a certain Jewish dignitary called Gamaliel laid down a general rule punishing attempts to convert Christian, or other non-Jewish slaves or freemen, and circumcising them. The enactment added that, in accordance with a certain enactment of Constantine, any Christian slaves held by him could be claimed by the *ecclesia*. The concluding provision seems to refer only to Gamaliel's own slaves and to take them away, not because he had them, but because he had tried to convert and circumcise them. The enactment of Constantine to which the law refers has not been traced: it has been suggested[3] that the reference should be to a law already mentioned of the sons of Constantine. But we have not such a complete knowledge of Constantine's legislation that this correction is forced on us. It is unlikely indeed that the reference is to the rule, above cited, laid down in 335[4], since that confers freedom, and there is no real reason to suppose that the expression *ecclesiae mancipentur*[5] implies a gift of freedom, any more than the expression *fisco vindicetur*[6] does. But it is quite likely that in the same or another enactment Constantine provided in addition to his rule that circumcision involved liberty, another rule to the effect that any attempt to proselytise a Christian slave involved loss of him, just as it was clearly laid down in A.D. 384[7]. In the same year (A.D. 415) it was enacted that Jews might have Christian slaves (though they could not acquire them), provided they did not interfere with their religion: any attempt to do so was punished as sacrilege[8]. In A.D. 417 a new enactment elaborated this with some distinctions. No Jew was to acquire a Christian slave, *inter vivos*, on pain of forfeiture, the slave being entitled to liberty if he denounced the fact. Those a Jew had, or acquired by death, he might keep, being capitally punishable if he attempted to convert them to the Jewish faith[9]. An enactment of A.D. 428 enumerated over twenty different kinds of heresy, and punished them in various ways, prohibiting, *inter alia*, any attempt to proselytise orthodox slaves, or to hinder them in the exercise of their religious observances[10]. In A.D. 438 a similar prohibition was directed at all Jews, Samaritans, heretics or pagans[11].

It is noticeable that in all this considerable surviving mass of prae-Justinianian legislation there is only one statute which, dealing

---

[1] C. Th. 16. 5. 52. 4, 54. 8.
[3] For reff. see Haenel, *ad h. l.*
[5] C. Th. 16. 8. 22; cp. C. Th. 3. 1. 5.
[7] C. Th. 3. 1. 5.
[9] *h. t.* 4. Confirmed as to its main prohibition, in A.D. 423, *h. t.* 5.
[10] C. Th. 16. 5. 65 = C. 1. 6. 3.

[2] C. Th. 16. 8. 22.
[4] C. Th. 16. 9. 1.
[6] C. Th. 16. 9. 2.
[8] C. Th. 16. 9. 3.
[11] Nov. Theod. 3. 4 = C. 1. 7. 5.

with the slaves of heretics gives them freedom in any event[1]. On the other hand there are two[2] dealing with Jews which do so, and some others[3] the ambiguous language of which has led some commentators to understand their effect to have been to give liberty. It is quite possible that liberty may, as a matter of policy, have been more freely given in connexion with Jews. Judaism was necessarily tolerated while heresy was not, and it may have been necessary to use stronger inducements to prevent slaves from adhering to a faith which was allowed to exist. However this may be, the distinction is not traceable under Justinian, from whom the rest of our authorities come.

He inserts in his Code[4], in an altered form, the enactment of Constantine's sons of 339[5], incorporating in it part of that of Honorius in 417[6], and putting the result under the name of the latter. It now provides that no Jew is to acquire a Christian slave by any title whatsoever, and that if he does and circumcises him, or any non-Jewish slave, he is capitally punishable and the slave is free[7]. He also includes some other provisions which have been mentioned[8], but these have no direct connexion with liberty. He provides in two enactments[9] that no pagan, Jew, Samaritan or unorthodox person is to have any Christian slave. The slave is free and a money penalty is payable to the Fisc[10]. Jews circumcising any non-Jews are to be punished like castrators[11]. Whether this means that the slave would become free as he did in the case of castration[12] is not clear, but the affirmative seems most probable. Finally, by an enactment already mentioned, he provides that if any non-Christian slave of a Jew or heretic joins the Christian church the slave thereby becomes free, no compensation being payable to the *dominus*[13].

(iii) Miscellaneous cases.

Here it is necessary to do little more than to refer to a number of cases which have already been discussed.

(*a*) *Captivi.* These were true slaves during their captivity, but they became free (retrospectively) by the mere operation of *postliminium*, with no process of manumission[14].

(*b*) *Servi Poenae.* A convict might, during his life, cease to be a slave in either of two ways. He might be simply pardoned, or he might

---

[1] C. Th. 16. 6. 4. 2.
[2] C. Th. 16. 9. 1, 4.
[3] *e.g.* C. Th. 16. 8. 22; 3. 1. 5.
[4] C. 1. 10. 1.
[5] C. Th. 16. 9. 2.
[6] *h. t.* 4.
[7] C. 1. 10. 1.   Presumably inheritance is not meant to be included.
[8] C. Th. 16. 5. 40. 6 = C. 1. 5. 4. 8; C. Th. 16. 5. 65 = C. 1. 6. 3; Nov. Theod. 3. 4 = C. 1. 7. 5.
[9] C. 1. 10. 2; 1. 3. 54. 8; see also C. 1. 5. 20. 6.   [10] *Ante*, p. 319; C. 1. 10. 2.
[11] 48. 8. 11. *pr.*   [12] *Ante*, p. 602.
[13] C. 1. 3. 54. 9, 10.   The master does not reacquire the man by conforming.   It is difficult to imagine a more effective defence of orthodoxy.
[14] *Ante*, pp. 304 *sqq.* See, however, Mitteis, Röm. Privatr. 1. 128.

be *restitutus*, with retrospective effect, and there were intermediate cases. These different modes of release had very different effects, already considered. Justinian abolished this form of slavery[1].

(c) Slaves noxally surrendered. Under the law as stated in the Institutes[2], if a slave was noxally surrendered by his master, and he had by acquisitions recouped the injured person for the damage done, *auxilio praetoris invito domino manumittetur*. The rule is clearly new and is not mentioned in the Digest. Its language shews some hastiness, for a person freed by the help of the Praetor *invito domino* is not properly said to have been manumitted[3]. It is a sort of happy thought of the compilers, an extension to slaves of the rule—obsolete in Justinian's time—that a *filiusfamilias* noxally surrendered can claim release from *mancipium* when he has made good the damage[4]. Even if it be understood to mean that the Praetor will compel the owner to free, the rule is still open to the objection pointed out by Girard[5] that such a man is better off than a slave who has committed no wrong, since he can compel his manumission.

(d) *Liberi Expositi.* The rules already stated shew that after Constantine, if an owner ordered the exposure of a child who was in fact a slave, a charitable person who picked him up had the right to rear him either as slave or as free[6]. If he took the latter course this was a case of a slave becoming free without manumission. The prohibition of exposure[7] must have been disregarded. In A.D. 412 it was provided that the previous owner had no right to recover him, if the finder formally proved the facts before the Bishop[8]. Justinian in his enactment dealing with the matter definitely contemplates the case of a slave so exposed, and declares that if anyone takes charge of him and rears him, he shall be in all cases free; and further that he shall be *ingenuus*, so that the charitable rearer has no patronal rights over him. The reason given is, lest charity degenerate into commercial calculation[9], but it may be doubted whether the new rule made for charity. A later enactment punishes the exposing owner who seeks to recover the slave[10].

(e) *Sanguinolenti.* The rules as to sale of young children, slave or free, have already been considered[11]. It is enough to point out that so far as the institution created true slavery, the power of redemption into *ingenuitas* involves a release from slavery without manumission. How far it did amount to actual slavery was considered in the earlier discussion.

---

[1] *Ante*, pp. 409 *sqq.*   [2] In. 4. 8. 3.   [3] Cp. *post*, p. 612.
[4] Coll. 2. 3. 1.   [5] Girard, Manuel, 680.   [6] *Ante*, p. 402.   [7] C. 8. 51. 2.
[8] C. Th. 5. 9. 2. The wording is almost identical with part of that of the last-mentioned enactment, which is dated 38 years earlier, addressed to a different person and by a different Emperor. They are treated as the same by Haenel and Mommsen. It seems more probable that it was a reenactment, with the significant omission of the prohibitory clause. See *ante*, p. 402.
[9] C. 8. 51. 3.   [10] Nov. 153.   [11] *Ante*, pp. 420 *sq.*

CHAPTER XXVII.

FREEDOM WITHOUT MANUMISSION.
CASES OF UNCOMPLETED MANUMISSION.

THERE are several types of case to consider.

I. *Concubina.* Justinian provided that if a man having no wife made a slave his concubine, and she so remained till his death, he saying nothing as to her status, she became free and her children *ingenui*, keeping their *peculia*, and subject to no patronal rights in the *heres*[1]. This applied only if the will contained no provisions, *e.g.* a legacy of them, shewing a contrary intent[2]. After varying legislation on legitimation[3] he further provided that if the *dominus* freed an *ancilla* and afterwards married her with written *instrumenta dotis*, the children already born should be *ingenui* for all purposes[4]. It is idle to look for legal principle under these rules.

II. Cases of *prima facie* abortive gift. We have already considered the cases in which a beneficiary could be compelled to accept, so that gifts took effect, and we shall soon consider the effect of refusal to carry out the gift after acceptance[5]. Apart from this a gift failed if the gift or instrument on which it depended failed to take effect. But cases of exceptional relief were rather numerous. The following list cannot claim completeness.

(*a*) Relief against failure to enter under the will.

(i) An *institutus* enters *ab intestato, omissa causa testamenti*[6]. The gift is good, retaining its modalities[7].

(ii) *Suus heres institutus* abstains. The gift is good if not *in fraudem creditorum*, which on such facts it is likely to be[8].

(iii) If the *heres* abstains for a price, he is compellable to buy the slave and free him[9].

---

[1] C. 6. 4. 4. 3.   [2] C. 7. 15. 3.   [3] *e.g.* Novv. 38, 74.
[4] Nov. 78. 3.   [5] *Post*, p. 611.   [6] 40. 4. 23. *pr.*; C. 6. 39. 2.
[7] 29. 4. 6. 10; *h. t.* 22. 1 is an apparent exception. *Quisquis mihi ex supra scriptis heres erit S liber heresque esto.* The *heres* omits and takes on intestacy. The liberty fails: its condition is not satisfied.
[8] 40. 4. 32.   [9] C. 7. 4. 1. 1, A.D. 197.

(iv)   A will is upset by collusion in order to defeat legacies, *etc.*
All are good.   Someone can appeal on the slave's behalf—himself if he
can get no one.   The text[1] refers to *fideicommissa*, but the rule is
applicable to direct gifts.   An enactment of 293[2] observes that if a will
is upset by collusion the Consul will look after liberty, under the rules
of Antoninus Pius.   This seems to connect the rule with those as to
defaulting fiduciaries[3].

(v)   A testator gives a man liberty directly and *hereditas* by *fideicommissum*: the will fails owing to death of *institutus* and *substitutus*.
Antoninus provides that the gift shall take effect apparently, in
ordinary cases, as a *fideicommissum,* binding on the *heres ab intestato*[4].

(vi)   A Jew who disinherits his Christian son is intestate by a
provision of Theodosius, which Justinian does not adopt, but his manumissions are to stand[5].

(vii)   The case of the *Querela* brought after five years[6].

(viii)   Ulpian says that if a *hereditas* is *caduca,* legacies and liberties
are good[7].   The rule is not here important except where there is a gift
charged only on a person who does not take.

(ix)   Where there has been undue delay in entry, and one to whom
liberty was given by the will is usucapted by a third person.   The
liberty is protected by the Praetor, somewhat as in the case of delayed
fideicommissary gifts[8].

(x)   Where a will is upset by a son, whose existence was unknown
to the testator, after five years from the death, slaves freed retain their
liberty, at any rate in later law, *favore libertatis*[9].

(xi)   One text seems to say that where a will is upset *iniuria
iudicis,* liberties are good, but this text is probably corrupt[10].

(*b*)   Case of judge ordering damages instead of delivery of slave.
A slave is left to A to free and the *heres* does not hand him over.
When A sues the judge orders damages instead of delivery.   Justinian
remarks on the foolishness of the judge and orders that in future, if
judgment for delivery is not brought within two months of action
brought, the man is to be free and *libertus* of the legatee, the *heres*
paying fourfold costs[11].   He is settling ancient doubts by this slapdash
piece of legislation.

(*c*)   Case of *heres* failing to choose.   A *heres* or other beneficiary is
directed to choose and free a child of an *ancilla* who has several.   He
dies without having chosen, owing to his own fault.   Justinian settles

1 49. 1. 14, 15.   2 C. 7. 2. 12. 2.   3 *Post*, p. 611.
4 29. 1. 13. 4; 40. 5. 42.   5 C. Th. 16. 8. 28.
6 *Ante*, p. 568; *post*, p. 650.   7 Ulp. 17. 3.
8 40. 5. 55. 1.   As to the possibility that he may have been only a latin, *ante*, p. 551.
9 40. 4. 29.
10 40. 7. 29. 1.   Appleton, Testament Romain, 87; Krüger, Z. S. S. 24. 193; *ante*, p. 502.
11 C. 7. 4. 17.

old doubts as to the effect by deciding that all are free[1]. Nothing is said of tho caso in which there is no fault. Probably his *heres* could choose[2].

(*d*) Case of *hereditatis petitio*. Where a *hereditas* changes hands by *hereditatis petitio*, Justinian enacts that the common law rule, according to which the gift fails, as the defeated possessor was not owner, is to apply only if the *petitio* is decided within one year from the death of the testator. If it is then still pending, direct gifts are good and *fideicommissa* are binding on the successor, subject to render of accounts. But if the will is a *falsum* all are of course void[3].

(*e*) Intervention of the Fisc. There is a general rule that where the estate falls into the hands of the Fisc, it must give effect to all liberties. The case will recur[4]: here it is enough to point out some cases. Where a succession is taken away for *indignitas*, and falls to the Fisc, liberty directed to be given to a slave of the *heres* will be given if the *heres* will sell him, which he need not do as he does not benefit under the will[5]. Where a will had given legacies and liberties, and failed because the testator struck out the names of the *heredes*, Caracalla decided that the Fisc, to whom the estate went, must give effect to all gifts[6].

These various solutions are the result of express legislation: they do not seem to express any legal principle other than an attempt to do equity in certain specific cases. As to give the liberty is to deprive some innocent person of what is legally his, the equity is often doubtful, and the rules express *favor libertatis* rather than anything else. The decisions give, approximately, the result that the gift, if validly made by the testator and affecting his own slave, would take effect if the testator died solvent in all cases 'which were at all likely to occur, subject to the limitation which has already been noted, that a *heres* was not compelled to enter, in general, for the sake of a *fideicommissum* of liberty alone[7].

III. The case of fideicommissary liberty overdue. Early in the Empire a set of rules developed, giving a slave to whom fideicommissary liberty was due, the right to apply to the Praetor to have himself declared free, if the fiduciary refused or neglected to complete the gift. The rules applied even if the gift were conditional, provided the condition was satisfied[8], or, even if it were not, if the circumstances were such that the man was entitled to his liberty nevertheless according to the rules already laid down[9].

---

[1] C. 7. 4. 16.　　　　　[2] C. 6. 43. 3; In. 2. 20. 23.
[3] C. 3. 31. 12.　　　　[4] *Post*, p. 626.　　　　[5] 34. 9. 5. 4.
[6] 28. 4. 3.　In the same case the name of one slave was struck out, but here too the Emperor decided, *favore libertatis*, that the liberty should take effect.　It is difficult to justify this.
[7] *Ante*, p. 523.　　　　[8] 40. 4. 20.　　　　[9] 40. 5. 33. 1, 47. 2; *ante*, p. 496.

The earliest known legislation on the matter is the *sc.* Rubrianum, of A.D. 103, under Trajan. It provides that if those from whom the liberty is due, on being summoned before the Praetor, decline to appear, the Praetor will on enquiry declare the claimant free, and he will then be regarded as having been freed *directo* by the testator[1]. To bring the senatusconsult into operation the persons liable must have been summoned with notice—*edictis literisque*[2]. The matter being an important one, *favore libertatis*, it must go before *maiores iudices*[3]. Severus and Caracalla provide that if the liberty is not really due the Praetor's decree is a nullity[4]; in other words the magistrate is not trying the question whether the gift is valid, but only whether, assuming liberty due, the fiduciary has done his duty. The rule applies to all fiduciaries, *heres* or third party[5]. On appearance before the Praetor the fiduciary is given the chance to free there and then, so as to avoid the praetorian decree and its privative results[6]. The *sc.* Rubrianum is an imperfect piece of legislation since it does not provide for the case of inability from any cause to appear, and further, in that it does not cover all cases of fideicommissary liberty. Further enactments deal with these matters, though the Rubrianum remains the principal statute.

The *sc.* Dasumianum, of unknown date, but apparently earlier than the Iuncianum[7], provides for the case in which the failure to appear is not blameable, and enacts that in such cases the freedom shall take effect on the Praetor's decree as if the man had been duly freed *ex fideicommisso*[8]. Hence follow a number of distinctions as to what is and what is not absence *iusta causa*, the result of the difference being usually expressed by saying that if the fiduciary is absent *iusta causa* he does not lose his *libertus*[9], while in the other case he does[10]. A person who hides, or simply refuses to come to the tribunal, or who, being present, refuses to free, comes under the *sc.* Rubrianum[11], as does one who imposes hindrances and delays[12]. Absence *iusta causa* includes any reasonable ground of absence, not necessarily on public affairs[13].

---

[1] 40. 5. 26. 7.　　　　　　[2] *h. t.* 26. 9.

[3] And thus an *arbiter* need not decide a reference on such a matter, 4. 8. 32. 7. No local or personal privilege bars the *sc.* 40. 5. 36. 2. The *sc.* Articuleianum (A.D. 128) provided that the *Praeses* might try the case though the *heres* was of another province, *h. t.* 51. 7. Marcus Aurelius provided that like many other *cognitiones* it might be tried on holidays, 2. 12. 2.

[4] 40. 5. 26. 8.　　　　　　[5] *h. t.* 26. 10.　　　　　　[6] 40. 5. 51. 9; C. 7. 4. 11.

[7] *Post,* p. 613. The Rubrianum seems to deal only with wrongful delay; the Iuncianum deals with both cases; the Dasumianum creates the distinction and seems thus to have come between the others.

[8] 40. 5. 36. *pr.,* 51. 4.　　　　[9] 40. 5. 30. 3, 33. 1, 36. *pr.,* 1.

[10] C. 7. 4. 15.　　　　　　[11] 40. 5. 22. 2, 28. 1, 49, 51. 9.

[12] C. 7. 4. 15, Justinian.

[13] Residence at a distance and consenting, 40. 5. 28. 5; infancy, lunacy, captivity, important affairs, great danger to person or property, being a *pupillus* with no *tutor* or whose *tutor* is detained in one of these ways, *tutor* refusing to act, being represented by *procurator, h. t.* 30. 1, 2, 3, 7; *h. t.* 36. *pr.,* 1. Some are directly under the *sc.,* some by imperial rescript, and some by juristic extension, *h. t.* 30. 3, 4, 5.

If the gift was conditional and the fiduciary has prevented fulfilment of the condition, he loses his *libertus* as for latitation[1]. A senatusconsult declares the Praetor entitled to decree freedom, if the *rogatus* has died without successors, as also if there is a *suus heres* who abstains, or a *heres* under 25 who having accepted is *restitutus in integrum*, and in all these cases the man is, for obvious reasons, a *libertus orcinus* of the original testator.   But the Praetor must not act in such a case till it is quite clear that there will be no *heres* or *bonorum possessor*[2].

The *senatusconsultum* Iuncianum, of A.D. 127, under Hadrian, provides for the case in which the slave to be freed did not belong to the testator.   In any such case if the fiduciary *adesse negabitur*, the Praetor declares the slave free as if he had been freed *ex fideicommisso*[3]. The case primarily contemplated by this senatusconsult is no doubt that of a slave of the fiduciary[4], but it expressly covers any case in which any person is under a *fideicommissum* to free any slave other than a slave of the *hereditas*[5].   Thus the *heres* who has bought a slave whom he was under a *fideicommissum* to free is within its terms[6].   It draws no distinction as to whether there is or is not any just ground for the absence: a fact which is no doubt due to the fact that any such slave could not under any circumstances be a *libertus orcinus*[7].

If the slave entitled to freedom is alienated, we know that he does not lose his right to be freed[8].   Accordingly these provisions apply also[9].   Where the fiduciary sells the slave, and on the slave's petition, he appears, but the vendee *latitat*, the Rubrianum applies, since he who should free absents himself[10]: it is the buyer who is under a duty to free.   So when the *rogatus* is compelled by death or *publicatio* to pass the slave on to another, Ulpian holds that the "constitutions" apply, lest the conditions of liberty be made worse[11].   This does not refer directly to these senatusconsults, but to the rules, shortly to be considered, as to whose *libertus* the freedman will be.   But it assumes the application of the senatusconsults.   Julian is quoted by Pomponius as discussing a difficult case.   A *heres*, directed to free a certain slave and to hand over the *hereditas* to X, hands it over without freeing.   On such a will the better view is (so say Octavenus and Aristo, and Julian is in substantial accord), that the slave did not constitute part of the *hereditas* within

---

[1] 40. 5. 33. 1.   A man was to be free on rendering accounts.   If the *heres* was wilfully absent, the man was declared free, the *heres* losing the *libertus*.   If absent *ex iusta causa*, the man would be declared free if the accounts satisfied an *arbiter*, *h. t.* 47. 2.
[2] *h. t.* 30. 9—14.   [3] *h. t.* 28. 4.   [4] *h. t.* 51. 8.
[5] *h. t.* 28. 4.   [6] *h. t.* 51. 10.
[7] A text set down to Julian says that the *sc.* applies if the direction is to free a *servus alienus* or a common or fructuary slave, *h. t.* 47. 1.   As to the latter cases, in view of the other rights, the rule is probably Tribonian's.
[8] *Ante,* p. 524.
[9] The jurists are not always at the pains to refer each case to its appropriate *sc.*
[10] 40. 5. 28. *pr.*   [11] *h. t.* 26. *pr.*

the testator's meaning, and therefore if there has been nothing but a general handing over of the *hereditas*, the *heres* is still owner and can free, being therefore liable to the proceedings under the senatusconsults. If, however, the slave has been long enough in the possession of the transferee to have been acquired by usucapion, then the transferee is owner and is bound to free, the rules applicable being those just laid down in the case of a buyer[1].

The rules which determine whose *libertus* the man will be are not altogether clear. In the case of *servus hereditarius*, apart from alienation, if the fiduciary is absent without reasonable cause, the man is *libertus orcinus*[2]: if the fiduciary was not in fault he does not lose the *libertus*[3]. If the slave was not the property of the testator, then, apart from alienation, he is the *libertus* of the fiduciary, in fault or not[4].

Alienation creates difficulty. There are several allusions to constitutions of Hadrian, Antoninus Pius and Marcus Aurelius affecting the matter, but the scope of these enactments is not clear[5]. If the *rogatus* is dead, then so far as *servi hereditarii* are concerned his *heres* assumes his duties[6]. But if it was not a *servus hereditarius* and the *rogatus* dies (or is *publicatus*) we are told that the constitutions apply, with the result that when the man is declared free he will be *libertus* (*orcinus*) of the *rogatus* as if he had freed[7]. If the *rogatus* dies without a successor the liberty is still good[8]. Paul asks the question whose *libertus* he will be, and answers, or is made by the compilers to answer, by reference to the *sc.* Rubrianum, applicable in strictness only where he was in fault, that the man is a *libertus orcinus* of the original testator. This is clearly *ex necessitate*[9].

It was clear law, apart from these constitutions, that the *rogatus* must not do anything to make the slave's position worse[10], and there are texts discussing this in relation to sale. Julian lays it down[11] that one conditionally so freed ought not to be sold without a condition for reconveyance on arrival of the condition. Pomponius says[12] that one to whom such liberty is left is not to be sold without his consent to be the *libertus* of another rather than of the *rogatus*. While Ulpian says[13] that such a slave can be sold before *mora*, *cum sua causa*, Marcian tells

---

[1] 40. 5. 20. Where there has been no entry, *fcc.* are not in general binding on successors *ab intestato*. Exceptions, *ante*, p. 609.
[2] 26. 4. 3. 3 ; 40. 5. 26. 7, 33. 1, 49 ; C. 7. 4. 15, *etc.*
[3] 40. 5. 30. 3, 36. *pr.*, 51. 4. In *h. t.* 30. *pr.* it is said that Caracalla provided that if the Praetor declared absent *iusta causa* one in fact dead, the decree stood for the benefit of his *heres*, whose *libertus* the man would be.
[4] 40. 5. 5, 28. 4. This assumes that he has acquired the slave, if not his own, *ante*, p. 531.
[5] 19. 1. 43; 40. 5. 24. 21, 26. *pr.*, 30. 12, 30. 16; C. 7. 4. 4.   [6] 40. 5. 20, 23. 1.
[7] *h. t.* 26. *pr.* If the man vests in the Fisc effect is given to the trust, *ante*, p. 611, *post*, p. 626.
[8] 40. 5. 5. A *sc.* under Hadrian.
[9] 40. 5. 30. 9—12. The text speaks of the rule as *ex constitutione*, but it is the *scc.* which are in question.
[10] *Ante*, p. 525.   [11] 40. 5. 47. 3.   [12] *h. t.* 34. *pr.*   [13] *h. t.* 45. 2.

us[1] that one to whom liberty is due cannot be alienated to another so as to bar his liberty or make his position worse[2].

How far these texts are influenced by the constitutions is not clear: so far as these are known they do not nullify the sale, but merely enact that the man may choose whether he will be freed by the buyer or the *rogatus*; if by the latter, he must be bought back for the purpose[3]. Pius added that if already freed he could claim to be the *libertus* of the *rogatus*[4]. But the constitutions seem to have used general language which the jurists interpreted widely. They were to apply though the sale was while the liberty was still conditional, and though the person who alienated was not the original *rogatus*, but his successor, and though the man had not been the testator's[5]. In considering the ultimate position it must be remembered that the request to be freed by one or the other brings the *senatusconsulta* into operation. If having belonged to the testator he desires to be freed by the *rogatus*, and he makes default, or the buyer will not reconvey, the Rubrianum applies and the man will be *orcinus*[6]. If he was not *hereditarius* it is the Iuncianum which applies and whether there is default or not he will be the *libertus* of the person he chooses[7]. The fact that in a given case he can claim to be *orcinus* does not prevent him from asking to be freed by the *heres* if he prefers[8]. If the *rogatus* dies without a successor, after the sale, the man must be the *libertus* of the vendee in any case, since otherwise he would lose both the man and his price, as he has no remedy over[9]. One text observes[10] that the choice did not exist if the testator did not wish it, but this is probably Tribonian[11].

In considering what is involved in the question whose *libertus* the man is, it must be remembered that in all cases of fideicommissary gift the patron has but a truncated right. The liberty is, as we have seen, somewhat independent of the fiduciary[12]. Thus the fiduciary manumitter has no personal patronal rights, except that he cannot be *in ius vocatus*[13]. Hadrian provides that he cannot exact any *operae*[14]. A person so freed can plead excuses from *tutela* as against the patron[15].

---

[1] *h. t.* 51. 3. [2] As being potentially free, see also *h. t.* 26. *pr.*
[3] *h. t.* 15, 24. 21.
[4] *Ib.* The texts suggest that they used language to the effect that if he wished he might be free as if it had been done as directed by the will. See *h. t.* 26. *pr.*, 30. 12.
[5] 19. 1. 43; 40. 5. 10. 1, 24. 21, 26. *pr.* [6] 40. 5. 28. *pr.*
[7] *h. t.* 29, 51. 10. [8] *h. t.* 10. 1, Pothier, *ad h. l.*
[9] *h. t.* 25.
[10] *h. t.* 24. 21. The text contains another interpolation or corruption apparently giving the *rogatus* the choice.
[11] It should be added that if the *rogatus* has handed him on *ex* Trebelliano, this is for this purpose an alienation. But if there has been a mere general transfer of the *hereditas*, *ex* Trebelliano, however formal, this would not, on construction, include a man so freed, so that in the better view there was no alienation till usucapion, *h. t.* 20, 23. 1.
[12] Illustrated by the rule of Caracalla that the fiduciary can make a legacy to such a man with no gift of freedom, *h. t.* 30. 15.
[13] 2. 4. 9; 27. 1. 24; Vat. Fr. 225. [14] 38. 1. 7. 4. *Ante*, p. 525.
[15] 27. 1. 24; Vat. Fr. 225.

On the other hand the fiduciary has *iura in bonis*[1] and, what is a consequence of this, *tutela*[2]. If he loses the *libertus*, he loses all these rights[3], except in so far as he may inherit them as *heres patroni*[4]. The matter is more complicated if there are several *heredes*, some or all of whom are *rogati*. If several are *rogati*, and they are all in default, the Rubrianum applies[5]. If of the *rogati* some are present and some absent, the senatusconsult (presumably the Dasumianum) requires the Praetor to pronounce which are in default[6]. The slave will then be the *libertus* of those not so pronounced, as if they alone had been *rogati*[7], the shares of the defaulters vesting in the others[8]. Where one *rogatus* was absent with cause, and one was dead without any successors, it was provided by Marcus Aurelius and Verus that the slave would be declared free as if duly freed by both[9]. This is a curious decision in view of the fact that if the *heres* who died *sine successore* had been alone, the slave would have been a *libertus orcinus*, *i.e.* of the testator[10]. As, however, that rule was clearly adopted *ex necessitate*, it may have been thought that the other rule met the testator's intent more nearly in the present case, since the effect would be, not to make a share of the *bona* vest in the Fisc, but to vest it all in the other owner. If there are several *heredes*, of whom some are *rogati*, and these make default, the rules determining to whom the *libertus* belongs are the same, but all the *rogati* are nevertheless liable to those not *rogati* for their shares of the slave's value, either by the *iudicium familiae erciscundae* or by a *utilis actio*[11]. If one of the *heredes non rogati* is an *infans*, then, even though there be no latitation, there is the difficulty that the *infans* cannot sell his share. For such a case it is provided by the *sc.* Vitrasianum, and a later rescript of Pius, that the slave is to be valued, and the shares of the *non rogati* are to pass automatically, the *rogati* being bound to the others to the extent of their shares, as if there were a judgment against them[12]. Where a man has two *heredes* and three slaves and directs the *heredes* to free whichever two they like, and one *heres* makes his choice, but the other wrongly refrains, Papinian lays it down that these two can be declared free as if the one *heres* had been able to free them, while if one slave dies the

---

[1] Vat. Fr. 225.   [2] 26. 4. 3. *pr.*, 1.   [3] *h. t.* 1. 3, 3. 3.
[4] Even thus he may lose *iura in bonis* if he wrongs the man in serious ways, as a patron would in like case, 40. 5. 33. 1; 37. 14. 10. *pr.*, 1.
[5] 40. 5. 28. 2.   [6] *h. t.* 22. 2.   [7] *h. t.* 28. 3.
[8] *h. t.* 1.   Pius enacts that a *rogatus infans* is absent with good cause, *h. t.* 30. 5.   He says also that the presence of *infans* makes the man the *libertus*, not of all, but only of those present or absent *iusta causa*.   The point is that as *infans* could not free, this would prevent actual manumission by the co-owners, and thus it could not strictly be said that they had wrongfully abstained from freeing.   And a Senatusconsult had expressly enacted that where the existence of an *infans rogatus* barred the manumission the slave was to be free, in terms so general that it might have been thought to make attendance needless.   Hence the rescript which negatives these otherwise strong arguments, *h. t.* 30. 1.
[9] *h. t.* 30. 13.   [10] *Ante*, p. 614.   [11] 40. 5. 49.
[12] 40. 5. 30. 6; cp. *h. t.* 51. 11.

others will be declared free, whatever the cause of non-assent of the
other *heres*[1].

One case remains unprovided for. If a legatee is directed to free
a *servus hereditarius* but has not yet become owner of him and is
willing to free, while the *heres latitat*, the Praetor can do nothing on
the slave's petition : the *senatusconsulta* apply only to failure by the
person bound to free. Accordingly there is no resource but to petition
the Emperor[2].

The system was apparently remodelled by Justinian, in a Novel.
He provided that if the *heres* or other person charged failed to carry
out any direction for one year from monition by a *iudex*, other beneficiaries in an order prescribed by the Novel might enter and take
some or all of what was given to him, giving security to carry out the
direction[3].

It remains to consider the effect of the decree on intervening
events. In effect the liberty relates back. Everything the slave has
acquired to his master after *mora* must be accounted for to the freedman[4]. Both the texts which say this are from Paul : the second deals
with a legacy to the slave. They are quite general in their terms : one
must, however, suppose an *exceptio doli* available where the acquisition
was plainly *ex re domini*[5]. Where monthly payments were to be made
manumissis, and the slave became free *absente herede*, Scaevola held
that the payments were due only from the actual freedom. But the
writer is clearly treating the matter as purely one of construction[6].

In the case of an *ancilla* difficult questions arise as to the status of
her child born before the Praetor's declaration. On strict principle he
is a slave, but there are progressive relaxations of this rule, dating
apparently from Antoninus Pius and continuing till the age of Justinian. The general effect of them is, as Paul can already say, that a
child born after there was *mora* in giving fideicommissary liberty is
an *ingenuus*[7]. If he was born before the liberty was due, *e.g.* while
a condition was unsatisfied, or a day not yet reached[8], or it was charged
on a pupillary substitute, and the *pupillus* is still alive, the child is a
slave and there is in general no relief[9].

The first difficulty in dealing with the rules, is in connexion with
the word *mora*. It appears to contemplate what is sometimes called

---

[1] *h. t.* 22. 1.
[2] *h. t.* 26. 10, 11, 27. So the *scc.* did not apply where the fiduciary was directed to buy and
free but did not buy. But he could be compelled to buy and when this was complete the *scc.*
might be applied. *Ante*, p. 531.
[3] Nov. 1. 1. Not set out in detail, since it is far from clear that it was intended to supersede
these provisions.
[4] 31. 84 ; 48. 10. 22. 3.
[5] Ulpian illustrates the retroactivity : where a *liberandus* under 25 was cheated, after *mora*,
he could get *restitutio in integrum*, 4. 4. 5.
[6] 36. 2. 27. 1.   [7] P. 2. 24. 4.
[8] C. 7. 4. 3 ; D. 40. 5. 26. 5. But see *post*, p. 618.   [9] 40. 5. 26. 5.

mora ex persona[1], *i.e.* not only is the freedom due, but the woman has actually demanded it. In this case it seems clear that the child will be *ingenuus*[2]. If the woman has not demanded it there is some difficulty on the texts. If she is a minor it is clear that she has some excuse for not having asked: in such a case the mere elapsing of the time is sufficient *mora*, and the child is *ingenuus*[3]. But where she is not a minor the majority of the texts lay down the rule that if there is delay and no demand made, the child is born a slave but the mother can claim, apparently by real action, to have the child handed over to her to be freed; the idea being that the *heres*, not having done his duty, ought not to have the benefit of the *libertus*[4]. But some of the texts go further. Ulpian, in a text in which he has said that on such facts they must be handed to the mother to be freed, remarks that since fear, or ignorance, *etc.*, may deter a woman from asking, there ought to be some relief in such a case, and then repeats the rule. But he then proceeds to cite a case which will be discussed later, and, on facts in which nothing is said of any demand by the mother, declares the children *ingenui*[5]. This is not perhaps to be regarded as laying down any different rule. But Marcian[6], after laying down the rule that if born after demand they are *ingenui*, adds that there are constitutions which lay it down that the child is *ingenuus* if born at any time after the liberty ought to have been conferred, and adds in somewhat clumsy latin that this is no doubt the right view, since liberty is a matter of public interest, and the person liable ought to offer it. It seems hardly necessary to give reasons for following the rule laid down in *constitutiones*, and it is not unlikely that these remarks emanate from Tribonian. We are told in the same extract[7] that in the opinion of Severus, Pius and Caracalla, it is immaterial whether the delay was wilful or accidental, and it is possible that there may have been constitutions, now lost, putting the case of wilful delay on the same level as that of failure on demand.

Even where the liberty is not in strictness due there may be relief in some cases. Where an *ancilla* was pledged and the owner, by will, ordered the *heres* to free her when the creditors were paid, the *heres* delayed paying, and the creditors sold children born after the debts ought to have been paid. Severus and Caracalla provided, following Antoninus Pius, that the price was to be repaid to the buyer, and

---

[1] Nothing else is properly called *mora*, Girard, Manuel, 646.
[2] 38. 16. 1. 1; 40. 5. 26. 1, 2, 4, 53; C. 6. 57. 6; 7. 4. 3.   Pius, Marcus Aurelius, Verus and Caracalla.
[3] 40. 5. 26. 1, Ulpian's deduction from a rescript of Severus to the effect that mere delay in paying a *fc.* of money to a minor was *mora* without demand; cp. 31. 87. 1; 22. 1. 17. 3; C. 2. 40. 3. Accarias, Précis, § 714.
[4] 40. 5. 13, 26. 1, 55. 1; C. 7. 4. 4, retouched by Justinian.   [5] 40. 5. 26. 2.
[6] *h. t.* 53.   [7] *h. t.* 26. 4.

they were to be *ingenui* as if the mother had been freed[1]. It is not said that the mother applied for the freedom. Where the *heres* was directed to buy and free an *ancilla cum filiis*, and the *ancilla* and her children were valued, and another child was born before the price was paid, Scaevola held that if the *heres* was *in mora*, he had to buy and free the last child also[2]. Here as the *ancilla* is to be bought and the purchase is not yet complete, the *senatusconsulta* do not yet apply : it is presumably for this reason that notwithstanding the *mora*, which seems to imply demand, the child is not *ingenuus*. Marcian tells us that if the liberty is not due and this is due to the delay of the *heres*, whether intentional or not, any child born in the meantime is to be handed to the mother to be freed[3]. The case he is dealing with is delay in entry, and he adds that if there was no wilful delay on the part of the *heres*, but he did not know that he was *heres*, even in this case the child is to be freed, but here as the *heres* is in no way to blame, he may free the child himself and so acquire a *libertus*[4]. Ulpian quotes a rescript of Severus and Caracalla to the effect that if the will or codicil is opened only *post quinquennium* from the death, and there is a *fideicommissum* of liberty to a woman, children born meanwhile are to be handed over to their mother to be freed, and he adds that this, and the rescript of Antoninus Pius, already mentioned[5], shew that the emperors did not mean even accidental delay to prejudice the freedom of the child[6]. One would have expected the *heres* to be allowed to free in this case[7], as the delay is accidental, but it must be noted that the case under discussion is one in which entry was postponed under the *scc.* Silanianum and Taurianum[8], and it may well have been thought that the *heres* ought not to obtain an incidental advantage from the operation of a statute which had no such aim[9].

If the mother (or her successor) having received the child, fails to free, she can be compelled to do so[10]. Nothing is said as to the means. As she is compelled actually to free, it is clear the *senatusconsulta* are not considered to apply, and indeed she hardly comes within the notion

---

[1] *h. t.* 26. 2.   [2] *h. t.* 41. 5.
[3] *h. t.* 53, 55. *pr.*
[4] Marcian applies a similar rule to direct gifts, though he observes that no application is needed to put the Praetor in seisin of the case, but he thinks the Praetor ought to allow a similar claim to the mother here, *h. t.* 55. 1. His basis is a statement of Marcellus that a slave directly freed, and usucapted before entry, has his liberty preserved by the Praetor, though he may be to blame, while in the present case there is no blame, *ante*, p. 291.
[5] 40. 5. 26. 2.   [6] *h. t.* 26. 3, 4.
[7] *Arg.*, *h. t.* 55. *pr.*
[8] 29. 5. 13 ; *ante*, p. 96.
[9] Haymann, Freilassungspflicht, 46, holds, largely on grammatical evidence, that many of these texts have been altered (*e. g.* 40. 5. 13, 26. 3, 54, 55). In some of them rehandling is clear, but the inference which he appears to draw, *i.e.*, that the rules as to the handing of the child to the mother are almost entirely due to the compilers, seems rather too drastic. The distinctions are rational and the story told in the texts is in the main consistent.
[10] 40. 5. 54.

of one bound to free under a *fideicommissum*. The child is not one to whom the *fideicommissum* referred[1].

In the same text[2] Maecianus adds, apparently without any authority, that if the mother refuses to receive the child, or is dead without any successor, a reasonable way out of the difficulty is that the *heres* should free. The case of a child in the possession of the *heres* is here considered. Nothing is said as to the mode of compulsion, or indeed on the question whether he can be compelled. Presumably here too the Praetor's order would come into play.

The rule, that, in some cases, these children were *ingenui*, brought with it the question whether they had rights of succession to their mother and father. As to the mother, the ancients doubted[3]. Ulpian, in a text probably genuine[4], takes a favourable view. He holds that, just as the issue of a *captiva*, returning with her, could succeed to her by a rescript of Severus and Caracalla, *quasi volgo quaesiti*[5], so persons declared *ingenui*, under the *sc.* Rubrianum, ought to succeed to their mother. The ground of analogy is apparently that in both cases they are alike freed from slavery by the operation of a rule of law. Justinian settles the doubt by providing[6] that, saving the right of those otherwise entitled under the *sc.* Orfitianum, there are mutual rights of succession under that senatusconsult and the *sc.* Tertullianum. But what of succession to the father? In another text Ulpian appears as still arguing from the case of *captivitas*, and holding that if both father and mother are entitled to freedom and there is *mora* affecting each, and thereafter a child is born, he is *suus heres* to his father[7]. His language suggests that he would hold this *a fortiori* if the father had been an ordinary *civis—etsi pater eiusdem sortis fuerit...ipseque moram passus sit*. In that case the analogy would seem to be with the case of children of whom a woman had been pregnant at the date of captivity. The rule is interesting as shewing that even slaves were capable of *affectio maritalis*.

IV. *Addictio Bonorum Libertatium Conservandarum Causa.* The rules of this institution were of gradual development, beginning with Marcus Aurelius and completed by Justinian. The general principle is that if an inheritance is refused an applicant may have the goods assigned to him on giving security to the creditors : he then steps into

---

[1] The rules of transfer *ut manumittatur* might have been applied, but the text of Maecian was probably written before Marcus Aurelius framed the rule which, with connected legislation, ended the rather chaotic state of the law on these points.
[2] 40. 5. 54. [3] C. 6. 57. 6.
[4] 38. 17. 1. 3.
[5] 49. 15. 9, 25 ; C. 8. 50. 1; *ante*, p. 308. [6] C. 6. 57. 6.
[7] 38. 16. 1. 1.

the position of a *bonorum possessor*, and any liberties given by will or codicil take effect[1].

By the rescript of Marcus Aurelius, such an application could be made, and security given, where there was no successor and the goods were in danger of sale by the creditors, if liberties were given in the will, by any one of the slaves who were to have freedom. The right was extended, apparently by Gordian, to *extranei*[2]. Justinian allowed even slaves not entitled to freedom to make the application[3]. It seems at first to have been allowed only if there were liberties, direct or fideicommissary, by the will, but to have been extended by juristic interpretation to the case of an intestate imposing liberties on the *heres ab intestato*, by way of *fideicommissum* in a codicil[4].

In later law it was enough if there were liberties given *mortis causa* or even *inter vivos*, if there was any possibility that they might be set aside as being in fraud of creditors : the goods might be *addicta* so as to avoid raising this question[5].

If some of the liberties were simple and others conditional or *ex die*, the *addictio* could proceed at once, the deferred liberties taking effect only if and when the day or condition occurred[6]. It could not be made if there were no liberties[7], and the older view seems to have been that if all the liberties were conditional or *ex die*, nothing could be done till there was one capable of taking effect. But the text which states this rule, at least for *dies*, proceeds to argue the matter, and comes ultimately to the conclusion that it may proceed at once. Clearly where no liberty could yet take effect there could have been no present *addictio* till after Gordian, (if it was due to him,) had authorised *addictio* to *extranei*. As Ulpian, the writer of the text, was dead before Gordian came to the throne, and the text contradicts itself, it is probable that the compilers had a hand in it as it stands[8], but it must not be inferred from this that they were making a new rule. If *addictio* to *extranei* really dates from Gordian, they may merely have incorporated a long established practice. On the other hand the origin of the rule that there could be *addictio* to *extranei* is obscure. The remark is added at the end of Gordian's constitution, the main part of which is concerned with addiction to a slave[9]. But in one of Justinian's constitutions, it is said[10] that under the constitution of Marcus Aurelius there could be *addictio* to an *extraneus*. And the rescript itself is addressed to

---

[1] Justinian observes that it benefits both the slaves and the deceased, as the goods will not be sold, In. 3. 11. 2. He might have added the creditors.
[2] In. 3. 11. 1; D. 40. 4. 50; C. 7. 2. 6.
[3] C. 7. 2. 15. 5.
[4] In. 3. 11. 3; D. 40. 5. 2. The language of C. 7. 2. 15. 5 makes it unlikely that this extension is due to Justinian.
[5] In. 3. 11. 2, 6. [6] 40. 5. 4. 5. [7] In. 3. 11. 6.
[8] 40. 5. 4. 5. [9] C. 7. 2. 6. [10] *h. t.* 15.

Popilius Rufus[1] and authorises *addictio* to him.   Such a name denotes a
freeman, and it is only Theophilus[2] who tell us he was a slave.   Moreover where no one was yet entitled to freedom, it is difficult to see
how Ulpian can have had any doubts as to the impossibility of *addictio*,
unless *addictio* to *extranei* was already admitted.

The first effect of the *addictio* was to prevent *bonorum venditio*, and
it might be made either after security had been given to the creditors, or
conditionally on security being afterwards given[3].   Strictly, as Severus
interpreted the rescript, there could be no *addictio* if the goods had
been already sold by the creditors[4].   Ulpian appears to have suggested
a more liberal view.   He says that when a creditor has sold the slaves,
one to whom fideicommissary liberty was due can get relief against
the *heres* only *ex iusta causa*[5].   This may not refer to our case : the
language does not suggest *bonorum venditio*, and the allusion may be
to sale under a pledge, or seizure under a judgment in the life of the
testator.   But he must have held a broad view in our case, for Justinian,
expressly following him, provided that *addictio* might be allowed within
one year after the sale[6].   The *addictio* is allowed only where it is certain
that there is no successor either by will or *ab intestato*[7].   If a *heres* who
has refused is granted *restitutio in integrum*, the *addictio* at once becomes
void, but, liberty being irrevocable, those gifts which have already taken
effect stand good[8].   Conversely if a *heres* has accepted but is afterwards
restitutus, there may be *addictio*[9].   Even though the *heres* is a *suus*,
and therefore, in strictness, must be *heres*, still, if he has abstained,
there may be *addictio*[10].   Here direct liberties take effect *ipso facto*, so
that it is only fideicommissary gifts which need the *addictio*[11], except
that even where the gift is direct, the *addictio* avoids the question
whether it is in fraud of creditors[12].   Direct liberties take effect immediately on the *addictio* : all others must be carried out by the addictee[13].

The security which must be given in all cases must be for the debt
and interest[14].   The presence or consent of the slaves affected is not
necessary[15].   If the *addictio* is to two, they will have the rights and
liabilities in common.   They will both have to free those in favour of
whom there is a *fideicommissum*, and the *liberti* will be common[16].

Upon the rule that all the liberties take effect, there is the restriction that if the testator was a minor under 20, the liberty will not
take effect *nisi si fideicommissam : haec enim competeret, si modo potuit*

---

[1] In. 3. 11. *pr.*, 1.   [2] Theoph., *ad* In. 3. 11. *pr.*   [3] 40. 5. 4. 10.
[4] C. 7. 2. 15. 1a.   [5] 40. 5. 52.   [6] C. 7. 2. 15. 1.
[7] 40. 5. 4. *pr.*; In. 3. 11. 4 ; C. 7. 2. 15. *pr.*   [8] 40. 5. 4. 2 ; In. 3. 11. 5.
[9] 40. 5. 4. 1.   [10] In. 3. 11. 5.
[11] The case in 40. 5. 30. 10 is one in which there was a *fc.* binding the testator.
[12] In. 3. 11. 6.   [13] 40. 5. 4. 7 ; In. 3. 11. 1.
[14] 40. 5. 4. 11.   Any form of security may suffice, and the *iudex* must summon the creditors
to nominate one to receive it on their behalf, *h. l.* 8, 9.
[15] *h. l.* 3, 4.   [16] *h. l.* 23.   *Familiae erciscundae, inter se.*

causam probare minor...si vivus manumitteret[1]. This is somewhat obscure: the meaning is probably, as has already been said, that it would stand good if the minor could have freed *inter vivos*[2]. If a gift of liberty were conditional on payment, simply, or to the *heres*, payment might be made to the addictee, but if it were in favour of a third person, the payment must still be made to him[3]. If liberty was to be given to slaves of a third person, the addictee must buy and free them. Even though legatees were to free, and the legacy of course failed, the addictee must free[4].

The addictee will be the tutor of any minor slave so freed[5]. The constitution provides that those to whom direct freedom was given will be *liberti orcini*, except where the addictee, at the time of taking the *addictio*, makes it a condition that the slaves shall be his *liberti*. They will then be his[6], and this, by interpretation of the constitution, without any act of manumission by him[7]. But though these and, in any case, those freed by him, are his *liberti*, he cannot impose services on them, since they are not exactly freed voluntarily by him[8].

The main text which tells us that on *addictio* gifts of liberty in fraud of creditors take effect, comes to that conclusion only after argument[9]. It remarks that in favour of this view there is the fact that the addictee has the facts before him, and it adds some obscure remarks as to the effect where the goods pass to the Fisc[10], which will be considered shortly. Other considerations leave no doubt about the rule. No text says or suggests that they do not. Such gifts are declared void in the interest of the creditors[11]. Here they do not suffer. The *heres* himself may not dispute the gifts[12]. We are told that *addictio* bars the action on fraudulent alienation, to which the present case is very near akin, and the reason assigned is *ut rata sint quod (testator) gesserat*, which covers this case[13]. Moreover we are told that the *addictio* had precisely the effect of avoiding the question whether such gifts were valid or not, which it would not do unless it confirmed them all[14].

The exact position of the addictee is not quite clear on the texts. We are told that he is assimilated to a *bonorum possessor*, and that the rights of the deceased, even the *iura sepulchrorum*, pass to him in the

---

[1] *h. l.* 18.
[2] *Ante*, p. 541. Justinian's changes as to age must be borne in mind, *ante*, p. 555.
[3] 40. 5. 4. 6.   [4] *h. l.* 15, 16 ; probably both late developments.
[5] 40. 5. 4. 14.   He would be a latin before Justinian.   As to *tutela* of latins, G. 1. 167.
[6] 40. 5. 4. 12 ; In. 3. 11. 1.
[7] 40. 5. 4. 13.   Justinian's recital of the rescript of Marcus makes it appear that the slaves must consent in this case (In. 3. 11. 1) and the Digest text suggests the same. This may be genuine but it is rather in Justinian's way of thought.
[8] 38. 1. 13. 1.   [9] 40. 5. 4. 19.
[10] To the effect that if the goods had gone to the Fisc, such liberties would have failed.
[11] 40. 7. 1. 1 ; 40. 9. 10 ; *ante*, p. 565.
[12] C. 7. 16. 7.   As to the fact that they are void though *heres* enters and creditors do not suffer, *ante*, p. 565.
[13] 42. 8. 10. 17.   [14] In. 3. 11. 6.

circumstances in which they would pass to a *bonorum possessor*[1]. His
remedies against debtors are thus indicated. We are also told, by
Ulpian, that he can be sued on his *cautio*, but that the better view was
that he can be sued only thereon, and not by the *actiones hereditariae*[2].
Elsewhere we are told, also by Ulpian, that, *plerumque*, the creditors
have *utiles actiones* against him[3]. This might conceivably mean merely
that creditors other than the one to whom the *cautio* was given might
be admitted to sue on it, and thus not be exactly in contradiction to
the other statement of Ulpian. But it is more likely that it is a
contradiction, and that it means that creditors could sue him on their
claims, but only by *actiones utiles*. This development would be so
much on the common lines as to be almost inevitable. It agrees with
what is now the accepted view as to actions against the *bonorum
emptor*[4]. There is no reason to accuse Ulpian of contradicting himself.
This particular text was originally written by him of an entirely
different person—the *curator bonis datus*[5]. It is the compilers who
apply it to the present case, and in all probability they are responsible for the word *plerumque*. But there is one respect in which the
position of the addictee differs from that of the *bonorum possessor*.
The title of the latter is purely praetorian : the addictee holds under
an enactment of the Emperor. His title therefore is good at civil law.
So far as obligations are concerned this is not very material, since these
are not transferable in any case at strict law. But as to property it
is important. For if the addictee had only a bonitary title he could
not free so as to make the slave more than a latin, till the period of
usucapio had elapsed.

Justinian observes in his Institutes[6] that he has made a complete
enactment reorganising and completing the institution. Some of the
changes made by this enactment[7] have been stated, but it will be well
to set out its gist in a systematic form. It provides :

(i) In accordance with Ulpian's suggestion, there may be *addictio*
even after the goods are sold, within one year[8].

(ii) Securities must be given for the debts and the liberties[9].
This is the first appearance of security for the latter : in the other
texts there is no sign of it. Probably it was not necessary, there being
the same remedies against the addictee as against any other person
bound by *fideicommissum*[10]. The security for debts was given as we

[1] 40. 5. 4. 21 ; cp. 47. 12. [2] 40. 5. 4. 22. [3] 40. 5. 3.
[4] Lenel, Ed. Perp. § 218. [5] Lenel, Ed. Perp. § 224. [6] In. 3. 11. 7.
[7] C. 7. 2. 15.
[8] *h. l.* 1. Justinian remarks that the *actio* Pauliana has made buyers familiar with a rule of rescission within one year, 42. 8. 6. 14, *etc.*
[9] C. 7. 2. 15. 1a.
[10] It is possible that the rules as to conveyance *ut manumittatur*, framed by the same author, were applied.

have seen[1] to a nominated creditor, but it is not likely that he would be burdened with the duty of looking after the liberties. Probably in this case the security, if any was really needed, was given to a *publica persona*, a *tabellio* or the like.

(iii) If security is given for all the liberties, *addictio* may be made, if the creditors agree, on security for only a part of the debts[2].

(iv) A slave may refuse the liberty. He will then be the slave of the applicant, but the *addictio* will proceed for the benefit of the others[3]. If all refuse there will be apparently no *addictio*. Justinian seems first of all to allow a slave to refuse the liberty and then to discourage his taking advantage of the right by providing that if he refuses he shall have for a master, *forsitan acerbum*, the man whom he has refused to have as patron.

(v) There may be *addictio* on an undertaking to free only some of the slaves. But in this case if the estate proves solvent, all must still be freed[4]. It seems thus that if all debts are secured, some only of the liberties may be given, and if all the liberties are secured, some of the debts, but both relaxations cannot occur together[5].

(vi) If several apply together they get *addictio* in common, giving security in common both for debts and liberties[6]. If they apply at different times, the *addictio* will be made to him who first, within the year, gives security for all the debts and liberties. On this matter the text says there had been doubts.

(vii) If there has been a grant to one who promised to free some and a later appears, whose undertaking applies to all, or to more than the first provided for, a grant will be made to him. And so also if there is a third. If the earlier grant has not yet taken effect this will supersede it. But if the first grantee has taken possession, and some liberties have taken effect, he will not lose his right of patronage though the goods and other rights and liabilities pass to the new demander. But all must be within the *annus utilis*[7].

(viii) If no freed slave, or *extraneus*, gives full security, even a slave not entitled to liberty may take *addictio*, with what Justinian calls the *venustum* outcome, that one not entitled to freedom gives liberty to the others. Of course he himself gets freedom. The application here too must of course be within the year[8].

---

[1] *Ante*, p. 622.   [2] C. 7. 2. 15. 1b.   [3] *h. l.* 2.   [4] *h. l.* 3.
[5] This language and that of the warning in the last rule seems to imply that under this system even slaves freed directly had to be freed by the addictee and became his *liberti*, though by the older rule those directly freed were *ipso facto* free and *liberti orcini*, In. 3. 11. 1.
[6] C. 7. 2. 15. 4; cp. D. 40. 5. 4. 23.
[7] C. 7. 2. 15. 4—7. *A fortiori* if there had been application but no grant.
[8] *h. l.* 5. Justinian calls the enactment *plenissima* (In. 3. 11. 7), but it leaves much obscure. The spirit of the institution is changed: it is not a means of giving effect to liberties in the will, but, to a great extent, of gifts in substitution, with different effects. As we have just seen it seems that no gift takes effect *ipso facto*, but this may not be meant: the law may be hastily drawn.

V. *Hereditates* passing to the *Fiscus*. There are many circumstances under which this may happen, set forth in the title *de iure fisci*[1]. We are not concerned with these in detail, but only with the effect of such an acquisition by the Fisc on liberties given by the deceased. The topic is discussed in close connexion with that of *addictio bonorum*, because when an inheritance lies vacant, any of three things may happen to it: it may be sold by the creditors; the goods may be *addicta* according to the rules just discussed; it may pass to the Fisc.

The general proposition is laid down that wherever the estate goes to the Fisc, all liberties take effect which would have been valid if the *heres* had entered[2]. Other texts say the same as to specific cases. Thus Caracalla and Pertinax decide that if the property passes to the Fisc on account of an unlawful tacit *fideicommissum*, all liberties, both direct and fideicommissary, are due[3]. Julian tells us that if *bona vacantia* go to the *fiscus* under the *lex* Iulia (*scil. de maritandis*), all *fideicommissa* binding on the *heres* will take effect[4]. Gaius tells us that when the *fiscus* acquires under the sc. Silanianum, all liberties are good[5]. In another text he says that some have doubted this, and remarks that there can be no reason for the doubt, since in all other cases in which the *fiscus* takes the property, liberties are good[6].

Notwithstanding these strong texts, a different view is now commonly held. In one text it is said by Papinian[7] that the enactment of Marcus Aurelius, for the preservation of liberties, applies if, the will being *irritum*, the goods are about to be sold, but if the goods are taken by the *fiscus* as *vacantia, non habere constitutionem locum aperte cavetur.* Cujas[8] takes these words to mean that where there was no claim by the creditors and the goods were simply unclaimed, the Fisc took the property and all liberties failed. This interpretation appears to have been widely accepted[9]. It seems, however, to be based on a misapprehension as to the purpose of Papinian's remark. Even if the supposed rule were clearly stated in the text, doubt would be thrown on it by the very clear and specific contrary rule stated in the foregoing texts, and, even apart from them, by the fact that the acceptance of it compels us to make an irrational distinction. We know that the right of the Fisc is subject to that of creditors. The goods go to the treasury only in so far as they are in excess of debts: the *bona* are the nett balance[10], a fact expressed in the Edictal rule that the goods are sold, *si ex his*

---

[1] 49. 14, especially *h. t.* 1. See also 48. 10. 24.
[2] 40. 5. 51; Haymann, Freilassungspflicht, 52.
[3] 40. 5. 12. 2; cp. 34. 9. 16. 2. See also the cases on p. 611, and Ulp. 17. 2, 3.
[4] 30. 96. 1. Esmein, see below, points out that the text does not mention liberties.
[5] 29. 5. 9, *i.e.* those not destroyed by operation of the *sc.*
[6] 49. 14. 14; see also 28. 4. 3.   [7] 40. 4. 50. *pr.* = Pap. Resp. 9. 13.
[8] Cited Esmein, Mélanges, 349.   [9] Esmein, *loc. cit.*; Accarias, Précis, § 475.
[10] 49. 14. 11.

fisco nihil adquiri possit[1]. Ulpian tells us that, if the goods are taken by the Fisc, the liberties will still take effect, by an express provision of the Constitution[2] as to *addictio*, and the words of the enactment as set out in the Institutes say the same thing[3]. This contradicts the interpretation we are discussing. To harmonise the views it must be assumed that the rule of the *constitutio* applied only where the estate was insolvent, so that the Fisc, though it had taken the goods and was liable to the creditors, had no prospect of getting any benefit, but that where there was a nett balance the Fisc could disregard the liberties. So absurd a distinction could only be accepted on very strong textual evidence, which does not in fact exist. It cannot be supported on the ground that the Fisc "comme tout autre successeur ab intestat[4]" can ignore the provisions of the will. The texts cited shew clearly enough that the Fisc cannot ignore the provisions of the will. In fact it is not like any other successor *ab intestato*. In the very case to which this interpretation is made to apply we are told that all legacies and *fideicommissa* binding on the *heres* take effect[5], but they would not be binding on the *heres ab intestato*. From all this it is clear that if the text of Papinian did say what Cujas understands it to say it would be in conflict with such overwhelming authority that it would have to be rejected. But in fact it says nothing of the kind. Cujas assumes that *non habere constitutionem locum* means "the liberties are void." But all it means is that, whatever happens to the liberties, the provisions about *addictio* have no bearing on the case. It by no means follows that the liberties fail: they may, (we have seen that they do[6],) take effect, but it is not by the operation of this provision. There exists another text, already cited[7], in which the same distinction is made in very similar language. Ulpian tells us that in the case of an insolvent estate, the liberties take effect and *constitutio locum habet*. But if *alia ratione (fiscus) agnoscat apparet cessare debere constitutionem*. In view of the foregoing texts[8] no one can contend that if the *fiscus* acquires the property *alia ratione* (*e.g.*, by forfeiture), the liberties fail. It is in fact the comparison of this text with that of Papinian which has created the difficulty. Papinian says[9] that if the *fiscus* takes the property, *non habere constitutionem locum aperte cavetur*. Ulpian[10] says: *sive iacent bona fisco spernente, sive agnoverit, constitutio locum habet*. The apparent contradiction is avoided by the distinction as to solvency and insolvency above adverted to and rejected. In fact there is no contradiction. The enactment of Marcus Aurelius[11] contains two distinct

---

[1] *h. t.* 1. 1.   [2] 40. 5. 4. 17.   [3] In. 3. 11. 1.
[4] Accarias, *loc. cit.*   [5] 30. 96. 1.   [6] *Ante*, p. 626.
[7] 40. 5. 4. 17.
[8] *Ante*, p. 626. See especially the very strong language of 49. 14. 14.
[9] 40. 4. 50. *pr.*   [10] 40. 5. 4. 17.   [11] In. 3. 11. 1.

provisions. The first is that in a certain event there may be an *addictio bonorum* to save liberties. The second is that if the Fisc takes the goods there will be no *addictio*, but the liberties will stand good. Papinian tells us, and any reader of the enactment can see for himself, that the constitution expressly provides (*aperte cavetur*) that the rule about *addictio* is not applicable where the Fisc takes the goods. Ulpian tells us that where the goods are taken by the Fisc, as *vacantia*, the second part of the enactment applies, but that if the *fiscus* takes the property on some other ground, such as forfeiture, the constitution has no application. Both these statements are correct and there is nothing in either which contradicts the other[1].

At first sight it might seem that if the *fiscus* is bound to give effect to the liberties, there is no point in *addictio*. There is not, if the estate is solvent. But in these cases it is usually insolvent, and sale by the creditors would destroy all the liberties. In the very unlikely case of acceptance by the Fisc of an insolvent estate, the liberties will be good, but while under *addictio* all would be good, those *in fraudem creditorum* would fail if the Fisc took the estate[2].

It may be noted that if a vacant *hereditas* has been reported to the Fisc, and not taken by it, there may be an *addictio*, and no subsequent intervention by the Fisc can upset it. But if the *addictio* took place before the estate was reported, and it proves solvent, so that the *fiscus* claims it, the *addictio* will be set aside. This would create a difficulty on the view here rejected, as liberties would have taken effect. No doubt it could be met by a rule similar to that in the case of *restitutio* by a *heres* who had refused: the liberties would stand good. But the texts do not advert to any such difficulty in this connexion, and on the view here adopted the question would not arise.

VI. A slave transferred *ut manumittatur*. Where a slave was sold or given[3], to be freed either at once[4], or within a certain time[5], or after a certain time[6], a constitution of Marcus Aurelius provided that if he was not duly freed by the receiver, he should become free by virtue of the original transaction, without more. There was no occasion for decree—*non de praestanda libertate...litigare debuisti, sed libertatem quam obtinueras defendere*[7]. It seems probable that the constitution did not in terms apply to gift, but that this was an early extension, *ex*

---

[1] See, for a different view and some references, Otto and Schilling's translation, note to 40. 5. 4. 17.
[2] 40. 5. 4. 19.
[3] 38. 1. 13. *pr.*; 40. 9. 30. *pr.*; C. 4. 57. 1, 2; 5. 16. 22, *etc.*
[4] 40. 1. 20. *pr.*; 24. 1. 7. 9; 40. 8. 9; C. 6. 61. 8. 7, *etc.*
[5] 37. 14. 8. 1; 40. 8. 1; 29. 2. 71. 1.
[6] C. 4. 57. 6; D. 18. 7. 10; 24. 1. 7. 9; 40. 1. 20. 2; 40. 12. 38. 1, 3, *etc.*
[7] C. 4. 57. 1.

sententia[1]. The constitution is addressed to Aufidius Victorinus, and it is at least twice described as issued by Marcus Aurelius *et filius, i.e.,* Commodus[2]. The exact words *ut manumittatur* are not necessary[3]. It is essential that the proceedings have been declared *ab initio* to be for this purpose. Thus the mere fact that after the transfer the buyer wrote a letter undertaking to free would not bring the constitution into operation[4]. The direction is good against all successors, operating independently of them, so that one sold to be freed before a certain time, becomes free when the time expires, though in the meantime both vendor and vendee have died leaving no successors[5]. If it is to be done at once the constitution takes effect so soon as the holder, being able to free, fails to do so[6].

As the freedom takes effect whether the receiver frees or not, defects in him are immaterial. Thus where one who had made an express pledge of all his goods, present or future, bought a slave on this condition, the constitution took effect, even though the vendee were insolvent. A debtor to the Fisc could free in such a case, even though insolvent[7]; a text tells us that as the man would be free anyhow, the Fisc loses nothing by his being freed[8]. Under Justinian, slaves given to a *filiusfamilias* to be freed, were free and were not affected by the father's usufruct in *bona adventitia*[9]. The case of a minor owner is dealt with in many texts. The fact that the receiver is a minor is no bar. In one text we are told by Ulpian that the condition on which he receives is a sufficient *causa*[10]. In another Papinian tells us that there is no reason to shew *causa* at all, since he becomes free by the constitution[11]. The latter is the more reasonable rule, and Ulpian himself seems to lay it down in another text[12], but the reasoning there does not look genuine. Where the vendor is a minor, we are told by Marcellus that if he sells and conveys a slave *ut manumittatur*, even with the intention that the freeing shall not be done till the transferror is over

---

[1] 40. 8. 8; see also Pernice, Labeo, 3. 1. 133, and Naber, Mnemosyne, 22. 443. Haymann (*op. cit.* 35) holds that the application of the rule to gifts on trust to free is due to the compilers. He infers from 39. 5. 18. 1 that Ulpian knew of no such application, since he speaks of the donor as having an action, after the time agreed for the gift of liberty has arrived, when, if the rule applied, the man would be free. But the action is one for recovery, otherwise there could be no talk of bringing it before the time. If in a case of *fiducia* the donor revoked the trust the constitution would not apply (*post,* p. 633) and the action could still be brought after the time fixed. The language of 40. 8. 8 and C. 4. 57. 1 is, so far as this point is concerned, what would be expected if there was an extension. And 40. 1. 20. *pr.* looks quite genuine.
[2] 40. 1. 20. *pr.*; 40. 8. 3; C. 4. 57. 2. Thus its date must be about 178: it has been suggested that there were two of nearly equal date, one extending the other.
[3] Thus *ut libera esset* (C. 4. 57. 3) or even *in libertate moretur* (18. 7. 10) will suffice.
[4] 40. 12. 38. *pr.*   [5] 40. 1. 23; 40. 8. 1.
[6] 40. 8. 9. If it is at, or after, or within, a certain time the rule applies when that time has expired (18. 7. 3; 40. 1. 20. 2; 40. 8. 3). If it is *vivo emptore,* or the like, the man is free at the acquirer's death, 40. 8. 4, 8. In *h. t.* 9 Paul is made to say that if it is doubtful whether it is at the holder's discretion or at once, *favor* induces the rule that it is at once, which is defined to be within two months or four if the slave is away.
[7] 49. 14. 45. 3.   [8] 40. 1. 10.   [9] C. 6. 61. 8. 7.
[10] 40. 2. 16. 1.   [11] 40. 1. 20. *pr.*   [12] 40. 2. 20. 1; *ante,* p. 541.

20, not only does the constitution not apply, since the rule of the *lex* Aelia Sentia was intended to protect owners of immature judgment, but the whole transaction is void[1]. This is declared to have been provided by senatusconsult[2]. Accordingly Ulpian, quoting Scaevola, says that the constitution has no application if the vendor is under 20, but that it does apply if he is between 20 and 25, except that he has *restitutio in integrum* till the man is actually free. The text adds 'that the same rule applies where the transferee is a minor[3].

Presumably though the textual authority is not strong, a gift, with this purpose, of a slave who cannot be freed, is void[4].

A gift *ut manumittatur* is permitted between husband and wife[5], perhaps, as Paul says, either *favore libertatis,* or because there was no real gift to the other party involved[6]. It might be at once or *post tempus* or *intra tempus,* a rule which is squared with the law as to gifts between husband and wife by a principle, laid down by Sabinus and accepted by Papinian and Ulpian, that in this case the slave does not vest in the donee until he or she proceeds to manumit according to instructions. It follows that the donee, where it is a wife, cannot free till the time appointed arrives, nor if it was to be *intra tempus,* after this has expired. From this several results follow. As the ownership has not passed out of the *vir,* it is possible for him to free at any time if he wishes: accordingly there is no reason for the automatic liberty under the constitution, which therefore we are told does not apply[7]. The conditions, being entirely different from those in an ordinary gift *ut manumittatur,* would be changed by a determination of the marriage: accordingly it is held that such an event absolutely destroys the gift[8]. Moreover as the gift is not compellable, and does not operate unless the woman carries it out, her position as patron is not quite ordinary. We are told that she can exact *operae,* and that this is not *ex re mariti,* since the promise is made by the man as a *libertus,* and further, that if she takes money to free, it is hers unless it is *ex peculio,* in which case it belongs to the husband[9]. We may also note that as the gift did not operate unless and until she freed, it was a nullity if the slave was one who could not be freed[10]. These rules are not peculiar to this form of gift: they are here worked out in special detail, but

---

[1] 18. 7. 4; 40. 9. 7. 1.   [2] C. 7. 11. 4.
[3] 4. 4. 11. 1.   The language of this provision (*libertas imponitur*) has led to the view that it is an interpolation. Gradenwitz, Z. S. S. 23. 346; Kalb, Juristenlatein, 75; Haymann, *op. cit.* 21.
[4] 24. 1. 9. *pr.* depends on the relation of *vir et uxor.* In case of such a *fc.* the receiver need not free, but while Modestinus thinks the gift void, Paul and (apparently) Neratius think it good, 31. 31; 35. 1. 37. Pernice, Labeo, 3. 1. 293, suggests that in one case there is intent to benefit the receiver while in the other it is a mere mandate.
[5] Ulp. 7. 1; C. 5. 16. 22; D. 24. 1. 7. 9; 24. 3. 63, *etc.*   [6] P. 2. 23. 2.
[7] 24. 1. 7. 8, 9.   There are interpolations but not material, Gradenwitz, Z. S. S. 23. 345.
[8] 24. 1. 8.   [9] 24. 1. 9. 1.
[10] *h. l. pr.*

they seem, *mutatis mutandis,* to be equally applicable to other licit gifts between *vir et uxor*[1].

There is nothing to prevent ordinary commercial transactions between husband and wife, and thus these special restrictions apply only to cases of *donatio ut manumittatur,* not to sale with the same intention.

In an ordinary case, the liberty takes effect automatically, at the agreed time and thus children born thereafter are *ingenui*[2]: their position is not affected by any subsequent manumission of their mother, which is in itself a nullity[3]. The receiver becomes patron whether he frees or allows the constitution to operate[4]. His position is not, however, quite that of an ordinary patron[5]. Marcellus says that as the receiver takes him under a trust to manumit he does not confer any real benefit in him, and thus cannot accuse him as *ingratus*[6]. Another text, of Ulpian, seems, however, to imply that he would have such a right if he freed, but not if he allowed the constitution to operate, *cum non sit manumissor*[7]. But the other rule was apparently expressed in an enactment of Severus and Caracalla, which prevents the manumitter from reenslaving the man[8], and this must be taken to be the law, at least thereafter. Whether the man be freed or allowed to become free, no *operae* may be imposed[9]. On the other hand in both cases the patron is protected against *in ius vocatio*[10], will be tutor of the slave, if the latter is a minor[11], and has the ordinary *iura in bonis*[12], this being expressly provided for in the constitution[13]. In the case in which the buyer institutes the man *cum libertate,* an important distinction is drawn. If this is done before the time at which he was entitled to liberty, he is a *necessarius heres.* If it is afterwards, says Ulpian, he can abstain[14]. Paul appears to say that he can abstain in any case[15], but his remarks in an earlier part of the text suggest a limitation to the case where the slave *nihil commodi sensit,* which would agree with Ulpian[16].

Such a gift may be conditional. In one text we have the case of a man who is to be free at the end of three years, *si continuo triennio servisset.* The man runs away before three years are over. Paul holds that he will

---

[1] *e.g.* 24. 1. 5. 9, 11. It will be observed that as the conveyance is by way of *mancipatio,* this is an instance of *mancipatio* subject to tacit condition or *dies.* But the modality *inest*: it does not spring from the will of a party. The gift cannot operate unless and until the wife is not profited, *ante,* p. 455. There is some difficulty in the rule that if the marriage ends while the manumission is still unperformed, the gift is null, but even this is said, by Gaius, *inesse,* 24. 1. 8. The jurists utilise the *primafacie* invalidity of the gift to produce these results: they could not result from convention *inter capaces.*

[2] 1. 5. 22.   [3] C. 4. 57. 3.   [4] 37. 14. 8. 1.
[5] Incomplete patronal rights occur in other cases, *e.g.* 37. 14. 3, 5. 1, *etc.*
[6] 37. 15. 3, *in fin.*   [7] 40. 9. 30. *pr.*   [8] C. 6. 3. 2.
[9] *Ib.*; D. 38. 1. 13. *pr.*   [10] 2. 4. 10. *pr.*   [11] 26. 4. 3. 2.
[12] 38. 2. 3. 3.
[13] 38. 16. 3. 3. He has the usual control over the marriage of the *liberta* freed *matrimonii causa,* 23. 2. 45. *pr.*
[14] 28. 2. 71. 1.   [15] 28. 5. 85. 1.
[16] *h. l. pr.* The time is that of operation of the will, not of making.

be free at the end of the three years: apparently he treats *servire* as meaning "be a slave[1]." In another case the slave is to be freed after five years and to pay a sum monthly meanwhile. Papinian holds that this is not a condition, but a mere direction as to what is expected of him during his temporary slavery[2].

It has been suggested that the constitution may have provided that the slave freed by its rules should be a latin[3]. There seems to be little evidence for this and it is negatived, as Gradenwitz shews, by a text already cited to the effect that the result is the same whether the man is freed by the receiver or becomes free by operation of the constitution[4]. The same result follows from the texts which say that the stipulation penalty cannot be recovered, since he becomes free by the constitution[5]. Still stronger is the text which says that the constitution itself declares that the man *meus libertus est, et legitima eius hereditas mihi deferetur.* Such language could not be used of a latin[6].

The mechanism of the transaction is not easily made out from the texts. In the time of Justinian it is clear, formal conveyances having disappeared, that any expression of intent either in the contract or in the conveyance, sufficed.

It may be noted that the transaction is sometimes a mere employment, *e.g.* where the receiver is to free at once or *intra tempus*[7], sometimes coupled with a benefit to the donee, *e.g.* where he is to free after a certain time[8], and sometimes a sale in which the price, though real, may be reduced by reason of the modality[9]. In the cases of employment and gift, *mancipatio cum fiducia* would be the appropriate mode, and it is clear that it occurs in some of the texts[10]. It is probable that it was the mode employed in nearly all the cases in which the texts associate the undertaking that the man shall be freed with the actual conveyance[11]. In the case of sale, with which the constitution directly deals, there is nothing to suggest *fiducia*[12]. We have in one case an agreed right of seizure with an alternative money penalty. No doubt the pact associated with the sale may have been sometimes

---

[1] 40. 12. 38. 3.   Cp. C. 4. 57. 1.   It is *servire* not *heredi servire*.   See *ante*, p. 487.
[2] 40. 1. 20. 3.   These are not terms in the mancipation, but in the agreement for sale.   The rather inept concluding clause is probably due to Tribonian.
[3] See Gradenwitz, Z. S. S. 23. 347.   [4] 40. 1. 20. *pr.*, 1.
[5] 18. 7. 10; 40. 1. 20. 2; C. 7. 57. 6.
[6] 38. 16. 3. 3.   It is hardly likely that Justinian would have omitted the case in his abolishing enactment, C. 7. 6.
[7] *e.g.* C. 4. 57. 2; D. 40. 8. 3; 40. 8. 9; *ante*, p. 628.
[8] *e.g.* 40. 8. 8; C. 4. 57. 1; *ante*, p. 628.   [9] 18. 7. 10.
[10] Lenel shews, Z. S. S. 9. 182, that 17. 1. 30 is from the 13th book of Julian's Digesta, which dealt with *fiducia*, and is probably identical with Fr. Vat. 334 a, which mentions *fiducia*, and he points out that 17. 1. 27. 1 deals with mandate after death and is by Gaius, who expressly repudiates such mandate.
[11] *e.g.* 12. 4. 5. 1; 17. 1. 27. 1, 30; 39. 5. 18. 1; 40. 8. 8; C. 4. 57. 1.   But in 45. 1. 122. 2 there is *donatio* and stipulation for a penalty.
[12] In 18. 7. 8, a sale, it is clear that there is no *fiducia*: the *actio fiduciae* would have been obvious.

fortified by a *fiducia* attached to the conveyance[1]. In any case it is clear that the transaction sometimes contained a *fiducia* and sometimes did not.

This fact is material in connexion with the much debated question as to the effect of change of mind on the part of the transferor[2]. Many of these texts tell us that the constitution applies only if the transferor has not altered his mind. Others ignore this point[3]. Most of the texts which speak of a right of revocation have obvious marks of interpolation[4]. Hence have arisen the most diverse opinions as to the history of this right of withdrawal. The texts seem to indicate a historical development somewhat as follows. Before the date of the constitution, if there was a *fiducia* the donor could recall the man at any time by an *actio fiduciae*, and free him, if the receiver had failed to do so, or keep the man, if he had changed his mind. If there was no *fiducia*, but a sale with a *pactum adiectum*[5], there might be agreements for return if the manumission were not carried out, or for a penalty or the like. There is no evidence of any right of pursuing the man in the hands of a third party[6], and it is clear that there is no right of recovery on mere change of mind[7]. The *constitutio* dealt only with this case and provided that the man should be free *ipso iure* when the agreed time arrived. It did not deal with the case of *donatio*, where the difficulty did not exist, but was soon extended thereto in practice[8]. The *constitutio* said nothing about revocation, but it did not abolish the principles of *fiducia*, and thus it did not apply if the donor had revoked the *fiducia*, whether he had reclaimed the man or not. Ultimately the practice grew of allowing revocation in all cases, to the exclusion of the constitution, but this is post-classical and is introduced into the texts by the compilers. It does not of course follow that it was new.

This opinion rests mainly on the following considerations. We have seen that though the *constitutio* did not at first cover fiduciary gifts there is reason to think it was soon applied to them. To put the *constitutio* out of operation is not necessarily to give any right of action, and every text which gives the transferor a right of recovery, or

---

[1] Yet the remark of Tryphoninus that the constitution makes the man free even though the gift were delayed to death of vendee may be a hint of the ancient doubt whether *fiducia* bound the *heres*, Pernice, Labeo, 3. 121.

[2] See *inter alios*, Gradenwitz, Interpolationen, 146 *sqq.*; Z. S. S. 14. 121; 23. 346; Lenel, Z. S. S. 9. 182; Pernice, Labeo, 3. 1. 134, 262; Monnier, N. R. H. 24. 185; Haymann, Freilassungspflicht, *pass.* All these admit large interpolations. For more conservative views, Karlowa, R. R. G. 2. 772; Heck, Z. S. S. 10. 119. The chief texts are: C. 4. 5. 7. 1, 6; 6. 6. 29; D. 4. 4. 11. 1; 12. 4. 5. 1; 17. 1. 27. 1, 30; 18. 7. 3, 8, 10; 39. 5. 18. 1; 40. 1. 20. 2; 40. 8. 1, 3, 8; 45. 1. 122. 2.

[3] See especially 40. 8. 1; 37. 14. 8. 1; C. 4. 57. 2, 3.

[4] See Haymann, *op. cit.* 25 *sqq.*   [5] Pernice, Labeo, 3. 1. 134.

[6] The *constitutio* applied, 40. 1. 23.

[7] Haymann, *op. cit.* 20, points out that it is possible the man may have had a right to invoke the Praetor before the *constitutio*. He cites 36. 1. 23. 1.

[8] *Ante*, p. 629.

anything which implies it, associates the undertaking with the conveyance, not with a contract of sale[1]. Conversely it has been pointed out that every text that sets out the constitution in detail refers to sale[2], and it may be added that most of the texts which ignore any right of revocation are cases of sale[3]. The general result seems to be that, where the compilers found in the text a reference to a right of recovery *ex fiducia*, they converted this into an *actio ex poenitentia* or the like[4], but if there was no sign of this they inserted, not consistently, but commonly, a provision for excluding the operation of the *constitutio*. That the power of recovery where it existed was independent of the *constitutio* appears from what seems the only text on this matter which mentions both the *constitutio*, and the right of recovery on change of mind. It deals with the *constitutio* in a separate clause and there mentions only the exclusion of its operation[5].

The foregoing conclusions differ from the verdict of Haymann mainly in that they attach significance to the fact that the right of recovery is never mentioned except in the cases which suggest *fiducia* (*i.e.* never in connexion with sale), so that the right of recovery is independent of the *constitutio*[6]. In the main the whole rests on 40. 8. 1. If that is genuine the other texts must be interpolated, and it is impossible to resist Haymann's arguments directed to shewing that they are in fact altered, and the failure of the many attempts to get the text 40. 8. 1 out of the way[7].

Some of the texts raise other questions which call for short discussion. In four texts it is laid down that if the alienor has died without changing his mind, the intent of the *heres* is immaterial[8]. On the view here accepted that the allusions to *ius poenitentiae*, though attributed here and there to the *constitutio*, are really due to the compilers, it is not necessary to say more of this limitation than that there exist obvious analogies which seem to have suggested it[9].

In one text Papinian is consulted on the question whether there is any action in a case in which there was a sale for manumission within a certain time, but before that time arrived the vendor changed his mind, and notified the vendee, who nevertheless freed the man. His somewhat cryptic answer is: *ex vendito actionem manumisso servo vel mutata*

---

[1] 12. 4. 5. 1; 17. 1. 27. 1, 30; 39. 5. 18. 1. Cp. 12. 4. 3. 2, 3. See Pernice, Labeo, 3. 1. 128.
[2] Haymann, *op. cit.* 36.   [3] Some are not, *e.g.*, 40. 2. 16. 1, 20.
[4] See Gradenwitz, Interpolationen, 146 *sqq.*
[5] 12. 4. 5. 1. It is of course much altered.
[6] Gradenwitz, Interp. 169. The case of payment to secure a manumission, which is the subject of many of his texts is on a different footing, *post*, p. 640.
[7] *Op. cit.* 6 *sqq.*, 25 *sqq.* He points out (p. 21) that 4. 4. 11. 1, interpolated as to the answers, contains questions which would be absurd if there was a right of withdrawal in any case.
[8] 18. 7. 3; 40. 8. 3, 8; C. 4. 57. 1.
[9] *Heres* cannot attack his ancestor's manumission as fraudulent (*ante*, p. 565) or his gift, Vat. Fr. 259, *etc.* Is a fiduciary gift revocable by the *heres*?

venditoris voluntate evanuit[1]. This is certainly not the whole of the answer. Probably it was to the effect that if there had been a *fiducia* there would have been a right of claim, but that on the facts the only right is to the enforcement of the contract made. This is ended if the man is freed or if you have notified a change of mind[2].

A text of Julian[3], written almost certainly before the constitution, considers the effect of notice given by an agent, and lays it down that if the procurator had good reason, in the misconduct of the slave, for intervening, the receiver is liable if he disobeys the injunction. The text was probably written of *fiducia*[4], and is, it seems, identical with one in the Vatican Fragments[5] restored by Mommsen. It has nothing to do with the constitution. In its earlier form it says nothing about cause for intervention, this limitation being probably due to the compilers[6].

Some texts raise the question whether *animus donandi* is material. Ulpian[7] quotes Aristo, who wrote before the constitution, as holding that if the manumission was to be at a later time there was a gift implied, and the man could in no case be claimed till the time had run. Pomponius is more precise: he remarks that even if the gift is not to take effect at once, circumstances may negative any intent to benefit the alienee[8]. That this text is written of *fiducia* appears from the next following passage[9], where Aristo asks whether in a case in which the element of *donatio* enters there can be *usucapio* if the slave was in fact *alienus*. Pomponius settles Aristo's doubt by saying that there could be, as in the case of *donatio mortis causa*. This suggests *fiducia*[10] for if it was a simple conveyance it is not easy to see reason for doubt. But in one text where the manumission was to be *intra tempus*, the alienor is entitled to reclaim the man at once. Presumably such a form was not here held to imply any intent to benefit the donee. In another it was to be *post mortem*, but here there was direct disregard of notice not to free, which would at once give rise to an action, in the case of *fiducia*. And both the texts seem to deal with *fiducia*[11].

It has been suggested[12] that even before the *constitutio* was enacted it may have been possible for the slave to appeal to the magistrate for an order that the manumission be carried out. In Hadrian's time[13] there seems to have been some enactment on the point, but if such a

---

[1] 18. 7. 8.
[2] It is still stronger if understood to mean "even if," as Haymann (*op. cit.* 16) takes it, rather than "or if."
[3] 17. 1. 30.   [4] Lenel, Z. S. S. 9. 182.   [5] Fr. Vat. ˵34 a.
[6] Haymann, *op. cit.* 48 *sqq.* Not, however, certainly: the Fr. Vat. may be abridged. The rule is not without analogies, though from another point of view. See 15. 1. 46.
[7] 39. 5. 18. 1.   [8] Cp. 40. 8. 9.   [9] 39. 5. 18. 2.
[10] Lenel, *loc. cit.*; Heck, *loc. cit.*
[11] Haymann, *op. cit.* 16, 35; Gradenwitz, Interp. 168; D. 12. 4. 5. 1; 17. 1. 27. 1.
[12] Haymann, *op. cit.* 20.   [13] 18. 7. 10.

right had existed the constitution would hardly have served any purpose. It is clear that stipulations for seizure and penalties were employed, until they were superseded and declared nugatory under the system of the constitution[1]. They were not effective as protections to the slave, but they were better for the late owner than an *actio mandati*, in which it might be difficult to shew any *interesse*. But a *condictio ob causam dati* might have sufficed[2].

It has been said that the rules afford a means of evading the statutory restrictions on manumission. But the texts nullifying trans-actions *in fraudem legis* prevent this[3]. On the other hand a sale *ut manumittatur*, after, *e.g.*, one day, would seem a ready means of substi-tuting mancipation for *cessio in iure* as a mode of conferring *civitas*, but it would involve loss of the *libertus*.

The form of the rule, which makes the liberty date from the breach of duty without any need of claim[4], puts the man in a rather better position than that of one entitled to fideicommissary liberty. It was perhaps designedly adopted to avoid some of the questions which had given the Emperor's predecessor trouble in that case[5]. The remedy might seem worse than the disease, since it may have often been difficult to determine the earliest date at which it was possible to free. But similar difficulties arose in many other cases, and the texts say very little about them : where the question is one of fact the sources deal very lightly with difficulties of proof.

VII.   *Servus suis nummis emptus.* The rules of this matter are based on a rescript of Divi Fratres, *i.e.* Marcus Aurelius and Verus, and therefore date from between A.D. 161 and A.D. 169. The general principle is that a slave *suis nummis emptus* is entitled to claim imme-diate manumission[6], and if this is not done he can claim his liberty before the *Praefectus Urbi* at Rome, or the *Praeses* of the province[7]. If he proves his case, the Court will order the owner to free, and if he *latitat*, or refuses, will proceed exactly as in the case of an overdue fiduciary manumission[8]. It does not appear that the decree is in any way declaratory : it orders the owner to free. The text last cited says, indeed, that it makes him free from the date of the purchase, but its whole argument is inconsistent with this, and it is most probable that a *non* has dropped out[9]. This view is supported by the fact that no

---

[1] 40. 1. 20. 2 ; 45. 1. 122. 2 ; C. 4. 57. 6 ; *ante*, p. 71.   [2] Cp. C. 4. 6. 6.
[3] Haymann, *op. cit.* 36 ; *ante*, p. 538.
[4] C. 4. 57. 1.   An enquirer is told that he has not to claim, *sed libertatem quam obtinueras defendere*.   This does not seem to mean that he will be defendant in any *causa liberalis* (*post*, pp. 654 *sqq.*) : this will depend on his apparent position.   It is only emphasising the absence of need to claim.
[5] *Ante*, p. 618.   [6] 40. 1. 4. *pr.*   [7] *h. t.* 5. *pr.*; 1. 12. 1. 1.
[8] 5. 1. 67.   [9] Mommsen, *ad h. l.*

text speaks of him as being free *ex decreto* or *ex constitutione*—every text contemplates his being freed by the owner. And there is no text which raises the question of the status of children born before the decree. The fair inference seems to be that if freed they were free from the manumission, and if the holder neglected to free, then they were decreed free as in the case of fiduciary manumission, and the status of children was similarly determined[1].

The expression *suis nummis emptus* is found long before the rules now to be considered were developed[2]. It is not strictly correct, since a slave can have no money: the real point is that it must not be the money of the buyer. So long as he gives only his name, it is immaterial where the money comes from. Thus it may be *ex adventitio lucro*, or from a friend, or borrowed on any form of security. It may even be *ex peculio venditoris*[3]. If, as may be the case, the buyer has advanced the money with this purpose, the right arises as soon as accounts have been squared[4]. It is essential that the sale have been of this *imaginaria* character from the beginning[5]. Accordingly the mere fact that the slave, after an ordinary sale, restores his price to the buyer will not bring the constitution into operation[6]; the point being that the owner must have no ownership but what is taken under this confidential arrangement. Conversely, if it was originally for this purpose, but the slave fails to refund the price, the constitution does not apply. On the other hand if one who has bought under this arrangement pays the money himself before the slave has provided it, this does not prevent the rule from applying, if and when he has been satisfied[7]. It is immaterial how the slave makes up the price, whether by money or by services or in any other way[8]. Where the sale is of this imaginary kind, the mere fact that the buyer agrees with the vendor that he will not free the man does not bar the operation of the rule : the buyer has no real interest[9]. But of course any preexisting bar to liberty, such as conditions on legacy or sale will prevent the constitution from applying[10].

The buyer may be anyone, male or female, private person, city or state, a pupil, or even a slave, there being no personal interest or risk of loss. The text adds the rule that the age of the vendor is immaterial[11].

---

[1] If the claim failed there might be condemnation *in metallum* or *opus metalli*, or the master might have him back and punish him, by chains *etc.*, not more severely than was involved in *opus metalli*, 40. 1. 5. *pr.*; 48. 19. 38. 4; *ante*, p. 404.

[2] Suetonius, de Gramm. 13, speaks of a slave in the time of Sulla, bought *de catasta, suo aere*, and freed by the buyer, *propter literarum studium*. This is a sort of bargain: the slave is to recoup the buyer out of future earnings. As to sale *de catasta, ante*, p. 39.

[3] 40. 1. 4. 1.   [4] *h. l.* 5.   [5] Not necessarily so expressly stated, *h. l.* 6.

[6] *h. l.* 2; *cp.* C. 7. 16. 12.

[7] 40. 1. 4. 3, 4.   The buyer having, perhaps in order to release the slave, paid with his own money.

[8] *h. l.* 10.   [9] *h. l.* 7.   [10] *h. l.* 9; *ante*, p. 585.

[11] *h. l.* 8.

Such sales being in their very nature collusive, this rule seems at first sight to provide an obvious means of evading the rule forbidding a master under 20 to free. We have seen that a master under 20 could not sell *ut manumittatur*[1] but this case is essentially different. There no real price need be paid : here there must be a full price. There the freedom is automatic : here it is only after decree, and the Court will see that a full price has been paid. We are told that the reason of the 20 year rule is to guard against damage due to immaturity of judgment[2], and the safeguard seems sufficient.

If the buyer already was part owner, or the owner bought in an outstanding usufruct, the rule did not apply for reasons already stated. But if a fructuary bought the *dominium, servi nummis,* the rule applied[3], a distinction which seems more logical than reasonable. A case rather on *apices iuris* arose where two bought—one with his own money, the other with that of the slave. We are told that the constitution did not apply, unless the buyer with his own money was willing to manumit[4]. One might rather have expected that the rule would not apply, since the whole value of the slave has not been paid *servi nummis,* but the fact that the institution was in favour of liberty may account for the rule laid down. Obviously Justinian's rule for joint owners cannot apply as this would require the nominal buyer to compensate the other owner[5]. Another somewhat remarkable case is put in the next text. If one buys a share of the slave *servi nummis,* and afterwards acquires the rest, *e causa lucrativa,* the rule applies. This gives a very odd result. So long as the acquirer owns only a part of the slave he has the use of him, *pro parte,* though he gave nothing for him, and in fact only holds by virtue of the slave's wish and provision of money. If anyone desiring to benefit him, gives him the rest, he at once loses the whole. This seems to be the work of Tribonian : its grammar is eccentric[6], and it imposes the obligation on an owner, part of whose interest is not of the imaginary kind contemplated by the rule. Other texts state some other complications of no great importance. If A gives T money to buy and free a slave, he can recover the money on notice before the slave is actually bought[7]. This is an application of the ordinary principles of mandate. But if the man be already bought and A does not wish him freed, he can still withdraw, (having paid the money,) taking the slave, whom T is bound to hand over to A unless he is dead or has run away without the fault of T, in which last case, T must promise to restore him if and when he returns to his *potestas.*

---

[1] *Ante,* p. 538.   [2] 18. 7. 4.   [3] 40. 1. 4. 11, 12.   [4] *h. l.* 13.
[5] *Ante,* p. 577.   No doubt full patronal rights, *pro parte,* are reserved to the other owner.
[6] 40. 1. 4. 14: *Sed et si partem quis redemit pars altera ex causa lucrativa accesserit dicendum erit constitutionem locum habere.*
[7] 12. 4. 5. 2.   The text gives a *condictio ex poenitentia, post,* p. 645.

It does not seem clear that this is compilers' work, though some details are interpolated[1]. The remark towards the end of the next passage that if the giver of the money prefers to have the slave, either the man or the money must be given to him, belongs, no doubt, as Gradenwitz says, to this case. All this looks a little hard on the slave. But it must be borne in mind that the case has nothing to do with the constitution we are discussing. This is merely a piece of philanthropy on the part of A of which he repents before it is carried out: the case to which the constitution applies is that of a purchase made as the result of a confidential arrangement to which the slave is a party—*ut imaginaria fieret emptio, et per fidem contractus inter emptorem et servum agatur*[2]. Of all this there is no indication in the present case: the rule as stated is normal, though one would have expected an *actio mandati* instead of a *condictio ex poenitentia*—a thing probably unknown to classical law.

Some nice points arise where the price is really provided by the vendor, as it might be[3]. It must of course be with his knowledge. Payment out of the *peculium* belonging to him, without his knowledge, is no payment and he can recover the money[4]. It follows that the buyer is not released[5]: the ownership has not passed and there can be no question of any right to demand freedom. A case which might very well happen was that of a slave who gave a mandate to buy him, the underlying intention being that he should be freed. Such a mandate would be absolutely void if there were no such intent, and the *mandatarius* would have no *actio mandati (contraria) de peculio*[6]. If, however, there was such an intention, we are told that if after sale and delivery the manumission is not carried out, the vendor can sue for the price[7], and even, *affectus ratione*[8], on the mandate. The text has been much discussed[9]. As the slave has not paid the price, the *constitutio* does not apply. Papinian seems to mean that the mandate to buy is essentially null, but the resulting sale is not, and the transaction may thus be treated as a sale coupled with a mandate to free the slave bought. If he is not freed there is an *actio mandati*, the difficulty as to *interesse* being met by confining the rule to a case in which the slave is related in some way to the vendor. There is presumably an *actio mandati contraria* for reimbursement if the man is freed. As the mandate is by the slave, *i.e.* to free him if bought, this is *de peculio* and may be useless[10]. But there may be an *actio doli* against the freedman for reimbursement[11].

[1] Gradenwitz, Interp. 166.   [2] 40. 1. 4. 2.   [3] *h. l.* 1.
[4] C. 4. 49. 7; *ante*, p. 201.   [5] C. 4. 36. 1. 2.   [6] *Ante*, p. 216.
[7] 17. 1. 54. *pr.*   [8] *e.g.* if the man is a natural son.
[9] *e.g.*, Pernice, Labeo, 3. 1. 185 ; Van Wetter, Obligations, 1. 82 ; 2. 58.
[10] It is not contemplated as a sale *ut manumittatur*: the consent of the owner was of course necessary for this.   [11] Cp. 4. 3. 7. 8.

Diocletian decides a similar problem in terms which seem to shew that he had this text before him[1]. He gives further reasons for holding the mandate to be essentially void[2]. But he says that, nevertheless, the *dominus* acquires an *obligatio*, as the object was to create a right of action not on the mandate, but on another contract, *i.e.* the sale, made on account of the mandate. This explains nothing, but it seems to be used as a reason for generalising the owner's right *ex mandato*, at any rate nothing is said of *affectus*. Here the slave pays *ex peculio* without authority, but ownership is regarded as having passed, which is not impossible. The emperor decides that if the man is not freed, the old owner may sue either for the price, *ex vendito*, or for the man, *ex mandato*, the actions being treated as mutually exclusive. The practical outcome would be much the same. Nothing is said as to the resulting rights if he is actually freed[3].

If the person who bought the slave, *servi nummis*, breaks his faith, so that the man is declared free by the magistrate, he is not patron for any purpose[4]. But even if he duly frees him his patronal rights are very restricted. Such a *libertus* is, we are told, in no respect like other *liberti*[5]. The manumitter is in this case a mere instrument[6]: he has therefore no right to accuse the freedman for ingratitude or to impose *operae*[7]. He can never veto marriage[8]. If the slave is instituted by him, with liberty, he is not a *heres necessarius*, since he was in a position to compel manumission[9]. He has no right of *bonorum possessio contra tabulas*[10]. Yet he certainly is patron[11], and this position has some results. Thus his civil law right of succession is not denied[12], so that he will succeed on intestacy, and if instituted. And he is protected against *in ius vocatio*[13].

VIII.   The slave whose master has taken money to free him[14]. This case presents close analogies with both of the two cases last discussed, and it is clear that rules developed as to the enforcement of the liberty here too. But the remarkable state of the texts makes it difficult to say what the rules were, or when they developed. The transaction is referred to in many texts. Of those in the Digest, apparently only two refer to any compulsory completion of the manumission. One of these, by Paul[15], says that the Constitution of Marcus Aurelius as to one sold *ut manumittatur* applies here too, *i.e.* the liberty takes effect auto-

---

[1] C. 4. 36. 1.   [2] *Ante*, p. 216.
[3] The case gave the early commentators a good deal of trouble, Haenel, Diss. Domm. 425.
[4] 2. 4. 10. *pr.*   [5] 27. 1. 14. 3.   [6] 37. 15. 3; cp. 40. 1. 5.
[7] 37. 15. 3; C. 6. 3. 8.   [8] 23. 2. 45. 2.   [9] 28. 5. 85. 2.
[10] C. 6. 4. 1. 4.   [11] C. 6. 3. 8, notwithstanding the language of C. 6. 4. 1. 4.
[12] Cp. 37. 14. 10, 11; 38. 2. 29. *pr.*   [13] 2. 4. 10. *pr.*
[14] See for an illustrative surviving case, Girard, Textes, Appendice.
[15] 40. 12. 38. 1.

matically. The other, by Papinian, says that in such a case the liberty can be compelled *ab invito*, as in the case of a *servus suis nummis redemptus, i.e.* on appeal to a magistrate the owner will be ordered to free[1]. The same conflict occurs in the Code. Here three texts refer to enforced completion. An enactment of A.D. 240, of Gordian[2], says that where a master took money to free his slave at a certain time, and did not free him, the liberty took effect automatically at the time when it should have been given. But two enactments of Diocletian say in very similar language, that on such facts the Governor of the province will make the owner keep his word, *i.e.* the liberty does not take effect automatically[3]. The difficulty does not stop here. Paul, who tells us that the liberty takes effect automatically[4] tells us elsewhere[5] that if the freedom is not given, the money paid can be condicted, *i.e.* the *causa* has failed, and one of the constitutions of Diocletian, which says at the end that the manumission can be compelled, says at the beginning that the money can be recovered if the liberty is not given[6]. Papinian who tells us the liberty[7] can be compelled, tells us also that if the owner does not free, the donor of the money can recover it, and has other remedies[8], but there is no hint that, after all, he can have it carried out if he likes.

What conclusion is to be drawn from all this? The fact that in some cases the money is paid by or on behalf of the slave and in others purely by an outsider suggests a distinction, but it proves useless. In the texts in which the liberty is not given and which ignore the constitutions, the payment is *ab alio*[9], but so it is in some of the cases in which the liberty can be enforced: in most of these it is merely enforceable, in one at least it takes effect automatically[10]. In one of these which contemplate enforcement the money seems to have come from the slave[11]. The fact that the texts which ignore the constitution deal almost entirely with payment *ab alio*, is due to the fact that the question in them is whether the money could be condicted—a point which could hardly arise between master and slave[12]. With the exception just cited the texts which deal with the case in which the money is provided by the slave do not speak of enforcement: they all assume him to have been simply freed. One text speaking perfectly generally says that where the freedom results from the giving of money for it, the patron has *omnia iura patronatus*[13]. So we learn that he could accuse as *ingratus*, which he could not do in the other two cases[14].

---

1 40. 1. 19.   2 C. 4. 57. 4.   3 C. 4. 6. 9; 7. 16. 8.
4 40. 12. 38. 1.   5 19. 5. 5. 2.   6 C. 4. 6. 9.
7 40. 1. 19.   8 19. 5. 7.
9 *e.g.* 12. 1. 19. *pr.*; 12. 4. 5. 3, 4; 19. 5. 5. 2, *etc.*   10 40. 1. 19; C. 4. 57. 4, *etc.*
11 C. 7. 16. 8.   12 C. 4. 6. 9.
13 C. 6. 4. 1; cp. C. 4. 6. 9; 6. 6. 3; 7. 16. 8.
14 37. 15. 3; C. 6. 3. 2. Taking money does not destroy *iura in bonis*, 38. 2. 3. 4 (Mommsen).

The manumitter could not exact services, or money in lieu of them[1], but this is a result of the fact that the manumission was not gratuitous: having agreed to free for a certain emolument, the *dominus* has no right to burden the liberty further[2]. An enactment of Diocletian tells us that even though the manumission were done *pecunia accepta*, it could not be revoked[3]. It is hardly credible that if such a gift operated automatically or could be enforced, such a question could have been asked[4]. We are told that a promise by the owner to free when certain services were rendered was in no way binding on him[5], and one would have thought that they would have been on the same level as money. On the other hand, in one text the question is raised whether if one has given money to be freed, and is instituted *heres* with liberty, he is a *necessarius heres*. Ulpian says *puto huic omnimodo esse succurrendum*. If this is genuine[6], guarded as the language is, it puts the person so freed on a level with the other two cases. And the allusion to the matter in Justinian's constitution abolishing latinity[7] is at least consistent with automatic operation of the gift, before his changes.

The case differs in one fundamental point from both the others. There the owner who is to free has no ownership at all except such as is conferred on him, at another's cost, for the purpose of the manumission: here he is the real owner of the slave. The importance of the distinction is brought out in several of the texts[8]. They point out that in our case the manumitter has conferred a real benefit on the man (for the gift of liberty in the beginning depended on his good will), while in the other cases—that of the fiduciary, the person who receives *ut manumittatur*, and him who buys *servi nummis*—they do nothing but lend their services. It seems probable that the whole law of enforcement is post-classical, and that the texts of Paul and Papinian are interpolated. This can hardly be doubted of Paul's text, which Haymann gives good reasons, not all of equal weight, for thinking not genuine[9]. The same is probably true of that of Papinian. Haymann, indeed[10], while shewing that there is alteration, considers the rule authentic but confined to the case of payment by a fellow-slave related to the *liberandus*, the rule being an analogous extension of the rule for *servus suis nummis emptus*.

---

[1] C. 6. 3. 3.   [2] 38. 1. 32, *etc.*   [3] C. 7. 16. 33.
[4] The question is surprising in any case: it is perhaps due to local usages. In the extant memorandum from Egypt in A.D. 221 the manumitter agrees that he will not reclaim the slave. See the document, Girard, Textes, Appendice.
[5] C. 7. 16. 36, Diocletian. *I.e.* it cannot be enforced by the slave.
[6] 29. 2. 71. 2. But the form of the remark, its vagueness, and the rather summary manner in which what must have been a difficult question is disposed of, all suggest that the whole passage is from Tribonian.
[7] C. 7. 6. 1. 8.   [8] 37. 15. 3; C. 6. 4. 1. They say nothing of enforcement.
[9] 40. 12. 38. 1; Haymann, Freilassungspflicht, 41 *sqq.*
[10] 40. 1. 19; Haymann, *op. cit.* 40.

It is clear that Papinian knew of no general rule[1]. But it is hardly credible that he should have held that a man who bargained with his own slave came under an obligation which would not have resulted from a similar bargain with a freeman. Nor is it likely that he would of his own authority have extended the rule for slaves *suis nummis empti* to a case so fundamentally different. The inference is that enforcement was not known to the classical law. As to the texts in the Code, there is some difficulty. Gordian's text is no doubt mainly due to the compilers[2], but there may be a question as to those of Diocletian[3]. They are both cases of payment by relatives, but the rule laid down is quite general, and though they are years apart the terms of the rule are identical, except that one inserts *favore scilicet libertatis*[4]. Haymann while accepting the rule, but as confined to the case of relatives, shews that this text has been fundamentally altered at the beginning: the other is grammatically defective[5]. The difficulty of principle which Papinian must have seen is less certain to have occurred to Diocletian's adviser, but on the whole, in view of the state of the texts and of the intermittent way in which the rule is recognised in the Digest, it is probable that the whole enforcement is due to Justinian.

The truth seems to be that this institution is an exotic in Roman Law, though the frequency of allusions to it suggests that it was common in later classical times. On the other hand it is a well-known Greek practice. Extant documents give plenty of evidence that it was common for an outsider to provide the price of the manumission without taking a conveyance of the man, retaining a right to his services after the manumission till the money was in some way repaid. Often too it was done in the way indicated by the Roman texts, *i.e.* with no reservation of rights[6]. This suggests that it is an importation from provinces under Greek influence. The case above cited is from Egypt and contains clear evidence of Greek influence. The fact that it is not referred to by the Constitutions which enact compulsion suggests that as a common institution it is of a later day. The probable inference is that the references to compulsion in the Digest are, as is above suggested, interpolated[7].

The money might with the master's consent be his own, but if his own money were used without his consent, an action was available

---

[1] 19. 5. 7.

[2] C. 4. 57. 4; Haymann, *op. cit.* 42. Apart from textual points of varying importance he remarks that though a time was fixed the automatic acquisition of liberty occurs only on *mora*, which was not the rule of the *constitutio, ante,* p. 631.

[3] C. 4. 6. 9; 7. 16. 8.　　　　　　[4] C. 4. 6. 9.

[5] C. 7. 16. 8: *Cum adfirmes placuisse domino tuo ut . . . . vos manumitteret, et te tantummodo liberavit.*

[6] Dareste, Recueil des inscriptions juridiques grecques, Série II, 236 *sqq.* See the discussions at pp. 252 *sqq.*, 273 *sqq.*

[7] As it is uncertain whether a decree was necessary, it is uncertain what rules were applied as to the *ingenuitas* of children.

against the person who paid it, if he was acting fraudulently[1]. Conversely where a slave induced a third party to become responsible to his *dominus* for his value, undertaking to take over the obligation as soon as he was free, and then not doing so, he was liable to an *actio doli*[2].

Most of the texts dealing with the transaction have no reference to enforcement: they lay down rules for it regarded as an ordinary innominate contract of the form "*do* (or *facio*) *ut facias.*" For the most part they present little difficulty and may be shortly stated. If the money has been paid and the liberty is not given, there is a *condictio* to recover it[3], or if he has any interest in the manumission he can sue *praescriptis verbis* for *quanti interest*[4]. The right to condict arises only where there has been some wrongful delay[5]. The death of the slave after *mora* does not destroy the *condictio*[6]. If it was before *mora*, Proculus says generally that there is no *condictio*[7]. Ulpian distinguishes[8]. The loss falls on the slave owner (*i.e.* the money can be condicted) unless some action reasonably caused by the bargain led to the death, *e.g.* the man was killed on the way to the magistrate, or he would have been sold or differently employed but for the bargain. It is likely that a good deal of this is Tribonian[9]. In a case in which the slave who was to be freed ran away, there is a similar discussion of hypotheses[10]. If the owner was going to sell the slave but did not because of this bargain, there is no *condictio*, but security must be given for the return of the money, less any diminution in value of the slave, if he came back. But if the payer still wished him freed, this must be done or all the money returned. If he was not going to sell him, he must return all the money unless he would have kept him more carefully but for the bargain: it is not fair that he should lose both slave and price. Here too Tribonian has clearly been at work[11].

If one slave was given that another might be freed, and after this was done, the slave given was evicted, there was an *actio doli* or *in factum* according to the state of mind of the person who gave him[12]. Conversely if a slave was given to secure the freeing of one who was not in fact a slave, the value of the slave given could be recovered by *condictio ob rem dati*[13]. But where money was promised to secure the freeing of a slave, and he was in fact freed, but by some other person,

---

[1] 16. 3. 1. 33.   On the facts, *actio depositi*.   The manumission is apparently completed.
[2] 4. 3. 7. 8.   Even where it had not been the master's, he sometimes left it with the slave as part of the *peculium*, 40. 1. 6.
[3] 12. 4. 3. 2; C. 4. 6. 9.   Where each agreed to free a slave, and one did while the other did not, there was a claim for the value of the slave freed, 19. 5. 5. *pr.*, 5.
[4] 19. 5. 7.
[5] 12. 1. 19. *pr.*; 12. 4. 3. 3; 19. 5. 5. 2.   The wider questions as to the scope of this *condictio* do not concern us.   See Haymann, Schenkung unter Auflage, 125 *sqq.*
[6] 12. 4. 3. 3, 5. 4.   [7] 12. 4. 3. 3.   [8] *h. t.* 5. 4.
[9] Gradenwitz, Interp. 167.   [10] 12. 4. 5. 3.
[11] Gradenwitz, *loc. cit.*   He remarks that the clause *sed si eligat*, etc., belongs to the discussion in the next preceding passage.
[12] 19. 5. 5. 2.   [13] C. 4. 6. 6.

the money was still due : nothing was said as to the personality of the manumitter[1].
The agreement was not always that he should be a *civis*. In a recorded case[2] the man was made a latin. The manumitter here was a *civis* who had been a peregrine. Probably in such cases and in manumission *inter vivos* by *libertini* the slave was usually made a latin : otherwise there would have been no mark of inferiority as there was where the manumitter was a *civis ingenuus*.

If the freedom is carried out there can be of course no condiction of the money[3]. But if the slave is not yet freed, and there has been no breach, two texts tell us that there is a *condictio ex poenitentia*[4]. It has been urged by Gradenwitz, not without predecessors, but with new and strong argument[5], that this particular *condictio* is an invention of the compilers. His view has been widely accepted[6], and at least so far as the present case is concerned hardly admits of a doubt. The texts themselves are so expressed as to make certain the fact that they are altered in some way, and they are definitely contradicted on the point[7]. It is not necessary to restate the arguments, or to enter on the wider question, which does not concern us, as to the extent to which the classical law admitted a *ius poenitentiae*.

It may be well to point out the essential differences between these last three cases, which do not seem always to be distinguished with sufficient clearness in current discussion. In the first case—transfer *ut manumittatur*—the transaction is expressly for that purpose and is initiated by the *dominus*. In the case of sale *servi nummis* the purpose is not necessarily express, and the initiative is in the slave. So far as appears the master receives a full price, and is merely a consenting party, who does not stand to lose anything by the transaction. In the first case the manumission is not necessarily, or so far as the texts go, normally, to take effect at once. In sale *suis nummis* it is always so. There is no suggestion in the second case of any right of withdrawal— a natural result of the fact that the initiative is in the slave, and no *fiducia* is imposed, or could be imposed, on the vendee. The various differences of rule which have been treated in this chapter are all fairly deducible from these differences.

---

[1] 45. 1. 104. A slave promised money for freedom, and when free promised it again : this was good. It was not *onerandae libertatis causa*, but merely deferred payment, 44. 5. 2. 2. There was an *actio in factum* against him if he refused to renew his promise, 4. 3. 7. 8; C. 4. 14. 3. See *post*, p. 692.
[2] Girard, Textes, Appendice.   [3] 12. 1. 19. *pr.*; 12. 4. 3. 3.
[4] 12. 4. 3. 2, 3.
[5] Gradenwitz, Interp. *loc. cit.* See also Haymann, Freilassungspflicht, 57, who points out the irrational character of the right.
[6] See, however, Heck, Z. S. S. 10. 119; Karlowa, R. R. G. 2. 772; Naber, Mnemosyne, 22. 432.
[7] 12. 1. 19. *pr.*

In the third case the manumitter is the real owner of the slave. No text speaks of a postponed manumission[1] (*i.e.* manumission *post tempus*) in this case, though there are cases in which the manumission is to be *intra tempus*. The initiative may be from the slave or an *extraneus*: it can hardly be from the *dominus*. There is no question of *fiducia*, but the money has been handed over for the express purpose[2].

---

[1] In C. 4. 57. 4 it may well be *intra tempus*.

[2] The case of fideicommissary liberty to a slave the property of the fiduciary, enforced by the *Sc.* Iuncianum, *ante*, p. 613, somewhat resembles the present case. But that legislation rests on the idea that the trust is itself an inchoate manumission (see, *e.g.*, 40. 5. 17, 26. *pr.*, 51. 3), on the fiduciary nature of the transaction, and the sanctity of a testator's wishes. These considerations are not applicable in the present case.

CHAPTER XXVIII.

EFFECT ON QUESTIONS OF STATUS, OF LAPSE OF TIME, DEATH, JUDICIAL DECISION.

In general an owner can free, but no pact or agreement can make a freeman a slave[1], or endow a slave or *libertinus* with *ingenuitas*[2], or make an *ingenuus* a *libertinus*[3]. Acting as a slave will not make a free person a slave[4]. An acknowledgment by a man that he is a slave, whether it be voluntary or compelled, does not make him one[5], even if it be formally made *apud acta praesidis*. Paul's language may confine this rule to the case in which the admission was compelled by fear[6]. But in the later law this restriction has disappeared if it ever existed, and it is most probable that Paul is merely giving an illustration of the circumstances under which such a false admission is likely to be made. In what purport to be two enactments of Diocletian[7], we are told generally, that acknowledgment of slavery *apud acta* or by *professio* is no bar. Similarly, whatever may have been the law under the old system of the Census, a failure to make proper *professio* as a *civis* does not cause enslavement[8]. The fact that a free person has been sold as a slave by his parents, or an apparent owner, or by the Fisc or by rebels is no bar to his claim of freedom[9]. A similar statement is made in an enactment of A.D. 293 as to one who, being under 20, allows himself to be given as part of a *dos*[10]. The same rule is laid down in an enactment of the following year without limit of age where the person sold was not aware of his freedom[11]. An enactment of Constantine[12] provides

---

[1] 40. 12. 37; C. 7. 16. 10. [2] C. 7. 14. 8.
[3] 40. 12. 37. Apparent exception under *sc.* Claudianum, *ante*, p. 412. *Transactio* might have been expected to be on the same level as pact, but as to this see *post*, p. 657.
[4] C. 7. 14. 2, 6; 7. 16. 20, 22; 7. 16. 23. That the Fisc has treated a man as *inter familiam fisci* does not make him a slave, P. 5. 1. 3.
[5] C. 7. 16. 6, 15, 23. [6] P. 5. 1. 4.
[7] C. 7. 16. 24, 39. [8] *h. t.* 15.
[9] P. 5. 1. 1; C. Th. 4. 8. 6 (= C. 8. 46. 10); C. Th. 5. 8. 1; C. 7. 14. 4; 7. 16. 1, 5, 12.
[10] C. 7. 16. 16. [11] C. 7. 14. 14.
[12] C. Th. 4. 8. 6. As to the bearing of these texts on the question of sharing price in fraudulent sale, *ante*, p. 432.

that one sold under 20 is not barred, by afterwards acting as a slave, from claiming his liberty. This text raises, however, a distinction not elsewhere traceable. If a person who has actually been freed under 14 allows himself afterwards to be sold as a slave, this is no bar, for he may reasonably have failed to understand the transaction of manumission. But if he was freed after puberty, he cannot be supposed not to know that he is a freeman, and is barred apparently at once from claiming his liberty. This rule is dropped in Justinian's Code[1].

Just as these various facts go but a little way towards proof of slavery, so facts of the same class but of contrary tendency weigh but little in proof of liberty. The fact that a man has been allowed to hold a public office does not exclude the possibility of his being a slave[2]. Letters and acknowledgments of freedom, even from the person now claiming him as a slave, are no bar to the claim[3]. Proof that the father is *ingenuus* is no proof that the child is, since the mother may have been a slave[4], and while the fact that the child was born after his mother's manumission is evidence of his freedom, nothing[5] can be inferred from the fact that his brother is free.

There were, however, some cases in which what may be called extraneous factors did affect a man's status. The most important are the following.

A. Lapse of Time. It seems fairly clear that in the time of Justinian lapse of time in apparent slavery, even though for as much as 60 years, was no bar to a claim of liberty[6]. So far as the classical law is known to us independently of the Corpus Iuris there is no trace of any other rule. It seems, however, from the *interpretatio* of an enactment in the Codex Theodosianus[7], and from Theodore in the Scholia in the Basilica[8], that the lawyers who advised Alaric, and the post-Justinianian lawyers, regarded the rule of *longissimi temporis praescriptio* of 30 or 40 years, laid down by Theodosius for all real and personal actions[9], as being applicable to *adsertiones libertatis*. But no sign of this appears in the Corpus Iuris[10].

---

[1] C. 7. 18. 3; 8. 46. 10. (Much of C. 7. 18. 3 is from C. Th. 4. 8. 6 as to disposal of the apparent *peculium*.) To begin an action claiming a man as a slave does not affect his position, C. 7. 14. 7. A man is *ingenuus* though born when his parents bore slave names to lead to the belief that they were slaves, *h. t.* 10. Failure to receive the proper *instrumenta*, or loss of them, affects only ease of proof, 4. 2. 8. 1; C. 7. 16. 25; *ante*, p. 453. See for similar rules, C. 7. 14. 10—13; C. 7. 16. 18, 34. Proof that relatives are slaves is not conclusive. See C. 4. 19. 22; 7. 16. 17, 28.   [2] C. 7. 16. 11, 38.

[3] *h. t.* 41. That the claimant has described the person claimed as a sister, or has lived on terms of equality, is not proof of freedom, unless it amounts to manumission, *inter amicos*, C. 4. 19. 13; C. 7. 16. 20. Purchase by natural father does not itself free, C. 7. 16. 29. To have repaid the purchaser the price does not free the man purchased, *h. t.* 12. To prove that you have contracted with the man whose *heres* now claims you is no answer, *h. t.* 18.

[4] C. 4. 19. 10.   [5] *h. t.* 17.   [6] C. 7. 14. 6; 7. 16. 5. 1; 7. 22. 3.

[7] C. Th. 4. 8. 6.   [8] Bas. Sch. 48. 24. 1.   [9] C. 7. 39. 3, 4.

[10] The rubric of C. 7. 22 is *de longi temporis praescriptione quae pro libertate et non adversus libertatem opponitur*.

There is more difficulty as to the acquisition of liberty by lapse of time. Such a lapse was no protection if the liberty had begun in bad faith, for instance, by *fuga*, which of course would have to be proved[1]. But an enactment of A.D. 300, in Justinian's Code, lays down the principle that long possession of liberty *iusto initio* is protected, and gives the concrete rule based on *favor libertatis*, that 20 years' *bona fide* possession of liberty *sine interpellatione* (*i.e.* not judicially disputed) makes the man free and a *civis*[2]. It may be noted that while the abstract proposition at the beginning of the enactment requires only *iustum initium*, the rule stated in the actual case seems to require good faith throughout the qualifying time. It is probable that the law is not quite in its original state. Another enactment of A.D. 491, which may possibly be genuine provides that a man whose condition has not been judicially disputed for 40 years, is free in any case[3].

But though the law of Justinian's time is fairly clear, the texts make some difficulty as to earlier law. An enactment of A.D. 331[4], which says that prescription does not protect children of a slave mother and free father living in an equivocal quasi-free position with their parents (precisely because it is equivocal, has no *iustum initium*, no gift of substitute or money to the master, or other indication that they were meant to be free) says, incidentally, that the period of prescription for liberty was already fixed at 16 years, by a *lex*. This statute is not extant, and there is no other trace of this term of 16 years. The way in which the rule is stated does not indicate that it was ancient, and it is probable that, as Gothofredus[5] suggests, the reference is to a lost enactment of Constantine. He also suggests, tentatively, that it might conceivably be the *lex* Aelia Sentia, basing this on the fact that the rule that the Fisc could annul a gift of liberty for fraud, within 10 years, is stated in a book of Paul *ad legem* Aeliam Sentiam[6]. But there is no probability that the *lex* dealt in any way with this sort of question[7].

Whether there was any rule on the matter in classical times may be doubted. The law of usucapion clearly did not affect the matter, nor is there any sign of, or probability in favour of, a praetorian form of liberty protected by *actiones utiles*[8]. On the whole it seems likely that liberty could not be acquired by lapse of time in classical law.

---

[1] C. 7. 22. 1.   [2] *h. t.* 2.

[3] C. 7. 39. 4. 2, the general rule of *longissimi temporis praescriptio*. It says nothing of *bona fides*. Presumably *iustum initium* is really assumed.

[4] C. Th. 4. 8. 7.   [5] *Ad* C. Th. 4. 8. 5.

[6] 40. 9. 16. 3.

[7] C. Th. 4. 8. 9 (393) says that those who have lived 20 years openly as free in the enjoyment of some public post need no *adsertores*. But this is not prescription for liberty.

[8] To suppose latinity is difficult: the case is not traceable in Justinian's Code (7. 6), and in those cases in which the Praetor protected liberty, the *voluntas domini* was the determining factor, cp. Fr. Dos. 7.

B. Lapse of time after a traceable manumission. A person who has been freed is obviously *prima facie* free and a *libertinus*. It is, however, over and over again laid down that the mere fact of manumission does not bar a man from asserting that he is an *ingenuus*[1]. But it seems clear that, up to the time of Justinian, a *manumissus* could not claim *ingenuitas* before the ordinary courts (*i.e.* those of the Consul or Praeses), unless the whole hearing were concluded within five years from the manumission[2]. There were no exceptions from this rule[3], but if important things came to light (*e.g.* discovery of *instrumenta ingenuitatis*), after the five years were over, it was always possible for the man affected to go to the Emperor[4]. The language of the text shews this to have been an extraordinary measure, but Justinian, regarding it as the mere substitution of one tribunal for another, abolishes the rule, and provides that *ingenuitas* can be claimed before the ordinary courts, without any limit of time[5].

From the other point of view, there is some difficulty in the rules. It is laid down that the *heres* cannot dispute his ancestor's manumission[6]. The scope of this rule is doubtful. The texts make it clear that their basis is the respect due from the *heres* to the *voluntas domini*, and they seem to mean merely that the *heres* might not object on technical grounds (or on account of *fraus creditorum*) to a manumission *prima facie* valid and having the dead man's full and real assent. Probably it did not prevent his opposing the claim of freedom, where the manumission had been compelled by force[7]. The manumission itself was no protection against a third party owner: he could still claim his slave[8]. It is clear, however, from the conclusion of the *lex* that there was some prescriptive period which would protect such a slave[9], but it is not easy to say whether this differed from the period in the case of ordinary apparent liberty. Analogy suggests that in such a case the liberty would be indisputable after five years, if the manumission proceeded from the owner. Rules suggesting this analogy are the following. A man's status could not be disputed after five years from his death[10]. If a will were upset by the *querela* more than five years from the death, all liberties which had taken effect remained valid[11]. Where a will was upset by a son whose existence was not known to the testator, persons freed by the will retained their liberty *favore libertatis*, if they had remained in liberty for five years[12]. So, quite apart from questions of death, where a judgment of *ingenuitas* was retracted for collusion within

[1] In. 1. 4. 1; P. 5. 1. 2; C. 4. 55. 4; 7. 14. 1, 2, 3.   [2] 40. 14. 2. 1; 40. 16. 2. 3.
[3] 40. 14. 4.   [4] *h. t.* 2. 2.   [5] C. 3. 22. 6.
[6] 40. 12. 31; C. 7. 16. 7.   [7] 40. 9. 17; cp. Fr. Dos. 7.
[8] C. 7. 10. 7. *pr.* There are penalties.   [9] C. 7. 10. 7. 2 = C. Th. 4. 9. 1.
[10] *Post*, p. 651.   [11] 5. 2. 9; *ante*, p. 568.
[12] 40. 4. 29.

five years, the man was handed back to his old owner[1]. These last texts shew signs of interpolation, and rather suggest that some such five-year limit was developed by the compilers, for cases in which the manumission, though by the *dominus*, was defective, but that there was no rule other than the ordinary prescription where the manumitter was not the real *dominus*.

C. Death. The mere fact of death does not put an end to questions of status. They may not, indeed, be raised *principaliter* after the death, *i.e.* where that is the substantial issue[2]. But that would be a rare case, for it is usually at bottom a property question. Thus where goods which were part of his estate are claimed as *peculium*, or the status of his or her child is in question, the action may be brought notwithstanding the death[3].

But lapse of five years from the death produces much more effect. The general rule of later law was that a man's status might not be attacked after he had been dead five years[4]. Callistratus tells us that this rule was first laid down by Nerva in an Edict[5]. Nerva's enactment was probably a statement of a general principle which was supplemented by a senatusconsult referred to in several texts[6]. It is clear that the rule is classical, but its application involves the settlement of details, and, for the most part, it is not possible to state the exact origin of each rule.

There are no exceptions from the general rule that a man's status may not be attacked more than five years after his death[7]. For the application of the rule it is essential that the person in question was in undisputed possession of the status at the time of his death[8]. It may be necessary to enquire as to whether the status was in fact undisputed at the death, and if the evidence leaves this doubtful, later times may be looked at[9]. Apparently the prescription is not barred by bringing proceedings within the time before a magistrate who has no jurisdiction[10]. However, if the man died *in fuga*, or *latitans*, he could

---

[1] 40. 12. 29. 1; *post*, p. 675.　　　　　[2] C. 7. 16. 13.
[3] C. 7. 16. 13, 27, Diocletian, but the rule is older. Alexander decided that the question of a man's status was not determined by his death, in an apparent status, but would be heard by the *iudex* who was adjudicating on the property questions, C. 7. 21. 3.
[4] 40. 15. 1. *pr.*, *etc.*
[5] *h. t.* 4. The rescript of Claudius is immaterial to us here: it is to the effect that a financial question must not prejudice one of status.
[6] C. 7. 21. 4. *pr.*, 7, 8. Perhaps the same as an enactment of Hadrian also mentioned, D. 40. 15. 1. 2.
[7] 40. 15. 1. *pr.*; *h. t.* 4. The rule barred even *incapaces* and the Fisc, 40. 15. 1. *pr.*, 2. 1; C. 7. 21. 6. *pr.* The proceeding must be begun but need not be ended within the time, C. 7. 21. 4. 1. Cp. D. 40. 16. 2. 3. The rule applied also to questions of *ingenuitas* and *civitas*, but not to questions of *patria potestas*, C. 7. 21. 2, 5, *etc.* See also C. 7. 21. 4. *pr.*, 7 and the rubrics of D. 40. 15 and C. 7. 21.
[8] C. 7. 21. 2, 4. *pr.*, 6. *pr.*, 7. The rule applies where an action begun before the time is clearly abandoned, D. 40. 15. 2. 2.
[9] C. 7. 21. 6. 1.　　　　　　[10] *h. t.* 7.

not be said to be living in undisputed possession of his status, and the rule did not apply[1].

It is plain that a dead man's status is not likely to be disputed if he is the only person concerned: it is in connexion with his property and successors that the question will arise. To defeat A's claim to certain property, it may suffice to shew that he claims it, e.g., as *heres* to X, who was in fact a slave. It is this that really needs prevention. Accordingly the rule is stated that even if the man has not been dead for five years, his status cannot be called in question if such an enquiry may affect the status of one who has been dead for that time. This is an odd sort of half-way house. Hadrian provides that a living person's status cannot be disputed if the enquiry will affect that of a person who has been dead for five years[2]. Papinian declares the same rule: the status of a father or mother dead more than five years cannot be called in dispute, by raising a question as to that of a child[3]. Severus and Caracalla also say that if X's patron has been dead for five years, the status of X may not be attacked through that of the patron[4]. In A.D. 205 it was laid down that where X was made *heres* by B, his right was not to be disputed by shewing that B's mother who had been dead more than five years was in fact a slave[5]. The rule is then, not that the status of these living people may not be disputed, but that, if it is disputed, evidence affecting the status of persons dead more than five years will not be admitted[6].

The rule applies only to attacks on status: there is nothing to prevent evidence at any time that the status was better than had been supposed. Marcian, Marcellus and Hermogenianus agree that evidence may be brought at any time to shew that a dead person was really a *libertina* and not an *ancilla*[7]. It is noticeable that these three jurists are very late: it is possible that the rule above stated had been couched in such general terms as to cover, in the opinion of some writers, this case also[8].

D. *Res Iudicata.* This topic will serve to introduce what is essential to a comprehensive view of the topic of slavery, *i.e.* the procedure in claims of liberty and in claims of a man, apparently free, as a slave. Both types of proceeding are called *causae liberales.* They

---

[1] C. 7. 21. 8.   [2] 40. 15. 1. 1, 2.   [3] 40. 15. 2. *pr.*
[4] C. 7. 21. 1.   [5] C. 7. 21. 2.

[6] The rule attributed to Claudius in 40. 15. 4 may conceivably be the same, but this would give rise to great difficulties of date. More probably it has nothing to do with death, but deals with the matter discussed *post*, p. 671.

[7] 40. 15. 1. 4, 3.

[8] Cases might occur in which the establishment of the fact that A, supposed to be a slave, was really free, might involve the conclusion that another supposed to be free was really a slave, *e.g.* where a mistake of identity had been made. How was this dealt with if both had been dead five years? Probably both would be treated as having been free. Cp. 50. 17. 20.

are civil suits[1], and as is the case with all suits, their form underwent historical changes, and had its own peculiar characteristics. It is clear that under the system of *legis actio*, the procedure in such cases was by way of *sacramentum*. We learn from Gaius, that, *favore libertatis*, in order not to be oppressive to *adsertores*, the *sacramentum* in such cases was fixed at 50 *asses*[2]. The dominant opinion is that in *causae liberales* the *vindiciae* were always given *secundum libertatem*, which would practically appear to mean that not only the man whose status was in question was *pro tempore* treated as free, but also that the burden of proof was with him who claimed him as a slave. For though in *sacramentum* each side must claim and prove, the *status quo* would it seems be determining if neither proved his case[3].

We are left in the dark as to the mode of trial under the system which superseded that of *legis actio*. It is generally held that the trial was by *praeiudicium*, a view which rests mainly on the fact that we are expressly told that this was so in later law[4]. There is, however, no direct evidence for this in earlier law. The opinion has in its favour the fact that *praeiudicia* had no *condemnatio*, and under the formulary system, when every action sounded in damages, a condemnation in such a case seems out of place. Nevertheless Lenel[5] remarks that it is very doubtful whether it was in fact a *praeiudicium*. He points out that Gaius does not mention it in speaking of *praeiudicia*[6]. His main illustration is *an libertus sit*, a very much less important affair. Further, he points out that a *praeiudicium* as such is essentially a preliminary matter affecting only indirectly the pecuniary interests of the parties. But this is one which directly affects them. We know that it was occasionally called a *vindicatio in libertatem*[7]. He admits the existence of texts which declare it to be a *praeiudicium*[8], and in relation to the text in the Code[9] he rejects as inadmissible the rendering of the word *praeiudicium* as meaning "disadvantage[10]," which would destroy the force of this text. Even if these texts be accepted they would shew only that the process was a *praeiudicium* in later law, after it had become a *cognitio*, and, for Justinian's time, this is generally accepted. Lenel has no substantial doubt but that in the case of a claim *in servitutem* it was an ordinary vindication, resting his view on the fact

---

[1] C. Th. 2. 7. 3.　　　　[2] G. 4. 14.

[3] As to the general question, see Jobbé-Duval, Procédure Civile, 355 *sqq.* The dominant view on the immediate question rests on the accounts of the case of Virginia (D. 1. 2. 2. 24; Livy, 3. 44 *sqq.*; Dion. Hal. 11; Diodor. Sic. 12. 24). The accounts have been much debated (Maschke, Der Freiheitsprozess, and earlier literature cited by him; Lenel, Ed. Perp. (2) p. 367; Schlossmann, Z. S. S. 13. 236 *sqq.*, etc.). Perhaps no conclusion can safely be drawn from narratives none of which is nearly contemporary, but Maschke seems to have shewn that it is possible to doubt whether the rule went further than that *vindiciae* were *secundum libertatem* if the man was *in libertate* when the issue was raised.

[4] In. 4. 6. 13; C. 7. 16. 21.　　　　　　[5] Lenel, Ed. Perp. (2) pp. 367 *sqq.*
[6] G. 4. 44.　　　　　　　　　　　　　[7] 10. 4. 12. *pr.*
[8] In. 4. 6. 13; Theoph. *ad h. l.*; C. 7. 16. 21.　　[9] C. 7. 16. 21.
[10] Sintenis, Otto and Schilling, *ad h. l.*; Wlassak, Z. S. S. 25. 395.

that there exist several texts shewing that there was or might be an actual *condemnatio*[1]. It may be doubted whether the process was tried by *formula* for any long time. It became a *cognitio* very early[2], at latest under Antoninus Pius. In the time of Cicero it was still tried by *sacramentum,* and went before the decemviral court[3]. Mommsen thinks on negative evidence[4] (*i.e.* that Dio and Pomponius do not say that they kept it, while they do record the fact in other matters) that Augustus took away this jurisdiction from them. Cuq thinks[5] that it was transferred to the *centumviri,* which gives the same results, since all centumviral causes were tried by *legis actio.* Karlowa says that the citations from Ulpian *de officio consulis* leave no doubt that the Consuls had jurisdiction perhaps concurrently with, perhaps in lieu of, that of the Praetor[6]. He thinks the *consilium* sat and voted—hence such rules as that of the *lex* Iunia Petronia, *etc.*[7]—and that[8] the Decemviri had jurisdiction where an apparent *civis* was claimed as a slave, in other cases either *recuperatores* or *unus iudex*[9]. Lenel considers the formulary process to have continued as an admissible alternative to the *cognitio,* and he cites texts in which the *iudex* appears[10]. It may be doubted whether the *iudex* here is the old *unus iudex* or the magistrate's deputy[11]. The view that the magistrate habitually appointed permanent deputies to try particular types of case, especially outside Rome, probable in itself, would harmonise these texts and those dealing with the closely similar case of the *querela*[12].

In Justinian's time it is of course a *cognitio.* It is sometimes described as a *praeiudicium,* but that means little under the system of pleading then in operation, under which a *condemnatio* need not be for money in any case. Perhaps the chief text means[13] merely that it might be an *actio praeiudicialis,* as it certainly might, *i.e.* a matter to be settled as a preliminary to some other issue, *e.g.* to a claim of a *hereditas*[14]. But it is frequently brought *principaliter*[15], when it is not easy to see anything *praeiudicialis* about it.

We shall see[16] that the *de facto* position of the slave when the question was raised, *i.e. in libertate* or *in servitute,* decided the burden of

---

[1] 7. 7. 4, 6 ; 40. 12. 36. There seems no sufficient reason for distinguishing the two cases. A formula *per sponsionem* for a *vindicatio in libertatem* is simple. And see Lenel, *op. cit.* p. 371.
[2] See Girard, Manuel, 102, where the literature is cited.
[3] Cicero, Pro Caecina, 33. 97; Mommsen, Staatsrecht (3) 2. 1. 605; D. P. R. 4. 315.
[4] Mommsen, Staatsr. (3) 2. 1. 608 ; D. P. R. 4. 318.   [5] Cuq, Instit. Jurid. 2. 141.
[6] There was a Praetor *de liberalibus causis* from about A.D. 200.
[7] 40. 1. 24.   [8] R. R. G. 2. 1108 *sqq.*
[9] The references to *recuperatores,* however, suggest general competence : see Girard, Manuel, 1104, and Textes, 127. The texts commonly contemplate a plurality of judges, and this may be one of the many precautions to secure a fair decision of so important a matter, 40. 1. 24; Karlowa, *loc. cit.*
[10] Lenel, Ed. Perp. (2) p. 372; D. 5. 3. 7. 1, 2 ; 40. 12. 8. 1, 2, 9. *pr.,* 23. 2, 42.
[11] See 40. 12. 41, *iudex qui de libertate cognoscat.*   [12] Girard, Manuel, *loc. cit.*
[13] In. 4. 6. 13.   [14] *e.g.,* C. 3. 31. 8.
[15] *e.g.,* 37. 10. 3. 2, 6. 3 ; 43. 29. 3. 7 ; 40. 12. 4.   [16] *Post,* p. 660.

proof. The fact might be doubtful and there was an edictal machinery for a preliminary enquiry on this point[1]. So far as can be gathered from the Digest[2] this was also a *cognitio*. Whether this was the case in classical law cannot be said. As Wlassak says[3], the question of fact might have been referred to an *arbiter* by the magistrate who had charge of the case.

The action has a good many preliminaries, a fact alluded to in the various texts which use the expression *sollennibus ordinatis* in this connexion[4]. The first point to note is that a person whose status is doubtful cannot *postulare in iure*, and therefore the action is brought, or defended, on the part of the person concerned, by an *adsertor libertatis*. This is expressed by the well-known rule that among the few cases in which it was possible *lege agere, alieno nomine*, was that *pro libertate*[5]. The *adsertor* was something like a *procurator* or *cognitor*, but under exceptional rules, somewhat favourable to liberty. Thus it was no objection to an *adsertor* that he was disqualified by *turpitudo* or the like from acting as *procurator*, unless indeed the Praetor thought fit to reject him on his own authority, as suspect[6]. If an *adsertor* abandoned the case, the whole matter might be transferred to another, but if the one who abandoned the case did it without good reason, and in order to betray the claimant, he would be dealt with *extra ordinem*[7]. There is an obscure enactment in the Codex Theodosianus, which may mean that if a second assertor presented himself when there was one already, he was admitted to the suit, but was liable to a severe penalty in case of failure[8]. It is plain, however, that in the later Empire there were difficulties in procuring *adsertores*: Constantine legislated elaborately on the matter[9]. He provided that if one in apparent liberty were claimed as a slave and could find no *adsertor*, he was to be taken about his province (*circumductus*) bearing a label, shewing that he needed an *adsertor*. If he failed to get one he would be handed over to the claimant. But if afterwards he could secure an *adsertor*, he could renew his defence, retaining the advantage that the burden of proof was on the other side. If at that hearing judgment was in favour of the alleged slave, he was entitled to claim, by way of compensation, a *servus mulctatitius*, although if the slave were a woman and had a child during the hearing, though his fate would be determined by the judgment, she could not claim one for him[10]. If the alleged slave died during the

---

[1] Lenel, Ed. Perp. (2) p. 371.
[2] The chief text is 40. 12. 7. 5.
[3] Wlassak, Z. S. S. 25. 395.
[4] C. 7. 16. 11, 15 ; C. 7. 19. 5 ; C. 8. 44. 18.
[5] In. 4. 10. *pr.*; G. 4. 82.
[6] Fr. Vat. 324.
[7] P. 5. 1. 5.   See also C. Th. 4. 8. 8 *in fin.*   An *adsertor* acting in bad faith was liable for *calumnia* on a high scale, for one-third of the value of the slave, G. 4. 175.
[8] C. Th. 4. 8. 8.   So understood by Gothofredus.   But this part of the *lex* may refer to a second claimant of the slave.
[9] C. Th. 4. 8. 5.
[10] C. Th. 4. 8. 4.

hearing the case went on and the *servus mulctatitius* went to his *heres*. If the claimant of the slave died, and his *heres* continued the suit, there would be the same penalty, but not if he withdrew. If the *adsertor* acted at his own risk, guaranteeing return of the *peculium* in case of failure, he was entitled to take security for the possible penalty[1]. The text says that this *circumductio* is a substitute for the idle proclamation. It may thus be assumed that until this time, if an *adsertor* did not appear there was a proclamation in court. It is probable that the whole legislation is part of the protection of the weak against the *potentiores* which is so marked a feature of legislation in the later Empire[2]. The word *proclamare* appears in the Digest in the expression *proclamare in* (or *ad*) *libertatem*, the regular expression for the case of one *in servitute* claiming liberty[3].

To the rule requiring an *adsertor* in all cases an exception was made in A.D. 393, by Theodosius, who provided that if a question of status was raised against one who had been living *in libertate* for 20 years, irrespective of *bona fide* origin of the condition (*iustum initium*[4]), and had to the knowledge of the claimant held some public office without objection during that time, he could defend his liberty without an *adsertor*[5]. Under Justinian the need for an *adsertor* was wholly swept away. He provided that the person concerned might appear personally and that if the claim was one *ex libertate in servitutem*, he might appear by procurator, though not in the other case. Under the new system, the *peculium* and other property which may be affected by the result is to be assigned to safe keeping by the *iudex*, at least in the case of a claim *ex servitute*. Those who can give a *fideiussor* must do so, but if the *iudex* is satisfied that this is impossible they must give a *cautio iuratoria*[6]. Before Justinian it is not clear what the law as to security was. His enactment shews that he altered the law on the matter and suggests also that the earlier rules were more severe than those established by him. So far as *peculium* and similar matters were concerned, his language seems to imply that the *adsertor* had had to give security for these in all cases. The same consideration would cover the case of the man himself, which suggests that the same rule applied there. It is true that the analogy of the ordinary real action suggests that it was only where the *adsertor* was defendant that security needed

---

[1] C. Th. 4. 8. 5.   [2] See Monnier, N. R. H. 24, pp. 62 *sqq*.
[3] As to the history of this expression and the extent to which the form *Proc. in libertatem* is interpolated, see Gradenwitz, Interp. 101; Z. S. S. 14. 118; Wlassak, Grünhut's Zeitsch. 19. 715; Schlossmann, Z. S. S. 13. 225. Schl. thinks *proclamatio* was originally an appeal to the bystanders for an *adsertor* (see the story of Virginia, and the rules as to *vindex* in *manus iniectio*) but that in the sources it is merely setting up his claim.
[4] *Ante*, p. 649.
[5] C. Th. 4. 8. 9. So explained by the *interpretatio*, but time and service may be alternatives: if not it is not clear whether the service must have been throughout the time.
[6] C. 7. 17. 1.

to be given[1], and so Wlassak holds[2]. But the reason assigned by Gaius for requiring security, *i.e.* that the defendant is in possession of the disputed thing, applies in every case of *adsertio libertatis*, since, as we know, the man was in all cases *pro libero* during the hearing, whether the alleged *dominus* was plaintiff or defendant. Wlassak also considers it possible, though not proved, that no security was exacted if the man was *in libertate voluntate domini*, and he attaches to this hypothesis the discussion in two texts, which are concerned with the question whether in given circumstances a man can be said to be *in libertate voluntate domini*. But it is not easy to see why the fact that the *dominus*, either in error or out of kindness, had allowed the man to run loose, should have deprived him of his right to exact security. Wlassak, however, seems right in refusing to apply these texts to the hypothesis of an informal manumission. They appear, however, to admit of another interpretation, elsewhere considered[3].

Causae liberales were required—*favore libertatis*[4]—to go before *maiores iudices*. In the provinces this would be the *Praeses*[5]. The *Procurator* Caesaris had no jurisdiction in such matters[6].

A *causa liberalis* was not a fitting subject for arbitration, and if one was submitted, *ex compromisso*, to an arbitrator, he would not be compelled to issue a *sententia*[7], and probably his decision if given would be in no way binding. It must be borne in mind that his decision would not in any case be a judgment: it might give a right to an agreed *poena*, but it did not prevent the question from being again raised[8]. The law as to the effect of a *transactio* on such a matter is not quite clear. In one text, a constitution of Diocletian, we are told that no *transactio* between a *dominus* and his slave could be in any way binding on the *dominus*[9]. On the other hand we are told that Anastasius provided that *transactiones* as to status should be good and should not *titubare*, merely because they decided for slavery[10]. Elsewhere Diocletian had decided that pact could not make a slave free, *nec his qui transactioni non consenserunt quicquam praeiudicare potest*[11]. This seems to be an allusion to a case in which a mother had, under a compromise, been admitted to be free, her children remaining slaves, or some case of this kind[12]. Nothing in Diocletian's enactments[13] suggests a positive force in a *transactio*, but it would seem that a little later such compromises were made, and were regarded as binding on the parties

[1] G. 4. 89, 96.   [2] Wlassak, Z. S. S. 26. 400.   [3] *Post*, p. 661.
[4] 4. 8. 32. 7.   [5] C. 3. 3. 2; 7. 14. 1, 9; 7. 16. 11, 15.
[6] C. 3. 22. 2. Whether the rule of 315 requiring cases in which the Fisc was concerned to go before the *Rationabilis* applied to *causae liberales* is not clear (C. 3. 26. 5). The older rules of Hadrian and Marcus Aurelius requiring fiscal officers to be present (49. 14. 3. 9, 7) are unnecessary in that case, but in the Digest they may be anachronisms.
[7] 4. 8. 32. 7.   [8] 4. 8. 29, 30; P. 5. 5a. 1, *etc.*
[9] C. 2. 4. 13; cp. *h. t.* 26.   [10] C. 2. 4. 43.
[11] C. 7. 14. 8; cp. C. 2. 4. 26.   [12] C. 2. 4. 26.
[13] C. 2. 4. 13, 26; C. 7. 14. 8.

so far at least as the result was in favour of liberty. The practical outcome of the enactment of Anastasius[1] seems to be that a *transactio* would now be valid, to the extent of preventing the owner from claiming the man as a slave, or in the converse case, of preventing the man from claiming liberty against that defendant or claimant, but not beyond[2]. There is no sign that the rule was carefully worked out: it does not appear in the Institutes or Digest, and in the Basilica where the matter is discussed[3], the rule is made out that *transactio* is effective, after *litis contestatio* in the *causa*, but not before.

Causae liberales might be tried and decided on privileged days, not open for ordinary litigation[4]. If the claim was one *e libertate in servitutem* it must be tried at the domicil of the alleged slave[5]. If it was *e servitute* it would be at the domicil of the alleged *dominus*[6].

Under the system of *legis actio* the person in question was of necessity present, and the *adsertio* appears to involve his presence in any case[7]. The machinery by which it was compelled is not very clear. The interdict *quem liberum* was not available because this assumes freedom, and to decide it would prejudge the *causa liberalis*[8]. We are told that the *actio ad exhibendum* was available to one who wished *vindicare in libertatem*[9], but it is not easy to see the pecuniary interest needed[10]. There is no need for compulsion where the man himself is raising the question. The Institutes mention an *interdictum exhibitorium*[11], for the production of one, *cuius de libertate agitur*. It is not mentioned by Gaius from whom the next interdict mentioned, *libertum cui patronus operas indicere velit*[12], seems to be taken. Lenel does not appear to think that the Edict contained such an interdict. It may be a late introduction, perhaps alternative to *actio ad exhibendum*, perhaps designed to meet the objection that an *adsertor* had not the pecuniary interest, which, according to the Digest, the *actio ad exhibendum* required[13].

At least after Constantine, the case could be continued and decided in the absence of one party[14]. Justinian's enactment abolishing *adsertores* provided that if the alleged slave failed to appear for a year after summons by the claimant, judgment should go against him[15]. But there is nothing to shew, apart from this, that action could ever have been begun in his absence.

---

[1] C. 2. 4. 43.   [2] See *ante*, p. 647.   [3] Heimbach, 1. 726.
[4] 2. 12. 3. 1.   [5] C. 3. 22. 3.
[6] *h. t.* 4. One *dolo malo in libertate* is treated for this purpose as *in servitute*, *h. t.* 1. Justinian seems to contemplate a double jurisdiction by providing that one who having begun suit in one jurisdiction starts another elsewhere, forfeits any right in the man, C. 7. 17. 1. 3. The text suggests that one is brought *ex divali iussione* in what would not otherwise be a competent jurisdiction.   [7] Varro, de l. l. 6. 64; cp. Accarias, Précis, § 797.
[8] 43. 29. 3. 7.   [9] 19. 4. 12. *pr.*   [10] *h. t.* 13.
[11] In. 4. 15. 1.   [12] G. 4. 162.   [13] 10. 4. 13.
[14] 40. 12. 27. 2; C. 7. 16. 4, 40. Presumably of the man himself, though he is not a party.
[15] C. 7. 17. 1.

Subject to the possibility of being already barred by res iudicata[1] anyone interested in the matter may raise the question of a man's status. The normal case is that of one claiming to own him, but a usufructuary may bring the action[2]. It is presumably barred to one who may not *postulare in iure*, and a freedman cannot bring it against his patron, but, apart from these cases, exclusions do not seem to be numerous. A pupil can bring it against his *tutor*[3], but not *tutores* and *curatores* against their former wards. A husband can dispute the status of his *liberta* whom he has married[4], as, indeed, a manumitter could in general prove his manumission invalid[5].

On the other side-the natural person to move is the alleged slave himself, and he can choose his *adsertor* freely. But, though he is not inclined to move, others may do so on his behalf, even against his will. Thus we learn that if he assents to the slavery to annoy his relatives, his parents may bring a *causa liberalis*, whether there is *potestas* or not. So children can for their parents, and even cognates can, for the slur extends to them. So too can 'natural' relatives, *e.g.* the parents of a freedman[6]. In general the right applies to all *necessariae*, *i.e.* related or connected people[7]. If the person concerned is mad or *infans*, not only relatives, but other people, may proceed[8]. A patron has an interest in the freedom of his *libertus* either on the ground of succession or on that of *operae*, and can thus bring a *causa liberalis* on his account[9]. The man's consent is immaterial[10], and thus the patron may do it even where the man himself has sold himself into slavery[11], though not, presumably, where the man himself would be barred. It must be added that, if there are several relatives or patrons claiming to act, the Praetor must choose the most suitable[12].

We shall have to deal later with cases in which the *causa liberalis* may have to be postponed owing to the existence of other questions with which it is connected. But Ulpian tells us that there are constitutions which provide for postponement, if necessary[13], even where it stands alone, and that Hadrian provided that there might be such postponement in the case of an *impubes*, if his interests required it, but not if he was sufficiently defended[14].

---

[1] *Post*, pp. 667 *sqq*.
[2] 40. 12. 8, 9. In later law, perhaps not in classical, pledge creditor, *h. t.* 8. 2.
[3] C. 7. 16. 35.   [4] 40. 12. 39. 23; P. 5. 1. 8, 9.
[5] The status of one made *limenarcha* may be attacked by the appointing authority, C. 7. 16. 38.
[6] 40. 12. 1—3. Even a parent who has sold the child may afterwards proceed, C. 7. 16. 1.
[7] Dirksen, Manuale, *s.v. necessarius*. If there is no one else, female relatives or a wife may proceed, 40. 12. 3. 2.
[8] *h. t.* 6. A *miles* may proceed for *necessariae personae* (*h. t.* 3. 1).
[9] 40. 12. 3. 3, 5. *pr.*, 12. 5.   [10] C. 7. 16. 19.   [11] 40. 12. 4.
[12] *h. t.* 5. 1.   [13] 37. 10. 3. 2.
[14] *h. l.* 5. He attributes a similar rule to Divi Fratres, 40. 12. 27. *pr.* Augustus provides that where mother and child are claiming before different judges the mother's case must be tried first. Hadrian says it must be so tried in any case unless they are taken together, 40. 12. 23. 2.

Whether the claim is *ex libertate* or *ex servitute* the action is essentially the same, but in the former case the man is defendant, while in the latter he is plaintiff and is thus under the burden of proof[1]. Upon this matter very precise rules are laid down. If the alleged slave was *in servitute* or *dolo malo in libertate* at the time the issue was raised, the claim is *ex servitute* and the burden of proof is on him[2]. If his *de facto* status is uncertain, the edict provides that there snall be an enquiry whether he was *in servitute* or *in libertate*, ahd if the latter, then whether it was or was not *dolo malo*. If it was, he is treated as *in servitute*[3]. There was evidently a good deal of discussion as to what was being *in libertate sine dolo malo*. Julian cited by Ulpian[4] lays down the simple rule that one who thinks he is free and acts as if he were free satisfies the rule. Varus is cited as making what purports to be a modification, but is in fact no more than a fuller statement. He says that even if the man thinks he is a freeman, so long as he acts as a *fugitivus* and hides, he is not *sine dolo malo* : indeed one who acts *pro fugitivo* acts *pro servo*, and in fact is not *in libertate* at all. Gaius adds[5] what seems to mean that if he fled so as to hide from his master, and then in his distant place acted *pro libero* he is still *pro fugitivo* and at any rate not *in libertate sine dolo malo*. It follows, as Ulpian says, that a freeman may be *dolo malo in libertate*, and a slave may be so *sine dolo malo*[6]. In fact, anyone who without fraud lived in liberty, and, with or without good reason, thought himself free, was *bona fide in libertate* and had the *commoda possessoris*[7], *i.e.* is not under the burden of proof[8]. But just as a man might be *in libertate mala fide*, so he might be *in servitute mala fide*. Two texts which leave something to be desired on the point of clearness seem, when fairly read, to mean that if one *bona fide in libertate* were about to be claimed as a slave, and the intending claimant, as a preliminary, seized the man and kept him in confinement, this would not settle the burden of proof, but that if it were substantially a claim *ex libertate*, it would still be so : the claimant by this act of brigandage would not have acquired to himself the position of defendant[9].

---

[1] C. 4. 19. 15; C. 7. 16. 5. 2. [2] 22. 3. 14; 40. 12. 7. 5.
[3] *Ib*. Apparently the burden of proof that he was *in libertate* was on him, 40. 12. 41. *pr.* Proof that it was *dolo malo* would be on the other side. It does not seem certain that the words *dolo malo* were actually in the Edict. This would make the enquiry in C. 7. 16. 21 unlikely, and Ulpian seems to find it necessary to explain that *in libertate* means *in libertate sine dolo malo*, 40. 12. 10. But he may be explaining only his own words. As to the mode of trial of this preliminary issue, see *ante*, p. 655.
[4] 40. 12. 10. [5] *h. t.* 11.
[6] *h. t.* 12. *pr.* He gives illustrations. An infant really free but stolen was *bona fide in servitute*. Not knowing his freedom he ran away and hid : he was *dolo malo in libertate*. One brought up as free, or freed under a false will which he thought good, or by one who was not his *dominus*, is *in libertate sine dolo malo*, 40. 12. 12. 1, 2.
[7] 40. 12. 12. 3.
[8] *h. t.* 4. The critical date is that at which application is first made to the court.
[9] 22. 3. 20; C. 4. 19. 15.

It is, however, nowhere said that a man could not be *in libertate sine dolo malo*, except in the cases laid down in the foregoing texts[1]. Two texts which have never been conclusively explained[2], discuss the question whether a particular man can be said to have been *in libertate voluntate domini*. It has been shewn by Wlassak that they cannot be applied to the question whether there has been an informal manumission, since there is no evidence of any *animus manumittendi*. He applies them to another hypothesis, elsewhere considered[3], but it may be suggested that their application is, possibly, to our present topic. They give perfectly good sense if they are understood as resting on the view, which may well have been held by some jurists, that a man was *in libertate sine dolo malo*, if he was in that position *voluntate domini*. The fact that in one of the cases the event under discussion happens after the *ordinatio litis*, is not material. If a man who had not been *in libertate* became so *sine dolo malo* after *ordinatio litis*, the only effect would be, if the classical law as to security was, as we have supposed[4], to shift the burden of proof, a matter involving no change in the mechanism[5].

Caracalla provided that there could be no proclamation *in libertatem* until proper accounts had been rendered as to past administration[6], so that from his time onward this must be regarded as another preliminary to the action.

The completion of the organisation of the case brings another and very important rule into play. As soon as the *lis* is *ordinata*, the man ceases to be *in servitute* if he was so before, and is treated pending the hearing as *liberi loco* or *pro libero*[7]. The origin of this rule is doubtful. It is sometimes said to be based on the rule of the XII Tables that *vindiciae* were to be *secundum libertatem*, and the fact that the rule is treated by Gaius as merely traditional—*volgo dicitur*[8]—which shews that it is not edictal, does not shew that it is not based on the XII Tables, since in any case it is a mere evolution from the supposed rule and not itself an express provision. It must be noted that its scope is less than that of the older rule: it has no relation to the question of proof. A person claiming *ex servitute* is *pro libero*, but must prove his case[9].

The rule applies from the moment when the *lis* is *ordinata* or *inchoata* or *coepta*[10]. The exact point of time meant by these expressions is

---

[1] No text gives any other case, but in the illustration in 40. 12. 12. 1 it is difficult to see why a point is made of the concealment if the state of mind was decisive.
[2] 40. 12. 24. 3, 28.   [3] Wlassak, Z. S. S. 26. 391 *sqq*. *Ante*, p. 657. See Buckland, N. R. H. 32. 235.   [4] *Ante*, p. 657.
[5] It does not appear that the question of *dolus malus* or not could be disposed of by oath, though this is allowed where a *libertinus* is claiming *ingenuitas*, C. 4. 1. 6. In C. 4. 19. 20 the effect is considered of the presence or absence of *instrumenta emptionis*.
[6] 40. 12. 34.   [7] 4. 6. 12; 40. 12. 24. *pr*., 3, 25. 2; C. 7. 16. 14.
[8] 40. 12. 25. 2.   [9] See, however, Maschke, *op. cit.* 34.
[10] 4. 6. 12; 40. 12. 24. *pr*., 25. 2; 43. 16. 1. 21.

nowhere indicated[1]. Karlowa thinks the cause is *ordinata* at the moment at which the distribution of parts is determined[2]. Cujas thinks it is at the absolute beginning[3], but the expression *ordinata* seems to imply that some matters have already been arranged[4].

The effect of this quasi-liberty is indicated in many texts. Thus a *tutor* can be appointed to the person in question, and the appointment will be valid or not, according as he is judged free or not[5]. He may not be put to the torture on the question of his liberty[6]. He may have actions even against his alleged *dominus*, lest they be barred by death or lapse of time[7], Servius holding that in all *actiones annuae*—the only ones in which in his day the point would have been material—time began to run from the moment the *lis* was *ordinata*[8]. This must presumably apply only where it is *ex servitute*, and thus the rule forms some support to the view that the *ordinatio* is the distribution of parts. If he wishes to sue a third person, we are told that the question whether the *lis* is *ordinata* or not is immaterial, lest any person liable to action have the power to postpone such action by getting someone to raise a question of status. Any judgment will be valid or void according to the result of the *causa*[9]. The main argument of this text is not very clear. This last rule seems to refer to the case of one claimed *e libertate*, while as we have seen the primary rule itself can hardly have any bearing except on the case of a claimant *ex servitute*.

The rule is, or may be, somewhat different if it is sought to make him defendant in an action. We are told that if the *dominus* (*i.e.* the other party to the *causa*) wishes to sue him in any personal action, the action will proceed to *litis contestatio*, but the hearing will be suspended till after judgment in the *causa liberalis*, according to the event of which the *iudicium* will proceed or be useless[10]. So if a third party wishes to charge him with theft or *damnum*, he must give security *se iudicio sisti* lest he should be in a better position than one whose status was not in dispute, but the hearing must be postponed to avoid prejudicing the *causa liberalis*[11]. So, if his alleged *dominus* is charged with *furtum* committed by him, and he *proclamat in libertatem*, the trial is postponed so that it

---

[1] See as to *lis inchoata*, Fr. Vat. 263; Cons. 6. 8. 9; see Roby, R. P. L. 2. 402. It is clear that this expression sometimes means *lis contestata*.

[2] Karlowa, R. R. G. 2. 1112.   [3] Cujas, Observ. 18. 23.

[4] See the language of 40. 12. 24. 2. It does not seem probable that the time is that of *litis contestatio*, at whatever time in the proceedings that occurred, as to which see Girard, Manuel, 1004.

[5] 26. 5. 17.

[6] 48. 18. 10. 6. If one liable to torture on any matter claims to be free, Hadrian rules that this must be settled before torture, *h. t.* 12.

[7] 40. 12. 24. *pr.*   [8] *h. t.* 24. 1.

[9] *h. l.* 2. He may have procurators in business or litigation and may be a procurator, 3. 3. 33. 1.

[10] 40. 12. 24. 3. The text remarks that this does not prejudice the *causa liberalis*, and the man is not *in libertate voluntate domini*, *ante*, p. 660.

[11] 40. 12. 24. 4.

may be transferred to him if he is really free, and the *actio iudicati* may go against him[1]. So an interdict *unde vi* brought against him, while he is proclaiming, can result in a judgment of restitution after he is declared free[2]. The difference of rule may be only apparent, since the main text dealing with action by the man does not say that it is to be fought out before judgment in the *causa*, and emphasises the importance of getting it as far as *litis contestatio*[3].

But the rule that he is *pro libero* has limitations. Thus a person whose *status* is in question may not enter any *militia*, whichever way the claim is made[4]. If a person claiming *ex servitute* does so become a *miles*, he will be expelled, and as the text says he is to be treated like other slaves[5] he is presumably liable to capital punishment if he proves to be a slave[6]. Our text adds that a *miles calumnia petitus in servitutem* is not expelled, but *retinetur in castris*[5]. As it would be impossible to say whether there was *calumnia*, till the *causa* was decided, the rule deducible from the texts would seem to be that a man claimed *e libertate* was not expelled from a *militia* unless and until declared a slave, but that no such person could become a *miles* pending the *causa*.

The law as to his relation with his master presents some difficulty. Gaius tells us that he still acquires to his master if he really is a slave. He adds a doubt for the case of possession, since he is not now possessed by the *dominus*, but disposes of it with the remark that there is no more difficulty in this case than in that of a *fugitivus*, by whom his master can certainly acquire possession[7]. It may, however, be remembered that a *fugitivus* is still possessed, and though this doctrine was disputed, and rests mainly on the authority of Nerva *filius*, a Proculian[8], it is certainly held by Cassius and Julian[9], leaders of the school to which Gaius belongs. Paul discusses the matter in two texts[10], the conclusions of which are that in a claim *ex servitute*, where there is no suggestion that the man was *in libertáte* before the issue was raised, the *dominus* continues to possess the man unless he is declared free. So also if he has run away, but has been away for so short a time or in such a manner that he has not before his capture established himself *in libertate*. But if he has definitely attained the position of apparent freedom, and on capture, or without capture, raises, or is ready to raise, the question of status, the master no longer possesses him. It is clear that for Paul the decisive point is the definite and express repudiation of the master's authority. This is more than is involved in *fuga* or even in acting *pro*

---

1 *Ibid.* See also 9. 4. 42. *pr.*; Koschaker, Translatio iudicii, 220.
2 43. 16. 1. 21.
3 40. 12. 24. *pr.* Nothing is said as to actions *in rem*, in which, as to claims *e libertate*, the risk must have been the same.
4 49. 16. 8. 5 40. 12. 29. *pr.* 6 49. 16. 11.
7 40. 12. 25. 2. 8 *Ante*, p. 270. 9 41. 2. 1. 14.
10 49. 2. 3. 10; 49. 3. 15. 1.

libero, and we have seen that even in that case many jurists thought the master lost possession[1]. Paul does not actually consider whether possession could be acquired through such a man: probably it could where the master still possessed, and could not where he did not[2].

It is clear that there were disputes. Traces of these are left in the case of an acquisition which required *iussum*, where that *iussum* was given and disobeyed. Justinian discusses the case in which X, claiming freedom from A, is instituted by B. A orders him to enter but he refuses. A cannot treat him as his slave: he is *pro libero*. Can any penalty or pressure be imposed? Justinian tells us there had been much doubt on this matter and he decides it by what he calls a subtle distinction. If in the institution the man was described as the slave of A, he can be made to enter and in that case whatever the issue of the *causa liberalis* he will get no benefit and incur no risk. If he was instituted as a freeman he will not be compelled to enter, whether the *causa liberalis* were *e libertate* or *e servitute*; the *hereditas* will await the issue, and he will enter at his master's *iussum* or, if he likes, on his own account, according to the result[3]. In the first case the decision may result in an acquisition by A through a slave in whom he had no right or possession.

The issue affects only the parties, and thus does not decide the status of anyone else. Thus if a woman's status is being tried, the decision of it will not determine the status of her children born before the hearing. But Constantine enacted that if a child were born to her during the *causa*, it should have the same fate as the mother, *i.e.* its status would be governed by the decision in her case[4].

Though the person whose status is in question should die *pendente lite*, other matters may ultimately be affected by the decision. Thus he may have made a will, or the man who bought him may have a claim for eviction against the vendor. Accordingly the *adsertor* is bound to go on with the case, and in Justinian's law, *adsertores* being abolished, the buyer can take up his claim, and require the vendor to prove the slavery[5].

The *lex* Iunia Petronia provided (A.D. 19) that if the *iudices* were equally divided the judgment must be in favour of liberty, though in other cases of equality it would be for the defence[6]. There were also

---

[1] *Ante*, pp. 270 *sqq.*, where we have already considered the shifting views held on this point, so critical for any theory of possession. Paul's texts may represent uncertain views. See Koschaker, Translatio Iudicii, 220.
[2] The master may be in other positions than that of owner, a point material in all these questions of acquisition.
[3] C. 6. 30. 21.
[4] C. Th. 4. 8. 4 = C. 7. 16. 42; cp. C. 7. 16. 17. 1.
[5] C. 7. 17. 2; 7. 21. 3. Burden of proof on vendor, in conformity with the rule where a slave bought claims liberty, C. 8. 44. 21.
[6] 40. 1. 24. *pr.*; 42. 1. 38. *pr.*

many constitutions directing them to decide in favour of liberty if the evidence seemed equal[1].

If the judgment is against the slave it will be simply *eum servum esse*[2]. But if it is in his favour the form of the proceeding affects the judgment. If he is defendant, and the plaintiff fails to prove his case, the judgment is *eum servum* (*Agerii*) *non esse, i.e.* that he is not the slave of the plaintiff. If the person claiming liberty is the plaintiff, the judgment will be *eum liberum* or (*ingenuum*) *esse*, which besides that it bars the defendant, puts the plaintiff into the position of one *bona fide in libertate*[3]. A result of this distinction is stated in a text which says that if the person claimed desires to take the burden of proof on himself he is to be allowed to do so ; the point being that, if successful, he will get a more satisfactory judgment[4]. In one text we are told that if judgment goes in favour of the alleged slave because the claimant of him does not attend, the effect is to bar the claimant, but in no case to make the man an *ingenuus*. Ulpian thinks indeed the wiser course in such a case is to give the man his choice of a postponement, or a hearing there and then. If he chooses the latter and wins, the judgment will be *eum servum* (*Agerii*) *non esse* but not *ingenuum esse*. This can injure no one but the absent claimant. If, however, the man is claiming *ex servitute*, there should be an adjournment, to avoid a judgment *eum ingenuum esse*, unless, as Hadrian is reported as saying, there is some special reason, and a very clear case[5].

If the *dominus* wins he need not accept damages, but may take away the slave[6], and conversely, damages to the slave, in lieu of liberty, are inconceivable, since they will not go to him, and, moreover, liberty is not capable of estimation in money[7]. But the pleadings may entitle him to an *actio iniuriarum*, or *calumniae*. To found such a claim the attack on his status must have been unjustified and *improbus, i.e.* made in knowledge that it was unfounded. Paul tells us that those trying such cases (in his day they were *cognitiones*) might punish *calumnia* with exile[8]. It was immaterial which way the action was brought[9]. It was *iniuria* to call a freeman a slave[10]: *a fortiori*, if, when called on to support the allegation, the person so speaking failed to do so[11].

---

[1] 40. 1. 24. 1.   Paul cites Pomponius as saying that if one *iudex* takes refuge in a *rem non liquere*, the others, agreeing, can give judgment, since in any case the majority decide, 42. 1. 36. As to the *iudices*, *ante*, p. 654.
[2] C. 8. 44. 18.
[3] *h. t.* 21 ; C. 7. 19. 5, 6 ; C. 9. 35. 10.   His proof must shew how he is free and thus may shew his *ingenuitas*, *post*, pp. 672 *sq.*
[4] 40. 12. 39. *pr.* ; P. 5. 1. 6.   As to absence of a party, *ante*, p. 658.
[5] 40. 12. 27. 1.   [6] *h. t.* 36.   [7] 50. 17. 176. 1.
[8] P. 5. 1. 7 ; D. 40. 12. 39. 1 ; 47. 10. 12 ; C. 7. 16. 31.   [9] 47. 10. 11. 9, 12.
[10] *h. t.* 1. 2.
[11] C. 9. 35. 10.   But a buyer continuing to oppose the claim in order that he may recover the eviction penalty, which he might not be able to get if he let the case go by default, was not liable *ex iniuria*, 40. 12. 26 ; 47. 10. 12.

The alleged slave on getting judgment will be able to recover any property which the soi-disant *dominus* has detained[1]. There may obviously be difficulties as to what this amounts to. In general one would suppose he would in any case take all but what his holder could claim to have acquired as a *bonae fidei possessor* of him. But there is a dark text credited to ·Paul, which says that a certain *senatusconsultum* provides that he shall keep only those things which *in domo cuiusque intulisset.* It is not clear whether this means brought in with him or took away with him[2]. The statement looks like a rule of thumb way of avoiding the difficult questions which might arise. Taken in conjunction with the cognate rules we have already considered[3], the text, if it is to be taken as genuine, seems to imply that where possession of a slave ended by a *causa liberalis,* the traditional rules as to acquisition were set aside. But as to what the rule really was we have no information beyond this meagre text[4].

The rights created would not necessarily be all on that side. The late master might well have claims against the quasi-slave for damage done to him in various ways. Gaius and Ulpian tell us that an *actio in factum* lay against the man for *damnum* done by him while *bona fide* possessed by his putative master, the former expressly limiting the action to the case of *dolus malus*[5]. Lenel holds[6], on account of the remark of Gaius[7] that the existence of the limit *certum est,* that the limitation to damage done *dolo malo* was not in the Edict. He seems indeed to think the limitation non-existent in classical law, since the illustration given by Ulpian is certainly not one of *damnum dolo datum*[8]. But this seems to be an interpolation : it purports to be a case of *damnum* to the possessor and is in fact nothing of the kind. And it speaks of the holder as *bona fide dominus,* which hardly looks genuine. There is no such remedy for *furtum,* perhaps because the possessor, being noxally liable for him, for theft, cannot have an action for theft by him[9]. For this purpose the holder is *pro domino.* The limitation to the case of *dolus* may mean no more than that the special remedy was aimed at misconduct.

Paul tells us[10] that in the actual *causa liberalis* the *iudex* may cast the man in damages for theft or *damnum,* and there is no limitation to *dolus.* He is speaking of a *cognitio* and in all probability of wrongs done pending the *causa.* There is no difficulty in the claim for *furtum* here as the possession has ceased. It does not seem that under the formulary system the *iudex* would have had the same power[11].

[1] C. 7. 16. 31.
[2] 40. 12. 32. The words *in domo cuiusque intulissent* are commonly taken to mean brought into the master's house, and to express the ordinary rule as to acquisitions *ex re* or *operis.*
[3] *Ante,* p. 664.　　　[4] See *post,* p. 674.　　　[5] 40. 12. 12. 6, 13.
[6] Ed. Perp. (2) § 181.　[7] 40. 12. 13.　　　[8] 40. 12. 12. 6.
[9] *Ante,* p. 107.　　　[10] 40. 12. 41.　　　[11] See Girard, Manuel, 705.

In addition to any claim against the man who has recovered his freedom, the putative owner may, as we have seen, have an eviction claim against his vendor, if he continues the *causa* to judgment[1]. If, however, the judgment is in his favour, he can in an appropriate case proceed for *calumnia* against the *adsertor* or any other person who set up the claim on behalf of the slave[2].

There are other results, outside the field of *obligatio*. There is a general rule that any person who attacks a testator's status forfeits any benefit under his will[3]. On the same principle, a patron of full age who claims his *libertus* as a slave has no *bonorum possessio contra tabulas*[4], and one who so claims the *libertus* of his father cannot claim, *unde liberi patroni* or *contra tabulas*[5]. If the attack was begun before the patron was 25 the penal consequence does not result, whether it was he or his *tutor* or his *curator* who made it[6]. It does not result if the claim is abandoned before judgment, or if, where a judgment is actually gained, wrongly, in the patron's favour, he learns the truth and allows the apparent slave to go free—*in libertate morari*. Even where the patron is excluded, his children not in *potestas* are not affected, at least after a rescript of Divi Fratres[7]. Most of these texts are expressed of the *patroni filius*, the commonest case, but the rule is equally applicable to the patron himself. It is edictal and thus does not directly affect civil law rights of succession, but they are no doubt sufficiently provided for under the general rule above stated, laid down in, or in connexion with, the *lex* Papia Poppaea.

The effect of the judgment on the man's status has already been incidentally considered, but it is necessary to examine it more in detail.

(*a*) Where the judgment is in favour of the man whose status is attacked. The main rule is that the judgment finally bars that particular claimant : he cannot proceed again[8], and there is no *restitutio in integrum*, or rescission even on the ground of minority[9]. There may of course be an appeal, and as the court which tries the case is the highest, the appeal is to the *Auditorium*[10]. We have already considered the case in which the judgment is rescinded after five years[11]. One text, of Macer[12], tells us that if my *libertus* is adjudicated the slave of another, *me inter-*

---

[1] C. 8. 44. 18, 21, 25.   [2] G. 4. 175.
[3] 34. 9. 9. 1.   The rule applies only where the claim is *e libertate*.   The other is unlikely, Ulp. 20. 11 ; D. 28. 1. 14, 15.
[4] 38. 2. 14. *pr.*
[5] *h. t.* 9, so where the claim is of a share or of any right involving slavery, *h. t.* 16. 1, where the claim is *e libertate*, *h. l. pr.*   It does not apply where the claim is merely to secure the eviction penalty, *h. t.* 30.
[6] *h. t.* 14. 1, 2.   [7] *h. t.* 16. 2—4.   [8] C. 7. 16. 4, 27.
[9] 4. 3. 24 ; C. 2. 30. 4.   [10] C. 2. 30. 4 ; 7. 16. 4.
[11] 40. 12. 29. 1 ; *ante*, p. 650.   A man who has won in a *causa liberalis* brings a claim against his late claimant.   The defence is raised that he is the slave of a third party.   There can be no *causa liberalis* between these parties, but the judge in the action will look into the matter, C. 7. 19. 4.   There is of course nothing to prevent a claim by the alleged owner.
[12] 42. 1. 63.

veniente, the effect is to bar me from any claim. The case is given as an illustration of the rule that one is barred by a judgment which is the result of his assent whether he is an actual party or not. In what capacity the patron is contemplated as intervening does not appear: it may be that he is *adsertor*.

We have seen that the claimant of the man may appear by *procurator*. There is here some risk, since *res iudicata* against a *procurator* is not necessarily so against his principal. And as there is virtually a claim of ownership in all cases, the security *de rato* is always exacted, though in general it is given only by the plaintiff's *procurator*[1]. The barring effect is only that of an ordinary judgment, and thus no one is barred who would not be barred by a judgment, and the bar applies only to claims under the old title, and not to a new title acquired from a third person, in no way affected by the judgment. Where judgment had been given for the slave, and the real owner of the slave, after the judgment, made the defeated litigant his *heres*, it was clear on the authority of Labeo and Iavolenus, that the old judgment was no bar[2].

(b) Case in which the judgment was against the person claiming liberty. Merely bringing a claim, and abandoning it, has no effect on status either way[3]. Texts dealing with the effect of judgment are few and are in at least apparent conflict. Gaius says that sometimes a claim may be renewed *ex integro*, as, for instance, where a condition is now satisfied which was not so at the first hearing[4]. The nature of the illustration shews that in the opinion of the writer, the decision was final between the parties. On the other hand Cicero says[5] that where the Decemviri had decided wrongly on such a case it could be renewed as often as was desired—a solitary exception to the general rule as to *res iudicata*, based on the view that none could lose his liberty without his own consent. Quintilian in one text speaks of *adsertio secunda*, the case having been heard before[6], and in another of *secunda adsertio*, tried before other *judices*[7]. Martial[8] speaks loosely and allusively of a third or fourth hearing which is to have a decisive effect. Finally Justinian in his constitution[9] by which he abolishes the need of *adsertores*, declares that the *leges* which formerly required such cases to be examined a second and third time are for the future to be out of application. He adds that the requirement was due to the absence of an appeal which he has now provided, and which, in turn, *ad secundam inquisitionem minime deducetur*, by colour of the aforesaid laws. With this collection

---

[1] 3. 3. 39. 5. For the remedy where the alleged *dominus* does not ratify the intervention of a *procurator* on his behalf, so that he can again claim, see 46. 8. 8. 2.

[2] 40. 12. 42. It should be noted that a judgment, *eum ingenuum esse* (*ante*, p. 665), has the advantage that thereafter he is *in possessione ingenuitatis*.

[3] C. 7. 14. 7.   [4] 40. 12. 25. 1.   [5] Cicero, de domo, 29. 78.

[6] Quintil. Inst. Orat. 5. 2. 1.   [7] *Id.* 11. 1. 78.   [8] Martial, Epig. 1. 52.

[9] C. 7. 17. 1. *pr.*

of statements telling a similar story, but differing in details, it is not easy to say what the law really was. One hypothesis is that up to the time of Justinian there was a right in the defeated claimant of liberty to bring the matter up again, either as often as he liked, or for a limited number of times, and that Justinian provided a regular system of appeal, and suppressed the rule, inserting the text of Gaius in a modified form so as to make it represent the current law[1]. Schlossmann[2] observes, with reason, that the text of Gaius looks perfectly genuine, and he distinguishes. He thinks that Justinian, Cicero, and Quintilian, are considering a claim *e libertate*, and laying down the rule that this case could be brought up again if the decision was against liberty, while Gaius is certainly dealing with one *e servitute*. But there are some difficulties in this, perhaps in any, solution. It is not advisable to attach much weight to Cicero's text[3]. He bases his rule on the ancient tradition that *civitas* could not be taken away, but if lost at all was always voluntarily resigned, a principle of which little is left in the Empire. His allusion is to a rule which differs materially in substance from that suggested by the other texts. He speaks of a privilege by which one who has, so to speak, become a slave by judgment, may yet repeatedly make his claim to liberty and *civitas*. Justinian bases the rule he is abolishing on certain *leges*[4], and the language of Martial[5], Quintilian[6] and Justinian seems rather to refer to a necessary precautionary repetition which every *adsertio* had to go through, and none of these texts contains any hint that the rule was confined to the case in which the alleged slave had been defeated. Moreover Justinian's abolition of a rule which gave an alleged slave several chances, if that is what he did, is an odd provision to call a *clementior terminus*. This all points to a conjecture that there was a rule, of which the source is now lost, requiring all *adsertoriae lites* to be gone through twice (or more) before different *iudices*[7], before a decision was come to. The whole thing would be one trial, and would amount to *res iudicata* whichever lost[8]. Such a rule would be a natural descendant of the principle invoked by Cicero. It avoids the apparent conflict created by the text of Gaius, and it gets rid of another difficulty observed by Schlossmann[9]. Constantine, in his enactment as to *circumductio*[10], provided that the slave handed over to the claimant by decree of the magistrate, for lack of an *adsertor*, could renew his claim if he ever found an *adsertor*. There is little point in

---

[1] 40. 12. 25. 1.   So Bethmann-Hollweg, cited Schlossmann, Z. S. S. 13. 228.
[2] *loc. cit.*   [3] Cicero, de domo, 29. 78.
[4] C. 7. 17. 1. *pr.*   Probably not the XII Tables; see his similar language in C. 3. 22. 6.
[5] Epig. 1. 52.   [6] Inst. Orat. 5. 2. 1; 11. 1. 78.
[7] See Quint. Inst. Orat. 11. 1. 78.   *Parte victa* in this text does not imply defeat of the adsertor.
[8] C. 7. 14. 5 appears to refer to a case not proceeded with.   [9] *loc. cit.*
[10] C. Th. 4. 8. 5; *ante*, p. 655. It is possible that the repetition was not required in all cases.

this if he could always do so, since there is no reason to suppose the decree more binding than a judgment. But it is quite intelligible on the view here adopted. It must, however, be admitted that it does not express the same law as that Cicero is discussing : it is necessary to the present contention to suppose that his principle was superseded by express legislation, providing for exceptionally careful trial.

There might be more than one claimant. It is clear that persons claiming lesser rights, such as usufruct or pledge, can raise a *causa liberalis*, although some one is already doing so as owner[1]. In such a case both claims are sent to the same *iudex*, and it is immaterial whether the lesser right is claimed through the same owner or another[2]. If claimants of usufruct and ownership are acting together and one is absent, Gaius doubts whether the case ought to proceed, since the one present may be injured by the carelessness or collusion of the other. He, or more probably Tribonian, settles the point by saying that one case will go on without prejudice to the other, and, if the other claimant appears soon enough, the same *iudex* will hear them both, unless the litigant who appears late has some objection to that *iudex* on the ground, *e.g.*, of enmity[3]. So where two are claiming common ownership a senatusconsult provides that they shall ordinarily go to the same *iudex*. But if two claim separately, each *in solidum*, this is not necessary, since there is not the same danger of a conflicting decision[4].

If there are two claimants of a common ownership and, for some cause, their cases are not tried together, it may happen that one loses and the other wins. What is the result ? Gaius asks the question if the victory of one ought to benefit the other, and says that, if you hold that it does, then the defeated one can sue again, meeting the *exceptio rei iudicatae* by a *replicatio*. If it does not benefit him, to whom does the share go ? Does all go to the one who gained the action ? Does part vest in the opposite party to the suit ? Is it a *res nullius* ? Gaius appears to think it all vests in the winner[5], the reason assigned being that a man cannot be *pro parte* free. In form, Gaius is merely settling the question what is to happen if we reject the view that it may go to the loser. It is to be presumed that he does reject this view, though he does not exactly say so[6]. Julian discusses a similar case[7]: that of two separate claimants *pro parte*, and opposing judgments. The text remarks that the best plan is *eo usque cogi iudices donec consentiant*, but it does not appear how or by whom this is to be done. If it proves

[1] 40. 12. 8. *pr.*   [2] *h. t.* 8. 2.   The claims might be hostile.
[3] *h. t.* 9. *pr.*   [4] *h. t.* 8. 1, 9. 1.
[5] *h. t.* 9. 2, he will have an *actio utilis* to recover it.
[6] 40. 12. 9. 2.   Ulpian gives a like decision in the somewhat similar case of a free man selling himself to two men, one of whom knows of the fraud (*h. t.* 7. 3), but here the loser is a wrongdoer.   [7] 40. 12. 30.

impossible, Sabinus Cassius and Julian agree that all goes to the winner, since it is absurd to talk of a man being half free. The possibility of the loser benefiting by the judgment is not considered. The text adds that, *favore libertatis*, the man is to be free, paying a fair proportion of his value to the winner. Mommsen thinks this last remark is Julian's, but the contrast between this and the earlier part of the text, and the nature of the rule itself strongly suggest the hand of Tribonian. The remark in the beginning of the text that the *iudices*, who have already given judgment, are to have pressure put on them, *donec consentiant*, may be from the same source.

The question of liberty might be entangled or combined with some other question. We have already had occasion to advert to the general rule as to pecuniary causes, not connected with *hereditas* : they are to be suspended so as not to prejudice the *causa liberalis*[1]. If by chance such a case has been tried first it must not be allowed to produce any prejudicial effect[2]. The rule is illustrated in many texts, of which the majority are in one title of the Code. Where A has a complaint against B, who alleges that A is a slave, the Praeses decides the *causa liberalis* first, and then, if the man is declared free, proceeds with the other matter[3]. An accusation is made against a woman. It is claimed, but disputed, that she is an *ingenua*. The *causa liberalis* must be brought first, in order that it may be known how she should be punished[4]. A *causa liberalis* is pending : the alleged dominus seizes something said to belong to the man claimed as a slave. It is clear that the *causa* must be tried before the *furtum*, and if it is *e servitute*, no rule is necessary. But if it is *e libertate*, he must give the thing back, security being given *rem salvam fore*. If no security can be obtained, the thing must be given to a *sequester* till the decision, an allowance being made, if necessary, out of it, for the man's expenses. If it was stolen before any question of status was raised and, a decision being given that the taker is bound to return it, he raises the question of status to avoid doing so, he will have to restore it without any security[5].

On the same principle, if a *hereditas* is claimed, the question of the testator's status, if raised, must be settled first[6], though an interdict for the production of his will may issue meanwhile, as this can have no prejudicing effect[7]. Where a man is claiming an inheritance, and his claim is disputed on the allegation that he is a slave, but his freedom is

---

1 Laid down as a general rule by Claudius, 40. 15. 4.
2 C. 7. 16. 2.   3 C. 7. 19. 1.
4 *h. t.* 3. Other illustrations shew that it was immaterial whether the *causa* is first set up and the other issue raised before it is decided, or the question of status is raised as a reply to a claim : in both cases the *causa* must be decided first. See, *e.g.*, C. 7. 19. 5, 6 ; C. 9. 35. 10 ; D. 40. 12. 24. 4 ; 9. 4. 42. *pr.* These last are noxal cases : as to certain questions of procedure herein, *ante*, p. 108.
5 C. 7. 19. 7, *fin.*   6 C. 3. 31. 8.   7 43. 5. 1. 7.

not claimed under that will, the *causa liberalis* must be tried, and the will may not be used as evidence that he is free[1]. A similar rule is laid down in the Code, but the text goes on to say that if a claim for a *hereditas* is pending, and the defence is raised that the plaintiff is really a slave, a *causa liberalis* is to be set on foot. But, it seems, the action for the *hereditas* is to proceed and if judgment is now given for him in that action, he need prove no more in the *causa liberalis*. The point seems to be that as he is really *in libertate* the burden of proof is not on him. The text is obscure[2] and it may mean that the court will decide the issue of status incidentally[3].

Where the liberty is claimed under the will, new rules apply. The validity of the will must be decided first: this is provided by senatus-consult, to avoid prejudicing that question by the decision of the *causa liberalis*[4]. Thus if the testator has been killed the *causa liberalis* will not be decided till the cause of death has been investigated[5]. Of course, *res iudicata* on a point arising out of the will will not affect the liberty[6]. Trajan provides that a *causa liberalis* must be postponed till a pending *querela* is decided[7], but Pius lays it down that there need be no postponement to await a *querela*. He enacts that where a man, freed and instituted by will, has his status disputed, and is in *de facto* possession of the *hereditas*, he can refuse to meet the *liberalis causa* on the ground that he is prepared to meet, first, claims affecting the validity of the will. This, says Pius, is because the other side can at once hasten matters by bringing the *querela*. But, if he is not in possession, a reasonable time must be allowed him in which to bring the *hereditatis petitio*, and if he does not, the *causa liberalis* will proceed[8].

The matter might be further complicated by the Carbonian edict. If the claimant is alleged to be a supposititious child, and in fact a slave, the Carbonian edict requires the whole matter to be postponed till he is *pubes*. But this has nothing to do with the *causa liberalis*: it would be equally true if he were not alleged to be a slave[9].

Claims of *Ingenuitas e libertinitate* are not within our real subject, but they are so closely connected with it, and so similar in principle, that it may be well to say a word or two about them. We have already seen

---

[1] 5. 3. 7. 2, Pius. Probably declaratory.　　[2] C. 7. 19. 2. It may be corrupt.
[3] Gaius tells us (40. 12. 25. *pr.*) that if a *legatum optionis* is left to a man who is claiming liberty, *aliunde*, the same rule applies as if it were a *hereditas*. The question is whether he can be compelled to exercise the *optio*. We have already discussed the doubt and Justinian's solution in the case of *hereditas* (*ante*, p. 664); the rule is to apply here, *mutatis mutandis*.
[4] 5. 3. 7. *pr.*　　[5] 40. 12. 7. 4.
[6] Thus where an action claiming a legacy has been lost, this is immaterial in the *causa liberalis*, as *res inter alios acta*, 44. 2. 1; C. 7. 16. 2; cp. C. 7. 19. 2.
[7] 5. 3. 7. *pr.*　　[8] *h. l.* 1.
[9] 37. 10. 3. 11, 6. 3. We have already seen that in any case the trial may, for cause shewn, be postponed to puberty, 37. 10. 3. 11; *ante*, p. 659.

that no such claim could in any case be made, after a lapse of five years from a traceable manumission[1]. Such cases would normally arise in connexion with property questions, and, apparently, they were always tried by *praeiudicium*[2]. Suetonius speaks of a recuperatory procedure[3], but probably the reference to *recuperatores* was made only when, as in the case he records, the claim was *e latinitate*. The earliest traceable case of one is of Nero's time, where the forced nature of the transaction suggests a *cognitio*[4]. Gaius speaks, however, of a *formula*[5], and Justinian uses language with the same implication[6]. But it is clear from the language of Diocletian, who directed it to be tried without any deputy, by the *Praeses*, that this was already a possible mode of trial[7]. It was of less social importance than a *causa liberalis* and thus, though there is no evidence about arbitration, it is clear that it might be decided by *iusiurandum*[8]. Though a pact could not give *ingenuitas*, it is clear that a *transactio* would bind the patron to regard the man as an *ingenuus*, though it would not bind any other person[9]. We have seen that *ingenuitas* could not be disputed after a man's death[10], though the question might be raised to shew that an apparent *libertinus* was really an *ingenuus*[11]. Conversely, one who had allowed himself to be sold and had afterwards been freed could not claim *ingenuitas*[12]. In the case of unwillingness, of the party directly affected, to proceed, others might act for him as in a *causa liberalis*[13], and if, a decision having been given against him, he declined to appeal, his *paterfamilias* might do so, within the proper time, as if it had been his own case[14]. The burden of proof, says Ulpian, is on him if he is claiming *e libertinitate*, and on the claimant if it is *ex ingenuitate*, but if he wishes to take the burden of proof in order to obtain a more favourable judgment, he is to be permitted to do so[15]. Elsewhere he tells us that if the man admits being a *libertus*, but alleges that he is a *libertus* of another person, the ordinary *praeiudicium* will be given whichever party asks for it, and that in such a case the burden of proof is always on the patron[16]. There seems little

[1] *Ante*, p. 650.
[2] 40. 14. 6.   Based on the Edict, In. 4. 6. 13.   See Lenel, Ed. Perp. (2) § 141.
[3] Suetonius, Vesp. 3.   [4] Tac. Ann. 13. 27; D. 12. 4. 3. 5.
[5] G. 4. 44.   [6] In. 4. 6. 13.
[7] C. 3. 3. 2; cp. C. 4. 1. 6; 7. 14. 5.   [8] C. 4. 1. 6.
[9] C. 7. 14. 8.   [10] 40. 15. 1. 3.   At least after a *pronuntiatio* of *ingenuitas*.
[11] *h. l.* 4.
[12] 40. 12. 40. Mommsen.   The case might be tried in absence of a party, duly summoned, but in case of absence beyond seas there might be nine months delay to allow of his appearance, C. 7. 16. 40; C. Th. 2. 7. 3 = C. 3. 11. 7.
[13] 40. 12. 3. 3.   [14] 49. 4. 2. 2.
[15] 22. 3. 14.   As to amount of proof, we are told that *instrumenta* and *argumenta* are to be used, as *soli testes non sufficiunt*, C. 4. 20. 2.   This rule, which may have applied to *causae liberales*, has many possible meanings which are discussed at great length by the early commentators (see Haenel, Diss. Domm. 406).   No doubt here as in *causae liberales*, lost *instrumenta* would suffice, C. 4. 19. 20.   The loss would be proved by *soli testes*.   Probably the rule means no more than that the oath of his friends that he was *ingenuus* would not suffice.
[16] 40. 14. 6.

reason for the exception if the claim is *e libertinitate,* which perhaps it would rarely be.

Pending the hearing he is in the position in which he apparently was when the issue was raised[1]. The judgment will be *ingenuum esse* or *non esse libertum Auli Agerii,* according as he or the claimant had the burden of proof[2]. There was a right of appeal[3]: apart from this there is no evidence of any right or need of rehearing[4]. As between the parties it was a *res iudicata,* and *pro veritate* however false[5]. And thus in the case of Paris where the judgment was glaringly false and compelled by the Emperor, he could recover what he had paid to secure his manumission[6].

It is clear that property relations would need adjustment. Paul and Pomponius tell[7] us that the successful claimant of *ingenuitas* could keep what he had acquired unless it was *ex re manumissoris,* but must return what was *ex re,* together with gifts from him, and of course what had been taken without his consent. Both of them are commenting on the words of a senatusconsult which dealt with the matter, shortly stated elsewhere as enacting that *quae de domo manumissoris habent ibi relinquant,* words which there too are explained as covering even legacies by the late owner to the *libertus* as such[8]. A rule of this kind was necessary, in view of the fact that all that such apparent *liberti* acquired was their own, while their position in their supposed patron's household gave them opportunities of acquisition through him, and in matters which really concerned him, somewhat to his detriment, and such as they certainly would not have enjoyed as *ingenui.* The rule is not, here, open to any such objection as that which can be made to it as applied to claims of *ingenuitas ex servitute*[9].

These claims of liberty and *ingenuitas* were of course mere nullities if there was no *iustus contradictor, i.e.* the other side made no genuine claim to be patron or *dominus*[10]. But, apart from this there was obvious room for collusion, and there were severe rules dealing with this possibility. In one text we are told that where a slave committed *stuprum* with his *domina,* and was by her collusion, with a pretence of captivity, declared free and *ingenuus,* this was void[11]. And Gaius says that anyone who proved that a *causa liberalis* had been gone through collusively, and the man declared free, had a right, by a senatusconsult of Domitian's

---

1 C. 4. 55. 4.   2 22. 3. 14.   3 49. 4. 2. 2.
4 C. 7. 14. 5 does not speak of rehearing.   5 1. 5. 25.
6 12. 4. 3. 5; Tac. Ann. 13. 27.   7 40. 12. 32; 40. 14. 3.
8 C. 7. 14. 1.
9 *Ante,* p. 666. It is quite possible that the whole allusion to slavery in 40. 12. 32 is interpolated. It may be added that a *libertinus* who loses his case does not lose his position as a *libertinus,* C. 7. 14. 13, and it is an *iniuria* to attack *ingenuitas* without reason, *h. t.* 5.
10 *h. t.* 1.   11 C. 7. 20. 1.

time, to claim the slave[1]. In the case of claims of *ingenuitas e liberti-nitate* texts are more numerous. A *senatusconsultum* Ninnianum provided penalties for such collusion, and a reward for the detector[2]. Marcus Aurelius seems to have legislated freely on the matter. He provides that collusion as to *ingenuitas* can be shewn at any time within five years from the judgment[3]: the *quinquennium* being *continuum*, but not running till the person whose collusion is in question is *pubes*, as, otherwise, since he could postpone the case, the proceeding might be rendered impossible. It is enough that it be begun within the five years[4], and time does not run to bar the real patron, if the original decree was given without his knowledge, *alio agente*[5]. The collusion may be shewn even by an *extraneus*, if he is a person who is qualified *postulare pro alio*[6], and if several come together to shew collusion there must be an enquiry to see which is the proper person on grounds of *mores*, age, and interest[7]. We are told by Hermogenianus that a judgment in favour of *ingenuitas* can be retracted for collusion only once[8]. This remark may mean that it can be attacked only once[9], but this is open to the objection that it would provide a way to new collusion. As the same judgment could hardly be retracted twice, it is possible that the meaning may be, that if, after a decree has been "retracted" for collusion, the claim of *ingenuitas* is set up again, and the decision repeated, there can now be no further attack on the ground of collusion[10].

When the judgment is retracted, the detector becomes patron[11], and the original patron loses all patronal rights[12]. The man becomes a *libertinus* again, but only from the decision[13], for this is not an appeal, and the *res iudicata* is *pro veritate* till rescinded. He loses the *ius anuli aurei*, if he had it before the collusive decree[14].

The normal case is of course of one patron and we hear little of the more complex case. Papinian, however, discusses the case of one declared *ingenuus* by the collusion of one of his patrons, the collusion being detected by another. He decides that the alleged *ingenuus* loses the *ius anuli aurei*, and certain *alimenta* due to him from a third patron[15], and it may be presumed that for the future two parts of the *iura patronatus* vest in the detector.

[1] 40. 16. 1. Ninnianum? C. 7. 20. 2.   [2] C. 7. 20. 2.
[3] 40. 10. 2; 40. 16. 2. *pr.*   [4] 40. 16. 2. 1—3.
[5] 40. 14. 1, 5.   [6] 40. 16. 2. 4.
[7] *h. t.* 5. 1.   [8] *h. l. pr.*
[9] Otto and Schilling, *ad h. l.*
[10] Death of the man affected ends the matter, 40. 15. 1. 3.
[11] 2. 4. 8. 1.   [12] C. 6. 4. 4. 6.   [13] 40. 16. 4.
[14] 40. 10. 2.   [15] *h. t.* 1. 1.

CHAPTER XXIX.

EFFECT AFTER MANUMISSION OF EVENTS DURING SLAVERY.
NATURALIS OBLIGATIO.

THE rules affecting this matter are of gradual development: they are, in the main, a result of three principles, not wholly consistent with each other, and are themselves modified by the increasing recognition of the individuality of the slave. The three principles are:

1. *Noxa caput sequitur,* a rule applied to delicts[1].
2. In matter of contract, the slave *naturaliter obligat et obligatur*[2].
3. The slave on manumission becomes a new man (and on re-enslavement, another man again[3]). The change is analogous to *capitis deminutio,* but it does not amount to this, as a slave has no *caput. Servile caput nullum ius habet, ideo nec minui potest*[4] *: servus manumissus capite non minuitur, quia nullum caput habet*[5].

So[6] far as concerns delicts to the slave, there is not much to be said. The only one which can well be conceived is *iniuria,* and we are told, emphatically, that he can have no remedy for that after manumission[7]. A theft of the man, or *damnum* to him, is a delict against his *dominus,* with whom the right of action remains, notwithstanding manumission of the slave[8]. If the slave stolen or injured were instituted and freed by his *dominus,* he would presumably acquire these rights of action as he did others. This is implied by two texts which deal with an exceptional case[9]. We are told by Ulpian, Marcian and Marcellus that if a slave who has been injured is instituted by his *dominus,* with liberty, and then dies, his *heres* will have no *actio* Aquilia. Marcian gives as the reason the fact that the case is now in a position in which the right of action could not possibly have arisen. Marcellus cites from Sabinus the reason that the *heres* could not have an action which

---

[1] *Ante,* pp. 106 *sqq.*   [2] 44. 7. 14.   [3] 46. 3. 98. 8.
[4] 4. 5. 3. 1.   [5] In. 1. 16. 4.
[6] As to servile cognation, *ante,* pp. 76 *sqq.*
[7] 47. 10. 30. *pr.* As to delicts to the *peculium, ante,* p. 194.
[8] 47. 2. 46. *pr.* So of *damnum* to the man, 9. 2. 15. 1.   [9] 9. 2. 15. 1—16, 36. 1.

would not have been available to the deceased. The reasons are the same : a man cannot have or transmit an action for his own death. The reasoning implies that he would have had an action for injury short of death, or for theft. There may be actions for injury to[1], or theft of[2], a freeman. There is thus no reason why the instituted slave should not inherit the action. The text of Marcellus goes on to say that if the slave instituted after injury, who died, had had a *coheres*, the *coheres* would have had the action[3].

The law as to the liability after manumission for a delict committed against a third person without the master's authority presents little difficulty. The general rule is that a slave who commits such a delict is liable, personally, and remains so, by virtue of the rule, *noxa caput sequitur*, after he is freed. As Ulpian says, *servi ex delicto obligantur et si manumittantur obligati remanent*[4]. The word *remanent* shews that it is the same obligation: there is here no question of a *naturalis obligatio* distinct from the *obligatio civilis*, and surviving the manumission. It may be remembered that *capite minuti* were still liable for their delicts[5]. But though he may thus be liable for *furtum*, he is not liable as a *fur manifestus*, even though he is found with the thing, for though it is the beginning of his liability to action, it is not the beginning of the theft[6]. The rule applies not only to what are expressly called *delicta*, but to anything which created a noxal obligation. Thus it applies to cases of *dolus*[7] and *opus novum*[8]. Here, as elsewhere, the liability for *dolus* depends on the absence of another remedy. Where a *libertus* contracted *in fraudem patroni* with a certain slave, and the slave was afterwards freed, the remedy was not against him but against the *libertus*, he being the person whose fraud is contemplated in the *actio* Faviana[9]. Pernice[10], while he recognises that the liability of a slave for a delict committed under *iussum* existed in the republic, considers that his liability in the same way for what he did without *iussum*, was an introduction of Labeo. This way of putting the matter seems to be due to his thesis of the gradual recognition of the capacity of a slave independently of his master. But this view has no a priori probability. It does not really make any less demand on recognition of the slave's individuality, which, for that matter, was already so fully recognised

---

[1] *h. t.* 13. *pr.*
[2] 47. 2. 14. 13, 38. 1.
[3] 9. 2. 36. 1.   *Pro parte*, see the Gloss.
[4] 9. 4. 24 ; 44. 7. 14 ; G. 4. 77 ; P. 2. 31. 8.
[5] 4. 5. 2. 3.   Liability after manumission for *furtum*, C. 4. 14. 4 ; D. 13. 1. 15 ; 47. 2. 44. 2, 65 ; *Damnum*, 9. 2. 48 ; *post*, p. 680.
[6] 47. 2. 7. *pr.*
[7] 16. 3. 21.
[8] 43. 24. 14.   An owner, misled by his slave as to the latter's qualities, sold him. The buyer freed him. The freedman is liable *de dolo*, unless the fraud was such, and so connected with the sale, as to avoid it, 4. 3. 7. *pr.*   One entitled to freedom who allowed himself to be sold to a *bona fide* buyer was liable when freed to the *actio in factum, ante,* p. 433 ; D. 40. 5. 10. 2. One who prostituted an *ancilla peculiaris* could be noted after he was free, 3. 2. 4. 3.
[9] 38. 5. 1. 24 ; cp. 4. 3. 1. 8—5.
[10] Pernice, Labeo, 1. 119.

in criminal and religious law[1], that, long before Labeo, nothing new was involved in a recognition of his personal capacity for delict. Moreover liability for what was done *mero motu* corresponded to a much greater need. In the other case, there was always, after the manumission, the liability of the master, and he would prove, in most cases, the better defendant: in this case the master would absolutely destroy any chance of compensation to the injured person by freeing the slave, if the man's liability were not recognised. And, as we have seen, this manumission need involve no loss to him: he could agree for a payment. The texts on which Pernice mainly rests his view do not really support it. That of Alfenus[2], which is a little confused, and deals with both crime and civil injury, hints at no difference of principle, and says *quamvis domini iussu servus piraticam fecisset, iudicium in eum post libertatem reddi oportet*. This implies clearly that the liability was more obvious if there had been no *iussum* by the *dominus*. The text of Ulpian[3] in which Labeo is cited as having laid it down that a man is liable after manumission for *iniuria* committed *iussu domini*, argues that he has committed a *noxa*, that *noxa caput sequitur;* and that he ought not to obey his master in everything, *i.e.* that obedience to *iussum* is not necessarily a defence. Here the rule that *noxa caput sequitur*, even to freedom, is treated as a standing rule, and liability for what is done without *iussum* regarded as the more obvious. What Labeo laid down, perhaps for the first time, was that *atrox iniuria* was one of those things in which it was no excuse to the *manumissus* to plead his master's authorisation or command.

In one case there is a special praetorian remedy, an *actio annalis in factum*, for twofold damages, *i.e.* where a slave, freed by the will, deals in any way with the estate so as to lessen what will come to the *heres*[4]. The reason for the existence of this remedy is that he has not committed *furtum*[5], since the act must have been after the death of the *dominus* and before any entry[6]. As he will be free at the moment of entry the *heres* will be able to do nothing to him, unless indeed he so "contrects" after the *aditio*, as to make himself guilty of *furtum*[7]. It is essential that he has been guilty of *dolus* or at least of *culpa lata*[8]. In strictness the action is available only if there is an immediate gift of liberty[9]; it is, however, immaterial whether it is direct or fideicommissary, since it is clearly laid down by M. Aurelius and others that a simple fideicommissary gift is not to be delayed on merely pecuniary grounds[10].

---

[1] *Ante*, pp. 73, 91.   [2] 44. 7. 20.   [3] 47. 10. 17. 7.
[4] 47. 4. 1. *pr.*   [5] 47. 2. 69.   [6] 47. 4. 1. 2, 8.
[7] *h. t.* 1. 1.
[8] *h. t.* 1. 2, 8.   The action is available only in absence of any other remedy (*h. t.* 1. 16), but covers all kinds of injury to the interest of the *heres*, details *h. t.* 1. 10—15.
[9] *h. t.* 1. 3.
[10] 47. 4. 1. 7.   As to the arbitration mentioned in the text, *ante*, p. 520.

Thus the action ought not to be available at all in cases of conditional manumission, and so the law is laid down by Gaius and Ulpian[1]. But elsewhere both Ulpian and a writer as early as Labeo[2] lay it down that, even in the case of conditional liberty, the action is available if the liberty supervenes very soon after the wrong was done.

A wholly different rule applies where the delict was committed against the slave's master. Here the *dominus* can bring no action against the slave after he is free[3]: in such a case *noxa non sequitur*[4]. If a slave stole from one of common owners the same rule was applied: there was no noxal action[5]. On the other hand it must be noted that in all these cases, if the man, after he was free, dealt with the thing he had stolen from his master, the ordinary liabilities for *furtum* arose[6]. The basis of this rule excluding action where the wrongdoer is or becomes the property of the injured person is not very clear. In most texts it is made to rest on the fact that there can be no *iudicium* between a man and his own slave[7], and on the consideration that one who can punish has no need to take legal proceedings[8], and the reason for its non-existence after alienation is put on the ground: *neque actio quae non fuit ab initio nata oriri potest*[9]. Mandry observes that these merely formal grounds would have been set aside if there had been no deeper reason. He concludes that it rests on the complete absence of legal effect in a delict, between master and slave, expressed in some texts by the statement that there is no obligation at all[10]. This might well be the basis of the Proculian distinction, since in the case of delicts to one who afterwards became *dominus* there certainly was an obligation to begin with. But this itself may be said to be little more than a formal ground, for the lawyers saw no difficulty in finding an *obligatio*, where there was a *peculium*, even to give an indemnification for delict[11], so far as the *peculium* would go. There was, however, no need to extend the conception: to have given an *actio* in the present case would have satisfied no economic necessity[12], and as it would have involved giving a noxal action against an alienee, it might have caused great injustice and abuse.

Fresh considerations arise if the master was in any way privy to the action of the slave he has since freed[13]. There is a general rule or maxim

---

[1] 47. 4. 1. 3, 2.   [2] *h. t.* 1. 3, 4; *h. t.* 3.   See also *ante*, p. 255.
[3] 47. 2. 17. 1; G. 4. 78; C. 4. 14. 6.   There seem to have been disputes.
[4] C. 3. 41. 1.   A rescript of Severus mentioned by Ulpian (4. 4. 11. *pr.*) must have been declaratory.   The school dispute as to the case of acquisition of the wrongdoer by the injured party after the fact shews that the main rule was older, 47. 2. 18; G. 4. 78; In. 4. 8. 6; *ante*, p. 107.
[5] 47. 2. 62. *pr.*; *ante*, pp. 107, 374.   [6] 4. 4. 11. *pr.*; 47. 2. 17. 1.
[7] See Mandry, Familiengüterrecht, 1. 354 *sqq.*
[8] 47. 2. 17. *pr.*; 47. 4. 1. 1; see Mandry, *loc. cit.*
[9] Mandry, *op. cit.* 1. 358.   [10] *e.g.* G. 4. 78.
[11] *Ante*, p. 223.   [12] As to the case of a duty to free, *ante*, p 520.
[13] *Ante*, pp. 114 *sqq.*

several times expressed that as a slave is bound to obey his master, he is not liable for what he has done under orders, though his master is[1]. But the exact limits of this exemption are not easily made out. It is probable that the law changed from time to time. The rule in crime may not have been in all respects the same as that in delict. The master's privity may in a given case have been something less than actual command. The act done may have been so serious as not to allow the excuse of obedience to the *dominus*. These factors are combined in the texts dealing with the matter.

Notwithstanding some loose language of Celsus, cited and corrected by Ulpian, it is fairly clear that we need consider nothing short of actual command: the master, *sciens, qui non prohibuit*, is personally liable but in no way excuses the slave[2].

The rule as recorded by Alfenus Varus at the end of the republic was that a slave is not excused by the order of his master in anything in the nature of a *facinus*. So, later, Paul[3] says that a slave must not obey his master *in facinoribus*, and Ulpian says[4] that slaves are excused for obeying their masters in matters *quae non habent atrocitatem*. But as to the exact position of the line between *atrocia* and trivial things it is not easy to be precise[5]. Ulpian quotes Labeo as holding that *iniuria, iussu domini*, rendered the slave liable after liberty—*noxa caput sequitur*[6]. It is probable that Labeo was speaking of *atrox iniuria*. Conversely Ulpian agrees with Celsus that command of the master excuses the slave for wrongs under the *lex* Aquilia[7]. Perhaps the true inference is that the distinction between *facinora* and lesser matters was not clearly defined at any time, and there was a tendency to narrow the exemption[8].

The remedies against the master and the slave are alternative, and thus if the master is sued, the freedman is released, not it would seem *ipso iure*, but by an *exceptio rei iudicatae*[9]. We have already considered the case of freedom supervening while a noxal action against the master is pending: the action was transferred, but there is, as we saw, much controversy as to the form of the transfer[10]. The matter of delict may be left with the remark that obedience to a *tutor* or *curator* is on the same level as obedience to a *dominus*[11].

---

[1] *e.g.* 9. 4. 2. 1; 35. 2. 13; 50. 17. 169. *pr.*
[2] 9. 4. 2. 1; *h. t.* 5, 6. As to distinction between *sciens* and *iubens, ante,* p. 114.
[3] 25. 2. 21. 1.   [4] 43. 24. 11. 7 = 50. 17. 157. *pr.*
[5] Alfenus gives as *facinora* (44. 7. 20), piracy, homicide, *furtum*, and *vis*, if there was *maleficium* in it, not a mere squabble in a claim of right.
[6] 47. 10. 17. 7.   [7] 9. 4. 2. 1.
[8] See Pernice, Labeo, 1. 118, and Mandry, *op. cit.* 1. 383; D. 9. 2. 37. *pr.* and 50. 17. 169. *pr.* are too general.
[9] 47. 8. 3; cp. 47. 2. 84. 1. It is not obvious why he should be released at all. Ordinarily where two are liable for a delict, judgment against one does not release the other. 9. 2. 11. 2.
[10] *Ante,* p. 108. See Koschaker, Translatio iudicii, pp. 199 *sqq.*
[11] 43. 24. 11. 7 = 50. 17. 157. *pr.*

The very similar rules in criminal law have already been considered[1]: all that need be said here is that if a criminal slave is freed and afterwards condemned, he is punished as he would have been had he been still a slave[2].

In relation to acquisition of property there is not much to be said, inasmuch as these transactions are, usually, so to speak, instantaneous. Acquisitions during slavery go to the master, even though *ex peculiari causa*. Those after liberty go to the man himself: the transition from slavery to freedom does not affect the matter, though there might be difficulties of fact as to the capacity in which the freedman received the *res*. *Mutatis mutandis*, the same is true of alienations. There are, however, a few exceptional cases. We know that a slave's possession *in re peculiari* is the master's[3]. If, however, he continues to possess secretly after he is free, his *peculium* not having been given to him, and his master subsequently gets the thing back, there is no *accessio possessionum*[4]. He is another man[5], and his possession is not dependent on, but adverse to, his master. The question arises whether if a slave acquires a *res* in good faith for the *peculium*, and is in process of usucapting it, and is freed and retains it secretly, he can complete the usucapion. If he receives an acquisition *ex re peculiari*, after he is freed without *peculium*, he does not usucapt: the *initium possessionis* was not in good faith[6]. Probably the decision would be the same in our present case, for it is only on freedom that he himself acquires possession: the earlier possession was his master's.

It is in connexion with wills that the most important questions arise in this matter. It is clear that an *alienus servus* instituted and freed during the testator's life can acquire the *hereditas* for himself[7]. The same rule applies to legacies and *fideicommissa*[8]. The extension of the principle to cover changes of status after the death and before entry, or *dies cedens*, is due to the desire to avoid intestacy. Its extension to legacies in the same case with no special reason is an instance of a common practice which we have already observed. The general rule here laid down is illustrated by some complex cases[9]. There were two *heredes*. A slave was left to one of them and money to the slave. The slave was freed *vivo testatore*. He acquires the whole legacy, although it might appear that the gift ought to have been valid only as

---

[1] *Ante*, p. 94.   [2] 48. 19. 1. 1.   [3] *Ante*, p. 200.
[4] 41. 2. 13. 8.   [5] 46. 3. 98. 8.   [6] 41. 4. 7. 2.
[7] G. 2. 189; Ulp. 22. 12, 13; In. 2. 14. 1.
[8] 30. 114. 10; 36. 2. 5. 7; Ulp. 24. 23. The fact that he is a new man is disregarded: the will operates only on death, being ambulatory till then.
[9] A is instituted and substituted. He enters, is enslaved and, later, freed. He can still take under the substitution, 28. 6. 43. 3. A legacy is left, *in annos singulos*, to a slave. If he is freed he still acquires: the gift cedes every year, 36. 2. 12. 2. A slave is legated and freed *inter vivos*. A later codicil gives a legacy to him: it is good, 30. 91. 5. A slave is left to T and money to the slave: there may be a valid *fc.* to give the money to the man when free, 30. 91. 4.

to half, inasmuch as it was, as to half, a legacy to the *heres*, of what
would have been his in any case, and it could not convalesce by the
manumission or alienation of the slave, by reason of the *regula* Catoniana. But Julian overrides these points by remarking[1] (by way of
proof that the whole vests *in persona servi*) that, if the *heres* to whom
he was *legatus* had not entered, he could have claimed the whole
from the other. The point for us, however, is the small one, that the
intervening manumission leaves him entitled to claim[2].

These rules preserving the provisions of a will are in sharp contrast
with those applied on intestacy. We have already seen how far servile
relationships were recognised after liberty[3]. Here we need consider
only the effect of enslavement followed by manumission. The rule is
clear and simple. One who is made a slave does not on manumission
reacquire cognatic rights[4], and, conversely, his relatives will reacquire
no rights of succession to him. His mother has ceased to be his mother,
though the text indicates that there had been doubts which were ended
by a rescript of Caracalla[5]. The same rule applied where the lapse
into slavery occurred after death and before entry on the *hereditas*[6].
Several texts deal with the matter of testation from the other point of
view. A person uncertain of his status, even though really freed or
ingenuus, could not make a will[7], and, consistently, a will made by a
slave could not be valid, even though he were freed before he died[8].
The same rules applied to *fideicommissa*, at any rate so far as they were
contained in wills. If, however, a slave makes a *fideicommissum* without
a will, and dies free, Ulpian appears to say that his *fideicommissum* is
valid, as operating only at his death, provided he has not changed his
mind[9]. The rule is a remarkable one. There is no hint that in
classical law a person who could not make a will could make a *fideicommissum*. The language of Justinian as to codicils is opposed to
such a view[10], and Gaius[11] mentions no such point in setting out the
existing and the obsolete points of difference between legacies and
fideicommissa. Ulpian[12] lays down a rule that those can make *fideicommissa* who can make wills. There is no sign that it is enough if
the maker is qualified before he dies. Our present text is also from
Ulpian. In other parts of it he says that *deportati* and those uncertain
of their status cannot make *fideicommissa*, because they cannot make

---

[1] 30. 91. 2.
[2] As to the case of two institutions of a slave, see 29. 2. 80. 2; discussed *ante*, p. 141. As
to the case of legacy of the slave and legacy to him, and ademption, see 34. 4. 27. 1; 18. 1. 6. *pr.*;
h. t. 34. 2; discussed *ante*, p. 149.
[3] *Ante*, p. 76.   [4] 38. 8. 7.   [5] 38. 17. 2. 2.
[6] *h. t.* 1. 4. An apparent exception stated in the text only confirms the rule: a *servus poenae*,
restitutus, is reintegrated in all his rights, *ante*, p. 411.
[7] 28. 1. 14, 15, Pius *rescripsit*.   [8] 28. 1. 19.
[9] 32. 1. *pr.*, 1. Yet he is another man, 46. 3. 98. 8.   [10] In. 2. 25. *pr.*
[11] G. 2. 284 *sqq.*   [12] Ulp. 25. 4.

wills[1]. A later passage in the text observes that if a *deportatus* does make a codicil and is *restitutus indulgentia principis*, the *fideicommissum* will be valid *si modo in eadem voluntate duravit*[2]. But this case is less significant than ours, since such a complete restoration would restore the validity of a will[3]. The style is rather that of a legislator, and the rule may be from the compilers[4].

Apart from *naturalis obligatio*, questions may arise as to payments to the man, after he is free, in respect of transactions during slavery[5]. Where a slave was appointed to collect debts and continued collecting them after he was free, this might be *furtum* in him[6], but if the debtors were not aware that he was free the payment was a good discharge, though the original transaction was by the *dominus*[7]. If it had been a transaction of the *peculium*, the payment discharged, even though the payer did know of the freedom, if he did not know that the *peculium* had been adeemed[8]. If he did know this, his handing over the money did not discharge his debt to the *dominus*: it was not a payment but a *donatio* to the freedman[9]. On the same principle we are told that, if there was in all respects good faith, return to the man of a thing deposited by him discharged the obligation, though he had been freed[10]. The rule is old: Paul cites Alfenus as saying that the test question is whether the transaction was either *peculiaris* or with consent of the master. If it was either, the money may be paid to the slave after freedom, provided there is no circumstance from which the other party ought to infer that the *dominus* did not wish it to be so paid[11]. So again, Ulpian rests on the authority of Sabinus the rule that good faith means ignorance that he has been freed[12]. There is here no case of *naturalis obligatio*, but this rule, like the recognition of such *obligatio*, is a result of the acceptance of the fact that a slave[13] is at natural law a man like another.

In the region of contract and the like the basis of the law is the conception of the slave as capable of *naturalis obligatio*. The exact method and period of the recognition of this principle have been much discussed, but they are points on which there can be little more than conjecture. The recognition is doubtless connected with that of debts to and from the *peculium*. Such debts were recognised even between slave and master, in republican times[14], but it is unlikely that any general theory of natural obligation of the slave is so old. Pernice[15] is

1 32. 1. *pr.*, 2.   2 *h. l.* 5.   3 28. 3. 6. 12.
4 Vangerow justifies it, arguing from the words *quasi nunc datum* (Pand. § 540), on the view that, at least originally, a *fideicommissum* needed no form, and its *initium* might be regarded as occurring at any moment, *e.g.* death, if the maker has not changed his mind.
5 *Ante*, pp. 158, 163, 202.   6 46. 3. 18.   7 *Ibid.*; 12. 1. 41.
8 46. 3. 18.   9 41. 4. 7. 2; cp. 17. 1. 12. 2.
10 16. 3. 11.   11 46. 3. 35; as to 44. 7. 14, *post*, p. 699.
12 16. 3. 11.   13 *Ante*, p. 73. See Machelard, Obligations naturelles, 188.
14 15. 1. 9. 3; Mandry, *op. cit.* 1. 370.   15 Pernice, Labeo, 1. 150 *sqq.*

of opinion that it is a development of the imperial lawyers and unknown
to Labeo. He is inclined to see distinct origins for the recognition of
naturalis obligatio in the slave. In relation to the *dominus* he thinks
it is merely the recognition of a long existing practice. As regards
extranei he considers it the result of a gradual change of doctrine, as the
result of which the *heres*, and not the *libertus*, was made liable *de
peculio* on earlier transactions[1]. The point is that this had the effect
of completely freeing the *libertus* from any liability, and the theory of
naturalis obligatio came in to modify this. This appears to be practically another way of saying that the *obligatio* was most important as
between slave and master during slavery and at the moment of release,
while in relation to *extranei* it was most important after the man was
free. Hence as against the master it is closely related to the *peculium* :
as regards *extranei* it soon frees itself from this association. In each
case it satisfies an obvious economic need[2]. The case of the slave is
the most frequently treated case of *naturalis obligatio*, and is in all
probability the original[3].

Whether Pernice's distinction be treated as fundamental or not, it
is clear that the two cases, subserving different needs, develop on somewhat different lines, and they can best be treated separately.

A. Transactions between the slave and his master. Such obligations can of course exist during the slavery[4]. They constitute additions
to, or deductions from, the *peculium*, for the purpose of the *actio de
peculio*[5], and it is not easy to see any other importance they could
have[6]. We are repeatedly told that there may be natural debts
between slave and master and that they are reckoned in the *peculium*[7].
It must be remembered that a debt to the *dominus* took precedence of
other debts[8]. Thus where the *res peculiares* were worth only 10, and
the slave owed his *dominus* 10 and an outsider 10, the *res peculiares*
belonged to the estate of the *dominus*[9]. But there was no debt unless
there was a *peculium*. Thus where a slave A owed a slave B, of the
same *dominus*, certain money, B could not claim anything on that
account from his *dominus*, until A had a *peculium*[10]. Such obligations
may arise from any transaction[11], even from payments in lieu of noxal

---

[1] *Ante*, pp. 230 *sqq.*
[2] Mandry remarks (*op. cit.* 1. 344) that 12. 6. 13, which says that payment of *fideiussor* of a
slave's debt is irrecoverable, because the slave is naturally liable, is giving the motive of the rule
in the guise of a consequence. On the question whether *naturalis obligatio* is the expression of
a new philosophy of legal duty, see Machelard, *op. cit.*, Généralisation, and authorities there
cited.
[3] As to this and the various uses of the word *naturalis*, see Gradenwitz, Natur und Sklave,
3, 26, 27, 35, 41.
[4] 33. 8. 16.   [5] *Ante*, pp. 220 *sqq.*   [6] Mandry, *op. cit.* 1. 157.
[7] 15. 1. 7. 6; 33. 8. 6. 4.   [8] *Ante*, p. 221.   [9] 35. 2. 56. 2.
[10] 15. 1. 7. 7. The *peculium* is left to a slave : he need not deduct debt from his *vicarius* to
the *dominus* unless the *vicarius* has a *peculium*, 15. 1. 18. The word debt is used though there
be no *peculium*, but the debt has only a potential existence.
[11] Payment by debtor of *dominus*, *h. t.* 11. 2 ; *promissio*, *h. t.* 56 ; loan, *h. t.* 49. 2.

surrender[1], *etc.* It is clear from this case that though for the time being the only importance of the debt is in relation to the *quantum* of the *peculium*, the transaction itself need have no relation to that fund. On the other hand, there is no text declaring indebtedness of the *dominus* to the slave except in connexion with a *peculium*, mentioned or assumed. Mandry shews that all the texts involve payments or the like by the slave, inconceivable without a *peculium*[2]. From this he infers not only that the debt had no importance except in relation to *peculium*, but also that no such debt could arise except out of a transaction in connexion with it. But there seems no reason for laying down any distinction in principle from the rule in the converse case. The only difference is that it is not easy to formulate a case in which a slave could become a creditor of his *dominus*, except in dealings connected with his *peculium*. The existence of a debt either way is declared by Pomponius to be estimated *ex civili causa*[3], an expression which he explains, by the remark that a mere entry in account of a debt, when there had been in fact no loan or other *causa*, will not make one. He does not appear to mean that the test as to addition or deduction is the question whether the state of things is such as between independent persons would have created an *obligatio civilis*, but rather that it must be such as would have created an obligation of some sort. The writer is considering the relation of *dominus* and *extraneus creditor* in an *actio de peculio*, and lays it down that the *dominus* cannot deduct from the *peculium*, or the creditor claim an addition, for anything but a real debt[4]. We are told elsewhere that the *dominus* was a debtor only as long as he liked, and could destroy his debt to the slave by merely cancelling it[5]. This is not inconsistent. It would leave a liability to the creditor *de in rem verso*, or under the *doli mali* clause in the edict *de peculio*[6]. It must be remembered that we are here considering only the rights of a creditor[7]. Two illustrative cases, slightly complex, but not otherwise difficult, may be taken from the texts. A slave exacts money from a debtor to his master. Ulpian, citing Julian[8], remarks that here, if the *dominus* ratifies the act, there is a debt from the slave to his *dominus*. If, however, the *dominus* does not ratify, the slave is not a debtor to him. He has collected an *indebitum*, which could be recovered by *condictio indebiti de peculio*. Obviously the debtor might not recover *in solidum*. It must be supposed on the one hand that there had been no circumstance justifying the debtor in supposing he might pay the slave, and on the other that the slave was

---

[1] *h. t.* 11. *pr.*; 33. 8. 16. *pr.*   [2] *Op. cit.* 1. 157, 374.   [3] 15. 1. 49. 2.
[4] 15. 1. 11. 2, Ulp., *naturalia enim debita spectamus in peculii deductionem.*
[5] 15. 1. 7. 6.   Probably interpolated.   [6] Pernice, Labeo, 1. 155; *ante*, p. 218.
[7] The natural obligation will revive if there is a new *peculium*, and see *post*, p. 690.
[8] 15. 1. 11. 2.

acting in good faith, so that there is no noxal action. A converse case is quoted by Paul from Neratius[1]. My slave makes an *expromissio* to me for my debtor. I can deduct the amount of the debt from the *peculium* in any *actio de peculio*. Nevertheless, as a slave's promise is not a *civilis obligatio*, and is, *qua* verbal contract, a nullity, the old *obligatio* is not destroyed : there has been no *novatio*[2]. Paul remarks that if the *dominus* deducts the amount of the *expromissio* in any *actio de peculio*, this makes the original debt vest in the *peculium* ; Neratius thought it possible that the mere *expromissio* might have made the claim against the original debtor vest in the *peculium*. This seems the more reasonable view : the *peculium* would be increased by the amount of this claim, and reduced by whatever amount was still due to the master on the *expromissio*. Here, as elsewhere, mere *deductio* would not be payment to the master[3].

There are many texts which appear to deny any obligation to or against slaves. Some speak in general terms : *in personam servilem nulla cadit obligatio*[4] ; *servus ex contractibus non obligatur*[5] ; *dominus cum servo paciscens ex placitis teneri et obligari non · potest*[6]. These texts are really laying down a rule in general terms which were no doubt correct before the introduction of *naturalis obligatio*, but which in later law are true only of *obligatio civilis*[7]. The transition is shewn by a text of Ulpian[8] which says that slaves cannot owe or be creditors, and that in using language implying that they can, we rather point out a state of fact *quam ad ius civile referimus obligationem*. The rule of later law is more clearly laid down by Paul[9], who tells us that *servus naturaliter obligat*, and by Ulpian himself[10] in the well-known text *ex contractibus (servi) civiliter non obligantur sed naturaliter et obligant et obligantur*. It is this habit of using language expressing the old principle, too wide for the contemporary state of things, but correct as applied to the actual case under discussion, which explains and enables us to harmonise texts in apparent conflict, dealing with specific types of transaction. Thus Paul tells us that sale to a man's own slave is no sale at all[11]. Ulpian says there can be no sale between father and son[12]. But elsewhere he says that where the *dominus* buys from the slave there is a sale though the *dominus* is not bound[13]. There is no conflict :

---

[1] *h. t.* 56.
[2] G. 3. 119, 176, 179. Nor will the debtor have an *exceptio doli*, since the state of the *peculium* may make it impossible to bring the right of *deductio* into effect, and as in practice the creditor can renew his action, the benefit is in any case rather illusory. See the case in 2. 14. 30. 1 ; *post*, p. 693.
[3] *Ante*, p. 224.   [4] 50. 17. 22.   [5] 44. 7. 43 ; cp. G. 3. 104.
[6] C. 2. 4. 13.
[7] Mandry, Familiengüterrecht, 1. 343 *sqq.* Could *votum* create a *naturalis obligatio*? 50. 12. 2. 1.
[8] 15. 1. 41. So Julian, 46. 1. 16. 4.   [9] 12. 6. 13. *pr.*
[10] 44. 7. 14.   [11] 18. 2. 14. 3.
[12] 18. 1. 2.   [13] 14. 3. 11. 8.

each text is giving on its facts a correct decision. Paul means that
there is no such sale as is contemplated by an agreement, in a contract
of sale, that it is to be void if the vendor can sell to another on better
terms before a certain day (*in diem addictio*): it is not such a sale as
involves alienation[1]. Ulpian in his first text means that there is no
actionable contract : in the second, that though this is so, there is a
sale for certain purposes, *e.g.* in the sense necessary to give a *iusta causa
usucapiendi* : there was a *naturalis obligatio* to deliver the thing.

Texts dealing with *novatio* give.a similar series of apparent conflicts.
Gaius tells us that a *stipulatio* from a slave is *inutilis*, whether the
promise be made to his *dominus* or to another, and, in conformity with
this, that if a slave stipulates, *novandi animo*, the old obligation stands
ac si a nullo postea stipulatus fuissem. This is because *novatio* needs
a verbal contract, and a slave's promise cannot have that force. *Novatio*
is a civil law conception, and at civil law there is no action on a slave's
promise. Another expression of Gaius, which may be that of Servius,
quia cum servo agi non potest, expresses the effect of a slave's promise
more correctly[2]. The difference between this view and that of later
law is as to the essentials of novation. As Theophilus says, there is a
naturalis obligatio, but this does not novate[3]. We have just considered
the effect of such a transaction[4]. *Fideiussio* gives rise to similar but
somewhat greater difficulties. We know that there may be *fideiussio*
on any obligation, natural or civil[5]. Accordingly there may be *fideiussio*
on a slave's *naturalis obligatio*, to his master or another[6], and we are
told that the very slave whose debt is in question may be the interro-
gator on behalf of the master[7]. On the other hand if the obligation is
the other way round, *i.e.* if the slave has stipulated from his master, we
are told that a *fideiussor* is not bound, the reason assigned being that a
surety cannot be liable for and to the same person[8], a rule frequently
laid down[9]. It is remarked by Pernice[10] that the reason is unsatisfactory,
since it would be equally true in the converse case. He is inclined to
see the reason in a refusal to recognise the reality of a debt from his
dominus to a slave[11]. But there is no reason to base the difference of
treatment of the two cases on a rigid conservatism which would ignore
the reality of an obligation which was in practice familiar. The reason

---

[1] Mandry, *op. cit.* 1. 152.
[2] G. 3. 104, 176, 179; In. 3. 19. 6; 3. 29. 3.   Gaius refers to an older exploded view, of
Servius Sulpicius, that there was *novatio*, with the result that in practice the right was
destroyed.
[3] *Ad* In. 3. 29. 3.
[4] 15. 1. 56; *ante*, p. 686.   See Machelard, Obligations naturelles, 165 *sqq.*
[5] 46. 1. 16. 3.   [6] 15. 1. 3. 7; 46. 1. 56. 1; G. 3. 119: In. 3. 20. 1.
[7] 46. 1. 70. 3.   [8] *h. t.* 56. 1.
[9] *h. t.* 71. *pr.*; 46. 3. 34. 8.   [10] Labeo, 1. 156.
[11] See also Machelard, *loc. cit.*   For texts expressing refusal to recognise such obligations,
see Gradenwitz, Natur und Sklave, 27.

assigned by the text is sufficient. It is hardly correct to say that it would apply equally to both cases. Where a *fideiussor* promises to a *dominus* on behalf of a slave, the transaction is real and intelligible. The *dominus* has a right against the slave's *peculium*, which may be made effective in an *actio de peculio* brought by any creditor of the slave, against whose claim a mere *ademptio* of the *peculium* would be no protection to the *dominus*, by reason of the *doli mali* clause of the edict. There may be no certainty of making it effective in this way, the *peculium* being already overloaded with debt to the *dominus*, or the slave, with *administratio*, having paid away all the liquid assets. Thus the *fideiussio* acquires something to the master. But in the other case, though the *naturalis obligatio* of the master to the slave is valid, the promise of the *fideiussor* to the slave on behalf of the *dominus* acquires nothing to the slave, but can operate only, if at all, in favour of the *dominus*. For, as we shall see shortly, rights acquired by a slave, by contract with *extranei*, vest absolutely in the *dominus*, and do not create any *naturalis obligatio*, in the ordinary sense, in favour of the slave[1]. Thus the surety's promise to the slave to pay the master's debt to him is in effect nothing more than a promise to the master to pay on behalf of the master to the master: it is for and to the same person in a sense in which this cannot be said of the converse case[2].

The situation is fundamentally changed by a manumission of the slave. So far as his rights are concerned, the resulting state of things is simple. The general rule is *quod quis dum servus est egit, proficere libero facto non potest*[3]. His right, such as it was, against his *dominus*, has no significance except in relation to his *peculium*, and, if he does not take that, there can be no question of any right[4]. If he does take the *peculium*, the natural obligation persists, and if the former *dominus* pays the debt he cannot recover[5]. In one text a curious rule is laid down. Ulpian says[6] that a *servus heres necessarius* who claims *bonorum separatio*, and does not intermeddle with the estate, can claim to keep a debt due from his master to him. Under such circumstances he cannot be entitled to his *peculium*, for it is part of the estate. But if he is not so entitled, there is no debt to him. Even though there were such a debt, he would be merely a creditor, and, assuredly, not entitled by virtue of what is a mere *naturalis obligatio*, to any priority over other creditors with claims at civil law. It has been suggested[7] that the debt must be one which became claimable only after the death of the

---

[1] 44. 7. 56; *post*, p. 698.
[2] It should be noted that the *fideiussor* has in any case an *actio mandati de peculio* against the *dominus*, 15. 1. 3. 7.
[3] 50. 17. 146; cp. 2. 14. 7. 18.
[4] The right of recovery by *statuliber* who has paid more than he was *dare iussus* is only an apparent exception, 12. 4. 3. 6; 40. 7. 3. 6.
[5] 12. 6. 64.   [6] 42. 6. 1. 18.   [7] Machelard, *op. cit.* 194.

dominus, e.g. where the *dominus* had taken a *hereditas* at some earlier date, with a conditional legacy to the slave, such a legacy being capable of taking effect, now that the slave has become *sui iuris*. The explanation is hardly satisfactory. The money is spoken of as a *debitum* : there is no suggestion of the sum having only now become due. Moreover the difficulty would still remain. There might be other legatees of the old *hereditas* still unpaid, but there is no hint of their having such a privilege. In the case supposed, they, and the slave legatee, would have been entitled to *bonorum separatio* against the creditors of the deceased heir of their testator[1], but that would apply only to the goods which formed part of the originally inherited estate, and could not have amounted to a general right of preference in the whole estate of the present deceased[2]. But a more serious objection is the general form of the language, which is not such as would have been used if such a remote hypothesis, as that suggested, had been in the writer's mind. He could hardly have thought the words *si quid ei a testatore debetur*, an apt form by which to describe a sum which was never in fact due from the master. On the whole it seems probable that it is a hasty Tribonianism, laid down without much reference to principle.

We have seen[3] that if the slave does not take his *peculium* his natural right against his *dominus* ceases on his manumission. This is not necessarily the case with his liabilities[4]. If he does not take the *peculium* he cannot be sued for *reliqua*[5]. If he does, it is subject to debts to the master[6], not actionable, but such that if he pays he cannot recover[7]. It is to be presumed, though we have no information, that his *fideiussor* is still liable. His position is awkward : he cannot sue the slave, his real principal, and his remedy *de peculio*, hardly worth anything in the circumstances, expires in any case in a year. He is in the position of one whose principal is insolvent, though in fact both slave and master may be wealthy.

The slave's liability comes into question mostly in connexion with his responsibility for past administration[8]. The texts need careful consideration. Where a slave, who has been engaged in administration for his *dominus*, is freed without his *peculium*, he cannot afterwards be sued for anything due on account of the *actus*[9]. If he is freed *directo*, there is a right to vindicate property in his possession, and if he is freed by *fideicommissum*, though the fiduciary must free without delaying the manumission on merely pecuniary grounds, an *arbiter* will

---

[1] 42. 6. 6. *pr.*
[2] There is the same difficulty if we treat it as an expression by Tribonian of the new rule as to a legatee's general hypothec.
[3] *Ante*, p. 688.   [4] Cp. 12. 6. 38.   [5] C. 4. 14. 5.
[6] 33. 8. 10.   [7] 46. 3. 83.   [8] 3. 5. 16.
[9] 3. 5. 44. 1, 16; 34. 3. 28. 7; 40. 5. 19. *pr.*, 37; 44. 5. 1. 4; C. 4. 14. 5.

be appointed, under rules already considered, to enquire into what is due. If this claim is satisfied, he need not fear further liability, apart from any benefit under the will[1]. We know that in all cases of manumission there is a general duty to render accounts, and if the investigation shews that moneys have been made away with in such a way as to create a liability, the amount can be deducted from any legacy[2]. There seems to be no text expressly dealing with the case in which the *peculium* is left to the man, his administration ceasing on the manumission, and the loss not being discovered till the *peculium* has been received by the legatee. As debts to the *dominus* automatically reduce the *peculium*, it might seem that the amount could be recovered, so far as the *peculium* would go, by a *condictio indebiti*[3], and this is suggested by at least óne text[4]. But most of them contemplate *retentio* as the obvious and only remedy. In fact to allow a *condictio indebiti* in such a case is to give an action to enforce a *naturalis obligatio*. It will be remembered that, apart from actual conveyance, the legacy vests in the legatee the ownership of the proper fraction only of each *res peculiaris*, so that *communi dividundo* is available. The texts to be considered in relation to the next point shew that, so far as this retention is concerned, the liability is estimated on the analogy of an ordinary *negotiorum gestio*, and extends to faults committed at any time during the *administratio*, irrespectively of the then state of the *peculium*. But no text extends it beyond benefits received under the will[5].

There is more difficulty in the case in which the freedman continues the administration which he began as a slave. He is of course liable in full for any misdoings after freedom, and there is a further rule, almost inevitable. If a transaction begun before, and continued after, he was free, is such that its parts cannot well be disentangled, all can be sued upon[6]. There are, however, some texts which seem to contemplate a wider liability in the case of a continued *administratio*. Paul cites[7] from three Proculians (Proculus, Pegasus and Neratius) a somewhat subtle doctrine. They say that a man who began to administer as a slave, and continues when free, is bound to shew good faith. At the moment when he became free, he knew that any further action was barred by the freedom. He ought then and there, before taking the

---

[1] 40. 5. 19. *pr.*, 37; 47. 4. 1. 7.
[2] 34. 3. 28. 7. Though during slavery the natural obligation to the master has no importance except in connexion with *peculium*, it has a potential existence apart from that fund. A legacy is given to an *actor* who is freed. *Reliqua* may be charged against it though there be no *peculium*. See *ante*, p. 684.
[3] It was only in a narrow class of cases that *condictio indebiti* was refused in case of legacy, G. 4. 9; In. 3. 27. 7.
[4] C. 4. 14. 5. [5] 3. 5. 16—18. 1.
[6] 3. 5. 16. A slave bought a site and built on it. The house fell. After he was free he let the land. In an *actio negotiorum gestorum* only the *locatio* can be considered.
[7] 3. 5. 17, 18.

peculium, to have debited himself with whatever losses had been caused by his fault at any time (*a capite rationem reddendum,* says Sabinus), and taken only the balance. Not to do this was a breach of his duty as a *negotiorum gestor,* and he is thus liable to an action, *ex negotiis gestis,* for the resulting loss, *i.e.* for what would have been saved had he then made the deduction. Neratius seems to require him to make the same allowance even out of after acquired assets[1]. Paul adds from Scaevola[2] the proposition that the maxim of Sabinus must not be understood to extend the liability beyond the then content of the *peculium,* or to enable the master *revocare in obligationem* losses incurred in slavery. This appears to repudiate the rule of Neratius of which there is no other trace, and which squares ill with the general language of the texts above cited[3]. The case differs from that of the ordinary *negotiorum gestor* with which it is equalised, in that the debt in that case was a full *obligatio civilis.* The action allowed by Proculus is to enforce a *naturalis obligatio.*

It is possible to release the slave even from the liability which attaches to him in the accepted doctrine. But it is also possible to increase the liability by special undertaking of the *manumissus.* He may specially promise *operae,* or money, or full compensation for waste during his slavery. A promise of this kind must be made or confirmed after the freedom is attained. Such a promise is valid and is not upset by the rule which forbade agreements *onerandae libertatis causa*[4]. These last are defined by Ulpian and Paul as such as are not *bona fide* intended to be enforced, but are to be held *in terrorem* over the *libertus* to be exacted if he offend, and so to secure obedience[5]. In the same way if a manumission was given on account of an agreement to give money, a promise to pay it, made after the man was free, is absolutely good, and not regarded as *onerandae libertatis causa*[6]. It is clear that the promise must be confirmed after freedom, whether it is for money or service. The rule is clearly laid down by Ulpian and Venuleius, though the latter shews that there had been doubts[7]. An enactment of A.D. 222[8] lays down, however, a different rule. Where a slave had promised money for liberty, and there was

---

[1] 3. 5. 17, 18. *pr.* The case is compared with that of a *negotiorum gestor* who fails to debit himself with a liability which has since become time-barred : he must make good the loss.

[2] 3. 5. 18. 1.

[3] As to the view that the freedom may not be burdened with old debt, see Machelard, Obl. Nat. 184.

[4] 44. 5. 1. 4.

[5] 44. 5. 1. 5, 2. 2. Agreements breaking the rule are not necessarily void, but there is an *exceptio,* see 44. 5, *passim.* But a *societas libertatis causa* between patron and *libertus* is absolutely void, *h. t.* 1. 7 ; 38. 1. 36. It is perhaps a fraud on the ' *lex Iulia et* Papia,' from a treatise on which one of the texts comes, 38. 1. 36.

[6] 44. 5. 2. 2.

[7] 38. 1. 7. *pr.,* 2 ; 40. 12. 44. *pr.*; *ante,* p. 442. Venuleius is clear that the oath puts only religious pressure on the man.

[8] C. 4. 14. 3.

44—2

no stipulation after liberty, it is said *adversus eum petitionem per in factum actionem habes.* The rule is strange and the language is at least unusual. If this is to be taken as law, it may be that, as Savigny says[1], it was treated as an innominate contract *facio ut des*, the intervening manumission being ignored. But this does not shew why it is ignored, and the rule is so inconsistent with that found in the other texts, that it seems most likely, in view of its clumsy language, that in its original form it advised a petition to the imperial court. Other texts shew the difficulty that was felt in dealing with this sort of case. A slave induced X to promise money for his freedom, undertaking to assume the liability after he was free. This he did not do. Pomponius, quoted by Ulpian, lays down the rule that the third party who promised has an *actio doli* against the *manumissus*, and if the patron has prevented the *libertus* from accepting the liability, the promisor has an *exceptio doli* against the patron[2]. This assumes that there is no other action, a point which Ulpian makes clear. Here the *dolus* is after manumission, and it must be remembered that *dolus* is a delict. A further difficulty arises if the slave has committed *dolus* to his *dominus* before he is free. We know that in general no action lies[3]. What is to happen if the manumission was itself procured by fraud? There can be no restitution, even though the manumitter were a minor, except by Imperial decree *ex magna causa*[4]. Several texts tell us, however, that when the owner was a minor, there is a remedy against the dolose slave. One gives an *actio doli* against him[5]: another gives *vel actio doli vel utilis*[6]. Another says that an indemnity can be obtained *ab eo cuius iuris dictio est, quatenus iuris ratio permittit*[7]. The *actio utilis*, whatever it may mean, may perhaps be neglected. It appears therefore that the later classical law allowed an *actio doli* on such facts. Yet as we know, and as one of these texts expressly says[8], no action lies to a master against his freed slave for a delict committed during slavery. The result seems to be a very strong recognition of the principle that the *actio doli* is available where a wrong has been done and there is no other remedy[9], eked out by the fact that the injured person is a minor[10], and by the consideration that the *dolus* may be said to have been committed at the very moment at which liberty was obtained. The amount recoverable is the *interesse* of the manumitter—what he would have had had the manumission not occurred[11].

[1] Savigny, System, Beilage IV *in fin.*
[3] *Ante*, p. 107.
[5] 4. 3. 7. *pr.*
[7] C. 2. 30. 2.   [8] 4. 4. 11. *pr.*
[2] 4. 3. 7. 8.
[4] 4. 4. 9. 6, 10.
[6] 4. 4. 11. *pr.*
[9] 4. 3. 1. 1.
[10] All the texts dealing with such *dolus* of the slave and most of those dealing with *dolus* of a third party, seem to discuss cases in which the owner is a minor. See the references, *ante*, p. 570.
[11] 4. 4. 11. *pr.* No deduction for the problematical value of the man as a *libertus*, 19. 5. 5. 5; cp. 50. 17. 126. 1.

B. Transactions between the slave and *extranei*. Most of the questions of principle which arise in this connexion have necessarily been discussed by anticipation—a fact which enables us to deal only briefly with some of the points.

In general where a slave contracts with an *extraneus*, he acquires the right to his master, and conversely, the *extraneus* will have, or may have, the *actio de peculio, etc.*, against the master. But the *naturalis obligatio* of the slave is something distinct from the rights represented by these rules. So far as a liability of the slave is concerned, this may certainly exist independently of his *peculium*: the transaction may have had no relation to that fund: there may indeed have been no *peculium* when it was made[1]. Some texts suggest it as arising where there could be no *actio de peculio*. Thus X stipulated from a slave of B for what was due from T to X. Gaius says, on Julian's authority, that if the slave had a *iusta causa interveniendi*, so that the *expromissio* gave X an *actio de peculio* against B, X is barred from suing T by the *exceptio pacti conventi*, but not if there was no such *causa interveniendi* or if he thought the slave free[2]. The debt is not novated, even in the first case, for the slave's promise is not a verbal contract[3], but the facts are construed as a pactum *ne a T peteretur*. It will be noticed that this effect differs from that in a case already considered in which the *expromissio* is to the slave's own master[4]. There the benefit to the person to whom the promise was made, the master, was unreal if the *peculium* was solvent: it depended on the possibility of making certain deductions for which there might never be occasion: here the promisee has in any case acquired an *actio de peculio*. In this case it can hardly be doubted that the slave would be under a *naturalis obligatio* whether there were an *actio de peculio* or not. In another text a *filiusfamilias* is liable under circumstances which give no *actio de peculio* against his father[5].

The independence of the obligation is shewn by the fact that there may be pledge or *fideiussio* for the slave's natural obligation independently of that *de peculio*. Thus, if a slave, having *administratio peculii*, gives a pledge for his natural obligation, this entitles the owner to regain possession of the thing pledged by an *actio pigneraticia utilis*[6]. It must be assumed here that there was also a "peculiar" obligation (as would ordinarily be the case), since otherwise the power of *administratio* would not have authorised any, even partial, alienation[7].

---

[1] The *actio de peculio* lay on such facts: the *naturalis obligatio* can hardly be narrower. Mandry, *op. cit.* 1. 374; Illustrations, *ante*, p. 212.
[2] 2. 14. 30. 1; *ante*, p. 215.   [3] *Ante*, pp. 215, 685.
[4] 15. 1. 56; *ante*, p. 686.
[5] 15. 1. 3. 11. See also 46. 4. 8. 4, *et tolluntur etiam obligationes honorariae si quae sunt.*
[6] 12. 6. 13. *pr.*   [7] *Ante*, pp. 201 *sqq.*

The case of *fideiussio* for such an obligation is considered in several texts. It may be either only for the *obligatio honoraria*, in which case it is *dumtaxat de peculio*, or for the natural obligation, in which case it is *in solidum*, whatever the state of the *peculium*[1]. An *actio de peculio* does not release the *fideiussor* on the natural obligation, the obligations being distinct[2]. Such a *fideiussio* may even be created after an *actio de peculio* has been brought, *quia naturalis obligatio, quam etiam servus suscipere videtur, in litem translata non est*[3]. Though payment discharges both, they are *plures causae*[4].

But though they are distinct obligations the money due is the same and payment will put an end to both. And the *naturalis obligatio* must in every case be at least as great as the *obligatio honoraria*. These points are illustrated in several texts. Thus if the slave pays, out of the *peculium*, having the necessary *administratio*, it is a valid *solutio*, even though an *actio de peculio* is pending, and the *dominus* will be released by the payment[5]. Conversely if the *dominus* pays under an *actio de peculio*, this releases the *fideiussores* of the slave's obligation, Africanus observing that the one payment has ended the two obligations[6]. The same result follows from an *acceptilatio* to the slave. Thus Paul says that if I have given an *acceptilatio* to the slave, the *actiones honorariae* become *inutiles*[7], and Ulpian says *et servus accepto liberari potest, et tolluntur etiam honorariae obligationes si quae sunt*[8]. Ulpian gives as the reason why both parties bound by an obligation are released by an *acceptilatio* to one: *non quoniam ipsis accepto latum est, sed quoniam velut solvisse videtur is qui acceptilatione solutus est*[9]. It seems that *acceptilatio* could not be effectively made to the *dominus*. Ulpian's text, in which he says that *acceptilatio* to the slave releases the *dominus*[10], begins with the remarks that *acceptilatio* to a son releases the honorary obligation of the father, and that *acceptilatio* to the father would be a mere nullity. Then he adds *idem erit in servo dicendum*. This is followed by the rule that the slave can take *acceptilatio*. One might expect *a fortiori* that the other part of the rule is to apply, for while it might be contended that the obligation of father and son could conceivably be regarded as one, since both are civil[11] (*i.e.* actionable), it

---

[1] 46. 1. 35.   [2] 46. 3. 84; *post*, p. 695.   [3] 15. 1. 50. 2.
[4] 46. 3. 38. 2. X lent money to S the slave of Y, who freed him. S then became *fideiussor* to X. If this was for the *obligatio annalis* it is good, but if for the natural obligation it is null, for a man cannot become *fideiussor* for himself. If he becomes *heres* to a *fideiussor* of the natural obligation or *vice versa*, both obligations persist, one being natural and the other civil, though in the case of a *filiusfamilias* there would have been merger, both being civil, 46. 1. 21. 2. See *ante*, p. 217 and *post*, p. 696. See also App. II.
[5] The slave's *fideiussores* are released, 12. 6. 13. *pr.*; 15. 1. 50. 2; 46. 3. 84.
[6] 46. 3. 38. 2.   [7] 46. 4. 11. 1.
[8] 46. 4. 8. 4; cp. 34. 3. 5. 3. There is no *obligatio de peculio* if the slave no longer owes. The converse is not necessarily true, *post*, p. 697.
[9] 46. 4. 16, *eiusdem obligationis participes*; cp. G. 3. 169; In. 3. 29. 1; *post*, p. 697.
[10] 46. 4. 8. 4.
[11] Cp. 5. 1. 57; 15. 1. 3. 11.

is clear that those of slave and *dominus* are not. One is natural: the other civil. Moreover the promise of the son is a verbal contract, while that of the slave is not, but has only the force of a pact, so that the *acceptilatio* cannot be in essence more than a pact[1]. The fact that son or slave can take *acceptilatio* for the father creates no difficulty[2]: they are mere expressions of his personality for the purpose of acquisi tion, but the converse is not true.

There is some difficulty about informal releases. The *dominus* can take a *pactum de non petendo*, but this will not release the slave[3]. On the other hand the liability of the *dominus* depends on the existence of that of the slave, and thus any pact which releases the latter will release the *dominus*. The *acceptilatio* to the slave is no more than such a pact[4]. But a slave's express pact, *ne a se peteretur*, is in strictness meaningless. The rule arrived at is that if the slave takes a pact *in rem, e.g. ne peteretur*, this destroys the natural obligation and thus gives the *dominus* also an *exceptio pacti*, but if he agrees *ne a se (servo) peteretur*, this is in strictness a nullity. Paul seems to have reluctantly allowed an *exceptio doli* to the *dominus* in such a case[5], and we must presume that the slave's obligation is destroyed. In like manner it appears that a pact to the *dominus, ne a se servove peteretur*, would destroy the natural obligation, though strictly it means nothing so far as the slave is concerned[6].

It is clear that merely bringing an *actio de peculio* does not release the slave or his *fideiussor*. But Pomponius tells us[7] that where an *actio de peculio* has proceeded to judgment, *fideiussores* for the slave have an *exceptio rei iudicatae*. This would be more intelligible if the *fideiussio* were for the *obligatio honoraria*, but this case is not commonly called a *fideiussio pro servo*, and if it be understood of the *obligatio naturalis* the rule conflicts with those just laid down and with their reason, *i.e.* that the *obligatio naturalis* has not been brought into issue[8]. The texts which deal with this question[9] have recently been very fully considered by Erman[10]. Most of them clearly express the view that the natural obligation and that *de peculio* are not *eadem res*, and this may

---

1 But Ulpian elsewhere (34. 3. 5. 2) cites, and it seems approves, Julian's view that if the father has a legacy of *liberatio* of the son's debt he should be released by pact lest the son be also released. This implies, in its context, that *acceptilatio* to the father would be effective and would release the son. He may be thinking of *novatio* followed by *acceptilatio*.
2 *Ante*, p. 154. As to *pactum de non petendo*, 2. 14. 17. 7—18.
3 34. 3. 5. 2; cp. 2. 14. 17. 7.
4 His promise is not a verbal obligation which is essential to true *acceptilatio*, *ante*, p. 216.
5 2. 14. 21. 1, 2.
6 Arg. 2. 14. 21. 2. *in fin.* A slave's pact *ne a domino peteretur* gave an *exceptio* whether the original transaction was by the slave or the master, *h. l.* 1.
7 44. 2. 21. 4.
8 15. 1. 50. 2.
9 15. 1. 50. 2; 46. 3. 38. 2, 84; 44. 2. 21. 4 *etc.*
10 Mélanges Appleton, 203 *sqq.*, esp. 266 *sqq.*

be justified on obvious practical grounds[1]. And if, as Julian holds, a natural obligation in the actual defendant can survive an adverse judgment[2], *a fortiori* would it survive in the case of another person. This is not the only case in which a *fideiussor* can be taken for a natural obligation surviving *litis contestatio*[3]. All this makes it difficult to understand the text which makes the judgment release the slave's *fideiussor*, and this not *ipso iure*, as might have been expected, but *ope exceptionis*[4].

The last point is perhaps unimportant in the Digest where the distinction no longer exists. Apart from possible interpolation[5] it may perhaps be explained on the ground that the *exceptio* was not excluded by the presence of *ipso iure consumptio*[6]. The more serious conflict remains. It may be set down to a difference of opinion, readily conceivable on such a point, preserved in the Digest by oversight[7]. The view that here the judgment was an absolution, while in both the other texts it was a condemnation, has met with some acceptance. Krüger[8] supposes that the was no *consumptio* and not an ordinary *exceptio rei iudicatae*, but a "positive" *exceptio rei contra A. A. iudicatae*. This is an appeal to the "praejudicial" effect of judgment. And Erman observes[9] that there is no sign of such an *exceptio* in classical law. Affolter[10], taking the same view of the judgment, holds that it is an ordinary *exceptio*, based not on a real identity, but on a "synthetic" identity resting on a relation of premiss and consequence. Judgment for the debt would not prove the natural obligation, but judgment that there was no debt would disprove it. This view Erman is inclined to accept[11], but it is much the same as the other, in effect: it requires the same enquiry into the content of the judgment, for only a judgment denying the transaction altogether would negative the natural obligation. And it is difficult to see how the nature of the judgment can affect the identity of the *res*, for this identity, however defined, is something already existing[12]. Here too the texts give no evidence of any such function of the *exceptio*[13], in fact it seems that every

---

[1] Cp. the case of *constitutum*, in which bringing the praetorian action did not destroy the other obligation, 13. 5. 18. 3, *vetus dubitatio*.
[2] 12. 6. 60 ; cp. *h. t.* 28.   [3] 46. 1. 8. 3. See Machelard, Obl. Nat. 363.
[4] 44. 2. 21. 4. See App. II.
[5] Erman, *op. cit.* 269, remarks that *excipiendum est* is an unusual form. He cites in support of its genuineness, 3. 5. 7. 2 *Agi...non posse quia exceptio r. i. opponenda est.* But this is strictly speaking self-contradictory and the last clause is probably Tribonian.
[6] So Erman, *op. cit.* 298, citing 44. 7. 34. 1.
[7] As to the possible influence of the actual form of the *fideiussio*, see Erman, *op. cit.* 270 *sqq.*
[8] Krüger, Processualische Consumption, 200, cited Erman, *op. cit.* 204.
[9] *op. cit.* 288.
[10] Affolter, Institutionensystem, 279 *sqq.*, cited Erman, *op. cit.* 290 *sqq.*
[11] *loc. cit.*
[12] Affolter's view cannot rest on the principle *non bis in idem*, for there was the risk of an adverse judgment, whether one was given or not.
[13] Such distinctions are plentiful in relation to *iusiurandum*, where the matter could be tested more readily, see, *e.g.*, 12. 2. 26. But there is here no question of *consumptio*.

argument which Erman urges against the view which he rejects applies equally here¹.
Of the *naturalis obligatio* to the slave we hear little during the slavery. Everything he acquires is acquired to the *dominus*, who can sue on his contracts². The slave's natural obligation survives manumission. Thus, if after he is free, he promises to pay the debt, this is not a *donatio* but a *solutio*³, and if he pays it he cannot recover⁴. But it is still only a *naturalis obligatio*, and thus a *manumissus* cannot be sued on his contract made as a slave⁵, even as a *statuliber*⁶, unless he has acquired the liability *de peculio*⁷ or the like, on account of his still having the *peculium*. Here too we have, however, to except the case in which a transaction, begun when he was a slave, is completed after manumission, and its parts are not readily separable. In that case he can be sued on the whole transaction, though it does not appear that this anomalous rule can have any application beyond *mandatum* and *negotiorum gestio*⁸.

In the case of deposit there is a difficulty. Where a thing is deposited with a slave, Ulpian quotes Marcellus as saying that, after he is free, he cannot be sued on his contract of deposit, and it is necessary therefore to fall back on other actions⁹, *e.g. vindicatio* or any delictal actions which may arise. But Paul cites Trebatius as holding that if he still has the thing it is he who must be sued and not the *dominus*, though in general action does not lie against the *manumissus*¹⁰. It is clear from the preceding clause¹¹ that he is not referring to the liability *de peculio*. Mandry¹² appears to regard this as resting on the principle already mentioned of a continuing *negotium* not separable in its parts¹³. But this leaves the conflict with Ulpian and Marcellus, and the mere

¹ Given natural obligation, the slave's obligation is a premiss, not the consequence of the *obligatio de peculio*, as Affolter and Erman make it. It may exist without the *obligatio de peculio*: the converse is not true.
² 15. 1. 41. As to the meaning of the words *servi ex contractibus naturaliter obligant* (44. 7. 14), *post*, p. 699.
³ 39. 5. 19. 4.
⁴ 12. 6. 13. *pr.* as ordinarily read. I lend to your slave, buy him and free him: if he now pays me the payment cannot be recovered, 46. 3. 83.
⁵ P. 2. 13. 9; C. 4. 14. 2.   ⁶ C. 4. 14. 1.
⁷ *h. t.* 2; D. 15. 1. 3. 1; 15. 2. 1. 7; 14. 4. 9. 2.
⁸ 3. 5. 16, 17. Africanus says (46. 1. 21. 2; *ante*, p. 694) that if the liability of *fideiussor* and the natural liability of the former slave fall on the same person by inheritance, both persist, so that if the civil obligation *perit* the money is still due under the other obligation, *naturaliter*. Machelard (*op. cit.* 176) thinks the word *perit* contemplates a loss by defect in procedure, leaving a natural obligation which would merge in the other. But the text contemplates a survival which would serve a purpose: here it would not. He cites Cujas as holding that it is a case of *fideiussio ad tempus*, but he remarks that there the civil obligation has not perished: it subsists but is met by an *exceptio*. He notes that it cannot be a case of *fideipromissio*, expiring in two years, for the principal debt is a *mutuum*. But *novatio* followed by *acceptilatio* may perhaps be contemplated, for though *acceptilatio* is a quasi-payment, it is not a payment, and it does not appear to be anywhere said that it would destroy an independent natural obligation.
⁹ 16. 3. 1. 18.   ¹⁰ 16. 3. 21. 1.   ¹¹ *h. l. pr.*, 1 *in fin.*
¹² *op. cit.* 1. 395.   ¹³ *Ante*, pp. 690, 696.

continuing to hold a thing is a very different matter from continuing to look after business relations, as in the other texts. He suggests also that it may rest on grounds of utility, but this is an unlikely basis for a rule which dates from Trebatius. It may be suggested that the view, established as it was in pre-classical days, fails to distinguish between contract and quasi-contract in obligation *re contracta*. If the obligation is regarded as resting not on any agreement, but on the mere holding of the property, it is easy to see that Trebatius may well have regarded the liability as continuing. If it be contended that this ignores the fact that the text itself regards the rule as exceptional, the answer is that the concluding words, *licet ex ceteris causis in manumissum actio non datur*, are not from Trebatius, or probably even from Ulpian[1]. It is likely that Trebatius was not discussing the *actio depositi* in its developed form at all[2].

As to rights arising out of the slave's transactions, it is clear that these remain with the *dominus*. What he does as a slave *proficere libero facto non potest*[3]. Actions acquired to the master remain with him, notwithstanding manumission of the slave[4]. This holds good even though the contract was so framed, by condition or the like, as to postpone the actual acquisition or right of action to alienation or manumission: *initium spectandum est*[5]. Where a slave conditionally instituted came to terms with creditors, as to dividend, before satisfying the condition, it was held that his pact made while he was a slave was not available to him after he was free. After doubts, Marcellus came to the conclusion that he had an *exceptio doli*[6]. The reason for the doubt may be that the *dolus* was committed to the man as a slave, and he can have no rights arising out of such a delict[7]. The difficulty may have been got over by regarding the *dolus* as consisting in the refusal to recognise the agreement after the man was free[8]. But to give an *exceptio doli* in such cases is to go a long way towards doing away with the rule that what he does in slavery *non potest proficere libero facto*. Marcellus adds a remark that if he had been instituted *pure*, and agreed before intermeddling, this would have been effective: he was free at the time, and as a result of the pact has lost his right of *bonorum separatio*, which must be claimed before he touches the property[9].

If the slave takes the *peculium*, he may of course have the right to have the actions attaching to it transferred to him, but this is no real exception[10]. The same is true of the conditions under which a payment may be validly made to a *manumissus* under a *negotium* conducted

1 Kalb, Juristenlatein, 66.
2 For some remarks on the text see Savigny, System, 2. 141 and Beilage IV (2. 426).
3 50. 17. 146.   4 44. 7. 56.   5 16. 3. 1. 30; 45. 3. 40; 50. 17. 18.
6 2. 14. 7. 18.   7 *Ante*, p. 676.   8 Cp. 4. 3. 7. 8; *ante*, p. 692.
9 42. 6. 1. 18.   10 33. 8. 19. 1.

while he was a slave[1]. The rule gives him no right to claim such payment, nor does it release him from a duty to account to his former owner. But these rules as to *solutio* are not without importance in this connexion. For if, in view of the foregoing principles, the question be asked, what is meant by such statements as that *servus sibi naturaliter...alium obligat*, or *naturaliter obligat* (*et obligatur*)?, the rules as to *solutio* seem to afford the best answer: in the principal text they are expressly based on the natural obligation[2].

Another question which has given rise to some controversy is that why the obligation of the slave remained natural after manumission, and did not become actionable. Schwanert[3] gives the plain reason that it was natural before, and that there is nothing in the act of manumission to make it actionable. To this Pernice[4] objects that it is not consistent with other opinions of Schwanert, but that is no objection to the opinion standing by itself. Savigny[5] says it is because, as the slave's contract was made in view of the *peculium*, which has gone to the *dominus*, it would be unfair to make him liable to an action. But this, as Pernice remarks, would equally negative a natural obligation. On Schwanert's solution, Pernice makes the further observation that it is a sophism, by which he presumably means that it is little more than giving the rule as a reason for itself, the real question being: why was this so? Why was not the manumission treated as creative of some type of action? But this is hardly surprising. The creditor contracts in view of the facts: to have given him an action against the slave as well as, in ordinary cases, against the master would have been to give him a great advantage which he could not have anticipated when he made the contract. Sell[6] takes much the same view as Schwanert: he rests the rule on the fundamental principle of procedure: *neque enim actio quae non fuit ab initio nata oriri potest*[7]. Pernice himself seems to rest it on the view that the whole conception of natural obligation of the slave was a late development, not thoroughly worked out. In fact the reason why a particular step in advance was not taken by jurisprudence cannot often be answered on juristic grounds: no doubt in this case the *actio annalis* met all needs. It must be observed that any such development would be unique: there is no other case in which an obligation which was natural owing to defective capacity of the debtor, became civil when that incapacity ceased. But the different cases of natural obligation have so little in common that this counts for little.

---

[1] *Ante*, pp. 158, 163, 203, 683.
[2] 44. 7. 14. Machelard, *op. cit.* 186, shews reason against inserting *meo* before *servo*. See Gradenwitz, Natur und Sklave, 35.
[3] Naturaloblig. cited Pernice, Labeo, 1. 150.
[4] *loc. cit.*
[5] System, 2. 426, cited Pernice, *loc. cit.*
[6] Sell, Aus d. Noxalrecht, 34, 35.
[7] 47. 2. 17. 1.

A more promising enquiry may be: why is the obligation of the slave *ex contractu* natural *ab initio*, whether his *dominus* is liable or not, while his obligation *ex delicto* is civil in all cases[1]? The distinction is allied with the well-known and ancient rule: *nemo delictis exuitur quamvis capite minutus sit*[2]. Both appear to rest on the close relation between delict and crime. A slave was always liable to punishment by judicial process for crime. Criminal law had a religious basis, and the fact that a man was a slave, or had, since his act, changed his status, could not protect him against the wrath of the gods. This connexion is very clearly shewn in one set of rules. The language used in discussing the question whether a slave is liable, after his manumission, for a delict committed at his master's order, is identical with that used in determining whether a slave is criminally liable for what he has done under the same conditions. Some of the texts do not distinguish the two cases[3].

All natural obligations were not necessarily enforceable to the same degree. We have seen that those with which we are here concerned admitted of pledge and *fideiussio*, and that a payment was not recoverable as an *indebitum*. But all these involve the consent of the slave. A question arises whether the obligation could be enforced against him by *compensatio*. No text answers the question either way. Savigny[4] thinks *compensatio* was applicable, on the very doubtful evidence of a text which says that one who is directed to pay and be free can *compensare*[5]. But, as Machelard[6] points out, there is here no question of *compensatio* in the judicial sense; and a rule introduced *favore libertatis* cannot be extended, without authority, to a somewhat contrary effect. Machelard thinks compensation inadmissible as being contrary to the tendency shewn in the texts dealing with *negotiorum gestio* to release him from any liability for things done in slavery[7]. Mandry[8] takes a similar view, citing the same and other texts which indicate the tendency against compulsory methods[9]. He observes that, in texts which seem to have a different tendency, there is always some fact after the freedom accounting for the liability[10]. This seems the most probable view. The fact that the *dominus*, in handing over the *peculium*, could deduct for what was due to him on a natural obligation is clearly very slight evidence for the contrary opinion. Such debts were on an entirely different footing from those to outsiders. They were *ipso facto* deducted from the *peculium*. This fund being the creature of the master's will was automatically lessened by their amount. A legatee

---

1 44. 7. 14.   2 4. 5. 2. 3.   3 *Ante*, pp. 91 *sqq*., 108, 678 *sqq*.
4 System, 1. 60.   5 40. 7. 20. 2.   6 *op. cit.* 183.
7 3. 5. 17, 18.   8 Mandry, *op. cit.* 1. 380 *sqq*.
9 3. 5. 16, 18. 1; C. 4. 14. 5.
10 3. 5. 14, 16; 4. 3. 7. 8; C. 2. 18. 21; 4. 14. 3.

of the *peculium* could not vindicate the *peculiares res* except subject to a proportionate deduction for these. Nothing of the sort was true of debts to outsiders[1]. One text observes: *etiam quod natura debetur venit in compensationem*[2]. It has been shewn[3] that this text refers to the obligation resulting from a partnership with a slave. The allusion is no doubt to the adjustment in the *actio pro socio*. Thus even where the *societas* is continued after freedom and the adjustment takes place then, it is not a question of true *compensatio*, of setting off a debt on one obligation against another, but of the interpretation to be given to the agreement of *societas*. It is in fact laying down the rule that even such natural obligations as cannot be used by way of *compensatio* must in such a case be brought into account.

It has been noted that the fact that the transaction gave no right to the *actio de peculio* did not prevent the arising of a natural obligation[4]: it is indeed in the absence of this action that the right would be most valuable. Its importance may easily be exaggerated: a right which was available only after manumission, and then not by action or set off, cannot have been very highly valued by creditors. It does not appear from the texts that a slave could so contract as to exclude the natural obligation. Classical law would perhaps have treated as a nullity the provision in his agreement that he was to be in no way personally liable. Whether any notice would have been taken of his proviso that the creditor was never to claim except by the *actiones honorariae* cannot be said, but on the analogy of what followed from a subsequent *pactum de non petendo*[5], it seems likely that an *exceptio doli* might have been allowed.

In this chapter it has been assumed that a normal slave has been normally freed. There were other cases, which have been discussed in their places. Such are the captives returning with *postliminium*[6], the *servus poenae plene restitutus* or pardoned *ex indulgentia principis*[7]. In the case of the slave freed by the public authority by way of reward or of punishment to his master[8], there is little authority: probably the rules were normal.

---

1 *Ante*, pp. 193, 221 *sqq.*
4 *Ante*, pp. 693 *sqq.*
7 *Ante*, pp. 410 *sq.*

2 16. 2. 6.
5 *Ante*, p. 695.
8 *Ante*, pp. 599 *sqq.*

3 Lenel, Paling., *ad h. l.*
6 *Ante*, pp. 307 *sqq.*

APPENDIX I.

THE RELATION OF THE CONTRACTUAL ACTIONS *ADIECTITIAE QUALITATIS* TO THE THEORY OF REPRESENTATION.

THESE praetorian actions appear to be a partial correction of what looks like a glaring injustice[1]. By the civil law a *dominus* acquired freely through his slave, but was in no way liable on his transactions. Doubtless the injustice had not been so great as it might appear, for in earlier law the slave was not the important instrument of commerce he afterwards became. Moreover in sale to a slave the ownership did not pass till the price was paid, so that the vendor could recover the thing by *vindicatio*, while the *dominus* could not enforce the completion of an unfulfilled undertaking to the slave without tendering what was due[2]. In fact a well-known analogous case suggests that the difficulty was the other way. When the *lex* Plaetoria allowed minors to set aside their agreements the result was that no one would deal with them[3]. Here, also, this may well have been the real difficulty : if any commercial use was to be made of slaves, a remedy against the *dominus* was essential[4]. So soon as these actions were evolved the slave became a much more useful person. He may be said to have fulfilled much the same function as the modern limited liability company. A person who has money to invest, and does not himself want to engage in trade, can invest his money in shares in such a concern. He runs a certain risk but he knows exactly how much he can lose. The slave owner in entrusting the slave with a *peculium* does much the same thing : his position is in one respect better since, if things are going wrong, he can always put a stop to further losses by withdrawing the *peculium*. It is not always possible to sell shares.

Whichever side suffered, and however the injustice may have been limited, these actions may be regarded as progressive stages in the adjustment of the matter. The Romans never reached any comprehensive principle which would cover all cases. It cannot even be said with certainty that any one principle underlies all these actions. It is not possible to be sure how the

---

[1] Cp. 50. 17. 206.   [2] See *ante*, p. 157.   [3] See Girard, Manuel, 227.
[4] So, in English Law, the remedies against infants are designed in their interest, not in that of creditors.

Praetor and his advisers looked at the matter, what need, exactly, he set himself to satisfy, what considerations would be most likely to define his rules, and what analogies would be likely to present themselves to his mind. For moderns the matter is simple; the notion of representation can easily be made to cover the whole ground. But it is not easy to apply this to the classical law of Rome. As has been said by Mitteis[1] our law is so saturated by the conception of representation in contract that we find it difficult to admit a legal system which ignores it. Yet it is common knowledge that the classical law did not admit of representation, to create liability in contract, at least (to beg no question), apart from these actions. Nevertheless, the opinions held by modern commentators on them make a constant appeal to this principle. No doubt all notion of representation is not to be summarily rejected. But in view of the intensely personal nature of obligation in Roman law, evidenced by a number of limitations which modern law rejects[2], it is difficult to believe that the Romans built up these actions on any theory of representation, and still more so to suppose that that theory was the one held in any particular modern system. This last point is not unimportant. In relation to the *actio institoria*, Karlowa remarks[3] that the fact of the appointment must be known to the third party, as an unknown principal could have no juristic importance. This consideration would not be convincing to one who was familiar with the English law as to the rights and liabilities of an undisclosed principal.

As we have seen[4] it is almost universally held that in the *actio quod iussu* the *iussum* must have been in some way published to the third party. The texts indeed are far from proving this. They suggest that this was, as it would naturally be, the common case, but no more. But modern law usually requires[5] that, for the third party to have an action against the principal, there must have been some form of notice that he was in the background, and this has at least helped in the acceptance of that requirement for Roman law. Yet, as we saw in discussing the action, there is no presumption to be drawn from analogous cases in favour of this view. The fact is that the rules of the action are based on the words of the relative edict, interpreted in the light of current habits of thought. There was no theory of representation to be utilised. Notice would not make it more or less reasonable that a contract between A and B should bind C. And if the analogy of acquisition of *iura in rem* involving liabilities had occurred to the jurists it might have led them to the idea of notice to the person liable, but not to that of notice to the person claiming[6].

In relation to the *actio institoria* and the *actio exercitoria* there is a similar tendency. The question whether notice of the appointment was necessary had, it appears, some importance in modern German law till the enactment of

---

[1] Stellvertretung, 9.
[2] See, *e.g., ante*, pp. 162 *sqq.* The power of acquisition through a slave has little or no relation to agency. It is independent of authorisation: the slave seems to be contemplated rather as a mere receptacle or receiver.
[3] R. R. G. 2. 1128, 9.
[4] *Ante*, p. 167.
[5] See, *e.g.*, Bürg. Ges. B. §§ 164, 171; Mourlon, Code Civil, 3. 489.
[6] *Ante*, p. 155.

the new Code, for, if notice was necessary, the rule went no further than that of the Handelsgesetzbuch which had within its field superseded the Roman law.   But if the third party could sue though he had made the contract in ignorance of the *praepositio*, the rule still existed and might be applied in German courts.   Accordingly there has been controversy.   But the dominant view has been that the contract must have been made in view of the *praepositio*.   We have already seen that there is no warrant in the texts for that[1] : this is indeed usually admitted, and though texts are freely cited they are always reinforced by fixed juristic principles which in the view of the writer compel this conclusion.   Thus, Lenel, who states the edict in terms which do not seem to express any such requirement[2], discusses the matter elsewhere[3], and proceeds to set and to answer the question : did this praetorian action assume a state of facts in which a modern lawyer would see agency? He holds, no doubt correctly, that the edict says *" cum institore gestum erit eius rei nomine cui praepositus fuerit,"* and infers that the third person must therefore have known of the *praepositio*.   But at most the words only shew that he must have known of the business not of the *praepositio*, and this is a different matter.   After discussing some other texts, already considered, he goes on to say that general considerations lead him to the conclusion that notice was necessary[4].   We must consider, he urges, the need the Praetor was satisfying, the existing practice to which he was giving a legal sanction. He says that masters were in the habit of honouring such contracts in certain cases, and those cases were what the Praetor protected.   These, he says, were the cases in which the third party knew that the affair concerned the principal, for it was only in that case that failure to honour the contract would affect the principal's credit, and thus only in that case that he had been in the habit of honouring the contract.   This conjectural argument is imperfect, since the failure to honour the contract would affect the credit of the business, whether it was known to belong to him or not.   Lenel goes on to say that to require only objective connexion would be to create an impossibly wide extension of the *actio de in rem verso*, but this contention, like the former, only goes to shew that the third person must know that the affair concerned the business, not that he must know that behind the actual dealer there was a principal or, still less, an identified principal.   And this last is what at the beginning of his article he sets out to prove.   Indeed he seems to regard the points as the same, but it is clear that this is not the case[5].

Dernburg[6] thinks the requirement rests on the ". Wesen der Sache," since one who does not know of the agency trusts the agent, and there is no reason for giving him an advantage he did not contemplate when he made the contract.   Doubtless there is some reason in this if we think of the matter in terms of agency (though our English law ignores the point), but that is precisely what we are not entitled to do.   In fact in such a case what the

---

[1] *Ante*, p. 173.
[3] Iherings Jahrbücher, 24. 134 *sqq.*
[5] The distinction is clearly brought out in 14. 3. 17. 3.

[2] Ed. Perp. § 102.
[4] *op. cit.* 142.
[6] Pand. 2. § 13, n. 13.

third party trusts is the show of capital. Karlowa, besides making the same assimilation of the trade with the *praepositio*[1], says that the principal, standing behind, of whom the third party knows nothing, could have no juristic importance. Mitteis[2] does not confuse the two kinds of knowledge, but, admitting the uncertainty of the texts, concludes that knowledge is necessary, because subsequent discovery that there is a principal behind ought not to benefit the third person. For the present purpose all these positions are substantially the same.

Among the vexed questions arising in connexion with the *actio de in rem verso* there are two which raise a similar point. Will the action lie only where a free man would have an action on *gestio*? Must the third party have handed over the property in view of the intended *versio*? These have been fully discussed[3]. Here it is enough to say that the widely held affirmative opinions rest in the main not on the texts but on a certain modern theory of representation.

All this seems somewhat misleading: it is not in the law of agency that we must expect to find the hints which will help us to solve the question. No doubt it is practical needs that have created the law of agency on the lines followed in most continental systems, but in view of our English practice these cannot be called so inevitable that no other lines can be imagined. It must not be forgotten that the *actio de peculio* is the original one of these actions, and it may fairly be regarded as in a certain sense supplying the type, but there is scarcely a principle of the law of agency which this action does not defy. We are told indeed that the other party contracts in view of the *peculium*[4]. But the action lies even though the contract (or all contracts) were prohibited by the *dominus* to the knowledge of the other party[5]. It lies against a master who acquired the slave only after the contract and who knew nothing of it[6]. It appears even that it lies though the contract was made even before there was a *peculium*[7] No doubt these rules were gradually reached[8], but so, in view of the words of the Edict, must those have been which are attributed to the other actions. It is not easy to see why in one case the liability should have been steadily widened while in the other it was being artificially narrowed. No doubt it might be contended that it was precisely the limitations set on these actions which called for an extensive interpretation of the Edict *de peculio*. But while this hypothesis might fairly be used to explain a divergence of practice apparent on the texts, it is a different and less legitimate course to use it as evidence of a divergence which the sources nowhere indicate. Indeed the supposed narrow interpretation is negatived by the texts. If the right of the third party rests, in the *actio institoria*, on the knowledge of the authorisation, it is difficult to see how the rule is arrived at that he has the action even though the principal was to the third party's knowledge dead when the contract was made[9]. The actions *de in rem verso* and *de peculio*

---

[1] R. R. G. 2. 1128, 9; *ante*, p. 173.   [2] Stellvertretung, 25 *sqq*.   [3] *Ante*, pp. 179 *sqq*.
[4] 15. 1. 19. 1, 32. *pr*.   [5] 15. 1. 47. *pr*.   [6] 15. 1. 27. 2, 42.
[7] See Mandry, Familiengüterrecht, 2. 133.   [8] *Ante*, pp. 212 *sqq*.   [9] 14. 3. 17. 3.

B. R. L.   45

are one: why should it be supposed to have embodied such a notion as *negotii gestio* in the one case, while in the other it excluded it so completely that, to prevent enforcement against the master of obligations utterly opposed to any possible interest of his, it was necessary to fall back on the view that the Praetor could not have been thinking of such contracts[1].

With regard to the *actio institoria* the views that are here combated start, rightly, from the principle that in interpreting the scanty words of the Edict it is necessary to consider what the need was that the Praetor set himself to satisfy. But in considering this question the writers above cited seem to treat it as equivalent to another question: what might the third party reasonably expect? What were his moral rights? They consider, indeed, another question also: what did the commercial interests of the principal require? But this is the same question: it is his interest for the credit of the business to satisfy the reasonable expectations of the third party. How will the matter stand if we formulate our question in another way and ask: what risks should a master who provides his servant with the means of trading, and gives him his authority to trade, be reasonably expected to undertake? To the question so stated a very different answer is possible. We may notice that in the *actio tributoria* where there is *scientia* but no authority the liability of the master is a little increased, and the increased liability is due to his knowledge, and not to any knowledge of the facts by the creditor[2]. It is clear that the extension depends on a conception of the master's duty rather than of the creditor's right. Similarly in English law a principal is liable on a contract made by his authorised agent though the agent did not disclose the fact that there was a principal. In the same way it seems most probable that in the *actio institoria*, where there was general authority and provision of capital, as opposed to mere *scientia*, the liability of the master *in solidum* was independent of the creditor's knowledge of the facts[3]. This is also the conclusion that we considered to be indicated by the texts, as we did also in the *actio quod iussu*, where there was authorisation of a specific contract.

APPENDIX II.

FORMULATION AND *LITIS CONSUMPTIO* IN THE ACTIONS *ADIECTITIAE QUALITATIS*.

THESE intimately connected topics have been the subject of much controversy in recent years. No generally accepted solution of all the problems has been produced. In the following paragraphs space allows of no more than a general account of the matter.

The most accepted view as to formulation is that of Keller[4]. He holds that in the *actio de peculio* the *intentio* was *in ius*, with a fiction of liberty,

---

[1] *Ante*, p. 214.   [2] *Ante*, p. 233.
[3] See Ulpian in 13. 3. 1. *pr.*   [4] Litis contestatio, 432.

where the contract was by a slave, and assuming of course that the claim is one which ordinarily gave an *intentio in ius*. This view is adopted with new argument by Lenel[1]. For ordinary *formulae in ius* the suggested form is the simplest way in which to raise the issue, all that is needed being a change of name in the *condemnatio*, and the fiction of liberty in the case of a slave. It is clear on the texts that there was a fiction of liberty[2], and this would not be needed in a *formula in factum*. And a text dealing with the novation of the obligation strongly suggests that the *intentio* was *in ius*[3]. But the chief argument is the *ipso iure consumptio* which appears in some of the texts[4].

The *intentio* thus framed, stating the transaction between the parties, brings into issue the whole obligation, but we know that the defendant could not be condemned beyond the extent of the *peculium* and any *versio*. It is not quite clear how this restriction was expressed in the *formula*. It has been supposed that there was a *praescriptio* limiting the issue[5], but the language of many texts[6] leads Lenel to the opinion, now usually accepted, that there was a *taxatio* in the *condemnatio—dumtaxat de peculio et in rem verso*, or the like[7].

From this formulation it would follow, since a *iudicium* is none the less *legitimum* because the liability is praetorian[8], that the action once brought could not be renewed except by some form of praetorian relief. But the texts tell a confused story, a fact which is not surprising, since there were disputes on points which might have been expected to affect the matter. The jurists were hardly agreed as to whether the master could be said to owe at any moment more than was then in the *peculium*[9]. There was disagreement as to whether the natural obligation of the slave was *eadem res* with the praetorian obligation of the master[10], and there are other signs of doubt as to the exact nature of the *res* intended in the proposition that after *litis contestatio* in a *iudicium legitimum in ius* there could be no new *formula* for *eadem res*. Further, we have to do with texts edited after the *formula* and *iudicia legitima* had disappeared. When it is added that there is not yet unanimity on the point of formulation, and that the view has recently been broached that notwithstanding Gaius, the expressions *actio praetoria* and *actio in factum* mean much the same thing[11], it is easy to see that we cannot expect a very simple tale from the texts. One fact does tend to simplify matters : a text of Ulpian, citing Julian, and dealing with the case of action against one of two persons liable, declares that where one is only liable for a

[1] Ed. Perp. (2) §§ 102, 104; Girard, Manuel, 663. Gradenwitz (Z. S. S. 27. 229 *sqq.*) doubts the possibility of the crude fiction : "si liber esset," and supposes a fiction of manumission at the date of the transaction.
[2] 19. 1. 24. 2 ; 45. 2. 12.   [3] 14. 3. 13. 1.
[4] Lenel, *loc. cit.*, states and discusses the views of Mandry (Familiengüterrecht, 2. 259) and Brinz (Pand. 2. 203), who argue for a *formula in factum*, and of Baron (Adject. Klag. 136 *sqq.*), who supposes an *intentio* expressing a duty (*dare oportere*) in the *dominus*.
[5] Bekker, Aktionen, 333, 341 *sqq.*
[6] In. 4. 7. 4 b ; D. 5. 1. 57; 15. 1. 41; 15. 2. 1. 10; 18. 4. 2. 6; 19. 2. 60. 7; 23. 3. 57; 24. 3. 22. 12; 42. 8. 6. 12 ; C. 4. 26. 12.
[7] Ed. Perp. (2) § 104.   [8] G. 4. 109.   [9] *Ante*, p. 217.
[10] *Ante*, p. 695.   [11] Pokrowsky, Z. S. S. 16. 7.

part, action against him releases the other, but on equitable grounds the Praetor restores the action[1]. This text, much suspected on linguistic grounds, is now proved by the discovery of a scrap of the original to be in the main genuine, the word *rescissorium* having been omitted[2].

Prima facie, the simplest case is that of renewal of the action against the same defendant, *aucto peculio*. Ulpian tells us that the action lies[3]. Paul, dealing with the case in which the *peculium* is insufficient, observes that security cannot be claimed for subsequent accessions, though it can be in the *actio pro socio*, giving as his reason for the difference, that in *pro socio* the defendant owes the whole amount[4]. The parallel is pointless unless further *actio de peculio* was barred at strict law. Erman indeed[5] takes a very different view of this text. According to him Paul and Plautius are not concerned with *consumptio*, but exclude the *cautio* only because, as the *dominus* owes only *de peculio*, there can be no question of *consumptio* beyond this, so that the *cautio* is useless. Paul's language is indeed ill chosen if he was thinking of *consumptio*. It is ill chosen in any case. But the point of the parallel with *pro socio* is the fact that there is *consumptio*. The gist of the allusion is that, though the cases are alike in this respect, they differ in that in the case of the *socius* there is a civil *obligatio* for the whole, while in the other there is no obligation but that stated in the Edict, and that does not exceed the *peculium*. Elsewhere Ulpian tells us on the authority of Labeo[6] that where the *actio annalis* has been brought in error and lost on grounds which do not negative the debt, and it afterwards appears that the slave was not dead, the plaintiff is to be allowed to sue again. Earlier in this book[7] the view was expressed that this was due to independence of the obligations, but it seems rather to be a case of restitution for error : there is no word of an increase in the *peculium*, and, apart from error, the claim would certainly be barred as to the existing *peculium*. The text thus does not bear on the present point. There is, however, a sharp conflict between Paul and Ulpian. Many ways of dealing with it have been suggested. The simplest view is to suppose that *non* has been struck out from Ulpian's text[8]. Gradenwitz remarks[9] that this text is the only one which having spoken of a right of action as once exercised, with the emphatic word *semel*, goes on to say clearly that it can be renewed. This of course is far from conclusive, and while it is true that a *non* is easily dropped, it is also true that it is an important word not to be lightly introduced to create a harmony which does not exist. Accordingly it has been said[10] that there was a difference of opinion as to the extent of the *consumptio* operated by the *litis contestatio*, some jurists holding that the whole obligation, being expressed in the *intentio*, was consumed,

15. 1. 32. *pr.* Erman, see below, has held its doctrine classical.

[2] Z. S. S. 27. 369. Much of the controversial literature is rendered obsolete by this discovery. Apart from the literature cited by Lenel, Ed. Perp. (2) 278, n. 2, see Keller, Civ. Proz. n. 927; Karlowa, R. R. G. 2. 1142; Pokrowsky, Z. S. S. 20. 115; Ferrini, Z. S. S. 21. 190; Affolter, Institut. 214, 280 *etc.*; Gradenwitz, Z. S. S. 27. 229; Erman, Servus Vicarius, 498; Mélanges Appleton, 203 *sqq.*

[3] 15. 1. 30. 4.   [4] 15. 1. 47. 2.   [5] Mélanges Appleton, 241.
[6] 15. 2. 1. 10.   [7] *Ante*, p. 227.   [8] Ferrini, *loc. cit.*
[9] Z. S. S. 27. 229.   [10] Erman, Mél. Appleton, 229, following Affolter.

others, *e.g.* Ulpian, that the liability and the *consumptio* were only to the extent of the existing *peculium*. There is nothing *a priori* improbable in this, in view of the fact that there might well be, and in fact were in other connexions, doubts as to the exact nature of the *eadem res*, further claim on which was barred. It might well be held that what was barred was what might be effectively claimed in that action. The *intentio* is not the whole *formula*. A *praescriptio* could limit its consumptive force[1], and some may have thought a *condemnatio* might do so, particularly in view of the fact that the only existing obligation is that expressed in the Edict, limited to the *peculium*. But we know from Gaius[2] that in ordinary cases a limited *condemnatio* did not in fact limit the consumptive effect of the *intentio*. No doubts appear on this point, and, except for the text of Ulpian, there is no text suggesting limited *consumptio* in case of the renewed *actio de peculio*, *aucto peculio*. It may be noted that Papinian holds the whole *obligatio* to be brought into issue[3], and that the jurists who refuse *condictio* for payment in excess of *peculium*[4], are not authorities for the view expressed in Ulpian's text as it stands[5]. They shew that these jurists thought the Edict created a natural obligation for the whole, beyond the actionable obligation to the extent of the existing *peculium*, not that they held that there was an actionable obligation after *de peculio* had been brought. There were other cases in which a natural obligation survived a judgment[6].

On the whole the more probable view seems to be that in classical law the action was not renewable without relief, and that Ulpian[7] either wrote *non potest* or, more probably, added a requirement of *restitutio*[8]. In another case in which the question was of the renewal of action in regard to the same *peculium*, so that there is no doubt of the *consumptio*, Ulpian, in declaring that the action may be renewed, does not expressly mention *restitutio*, but uses the equivalent expression, *permittendum est*[9]. The same conclusion is deducible from the rule that in the case now to be considered of claim against one owner, after action against another, the plaintiff might proceed as if the earlier *iudicium* were rescinded and could recover not only what existed, but further accessions, not being bound to sue the other as at the time of the first action[10]. The language is significant and it is Ulpian who is speaking.

In relation to the renewal of the action against another person there are several cases to be considered. In those of common owners, and *coheredes* who have succeeded to the slave, either could be sued for the whole, was liable to the extent of the whole *peculium*, and could deduct for debts due to the other[11]. As we learn that of two owners he could be sued in respect of whom there was no *peculium*[12], the rule was no doubt as in the last case, and it would be immaterial whether the renewed action was against the same or another owner.

---

[1] See, *e.g.*, 21. 1. 48. 7.
[4] 12. 6. 11; 34. 3. 5. 2; *ante*, p. 217.
[6] 12. 6. 60. *pr.*; *ante*, p. 696.
[9] 15. 2. 1. 10.
[11] 15. 1. 11. 9, 27. 8; *ante*, p. 378.

[2] G. 4. 57.
[5] See, however, Erman, Mélanges Appleton, 229, 242.
[7] 15. 1. 30. 4.
[10] 15. 1. 32. 1.
[12] 15. 1. 12.

[3] 15. 1. 50. 2.
[8] Cp. 3. 5. 46. 1.

It is odd to find another rule applied as between two fructuaries or *bonae fidei possessores*, since they had the same remedies as common owners for adjustment[1]. But Ulpian, quoting Julian, tells us in a suspected text, now proved, by discovery of a fragment of the original, to. be substantially genuine[2], that neither could be condemned for more than he held, or deduct except for what was due to himself[3], that suing one freed the other, and that on equitable grounds a remedy was given by *restitutio actionis*. In fact there was a change of view as to the fructuary's liability *de peculio*[4]. The earlier lawyers held him liable only so far as he acquired. On that view the present question could not have arisen, except in a common undertaking. Then the view appeared that the acquirer must be sued first, and that is the rule from which the present text starts, since Julian, who favoured that view[5], is the source of this text. When the rule was accepted that either could be sued on any contract, the present restriction became unnecessary. But as between owner and fructuary Justinian's rule is still that the fructuary can be sued primarily only for what concerns him, but the action is restored against the owner and *vice versa*[6]. There is no *communi dividundo* between them. A similar limitation of the right of action and deduction, with *restitutio actionis*, occurs in the case of *coheredes* liable only to the *actio annalis*[7], but here the division is due to the express provision of the XII Tables.

In the case of vendor and buyer, within the *annus utilis*, the rule applied is due to the fact that neither, if he is sued, and has paid in full, can recover from the other. Thus, though either can be sued for the whole, he is liable only to the extent of the *peculium* he holds. Though the other is freed, the claimant has *restitutio actionis*, to recover any balance still due[8].

The relief is sometimes called *restauratio* of the old action[9]. There are signs of dispute as to the effect of this. Strictly it might seem to restore the action only against the old defendant. This would be useless in the present case. Some seem to have held that it only went so far as to give the claimant what he could have recovered in the earlier action if the present defendant had been a party. The view which prevailed was that the *condemnatio* would bę based on the present state of the *peculium*[10]. It is in fact *restitutio in integrum*. It is elsewhere called *rescissio iudicii*[11], which expresses the same idea. It has been said that this makes what has been paid an *indebitum*[12]. But the debt is not rescinded : what was paid was due and cannot be recovered. Nor indeed is the old judgment rescinded : the new judge is merely directed to proceed as if the matter had not been before the court.

We have assumed that the earlier action has proceeded to judgment. But there are cases of *translatio iudicii*, in which a pending action is transferred. If a *dominus* dies, pending the action, the *iudicium* is transferred

---

[1] 10. 3. 7. 6, 7.
[2] 15. 1. 32. *pr.*; cp. Z. S. S. 27. 369 and D. 15. 1. 19. 1.
[3] 15. 1. 15.
[4] *Ante*, p. 339.
[5] 15. 1. 37. 3; *ante*, p. 340.
[6] 15. 1. 19. 1, 37. 3.
[7] 11. 1. 18; 15. 1. 14. 1, 32. *pr.*
[8] 15. 1. 30. 5, 37. 2, 47. 3.
[9] 15. 1. 32. *pr.*
[10] 15. 1. 32; cp. 12. 2. 26. 1.
[11] 15. 1. 47. 3.
[12] Ferrini, cit. Erman, Mél. Appleton, 355.

to the *heres*. Is this mere succession or *rescissio iudicii*? The point might be very material, as, if the claim were liable to be barred by time, the second action, regarded as a new one, might be too late. The material texts do not deal with slaves : it is enough to say that Koschaker has shewn[1] that it is a mere case of succession. He has also shewn, however[2], that no inference for the identity of the two *iudicia* can be drawn from use of the term *translatio iudicii*. The point has already been considered in connexion with noxal actions[3], and the view adopted that transfer of a pending noxal action against the slave, freed, or against a new owner, is a case of mere succession. Koschaker takes a different view[4], at least in the case of the man himself. He shews that Ulpian calls the noxal *iudicium inutile*, while Paul says the *iudex* must *transferre iudicium*[5]. As a void *iudicium* cannot be transferred, he holds that the second must be new. Admitting the possibility of disagreement, he yet thinks that Paul agrees with Ulpian. It is quite possible, however, that Ulpian agrees with Paul, merely holding that there can be no valid judgment against the alleged *dominus*. But in view of the doubts which certainly existed[6], no stress can be laid on Ulpian's mode of expression.

We have hitherto assumed that where *litis contestatio* has occurred, what is consumed is the *obligatio* stated in the *intentio*, limited sometimes by *praescriptio*. This agrees with the language of the texts[7] and accounts for the rules arrived at. But the matter is less clear when we turn to the other *actiones adiectitiae qualitatis*. The *intentio* being the same in all cases the bringing of one action ought to bar any other except for relief, and this is the result deducible from most of the texts. All possible combinations are not represented, and, apart from the institutional books, Ulpian is the sole authority. We learn that *de peculio* and *tributoria* barred each other[8], and that *de peculio* barred *quod iussu*[9]. As to *de in rem verso* there is a text which seems to imply that it did not bar *de peculio*, and is so treated earlier in this book[10]. But it is more probably a case of praetorian relief against error in the *actio de peculio*, ignoring the fact that there has been a valid trial of the same issue under the *de in rem verso* clause.

Another text raises another apparent difficulty of the same kind. A *filiusfamilias* accepts a *iudicium* as *defensor* of his father in an *actio de peculio*, as it seems, on his own debt. The effect is to release his father. This, we are told, is a *versio*, to the amount of the *peculium*[11], even before judgment. This excludes the possibility of the view that it is in the *actio iudicati de peculio* that the *versio* is made effective. But any new action is presumably barred. Von Tuhr shews reason for supposing the action to be one by the surety *iudicatum solvi*, which the *defensor* must have had[12]. On this view the text has nothing to do with *consumptio*.

[1] Translatio Iudicii, 239 *sqq.*, in opposition to Krüger, Z. S. S. 15. 140.
[2] *op. cit.* 15. The distinction is, however, sometimes brought out, *e.g.* in 5. 1. 57.
[3] *Ante*, p. 108.   [4] *op. cit.* 220.   [5] 9. 4. 42; 40. 12. 24. 4.
[6] *Ante*, p. 109.   [7] G. 4. 53, 68, 107 *etc.*
[8] G. 4. 74; Inst. 4. 7. 5; D. 14. 4. 9. 1.   [9] 14. 5. 4. 5.
[10] *Ante*, p. 228.   [11] 15. 3. 10. 3.   [12] Actio de in rem verso, 147.

In relation to the *actio institoria* (and *executoria*) there is difficulty. It is clear that the primary obligation is brought into issue, for it bars action against the representative, and is said to lie *ex persona magistri*[1]. And it bars another *actio institoria*, where the first was lost through a mistake as to the business for which the loan was made[2]. But the same writer, Ulpian, says in the same context, that if *institoria* has been brought on what is in fact a *peculiare negotium*, and thus lost, the *actio tributoria* is still available[3]. This seems to mean that *institoria* does not bar *tributoria*. Erman[4] is inclined to explain the texts as expressing a difference of view, some jurists holding the primitive (Proculian) view that *intentio consumitur*; others taking all the conditions of the *condemnatio* into account, the claim being barred only where all are identical. He cites certain texts in support, but they refer to real actions[5], where there is no question of the *novatio necessaria* produced by *litis contestatio*[6]. And the frequent appeal to *restitutio* shews that it was not in this way that relief was found. It is possible in view of the language of the texts that Ulpian allowed *restitutio*, and that the present form of the text is due to the compilers[7]. There is, however, another possibility. The *formula* of the *actio tributoria* is uncertain. It differs from the other actions in that the liability depends on the master's *dolus*. It is not certain whether the bar of *de peculio* by *tributoria* depends on *consumptio*[8], or on fairness[9], or on express provision, as is suggested by one of the texts[10]. If the *formula* alleged an obligation of the *dominus* other than that of the representative there is no reason why it should not survive so far as *consumptio* is concerned. This would explain why *tributoria* is mentioned and not *de peculio*. But this solution seems to require that it be *dolus* not to admit, in the *tributio*, a debt now reduced to, at best, a *naturalis obligatio*.

APPENDIX III.

FORM USED BY SLAVE IN ACQUISITION BY *MANCIPATIO*, ETC.

In an essay in the Zeitschrift der Savigny Stiftung for 1905 with the chief thesis of which we are not here concerned[11], Professor Eisele makes some interesting remarks on the form of *mancipatio*. As Gaius shews[12], it contained in ordinary cases, two members; first an assertion of ownership in the acquirer, and secondly, what looks like the chief operative part, *esto mihi empta hoc aere aeneaque libra*. With the odd fact that at the time when the

---

[1] 14. 1. 1. 17, 24. [2] 14. 3. 13. *pr.* [3] *h. t.* 11. 7.
[4] Mélanges Appleton, 234 *sqq.* [5] 44. 2. 9. 1, 18; 46. 8. 8. *pr.* [6] G. 3. 180.
[7] The action was just that one not confined to the household relation. Lenel (Ed. Perp. § 102) shews that the fact that the contracting party was a representative was prominently stated, as he thinks in a *demonstratio*. But it is difficult to suggest a formulation which, resting on this idea, shall leave intact the *actio tributoria* (14. 3. 11. 7) while destroying the action against the representative (14. 1. 1. 17, 24).
[8] Mandry, Familiengüterr. 2. 448, 9. [9] Karlowa, R. R. G. 2. 1163.
[10] 14. 4. 9. 1: *cum scit sibi regressum ad alium non futurum.*
[11] Z. S. S. 26. 66 *sqq.* [12] G. 1. 119; 3. 167.

assertion of ownership is made it is not true we need not here deal[1]. Our difficulty is to see how far the form was modified if the acquisition was by a slave. It is clear that he could say *hanc rem domini mei ex iure Quiritium esse aio*[2]. But he did not always say this, as there might be doubt as to the person to whom he acquired, *e.g.* in the case of usufruct[3]. Eisele thinks that he said *meum esse aio*. This is improbable on the face of it, and cannot really be made to agree with the remark of Gaius that the reason why he could not claim in a *cessio in iure* was that he could have nothing of his own[4]. Eisele supposes that Gaius is really referring to incapacity to appear in court, but that is not what Gaius says, and it is scarcely credible that he could have expressed himself as he does, if slaves had been constantly using that exact formula in *mancipatio*. Eisele adverts to the well-known rule laid down, *e.g.* by Julian[5], that a slave could stipulate *sibi dari*. But Julian is also clear that a slave cannot stipulate for a right for himself[6]. A way out is found by understanding such words in a loose, *de facto*, sense[7], but this resource is useless in the case of such words as *meum ex iure Quiritium esse aio*. On the other hand the form absolutely requires the naming of someone in whom the right is to vest.

A text already briefly considered[8] discusses the case of a slave who buys a thing and pays for it by handing over a bag containing twice the price, half being his owner's, half his fructuary's[9]. Ulpian decides that there is no transfer of the money, so that the property is not acquired to either. It is hardly possible that in this case he can have named both, since the naming of each would have had a privative effect[10] on the other, as to half, so that each would have acquired half and it would have been indifferent which money was paid first. He can hardly have named no one. The decision would conflict in a quite unnecessary way with principle, and indeed with Ulpian's own views[11]. But the result in the text would appear to follow if he had said *domino aut fructuario* and there was no evidence other than this payment as to whether it was or was not within the *causae*. It is analogous to a *stipulatio* "to A or B," both being *domini*. It is of course an improbable form, but there are many similar illustrations : the whole case is imaginary. These events never happened[12].

---

[1] See Wlassak, Z. S. S. 28. 71 *sqq.* Nor need we consider whether *est* or *esto* is to be preferred in the second member.

[2] G. 3. 167. [3] 7. 1. 25. 1. [4] G. 2. 96.

[5] 45. 3. 1. [6] 45. 1. 38. 6 *sqq.* [7] *h. t.* 38. 3—9.

[8] 7. 1. 25. 1; *ante*, p. 364.

[9] It is for the purpose of the text indifferent whether the transfer of the thing bought was by *traditio* or by *mancipatio*.

[10] *Ante*, p. 380. [11] *Ante*, p. 364.

[12] See Eisele, *loc. cit.*, and Buckland, N. R. H. 32. 226. Absurd as looks the form, *Hanc rem Titii aut Seii ex i. Q. esse aio*, it does not seem to conflict with anything that is known of the rules of *mancipatio*. If T was *dominus* and S a stranger, it is not unlikely that there may have been speculative discussion on the question whether the insertion, *aut Seii*, vitiated the transaction or was mere surplusage. And the decisive effect of payment in connexion with the theory of the two *causae* (*ante*, p. 364) makes the case suggested one of speculative interest, though hardly of practical importance. But the transfer may have been by *traditio*, or the expression may have been used in the contract of sale.

APPENDIX IV.

THE ESSENTIAL CHARACTER OF MANUMISSION[1].   *ITERATIO.*

To analyse the conception of manumission so as to express it in terms of other institutions is perhaps impossible.   It has an obvious affinity with conveyance, and Vangerow[2], treating it as essentially an act of transfer, deduces from this character its main rules, so far as they are concerned with latinity.   But though this affinity is clear, it is no more than an analogy, and it is not alone.   What was given to the man was not *dominium* over himself: no man has that.   The *lex* Aquilia gave no action to a man for personal damage, precisely for this reason.   It is true that Vangerow[3] holds this text[4] of no force in this connexion; he says that what Ulpian means is that the *lex* applies only to ownership of things in the ordinary sense, and this does not cover his ownership of himself.   But what Ulpian says is that the man has no *actio* Aquilia, because he is not *dominus* of his members. That is, his right is not *dominium*.   That it is analogous to ownership is true, but this does not justify Vangerow's inferences.   Personal independence is not ownership of one's person[5].   We know that manumission by will is not a legacy[6].   What is conferred is liberty with citizenship.   If the analogy with transfer of ownership were identity, or had been the most prominent factor in the minds of the lawyers, we might have expected a development of mancipation with safeguards; we should have looked for discussion of the question whether one freed informally or under 30 (thinking he was older), would acquire *libertas ex iure Quiritium* by one year's usucapion.   The modes employed *inter vivos* are not those of ordinary conveyance.   *Census* has little relation to them, and though manumission *vindicta* is in all probability a case of *cessio in iure*, it must be noted that that form is usually employed, precisely because the subject of the transaction is not *dominium*. It is true that Schlossmann holds that *cessio in iure* is the primitive conveyance and that *mancipatio* is a development from it[7], but though there are early references to *cessio in iure*, there seems to be no evidence earlier than Gaius for its use in conveyance of a specific thing.   The text of Varro[8] sometimes cited may refer only to *cessio in iure hereditatis.*

What passes to the man is not what belonged to the master: his liberty and *civitas* are not subtractions from those of the *dominus*.   There are other cases in which *cessio in iure* is applied in the same way: the *potestas* which is acquired by the *cessio in iure* which is the last step in *adoptio*[9] is not identical with the right which is destroyed.   The cases seem parallel: what

---

[1] See Wlassak, Z. S. S. 25. 84 *sqq.*, 28. 1 *sqq.*; Karlowa, R. R. G. 2. 128; Rabel, Z. S. S. 27. 290 *sqq.*; Vangerow, Latini Iuniani, §§ 16, 28—30.
[2] *loc. cit.*   [3] *op. cit.* 70.   [4] 9. 2. 13. *pr.*
[5] Karlowa, *loc. cit.*   [6] *Ante*, p. 466.
[7] Schlossmann, Cessio in Iure und Mancipatio.
[8] Varro, R. R. 2. 10. 4.   [9] G. 1. 134.

is released is something other than what is acquired. Rabel[1] holds this to be a disregard of logic, intelligible in adoption, but not admissible in manumission. But it is clear from the doubts as to the effect of an attempt to cede usufruct to an *extraneus*[2], and as to *cessio hereditatis* by a *necessarius*[3], and perhaps still more from the rule that *cessio* after entry released debtors to the estate[4] and from that as to the effect of attempted *cessio* by a *tutor cessicius*[5], that there was no very certain logical doctrine, as to the juristic nature of *cessio in iure*.

Manumission is not transfer of *dominium* : it is creation of a *civis*, and release not merely from ownership, but from the capacity of being owned. This seems a better way in which to express the matter than to speak, as Karlowa does[6], of the acquisition of personality. The Romans of an early age did not so think of the matter, still less would they have felt Karlowa's difficulty that if the slave is a mere *res* he cannot acquire, and manumission is an impossibility. This sort of subtlety is of a later time, as is his solution that the man acquires by virtue of a derivative personality, based on that of his master.

Manumission *inter vivos* is probably due to the Pontiffs, who applied such analogies as presented themselves and, so far as their activity is known, do not appear to have been bound by a very strict logic[7]. In the case of *census*, there is no element of conveyance, and in manumission *vindicta* it is rather the fact that the case is not one of *dominium* which prompts the use of the form. It has indeed been contended that this is not a case of *cessio in iure*[8], but a comparison of the accounts of the two transactions[9] shews the closest similarity. It is true that there are differences : the prominence of the *festuca* is the most important. But nothing is more to be expected than distinctions of detail expressive of the particular application ; there is no reason to treat them as shewing a difference of underlying principle, and it must be noted that we have a description not of *cessio in iure* in general, but of *cessio in iure* of the *dominium* in a specific thing.

There is no doubt difficulty in the question whether *cessio in iure*, and therefore manumission *vindicta* is properly called a piece of fictitious litigation. Discussion of that wider question is not in place here. It has recently been thoroughly examined by Wlassak[10] : he declares against this view, holding that it is *ab initio* not an act of litigation, but of release by the *dominus* with official sanction, given in the form of *addictio*. He shews reason for thinking that there was no *addictio* where a defendant in a real action refused to defend, or admitted his liability ; indeed he denies the applicability of the notion of *confessio* to a real action, and considers that the form *ad-dicto* shews that what is done is in supplement to the act of another[11].

From this point of view the question whether it is fictitious litigation or not is rather a matter of words. Wlassak suggests that it is of the essence

1 *op. cit.* 325.   2 G. 1. 30.   3 G. 1. 35 *sqq.*
4 *Ibid.*   5 Ulp. 11. 7. As to death of *cessicius*, see Rabel, *loc. cit.*
6 *loc. cit.*   7 G. 1. 134, 2. 53.
8 See reff. in Wlassak, Z. S. S. 28. 1—3.   9 See G. 1. 24, and *ante*, p. 451.
10 Z. S. S. 25. 84 *sqq.*   11 Z. S. S. 25. 91.

of a "Scheinprozess" that the true drift of the proceedings shall be concealed from the parties or the public. But this is hardly essential: our own "common recovery" was assuredly fictitious litigation, though everyone was aware that it was a mere device of conveyancing to enable a man to convey what in fact he had not. It is not deceit, but evasion of legal difficulties, at which the transaction aims. Wlassak has made it extremely probable that the *addictio* is a characteristic part of the *cessio*, and does not occur in real actions even on admission of the claim. It indicates that what is in hand is not true litigation. The nature of the transaction is evident from the beginning, and in that sense it may be said to have nothing fictitious about it. But this is to ignore the equally notable fact that it borrows the form of a *causa liberalis*, the *vindicatio* and the *assertor*, and is plainly based thereon[1]. The question as to the exact significance, and place in the proceedings, of the master's touch with the wand, and as to the essentiality of the blow on the cheek, *etc.*, are matters on which the evidence permits little but conjecture. And even on Wlassak's view, that *addictio* is characteristic, it is not possible to say with certainty whether it is, as some say, a mere recognition by the magistrate, or as others say, an act of grant by the magistrate[2], or as he holds, and, as it seems, with much probability, an act of sanction. But on the view here taken of the nature of manumission, these points are of small importance. If conveyance, gift of *civitas*, release from the position of a *res* are all present to the minds of the framers, and these are by no means slaves to logic, any one of these analogies may be the determining cause of a particular part of the form without entitling us to draw any inferences from the existence of that detail, as to the real nature of the transaction.

The law of *iteratio* might be expected to provide a touchstone for some at any rate of these opinions. The texts are few and somewhat obscure[3]. Vangerow[4], starting from his view that *manumissio* is essentially conveyance (and *iteratio* must of course proceed from a quiritary owner), holds that there may be *iteratio* after informal manumission, though the original manumission was before the slave was 30, and after manumission by the bonitary owner, in each case by the quiritary owner for the time being, even a transferee or heir. He refutes the opinion of Bethmann-Hollweg and others[5], who hold that only the original quiritary owner can iterate, not his heir or assignee, and not even he, if, before the first manumission, the man was in the bonitary ownership of another. He shews that this last view is plainly contradicted by the texts[6] and that the textual support of the others is only apparent[7]. But he holds that one who has formally freed a man under 30 cannot iterate, as he has by the formal act abandoned the *ius Quiritium*, though circumstances prevent the slave from acquiring it. He does not distinguish between *vindicta* and will. He accounts for the language of Ulp. 3. 4, which requires

---

[1] Livy, 41. 9.   [2] See the reff., Wlassak, Z. S. S. 25. 104 *sqq*.
[3] The chief are G. 1. 35, 167; 2. 195; Gai. Ep. 1. 1. 4; Ulp. 1. 12; 3. 1; 3. 4; 11. 19; Fr. Dos. 14; Vat. Fr. 221; Plin. Litt. 7. 16; Tacit. Ann. 13. 26.
[4] *loc. cit.*   [5] Reff., Vangerow, *op. cit.* 152.
[6] G. 1. 167; Vat. Fr. 221.   [7] Ulp. 3. 4, *fuit*, and Plin. Litt. Traj. 105.

the man to be 30 at the first manumission, on the ground that it is only of a slave first freed over 30 that the proposition he lays down as to *iteratio* is true generally. The texts[1] seem to leave no doubt as to the justice of his view in the case of informal manumission of a man under 30. Indeed since iteration in this case dates from before the *lex* Aelia, any other view requires this law or the *lex* Iunia to have contained an express provision forbidding *iteratio* in this case. But his opinion as to formal manumission seems less certain. The textual authority is small : there is only the doubtful inference from Ulpian[2], and some indications in Gaius 1. 35, so defective that reconstitution of the text is hopeless. On the other hand it must be admitted that while there are texts speaking of *iteratio* as applicable to junian latins generally[3], there is none which unequivocally applies it to a latin freed *vindicta* or *testamento*.

Vangerow bases his opinion mainly on the view that as manumission implies ownership, it is impossible where there has been a formal manumission, since the formal act of conveyance, though the provisions of the *lex* Aelia prevent it from giving *civitas*, produces nevertheless the other effects of which it is capable. Thus it causes the *dominium* to pass out of the manumitter, though it does not pass to the *manumissus*. He supports this view by reference to the cases above mentioned in which *cessio in iure tutelae*, *ususfructus* and *hereditatis*, were treated as depriving the *cedens* though the primary purpose was not realised. But, apart from the fact that these texts shew evident signs of dispute, they appear to turn, not on the principle invoked by Vangerow, but upon the notion that *cessio* is an acknowledgment in court that the *cedens* has no right. This could have no bearing on manumission by will[4]. It may be observed that in some cases, and in the opinion of some jurists, the *cessio* might be pleaded by persons who were not parties to it[5], and it is also noticeable that in every recorded case it is used as a defence to a claim set up by the *cedens*. It may also be noted that Vangerow's theory leads to the result that if an owner under 20 manumitted *vindicta*, though the manumission did not take effect, it would be impossible for the owner ever to make the man a *civis*. For the texts do not say that his act is a nullity but only that the statute bars the freedom[6]. Indeed on Vangerow's view it seems that the man should have become a *servus sine domino*, for it is not merely the *ius Quiritium* which is affected by a *cessio in iure*. Analogous difficulties arise in the case of manumission by will. As we have seen, it is by no means clear that a manumission *vindicta* could make a man a latin in classical law[7], and it may be that this is the real reason of the silence of the texts. As to manumission by will Ulpian tells

---

1 G. 1. 167 ; Vat. Fr. 221. 2 Ulp. 3. 4, referring only to latins over 30.
3 Ulp. 3. 1 ; Fr. Vat. 221.
4 The rule of accrual when a common slave is freed *vindicta* or *testamento* by one owner (*ante*, p. 575) may seem to throw doubt on this. But the principle on which this accrual rested was very doubtful. Some thought it operated even in informal manumission. The view which prevailed seems to have been that it was confined not only to a formal manumission but to one which satisfied all the requirements of manumission (40. 2. 4. 2). Justinian observes (C. 7. 7. 1. *pr.*) that, as to the rules of accrual in this case, *multa ambiguitas exorta est apud veteres iuris auctores.*
5 G. 1. 35 ; Ulp. 11. 7.   6 Reff., *ante*, p. 542.   7 *Ante*, p. 543.

us expressly that the *lex* Aelia treats a man manumitted under 30 by will as if he had been freed informally, which he would hardly have said if there was the fundamental difference that *iteratio* was impossible in the case of the former. The result seems to be that any Junian latin could, when he was over 30, be made a *civis* by *iteratio*, by the person in whom the quiritary ownership of him was now vested. But it is an open question whether in classical law a person freed *vindicta* could be a latin.

APPENDIX V.

MANUMISSION *VINDICTA* BY A *FILIUSFAMILIAS*.

It is clear that manumission *vindicta* was a *legis actio*[1]. It is also most probable that a *filiusfamilias* was incapable of *legis actio*. It appears to follow that he could not free *vindicta*, even *iussu patris*. Yet this power is repeatedly credited to him, and is nowhere expressly denied. On the texts as they stand there is therefore something like an absolute contradiction.

There seem to be two ways of dealing with the matter, assuming the truth of the proposition that a *filiusfamilias* cannot *lege agere*. One of these is that of Mitteis[2], to refer all the texts which do not specify the form to the informal methods and to treat the others as in some way interpolated. The other course is to accept the texts and to treat their rule as one more case in which the character of the process was disregarded. The following pages state as briefly as possible the grounds on which the present writer has held[3], and holds, this the better view.

The relaxations stated on p. 452 are no doubt for the most part merely evidences that the process was not really regarded as judicial. Some can hardly be so disposed of[4], but they are much less important than the texts directly touching the question, of which the chief are set out and discussed in the following pages.

I. Schol. Sin. 18. 49 (Krüger): ...ὁ ὑπεξούσιος ὡς μὴ ὢν *legis* (   ) δεκτικὸς οὐ δύναται *in iure cedere* ἑτέρῳ τὴν ἐπιτροπήν.

This text leads Mitteis to reject all the others. He infers that in the judgment of Ulpian a *filiusfamilias* could not *lege agere*, and that thus all the texts which speak of him as freeing *vindicta* must be in part post-classical. Fifth century greek scholia are not perhaps the best evidence of what Ulpian said, and it may well be that the rule is Ulpian's, the reason the scholiast's. But admitting that it is in effect Ulpian who speaks, the text is but a doubtful starting-point. It gives an odd result. The *tutela* in

---

[1] *Ante*, p. 451.
[3] N. R. H. 27. 737.
[2] Mitteis, Z. S. S. 21. 199; 25. 379; Röm. Privatrecht, 1. 2. 11.
[4] 40. 2. 8; 40. 2. 23.

question must be *legitima*, for Ulpian allows only *legitimi tutores* to cede[1]. The case is thus one of a patron, *i.e.* a *miles* or former *miles*, who can, as we know, free *vindicta*. The proposition thus is : certain persons who can certainly free by *legis actio* cannot cede the *tutela* acquired by the manumission, because they are incapable of *legis actio*. This is at least something like a contradiction, and such a text seems hardly clear enough to put all the others out of court.

II. P. Sentt. 1. 13 a. *Filiusfamilias iussu patris manumittere potest, matris non potest.*

This text is perfectly genuine and thus ought to cover all cases of manumission *inter vivos*. Mitteis considers it arbitrary to apply it to manumission *vindicta*. It seems more arbitrary to understand a tacit limitation to manumissions which produce only a truncated result. The effect is to make the text give a misleading result, which Paul elsewhere carefully avoids. In view of the language of P. Sentt. 4. 12. 2, it is difficult to understand our text of a manumission which did not give *iusta libertas*. It is one thing to state a general rule ignoring exceptions : it is another to lay down in general terms a rule which does not apply to the normal case at all.

III. C. 7. 15. 1. 3. In this enactment Justinian extends the power of authorising manumission to ascendants of either sex in respect of any descendants. He says he is abolishing the old restrictions of persons, but he says nothing of any extension in point of form. The first case he names is *per iudicem*.

IV. 37. 14. 13, Modest.; 40. 1. 16, Idem ; 40. 1. 22, Papin. These texts are general and if written as they stand must fairly be applied to all manumission *inter vivos*. They may have been abridged, but there is no sign of this, and, at least as to 40. 1. 16, the reference to manumission *vindicta* is strongly suggested.

V. 38. 2. 22, Marcian. *Si filiusfamilias miles manumittat, secundum Iuliani sententiam...patris libertum faciet: sed quamdiu, inquit, vivit, praefertur filius in bona eius patri. Sed divus Hadrianus Flavio Apro rescripsit suum libertum eum facere non patris.*

This text, adduced by Mitteis, deals with a *miles* and is not strictly in point. Its only importance is that its language shews the practice to have been older than Hadrian's enactment[2], and that as it is not easy to see how the father can have been thought entitled to the goods of such a man otherwise than by descent, the manumission must have given *civitas* and thus been formal. The possible but uncertain inferences need not be entered on.

VI. 40. 1. 7, Alfenus Varus. This text mentioned by Mitteis has been so maltreated that little can be inferred from it. What can be made of the *libertus* who becomes a slave again at the end of the text? The fragment seems of little importance in the present connexion[3].

VII. 40. 2. 4. *pr.*, Julian. *Si pater filio permiserit servum manumittere et interim decesserit intestato, deinde filius ignorans patrem suum*

[1] Ulp. 11. 6, 8.
[3] *Ante*, p. 459.

[2] See 37. 14. 8. *pr.*; 38. 2. 3. 8 and *ante*, p. 459.

mortuum, libertatem imposuerit, libertas servo favore libertatis contingit, cum non appareat mutata esse domini voluntas, sin autem ignorante filio vetuisset pater per nuntium et antequam filius certior fieret, servum manumisisset, liber non fit. nam ut filio manumittente servus ad libertatem perveniat durare oportet patris voluntatem : nam si mutata fuerit non erit verum volente patre filium manumisisse.

This text has been profoundly altered. It does not express Julian's view[1], and some at least of the talk about *voluntas* seems to be due to Tribonian. It is difficult to see why it should have been placed under the heading *de manumissione vindicta*, unless originally written of this, since it contains no reference to form. Mitteis holds that it was written of informal manumission, mainly it seems, because *h. l.* 1 was. The force of this is weakened by the fact that *h. l.* 2 was certainly written of formal manumission, and, if contiguity is decisive, settles the question the other way for the whole *lex*. There is indeed little reason to think that *h. l.* 1 was written of informal manumission. The needlessly duplicated talk about *voluntas* looks like Tribonian seeking a reason good for all manumission. And though, as Mitteis has elsewhere shewn[2], it is dangerous to be dogmatic as to what Julian cannot have written, he can hardly have written the reasoning put before us. He is supposed to have said that when Titius declares *inter amicos* that he frees a man, whom he thinks, in fact, to be the property of another, but who is his own, *verum est voluntate domini servum manumissum esse*. But that is not the case : the needed *voluntas* is not present. He intended a joke to deceive the man or his own friends : *lex enim Iunia eos fieri latinos iubet quos dominus liberos esse voluit*[3]. On the other hand, as applied to manumission *vindicta* the decision is perfectly sound. As has been said by Wlassak[4] : "bei allen Formalgeschäften des alten Rechts, so auch bei der manumissio vindicta, die rechtliche Geltung unabhängig war vom Dasein des durch die Wortformel...der Partei angezeigten Willens." This is surely what Julian is laying down. There are other texts which shew that formal acts produced their effects irrespective of state of mind[5], and others which shew that, apart from form, the transaction was null in such a case of mistake unless there was a real *voluntas* which the transaction realised[6]. Some of them refer to informal manumission.

VIII. 40. 2. 10, Marcian. *Surdi vel muti patris filius iussu eius manumittere potest : furiosi vero filius non potest manumittere.*

It is not easy to see why this text is placed in this title, unless it was originally written of manumission *vindicta*. Here too there may have been alteration : apart from this its general form would have been misleading. Mitteis observes that it was of course necessary to mention here and there the powers of *muti* and *surdi*, and he cites three other examples. It may

---

[1] 40. 9. 15. 1; *post*, p. 722.   [2] Z. S. S. 27. 369.
[3] Fr. Dos. 7, 8.
[4] Z. S. S. 26. 403. As to the interpolation of this text he agrees with Mitteis.
[5] Cp. P. 1. 7. 6, 8; G. 4. 117.
[6] 17. 1. 49; 29. 2. 15; 22. 6. 9. 4; 41. 1. 35; 40. 9. 9. *pr.*, 17. 1; 40. 12. 28; 41. 2. 4. 15; In. 2. 20. 11. See also Buckland, N. R. H. 32. 236.

not be altogether insignificant that in two of these[1] the limit of the power is clearly stated, while in the third[2] the negative form of the proposition makes this unnecessary.

IX. 40. 2. 18. 2, Paul. *Filius quoque voluntate patris apud patrem manumittere potest.*

As it stands this text is conclusive. Mitteis holds that there has been alteration and that Paul actually wrote: *Filius miles apud patrem, etc.* There is no evidence of change and indeed that remark seems hardly worth making. The point actually made is more important. If the manumission was *voluntate patris*, it was his own manumission and he was judge in his own cause. The words *voluntate patris*, redundant as they look, are essential to the statement of this point.

X. 40. 2. 22, Paul. *Pater ex provincia ad filium sciens Romae agentem epistulam fecit quae permisit ei quem vellet ex servis quos in ministerio secum hic habebat vindicta liberare: post quam filius Stichum manumisit apud Praetorem: quaero an fecerit liberum. respondi: quare non hoc concessum credamus patri ut permittere possit filio ex his quos in ministerio haberet manumittere? solam enim electionem filio concessit, ceterum ipse manumittit.*

Mitteis supposes the compilers to have here interpolated the references to form, though they have omitted to do so in the other texts in this title which we have discussed. He considers the expression *apud praetorem* ill placed and redundant in view of the word *vindicta* earlier in the passage. But the expression is inserted precisely because the authorisation was to proceed in a certain way, and the statement shews that the direction was followed. The form *vindicta liberare* is the usual classical form[3]. In 40. 1. 15 and 45. 1. 122. 2 it is clearly genuine, but it does not seem common in the Digest. In our text the words have all the appearance of being a quotation from the letter.

XI. 40. 9. 15. 1, Paul. *Iulianus ait si postea quam filio permisit pater manumittere filius ignorans patrem decessisse manumisit vindicta non fieri eum liberum, sed et si vivit pater et voluntas mutata erit non videri volente patre filium manumisisse.*

Mitteis supposes the compilers to have interpolated the word *vindicta*. It is not clear why they should have so done. If the original text contained no reference to form the insertion would be misleading. If it did, it would be still more misleading to strike out that reference and also insert the word *vindicta*, though to do either without the other would be reasonable. The chief positive sign of interpolation is the fact that, in the Florentine *index*, the corrector of the MS. has altered a heading *ad legem* Iuliam, and made it Iuniam. I have suggested that the corrector was wrong, as he was far from infallible, and though Mitteis attaches no weight to this, the suggestion may not look quite absurd to one who will look at the surroundings of the correction at the place where it occurs. That is the Florentine *index* and not in the inscription of this *lex*. It is not indeed certain that it refers to

[1] 3. 3. 43. *pr.*; 29. 2. 5.   [2] 39. 5. 33. 2.
[3] G. 1. 17, 18, 44; P. 4. 12. 2; Fr. Dos. 10. Cp. Brissonius and Dirksen, *s.v. liberare.*

the same book. There is no sign of correction in the inscription. It must be observed that the mistake, if it is a mistake, occurs twice quite independently, and that there is no trace but the correction in the *index* of any writing by Paul on the *lex* Iunia. Moreover this text has not been generally overhauled, for it retains a view of Julian's, which is elsewhere set aside[1]. And the word *vindicta*, useless or worse under Justinian, may have served a purpose in the original. An informal manumission would be null if the authorising *pater* were dead, but some may have doubted if this was equally true where a *legis actio* had been gone through without notice of the death. It is easy to see many complications which Julian's decision avoids.

Mitteis observes also that there is no known *lex* Iulia which deals with manumission. The *leges* Iuliae *iudiciariae* must have given occasion for the discussion of those quasi litigations which were still tried by *legis actio*, of which manumission *vindicta* was one. It is always difficult to say what a book may have contained.

XII. 49. 17. 6, Ulpian. *Si militi filiofamilias uxor servum manumittendi causa donaverit an suum libertum fecerit videamus, quia peculiares et servos et libertos potuit habere, et magis est ut hoc (?) castrensi peculio non adnumeretur, quia uxor ei non propter militiam nota esset. plane si mihi proponas ad castra eunti marito uxorem servos donasse ut manumittat et habiles ad militiam libertos habeat potest dici sua voluntate sine patris permissu manumittentem ad libertatem perducere.*

The concluding words imply without actually saying it that where the slave was not in the *peculium castrense*, the *filius* with the father's consent might have done what he is contemplated as doing without it if the slave is in the *peculium castrense*. And this is so to free a man as to make him *habilis ad militiam*. This must be formal manumission since a latin would not be qualified.

Texts in general terms, and thus applicable to latins, have not been cited, except where they contain something to suggest that they were intended to refer to formal manumission, and no doubt some relevant texts have been missed. Some, discussed elsewhere, have been omitted[2], as having less weight than I had attached to them. No text in the Digest can be absolutely conclusive for classical law, since there may always have been alteration. But these seem rather a strong body, and if their force for classical law is to be destroyed it must be by the assumption of systematic interpolation, of which there is in many cases no trace and in most of these no purpose. The texts are in all parts of the Digest and the compilers never seem to have made a mistake: they have left so far as appears, no trace, no suggestion, of the older doctrine. They are not often so exact in their workmanship. And the main reason for this opinion is a fifth century Greek scholion which does not directly deal with the point and is itself in somewhat

---

[1] *Ante*, p. 719, no. VII.
[2] 28. 2. 51. 1 (which, as Mitteis says, may have to do with *matrimonium iuris gentium* though this seems unlikely) and 40. 9. 16. 5, in connexion with which the distinction relied on in my discussion is far from clear on the texts.

self-contradictory form. After all there is a presumption in favour of the genuineness of a text even in the Digest.

I venture to suggest that Professor Mitteis in studying these texts is giving them an importance they do not deserve in relation to his general theory. He has shewn us how inadmissible the idea of representation in formal acts was to the classical lawyer. But the foregoing chapters shew that *favor libertatis* led to the doing of things, the acceptance of interpretations, and the laying down of rules, quite inadmissible in other branches of the law. *Nec enim ignotum est quod multa contra iuris rigorem pro libertate sint constituta*[1].

---

[1] 40. 5. 24. 10.

INDEX

A HISTORY OF THE FEDERAL RESERVE

ALLAN H. MELTZER

A HISTORY OF THE

Federal Reserve

VOLUME I, 1913–1951

WITH A FOREWORD BY ALAN GREENSPAN

THE UNIVERSITY OF CHICAGO PRESS • CHICAGO AND LONDON

ALLAN H. MELTZER is the Allan H. Meltzer University Professor of Political Economy at Carnegie Mellon University and Visiting Scholar at the American Enterprise Institute, Washington, D.C. He is the author or coauthor of several books, most recently *Money, Credit, and Policy,* and served on the President's Council of Economic Advisers from 1988 to 1989.

The University of Chicago Press, Chicago 60637
The University of Chicago Press, Ltd., London
© 2003 by The University of Chicago
All rights reserved. Published 2003
Printed in the United States of America

12 11 10 09 08 07 06 05 04 03   2 3 4 5
ISBN: 0-226-51999-6 (cloth)

Library of Congress Cataloging-in-Publication Data

Meltzer, Allan H.
    A history of the Federal Reserve / Allan H. Meltzer.
        p. cm.
    Includes bibliographical references and index.
    Contents: v. 1. 1913–1951 —
    ISBN 0-226-51999-6 (v. 1 : alk. paper)
        1. Federal Reserve banks.   2. Board of Governors of the Federal Reserve System (U.S.)
    I. Title

HG2563 .M383 2003
332.1′1′0973—dc21

                                                                    2002072007

♾ The paper used in this publication meets the minimum requirements of the American National Standard for Information Sciences—Permanence of Paper for Printed Library Materials, ANSI Z39.48-1992.

To Marilyn

CONTENTS

FOREWORD

Allan Meltzer, who undertakes projects that to most appear daunting, has delved deeply into the history of the Federal Reserve System, with a result that will add substantially to the discourse on the institution's role and development. He has reviewed the records of policy discussion at an extraordinary level of detail, and his analysis illuminates the contributions of the many fascinating individuals who shaped the Federal Reserve System we know today.

Beginning with a history of developments that underlay the initiation of America's most recent experiment in central banking, Meltzer carries the reader through the challenges of a developing institution faced with enormous economic upheaval, aptly describing the strong personalities that influenced both policy and culture in the System.

His work explores the Federal Reserve's inadequate response to the Great Depression and the struggle for dominance in the System. According to Meltzer, the struggle did not wholly preclude agreement in times of crisis; nevertheless, the well-known exhortations of Bagehot and Thornton that a central bank must act to counter a banking crisis and currency drain without regard for the gold reserve were ignored. In Meltzer's view, the System's adherence to the real bills doctrine, combined with a belief that the purging of speculative excess was necessary to set the stage for price stability, led to the failure of monetary policy to lessen the decline.

The book describes in detail the roles played by Federal Reserve bank presidents, which have evolved substantially over the years, as has the relationship between the reserve banks and the Board of Governors. The early dominance of the Federal Reserve System by Benjamin Strong, governor of the Federal Reserve Bank of New York, is an interesting episode.

Strong was credited more than anyone else with recognizing in the years after World War I the financial and economic impact of reserve bank purchases and sales of Treasury debt and the need to coordinate those transactions. Meltzer depicts Governor Strong's opposition to a 1926–27 congressional proposal to amend the Federal Reserve Act to make price stability an explicit policy goal. He describes Governor Strong's concern that the bill offered by another Mr. Strong—Kansas Republican congressman James A. Strong—would be interpreted to mandate the stability of individual prices, particularly of agricultural products. In a clear example of his willingness to take sides, Meltzer says here that had a mandate for price stability been approved, the Fed "could not have permitted the Great Depression of 1929–33 or the Great Inflation of 1965–80."

Ultimately the Banking Act of 1935, largely adopting reforms proposed by Marriner Eccles, resulted with some subsequent refinement in the structure of the Federal Open Market Committee. Eccles had sought an FOMC wholly controlled by the Board rather than so-called private interests. However, Senator Carter Glass of Virginia and others were leery of monetary policy dominated by what they saw as "political interests." The compromise that emerged mandated that monetary policy be conducted with a broader vision than if either Eccles or Glass had prevailed.

Meltzer's book covers with the same methodical illumination the events of more recent years, completing a work both stimulating and provocative. Readers will have substantial material for continued reflection and discussion.

Allan Meltzer has spent a lifetime inquiring into monetary economics, and he calls the evidence as he sees it. His combination of interests and experience makes him most qualified for this undertaking, and he brings to the endeavor a closeness of analysis that makes his conclusions both fascinating and valuable. Those of us who enjoy the debates he inspires will find much satisfaction in this book, as in his other important works.

Alan Greenspan

The project that eventually became this book began in 1963–64, when the late Congressman Wright Patman asked me to extend a study I had done for the Joint Economic Committee. That study described operations in the dealer market for government securities—the market in which the Federal Reserve conducts its open-market operations. When I explained that the problems that concerned him arose at the Federal Reserve and not in the market, he asked me to undertake a study of the Federal Reserve.

My former teacher Karl Brunner, later my friend and lifetime collaborator, joined the project. Together we wrote a lengthy study of Federal Reserve operations, emphasizing their use of free reserves as a target and indicator of the thrust of policy. We showed that these procedures were faulty—that the Federal Reserve's analysis did not go beyond the money market to the broader objectives required by an efficient and effective monetary policy. We proposed an alternative framework.

The late Harry G. Johnson proposed to the University of Chicago Press that it republish the study. The original studies were hastily written to meet congressional deadlines. I started to rewrite several sections but decided instead to extend the analysis. One set of questions in particular warranted attention: Why had the Federal Reserve acted as it did? Why had it failed to respond to the Great Depression or the deep recession of 1937–38? Why was monetary policy often pro-cyclical?

This book tries to answer those questions. At various times in the late 1960s and early 1970s, I began to revise the manuscript to complete the history. Karl Brunner always expressed interest, but he never devoted any time to working on the manuscript or commenting on what I had written.

In the fall of 1994 I returned to work on this book while on leave from

Carnegie Mellon at Harvard University and the National Bureau of Economic Research. My thanks to Martin Feldstein for the hospitality and pleasant working conditions at the Bureau.

In the nearly thirty years since I first started on this project, both the Federal Reserve and my ideas have changed. Some of the ideas in the original study remain, but much of this material is new.

The most important influence on my thinking and conclusions has come from reading the minutes, correspondence, and other internal documents developed at the time. Records for the Federal Reserve Board and the Board of Governors became available as a result of the Freedom of Information Act in the 1970s. The cooperation of Chairman Alan Greenspan, the secretary of the Federal Open Market Committee, Normand Bernard, and the library staff went far beyond legal requirements. I am indebted to them, to Susan Vincent and Kathy Tunis at the Board of Governors library, and to Elizabeth Jones of the Board's staff for their helpful assistance.

I began by reading all the archival material. It soon became apparent that the amount was too great for one person to summarize the material and complete the manuscript in reasonable time. Several researchers have reviewed and summarized material, collected data, and assisted in other ways. I am particularly grateful to Randolph Stempski, Sean Trende, Catherine Pharris, Matthew Korn, and Jessie Gabriel for their perseverance, diligence, and thoughtful selection of material.

To supplement their efforts, I continue to read and summarize materials at the Federal Reserve Bank of New York. The bank has collections of papers left by its governors and later presidents, Benjamin Strong, George Harrison, and Allan Sproul. These include memos, correspondence, and records of conversations. Lester Chandler used Benjamin Strong's papers for his biography of Strong. Instead of rereading all the Strong papers, I relied on the quotations in Chandler's biography. Where I differed on interpretation, I referred to primary sources.

The New York board of directors, or its executive committee, met weekly. The weekly minutes often have more detail than the daily minutes of the Federal Reserve Board's meetings. The New York archives directed me to topics in the board's records and conversely. The New York bank has been extremely helpful not only by providing access to materials but by offering pleasant working arrangements. Although not covered by the Freedom of Information Act, the bank provided materials without hesitation or restriction. I am indebted to President William McDonough for his assistance and to Rosemary Lazenby, the bank's gracious and ever helpful archivist and her staff.

Many people read and commented on parts of the manuscript. I am grateful to all of them and particularly to Robert Aliber, Michael Bordo, Kevin Dowd, Milton Friedman, Alan Greenspan, Jerry Jordan, David Laidler, Athanasios Orphanides, Robert Rasche, and Elmus Wicker.

I owe a special debt to Anna Schwartz, who encouraged and prodded me. Anna commented fully and helpfully on each chapter from her vast store of knowledge. Bennett McCallum listened patiently at lunches over many years and commented with his usual economic insight. Alberta Ragan typed the several revisions and proofread the entire manuscript with her usual care, efficiency, and good humor.

Several readers have asked why I included the years covered in Friedman and Schwartz's now classic monetary history. In one respect this is a strange question: in the physical sciences, replication of experiments is the norm. No one appreciates their work more than I, but its quality and importance should encourage, not deter, replication.

There are additional good reasons for revisiting the early years. First, I had unlimited access to material that they did not have. To the extent that I reach the same conclusions, as I often do, my work strengthens theirs. Where I find differences, as I sometimes do, my work supplements theirs by giving a more complete or more accurate account. Second, I am interested in some different questions, such as those listed above and others.

To answer those questions, I let the Board members, governors, presidents, and others explain their actions in their own words. Although personal animosities and indecisiveness play a role, there is a remarkable consistency in the statements and explanations. Using the earlier studies for the House Banking Committee, I develop the framework that guided many of their decisions.

The research for this book required much time in Washington, D.C., and at National Archives II in College Park, Maryland. My continuing association as a Visiting Scholar at the American Enterprise Institute was invaluable. I am greatly indebted to Christopher DeMuth for his generous hospitality and assistance and to my colleagues there, especially Douglas Besharov, for support and encouragement. I am indebted also to Dean Douglas Dunn and others at Carnegie Mellon University. They have encouraged me through more than forty years of an active life.

The Sarah Scaife Foundation, the Lynde and Harry Bradley Foundation, and the Smith Richardson Foundation have given generously to finance the project. It has taken six years to get to this point. Without their backing, it might never have happened.

My largest debt is to Marilyn, my wife, whose support, encouragement, and love have always been there during a lifetime of often hectic but always absorbing activities.

ONE

Introduction

This book is the biography of an institution, the Federal Reserve System, much of it told by its principals. The Federal Reserve is now the United States' powerful central bank. The founders did not intend to create either a central bank or a powerful institution; had they been able to foresee the future accurately, they might not have acted.

Institutions, no less than individuals, change as they mature and as the conditions that led to their creation change. In 1913 the United States was a developing country, with agriculture its largest occupation. The enormous shift in political and economic power and responsibility toward the United States that occurred in the twentieth century was at an early stage. The founders did not design or contemplate the Federal Reserve System we have today. They hoped to reduce financial instability, improve the quality of financial services, and strengthen the payments system.

The leading central banks in 1913 were privately owned institutions vested with responsibility for such public activities as providing currency, maintaining domestic payments systems and international payments, and serving as lenders of last resort in periods of financial disturbance following threat of failure by major banks or financial institutions. Depositors were not insured against these risks, so the threat of financial disruption set off a shift from bank deposits to gold or currency issued by the government. The drain of gold and currency into private hands forced multiple reductions in bank assets and liabilities and threatened additional bank failures. Interest rates on short-term loans rose with the increased demand to borrow and the reduced supply of loans.

By the late nineteenth century, central bankers in principal countries understood that their responsibility to lend at times of financial panic

made them unique. Their public responsibility to prevent widespread failure of banks and financial institutions that would otherwise remain solvent had to dominate the private interests of their stockholders. Private interests would lead them to contract lending, call loans, and shrink their
balance sheets. Such action would force unneeded bankruptcies and increase the risks the public had to bear.

In a well-managed panic under the gold standard, the government suspended the central bank's requirement to pay out gold or silver on demand.
Relieved of the requirement to hold a fixed percentage of the note issue in
metallic reserves, the central bank could expand the currency issue to satisfy any increase in the demand for currency. Privately owned banks with
good collateral could borrow from the central bank instead of calling loans,
reducing deposits, and forcing economic contraction and bankruptcies.
When the system worked in this way, financial panics ended quickly. The
additions to currency returned to the banks as deposits. Banks repaid their
loans at the central bank. As the central bank's liabilities fell, the government could restore the requirement to pay out gold on demand.

This system of public-private cooperation, combining suspension of
gold payments with a lender of last resort facility, did not survive the economic, political, and financial disturbances later in the twentieth century.[1]
By the 1950s, privately owned central banks had disappeared. Governments looked to public institutions to manage money and credit.

Public control of money raised a new issue or, more accurately, reopened an old one—preventing governments from abusing their power to
create money and credit for temporary political advantage. After a decade
or more of rising inflation, central banks became more independent of
political control. By the end of the twentieth century, principal countries
accepted two organizing principles—public ownership and "independence." The latter term has many different specific meanings; their common element is limitation of the government's power to use monetary
policy to gain political advantage.

The structure of the early Federal Reserve System reflected these concerns about reconciling the public nature of the central bank's task with responsible control of money and credit. Writers and commentators at the
time did not use terms like "public goods" and "central bank independence," but they recognized the problem of designing an organization with
proper incentives. Fears that a privately owned bank would place the bank's
interest above the public interest had to be reconciled with concerns about
empowering the government to control money. In addition, the new insti-

---

1. Reasons other than effectiveness played a role in this transformation.

tution was supposed to provide a currency with stable value, capable of expanding and contracting in response to demand; a payments system that efficiently transferred money and cleared checks in a growing national economy; and the services of a lender of last resort.[2]

President Woodrow Wilson offered a solution that appeared to reconcile competing public and private interests. He proposed a public-private partnership with semiautonomous, privately funded reserve banks supervised by a public board. The directors of the twelve reserve banks, representing commercial, agricultural, industrial, and financial interests within each region, controlled each bank's portfolio. The new rules sought to pool the country's gold reserves to strengthen the individual parts by making the total reserve available in a crisis. Reserve banks could lend gold to other reserve banks. No formal provision required coordination or cooperation of the various parts, however. In practice this meant that if the system was to serve as a lender of last resort, it would have to coordinate the actions of the semiautonomous reserve banks.

President Wilson was proud of his achievement.

> It provides a currency which expands as it is needed and contracts when it is not needed, a currency which comes into existence in response to the call of every man who can show a going business and a concrete basis for extending credit to him, however obscure or prominent he may be, however big or little his business transactions. More than that, the power to direct this system of credits is put into the hands of a public board of disinterested officers of the Government itself who can make no money out of anything they do in connection with it. No group of bankers anywhere can get control; not one part of the country can concentrate the advantages and conveniences of the system upon itself for its own selfish advantage. (Wilson as quoted in Kettl 1986, 22)

LAW AND PRACTICE

President Wilson's compromise resolved the immediate political conflicts and established an institution, but it left major economic and organizational issues unresolved. The structure of the new system did not concentrate decision-making authority and responsibility. A struggle for power and control broke out early and continued until resolved by the Banking Act of 1935.

---

2. Wicker (2000) shows that perceptive writers understood the need for a lender of last resort by the 1860s, but attempts by the New York clearinghouse to provide the service often failed because of the conflict between the collective interest in system stability and the members' individual concerns for the safety of their own institutions.

Although the Federal Reserve was an independent agency from the start, in practice two political appointees—the secretary of the treasury and the comptroller of the currency—served as ex officio members of its board, with the secretary as board chairman.[3] Before the 1930s, treasury secretaries rarely participated actively.

The 1935 act resolved this organizational anomaly by removing the secretary and the comptroller from the Federal Reserve Board. By that time the secretary took an active part in monetary policy and often influenced decisions. The legal change did not change the locus of decision-making power. The Treasury retained its strong influence until 1951.

The 1913 legislation did not ensure that the new system would respond to crises better than the old. On the recommendation of the officers, or on their own initiative, the directors of individual reserve banks could decide not to participate in System operations. The officers who headed the reserve banks were mainly bankers, the same types of individuals that had run banks or clearinghouses in the past. A change of location to the reserve banks was not enough to ensure that concern for financial stability would outweigh other interests. Some did not recognize that the lender of last resort had to place the interests of the financial system above the interests of the individual reserve banks.

Institutions both shape the society of which they are part and adapt to the dominant views in that society. Although the Federal Reserve was independent of the day-to-day political process, the public, acting through its representatives, could insist on structural changes or, without formally changing structures, demand that the Federal Reserve undertake new responsibilities or give up old ones. No institution can be independent of this pressure for change.

In the 1920s the reserve banks learned to coordinate actions that affected interest rates and the stocks of money and credit. A committee, led by the New York reserve bank, took responsibility for securities purchases and sales. The reserve banks adopted a formula for allocating the System's portfolio among the reserve banks. The reserve banks retained the right to reject participation.

The committee was an informal, extralegal arrangement. The Board, acting in its supervisory role, had to approve purchases and sales. The line between supervision and decision making was never clear, so the procedures irritated some Board members and became a source of friction. Friction increased as open market operations became the principal policy instrument.

3. The comptroller is a Treasury official responsible for regulating banks with national charters.

The Banking Act of 1935 resolved this conflict also. Board members became members of the Federal Open Market Committee for the first time and held seven of the twelve seats and chairmanship of the committee. New York lost its leadership role. The New York bank did not regain a permanent seat on the committee until 1942. Since that time, the president of the New York bank has served as the committee's vice chairman.

The 1935 act permanently shifted the locus of power to the Board. The Federal Reserve became a central bank. The twelve regional reserve banks lost their semiautonomous status and much of their original independence.

The history of the Federal Reserve is in part the story of how social, political, economic, and technological changes affected the institution. The Federal Reserve began operations not in the heyday of the gold standard but near its end. At the time, acceptance of the standard by bankers, economists, leading businessmen, and others, at home and abroad, was so great that the standard seemed to many the social manifestation of a natural order. The standard did not work in the smooth, orderly way that its proponents imagined, but it provided an internationally acceptable means of payment and store of value (Bordo and Schwartz 1984). Debts were settled and payments made without conflict. The movement of gold balances and their effect on domestic prices gave the standard the automaticity for which it is famous.

The gold standard required countries to use monetary policy to keep exchange rates fixed and thus to allow prices, output, and employment to vary as required by the movements of gold and the country's exchange rate. Debtor countries had to pay their obligations in gold even if the price of gold rose relative to commodity prices, and creditors had to accept gold in settlement if commodity prices rose relative to the price of gold. Exporters and importers had reasonable certainty about the payments they would make or receive, since the rate of inflation remained bounded except in wartime, when the standard did not operate.

Efforts at international monetary coordination in the 1920s and 1930s foundered on the conflict between a fixed exchange rate and goals for inflation or employment. The Federal Reserve worked actively to restore the international gold standard in the 1920s, first in Germany, than in Britain, France, Holland, Poland, and elsewhere. It sought to maintain domestic price stability also. The two goals were incompatible once other countries fixed their currencies to gold. Coordination could not resolve the conflict. In the end, the Federal Reserve failed to achieve either its domestic or its international goal.

Again in the 1930s, Britain, France, and the United States renewed efforts to coordinate exchange rate policy. The new approach, known as the Tripartite Agreement, failed also. Countries would not subordinate domestic policy to the exchange rate goal.

The lesson drawn from these experiences by policymakers in Washington, London, and elsewhere was that previous attempts lacked effective mechanisms for enforcing coordination while achieving price stability. In 1944 the Bretton Woods Agreement sought to retain exchange rate stability as a goal of economic policy and to reconcile external and internal monetary stability. The agreement had fixed but adjustable rates in place of the rigid exchange rates under the gold standard. Countries did not have to reduce their price level to remove external imbalances. They could respond to permanent changes in competitive position by devaluing and could borrow from a central facility, the International Monetary Fund (IMF), when facing cyclical or temporary balance of payments deficits. The Fund would lend balance of payments surpluses to countries in deficit. In the early postwar years to 1951, the Fund did little. Most countries had wartime exchange controls and inconvertible currencies.

The Bretton Woods system of fixed but adjustable exchange rates, like the interwar gold exchange standard, tried to supplement the stock of gold by using foreign exchange—dollars and pounds—as reserve currencies. The two differed fundamentally. The stock of gold grew slowly; the stocks of dollars and pounds could grow without limit. Member countries accepted an obligation to treat the two alike. In practice this meant they had to accept inflation or appreciate their exchange rate.

The new system recognized a lasting change in beliefs about the responsibilities of government. As the population moved from rural to urban areas and from agriculture to manufacturing and service industries, governments assumed new responsibilities for social welfare and economic stabilization. The public in many countries would not accept the level of unemployment, deflation, or inflation needed to maintain the exchange rate. Adjusting the exchange rate seemed to be a less costly solution in 1944. At first the IMF had to approve exchange rate changes, but this restriction was not enforced.

President Wilson wanted the Federal Reserve to remain independent of government. Except for wartime and postwar subservience to the Treasury, independence developed in the early years and continued through the Harding, Coolidge, and Hoover administrations.

President Roosevelt and his treasury secretary, Henry Morgenthau, believed that the reserve banks represented bankers, many of whom opposed the president's programs. Devaluation of the dollar in 1934 gave the Treasury the financial resources to affect interest rates by buying securities, and it did so. Also, the Treasury sterilized and desterilized gold, affecting the rate at which monetary aggregates rose.

The Federal Reserve chairman, Marriner S. Eccles, expressed concern about the Treasury's actions but felt powerless to prevent them. And faced with relatively large gold inflows, he wanted to prevent inflation. Equally, he believed that at the interest rates prevailing during the 1930s, monetary policy could do little to stimulate expansion.

The head of the fiscal authority favored an activist monetary policy. The head of the monetary authority proposed more activist fiscal policies. Secretary Morgenthau wanted interest rates to remain low so that he could finance peacetime deficits and much larger wartime deficits. Monetary policy had the important role in his scheme of keeping market rates from rising. Eccles wanted larger budget deficits during the depression and large surpluses after the war.

Eccles, like Morgenthau, did not respect Federal Reserve independence. Although he disliked Treasury interference in monetary matters, he did little to prevent it. He advised and testified on a broad range of government policies including budget, tax, and housing policy. At times he opposed Morgenthau's policies, and on one occasion he proposed an excess profits tax that differed from administration policy.

A most unusual breach of independence occurred in January 1951 when the entire open market committee met in President Truman's office. The president and Secretary John Snyder wanted the Federal Reserve to maintain the long-term interest rate on Treasury bonds at the wartime peg. The president did not ask for a commitment, and the committee did not offer one. Nevertheless, meeting the president in the White House to discuss monetary policy was a long way from the tradition of independence that President Wilson had tried to foster.

IDEAS AND DECISIONS

A history of the Federal Reserve is a history of the decisions made and the ideas that prompted them. The chapters that follow allow the participants to explain their actions, and the reasons for them, in their own words. These decisions produced very different results: a steep postwar recession in 1920–21, a period of stability in the 1920s followed by the Great Depression of the 1930s and, much later, the Great Inflation of the 1970s.

The men who made these decisions were not chicane or evil. They did not directly seek the outcomes that their decisions helped to bring about. They did not fail to stop the depression because they liked the outcome and wanted it to continue. They acted as they did because of the beliefs they held about their responsibilities and about the way their actions affected the economy. Much of this history is about their reasons and their reasoning—what it was and how it changed in response to events and new ideas.

Men and women interpret events using the theories or beliefs they learned earlier. The beliefs or theories that guided the Federal Reserve were mostly mainstream beliefs at the time they were held. Individual leaders influenced decisions most effectively by introducing new or different ideas or new interpretations. Benjamin Strong in the 1920s recognized the need to replace the gold standard rules and the commercial loan theory, on which the founders based the Federal Reserve Act. Marriner Eccles believed monetary policy could do nothing in the 1930s when short-term interest rates were low, so he did nothing to lift the economy from the depression. Later he believed that the Federal Reserve did not have the political support to use general monetary policy to prevent inflation after World War II. He proposed selective credit controls to substitute for higher interest rates and slower money growth.

Individuals matter most when they are able to lead others to act in ways that do not fit comfortably within the prevailing orthodoxy. Strong led the Federal Reserve to support Britain's return to the gold standard in 1924–25. In 1927 he lowered interest rates and expanded money to help Britain maintain the gold standard. Allan Sproul led the Federal Reserve toward independence from the Treasury in 1950–51.

These and other episodes show that leadership was important at times. Events of this kind are rare. Most policy decisions and actions apply a framework or theory based on prevailing beliefs.

This volume starts with the founding of the Federal Reserve in December 1913 and ends with the Treasury–Federal Reserve Accord in March 1951. In many respects the accord marks the beginning of a larger, and greatly changed, institution. In 1913 the United States was an emerging economy. Great Britain was the financial power and the center of the international financial system. Approximately 30 percent of the labor force worked in agriculture. By 1951 only 11 percent remained in agriculture (U.S. Department of Commerce 1966, 178–79). The United States had become the financial leader, the dominant economy, and the technological and managerial leader as well.

In 1913 the London market financed most United States exports. Since the exports included mainly agricultural products, there was a large seasonal demand for financing in the fall, so interest rates rose each fall. United States bankers wanted to replace London bankers. They believed they were at a disadvantage, since they could not discount export credits at a central bank. Politicians wanted to reduce the seasonal fluctuation in interest rates. A bank that could expand credit and reduce interest rates seasonally satisfied both groups.

Seasonal credit expansion was not the only reason for establishing the Federal Reserve. Recessions in 1893–94, 1895–97, 1899–1900, 1902–4, 1907–8, and 1910–12 averaged nineteen months, according to the National Bureau of Economic Research. In all, there were 113 months of recession from December 1895 to January 1912—55 percent of the time. Several of the recessions were severe. Financial panics, interest rates temporarily at an annual rate of 100 percent or more, financial failures, and bankruptcies were much too frequent. Other countries had a lender of last resort to ameliorate financial crises or even prevent them. The series of crises and financial panics increased support for creation of a new institution.

In the 1920s the Federal Reserve received credit for improving economic performance. It eliminated both the seasonal and the extreme changes in interest rates characteristic of financial panics. Although the economy continued to experience relatively large cyclical fluctuations and many banks failed, old-style financial panics did not return in the three recessions from 1920 through 1927.

THE ECONOMY 1913–51

In first quarter 1951, real GNP was nearly three times greater than at the start of System operations in 1914, a compound annual growth rate of 2.8 percent. Growth was far from uniform. Chart 1.1 shows the many cyclical swings. Quarterly values of annual GNP growth range from 20 percent to −20 percent, associated with war and the Great Depression, but many years show changes of 10 percent or more.

Stable growth was not part of the Federal Reserve's formal mandate in the early years. Most of the System's leadership would have denied any responsibility for economic activity or employment.

Chart 1.1 shows the main events and experiences that shaped the Federal Reserve and were shaped by it. Two postwar contractions followed the two wartime expansions. The three and a half years of contraction from 1929 to 1933 stand out, as do the recovery following devaluation of the dollar against gold in 1933–34 and the wartime expansions from 1941 to 1945.

Also, the price level in first quarter 1951 was approximately three times its early 1914 value. Prices rose at a compound annual rate of 2.8 percent a year. As chart 1.2 shows, wartime inflations contributed greatly to the average rate of change, so the average for the period is misleading. In both world wars, the Federal Reserve issued money, as required to support the Treasury's interest rate policy. After increasing in response to gold inflows from 1914 to 1917, the price level fluctuated widely from 1917 to 1939 around a constant value. The price level was approximately the same in 1939 as in 1917, before the United States participated as a combatant in World War I. The price level then doubled between 1940 and 1951, a more than 6 percent annual rate of increase. Most of the increase occurred during World War II, but part of it appears after the war, when price controls ended.

In the early years, 1914–16, the Federal Reserve's portfolio remained small. The Federal Reserve's nongold assets were too small to offset gold

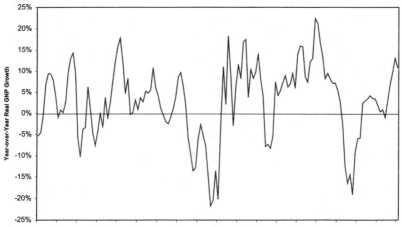

Chart 1.1 Year-over-year real GNP growth, 1915.1 to 1951.1.

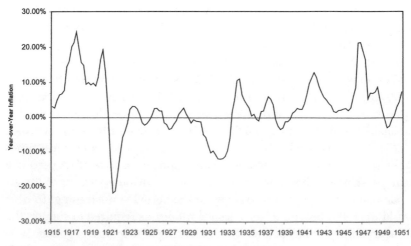

Chart 1.2 Year-over-year change in GNP deflator, 1915.1 to 1951.1.

Table 1.1   Federal Reserve Performance, 1917–51

TREASURY DOMINANCE	INFLATION OR DEFLATION	STABILITY AND LOW INFLATION
1917–20	1920–22	1922–29
1934–51	1929–33	

inflows. Since the United States was on the gold standard the rules required higher prices, so it is not clear that a larger portfolio would have been used at the time to cancel the effect of gold flows on money and prices. Principal gold standard countries had suspended the standard during wartime, but the belligerents and others used gold to pay for imports, and some foreigners sought safety in dollar securities.

Putting aside these early years, table 1.1 summarizes outcomes in the years 1917 to 1951. The table shows that in this period the country rarely experienced price and output stability. The Treasury dominated the Federal Reserve more than half the time. The seven years of stability, 1922–29, are exceptional, not the rule.

The founders of the Federal Reserve expected the new institution to follow gold standard rules. Gold movements would determine long-run price changes. Chart 1.3 shows that the stock of monetary gold rose in the 1920s, particularly from 1920 to 1925, when the dollar was the only major currency convertible into gold. Restoration of the international gold standard increased the demand for gold, contributing to the gradual fall in the United States price level after 1926. Federal Reserve officials worried that the gold flow would reverse. They were reluctant to monetize inflows or permit prices to rise. Despite the gold inflow, prices fell in the 1920s.

Chart 1.3 shows the dollar value of the monetary gold stock. The vertical line at the beginning of 1934 shows the revaluation of gold to $35 an ounce (devaluation of the dollar against gold). At the $35 price, gold flowed to the United States at a rapid rate that slowed during the 1937–38 recession but accelerated after the recession as Europe moved toward war.

The monetary gold stock increased nearly eightfold during the thirty-seven-year period, using troy ounces to abstract from the 1934 revaluation. At its start in late 1914, the Federal Reserve held 74 million ounces of gold, valued at $1.5 billion. After 1934 United States citizens and corporations could not own gold. Only the Treasury held gold. At the peak in 1949 the Treasury held more than 700 million troy ounces, valued at over $24 billion.

The main contribution to this growth came between 1934 and 1939, following the revaluation. The rising gold stock was the dominant force increasing money and credit, keeping nominal interest rates low, and promoting economic expansion with modest inflation. Rising income, rising

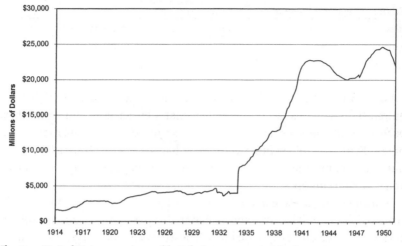

Chart 1.3 United States monetary gold stock, January 1914 to March 1951.

stock prices, low inflation, and concerns about a European war sustained the gold inflow until 1941.

Potential inflation, driven by gold inflows, was the Federal Reserve's main concern in the 1930s. Gold certificates representing the monetary gold stock became the largest asset on the System's balance sheet. Bank reserves rose rapidly; banks held large stocks of excess reserves. As in 1914–17, the Federal Reserve was concerned that its nongold assets were too small to counter the inflationary effects of the gold inflow. In 1936 it persuaded the Treasury to sterilize the gold inflow, ending the increase in reserves. And at about the same time, it used its newly acquired power to double reserve requirement ratios over a nine-month period in 1936–37. These actions contributed to a new, severe recession in 1937–38.

Chart 1.4 shows the sudden reduction in monetary base growth in 1936–37 resulting from these policy errors. The rate of base growth fell from 19 percent in December 1935 to –11 percent a year later. As chart 1.4 shows, the reversal, when it came, was just as sudden and sharp. The Federal Reserve reversed part of the increase in reserve requirement ratios, and the Treasury stopped sterilizing gold inflows. The only declines comparable to the 1937 experience came in 1920–21 and in 1946. Both contributed to severe postwar recessions.

The monetary base is the amount of reserves and currency supplied by the Federal Reserve.[4] The principal counterparts or sources of the base are gold and Federal Reserve credit, the latter consisting mainly of member

4. Reserves are adjusted for changes in reserve requirement ratios.

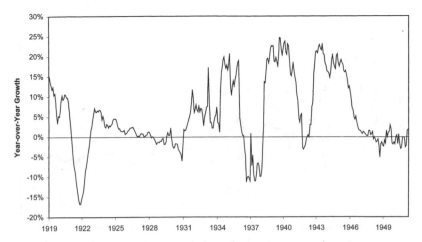

Chart 1.4 Year-over-year growth, nominal adjusted St. Louis monetary base, January 1919 to March 1951.

bank discounts and Federal Reserve purchases of government securities. Growth of the monetary base shows the monetary actions that the Federal Reserve permits or takes.

The data in chart 1.4 suggest the central role of monetary actions in this period. As noted, the economic contractions of 1920–21 and 1937–38 followed monetary contractions. Although committed to restoration of the gold standard in the 1920s, the Federal Reserve followed a deflationary policy that drained gold from other gold standard countries. In the first half of the 1940s, the Federal Reserve helped to finance World War II by purchasing government securities at fixed interest rates. It continued this policy after the war ended. Although the Federal Reserve complained that it had become an "engine of inflation," the monetary base fell in the early postwar years. By late 1948 the economy was in recession with falling prices, as shown in earlier charts.

Interest rates are the more conventional way to describe monetary policy actions. Chart 1.5 shows short- and long-term interest rates for most of the period. Long-term rates decline over the entire period with brief interruptions, notably in 1931, following Britain's departure from the gold standard. Most subsequent movements are relatively small.

Both short- and long-term rates are highest in 1920–21. This was the Federal Reserve's first attempt to use monetary policy to control inflation. High interest rates were very unpopular with Congress and large parts of the public. The Federal Reserve did not raise rates to this level again for a generation.

Changes in short-term rates from 1922 to 1930 show the beginning of

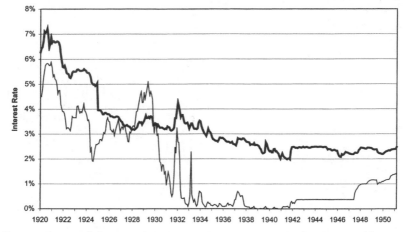

Chart 1.5 Long- and short-term interest rates, January 1920 to March 1951: —————— long rate
—————— short rate

active monetary policy. Short-term rates are highest at the peak of expansions in 1923, 1926, and 1929 and lowest near business cycle troughs in 1924 and 1927. The modest reductions in interest rates in 1927 took on importance well beyond the size of the change. Under the influence of Benjamin Strong, the Federal Reserve lowered interest rates, in part to help Britain remain on the gold standard. Critics within and outside the System blamed the reduction for the subsequent stock market boom and the depression that followed.

Policy changed after 1932. With interest rates near zero, Federal Reserve officials believed that policy was "easy" and that additional monetary ease would not contribute to expansion. During World War II the short-term interest rate remained at 0.375 percent until November 1947. The Federal Reserve would not change rates without Treasury approval until the March 1951 accord.

The Treasury's reluctance to let interest rates rise after World War II was the traditional reluctance of a large borrower to experience an increase in interest cost. The Federal Reserve had the same problem after World War I. To the treasury secretaries in both periods the debt seemed very large, and it was compared to their previous experience.

Andrew Mellon became treasury secretary after the 1920 election. During his term of office, he retired debt and reduced tax rates. Government debt declined from 34 percent to 16 percent of GNP and from $25 million to $16 million. By 1932 the debt to GNP ratio was above its wartime peak, mainly the result of a decline in GNP. Chart 1.6 shows these data.

New Deal deficits seemed large to contemporaries accustomed to Mel-

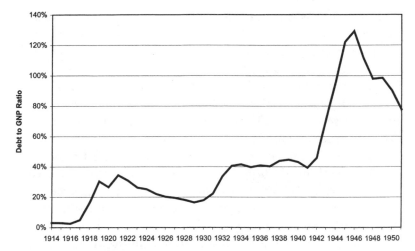

Chart 1.6 Ratio of public debt of the federal government to GNP, 1914–51.

lon's policy and earlier peacetime policies. The chart shows that the debt to GNP ratio was approximately constant from 1933 to 1941 at about 40 percent. Wartime finance brought the debt to nearly $300 billion by the end of 1946, a peak of 129 percent of GNP. The large outstanding stock of debt raised new fears about the operation of monetary policy. A large literature claimed that higher interest rates would cause losses to creditors (debt owners) and that such losses would have severe negative effects on the economy. Arguments of this kind became popular in government, but not just in government. This literature neglected to mention either the gains that debtors received or the losses that creditors would experience if inflation resulted. The argument became part of the case against higher interest rates and an end to the wartime pegging policy.

PLAN OF THE VOLUME

Central banking institutions developed and spread in the nineteenth century. Understanding of the role of money and monetary institutions followed. Chapter 2 traces major developments in central banking and monetary theory using the work of Henry Thornton, Walter Bagehot, and Irving Fisher. If the Federal Reserve had followed the policies these authors advocated, it would have avoided the most serious and socially costly errors.

The rest of the volume divides the thirty-seven-year history into five chapters. Each chapter covers a major event and the environment in which it occurred. Chapter 3 treats the founding of the System and the early years. The conflict over political versus financial control that delayed the Federal Reserve's founding began almost immediately. Problems of war finance soon took precedence. During the war, the Treasury's financial demands controlled monetary policy. After the war, the Federal Reserve faced the problem of freeing itself from Treasury control. Once freed, the System raised interest rates to end inflation. It was more than successful, but at a high cost. Prices and output fell sharply in the 1920–21 recession.

The 1920–21 recession and deflation constituted an important milestone. The severe contraction was costly economically and politically. The severity of the decline raised doubts about the applicability of the operating principles in the Federal Reserve Act. Chapter 4 traces the development of a new framework and the beginning of a more activist role. Instead of depending on banks' decisions to discount or repay borrowings, the new approach used open market operations to force banks to borrow or repay.

Open market operations required the reserve banks to work together. Portfolio decisions remained with the directors of the individual reserve banks, but the New York reserve bank, aided by a System committee, guided and implemented System decisions to purchase and sell. The Federal Reserve Board had supervisory responsibility only.

The new procedures radically changed the System's original structure. The reserve banks sacrificed part of their autonomy to the System committee. Control of operations shifted toward the New York bank. Members of the Board resented New York's increased authority, but they were powerless to combat it. These substantive differences combined with personal antipathies to heighten conflict between Benjamin Strong of the New York bank and members of the Board, particularly Adolph C. Miller. After Strong died, the conflict contributed to the delay in responding to the rapid expansion in the first half of 1929.

Chapter 4 ends at the start of the Great Depression. Chapter 5 follows the decisions and reasoning from meeting to meeting during the depression. It shows why the Federal Reserve remained passive through most of the decline and why it undertook major purchases in 1932 but stopped purchases before recovery was under way. The chapter ends with the financial collapse in March 1933.

President Franklin Roosevelt took office at the climax of the financial collapse. The new administration transformed many institutions, including the Federal Reserve. At the time, the dominant explanation regarded the depression as an inevitable consequence of speculation financed by speculators' easy access to credit. Legislation separated commercial and investment banking and gave the Federal Reserve authority to set stock market margin requirements. In these and other ways, Congress absolved the Federal Reserve of responsibility for the debacle.

Legislation also corrected deficiencies in the 1913 Federal Reserve Act.

That act barred the use of government securities as collateral for the currency. In 1932 the Glass-Steagall Act ended the prohibition as a temporary measure that later became permanent. The Banking Act of 1935 settled the long dispute over the locus of power by greatly increasing the Board's power and by giving the Board a majority on the open market committee. The act ended the reserve banks' ability to control their portfolios independently, creating the structure we know today.

Treasury requirements and gold inflows were major influences on money growth and interest rates from 1933 to 1941. The Federal Reserve's main decision was to double reserve requirement ratios in three steps between August 1936 and March 1937. These actions, along with the Treasury's decision to sterilize gold inflows, produced a steep monetary contraction. The 1937–38 recession followed.

Chapter 6 reports these events and the reasoning that produced them. The chapter also develops the attempts to reestablish an international financial system at the London Monetary and Economic Conference in 1933 and in the Tripartite Agreement of 1936 to limit exchange rate changes.

President Roosevelt called his programs the New Deal. Economic policy did not follow a consistent strategy. Before World War II, New Deal programs and actions had not restored prosperity or ended high unemployment. Wartime expansion achieved what New Deal policies did not.

The war and early postwar years (chapter 7) bring the volume to 1951. As in World War I, the Federal Reserve took an active part in administering wartime regulations and selling bonds. Its pledge to maintain a "pattern of rates" in effect fixed maximum rates at all maturities. The pledge ended any possibility of using monetary policy to control wartime or postwar inflation. In the postwar years to 1951, Federal Reserve officials became increasingly unhappy with the fixed pattern of interest rates, but they did not believe they could change policy without Treasury consent or support in Congress.

Chapter 7 also traces the development of postwar domestic and international legislation such as the Full Employment Act of 1946, the Bretton Woods Agreement establishing the International Monetary Fund and the World Bank, and the United States decision to finance European recovery. The chapter ends with the financing of the Korean War and the threat of renewed inflation that pushed the Federal Reserve into open conflict with the Treasury and brought about the March 1951 accord.

The concluding chapter summarizes the main findings and the lessons for monetary theory and policy.

TWO

Central Banking Theory and Practice before the Federal Reserve Act

Modern central banking theory began to develop in the eighteenth and nineteenth centuries under the gold standard. Because of the dominant position of England in trade, finance, and economic theory, much of the development took place either at the Bank of England or in response to its actions. The designers of the Federal Reserve System accepted a theory of central banking and a framework for policy operations that reflected the prevailing practices of European central banks, particularly the Bank of England. More important, the developers of the Federal Reserve System in the 1920s imported many of their aims and much of their understanding from the pre–World War I Bank of England. The blending of these imported elements with practices or principles from United States experience created the broad framework that guided Federal Reserve policy operations at its start and for many years after.[1]

It would be comforting to find in the history of central banking a record of steady progress and orderly development from earliest antecedents to present knowledge. The facts are different. The discussion reached a high point very near its start in the first decades of the nineteenth century. Thereafter, the level of discussion drifted lower. Some of the subtle points were lost and, more important, the focus of the discussion shifted.

At the start of the nineteenth century Henry Thornton, building on his own earlier work and pieces of analysis taken from Smith, Locke, and Hume, developed some guiding principles for the conduct of monetary

---

1. This refers to the economic framework, not the political and administrative framework. The latter is perhaps uniquely American in its blend of public and private enterprise, of centralism and decentralism. A brief description of some of the domestic political forces shaping the Federal Reserve Act is in Dunne 1963.

policy from an analysis of the relation of money, economic activity, prices, and balance of payments under fixed and flexible exchange rates. This framework was lost between David Ricardo's emphasis on long-run comparative statics and the concern of men of affairs with short-term fluctuations in market variables. After two nineteenth-century experiments with what they regarded as the essential principles of Ricardian monetary theory, bankers and men of affairs became skeptical about the applicability of economic theory to their problems. Early work was ignored or lost.

At their best, as in Walter Bagehot's *Lombard Street*, the discussions by men of affairs of the principles by which monetary policy should be conducted reached a very high level. Strict adherence to these principles would have avoided some of the worst errors of monetary policy in later years. Nevertheless, neither Bagehot nor those who followed his lead attempted to combine the theory of central banking or monetary policy with what is now called macroeconomic theory, as Thornton had done. Until Wicksell, Fisher, Marshall, Hawtrey, and later Keynes and Friedman reopened the discussion, very little was done to extend Thornton's analysis or to develop an alternative framework connecting monetary policy to output, employment, prices, and balance of payments. Monetary policy—or bank rate policy as it came to be known in England—was assigned the task of regulating the gold flow.[2]

Why did Thornton's rich and promising analysis degenerate first into a Bank of England policy of using bank rate mainly to protect the gold reserve and later into the Federal Reserve's concern for short-term market interest rates and money market conditions? Three reasons appear to be important. First is the "automatic" gold standard. The gold standard gave monetary policy a clear and definite objective. Writers such as William Jevons and Alfred Marshall wanted to make improvements in the standard to eliminate or reduce procyclicality of money, but they paid little attention to implementation. Second, much of Thornton's analysis considers an economy with an inconvertible currency. After the return to the gold standard, the continued relevance of other parts of his work was overlooked. Third, Ricardo and many of his followers not only failed to address the questions uppermost in the minds of the practitioners but failed to make clear that they were not addressing these questions. Ricardo's analysis is almost entirely long-run comparative statics, and his policy recommendations consisted mainly of a set of rules for restoring and maintaining convertibility of pounds into gold at a fixed exchange rate. Important as is his

2. A similar idea returned in the 1960s, when monetary policy was "assigned" to control the gold flow or balance of payments under fixed exchange rates.

work for economic theory, it gave very little guidance to the Bank of England on the issues of greatest concern to its directors. The governors and directors of the Bank of England were concerned with the profits of the bank, the avoidance of panic, and the appropriate response to short-term changes—for example, an increased demand for borrowing by the country banks or from banks abroad.

The wide gap between monetary theory and the practice of monetary policy, familiar to observers of the contemporary discussion of policy, had opened by the 1830s. The most able economists of the period participated in the discussion, and though they focused mainly on the longer-run consequences of policy actions and ignored short-term effects, they did not hesitate to recommend policy actions. Those bankers and economists whose writings show greatest interest in and knowledge of short-term operations and practices neglected, for the most part, the longer-run consequences of the policies and procedures they espoused. They tended to concentrate on the initial effects of policy actions and to ignore the longer-term consequences.[3]

In the history of economic thought, the participants in these discussions are grouped into schools known as bullionists and antibullionists for the first quarter of the nineteenth century and into currency and banking schools for the second quarter and into the third. While the groupings may be useful for certain purposes, they suggest more direct confrontation of ideas than appears to have taken place or than could have taken place given that one side was concerned much more with ultimate effects, the other mainly with initial effects.[4] Indeed, the "disputants" most often failed to agree on the subject under discussion or even to mention whether they were concerned with short- or long-run consequences. One main result is that the link between short- and long-run effects of policy remained unanalyzed (Viner 1965, 139–40).

A second reason for the decline in the level of the discussion is related to the first. Throughout monetary history, the belief recurs that monetary policy has very limited effects on employment, expenditure, and output. Lacking an explicit theory of the transmission of policy changes, it was easy for the men who guided the Bank of England to mistake initial effects of a

---

3. Viner's 1965 discussion of Ricardo's analysis brings out this point and its importance for the policy discussion of the time.

4. A central issue returns many times in monetary history: What is to be included as money? Bullionists and the currency school chose narrow definitions. The bullionists argued that the stock of gold (or silver) bullion determined the price level and the exchange rate. The currency school emphasized the note issue. They wanted a rule tying the note issue to the Bank of England's gold reserve. See Schwartz 1987a.

change in bank rate for the ultimate effect. Many of the writers in the so-called banking school, and many others in later generations, contributed to this belief by equating the effect of monetary policy with the change in the supply of "funds" in the money market. No reader of the discussions or interpretative accounts of nineteenth-century (or twentieth-century) monetary theory and policy can fail to be impressed by the frequency with which the idea reappears that any effect of monetary policy on the real economy is adventitious, the result of a particular and special conjuncture of forces that was either unlikely to be repeated or unlikely in the future to spread the effect far beyond the money market. Or if monetary actions had short-term consequences for the real economy, the effects were limited to specific sectors. Arguments about the "ineffectiveness" or noneffectiveness of monetary policy on the real economy became the official view of the working of policy.[5]

Ricardo's dominant position and his failure to build on Thornton's analysis of the ways in which the effects of monetary policy spread from the money market to economic activity, prices, and balance of payments meant that most of Thornton's analysis was neglected. A century after Thornton's promising start on a theory of money, his analysis leading to a statement of the principles by which monetary policy should be conducted to stabilize the economy had degenerated into the three main rules or principles for setting bank rate. These rules were accepted as basic at the start of the Federal Reserve System. First, there was the core principle of the gold standard: the central bank must raise or lower the discount rate as required to protect the gold stock and the exchange rate. Second, the central bank served as lender of last resort by offering to lend in a panic when markets did not function. Third, the central bank was to accommodate the needs of trade and agriculture by discounting only (or mainly) commercial paper, a principle known as the productive credit or real bills doctrine. This principle prevented purchases of government securities, mortgages, other long-term debt and the use of these instruments or equities as collateral for borrowing from the central bank.

The details of doctrinal history are less important than their consequences for the theory and practice of central banking. A number of excellent summaries of the literature of the period are available: Bagehot 1962, Clapham 1945, Hawtrey 1962, Keynes 1930, Rist 1940, Sayers 1957,

---

5. Laidler (1992, 4) argues that Thornton was perhaps the only classical economist to recognize that monetary impulses contributed to a business cycle, not just a "credit" cycle. Several earlier writers discussed the transitional real effects of monetary changes on real output. Indeed, analyses of monetary effects are among the oldest propositions in economic theory. See Hegeland 1951.

Schumpeter 1955, Thornton 1965, Viner 1965, and Wood 1939. Since many of the issues that arose, and their solutions, reflect the economic events of the period, the chapter begins with a description of the background events. The rest discusses three major contributions to monetary and central banking theory that were ignored, at great cost, during most of the twentieth century. First is Henry Thornton's analysis of the control of money and credit under either a fluctuating or a fixed exchange rate. Second is Walter Bagehot's discussion of the responsibility of the central bank as lender of last resort. Third is Irving Fisher's distinction between real and nominal interest rates. Thornton's work was not well known. Bagehot's work was well known at central banks, and Fisher was active until the middle of the twentieth century. Yet none of the three had a major influence on the conduct of policy. If they had, monetary history would have been much different.

The main issues in dispute during the period are familiar to contemporary economists. Can the monetary system be controlled? If so, which variables should be controlled, and how should this be done? What are the consequences of alternative systems of control? Did the central bank have an opportunity to exercise discretion, or is the real stock of money constant, so that central bank policy ultimately determined only the division of the real stock of money between gold (foreign exchange) or specie and paper? Should the central bank protect its own reserve, or is its main responsibility to protect the financial system in time of crisis? How could either or both of these ends be achieved? The answers to these and other questions given by central bankers and economists reveal the way the theory of central banking developed in the nineteenth century and the state of the art in the early twentieth century when the Federal Reserve was founded.

BACKGROUND EVENTS AND ARRANGEMENTS

During most of the eighteenth century the main policy actions involved the choice of standards, the establishment of de facto or de jure rules, and the provision of currency. By the end of the century England was on a de facto bimetallic standard at a ratio that undervalued silver, so full-weight silver coins did not circulate, and the currency consisted of gold, underweight silver coins of small denomination, and note issues of the Bank of England and other banks.[6] Bills of exchange had come into use, and in some areas endorsed bills served as a medium of exchange. Usury laws restricted interest rates, including the rate on advances from the Bank of England

---

6. The Bank of England received its charter in 1694 to assist in the financing of war with France. See Dowd 1991 for a brief history of the bank and Clapham 1944 for a detailed history.

(bank rate), to a 5 percent maximum. Bank rate for inland bills was put at 5 percent in 1746. The rate on foreign bills rose from 4 to 5 percent in 1773 and did not change again until 1822.

In 1697 the Bank of England was granted a charter to operate as a joint stock bank, but until 1826 other banks could not have more than six partners. The restriction of joint stock banking meant that partners were required to pledge their personal fortunes in periods of crisis. Consequently there were numerous small individually owned banks and very few branch banks.[7]

The main business of a banker consisted in issuing notes and discounting bills of exchange.[8] Since a large number of country banks accepted bills and issued banknotes, and since many of the bills were drawn by small local merchants in payment for merchandise, it became common for country bankers to develop correspondent relationships with London bankers to provide information and clearing arrangements. This tendency strengthened because the supply of bills of exchange did not grow at a uniform rate throughout the country. London became the financial center through which deficit areas were able to sell bills to surplus areas. Country bankers held deposits with their London correspondents and purchased or sold bills. The continued increase in the number of country banks during the early nineteenth century made it increasingly difficult for London bankers to clear the bill market by operations between correspondents. A new institution, the bill broker, arose in London to perform part of the market clearing function.

The growing importance of the bill broker resulted also from the arrangements prevailing at the time. First, the usury laws prevented the London banks from changing rates to attract a larger volume of Bank of England notes and gold from country banks and to reduce the supply of bills. Second, the Bank of England adopted rules designed to reduce the demand for discounts from country bankers. To be eligible for discount at the Bank of England, bills had to be endorsed by two London names, one of which was the merchant or manufacturer accepting the bill. Many of the bills originating in the country did not meet this requirement.

As the system functioned at the start of the 1790s, the country banks

---

7. There are a number of estimates for the earlier years. After 1808, country banks required a license to issue notes, so the number of licensees gives a more accurate estimate. The number rose from approximately 700 in 1809 to a peak of 940 in 1814. Thereafter the number of country banks declined, at first because of losses from deflation and after 1826 because of the growth of joint stock and branch banking. By 1842 the number had fallen to 429. See Wood 1939, 14.

8. Bank of England notes did not become legal tender until 1833. London banks stopped issuing notes in 1793.

maintained deposits and bought or sold bills from correspondent bankers in London. Bill brokers operated in the market in much the same way that a federal funds broker operates in the present New York money market. When the quantity of money demanded in London (bills supplied to London) exceeded the quantity of money supplied, bill brokers searched for buyers in the sections known to have surplus reserves. Just as the present-day federal funds market redistributes reserves from surplus to deficit banks, the bill brokers and correspondent banking system of the time drew bills and money to and through the London money market. The Bank of England participated in the market process as a banker. In addition, the bank absorbed gold and its own note issues as the market required and, without formally committing itself to do so, functioned as lender of last resort by advancing to banks on eligible paper.[9]

The system had an obvious flaw. With the rate of discount set at the maximum permitted under the usury law of 1714, the bank could not keep the market price of gold equal to the mint price of gold, maintain convertibility, and discount all of the eligible paper offered in periods of expansion. The reason is that the bank had only one means, and that a very ineffective means, of limiting or reducing the rate of monetary expansion: using qualitative controls or eligibility requirements to reduce the amount of discounts. After 1793 the government chose to finance the budget deficit incurred to wage the Napoleonic Wars by borrowing from the bank, so the bank's notes and deposits increased. The monetary expansion and deficit spending generated an increase in private expenditure. Under the prevailing payments system, this meant an increase in the number of bills of exchange drawn, including bills eligible for discount at the bank.

From 1790 to 1795 the bank saw total securities (private and public) rise from approximately £8 million to £16 million and bullion reserves decline from £8 million to £4 million. The price index (base 100 in 1821–25) started to rise in 1793. Between 1792 and 1795, prices increased by 30 percent, a 9.9 percent compound annual rate of increase (Gayer, Rostow, and Schwartz 1978). To stem the gold outflow, the bank attempted to reduce the size, or perhaps the portfolio's growth rate, by restricting the banks' right to discount. Any step of this kind, however, raised fears that the resources

9. After the crisis of 1825, there were two changes in the arrangements just described. The responsibilities of the Bank of England were more widely recognized, although not acknowledged officially, and bill brokers performed many of the market functions previously performed by London banks, especially the function of absorbing and holding or supplying bills as the market demanded. In recognition of the changed roles of brokers and banks, by 1830 the Bank of England accepted deposits and made advances to the largest brokers. As the system evolved, the London banks no longer borrowed from the Bank of England; instead, the bill brokers borrowed, often for months. See Scammell 1968, 134–42.

of the financial system would prove inadequate to redeem outstanding bills at the fixed rate of interest. The policy of controlling the quantity of discounts by rationing, exhortation, and eligibility requirements failed on this occasion, as on many subsequent occasions. With the gold reserve reduced to less than £1.5 million, the bank asked the government to order an end to convertibility. From 1797 to 1821, the pound was an inconvertible currency.

LESSONS FROM RESTRICTION AND RESUMPTION

The events of the next twenty-five years and the analysis they engendered make the period known as Restriction and Resumption a remarkable epoch in the histories of money, monetary theory, and of particular interest here, the theory and practice of central banking. A key figure in the early discussion is Henry Thornton, whose contributions to monetary and banking theory reveal an understanding of monetary process and policy that is far better than can be found in much of the professional writing a century or more after his death.

Thornton's contributions fall into five main areas. First, he provided a thorough discussion of the way the monetary arrangements of his day worked in practice and discussed some of the main implications of alternative arrangements and alternative monetary standards, including an inconvertible paper currency. He recognized that money produced by the banking system, paper credit, was part of the (circulating medium) means of payment. The effect of bank deposits on prices was the same as an increase in currency or gold. Second, he analyzed the monetary aspects of international exchange. David Hume had developed the basic flow analysis of monetary changes acting on home prices relative to foreign prices, thus on gold flows. Thornton for the first time used this analysis to explain the effects of actual price changes on international currency movements and the domestic economy. His discussion of currency movements is superior to the work on the same subject for the next century. Third, he saw clearly the difference between nominal and real interest rates, distinguished expected from actual rates, and offered an explanation of the rise in interest rates during an unanticipated inflation that is superior to the discussion in many later textbooks.[10] In his testimony of 1797 and in his book, he at-

10. Hawtrey (1962, 16) argues that Thornton failed to recognize the time dimension in real rates of return (or mercantile profit). This conclusion is based on an incomplete examination. In a speech on the Bullion Report, Thornton (1965, 336 and elsewhere) computes a net rate of return with dimension dollars per dollar per year in the course of his explanation of why an unanticipated inflation increases the realized profits of the borrower. Speaking of the merchants during an inflation, he wrote (336): "There was an apparent profit over and

tacked both the usury law and a fixed rate of discount on the grounds that by fixing the rate the bank relinquished control of money (the circulation). He argued that the discount rate had to be changed to raise or lower the cost of borrowing when the (anticipated) rate of return to real assets changed (Thornton 1965, 253–54). Thornton saw that the absolute level of the rate was not a proper criterion. The nominal rate had to be judged relative to the nominal rate of profit or, in modern usage, the return to capital. Fourth, his contributions do not appear as vague suggestions or dimly perceived truths occurring in the midst of an otherwise flawed argument. They are part of a carefully articulated explanation of the relation of money, prices, output, interest rates, credit, and balance of payments.

An important key to Thornton's analysis is the distinction between the demand for bank credit (indebtedness to the banking system) and the demand for money. At the start of an (unanticipated) inflation, the demand for bank credit and the demand for money move in opposite directions. These movements reflect a common cause, changed anticipations of the return to real assets and the rate of change of prices. Increases in the stock of money, resulting from an issue of paper or a gold inflow, increase the demand for goods, raising the prices of the goods demanded and encouraging borrowing by businessmen, whose sales and prospective profits rise. Velocity increases—the demand for money falls—not only because (some) businessmen are for a time more optimistic and velocity depends on "confidence" (ibid., 96), and thus on anticipations of the future, but also because inventories decline (237). These are short-term cyclical effects, but for a time they persist and generate additional increases in the demand for credit and in velocity. One reason the demands persist is that not all prices adjust at the same rate. Some are fixed by contract in nominal

---

above the natural and ordinary profit on mercantile transactions. This apparent profit was nominal, as to persons who traded on their own capital, but not nominal as to those who traded with borrowed money, the borrower, therefore, derived every year from his trade, not only the common mercantile profit . . . but likewise the extra profit which he [Thornton] had spoken of. This extra profit was exactly so much additional advantage, derived from being a trader on borrowed capital *and was so much additional temptation to borrow.* Accordingly, in countries in which currency was in a rapid course of depreciation, supposing that there were no usury laws, the *current rate of interest was* often, . . . *proportionably augmented.* Thus, for example, at Petersburgh, at this time, the current interest was 20 or 25 percent, which he [Thornton] conceived to be partly compensation for an expected *increase of depreciation of the currency*" (italics added). Thornton then gave examples of the working of this principle from the experiences of Russia, Sweden, France, and America. In his book, (1965, 254) Thornton wrote: "The temptation to borrow, in time of war, too largely at the bank [of England] arises, as has been observed, from the high rate of mercantile profit. . . . [C]apital, by which the term *bona fide* property was intended, cannot be suddenly and materially increased by any emission of paper. That the rate of mercantile profit depends on the quantity of this *bona fide* capital and not on the amount of the nominal value . . . [is] easy to point out."

terms and rise or fall more slowly than others. Thornton used money wages as an example of a price that was fixed in nominal amount and argued that, as a result, real profits rise and real wages fall in periods of (unanticipated) inflation. Once real balances adjust to their desired level, total wealth is "nearly the same," but there has been a once and for all redistribution from workers and other creditors to debtors (189–90).[11]

Thornton saw that short-term monetary disturbances had no lasting real effect. Money is neutral in the long run. One of his main reasons for short-run nonneutrality is that it is difficult to distinguish between permanent and transitory changes when they occur.[12]

In contrast to Ricardo, Thornton argued that replacing a convertible currency with inconvertible paper causes the market price of gold to rise above the mint price even if the nominal amount of paper money remains unchanged. His reasoning is that if money holders anticipate a decline in the purchasing power of money, they attempt to shift out of money. This argument makes the demand for money and short-run price changes depend on the anticipated rate of price change.[13]

Thornton's fifth contribution to the theory of central banking is a part of his theory of money and in this respect also stands in marked contrast to much of the literature on monetary theory and policy that followed. By combining short-run and long-run adjustment, he was able to deal with issues that Ricardo neglected or dismissed. In all important respects, his analysis of the long-run consequences fully anticipated Ricardo's.[14]

Neglect of Thornton's work and reliance on Ricardo's meant that the di-

11. On the following pages, 97–100, Thornton offers as one example the panic of 1793 when "many country banks failed. The stock of Bank of England notes, at the start, were not fewer than usual," but the number became "insufficient for giving punctuality to the payments." The effect was "to lessen the rapidity of the circulation of notes on the whole, and thus to increase the number of notes wanted." The remedy was found in issuing Exchequer bills discountable at the Bank of England. Thornton points out as a "fact worthy of serious attention" that the crisis was started by a demand to convert country notes into gold but was brought to an end by an issue of paper (Exchequer bills) that could be turned into banknotes or gold and that "created an idea of general solvency." In this passage Thornton anticipated Bagehot's 1962 work on the lender of last resort.

12. See also Thornton 1965, 236–41, where he traces the consequences of an injection of new money for the borrower and for the community. See especially 239 for a brief statement relating the fall in real wages during inflation to forced saving.

13. The idea appears several times. He discusses (1965, 119) the greater variance of nominal prices than of nominal wages that leads agents to regard a fall in price as temporary. The same misperception of a permanent change is used to explain the real effect of currency depreciation. In this case Thornton also invokes misperception of relative and aggregate changes (340).

14. See Viner 1965, 134, for a comparison of Thornton's views and those of his contemporaries. Keynes was apparently unaware of the extent to which Thornton anticipated his discussion of the demand for money.

rectors of the Bank of England, after periodically facing large changes in gold stocks and several threats to convertibility at the fixed exchange rate, concluded that Ricardian theory was inapplicable or useless. They therefore abandoned monetary theory as a basis for monetary policy and substituted ad hoc notions about money markets. These notions are at their best in the brilliant essays of Walter Bagehot and perhaps at their worst in the writings of central bankers during and after the depression of the 1930s. But either at their best or at their worst, the principles and practices of monetary policy became divorced from any analysis of the mechanism linking changes in money to short- and long-run changes in output and employment.

As part of his development of the price-specie flow mechanism, Thornton analyzed the effects of price changes on the gold stock of the Bank of England under convertible and inconvertible paper standards. Although he recognized the short-term effects of anticipations on the demand for money, he placed responsibility on the Bank of England for long-run inflation and any permanent divergence of the market from the mint price of gold. In a lengthy discussion of the relation of the country banks to the Bank of England, he argued persuasively that the expansion of country banknotes depended on expansion by the Bank of England and that the expansion of money was a necessary condition for inflation. But unlike the currency school, he emphasized that neither the total stock of notes in circulation nor the price level rose and fell in direct proportion to the note issue of the Bank of England (Thornton 1965, 219–29). If some resources are idle, the Bank of England can increase their employment by increasing the note issue, but "the increase of industry will by no means keep pace with the augmentation of paper," and inflation results (239).

The three duties of the Bank of England were to protect the gold reserve, function as lender of last resort, and control the note issue. These duties were best performed, Thornton thought, by keeping the market price of gold equal to the mint price, limiting the note issue by discount rate policy, except in periods of crisis when the bank must expand the note issue and lend more freely. Any attempt to limit the note issue by rules controlling the quality of credit as proposed in the real bills doctrine was to lend "countenance to the error . . . of imagining that a proper limitation of bank notes may be sufficiently secured by attending merely to the nature of the security for which they are given" (ibid., 244 and elsewhere in chap. 10).[15] The

15. The "real bills" notion, that credits advanced for productive purposes could not be a cause of inflation, had been proposed by several writers including James Stewart and had been used unsuccessfully to limit the note issue of the Bank of England before the Restriction. Mints (1945, 1) finds the real bills doctrine in writings during the 1770s. He notes (48)

appropriate policy for the bank was to change the discount rate so as to control the quantity of money. In Thornton's words, the policy should be

> to limit the total amount of paper issued, and to resort for this purpose, whenever the temptation to borrow is strong, to some effectual principle of restriction; in no case, however, materially to diminish the sum in circulation, but to let it vibrate only within certain limits; to allow a slow and cautious extension of it, as the general trade of the kingdom enlarges itself; to allow of some special, though temporary, increase in the event of an extraordinary alarm or difficulty, as the best means of preventing a great demand at home for guineas; and to lean on the side of diminution, in the case of gold going abroad, and of the general exchanges continuing long unfavorable; this seems to be the true policy of the directors of an institution circumstanced like that of the Bank of England. To suffer the solicitations of the merchants, or the wishes of government, to determine the measure of the bank issues, is unquestionably to adopt a very false principle of conduct. (259; italics added)[16]

The bank did not accept Thornton's prescriptions. From 1797 to 1815, the securities portfolio of the Bank of England increased threefold, and in the next seven years it declined as much as it had risen in the previous fifteen.[17] At the end of the period as at the beginning, the Bank of England's portfolio was approximately £15 million.[18] Most of the increase in money during 1800 to 1810 resulted from the increase of commercial paper at the Bank of England. At its maximum of approximately £23 million in 1810, the bank's portfolio of "private securities" was larger than at any time in the next hundred years. From 1810 to 1815, by far the largest part of the increase in money resulted from the bank's acquisition of government securities to finance wars with France and the United States. The Gayer, Rostow, and Schwartz (1978) price index shows that the price level (December 1790 = 100) follows a similar course. Prices rose to 198 in May 1813, then fell to 94 in mid-1822.

---

that even the earliest statements of the doctrine relate real bills to "elasticity" of the stocks of money or credit and to effective limitation of the note issue.

16. Note Thornton's careful distinction between credit (borrowing) and money. This distinction was neglected by most writers until Lauchlin Currie wrote in the early 1930s. Notable also in his monetary policy are the principles that the stock of money should grow as the economy expands and that the bank should make temporary advances when there are internal drains. The complete argument of his book makes clear that by the "general trade" he means real output, not "real bills."

17. Suspension of convertibility came in 1797 following France's attempt to land troops in Wales. See Dowd 1991.

18. Data in this and in the next several paragraphs are from Wood 1939, 191, and Viner 1965, 174. Viner uses price indexes developed in Silberling 1923, 232–33. I use the data from Gayer, Rostow, Schwartz 1978 instead.

There are several important developments for central banking theory and practice during the period.[19] One is that bankers found, as Thornton had insisted, that the Bank of England had no effective means of limiting its portfolio and the rate of monetary expansion in a period of inflation. With prices doubling from 1790 to 1812, the average rate of inflation is 5 percent, but at times it was much higher.[20] Since the usury law fixed the discount rate at 5 percent, the realized cost of borrowing was zero on average. There was no previous experience with managing a paper currency and, even neglecting the usury law, no tradition of limiting the volume of discounts and allowing the market to determine the rate on bills of exchange. The bank, in an early application of the "real bills" approach, attempted to control the quantity by controlling the "quality" and restricted commercial discounts to short and "sound" bills. The policy failed on this occasion, as on many future occasions.

At the end of the Napoleonic Wars, the government deficit declined from £35 million in 1814 and 1815 to £2 million in 1817. After 1816 the Treasury retired debt, and the bank's holdings of public securities declined. The monetary base measured as the sum of gold and total securities appears to have fallen after 1815. At first the bank's holdings of private securities continued to rise, presumably because the anticipated cost of borrowing remained far below the anticipated rate of return on real assets after fifteen years of inflation. But the anticipations probably changed quickly. From mid-1814 to late 1815, the price index fell about one-third, and the bank's holdings of private securities dropped to the low levels of the early 1790s. By March 1816 the Treasury was able to issue exchequer bills below the 5 percent usury rate. In the severe postwar deflation, the bank accumulated gold and lost earning assets. Thus it came to recognize a second problem of monetary management, a problem that was in fact the mirror image of the first. As long as the discount rate remained above the market rate, the bank could not take action to expand its portfolio. It eventually resolved this problem. Under pressure from the prime minister, it lowered the discount rate to 4 percent in 1822, the first change in fifty years. For a time the bank's holdings of private securities, the note issue, and the bank's deposit liabilities expanded.[21]

The third main problem of monetary management that the bank faced during these years was the restoration of convertibility, or Resumption. As

19. For the developments of the theory of money see especially Viner 1965, chaps. 3 and 4.

20. The peak rate of inflation is 20 percent a year compounded from 1798 to 1800. Prices fell an astonishing 20 percent in 1801.

21. The reduction of bank rate was not the only action taken. The gold standard became the legal (de jure) standard in 1821. Also, the bank's holdings of government securities ex-

early as 1810, the Committee on the High Price of Bullion, under the influence of Thornton, who was a member of the committee, and of Ricardo, who was not, urged a resumption of cash payments at the price of gold that had prevailed in 1797. Since prices had increased, the market price of specie was above the former mint price. To resume specie payments at the old mint price, the Bank of England had to engineer a deflation. On May 1, 1821, Britain returned to the gold standard at the historical mint price.

A century later, the Bank of England faced a similar problem and made a similar decision. Both decisions were followed within a few years by severe and prolonged depressions. The decision to resume specie payments (1819) allowed for a four-year delay and came after a deflationary policy had been in effect for six years. After the decision to resume cash payments was announced, gold flowed into the Bank of England. Much of the gold inflow occurred because the deflationary policy had pushed the price of silver and the exchange rate for the paper pound close to the mint price.[22] Between 1821 and 1824, the bank's holding of gold never fell below £10 million.

The years from 1820–24 are one of the more interesting episodes in early monetary history. The Bank of England's holdings of bullion tripled in the brief span of seventeen months and reached £12 million, the highest level attained to that time. Prices continued to fall until 1822, then rose, on average, 8 percent a year for the next three years. Part of the rise was the result of an agreement between the bank and the Treasury calling for the bank to advance £13 million to the Treasury in exchange for a forty-four-year annuity, known as the Dead Weight debt. These and other special advances combined with the gold inflow to increase the bank's deposit liabilities and note issue. Private borrowing expanded, and with bank rate reduced to 4 percent in 1822, the bank acquired bills and issued money.

Throughout the period, the government ran an almost constant budget

---

panded and the bank lengthened the maturity of eligible private bills from sixty-five to ninety-five days.

Some indication of the effect on the bank of the changes in activity during these years is given by its income from discounts. Scammell (1968, 145) shows the following:

Year	Bank of England Income from Discounts (in thousands of £)
1795–96	147
1809–10	914
1815–16	646
1820–21	150
1925–26	303

The figures are, of course, nominal values and therefore overstate the size of the changes in the bank's real income.

22. See Viner 1965, chart 1 and table 1, 143–44. For Ricardo's views on devaluation of the pound see Viner 1965, 204. The Gold Standard Act of 1816 repealed bimetallism in England.

surplus of £3 million to £4 million per year and used the surplus to retire debt. The net effect of the Treasury's debt retirements and the special issues to the Bank of England was the same as would have occurred had the bank engaged in open market purchases. The expansive effect of the open market operation on the monetary base and the economy was not entirely unexpected. The prime minister, Lord Liverpool, informed the bank in 1822 that he wanted to increase the circulation, and it is likely that the bank's purchases of Dead Weight debt were part of a plan to expand the stock of money and slow or stop the fall in (agricultural) prices. There is additional evidence that the idea of using open market operations to expand the note or monetary liabilities of the bank was understood, though the term open market operation was not used. At about the same time the bank purchased exchequer bills in the market at the request of the Treasury.[23]

Judging from the increase in the bank's holdings of private securities from 1822 to 1824 and particularly in the latter year, the economy expanded. The data are not sufficiently accurate to conclude that the expansion of the economy and the return of inflation can be attributed solely to the rise in the monetary base and the reduced discount rate at the Bank of England. However, the timing and direction of changes are consistent with the hypothesis that the deflationary policy before 1820 (1) induced a subsequent inflow of gold that increased spending, (2) thereby raising realized returns in agriculture and trade above previously anticipated rates, (3) stimulating additional borrowing, and (4) resulting in a further expansion of the monetary base. The reduction in bank rate and the open market purchases added to this process by increasing the growth rate of the base.

Ricardo had urged that paper money be kept in circulation. He recommended that bullion be held in ingots at the bank and the mint or held by private owners when demanded. The directors of the bank preferred bullion to paper for coins and notes of small denomination. English notes of less than five pounds, issued during the Restriction, were withdrawn from circulation after the Resumption. The effect was to raise the demand for gold in England and increase both the resource cost of maintaining the money stock and the rate of deflation required to restore convertibility at the previous fixed rate. By the winter of 1823–24, the bank's gold stock reached a maximum and started to decline. The decline continued throughout 1824, accelerated in 1825, and reached a trough early in 1826. At the trough, the bank held only £2 million pounds after suffering a drain of £12 million in two years.

---

23. The government's budget surplus and deficits are from Wood 1939, table 6, 74–75. A brief discussion of the Dead Weight debt and open market operations is Wood 1939, 80–83.

To stem the decline and protect the gold reserve, the bank refused to discount eligible paper, but it did not at first raise bank rate. Hawtrey (1962, 14–15) argues that raising the rate would not have been effective because short-term interest rates rose above 70 percent per annum. He overlooks the fact that before this occurred the crisis had intensified for several months and had become a panic after the bank restricted its loans. Bagehot, in a graphic passage, describes the money market in December 1825.

> In the panic of 1825, the Bank of England at first acted as unwisely as it was possible to act. By every means it tried to restrict its advances. The reserve being very small, it endeavored to protect the reserve by lending as little as possible. The result was a period of frantic and almost inconceivable violence; scarcely anyone knew whom to trust; credit was almost suspended; the country was, as Mr. Huskisson expressed it, within twenty-four hours of a state of barter. Applications for assistance were made to the Government, but . . . the Government refused to act. (1962, 98)[24]

In previous crises, such as 1793 and 1811, the government had issued exchequer bills to the merchants. Sir Robert Peel believed that issuing bills would help only if the bank agreed to purchase them from the market. Since "intervention would be chiefly useful by the effect which it would have in increasing the circulating medium, we [Peel] advised the Bank to take the whole affair into their own hands at once, to issue their notes on the security of goods, instead of issuing them on Exchequer Bills, such bills being themselves issued on that security" (ibid., 99). With the government's guarantee in hand, the bank raised the discount rate to 5 percent and resumed lending. Bagehot describes the turnaround:[25]

> "We lent it," said Mr. Harman, on behalf of the Bank of England, "by every possible means and in modes we had never adopted before; we took in stock on security, we purchased Exchequer bills, we made advances on Exchequer bills, we not only discounted outright, but we made advances on the deposit of bills of exchange to an immense amount, in short, by every possible

24. William Huskisson was a director of the bank and had been president of the Board of Trade. He was an active reformer who opposed mercantilism and favored the reforms advocated by Smith and Ricardo.

25. Bagehot called this turnaround "classical" and liked the example so well he repeated much of the passage (1962, 99). Among the many bank failures of the period was Henry Thornton's bank, Pole, Thornton, and Company, in which his son remained active after Thornton's death in 1815. Bagehot's analysis is, of course, similar to Thornton's discussion of the panic of 1793. See note 11 above.

means consistent with the safety of the Bank, and we were not on some occasions over-nice. Seeing the dreadful state in which the public were, we rendered every assistance in our power." After a day or two of this treatment, the entire panic subsided, and the "City" was quite calm. (Ibid., 25)

The crisis, coming at the end of a period of alternating inflation, deflation, expansion, and depression that characterized the first quarter of the century, provided the impetus for an examination of monetary arrangements and produced some major changes in banking and central banking practices. Repeal of the usury law (1833) permitted the bank to raise the discount rate on short-term bills above the 5 percent limit, a very important step for the future development of central bank policy. Other changes made to improve the functioning of the banking system included the opening of branches of the Bank of England, the extension of the joint stock form of organization to commercial banks, and the granting of legal tender status to Bank of England notes. The latter changes show the tendency of governments (repeated on many subsequent occasions) to adopt new arrangements after a crisis even if there is little reason to believe that the previous arrangement was a major contributing cause of the crisis.

As is often the case, changes in informal arrangements were far more important than the new laws. Of particular interest here are the changes in central banking practices, since they reveal the attitudes and understanding of the directors. But there were also important changes in the practices of bankers and bill brokers.

The Bank of England was forced to accept, or at least to share, the responsibility for maintaining the payments mechanism and to function as lender of last resort to the economy. The bank did not publicly acknowledge the responsibility, and during the crisis the government had been forced to prod the bank and offer guarantees. A tradition was established thereby, and the bank was able to demand and get similar guarantees in later crises. The bank's caution was partly a consequence of private ownership, as was alleged at the time, and perhaps partly of bureaucratic slowness resulting from its monopoly position, but it was partly lack of understanding of the responsibility of a central bank to serve as lender of last resort.

The basic cause of the crisis, however, was the bank's inability or failure to slow the rate of monetary expansion in 1823–24. Many of the bank's directors believed that the expansion had been partly the result of "speculation" and the panic a result of "overspeculation." Influenced by the real bills doctrine, some directors attributed the start of speculation to the bank's purchase of government securities, that is, the purchases of Dead Weight debt and other issues. But most of the directors recognized that the problem arose because of the expansion of the circulation or, as some of them put it, the reduction in interest rates.[26]

The experience led many of the directors to conclude that the bank had been too ambitious when it agreed in 1822 to assist the government in a policy of reversing the price level decline. The bullion reserve had been at one of the highest points in the bank's history when the policy started, but even so large a reserve had proved insufficient to satisfy the demand for bullion during the crisis. The experience seemed to support the extreme bullionist view that the combined circulation of gold and paper currency had to be kept equal to the amount of gold that would otherwise have circulated. Any excess would raise the price level in proportion to the excess issue, causing a fall in the exchange rate and a loss of bullion. This point was well known because Ricardo had stressed it in his writings and testimony, and it had become a main point of emphasis for the writers in what came to be known as the currency school. By accepting this point from Ricardo and the members of the currency school, the directors in effect rejected Thornton's earlier stress on the effect of business conditions on confidence and of confidence on the demand for money. Neglect of Thornton's promising start on an analysis that combined short- and long-run consequences of a change in gold or money closed off one of the few opportunities in a century to develop a general equilibrium analysis of money, bank credit, output, prices, and balance of payments.

The wave of bank failures profoundly affected London bankers and bill brokers, just as a similar experience was to affect their American counterparts a century later. Innovation and changes in practices followed. The risks inherent in the previous practice of holding very low ratios of reserves to deposits and relying on the sale of bills, or in some instances advances from the Bank of England, had proved larger than anticipated. The banks were partnerships at the time, so failure often meant the loss of a personal fortune. For a time the banks increased their reserve ratios by increasing their holding of bullion and deposits at the Bank of England relative to their deposits. They no longer relied on the purchase and sale of bills of exchange to adjust portfolios but held bills to maturity and adjusted port-

26. Very similar views about speculation are repeated in the Great Depression of the 1930s. Wood (1939, 83–84) presents a number of quotations from the parliamentary hearings of 1832 to show that the predominant view at this time was that it made very little difference whether the bank increased the circulation by a purchase of Treasury bills or by discounting commercial paper. This view contrasts with the views held by the bank's directors earlier and criticized by Thornton and the views held by members of the Federal Reserve Board in the 1920s.

folios by making or calling loans to bill brokers. As the banks withdrew from the bill market, some of the larger brokers accepted many of the functions the banks had performed. They bought and sold bills from their portfolios instead of acting as brokers (Scammell 1968, 133). Others continued a brokerage operation as before the panic.

Just as the United States banks in the 1930s virtually stopped all borrowing from the Federal Reserve, after 1825 English banks no longer relied on advances from the Bank of England. To increase cash, banks reduced call loans to the bill brokers. After 1830 the brokers were allowed to discount at the Bank of England, and they did so when the banks reduced call loans.

Some may find in these developments the origin of a "tradition against borrowing." Wood (1939, 90–104) points out that the facts do not support that hypothesis. Generally the bank's discount rate was a penalty rate, above the rate on bills of highest quality, the only type eligible for discount. London banks did not borrow even in periods of crisis but relied on call loans to adjust their cash position. When the banks' demand for cash assets increased, the country banks sent more bills to the bill brokers and surplus areas purchased fewer. London banks reduced call loans, and the bill brokers borrowed from the Bank of England. The so-called tradition against borrowing by banks should be seen, therefore, as a tradition of borrowing by the bill brokers and dealers who supplied reserves to the banks.

Furthermore, there were other ways the bank's rate policy affected the market. There were seasonal swings in the volume of exchequer bills. If the market refused to absorb the bills at existing rates, the bank was asked to lend to the Treasury or purchase bills in the open market. By raising bank rate, the bank induced the market to hold more bills. With the usury law repealed, the bank experimented with the use of bank rate as a means of controlling base money.

FROM PALMER'S RULE TO PEEL'S ACT

By the 1830s the main features of the monetary system were in place.[27] A money market had developed, and the principal institutions had accepted distinctive roles. The Bank of England had a set of social objectives, some partial understanding of the steps required to achieve these objectives, and glimmerings of an understanding of the short-run consequences of its actions. Both the market and the bank realized that the bank's responsibilities went beyond those of an ordinary bank to include the role of lender of

---

27. Bordo and Schwartz 1984 has a thorough discussion of the operation of the gold standard in Britain and other countries during the nineteenth century.

last resort. Moreover, the bank accepted responsibility for maintaining specie payments at a fixed pound price of gold and had become familiar with the traditional central banking control techniques—discount rate changes, qualitative restrictions, and in a limited sense, open market operations.

In 1827 the bank added a rule of procedure to guide policy actions, known as Palmer's rule after the governor who announced it at the parliamentary hearings of 1832. John Horsley Palmer saw the rule as a means of reducing the variability of the quantity of money in circulation and the exchange rate, and he apparently regarded such smoothing operations as part of the responsibility of a central bank.

Palmer's rule attempted to tie the liabilities of the Bank of England to the stock of bullion. When the exchange rate was at par, the sources of the monetary base were to consist of one-third bullion and two-thirds securities. Except for seasonal adjustments, discussed below, the security portfolio would be kept constant, and the bank would increase or decrease the note issue as gold flowed in or out.

Every monetary rule is based on a theory of the monetary process, Palmer's rule no less than those that came later. The theory behind the rule was the Hume-Thornton-Ricardo theory of the long-run consequences for prices, gold stock, and the exchange rate of changes in money. The rule accepts two propositions from that analysis. One, emphasized during the Restriction, is that depreciation of the exchange rate is evidence of an excessive issue of notes. The second is that the gold reserve is held against the bank's notes and deposits, not just notes as the currency school proposed (Mints 1945, 83).[28]

The main defects of Palmer's rule as a guide to operating policy bring out some differences between the monetary theories of Thornton and Ricardo. First, Thornton accepted proposition one as a long-run proposition, but he argued at length that, in the short-run, changes in the demand for money (or monetary velocity) cannot be neglected. Such changes occur when new substitutes for money appear or their use expands. Thornton was clear that "paper credit," which is to say bank deposits, differs from gold but that both are part of the "circulating medium" and both affect the price level. Second, Thornton urged the Bank of England to expand the monetary base with the long-run growth of trade. Third, he stressed the effects on money, output, and prices of temporary changes in the demand for currency. Under Palmer's rule, expansion and contraction of money

28. The modern version is known as the monetary theory of the balance of payments.

(currency and deposits) were tied to gold flows. However, the rule made no provision for changes in the amount of currency produced by country banks and no provision for changes in the distribution of the liabilities of the Bank of England between government deposits and base money.

The members of the currency school attacked Palmer's rule on two grounds, both familiar. The rule allowed the bank discretion, not only because it had been adopted voluntarily but because in practice the rule was sufficiently complex that the bank could abandon it or make exceptions whenever it wished. A second, and more frequent, criticism concerned the definition of money. Palmer's statement of the rule allowed the bank's total liabilities—deposits and currency—to rise and fall with gold movements. Since the bank offset the effect of quarterly fluctuations in Treasury deposits on the base, it had to raise or lower the monetary base as gold flowed in and out. The currency school defined money as the sum of currency (notes) and bullion but excluded deposits. It argued that gold movements would have their expected effect on the price level and exchange rate only if changes in currency matched the changes in gold, and it urged the Bank of England to operate as if the source of the monetary base consisted entirely of bullion.

Some of the issues raised by the currency school have had a long life. The issues resurface periodically when there are changes in the types of financial institutions or their activities. One part of the currency school position is that the price level depends on the type of liabilities or assets issued and repurchased by the central bank. These writers understood that money was neutral in the long run, but they emphasized a narrow definition of money. To maintain stable prices they believed the central bank should limit currency issues. The modern statement of the proposition usually assigns importance to a broader definition of money that includes checkable deposits and often time and saving deposits as well as some additional items.

From 1827 to 1836 bank rate remained constant (at 4 percent), and the base fluctuated with market forces. The stock of bullion varied between £4 million and £12 million and the security portfolio between £20 million and £34 million, both narrower ranges than in the previous decade. For this reason the rule might be regarded as a partial success. Some small portion of the fluctuations consisted of seasonal movements resulting from continuation of the bank's practice of offsetting seasonal fluctuations in market interest rates caused by differences in the timing of Treasury payments and receipts. Apparently Palmer's rule was never intended to apply to short-term portfolio changes of this kind, because neither Palmer nor most of the other directors believed at the time that short-term fluctuations in money (however defined) had a permanent effect on the exchange rate. The bank had not yet accepted the state of the money market as an indicator of bank policy, but it had started a move that would bring it to that position within a decade (Wood 1939, 45).

Wood (1939, 102–3) argues that Palmer adopted the rule because he did not believe discount rate changes provided an effective means of controlling the bank's portfolio, a point that Hawtrey repeats (1962, 14–15). These writers neglect that the rule was promulgated in 1827 and announced in 1832 when the bank still operated under the usury law.[29] Whatever Palmer's earlier views on the effectiveness of rate changes may have been, the bank under his leadership changed the discount rate seven times between the summer of 1836 and the winter of 1839–40 in response to a series of crises, first in the United States and later in Belgium. Equally important, the bank raised the discount rate above 5 percent, first to 5.5 and then to 6 percent, to stem the outflow of gold in 1839. By changing the rate and borrowing abroad to increase its bullion holdings, the bank was able to maintain specie payments throughout the period despite the loss of two-thirds of its bullion in 1839.

The experience convinced most observers that monetary problems had been exacerbated by the defects of Palmer's rule. The bank lost gold when deposits were withdrawn, and although currency remained unchanged, it had acted to increase security holdings so as to restore deposits despite the loss of gold. The currency school and the bankers drew very different conclusions, however. Anticipating a dispute that continued for the next century and beyond, Palmer and the group of writers known collectively as the banking school, generalizing from their experience with the rule and the events of the previous half century, concluded that no set of rules could guide the bank adequately. To the extent that they proposed solutions, they favored changes in the discount rate, to be made at the discretion of the bank, as required to protect the bullion stock and the exchange rate. The currency school, on the other hand, blamed the failures of the rule on the exercise of discretion by the bank and particularly the failure of the bank to keep a constant stock of gold and notes.

The proponents of rules triumphed over the advocates of discretion. With the passage of Peel's Act in 1844, the currency principle was established as the governing principle of the monetary system.

29. The belief appears to rest on statements like the one by Palmer that a 5 percent rate was an offer to lend as much as the market wished to borrow at that rate. Under the usury law, the bank could limit borrowing only by imposing quantitative restrictions once bank rate was at 5 percent.

NEW LESSONS FROM RENEWED CRISES

The Bank Charter Act of 1844 (Peel's Act) accepted a main point in Ricardo's plan for a central bank: separation of monetary operations (the control of the note issue) from banking operations (control of deposits and lending). The bank was to have two departments, an Issue Department and a Banking Department. The Issue Department carried out the monetary operations under a formula that tied the note issue to the stock of gold, as the currency principle required. The bank's maximum note issue was set at £14 million plus the stock of gold coin and bullion held by the Issue Department. The bank gained a monopoly of the note issue.[30]

The Banking Department was expected to function in much the same way as any other private bank. Its reserves consisted of the notes of the Issue Department and a small stock of gold held to facilitate exchange of notes and deposits into gold. Whenever the Banking Department accumulated more notes than it wished to hold, the Issue Department redeemed them by paying out gold. The proponents of the act expected the bank to compete for discounts and to hold deposits for other London banks, and they saw no conflict of interest in these functions. The custom of country banks' keeping deposits in London and of London banks' keeping deposits at the Bank of England was well established. More important, the proponents of the act denied that deposits were money.

The bank apparently welcomed its new freedom of action. Prices had fallen 20 percent in four years, and the gold stock had increased by £11 million to £12 million. It reduced bank rate from 4 percent to 2.5 percent within the month that the act passed, and the bank aggressively competed for discounts in London and at its branches. From the low level of £2.6 million in 1844, the discount portfolio jumped to £18.5 million in 1845, £34 million in 1846, and £38 million in 1847 while the bank's income from discounts rose from £80,000 to £380,000 (Wood 1939, table 9, 137; Scammell 1968, 145).

With the decline in British prices, gold had come to England at a steady rate during 1842 and 1843, increasing the bank's gold holdings and expanding the monetary base. The 1844 act required the bank to follow the currency principle by issuing or withdrawing currency (notes) as gold held by the Issue Department rose and fell. The Banking Department could use all the gold it acquired to expand deposits. As a result the directors, for a time, took no action to control deposit expansion. Bank rate remained at the market rate of discount on bills of highest quality, whereas before it had

---

30. Outstanding country notes were counted as currency for the first time. Further issues were banned, and outstanding issues had to be retired and replaced by Bank of England notes (Wood 1939, 111).

served as a penalty rate. Prices started to rise in the second half of 1845. The gold flow reversed, so the bank raised the discount rate to 3.5 percent. The following year the rate was reduced to 3 percent, where it remained during the fall while gold flowed out.[31] Between 1844 and 1847, prices rose by more than 20 percent, with much of the increase in 1847.

The panic of 1847 is in many respects similar to the panic of 1825.[32] The bank raised the discount rate, first by steps of 0.5 percent and in April by 1 percent. When gold continued to flow out, the bank limited discounts and called advances. The brief panic that ensued ended when the gold flow reversed. During May and June the bank accumulated about £1 million of gold, and the reserves of the Banking Department increased by £3.5 million. In July the gold drain resumed. The bank met the new threat by raising bank rate to 5.5 percent and again placing restrictions on the type of discounts it would accept. A series of bank failures called forth new restrictions, and although the bank did not refuse to lend, it raised substantial doubt about its intentions by announcing that after October 15 bills could be discounted only at rates to be decided at the time of application. The currency drain intensified and produced a new wave of bank failures. The internal and external drain of £1 million pounds in the following week reduced the reserves of the Banking Department to £2 million and raised the fear that the bank would soon be unable to issue notes or accept deposits.[33]

The bank looked to the government for assistance, just as it had in 1793, 1811, and 1825. This time assistance took the form of a letter indemnifying the bank for damages arising from violation of the 1844 act and empowering it to expand its discounts provided it raised the minimum discount rate to 8 percent. The bank quickly adopted the policy later known as "lend freely at a high rate." Within a few days, the panic ended; bank rate was lowered to 7 percent within a month, and by late December it was back to 5 percent.

The panic was mainly a monetary crisis, as that term is now understood, brought on by the tardy and hesitant actions of the Bank of England during the period of rising prices after 1844, followed by a very restrictive policy in 1846–47. The bank seems to have recognized that its policy had either caused or contributed to the crisis. During the next few years the se-

---

31. The price increase and gold flow were not entirely monetary in origin. The famous Irish potato blight required increased food imports, at higher prices, draining the gold stock.

32. A thorough analysis of the 1847 panic is Dornbusch and Frenkel 1984.

33. The act of 1844 required the bank to publish a weekly statement showing the principal assets and liabilities of the Issue and Banking Departments separately, so the bank's situation was known within a few days.

curities portfolio fluctuated much less than in the past, and the bank was able to reduce the discount rate in a series of steps to 2.5 percent by 1849. At the time the bank had £17 million in gold, and the Banking Department had £12 million in reserves and only £25 million in securities.

The panic helped to resolve some disputes about the role of a central bank. The currency school argued that before the act there was no effective limit on the note issue. The Bank of England was not required to maintain a fixed gold reserve ratio, and the regional banks could issue notes in response to demand. The currency school claimed that, as a consequence, money growth was procyclical in the early stages of an expansion. The increase in currency raised the price level, causing a loss of gold and a crisis.

The so-called banking school differed about the importance of currency and did not rely on any of the monetary aggregates. Its proponents wanted the bank to discount only real bills, and they claimed that a real bills policy would prevent over- and underissue of money and credit. To the extent that they had a uniform view, they emphasized real events at home or abroad as the principal cause of crises. In their view, the role of the Bank of England was to serve as lender of last resort to the financial system. This distinguished the bank from other banks. (See Laidler 1988, 100–102.)[34]

The crisis showed that the system had not worked as the currency school predicted. The Banking Department had not been able to operate as an ordinary bank. At the beginning of the expansion, as in 1824–25, the bank held a stock of gold that was much larger than the stock usually held. Yet the gold stock and the reserve of the Banking Department had proved insufficient, and the bank had been forced to appeal to the government to suspend provisions of Peel's Act. The currency school interpreted the crisis of 1825 as the consequence of the bank's failure to keep note issue tied to gold. Prominent members of the banking school, who had opposed the act of 1844, interpreted the crisis of 1847 as evidence of the failure of the currency principle. These writers now urged the bank to adopt a more effective means of maintaining the exchange rate, protecting the gold reserve, and avoiding crises.

Evidence of the change in policy and in the approach to policy is shown by the variability of the discount rate. Between 1793 and 1844 the bank changed the discount rate only eleven times, and except for a brief period in 1839, the rate was never less than 4 percent or more than 5 percent. Between 1844 and 1849 the rate changed sixteen times and varied between 2.5 percent and 8 percent, eight of the changes occurring in the crisis year 1847. During the quarter century beginning in 1850, bank rate changed

---

34. Hetzel (1987) finds references to the lender of last resort function as early as 1797.

more than 225 times, an average of once each five or six weeks. There are only three years from 1844 to 1914 in which the discount rate did not change. In two of them, 1895 and 1896, the rate remained constant at 2 percent, a rate that tradition had by that time established as a minimum.

If the act of 1844 was a victory for the currency school, the victory was short-lived. We do not know the precise date on which the bank's policy changed from reliance on the currency rule to reliance on discretion, but there can be no doubt that it pursued a less aggressive lending policy and a more variable bank rate policy after the panic. Bank rate remained above the market rate, and the bank's stated policy was "to follow the market" (Wood 1939, 138). Attention shifted away from the theoretical issues raised by Thornton or Ricardo and toward the solution of so-called practical, or managerial, questions about how best to operate under the gold standard and how to avoid suspension and inconvertibility. The bank learned to use the discount rate to attract balances to London from country banks and from abroad or, when required, to send balances to the country or abroad. Gradually, the bank accepted responsibility for maintaining convertibility at the fixed mint price of gold and relied on changes in bank rate to attract and repel balances.[35]

Thornton had described the relation between capital movements, exchange rates, and demand for gold and pounds. He recognized also that changes in the quantity of gold affected the monetary base, the volume of currency and deposits, expenditure, and prices. Most writers accepted the general framework, but many failed to emphasize the effects of gold movements on the prices of goods, on output, and on the price level that Thornton had stressed.

By the 1850s most discussions of central bank policy that mentioned long-run (or general equilibrium) effects acknowledged that increases or decreases in money (however defined) changed prices in the same direction. However, many policy discussions ignored long-run effects and emphasized short-run changes in the money market and short-term capital flows. Effects of relative price changes on the balance of trade were said to operate slowly and as a consequence received much less attention than they had earlier. Critics of these orthodox views raised many of the objections that have been repeated ever since. Announcement effects and destabilizing speculation are common in the writing of the period. Some claimed that an increase in bank rate encouraged a withdrawal of gold from England because speculators anticipated a further increase; others claimed

35. At about the same time, the Bank of France also began to change the discount rate more frequently.

that monetary policy was counterproductive because exports had to be financed at a higher interest rate, whereas imports were not reduced until later, so gold was withdrawn (Wood 1939, 125–26; Viner 1965, 278–79).

Hawtrey (1962) notes that bank rate policy was more variable from 1860 to 1880 than after 1880. He explains the greater variability during the earlier period as a consequence of the interaction between the bank and the market and argues that during this period a change in bank rate had a substantial effect on the balances country bankers held in London. A rise in bank rate restored the bank's reserve by drawing balances from the country and permitted it to lower the rate. Once the bank lowered the rate, the balances went back to the country, forcing it to raise the rate again. The process continued until the bank's reserve was restored. According to Hawtrey (xii), London banks acquired many of the country banks as branches after 1880 and centralized reserves at the head office, so a rise in bank rate drew fewer balances to London and a fall drew fewer balances out.

The argument is of interest for two reasons. First, Hawtrey's argument that institutional changes weaken the effectiveness of monetary policy returns many times. Second, his argument is opposite to the argument, frequently made in the United States, that a decentralized banking system is less responsive to interest rate changes. Most arguments of this kind confuse levels and changes. If banks holding negative excess reserves are penalized or incur a loss of utility greater than the cost of adjusting (by borrowing or by other means), on average each bank will hold positive excess reserves. Centralizing the banking system reduces the average level of reserves. Neither centralization nor decentralization, however, implies that the response to a change in the discount rate is larger before or after the change, only that variations take place around a new level. Moreover, the evidence for the period does not support Hawtrey. His argument requires the time series on bank rate to show advances followed by declines more frequently in the earlier years than in the later years. Most of the changes are unidirectional movements in both periods, contrary to Hawtrey's hypothesis.

A more plausible partial explanation of the higher variability in the ten to fifteen years before 1880 than after 1880 is that trade expanded and in the 1870s several countries accumulated gold to prepare for a resumption of specie payments. Gold production was considerably smaller and more variable than it had been in the decade following the discoveries of gold in California and Australia. The growth in world demand for gold meant that the Bank of England had to either pursue a more deflationary policy than in earlier years or let its reserve ratio of gold to monetary liabilities decline. The bank chose the latter course. The monetary base, deposits and notes at the Bank of England, rose relative to gold during the sixties and seventies. As a result, a given change in gold both permitted a larger expansion and required a larger contraction in the monetary base and the stock of money.

The variability of the bank's policy meant that the economy had to adjust frequently to large swings in monetary policy. Table 2.1 gives the data on the size and frequency of changes in bank rate. When reading these data, it is important to keep in mind that the changes were always made in a series of steps; most often the rate increased in steps of one percentage point and decreased in steps of one-half point. The data understate, to a considerable extent, the frequency with which the economy had to adjust to changes in bank rate.

A key difference between the earlier and later policies appears in the data at the end of table 2.1. After 1873 bank rate remained within a narrower range than before. More often than not, the rate was between 2 and 6 percent, and until 1907 it did not exceed 6 percent again, and then only for a short time. There is little doubt that the Bank of England's discount policy became less variable. The reason is that between 1876 and 1886 the price level fell at a compound rate of nearly 4 percent a year. Since the bank did not set bank rate below 2 percent, the economy had to undergo enough deflation to equilibrate the balance of payments and maintain the bank's reserve position. When economic expansion took place and gold was withdrawn, the bank raised the rate by steps of 1 percent just as it had done during the period of inflation. The bank did not recognize that a 5 or 6 percent bank rate was a much more restrictive policy with 4 percent average deflation than during years with positive average inflation. A short period with bank rate above 5 percent brought contraction, renewed deflation, and an inflow of gold. During the last quarter of the nineteenth century as a whole, bank rate remained above 5 percent a combined total of only twenty-six weeks.

The bank failed to recognize the effect of inflation on interest rates or to distinguish between market rates and real rates of interest. Thornton's recognition of this distinction was lost. For the next century, during wars, depressions, inflations, and deflations, central bankers used the absolute value of market rates to judge whether rates were high or low and monetary policy tight or easy. Many of their most serious mistakes resulted from this error.[36]

We can only speculate on other reasons for reduced variability, but one

---

36. The belief that the gold standard maintained price stability may have contributed to the error, but that would not explain why the error persisted. I am inclined to the view that central banks, influenced at first by the real bills doctrine and later by habit, looked mainly at money market responses and ignored longer-term effects of their actions.

Table 2.1 Main Swings in Discount Rates of the Bank of England, 1853–79 (percent)

LOW POINT		HIGH POINT	
LEVEL	DATE	LEVEL	DATE
2.5	January 1853	5.5	May 1854
3.5	June 1855	6	October 1855
4.5	June 1856	7	October 1856
5.5	July 1857	10	November 1857
2.5	December 1858	4.5	May 1859
2.5	July 1859	5	April 1860
4	May 1860	8	February 1861
2	July 1862	5	January 1863
3	April 1863	8	December 1863
6	February 1864	9	May 1864
6	June 1864	9	September 1864
3	June 1865	10	May 1866
2	July 1867	4.5	May 1869
2.5	August 1869	6	August 1870
2	July 1871	5	October 1871
3	December 1871	5	May 1872
3	June 1872	7	November 1872
3.5	January 1873	7	June 1873
3	August 1873	9	November 1873
2.5	June 1874	6	November 1874
2	August 1875	5	January 1876
2	April 1876	5	October 1877
2	January 1878	6	October 1878
2	April 1879		

Source: Hawtrey 1962, 281–88.

plausible reason is that the variable policy was followed by a series of disturbances and some crises. In 1857, 1866, 1873, 1878, and 1890 the Bank of England was forced to respond to an internal, external, or combined internal and external demand for gold. These disturbances to financial stability were by no means wholly a result of the bank's policy. In 1857 the expansion of the economy was brought to an end by an external drain to the United States to satisfy the demand for gold during the United States panic of 1857. The disturbance was made worse by the failure of a large discount house, Sanderson and Company. In 1866 a crisis occurred, intensified by the failure of several banks and discount houses—including the largest discount house, Overend, Gurney and Company—a failure often attributed to poor management but no doubt intensified by the balance of payments deficit of 1865. In 1873 there were drains of gold to Germany, Austria, and the United States owing to crises in those countries, and in 1878 the failure of a large Scottish bank—the City of Glasgow Bank—induced an internal demand for gold and Bank of England notes as well as a series of bank failures. The problem in 1890 involved one of the largest and most prestigious merchant banks, Baring Brothers (see Schwartz 1987b, 272–74).

During the crises of 1857 and 1866, the bank relied entirely on bank rate until the government announced that it would indemnify the bank against issuance of currency in excess of its gold holdings. As table 2.1 shows, the rate was raised from 3 percent or 5.5 percent to 10 percent. During the Baring disturbance the maximum rate was 6 percent, and this rate remained in effect only four weeks. A considerable part of the difference in the discount policies of the two periods is explained by the alternative policies the bank developed. On receipt of the news that Baring would have to suspend payments, the bank increased its gold reserves by borrowing abroad, as it had done in 1839, and by purchasing gold. The governor of the bank then organized a syndicate of leading London banks to guarantee Baring's liabilities. The disruption was short, and the sizable reduction in output that occurred several years later cannot be attributed to the Baring crisis.

Several important changes in the bank's policies took place after the panic of 1847. In the panics of 1825 and 1847 the bank attempted to restrict the volume of loans. In 1857 and again in 1866 it made large loans at ever higher rates and made no attempt to restrict the volume. Within a few weeks of the start of the 1857 panic, the bank's discounts doubled. The loss of gold was so great that it was forced to make use of the temporary power to issue notes without gold backing, that is, to temporarily suspend the provisions of the act of 1844. At the start of the 1866 panic in January, the bank had a larger reserve and did not have to suspend the act until March.

A second important change occurred between 1857 and 1866. The bank sold government securities during the crisis of 1857 in an attempt to reduce the growth of its portfolio. By 1866 the bank recognized the role of lender of last resort more clearly; it increased "private securities held" by a larger amount than in 1857 and made no attempt to sell government securities. Bagehot, a major critic of the bank's directors, congratulated them for at last recognizing that the Banking Department was not an ordinary bank but the protector of the country's reserve and the lender of last resort for the financial system.[37]

The series of panics from 1847 to 1866 also contributed a classic to the

---

37. See Bagehot 1962, 80–81 and appendix D. Bagehot recognized that as lender of last resort, the bank should not sell at a time of panic. Exactly one hundred years later, the Federal Reserve at last recognized similar responsibilities. Faced with the prospect of failures by savings and loan associations, the System authorized the reserve banks to lend to the associations if required to prevent failures. The Federal Reserve came to recognize its role as lender of last resort to the entire financial system and thus to the economy. For the contrast with System thinking in 1929, see below, chapter 5.

banking literature: Walter Bagehot's book *Lombard Street: A Description of the Money Market* (1873). The book gives a clear description of the institutional arrangements of the time and proposes rules for the conduct of monetary policy. Bagehot did not criticize the bank for failing to respond to crises. Long before economists emphasized anticipations and policy credibility, Bagehot criticized the bank for failing to announce its policy in advance. A main point of the book is that directors of a central bank must publicly acknowledge their responsibility as lender of last resort and prepare for future crises under a commodity standard by holding a larger reserve than ordinary banks. Failure to do so creates and intensifies panics. In the course of the argument, Bagehot reveals a clear understanding of fractional reserve banking.

Like Thornton, Bagehot distinguished between the appropriate response to an internal drain and an external drain. If an internal drain increased the demand for gold or Bank of England notes and there was no reason to be concerned about the exchange rate, the drain should be met by substantial loans from the bank. But if large amounts of gold went abroad, the crisis was external and should be met by raising the lending rate of the Bank of England. A rise in bank rate encouraged foreign lenders to buy bills in London and, by reducing internal demand and the price level in England, encouraged exports and reduced imports: "The rise in the rate of discount acts immediately on the trade of this country. Prices fall here; in consequence imports are diminished, exports are increased, and, therefore, there is more likelihood of a balance in bullion coming to this country after the rise in the rate than there was before" (Bagehot 1962, 23).[38] Later the gold attracted by the higher rate reversed the decline in domestic demand and the price level.

Bagehot recognized that if the bank allowed an external drain to persist, it would face an internal drain as well. The domestic public, seeing the decline in the gold reserve, would exchange deposits and the note issues of country banks for gold and Bank of England notes. If the two drains occurred together, the Bank of England must discount willingly at a high rate.

> Before we had much specific experience, it was not easy to prescribe for this compound disease; but now we know how to deal with it. We must look first

---

38. Bagehot (1962, 22) referred to evidence of the effect of interest rates on short-term capital movements: "If the interest of money be raised, it is proved by experience that money *does* come to Lombard Street, and the theory shows that it ought to come . . . as soon as the rate of interest shows that it can be done profitably" (italics in the original). Bagehot did not offer comparable evidence of the effect of price changes on the balance of trade, although he discussed some related matters on 69–78 and suggested there that the effect on prices would be delayed.

to the foreign drain, and raise the rate of interest as high as may be necessary. Unless you can stop the foreign export, you cannot allay the domestic
alarm. . . . And at the rate of interest so raised, the holders—one or more—
of the final Bank reserve must lend freely. Very large loans at very high rates
are the best remedy for the worst malady of the money market when a foreign drain is added to a domestic drain. Any notion that money is not to be
had, or that it may not be had at any price, only raises alarm to panic, and en-
hances panic to madness. (Ibid., 27–28)[39]

Throughout his book, Bagehot (1962, 31–32, 79–82) made it clear that by
"very large loans" he meant the absolute volume and not the volume of
loans relative to the gold reserve.

Lombard Street is a clear and definite statement of some important principles of central banking. Consistent application of these principles would
have avoided many of the worst consequences of monetary policy in the
century that followed its publication. The book is a high point in the statement of the banking school view of the role of a central bank and its responsibilities.

The weakness of the book is the weakness of the bankers' approach.
Bagehot's analysis of the relation between the operations on the money
market and their consequences for the economy never reaches the level of
Thornton's. Throughout his book he shows an awareness of the feedback
and response between monetary policy and the economy, but his astute observations never produce an incisive analysis of these effects to stand beside and supplement his analysis of the money market. Nowhere in the
book does he attempt an analysis of the relation between discount rate and
market rate that would be required to carry out his policy of increasing the
gold reserve of the Bank of England. Nowhere does he mention that his
policy of increasing the gold reserve at times requires deflation, although
he was aware of this possibility. The appearance of the book before the start
of a long period of deflation helps to explain this lack of attention, but examination of the many proposals to increase the bank's reserve ratio, produced in response to his book, shows no recognition of the deflationary effect of the policies required to increase the bank's gold reserve.

Bagehot's book makes it clear that bankers and the banking school did
not regard the international gold standard as a completely self-regulating
system, and the data in table 2.1 show that their actions were consistent

39. Note that Bagehot assigns priority to maintaining the exchange rate. See also Thornton 1965, 93–99, for a similar argument and analysis of the crisis of 1793. Charles Rist (1940,
404–6) quotes several Frenchmen (Thiers, Burdeau, Vuitry) who recognized, in the middle
of the nineteenth century, the role of a central bank as lender of last resort and holder of the
reserve and also recognized some of the policies required to carry out these functions.

with their views in this respect. The bank was expected to regulate the money market. Indeed, the views of the period erred far more on the side of minimizing or ignoring the consequences of variability for the economy than of overlooking the role of a central bank in keeping the exchange rate between the gold points.

By automaticity of the gold standard, bankers most often meant that in the long run a central bank could not both keep the exchange rate fixed and prevent prices from rising or falling. Virtually every English nineteenth-century writer on banking understood that inflation or deflation must be accepted as the cost of keeping the market price of gold equal to the mint price. The statements of United States bankers and world central bankers during the 1960s on the importance of "discipline" and "confidence" could just as well have been made by English writers a century earlier.

The series of panics and disturbances after 1857 silenced any remaining adherents of the currency school view. Although the act of 1844 remained on the statute books, the Bank of England accepted de facto responsibility for controlling the reserves of the Banking Department and the broader responsibility for the functioning of the international monetary system. After 1870, world demand for gold rose as other countries joined England on the gold standard. The Bank of England accepted the resulting deflation as the price of maintaining convertibility, just as it accepted deflation after 1815 and 1919 as the price of restoring convertibility at the previous mint price.

The actions of the Bank of England after 1844 make it clear that the bank gradually accepted money market rates as the principal indicator of current monetary policy. Bank rate was set in relation to money market rates, and without any distinction between nominal and real rates. In both the inflation of the 1850s and 1860s and the deflation of the 1870s, 1880s, and early 1890s, the bank kept 2 percent as the minimum rate of discount. Neither the bank's management nor the economists of the period recognized that under the gold standard, the bank's refusal to lower the discount rate below 2 percent meant that the only equilibrium was at an anticipated rate of deflation equal to the actual rate. Alfred Marshall's testimony before the Gold and Silver Commission of 1887–88 shows him to be struggling toward such an explanation without reaching it.[40]

One aspect of the act of 1844 that should not be overlooked is that the

---

40. Rist (1940, 291–97) and Hawtrey (1962, 227–31) discuss Marshall's testimony but fail to see clearly the distinction he tries to draw between nominal and real rates. In the *Treatise*, Keynes also admits to finding Marshall's statement to the commission unclear (Keynes 1930, 1:191–92). Fisher (1930b, 1:43 n. 7) recognizes Marshall's proposition as a weak association between inflation and nominal interest rates.

Bank of England was forced to respond to internal as well as external drains. The bank did not—and could not—ignore the series of bank failures and the internal drains as the Federal Reserve did in the 1930s. Any failure or hesitation to assist the banks by refusing to lend or restricting discounts increased the demand for loans, gold, and Bank of England notes. Wood (1939) summarizes the period up to 1858: "The principle was thoroughly engrained in the minds of the business community that good bills were convertible into Bank funds and, regardless of the state of the reserve, there were only two occasions (1825 and 1847) when the principle was called into question. On these occasions the Bank's action was quickly reversed after an understanding with the Government."

The bank's understanding of its responsibilities during crises improved so much after 1858 that it organized the banking community and participated in the guarantee of Baring's assets in 1890 in full knowledge that these were illiquid. "Good bills" were, of course, preferred, but the bank showed by this action that convertibility could be maintained and the crisis ended if it acted promptly and did not refuse to lend.

FISHER ON REAL AND NOMINAL RATES

At the end of the nineteenth century, Irving Fisher (1896) analyzed the relations between real and nominal interest rates using a number of examples to illustrate his argument. He repeated and extended the argument in subsequent work. His economic writings and policy campaign for a stable standard of value recognized that stable purchasing power of money would remove most of the problem.

Fisher's discussion (1930b) is much clearer than Thornton's.[41] He distinguishes between perfect and imperfect foresight. Under perfect foresight, expected appreciation or depreciation of purchasing power is fully reflected in the market rates (39, 41–42). People do not anticipate correctly: "When the cost of living is not stable, the rate of interest takes the appreciation and depreciation into account to some extent, but only slightly and, in general, indirectly." Fisher does not fully explain why the public always underestimates the rate of price change.[42]

Fisher's explanation of the relation (1930b, 439) is similar to Thornton's:

41. I use his last complete statement (Fisher 1930b), but the argument is not very different from his 1896 tract or his 1907 book. The same argument is made in Fisher 1920, 56–58.

42. The conclusion rests partly on correlation between interest rates and price changes reported later in his book (Fisher 1930b, 410–11) and partly on his finding that nominal rates are less variable than calculated real rates (413–15). His empirical work does not take account of the constraint on sustained inflation imposed by the gold standard.

"Rising prices increase profits both actual and prospective, and so the profit taker expands his business. His expanding or rising income stream requires financing and increases the demand for loans."

Fisher was not an obscure author of unread economic tracts. He was the leading American academic economist and an active participant in policy discussions. He worked hard to get his ideas about money and monetary standards adopted. In the 1920s a citizens' league promoted his ideas. Congress considered legislation to mandate his monetary standard. Yet I have found no mention of the distinction between real and nominal interest rates in Federal Reserve minutes during the deflation from 1929 to 1933 or until late in the inflation of the 1960s and 1970s. In both periods, and in many others, the Federal Reserve (and other central banks) used an absolute standard to judge whether interest rates were high or low and associated high and low market rates with tight and easy money.

Why was the distinction between nominal and real interest rates lost? Central bankers seem generally to have regarded Fisher as a bright but annoying crank. The Federal Reserve Board was dominated throughout the 1920s and early 1930s by advocates of the real bills doctrines who, like their predecessors, denied any relation between their actions and inflation or output. They ignored Fisher's emphasis on the role of money, much as the banking school dismissed the arguments of the currency school without meeting them.

Further, Fisher often minimized the empirical relevance of the distinction between real and nominal rates. He viewed foresight as typically poor, so that interest rates did not reflect anticipations very accurately, if at all. But lack of foresight does not eliminate the importance of the effect of inflation on interest rates. The more myopic the public is, the larger are the losses and gains, and the effects on realized returns, when inflation or deflation occurs.

Fisher's writings are also exemplary for the clear distinction he makes between permanent effects and temporary, transitional changes. Chapter 4 of his *Purchasing Power of Money* (1920) is concerned entirely with transitional effects. The same is true of his paper later in that decade relating inflation to unemployment. This insightful work had no influence on or meaning for adherents of the real bills doctrine, so it had no influence on policy decisions in the first twenty-five or thirty years of the Federal Reserve's history. Later much of the staff and many of the policymakers adopted a type of Keynesian analysis that emphasized short-term or transitional effects and ignored long-term, permanent effects.

MONEY, CREDIT, VELOCITY, AND INTEREST RATES

Perhaps the most disconcerting aspect of the nineteenth-century discussion is that as central bankers improved their understanding of the effects of their actions, the techniques of central banking, and the responsibilities of the central bank during crises, their understanding of how their actions affected economic activity declined. The distinction between nominal and real magnitudes is more carefully observed at the beginning of the century than at the end. There is a clearer analysis at the start than at the end of the effect of substituting one means of payment for another. The distinction between money and credit blurred during the century, and most of the now familiar arguments about the "ineffectiveness of monetary policy" appeared. Although these issues returned to the academic literature at the end of the century, there is no evidence that academic writing had much influence on central banking. The gold standard and the real bills doctrine dominated policy action.

During the course of the century, the Bank of England (and others) learned to offset panics by serving as lender of last resort, to prevent large inflations or deflations by adopting the gold standard, and to manage short-term demands for credit by adjusting the discount rate to limit or increase the amount of discounts. Twentieth-century concerns about employment and economic growth were heard but had little effect.

Much of the academic writing failed the operational test that central bankers required. Definitions were not tight. There was little agreement and, with a few exceptions, no attention to the distinctions between temporary and persistent or transitional and permanent effects.

Ricardo, a leader of the bullionists, argued that the depreciation of the paper pound during the early years of the century could not be explained by the actual increase in paper money. The relevant change was the increase or decrease in paper money over the amount that would have circulated had there been convertibility. For this reason he tended to deny the validity of any simple comparisons between changes in paper money and changes in exchange rates. His argument, of course, allows for an effect of changes in the demand for money arising, as in Thornton, from changes in confidence and anticipated changes in the volume of transactions. Ricardo denied that these factors had operated between 1797 and 1810, however, and he offered no other explanation of changes in the demand for money. Further, like Thornton, Ricardo recognized that a change in the stock of money does not immediately affect prices and exchange rates, and he criticized his opponents for expecting immediate effects (Viner 1965, 135–42). Some of the other bullionists ignored these subtleties and wrote as if they too expected a very prompt and close adjustment between changes in money and changes in prices and exchange rates. A century later, rational expectationists also erred by understating the time required for the price level to respond to money.

By extension, the name bullionists is given to another group, those willing to extend the definition of money to include paper currency issued in fixed proportion to the stock of gold or specie. The Ricardians and their intellectual descendants in the currency school presented both views, and they inspired Sir Robert Peel, the author of the act of 1844. When writers in this tradition referred to deposits at the Bank of England or at other banks, they did not use the term money; they talked about means of payment, bills, credit, and sometimes the circulating media.

The group known as antibullionists generally denied that there could be an excess issue of paper money if banks restricted issues to the amount issued as part of the process of discounting commercial paper—at the time, bills of exchange. The core of their argument is that as long as the sources of the monetary base consist of gold and commercial paper, money cannot be overissued. The explanation they gave is that "no one would borrow at interest funds he did not need" (ibid., 148). If by chance a bank overexpanded notes or deposits, the excess issue would return to the bank either to reduce loans or, under convertibility, to acquire specie.[43]

The central argument of the antibullionists reappears periodically and had a powerful influence in the early days of the Federal Reserve System. The influence has become a less important cause of errors in policy, but it still survives in two distinct ways. One is the belief that some increases in "credit" are productive while others are "speculative," a belief that in its milder form generates periodic concern about the "quality" of credit as an independent factor. The second is the notion that the monetary base is demand determined, an argument that has been used at times to absolve central banks of responsibility for their errors and even for their policies.

The antibullionists, and all later adherents of the real bills doctrine, failed to distinguish between propositions that superficially appear similar. The first is the proposition that in the long run there can be no infla-

43. After praising central bankers' decisions for their "singular judgment and moderation," Bagehot calls their responses to questions about why they acted as they did "almost classical by their nonsense." Bagehot (1962, 86) quotes from testimony of the bank's directors in 1810: "I cannot see how the amount of bank-notes issued can operate upon the price of bullion, or the state of the exchanges; and therefore I am individually of the opinion that the price of bullion, or the state of the exchanges, can never be a reason for lessening the amount of bank-notes to be issued. . . . Is the Governor of the Bank of the same opinion which has now been expressed by the Deputy-governor? Mr. Whitmore: I am so much of the same opinion, that I never think it necessary to advert to the price of gold, or the state of the exchanges, on the days on which we make our advances."

tion if the stock of money grows at the growth rate of real output. The second is that changes in output induce changes in the demand for bank credit and the stock of money but that if the credit is limited to the change in output, expenditures cannot increase more than output and therefore inflation cannot result.

Thornton was the first to distinguish these two arguments and to recognize that the fallacy in the second argument resulted from the failure to differentiate nominal quantities and rates of interest from real quantities and rates of interest. The error, said Thornton, was the error of John Law, who "considered security as everything and quantity as nothing."[44] Under an inconvertible paper currency, real bills provide no effective limitation of the currency and no defense against depreciation of the exchange rate. With a convertible currency the situation is no better, because the bank could not maintain convertibility if it allowed the base to be determined by the demands of the merchants. Thornton's argument against the usury laws, discussed above, is a trenchant criticism of the real bills doctrine for the failure to distinguish between nominal and real rates. The antibullionists never replied to this argument.

Neither the antibullionists nor other proponents of the real bills doctrine recognized that it is the total quantity of notes, not their backing, that affects the price level. Commodities are sold and resold; each sale gives rise to a real bill. In the limit, there may be one increase in output backing many real bills.

As long as the payments system remained relatively simple, there was very little discussion of the definitions of money and the monetary base. Disputes about the definition start after the development of a market for bills of exchange and their use as a medium of exchange, the growth of deposit banking, and the increased use of banknotes in place of specie. Many of these disputes came to the fore during the Restriction period. Under convertibility, the requirement to pay gold on demand limited the quantity of money. The use of inconvertible paper raised questions about the effect of paper money on prices and exchange rates. In fact several different, but related, questions arose. One was whether the deposits at the Bank of England were money, and if they were money why they differed, if at all, from deposits at any other bank. To some writers if seemed obvious that because one liability is a substitute for another, there is no reason to draw fine distinctions between types of liabilities. A related issue is the possibility of controlling the stock. Those who emphasized substitutability generally

---

44. See Viner 1965, 150–51, for the quotation in the text, the comparison of Thornton and Ricardo on this point, and the views of the directors of the Bank of England.

concluded that efforts to control the stock of money, however defined, were a waste of time. Others focused on the gold stock and currency, items they believed to be money. Other items they regarded as part of the "circulating medium." Related to these issues were disputes about the appropriate indicator of Bank of England policy—exchange rates, gold stock, gold flows, interest rates, or balance of payments—and about the variables that determined prices and exchange rates.

One long-lasting source of confusion in the monetary literature can be traced to the absence of accepted definitions. Since money originally meant gold or bullion, an increase in paper money was described as an increase in velocity. The reasoning was that the gold was held as a reserve by the issuer of notes, who thereby increased the "circulation" of the reserves he held (see Schumpeter 1955, 319). The source of this confusion lies in the origins of the banking system, particularly the "goldsmith" principle, under which goldsmiths could hold gold but could not increase its "circulation" by issuing claims in excess of the amount held. When the definition of money broadened to include notes as well as specie, the definition of monetary velocity changed also. Velocity included the "turnover" of notes, including the notes that might have been issued had bankers not elected to hold deposits at the Bank of England. The spread of deposit banking was often described, therefore, as an increase in monetary velocity.

Adding to the confusion was the practice of referring to an increase in deposits as an increase in credit, or sometimes as an increase in bank credit, and the related practice of referring to the stock of deposits as a stock of credit. For example, when Hawtrey discusses currency and credit, he means what is now called currency and deposits. Many of the writers who wrote that velocity declined secularly meant the same thing that others meant when they wrote that in the long run the ratio of currency to deposits declined with habits of payment.

A difficulty with any attempt to interpret parts of the discussion is that writers who denied that some asset or group of assets should be labeled money often did not make it clear whether they meant there was no point to defining the assets that serve as medium of exchange or that prices and the exchange rate did not depend on the quantity of money, however defined. Thomas Tooke, an early and prolific writer of the banking school, appears to have believed that the bank could affect the price level and exchange rate by changing market interest rates. But he also believed there was no need for interference by the Bank of England if bankers discounted real bills and notes and deposits remained convertible. For him the world price level was determined by the world's gold stock, but he offered no explanation of English prices and denied that money, credit, or base money bore any consistent relation to prices. Most Federal Reserve officials remained in this tradition in the 1920s. They denied that their actions affected prices. A modern version of Tooke's argument is found in Sayers 1957, 5, which argues that "to label something as 'money' . . . is to build on shifting sand."[45]

Later writers in the banking school tradition (Bagehot, for example) believed that the exchange rate and gold flows could and should be regulated by the bank. Bagehot emphasized that the bank had to regulate reserves, but a main reason for his emphasis is that the point was often denied. Under the act of 1844, currency issues were tied closely to gold movements, and it seems likely that if the currency issues were not regulated, Bagehot would have argued for control of both uses of the base—reserves and currency. Viner (1965, 243–44) points out that many in the banking school thought of banknotes and bank deposits as money, meaning mediums of exchange, even if they were vague about the effect of money on prices.[46]

All of this was a far cry from Thornton, who recognized that the "possession of a right to draw [deposit] obtained in the one case, is exactly equivalent to the possession of the note [banknote] obtained in the other" (1965, 134). But few later writers saw that both reserves and currency affected market rates, money, and prices; most did not or, if they did, were inclined to emphasize one type of money rather than another.

The two points that the banking school emphasized most were the determination of interest rates in the money market and the determination of the exchange rate by the demand for and supply of pounds. If they saw beyond these points to the effect of changes in the base on money and of money on prices, market interest rates, and exchange rates, they did not stress the latter relations, and some denied them vigorously. As early as the 1830s John Horsley Palmer, a governor of the bank, had testified that the bank affected market rates by changing the "circulation" and suggested that during periods of crisis, market indicators are useful indicators of the state of the money market (Wood 1939, 45–47). With the passage of time and a series of crises and disturbances, this view gained adherents. The avoidance of panics seemed a more attainable goal if bank failures and internal drains could be avoided. Panics appeared to be money market re-

---

45. My interpretation of Tooke is based on the discussion in Wood 1939, 56–58. A succinct statement of Sayers's views is in Sayers 1957. This point and the notion that the relation between components of "liquidity" is ever changing catch essential points of Sayers's argument on this issue. Most of these issues returned in the early years of the Federal Reserve.

46. Viner notes (1965, 246) that Mill included potential borrowing power as a part of credit.

sponses, so avoiding panics required stability of the money market. Moreover, with the increased size and growing emphasis on short-term capital movements under the gold standard, market interest rates and other money market variables gained acceptance as indicators of near-term gold flows. As maintenance of the exchange rate and the bank's reserve became the principal goal of bank policy, stability of the money market became its primary concern, the best means of ensuring exchange rate stability and avoiding domestic crises.

Some of the writers in the banking school deserve praise, however, for recognizing that the private sector is able to produce a variety of substitute means of payment. They described the development of branch banking, the pooling and centralization of bank reserves, and the use of deposits and bills of exchange as innovations that increased credit by finding more efficient uses of a given monetary base. They failed to see that the introduction and use of deposits and other substitutes for base money are limited by the return from producing substitutes. Nor did they see the related point that more efficient use of a given stock of base money does not imply loss of control of the stock of means of payment by the central bank.[47]

The failures of the banking school included a failure to analyze the monetary system as part of the economy and often to define terms. Its adherents made no attempt to distinguish substitution in demand from substitution in supply, the use of substitutes from the production of substitutes. As late as 1867 Thomas Hankey, a director of the Bank of England, denied that either the bank or the banking system could create or destroy means of payment (Viner 1965, 255 n. 3). His argument repeats the central notion on which the act of 1844 rested and shows that Hankey was unable to distinguish partial substitutes from perfect substitutes. Bagehot's criticism of Hankey and those who shared his view stresses the difference between bank reserves and bank deposits but not the difference between partial and perfect substitutes or between substitutes in demand and substitutes in supply.

The fundamental relation governing substitution on the demand side is that for each type of "money" the sum of the marginal product per dollar (or other unit) and the anticipated rate of deflation must equal the return per dollar (unit) in services and income. If two means of payment are rela-

---

47. The substance of banking school views on these matters (and on many others) is not strikingly different from the discussion of banking and financial innovation by many contemporary bankers and financial writers. Each major innovation in financial markets brings forth comments designed to establish that the central bank has lost (or will lose) control, so that monetary policy is "impossible" or ineffective. Recall the discussion of Eurodollars in the 1960s.

tively poor substitutes in supply, equilibrium is reestablished mainly by relative price changes, with little change in relative supplies. At the opposite pole, if the two are relatively close substitutes in supply, equilibrium is reestablished by changes in the respective outputs, with little change in relative returns to the two assets.

In the British monetary system, in our own, and in most others, currency and checking deposits are close substitutes in supply at a fixed supply price. Anyone who wishes to exchange one means of payment for the other does so at a fixed exchange rate. Technological change or other change in the relative cost or relative return from using one means of payment rather than the other affects relative demands. The return received by holders and users of these assets and the (real) demand for the sum changes. However, under a fractional reserve banking system, changes in relative demand for currency and deposits mainly change the combined nominal stock of the two and the price level at which the combined stocks are held.

The writers of the banking school, and many of those who repeated their arguments, observed the use of substitute means of payment and concluded, incorrectly, that the use of substitutes meant that each substitute means of payment had the same effect on the price level or the exchange rate as any other. Or if they were more sophisticated, they regarded changes in "credit" as changes in the "velocity" of the existing means of payment. They argued that the changes in velocity permanently changed the price level, the exchange rate, or the gold stock. For them money was a weighted average with the weights equal to the respective, but ever changing, velocities. Hence, they concluded, there was no point to defining money and no prospect of controlling money. These notions survive in discussions of "unstable velocity," the impossibility of defining money, or the importance of controlling total "liquid assets," credit, or the total liabilities of all financial institutions.

The currency school did not respond to the banking school arguments correctly or even uniformly. Some argued that the currency to deposit ratio was approximately constant, so control of currency issues meant control of money. Others argued that deposits could not be controlled because of substitution. Still others contended that the velocity of deposits was much lower than the velocity of currency and that the velocity of bills of exchange was lowest of all.

Improved understanding of the reasons for the failure of the currency principle had to await Fisher and Keynes. Fisher argued that the currency principle worked badly because currency was a poor indicator of monetary expansion and inflation. According to Fisher (1920, chap. 4), bank loans and bank deposits increased much more than currency during the early stages of the expansion. In his notation, M' (deposits) rose relative to M (currency) following an inflow of gold or other source of base money. Later in the expansion, consumer expenditures increased and the ratio of currency to deposits rose. This rise forced fractional reserve banks, operating under gold standard rules, to surrender reserves. Faced with a loss of reserves, the banks raised loan rates, called loans, and reduced deposits. By redistributing the monetary base between reserves and currency, the rise in the currency ratio reduced the circulating medium, M + M', or in current terminology, reduced money, currency and deposits. The reduction in money brought the expansion to an end and started the contraction.

Fisher's explanation links short-term changes to the long-term value. The key element in his explanation of cycles is that businesses, banks, and households failed to anticipate promptly the inflation caused by monetary expansion. A central bank operating on the currency principle (or gold standard rules) would always react too slowly to prevent inflation. Since currency increased for a time by less than the inflow of gold, the central bank did not increase the discount rate or take action to slow the monetary expansion. As a result, commercial banks expanded deposits and loans by more than the amount consistent with the given gold stock and the long-run average ratio of currency to deposits. Inflation was under way before currency increased relative to gold. Changes in money and credit were therefore procyclical.

Fisher was one of the first to emphasize that differences in the timing of cyclical changes in the stocks of currency and deposits caused the currency ratio to fluctuate around its long-run trend. Others commented on the fluctuations but failed to see that they were systematic, not random events. However, Fisher did not draw the implications for central bank policy of adherence to the currency principle. This was done by Keynes, in rather picturesque language.[48]

Most nineteenth-century writers not only failed to analyze the timing and proximate causes of changes in money but did not consider the failures of monetary policy as a main cause of fluctuations in output. Neither the fluctuations under Palmer's rule nor the series of crises under the act

48. "For in the event of an inflation developing, the note issue is in modern conditions the *latest* phenomenon in point of time to exhibit symptoms of the disorder which is at work in the economic system. To attempt to maintain monetary health by regulating the volume of the note issue is like attempting to maintain physical health by ordering a drastic operation or amputation after the affliction has run its full course and mortification is setting in. For, generally speaking, the note-issue will not expand—for reasons other than increase in the volume of employment—until the inflationary influences have had time to raise the money-rates of remuneration of the factors of production" (Keynes 1930, 2:273, 2:264).

of 1844 stimulated anyone to analyze the relation of the Bank of England's policy to interest rates, output, prices, and specie flows. A few writers in the currency school accused the bank of overexpanding its discounts in 1844, but they did not follow the charge far enough to see the conflict with the currency principle. Had they considered the implications of their argument, they would have been forced to recognize that a central bank should keep control of both uses of the monetary base—reserves and currency—not currency alone. Almost certainly, some would have recognized that the way to control the uses was to control the total sources. Again, this point was not recognized until John Maynard Keynes's *Treatise on Money* (1930, 2:225–26).

Thomas Tooke, testifying before Parliament in 1832, anticipated Marriner Eccles's "pushing on a string."[49] Wood (1939, 48) summarizes a part of his statement: "An increased issue of notes might only swell the note reserves of the London bankers or be deposited by them in the Bank." Samuel Gurney, a leading banker of the period, testified that if there was an abundance of notes, extra notes would remain in the tills of the bankers, the "natural depository" of surplus notes. If there were ample means for speculation, mere idle funds would not encourage speculation (54).

William Blake argued in 1823 that inflation was caused by fiscal policy (government purchases) financed by new debt issues. The debt issues activated previously idle balances, that is, increased velocity. And Lord Lauderdale blamed the contraction before 1820 on the government's budget surplus. A surplus reduced "effectual demand," so production declined. Lauderdale wanted the government to replace the war expenditures that ended in 1815 with expenditures on public works (Viner 1965, 192–94).[50]

CONCLUSION

Every complete theory of the monetary system must provide answers to a number of related questions. What is the monetary standard, and what are

49. Eccles's statement is in the congressional hearings before the Banking Act of 1935. See , House Committee on Banking and Currency 1935, 321. Asked what would happen if the Federal Reserve printed currency and paid off debt, Eccles replied, "The currency would increase the reserves of the banking system . . . but the currency would immediately go into the banks and from the banks into the Federal Reserve banks—and you would have—additional excess reserves."

50. Some, of course, recognized that among all the arguments, there were none that showed an increase in money would not raise prices. See Wood's discussion of Thomas Attwood (1939, 52–53). Attwood wrote of a depression: "Let them [the public] be glutted with money. They will then seek prosperity and the prosperity of the country will return." Attwood elsewhere recognized that an unanticipated fall in prices redistributed wealth and intensified depression because prices did not all fall at a uniform rate. Like Thornton, Attwood noted that wages were slow to fall and used this observation to explain unemployment of labor.

the source components of the monetary base? Why do the source components expand and contract? Which items are included as uses of the monetary base? If the uses of the base consist of more than one item, what effect does the substitution of one item for another produce on the monetary system? By what means and to what end should the government or a central bank seek to control the base? What are the short- and longer-term consequences of a change in the base on the stock of means of payment? What are the short- and longer-term consequences of changes in the means of payment on prices, output, employment, and balance of payments? What, if any, is the feedback from the changes in prices and real variables to the source components of the base?

In practice, there have been three distinct types of answers. One, following Thornton, stresses the relation of the base to the stock of money, the effects of money on economic activity, prices, balance of payments, and specie flows or exchange rates. A second approach, following Ricardo, puts aside questions of the relation of the base to the stock of money or means of payment and avoids analyzing the effects of substituting one means of payment for another. For the purposes of analysis, money and the base are identical or proportional. In both of these approaches, the monetary base stands at the bottom of a pyramid. Substitution of one type of credit instrument for another is of secondary importance, or no importance at all, once the determinants of the base and the stock of money have been specified and the relation between the two analyzed or dismissed. Corresponding to each set of tastes, state of technology, and anticipation of the future, the economy has a real rate of return at which the public willingly holds the stocks of money and real capital. The variety of claims and debts cancel each other out and affect the solution only to the extent that they represent changes in taste or technology, and then only as much as any other change in taste or technology. Corresponding to the real rate of interest, there is a market rate that differs from the real rate by the anticipated rate of price change. When anticipated and actual rates of price change remain equal, the economy reaches and remains in long-run equilibrium.

A third approach looks at the credit system as one that issues a variety of claims and debts that substitute for money or more generally for means of payment. In this approach, money lacks fundamental importance in the explanation of price and output changes or specie flows. Credit, interest rates, or more recently "flows of funds" become the main indicators of the state of the credit markets. The banking school developed this notion, if such a loose and amorphous collection of ideas can be described as "developed."

Each of the three types of monetary analysis was known in the nineteenth century, and for a time each had a dominant influence on the development of central banking theory and practice. But in the end the banking school view became the established view among bankers and central bankers and was challenged by only a few economists. When the Aldrich Commission in the United States received the testimony of leading bankers and experts on central banking in 1912, the members heard very little about the effects of changes in money on domestic economies and a great deal about the "needs of trade," "self-regulating productive credit," and the use of the discount rate to stop an outflow of gold.

They learned, too, about the role of the Bank of England in smoothing the money market to eliminate seasonal fluctuations and its practice, well established by the 1840s, of offsetting the effects of Treasury operations on interest rates. These policies focused attention on short-term market interest rates and were the forerunner of so-called defensive open market operations. Among the by-products of the focus on short-term changes was the increased frequency of discount rate changes and, considerably more important, the belief or opinion that such operations were a main responsibility of central banks.

The promising analysis started by Henry Thornton recognized that money was neutral in the long run but not in the short run. Thornton's work opened the way to a careful analysis of the differences between central banks and intermediaries, between money and credit, between real and nominal rates of interest, between relative and absolute price changes, and between permanent and transitory changes. He recognized the errors in the real bills doctrine. Later Irving Fisher revived and added to the understanding of these issues, but, like Thornton's, his work did not influence central bankers until the Great Inflation of the 1970s.

Walter Bagehot did not have a theoretical framework to match Thornton's. He understood, however, the importance of a lender of last resort. And he emphasized the importance of precommitment by the central bank and of following precommitment with action.

The Federal Reserve's approach to policy originated in the Bank of England's nineteenth-century practices and the partially developed theory or framework that the practices attempted to apply. By the end of that century, discussions of central banking confused credit and money, used money market variables as indicators of monetary policy, and denied or cast doubt on the ability of a central bank to induce short-term changes in output or employment by monetary means. Although stabilization of prices and employment was mentioned as a goal of monetary policy in the literature of the early and late nineteenth century, virtually every discussion of the policy of the period concluded that monetary policy was guided by the state of the reserves, not by output, employment, or economic stability.

THREE

In the Beginning, 1914 to 1922

On December 23, 1913, Congress approved the Federal Reserve Act. Final passage came after several lengthy disputes and many pages of testimony favoring and opposing a central bank. More than thirty volumes of research reported on the findings of the National Monetary Commission.[1] Despite the intense discussions, detailed investigation of financial systems that preceded the act, and the number of alternative bills drafted, considered, and dismissed, the act says very little about the broader purposes of the legislation. The title talks of furnishing an elastic currency, affording means of rediscounting commercial paper, and improving the supervision of banking; the act speaks of setting discount rates "with a view of accommodating commerce and business" but mentions no other objectives.

Omission of a broad statement of purpose or policy objective was not an oversight. The act represented a compromise between many different groups that had very different purposes in mind. At one extreme were the proponents of a single central bank, owned by the commercial banks and run by bankers. The group favoring this alternative looked to the European central banks as a model, particularly the Bank of England. Many of the group's members were bankers or "practical" men, which often meant in the context of the time that they had some idea of the services that central banks rendered to banks but less understanding of the longer-run consequences of central bank operations. They wanted the central bank to damp fluctuations in market interest rates, particularly those caused by the seasonal demand for currency and the financing of crop harvests, and to en-

---

1. The commission was created by act of Congress following the 1907–8 recession that produced more than 240 bank suspensions (Board of Governors of the Federal Reserve System 1943, table 66, 283).

courage the development of a broad national market in commercial paper
and bills of exchange patterned on the London market. One of their principal aims was to increase the seasonal response, or elasticity, of the note
issue by eliminating the provisions of the National Banking Act that tied
the amount of currency to the stock of government bonds.[2] They believed
firmly that a central bank could reduce panics by serving as lender of last
resort in periods of distress. The record of the Bank of England in the previous fifty years reassured them that their beliefs were well founded.

At the opposite extreme were those who opposed a central bank of any
kind. The main economic content of their argument was that a central
bank is a monopoly, but they did not oppose monopoly as such. They feared
or claimed that the monopoly would be run for the benefit of the bankers, particularly J. P. Morgan and other New York bankers. Instead of proposals to avoid a "bankers' monopoly" they produced evidence of concentration, interlocking directorates, and control of financial institutions,
railroads, and other enterprises in hearings before the Pujo Committee
and in that committee's final report.[3] However, the Pujo report made few
recommendations, was silent on the main issues involved in the discussions of banking reform, and had greater influence on the designers of the
Federal Trade Commission than on the designers of the Federal Reserve
System.

Proponents and opponents of a central bank clashed over the recommendations of the National Monetary Commission. Legislation drafted at
the end of the Taft administration in 1912 embodied many of the principles
proposed by the commission. The chairman of the commission, Senator
Nelson Aldrich, was a New York Republican. His plan, the Aldrich plan,
was unacceptable to the Democrats and opposed in their platform for the
1912 election. They objected much more to the organization of the system
and the centralization of power in the hands of the larger banks than to the
chartering of a bank to discount commercial paper and issue currency not
tied to government securities.

The 1912 election shifted control of Congress to the Democrats. Many
Democrats were willing to accept a central bank only if it was under political control. Some members wanted semi-independent regional banks. A

---

2. Government bonds were used as collateral or security for national banknotes, the principal currency or note issue under the 1863 National Bank Act. As the government debt declined, pressure to reduce the note issue rose. The Federal Reserve Act initially removed this
tie by eliminating government securities as collateral for Federal Reserve notes.

3. Arsene P. Pujo was chairman of the House Committee on Banking and Currency. See
62d Cong., 3d sess., February 28, 1913, H. Rept. 1593, in Krooss 1969, 3:2143–95.

month after his election, President-Elect Wilson met with Carter Glass, the new chairman of the House Committee on Banking and Currency. Wilson proposed a mixture of private and public control (Glass 1927, 81–82).[4] His legislative proposal to Congress, on June 23, 1913, included that recommendation and urged that control "be vested in the Government itself, so that the banks may be the instruments not the masters of business and of individual enterprise and initiative." The final structure included Wilson's compromise—a politically appointed Federal Reserve Board in Washington and regional banks in principal centers, run by bankers, with no clear division of authority between the two. As part of the compromise, Wilson proposed a Federal Advisory Council consisting of bankers, appointed by the reserve banks, to serve as advisers to the Board. As with the First Bank and Second Bank of the United States, Congress did not want to grant a permanent charter, so the initial charter was for twenty years. Permanence was not granted until the McFadden Act of 1927.

In its early years the Federal Reserve faced three major challenges. First, an unanticipated war brought a large increase in gold and removed the gold standard as the monetary system of the developed world. The Federal Reserve had a small portfolio, so it had no means of controlling the resulting inflation, even if it wished to sterilize the inflow. Second, the compromises that enabled a majority to support passage of the act shifted the argument over government or private control without resolving it. In the System's early years, frequent conflicts broke out between the reserve banks and the Board as both sides struggled to gain control. Third, the intent of the principal proponents was not realized. They expected to create an institution capable of preventing inflation, responding to banking crises, and financing exports of grain, cotton, and other primary products. Instead they created a largely passive bank, dependent on revenues from member bank discounts but with limited influence over the volume of discounts. The real bills doctrine left the initiative to commercial banks. The Federal Reserve's main channel of influence—the discount rate—was a penalty rate. But raising interest rates was unpopular and provoked concerns about bankers' domination of the economy.

The early experience of the Federal Reserve induced it to abandon, or modify, the principles underlying the act. As noted, the international gold standard ended when the war started. War finance conflicted with the

---

4. Carter Glass was a Virginia country newspaper publisher. He was elected to the House from Virginia in 1902 and served as chairman of the Banking Committee from 1914 to 1918. In 1918 he replaced William G. McAdoo as secretary of the treasury. In 1920 he was appointed, then elected, to the Senate, where he served until 1946.

penalty rate, so the Federal Reserve abandoned it. Political concerns and mistaken policies prevented return to a penalty rate. And the more thoughtful among the early leaders began to question the central tenets of the real bills doctrine.

Wartime experience and the postwar boom, recession, inflation, and deflation convinced many that a passive strategy was inappropriate. Less than a decade after it was established, the Federal Reserve began to search for a more active approach.

THE FOUNDERS' RATIONALE

The House report on the Glass bill accepted that centralization of banking resources is the "root of the central banking argument" but concluded that in a country as large as the United States "equally good results can be obtained" by several federations.[5] The report makes it clear that the House Banking Committee expected the regional reserve banks to function cooperatively but independently and to achieve the advantages of central banking without acquiring the monopoly powers of a single central bank. The striking feature of the report, however, is the extent to which the congressmen who approved it viewed the proposed system as a large association of banks able by pooling gold reserves to take better advantage than the individual national banks of the note issuing and discounting privileges that the national banks possessed. In addition to providing a new bank of issue, Congress made sure that the act improved the procedures for issuing notes by both broadening the definition of acceptable collateral and removing government bonds from the list of acceptable collateral.

Virtually every discussion of banking reform commented on the frequency and severity of United States banking crises. The desire to reduce

5. See 63d Cong., 1st sess., September 9, 1913, H. Rept. 69, in Krooss 1969, 3:2275–2342. The quotations are from Krooss 1969, 3:2284. Some of the passion aroused by the different views can be judged from the reference to the work of the National Monetary Commission. The commission's work is described as costly, lacking in originality, of historical interest only, and with no value for or direct bearing on legislative issues (Krooss 1969, 3:2280–81). Although Glass claimed credit for the final bill, much of the substance had been worked out earlier by Nelson Aldrich based on proposals made by Paul Warburg, a partner in Kuhn, Loeb and Company. Also, Glass gave no credit to Senator Robert Owen (Oklahoma), chairman of the Senate Banking Committee (Friedman and Schwartz 1963; Chernow 1993). Warburg (1930, 2:238) found five main differences between the Aldrich bill and the Owen-Glass bill. The most important of these concerned the greater role of the federal government in the Owen-Glass bill and the provision allowing each reserve bank to set its own discount rate. Owen-Glass also prescribed the size of reserve requirement ratios, a matter left to the central bankers in the Aldrich plan. The act specified that two members of the board were to come from banking and finance. The principal difference between the Glass-Owen and Aldrich proposals is the size and power of the Federal Reserve Board. The Aldrich plan called for a single central bank with fifteen branches and a board with forty-five members.

the frequency and severity of crises—five in the previous thirty years—is a main point of agreement in all the reform plans. All proposals recognized that a central bank could serve as lender of last resort in a banking crisis.

Since there was no established lender of last resort under the National Banking Act, banks attempted to protect themselves against runs or currency demands by holding gold or currency reserves.[6] If all banks sought to increase their gold holdings simultaneously, short-term interest rose as high as 100 percent annually. To reduce the demand for gold, clearinghouse associations or groups of bankers pooled resources to provide payment facilities during periods of stress. Such private facilities had to assume the risk of defaults. A central bank that pooled reserves and lent during a panic would provide "elasticity" at lower cost. Hence bankers were eager to shift responsibility for maintaining the payments and clearing mechanism to a central bank, and there was wide support for this reform.

A second meaning of elasticity referred to seasonal fluctuations. Proponents expected a central bank to reduce seasonal fluctuations in interest rates, principally during the autumn marketing of the harvest. Under the prevailing system, interest rates rose and the dollar appreciated within the gold points when foreigners borrowed and purchased dollars to buy grain. New York banks sold holdings of British bills to smooth the seasonal fluctuation in exchange rates, but large seasonal swings remained until after the Federal Reserve was established (Warburg 1930; Myers 1931; Miron 1986).

The two types of inelasticity had a common source. The National Banking Act tied note issues to government bonds. Hence if banks expanded up to the limit set by the note issue, note issues could not expand further in response to seasonal or cyclical demands. A central bank empowered to dis-

---

6. In the panic of 1907, call money rates in New York reached a 100 percent annual rate on October 24. There were no offers earlier in the day at 60 percent (Tallman and Moen 1990, 8). J. P. Morgan and others organized loans to the stock exchange, and on October 26 the Clearinghouse Association began to issue certificates. The certificates served principally as a means of settlement between banks, releasing gold and currency for use by the public. Other currency substitutes were also introduced (9–10). Tallman and Moen (1995) point to an important difference between New York and Chicago during the panic of 1907. The Chicago clearinghouse treated trusts similar to banks and permitted them to be members of the clearinghouse. New York did not. When concerns arose about the safety of depositors at Knickerbocker Trust, the New York clearinghouse did not have much information about, or responsibility for, payments drawn on Knickerbocker. Chicago did not experience failures, but New York did. Although there was no lender of last resort, this experience suggests how anticipations or uncertainty about the payments function can induce bank runs and failures. The experience also points up the importance of defining financial institutions broadly at a time of panic.

count real bills would remove this inelasticity and finance the crop movement. Currency would be more elastic.[7] John U. Calkins, later governor of the Federal Reserve Bank of San Francisco, subsequently stated the contemporary view of the relation between elasticity and real bills: "Probably the most important effect of the Federal Reserve Act was to set up the machinery necessary to provide elastic currency; elastic in that it would be based on self-liquidating credit instruments arising out of the production and distribution of commodities. An obligation of the United States does not represent a transaction of this character . . . to the extent such obligations back the currency such currency is fiat currency" (Federal Reserve Governors Conference, May 1922, 143–44 [hereafter cited as Governors Conference]).

Authority to discount real bills was seen by many at the time as the main improvement of the new legislation.[8] Many bankers shared Paul M. Warburg's view that the Federal Reserve could prevent wide swings in interest rates without risking inflation if it purchased real bills.[9] Reliance on real bills also freed the credit system from dependence on the call money market and thus on credit to stock exchange brokers and dealers who financed their positions in that market. Leading economists such as A. Piatt Andrew, H. Parker Willis, J. Laurence Laughlin, and Horace White also advocated the real bills doctrine.[10] These economists believed that credit would be adjusted to the needs of trade if banks invested in commercial and agri-

7. The outright prohibition against government securities as backing or collateral for note issue was written into the Federal Reserve Act. Paradoxically, the Glass-Steagall Act of February 1932 temporarily removed the restriction as a means of encouraging expansion of the note issue and preventing bank runs during the Great Depression. It was never restored. In June 1945 the use of government securities as collateral became permanent. See chapter 5.

8. Attempts to include deposit insurance in the Senate bill failed in the House. Glass opposed these efforts, and they were removed in conference (Glass 1927, 208–9). United States economic history would have been very different had the provision been in place after 1930.

9. Warburg was a New York banker who had taken a strong interest in central banking. He was born in Germany into a family of German-Jewish bankers, so he was familiar with practices abroad. After the 1907–8 crisis, he discussed his views with Senator Nelson Aldrich and subsequently took a leading role in drafting the Aldrich plan. One of his major contributions was to convince Aldrich that the problem of elasticity was not primarily a problem of providing currency. He saw the need for a discount bank to provide reserves seasonally and cyclically. He repeated this point many times. See Warburg 1930, vol. 2. He also worked with the House and Senate committees that drafted the Federal Reserve Act and served a four-year term from 1914 to 1918 (vice chairman in 1916–18) as a member of the first Federal Reserve Board. He was not reappointed during World War I, allegedly because of his German origin and his close ties to German bankers (Chernow 1993, 44). In the 1920s he served as an influential member of the Federal Advisory Council.

10. Of these, the most important in practice was Willis. Willis collaborated with Glass, served on his staff at the House Banking Committee, and drafted much of the act. Later he served as secretary of the organizing committee and as secretary of the Federal Reserve Board. In later years he was highly critical of the way the System developed and made his views known as editor of a leading business paper, the *Commercial and Financial Chronicle*.

cultural loans and avoided bonds, real estate, call money, and other speculative assets (Mints 1945, 206–7).

Mints (1945, 251–53) adds three additional benefits the founders expected the Federal Reserve to bring. First, bank reserves, mainly gold reserves, would be pooled and therefore available for lending when needed.
Second, a bill market would replace the call money market, as in London.
The call money market provided credit based on stock exchange collateral
and hence depended on a speculative asset. The bill market depended on
real bills, particularly bills arising from the financing of foreign trade.
Third, improvement in the check clearing system would reduce the number of banks charging fees for clearing checks. The Federal Reserve instituted collection at par at the reserve banks but did not, initially, make par
collection a condition of membership.

Section 15 of the Glass bill (section 14 of the act), titled "Open Market Operations," authorized the Federal Reserve banks to engage in such operations in any of the assets acceptable as collateral for rediscounts and to purchase and sell gold and government bonds. The House report on the Glass
bill noted that the purpose of open market operations was to enable the
"Federal Reserve banks to make their rate of discount effective in the general market at those times and under those conditions when rediscounts
were slack and when therefore there might have been accumulation of
funds in the Reserve banks without any motive on the part of member
banks to apply for rediscounts or perhaps with a strong motive on their part
not to do so" (Krooss 1969, 3:2317–18). The Senate report saw open market
operations as a means of developing a market for bills, thereby reducing the
variability of rates, the risk premium, and the average level of market rates.[11]

---

11. Glass (1927, 90) records that H. Parker Willis, his chief adviser, proposed open market operations. Willis was later highly critical of the use of open market operations as the principal policy tool. The perceived tie between open market operations and discount rates was so
close that authority for setting discount rates is in (the same) section 14 of the act. The Senate
committee could not agree and issued two separate reports. One report refers to open market
operations as one of the main benefits of the bill. The source of the gain is the development
of a market for bills and not the power to affect market rates of interest and expand or contract the monetary base. See 63d Cong., 1st sess., November 22, 1913, S. Rept. 133, in Krooss
1969, 3:2377–2416. The discussion of open market operations is on 2398–2400. On 2395 the
report discusses the stability of interest rates and notes that in 1907 interest rates had been
highly variable using the following figures for money rates in selected months of 1907:

Month	Range of Rates
January	2%–45%
March	3%–25%
October	5%–125%

The extreme variability of rates may explain the great concern in the Senate report with
reducing the variability of market rates. However, the report anticipates that there will be "a

None of the reports discusses the effect of changes in money on prices or pays much attention to problems of inflation or deflation. The effects of money on prices were not unknown to Congress. Silver agitators had pressed the point during the deflation of the seventies and eighties. The lengthy report of the Jones Commission (1877) had discussed the issue and concluded that an inconvertible paper money was subject to government control and should be allowed to expand with population so as to keep the price level constant.[12] The quantity of gold or convertible currency, on the other hand, could not "be greater than such an amount as may be requisite to maintain the prices . . . at a substantial parity with the prices of all other countries using the same kind of money" (Krooss 1969, 3:1866).[13] Yet none of this found its way into the act or influenced the reports of the House or Senate committee on the amended Glass bill.[14]

A principal reason for the omission is the Gold Standard Act of 1900 that legally established the gold standard as the United States monetary standard. The United States was thought to be part of the international gold standard that determined the stocks of money and the price levels in all member countries. However, after the start of the European war but before the effective beginning of the Federal Reserve System, all the princi-

---

comparatively stable rate of interest upon a lower basis than heretofore, because the element of hazard of panic and of financial stringency will be removed by the proposed system" (2395).

12. The proposal is, of course, similar to Henry Thornton's. Krooss (1969, 3:1798–1911) reprints the report of the chairman of the Senate Monetary Commission (45th Cong., 1st sess., March 1877, S. Doc. 703). The report offers, as a sideline, a monetary explanation of history and points out that from the end of the Roman Empire to the fifteenth century, the stock of money in the (former) empire shrank from $1.8 billion to $200 million. It asserts a large effect of the decline in money and prices: "The crumbling of institutions kept even step and pace with the shrinkage in the stock of money and the falling of prices. All other attendant circumstances than these last have occurred in other historical periods unaccompanied and unfollowed by any such mighty disasters. It is a suggestive coincidence that the first glimmer of light only came with the invention of bills of exchange and paper substitutes, through which the scanty stock of the precious metals was increased in efficiency" (3:1863). Other periods are interpreted in a similar way. However, the report does not argue for inflation but generally favors stable prices.

13. The following was written before Irving Fisher's analysis of interest rates: "Equally fanciful and erroneous is the proposition that the rates of interest for money can be lowered by increasing its quantity. . . . [T]he rates for the use of loanable capital depend upon . . . the current rates of business profits . . . and the fiscal policies [sic] of governments. . . . In truth, *increasing the amount of money tends indirectly to raise the rate of interest* by stimulating business activity, while *decreasing the amount of money reduces the rate of interest* by checking enterprises and thereby curtailing the demand for loans" (3:1866–67; italics added). The report did not, however, distinguish anticipated from actual price changes, as Thornton had done.

14. There was a general belief, however, that centralization of reserves and development of a money market would reduce interest rates and make rates more uniform within the country. This was expected to contribute to economic development (U.S. Treasury Department 1915, 12; Warburg 1930).

pal gold standard countries suspended the gold standard. It was never reestablished in its prewar form.

The intent of the legislation was very different from the way the System evolved. The original conception was of a relatively passive system. The price level would be controlled mainly by gold movements and changes in foreign exchange. Seasonal and cyclical movements in demand for credit would increase or reduce demand for rediscounts at Federal Reserve banks. Much of this activity, it was believed, would take the form of changes in the volume of rediscounts of bills of exchange or acceptances initiated by banks. The Federal Reserve would not be entirely passive, however. Its active role, like that of the Bank of England, would consist mainly of raising or lowering the discount rate in ordinary times and providing emergency credit to prevent or respond to a financial panic. The discount rate would be a penalty rate, so in ordinary times bankers would keep discounts to a minimum.

FIRST STEPS AND CONFLICTS

The new system took nearly eight months to get organized. A main reason for the delay was that members of the Board and governors of the reserve banks could not be appointed until the size and number of Federal Reserve districts had been set. The act specified that no two members should come from the same district and required that there be at least eight and not more than twelve districts, each with a Federal Reserve bank in a principal city. Decisions about size, location, number, and boundaries were left to an organizing committee consisting of the secretaries of the treasury and agriculture and the comptroller of the currency.[15]

These decisions were contentious, political, and time consuming.[16] By April 2, 1914, the locations were decided, although appeals continued for more than a year.[17] By mid-May the twelve reserve banks began to organize. Almost ninety days passed, however, before Charles S. Hamlin, Paul M. Warburg, Frederic A. Delano, W. P. G. Harding, and Adolph C. Miller took

15. The committee used data on trading areas and size and growth of banking facilities. It also took a poll of national banks and usually chose the most popular city. Cleveland was the exception; it came third in the voting after Pittsburgh and Cincinnati. The committee also held hearings in eighteen cities (Reserve Bank Organizing Committee 1914).

16. Warburg's account of the choice of number of districts and their boundaries shows the importance attached to these issues at the time. Those, like Warburg, who wanted a European-type central bank appear to have resented greatly the decision to create twelve instead of eight districts. See Warburg 1930, vol. 1, chap. 11. Earlier, Warburg had wanted only four districts with multiple branches (Warburg 1930, 2:275).

17. In 1916 the attorney general ruled that the Board could not reduce the number of reserve banks or change the location of reserve bank cities.

their oaths of office on August 10 as the first appointed members of the Federal Reserve Board.[18] The president designated one of the members as governor and one as vice governor for renewable one-year terms. The secretary of the treasury was ex officio chairman of the Board, but the governor was the chief operating official of the Board. Hamlin served as governor until 1916, when Harding replaced him. The two remaining members of the seven-person board, Secretary of the Treasury William G. McAdoo and Comptroller of the Currency John Skelton Williams, were ex officio members who had taken office earlier.[19]

The twelve reserve banks opened on November 16, 1914, eleven months after passage of the act.[20] Secretary McAdoo's announcement of the opening said in part: "They will put an end to the annual anxiety from which the country has suffered and would give such stability to the banking business

18. Charles S. Hamlin, the first governor, was a Boston lawyer who was serving as assistant secretary of the treasury. He was a last-minute substitute for Richard Olney, a former secretary of state, who declined because of age (Warburg 1930, 2:143). He is described as organized and conciliatory but a weak leader who was too responsive to the requests of Secretary McAdoo (Katz 1992). Delano, a railroad executive from Chicago, was designated vice governor. Harding was a banker from Birmingham who served as governor from 1916 to 1922. Miller, an economics professor who had taught at Chicago and Berkeley, served as assistant secretary of interior in the early Wilson administration. Miller was also the brother-in-law of Wesley C. Mitchell, a leading economist and founder of the National Bureau of Economic Research (NBER) (Katz 1992). Hamlin and Miller were reappointed twice. Both served until February 3, 1936. By law two of the members were to represent banking and finance. In 1922 this requirement was removed and an eighth member, representing agriculture, was added. Members had ten-year terms with two-year staggered appointments. Other requirements for membership were geographical diversity to satisfy sectional interests and prevent eastern control. The initial salary was $12,000, at the time equal to the salary of a cabinet member. In 1995 prices, the salary before taxes would be approximately $175,000, 40 percent more than the salary in 1995.

19. Charles J. Rhoads, first governor of the Philadelphia reserve bank, described Williams as "the only man I ever knew who could strut sitting down" (Rhoads, CHFRS, June 29, 1955, 4). Rhoads was a Quaker, opposed war, and left the system rather than sell war bonds.

20. Secretary McAdoo was authorized to choose the date on which the reserve banks opened. Under pressure from agricultural groups, he chose November 2 against the advice of Strong and Warburg. The opening was delayed because Federal Reserve notes were not ready for distribution. Also, not much capital had been paid in, so the System had very little gold (Harding and Warburg to McAdoo, Board of Governors File, box 659, October 13, 1914). I will use this reference with box number, date, and page where applicable to identify unpublished records in the "Central Subject File, 1913–54," stored at National Archives II in College Park, Maryland.

Many in the South and West criticized the delay in opening. The Texas legislature passed a resolution urging prompt opening. The System was expected to release gold by lowering reserve requirement ratios and thus lower interest rates. Rates had increased after August, when war started in Europe. (Prime commercial paper increased from 4.5 percent in May to 7.6 percent in September, and other rates rose commensurately.) Large banks were less eager to rush the opening because the gold outflow at the start of the war made it more costly to deposit reserves and subscribe.

that the extreme fluctuations in interest rates and available credits which have characterized banking in the past will be destroyed permanently" (Board of Governors File, box 659, November 15, 1914).

Tension between the Board and the reserve banks began before the System opened for business. Two factions formed within the Board. Delano, Miller, and Warburg worried about Treasury control and loss of independence. They distrusted the Treasury group—Hamlin, McAdoo, and Williams. Harding was in the middle. Typical of the reserve banks' concerns is a letter from a Chicago director H. B. Joy (president of Packard Motor Company), to Frederic Delano: "I have a little feeling—in fact it is growing on me—that the Federal Reserve Board in Washington is inclined toward dominating the District Banks" (Board of Governors File, box 659 October 10, 1914). Warburg described the problem. Dominance by the Board would allow political considerations to dominate decisions about interest rates. Dominance by the reserve banks "would render a concerted discount policy . . . an impossibility and reduce the Board to a position of impotence" (Warburg 1930, 1:473–74). To resolve some of the issues and coordinate the reserve banks' activities, the organizing committee recommended appointment of an executive council of the banks' governors. This is the origin of the Conference of Governors, later the Presidents Conference, that still continues (Board of Governors File, box 659, October 13, 1914).

The dominant personality in the early days of the System was Benjamin Strong, first governor of the Federal Reserve Bank of New York. Strong's early views were the views of a sophisticated banker, with little formal training, who had gained enough understanding of the functioning of the domestic and international payments mechanisms to be ahead of most of his contemporaries. He saw the Federal Reserve Act as an opportunity to expand the international operations of United States banks, particularly New York banks, and like Warburg, he believed that the development of the market for bills of exchange and acceptances was the means to accomplish this end in a manner consistent with the act. Throughout his life he remained a proponent of fixed exchange rates and the gold standard and an opponent of devaluation or revaluation of currencies and of inflation. In practice, this meant that he accepted deflation when required and came to regard it as the price of international stability.[21]

Strong's mature views on the gold standard and on monetary policy reflected his experience in the twenties. His prewar policies can be described succinctly as an attempt to recreate Lombard Street on Wall Street, with the

21. Strong's views and actions are described in a favorable biography (see Chandler 1958). His starting salary as governor was $30,000, equal to more than $400,000 in 1995. The governors of Boston and San Francisco banks received $15,000 as initial salary.

Federal Reserve System, particularly the New York bank, playing the role of the Bank of England.[22] He regarded the twelve reserve banks as eleven too many. The appropriate number was one, he wrote. And he believed it was a major defect to issue Federal Reserve notes as obligations of the government. Government note issues were too reminiscent of greenbacks and other fiat money (Chandler 1958, 34–35, 37).[23] Like Warburg, he accepted that real bills should be the base for expansion. To that end he worked to develop and strengthen the money market. One of his first appointees to the New York bank was an American expert on the operation of the London bill market. This effort to develop a market for banker's acceptances and bills of exchange as the principal means of affecting money market interest rates and to replace the call money market was renewed in the 1920s but did not succeed (Warburg 1930, vol. 2, chap. 12; Burgess 1964, 219). Early in his career as governor, he favored compulsory membership of state banks as a means of centralizing reserves. His views on discount policy read very much like pages from Bagehot and are not noticeably different from British views at the time.[24]

The first task was to organize and begin operations. For Strong this meant not only staffing the New York bank but organizing the System. Since he regarded the Board as a political agency and saw the banks as the business end of the System,[25] Strong moved to enlist the support and co-

22. See his letters to Adolph Miller and to Paul Warburg, both of the Board, quoted in Chandler 1958, 90–91. Warburg's views on real bills, discussed earlier, were similar to Strong's. The two had worked together on the Aldrich bill. One of the first statements issued by the Federal Reserve appears in the *Commercial and Financial Chronicle* for November 14, 1914. The statement declares that discount policy is for the purpose of financing self-liquidating loans, or real bills (Mints 1945, 266).

23. In a letter to Warburg, Strong explained that he would decline the offer to serve as governor of the New York bank because of his disagreement over two features of the act—failure to create a central bank and vesting the note issue in a government institution. He accepted the appointment only after a weekend of persuasion by banking friends including Warburg (Chandler 1958, 39).

24. There are many references to Bagehot and Bagehotian principles in speeches at the time of passage. One proposal that did not become law would have made discounting up to twice the amount of the banks capital and surplus a right and not a privilege of membership. This proposal was defeated in the Senate by a vote of thirty-seven to thirty-one (Timberlake 1978, 202). Had it been approved, Federal Reserve history, particularly during the Great Depression, might have been very different.

25. Strong, like Warburg, had favored the Aldrich plan based on foreign central banks. The political role of the Board referred to the presence of the secretary and the comptroller on the Board, its presence in Washington, and the legal requirement that the Board's accounts were subject to audit (until 1933) by the General Accounting Office. On the other hand, the attorney general ruled in December 1914 that the Board was independent of the Treasury (Beckhart 1972, 31). The Federal Reserve Act was unclear about the specific function and responsibilities of the treasury secretary. He was chairman of the Board by law, but the duties of the chairman and his relation to the governor of the Board were not spelled out (Dykes and Whitehouse 1989).

operation of the other reserve bank governors so as to make the banks the dominant partner. His opportunity came very quickly. The Board called a meeting of the governors for December 10–12 to discuss common problems. The governors used the meeting to organize a permanent Governors Conference, with Strong as chairman.

From the start, the Governors Conference tried to control operations. At its first meeting, the governors discussed how the reserve banks would conduct open market operations.[26] One of the main issues was whether each bank would operate independently, as prescribed in the law, or whether they would operate collectively, as required for centralized control. Early in 1915, at Strong's suggestion, the banks agreed to combine operations in both the open market and acceptance accounts to avoid any effect of competitive purchases on market rates. Although effects on the market were recognized, purchases were made principally to increase the earnings of the reserve banks and were allocated to the individual banks in part based on their need for earnings. Reserve banks retained the right to purchase independently (Anderson 1965, 8; D'Arista 1994, 22). Not all the governors were satisfied. Some claimed that New York did not buy enough, so their earnings were held down.

The reserve banks also purchased the 2 percent bonds that continued to serve as collateral for national banknotes. The aim was to replace national banknotes with Federal Reserve notes. At first purchases were made by the individual reserve banks for their own accounts. By 1917 wartime expansion of the reserve banks reduced pressures to increase earnings, so the banks centralized open market purchases of the 2 percent bonds in New York. Concern for earnings returned, however, in the early 1920s and in the mid-1930s. The reserve banks again acted independently in the early 1920s until a new agreement was reached. Centralization of open market operations and the decision about participation remained as problems until the Banking Act of 1933 amended section 14.

The Board also sought control. One of its earliest acts was to rule that the reserve banks could not announce or change discount rates until they had been approved by the Board (letter of Parker Willis to all reserve banks, Board of Governors File, box 1239, November 18, 1914). The Board based its order on the provision of section 13 that gave the reserve banks power to establish rates "subject to review and determination of the Reserve Board." The governors chose to interpret "review and determination" as pro forma but the Board insisted that discount rates were subject to the Board's "de-

26. The first open market purchase of $5 million of New York City tax anticipation notes was made by the New York bank on December 31, 1914.

termination."[27] Early in 1915 the Governors Conference approved a resolution giving the reserve banks sole power to initiate discount rate changes "without pressure from the Federal Reserve Board" (Chandler 1958, 71).

Initially, discount rates were set above prevailing market rates; they were penalty rates to provide discount facilities in periods of market malfunction, as proposed by Bagehot.[28] This principle was in conflict both with the political desire for lower interest rates during the 1914–15 recession and with the desire of the reserve banks to increase earnings.[29]

Earnings depended on membership. The act required approximately 7,500 national banks to be members, but state-chartered banks had a choice. Among the obstacles to membership were requirements for par collection of checks cleared at Federal Reserve banks and for holding reserves at Federal Reserve banks without earning interest. As of June 30, 1915, only seventeen of nearly twenty thousand state banks had elected to join. A year later state bank membership had increased only to thirty-four.

Partially offsetting these increased costs of membership, the act broadened the powers and reduced the reserve requirement ratio for national banks.[30] Cagan (1965, 140) estimates the reduction as 13 percent in No-

27. This clause continued as a source of friction. In 1919 and again in 1927, the Board considered or ordered a change in a discount rate without prior action by one of the reserve banks.

28. Until the early 1920s penalty rates were considered the normal arrangement. Warburg wrote to John Perrin, Federal Reserve chairman and agent at San Francisco: "Whenever the market rate approaches the bank rate, the bank rate will be increased" (Board of Governors File, box 1239, December 13, 1914).

29. The latter was a legitimate concern. The reserve banks were required to cover expenses, including salaries for the Board and its staff and a cumulative dividend for the member banks. Section 10 of the act authorized the Board to assess the reserve banks in proportion to their capital and surplus. The reserve banks as a group had negative earnings (– $141,000 before dividends) for the period from their organization in November 1914 to December 1915. The reserve banks were authorized to assess member banks if necessary to meet expenses. In 1915 the Board discussed an assessment to cover losses and voted in favor, but the reserve banks recognized the effect on membership and were reluctant to choose this option (Board of Governors of the Federal Reserve System, Board Minutes, September 21, 1915, 1154 [hereafter cited as Board Minutes]). Moreover, with the gold inflow providing reserves, banks had little reason to discount. Further, the reserve banks were obligated to pay a 6 percent cumulative dividend on capital stock owned by member banks. Any net earnings in excess of dividend were divided between payments to the Treasury and the surplus account of the reserve banks. (When the surplus account reached 40 percent of paid-in capital, the entire net earnings were to be paid to the Treasury as a franchise tax on the note issue.) The law changed in March 1919 to permit the reserve banks to keep all net earnings after dividends until the surplus reached 100 percent of subscribed capital, after which 90 percent of earnings was paid as a franchise tax and the remaining 10 percent was added to surplus. The franchise tax was repealed in 1933 and restored after World War II (Board of Governors of the Federal Reserve System 1943, 329 n. 7).

30. Under the National Bank Act, there were three classes of banks. Central reserve city banks in New York, Chicago, and St. Louis were required to hold 25 percent of deposits as re-

vember 1914, when the System started operations. This reduction was partially offset in subsequent years by the requirement that member banks deposit more of their required reserves at Federal Reserve banks. In June 1917, by law all required reserves were held at Federal Reserve banks; vault cash was excluded from reserve computation.[31] The legislation increased gold held by the Federal Reserve in excess of requirements by $300 million.[32]

Strong, and also Warburg (1930, 2:150–52), regarded the centralization of reserves as critical to the success of the System. Failure to deposit reserves at the reserve banks meant that gold holdings were dispersed, as they had been before the act. Without centralization, the System would be in a weak position to respond if the gold inflow from Europe reversed at the end of the war. Even if the gold remained, Warburg believed, the System required a larger gold reserve so that it would not be forced to contract the note issue in recessions as eligible paper declined. A larger stock of gold

serves in gold, government currency issues, or gold certificates issued by a clearinghouse. National banknotes could not be used as reserves. Reserve city banks also had a 25 percent reserve requirement, but half could be held at central reserve city banks at prevailing interest rates. Country banks had a 15 percent reserve requirement ratio, of which 60 percent could be deposits at reserve city or central reserve city banks. These requirements applied to all deposits, demand and time. Treasury deposits were exempted in 1908. The Federal Reserve Act set different reserve requirement ratios for time and demand deposits. For demand deposits, the initial reserve requirement ratios were 18 percent for central reserve city banks, 15 percent for reserve city banks, and 12 percent for country banks. For time deposits, the ratio was a uniform 5 percent. Initially, vault cash and correspondent balances counted as reserves, up to 6, 5, and 4 percent at the three groups of banks respectively.

31. At the same time, requirement ratios were reduced to 13 percent, 10 percent, and 7 percent for central reserve city, reserve city, and country banks and to 3 percent for time deposits, greatly expanding the money multiplier. Cagan (1965, 190) estimates that the 1917 amendment was a 21 percent increase in the monetary base. The increase was partly offset by reductions in the amounts discounted. These 1917 ratios remained unchanged until August 1936. In 1922 St. Louis changed from central reserve to reserve city classification, releasing a modest amount of required reserves. Vault cash did not again count as part of reserves until 1959. Miller (1921, 180) explains the 1917 legislation as a wartime measure to centralize gold reserves and provide for expansion of money and credit to finance the war. Sprague (1921, 19) estimates that the Federal Reserve increased the base money multiplier by 50 to 100 percent compared with the pre–Federal Reserve period.

32. The legislation also made membership more attractive for state banks by permitting them to withdraw on six months' notice. Warburg also wanted the Board to have authority to raise reserve requirements in case of a large gold inflow. This authority was not granted until the 1930s. Reserve requirement ratios could be reduced for central reserve and reserve city banks if five of the seven members of the Board approved. State banks also disliked having the comptroller of the currency as a member (ex officio) of the Board. They feared he would favor national banks. In 1915 the Federal Advisory Council urged an amendment removing the comptroller, but no action was taken (Board Minutes, 1915, 1158). The Federal Advisory Council consisted of bankers from each of the districts. It was authorized by the Federal Reserve Act and continues to the present as an advisory group to the Board.

could be used to maintain the note issue.[33] After June 1917, vault cash no longer counted as part of reserves, so banks deposited more of their gold at the reserve banks.

Gold flows in 1915 reversed the direction of change in interest rates. Early in January, discount rates followed market rates down. Interest rates continued to fall slowly through the first year of operations. The Board was quick to claim credit. Governor Hamlin wrote that by merely opening the doors, the steadying effect of the act became apparent in the market (Board of Governors File, box 1239, December 17, 1915). The reserve bank governors were more skeptical. When the Board asked all reserve banks to describe the effect of the new system, most attributed the decline in interest rates to gold inflows and the increase in gold reserves. Chairman John Perrin (San Francisco) wrote that there was "very little tangible evidence that the establishment and operation of the Federal Reserve bank has influenced rates in any important way." Pierre Jay, chairman at New York, wrote that the new system had "no effect whatever" (letters, Board of Governors File, box 1239, December 11 and 13, 1915).

Although the governors invited the Board to send representatives to their meetings, and they sent summaries to the Board, the Board regarded the Governors Conference as a rival organization that weakened its authority by operating independently. It resented decisions by the governors to meet at reserve banks instead of in Washington. It was determined to prevent the governors from meeting too frequently or acting independently.

The Board decided to take control after the Governors Conference criticized the Board for "an exercise of pressure" on the reserve banks. It sent a letter to each of the governors suggesting that the governors hold no more than three or four meetings that year. Although the Board approved $12,900 in expenses for the most recent meeting, it told the governors that their expenditures were too large. The Board did not object to informal discussions among the governors, but "a permanent organization, the appointment of an executive committee, and the election of a paid secretary, are matters . . . of doubtful propriety and beyond the scope and powers of the Federal Reserve banks as defined in the Federal Reserve Act" (Board Minutes, January 20, 1916, 79). The creation of a standing executive committee "might create the impression that certain banks . . . had delegated certain powers to a definite committee" (80). Responding to the governors' criticism, the Board replied that the governors had "assumed powers which they do not possess . . . when they undertook collectively to direct or

33. Under Warburg's proposal, the Federal Reserve would not follow gold standard rules.

to suggest to the Federal Reserve Board the manner of its exercise of the powers conferred upon it by the Act" (81).[34]

The Board won the first contest, but the issues of control and power were put aside, not resolved. Late in July the secretary of the Governors Conference notified the Board that the governors planned to meet on August 15. By this time Harding had replaced the conciliatory Hamlin as governor (Katz 1992, 119). Harding responded that the Board did not want a conference held and that in the future conferences could be held only if called by the Board. The Treasury opposed a conference, Harding wrote, and, he added, "plans for the proposed meeting should be abandoned. . . . [I]n matters which concern interbank relations and operation of the Federal Reserve banks as a system, authority is vested by law solely in the Federal Reserve Board" (Board Minutes, July 25, 1917, 99–101). McAdoo attended the meeting and concurred in the decision. He urged the Board to keep the Federal Reserve banks in hand. To rein in the banks, he had considered appointing five additional government directors to the banks' boards, but he postponed the decision pending a favorable resolution of the dispute.

The following week the Board formally adopted the resolution discussed in the letter to the reserve banks. There was to be no permanent organization and no Governors Conferences unless called by the Board. No further conferences were held until November 1917.[35]

The Board and the reserve banks also clashed over the obligation of one reserve bank to discount for another and the rate to be charged for interdistrict borrowing. The intent of the act was to pool gold reserves by permitting interdistrict borrowing, thereby smoothing regional demands for reserves and borrowing associated with crop movements. The Board had authority under the act to set the rates for interdistrict loans. Strong disliked the provision and sought to limit its scope by permitting the lending bank to set the rate on borrowings (D'Arista 1994, 19). The Board members insisted that this was their responsibility, and they prevailed.

34. On March 9 the Board voted to publish expenses of the Governors Conference in the *Federal Reserve Bulletin,* but they reconsidered on April 21 and voted to include these expenditures in the accounts of the reserve banks (Board Minutes, 1916).

35. In March 1918, Strong proposed a Governors Conference to act on interest rates. The Board responded that if a meeting was held, it would be confined to Treasury security sales and a few technical matters. Strong held an informal meeting in New York with about six governors (Board Minutes, March 8 and June 22, 1918). As late as May 1921, Governor Harding appointed a committee of governors to consider whether the Governors Conferences should be continued. The governors responded that they wanted more frequent conferences, with some held at reserve banks. Harding remained opposed to meetings outside Washington, and none were held (Federal Reserve Governors Conference, May 28, 1921 [hereafter cited as Governors Conference]).

In March 1915 the Board established interdistrict rates. No transactions were made until 1916, when rates were set by the Board on each transaction. In the fall of 1920 the Board reestablished a common rate for interbank rediscounts related to the discount rate on member bank borrowing.

POLICY PROBLEMS

Almost from its founding, the System faced a series of major policy problems. First there was an outflow of gold before the reserve banks opened, as foreigners sold dollar securities at the start of the war in August 1914. Exports declined for lack of shipping because German and British ships that had carried much of the freight withdrew. Commodity prices, particularly for exportables, fell sharply. The initial wartime problems were severe enough to send the dollar above five dollars per pound sterling, well above its intervention point. The New York Stock Exchange and most foreign stock markets closed to hinder sales of securities and demands for gold.

Soon after the reserve banks began operations in November, a gold inflow replaced the outflow and produced monetary expansion and inflation. Wartime inflation, resulting from the financing of Treasury bond sales, soon followed. After the war there was the difficult task of establishing independence from the Treasury and developing an anti-inflation policy. By 1920 the System had to deal with its first recession. The System's response to this series of events—the discussions, the proposals for action, and the actions themselves—reveals the policy approaches and understanding of the Board members and governors at the time and the flaws in the act.

The Federal Reserve System was not fully organized when war started in Europe, so it had a minor role in responding to the gold outflow. In September the Treasury issued emergency currency, authorized under the Aldrich-Vreeland Act of 1908.[36] One of the Federal Reserve's first actions was to oppose issuance of additional Aldrich-Vreeland currency. It worked with the Treasury to organize a group of bankers that subscribed $108 million to redeem United States loans abroad. The organization of the fund may have helped to restore calm; only $10 million was drawn.

---

36. The act expired in June 1915 and was not renewed. The emergency currency issue helped to prevent a panic (Friedman and Schwartz 1963, 196; Dykes and Whitehouse 1989, 237). At its peak in October, $308 million of emergency currency was outstanding, approximately 15 percent of total currency. In addition, banks issued clearinghouse certificates to pay their adverse balances (Chandler 1958, 56). There were no bank runs and the crisis was overcome, a marked contrast to experiences in 1929 to 1933.

Gold Flows

Within a few months of the start of the European war, exports increased and gold flowed to the United States in payment. In 1914 the United States held 19 percent of the world's monetary gold stock. By 1918 its monetary gold stock had increased by 65 million ounces, more than $1.3 billion at the official gold price, $20.67 per fine ounce. The increase was 88 percent of the United States monetary gold stock in 1914 and more than 16 percent of the world's prewar monetary gold (Schwartz 1982, tables SC7 and SC10).[37]

The Federal Reserve followed gold standard and penalty rate rules by reducing discount rates as market rates fell. By mid-December 1914 it had lowered discount rates at all reserve banks. By February 1915, rates at most reserve banks were two percentage points lower than on opening day.[38] Market rates rose briefly in the spring, perhaps in anticipation of the expiration of Aldrich-Vreeland currency issues on June 30. The Board issued a press release urging the reserve banks to "discount as liberally as prudent" (Board of Governors File, box 1239, January 21, 1915). No problems occurred, and interest rates resumed their decline.

The gold inflows substantially increased the monetary base. Table 3.1 shows annual rates of increase in the base from 1915 to 1922. The Federal Reserve was at first powerless to stop or offset the increases even if it had chosen to abrogate gold standard rules by selling securities. The open market portfolio of government securities at the end of 1916 was only $55 million.[39] In fact, the System made small net purchases of government securities in 1915 and 1916 and larger net purchases after the United States entered the war in April 1917.[40] Many of these purchases were made to increase the reserve banks earnings.[41]

37. In addition, foreigners sold $2 billion of American securities and borrowed $2.4 billion. The United States became a net creditor.

38. In the early years, discount rates differed by maturity and by district. I have used the rates on thirty-one- to sixty-day commercial and agricultural paper.

39. The Federal Reserve requested authority to increase reserve requirements of member banks, but Congress did not approve. Increases in reserve requirement ratios were often politically unpalatable. Congress resisted or ignored proposals to increase statutory authority both at this time and after World War II.

40. Net earnings before payments to the Treasury rose from $2.7 million in 1916 to a peak of $149 million in 1920. The 1920 earnings were not surpassed in nominal value until 1948. Most of the increase at the end of World War I came from the increased volume of discounts.

41. One achievement of the early years was a reduction of the seasonal swing in interest rates. Warburg (1930, 2:357–58) emphasizes this result. For a modern analysis supporting his view, see Mankiw, Miron, and Weil 1987.

Table 3.1   Annual Growth of the Monetary Base, 1915–22,
December to December (percent)

YEAR	GROWTH RATE	YEAR	GROWTH RATE
1915	11.2	1919	5.0
1916	15.2	1920	3.6
1917	20.6	1921	−15.5
1918	16.2	1922	4.2

Source: 1915–18, Friedman and Schwartz 1963, table 33; 1919–22, Anderson and Rasche 1999.

Alarmed at the increase in bank reserves and unable to get Congress to permit changes in reserve requirement ratios, the Board began 1917 by urging all reserve banks to let their aggregate acceptances decline by $40 million to $50 million, 20 to 25 percent of their holdings (Board of Governors File, box 1239, January 19, 1917). Several of the reserve banks ignored the request to maintain earnings.

Discount rates remained mostly unchanged until late in the year. The Board confined its activity to simplifying the rate structure. Reserve banks were requested to post no more than seven discount rates by type and maturity and to unify the rate structure across districts. The reserve banks' responses to the request show the diversity that prevailed at the time in the United States.[42]

Wartime Finance

Once the United States entered the war, government spending increased. The nation advanced $7.3 billion to its allies during the war and an additional $2.2 billion after the war (Friedman and Schwartz 1963, 216). Effective income tax rates increased sixfold from 1916 to 1918, but the increased revenue was much less than the increased spending, so the Treasury had to finance relatively large deficits (Bureau of the Census 1960, 716).[43] Military spending increased from less than $1 billion in fiscal 1916 to an average of $15 billion a year for the fiscal years ending June 1918 and 1919.

The war reshaped the Federal Reserve System in many ways. Most for-

42. For example, the New Orleans branch of the Atlanta reserve bank had a different structure of rates than Atlanta. Many banks had more than seven rates. Schedules differed by number of rates, type of discount, and maturity.

43. Gross public debt rose from $1.2 billion on June 30, 1916, to $25.5 billion on June 30, 1919 (Bureau of the Census 1960, 720). Deficits for the two fiscal years 1918 and 1919 were $22.3 billion, a large fraction of GNP but not as large as the 50 percent share estimated at the time. Average nominal GNP for the two years is $73.5 billion (Balke and Gordon 1986, 793). Friedman and Schwartz (1963, 221) put the total cost of wartime outlays at $32 billion, with 70 percent financed by borrowing, 25 percent by explicit taxation, and 5 percent by money creation. Their estimate implies a $22.4 billion increase in debt for war finance.

eign governments suspended the gold standard, so it no longer served as a guide to policy. The System abandoned the penalty discount rate in the interest of war finance. The number of state member banks rose to more than a thousand by 1919, and they included the largest state-chartered banks, with 40 percent of the assets of all state-chartered banks (Bureau of the Census 1960, 633). Wartime (and prewar) changes made the System more like a central bank, as in World War II. Independence was sacrificed to maintain interest rates that lowered the Treasury's cost of debt finance. The System became subservient to the Treasury's perceived needs.

The Federal Reserve's main wartime activity was selling Treasury bonds. The New York bank wanted to replace the existing Independent Treasury System, carried over from the nineteenth century, by serving as fiscal agent for the government. Its wartime activities, and those of the other reserve banks, included selling almost half of the debt issues. It succeeded in convincing the Treasury that the Independent Treasury System was redundant. In 1920 the New York bank was designated fiscal agent, and the Independent Treasury System ended.

Wartime finance consisted principally of a series of Treasury bond drives or Liberty Loans. The governors of the reserve banks served as chairmen of the committees organized in each district to sell Treasury bonds to the nonbank public. Since the amount borrowed was large relative to the size of the country or previous credit demands, the System ensured the success of the four wartime Liberty Loans by making two types of loans. Short-term loans at preferential discount rates encouraged banks to buy short-term Treasury certificates during the interval between bond drives. Initially the discount rate on these loans in New York was 3 percent for fifteen days and 3.5 percent for sixteen to ninety days. Rates rose to 3.5 and 4 percent in December 1917 and to 4 and 4.5 percent in April 1918, where they remained until November 1919.[44] Loans were also made to encourage banks to stretch out the public's payments for purchases of Liberty Loan bonds over $1,000. The latter was known as the "borrow and buy" policy. Its original intent was to avoid a short-term contractive effect on the money stock and interest rates as buyers drew down their balances to make pay-

---

44. Discount rates were discussed at a meeting of the Board and the governors on November 9, 1917. New York saw no need for a change in rates, but Boston wanted higher rates to prevent borrowing for profit. Chicago wanted uniform rates at all reserve banks. On November 21, Harding telegraphed the reserve banks that the Board had concluded that rates should be raised by 0.5 percent. Rate increases were approved in late November for all banks except Boston and New York. New York did not increase its rate to 3.5 percent until December 21. At the time all other banks were at 4 percent (Board Minutes, November 9, 21, 26 and December 21, 1917).

ments to the Treasury (Governors Conference 1917, 233). Later it became a marketing device for the bonds, since buyers could defer payments for as much as a year from time of purchase.

The Treasury's borrowing tested the System's ability to pool reserves. By far the largest part of the Treasury's short-term borrowing was in New York, so the New York bank was under pressure to finance the purchases. The Board urged other reserve banks to buy acceptances from New York to relieve the strain on its reserve position, and New York renewed the request at the November Governors Conference. All banks except Kansas City, Chicago, and Atlanta agreed to buy acceptances to earn interest for their banks and thereby supply additional gold reserves to New York.

The intent of the Treasury's policy was that sales of certificates would be retired out of the proceeds of the Liberty Loans. From April 1917 to October 1919, the Treasury sold $6 billion of tax anticipation certificates and $19 billion in anticipation of bond and note sales. The intent was not realized. A large volume of certificates remained outstanding at the end of the war. The Treasury opposed raising short-term rates to refund the certificates as they came due. It expressed concern not only that higher short-term rates on certificates would carry over to long rates, lowering bond prices, but also that an increase in rates would abrogate commitments made to purchasers of Treasury bonds under the borrow and buy policy.

By offering discounts at a preferential rate on Treasury certificates, the Federal Reserve abandoned the penalty rate, one of the main principles on which it was founded. Member banks could borrow at a preferential rate below the rate paid on the Treasury certificates or Liberty bonds, so borrowing became profitable.[45] Penalty rates for other types of borrowing remained, but most borrowing was at the preferential rate, so higher rates had no effect. One consequence was that state banks membership increased, as noted earlier. Another consequence was that much of the collateral for borrowing was Treasury debt, contrary to the spirit of the Federal Reserve Act.

Table 3.2 compares the interest rates at which the Treasury sold Liberty bonds to the preferential discount rates at New York. Congress set the rate on the First Liberty Loan below the market rate on savings deposits. The intention was to avoid a drain of existing savings into war bonds (Warburg

---

45. The Board objected to the low rate paid by the Treasury on the initial certificates, $50 billion at 2 percent interest. Secretary McAdoo responded by threatening to invoke the Overman Act, under which the president could give the secretary (or other official) authority to carry out any of the functions of the reserve banks. The Board withdrew its objections. McAdoo was President Wilson's son-in-law. This was the first clash with the Treasury over wartime finance. It was a preview of experience during and after the two world wars.

Table 3.2   War Finance (millions of dollars)

DATE	LOAN	INTEREST RATE (%)	PREFERENTIAL DISCOUNT, NEW YORK[a] (%)	SIZE OF ISSUE
May–June 1917	First Liberty	3.5	3–3.5	1,989
October 1917	Second Liberty	4	3–3.5	3,808
April–May 1918	Third Liberty	4.5	4–4.5	4,177
September–October 1918	Fourth Liberty	4.25	4–4.5	6,993
April–May 1919	Victory	4.75[b]	4–4.5	4,498

[a]Lower rate for fifteen days or less; higher rate for sixteen to ninety days.
[b]Tax-exempt bonds offered at 3.75 percent.

1930, 2:12). On May 22, 1917, a week after the borrowing campaign began, New York introduced the preferential discount rate. The other banks followed within a few weeks. The decision reflected concern about the ability to sell the issue at the low interest rate Congress set (Wicker 1966, 14).[46]

The preferential rate enabled the Treasury to borrow on favorable terms between bond drives. The Treasury sold short-term certificates to the banks. The member banks paid by crediting the Treasury's account at their banks and retained the deposits until the Treasury drew on its balances. Treasury balances were not subject to reserve requirements, but after they were spent, the money returned as private deposits subject to reserve requirements.[47] The preferential discount rate allowed the banks to meet this obligation at low cost. The preferential rate soon became the modal borrowing rate. The Federal Reserve continued the practice until December 1919, after the war ended and the fifth and final war loan, the so-called Victory Loan, had been sold.[48]

The System considered direct purchases to be "inflationary." To avoid making open market purchases, it encouraged banks to offer installment loans to nonbank purchasers on favorable terms. Most commentators point out (correctly) that it is no more inflationary for the Federal Reserve to buy the bonds directly (or in the open market) than to lend money to the banks at below market rates so that banks can either purchase the bonds or finance the public's purchases. The increase in the monetary base is the same in both cases. However, the distinction was important to the

46. The governors' recommendation was that the first Liberty Loan should be for $1 billion, a sum they considered very large (Governors Conference 1917, 317–20). The Treasury ignored this advice also. See table 3.2.

47. This change was made in April 1917 as part of Federal Reserve support of war finance.

48. During and after World War II, Secretary Henry Morgenthau pointed out frequently that Liberty Loans had been sold at rising interest rates, whereas he financed World War II at constant rates. Another major difference is that in World War II the Treasury offered the public nonmarketable bonds, with fixed nominal redemption value. These were used to attract small savers and avoid the losses of nominal value that followed World War I.

Federal Reserve and many others who shared the real bills framework. Central bank purchases of government securities expand money (or credit) based on speculative paper. This paper would have to be eliminated after the war to restore the central bank's reputation. Although the members recognized that it would be difficult to reduce member bank indebtedness by restoring a penalty rate in the face of almost certain Treasury opposition, far more difficult would be postwar direct sales of Treasury obligations by the reserve banks with the secretary and the comptroller on the Board. Further, currency issues had to be backed by gold and real bills. Treasury securities and commercial paper were not close substitutes for this reason.

By 1918 most of the Liberty Loans sold in the secondary market at a small discount. To raise their prices, Congress, in approving the Third Liberty Loan, permitted the Treasury to purchase not more than 5 percent of each outstanding issue in the market. Purchases were made at the market price and financed by short-term certificates subject to preferential rates for borrowing from the reserve banks. The effect was to lower the average maturity of the debt and to increase the incentive for the Treasury to maintain low interest rates on Treasury certificates and the preferential discount rate after the war. The purchase operations ended on June 30, 1920, when a sinking fund replaced the purchase program. In all, the Treasury purchased $1.7 billion under the program, with most of the purchases made after the war. The program did not succeed in bringing taxable bonds to par value.

Since the commercial banks could use the certificates at their option to borrow at preferential rates, the reserve banks were the source of the financing no more and no less than if they undertook the same volume of purchases directly. Despite a rising rate of inflation, Liberty bonds remained only slightly below par throughout the war. For example, at the time of the Third Liberty Loan, in spring 1918, the GNP deflator rose at an annual rate of about 7.5 percent. For the year 1918 as a whole, the deflator rose by 10 percent (Balke and Gordon 1986) and the consumer price index by 18 percent. Yet the Treasury was able to sell bonds at par with a 4.5 percent coupon and to keep its outstanding debt close to par by making occasional purchases. One partial explanation is that the market did not anticipate continued inflation over the life of the bonds. Although there was an embargo on sales of gold abroad, the United States remained legally on the gold standard, and the bonds contained a gold clause, permitting the holder to demand gold at redemption. Further, the common anticipation, based on experience in previous wars, was that budget deficits would end and the gold standard would be restored at the end of the war. Evidence of this disinflationary anticipation is given by the inverted yield curve: commercial paper with a maximum of 180 days maturity yielded 6 percent.[49]

Unlike its World War II policy, the Federal Reserve did not agree to purchase all government securities at fixed rates. In keeping with its mostly passive policy orientation, it achieved the same end by setting the discount rate on Treasury securities below the market rate on the securities. Bank reserves and the monetary base were thus set by the banks' demand to borrow. Any bank with Treasury certificates could borrow profitably. The price of Treasury securities was kept relatively stable by this arrangement at the cost of supplying reserves and money at the market's demand. As in World War II, the Federal Reserve became the "engine of inflation."

The wartime policy achieved the Treasury's objective of marketing an extraordinary increase in debt at relatively low direct cost to the Treasury.[50] The public bought most of the debt, but between 1916 and 1919 commercial banks bought almost $5 billion, approximately 20 percent of the total issued. The banks financed their purchases in part by borrowing $2 billion from the Federal Reserve.

In June 1917 Congress amended section 13 of the Federal Reserve Act by reducing collateral behind the note issue. Initially, a reserve bank had to deposit with the Federal Reserve agent (at the reserve bank) 40 percent of the issue in gold and 100 percent in commercial paper and bills of exchange with less than ninety days to maturity. The new requirement reduced the total of real bills and gold to 100 percent of the note issue, 40 percent in gold. A year earlier, banker's acceptances became eligible as collateral and, slightly altering a premise of the act, reserve banks could also use as collateral promissory notes of member banks secured by government bonds or notes.

Gold inflows slowed after 1917 (Schwartz 1982, table SC14). For the next three years Federal Reserve credit—mainly discounts—became the driving force in the expansion of the monetary base and inflation. The Federal Reserve Board's annual report for 1918 looked forward to the time when "the invested assets of the Federal Reserve Banks have been restored to a commercial basis" (Board of Governors of the Federal Reserve System, *Annual Report*, 1918, 87). This appeal to the real bills standard gives a mis-

---

49. This does not explain why short-term rates rose so little, hence it can only be a partial explanation of interest rate changes.

50. Congress approved the Third Liberty Loan with a 4.25 percent maximum interest rate. This restriction on the interest rate remained for all government bonds issued until the 1960s. The restriction did not apply to notes.

leading impression of what had happened. From December 1916 to December 1918, Federal Reserve notes outstanding increased by $1.7 billion and bank reserves increased by $400 million. On the asset aside, discounts for member banks rose by $1.5 billion, gold by $200 million, and government securities by $180 million. Nearly all of the discounts, however, were secured by government obligations (Board of Governors of the Federal Reserve System 1943, 340).

THE POSTWAR STRUGGLE FOR INDEPENDENCE

The history of the early postwar years is principally the story of the Federal Reserve's struggle for independence from the Treasury and the deflationary consequences of its policies after it obtained independence. This was the System's first opportunity to take independent policy action. It made several mistakes, some avoidable, some unavoidable in the circumstances. By promising not to raise interest rates during the last wartime bond drive, the System relinquished a chance to moderate the postwar inflation. By raising discount rates from 4 percent to 6 percent and then to 7 percent in the space of a few months, it contributed to the postwar contraction.[51] By failing to lower discount rates for more than a year after the cyclic peak, the System prolonged the recession and contributed to its severity.

In the first four years of Federal Reserve operations, the compound average rate of inflation was 12 to 13 percent, using consumer prices and the GNP deflator. Table 3.3 shows the annual data. The peak in the quarterly rate of inflation is in third quarter 1918, at the end of the war, but the price level did not reach a peak until second quarter 1920. For the first two quarters of the latter year, the deflator rose at a 20 percent annual rate. For the last two quarters, it fell at a 15 percent annual rate. The price level continued to fall throughout 1921, although the rate of decline slowed after midyear.

The inflation period has two phases. At first the Treasury dominated the Federal Reserve, aided by the System's commitment to assist in war finance and, after the war, commitments under the borrow and buy policy. In the second phase, the commitments had expired. The System was free to act but uncertain about what to do.

---

51. The 7 percent discount rate was posted (as the lowest available rate for commercial and agricultural discounts) at only six of the twelve reserve banks. Philadelphia, Cleveland, Richmond, St. Louis, Kansas City, and San Francisco held the minimum discount rate at 6 percent, but some of these banks adopted progressive rates to penalize heavy borrowers. Dallas did not adopt the 7 percent rate until February 1921, more than a year after the NBER date for the cyclic peak, January 1920. Less than two months later, Boston lowered the discount rate to 6 percent on April 15, followed by New York on May 5. The 7 percent rate applied to commercial paper. A 5.5 percent rate for borrowing on Treasury certificates remained in effect throughout the period. The latter was the applicable rate for most borrowing.

Table 3.3   Inflation Rates, 1915–20 (percent)

YEAR	RATE	YEAR	RATE
1915	2.0	1918	18.6
1916	11.0	1919	13.8
1917	17.0	1920	2.3

Source: Balke and Gordon 1986. Rates are from fourth quarter to fourth quarter.

The Inflation Phase, Part 1

The Board's annual report for 1920 blamed the inflation on "an unprecedented orgy of extravagance, a mania for speculation, overextended business in nearly all lines and in every section of the country" (Board of Governors of the Federal Reserve System, *Annual Report,* 1920, 1). At best this was disingenuous, as the Board had recognized in its annual report for 1919. The Board wrote there that the absence of a penalty rate "is enough to prevent a normal functioning of a Federal Reserve Bank, whose rates should be so fixed that resort thereto is unprofitable . . . and thus has a tendency to check expansion" (Board of Governors of the Federal Reserve System, *Annual Report,* 1919, 2).

In fact, the Federal Reserve lacked any consensus on a policy regarding rates. A return to penalty rates might be sufficient to stop the inflation but was likely to conflict with accommodating the needs of trade and commerce. This was a principal concern for several governors. Others viewed the wartime policy as a violation of the real bills basis for credit expansion, hence inflationary. Insisting on a return to a real bills policy meant that the preferential discount rate on Treasury securities had to be raised. As long as the preferential rate remained in effect, the discount rate would be controlled by the Treasury when it set the rate on Treasury issues.[52] Thus there was an issue of control or independence as well as a policy issue about rates. Members were aware, however, that the president could invoke the

52. The first restive sign came early. Chairman Perrin (San Francisco) wrote on October 3, 1917, to ask whether the discount rate should be raised to 4 percent for loans on 4 percent certificates and 4 percent Liberty bonds. Miller replied for the Board, saying that an increase in rates would hurt the Second Liberty Loan. Two weeks later, in a lengthy memo, Miller argued that rates should have been raised after the First Liberty Loan so they could be reduced to support the Second Liberty Loan. Miller defended the policy as part of the Federal Reserve's responsibility to help the government finance the war "with a minimum of injury to the health and strength of the banking situation" (Board of Governors File, box 1239, October 3 and 17, 1917). Miller also stressed the need to modify the System's real bills orientation by reducing commercial loans to nonessential industries. On December 12 Warburg responded, noting the Board had no power to discriminate against particular borrowers. Rates were raised by 0.5 percent after first payments were made on the Second Liberty Loan. This established a precedent that the Treasury was not willing to follow in 1919.

Overman Act and assign their responsibilities to another agency. This act did not expire until six months after the end of the war, in April 1919.

The division of opinion remained throughout the war and beyond. In February 1918 Governor Harding suggested an increase to 4 percent on commercial discounts with less than fifteen days to maturity. Opinion was mixed, and the rate remained unchanged. In June Adolph Miller wrote a long memo pointing out that the government had spent less than planned in fiscal 1918 but would increase spending to $24 billion in fiscal 1919. He estimated that this would be half of current GNP, and he urged an immediate increase in rates to curtail commercial lending. He included an increase in rates on loans secured by Treasury certificates. Hamlin replied in a letter to Harding, opposing Miller's proposal and recommending "rationing credit as we now ration food." Raising rates would be "bad faith" with the banks that bought certificates (Board of Governors File, box 1239, February 21 and 25, June 27 and 28, 1918).[53] The only action was a decision by the Cleveland and Richmond banks to raise the discount rate from 4 to 4.25 percent in April. Kansas City followed in May, raising its rate to 4.5 percent. The others remained at 4 percent.

Government spending continued to exceed revenues at the end of the war, so the Treasury's problem of financing the deficit continued through the winter and spring of 1919. This was one source, but not the only source, of contention between the Treasury and the Federal Reserve and within the Federal Reserve. Carter Glass, who replaced McAdoo as treasury secretary in January 1919, preferred qualitative controls and moral suasion to rate increases as a means of controlling credit. In the first of many differences about qualitative controls, governors of many of the Federal Reserve banks argued that exhortation or moral suasion would work, if at all, only if rates increased.[54] Missing from the discussion of qualitative controls, as from Hamlin's proposal to ration credit, was the role of interest rates in resource allocation. Wartime expenditures required a shift of real resources equal to almost 20 percent of GNP. Several Board members and Treasury officials seem unaware that their proposals raised the cost of the transfer and added to the burden of financing the war.

In addition to deficit finance, the Treasury faced the problem of rolling over the outstanding stock of short-term certificates. Before leaving office,

53. A few months later, Governor Joseph A. McCord (Atlanta) wrote to Harding warning that banks were recycling fifteen-day paper to avoid the 0.5 percent difference between fifteen- and ninety-day paper. The Federal Reserve ignored evidence of this kind when it decided that there was a tradition against borrowing for profit.

54. No one pointed out that urging a bank to repay borrowing could shift the borrowing to another bank.

McAdoo had sent a letter to all banks urging them to purchase short-term Treasury certificates. Glass continued this policy of moral suasion. Moreover, to sell the Fourth Liberty Loan (in September and October 1918), national banks had promised as part of the borrow and buy program to lend at 4.25 percent for ninety days with renewal guaranteed for a year at the 4.25 percent rate. These commitments did not expire until the end of October 1919. And to sell the Victory Loan, in April–May 1919, banks had offered customers installment loans at a 4.25 percent rate for six months.

The shorter period for financing the Victory Loan reflected a telegram from the Board to the reserve banks on April 16 suggesting that member banks be discouraged from "leaving the situation with respect to loans secured by Government bonds entirely clear after November" (Board Minutes, April 16, 1919, 297).

The Board and the reserve banks were parties to the borrow and buy policy. As heads of the Liberty and Victory Loan committees, the governors had wanted this commitment to make the bond drives successful and to avoid large changes in money and interest rates following Treasury bond drives. Treasury took the position that honoring the commitments took precedence over credit and monetary control (Board Minutes, April 16, 1919). With this stance, the Treasury also hoped to fund its outstanding short-term debt at the prevailing interest rate.

Behind the subsequent struggle lay the governors' concern about independence. Wartime policy had prevented Strong and other governors from establishing an independent institution that was free of political control. A strong Board subject to political pressures, or dominated by the Treasury, was a long-standing concern.

In January Strong took another leave to rest and recuperate from tuberculosis. The Board approved a three-month leave with full pay. Strong was away from the bank during January and February and in Europe from mid-July to late September. He participated in the discussion only by letter. Early in February he wrote to Adolph Miller and to Russell Leffingwell, the undersecretary of the treasury, about the need to liquidate the banks' borrowings secured by Treasury certificates. In his letter to Miller he is undecided about the speed with which the Federal Reserve should act and the consequences of a rapid liquidation. The letter to Leffingwell is more decisive about the need to deflate, although he recognized that "the process of deflation is a painful one, involving loss, unemployment, bankruptcy, and social and political disorders" (Chandler 1958, 138–39).

When the Governors Conference met with the Federal Reserve Board on March 20–22, three main considerations were the forthcoming sale of the Victory Loan, the French and British decisions to allow their currencies to depreciate against gold and the dollar, and the end of the gold embargo with the expiration of the Trading with the Enemy Act in June.[55] Discussion of the size and pricing of the Victory Loan presumed that discount rates would remain unchanged. Large foreign balances had built up during the war, currency exports had increased, and there was concern that a higher discount rate would be needed to slow the gold export.

Leffingwell argued that Europe lacked effective demand. Although the gold reserve ratio had fallen from 61 percent to 49 percent in the year to March and seven reserve banks including New York and Philadelphia had recourse to interbank loans to supplement their reserves, he did not "see anything in the international situation to justify an apprehension about the protection of our gold reserves" (Governors Conference, March 20, 1919, 156). He would soon reverse that forecast. Strong responded that British and French devaluations effectively raised prices in the United States, so it was equivalent in its effect on spending to an increase in the discount rate. He feared that raising the discount rate would cause too rapid liquidation of inventories (162).

The next day the Conference voted to maintain the discount rate until after the Victory Loan was placed and "for such reasonable period thereafter as will permit a considerable liquidation of such borrowing [to buy the bonds] without imposing undue penalties upon the banks" (Governors Conference, March 21, 1919, 354–55). It would soon regret this decision. The Conference also voted to recommend a 5 percent interest rate on the Victory Loan.[56] The Treasury set the rate at 4.75 percent.

The inflation rate increased sharply during the summer and fall of 1919. Part of the increase is mainly measurement, the release of prices that had been controlled in wartime, but this explains only a small part of the surge in the inflation rate. Balke and Gordon's (1986) estimate of the deflator rose from 4.3 percent annual rate in first quarter 1919 to 15.8 percent for the last two quarters. The consumer price index shows an even larger increase.

Interest rates on government bonds and commercial paper remained steady through the spring and summer. The Treasury continued to support the bond price by purchasing in the open market. From June to year end,

55. Some of the meetings in this period included outsiders. Present on the first day of the meeting were members of the executive committee of the Federal Advisory Council and two senior members of Congress, Senator Robert Owen, chairman of the Senate Banking Committee, and Congressman Edmund Platt, the ranking minority member of the House Banking Committee. Platt subsequently became a member of the Board.

56. The conference agreed also to hold the buying rate on acceptances below the discount rate to encourage the market for dollar acceptances. This policy, favored by Strong, later infuriated Glass.

the Treasury purchased $500 million, with more than half the purchases in late November and early December (Wicker 1966, 35).

By June, an outflow of gold and rising inflation revived interest in eliminating the preferential rate for Treasury securities and raising the discount rate. On June 9 the Treasury removed the embargo on gold exports. Despite the subsequent gold outflow, bank reserves and currency continued to rise in response to member bank borrowing. Rising monetary liabilities and falling gold stock reduced the ratio of gold to monetary liabilities from 50.6 percent in June to 47.3 percent in September. The fall in the gold reserve ratio was the traditional signal to raise interest rates. The Federal Reserve had urged an end to the wartime embargo so that the United States would lose gold. Adolph Miller describes the decision as helping "to bring nearer the day when the Federal Reserve must be permitted to resume their normal relations to the money market and to exercise control through discount rates" (1921, 182).

The Treasury was in charge, and it continued to oppose a rate increase. In July, Boston requested a general increase in its discount rates. The Board rejected the request as "inadvisable from the point of view of Treasury plans." Government debt outstanding reached a peak in August, but the Treasury was not yet ready to raise rates. At a September 4 meeting with the Board, Leffingwell explained that he shared the view that rates must rise. He was not primarily interested in borrowing money cheaply for the government. His purpose, he said, was to refund the debt and eliminate the Treasury certificates that were subject to the preferential discount rate. He thought that higher rates would make that task more difficult in two ways. First, Liberty and Victory bonds would fall below 90, and if this occurred, Congress might require the Treasury to refund the entire debt and absorb the loss. Second, banks were obligated to renew loans to carry securities at unchanged rates. A rise in rates would put more of the debt into the banking system, so speculative credit expansion would increase at the expense of commercial and agricultural credit. This he viewed as contrary to real bills principles, hence inflationary.

In response to a question from Governor Harding, Leffingwell indicated that the Treasury did not oppose an increase in rates on commercial loans: "I ask that you do not increase your rates on paper secured by Government obligations" (Board Minutes, September 4, 1919).

Despite Leffingwell's comment, some of the differences at the meeting reflected the commitment to keep rates unchanged at least until November. A second issue concerned debt management. Strong wanted the Treasury to borrow at market rates, in smaller amounts, more frequently. His reasoning was that Treasury borrowing created a large volume of Treasury deposits not subject to reserve requirements. When the Treasury spent the proceeds, private deposits increased. Banks borrowed at the prevailing preferential discount rate to meet the reserve requirement. The Treasury's view was that the reserve banks should discourage borrowing by the banks without raising rates. Strong, supported by several of the reserve banks, argued that inflation could not be controlled as long as borrowing at the preferential discount rate remained profitable.[57]

At an October 28 meeting, Strong urged the Board to approve an increase in the minimum discount rate to 4.5 percent. Leffingwell objected that such a move would hurt the Treasury's planned refunding. He again favored higher rates for commercial and agricultural borrowers and greater use of moral suasion to prevent "speculation." Secretary Glass strongly favored moral suasion and opposed rate increases.[58]

Glass, and others, argued as if demand were completely inelastic. By raising rates, the reserve banks would encourage commercial banks to raise their rates with no effect on the amount borrowed. He agreed, however, to increase the rate for borrowing against Treasury certificates to 4.25 percent and voted for the increase at the November 1 Board meeting.

Table 3.4 shows the interest rates prevailing during the years 1919 and 1920. In October 1919, just before the first increase in discount rates, short-term rates were above long-term rates. Both had changed little during the year; bond prices, on average, had remained in a narrow range below par, 91.3 to 92.9, sustained in part by Treasury purchases.

At the end of October 1919 the outstanding debt was $26 billion, with $3.7 billion in certificates of indebtedness subject to a preferential rate. At the nearest call date, November 17, member banks held $3.5 billion in United States government obligations, mainly Treasury certificates, and had borrowed $2.2 billion from Federal Reserve banks, mainly at prefer-

57. For example, Governor Perrin (San Francisco) wrote to the Board on September 16 to report that his directors favored a gradual increase in discount rates, first eliminating the preferential rate for Treasury certificates, then "fixing higher rates for loans based on government securities than for those growing out of commerce." Harding replied that "it was not advisable to make any change in rates until after Christmas" (Board of Governors File, box 1239, September 16 and 24, 1919).

58. The chairmen of the reserve banks, who also served as Federal Reserve agents, met in conference periodically. The views expressed at their October 1919 meeting suggest the ambivalence that prevailed at the time. The chairmen concluded: "The normal check [against inflation] . . . is a higher discount rate. But in the opinion of your Committee the conditions prevailing at home and abroad are so abnormal as to render this method not wholly effective of itself. . . . Some increase in bank rate, however, seems the necessary first step in any program for the restraint of undesirable credit expansion" (Federal Reserve Agents Conference, October 1919, 6). The agents favored a small increase in rates accompanied by a campaign to moderate speculative uses of borrowing (7). Talk of "special conditions" and the problems of refinancing debt produced a very similar lack of response after World War II.

Table 3.4   Market Interest Rates, 1919–20 (percent)

DATE	U.S. GOVERNMENT BONDS[a]	PRIME COMMERCIAL PAPER	MINIMUM DISCOUNT RATE, NEW YORK
1919			
January	4.63	5.25	4.00
April	4.72	5.38	4.00
July	4.72	5.38	4.00
October	4.71	5.25	4.00
1920			
January	4.93	6.00	4.75[b]
April	5.28	6.88	5.00
July	5.57	8.13	5.50
October	5.08	8.13	5.50

Source: Board of Governors of the Federal Reserve System 1943.
[a]Eight years or more to maturity.
[b]Increased by steps in November and December 1919.

ential rates (Board of Governors of the Federal Reserve System 1943).[59] An important change had occurred, however. Commercial bank commitments to lend at a fixed rate on the Fourth Liberty Loan and the Victory Loan issues had expired.

On November 3 the directors of the New York bank voted to increase the discount rate by 0.25 percent, putting the discount rate for borrowing on certificates (4.25 percent) equal to the rate on the certificates. The discount rate on commercial paper increased by 0.75 percent to 4.75 percent and to 4.5 percent on paper secured by Liberty Loans. However, the Bank retained the preferential rate for borrowing collateralized by Treasury certificates, so the new minimum effective rate was 4.25 percent for up to fifteen days maturity.[60] This was the first increase in the discount rate for more than a year. The Board immediately approved increases at New York, Boston, and Chicago and, on the next day, at Kansas City. Other banks followed later.

Member bank borrowing continued to increase, but government bond yields rose and stock prices fell. The monthly index of common stock prices, at 80.5, was close to a peak in October. It did not pass the monthly October level in the next five years. Loans to brokers and dealers on the New York Stock Exchange declined, suggesting reduced demand for "speculative" credit. The rate of inflation increased, however.

Although Glass voted for the increase in rates, he was far from enthusiastic about the decision. He had always favored the real bills doctrine, and

59. Reserve bank holdings are available for June 30 and December 31, 1919. On these dates, 86 percent and 68 percent of borrowings were secured by Treasury obligations. The December data came after the increase in discount rates, so they probably understate the importance of Treasury debt at the October meeting.

60. The preferential rate remained until June 1921.

he now forcefully urged the reserve banks to rely on qualitative control. On November 5 he wrote a five-page letter to Governor Harding arguing that the Federal Reserve could not rely on interest rates alone. In principle he accepted that discount rates should be above commercial rates, but these were difficult times. A rise in Federal Reserve rates would only raise other rates. Wartime embargoes remained, so gold would not be imported. Higher rates would curtail domestic production, raise prices, and stimulate speculation. Then he added:

> We cannot trust to copybook texts. Making credit more expensive will not suffice. . . . The Reserve Bank Governor must raise his mind above the language of the textbooks and face the situation which exists. . . .
>
> Speculation in stocks on the New York Stock Exchange is no more vicious in its effect upon the welfare of the people and upon our credit structure than speculation in cotton or in land or in commodities generally. But the New York Stock Exchange is the greatest single organized user of credit for speculative purposes." (Board of Governors File, box 1239, November 5, 1919)

Glass praised the Federal Reserve for accepting Treasury leadership during the war. Now the Board must provide the leadership. Governor Harding replied that he was "in hearty agreement" with the letter. The Board sent a copy to each of the reserve banks "with the injunction that the policy outlined be carried into effect" with reliance on direct action to prevent excessive borrowing and improper use of "bank credit."[61] The emphasis on direct action continued. As late as April 1920, the Board commented on the use of credit for speculation.[62]

61. Leffingwell stated the Treasury's case for moral suasion as a solution to the wartime and postwar problem at a symposium held at the American Economic Association meeting in December 1920 (Leffingwell 1921). Wartime inflation reflected excess demand and the waste of those goods in a wartime "debauch." "To control credit through rates would have been futile" (31). The Treasury would have had to pay higher rates. Since gold movements were controlled by all governments, this would have had no effect unless rates were so high that "we would have lost the war and would have to inflate afterwards to pay the indemnity which Germany would have imposed" (31). The same conditions continued after the war. Invoking an argument reinvented after World War II, he argued: "You cannot have credit control with an unmanageable floating government debt" (32). "An increase in rates would operate solely on the domestic situation, and with painful results" (34). Leffingwell concluded that the Federal Reserve was "bound to make the effort to deal with the problem by direct action" (34). In fact, the failure of higher rates to attract a gold inflow because foreign governments were off the gold standard, if true, would have helped, not hindered, Federal Reserve control of inflation. In fact, deflation soon attracted a gold inflow despite restrictions abroad.

62. Later Strong amplified his view about the difficulty of implementing control in testimony before the Joint Congressional Commission on Agricultural Inquiry (1921, pt. 13, 693–98). He argued that qualitative control would require examining each loan by each member bank, so it was not feasible in practice. Governor Harding recognized that the policy had not

A new element now entered. Inflation reduced the real value of cash balances, inducing conversion of dollars to gold. The continuing fall in the gold reserve threatened to force suspension. The problem was most acute in New York, where most foreign balances were held. New York's reserve ratio fell to 40.2 percent.

On November 7 the Board voted to suspend for ten days, if necessary, the reserve requirement against deposits at the New York bank.[63] Adolph Miller opposed the action, arguing that New York had available $150 million in gold from the other reserve banks. Further, Miller noted, New York had allowed its credit facilities to be used for speculative borrowing. The Board was reluctant to let New York borrow gold by rediscounting in other districts. It had to be punished for permitting the increase in speculative credit.

The Federal Advisory Council met on November 19. A majority favored a rate increase, but Leffingwell convinced the members that a rate increase would be harmful. Their report to the Governors Conference the following day recommended no change. Many of the governors disagreed. They wanted a prompt increase in rates. Governor Charles A. Morss (Boston) expressed concern about speculative activity. The gold reserve ratio was approaching 40 percent. He "strongly advocated higher rates, even for commercial paper." Governor Maximillian B. Wellborn (Atlanta) saw the credit situation in the country as more important than Treasury borrowing rates. But others were hesitant and preferred to hear the Treasury's arguments before deciding (Governors Conference, November 19, 1919, 59–71).

When the governors meeting resumed after hearing Glass and Leffingwell, Strong asked each of the governors whether control could be achieved by moral suasion and admonition and what would happen to market rates if moral suasion succeeded in controlling credit. Although Strong was a proponent of the real bills view at the time, he did not believe that qualitative controls and moral suasion could replace quantitative controls. He believed that direct action to control the quality of credit would not work without an increase in rates. Even if the New York bank succeeded in getting its members to withdraw loans for stock exchange credit, loans would be available from banks in other districts. Many of the lending banks did not bor-

---

worked (Harris 1933, 1:224). Nevertheless, the Board returned to the policy at the end of the decade. With hindsight, several Board members concluded that September 1919 had been the time to increase rates (Miller 1921, 188). Recognition came after the Federal Reserve was blamed for the subsequent deflation.

63. This action contrasts with the inaction in 1931–32 when faced with the alleged free gold problem. The law required a 35 percent reserve against deposits and 40 percent against notes. The note issue was about three times the amount of reserves, so the 40 percent reserve was considered a minimum for the sum.

row from their reserve banks, so they were not subject to direct pressure. Several governors accepted that direct pressure could have an effect but doubted that it would work without an increase in rates. Governor Roy Young (Minneapolis), in particular, recognized that money and credit are fungible; the lender does not truly know what is financed at the margin. Governors who took this position argued that substituting one type of credit for another undermined the effects of direct action. These governors concluded that, if effective, moral suasion would raise interest rates.[64]

The conclusion was not unanimous, however. Governor George Seay (Richmond) claimed that moral suasion had a "very widespread effect." A concerted effort would, he claimed, reduce credit demand and interest rates. Some shared this view, at least in part, qualifying their answers in various ways (Federal Reserve Governors Conference, November 19, 1919, 74–88).

The Board wanted to avoid harming the Treasury's January refunding of $1.5 billion in certificates. Leffingwell agreed that rates should rise, but not until after the refunding. Miller expressed a common concern about the effects on the prices of government bonds. He favored an increase in rates only after the Treasury refunding.[65] Strong argued that it was wrong to follow certificate sales with an increase in rates and compared this proposal to a "sharp" commercial practice. Strong's position was weakened, however, by his own and the New York directors' concern, earlier in the month, about the effect of a discount rate increase on bond prices and by his apparent ambivalence on the issue of a preferential rate.[66]

Strong recognized, correctly, that banks would borrow at the lowest rate available. He weakened his argument for higher rates, however, by buying

64. Young's position is of interest because he was governor of the Board during the 1928–29 period of qualitative controls. Many have noted that the dispute over policy in 1919–20 was a prelude to the policy dispute in 1928–29 when the Board again favored moral suasion and direct pressure to control speculative credit without raising interest rates and most of the reserve banks wanted to raise rates as a supplement to direct pressure. In both periods the Board was able to delay an increase in rates. An important difference between the two episodes is often overlooked. In 1919–20, monetary growth was fueling inflation, and ex post real interest rates were negative. Balke and Gordon's (1986) data show the price deflator rising at a 16 percent annual rate at the end of 1919 and nearly 25 percent in the first quarter of 1920. In 1928 the deflator rose only 4 percent, and the consumer price index fell. In the first half of 1929, the price level appears to have been stable or falling.

65. Miller (1921, 188) later admitted that it was wrong not to raise rates in September 1919.

66. Wicker (1966, 39) quotes Hamlin's diary: "I cannot help feeling some lack of confidence in Strong—his health is bad and he is inclined to be panicky." In October, Strong had insisted on a minimum rate of 4.75 percent. Two days later, he phoned saying that any increase would hurt Liberty bonds and finally accepted Leffingwell's proposal to increase the rate to 4.25 percent. See also Friedman and Schwartz 1963, 226.

banker's acceptances at a 4 percent rate even after the discount rate on Treasury certificates was raised to 4.25 percent. Strong considered this preferential rate necessary to encourage the market for banker's acceptances, one of his main aims. He wrote to Governor Harding that it was

> essential to the Federal Reserve System and, particularly, to the financing of the foreign commerce of the United States by American banks instead of, as heretofore, by foreign banks. But this preferential rate was also established in recognition of the fact that a bill drawn against an actual shipment of commodities and accepted by the largest and richest bankers of the country was a credit instrument of greater value commanding a lower rate than the average of the commercial paper which would reach us. (Chandler 1958, 160)

This argument for a preferential rate has some similarities to the Treasury's argument. The principal difference is that Strong wanted a preferential rate for a particular type of real bill. The Treasury wanted the preferential rate for itself, based on its claim that its debt had lower risk because the government would not default. A central issue was whether the rate structure should give preference to real (commercial) or speculative (government) borrowers. Beneath the surface was the continuing struggle over the control of policy and the requirements of Treasury finance.

The November Governors Conference made no decision.[67] On November 24 New York and Boston voted to increase their discount rates. When the Board met two days later to consider the request, Leffingwell attacked Strong both personally and for several of his actions and policies.[68] He accused Strong of making "a direct attempt to punish the Treasury of the United States for not submitting to dictation on the part of the Governor of the Federal Reserve Bank of New York even though it be at the cost of a shortage of funds of the Treasury to meet its outstanding obligations." Treasury had consented to a rate increase early in November because Governor Strong had agreed to do three things: insist that stock exchange accounts be adequately covered; prevent a scramble for deposits (higher rates on deposits) by New York banks; and raise the buying rate on acceptances. Strong had done none of the three. Further, he said, Strong had made an agreement with the governor of the Bank of England to increase rates for Treasury borrowing. The Bank of England had forced the British Treasury

67. The governors also noted but took no action against the effects of inflation on the melting of silver coinage and the reduction in silver certificates outstanding.

68. Glass told Hamlin that he had almost made up his mind that Strong should be removed. The section of Hamlin's diary is in Board of Governors File, box 1240, November 26, 1919.

to raise rates, thus encouraging a gold outflow and the fall in the gold reserve. The United States Treasury had to borrow $500 million every two weeks until January 15. Leffingwell urged the Board to wait until January 15, when Treasury borrowing would be completed.

The Board disapproved the increases by New York and Boston. Miller said that he believed rates should rise, but he would not vote against the Treasury. Albert Strauss, a New York investment banker who had replaced Warburg, saw "no occasion for an increase in rates" that would only add to the cost of credit with no effect on the credit situation. Williams opposed a rate increase because of heavy borrowing by banks that lent to Wall Street. The Board rejected the increase in discount rates and voted to advise Boston and New York that acceptance rates were too low (Board Minutes, November 26, 1919).[69]

The criticism found its mark. Strong at last fulfilled his commitment by raising buying rates on acceptances to 4.375 percent on November 26 and to 4.5 percent on December 4.[70] Within a month, the rate was 4.75 percent. At a meeting in Secretary Glass's office, Strong threatened to increase the discount rate without Board approval, claiming that section 14 of the Federal Reserve Act gave power over discount rates to the reserve banks. This was too much for Glass. He threatened to have the president remove Strong, and in a lengthy letter to the attorney general that left no doubt about his view, he requested an interpretation of section 14.[71]

On December 9, the Justice Department responded: "I am of the opinion that the Federal Reserve Board has the right, under the powers conferred by the Federal Reserve Act, to determine what rates of discount should be charged from time to time by a Federal Reserve bank, and under their powers of review and supervision, to require such rates to be put into effect by such bank" (quoted in Warburg 1930, 2:822).

69. The criticism of acceptance policy had merit. Acceptance rates in October and November were almost a full percentage point below rates on prime commercial paper. Banks therefore sold acceptances to the reserve banks at the preferential rate and bought commercial paper. Acceptances held by the reserve banks increased from a low of $187 million in May 1919 to $570 million in January 1920. During the same period discounts, although a much larger stock, increased only $160 million.

70. Hamlin wrote in his diary for November 29 that Strong was "in a panic." He "feared an industrial panic." Raising rates might bring on a crisis. Rates should have been raised "long ago" (Board of Governors File, box 1240, November 29, 1919).

71. A month earlier the Board's legal staff had concluded that the act gave the Board wide authority, so the Board could require a reserve bank to change discount rates. Glass sent the staff opinion to the attorney general and added his recollection that it was the "intent of Congress to give the Federal Reserve Board complete power in the matter of fixing the rate of discount." Attorney General King's opinion repeated many of the arguments in Glass's letter to him (Board of Governors File, box 1239, October 29, November 14, and December 9, 1919).

The Treasury won the point, and the Board won another round in the continuing dispute about the locus of power in the System.[72] The Federal Reserve System had shown itself divided, hesitant, and unable to move promptly against inflation in the face of Treasury opposition, a situation that was repeated in different circumstances after World War II.

The Inflation Phase, Part 2

The attorney general's opinion came just as the Treasury's cash position improved. On December 9 Leffingwell wrote to Glass: "I do not think that a moderate further increase in rates at the present time would have a disastrous effect upon the Treasury's position" (quoted in Wicker 1966, 42). On the following day he gave a similar message to the Board, offering several reasons for the change in position. Recent Treasury issues had been successful; the chance of a coal strike had diminished; and he was concerned about renewed speculation. He no longer objected to an increase in rates or the elimination of the preferential rate for debt secured by Liberty and Victory bonds. The preference for certificates should remain (Board of Governors File, box 1239, December 10, 1919).

The Board immediately sent a telegram to the reserve banks informing them that they could now propose a rate increase. New York and Richmond responded at once, raising rates on paper collateralized by Treasury certificates and Liberty bonds by 0.25 percent to 4.5 percent and 4.75 percent, respectively. The minimum discount rate, 4.5 percent, was now above the rate on the Treasury's latest certificates. Most other banks followed within the week. On December 30 New York voted to increase the rate on certificates to 4.75 percent. Despite the Treasury's sale of certificates on the same day, Leffingwell permitted the increase, although he described the change as unwise.[73] Other banks followed.

72. Less than eight years later, the Board used the ruling to lower the discount rate at Chicago without a vote by the Chicago directors. Glass, then a senator, opposed the move as an unwarranted centralization of authority, "a long stride in the direction of making the Federal Reserve Board a central bank, with the Reserve banks as mere branches" (quoted in Warburg 1930, 2:493). Hamlin wrote to Glass reminding him of his position in 1919. Glass responded that his request for a ruling from the attorney general in 1919 was opportunistic, done "more in anger than in reason" (Chandler 1958, 104).

73. Strong went on a year's leave soon after. On December 31 the Board met to decide whether Strong could have a year's leave of absence (for health reasons) at half salary as recommended by the New York directors. The Board's discussion shows the divisions and controversy within the System. Glass favored an indefinite leave, saying that if Strong were well he would favor calling for his resignation. Harding, Strauss, and Hamlin voted for the resolution; Miller and Comptroller Williams voted no. Miller urged the Board to demand Strong's resignation, "in view of the conditions existing in the Second Federal Reserve District." This motion was tabled. The reference was to the use of speculative credit, the need to borrow from other reserve banks, and continuous heavy borrowing by some member banks.

By mid-January the Treasury had completed its current financing operations. Leffingwell now became a proponent of higher rates on commercial loans but continued to demand a preferential rate for borrowing on Treasury certificates.[74] He proposed a 6 percent rate on commercial paper and a 5.5 percent rate on Liberty bonds but wanted to retain the 4.75 percent rate on certificates. Comptroller Williams offered a substitute motion with a lower rate schedule. Williams's proposal was approved by a vote of four to three. After further discussion, the Board voted to reconsider; Adolph Miller changed sides, and the Board approved Leffingwell's proposal for Boston, New York, and Philadelphia (Board Minutes, January 21, 1920, 79–81). The new schedule put rates on commercial paper above the rates proposed by the New York directors. Relying on the earlier letter from the acting attorney general, the Board interpreted section 14 of the Federal Reserve Act as giving the Board authority to initiate increases in the discount rate and require reserve banks to adopt them.[75]

Why did the Board change its views about rates at this time? Years later, Adolph Miller answered: "It is a terrible thing to admit that the only thing that really awakened us was the fact that we were in sight of the 40 percent [gold reserve] ratio" (Governors Conference, March 1923, 766). In 1924 the Board's staff gave several reasons. The gold reserve ratio is mentioned first, but the staff also cites data on gold exports following the end of the embargo, borrowing from the Federal Reserve banks, the increase in note circulation, and the rise in the wholesale price index (Board of Governors File, box 1240, July 28, 1924). The staff did not mention the change in the Treasury's view.

The Treasury's change of view was not adventitious. It had completed its borrowing, and inflation had increased with no sign of credit liquidation yet visible. Treasury debt outstanding was past its peak and continued to fall. The monthly average gold reserve ratio was probably most important. The ratio had continued to fall after the wartime gold export embargo ended the previous June. By January the monthly average reserve ratio for the System was 42.7 percent, down five percentage points in a year. Gold reserves in excess of statutory requirements had fallen to $233 million, a 50 percent decline in twelve months. Several reserve banks had less than a 40 percent reserve. They had to either suspend gold reserve requirements or rediscount acceptances with other reserve banks.

---

74. Leffingwell wrote to Strong: "I became an earnest and, in some respects, successful advocate of dear money" (quoted in Chandler 1958, 167).

75. The New York directors hired a law firm to give an opinion on section 14. The opinion said that the initiation of a rate change was the responsibility of the reserve banks, but the Board had authority to change the recommendation.

The Federal Reserve overcame the problem by using interbank loans to pool System reserves.[76] The risk of suspension was greater than at any time in the next fifty years. Even in the fall and winter of 1931–32, after the British devaluation, the gold reserve ratio never fell below 60 percent, and excess reserves remained above $1.2 billion.[77] The System's later claim that the gold reserve prevented them from acting in 1931–32 is belied by the actions taken in 1920.[78] Although the problem was inflation in 1920 and deflation in 1931–32, the remedy of pooling reserves to meet a deficiency at one or more banks applied in both periods.

The January rise in the discount rate did not change the minimum borrowing rate. Bank lending and reserve bank discounts continued to increase, and the gold reserve ratio continued to fall. At the end of February the minimum discount rate increased to 5 percent. In March, Boston, New York, and Cleveland asked to raise the minimum rate (collateralized by Treasury certificates) to 5.5 percent. The motion was tabled by the Board, with Harding and Miller opposed (Board Minutes, March 9, 1920, 250–51). The reserve banks continued to lose gold, so the Federal Reserve Board approved an increase in the discount rate at New York, Chicago, and Minneapolis to 7 percent on commercial credit and from 4.75 to 5.5 percent on Treasury certificates at seven banks effective June 1. Boston soon followed. This increase in interest rates, and the start of deflation in July, reversed the gold flow.

To supplement the increase in rates, Congress passed the Phelan Act in April 1920. The act authorized progressive discount rates on a member bank that borrowed relatively large amounts from its reserve bank. In districts that adopted progressive rates, each bank was given a line of credit, or normal rediscount. The governors agreed in principle that a member bank's contribution to the lending power of the System increased with its reserve deposits and paid-in capital. They could not agree on a formula to apply the principle, so the choice of formula was left to the reserve banks (Governors Conference, April 1920, 388). Borrowing in excess of the normal line was subject to progressively higher discount rates.

---

76. On October 12, 1920, four of the reserve banks had $231.8 million in loans outstanding to the other reserve banks. Banks in the South and West did most of the borrowing; Cleveland, Boston, and Philadelphia were the principal lenders. Other unusual arrangements included counting deposits abroad as part of reserves and including deposits of silver from the Treasury's holdings. The Federal Reserve Act authorized interdistrict lending at rates set by the Federal Reserve Board.

77. The monthly average reserve ratio fell to 56.3 percent in July 1932 and 51.3 percent in March 1933 (Board of Governors of the Federal Reserve System 1943, 348–49). New York had a reserve deficiency in early March 1933.

78. Several of the governors and Board members served in both periods.

There was considerable difference of opinion about how and when to use the new powers. Governor Wellborn (Atlanta) wanted progressive rates to be applied in all districts. Others wanted these rates used only as a last resort, mainly to reinforce efforts to discourage banks that borrowed heavily. A resolution to that effect was defeated at the April Governors Conference, in part because several governors opposed any effort to bind their directors or limit local authority over discount rates (Governors Conference, April 1920, 269, 279).

Rates were considerably higher in agricultural districts. The reserve banks in these districts saw that their members could lend at rates of 10 or 12 percent or more, so they would not be deterred by discount rates of 5 to 6 percent.[79] Unable to get an agreement to use a progressive rate, the four agricultural districts in the South and West—Atlanta, St. Louis, Dallas, and Kansas City—acted on their own. The details of the formulas for computing borrowing lines differed, but in each of the districts the progressive rate was tied to the member's reserve position, stock in the reserve bank, and the amount borrowed. Loans on government securities were excluded.[80] Each 25 percent above the borrowing line was subject to a progressive or marginal rate of 0.5 percent a month. A bank with a borrowing line of $150,000 and excess borrowing of $150,000 subject to progressive rates would pay 2 percent above the standard discount rate for agricultural paper on borrowing above $112,500 and up to $150,000.

The aim of the program was to make the discount rate "effective" and penalize banks that borrowed heavily.[81] Although Congress had authorized the program, it did not like its application. Since only banks in agricultural regions used progressive rates, the program seemed to confirm populist claims that a central bank would be run for the benefit of eastern bankers, especially Wall Street. Congress and the press pointed to marginal rates as high as 81.5 percent charged by the Atlanta Federal Reserve Bank on agri-

79. "The margin of profit to a member bank in the western regions of this district . . . is so great as to tempt even the most conservative bankers to make loans which they know their bank is not able to carry" (R. L. Van Zandt [Dallas] to Governor Harding, Board of Governors File, box 1470, December 8, 1920). Richard L. Van Zandt was governor at Dallas. The letter goes on to recognize that a penalty rate should be based "on the rate actually received by the member bank from its customers on the identical item." This was a rare recognition of differences in risk.

80. If a bank with a borrowing line of $100,000 borrowed $400,000 with $150,000 secured by government securities, the amount subject to a progressive rate was $400,000 − $100,000 − $150,000 = $150,000.

81. The annual report (Board of Governors of the Federal Reserve System, *Annual Report,* 1921, 3) reports that 906 member banks had borrowed 494 percent of their basic lines, while all member banks borrowed 40 percent of their basic lines.

cultural paper (Board of Governors File, box 1240, 1920).[82] The System was also criticized for not applying the progressive rate at all reserve banks.

Political issues aside, progressive rates applied selectively shifted borrowing from reserve banks with high rates to those with lower rates. Member banks in an agricultural district could borrow from correspondent banks in other districts to repay their borrowing at the district reserve bank. Often the correspondent bank then borrowed from its reserve bank. The Board was aware that this kind of substitution took place, and the Joint Commission of Agricultural Inquiry gave examples, but the Board made no systematic effort to estimate the extent of the problem.[83]

Progressive rates remained in effect from six to fifteen months depending on the district. The main lessons the System learned were to be wary of political criticism of high marginal rates and to avoid the appearance of favoring financial over agricultural interests. Progressive rates were never used again. In March 1923 Congress repealed the provisions of the Phelan Act authorizing progressive rates.[84]

Glass left the Treasury early in 1920 and was elected to the Senate. His successor for the remaining months of the Wilson administration was David Houston and, after the presidential election, Andrew Mellon.[85] Houston adopted Strong's earlier plan of selling and refunding certificates more frequently, so in smaller volume. The Treasury intervened in the Board's policy much less. For the first time in its brief history, the System had control of its policy and sufficient resources to carry it out. But it lacked enough determination and coherence of views to act. Although several governors complained about the preferential rate for Treasury securities, the April 1920 Conference voted nine to three to retain the preferential rate.

For nearly a year after the June 1920 increase in rates, the Federal Reserve did very little. Minimum borrowing rates on Treasury certificates

---

82. The borrowing bank had a small reserve position, hence a small borrowing line. The 81.5 percent rate applied to a loan of $112,000 for two weeks. Maximum rates at St. Louis, Dallas and Kansas City were 16 percent, 7 percent, and 22.5 percent, respectively, all on relatively small amounts for short periods (Board of Governors File, box 1240, December 1, 1920).

83. To mute criticism of the effect on agricultural districts, the Board did a study of borrowing rates at the twelve reserve banks. The study compared average rates charged in New York with the average rates charged in the four districts with penalty rates. The study ignored differences in marginal rates and found similar average rates.

84. Progressive rates were not the only problem. Congressional criticism of the System's policy was followed by bills in December 1920 and April 1921 to impose ceiling rates of 5 percent. Senator Robert Owen (Oklahoma), an author of the Federal Reserve Act, took a leading role in criticizing policy and urging lower rates (Board of Governors File, box 1246, November 1919, October 1920).

85. Houston was the secretary of agriculture in 1914, so he had served on the organizing committee for the System.

Table 3.5   Amount and Types of Discounts, 1918–20 (millions of dollars)

DATE (LAST FRIDAY OF)	SECURED BY GOVERNMENT SECURITIES	SECURED BY COMMERCIAL PAPER	MINIMUM DISCOUNT RATES, NEW YORK		OPEN MARKET RATE, COMMERCIAL PAPER, NEW YORK (%)
			Governments	*Commercial*	
December 1918	1,300	303	4	4	6
June 1919	1,574	244	4	4	$5^3/_8$
December 1919	1,510	684	$4^1/_4$	$4^3/_4$	$5^7/_8$
June 1920	1,278	1,154	$5^1/_2$	7	$7^7/_8$
December 1920	1,142	1,578	$5^1/_2$	7	8

Source: Board of Governors of the Federal Reserve System 1943, 340, 450.

remained at 5.5 percent in New York, Boston, and most other banks. Several reserve banks, however, kept the minimum, preferential rate on Treasury certificates at 5 percent until January or February 1921, when it was raised at all banks to 5.5 or 6 percent. Large-scale borrowing by member banks continued in 1920. Not surprisingly, much of the borrowing was at the minimum rate. Continuing the preferential rate severely reduced the effect of discount rate increases for commercial borrowers.

Table 3.5 shows the amount borrowed by type of collateral in the first two postwar years. The table makes clear that it was profitable for banks to borrow even at the higher rate on commercial paper.[86]

The gold reserve percentage continued to increase throughout the summer and fall, but it did not reach 50 percent until March 1921. Rates on commercial paper reached a peak early in January 1921 and remained above the 7 percent discount rate until late April. The Federal Reserve watched and waited but did not begin to reduce rates until open market rates began to fall.[87] It made no effort to restore a penalty rate but followed

86. Banks in the largest cities did most of the borrowing, so the discount rates at New York are a useful benchmark. For example, at December 30, 1920, all member banks had borrowed $3.04 billion, of which $2.1 billion was for banks in 101 leading cities. New York banks owed more than one-quarter of the total outstanding (Board of Governors of the Federal Reserve System 1943, table 48). Friedman and Schwartz (1963, 233) neglect the 5.5 percent borrowing rate on Treasury certificates and conclude that banks continued to borrow at a loss. This leads them to overstate the role of the 7 percent discount rate and the lag in response to discount rate increases during this period.

87. The October 1920 Governors Conference voted to eliminate the preferential rate on Treasury certificates, but the Board did not act. In place of policy discussion, the governors considered, at length, the development of an acceptance market in each district. The discussion brings out the rivalry between reserve banks. With Strong on leave, Acting Governor J. Herbert Case argued that New York's purchases should "unreservedly" bind other banks to participate in the purchase. Chicago and Boston were unwilling, and Boston argued that if New York wanted to limit purchases, it could raise it rate and let acceptances go to other markets. Charles A. Morss (Boston) accused New York of being too protective of the buyers and too hesitant to change buying rates: "We think you protect them too much; that they do not take any chances at all" (Governors Conference, October 14, 1920, 65). The Conference voted,

the market, reducing the discount rate on commercial paper to 6.5 percent in May and 6 percent in June. Rates in New York were now uniform for all collateral.

The National Bureau of Economic Research (NBER) chose January 1920 as the peak of the postwar expansion. Industrial production reached a peak in that month, but consumer prices continued to increase until July. Using this measure of the start of recession, the recession was a year old before the Federal Reserve acted to stem the decline.

POLICY IN RECESSION AND RECOVERY

Virtually every statistical indicator shows the 1920–21 recession as a sharp decline. The measured unemployment rate rose from a 4 percent average for 1920 to 12 percent in 1921. The Federal Reserve Board's index of industrial production (base 100 in 1947–1949) fell 23 percent, from 39 in 1920 to 30 in 1921 before returning to 39 in 1922. Agricultural production fell from 83 to 71 between 1920 and 1921, a much more severe decline than in the early years of the 1929–33 depression.[88] The Bureau of Labor Statistics wholesale price index (base 100 in 1947–1949) fell 37 percent, a much sharper percentage decline than in any single year of the 1929–33 depression and a total percentage decline of comparable magnitude. Yet throughout the period the Federal Reserve maintained and even raised its discount rates.[89]

In its annual report for 1920, the Board defended the sharp rise in discount rates as necessary to "maintain the strength of the Federal Reserve Banks, which are the custodians of the lawful reserves of the member banks," a reference to the gold reserve ratio. It denied that Federal Reserve policy had been the cause of the contraction (Board of Governors of the Federal Reserve System, *Annual Report*, 1920, 12–14). The dominant view, which reappears again in 1929–33, was that the deflation was an inevitable consequence of the previous inflation. Federal Reserve officials defended the deflationary policy as a means of reversing the effects of the previous inflation and restoring the gold standard at the prewar gold price.

Since prices had risen in virtually every country, a less costly means of

---

however, to establish a centralized committee on acceptances, with a secretary in New York. The committee was to develop uniform policies, suggest buying rates, and receive weekly reports on activity from each reserve bank. Much of the discussion foreshadows issues that arose about the management of the open market account.

88. Comparable figures for 1929–33 show agricultural production relatively flat from 1929 through 1932, then falling from 80 to 58 between 1932 and 1934.

89. Balke and Gordon 1986 shows a 27.5 percent peak to trough decline in the GNP deflator. The wholesale price index available at the time, base 100 in 1913, declined 44 percent from May 1920 to January 1922.

restoring the standard would have been to adjust exchange rates to reflect differences in recorded rates of inflation. The United States, as the principal gold standard country, was in a position to negotiate buying and selling prices that would have avoided much of the adjustment of domestic and foreign prices. Although several European countries devalued against gold, there is no evidence that the Federal Reserve discussed devaluation or any other alternative to domestic deflation. To the governors and board members, gold standard rules called for a fixed gold price.

Both Strong and the governor of the Bank of England, Montagu Norman, regarded the restoration of the prewar gold standard as a necessary condition for reestablishing international stability. To restore "stability," they were willing to deflate, just as the governors of the Bank of England had been willing to deflate to achieve resumption a century earlier and the United States had accepted deflation as necessary for resumption after the Civil War. However, there are few clues to why Strong, Norman, and others believed that both countries should deflate to restore prewar exchange rates.

Strong knew there were real costs of deflation. He predicted that the deflation would be "accompanied by a considerable degree of unemployment, but not for very long, and that after a year or two of discomfort, embarrassment, some losses, some disorders caused by unemployment, we will emerge with an almost invincible banking position, prices more nearly at competitive levels with other nations, and be able to exercise a wide and important influence in restoring the world to a normal and livable condition" (letter to Professor Kemmerer, February 1919, quoted in Chandler 1958, 122–24).[90] There is no suggestion in his writings or speeches that the goals Strong sought to achieve required adjustment of the relative rates of inflation and not a reduction of the absolute price levels to their prewar values.

The size of the deflation during 1920–22 shows the extent to which the Federal Reserve saw the problem of restoring the gold standard as a problem of reducing the absolute price index to its prewar level. There had been two periods of rising prices in the United States between 1914 and 1920. The first, mainly due to gold movements, ended early in 1917; the second, mainly due to the Federal Reserve policy of assisting Treasury debt operations, continued until 1920. The prevailing view of the gold standard and

90. This was very much the conventional view. At the time, Keynes was a strong proponent of rapid deflation in the United Kingdom. He favored a 10 percent bank rate for up to three years to eliminate inflation (Meltzer 1988, 45–46). At the time, Keynes also favored a return to the prewar gold parity for Britain on grounds of national prestige and confidence (49).

Table 3.6   Wholesale Price Index (base 100 in 1947–49)

YEAR	INDEX
1914	44.3
1915	45.2
1916	55.6
1917	76.4
—	—
1920	100.3
1921	63.4
1922	62.8

Source: Bureau of Labor Statistics.

the real bills doctrine treated these price increases very differently. Only the increases in price level resulting from the wartime and postwar policies had to be rolled back by eliminating the effects of speculative credit based on government securities or stock exchange loans.

Table 3.6 shows the values of the wholesale price index during the period. By 1921–22, the wholesale price level was approximately the same as the average for the years 1916–17.[91] The United States gold stock was slightly higher than it had been at the start of the war, and at 70 percent the gold reserve ratio was within a few percentage points of its April 1917 value. If the Federal Reserve intended to eliminate the effects of wartime inflation, these indicators suggest that the policy was successful. The effect of the policy, however, was to reduce the United States price level relative to the price levels in other trading countries, so the commitment to fixed exchange rates became a commitment to deflation abroad as well as at home.[92]

The 1920–21 recession is one of the few recessions in which published market interest rates were higher at the NBER trough (by three-eighths to three-quarters of a percentage point) than at the previous peak. As long as market rates remained above the discount rates, many Federal Reserve officials opposed reductions in discount rates. Their arguments are very similar to the arguments put forward in England a half century earlier. Any at-

91. Balke and Gordon's deflator returns to the level of mid-1918, the consumer price index to the level of early 1919. These data were not available, of course.

92. Friedman and Schwartz (1963, 770) suggest how much the size of the disequilibrium increased from 1920 to 1921. The ratios of United States prices to British, Swedish, and Swiss prices (each base 100 in 1929 and each adjusted for exchange rate changes) are:

Year	Britain	Sweden	Switzerland
1920	106.5	102.8	99.8
1921	95.4	85.4	92.8

The deflationary policy turned the terms of trade in favor of the United States and required revaluation or deflation in the rest of the world.

tempt to encourage expansion by reducing discount rates or allowing discount rates to remain below market rates was an encouragement to borrowing for profit, speculation, and therefore was inflationary.[93] They believed the discount rate should be a penalty rate.

At the start of 1921, rates for borrowing collateralized by Treasury certificates and Liberty bonds were generally 5.5 percent to 6 percent, and for agricultural and commercial paper 6 to 7 percent. On January 12 the Board sent a telegram to each of the reserve banks suggesting a uniform rate of 6 percent on all types of borrowing. The responses were mixed. The southern and western banks mainly favored the proposal; the larger eastern reserve banks opposed it. New York and Cleveland cited as reasons for their opposition that market rates were about to stabilize or fall below prevailing discount rates. Governor Richard L. Van Zandt of Dallas reported on the unsatisfactory and illiquid position of the Dallas bank. He suggested that discount rates be raised to correspond to market rates. The Board replied that the bank's "condition . . . constitutes a serious reflection upon the management" and ordered the bank to set discount rates at 6 percent for government securities used as collateral and 7 percent for commercial paper (Board Minutes, January 24, 1921, 72).[94]

The outgoing Wilson Treasury at last agreed to end preferential rates on certificates of indebtedness. In late January, Undersecretary Parker Gilbert wrote to Governor Harding urging the reserve banks to raise their minimum rates to 6 percent. Between January 19 and February 9 several banks, including New York, adopted the 6 percent minimum rate on Treasury obligations.

President Harding's administration had a different attitude than its predecessor. Pressure for lower discount rates came from farmers, Congress, the Treasury, and particularly Andrew Mellon, who had become secretary of the treasury in the new administration and was therefore ex officio chairman of the Federal Reserve Board. Mellon favored a reduction in the discount rate from the time he took office, March 1921.[95]

93. Chandler (1958, 174) quotes Strong's letter to Parker Gilbert of July 1920 to this effect. Strong wrote in a very similar vein to Montagu Norman almost nine months later—April 1921—after he had been pressured to reduce the New York bank's discount rate by Secretary Mellon and the Federal Reserve Board.

94. Within a year the Dallas bank replaced Governor Van Zandt. The problems at the Dallas bank arose from the agricultural depression. Later recollections by officers of the Dallas bank describe their memories of the period. They recall that cotton prices fell from 60 cents to 5 cents a bale. All eleven banks in El Paso, Texas, failed in 1920; eight hundred banks failed in Texas the same year (CHFRS, interviews with William D. Gentry and Joseph Dreibilbis, March 4 and 31, 1955).

95. In 1921 Secretary Mellon also proposed, and Congress agreed to, a reduction of $835 billion in tax revenues out of a budget of approximately $5 billion (17 percent).

Mellon took office with the volume of discounts below its peak but above $2.3 billion and with prices falling at a 25 percent annual rate.[96] Banks still held $2.5 billion of government securities, and their outstanding loans had declined very little from the peak. To the Federal Reserve, at the time, the banking data indicated inflationary pressure, both because the banks were borrowing heavily and because they continued to hold government securities. Hence banks could be regarded as financing speculative holdings by borrowing at the reserve banks. Moreover, the gold reserve ratio had increased only to 50 percent, and three of the reserve banks—Dallas, Richmond, and Minneapolis—continued to rediscount with other banks to maintain the legal reserve ratio behind their note issue.[97]

At his first meeting with the Board, in April, Secretary Mellon urged reducing rates at all reserve banks to a 6 percent maximum. Miller was opposed, arguing that wages had not been reduced enough. Other Board members did not want to dictate rate changes to the reserve banks again. Boston then proposed a reduction from 7 to 6 percent, but the request was denied pending a meeting of the Governors Conference the following week.

At the Conference, April 12–15, only Boston and Atlanta favored lower rates. Strong was opposed on grounds that a penalty rate had not yet been established. He claimed that a reduction in rates would encourage speculation on the stock exchange that "might very well extend to commodities. . . . I think the sound policy is to leave the rate unchanged" (Governors Conference, April 1921, 28–29).

Strong's reasons for opposing rate reduction are set out more clearly in a March letter to Montagu Norman: "What I have written to you . . . is absolutely the fundamental and controlling factor, that is, the debt of member banks to the Reserve Bank" (quoted in Chandler 1958, 172). Bank loans had fallen only 4 percent, not the 20 percent reduction Strong believed necessary to reestablish sound conditions. During a period of liquidation, rate reduction would not encourage business. Businesses were liquidating inventories. Banks would not increase their borrowing at the reserve banks unless the Federal Reserve encouraged "a period of inflation with all the accompanying evils of speculation and extravagance." The proper policy, he believed, was to follow "Bagehot's golden rule" (Chandler 1958, 173–74).

---

96. The March 1920 volume of discounts was not reached again until 1980, when the price level, the economy, and the size of the banking system had increased manyfold.

97. The system hailed the interdistrict lending as evidence of the importance of the new system. After 1921, however, the system relied much more on open market operations and could use the allocation of the open market portfolio among banks to smooth earnings and gold reserves.

On one of the four meeting days, the Board and the governors met with representatives of the American Farm Bureau Federation. This group told them that "the farmers feel that they have no financial system designed to meet their needs" (Governors Conference, April 13, 1921, 468). "Money is borrowed from Federal Reserve banks to be reloaned on Wall Street" (477). The farm representatives asked, "Who decided that deflation was necessary?" (472).

Strong replied that the deflation was an inevitable consequence of the previous inflation: "No one could have stopped it, and no one could have started it. In our opinion, it was bound to come" (ibid., 496). Governor George W. Norris (Philadelphia) supported him. Ignoring the effect of the gold standard, he said deflation was not confined to the United States. All countries had inflated during the war, and all must deflate.

Pressure for rate reduction was rising, however. Unlike some banks, the Board no longer argued for penalty rates or elimination of Treasury certificates from the banks' portfolios. The 1920 annual report comments that "the Board's purpose [in raising rates in 1920] was to maintain the strength of the Federal Reserve banks," a reference to the gold reserve (Board of Governors of the Federal Reserve System, *Annual Report*, 1920, 12). Harding expanded the argument in a May letter to the Atlanta reserve bank. The 7 percent rates were emergency rates. He denied that the Federal Reserve responded to political pressure. Rates had been reduced because the emergency was over (Board of Governors File, box 1240, 1921).

At the end of the meeting, on April 15, Boston lowered its rate by one percentage point to 6 percent. The reduction and political pressure from Congress led New York to lower rates by 0.5 percent in early May. The following day, Strong wrote to Norman:

> So far as I can discover, the demand [for lower rates] comes from no other class than those engaged in agriculture. They made an impressive showing, and their complaints reached all classes of Congressmen and executive officers of the government right up to the President.
>
> . . . The general feeling prevailed that the New York Bank was causing the deadlock. My own belief is that the principle followed so long by your institution, and . . . first enunciated by Bagehot, that in such times as these, money should be loaned freely, but at high rates, is the principle which should now govern our operation. (Ibid., 175)

This was not the unanimous view of System officials. The Board was more responsive to political pressure. On June 10 the Board sent a telegram to all reserve banks recommending that "rates on paper secured by new Treasury notes should be 6 percent flat at all banks" (Board of Governors File, box 1240, 1921). Within a week, several banks (including New York) lowered rates to 6 percent. By June all the major banks had reduced their rates, and in July New York, Boston, Philadelphia, and San Francisco again lowered rates to 5.5 percent. Criticism of the Federal Reserve did not stop. On July 25 Harding wrote John Perrin (Federal Reserve agent in San Francisco): "I do not know whether you appreciate how violent the attacks are which are now being made upon the Board and the system" (Board of Governors File, box 1240, 1921).

Complaints were not limited to speeches and editorials.[98] State legislatures, and Congress, considered legal limits on interest rates. In August 1922 the Senate approved a resolution criticizing the use of progressive rates only in agricultural districts and asking the Federal Reserve to refund any excess over the amounts that would have been paid at a 10 percent annual interest rate. It authorized Federal Land Bank to lend to farmers in distress but restricted loans to farmers who owned their land.

Those who had opposed a central bank on grounds that it would penalize agriculture by keeping rates high to benefit bankers and lenders believed that the Federal Reserve System had acted like the central bank they thought they had prevented. Typical of the criticism was a letter from the governor of Nebraska: "The War Finance Corporation promised relief to the . . . corn belt, but this relief should have come from the Federal Reserve. . . . [T]he tremendous reserves of the Federal Reserve Banks at a time when there was much need for credit in essentials [remained unused]" (Governors Conference, October 27, 1920, 580).

The Federal Reserve was torn between concern for the political power of the farmers and belief that the farmers' problems were not of their making. They pointed to the worldwide decline in agricultural prices but made no mention of the deflationary effect of renewed United States accumulation of gold on other countries attempting to return to the gold standard. Their defense was that credit to agriculture had fallen very little. The much greater reduction was in nonfarm regions. Reserve banks had not called agricultural loans. Farmers had borrowed to buy land and increase output during the war and postwar inflation. Worldwide deflation had now reduced the value of farm assets while leaving loan liabilities un-

98. The Board's records for the period contain many editorials, especially from agricultural areas, denouncing and criticizing the Federal Reserve. To meet the criticisms, the Board requested the reserve banks' opinions on a proposal to establish a preferential rate for commodity paper. The banks opposed it, and the proposal died (Board of Governors File, box 1240, August, 1922).

changed. This forced liquidation, low prices, and bankruptcy. The governors were relieved when this interpretation was accepted by Congress's Joint Commission of Agricultural Inquiry (Governors Conference, October 27, 1921, 567).

Livestock farmers faced particularly severe distress as prices fell and loans came due. Congress responded by extending the life of the War Loan Corporation to help livestock producers. In October the governors and Board members met with a group of senators who described at length the problems faced by farmers and ranchers. The governors responded that the Federal Reserve could not make long-term loans and was not authorized to direct credit to particular uses. Part of Strong's response is a firm denial of the efficacy of direct pressure, or qualitative credit control, that played such a large role in the Board's approach and was to return at the end of the decade. The Federal Reserve, Strong said, "has no power to tell any of its members what kind of loan it shall make, nor to restrain it from making any loan it wants to make" (Governors Conference, October 27, 1921, 390–91). He was concerned, however, that state member banks would withdraw from the system if Congress permitted the Federal Land Bank to make long-term loans. He urged the senators to confine such loans to member banks (392–93).

Deflation brought a large gold inflow. Strong's first reaction was to favor keeping the gold abroad, earmarked at the Bank of England and thus not counted as part of the gold reserve (Governors Conference, April 15, 1921, 1083). This would avoid the need for monetary expansion. Others pointed out that this was politically risky. The system would be criticized for refusing to expand.[99]

By late October New York's gold reserve ratio reached 82 percent. Strong told the October Governors Conference that if the gold reserve was the only factor, as at the prewar Bank of England, the discount rate would be 2 percent (Governors Conference, October 28, 1921, 622–24). He favored lower rates, and he urged the other governors to keep downward pressure on rates. Although a penalty rate had not been restored, he favored faster reductions in discount rates "as long as speculative fever is not on." The New York bank intended to keep downward pressure on rates by remaining in the acceptance market and by making small purchases of new issues of Treasury certificates to keep them at a premium price (Governors Conference, October 28, 1921, 634–36).

99. Miller asked Strong whether he could maintain a 7 percent interest rate if the gold reserve reached 60 or 65 percent. Strong replied, "Yes, I think we ought to fight that out right now" (Board of Governors File, box 1102, April 15, 1921).

Shortly after the meeting, most reserve banks reduced discount rates by 0.5 percent. The more important change was in the open market portfolio. That portfolio had remained in a narrow range since the summer of 1919. In November it began to increase. In the next seven months the portfolio increased threefold, an addition of more than $400 million.

During the winter and spring of 1922, open market rates continued to fall. As the discount portfolio fell, the reserve banks bought acceptances and Treasury certificates principally to improve their earnings. But Strong's revised view had gained acceptance. At the Governors Conference in May, Morss (Boston) noted that a reserve bank could increase "momentum" by purchasing in the open market and then reducing the discount rate. And Strong pointed out that buying in the open market is equivalent to member bank borrowing (Governors Conference, May 2, 1922, 155–56). Some at the Federal Reserve had found virtue in activist policy, but the view was far from unanimous.

END OF THE RECESSION
The NBER dates the trough of the business cycle at July 1921, four months before the activist policy began. Industrial production turned in August and rose strongly. By March 1922 production was more than 20 percent above the previous year. Perhaps influenced by continuing agricultural problems, Balke and Gordon's (1986) real GNP series shows a mixed pattern. A strong recovery in fourth quarter 1921 is followed by renewed contraction after the start of 1922. Averaging the two quarters suggests continued contraction. On this basis, real GNP does not return to expansion until second quarter 1922. Stock prices, however, reached a bottom in August 1922, and by December they were 13 percent above their trough.

The monetary base was subject to two principal countervailing forces. Federal Reserve discounts and advances continued to decline until September 1922, at times offsetting the continued strong inflows of gold. Quarterly average growth of the base did not become positive until second quarter 1922, nine months after the NBER trough. Quarterly average growth of M_1 was weakly positive after fourth quarter 1921 but did not increase strongly until two quarters later. The New York discount rate remained at 4.50 percent until late in June 1922. This is the only business cycle in Federal Reserve history where market interest rates on many instruments—including commercial paper, long-term Treasury and corporate bonds—were higher at the NBER trough than at the preceding peak. Since prices fell throughout 1921, ex post real interest rates were far above nominal rates. Using Balke and Gordon's (1986) deflator, real rates on

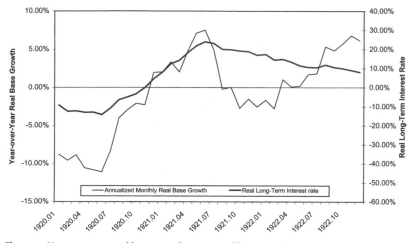

Chart 3.1 Year-over-year real base growth versus real long-term interest rate, January 1920 to December 1922.

commercial paper were between 13 percent and 26 percent around the recession trough.[100]

The economy recovered despite these high rates and the restrictive Federal Reserve policy. Two forces were at work. The monetary gold stock rose 28 percent in 1921 and 18 percent in 1922, moderating and finally reversing the effects of falling discounts on the monetary base and the money stock. Falling prices raised the value of the public's real balances as well as real interest rates. Of the two, the rise in real money balances was the more potent.

Chart 3.1 compares the growth of the real value of the monetary base with the real long-term interest rate.[101] The two series reach a peak just before the NBER trough in the economy. The recovery occurs despite an (ex post) real interest rate of more than 20 percent. Although the real interest rate fell after June 1921, the decline was gradual.

Real money balances show a very different pattern, surging during the early months of 1921 and, after a brief decline, rising in 1922. Chart 3.2 shows that this pattern is similar to the growth of real GNP two quarters later.

Growth of real money balances predicts the start and end of the recession; the growth rate declines precipitately before the recession, remains negative during 1920, and starts to rise five months before the trough

---

100. Consumer prices show a similar pattern. They fell until March 1922. Their annual growth rate did not turn positive until early 1923, in part as the result of a large negative value in August 1922.

101. Real base growth is the annual rate of change of the monetary base deflated by Balke and Gordon's (1986) GNP deflator. Real long-term interest rates are rates on Treasury debt minus the annual rate of change of the deflator.

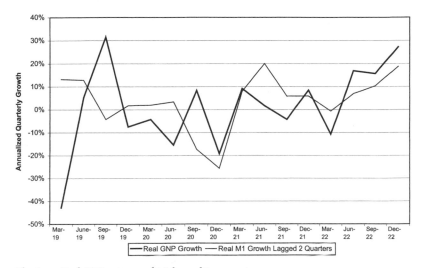

Chart 3.2 Real GNP versus real M₁ lagged two quarters.

(chart 3.2). Real interest rates show almost the opposite pattern, falling before the recession and rising during the recession. The reason is that both series have a common element—the annual rate of price change.

Falling prices raised real balances and attracted gold from abroad. The public used its increase in money balances to purchase goods and assets. Judging from stock market prices, after July 1921 asset prices rose absolutely and relative to prices of new production, stimulating the demand for new production. The change in relative prices and real wealth more than offset the negative effect of high real interest rates on spending.

The recovery from the 1920–21 recession provides some evidence on the way money and monetary policy influence the economy.[102] Relative price changes are not limited to market interest rates. Prices of housing, autos, buildings, and many other assets change relative to the price of new production of substitutes. The relative price change stimulates or retards production (Brunner and Meltzer 1976).

POLICY FRAMEWORK

The 1920–21 recession was the first test of the policy conception implicit in the Federal Reserve Act. The act provided three principal means of regulating money—gold flows, discounting, and the discount rate.[103] The

102. Real money balances are M₁ balances deflated by Balke and Gordon's (1986) deflator.
103. Acceptances and open market security purchases or sales had a smaller policy role at the time. Acceptances, like discounts, were at the discretion of holders, given the rate posted by the reserve banks. The Federal Reserve wanted to expand the role of acceptance

Federal Reserve was expected to follow gold standard rules, allowing money and interest rates to rise and fall with gold movements. Discounts were at the discretion of the banks; they presented or paid off real bills at the given discount rate. The Federal Reserve responded by issuing or withdrawing base money. The discount rate was intended to be a penalty rate that changed in response to market rates.

Whether judged by money, interest rates, or economic activity, policy failed in 1920–22. The recession was long and deep; two years after the NBER peak, real GDP was 8.4 percent below its peak value. Principal monetary aggregates fell throughout the recession, and as noted, nominal interest rates were higher at the trough than at the previous peak. Table 3.7 shows the peaks and troughs in several of these series and the changes from the NBER peak to trough.

The monetary base and the money stock declined from peak to trough despite the heavy gold inflow in 1921. Measured by either the deflator or the consumer price index, prices fell after midyear 1920; the rate of deflation remained between 20 and 30 percent from fourth quarter 1920 through second quarter 1921. Thereafter, prices declined more slowly until mid-1922.

The movements of gold, discounts, and money were a response to a common cause. Federal Reserve policy held nominal interest rates high. With prices falling, real interest rose, reducing discounts and attracting a gold inflow that continued after nominal interest rates declined from their peaks. The relatively high real interest rates and declining activity also reduced the supply of acceptances offered to the Federal Reserve. The net flow of discounts, gold, and acceptances accounts for the peak to trough decline in the monetary base. Federal Reserve open market sales and redemptions of government securities made a further small negative contribution to the base.

Charts 3.3 and 3.4 show the relation of monthly values of the gold stock and the monetary base during the recession and recovery. Despite the gold inflow from October 1920 to January 1922, the Federal Reserve kept interest rates unchanged until September, contrary to gold standard rules, and allowed the monetary base to decline. After January 1921, the relation of gold to the monetary base reversed. Gold inflows supplemented by Federal

---

markets but did not succeed. Warburg (1930, 1:457) regarded the failure to develop markets for discounts outside New York as the System's biggest failure. In his view, this failure left the banks dependent on the call money market and thus on the daily movements of the New York Stock Exchange. After he left the Board, Warburg returned to Wall Street. He became the representative of the New York Federal Reserve bank to the American Acceptance Council. In 1922 he proposed a preferential discount rate for trade acceptances. The Federal Reserve disliked preferential discount rates and voted to treat acceptances as open market paper, where they would have a lower rate only if endorsed by a bank.

Table 3.7 Cyclical Changes in Money, Interest Rates, and Prices, 1920–22

PEAK OR TROUGH AND DATE	GOLD	DISCOUNTS	BASE	M_1	i_s	i_L	DEFLATOR
Cycle peak, January 1920	$2.67	$2.14	6.91	23.26	6.00	4.93	38.15
Series peak	2.53*	2.78	7.33	23.91	8.13	5.67	42.71
Date	1920/4	1920/10	1920/10	1920/3	1920/9	1920/8	1920/2
Cycle trough, July 1921	3.02	1.72	6.47	20.73	6.38	5.26	33.74
Series trough	NA	0.40	6.08	20.45	4.13	4.12	32.43
Date		1922/8	1922/1	1922/1	1922/8	1922/8	1922/2
Change cycle P to T	0.37	−0.42	−0.44	−2.51	0.38	0.32	−4.41
%	13.8	−19.6	−6.4	−10.9			−11.6
Change, series P to T %	NA	−85.6	−17.0	−14.4			−24.1

Source: Board of Governors of the Federal Reserve System 1943; Friedman and Schwartz 1963; Balke and Gordon 1986.
Note: Dollar amounts are billions.
i_s, prime commercial paper, four to six months.
i_L, government bond rate.
NA, no peak in this period, series rises throughout 1922.
*trough.

Reserve open market purchases more than offset the continued decline in discounts, producing a rise in the monetary base.

At the time, the Federal Reserve did not use the gold reserve ratio as a guide to discount policy. To reduce pressure for reductions in discount rates, it excluded gold held abroad from the gold reserve in February, as Strong had proposed (Board Minutes, January 28, 1921, 94). By May 1921, the gold reserve ratio was above 55 percent. A classical response required reductions in discount rates despite member bank borrowing in excess of $2 billion. Although a reduction in discount rates would have helped Britain and others to accumulate gold for a return to the gold standard, as noted earlier, the Federal Reserve required prodding from the new administration and Congress to reduce its rates in May and June.[104]

Failure to respond to the reserve ratio was not the only departure from the classical gold standard. At the May meeting, Strong reported on a recent conversation with Montagu Norman in New York. Their concern was exchange rate instability. They had considered a plan to stabilize exchange

104. In a speech delivered late in 1922, Strong recognized that the gold reserve ratio was not likely to be useful as a policy indicator or guide: "The present banking system has created a situation where there is a surplus of banking reserves (gold and foreign exchange) in the country, and where there is not likely to be a deficiency. The real reserve barometer is the reserve percentage of reserve banks. The impulse, which led the Reserve System to change rates, must for the present largely arise from general conditions, and it cannot be expected that the impulse to advance rates will be given by gold exports for a long time to come. Therefore, the regulation of the volume of credit which is the chief function of the Reserve System must be effected by a combination of rate changes and due caution as to members' borrowings" (Strong 1930, 197).

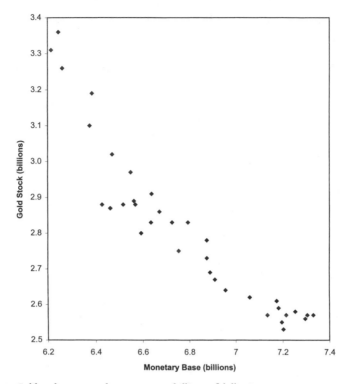

Chart 3.3 Gold and monetary base, 1919–21 (billions of dollars).

rates among eight countries—the United States, Britain, Switzerland, Holland, Denmark, Norway, Sweden, and Japan. The participating countries would establish a trading account of about $300 million to buy and sell foreign exchange. Risks would be limited by an agreement to ship gold to pay for losses. To overcome legal obstacles, Strong proposed to implement the policy by buying foreign bills instead of currencies. Strong believed the operations would be highly profitable. The proposal was never adopted (Governors Conference, May 28, 1921, 721–41).[105]

By October 1921, the gold reserve ratio was above 69 percent and still rising. At the Governors Conference, the Treasury proposed putting gold into circulation. The governors objected on two grounds. The proposal was contrary to the System's policies of centralizing gold reserves at reserve banks and encouraging the use of Federal Reserve notes. And the policy would be viewed as a subterfuge to avoid reducing discount rates. The action would raise new concerns about the System's responsibility for deflation and high interest rates (Governors Conference, October 25, 1921, 90–

105. The plan is a forerunner of the swap arrangements developed after 1960.

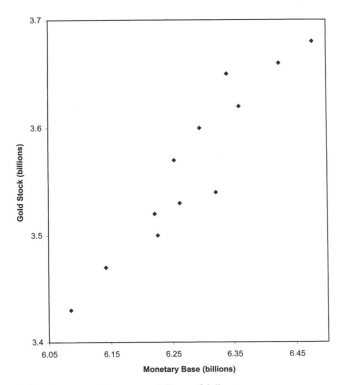

Chart 3.4 Gold and monetary base, 1922 (billions of dollars).

91, 374–77). In March 1922 the Treasury, on its own, announced a policy of unrestricted gold circulation. New York followed later.

The Treasury's action put more gold into circulation but did not keep the reserve ratio from rising. The ratio reached a peak of almost 80 percent in August 1922 and did not fall below 75 percent until late in 1924.

The governors were not alone in rejecting the gold reserve ratio as a guide to policy. Many academic economists also held that view. For example, Oliver M. W. Sprague (1921) argued that the Federal Reserve could not adopt traditional Bank of England practices. Most countries had left the gold standard and would not soon return. Hence moderate credit expansion would not automatically induce an outflow of gold to limit credit expansion. Sprague urged the Federal Reserve to adopt a domestic standard, based on discretionary judgment. He favored a modestly countercyclical policy of "lessening price fluctuations within particular business cycles, checking somewhat the upward movement, and thereby lessening the subsequent decline" (ibid., 26). A policy of this kind could work, provided there was support from public opinion and "general confidence in the wisdom of the policies" (29).

Sprague wanted to substitute price stability for the reserve ratio as a guide to action. The price level should change "with permanent changes in prices associated with variations in the world's supply of gold" (ibid., 28), but fluctuations around this level should be damped by the Federal Reserve acting on its best judgment.

This view was strongly criticized externally in papers or comments by Russell Leffingwell (1921) and Adolph Miller (1921). Leffingwell agreed that the reserve ratio was not an adequate guide when most countries had left the gold standard. He favored a penalty discount rate, to get the banks out of debt to the Federal Reserve, and circulation of gold to reduce the gold reserve ratio at the reserve banks. Miller recognized that, in principle, price stability could be a guide to policy. He found no practical merit in the proposal, however. Nothing in the Federal Reserve Act authorized such a policy, while both the act and tradition favored continued reliance on the reserve ratio. The problem was not one of finding a substitute for the reserve ratio, it was finding ways to make the "reserve ratio a more sensitive and immediate indicator" (Miller 1921, 195). Like Leffingwell, Miller blamed the 1917 amendments that centralized gold holdings at Federal Reserve banks for the reserve banks' slow response to gold.[106]

Price stability as the goal of policy is a recurrent issue for the rest of the decade and again in later years. The internal discussion of price stability as a goal contains much that is repeated in these later episodes. Frederic H. Curtiss, chairman of the Boston reserve bank, accepted price stability as an important aim of policy. He argued that an explicit price level objective would have several defects. First, it would open the System to irresistible political pressure to create prosperity. Second, the public would not distinguish relative and absolute price changes. The farm bloc in particular would want the index to reflect its concerns. Third, changes in the price level are not entirely the result of monetary changes: the relation between money and the price index was looser, he thought, than quantity theorists like Irving Fisher and Knut Wicksell believed.

---

106. Miller favored a system more like the Bank of England's, in which gold reserves were held separately against notes and bank reserves with a higher percentage against currency than under the Federal Reserve Act. The aim was to absorb some of the excess gold and restore the gold reserve ratio as a policy indicator. At about the time this public statement was published, Miller argued internally that the reserve ratio was a faulty indicator that was inconsistent with the prevailing discount rate. His proposal was intended to remove the problem (Governors Conference, April 1921, 1098–99). The Governors Conference did not accept his proposal. A principal counterargument was the uncertainty about whether or when the gold reserve would fall. The members were unwilling to make a permanent policy change based on a gold stock that might prove to be temporarily high.

As usual, Strong was more forceful. He opposed price stability as a guide to policy: "It is not the business, the duty, or the function of the Federal Reserve System, or of central banks generally, to deal with prices" (Governors Conference, May 28, 1921, 629). For Strong, price stability was a desirable outcome of a proper monetary policy, not a policy objective. He continued to hold this position throughout the 1920s. Although his opposition lessened in 1928, he preferred to reconstruct the international gold standard, in the belief that the standard would maintain price stability, and he worked to that end.

If the reserve ratio was no longer useful, what principles should govern policy? At the October Governors Conference, the Board asked the governors to state how interest rates should be set.

Governor Norris expressed the confused state: "No two of us would write exactly the same essay. . . . The only thing we could agree on would be absolutely nothing" (Governors Conference, October 27, 1921, 591). The Federal Advisory Council had been asked to discuss the issue. It provided a list of factors affecting decisions, such as gold reserves, conditions of banks, or national, district, and world business conditions. The governors recognized that these were guides, not principles.

Roy Young (Minneapolis) proposed that discount rates should be penalty rates, "equal or slightly in excess of what the customer pays the member bank" (ibid., 599). Several governors agreed with this principle, none more than James McDougal (Chicago): "If the reserves of the Federal Reserve System were to be safeguarded against misuse and to be held available for legitimate seasonal requirements, as the law contemplated they should be held, the discount rate policy should be one which should hold those rates as high or slightly higher than the prevailing rates in the commercial centers" (619–20). George W. Norris (Philadelphia) and George Seay (Richmond) strongly agreed.

Strong's reply is a sharp break from his earlier views favoring a penalty rate. In a March 1921 letter to Norman, he called the indebtedness of the member banks "absolutely the fundamental and controlling factor" (Chandler 1958, 172). He estimated that there would have to be a $6 billion to $7 billion reduction in lending, a decline equal to 20 percent of the outstanding stock, a contraction of lending five times greater than the contraction that he estimated had occurred to that time. A different signal had to be found, at least for the present.

The following month he told the Governors Conference that he opposed putting undue pressure on banks to liquidate debt. The effect would be to force inventory liquidation and additional deflation. He believed the correct policy was to lend freely at a penalty rate, and he again cited Bagehot's rule.[107] In July he continued to favor a penalty rate in principle, but he recognized that the principle had to give way. He told Norman that money market conditions "hardly justified . . . making a further reduction." There were other considerations, however, that made classical methods "not always the wisest," and he added, there were "political considerations brought about by the change of administration" (Chandler 1956, 176).[108]

At the October Governors Conference, Strong noted that the reserve ratio at the New York bank was 82 percent. If he followed Bagehot's formula, the discount rate would be 2 percent. Further, he now saw that United States markets differed from Britain's. Only one type of paper, acceptances, mattered for the Bank of England. The Federal Reserve bought many types of paper, each with its own rate, so the same procedures could not be applied. The problem was to keep the banks from borrowing for profit. This problem, he now believed, was more acute when the outlook for business was good and the community was more inclined to speculate (Governors Conference, October 27, 1921, 624–29).

Strong offered an observation that was to have an important role in shaping future policy operations and the policy framework. When banks were in debt, they used surplus reserves to reduce borrowing. Once some were out of debt, they reduced rates to put surplus funds to work: "The reduction in our rate had no influence in the market. It was the competition to lend money that did it" (ibid., 634).

Weekly data for 1921 and 1922 show that reductions in the discount rate at New York preceded declines in interest rates on four- to six-month commercial paper. All the reductions occurred with market rates on commercial paper above the discount rate. The timing was contrary to the penalty rate conception and suggests that the Federal Reserve had abandoned the idea of a penalty rate as a rule for setting the discount rate without making an explicit decision to do so.[109]

107. He seemed unaware that Bagehot's argument for maintaining a high discount rate was offered as a means of reversing a temporary gold drain and was inappropriate in 1921 with the gold reserve rising and the price level falling.

108. Classical conditions meant maintaining a penalty rate and following market rates down. Strong mentions five factors that guided his policy. Four were short-term interest rates—the rates on banker's bills, short-term Treasury certificates, commercial paper, and stock exchange call loans. The fifth factor was the Treasury's success in selling three-year notes and the rate at which they sold. He does not mention that these are nominal rates and that real rates were much higher.

109. In contrast, rates on short-term Treasury certificates led market rates down. At each of the reductions in the New York discount rate during 1921 and 1922, open market rates on certificates were from 0.5 percent to 0.75 percent below the discount rate in the month before the discount rate reduction. For these securities, the penalty rate was in effect. However, the

Perhaps the main force producing a major policy change was the political response to the 1920–21 experience. Congress began to discuss legislation limiting the Federal Reserve's power to raise discount rates beyond a ceiling rate without congressional approval. In January 1921 Congress revived the War Finance Corporation to finance agricultural and other exports. Eugene Meyer, later governor of the Federal Reserve Board, returned as head of the corporation. In August 1921 Congress appointed the congressional Joint Commission of Agricultural Inquiry to investigate the reasons for agricultural distress, the protracted economic decline, and the level of interest rates.

The commission was organized in response to a request by the Board to consider charges against the Board and Strong by John Skelton Williams, the comptroller of the currency in the Wilson administration and an ex officio member of the Board until March 1921. Williams claimed that the Federal Reserve had deliberately created a deflation to the detriment of farmers and small banks.

In December 1920, with the election over and his term about to end, Williams wrote a letter to the Board advocating lower rates. After an exchange of letters with Governor Harding, he brought his proposals before the Board on January 25 (Board Minutes, January 3, 13, 17, and 25, 1921). His principal motion, at the time, called on the Board to prepare a press release showing the unused lending power resulting from gold inflows and stating the Board's intention to reduce interest rates. The motion was defeated five to one, with Secretary Houston absent. A second motion, to suspend progressive rates, was tabled at Williams's request when the Board produced a letter from the Dallas bank suspending its progressive rate.

On February 26 the Board considered some additional motions and charges.[110] This time Williams demanded discount rate reductions to 6 percent at all reserve banks effective March 1 and the elimination of the remaining progressive rates. (Six banks were at 7 percent, the others at 6 percent.) Ignoring its own precedent, the Board objected that discount rate policy actions should be taken by reserve bank directors. Williams also moved that 4.5 percent Liberty bonds be purchased at par if the money was used for "essential purposes." None of the proposals was approved.

Federal Reserve had no intention of allowing these securities to be used as collateral. That was contrary to their real bills view and the principles of the act. Long-term governments with a minimum of eight years to maturity or first call were also below the discount rate in July 1921 but 0.25 percent above at the other reductions.

110. This meeting was considered so confidential that the Board's copy of the minutes is written in longhand. The minutes for the meeting were stored in Governor Harding's office and never transcribed. These are the only handwritten minutes I have found.

Williams charged that the New York bank had lent to the Chase National Bank and that Chase had made "unsafe and improper advances to the officers of the member bank and to companies and corporations in which such officers were interested" (Board Minutes, January 25, 1921, 173). New York had continued the policy after the comptroller's examinations in October 1919 and August 1920.

Strong was present for this part of the meeting and replied that there was nothing in the comptroller's 1919 report to warn the Federal Reserve bank. A report of the August 1920 examination had not been received until January 1921. Moreover, the comptroller was required by law to make two examinations a year but had made only one.[111]

Williams's charges and the complaints of farmers and small businessmen were aired by the Joint Commission at the first congressional hearing on Federal Reserve policy. Strong acted as the System's principal witness. In three days of testimony, he defended the deflationary policies and urged the commission to accept that deflation was an inevitable response to the previous excessive expansion. The System had been unable to control the expansion because of wartime exigencies and subservience to the Treasury. "Nature" had brought on the deflation, and there was little the Federal Reserve could have done to prevent it.[112] The reserve banks had been willing to lend on real bills. Without the reserve banks, there would have been liquidation and financial panic, as experience before 1914 showed. In the same hearings, Harding denied that the Federal Reserve had anything to do with the deflation and could not have prevented it (Joint Commission of Agricultural Inquiry 1921, 363).

The commission accepted most of Strong's argument and concluded that the Federal Reserve was most at fault when it yielded to Treasury pressure during the summer and fall of 1919. The commission argued, correctly, that the System should have been more concerned about inflation and less concerned about Treasury refunding operations. To a considerable extent the final report reflects Strong's ability to shift responsibility from the

111. Williams sent copies of his charges to some members of Congress but refused to give the Board their names (Board Minutes, March 2, 1921, 184). The Board and the reserve banks retaliated by asking the Treasury to transfer the comptroller's functions to the Board (Board Minutes, March 11, 1921, 205).

112. Strong's testimony is reprinted in Strong 1930; see esp. 135–38. The claim about inevitability was widely held at the time. See, e.g., Sprague 1921, 20–22, or Miller 1921. The same claim returns at the end of the decade. "Nature" in this case is the combination of the real bills doctrine, the gold standard, and agricultural production. The Federal Reserve and the Bank of England wanted to restore the prewar gold standard at unchanged gold parities. The Federal Reserve also wanted to eliminate speculative credit as collateral for discounts to banks and to eliminate most Treasury securities from the portfolios of borrowing member banks. They did not achieve the last objective.

Federal Reserve to the Treasury, as well as the absence of any witness for the Treasury and perhaps the commission's desire to dispose of the issues by blaming the previous Democratic administration. The System's case was strengthened because the Treasury could have invoked the Overman Act and had threatened to do so. Moreover, the hearings came at the end of the deflation and the beginning of recovery. On the indexes used at the time, industrial production rose from 75 (1919 = 100) in the summer of 1921 to 87 by January 1922 and 100 by September 1922 (Reed 1930, 16).[113]

The commission led to only one important change in the Federal Reserve's structure—the addition of one member to the Board to represent agricultural interests. Beginning in 1923, the Board had six appointed members plus two ex officio members. The first appointee to the new position died after eight days. He was replaced by Edward H. Cunningham, a farmer, leader of the Iowa Farm Bureau, and a Republican legislator. Cunningham served until his death in November 1930.

The problem of when to change the discount rate and the more basic problem of how to conduct monetary policy had not been resolved. Studies by Federal Reserve staff concluded that member banks borrowed for profit or at least profited while borrowing. The 1921 annual report compared the average rates charged on rediscounts at each Federal Reserve bank with the average rates charged by member banks on the paper used as collateral during December 1921. At a time when discount rates at the reserve banks ranged from 4.5 percent in the large eastern centers to 5.5 percent at Dallas and Minneapolis and rates on open market paper at New York were between 4 and 4.5 percent, the rates on the rediscounted paper ranged from 4 percent to 12 percent. Instead of a net cost, or penalty, the data show an average net return to the borrowing banks ranging from 1.27 percent (Cleveland) to 2.87 percent (Kansas City). Almost one-third of the items rediscounted had rates of 8 percent or above, and on 20 percent of the items the reported rates were at least 10 percent, almost twice as high as the highest rate of discount at any of the reserve banks. The study made no allowance for differences in risk on the different rediscounts. Further, the highest rates of recorded profit appear to have been on relatively small items, so the data overstate the marginal net return from borrowing by neglecting the cost of arranging and collecting loans and depositing collateral at the reserve banks.[114]

113. The recent Federal Reserve index shows a more rapid initial recovery from 6.03 in July 1921 to 6.53 in January 1922 followed by a 26 percent increase to 8.22 in September 1922. Miron and Romer (1989) have a very different pattern, based on a smaller sample.

114. More than 80 percent of the total *volume* of rediscounts carried rates of 6.5 percent or less, but this volume was accounted for by only 25 percent of the number of items redis-

A second type of evidence on the effect of rediscount rates on member bank borrowing came from a study of progressive discount rates. Although only four of the reserve banks used progressive discount rates, all of them accumulated information on the number of banks borrowing in excess of their basic line and the average amounts borrowed.[115] These data showed that during the contraction of 1920–21 the volume of borrowing in excess of basic discount lines rose at first, then declined as the larger banks reduced their borrowing. But the number of banks borrowing in excess of their lines continued to increase—from 1,800 in May 1920 to 3,000 in December 1921—and the increase was particularly great in the agricultural sections (Board of Governors of the Federal Reserve System, *Annual Report*, 1921, 67). These data furnished the main empirical basis for the conclusion that the use of a penalty discount rate did not reduce borrowing in the agricultural and rural sections of the country. Yet the report offered no analysis of the effect on borrowing of removing the progressive rates and made no effort to separate the volume of borrowing secured by Treasury securities that, during most of the period, could be used by banks subject to progressive rates to obtain discounts at a preferential rate. Perhaps most important of all, the Board's report made no attempt to compare the marginal rates on loans at banks subject to progressive rates with marginal rates at other banks. Data collected in December 1921, long after the peaks in borrowing and interest rates, showed that lending rates on eligible paper rose to 12 percent or more, suggesting that marginal loan rates at the peak were well over 12 percent. The borrowing data, on the other hand, showed that fewer than 250 banks paid progressive rates of 10 percent or more (Wallace 1956, 61). Nevertheless, the Board concluded that progressive rates were not effective, and this conclusion has been repeated in subsequent System studies (see Anderson 1966, passim).

A third source of evidence came from examining the effect of removing the preferential discount rate for borrowing secured by government obligations. The elimination of the preferential rate at various times during 1921 was reflected in a rapid decline in the volume of borrowing secured by such obligations, but total borrowing continued to rise, and as late as May 1921, borrowing was above the level at the start of the recession. The Board's 1921 annual report clearly conveys its inability to find a satisfactory

---

counted. The average value of the notes rediscounted during the month was about $14,000; the average value of the notes bearing 6 percent interest was about $40,000; the average size of notes bearing 10 percent interest was about $1,000.

115. Most of the reserve banks computed the borrowing lines by taking 65 percent of the balances maintained with the reserve bank, adding the amount paid in subscription to the reserve bank's capital stock, and multiplying the total by 2.5.

explanation for the movements in member bank earning assets and member bank borrowing during the recession. After noting that the principle of maintaining central bank discount rates above market rates was well established, the report compared the Bank of England and the Federal Reserve System. The Bank of England accepted only one class of paper for rediscount—bills of exchange. Federal Reserve banks accepted a wide variety of paper, so that it is "exceedingly difficult to determine just what current market rates are" (Board of Governors of the Federal Reserve System, *Annual Report*,1921, 30). Neither the studies nor the discussion suggested setting the penalty rate in relation to the rate changed for the loan.

To many in the System, the 1920–21 experience showed the need to replace or supplement the discount rate as a main instrument of Federal Reserve policy and to speed the process by which policy changes reduced market interest rates. Using the discount rate as a penalty rate, applying the Bank of England's system under American conditions, did not seem to work in the way they had expected. The System had tried progressive rates, nonuniform rates, uniform rates, preferential rates, and moral suasion. None of these methods seemed to them to be an effective means of controlling member bank borrowing. Years later Ralph Young, a director of research at the Board, summarized the experience: "The broad conclusions of System experience in the '20's, the record shows, was that in this country it was not feasible to attempt to make the discount rate function as a penalty rate. Our banking conditions were too unique. It was more practical to rely on the bankers' tradition against borrowing and reluctance to remain continuously in debt" (Minutes, Federal Open Market Committee, August 23, 1955).[116]

The political attacks on the Board and the System for the high rates charged at a few banks during the period of progressive discount rates, and also the criticisms of the Board and the System for having caused a decline in agricultural prices and incomes, must be viewed against the background of hostility to high interest rates in the South and West, where the highest rates were charged, and the long debate before Congress agreed to establish the Federal Reserve System. Fears of political reprisal, combined with doubts about the effectiveness of the penalty rate policy, stimulated the search for a new approach to policy.[117]

116. The Board's tenth annual report comments that the outlook for credit regulation would be "unpromising . . . if the Reserve banks had no other means than discount rates to regulate the volume of their credit" and had to rely on penalty rates (Board of Governors of the Federal Reserve System, *Annual Report*, 1923, 9).

117. The 1920–21 experience and its political repercussion helps to explain why the Board was reluctant to raise interest rates above 6 percent during the stock market boom at the end of the decade.

CONCLUSION

The first annual report of the Federal Reserve Board, published within six months of its founding, saw the role of the Federal Reserve as preemptive. Its duty was "not to await emergencies but, by anticipation, to do what it can to prevent them" (Board of Governors of the Federal Reserve System, *Annual Report*, 1915, 17). Practice was far from that intent. In its early years the Federal Reserve financed the war by indirectly monetizing the Treasury's debt. It was too weak politically to slow or stop the postwar inflation and too uncertain about the political consequences of its actions to act decisively when the Treasury allowed it to act. Thereafter the Federal Reserve pursued a deflationary policy throughout the deep postwar recession.

Wartime political weakness is certainly part of the explanation for the inauspicious beginning. Beliefs, or theories, also had a large role. Notwithstanding the intention to be preemptive, expressed in the first annual report, the policy conception embedded in the Federal Reserve Act and in the minds of the principals was passive. The gold standard was expected to maintain long-term price stability. The discount rate was a penalty rate that followed the market and the gold reserve. The principal asset, other than gold, was the discount portfolio. The real bills doctrine gave the borrowers responsibility for deciding on the volume of discounts.

This conception proved inadequate in the early years, particularly in the 1920–21 recession. Freed of Treasury controls in 1920, the Federal Reserve soon found its policy guides giving directions it did not wish to follow. The gold reserve rose, signaling a reduction in the discount rate at a time when member banks remained heavily in debt to the Federal Reserve, when member banks held large portfolios of Treasury securities, and when the penalty discount rate had not been restored. The real bills doctrine required higher interest rates and a reduction in borrowing. The gold reserve ratio sent the opposite signal.

In the event, political considerations tipped the balance in favor of lower discount rates. Secretary Mellon and the new Republican Congress were eager to show improved economic conditions, particularly before the 1922 congressional elections. Congressmen from agricultural areas, particularly in the South and West, were highly critical of the higher discount rates in those regions. Bills were introduced limiting the System's ability to increase rates. The Federal Reserve yielded to this political pressure by lowering discount rates. More important for the recovery, however, was the gold inflow and the rise in real money balances resulting from almost two years of severe deflation.

The experience convinced the Federal Reserve that the original policy conception was flawed: the Bank of England's use of the discount rate as a penalty rate and its limitation on discounts to one type of eligible paper were not the model for the United States. This conclusion appears to have been based more on conjecture than on careful analysis, the conclusion itself being as much political as economic. The discount rate worked "too slowly," hampered by the diversity of the economy, by the alleged profitability of borrowing, and by the many types of paper eligible for discount. The evidence, such as it was, came from comparing average gross returns to banks on a wide variety of risky loans with the risk-free rate and from the fact that discounts had continued to rise long after the recession began. This suggested to the governors that much larger increases in discount rates would be needed during recessions. The political response to such rates was not something they wanted to experience.

Bank portfolio choices appeared to support the conclusion. There was no sign of a return to real bills. In both January 1920, when the discount rates were raised, and June 1922, when the rates were reduced, the 101 weekly reporting banks held $2 billion in government securities and $4 billion or more in total investments. Loans on securities had fallen by less than $1 billion. In fact, the low point for bank investment in "speculative" instruments and loans on securities had come in summer 1921, at the trough of the recession. The prospect of shifting portfolios of borrowing banks mainly to real bills by discount rate policy appeared unattainable.

By the end of 1922, in a speech at Harvard, Strong recognized that the real bills doctrine provided no effective limitation. He had seen early on that a bank may use its borrowings for many purposes. Now he saw clearly that the doctrine was flawed. Although he did not fully recognize the distinction between an individual bank and the banking or financial system, he was far ahead of his contemporaries on the Board and at the other banks.

Now as to the limitations which the Federal Reserve Act seeks to impose as to the character of the paper which a Reserve bank may discount. When a member bank's reserve balance is impaired, it borrows to make it good, and it is quite impossible to determine to what particular purpose the money so borrowed may have been applied. It is simply the net reserve deficiency caused by a great mass of transactions. The borrowing member selects the paper which it brings to the Reserve bank for discount not with regard to the rate which it bears, but with regard to various elements of convenience. . . . [S]uppose a member bank's reserve became impaired solely because on a given day it had made a number of loans on the stock exchange; it might then come to us with commercial paper which it had discounted two months before. . . . If it were the design of the authors of the Federal Reserve Act to prevent these funds . . . from being loaned on the Stock Exchange or to non-member state banks or in any other type of ineligible loan, there would be only one way to prevent the funds from being so used, and that is by preventing member banks from making any ineligible loans whatsoever, or deny it loans if it had.

The eligible paper we discount is simply the vehicle through which the credit of the Reserve System is conveyed to the members. But the definition of eligibility does not effect the slightest control over the use to which the proceeds are put. (Chandler 1958, 197–98)

Important as the policy issues were, they were not the only problems. The Federal Reserve Act left the lines of authority unclear. Political trading had not resolved the dispute between those who wanted a central bank modeled as closely as possible on the Bank of England and those who wanted the political authorities to protect the public against bankers. Lines of authority were unclear not only between the Board and the reserve banks, but between Washington, New York, and the other banks. Early conflicts did not resolve the issue. Throughout the early 1920s letters and memorandums from the reserve banks complained that the impression in the districts was that discount rates were set in Washington and that the Board controlled discount policy. The Board, in turn, complained that the reserve banks leaked information about rate changes before they had been approved by the Board. In addition, personal antipathies between Strong and Miller, or between Strong and Glass, sometimes affected judgments and decisions.

The long delay in reducing interest rates provided a test of two long-standing conceptions about monetary policy. Nominal interest rates were higher at the trough of the recession than at the preceding peak, the only time this has occurred in Federal Reserve history to date. With prices falling at the trough, real interest rates rose more than nominal rates during the contraction. The economy recovered in large part because falling prices combined with an inflow of gold to increase real money balances. The rise in real money balances overcame the effect of high real interest rates, increasing spending and output. This experience contrasts with experience in the early 1930s when real balances fell as real interest rates rose.

Although there were many mistakes, the first eight years produced some successes as well. The System was able to pool the gold reserve and to make interdistrict loans when the gold reserve ratio fell. Although more banks failed in 1921 than in the recessions of 1893 or 1907 and 1908, there was no banking panic. Also, the Federal Reserve pressed the banks, particularly rural banks, to establish par collection. It improved the system for issuing currency, eliminated the effects of seasonal swings in currency demand, and nurtured a market in banker's acceptances with the aim of reducing the influence of the stock exchange and the call money market on the banking system.

The System had survived its first mistakes. The central task of developing a policy framework and useful operating guides remained.

FOUR

New Procedures, New Problems, 1923 to 1929

The years 1923 to 1929 are often described as one of the best periods in Federal Reserve history. Inflation, though highly variable from quarter to quarter, averaged close to zero for the period as a whole. Economic growth was variable but robust. The economy grew at a 3.3 percent average rate, despite two recessions in six years.[1] Labor productivity in manufacturing rose 4 percent a year, and the index of stock prices rose 20 percent a year.

Whether judged by money growth or by interest rates, Federal Reserve policy avoided the sharply inflationary and deflationary actions of earlier and later years. Interest rates on both long-term Treasury bonds and commercial paper averaged about 4.5 percent. The monetary base rose about 1.5 percent a year. Although the United States was on the gold standard for the period as a whole, variations in money growth were not much affected by gold movements.

Membership in the Federal Reserve System was far from complete. Fewer than 10 percent of state banks were members. The number of state member banks declined, but deposits of member banks increased both absolutely and relative to deposits of nonmember banks.

The Federal Reserve developed much more activist procedures than envisaged by the authors of the Federal Reserve Act or practiced in earlier years, and policy actions became more centralized. The reserve banks, par-

---

1. Real growth is computed from third quarter 1923 through third quarter 1929 to omit the recovery early in 1923 and the start of the 1929 recession. Using annual data, growth is 4.7 percent for the seven years 1923 through 1929. The difference is due principally to the strong recovery reported for second quarter 1923. Quarterly and annual data for inflation give very similar results.

ticularly New York, gained more control over decisions, but disputes about the locus of power continued and at times became intense.

The problem was partly personal, partly substantive. Adolph Miller, the dominant personality at the Board, was indecisive, inclined to shift his position in debate, and unwilling to take responsibility. Miller envied the power and influence of Benjamin Strong and the New York reserve bank that Strong headed. As the only economist in a decision-making position, he expected Strong and others to defer to him on economic issues. Strong was decisive, commanding, and eager to exercise leadership. Intended ambiguity in the Federal Reserve Act, a result of the compromise President Wilson crafted, heightened the personal controversy. To Strong and other bank governors, the System was an association of reserve banks supervised by the Board. To Miller and others in Washington, the Board was responsible for directing the System to a common policy goal and steering away from bankers' interests. As open market operations increased in importance and discount policy declined, Miller tried repeatedly to shift control of open market policy from Strong and his colleagues to the Board. He was unsuccessful while Strong was alive.

Substantive differences also reflected problems in the Federal Reserve Act. Miller and the Board emphasized control of the quality of credit by discounting real bills. The act supported their position; this was the intent of Carter Glass and others who drafted the act. Strong held this view before the 1920–21 recession, but the policy failures of that period and the political response to interest rate increases changed his mind. Further, unlike Miller and the Board, he recognized that the type of credit instrument discounted by the borrowing bank did not restrict the volume of borrowing or give information about the use of new loans. He saw that under the real bills doctrine, money and credit would expand as long as banks had eligible paper and could discount profitably. To be effective, the System had to control the quantity of credit.

Initially, policy action responded to the gold reserve ratio. A decline in the ratio signaled that interest rates should rise, a rise that rates should decline. With few countries on the gold standard during and after the war, the signal was less reliable.

What should replace it? The Board's annual report for 1923 set out the new operating framework. By carefully sifting through the responses to open market purchases and sales, economists at the New York bank and the Board developed a new set of signals to guide operations. I call this analysis the Riefler-Burgess doctrine. The doctrine played a major role in the 1920s and beyond.

Governor Strong's efforts to support the British by easing policy in the summer and fall of 1927 brought differences between New York and the Board into sharp focus. Under Strong's leadership, the open market committee lowered United States interest rates by buying government securities after member bank borrowing declined. Advocates of real bills, such as Miller, criticized the action as inflationary, by which they meant that the increased credit was not backed by productive assets. They, and most others, believed that inflationary credit expansion, like wartime expansion, must inevitably be followed by contraction and deflation. For the real bills advocates, the deflation and depression that started in 1929 were the inevitable consequence of Strong's policies in 1927.

Conflict between New York and the Board reached new heights in 1928 and 1929. New York, operating on Riefler-Burgess rules, favored a higher discount rate to reduce member bank borrowing and the quantity of credit. On their interpretation, reduced borrowing would indicate greater ease. The Board, fearful of a return to the high discount rates at the start of the decade and wanting to limit credit to stock market speculators, favored controlling the quality of credit by moral suasion, direct pressure, and exhortation against speculation. It opposed increases in discount rates. The result was delay and inaction; the more serious problem on both sides was failure to recognize that monetary policy was deflationary.

The Federal Reserve had three principal aims during the 1920s: to reestablish the gold standard as an international exchange system; to maintain price stability at least as well as if the country remained on the prewar gold standard; and to prevent or slow the growth of speculative credit, particularly credit used to carry securities traded on the New York Stock Exchange. A fourth aim, though rarely stated, was present also: the Federal Reserve wanted to avoid a return to the level of interest rates and deflationary policies of 1920–21 that had damaged agriculture and commerce and heightened criticism of the System.

The different aims often gave conflicting signals. Higher interest rates to prevent growth of stock exchange lending exposed the System to renewed criticism and attracted gold. Mindful of those criticisms, some officials preferred to rely on exhortation or qualitative control instead of quantitative control. This produced conflict within the System.

At a more basic level was the conflict between price stability and restoration of the world gold standard. In part to maintain price stability, the Federal Reserve System sterilized gold inflows and, reversing its earlier policy, put gold and gold certificates into circulation. This policy reduced the monetary expansion resulting from gold inflows, thereby shifting more of the burden of adjustment to Britain and other countries seeking to reestablish and sustain a type of gold standard. Once Britain returned to the gold standard, it had to raise interest rates and deflate to defend its exchange rate. A more classical gold standard policy of lowering United States interest rates and allowing the country's prices to rise in response to gold inflows would have reversed some of the gold flows and reduced the need for deflationary policies abroad, at the cost of higher inflation in the United States.[2]

French policy added to the problems faced by Britain and others. France returned to the gold standard in 1927 at a rate that undervalued the franc; Britain returned in 1925 at an exchange rate that overvalued the pound. Under the rules of a full gold standard, gold would have flowed from Britain to France, the United States, and perhaps elsewhere. The countries receiving gold would have allowed prices to rise, and British prices would have fallen. But France and the United States were as reluctant to permit prices to rise as Britain was to let them fall. Without this mechanism, or a substitute, the gold standard could not work to adjust gold stocks and prices.

In practice, after 1927 the United States and France pursued mildly deflationary policies that drained gold from Britain, Latin America, and elsewhere. The collapse of the gold standard came in the 1930s, foreshadowed by the policies of the 1920s.

The result was failure to achieve three of the four aims. Qualitative controls failed to prevent a rise in stock prices and brokers' loans. The international gold (or gold exchange) standard collapsed, never to be restored. And the relative stability of the 1920s was followed by severe deflation and economic depression throughout the world.

NEW PROCEDURES

A more activist policy required more and better information, new procedures, and a new framework for deciding on policy actions. The procedures began to take shape after 1921, and though they evolved through the first half of the decade, the System had the main outlines in place by the end of 1923.

The prewar gold reserve had served as a signal for timing changes in the thrust of policy. That signal was now muted. During the first part of the decade, the United States was the only major country on the gold standard. The governors agreed that they could not rely on the gold standard mechanism to maintain price stability until currencies became convertible and countries restored the international standard. They favored restoration and worked toward that end, but until countries readopted the gold standard,

2. Between 1922 and 1926, the United States share of the world monetary gold stock rose from 43.3 percent to 45.5 percent, while the share held by the Treasury and Federal Reserve fell. The difference is explained by gold and gold certificates in circulation (Schwartz 1982, vol. 1, tables SC8 and SC10).

they needed a new guide for policy. Hence they developed the research function, first in New York and later at the Board, to provide indexes of industrial production, prices, interest rates, credit, and other measures of current and prospective economic activity.[3] These measures, and the volume of discounts, replaced the gold reserve ratio as guides to policy action.

Development of Open Market Policy

Section 14 of the Federal Reserve Act authorized open market operations to make discount rates effective. The section reflected the belief that if banks were out of debt to the reserve banks, changes in discount rates would be ineffective.[4] By selling in the open market, the reserve banks could reduce bank reserves and force banks to borrow, thereby restoring the effectiveness of discount policy.

Open market operations were not new. They had been known for at least one hundred years in England. As early as 1822, the Bank of England purchased and sold government securities to assist the Treasury in refunding the public debt by maintaining a particular market rate (Wood 1939, 5).[5] After 1830, the bank bought and sold Exchequer bills at its own initiative on a limited scale.[6]

3. Adolph Miller, the only economist on the Board, urged creation of a statistical office. The office was located in New York mainly to accommodate Parker Willis, its director. It began publication of the *Federal Reserve Bulletin* in 1914. Willis took charge in 1918 after he resigned as secretary of the Board. The New York bank started its own publication, the *Monthly Review of Credit and Business Conditions*, and in 1920 it hired W. Randolph Burgess as its first editor. New York also had a statistics department led by Carl Snyder. In 1922 the Board's research office moved to Washington, D.C., when Walter Stewart was appointed director in July. See Burgess 1964 and Yohe 1982. Stewart left the Board in 1926 to enter private business, but he continued to serve as an adviser to Strong until Strong's death. He then served as economic adviser to the governor of the Bank of England from 1928 to 1930, where he initiated construction of statistical series similar to his work at the Board. During this period, the Board's staff developed the statistical data for the table called "Member Bank Reserves and Related Items." The "Index of Industrial Production" first appeared in 1922 as the "Index of Production in Basic Industries" and later (1927) as "A New Index of Industrial Production." Between 1922 and 1925, the statistical section of the *Federal Reserve Bulletin* introduced, among others, series on department store sales, agricultural movements, department store stocks, wholesale trade, factor employment, factory payrolls, and building contracts (House Committee on Banking and Currency 1926, 698). Yohe (1990) discusses the early history of the Research Division.

4. The House report on the Glass bill mentions two reasons for open market operations in "the classes of bills which it is authorized to rediscount" (Krooss 1969, 3:2318). The first is to make the discount rate effective. The second is to provide an outlet for investment of funds "when it was sought to facilitate transactions in foreign exchanges or to regulate gold movements" (ibid.).

5. Before 1819, the bank seldom bought Exchequer bills except at the Treasury's request (Wood 1939, 5). Other bills were bought, however.

6. Keynes (1930, 2:170, 229) is misinformed when he writes that in 1890 "open market policy had not been heard of." Sayers (1957, 49) claims that before 1914 the bank purchased

Open market purchases and sales were also well known in the United States before 1920. A few weeks after the reserve banks began operations, the Board authorized them to purchase government securities "within the limits of prudence as they might see fit" (Board of Governors of the Federal Reserve System, *Annual Report*, 1914, 16). The first Governors Conference in 1915 discussed whether each reserve bank should purchase and sell independently or as part of a coordinated effort.[7] The reserve banks retained the right to purchase independently but agreed to combine operations in government securities and acceptances under New York's supervision.

The Board's hostility to the Governors Conference and the demands of wartime finance ended the first coordination effort. Although San Francisco, Chicago, and Cleveland continued to coordinate actions with New York in the acceptance market, the System did not have a common policy (D'Arista 1994, 82). After the war, the reserve banks renewed efforts to coordinate operations at the March 1919 Governors Conference. New York proposed centralization of acceptance purchases in New York and rules for reserve bank operations. New York wanted a no resale rule for acceptances, to avoid competition with member banks, and common rules for purchases made outside a reserve bank's home market to restrict competition. Nothing happened. A year later New York tried again, this time urging a common program in which everyone would share and all would be obligated "unreservedly." Boston argued for developing local markets, and Chicago argued that New York held acceptance rates too low, reducing reserve bank earnings.

The governors could not agree at the time on rules for allocating acceptances purchased commonly. The main decision in 1920 was to appoint a committee to develop a basis for dividing costs and income from joint operations in the acceptance market. A year later the committee recommended a uniform purchase rate and urged that purchases be made only from dealers and only after bills had been endorsed.[8]

Coordinated operations in acceptances laid the groundwork for coordi-

---

but never sold. Hawtrey (1932, 151) cites the 1847 experience when the bank sold current bills for specie and bought forward bills, thereby removing cash from the market at a time of stress. Testifying before the Lords in 1797, Thornton said it was immaterial whether the bank relieved market strain by discounting or by purchasing government securities.

7. The Federal Reserve Act gave each reserve bank responsibility for its own portfolio. Without voluntary agreement, the System could not have a common policy.

8. The committee included Governors Morss and Fancher and Edwin Kenzel, New York's expert on acceptances and one of the first appointments Strong made in 1914. The recommendations were not entirely welcome at several of the reserve banks, so frictions about acceptance market practices continued.

nated government securities purchases. Three factors worked to force the next step. First, the New York bank, as the main fiscal agent, was responsible for distributing and refunding government debt. The Treasury complained that uncoordinated market activity by the reserve banks interfered with debt management operations, and some commercial banks complained about competition from the reserve banks in the debt market. Second, the reserve banks purchased heavily in 1921–22 to replace income from discounts during the recession and recovery. The Treasury objected both to the timing of purchases and to the magnitude of the reserve banks' holdings. Third, the New York bank observed that when the regional reserve banks purchased, New York member banks repaid some of their borrowings. The result was a transfer of earnings to the regional reserve banks at New York's expense.

The main impetus for coordination came from the Treasury following the large-scale purchases by the reserve banks. Between October 1921 and May 1922, the reserve banks added almost $400 million to their holdings of government securities as partial replacement for the $900 million reduction in discounts during the same period. Purchases were particularly heavy in February and March, when the reserve banks purchased $200 million, doubling their holdings.[9]

The desire to avoid losses overcame scruples about real bills (Parthemos 1990, 12). In 1920, with high discount rates and heavy discounting, the reserve banks added $83 million to surplus after paying a franchise tax of $60.7 million and dividends of $5.6 million. In 1921 the addition to surplus fell to $16 million after similar franchise tax and dividend payments. By early 1922 all the reserve banks recognized that income would not be enough to cover their banks' expenses, franchise tax, and dividends. The volume of acceptances had declined along with discounts and discount rates, reducing earnings. Even with the large increase in their government portfolios early in the year, some of the reserve banks had to pay dividends in 1922 from their accumulated surplus.[10]

Secretary Andrew Mellon asked the Federal Advisory Council in November 1921 to recommend a policy for the reserve banks. On April 29, 1922, he sent Governor Harding the council's recommendations, opposing any use of the Federal Reserve System "for the purpose of carrying the

9. Purchases were not uniform. New York, Chicago, Cleveland, Boston, and Kansas City were heavy buyers (Board of Governors File, box 1441, March 8, 1922).

10. Inflation and expanded operations had greatly increased expenses. By 1921–22 the reserve banks' expenses were close to $50 million, nearly ten times expenses in 1916. The general price level was about 50 percent higher, so in constant dollars expenses had increased about sevenfold while the number of member banks increased by 30 percent.

Government's obligations" and recommending that the reserve banks confine their purchases to bills of exchange and acceptances (Governors Conference, May 1922, 13–14). Undersecretary Parker Gilbert pursued the issue with great force in 1922 by writing and speaking to the governors, rejecting their argument about covering expenses, and repeatedly urging them to sell their holdings (Board of Governors File, box 1441, January, March, and April 1922).

Strong undertook three main tasks at the May 1922 governors' meeting. He wanted to coordinate purchases and sales and centralize responsibility in his hands and away from the Board. He had to satisfy the Treasury that the reserve banks would not interfere with fiscal operations and would reduce their holdings. And he had to satisfy the other governors that their autonomy and earnings would be maintained. The governors regarded government securities as a substitute for discounts and acceptances, hence subject to decisions by their directors.

At the May 1922 Conference, Strong read a letter from Secretary Mellon to Governor Harding, dated April 25, objecting to reserve bank purchases. The Treasury's policy was to not ask Federal Reserve banks for assistance. Mellon's letter recognized the desire for earnings, but policy was more important: "I should regard it as particularly unfortunate if incidental questions of expenses and dividends were to be permitted to control on questions of major policy" (Governors Conference, May 1922, 519). He reminded the governors that the reserve banks were not created to make a profit.

Treasury Undersecretary Gilbert wanted the reserve banks to liquidate all their current holdings of governments. To partially compensate for the reduced income, he offered to pay the reserve banks for their fiscal services. And he reminded them that the attorney general had ruled that they could pay dividends out of accumulated earnings when they had insufficient current income.

Most of the governors admitted they were investing for earnings. George W. Norris (Philadelphia) favored buying longer-term bonds to increase yield. Others argued, incorrectly, that since they bought mainly from district banks, they had no effect on the national market. David C. Biggs (St. Louis) reported that one of the reasons his directors agreed to purchase Treasuries was to keep the gold reserve ratio from rising.

Although New York was by far the largest investor in Treasury debt issues, Strong used the Treasury's complaints to advance his program. The reserve banks were fiscal agents of the Treasury. And, he insisted, the Treasury's complaints were correct. The reserve banks had a legal right to purchase securities, but the Treasury wanted a policy of noninterference.[11] Not only was it their duty to meet these demands, Strong said, but the Federal Reserve Board could require them to do so.

James McDougal (Chicago) resisted centralization as an attack on the regional character of the System. Open market purchases were local decisions to be decided locally. If the Treasury was in the market, the reserve banks would stay out if notified. He offered a resolution expressing willingness to work with the Treasury but retaining local decision making (Governors Conference, May 1922, 113, 129).

Strong had no interest in solving the problem so simply. He saw the opportunity for a coordinated policy under his guidance. He wanted to build a portfolio that they could use later to prevent a repeat of the 1919–20 (or 1915) experience: "The first thing we know we will suddenly break into a run-away market such as occurred in 1919, with no means of checking it. It is not the intention of this bank to let go its hold upon the situation at the present time, and we would regard ourselves as derelict in our duty were we to do so" (quoted in Chandler 1958, 211).[12]

The main concern of most governors was their banks' earnings, not System policy. McDougal moved, and the Conference agreed, that "each governor recommend to his directors that it be the policy of the bank to invest in Government securities only to the extent it may be necessary from time to time to maintain earnings in amounts sufficient to meet expenses including dividends and necessary reserves" (Board of Governors File, box 1434, May 2–4, 1922). The governors also agreed to allow their investment accounts to decline at maturity until they had eliminated earnings in excess of expenses and dividends.

Strong was able to gain approval for creation of a committee that would execute centrally all orders to buy or sell for the account of any of the Fed-

---

11. The Treasury's policy seems a reversal of typical government finance. A reason for the Treasury's desire to keep the reserve banks from buying or holding governments was that the Treasury had started to run surpluses in fiscal year 1920 and continued to run large budget surpluses throughout the decade. (At its peak in 1927, the budget surplus was 28 percent of Treasury receipts.) The Treasury used the surplus to retire debt. Between June 30, 1922, and 1929, the gross debt declined $6 billion, 26 percent of the amount outstanding in June 1922. Hence the Treasury had no interest in having the Federal Reserve banks bid for and raise prices on outstanding debt that it would buy. The Treasury did not invoke the real bills view that the central bank should hold gold and real bills.

12. Strong added: "I would view the future with apprehension were we to commence now to liquidate the $150 million or $160 million of investments" (Chandler 1958, 211). These amounts refer to holdings at New York. The System held over $500 million but began to liquidate in June when prices started to rise. Within a year, System holdings were less than $100 million.

eral Reserve Banks. He saw this as a way of laying "a foundation for an investment policy" (ibid., 497). The banks were to draw up statements of projected earnings and expenses including dividends. All agreed to stay out of the market when the Treasury issued or redeemed securities. This was the beginning of what was later called an "even keel" policy—keeping interest rates unchanged during Treasury operations.

The agreement did not satisfy McDougal, Norris, and Charles A. Morss (Boston). Chicago had nurtured a local market for government securities. A central committee in New York would favor the New York market. Strong offered to buy and sell in all active markets and suggested that decisions to purchase and sell be controlled by a committee consisting of himself, McDougal, Norris, and Morss. The governors voted to establish the Committee of Governors on the Centralized Execution of Purchases and Sales of Government Securities with the four members Strong had proposed. In October the committee added Governor Elvadore R. Fancher (Cleveland). Governors of these banks continued to serve as the executive committee during the 1920s.

As the committee's name suggests, its role was limited to recommendations and to execution of orders sent by the reserve banks. Responsibility for decisions remained with the individual banks and their directors, who retained the right to purchase and sell at their discretion and to buy directly from member banks in their districts.

At the first meeting, the committee elected Strong chairman, with Deputy Governor J. Herbert Case of New York as his alternate. The committee began coordinated sales of securities in response to the Treasury's request to reduce holdings and the reserve banks' agreement to limit holdings to cover expenses. The sales occurred at a time of recovery and expansion. The Board's index of industrial production rose 35 percent in 1922, and GNP increased at a 13 percent average annual rate for the four quarters of 1922, despite a decline at the start of the year. In June Boston, New York, and San Francisco responded to the continuing decline in open market rates by reducing their discount rates by 0.5 percent to 4 percent despite the expansion.

Undersecretary Gilbert wrote to Strong in mid-September, again urging that the reserve banks liquidate all their government securities. Sales would permit increased member bank borrowing, he said, expressing what was soon to be the System's policy view. The reserve banks should reduce discount rates to encourage the additional borrowing. Further, he complained that even with the Committee on Centralized Purchases and Sales, reserve banks were purchasing independently to increase earnings. Strong replied that since May the reserve banks had sold $150 million, one-third of the account. The committee had no power to do more than act as agents for the individual reserve banks. And, Strong added, he opposed a reduction in the discount rate, since additional borrowing might prove to be inflationary (Board of Governors File, box 1434, September 13 and 15, 1922).

When the governors met in October, Gilbert continued to press for reductions in reserve bank holdings to be carried out without disturbing Treasury operations (Governors Conference, October 10–12, 1922, 425). The governors recommended no further purchases and modified their objectives.[13] Henceforth they would conduct open market operations with less attention to earnings and dividends and more to the effects on the money market. Governor McDougal, though a member of the Committee on Centralized Purchases and Sales, spoke against the recommendation as a radical departure from practice and from the principle that made directors responsible for portfolio decisions. George J. Seay (Richmond) also objected. He was hesitant to give any committee the power to override the judgment of the individual reserve banks. Strong replied, perhaps disingenuously, that nothing of that kind was intended. The committee would make recommendations to the individual banks. The reserve banks' directors would make portfolio decisions. The committee had a "purely ministerial function"; it would not decide policy.[14]

The governors also took a major step away from the original plan for semiautonomous banks and toward a unified System. The Committee on Centralized Purchases and Sales now had responsibility for recommending to the reserve banks the advisability of purchases and sales.[15] Decisions remained with the individual banks; they could refuse to participate, so

13. An exception to the decision allowed reserve banks to purchase so-called Pittman Act securities that the Treasury wanted to withdraw. Richmond, Atlanta, and Dallas purchased only these securities. Pittman Act securities had been issued under an April 1918 act that permitted the Treasury to withdraw silver certificates from circulation and replace them with Federal Reserve banknotes backed by Pittman Act certificates. The Treasury sold the silver to Britain to support India's silver standard. After the war, the Treasury repurchased silver and reissued silver certificates, and the reserve banks reduced Pittman Act certificates and the corresponding currency issues (Friedman and Schwartz 1963, 217n).

14. Strong recognized, however, that unless the directors objected, an individual reserve bank would receive securities under the formula for allocating purchases and sales. Hence a bank's portfolio would change with decisions by other banks, including particularly the decisions by the five largest banks, whose governors constituted the committee. But he did not mention this point in response to Seay.

15. Burgess (1964, 220) cites Strong's discussion of "credit control" at Harvard in October 1922, in which he does not mention open market operations, as evidence that there was no open market policy. The May and October 1922 meetings, however, show that Strong was clearly aware of the opportunity. The only coordinated action to that point had been sales at the behest of the Treasury.

centralization had not yet been realized. This is clear from the responses to a letter sent by Vice Governor Edmund Platt of the Federal Reserve Board early in February 1923.[16] The letter asked each governor to explain his bank's policy with respect to purchases of acceptances and governments.[17]

The question is surprising. The reserve banks, by unanimous vote, had adopted a common policy statement at the October 1922 Governors Conference. The statement said that discount policy and "open market operations should be administered in each district in such manner as to assist the system in discharging, as far as it may be able, its national responsibility to prevent credit expansion from developing into credit inflation." The statement was included again in the minutes of the Committee on Centralized Purchases and Sales on February 5, 1923, when it decided not to make further purchases (Board of Governors File, box 1434, February 5, 1923). Except for New York, none of the responses to Platt's letter referred to the policy statement. The eleven banks gave no recognition to systemic or market effects. There were three types of responses.

Several banks reported that they executed all their purchases through the centralized committee. There were not many discounts, so purchases were made to increase earnings. Chicago acknowledged that the System's policy was to assist the Treasury by buying acceptances instead of governments. However, "the volume of bills . . . is at times inadequate to supply the Federal Reserve Banks with sufficient investments" (Board of Governors File, box 1434, February 7, 1923). Relying only on acceptances would depress rates and drive the commercial banks out of the market. A few banks wrote that they did not participate in the governors' centralized purchases. They bought governments from district member banks, at prices quoted in New York, as an accommodation because there was no market in their district. Only New York wrote that purchases were made as part of

---

16. Edmund Platt served as a member of the Board from June 1920 to September 1930 and was vice governor after July 1920. Platt trained as a lawyer but had worked as a journalist and an editor. In 1912 he was elected to Congress as a Republican when his opponent died. He voted against the Federal Reserve Act. In 1919 he became chairman of the Banking Committee (Katz 1982, 216–17). Platt was the senior operating official of the Board from August 9, 1922, when Governor Harding's term as a Board member ended, to May 1, 1923, when Congress confirmed Daniel R. Crissinger as governor. The most likely reason for the change was that Governor Harding was a Democrat, appointed by President Wilson. The New York Times wrote at the time that "his forced retirement would give a shock to the financial community," a comment repeated about many of his successors (Kettl 1986, 28). Subsequently, Harding became governor of the Federal Reserve Bank of Boston, where he served from 1923 to 1930.

17. The letter appears to have been sent after Adolph Miller raised the issue at the January 8 Board meeting. Miller understood that open market operations had a monetary effect. He wanted the banks to explain the reasons for their purchases and their plans for 1923 (Board Minutes, January 8, 1923).

a policy of keeping the volume of credit as stable as possible after allowing for seasonal demands.[18]

The Board's Response

From the very beginning of centralized purchases, the Board tried to find ways to control operations. Soon after the Treasury began to express concern about purchases, the Board asked its general counsel for an opinion about its powers. The counsel's report concluded that the "Board has legal right to impose any restrictions and limitations it may deem proper" (Board of Governors File, box 1434, April 14, 1922, 190). The memo left decisions to purchase and sell up to the reserve banks; the Board had general supervisory powers.

During the winter of 1923, the Board was pressed to adopt a policy from one side by Secretaries Mellon and Gilbert and from the other by Adolph Miller. The Treasury wanted the Board to stop the reserve banks' open market purchases and get the banks to liquidate their holdings (letter Mellon to the Federal Reserve Board, Board of Governors File, box 1434, March 10, 1923). Vice Governor Platt's response expressed general agreement with Mellon's concerns, but he noted that the Board could coordinate actions by the reserve banks but did not have authority to stop all purchases. Mellon's reply did not accept the Board's argument. Under its power of general supervision (section 11[j]), he wrote, the Board had ample authority to prohibit the reserve banks from investing in government securities. Mellon sharply distinguished investments from credit market transactions. Only the former should be prohibited. Credit market transactions "should not be hampered by regulations any more than is absolutely necessary" (Mellon to Platt, Board of Governors File, box 1434, March 15, 1923).

Miller wanted open market policy to be made with regard to the general credit situation. On March 8 the Board voted to ask Miller to draft a policy statement, and meanwhile it wrote to all the reserve banks urging them to allow their certificate holdings to run off without replacement. Two weeks later the Board considered Miller's proposed resolution. Citing its powers of general supervision of investments under sections 13 and 14 "to limit and otherwise determine the securities and investments purchased," the need to maintain a proper relation between discount and open market op-

---

18. The reserve bank governors' concern for earnings is shown by the votes on the resolutions offered at the October 1922 meeting. The governors defeated Strong's proposal that open market operations be used to regulate discounts and gold imports. When the resolution omitted "gold imports," the proposal passed unanimously. The difference affected earnings. Substituting securities for discounts leaves earnings unchanged; substituting securities for gold changes the earnings flow.

erations, and the embarrassment that past operations had caused the Treasury, the Board ruled that the reserve banks should conduct open market operations "with primary regard to the accommodation of commerce and business, and to the effect of such purchases or sales on the general credit situation" (Board Minutes, March 22, 1923, 177–78). The resolution abolished the Committee on Centralized Purchases and Sales and appointed the five members of that committee as the Open Market Investment Committee (OMIC). Miller's resolution placed the committee under the Board's control.[19]

To placate the Treasury, the Board's resolution required the committee to conduct most of its operations in the acceptance market. Reflecting the real bills view incorporated in the act, the resolution instructed the committee to take account of the effect of purchases of government securities, "especially short-dated issues, upon the market for such securities, and to restrict open market purchases to *primarily commercial investments,* except that Treasury certificates be dealt in, as at present, under so-called repurchase agreement" (Board Minutes, March 22, 1923, 177–78; emphasis added).

The governors were meeting down the hall. A joint meeting with the Board, which Burgess (1964, 221) describes as "stormy," discussed the Board's resolution and its claim to general powers over portfolio decisions. W. P. G. Harding had replaced Morss as governor at Boston. Perhaps because he was the former governor of the Board and Strong was on leave, Harding led the governors' criticism of the proposed resolution. He was not opposed to selling government securities, but he opposed doing so on the Treasury's orders. This gave the Treasury a voice in open market policy and set a bad precedent. Further, he objected to the part of the resolution that severely restricted the banks' right to buy government securities. The Board did not have power to prevent the reserve banks from buying securities. Its power was supervisory only, and the Treasury had no power at all (Joint Meeting of Governors and Board, Governors Conference, vol. 2, March 22, 1923, 669–70).

Miller responded that the banks' purchases in 1922 had not been coordinated by the Committee on Centralized Purchases and Sales. The banks

19. Miller's recommendation had the open market committee chaired by the Board. The Board removed this phrase to meet the objections expressed at the Governors Conference. Miller was not satisfied with the Board's role. In the 1926 Stabilization Hearings, he urged the House Banking Committee to strengthen the Board's role by making open market operations "subject to the approval and the orders of the Federal Reserve Board" (House Committee on Banking and Currency 1926, 866), and he proposed Board control again in 1928–30, when the committee's size increased to twelve members. The Banking Act of 1935 transferred control to the Board.

had purchased $400 million more than needed to meet expenses and dividends. This criticism angered McDougal, who argued that the additional purchases were made because discounts had increased more than expected as the economy recovered.[20]

The Federal Reserve Act gave the Board general powers of supervision. None of the governors questioned the extension of these powers to open market operations. Harding, joined by Case and Norris, objected to the Board's claim that it would "limit and otherwise determine" the amount and type of open market purchases and sales. Norris said the Board lacked general authority over a reserve bank's portfolio decision. General authority would mean that the law created a central bank, in Washington, with the reserve banks as operating branches.

Miller's response recognized the importance of open market operations: "The open market operations of the system are going to be the most important part of the system, largely because it is through the open market clause of the Act that the reserve banks are in a position to take the initiative" (ibid., 700).

The Board was the proper authority, Miller argued, because it had a national, not a regional, perspective. Harding replied that there was no general power in the Federal Reserve Act. The Board's counsel could not point to any place where the Board was empowered to limit the amount of government securities that the reserve banks could purchase.

Miller's response recognized the law's limitations but chose to ignore them. Without intending to prophesy, he foresaw what would happen: "The powers of the Board have been challenged in this matter. I regret to say that there has even been some question in the Board itself as to whether it had the power. A Board that doubts its power doubts its responsibility, and a Board that doubts its responsibility is very apt to be charged with responsibility later. . . . I think we have got the power; to me it is almost as clear as though it were there" (ibid., 694).

Miller found no support for his interpretation among either the governors or his Board colleagues. The governors, on their side, did not question the Board's supervisory role or its power to replace the Committee on Centralized Purchases and Sales with the OMIC. Hamlin proposed that the offending paragraphs claiming general authority be stricken. With that change, the Board and the banks reached agreement. On April 7 the Board approved an amended version of Miller's resolution that omitted the offending language. The Board also issued a statement of objectives for open

20. Undersecretary Gilbert was present at the meeting. He did not participate in the heated exchanges, confining his remarks to urging additional liquidation first of certificates and then of notes (House Committee on Banking and Currency 1929, 741).

market policy. Open market investments were to be "governed with primary regard to the accommodation of commerce and business, and to the effect of such purchases or sales on the general credit situation." Thus the new procedure was blended with the old and brought under the congressional mandate. The banks had thwarted the Board's attempt to control policy operations, but the issue would return.

The compromise did not satisfy either side. Before the first meeting of the OMIC on April 13 at Philadelphia, Miller proposed that Vice Governor Platt tell the governors they must sell all their government securities before the Board would approve an increase in discount rates. Strong was annoyed repeatedly by the Board's failure to endorse OMIC decisions and by the frequent delays and changes in the decisions reached by the committee. Miller continued to press for more control. As chairman of the Board's Committee on Discounts and Open Market Operations, Miller was well placed to interpose his views of proper actions. Further, he tried unsuccessfully to reduce the committee's power. Early in 1925 he proposed that the Board outlaw repurchase agreements. In 1928 he again asked the Board's counsel to review the Board's authority over open market operations. The resulting memo left no doubt that the Board lacked the power Miller sought. The memo also made it clear that the open market agreement was voluntary—that any bank could withdraw if it chose to do so:

> The Board, under this Section [14(b)], is given the power to regulate, and probably it could prescribe, maximum and minimum amounts which could be sold during any one period, but it could not forbid sales or purchases absolutely, for the power to regulate is not the power to destroy. . . .
>
> The formation of the Open Market Investment Committee grew out of a voluntary agreement entered into between the Federal Reserve Board and the Federal Reserve banks. Under this agreement, the individual authority and discretion of each Federal Reserve bank to buy and sell Government securities is taken away, and the power is given to the Open Market Investment Committee and the Federal Reserve Board. I believe a Federal Reserve bank could withdraw from this agreement at any time. . . .
>
> In my opinion, the Federal Reserve Board has no legal right under the Federal Reserve Act to create such a Committee, or to take over to itself such functions, except by voluntary agreement. (Board of Governors File, box 1435, April 25, 1928)

What Changed?

The decision to create an open market committee did not introduce a new policy instrument. Open market operations had been used for more than a century, and it was widely believed that purchases and sales could be used to change interest rates and expand credit and money.[21]

The principal changes were in interpretation or beliefs about the effect of open market purchases and sales, the role of the reserve banks, and their influence on national, as opposed to regional, financial conditions. Strong's view that the principal effect of open market operations fell on member bank borrowing, not interest rates or credit, became the foundation of a revised view of how monetary operations worked. The new view changed the role of the reserve banks in two ways. Burgess (1964, 220) reports the two conclusions drawn at the time:

> First, as fast as the Reserve banks bought government securities in the market, member banks paid off more of their borrowings; and, as a result, earning assets and earnings of the Reserve bank remained unchanged. Second, they [the reserve banks] discovered that the country's pool of credit is all one pool and money flows like water throughout the country. . . . These funds coming into the hands of banks enabled them to pay off their borrowings and feel able to lend more freely.

Burgess (1964) recognized that the new policy view depended on the large gold reserve. This allowed policymakers to ignore any gold movements induced by purchases or sales. Reserve banks did not have to wait for gold movements or for member banks to borrow or repay; they could take an active role, forcing borrowing or encouraging repayment by reduc-

21. In September 1921 a private citizen, Albert Russell, wrote to Governor Harding urging action to stop the deflation. Russell wanted the Board to authorize purchases of bills, acceptances, and government securities to expand credit, lower interest rates, and reduce unemployment. Russell also wanted to let New York buy securities in districts with higher rates to bring rates toward equality in the various districts. Harding's reply did not disagree but claimed that the Board lacked authority. The "Board does not have the power to compel a Federal Reserve bank to make any investment which its own directors may deem inadvisable." Harding urged Russell to write to the reserve banks, "particularly the Federal Reserve Bank of Chicago," but he asked that the letter not mention Harding's reply. Russell wrote to both McDougal and Strong (and perhaps to others). The letters urged that "the Federal Reserve Banks force lower commercial rates by increasing on their own initiative the reserve funds of commercial banks." The letter went on to argue that there would be a multiple expansion of money and credit. McDougal replied that he could not comment because "I prefer not to be quoted" (Board of Governors File, box 1433, September 26 and 28, October 1 and 6, 1921). Strong replied that purchases would not lower interest rates or expand credit "but would probably result in the immediate repayment of borrowings for a like amount by the member banks." Strong added: "I agree that ultimately in more normal times . . . the operations of the Reserve banks will be principally through open-market purchases rather than discounting for member banks" (Chandler 1958, 207–8). Chandler criticizes this passage for its lack of understanding and comments on the change that occurred in Strong's thinking in the next two years (by 1923). In fact, the passage shows that Strong had already formed the main new idea he held in the 1920s—that open market operations drove banks to borrow or repay discounts.

ing or increasing bank reserves. Further, discount rates now had at best a secondary role of supporting open market policy. The System could curtail borrowing without raising rates to levels that brought political and public criticism.

The new view, developed in New York, was based partly on observation of the effects of open market purchases in 1921–22 and partly on empirical studies. At the time, Burgess summarized the empirical findings about interest rates from 1831 to 1922 as showing that the System's main effect on rates would be less seasonal variation. He reported that

> (1) there is no long-term effect of Federal Reserve operations on interest rates; in the long-run rates depend on the productivity of capital;
>
> (2) changes in the demand for and supply of money cause fluctuations around the long-term rate;
>
> (3) the Federal Reserve is one factor reducing interest rate variability; other factors include reduced speculation on natural resources, other improvements in money market organization, and increased wealth and saving;
>
> (4) a main effect of the Federal Reserve was a change in the seasonal; rates were lower in October to December, and higher in April to July, after 1914. (Board of Governors File, box 1240, December 1923)

As was customary at the time, and long after, Burgess did not distinguish between real and nominal interest rates.

The Board's Tenth Annual Report

Studies of policy actions and development of statistical series by the Board's staff, led by Walter Stewart, complemented the findings at New York. Stewart's work formed the basis for the most important policy statement of the period—the Board's tenth annual report—offering substitutes for the gold reserve ratio as a guide to Federal Reserve policy (Board of Governors of the Federal Reserve System, *Annual Report*, 1923, 29–39).

The report, written mainly by Stewart with Miller's support, blends the old and the new policy views by joining the real bills doctrine underlying the Federal Reserve Act with the more activist policy of responding to current and anticipated changes in the credit market.[22] Instead of waiting for member banks to borrow or repay, the reserve banks could influence the supply of real bills. Instead of a portfolio consisting of real bills and gold,

---

22. "The discussion had moved away from the concept of the Reserve system as a mechanism responding semiautomatically to the demands made upon it to that of an organization responsible for taking the initiative" (Burgess 1964, 222).

the reserve banks would now choose to hold government securities as part of their portfolios.[23]

The report offered two "tests" of policy, qualitative and quantitative. The qualitative test, as before, was whether credit was used for productive purposes. The new quantitative test replaced the gold reserve ratio with measures showing how credit changed relative to production. The report argued that the qualitative test alone could not be sufficient. Credit is fungible. A bank could offer real bills while financing speculative activities. Or a bank could borrow on government securities to finance production.

Both tests required judgment. The assets used to support bank borrowing need have no relation to the marginal extension of credit. Judgments about quantity could be made only by looking at many indications of business conditions, including indexes of production and employment.

The report rejected both the gold reserve ratio and the price level as the principal quantitative guides. The gold reserve ratio had the benefit of tradition and wide acceptance, but its usefulness depended on the reestablishment of the international gold standard. In response to critics who urged the Federal Reserve to adopt price level stability as its main objective, the report argued that there are many causes of price level changes. Several of the causes are independent of "the credit system," so a central bank that tried to control the price level would fail. The quantity theory of money was brushed aside: "The interrelationship of prices and credit is too complex to admit of any simple statement." The discussion of the price level ended with the following: "Credit is an intensely human institution and as such reflects the moods and impulses of the community—its hopes, it fears, its expectations" (Board of Governors of the Federal Reserve System, *Annual Report*, 1923, 32). Credit administration cannot be done by "mechanical rules." It must be done by judgment guided by the principles of the Federal Reserve Act.[24]

Some members of the Board, particularly Miller and Hamlin, did not accept the activist view of policy and the quantitative guides. They could accept the new policy as a means of getting banks to discount or repay, since that was consistent with the Federal Reserve Act and the real bills doctrine.

23. The report does not recognize, however, that making the latter change without changing the authorized backing for currency created a potential mismatch between assets and liabilities. If government securities became a relatively large part of the asset portfolio, there would be fewer real bills to back currency and bank reserves. The Glass-Steagall Act removed the problem temporarily in 1932. Permanent authority waited until 1945.

24. These statements reflect the strong belief that monetary (or credit) velocity was unstable. This was the basis of the statements by Miller and others that the Federal Reserve could control credit but not the price level.

Further, to satisfy proponents of real bills the report advocated a policy of qualitative control by "direct supervision" of the use of credit by member banks, contradicting the clear statement about the fungibility of credit.

These different statements became the basis later in the decade for disputes between the Board and the reserve banks. In 1924 and 1927, Miller objected to open market purchases made not to reduce discounts but to expand money and credit. In 1929, the Board and the reserve banks quarreled over reliance on direct supervision (qualitative control) to prevent increases in stock exchange credit.[25]

Differences of Opinion

Burgess later claimed that most of the reserve banks regarded direct supervision of the use of credit as "theoretical and impractical" (1964, 222 n. 2). Clearly there was little enthusiasm for direct controls at some of the larger reserve banks, and New York was opposed. Governors of several reserve banks held to the real bills view, however, and accepted qualitative controls. They disliked Board interference in lending as a violation of their autonomy, but their views were closer to Miller's than to Strong's.

Case praised the discussion in the tenth annual report, calling it "a most excellent report and a good set of principles to follow" (Governors Conference, May 6, 1924, 240).[26] New York had applied the quantitative principles on April 30, lowering its discount rate in recognition of what appeared to be the start of a recession. At a joint conference of the Board and the Governors on May 7, Governor Daniel R. Crissinger[27] of the Board asked New York "on what theory they acted" (Joint Conference, Governors

25. Concerns about the quality of credit and real bills were common in the academic profession, the financial community, and Congress. Beckhart (1972, 214) quotes congressional testimony by leading academics who refer to "diversion of large amounts of credit into speculative enterprises which are bound to breed ultimate collapse." This view is closely related to the alleged inevitability of depressions following increases in speculative credit that the System used to absolve itself of responsibility for the Great Depression.

26. At the time, J. Herbert Case was deputy governor at New York. Later he served as chairman and Federal Reserve agent. Case substituted for Strong on the Open Market Investment Committee (OMIC) in the 1920s when Strong was absent.

27. Daniel R. Crissinger was a boyhood friend and neighbor of President Warren Harding. He served as Comptroller of the Currency, and ex officio member of the Board, from March 1921 to April 1923. On May 1 he became governor of the Board. Crissinger was a small-town lawyer who had served as president of a small bank. Secretary Mellon opposed his appointment as governor, but President Harding insisted and he was confirmed, perhaps because he came from a rural and agricultural background (Katz 1992, 62). He is generally regarded as an ineffectual manager who could not achieve agreement within the Board or control Strong and the reserve bank governors. He resigned to join a mortgage loan firm in November 1927 after the Chicago discount rate controversy discussed later in this chapter.

Conference, May 7, 1924, 1).[28] This question started a lengthy discussion of discount rate policy that gives insight into prevalent views. Some of the differences reflected in the discussion became central issues later in the decade and help to explain the failure to act during the depression.[29]

The governors had agreed at an earlier meeting that in place of a penalty discount rate, the discount rate should be held at the average of commercial paper rates and the lending rates at banks in the principal cities of the district (Governors Conference, May 6, 1924, 240). This set the level of the discount rate relative to a market rate, but it left the decision to the market, in contrast to the part of the tenth annual report that proposed activist Federal Reserve policy.

Case used this agreement to justify the New York decision. The decision was taken to align the discount rate with market rates and with the principles of the tenth annual report. Several governors, who disliked the lower discount rate, challenged the decision as an unduly activist policy out of keeping with the Federal Reserve Act. One reason for the criticism is that the lower discount rate in New York drew borrowing to New York, reducing the earnings of other reserve banks and encouraging Boston, Philadelphia, and others to lower their rates, further reducing their earnings. Governor Harding of Boston described business conditions in New England as showing "a very distinct recession," but he did not want to lower the discount rate. A reduction would not stimulate business but would probably encourage speculation. Further, the member banks did not want a reduction because they did not want to reduce their lending rates (Joint Conference, Governors Conference, May 7, 1924, 9–11). Governor Norris supported Harding's statement. Banks in the Philadelphia district also opposed a reduction in discount rates. Norris believed that any recession "should be allowed to run its course, provided it does not become too violent" (ibid., 19 and 20).

Neither Norris nor Harding gave either recognition or support to the new policy principles. McDougal also opposed activist policy. In an exchange with Miller, he argued that lowering the discount rate was "squarely against the policy that Federal Reserve banks should pursue." It would lead to an "abuse of credit [and] . . . encourage inflation." The discount rate reduction was wrong because "it is not reflected in the demands

28. This particular report of the Joint Conference was treated as confidential within the System. It was not circulated to the governors or included with the report of the meeting. The report is filed at the end of the report of the Governors Conference, but the pages are numbered independently.

29. Wicker (1965) correctly distinguishes between quantitative and qualitative guides but separates their application by time period. A closer reading suggests that some members relied on one, some on the other, throughout the period.

upon the Reserve banks." "I think we should not lead the rates down, and that is what has been done recently by one bank" (ibid., 38–40). Although they were members of the OMIC, McDougal and Norris threatened to purchase securities for their banks to increase earnings.

John U. Calkins (San Francisco) and Fancher (Cleveland) criticized New York's action also. Calkins took a standard real bills approach. The open market committee "has put money into the market when it is unduly easy and it will . . . be taking money out of the market when the market is beginning to tighten" (ibid., 19). He did not oppose Strong's purchases in principle, but the purchases had not lowered market rates. The failure was evident in New York's decision to lower rates by reducing its discount rate. The only reason for reducing the discount rate that he had heard from Case was that it could be raised later.

Stewart then reported on business conditions. Wholesale prices had fallen by 6 percent in three months, and employment by 2 percent, since the start of 1924. Other indicators also showed the beginning of a moderate to steep decline.[30] The report had no perceptible effect on the discussion. The Board and the New York bank continued to argue for lower interest rates; the other reserve bank governors continued to oppose them. Seay (Richmond) thought 4.5 percent was attractive, since banks in his district paid 5 percent for time deposits. He challenged Miller to explain why a reserve bank should try to lead rates down (ibid., 57). Roy A. Young (Minneapolis) and David C. Biggs (St. Louis) saw no reason for lower rates. Willis J. Bailey (Kansas City) put forward an argument that some of the others may have been hesitant to make—the effect on reserve bank income: "How are we going to pay dividends and salaries?" (80).

Miller and Crissinger said that rates should have been reduced in January or February. Miller made the argument for the Board, but all the Board members concurred (ibid., 80, 83–84). Leading the market to rate reduction was the right policy unless the increase in credit was for speculation. Policy actions must be symmetrical. When the Federal Reserve "undertakes to use its rates for the purpose of restricting credit, it has got to show that it is also willing to do what it can to give the public and the borrowing community the benefit of lower rates when conditions warrant it" (59). If the recession continued or deepened, Miller said, New York should reduce

---

30. Industrial production reached a peak in May 1923, then fell until August 1924. The annual rate of decline reached 18 percent in July. At the time of the meeting, the year-to-year decline was 13 percent. Balke and Gordon's GNP data show a 7 percent decline in the price level and an 8.6 percent decline in real GNP for the second quarter of 1924. The recession had started a year earlier but had been interrupted by a strong recovery early in 1924. The recovery ended, however, and the decline in the price level and real GNP resumed.

its rate to 3.5 percent: "It will be very much easier for the directors of the New York reserve bank and its officers to bring the rate up if they move from 3.5 percent than if they had stuck at 4.5 and desired to raise it from 4.5 to 5" (60–61). Miller concluded: "The Federal Reserve is on trial, and I do not want to acutely attract destructive attention to us through niggardly, parsimonious or hesitant action with respect to the discount policy" (75).

Much of this argument was political, so it was unlikely to persuade the governors who thought the Board was overly responsive to political pressures. The argument hardly spoke to the main concerns felt by most of the governors—concerns about earnings and dividends and what later became known as "elasticity pessimism," the belief that demand did not respond much to changes in interest rates. Although Miller claimed that rate reductions could have sizable effects on the amount of borrowing, many of the governors contended the opposite. This was particularly true of the governors from the agricultural regions, but the point was voiced by others, including Norris, McDougal, and Harding.[31] None of the principals except Case (New York) made any reference to, or expressed support for, the principles in the tenth annual report.

Meeting in conference without the Board, the governors discussed whether to continue centralized purchases through the OMIC and, if so, the principles that should guide the OMIC. Calkins argued that reserve bank earnings were an inappropriate guide. Earnings would be low when borrowing and interest rates had fallen. If earnings were the guide, the reserve banks would purchase and ease the money market when the market was "easy" and conversely. Policy would be countercyclical. This, he said, is "exactly the reverse of what is desired" (Governors Conference, May 1924, 17). The reserve banks were supposed to take money out of the market in recession when the market was "unduly easy" because the supply of real bills had declined (19). This policy was procyclical.

McDougal, Fancher, and others criticized earlier decisions, taken in response to Treasury pressure, requiring reserve banks to sell all government securities. McDougal wanted to purchase long-term bonds to increase earnings (ibid., 20). Case acknowledged that selling off most of the portfolio in 1923 was a mistake, but recently the Open Market Investment Committee had bought back $235 million. The purchases had not increased reserve bank credit as Calkins implied. Reserve bank credit declined as purchases were made in recession. The effect of purchases, he said, was much more on the volume of discounts than on the aggregate portfolio.

---

31. These claims that the discount rate had only modest effect were not forgotten when the reserve banks wanted to increase discount rates in 1929 and the Board opposed.

The discussion turned again to earnings. The governors discussed three options: If earnings fell below expenses plus dividends, the reserve banks could curtail check processing, currency deliveries, and other services, purchase securities, or pay dividends from their accumulated surpluses. Three governors favored curtailing services. Nine favored paying dividends from surplus. The consensus was that open market operations should be conducted independently of earnings and dividend requirements and that the OMIC should continue. The governors retained the right to purchase or sell independently of the OMIC if their directors decided to do so.

Economists' Views

The tenth annual report marks a turning point in Federal Reserve policy and, later, in the policies of other monetary authorities. Leading economists commented on the development of more activist policy and the use of open market operations to adjust bank borrowing.

The British economist Ralph Hawtrey found the new view of open market operations "highly encouraging to those who hope for enlightened management of credit with a view to the stabilization of prices" (1924, 284). He praised the report for its contribution to solving some of the practical problems of monetary control. He found the analysis flawed in two respects, however. First was the continued reliance on real bills and the qualitative test. These are "time-honored fallacies from which practical bankers seem to be quite incapable of emancipating themselves." (285) Second was the "delusion" that the United States received gold because of its balance of payments: "Apparently they have not yet learnt that they receive all this gold simply because they offer a higher price for it" (286). However, Hawtrey did not go on to say that, at the current gold price, the Federal Reserve's aims of achieving price stability and restoring the international gold standard required continued deflation abroad or changes in exchange rates.

John Maynard Keynes (1930, 2:225–21) accepted the new role for open market operations but thought that Federal Reserve officials underestimated their effectiveness (2:231). He praised the Federal Reserve for its policy from 1923 to 1928. It had shown "that currency management is feasible in conditions which are virtually independent of the movement of gold" (2:231). Although he recognized that the policy failed after 1929, he did not relate the failure to the previous policy.[32]

Charles O. Hardy (1932, 27, 273) was more representative of contempo-

---

32. One reason is that he misinterprets Federal Reserve policy in the 1920s. Keynes claimed that the policy worked because the United States public was willing to absorb "the remarkable growth in the volume of bank money." In fact, base money and M_1 rose at average rates of 2 to 3 percent a year, slightly less than output growth.

rary views. He argued that the new approach missed an important difference between discounts and open market operations. Control of discounts provided quantitative and qualitative control, whereas open market operations controlled only the quantity of credit. Like many of his contemporaries, he accepted the central idea of the real bills doctrine.

THE RIEFLER-BURGESS DOCTRINE

The tenth annual report does little more than sketch a new framework for monetary policy.[33] During the 1920s, many people contributed to filling in the details. The best of this work was contained in two remarkable books by Winfield Riefler, an economist at the Board, and W. Randolph Burgess at the New York bank (Riefler 1930; Burgess 1936). I refer to the framework they developed as the Riefler-Burgess doctrine.[34]

The central relation was the member bank borrowing function. Although the reserve banks had tried in the early years to operate an English system with a penalty rate, Riefler and Burgess discarded that approach; they explained that banks were reluctant to borrow, borrowed only if reserves were deficient, and repaid promptly.[35] To repay borrowing, banks called loans, raised lending rates, and sold government securities.[36] Discount rate policy reinforced open market policy. A rise in the discount rate lowered the level of member bank borrowing, reduced credit and money, and raised market interest rates; a reduction in discount rates lowered market rates. Thus policy actions influenced market rates by changing the level of member bank borrowing and the discount rate.

Riefler presented the reluctance view as a central element of his theory. The importance of bank indebtedness in the transmission of policy reflected the banks' inability to control borrowing and their unwillingness to remain in debt.

---

33. A complete statement of the Riefler-Burgess framework is part of Brunner and Meltzer 1964a. This section is based partly on that paper.

34. As already noted, Strong and Stewart contributed independently. Strong read and commented on an earlier edition of Burgess's book. The framework evolved to reflect major changes, notably the large increase in excess reserves in the 1930s. It remained as a guide to policy into the 1950s.

35. Riefler (1930, 21–22) compared the behavior of borrowing under the "reluctance" and "for profit" motives. Banks could have borrowed to equalize rates during the 1920s. When open market rates were above discount rates, banks would have brought them down if they borrowed for profit. This argument ignored risk elements.

36. "When the member banks find themselves continuously in debt at the Reserve banks, they take steps to pay off the indebtedness. . . . Conversely, when most member banks are out of debt at the Reserve banks, they are in a position to invest their funds; and money rates, including commercial paper rates become easier. The relationship rests largely on the unwillingness of the banks to remain in debt at the Reserve banks" (Burgess 1936, 220).

The most obvious theory is that member banks, on the whole, borrow at the reserve banks when it is profitable to do so and repay their indebtedness as soon as the operation proves costly. The cost of borrowing at the reserve banks, accordingly, is held to be the determining factor in the relation between the reserve bank operations to money rates, and the discount policy adopted by the reserve banks to be the most important factor in making reserve bank policy effective in the money markets. At the other extreme, there is the theory that member banks borrow at reserve banks only in case of necessity and endeavor to repay their borrowing as soon as possible. According to this theory the fact of borrowing in and of itself—the necessity imposed by circumstances on member banks for resorting to the resources of the reserve banks—is a more important factor in the money market than the discount rate . . . open market operations . . . contribute more directly to the effectiveness of the reserve bank credit policy than changes in discount rate. (Riefler 1930, 19–20)[37]

Chart 4.1 shows that the relation between discounts and government securities is negative in the 1920s. The bivariate relation is much less than one-to-one, however. On average, open market purchases reduce discounts by less than the amount of the purchase. A more complete analysis in appendix A allows for other relevant factors and casts doubt on the posited relationship.[38]

The discount rate has an ambiguous role in Riefler-Burgess. At times its role is modest; open market operations drive banks to borrow and repay at the prevailing rate. More often, open market operations prepare the way for discount rate changes. Strong testified in 1926 that the Federal Reserve continued to study and learn but had reached some preliminary conclusions:

If speculation arises, prices are rising, and possibly other considerations move the Reserve banks to tighten up a bit on the use of their credit, and we own a large amount of Government securities, it is a more effective program, we find by actual experience, to begin to sell our Government securities. It lays a foundation for an advance in our discount rate.

If the reverse condition appears, . . . then the purchase of securities eases the money market and permits the reduction of our discount rate. (House Committee on Banking and Currency 1926, 332–33)

37. The acceptance market differed from the market for borrowed reserves. The Federal Reserve announced a price, the discount charged on acceptances. Banks sold to the Federal Reserve, at their initiative, only if it offered a price above the going market rate.

38. The points at the upper right of chart 4.1 are for second quarter 1928 to third quarter 1929.

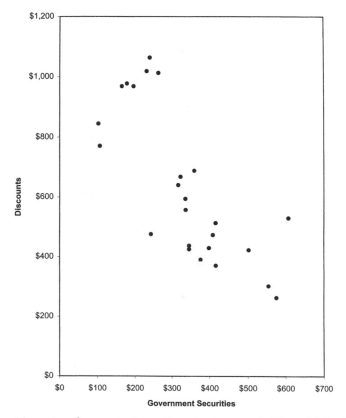

Chart 4.1 Discounts and government securities 1923.3 to 1929.3 (millions of dollars).

The Riefler-Burgess doctrine was compatible with the real bills doctrine and the Federal Reserve Act, but it permitted activist policymaking. Open market operations could be conducted so as to accommodate agriculture and commerce, as the act prescribed, but they could also be used for other purposes. However, nothing in either the Riefler-Burgess or real bills doctrine distinguished between real and nominal interest rates, a major reason for later misinterpretation of policy.

The "reluctance" view of borrowing is the weak link in the Riefler-Burgess doctrine. Banks borrowed heavily in 1920–21, when it was profitable. The Board's annual reports and statements of members during the next few years seem intended to inform banks of the "tradition" against borrowing or to impose it on them through the administration of the discount window.[39]

39. In 1922 Strong discussed borrowing in a talk at the Harvard Economics Club. He placed considerable emphasis on profitability. Banks repaid borrowing when other opportunities were less attractive: "Now, in the long run, it is my belief that the greatest influence

Being able to control borrowing without large changes in discount rates had strong appeal. If interest rates could be held in a narrow range without jeopardizing control of inflation, System policy would be effective and criticism would be muted. Until the end of the decade, discount rates stayed within a narrow range, 3.5 percent to 4.5 percent at New York.

Neither Riefler nor Burgess completed the framework to link money, credit, interest rates, and borrowing to income and the price level. Instead, they relied on the real bills notion that if productive lending expanded at about the same rate as production, prices would be stable. It was an easy, but invalid, inference to rely on member banks' borrowing or a market interest rate as the proper measure of the thrust of monetary policy. If borrowing and interest rates were low, policy was easy; if the two were high, policy was tight. By the mid-1920s, high and low borrowing were defined as member banks' borrowing above and below $500 million.

The System had adopted measures of tightness and ease that misled them at critical times. A principal problem was the failure to distinguish between an individual bank and the banking system. An open market sale removed reserves, but if banks were induced to borrow, reserve bank credit and the monetary base remained unchanged. The increase in borrowing may have induced some banks to repay, as Riefler-Burgess claimed. But unless all banks behaved that way, others borrowed at the unchanged discount rate.

During many of the cycles in Federal Reserve history, both member bank borrowing and the monetary base moved procyclically, rising relative to trend in expansions and falling relative to trend in contractions. The Federal Reserve interpreted increased (reduced) aggregate borrowing as evidence of restrictive (expansive) policy even if the monetary base and the money stock accelerated (decelerated).

Differences in regional discount rates and in the reserve position of member banks produced a market innovation. In 1921 banks with surplus reserves—reserves above current and near-term requirements—began to sell reserves to banks with deficient reserves. These sales (or loans) and purchases made better use of existing reserve balances and supplemented the correspondent banking system as a means of putting idle balances to work. The market also supplemented the discount facilities.

The new market was known as the federal funds market (Board of Governors of the Federal Reserve System 1959). Banks with surplus reserves

---

upon the member bank in adjusting its daily position is the influence of profit or loss" (Strong 1930, 181). Possibly Strong and others revised their earlier opinion. An alternative explanation is that policy changed, and the reluctance theory of borrowing reflected constraints that reserve banks imposed on borrowers. The "reluctance theory" failed later in the decade when the Board tried to reduce borrowing by exhortation.

exchanged checks drawn on their accounts at a reserve bank for checks drawn on the purchasing bank payable through the clearinghouse the following day (or later). The difference between the two checks included interest for the term of the sale. Most transactions were made in New York, and transfers occurred on the books of the New York Federal Reserve bank.

Once the banks established the market, its convenience attracted other users. Acceptance dealers, commercial paper dealers, and others settled transactions in federal funds—reserve balances at Federal Reserve banks. Brokers began to canvass regularly.

The market languished in the 1930s. Early in the decade, risk increased as bank failures rose, so far fewer banks were willing to accept the default risk. Later, gold flowed in and excess reserves accumulated. The market disappeared until after World War II (ibid., 29–30).

GOLD POLICY

Although the United States remained on the gold standard, Riefler and Burgess did not dwell on the role of gold and did not state a policy with respect to gold. The explanation may be that both authors sought to develop policy guidelines in place of the gold reserve ratio. Nevertheless, gold policy played a secondary, but important, role in the 1920s.

A contemporary reader has difficulty comprehending the strength of commitment to the gold standard by bankers, officials, and many economists. Federal Reserve officials were unanimous in their commitment to restore some form of gold standard. Strong and others took many trips abroad, motivated in part by efforts to restore fixed parities tied to gold.

Montagu Norman, governor of the Bank of England, expressed an opinion representative of the ideas of informed central bankers. Failure to restore the gold standard would mean "violent fluctuations in the exchanges, with probably progressive deterioration of the values of foreign currencies vis-a-vis the dollar; it would prove an incentive to all of those who were advancing novel ideas for nostrums and expedients other than the gold standard to sell their wares; and incentives to governments at times to undertake various types of paper money expedients and inflation" (Chandler 1958, 311).

The ruling orthodoxy of the period sharply separated governments and central banks. The decision to fix the exchange rate was typically taken by the government. Central bankers negotiated support operations among themselves, usually keeping their governments informed about their progress. Continuing prewar practice, Strong was the principal negotiator of these agreements for the United States.

It is convenient to treat gold policy in the 1920 as three separate topics: the monetary response to changes in gold; circulation of gold and gold certificates; and actions to foster or sustain the gold standard. The last of these raises the issue of international cooperation, about which much has been written (Nurkse 1944; Clarke 1967; Eichengreen 1992).

Gold and Money

The Federal Reserve has been both criticized and praised for not following gold standard rules during the 1920s (Brown 1940; Keynes 1930). To contemporary observers at the Federal Reserve, the rules did not apply in the circumstances of the period. These officials believed that the gold reserve ratio was not an adequate policy indicator as long as no international gold standard existed. New procedures had to be found while they waited for, and worked toward, convertibility of the principal European currencies into gold and elimination of embargoes and other impediments to gold flows.

The problem, as seen in the early 1920s, was that the United States gold stock had increased much more than expected. By the end of 1921, the System's gold reserve ratio reached 72 percent; it continued to rise in 1922, and by midyear it had nearly doubled from its low point in 1920. The Federal Reserve did not want to monetize the entire increase, as required under gold standard rules, both from fear of a new inflation and from concern about subsequent deflation if gold should leave when foreign governments restored an international gold standard. The Federal Reserve had used the fall in the gold reserve ratio as a main reason for raising interest rates in 1920. Many in Congress and the public interpreted the rising gold ratio as a signal that the Federal Reserve banks should lower interest rates in 1922.

At the beginning of 1923, discount rates at New York, Boston, and San Francisco were 4 percent, 0.5 percent below the rates at other banks. Concerns about inflation prompted these banks to consider raising the discount rate, as they subsequently did, despite their gold reserves. Concerns about public interpretations of the gold reserve ratio prompted the Governors Conference to approve a resolution urging the Board to issue a statement about the diminished importance of the gold reserve ratio (Governors Conference, March 28, 1923, 379). Case (New York) expressed the dominant view: "The average person cannot understand why we should be thinking of high rates with that reserve ratio" (ibid., 768).[40]

Contemporary observers report a difference in the Federal Reserve's response to gold movements before and after 1925 (Hardy 1932, 148). Table

---

40. Once again, Adolph Miller had a different view. He asked: "Suppose it [gold] doesn't presently flow back?" And he warned that it was risky "to predicate a policy upon a possibility that may or may not materialize" (Governors Conference, March 28, 1923, 769). The Board did not follow the governors' recommendation. It did little to change opinion about the gold reserve ratio. Chandler (1958, 191) reports that this irritated Strong and other governors,

Table 4.1   Changes in Gold, Base, and Discounts, 1923–29 (millions of dollars)

PERIOD	GOLD	MONETARY BASE	DISCOUNTS	GOVERNMENT SECURITIES
1923.1–1925.2	+393	+406	–182	–10
1925.2–1929.3	0	+145	+624	–198

Source: Board of Governors of the Federal Reserve System 1943.
Note: Quarterly dates.

4.1 divides the period 1923–29 at the second quarter of 1925, the date at which Britain returned to the gold standard. These data support Hardy; the monetary base more fully reflected the gold flow in the earlier period, before the Europeans returned to the standard. Chart 4.2 gives more detail, using quarterly data for the period.[41]

If the Federal Reserve had followed strict gold standard rules, gold movements would be fully reflected as changes in the base, and changes in the base would reflect only changes in gold. All points in chart 4.2 would lie on a straight line through the origin with a unit slope. We know that the Federal Reserve allowed discounts and open market operations to change the base. The points in the upper left quadrant suggest that large gold inflows were more than offset at times; the lower right quadrant shows that the base could rise while gold flowed out, contrary to gold standard rules. Nevertheless, there is a weak but clear positive relation between current quarterly gold movements and current quarterly changes in the base for the period as a whole. The Federal Reserve did not follow gold standard rules, but it did not ignore them entirely in the short run.

Together the data in chart 4.2 and table 4.1 suggest that gold flows often affected the base on arrival. In this sense the Federal Reserve "followed the rules" to a degree, most likely as a result of fixing the interest rate on discounts and acceptances and allowing reserves to respond to unanticipated gold flows. After Britain returned to the gold standard, the long-term change in the base was independent of gold flows.[42]

---

who faced this issue when talking to bankers, businessmen, and farmers. It seems likely, however, that the Board produced the policy statement in the tenth annual report partly in response to these demands. Friedman and Schwartz (1963, 283) point out the Federal Reserve continued to cite the possible withdrawal of gold as a reason for sterilization after the gold standard was restored, when the argument was no longer valid.

41. Appendix 4B describes the monetary base and its relation to Federal Reserve policy operations. Appendix 4A analyzes the statistical relation between gold and the base.

42. Short-term and lagged responses are shown in appendix 4B. The long-term relation is positive but small. Criticism of gold sterilization was common abroad. Criticism of the United States and France is a main point of the League of Nations (1932) retrospective study of the interwar gold exchange standard. On the other hand, Keynes (1930, 2:258) praised the Federal Reserve for showing that "currency management is feasible in conditions which are virtually independent of the movements of gold."

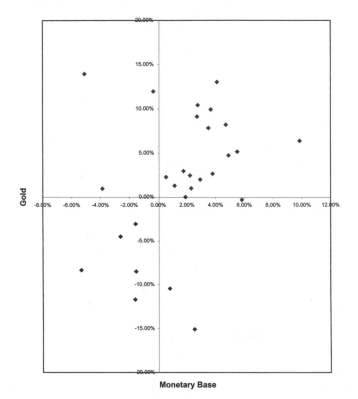

Chart 4.2 Rates of change, gold and monetary base 1923–29.

Gold as Currency

One aim of the Federal Reserve Act was to pool reserves by centralizing gold holdings in the reserve banks. In its first decade, the System worked to achieve this objective by replacing gold certificates with Federal Reserve notes.

Policy changed in the 1920s. Unwilling to allow prices to rise and concerned about the political pressures to expand as a consequence of a high reserve ratio, the governors looked for ways to reduce the reserve ratio without inflating. Early in 1922 Secretary Mellon proposed to substitute gold certificates for Federal Reserve notes. Gold certificates had 100 percent gold backing instead of the 40 percent behind Federal Reserve notes, so they reduced the gold reserve but had no effect on money or inflation.

The Federal Reserve was at first reluctant to change its policy of centralizing the gold reserve. Miller proposed instead raising the 40 percent gold reserve behind currency issues. This proposal, like Mellon's, seemed too transparent to defuse political pressure. A second alternative kept the gold in Europe on "earmark" and, by ruling of the Board, excluded from reported gold reserves. At first the amount earmarked was relatively small, $20 million or less. Earmarked gold rose to $50 million in 1924–25 and again in the first half of 1926. The maximum during the decade was $200 million, about 5 percent of the monetary gold stock.

Despite Mellon's request, in May 1922 the Governors Conference approved a proposal that made issuing gold certificates to the public a last resort. Gold inflows continued. In August, New York began issuing gold certificates and sent a letter to the Board asking all reserve banks to do the same. The other large bank, Chicago, did not accept the policy until February 1924, after repeated requests from Undersecretary Gilbert at the 1923 Governors Conference and by letters. The two banks had issued over $700 million in certificates by the end of 1924. The gold flow then reversed, so after discussion with the Treasury, Strong changed policy. The new policy kept total gold certificates equal to $1 billion, the amount outstanding in 1925. This policy remained in effect until mid-1928 (Governors Conference, March 1926, 126–29).[43]

In testimony before the Royal Commission on Indian Currency and Finance in 1926, Strong gave four reasons for changing gold certificate policy in 1922. First, the amount of gold certificates in circulation had fallen to $170 million; continued reduction might give gold certificates a scarcity value relative to Federal Reserve notes. Second, although the economy was recovering from the 1920–21 recession, "there was prevalent, especially in the agricultural sections, a feeling that possibly it would be a good thing for the country to have some expansion of credit" (Strong 1930, 301). Third, to restore the working of the gold standard, a country like the United States could fix the amount of gold in domestic circulation and permit inflows and outflows to be reflected in the monetary base. Fourth, he feared that the high reserve ratio would become the norm, so that a reduction from 85 percent to 65 percent would be considered serious (301–2).

Strong gave greatest weight to his third reason, letting the monetary base respond to gold movements, although the Federal Reserve did not follow this policy subsequently. His reasoning probably reflects the period in which he spoke, after Britain had returned to gold. Initially, the princi-

---

43. The $1 billion was about equal to the value of gold certificates in circulation at the start of the Federal Reserve System. The Treasury also tried to increase the circulation of gold coins, but this policy was not successful, suggesting that the reserve banks were now sufficiently established in the public's mind as the main source of money that the public was unwilling to bear the costs of using gold coins.

pal concern was the pressure from agricultural representatives to expand credit.[44]

The net new issues of gold certificates, about $800 million from 1922 to 1926, equaled about 20 percent of the gold reserve. Together, the policies of earmarking gold and issuing certificates reduced the gold reserve by about 25 percent at peak issuance.

Restoring the Gold Standard

The Federal Reserve consistently favored restoration of the gold standard in the principal countries, and it worked toward that end as long as it was consistent with domestic policy.[45] At the end of the war, this meant that foreign governments had to either deflate or devalue prewar parities. Britain chose deflation; France, Germany (and others) chose devaluation.

Wholesale prices in Britain had increased 115 percent from the beginning of the war (August 1914) to March 1919, when the pound was allowed to float. In the following year, the pound declined 30 percent against the dollar. Devaluation and the effect of removing wartime price controls contributed an additional 40 percent price increase. From this inauspicious starting point, the Bank of England began to reestablish the prewar parity at $4.86 per pound by deflating rapidly. By the end of 1922 the Sauerbeck index (1867–77 = 100) had fallen almost 50 percent, from 251 to 131. At the 1922 level, the index was lower than in 1925, when Britain restored convertibility. The dollar exchange rate reached $4.61 per pound.

Achieving the remaining 5 percent appreciation took more than two additional years. Political and economic tension over reparations, including occupation of the Ruhr by French and Belgian troops, contributed to the fluctuation in the European exchange rates against the dollar during this period. The Dawes Plan of 1924 rescheduled reparations payments and provided loans to Germany that removed a major source of instability, at least for a time, by ensuring prompt payment of reparations and wartime debts.[46]

44. McDougal had a very different reason for issuing gold certificates—they reduced expenses by the reserve banks for issuing and replacing currency. In 1928 he proposed replacing all Federal Reserve notes with gold certificates to save $700,000. All other governors were opposed (Governors Conference, April 1928, 199–213).

45. The 1924 annual report relates the opinion of the Federal Advisory Council that it was "imperative" that England and Germany return to the gold standard. At the time, French restoration seemed unlikely.

46. The Dawes Plan removed reparations as a source of current instability but did not resolve either the reparations problem or the transfer problem. The latter problem arose because German reparations payments required a surplus on the German current account. Hence other countries collectively had to be in deficit relative to Germany. The Dawes Plan did not settle the total reparations to be paid by Germany. Instead, the plan required Germany to pay reparations of £50 million, rising to £125 million in the next five years. To stabilize the

Germany's return to the gold standard, or more accurately, the gold exchange standard, put pressure on Britain.[47] Further, the British embargo on gold exports expired at the end of 1925. Aided by lower rates in the United States and speculation that the embargo would not be renewed, the pound rose toward its prewar parity (Howson 1975). On April 28 Winston Churchill, chancellor of the Exchequer, announced that Britain would not extend the embargo. This decision made the pound convertible de facto. Two weeks later Parliament passed the Gold Standard Act of 1925, restoring the prewar parity de jure.[48]

To achieve and maintain the $4.86 parity, the Federal Reserve offered the Bank of England a two-year standby loan of $200 million. On two occasions, 1924 and 1927, to help Britain it encouraged gold exports from the United States by lowering interest rates.[49]

The financial press and Congress criticized the loan as beyond the authority of the New York Federal Reserve bank.[50] Strong responded at length

----

German mark against gold, loans of $190 million were offered to support the currency. The plan did not restrict import tariffs by the receiving countries or assess Germany's ability to pay. However, by limiting and rescheduling German payments and stabilizing the mark, the plan removed a major source of European instability. The Dawes Plan achieved its reparations targets because stabilization encouraged foreign loans to Germany, principally from the United States, but also from Britain. Germany received more loans than the amount of its reparations payments under the Dawes Plan, so foreigners financed the reparations payments that Germany made. According to Hjalmar Schacht (1955, 211), governor of the Reichsbank between 1924 and 1932, Germany paid only $10 billion to $12 billion of the $120 billion promised. Germany never achieved a current account surplus; all the payments were made from the proceeds of $20 billion in loans that foreigners "pressed upon her to such an extent that in 1931 it transpired she could no longer meet even the interest on them" (211). The result was that foreign governments received the $10 billion to $12 billion, and the lenders lost their money.

47. To conserve limited gold stocks (and earn interest on reserve balances) countries other than the United States, Britain, and later France held part or all of their reserves in dollar or pound securities, exchangeable for gold. These dollar or pound claims could be exchanged for gold reserves on demand as long as the United States and Britain maintained convertibility; hence the name gold exchange standard.

48. Norman was the main proponent; Churchill was a reluctant follower of his advice and the advice of Otto Niemeyer in the Treasury. Churchill, influenced by Keynes, was concerned about the effect on industry and employment.

49. Strong negotiated the loan to the Bank of England on behalf of the Federal Reserve, not the United States government. This was a standard feature of international monetary policy at the time; central bankers negotiated with other central bankers. Typically they informed their governments and kept them apprised of foreign developments and negotiations. Governments borrowed in the market using investment bankers as agents. Britain used J. P. Morgan.

50. Parker Willis, former secretary of the Board and editor of the *Commercial and Financial Chronicle,* was a main critic. He had worked for Carter Glass at the House Banking Committee in writing the act, so his criticisms were taken up by members of Congress. Willis favored Britain's return to the gold standard and recognized that section 14 authorized

in congressional hearings (House Committee on Banking and Currency 1926). The loan was secured by British Treasury obligations, payable in dollars. Governor Crissinger of the Federal Reserve Board had been present when it was discussed, and he had asked for and received approval from all members of the Board. The Open Market Investment Committee approved the loan unanimously, with Secretary Mellon present: "Mr. Mellon asked specifically if there were any objections to the arrangement . . . and the making of the commitment, and no objection being made, he stated it was understood that I was to go ahead" (Chandler 1958, 315).[51]

International Cooperation

As part of its policy to help countries return to the gold standard, the Federal Reserve lowered discount rates in August 1924. The United States was in recession, so the System had a domestic as well as an international reason for acting. Wicker (1966, 77) claimed that "the desire of the Federal Reserve Bank of New York to establish a rate spread between New York and London to encourage capital outflows and reduce gold imports was indeed the chief determinant of policy. It was not, however, the only one."[52] Chandler (1958, 241) was at the opposite pole, claiming that the policy was mainly an anticyclical policy that also was expected to encourage a capital outflow. This was also the view of Hardy (1932, 108), who found "a great deal of exaggeration" about the attention given to international considerations in setting Federal Reserve policy. Hardy recognized that Strong held

---

transactions with foreign banks. He criticized the size of the loan and the use of section 14 to aid a foreign government. Willis interpreted the act narrowly. He wanted a penalty discount rate, and he opposed the issuance of gold certificates as a violation of the principle that the act intended to centralize gold holdings. Currency should be backed by gold and commercial paper only, and the Federal Reserve should limit its activity to discounting real bills. Similar views were held, perhaps not independently, by Senator Carter Glass.

51. The loan was fuel for Strong's critics, who feared that Strong acted like the head of a central bank instead of being one member of a system of semiautonomous banks. After the loan commitment was announced, Miller changed his opinion about the legal authority for the loan. He is recorded as "not voting" when the Board approved a resolution confirming the transaction (Board Minutes, May 19, 1925). The credit expired after two years and was never drawn upon. Miller was a strong supporter of the gold standard and a partisan of the policy of restoring the standard. He described restoration this way: "The fantastic vagaries which a certain school of economics on both sides of the Atlantic embraced in their efforts to find a substitute for the gold standard have given way before the world's resolution to tie its fate in monetary matters . . . to something more objective and less capricious than fallible human discretion" (Miller 1925b, 4).

52. Wicker (1966, 90) based much of his argument on the decline in New York member bank borrowing after February or March 1924. Total system borrowing remained above $400 million until June and did not fall below $300 million until August. Open market purchases began in March and ended in November. These data are consistent with the Riefler-Burgess view that high borrowing in recession called for open market purchases.

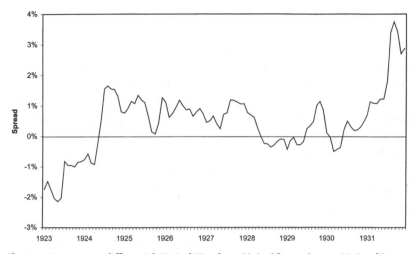

Chart 4.3 Interest rate differential, United Kingdom–United States. Source: National Bureau of Economic Research. Three-month banker's bills, London, minus banker's acceptances, New York, monthly.

such views, and stated them often, but he noted correctly that there was little evidence that other members of the OMIC shared them. They agreed on the desirability of reestablishing the gold standard but were more skeptical about using policy actions to help the British. Friedman and Schwartz (1963, 269) agreed with Hardy.

Chart 4.3 leaves no doubt that the spread between short-term rates in London and New York turned sharply in favor of capital flows to London during the summer and fall of 1924. The spread again moved in favor of Britain in the summer of 1927, the second occasion that some observers cite as evidence that international considerations had an important influence on United States policy. The covered interest parity shows the same general pattern, though the changes are smaller (Clarke 1967, 129). The difficult problem for an international explanation of policy action is that the spread reversed early in 1925, just as Britain was about to restore the gold standard. The reason for the reversal was a rise in the discount rate in New York on February 27, two months before the British decision. The reversal came for domestic reasons. The trough of the recession had occurred the previous July. By early 1925, recovery and expansion were well under way and the price level was rising. Despite the emphasis Strong gave to capital movements and restoration of the gold standard, he did not hesitate to raise the New York discount rate. This action required Norman to raise rates in London by 1 percent in early March to keep the spread in favor of London. Strong was fully aware that the British decision on gold was imminent; he was negotiating the standby credit at the time.

With hindsight, Strong told Congress in 1926 that policy in the summer of 1924 might have been too expansive for too long: "I think myself, if it were to be done over again, we might have stopped a month earlier or even sixty days earlier. We might have bought $50 million or even $100 million less, but there is no mathematical formula that will tell you where to stop or to begin" (House Committee on Banking and Currency 1926, 336). In a memo to his files written in December 1924, he defended the policy as a response to the recession in business starting in the fall of 1923 and problems in the farming and cattle industries. These "became perilously near a national disaster, and feeling became so strong throughout the West that all sorts of radical proposals for legislation and other government relief were being urged" (quoted in Chandler 1958, 242). The memo mentioned international considerations as a third reason for open market purchases "when [domestic] prices were falling generally and when the danger of a disorganizing price advance in commodities was at a minimum and remote" (243).

What remains of the role of international cooperation as a reason for easing policy in 1924? In his testimony to Congress, and in his conversations with Norman about the stabilization credit, Strong always insisted that international cooperation could not run counter to domestic policy considerations.[53] Control of domestic inflation had priority for both political and economic reasons. Strong and others understood that a 10 percent United States price increase would make restoring the international gold standard easier, particularly for Britain. The Federal Reserve might have defended such action by appeal to gold standard rules or to the gold reserve ratio. Instead, Strong made price stability a more important goal and sought to avoid a repetition of the damaging 1920–21 inflation cycle.

Again in the summer of 1927, international cooperation played a role during a recession and at a time of falling prices. The Federal Reserve made larger than seasonal open market purchases during the fall, and all reserve banks reduced discount rates by 0.5 percent, to 3.5 percent, in August and September.[54] Once again, the gold inflow reversed after the policy change.

---

53. One of many examples of Strong's view of limited international cooperation is in a letter to Norman in March 1921: "I have always taken the position that both you and we had three possible courses in our relations with each other. One was to deal wholly independently with our respective problems . . . in other words to ignore each other; another might be to pursue a wholly selfish policy . . . ; and the third might be to adopt a policy of complete understanding, and exchange of information and views, and to cooperate where our respective interests made it possible" (Chandler 1958, 247).

54. Chicago at first refused to reduce its rate. The Board ordered the reduction. The incident is discussed more fully below.

The 1927 reduction in discount rates was part of an agreement between Strong, Norman, Governor Hjalmar Schacht of the Reichsbank, and Deputy Governor Charles Rist, acting for Governor Émile Moreau of the Bank of France, made at a secret meeting in New York held in July.[55] Capital flows to Germany, fiscal reform and stabilization in France in the summer of 1926, the aftermath of the 1926 British general strike (implying that further deflation was unlikely), and continued gold flows to the United States weakened the British position. French interest rates were considerably above rates in Germany, Britain, or the United States, adding to the British problem of attracting short-term balances from abroad. Between January 1926 and February 1927, the Reichsbank reduced its discount rate in steps from 9 percent to 5 percent to slow its capital inflow (Board of Governors of the Federal Reserve System 1943, 656). The reductions soon produced a short-term capital outflow and a fall in the Reichsbank's gold reserve that threatened its gold parity. Higher German rates, widely expected, implied increased short-term capital flows from Britain to Germany (Clarke 1967, 114). By the end of 1927, the German discount rate was back to 7 percent.

In May the Bank of France began to sell pounds against gold, withdrawing gold from the Bank of England and weakening the British position. Both central banks wanted the capital flow to slow or stop, Moreau because he resisted both appreciation of the franc and inflation, Norman because a large loss of reserves would force Britain to raise interest rates or suspend gold convertibility. At a meeting in late May at the Bank of France, Moreau told Norman that France would stop exchanging pounds for gold if Britain increased its discount rate. Norman responded that an increase was difficult given the weak state of the British economy. He told Moreau that the French capital inflow would not be solved by higher rates abroad. Moreau's notes of the meeting record Norman's comments:

> Is it surprising that . . . you have an influx of capital! . . . Never before have such favorable conditions existed. 6½% for life with, in addition, the hope of a premium on the revalorization of the currency which may be considerable! In these circumstances, it is a hopeless task to check the influx of foreign exchange whatever you do. . . .
>
> If you buy gold in order to cut short credits for speculation, people will say: "The franc has more gold behind it, it is therefore worth more." If you

---

55. The meeting had been planned before the crisis began in May. Norman had wanted a meeting of the principal banks for a long time. Strong had been hesitant but changed his mind. The location of the meeting, New York, shows the shift in power toward the United States.

abolish the law on the export of capital, many Frenchmen will conclude that there is no longer any risk in repatriating and they will bring their money back. . . .

At all costs reduce the price of money. (Moreau 1954, as quoted in Clay 1957, 231)[56]

Norman hoped to end speculation that the franc would appreciate by having Moreau announce that France would maintain its exchange rate. Instead, the Bank of France lowered its official discount rate to 5 percent. By late summer, open market rates had fallen to 2 percent (Board of Governors of the Federal Reserve System 1943, 656). Norman argued that any British rate increase must come later, after the British economy improved. He feared riots if he raised interest rates at once, but he promised to raise the discount rate a full 1 percent if conditions in industry improved (Clay 1957, 231).

The central bankers' meeting in New York began on July 2 and continued through the week. To maintain secrecy about decisions, the group met at the summer home of Ogden Mills, undersecretary of the treasury.[57] It did not keep minutes, and members of the Board were not informed about the agreements.[58] After the meeting, on July 9, the central bankers met with the Board and Treasury officials in Washington but did not discuss details of the agreement.

Strong did not make notes of the New York meeting. Our information

56. Moreau published the account in the late 1930s; 6.5 percent was the French long-term interest rate at the time of the Paris meeting.

57. Norman and Schacht traveled to the United States incognito, but their arrival in New York was well known and the subject of much speculation. Mrs. Ogden Mills describes Norman at the meeting. Despite warm July weather, Norman dressed in a large velvet-collared cloak and sat in a fan-back chair placed at the end of the room (CHFRS, March 1, 1954). The Committee on the History of the Federal Reserve, organized at the Brookings Institution in the mid-1950s under the direction of Allan Sproul, interviewed several participants in Federal Reserve policymaking and administration. The unpublished notes are at the Brookings Institution. The principal publication from the project is Chandler's book on Strong. At the time, Sproul was president of the Federal Reserve Bank of New York.

58. After these meetings, the Open Market Investment Committee met with Norman. Governor Crissinger represented the Federal Reserve Board, but no other members were invited. Wicker (1966, 111), relying on Hamlin's diary, reports that their exclusion irritated members of the Board and added to their animosity toward Strong. We know most about Miller's irritation because he testified at length about the 1927 meetings and his own meeting with Schacht before the luncheon. He described the luncheon at the Board as a "social" event (House Committee on Banking and Currency 1928, 216–220). On June 15, in advance of the meeting but after it was scheduled, the Board reviewed the authority of reserve banks to conduct foreign business and the Board's supervisory role. The secretary was instructed to open and read the sealed agreement with the Bank of England, signed in December 1916. The legal opinion of the Board's counsel was that the act authorized the reserve banks to enter into such agreements and to lend abroad.

comes from Moreau (1954, 367–72) and Clay (1957, 237). The conference considered four problems: discount rates, gold movements, the pound-franc relation, and the worldwide decline in commodity prices. Strong offered to lower the discount rate to 3.5 percent, citing domestic reasons for the action. This pleased the British and Germans but not the French, who favored higher rates in Britain and Germany as a classical response to a weakening currency.[59] Strong offered to sell gold to France and Germany at a price equal to the London price and absorb the extra transport cost; Germany and France agreed to buy gold in New York under these conditions.[60]

After the meeting, the Federal Reserve banks reduced discount rates and began large-scale purchases of acceptances and government securities, and the Bank of France began forward sales of French francs and purchases of pounds in the Paris market.[61] The capital flow reversed. The pound rose to the highest value reached since the war, and gold flowed to London. By year end, cooperation—both Federal Reserve and French action—appeared to have improved the foreign exchange position of the Europeans and encouraged domestic expansion in the United States. Despite Norman's statements to Moreau in May, Britain maintained the 4.5 percent discount rate unchanged until February 1929. France lowered its discount rate to 4.5 percent in December.

Eichengreen (1992, 213) regards this episode as "an admirable instance of international cooperation." There is ample evidence in the minutes that international considerations influenced the decisions as to timing and magnitude of the actions and the uniform reduction in discount rates at reserve banks. Although some officials justified their votes by appeals to the beneficial effects on the sale of United States crops abroad and others were influenced by falling commodity prices, the minutes report that

the most important consideration at the meeting was undoubtedly the fact that the differential between the rates in New York and the rates in London was not today sufficient to enable London, and therefore the rest of Europe, to avoid general advances in rates this autumn unless rates here were lowered, and the consequence of such high rates as would result in Europe would be unfavorable to the marketing of our export produce abroad and

59. Goldenweiser's diary reports on a 1949 letter from Rist that claims the reduction was agreed to in a meeting between Norman and Strong by themselves. Schacht and Rist approved it after the fact. See Wicker 1966, 112.

60. In late June 1927 the London price (in dollars) was $20.64 per fine ounce, above the price in the Netherlands or Switzerland but below the $20.669 in the United States. Strong's offer lowered the price in New York and absorbed shipping costs (memorandum, Harrison to Strong, Sproul files, December 2, 1927).

61. Kindleberger (1986, 51) reports the total of these transactions as $440 million in May 1928 and almost $600 million in June 1928.

would have an adverse effect generally on world trade. (OMIC Minutes, Board of Governors File, July 27, 1927)[62]

Federal Reserve action improved the short-term problem but did nothing about the long-term problem.[63] French and British exchange rates were misaligned relative to gold, the dollar, and each other. The franc had depreciated officially by 80 percent, the pound not at all. After adjusting for price level changes, the franc was undervalued, the pound overvalued. Sooner or later, capital was bound to flow from Britain to France, the United States, and elsewhere.

Cooperation had not resolved the basic problem. Although the governors discussed falling commodity prices at the July meeting, they did not discuss a policy to stabilize price levels and exchange rates. Short-term concerns dominated a long-term solution. A choice had to be made between parity changes and price level changes. Both were ruled out politically. Neither France nor Britain was willing to adjust its exchange rate. Britain was unwilling to deflate further; France and the United States were unwilling to inflate. Temporary United States interest rate reductions, United States loans to Europe, or French decisions to buy gold in New York rather than London, as in 1927, could postpone but not prevent a long-term solution. If governments maintained the misalignment, the only issue was when financial markets would begin to force price level or parity changes.[64] The answer, we know, was September 1931, when Britain left the gold standard.

Breakdown

The Board's annual report for 1928 defended the 1924 and 1927 actions as factors "favoring the redistribution of gold [that] . . . contributed to the maintenance of the gold standard [and] . . . reduced the fluctuations of the exchanges to a range within the gold points" (Board of Governors of the Federal Reserve System, *Annual Report,* 1928, 16).[65] By emphasizing the

---

62. Goldenweiser's summary of policy from mid-1927 to 1929, based on his records but written later, repeats this argument but adds that higher rates abroad "would have endangered the maintenance of the gold standard" (Goldenweiser to Miller, Board of Governors File, box 1449, October 30, 1934).

63. The gold flow reversed quickly. In the first six months, the United States received $200 million in gold. From July 27 to December 28, 1927, it sold $193 million. Open market purchases offset the domestic effect of the gold outflow.

64. The problem was repeated in slightly different form in the 1960s with similar outcome—the breakdown of the standard.

65. Board members, governors, and leading members of Congress shifted their views in the 1930s. They blamed Strong's policy change for subsequent credit expansion, and they blamed the rise in stock prices on the credit expansion. The result, they said, was an inevitable collapse.

distribution of gold instead of the exchange rate misalignment, the Board's statement overemphasized the benefits of short-term activist policies while neglecting the long-term problem. The same mistake was repeated in the 1960s in the efforts to "save" the Bretton Woods system of fixed exchange rates without correcting the misalignment of exchange rates.

The Board was not alone. Many observers at the time saw the maldistribution of gold as the core problem, just as they were to regard the "shortage" of gold as the core problem of Bretton Woods (League of Nations 1932).[66]

The distribution of monetary gold stocks had changed from prewar values. Table 4.2 shows the principal changes for the United States, Britain, and France. Estimates for the world are imprecise, but greater precision is unlikely to change main conclusions: Britain had a larger relative share in the 1920s than in 1913; France had restored its 1913 share by 1928; the combined United States and French shares rose from 50 to 55 percent in 1929, draining gold from the rest of the world; and the most significant change during the years 1926 to 1931 was the relative and absolute increase in French gold holdings.

The French view of the period 1927 to 1929 claimed that purchases by the Bank of France "tended to establish a better balance in the world's distribution of gold" (Aftalion 1931, 8). After the de jure stabilization of the franc in June 1928, the Bank of France was no longer permitted to purchase foreign exchange. Foreigners had to pay in gold: "It was hoped, however, that foreign banks of issue, by raising their discount rates, would prevent the flight of their gold to France." Writing soon after these events, Aftalion recognized the overvaluation of the franc, but he saw the solution as coming principally from an end to British investment abroad, not a change in French policy (8–10).

Despite the gold inflow, French wholesale prices, after declining rapidly in 1926, remained unchanged between the de facto stabilization in December 1926 and March 1929. In the next eighteen months, wholesale prices fell 16 percent, a compound annual rate of 11 percent a year, somewhat faster than the decline in the United States during the same period (League of Nations 1932, 46; Aftalion 1931, 10). Stable or falling prices re-

---

66. Perhaps one reason for the emphasis on maldistribution in the 1920s is that the stock of monetary gold increased much more than commodity prices. The 1925 commodity price index for the world increased 60 percent from 1913 to 1925; the world monetary gold stock doubled. For the rest of the decade, the commodity price index fell and the monetary gold stock rose. The world's price index is the wholesale price of commodities from League of Nations (1930, 84). The stock of monetary gold is from Board of Governors of the Federal Reserve System (1943, 544).

Table 4.2   Monetary Gold Stocks and Shares, 1913–31

	MILLIONS OF DOLLARS				SHARES (%)		
YEAR END	UNITED STATES	FRANCE	BRITAIN	WORLD	UNITED STATES	FRANCE	BRITAIN
1913	1,290	679	165	4,589	28.1	14.8	3.6
1926	4,083	711	729	9,234	44.2	7.7	7.9
1927	3,977	954	737	9,593	41.4	9.9	7.7
1928	3,746	1,254	748	10,058	37.2	12.5	7.4
1929	3,900	1,633	710	10,336	38.9	16.3	7.1
1930	4,225	2,100	718	10,945	38.6	19.2	6.6
1931	4,051	2,699	588	11,325	35.7	23.8	5.2

Source: Board of Governors of the Federal Reserve System 1943, 544, 545, 551.

flected the combined effect of increased demand for francs by domestic and foreign holders after stabilization and the policy of the Bank of France.[67]

The law required the Bank of France to stop purchases of foreign exchange after June 1928. It did not require sales. Between 1928 and 1932, France reduced the share of foreign exchange in central bank reserves from 51 percent to 5 percent, an aggregate sale of more than $1 billion, 9 to 10 percent of the world gold stock. Many other countries reduced foreign exchange reserves in 1931, anticipating or following the British devaluation. France began large-scale sales of foreign exchange for gold in 1929 and continued to sell throughout the period (Nurkse 1944, app. 2, 234–35).[68]

French policy and French growth redistributed gold from the United States to France in 1928. In the next three years, France and the United States absorbed gold from the rest of the world. The redistribution toward France made the gold standard more deflationary after the French stabilization than before.

The French response to criticism denied the relevance of the quantity theory of money, linking prices to past or current changes in money and gold, and cast doubt on any effect of higher discount rates on price levels. The Bank of France kept its discount rate below the levels in other countries, and the government reduced taxes on sales of foreign securities in

67. The increased demand for francs despite falling interest rates reflected not only stabilization but the rapid growth of the French economy after 1927. Between 1927 and 1929, GDP rose 13 percent and industrial production 17 percent compared with GDP growth of 4 percent in Britain and 7 percent in the United States. French M_1 growth was 15 percent, approximately equal to growth of production (data from St. Etienne 1984).

68. Nurkse's data differ slightly from the data in table 4.2. French sales were usually made in the forward market by selling pounds forward. This policy began in August 1927, possibly reflecting an understanding at the New York meeting in July, to avoid sales in the spot market that were more easily monitored by private speculators and the Bank of England.

the French market to stimulate capital exports (Aftalion (1931, 11–13). But the bank's sales of foreign exchange dwarfed any effect of these efforts.[69]

The particular crises that ended the interwar gold standard, in the summer and fall of 1931, have been analyzed many times, for example in Eichengreen (1992). The timing of these crises depended on the patterns of lending and borrowing that helped to sustain the system in the late 1920s and the subsequent reduction in lending. In this sense, international cooperation to "rescue" currencies by larger loans from surplus countries could have kept the system viable for a longer time. Without a willingness to permit price levels and exchange rates to adjust, crises seem to be the inevitable, but costly, means of adjusting exchange rates.

Federal Reserve policy of restoring the gold standard and maintaining stable prices failed. The principal fault was not insufficient cooperation but failure to follow the rules.[70] The United States and France shared responsibility, but Britain's (and other countries') unwillingness to deflate also contributed. When Britain abandoned the gold standard on September 21, 1931, the *London Times* wrote:

> The international economic crisis has played a large part in the temporary abandonment of the gold standard. The responsibility for this belongs to those countries that have hoarded gold on an unprecedented scale. . . . Prohibitive tariffs keep out goods, and unless the creditor nations relend the credits due to them, the debtor nations must pay in gold to the extent of their resources and then default. The gold standard game can only be played according to its well-proven rules. It cannot be played on the new rules practiced since the War by France and the United States. (Quoted in Crabbe 1989, 434)

PRICE STABILITY AND POLICY RULES

Inflation and deflation in 1920–21 heightened interest in the Federal Reserve's choice of policy objectives. Some economists, influenced by Irving Fisher's work on the purchasing power of money, favored price level stability as the main goal of Federal Reserve policy. Others supported price

---

69. Like Strong, Moreau wanted to build his country's financial center at Britain's expense. One part of this policy was to shift French reserves into gold until France, like Britain and the United States, held only gold as a reserve. See Chandler 1958, 379–80. There was in addition France's desire to divide Europe into two spheres of financial influence, one British, one French. See Moreau 1954, 489. Personal relations may also have been a factor. Moreau and Norman did not have a warm or cordial relationship. There is a parallel in the 1960s when France insisted on converting dollar reserves into gold to reduce "American hegemony."

70. For a different view, stressing the absence of international cooperation, see Eichengreen 1992.

stability as an interim solution, pending the return to an international gold standard.

The severity of the inflation-deflation cycle, particularly in the heavily agricultural regions, gave popular support and created political pressure for stable prices. Stable money societies, influenced and encouraged by Fisher, campaigned actively for price stability. With the return of price stability during the 1920s, the Federal Reserve received credit for the more stable conditions; this encouraged advocates of a congressional mandate to believe that a stable price level rule was feasible.[71]

Congress held hearings on legislation setting price stability as the policy goal in 1922–23, 1926–27, and 1928. With the important exception of Benjamin Strong in 1928, all Federal Reserve officials and staff opposed the legislation, and it never became law.[72] The extensive hearings go much beyond the reasons for the Federal Reserve's opposition; Strong, Miller, and others from the Board and the reserve banks explained how monetary policy worked and the reasons for specific policy actions. The testimony showed the deep divisions and confusion within the system about how to conduct monetary policy.

In 1922–23, the Banking Committee considered House Resolution 11788, Irving Fisher's proposal for a compensated gold dollar. The resolution, offered by Congressman T. Alan Goldsborough of Maryland, would have replaced the fixed price of gold, $20.67 per fine ounce, with a fixed number of grains of gold, the number of grains to be adjusted every two months based on changes in a basket of one hundred wholesale prices. The proposal restricted the maximum adjustment at each two-month period to 1 percent. If the wholesale price index rose, the relative value of gold declined, so the number of grains of gold had to increase to keep the real purchasing power of money constant. Conversely, a decline in the price index required a reduction in the number of grains of gold in a dollar.

Fisher testified at length, explaining the proposal, the benefits of the standard, and the advantages of price stability. He lectured on the differences between nominal and real interest rates and the effect of inflation on nominal rates, a topic that does not appear in Federal Reserve discussions for the next forty or fifty years (House Committee on Banking and Currency 1922–23, 13–14).[73]

71. Berg and Jonung (1998) report on the successful efforts of the Swedish Riksbank to stabilize the price level after 1931 using a price level rule.

72. Legislation passed the House in 1932 by a vote of 289 to 60 but was defeated in the Senate, owing largely to opposition by Carter Glass. The Federal Reserve opposed the bill.

73. E. W. Kemmerer, John Bates Clark, Henry Wallace, and many others testified for the proposal.

The witnesses who criticized the proposal emphasized the uncertainty and unreliability of price index numbers. Federal Reserve officials did not testify at these hearings. At the time they had not formulated either the Riefler-Burgess doctrine or the policy statement in the tenth annual report. The hearings forced them to recognize the need for publicly stated guides or policy indicators to replace the gold reserve ratio.

Soon after the congressional hearings ended, the governors discussed a proposal by Professor Charles Bullock of Harvard that they announce the factors affecting discount rate changes. Anticipating later arguments about the importance of credibility, Bullock argued that the announcement would benefit businesses by letting them know how the discount rate would change in the near term. The statement would not be a precise rule, but it would require the System to name the factors that replaced the gold reserve ratio as an indicator of policy action.

Case, who substituted for Strong at the meeting, favored the proposal. He listed the main factors: the volume of credit relative to production, interest rates on various classes of paper, and gold movements. Most others opposed. Governor Seay (Richmond) expressed the dominant (and classic) view: "It is never the custom . . . for central banks to give out to the public their reasons for raising rates" (Governors Conference, March 1923, 46).

Nothing more was done until Congress called for hearings on stabilization policy in 1926–27 and 1928 to discuss an amendment to the Federal Reserve Act making price stability an explicit policy goal. The proposed legislation in 1926 added the words "promoting a stable price level for commodities in general" to section 14 of the act. The resolution also amended the purposes of the act by adding: "All the powers of the Federal Reserve System shall be used for promoting stability in the price level" (House Committee on Banking and Currency 1926).

The legislation was the work of Congressman James Strong, a Kansas Republican, who was influenced both by the events of 1920–21 and by Fisher's work.[74] In addition to Congressman Strong, members of the House Banking Committee included eight Democrats, five from cotton-growing states, and thirteen Republicans, about half from other heavily agricultural states. Their presence on the committee contributed to the wariness with which Federal Reserve officials considered the legislation.[75]

74. Congressman James A. Strong was not related to Governor Benjamin Strong. I will refer to the congressman as Strong (Kansas) when needed to avoid confusion. The wording of the mandate changed many times to respond to objections from Federal Reserve officials and others.

75. Cotton was by far the most important export crop at the time. In most years the value of cotton exports exceeded the combined value of the next four or five export items. The Sys-

The bill generated unanimity within the Federal Reserve on the need to avoid any "mechanical formula" for setting policy and on the inapplicability of the quantity equation as a guide to price stability. Beyond that, there was not much agreement about how policy should be conducted. Although the spokesmen for the Board and the reserve banks opposed the bill, their reasons differed in several ways.

Strong's Testimony

Governor Strong gave three main reasons for opposing the Strong bill. First, the mandate was difficult to carry out precisely because monetary velocity was unstable. The price level depended on velocity, and velocity depended on confidence or, in modern terms, anticipations (House Committee on Banking and Currency 1926, 482).[76] Second, changes in money, or credit, were one of many factors affecting the price level.[77] Third, as noted, he feared that price stability would be interpreted as the stability of individual prices, particularly agricultural prices: "Much of the discussion of prices recently has arisen from the great misfortune which the farmers of the country have suffered, which we all recognize and deplore. If the Federal Reserve Act is amended in these words, is it possible that the farmers of the country will be advised, or will be led to believe upon reading it, that a mandate has been handed to the Federal Reserve System to fix up the matter of farm prices?" (House Committee on Banking and Currency 1926, 293).

---

tem was concerned that it would be expected to stabilize the prices of individual commodities, especially cotton.

76. Strong had written many of the same objections to Professor Bullock in 1923. His first objection criticized "quantity theory extremists," by which he almost certainly meant to include Fisher (Chandler 1958, 203–5).

77. "Mr. Goldsborough: . . . You [Strong] have said that the Federal Reserve System, by its open market operations and by changes in the discount rate, would influence the supply of credit, which, of course, influences the price level. Now, that being so, what is the objection to a general direction of the Federal Reserve System to use such powers as it has for the purpose of stabilizing the general price level? That is certainly one question in which the committee is deeply interested. Governor Strong: It might be possible, Mr. Goldsborough, to frame some language as an amendment to the act . . . that would safeguard the system against misinterpretation of the intention of that declaration. . . . [I]t certainly would need to contain the limitation, or the recognition of the fact, that credit alone does not control prices. Mr. Goldsborough: Is not that generally understood? Do you not think that is generally understood? . . . Governor Strong: No. If I felt so, I would not feel as strongly as I do about this amendment, which I would fear on that account principally" (House Committee on Banking and Currency 1926, 299). Goldsborough persisted, citing evidence from farm publications. Strong responded by citing the blame heaped on Federal Reserve policy for agricultural problems in 1920–21. This was a non sequitur. The Federal Reserve had contributed to the problems, but Goldsborough did not make that point.

A member of the committee reminded Strong that the bill referred to the price level, not prices in general. Strong was not persuaded. He doubted that noneconomists would recognize the distinction (ibid., 293).

Strong used the opportunity to cite the accomplishments of the Federal Reserve System and to criticize the real bills doctrine as a guide to policy. Using charts to drive home his points, Strong pointed out that the System had eliminated seasonal swings in interest rates, reduced the spread in rates between New York and Chicago (and by inference the spread with other regions) and between different maturities of commercial paper, and lowered the amplitude of interest rate fluctuations (ibid., 426).

The real bills doctrine offered no guidance. He insisted, repeatedly, that the Federal Reserve could control the quantity of credit, not the type of credit outstanding. Asked by a congressman whether the Federal Reserve could direct the way credit was used, Strong replied: "We have no power to do that" (ibid., 260).[78]

Although Strong opposed the bill, he favored the principle that the bill represented. His testimony included several offers to help the committee redraft the bill and remove his objections, despite his conviction that the legislation was unnecessary (see, inter alia, House Committee on Banking and Currency 1926, 517–18). He told the committee that restoring the international gold standard was a better solution to the problem that concerned them: "I earnestly believe that the greatest service that the Federal Reserve System is capable of performing today in this matter, is to hasten . . . monetary reform in the countries that have suffered from the war. We can not do it until the time is ripe, and the conditions are favorable in each country" (518).[79]

---

78. In contrast to Miller's testimony (see below), Strong described the Board as solely a supervisory body. Operations were conducted "in cooperation with the Board, and subject to their review." "Policy results from the discussions and recommendations that are made by the operating officials of the banks; that would necessarily be so." Strong recognized a change in his own views: "I believe in this regional system. . . . Textbook knowledge had always led me to believe that a central bank was the proper thing. This system suits the needs and feelings of the country much better socially, politically, and in every way." Then he warned: "The danger in a regional system might be that if each Reserve bank goes its own way, the system as a system would have no policy" (House Committee on Banking and Currency 1926, 341).

79. The gold standard also removed power over the price level from central banks and governments: "When you speak of a gold standard, you are speaking of something where the limitation upon judgment is very exact and precise and the penalty for bad judgment is immediate" (House Committee on Banking and Currency 1926, 295). Like many of his contemporaries, Strong did not recognize that the gold standard did not guarantee a stable long-run price level.

Miller's Testimony

Miller's testimony differed markedly from Strong's. He emphasized accommodating the needs of commerce and preventing speculative uses of credit. He rejected the price level as a policy objective, and he used the opportunity to urge Congress to increase the authority of the Federal Reserve Board over credit decisions. Where Strong, the practical banker, looked for principles to guide policy, Miller, the trained economist, came close to denying that such principles existed.

Miller's response to the central issue before the committee used a quotation from the Board's tenth annual report: "No credit system could undertake to perform the function of regulating credit by reference to prices without failing in the endeavor" (House Committee on Banking and Currency 1926, 634). The reason he gave was that the price index records an "accomplished fact." Credit administration could be based only on judgment. He quoted from the tenth annual report on the role of judgment and the importance of judging each set of circumstances separately:

> The Chairman: You [the Federal Reserve] have not, I understand from what you have just said, a definite plan on which you work in dealing with the question of stabilization?
> Doctor Miller: We have nothing with reference to stabilization of prices as such.
> The Chairman: You deal with the situation as the conditions are presented to you?
> Doctor Miller: We deal with the credit situation.
> The Chairman: And there is a good bit of human equation there in dealing with the subject, is there not?
> Doctor Miller: Yes. . . . I think it is important to realize that no two situations are identical. They do not repeat themselves with such accuracy that the method by which you successfully deal with one situation will insure an equally satisfactory result in another situation. (Ibid., 636)

Asked for what end the System regulated credit, Miller replied: "To the end of 'accommodating commerce and business' as the act instructs" (ibid., 637). How did it decide when to act? "I should say, gentlemen, that action by the Federal Reserve Board usually lies midway between a deliberate or calculated action, such as is taken with full appreciation of the consequences, and what you may call unconscious action. I could not undertake to give any clear definition of just what considerations move my colleagues from time to time" (647).

Miller, like Strong, argued that restoring the international gold standard would restore price stability.[80] But he saw risks in restoring the gold standard that Strong neglected. The principal risk he cited was that the demand for gold by countries restoring gold convertibility could cause a worldwide tightening of credit. Miller compared the current period to the years 1870 to 1880, when many governments restored or joined the gold standard. He concluded: "While the gold standard had very much of the quality of an automatic regulator before the war, it would never do to trust purely and in all situations to devices automatic or quasi automatic in their qualities" (ibid., 695). Miller thought that the price index was the wrong target. Price increases came late.

> To the extent that the Federal Reserve System can do something useful and constructive . . . , it has got to have a far more competent guide than the price index offers. . . .
>
> Assuming that we want price stability—I prefer to put it as I have already put it, economic stability with price stability as a concomitant or resultant of that—in order to obtain it we have to look at things closer to the source or beginning of troubles than the price index. . . .
>
> If you are to have competent control of credit, you cannot wait until inflationary developments register themselves in the price index. By that time the thing will have already gotten considerable momentum. (Ibid., 837–38)

Controlling inflation did not depend on the quantity of money or credit. Miller's remarks on expectations and speculation paralleled many statements by Latin American officials and economists in the inflating economies of the 1970s and 1980s. Inflation was a "vague term" without "precise or generally accepted meaning." He discussed one type of inflation, inflation due to rising expectations. Businessmen observed "a disturbance in the market for a commodity or group of commodities. . . . You have an inflated state of commercial expectation that leads men to make plans and conceive projects and then make commitments and then, only after a lapse of considerable interval, does [the] thing [inflation] show itself in the form of a demand for increased credit. . . . By that time the thing will have already gotten considerable momentum" (ibid., 838).

Miller had rejected the quantity theory in the tenth annual report. In the 1928 hearings on a revised version of the Strong (Kansas) bill, Miller rejected the theory because it had two incorrect assumptions: "Changes in the level of prices are caused by changes in the volume of credit and cur-

---

80. "It will not be a great while before we shall see restored this condition of price stability that was insured to the commercial world before the outbreak of the great war, under the operation of the gold standard" (House Committee on Banking and Currency 1926, 694).

rency; . . . [And] changes in the volume of credit and currency are caused by Federal Reserve policy. Neither one of those assumptions is true of the facts or the realities" (House Committee on Banking and Currency 1928, 109).

Later, returning to the role of money, Miller explained the irrelevance of the money stock in words that Federal Reserve officials repeated many times in the next fifty years: "The total volume of money in circulation is determined by the community. The Federal Reserve System has no appreciable control over that and no disposition to interfere with it" (ibid., 180).

For Miller, the way to provide economic and price stability was to prevent speculation based on credit. The Federal Reserve must "stop and absolutely foreclose the diversion of any Federal Reserve credit to speculative purposes" (ibid., 671).

Miller used the two hearings to comment on his colleagues, the role of the Board, policy in 1927, and the role of open market operations. Unlike Strong and the reserve bank governors, he claimed not to fear political influence on the Federal Reserve Board. Washington was the right place for the Board. The threat to good Federal Reserve policy came from bankers, not politicians: "The atmosphere of Washington keeps an administrative body on its feet, keeps them alert . . . I am not at all afraid of politics getting into the Federal Reserve Board because the Federal Reserve Board has its headquarters in Washington. I would be afraid of banking and financial interests getting undue preponderance in the deliberations of the board if the board were located in one of our great financial cities" (House Committee on Banking and Currency 1926, 727).[81]

Miller urged the committee to strengthen the Board's role in policymaking, especially over open market operations (ibid., 678–79, 865–66). To strengthen his case, he criticized Strong's 1927 open market purchases and blamed the policy for stock exchange speculation, neglecting to note that he had voted for the policy: "The money that was released by the Federal Reserve banks to the market through its policy of open market purchases had to go somewhere. . . . [T]he low money rates that resulted from Federal Reserve policy, in the light of subsequent developments, appear to have been particularly effective in stimulating the absorption of credit in stock speculation" (House Committee on Banking and Currency 1928, 172).

Earlier in the hearings he had urged a return to reliance on the discount rate as the principal policy instrument: "I am of the opinion that open-market operations have been the cause of almost as much mischief in credit and economic situations as of good" (ibid., 125).

81. The context makes it difficult to judge whether this statement was a reflection of Miller's beliefs or a pandering to southern and western congressmen with their traditional fear of "Wall Street." Perhaps both.

This was not a new view. Miller had written much the same in an article explaining Federal Reserve operations (Miller 1928). There he restated the "needs and reluctance" view of borrowing. The economy required "a credit control device less leisurely in character and less openly deliberate than that of the discount rate" (75). This was an "expedient solution" to a temporary problem. With the restoration of the international gold standard and recovery of the world economy, "primary reliance in the future will be [on] the discount rate rather than the open market operation" (75).

Other Testimony

The committee heard from many other witnesses, including other Federal Reserve officers and officials, economists, and bankers. Irving Fisher supported the bill but urged the committee to attach the Goldsborough bill for a compensated dollar.[82] Price stability could not be achieved without a rule of that kind. Fisher argued that the Federal Reserve had worked to stabilize the price level but refused to admit it. Oliver M. W. Sprague opposed the bill but favored "avoidance of considerable advance in the general level of prices" (House Committee on Banking and Currency 1926, 415). He opposed Fisher's rule, or any other, on the usual ground that good policy required judgments not formulas.[83]

Governor Norris (Philadelphia) and Emanuel A. Goldenweiser were two of the more interesting witnesses. Their testimony suggests the level of understanding reached by officials and advisers outside New York. Norris testified against the bill. He regarded the bill as a doubtful and dangerous experiment (ibid., 395) The Federal Reserve dealt with currency and credit. Why was it asked to stabilize the price level? (384). Price stabilization, if it were to be done, should be left to the Commerce Department or the Bureau of Labor Statistics (395). Though a permanent member of the OMIC, he thought open market operations were too small to have an effect on credit supply. A committee member questioned his judgment:

> Mr. Beedy: You would not deny that the purchase of Government securities, or the refraining from purchase . . . would either accelerate or retard the tendency [of prices and interest rates to change]?

82. Fisher paid the salary of John R. Commons, who stayed in Washington to work on the Strong (Kansas) bill (Fisher 1946, 8). I am indebted to Wayne Angell for providing a copy of Fisher's 1946 letter to Clark Warburton.

83. Sprague defined inflation as "a rapid rise in prices continued for a number of years," thereby distinguishing persistent from temporary price level movements much more clearly than his friend Benjamin Strong (House Committee on Banking and Currency 1926, 404). Like Strong, he recognized that real bills failed as a regulatory principle because the type of collateral could not change the (marginal) use of credit.

Mr. Norris: It has an immediate effect on the volume and, therefore, to a certain extent on the price.

Mr. Beedy: It has a consequent proportional effect on the price.

Mr. Norris: I think before you translate those operations into an effect on credit and further dilute it by considering the effect of the cost of credit upon the cost of goods, it is very much like the homeopathic prescription of putting a drop of medicine in the Mediterranean and then a drop of that mixture in the Atlantic Ocean." (Ibid., 391)

Other members of the committee joined the discussion, reminding Norris that changes in reserves increased credit by a multiple of the change in reserves. At last Norris admitted that open market operations could have an effect on credit supply, but he said they had been used "to take care of more or less temporary or local conditions" (ibid.).

Goldenweiser was the longtime director of the Board's research division and one of its leading economists. Like Norris, he doubted there was any relation between open market operations and the price level. Asked by a committee member if supplying more credit would have "no appreciable effect on the price level," Goldenweiser replied: "In general, I should say that is correct" (House Committee on Banking and Currency 1928, 46).

The 1928 Act

Irving Fisher wrote that Governor Strong favored the principle of the 1926 Strong (Kansas) bill but feared that legislation would be harmful. Fisher reported on a private conversation with Strong in which Strong threatened to resign if the bill became law: "If you will let me alone, I will try to do the best I can, but if you make me do by law what I am trying to do without legislative control, I will be so afraid that I cannot fill the bill that I will not accept the responsibility" (Fisher 1946, 3).[84]

Strong changed his mind in 1928, according to Fisher.[85] He worked with Congressman Strong to redraft the 1926 bill and remove his three principal objections. As a result, the preamble to the revised bill included "to further promote the maintenance of a stable gold standard" and "to assist in re-

---

84. Fisher claims to have responded: "I will trust you as long as you live but you will not live forever and when you die I fear your policies will die with you." Fisher says that Strong replied: "I have trained my assistants so that they know these policies and they will be continued" (Fisher 1946, 3). Hetzel (1985, 8) reports very similar statements in Fisher 1934, 151. Fisher's recollection is probably correct. Very similar statements were made by Congressman Strong in the 1926 hearings (House Committee on Banking and Currency 1926, 569, 601).

85. Fisher (1946, 5) claims that Strong could not favor the bill in public without the approval of the Federal Reserve Board. Strong asked the Board if he could favor the legislation, but they refused.

alizing a more stable purchasing power of the dollar." The bill itself directed the Federal Reserve to use its powers "to maintain a stable gold standard . . . [a]nd a more stable purchasing power of the dollar, so far as such purposes may be accomplished by monetary and credit policy" (House Committee on Banking and Currency 1928, 1, 5, 6). Congressman Strong met with the Reserve Board accompanied by Professor John R. Commons and, after discussion, made other changes to meet their objections.

Congressman Strong concluded his opening remarks at the hearings with a warning that was prophetic: "There is but one principal objection . . . that I would not meet in this bill . . . that the American people will not understand what is meant by the powers that they have given to the Federal Reserve System. . . . To my mind . . . that is not to be compared with the danger that may result from the failure to use these powers for the stabilization of the purchasing power" (ibid., 8).

The Board resolutely opposed the bill. Governor Strong began his testimony by noting that he spoke only for himself, not the System. He recognized that the new bill removed many of his earlier objections. Nevertheless, he did not endorse it. He preferred "a scientific application of the well-known principles of the gold standard" (ibid., 13). This would achieve "everything in the act" (17). He favored the gold standard because it was a rule that did not depend on human judgment: "When you are speaking of efforts to stabilize commerce, industry, agriculture, employment, and so on, without regard to the penalties of violation of the gold standard, you are talking about human judgment and the management of prices which I do not believe in at all" (21).

Governor Young of the Board testified for the Board, opposing the bill as requiring a central bank instead of an association of regional banks; reversal of the increases in agricultural prices that had recently occurred; and price fixing by the Federal Reserve. His arguments were superficial and showed little understanding. The first two arguments, however, appealed to widely held political views about a central bank and to the representatives of agricultural districts. Congressman Strong answered at length, denying Young's claims by reading from the bill (ibid., 413–22). Young also defended the 1927 policy as "purely an American policy" to assist exports (415).

Miller's testimony repeated many of the ideas he advanced at great length in the 1926–27 hearings. He continued to oppose the Strong (Kansas) bill. At one point he accused Governor Strong of not understanding the relation of Federal Reserve policy to price stability:

> Mr. Strong: [T]he language you refer to has been dictated and suggested by members of the Federal Reserve System.

Doctor Miller: . . . The Federal Reserve System is a pretty big organization. There are many persons in it. We have a considerable number of amateur economists, and from my point of view they constitute one of its dangerous elements. . . . I venture to say that some of the men you have consulted do not know what this is all about. These are high sounding and captivating words you are using in your proposed statement.

Mr. Strong: Of course, one of them has been Governor Strong.

Doctor Miller: Of course, he is a very able man. But when it comes to economic insight and understanding . . . that is very unusual in any group of men anywhere. (Ibid., 212–13)

Miller's views prevailed. The committee did not report the bill to the House. It is an understatement to say this was a missed opportunity. If the mandate for price stability had been passed and followed, the Federal Reserve could not have permitted deflation during the Great Depression of 1929–33 or inflation during the Great Inflation of 1965–80. Possibly a recession would have occurred in 1929, but the United States and the world would have avoided the deflationary policy and its consequences. The Federal Reserve would have had to choose price stability over the real bills doctrine and to lose gold, thereby reducing or preventing deflation elsewhere.

PERSONALITIES AND CONFLICTS

Miller's testimony about Governor Strong suggests some of the rivalry and animosity between the two. As is often the case, the causes of the dispute were both substantive and personal, but it is not clear from the record which came first. Some of the differences had roots in the Federal Reserve Act itself. Miller resented Strong's leadership in domestic and international policy, but he also believed that the Board, not the reserve banks, should lead the System. Only the Board considered the whole system.

Some of the substantive issues were the type that arise in many organizations. Particularly when discount rates were reduced, reserve bank governors often announced the changes, or leaked them to the press, before the Board acted. The Board believed that it was its prerogative to make these announcements. The governors complained that the Board acted as if it controlled rate changes, while the Board complained that the governors blamed the Board for discount rate increases when talking to member banks. The Board often irritated Strong and some of the other governors by delaying or modifying decisions about open market purchases.

The governors complained that the Board was not well organized, delayed decisions, failed to answer questions, and lost communications. Governor Crissinger, appointed by President Harding to head the Board, had no knowledge of central banking. William McChesney Martin Sr., who served at first as chairman and then as governor of the St. Louis bank from 1914 to 1941, described Crissinger as a "good natured man" but added that that was the only good thing that could be said of him (CHFRS, Martin, August 4, 1954, 2). Strong complained to Mellon about the Board's functioning, but nothing was done until Crissinger resigned in September 1927 (Chandler 1958, 257).

Three more substantive issues underlay the antagonism between Strong and Miller. First, Miller was a firm believer in the power of the real bills doctrine and the importance of the quality of credit for controlling the quantity of credit and inflation. Strong recognized early in the decade that the marginal use of credit was unrelated to the type of paper a bank discounted. Second, Miller opposed reliance on open market operations to control the amount of credit and money. He favored reliance on discount policy and classical (British) central banking. Strong regarded the discount rate as a secondary instrument. He preferred to force bank borrowing and repayment by using open market operations. The Riefler-Burgess doctrine, with its emphasis on open market operations and quantitative control, could be called the Strong-Riefler-Burgess doctrine, to recognize Strong's role in developing a policy framework based on observation and experience. Third, both Strong and Miller favored the restoration of the international gold standard, but Miller was skeptical about the relationship between Strong and Governor Norman of the Bank of England. He believed that Strong at times altered United States policy to benefit Britain, allowing the quantity and quality of credit to change unfavorably and inappropriately.[86] This probably meant that Strong did not wait for banks to borrow or repay.

Oral transcripts of the recollections of Federal Reserve officers show Miller and Strong with powerful personalities. It is not hard to see why they would clash even if there had been no substantive issues. Both wanted to dominate decisions, but Strong was a decisive leader and Miller was not.

Charles J. Rhoads, the first governor at Philadelphia, who admired Miller, described him as "didactic," "quite sure he knew the answer to every question" (CHFRS, Rhoads, June 29, 1955, 3). George L. Harrison, who

86. Chandler (1958, 255) reports Herbert Hoover's references to Strong as a "mental annex to Europe" and "Strong and his European allies." Hoover was friendly with Miller. Chandler claims that Hoover took these views from Miller.

worked at the Board as an attorney from 1914 to the mid-1920s before moving to New York, described Miller as unwilling "to admit that he was ever
wrong" and difficult to persuade about the worth of an idea that was not his
own (CHFRS, Harrison, April 19, 1955, 2).[87]

Unlike Miller, Strong had not gone to college and had not formally studied economics, but he had learned a great deal from his experience as a
banker and central banker and from discussion with leading economists.
Miller distrusted and possibly disdained this type of learning, and he envied the respect and acclaim that Strong received from economists such as
Fisher, Sprague, and Bullock.

William McChesney Martin Sr. described Strong as ambitious personally and determined to make the New York bank the dominant force in the
system. According to Martin, if the Aldrich bill had passed, Strong would
have been the head of the central bank. The Glass bill created a regional
system instead of a central bank, but Strong succeeded for a time in getting control (CHFRS, Martin, August 5, 1954, 2). Jay Crane, who worked
in the New York bank from 1913 to 1935 and later became its chairman, described Strong as a powerful leader. He talked frequently about central
banking with the junior staff who "sat at his feet and worshipped him"
(CHFRS, Crane, March 5, 1954, 1). He was the only governor who tried to
learn about central banking from European experience. Another officer of
the New York bank, Leslie Rounds, referred to Strong's great influence
over policy and his clashes with Adolph Miller. But he also described
Strong as certain that "he knew what was right" (CHFRS, Rounds, January 29, 1954, 3).[88]

George Harrison, who replaced Strong as governor, had a very different
personality. Rounds described Harrison as diplomatic and thoughtful.
Strong, he said, "moved directly from thought to speech," whereas Harrison "thought first and talked afterward" (CHFRS, Rounds, January 29,
1954, 4).

On the critical question of whether Strong would have forced a change
in policy in 1929 or after if he had lived, his contemporaries have mixed
opinions. Rounds (CHFRS, May 2, 1955, 3) was uncertain whether Strong
could have changed policy in 1928–29, but he believed that Strong would

87. Young described Miller's love of argument: "If no one on the Board started arguing
with Mr. Miller, he would argue with himself" (CHFRS, Young, March 1, 1954, 2).

88. Eugene Meyer, governor of the Board from 1930 to 1933, did not share in the adula-
tion. He described Strong as "an ignoramus in international banking" (CHFRS, Meyer, February 16, 1954, 3). Irving Fisher thought highly of Strong and believed he would have prevented the deflationary policy of the 1930s. Fisher had contempt for Meyer. He claimed that
in 1931, when told that demand deposits were falling, Meyer did not know what a demand deposit was and did not know that they had fallen (Fisher 1946, 4).

have insisted on an increase in the discount rate in 1929 (13).[89] Roy Young was doubtful. Strong "thought he had more power in the System than he really had" (CHFRS, Young, March 1, 1954, 3). J. Herbert Case, one of Strong's deputies, asserted the opposite (CHFRS, Case, February 24, 1954, 7). Several governors, led by Miller, blamed Strong's policies, particularly the 1927 open market purchases, for the increase in speculative activity and the growth of stock exchange credit.[90] He would have had difficulty persuading them to follow his (nonreal bills) policies again.[91]

Other active members of the Board and the banks at the time included Charles S. Hamlin, the first governor, who served on the Board from 1914 to 1936; Roy A. Young, governor of the Board from 1927 to 1930 and governor at Boston from 1930 to 1942; James B. McDougal, governor at Chicago from 1914 to 1934; and George R. James, a member of the Board from 1923 to 1936. Contemporary descriptions of these men give no evidence of leadership, understanding, or an ability to resolve the conflict between Miller and Strong.

Paul Warburg described Hamlin as a "second class Governor" (quoted in Yohe 1990, 479). Young reported that Hamlin seldom spoke at Board meetings: "He sat with his diary at hand and made notes" (CHFRS, Young, March 1, 1954, 1). Chester Morrill, in the Board's Secretariat (secretary after 1930), claimed that Hamlin's diary is "far from accurate as he grew older" (CHFRS, Morrill, May 20, 1954, 9). Others described him as "a man of no particular force who usually went with the majority" (CHFRS, Morgan, April 23, 1954, 5).

Harrison described Young as extremely stubborn and very vocal, and Young described James as "a diamond in the rough." Meyer thought James lacked financial ability but was otherwise all right. Morrill held a very different view. He thought James had great respect for authority. Since Meyer

89. Leslie Rounds compared Strong with Gates McGarrah, who served as acting governor for a few months after Strong died: "McGarrah could present a case quite effectively, but when it got to the arguments, he was through. . . . McGarrah just wasn't built on a plan to permit him to argue and win. Strong loved it. He thoroughly enjoyed getting into a fight and coming out on top, as he always did" (CHFRS, Rounds, 13). McGarrah and the New York directors voted for discount rate increases repeatedly in the spring of 1929, but the Board would not approve.

90. Early in 1928, Miller and others at the Board worked to dilute Strong's authority by replacing the five-person OMIC, dominated by Strong, with a twelve-person committee consisting of all reserve bank governors. The change, discussed below, was made in 1930 after Strong died.

91. There are two issues. First is whether Strong would have convinced the Board to raise the discount rate early in 1929. The other, more important issue, is whether he would have convinced the open market committee to expand in 1930 or 1931. I return to that issue in chapter 5.

was governor, James took Meyer's word and spent no time studying issues. In return, Meyer sponsored his reappointment (CHFRS, Harrison, April 19, 1955, 2; Young, March 1, 1954, 1; Meyer, February 16, 1954, 6; Morrill, May 20, 1954, 6).[92]

James McDougal, the governor at Chicago, was a man of few words. Bentley McCloud, who served as McDougal's assistant governor, said that if he was asked the time of day, he would not answer but would show you his watch. McDougal came to the Federal Reserve from the Chicago clearinghouse, where he had worked as an examiner. Meyer described him as "a mere bookkeeper" (CHFRS, McCloud, July 27, 1954, 5; Meyer, February 16, 1954, 5).

The other Board members during most of the 1920s were Edward H. Cunningham and Edmund Platt, the vice governor. Cunningham was a farmer who went into Iowa politics and was active in the American Farm Bureau. He filled the agricultural seat created after the 1920–21 deflation. He often opposed rate increases because he believed they hurt farmers and small businesses (Katz 1992, 67). He served from 1923 to his death in 1930. Platt's biography appears above (see note 16). He was usually in favor of raising interest rates during 1927–29.

The general picture that emerges has two features. Many of the principals responsible for policy in the 1920s, and during 1929 to 1933, were weak men with little knowledge of central banking and not much interest in developing their knowledge. There were a few strong-minded individuals, but they were often at loggerheads. Policy decisions became a contest of wills between Strong and Miller and later between Miller, Meyer, and Harrison or Burgess.

Edward Smead, who served throughout the period as head of the Division of Reports and Statistics, described the scene. At first "Benjamin Strong was more powerful than anybody on the stage." Later "Eugene Meyer was in constant opposition to Harrison in the New York bank" (CHFRS, Smead, June 14, 1954, 2).[93] Meyer confirmed and strengthened Smead's comments. During his period of service at the Board, he claimed, there was constant strife at the Board and ill feeling between the Board, New York, and Chicago. The "New York bank had built up its power entirely out of proportion with the intent of the Act" (CHFRS, Meyer, February 16, 1954, 4).

92. Morrill reports that James was from Tennessee and believed that the mule, the horse, and hay were "the basic elements of any economy." He was "wrapped up in organic fertilizer." He disliked the automobile and believed that by doing away with the horse and the mule, automobiles contributed to the "decay of the country" (CHFRS, Morrill, May 20, 1954, 6).

93. Smead added that in the 1940s the "New York–Washington feud" continued under Allan Sproul and Marriner Eccles.

The struggle for power and control that was inherent in Wilson's compromise had gathered momentum by the late 1920s. The Federal Reserve entered a critical period for policy decisions with a conflict that made decisions easy to postpone and left basic policy issues unresolved.

POLICY ACTIONS

New York and some of the Board's staff followed the Riefler-Burgess doctrine as a general guide to policy actions. Miller relied mainly on the qualitative test, based on the real bills doctrine, underlying one part of the tenth annual report. Regional reserve bank governors were often more interested in their bank's earnings than in issues of money or credit management. They were more willing to follow Strong's leadership and participate in System policy when policy increased earnings. Those who voiced opinions about System policy usually held orthodox gold standard and real bills views.

The deflation of the early 1920s ended by 1922, but it continued to shape interpretations and actions. Many of the banks in the South and Middle West held distressed agricultural and livestock loans. The problem was particularly acute in the upper Middle West and in the northern plains states. Bank suspensions continued to rise, particularly in these states, during the middle twenties. As late as 1926, the peak year for suspensions in that decade, 976 banks with deposits of $260 million closed. More than one-third of the number of suspensions occurred in three states: Minnesota, Iowa, and South Dakota.

The potential political impact of agricultural interests heightened the effect of the regional economic problem. Since deflation was widely regarded as the inevitable consequence of prior inflation, avoiding inflation became a paramount interest. Strong had been impressed, however, by the reports of distress in agricultural regions during his appearance before the Joint Commission on Agricultural Inquiry and, despite concerns about inflation, he believed it was prudent to lean to the side of ease in 1922 (Burgess 1964, 223).

The 1923–24 Recession

The wholesale price index rose during most of 1922, sharply in the early part of the year, more slowly later. In the fifteen months ending in March–April 1923, the index (base 100 in 1913) increased from 140 to 160. Concern spread that inflation had returned.[94]

94. In late April 1923 the National Bureau of Economic Research wrote: "We will soon have a boom, with the standard trimmings and the standard ending" (quoted by Miller in House Committee on Banking and Currency 1926, 701).

Although it was eager to take credit later, the Federal Reserve's response was largely fortuitous. Under pressure from the Treasury, the reserve banks began to sell securities after May 1922. By the end of the year they had sold more than one-third of their holdings, $220 million. Sales continued in the first half of 1923. By June, System holdings were $150 million, one-fourth of their peak in May 1922. The System relied on discounts to satisfy seasonal credit demand in the fall. To the surprise of many in the System, after a small seasonal decline in January, member bank discounts continued to rise throughout the spring and summer.

The Federal Reserve increased discount rates at Boston, New York, and San Francisco by 0.5 percent in late February and early March. Rates were now uniform for all classes of paper, at 4.5 percent, at all reserve banks. Open market rates rose following the rise in discount rates.[95]

With market rates above the discount rate, prices and production rising, and speculation developing in stocks and commodities, Platt, the acting governor, wrote to Treasury Undersecretary Gilbert on March 24, 1923, reflecting the general uncertainty about how to conduct policy: "The old Bank of England guides appear to be inapplicable. . . . It may not always be necessary to have reserve bank rates above or exactly even with open market rates, but an increasing spread between them is certainly an invitation to inflation" (Board of Governors File, box 1240, March 24, 1923).

The March Governors Conference discussed additional discount rate increases. McDougal thought that economic conditions were similar to 1919–20. He favored an advance of 1 percent, to 5.5 percent, at all reserve banks. Calkins (San Francisco) and Norris (Philadelphia) were less aggressive, but both favored rate increases. Case thought another increase would be appropriate by mid-April. All other governors saw no reason for change. Chicago voted on April 6 to raise the discount rate to 5 percent, but the Board refused to approve the increase. The next day the Board sent a letter, proposed by Miller, to all reserve banks saying that discount rates should not be increased until the reserve banks had substantially liquidated their portfolios of governments. This was a reversal of traditional policy; open market sales were supposed to make discount rates effective. The new policy, under pressure from the Treasury, had the sales precede any increase in discount rates.

The Board's correspondence leaves no doubt about the reason for the policy change. The Treasury continued to press the reserve banks to elim-

95. Strong wrote to Norman that the discount rate increases had been delayed until it was clear that Congress would approve a loan to Britain. As reason for the increase in the discount rate, Strong cited the increase in borrowing, market rates 1 percent above the discount rate, rising stock market loans, and production "practically at a maximum" (Chandler 1958, 221).

inate all government securities. On April 20 Platt wrote to Secretary Mellon, calling attention to the large open market sales in the previous year and pointing out that the System holdings of governments were about equal to the capital and surplus of the reserve banks. The reserve banks were eager to hold governments at this level to ensure sufficient earnings to pay dividends on their capital stock. They wanted the Treasury to agree that additions to surplus could be matched by increases in government securities. Mellon opposed, and Undersecretary Gilbert continued to press for additional sales (Board of Governors File, box 1434, April 20 and 27, 1923, and box 1433, May 3, 1923). Platt replied that additional sales would force higher discount rates and, by eliminating the portfolio, reduce the reserve banks' ability to influence the market and prevent inflation should it occur.

The Board had abolished the governors' Committee on Centralized Purchases and Sales and established the Open Market Investment Committee (OMIC), with the same membership but operating under regulations and subject to supervision by the Board. The Board's resolution gave two guidelines to the OMIC. First was the effect on commerce, business, and credit markets. Second was the effect on the market for Treasury securities. At its first meeting, April 13, the OMIC adopted a statement, similar to the Board's, directing open market operations to "the accommodation of commerce and business." The statement added that a penalty rate of discount "is not always suited to the American bill market" and expressed concern that attempts to maintain a penalty rate "would quickly drive the dollar credit from those [bill] markets" and benefit London. The statement indicated that, although government securities would be bought and sold in the market, acceptances, once bought, would be sold only to another reserve bank. The latter policy represented New York's view that sales should be avoided to prevent competition with member banks and encourage a domestic bill market (Policy Governing Open Market Purchases by Federal Reserve Banks, Exhibit A, Board of Governors File, box 1436, April 13, 1923).

Strong was on leave for health reasons from March to November 1923, so he missed the first OMIC meeting, in April. The meeting elected him chairman and selected Case, his deputy, to act in his place. Acceding to the Treasury, the OMIC allowed $36 million of maturing securities to run off and proposed raising the buying rate on acceptances by 0.125 percent. Four days later, New York raised the buying rate.[96]

96. The meeting also considered an issue that continued throughout the decade. Banks in California allowed a limited amount of check writing against "special savings deposits, subject to a 3 percent reserve requirement ratio." By a vote of seven to five, the governors agreed

The following month the OMIC recommended open market sales of $50 million, about one-quarter of remaining holdings, with sales distributed among the reserve banks in inverse relation to a bank's earnings. Crissinger had become governor of the Board at the beginning of May. On May 31 he wrote to Case reversing Platt's position and expressing concern at the restriction to $50 million: "The Board sees no reason why there should be any limitation. . . . [G]overnment securities should be disposed of as rapidly as possible until they are out of the banks" (Crissinger to Case, Board of Governors File, box 1434, May 31, 1923).

Case's reply expressed surprise that the Board had not objected to the limitation at the time of the meeting, but his tone was conciliatory. His only criticism of the Board's action was its timing, coming so soon after the Board had not objected to the decision. But he appended to his letter a letter from Philadelphia denying the Board's authority to specify the volume of sales (Case to Crissinger, Board of Governors File, box 1434, June 11, 1923).[97] Strong was more forceful. From Colorado, he wrote to Miller using the economic arguments of the Riefler-Burgess doctrine. Additional sales of $130 million would force the banks to borrow $130 million, reducing bank profits and increasing pressure to liquidate loans. There were signs of "hesitation in business" and rising bank failures: "Had I been home recently when these failures were popping, I would have bought $25 to $50 million" (Chandler 1958, 232).

The Treasury continued to urge the OMIC to get rid of all government securities. Despite the OMIC's decision to support the acceptance market, the Treasury urged that the acceptance market be allowed to develop on its own "without artificial support from the Federal Reserve Banks." The Treasury wanted the OMIC to limit its actions to the acceptance market, arguing that this could be done if the acceptance rate was a market rate and the reserve banks sold as well as bought (Letter Gilbert to Case, Board of Governors File, box 1434, May 25, 1923). Strong did not share this view, and the Treasury did not press it further.[98]

---

to keep the prevailing policy. The problem spread to other states, and though it was discussed many times, the policy was not changed. The policy allowed banks to lower the applicable reserve requirement ratio and blur the distinction between demand and time deposits.

97. Case circulated Crissinger's letter to the members of the OMIC. Philadelphia's reply suggests the way many of the reserve banks looked at the issue. The Philadelphia directors had approved sharing in the sale only to accommodate the Treasury. The Board's program would require selling securities at a loss. Decisions about purchases and sales were not the province of the Board, and the Board lacked authority to have a policy about sales. His directors reserved the right to dissent from future OMIC recommendations (Norris to Case, Board of Governors File, box 1434, June 8, 1923).

98. Gilbert continued to develop and modify this view and to urge it on the Board until August. (See Letter Gilbert to Crissinger, Board of Governors File, box 1434, August 3, 1923.)

By fall the country was in a deep recession. The National Bureau of Economic Research ranks the recession as one of the most severe in the years 1920 to 1982, surpassed by only three others. The Board's index of industrial production (1919 = 100) reached a peak of 127 in May 1923. The NBER trough is in July 1924, with the index at 94, a 23 percent decline (Reed 1930, 45).[99] Balke and Gordon's (1986) real GNP declined 4.1 percent. The decline was irregular, with some recovery in the fall.

At its November 1923 meeting, the OMIC mentioned "the possibility of harm to business when business is hesitating" but took no action to expand. Most of its attention was on the continued imports of gold and the seasonal increase in borrowing. A principal policy concern at the time was the small size of the open market portfolio available for sale if gold imports continued.

Strong had returned. His report to the committee, as chairman, noted that purchases would not be inflationary if total earning assets did not increase. He did not urge purchases at that time, however, because he did "not think the Federal Reserve Board would consider that" (Report of OMIC, Board of Governors File, box 1436, November 10, 1923, 29–35).[100]

A few weeks later, the OMIC voted to make its first purchases but, mindful of Treasury concerns, added that purchases should not disturb the money market. The Board approved purchases of no more than $100 million on December 3, but it reserved the right to discontinue purchases and resume sales if market conditions changed (Board Minutes, December 3, 1923).[101]

Although New York favored the decision to purchase, Strong and his directors feared that purchases of governments would be regarded as inflationary. They wanted the Board to issue a statement endorsing the view

The Federal Advisory Council accepted Gilbert's suggestions in principle but decided that the time was not right for further sales. In August Gilbert accepted that the reserve banks' position was "well liquidated," ending the issue.

99. A later index, base 100 in 1992, puts the decline at 18 percent. The Miron-Romer index has an overall decline of 36 percent for the period. Their index has an initial decline of 38 percent between May and September 1923, followed by a rise to February 1924 and a renewed decline to July 1924.

100. In September the Board approved a request from Dallas to purchase $10 million of long-term Treasury bonds for income. The Board approved because of the weak earnings of the Dallas bank. It denied a similar request from Boston in November. These incidents suggest, correctly, that much of the interest in open market purchases at the reserve banks continued to be for earnings. The tenth annual report had not been written. Strong's statement at the meeting anticipated part of the report.

101. Purchases were made for a new Special System Investment Account to be used for all purchases and sales by the committee. Allocation to individual reserve banks was based on earnings needs of the reserve banks. The reserve banks paid or received payment by transferring gold on the books of the gold settlement fund.

that open market operations changed the composition, but not the size, of the Federal Reserve's earning assets. The Board adopted a statement prepared by Strong, Walter Stewart, and Pierre Jay (chairman at New York) that reviewed evidence of the close negative relation between open market operations and member bank borrowing in 1922 and 1923 and emphasized the relation between discount policy and open market policy as a means of accommodating commerce and business (Board Minutes, December 19, 1923). Although the act authorized open market purchases, the emphasis on commerce and business appealed to beliefs about real bills. The Board published the statement in the *Federal Reserve Bulletin*.

Strong was cautious. The System bought only $30 million in December. At its January 1924 meeting, the OMIC adopted a "waiting policy" at a time of "extreme caution" (Board of Governors File, box 1436, January 14, 1924). The committee purchased only $15 million. The reason for caution was the fear of inflation caused by adding securities purchases to a continued gold inflow.[102] The background memo prepared for the meeting mentioned stock market speculation as a possible sign of inflation but noted that commodity prices showed no sign of inflation. In February, with a renewed decline in industrial production, the OMIC resumed purchases. On February 25 the Board approved purchases of an additional $100 million. By November 1924, the OMIC had bought more than $500 million in twelve months, with the bulk of the purchases between February and August, nine to fifteen months after the recession started.[103]

The reserve banks easily reached agreement on purchases. Nine of them, including New York, had negative earnings. In May, the OMIC revised the allocation formula to reflect the projected earnings positions. New York took 51 percent of purchases in June (instead of its previous 29 percent), and Chicago took 10 percent. Thereafter, allocations changed monthly.

Treasury officials did not oppose purchases by the reserve banks, but they asked for a limit on the size of the System account (OMIC Minutes, Board of Governors File, box 1436, April 22, 1924). The Board and the Treasury continued to resist purchases of long-term securities. The Federal Advisory Council supported the Board's position, and the Board used the

102. The bulk of the gold was in bullion. Beginning in January, governors agreed to ask the Treasury to increase gold coinage and to issue more gold certificates until coins and certificates equaled 20 percent of notes and deposits, 6 percent in coin and 14 percent in certificates (Governors Conference, May 6, 1924, 340–47; November 10–14, 1924).

103. Wicker (1966) interprets the 1924 purchases as made mainly for international reasons. He dates the principal purchases as occurring between June and August (88). This neglects $100 million made in March 1924. As noted below, Strong later testified that purchases should have stopped in June.

council's opinion to reject Chicago's request to purchase long-term securities for income (Letter Board to McDougal, Board of Governors File, box
1434, May 23, 1924).[104] The issue did not die. In November 1924, with most
of the reserve banks in deficit, the governors voted on a proposal to defy the
Board by purchasing long-term governments to increase earnings. The
motion was defeated on a tie vote.

Early in May 1924, New York reduced its discount rate to 3.5 percent in
two steps.[105] By July only Minneapolis remained at 4.5 percent. Open market rates for commercial paper fell to 2 percent. For the first time, some
member banks began to report rising excess reserves. The difference in
discount rates suggests, correctly, that there were sizable regional differences. Excess reserves at banks in large cities accompanied heavy borrowing in agricultural districts, particularly in June and July. A large United
States crop and small crops abroad raised farm prices and improved the
farmers' position, so discounts declined in the fall, counter to the usual
seasonal pattern. Strong later described the effect on the United States
market:[106] "The outcome of the crops made it necessary for Europe to make
unprecedented purchases of our small grains at very high prices compared
to recent years. But the coincidence of low rates for money in this market
and higher rates in London enabled foreign . . . borrowers to place a billion
and a quarter of loans in this market" (House Committee on Banking and
Currency 1926, 337).[107]

The recession ended in July, but open market purchases continued. As
noted earlier, gold outflow from Britain threatened Britain's return to the
gold standard. With United States interest rates below British rates, the
United States gold stock reached a peak in June 1924 and declined slowly
through the fall. Following a recommendation of the Federal Advisory Council, the OMIC discussed purchases of future sterling bills at its October meet-

104. The Board was divided on the issue. The vote was three to two to reject Chicago's request. Crissinger abstained. Hamlin believed the Board exceeded its authority.

105. This was a year after the start of the recession. The only discount rate change in 1923
was a 0.5 percent increase by San Francisco two months before the cyclical peak. Chandler's
claim (1958) that the Federal Reserve, particularly Strong, had discovered countercyclical
policy (along Keynesian lines) is not consistent with the long delay at the start of the 1923–24
and 1927 recessions. What Strong and other proposed, and did, depended mainly on credit
markets, particularly the level of borrowing. Although Strong talked about measures of production, his actions were based on discounts and interest rates as suggested by the Riefler-
Burgess doctrine.

106. In July, the OMIC voted to allow its chairman to sell and repurchase securities in the
new Special System Investment Account to smooth the market during tax payment periods.
New York and Chicago had been smoothing on their own earlier.

107. The statement is based on a memo that Strong wrote in December 1924 and read to
the Banking Committee at the 1926 hearings.

ing but decided that the futures market was too small. The committee was uncertain about its next move. It voted to give the chairman authority to buy or sell up to $100 million, but the Board would not consider giving the decision to Strong. By November, market rates were rising. The reserve banks' acceptance rates were below market rates, so they supplied the usual seasonal demand for reserves and currency through the acceptance market.

Strong prepared a lengthy congratulatory report for the November meeting on the first full year of the OMIC's operations. Purchases had added $500 million to the System account without adding directly to the volume of credit. Credit had shifted from discounts to government securities with little change in the total. As a result, gold imports and currency had their full effect on the credit markets and contributed to ease markets during the recession, and later a gold outflow contributed to the "readjustment of world finance" (Riefler 1956, 26).[108]

Further, Strong said, the System had built its portfolio so that it was now in a position to offset gold inflation. All of this had been achieved "without business disturbance or price inflation but rather with considerable benefit to business" (ibid., 26). The report argued that by changing the amount of credit available the Federal Reserve could smooth the business cycle, and that by reducing interest rates in recession it could help foreigners to finance recovery abroad. The report cited the financing of the Dawes loan to Germany that year as an example.[109]

Within a few weeks, the atmosphere at the meetings changed. The early months of recovery were very strong. Consumer prices rose at a 4.5 percent annual rate in October and November, and stock prices were 25 percent above 1923. At the December 2, 1924, Board meeting, Adolph Miller introduced a resolution calling on the reserve banks to raise discount rates by 0.25 percent above open market rates, restoring a penalty rate. The motion failed four to two. Reserve bank credit and the monetary base continued to increase despite the redemption of $65 million from the open market account. The M_1 money stock rose at an annual rate of 10 percent for the quarter and 12 percent for the second half of the year. When the OMIC met with the Board on December 19, Miller favored an increase in the acceptance rate to 3 percent to slow the rise in stock prices and brokers' loans. He

108. W. W. Riefler prepared a summary of open market decisions for 1923 to 1931 based on the principal documents for the period. His summaries are in the Board's files.

109. Strong also responded to criticism of the policy by the American Bankers Association. The bankers accused the Federal Reserve of accentuating financial swings and competing for securities with member banks. They suggested that Federal Reserve banks return "to their primary functions as banks of issue and rediscount" (Riefler 1956, 30). Strong recommended that the Board reply in the *Federal Reserve Bulletin*. The Dawes loan was part of the Dawes Plan to reduce German reparations payments and restore convertibility of the mark.

feared that businesses would start to borrow, requiring a rapid increase in interest rates: "We have an enormous volume of credit poured into the market, and member banks are going to be put to it to meet demands. They will go to the reserve banks to get it" (OMIC Minutes, Board of Governors File, box 1436, December 19, 1924, 11).

Strong urged caution. December was not the time for a shift in policy. He wanted the Board and the OMIC to wait for the January meeting, when the market situation would be clearer, but he did not oppose an increase in the acceptance rate to 3 percent on ninety-day paper. Within a few days, New York increased the rate. During the rest of December discounts rose, and the System allowed government securities to mature without replacement. At year end the System account stood at $540 million—about $50 million below its peak but $40 million above the amount set as a maximum in November.

The minutes have no evidence that Strong wanted to delay sales in December to assist Britain's return to the gold standard. Foreign borrowing and low rates in the United States helped the pound to appreciate nearly 9 percent against the dollar from the summer low, with no further increase in the Bank of England's discount rate. In January the pound appreciated further, driven by rumors of a return to gold. On the record, Strong's position at the December meeting is not very different from Miller's and others'. All shared some uncertainty about the strength of the recovery and the size of the seasonal movement at the end of the year. The committee voted not to increase the OMIC account and to respond to demand for reserves by discounting.[110]

Recovery and Expansion

Despite a mild recession beginning in October 1926, real GNP grew at an average rate of 6 percent a year in 1925 and 1926. Prices remained within a band from −2 percent to +4 percent monthly, at annual rates. Common stock prices rose 24 percent in 1925, and total return to equities reached nearly 12 percent in 1926.[111] These figures suggest a strong and steady expansion. Closer examination shows a much more variable pattern in 1925.

---

110. The following week, Strong wrote a lengthy memo to the files summarizing the events of 1923–24. Subsequently he read from this memo at a congressional hearing, as cited above. One part of the memo refers to the gold inflow as "one of the greatest menaces to our ultimate security against inflation." Recognizing the role of United States interest rates as helpful for the recovery of the pound, he concluded that Britain was now able to resume gold payments: "A lower interest level . . . was a further influence in turning the tide of gold away from the United States" (House Committee on Banking and Currency 1926, 337).

111. Beginning in 1926, I rely on appendix table A-1 in Ibbotson and Sinquefeld 1989 for annual returns on common stocks.

Industrial production rose rapidly in January, then declined unevenly until late summer, so much of the rise for the year was completed in the first month. Balke and Gordon's (1986) data on real GNP shows strong positive growth in the first and fourth quarters of 1925, declines during the second and third quarters, and renewed growth in 1926. Prices rose in 1925 and fell in 1926 following a decline in money (M_1).

The OMIC met in Philadelphia on January 9, 1925, with Crissinger and Platt present. The secretary's report showed that since the December meeting the open market committee had sold $57 million of governments and bought $125 million of acceptances, mainly in December. In the first week of January, as market rates fell, acceptances ran off. The committee anticipated that the market would firm in February and March. It voted to continue sales to prevent undue ease (OMIC Minutes, Board of Governors File, box 1436, January 9 and 10, 1925).

The February meeting renewed the decision to sell. Between November and March, the System sold $210 million. In the same period, member bank discounts rose $170 million and acceptances rose $30 million, offsetting the sale, as Riefler-Burgess implied. The gold stock fell almost $200 million, and open market rates rose. New York responded in late February by raising the discount rate from 3 to 3.5 percent, where it remained for the rest of the year. Strong coordinated the increase with Norman both during his visit in January and by cable (Governors Conference, April 6–7, 1925, 21).[112]

Strong credited the open market sales and the rise in the discount rate with reducing speculative activity on the stock exchange and lowering stock prices. He made no mention of the decline in business that occurred about the same time (Riefler 1956, 44).[113]

At the April 1925 meeting of the Governors Conference the governors considered a problem that continued for the rest of the decade—the use of credit by securities brokers and dealers. Strong explained how New York analyzed the problem. A tightening of the money market reduced loans by brokers to their customers if the New York banks were in debt to the reserve bank. Higher money market rates in New York also brought loans from banks in the interior. Governor Willis J. Bailey (Kansas City) asked

112. Strong wanted to increase the rate before the British resumed gold convertibility (Governors Conference, April 6–7, 1925). The Bank of England preceded New York by raising its discount rate in February and again in April (to 5 percent). Board of Governors of the Federal Reserve System 1943, 656, shows the British increase in April but not in February. This record is not consistent with discussion at the time.

113. Reed (1930, 93) suggested that the slow shift to tighter policy and the aggressive ease in 1924 were the forerunners of the aggressive policy of ease in 1927 and the slow reversal in 1928.

how the interior banks could be prevented from sending money to the call money market. Strong replied: "I do not know that it can be done" (Governors Conference, April 6–7, 1925, 16).

Adolph Miller pressed Strong on the role of the discount rate as a factor affecting member bank borrowing and the volume of stock exchange lending. Strong, as usual, said he was uncertain about the effect of the discount rate. Gold flows and open market operations were the factors he cited as driving banks to borrow or repay discounts. Strong's reasoning later made it difficult to persuade the Board to increase the discount rate in 1929, when New York wanted a 6 percent rate (Joint Meeting, Governors Conference and Board, Governors Conference April 8, 1925, 27–29).[114]

The April 1925 meeting reversed direction by purchasing up to $50 million to offset continuing gold outflows. This decision brought the power struggle into the open. The Board did not consider the action for two weeks and neither approved nor rejected it.[115] No purchases were made. On May 21, 1925, the Board revoked the authority to purchase without its approval.

The OMIC met again on April 30 but devoted most of its attention to the reserve banks' earnings. Strong defused pressure for purchases of long-term securities by agreeing to reapportion $83 million of the existing portfolio to increase the earnings at reserve banks with losses. Payments were made through the gold settlement fund.[116]

114. At its April joint meeting the Board and governors also appointed a committee to consider legislation introduced by Congressman Louis T. McFadden. The legislation included renewal of the Federal Reserve's charter. The Board appointed O. M. W. Sprague of Harvard and Walter Stewart, a former research director, to work with the Board. Sprague also undertook a study of member bank borrowing. He found that, contrary to the "reluctance" theory, a large number of member banks in agricultural areas continued to borrow, to carry loans made in 1918–20. He urged the reserve banks to notify members that continuous borrowing was not permitted.

115. The authorization to buy or sell up to $100 million, agreed to in November 1924, was still in effect. Critics of Strong's policies in 1924 and 1927 never mentioned this decision to sterilize the gold outflow just at the time Britain resumed convertibility.

116. After the April 6 meeting, Adolph Miller challenged the argument that System purchases should be made to prevent individual bank purchases. That undermined the case for a System account and a System policy. Miller added that purchases should not be made to increase earnings. Strong and McDougal defended the purchases as consistent with the agreement under which they participated in the OMIC. Although the OMIC made no purchases, the incident brings out the concern of many governors for their earnings and the pressure on Strong to accede to these demands in the interest of maintaining a System policy. The pressure came mainly from the reserve banks in the South and West. In March, Dallas had made purchases for its own account until March 26, when the Board ordered it to stop. Governor Lynn P. Talley of Dallas replied that the Board had approved purchases in October 1923 and never revoked the authority. Chicago, Kansas City, and Minneapolis made small purchases also. At the time, Dallas and some of the others were probably below efficient size. They owed their existence to the decision to establish twelve reserve banks rather than eight.

In late June 1925, the OMIC described the economy as in recession but above the level reached a year earlier. In the same month, the stock market reached a new high. The committee ignored the possible recession; it discussed sales to tighten the money market seasonally, if needed during the summer.

Stock prices continued to increase. When the OMIC met on September 21, the Standard and Poor's index had risen 24 percent in twelve months, and volume was at a record level. Brokers' loans to September 30 had increased more than $1 billion in a year, a 50 percent increase, and so-called street loans to finance stock purchases were $700 million above the previous year. Much of the increased lending to brokers and dealers came from outside New York.

Miller proposed open market sales, to be followed by an increase in the New York discount rate if discounts increased seasonally, as they were likely to do. The motion was defeated. The OMIC suggested that purchases might be needed in December, followed by sales in January, for seasonal reasons. The only action at the meeting was to suggest that reserve banks carefully consider whether discount rates should be raised (OMIC Minutes, Board of Governors File, box 1436, September 22, 1925; Board memo, box 1434, July 1, 1927). The following day, Boston voted to increase its discount rate to 4 percent. Miller was strongly in favor, but the Board was not, so it tabled the increase and did not approve it until November 10, 1925, six weeks later.

The semiannual Governors Conference met from November 2 to 4. The agenda included McDougal's (Chicago) proposal to discuss discount rates, normally reserved for the individual banks. He believed New York's rate was too low. Other governors shared his view, possibly to increase earnings. Norris (Philadelphia) argued that if the 3.5 percent rate in New York had been appropriate in midsummer, it was now too low because business conditions had improved and open market rates had increased. Others supported the increase, using as a main reason the increase in stock exchange credit.

Strong defended New York's policy. He saw no sign of speculative borrowing for inventory accumulation.[117] The main problems were local— real estate speculation in Florida and stock exchange speculation in New York. He then made the argument that he had made earlier and that New York would repeat many times in the next four years: loans to finance stock

---

117. At about this time, Miller (1925a) publicly criticized the financing of speculation and urged his readers to accept greater variability in discount rates, as in England. To real bills advocates like Miller, increases in speculative credit were evidence of inflation even if commodity prices remained unchanged.

market accounts came from all over the country. A rise in the New York discount rate would reduce discounting in New York but increase discounting in the rest of the country without any effect on the call money market. Strong argued that at $210 million, the open market account was too small for additional sales to be useful. Member banks were already in debt to the reserve banks; increased indebtedness would not matter much. Higher rates would bring more gold to the United States, and that "would make the situation worse" (Governors Conference, November 2–4, 1925, 353).

Harding (Boston) urged a general increase in rates, to 4 percent at Boston, New York, Philadelphia, Cleveland, and San Francisco, but Calkins and Norris argued that the effect on speculative credit would be small. Fancher (Cleveland) and Norris agreed, however, that their rates should go to 4 percent. In the next two or three weeks the Board approved increases in discount rates to 4 percent at Boston, Philadelphia, Cleveland, and San Francisco. New York remained at 3.5 percent until early January 1926.

Underlying the discussion was the widely held belief that Strong was holding New York's rate at 3.5 percent to help the Bank of England. Under pressure from British industry, the bank had lowered its rate from 5 percent to 4 percent in September and October. Gold flows to the United States stabilized during the summer and began to reverse. With United States commodity prices falling, Strong could help Norman without sacrificing price stability at home. This was always his policy, as he told Norman many times. Norman agreed and accepted it.[118]

In November 1925, after Britain removed restrictions on foreign lending, the gold flow reversed again. Norman was not disturbed. The size of Britain's gold stock was now large enough to absorb the loss. In correspondence with Strong, he expressed concern about the effects of gold inflows on future inflation, either directly or through public pressure to reduce interest rates. The loss of gold gave him the opportunity to raise interest rates back to 5 percent in early December 1925.

Strong was in Europe during the summer of 1925. His correspondence with Norman and with the New York bank showed him shifting between two positions. Growing stock exchange speculation and concern about possible commodity price speculation and future inflation suggested the time had come for an increase in the New York discount rate, but higher rates would reverse the gold outflow and force higher rates in countries that had restored gold payments—Britain, Germany, Switzerland, and

---

118. In his 1926 testimony to Congress, Strong said (about the standby credit to the Bank of England): "[The New York bank] is free to raise and lower its discount rate; quite as free, in fact, as though no such arrangement had been made" (quoted in Chandler 1958, 320).

Holland. From Europe he explained the dilemma as seen by the four European banks. They were concerned about having gold forced on them and the inflation that would follow. They believed "that their own future depends upon establishing lower prices for what they produce and consume, especially what they produce for export" (Chandler 1958, 325).

The United States faced a classical central banking problem under a fixed exchange rate system. The gold outflow was deflationary but not large enough to offset increased borrowing. Higher rates seemed called for, but they would attract more gold, with longer-term inflationary consequences. Further, stock market speculation had increased. From New York, Strong wrote to Norman in November 1925: "Now all of this reads very much like an attempt to manipulate the stock market. I confess I hate it. It is repugnant to me in every possible aspect. It is the sort of thing that would not be necessary at all if general resumption of gold payment had been effected throughout the world and we had been able to effect some distribution of our excess vault reserve. . . . It is merely another chapter in the argument against a managed currency" (ibid., 329).

I believe this statement is as close as Strong ever came to recognition that he, Norman, and others had to choose between short- and long-term objectives. To get the gold standard operating as automatically as before World War I, either Britain had to deflate or the United States had to inflate. Reaching this long-term solution involved short-term changes that neither country would accept.

The problem was not, as is often suggested, lack of cooperation or unwillingness to cooperate. The failure was a failure of a managed system operating under inconsistent objectives on both sides. Forecast errors about short-term responses added to the problem, but these errors were minor compared with the inconsistent objectives: restoring the prewar gold standard at prevailing exchange rates without additional adjustment of the relative prices of traded goods on both sides of the Atlantic. European countries wanted to lower the real cost of exports, and the United States wanted to avoid inflation. All of them wanted the gold standard, but none wanted more gold. Coordination could not solve this problem; the countries' objectives were incompatible with the international monetary system they had adopted.

Strong was more than a little misleading when he complained to the November 1925 Governors Conference about the "unjustified assumption that there was some arrangement with the British which made it impossible for us to increase our rates." The key word is impossible. He had not pledged to keep rates unchanged. His correspondence with Norman during this period shows, however, that foreign considerations were important. His report on open market policy at the November meeting stated that "this country has a definite responsibility to determine its monetary policy with some regard to the effects of such policy outside of our own borders."

Some of the governors were openly skeptical about Strong's commitment. To Strong's statement denying an arrangement with the British, Governor Calkins replied: "It is an assumption that still prevails, I believe" (Governors Conference, November 2–4, 1925, 351–52). Soon after, Calkins added: "I believe there is a widespread belief throughout the country that the Federal Reserve banks will not raise their rates because of some understanding with England." Strong did not reply on the record. Discussion went off the record at this point.[119]

With the recovery and increased borrowing, all reserve banks could cover expenses and pay dividends. The November 1925 meeting, however, reconsidered the apportionment of the portfolio. The OMIC approved a resolution apportioning acceptances among the banks, based, first, on estimated expenses and dividends and, second, after these expenditures were covered, to take account of charge-offs for loan losses. By accommodating some of the regional reserve banks, Strong was able to maintain support for his policy actions. The November meeting suggests, however, that this support could not be taken for granted. The real bills view was firmly held, and several of the governors were openly critical of a policy they regarded as inflationary.[120]

The November conference also discussed an issue that continued to irritate some of the governors. Differences in reserve requirement ratios, combined with nonpayment of interest on required reserve balances, gave banks an incentive to minimize required reserves by encouraging customers to shift deposits from demand to time account. The customer received higher interest payments on the deposit, and the bank reduced its required reserves. The reserve banks' desire to increase membership worked in the opposite direction. Oliver M. W. Sprague, as part of his work with the

119. Short-term changes at year end induced New York to purchase $50 million to prevent an increase in call money rates to 6 percent. The Board agreed reluctantly when New York explained that it had bought $18 million and would put the purchases in its own portfolio instead of the System account (Board memo, Board of Governors File, box 1434, July 1, 1927; Riefler 1956, 63–64).

120. At the November 1925 Governors Conference, Strong raised the issue of charter renewal. Although the original charter did not expire until 1933, Congress had started consideration. Strong urged the governors to make sure that no scandals would be uncovered if Congress examined the System's operations before renewal. His list includes issues of discrimination for religious or political belief, nepotism, favoritism for one or another person or group in purchasing, dealing in securities, and similar matters. No officer at the New York bank was allowed to borrow money without Strong's approval. He urged the other governors to adopt similar standards.

legislative committee, proposed a reduction to 2 percent in reserve requirements on savings deposits, with time deposits remaining at the 3 percent
rate. The objective was to strengthen the System's political base by increasing membership by savings banks. The reserve banks overwhelmingly rejected the proposal. Although the issue did not die, they took no action in
the 1920s.[121] Partly as a result of inaction, the ratio of time to demand deposits increased by 10.8 percentage points from 1920 to 1929. Inaction permitted bank credit to grow relative to money by about $1.5 billion.

The OMIC held meetings in January, March, June, August, September,
and November 1926, but it made few decisions to purchase or sell government securities other than temporary changes to smooth the money
market or replace maturing issues. Concern about renewed recession
prompted purchases of $65 million in May and a reduction in New York's
discount rate to 3.5 percent. These decisions were soon reversed: in August
New York restored the 4 percent rate, and the OMIC voted to sell $80 mil-
lion.

Inactivity reflected an atypical year of general consensus on appropriate
actions.[122] Total return on common stocks was less than 12 percent, so total
brokers' loans and the stock exchange rose modestly, satisfying the real
bills faction. Reserve bank earnings not only covered expenses and dividends but increased earned surplus by $8.5 million, satisfying those for
whom earnings were the primary concern. The gold stock increased modestly, and member bank discounts remained between $500 million and
$650 million throughout the year. This range reflected moderate pressure.
Strong reminded the governors of the Riefler-Burgess principle:

> Experience in the past has indicated that member banks when in debt to the
> Federal Reserve Bank of New York, and in less[er] degree at other money cen-
> ters, constantly endeavor to free themselves from that indebtedness, and as
> a consequence such pressure as arises is in the direction of curtailing
> loans. . . .
>
> The total volume of borrowing undoubtedly exerts some pressure upon
> the business community. Should we go into a business recession while the
> member banks were continuing to borrow directly 500 or 600 million dol-

---

121. Seventy years later, banks used computer programs to shift deposits from demand
to time account overnight, reducing bank reserves. The System reduced the reserve requirement ratio against time deposits to zero.

122. Agricultural problems continued. A drought in Texas increased the demand for discounts at the Dallas reserve bank. Governor Talley tried to be selective, angering local bankers
who thought they had a right to borrow. A local congressman introduced a bill to remove Talley, and there was a congressional hearing in 1928. Talley remained (CHFRS, Dreibilbis,
March 4, 1955).

lars, (if bills [acceptances] are included nearly 800 million dollars,) we should continue taking steps to relieve some of the pressure which this borrowing induces by purchasing government securities and thus enabling member banks to reduce their indebtedness. (OMIC Minutes, Board of Governors File, box 1436, March 20, 1926, 3–4)[123]

Notwithstanding general agreement on actions, conflict between the Board and the OMIC continued. The Board was often reluctant to give the OMIC standby discretion to purchase or sell without prior approval by the Board. For example, in November 1925 the OMIC voted no change in open market policy but asked for authority to purchase up to $100 million, if necessary, to offset near-term seasonal movements. Purchases would reverse in January if business conditions warranted. The Board rejected the request.

The Board continued to press the governors about continuous borrowing and stock exchange lending by member banks, particularly banks that discounted at the reserve banks.[124] Despite his frequent claim that banks were reluctant to borrow, Strong agreed that governors should stop "continuous borrowing." He reported that nine hundred banks had borrowed continuously for at least one year. The reasons differed. Some were problem banks, others were heavy seasonal borrowers or large borrowers that repaid.

Strong recognized that pressure on small banks to repay borrowing would shift the borrowing without affecting the total. Small banks would borrow from their correspondents. Given the stock of reserves, the correspondents would borrow from the Federal Reserve or, if the Federal Reserve would not lend, credit would contract. The question, he said, is, "Who is going to borrow this money from us to make good the reserves of the banking system as a whole? Somebody has got to do it" (Governors Conference, March 1926, 53).

Strong's answers did not satisfy the Board. In April it asked the governors to supply the names of banks that borrowed continuously in 1925 and to identify those that could liquidate loans by selling government securities or other securities—nonreal bills. The Board justified this intervention in the management of the reserve banks as a means of helping individual

123. Later in the same report, Strong added an additional condition—borrowing by New York City banks of $100 million or more. With only $50 million borrowed, there is less tendency for credit to flow to New York (in the form of call loans). Thus, for Strong, the key to reducing call loans was to reduce borrowing by New York banks without increasing borrowing elsewhere.

124. Stock prices fell sharply from February to April, then renewed their rise. Every month in 1926 is above the corresponding month of 1925.

member banks "to conserve their capacity to borrow at the Reserve banks" (Board of Governors of the Federal Reserve System, *Annual Report*, 1926). The reserve banks did not welcome the interference. The policy difference that paralyzed decision making in 1929 had begun.

Member bank borrowing rose to $650 million in the fourth quarter, about 30 percent of total reserves. The Board continued to press the reserve banks. In November some governors proposed that members be required to repay all borrowing at least once a year, but the only decision was to review the issue at the next meeting in spring 1927. By that time, borrowing had declined.

The Board took an additional step; it urged New York to collect data on loans to New York Stock Exchange members. Strong was reluctant, but he discussed the issue with the governors of the stock exchange. They agreed to collect and publish the data, but the published data included only borrowings in New York. A stock exchange firm that borrowed at a branch outside New York did not include those borrowings in its report (Governors Conference, March 1926, 83–85).[125] The report also excluded non-member firms (124).

Differences between New York and Washington on this issue continued for the rest of the decade. The Board wanted the governors to reduce loans for speculative, stock exchange credit. New York replied that the uses of Federal Reserve credit could not be controlled "once it leaves our doors" (ibid., 122).

In addition to these substantive issues, there were minor irritants. In March, just before the Governors Conference, the Board tried to return to the policy it had enforced before 1920. It voted to require that all meetings be held in Washington. The governors responded by voting that the action was an "inadvisable restriction upon the freedom of the Committee" (OMIC Final Minutes, Board of Governors File, box 1436, May 20, 1926).

Banks could choose to participate in open market purchases. Even if a governor voted to approve purchases at the Governors Conference, the directors of the bank did not always agree to share in the purchases. Several banks did not participate unless they were operating at a loss. Other banks—Dallas, Kansas City, and Minneapolis—were usually short of earnings, so they participated more than proportionally in the System portfolio. Table 4.3 compares the relative size of the open market portfolio at each bank in December 1926 and 1928 with the bank's relative size.

The table suggests that Strong used New York's portfolio to increase

125. Strong admitted, however, that he was startled by the amount, more than $1 billion, above the highest estimates before the data were reported (Governors Conference, March 1926, 124).

Table 4.3   Government Securities and Reserve Bank Size, December 1926 and 1928 (percent)

BANK	1926 GOVERNMENT SECURITIES	1926 NOTES AND DEPOSITS	1928 GOVERNMENT SECURITIES	1928 NOTES AND DEPOSITS
Boston	3.2	7.4	3.6	7.2
New York	18.7	31.2	21.6	31.3
Philadelphia	6.4	6.7	9.4	6.5
Cleveland	11.5	9.8	14.4	9.4
Richmond	2.4	3.8	1.5	3.6
Atlanta	0.6	5.7	3.2	4.7
Chicago	15.5	13.8	15.7	15.7
St. Louis	6.7	3.2	9.2	3.5
Minneapolis	5.4	3.0	4.8	2.9
Kansas City	9.3	3.9	4.6	3.8
Dallas	7.4	2.8	4.4	2.8
San Francisco	12.9	8.7	7.5	8.5

earnings at the regional banks. In December 1926 and 1928, New York's holdings were ten to twelve percentage points below its proportional share.[126] Together, St. Louis, Kansas City, and Dallas held ten to thirteen percentage points more than their proportional share. These banks were not members of the OMIC, but they had an incentive to support Strong's policies at the Governors Conferences, particularly when he wanted to purchase. On the other hand, Richmond and Atlanta typically participated much less than proportionally, often not at all.

Rising Conflict

A turbulent 1927 followed the relative calm of 1926. Weaknesses of the Federal Reserve Act and the inconsistent objectives and divergent beliefs of officials hindered the System in choosing and maintaining policies. The

126. Comparison of bank participation in the System account in 1928 with the initial distribution of securities when the System account started in 1924 shows that Boston, New York, Richmond, and Atlanta reduced their shares while Cleveland, St. Louis, Minneapolis, Kansas City, and Dallas increased by relatively large percentages. As suggested above, New York, possibly assisted by Boston, appears to have worked systematically to redistribute income within the System toward the small, mainly agricultural regional reserve banks. For comparison with table 4.3, the distribution in January 1924 is as follows (percentage):

Boston	8.4	Chicago	16.3
New York	27.0	St. Louis	3.5
Philadelphia	8.1	Minneapolis	2.7
Cleveland	9.7	Kansas City	3.4
Atlanta	4.8	San Francisco	9.1

Source: Letter Rounds to Smead, System Open Market Account (Board of Governors File, box 1452, January 3, 1924).

recession that started in October 1926 called for open market purchases and lower discount rates to expand money and credit. Bond yields declined and stock prices rose throughout the year. Credit to carry securities rose, renewing and strengthening concerns about speculative credit expansion. The pound depreciated against the dollar, particularly in the winter and spring. Renewed gold flows to the United States increased the gold reserve ratio. Beginning in April, the Federal Reserve tried to hide the gold inflow by keeping the gold on deposit under earmark abroad.[127]

The Board, the New York bank, and the open market committee could not agree on which of these changes was most important. Strong's views finally dominated; the System reduced interest rates during the summer and early fall, long after the recession had started, in part to support the pound. Miller blamed Strong for making a serious error, and he later told Herbert Hoover that Strong bore "a large measure of responsibility" for the 1927 increase in reserves (quoted in Kettl 1986, 34). Many contemporary observers shared this view. Reed (1930) called the credit expansion in 1927 excessive and argued that it contributed to a sustained rise in share prices.

In fact, growth of the monetary base was only slightly above 1 percent for the year; modest positive base growth in the first half turned negative in the second half. Growth of the money stock, currency, and demand deposits was slightly faster, about 1.5 percent for the year. More rapid growth of bank lending was achieved by growth of time deposits, in part encouraged by bankers' efforts to reduce required reserves while increasing deposits.

The 1926–27 recession did not reach its trough until November 1927, thirteen months after it began. The National Bureau of Economic Research ranks the recession as one of the mildest in the years since 1920. Industrial production fell only 7 percent from peak to trough, one of the smallest reductions on record.

The Federal Reserve began open market purchases in May 1927, about halfway through the recession. Purchases added a total of $240 million to reserves, but much of the increase was offset by a decline in borrowing and in the reported gold stock.

On February 25, Congress passed the McFadden Act.[128] Section 18

127. Earmarked holdings were excluded from reported gold holdings, so they did not appear in the Federal Reserve published reports or in the monetary base. In 1927 earmarked gold rose $160 million, but the Federal Reserve was able to report a decline in gold holdings of $113 million for the year (Board of Governors of the Federal Reserve System 1943, 536).

128. The McFadden Act began as an effort by the comptroller to revitalize the national banking system. To escape restrictions in the national banking laws, national banks converted to state banks in the mid-1920s. Before the McFadden Act, national banks could not establish branches or purchase investment securities.

renewed the Federal Reserve's charter and extended its term "until dissolved by Act of Congress" (Krooss 1969, 4:2656). The act also expanded the powers of national banks by permitting them to make loans on real estate for more than one year.[129] And it permitted national banks to establish branches under the rules that applied to state-chartered banks in the state of domicile. This effectively prevented the spread of interstate and, in many states, intrastate banking for more than fifty years.

Despite the recession, the February meeting of the Federal Advisory Council found no reason to reduce discount rates or change open market policy. The OMIC did not meet until March 1927. With Strong once again on leave for health reasons,[130] the committee voted to replace $25 million of expiring securities and to purchase an additional $50 million if the situation required. The preliminary memo prepared for the meeting offered three reasons for not selling securities or permitting them to expire without replacement: to hold the portfolio to protect against future inflation; to avoid attracting more foreign balances and gold "from countries who need them, to us who do not want them"; and to prevent higher interest rates worldwide in a period of falling commodity prices (OMIC Final Minutes, Board of Governors File, box 1436, March 21, 1927).[131]

Hamlin moved that the Board accept the OMIC's recommendations. Miller offered a substitute motion permitting replacement of the $25 million but rejecting standby authority to purchase up to $50 million. The Board approved the substitute, keeping decision power at the Board; only Hamlin voted no (Board Minutes, March 21, 1927, 235–37).

Strong returned at the end of April. Early in May, he informed the Board that the Bank of France was in the process of shipping $90 million in gold

129. Before the change, loans were for one year, renewable at the one-year rate. Telser (1996, 19) claims this change contributed to the severity of the depression by increasing bankers' risk. In fact, real estate loans by national banks were a modest share of national bank portfolios and did not increase rapidly after February 1927.

130. His deputy at the OMIC, Pierre Jay, resigned as chairman of the New York bank in December 1926. His replacement was Gates McGarrah, who served from May 1927 to February 1930, when he resigned to become president of the Bank for International Settlements. McGarrah would not accept appointment as chairman until the Federal Reserve Board agreed that he could remain a member of the general council of the Reichsbank set up as part of the Dawes agreement.

131. This was a change of mind. In February, New York had concurred with the Federal Advisory Council's recommendation that the March maturities should not be replaced. The change reflected the increase in securities market activity and rise in stock prices (Riefler 1956, 95). The Board staff's memo for the meeting gave an additional reason for inaction: belief that the recession had ended. The memo shows industrial production back to the level of the previous year. The National Bureau of Economic Research dates the end of the recession eight months later. The memo reports the price level as 6 percent below the previous year (Board of Governors File, box 2461, March 18, 1927).

to a New York bank: $30 million had already been shipped. The gold had served as collateral for a loan from the Bank of England. The Bank of France prepaid the loan, releasing the gold for sale. After discussion with the other members of the OMIC, Strong bought the remaining $60 million from France and held it on earmark at the Bank of England. New York offset the effect of the purchase on the New York market by selling the Bank of France securities from the open market account.[132]

The preliminary memo, prepared for the May 9 OMIC meeting, mentioned a number of special factors—floods, problems in the oil industry, collapse of some real estate speculation—but made no reference to the general recession, then six months old. The report noted that a considerable fall in commodity prices had affected agricultural and nonagricultural prices and expressed concern about the growth of total credit (estimated to have increased $1.5 billion in the past twelve months), renewed gold flows to the United States, and the reduced size of the open market account after sales to France. The Federal Reserve had the same problem as in 1916; the remaining balance in the OMIC account, about $100 million, was too small to prevent future inflation or sterilize additional gold inflows.

Chart 4.3 (p. 173) shows a main source of the problem. The difference between New York and London rates had decreased, along with the covered spread, so New York was a relatively more attractive market for foreign and domestic accounts. Moreover, the Treasury paid up to 98 percent of the value of imported gold when it acquired the gold. This gave sellers a few additional days to earn interest, raising the effective price above prices abroad.[133]

Strong presented twelve ways of responding to the problem but did not recommend any action pending a meeting with the Board (OMIC Minutes, Board of Governors File, box 1434, May 11, 1927). The following day the OMIC voted unanimously to stop selling securities to offset gold inflows and to begin seasonal purchases no later than August 1 to bring the account up to $250 million, if it could be done "without undue effect on the money market" (OMIC Final Minutes, Board of Governors File, box 1436, May 11, 1927). The committee defined "undue effect" to mean that interest rates and borrowing would remain approximately unchanged during the summer. The decision permitted purchases of $150 million.

132. These actions avoided showing an increase in the gold stock on the weekly release. The bank reported the earmarked gold on the published statement as "gold held abroad," a new item. Since the gold had originally been offered to the Irving Trust, there was no secret about the Bank of England's changed position.

133. One of twelve possible actions discussed at the meeting was to stop this practice, thereby lowering the gold price by the amount of interest lost on delayed payment.

Once again, Hamlin moved for approval by the Board and Miller offered a substitute that delayed the decision. Miller's substitute passed on a close vote. The next day, with Mellon present, the Board reconsidered. Hamlin again moved for approval; Miller again proposed delay, and Vice Governor Platt proposed to permit purchases up to $250 million but at a slower rate. Platt's motion passed seven to one.[134]

The Board staff's presentation to the May Governors Conference noted that the Bureau of Labor Statistics price index had fallen 10 percent in two years and was approaching its postwar low. The staff report mentioned the return of many countries to the gold standard, but it rejected this reason for the price decline. Although the staff produced no evidence to support its argument, it concluded that the price decline resulted from increased productivity (Governors Conference, May 9–12, 1927, 506). The Board made no mention of falling prices as a reason for open market purchases. Miller was generally opposed to using open market operations for such purposes. He preferred to let prices result from the ebb and flow of real bills relative to output.

Surprisingly, none of the governors disagreed with the staff argument that a return to gold convertibility by many countries had not lowered prices by increasing the world demand for gold. The price declines of the 1880s, when several countries adopted the gold standard, were well known. Even Miller, who had made this point in the 1926 hearings, did not insist on the deflationary effect of restoration.

Between May 16 and June 8, the System's portfolio increased $180 million to $316 million, well above the limit established by the Board. On June 9, Strong wrote to Crissinger explaining that only $16 million of the $180 million was for the System account.[135] The rest had been purchased to offset gold movements, changes in earmarked gold, and Treasury overdrafts. Later in the week, New York sold the Bank of France the $60 million in gold that it had acquired from the Bank of England. Britain's gold sales renewed pressure on the pound.

Strong had considerable difficulty explaining the purchases to the Board. In letters written in mid-June, he described the technical changes in the money market resulting from Treasury operations, seasonal factors, gold flows, and actions of the Bank of France. France had withdrawn

---

134. Miller's principal concern was the rising stock market. The vote on his proposal to delay was five to three against. He argued that the Federal Advisory Council was to meet and report on its proposal to change the OMIC's methods and objectives and that delay would give an opportunity to purchase after trade (and discounts) expanded. The last, real bills view was repeated frequently during 1929–33 as a reason for delaying purchases.

135. The monetary base increased less than 1 percent in the twelve months ending in May.

$100 million of deposits, converted them to gold, and shipped the gold. This alone would have reduced reserves and base money by $100 million if Strong had not purchased securities. Strong did not want to count the purchases made to offset these disturbances against the purchases authorized in May. His aim was to lower, not raise, market rates in New York (Strong to Crissinger, Board of Governors File, box 1434, June 9, 16, 20, 1927).

Strong argued that if open market rates increased, acceptances would come to the bank. To avoid the increase, the bank's discount on acceptances would have to increase, followed by an increase in the discount rate to restore the rate spread. He gave three reasons for opposing higher rates. Higher rates would hurt business, reduce the sterling exchange rate and other foreign rates, thereby renewing the gold inflow, and interfere with a large Treasury refunding operation then in process (ibid., June 20, 1927).

Miller prepared the Board's response. He acknowledged Strong's argument about Treasury operations, made no mention of the other reasons Strong gave, and insisted on holding the System account within the limits agreed on in May. Additional purchases would have to be approved by the Board (Crissinger to Strong, Board of Governors File, box 1434, June 22, 1927).

By going to Washington to discuss the issue, Strong was able to get a majority of the Board to exclude the $100 million of purchases made to offset the gold outflow. Miller, joined by Edward Cunningham, did not agree; both voted against the resolution. Miller explained that he believed all authorizations to purchase and sell should be approved explicitly by the Board. He was not in favor of higher rates; his concern was the Board's control of open market policy.

Shortly after the New York meeting between Norman, Schacht, Rist, and Strong, the OMIC met with the Board in Washington. Miller was on vacation. The meeting was free of conflict. The Board unanimously approved an additional $50 million of purchases. The members also discussed discount rate reductions:

> There was no exception to the view that the time had arrived, or was approaching, when the discount rate in New York should be reduced, and with one or two exceptions, there was no dissent from the view that a System policy of lower discount rates should in general prevail. It was pointed out, however, that local conditions in some of the interior reserve districts did not indicate any demand for rate reductions in those districts. . . .
>
> The most important consideration at the meeting was undoubtedly the fact that the differential between the rates in New York and the rates in London was not today sufficient to enable London, and therefore the rest of Eu-

rope, to avoid general advances in rates this autumn unless rates here were lowered, and that the consequences of such high rates as would result in Europe would be unfavorable to the marketing of our export produce abroad and would have an adverse effect generally on world trade. (OMIC Final Minutes, Board of Governors File, box 1436, July 27, 1927, 2)

The reasoning taken from the minutes shows that, at the time, the Board accepted Strong's policy of helping Britain. Although the statement mentions domestic factors, they are not the main reason for acting. Later, many of those who voted for the rate reduction disavowed the decision and blamed Strong for the stock market boom that followed.

The background memo showed that the spread between market rates and the (penalty) discount rate had narrowed in London and Berlin and that the discount rate had increased in Berlin, drawing gold from London. At home, commodity prices continued to fall and, the committee noted, "there was some slackening in business" (ibid, 2).[136] The System had continued to purchase in July; the System account increased to $265 million, but gold and foreign exchange changes, and reduced borrowing, canceled much of the effect on bank reserves and the monetary base.[137]

Discount rate reductions (to 3.5 percent) began in Kansas City, acting on Strong's request. Four other banks followed within the next two weeks. By mid-August only four banks—Philadelphia, Chicago, Minneapolis, and San Francisco—kept their rates at 4 percent.

THE CHICAGO RATE CONTROVERSY The *Wall Street Journal* reported on August 4 that the Federal Reserve Board had asked Chicago to reduce its discount rate, following reductions by Boston and Cleveland. Chicago replied that "there was no basis or necessity." Governor Crissinger and two other Board members responded by notifying Chicago that the Board, acting under the authority of the attorney general's opinion in 1919, would lower the rate without waiting for the Chicago directors to act (Letter Platt to Hamlin, Board of Governors File, box 1434, August 4, 1927).[138]

---

136. The Board staff's background memo notes that industrial production in July was the lowest for the year and back to the 1925 level. Preliminary figures for August were weak also (Board of Governors File, box 2461, August 19, 1927).

137. The London market strengthened in August. Strong sold sterling bills in London and, to offset the effect on the base, purchased governments in New York. By mid-August the System account was at $347 million, more than $20 million above the ceiling approved at the July 27 meeting. Strong kept Crissinger and the Board informed, and there was no criticism of his decisions at the time. Nor is there any record that the Board approved the additional purchases.

138. Hamlin was on vacation in Massachusetts and so ineligible to vote. Platt's letter identifies Crissinger, James, and Comptroller Joseph W. McIntosh as favoring action, but James

With New York's rate below the rates in other financial centers, regional banks borrowed in New York and lent at home. These actions, and the normal seasonal pattern, drained New York's gold reserve by $120 million through mid-August. On August 19, Strong wrote to Crissinger about the higher discount rates in Philadelphia and Chicago but added "that is a matter for them to decide" (Strong to Crissinger, Open Market Policy, Board of Governors File, box 1434, August 19, 1927, 24).

The August 19 letter is the only mention of Chicago's rate in Strong's many letters to the Board during August. He wrote directly to Norris and McDougal, making the case for rate reductions in terms of the benefits achieved abroad by lower rates in New York.[139] If the gold drain from New York to the districts with higher rates continued, New York would have to raise rates to stop it. Strong concluded with an argument that appealed to Norris's and McDougal's views about commerce and industry: "That orgy [stock market speculation] will always be with us and if the Federal Reserve System is to be run solely with a view to regulating stock speculation instead of being devoted to the interests of the industry and commerce of the country, then its policy will degenerate simply to regulating the affairs of gamblers. I have no hesitation in expressing my impatience with such a view of our role" (quoted in Chandler 1958, 444).

McDougal replied on August 24, saying that Chicago would decide by itself when it was appropriate to change rates. Strong responded, now citing issues that were important to the Chicago district—the benefits to crop movements and the need for System policy—but McDougal and the Chicago directors were not persuaded. On August 29, for the third time in a month, they voted to retain the 4 percent rate (ibid., 445–46).

Chicago's inaction angered Crissinger. He demanded that Chicago reduce its rate by September 2 or the Board would act without a recommendation. Chicago's chairman, William A. Heath, asked for a delay until September 9, when the Chicago directors would meet again. Heath explained that only the directors could act, not the executive committee, and they would not meet until September 9.

Although Crissinger waited for Philadelphia and San Francisco, he would not wait any longer for Chicago. At a September 6 Board meeting, Vice Governor Platt argued that the Board could not disapprove an existing rate. Crissinger overruled him. A motion was made to reduce Chicago's rate to 3.5 percent effective the following day, September 7. Hamlin moved

subsequently reversed his position, making action unlikely. Cunningham and Miller were on vacation also.

139. The benefits included postponement of rate increases abroad and a strengthening of sterling that permitted New York to sell some of the sterling bills held in London.

to substitute continuation of the 4 percent rate until September 9 to give Chicago time to reconsider. The substitute failed on a three to three vote with Miller abstaining and Mellon absent. The Board voted four to three to reduce the rate, with Platt, Hamlin, and Miller voting no and Cunningham, James, and McIntosh supporting Crissinger.[140] By the same one-vote margin, the Board then voted to notify San Francisco to reduce its rate. By the middle of September, all rates were 3.5 percent.

The Board had seized power from a reserve bank despite the bank directors' opposition. Strong wrote to Senator Carter Glass expressing concern about the strengthening of a central bank in Washington, subject to political control (Chandler 1958, 449). Glass disliked the Board's action. He dismissed its argument that it acted on the principle he had established in 1919, claiming that his earlier decision, and the supporting opinion of the acting attorney general, was not the correct interpretation of the Federal Reserve Act.[141] But Glass was more concerned about New York's role than about the board's action. In a letter to Hamlin, he expressed most concern about "the New York Bank being regarded [as] the Central bank of the Reserve System, with the other eleven banks merely branches" (Glass to Hamlin, Board of Governors File, box 1434, September 29, 1927).[142] Congress took no action.

The gold flows reversed after the rate reduction. In the next year, the gold stock declined more then $460 million to the lowest level in five years. By October, Strong suggested to the Board that an increase in the discount rate might soon be advisable. He also asked for the views of foreign central bankers. Governor Gerard Vissering of the Netherlands Bank urged caution (Board of Governors File, box 1434, October 20, 1927). The Board took no action; the 3.5 percent rate remained for the rest of the year. In November, New York proposed to set interest rates in relation to Europe that would allow newly mined gold to flow abroad "where the reserves are most

140. According to Hamlin, Crissinger did not report to the Board that Mellon had asked to delay a decision until he returned to Washington on the following day. Strong took no part in the decision. Although he wanted the rate reduced, he disliked the Board's action (Chandler 1958, 449).

141. Glass wrote in 1927: "Neither the spirit nor the text of the Act sanction[s] interferences by the central board except in unusual circumstances" (quoted in Warburg 1930, 2:493).

142. Warburg (1930, 2:493–95) shows that the only support for reserve bank autonomy with respect to discount rates in 1914 was in an amendment offered by Senator Owen that was not included in the final bill. He criticized Owen, Glass, and Parker Willis for taking opposing positions on what the act intended. The final wording was "subject to review and determination" by the Federal Reserve Board. In the early days, reserve banks resubmitted rates weekly, so the Board could influence changes by rejecting a submission (ibid., 491). This practice resumed in the 1930s.

in need of reinforcement" (OMIC Minutes, Board of Governors File, box 1436, preliminary memo for November 2, 1927, 11).

CONFLICT ABOUT STOCK PRICES   Crissinger resigned as governor on September 15, 1927, to accept private employment. Roy A. Young succeeded him as governor. Young had been governor of the Minneapolis bank for eight years.[143] Strong quickly wrote to foreign central bankers to assure them that Crissinger's resignation was unrelated to the Chicago controversy (Chandler 1958, 450).

Chandler reports that Strong was enthusiastic about the appointment (ibid., 450). If so, it was a mistake. Young shared Strong's enthusiasm for the gold standard but little else. He had sided with McDougal in the rate controversy, and he would later side with Miller in relying on direct action. Nothing in his record as governor of the Board suggests that he shared Strong's enthusiasm for a systematic policy to moderate deflation. He was, first and last, a real bills advocate with a good understanding of banking and little appreciation of the role that the Federal Reserve could have taken to alleviate the depression by preventing deflation.

By mid-1927, stock exchange speculation began to take a more prominent place in policy discussions. Common stocks returned 37.5 percent in 1927, one of the largest returns on record. Returns in 1928 were larger still, 43.6 percent, so the compound total return for these two years was 98 percent. Between July and November 1927, loans to brokers and dealers in New York increased more than $300 million. The Board and the reserve banks faced a question that has often plagued central bankers: Should they respond to large increases in asset prices or confine their attention to prices, output, money, or foreign exchange rates?

At Strong's request, Burgess prepared a background memo on the stock market for a meeting of the Governors Conference and the OMIC early in November.[144] The memo showed that security loans had increased mod-

143. Young served until April 1930, when he became governor of the Boston bank. Young started in banking as a bank messenger but rose quickly. In 1927 he supported McDougal in the rate controversy and was the last to lower his discount rate. He had extensive experience with agricultural credit and had handled many defaults, so he was welcomed by the farm bloc as an antidote to eastern (New York) influence.

144. The meeting had been discussed for more than a month. In late September Strong asked the members of the OMIC if they wanted to meet. Opinions differed. All favored a meeting and approved sterilizing gold outflows. Norris and McDougal expressed concern about stock market speculation. Harding and Fancher favored seasonal purchases to be reversed in January. Strong favored seasonal purchases also. At the time, the System held about $375 million. Strong expected purchases of an additional $25 million, made to offset sales of sterling bills, to bring the account to $400 million, far above the authorized $325 million. However $95 million of the total had been purchased to offset gold outflows.

estly as a percentage of total loans, rising from 25 percent in 1922 to 1924 to 28 or 29 percent in 1926–27. The stock market increase occurred worldwide, but United States stock prices rose somewhat more than prices abroad (OMIC Minutes, Board of Governors File, box 1436, November 2, 1927).

Earlier, Strong had written to Governor Young sending a draft of Burgess's memo and commenting on the longer-term growth of bank credit. In the past three years, Strong wrote, bank credit had increased by about $5 billion, with about $3 billion at member banks, while the gold stock had increased only $18 million. The System had supplied about $200 million of additional reserves, a credit multiplier of fifteen. The large multiplier had been achieved by a reduction in the average reserve requirement ratio resulting from more rapid growth of time and savings deposits relative to demand deposits.

Some favored security sales and higher interest rates to reduce stock exchange lending. Strong opposed using an argument that the Board used later against New York: "I have not felt that such a policy was justified by the facts, that any effort through higher rates directed especially at stock speculation would have an unfavorable effect upon business generally, and that this would be particularly unfortunate at a time when we are producing a surplus of exportable farm products which cannot be marketed abroad unless the country remains a free loaning market for the rest of the world" (Strong to Young, Board of Governors File, box 1436, October 19, 1927).

The Governors Conference coincided with the end of the mild recession. Newspapers at the time commented on the "low rate policy" and urged the Federal Reserve to tighten. Others expressed concern about the loss of gold to Argentina, Brazil, and Canada (Reed 1930, 124–26).

Although all banks had reduced their rates to 3.5 percent and the Board had urged or forced some of the reductions, the governors grumbled but agreed to keep open market rates unchanged until March and to offset gold movements by open market purchases and sales. George Seay (Richmond) said: "I think it is too low a rate, and I thought so from the beginning." Maximillian B. Wellborn (Atlanta) said he was compelled to lower rates because Kansas City, St. Louis, and Dallas had lowered theirs. Even Willis J. Bailey (Kansas City), who had been the first to reduce the rate (at Strong's urging), wanted to return to the 4 percent rate. McDougal, of course, favored an increase (Governors Conference, November 2–3, 1927, 31–46).

The committee endorsed three policy guidelines: member bank borrowing, the general level of interest rates, and the movement of foreign exchange rates, the last as a guide to future gold movements. Adolph Miller proposed making all purchases or sales of foreign exchange subject to prior approval by the Board. The Board rejected his motion and accepted the OMIC proposal. Strong now had authorization to offset gold flows without limit, and he moved quickly. In the following two weeks, the System partially sterilized large gold movements to France and Argentina and from Brazil and Poland. The net effect was an increase in the System account but little change in the money market. When New York stopped sterilizing gold losses, discounts rose to more than $600 million for the month. Despite the increased discounting, the monetary base continued to fall. By year end, call money rates began to increase.

The November meeting shows both Strong's ability to get approval for his policies and the growing restlessness of several governors and Board members. Miller was, as usual, opposed to giving Strong discretionary authority. McDougal and Norris wanted higher rates and a tighter policy. They were now joined openly by governors of smaller banks, who wanted to increase their earnings. Strong had answered, but not satisfied, the critics of his policy, who blamed him for the increase in loans to the stock market and in speculative credit.

Thus the discount rate and open market decisions of 1927 further divided the System's policymakers. Those, like Strong, who favored a System policy that took account of domestic and international objectives were generally pleased by the outcome.[145] International cooperation, though restricted by domestic considerations, had prevented a threat to the gold exchange standard. Strong now recognized more clearly the weaknesses in that system: any central bank holding a large stock of dollars or pounds instead of gold could precipitate a crisis or a serious problem by calling for gold.

Miller later blamed Strong for the easy policy. In congressional testimony and elsewhere, he described the 1927 actions as the beginning of an inflationary policy that produced an "inevitable" reaction culminating in the "breakdown of the autumn of 1929" (Miller 1931, 124; 1935). He described the policy in harsh words as based on an illusion that the Federal Reserve could correct "the maldistribution of gold in the world. . . . It is one of the most misleading illusions that any body of men charged with the responsibility of administering the fundamental credit mechanism of the country could allow to enter its mind" (Miller 1931, 134): "In my judgment [the policy] resulted in one of the most costly errors committed by it or any other banking system in the last 75 years" (134).

The mistake, according to Miller, was to expand reserves when there was no demand for additional reserves. Banks don't hold idle reserves. The money flows into the stock market and brokers' loans in the call money market.[146]

Miller's statement reflected the theory he and others relied on. His statement is correct when it claims that the additional reserves would not remain idle, but the implication he drew was incorrect. Monetary expansion encourages stock purchases and raises stock prices by changing expected (nominal) earnings and lowering interest rates. This was part of the transmission process, as Miller recognized. He was wrong to oppose monetary expansion for this reason and to assert the real bills position that the Federal Reserve should respond only to banks' increased demand to borrow on real bills.

Miller's statement conflicted also with Strong's Riefler-Burgess views. That analysis was flawed also, as events at the time, fall 1927, suggest. Discounts rose in December despite increased open market purchases of acceptances and securities. Contrary to Riefler-Burgess, banks did not show the reluctance to borrow that Strong's interpretation relied on. Borrowing to buy shares had become unusually profitable. By holding rates down seasonally and to help Britain, the System permitted market rates to rise above the discount rate. The central problem of the next two years had begun.

Thus the System entered 1928–29 with divided views about its responsibilities and mistaken ideas about the appropriate course of action. Strong was now terminally ill. The Board had new, but weak, leadership in Young. Miller was an active critic, eager to take control but without much ability to persuade. Most of the others lacked an understanding of central banking and financial markets. They agreed on the desirability of an international gold standard, but they were unwilling to permit domestic prices to rise when gold flowed in, and they all seemed unaware, or at least never mentioned, that falling United States prices from 1926 to 1929 signaled that the gold exchange standard had a serious inconsistency.[147]

Hesitant and Uncertain Direction

Net gold exports continued in early 1928. The Federal Reserve sterilized part of the net outflow and allowed part to balance the seasonal reduction in bank reserves. Deputy Governors Case and Harrison kept the Board in-

146. Kettl (1986, 34) reports on a 1934 letter from Miller to Herbert Hoover claiming that Montagu Norman exerted great influence on Strong. I have found nothing in the record that contradicts Strong's statements that he cooperated only to the extent that it did not conflict with domestic objectives. United States prices had fallen at the time of the July 1927 agreement.

147. Burgess (1964, 224) mentions discussions in the twenties about the desirability of United States inflation to help Europe recover. Strong was opposed.

formed about the ebb and flow and the size of open market purchases and sales.

The OMIC met in mid-January. The preliminary memo described the 8 percent growth of bank credit in 1927 as the largest in three years and, despite the recession, 2 percent above "normal" growth. Loans on stocks and bonds showed the most rapid increase.[148]

The recession appeared to have ended. Also, system policy was now "much more independent of the European situation." The current problem was to control credit expansion without harming business. The OMIC proposed, and the Board approved, authorization to sell securities to offset gold movements (OMIC Minutes, Board of Governors File, box 1436, January 12, 1928). In the three weeks ending January 25, the System sold $80 million and reduced advances to dealers by $76 million. Those actions offset the seasonal decline in currency. Market rates declined, so the OMIC voted to tighten by selling an additional $50 million.[149]

Chicago led the increase in discount rates back to 4 percent. Between January 25 and March 1, the other banks followed. The reason for the higher rates puzzled some officials. R. L. Austin, chairman at Philadelphia, requested an explanation of Chicago's action and the Board's approval. Young replied that the Board's action was almost unanimous. The members had acted because open market sales in January had not raised rates very much. Young later repeated that credit extension had increased more than normal (Letters Young to Austin, Board of Governors File, box 1240, January 28 and 31, 1928). At this point, both the Board and the reserve banks agreed that the Federal Reserve could control credit expansion by open market operations and discount rate changes.

Agreement did not last. Early in February, Harrison told Young that discounts by New York banks had reached $156 million, indicating a modest increase in market tightness. New York wanted to suspend sales for a few days. The Board accepted the proposal with some members urging an indefinite suspension (Riefler 1956, 182).[150]

---

148. President Coolidge found nothing alarming about the stock market. His statement to this effect shocked Hoover, who was about to campaign for the presidency (Kettl 1986, 34).

149. Strong was not present at the time, but he favored sales. Burgess (1964, 219) reports a visit early in 1928 to Strong, who was recuperating in Atlantic City. Strong was concerned that the New York banks had reduced borrowings from the Fed. He favored greater restraint (increased borrowing) to prevent inflation. The wholesale price level, recorded at the time, was 97 (base 100 in 1926). See also Chandler 1958, 454–55.

150. At about this time, Hamlin asked the research division what open market operations accomplished. The reply was that open market operations support discount rate changes, but their effects "are not as great as is generally believed" (memo, Goldenweiser to Hamlin, Board of Governors File, box 1435, February 17, 1928).

The OMIC met again in late March and noted that recovery was under way. Net sales of $150 million since January had reduced the System account to $273 million, but the New York money market did not show evidence that the discount rate was effective. The Board accepted a proposal for additional sales but exacted a promise that sales would be used to make discount rates effective without raising rates (Open Market, Board of Governors File, box 1436, March 26, 1928). Miller voted against the resolution, citing no evidence of increased borrowing for commercial purposes and uncertainty about business conditions (ibid.).

In April, credit expansion continued to exceed growth of output. The recovery from recession was complete, and there was no sign of price inflation.[151] The main concern was that after a lull during the winter, security loans had increased. The OMIC continued to sell securities. Late in the month, Boston and Chicago raised their discount rates to 4.5 percent. Richmond, St. Louis, and Minneapolis promptly followed. New York waited a month.

Case was optimistic when the Governors Conference met at the end of April (1928). With call money rates at 5 percent and discount rates at 4.5 percent at several banks, the credit situation seemed well in hand. The French elections had been won by Raymond Poincaré, so French stabilization and continued United States gold outflow seemed likely. The governors discussed the possibility that some countries (France) would want to return to selling foreign exchange holdings to restore a full gold standard. Harrison dismissed this possibility as unlikely. He was soon proved wrong.

The committee once again discussed the continuing shift from demand to time deposits that lowered the average reserve requirement ratio and expanded bank credit. Bank credit was 9 percent above the previous year, production 2.5 percent. This was far from the norm proposed in the tenth annual report, but the governors could not agree on what should be done about time deposits (Governors Conference, April 30–May 2, 1928).

Between the April Governors Conference and the May 25 OMIC meeting, France withdrew $97 million in gold. Bank borrowing in New York increased to between $200 million and $300 million. New York now raised its discount rate with the intention of reducing borrowing. By May 25 the System account had fallen to $100 million, so it was no longer of much use (Riefler 1956, 202).[152] System sales and gold outflows continued to reduce

151. The year-to-year change in stock prices (S&P) was 33 percent, in consumer prices – 1 percent.

152. The reserve banks continued to hold about $150 million on their own account for income, so total holdings of governments were about $250 million.

the monetary base, and member bank borrowing continued to rise; New York banks had borrowed $272 million, the System $880 million, far above the $100 million and $500 million that Strong regarded as "tight." Market interest rates reached the highest level since 1923, with call money at 6 percent.

The preliminary memo recognized that discount rate changes in New York relative to the rest of the country changed the place where banks borrowed without much effect on the total amount borrowed. With call money 1.5 percent to 2 percent above discount rates, banks found borrowing profitable. The committee voted to continue open market sales.

June brought renewed, large gold outflows, almost $150 million to France alone, that reduced the reported gold stock to the lowest level since 1923. Chicago voted to increase its discount rate to 5 percent in early July. The Board was divided and delayed action. New York opposed an increase. With the call money rate at 10 percent, Case wrote to Young that the rise in call money rates was a more effective response than a new round of discount rate increases (Case to Young, Board of Governors File, box 1240 July 3, 1928). The following week the Board approved the Chicago increase, with James and McIntosh opposed. Despite the presidential election, Mellon favored the increase: "The sooner the rate increases come, the better" (Letter Platt to Young [on vacation], Board of Governors File, Box 1240, July 10, 1928). New York followed. By the end of July seven banks were at 5 percent, but the rate did not become uniform until the following May.

By the time the Board approved the higher rates, stock exchange trading had slowed to the level of previous years. Call money rates fell from 10 percent to 5 percent, and the Standard and Poor's index was below the May level. These changes were seen as hopeful signs that the speculative boom was over. The OMIC met on July 18 but took no further action. Table 4.4 shows, however, that stock exchange volume soon increased.[153]

The mood was not entirely cheerful. The memo prepared for the July 18 OMIC meeting compared business activity with interest rates since 1900 and concluded with a prophetic warning: "High [interest] rates have almost invariably been followed by business declines after a lag of six months to a year" (Memo to OMIC, Board of Governors File, box 1436, July 17, 1928). The memo suggested that the restriction worked by slowing construction and new financing. It noted, however, that there was no current evidence of slower domestic activity or of adverse effects abroad. These circumstances did not last.

---

153. Market acceptance rates had fallen below the Federal Reserve's minimum buying rate, so the acceptance portfolio declined. One reason was a change in tax laws exempting foreign central banks from tax on interest received on acceptances.

Table 4.4   Shares Traded on the New York Stock Exchange (millions of dollars)

YEAR	1926	1927	1928	1929
January	39.0	34.3	56.9	110.8
February	35.7	44.2	47.0	78.0
March	52.3	49.2	85.0	105.7
April	30.3	49.8	80.5	82.6
May	23.3	46.6	82.4	91.3
June	38.2	47.8	63.9	69.5
July	36.7	38.6	39.2	93.4
August	44.5	51.2	67.2	95.7
September	37.0	51.6	90.6	100.0
October	40.4	50.3	98.8	141.7
November	31.3	51.0	115.4	72.4
December	42.0	62.1	92.8	83.9
Year	450.8	576.6	919.7	1,125.0

Source: Reed 1930, 163.

By mid-August, some exchange rates abroad had moved toward the gold export point. The OMIC did not want to absorb more gold but also did not want foreign banks to sell their short-term bill or security holdings at a time when the Federal Reserve provided additional credit to assist the seasonal crop movement. The reserve banks bought bills from foreign central banks to prevent a rise in market interest rates.

Miller proposed that the Board send a letter to all the reserve banks setting a preferential rate for seasonal crop marketing paper at 0.5 percent to 1 percent below market rates. James suggested, instead, a preferential rate on all acceptances to help move the crops (OMIC Minutes, Board of Governors File, box 1436, August 13, 1928). Only Governor Harding (Boston) favored the proposals, and they were not adopted.[154] The principal objections were that without a general reduction in rates, member banks would not reduce their lending rates to farmers. The governors did not believe that preferential rates would affect the distribution of credit (ibid.).

The OMIC voted to ease money and credit through open market purchases, if necessary, to prevent "an emergency situation." Young proposed that the Board purchase only to relieve a strain "which may react unfavorably upon commerce and industry," but he also proposed allowing the OMIC to buy securities from foreign governments to prevent higher rates. He again suggested a preferential rate on crop-moving paper (draft letter, Young to Harrison, Board of Governors File, box 1436, August 15, 1928). The Board considered but rejected Miller's proposal for a preferential rate for agriculture and also rejected a grant of discretionary authority to New York.

154. Harding (Boston) was the principal advocate of preferential rates in 1920–21.

Typical seasonal credit expansion added $100 million to $200 million during the fall. With prices falling, Young thought many producers would hold inventories, so credit demand could be as much as "$300 million or more" (Letter Young to Cunningham, Board of Governors File, Box 1436, August 17, 1928). Member banks were heavily in debt; the concern was that they would not borrow enough to prevent a sharp increase in interest rates. Recalling the 1920–21 experience and the political influence of agriculture, some Board and OMIC members agreed to open market purchases as a last resort to prevent a substantial increase in market rates.[155] By a three to two vote, the Board approved a limit of $100 million in purchases, only as a last resort. It urged the reserve banks to ease through purchases of acceptances only if ease was "unavoidable" (Open Market, Board of Governors File, box 1436, August 16, 1928).[156]

Although the August decision was cautious about purchases, it was not cautious enough to satisfy some of the reserve banks. C. R. McKay, deputy governor at Chicago, reported that the Chicago directors opposed any open market purchases and expressed "very little concern" about moving the harvest to market. The banks could rediscount if a problem arose. Governor Seay (Richmond) opposed open market purchases also: "Our directors are on record that this bank should not only not purchase government securities but that it should sell those which it has. . . . [T]his bank will not participate in any purchase of government securities." Seay recommended a reallocation of credit from "those who have absorbed credit for other than business purposes." His letter explicitly reflects a recurring issue—loans by large corporations to the securities market. R. L. Austin, chairman at Philadelphia, approved of the decision to supply seasonal credit but urged the Board to state its policy publicly (McKay to Young, Seay to Harrison, Austin to Young, Board of Governors File, box 1436, August 17, 20, 23, 1928).[157]

155. The OMIC also discussed reductions in discount rates to encourage borrowing. Opinion was unanimous that reductions should be avoided but that the lower (4.5 percent) rates should be maintained in dominantly agricultural districts (Letter Young to Cunningham, Board of Governors File, box 1436, August 17, 1928).

156. Hamlin and Cunningham were on vacation (Young to Cunningham, Board of Governors File, box 1436, August 17, 1928). Miller and James voted no. Miller (1935, 451–52) claimed the easy policy in the second half of 1928 was "lacking in strong conviction" (452), but he did not say what he wanted to do at the time. Seasonal factors favored an increase in credit. The gold stock and the gold reserve percentage fell. Discounts remained near $1 billion, evidence of tight, not easy policy on the Riefler-Burgess interpretation. The main evidence of ease was the rise in acceptances. Acceptance rates remained below discount rates.

157. Strong returned from Europe in early August but was too ill to resume his duties. Soon after, he offered to resign, but the directors refused. He no longer had an active role. He received a memo from Walter Stewart, at the time an adviser to the Bank of England. Stewart

The Board was in no position to issue a policy statement, since it had no policy and focused only on the short term. One financial journalist described the problem as a choice between three risky options. First, the System could ease to finance seasonal agricultural inventories. The risk was that the additional credit would lead to "another boiling stock market with ultimate danger to business." Second, the System could tighten enough to reduce stock prices. This path led to deflation, recession, and accusations that policy was influenced by "the money power." Third, the System could continue the status quo (Temple 1928).[158]

The presidential election made an additional complication. Early in January, the Treasury announced its intention to refund the Second Liberty Loan in September at 3.5 percent interest (Reed 1930, 136). This put the Federal Reserve on notice nine months in advance. No less important was the expected effect of higher interest rates in the midst of congressional and presidential campaigns. Temple (1928) quotes as the opinions of "Chicago bankers" that "the fall will see the greatest political market in history" and of an eastern investment banker that "there will be the greatest bull market in history from the middle of September until November."

In the event, when commercial paper rates rose to 5.625 percent in September, the System bought acceptances to lower rates. In effect, it pegged the acceptance rate at 4.5 percent by buying $300 million of acceptances between August and November.[159] The increase in acceptances and a small renewed inflow of gold offset a decline in discounts. The monetary base fell at an 8 to 10 percent rate in July and August, then increased in the fall. Nevertheless, the annual rate of change remained between 0 and –2 per-

---

warned that money was tight in New York. Concerning the large volume of borrowing, Stewart wrote: "Surely it was never intended that member banks should bear the full burden of gold exports for currency stabilization in France" (quoted in Chandler 1958, 459–60). Strong was less concerned about the short term than the long. He replied that the Federal Reserve could reduce short-term pressure by open market purchases and discount rate reductions. Then he added: "If the System is unwilling to do it, then I presume the New York Bank must do it alone" (ibid., 460). With respect to the stock market, he wrote: "I fear voluntary assumption of responsibility for this matter just as much as I fear voluntary assumption of responsibility for the prices of commodities" (ibid., 460–61). At the time, he believed New York's discount rate was too high. He preferred a 4.5 percent rate in New York, with 5 percent elsewhere, to push discounting toward New York. However, he avoided mentioning the System's major problem—reaching several inconsistent goals simultaneously.

158. Alan Temple was managing editor of a business weekly. His memo brings out the political, and policy, conflict between support of the crop movement and concerns about Wall Street and the stock market.

159. This policy was not accidental. In a letter to the Board dated September 26, Harrison proposed the policy that they followed (Riefler 1956, 338). In December, Miller proposed an increase in the acceptance rate, but the motion failed. Hamlin and Platt joined Miller in voting to approve. This was a bold interference, since the reserve banks set acceptance rates.

cent from March 1928 to August 1929. Long-term rates remained unchanged in the fall of 1928, but rates for new stock exchange loans increased almost three percentage points (to 8.9 percent) between August and December, the highest rate since 1920. The preliminary report for the November 13–16 OMIC meeting referred to "the presence of few other buyers of bills [acceptances]" and the reduction in discounts as banks borrowed at the lower acceptance rate to repay discounts.

The memo mentioned three guides to current policy: ending expansion of credit for speculation; limiting effects of interest rates on the volume of business; and limiting effects on world rates and world trade. The report noted that new stock and bond offerings through October were about the same in 1928 as in 1927. An increase in new stock issues almost offset an $800 million decline in bond issues. On September 28, the Federal Advisory Council agreed that the 5 percent discount rates had delayed some permanent financing but had not harmed business. All in all, the current situation seemed favorable for continued expansion and credit availability. The Board staff's memo on the business situation is about expansion in production and sales without inflation (Board of Governors File, box 2461, November 8, 1928).

The situation abroad was more disturbing. The Bank of England began to lose gold in September 1928. Losses continued, with only brief interruption, throughout the fall and in 1929. The report for the OMIC meeting noted that earlier gold outflows from the United States improved countries' ability to defend exchange rates, but continued high rates at home would force higher rates abroad. They soon did.

The OMIC congratulated itself for providing seasonal credit expansion at relatively low interest rates. The committee proposed that New York consider a 0.125 percent increase in the buying rate for acceptances. The Board accepted the recommendation, but the New York directors rejected the proposal. The acceptance rate remained at 4.5 percent until January. Adolph Miller later criticized New York for failing to tighten in the fall of 1928.

Balke and Gordon's (1986) quarterly data show a small decline in the GNP deflator in third quarter 1928, the first such decline after three quarters in which the price level rose at an annual rate of 3.8 percent. It was not the last decline; the deflator fell persistently for the next eighteen quarters with only one exception.[160] Thus ex post real interest rates remained above market rates during the 1929 expansion. And despite a sharp reversal of

---

160. The twelve-month percentage change in the consumer price index is negative from July 1926 to May 1929. Between June 1929 and January 1930, the annual change is between 0 and 1 percent. It then turns negative for more than three years.

the gold outflow, beginning in fourth quarter 1928 (and continuing for the next three years) the monetary base declined at an average annual rate of 1.3 percent in the year ending June 1929.

These indicators suggest that monetary policy was deflationary. The Federal Reserve considered policy expansive, based on the 43 percent increase in stock prices in 1928, the use of credit to support leveraged positions, faster growth of credit than of output, and the large volume of member bank borrowing. Misled by its indicators, it believed the challenge as 1929 started was to restrain "speculation." Disagreement, though sharp, was limited to how this could be best accomplished—how monetary policy should be tightened. All parties ignored the deflation.

Discount Rates and Direct Action

The new year's first conflict between the Board and the New York bank came on January 3. With seasonal credit demands completed, New York raised its acceptance buying rate to 4.75 percent, effective at 10:00 A.M. the next day. This was the first change since July.

Following the procedure used since 1918, Harrison publicly announced the change and notified the Board. Young responded that the Board was not a "rubber stamp." Early on January 4, Young reminded Harrison that the Board had changed procedural rules in 1926 to require Board approval of all acceptance rate changes. He allowed the higher rate to remain, since it had been announced, but he told Harrison that new regulations would be drafted (Conversations 1926–31, Harrison Papers, January 3 and 4, 1929).[161]

Three days later, the OMIC met in Washington. The preliminary memo commented on the growth of credit relative to output and the rise in open market rates. Harrison reported on the international effect of United States interest rates. Foreign central banks had reduced dollar balances to support exchange rates, and some—notably England—had sold gold heavily (Board of Governors File, box 1436, January 12, 1929).

With Young present, the committee discussed the Board's responsibilities. The Board had not approved the November decision to purchase up to $25 million in an emergency because in its view the request was open ended and gave the OMIC too much discretion. Henceforth the Board

---

161. Procedure did not change. Harrison pointed out that the 1926 rules had never taken effect. New York had changed the rate on ninety-day acceptances fourteen times in the interim. On January 21, New York raised the rate to 5 percent. Miller (1935) ignored this incident when he blamed New York for the "easy policy" and insisted that New York failed to act in 1929 until after the Board announced its "direct action" policy. Miller described New York's policy in late 1928 as "complete abandonment of restraining action" (453). He concluded that the Board should have taken control sooner.

would approve specific decisions to purchase or sell a specified amount. It would no longer approve requests to be executed when, or if, the chairman or the committee chose.

This exchange, coming shortly after Strong's death the previous October, showed that the Board had renewed its effort to increase control over open market operations. The committee resisted. Harrison defended the procedures that had been in effect since 1923 and argued that the Board's proposal would eliminate the usefulness of the OMIC. The Board's reply is not reported in the minutes, but it is likely to have followed the lines of a letter that Young drafted after the meeting but did not send. The letter said that the Board would approve definite decisions. However, the future is indefinite, so the Board would henceforth make its decision whenever the OMIC proposed to purchase or sell (Young to Harrison, Board of Governors File, box 1436, January 12, 1929).[162] The OMIC also considered selling up to $50 million in January or February if discounts and market rates declined. Since there was no definite recommendation, the OMIC did not test the Board's new procedures.

By the end of January, System holdings of governments were down to $200 million, including both the open market account and approximately $150 million held by individual reserve banks for revenue.[163] Discounts were nearly $900 million, below their peak but almost twice the level of the previous year. There was little prospect that open market sales could reduce borrowing substantially. For the first time in many years, the discount rate became the principal policy instrument available.

The Board was reluctant to use a general instrument to deal with what it regarded as special circumstances. Credit had increased 8 percent in 1928, and output only 3 percent.[164] The Board believed much of the credit

162. The Board also had under consideration a proposal to replace the OMIC with a committee of twelve reserve bank governors chaired by the governor of the Board. See below.

163. The open market account changed during this period when the System purchased from foreign central banks and attempted to dispose of the purchases in the market without affecting rates. Also, securities matured.

164. There is considerable difference in measures of output growth for the period. The 3 percent estimate in the minutes and correspondence lies between the 2.2 percent later estimated as the annual average by the Department of Commerce and the 4.1 percent from the (base 1982) index of industrial production based on yearly averages. Growth rates for the four quarters or twelve months ending in December suggest substantial acceleration during the year, more in keeping with credit growth. Balke and Gordon's (1986) average GNP growth for the four quarters of 1928 is 9 percent; Kendrick reports a 10 percent increase in manufacturing output; Miron and Romer (1989) report a 26 percent increase in industrial production for December 1927 to December 1928; and the Federal Reserve's (1982) index shows a 15 percent rate of increase. Balke and Gordon's data show no growth in the first quarter and 16 percent (a.r.) in the fourth quarter. Miron and Romer are at the extreme with 14.4 percent (a.r.) for the first half and 36.5 percent for the second half. The high growth rates of output are more

had financed stock purchases on margin. It aimed to reduce this use of credit without raising interest rates to the level reached in 1920–21 and to shift credit from financing speculative ventures to financing productive assets.[165]

Pressed by Adolph Miller to stop the speculative use of credit, on December 31, 1928, the Board adopted a resolution that blamed the spread between discount rates and rates for stock exchange loans for the temptation to borrow from the Federal Reserve and lend to help buy or carry securities. The Board decided to learn what the reserve banks were doing to prevent "improper use of Federal Reserve credit facilities by their member banks" (Riefler 1956, 263).

On February 2 the Board revised and approved a letter originally drafted by Miller. The letter noted that interest rates had increased, counter to the typical seasonal pattern. Since the available data underestimated the strength of the expansion, the Board blamed the rise in market rates on the absorption of funds in speculative loans. Continued growth of these loans would further increase interest rates, "to the prejudice of the country's commercial interests." The aim of the Board's policy was to prevent credit expansion for uses not contemplated by the Federal Reserve Act. "The Board has no disposition to assume authority to interfere with the loan practices of member banks so long as they do not involve the Federal Reserve banks. It has, however, a grave responsibility whenever there is evidence that member banks are maintaining speculative security loans with the aid of Federal Reserve credit" (Board Minutes, February 2, 1929). On February 7 the Board issued a press release to the general public, quoting its letter.

The policy conflict between the Board and the banks intensified. After abandoning the penalty discount rate early in the decade, the System had kept the discount rate above the acceptance rate. The two were now equal, so banks and market participants believed an increase in the discount rate was imminent.[166] Responding to the Board's action, Boston notified the

---

consistent with Harold Barger's (1942) reported 23 percent increase in corporate net profits and the 37 percent return to equities.

165. Harrison also used the 3 percent and 8 percent numbers in his preliminary memo for the January 7 OMIC meeting. He estimated the change in deposits times their velocity (MV) as 25 percent in 1928 versus 15 percent in 1927. The probable underestimate of output growth and overestimate of money growth (or growth of aggregate demand) contributed to the belief that policy was inflationary.

166. In its 1928 annual report and elsewhere, the Board criticized the reserve banks for their policy. The banks' "liberal purchase of bills [acceptances] in excess of credit needs was a factor in the revival of speculation and in the growth of broker loans" (Discount Rate Controversy, 11, Board of Governors File, box 1246, undated). The Board charged that the acceptance purchases nullified the discount rate increases (12).

Board on February 4 that it voted to increase its discount rate. The Board asked that the Board's program be implemented instead. The following day Harrison told the Board that its program "does not have any substantial effect upon the total volume of credit outstanding but that is a matter which . . . can be controlled properly only through the rate" (Conversations 1926–31, Harrison Papers, February 5, 1929, 8). Nevertheless, Harrison agreed to try the Board's program.[167]

Within a week, the New York directors voted unanimously to increase the discount rate by a full percentage point to 6 percent. The Board voted seven to one to reject the request on the grounds that New York made the request by telephone and had not given any reason for the increase. Young explained that the increase would force other banks to follow. A general increase might seriously affect agriculture and commerce.

Market rates continued to increase in March. Commercial paper reached 6 percent; banks offered 8 percent for time deposits. New York again raised the buying rate for acceptances, in two steps, to 5.5 percent. The rise had the expected effect. The System's acceptance portfolio declined while its discounts rose, contrary to the "reluctance" theory of borrowing.

Propelled by higher interest rates, rising stock prices, and deflation, capital flowed to the United States. New York sterilized gold inflows by selling securities from the System account, reducing the account to $40 million in early March. To stem the gold flow to the United States and France, the Bank of England raised its discount rate a full percentage point to 5.5 percent. Holland, Italy, and others soon followed.[168]

New York's directors voted to increase the discount rate on March 4 and March 21. The Board did not approve, citing in the latter case the decline in Federal Reserve credit. Unable to convince the Board, Harrison appealed to Secretary Mellon on March 21. Mellon agreed, but the Board insisted that direct action was the correct policy and rejected the request. Boston, Philadelphia, and Chicago discussed or voted for 6 percent rates; the requests were rejected, tabled, or withdrawn to avoid rejection (Riefler 1956, 282–84).

Standard and Poor's index of common stocks rose more than 10 percent in the first three months of 1929. The Board's policy succeeded in reducing bank lending to brokers, but total loans to brokers secured by stocks

167. On February 7, the Board tabled a request by the Dallas bank to raise its discount rate to 5 percent. Dallas was one of four banks with a 4.5 percent rate. The Board permitted the increase early in March.

168. The Bank of France kept its discount rate at 3.5 percent and sterilized its gold inflow by selling foreign exchange.

and bonds rose.[169] Most of the lending came from corporations and other nonbanks, attracted by call rates of 9 or 10 percent. Nothing in the program prevented individuals or corporations from borrowing from banks while lending to brokers and dealers. This pattern continued through the first three quarters of the year.

The April meeting of the Governors Conference had a thorough discussion of market rates. Boston, New York, Chicago, Philadelphia, and Richmond said they had exhausted the possibility of credit control through the Board's program of direct action against speculative uses of credit. Some of the regional banks said that local businesses had difficulty borrowing because credit was going into brokers' loans. Several of the governors warned of an impending crisis if the current policy continued (Governors Conference, Board of Governors File, box 1436, April 4, 1929).

Policy was beginning to affect economic activity without reducing stock prices. Harrison's preliminary memorandum reports call loan rates of 8 to 20 percent at the end of March and commercial paper at 6 percent. The memo reported building activity in decline, state and local government projects postponed, and foreign borrowing curtailed. Gold continued to flow to the United States. Conditions abroad would soon reduce exports. Business conditions were sustained by automobile production "considerably in excess of retail purchases." "Present money conditions, if long continued, will have a *seriously detrimental effect* upon business conditions, and the longer they are continued, the more serious will be the effect" (OMIC, Board of Governors File, box 1436, preliminary memo for April 1, 1929; emphasis added).

A rate increase now was seen as a step toward lower rates later. Boston and New York argued for a 6 percent rate immediately and perhaps 7 percent later. Philadelphia talked about a possible 8 percent rate. By raising discount rates, the reserve banks expected to reduce discounts, paving the way for a lower discount rate. The Board rejected this reasoning when it turned down New York's sixth request in mid-April. The Board noted that New York had used the same evidence—declining exports, difficulty in placing foreign loans—when it asked to lower the discount rate in 1917.

The warnings about declining activity and a possible crisis ahead (if

169. In the first quarter brokers' loans by New York banks fell 33 percent and those by other banks 18 percent. Nonbanks increased lending by 27 percent. Total brokers' loans rose 6 percent (Board of Governors of the Federal Reserve System 1943, 494). Miller (1935, 456) recognized the substitution of loans by nonbanks but claimed success for direct action because, he said, total brokers' loans decreased and loan rates increased sharply. A chart in his paper showed a small decline in total brokers' loans in the spring followed by a much larger increase after the Board "relaxed" direct action in June (448).

countries were forced off the gold standard) had no effect on Young or Miller. Young recognized that policy "has had a detrimental effect on business," but he told the governors there was no occasion to raise rates: "There is one factor you have been unable to control, which is speculative credit. As the Board sees it, the discount rate will have no effect" (Governors Conference, Board of Governors file, box 1436, April 4, 1929). Miller said he would favor lower rates if the "abuse of Federal Reserve credit" ended (ibid.).[170]

The governors did not speak with one voice. Governor Fancher cited the large gold reserve as a reason for not raising rates. Cleveland would raise its rate, defensively, only if New York and Chicago increased theirs. Seay (Richmond), Eugene R. Black (Atlanta), and other governors of small banks either opposed raising discount rates or were ambivalent.

The governors agreed, informally, on a policy statement. To lower interest rates, they first had to raise discount rates. The minimum discount rate at any reserve bank should be 5 percent, with a 6 percent rate in the principal financial centers. Since the Board had to approve these rates and was certain not to do so, the governors who disagreed could accept the policy statement.

Gold continued to flow to the United States, much of it from Germany.[171] Between March 6 and April 30, the Reichsbank lost $215 million in gold reserves, one-third of the stock held at the end of 1928. The Federal Reserve sold most of the gold to the Bank of France, which paid partly by selling foreign exchange, mostly dollars, and by sterilizing most of the remainder by reducing its holdings of governments. The Federal Reserve reinforced the gold outflows by reducing government securities. By the end of April the Federal Reserve's government security holdings had fallen to $150 million, of which only $17.5 million was held in the System account. Thus, as France acquired gold, both the buying and selling countries took deflationary action. Moreover, acceptances continued to run off, further reducing the monetary base.

New York again voted to increase its discount rate, and again the Board refused. At times Boston, Philadelphia, and Chicago joined New York. On April 25, Harrison appealed to Secretary Mellon to intervene. Mellon pleaded for an increase that day, but only Platt supported him. Instead, the

170. Harrison asked, "Are we getting what we want?" The minutes report that Miller answered: "What it is that the System wants. Considerable discussion ensued, but no definite statement was made" (Governors Conference, box 1436, April 4, 1929).

171. Part of the German gold outflow resulted from the failure to reach agreement about reparations payments.

following week the Board sent letters to the reserve banks listing member banks that borrowed continuously while lending to security brokers and dealers. The Board threatened to stop all discounting by these banks.

May saw a slight change in the stalemate.[172] The Board approved increases in discount rates to 5 percent at Kansas City, Minneapolis, and San Francisco. The 5 percent rate was now uniform throughout the System. The Board continued to disapprove or table requests for a 6 percent rate, but on May 15 Governor Young changed sides to vote for approval of New York's request. With the fall approaching, he now shared Harrison's view that to reduce rates, they must first be raised. The vote was four to four, rejecting the request (Office Correspondence and Memos, Harrison Papers, May 14 and 15, 1929).[173]

End of the Stalemate

The next move came from New York. Instead of again voting to increase the discount rate, the New York directors sent a letter to the Board on May 31. The letter called attention to the uncertainty created by the continuing policy conflict and rumors that all discounting would be denied. It urged agreement on a mutually satisfactory program. The letter made clear that the directors had not changed their opinion about the rate increase but decided to "refrain from rate action in the hope that a general policy . . . may be quickly determined" (Riefler 1956, 315).

The New York directors proposed three changes to avoid further tightening when seasonal demands appeared: relax qualitative controls to permit banks to borrow freely; end the Board's policy of opposition to collateral loans (secured by marketable securities); and allow reserve banks to expand credit if needed.

The Board met with several New York directors on June 5. Each side appeared willing to compromise but unwilling to fully abandon its previous position. New York stressed that it wanted to increase the discount rate. The Board stressed that any relaxation of its direct action policy would be "merely a suspension" (Riefler 1956, 316). A week later the Board proposed temporarily suspending the direct action program during the months in which banks would be discounting heavily to market the harvest, and it

---

172. In all, New York voted nine times to raise the discount rate. Leslie Rounds, the first vice president at New York, explained the persistence as an effort by Chairman McGarrah to "show the bank had been on the job and had done what it could, but perhaps he did not sense how great a calamity was building up" (CHFRS, Rounds, May 2, 1955, 13).

173. A week later, the Federal Advisory Council changed sides also, recommending a 6 percent rate.

recognized that purchases of acceptances and possibly governments might be needed if discounts increased substantially.[174]

By July 10 the System's acceptance portfolio had declined to $66 million, more than $100 million below the previous year and the lowest level since the 1924 recession. Call loan rates reached 11 percent in the first week of July. Responding to the pressure, New York lowered its acceptance buying rate by 0.25 percent to 5.25 percent. Acceptance rates in the market quickly fell to 5.125 percent, where they remained until mid-October. New York followed, reducing by 0.125 percent on August 9. Acceptance purchases now began to add reserves.

Harrison met with the Board on August 2 to discuss a discount rate increase. Business now "appears to be on a sound basis." "The time has passed for the adoption of a policy of higher rates." Nevertheless, he proposed combining an increase in the discount rate to 6 percent with a small reduction in the acceptance rate to help finance domestic business and exports (Harrison Papers, Board Meetings, August 2, 1929). George R. James, a member of the Board, suggested a preferential rate for commodities. The only agreement was to call a meeting of all governors for August 7 and 8.

The governors accepted Harrison's proposal by a vote of eleven to one. Their resolution looked forward to supplying the seasonal increase by buying acceptances and explicitly ruled out a general increase in discount rates at reserve banks outside New York. The Board approved the resolution and a 6 percent discount rate at New York. No other bank followed.

The reasoning behind the policy action was confused, its effect modest. In the Board's view, which New York accepted to reach the seasonal compromise, credit allocation mattered. Acceptances were real bills, whereas discounts could support speculative credit. Hence encouraging acceptance purchases while reducing discounts helped commerce and agriculture and discouraged speculation. In contrast, under Riefler-Burgess, a reduction in discounts was a move toward easier policy, since banks borrowed reluctantly, not for profit.

174. After the Board relaxed its policy of direct action in June, Seay (Richmond) wrote to Harrison: "It is a rather strange or mixed course or procedure which the Board expects Federal Reserve banks to follow. Having told member banks that they were not within their reasonable rights for rediscounts while they are lending under certain conditions, we are now not to abandon that position but to temper it . . . then if they overdo the matter, we are to tell them that they have overdone it and resume pressure. It is difficult to pilot the ship with such a variable compass" (Seay to Harrison, June 27, 1929; quoted in Chandler 1958, 469).

The Board communicated the agreement in a letter to each of the reserve banks. The letter described its earlier decision to take direct action as deliberate, its current position as holding fast to its belief that it was necessary. The present suspension was temporary to assist banks "that have not found it practicable to readjust their position in accordance with the Board's principle."

Banks responded to the rate switch by lowering their costs. In the ten weeks from August 16 to the stock market break on October 23, discounts declined and acceptances increased. The net effect was $29 million in additional Federal Reserve credit, far below the $200 million estimated as the required seasonal increase through October (OMIC Minutes, Board of Governors File, box 1436, September 24, 1929).[175]

The discount rate increase had little effect on market rates. Bond yields increased at first but then reversed. After six weeks, Harrison reported very small effects on rates except abroad. Britain continued to lose gold to France and Germany. New York bought sterling bills to stabilize the pound.

The National Bureau of Economic Research puts the peak of the expansion in August. At the September 24 OMIC meeting, Harrison reported that though business was at a "high level . . . [t]here has been a declining tendency in a number of basic industries." The committee proposed open market purchases of acceptances and, if necessary, up to $25 million of short-term government securities each week. The aim was to prevent an increase in borrowing if acceptance purchases proved insufficient for seasonal expansion. A week later the Board approved the resolution, noting in its letter that the approval should not be seen as a change in Board policy. No purchases were made in the month before the stock market break.

The OMIC did not meet again until November, after the market break. For the week ending October 12, call loan rates were below 6 percent, for the first time in more than a year, and half the level reached in early May. October 24 was "black Thursday," a day of climactic decline in share prices. The Board approved a reduction in the acceptance rate to follow the market but rejected New York's request to lower its discount rate to 5.5 percent.

Acceptance rates continued to fall as banks scrambled for short-term liquid assets. On October 28 New York told Young that "there has been a large reduction in brokers loans and that corporations and bankers in the interior are calling such loans and investing in bills, Governments and commercial paper" (Riefler 1956, 355). To meet the demand, New York banks borrowed heavily from the reserve bank. With the market rate down to 4.625 percent, New York asked for a further reduction in its acceptance buying rate. The Board refused: "No further reductions in the bill rate should be made at this time as the easing program of the System seems to be progressing satisfactorily." Riefler added: "At this time, conditions in the money market were threatened by reason of drastic liquidation in the securities markets" (Riefler 1956, 356).

175. The full seasonal swing from early August through the end of December was estimated at $500 million (OMIC Minutes, Board of Governors File, box 1436, September 24, 1929). The actual was half the estimate.

The Federal Reserve was established, in part, to prevent a panic in the money market. The Board's response to New York ignored the scramble to reduce loans to the call market then in progress. Table 4.5 shows the large changes in lending as the stock market fell.

In the week ending October 30, the New York reserve bank opened its discount window. System discounts rose $200 million for the week. By October 28 the New York directors, tired of haggling with the Board, gave Harrison discretion to purchase governments without any limit.

Harrison informed the Board but began purchases of $50 million before the stock market opened on October 29. The Board accepted the result reluctantly, since the purchases had been made before its meeting, but it noted that New York had not consulted the OMIC or the Board.[176] In all, New York purchased $133 million, $25 million for the System account and $108 million on its own.

Later in the day Harrison telephoned to hear the Board's response to a proposed reduction in the discount rate to 5 percent. The Board agreed to the reduction if New York would suspend open market purchases. On November 1, New York's rate went to the 5 percent rate maintained at other reserve banks.

The decline that became the Great Depression was under way. Balke and Gordon (1986) show real GNP rising only 0.5 percent in the third quarter before falling at an annual rate in excess of 11 percent in the fourth quarter. After rising at an 11 percent rate in the first nine months, industrial production (as reported at the time) declined in the fourth quarter (Reed 1930, 171).[177] Although the initial decline in output was steep, it was less steep than at the start of the 1920–21 recession. Federal Reserve documents in October noted the beginning of the decline within two months of the NBER peak. The rapid fall in stock prices in late October suggests a rather sudden shift in anticipations about future profits and economic growth.

Knowledge of events was not a problem at the time or later. Misinter-

176. The Board regarded New York's action as a violation of the 1923 agreement establishing the OMIC. The following week the Board approved a resolution denying Federal Reserve banks the right to buy or sell government securities without Board approval. Counsel advised them that there was considerable doubt about its legality, so it did not become effective (Riefler 1956, 359).

177. For the period 1922 to 1929 as a whole, the Board's contemporary measure of industrial production rose at a compound average annual rate of 7.5 percent (Miller 1935, 443, chart 1). The Miron-Romer data show a growth rate above 8 percent from January 1922 to February 1929, the peak in their data. Extended to August, their average is close to the Federal Reserve data. Recent Federal Reserve data (base 100 in 1982) show a peak in July 1929 and a 3.3 percent decline in the next three months (a 13.5 percent annual rate). These data show industrial production doubling between the 1921 trough and the 1929 peak, a 9 percent compound annual rate of increase.

Table 4.5   Loans to Brokers and Dealers, 1929 (millions of dollars)

DATE	TOTAL	NEW YORK BANKS	OTHER BANKS	OTHER
October 16	6,801	1,095	1,831	3.875
October 23	6,634	1,077	1,733	3,823
October 30	5,538	2,069	1,005	2,464

Source: Board of Governors of the Federal Reserve System 1943, 498.

pretation, incorrect analysis, lack of agreement, and concern about letting the discount rate rise without limit—not ignorance of events—prevented action. The Board was unwilling to accept the political cost of raising rates to levels that would renew the concerns and criticisms in 1920–21. Young asked repeatedly how much Harrison and the other governors proposed to increase discount rates. The answers did not reassure him or other Board members.[178]

CONFLICTING INTERPRETATIONS

Ambiguity in the Federal Reserve Act was one reason for the policy conflict. Lines of authority and responsibility between the individual reserve banks and the Board were unclear, hence a source of the periodic frictions and disputes. At a deeper level was the conflict over how policy operated and what it should and could accomplish.

This conflict showed through in the Board's tenth annual report. As noted earlier, although the report was the work of Walter Stewart, Adolph Miller had considerable influence on the drafting. Yet New York praised the report at the time. The reason for this anomaly was that the report, like the Federal Reserve Act, had two policy conceptions that had not been reconciled. One was the real bills doctrine, calling for the control of speculation and restrictions on the use of credit to encourage commerce, agriculture, and industry. The other was first the gold standard and later the Riefler-Burgess doctrine. Under Riefler-Burgess, the volume of discounts replaced the gold reserve ratio as the principal signal for expansive or contractive action.

Both policy rules or procedures had the same objective—to prevent inflation by changing the amount of bank credit (and money) as output

178. The Board prepared a summary (unsigned) that appears to have been written by Young based on his personal records. The summary contrasts the Board's direct action with New York's policy, which it characterized as a request for repeated increases in rates. The summary quotes an April 9, 1929, letter from Harrison: "The discount rate would be employed incisively and repeatedly, if necessary" (Discount Rate Controversy, 21, Board of Governors File, box 1246, undated). Several other quotations from Harrison and McGarrah's comments refer to higher rates, even 8 percent or more (22).

changed. Proponents of real bills saw the financial system as largely self-regulating. If banks created credit only on real bills, they believed it would grow or decline with production and trade. Adherents of Riefler-Burgess agreed that money (bank credit) should grow at the same rate as output in the long run, but they regarded the short-run relation of money to output as highly variable. They wanted to manage the relation by using open market operations to control the volume of member bank borrowing.

Miller was the System's most outspoken proponent of real bills, but he was not alone. Several of the bank governors—Norris, McDougal, Seay, and Calkins—held similar views, and they were joined by some, perhaps most, of the Board.[179] They had strong support in Congress, from Carter Glass and others, and in much of the financial press. No less important, they had the text of the Federal Reserve Act with its injunctions against the use of credit for speculation and its emphasis on discounting real bills.[180]

Although the real bills advocates agreed on the importance of preventing speculation, they did not agree on the means. For example, Norris wrote: "This whole process of 'direct action' is wearing, friction producing, and futile. We are following it honestly and energetically, but it is manifest beyond the peradventure of doubt, that it will never get us anywhere. . . . Our 5 percent [discount rate] is equivalent to hanging a sign over our door 'Come In' and then we have to stand in the doorway and shout 'Keep Out.' It puts us in an absurd and impossible position" (Norris to Hamlin, April 2, 1929; quoted in Chandler 1958, 467–68).

Strong, and others at New York, did not disagree that preventing speculation was part of their mandate. Like Norris, they believed that persuasion or direct action was unavailing without an increase in interest rates. Strong went further. He had learned from the experience of 1919–20 that qualitative control could not work because there is no way to identify how additions to reserves and loans would be used at the margin. Repeatedly New York explained that the collateral used for loans from a bank or from a reserve bank bore no relation to the purchase or loan financed by the addition to reserves and that the bank had no way to discover how credit was used in practice. The only effective way to prevent credit expansion, New York said, was to reduce the total by open market sales or discount rate increases. But it never stated, and perhaps did not recognize, that the rise in

179. Leslie Rounds remarked that "without Miller there never would have been any great difference of opinion. I don't think anybody else down there would have . . . trusted their own judgment enough to take such a stand" (CHFRS, Rounds, May 2, 1955, 6).

180. In the 1960s, Clay Anderson (1965, 57) gave these same reasons for reliance on "direct action" in 1929 and added concern that an increase in rates would harm commerce and agriculture. Anderson was an officer of the Philadelphia reserve bank.

stock prices was at least partly a response to the policy of inaction[181] and the robust economic expansion.[182]

Another part of the controversy was as old as the Federal Reserve. The Board's first annual report (Board of Governors of the Federal Reserve System, *Annual Report*, 1914, 53) discussed limiting discounts by the purpose of the loan and concluded that it was not possible to know what each bank did with its loans. The issue arose again after World War I when the Treasury, opposed to higher market rates, had the Board ask the reserve banks to ascertain which banks were borrowing on government securities for speculative purposes. In 1925, as again in 1929, the Board was reluctant to increase rates when faced with increased borrowing. The 1925 annual report, however, recognized the futility of qualitative control: "It was seldom possible to trace the connection between borrowings of a member bank at the Reserve bank and the specific transactions that gave rise to the necessity for borrowing" (*Annual Report*, 1925, 16). It is only in the 1929 report that we find: A bank is not "within its reasonable claims for rediscount facilities" when borrowing to make or maintain speculative loans (*Annual Report*, 1929, 3). This statement is unobjectionable as a comment on the intent of the law; however, it does not make a case for the effectiveness of direct action.

The legal basis for the Board's "direct action" was unclear. In 1925 Miller justified his proposed policy on the grounds that "the use of credit for speculative or investment purposes is precluded by specific provisions of the Federal Reserve Act" (quoted in Harris 1933, 1:225). He later modified the position, finding support for direct action in the references to real bills as the proper collateral for discounts. The Board's legal counsel found support for the February 1929 letter to member banks in section 13, which made rediscounts subject to the restrictions and regulations of the Board.[183]

---

181. One month after announcement of the policy of direct action, National City Bank offered to lend $25 million to the call market while borrowing from the Federal Reserve. The president of the bank was a Federal Reserve director. He justified the policy as necessary to prevent panic in the money market. His defiance made the System appear weak even to those who understood that direct action could not prevent credit expansion. Neutral observers saw loans at rates of 20 percent or more financed by borrowing at 5 percent.

182. Strong agreed that the problem was "speculation" in Florida land in 1925 and in stocks in 1927–28. Like the others, he saw these more as manias than as endogenous responses to strong economic growth and low inflation. See, for example, Chandler 1958, 460–61.

183. Burgess (1964, 224) suggested a different reason for the program—reluctance to raise interest rates after the 1920–21 experience: "The disagreement was not as to the dangers of the situation but as to the methods of dealing with it. . . . Back of this was, I believe, reluctance to take the responsibility for decisive action, having in mind the criticism incurred by the Board for increasing the discount rate in 1920."

The principal antagonists learned nothing from the experience. Carter Glass and Miller blamed Strong's 1927 policy for the speculative boom and the 1929 collapse. Using a phrase that was repeated many times in the next few years, they described the collapse as an *inevitable* consequence of the preceding expansion. For them, the problem was the violation of real bills by financing speculation. They believed the speculative boom had started when excessive open market purchases were used to help Britain in 1927. They usually neglected the Board's supporting role, including its insistence on forcing Chicago and others to reduce their discount rates.

Miller (1935) set out to show why it was wrong to conclude that in 1927–29 the reserve banks had been right and the Board wrong.[184] He made three claims: that the New York Federal Reserve bank initiated the 1927 reduction in discount rates; that between August 1928 and February 1929 the reserve banks took no action to check speculation; and that the first attempt to increase the New York discount rate in 1929 came after the Board announced its policy of direct action. The timing of New York's action was important to Miller. The Board's February 2 statement said: "There are elements in the situation which are not readily amenable to recognized methods of banking control." This meant, he said, that the time for a rate change had passed (Senate Committee on Banking and Currency 1931, 142).

At first New York's 1927 policy seemed to work. The pound strengthened, and the economy recovered from recession. Many people praised this result as the beginning of a "new era" in which "well timed monetary policy" would substantially reduce "the terrors of the business cycle" while ensuring price stability Miller (1935, 447).

Unfortunately, he continued, the policy had other effects:[185] "Cheap credit gave a further great and dangerous impetus to an already overexpanded credit situation, notably to the volume of credit used on the stock exchanges" (1935, 449).[186] The reserve banks tightened in the spring of 1928 by selling securities and raising interest rates, but this had only a

184. The specific references are to Lionel Robbins and a *New York Times* editorial. Miller recognized that the Board approved some of the policies he cites, so he assigned it secondary responsibility for the outcome.

185. The policy was originated by "the distinguished Governor, the late Benjamin Strong. Brilliant of mind, engaging of personality, fertile of resource, strong of will, ambitious of spirit, he had extraordinary skill in impressing his views and purposes on his associates in the Federal Reserve System" (Miller 1935, 447). Miller ignored not only Strong's absence during most of 1928 and the increase in the acceptance rate that came before the Board's announcement in February 1929 but also his own initial praise of the operation.

186. Miller cited a secondary factor in 1927—larger than expected redemptions of the Second Liberty Loan. Federal Reserve banks supported the issue to help the Treasury.

brief, temporary effect on the stock market. In Miller's view the policy did not work for three reasons. First, "the astonishing increase in the earnings of large corporations and the extremely low rate of interest . . . appeared to supply a basis for the high prices that were being paid for stock of companies whose earnings were rising and whose dividend disbursements . . . were far above the going price for money" (451). Second, banks believed there would be no classical money panic because the Federal Reserve would rediscount in an emergency. Third, nonbank funds supplied large amounts of credit for the stock market.

The reserve banks failed to tighten in the fall of 1928 partly because they expected normal seasonal demands to raise rates and partly because they did not want to be blamed for harming agriculture. Banks sold acceptances to the reserve banks, then used the proceeds to finance stock purchases. Miller characterized this policy as "lacking in strong conviction" (451–52).

The mistaken policy was the work of the New York Federal Reserve bank.[187] The Board's role was secondary; its mistake was a delay in taking leadership. The error reflected the division of responsibility in the Federal Reserve Act and the primary role given to the reserve banks to propose policy action.[188]

By early 1929 "the rate of speculative expansion had attained such speed and the thirst for credit had attained such intensity . . . [that] control through discount rate increase . . . is at best to be regarded as a frail reliance and a dubious expedient" (Miller 1935, 455). Direct pressure, on the other hand, was a more flexible method of control of the particular banks and type of credit that had to be controlled.

Miller, writing in 1935, cited the provisions of the Banking Act of 1933 (and the Securities and Exchange Act) as evidence that Congress had accepted the Board's view. The specific features included control of margin requirements and restrictions on brokers' loans. These changes were made to prevent credit from being diverted from commercial to speculative uses. In the real bills view, financing the stock market did not lead to

187. "The incontrovertible fact is that during this period . . . the leadership of the Federal Reserve System rested with the Federal Reserve Bank of New York" (Miller 1935, 452).

188. Miller cited the public outcry against the Board for its actions in the 1927 Chicago rate controversy as a reason for the Board's failure to act in 1928. This is a weak defense. Nothing prevented the Board from suggesting discount rate changes, as it had done several times. Also, he failed to recall his statement to the Strong (Kansas) hearings on stabilization, where he gave the Board credit for initiating "most of the changes in the discount policy" and credited the Board with a longer view. See House Committee on Banking and Currency 1926, 640–41. Although Miller defended the Board and criticized the reserve banks, particularly New York, he never explained why the Board waited until it believed the time for a discount rate increase had passed. Nor did he explain his vote in March 1928 against an increase in the discount rate.

new output, hence it "diverted" credit from productive to unproductive uses.[189]

Earlier, Miller had testified on the reasons for the Board's refusal to raise rates in 1929: "It was our belief that an increase to 6 percent in February, 1929, would have been nothing but a futile gesture; that it would have been a practical declaration to the speculative markets of the country that the doors of the Federal Reserve System were open to all comers. . . . With call rates mounting to 8, 9, 10, 15, and 20 percent, a 6 percent discount rate would have been an admission of defeat and given great relief to the speculating public" (Senate Committee on Banking and Currency 1931, 143).[190]

Harrison made a weak defense of New York's policy. He didn't question that the growth of speculative loans was a major problem, but he was more confident than Strong had been earlier that raising the discount rate would have been an effective response. His difference with Miller was mainly about whether "direct action" was, or could be, effective without an increase in rates. He was ambivalent about whether the Federal Reserve should lend only on productive credit, but he understood, as Miller and Glass did not, that limiting rediscounts to real bills did not change the marginal loan at member banks or the volume of credit outstanding.[191]

Harrison stated the quantitative guide: When credit expands faster than

189. Woodlief Thomas (1935) argued that more effective control of stock market credit was necessary for economic stability. Thomas was a leading economist on the Board's staff and later an adviser to the Board. Credit control prevented diversion of credit, which he took to be a major reason for policy failure in 1928–29. This was a widely held view. Reed (1930) devoted many pages to analysis of whether there was diversion. The idea of "absorption and diversion of credit" lacks analytic content except, perhaps, in a real bills framework.

190. Senator Carter Glass chaired the hearing and heartily agreed with Miller's testimony. The following exchange is representative: "Mr. Miller: An alternative use of discount policy would have been what you alluded to yesterday, Mr. Chairman . . . successive increases to 6, 7, 8 or 9 percent, in other words, a race between the call rate and the discount rate. The Chairman [Glass]: With legitimate commerce the victim" (Senate Committee on Banking and Currency 1931, 143).

This position was not uniformly held in Congress. Warburg (1930, 514) reported that the chairman of the House Banking Committee, Henry Steagall, did not share Glass's views and wanted the Board to stop interfering with stock exchange loans. Former senator Robert Owen was counsel for plaintiffs in a suit to stop the Federal Reserve from restricting the credit supply.

191. His difference with Glass became clear in this exchange: "Governor Harrison: If we have to go beyond the paper presented and determine the loan not on the character of the paper but the business of that bank— The Chairman: You have to determine it upon the purpose for which the borrowing bank wants money from you. Governor Harrison: In the usual case, I will have to say that I could not tell. The Chairman: What are your examiners for if you cannot tell? . . . Governor Harrison: At times, the banks themselves do not know whether the borrower is speculating. The Chairman: But ought they not to know that? Governor Harrison: It is sometimes pretty difficult to find out" (Senate Committee on Banking and Currency 1931, 54).

trade or business, the Federal Reserve System should raise rates, "whether the expansion is due to speculation in real estate, securities, or commodities, or whether it is due to abnormal growth of business" (Senate Committee on Banking and Currency 1931, 55). The task of deciding who borrows was the job of the member banks, and he insisted that the New York Federal Reserve bank did not admonish its members to reduce brokers' loans in 1929. These statements puzzled, and infuriated, Chairman Glass.

> The Chairman: It [the act] says expressly that you are not to permit the facilities of the Federal Reserve banks to be used to purchase or to carry—
> Governor Harrison: We do not—
> The Chairman: To purchase or to carry—oh, you may not do it directly, but you practically vitiate this act in the way you do it.
> Senator Walcott: The borrowing bank does it.
> The Chairman: The Federal Reserve bank permits the borrowing bank to do it. It is the business of the Federal Reserve bank to know what the borrowing bank is doing and for what purpose it is doing it. If this is not the meaning of this act, why should . . . your board of directors ever feel—in any sense or degree—warranted in admonishing member banks in New York to reduce their loans to brokers?
> Governor Harrison: Senator, we never did it.
> The Chairman: You did not?
> Governor Harrison: No, sir. (55)

Harrison then gave two reasons. First, brokers' loans did not increase at New York banks. Second, the directors believed that the correct policy was to raise rates, not admonish individual banks. He explained again why rate increases would work where direct action would fail to control the amount of lending. None of his arguments reached Glass.[192]

Harrison acknowledged two mistakes in 1928–29: "First we raised our rate the first time too late, and, second, we did not raise it enough. I mean that had we had at that time the light of the experience we have since had, it would have been better perhaps to have raised the rate 1 percent in December of 1927" (ibid., 66). Harrison went on to blame the "bootleg banking system" through which corporations and individuals lent to brokers and dealers outside the regular banking system.

J. Herbert Case also testified about the New York bank's position. He ex-

---

192. Glass responded: "I have never been able to see, and I did not see in 1920, either the fairness or the effectiveness of increasing the discount rate and thereby imposing a penalty upon the ordinary business of the country, commercial or industrial, in order to control the activities of the stock market" (ibid., 57).

plained that the collapse was regarded as inevitable because speculation in farmlands during the war and postwar inflation were followed by speculation in Florida real estate and, finally, in the stock market, "which adversely affected the general business of the country. These movements have each in turn culminated as they inevitably must in a deflation" (ibid., 111).

THE STOCK MARKET BOOM

The rise in stock prices that ended in 1929 is extraordinary by almost any standard except 1998–2000. From the end of 1924 to September 1929, Standard and Poor's index rose at a 21 percent compound annual rate. The Dow Jones industrial average, at its peak of 381 in September 1929, had doubled in less than two years. The rise was propelled in part by rising profits and economic activity. Real GNP and corporate profits rose at annual rates of 4 percent and 12 percent, respectively, with only one mild recession during the nearly five-year period. The increase in market capitalization relative to nominal GNP brought the ratio of the two to a level that was not surpassed until 1996.

The rate of rise in corporate profits was much greater than the rate of increase in GNP but only half the rate of increase in the value of traded stocks (market capitalization). Chart 4.4 shows that between 1925 and 1929 the ratio of market capitalization to corporate profits doubled.[193] In absolute value, the ratio rose from 6.2 in 1925 to 12.7 at its peak in 1929.

For those brought up on the belief that the 1929 stock market was a wild speculative orgy, chart 4.4 is surprising. It shows that the capitalization rate rose most rapidly in 1926, with rising profit anticipations.[194] The rate then remained between 10 and 12 until the market break in 1929. These data suggest that the so-called speculative boom of 1927–29 was driven by rising profits and, most likely, by anticipations of further increases to come. The 17 percent decline in corporate profits in fourth quarter 1929 and the 30 percent decline in first quarter 1930, or anticipation of the decline, must have reversed some of the beliefs built up during the expansion. At the time, many could vividly recall the volatility of the late nineteenth century and the frequent banking panics that Congress intended the Federal Reserve to prevent. Call money rates briefly reached 20 percent (a year) in 1929. Rates of 100 percent or more had not occurred in the fifteen years of the Federal Reserve's existence. There had been recessions, but the only

193. Market capitalization includes new issues and valuations of shares not included in the S&P index.

194. In the nearly seventy following years, there were only two periods when the ratio came close to its 1929 peak. One was in the latter part of 1936, just before a steep recession. The other was 1965 to 1968, just before the Great Inflation of the 1970s.

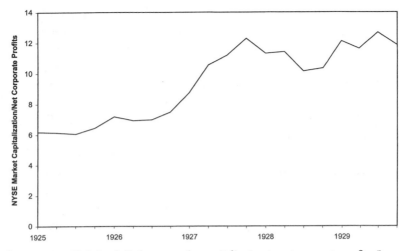

Chart 4.4 New York Stock Exchange market capitalization to net corporate profits. Source: Profits from Barger 1942 quarterly values at annual rates.

major deflation, in 1921, was universally attributed to the end of wartime excesses. The belief spread that the Federal Reserve had learned how to maintain prosperity, damp recessions, and prevent inflation. The return of many countries to the gold standard by 1927 reinforced the view that the world economy was on a stable foundation and that inflation and deflation were unlikely to occur.

In the 1920s, low inflation, sustained growth, and technological change convinced many that the United States had a "new economy." At the time, Irving Fisher commented that the stock market "went up principally because of sound, justified expectations of earnings, and only partly because of unreasoning and unintelligent mania for buying" Fisher (1930b, 53). He credited increased profits to the application of science, technology, and new management methods.

Annual rates of inflation (consumer price index) remained negative from July 1926 to May 1929. Restoration of the international gold standard—raising the demand for gold—and Federal Reserve actions were the main reasons for the sustained, mild deflation. The twelve-month moving average of monetary base growth fell below 1 percent in November 1926, turned negative in May 1928, and remained negative through June 1929. In this period of rapid economic growth, monetary policy was deflationary.

Federal Reserve records show that the 1929 increase in output and fall in prices was known at the time. The United States economy had a spectacular performance in the first half of the year. Corporate earnings increased about 30 percent in the first nine months: "Large corporate earnings, together with the ability of corporations to float stocks at high [stock] prices . . . put them in possession of funds with which to complete contemplated expansion programs" ("Review of Business in 1929," preliminary, Board of Governors File, box 2461, January 15, 1930, 4).[195] The only negative influence reported at the time was a decline in residential structures. Industrial and commercial building was at a record level. Exports of manufactured goods increased 50 percent for the year, despite the recession in the last four to six months (ibid., 2).

These data suggest that the optimistic projections underlying the rise in stock prices had a factual base. Even after the severe decline at the end of 1929, the Board's staff described the first six months of 1929 as "the continuation of the steady expansion throughout the year 1928" (ibid., 5). It reported industrial production as 26 percent above the trough in the 1927 recession.

Some questioned or dissented from these optimistic beliefs. Allyn Young warned about deflation early in 1929.[196] Unlike many of his contemporaries who blamed deflation on either a decline in the gold stock or a maldistribution of gold holdings, Young blamed central bank gold hoarding. He saw that central bank policies forced deflation.

Paul Warburg was critical of Federal Reserve policies from a technical perspective. A thoughtful representative of the real bills view, Warburg believed that the Federal Reserve System had serious flaws. He saw the principal flaw as short-term investment in call loans instead of real bills. The problem was that call loans made the banking and financial system depend on the stock exchange. Since call loans could be called daily, a sudden decline in stock prices would weaken the banking system. Warburg favored a secondary reserve against call loans as a temporary expedient and the development of the acceptance market to replace the call market (Warburg 1930, 1:457–58, 501–18).[197]

195. The report showed the peak in the index of industrial production in June 1929, up at a 19 percent annual rate for the first six months. Automobile production peaked in April, 67 percent above its 1928 average. Agricultural prices continued to fall in 1929, at a 4.5 percent annual rate from December 1928 to September 1929 (Board of Governors File, box 2461, January 15, 1930, 10–11).

196. Allyn Young was a leading economist of his time. He finished college at seventeen. He was the first American to be president of the Royal Economic Society. He was also president of the American Economic Association and the American Statistical Association. He served as an adviser to President Wilson at the Versailles conference.

197. Warburg (1930, 1:506–7) blamed the Board for "the most anomalous rate structure ever devised by any powerful central bank." This refers to the refusal to raise the discount rate in 1929. In the annual report of his bank, published in March 1929, Warburg accused the Federal Reserve of "tossing about today without its helm being under the control of its pilots" (ibid., 826). Kindleberger (1986, 96) recognizes that prices were not at extraordinary levels

By the spring of 1929, recession had started abroad. It was probably too late to stop a worldwide recession, but there was ample time to stop the severe deflation that followed. The National Bureau of Economic Research marked a cycle peak in April for Germany and in July for Britain. March was the peak month for production in Belgium; Canada's peak came in the spring. By fall, financial and business failures had increased in Britain, Germany, and elsewhere (Kindleberger 1986, 102–4). The Federal Reserve's production index, available at the time, peaked in June. By October it was 8 percent below the peak. Monthly peaks in the stock markets in the United States, Canada, and France came in September 1929, but markets in Germany, Sweden, and Switzerland reached peaks in 1928, and in Britain the peak came in January 1929[198] (Kindleberger 1986, 110–11, based on League of Nations data).[199]

Kindleberger (1986) and Galbraith (1955) propose that causality went from the stock market crash to the economy. Kindleberger wrote: "It is hard to avoid the conclusion that there is something to the conventional wisdom that characterized the crash as the start of a process. . . . The stock market crash is less interesting for the irony it permits the historian, bemused by the fables of greedy men, than the start of a process that took on a dynamic of its own" (116).

Charles O. Hardy, a contemporary observer, was skeptical about arguments of this kind.

> In my judgment, the case for the campaign against speculation was weak. It is easy now to see the evidence of over-optimism in the judgment of those who made the stock prices of 1929—though today's appraisals may look just as absurd three years hence. . . . There was no evidence in 1928 or 1929 that business and agriculture were suffering from the competition of the stock market—there was only apprehension that such suffering might ensue. . . .

---

relative to profits. Like Warburg, he located the problem in the financing on the call money market: "The danger posed by the market was not inherent in the level of prices and turnover so much as in the precarious credit mechanism that supported it." Warburg did not criticize Strong or the Federal Reserve for helping Britain remain on the gold standard. He criticized the failure to promptly reverse policy (raise interest rates). He did not speculate on whether a prompt reversal would have reversed the gold flow.

198. Beckhart (1972, 227) listed as proximate causes of the October decline: reports of smaller corporate earnings, the flooding of the market with new security issues, the rise of London bank rate to 6.5 percent, the Hatry failure in London, and a decline in business activity clearly evident by October.

199. These data suggest that between January 1926 and September 1929, Canada and France experienced a stock market boom greater than in the United States. United States stock prices rose 112 percent, Canadian prices 243 percent, and French prices 156 percent (Kindleberger 1986, 110–11).

> There was no evidence in 1928 or 1929 that brokers' loans were too high
> for safety, except that they were higher than a few years before. (Hardy 1932,
> 177–78)

Friedman and Schwartz (1963, 306–7) described the stock market crash as partly "a symptom of the underlying forces making for a severe contraction in economic activity. But, partly also, its occurrence must have helped to deepen the contraction." They suggested tentatively that the decline in velocity and interest rates in 1929–30 was consistent with a desired reduction in spending and the ownership of financial assets and a desired increase in the demand for money. This effect, they said, was dwarfed over the next two years by the decline in the money stock.[200]

A puzzling aspect of Kindleberger's argument is that the association between falling stock prices and recession differed across countries and time. Kindleberger showed that the stock price index he used for the United States had an initial decline of 28 percent between September 1929 and February 1930. It then recovered 10 percent, with evidence of economic recovery in early spring 1930. The French index dropped by 25 percent between September 1929 and October 1930. France did not experience the severe recession for more than five years. Nor did the United States experience a recession after a similar fall in 1987. The difference in these experiences resulted in part from the policies followed at the time.[201]

Far from being the expansive agent that Miller and others alleged, the Federal Reserve followed a generally deflationary policy from mid-1927 on. Growth of the real value of the monetary base increased briefly in spring 1927, but it reversed quickly. Assistance to Britain produced a modest increase in the fall, but that too reversed quickly. Growth of the real base was negative for more than a year before the stock market crash. Chart 4.5 shows these data. The data suggest that if the Federal Reserve had used the monetary base as an indicator of policy thrust instead of the interest rates or bank credit, it would leave increased monetary growth.

Chart 4.5 shows that monetary growth remained in a narrow range during 1927 to 1929. The same is true of real interest rates; they too remained in a narrow range until summer 1929, then fell after industrial production

---

200. The decline in the demand for money in 1929 and 1930 is largely consistent with contemporary changes in interest rates and wealth. Annual estimates for these years do not show large residuals. Relatively large residuals are found in 1926 to 1928. See appendix to chapter 5 below and Field 1984.

201. After reading an earlier version of this chapter, Michael Bordo referred me to Sirkin 1975. Sirkin used a valuation model to show that, although individual companies may have been valued optimistically, "the marked overvaluation of stocks was not general" (231).

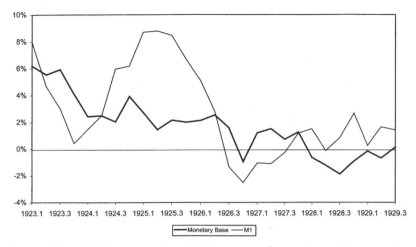

Chart 4.5 Growth of the monetary base and M_1, 1923–29 (four-quarter moving averages).

peaked and the economy moved toward recession. These data deny that a rise in (ex post) real interest rates ended the stock market boom. Rather, the evidence suggests that deflationary monetary policies in all the gold standard countries induced reductions in output abroad that later spread to the United States and other countries. The stock market responded to the actual and anticipated decline in corporate profits. The fall in stock prices lowered the price of existing capital relative to replacement cost, reducing investment, output, and income and increasing the demand for money. (See Brunner and Meltzer 1968b, 1993.)

POLICY ACTIONS AND EFFECTS

Federal Reserve policy remained deflationary in the 1920s when judged by growth of the nominal monetary base.[202] Accelerations of the base were typically short-lived, followed by renewed declines. In the two years ending June 1929, the monetary base fell 2 percent.

Growth of the money supply, M_1, currency and demand deposits, generally moved with the growth of the base during the years 1927 to 1929. Chart 4.5 above shows these series. Real GNP rose 9.2 percent during these years. Rising output with slow or falling money growth produced deflation.[203] As noted earlier, Balke and Gordon's (1986) GNP deflator started

202. Appendix A shows the statistical relationships discussed in this section.

203. Narrow monetary aggregates such as the base and M_1 are more revealing of the deflationary policy than broader aggregates (M_2) in this period. M_2 rose 3.6 percent in the two years ending in second quarter 1929 (based on quarterly averages) (Friedman and Schwartz 1963, table A-1). One reason for the difference is that, as noted several times, banks encour-

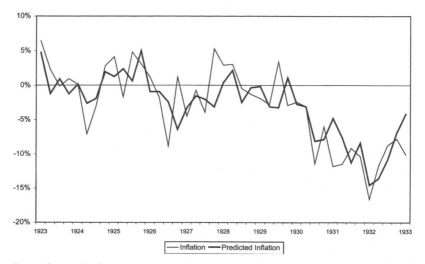

Chart 4.6 Actual inflation versus predicted inflation: Inflation regressed on inflation (−1) and M_1 (−1), 1923–33, quarterly.

to fall in third quarter 1928, five quarters after the local peak in the monetary base.[204]

Actual and Predicted Inflation

The Federal Reserve was responsible for sterilizing gold inflows and for the deflationary policy in the United States. Chart 4.6 compares predicted and actual inflation, quarterly, from 1916 to 1930. The predictions come from estimates of the response of current inflation to past inflation and past money balances.[205]

Predicted and actual values generally move together, most notably in the quarters preceding the depression. Actual or measured inflation is much less variable quarterly than in the years after World War I. The data predict deflation or price stability at the end of the decade.

---

aged depositors to shift from demand to time deposits, reducing the average reserve requirement ratio and permitting bank assets to rise relative to M_1. I interpret the shift of deposits as a response to the restrictive policy. Banks could not obtain desired reserves from the Federal Reserve, so they "innovated," sharing some of their gains with their customers by paying higher interest rates on time deposits.

204. GNP data were not available at the time. The Bureau of Labor Statistics (BLS) index of wholesale prices declined also. By 1928 the BLS index was 6.6 percent below its peak in 1925, a larger decline than Balke and Gordon's (1986) index for the same period. The BLS index declined an additional 1.5 percent in 1929. These data were available at the time and are at times cited in the minutes. The annual rate of change of consumer prices lies between 0 and −3 percent from July 1926 to June 1929.

205. Appendix A reports the equation used for these estimates.

Fiscal Actions

Budget surpluses from 1921 to 1929 averaged 20 percent of tax revenues a year; for 1927 to 1929 the average is 23 percent. These data suggest that the government followed fiscal policies usually described as "restrictive." This characterization ignores the stimulus to enterprise from debt retirement and tax rate reduction. The Treasury retired almost 30 percent of the debt outstanding in 1921 as part of Secretary Mellon's program to reduce the wartime debt. The large surpluses permitted the Mellon Treasury to reduce income tax rates in 1922, 1923, 1924, 1925, 1928, and 1929, the last a temporary reduction. The maximum tax rate on $1 million or more declined from 66 percent to 23 percent; the rate on incomes of $2,000 to $3,000 fell from 2 percent to 0.1 percent.

REORGANIZATION OF THE OPEN MARKET INVESTMENT COMMITTEE

As open market operation increased in importance and discount rate policy declined, the Board lost influence. Control of policy shifted to the five reserve banks represented on the OMIC and particularly to Strong, its chairman. Once Strong left the New York bank, the Board undertook to change the balance of influence.

Miller especially resented Strong's influence, but he was not alone. Other members of the Board, including Young, the Board's governor from 1927 to 1930, also wanted to shift power from the banks to the Board.[206]

The strength of feeling and, at times, irrational character of the arguments came out in a conversation between Young and Harrison in 1929. Harrison began the conversation by referring to the dispute between Washington and New York over open market purchases after the 1929 market crash. The Board objected to New York's decision to act on its own and, despite the crisis, required New York to stop purchases before it would agree to reduce the discount rate. He soon put the issue into a larger context, warning Young that failure to reach a compromise would have "very serious consequences" for the System. The Board had gradually but steadily restricted the role of the reserve banks by taking "not supervisory powers but the equivalent of operating functions." Harrison cited conflicts over discount policy, acceptance policy, and open market policy to illustrate his point. The Board delayed for months raising discount rates at New York and other banks in 1929, despite repeated requests from the reserve banks and agreement of all reserve bank governors. The Board had increased its

206. Young's view is more surprising because he had been governor at Minneapolis before moving to Washington.

role in setting acceptance rates so much that it was now difficult to make rates effective in the market. The New York directors did not want to be "a rubber stamp." He recognized that the Board also should not be a rubber stamp. The path they were on would lead to "a central bank operating in Washington" (Harrison Papers, Confidential Memoranda, conversation with Roy Young, November 15, 1929).

Governor Young replied, "I think that is so." Harrison was surprised at this frank expression. Young continued, "the Federal Reserve Board has been given most extraordinarily wide powers. . . . They would feel free to exercise them and Congress could determine whether they objected to having a central bank operating in Washington."

The shift of control over open market operations had been under way for more than a year before the conversation between Young and Harrison took place. In August 1928 the Board voted to consider expansion of the OMIC to include all the reserve banks. Miller had long favored a further step, making the Board's governor chairman of the reconstituted committee (OMIC Minutes, Board of Governors File, box 1437, August 16, 1928). In September the Federal Advisory Council approved a resolution to expand the OMIC to include the twelve governors but did not include any Board members. The resolution called for a five-person executive committee to carry out the policies, thereby reducing any discretionary action by the five members of the original OMIC.

A few days later the Board appointed Miller and Platt to draft a revision of the rules governing the OMIC. Their proposal followed Miller's 1923 proposal (see above) to replace the OMIC with an Open Market Policy Conference (OMPC), chaired by the governor of the Board, to meet at the call of the Board. Purchases and sales would be made mainly in the acceptance market (ibid., October 30, 1928). The Board approved a slightly weaker proposal for consideration by the Governors Conference. The governors rejected the proposal and called on the Board to keep the 1923 resolution but expand the committee by including all reserve bank governors (ibid., December 3, 1928).

In January 1930 the Board approved a proposal replacing the OMIC with the OMPC, the latter consisting of twelve reserve bank governors. An executive committee could carry out only those decisions of the OMPC "as have been approved" by the Board. Atlanta, St. Louis, Minneapolis, and San Francisco approved the proposal.[207] The members of the OMIC—

207. Richmond, Kansas City, and Dallas did not reply by the date of the meeting, so their positions are not included. There were objections also to other sections not discussed in the text. A summary of the responses by Hamlin is part of the minutes of a meeting of the governors (Open Market, Board of Governors File, box 1437, March 24, 1930).

Cleveland, Chicago, Philadelphia, Boston, and New York—either opposed the proposal or opposed the Board's veto power over committee decisions. Chairman Gates McGarrah wrote for New York that "they would continue membership on the committee, provided it is not inconsistent with these [their] general views." Most banks reserved the right to conduct open market operations outside the committee framework, as permitted by law. Only New York reserved the right of any reserve bank to "withdraw from the Committee procedure altogether, if it deems it advisable" (Organization of OMPC, Board of Governors File, box 1437, March 24, 1930). It would soon regret this insistence.

The twelve-member OMPC began operations soon after the meeting. The Board gave way on the issue of control but did not abandon its efforts until the Banking Act of 1935 centralized power and control in Washington.

CONCLUSION

The 1920s began and ended with major recessions. The 1920–21 recession was the first test of Federal Reserve policy in recession. The depth of the recession, the belief that discount policy had not worked as expected, and the political response to higher interest rates encouraged Federal Reserve officials to search for new policy procedures. Suspension of the gold standard abroad reduced the usefulness of the gold reserve ratio as a measure guiding policy action. This too suggested the need for new procedures. By 1923 the Federal Reserve had developed a more activist policy stance. The new procedures seemed successful. Confidence rose in the Federal Reserve's ability to moderate the business cycle and prevent inflation. These hopes or beliefs were reinforced by restoration of gold convertibility, within a gold exchange standard, in all major countries. The recession that began in 1929 destroyed these beliefs.

The new activist policy was supposed to achieve three ends: mitigate business fluctuations, prevent inflation, and restore the international gold standard. From 1923 to 1929 the United States economy experienced growth, with brief recessions and low inflation before 1925 and modest deflation thereafter. The apparent success of postwar policies in achieving the three main objectives and preventing financial panics increased the credibility of policies and the belief that a new more stable era had begun. The rise in United States stock prices relative to earnings in 1926 supports this interpretation.

In retrospect, we know that the years 1923 to 1929 were one of the best periods in the first eighty years of Federal Reserve experience. The good results were not permanent, however. A severe recession began in Europe in 1929. In August, the United States economy followed. The gold standard also showed signs of strain: Canada left the standard in January 1929; although it continued to maintain a fixed exchange rate against the dollar and the pound, it did not have an official gold price (Bordo and Redish 1988).

The good years could not last. The three aims of Federal Reserve policy were incompatible. As Adolph Miller foresaw, restoration of the gold standard increased the demand for gold; with gold prices fixed in nominal value, commodity prices had to fall. Britain was unwilling to continue the restrictive policies required to lower domestic price and wage levels until they were consistent with its exchange rate and prices abroad. France wanted Britain to increase interest rates and deflate to slow or stop the loss of gold; it was motivated partly by classical gold standard reasoning, partly by its political aim of making Paris a financial center rivaling London and New York. The United States and France drained gold from many of the other gold standard countries, forcing them to contract, but both countries sterilized the gold inflow to prevent domestic inflation. The international system therefore had no way to make an orderly transition by adjusting price levels or exchange rates.

Eichengreen (1992), Clarke (1967), and others attribute the policy failures to insufficient cooperation among central banks. This charge is more true of France than of the United States, but it was not wholly true of either country. The Federal Reserve, principally the New York reserve bank as agent for the System, actively aided Britain and other countries to restore gold convertibility. It lent dollars to Britain and changed domestic policy in 1924 and again in 1927 partly for international purposes—to restore or maintain gold convertibility. These actions were always taken with an understanding, on both sides of the Atlantic, that cooperation would not be allowed to affect domestic inflation. The latter restriction meant that cooperation could not succeed. Exchange rates were misaligned: the pound was overvalued, the franc undervalued. Ruling out inflation in the creditor countries and deflation in Britain left only one course—exchange rate changes—to adjust the system.

The New York reserve bank and its governor, Benjamin Strong, received much criticism at the time and subsequently for lowering interest rates in 1924 and 1927 partly to assist Britain. Although United States prices generally declined, New York's policy was considered inflationary by the financial press, the Federal Reserve Board, and leading members of Congress. Strong was charged with allowing credit expansion based on purchases of government securities. That the price level fell after 1925 did not mute this criticism.

The conflict over policy in 1928 and 1929 was part of the continuing struggle between the Board and the reserve banks and mainly between

New York and Washington. Strong was convinced of the correctness of his policy views and his ability to manage the system. The Board, particularly Adolph Miller, wanted to use the supervisory powers granted in the Federal Reserve Act to gain control of policy decisions. Decisions to change discount rates or purchase and sell remained under the control of the reserve banks, subject to the Board's approval.

The Board wanted to expand its power to approve changes into the power to make changes. By 1929 the System's holding of securities had been reduced to a level too low to be useful. The System had to rely on other policies, but the reserve banks and the Board could not agree on what the policies should be. New York and other reserve banks wanted to raise discount rates. The Board believed that higher rates would penalize industry and trade without deterring stock exchange speculators. It insisted on selective controls implemented by direct pressure or moral suasion and would not approve a 6 percent discount rate.

Disputes were not limited to personal and power conflicts. A main substantive issue was central to the dispute. Miller, other Board members, and several reserve bank governors accepted the real bills doctrine as the only correct guide to policy action. The Federal Reserve Act was written by people who accepted "real bills" and the gold standard as proper guides, so there was a firm legal basis for the positions held by the proponents of real bills.

The central tenet of the real bills doctrine is that increases in credit achieved by discounting real bills finance production and output. Hence credit and output expand together, and there is no inflation. Credit expansion based on government securities (or real estate) is speculative credit. No new production results, so the expansion is inflationary. The proponents of this view disliked open market purchases of government securities. They wanted such purchases to be limited to bills of exchange or banker's acceptances arising from financing trade or production. They might tolerate using open market operations to affect discounts, but not to change the amount of money or credit outstanding.

Strong was the chief spokesman for the opposing view. He did not dispute the importance of discounting. Strong, Warburg, and others wanted an acceptance market, like the British bill market, to replace the call loan market as a short-term credit market. Differences with the Board on these issues were small.

The major difference and substantive source of dispute concerned the ability of a reserve bank to control the volume of credit or money, hence inflation, by limiting discounts to real bills. Strong understood that the collateral offered to the reserve banks had no fixed or logical connection to the marginal use of bank credit. Banks borrowed in the most efficient way and lent for the most profitable uses. Miller and other Board members, Carter Glass and other members of Congress, and many bankers and economists did not accept this conclusion.

In the early years of the decade, research at the Board and the New York bank uncovered a negative relation between open market operations and member bank discounts. They gave a causal interpretation to the relationship: open market sales caused banks to borrow; open market purchases caused repayments. At times the relation was viewed as one-to-one or dollar-for-dollar. On this interpretation, open market operations could be used to control the volume of member bank borrowing. I have called this relation the Riefler-Burgess doctrine.

The Riefler-Burgess doctrine is ambivalent about the role of the discount rate. At most, it has a supporting role; at worst, it has little supplementary effect. Strong, who used the doctrine as a guide to policy, was ambivalent about the independent effect of discount rate changes.

For a time, the emphasis given to control of discounting at New York fit well with the real bills views in Washington. Conflict was muted as long as the governors used open market operations mainly to force borrowing or repayment of discounts based on real bills. Purchases for other reasons, as in 1924 and 1927, were more contentious.

Strong died in October 1928 and was ill and absent for months before his death. His commanding influence during the 1920s invites speculation about what he might have done in 1929 to reverse the Board's policy. Leslie Rounds, a vice president of the New York bank, conjectured that Strong would have succeeded in raising the discount rate early that year (CHFRS, Rounds, May 2, 1955, 13). If this inference is correct, policy would have been more deflationary at an earlier date. With the open market portfolio at a minimum, raising the discount rate was the only remaining way to reduce borrowing.

In Strong's absence, traditional ambivalence about the power of discount rate changes left New York in a weak position to urge such changes as an alternative to direct action in 1929. New York and other reserve banks nevertheless voted to raise the discount rate to control credit expansion. The Board vetoed all requests for four months in the winter and spring; it insisted on using direct action to control speculative credit by urging banks not to make loans to finance stock exchange purchases.

Political concerns reinforced the Board's desire to hold the discount rate at 5 percent. Higher discount rates in the early twenties had been extremely unpopular in Congress and in agricultural areas. Neither the Board nor the reserve banks wanted to repeat that experience. The Board felt the pressure directly from members of Congress, many of whom, like Carter Glass, believed that credit was financing speculation, not commerce and agriculture. Higher rates, they believed, would deprive legitimate users of credit without deterring speculators. Miller and other Board members shared this view.

Both sides in this dispute were misled by the rise in interest rates, particularly call money rates, the relatively high volume of discounts, and the growth of loans to finance securities. Based on these indicators, they regarded policy as highly expansive and inflationary. Since they did not distinguish between real and nominal interest rates, they remained unaware that real rates remained above market rates after 1925.

Growth of the monetary base or the money stock tells a different story. These indicators implied that policy was deflationary. In 1920–21, deflationary policy attracted gold imports and raised real money balances, thereby contributing to expansion despite relatively high real interest rates. In 1927–29 the Federal Reserve followed a more activist policy by sterilizing the gold inflow to prevent monetary expansion. Misled by the level of discounts and the growth of borrowing, the System forced further deflation instead of moderating policy to prevent deflation. The evidence suggests that a less restrictive policy that avoided deflation would have ameliorated or possibly prevented the 1929 recession.

Experiences in the 1920s also show that the Federal Reserve was misled by the stock market. A rapid rise in stock market prices does not permit a central bank to distinguish between well-founded anticipations of increased productivity and output growth and mistaken speculation. Rising expenditure and output, with falling prices, suggests that the public reduced desired real balances to buy claims to real assets. If it had given attention to deflation instead of the booming stock market, the Federal Reserve could have recognized the symptoms of an excess demand for money and increased money growth. Or it could have achieved the same result by ending gold sterilization. The latter course would have required similar action by the Bank of France—an end to gold sterilization.

The 1923–29 experience highlights a major flaw in activist policy, a flaw that reappears in many subsequent periods. Increasingly, policy focused on short-term changes, smoothing the money market, gold inflows and outflows, or Treasury operations. These concerns were visible; longer-term considerations were more remote and conjectural. Hence longer-term aims tended to be sacrificed or postponed to satisfy immediate concerns.

The 1929 recession began with the Federal Reserve System divided on personal and substantive issues. With Strong dead, the Board was in a better position to shift power from New York and the other banks to Washington. The shift of power strengthened Miller and the real bills faction. The financial system entered the Great Depression divided, unprepared to take decisive action, and uncertain whether policy action was useful or desirable to stop economic decline and price deflation.

APPENDIX A: DETERMINANTS OF INFLATION—RELATION OF THE MONETARY BASE AND ITS COMPONENTS

Data are quarterly values at annual rates. The first equation is used in the text. The others are for comparison.

Inflation

Table 4.A1 shows some regressions used to estimate the relation between inflation and money growth for different periods. The text reports on predictions of inflation in the 1920s using quarterly data for 1923 to 1933, regression (1). Regressions (2) and (3) are for comparison. The similarity of the coefficients in equations (2) and (3) suggests that the relation of money to inflation remained the same in the two periods.

Relation of the Monetary Base and Its Components

Chart 4.A1 shows the relation between the monetary base, discounts, gold, and government securities held by the Federal Reserve. The estimates come from a four-variable vector autoregression (VAR) using the following order: discounts, gold stock, monetary base, government securities. Data are monthly from March 1922 to October 1929.

The estimates are based on two lags, eleven seasonal dummy variables, and a constant. Alternative estimates use twelve lags of each of the four variables and no seasonal correction. Main conclusions are the same for both VARs.

The Riefler-Burgess hypothesis specifies a causal relation relating open

Table 4.A1　Regressions for Inflation

	VARIABLE	COEFFICIENT	T-STATISTIC	R^2	DW	PERIOD
(1)	Constant	−0.02	−2.48	0.63	2.36	1923.1–1933.1
	Inflation (−1)	0.44	3.88			
	M_1 (−1)	0.32	4.19			
(2)	Constant	−0.01	−0.52	0.43	2.28	1915.2–1922.4
	Inflation (−1)	0.31	2.20			
	M_1 (−1)	0.57	2.98			
(3)	Constant	−0.00	−0.02	0.38	2.26	1923.1–1929.4
	Inflation (−1)	0.29	1.38			
	M_1(−1)	0.59	1.92			

Note: Data are quarterly values at annual rates. The first equation is used in the text. The others are for comparison.

market purchases and sales to discounts. Open market operations are said to force banks to borrow or permit them to repay. The VARs find no effect of government securities on discounts. To the extent that there is a relation between the two, the data suggest that Federal Reserve operations responded to higher discounts by selling.

Gold has no significant effect on discounting in the short term and a negative relation after a quarter. Over the longer term, government securities have a modest negative effect on gold. Nevertheless, the variance decomposition (not shown) suggests that past gold movements dominate all other influences on the gold stock.

The monetary base appears to be relatively independent of its asset components. The exception is a longer-term positive effect of gold flows on the base. The short-run response of gold to the base is small and insignificant, suggesting the active program of short-run gold sterilization during these years. Chart 4.2 above shows that the contemporaneous relationship is weak also.

The very weak association between the base and its principal components suggests that the deflationary policy of the period was a consequence of Federal Reserve actions. Over the longer term, the base moved with net gold inflows; for the period as a whole, the gold stock increased by $650 million, and the monetary base rose $970 million. These increases were produced by compound average annual growth rates of 2 percent and 1.7 percent, respectively. All of the increase occurred before summer 1927.

APPENDIX B: SOURCES AND USES OF THE MONETARY BASE AND OPEN MARKET OPERATIONS

The basic statement of the Federal Reserve's monetary position is the table Member Bank Reserve, Reserve Bank Credit, and Related Items, published in the *Federal Reserve Bulletin*. The table was developed at the Board in the 1920s by combining the balance sheets of the twelve reserve banks and the monetary accounts of the Treasury. This appendix rearranges these data as sources and uses of the monetary base.

The principal sources of the monetary base are Reserve Bank credit and gold and foreign exchange assets. Under a pure gold standard or a fixed exchange rate system without intervention, gold and foreign exchange are the principal sources of the monetary base. Under a fluctuating rate system, without intervention, gold and foreign exchange is constant. Reserve bank credit is the principal source item.

Other source items are mainly small positive and negative accounts. Historically, the principal positive item here has been treasury currency outstanding, because the Treasury formerly issued currency. During much

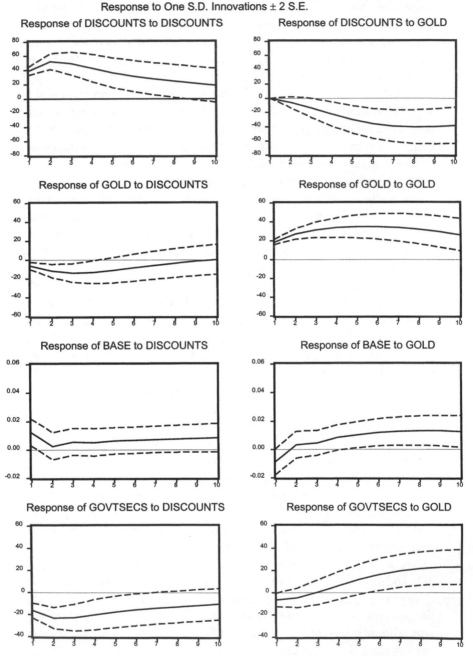

Chart 4A.1 Based on VAR with two lags and eleven seasonal dummies, monthly, March 1922 to October 1929.

Response to One S.D. Innovations ± 2 S.E.

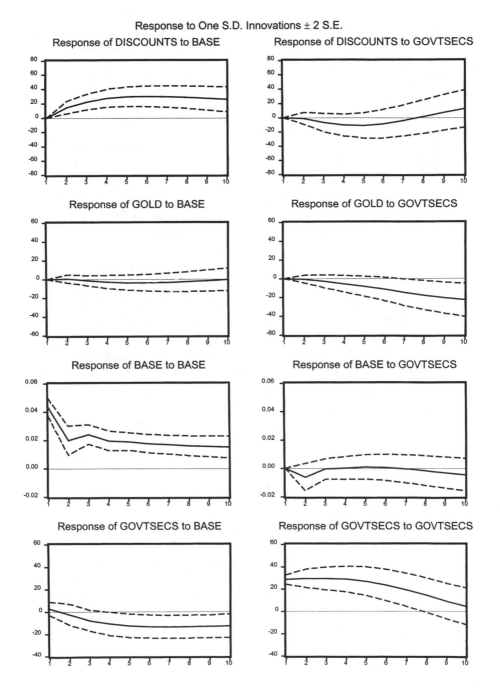

Table 4.A2   Monetary Base (millions of dollars)

SOURCES		USES	
Discounts	465	2,426	Bank Reserves
Acceptances	373	4,498	Currency[a]
Governments	512	6,924 =	Monetary base
Reserve bank credit[b]	1,388		
Gold	4,090		
Other items net	1,648		
= Monetary base	6,924		

[a]Called "money in circulation."
[b]Includes additional minor items.

of Federal Reserve history, these were small-denomination notes.[208] The principal liabilities here are Treasury deposits with Federal Reserve banks and deposits of foreign governments and central banks.

Reserve bank credit consists of three principal items: bills discounted, bills bought, and United States government securities. The first is usually referred to as discounts and advances. These are made at the option of the member bank, under rules prescribed by the Federal Reserve. The founders of the Federal Reserve believed this item would be the major source of short-term changes. The text refers to "bills bought" as acceptances. The founders intended this source to become an important item and the main source of adjustment and policy operations, as in London. From the 1920s on, its role was taken by the third source—United States government securities.

The uses of the monetary base include member bank reserves and currency held by the nonbank public. Rules permitting member banks to count vault cash as part of reserves add to the base by including currency held by banks as a use of the monetary base.

In January 1928 the statement of sources and use of the monetary base, appeared as in table 4.A2.

An open market purchase of acceptances or government securities increases one of the items on the sources side and balances the increase by adding to member bank reserves. An open market sale of government securities reduces this source and, correspondingly, reduces bank reserves.

By law the Federal Reserve cannot buy securities directly from the Treasury (with some minor exceptions). Open market operations are therefore conducted in the credit markets.

208. For more detail, see Friedman and Schwartz 1970.

FIVE

Why Did Monetary Policy Fail
in the Thirties?

From the peak of the cycle in the summer of 1929 to the bottom of the depression in March 1933, the stock of money—currency and demand deposits—fell by 28 percent and industrial production fell by 50 percent. The sizable declines in the two series merit attention not only because the social consequences of the decline in output were large and pervasive, but because the policies pursued during the period and the justification of them provide considerable evidence about the framework that guided Federal Reserve policy and the response of the Federal Reserve to a crisis.

This chapter gives special attention to the Federal Reserve's response to the contraction, considers some previous explanations of its actions and inaction, and uses the history of the periods and the statements of participants to discriminate among alternative explanations of Federal Reserve behavior. Inevitably, this leads to a central issue about the 1929–33 decline: why the decline was so severe. There is no doubt that early in the decline the Federal Reserve knew a major contraction was under way. Whatever its causes, monetary policy could have lessened the decline. At issue here is why it failed to do so.[1]

The chapter does not attempt to resolve the more difficult problem of assessing the relative contribution of nonmonetary factors to the start of the Great Depression. It is now generally accepted that the depth of the depression, its duration, and its spread through the world economy are mainly the result of monetary actions or inactions. Warburton (1966), Friedman and Schwartz (1963), and at an earlier date Currie (1934) high-

---

1. There are several nonmonetary changes that supplement the monetary forces. The papers in Brunner 1981 discuss many of these explanations.

lighted the role of monetary forces in the United States. More recent work by Eichengreen (1992) and Bernanke (1994) accepts the role of money and concentrates on the international character of the decline and the influence of the international gold standard. Agreement is limited, however. There are several different, and at times conflicting, explanations of the severity of the decline.

DIFFERENT INTERPRETATIONS

Following Bernanke (1994) and Mishkin (1976), several authors have revived a version of Irving Fisher's (1933) debt-deflation explanation of the severity of the Great Depression.[2] These authors supplement the monetary explanation by highlighting the role of capital market imperfections resulting from differences in borrowers' net worth. Borrowers with relatively low net worth face more restricted opportunities to borrow, so they depend more on banks. As firms' net worth fell during the depression, banks refused additional loans. Also, bank failures removed the principal lenders for businesses with moderate net worth. On this explanation, bank failures contributed to the depression not only by reducing the money stock, as claimed by Currie (1934), Warburton (1966), and Friedman and Schwartz (1963), but by raising the cost and availability of loans more than would have occurred based on the monetary and credit contraction resulting from Federal Reserve policies.

Friedman and Schwartz (1963, 407–19) attributed the Federal Reserve's behavior in the early thirties to the death of Benjamin Strong in 1928 and the shift of power from the Federal Reserve Bank of New York to other parts of the System. George L. Harrison, who replaced Strong as governor of the New York bank, lacked Strong's ability to organize and lead other members of the open market committee. In this interpretation, the period is unique not only because of the severity of the contraction but because the Federal Reserve behaved as it had not behaved earlier and should not be expected to behave again.

In his history of the interwar gold standard, Barry Eichengreen (1992) revived the idea that lack of central bank cooperation, the workings of the interwar gold exchange standard, and the requirement that Federal Reserve notes be backed 40 percent by gold produced and prolonged the decline. Lack of cooperation weakened the operation of the interwar gold standard Eichengreen (1992, 213). Cooperation would have enhanced the credibility of the System by encouraging speculators to believe that gold

2. Calomiris (1993) surveys this literature, and Bernanke (1994) refers explicitly to Fisher's debt-deflation theory.

parities would be defended with the help of foreign central banks (xi, 257, 390). Monetary contraction in the United States and a decline in its international lending in 1928 put unsupportable strain on a fragile system, necessitated contraction in many countries, and "set the stage for the 1929 downturn" (392).[3] Gold stocks were most heavily concentrated at the Bank of France and the Federal Reserve, but even these banks "had very limited room for maneuver" (393).

Elmus Wicker (1966, ix, 155, 195) attributed the Federal Reserve's failure to its incomplete understanding of how monetary policy influenced economic activity and the price level. The Federal Reserve Board and the governors of the reserve banks were confused and misled by their interpretation of the events they watched. Power within the System was so diffused that leadership from New York or Washington was not possible (195). Even if there had been strong leadership, the uniqueness of the events of 1932 and 1933 immobilized the policymakers.

Wicker argues that Federal Reserve policy in 1929–33 was consistent with its actions in the 1923–24 and 1926–27 recessions. The Federal Reserve followed the practices laid down by Governor Benjamin Strong: use open market operations to reduce member bank borrowing below $500 million and reduce borrowing by New York banks commensurately. Once this was done, policy would be "easy." Wicker added that international cooperation motivated open market purchases in 1924 and 1927, specifically to help Britain return to and remain on the gold standard.

A problem with some of these explanations is that the Federal Reserve was not entirely passive for the three and a half years of the decline. More than once it purchased securities or lowered the rediscount rate. It actively responded to events such as the departure of Britain from the gold standard in October 1931 by raising the rediscount rate to stem a gold outflow, as gold standard rules required. Although disputes persisted about the locus of power within the System and there were clashes between personalities, these are overtones that do not adequately explain the dismal record. If the crisis was largely due to an absence of leadership, more effective action would have been taken later, after the System reorganized, given additional authority and a strong chairman. But in the middle and late thirties, just as in the early thirties, the Federal Reserve did next to nothing to foster recovery. In a period of prolonged and widespread unemployment,

---

3. Clarke (1967) surveys experience with central bank cooperation in the interwar period. Clarke too concludes that cooperation failed after 1928, but he describes the failure differently. "The failure stemmed not so much from the deficiencies of central bank cooperation itself as from the inability of the authorities—including particularly those in the United States—to manage their domestic economies successfully" (220).

the Federal Reserve's principal policy action was the 1937–38 series of deflationary and contractive increases in reserve requirement ratios taken to forestall a possible future inflation.

Although Friedman and Schwartz offered an interpretive history based on what might have happened if Governor Strong had lived, a main point of their explanation is of doubtful validity. It is true that W. Randolph Burgess, and others at the New York bank, proposed expansive policies, and at times Harrison suggested purchases. In fact, Harrison argued vigorously for open market purchases at times, but at other times he was a leading proponent of open market sales. The timing of Harrison's decisions to purchase or sell can be explained (approximately) by the conjunction of the Riefler-Burgess and real bills doctrines. These ideas or beliefs misled Harrison and others in the Federal Reserve at critical points in the early thirties and thereafter. As noted by Wicker (1966), Brunner and Meltzer (1968b), and Wheelock (1990, 1992), Federal Reserve officials behaved consistently in the 1923–24, 1926–27, and 1929–33 declines.[4]

The difficult issue to resolve is whether Strong's colleagues on the Open Market Policy Conference (OMPC) would have supported expansive policies had he proposed them.[5] Many of his fellow governors had been persuaded to go along but were not convinced that his arguments were correct in 1924 and 1927. Moreover, member bank borrowing remained high in 1924 and 1927, so domestic concerns (and the desire for earnings) reinforced international reasons for purchasing government securities. During most of 1929–33, member bank borrowing remained low; on Riefler-Burgess views, domestic policy was easy. Further, Adolph Miller and others at the Board blamed Strong's policies for the depression. They interpreted the depression as the inevitable consequence of the preceding growth of bank credit and asset prices that followed the 1927 policy actions Strong had urged. Because credit expansion had increased without equivalent purchases of real bills, this policy was inflationary. Deflationary policy should have followed in 1928. That mistake had to be corrected.

Several governors agreed with this interpretation. Although the price

4. Wheelock (1990) estimates an equation for borrowing by member banks. He shows that increases in nonborrowed reserves, (through gold inflows or Federal Reserve purchases) reduce borrowing, but the reduction is approximately 0.5, not 1 as in Riefler-Burgess. See also the appendix A to chapter 4.

5. Strong was more persuasive than Harrison and more convinced by the logic of his arguments. Harrison seems more of a diplomat, without strongly held views. Moreover, the OMPC included all twelve governors instead of the five members that Strong dealt with. A serious problem, discussed below, was that Harrison could not persuade the Boston and Chicago reserve banks to participate in open market purchases.

level had fallen, Strong's policy had violated the rules of the real bills doctrine. The violation had to be purged.[6]

Eichengreen's claim that the gold standard prevented action is difficult to reconcile with the System's responses in the 1923–24 and 1926–27 recessions. These actions had received praise at the time and encouraged the belief that the System had taken countercyclical action to lessen the downturn. If the Federal Reserve had risked the temporary loss of gold on these occasions, why would it fail to run the same risk in the much steeper decline after August 1929?

The Federal Reserve was in no danger of abrogating its gold reserve requirements in 1929, 1930, or early 1931. In fact, the System experienced a gold inflow in 1930 and early 1931. By June 1931, the monetary gold stock was almost 15 percent above the August 1929 level, whereas gold collateral required for notes had increased no more than 2 percent and collateral for bank reserves had increased only $40 million—less than 2 percent.

Eichengreen (1992, 297–98) accepts the argument in the Federal Reserve's 1932 annual report that its response in 1931 was limited by the decline in the gold stock and the requirement to use gold as backing for Federal Reserve notes, the so-called free gold problem.[7] Although there is some dispute about the relevance of the problem, any relevance is limited to the period following Britain's departure from gold on September 20, 1931, and the passage of the Glass-Steagall Act on February 27, 1932. During the rest of the decline, gold cover for the notes was not an issue.[8] The

6. The same reasoning applied to wartime inflation. Wartime inflation had to be followed by deflation, and it was until World War II.

7. Federal Reserve notes were backed by a minimum of 40 percent in gold. Eligible paper made up the remainder. The decline in eligible paper at the Federal Reserve required the reserve banks to substitute gold for eligible paper. Government securities could not be used as collateral until the passage of the Glass-Steagall Act in February 1932. All notes issued, including notes held at other Federal Reserve banks, required gold and eligible paper as backing. The collateral requirements applied to each reserve bank separately, so the distribution of notes and gold affected free gold—the gold that was not used as collateral for notes and deposits at reserve banks. Friedman and Schwartz (1963, 400–404) argue that free gold was never a problem and suggest several ways any problem could have been relieved. For example, the reserve banks could have lowered the acceptance rate to acquire eligible paper and free gold for expansion of the note issue.

8. The *Federal Reserve Bulletin* for 1932 shows notes outstanding and collateral for each reserve bank on February 28, 1932. Gold was used as collateral for 71 percent of the total note issue. Chicago was at the extreme position with 88 percent gold and 14 percent commercial paper. The largest issuer, New York, had 75 percent gold and 25 percent commercial paper. The third largest bank, Cleveland, had 63 percent gold and 40 percent commercial paper. Open market purchases could have been made by the banks with sufficient gold to issue notes. Since there was no requirement at the time for all reserve banks to participate in an open market purchase, some abstained at times.

Federal Reserve did not use government securities as collateral for notes until May 1932, after increasing its holdings of governments more than $650 million between February and May.

Stripped of its technical details, the free gold explanation asserts that System open market purchases would have reduced the ratio of gold to notes and deposits below the required ratios of 40 percent and 35 percent. Technical restrictions seem a weak explanation for the lack of response. Bagehot's well-known writings had instructed the Bank of England that it could not protect its gold reserve by failing to expand. On several occasions in the nineteenth century, the Bank of England had suspended the gold reserve requirement and relaxed restrictions on eligible paper for discounts when required to stop a panic. When necessary, the government had indemnified the bank against claims arising as a result of the suspension. This history was known within the Federal Reserve and referred to on more than one occasion.

Charles S. Hamlin, a member of the Federal Reserve Board from 1914 to 1936, discussed the loss of gold at a meeting in Boston on November 20, 1931, two months after Britain had suspended convertibility (Federal Reserve Bank of Boston 1931, 13–16). Hamlin began by summarizing the main movements of gold into and out of the United States since 1914. He described the $750 million outflow from September 17 to October 30, 1931, as "the largest ever sustained by any country in such a short space of time" (15). Nevertheless, the Federal Reserve, he said, held more than $1 billion of gold reserves above the amounts required for Federal Reserve notes and member bank balances. Then he added: "In addition, there is about $1,000,000,000 in gold certificates in circulation in this country, a considerable part of which could if desired be replaced with other forms of currency. We not only have ample gold to cover the legal requirements but our monetary gold stocks, even after the heavy withdrawals, are only slightly below the prosperous years of 1928 and 1929" (16).

Hamlin next commented on the reason for protecting the gold reserve: "The experience of recent weeks brings home to Federal Reserve officials their heavy responsibility, the necessity for *keeping their powder dry,* so that in these troublous times they may remain the rock that can withstand all storms and upon which world confidence may once more be reconstructed" (ibid.; emphasis added).[9]

Eichengreen correctly points out that before and during the world economic decline, France contributed to the onset and the severity of the

___

9. Eichengreen's figure 4.4 (1992, 119) shows that free gold in late 1931 remained well above the levels of 1920–21. Bordo (1994) notes that Eichengreen misstates the amount of open market operations necessary to restore the money stock.

world depression by sterilizing much of its gold inflow. From June 1928 to September 1929, the French bought $2.6 billion in gold and, in the same period, reduced their foreign exchange reserves by an equal amount.[10] From September 1929 to March 1933, the Bank of France acquired an additional $1.6 billion in gold while reducing foreign exchange reserves by $800 million. For the period September 1928 to March 1933 as a whole, French gold reserves increased by 2.8 times while French holdings of gold and foreign exchange increased only 30 percent.

The French money stock rose 18 percent in the two years 1930 and 1931. Greater expansion and less sterilization by the Bank of France would have lessened the severity and scope of the world decline. At issue is whether the failure to expand more resulted from a lack of coordination. The Bank of France was not obliged to sterilize much of the gold inflow. The United States was not obliged to contract as France sterilized.

The critical flaw was not the absence of international coordination but domestic decisions at critical times to not interfere with the contraction of money and credit and the resulting deflation. Protecting the United States gold reserve was at most a secondary effect of the principal decision. Leading central bankers and their advisers believed that credit expansion to finance stock market speculation in 1928–29 was a misuse of credit that had to be eliminated. Bankers, economists, and others stated this view repeatedly during the contraction.

Writing at the time, Oliver M. W. Sprague explicitly rejected both the idea that monetary expansion was desirable and the idea that absence of international cooperation contributed to or exacerbated the depression. Sprague was an expert on banking crises and a close adviser to the Federal Reserve. He also served as economic adviser to the Bank of England from 1930 to 1933.[11] In a May 1931 speech in London, Sprague discussed the causes of the depression and the role of international coordination (Board of Governors of the Federal Reserve System, Weekly Review of Periodicals, June 2, 1931, 1–2).[12] He began by noting that the depression had become more acute. There was no agreement on its causes or on appropriate reme-

---

10. Data on French gold stocks and reserves are from *Banking and Monetary Statistics* (Board of Governors of the Federal Reserve System 1943, 641–42). Data are converted from francs to dollars using 3.92 francs per dollar. Sterilization of the gold inflow was similar to the policy followed by the Federal Reserve in 1921–22. See Strong 1927.

11. Sprague was a professor at Harvard from 1913 to 1941. He had written an influential study for the National Monetary Commission and was active in policy discussions throughout his career.

12. The Federal Reserve staff prepared a summary of press discussion. It included the *Economist*, other financial journals, market letters, and foreign and domestic newspapers. The 1931 Weekly Reviews are available in the Widener Library at Harvard.

dies. He summarized two divergent views. The "monetary school" wanted the leading central banks to "flood the market with a great amount of additional credit and currency." The "industrial or economic equilibrium school included all the responsible [sic] people connected with the great central banks of the world." This school held that falling prices were a symptom, not a cause: "When prices did advance, more currency and credit would be employed, but they did not believe that simply by injecting more currency and credit into the situation they could certainly bring about the desirable rise in prices and business activity."

The problem was not lack of agreement between the principal central bankers: "It was not because of any difficulty of securing agreement among the three banks, (France, U.K., U.S.) but because none of them harbored the belief that it was the appropriate remedy" (ibid., 1–2).

Sprague, like the central bankers in France, England, and the United States that he described, accepted the "industrial equilibrium" explanation. The world's economies would reach a new equilibrium at lower prices and wages. It would take time, they recognized, but they believed deflation was the correct solution to the mistakes of 1928–29.

In a speech to the Royal Statistical Society a few weeks later, Sprague explained why the deflationary solution was proper. There had been over-production particularly in the American automobile industry. Further, there had been a speculative boom. He blamed Federal Reserve policy in 1928, when it would have been "possible to check the speculative wave on the New York Stock Exchange" (Weekly Review, June 24, 1931, 1).

Paul Warburg wrote in the *American Banker* for January 20, 1931, "The way to avoid a depression (or lessen its severity and duration) is to 'sit on the bulge' during an excessive upward swing. Once acute over-expansion has taken place, acute overcontraction must follow with inexorable certainty. Unfortunately, it would seem politically impossible for any government to use its influence toward checking a wave of prosperity, even though it was clearly a fake prosperity destined to end in a crash" (Weekly Review, January 27, 1931, 5).

These were not the only views, but they were common views of central bankers. M. H. deKock of the South African Reserve Bank thought that the "maintenance of pronounced monetary ease for any length of time almost inevitably leads to inflation and speculation in one form or another" (Weekly Review, February 3, 1931). In the same report, the noted British economist Lionel Robbins argued against the view that there was a world-wide shortage of gold. Like most others, he failed to distinguish between real and nominal interest rates: "If insufficiency of gold is the main cause of depression, why is there a depression in America. And with a 2 percent discount rate in New York, it is hard to contend that credit conditions are stringent" (2–3).

Robbins also mentioned the maldistribution of the gold stock, a common complaint at the time. However, he assigned more importance to the unhealthy character of the boom in 1928. Money rates had been held too low for too long.[13]

Charles S. Hamlin shared the view that speculative excesses had to be purged from the financial system and the economy. On November 8, 1929, shortly after the 1929 stock market break, he told a group of New England bankers:

> The present crisis through which we are passing is typical of the kind of crisis that the framers of the Federal Reserve Act had in mind. The Act was designed to prevent the close dependence or interdependence of American industry upon speculative activity throughout the community. . . . The Federal Reserve System was designed to break up the vicious circle under which a speculative orgy accompanied every forward step of industry. . . .
>
> The success of the Federal Reserve System is apparent today. . . . These events [losses] are deplorable, but they were of course inevitable and could not have been avoided. (Federal Reserve Bank of Boston 1929, 28)

The opinions of bankers and central bankers at the time are similar to the statement of Federal Reserve policy in the tenth annual report (Board of Governors of the Federal Reserve System, *Annual Report*, 1923). As Friedman and Schwartz note, the statement was compatible with two interpretations. One, the "real bills" or "productive credit" view of policy, required the Federal Reserve to provide "credit" for the "needs of trade" but not for "speculative" uses. The second interpretation is that the Federal Reserve would attempt to counteract inflation and deflation by counter-cyclical open market operations.

Only the first interpretation, the real bills view, appears in the minutes of the Open Market Policy Conference for the early thirties and in the statements of bankers and central bankers above. It is possible that the references to statements in the tenth annual report were made to justify views that were held for other reasons. Even if this was true, however, it is striking that none of the governors objected to the interpretation or presented an alternative. Even more striking is the absence, at most of the meetings of the OMPC, of any statement favoring an expansive policy. Even those

---

13. J. M. Keynes is quoted in the February 3, 1931, Weekly Review as opposing reductions in money wages. Keynes blamed low investment, which he attributed to uncertainty, high interest rates, high-risk premiums, and borrowers' fears. Keynes also noted that falling prices increased the burden of outstanding debts.

governors who occasionally pressed for open market purchases and re-ductions in the discount rate expressed doubt that monetary (or credit) policy *alone* would have much effect on output. They too appear to have been greatly influenced by the notion that the prevalence of low nominal interest rates and low borrowing showed that policy was "easy."

Benjamin Strong shared many of these interpretations. He often relied on the volume of member bank borrowing as a measure of ease or re-straint.[14] Nothing in either the Riefler-Burgess doctrine or the real bills doctrine distinguished between real and nominal rates of interest or rec-ognized that the level of borrowing depends on anticipated income and in-flation.

The minutes of the Open Market Investment Committee, the Federal Reserve Board, and the Conference of Governors of the Reserve Banks, considered below, show that most of the policy decisions remained consis-tent with the Riefler-Burgess and real bills frameworks. This should not suggest that everyone slavishly followed a formula. Many other inherited notions, mentioned in the minutes, contributed to the Federal Reserve's failure to act or justified inaction. Concerns about "redundant reserves" or "excessive liquidity in the banking system" are variations on the real bills theme but may have other origins. Whatever the source of these ideas, many of the policymakers opposed expansive policy action because they believed that expansive action was inappropriate. Concern about future in-flation caused several governors to hesitate to act, to regard deflation as the inevitable consequence of previous speculative excesses, for much the same reasons that Strong and others had viewed the severe deflation of 1920–21 as a consequence of inflationary wartime policies and a necessary prelude to the price stability of the middle twenties. Speculative credit and nonreal bills had to be purged. This was the message of Hamlin, Warburg, Robbins, Sprague, and many other bankers and central bankers.

Once borrowing and short-term market rates had fallen below the range familiar to governors and commercial bankers, policy was "easy."[15] They saw no reason for further additions to reserves and further reductions in market rates. Expansive policy would finance speculative credit and be-come the source of a future inflation that, once under way, would be diffi-

14. "As a guide to the timing and extent of any purchase which might appear desir-able, one of our best guides would be the amount of borrowing by member banks" quoted in Chandler 1958, 239–40.

15. The range usually mentioned for the United States was aggregate member bank bor-rowing of $500 million to $600 million in recession. During the deflation after 1870, the Bank of England never adjusted the discount rate to prevent continued deflation once the dis-count rate reached 2 percent.

cult to stop. The System's holdings of government securities were much smaller than the level of member bank borrowing during much of the twenties and were not substantially larger than the level of borrowings in the early thirties. Not having enough securities on hand to prevent a future inflation had been a recurring concern since the start of the Federal Reserve System. The concern seems a ludicrous reason for not expanding, but it appeared very real to several of the governors at the time. Since nominal interest rates had been reduced to levels that were comparatively low by the historical standards or experience the governors and members relied on, they saw little reason to increase speculative credit and accept the risk of inflation.

Some officials either did not fully share the dominant view or differed about particular events. At times some showed clear understanding of the role the System might play, although they did little to promote their views against the dominant view in the System. Included in this group are two members of the Federal Reserve Board—Eugene Meyer and Adolph Miller—who at times questioned Harrison and the other members of the open market committee about their reasons for not pursuing a more expansive policy. W. Randolph Burgess at the Federal Reserve Bank of New York urged more expansive policies at critical times, with support from the directors of the New York bank.

The policy problems of the early thirties were not unique. Books discussing the appropriate means of handling these problems were known to some of the members of the open market committee or their staffs. The effect of changes in the quantity of money had been discussed for more than a century, and many outstanding economists had contributed to the analysis. Some, like Henry Thornton (1965) and Walter Bagehot (1962), whose works are discussed in chapter 2, had described the appropriate response of a central bank to a crisis. Both Thornton and Bagehot suggested some of the principal reasons for large-scale currency withdrawals, and both had indicated that during a currency drain the central bank should expand.

Three of Thornton's recommendations to the Bank of England are particularly relevant to—and contrast sharply with—the behavior of the Federal Reserve during the thirties. First, he argued repeatedly that there was rarely any reason for reducing the quantity of money (Thornton 1965, 259). Second, he urged the governors of the bank to meet an increase in the demand for currency by temporarily increasing the bank's liabilities (259). Third, he recommended that the bank use the quantity of money—and not the volume of commercial bank borrowing from the central bank or of private borrowing from commercial banks—as a measure of its policy and the influence it would have on prices and output (271).

It is possible, but unlikely, that Thornton's work was entirely un-known.[16] However, there is no doubt that officials knew Bagehot's work, since references to his book, *Lombard Street*, appear in the OMPC minutes. Bagehot had demanded repeatedly that the Bank of England acknowledge publicly that it served as lender of last resort, and subsequently the bank had done so. And Bagehot had discussed fully why it was a mistake for a central bank to seek to protect its gold reserve by failing to lend during a run on commercial banks.

Numerous other writers had analyzed the effects of changes in the quantity of money and the responsibilities of central banks in a crisis. Two of the most able monetary economists of all time, Irving Fisher (1920, esp. chap. 4) and John Maynard Keynes (1930, 1931), had argued in scholarly books, in pamphlets, and in newspaper articles of the period that a decline in the quantity of money would first affect the level of output and employ-ment and only later affect the price level.[17] Neither the absence of relatively simple, comprehensible alternative theories, nor the absence of facts about developments in the economy, nor the absence of strong leadership can ex-plain the dismal record. The main reason for the failure of monetary policy in the depression was the reliance on an inappropriate set of beliefs about speculative excesses and real bills. This set of beliefs, embodied in the Riefler-Burgess framework, directed attention to short-term market inter-est rates and member bank borrowing and encouraged their use as indica-tors of the magnitude and direction of monetary stimulus.

THE FIRST YEAR OF DECLINE: POLICY FROM AUGUST 1929 TO SEPTEMBER 1930

To show how policy responded to the economic decline, the discussion comments on each meeting of the Open Market Investment Committee and its successor the Open Market Policy Conference, or their executive committees, between the peak of the expansion in August 1929 and the trough of the recession in March 1933. A series of twenty tables shows some of the information available at each meeting. Three types of data sug-gest the direction of monetary policy and the levels or changes in other variables that the committee discussed from time to time at its meetings or that influenced its decisions. One type of data shows cumulative change from the peak of the expansion to the nearest month. A second type, called

16. Jacob Viner, a distinguished economist of the period, had paid considerable attention to Thornton's work. See Viner 1924.

17. In the *Treatise*, Keynes argued for sizable open market operations in the United States. See Keynes 1931, 2:371–74 and 304–37. Charles Rist (1940, 404–6) points out that by 1840 the Bank of France had recognized the responsibility of a central bank to act as lender of last resort.

"recent changes," shows the change in various measures between meetings. The third group shows the levels of variables that are of interest, again dated to the nearest month.[18] Data for the money supply were not available at the time, but currency and demand deposits were available separately.

Responses to the Financial Panic

At the peak of the cycle in August 1929, the level of member bank borrowing exceeded $1 billion, the highest level reached since 1921. The interest rate on new stock exchange call loans was 8.15 percent, more than 1.5 percent below the high for the year in March. Other short-term market rates had passed their peak, while long-term rates were generally at the highest levels of the expansion. The seasonally adjusted monetary base was 1 percent below the peak reached more than a year earlier.

In the first six weeks the policy, agreed on in August, worked as planned; the System provided seasonal credit expansion by lowering the acceptance rate while raising the discount rate. Harrison told the Board that the total seasonal increase was about average. The acceptance portfolio increased $162 million, more than offsetting the $130 million decline in discounts. In addition the System purchased $20 million in the open market. Harrison asked for an OMIC meeting in September to consider open market purchases to supplement acceptance purchases (Board of Governors File, box 1435, November 12, 1929; these are minutes of the September meeting).

Brokers' loans continued to increase. Banks used all the reserves obtained from sales of acceptances to the reserve banks to repay discounts, so total bank credit remained unchanged. Interest rates changed little.[19]

18. Most of the data are taken from *Banking and Monetary Statistics* (Board of Governors of the Federal Reserve System 1943). An index of industrial production is available in the *Federal Reserve Bulletins* at the time, but I have used the revised index of industrial production from *Industrial Production 1957–59 Base* (Board of Governors of the Federal Reserve System [1962?], 5–149). These data are seasonally adjusted. Data on money supply are from Friedman and Schwartz 1963. The money supply is the sum of currency and demand deposits of the public. The monetary base is from Anderson and Rasche 1999. The base is the sum of total currency and reserves outstanding adjusted for changes in reserve requirement ratios. In addition to the changes in the monetary base, I present data on changes in some of the principal sources of the base: changes in government securities held in the Federal Reserve portfolio, changes in bills bought (acceptances), and changes in the gold stock. These data are from *Banking and Monetary Statistics*. Data on wholesale prices are from various issues of the *Federal Reserve Bulletin* for the period. Other data that were available regularly include department store sales and inventories, money rates abroad, and a breakdown of member bank loans and investments. See data sources, pp. 761–64.

19. The report notes that England continued to lose gold reserves to France and Germany. Pressure from high rates "is becoming constantly more intense and is tending to retard industrial and business developments" (Open Market, Board of Governors File, box 1435, November 12, 1929, 7). The report (written for the September 24 meeting) also notes a more than seasonal drop in exports and declines in several basic industries.

At the September 24 meeting, the governors expressed concern about the levels of discounts and rates of interest. To reduce both while acting against an impending recession, the committee voted to purchase up to $25 million of government securities weekly, if acceptances could not be obtained at the posted buying rates of 5.125 percent. When presenting the proposal to the Board, Harrison, the chairman of the OMIC, noted that "some reduction in this [member bank] indebtedness would be a necessary prerequisite to any further easing of interest rates," as implied by Riefler-Burgess. The Board delayed accepting the proposal until its members returned from vacation. On September 30 Harrison wrote to Governor Roy A. Young at the Board to report the favorable response of the New York directors to the purchase program and again stressed the importance of reducing interest rates.

The Board approved the committee's recommendations on October 1. In his reply to Harrison, however, Young noted that the Board's approval was mainly for seasonal reasons, not a reversal of prevailing policy. There was no suggestion in the monetary indicators the Board and the committee watched, and no recognition in their discussions or letters, that the financial system was about to experience the first of a series of shocks in the following weeks. The committee made no open market purchases until the week of October 30.

The indexes of prices on the New York Stock Exchange reached peaks in September and plummeted in the last week of October. The Federal Reserve lowered the buying rate on banker's acceptances by 0.125 percent (to 5 percent) on October 25. By October 28, with the decline on the stock exchange continuing, the members of the Board were of the opinion that "no further easing of the bill rate should be made at this time as the easing program of the system seems to be progressing satisfactorily." The next day the market plunged downward on volume in excess of 16 million shares, nearly five times the average daily volume.

The following day Governor Young reported on his conversation with Harrison. Harrison informed him that the directors of the New York bank had given him authority to purchase government securities for the bank's account without any stated limit, and he had used this authority to purchase $50 million. Inasmuch as the purchases had been completed, Young concluded: "There was nothing before the Board at that time requiring immediate action."

The Board was piqued at Harrison and the New York bank for undertaking purchases without prior approval (as was customary), but decided to defer discussion of Harrison's assumption of responsibility until later. Instead, the discussion turned to action that "might appropriately [sic] be taken." Cunningham suggested, and the majority agreed, that it would be best to reduce the discount rate at the New York Bank from 6 to 5 percent, "with the understanding that the System will suspend, for the time being, any purchases of government securities, pending further developments in the credit situation as a result of the rate reduction, and further consideration and approval by the Federal Reserve Board."

Harrison then called to inform the Board that he had purchased an additional $65 million, a total of $115 million for the day. There was no further discussion of policy at the Board meeting.

On the following day, October 30, Young reported to the Board on his conversations with Harrison and James B. McDougal (Chicago). Young's position was classical; the System should encourage discounting by member banks, and he had told McDougal that "while he could not commit his board, he thought loans should be made freely and liberally." The conversation with Harrison had apparently been lengthy, owing to a difference of opinion between New York and Washington on the policy that was appropriate for the day. Harrison informed Young that he was planning further purchases of securities. Young reported to the Board that he had advised Harrison that further purchases would "probably lead to the eventual promulgation of a regulation on the subject" by the Board.

The difference of opinion between New York and Washington was another round in the dispute about who had responsibility for decisions. Young reported that he had "advised Governor Harrison that he would not hesitate about lending to a member bank." He told the Board that "he would go farther and purchase government securities liberally using any resource that the System has in an attempt to minimize the effects of conditions that may develop." Other members of the Board—Edmund Platt, Hamlin, and Miller—agreed with Young's position and urged him to communicate these views to the reserve banks.

Young informed Harrison on October 31 that the Board was in favor of reducing the discount rate at New York from 6 to 5 percent and that the "majority appeared to have changed their views with respect to coupling the reduction in the discount rate with an agreement to suspend purchases of government securities for the time being, feeling that the Federal Reserve banks should be prepared to pursue a liberal policy."

The positions now reversed. Banks had reduced their discounts by more than $150 billion since the cyclic peak. The gold stock had increased, and banks continued to lend on commercial paper, real bills, with only modest changes in interest rates. Harrison told the Board that he had made no purchases on October 30, that he did not plan to make any purchases that day, and that he could see no reason for additional purchases, "although it might become necessary to take on additional amounts later." His directors had adopted a resolution, unanimously, "that, in the interest of maintaining business and employment, the policy . . . for the coming weeks should be to keep a plentiful supply of money in the market . . . in order that discounts of the Federal Reserve System may be reduced and at the proper time a further reduction of the discount rate effected with the objective of securing lower interest rates for business throughout the country."

The prompt and rapid response by the New York bank undoubtedly prevented the rapid decline in stock prices from affecting interest rates in the money market. The monthly data show a slight rise in the interest rates on short-term Treasury notes and longer-term corporate bonds and a substantial decline in the rate charged for new stock exchange call loans. Weekly data on open market rates for the last week of October 1929 show a slight rise in the rate on new stock exchange call loans and a decline in other quoted market rates. Commercial banks in New York made the largest volume of new loans to brokers and dealers shown in any week up to that time and offset to a large extent the reduction in call loans by banks outside New York. Although the average of daily figures in table 5.2 shows the Federal Reserve as a net seller of government securities for the month as a whole, the System purchased $157 million of government securities during the last week of the month, more than doubling the size of its portfolio of governments. In addition, the discounts of member banks with the System increased by $200 million for the week.

Although the Board was in favor of continuing the policy Harrison had started, the committee made no purchases in the following week. On November 1, New York reduced its discount rate to 5 percent and also reduced the buying rate on banker's acceptances. The monetary base declined by $50 million, almost one-sixth of the increase in the previous week. Open market rates changed very little, and both the market and the System appear to have decided that the crisis had passed. The Board did not press New York to make further purchases. During the rest of 1929, the Board met almost every day, generally discussed routine matters, and rarely mentioned open market policy.

The Board's minutes for the week of the crisis make it clear that the members were slower than the New York bank to recognize the desirability of large-scale open market purchases. But the lag, or delay, was at most two days. By October 31, Governor Young and most of the Board members wanted further purchases to offset rising discounts, while Harrison and the directors of the New York bank, knowing that the panic had not affected the money market, favored a less aggressive approach.

Part of the dispute about whether the System should act through open

Table 5.1 OMIC Meeting, September 24, 1929

COMMERCIAL PAPER AND ACCEPTANCES	LOANS OF 101 WEEKLY REPORTING BANKS	GOLD STOCK	BORROWING	BILLS BOUGHT	GOVERNMENT SECURITIES	CURRENCY	MONETARY BASE	MONEY (M_1)
			Current Changes to September 30, 1929					
+$69	+$228	+$12	−$74	+$105	+$10	−$97	−$15	−$56
			Cumulative Changes from August 1929					
4.7%	1.3%	0.3%	−$74	+$105	+$10	−2.5%	−0.2%	−0.2%

BORROWING	EXCESS RESERVES	DISCOUNT RATE (N.Y. AND RANGE)	AAA RATES	AAA ACCEPTANCES	BAA-AAA	WPI ALL ITEMS (1926 = 100)	WPI FARM (1926 = 100)	INDUSTRIAL PRODUCTION (AUGUST 1929 = 100)
			Levels as of September 1929					
$969	$34	6 (5–6)	4.80%	−0.33%	1.32%	98	107	98.9

Note: Dollar amounts are millions.
WPI = wholesale price index.

Table 5.2 Meetings of the Federal Reserve Board, October 28–31, 1929

COMMERCIAL PAPER AND ACCEPTANCES	LOANS OF 101 WEEKLY REPORTING BANKS	GOLD STOCK	BORROWING	BILLS BOUGHT	GOVERNMENT SECURITIES	CURRENCY	MONETARY BASE	MONEY (M_1)
			Current Changes to October 31, 1929					
+$289	+$509	+$14	−$84	+$108	−$11	+$10	+$270	+$1,849
			Cumulative Changes from August 1929					
24.4%	4.3%	0.6%	−$158	+$213	−$1	−2.2%	−2.6%	+6.8%

BORROWING	EXCESS RESERVES	DISCOUNT RATE (N.Y. AND RANGE)	AAA RATES	AAA- ACCEPTANCES	BAA-AAA	WPI ALL ITEMS (1926 = 100)	WPI FARM (1926 = 100)	INDUSTRIAL PRODUCTION (AUGUST 1929 = 100)
			Levels as of October 31, 1929					
$885	$42	6 (5–6)	4.77%	−0.36%	1.34%	96	104	97.4

Note: Dollar amounts are millions.

market operations or by discounting reflects the entrenched "real bills" doctrine. Those who favored discounting as a means of supplying reserves generally wanted to leave the initiative with the member banks and favored using the "needs of trade" as a guide to appropriate policy. Even in periods of crisis, their discussion contains repeated references to the "demand for Reserve bank credit," in contexts suggesting that the Federal Reserve should supply the quantity of reserves demanded to meet the "needs of trade" but should avoid using open market operations to supply "redundant reserves" that would generate "speculative excesses."

The reactions in New York and Washington are consistent with the Riefler-Burgess view. The pressure on the commercial banks in New York became intense at the time of the stock market decline, in large part because banks outside New York reduced their loans to the call money market. The security purchases by the New York bank undoubtedly prevented both a sharp rise in interest rates during the week and additional borrowing from the Federal Reserve by banks in New York and other large cities. Since the Open Market Investment Committee had decided at the September 24 meeting to reduce borrowing, by open market purchases if necessary, the response by the New York bank is not a deviation from the prevailing policy or from the concentration on interest rates and money market conditions. The reluctance to continue purchasing once borrowing and upward pressure on interest rates declined is further evidence that its behavior at the time was consistent with the Riefler-Burgess framework.[20]

Friedman and Schwartz (1963, 367) offer a different interpretation of these events. Their discussion, based on Harrison's papers, makes no mention of the change in responses by Washington and New York after October 29. In their view, New York stopped purchasing securities because of the strong reaction at the Board. More important, they suggest that this episode had a permanent effect on Harrison and that thereafter he was reluctant to engage in open market operations without the consent of the Board or the Open Market Investment Committee. The Board's records suggest, on the other hand, that the Board members conceded Harrison

20. Harrison made a very similar point on November 13 in a letter to Governor Black of the Atlanta Federal Reserve bank. "We had only commenced operations at the rate of $25 million a week in accordance with the recommendation of the Open Market Investment Committee, when the severe collapse in stock prices at the end of October and the consequent immense shifting in loans to the New York City banks made it imperative that we purchase very substantial sums of Governments to minimize the risk of an up-swing in rates." He now (mid-November) favored a policy of continuing the "purchases of Governments as rapidly as opportunity offers in order that we may avoid any further large increase in the total volume of discounts in the System and, if possible, to facilitate the reduction of those discounts" (Harrison Papers, Letters and Reports, vol. 1, November 13, 1929).

had been correct in making large-scale purchases of government securities and in encouraging the additional discounts that the Board had urged from the start as a means of meeting the crisis. They disliked New York's decision to act alone.

The dispute was mainly about procedure, not about substance. Nor was the procedural issue a new one. The Board and the New York bank had differed about the division of responsibility and particularly about the Board's role in open market policy from the very first years of the System and particularly after 1923, when the importance of open market operations increased. The Board had discussed reorganization of the committee responsible for policy recommendations at meetings in 1928 and 1929.

Harrison wrote to Young on November 7. The New York directors had voted that day to purchase government securities if they did not acquire sufficient acceptances. Their aim was to provide a seasonal increase in reserves while reducing the volume of discounts and open market rates. His letter mentions the directors' concern "that there may be a greater danger of recession in business with consequent depression and unemployment, which we should do all in our power to prevent" (Open Market, Board of Governors File, box 1435, November 7, 1929).

No purchases were made. Between September 24 and November 8, the System account increased $80 million, by purchases of $30 million and acquisition of $50 million purchased by New York during late October. New York increased its holdings (net) by $108.8 million. Only seven reserve banks participated in the purchases.[21]

John U. Calkins, president of the San Francisco reserve bank, explained his reasons for not participating in open market purchases.[22] He was not "in entire sympathy with the course of open market policy." He was opposed to the view that "artificial conditions should be created for the purpose of promoting a bond market. . . . We can not see that this policy can be continuously followed without unfavorable results" (Letter Calkins to Harrison, Board of Governors File, box 1435, January 7, 1930).

Calkins then commented on Strong's 1927 purchases: "We are unable to see that the 1927 experiment, now quite generally . . . admitted to have

21. Cleveland, Richmond, Minneapolis, Kansas City, and San Francisco did not participate. These banks had lower gold reserve ratios than several of the participating banks, but the ratios ranged from 52 percent to 66 percent (Board of Governors File, box 1436, November 12, 1929).

22. Calkins served as governor of the San Francisco bank from May 1919 to February 1936, when he was required to retire after passage of the Banking Act of 1935. Governor Seay (Richmond) expressed similar views. At the December meetings of the Governors Conference, the governors voted on whether they agreed with the OMIC's policies. Governor Talley (Dallas) voted no, and Norris and Calkins abstained.

been *disastrous,* contributed very materially to the welfare of this country by providing or supporting a market for our exports. . . . [T]he purpose of the Federal Reserve System is to provide and assure adequate finance for trade . . . at a cost conducive to stability" (ibid., 2; emphasis added).

This letter, written within a few months of a major financial panic and at a time of deepening recession, represented a substantial body of opinion within and outside the Federal Reserve System. To these real bills advocates, Strong's 1927 policy had failed on the narrow grounds of expanding exports, on which it had been offered, but it also had been a main cause of the increase in stock prices and brokers' loans. They wanted no more. They believed that crises and recession were inevitable after speculative lending; they had to be endured to reestablish a sound basis for expansion.[23]

The data in table 5.3 are for the end of November, hence they overstate somewhat the changes that had taken place at the time the committee met. The sizable reduction in the money supply is a reversal of the very large rise in deposits in the last week of October. At the time of the meeting, industrial production was 5 percent below its level at the peak, and by month's end it was more than 7 percent below the August peak. Short-term interest rates and wholesale prices had continued to decline, but member bank borrowing was higher on average than in the preceding month.

The committee noted that a turning point had occurred and that there had been a "severe liquidation of credit against securities under circumstances which constitute a serious threat to business stability at a time when there were already indications of a business recession." The time had come for the Federal Reserve System to "do all within its power toward assuring the ready availability of money for business, at reasonable rates." In the Riefler-Burgess framework, the committee's statement meant that the discounts of member banks should be reduced. The governors voted to do just that by purchasing bills (acceptances) and, if necessary, by purchasing government securities. At Harrison's suggestion, the committee changed the limit on purchases from $25 million per week to a total of $200 million between the November and January meetings.

This meeting, within three months of the turning point, showed little disagreement about the interpretation to be placed on the events that had occurred or on the proper means of meeting the expected recession. The committee clearly regarded the fall in security prices and the decline in the public's wealth as factors intensifying a recession that was already under way. The record in 1929, as at the start of most subsequent recessions, is

---

23. Calkins's letter suggested a $150 million (16 percent) reduction in the open market portfolio.

inconsistent with the often-repeated view that the Federal Reserve is slow to take countercyclical action because it is slow to recognize the onset of a recession. The reluctance to take expansive action that many of the governors showed at subsequent meetings of the committee cannot be explained as a misinterpretation of the then current economic conditions or a failure to recognize that the economy had turned from expansion to recession.

At first the Board refused to approve the committee's decision. Young wrote to Harrison on November 13 that the Board was willing to authorize purchases for emergencies but would not grant authority to purchase up to the $200 million approved by the committee. Harrison's memo, recording his subsequent conversation with Young, makes it clear that he viewed the Board's objection as an opposition to the grant of discretion, not to the purchase policy. He accused Young of wanting to have a central bank operating in Washington and was surprised when Young agreed (Harrison Papers, Conversations, vol. 1, November 15, 1929).

To obtain approval of the purchase program, Harrison offered a temporary solution to the procedural issue. New York agreed to stop purchasing for its own account if the Board approved the committee's decision without qualification. The Board accepted on November 25. In the first three weeks of December, the System purchased $207 million of securities and $52 million in acceptances. In the remaining weeks of December, market rates fell, acceptances came to the bank at a faster rate, and the System sold nearly $50 million of government securities. The initial crisis was over.

Response to Recession

Changes in many of the monetary variables at the time of the January meeting are not markedly different from the changes that characterize other recessions.[24] Gold and bank loans had fallen, the latter partly a reflection of the reduction in stock exchange credit. The monetary base had fallen also, but more of the base was held as bank reserves, so the money supply had increased. Short-term interest rates were below the levels reached at the peak and had declined since the previous meeting; the term structure sloped up. (The term premium between Aaa rates and ninety-day acceptances had increased from 0.57 to 0.72.) Member bank borrowing was 50 percent below its peak, the lowest level since early 1928.

The January meeting was the first meeting after issuance of the Board's

---

24. See Cagan 1965. An exception is the decline in currency, which began earlier than the average for the cycles up to 1960 that Cagan studied.

Table 5.3 OMIC Meeting, November 12, 1929

COMMERCIAL PAPER AND ACCEPTANCES	LOANS OF 101 WEEKLY REPORTING BANKS	GOLD STOCK	BORROWING	BILLS BOUGHT	GOVERNMENT SECURITIES	CURRENCY	MONETARY BASE	MONEY (M₁)
			Current Changes to November 30, 1929					
+$147	+$335	−$19	+$68	−$41	+$161	+$20	−$193	−$2,761
			Cumulative Changes from August 1929					
34.4%	6.3%	0.2%	−$90	+$172	+$160	−1.7%	0%	−3.6%

BORROWING	EXCESS RESERVES	DISCOUNT RATE (N.Y. AND RANGE)	AAA RATES	AAA-ACCEPTANCES	BAA-AAA	WPI ALL ITEMS (1926 = 100)	WPI FARM (1926 = 100)	INDUSTRIAL PRODUCTION (AUGUST 1929 = 100)
				Levels as of November 30, 1929				
$953	$65	4.5–5 (4.5–5)	4.76%	−0.57%	1.27%	94	101	92.7

Note: Dollar amounts are millions.

Table 5.4 OMIC Meeting, January 28–29, 1930

COMMERCIAL PAPER AND ACCEPTANCES	LOANS OF 101 WEEKLY REPORTING BANKS	GOLD STOCK	BORROWING	BILLS BOUGHT	GOVERNMENT SECURITIES	CURRENCY	MONETARY BASE	MONEY (M₁)
			Current Changes to January 31, 1930					
+$124	−$1,220	−$76	−$452	+$18	+$170	−$100	−$172	+$174
			Cumulative Changes from August 1929					
42.8%	−0.1%	−1.7%	−$542	+$190	+$330	−4.3%	−2.4%	−3.0%

BORROWING	EXCESS RESERVES	DISCOUNT RATE (N.Y. AND RANGE)	AAA RATES	AAA-ACCEPTANCES	BAA-AAA	WPI ALL ITEMS (1926 = 100)	WPI FARM (1926 = 100)	INDUSTRIAL PRODUCTION (AUGUST 1929 = 100)
				Levels as of January 1930				
$501	$44	4.5 (4.5–5)	4.66%	0.72%	1.26%	93	101	88.7

Note: Dollar amounts are millions.

order replacing the OMIC with a new Open Market Policy Conference (OMPC) on which all reserve banks would serve. Although all governors participated in the January meeting, there was substantial disagreement about the new procedure, and it was not adopted until March 31.[25]

The new committee recognized that "a business recession has taken place, the extent or duration of which is not yet possible to determine" and that "liquidation is progressing in an orderly fashion." However, the members were divided about the policy that should be pursued in the coming months. Governor Eugene R. Black (Atlanta) "desired a continuation of credit ease," arguing that neither business nor the mental attitude of businessmen in his district was conducive to expansion. At the other pole, "Governor McDougal (Chicago) indicated that an easing policy would be worth considering if it would benefit business, but he felt present rates were not restrictive." "Governor Norris (Philadelphia) believed that open market operations had been carried far enough, that the object of the November policy had been achieved, and he would rather see lower interest rates come of their own accord than as a result of Federal Reserve interference."

Governors Lynn P. Talley (Dallas), William McChesney Martin Sr. (St. Louis), and John Calkins (San Francisco) joined Norris and McDougal. Calkins noted that there had been "more than the usual liquidation in his district," but he could see no reason for further changes in interest rates. Others took intermediate positions, several favoring Harrison's proposed reduction in the buying rate for acceptances.[26] No one argued for a pro-

25. The Board's March order differs from the January order by recognizing that the OMPC was a voluntary association, that banks could withdraw or refuse to participate in purchases and sales, and that members of the OMPC would be appointed by each bank's board of directors (Board of Governors File, box 1452, March 31, 1930). These were the conditions New York had demanded earlier.

26. Harrison's position at this meeting does not fit well with the view that he recognized the need for expansion at an early date but was hampered by the Board. The minutes state: "Governor Harrison stated that the proposal for a reduction in the buying rate for bills was made by the Federal Reserve Bank of New York in order to prevent a decrease in the bill portfolio and an increase in rediscounts such as might lead to a firming of money rates or at least an interruption to the natural downward trend of interest rates. It was not suggested as a program which would *artificially force a more rapid easing of credit conditions,* although it seemed likely that the directors of the New York bank might also wish soon to reduce the discount rate" (italics added). The italicized statements might be interpreted as an attempt to win support from those governors who viewed the contraction as a "natural" reaction. But Harrison did not couple his statement with a proposal for purchases after he obtained the support of the committee for the proposed reduction in the buying rate on acceptances. In January Harrison had written to one of the governors that "in view of the progress we have already made and in view of the uncertainties . . . there is no need at this time for any further purchases" (Harrison to Governor Seay [Richmond; copy sent to all Governors], Harrison Papers, Letters and Reports, vol. 1, January 10, 1930).

gram of substantial or even moderate open market purchases. It was "the judgment of the Committee that no open market operations in government securities are necessary at this time either to halt or expedite the present trend of credit."

Although the committee recognized that changes in loans and investments of reporting member banks were smaller "than the usual growth of credit required by the country's business," it voted only to "avoid the hardening of rates which might result from a seasonal demand for additional reserve credit." Its statement urged caution and restraint. The reasons that prompted most members to proceed cautiously are developed more fully in the committee's policy statement:

> The majority opinion was that what had already been done has set in motion a trend which should result in lower rates. Between a reduction of discounts and large purchases of securities and a reduction of rates to business there is always a lag and that lag is likely to be greater at this time because the appetite of the bankers has been whetted during recent months, and they are slower about coming down. There is every reason to anticipate that the reduction will occur, so that it is believed that the current is set in the direction of easier rates.
>
> We feel we should not interfere in that movement either in the direction of halting it or attempting to expedite it. . . . [It] is inexpedient to exhaust at the present time any part of our ammunition in an attempt to stimulate business when it is perhaps on a downward curve . . . in a vain attempt to stem an inevitable recession. . . . The majority of the Committee is not in favor of any radical reduction in the bill rate or radical buying of bills which would create an artificial ease or necessitate a reduction in the discount rate. (Open Market, Board of Governors File, box 1436, January 30, 1930)

The empirical basis for the committee's conclusions is more clearly set forth in a memo that Harrison had read to the Governors Conference more than a month earlier.[27] The memo contained two charts. One showed the relation between member bank borrowing and market interest rates. The other compared the rate of increase in bank credit with the volume of member bank borrowing. Harrison interpreted the charts as showing that "generally speaking the trade and business of the country require an increase in bank credit somewhere in the neighborhood of 4 to 5% a year, and the chart indicates that the rate of increase in bank credit has usually ex-

27. Report of the Chairman of the Open Market Committee to the Governors Conference, December 11, 1929. The memo dated December 4 is in Governors Conference, vol. 1, December 11, 1929. Here as elsewhere, Harrison does not distinguish real and nominal rates.

ceeded this rate when the Federal Reserve discounts were under 400 to 500 million dollars, and usually falls under this rate when discounts are over 500 to 600 million dollars." The memo goes on to spell out these central notions of the Riefler-Burgess framework and, after mentioning some qualifications, concludes that "these charts show in general that under conditions that have prevailed in recent years an amount of member bank borrowing somewhere in the neighborhood of 500 million dollars [the level then current] may be considered a normal at which commercial paper rates have tended to average 4¹/₂% and at which the volume of bank credit has tended to increase at the rate generally proportionate to the needs of business." Since the volume of member bank borrowing had been reduced by $450 million in less than two months and was now within the range Harrison spoke of, it is not surprising that he did not favor or propose an aggressive policy of open market purchases.

When the Board met the next day to discuss the committee's recommendations, Treasury Secretary Andrew Mellon repeated several of the arguments that had been made in the policy statement. The Board voted to carry out the policy recommendation and approved a minimum effective buying rate of 3.875 percent for any Federal Reserve bank wishing to establish that rate. By a tie vote, the Board followed the OMIC majority and refused to reduce the discount rate at the New York bank to 4 percent. The reasons for the Board's refusal are not clearly stated in the report, although there is some indication that it regarded the request as premature.

The governors' statements at this meeting provide a clear indication of their reasons for failing to take more expansive action at the time and throughout the period. Since short-term market interest rates had fallen and were expected to fall further as member bank discounts declined, most governors saw little reason for the Federal Reserve to "interfere" or to hasten the decline in rates. Words like "artificial stimulus" and "inevitable decline" reflect the dominant view that speculative excesses had to be purged. Once that happened, the economy would recover, and the System would be able to expand based on rediscounting of real bills.

Virtually all the governors used the level of market interest rates as an indicator of current policy. Differences between them at the meeting were largely matters of detail. Some opposed the 0.125 percent reduction in the buying rate for bills on the grounds that the reduction would cause the System to acquire bills in much larger quantities temporarily and thus cause market rates to fall faster than they believed desirable. Others opposed the reduction on the similar grounds that the reduction in the buying rate for bills would "force" a decline in the discount rate by contracting the amount of member bank discounts (reducing the demand for reserve bank credit). Only Governor Black advocated a policy of open market purchases.[28]

After the January meeting the Board approved reductions in the minimum buying rate for bills on February 11 and 24 and on March 5, 6, 11, 14, 17, 19, and 20. By the March meeting, the buying rate was 3 percent. The Board also approved further reductions in the discount rate to 3.5 percent at New York and to 4 or 4.5 percent at the other banks. These changes did not receive the unanimous support of the Board members, and those who voted for the reductions often expressed doubt about the efficacy of a "cheap money" policy.[29] No one mentioned that wholesale prices had fallen 7 percent in seven months or that real rates had increased more than nominal rates had fallen.

Despite the nominal rate reductions, the System's holdings of acceptances had declined since the January meeting, and the volume of member bank discounts was at the lowest level since early in World War I. Long- and short-term interest rates continued to decline, as shown in table 5.5. Although nominal short- and long-term rates had fallen to the levels reached in the recessions of 1924 and 1927, the term spread between short- and long-rates had doubled in the two months to March.

This was the last meeting of the committee for more than two years at which the seasonally adjusted money supply showed a rise from the previous meeting. The increase in money from January to March was largely the result of a gold inflow from Brazil and Japan and the higher base money multiplier produced by the continued decline in the public's demand for currency in both nominal and real terms.

Much of the discussion at the meeting was about New York's decision to purchase $50 million of government securities early in March. Although the committee had voted against further purchases at the January meeting, New York explained, as it had in a letter earlier in the month, that the purchases had been made, after consultation with the Federal Reserve Board, because it had been "impossible to maintain the bill portfolio" in the face of an increasing demand for bills by banks and financial institutions. The "unfavorable business situation" was also mentioned as a factor in the decision to purchase.[30]

28. The new OMPC overrepresented the smaller banks in the System, but it is not clear that it was more or less inclined toward expansion. Black (Atlanta) was the most expansionist of the new members, but the new committee also included Calkins and Talley, who usually opposed purchases as "artificial" stimulus. At the time, the seven new members held only 25 percent of the System's portfolio.

29. For example, one Board member, Cunningham, stated that he voted aye but had hesitated to do so because at 4 percent "money is cheap."

30. In fact, the Board proposed the purchases on the grounds that "no harm and some good might be accomplished" (Case to Young, Board of Governors File, box 1435, March 7,

The discussion makes it clear that the main reason for the purchases was to correct a problem that the members regarded as technical. An inflow of gold—from Japan and South America according to the minutes—had increased the reserves of the New York banks. The banks used the new reserves to purchase acceptances, forcing the Board to lower the buying rate for acceptances or allow the acceptance portfolio to decline. At first the Board reduced the acceptance rate, but the acceptance portfolio continued to fall in early March because the gold imports continued and the Treasury's balance at the reserve banks declined. The falling acceptance rate was regarded as a technical reaction because a rise in the rate on other short-term instruments—for example, stock exchange collateral loans, particularly brokers' and dealers' loans—accompanied the decline.[31]

The preliminary memorandum prepared for the meeting noted that the recession was probably more severe than the recessions of 1924 or 1927 and that unemployment had increased. However, it also observed that "the effects of easy money and freely available credit have been, in the first place, to stimulate a vigorous recovery in the bond market. Bond prices have risen to the highest points in more than a year." This was a particularly important piece of information within the framework that most of the members used. The rise in bond prices and the reduction in member bank borrowing seem to have provided the entire basis for the decision to make no further purchases of government securities. In the committee's words, "The steps already taken by the Federal Reserve System in easing the money market through open market operations have gone as far in providing the stimulus of easy money for business use as seems desirable at this time."

With hindsight, it is clear that this was an important meeting. The decision to avoid further expansive action because monetary policy was judged to be "easy" came just as there were signs of a turning point or a bottom of the recession. The preliminary memorandum prepared for the meeting noted a slight improvement in "business and trade" between December and January and further slight improvement from January to February. The data now available partly confirm the observations made at the time. Industrial production, seasonally adjusted, rose in January and declined very little in February. More important, there was a slight drop in in-

---

1930). J. Herbert Case replaced Gates McGarrah as chairman at New York on February 28. Case had long been an officer of the New York bank.

31. Total bank credit had risen by $300 million from the end of February to the date of the meeting. Loans to brokers and dealers had risen to the level of the previous November, but more of the loans were held by New York banks. The rise in brokers' loans was accompanied by a rise in stock prices. Standard and Poor's Index (1935–39 = 100) increased from 159.6 in November to 182.0 in March. Data on total bank credit are from the minutes; other data are from Board of Governors of the Federal Reserve System 1943, 498, 481.

dustrial production from March to April and larger declines in May and June. The index of common stock prices had restored approximately 25 percent of the October decline in the value of common stocks by the end of March, but the rise in stock prices ended in April.

If the governors of the Federal Reserve had used the stock of money instead of interest rates as an indicator of monetary policy, they would not have concluded that monetary policy was "easy." Additional open market purchases at this time would have contributed to the expansion. Instead, the further contraction of money contributed to the decline in output and to the bank failures that came with increased frequency after this meeting.

The striking fact about the meeting is that although there was little dissent about the size of the recession, there was little support for a policy of monetary expansion. The committee's main recommendations were designed to prevent a further reduction in bills: it voted to reduce the buying rate for bills to 2.5 percent, but not to purchase below 3 percent except in an emergency, and to engage in no open market purchases. A memo prepared for the meeting and made part of the record showed that the System's earning assets were lower than in the previous year, largely as a result of the fall in member bank discounts.

The discussion at the meeting showed no evidence of disagreement between New York and Washington. On March 14 New York reduced its discount rate to 3.5 percent, with Board approval. Other banks remained at 4 to 4.5 percent. In a letter to Governor Young, J. Herbert Case described the 3.5 percent rate as a possible danger, but he urged the Board to approve the step "in the hope that business may be benefited" (Board of Governors File, box 1435, March 17, 1930). He hoped that the System would act promptly to prevent excessive credit expansion.

Outside New York, reserve banks remained skeptical about additional ease. Although he saw "plenty of evidence . . . that what had appeared to be an upturn in January has not held," Governor Talley (Dallas) wrote opposing any additional expansive actions.[32] "Everyone seems to want to keep business jazzed up all the time and have it run along at boom figures. . . . [T]he sounder course to pursue . . . is to catch up and let the public pay some of its debts or at least acquire larger equities in its automobiles, radios, and real estate (Talley to Case, Board of Governors File, box 1435, March 13, 1930, 3).[33]

32. "Frankly, we were very much disappointed over your reduction [of discount rate] to 3.5 percent last Thursday. We feel a little bit better about it today, because the stock market has regarded the action as an unfavorable symptom and seems to recognize it as a panacea for business depression (Talley to Case, board of Governors File, box 1435, March 13, 1930, 2).

33. Talley also refers to governors who vote for open market purchases, then refuse to participate in the purchase. (Only eight of the twelve banks participated in the purchase of

Between the March and May meetings of the Open Market Policy Conference, the Board considered a request from New York to lower the discount rate from 3.5 percent to 3 percent. At first the Board unanimously disapproved. The Board's minutes for April 24 record a "considerable variance of opinion between the New York Bank and the Federal Reserve Board with regard to Federal Reserve policy." The Board favored "the maintenance of stability rather than further easing through Federal Reserve action." Within a week, however, Governor Young changed his mind and announced that he favored reducing the discount rate and the buying rate for bills. On May 2 the Board approved New York's request, and in the following weeks the effective buying rate for bills declined to 2.5 percent, below the rate that the March conference had suggested as a minimum.

New York's request was a response to the deteriorating economy. At a meeting on April 24, Harrison reported to his directors that production and trade had declined in March and that preliminary figures for April, covering building contract awards and railroad car loadings, showed a further decline. Harrison also reported that commodity prices had fallen, that foreign trade had declined during the first quarter, and that gold continued to flow in. He recommended a reduction in the discount rate as a means of improving the bond and mortgage markets, which "historically and logically appear to be a precedent or a necessary accompaniment of recovery in business and prices after a period of depression." The following week Harrison again discussed a discount rate reduction with the directors. This time the Board approved.[34]

The data for this meeting, in table 5.6, show the renewed decline in industrial production and the fall in wholesale and farm prices. Although bank lending (at weekly reporting banks) had increased since March, commercial paper and banker's acceptances had fallen. The data also show that standard policy actions were not having their expected effect. Lowering short rates had not reduced long rates. Rates on Aaa bonds were only twenty-four basis points below the August 1929 peak, while prime banker's acceptances had been reduced by 2.625 percent. The term premium had increased by a factor of three, from 0.7 to 2.1 percent since the end of January.

Some of the New York directors continued to press for expansive action.

$50 million in March.) His bank participated fully. As a result, they had taken 7 percent of the allocation instead of their usual 3.3 percent. He withdrew from his pro rata share of the non-participating banks acquisition by limiting Dallas's purchases to its standard 3.3 percent (Talley to Case, Board of Governors File, box 1435, March 13, 1930, 3).

34. At a May 1 meeting with his directors, Harrison discussed an ambiguity in the (March) agreement with the Board. The agreement did not make clear whether the new procedure applied to bill purchases (acceptances). This oversight is surprising given previous disputes about whether the Board's approval must be secured before an announcement could be made.

Table 5.5 OMPC Meeting, March 24, 1930

COMMERCIAL PAPER AND ACCEPTANCES	LOANS OF 101 WEEKLY REPORTING BANKS	GOLD STOCK	BORROWING	BILLS BOUGHT	GOVERNMENT SECURITIES	CURRENCY	MONETARY BASE	MONEY (M_1)
Current Changes to March 31, 1930								
-$29	-$75	+$132	-$227	-$68	+$55	-$35	-$17	+$659
Cumulative Changes from August 1929								
40.9%	-1.3%	+1.5%	-$769	+$122	+$385	-5.1%	-207%	-0.5%

BORROWING	EXCESS RESERVES	DISCOUNT RATE (N.Y. AND RANGE)	AAA RATES	AAA-ACCEPTANCES	BAA-AAA	WPI ALL ITEMS (1926 = 100)	WPI FARM (1926 = 100)	INDUSTRIAL PRODUCTION (AUGUST 1929 = 100)
Levels as of March 1930								
$274	$56	3.5 (3.5–4.5)	4.62%	1.51%	1.11%	91	95	86.7

Note: Dollar amounts are millions.

Table 5.6 OMPC Meeting, May 21–22, 1930

COMMERCIAL PAPER AND ACCEPTANCES	LOANS OF 101 WEEKLY REPORTING BANKS	GOLD STOCK	BORROWING	BILLS BOUGHT	GOVERNMENT SECURITIES	CURRENCY	MONETARY BASE	MONEY (M_1)
Current Changes to May 31, 1930								
-$145	+$79	+$94	-$27	-$64	-$11	-$23	-$58	-$1,011
Cumulative Changes from August 1929								
31.0%	-0.1%	3.8%	-$796	+$58	+$374	-5.7%	-3.5%	-4.3%

BORROWING	EXCESS RESERVES	DISCOUNT RATE (N.Y. AND RANGE)	AAA RATES	AAA-ACCEPTANCES	BAA-AAA	WPI ALL ITEMS (1926 = 100)	WPI FARM (1926 = 100)	INDUSTRIAL PRODUCTION (AUGUST 1929 = 100)
Levels as of May 1930								
$247	$56	3 (3–4)	4.57%	2.07%	1.21%	89	93	84.9

Note: Dollar amounts are millions.

They instructed Harrison to inform the Board that they wished to purchase government securities. Governor Young suggested a meeting of the conference so that "all Federal Reserve Banks may be informed of the program which the New York Bank seems to have in mind" (Board Minutes, May 15, 1930).

New York was not the only bank dissatisfied with the conduct and achievements of open market policy. At the May meeting, Governor Young presented five suggestions that had come before the Board. Two called for open market sales; two called for purchases; and one bank wanted to maintain the prevailing policy but provide from $350 million to $400 million for seasonal requirements through open market purchases and increases in bill holdings during the fall.

Several features of the Federal Reserve's approach to policymaking are mentioned to support or justify the three proposals. Some governors, following one aspect of the real bills doctrine, regarded the end use of credit as the most useful guide to appropriate policy. They believed open market sales would "check speculation" and help the banks to liquidate security loans. Their main evidence of speculation at this time was the increased volume of brokers' and dealers' loans that had accompanied the increased volume of security purchases and rising stock prices in the months before the meeting. Others, concerned about the distribution of the Federal Reserve's earning assets, wanted to sell $200 million of securities and reduce discount rates "so that rediscounts might be approximately equal to the total of government securities and bankers acceptances held." This proposal reflected a different aspect of the real bills doctrine, the view that a main purpose of monetary policy was to respond to changes in the demand for reserve bank credit. Some governors believed that open market sales would ease credit by encouraging banks to reduce interest rates and force them to borrow on real bills. The proper policy, they claimed, was to lower discount rates and sell securities.

Poor timing was one reason the proposal for open market sales and lower discount rates did not receive more widespread support. The provision of the Federal Reserve Act calling for an "elastic currency" was interpreted as a requirement to meet the seasonal "needs of trade." One governor who favored seasonal expansion in the fall expected the seasonal demand for bank credit to be larger than the current (May) demand. He expressed the view of several governors when he suggested that open market purchases would have more effect if they were made at a time of increased demand for bank credit and for reserve bank credit.[35]

---

35. By fall the contraction had become more severe. The System's purchases were smaller than the $350 million to $400 million estimate of seasonal demand. They were made mainly in response to the bank failures that came late in the year.

Of the two banks proposing purchases, one favored monetary expansion and the other had the traditional concern about reserve bank earnings. Since interest rates had fallen and member bank borrowing had not been fully offset by an increase in bills and securities, the reserve banks' income had fallen. Some of the banks faced losses. The conference agreed that supplementing the income of a reserve bank was not a "proper reason for the purchase of government securities," and the matter ended. This issue arose again in the middle thirties.

The committee could not find any "proper reason" for engaging in either purchases or sales at the time. It was too early to provide for a seasonal demand that would not arise until fall. The only agreement reached was the empty statement that "conditions merit continuous careful observation of the Federal Reserve System in order that the System will be prepared to act promptly in the event that conditions further develop in such a way as to make actions seem advisable."

No one attempted to set out the conditions that would make open market purchases advisable. Nevertheless, Harrison's advocacy of purchases contrasts with the views expressed by several others. He believed that the "possible necessity for the purchase of government securities might be imminent at any time." Another member called for immediate purchases "to remove every possible restraint from business as far as credit was concerned." Still another suggested that the conference agree on a formula for the total amount of reserve bank credit as a guide to the desirable volume of purchases. None of these suggestions received much attention.

The minutes described money conditions as slightly "easier" because of the inflow of gold, the further decline in the amount of currency in circulation, and the reduction in member bank borrowing. But no one mentioned or appears to have noticed that the money supply (or demand deposits) had declined by more than $1 billion in the previous two months. Since most of the decline was in deposits, there must have been some recognition of the decline at major banks.

The governors not only were aware of the worldwide scope of the depression, they sensed that there was a connection between the depression and the New York money market. Harrison gave the standard explanation of the economic decline and the central role of real bills. There had been overproduction of "certain principal commodities," accompanied by a "shortage of working capital and thus a restriction of purchasing power." In the previous year, funds had been used for speculation, mainly in New York but in other markets as well. The recovery of world trade appeared to depend "in no small degree on a restoration of purchasing power through the medium of foreign borrowers on the New York money market, just as the recent recovery of domestic trade appeared to be much dependent on the new financing for domestic enterprise in the United States."

This statement places Harrison well within the mainstream of Federal Reserve thinking and accounts for his failure to mention the substantial decline in demand deposits. However, within the common framework there are two main differences between New York and other parts of the System.

One is the minor point that New York developed more information and expressed more concern about current money market conditions and was more eager to take action to correct or offset money market changes. The second and more important difference within the committee concerns the interpretation of changes in member bank borrowing and interest rates and the System's responsibility for bringing about further reductions in both. Some governors argued that the Federal Reserve should attempt to lower interest rates further by reducing discount rates and, if that failed, to lower interest rates and encourage member bank borrowing by engaging in open market purchases. Others—McDougal of Chicago and Norris of Philadelphia were leaders of this group—wanted to wait for the member banks to demand more reserve bank credit. In their view, the decline in borrowing meant that the System should sell securities to force an increase in member bank borrowing. With the possible exception of Governor Black, none of the governors argued for an aggressive purchase policy, and none professed a belief that such a policy would succeed.

Although the Board's minutes indicate that the meeting was called to discuss New York's program, Harrison did not present a program and, at the meeting, seemed most concerned about matters of timing and procedure, particularly the Board's failure to agree quickly to requests for reductions in the buying rate on acceptances and discount rate changes. Young told the committee that "he had hesitated to vote favorably on the New York application for a three percent discount rate because of the position of the governors at the OMPC meeting on March 25." This reopened a continuing disagreement. Harrison replied that decisions about discount rates were primarily the responsibility of the individual reserve banks and that "he did not believe the action of the Open Market Policy Conference should be regarded as in any way restricting freedom of action on discount rates." Several governors agreed with Harrison, and the conference voted that discount rates "were not within its proper province and that the directors of any Federal Reserve Bank must feel free at any time to change the discount rate of their bank subject only to the review and determination of the Federal Reserve Board."

This was a partial victory for New York. It removed any control that McDougal, Norris, or other governors might have had over the decisions about the discount rate at New York. Since New York's 3 percent rate was one percentage point lower than the rates at ten of the eleven other banks, the banks with higher rates could not press New York to raise its rate by a formal vote of the conference. But it left New York, as before, dependent on the decisions of the Board.

To further strengthen New York's position, Harrison argued for greater control of the acceptance rate by the reserve banks. The Board's delays in approving applications for lower bill buying rates had left New York without "downward flexibility." The committee voted to support Harrison, and after the meeting the Board sent a letter to all the reserve banks accepting the conference's decision.

Although most of the decisions at the May meetings concerned operating procedures, they show that New York was no more isolated from the rest of the System in regard to procedure than in regard to policy. The conference was willing to support New York on day-to-day policy and to provide discretionary "flexibility" in managing the account. The Board and the conference were unwilling to allow New York to purchase and sell government securities on its own initiative and for its own account, but it is not clear that most would have opposed a program of open market purchases for the System if Harrison had supported the program vigorously. In fact, the members responded to Harrison's statement that "the possible necessity for the purchase of government securities might be imminent at any time" by voting to reconvene or to act promptly on the recommendations of its five-man executive committee, which Harrison headed. When Harrison proposed open market purchases only ten days later, a majority of the conference voted in favor.

New York Seeks Expansion

Harrison's approach to policy comes out clearly in the decision to purchase $50 million of securities early in June 1930. The discussions leading to the decision show the importance he attached to short-term factors affecting interest rates and money market conditions and his failure to develop a long-term program.[36] They also show Harrison as a broker trying to reconcile differences between opposing groups. Three points stand out. First, Harrison twice changed his mind about the desirability of purchases. Both changes coincide with changes in the technical position of the money market. Second, Harrison did not suggest a program of steady expansion. In fact, he did not propose as expansive a policy as some of the New York

36. My interpretation of this episode is based on the minutes of the New York directors for May 8, 19, and 26 and June 5, the Board's minutes for June 3, 1930, and a telegram on June 5 from Harrison to the Board that is part of the Board's minutes.

directors urged on him. Third, Harrison never answered, and at times appears to have accepted, the main criticisms of the policy of expansion made by Norris and other opponents.

The first suggestion that purchases should be made came at the May 8 meeting of the directors of the New York Federal Reserve bank. Several of the directors spoke in favor, but others opposed on grounds that recovery in bond prices had been delayed by the floating of a large foreign loan—the $300 million German annuities loan. The directors who opposed purchases expected interest rates to resume their decline once the offering was sold. The directive recommended that Harrison discuss the possibility that open market purchases "may become desirable" with other governors and the Board. On May 19, two days before the Governors Conference, the executive committee of the New York directors remained divided. Most agreed that purchases of open market securities would be "inflationary" (which to them often meant that bond prices would rise), but some believed this danger should be faced "to check a decline in commodity prices."

The following week, Harrison reported on the results of the Governors Conference to the executive committee of the New York directors. One of the directors remarked that there had been a net withdrawal of Federal Reserve funds from the money market during the preceding six months.[37] He urged that these funds should "now be restored to the market by the purchase of government securities," and he suggested that if this were done bankers would be encouraged to make loans to business borrowers. Then, in a statement that is considerably at variance with the real bills and Riefler-Burgess doctrines, a director pointed out that "if government securities should now be purchased in sufficient amount so that member banks would no longer be able to use the funds thus made available to pay off advances and rediscounts, expansion of bank investments would be forced and business would perhaps be stimulated."

Support for purchases was rising in New York. Harrison reminded the directors that the governors had considered purchases but had voted not to take any action. Some of the directors disagreed with this policy. In their opinion, "it would be unfortunate if the banking system would not be used to facilitate recovery." Three days later, on May 29, the full meeting of New York's directors unanimously approved the report of the Open Market Policy Conference, then seized on the section that permitted the committee's decision about open market policy to be reopened. Although only a

37. Member bank borrowing had fallen $800 million since August. See table 5.6. These and similar remarks suggest that some directors did not equate low borrowing with monetary ease.

week had passed, they voted that "it now seems desirable to undertake the purchase of government securities in moderate amounts."

During the next few days, Harrison and Burgess telephoned the other governors to discuss their directors' recommendation. Frederic H. Curtiss (Boston) believed that the situation had "retrogressed," so he favored purchases of $20 million to $25 million for the next few weeks to test out the situation, "feeling that no harm would result and some good might be accomplished." E.R. Fancher (Cleveland) also favored purchases, "believing that it might possibly help and that in any event it would be preferable to err on the side of ease rather than on the other side." McDougal (Chicago) believed purchases would "do little or no good," so he preferred not to purchase. Black (Atlanta) was very much in favor; Norris and Calkins were opposed.

Early in June, Harrison telegraphed the results of the canvass to the Board. Seven of the governors favored purchases if limited in magnitude and duration, four were opposed, and one "interposed no objection." On a divided vote, the Board approved purchases of not more than $25 million per week for two weeks, the first open market purchases since the middle of March.[38] New York began purchasing almost at once.

Four main reasons tipped the balance in favor of limited purchases. First, some long-term bond yields, particularly on lower-rated bonds, had risen at the time the German annuity was announced and had not returned to the April level. Second, discounts show a sharp increase during the week ending May 28. On the Riefler-Burgess interpretation, the rise in discounts meant that demand for reserve bank credit had increased, so open market purchases were justified as a means of providing "productive credit" and preventing an increase in short-term rates. Third, as Harrison explained to the Board on June 16, the directors at New York believed recovery would not occur for several months and perhaps not for a year, but they "are particularly concerned about the export trade which has such a direct effect upon commodity prices and feel that a revival of our foreign trade depends largely upon the bond market and that hopes of getting a strong bond market rest upon the continued ease in the short time money market more than anything else." Fourth, and possibly most important,

38. The original vote, three to three with Vice Governor Platt abstaining, would have defeated the motion. After further discussion, Platt voted in favor. The executive committee of governors was more evenly divided than the full committee, since two of the opponents, McDougal of Chicago and Norris of Philadelphia, were members of the five-man executive committee. Another opponent of the purchase program, Governor Calkins of San Francisco, refused to participate, so the San Francisco bank did not accept a pro rata share of securities. The positions taken by the individual governors and their reasons are taken from a memo Harrison wrote to his files on June 30 (Harrison Papers, Office Memoranda, vol. 2).

none of the opponents of expansion believed that the purchases, if limited, would be "inflationary" in the circumstances then prevailing in the money market, that is, the increased volume of member bank borrowing.

Harrison's reasons for supporting a limited program of purchases and his opposition to a more expansive program came out clearly at a June 5 meeting with the New York directors. To a director who urged a reduction in the discount rate to 2.5 percent as a means of encouraging banks to reduce the rates charged on bank loans, Harrison replied that banks already had "sufficient reasons for lowering rates." To another who pointed out that the decline in the New York bank's bill portfolio in the most recent week more than nullified the $50 million purchase of securities, Harrison gave the standard Riefler-Burgess argument that the banks had been "placed in the position to pay off a substantial part of their borrowings, . . . the money market is definitely easier than it was before our purchases." He reminded the directors that the quarterly Treasury financing and the German loan made the timing unfavorable.

At least one of the directors was dissatisfied with the policy of delay and hesitation. He urged purchases of at least $100 million, and in a prophetic statement he made it clear that Harrison's was not the only view.[39] "Unless the banks take initiative in affording the relief of very cheap money, however, he foresaw a relatively long period of business depression and severe unemployment. The first step in the program, as he viewed it, might be to get the call money rate down to a dramatically low level."

The decline in short-term market rates and the return of borrowing to the level of mid-May helped to convince the Boston and Cleveland banks that no further purchases should be made. They now sided with Philadelphia and Chicago, so the vote in the executive committee on June 23 was four to one against the purchase program. Harrison was the lone dissenter, arguing as before that there was a maldistribution of credit between short- and long-term markets and that further purchases of securities would lower long-term rates, increase loans to foreigners, and thus stimulate exports. Harrison's argument—which he attributed to the directors of the New York bank—repeated the directors' earlier statements about "lack of purchasing power in various parts of the world." Prices had fallen because countries "are not in a position to purchase commodities." Reversing the position he had taken at the directors' meeting, he now argued that the effect of recent purchases of securities had been offset by a decline in the System's bill holdings (see table 5.7).

39. Adolph Miller was present at the June 5 meeting in New York. He favored a reduction in the discount rate in lieu of additional purchases. He viewed the current recession as part of a long-term postwar readjustment to lower prices following wartime inflation.

Table 5.7 OMPC Executive Committee Meeting, June 23, 1930

COMMERCIAL PAPER AND ACCEPTANCES	LOANS OF 101 WEEKLY REPORTING BANKS	GOLD STOCK	BORROWING	BILLS BOUGHT	GOVERNMENT SECURITIES	CURRENCY	MONETARY BASE	MONEY (M_1)
Current Changes to June 30, 1930								
-$91	+$223	+$18	+$4	-$41	+$42	-$13	+$3	-$32
Cumulative Changes from August 1929								
24.8%	0.4%	4.3%	-$792	+$17	+$416	-6.1%	-3.4%	-0.4%

BORROWING	EXCESS RESERVES	DISCOUNT RATE (N.Y. AND RANGE)	AAA RATES	AAA-ACCEPTANCES	BAA-AAA	WPI ALL ITEMS (1926 = 100)	WPI FARM (1926 = 100)	INDUSTRIAL PRODUCTION (AUGUST 1929 = 100)
Levels as of June 1930								
$251	$54	2.5 (2.5–4)	4.52%	2.39%	1.25%	87	89	82.4

Note: Dollar amounts are millions.

Unfortunately, Harrison failed to respond to the main points raised by some of the other members on the committee. They argued that "easy money" and the low interest rates on the short-term markets had not had any effect on longer-term markets. The term spread had continued to widen. Some now interpreted the purchases in early June as an experiment that had failed to lower long-term rates. Harrison agreed that the short-term money market was "easy." He told the group "that he did not want to leave the thought that there is any feeling in New York different from that expressed by the other members of the Committee that there is an adequate supply of short-term credit available for business. This is not the difficulty today, . . . and it has not been for months" (Board Minutes, June 23, 1930).

Governor Fancher (Cleveland) pointed out that since short-term rates had fallen, there was very little more that the System could do. Money would flow from the short-term market to the bond market as soon as banks attempted to increase their earnings. This would revive the bond market and lower long-term rates. Early in June he had favored a purchase program (to reduce short-term rates), but he now believed that additional purchases would accomplish little.

McDougal and Norris led the opposition to purchases in the executive committee with support from a letter that Governor Calkins wrote to Governor Young explaining why San Francisco did not share in the June purchases. The basis of their position was that "credit is cheap" and that nothing could be gained by making it cheaper. Further increases would not stimulate production, but a large security portfolio would make the committee hesitant to purchase when an opportune time came.

Harrison's opponents agreed on one point—no further purchases should be made. McDougal wanted to sell securities and allow the acceptance portfolio to run off. Norris told the executive committee that he opposed the purchase program because the recession was due to excess capacity and overproduction that had caused a fall in the price of commodities. His examination showed that "the commodities on which the reduction of prices had been most marked disclosed in almost every case a specific reason which has nothing to do with credit." Easier money, by which he meant lower interest rates, "might lead to further increases in productive capacity and further overproduction." On the same day, he told the Board that he opposed a reduction in the discount rate at the Philadelphia bank because the only effect of a reduction would be "to increase the margin of profit for those banks which are chronic borrowers . . . and make it more difficult for the well managed bank to show any earnings at all." As for open market purchases, Norris said that he and other members

of the executive committee "cannot bring themselves to believe that a further purchase of government securities would help, but feel that such purchases would be an interference with the natural effect at this time and
would not be productive of any good, and might be embarrassing at the
time when business starts to pick up, at which time this System would find
itself with a large amount of government securities and low discount rates."
The majority of the executive committee could not see any benefit to be
derived from "affirmative action" (Harrison Papers, Office Memoranda,
vol. 2, June 1930).

Harrison consistently evaded the question of how or why the policy of
relatively small weekly purchases would work. He agreed that short-term
funds must be regarded as "abundant," since short-term rates were in the
lowest ranges reached in previous recessions.[40] Several of the other members—despite their differences—believed that recovery would not come
until there was an increase in member bank borrowing and an increased
demand for bank loans to finance trade and other productive activities.
Harrison appears to have shared large parts of this real bills view. He made
no effort to present an alternative.

Three days later, on June 26, Harrison discussed the response to the
OMPC's decision with the New York directors. They could wait for a
change in sentiment at the other banks; withdraw from the OMPC and
purchase for their own bank; or attempt to persuade the boards at other
reserve banks by circulating a statement of their position. The bank's officers favored the third proposal. The directors were reluctant to agree because they believed delay was "tantamount to retarding business recovery. . . . [T]hey indicated their belief in the power of credit to bring about a
revival in the bond market and, through it, to bring about an improvement
in business" (Minutes, New York Directors, June 26, 1930).

Harrison put the issue sharply. Was the bank "so firmly convinced of the
soundness of its position as to be willing to withdraw from the System
Open Market Policy Conference?" He preferred delay. He was not convinced of "the power of cheap and abundant credit, alone, to bring about
improvement in business" (ibid., 2). New York either had to act alone or
had to persuade other banks to change their position. He was unwilling to
do the first, unable to do the other.

Those who argue that Harrison saw the need for more expansive policy
but was prevented from carrying it out by the other members of the conference and by the Board point to the events of this period to support their

40. By June the wholesale price index used by the Board had fallen 11 percent since August 1929, a 13 percent annual rate of decline. Ex post, short-term real rates were approximately 15 percent.

position. The claim is more true of the New York directors than of Harrison. Harrison seems pushed and pulled by the opposing views of his directors and his colleagues on the OMPC. He showed no intention of seeking a sustained rate of increase in money or bank credit. He had the much more limited aim of offsetting an increase in short-term rates and planned to stop purchases once he achieved this objective.

After the June 26 meeting, he wrote to the other governors suggesting that the Federal Reserve resume purchases of $25 million a week. The letter described the situation in the economy and in the money and bond markets in enough detail to convince even the most skeptical that the failure to act cannot be explained by lack of information. Commodity prices had suffered the most severe and rapid decline since 1921. These prices, he said, were now 12 percent below the previous year, and the decline had accelerated (see table 5.7). Profit margins and purchasing power had fallen, and many people were facing unemployment and distress. Although money market rates had come down, the long-term bond market had not eased sufficiently: "Purchases of securities which had been made thus far have aided in relieving the member banks from a pressure of indebtedness at the Reserve banks and in a measure had provided the market with surplus funds available for use on the bond and mortgage market. But to a large extent these purchases . . . had been offset by declines in rediscounts and in the bill portfolios of the Federal Reserve Banks so that the total Federal Reserve credit has shown a net decline, even making allowance for gold imports." Emphasizing that the opinions he expressed were those of his directors, Harrison recommended that the System resume purchases and concluded, "While there may be no definite assurance that the market operations and government securities will of themselves promote any immediate recovery, we cannot foresee any appreciable harm that can result from such a policy" (Harrison Papers, Correspondence, July 3, 1930).

This weak proposal brought some strong responses. Calkins (San Francisco) wrote that his bank's executive committee believed that "the volume of credit forcibly fed to the market up to this time has had no considerable good effect. . . . [E]very time we inject further credit without appreciable effect, we diminish the probable advantage of feeding more to the market at an opportune moment which may come" (Harrison Papers, Correspondence, July 10, 1930, 2).

At the July 10 New York directors' meeting, Harrison discussed the Board's response to New York's proposal. At first Vice Governor Platt indicated that the Board would approve a recommendation by the New York directors to purchase $50 million for the bank's own account. Later Platt suggested that New York should wait until it received replies from the other governors. Harrison said he agreed with Platt's suggestion to await replies from the other banks because they had been able to accomplish at least part of what they hoped to achieve by their operations in the accept-ance market.[41]

A week later Harrison told the directors that an unanticipated increase in the offering of acceptances had enabled the bank to increase reserves by approximately $70 million: "This increase in the System's holding of bills had, in considerable measure, accomplished what we had hoped to ac-complish by further purchase of government securities." He did not be-lieve New York would be justified in "forcing further funds upon the mar-ket." Then Harrison made a clear statement of the Riefler-Burgess doctrine to explain his reason for first favoring and now opposing purchases: "If the program of purchases of government securities advocated by this bank at the beginning of July had been approved by the Federal Reserve System, that approval *would not have resulted* in further purchases of government securities in view of the money market conditions which later developed" (emphasis added).

The next day, Harrison sent a letter to all the other governors repeating this position.

> Since the end of June, even since my letter of July 3, conditions in the money market have changed with rapidity. . . . The principal New York City banks have paid off all their discounts here and at present have a surplus of reserves. Thus, the condition which we have desired, and for the attainment of which we believed purchases of government securities might be necessary, has been achieved during the past ten days in the natural course of developments in the bill market which could hardly have been anticipated. . . . As we pointed out in our letter of July 3, we believe that the important thing to be achieved in present circumstances is that the money center banks should be substantially out of debt and that there should now be some surplus funds available. As just stated, this condition now exists largely as a result of the increase in the Sys-tem bill portfolio. (Minutes, New York Directors, July 17, 1930)

41. The bill purchases reflected mainly changes in market rates relative to the posted ac-ceptance rate. Harrison summarized the governors' replies in a memo included as part of the minutes of the directors' meeting of July 17. An example of the importance given to real bills and the need to avoid "speculative" credit is the letter Harrison received from Governor Tal-ley of Dallas (Harrison Papers, Letters and Reports, vol. 1). Talley wrote that "if rediscount rates are reduced beyond their natural point and open market transactions are used to force the rediscount rate below that point to which it would naturally fall, then reserve credit would be forced into illegitimate channels and the total amount of credit, based upon the excess reserve credit released, would find its way into a long-term investment where it does not be-long, and the tendency would be for another period of inflation to ensue without stopping at the natural point of readjustment from which recovery would proceed in the natural way."

The committee did not meet again during the summer of 1930. On August 7 the executive committee and the conference agreed by telephone, without much dissent, to purchase $25 million so as to offset part of the gold export. At the end of August it approved $50 million of additional purchases by telephone to reverse the money market effect of a seasonal increase in member bank borrowing or a further decline in the gold stock if these should occur.

The Board granted the authority but, still concerned about prerogatives, noted that the Open Market Policy Conference had not held a meeting as required by the resolutions it operated under. Harrison replied that the purchase program had been entirely for seasonal purposes. He had consulted members of the executive committee of the conference, and "we are all in agreement that at the moment there does not appear any need to purchase government securities." He explained that the demand for currency and credit for the Labor Day weekend had subsided; the New York City banks had reduced their indebtedness to $8 million; reserves were in excess of requirements. "Money" was easy.

On August 30 Governor Young expressed the same opinion in a letter to President Hoover tendering his resignation as governor of the Federal Reserve Board to accept appointment as governor of the Boston bank: "Now, however, it is clearly evident that the credit structure of the country is in an easy and exceptionally strong position" (Young to Hoover, Board Minutes, August 30, 1930).

Young did not give the basis for this claim. The data show a further decline in June for the sum of banker's acceptances and commercial paper. In fact, both had fallen, while loans at reporting member banks had increased. Although table 5.7 shows commercial paper and banker's acceptances outstanding above the August 1929 level, the peak occurred in January 1930. By June, acceptances and commercial paper were 13 percent below the January total, while bank lending had increased 1.3 percent since January and was slightly above the level at the cyclic peak in August 1929. However, member bank borrowing and short-term market rates were in the range considered easy.

Bernanke (1983, 1994) and Calomiris (1993) claim the decline in bank lending was an independent cause of the economic decline that supplemented the decline in the money stock. They argue that small firms that depended most on banks for credit were forced to contract by the decline in bank lending. Bank failures increased the costs of intermediation, making credit more difficult to obtain for borrowers too small or too risky to use open credit markets.

A cursory examination of the data in table 5.7 seems to support this claim. Bank loans, acceptances, and commercial paper increased in the first ten months of recession, but the cumulative increase in open market lending far exceeds the increase in bank loans. This is misleading. Most of the increase in open market lending occurred from August to November 1929. Loans at weekly reporting banks also rose in this period, but by a smaller amount. In the first half of 1930, Bernanke's hypothesis fails. From January 31 to June 30, commercial paper outstanding fell by 12.6 percent, while loans at weekly reporting banks rose by 1.3 percent. Weekly reporting member banks are above average size and lend to larger customers. For all member banks, call data on December 31, 1929, and June 30, 1930, show a decline of 3.6 percent in total loans, much less than the decline in commercial paper.

Changing Character of the Decline

By the next OMPC meeting, more than a year had passed since the cyclical peak. Industrial production had fallen 25 percent, and the stock of money and the monetary base had fallen 4 to 5 percent. Member bank borrowing had fallen $850 million from the peak and was at a comparatively low level, and short-term interest rates were less than half the levels of the previous year. Long-term interest rates on Aaa bonds had fallen much less, as is typical in a cyclical downswing (table 5.8).

A new element appeared for the first time in the September data: the spread between Aaa and Baa rates widened. Baa rates rose while Aaa fell, so the risk premium increased from both ends, suggesting flight to quality. In June the risk spread was the same as at the August 1929 peak; in September it was wider by 0.27 percent.

A comparison of the decline in money, output, and prices during the first year with the changes in later years shows how the character of the contraction changed. At first, industrial production declined by a much larger percentage than the stock of money or the price level. After the first year of contraction, industrial production was midway between peak and ultimate trough; the stock of money and the price deflator were no more than a quarter of the way from peak to trough. A severe deflation now combined with a severe contraction. Even on the Federal Reserve's interpretation that the contraction was brought on by the speculative excesses of the late twenties, it is clear that the speculative excesses had been obliterated after one year by the precipitous decline in output. From this point on, output declined at a slower rate; money and prices declined faster. During the next thirty months, the average percentage declines in money, industrial production, and prices were more nearly the same.

Most of the policymakers regarded the substantial decline in short-term market interest rates and the attendant decline in member bank borrowing as the main—and perhaps the only important—indicators of the current position of the monetary system. On the Riefler-Burgess view, policy was "easy" and had never been easier in the experience of the policymakers or of the Federal Reserve System. However, table 5.8 makes clear that the decline in interest rates was not principally a result of Federal Reserve operations. The Federal Reserve had partially offset the decline in interest rates resulting from the reduction in the public's currency holdings, the demand for loans and other forms of bank credit, and deflation.

There can be no doubt that the Federal Reserve was aware of the severity of the depression. The preliminary memorandum prepared for the September meeting compared the then current depression to the depression of the 1880s, described it as one of the worst in the country's history, and named lack of purchasing power as a main cause. The memorandum also referred to the cautious approach being taken by the banks, particularly banks in New York, a reference to the fact that member banks' borrowing had fallen.

At the September meeting, Harrison again described the monetary and economic situation, called attention to the fact that most central banks had increased their gold reserves during the year, and for the first time mentioned the reduction in the monetary base. The ratio of gold to central bank liabilities had increased because of the "very substantial" decline in note and deposit liabilities.[42]

Traditionally, the committee devoted much of its attention in the early fall to the seasonal increase in bank credit and bank reserves. This year, however, member bank borrowing and short-term interest rates had fallen, contrary to the seasonal pattern, so the governors considered selling securities. After some discussion, the committee approved Harrison's motion that "it

42. "For the past year, this country has been in a business recession. At first it was hoped that the recession would be relatively brief reflecting the temporary disturbance of the stock market inflation and decline. But in recent months the recession was extended until, even if the bottom has now been reached, it will rank as one of the country's major business recessions both in extent and duration. The duration of the recession has already been as long as any recession since the 1880s. The causes of the recession are deep seated and broad in their scope and involved, in part at least, a serious shortage or working capital and curtailment of purchasing power in a number of countries and some over-production in basic world industries accompanying under-consumption. . . . The end of the recession does not yet appear by any concrete evidence to be definitely in sight though there have been of late some indications of a check in the downward movement. Generally speaking the banks have pursued an extremely cautious lending and investment policy seeking to keep themselves in the most liquid position" (Harrison Papers, Open Market, September 25, 1930).

Table 5.8 OMPC Meeting, September 25, 1930

COMMERCIAL PAPER AND ACCEPTANCES	LOANS OF 101 WEEKLY REPORTING BANKS	GOLD STOCK	BORROWING	BILLS BOUGHT	GOVERNMENT SECURITIES	CURRENCY	MONETARY BASE	MONEY (M_1)
				Current Changes to September 30, 1930				
+$48	-$189	$0	-$62	+$56	+$26	-$47	-$79	-$251
				Cumulative Changes from August 1929				
28.1%	-0.1%	4.3%	-$854	+$73	+$442	-7.3%	-4.6%	-5.4%

BORROWING	EXCESS RESERVES	DISCOUNT RATE (N.Y. AND RANGE)	AAA RATES	AAA-ACCEPTANCES	BAA-AAA	WPI ALL ITEMS (1926 = 100)	WPI FARM (1926 = 100)	INDUSTRIAL PRODUCTION (AUGUST 1929 = 100)
				Levels as of September 1930				
$189	$59	2.5 (2.5-3.5)	4.42%	2.54%	1.52%	84	85	75.6

Note: Dollar amounts are millions.

should be the policy of the System to maintain the present easy money rate position in the principal money centers . . . that . . . no further easing of such money rates would be advisable and that no firming of rates would be desirable whether because of seasonal requirements, gold exports, or other causes." The OMPC approved this motion nine to two with one abstention.[43]

The minutes then refer to a general discussion between the members of the OMPC and the Board at which members of the Board asked why the conference had not requested authority to engage in substantial purchases so as to force more credit on the country.[44]

Governor McDougal restated his position at length. He was opposed to maintaining the present low rates that prevailed in the market because they were "artificial," "too low." Banks were now unwilling to pay a 2 percent rate to buy new Treasury issues on credit because money was not worth 2 percent. In an apparent reference to the open market purchase of $50 million the previous spring, which he had opposed, he reminded the governors that easy money had been tried, and while it could not be said that the policy had achieved nothing, "it has not done what we hoped." And he added, "We are all in agreement that nothing should be done to make things easier."

Governor Calkins explained that he had voted against the resolution for reasons he described as "trivial." He had written the background memorandum, but he opposed the section, added at the meeting, authorizing purchases or sales of $100 million instead of $50 million. He did not want any action to ease the money market, but he could not agree with Governor McDougal that this was an opportune time to "firm the money market." "We have every reason to anticipate the usual seasonal increase, and I think we should go through that period, the remainder of this year, before we take any action to bring about a less sloppy condition."

Governor Norris voiced an opinion similar to McDougal's: "I think the large majority felt that money conditions were unduly and unwholesomely easy and that there might be some little hardening in some rates without

43. The conference also voted to raise the limit on purchases and sales by the executive committee from $50 million to $100 million without further approval of the conference. Governor Calkins believed this would be interpreted as a move to greater ease, so he voted against the resolution. Governor McDougal gave the other negative vote. He explained that "he thought some firming of rates might be advisable."

44. The details of this discussion are not contained in the minutes, but they are available from the Board's correspondence. They reveal most clearly the positions, beliefs, and attitudes held by leading members of the System. The quotations and source material that follow in the text are from a letter to Eugene Meyer, dated September 30. Meyer had replaced Young as governor of the Federal Reserve Board. He served from 1930 to 1933. The memo notes that the remarks are not verbatim.

doing any harm and possibly doing some good." He had voted for the resolution as Harrison presented it, because he did not want to take responsibility for a firmer policy at that time in view of the seasonal problem. His
views were more fully expressed in a memorandum from the directors and
officers in Philadelphia that he had read to the conference. The memo restated the dangers of low interest rates and argued that low interest rates
could not bring about recovery. The problem, as they saw it, was one of excess capacity and not one of underconsumption.

The Philadelphia memo appealed to the real bills doctrine that most of
the governors regarded as their guiding principle:

> We have always believed that the proper function of the System was well ex-
> pressed in the phrase used in the Tenth Annual Report of the Federal
> Reserve Board—"The Federal Reserve supplies needed additions to credit
> and takes up the slack in times of business recession." We have, therefore,
> necessarily found ourselves out of harmony with the policy recently followed
> of supplying unneeded additions to credit in a time of business recession,
> which is the exact antithesis of the rules stated above.
>
> The suggestion has been made that we should be prompt to "go into re-
> verse" and dispose of these governments when business picks up. This is a
> complete and literal reversal of the policies stated in the Board's Tenth An-
> nual Report, already quoted. We have been putting out credit in a period of
> depression, when it is not wanted and cannot be used, and we will have to
> withdraw credit when it is wanted and can be used. (Open Market Policy
> Conference, Board of Governors File, September 25, 1930)

Norris and his directors believed that "correction must come about
through reduced production, reduced inventories, . . . and the accumulation of savings through the exercise of thrift." The burden was on those
who wished to deviate from the established principles of policymaking to
show that some benefit would result. None of the members of the Open
Market Policy Conference openly disagreed with Norris's interpretation of
the policy statement in the Board's tenth annual report. None of them offered an alternative interpretation or argued that he had misinterpreted
that report, as Chandler (1958) has suggested.

Adolph Miller of the Board urged the members of the committee to consider a more expansive policy and stated the case for countercyclical policy
as clearly as it was ever done in the minutes for the period. He began by
asking whether the governors' recommendations related to the economic
situation and to the depressing conditions the System faced. He questioned whether they misinterpreted money market conditions because
they relied on a faulty indicator:

Is this your program for handling whatever problems of a financial or credit character that originate in this present condition of depression? I ask that because in times of depression, particularly, a money rate is a very imperfect indicator of the true state of credit. . . . You have lower rates precisely because business is stagnant. . . . I expected the Committee might come along with a proposal not to maintain the existing program, but to alter the situation by a bold buying away from the public or banks 50 million or 100 million dollars of bonds and make them turn around and look for some other avenue of investment.

After an exchange with Harrison, Miller continued:

The fellow who sells me his corporate bonds which I buy with the money the Reserve bank has given me in exchange for my government bonds turns around and eventually has got to find something in the field of some new undertaking. I think the real meat of this matter is that in a condition of this kind the fellow who is tempted to sell a security, a government bond in the first instance, does it because he sees somewhere an opportunity where he can replace his investment to his own advantage. In the meantime you have started a movement which causes a revision of the relative scale of investment desirability and values which may work some benefit in a stagnant situation. (Open Market Policy Conference, Board of Governors File, September 25, 1930)

In reply, Harrison argued that Miller's policy was the policy of deliberate inflation, a policy that was "fraught with a great many dangers." There were "some in the organization of the New York bank," who wanted to pursue the policy Miller now urged upon them, but the governors had not considered this alternative. One of the great dangers in this policy was that it would fail to generate much expansion but would instead cause a gold outflow. After they used all their reserve bank credit, they "would be stumped."

Harrison's reference to "some in the organization of the New York Bank" is to two officers of the New York bank, Carl Snyder and W. Randolph Burgess, and perhaps to some of the directors. At a meeting of the officers' council on September 17, Snyder urged Harrison to support an aggressive policy of expansion.[45] Snyder pointed out that the call report data for June 30 showed that the volume of bank credit at all member banks was the same as in 1928, and that credit had actually declined compared with 1929. The city member banks had reported an increase during this period so, he rea-

---

45. At the New York directors' meeting on October 23, Harrison mentioned again that a majority of the officers of the New York bank favored additional purchases. Harrison opposed on grounds that the market was easy and the OMPC would not agree (Minutes, New York Directors, October 23, 1930).

soned, the approximately eight thousand nonreporting member banks must have curtailed the amount of credit outstanding. In his opinion this was deflationary. He favored an aggressive policy of purchases to stimulate business and avoid the winter of depression that now seemed likely.

Harrison replied that since the banks borrowed only minimum amounts from the Federal Reserve, additional purchases would force them to invest in securities instead of real bills. The dangers of such an inflationary policy were "great" and the advantages "doubtful."

Burgess argued that the attempt to correct a previous deflation was not inflationary. He believed that New York should favor a policy that involved more than merely maintaining easy money rates and keeping the New York City banks out of debt. By increasing the pressure on the banks to employ their surplus funds, open market policy could give a little impetus to business recovery. Later, if inflation developed, there would be ample opportunity to slow it down.

Harrison replied that the present economic difficulties could no more be remedied by a "heavy dose of easy credit" than by the small dose that had already been administered. He repeated the stock argument: when the New York City banks are continuously out of debt to the reserve bank over any considerable period of time, it means a very easy reserve position. Harrison added that most of the other Federal Reserve Banks would not agree to additional purchases (Harrison Papers, Discussion Notes, "Credit Policy in the Business Situation").

At the OMPC, Governor Meyer agreed with Harrison that any increase in reserve bank credit beyond what he called the "status quo" would lead to a gold outflow. Miller then urged that they at least consider an exploratory operation, but he was unable to counter the arguments of Harrison and Meyer that the proposed policy was inflationary, that the conference felt it had "gone too far."

Norris closed the discussion with the type of argument that often appeals to "practical men." He had talked to a partner of Morgan and Company, who assured him they had "no trouble at all in selling high grade bonds but that there was difficulty in selling second grade bonds, because buying was institutional." Further purchases by the Federal Reserve would succeed in marking bond prices up only temporarily; as soon as the purchases stopped, prices would fall, and the customers would be disgruntled.

Summary: Policy in the First Year

The September meeting was the last scheduled meeting of the full Open Market Policy Conference in 1930 and the last opportunity the Federal Reserve had to prevent the wave of bank failures and currency drains that started late in the year. With the exception of Miller's plea for a more expansionist policy and the Snyder-Burgess suggestions a few weeks earlier, there had been no serious consideration of an alternative to the existing policy. Of those present at the OMPC meeting, only Miller appears to have dissented from the view that "ease" was best measured by member bank borrowing and short-term market interest rates, and only Miller questioned the notion that policy could do nothing more until there was an increase in the demand for credit. No one suggested that the severe deflation had increased real rates.[46]

As usual, the quixotic Miller did not convert others to his view. It seems unlikely, however, that the more persuasive Strong would have succeeded if he had lived. The dominant view among the governors was that open market purchases and easy money had failed to revive the economy. The System had purchased more than $500 million of securities and acceptances in the previous twelve months. Short-term rates were at historical lows. The Riefler-Burgess doctrine suggested that policy was easy. The real bills doctrine implied that the correct policy was a passive one. Most governors had always held these views; Harrison shared many of them.

The economies of the United States and much of the rest of the world became victims of the Federal Reserve's adherence to an inappropriate theory and the absence of basic economic understanding such as that developed by Thornton and Fisher (chapter 2 above). The alternative interpretation, that monetary policy failed because no one suggested the appropriate action to take, is contradicted by the arguments that Miller, Burgess, and Snyder advanced at the September meetings in New York and Washington and by the arguments of several New York directors in May and June.

Although Harrison mentioned a future loss of gold as a reason for not expanding, gold movements had little impact on policy decisions and actions. In the year to September, bank reserves had increased by less than the increase in gold stocks and the monetary base had declined, so gold standard reasoning supported expansion.[47]

46. Snyder and Burgess continued their efforts. At the October 23 meeting of the New York directors, Harrison reported that the officers were in favor of further purchases. One of the directors urged Harrison to make these views known to the Board. Harrison again referred to the very low level of member bank borrowing but now argued that "he was doubtful of the advisability of forcing more funds into the market where they might back up and cause an unwise inflation of credit." In a letter to Governor McDougal written at about this time, Harrison interprets the 1928–29 experience as "speculative excess" with insufficient credit restraint, the view taken by Strong's critics.

47. On both October 9 and October 30, New York voted to purchase $25 million of sterling bills for its own account. New York acted to strengthen the pound, but discussion of the assistance to cotton exports may have influenced some directors (Minutes, New York Directors, October 9 and 30, 1930).

The discussion at the September 1930 meeting shows that the Federal Reserve's decisions followed the real bills doctrine, as expressed in the tenth annual report, and failed to distinguish between real and nominal interest rates. Consumer and wholesale prices had fallen 14 to 15 percent in the year to September, so the 3.25 percent reduction in acceptance rates, the 3.5 percent reduction in the discount rates at New York, and other rate reductions left short-term real interest rates more than ten percentage points above the level of the earlier year.

Eichengreen's (1992) claim that lack of international coordination prevented expansion finds no mention in the discussion. With few exceptions, the governors, members, and officers of the Federal Reserve believed they had acted appropriately—that any additional purchases would fuel speculative growth. They did not look to foreign central banks for guidance or leadership, and they did not consider coordination necessary for expansion.

In the year since the peak, the Federal Reserve had purchased $442 million of government securities and acquired $73 million of acceptances. Borrowing had declined $854 million and was well below the minimum levels reached in the 1923–24 and 1926–27 recessions. To a modern observer, these changes suggest that the Federal Reserve had failed to offset the decline in borrowing. The Riefler-Burgess doctrine provided a different interpretation: Federal Reserve purchases had permitted the banks to repay borrowings. The financial system was in a position to expand if the private sector wanted to borrow.

Two months after the September meeting, Charles S. Hamlin of the Board talked about changes needed in the Federal Reserve Act. The proposed changes were modest and, Hamlin said, were considered nonpartisan by the Board and Congress. Hamlin talked about the Board's cordial relations with Congress. He made no mention of changes in gold reserves or requirements as a restriction the Board wanted removed.

Hamlin's speech showed no evidence of the need for stimulus. He accurately described the magnitude of the decline in industrial production and prices in the first year of recession. The decline in bank credit was the usual occurrence in a recession. He noted the reduction in bank borrowing and in the ratio of loans to deposits (Federal Reserve Bank of Boston 1928–31, 1930, 19). After discussing quantitative changes in the distribution of credit between New York and the rest of the country, Hamlin concluded by comparing 1929–30 and 1920–21. "The Federal Reserve Banks are not now, as they were then, close to the limits of their lending power. On the contrary, they have ample reserves and stand ready to finance a growing volume of business as soon as signs of recovery express themselves in an increasing demand for credit. That day cannot arrive too soon to please any of us" (21).

WATCHING AND WAITING: POLICY IN THE SECOND YEAR

By November–December 1930, a radically new element had emerged. The eruption of serious bank failures shifted the balance of relative advantage toward increased currency holdings. The risk attached to holding demand deposits increased substantially, lowering the relative inconvenience of holding currency. With Federal Reserve policy unchanged, the public's increased demand for currency forced a further contraction in the money supply and in the banks' demand for earning assets. But until mid-December, member bank borrowing remained virtually unchanged, and short-term interest rates did not rise, so the executive committee did not meet and made no purchases of securities for seasonal or other reasons.

Bank failures began in the Southeast after the collapse in November 1930 of Caldwell and Company, a large Tennessee investment bank (Wicker 1996). Runs on 120 banks followed the collapse, but most were small. Wicker (1996, 32) concluded that the effect of the failures did not spread beyond the region, and Calomiris and Mason (2000) support this conclusion. Since money market interest rates did not rise, the Federal Reserve took no action.

On December 11 the New York State superintendent of banking closed the Bank of the United States, a New York City member bank. More than half a million depositors found their deposits unavailable.[48] The proximate reason for closing the bank was failure to merge the bank with two others—the Public National Bank and the Manufacturers' Trust Company. Neither of the latter banks closed. All three banks had Jewish owners, and each lent to small and medium-sized clothing and textile manufacturers. None was a member of the New York clearinghouse at the time.

After two weeks of late-night meetings, a group including J. Herbert Case, chairman of the New York reserve bank, Leslie Rounds, Federal Reserve officer responsible for banking, and Mortimer Buckner, head of the New York Trust Company and chairman of the relevant clearinghouse committee, agreed to merge the three banks with Case as chairman of the new board. The agreement required the clearinghouse banks to advance $20 million: "The Public was in fine shape, the Manufacturers' was in good

---

48. Two smaller banks closed also—the Chelsea Bank in New York and the Binghamton State Bank.

shape, and the Bank of the United States was generally supposed to be in pretty poor shape" (CHFRS, Rounds, May 2, 1955, 15).

Rounds and Case give different explanations of the failure to merge. According to Rounds, Harrison returned from Europe just as the agreement was reached. Harrison was cool to the idea. The Manufacturers' Trust was hesitant and would agree only if the clearinghouse banks would guarantee up to $20 million of Bank of the United States assets: "Quite a few of those representing the clearinghouse banks cooled off and George [Harrison] was not disposed to warm them up any, so it all fell through; at about 5:30 that morning it was decided to close the bank" (ibid., 16).[49]

Case's version has Harrison in Europe throughout.[50] Case attributed the failure of the merger to a decision by the Public National Bank to withdraw from the merger. The governor, Franklin Roosevelt, "sent Lehman down to plead that the consolidation should go through. One of the distinguished bankers [a clearinghouse member] shook his head and said 'let it fail, draw a ring around it, so that the infection will not spread.' Obviously any such idea was impossible" (CHFRS, Case, February 26, 1954, 7).[51]

To ease the burden of the closing of a medium-sized member bank and to slow the currency drain, the New York clearinghouse admitted the Manufacturers' Trust and the Public National Bank to membership. The own-

49. Rounds had looked over the bank's records for several days and nights. He claimed the bank was solvent at the time it closed. "We had discounted the doubtful items very heavily. They had a pretty good bond account, they had $35 or $40 million of capital to be exhausted before they became insolvent" (CHFRS, Rounds, May 2, 1955, 17). Friedman and Schwartz (1963, 311) report that the Bank of the United States paid out 83.5 percent of its adjusted liabilities despite declining asset prices in the following two years.

50. Case described a conversation with Harrison in Germany in which Harrison agreed that Case should be chairman of the merged bank (Case, CHFRS, February 26, 1954, 7). The conversation must have occurred earlier. Harrison was in New York on December 4 for the New York directors' meeting.

51. The issue of Harrison's presence or absence aside, Case's story emphasizes a different side of a very similar story. Both the Manufacturers' and the Public National demanded the clearinghouse guarantee. Failure to get the guarantee caused them to withdraw. One reason the clearinghouse banks were unwilling to guarantee the $20 million was that they had lost heavily when they guaranteed the Harrison National Bank. The Harrison bank went bankrupt, and stockholders lost most of their equity. Another reason, offered by Friedman and Schwartz (1963, 309–10), is that the Jewish ownership of these banks played a role in the clearinghouse decision. Earlier, Rounds denied the story in a way that suggests it was a consideration. "I don't think anti-Jewish feeling was too important so far as the clearinghouse banks were concerned. Of course, it contributed to the feeling that they all had of doubt about how bad the situation was. . . . There was a definite feeling in the minds of the public regarding banks that was anti-Jewish. As far as the clearinghouse banks were concerned, I don't think they thought in terms of race. . . . There was a certain amount of feeling about the Jewish banks but I don't think it was based on race. I do think that in the public mind there was a strong aversion to Jewish banks and that many of the Jewish bankers felt that the public had made that decision" (CHFRS, Rounds, May 2, 1955, 19).

ers of the Manufacturers' Trust sold controlling shares to a non-Jewish banker (CHFRS, Rounds, May 2, 1955, 21).[52]

The December 1930 OMPC meeting was one of the briefest on record. The minutes cover only two pages. Harrison reported on the closing of the Bank of the United States nine days earlier and informed the conference that he had made some emergency purchases of securities from particular banks in New York after the failure. In fact, New York had purchased $100 million of securities and $75 million of acceptances between November 30 and December 17; the System's discounts and the monetary base increased by $80 million and $250 million, respectively. Most of the increase in the base reflected the currency drain, a subject discussed at length in the preliminary memorandum prepared for the meeting and all but completely ignored by the governors.[53]

Borrowing, currency, and the base continued to rise to the end of the month but, contrary to the normal seasonal increase, loans at weekly reporting banks fell $500 million in two months (see table 5.9). The risk spread between higher- and lower-rated bonds rose 0.67 to 2.19 in the same period and was almost one percentage point above the August 1929 level by the end of the year.

The conference was willing to leave any decision about further purchases to Harrison but stipulated that the purchases would have to remain within the $100 million limit set by the OMPC in September. It is not clear whether this was intended as a vote of confidence in New York's ability to handle the crisis or whether the governors were aware that New York had purchased most of the $100 million for its own account before the meeting and had little remaining authority. During the week of the meeting, discounts rose more than $100 million to the highest level since the start of the year. New York sold $50 million, and at the end of the week it reduced its discount and acceptance rates. When the pressure increased in the last week of the year, New York temporarily exceeded its authority by purchasing more securities than the conference had authorized.[54]

---

52. "The feeling of the Clearinghouse was that the bank could not survive as a Jewish bank" (CHFRS, Rounds, May 2, 1955, 22).

53. Case reported that in the single week ending December 13, 1930, the New York Federal Reserve Bank supplied $170 billion in currency, 4 percent of the total stock outstanding. For the country as a whole, currency increased $300 million, about 7.5 percent of the outstanding stock. Part of the increase was seasonal (testimony of J. H. Case, Senate Committee on Banking and Currency 1931, 108–9).

54. During the week ending December 24, a fortuitous increase of $50 million in float eased the money market and offset the System's open market sales. In the following week, float declined and the pressure on the money market increased. New York purchased more than $100 million of acceptances and $85 million in securities during the week; at $729 million in securities and $364 in acceptances, the account was more than $300 million higher

Before December, most failed banks were rural nonmember banks. The Bank of the United States was a medium-sized member bank in the country's main financial center. After calm returned to the markets, evidence of concern remained. Risk spreads between Baa and Aaa bonds remained above the levels customary before the failure, and currency outstanding continued to increase absolutely and relative to the money stock.

The background memo prepared for the December meeting painted a gloomy picture. Industrial production had declined "to the lowest level relative to normal ever reached"; factory employment had declined further; agricultural prices had fallen; the autumn expansion was below average. The memo mentions a decline from 92 to 85 between August and November in the seasonally adjusted production index and a decline in the price index from 85 to 81. Yet these facts had no apparent effect on the OMPC's decision. Member bank borrowing remained below $500 million; on Riefler-Burgess grounds, the market did not require further support.

Once the money market disturbance subsided, the System began to sell securities and to reduce its acceptance portfolio, following the usual seasonal pattern. Bank loans had declined by almost $1 billion, nearly 6 percent, in the four months to January 31. Industrial production, prices, and the stock of money continued to decline. Currency held by the public rose from December to January, reversing the standard seasonal movement and suggesting public concern about the financial system. A new element appeared for the first time: member bank excess reserves were above $100 million, twice the average level of the preceding year.

The rise in excess reserves could have been a signal to the members of the Open Market Policy Conference or to their staffs. In their analysis, excess reserves were small and approximately constant, so the relatively large increase from December to January was inconsistent with the Riefler-Burgess framework. Miller was aware of the inconsistency. He asked why the banks were acquiring surplus reserves and how widespread the practice had become. Harrison replied that excess reserves were most likely a sign of lack of demand by borrowers and of banks' reluctance to use funds; McDougal and Young replied that most of the banks in Chicago and Boston did not have surplus reserves but that the banks were "very liquid." Miller pressed his point, suggesting that the "banking system might be suffering just now from excessive caution and excessive desire for liquidity." Harrison replied that "that was one reason why our easy

than at the time of the OMPC meeting. All of the increase came in December. These figures are higher than those shown by the change in securities in table 5.9, which are based on monthly averages of daily figures. Approximately $45 million of the purchases were made (net) by New York for its own account.

Table 5.9 OMPC Meeting, December 20, 1930

COMMERCIAL PAPER AND ACCEPTANCES	LOANS OF 101 WEEKLY REPORTING BANKS	GOLD STOCK	BORROWING	BILLS BOUGHT	GOVERNMENT SECURITIES	CURRENCY	MONETARY BASE	MONEY (M₁)
Current Changes to December 31, 1930								
+$34	-$527	+$58	+$149	+$60	+$57	+$175	+$296	-$120
Cumulative Changes from August 1929								
30.4%	-3.8%	5.7%	-$705	+$133	+$489	-2.8%	-0.4%	-5.8%

BORROWING	EXCESS RESERVES	DISCOUNT RATE (N.Y. AND RANGE)	AAA RATES	AAA-ACCEPTANCES	BAA-AAA	WPI ALL ITEMS (1926 = 100)	WPI FARM (1926 = 100)	INDUSTRIAL PRODUCTION (AUGUST 1929 = 100)
Levels as of December 1930								
$388	$73	2 (2–3.5)	4.52%	2.64%	2.19%	78	75	70.1

Note: Dollar amounts are millions.

Table 5.10 OMPC Meeting, January 21, 1931

COMMERCIAL PAPER AND ACCEPTANCES	LOANS OF 101 WEEKLY REPORTING BANKS	GOLD STOCK	BORROWING	BILLS BOUGHT	GOVERNMENT SECURITIES	CURRENCY	MONETARY BASE	MONEY (M₁)
Current Changes to January 31, 1931								
-$67	-$438	+$50	-$85	-$51	+$3	+$9	+$27	-$361
Cumulative Changes from August 1929								
25.8%	-6.3%	6.9%	-$790	+$82	+$492	-2.6%	0%	-7.2%

BORROWING	EXCESS RESERVES	DISCOUNT RATE (N.Y. AND RANGE)	AAA RATES	AAA-ACCEPTANCES	BAA-AAA	WPI ALL ITEMS (1926 = 100)	WPI FARM (1926 = 100)	INDUSTRIAL PRODUCTION (AUGUST 1929 = 100)
Levels as of January 1931								
$253	$105	2 (2–3.5)	4.42%	2.86%	1.99%	77	74	69.8

Note: Dollar amounts are millions.

money policy [*sic*] has not proved more effective." No one suggested that the excess reserves could be eliminated by an aggressive policy of monetary expansion or that the banks' "desire for liquidity" should be satisfied by the System.[55]

Although borrowing was only $250 million, the main discussion at the meeting was not, as in September, about whether there should be sales but about how much should be sold. McDougal suggested they sell $100 million; George Seay (Richmond) suggested they sell $200 million; Harrison reported that the directors at New York wanted to sell $35 million.[56] Only Meyer suggested that sales might be interpreted as a change to a more restrictive policy. And Meyer added, "The Reserve System has been accused in a number of quarters of pursuing a deflationary policy in the past year." In the end, the governors did not decide on the amount to be sold, but they agreed unanimously that it "would be desirable to dispose of some of the System holdings of government securities."

The tone of the minutes was more pessimistic than it had been at previous meetings. For the first time there was a lengthy discussion of gold, but the problem was an inflow, not an outflow. Harrison had returned from Europe in December. He reported that the European countries were planning to reduce imports from the United States because they could not afford to pay $600 million in gold each year. Britain, Germany, and Italy had experienced a decline in gold reserves during 1930. With the decline in exports, these countries reduced borrowing. The Smoot-Hawley Tariff had added to the decline in world trade and particularly to reduced exports and imports by the United States.

International cooperation continued. The New York bank purchased sterling bills during the fall because of the "weakness in sterling." Harrison added that in December he had "been urged from many quarters to make a reassuring statement which might aid in quieting the banking situation," but he had declined to do so for fear it might be contradicted by any small bank failure that occurred. McDougal noted that the recent reduction of the discount rate at Chicago had been made without any belief that it would encourage business activity.

Despite these gloomy prospects, the meeting had no recommendation or even discussion of expansive Federal Reserve action. All the members

55. Harrison's response neglected to mention his officers' discussion earlier in the month. At that meeting, one of the officers described the excess reserves as "a result of a period of country-wide apprehension concerning the banking situation" (Harrison Papers, Meeting of Officers Council, January 14, 1931).

56. He did not explain that he proposed selling $45 million but some of the directors objected that they should not sell (Minutes, New York Directors, January 15, 1931).

believed that policy was easy. There was only one type of evidence to support this belief at the time. Between December and January, member bank borrowing had declined and short-term interest rates had fallen to the lowest point recorded up to that time. To the governors of the Federal Reserve System, nothing was more indicative of the direction of policy and its effect.

Again, an alternative view was presented and rejected. W. Randolph Burgess told the New York directors at their meeting on January 15 that selling securities meant reversing current policy and suggested that they delay the change. Two of the directors recommended that Harrison continue the "easy money policy," but they were unable to persuade him that selling securities would have an adverse effect. However, when the sale of only $20 million was followed by a much larger decline of excess reserves, sales were suspended.

A week later, Burgess reported to the directors that Harrison suggested resumption of selling, but "a majority of the Officers Council was of the opinion that it would be better to defer further sales." One of the directors again urged a policy of expansion; as a compromise, they postponed further sales.

Between the end of January and the end of April, the risk spread on long-term bonds increased by 0.875 percent, but excess reserves declined and the index of industrial production rose by almost two percentage points. The minutes note the rise as early as the February 26 meeting of the New York directors.

The Federal Reserve never discussed using monetary policy to support the modest recovery. On March 5, Harrison advised "maintaining the status quo," which at the time meant no change in the discount rate, in the buying rate on acceptances, or in open market policy. Meyer, who was present, agreed that it was unwise to take any small steps that might be interpreted as a change in policy when none was intended.

Nor did the rise in industrial production receive much attention at the OMPC meeting. The committee focused on three changes in the data for the monetary system—the continued gold inflow, the decline in the System's acceptances, and the decline in member bank excess reserves.[57] At the time of the meeting, the gold stock had increased nearly 5 percent since the previous August, and the rate of increase had quickened during the winter.

57. Much of the gold now came from France. Meyer asked why the Bank of France sold gold. Harrison responded that it probably had more than it needed. Meyer urged that the increased gold be allowed to lower interest rates and expand credit (Minutes, New York Directors, April 23, 1931).

The governors were concerned because the gold imports were not having "their normal and natural effect on the loans and investments of member banks." The banks were bidding for acceptances in the market and were offering a higher price (lower yield) than the System. There is no mention of the System's open market sales. Table 5.11 shows that, between January and April, the expansive effect of a gold inflow was balanced by a reduction in acceptances (bills bought) and open market sales of government securities. Despite the increase in currency, the base fell as the banks reduced their discounts. The money stock continued to fall.

Harrison's report to the Governors Conference argued again that recovery would not occur without an increase in borrowing by foreigners. His analysis of the monetary situation at this meeting differed substantially from those he had offered previously. He noted that the Federal Reserve's policy between October 1929 and August 1930 had not provided a "vigorous stimulant" to the market and that, although recently "money rates have been at very low levels, there has not been over a period of months any consistent surplus of Federal Reserve funds pressing for use upon the market" (Governors Conference, April 23, 1931).

Friedman and Schwartz (1963, 378) interpret this passage as evidence that Harrison's understanding of the effects of open market operations was superior to that of the other governors and as an indication that he was not bemused by the decline in short-term market interest rates. There is at best a tenuous basis for this interpretation. The statement probably refers to the failure of long-term interest rates to decline. First, Harrison's analysis at most of the previous meetings—and particularly at the meeting in September 1930—differed little from the analyses offered by most of the other governors. Second, he did not press for large-scale open market purchases at the time of his statement but argued for open market purchases only if necessary and as a last resort. Third, between April and June he did not use existing authority to purchase securities, despite a renewal of the currency drain and a new wave of bank failures. Fourth, the proposal to purchase appears to have originated with Meyer and Miller. Both had come to the April 23 meeting of the New York directors and had argued for a change in policy. Miller said that a reduction in interest rates in New York would force a redistribution of reserves between New York and the rest of the country, thereby lowering rates generally. Meyer made a more forceful statement urging the bank to reduce rates "no matter how low rates already seem to be." To the standard plaint that rates were "very low," Meyer replied, "The whole history of investment showed that money would go from short-term into long-term channels at a price. The problem is to find the price." Harrison expressed a supporting view only after Meyer's strong statement and, characteristically, favored a cautious policy of reducing the buying rate on acceptances by 0.125 percent and observing its effect.[58]

Harrison had no difficulty obtaining approval for the proposed purchases. Because of the gold inflow, several governors spoke in favor of expansion. Governor Fancher stated that the "System can lend its efforts to make money so cheap as to put it to work." Governor Talley said that he still had "confidence that gold will finally express itself in an expansion of bank credit" and that Harrison's program would help to bring this about. Even McDougal supported the motion to purchase up to $100 million in the open market.

Why could the governors agree to purchase bills and securities at this meeting when they had been unwilling to consider purchases at earlier meetings? The minutes furnish a very clear and simple answer. The gold inflow was a "real" force that should have the effect of lowering market interest rates. Since the expected effect had not occurred, most of the governors were willing to help bring it about. Harrison summarized the widely shared belief. If the banks could be discouraged from acquiring acceptances from the System, they would make loans or acquire securities in the market and thus expand bank credit. Like the others, he regarded an expansion of bank credit and a reduction of interest rates as a "natural" response to the gold inflow, with different consequences than a reduction of interest rates brought about solely by open market purchases. Under gold standard rules, countries were expected to allow interest rates to fall and to encourage expansion in response to gold inflows. To do otherwise was a violation of the accepted rules.

58. The first hint that a policy of purchasing securities was being considered came at the New York directors' meeting of April 9. Harrison was opposed. He noted that he had opposed purchases in the fall because of his fear of a gold drain to France; he now opposed purchases because member banks would not be able to use the reserves to retire indebtedness (a reference to the low level of indebtedness). Moreover, he viewed the risk of "inflation" as a serious danger: "In the absence of an ability to quickly reverse our position, inflation would probably do more harm than good." Meeting with the officers of the New York bank on April 15, Harrison again opposed purchases of government securities but favored purchases of bills because they could be more quickly reversed.

Harrison's argument for open market purchases of $100 million at the April meeting was based on the decline in the bill (acceptance) portfolio to about $175 billion at the time of the meeting. Harrison noted that "it was the purpose of the New York bank, if necessary, to reduce its bill rate as low as one percent in the hope of accomplishing its objectives of maintaining or even increasing the bill portfolio in the face of gold imports. . . . It was felt that this policy sooner or later would necessarily [sic], because of its effect upon the short time money rates, encourage banks and depositors, in spite of their present liquidity, to employ their money, which is now becoming relatively so unprofitable." He repeated this argument to the New York directors on May 14, but as late as May 26 he opposed using the authority to purchase because of the danger of inflation.

Early in May, New York reduced the buying rate on acceptances, and during the month ten of the twelve reserve banks reduced their discount rates. The Philadelphia and Chicago banks, which had been most strongly opposed to expansive actions or to further reductions in interest rates, were among the first to approve reductions. Nevertheless, member bank borrowing remained virtually unchanged throughout May; the market's acceptance rate fell below the Federal Reserve's buying rate, and the System's holdings of acceptances continued to decline. Although the gold inflow continued, the executive committee did not meet to discuss open market purchases until late in June.

One puzzling aspect of the discussion that took place during the spring concerns the relation of the currency drain, the deposit rates, and bank failures. The New York directors discussed several proposals aimed at reducing the interest rates New York banks paid on deposits. Most agreed on the desirability of reducing deposit rates, but there is no indication in the minutes that the probable reason the New York banks maintained deposit rates was to hold deposits in the face of a renewed wave of bank failures and a renewed currency drain. Nor is there evidence that the directors saw the relation between the public's rising demand for currency, bank failures, and the growing spread between higher- and lower-quality bonds. By May, yields on Baa bonds were much higher than they had been at the peak of the expansion in August 1929, whereas Aaa yields were lower. Throughout the winter the two yields had moved in opposite directions until they differed by 2.78 percent (table 5.11).

At their March 5 meeting the New York directors considered the increased number of bank failures. Many banks had been forced to close because the decline in the market value of their bond portfolios made them insolvent. Among the proposals made to reduce or prevent failures, none involved open market purchases or monetary expansion.

From April to June $230 million in gold flowed into the Federal Reserve banks. Half of the increase in the base produced by the rise in gold holdings was taken as currency. Borrowing increased and excess reserves of member banks rose by $73 million. The rising demand for currency by the public had a contractive effect, so the money stock declined. The rise in currency holdings and in excess reserves are related. Both reflect the increased number of bank failures during the period.

Interest rate changes also show the effect of the currency drain and the series of bank failures during the period. Rates on short-term securities fell to the lowest levels of the contraction. The rate on prime banker's acceptances reached a level (0.88 percent) more than four percentage points below the rate prevailing at the NBER peak in August 1929. Yields on bonds

Table 5.11 OMPC Meeting, April 27–29, 1931

COMMERCIAL PAPER AND ACCEPTANCES	LOANS OF 101 WEEKLY REPORTING BANKS	GOLD STOCK	BORROWING	BILLS BOUGHT	GOVERNMENT SECURITIES	CURRENCY	MONETARY BASE	MONEY (M_1)
Current Changes to April 30, 1931								
−$118	−$697	+$83	−$98	−$33	−$47	+$79	−$33	−$311
Cumulative Changes from August 1929								
17.8%	−10.5%	+9.0%	−$888	+$49	+$445	−0.6%	−0.5%	−8.3%

BORROWING	EXCESS RESERVES	DISCOUNT RATE (N.Y. AND RANGE)	AAA RATES	AAA-ACCEPTANCES	BAA-AAA	WPI ALL ITEMS (1926 = 100)	WPI FARM (1926 = 100)	INDUSTRIAL PRODUCTION (AUGUST 1929 = 100)
Levels as of April 1931								
$155	$56	2 (2–3.5)	4.37%	2.87%	2.78%	73	70	71.6

Note: Dollar amounts are millions.

Table 5.12 Meeting, Executive Committee, June 22, 1931

COMMERCIAL PAPER AND ACCEPTANCES	LOANS OF 101 WEEKLY REPORTING BANKS	GOLD STOCK	BORROWING	BILLS BOUGHT	GOVERNMENT SECURITIES	CURRENCY	MONETARY BASE	MONEY (M_1)
Current Changes to June 30, 1931								
−$63	−$574	+$230	+$35	−$52	+$10	+$98	+$183	−$367
Cumulative Changes from August 1929								
13.5%	−13.8%	14.6%	−$853	−$3	+$455	+1.9%	+2.0%	−9.8%

BORROWING	EXCESS RESERVES	DISCOUNT RATE (N.Y. AND RANGE)	AAA RATES	AAA-ACCEPTANCES	BAA-AAA	WPI ALL ITEMS (1926 = 100)	WPI FARM (1926 = 100)	INDUSTRIAL PRODUCTION (AUGUST 1929 = 100)
Levels as of June 1931								
$190	$129	1.5 (1.5–3.5)	4.36%	3.48%	2.72%	70	65	69.1

Note: Dollar amounts are millions.

rated less than Aaa continued to show the relatively large risk premiums that first appeared in the April 1931 data.[59]

Despite the decline in nominal rates on short-term loans, real rates continued to rise. Wholesale prices had fallen at an annualized rate of nearly 25 percent in two months and a 20 percent annual rate since the start of the year. Farm prices had fallen faster. In response to the high real rates and the declining economy, bank lending fell at an annualized 20 percent rate in the first six months of 1931.

At the June meeting, members of the executive committee commented on the changes that had occurred since the previous meeting. Harrison referred to the currency withdrawals, and several governors referred to the "banking situation." Governor Meyer reported that the Board's staff estimated that from $300 million to $375 million of currency "was now hoarded."[60] Moreover, none of the governors disagreed with Harrison's appraisal of the economic situation or with his judgment that the prospects for a revival were now poorer than they had been only a few weeks before.

A new element was the "threat of a general moratorium and a possible breakdown of capitalism in Europe," a reference to the series of coups in Eastern Europe and the rise of the Nazi Party in Germany.[61] There was also a possible moratorium on payments by some South American countries. These comments, and other more explicit statements, show that the governors recognized that the gold inflows were not solely the result of short-term capital movements in response to interest rate differences but were indications of a flight of capital from foreign countries and signs of a possible breakdown in the international payments mechanism.[62]

Harrison proposed purchases up to $50 million to his directors on June 18, hoping that lower interest rates would slow the gold inflow.[63] During May and the first half of June, the United States received $170 million in

59. Bank failures were so severe that the Governors Conference voted to seek legislation permitting Federal Reserve banks to make advances in emergencies against securities of Federal Intermediate Credit Banks. Governors Calkins, Martin, and Talley voted against.

60. This is approximately the result one would get by assuming a constant ratio of currency to money stock and measuring the decline from the peak in August 1929. Currency had increased by $75 million since the peak instead of declining as the money stock declined.

61. On June 4, Harrison discussed the problem of Credit Anstalt in Austria and its likely effect on Germany. He favored a loan to Germany (Harrison Papers, Memoranda, New York Executive Committee, June 4, 1931).

62. During 1930 Brazil lost its entire gold holding, more than $150 million when valued at $20.67 per ounce. From early 1929 to June 1931, Argentina lost $300 million in gold, half of its gold holdings. The outflow of gold from Germany during June had reduced the German stock by 40 percent, more than $200 million, and had prompted President Hoover on June 20 to propose a moratorium on intergovernmental payments for reparations and war debts.

63. Harrison said that "we should not heedlessly embark upon a program of purchasing Government securities . . . he thought that the arguments in favor of such purchases now out-

gold, with more on the way. The directors agreed that the gold inflow had not been put to work. They differed over whether additional purchases would help, but they voted their support.

When the OMPC executive committee met in June, governors were divided about the action to be taken. Neither Black nor Meyer was a member of the executive committee, but both were present at the meeting and advocated purchases in the strongest terms. Meyer stated that the Board would be sympathetic to the purchase of governments and added that he personally favored a larger program than the $50 million Harrison proposed. Black regarded the purchase program as a "logical continuation of the affirmative policy" adopted at the April meeting. Harrison took an intermediate position. Although he had proposed the program of purchases and supported it at the meeting, he was doubtful about buying governments unless there was at least an informal understanding with the principal member banks concerning "the employment of excess reserves." He hoped the banks would place bids for lower-quality bonds to prevent price quotations from falling.[64] Talley supported Harrison's proposal in the hope that the banks would be encouraged to "use their funds courageously." McDougal, Norris, and Young believed that money was easy and that further purchases would make it even easier. All three agreed that something should be done in support of the president's proposal for a one-year moratorium on reparations and intergovernment repayments of debt and interest. They did not believe further reductions in interest rates would accomplish much. McDougal voted to support the purchases because he believed positive action would have a beneficial effect on the public's state of mind. Norris abstained, and Young (Boston) opposed the purchase program because he "believed that (gold) sterilization had been and was natural and inevitable under the operation of the Federal Reserve System" (Open Market Policy Conference, Board of Governors File, June 22, 1931).

On the same day, the New York directors agreed to make advances to the central banks of Hungary and Germany as part of an international central bank consortium. New York provided $2 million of the $10 million loan to Hungary and $25 million of the $100 million loan to the Reichsbank. Late

---

weighed the arguments against them. . . . [T]he Board was of the opinion that now is the time to purchase Government securities" (Minutes, New York Directors, June 18, 1931).

64. Harrison thought the problem of falling bond prices on lower-quality bonds might be solved if the banks placed bids in the market. The difficulty, as he saw it, was not so much that bonds were "being pressed for sale as that in many cases, there are no bids whatsoever." Meyer assured him that a program of open market purchases would "be more effective in preventing losses by the banks than anything that could be done to improve their income." Meyer continued, "There is a question whether the Reserve System can be said to have done everything within its power, until it has tried that policy [purchases of securities] more vigorously."

in May, and again in June, New York agreed to participate in two $14 million credits to the Credit Anstalt, a private Austrian bank with large foreign liabilities, and lent $1.08 million to the Austrian National Bank. The loans were less than 10 percent of Germany's short-term liabilities. The assistance proved insufficient to stem the flight of capital from any of the countries for more than a few days or weeks or to prevent these countries, and later the British, from suspending convertibility.[65]

Although Eichengreen (1992) repeats the argument that international cooperation failed, there is a remarkable difference between the flurry of activity set off by the foreign exchange crisis and the continuing failure to respond to the domestic crisis.[66] Harrison was willing to risk having some of the New York bank's assets "frozen" in Central Europe to maintain the prevailing exchange rates and the gold exchange standard, but he had been unwilling to offer assistance to prevent bank failures at home (Harrison Papers, Conversation with Meyer, June 23, 1931). In the fall he refused to offer rediscounts to banks that were willing to participate in a lending pool designed to prevent the spread of domestic bank failures. The difference was not ignored at the time. One of the directors questioned Harrison about the difference in approach to domestic and international crises, but there is no record of an explicit reply (Harrison Papers, Meeting of the Executive Committee, June 22, 1931).

The contrast between domestic and international policy was particularly sharp during the summer. Although the executive committee of the OMPC approved purchases of up to $50 million on July 6, the System purchased only $30 million. Harrison favored delaying further purchases, at first because the international monetary system had deteriorated and he believed the timing was poor, later because the banks held excess reserves. Although he fully discussed the rising rate of failure and insolvency among New York banks, he never mentioned the relation between rising excess reserves and rising failure rates. He believed that open market purchases would be useful only if the banks acquiring reserves used them to acquire lower-quality bonds, and he attributed the increased bank insolvency to

---

65. Clarke (1967, 182–219) reports on the series of crises discussed in the minutes and the Harrison Papers. Eichengreen (1992, 265) lists public and private short-term debts of these countries. Central banks in Hungary, Germany, and Austria owed $25 million, $194 million, and $122 million. The Austrian figure includes banks, of which the Credit Anstalt amount was $100 million (Clarke 1967, 187). In his memoirs, President Hoover is critical of the Federal Reserve for being unhelpful and even obstructionist in arranging the moratorium on intergovernment debt payments (Hoover 1952, 73–80; Todd 1994, 9).

66. It is, of course, true that the United States, France, and Britain did not lend the $1 billion that Germany requested in July, but as Eichengreen notes (1992, 276), domestic German firms would not lend half that amount.

bad management and more careful examination.[67] He favored open market purchases to relieve a sudden change in pressure on the New York money market only after the Bank of France withdrew $50 million from the money market and only to the amount of $50 million (Harrison Papers, Open Market II, August 10, 1931).

The decision to purchase $50 million, made at the June meeting of the executive committee, went into effect at once. The System made additional purchases of $30 million after Harrison conferred with other members of the executive committee. In July excess reserves stopped rising, and member bank borrowing declined. Both long- and short-term interest rates fell during the month. By the usual money market indicators, the money market was easier during July than in June, and no purchases were made between July 8 and early August.

Harrison told his directors that Meyer wanted to make additional purchases. Harrison opposed because the System was likely to extend additional credit to foreigners. He favored waiting (Minutes, New York Directors, July 23, 1931). The following week the directors approved purchase of $125 million of prime commercial bills, endorsed or guaranteed by the Bank of England, for three months.[68]

67. The lower-quality bonds were mainly railroad bonds that banks held. At the time, banks' bond portfolios were marked to market value under examination rules. As railroad earnings fell, many railroad bonds became ineligible for bank portfolios. In anticipation of the ineligibility expected to occur when railroads released their 1931 earnings reports, the banks sold bonds, lowering their price. Bank examiners, using the market value of the bonds to value the bank's assets, found many banks insolvent. The minutes record that 222 banks were threatened with insolvency. Harrison favored methods of revaluing the bonds and changes in the examination procedures used by the state and the Comptroller of the Currency.

Harrison's response to the domestic banking crisis was very different from the response of Owen Young, one of his directors. At the August 10 meeting, Young noted that "the country looked to the Federal Reserve System and not to the Comptroller of the Currency to assume leadership in banking crises." His suggestion for a series of strong measures to assist the banks appears to have been ignored. On August 13, Harrison told his directors that "the events of the past year have made bank examiners much more critical and have brought to light weaknesses in management and in assets which previously were not so apparent."

Contrast with insurance companies suggests what might have been done. The National Association of Insurance Administrators agreed not to revalue the bonds in life insurance portfolios by the full decline in price if the bonds were not in default. As a result, many fewer insurance companies failed.

68. The Bank of France made an identical purchase, so in total the Bank of England received $250 million. Owen Young, a New York director, urged making a larger purchase. He argued that the larger the credit, the more effective it would be because announcement of a large credit would deter speculation. Harrison then talked to Meyer. Meyer doubted the Board would approve more than $125 million. He "thought that England's present difficulties were so fundamental that much of the help needed should be obtained through a Government loan in this market" (Minutes, New York Directors, July 30, 1931).

Table 5.13   OMPC Meeting, August 11, 1931

COMMERCIAL PAPER AND ACCEPTANCES	LOANS OF 101 WEEKLY REPORTING BANKS	GOLD STOCK	BORROWING	BILLS BOUGHT	GOVERNMENT SECURITIES	CURRENCY	MONETARY BASE	MONEY (M₁)
				Current Changes to July 31, 1931				
-$143	-$28	-$7	-$21	-$42	+$64	+$63	+$19	-$81
				Cumulative Changes from August 1929				
3.7%	-14.0%	+14.5%	-$874	-$45	+$19	3.5%	2.3%	-10.1%

BORROWING	EXCESS RESERVES	DISCOUNT RATE (N.Y. AND RANGE)	AAA RATES	AAA-ACCEPTANCES	BAA-AAA	WPI ALL ITEMS (1926=100)	WPI FARM (1926=100)	INDUSTRIAL PRODUCTION (AUGUST 1929=100)
				Levels as of July 1931				
$169	$124	1.5 (1.5–3.5)	4.40%	3.52%	3.07%	70	65	68.1

Note: Dollar amounts are millions.

Purchases resumed early in August. Harrison explained the August purchases by first noting that the banks in New York had held excess reserves of $60 million to $80 million during the past two months: "In the past few days, due to currency withdrawals and the action of the Bank of France in allowing Treasury bills and bankers bills to run off, this excess had been wiped out and the banks had been obliged to borrow at the Reserve bank from $40 to $80 million. . . . In view of this sudden and unusual change, and to avoid a disturbance to the money situation, the New York Reserve Bank had made purchases on August 10 and 11, for its own account, of $50 million of government securities."[69]

The Open Market Policy Conference held a lengthy discussion of open market policy. Harrison described the economic situation and talked of the prospect of economic, social, and political upheavals and of the high rate of unemployment expected in the winter. He introduced a motion to authorize the executive committee to buy up to $300 million "when they thought it was necessary," but he indicated that the time for purchases had not yet come because "the attitude of the banks and the investors was such that funds thus made available" would be held idle. Authority to purchase up to the larger amount was necessary he thought, because of the currency drains and the recent action of the Bank of France.[70] Calkins introduced an amendment reducing the authorization to $120 million, an amount equal to the estimated autumn seasonal. Harrison and Young (Boston) opposed the amendment, the latter because he opposed further purchases. The amended motion passed, Governor Young dissenting.

A preliminary memorandum prepared for the meeting explained that in the typical seasonal pattern currency reached a low point near the end of July. The memo noted that the increase in currency during the autumn months would be superimposed on the estimated hoarding, $500 million in currency, and that there would be further increases in the demand for currency. Harrison, Meyer, and Black wanted authority to offset the cur-

69. These purchases are not shown in table 5.13 because they came after the end of July. On August 6, Leslie Rounds reported on bank failures in the district. Owen Young asked: "Must we stand by and see these banks fail?" Harrison replied that "there is no alternative" (Minutes, New York Directors, August 6, 1931).

70. The memo prepared for the August 11 meeting refers to 166 bank failures in the country in June, the largest number since January. Total deposits in failed banks reached $218 million, the largest since December 1930. A table showed the number of suspended banks and their deposits from January 1930 through July 1931. The big months are November and December 1930, January and June 1931. Totals for 1930 were 273 and $865 million, and for 1931 through July, 773 and $498 million. The memo concluded, however, that financial difficulties abroad were more severe than the difficulties at home. The principal concerns abroad were the loss of $150 million in gold from the London market and the suspension of debt payments by South American countries.

rency drain and the seasonal movement if it developed. The other governors raised two related arguments, both of which were answered to no avail.

Governor Calkins argued that not all the reserve banks could participate in the purchase program, hence not all would benefit from the higher earnings if the System undertook large-scale purchases. Gold holdings were not distributed in the same proportion as the liabilities of the System, so not every bank had reserves to cover its share of the additional deposits and currency. The second argument was about the System's volume of "free gold." Governor Meyer presented a detailed analysis showing over $800 million of "free gold" was available and that the key problem was not gold but currency hoarding and bank failures.[71]

Once again the Board favored a more expansive policy than the Governors Conference. Meyer and other Board members expressed disappointment at the small volume of purchases authorized and urged the members to undertake an effective program of purchases. This discussion was in vain. Money market pressures did not increase during the month, the System's holdings of acceptances increased slightly, and the inflow of gold slowed. Despite the continued increase in currency held by the public, the System did not use its authority to purchase securities.

Although Harrison argued for a more expansive policy than the OMPC approved, he made it clear that he did not plan to put the purchase program into effect even if approved. His argument for standby authority is very

71. The Federal Reserve defined free gold in terms of the excess gold reserves of the reserve banks. Two definitions were sent to all the reserve banks in 1930. "Excess reserves: deduct from cash reserves the thirty-five percent required reserves against deposits and the forty percent against Federal reserve notes in circulation. Free gold: deduct from excess reserves the amount by which gold required as collateral against outstanding notes and for the Gold Redemption Fund exceeds forty percent of the notes in circulation."

On August 21, Harrison followed up Meyer's discussion of "free gold" in a letter to McDougal. With the letter, Harrison sent a memo showing the effect of $300 million in purchases on the ability of the System to maintain gold reserves sufficient for the additional note issue. The memo showed that after the purchase, there would be $600 million of "free gold" and that the amount could be increased to $900 million by reducing the amount of Federal Reserve notes issued but not in circulation. (These notes were held at reserve banks and could be canceled.) The memo argued that with the increased demand for currency, the banks would discount eligible paper that could replace gold as collateral for outstanding notes.

The "free gold" problem is similar to the problem the Bank of England periodically encountered during the nineteenth century. Friedman and Schwartz's useful discussion of the "free gold" problem in 1931–32 suggests that the problem had not been discussed before the thirties. Traditional central bank concern with the gold reserve ratio and with the effect of monetary expansion on the demand for currency shows that the issue was an old one. During the twenties, the Board used the "free gold" position to argue against expansion in 1928, and Burgess had discussed the "free gold" position in a published paper. For references to these discussions, see Harris 1933, 1:377–81. See also Friedman and Schwartz 1963, 399–406.

similar to the statements he made in his discussion with Governor Miller of the Board almost a year earlier. A program of purchases would not be effective, in his view, if it added to the excess reserves of the member banks. He did not see any prospect that reserves would be used to purchase securities or to expand credit, and he did not urge the executive committee to make the limited volume of purchases that the OMPC authorized.

Friedman and Schwartz gave considerable attention to this meeting. On their interpretation, Harrison desired a more expansive policy but was unable to convince the other members to support his position and therefore failed to carry out the expansive policy that Governor Strong would have followed had he lived. In fact, Governor Meyer made the case for expansion.[72] Harrison's statements at the meeting and his actions during the summer show little interest in an expansive policy. He told the other governors that he did not intend to undertake large-scale purchases based on the increased authority to purchase; he desired standby authority to offset the effect of larger than usual demands for currency and renewed gold flows that he expected because of the weakened position of many of the banks and the repeated crises in the markets for foreign currencies.

When Harrison discussed the OMPC report with the New York directors on August 20, he complained only about procedure. The Board and the OMPC had agreed to a procedure under which the Board approved a general program proposed by the governors, and the executive committee of the Governors Conference decided on the timing and amount of purchases or sales. This time the Board had not approved the program but had delegated to Governor Meyer the right to approve purchases (but not sales) recommended by the executive committee. Meyer was present in New York and replied that the OMPC had not presented a program. The Board would have approved a "real program" of purchases but was opposed to sales and did not approve the OMPC report because it permitted the executive committee to buy or sell at its own discretion without limit as to time. Harrison's complaints about the difficulty of obtaining the agreement of

---

72. Charles Hamlin, a member of the Board, testified about the August decision: "Governor Meyer . . . went before the committee for 2 hours explaining that under existing conditions nothing but a major stroke would help the situation, and perhaps that would not; but that it was vitally important that the System should make a bold stroke and buy, say, 300 millions or 400 millions of Government securities hoping that might turn the tide. For 2 hours he discussed the math with the governors. We then came together in a conference and we found, after their meeting by themselves, . . . [they] cut the power from $300,000,000 to $120,000,000. The $20,000,000 was an unexpended balance. . . . [This] naturally would destroy the effect because it would cease to be a major operation" (Senate Committee on Banking and Currency 1935, 945–46). In September Meyer told the New York directors they should raise interest rates but purchase securities to show that policy had not changed (Harrison Papers, Memorandum, September 3, 1931).

the other governors seem hollow in view of his failure to carry out or even recommend a regular program of monetary expansion.

Why did Harrison fail to press for purchases under the August decision? He told the executive committee of his directors on September 1 that he expected the seasonal requirements for credit to be small, but he anticipated a continued demand for currency. In keeping with Riefler-Burgess doctrine, he saw no advantage in making purchases unless an expansion of member bank credit would result; he had discussed the matter with bankers, and they indicated that any increase in excess reserves would remain idle. There would be no increase in real bills, hence no reason to provide reserves.

In fact, Federal Reserve credit increased $200 million during August as banks sold bills to obtain currency. Harrison at first favored purchases to offset any increase in market rates, but after listening to several directors argue that higher rates might be interpreted as a sign of recovery, he concluded—inconsistently—that "no action should be taken . . . to prevent such a seasonal firming of money rates."

At the next two directors' meetings, attention shifted to the prospects for selling the $50 million in securities that the New York bank had acquired early in August. Both Harrison and Meyer opposed the sale, fearing misinterpretation of any move toward tightness. Meyer added, "The opinion was being expressed by substantial people that the System had not taken sufficiently aggressive action to maintain the volume of credit as a support for the commodity price level," an indication of congressional attention that introduced a new element, fear of "inflationary legislation," into the Federal Reserve's discussions during the winter of 1932.

FROM THE BRITISH DEVALUATION TO THE BANKING HOLIDAY

Two years had passed since the cyclical peak, but the end of the decline was not in sight. Two events were about to happen that permanently changed beliefs and attitudes. First came the British decision to leave the gold standard. In less than two years, most gold standard countries followed.[73] In retrospect, these decisions led a majority of the public, economists, and eventually central bankers to reconsider the alleged virtues of the gold standard, by first questioning the gold exchange standard and later the gold standard in its various forms.

73. The British Empire and all British dominions except South Africa followed Britain. Three Scandinavian countries also suspended gold payments immediately. By the end of the year, they were joined by Portugal, Egypt, Bolivia, Finland, and Japan. Several South American countries had suspended gold payments in 1929 and 1930.

Second, in many countries, including the United States, government took more responsibility for managing the economy through regulation and controls. In the United States the first steps came within a few weeks of the British devaluation. Concerned about a renewed wave of bank failures, President Hoover pressed for the formation of a public-private partnership, the National Credit Corporation, to support the banks by supporting the bond market. This was a forerunner of the Reconstruction Finance Corporation.

Britain Leaves the Gold Standard

Britain had remained on the gold standard for most of the preceding two hundred years. The Bank of England had suspended specie payments in crises but had always returned to convertibility at the former gold price. After the Napoleonic Wars and again after World War I, the government and the bank engineered socially costly deflations to restore gold parity. The decision to suspend gold payments and allow the pound to float was therefore a climactic event for Britain and, given Britain's important international role in lending and borrowing, a major event for the world economy.

Conventional opinion at the time criticized the government and the bank for offering only a weak defense. Bank rate had remained at 4.5 percent. In many previous crises the bank had raised the discount rate to 10 percent to attract gold.[74] Many of these comments reflected the prevailing orthodoxy—suspension was evidence of failure to follow proper policies. The freedom to end deflation, gained by suspension, represented the choice of inflation over sound, proper policies.[75]

Although the Bank of England did not raise its discount rate, Britain had not been idle. The British announcement on September 20 came after six months of recurrent payments difficulties that started in Austria and Hungary, then shifted to Germany and later to London. Resort to exchange controls and blocked balances on the Continent increased the magnitude of the problem confronting the Bank of England by freezing British balances abroad.

74. Harrison reported a comment by officers of the Bank of France, who described "tremendous feeling in Paris" against the weak British action (Harrison Papers, Memoranda, September 3, 1931); memo, Consequences of the British Suspension of Gold Payments, Minutes, New York Directors, October 15, 1931). There was no mention of the severe deflation or the very high real interest rate then in effect.

75. Kindleberger (1986, tables 12 and 19) permits comparison of the depreciation of the pound (relative to the French franc) and the change in French and British prices as recorded during this period. Between August and December, the pound exchange rate in France fell 31 percent, and British prices rose 37 percent relative to French prices. These data suggest that Britain did not "beggar its neighbor." It was able to lower its interest rate and stop deflation.

During the two months from July 23 to September 19, Britain paid out $972 million of reserves. To finance the reserve loss, the Bank of England borrowed $650 million in New York and Paris during July and September. The Federal Reserve, with the approval of the Board, agreed to lend $125 million on July 30, and the Bank of France lent a similar amount. Throughout August and into September, Harrison negotiated with the Bank of France and acted as intermediary for the Bank of England with the New York bankers to find a set of terms for a one-year private loan (Clarke 1967, 201–8).

The Federal Reserve's assistance to the Bank of England and its earlier assistance to the Austrian, German, and Hungarian central banks showed an ability to respond promptly to events it understood.[76] Treasury Secretary Andrew Mellon, who served ex officio as chairman of the Federal Reserve, at first opposed aid to European banks, but he changed his views as the crisis spread from Austria and Hungary to Germany (Todd 1994, 8). Perhaps as a result, policy toward international and domestic troubled banks differed markedly. Harrison and other central bankers lent money to support Credit Anstalt, a private Austrian bank. Under the leadership of Gates McGarrah, a former chairman of the New York bank who had become president of the Bank for International Settlements, central banks in June had made available a second $14 million credit to the Austrian National Bank contingent on an agreement by the Austrian government to negotiate a $21 million, two- to three-year foreign loan to strengthen the position of Credit Anstalt. Yet the Federal Reserve was unwilling to take any new steps to prevent the failure of United States banks.

The Federal Reserve's first response to the international monetary crisis was to raise the buying rate on acceptances to 1.25 percent on September 25 and to purchase $14 million in the open market. On October 8 the New York directors approved an increase in the discount rate of 1 percent (to 2.5 percent).[77]

Harrison gave two reasons. First was the gold export. Second was his

76. Harrison remained cautious toward countries with structural problems. "Governor Harrison raised the question as to what this bank could best do. . . . He expressed the opinion that this bank should not dissipate its resources by making loans to various countries to help them stay on the gold standard when it appeared doubtful whether such loans would be adequate for the purpose" (Consequence of the British Suspension of Gold Payments, Minutes, New York Directors, September 24, 1931). The countries mentioned are Uruguay, Bolivia, and Colombia. These central banks needed more than short-term credits so, Harrison said, they should borrow from commercial banks.

77. A comparison of the loans made to the United Kingdom in the weeks before suspension and open market operations casts doubt on Eichengreen's argument about lack of cooperation. In July the Federal Reserve and the Bank of France each lent £25 million (approximately $120 million). Later J. P. Morgan and a French bank each lent $200 million additional,

conversation with Governor Clement Moret of the Bank of France. Moret complained that rates were too low; this contributed to a lack of confidence.[78] Harrison explicitly dismissed a shortage of "free gold," the argument subsequently used by Federal Reserve officials to explain policy inaction. He "pointed out that the amount of free gold held by the System had not been materially affected by the recent loss of gold, so that there was still considerable leeway for purchases of Government securities (Discount Rate Advance, Minutes, New York Directors, October 8, 1931). A week later the bank set the rate at 3.5 percent and the System sold the purchased securities.[79] Before the second increase, New York's rate had been the lowest in the System. Once New York put its rate at 3.5 percent, the other reserve banks followed. Table 5.14 shows some of the principal money market changes during the period.

The Federal Reserve responded to the gold outflow by increasing interest rates. It ignored the currency drain and the banking failures. Again, a main reason for the difference is that the gold stock fell, market interest rates rose, and the money market indicators the governors relied on revealed the changes accompanying the gold and currency movements. As table 5.14 shows and as Harrison's comment made clear, market interest rates rose slowly at first. Not until late October did the market rate on banker's acceptances rise above the posted acceptance rate. The increase in the market rate forced the System to buy bills or raise its buying rate.

Start of the Reconstruction Finance Corporation

Alarmed by spreading failures and continued declines, President Hoover called a meeting of nineteen bankers at Secretary Mellon's apartment in Washington on October 4 to discuss steps that might be taken to prevent bank failures. A memo read at the meeting noted that 1,215 banks with $967 million in deposits had failed in the first nine months of the year, most of them during the summer. The memo interpreted these and other data on currency hoarding and bank failures as showing that bankers and the public had lost confidence in the banking system. Then Hoover's memo continued: "Prior to the establishment of the Federal Reserve Bank System, it [the banks' demand for liquidity] would probably have been met

---

a total of $640 million. Federal Reserve open market purchases for the two years following the August 1929 peak were only $519 million (table 5.13).

78. From England, W. Randolph Burgess cabled recommending against any action to increase rates. Harrison read the cable to the directors, but it had no effect.

79. Meyer was at the meeting. He said that "the advance in the rate was called for by every known rule, and believed foreigners would regard it as lack of courage if the rate were not advanced. . . . [H]e did not see how it could affect depositors in this country" (Discount Rate Advance, Minutes, New York Directors, October 15, 1931, 2).

Table 5.14   Money Market Variables and Changes in Gold and Currency,
Weekly September–October 1931

| | FEDERAL RESERVE BANK OF NEW YORK | | | | TOTAL FEDERAL RESERVE SYSTEM | | |
WEEK ENDING	DISCOUNT RATE (%)	ACCEPTANCE RATE (%)	MARKET RATE ON PRIME ACCEPTANCES (%)	WEEK ENDING	DISCOUNTS	BILLS BOUGHT	GOLD OUTFLOW PLUS CURRENCY DRAIN
9/26	1.50	1.25	1.06	9/23	+$47	+$25	+$186
10/3	1.50	1.25	1.25	9/30	+23	+226	+238
10/10	2.50	1.75	1.25	10/7	+135	+112	+284
10/17	3.50	3.12	2.75	10/14	+160	+149	+260
10/24	3.50	3.12	3.25	10/21	+70	+39	+119
10/31	3.50	3.12	3.25	10/28	+19	−44	+24
				Total	$454	$507	$1,111

Source: Board of Governors of the Federal Reserve System 1943.
Note: Dollar amounts are millions.

through the relationship between the banks in the principal centers and their out of town correspondents, but, with the establishment of the Federal Reserve System, there grew up a tendency to feel that it was to the Federal Reserve System rather than to the banks in central reserve cities that all other banks should look" (Harrison Papers, Miscellaneous Letters and Reports). President Hoover then proposed a central organization, the National Credit Corporation (NCC), to rediscount assets not legally eligible for discount at the Federal Reserve banks and purchase marketable assets of insolvent banks.[80] To provide capital, commercial banks would subscribe $500 million. The corporation would have the power to borrow an additional $1 billion.

The New York clearinghouse bankers agreed on the following day to subscribe $150 million of the $500 million. Harrison notified the president on October 7 that "there was quite general and enthusiastic support

---

80. Railroad bonds posed the main problem. During the 1920s, small banks with insufficient local loan demand bought railroad bonds to increase earnings. Also, many banks invested savings deposits in bonds (CHFRS, Rounds, May 2, 1944, 20). Interest payments became uncertain as railroad earnings declined, so bond prices fell. Examiners priced the bonds according to a scale based on bond ratings. If the average (dollar weighted) rating fell below 80 (a BBB bond), the bank could be declared insolvent (ibid.). The examiner closed the bank and sold the bonds, depressing their prices. At the October 4 meeting, Harrison proposed raising freight rates to increase earnings. President Hoover dismissed that proposal as not likely to help. Railroad unions opposed wage reductions on the grounds that employed workers contributed 20 percent of their income for relief of unemployed members. The president then suggested that the NCC buy bonds from solvent but illiquid banks and pay depositors of insolvent banks. He proposed also making NCC obligations eligible for discount at the reserve banks and increasing the capital of the Farm Loan banks (Minutes, New York Directors, October 5, 1931).

throughout New York for your proposal, not merely to the formation of a $500 million corporation but also to the enlargement of the rediscount facilities of the Reserve System." Support in the Federal Reserve was more restrained. Harrison's report on Hoover's proposal to the executive committee of his directors on October 5 mentions his own proposal to increase the market value of railroad bonds by raising railroad freight rates or reducing railroad wages but does not record his opposition to broader lending powers for Federal Reserve banks. However, he had made his opposition to such proposals clear on October 1, and at an October 26 meeting he firmly opposed any plan that allowed Federal Reserve banks to acquire assets that were not self-liquidating (Harrison Papers, Miscellaneous Letters and Reports, October 5, 1931). The NCC was organized without a Federal Reserve commitment.[81]

Hoover proposed the NCC as a temporary measure during the emergency.[82] Once Congress reconvened in December, he intended to ask it to broaden the powers of the Federal Reserve to discount paper secured by government securities (Hoover 1952, 84–88). In January Congress passed the Reconstruction Finance Corporation Act, and in February it extended Federal Reserve powers to discount in the first Glass-Steagall Act.[83] The Treasury provided $500 million as capital for the Reconstruction Finance Corporation. The RFC could borrow $1.5 billion either from the Treasury or from private sources. In July 1932 Congress increased the borrowing line to $3 billion.

Return to Inaction

Monetary and economic conditions deteriorated considerably between the July OMPC meeting and the executive committee meeting on October 26

81. Todd (1994, 11–13) reports that Eugene Meyer was one of the principal proponents of the NCC and later of the Reconstruction Finance Corporation. Todd credits Meyer with obtaining the support of the commercial bankers. Meyer became chairman of the new organization while remaining governor of the Board. The only other instance of a Federal Reserve chairman accepting an administration position while remaining chairman came with Arthur Burns in the 1970s.

82. The NCC advanced only $15 million between October and mid-December, an inconsequential amount in relation to the shrinkage of capital values (see table 5.17, p. 352) The data on advances are from a cable Harrison sent to Governor Moret of the Bank of France. The French feared that Congress was about to pass "inflationary legislation." The cable restates Harrison's opposition to making obligations of the National Credit Corporation or the proposed Reconstruction Finance Corporation eligible for discount at the reserve banks.

83. Hoover's report of the meeting with congressional leaders recalls a past era. "The group seemed stunned. Only Garner [Speaker of the House] and Borah [Senate majority leader] voiced approval. The others seemed shocked at the revelation that our government for the first time in peacetime history might have to intervene to support private enterprise" (Hoover 1952, 90, as quoted in Todd 1995, 7).

(table 5.15). Industrial production fell 12 percent, the index of stock prices more than 25 percent. Bank loans and money also fell by $1 billion. The risk spread was one percentage point higher than in July as bank failures and the currency drain returned.

In the five weeks following the British suspension, new member bank borrowing offset 85 percent of the direct effect of the gold outflow. Although the OMPC had approved purchases of up to $120 million, Harrison saw no reason to undertake any large volume of purchases, and none was made. McDougal, supported by a telegram from Calkins, favored sales.

The preliminary memorandum prepared for the October 26 meeting and the minutes of the meeting pay far less attention to the British decision than to the renewed bank failures and currency "hoarding." Harrison noted that four hundred banks closed during the first three weeks of October. Banking problems are described as "the most important" problems facing the System, and the preliminary memorandum suggested that all actions be considered in terms of their effect on bank failures.[84]

What action was appropriate? The consensus of the meeting was that "everything should be done to persuade the (city) banks to adopt a liberal policy" of lending to banks in difficulty and rediscounting at the Federal Reserve banks. Despite the references to bank failures in the minutes, the Federal Reserve gave less assistance to the banking system than it had arranged for the Bank of England. Nor did it contribute the type of support for the commercial banks that it and other central bankers had urged the Austrian government to give to Credit Anstalt.

Within a month, the Federal Reserve allowed acceptances to run off. The preliminary memorandum prepared for the November meeting conveyed the sense of satisfaction about the System's response to the "largest gold export . . . and a heavy domestic withdrawal of currency continuing a movement of almost a year's duration." The memorandum described the response as "classic" and, to reinforce the point, quoted heavily from Bagehot. By lending freely at an increased discount rate, the System had followed Bagehot's advice for central banks confronting a crisis. The preliminary memorandum referred to the fact that Federal Reserve credit had expanded by $1 billion during the weeks of the crisis. The maximum amount outstanding, more than $2 billion in the week ending October 14, was the largest total in more than ten years, and the rate of increase—doubling in less than two months—was the largest change in Federal

---

84. Harrison explained that the receivers of closed banks liquidate marketable assets quickly, depressing the bond market. The Comptroller had proposed that certificates backed by the assets of closed banks be eligible for rediscount. Harrison opposed because the assets were not self-liquidating (memo, Executive Committee, Minutes, OMPC, October 26, 1931).

Table 5.15 Meeting, Executive Committee, October 26, 1931

COMMERCIAL PAPER AND ACCEPTANCES	LOANS OF 101 WEEKLY REPORTING BANKS	GOLD STOCK	BORROWING	BILLS BOUGHT	GOVERNMENT SECURITIES	CURRENCY	MONETARY BASE	MONEY (M_1)
			Current Changes to October 31, 1931					
-$270	-$945	-$657	+$445	+$613	+$59*	$479	$249	-$1,092
-14.6%	-19.6%	-1.6%				+15.8%	5.8%	-14.2%
			Cumulative Changes from August 1929					
			-$429	+$568	+$578			

BORROWING	EXCESS RESERVES	DISCOUNT RATE (N.Y. AND RANGE)	AAA RATES	AAA-ACCEPTANCES	BAA-AAA	WPI ALL ITEMS (1926 = 100)	WPI FARM (1926 = 100)	INDUSTRIAL PRODUCTION (AUGUST 1929 = 100)
					Levels as of October 1931			
$614	$129	3.5 (3-4)	4.99%	2.74%	4.05%	70	59	60.3

Note: Dollar amounts are millions.
*Purchases were made during the first two weeks of August, none thereafter.

Table 5.16 OMPC Meeting, November 30, 1931

COMMERCIAL PAPER AND ACCEPTANCES	LOANS OF 101 WEEKLY REPORTING BANKS	GOLD STOCK	BORROWING	BILLS BOUGHT	GOVERNMENT SECURITIES	CURRENCY	MONETARY BASE	MONEY (M_1)
			Current Changes to November 30, 1931					
-$75	-$205	+$122	+$81	-$132	-$6	-$34	-$112	-$355
-19.8%	-20.8%	+1.3%				14.9%	4.2%	-15.5%
			Cumulative Changes from August 1929					
			-$348	+$436	+$572			

BORROWING	EXCESS RESERVES	DISCOUNT RATE (N.Y. AND RANGE)	AAA RATES	AAA-ACCEPTANCES	BAA-AAA	WPI ALL ITEMS (1926 = 100)	WPI FARM (1926 = 100)	INDUSTRIAL PRODUCTION (AUGUST 1929 = 100)
					Levels as of November 1931			
$695	$57	3.5 (3.5-4)	4.94%	1.78%	3.99%	70	59	59.5

Note: Dollar amounts are millions.

Reserve credit in any two-month period up to that time. Bank failures and currency movements received little attention.

The immediate crisis had passed without reliance on open market purchases, and the governors expressed little interest in a purchase program during the following months. Miller's suggestion that they start a bold program received very little support. The data on member bank borrowing show that at last an increase in real bills could be used to justify open market purchases. Harrison argued for delay, although he recognized that the volume of borrowing had increased substantially and expected the New York banks to borrow heavily during December. Others saw no reason to keep New York and Chicago banks out of debt.

The OMPC gave the executive committee authority to purchase up to $200 million in securities during December to be sold after the start of the year. Clearly intended as a seasonal adjustment, the authority was used in precisely that way. The weekly figures show changes ranging from +$200 million to –$150 million during December and early January and a net increase of less than $50 million during the month.

Why was the increased borrowing ignored? Harrison made his position clear at meetings with his directors in November and December. His first argument opposed purchases because the gold flow had reversed. Gold had come into the country during November, but the reduction in Federal Reserve credit exceeded the gain in gold mainly because acceptances had run off and had not been replaced. This showed "disinclination on the part of member banks to use Federal Reserve credit for the purpose of extending credit to their customers." Several of the directors urged purchases; Owen Young pointed out that it was the end of the year and a "bad time to impose any further load of indebtedness on member banks." Harrison dismissed this argument, and when Young persisted in urging purchases, Harrison offered a whole catalog of arguments purporting to show that the purchases would be badly timed and would do no good.

A month later, on December 24, Harrison showed the directors a chart of the relation between bank credit, business activity, and the price level. Based on past relations, he predicted a further deflation and "commented on the serious aspects of any further deflation of prices." Still, he urged no purchases because of the "present free gold position and the potential demands which may be made on us at home and abroad." Some of the directors pointed out that the New York City bankers were almost unanimous in opposing purchases. After a brief discussion, the directors agreed to wait until after the first of the year and to observe the progress of the bill to replace the privately financed National Credit Corporation with a publicly financed Reconstruction Finance Corporation (RFC).

Again, Harrison's discussion shows that he knew the crisis had deepened. He referred to the decline in bank credit as the largest in the history of the country and reported that his staff had estimated its size at $5 billion in the first two years of contraction. Further, he noted that the rate of decline had increased during the fall.[85] He was aware, also, that the effect of a further decline would be a further contraction in business activity and further deflation, and he discussed these problems with his directors. Moreover, he had received a confidential memo in early December showing the position of the banks in the New York Federal Reserve district (Harrison Papers, Memoranda, December 24, 1931). Table 5.17, taken from the memo, points up that he knew, in considerable detail, how much the position of the banking system had deteriorated between November and the first week of December. However, yields on lower-rated bonds increased during the autumn, as shown by the yield spread in table 5.16. The estimated "shrinkage" of capital funds in table 5.17 is the amount the banks lost mainly as a result of the decline in the market value of their bond portfolios. The memo notes that 300 of the approximately 800 banks had losses nearly equal to their capital funds and that an additional 150 to 200 had some capital impairment. The table included all banks in the New York district except 23 money market banks.

On January 4, Harrison again discussed purchases with his directors. He believed the time had come for the Federal Reserve to consider substantial purchases of government bonds: "His only hesitation in recommending such a program . . . [was] . . . the relatively small amount of 'free gold'" (Minutes, New York Directors, January 4, 1932).[86] Congress was considering legislation that would permit the Federal Reserve to pledge all of its assets as collateral for the note issue. Once the legislation passed, it would be able to supplement the legislative program by taking action in the open market.

One of the directors (Clarence M. Woolley) asked Harrison whether there was nothing that so great an organization could do to stem the tide of disaster. He was not satisfied with the usual answer that the banks would not make use of the reserves created by the purchase of government securities. Harrison pointed to the "free gold" position. "We must," said Harrison, "be

---

85. *Banking and Monetary Statistics* (Board of Governors of the Federal Reserve System 1943) shows the decline at weekly reporting banks as more than $3.7 billion (20 percent) from August 1929 to December 1931 and an additional $374 million (20 percent) in commercial paper and acceptances. Call reports show nearly $7 billion (26 percent) decline in total loans at all member banks from October 4, 1929, to December 31, 1931. Weekly reporting banks gained relatively, no doubt influenced by fewer failures.

86. Harrison later revised this view. See below.

Table 5.17   Capital Shrinkage, New York Federal Reserve District

CLASS	NUMBER OF BANKS	DEPOSITS	CAPITAL AND SURPLUS	SHRINKAGE OF CAPITAL ON THE DATE OF EXAMINATION (NOVEMBER–DECEMBER 1931)	SHRINKAGE AS OF DECEMBER 7, 1931
I	245	1,192	226	26	125
2	245	943	167	47	126
3	174	687	123	60	117
4	89	352	60	47	77
5	83	176	22	30	44

Source: Harrison Papers, Memoranda, December 1931. Excludes money market banks.
Note: Dollar amounts are millions.

on relatively safe ground before we embark on a program of government security purchases, which is not the case at the moment when banks are failing by the score, the renewal of currency hoarding is a probability, and substantial gold withdrawals by foreign holders of dollars are quite possible."

The directors did not accept Harrison's answer. But Harrison held firm and urged delay so that actions could be synchronized with the passage of Reconstruction Finance Corporation legislation (passed at the end of January), the (downward) adjustment of railroad wages, and other pending changes. Then they could reduce the discount rate to encourage borrowing and begin open market operations.

Delay during the fall allowed a large part of the banking system to fail. In two months, September and October 1931, the deposits of suspended banks rose to $705 million, as much as in the entire year 1932 yet to come. Nearly 30 percent of the bank suspensions between August 1929 and February 1933 came in the last four months of 1931.

Member bank borrowing had fallen at the time of the January meeting from the seasonal peak at the end of December, and short-term open market rates had fallen also. As borrowing fell, the Federal Reserve sold some of the securities acquired in December. The amount of borrowed reserves and market rates on both short- and long-term securities remained high relative to the recent past. The money stock continued to decline, reflecting the additional increase in demand for currency and the contractive policy of the Federal Reserve.

In the six months between June and December 1931, the money stock fell about 6 percent and industrial production about 14 percent. The risk premium on bonds rose nearly four percentage points above their level at the peak of the expansion in 1929, and even rates on Aaa bonds were above the August 1929 level. With wholesale prices 11 percent below the December 1930 level, real yields on Baa bonds were above 20 percent. The risk spread was above five percentage points.

Table 5.18   OMPC Meeting, January 11, 1932

COMMERCIAL PAPER AND ACCEPTANCES	LOANS OF 101 WEEKLY REPORTING BANKS	GOLD STOCK	BORROWING	BILLS BOUGHT	GOVERNMENT SECURITIES	CURRENCY	MONETARY BASE	MONEY (M_1)
				Current Changes to December 31, 1931				
–$84	–$241	+$46	+$79	–$220	+$50	+$101	+$277	–$461
				Cumulative Changes from August 1929				
–25.5%	–22.2%	+2.4%	–$269	+$216	+$622	+17.5%	+8.1%	–17.2%

BORROWING	EXCESS RESERVES	DISCOUNT RATE (N.Y. AND RANGE)	AAA RATES	AAA-ACCEPTANCES	BAA-AAA	WPI ALL ITEMS (1926 = 100)	WPI FARM (1926 = 100)	INDUSTRIAL PRODUCTION (AUGUST 1929 = 100)
				Levels as of December 1931				
$774	$60	3.5 (3.5–4)	5.32%	2.32%	5.10%	69	56	59.0

Note: Dollar amounts are millions.

The gold outflow stopped in November and reversed in December. The Open Market Policy Conference decided that the time had come for a reduction in bill rates and in discount rates. Much of the discussion at the meeting concerned the government's budget and the desirability of a balanced budget as a means of reducing pressure on market interest rates. The members apparently continued to favor a reduction in member bank borrowing brought about by a continuation of gold inflows. They hoped the currency drain would reverse.

Despite his statements at the directors' meetings earlier in the month, Harrison neither urged open market purchases on the other governors nor advocated any other expansive action. Nor did he urge the directors to reduce the discount rate when he returned to New York. When two of the directors, Clarence M. Woolley and Theodore F. Whitmarsh, pressed for immediate action at the January 14 meeting, Harrison advocated caution and delay. Again, on January 21, Whitmarsh urged Harrison to reduce the discount rate, and again Harrison urged delay and caution. The following week Owen Young joined Whitmarsh and Woolley in urging Harrison to take some expansive action, but Harrison pointed to the "free gold" position as a reason for delay. Young was not deterred and pressed Harrison to purchase $50 million while maintaining the discount rate unchanged to stem any outflow of gold. The only concessions Harrison made were an agreement that purchases would be considered in an emergency and that a change in the discount rate would be reconsidered the following week. At the next meeting, February 4, the gold outflow had stopped temporarily, and the "foreign situation" was no longer an excuse for inaction. Harrison now cited a "bad banking situation on the Pacific Coast" as a reason for delaying any decision to reduce the discount rate.

At each weekly meeting with his directors, Harrison urged delay. Before Congress passed the RFC legislation, he argued for an expansive program to accompany congressional approval of the RFC. Later he wanted to wait for the Glass-Steagall Act, or similar legislation removing the restrictions on the assets eligible for discount and the use of government securities as collateral for the note issue. Once such legislation appeared likely to pass, he favored delay because the proposed legislation might alarm foreigners. When Owen Young pointed out that Harrison had offered a variety of reasons for postponing action and urged an end to the "ruinous" decline in bank credit, Harrison modified his position and agreed that, once the Glass-Steagall Act passed, they could both reduce the discount rate and buy government securities.

Free Gold

One of the reasons given for delay was that the System either lacked free gold or was at risk of doing so.[87] The Board made this argument in its 1932 annual report, and Goldenweiser (1951), Thomas (1941), Burgess (1964), and other Federal Reserve officials used the argument later to explain delay and inaction.[88] As noted earlier, Eichengreen (1992) accepted the System's argument, but Friedman and Schwartz (1963) rejected it. The next two sections present the case for and against the importance of free gold as a reason for delaying open market purchases.

THE CASE FOR FREE GOLD Harrison cited the free gold position several times in the four months between the British suspension and the passage in February 1932 of the Glass-Steagall Act, removing the free gold problem. Most of these citations are in months with relatively large gold outflows, October 1931 and January 1932.[89] Taken alone, these statements support the Federal Reserve's explanation of its inaction.

With the benefit of hindsight, Harrison rejected the argument he made at the time. A year later he told Gates McGarrah that when the Glass-Steagall Act passed, the System "had around $350 million of excess gold; that even if there had been a further drain, the $350 million did not represent the maximum of our capacity to export gold since additional borrowings would have been forced upon the banks which would have given us

87. Free gold was the amount of gold held by reserve banks that was not required as a reserve against outstanding base money. Note issues required 40 percent gold and 60 percent eligible paper as backing. In addition, reserve banks had to hold 5 percent of the difference between notes outstanding and notes in circulation (Harris 1933, 2:770). The decline in borrowing and the rise in currency more than exhausted the stock of eligible paper, so reserve banks substituted gold as backing. This reduced free gold. As noted earlier, each reserve bank met the requirement from its own resources (but could borrow gold from other banks). For the System, the ratio on February 28, 1932, was 71 percent, implying free gold of about $300 million. This number is approximate because each reserve bank had its own free gold. As noted in the text below, Federal Reserve banks could have increased the amount by canceling notes in their vaults.

88. Thomas's statement is ambiguous (1941, 33): "Had the Reserve banks bought Government securities . . . then it would have been necessary to substitute gold as collateral, and there might not have been sufficient gold."

89. Harrison Papers, Open Market, October 5, 1931: "He considered the gold position of the System paramount at this time, and on that account would not be inclined to purchase government securities." Ibid., January 4, 1932: "His only hesitancy in recommending such a program at the moment, he said, was on account of the relatively small amount of free gold." January 28, 1932: Governor Harrison pointed out that our free gold position must still be considered in relation to further purchases of Government securities." All references are to Harrison's statements to the New York directors.

additional collateral which would have released gold"[90] (Harrison Papers, Confidential Files, Telephone Conversation with Mr. McGarrah, October 10, 1932).

To reconcile these contradictory statements, note that Harrison made the last statement months after the event. His expressions of concern about free gold came when the gold outflow was large, and no one could predict how long the outflow would last or how large it would be. These were real concerns at the time. Between late September and late February, the Federal Reserve's gold stock declined by 8.7 percent, reversing the entire inflow received since the August 1929 peak.

The free gold problem affected New York, Chicago, Boston, and Philadelphia. By November 1931, reserve banks in Richmond, Atlanta, Dallas, Minneapolis, and Kansas City together had sold almost $50 million of securities to other reserve banks to meet gold reserve requirements.[91] In addition, several of the regional banks stopped participating in the System's acceptance (bill) purchases, thereby shifting purchases to the other reserve banks.

THE CASE AGAINST FREE GOLD   Section 10c of the Federal Reserve Act permitted the Board to suspend any reserve requirement for thirty days followed by an additional fifteen days if needed. Suspension of the gold reserve against note issues required the reserve bank to pay a small tax; for reductions from 40 to 32.5 percent, the tax rate was 1.5 percent. Miller (1925a) referred to this provision.

This was not the only recourse. The System could have reduced the discount rate on acceptances to increase its holdings of the $1 billion of acceptances outstanding in November 1931 (Board of Governors of the Federal Reserve System 1943, 465). It could have canceled currency in its vaults to save a 5 percent gold reserve against unissued notes. It could have speeded the return of notes issued by other reserve banks.[92] It could have issued other currency not subject to a gold reserve. It could have asked Congress to suspend gold reserve requirements, as Britain often did in the nineteenth century.

More important, free gold can explain inaction for only a very short pe-

90. The commercial banks would lose reserves, so they would borrow from the reserve banks, increasing eligible paper (real bills).

91. New York took more than half of the acceptances. Its relative size was about 30 percent at the time.

92. Until 1954, a reserve bank paid a tax for reissuing notes of other reserve banks, so it returned these notes. The notes in transit were considered outstanding, thus subject to the 40 percent gold reserve requirement and, under prevailing conditions, the substitution of gold for eligible paper.

riod, October 1931 to March 1932. The Federal Reserve had ample gold to support expansion before the British suspension, and the constraint was not binding after February. Further, the Federal Reserve did not find it necessary to invoke the Glass-Steagall Act when it began large-scale purchases in March.

Did the free gold problem delay open market purchases? The answer is certainly yes. Harrison gave several reasons for delay, and several governors opposed purchases generally, so the System might have delayed in any case. Nevertheless, the many references to free gold as a reason for delay, and the initiation of purchases as soon as the Glass-Steagall Act passed, support the case if only in the limited sense that passage of Glass-Steagall put the administration and Congress, including Senator Carter Glass, on record as favoring purchases. The System could not ignore the message in this action.[93]

THE 1932 PURCHASE PROGRAM

Passage of Glass-Steagall temporarily suspended the collateral requirement for notes by permitting reserve banks to substitute government securities for commercial paper or real bills.[94] Though intended to be temporary, this was a major retreat from the principles underlying the Federal Reserve Act. Passage of the 1932 legislation recognized that the real bills doctrine did not provide the flexibility (elasticity) to expand the note issue or prevent the crisis from deepening.[95]

Despite worsening business and financial conditions, only two banks reduced discount rates between the meetings on January 11 and February 24. In late January, Richmond and Dallas lowered their rates from 4 percent to 3.5 percent. The system took no other expansive action despite a 20 percent decline in loans of member banks, a 35 percent decline in open market paper outstanding, and a 15 percent increase in the public's currency holdings during the last six months of 1931. The buying rate on acceptances remained below the market rate, so the bill portfolio declined.

93. Harrison gave three reasons for not using the authority to purchase that had been agreed on at the January OMPC meeting: "various elements in the domestic situation had developed more slowly than had been anticipated, . . . gold withdrawals to Europe, and . . . the limited amount of free gold held by the System" (Harrison Papers, Open Market, February 24, 1932).

94. Congress renewed the temporary provision several times before making it permanent.

95. Glass recognized what had happened. He told Burgess: "You tell George Harrison that I am now just a corn-tassel Greenbacker" (Burgess 1964, 226). The act was prepared mainly by Walter Wyatt, the Board's general counsel.

The Glass-Steagall Act

The Glass-Steagall Act relaxed Federal Reserve collateral requirements in three ways. First, government securities became eligible as collateral for note issues, as discussed previously. Second, reserve banks could lend on previously ineligible commercial paper at a rate 1 percent above the discount rate. This provision permitted banks to borrow against a much broader range of assets. Third, groups of five or more banks could borrow on the group's credit. This provision permitted clearinghouses to borrow directly and encouraged the formation of county clearinghouses in rural areas.

Exchange rates and bond yields responded almost at once to the new provisions and the start of the RFC. The dollar weakened against the pound, falling 5 percent between December and February and an additional 8 percent by its trough in April. Yields on government bonds rose between December and February, but yields on corporate bonds fell, particularly on lower-rated bonds, as perceived risks declined. Both changes suggest that markets interpreted the change as a less deflationary policy.

Glass-Steagall was a temporary change, scheduled to last a year. Several New York directors criticized the one-year limit. Some noted that if the gold outflow continued, the System would be in crisis at year end, unable to replace government securities with gold or commercial paper. Harrison responded that he hoped hoarded currency would return to the banks, releasing gold reserves (Minutes, New York Directors, February 11, 1932).

Permitting banks to borrow on ineligible paper alarmed the governors: "A number of governors pointed out the dangers in the Federal Reserve System's becoming loaded down with loans of this sort" (Governors Conference, February 24, 1932, 2). Talk shifted to ways of limiting the volume of ineligible paper. Governor Meyer suggested a 5.5 percent rate, the rate charged by the RFC (4); Governor Black (Atlanta) warned against thwarting the will of Congress.

Purchases Begin

By the time the Open Market Policy Conference met late in February, it had become clear that neither a decline in the demand for currency nor an inflow of gold could be counted on to reduce the level of member bank borrowing and short-term market interest rates. As table 5.19 shows, gold flowed out during January and February, and the demand for currency again increased. In fact Harrison told the members of the OMPC to expect additional reductions in the gold stock of about $50 million a month. Further, he thought "it seemed unnecessary for the banking position to be subjected to severe strain" because of the hoarding of currency. The Glass-Steagall Act, which Congress was about to pass, gave them the power "to purchase government securities to relieve the banks of some of their indebtedness to the Reserve banks."

As on most previous occasions, the OMPC followed Harrison's recommendation. By a vote of ten to two, it approved purchases of $250 million; the executive committee, three to two, authorized purchases at the rate of $25 million a week. The Board approved immediately. The magnitude of the operation, though small compared with the decline in money, bank loans, output, or prices, should not be underrated. At the time the decision was taken, the Federal Reserve held $741 million in securities, so the decision permitted the System's security holding to increase by one-third. The addition to the security portfolio during the next few weeks was equal to 50 percent of the securities purchased during the two and one-half years since the August 1929 peak in economic activity.

Many of the banks that voted to purchase did not take part in the program. Only four banks—New York, Philadelphia, Cleveland, and Kansas City—participated in the initial purchases, with New York taking 80 percent of the first $70 million.[96] Some banks had sold part of their portfolio to others, but Chicago and Boston did not participate because they opposed purchases. James B. McDougal (Chicago) said the new legislation encouraged borrowing, so there was no reason for purchases. George W. Norris (Philadelphia) preferred to wait until "all serious troubles are behind us. . . . [H]e feared further possible bank failures, further commercial failures and possible municipal defaults" (Harrison Papers, Open Market, February 24, 1932, 6). He voted for purchases after being assured that New York would buy most of the securities but that the money would flow all over the country. If he had voted against, a majority of the five-person executive committee would not have supported purchases.

Why did the System finally decide to act in a way that, at the time, seemed bold? There are at least three reasons. First, the action was consistent with the Riefler-Burgess framework. Member bank borrowing and short-term rates had not declined. Borrowing was well above the $500 million range considered high in an ordinary recession and was almost back to the 1929 peak. A program to reduce the volume of borrowing by undertaking purchases was consistent with the dominant view that credit markets could be eased by forcing a reduction in the System's portfolio of real bills. The preliminary memorandum prepared for the meeting talks about

96. At the time, New York owned 33 percent of the System portfolio and was expected to buy 27 percent under the formula used to allocate System securities to individual reserve banks (Board of Governors File, box 1452, March 16, 1932).

the deflationary effect of the large volume of member bank borrowing and compares the borrowings of banks outside principal money market cities with the amount borrowed in 1929 when the "Reserve System was exerting the maximum pressure for deflation." Gold flows to the United States or a return of currency to banks had not occurred, so borrowing had remained high. System action would not be seen as inflationary.

Second was passage of the Glass-Steagall Act on February 27, 1932, and the start of Reconstruction Finance Corporation purchases on February 2, 1932. Third was the threat of additional legislation, particularly the passage of two bills that had been introduced in Congress, one calling for a soldiers' bonus, the other for an issue of paper currency, or "greenbacks." When some directors expressed concern about the inflationary effect of the purchase program, Harrison replied that "the only way to forestall some sort of radical financial legislation by Congress" was an expanded program of purchases.

The New York directors had urged Harrison to purchase for weeks. Woolley was enthusiastic and urged purchases of $100 million a week instead of $25 million. Roy A. Young (Boston) expressed fears that an inflationary policy would drive the country off the gold standard, but after receiving assurances from Treasury Secretary Ogden Mills that the next budget would be balanced unless Congress passed the bonus bill, Young conceded that "by working toward controlled inflation we would be working against uncontrolled inflation by the Congress." He then shifted his position and urged Harrison to double the weekly rate of purchase and get an agreement from the other governors to purchase $500 million at a rate not less than $50 million a week. "If we are going into this program," he said, "the more vigorously and promptly we act, the less we shall have to do."[97]

Harrison's principal concern was that Congress would approve "inflationary policies" before Federal Reserve purchases could help the economy. During the Coolidge administration, the government had promised a bonus to World War I veterans, payable in 1945. One group in Congress wanted to pay the soldiers' bonus at once. Another group, led by Senator Thomas, wanted to print $2.4 billion of Federal Reserve banknotes, collateralized by 2 percent government bonds sold to the Federal Reserve banks. Neither group could get its bill passed, but the two groups had started to work together. Their plan was to use Federal Reserve banknotes to pay the bonus. This would stimulate spending. Senator Elmer Thomas, author of the bonus bill, told Harrison that "if his bill is not favorably received, even

97. Both Young's use of "we" and his demand for a more expansive program contrast with his bank's failure to participate in the purchase program.

more radical proposals will be forthcoming from Congress" (Minutes, New York Directors, April 4, 1932).

Political concerns accomplished what economic disaster could not. The Thomas bill, and the threat of other legislation, aroused Harrison to action. He told his directors, "The only way to forestall some sort of radical financial legislation . . . is to go further and faster with our own program" (ibid., 2).[98] He proposed purchasing $500 million in the next month, an extraordinary amount and rate of purchase and completely out of character for Harrison.

Although the purchase program had been in effect for five weeks when the OMPC met in April, System policy had not yet become expansive. The money supply fell during March, as table 5.20 shows. The preliminary memorandum prepared for the April 5 meeting of the executive committee noted, on Riefler-Burgess grounds, that the "program of security purchases has been even more successful than had been hoped . . . as member bank indebtedness has been reduced by more than $200 million." The memorandum correctly noted the contribution made by the reversal of the currency flow and by the small gold inflow. Moreover, the risk premium had fallen two percentage points since the end of 1931.

On April 5, the OMPC's executive committee unanimously approved continuing the purchase program. Even McDougal and Young, who had opposed the program when it started in February, voted to continue purchasing because they did not believe that the executive committee should stop a program adopted by the full Open Market Policy Conference. But the executive committee did not accept Harrison's argument to expand the program. It deferred action pending a meeting of the full OMPC the following week.

The New York directors wanted a more aggressive program. At their meeting on April 7, they talked about a "race against time" and urged Harrison to take "dramatic action," to make "emergency purchases" for their own account immediately, and to "go it alone" without waiting for the other reserve banks. When Harrison reported that Senator Thomas had told him

---

98. He seemed to describe himself. "There will always be some reason for postponing action, and we shall never do the courageous thing if we wait for absolutely clear skies" (Board of Governors File, box 1452, March 16, 1932, 2). He then described four difficulties: System approval would be needed; New York might have to buy most of the securities; New York would have to invoke the Glass-Steagall provision; and the critics would call New York's policy inflationary. He did not mention the loss of gold, a major offset to the expansion. France held approximately $80 million in short-term acceptances. By late March it had adopted a policy of withdrawing $12.5 million in gold each week. Governor Moret of the Bank of France wanted to increase the rate. Harrison told him that the New York bank did not object to any gold purchase and export program he chose.

Table 5.19 OMPC Meeting, February 24, 1932

COMMERCIAL PAPER AND ACCEPTANCES	LOANS OF 101 WEEKLY REPORTING BANKS	GOLD STOCK	BORROWING	BILLS BOUGHT	GOVERNMENT SECURITIES	CURRENCY	MONETARY BASE	MONEY (M_1)
				Current Changes to February 28, 1932				
−$71	−$493	−$106	+$74	−$189	−$34	+$220	−$198	−$584
				Cumulative Changes from August 1929				
−30.4%	−25.1%	−0.2%	−$195	+$27	+$588	+23.1%	+5.3%	−19.5%

BORROWING	EXCESS RESERVES	DISCOUNT RATE (N.Y. AND RANGE)	AAA RATES	AAA-ACCEPTANCES	BAA-AAA	WPI ALL ITEMS (1926 = 100)	WPI FARM (1926 = 100)	INDUSTRIAL PRODUCTION (AUGUST 1929 = 100)
				Levels as of February 1932				
$848	$44	3 (3–3.5)	5.23%	2.42%	3.64%	66	51	56.0

Note: Dollar amounts are millions.

COMMERCIAL PAPER AND ACCEPTANCES	LOANS OF 101 WEEKLY REPORTING BANKS	GOLD STOCK	BORROWING	BILLS BOUGHT	GOVERNMENT SECURITIES	CURRENCY	MONETARY BASE	MONEY (M_1)
				Current Changes to March 31, 1932				
−$5	−$336	+$36	−$134	−$46	+$66	−$81	+$2	−$200
				Cumulative Changes from August 1929				
−30.7%	−27.1%	0.7%	−$329	−$19	+$654	+21.0%	5.4%	−20.2%

BORROWING	EXCESS RESERVES	DISCOUNT RATE (N.Y. AND RANGE)	AAA RATES	AAA-ACCEPTANCES	BAA-AAA	WPI ALL ITEMS (1926 = 100)	WPI FARM (1926 = 100)	INDUSTRIAL PRODUCTION (AUGUST 1929 = 100)
				Levels as of March 1932				
$714	$59	3 (3–3.5)	4.98%	2.48%	3.05%	66	50	55.0

Note: Dollar amounts are millions.

he "might be satisfied not to press for congressional action [on the bonus bill] if the System would proceed more vigorously," one of the directors urged an immediate purchase of $100 million.

Thus prodded by Senator Thomas and his directors, Harrison introduced a resolution at the April 12 OMPC meeting calling for purchases of up to $500 million in addition to the unexpired authority under the February 24 decision. Purchases were to be made as rapidly as practicable with at least $100 million purchased in the current week. The OMPC approved the program ten to one, and the Board added its approval on the same day.

Governor Young of Boston was the main opponent. His argument was very similar to the argument made by Governor Norris eighteen months earlier. A purchase program could not be successful unless the commercial bankers approved. Previous programs had failed; he saw little point in continuing the program.

Meyer replied to each of Young's arguments. The country was not in a favorable position to take advantage of the funds made available. He believed the program would inspire confidence and would not be opposed by the banks. Governor Harrison reinforced this view: "The uncertainty as to the budget and bonus legislation had constituted obstacles," but it was not necessary to wait for these questions to be resolved. He believed the success of the program depended on the use member banks made of their excess reserves, but he thought the wisest course was vigorous action by the Federal Reserve.

Several governors said they regarded the purchase program as a success, supporting their statements with references to various measures. The minutes note that open market rates had fallen, that government security prices had fallen markedly, and that banks had reduced borrowing and accumulated excess reserves. Some hoped that the decline in member bank loans and investments had ended, as suggested by the data for weekly reporting banks early in May.[99]

Purchases Slow

The signs of improvement quickly disappeared. The data in table 5.21 show that by the end of May the risk premium had risen to the highest level experienced in the depression. Despite open market purchases of more than $100 million a week, Aaa rates were back to the December level, and Baa rates were at a new high. The gold outflow to Europe, mainly to France, increased during the spring. The gold stock was now below the level at the

99. Seasonally unadjusted data show a small increase in loans and investments for the week ending May 4. Loans declined at a slower rate (Board of Governors of the Federal Reserve System 1943, 145).

previous peak in 1929, one of the few times this had occurred during the downswing. Perhaps influenced by the new rules for collateral or fear of congressional action, the members of the OMPC paid little attention to the gold movement and authorized additional purchases of $500 million, at a reduced weekly rate.

Bank lending, commercial paper, and acceptances continued to fall. Industrial production fell five percentage points in May to a level nine percentage points (15 percent) below the December 1931 level and 50 percent below its value at the 1929 peak. Wholesale and consumer prices continued to decline; the wholesale price index reached 64 (base 100 in 1926). The index of farm prices was 16 percent below the previous December level, a 38 percent annual rate of decline.

Governors Young and Martin could find no beneficial effect of the past purchases. Both thought that the Reconstruction Finance Corporation had helped but that open market purchases had had no effect. Adolph Miller also believed the purchase program had failed. McDougal favored slowing the program down until the large excess reserves were put to work.[100] He hoped there would be no specified amount of security purchases fixed in advance, and he expressed his fears that the System would dissipate its resources and not be in a position to meet a crisis.

Pulled in different directions by opposition within the OMPC, concerns about congressional and public reaction, and his characteristic indecisiveness, Harrison took a position midway between McDougal and the New York directors. On May 5 he opposed the proposal by one of his directors, supported by Burgess, that the System buy longer-term securities. A week later he talked about setting an objective, a terminal point such as a specific level of member bank reserves. He again opposed proposals to purchase longer-term securities and a suggestion that New York reduce its discount rate from 3 percent to 2.5 percent. On May 16, with Harrison absent, Burgess told the executive committee of the directors that the System was trying to find an objective for the purchase policy, perhaps by tying the volume of purchases to the volume of reserves. He expressed his own view that after a long period of credit contraction, credit expansion required larger reserves than in normal times.

Bank reserves had increased by $725 million between February and May, mainly as a result of System purchases. Member banks had reduced borrowing or increased excess reserves by almost $600 million. When Harrison reported to his directors on May 26, he favored a slower rate of

---

100. More than one-third of the $600 million purchased in April and May was held as additions to excess reserves at the end of May.

purchase. He reasoned that the "best policy would be to keep our program alive for a considerable period rather than to fire all of our ammunition at once." In the previous two weeks, the rate of purchase had declined from $100 million to $86 million and then to $58 million. Currently, he thought, $50 million to $60 million was sufficient to offset gold exports, month-end and holiday currency withdrawals, and other demands for reserve bank credit. On June 9 he opposed the proposal by one of the directors to increase the rate of purchase, again stressing the importance of stretching out the program instead of using up "ammunition."

The rate of purchase continued to slow after the May meeting. By the June meeting of the executive committee purchases had fallen to about $40 million a week. Some governors claimed they had achieved the aims of the purchase program. The volume of member bank borrowing was $350 million below the late February level. Although the risk premium had risen to more than six percentage points, short-term market interest rates had fallen. At the end of June, loans at weekly reporting member banks were 13.5 percent lower than at the start of the year. Late in June the Federal Reserve lowered the buying rate on acceptances from 2.5 percent to 1 percent and set the discount rate at New York at 2.5 percent. The Federal Reserve's discount on acceptances remained above the market's discount, so the System did not expect acceptance holding to increase.

All the accustomed indicators of Federal Reserve policy showed that policy was "easy" and suggested to the governors that the time had come for a less active policy. At the June meeting of the executive committee, Governor Meyer noted that the weekly telephone discussion about the volume of purchases could be avoided by agreeing on a policy target. He suggested that member bank excess reserves be kept between $250 million and $300 million, approximately the amount held by banks at the time of the meeting. The committee decided that the System should continue to purchase securities so as to avoid any indication that policy had changed. The purchases, however, were to be as small as required to maintain the volume of excess reserves.

Another reason for slowing purchases was the absence of a System policy. Most of the reserve banks did not accept their allotment of securities, and some did not participate at all. New York took more than half, at times 75 to 80 percent of purchases. Gold exports to Europe drained New York's gold reserves disproportionately, and banking problems in the country drained correspondent balances of New York banks. With his gold reserves falling, Harrison became reluctant to continue purchases without more support from other reserve banks, particularly large banks such as Boston and Chicago: "Given the comparative reserve positions of the two

Table 5.21 OMPC Meeting, May 17, 1932

	COMMERCIAL PAPER AND ACCEPTANCES	LOANS OF 101 WEEKLY REPORTING BANKS	GOLD STOCK	BORROWING	BILLS BOUGHT	GOVERNMENT SECURITIES	CURRENCY	MONETARY BASE	MONEY (M$_1$)
Current Changes to May 31, 1932	-$120	-$673	-$238	-$228	-$64	+$604	+$3	+$171	-$579
Cumulative Changes from August 1929	-38.8%	-31.0%	-5.1%	-$557	-$83	+$1,258	21.1%	7.8%	-22.4%

	BORROWING	EXCESS RESERVES	DISCOUNT RATE (N.Y. AND RANGE)	AAA RATES	AAA-ACCEPTANCES	BAA-AAA	WPI ALL ITEMS (1926=100)	WPI FARM (1926=100)	INDUSTRIAL PRODUCTION (AUGUST 1929=100)
Levels as of May 1932	$486	$277	3 (3-3.5)	5.36%	4.36%	6.27%	64	47	50.0

Note: Dollar amounts are millions.

Table 5.22 Meetings, Executive Committee, June 16, 1932, and OMPC, July 14, 1932

	COMMERCIAL PAPER AND ACCEPTANCES	LOANS OF 101 WEEKLY REPORTING BANKS	GOLD STOCK	BORROWING	BILLS BOUGHT	GOVERNMENT SECURITIES	CURRENCY	MONETARY BASE	MONEY (M$_1$)
Current Changes to June 30, 1932	-$48	-$282	-$233	+$9	+$9	+$284	+$213	+$78	-$82
Cumulative Changes from August 1929	-42.1%	-32.7%	-10.1%	-$548	-$74	+$1,542	26.5%	8.8%	-22.7%

	BORROWING	EXCESS RESERVES	DISCOUNT RATE (N.Y. AND RANGE)	AAA RATES	AAA-ACCEPTANCES	BAA-AAA	WPI ALL ITEMS (1926=100)	WPI FARM (1926=100)	INDUSTRIAL PRODUCTION (AUGUST 1929=100)
Levels as of June 1932	$495	$234	2.5 (2.5-3.5)	5.41%	4.53%	6.11%	64	46	48.2

Note: Dollar amounts are millions.

banks, he said, it is difficult to see why we should pump funds into the market which will then be siphoned off to Chicago" (Minutes, New York Directors, June 23, 1932, 2).[101] A new round of bank failures in Chicago made him hesitant to stop purchases entirely, so the directors agreed to purchase up to $30 million in the last week of June.

The following week, Owen Young described the purchase program as having "served to check a contraction of credit rather than stimulate an expansion of credit. We have been clearing away for action, rather than taking action."[102] Harrison agreed, citing the decline in borrowing "to a minimum" and the withdrawal of gold by France and other large holders. He added that "our program is only now getting a real test as an agency for recovery" (Minutes, New York Directors, June 30, 1932).

That test did not come. Harrison favored continued purchases, possibly at a higher rate, only if "the program be made a real system program and that the Federal Reserve banks of Boston and Chicago, in particular, give it their affirmative support" (ibid.). Further, he wanted to transfer securities to these banks to acquire gold, and he wanted the Federal Reserve Board to get Chicago and Boston to agree.[103] In response to a director's question, he proposed a $250 million to $300 million target for excess reserves, as much as $80 million above the prevailing level.

Chicago Banking Problems

Bank failures continued in the Chicago district throughout June, rising to a peak in the last full week of June, when twenty-six banks failed (Calomiris and Mason 1997). Fearing that the crisis would spread, the public withdrew deposits from some of the leading banks that held relatively large portfolios of municipal warrants, real estate mortgages, or loans to electric

101. New York had a 50 percent gold reserve ratio compared with 58 percent for the System and 75 percent for Chicago. Excess reserves of the Chicago reserve bank were now larger than New York's (Minutes, New York Directors, June 23, 1932).

102. He based his statements on a report showing that $1 billion of purchases had offset a gold loss of $500 million, reduced discounts by $400 million, and increased reserve bank credit by $100 million.

103. It is difficult to know whether this was a serious recommendation or simply a response to those New York directors (and Burgess) who wanted to continue or expand the purchase program. Harrison knew that Young and McDougal opposed the program and that Boston (Young) had not participated at all. Harrison then added the condition that the RFC become more active in stopping bank failures. He accused it of being too cautious. On the other hand, Charles Hamlin probably described this meeting in testimony several years later: "The Governor delivered an oration worthy of Demosthenes. He nearly drew tears to my eyes, when he told us it was the duty of the Board to force Boston and Chicago into line. I agreed with him entirely." Hamlin promised to try to get the Board to either force the two banks to purchase or rediscount for New York (Senate Committee on Banking and Currency 1935, 948). Hamlin gives the date as the fall of 1933, but that is clearly incorrect.

utilities, particularly those associated with Samuel Insull's collapsed holding company. The City of Chicago had stopped paying interest on its bonds, paid wages and salaries intermittently, and sold illiquid tax warrants to local banks to finance payments to suppliers and some creditors (ibid.).

The Central Republic Bank was one of the threatened banks.[104] On Sunday, June 26, Harrison, Burgess, and Meyer talked with Treasury and RFC officials. These officials reported that the bank was insolvent, an assessment some Chicago bankers did not share. Afraid to close the bank for fear of additional runs, the RFC lent $90 million (and Chicago banks lent $5 million), sufficient to cover all the Central Republic Bank's deposits. This was the largest loan by the RFC to that time. It permitted the bank to pay its depositors and go into voluntary liquidation (see Upham and Lamke 1934, 158–60).[105]

Purchases End

In the month following the June meeting of its executive committee, the System purchased less than $150 million. The July meeting of the Open Market Policy Conference authorized purchases of at least $5 million a week for four weeks and no more than $15 million per week until the time of the next meeting. The OMPC agreed unanimously to hold excess reserves at approximately $200 million and limit total purchases between July and January to the $207 million remaining from the authorization given at the May meeting.

Harrison supported the recommendation and argued against a proposal to sell $150 million provided excess reserves did not fall below $250 million. No strong support for sales developed, so the committee postponed discussion of sales until the next meeting, scheduled for January 1933.

104. The bank's head was General Charles G. Dawes, author of the Dawes Plan for German reparations and vice president of the United States in the Coolidge administration. Dawes was a prominent citizen who received the Nobel Peace Prize for his work on German reparations. But Dawes had been administrative head of the RFC until June 1932. A few days after leaving the RFC, the RFC made its largest loan to Dawes's bank. To embarrass Hoover and Dawes, the Democrats in Congress forced the RFC to publish the names of banks that received assistance to show that Dawes's bank received the largest loan up to that time. Publication of names weakened the listed banks and made banks reluctant to apply for RFC assistance.

105. Hoover had asked Congress to appropriate $500 million and permit the RFC to borrow an additional $3 billion. Congress set initial borrowing authority at $1.5 billion. After the Chicago failures, on July 21, 1932, it increased borrowing authority to $3.3 billion. In March 1933, Congress increased the RFC's powers and permitted it to acquire preferred stock in weak or failing banks.

In the last two weeks of July and the first weeks of August the System made its maximum authorized purchase ($15 million) when discounts increased and its minimum required purchase ($5 million) when discounts fell. After mid-August, the requirement to purchase expired. Since member bank discounts were near the level of the previous autumn and continued to decline, the Riefler-Burgess framework suggested that the market had returned to the "degree of ease" prevailing before Britain left the gold standard. After mid-August, the acceptance portfolio remained unchanged. The System did not undertake any additional purchases even though the executive committee had not yet made all the purchases authorized in May. Short-term open market rates remained below the levels of summer 1931. On the Riefler-Burgess interpretation, there was no reason to purchase.

Riefler-Burgess reasoning was not the only motivation for ending purchases. As is often the case in committee decisions, no single argument appealed to all the members. That the program did not trigger a rapid expansion in bank credit, however, strengthened the opponents and weakened the supporters. Governor Young of Boston had opposed the program from the start, and Norris of Philadelphia had voted for the program without any belief that it would succeed. Boston and Chicago refused to participate in further purchases. Although Harrison recognized that purchases had offset a gold outflow, permitted member banks to repay borrowing, and greatly reduced the rate of decline in bank credit, the demand for credit had not increased. Foreign governments had sold their United States securities and taken gold. Continued purchases would have a more expansive effect. Harrison told his directors that he was willing to continue purchasing provided that other banks, particularly Boston and Chicago, participated and that the RFC liberalized its operations so as to stop further bank closings (Minutes, New York Directors, July 7, 1932). Since Harrison knew neither condition would be met, his proposal seems disingenuous, more an effort to placate some of his directors than a program for open market purchases.

Harrison wanted to protect New York's gold reserve. The New York bank had taken 55 percent of the System's purchases between April 13 and July 13, slightly more than twice its standard allotment. Boston, Richmond, Kansas City, and Dallas had taken much less than their standard allotment. One result was that New York had the second smallest gold reserve ratio in the System even after selling securities worth more than $164 million to other reserve banks for gold. Table 5.23 shows these data.

On July 9 McDougal wrote to Harrison to explain his bank's decision not to purchase. He noted that between February and June, Chicago and New York had taken a much larger share of the securities than required by

Table 5.23   Purchases, Allotments, and Adjustments, April 13 to July 13, 1932

CITY	PARTICIPATION AT TIME OF PURCHASE (%)	RESALES (−) OR PURCHASES (+) (MILLIONS OF DOLLARS)	STANDARD ALLOCATION RATES (%)	OVER (+) OR UNDER (−) PRO RATA SHARE (MILLIONS OF DOLLARS)	GOLD RESERVE RATIO 7/11/32 (%)
Boston	1.1	+30.6	7.25	−22.7	64.4
New York	55.2	−164.3	27.0	+81.4	49.1
Philadelphia	7.9	0.0	7.75	+1.1	53.9
Cleveland	8.7	+15.5	10.50	0.0	55.1
Richmond	1.5	+15.2	5.00	−15.6	50.6
Atlanta	2.4	+18.0	4.75	−2.4	46.3
Chicago	12.8	0.0	12.75	0.0	71.2
St. Louis	2.2	+16.6	4.25	−0.8	54.2
Minneapolis	1.7	+11.4	3.00	0.0	50.6
Kansas City	1.4	+19.9	5.50	−15.6	53.9
Dallas	1.0	0.0	3.75	−24.4	53.8
San Francisco	4.1	+37.0	8.50	−1.0	49.3
	100.0	0	100.0	0.2	

Source: Open Market, Board of Governors File, box 1452, July 14, 1932.
Note: Total purchases $872.77 million.

the allotment formula. This was particularly difficult for the Chicago bank, which had an "abnormally large amount of circulation . . . over 25 percent of the entire [currency] circulation of all the Reserve banks."[106] McDougal then expressed concern about the integrity of the note issue and the dangers that might arise because of reliance on the provisions of the Glass-Steagall Act permitting the reserve banks to use government securities as collateral.

The Chicago bank had faced an increased demand for currency after the Chicago bank failures. The failures may have convinced a skeptical and reluctant McDougal to stop participating in the purchase program. Harrison told his directors on July 25 that McDougal feared the newly issued currency would later return to the banks, producing excess reserves that would flow to New York. Chicago would have to settle the balance with

---

106. Letter dated July 9, 1932, from McDougal to Harrison. McDougal supported his argument with data showing that in the Chicago district, member bank reserves were only about one-third of the note issue, whereas in New York, member bank reserves were more than 1.4 times currency outstanding. The implicit point was that his bank was more vulnerable because the demand for currency was much greater in his district. In fact, Chicago also had a much higher ratio of gold to monetary liabilities than New York. The Glass-Steagall Act had removed the requirement that currency had to be backed by real bills and gold, but as noted in the text, McDougal did not want to use government securities as backing for the note issue. Epstein and Ferguson (1984) argue that commercial banks wanted purchases to end because lower interest rates reduced their profits. Coelho and Santoni (1991) dispute this claim by showing that Federal Reserve purchases did not contribute to lower bank profits.

New York in gold. McDougal did not want to further reduce Chicago's gold reserve by increasing currency (Harrison Papers, Memoranda, New York Executive Committee, July 25, 1932).

Concern at the New York and Chicago banks about their gold reserves represents another failure of the Federal Reserve Act. Chicago acted as banks had acted before the act. The Federal Reserve Board did not force banks to pool their reserves, as the act intended. Knowing that it could not rely on support from other banks, New York also acted to protect its gold reserve by first limiting, then ending, open market purchases.

By late June, Harrison's interest in purchases had become conditional on actions by Chicago and Boston and more aggressive efforts by the RFC. On July 11 he reported to his directors on his conversation with Meyer.[107] Meyer agreed that the RFC had been "defensive" but made no commitment about future policies. Meyer wanted the System to continue the purchase program: "If for no other reason, it is politically impossible to stop at this particular time. . . . If the program were terminated just as Congress adjourned, we would be crucified next winter."[108]

A decline in excess reserves early in July proved to be temporary. By late July, excess reserves were again above $250 million. With the rise in excess reserves, Harrison's interest in the purchase program disappeared. He told the executive committee of his directors that the "need for further purchases is subsiding." Purchases ended in early August.

The rise in excess reserves reflected the return flow of gold during July, a flow that continued throughout the fall. After August, excess reserves generally remained above $400 million, member bank borrowing was less than excess reserves, and short-term interest rates remained below the discount rate and in the range traditionally regarded as "low."

Results of the Purchase Program

In the year following the British decision to suspend gold payments—from September 1931 through August 1932—the System's balance sheet showed the following changes:

---

107. Eugene Meyer, governor of the Federal Reserve Board, served ex officio as first director of the Reconstruction Finance Corporation until July 1932, when he asked to be replaced at the RFC for health reasons. This is one of several examples of a Federal Reserve governor or (later) chairman taking an active role in economic policy. Federal Reserve directors also served on regional branches of the RFC (Todd 1994, 16).

108. Congress had considered, but not passed, legislation to reflate, principally the Goldsborough bill mandating a return to the 1920s average price level. The Federal Reserve opposed it, as it had opposed similar efforts by Congressmen T. Alan Goldsborough and James A. Strong to stabilize the price level in the 1920s. Congress approved issuance of $500 million in Federal Reserve banknotes (greenbacks) at the discretion of the president.

Securities	Other Portfolio	Gold Stock (in millions)	Other	Reserves	Currency
+1,124	−14	−911	−229	−228	+656

Expressed in terms of a change in the monetary base, the data show that the monetary base increased approximately $400 million. The sources of the increase were the excess of security purchases over the gold outflow ($213 million) and the change in "other," mainly a decline in deposits of nonmember banks at Federal Reserve banks.

Chart 5.1 shows that the gold outflow followed open market purchases after a brief lag. This was the classical reaction, substitution of domestic assets for gold on the central bank's balance sheet. Substitution was incomplete, however. During March, gold flows were small and positive. From March 30 to early July, the period of large-scale open market purchases, gold losses were more than half the size of open market purchases. The gold flow reversed before purchases ended. By mid-January 1933, the Federal Reserve's gold holdings had returned to the level reached before the British devaluation.

Gold losses did not force an end to the purchases program. The System's gold reserve ratio did not fall below 56 percent, well above the minimum requirement. To a limited extent, individual reserve banks transferred security holdings to others to meet the gold reserve requirement.

Reductions in discounts and advances were the other main offset to purchases. These also remained far below the volume of open market purchases. During the peak purchase period, from March to July, member bank discounts declined $133 million, 14 percent of open market purchases. Together gold and discounts offset 64 percent of purchases. With discounts reduced and many foreign balances withdrawn, the offset would have fallen had purchases continued. Economic recovery would have reversed the gold flow and the reduction in member bank borrowing.

As these comparisons suggest, seasonally adjusted data show that the stock of money—currency and demand deposits—increased during the summer and fall (Friedman and Schwartz 1963, table A-1). Output responded to the increase in money. After falling to 47 in July, the seasonally adjusted index of industrial production (August 1929 = 100) rose to 53 in October, an increase of more than 12 percent.[109] It seems likely that had

109. The index went from a 20 to 30 percent annualized rate of decline in the winter and spring to a 50 percent annualized rate of increase from July to October. Growth stopped in November, and decline resumed in December.

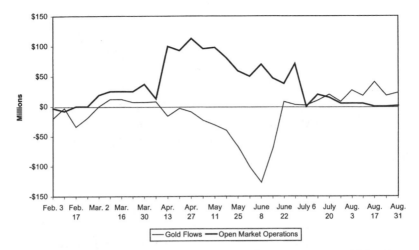

Chart 5.1 Gold flows versus open market operations, February–August 1932, Wednesday series. Source: *Federal Reserve Bulletin* (various issues).

purchases continued, the collapse of the monetary system during the winter of 1933 might have been avoided.[110]

The Federal Reserve recognized the improvement at the time. At the August 11 meeting of the New York directors, Meyer described the rise in commodity and security prices as the best in nearly three years. He then dismissed "those who think things are going too fast; they are not going fast enough." Meyer saw a continued rise in commodity prices as the chief hope for banks and the economy.[111]

The Federal Reserve's purchase program was not the only factor working toward improvement in the financial system and the economy. From

110. A memo prepared for the July 14 meeting of the OMPC compared the current recession with previous deep recessions. Previous deep declines in industrial activity, 1873–78, 1892–94, 1920–21, and 1923–24, measured 24 to 34 percent from peak to trough. The current decline was 56 percent from June 1929 to June 1932. Payrolls had fallen by more than two-thirds in several durable goods industries, where employment had fallen by 50 percent or more. Unemployment had increased to 10 million, a rise of 3 to 4 million in a year. The memo mentions the threat of social disturbance and radical legislation. It also recognizes some signs of improvement—the nearly complete withdrawal of foreign short-term balances, an end to domestic gold hoarding, passage of tax increases to balance the budget (*sic*), and expanded powers for the RFC. Banks had stopped reducing credit, "since the Reserve System began its policy of vigorous purchases of government securities" (Open Market, Board of Governors File, box 1452, July 14, 1932). The OMPC did not use this analysis as a reason for continuing purchases.

111. The index of common stock prices (base 100 in 1935–39) confirms Meyer's statement. The low point of the index is 35.9 in June 1932. By August the index reached 56.3, more than 50 percent above its low point. The performance of the index of railroad stocks is even more dramatic. After reaching a low of 37.5 in June, the index rose to 91.5 in September. None of the com-

the date of its inception, January 22, 1932, to the end of August, the Reconstruction Finance Corporation authorized loans of $784 million to more than 4,000 banks as compared with only $155 million lent to 575 banks by the National Credit Corporation in the three months ending January 1932. Under the impact of monetary expansion and RFC lending, the bank failure rate declined markedly. The improvement was so great that by October 1932, repayments to RFC exceeded new loans. The improvement did not last, however. In December the number and deposits of suspended banks rose once again.[112]

At the July 1932 meeting, a majority of the reserve banks were in favor of continuing the purchase program on a limited scale. Only one governor, George Seay of Richmond, joined Young and McDougal in opposing purchases.[113] It seems likely that if Harrison had urged continued expansion, he would have had the support of the smaller banks and the Board. Harrison failed to continue the program, ostensibly because he did not have the support of two banks that had taken less than 20 percent of the previous purchases. To protect New York's reserve, he did precisely what Bagehot had warned central bankers to avoid.

THE FINAL COLLAPSE

The standard seasonal pattern called for an increase in reserves to prevent a seasonal increase in interest rates. With little upward pressure on interest rates and declines in November and December, the System was inactive throughout the fall. The main discussion was the timing of sales.

Gold continued to flow in, adding to excess reserves. The System remained passive despite a resumption of banking failures, the beginning of state or area bank closures, and the renewed gold outflow during the winter. Despite requests for assistance from President Hoover, it remained almost passive as the financial system collapsed, stirring itself only at the very last moment.

---

mon stock indexes ever returned to the June 1932 low point. Bond yields also reversed direction. Moody's corporate bond yields reached 8.01 in June, then declined to 6.45 in August and 6.08 in September. Yields on lower-quality Baa bonds declined more than one-third, from 11.63 in May to 7.61 in September, in part a result of Reconstruction Finance Corporation activities.

112. In the four months through January 1932, deposits of suspended banks exceeded $1 billion. In the remaining eleven months of 1932 deposits of suspended banks declined to just under $500 million. See *Federal Reserve Bulletin*, December 1933, 664.

113. The vote differs from Harrison's report to the executive committee of his directors (July 9) that the majority of the executive committee of the OMPC would like to stop purchases but that they were not able to do so without a vote of the full committee. At the time, he described McDougal and Young as opposed to further purchases and Norris (Philadelphia) as "lukewarm." The other members of the committee were Fancher (Cleveland) and Harrison. Philadelphia voted with the majority in mid-July.

Open Market Policy Discussions

Once the purchase program ended in August, Harrison showed no interest in a new program. Burgess spoke in favor of continuing the purchase program in early August, but Harrison preferred to rely on the gold inflow to maintain excess reserves and talked about the prospects for reducing System holdings of government securities by allowing Treasury bills to run off. In September and October, Burgess proposed additional purchases; Harrison discussed the appropriate time for sales.[114] Governor Norris expressed the view of many when he told the New York directors on September 13, "The only question to be decided is when and how we shall reduce our portfolio." Harrison agreed that securities should be sold but was uncertain about the appropriate timing. He was concerned that "too large an amount of excess reserves would mean that the credit situation might get out of control" (Harrison Papers, Meeting of the Officers' Council, September 13, 1932). His discussion presages the deflationary policy action later in the decade, when the System raised reserve requirements.

Burgess responded, opposed sales, and argued for additional purchases. The Federal Reserve should "keep on all possible upward pressure in order to stimulate business improvement." There was "plenty of time for us to turn around" because there would be no sudden upsurge that would restore employment and output. He thought recovery would take months and perhaps years, so he favored continued purchases.[115] Governor Norris was present at the New York meeting and expressed the dominant opinion. He could not "see that it would be worthwhile to burden the city banks much longer with large accumulations of excess reserves."

The November meeting of the Open Market Policy Conference considered a proposal to sell up to $150 million of securities provided that excess

114. Harrison called a meeting of the principal New York officers on September 13 to discuss when sales should begin. He said that the traditional indicator of the monetary situation, the rate of increase in bank credit relative to business activity, did not suggest the need for sales. Some of the officers challenged the use of that indicator, suggesting that it had misled them. Burgess defended it. "If we had acted in the light of the bank credit-business activity index in the past, we would have acted promptly enough for our purposes and in the right direction" (Harrison Papers, Meeting of the Officers' Council, September 13, 1932, 2). Harrison expressed concern about the risk of inflation. Burgess pleaded for an expansive policy, citing "the fact that we are approaching a terrible winter from the standpoint of unemployment and widespread social distress" (3).

115. A month later, Burgess expressed very similar views at a meeting of the New York directors. He declared that "the time has not yet come for a reversal of our System open market policy." He then analyzed the policy of the previous year as one that had encouraged people to switch from cash or liquid assets to short-term securities. By continuing to purchase, they could now force a switch from short- to long-term securities. This would lead to the employment of men and machinery.

reserves remained above $250 million. There was general agreement that the recent election, the choice of a new Congress, and other uncertainties made it appropriate to delay sales. The OMPC voted to reopen the question during the first week of January after defeating a motion by Governor Seay, supported by McDougal, to reconvene in December. The only action was to ask Congress to extend the Glass-Steagall provisions for a second year.

Harrison and Meyer stated the prevalent arguments for and against sales at a meeting of the New York directors on December 22. Harrison rested the case for selling on two main points. In both, he treated excess reserves as a redundant surplus and ignored Burgess's earlier argument. (1) The purchase program had accomplished the objective of stopping a "drastic deflation" but not the secondary and "unavowed objective" of stimulating business recovery. However, it was unclear whether the $700 million to $800 million of excess reserves was any more effective in stimulating recovery than $400 million. (2) The accumulation of excess reserves created a risk: "We do not have real control as contrasted with psychological control until member banks are forced to borrow at the reserve banks. If excess reserves pile up, . . . we must remember that we are relinquishing a lever of immediate control."

Meyer's response emphasized political as well as economic factors. The inflationists in Congress were looking for a reason to inflate. Sales would be interpreted as deflationary and would fly in the face of predominant congressional sentiment. Also, sales would attract a gold inflow by raising interest rates. The present inflow was "embarrassing"; a further inflow generated by a deliberate policy of raising interest rates was hard to justify to foreign governments.[116]

It is impossible to reconcile Meyer's statement that sales would raise interest rates with Harrison's treatment of excess reserves as a redundant surplus. Meyer's comments on the level of excess reserves correctly interpret the increase as a response to expected System policy. He suggested that the variability of excess reserves was as important as the level and that the banks had failed to use the excess reserves as a basis for expansion of deposits and earning assets because of uncertainty about future Federal Reserve policy.[117] The banks expected sales, and Meyer did not strongly op-

116. Owen Young, a director, offered a succinct statement of a major problem. "There is deflation in the country which loses the gold and no inflation in the country which receives it" (Minutes, New York Directors, December 22, 1932, 2).

117. Meyer's statement is in the minutes of the directors' meeting. At the time, Treasury bill yields had been driven almost to zero—an average of 0.085 percent for the month. "Concerning the most effective pressure of excess reserves, Governor Meyer said that if the banks knew that there is a constant amount of excess reserves over a long period, the amount can be relatively small and still be more effective than a much larger but uncertain

pose selling. He believed that if sales were to be made, the time for it would be January, when currency would return to the banks.

The background memo for the January 4, 1933, OMPC meeting showed that bank credit (loans and investments) was 2 to 3 percent above the July low point, but growth had stopped in October. Loans at weekly reporting banks were below the July level (table 5.24). Member bank borrowing had fallen about $600 million. Excess reserves, mainly at New York and Chicago banks, continued to increase. Most of these funds came from regional and rural banks seeking investment in the New York and Chicago markets. The memo noted also that the rise in commodity prices and industrial production during the spring and summer had reversed.[118]

The OMPC members had different interpretations of excess reserves, but there was general agreement on a policy of purchases or sales to maintain the level of excess reserves no higher than $500 million, slightly less than the amount that prevailed at the time of the meeting. Seay and McDougal wanted the System to reduce excess reserves by $125 million at once, but they voted for the resolution and it passed unanimously.

During the next few weeks New York followed the instructions almost to the letter. It sold approximately $60 million and maintained the banks' excess reserves close to $500 million. By early February, currency drains had reduced excess reserves below the target. Burgess wanted to return to the target, but Harrison was cautious and limited purchases to $25 million. After February 8, the committee ignored the instructions. Purchases failed to offset the increase in currency, so excess reserves fell. Between mid-February and the banking "holiday" of early March, weekly purchases did not exceed $25 million. On February 16, New York reduced its acceptance rate to 0.5 percent and purchased $27 million.

The final bank runs had started. Harrison told his directors on February 16 that the OMPC could not meet because reserve bank governors could not leave their districts. New York might have to purchase securities for its own account, offering participation to other reserve banks later. He reported increased gold withdrawals by domestic residents and foreigners. In the second half of February, Michigan, New Jersey, Missouri, Maryland,

---

amount. To be effective, he said, the pressure of excess reserves has to enter into the calculations of people who are going to use the money over a period of time. We have not obtained the full effect of recent large excess reserves because of uncertainty as to our future policy" (Minutes, New York Directors, December 22, 1932).

118. A table in the memo compared levels of excess reserves in previous deep recessions back to 1884–85. The table showed that in previous recessions excess reserves had been larger relative to requirements, that business activity lagged six to eighteen months behind the increase in excess reserves, and that there was little risk of a sudden rise in commodity prices.

Table 5.24 OMPC Meeting, January 4, 1933

COMMERCIAL PAPER AND ACCEPTANCES	LOANS OF 101 WEEKLY REPORTING BANKS	GOLD STOCK	BORROWING	BILLS BOUGHT	GOVERNMENT SECURITIES	CURRENCY	MONETARY BASE	MONEY (M_1)
Current Changes to December 31, 1932								
−$59	−$1,080	+$594	−$213	−$16	+$157	−$129	+$240	−$108
Cumulative Changes from August 1929								
−46.1%	−39.1%	+38%	−$761	−$90	+$1,699	23.2%	12.2%	−23.2%

BORROWING	EXCESS RESERVES	DISCOUNT RATE (N.Y. AND RANGE)	AAA RATES	AAA-ACCEPTANCES	BAA-AAA	WPI ALL ITEMS (1926 = 100)	WPI FARM (1926 = 100)	INDUSTRIAL PRODUCTION (AUGUST 1929 = 100)
Levels as of December 1932								
$282	$526	2.5 (2.5–3.5)	4.59%	4.21%	3.83%	63	44	51.8

Note: Dollar amounts are millions.

Ohio, Pennsylvania, Indiana, and Kentucky either authorized banks to close as required or declared bank holidays.[119]

Once again, the Federal Reserve watched events take place and failed to respond as long as the level of market interest rates remained low. Once again, when market interest rates rose the System responded by discounting "freely" at a higher rate, by raising the acceptance rate at the New York bank, and by purchasing very little in the open market. Even Governor Meyer shared the dominant view. He told the Board on February 27 to follow gold standard rules: "Continued purchases of government securities at the present time would be inconsistent from a monetary standpoint . . . the New York money market should protect itself against the higher rates abroad by increased rates and not through open market purchases of governments by the Federal Reserve Banks. . . . Any reasonable amount of open market purchases at this time would prove to be ineffective and appear to be a vain attempt to prevent a readjustment of rates which is inevitable."

Renewed currency demand, "hoarding of gold coins in aggravated form," weakness in the foreign exchanges, and foreign demand for gold produced almost no response.[120] During February, reserve bank credit increased only $284 million, mainly by bill purchases in the last week. In the same period, currency circulation increased by almost $400 million. Table 5.25 shows some principal financial measures at the end of February and the changes from the August 1929 peak.

Final Currency and Gold Drains

The banking crisis was not a sudden, unanticipated event. It developed over months, spreading from state to state, and when it was left unattended, spread fear throughout the country. Failure to stop the growing crisis arose at many levels. Boston and Chicago would not participate in purchases, so New York did not ask for a System policy. The Board would not insist on a Systemwide program. It watched passively while its staff prepared for a financial collapse. The political system was in transition from

119. Rockoff (1993, table 2) lists the restrictions by date and state beginning in October 1932. He notes that restrictions had begun earlier. His data are from the *Commercial and Financial Chronicle* (1933). See also his table 3, showing the restrictions in place on Sunday, March 5, just before the national bank holiday.

120. The only major action discussed in the minutes was purchase of Treasury securities to prevent "violent price fluctuations" when the Treasury had to borrow $350 million and refinance $650 million on March 15. Harrison urged his directors to agree to support the Treasury market during the sale if needed. One director dissented but changed his vote to make the decision unanimous (Harrison Papers, New York Executive Committee, February 27, 1933).

Table 5.25   Financial Conditions, February 1933

LOANS IOI WEEKLY REPORTING BANKS	COMMERCIAL PAPER AND BANKER'S ACCEPTANCES	BILLS BOUGHT	GOVERNMENT SECURITIES	DISCOUNTS	CURRENCY	MONEY (M_1)
$10,036	$755	$336	$1,866	$582	$5,588	$19,982
			Change from August 1929			
−$6,933	−$713	+$160	+$1,716	−$464	+$1,669	−$6,489
			Percent Change			
−40.8	−48.6				+23.0	−24.5

INTEREST RATES (%)			
DISCOUNT RATE (NEW YORK AND RANGE)	RATE	ACCEPTANCE AAA RATE	BAA RATE
2.5 (2.5–3.5)	0.88	4.48	8.37

Note: Dollar amounts are in millions.

Hoover to Roosevelt. Without Roosevelt's agreement, Hoover would not take responsibility for actions whose legality he suspected. Roosevelt would not accept responsibility until he was inaugurated and had authority to act. Clearinghouse banks would not issue currency substitutes, scrip or clearinghouse certificates, because they believed the crisis differed from the crises in the 1890s or 1907, when they had last issued clearinghouse certificates.[121]

Roosevelt was elected without commitment to a specific program. His advisers included people with known views, but these views covered several different policies. Roosevelt would not commit to balance the budget or maintain the gold value of the dollar during the four months between his election and inauguration on March 4, 1933. Several senators and congressmen proposed legislation to raise prices by increasing money. The proposals, if enacted, would have made devaluation a likely outcome.[122] These proposals, speculation about Roosevelt's plans and intentions, a con-

121. The three main arguments were that the crisis was not caused by a shortage of currency (as in the past) but by insolvent banks; that scrip would exchange at a discount against Federal Reserve notes; and that checks payable in scrip could not be transferred through Federal Reserve banks. At best such checks would be noncash items, but only if they contained the words "payable in scrip" on their face (Memorandum re: Proposed Plan for the Issuance of Secured or Unsecured Bank Scrip, Board of Governors File, box 2222, February 15, 1933). The source contains analyses of the programs used in 1890, 1893, and 1907 and for the possible use of scrip in 1907 and 1914.

122. Eichengreen (1992, 327) cites press accounts at the time showing recognition of the threat to the dollar's gold value. The proposals included calls for stabilizing the price level at the 1920s level and for printing greenbacks. See discussion of the Thomas amendment in chapter 6. Federal Reserve discussions did not distinguish between proposals to raise the price level and to print fiat money.

gressional mandate requiring the RFC to publish the names of banks it assisted, and the long delay between election and inauguration heightened uncertainty, adding to the crisis.

Between February 1 and March 4, the demand for Federal Reserve notes and gold increased $1.43 billion and $320 million respectively. In the same period, foreigners moved $300 million in gold into earmarked accounts, $200 million in the week before the inauguration (Eccles 1951, 115).[123] The public's increase in note and gold holdings was about one-third of the outstanding stock at the end of December 1932, the gold loss, 6 percent of the December 1932 stock.

These data suggest that most of the gold purchases were made by foreigners, including foreign central banks. If we attribute all or most of the currency drain to domestic demand, foreigners account for about 10 percent to 20 percent of the run on the monetary system in early 1933 and about the same percentage in the climactic two weeks from February 22 to March 8, when currency outstanding increased $1.55 billion and the gold stock fell $2.7 million (Board of Governors of the Federal Reserve System 1943, 387).

Bagehot (1962) describes the remedy for an internal and external drain as lending freely at a high rate. The Federal Reserve continued to ignore this advice. Banks therefore could not meet demands for currency and gold. In the four months between election and inauguration, the Hoover administration tried unsuccessfully both to activate the Federal Reserve and to cooperate with the incoming administration.

Burdened by its history of crises, a lame duck administration, Federal Reserve inaction, and Roosevelt's silence, the financial system collapsed.

---

123. These data are not entirely consistent, as is shown by the comparisons of Eccles's and the board's estimates of currency withdrawals. Combining the end of January data and weekly data ending March 8, official figures show a $310 million fall in the gold stock and a $41.9 billion increase in "money in circulation" (Board of Governors of the Federal Reserve System 1943, 376, 387). The latter figure includes vault cash. Gold sales are close to Eccles's claim, so I use his numbers with Federal Reserve data for Federal Reserve notes, gold coin, and gold certificates (412). These items show a combined increase of $850 million in the month of February, suggesting that the demand for Federal Reserve notes, gold coins, and currency increased $580 million in the critical days of early March. New York reserve bank estimates show an increase of $162 million in gold coin between January 11 and March 4 and $172 million in gold certificates from February 8 to March 4 (Sproul Files, memo E. Despres to Burgess, March 18, 1933).

Weekly data on earmarked gold are not available. Monthly data show transfers to earmarked gold in early 1933.

January	$91.5 million
February	$178.3
March	$100.1
Total	$369.9

By inauguration day, thirty-five states had declared bank holidays, closing all banks. Closings typically were for limited periods, but some were indefinite. In the states without declared holidays, withdrawals were severely restricted; often no more than 5 percent of deposits could be withdrawn (Board of Governors File, box 2166, March 1933).

The final crisis did not come suddenly. In November, Harrison and Secretary Mills discussed a likely December default on intergovernmental debt payments. Greece had defaulted earlier in the month; Britain wanted an international meeting to discuss intergovernmental debt payments and had asked to postpone its December payment. Harrison and Mills thought Roosevelt would probably not accept a private invitation to discuss problems with President Hoover. The best available course was an open letter, discussing the problems and inviting cooperation. The letter appeared on November 3, 1932. Roosevelt accepted the invitation the following day, but the meeting achieved nothing.[124]

In late November, Harrison warned Mills about the beginning of flight from the dollar. Although the gold stock continued to increase, Harrison explained that Britain had stopped buying dollars and started using them to strengthen its exchange rate against the French franc. This involved selling dollars for francs in Paris and selling francs for pounds in London.

By December the staff began informing the New York directors about the number of banks in the United States that had closed since the previous week. In mid-February Michigan joined the several states that had declared banking holidays, closing all banks. Michigan's action closed the Detroit banks.[125] To avoid loss of deposits, corporations moved their balances to New York banks, thereby draining reserves from small and medium-sized cities. New York made a feeble effort to relieve the pressure by lowering the buying rate for bills to 0.5 percent on February 16. The directors

124. The campaign had been bitter, so there was not much spirit of cooperation. Mills's discussion shows that the administration believed the election repudiated its program, so it was reluctant to act alone and uncertain about how a Democratic-controlled Congress would receive its proposals (Harrison Papers, Conversations with Ogden Mills, November 11, 13, 14, 1932).

125. Awalt (1969) describes negotiations with Henry Ford before the failure of one of the large Detroit banks. Ford's company was a large depositor, and members of the Ford family were principal stockholders in one of the banks. Ford believed the collapse was "inevitable" (354). He refused to subordinate his deposit liability in exchange for additional capital from the RFC. Instead he threatened to withdraw $7.5 million in deposits from the trust company, forcing it to close, and $25 million from one of the banks, putting it at risk. The secretary of commerce warned him that his actions would cause a run on other Michigan banks, force bank closures, and cause great distress. Ford persisted, so the governor of Michigan closed the banks before they opened on February 14, 1933. Awalt was the acting comptroller of the currency in 1932–33. He participated in meetings in Detroit with Henry Ford, Secretary Roy D. Chapin, and others.

approved purchases of $20 billion to $25 billion of government securities a week during February and bought $350 million in commercial bills for the month.

In mid-February, President Hoover wrote to Roosevelt to inform him about capital flight, currency drains, and the threat to the exchange rate and the gold standard. Hoover's letter blamed the problem on agitation to tinker with the financial system, publication of RFC loans, and the like. The letter asked Roosevelt to commit to a policy based on the gold standard and a balanced budget and to reassure the public that the country would recover if the government followed sound policies. Roosevelt replied that "mere statements" would do nothing to stop the runs (Moley 1939, 141–42).[126]

Hoover next wrote to the Board on February 22, referring to capital flight and to the "hoarding of currency, and to some minor extent of gold, [that] has now risen to unprecedented dimensions," and asked whether there was a need for some action, or some additional powers (Hoover to the Board, Board of Governors File, box 2158, February 22, 1933). The Board replied on Saturday, February 25, that it was watching the situation develop but "did not desire to make any specific proposals for additional measures or authority" (Meyer to Hoover, Board of Governors File, box 2158, February 25, 1933).

The following Monday the Board met with Ogden Mills present.[127] Mills referred to the pressures in the market and on the Treasury arising from the Treasury's debt sales to finance the Reconstruction Finance Corporation's assistance to failed banks. He urged the Board to arrange for open market purchases of up to $100 million that week.

Governor Meyer saw no reason for purchases. The rise in bond yields was a "necessary readjustment in a market which has been too high" for current conditions. The proper response was for the New York market to increase money rates and for the Federal Reserve to increase bill rates to protect against higher rates abroad: "Purchases of Government securities at the present time would be inconsistent from a monetary standpoint," although the Treasury might wish to purchase some long-term securities for

---

126. The reply was not sent for eleven days. Raymond Moley (1939, 142 n. 5) blames an oversight by one of Roosevelt's secretaries. Hoover's letter reached Roosevelt when he returned to New York, after an attempted assassination killed Chicago's Mayor Anton Cermak, who was riding beside Roosevelt. Moley comments on Roosevelt's calm following the attempted assassination. He spent the evening discussing the financial crisis and his response to Hoover. "I detected nothing but the most complete confidence in his own ability to deal with any situation" (142).

127. Mills had replaced Andrew Mellon as secretary of the treasury and ex officio chairman of the Federal Reserve Board a year earlier.

the postal savings account. A readjustment of rates was "inevitable," so it was wrong for the Federal Reserve to try to prevent it (Minutes, Board of Governors File, box 2158, February 27, 1933, 2–3).

President Hoover wrote again on February 28. This time the letter was more urgent. He noted that the Board was not an adviser to the president, but he wanted its advice on three proposals in the "emergency": federal guarantee of bank deposits; issuance of clearinghouse certificates by established clearinghouses in the affected areas; and "allow[ing] the situation to drift along under the sporadic state and community solutions now in progress" (Hoover to Board, Board of Governors File, box 2158, February 28, 1933).

The Board did not reply until March 2, two days later. It was "not at this time prepared to recommend any form of Federal guarantee of banking deposits."[128] Clearinghouse certificates present "a number of complications from the standpoint of practical operation." The Board discussed the actions under consideration in several cities but made no recommendation. As to Hoover's third suggestion, "the question is not whether the situation should be allowed to drift along under the sporadic state and community solutions now in progress," but whether there was something better to be done: "No additional measures or authority have developed in concrete form which . . . the Board feels it would be justified in urging" (Board to Hoover, Board of Governors File, box 2158, February 28, 1933).[129]

Soon after the letter was delivered, the situation changed. The attorney general had met with the Treasury and Board counsels and now opined that section 5 of the (World War I) Trading with the Enemy Act justified declaring a national bank holiday if the president believed the emergency justified it.[130] Secretary Mills told the Board that "the matter was not free from doubt and he did not feel that he should advise the President to do so without the consent and approval of the incoming administration." Nevertheless the Board voted unanimously that a banking holiday be declared for March 3, 4, and 6 and recommended that Congress be called into session to pass legislation supporting the president's order. The president had

128. Once the banks had closed, Harrison favored deposit guarantees to get them reopened. Roosevelt opposed the plan.

129. At the same meeting, the Board approved an increase in the New York discount rate to 3.5 percent. Miller voted no. On March 2, New York sold $142 million of its portfolio to Boston and $95 million to Chicago to keep its gold reserve ratio above 40 percent (Minutes, New York Directors, March 2, 1933, 142). Meyer reported to the Board meeting that he had talked to all governors except San Francisco. They reported that "the situation on the whole is comparatively quiet" (Board Minutes, February 28, 1933, 1).

130. Awalt (1969, 357) was present at the meeting after 10 P.M. on March 2. Hoover asked the Board whether he should declare a bank holiday and, if so, requested it to draft a proclamation. Mills and Meyer favored a three-day holiday, from March 3 to 5, followed by congressional approval of emergency legislation. Miller and Hamlin opposed the holiday (357–58).

gone to bed by the time the decision was reached, so the meeting adjourned (Board of Governors File, box 2158, March 2, 1933).[131]

At its March 3 meeting the Federal Reserve Board discussed the growing number of states with bank holidays. Miller advocated the use of clearinghouse certificates, but he opposed any plan to guarantee bank deposits.[132] Others proposed legislation. No one suggested additional open market purchases to provide reserves that banks could exchange for currency. The only decision was that Governor Meyer should talk to the president and recommend a nationwide bank holiday.

Earlier in the evening, Hoover actively considered plans for a holiday. Meyer reported to the Board that Hoover agreed to the holiday provided Roosevelt would approve the action (Board of Governors File, box 2158, March 3, 1933, afternoon meeting).[133]

---

131. Mills's desire to have Roosevelt agree to the bank holiday was not a new idea and was not likely to succeed. Governor Harrison had approached Roosevelt's adviser, William Woodin, in mid-February with an offer to brief the president-elect on the banking and monetary situation. Roosevelt declined to meet Harrison. Woodin became secretary of the treasury at the start of the Roosevelt administration. He had been president of American Locomotive Company. He had served as a director of the New York bank, so he was acquainted with Harrison. Harrison also met with Raymond Moley, one of Roosevelt's advisers from Columbia University, to urge a balanced budget. Woodin urged Harrison to persuade Carter Glass to accept appointment as treasury secretary, a position he held after World War I. Glass wanted Roosevelt to commit to a balanced budget and the gold standard. Roosevelt had campaigned on both issues, but he would not commit to either for the long term (Harrison Papers, New York Federal Reserve Bank, file 2010.2. Moley (1939, 118–21) handled the negotiations with Glass after Roosevelt offered the appointment. When Glass asked for assurance about Roosevelt's policy on the gold standard, Moley delivered Roosevelt's reply: "We're not going to throw ideas out of the window simply because they're labeled inflation." Glass then mentioned his health problems and, after a few days, declined. Moley believed it was unlikely that Roosevelt and Glass would have gotten along. He did not know Roosevelt's monetary plans at the time, but he described Roosevelt as "experimental, tentative, and unorthodox," the very opposite of Glass (1939, 121). Moley served as an assistant secretary of state early in the administration, with principal duties as presidential policy adviser. He resigned within a few months.

132. The New York Clearinghouse also considered issuing clearinghouse certificates, as it had done in 1907. Leslie Rounds, a deputy governor of the New York reserve bank, dismissed the proposal because it was impossible to substitute clearinghouse certificates for the entire stock of bank deposits. The earlier use of certificates to substitute for banknotes required many fewer certificates. This argument presumes that most of the stock of deposits would be exchanged for certificates. No further discussion is reported (Minutes, New York Directors, March 4, 1933, 154).

133. Moley's account (1939, 145–47) of the March 3 meeting with Hoover, at which Meyer and Mills were present, is somewhat different. Roosevelt came to pay a courtesy call on President Hoover but was warned at the last minute by a White House staff member that substance would be discussed. He sent for Moley. Hoover proposed a proclamation giving government control of foreign exchange withdrawals but leaving the banks open. Hoover reported that his attorney general doubted the legality of closing banks, so he was concerned that Congress would challenge the closure. He wanted Roosevelt's assurance to prevent this challenge. Roosevelt replied that his designated attorney general believed the president had

At a special meeting of the New York directors in the afternoon and evening of March 3, Harrison reported that the overall gold reserve ratio for the system remained above 40 percent, but the New York reserve bank's ratio had fallen to about 24 percent.[134] Normally the deficiency could be covered by rediscounting with other reserve banks, but an internal drain of gold now supplemented the external drain.[135] Harrison told Governor Meyer that "he would not take the responsibility of running this bank with deficient reserves" (Special Meeting, Minutes, New York Directors, March 3, 1933, 2).

---

adequate authority. He told Hoover to declare a holiday for his remaining term if he wished. Roosevelt would decide once he was in office (Awalt 1969, 359). That was as far as Roosevelt would go. The meeting ended with Roosevelt telling Hoover: "I shall be waiting at my hotel, Mr. President, to learn what you decide" (Moley 1939, 146). The source of the problem was doubt about whether the 1917 act expired at the end of World War I.

134. The estimates are from Burgess's statements to the New York directors (March 7, 1933, 160). Awalt (1969, 358) reports that New York sold $200 million of gold on March 3. It was short about $250 million. Chicago also faced a run. It had orders for $100 million of gold from banks in its district. Awalt claims that part of the demand in Chicago was an effort to prevent the New York reserve bank from borrowing in Chicago.

The New York directors met for about ten hours between 3:00 P.M. and 2:40 A.M. on the morning of March 4. Herbert Lehman, who replaced Roosevelt as governor, considered declaring a bank holiday for New York. As usual, Harrison was indecisive. A holiday "would not solve the problem in other parts of the country nor with respect to foreign countries where the Federal Reserve Bank of New York acts . . . for the whole Federal Reserve System" (Minutes, New York Directors, March 3, 1933, 146). Deputy Governor Case informed them that the Chicago board had voted that a national holiday should be called but, failing that, holidays should be declared in New York and Illinois. Harrison explained that New York could not declare an embargo on gold. That would be a "usurpation of a government function" (147). The directors agreed. The directors then voted in favor of immediate passage by Congress of legislation remedying banking problems; if that could not be done, they favored a national holiday and suspension of specie payments if a holiday was not declared. Harrison telephoned this decision to the Board. The Board explained that banking legislation was impossible.

135. Most of the speculation against the dollar in London and Paris came from London and included the Bank of England. The bank sold sterling and bought francs in New York, sold francs for dollars in Paris "in fairly substantial amounts," and used the dollars to buy gold in London. Harrison learned about these transactions from bankers in New York who executed some of them (Harrison Papers, Memo Crane to files, file 2610.1, February 28, 1933). He mentioned these operations to Montagu Norman of the Bank of England in late February and urged him to let the pound rise (from about 3.4 to the dollar). Norman was noncommittal about his purchase and sale operations but "emphatically . . . said that it was their intention to continue their present policy and to keep the sterling rate about its present level" (Harrison Papers, Conversations with Norman, file 3115.4, March 1, 1933, 1–2). (From December to March the pound appreciated about 4.5 percent against the dollar.) Norman also did not respond to Harrison's suggestion that he seek to lower the rate London banks were offering for dollar deposits. Robbins (1934, 221) shows the Bank of England's gold reserve rising from a low of £120.6 million in December 1932 to £172.7 million in March 1933, a 43 percent increase, somewhat less than the £253 million reported in Board of Governors of the Federal Reserve System (1943, 551). The December value is the lowest since the early 1920s; the March value is exceeded only by values for a few months in 1928. France and Germany show modest reductions in official holdings from December to March.

The Board suspended the gold reserve requirement. That action removed the legal issue, but the bank was open, so the gold drain continued. Harrison told Meyer and Mills that at current rates of loss the gold reserve would be depleted. There were three courses of action: declare a bank holiday; suspend specie payments; or suspend reserve requirements for the entire System.[136] Harrison considered suspension of reserve requirements least attractive, since it would continue payments to speculators and hoarders. Suspension of specie payments was "almost equally unattractive . . . [H]ysteria and panic might result, and there probably would be a run on the banks" (ibid., 3).

That left a national bank holiday. He gave this recommendation to Meyer and Mills. They had suggested instead that Governor Herbert Lehman of New York declare a holiday for the state, but Harrison was not sure a state bank holiday was sufficient basis for refusing to pay out gold to foreigners. He was reluctant to continue losing gold, but he saw no alternative without a holiday.[137] After further discussion, the directors learned that both Hoover and Roosevelt had retired for the night. Secretary Mills called to say that President Hoover would not declare a national holiday. Harrison went to meet with Governor Lehman to discuss a state holiday.[138]

136. Although one of the main purposes of the Federal Reserve Act was to permit gold reserves to be pooled in an emergency, New York had difficulty borrowing from Chicago. On March 3, Chicago refused to purchase $410 million of government securities from New York in exchange for gold. On March 4, Harrison asked Governor Meyer for help, specifically to use the interdistrict settlement fund to transfer gold to New York against securities. Under section 11a, this required the votes of five Board members and, Meyer later reported, the Board did not agree. The transfer was finally agreed to on March 7, after the New York directors adopted a resolution requesting the Board to require other reserve banks to rediscount for New York (Minutes, New York Directors, March 7, 1933, 160–62). The same day, the Board instructed Boston, Cleveland, Richmond, Chicago, and St. Louis to rediscount for New York at 3.5 percent. This was the first time since 1922 that the System used interbank rediscounts. In all, New York made $210 million in rediscounts, $150 million with Chicago. New York raised an additional $230 million by selling government securities and acceptances to the five banks plus San Francisco. Philadelphia also required assistance. New York paid a $10,000 tax for its reserve deficiencies. Data are from McCalmont 1963, 76–77. On March 9 the reserve banks reopened. New York's gold reserve ratio was 41.3 percent, including $245 million obtained from other reserve banks (Minutes, New York Directors, March 9, 1933, 168). The Board later waived penalties on member banks that were unable to meet reserve requirements on deposits, but it collected the penalty from the reserve banks (Board Minutes, April 1, 1933, 4).

137. At this point in the meeting, Deputy Governor Case told the meeting that the Chicago bank directors had voted to ask the Board to recommend a national holiday. The New York banking superintendent announced a sixty-day notice of withdrawal at savings banks.

138. Governor Lehman wanted the Clearinghouse Association or the Federal Reserve or both to request the bank holiday. The clearinghouse bankers did not want to request the holiday, because they were solvent and still liquid. They told the governor they would cooperate if he acted. Harrison was also reluctant to ask for the holiday without a request by the banks.

Later he phoned the meeting to report that the clearinghouse banks and the state superintendent had asked for a state holiday. Governor Lehman wanted a request by the Federal Reserve also. The directors voted the recommendation, and the governor declared the holiday.[139] Illinois, Pennsylvania, Massachusetts, and New Jersey also declared holidays.

Finally, after midnight the Federal Reserve Board voted to recommend a three-day banking holiday. Aides woke Hoover, but he did not act. One of his last acts in office was an angry letter to the Board, on March 4, stating that he had received their letter at half past one in the morning. He was "at a loss to understand why such a communication should have been sent to me in the last few hours of this administration." The Board's letter, Hoover said, had been written after the Board was aware that Roosevelt "did not wish such a proclamation issued" and while the states of New York and Illinois were in process of declaring state holidays, "thus accomplishing the major purpose which the Board apparently had in mind" (Hoover to Meyer, Board of Governors File, box 2158, March 4, 1933).[140]

The Board remained in session until after 3:00 A.M. Before adjourning, it received word of the decisions by the governors of Illinois and New York to close banks in those states. The Board could not decide whether to order Federal Reserve banks to close, so in a final lack of decision, it voted not to object if the directors voted to close.

On his first day in office, Sunday, March 5, President Roosevelt declared an emergency to meet "heavy and unwarranted withdrawals of gold and currency" and "increasingly extensive speculative activity." His proclamation used the recommendation the Board had made to President Hoover

139. Early in the morning of March 4, Governor Lehman, acting "on the request of the New York Clearinghouse banks and with the advice and recommendation of the Federal Reserve of New York" declared a state bank holiday for March 4 and 6. Federal Reserve banks closed along with commercial banks. This posed a problem. Ohio had not declared a holiday on March 4, so the Cleveland reserve bank remained open. Dallas also remained open until it received a wire from a bank in Pittsburgh asking for $10 million in cash. Told that a plane was on its way, Dallas closed (CHFRS, interview with Joseph P. Dreibilbis, March 9, 1954). Dreibilbis was counsel to the Dallas bank.

140. Hoover's letter also said that the "authorities on which you were relying were inadequate unless supported by the incoming administration." This point had been made forcefully by Secretary Mills on many occasions, most recently at the midnight meeting of the Board. Mills reported that the attorney general had advised the president not to issue the proclamation. Todd (1995, 21–22) reports a conversation between Glass and Roosevelt in Roosevelt's hotel room at 11:30 P.M. on March 3. Roosevelt told Glass he had rejected Hoover's request that they act jointly. Glass then asked Roosevelt what he planned to do. Roosevelt replied: "Planning to close them, of course." Glass pointed out that Roosevelt lacked the authority to close any banks and especially state banks, but Roosevelt insisted he would have the authority as president.

the day before, citing the 1917 Trading with the Enemy Act as authority to prevent the export, hoarding, or earmarking of gold or silver.[141] The proclamation closed all banks first from March 6 to March 9, then later for two additional days. On March 9 Congress approved the holiday, and strengthened its legal foundation, by passing the Emergency Banking Act.[142]

The act extended and broadened the president's powers to close, liquidate, license, and reopen banks under the Trading with the Enemy Act, removing any possible challenge to the legality of his proclamation. The act also strengthened the Reconstruction Finance Corporation, authorized national banks to issue preferred stock, and permitted the RFC to purchase shares in national and state banks. And it prepared for the nationalization of gold holdings by empowering the secretary of the treasury to order all domestic gold owners to sell their holdings to the Treasury.

The bank holiday was a climax to the depression because it forced the government and the Federal Reserve System to respond to the domestic financial and economic collapse. Actions that had seemed beyond consideration were no longer unthinkable. In the next few months the administration chose domestic expansion over fixed exchange rates and dismissed the opportunity to return to the gold standard. Employment, agricultural prices, and other domestic concerns replaced the gold price and real bills as guides to economic policy.

EMPIRICAL STUDIES: THE ROLE OF MONEY

The Great Depression was mainly a monetary event in two senses. Monetary policy could have mitigated or prevented the decline but failed to do so. A different set of Federal Reserve policy actions could have avoided the severe deflation and reduced the depth and severity of the economic decline. In this sense the Great Depression was a response to monetary policy.

There is another sense in which the depression was a monetary event. The initial decline could have been a response to a negative monetary impulse or sequence of impulses. A few writers have taken this view (Anderson, Shugart, and Tollison 1988). Other students of the period suggest that monetary forces had no role (Temin 1976).

The extreme positions—that monetary policy was the only cause or that

---

141. There were few legal challenges. South Carolina's decision to close its banks was upheld by the Supreme Court in December 1933 (Board of Governors File, box 2165, December 5, 1933).

142. Walter Wyatt, the Board's legal counsel, prepared the act. According to Joseph Dreibilbis, one of the Federal Reserve attorneys, there was only one copy of the act when it passed (CHFRS, Dreibilbis, March 9, 1954).

monetary policy played no role—are difficult to sustain.[143] A more plausible explanation is that the depth and severity of the Great Depression were the consequence of a series of shocks that the Federal Reserve neglected or failed to offset completely. The shocks include French gold policy, banking panics, increased demand for currency, departure of Britain from the gold standard, the stock market decline, failure of banks in Austria and Germany, collapse of United States export markets in Latin America, the effects of tariffs and retaliation on prices and thus on gold movements, and other events. Some of these events are both the effect of prior changes and the proximate cause of subsequent changes. We are unlikely to develop a complete list of "true" causes that operated independently of other events.

One alternative is to look for outliers, or large changes, in output and the money stock. A Kalman filter, developed by Bomhoff (1983), uses the past history of a series to predict future values. The difference between predicted and actual values is a measure of changes that could not have been foreseen from the history of the series. Using quarterly data reported in Balke and Gordon (1986) from 1890 or 1915 through 1984, the filter predicts each quarterly observation, then uses the error to revise subsequent predictions. Predictions of GNP, money, and prices are made independently, so it is possible to check on the consistency of the predictions of GNP by summing the errors in predicting real output and prices. For 1928–33, these sums are generally in the same direction and have similar magnitude as the error in GNP. Table 5.26 shows all errors in M_1 and errors in GNP and prices greater than or equal to 1 percent for this period.

The data support five principal implications. First, the depression was caused by a series of unanticipated changes or shocks, not by a single event. There were large shocks to nominal and real GNP, both positive and negative, throughout the period. Despite the reversals in sign, the cumulative sum of the shocks to nominal GNP from the peak in third quarter 1929 to the trough in first quarter 1933 (17.4 percent) represents about one-third of the decline in nominal GNP.[144]

Second, most of the large shocks to nominal GNP were also large shocks to real GNP in the same direction. There are fewer large shocks to the price level, suggesting that price changes were mainly the result of sys-

143. After a thorough examination of several types of data, Hamilton (1987) draws a similar conclusion. He interprets much of the deflation as unanticipated based on commodity prices, interest rates, and newspaper accounts.

144. This calculation excludes the continuing effects of the shocks in subsequent quarters, hence it understates their impact. Ohanian (2001) attempted a nonmonetary explanation of the decline in productivity. He concludes that nonmonetary factors explain only one-third of the decline.

Table 5.26 Large Prediction Errors for United States GNP, Prices, and Money, 1928–33 (percent)

DATE	NOMINAL GNP	PRICES	REAL GNP	MONEY (M_1)
1928.3	+2.88		+3.84	−1.44
1928.4				2.44
1929.1	+1.73		+2.23	−1.57
1929.2	−2.09		−1.64	0.20
1929.3		1.47	−1.87	1.35
1929.4	−4.68	−1.23	−4.02	−0.13
1930.1	−3.68		−3.22	−3.71
1930.2				0.60
1930.3	−3.00	−2.19		0.64
1930.4	1.71		1.33	0.72
1931.1	4.02	−1.56	5.55	−0.34
1931.2				−1.62
1931.3	−6.25		−7.84	0.49
1931.4	−3.47		1.16	−3.18
1932.1	−1.48	−1.62	1.17	0.56
1932.2	−1.82		−2.26	1.44
1932.3	1.10			1.37
1932.4	8.38		7.92	3.27
1933.1	−8.25		−12.18	−3.43
1933.2	21.78		19.62	−0.91

tem response to current and past shocks acting on output and spending. Large price-level shocks typically have the opposite sign from contemporary output shocks, suggesting that the shock affected supply. Since most of the supply shocks are positive, they cannot explain the long and deep decline in output.

Third, shocks to money either are contemporaneous or lead shocks to GNP by a quarter or more. The largest monetary shock comes early in 1930, when M_1 fell 11 percent (annual rate), the largest decline in any quarter since 1921. Negative shocks to money dominate 1931, particularly following the Federal Reserve's response to the British devaluation. The monetary shocks change sign in 1932 following (or accompanying) the relatively large open market purchases in second and third quarter 1932. Positive shocks to real and nominal GNP follow. Although the money stock continued to fall during most of that year, the rate of decline slowed for a time and money stock rose in the fourth quarter. Industrial production and stock prices rose in fall 1932. These data suggest that, contrary to some Federal Reserve interpretations, the 1932 open market purchases did not fail. Continuation of the positive shocks by more expansive actions in 1931 and 1932 or earlier would likely have changed the course of the depression.

Fourth, some periods show negative shocks to output that are large relative to current or past shocks to money. Fourth quarter 1929 and third quarter 1931 are prominent examples. In both quarters there was some prominent event: for third and fourth quarter 1929 we have the peak in the economy in August 1929, the spread of recession abroad, and the fall in United States stock prices in October 1929; in third quarter 1931 there were banking problems in Germany and the suspension of gold payments by the Bank of England in September 1931. These changes may have affected monetary velocity.[145] Waves of bank failures and suspensions in 1930.4, 1931.2, 1931.3, 1931.4, and 1932.1 had mixed effects. Shocks to money and nominal GDP were positive in 1930.4, relatively small but positive for nominal GDP in 1931.2, commingled with the effect of the British suspension of gold payments in 1931.3, and accompanied by a large negative shock to money and nominal GDP in 1931.4. Only the bank closings in 1932.1 are accompanied by negative shocks to output and a positive monetary shock that would support a major role for nonmonetary factors associated with bank suspensions. None of this evidence rules out a nonmonetary channel, but it does not suggest a dominant effect of nonmonetary shocks.

Fifth, there is not much evidence of a decisive monetary surprise, or series of surprises, in the year preceding the start of the depression. The cumulated monetary shocks in the year ending 1929.2 is a small negative value. Price data show a sequence of small deflationary shocks (or errors) for the year ending 1929.2. Nonmonetary factors may have contributed to the deflation and the start of the depression.

An alternative for investigating nonmonetary shocks uses errors computed from a demand function for money to see if there were large unexplained increases in the demand for money as suggested by Temin (1976). Table 5.27 shows the percentage errors from a demand function in which the logarithm of real money balances depends on the logarithms of interest rates and wealth or expected income. The equation is estimated separately for the logarithms of levels and changes of real money balances, using annual data for 1902 or 1903 to 1958. An appendix shows the equations. Errors are actual values minus estimates from the equation.

For both equations, most of the errors are comparatively small. These data give no evidence of a sudden large, unexplained desire to accumulate real money balances. Most of the errors in log levels are negative, suggesting that real money balances fell below predicted values. This typically occurs when money growth falls more than anticipated. The years 1928 and 1930 are notable in that regard.

---

145. Since monetary velocity is measured by GNP/M_1, the numerator reflects the fall in nominal GNP. It is not possible to measure velocity shocks independently using the Kalman filter. An alternative procedure is discussed below.

Table 5.27   Errors in the Demand for Money, 1928–33

YEAR	LOG LEVEL	CHANGE
1928	–.063	–.067
1929	–.027	.027
1930	–.041	.013
1931	–.024	.045
1932	+.009	–.095
1933	–.038	.014
Standard error of estimate	.046	.049

The years 1928 and 1932 are the only ones before the middle 1930s with relatively large errors in the change in real balances. Chart 5.2 shows that real balances fell much more in 1928, and rose much more in 1932, than anticipated by the demand equation. The negative error in 1928, for both levels and changes, suggests that before the recession demand for real balances fell more than actual balances.[146] Factors other than income, wealth, and interest rates played a role in reducing growth of desired real money balances. In 1932 actual growth of real balances is 6 percent above the growth expected at a time of increased nominal money following several years of falling nominal money. Chart 5.2 shows the prediction errors for 1922–40.

Gandolfi and Lothian (1977) estimated a demand for money equation using data for a cross section of states for the years 1929–68. Their findings also suggest that the demand function for money remained relatively stable during the Great Depression. They reject the presence of a liquidity trap. Their measure of the interest elasticity declined as interest rates fell, contrary to the liquidity trap. (See also Brunner and Meltzer 1968a.)

Would a more expansive monetary policy have prevented the Great Depression or reduced it to a typical recession? McCallum (1990) simulated the response of nominal GNP assuming the Federal Reserve followed a monetary base rule from 1923 to 1941.[147] McCallum's rule is activist but not discretionary. The Federal Reserve adjusts the growth of the monetary base each quarter to reflect past changes in base velocity and deviations from a 3 percent growth rate.[148]

146. This finding contradicts Field's (1984) claim that stock market speculation increased the demand for money. A more likely explanation is the unanticipated decline in money growth following the French stabilization. Typically in periods of unanticipated decline in money growth, velocity (the ratio of income to money) rises. Consequently, the demand for money (per unit of income) falls.

147. Bordo, Chaudri, and Schwartz (1995) take a similar approach using a rule that keeps growth of M_2 constant. In some of their simulations, there is no depression. In others, as in McCallum's, a typical recession would have occurred.

148. McCallum adjusts his rule to allow for differences between the growth rates of M_1 and the monetary base arising from currency drains and bank failures and suspensions.

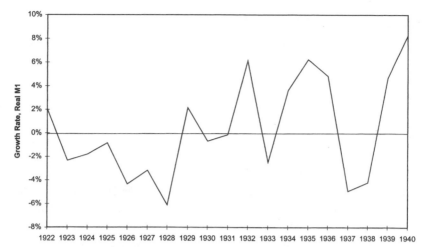

Chart 5.2 Errors in growth of demand for money, 1922–40. Source: See chapter appendix.

The simulations by McCallum (1990) and by Bordo, Chaudri, and Schwartz (1993) support two propositions. First, the Federal Reserve's inaction converted a modest or possibly moderate recession into the Great Depression. In this limited sense, the depression was caused by monetary policy. Second, nonmonetary events contributed to the decline. All of McCallum's simulations, and most of the simulations by Bordo, Chaudri, and Schwartz, show a recession in 1929 and 1930.

Taken together, the estimates of the role of money in 1929–33 point to a relatively large role for money growth both as a factor deepening the recession and, at times, reversing the fall in output. There is no evidence that money was the unique cause of the decline. Systematic effects of other factors, including tax increases or expenditure reductions to balance the budget or tariff increases and retaliation abroad, have not been ruled out.

Sweden avoided severe deflation. Its central bank, the Riksbank, followed the policy advocated by some members of Congress in the 1920s and at the time; acting under parliamentary guidance, the Riksbank worked to stabilize the domestic price level. Sweden could not offset the real effects of an international decline, but after leaving the gold standard in 1931, the country avoided the deflation and its effects on output, financial institutions, firms, and households (Berg and Jonung 1998). The Swedish recession was comparatively mild.

Bernanke (1983, 1994), Bernanke and James (1991), and others link monetary and nonmonetary factors in the Great Depression and at other times. These authors accept that bank failures and suspensions during the depression reduced the money stock. They propose, in addition, that

Table 5.28   Ratio of Open Market to Bank Lending, 1929–33 (percent)

DATE	RATIO	COMMENT	DATE	RATIO	COMMENT
August 1929	8.6	Expansion peak	August 1931	9.5	
November 1929	10.9		November 1931	8.8	
February 1930	12.6	Peak ratio	February 1932	8.0	RFC begins
May 1930	11.4		May 1932	7.7	
August 1930	11.0		August 1932	7.2	Trough
November 1930	12.1	Bank suspensions rise	November 1932	8.0	
February 1931	11.8		February 1933	7.5	
May 1931	11.6				

Source: Board of Governors of the Federal Reserve System 1943, 142, 143, 144, 145, 465.

bank failures and suspensions reduced bank lending. Since small and medium-sized firms depend disproportionately on bank loans to produce and finance output or sales, reductions in bank lending have a large impact. Further, during the depression, these authors claim, deflation had a nonneutral effect on debtors by forcing contraction, lowering net worth, and reducing access to bank credit. The last of these effects, debt deflation, requires borrowers to be affected more, or more quickly, than creditors.

Bernanke does not dispute the monetary effect of the Federal Reserve's failure to stop the bank runs by open market operations. That bank loans declined with bank deposits is an expected consequence of monetary contraction. The extraordinary real rates of interest and high-risk premiums on Baa bonds after late 1930 testify to a general reluctance to extend credit to any borrowers, particularly lower-rated or unrated borrowers.

More problematic is the particular, nonneutral effect of the decline in bank loans on smaller firms. For this effect to have aggregate consequences, bank loans must decline relative to open market lending by nonbank firms. The data for the second half of the depression show the opposite. Short-term open market lending fell relative to bank lending. Table 5.28 shows the ratio of commercial paper plus banker's acceptances to loans at 101 weekly reporting member banks at each three-month interval from the peak in August 1929 to February 1933.

The data show a relative expansion of open market lending during the early months of the decline. The ratio reached a peak in the first six months; thereafter open market lending declined relative to bank lending. The relative decline accelerated when suspensions (measured by deposits of suspended banks) rose beginning in November 1930. During the peak period of bank suspensions in second half 1931, the ratio fell below its value in August 1929.[149]

149. Commenting on this section in oral discussion, Bernanke attributed the result to a change in the commercial paper market. This does not explain banker's acceptances. Further, as shown in Greef 1938, most of the change occurred before the 1930s.

Table 5.29   Percentage Decline in Lending, December 1929 to December 1932

Weekly reporting banks	18.1
All member banks	41.8
All banks	37.6
All banks minus weekly banks	61.4
Banker's acceptances	59.0
Commercial paper	75.7

Source: Board of Governors of the Federal Reserve System 1943, 18, 76, 142, 146, 465.

Table 5.28 gives little support to the argument that the decline in bank lending had a nonneutral effect that augmented the monetary effect. The common decline in lending by banks and nonbanks suggests a reduction in desired borrowing in response to poor opportunities and widespread beliefs that the recession would continue. These beliefs are documented in the minutes of the Federal Reserve.

Table 5.29 compares the percentage decline in lending for different groups of banks to the decline in external finance. Weekly reporting banks show the smallest percentage decline. To get a better measure of small banks, subtract weekly reporting banks from all banks. Line 4 of the table shows that this class declined by about the same percentage as banker's acceptances and less than commercial paper.

The relative share of credit by large banks rose despite the sharp decline in acceptances and commercial paper. These markets were much smaller than the bank loan market in absolute size. If we assume that large banks lend mainly to large firms, the evidence suggests that credit to large firms declined less than credit to other firms. This conclusion is tempered, however, by the comparison of all member banks and all banks. These groups declined in the same proportion.

These data do not separate a decline in the demand for loans from restrictions on supply to small firms. The data are entirely consistent with a relative decline in loans demanded by small firms. Data are not available on sales by size of firm, so an examination of the proposition is incomplete.

Chart 5.3 shows, however, that total loan volume declined with GNP. Predicted loans are estimated from a simple regression in which loans depend only on nominal GNP. The decline in loans differed little from the decline in GNP. It seems fanciful to suggest that the decline in loans caused an immediate decline in GNP in each period. The more likely explanation is that households and businesses reduced borrowing as their incomes fell. Falling demand explains most of the decline in loans. Given the real return to lending, banks should have been eager to lend to solvent borrowers.

Haubrich (1990) tested Bernanke's nonneutrality hypothesis for Canada. Canada had no bank failures, but banks closed many of their

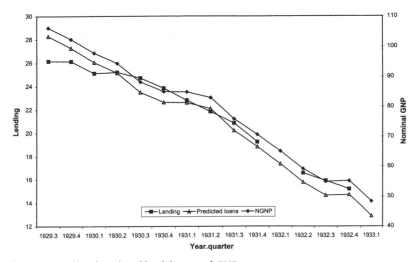

Chart 5.3 Actual and predicted bank loans and GNP, 1929–33.

branches, probably disrupting lending arrangements. Canada also had a smaller share of interest payments on loans past due, but Canadian commercial failures were a larger fraction of GNP. Canada was effectively off the gold standard after January 1929. Haubrich finds no support for bank closings and commercial failures in Canada as a reason for decline.

The United States was not the only country experiencing bank runs and failures. The public in many countries expressed its fear of bank failures by withdrawing deposits and holding currency. Spain and the Netherlands experienced large increases in the ratio of currency to deposits. Austria, France, Norway, and Canada had smaller, but not negligible, increases. A central bank can offset the effect on the economy of an increased demand for currency by expanding the monetary base by more than the increase in currency demand. Under the gold standard, the government may have to temporarily suspend convertibility, as Britain did in such circumstances several times in the nineteenth century.

To study the effect of currency drains (or bank runs) on real income during the decline, 1929–32, I regressed percentage changes in the real value of the monetary base, the ratio of currency to deposits, and base velocity on the percentage change in real income for twenty countries in Europe, North America, and South America. The twenty countries for which data are available report very different experiences. Denmark, Greece, Hungary, Norway, and Spain show a rise in real income for the period as a whole. The United States, Canada, Brazil, Mexico, Austria, France, and Germany show double-digit declines in real income for the three-year period. Estimates and a list of the countries are given in appendix B.

The data attribute about half of the decline in real income in these countries to the combined effects of the change in the real value of the country's monetary base and the change in base velocity. The change in base velocity includes changes in the demand for currency per unit of income. The larger the currency drain, other things equal, the larger the decline in base velocity. Currency drains and bank runs do not appear to have had any significant effects through a lending channel or other channel, independent of their effects on the real value of the monetary base and base velocity. The statistical results again suggest that monetary factors had an important role in the decline, but other factors affecting the demand for money were also significant for the twenty countries. I return to the role of gold in the concluding section.

Federal Reserve records suggest that the real bills or Riefler-Burgess doctrine is the main reason for the Federal Reserve's response, or lack of response, to the depression. With few exceptions, the Federal Reserve governors accepted this framework as a guide to decisions. They believed that a low level of member bank borrowing and low nominal interest rates suggested there was no reason to make additional purchases. Additional purchases of government securities would expand credit based on speculative assets, which was inconsistent with the real bills doctrine and the gold standard.

Federal Reserve purchases at the start of the 1929 recession were much larger than at the start of previous recessions. One reason is that New York started to purchase at the time of the stock market break. Also, member bank borrowing was over $1 billion, far above the range that the Federal Reserve regarded as restrictive. At a March 1926 meeting of the Governors Conference, Strong restated the Riefler-Burgess doctrine and described how it would be applied at the start of a recession: "Should we go into a business recession while the member banks were continuing to borrow directly $500 or $600 million (if bills are included nearly $800 million) we should consider taking steps to relieve some of the pressure which the borrowing induces by purchasing government securities and thus enabling member banks to reduce their indebtedness" (quoted in Chandler 1958, 239).

Table 5.30 compares member bank borrowing and interest rates at the beginning and one year after the start of three recessions. The 1929–33 recession started with more member bank borrowing and higher interest rates than the others. By the end of the first year, the Federal Reserve had purchased $350 million to $400 million more than in the two previous recessions. In the 1923–24 recession, the Federal Reserve made seasonal securities purchases in December, seven months after the peak, but sold in January. Sustained purchases did not begin until February 1924, nine

Table 5.30 Borrowing and System Purchases in Three Recessions (millions of dollars)

PEAK	MAY 1923	OCTOBER 1927	AUGUST 1929
Length of recession	14 months	13 months	42 months
Acceptance rate			
At peak	4.13	3.88	5.13
Peak + 12 months	3.25	3.19	1.88
Peak + 18 months	2.38	3.75	1.44
Borrowing			
At peak	771	690	1,046
Peak + 12 months	441	412	215
Peak + 18 months	242	834	198
Borrowing plus:			
Acceptances			
At peak	1,030	1,013	1,222
Peak + 12 months	524	754	383
Peak + 18 months	556	1,191	307
Securities purchased			
First 12 months	+161	+221	+578
First 18 months	+392	−5	+449

months after the cyclical peak. In 1926–27 the System made small-scale securities purchases at once, partly for seasonal reasons, since the recession started in October. Sustained purchases began in February, four months after the cyclical peak.

The earlier recessions reached a trough after thirteen or fourteen months. Eighteen months after the peak, the levels of borrowing or borrowing plus acceptances on the Federal Reserve balance sheet were very different after 1929 than after the earlier recessions. Interest rates on ninety-day acceptances are highest in the October 1926 cycle, lowest in the August 1929 cycle. Securities purchased show the same ordering. Judged by the measures that Riefler, Burgess, and Strong emphasized, Federal Reserve policy shifted from restraint to ease and back to restraint in the 1923–24 and 1926–27 cycles. In 1929–30 these measures indicated that credit conditions had eased substantially.

The monetary base shows a different pattern, largely unrelated to the Federal Reserve's measures of credit conditions. In 1923–24 the base started to rise six months after the cyclical peak and continued to rise through the first six months of the recovery. Three months after the 1929 peak, the base was below the level reached at the August peak, and it continued to fall through the spring and summer of 1930, as shown in tables 5.5 to 5.8 above.[150]

150. In 1926–27, the base changed very little in the recession and in the early months of recovery.

CONCLUSION

People see most clearly what they are trained or disposed to see. The Riefler-Burgess version of the real bills doctrine was not a mechanical formula directing Federal Reserve policy, but it directed attention to member bank borrowing and market interest rates as measures of tightness and ease. In 1929–30, most members of the Federal Reserve Board and governors of the reserve banks accepted this framework. They believed they had acted decisively to ease credit conditions, and on their measures they had.

The real bills doctrine taught that central bank credit should finance self-liquidating commercial loans. Government paper, stock market loans, and real estate mortgages were "speculative" investments that had no place on a central bank's balance sheet. Since speculative loans were not self-liquidating, they were considered inflationary finance.

To a modern reader, fear of inflation seems a strange concern after a year or more of falling prices. Yet there are surprisingly few proposals to restore the price level. The comments of W. Randolph Burgess, occasional comments by Governor Meyer or some New York directors, and the efforts of a few members of Congress are the only official comments to that effect that I have found.

Eichengreen (1992, 251–53) contrasts the Riefler-Burgess emphasis on borrowing and interest rates with the "liquidationist view," so called because Treasury Secretary Mellon is said to have advised President Hoover to "liquidate labor, liquidate stocks, liquidate the farmers, liquidate real estate" (251). Mellon's advice is entirely consistent with the real bills doctrine and the firm belief that Federal Reserve policy had financed speculative lending; its effects had to be purged (liquidated). An increased demand for borrowing to finance real bills would, on this view, show that liquidation was complete and that recovery could occur without inflation. That is why the most extreme proponents of the real bills doctrine—Governors Mc-Dougal, Norris, and Young—typically opposed purchases. These men, and many others, repeatedly referred to the contraction as "inevitable"—the inevitable consequence of providing speculative credit.[151] In 1929–33 their principles told them that deflation was both necessary and inevitable. For much the same reason, the Federal Reserve deflated in 1920–21 to eliminate the credit expansion based on war finance.

The volume of loans on securities by banks in New York and in the rest of the country did not increase disproportionately during the stock market

---

151. Senator Carter Glass held this view firmly. In hearings before his subcommittee, he attributed the financial collapse to neglect of the real bills principles (Senate Committee on Banking and Currency 1931).

Table 5.31 Bank Loans and Stock Market Lending, 1927–29 (billions of dollars)

	LOANS ON SECURITIES[a]		TOTAL LOANS	
DATE	NEW YORK	101 BANKS	NEW YORK	101 BANKS
December 1927	2.6	6.7	5.1	15.4
December 1928	2.7	7.2	5.3	16.2
August 1929	2.8	7.7	5.7	17.0
October 1929	3.2	8.1	6.1	17.7
	LOANS TO BROKERS AND DEALERS BY NEW YORK BANKS[b]			
December 28, 1927	3.7			
December 26, 1928	5.1			
October 2, 1929	6.8			

[a]Weekly reporting banks from Board of Governors of the Federal Reserve System 1943, tables 48 and 49.
[b]Ibid., table 141.

boom. The main evidence of expanding stock market lending is the relatively large increase in loans to brokers and dealers, not to the public. At its
peak, in the week ending October 2, 1929, total lending of this kind was
$6.8 billion; the volume had nearly doubled since the end of 1927. Table
5.31 shows these data.

Eichengreen and Bernanke correctly emphasize the transmission of deflationary impulses by the gold exchange standard. Falling gold stocks in
many countries reduced the monetary base in countries that lost gold. Appendix B recognizes the importance of the decline in the real stock of base
money as a factor reducing real income, but it also recognizes that the gold
did not disappear. Some countries, including the United States and several
members of the gold bloc, acquired gold reserves.

The United States experienced a gold inflow in the first year of the decline. Under gold standard rules, the increase in gold should have increased the monetary base. If the Federal Reserve had followed the rules,
the money stock would have expanded by 14.6 percent from August 1929
to June 1930. This, of course, overstates the amount of gold inflow that
would have occurred. However, an expansive monetary policy would have
prevented at least some of the deflation and recession, so falling prices and
fears of collapse would have been absent. The world would have been
spared much of what followed.

The principles of the Federal Reserve Act called for passive policies. The
founders intended the System mainly to respond to gold movements and
offers of real bills. No one discussed what the System should do if the two
signals gave conflicting commands, as in 1930 when gold flowed in and
real bills declined. The Federal Reserve had abandoned strict adherence to
the gold standard in World War I and in the 1920s. It followed the real bills

guide. Policy was deflationary in 1930 when adherence to gold standard rules called for expansion.[152]

Eichengreen (1992, table 8.6) compared the behavior of surplus and deficit countries from 1929 to 1931. He showed that in 1929 and 1930 the twenty-six countries losing gold contracted reserves as they paid out gold. Surplus countries like the United States contracted also, so the well-known stabilizing process did not work. We can only speculate on why deficit countries followed deflationary policies instead of leaving the gold standard. One reason is that most policymakers, economists, and businessmen in these countries also believed that deflation was an inevitable consequence of the previous speculative boom in the United States. The world economic system could not return to stability until these "excesses" had been purged. Also, many countries attempted to protect their gold reserves by deflating, contrary to the advice of Bagehot and Thornton.

The data suggest that the United States economy and its monetary system experienced not one but a series of monetary and nonmonetary shocks in the forty-two months following the August 1929 peak in economic activity. Seasonally adjusted industrial production declined more than 50 percent, and the money supply declined by over 25 percent. Of the banks operating at the time of the peak, more than 25 percent—6,704 banks—failed or were merged into other banks.[153]

One long-popular belief is that the fall in output and the financial collapse were caused by a prior decline in stock prices. The decline in money and the waves of bank failures are attributed to the decline in loan demand. To be more than an example of the post hoc, ergo propter hoc fallacy, there must be some connection between the initial decline in stock prices and the series of shocks to the United States economy.

Prices of industrial shares had declined by percentages similar to the

152. Fremling (1985) notes that the United States was not the only country that did not follow gold standard rules. As noted above, France sterilized much of its inflow. Fremling's conclusion that the rest of the world increased its holdings of foreign reserves and gold does not separate France from other countries, many of which were forced to deflate.

153. During the entire period 1864 to 1896, there were 1,562 bank failures—328 national and 1,234 state banks. In the worst year, 1893, 326 banks—approximately 4 percent of the total—failed. During the banking panic of 1907–8 there were 172 failures; fewer than 1 percent of the banks in existence on June 30, 1907, closed in the next two years. The number of active banks increased from 16,266 in 1906 to 17,891 in 1907 and 19,620 in 1908.

The number of suspensions per one hundred active banks during the early thirties was: 5.61 in 1930; 10.48 in 1931; 7.75 in 1932; and 12.86 in 1933. Banks that suspended operations between December 1929 and March 1933 had gross deposits of $5.5 billion, approximately one-third of the decline in total deposits for the period. All data are from Upham and Lamke 1934, 245, 247, and 250.

Table 5.32 Net Demand Deposits, 1929–33 (millions of dollars)

DATE	WEEKLY REPORTING BANKS IN NEW YORK	WEEKLY REPORTING BANKS IN 101 CITIES
August 1929	5,154	13,120
August 1930	5,595	13,651
August 1931	5,674	13,290
August 1932	4,996	10,842
March 1933	4,690	9927

Source: Board of Governors of the Federal Reserve System 1943.

1929 decline in the recessions of 1906–7 and 1919–20 without producing depressions of the same length and magnitude, although the earlier declines in the stock prices had been spread over a longer time. Following the October–November decline, stock prices rose in winter 1930 and summer 1932. By April 1930 the Standard and Poor's index was only 3 percent below April 1929. It had recovered almost 40 percent of the decline from the September 1929 peak. Stock prices rose again in the summer of 1932 following the expansive monetary policy and despite an increase in tax rates during the spring.

Banking data show little evidence of a prolonged effect of the October decline in stock prices. The data in table 5.32, and similar data on bank loans or loans and investments, show that in the first two years of the contraction, demand deposits in the larger New York banks rose approximately 10 percent, while deposits in all other banks rose about 1 percent. For the decline in money to result from the fall in stock prices, New York banks would have to have experienced a large loss of deposits. In fact, New York banks increased loans and deposits absolutely and relative to other banks for more than a year following the stock market break.

The data in the table support an alternative explanation. During the first two years of the contraction, gold flows and currency movements dominated the behavior of the monetary system. Deflation in the United States and risks abroad brought gold to the United States, as in 1920–21. The gold flows supplied relatively more reserves to the New York banks than to the small or regional banks in the interior. In part for this reason, the internal currency drains and rates of bank failures were much larger in the midwestern Federal Reserve districts than in others. Approximating the regional impact of the currency drains by the changes in the note issue of the various reserve banks shows that between December 1930 and December 1931 the total note issue of the reserve banks increased approximately 60 percent while the note issue of the Federal Reserve Bank of Chicago increased 275 percent and the note issue of the Federal Reserve Bank of

Atlanta declined (Board of Governors of the Federal Reserve System 1943, 338).[154]

On the alternative explanation, the absolute and relative increase in deposits at large New York banks was mainly the result of the Federal Reserve's contractive policy and the gold and currency movements of the period. When the gold flow reversed and the currency drains resumed after August 1931, deposits at New York banks declined, and the experience of the New York banks was more like the experience of banks in the interior.

Stock prices are one among many measures of asset prices. Since shares are traded on open securities markets, share prices respond promptly to changes in anticipated future earnings and dividends. Suitably deflated by current output prices, share prices offer an approximate measure of the cost of available assets relative to the production cost of new assets.

Standard and Poor's index of stock prices deflated by the GNP deflator reached a peak in third quarter 1929. The deflated stock price index was only 23 percent below its peak in second quarter 1930. If the decline had stopped there, deflated stock prices would have been more than twice their level four years earlier. Three quarters after the cyclical peak, stock prices showed no evidence that asset owners believed a further decline was inevitable, to use the term central bankers overworked so much at the time.

The decline in deflated stock prices is not a uniform or even a unidirectional movement that would characterize transmission of a single shock. Like the data on money and GNP, the movement of stock prices suggests a sequence of shocks. In addition to the initial 24.3 percent decline in fourth quarter 1929, three other quarters show declines of 20 percent or more—fourth quarter 1930, fourth quarter 1931, and a decline of nearly 38 percent in second quarter 1932, when bank failures reached a temporary peak. The last of these shocks brought the deflated index to its lowest point of the depression, three calendar quarters before the bank holiday. The earlier chronology identifies these quarters as periods of financial stress.

A second explanation attributes the decline in money to the operation of the gold standard, to the desire to maintain the gold reserve, or to the desire to maintain convertibility of foreign currencies. This argument takes various forms. One claim is that under the conditions of the period, gold and international reserves flowed toward the countries with surpluses on current account of the balance of payments, principally the United States

---

154. For the four years December 1929 to December 1933, the total note issue increased $1.17 billion. Currency held by the public increased $1.04 billion. The Chicago district had by far the largest absolute and percentage increase.

and France. This forced contraction in the deficit countries without producing expansion in the surplus countries.

Eichengreen (1992) makes this argument forcefully. His descriptive statement is correct, but it does not explain why both deficit and surplus countries behaved as they did. Temporary or long-lasting suspension of gold convertibility had occurred under the gold standard many times and in many countries. Great Britain had suspended convertibility several times in the nineteenth century. Yet most deficit countries chose to deflate and protect their gold reserves rather than suspend convertibility. One reason is that policymakers in many of these countries also believed that contraction and deflation were the inevitable consequences of the speculative excesses that had gone before.

The French government was not immune to this view. Far more important, it disliked the gold exchange standard. The French preferred to hold gold rather than foreign exchange as an international reserve, an attitude and policy that reappeared under the Bretton Woods system in the late 1960s. Eichengreen and others point out that the Bank of France was prohibited from undertaking open market operations. This claim fails to recognize that the bank engaged in open market sales of foreign exchange as part of its policy of holding only gold reserves. Under this policy, France sterilized a large part of its gold inflows.

The Federal Reserve did not depend on foreign central banks and governments and did not follow gold standard rules. The large inflow of gold in spring and summer 1930 did not expand bank reserves or the monetary base. With a few exceptions, such as the British suspension, gold flows received little attention in the minutes for the period.[155]

Concern about the size of the gold reserve relative to the reserve requirements for currency and bank reserves—the problem of "free gold"—has limited applicability. Goldenweiser (1951) argued that the Federal Reserve "could not proceed to buy securities in the market because member banks were likely to use the proceeds to reduce their indebtedness to the Federal Reserve Banks. These banks would then have to put up more gold as collateral against notes and there would soon not be enough gold to meet

155. Much the same can be said about the failure of international cooperation. Earlier in the chapter, Oliver M. W. Sprague, an adviser to the Bank of England, is quoted as saying that when cooperation was desirable, central banks could agree (Board of Governors of the Federal Reserve System, Weekly Review of Periodicals, June 2, 1931, 1–2). Clarke (1967, 42) makes a more accurate statement. "Monetary policy could be brought into play [for international cooperation] only when the central bank's international aims happened to coincide, or at least not conflict, with its domestic ones." Eichengreen (1992, 247 ff.) also uses "deflationist" views as an explanation of Federal Reserve actions in 1929–31. As discussed earlier, "deflationist" views arose because the Federal Reserve permitted an expansion based on speculative credit.

the requirements against deposits."[156] Harrison and others mentioned free gold at times during summer and fall 1931, but after the fact Harrison recognized that free gold had not constrained action. Nevertheless, the Open Market Policy Conference waited for the passage of the Glass-Steagall Act in 1932, permitting government securities to serve as collateral for notes, before beginning large-scale purchases. However, the argument is not credible as an explanation of the System's inaction between January 1930 and October 1931. During these months the System's reserve ratio never fell below 75 percent, was always above the average for the decade of the twenties, and generally was more than twice the required ratio. Open market purchases had been made in 1924 and again in 1927 when the reserve ratio was similar to or lower than that in 1930 and most of 1931.

The greater puzzle about the reserve ratio or alleged "free gold" problem is that traditionally countries suspended the reserve ratio whenever a fall in the ratio would have prevented a central bank from acting against an internal drain. Bagehot's dictum, "lend freely at a high rate," had been the unstated policy of the Bank of England through most of the nineteenth century. The bank had suspended its gold reserve requirement rather than force contraction. The Federal Reserve followed a similar policy in 1920, suspending reserve requirements for the New York bank rather than forcing the System into a more contractive policy. Other reserve banks had avoided suspension during and after the war only by selling acceptances and rediscounting commercial paper with other reserve banks.[157] This option remained open throughout the period. Although Boston and Chicago refused to participate in open market purchases, Boston had offered to rediscount for New York during the summer of 1932 if New York continued the purchase policy of the previous spring.

Even if "free gold" had prevented purchases of government securities, it did not prevent monetary expansion. An aggressive policy of acquiring some of the outstanding commercial paper and acceptances would have provided eligible paper and freed up gold for use as a reserve against currency issues. Nor does the free gold argument account for the failure to redefine eligible paper to include notes secured by high-grade corporate bonds or even the bonds themselves or to press for a change in legal requirements.[158]

---

156. Emanuel Goldenweiser was director of research at the Board of Governors. Anderson (1965, 67–69) repeats this argument.

157. Chandler (1958, 184–85) shows that in October 1920 eight of the Reserve banks remained below the required reserve ratio, some by more than twenty percentage points.

158. In spring 1930, W. P. G. Harding, governor of the Boston bank until April 1930, proposed redefinition of eligible paper to permit discounts secured by high-grade bonds. See Harris 1933, 1:304. There is no record of a System response.

The most that can be said for the "free gold" argument is that it was one of a number of reasons Harrison and others used to delay the start of the purchase program in January and February 1932. The "free gold" position cannot explain the System's failures to pursue expansive policies during 1930 and most of 1931 or during the fall of 1932. To explain these we must look elsewhere.

The third explanation of Federal Reserve inaction is lack of knowledge. Bach (1967, 346–56) and Stein (1969, 15) suggest that the System either lacked information about contemporary movements or acquired information too slowly to act in time to prevent a catastrophe. The discussion and tables in the chapter give only a few of many examples showing that the members knew about gold movements, currency changes, interest rate movements, changes in bank earning assets, industrial production, and employment. The minutes and memos of the time frequently contain accurate estimates of current gold flows, the volume of currency "hoarded" by the public, changes in industrial production, and commodity prices. The severity of the crisis would have been lessened if the governors had allowed the monetary base to rise by the full amount of their estimate of the increased demand for currency. Information on output, employment, prices, and lending is available in the minutes, in the *Federal Reserve Bulletin,* in the Board's annual reports, and in speeches by officials at the time. Intelligence gathered within the System and available at the time was entirely adequate for the improvement in policy that would have substantially reduced the severity of the contraction or eliminated it entirely. Much the same can be said for the available theories. Indeed, if the System had done no more than follow the principles established in the nineteenth century, it would have prevented the internal drain and the greater part of the monetary crisis.

There can be no doubt that most of these principles were known at the time. Some of the governors refer to Bagehot's work. Keynes (1930, 2:225–26) describes as the "first necessity of a Central Bank" the control of the deposits created by the member banks. The way to control the deposits, he said, was to control the total stock of money, currency and deposits, by controlling the monetary base. Within the system, several of the New York directors, W. Randolph Burgess, and Eugene Meyer often favored purchases, opposed sales, and at times pointed out the consequences of the System's policies for employment, prices, and production. Outside the System, Seymour Harris (1933, 2:175–92) criticized the central relation of the Riefler-Burgess analysis—that the Federal Reserve controlled member bank borrowing by open market operations—and pointed out that the analysis neglected changes in currency, Treasury operations, and gold movements.

From his detailed examination of various periods during the twenties, Harris concluded that the inverse relation between borrowing and open market operations was much weaker than Riefler, Burgess, and Strong claimed.[159]

A fourth explanation is that the monetary system collapsed because the Federal Reserve lacked leadership. With the death of Benjamin Strong, leadership of the Federal Reserve Bank of New York passed to George Harrison. According to Friedman and Schwartz (1963, 411–19), Harrison lacked Strong's ability to lead and was unable to get other members of the Open Market Policy Conference to follow his suggestions.[160]

There is ample reason to believe that Strong would have regarded the policy action from August 1929 to the summer of 1931 as an "easy policy."[161] His statements on open market operations repeatedly emphasized the importance of the volume of member bank borrowing as the most important indicator of the desirability of purchases and sales. His March 1926 statement, quoted earlier, uses $500 million to $600 million as a tight policy at the start of a recession.

Strong approved of the policy of selling securities during the winter of 1928 and the increases in the discount rate during the spring, despite the very slow rate of increase in money and the slow decline in the monetary base during the recovery from the 1927 recession. We know that Strong approved of the deflationary policy of 1920–21, but this decision antedates his understanding of the role of open market operations.

Burgess changed his views after 1930, arguing for expansion. Burgess

159. Harris comes close to recognizing that the Federal Reserve must control the monetary base. His criticism of Keynes (Harris 1933, 2:192–95) for insisting that a central bank must control the stock of money, however, shows that he did not fully understand this point. Instead, he reached a conclusion that the System was only too willing to adopt later; the Board members and governors had less control than they claimed. Harris had access to the Board's files and internal memorandums, and his discussion gives an excellent account of the changing views of the Board members.

160. Wheelock (1992) notes that this view goes back at least to Irving Fisher. He quotes Fisher's testimony in hearings on the Banking Act of 1935 that if Strong had lived, "we would have had a different situation"—stable prices (12). Fisher (1946) repeated his view in a letter to Clark Warburton, dated July 23, 1946, 3. I am grateful to Wayne Angell for providing a copy of the letter.

161. We know that Strong used the Riefler-Burgess framework and paid no attention to monetary aggregates in conducting policy during the 1923–24 and 1926–27 recessions. See table 5.30 above. In his 1926 testimony to the House Committee on Banking and Currency, reprinted in Strong 1930, 257–58, Strong described the elimination of indebtedness of the New York banks as the main objective of the 1924 purchase policy. He listed six aims of monetary actions including, as number five, assisting when possible "the recovery of sterling and the resumption of gold payment by Great Britain." Then he added, "I think the guide, looking back now, was whether the New York banks were completely out of debt or not, or whether they still owed us a small amount as a regulator."

was a main proponent of continued expansion in summer and fall 1932. Clearly, Burgess put aside the Riefler-Burgess framework. It seems probable that Strong would have done the same. On this point, Fisher and Friedman and Schwartz seem correct. Strong was by far the most knowledgeable and thoughtful of the governors or Board members.

Would Strong have succeeded in persuading a majority of the committee? After April 1930, the five-member executive committee included a majority—McDougal, Norris, and Young—who insisted that deflation was an inevitable consequence of the speculative boom that had gone before. These governors, and others, blamed Strong for the expansive purchases in the fall of 1927 when member banks were only $400 million in debt. And they repeatedly cited the real bills interpretation of the tenth annual report to support their position. Some of them had opposed Strong's policies in 1927. McDougal in particular was hostile to Strong's policy of reducing the discount rate and acted only after the Board forced the reduction.

The recalcitrant governors made an internally consistent argument. Moreover, they could appeal to the intent of the Federal Reserve Act. Carter Glass, who never tired of pointing out that he had written the act, shared their view. Even Eugene Meyer believed that "the New York bank had built up its power entirely out of proportion with the intent of the Act" (CHFRS, Meyer, February 16, 1954, 4).[162]

Even when the OMPC voted to purchase, Boston and Chicago did not always participate in purchase programs. One reason New York stopped purchases in 1932 was that it lost gold reserves to other banks. Unless Strong could have persuaded McDougal and Young to participate, or convinced the Board it should force other banks to sell gold to New York, Strong would have faced a loss of gold and a fall in the gold reserve ratio. Although Meyer at times favored continuing purchases, he was unable to get the Board to insist on a System program. Miller, often joined by Hamlin, opposed purchases. Strong would have faced the same resistance.

Many of the other governors and Board members blamed Strong's policies in 1924 and 1927 for starting the speculative expansion. The contraction was an "inevitable consequence" of the expansion. When speculative credit expansion produced a boom, a collapse must follow. Despite a falling price level before the collapse and an accelerating price decline after, there is far more concern about potential inflation than about deflation. Strong would have had to convince his colleagues that another round of speculative credit expansion could succeed.

---

162. Meyer refers to "ill feeling between the Board, New York and Chicago," no doubt a contributing factor in the inability to reach agreement (CHFRS, Meyer, February 16, 1954, 4).

Quite independent of the role Strong might have played, there is little evidence that Harrison generally favored an expansive policy. The two strongest pieces of evidence Friedman and Schwartz present to suggest that Harrison favored such a policy fail to support that interpretation when examined more closely. Although Harrison received little support for his proposal to purchase, sent to all the governors in July 1930, there is no evidence that he intended to steadily expand the portfolio or the stock of money. In a reply written to the governors of the other reserve banks in mid-July, Harrison noted that there had been an unanticipated increase of $100 million in the bill portfolio and that the money market banks had reduced their borrowing from the reserve banks. This, he said, removed the necessity for purchases. In summer 1931 Harrison, urged on by Meyer and his directors, again tried to persuade the other governors to expand the executive committee's authority to purchase $300 million. Other members of the Open Market Policy Conference opposed and authorized purchases of $120 million. Another improvement in money market conditions occurred shortly after the meeting, and Harrison failed to use the more limited authority given to the executive committee.

In September 1930 W. Randolph Burgess, Carl Snyder, and several members of the Board supported purchases; Harrison opposed.[163] In January 1931 Harrison favored a policy of sales. In January and February 1932 he talked about the need for delay and the danger of wasting ammunition. On these and other occasions, Harrison's views do not differ from the views of the other governors. The minutes provide some evidence that the majority of the committee would not have opposed Harrison if he had encouraged them to continue the purchase program during summer and fall 1932, as Burgess wished. But those who opposed strongly would not have taken their share of the securities. The sample of his views, quoted throughout the chapter, does not show Harrison as repeatedly rebuffed. More often, Governor Meyer of the Board, or some of the New York directors, urged a cautious Harrison to expand.

Harrison's behavior, and the behavior of most of the other governors, is consistent with their understanding of the Riefler-Burgess framework. If, on the Federal Reserve interpretation, the market was "easy," purchases were not authorized or made. Because the governors believed monetary policy was best judged by money market variables, most of them believed they had done all that could be done to prevent a collapse of the monetary

163. In a revised edition of his book, published in 1946, Burgess comments that during the depression borrowing, interest rates, and bank lending responded to Federal Reserve actions but the economy didn't respond. See Wheelock 1990, 415.

system. They did not regard the declines in money and bank credit as consequences of their actions. On their interpretation, the demand for credit had fallen as a "natural" result of the previous speculative boom. This reduced the demand for reserve bank credit. In 1932 they tried a policy that many of them described as credit inflation, and it failed to revive the economy, as several of them expected it would.

Later statements of the reasons for the failure of the 1932 purchase policy differ little from the reasons given in fall 1932 to justify ending the program of open market purchases: "The success of the enlarged open market program (in 1932) depended on the use of excess reserves by member banks" (Anderson 1965, 71). "In October [1933], there was a full-scale review of policy. Excess reserves were about $760 million, member bank indebtedness to the Reserve banks was at the lowest level since August, 1917, and short-term interest rates were at an all-time low. There was general agreement that additional purchases were not needed for monetary reasons" (73).

Federal Reserve officials were not alone in their acceptance of the real bills doctrine. Seymour Harris (1933, 1:365) describes "the heroic efforts made by the Reserve banks in the years 1929–32 to stimulate the expansion of bank credit and (later) to stop the decline." Mints (1945, 264) quotes a 1935 statement by sixty-nine members of the Economists' National Committee on Monetary Policy opposing liberalization of the rediscount provisions of the Federal Reserve Act. The statement expresses concern about illiquidity and inelasticity if the Federal Reserve issues "notes against frozen or illiquid assets." The committee argued that "the supply of non-commercial paper eligible for rediscount should be further restricted, not enlarged."

Looking back on the experience at the end of the 1930s, a *Federal Reserve Bulletin* described the 1929–33 collapse as caused by the speculative situation that developed between 1921 and 1929. The experience also showed that the price level does not respond to the cost of money: "When the cost of money was so drastically cut, prices went down by about one-fourth" (quoted in Mints 1945, 273–74, from the 1939 *Federal Reserve Bulletin*, 363–64).

Wicker (1966) concluded that Federal Reserve officials were ignorant of the proper role of a central bank. This is correct but incomplete. A more complete statement is that most of the governors accepted the real bills doctrine, failed to function as lender of last resort, and failed to distinguish between nominal and real rates of interest.

Ex post real interest rates rose in 1930 and 1931 and remained at histor-

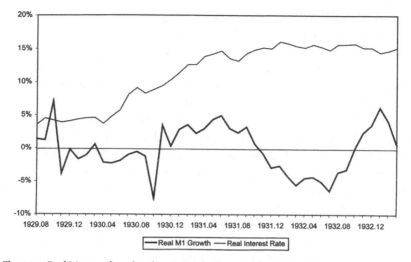

Chart 5.4 Real M$_1$ growth and real interest rate, August 1929 to March 1933.

ically high levels in 1932. Chart 5.4 compares real interest rates to growth of the real money stock.[164] In the previous deflation, 1920–21, falling prices raised real balances and stimulated spending despite relatively high real interest rates. Falling prices also attracted gold, increasing money balances. (See chart 3.1.)[165]

The principal difference in 1929–33 is that the falling money stock more than offset the expansive effect of falling prices on real balances. If the Federal Reserve had prevented the decline in money, falling prices would have raised real balances, created an excess supply of money, stimulated spending, and limited or ended the decline when the economy began to recover in spring 1930; rising real balances and an excess supply of money would have increased aggregate spending. Or if the Federal Reserve had followed gold standard rules, the gold inflow would have increased nominal and real money balances from 1927 to 1929 and from 1929 to the British devaluation in the fall of 1931.

The minutes of the period, statements by Federal Reserve officials, and outside commentary by economists and others do not distinguish between

164. The rate of inflation is common to both series. Ex post real rates are computed using long-term bond yield minus four-quarter moving average inflation. Growth of real money balance is a four-quarter moving average using M$_1$ as the measure of money. The large currency drain makes the monetary base misleading for this period.

165. The same mechanism, deflation, worked subsequently in the deflation of 1937–38 and 1947–48 to raise real balances.

real and nominal interest rates. Surprisingly, even Irving Fisher did not insist on this distinction. Although Fisher pointed to the decline in demand deposits in conversation with Meyer, his preferred explanation of the prolonged decline was the asymmetric effect of deflation on debtors.

Not every official of the Federal Reserve slavishly followed the real bills doctrine or the Riefler-Burgess version of that doctrine. Nor did they all interpret the doctrine in precisely the same way. Some would have preferred a more deflationary policy. Some believed the time for expansion would come in the future, when credit increased and banks offered discounts to the reserve banks. All could agree, much of the time, that purchases should not be made.

In his memoirs many years later, President Hoover expressed his frustration and anger. The Federal Reserve, he wrote, "was indeed a weak reed for a nation to lean on in time of trouble" (Hoover 1952, 212). This was not the accepted view at the time. So certain was the System about the correctness of its actions and its lack of responsibility for the collapse that I have found no evidence the Board undertook an official study of the reasons for the policy failure. Legislative action expanded and centralized the Board's authority. The Riefler-Burgess framework continued as a general guide to policy action and interpretation for many years, and return to the gold standard remained the accepted goal of governments everywhere.

APPENDIX A: DEMAND FOR MONEY

The equations for $\ln M/p$ and $\Delta \ln M/p$ are from Meltzer and Rasche 1994.

	LOG LEVELS M/p 1902–58			FIRST DIFFERENCES $\Delta \ln M/p$ 1903–58	
Constant	−0.28	(0.91)		0.00	(0.38)
$\ln i$	−0.49	(5.61)	$\Delta \ln i$	−0.52	(4.68)
$\ln w$	0.20	(1.28)	$\Delta \ln w$	−0.55	(1.53)
$\ln y_p$	0.39	(2.52)	$\Delta \ln y_p$	0.28	(1.23)
$\ln M/p_{-1}$	0.42	(3.95)	$\Delta \ln M/p_{-1}$	0.12	(0.74)
AR(1)	0.22	(1.44)	AR(1)	−0.30	(1.56)
R^2	0.99		R^2	0.38	
DW	2.01		DW	2.05	

Note: t-statistics are in parentheses.
The variables are defined as:
i = long-term government bond rate
w = real wealth
y_p = expected income from first-order autoregressive equation

APPENDIX B: CROSS-SECTION RESPONSE OF REAL INCOME GROWTH TO GROWTH OF REAL BASE, BASE VELOCITY, AND CURRENCY-DEPOSIT RATIO, 1929–32

The twenty countries are Austria, France, Germany, Italy, Netherlands, Norway, Sweden, United Kingdom, United States, Bulgaria, Czechoslovakia, Denmark, Finland, Greece, Hungary, Spain, Yugoslavia, Mexico, Brazil, Canada. Data are from Mitchell 1992, 1993. Canada appears to be an outlier in the sample, so estimates were made with and without Canadian data. All data are percentage changes for the period. The wholesale price index is the available deflator. Standard errors are in parentheses.

CONSTANT	REAL BASE	BASE VELOCITY	CURRENCY	RATIO R^2 AND SEE
		Twenty countries		
	0.61	0.78	−0.02	0.43
0.05	(0.19)	(0.24)	(0.15)	0.14
		Omitting Canada		
	0.46	0.51	0.01	0.45
0.02	(0.13)	(0.17)	(0.11)	0.09

A simple regression of the growth of the currency-deposit ratio on the growth of income (excluding Canada) has an $R^2 = 0.003$ and a statistically insignificant coefficient = 0.04.

SIX

In the Backseat, 1933 to 1941

The Federal Reserve took few policy actions from 1933 to 1941. The open market portfolio and the discount rate rarely changed. Changes in the monetary base during these years reflect principally changes in the gold stock and the devaluation of the dollar against gold; after the gold standard broke down the United States more closely followed gold standard rules for the money stock.

Congress and the Treasury made the important decisions about gold, silver, and banking legislation. Early in the administration, President Roosevelt took an active part in setting gold policy and making decisions about gold and silver purchases and exchange rates. The Federal Reserve had a subsidiary role—the backseat. New York transacted for the Treasury, as fiscal agent, but the Board had little influence on the decisions and was often uninformed about Treasury actions and plans.

The Banking Act of 1935 permanently changed the Federal Reserve's structure and laid the foundation for the postwar Federal Reserve System. Out went the legal basis for semiautonomous, regional banks, each controlling its own portfolio. Reorganization shifted power and authority over the reserve banks to the Federal Reserve Board in Washington, where it remained. Although the Treasury controlled most decisions until after World War II, the 1935 act made possible the centralized system that developed once the Federal Reserve became free to pursue an independent policy.

Reorganization was mainly the work of Marriner S. Eccles, a Utah banker, aided by Lauchlin Currie, a young economist at the Treasury and later at the Board and in the White House as a presidential adviser. Eccles became governor of the Federal Reserve Board in November 1934 and, after reorganization, the first chairman of the Board of Governors in 1936. He was a strong proponent of government investment spending as a countercyclical policy and believed that the Federal Reserve should keep market rates low to facilitate private spending and government finance during a depression. He called his program "controlled inflation."

Despite these strongly held views, Eccles and the Board became convinced after 1935 that the growing volume of reserves at member banks posed the threat of future inflation. The Board's principal policy action in these years increased reserve requirement ratios as a preemptive act against inflation. Between August 1936 and May 1937, the Board doubled these ratios, thereby contributing to a steep recession in 1937–38.

Until 1937, recovery from the depression proceeded rapidly. In the four years following the trough in March 1933, using Balke and Gordon's (1986) data, real GNP rose at a compound annual rate of almost 12 percent. After a sharp decline in the 1937–38 recession, growth resumed in mid-1938. Real GDP did not reach its 1929 value until 1941, however, and per capita consumption did not regain its 1929 peak until 1942.[1]

Prices rose during the recovery, in part a result of deliberate policy to devalue the dollar so as to raise agricultural and commodity prices. The GNP deflator and the consumer price index remained below their 1929 levels, however, when the United States entered World War II.

Despite the strong recovery, many contemporary observers, including prominent administration officials, regarded President Roosevelt's New Deal as unsuccessful. The principal reason is that 8 million people, more than 14 percent of the labor force, were unemployed in 1940. In fact, the number employed in 1940 was the same as in 1929, and hours worked were lower. Viewed one way, there was a substantial increase in productivity, but part of the measured increase was a substitution of capital for labor to avoid costly New Deal legislation. These measures sought to raise wages, reduce hours of work, and encourage the growth of trade unions. Militant unionism, particularly in manufacturing industries such as autos, steel, and rubber, reduced current and expected profits in those industries and deterred investment.

Labor legislation was one part of President Roosevelt's New Deal. The period 1933–41, particularly the early years, was a time of intense legislative activity. The New Deal restructured society, permanently changing the role of government and the public's attitude toward the responsibilities of

1. GNP came very close to the 1929 peak in 1937, before the recession. Balke and Gordon's (1986) quarterly data (in billions) have a peak of $329.7 in third quarter 1929 and $329.3 in first quarter 1937. Annual data (in 1958 prices) show $203.6 billion for 1929 and $203.2 for 1937. The annual data in 1958 dollars pass the 1929 peak in 1939.

government. Lasting changes were made in the financial system and the Federal Reserve.

Much of the period's financial legislation reflected the judgments reached by the authors of the new legislation, often shared by much of society at the time, that speculation was responsible for financial collapse and the Great Depression. Taken as a whole or separately, much of the new financial legislation sought to prevent or limit speculation in common stocks, restrict banks from financing securities, and centralize authority and responsibility for monetary policy.[2] The Securities Exchange Act (1934) gave the Federal Reserve Board authority to set margin requirements in the belief that general monetary powers, such as open market operations or discount rate changes, cannot prevent a speculative boom in stock prices without harming the so-called legitimate needs of trade.[3] Parts of the Banking Act of 1933, generally referred to as the Glass-Steagall Act, separated commercial banking from investment banking. This section of the Banking Act was mainly the work of Senator Carter Glass. A leading proponent of the real bills doctrine, Glass was convinced that the boom and bust had been caused by commercial bankers' financing investment banking activities and other nonreal bills.[4]

In retrospect, the period marks the beginning of the decline in the importance of the real bills doctrine at the Federal Reserve. The 1932 Glass-Steagall Act permitted government securities to serve as backing for the note issue. Conceived as a temporary step, lack of discounts during the depression required renewal of temporary authority, later made permanent. At the end of the period, the beginning of wartime expansion restructured the Federal Reserve's balance sheet. Government securities became the principal source of reserve bank credit. Growth in the size of the balance sheet and wartime inflation made it less costly to reduce, and later elimi-

---

2. President Hoover partly shared this belief. In 1930 he asked the officers of the New York Stock Exchange to reform their rules to eliminate excessive speculation. He did not believe there was constitutional authority for legislation (Fusfeld 1956, 224).

3. Several studies, beginning with Moore 1966, find that margin requirements are ineffective and have little effect on stock prices or trading. Although not recognized by the financial community at the time, some of the legislation contributed to the development of financial markets. The 1933 Securities Act improved both the quantity and the quality of information about companies, thereby encouraging widespread ownership of common stocks after growth resumed in the postwar years.

4. Benston (1990) documents the charges made against bankers, including claims of criminal activity and disregard for the public. In a superb book, he shows that the claims were either false or unsupported by evidence. At the time, each citation of evidence of wrongdoing referred to previous citations, so a reader could believe that the changes had been thoroughly researched and documented. After World War II, the United States imposed a similar system on Japan. Congress repealed these provisions in 1999 after a major bank merged with an investment bank and an insurance company.

nate, reserve requirements behind the note issue and the monetary base than to shrink the base and force postwar deflation.

Other legislative changes reshaped the Federal Reserve by reducing the power of the New York Federal Reserve bank domestically and internationally. Glass and others believed that Benjamin Strong's assistance to Britain in 1924 and, even more, in 1927 initiated the speculative boom that ended in the collapse. A widely shared view held that the collapse was an inevitable consequence of previous speculative excesses and departures from real bills principles. Unorthodox policies, such as the Hoover budget deficits and Britain's departure from gold, sustained and deepened the collapse. Hence the remedy was to reduce the influence of those like Strong whose ideas, they believed, had failed.

None of this was lost on Adolph Miller. Miller, a friend of both Glass and Roosevelt, saw the Banking Acts of 1933 and 1935 as a vindication of his views (Miller 1935). He believed that by centralizing power in the Board, and eventually restoring the gold standard, the Federal Reserve would return to its original conception. In this he was mistaken.

A contemporary reader finds it difficult to reconstruct the prevailing orthodoxies of the past or to see events as they were seen at the time. Bernard Baruch, a financier who advised many presidents, perhaps typifies the views of the more articulate and influential bankers and financiers of the period. In testimony before the Senate Finance Committee in February 1933, Baruch blamed the depression on four factors, all the effects of war: inflation, debt and taxes, national self-containment, and excess productive capacity (Baruch 1933, 1). The "chief barrier" was wartime inflation. Only in 1933 could prices be said to have fallen to the 1913 level. Reflation by monetary means to restore prices to the 1929 level was the wrong policy. Prices could not be raised by increasing money: "If there is no confidence, no amount of tinkering with the currency can raise the price level. . . . Deficits and the finance of them by 'bank money' inflation . . . impair confidence and drive money deeper into hiding" (9). A main task of government was to reduce public spending. Although he favored relief of human suffering, he believed that "reduction in public expense is indispensable for recovery" (2). Reductions in spending and the budget deficit instill confidence and "the working of natural processes" (4). Baruch's views are similar to the views of the Economists' National Committee on Monetary Policy, a group that included prominent academic economists.

Views like these were not just wrong, they were influential. They appealed to beliefs that were widely shared. They called for more deflation and contraction in the mistaken belief that the 1913 price level (or some other) was correct. Restoration of that price level would somehow right whatever was wrong, but the proponents could not say how or why that would happen.

Not all financial legislation and action corrected past mistakes and alleged misdeeds. Roosevelt had campaigned as a financial conservative, critical of the Hoover administration's deficit spending, but he also wanted to end the depression and stop the fall in prices. He promised to balance the budget, except for emergency relief, but he offered few specific proposals during the 1932 campaign and had no coherent plan for the economy when he took office.[5] During the campaign, Roosevelt described himself as an advocate of experimentation: "The country needs and, unless I mistake its temper, the country demands bold, persistent experimentation. It is common sense to take a method and try it. If it fails, admit it frankly and try another. But above all, try something" (quoted in Sumner 1995, 1).

Between 1933 and the beginning of defense and war mobilization in 1940, the Roosevelt administration experimented with five main types of economic policy. The Supreme Court declared some of these actions unconstitutional. Some conflicted with others, for example, establishing cartels to fix prices and later strengthening antitrust action against price fixing. Roosevelt encouraged some advisers to advocate policies that others opposed so that he could gauge public reaction. He chose between them, tired of the policies when they did not work or were unpopular, and went to something different.

One group led by Agriculture Secretary Henry Wallace and two of Roosevelt's campaign advisers, Rexford Tugwell and Raymond Moley, wanted national planning.[6] In the administration's first months, Congress passed

---

5. Much of his campaign was an attack on Hoover's policies. His main charges were that the Hoover administration had encouraged speculation and overproduction, misled the public about the gravity of the collapse, blamed other countries for our problems, and delayed relief and forgotten reform (Fusfeld 1956, 223). During the campaign Roosevelt favored a larger measure of "social planning" but did not elaborate (204).

6. Tugwell was an economist and Moley a political scientist at Columbia University. Along with Adolf Berle, a lawyer, they were the principals of Roosevelt's campaign "brain trust." Moley coordinated campaign policy statements. His specialty was crime and the administration of justice, but he worked on all domestic policy issues during the campaign (Fusfeld 1956, 210–15). Tugwell was the main advocate of planning and a tax on undistributed corporate profits that the administration later tried. Berle was a student of economic concentration. He believed that corporations must serve not just stockholders but the community, a view that appears periodically in the literature critical of the modern corporation. Although he shared some of Tugwell's views, he was more favorable to antitrust as a solution to the economy's problem. Instead of forming cartels under government supervision, Berle favored breaking up large firms.

the National Industrial Recovery Act (NIRA) and the Agricultural Adjustment Act. Both were declared unconstitutional within three years.[7]

A second group wanted reductions in government spending and a balanced budget. During the campaign Roosevelt had promised a balanced budget, except for emergency relief, in a campaign speech in Pittsburgh, and he had criticized Hoover repeatedly for running deficits. In the first one hundred days Congress passed the Economy Act, reducing government employees' salaries by 15 percent and reducing veterans' pensions. Balancing the budget remained an unrealized goal of the administration until the 1938 recession, when the goal changed. Prominent advocates of balanced budgets, as a means of restoring confidence, included many economists and businessmen. Within the administration, the leaders of this group were Henry Morgenthau, who followed William Woodin as secretary of the treasury, serving from late 1933 to 1946, and Lewis Douglas, the first budget director.

A third group took the opposite position. This group included Marriner Eccles, Lauchlin Currie, Harold Ickes, and Harry Hopkins. Eccles and Currie, separately, developed the idea of countercyclical fiscal policy that later became identified with Keynes's *General Theory*.[8] Eccles, like Keynes, wanted not just spending but government investment to replace private investment during recessions. Roosevelt took this approach in 1938, but his change of view was partly, possibly mainly, a political decision about the 1938 election.

The fourth group wanted antitrust policy to break monopolies. Adolph Berle, an early adviser, was the leading proponent for many years, but he was supported in 1938 by the staff of the antitrust division of the Justice Department led by Thurman Arnold. As part of this policy, the Temporary National Economic Committee conducted a massive study of monopolies, trusts, and business practices beginning in 1938.

Fifth was the concerted effort to supplement NIRA codes of fair pricing by increasing the gold price and buying silver. These monetary operations to raise the price level are discussed more fully below.

Both the Democratic and Republican platforms, prepared for the 1932

7. Weinstein 1981 is a careful study of the macroeffects of NIRA. The act, signed by the president in June 1933, gave the administration power to regulate production in cooperation with business and labor unions. These groups adopted "codes" of conduct that had the force of law. In total, 557 codes were adopted (plus 188 supplementary codes), covering 95 percent of industry. The codes increased wages, reduced hours of work, and set "fair" prices (Arndt 1966, 42).

8. Keynes first advocated the plan (with Hubert Henderson) during the 1929 British election. Eccles and Currie did not seem to know that Keynes's advocacy predated their own. As Laidler (1999) shows, deficit finance had many advocates before Keynes, Currie, or Eccles.

campaign, called for an international conference to consider monetary questions. Both platforms mentioned silver explicitly, in deference to political pressures from western states. Both urged reform of bank supervision and action to prevent the use of credit for speculation (Krooss 1969, 4:2692–93). Both are short on specific recommendations.

The depression years were the beginning of the end of the international gold standard. Increasingly, domestic concerns dominated international concerns. Roosevelt had not committed to maintaining the gold standard during the campaign or after. He had not decided to devalue, either. In retrospect, July 1933 is the turning point, the time when the administration chose domestic recovery and an end to deflation over commitment to a fixed gold price. The Federal Reserve had sterilized gold flows in the past to achieve domestic objectives, but sterilization did not alter the commitment to a fixed exchange rate. Although the Roosevelt administration attempted to stabilize exchange rates by international agreement in 1936 and again in 1944, neither agreement required the Federal Reserve to subordinate domestic to international monetary objectives.

REOPENING THE BANKS
Most of the banks in the country had been closed before the national banking holiday in March 1933 as a defense against further bank runs. Federal Reserve staff had considered how to restore banking services. The administration, however, had no plan for reopening banks, and no program for what would come next. It had not planned whether the United States would leave the gold standard or reopen the reserve banks and pay out gold as necessary. On March 9 the Emergency Banking Act resolved the administrative issue by authorizing the secretary of the treasury and the state banking authorities to license banks. Implementing the program proved time consuming.[9]

The Federal Reserve had been indecisive and incompetent as the banking problem became a crisis. The Board now took a backseat.[10] The Trea-

---

9. Case describes procedures at New York (interviews with J. Herbert Case, CHFRS, February 26, 1954, 3–4). The New York district had 1,200 banks, of which 30 percent had problems. Leslie Rounds, a vice president, and his staff screened each bank. The directors met all day, every day, during the bank holiday to consider his recommendations. In some cases, the RFC purchased preferred stock to restore capital and permit reopening.

10. One active participant blames Meyer for the lack of leadership. Meyer did not get along with Roosevelt and resigned in May 1933 (CHFRS, interview with Edward Smead, June 14, 1954). Smead was head of Reports and Statistics at the Board. Smead claims that Ogden Mills took control of the banks' reopening. Awalt (1969, 361–63) also credits Mills with a leading role even though his term had ended. He reports that Meyer insisted on a stenographic record of all his conversations (and his staff's) with Secretary Woodin. Woodin refused to speak to him or the staff. Awalt (368) attributes this behavior to concern about future embarrassment.

sury and the new president made the policy decisions. Ogden Mills stayed on to assist the new secretary, William Woodin. The Board's senior staff took a leading role in drafting proposals to reopen the banks in stages. It also drafted legislation that became the Emergency Banking Act, based on earlier work. George Harrison came to Washington on March 5 to work with Mills, Woodin, Senator Carter Glass, Congressman Henry Steagall, the acting comptroller, Francis Awalt, Adolph Berle, one of the Columbia professors advising Roosevelt, Treasury staff, and others. Later, Adolph Miller joined the group.

The group could not reach a conclusion. Some wanted to guarantee all bank deposits. Others wanted to print currency and pay it out to all depositors. Glass shifted from favoring an end to gold payments to a proposal that they pay gold on demand without regard to the statutory reserve. The proposal to issue currency is the only mention of a readily available Bagehotian solution to the currency drain. Harrison opposed the proposal as inflationary, and it did not get much consideration (Harrison Papers, Memo to the Files, file 2010.2, March 12, 1933).

The discussion went on most of Sunday without reaching a conclusion. Woodin appointed a small subset to work out a plan. On Monday, this smaller group proposed to guarantee bank deposits either up to 50 percent or on a sliding scale depending on the bank's assets, but the administration, especially the president, opposed a guarantee.[11] They agreed to open the strongest banks first but could not agree on how to open the weaker banks without renewing bank runs or offering guarantees.[12] Finally Roosevelt decided to make all government bonds, $21 billion, convertible into currency on demand at par. Full conversion would have doubled the money stock, currency, and demand deposits. Mills and Harrison were aghast. Harrison regarded it as "completely destructive of government credit, such an inflation of the currency as to destroy the currency and offer no means of contraction" (ibid., 7).

The crisis got the Federal Reserve to do what it had failed to do earlier— relax its rules governing currency issues and credit expansion. To head off the president's proposal, Mills and Harrison proposed that the administration reopen the sound banks, reorganize those that could survive and

---

11. Harrison describes Adolph Miller at these meetings as "impossible . . . making long harangues—many of them quite academic and not pertinent." Miller refused to take a position because he was there unofficially (Harrison Papers, Memo to the Files, file 2010.2, March 12, 1933, 5).

12. Harrison proposed that individuals, corporations, and others that held government bonds be allowed to borrow currency against this collateral at Federal Reserve banks. This was a major departure from precedent, but it did not solve the larger problem of reopening banks.

support many of them in exchange for preferred stock held by the Reconstruction Finance Corporation (RFC), and close the rest. The Federal Reserve (1) would lend to any member bank that opened based on its sound assets and weaken the links between gold and note issue by (2) issuing Federal Reserve bank notes backed only by portfolio assets (not gold), and (3) would broaden the definition of eligible paper backing the new notes to include direct obligations of individuals and firms that borrowed from Federal Reserve banks against government securities. The president accepted the proposal, and it became part of the Emergency Banking Act (Harrison Papers, file 2010.2, March 12, 1933).[13]

Federal Reserve banks reopened on March 10 and 11 to provide cash for payrolls and to lend on government securities. Harrison told his directors that the new law "greatly extends the powers of the Reserve banks, and adds to their responsibilities and the risks, which they may incur" (Minutes, New York Directors, March 9, 1933, 172). They could now lend more freely and greatly expand the note issue. Since the objective was to prevent reopened banks from failing, "the Federal Reserve banks become in effect guarantors of the deposits of reopened banks" (172).[14]

In his first "fireside chat" to the public on March 12, the president explained the plan for reopening banks. Licensed banks in Federal Reserve cities reopened on Monday, March 13. On Tuesday, licensed banks reopened in 250 cities with clearinghouses. Reopening continued for months. The Federal Reserve banks sent the Treasury lists of banks recommended for reopening, and the Treasury licensed those it approved.[15] As late as October, bankers wrote to complain about the slow pace of reopenings (Board of Governors File, box 2185, October 2, 1933).

13. Joseph Dreibilbis gives principal credit to Walter Wyatt, the Board's counsel, and to various ideas that "had been thought up previously." He does not mention Harrison by name (CHFRS, Dreibilbis, March 9, 1954, 2). Awalt (1969) also credits Wyatt and Mills. Roosevelt's refusal to consider deposit guarantees may have been motivated by unwillingness to endorse Hoover's main proposal or by his belief that guarantees would increase risk.

14. A liberal reopening policy meant the reserve banks would have to lend to relatively weak banks but deflation would end. A conservative policy would leave many areas without banks; the shrinkage of money and credit would pose a risk. The directors chose a liberal reopening policy but wanted to restrict the public's access at first to 50 percent of its deposits, gradually increasing the percentage. The Treasury wanted 100 percent of the deposits available and agreed to indemnify the reserve banks against losses (Minutes, New York Directors, March 11, 1933, 179). Out of 5,938 national banks, 5,300 reopened on March 9 (Awalt 1969, 360–61, 367).

15. Authority for the secretary to license banks continued until April 1947, and some banks continued to operate under Treasury license in the 1940s. Government intermediaries such as the Reconstruction Finance Corporation, the Home Loan Banks, Intermediate Credit Banks, and Land Banks reopened on March 13. Some states permitted all banks to open at once, so there were wide differences in availability of banking facilities in the country.

Approximately 4,000 banks did not reopen.[16] This was nearly 40 percent of the banks that closed between June 1929 and June 1933. The Midwest was hit particularly hard, losing 2,500 of the 4,000 banks. The Cleveland Federal Reserve bank sent a telegram to the Board expressing concern about "many banking institutions the present condition of which precludes their reopening with governmental support . . . or otherwise" (telegram, Decamp to Meyer, Board of Governors File, box 2158, March 11, 1933). Other reserve banks wired concern about too few or too many banks being opened.

The president's announcement had assured the public that only sound banks would be reopened. Recognizing that the public would not distinguish between member and nonmember banks, Congress allowed state nonmember banks to borrow from Federal Reserve banks on acceptable collateral. This power expired after one year.[17]

Many of the banks that did not immediately reopen had borrowed from the Federal Reserve. Nearly nine hundred unlicensed and closed banks owed $125 million, almost 30 percent of outstanding borrowing in early April. Chicago had the largest number of such banks, 13 percent of the total, but Philadelphia, New York, and Cleveland each held about 20 percent of the now illiquid loans (Board of Governors File, box 1297, April 8, 1933).

The April meeting of the Governors Conference considered the many problems encountered in reopening and licensing banks. A week after the meeting, a committee of governors drafted a statement reporting the unanimous opinion that "if any member bank which had been licensed to reopen, is permitted to fail, it will prove a serious shock to the confidence

16. Data from Board of Governors of the Federal Reserve System (1943, 16) show a decline of 3,871 in the number of banks (including mutual savings banks) between December 1932 and June 1933. Friedman and Schwartz (1963, 423–27) give a detailed accounting. They report only 2,132 banks closed, suspended, or liquidated between March 15, 1933, and December 31, 1936. An additional 500 banks terminated during the bank holiday to March 15. Part of the discrepancy results from differences in the definition of a bank, but the main difference arises from the difference in dates; 1,334 banks reopened between June 1933 and December 1936.

17. The banks had to meet reserve requirements and other Federal Reserve regulations while in debt to a reserve bank. The history of this bill gives insight into the way government functioned during the crisis. The Federal Reserve learned about the bill by chance, when one of its senior staff overheard a conversation between the budget director and a treasury undersecretary. The Board believed the legislation unnecessary because the Reconstruction Finance Corporation could make the necessary loans or could purchase preferred stock under the Emergency Banking Act. Senator Huey Long (Louisiana) wanted to admit all banks to the Federal Reserve System, so the Board proposed to amend the pending bill by making state banks meet the reserve and other requirements of member banks. The Board notified Senator Glass, however, that it continued to oppose the legislation.

of the public, . . . and may well precipitate a banking crisis even more critical than the recent one" (Governors Conference, April 19, 1933, memo dated April 26, 1933).[18] The governors accepted a share of the responsibility for avoiding failures, but they were concerned that their efforts would reduce the capital and surplus of the Federal Reserve banks if banks failed while in debt to the reserve banks. The governors' subcommittee recommended that the Federal Reserve banks "adopt a liberal loan policy and be prepared to make loans on sound assets with little or no margin in cases where it is necessary to keep a bank open." To reduce risk to the reserve banks, the subcommittee urged that the Reconstruction Finance Corporation take over loans after an agreed period (ibid., 2–3).[19]

The subcommittee also suggested an alternative. The Federal Reserve could lend to the RFC, and the RFC could lend to the banks. The RFC's debentures carried a government guarantee, so the Federal Reserve would be protected against losses. The subcommittee wanted authorization to negotiate an agreement to this effect with the Treasury.

The remarkable feature of the memo is that, except for the guarantee, it recalls a proposal made by Secretary Mellon in 1931. At that time President Hoover and Secretary Mellon sought a nongovernment solution to prevent bank failures. Large banks were asked to underwrite a new intermediary, the National Credit Commission, that would buy up some of the assets of failing banks. The effort failed in part because the Federal Reserve refused to accept obligations of the proposed intermediary as eligible paper if the subscribing banks faced insolvency or illiquidity. If the earlier proposal had been implemented, many of the bank failures and the resulting financial crisis could have been avoided.

No less remarkable is that the subcommittee recommending the financial safety net had three members, George W. Norris, George Seay, and George L. Harrison, who had served throughout the decline. Norris was an especially strong proponent of real bills and an opponent of credit expansion by the Federal Reserve. It is hard to avoid the conclusion that the governors were not just chastened by their experience but were also fearful of the legislation that the new Congress and administration would support if they failed to cooperate with the recovery program.

The proclamations and orders closing and reopening banks also changed the role of gold in the monetary system. On March 6 banks were

18. The minutes of the April 19 Governors Conference also considered matters "of such a confidential nature that a written record seems to be undesirable."

19. Calomiris and White (1994) point out the importance of an agreement between Roosevelt and the RFC regarding deposit insurance as one of the key steps in the reopening process by reducing concerns of the reserve banks.

ordered not to pay out gold or gold certificates in connection with the few transactions authorized with foreigners during the bank holiday. After March 10, reopened banks or financial institutions could not pay out gold or gold certificates without authorization by the secretary of the treasury. The Board ordered the reserve banks to compile lists of all persons who purchased gold from the reserve banks after February 1 and had not redeposited the gold in a bank before March 13 (later extended to March 27).

The administration had not formulated a gold policy. Among those whose advice the president sought, Professors Irving Fisher, George Warren, and John R. Commons were the main proponents of devaluation or abandoning the gold standard. Roosevelt made no decision at the time, so it was not known whether the restrictions on gold payments would remain or prove temporary (Barber 1996, 24–25).

The banking position was a decisive factor in the decision to leave the gold standard. On April 5, the president forbade domestic gold holding. All gold coin, certificates, and bullion were ordered sold to the Federal Reserve banks by May 1.[20] On April 18 the president announced that the Treasury would cease issuing licenses to export gold (except to settle claims of foreign governments made before the moratorium).

The April 18 order took the country off the gold standard and ended any deflationary threat from adherence to gold standard rules. The president's announcement did not explain what would happen next. The president was no less obscure the next day, when he explained that he wanted to raise commodity prices and get the world back on the gold standard. This was followed on June 5 by a joint resolution abrogating the gold clause in all public and private contracts. Payments could be made only in legal tender.

The gold drain did not require a ban on domestic gold holding or repudiation of the gold clauses in private and public contracts. The president's April 18 decision would have stopped the gold outflow by making the dollar inconvertible into gold, a decision President Nixon made in 1971. This would have permanently removed the deflationary pressure that the embargo had ended temporarily. Banning private gold holdings and abrogating the gold clauses transferred the profit on the devaluation to the federal

20. Awalt (1969, n. 6) reports that Miller considered leaving the gold standard in the fall of 1932. Also, he notes that Adolph Miller discussed a gold embargo in June 1932. The discussion never went further. The Treasury agreed to repay the Federal Reserve for the expenses incurred in reopening the banks. Roosevelt had insisted on frugality, so the Treasury would not pay for the costs of shipping gold and for losses from abrasion. Some commercial banks refused to ship gold to the reserve banks unless the reserve banks paid for freight, insurance, and abrasion (memo to Morrill, Board of Governors File, box 745, October 10, 1933). The following April, the Treasury agreed to reimburse the reserve banks.

government. These steps seem unnecessary interventions into private contracts and asset decisions. Their purposes were mainly political, to show that bankers and wealthy individuals would not gain from the policy.

Since the United States held about one-third of the gold in all central banks, these moves puzzled Europeans and generated suspicion and distrust of United States policy in the negotiations leading up to the London economic summit scheduled to be held that summer. The suspicions remained when the administration later changed course and sought cooperation to stabilize the dollar exchange rate against the pound and the franc.

MONETARY AND OTHER LEGISLATION, 1933

The Hoover administration had done little to correct the perceived flaws in financial regulation. The Glass-Steagall Act granted authority to use government securities as collateral for the note issue as a temporary measure, later made permanent. Likewise the Reconstruction Finance Corporation started as a rescue operation for banks, insurance companies, and railroads, but initially loans had to have full collateral backing. The RFC had very limited resources. After Congress required release of the names of banks it helped, banks hesitated to ask the RFC for assistance. Mason (1994) notes that the RFC's constructive role in reorganization began in 1933, when it gained the power to acquire preferred stock in weak or failing banks.

Congress held hearings on reform proposals during 1931 and 1932 without reaching agreement or passing legislation.[21] The information collected proved useful, however. In 1933 the banking committees could proceed without new hearings. Their major problem was to avoid some of the more populist measures such as those calling for issuing greenbacks, coining silver, devaluing the dollar, and compensating depositors for part of their losses from bank failures.[22] Some of these proposals had considerable public support and support in Congress.

---

21. The 1931 hearings focused on branch, group, and chain banking. Congress could not agree on what regulation was needed. National banks were permitted to follow state rules on branching in 1927.

22. One bill (S. 806) abolished the Federal Reserve System. All deposits would be placed in a bank (with branches) authorized to issue $2 billion of new credit (approximately 25 percent of the monetary base at the time). The bank would be charged with restoring the price level to the 1915–25 range, a range that included wartime inflation (Woodin to Fletcher, Board of Governors File, box 136, May 3, 1933). The Home Loan Bank Act passed on July 16, 1932, permitted issuance of $917 million in national banknotes. Only $120 million was issued in the next year. On the same date legislation authorized Federal Reserve loans directly to individuals and businesses.

The Thomas Amendment

The wholesale price index, as recorded at the time, reached a low of 59.6 (base 100 in 1926) in early February and again in March. By early April the index had increased only one point. This was far too slow for many farmers and ranchers, hence for their representatives. They wanted prices for crops and livestock increased in time for the harvest.

Senator Burton Wheeler (Montana) offered an amendment requiring the Treasury to coin silver in the ratio of sixteen to one to gold. When Roosevelt threatened to veto the bill, Senator Elmer Thomas (Oklahoma) offered a substitute amendment to the Agricultural Adjustment Act (AAA) that permitted the Federal Reserve to purchase up to $3 billion of securities directly from the Treasury upon authorization by the president; gave the president discretionary authority to issue $3 billion in currency (United States notes or greenbacks) if the Federal Reserve refused to make direct purchases of Treasury securities; and permitted the president to devalue the dollar against gold and silver up to 50 percent of its value.[23] The amendment also permitted the Federal Reserve Board to raise or lower required reserve ratios by declaring an emergency, on a vote of five members and with the approval of the president, and it authorized silver purchases of up to $200 million (Krooss 1969, 4:2719–22).[24]

Roosevelt and his advisers did not agree about the amendment. Opponents believed it was inflationary and likely to raise concerns about the administration's direction. Roosevelt saw the issue in political terms. The amendment authorized action but did not require it. If he opposed the Thomas amendment, Congress could pass mandatory legislation to inflate. The hesitation suggests that the administration had not decided whether to return to the gold standard at the old parity, devalue, or inflate. When Roosevelt announced on April 18 that he would accept the amendment, his budget director, Lewis Douglas (a gold standard advocate), is reported to have said, "This is the end of western civilization" (Kindleberger 1986, 200).

The Federal Reserve did not participate in discussions with the president about the Thomas amendment (Todd 1995, 26). Nor did it raise objections or point out that prices of most agricultural products were set in

23. Originally the bill had no time limit. In January 1934 the Gold Reserve Act limited the authority to two years.

24. The legislation became part of the Agricultural Adjustment Act because the act sought to raise farm prices by restricting output. The Thomas amendment added a demand side policy to raise farm prices. The amendment passed the House 307 to 86 and the Senate 64 to 21, more than enough to override a veto.

world markets, so that any benefit to farmers resulting from inflation would be temporary, reversed by devaluation of the dollar and a rise in the prices farmers paid.

Meyer did not approve of the administration's direction and had limited contact with its officials. On May 10, he resigned. His replacement as governor was Eugene R. Black, governor of the Federal Reserve Bank of Atlanta since early 1928. Black had the shortest tenure as governor of the Board to date; he served only fifteen months before returning to the Atlanta bank. He died in December 1934, four months after his return.[25] Roosevelt also appointed J. F. T. O'Connor as comptroller and, ex officio, a member of the Board.

The Banking Act of 1933

As a senior member of Congress, Carter Glass had his choice of the chairmanship of two Senate committees—Appropriations and Banking. If Glass chose Banking, Kenneth McKellar (Tennessee) would be chairman of Appropriations. McKellar was a machine politician and, for this and other reasons, unattractive to the incoming administration as chairman of a key committee. The president prevailed on Glass to take the Appropriations post but, de facto, he retained control of banking legislation (Hyman 1976, 162).[26]

The 1933 act was the first major revision of the Federal Reserve Act. Glass submitted his first bill in December 1930. Shortly after, he appointed H. Parker Willis as technical adviser to the committee.[27] Willis had worked with Glass in 1913 and shared his views about the real bills doctrine, speculation, and decentralization. Hearings began in January 1931. Glass and Willis used the hearings to question Harrison, Case, Miller, and others

25. Black knew Roosevelt from Roosevelt's frequent trips to Warm Springs, Georgia. He did not intend to stay in Washington and went on leave from the Atlanta bank. His salary at the Board was about half his salary at Atlanta, and though he opposed deflation, he did not favor the administration's "inflationary policies." Unlike Meyer, he favored expansion, so he resumed open market purchases, but he opposed devaluation of the dollar (Katz 1992, 14–24).

26. Duncan Fletcher (Florida) became chairman of Banking and Currency, but power and authority rested with Glass. Glass became chairman of a subcommittee with authority to formulate banking and monetary policies. All members of the committee were also members of Glass's subcommittee, and all legislation affecting banking and the Federal Reserve went through his subcommittee. In the House, Henry Steagall remained as chairman of the Banking and Currency Committee. Before the 1932 election, the Republicans controlled the Senate but not the House after 1930. Senator Peter Norbeck (South Dakota) was chairman of the banking committee, but he allowed Glass to chair the subcommittee on banking legislation (Patrick 1993, 42–43).

27. Chester Morrill, for many years the Board's secretary, reports that bankers strongly opposed Willis's draft legislation. Early in 1932, "Meyer exposed his weakness as a draftsman." Willis resigned (CHFRS, interview with Chester Morrill, May 20, 1954, 4–5).

about what had gone wrong, whether speculation and the power of the New York bank in dealings with foreign central banks had contributed to bank failures, deflation, and depression, and whether the Board should have more control of open market operations.[28]

A second attempt to write a bill, in 1932, strengthened the Board's power over open market operations. All operations had to have the approval of the open market committee and the Board. The Board argued that that was too rigid.[29]

The 1933 act established a deposit insurance fund that became the Federal Deposit Insurance Corporation (FDIC), separated deposit and investment banking, restricted member banks from dealing in investment securities, and placed supervision of bank holding companies under the Board.[30] The act also lengthened the terms of the six appointed Board members to twelve years, increased the Board's power to remove bank officers or directors who violated banking laws, prohibited interest payments on demand deposits, and gave the Board power to set ceiling rates on time deposits.[31]

The Federal Open Market Committee, with all twelve banks as members, acquired legal status. Reserve banks could engage in open market operations only under Board regulations (Krooss (1969, 4:2725–69). To retain local directors' authority, the act permitted a reserve bank to refuse to participate in an open market operation on thirty days' notice to the Board and the committee (Kennedy 1973, 210). This was a step away from the idea of semiautonomous reserve banks, but it did not abandon local option.

Glass believed the New York bank and the secretary of the treasury had

28. The reference to "foreign central banks" referred mainly to Strong's assistance to the Bank of England, which Glass regarded as violating the principles of the Federal Reserve Act. Parts of the colloquy are summarized in chapter 4. Miller supported Glass's argument for greater Board supervision and responsibility for open market operations but did not argue for the Board's taking responsibility for relations with foreign central banks (Senate Committee on Banking and Currency 1931, 159).

29. In his letter to Congress about the proposed bill, Meyer offered a strange proposal suggesting that reserve requirements be based on deposits and deposit turnover—debits to deposit accounts. The intention was to penalize speculative credit by taxing overnight or short-term borrowing and repayments (Board of Governors File, box 142, March 29, 1932). The proposal penalized a bank for its customers' decisions.

30. One-bank holding companies were inadvertently omitted. This omission was corrected in 1956.

31. Restrictions on interest payments reflected the belief that banks had made speculative and unsound loans to increase earnings and pay interest. Benston (1964) shows there is no evidence for this belief. The Board opposed the prohibition of interest payments as a major change whose consequences could not be foreseen. Glass told them he did not need their views, since he knew them (Board Minutes, April 10, 1933, 24; April 13, 1933, 16).

too much power. He blamed New York, particularly Strong, for the expansion of speculative credit after 1927. He was suspicious of the relation between the New York bank and the Bank of England and determined to prevent relations of this kind from affecting the growth of credit. The act reduced New York's role in foreign transactions by shifting control to the Board. Glass also wanted to remove the treasury secretary from the Board, but the secretary objected strongly, and Glass did not prevail.

The act also eliminated the double liability of directors of national banks, specified in the National Banking Act.[32] Despite much testimony arguing that reserve banks could not control the use of credit, Glass inserted a provision that the banks must keep informed about "whether undue use is being made of bank credit for the speculative carrying or trading in securities, real estate or commodities" (Krooss 1969, 4:2726). The intent was to limit discounting and prevent financial speculation. Since discounts remained low in the 1930s, the provision had no effect. Glass also included a provision making the System's goal the accommodation of commerce, industry, and agriculture.

Writing at the time, Westerfield (1933, 727) reports that Glass believed the Federal Reserve had been dominated by the Treasury and had permitted securities speculation. The Board had been timid and vacillating. Power had shifted to New York. The Board, on its side, considered most of the legislation unnecessary. It wanted only an amendment clarifying its power of supervision over open market operations and relations with foreign banks (732).

Glass had larger plans. He wanted most of all to strengthen commercial lending by separating commercial and investment banking. Some bankers supported this change, among them Winthrop Aldrich, chairman of the Chase National Bank (Harrison Papers, Conversations, file 2500.1, March 8, 1933).[33] He wanted banks to retain powers to underwrite only municipal, state, and federal government bonds. After the Pecora investigation of investment banking exposed the alleged misdeeds of banks' investment affiliates, other bankers wrote to Roosevelt or Glass supporting separation (Kennedy 1973, 222–23).[34]

32. Kane and Wilson (1998) show that elimination of double liability helped shareholders of large banks during the recovery.

33. Winthrop Aldrich was the son of Senator Nelson Aldrich, who played a leading role in establishing the Federal Reserve. He had become chairman of Chase by opposing financing through an affiliate and favoring conservative banking. At Chase, he replaced Albert Wiggins, a longtime director of the New York reserve bank.

34. As noted above, Benston (1990) shows that there was little if any evidence to support the charges. Calomiris (1997, 11) summarizes research as showing "that securities underwriting by banks prior to 1933 was at least as honest as securities underwriting outside of

Section 20 of the Banking Act, known as the Glass-Steagall Act, gave banks one year to choose between commercial and investment banking, prohibited investment banks from taking deposits, and banned interlocking directorates for commercial and investment banks. Glass regarded this as the most important feature of the 1933 act. It took more than sixty years to reverse the mistake.

Henry Steagall (Alabama) had proposed some type of deposit insurance or guarantee for several years. The insurance provisions were his main contribution to the Banking Act.[35] Public pressure to get partial recompense for banking losses helped to move the legislation toward passage.

Opposition to deposit insurance came from two sources. First, past attempts by states had produced mixed results, in part because of problems of moral hazard, in part because local banks were not diversified. Second, many small banks wanted insurance, but large banks believed they would be forced to pay most of the cost and thus subsidize small, weak banks. The history of failures before the depression supported this argument. Opponents favored liberalized branching to produce more diversified financial institutions (White 1997, 3).

The 1933 provision started as a proposal to deal with the liquidation of failed member banks. The Federal Advisory Council argued that the government should pay the liquidation costs for member banks just as the RFC paid for nonmember banks. The compromise proposal took $150 million from the RFC and half the surplus of the reserve banks on January 1, 1933—$138 million—to establish the Temporary Deposit Insurance Fund, which opened in January 1934 (Todd 1995, 28). Insurance was limited to $2,500 of deposits. Large bankers wanted any fund restricted to member banks, but the legislation admitted nonmembers if they undertook to join the System within two years. This provision was unpopular with small banks, and it was removed in the Banking Act of 1935.[36] The latter act changed the fund's name to the Federal Deposit Insurance Corporation (FDIC), made it a permanent agency, and raised maximum insurance to

---

banks." Securities operations diversified bank risks, hence lowering risk. See also Rajan (1992), who points out that banks realize informational economies by combining lending and underwriting securities. If there is conflict of interest, this gain could be a loss to customers.

35. In 1932, with the help of Speaker John Nance Garner, later vice president, a deposit insurance bill passed the House. Glass was opposed, so the bill died (Kennedy 1973, 214). See Calomiris and White 1994 for a thorough discussion of Steagall's role.

36. The Banking Act of 1933 made the fund permanent beginning July 1934, but later amendments postponed the start of permanent operations. The fund had independent directors, one of whom was the comptroller of the currency. Hence, until 1936 the comptroller served as a member of the Federal Reserve Board and as a director of the FDIC.

$5,000 (White 1997, 4–5). By 1980 the government insured deposits up to $100,000, the equivalent of $16,000 at 1934 prices.

The Federal Reserve's failure to serve as lender of last resort, principally from 1931 to 1933, is the main reason for deposit insurance. Deposit insurance, however, is not a substitute for the lender of last resort; the insurance fund cannot protect against systemic or widespread failure. For that, the financial system required improvements in monetary policy that the 1930s legislation did not address. Without the many bank failures, the many depositors who lost money in failed banks, and others who feared such losses in the future, political pressure for deposit insurance most likely would have remained weak. Glass and Roosevelt would most likely have prevailed.

There is no record of the Federal Reserve's opinion about deposit insurance, but there is some evidence in the minutes of the executive committee of the New York directors for April 10, which Secretary Woodin attended. The dominant view was opposition, but some directors accepted insurance for national banks. Harrison opposed the plan and criticized the proposal to use the Federal Reserve banks' surplus to finance the insurance fund.[37]

Roosevelt had opposed guarantees and insurance in discussions about the bank holiday, and he did not quickly change his position. Glass opposed insurance, as he had earlier. The Senate bill provided only for a sinking fund limited to member banks. Change began after Senator Arthur Vandenberg (a Michigan Republican) offered a substitute amendment authorizing $2,500 of insurance. Most midwestern senators voted for the bill, urged on by thousands of telegrams and letters from citizens with deposits in failed banks.[38] At its start, on January 1, 1934, 13,201 institutions joined the new system. Only 1 percent of state banks that applied did not qualify at the opening (Patrick 1993, 179–81).

Deposit insurance seemed a great success until the banking failures of the 1980s once again highlighted the problems of moral hazard and ad-

37. Earlier, there is a Board staff memo that recognizes the need for a new policy because of failure to stop bank runs. The memo discusses a guarantee of deposits and a policy of marking deposits to the market value of bank assets. The memo also considers the use of clearinghouse certificates in a crisis (memo Riefler to Goldenweiser, Board of Governors File, box 2222, February 23, 1933). The memo, written during the crisis, is concerned mainly with current problems.

38. There are several histories of deposit insurance and the legislative battle. A main conclusion is that the proponents were mainly small rural banks and their representatives, who expected to gain; the opponents were led by large city banks who expected to subsidize the small banks. After the bank holiday, the public overwhelmingly supported insurance, partly in the hope of repayment of losses, partly because many blamed Wall Street and big bankers for the depression. With Vandenberg's intervention, the issue was likely to be a major issue in the 1934 campaign. Glass, who had opposed deposit insurance for years, urged Roosevelt to accept it. See Calomiris and White 1994 and Golembe 1960.

verse selection that were recognized at the time of passage.[39] Almost all banks have chosen to be insured, and insurance of savings and loans, credit unions, and stock market accounts followed. Most mutual savings banks stayed out of the federal system.

White (1997, 35) concludes that the FDIC did not reduce costs of bank failures from 1945 to 1994 and may have raised them. He places the cost of resolving bank failures in these years at $39 billion, with a present value of $7.8 billion. His estimates exclude the much larger costs of savings and loan failures in the 1980s and do not include the benefit of avoiding bank runs. Bank runs almost disappeared under the FDIC, in part because the FDIC absorbed part of the losses and encouraged mergers of failing banks into stronger banks. Instead of a run to currency, depositors in banks and savings and loans, with very few exceptions, held their insured deposits or moved them to another insured bank.

Although deposit insurance appears less successful now than before the 1980s, it retains broad public support. The failures of the 1980s convinced Congress that moral hazard was a real problem. Legislation strengthened capital requirements and required banks with less than minimum capital to close. After 1980, national and regional banking, proposed in the 1930s as an alternative to insurance, increased diversification of portfolios and the banks' average size.

Contemporary beliefs that speculation had caused financial collapse, and Senator Glass's powerful role in the Banking Act of 1933, greatly enhanced the Federal Reserve's ability to respond to speculation. The new legislation included the power to fix the percentage of a bank's capital and surplus invested in loans secured by stocks or bonds, restrict discount privileges by banks ordered to stop lending to customers using stock as collateral, warn banks not to lend to stock exchanges or loans from the Federal Reserve would come due immediately, and suspend a bank using its facilities for purposes not related to sound credit ("Power of the Federal Reserve System to Restrain Speculation in Stocks and Bonds," Board of Governors File, box 1297, July 6, 1933). Most of these powers were rarely, if ever, used. Their presence after 1933 shows that Congress accepted Glass's explanation of the financial collapse.[40]

---

39. Friedman and Schwartz (1963, 442) call deposit insurance far more important than reform of the Federal Reserve, but they recognize that some of the reduction in bank failures resulted from FDIC actions to merge failing banks rather than permit failures (440).

40. Glass's view was widely held. One of the Board's senior economists, Woodlief Thomas, claimed: "More effective control of stock-market credit is necessary for business stability. Adequate control may be exercised over the supply of funds only by making stock-market activity the principal guide of credit policy" (Thomas 1935, 21).

Operations of the Reconstruction Finance Corporation

Nonmember banks that failed or required capital infusion to survive became the responsibility of the RFC. After the Emergency Banking Act authorized banks to issue preferred stock, the RFC assisted banks by buying their preferred stock or debentures. During its twenty-five years of operation, the RFC made 15,400 loans, totaling more than $2 billion, to more than 7,300 banks and trust companies. It ended operations in 1957 (Beckhart 1972, 273).

Beginning in June 1934, Congress authorized the RFC to lend to business enterprises. The same statute added section 13b to the Federal Reserve Act authorizing commercial and industrial loans in cooperation with financial institutions or on its own. The volume of such loans outstanding and authorized was never large. It varied between $35 million and $60 million. The number of applications ranged from eight thousand to ten thousand a year (Board of Governors of the Federal Reserve System (1943, 345). Discussion of section 13b loans absorbed a considerable amount of time at directors' meetings.

OPEN MARKET POLICY IN 1933–34

The New York reserve bank closed with its gold reserve ratio about 25 percent, far below requirements. Although the Board had been unwilling to require Boston and Chicago to participate in open market operations, it now instructed five reserve banks to rediscount $245 million for New York at 3.5 percent. This was the first use of interdistrict lending since 1922 and the last use to date.[41] New York repaid its borrowings in mid-April.

The monetary base and the money stock continued to fall in March and April as banks repaid discounts made during the emergency. The Federal Reserve was busy reopening banks and preparing legislative proposals, so the Open Market Policy Conference did not meet. Early in April, New York lowered its discount rate by 0.5 percent to 3 percent. Late in May, it reduced the rate again to 2.5 percent, where it remained until October. Other banks followed, but Richmond, Minneapolis, and Dallas kept their rates at 3.5 percent until February 1934.

The Open Market Policy Conference met on April 21 and 22 and voted to purchase up to $1 billion in securities over time "to meet Treasury requirements." Harrison told his directors that the Governors Conference

---

41. Chicago supplied $150 million, Cleveland $50 million, Boston $20 million, St. Louis $15 million, and Richmond $10 million. Boston also bought $15 million from Philadelphia. New York paid a fine of $10,200 for violating the reserve requirement.

was not in favor of purchases, but referring to the Thomas bill, he was afraid of "undesirable legislation coming out of Congress" (Harrison Papers, Directors' Meeting, April 27, 1933). The Board deferred action and made no purchases. This was Meyer's last meeting. On May 12, with Meyer gone, the Board approved purchases of up to $1 billion. The amount was 60 percent of the portfolio held at the time.[42]

Governor Black first met with the executive committee on May 23. Under pressure from the administration, Black urged the members to purchase $100 million to $200 million. The OMPC favored $25 million. Before Black agreed to the lower amount, he obtained agreement that the committee would make heavy purchases if business activity and prices fell off. The committee agreed, subject to approval by a majority of the OMPC. Fears of a renewed decline did not materialize, but the purchases continued. In the next two months, the Federal Reserve purchased $200 million, at the rate of $20 million to $25 million per week.[43]

Most of the purchases were Treasury notes with up to five years maturity. Between May and December, note holdings increased by $700 million. The System sold shorter-term securities, mainly certificates (under one year), lengthening the portfolio's maturity. The increased risk alarmed some of the governors, who pointed out that a rise in interest rates could wipe out the reserve banks' capital.[44]

With the passage of the Banking Act of 1933, the Open Market Policy Conference became the Federal Open Market Committee (FOMC). At its first meeting on July 20, the FOMC chose an executive committee consisting of the same five members as before to carry out its instructions— Boston, New York, Philadelphia, Cleveland, and Chicago. Harrison remained as chairman. The committee voted unanimously to continue purchases and renewed the authority to purchase up to $1 billion.[45]

42. John H. Williams joined the New York bank as assistant Federal Reserve agent on May 1. Williams taught economics at Harvard. He had considerable influence on policy throughout a long career at the Federal Reserve and was an ardent proponent of international coordination under the gold standard (Tavlas 1997, 168–70).

43. Dallas did not participate in some of these purchases.

44. Letters and telegrams from Governor Seay (Richmond) to Burgess and Black make Richmond's reluctance to participate clear. He participated, nevertheless, because of the "inflation bill" (Thomas amendment) then in Congress. Seay wrote that he preferred to purchase securities directly from the Treasury because it would be "credit inflation pure and simple" (Seay to Burgess, Open Market, Board of Governors File, box 1437, May 8, 1933).

45. The meeting was held on the day the National Industrial Recovery Administration announced policies to raise prices and wages. The stock market broke under this news. The decision to purchase may have reflected these developments or renewed bank failures and rising demand for discounts (Minutes, New York Directors, July 20, 1933, 113–15).

As excess reserves rose, some members of the FOMC became more reluctant to continue purchases. The System continued purchases, however, to avoid displeasing the administration and from fear of new legislation. On June 8, W. Randolph Burgess used Riefler-Burgess reasoning at the New York directors' meeting to argue that there was not much reason, other than the psychological reaction, to continue purchases. On July 6 Harrison told his directors that Governor Black believed purchases should stop but that the president had said publicly that he wanted higher commodity prices, so this was a poor time to stop purchases. Oliver M. W. Sprague talked about the need to assist the Treasury in debt finance (Board Minutes, July 21, 1933, 1). On August 10 Harrison reported he had told Secretary Woodin that, with excess reserves at $500 million, the FOMC saw no reason for additional purchases. The Treasury responded that the president wanted purchases to continue.

Oliver Sprague was again present at the August 10 meeting. Sprague was working at the Treasury and served as an intermediary with the Federal Reserve. Asked to describe the administration's monetary policy, Sprague replied that he could not because no particular policy had been adopted. Various policies had adherents in the administration. He warned that some wanted more radical approaches, so they hoped Federal Reserve policies would fail. Harrison complained again that it was difficult to know what to do, since he didn't know what the administration's policy was. One of his directors disagreed: the Federal Reserve, he said, should pursue its own correct policy.

The following week, Harrison reported that the president wanted purchases of up to $50 million. After an initial recovery, the economy was slowing down and commodity prices had fallen. The directors were reluctant to approve large purchases. They authorized only $25 million.[46] A week later, Governor Black and Secretary Woodin came to New York. Black told the executive committee of the New York directors that purchases of $10 million or even $25 million a week would achieve little. He wanted purchases of $50 million a week. This was a relatively large rate of purchase, and Black would not say how long he thought it should continue. Much of the discussion at the meeting was not about the economy but about the risk of legislation to force inflation. The directors approved purchases of $50 million for that week with only one director voting against. Woodin

46. Roosevelt appointed a special committee to consider monetary policy. He asked the committee to recommend issuing greenbacks under the Thomas amendment. The committee did not want to go along, so the president withdrew the request and asked, instead, to have open market purchases of $50 million.

urged that the vote be unanimous so he could tell that to the president; the recalcitrant director reluctantly changed his vote.

The president knew how to keep the Federal Reserve under his control. He agreed not to issue greenbacks during September, but he did not offer a longer-term commitment. The New York directors' meeting of August 25 was reluctant to approve the $50 million rate of purchase agreed to by its executive committee. Owen Young of General Electric voiced the sentiment of many. He was opposed to directives from the government. If there was to be a policy of inflation, it should be a consistent policy, not one that changed every week.

Late in August, Governor John U. Calkins (San Francisco) wrote to Black suggesting larger purchases, up to $100 million a week. But he added that he did not expect them to be effective: "It is my view that the Federal Reserve System should do its full part [to encourage expansion], even at the risk of subsequently having to realize that its efforts were ineffective." Black replied that he agreed "with the expressions in your letter" (Calkins to Black and Black to Calkins, Board of Governors File, box 1449, August 23 and 31, 1933).

The FOMC continued to authorize purchases in September and October. Member bank borrowing declined to about $125 million, and excess reserves rose to between $700 million and $800 million. By Federal Reserve standards, policy was easy and there was no reason for further purchases. Harrison's memo for the September FOMC meeting referred to the volume of excess reserves as evidence of an easy money market position. The governors agreed that further purchases were unnecessary from a banking and credit perspective, but they feared an issue of greenbacks and for that reason wanted the Board to indicate that it favored further purchases. Governor Black gave that assurance, and the executive committee of the FOMC voted to maintain the $36 million per week rate of purchase for another week.[47]

Opposition to Purchases

Between the July and October meetings, the Federal Reserve purchased almost $300 million, bringing total purchases to $500 million of the $1 bil-

---

47. In a memo to his files, Harrison reports Black's statement more fully. "He said that there is persistent and insistent pressure in Washington for *immediate* inflation, not for inflation in two or three weeks, but for inflation at once" (Harrison Papers, file 2210.3, September 16, 1933, 2; emphasis in the original). Black named Senator Bryan P. (Pat) Harrison, the majority leader, and Senators Elmer Thomas, Ellison D. Smith, and Duncan Fletcher as proponents of inflation. He had talked to Senator Harrison, who wanted more done than the Federal Reserve was doing. Black also wrote to Jesse Jones at the RFC and urged him to purchase $600 million of preferred stock to reopen closed nonmember and member banks by January 1.

lion authorized in April. Prime commercial rates fell to 1.25 percent and acceptance rates to 0.25 percent, far below the discount rates at Federal Reserve banks.

Opposition to the purchase program increased. Disturbed by the decline in rates and loss of revenues and by the volume of government securities, the executive committee of the Chicago bank unanimously approved a resolution on September 29 calling for reduction in its share of open market purchases. Chicago continued to adhere to the real bills doctrine, citing not only the $700 million of excess reserves but the need to be in position to rediscount paper for commercial, agricultural, and industrial borrowers. Further, the directors saw "no need for further purchases" (Letter C. R. McKay to Eugene Black, Board of Governors File, box 1449, October 4, 1933). Since Chicago took the largest share of new purchases, its decision threatened the purchase program.[48]

The background memo for the October 10 meeting showed that "basic commodity prices" reached a peak in July, then fell back. By early October, the index was above April but substantially below mid-July. Governors Roy A. Young (Boston) and George W. Norris (Philadelphia) argued that market rates were so low that they deterred lending. Banks incurred costs with very little return. All the governors agreed that the credit and banking position gave no reason for purchases. The committee voted to continue purchases, however, to avoid political confrontation.

The minutes of the meeting give the governors' view of how open market operations work and why they had not worked on this occasion. Open market operations force funds into the short-term market and, as short-term rates decline, into the longer-term markets. The focus is on interest rates, not on the broader interplay of relative prices of assets and output. Some governors reported that banks were reluctant to lend because of their recent experience and concerns about some (inflationary) provisions of the Securities Act and the Banking Act. Borrowers were reluctant to take on debt. The governors believed that the inflationary program deterred lending and investment. They favored an administration program to strengthen confidence. The latter is probably a reference to the budget deficit and the uncertainty surrounding the administration's policy of buying gold to raise the price level and devalue the dollar (FOMC Minutes, Board of Governors File, box 1449, October 10, 1933).

48. In April the FOMC changed allocations of government securities to give more securities to banks with larger gold reserves. The change shifted the allotment by reducing New York, Kansas City, and Dallas. Chicago went from 12 percent to 36 percent. New York's percentage was 15.25 percent (McKay to Black, Board of Governors File, box 1449, September 12, 1933). Hitherto New York had always taken the largest share.

Harrison described the committee's position when presenting the recommendation to the Board. The committee found "little or no reason for further purchases." A reduction in purchases should be made if it could be carried out without harming the recovery program (Board Minutes, October 12, 1933, 3–4).

Chicago's directors voted to participate in 12 percent of the purchases, based on the allocation formula in effect before May 1933, instead of 36 percent under the new formula. This was a modest concession to the Board, since the directors had voted to participate only on the written request of the Federal Reserve Board (Letter McKay to Black, Board of Governors File, box 1449, October 16, 1933). The main reason for the concession was that the Banking Act of 1933 required a month's notice by reserve banks withdrawing from the purchase program (Letter Young to the Board, Board of Governors File, box 1449, November 6, 1933).

Chicago was not the only recalcitrant bank. After the FOMC voted to reduce the rate of purchase to $18 million on October 25, Boston voted on November 1 not to participate in the purchase. It cited the Chicago decision, the large amount ($581 million) remaining from the $1 billion commitment, and uncertainty about what its share would be. The formal rules required prior notification. The bank was willing to consider purchases weekly (ibid., 2).

In October and November the System purchased $55 million, then purchases stopped. The committee did not meet again until March 1934, when it voted to reduce the authorization to purchase from $1 billion to $100 million. Between November 1933 and April 1937, the open market portfolio remained at about $2.43 billion. Changes represent expiring maturities not immediately replaced.

The System's discussion of interest rates and credit conditions ignored the sustained upward movement of stock prices. During the spring and early summer of 1933, the Standard and Poor's index of stock prices nearly doubled, rising from 45 in March to 85 in July. Thereafter the index declined slightly to the end of the year. By July 1933 the index of industrial production reached the highest level in three years, more than 50 percent above its trough; the Board's index, available at the time, shows a larger increase, 70 percent above its trough, back to the level last experienced in May 1930. The index declined in the fall. By December much of the increase had reversed.

Just as in 1932, open market purchases stopped as the economy began to expand. Although the circumstances differed, the reasoning was much the same. Harrison explained the prevailing view in a memo to his files on November 20. Acting Treasury Secretary Henry Morgenthau wanted the reserve banks to purchase $25 million a week in advance of the December Treasury financing.[49] All the governors opposed. Harrison told Morgenthau that "it would not only do no good, but it might do some harm; it would be only another factor of uncertainty, tending toward inflation" (Harrison Papers, November 20, 1933). According to Harrison, Morgenthau agreed.[50]

Federal Reserve officials appear to have learned nothing from the experience of 1929–33. They continued to operate in established ways and to interpret events as they had in the past. The principal reason for large-scale purchases was fear—fear of legislation or of action by the new administration. Balancing this fear was fear of inflation, a concern more closely related to the real bills doctrine than to the fact that the price level was 25 percent below its 1929 level.

In 1920–21, gold movements and a falling price level raised real balances and ended the recession despite high real interest rates. The pattern was very different in 1933. The economy recovered strongly beginning in the second quarter, as banks reopened and the financial crisis ended. The deflator rose at an 11 percent average annual rate for the last three quarters of the year, mainly the effect of NRA codes approved in July. Growth of the monetary base remained negative throughout the spring and early summer, and real balances fell. The ex post real interest rate was negative. In the fourth quarter output fell, and the risk premium in interest rates rose by 0.75 percent from the low reached in May.[51]

Unlike Hoover, Roosevelt did not intend to be the victim of Federal Reserve inaction. He began buying gold and silver to raise their prices and the general price level. Although Federal Reserve credit declined slightly in 1934 as discounts and acceptances fell to insignificant levels, gold and silver purchases increased the monetary base. The base and the money stock resumed their increase, and recovery also resumed.

49. Woodin was ill and resigned. Morgenthau became secretary on January 1, 1934.

50. Harrison took a different attitude toward commercial bank bond purchases. In January he called on Winthrop Aldrich to discuss sales of governments by Chase National. He told Aldrich Washington believed that "New York banks were selling . . . as part of a conspiracy to depress government bonds and thus to defeat the government's program." Aldrich agreed to cooperate (Harrison Papers, file 2500.1, January 9, 1934).

51. The risk premium is the difference between Baa and Aaa bonds. Output data are from Balke and Gordon 1986. Monthly data for industrial production, wholesale prices, and common stocks show similar patterns. Industrial production rose 57 percent between March and July, then faltered. By November, half the initial rise was gone. Wholesale prices rose 18 percent between March and August, then remained unchanged for the rest of the year. The stock market peaked in July, 80 percent above the March average. By November the average was 16 percent below its peak. The NRA was the proximate cause of the stock market decline from its peak. Announcement of the first codes raising costs of production in mid-July, precipitated the decline (see below).

GOLD AND SILVER POLICY, 1933-34

From the banking holiday to April 11, the gold price remained within 15 cents (0.7 percent) of its par value, $20.67 an ounce. There is no sign of anticipated devaluation in either the gold price or the forward market. The Treasury granted export licenses without hindrance. Gold returned to the Federal Reserve banks.[52] These and other available data suggest that the markets regarded the suspension of convertibility as a temporary move. The relatively large United States gold holdings at the time gave no reason for permanent devaluation under "rules of the game."

Sentiment began to change in April. Discussions leading to the Thomas amendment and pressure for inflation or reflation increased requests for licenses to export gold. In mid-April, gold outflows increased. The liberal gold export policy ended abruptly on April 18, when Secretary Woodin refused to issue new export licenses. The following day, the president prohibited gold exports except for gold previously earmarked, and hence owned, by foreign governments.[53] The United States was no longer on the gold standard.[54]

Business and the public supported the decision. The stock market response was euphoric. The Dow Jones index of industrial stock prices rose 14 percent in the next two days and 55 percent in the next three months (Sumner 1995, 12). A daily index of the wholesale prices of seventeen commodities rose 76 percent, and the gold price rose to $30.18 in the next three months (Pearson, Myers, and Gans 1957, 5613).[55] J. P. Morgan praised the decision as an end to the deflationary policy (quoted in Crabbe 1989, 436).

52. Between March 4 and March 22, $250 million in gold coin and $310 million in gold certificates returned to Federal Reserve banks (Draft Statement of Executive Order Forbidding the Hoarding of Gold Coin, Board of Governors File, box 2160, April 2, 1933). The statement was issued on April 5.

53. The shift in policy appears to have been a sudden change, supporting the view that the Thomas amendment played a major role. Two weeks earlier, Harrison and the New York directors had discussed possible resumption of gold payments and a fixed parity. Harrison acknowledged, however, that he did not know the administration's plans (Minutes, New York Directors, April 3, 1933, 253-54).

54. April 19 is also the day Roosevelt agreed to accept the discretionary powers to print greenbacks granted by the Thomas amendment and talked about depreciating the dollar to raise the domestic price level.

55. The stock market boom ended on July 19. The Dow Jones average fell 4.8 percent that day and an additional 15.5 percent in the next two days, eliminating half the gain since April 18. On July 19 the NIRA announced an increase in wages and reductions in hours. Sumner (1995, 18-19) computes the increase in nominal and real wages as 20 percent in the two months from July to September 1933, using the wholesale price index as the deflator for average hourly earnings. Weinstein (1981, 267) estimates that the NIRA codes raised nominal wages 26 percent a year for the two years of NRA existence and raised prices by 14 percent a year.

Proponents of devaluation within the administration were delighted, as was the Committee for the Nation, a group of prominent citizens who favored reflation as a cure for depression (Pearson, Myers, and Gans 1957, 5610).[56]

Suspension of the gold standard was a decision to favor domestic over international considerations in the recovery. Most observers at the time presumed this was a temporary move, not a decision to float the dollar permanently. Roosevelt had not yet made a firm decision about either gold or the dollar.

Congress took a longer view. On June 5 the president signed legislation abrogating the gold clause in all contracts. The action redistributed wealth from creditors to debtors, including the government as a principal debtor. The clause applied to about $100 billion of public and private debt and to $1.6 billion of currency—gold certificates. Holders of mortgages, bonds, notes, and currency calling for payment in gold at 23.22 grains per dollar could not insist that their claims be enforced by the courts. Creditors challenged the action, but the Supreme Court upheld the government's action five to four in February 1935 (Pearson, Myers, and Gans 1957, 5598).[57]

The London Monetary and Economic Conference

Events soon forced President Roosevelt to choose between stabilization and devaluation. An international conference at Lausanne, Switzerland, in July 1932 agreed to call another conference to consider international capital movements, currency stabilization, tariffs, and trade policy.[58] London was chosen as the site and June 12 as the date. As the conference date approached, Roosevelt became active. Between April 22 and June 3, he met with ten prime ministers or presidents and cabled fifty-four others. His statements supported the aims of the London conference and an international solution, as pledged in the 1932 party platform (Pearson, Myers, and Gans 1957, 5617). In a fireside chat on May 7, he told the public that the conference "must succeed. The future of the world demands it" (quoted in Beckhart 1972, 306).

56. The group of three hundred included Henry Morgenthau Sr., father of one of Roosevelt's closest advisers, soon to become secretary of the treasury. Other members included the heads of Sears, Roebuck, Remington Rand, and several banks. Earlier, on April 5, an executive order prohibited domestic gold holding of more than $100 (except for industry and the arts).

57. Gold clauses became common after the Civil War, especially after de facto stabilization in 1879 at the gold price of $20.67 per ounce. The clause specified payment "in gold coins of present standard weight and fineness," that is, 23.22 grains of gold to the dollar (Pearson, Myers, and Gans 1957, 5598).

58. The Lausanne conference ended German reparations payments permanently.

Roosevelt's advisers were divided. George Warren was the leading advocate of devaluation within the administration. Outside, Irving Fisher favored devaluation based on his proposal for a compensated dollar and his belief that the rise in the real value of debt was a main obstacle to recovery. Both wanted the price level restored to the 1926 level.[59] Morgenthau supported Warren's views and used his charts comparing weekly changes in agricultural prices to changes in the world price of gold to convince Roosevelt. The president "was impressed" (Blum 1959, 64).

Conservatives within the administration opposed devaluation. Dean Acheson, later secretary of state in the Truman administration, was undersecretary of the treasury under Woodin. Woodin appointed Oliver Sprague of Harvard as his adviser on international economic policy. Sprague held traditional views; he favored deflation to reduce the price level as required under gold standard rules. Government could help by reducing "sticky" prices—wages, freight rates, and telephone charges.[60]

Secretary of State Cordell Hull headed the delegation to the London Monetary and Economic Conference. Hull's concern was multilateral tariff reduction, and he does not seem to have taken much interest in monetary or financial issues. Drafting the United States position on these issues was left to Sprague and James Warburg, who favored a return to a gold standard after a 15 to 25 percent devaluation of the dollar. This plan was unacceptable to the British and the French (Kindleberger 1986, 205–6).[61]

Harrison was the principal Federal Reserve official involved in the discussions. In May he talked to Montagu Norman about a French proposal

59. Warren was a professor of agricultural economics at Cornell, where Henry Morgenthau Jr. had been a student. Morgenthau introduced Warren to Roosevelt as an agricultural adviser in 1930. Warren kept a diary of his meetings with Roosevelt and others in 1933–34. The diary is the basis for large parts of the paper by Pearson, Myers, and Gans (1957) on which I draw heavily. Warren served as a consultant and did not hold any position in the administration. Fisher wrote to Roosevelt, sometimes by request, but he did not participate in the principal policy discussions within the administration, as Warren did, and he was not an adviser.

60. Sprague also favored increased government spending, especially on construction (Pearson, Myers, and Gans 1957, 5649). In the 1920s he testified in Congress against bills to make price stability a goal of the Federal Reserve. He was always skeptical of linkage between money and prices and opposed Fisher's compensated dollar. Other prominent opponents of devaluation included James Warburg, son of Paul Warburg, a member of the original Federal Reserve Board, Herbert Feis, economic adviser to the secretary of state, and the budget director, Lewis Douglas.

61. Kindleberger (1986) summarizes many of the proposals for tariffs, public works, and currency stabilization. The discussion shows disagreements on major issues that were unlikely to be resolved by a multinational conference. War debts were ruled out of the discussion, but they were important to Congress and to the United States public, so the United States delegation was unwilling to consider any of the proposals calling for additional international lending.

to stabilize the dollar, franc, and pound. Norman suggested that the franc and the dollar could remain at their current values but said the pound was likely to depreciate. He proposed that France and the United States accumulate sterling balances in London, to be paid in gold when the stabilization agreement ended. He doubted that the plan would work or would be helpful to Britain, but he promised to send a member of his staff to Paris to discuss the proposal (Harrison Papers, Memo, file 3115.4, May 18, 1933).

Four days later, Norman told Harrison that the Bank of England and the Bank of France had agreed on a joint reply to the United States. They favored a return to gold. In an indirect reference to uncertainty about United States monetary policy, he urged that the three governments "should make each other aware as to what policy they intended to follow in monetary matters" before agreement could be reached (Harrison Papers, Memo, Crane to Files, file 3115.4, May 22, 1933, 1). Norman insisted there was no point discussing Warburg's proposal or any other technical details until the three countries agreed on a policy.[62]

The problem for the United States delegation was that Roosevelt had not yet decided what to do. Devaluation and rising prices were politically popular. By June 2 the Board's weekly wholesale price index was five points higher (8.5 percent) than when the administration took office. The weekly price memo referred to "substantial increases" in several prices and no large declines.[63] Wallace, Tugwell, and the planners claimed credit for the price increases, as did the proponents of devaluation. Under the Agricultural Adjustment Act, approved on May 12, the Agriculture Department paid farmers to reduce supply by plowing under cotton and wheat and slaughtering pigs. Slaughtering little pigs proved politically unpopular, strengthening the proponents of devaluation as a means of raising prices (Pearson, Myers, and Gans 1957, 5623).

Roosevelt is often accused of scuttling the London conference and ending monetary cooperation working toward currency stabilization (Kindleberger 1986, 220–21; Beckhart 1972, 306). The truth to this charge is that Roosevelt's message to the conference, on July 3, rejected an agreement to return to an international gold standard. The agreement specified neither the time nor the parity at which countries would rejoin because the conference could not agree on exchange rates. Chart 6.1 suggests the principal

---

62. Warburg's proposal probably refers to the proposal drafted by James Warburg and Oliver Sprague, calling for a return to a gold standard with different rules. Gold would not circulate but would be held only by central banks and governments. Gold reserve ratios supporting currency would be adjustable, not fixed. Silver would supplement gold as a reserve metal.

63. Cotton and wheat prices were back to levels not seen since 1930 or 1931 (Kindleberger 1986, table 16).

Chart 6.1 Real exchange rates, dollar-pound and dollar-franc.

difficulty—the depreciation of the real dollar exchange rates for the pound and the French franc in 1933. France and Britain would not accept the 1933 rate; Roosevelt would not restore the earlier nominal rate and accept the implied deflation that would follow.[64]

In April, after floating the dollar, Roosevelt had offered to stabilize at a 15 percent devaluation against gold provided Britain and France would agree to a stabilization fund to keep exchange rates at the proposed levels. They refused. The British and French had been favorable to stabilization in the winter of 1933, before devaluation of the dollar brought the franc to a peak and the pound back to its traditional range, $4.86 per pound. By the time of the conference, the principal concern for Britain and France was that the dollar would continue to depreciate against the pound and the franc.

Harrison's notes record the jockeying for relative advantage of the British, French, and United States delegations to a conference called from June 9 to June 16 at the Bank of England to resolve trilateral issues outside the main London conference. James Warburg, representing the State Department, Oliver Sprague, representing the Treasury, and Harrison were members of the United States delegation. All three favored a return to the gold standard, and two of them resigned later in the year when Roosevelt

64. Real exchange rates are obtained using relative wholesale price indexes to adjust for differences in inflation. Eichengreen (1992, 318) agrees that Roosevelt was not wholly to blame for the failure. He blames differences in analysis of the problem and domestic political considerations. The latter have a role, but I believe there was a common view about the gold standard and fixed exchange rates. The hard issues were where new exchange rates would be set and whether prosperity could best be restored by reflation or further deflation.

forced further dollar devaluation. This agreement aside, the United States delegation did not have a common viewpoint. Harrison favored "de facto stabilization as soon as possible" but does not mention an exchange rate (Harrison Papers, Diary of Trip to London, file 3010.2, June 1933, 1). He reports Sprague as not favoring any definite arrangement until exchange rates stabilized, perhaps in three months, but willing to consider an interim agreement. Warburg worried about the domestic political consequences of stabilization, almost certainly a reference to congressional and agricultural interests and perhaps to Warren and Morgenthau also. By June 10 Warburg had changed his mind, at least to the extent of tactically favoring stabilization. He cabled the president that he would support gold exports to make stabilization effective, but he did not expect the British to agree. The onus for failure would then be on them (ibid., 2).

Norman refused to negotiate any agreements until Treasury and government officials agreed on the policies of the respective governments.[65] The governments agreed on the desirability of fixed exchange rates, but they could not agree on a policy. The French wanted a permanent agreement, based on gold. They considered an interim agreement useless or worse. Speculators would bet on the next step. Sprague said that "a permanent stabilization commitment was now entirely out of the question so far as the United States is concerned" (ibid., 3). The question to be considered was whether there should be a temporary agreement. He offered to forgo use of the Thomas amendment during the period of the agreement if the United States recovery continued. He favored stabilization but argued that it was impossible as long as unstable economic conditions persisted. Norman agreed with Sprague, but he viewed the pound as the weak currency. The United States and France had large stocks of gold; Britain did not: "He foresaw great difficulties and many quarrels" in a tripartite agreement (ibid., 7).

At the central bankers' meeting, Norman suggested an interim program under which the pound and dollar would be fixed to gold with settlement in gold. The commitment would be limited to the specific amount of gold committed. If a country paid out its entire commitment, a new agreement could be reached at adjusted gold parities. This process could continue until the countries reached stable parities.[66] Émile Moret preferred

65. The French Treasury delegation included Émile Moret, governor of the Bank of France, and Jacques Rueff, a strong proponent of the gold standard. In the 1960s, Rueff, as an adviser to President Charles de Gaulle, took positions similar to those he had taken in the 1930s. At London, government officials met separately to work out a government position, then met with the central bankers.

66. The working assumption was that they would. Chart 6.1 suggests that starting in 1933 might have required large changes in the relative price levels of the three countries.

this plan to Harrison's proposal to stabilize exchange rates, because the franc remained convertible into gold and the Bank of France was not allowed to buy foreign exchange. Harrison was skeptical because Washington favored stabilizing exchange rates, not the gold price. He considered daily or weekly announcements of gold movements a source of instability, so he wanted to avoid them. Exchange rate stabilization with gold settlement would show only net movements over a period. Further, he explained, the United States Treasury was unwilling to promise not to devalue after the London conference ended.

Moret rejected Harrison's proposal. Central banks could stabilize exchange rates without an agreement. What was needed was a statement about monetary policy, current and future. Announcing and maintaining a gold price would provide the information.

On June 15 the central bankers' meeting reached a modest, partial agreement to fix the dollar-pound rate within a 3 percent (12 cent) band around $4 per pound for a two-week period. The British government reserved the right to change the rate after two weeks, and the United States reserved the right to reject any British devaluation. Otherwise the contract would remain in force. The French would continue pegging to gold at a rate that equaled $0.04662 per franc. The United States promised not to invoke the Thomas amendment.

Financial markets greeted the announcements as a halt to reflation and recovery. Stock and commodity prices began to fall on June 12 as rumors of an agreement spread. Between June 12 and June 17 commodity and stock prices fell 3.5 and 8 percent, and the dollar appreciated against gold. Burgess told Harrison that even temporary stabilization was unacceptable. The delegation to the main London conference announced that "measures of temporary stabilization now would be untimely" (State Department files, quoted in Eichengreen 1992, 333). Roosevelt went on a sailing trip. The dollar fell, and commodity and stock prices resumed their rise.

That seemed to put an end to the main business of the London conference, but the conference continued. Roosevelt seems not yet to have made a final decision. Instead he sent one of his principal advisers, Raymond Moley, to London with instructions calling for a return to "stability in the international monetary field . . . as quickly as practicable," with gold "reestablished as the international measure of exchange values" (Moley 1939, app. F). Gold would not circulate but would be held by central banks or governments. Currencies would be subject to a uniform minimum gold reserve ratio. Silver could substitute partially for gold as a central bank reserve.

Based on these instructions, Moley negotiated a new agreement with

Britain and France to limit speculation and restore the gold standard, but the agreement did not specify either the date or the gold price at which countries would return to gold. This was left to the future.

The June experience helped to convince Roosevelt about the difficulty of reaching a meaningful agreement. The market response to the June 15 agreement seemed to confirm Warren's view that stabilization would bring back deflation. Morgenthau, who joined the president on his vacation, reinforced the latter view by showing Roosevelt Warren's charts of weekly changes in gold and commodity prices.[67]

On July 3 Roosevelt reversed direction, threw out the instructions given to Moley, and rejected Moley's agreement. In a strongly worded message to the conference favoring domestic over international action, the president said:

> The world will not long be lulled by a specious fallacy of achieving a temporary and probably an artificial stability in foreign exchange on the part of a few countries only. The sound internal economic system of a nation is a greater factor in its well-being than the price of its currency in terms of the currencies of other nations. . . . Our broad purpose is permanent stabilization of every nation's currency. Gold or gold and silver can well continue to be a metallic reserve behind currencies, but this is not the time to dissipate gold reserves. When the world works out concerted policies in the majority of nations to produce balanced budgets and living within their means, then we can properly discuss a better distribution of the world's gold and silver supply to act as a reserve base of national currencies. (Quoted in Crabbe 1989, 437–38)

Roosevelt had at last made up his mind to emphasize domestic over international considerations as many in Congress wanted. Reflation of the domestic commodity price level became a key element in a policy of domestic recovery.

The world, Roosevelt said, faced catastrophe if the conference limited its concerns to exchange rate stabilization. There was no visible prospect of successful international cooperation to restore prosperity. The British hesitated to enter more than a temporary agreement that gave them a temporary advantage. The Harrison diaries make clear that agreement with the French was possible only on their terms. By law France could not engage in expansive open market operations. By choice they would not do so, because French officials continued to believe that the only proper solution was for each country to force its prices down to the level implied by its gold

---

67. Morgenthau gives credit to Louis Howe and Eleanor Roosevelt (Blum 1959, 65).

holdings. If this policy forced deflation on other countries, they must restrict money growth and deflate also. Harrison, Black, Miller, and others at the Federal Reserve, and Acheson, Warburg, and Sprague at the Treasury, favored a gold standard policy for the United States. The Federal Reserve made open market purchases at the time, but mainly out of fear of the administration and congressional "inflationists." A commitment to restore the gold standard would soon end these purchases and restore deflationary policy.

By rejecting the London agreement, Roosevelt freed policy from the gold standard and kept the Federal Reserve in the backseat. He had moved, hesitantly, toward the policy of reflation advocated by Warren, Fisher, and Morgenthau. He did not decide to forever abandon the gold standard, as Fisher and Warren proposed. Long-term commitments had no special attraction and surely were not his concern at the time. The decision was to raise agricultural and commodity prices, to experiment, and to see where the experiment led.

Roosevelt's decision to choose domestic expansion over stabilization of the gold price was correct in the circumstances. Starting from the low levels of 1933, the income effect of domestic United States expansion would more than offset any effect on foreigners of a United States devaluation. Further, a return to the gold standard would have brought back deflation in those countries that lost gold. Even if the technicians could have adjusted exchange rates appropriately—an unlikely event—fixed exchange rates would again be misaligned as countries moved toward full employment at different rates and with different price changes. The London meetings show that policymakers could not agree on exchange rate changes. They were unlikely to pay the costs of maintaining fixed rates during the long period of adjustment that lay ahead.

Unilateral Action

Markets greeted Roosevelt's "bombshell," as it is often called, enthusiastically. They anticipated reflation, rising output, and a vigorous policy of domestic expansion. On July 3 the daily indexes of commodity and stock prices rose 2 and 3 percent respectively, and the dollar depreciated against the pound. The daily price indexes continued to rise until July 18, when the NIRA announced its first codes. The following day, the Dow Jones industrial average fell almost 5 percent. The cumulative decline in the next few days reached 18 percent for stocks and 10 percent for Moody's daily index of commodity prices. The dollar appreciated.

The president did not want the dollar to go above $4.86 per pound, the nominal rate prevailing before the 1931 British devaluation. On July 11 he asked the Federal Reserve to earmark $20 million in gold for the Bank of England, to be released two weeks later. Harrison explained to Norman that the intervention was intended to slow the dollar's appreciation; it was not an attempt to fix the dollar at the old rate. As chart 6.1 above suggests, the dollar had appreciated strongly in real terms since April; it reached a peak in July, then declined (Board Minutes, July 13, 1933, 1–3; Harrison Papers, file 2210.3, July 14, 1933).[68]

A week after his July 3 message to London, Roosevelt asked Morgenthau to invite Warren, Fisher, and Professor James Rogers of Yale for tea. Warren and Fisher met with Roosevelt at his home in Hyde Park, New York, on August 8. Roosevelt asked whether he should increase the price of gold to $29 an ounce. Warren urged at least $32 to $37. He showed Roosevelt charts showing the recent increases in prices of commodities, stocks, and gold and the level of employment (Pearson, Myers, and Gans 1957, 5626–27). Fisher, of course, agreed with Warren that buying gold would raise the price level (Barber 1996, 47, paraphrasing a letter from Fisher to his wife). Roosevelt was convinced and apparently pleased. He called a news conference the next day to show the press some of Warren's charts.

Warren divided the determinants of commodity prices into national and international factors. World supply and demand for gold determined a world price level. Domestic price levels depended on the world price level and the domestic price of gold. By changing the latter, the domestic price level could be made to rise or fall (Pearson, Myers, and Gans 1957, 5601).

Warren's conclusion was attractive to Roosevelt, since the charts showed that the effects occurred quickly (ibid., 5664). Farm prices had declined 64 percent from February 1929 to February 1933, while prices paid by farmers declined 36 percent. Devaluation, Warren concluded, would reverse this change in the price level and the relative price of farm products (5670–71). This was what Roosevelt wanted to accomplish for political as well as economic benefits.[69]

Roosevelt did not want the higher gold price to reward gold speculators and foreigners. On August 28 he used the emergency powers in the Trading with the Enemy Act and the Emergency Banking Act to extend the embargo on gold exports and call all outstanding gold into the Federal Reserve banks. The resolution abolished the domestic market for gold, hampering efforts to raise the gold price without making foreign purchases, contrary to Roo-

---

68. The authorization to intervene was for two weeks, ending July 28. By that time the dollar had fallen, so the authorization ended.

69. Warren recorded Viner as favoring a return to the gold standard following an international conference to fix the price of gold. Strangely, Warren did not believe that central banks could fix the price of gold by joint action (Pearson, Myers, and Gans 1957, 5628–29).

sevelt's intention. The next day the president authorized the Treasury to purchase all newly mined gold at a price set by the secretary. Ten days later, the Treasury set the price for newly mined gold at $29.62 an ounce. This decision formally abandoned the $20.67 price of gold.[70] By late October, the gold price had increased only to $29.80 (Pearson, Myers, and Gans 1957, 5632).

Farm prices continued to fall. As the harvest approached, political pressure from the farm states and memos from Warren pushed Roosevelt to be less concerned about profits to foreigners. By mid-August, he decided to buy gold in the open market above the open market price. The attorney general ruled that he did not have that power, but as usual Roosevelt was determined. He decided to set up a corporation within the Reconstruction Finance Corporation to buy gold, silver, cotton, and other commodities. The attorney general, the Treasury, and RFC lawyers discussed the legality for several weeks before reaching a conclusion (Blum 1959, 65–67). Acheson opposed the decision and soon after resigned.[71]

The plan called for the RFC to sell short-term notes and use the proceeds to buy domestic and foreign gold above the going market price. Roosevelt personally drafted the fireside chat he gave on October 22, highlighting the importance of restoring the price level nearer to the level at which debts had been incurred and reversing the relative decline in farm prices. Higher prices would restore employment, Roosevelt said, but the increase was to be a one-time change, achieved over two or three years, not the start of permanent inflation. Once the price level rose, his policy was to maintain the dollar's "purchasing and debt-paying power during the succeeding generation" (Krooss 1969, 4:2780). The option was not a temporary expedient, Roosevelt said. His policy moved toward a managed currency that "would not be influenced by the accidents of international trade, by the internal policies of other nations and by political disturbances in other continents" (4:2780).[72]

Roosevelt's speech notwithstanding, the immediate objective was more

70. The Treasury had established a committee on monetary policy under James Warburg. The committee included among its members Black and Harrison from the Federal Reserve and Walter Stewart. They opposed the devaluation policy but did not propose an alternative.

71. Pearson, Myers, and Gans (1957, 5633–34) report from Warren's diary that Roosevelt continued to talk about greenbacks and silver as well as gold. Warren warned against other methods as ineffective. The reason for Roosevelt's strong interest is the fall in commodity prices. Wheat at 75 cents a bushel was 50 cents below the summer peak, corn was back to the April price, and cotton, at 9 cents a pound, was 25 percent below its summer peak. The pressure from farm organizations and Congress for inflation rose as farm prices fell. Woodin objected, and the monetary committee including Sprague, Rogers, and Harrison tried to stop the planned devaluation.

72. Roosevelt bypassed the legal issue by citing "the clearly defined authority of existing law." Roosevelt seems to have accepted some part of Fisher's debt-deflation theory.

circumscribed. On October 29 he told Harrison that it was "imperative to get agricultural prices up before Congress meets and that if we did not, he was fearful of what Senator Thomas [Oklahoma] and the other inflationists might do" (Harrison Papers, file 2010.2, October 30, 1933, 3). He anticipated spending $100 million to get the dollar gold price to $33 or $34 before Congress met, and he again warned about the dangers of serious social disorder in the West.[73]

Markets and the public received Roosevelt's speech enthusiastically. Between the beginning and the end of the broadcast, wheat future prices rose 38 percent to more than 93 cents a bushel (Pearson, Myers, and Gans 1957, 5641). Telegrams gave overwhelming support. With a few exceptions, leading economists of that period opposed the plan, usually because they favored the gold standard at the traditional gold price and opposed devaluation.

Purchases began on October 25. Roosevelt personally decided on the daily price.[74] The initial objective was to have cotton at 10 cents a pound, corn at 50 cents a bushel, and wheat at 90 to 95 cents a bushel by January 1, 1934. (These prices were 10 to 20 percent above June 1933.) Originally the RFC made all gold purchases in the United States. Since gold exports had to be licensed, the United States gold price soon rose above the world price, so the policy changed by November 1 to include purchases abroad. Still, the purchases were limited to about $5 million a week, divided equally between London and Paris. A two-tier market developed, with the higher price set by United States purchases. After its initial successes in raising the domestic and international gold price to $34 an ounce, the program faltered. World gold prices fell, and commodity prices (in dollars) followed.

The gold buying program rewarded sellers able to sell to the RFC with little effect on its target, the prices of wheat, cotton, and corn. If the United States had been willing to buy in unlimited quantities, it would have eliminated the difference between domestic and international gold prices. Under the program, the difference persisted and widened. By mid-December, the

73. Governor Black, who was at the meeting, told the president that small purchases would not be effective and large purchases would have serious repercussions abroad. He offered to cooperate, however, if the president decided to proceed. Harrison seconded his statements. Neither man said what he would do (Harrison Papers, file 2010.2, October 30, 1933, 4–5).

74. Each morning Morgenthau, Warren, and Jesse Jones, head of the RFC, met in Roosevelt's bedroom. Morgenthau reported the previous day's prices of gold and commodities. Roosevelt chose a new gold price for the day. The aim was to keep the gold price rising. On Roosevelt's announcement the price in London rose from $29.01 to $31.02. Roosevelt set the first buying price at $31.36. The daily price changes were always positive, but the increments varied to fool the speculators (Blum 1959, 69). In fact, it made little sense to fool the speculators. One day he raised the price by 21 cents because that was a lucky number, three times seven (ibid., 70). Pearson, Myers, and Gans (1957, 5643) quote a slip Roosevelt gave to Warren with the words "Oct. 30. I think 31.96 is right for today. FDR."

United States gold price was 7 percent above the world price, but commodity prices were set in international markets. They fell from mid-November to mid-December. The Board's wholesale price index was 11 percent above the previous year but back to the level of early September.

Falling commodity prices weakened the program's support and strengthened opponents. Opposition intensified. Acheson, budget director Douglas, and Sprague resigned, the last after complaining that the "present policy threatens a complete breakdown of the credit of the government" (quoted in Pearson, Myers, and Gans 1957, 5649). Other prominent economists stressed the risk of inflation and damage to the government's credit.[75] These claims seemed to be validated by a small temporary, seasonal increase in short-term interest rates in December.[76] The American Federation of Labor (AFL), the Chamber of Commerce, the American Legion, and the Economists' National Committee on Monetary Policy opposed the policy. Farm groups and the Committee for the Nation approved.

Foreign central bankers vigorously opposed the policy also. Harrison described Norman as having "hit the ceiling" when first informed about RFC purchases. United States gold purchases might "undermine confidence in all currencies . . . [a]nd bring about currency and exchange chaos in Europe" (Harrison Papers, file 3115.4, November 2, 1933, 1). Harrison assured Norman repeatedly that Roosevelt acted for domestic reasons only.[77] With the dollar depreciated in mid-November, he offered to discuss stabilization of the pound at $5.25 to $5.35, even if it meant selling up to $25 million in gold. Nothing came of the discussion. The usual reason given was that French political problems made it difficult to discuss stabilization of the franc,[78] but Morgenthau told Harrison his main concern was that, even if the agreement lasted only a week, prices might fall.[79]

75. Six young Harvard instructors, led by Lauchlin Currie, sent a letter to Roosevelt supporting devaluation of the dollar as essential for Roosevelt's expansionist policies, but they dismissed Warren's argument closely linking the price of gold to commodity prices (Pearson, Myers, and Gans 1957, 5653; Sandilands 1990, 56–57).

76. On November 16, Roosevelt accepted Acheson's undated letter of resignation and appointed Morgenthau as his successor. Since Woodin was ill, Morgenthau became acting secretary and, after Woodin's resignation, secretary on January 1, 1934.

77. Norman recognized, as Harrison apparently did not, that, if successful, the "domestic operation" would raise the gold price and lead to increased United States exports, fewer imports, and a flow of gold to the United States. This would initially force appreciation and deflation on all gold standard countries.

78. Roosevelt blamed the French problems on their failure to balance their budget for three years. He told Harrison that he did not expect them to remain on the gold standard. Harrison urged him to stop gold purchases temporarily to help the French, and Roosevelt agreed (Harrison Papers, file 2012.4, November 22 and 23, 1933).

79. Harrison made several proposals, on his own initiative, to stabilize exchange rates (Harrison Papers, file 3115.4, November 15, 18, December 1). At one point (December 1) Nor-

Between September and December, the dollar depreciated against the pound and French franc by 9.6 and 5.3 percent, respectively, in nominal terms and by 8.6 and 7.8 percent in real terms. Harrison described Roosevelt in mid-November as "pleased with the gold experiment up to date" and "working up to around $34 at the end of the week when he will survey the situation and decide on the next move" (Harrison Papers, file 2012.4, November 13, 1933, 5). Harrison also described the president as uncertain what to do next. He was opposed to legal devaluation but might consider temporary de facto stabilization if the British would agree. But the president was also concerned that Congress would want wheat and cotton prices to reach $1.25 a bushel and 15 cents a pound (5).[80]

Depreciation awakened British interest in concerted action to stabilize currencies temporarily. As commodity prices fell, Roosevelt's interest in a joint agreement increased, and his interest in buying gold waned.[81] By December, RFC gold purchases slowed. Morgenthau asked Harrison to reopen discussions with Norman about a possible agreement to devalue jointly against gold, then stabilize. Agreement had to be reached before Congress reconvened.

The British would not consider joint devaluation against gold (Harrison Papers, file 2012.4, December 4, 1933, 4). Roosevelt blamed them for the dollar's failure to depreciate against gold in foreign markets (Blum 1959, 121).[82] Many bankers shared this view and claimed that the British used their Exchange Equalization Fund, set up after the 1931 devaluation, to prevent dollar devaluation. The bankers wanted a United States stabilization fund to counter the British fund (12).

---

man was willing to approach the British Treasury with a proposal to stabilize the exchange rate at the former rate, $4.86. Norman and Harrison also discussed the possibility of exchange controls. Harrison's concern was with inflationists in Congress when Congress returned in January.

80. The memo also reports that Roosevelt and Morgenthau were concerned about capital flight as rumors of an impending devaluation spread.

81. Morgenthau's evaluation was that success had been partial, but the changes "did not restore the balance between agricultural and industrial prices that Warren had hoped to redress" (Blum 1959, 75). Morgenthau's views are consistent with Harrison's reports suggesting that Roosevelt had achieved most of his objective. Warren cites criticism of the program at home and abroad by the AFL, the Chamber of Commerce, bankers, numerous economists including J. M. Keynes, and many members of Congress (Pearson, Myers, and Gans 1957, 5649–55).

82. Jacob Viner, on Morgenthau's staff, explained the differences between domestic and foreign gold prices in the same way Warren did (Blum 1959, 120). The United States gold purchases abroad were not large enough. Roosevelt and Morgenthau did not seem to understand that devaluation and a fixed gold price would bring the domestic and world gold prices together at the fixed price, and raise the dollar prices of commodities commensurately, if the United States maintained the higher gold price by buying all gold offered at the price. The United States gold price would become the world gold price, so dollar prices of commodities would rise.

Devaluation

Discussion of a formal devaluation started in late September.[83] The Federal Reserve's main concern, at first, was whether the profit on the gold stock belonged to the Federal Reserve or could be taken by the Treasury under existing legislation. The attorney general's staff considered the Thomas amendment possibly invalid because it delegated to the president congressional power "to coin money and regulate the value thereof." Further, even if the courts upheld the Thomas amendment, that amendment did not give the president the right to take the Federal Reserve's profit from the devaluation. When Congress discussed the Thomas amendment, it considered profits from devaluation, but it did not reach a conclusion (Memo on Taking Gold Profit, Board of Governors File, box 164, October 5, 1933).

The Board's staff repeated the arguments about legality and added others. The takings clause of the Fifth Amendment provided some protection. The staff argued also that the Federal Reserve could not maintain gold reserve requirements against Federal Reserve notes, and member bank reserve balances could not be maintained, if the Treasury took the gold in Federal Reserve banks.

In addition to legal concerns, the Board had policy concerns. A devaluation by 40 percent of the gold content would increase the value of monetary gold by almost $2.9 billion. If the profit accrued to the Treasury, the Treasury could retire all the debt held by Federal Reserve banks, depriving them of earnings and removing their ability to sell securities to contract credit. Further, the profit to the Treasury could be used to finance government spending (Memo Smead to Black, Board of Governors File, box 164, November 23, 1933).[84] The System's relations with the Treasury, and Morgenthau's attitude toward "bankers," did not permit the System to dismiss this possibility.

Early in December, Roosevelt appointed a committee consisting of the acting secretary of the treasury, the attorney general, and the governor of the

83. There was not much precedent. Congress had reduced the weight of the gold dollar by 6 percent and fixed its value in 1834. The dollar had floated during and after the Civil War, but the gold parity did not change.

84. The reserve banks, as legal owners of the gold, hired Newton Baker, a longtime outside counsel, to negotiate a compromise with the administration. The banks accepted that the profit belonged to the Treasury. They proposed that, at the time of devaluation, the Treasury should exchange gold for gold certificates. The profit would go to the Treasury, but the gold would be returned in exchange for the gold certificates once the devaluation was completed. Congress would pass legislation approving the devaluation and the exchange. Otherwise several banks would not surrender their gold and others would do so under protest unless the banks' directors approved the transfer. The banks' directors were concerned about their fiduciary responsibility as representatives of the shareholding banks.

Federal Reserve Board to consider how to resolve differences. The committee did not meet. Instead, the attorney general proposed that the Treasury take the System's gold, using the powers of the Board authorized in section 11 of the Federal Reserve Act, without public announcement or prior notice to the officers of the reserve banks. The reserve banks would receive a letter stating that they were entitled to gold certificates. Black objected that the proposal was probably illegal, unwarranted, unworkable, and unnecessary. The Thomas amendment was probably unconstitutional. It should be left to Congress to legislate the disposition of the Federal Reserve's gold holdings (Board of Governors File, box 164, December 22, 1933).

The directors of some of the reserve banks reinforced Black's position. Chicago's directors unanimously approved a resolution opposing the transfer. Citing the opinions of Newton Baker and their own counsel as the basis for doubts about their legal authority to surrender the gold, they declined to voluntarily comply with a request to turn over the gold (Letter Stevens to Black, Board of Governors File, box 164, December 27, 1933).

After much additional discussion by the reserve banks, by the Board, and within the administration, on December 28 the secretary ordered all gold delivered to the Treasury at $20.67 per ounce. The next day the Board agreed that the profit on revaluation belonged to the government, not the reserve banks. It urged the president to get congressional approval of the decision to take the gold and allocate the profit (Board Minutes, December 29, 1933; Letter Black to Roosevelt, same date).

Roosevelt yielded. On December 29 he offered Black a compromise. If the reserve banks would transfer their gold, he would propose legislation ratifying the transfer. If Congress did not approve the transfer in the next session, the Treasury would return the gold, excluding the profit on revaluation. He reserved the right to take over the gold at a later date (Letter Roosevelt to Black, Board of Governors File, box 164, December 29, 1933).

Two weeks later the president asked Congress for authority to acquire the gold held by the Federal Reserve banks, substitute gold certificates, permit devaluation up to 60 percent of the gold content, and use $2 billion of the profit of any revaluation to establish a fund for foreign exchange operations, later called the Exchange Stabilization Fund (Krooss 1969, 4:2789–92). The proposed fund was about the size of the Federal Reserve's open market portfolio. It operated secretly, under the control of the treasury secretary with the president's approval (Schwartz 1997). Moreover, the proposal gave the secretary "authority to assume complete control of general credit conditions and to negate any credit policies that the Federal Reserve System might adopt" (Memo, Smead to Black, Board of Governors File, box 164, January 17, 1934). The Exchange Stabilization Fund gave the Treasury the means to conduct monetary operations without getting approval for spending from Congress.

The Federal Reserve did not oppose the bill. Black testified against the transfer of gold.[85] Burgess and Young (Boston) urged Congress to limit the secretary's use of the Exchange Stabilization Fund to an emergency. Both pointed to the potential conflict between Treasury and System policy actions. Burgess also warned about the potential increase in excess reserves if the administration used the profits on devaluation to expand credit.

Several economists testified against passage. H. Parker Willis is representative. He opposed abandoning the gold standard and devaluation, but he recognized that the administration intended to devalue. He opposed transferring the gold to the Treasury, but he argued that if it was done, the dollar should be stabilized at some depreciated level by returning to the gold standard. Always an opponent of the quantity theory, Willis showed how little he knew about economics when he rejected the argument that devaluation would raise the domestic price level: "I refuse to accept the idea at all that a change in the theoretical weight of the dollar would have any effect whatever on prices" (Senate Committee on Banking and Currency 1934, 230).[86]

Congress passed the Gold Reserve Act on January 30, by votes of 370 to 40 in the House and 66 to 23 in the Senate.[87] The following day the president fixed the price of gold at $35 an ounce, a 59.06 percent devaluation against gold. Secretary Morgenthau announced that the New York Federal Reserve bank would buy gold for the Treasury at $34.75 and sell at $35.25, but purchases and sales were restricted to transactions with central banks and governments.[88] The nominal gold price remained fixed for more than thirty-seven years, until President Richard Nixon stopped gold sales and purchases on August 15, 1971.[89]

85. Black testified in executive session, so his criticisms are not part of the hearings on the bill. He read his testimony to the Board before presenting it. His statement outlines the dispute with the administration before the bill (Board Minutes, January 20, 1934, 280–81).

86. Other opponents believed there would be serious inflation if the dollar was devalued. Edwin W. Kemmerer of Princeton feared that insurance and endowments would be wiped out (Senate Committee on Banking and Currency 1934, 213). Walter Stewart said the bill would "scrap the Federal Reserve System" (358).

87. As the vote suggests, many Republicans voted for the bill on final passage. Robert A. Taft, son of a former president and a leading Republican member of Congress, was more active in defending the gold clause than opposing the devaluation (Patterson 1972, 152).

88. The official price of gold rose from $20.67 to $35, an increase of 69.3 percent. In terms of grains of gold, however, the devaluation is from 23.22 to 13.71 grains, or 59 percent of 23.22. This is the equivalent of a devaluation from 25.8 to 15.238 ounces, nine-tenths fine.

89. By the end of December 1933, gold coin in circulation had fallen to $24 million from $181 million a year earlier.

Devaluation raised the relative gold price and stimulated world gold production. Schwartz (1982, table SC2) reports that world gold production did not exceed 25.4 million fine ounces a year until 1934. World production rose each year of the 1930s, reaching a local peak of 41.8 million fine ounces in 1941. United States production rose from 2.28 to 4.86 million fine ounces in the same period. The United States share of world production rose from 9 percent to 11.6 percent, but the largest part of the production subsidy went to foreign producers (Schwartz 1982, tables SC2 and SC5).

The Treasury used $2 billion of the profit from devaluation to establish the Exchange Stabilization Fund, $650 million to retire national banknotes, and $27 million to finance industrial loans by reserve banks. The Federal Reserve received gold certificates for its gold. The initial effect was a one-time increase in the gold price and ultimately in the prices of goods and services.[90]

United States devaluation made life difficult for the countries remaining on the gold standard, France among them. Gold flowed toward the United States. Once the act passed, the Treasury started buying gold immediately and in relatively large quantities. It purchased $454 million in February, of which $239 million came from London and $124 million from France (Crabbe 1989, 439). In the three years 1934–36, before the Treasury began to sterilize inflows, the United States purchased more than $4 billion of gold, a 57 percent increase in the stock held on January 1934. By the end of 1936, the Treasury held more than half of all gold at central banks (Schwartz 1982, table SC8). Purchases were made directly, not through the Exchange Stabilization Fund. The latter did not begin operations until April 27, 1934, when the Treasury transferred $250 million from the capital of the fund for use in market transactions.

The Federal Reserve paid for its inactivity by losing control of monetary policy. The fund gave the Treasury a strong hand in setting policy toward interest rates, money, and debt, and it used its power. The Treasury remained the dominant partner for the next fifteen years, until the March 1951 accord released the Federal Reserve from Treasury control.

---

90. In addition, the Treasury issued $180 million in gold certificates to the Federal Reserve for gold that the Federal Reserve purchased in January. The Board's counsel ruled that the reserve banks could "safely comply" with the requirement to transfer their gold to the Treasury (Wyatt to Black, Board of Governors File, box 164, January 30, 1934). The transfers were made the same day, so that all domestic gold was held by the Treasury when the dollar price of gold changed. Devaluation did not change the monetary base. The increase of $2.8 billion in the value of gold certificates offset an increase in the liability "general fund in gold" included as part of the liability "Treasury cash."

Silver Policy

The Gold Reserve Act did not end either the agitation for reflation in Congress and the farm states or Roosevelt's interest in raising the price level. The focus shifted to silver, where the combined influence of senators from the silver mining states and the reflationists constituted a sizable bloc of votes.

Their first action, part of the Thomas amendment, authorized the president to accept silver in payment of foreign debts, coin silver, and issue silver certificates. Like other parts of the amendment, these actions were permissive, not mandated.

The silver interests wanted more. To accommodate some of their demands, Roosevelt appointed Key Pittman, a Nevada senator and chairman of the Foreign Relations Committee, as a delegate to the London Monetary and Economic Conference. Pittman was able to get an agreement to stop countries from melting silver coins, replace paper money with silver coins, and purchase an agreed minimum of 35 million ounces of silver a year for four years. The United States agreed to purchase about two-thirds of the total. In advance of the new congressional session, on December 21, Roosevelt committed the United States Treasury to buy silver produced in the United States at 64.5 cents an ounce and to coin silver dollars (Krooss 1969, 4:2782–85). The price was about 20 cents above the world market price.

The president's action did not appease the silver advocates. They failed by two votes to attach an amendment to the Gold Reserve Act requiring the government to buy 50 million ounces of silver a month to add 1 billion ounces to monetary reserves. The narrow defeat encouraged new approaches. By May, Roosevelt conceded and began work on the Pittman Silver Purchase Act of 1934, committing the Treasury to purchase silver until the silver reserve reached one-fourth of the gold reserve. The act became law on June 19. Unlike its predecessor, the act committed the Treasury to purchase silver from foreign as well as domestic sources at prices up to $1.29 an ounce.[91]

Since the Treasury purchased large volumes of gold, the required vol-

---

91. The price at which the Treasury coined silver, $1.29, was the equivalent at a sixteen-to-one ratio to $20.67 per ounce of gold. Warren claims that Morgenthau and Roosevelt believed silver purchases would raise commodity prices (Pearson, Myers, and Gans 1957, 5663). Seigniorage on silver (arising from the difference in the prices at which the Treasury purchased silver and issued coins and certificates) rose from $80 million in 1934 to $181 million in 1935. For the years 1934 to 1940, seigniorage on silver was $600 million (Board of Governors of the Federal Reserve System 1943, 515).

Table 6.1   Silver Prices, 1925–40 (cents per fine ounce)

YEAR	PRICE	YEAR	PRICE
1925	69.06	1934	47.97
1929	52.99	1935	64.27
1932	27.89	1938	43.22
1933	34.73	1940	34.77

Source: Bureau of the Census 1960, 371.

Table 6.2   Silver and Gold Production, 1925–39 (thousands of fine troy ounces)

PERIOD	GOLD	SILVER
1925–29	2,171	63,343
1930–34	1,941	31,251
1935–39	4,015	61,432

Source: Bureau of the Census 1960, 371.

ume of silver purchases rose substantially. The Treasury purchased silver and issued silver certificates up to the purchase price of the silver. The demand for currency did not increase as rapidly as the supply, so most of the new currency substituted for Federal Reserve and national banknotes (Blum 1959, 188–89). In July, Morgenthau used the Exchange Stabilization Fund to buy silver in London. Table 6.1 shows the price of silver in selected years. The price rose after the purchase program started but reached a peak in 1935 and subsequently declined. The price was high enough, however, to increase domestic silver production.[92]

There were two prices for silver, just as there had been for gold. Domestic producers received 64.5 cents an ounce. Foreign purchases by the New York Federal Reserve Bank were at the world market price. Treasury purchases were far in excess of domestic production in 1934 and 1935, so the world market price rose toward the domestic price. As the price rose, silver activists offered new legislation to raise the price. Table 6.2 shows production of gold and silver on five-year averages.

A new complication entered. China and Mexico were on a silver standard.[93] At 72 cents an ounce, it paid to melt Mexican pesos and sell the silver to the Treasury. Morgenthau fixed the domestic price at 71.11 cents. This did not satisfy the silver activists, and the price went to 77.57 cents. Pressure mounted for a $1.29 domestic price, but Roosevelt refused because he had the votes to prevent legislation that term (Blum 1959, 190–92). Spec-

92. On August 9, 1934, by proclamation, President Roosevelt ordered all silver not used as coins or in arts and manufacture to be sold to the Treasury (Krooss 1969, 4:2833–35).

93. The problem for China is discussed as early as December 1934 (Minutes, New York Directors, December 6, 1934, 29).

ulators acted on the presumption that the price would continue to rise, but Morgenthau sold silver from the Exchange Stabilization Fund to stop the rise at 81 cents in April 1935. By August the price was back to 65 cents. Prices did not reach this level again until after the World War II inflation.[94]

Silver activists argued that raising the silver price would help China and Mexico by raising commodity prices in countries on the silver standard. This was backward. The policy drew silver from these countries, forcing monetary contraction. In November 1935, China abandoned the silver standard and offered to sell the United States most of its remaining silver, 200 million ounces, for approximately $130 million at the Treasury's buying price, $50 million above the market price (Friedman 1992, 171–78).

That was too much for Morgenthau.[95] Silver sold in China for about 40 cents an ounce. He allowed the world price to fall toward 40 cents after an understanding with the silver state senators that he would continue to buy newly mined domestic silver at 64.5 cents.

The silver purchase policy hurt China more than Mexico, because Mexico had large silver mines and was able, for a time, to increase its exports to the United States. China was less fortunate. Forced off the silver standard and soon afterward attacked by Japan, China experienced a major inflation that a more rational silver policy would have avoided.

Domestically, the program was a waste of money. It subsidized a relatively small number of miners and companies at large cost. Like several of the experiments during these years, the program achieved very little. It continued until November 1961.

SUMMARY: INFLATIONARY POLICY IN 1933

Roosevelt was right to be concerned about congressional and public reaction to his policies. At the end of 1933, his experiments with the NRA, the AAA, gold, and silver had not succeeded. Prices were 20 percent or more below the 1929 or 1926 level. After a robust recovery in the second and third quarters, Balke and Gordon's (1986) quarterly real GNP growth declined at a 24 percent annual rate in the fourth quarter. Despite the low levels of employment and output, the GNP deflator continued to rise in the fourth quarter, although at a much lower rate than in the summer.[96]

94. On August 14, to hold the price near 65 cents, the Treasury purchased more silver in one day than the entire production in the United States in 1934 (Blum 1959, 195).

95. In his diary he called the policy "stupid." He was particularly incensed by the encouragement to smuggling of silver from China to Japan for sale to the United States (Blum 1959, 196).

96. Perhaps for reasons such as this, economists who associate inflation with low unemployment typically ignore the 1930s.

Market indicators showed continued anxiety and fear of inflation. The risk spread between Aaa and Baa bonds remained above 3 percent, not much lower than at the end of 1932. The term spread between long- and short-term securities was above 4 percent and had increased over the course of the year.

One reason for the aborted recovery was the change in the thrust of monetary policy. Annual growth of the monetary base remained low in the spring and summer. Growth in the money supply, M_1, had a similar pattern.

The Federal Reserve committed to an expansive policy, mainly for political reasons during the congressional session, but it failed to follow through. If it had made substantial open market purchases, the administration's gold (and silver) purchase policy would have been unnecessary. The 1926 price level could have been restored by domestic monetary expansion, particularly after April when the president suspended the gold standard. Instead, the administration bought gold at a fixed (but adjustable) price. The policy drained gold from countries in the gold bloc, forcing further deflation there without much domestic benefit until purchases became large enough to change the world gold price.

Early in 1934, devaluation brought an increase in money growth. The Gold Reserve Act devalued the dollar against gold and fixed the United States buying price above the world market price. Instead of limited purchases of 1933, the United States announced its willingness to buy all gold offered at the $35 price. Thus, disappointment at what appeared to be a failed policy produced a change that achieved the desired end of higher commodity prices and economic expansion that the administration sought.

ECCLES AND MORGENTHAU

The new year brought in a new economic team. Early in January 1934, Henry Morgenthau became secretary of the treasury. In June, Eugene Black resigned as governor of the Federal Reserve Board to return to the Atlanta bank.[97] The vice governor, J. J. Thomas, served as acting governor until November, when the president nominated Marriner S. Eccles to be governor of the Board.

---

97. He left in August. Hyman (1976, 154) attributes his resignation to the much lower salary at the Board. His lasting contribution to the Federal Reserve was to start planning for the Board's own building. The Board and its staff were scattered in offices at the Treasury Department and in buildings around Washington. In July 1934 the Board approved an assessment on the reserve banks to build the Board's building (Minutes, New York Directors, July 5, 1934, 11). Black died in December 1934, a few months after his return to Atlanta.

Eccles was a Utah banker and businessman whose father and grandfather had emigrated from Scotland in 1863. Though impoverished when he arrived, Eccles's father built a successful timber and sugar business. Like many self-made men, he was a strong believer in hard work, personal effort, and responsibility and an opponent of government involvement in the economy. His son, Marriner, inherited responsibility for the family business. With his brothers, he expanded the business and added banking. His banking corporation, the First Security Corporation, had branches throughout the region. Until the depression, he held many of the same political and social views that he learned from his father and mother.

Eccles first came to national prominence during the banking crises from 1931 to 1933. By pluck, boldness, and careful planning, all his banks remained open until ordered to close in March 1933. None of his depositors suffered a loss.

The experience had a lasting effect on Eccles's beliefs. The prevailing belief was that the depression was purgative.[98] Business leaders argued that "a depression was a scientific operation of economic laws" and could not be interfered with (Eccles 1951, 73). The 1920s had been a profligate era. The price of profligacy was (eventual) depression—the inevitable consequence of prior events.

Experience caused Eccles to reject these views. He recognized that many of the same people who had declared in the 1920s that depression could not occur again now found the seeds of depression in the excesses of that decade. Eccles recognized this argument as fallacious; in the 1920s the economy had produced in the aggregate more than it had consumed. There was no evidence of national overconsumption or indulgence (ibid., 74). Further, he convinced himself that there was nothing "natural" or preordained about what was happening. He believed the depression was caused by an overexpansion of debt and investment; the maldistribution of wealth—too much wealth concentrated in too few hands; and underconsumption by low-income earners (76–77). His solution was government spending for investment, timed countercyclically to take up the shortfall resulting from the depression. He accepted an unbalanced budget as a means of paying for public works—a result of the depression, not a cause. He favored redistribution to aid the poor and unemployed (78–81).

His views soon attracted national attention. In February 1933 he testified at hearings before the Senate Finance Committee that the economic system's failure was "due to the failure of our political and financial lead-

98. "As I looked to the business and financial leaders . . . their stock reply was that a deflation in values, and a scaling down of the debt structure to meet existing price levels, would in time create a self-corrective force" (Eccles 1951, 71).

ership." The problem was "purely of distribution." The cure was more purchasing power, to be achieved by deficit spending until prices and employment rose (Eccles 1933, 705, 708).

His views help to explain his decisions and his passivity as head of the
Federal Reserve. Eccles did not blame the Federal Reserve for the depression
or urge credit expansion. The Reconstruction Finance Corporation and the
Federal Reserve banks had expanded credit without result.[99] The "extension
of credit alone is not the solution" (ibid., 709). Nor was the solution a continued or deeper deflation, as many bankers and businessmen insisted.

Eccles opposed devaluation, silver purchases, or increases in money unless they increased consumers' purchasing power. He believed the money
stock, though 22 percent below 1929, was adequate to support higher
spending; the problem was low velocity of circulation resulting from hoarding currency. His program, calling for $2.5 billion of government spending
on public works (more than 4 percent of depressed GNP), financed by debt,
and cancellation of Allied war debts, did not appeal to most senators
(ibid., 712).[100] He also favored "a more equitable distribution of wealth"
(730) to increase purchasing power, unification of the banking system
under Federal Reserve supervision, high income and inheritance taxes, a
minimum wage, unemployment insurance, old age pensions, government
supervision of security issues, transport, and communications, and a national planning board to coordinate public and private activities (730–31).[101]

Eccles's views on budgets and deficits differed from Roosevelt's or Morgenthau's. Roosevelt advocated a balanced budget and reduced expenditure
as "the most direct and effective contribution that Government can make to
business" (Eccles 1951, 97, quoting Roosevelt's campaign speech of October
19, 1932).[102] Morgenthau was a strong advocate of a balanced budget, and
the difference became a source of friction between the two men.[103]

99. Eccles in 1935 accepted the much-used phrase "pushing on a string" to describe his
belief about expanding credit and money in deep recessions.

100. Gross investment had fallen $26 billion from the 1929 peak.

101. Although Eccles advocated a national planning board, he opposed the NRA price-
and wage-raising schemes. He was glad when the Supreme Court declared the NRA unconstitutional (Hyman 1976, 153).

102. As noted earlier, Roosevelt categorically rejected deficits but then added that he
would tolerate a deficit to relieve "starvation and dire need." Eccles (1951, 98) claims that
Samuel Rosenman, who edited Roosevelt's papers, tried to reconcile Roosevelt's deficits with
his 1932 speech by claiming that Roosevelt meant only the administrative costs. Eccles viewed
Roosevelt as a "budget-balancer" who regarded a balanced budget as "a self-contained good"
(98).

103. Eccles was highly critical of wartime deficits. He favored deficits only to make up for
a shortfall of private investment. Although his proposals for deficit finance are similar to
Keynes's views after 1928, Eccles claimed never to have read Keynes's main work.

Eccles's first job in the Roosevelt administration was as an assistant to Morgenthau for banking and monetary problems. He came to Washington early in February 1934 with the stated intention of staying sixteen months. He remained for seventeen years, most of the time as head of the Federal Reserve System.[104]

His initial meetings with Morgenthau were a prelude to their later relationship. The two men were very different in background, personality, and beliefs. Eccles described himself as blunt, and his biographer adds that his relationship with Morgenthau was "deeply troubled" (Eccles 1951, vii; Hyman 1976, 207). Morgenthau saw Eccles as talented and energetic but also as confident, assertive, and ambitious, with "an insatiable drive to gain personal power" (Hyman 1976, 207; Blum 1959, 279). Morgenthau was a country gentleman who had been drawn into government by the long-standing family friendship of the Roosevelt and Morgenthau families. His biography shows him to be cautious, rarely willing to make a decision without the president's approval. He distrusted bankers and opposed "bigness" and government deficits. Eccles attributed many of his disputes to the "quirks of Morgenthau's personality" (Hyman 1976, 207).[105] Both men tended to see substantive issues as personal, a fact that Eccles realized after Morgenthau resigned and his disputes and differences continued, and intensified, with Secretaries Fred M. Vinson and John W. Snyder, who followed.

Eccles's self-image was that he defended principles against expediency (Eccles 1951, 394). The role of government was to run deficits in depression to finance investment and to run surpluses during prosperity, even in wartime, to reduce debt. This view of government spending and deficits clashed with Morgenthau's belief that spending financed by deficits during

104. His service as head of the Federal Reserve ran from November 15, 1934, to January 31, 1948, when President Truman replaced him as chairman. He remained as a member of the Board until July 14, 1951. Eccles believed that his pursuit of antitrust charges against Transamerica Corporation angered powerful political and banking interests in California during the 1948 election year. This, combined with his antagonistic relationship with Treasury Secretary John W. Snyder, a friend of the owners of Transamerica, may have led to his dismissal (Eccles 1951, 450–53). The dismissal was the subject of a congressional hearing, but the reason was not firmly established.

105. A contemporary describes Morgenthau as "suspicious" and irritable, Eccles as a person of "contradictory enthusiasms." "He loved the freedom . . . which allowed him to get very rich, and at the same time, a born centralizer" (CHFRS, interview with Casimir Sienkiewicz, March 18, 1954, 3). Sienkiewicz worked in the Federal Reserve System from 1920 to 1947. Jacob Viner describes Eccles as a "voluble talker" who "talked for hours at a time." Morgenthau "had no patience with Eccles. The two men grated on each other." Viner, like Sienkiewicz, described Morgenthau as a "suspicious man" but also as decisive in the early days (CHFRS, interview with Jacob Viner, March 17, 1954, 3–5). Currie (1971, 2) adds that "Morgenthau disliked Eccles intensely."

depressions was a cause for alarm and hesitancy by business, leading to lower investment. Wartime deficits were, for Morgenthau and many others, a very different matter—a necessity. Eccles saw the inconsistency in this position and attributed it to the self-interest of those who benefited most from the spending.[106]

Appointment to the Federal Reserve

Despite their early differences, Morgenthau proposed Eccles to replace Eugene Black as governor of the Board. In September, when President Roosevelt interviewed him, Eccles told him that he would accept appointment only if the president agreed to change the System. He wanted a commitment to end President Wilson's compromise by centralizing power and authority in the Board and its chairman. The regional banks, particularly New York, representing "private interests," controlled the System. Their power had to be broken, or the job was not worth having (Hyman 1976, 155).

Eccles agreed to prepare a memo describing the changes he regarded as necessary. He presented it to Roosevelt shortly after the 1934 congressional election. The memo, prepared with the assistance of Lauchlin Currie, combined Eccles's and Currie's ideas of what went wrong at the Federal Reserve. Currie claimed to have drafted the memo (Sandilands 1990, 63); his views were well represented.[107] It seems highly likely that it was how Eccles learned about the role of the real bills doctrine as a cause of the depression. Currie had written extensively on that issue; Eccles never mentioned it in his testimony and speeches, before meeting Currie or after. The memo to Roosevelt, however, began with an explicit statement of the need to eliminate procyclicality of the money supply. Money supply should be used as "an instrument for the promotion of business stability" (Eccles

---

106. Clashes were not limited to spending and budgets. Eccles was often involved in government policy. One of the principal clashes with lasting effect arose in 1936 over the undistributed profits tax. Eccles proposed his own version and actively worked against the Treasury's proposals.

107. Currie (1968, 39) concluded that "there is no valid theoretical justification for the Commercial Loan Theory of Banking" (real bills). He found that the Federal Reserve had never defined "productive credit" or distinguished productive from nonproductive credit except by casual inference (39). Currie also favored 100 percent reserve requirements against demand deposits and zero against time and savings deposits (151). He favored control by a three- or four-person board, in Washington, with reserve banks reduced to branches of the central bank and with all banks required to be members of the System. He recognized that expanding the Board's control was useless (or worse) unless it gave up quality of credit (real bills) as a guiding principle. Its goal should be control of spending by controlling money—currency and demand deposits (157). He repeated some of these points in different form in a long memo to Secretary Morgenthau written in September 1934 (197–226). The memo contains many of the same points but differs from his book, notably by calling for government ownership of the reserve banks. Morgenthau's diary does not mention the memo.

1957, 173). The notion of eligible paper, a keystone of real bills, would be replaced by "sound assets."

The memo departed from the more extreme position on nationalization of the reserve banks that Currie took in his September memo to Morgenthau (Currie 1968). But he proposed to vest control of open market operations in the Board, with "banker interest" removed. Bank directors would no longer have power to refuse to participate in open market operations. Also, the Board would have the power to approve or disapprove appointment of governors of the reserve banks.[108] The memo met the usual complaint head-on. The Federal Reserve would become a central bank, centrally controlled: "Private ownership and local autonomy are preserved, but on really important questions of policy, authority and responsibility are concentrated in the Board" (quoted in Hyman 1976, 158).

In the two-hour meeting at which Eccles presented and discussed the memo, Eccles records that Roosevelt paid close attention, recognized the serious political obstacles, rejected the idea of national branch banking, and accepted the proposal as a blueprint for reform. Six days later, on November 10, Roosevelt nominated Eccles as governor of the Board.[109] The announcement emphasized Eccles's business and banking background and reported the capital value of each Eccles enterprise, its volume of business, and the fact that all his enterprises had survived the depression. In this way the administration hoped to defuse criticism of Eccles's radical ideas about budgets and show that not all the new appointees lacked business experience.

Perhaps because Carter Glass had not been notified of his appointment, Eccles served in a recess appointment for five months. He was not confirmed until the following April, by a four to three vote in Glass's banking subcommittee with Glass opposed, and by a unanimous vote in the full banking committee with Glass absent.

Much of the opposition to Eccles focused on the banking bill prepared by Eccles and Currie. Many bankers opposed the legislation, particularly the sections that shifted power from the New York bank to the Board. Har-

108. Until 1936, each bank's directors appointed the bank's governor without approval by the Board. The Board approved salaries, however.

109. Roosevelt failed to clear the appointment with Carter Glass, increasing the animosity that Glass held toward Eccles. Up to this time Eccles had not had to resign from any of his business activities. After the appointment, Eccles resigned as president of First Security Corporation and First Security Bank and sold his stock. But he was legally permitted to retain positions as chairman on leave of the Utah Construction Company, vice president and treasurer of the Amalgamated Sugar Company, and president of the Eccles Investment Company. He attended directors' meetings of the latter companies throughout his Washington career (Hyman 1976, 160).

rison was among them, firmly opposed to the legislation. Always ready to put an issue in personal terms, Eccles viewed this opposition as acting "on behalf of the private banking interests of New York" or out of personal pique (Eccles 1951, 178–79). He never mentions, and seems unaware, that the proposed move toward a central bank and the weakening of the System's regional structure was seen as a substantive issue of great importance in many sections of the country and by many groups.[110] Even bankers who favored a central bank did not want the bank controlled from Washington.

Further, Eccles irritated Glass by his brash manner, failing to pay a courtesy call until two months after the president announced his appointment and failing to keep his promise to give Glass an advance copy of the legislative proposal that became the Banking Act of 1935. Eccles, uncharacteristically, recognized the second failure as a mistake (ibid., 196).

Eccles's recess appointment did not deter him from taking charge. Three days after taking office, he met with the Federal Advisory Council, a group of twelve bankers legally constituted under the Federal Reserve Act to confer and advise the Board. The council had adopted the practice of issuing statements without submitting them to the Board.[111] Eccles threatened to ignore the council and deny them access to the staff unless they agreed to submit their statements to the Board before their release. This would allow the Board to reject the statements privately and, if it chose, publicly. The council reluctantly accepted the new arrangement.

Even before he was sworn in, Eccles clashed with Harrison. The immediate issue was the System Committee for Legislative Suggestions, established in spring 1934 at the request of the Federal Reserve bank chairmen. The Board approved the committee in June (Board Minutes, June 23, 1934, 4–5). Harrison was elected chairman. All but one of the members came from the reserve banks; Vice Governor J. J. Thomas represented the Board. To Eccles, control by the reserve banks was control by private interests, especially the reserve bank directors. Eccles determined to shift control to himself, representing the public interest.

When Harrison came to congratulate Eccles on his appointment and invite him to replace Thomas on the committee, Eccles replied: "I don't intend to be a member of your committee. And, moreover, one of my first acts after I'm sworn in as Governor will be to move the abolition of your

110. Eccles several times charged Glass with changing sides, from fighting the "interests" in 1913 to defending them in 1936 (Eccles 1951, 179, and elsewhere).

111. The statement that irritated Eccles was issued in September just before the 1934 congressional elections. The statement demanded a balanced budget. Eccles regarded the statement as a political document issued to embarrass the administration.

committee. . . . I have accepted the post of Governor primarily for the purpose of carrying out an important legislative program, which you in all
probability are going to oppose" (Eccles 1951, 192). Thus Eccles began his
tenure at the Board.[112]

THE BANKING ACT OF 1935

Planning for changes to the Federal Reserve Act started before Eccles became governor. A Treasury committee headed by Jacob Viner began work
on banking and currency legislation early in 1934. The Board's research director, Emanuel A. Goldenweiser, and the Federal Reserve agents (chairmen), recommended that a System committee work with the Treasury. On
June 25 the Board approved the recommendation and established the legislative committee, chaired by Harrison, that Eccles abolished on taking office. Also, Eccles and Currie had prepared recommendations for Eccles's
November meeting with Roosevelt.[113]

Eccles did not want the modest reforms and compromises expected
from a System committee. With Currie, he challenged two of the main
tenets underlying the Federal Reserve Act. First was the almost ritual restatement that the Federal Reserve was not a central bank. Eccles wanted a
central bank with authority concentrated in Washington, specifically in his
hands. Second, although he did not seem to share Currie's strong beliefs
about the need to abandon the real bills doctrine, he did not defend it. Eccles disliked rules such as the real bills doctrine. He preferred to rely on
judgment and wanted a large measure of authority to do what he believed
was in the public interest.

Glass held exactly the opposite view from Eccles on both main issues.
Financial collapse reinforced his commitment to the real bills doctrine. In
his view the collapse was the inevitable consequence of violating the doctrine, and he continued to favor a decentralized system. The fault was that
New York had acquired too much power. Centralization had gone far beyond original intent.

---

112. Relations were rarely good. In September, before Eccles's appointment, Harrison
discussed relations with the Board "and the possibility of their improvement" (Minutes, New
York Directors, September 17, 1934, 171).

113. There were many other proposals for change. One bill by Senator Elmer Thomas
(Oklahoma) established a government-controlled system by purchasing all stock of the
reserve banks. The System's objective would be to "control the price of commodities through
control of the purchasing power of money" (Board of Governors File, box 141, S. 433, undated). A bill offered by Senator Gerald P. Nye (North Dakota) created a central bank with representatives elected from each state for twelve-year terms. The bill also imposed 100 percent
reserves against demand deposits and 5 percent against time deposits (ibid., S. 2162, March
4, 1935).

Even if Eccles and Glass had had good personal relations, they would have clashed over substance. In the event, substance and personal feeling set up a clash between two strong-willed men.

Harrison and the System Committee

The work of Harrison's committee shows the internal view of what went wrong and the desirable changes.[114] There were, of course, differences of opinion and pressures to avoid contentious issues.[115]

The committee began to consider an ambitious agenda of reform of the banking system and Federal Reserve controls. A comparison of failure rates in the United States, Canada, and Britain led to a proposal for branch banking. The background paper for the meeting recognized that "England, with a central bank, and Canada, without a central bank, entirely escaped bank failures" and that United States banking failures explain "both the greater severity of the depression in this country, particularly from 1931 on, and the greater difficulty experienced in achieving recovery" (Memo on Banking Reform, Goldenweiser to Committee, Board of Governors File, box 142, September 6 and 7, 1934, 2). But the memo shifted away from this promising start by blaming the "soundness of bank assets" for the higher failure rate (3). Thus it missed the opportunity to rid the banking system of its greatest weakness—restricted portfolios and limited diversification.

The rest of the memo was defensive, aimed at preventing reorganization and a shift of power to the Board. The memo claims that the Federal Reserve had shown its effectiveness in financing World War I and in acting promptly in the recessions of 1924 and 1927. None of the existing central banks used credit or monetary control to stabilize prices, prevent booms or depressions, or hasten recovery; therefore the System should be credited for its successes and could not be blamed for the depression. Further, the Federal Reserve Act limited the Federal Reserve's mandate to "accommodat[e] the needs of industry, commerce and agriculture" (ibid., 4).

---

114. In addition to Harrison, the committee included two former governors of the Reserve Board, Black and Young, Norris (Philadelphia), two representatives of the Cleveland bank, and G. J. Schaller, who had replaced James McDougal at Chicago. The only Board member was J. J. Thomas, recently arrived as vice governor of the Board. Its advisers, Emanuel Goldenweiser and John H. Williams, were responsible for the drafting. Most members of the committee had participated actively in policymaking during the depression, so the committee was almost certain to find lack of power, not errors, as the reason for the System's failures.

115. An early draft drew a strong response from George James, a member of the Board (1923–36), who was not a committee member. Describing the drift as "one man's offhand opinion," James criticized most severely neglect of "investment speculation on the part of member banks. In my humble opinion this very factor was one of the major causes of the recent banking difficulties" (memo James to Board, Board of Governors File, box 142, October 2, 1934).

The Thomas amendment removed that restriction, so there is "no lack of power or of central banking machinery for carrying out whatever monetary and credit policies the *Government may deem desirable* for the promotion of recovery" (6; emphasis added).

The principal conclusion: System reorganization would not solve the problem of how to manage credit control policy. The memo proposed a broad study of banking, monetary, credit, and organizational changes. In October the committee reduced the scope of possible changes. The defensive tone and substance remained until the final report.

The preliminary report (October) located the "basic problem" in the quality of bank credit extended: "This lack of quality has been due to conflicting jurisdiction, to laxity of laws, to lack of uniformity . . . in supervision, and . . . to lack of skill and vision in [bank] management" (Preliminary Report of the Committee on Legislative Program, Board of Governors File, box 142, October 16, 1934, 1). There is not a word about Federal Reserve failures or inaction: "The depression which began in 1929 continued to develop notwithstanding the great volume of credit made available to the banks through open market operations by the Federal Reserve banks" (2).[116]

Perhaps reflecting the realities of the time, the final report made a brief reference to a new theme: the Federal Reserve banks have a responsibility to adjust their policies to "the need for expansion or restraint as conditions dictate" (Report, System Committee on the Legislative Program, Board of Governors File, box 142, December 17, 1934, 2). The report immediately shifted away, locating the main defects not in System failures to respond to economic conditions or bank failures, but in the "quality of bank assets and the soundness of banks" (ibid.). It failed to recognize that "quality" and "soundness" depend to a considerable extent on what happens to the economy.

The report proposed improved supervision and regulation, to be achieved by unifying examinations and supervision under the reserve banks and by subjecting all banks to unified standards.[117] The deposit insurance law required all insured banks to join the Federal Reserve System by July 1937. The report wanted this provision retained, but it was dropped.

The most important change proposed in the report called for increased authority to raise and lower reserve requirement ratios. Under the exist-

116. The section on credit control concludes: "The record of the System shows that it has always functioned in the spirit of its constitution as an institution vested with the public interest" (Preliminary Report of the Committee on Legislative Program, Board of Governors File, box 142, October 16, 1934, 5).

117. Unification of examination standards was not achieved until 1938. The report showed awareness of moral hazard. It recommended that liquidation of failed banks take place "before the equity has been absorbed," but it made no proposal about how this could be done or how to avoid dissipation of the assets of failed or failing banks.

ing power, in section 19 of the act, changes required approval of the president and declaration of an emergency. The committee proposed giving that authority to the Board. It also endorsed a staff proposal to make reserve requirements depend on both deposit turnover (velocity) and volume (ibid., 18).

The final report removed from the earlier draft the Board's defense of its policy from 1929 to 1933: "The Federal Reserve System has undertaken bolder and more extensive experiments in credit control than have ever been carried out by any other banking or Governmental authority" (Preliminary Report, Board of Governors File, box 142, October 16, 1934, 9). Failures and depression had occurred, of course, but not because of Federal Reserve failures. The problem was expansion of speculative credit, over which the Federal Reserve had more control after 1933. However, "sound banking is possible only under sound economic conditions. In the presence of profound national and international maladjustments that developed during the decade after the war, no banking system could function effectively" (10).[118] The report does not mention that some reserve banks refused to participate or that the Board did not force recalcitrant reserve banks to pool the gold stock by discounting for participating banks.

Currie's Treasury Proposal

Most of the work of Viner's committee at the Treasury reflected Currie's views.[119] Currie expanded the recommendations in his book (Currie 1968). The responsibility of the Federal Reserve, Currie wrote, is to control the quantity of money, not the quality of credit. The Federal Reserve Act took the opposite approach through its reliance on the real bills (commercial loan) doctrine.[120]

118. The preliminary report ignores the dispute between New York and Washington in October 1929, when New York acted independently, and the subsequent criticism by Young and the Board. See chapter 4. "The Federal Reserve promptly cushioned the decline [in stock prices] by promptly . . . buying securities on a large scale. During the depression it purchased . . . in unparalleled volume and thereby enabled the member banks not only to meet the drain of currency. . . . [but] to reduce their indebtedness to the Reserve banks to negligible proportions" (Preliminary Report, Board of Governors File, box 142, October 16, 1934, 8). The last statement shows the continuing influence of Riefler-Burgess views.

119. Currie had studied at the London School of Economics before receiving a Ph.D. at Harvard. At Harvard, he met Ralph Hawtrey, a visiting professor who had done pathbreaking work in monetary economics, emphasizing the role of money in cyclical fluctuations. Currie's work (1968) blamed the Federal Reserve for the depth and severity of the depression, anticipating the later critiques by Warburton (1948) and Friedman and Schwartz (1963). See Sandilands 1990, Laidler 1993, and Brunner 1968.

120. "By and large the concern of the banking authorities in this country has been with the composition of bank assets" (Currie 1968, 35). Currie pointed out that, probably because it was difficult to do, the Federal Reserve had never defined "productive credit" (39).

Currie concluded that "there exists no valid theoretical justification for the Commercial Loan Theory of Banking" (ibid., 39). "The drastic contraction of money from 1929 to 1932 can in large part be attributed to the failure of the reserve administration to appreciate the significance of changes in the supply of money" (44). And he added: "It is generally held that the reserve administration strove energetically to bring about expansion throughout the depression but that the contraction continued despite its efforts. Actually the reserve administration's policy was one of almost complete passivity and quiescence" (147).

To remedy these failures and control the money stock, Currie proposed 100 percent reserves against demand deposits and no reserve requirements for other deposits. The gold standard and open market operations would control the volume of reserves and deposits. Banks could expand or contract lending relative to money by bidding for time deposits.

Control of money was vested in a five-person board appointed by the president and confirmed by the Senate. Its charge was to maintain business stability, not to "accommodate commerce and business." It would have discretionary authority to alter gold reserves, within limits consistent with maintenance of the gold standard.

Currie expanded these proposals in his recommendations to Morgenthau mainly by adding detail and working out the transition to 100 percent reserves against demand deposits. One issue discussed at length was whether the Federal Reserve Board (called the Federal Monetary Authority) should be responsible to the administration. Currie recognized the possible inflationary consequences of this arrangement, but he chose political control under a general congressional mandate that set objectives. He suggested removing the secretary of the treasury from the Board.[121] Eccles took Currie onto the Board's staff as assistant director of research. Currie's main task initially was staff work leading to the 1935 act.

The Banking Act in Congress

The bill that was sent to Congress in February 1935 contained three sections. Roosevelt recognized that the proposed changes in the Federal Reserve Act calling for creation of a central bank, with headquarters in

121. The Board would consist of experts who would publish quarterly reports containing diagnosis of current conditions, expectations about future trends, "an account of its current policy which not only explains why it is being pursued but also what it hopes to accomplish thereby" (Currie 1968, 215). This proposal anticipated the decisions in New Zealand, Sweden, Britain, and elsewhere in the 1990s when central banks in these countries adopted inflation targets. It took many years before central banks surrendered enough secrecy to provide information about their current and prospective activities.

Washington, would not be popular with most bankers, many populists, and those who wanted to nationalize banking. He joined the Eccles-Currie proposals (title 2) to two other pieces of legislation. Title 1 liberalized FDIC assessments and required all member banks to join the deposit insurance fund.[122] Title 3 changed a section of the Banking Act of 1933 that required bank officers to resign if they had not repaid all loans to their banks by July 1. Title 3 extended the time limit for repayment, made technical adjustments to the Federal Reserve Act, and made permanent the use of government securities as collateral for the note issue. Thus Roosevelt put together a provision that many bankers wanted for personal reasons, and permanent deposit insurance, popular with Congress and the public, with a proposal that many disliked very much (Hyman 1976, 171).[123]

The House passed the bill almost as it had been submitted. The vote was 271 to 110. Eccles testified on ten days, presenting the proposal and responding to questions. Unlike Currie, he described the 1928–29 experience as a "speculative orgy," perhaps to appeal to Congress. The aim of the proposed legislation was both to control speculation and to "promote stability of employment and business." The latter was a decisive shift in goals, certain to be unpopular with Glass (House Committee on Banking and Currency 1935, 180).

To meet this new goal the Federal Reserve needed reorganization and new powers. Eccles emphasized four changes proposed in the bill: (1) subject the head of each reserve bank to approval by the Board, make the Board's governor the head, and eliminate the office of reserve bank chairman;[124] (2) vest control of open market operations in a five-person committee consisting of three Board members and two reserve bank governors; (3) transfer authority to specify eligible paper from the reserve banks to the Board; and (4) further liberalize provisions relating to real estate

122. The 1934 FDIC law provided permanent deposit insurance on July 1, 1935, up to $10,000, 75 percent insurance for accounts between $10,000 and $50,000, and 50 percent above $50,000. Title 1 limited insurance to $5,000. Title 1 also gave the FDIC power to restrict entry. Warburton (1966, xiii) explains that the premium for deposit insurance, 0.083 percent, was set to cover depositors' losses from bank failures except in deep depression of the 1870s, 1890s, and early 1930s.

123. Morgenthau saw the bill as a means of wresting control of monetary policy from bankers. Roosevelt shared this view. In October 1933 he said: "Some members of the banking fraternity . . . do not want to make loans to industry. They are in a sullen frame of mind hoping by remaining sullen to . . . force our hands" (quoted in Blum 1959, 343). See the earlier reference to Chase National Bank and Harrison's discussion with Winthrop Aldrich, its chairman. Morgenthau and Roosevelt saw this opposition of New York banks and large insurance companies as the dominant influence on the open market committee and the New York reserve bank (343).

124. The title of governor is not written into the Federal Reserve Act. The reserve bank directors created the position and gave the title to the banks' top officials.

lending. The last provision was included to attract bankers' support by increasing their opportunities at a time of relatively small loan demand.[125]

The proposed control of open market operations did not fully satisfy Eccles. In his testimony he went beyond his bill, asking the committee to remove the two reserve bank governors, eliminate the committee, and make the Board alone responsible for open market operations. A committee of five reserve bank governors would have a consultative or advisory role only.[126]

In the course of more than two hundred pages of testimony, Eccles both explained and defended sections of the proposed bill and offered his explanation of the causes of the depression and the path to recovery. The questions show the principal concerns of opponents and supporters, and Eccles's arguments give a preview of the policies he followed and advocated during the rest of the decade. The committee members expressed their fears of deficits and debt burdens that return again and again in the next sixty years. Many of the comments about debt and deficits would be repeated unchanged in the 1980s and 1990s.

CONGRESSIONAL CONCERNS Eccles chaired a committee, consisting mainly of Board staff, that prepared the bill without consultation or discussion with the reserve banks. The proposal then went to an Interdepartmental Loan Committee, chaired by Morgenthau, with representatives of other government agencies: "The Board was not asked to approve it. The Board was kept advised of the legislation" (Blum 1959, 352–53).

This method of drafting raised concern about the shift in power that the bill proposed. Repeatedly Eccles was asked about the dangers of consolidating power over discount rates, reserve requirements, and open market operations in a single agency, appointed by the president and subject to political control. Congressmen expressed concern about the potential for

125. Other provisions of title 2 reduced terms for reserve bank directors to six years, raised salaries and provided pensions for future members of the Board, repealed collateral requirements for Federal Reserve notes (extending the 1932 Glass-Steagall provisions), expanded authority to raise or lower reserve requirements, and made other technical changes (House Committee on Banking and Currency 1935, 185).

126. The House had already adopted this plan, but Eccles's testimony angered Morgenthau. He distrusted the Federal Reserve Board, in part because of its unwillingness to further reduce interest rates in 1934 (Blum 1959, 346–47). They "lacked courage" (348). Glass tried to use the opportunity to get Morgenthau to withdraw support, but after talking to Roosevelt, Morgenthau decided to support government ownership of the reserve banks and the principle of placing the open market committee under the Board's control. He did not endorse a specific compromise because Roosevelt had not yet made a decision (349). Throughout the spring Roosevelt was cautious about endorsing title 2. At one point he led Glass to believe that he did not care about title 2 (347, 349).

inflation and the use of monetary expansion by the executive branch to influence elections. And the old issue of regional autonomy remained (366–67). Eccles responded that "monetary policy is a national matter, and it cannot be dealt with regionally without having such situations as we have had in the past" (367).

THE ROLE OF MONETARY POLICY The colloquy with House members shows that Eccles knew the legislation was a long step away from the Glass-Wilson reserve system and toward a modern central bank with responsibility for economic stability. That step was not taken for many years, however. The main reason is that the Treasury held a commanding position during the 1930s and 1940s. Eccles's beliefs about monetary policy and his framework for analyzing the economy also played a role.

Eccles held a Keynesian view long before that view became dominant among academics and central bankers. Mixed with that view were vestiges of older ideas about underconsumption, overinvestment, borrowing, speculation, and income distribution. Eccles repeated many times, in the hearings and elsewhere, that the depression was due in part to inequality in income distribution. One of the fullest statements of this belief is: "One of the principal troubles or difficulties that brought about the depression was not the shortage in the supply of money altogether, but it was due in part to the inequitable distribution of income which contributed to the speculative situation in the security markets and to an expansion of productive capacity out of relationship to the ability of the people of the country to consume under the existing distribution of income" (House Committee on Banking and Currency 1935, 405).

He regarded the depression as "inevitable" given the distribution of income. The depression might have been deferred or delayed by increasing the stock of money in 1929, but it could not have been prevented: "As long as we had such an inequitable distribution of wealth production . . . a depression was inevitable" (ibid., 210).

The cure was therefore mainly fiscal. Eccles thought that "there is only one way by which we will get out of the depression, and that is through the process of budgetary deficits until such time as private credit and private spending expands. . . . Until private borrowing and spending expands, and puts people to work, the Government must do the borrowing and spending" (ibid., 403).

This view does not seem unusual now, but at the time it struck many of his listeners, both in and out of Congress, as radical. Eccles coupled his view with his belief that depressions were inevitable under capitalism. Debt built up in periods of expansion. Investment expanded production faster than consumption. When depression came, there were two choices: deflation, bankruptcy, and debt reduction or reflation to lower the real value of the debt (ibid., 346–48).[127]

The most quoted line in Eccles's testimony is "you cannot push on a string" (House Committee on Banking and Currency 1935, 377). Congressman T. Alan Goldsborough (Maryland),[128] a supporter of Eccles and the bill, introduced the phrase. Eccles accepted it immediately: "That is a good way to put it, one cannot push a string. . . . [T]here is very little, if anything that the reserve organization can do" (377). He had expressed the same pessimism earlier in his testimony several times. Monetary action was asymmetric; it was easier to stop an expansion than to end a contraction.[129] An attempt to flood the economy with currency by paying off the debt, as some congressmen proposed, would just create excess reserves (322).

Eccles's views fit well with those of Goldenweiser, Riefler, and other Board staff. Monetary expansion did not work in the depression because "you must have borrowers who are willing and able to borrow" (ibid., 216). Although he mentioned interest rates, and the effects of policy action on interest rates, these were far from central to his analysis. The liquidity trap—pushing on a string—dominated his view.[130] Hence the only role for monetary action was to keep rates low and to be alert to the risk of inflation inherent in the large volume of excess reserves held by the banking system. Several times Eccles warned about this problem and mentioned the large potential expansion in loans and money.

Eccles differed from his predecessors in his belief that government had to take responsibility for the economy. He devoted much of his time to ad-

127. Elsewhere in his testimony, he reaches the same conclusions by arguing that an inequitable distribution of wealth results in "excessive savings" in the expansion phase, hence too little consumption (House Committee on Banking and Currency 1935, 241). Government can help to stabilize by taxing away the excess saving, thereby increasing monetary velocity and spending.

128. In the 1920s, Goldsborough proposed Irving Fisher's rule for price stability. See chapter 4. In 1932 he proposed expansive operations to raise the price level. He took an active part in the hearings on the Banking Act of 1935. Commenting on Federal Reserve purchases in 1932, Goldsborough said, "They continued [purchases] until the danger of the passage of the Goldsborough bill was over, and then it immediately stopped" (House Committee on Banking and Currency 1935, 209).

129. This is a remarkable shift from the hand-wringing in 1928–29 about inability to stop the "speculative" excesses. Before testifying, Eccles held a press conference. Contrary to his testimony, he gave as two main reasons for the banking bill "to accelerate the rate of economic recovery . . . [and] to prevent the recurrence of conditions that led to the collapse of our entire banking structure" (Eccles 1934–37, press conference, February 8, 1935, 1).

130. Although the idea of a liquidity trap is now associated with Keynes (1936), Eccles's 1935 testimony shows that the idea was older. Keynes may have acquired the idea from bankers.

vocating fiscal measures, especially increased spending on investment financed by government borrowing to expand demand.[131]

THE BILL IN THE SENATE   Senator Glass intended to defeat the bill by separating title 2, containing Eccles's proposals, from the sections the bankers wanted.[132] July 1 was the critical date on which bankers would have to repay their loans and the (temporary) FDIC would expire. Glass hoped to delay passage until that time, get an agreement to separate the sections, pass titles 1 and 3, and later defeat title 2.

When the House in April appeared ready to pass a version of the bill, Glass held brief hearings on Eccles's nomination, hoping to defeat the nomination and be rid of Eccles.[133] The subcommittee approved the nomination four to three, with Glass opposed. On April 25 the Senate confirmed Eccles as governor. Glass then started hearings on the bill.[134]

The Republican minority on the House Banking Committee had ob-

131. Currie seems to have shared this view. Although he analyzed the Federal Reserve's failure to expand as a consequence of adherence to the real bills doctrine and neglect of the falling money stock, he does not seem to have pursued this view at the Federal Reserve. He devoted much of his research after 1935 to developing measures of fiscal thrust and the case for unbalanced budgets (Sandilands 1990, 68–78). Later, he described his 1934 book as "partly obsolete when it was published" (Currie 1971). The reason he gave was that money (deposits) depend on member bank borrowing, and there was no borrowing. This is an odd conclusion.

Currie worked as Goldenweiser's deputy, but he reported directly to Eccles. Goldenweiser could (and did) prevent him from publishing some of his work, but he could not prevent him from urging expansive monetary policies or avoiding the doubling of reserve requirement ratios in 1936–37 if he had chosen to do so. Currie described Goldenweiser as laying down "a rule that nothing can be published by the division which he does not understand, which limits the possibilities seriously" (Currie 1971, 79). It is difficult to understand why Eccles retained Goldenweiser in his position and adopted many of his ideas about excess reserves. Currie noted in a 1934 letter to Eccles that Goldenweiser believed that the Federal Reserve had been too *inflationary* in 1931. They (the staff) are "not interested in money and have never completed a series on money" (68–69). Of course, Goldenweiser disliked Currie's criticism of policy from 1929 to 1933 and thought it tainted by what would later be (loosely) called "monetarism." In a 1935 letter to Viner, Currie complained that Goldenweiser vetoed publication of an article on income-increasing government spending.

132. Roosevelt worked behind the scenes, but not openly, to assist passage. He had the Senate add three new members to the banking committee and secretly encouraged Senator Duncan Fletcher (Florida), chairman of the whole committee, to hold hearings with the whole committee instead of Glass's subcommittee. The latter effort failed. It violated the spirit and possibly the letter of the agreement under which Glass gave up the chair of the Banking Committee to take the Appropriations Committee.

133. He also began an investigation of whether Eccles remained connected to his banks and therefore ineligible (Hyman 1976, 174–75).

134. At first he ignored Eccles and invited Chairman Leo Crowley of the FDIC and Comptroller J. F. T. O'Connor. Both favored separating title 2 and promptly passing titles 1 and 3. Both Crowley and O'Connor opposed title 2. Morgenthau disliked both of them, but both had

jected to the bill on three main grounds. First, the minority claimed that the bill ended the private-public compromise arrangement in the 1913 act by changing the Board from a supervisory agency to a managing partner and by giving the Board authority to approve the appointment of reserve bank presidents. Second, the bill gave the Board control of open market operations and forced the reserve banks to buy or sell securities at the Board's initiative. Third, since there was no emergency, there was no reason to pass title 2 without further study. The last was Glass's plan, and the objective of the bill's opponents.

Eccles's testimony before Glass's subcommittee responded to the main criticisms in the minority report on the House bill, so it was largely defensive in character. He repeated the arguments he had made to the House committee about income redistribution, but most of his statement defended the shift of power to the Board. He claimed the shift did not increase political control over the financial system: "There is nothing in this bill that would increase the powers of a political administration over the Reserve Board" (Senate Committee on Banking and Currency 1935, 280).

Glass interrupted repeatedly. He disputed Eccles's claim that proposals to place the regulation of monetary policy under government control retained the spirit of the 1913 act. The 1913 act gave the Board supervisory responsibility, he said, not control of policy (ibid., 281).

Eccles offered to compromise. The American Bankers Association had proposed that five reserve bank governors should join with the Board to set open market policy. Eccles accepted this proposal in place of his earlier recommendation that the banks have only an advisory function (ibid., 287–89).

Senator James Couzens (Michigan) raised the most intriguing question: What would the Federal Reserve have done differently if the proposed changes had been law in 1928–29? Eccles first tried to evade the issue, but Couzens, joined by Glass, persisted. Eccles could not answer at the hearing but submitted his response in a letter to Senator Couzens.

"The banking bill of 1935 is not primarily proposed for meeting a situation such as existed in 1928 and 1929" he responded (Senate Committee on Banking and Currency 1935, 673). The Banking Act of 1933 and the Securities Act strengthened the Board's power to meet such situations. Then he added two arguments that reflect hindsight, not the views held at the time. First, despite the dominant view at the Board denying any ability to

---

support in Congress (Hyman 1976, 345–46). O'Connor had been a law partner of Senator William G. McAdoo (California) and was a friend of Glass and the president's son, James. Crowley had the support of James A. Farley, head of the Democratic Party. Eccles did not testify until May 10, a month after hearings began.

affect economic activity or prices, Eccles claimed, "The Federal Reserve Board felt that there was nothing in the business situation that required restraint" (674). Second, "It was not in 1929 that the powers contained in this bill would have been valuable but in 1931. . . . The System would have been in a much stronger position to adopt a vigorous open-market policy if this bill had been in effect" (674). Eccles added that the bill also would give the Federal Reserve power to counteract inflation if banks expanded based on their current excess reserves.

Adolph Miller was the next witness. Miller supported Eccles's argument about (August) 1931: "In 1931 some of the Reserve banks and the Reserve Board had reached the conclusion that it would be desirable to relieve the situation by an open-market operation of considerable extent. Strong opposition was encountered on the part of two or three of the reserve banks . . . [A]n open market operation was undertaken, but to a very much more limited extent" (ibid., 750).[135]

Miller defended the main provisions of the bill. He had favored, and worked for, Board control of open market operations since 1924. In his view the bill did not cause a massive redistribution of powers within the System (ibid., 699). His main objection was to the section making the 1932 Glass-Steagall provisions permanent. Limited powers to change eligibility requirements in an emergency would be sufficient.[136]

A colloquy with Glass brought out a main substantive issue between opponents and proponents. Glass viewed the reserve banks as acting in the interest of stockholders and depositors. He opposed giving the open market committee "the right to compel [reserve] banks to use their resources and the resources of their depositors, whether they thought it was prudent to do it or not" (ibid., 751). Miller responded that centralization was critical not only to affect the public interest but to concentrate responsibility: "Open market policy is peculiarly a national policy, and if it be kept as a

135. Hamlin's testimony confirmed that the reference was to August 1931 (Senate Committee on Banking and Currency 1935, 945–46). At that meeting, Meyer urged purchases of $300 million, and Harrison agreed. The committee voted to make seasonal purchases of only $120 million. Governor Young (Boston) opposed any purchases; Calkins (San Francisco) argued that not all the banks could participate because some lacked sufficient gold reserve. See chapter 5. Another occasion, not mentioned here, is November 1931, when Miller wanted a "bold" program of purchases, but the committee made only seasonal purchases. Hamlin also mentions the refusal by Boston and Chicago to participate in purchases in 1933, most likely a reference to 1932.

136. Glass, a former treasury secretary, observed that the Treasury would always consider it an emergency when it had bonds to sell (Senate Committee on Banking and Currency 1935, 729). With respect to the 1932 Glass-Steagall Act, he observed that "I never would have agreed to have reported that bill but for the fact that we were assured . . . that they did not expect to use it" (685).

national policy and operated only . . . when the indications of its need are clear, I do not think there is anything to fear in the way of bad action through withholding from any individual reserve bank the power of veto so far as itself is concerned" (751).[137]

Citing the Federal Reserve's inability to offset gold inflows in 1916, Miller favored increased power to change reserve requirement ratios. Like Eccles, Miller called attention to the problem of excess reserves and potential inflation that had begun to concern the Board. Glass opposed the change.

Miller proposed that the name of the Federal Reserve Board be changed to Board of Governors with the members as governors, as a "matter of prestige" (ibid., 756). He also proposed that the Board be permitted to elect its chairman and vice chairman, but the final bill gave the president that right, subject to Senate approval.

Harrison decided not to testify, but he helped Glass find witnesses who opposed the bill. Many of them urged the subcommittee to pass the bill without title 2. H. Parker Willis reaffirmed Glass's view that the bill subverted the Federal Reserve Act. Title 2 negated "everything in the theory of the Reserve Act" (ibid., 864). He thought open market operations should be phased out. An expanded definition of eligible paper would make it more difficult to enforce provisions against speculative credit. In Willis's view, "the Reserve System has been in the hands of Philistines a great deal of the time and has not lived up to its early promise. . . . [That] has nothing to do with the validity of the principles under which it was organized" (873).[138]

137. It is likely that Miller's statement was more persuasive than Eccles's had been. He was a proponent of the gold standard and real bills, had been a member of the Board from the start, and was a friend of many senators and of both Hoover and Roosevelt. He had opposed the increase in "speculative credit" that many senators blamed for the depression. Senator McAdoo, another former treasury secretary on the subcommittee, agreed with Miller's statement at the time (Senate Committee on Banking and Currency 1935, 751), but later in the hearing he proposed to give the Board authority to excuse a regional bank from participation in an open market operation (761).

138. A sample of views conveys some of the strong beliefs of the time. James Warburg of the Bank of Manhattan left the Roosevelt administration because of its gold policies. Like Willis, he was against open market operations and favored a return to the principles of the 1913 act that his father had helped to write. Oliver M. W. Sprague, of Harvard, testified that decentralization was no longer possible. There is one money market. The Federal Reserve Board should have more control, but the Board should be independent of the administration. Edwin W. Kemmerer of Princeton opposed the bill as too large a transfer of authority to the president over the Board and the Board over the reserve banks. He also opposed provisions to lower the quality of bank assets by abandoning real bills. Kemmerer ended his statement by reading a statement signed by the sixty-two members of the Economists' National Committee on Monetary Policy urging defeat of title 2.

Board members George R. James and Charles S. Hamlin testified also. James saw no need for a central bank or title 2. The present arrangement worked well. Bankers had caused problems by creating deposits "against prices rather than values" (Senate Committee on Banking and Currency 1935, 925). Hamlin favored several of the changes, including substitution of "sound assets" in place of the needs of trade as a criterion for discounts and centralized control of open market operations. He preferred to leave the power to appoint reserve bank governors to the directors, to leave the treasury secretary on the Board, and to keep current restrictions on changes in reserve requirement ratios. Hamlin concluded by affirming support of the Eccles bill.[139]

In all, Glass called about sixty witnesses. Most opposed title 2 as un-necessary. Several made the same argument that Eccles used to respond to Senator Couzens—that the important changes in powers were in the Banking Act of 1933 and the Securities Act.[140]

Glass was exultant after the hearings ended. He told Harrison, "I have them badly whipped both in the subcommittee and in the big committee" (Harrison Papers, Telephone Conversation with Senator Glass, file 2021.0, June 15, 1935). The subcommittee had voted to put off discussion of title 2 for a week, so Glass hoped to pass only titles 1 and 3 to meet the July 1 dead-line for bankers to repay their loans and continue deposit insurance. He planned to amend title 2 "to make it objectionable to the administration" (ibid., 1).[141]

Both tactics failed. Pressed by Roosevelt, Chairman Steagall insisted on a compromise, prepared by Eccles and Goldsborough, that extended title 1 for two months. The Senate accepted many of Glass's amendments, but the House did not, so the issue moved to a conference committee.[142]

The final bill was again a compromise between concerns about banker or political control. Congress accepted many of the changes Eccles pro-

139. Hamlin's argument for keeping the secretary on the Board stressed the need for co-operation and coordination of fiscal and monetary actions, a theme much discussed in the early postwar years (Senate Committee on Banking and Currency 1935, 949).

140. Eccles (1951, 206) is critical of this argument and fails to recognize that he had made a similar argument in response to Senator Couzens's question. A list of some principal wit-nesses is on 205–6.

141. Glass does not seem to have noticed that Eccles's testimony, defending the bill and its purposes, had changed opinions in the press and the public. The *Washington Post*, owned by Eugene Meyer, and the *New York Times*, both influential, changed from opposition to sup-port. Eccles was the subject of favorable articles in leading magazines (Hyman 1976, 181–82).

142. Glass's bill tried to prevent the executive branch from controlling the System. It re-quired the Federal Reserve to report to Congress on open market operations, required a su-permajority of five governors to change reserve requirement ratios, limited Board members to a single term, and required four members from one party and three from another.

posed, but not in the form he had suggested. The Board gained power and influence over policy and appointments at the reserve banks; however, Glass managed to get representation by the reserve banks on the new open market committee and authority for directors to choose a reserve bank's officers, subject to Board approval.[143]

Morgenthau supported the final bill because he anticipated large budget deficits and wanted to share responsibility for any future debacle that deficit finance might cause. Above all, he wanted a Board with power to keep interest rates low. He wrote in his diary: "I have been hoping and have not mentioned it to a soul that the Federal Reserve Board would be given additional powers and created more or less as a monetary authority so that they and the Treasury can share the responsibility and possibly help us in case we get into a financial jam" (Blum 1959, 352).[144]

The Act

The act changed the open market committee from a committee of twelve reserve bank governors to seven Board members and five members chosen by reserve bank directors.[145] The head of the bank had the title president, not governor, and was not ex officio a member of the open market committee. Reserve bank directors appointed the presidents and first vice presidents for five-year terms, with approval of the Board of Governors. As before, the Board set salaries. The act replaced the full-time office of chairman and Federal Reserve agent with a part-time chairman.[146]

As before, the president appointed members of the Board of Governors,

143. Subsequently, the new bylaws of the Federal Open Market Committee barred the presidents from divulging FOMC decisions to their directors.

144. Morgenthau continued along this line, citing his power over the present Board as stemming not from his seat on the Board but from the use of the Exchange Stabilization Fund "plus the many other funds I have at my disposal. . . . [T]his power has kept the open market committee in line and afraid of me" (Blum 1959, 352).

145. Section 205 of the 1935 act specified that the five presidents would be chosen from restricted groups as follows: Boston and New York; Philadelphia and Cleveland; Chicago and St. Louis; Richmond, Atlanta, and Dallas; Minneapolis, Kansas City, and San Francisco. Each year, a committee of directors met to choose the representative. The act did not require rotation among the reserve banks. Harrison was chosen from 1936 to 1940, with Boston's president always as alternate. Beginning in 1942, New York gained a permanent seat as vice chairman of the committee; Chicago alternated with Cleveland, and the remaining nine banks rotated within three triplets. New York's first vice president serves as the New York alternate.

146. The 1913 act intended the chairman and Federal Reserve agent to be the main contact with the Board. The position of governor is not mentioned in the act. Practice evolved so that the governor became the chief executive. The 1935 act recognized practice. Directors of reserve banks continued to receive $20 per meeting they attended plus travel (if over fifty miles), plus $10 per diem for expenses.

subject to Senate confirmation. The act reduced the size of the Board from eight to seven members, holding office for staggered fourteen-year terms beginning March 1, 1936, and removed the secretary of the treasury and the comptroller of the currency.[147] The chairman and vice chairman (formerly governor and vice governor) received four-year terms in those offices and fourteen-year terms as board members (or the remaining years of an unexpired term). No one could be appointed to more than one fourteen-year term.[148]

Accommodating commerce and business remained in the act, but the new law weakened the role of real bills by adding "with regard to the general credit situation of the country." Eccles did not get his choice of phrasing, but Glass could not keep unchanged the wording in the 1913 act. More important was the change in the definition of eligibility. Under the 1935 act, the Board could define eligibility as broadly as it wished. Although the real bills doctrine lived on, it no longer had the force of law behind it. This was a major step in the evolution of the System.

The Board also gained authority to change required reserve ratios up to twice the prevailing ratio by majority vote. Eccles lost the unlimited authority that he requested and Glass opposed. The act eased restrictions on mortgage loans by member banks. Reserve banks were required to vote on discount rates every two weeks; as before, changes required approval of the Board.

Eccles had tried to replace requirements for geographical representation on the Board with a vague reference to education and experience. Glass's views prevailed, so the bill retained the original restrictions.[149]

The bill passed on August 19, and the president signed it on August 23. Glass took credit for the final bill, as he had for the 1913 bill (Eccles 1951, 221). In fact, the compromise gave Eccles many of the changes he wanted.

147. Morgenthau agreed to the removal of the secretary but was piqued when he learned that the comptroller, his subordinate, would remain (Hyman 1976, 187). Glass favored removal of the secretary because he believed that, as secretary, he had too much influence after World War I.

148. The salary increased from $12,000 to $15,000 a year, more than $190,000 in 2001 dollars. The rule for service left either Miller or Hamlin, who had served since 1914, eligible for the fourteen-year term beginning in 1936. The other could receive a twelve-year term. Eccles persuaded Roosevelt not to reappoint either. Hamlin was given a staff position as special counsel, and Miller was given responsibility for supervising construction of the new Board of Governors building (Hyman 1976, 198). The building was financed from the Board's "profits" and by assessments on the reserve banks.

149. In the 1960s and after, several presidents bypassed sectional restrictions by appointing governors based on their birthplace, even if they had not lived there for twenty years or more.

Glass lost on the shift of power to the Board, the diminished powers of the regional reserve banks, and the weakened role of the real bills doctrine. The 1935 Act permitted the Federal Reserve to become a central bank, but the major changes in practice came only after World War II and the Korean War.[150]

OTHER PROPOSED CHANGES

Although pleased by the increased power granted by the Banking Act, Eccles was not satisfied with the extent of the Board's powers. He pressed Roosevelt to support legislation forcing all banks to become members of the Federal Reserve System. His reasoning is similar to claims made repeatedly by other Federal Reserve chairmen: the Reserve System "cannot function efficiently or effectively in the national interest as long as half of the banks are in it and the other half out. . . . [O]ne half . . . is free to negate management in the national interest" (Eccles 1951, 267–68; memo to President Roosevelt November 12, 1936, quoted in Hyman 1976, 275–76). Eccles wanted all banks with deposit insurance to be members of the Federal Reserve System and all bank examination and regulation to be under the Federal Reserve's control. Also, he wanted bank examiners to vary examination standards over the cycle in harmony with monetary policy, a result that could be achieved only if the Federal Reserve controlled the examinations.

Eccles greatly overstated his case. More than 50 percent of the banks were not members, as he said, but their share of deposits was down to 15 percent in 1936 from 27 percent in 1928 and nearly 17 percent in 1933. Bank failures in the depression, and the bank holiday, had eliminated many of the small, weak, mainly nonmember banks. New lending powers had encouraged growth in the number of state bank members and national banks. Table 6.3 shows these data for selected dates in the 1930s.

The proposal requiring membership, coming soon after the first increase in required reserve ratios, probably reflects Eccles's concern that the higher ratios would reduce Federal Reserve membership by increasing cost. This argument is more plausible than the argument Eccles—and subsequent chairmen—used. Contrary to their claims, control of money and bank credit or an interest rate does not require universal membership in the Federal Reserve System. There is no valid argument to this effect

150. The act also required the Board and the open market committee to keep a complete record of all action taken, the reasons for the action, and the votes. The record had to be published annually in the Board's report. Miller (1936, 11) describes this as a major innovation for central banking. He thought it would improve the reasoning given for votes.

Table 6.3   Number and Size of Member and Nonmember Banks on Selected Dates

	NUMBER			DEPOSITS (BILLIONS)			
DATE	ALL COMMERCIAL	NATIONAL	STATE MEMBER	NON-MEMBER	ALL COMMERCIAL	NATIONAL	STATE MEMBER	NON-MEMBER
June 1933	13,949	4,897	709	8,343	31.9	16.7	9.8	5.3
June 1936	15,243	5,368	1,032	8,843	47.9	26.2	14.6	7.2
June 1938	14,737	5,242	1,096	8,399	48.6	26.8	14.5	7.3

Source: Board of Governors of the Federal Reserve System 1943, 16–17.

and no evidence that control changed after all banks became subject to reserve requirements in the 1980s.

Examination Standards

Roosevelt did not endorse Eccles's proposal for Federal Reserve control of bank examination, but Eccles did not give up. He tried several more times to persuade Roosevelt to endorse his program. Finally, as part of a program to end the 1937–38 recession, Roosevelt endorsed unification and liberalization of bank examination policies in a message to Congress on April 14, 1938 (Hyman 1976, 247; Eccles 1951, 272).[151] Roosevelt then asked Morgenthau to establish a committee of federal and state banking agencies to agree on a more liberal bank examination policy.

All the banking agencies, except the Federal Reserve, quickly agreed on revision of examination procedures and a common set of standards. The National Association of State Bank Examiners accepted the changes. Eccles continued to argue over some technical details. What most disturbed him, perhaps, was that the new standards had been agreed to without legislation. Consolidation of all examination under the Federal Reserve would not be necessary, and he would not get countercyclical examination standards. Adding to Eccles's problem was strong support for the revision by the American Bankers Association and the financial press, and his own political blunder.[152] Morgenthau gave him an ultimatum:

151. Many of the same arguments about examination standards as a cause of recession or slow recovery reappeared in Federal Reserve and administration statements in 1991–92. Eccles's argument seems rather naive despite his experience in government. He compared the banking authority he wanted to create to the Interstate Commerce Commission—"a single, strong, independent, nonpolitical, but public body . . . that would make decisions free from the political winds" (Eccles 1951, 270).

152. Eccles made the mistake of complaining about "faulty examination procedures" in a long letter to Senator Arthur Vandenberg (Michigan), a potential rival to Roosevelt in the 1940 election. The letter urged countercyclical examination standards. Vandenberg published it in the *Congressional Record* and made it public. Eccles's criticism of administration banking policy, with the clear implication that it delayed the recovery, infuriated Morgenthau (Blum 1959, 430–31; Eccles 1951, 275–77).

agree to the committee's recommendations or he would go to the president without Federal Reserve agreement. Eccles agreed, and the standards were issued.[153]

The new standards allowed banks to invest in nonmarketable bonds issued by small corporations and reduced the size of the mandatory write-off of slow and doubtful loans. The standards used average value over several months in place of current market value to judge soundness of marketable assets. This moved away from mark-to-market accounting and increased examiner's discretion.

Eccles did not give up. A few months later he told Roosevelt that he would resign at the end of his term, February 1940, unless the Board of Governors gained new powers "to do the work expected of it" (Eccles 1951, 279). Knowing Roosevelt's reluctance to take up the membership issue, Eccles recommended that the president ask Congress to study the issue and draft legislation. Congress appropriated $25,000 for this purpose, one-fourth the amount Eccles had suggested. The matter died when the war in Europe shifted attention toward preparation for war. Eccles never realized this objective, nor did other chairmen who pursued it.

Nationalizing the Reserve Banks

Proposals to nationalize the reserve banks by having the government repurchase all outstanding shares continued after passage of the 1935 Banking Act. In May 1937 Congressman Wright Patman (Texas), who later chaired the House Banking Committee, proposed legislation that attracted 151 cosponsors. The legislation transferred ownership of the reserve banks to the government, returned the treasury secretary and the comptroller to the Board, and added the chairman of the FDIC and twelve members, one from each district. The enlarged Board would serve as the Federal Open Market Committee (FOMC). The bill also required the Federal Reserve to stabilize and maintain the purchasing power of money and gave all members of the FDIC the rights and privileges of member banks. At the time, the consumer price index was about 80 percent of its 1926 level. The act required the Federal Reserve to keep the price level within 2 percent of its 1926 value. Once again, some members urged price stabilization and a price level target.

The Board's staff dismissed the last proposal as unrealistic and impractical (Board of Governors File, box 141, undated). The reasons they gave

---

153. Eccles's version claims that Morgenthau adjusted the recommendations to meet Eccles's requirements (Eccles 1951, 276).

show some change of views. The staff no longer denied that the price level depends on money, but it recognized both monetary and nonmonetary causes of price changes. For example, a crop failure or taxes may raise prices. Also, there was no satisfactory measure of the price level. Index numbers differ.

The staff concluded that the Patman bill mistook ownership for control. The banks owned stock in the reserve banks but did not control the System. All the net earnings of the reserve banks after dividends of 6 percent went into a surplus fund. The excess was paid to the Treasury (or had been used for other purposes, e.g., to establish the FDIC). Congress could allocate the surplus, so it had final control.[154]

Raising Prices

The 1937–38 recession renewed proposals to raise the price level and thereafter keep it stable. Congressman Goldsborough again offered legislation to require the Federal Reserve to restore wholesale prices to the 1921–29 average. Other legislation (Board of Governors File, box 136, January 21, 1938) required the Federal Reserve to make social payments to aged and infirm adults and to dependent children and to finance farms and homes for lower income groups. Senator Elmer Thomas (Oklahoma) proposed to reconstitute the Federal Reserve as a monetary authority responsible for controlling the price level based on the values at home and abroad of tax payments, interest payments, outstanding debt, prices, and other factors (Board of Governors File, box 141, March 25, 1937, 7).

The staff responded to the price level proposals by sending out a published version of its response to the Patman bill. It accepted the desirability of economic stability, opposed using price stability as a goal, and opposed raising the price level 25 percent to restore the 1926 price level. The memo failed throughout to distinguish between individual prices and the price level (Wyatt to Congressman Kelly, Board of Governors File, box 141, June 17, 1938).

The lasting feature of these proposals is congressional interest in legis-

---

154. Other provisions of the Patman bill eliminated the restriction on changes in reserve requirements that mandated uniform changes for all reserve city and central reserve city banks, or all country banks. But it also removed the required reserve ratio from banks that did not borrow from a reserve bank. The staff memo liked the proposals to unify the Board and the open market committee (although the timing might be wrong) and eliminate the Federal Advisory Council of twelve bankers. The council "serves no useful purpose," and "its advice on monetary and credit matters is either useless or worse" (Board of Governors File, box 141, undated, section 7). But the report grudgingly accepted that there would probably have to be consultation with bankers, so it might be best to retain the council.

lation giving guidelines for improving the economy and maintaining price stability. These concerns eventually led to the Employment Act of 1946.[155] Legislative interest in price stability as a goal of monetary policy waxes and wanes, but Congress has not adopted it.

RESERVE REQUIREMENTS AND OPEN MARKET POLICY, 1935–37

By the time Eccles joined the Federal Reserve, Roosevelt's economic program was about to change. The Supreme Court soon declared the NRA and the AAA unconstitutional. Gold and silver purchases continued routinely, but hopes for reflation to the 1926 or 1929 price level were no longer widely held.[156] Agricultural prices (measured at the time) had increased absolutely and relative to other prices, as Warren had predicted, but they remained 25 percent below the 1926 average. The consumer price index was about 30 to 35 percent above its low but 25 percent below the 1929 level.

Roosevelt had not yet abandoned his hopes for a balanced budget, but the low level of activity and relief expenditures kept the hope unrealized. To finance the deficit while keeping interest rates from rising, Morgenthau bought bonds for the new Exchange Stabilization Fund and the Treasury trust funds—Postal Savings, Railroad Retirement, and others. The Federal Reserve, as fiscal agent, made purchases for the Treasury, limiting its own operation for most of 1934 to exchanges of long-term for short-term debt. The open market portfolio remained below $2.5 billion, about 25 percent larger than in March 1933.

Morgenthau recognized that using the stabilization and trust funds not only freed him from dependence on the Federal Reserve but gave him an opportunity to influence its decisions. Despite the legislative changes that had increased de jure Federal Reserve independence, the Federal Reserve was less independent of the administration from 1934 to 1941 than in any other peacetime period.

155. The Board also used Eccles's 1938 letter to Senator Vandenberg to respond to proposals for nationalizing Federal Reserve banks or repaying the government debt by issuing currency. On the latter issue, Eccles makes the extraordinary claim that issuing currency to buy back the federal debt would not raise prices or increase prosperity (Eccles to Senator Arthur Capper, Board of Governors File, box 141, June 5, 1939, 3). The claim is that the currency would return as excess reserves and remain idle. In the 1938 letter, this is followed by a contradictory claim that inflation would result (Eccles to Vandenberg, Board of Governors File, box 141, June 14, 1938, 5, 7).

156. Fisher continued to argue for a higher gold price, an increase to $41.34, the maximum permitted under the Thomas amendment. Roosevelt listened but did not act (Barber 1996, 81). The experiment had not worked in 1933 as Warren and Fisher promised, so Roosevelt had moved on.

Policy Issues, 1935–36

In January 1935 the Board approved reductions in discount rates to 2 percent at Philadelphia, Atlanta, and St. Louis and to 2.5 percent at Richmond, Minneapolis, and Dallas. These were the lowest rates at these banks up to that time, but further reductions in discount rates, open market rates, and deposit rates soon followed. The proximate cause of lower rates was the gold inflow in response to the $35 price. The Federal Reserve had not made any net open market purchases for more than a year.

THE GOLD CLAUSE On January 25, Eccles told the FOMC's executive committee about the Treasury's concern that prices of bonds carrying the gold clause had increased absolutely and relative to the prices of other bonds. On January 11 the price of Treasury bonds with the gold clause was 0.75 percent above bonds without the clause. The difference remained throughout the month. The price difference reflected the impending Supreme Court decision in *Perry v. United States,* known as the gold clause case.[157]

The New York directors responded to the spread in rates by authorizing sales of gold clause bonds in exchange for other bonds. The FOMC followed. On February 5, it approved purchases or sales of up to $250 million (FOMC Minutes, Board of Governors File, box 1451, January 25 and February 5, 1935).

The administration also prepared for the Court's decision. Harrison was told to stabilize the foreign exchange and gold markets by keeping the French franc within the gold points. The plan was to use the Exchange Sta-

---

157. There were several cases. The Court issued separate opinions for private bonds and pubic debt. The plaintiffs in the private bond cases asked to receive compensation for the 59 percent devaluation of the dollar against gold by payment in dollars at the old exchange rate of dollars for gold. They did not question the right to devalue or withdraw gold. The government claimed the right under its explicit power to coin money and regulate its value. The decision, expected in early February, was delayed until February 18. The Court found for the government by five to four, with Justices Hughes, Stone, Cardozo, Brandeis, and Roberts in the majority and Butler, Sutherland, Van Deventer, and McReynolds in the minority. Citing earlier decisions in the Legal Tender Cases (1871) and the Court's opinion following the 1834 6 percent reduction of the gold content of the dollar, Hughes's opinion found that the plaintiff had not been damaged and placed the constitutional power to regulate the value of money above the obligations of private contracts. Stone's decision, in the case involving government bonds, *Perry v. U.S.,* concluded that the plaintiffs had not suffered a loss. McReynolds's dissent denied that the Constitution gave Congress power to repudiate contracts. He found that Congress had acted to "destroy private obligations, repudiate national debts and drive into the Treasury all gold within the country in exchange for inconvertible promises to pay, of much less value" (Krooss 1969, 4:2865). The gold clauses in contracts did not prevent Congress from regulating the value of money. Justice McReynolds is reported to have said, "The Constitution is gone" (Pearson, Myers, and Gans 1957, 5618). The court ignored the higher market price of bonds with the gold clause, clear evidence that the option was valuable as protection against future inflation.

bilization Fund to buy francs by selling sterling "violently" if necessary (Harrison Papers, file 2012.5, February 18, 1935). The Court's decision, favorable to the government, required no action.[158]

DELAY AND INACTION   The System's inaction in 1935 was not accidental.[159] As excess reserves rose, members of the FOMC became concerned about potential credit expansion and uncertain what to do. A background memo prepared for the March 21 meeting addressed the issue by asking, What is the duty of a central bank in the present situation? (Excess Reserves and Federal Reserve Policy, Board of Governors File, box 1449, March 21, 1935).

The memo had two parts. The first traced the increase of excess reserves and discussed the reasons for their continued growth. It found that, initially, excess reserves were expected to pressure banks to expand private loans by pushing down the yield on government securities. This could happen, but there was little evidence so far. One reason given was that government deficits supply bonds that the banks bought (ibid., 2–3): "If this process should continue, should we not expect on the basis of the experience of other nations that eventually a point will be reached where the banks will be unable or unwilling to absorb the government debt, so that the government will be forced to expend its stabilization fund . . . or request the reserve banks to purchase more government securities . . . , or to borrow directly from the Reserve banks" (4).[160] The memo concluded that neither past experience nor central bank theory gave any guidance in pres-

158. Issues about the gold clause did not end with the cases. The decision for the government was based in part on the finding that, since prices had fallen, bondholders had not been harmed. This suggested that the decision might be reversed at a later date. In March 1935 Robert A. Taft, acting for the Dixie Terminal Company, demanded payment on a $50 bond with the gold clause at the value of gold in 1918, when the bond was issued. The Treasury refused, so Taft sued in the Court of Claims on behalf of Dixie Terminal and other clients. In November 1936 the Court of Claims rejected these suits. A year later, the Supreme Court agreed with the government (Patterson 1972, 152–54). I am indebted to Leonard Liggio for this reference.

159. The Federal Reserve was not alone in its inactivity and hesitancy. Harrison reports on a meeting with Roosevelt in late May. The NRA had been declared unconstitutional on May 27. Harrison describes Roosevelt as "harassed and stumped and for once I thought he had no definite plan and seemed quite hopeless and helpless" (Harrison Papers, memo to personal files, June 3, 1935, 3). The meeting came about after Morgenthau told Harrison that the president was concerned that Harrison might be angry about the banking bill and, for that reason, no longer called on him. Harrison made an appointment. The president "chided me for not having called on him and rather expected me to explain why I had not called" (3). They agreed that Harrison would call and visit when he was in Washington.

160. This presumes without explicit recognition that the gold inflow is less than the deficit. Otherwise banks would continue to gain reserves and purchase Treasury bonds. Eventually prices would rise, reversing the gold flow.

ent circumstances.[161] Previous inflations abroad had occurred with rising activity and government borrowing directly from the central bank.

The second issue was the course to follow. The memo considered open market sales to absorb excess reserves but rejected this course on economic and political grounds. The economic argument was that sales might cut off an incipient expansion by overweighting future dangers of inflation and not encouraging expansion enough. The political argument was that the government could offset Federal Reserve actions by using the stabilization fund or resort to issuing paper money under the Thomas amendment. Further, with the banking act in Congress, the government could change the entire financial system, including the central bank: "It seems clear that we could act effectively only with the consent and cooperation of the administration" (ibid., 8).[162]

The memo recommended no action for the present. The only policy change in the next two months followed a May 1 letter from the Board to the reserve banks, calling attention to discount rates and suggesting that the directors consider reductions. A week later the Board approved reductions at Dallas, Richmond, Cleveland, Minneapolis, and Kansas City. Discount rates were now 1.5 percent in New York and Cleveland, 2 percent at all other banks. Discount rates remained at these levels for the next two years.

The volume of discounts fell below $10 million in January 1934 and, except for a small increase in the 1937–38 recession, remained there until the war. The acceptance portfolio reached $10 million in spring 1934, then gradually faded away. Open market rates remained below the discount rate and the buying rate on acceptances. Prime commercial paper was at 0.75 percent, banker's acceptances were at 0.125 percent, and long-term Treasury bonds fluctuated around 2.75 percent.

CONCERNS ABOUT FUTURE INFLATION Propelled by gold inflows, the monetary base rose at an 18 percent annual rate for the first three quarters of 1935 and at a 25 percent annual rate in the fourth quarter. Chart 6.2 shows the very close relation between gold and the monetary base dur-

---

161. The memo has a rare acknowledgment of policy error. Looking back at September 1931, the memo commented that standard theory misled them following England's departure from the gold standard. The Federal Reserve raised the discount rate, a classic response. "The rate increase probably served more to add to the deflationary movement of succeeding months than to check the gold outflow" (Excess Reserves and Federal Reserve Policy, Board of Governors File, box 1449, March 21, 1935).

162. Governor Schaller of Chicago wrote on May 4 urging reduction of Treasury bill holdings, by allowing them to run off weekly, until the bill rate reached 0.5 percent. The Board responded: "Excess reserves should not be reduced until there is evidence of excessive borrowing or speculative expansion" (Board of Governors File, box 1451, May 4 and 17, 1935).

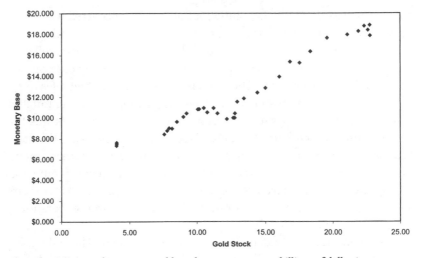

Chart 6.2 Monetary base versus gold stock 1933.2 to 1941.4 (billions of dollars).

ing the recovery. With the exception of a few periods, mainly in 1937–38, gold flows dominated changes in the base. The money stock rose and fell with the base.

The background memo for the October 1935 FOMC meeting noted the improvement in business conditions. But it noted also that member banks held almost $3 billion in excess reserves, an increase of $1 billion since March.[163] The volume of excess reserves now exceeded the size of the open market portfolio.

The memo was more anxious than the March memo. It asked whether the Federal Reserve should intervene to prevent further accommodation and the risk of inflation. Its conclusion: the System must coordinate with the Treasury. Monetary restraint without a reduction in the budget deficit would risk higher interest rates on Treasury financing (Memo for FOMC, Board of Governors File, box 1452, October 22, 1935, 11–12).

The memo raised two questions that the governors discussed at length: What was the appropriate time to reduce excess reserves, and should it be done by open market sales or by an increase in reserve requirement ratios? The governors were divided. Some saw no reason to act; some favored an increase in required reserves; some wanted open market sales. Eccles favored an increase in reserve requirements, but he was concerned about how it could be presented to the public.

The resolution adopted at the meeting recognized the risks of action

163. This figure is preliminary. The final figure was $3.6 billion. The difference suggests the large changes occurring at the time.

and rejected taking any immediate steps. It called for action "as promptly as possible" to reduce excess reserves, and it provided for purchases of up to $250 million in the event of a disturbance following an increase in required reserve ratios, the decision to be taken by telegraphic vote. The members generally preferred a change in the requirement ratios to open market sales, because open market sales had previously been used only to tighten credit. This was not the intention. The effect of increased reserve requirement ratios, they said, would depend on the distribution of excess reserves by class of banks and by geographical location. The governors recommended that the Board learn about these distributions (FOMC Resolutions, Board of Governors File, box 1450, October 23, 1935).[164]

THE ROLE OF EXCESS RESERVES With borrowing reduced almost to zero, the key relation of the Riefler-Burgess framework was inoperative. Member bank borrowing could not be an indicator of policy action. Instead, the System focused on the level of excess reserves. A high level indicated potential credit expansion; an increase was a sign of increased potential expansion.

This interpretation of excess reserves follows directly from the Riefler-Burgess theory, if excess reserves are treated as negative borrowing. Instead of reducing borrowing when the credit market eased, banks added excess reserves. In the System's view, beyond some point additional excess reserves were excess in the economic as well as in the accounting sense.

There is no evidence of a study by the Board or the reserve banks to understand why banks held large excess reserves. With short-term interest rates below 0.5 percent, the opportunity cost of holding excess reserves remained low, but banks had other options. Interest rates on long-term Treasury bonds fluctuated around 2.75 percent. The Board appears to have made no effort to understand or explain this puzzle. The common presumption was that unless excess reserves remained concentrated in one part of the banking system, they could be absorbed without consequence.[165] All Federal Reserve discussion at the time treated excess reserves as a redundant surplus.[166]

164. After the meeting, Harrison prepared the first of many draft statements explaining that the increase in reserve requirements was a precautionary move, not a change in policy. (Harrison to Eccles, Board of Governors File, box 1450, November 4, 1935).

165. There is remarkably little academic study of excess reserves. The best work (Frost 1966) attributes the increase in excess reserves to risk and the prevailing low level of opportunity cost. See also Brunner and Meltzer 1968a for conditions required for a liquidity trap in the banking system.

166. A staff study showed that at the last call report on June 29 only 897 banks out of 6,410 would have to increase their deposit balances at reserve banks if reserve requirements increased by 25 percent. The Federal Reserve would have to provide only $99 million of additional re-

The poor quality of the Board's analysis shows also in the estimates of potential credit or monetary expansion. Their usual estimate is ten to twelve times the volume of additional reserves, but some estimates put additional lending potential at twenty times excess reserves. Emanuel Goldenweiser's book, written many years later, repeats these estimates (Goldenweiser 1951, 175). To get these numbers, the staff used only the required reserve ratio, ignoring drains into currency holding and time deposits. A more accurate calculation, one that allowed for these concomitants of monetary and credit changes, would have estimated maximum credit expansion as seven or eight times the addition to reserves. And this calculation is almost certainly too high because, like the Board's staff, it assumes that none of the excess reserves were held for reasons of safety based on experience. The result was a large overestimate of potential monetary and credit expansion and prospective inflation and an underestimate of the effect of higher reserve requirement ratios.

A subsequent memo by the Board's staff considered the pros and cons of a reduction in excess reserve achieved by raising reserve requirement ratios. The pro case claimed there was no question that the Board would have to act; it was "merely a question of timing" (Memo, Board of Governors File, box 1450, November 5, 1935). Prompt action, before banks expand, based on outstanding excess reserves, was best because delay might force loan liquidation. Also, reserves were "ample," so increased reserve requirements would be less likely to lose members.

The memo recognized that the same reduction in excess reserves could be achieved by selling securities. Raising reserve requirements would not affect the government bond market, unlike open market sales, or diminish the earning assets of the reserve banks. It would begin a policy of using the new instrument to adjust to new conditions while reserving traditional methods to expand or contract bank credit. And it would put the Federal Reserve in a better position to control credit expansion by open market operations.

The con case was shorter. There was no evidence of a need for restraint. Policies of restraint should be used when restraint is required, or they risk misunderstanding. Both the open market portfolio and the effect of a max-

serves to offset the shortfall at banks with reserve deficiencies. All the banks had correspondent bank balances sufficient to cover the reserve deficiency. A 50 percent increase would require 2,041 banks to increase reserves by $528 million. All but 125 could meet the increase from correspondent balances. The memo makes clear that no further adjustment was expected following the increased requirements or the reduction in correspondent balances (Board Minutes, November 6, 1935, 5–6). Only James questioned whether some banks would adopt "less liberal lending policy" to restore excess reserves (6). The rest of the Board accepted the memo's conclusion. Eccles used the memo in his discussions with Morgenthau and left a copy.

imum increase in reserve requirement ratios would remove current, but not future, excess reserves. It might be better to wait to get the maximum effect "when the need comes." Action might retard recovery, although it should not.[167]

On November 15 the directors of the Chicago bank voted to advise the Board that they favored an increase in reserve requirements. One director opposed, preferring a sale of government securities. A month later, New York unanimously endorsed the change (Board of Governors File, box 1450, November 15 and December 16, 1935). The Board was ready to act. The next steps were to discuss the issue with Secretary Morgenthau and to prepare a press release announcing the increase, effective January 1, 1936.

Morgenthau was still chairman of the Federal Reserve Board, but he attended few meetings. On November 7 Eccles briefed him on the Board's decision to raise reserve requirement ratios. Morgenthau prepared for the meeting by getting opinions from former undersecretary Parker Gilbert, a partner at J. P. Morgan, Walter Stewart, and Jacob Viner. All three urged delay; the economy was recovering but needed stimulus, not contraction (Blum 1959, 354–55). Morgenthau added concerns about financing the 1937 budget deficit that would soon be sent to Congress, and he urged delay for three or four months. Eccles agreed that there was no reason for immediate action, but based on the staff memo about the distribution of reserves, he assured Morgenthau that the increase would have no market effect. Eccles reported his conversation to the Board. No action was taken (Board Minutes, November 8, 1935, 1–5).

In May, stock prices started to rise rapidly. After remaining unchanged through 1934, the Standard and Poor's index rose 40 percent in 1935, with much of the increase in the second half of the year. Many of those who believed that the 1927–29 stock market boom had caused the economic and financial collapse interpreted the 1935 increase as another speculative boom presaging another collapse.

Eccles had started to issue a press release after every FOMC meeting, announcing the decision, if any, and the main issues discussed. The release following the November 22 meeting discussed inflation and the stock market boom. It defined inflation as "a condition brought about when the means of payment in the hands that will spend them increases faster than goods will be produced" (Press Releases, Board of Governors File, box 1441, November 22, 1935, 1). The memo added that the economy was a long

167. The Federal Advisory Council opposed, preferring open market sales because of the "rigidity" of reserve requirements (Board of Governors File, box 1450, November 21, 1935). Open market sales would transfer earning assets to the market; increased reserve requirement ratios would reduce bank earnings.

way from inflation. It noted that the increase in stock prices was financed by cash, not credit, a reminder that concern about "speculative credit" remained widespread.

Many bankers criticized administration policy. Some used devaluation, continued budget deficits, large excess reserves, and rapidly rising stock prices to claim that the administration was bent on inflation.[168] As the election year approached, Morgenthau regarded much of this criticism, and many of the pressures to reduce excess reserves, as political efforts to hurt the administration (Blum 1959, 355–56). But he also accepted the argument that rising excess reserves permitted increased inflation. Resisting Harrison's argument for higher reserve requirement ratios to control the stock market, he recommended an increase in margin requirements instead. Harrison replied that the purchases were for cash, so increased margin requirements would not help. Higher reserve ratios were needed primarily to prevent future inflation and reassure foreigners that we recognized the danger (Memo, Conversation with Secretary Morgenthau, Harrison Papers, file 2012.5, November 21, 1935).

The Board reviewed its policy on December 17 with Harrison and Williams present. Goldenweiser presented the options, now including increased margin requirements. He favored an increase in required reserve ratios, but he warned of a possible bad psychological reaction. He recommended that a press release say that the Board wanted to foster recovery and that "if any action were taken on reserve requirements, it would be in the nature of a precautionary measure . . . rather than a reversal of the System's easy money policy" (Board Minutes, December 17, 1935, 5).

Goldenweiser was ambivalent about the need for action. He saw the threat of future inflation if the banks expanded but found "no need to worry about inflation at this time with the very large volume of unused plant capacity and unemployment" (ibid., 6).[169] He dismissed pressures from bankers to reduce excess reserves as based on a desire for higher interest rates (6).

John H. Williams supported Goldenweiser's analysis but strongly urged prompt action: "The present volume of excess reserves was considerably greater than anyone considered necessary for the furtherance of the present easy money policy" (6). He wanted to absorb the 1935 excess reserve in-

168. The extent of the hostility is suggested by the proposal at the American Bankers Association convention to boycott the government and, by refusing to purchase government bonds, force the government to reduce spending (Eccles 1951, 251).

169. He estimated industrial production as halfway between the depression low and the 1929 peak. (Current data put the recovery at two-thirds of the decline.) He put the gold inflow in the year to September at $900 million, and $3 billion since the devaluation.

crease, and he proposed that action be taken in January as soon as the administration announced the 1937 budget proposal.

The Board's only action was to issue a press release after the meeting emphasizing that the volume of reserves, reflecting gold inflows, "continues to be excessive" and warning that "appropriate action may be taken as soon as it appears to be in the public interest" (Press Statement, Board of Governors File, box 1441, December 17, 1935).

The FOMC met the following day. It adopted a resolution calling on the Board to act "as soon as possible without undue risk" to absorb part of the excess reserves. It left to the Board decisions about the timing and size of the increase (Sproul Papers, FOMC Resolution, Excess Reserves, December 18, 1935).

Excess reserves decreased seasonally in December but rose back to $3 billion in January. The relation of the reserve banks to the Board was in an important respect the reverse of the 1920s. The bank governors were the only members of the FOMC for a few remaining months, but having decided to avoid open market operations, the FOMC could only petition the Board to act. On January 21 the committee again adopted a resolution, marked "very confidential," recommending "a substantial reduction in excess reserves . . . as soon as this may be feasible" (Policy Record, Board of Governors File, box 291, January 21, 1936). The vote was nine to three in favor with Governors Roy A. Young (Boston), Oscar Newton (replacing the deceased Eugene R. Black at Atlanta), and William McChesney Martin Sr. (St. Louis) opposed.[170]

This was the last meeting of the full membership of the old FOMC. The Board ignored its principal recommendation, choosing instead to replay, in different form, the issue of general versus selective control. Three days later the Board voted to increase stock market margin requirements from 45 percent to 55 percent.[171] Two months later, it extended the increase in margin requirements to collateral loans made by banks.[172]

---

170. The Board replied by letter, citing the increase in margin requirements and insisting that there had been little change in the past month (Sproul Papers, Excess Reserves, January 31, 1936). Harrison told the New York directors that the Board would not act until the new Board took office.

171. Legal counsel advised the Board that it had no responsibility for stock prices or the volume of trading. It could act only on a finding that action was "necessary or appropriate to prevent the excessive use of credit to finance transactions in securities." Earlier in the same meeting the Board noted that the increase in loans on securities was "slight" and "the amount of borrowing at this time is low as compared with some past years." Most of the purchases—estimated at 80 percent—were for cash. Nevertheless, the Board cited increased borrowing to justify its action and used its decision to increase margin requirements to reject the FOMC's recommendation to increase reserve ratios (Board Minutes, January 24 and January 31, 1936).

172. Margin requirements are governed by Board regulation T, collateral requirements by regulation U.

These steps did not allay fears of inflation. In February the Federal Advisory Council concluded unanimously that the Board should increase required reserve ratios. The "present huge volume of excess reserves is a most serious menace." The council did not make a specific recommendation about the size of the increase, but it urged an increase large enough to prevent the country's credit structure from "being built on that part of the gold holdings which may be deemed to be transitory or temporary." The council released its recommendation to the public within a week (Board Minutes, Meeting with Advisory Council, February 12, 1936, 2–3).

Reorganization

The Banking Act of 1935 required the treasury secretary and the comptroller of the currency to resign from the Board. The act also reduced the number of Board members from eight to seven and changed the membership of the FOMC.

Eccles did not want to reappoint most members of the Board. J. J. Thomas resigned as vice chairman in February to return to Kansas City as chairman.[173] The new members included Ronald Ransom, a banker from the Atlanta district who had served on the legislative committee of the American Bankers Association. The bankers had split on the new legislation, but Ransom and the legislative committee had worked to get a compromise they could support. To gain Glass's support for Eccles's appointment, Roosevelt allowed him to choose three members of the new Board. He chose Ransom, John K. McKee, chief examiner of the Reconstruction Finance Corporation, and Joseph A. Broderick, New York state superintendent of banks. Roosevelt chose Eccles and Menc S. Szymczak from the old Board, and Ralph W. Morrison.[174] Disagreement about the member to represent agriculture delayed appointment of the seventh member until June, when Roosevelt appointed Chester C. Davis, head of the Agricultural Adjustment Administration. The four new members joined the Board in February 1936. Four of the seven served through the end of World War II. Broderick left in September 1937 and Davis in 1941.[175]

173. Thomas was paid a salary for three years to encourage his return to Kansas City. In hearings on Eccles's appointment, Glass again raised the issue of Eccles's financial interests. Eccles replied forcefully, denying the charges, and the matter ended.

174. Morrison remained only five months. His nomination was pushed by Vice President Garner. He was a Texas rancher but had legal and financial difficulties and fled to Mexico in July 1936 (Hyman 1976, 201).

175. Szymczak served twenty-eight years, twenty-five of them under the new rules. His twelve-year term ended in 1948. He was reappointed for a full term but resigned in 1961. He served also as United States director in charge of German rehabilitation in 1946, on leave from the Board and, in 1944, as an adviser to the Bretton Woods Conference (Katz 1992, 314–16).

As the March 1 date for the new FOMC approached, the Board voted not to approve appointment of any president who was over seventy or would become seventy during a five-year term. Four governors left the System. George Seay (Richmond) had started as a governor in 1914.[176] George W. Norris (Philadelphia) and John Calkins (San Francisco) had served since 1920. Of the old guard, only Roy A. Young (Boston), George L. Harrison (New York), and William McChesney Martin Sr. (St. Louis) remained.

The 1935 act did not specify who could be a member of the FOMC. Some reserve banks wanted to nominate people with wide experience in financial affairs who were not officers of the reserve banks. The Board voted that the non-Board FOMC members should be presidents of the reserve banks. At its organizational meeting on March 18 and 19, the new FOMC elected Eccles chairman and Harrison vice chairman and set March 1 of each year as the date for rotation of membership and election of an executive committee to execute transactions and allocate securities to the reserve banks. The new executive committee would have five members as before, but now three came from the Board.

The new bylaws changed the 1933 wording of the governing principle by omitting agriculture. More significant, the new statute now included "bearing upon the general credit situation," an open-ended commitment to discretionary action. The rules barred individual reserve banks from making purchases and sales except as part of the committee, and the committee reserved the right to require a reserve bank to sell or transfer to the System Open Market Account any securities held or purchased outside the committee. The old issue of individual bank earnings was put to rest. Earnings would now depend principally on shares in the open market portfolio (Open Market Regulations, Board of Governors File, box 1433, March 19, 1936).

The Board now had control. Perhaps recalling October 1929, Harrison moved to permit a reserve bank to purchase government securities in an emergency. The motion was defeated. Eccles was unwilling to have the issue considered.

In May, the Conference of Reserve Bank Presidents and the new FOMC discussed the allocation formula for allotment of securities and earnings to the reserve banks. They agreed to transfer all securities held by individual reserve banks to the System account, but the individual reserve banks retained the right to enter into temporary resale agreements for up to fif-

---

176. Governors Fancher (Cleveland) and McDougal (Chicago) had left in 1935 and 1934. As already noted, Black died at the end of 1934. His replacement (Newton) had served as chairman of the Atlanta bank.

teen days. The new FOMC retained the old formula for allocating profits and losses to individual banks (Board of Governors to Reserve Banks, Board of Governors File, box 1452, June 12, 1936).[177]

The First Increase and Its Aftermath

Although the gold stock continued to increase during the winter and spring, excess reserves fell about $500 million between January and April. The decline did not change the discussion. Harrison and the commercial bankers continued to agitate for an increase in requirements. Harrison, Burgess, and Williams pressed hard at an April Board meeting, but the Board deferred action pending receipt of new information on individual bank positions showing how many banks would lose all their excess reserves. Eccles agreed with Morgenthau, who wanted to delay action until the Treasury completed its June financing (Hyman 1976, 216).

Roosevelt had a different view. With the political conventions starting, he wanted to show that he was alert to the risks of inflation. He told Eccles he preferred the increase in May rather than July (Blum 1959, 356). The political problem was less important to Eccles. The decisive factor for him was the decline in interest rates. During the spring and early summer, government bond yields continued to fall. Eccles's concern was that banks would lend money and buy securities at low interest rates and suffer large losses in a future inflation (Eccles 1951, 289). Nevertheless, Morgenthau prevailed; the Board did not act.

On July 9 Eccles met with Roosevelt to explain that the Board was about to act and to discuss the political consequences of the action.[178] He assured the president that he would not act if he thought interest rates would rise and that the FOMC would purchase bonds if bond prices fell by one point or more (ibid.).

The Board voted on July 14 to increase reserve requirement ratios by 50 percent. The new ratios were 19.5, 15, and 10.5 percent for demand deposits at central reserve city, reserve city, and country banks and 4.5 percent for all time deposits. The new requirements became effective on August 15.

---

177. The formula, proposed by Harrison in December 1929, provided for interbank transfers at book value and for profits and losses distributed at year end based on average annual holdings of securities. Since interest rates had fallen, many of the securities were above purchase price. Reallocation at book value had major effects on individual bank earnings. Additional meetings and some adjustments were required before the transfer could be completed (Minutes, FOMC, Executive Committee, June 24, 1936).

178. Under the new law, Eccles did not need presidential approval, but he believed "the country would hold him responsible for whatever was done" (Eccles 1951, 289). As this and his subsequent actions show, Eccles was not greatly concerned about independence from the executive branch.

The vote was four to two, with McKee and Davis opposed.[179] The staff estimate showed that the increase would absorb $1.45 billion of excess reserves but would leave excess reserves of $1.95 billion with $400 million to $800 million in excess reserves at the three classes of banks (Board Minutes, Board of Governors File, box 291, July 14, 1936, 4). The press release described the reserves as "superfluous" and the action as preventive, not a change in policy (ibid., 2–3).

The market was not convinced, and Morgenthau was "furious that Eccles had not warned him about the action" (Blum 1959, 356). He did not believe Eccles's response that Roosevelt had been told the previous week. Bond yields rose by 0.01 percent in the week following the announcement. The Treasury ordered Harrison to buy long-term bonds for the trust and stabilization accounts. The Federal Reserve joined in, selling bills and buying bonds.[180] By late August, yields were lower than at the time of the announcement.

The Economy at the 1936 Election

The August increase had no perceptible effect on the economy in 1936. Expansion was robust as the country approached the presidential election. Industrial production increased 17 percent in the year ending in October, just before the election. Balke and Gordon's (1986) GNP data show 9 percent growth and 1.9 percent inflation for the four quarters of 1936. Contemporary data show national income produced in 1936 rising 15 percent, with wholesale prices almost unchanged (Barber 1996, 98–99). Based on these data, income had reached 80 percent of the 1929 level, but population and economic potential had increased since 1929, so there was considerable idle capacity. Currie estimated potential output at full employment as $85 billion to $90 billion. Using those values, national income was about 65 to 70 percent of its full employment level, but the unemployment rate was 17 percent (Memo, Board of Governors File, May 18, 1936). The private sector created fewer than 30 percent of the 5 million new jobs in 1936 (Barber 1996, 99). The rest were jobs in relief agencies like the Works Progress Administration (WPA).

PARTNERS WITH THE TREASURY Gold inflows continued, influenced in part by fears in Europe, in part by the gold price and economic expansion. By the time the new reserve requirement ratios took effect, some

---

179. Davis had joined the Board two weeks before, so he voted no because he lacked information. McKee wanted to postpone the decision until September.

180. Eccles claimed that in April Morgenthau agreed to the change. By August 15 the increase in required reserves was $1.79 billion, larger than the staff estimate.

of the expected decrease in excess reserves had been offset by the gold inflow. The monetary base fell (after adjusting for reserve requirement ratios). For the last six months of 1936, the base remained about 10 percent below the previous year.

Morgenthau's tongue lashing on July 15 was followed by efforts to improve the working relationship. Eccles complained that Morgenthau was very secretive about gold operations and did not inform the Board. Even New York (as fiscal agent) was better informed. Morgenthau agreed to release weekly data to the Board on net purchases and sales by the Exchange Stabilization Fund. In return, he asked Eccles to help with bond market stabilization. The Treasury had bought heavily to keep prices of recent issues above par. He asked Eccles to participate in the purchases. The Treasury would henceforth make purchases in the open market, instead of through the New York bank. At the end of each day, the open market committee could decide to take half the amount purchased. Eccles checked with the committee and agreed to the new arrangement. This arrangement made the Federal Reserve an adjunct of Treasury or, as Morgenthau put it, the Treasury's partner (Blum 1959, 358).

Morgenthau also urged Eccles to make an open market purchase or sale of $50 million in December. He thought the public should be accustomed to the idea that open market operations would be used, and it was best to get the market accustomed to purchases and sales after three years of inaction.

Gold Sterilization

By the end of October, excess reserves were above $2 billion, again almost equal to the size of the open market portfolio. The sustained gold inflow had three effects that worried the president and others.

First, foreigners bought United States securities, contributing to a rapid increase in stock prices. Total return to common stocks was 47.7 percent in 1935 and 33.9 percent in 1936. By the end of 1936, the total return on common stock since 1929 was again positive (Ibbotson and Sinquefeld 1989, 160–61). Second, the gold inflow added to reserves and base money, raising the price level. Inflation remained low, however. Consumer prices rose only 1 percent in 1936. Third, the United States was vulnerable to a gold outflow. A particular concern was that in a European war foreign governments would sequester private holdings of foreign securities, sell securities to finance the war, and export gold from the United States.

Similar concerns had arisen before World War I, when the Federal Reserve was unable to prevent a gold inflow, and in the early 1920s, when the Federal Reserve sterilized part of the inflow. Roosevelt wanted something done to remove speculative inflows without reducing long-term investment (Blum 1959, 359).

The November FOMC meeting came in the midst of these concerns. Eccles told Morgenthau that he proposed to sell $300 million to $400 million to offset the increase in excess reserves from August to November. Some FOMC members preferred to again increase required reserve ratios, and some preferred to wait until after the seasonal return of currency to banks in January. Others argued that, although the economy had recovered, the time for reversing policy still lay in the future. The consensus was to wait (Minutes FOMC, November 19 and 20, 1936). In the press release following the meeting, the Board alerted the country to its renewed concern about reserve growth.

Eccles soon shifted his position to favor a second 50 percent increase in required reserve ratios. The Treasury was not enthusiastic.[181] Morgenthau searched for an alternative.[182]

The Treasury staff proposed to sterilize the gold inflow to prevent it from increasing bank reserves and the monetary base. The Treasury would continue to issue gold certificates on receipt of gold. Instead of allowing the gold certificates to increase bank reserves, the Treasury would pay for the gold by selling debt. Later, if foreigners sold securities and withdrew gold, the Treasury could reverse the operation and avoid the deflationary effect. In accounting terms, the transaction differed little from a Federal Reserve sale of debt to the public combined with a gold purchase. The difference was that responsibility for the conduct of the operation remained with the Treasury.[183]

---

181. Nor were some reserve bank presidents and their members. An increase in the reserve ratio would make member banks pay the cost of offsetting the gold inflow, discouraging membership by country banks. George Hamilton, president of the Kansas City reserve bank, made this argument in a letter to Eccles after the November FOMC meeting. Eccles's reply did not respond to this point. Instead, Eccles pointed to the excess reserve holdings of country banks, showing that they held a higher proportion of total to required reserves than other classes of members (Hamilton to Eccles and Eccles to Hamilton, Board of Governors File, box 1450, November 24 and December 5, 1936). Hamilton warned also that "many banks are watching . . . with the idea of dumping [bonds] whenever there is a change made in our policy" (Hamilton to Eccles, Board of Governors File, box 1450, November 24, 1936, 2).

182. Toma (1982) explains the 1936–37 increases, and the recession that followed, as an effort by the Federal Reserve to increase seigniorage. There is no mention of a seigniorage or revenue motive, and as noted, the Treasury was displeased and in 1938 forced a reduction in reserve requirement ratios.

183. The accounts showed a Treasury purchase of gold paid for by drawing on its deposit account at the Federal Reserve and a sale of debt to the public to replenish its deposit. The net effect on the Treasury's balance sheet is a larger gold stock offset by increased debt outstanding. The Treasury issued gold certificates but held the gold in the "general fund in gold," part of Treasury cash. These operations neutralized the effect on the monetary base; no additional reserves were created.

Eccles could not make up his mind. He alternated between seeing the proposal as a way to avoid increasing reserves and concern about the shift in responsibility for monetary policy from the Federal Reserve to the Treasury.[184] He argued also that the timing was bad; reserve growth and the stock market had slowed. The Board could raise reserve requirement ratios, at no cost to the government, instead of selling short-term debt to sterilize gold inflows. In a letter to Morgenthau he demanded that the policy, if adopted, should be automatic, not left to the discretion of the Treasury to operate monetary policy.

The letter annoyed Morgenthau and led to another in the series of disputes that frequently disturbed their relationship. Eccles withdrew from the agreement to share in the Treasury's bond market support program. Morgenthau threatened to take control of monetary policy: "I think there is one more issue to be settled . . . that is whether the Government through the Treasury should control . . . monetary policy . . . or whether control should be exercised through the Federal Reserve Banks who are privately owned and dominated by individuals who are banker minded" (quoted in Blum 1959, 363).

Eccles then sent a conciliatory letter but followed it on December 10 with a more formal letter explaining that he would endorse the sterilization policy if the Treasury would agree not to run its own discretionary monetary policy (Hyman 1976, 221–22). As usual, Roosevelt listened to the two disputants. Instead of making his own case, Eccles changed sides, endorsed Morgenthau's case for sterilization, and declared his own preference for sterilization over the Board's proposal to use open market sales or higher required reserve ratios to neutralize the gold inflow (Hyman 1976, 223; Blum 1959, 364–65).

Roosevelt ordered the sterilization program to begin. On December 23 the Treasury began sterilizing gold inflows and newly mined United States gold. Between December 1936 and July 1937, when gold sterilization ended, gold certificates outstanding increased $1.3 billion and Treasury cash increased by a like amount. Bank reserves rose only $180 million in this period.

The FOMC's executive committee met on December 21 to discuss the System's role in smoothing the government securities market. There was general agreement that with short-term rates near zero, much of the market activity was in longer-term securities. Hence the long-term market was now "a huge part of the money market" (Minutes, FOMC Executive Com-

184. At the New York bank, Burgess wrote a strong objection to gold sterilization as putting additional monetary control in Treasury (political) hands (Sproul Papers, Excess Reserves, December 9, 1936).

mittee, December 21, 1936, 4). The committee agreed that it was responsible for smoothing the market, either alone or in partnership with the Treasury.

The committee then met with Secretary Morgenthau. They agreed to renew the partnership operation. The Treasury ended its own purchase operations, restoring the role of the manager of the System Open Market Account acting on orders from the Treasury. The Federal Reserve agreed to share in the purchases and sales up to the authority granted by the FOMC, $50 million at the time. If more purchases were needed, the FOMC would meet to discuss what action should be taken.

The Second and Third Increases in Reserve Requirements

By late 1936, short- and long-term interest rates were at the lowest levels experienced to that time. The economy and the stock market continued to recover, and gold stocks were at record levels. Many bankers believed that low rates would not persist in that environment. Strengthening that belief was the almost continuous discussion of policy actions to reduce excess reserves by open market operations or a change in reserve requirement ratios.

Perhaps typical of prevailing attitudes is the letter from a Missouri banker who wrote to the Kansas City reserve bank urging open market sales instead of a higher reserve requirement ratio for country banks.

> We are vitally interested in protecting our capital funds from depreciation *when the ultimate increase in interest rates comes* and brings along a depreciation in longer term securities. This being true the only chance we have to maintain earnings at all is through an increase in volume. Our deposits show a substantial increase but if reserve requirements were again substantially raised, it would limit our resort to this procedure in what seems to me a very serious way. (J. E. Garm to Hamilton, Board of Governors File, box 1450, November 23, 1936; emphasis added)

Morgenthau reported a similar view in his diary. Discussion of future inflation and proposals to increase reserve requirement ratios, he believed, convinced many bondholders that interest rates would rise (Blum 1959, 367). Morgenthau was concerned that higher interest rates would raise Treasury borrowing costs, increasing the deficit, and hurt the economy by reducing investment. He urged the Board to reach a decision before February 1. To help him plan the March 15 bond issue, he wanted the increase to be effective by March 1.

At Vice Chairman Ransom's suggestion, the Board met with Morgenthau to hear his opinion directly (Board Minutes, January 19, 1937, 2). Morgenthau expressed reservations about a second increase in reserve requirement ratios, but he gave his approval (Blum 1959, 368). A memo from Goldenweiser predicting only small increases in short- and long-term interest rates reassured him (Memo, Goldenweiser, Board of Governors File, box 418, January 12, 1937).[185]

Eccles and some of the Board's staff hesitated. On January 25, Currie prepared two memos. One warned that the proposed increase in the reserve requirement ratio for time deposits was too large. The second argued the opposite side at greater length (Currie to Eccles, Board Files, January 25, 1937.[186] He concluded that the current stock of money was sufficient to support full employment.

The reserve bank presidents received a briefing from Goldenweiser on the day of Currie's memos. There is no mention of Currie's estimates.[187] Goldenweiser urged the increase. He expected short-term rates to increase: "Short-term rates had been abnormally low in relation to long-term rates and some stiffening of the former would be desirable" (Board Minutes, January 26, 1937, 3). The Board or the FOMC would have to reduce excess reserves at some time in the future, and he believed that the "most effective time for action to prevent the development of unsound and speculative situations is in the early stages of such a movement when the situation is still susceptible of control . . . [S]uch a time had arrived" (3).[188]

Goldenweiser added that aggregate excess reserves of $2.1 billion could absorb the $1.5 billion increase in required reserves. However, 2,435 banks would have to draw on correspondent balances, and 197 would have a reserve deficiency that would require borrowing or asset sales (ibid., 4). He also dismissed concerns about loss of membership. John H. Williams reinforced Goldenweiser's arguments and urged prompt action. The longer the Board delayed, the greater the likelihood that future action would force liquidation of loans.

A majority of the presidents spoke in favor.[189] The following day, Golden-

185. Goldenweiser argued that rates on Treasury bills would be held down by rates of 0.5 percent on banker's acceptances and that rates on long-term bonds would remain low until short-term rates equaled or exceeded long-term rates (Board of Governors File, box 418, January 12, 1937, 3, 5). The prediction proved to be wrong.

186. Currie also computed the estimated nominal value of national income three years ahead, based on estimates of velocity and his belief that the price level would rise by 10 percent as the economy returned to full employment in 1939.

187. However, Goldenweiser dismissed the argument that time deposits be exempt from the increase.

188. This is probably a reference to a revised view of the 1927–29 stock market speculation.

189. Harrison again proposed that reserve banks be given emergency powers to purchase and sell securities in amounts up to $50 million without prior approval. The FOMC postponed discussion until January 26. Eccles opposed the motion, but it passed six to five, with

Table 6.4   Reserve Requirements

	DEMAND DEPOSITS (%)			
DATE	CENTRAL RESERVE CITY	RESERVE CITY	COUNTRY	TIME
Before 8/15/36	13	10	7	3
8/15–3/1/37	19.5	15	10.5	4.5
3/1–5/1/37	22.75	17.5	12.25	5.25
On 5/1/37	26	20	14	6

weiser assured the FOMC that the increase in required reserve ratios would not reverse the easy money policy but would place the System in a position to influence the market by open market operations when needed. Three days later, Eccles reported that Morgenthau had again not opposed the change, provided it was effective no later than the close of business on February 27 so that the market could adjust before the March 15 financing. Eccles and Morgenthau then discussed the issue with the president. Roosevelt left the decision to the Board but did not object to the increase (Board Minutes, January 28, 1937, 4).

Governor McKee proposed that the increase be made in two steps, half at the end of February and half in April or May. Eccles later asked Morgenthau and Burgess about this suggestion. Both found it acceptable. The following Saturday, January 30, 1937, the Board increased reserve requirement ratios by $33^1/_3$ percent of prevailing levels. The vote was five in favor, one (McKee) not voting. Deferring a bit to Treasury concerns, only half the increase became effective on March 6. The rest was scheduled for May 1. Table 6.4 shows the changes.

The Board's press release emphasized that policy had not changed and affirmed its view that the $1.5 billion of excess reserves was superfluous: "Member banks will have excess reserves of approximately $500 million, an amount ample to finance further recovery and to maintain easy conditions" (Press Release, Board of Governors File, box 291, January 30, 1937, 2). The release cited the earlier experience, warned about the risks of inaction, and repeated its earlier conclusion: "It is far better to sterilize a part of these superfluous reserves while they are still unused than to permit a credit structure to be erected upon them and then to withdraw the foundation of the structure" (4).

The Board had now used all of its new authority to raise reserve requirements. With gold sterilization limiting increases in reserves and an open market portfolio five times the estimated volume of excess reserves, the Board believed it had the power to control future inflation.

Governor Broderick voting with the five presidents. Broderick then changed his vote to abstain on grounds that motions of this character should not be carried by such a narrow margin (Minutes, FOMC, January 26, 1937, 15–16).

Burgess met with Morgenthau and the Treasury soon after the announcement. There were no complaints. The main discussion concerned Treasury issues in March and June.[190]

BOND MARKET JITTERS Neither the Federal Reserve nor the Treasury anticipated the break in the bond market on March 12. Government bond yields had remained between 2.46 and 2.48 since the start of the year, influenced partly by Treasury operations. Rates rose on March 12 and 13, ending at 2.52 percent on March 13.

Once again Morgenthau was furious. He described the decline as a "panic" and cut short his conversation with Harrison when Harrison pointed out that rates were at the lowest level in history and refused to agree that there was a panic. Morgenthau blamed the increase in reserve requirement ratios for the market break and insisted that the Federal Reserve make net purchases of bonds to support the market (Harrison Papers, file 2012.5, dictated March 31, 1937).[191] The Treasury had purchased $75 million in three days. It was time, Morgenthau said, for the System to help. Eccles agreed, but Morgenthau was doubtful that Eccles could get Harrison and Burgess to consent (Blum 1959, 369).

The FOMC's executive committee called an emergency meeting for March 13. Eccles reported on his meeting with Morgenthau, explaining that Morgenthau blamed the Federal Reserve and wanted outright purchases to bring the 2.5 percent bond to par (a difference of 0.02 percent). The executive committee refused to make a commitment to a particular interest rate but pledged its cooperation with the Treasury (Minutes, FOMC Executive Committee, March 13, 1937).

The entire executive committee then went to Morgenthau's office. Eccles reported the decision and, to strengthen his case, urged Morgenthau to balance the 1938 budget by raising tax rates and begin to retire debt. Morgenthau tried to get a commitment from the Federal Reserve about how much it would let interest rates rise, but Eccles would not go beyond a general commitment to continue an easy money policy. Morgenthau

190. The Senate approved a resolution on February 5 asking for the reasons leading to the increase in reserve requirement ratios. The Board's reply consisted of a copy of the press release announcing the change, and the reasons for it, and a longer article prepared for the *Federal Reserve Bulletin* showing the ability of the banking system to obtain the required reserves from correspondents if needed.

191. The Federal Reserve began sharing purchases with the Treasury on March 12, but it continued its usual practice of offsetting purchases by sales of Treasury bills. Morgenthau wanted an increase in reserves, which Harrison opposed. Total Treasury purchases for the day were $32 million.

threatened to end gold sterilization, in effect nullifying the Federal Reserve's action. The FOMC members urged him not to do that, since it would transfer responsibility for monetary policy to the Treasury (ibid., 1–2). The two sides agreed to continue operating as they had, placing bids under the market, sharing purchases without any change in the System Open Market Account. The Federal Reserve agreed to hold a full FOMC meeting on March 15 to extend its power to purchase.

At the March 15 meeting the FOMC voted unanimously to continue the policy of offsetting long-term purchases with sales of short-term bills. This increased earnings of the reserve banks, so it was popular with the presidents, and it avoided adding to the portfolio and offsetting part of the long-sought reduction in excess reserves.

Eccles argued at length that the market break was not caused by Federal Reserve policy. He cited instability in France, British rearmament, demand for war materials, increased union activity, inventory building, and concerns about another unbalanced budget. He told the FOMC he had prepared a press release saying that monetary policy remained easy and that "the time for adoption of a restrictive monetary policy does not arise until there is full production and employment" (Minutes, FOMC, March 15, 1937, 7). No one responded that a long-term commitment to "easy money" could contribute to the increase in long-term rates.

Harrison agreed with Eccles but took a less defensive stance, accepting that Board action was one cause of the market break, but not the principal cause. The policy change had been necessary to absorb excess reserves. He opposed open market purchases (unless offset by sales of other maturities) and attributed the bond market problem to concerns about inflation.

Goldenweiser discussed the economic situation. Expansion was under way everywhere. As to policy, the committee should be willing to undertake purchases to avoid disorderly markets. They could be offset later. His concern was political: if the System did not act, the Treasury would. The System would run the risk that action might be taken in another form that would complicate the machinery of credit control and divide responsibility for such control (ibid., 11). Williams disagreed. Like Eccles, he regarded the disturbances to the bond market as nonmonetary in character, then added, "Sooner or later the System will be forced to take restrictive monetary action to prevent dislocation" (12). Purchases would be seen as a reversal of policy.

Morgenthau called from Georgia to learn what the FOMC had decided. The minutes report that he was satisfied with the decision to continue bond market support, offset by short-term sales, and with authority to purchase up to $250 million in an emergency (ibid., 19).[192] The minutes show that the committee wanted to tell Morgenthau it saw no reason to increase its portfolio at that time (16).[193]

Eccles left for vacation. The committee had failed to specify what constituted a dire emergency, requiring purchases. When the bond market fell again on March 16 and 17, Morgenthau wanted to desterilize gold, but Roosevelt did not approve. The Treasury continued to purchase bonds for the trust funds, mainly the postal savings account, but purchases could not exceed the amount of uninvested cash in the fund.

Harrison bought $37 million on March 16 and 17 but offset the purchases by selling bills. On March 18 the market rose, and by the end of the week the bond yield was at 2.62 percent, an increase of 0.15 in two weeks. Harrison regarded the change as an orderly adjustment; Eccles and Morgenthau saw it as an emergency. Eccles, perhaps influenced by Morgenthau, wanted purchases of $250 million—a 10 percent increase in the portfolio, the maximum amount approved by the FOMC. If the banks wanted excess reserves instead of earning assets, he would let them have them. Harrison regarded this as partly vindictive (Harrison Papers, file 2140.2, April 2, 1937, 2). Vice Chairman Ransom agreed with Harrison that there was no emergency.

The executive committee met on Saturday, with Harrison presiding in Eccles's absence. Ransom said the meeting had been called because the Treasury had only $14 million left in the trust accounts. It wanted the System to take responsibility for purchases. Morgenthau had told him, he reported, that "if the Treasury were called upon to make additional purchases in order to prevent a disorderly market such purchases would have to be accomplished with funds derived from the transfer of gold certificates to the Federal Reserve banks or in some other manner" (Minutes, Executive Committee, FOMC, March 22, 1937, 2).

The threat did not perturb the members. Harrison thought the principal lesson from the recent experience was not to follow the market too closely or offset daily adjustments. He had purchased $121 million for the

---

192. In the 1960s, the Federal Reserve returned to the policy of offsetting long-term purchases with short-term sales in an effort to change the slope of the yield curve. Most studies of the later episode suggest it had no effect on relative yields.

193. Harrison reports that Eccles opposed a motion to renew authority of the executive committee to increase or decrease the portfolio by telephone conference. The reason was that "it would not satisfy the Secretary" (Harrison Papers, file 2012.5, March 31, 1937, 8). The motion was redrafted to mention emergency action. "It was clearly understood . . . that the emergency in mind must be a dire one" (8). The FOMC minutes report that Morgenthau was unhappy with Eccles's press release and with the decision to leave authority to purchase with the executive committee, where Harrison would have more influence (Blum 1959, 370).

Treasury and $68 million for the System. Ransom presented Eccles's case for immediate purchases. The committee disagreed. It did not see an emergency that required purchases; it was unwise to increase excess reserves; the best course was to continue Harrison's policy of placing bids beneath the market price and offsetting purchases with sales of bills.

The next day the FOMC considered a broader agenda: purchases; revocation of the May 1 increase; and ending gold sterilization. There was general agreement that none of these steps should be taken (Harrison Papers, file 2140.2, April 2, 1937).

Morgenthau wanted more action by the Federal Reserve but was dissuaded by a conversation with Roosevelt. The president, Morgenthau told his staff, was not worried about the bond market (Blum 1959, 371). But Morgenthau was, and his concern increased as the bond market continued to fall. Yields reached 2.72 in the week ending March 27. Eccles, still on vacation, wanted to act. He blamed Harrison for the failure.[194] But only Eccles and Morgenthau appear to have been disturbed.[195]

Eccles and Morgenthau met on April 6. Eccles was "apologetic." He proposed three alternatives. The Board could repeal the May 1 increase for country banks; the FOMC could begin outright purchases; or the System could ask the Treasury to desterilize some gold. The Treasury staff wanted some combination of the three actions to assist the Treasury at its next bond sale. Morgenthau told Eccles he wanted a "big, broad stroke," including release of $500 million of gold and beginning net open market purchases. Eccles was "very much in favor" (Blum 1959, 372).

If so, Eccles reconsidered. His proposed announcement of the joint program referred only to open market purchases "if necessary." Morgenthau threatened to ease by desterilizing gold if the System would not cooperate. Eccles, at last, agreed to endorse the original joint program, even if the FOMC did not want to purchase (ibid.).[196] He now had to sell the plan to the FOMC.

194. Eccles's biography says he hurried back to Washington (Eccles 1951, 292). In fact, he stayed on his fishing vacation in Florida for two weeks and was kept informed by telephone.

195. Ransom reported that the Treasury staff was not disturbed. Harrison and Ransom met with Eccles on Monday, March 29. Both favored doing nothing other than continuing the swap operation, but Eccles wanted more. Eccles favored net purchases but indicated that he would accept gold desterilization (Harrison Papers, file 2140.2, April 9, 1937).

196. Currie sent Eccles a memo that dismissed the reserve requirement change as a factor affecting interest rates. He blamed fears of inflation arising from price and wage increases. (Balke and Gordon's deflator shows a 10.76 percent increase for the quarter; Currie to Eccles, Board of Governors File, box 1433, April 2, 1937). However, the spread between Baa and Aaa bonds, a measure of risk, fell to the lowest level in seven years. Rates on four- to six-month prime commercial paper increased from 0.75 percent to 1 percent in April. They remained at 1 percent for a year.

The committee met on April 3. The bond yield was 2.78, 0.32 above its all-time low. Eccles began the meeting by reading the statement, prepared with the Treasury, announcing a program to release $400 million in gold from sterilization and open market purchases to increase Federal Reserve holdings[197] (Minutes, FOMC, April 3, 2).[198] He was willing to accept Treasury policy with the understanding that Morgenthau would again sterilize gold after the May 1 increase in reserve requirements.

The FOMC members, other than Eccles, argued that there was no emergency and no reason for System purchases. Harrison urged the FOMC to hold a free and open discussion. It was Saturday; markets had closed. There was no reason for hasty action. Eccles replied that the committee was wrong not to have declared the markets disorderly and begun purchases. Ransom responded that he had talked to the Treasury all through the week and had heard no complaints, even from Morgenthau.[199]

Perhaps without realizing it, Eccles shifted his argument. He had claimed throughout that excess reserves were redundant and could be removed without cost.[200] Now he recognized that

[the] banks have been accustomed for a long time to an extremely large amount of excess reserves, that by the actions of the Board this excess has been drastically reduced, and that it would take the banks some time to accustom themselves to operating with a smaller amount of excess, as evidenced by the fact that they had sold earning assets rather than reduce their balances with correspondents. He suggested that . . . the System would be justified in increasing the System portfolio in recognition of the fact that, because of the reluctance of banks to reduce their excess reserves, there had

197. Williams's memo to Harrison reporting on the meeting described the memorandum as "an ultimatum by the Treasury" (Williams to Harrison, Harrison Papers, Open Market, April 14, 1937).

198. The Federal Reserve proposed a sentence for the joint statement that attributed the fall in market rates to "developments wholly unjustified by underlying financial and economic conditions" (Blum 1959, 372). Morgenthau objected to the statement because he believed the increase in reserve requirements had caused the rise in interest rates. The System removed the words "developments wholly unjustified." Eccles also wanted to insert that open market purchases would be made "if necessary," but Morgenthau wanted no qualifications and threatened to act alone if the FOMC would not act (ibid.). Eccles had promised Morgenthau that the FOMC would decide by noon because the two of them would meet the president at 1:00, and Morgenthau had scheduled a press conference at 4:00.

199. Williams's memo to Harrison gives a somewhat different account of these events. He describes Eccles's statement as "an ultimatum by the Treasury" and reports Eccles as saying that a failure to agree to the program would be evidence that the System would not "play ball" (Williams to Harrison, Harrison Papers, file 2140.2, April 14, 1937, 1).

200. Eccles did not recognize the import of this statement, for he continued to deny responsibility for the rise in interest rates and voted that way at the next day's meeting. His biography also denies any responsibility.

been a larger amount of selling of government securities than was anticipated when reserve requirements were increased, and these offerings were coming into the market at a time when the market was already disturbed by other factors and there were practically no buyers. (Minutes, FOMC, April 3, 1937, 7)

It is difficult to know what to make of this statement. If Eccles believed what he said, he should have stopped the third increase in required reserve ratios. Although the members discussed cancellation at times, there is no suggestion that this was a real possibility. Cancellation would have recognized the System's responsibility for the rise in long-term rates. The main arguments against it were concern about the embarrassment of reversing a policy that had been announced and the belief that inflation remained a threat. The committee was reluctant to appear to have made an error.

The FOMC split between those who favored purchases because of the rise in interest rates, those who wanted to prevent the Treasury from taking monetary action alone, and those who favored letting the Treasury deposit gold certificates at the Federal Reserve. The main opponents of purchases, Ransom, Harrison, and John H. Williams, expressed fear of inflation, citing labor strife and the unbalanced budget.[201]

Harrison asked whether the FOMC considered purchases only to meet the Treasury's demand. In the classic New York–Washington split, he expressed a willingness to purchase if the economic situation required it, but not just to satisfy the secretary. Eccles's reply repeated his earlier argument; rates had increased more than the FOMC had anticipated. Williams supported Harrison. He saw no reason for purchases. The problem was that the Treasury had sterilized gold without waiting for the change in reserve requirements to take effect. They could now stop sterilizing. Eccles opposed this suggestion: "It was the responsibility of the System to take the leadership in meeting this problem" (ibid., 15).

Eccles then talked to Morgenthau, who agreed to wait until the following day for the FOMC's decision. Morgenthau believed the time had passed for action by the FOMC alone, but he was willing to wait a day for joint action on the program he had worked out with Eccles.[202] The FOMC decided to let the executive committee meet with Morgenthau at his home that evening.

201. The Congress of Industrial Organizations had broken off from the American Federation of Labor. At the time, there were seven strikes in the auto industry. Freeman (1998, 282) shows that in 1937 there were 2,200 strikes for union recognition, involving nearly a million workers. For comparison, 1935 had 560 strikes for union recognition involving 200,000 workers.

202. The FOMC's discussion of a reversal of the third increase in reserve requirements went beyond its authority and into the actions of the Board. It is clear that Eccles was not overly concerned about the separate roles of the Board and the FOMC.

Eccles and Morgenthau met with Roosevelt in the afternoon. Roosevelt asked whether it would be inflationary to desterilize gold. Morgenthau agreed that it would. The president proposed a compromise that pleased both men. Morgenthau would tell the Federal Reserve that if it did not fulfill the responsibilities Congress had given it, he would act alone. Eccles would have the opportunity to act alone; the Treasury would not desterilize gold if the Federal Reserve purchased enough to reduce the long-term rate (Blum 1959, 373–74).

At his home that evening, Morgenthau criticized the FOMC for allowing interest rates to rise. Harrison continued to balk. The meeting dragged on until Morgenthau exploded: "You people just don't want to admit that . . . you monkeyed with the carburetor and you got the mixture too thin . . . You give us the policy now" (ibid., 374). Harrison would not yield. Finally, Morgenthau ended the meeting with the warning that the president had suggested. Either the FOMC would act or the government would.[203]

The threat ended the controversy. After meeting for the whole next day, on Eccles's motion the FOMC voted to begin purchases at once, to purchase $25 million in the current week, and to purchase up to $250 million by May 1. If the FOMC refused to adopt the policy, or if it failed to lower interest rates, Eccles was willing to cancel the third increase in reserve requirements ratios. He believed it was most important for the System to remain in control of policy.

Harrison fought a rear-guard defense, urging that action not be taken solely to prevent Treasury action. He preferred to continue the policy of shifting maturities without changing the total portfolio, but once he recognized that he had little support, he favored giving the executive committee authority to prevent disorderly markets (Minutes, FOMC, April 4, 1937, 5).[204]

Only Governors Davis and McKee favored canceling the May 1 increase in reserve requirements. The dominant view was that inflation remained a threat. A majority supported open market purchases, some to prevent Treasury action, some to correct so-called disorderly market conditions.[205]

---

203. Eccles supported Morgenthau, agreed on the need for purchases, and at one point threatened to resign if the FOMC did not support him (Harrison Papers, file 2140.2, April 14, 1937).

204. Williams's memo conveys the intense feeling, even animosity, between Eccles and Harrison (Williams to Harrison, Harrison Papers, FOMC, April 14, 1937).

205. By a vote of nine to two, the FOMC agreed that the disorder in financial markets was not caused by the Board's policy action. Only McKee and Davis, both Board members, blamed the Board. Neither had voted for the increases. Despite Eccles's April 3 statement, quoted above, he continued to absolve himself and the Board of responsibility.

With Harrison abstaining, the rest of the committee voted to adopt Eccles's motion. Purchases began the next day. This was the first increase in the open market account since November 1933.

The committee's action was mainly political.[206] Only Eccles expressed strong support for purchases. He summarized the views of the other members as acting "on grounds of expediency, to avoid a break with the Treasury" (Harrison Papers, Supplementary Memo, Williams to Harrison, file 2140.2, April 14, 1937). Goldenweiser agreed with Eccles but regarded the decision as "not mainly an economic but a political question."[207]

The executive committee met again the following day, April 5, and voted to purchase up to $5 million of Treasury bills. Harrison voted no. Bond rates fell, so no purchases were made until the next day, when rates again rose. Burgess purchased $29 million for the week. No one objected that the account manager (Burgess) exceeded the authorization for the week's purchases.[208]

Bond yields reached a local peak of 2.80 percent at the end of the week. In all, rates increased 0.34 (14 percent) from the January low. The executive committee had set a limit to the open market account of $2.53 billion. The System continued to purchase until the portfolio reached $2.525 billion at the end of the month, an increase of $95 million for the month.[209]

The third increase in reserve requirements took effect on May 1. Banks had prepared adequately, so there were no additional repercussions. Bond yields reached 2.80 percent again, then declined. The Federal Reserve did not undertake additional purchases.

206. Harrison opposed the commitment to purchase a fixed amount in the next week, but he lost on a vote of eight to three. Only Szymczak and Sinclair (Philadelphia) supported him. The choice of a week reflected Morgenthau's warning that he would judge their actions after a week. Harrison subsequently changed his vote to support the motion.

207. Williams summarizes the difference in economic outlook between Eccles and Harrison. Eccles believed the economy had been hurt by the rise in interest rates, citing the virtual standstill in new issues on the capital market. Harrison (and Williams) saw the economy acquiring "increased momentum." They were more concerned about inflation, the budget deficit, wage settlements, and the beginning of armament demand (supplementary memo, Harrison Papers, file 2140.2, April 14, 1937, 2).

208. Eccles twice asked Harrison to reduce the acceptance-buying rate. Harrison took the issue to his directors but expressed his view that the reduction was not justified. The directors agreed (Sproul Papers, Open Market Policy, April 8, 1937).

209. Most of the purchases were made in periods of market breaks on April 6–8 and April 22–24. On the latter dates, the Federal Reserve was the principal buyer. The account also sold bonds when the bond market rose, for example, on April 10 (memo, Harrison to files, file 2012.7, April 10, 1937). Morgenthau was annoyed by the purchases on April 14 because he had to sell bills to continue gold sterilization and bill rates had increased a bit (Harrison Papers, file 2012.7, April 14, 1937). The sales were offset within the week by bill purchases so that the account would not decline.

Summary: Reserve Requirements and Monetary Policy

The response to doubling reserve requirement ratios in 1936–37 remains controversial. The controversy began when Morgenthau blamed the Federal Reserve for the rise in interest rates and for the recession that followed. He did not mention the Treasury's decision to sterilize gold inflows. Eccles and most Federal Reserve officials denied responsibility for both the increase in interest rates and the recession.[210] Roose's comprehensive study of the 1937–38 cycle includes monetary action as one factor affecting the decline (1954, 239). Friedman and Schwartz (1963, 526–31) argue for the importance of monetary policy acting on output and income by reducing the money stock. Calomiris and Wheelock (1996, 510) reject this explanation at least for the changes in reserve requirements. They give more attention to changes in reserve requirements than to gold sterilization, but they recognize both as factors affecting money growth.

Chart 6.3 compares the increase in the weighted average reserve requirement ratio in 1936–37 with subsequent changes in the years to 1953.[211] The 1936–37 changes removed $3.1 billion of reserves as a base for monetary expansion in a period of nine months. The reduction is approximately 28 percent of the level of reserves on June 30, 1936. After subsequent changes in reserve requirement ratios, the Federal Reserve held interest rates constant, so banks could sell securities and restore desired reserve positions at unchanged interest rates. The principal effect of later changes in reserve requirement ratios was to raise (or lower) the tax on bank profits without any significant effect on the money stock.

In 1937 Morgenthau and the Federal Reserve agreed to prevent disorderly market conditions without pegging interest rates. Interest rates rose, and the effective monetary base declined. Banks did not restore the reserves absorbed by the changes in reserve requirements; total reserves, the monetary base and, beginning in second quarter 1937, the M_1 money stock

210. McKee, who did not vote for the increases, is one exception, as noted earlier. The Board's staff undertook a study of reserve requirements but did not study the effect of the 1936–37 changes. Their report reconsiders proposals made in 1931 to count vault cash as part of reserves, to make reserve requirements uniform for all classes of banks and types of deposit, and to put reserve requirements on deposit turnover (debits). The report gave a mixed review to these proposals, and none was adopted at the time (Board of Governors File, box 107, February 5, 1938). In March the Conference of Reserve Bank Presidents endorsed the proposal to count vault cash as part of required reserves up to 50 percent of required reserves (Board of Governors File, box 136, March 19, 1938). The Board made the change in vault cash beginning in 1959.

211. The chart is computed using deposits subject to reserve requirements (net demand deposits and time deposits) from the call reports published in Board of Governors of the Federal Reserve System 1943. See Cagan 1965, 198–99.

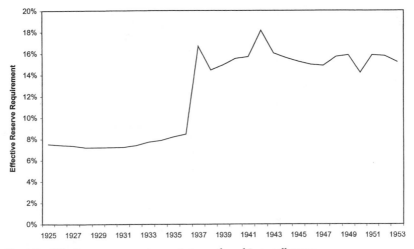

Chart 6.3 Effective reserve requirement at month-end June call report.

fell. In the four quarters of 1936, average M_1 growth was 12.8 percent, propelled by the increase in gold. Growth fell to 5 percent (annual rate) in first quarter 1937. For the remaining three quarters of 1937, the average annual growth rate of money was −6.5 percent.[212]

Interest rates on risky assets show relatively large increases. Table 6.5 shows the rates on Baa bonds and the spread between Baa and Aaa rates, a measure of the risk premium. The risk premium rose in 1937 and the first half of 1938. At its peak, the risk spread had returned to the level reached in third quarter 1931, when Britain left the gold standard.

The Federal Reserve's error was the belief that excess reserves could be reduced without consequence. Its denial of the effect of doing so is puzzling in light of the efforts that banks made to restore excess reserves, an effort Eccles and others commented on at the time. Since most short-term interest rates did not change, Harrison and others refused to believe that policy had tightened.

Table 6.6 shows the estimates of excess reserves at New York and other banks based on data available at the time. These data suggest that banks in New York and outside first restored, then increased excess reserve hold-

212. Changes in short- and long-term interest rates on government securities show only modest effects of the policy action. Rates on four-to-six-month prime commercial paper increased from 0.75 percent to 1.0 percent in April 1937 and were otherwise unchanged. Monthly average rates on ninety-day banker's acceptances moved steadily from 0.19 percent in December 1936 to a peak of 0.56 percent in April 1937 before declining again. As noted earlier, rates on long-term governments peaked at 2.80 percent in April 1937, then declined slowly. Although these relatively modest changes disturbed Morgenthau, they were much less than the annualized rate of inflation, 8.3 percent for the GNP deflator, in the first half of 1937.

Table 6.5   Risky Rates and the Risk Premium, 1936–38 (percent)

DATE	BAA RATE	RISK PREMIUM	DATE	BAA RATE	RISK PREMIUM
3/36	4.86	1.57	9/37	5.16	1.88
6/36	4.90	1.66	12/37	5.73	2.52
9/36	4.62	1.44	3/38	6.30	3.08
12/36	4.53	1.43	6/38	6.25	1.99
3/37	4.68	1.36	9/38	5.65	2.44
6/37	4.93	1.65	12/38	5.27	2.19

Source: Board of Governors of the Federal Reserve System 1943, 471.

Table 6.6   Estimated or Actual Excess Reserves, 1937–38 (millions of dollars)

DATE	TOTAL	NEW YORK	OTHER
1937			
June 14	902	156	745
September 14	800	70	720
December 14	1,150	360	800
1938			
March 14	1,400	500	900
June 14	2,730	1,040	1,690
September 14	3,150	1,480	1,670
December 14	3,520	1,850	1,670

Source: Board of Governors of the Federal Reserve System 1943.
Note: Detail does not add to total.

ings, so that banks held more excess reserves at the end of 1938 than they did when the System undertook to eliminate them in August 1936. New York banks added more to excess reserves during this period than banks outside New York.[213] The policy therefore did not achieve what the Federal Reserve set out to accomplish. It not only contributed to the recession but also failed to reduce the System's fear that it could not prevent future inflation.

The source of this concern is a slightly modified version of the Riefler-Burgess framework. The principle was unchanged. In the 1920s Riefler-Burgess suggested that once banks were out of debt, the Federal Reserve had little control. For it to exercise control, the banks had to be forced to borrow. Since borrowing had almost disappeared in the 1930s, the doctrine changed. Now excess reserves (negative borrowing) rendered the System incapable of preventing inflation. By reducing excess reserves below the size of the open market portfolio, the System believed it was in position to prevent runaway inflation; once excess reserves were smaller than the

213. The risk premiums in table 6.5 suggest the increase in uncertainty, as in Frost 1966. Despite the low interest rates on government bonds, Baa bonds were at about the same rates as in the 1920s, so the risk spreads were higher.

open market portfolio, open market sales could force banks to borrow. Under Riefler-Burgess, they would then want to pay off their indebtedness by contracting.[214]

The System ran the experiment of reducing excess reserves three times. Each time banks responded by restoring excess reserves. Partly out of unwillingness to admit policy error and partly under pressure from the Treasury, the Federal Reserve ignored this contradiction of Riefler-Burgess, much as it had ignored contrary evidence earlier. It continued to cling to its theory.

THE 1937–38 RECESSION

Did the increase in reserve requirement ratios cause the 1937–38 recession? Changes in reserve requirements were part of monetary policy, and monetary policy was part of government policy. The data on interest rates, risk premiums, and changes in the monetary base and money suggest that the Federal Reserve did not offset the effects of the change. Monetary policy became more restrictive. The proximate causes of the monetary policy change were the increase in reserve requirement ratios, not offset by open market purchases, and the shift in December 1936 to gold sterilization.

Monetary factors were not alone.[215] There were two large contractive changes in fiscal policy in 1937. One was the reduction of soldiers' bonus payments and passage of the undistributed profits tax; the other was the beginning of Social Security tax payments. Passed in 1935, Social Security taxes became effective in fiscal 1936 (calendar 1937).[216]

Congress had insisted, over the president's veto, on accelerating the soldiers' bonus, so that veterans would receive payment before the 1936 election.[217] Beginning in June 1936, the government issued $1.7 billion of

214. Concerns about membership appear to have been misplaced. The proportion of member banks among commercial banks increased annually from 1935 to 1939 and more rapidly in 1940 and 1941.

215. Romer (1992) estimates the effects of fiscal and monetary shocks using data for 1920 to 1937. She found no effect of fiscal shocks and attributed the 1937 recession to monetary shocks. Romer assumed a one-year lag of policy variables to recognize that the fiscal changes were known in advance. As the text shows, the Board gave advance notice of changes in reserve requirement ratios.

216. Concerns about the effect of Social Security taxes on the 1937–38 recession led to repeal of actuarial provisions and substitution of "pay as you go" or intergenerational transfer in 1939.

217. The bonus had been approved in 1924 for payment in 1945. Congressman Wright Patman (Texas) led the fight to have the bonus paid in 1936 (without discount). He proposed to finance the payment by printing greenbacks, and the bill passed the House and Senate with that provision. Roosevelt vetoed the bill but did not work to prevent an override after Congress omitted greenback financing. Bonds were issued to the veterans but could be sold immediately for cash (Blum 1959, 249–58).

bonds. By December veterans had cashed $1.4 billion of the bonds and spent the money. Balke and Gordon's (1986) quarterly data show an 18 percent average rate of increase in real GNP for the final three quarters of 1936. The deflator rose, and profits reached a peak for the recovery in fourth quarter 1936.[218]

Responding to criticism about deficit spending, and hoping to stimulate private spending, in March 1936 the administration promised to tax undistributed corporate profits (Eccles 1951, 260). The tax was based on the peculiar belief that corporations held funds idle instead of investing them. If these funds, like the excess reserves of the banks, could be put to work, the economy would expand faster.[219] The Treasury expected the tax to raise $620 million, about 5 percent of the prospective deficit (ibid.).

Roose (1954, 238–39) adds some additional factors influencing investment spending, of which the most important is the increase in labor costs following strikes to organize major industries. The combined effect of higher interest rates, fiscal contraction, rising costs, and the growing belief that the Roosevelt administration had become more hostile—as shown by the undistributed profits tax and Roosevelt's second-term rhetoric about "economic royalists"—raised current and prospective tax rates and costs of capital.[220]

The National Bureau of Economic Research ranks the 1937–38 recession as the third most severe in the years after World War I. Real GNP fell 18 percent and industrial production 32 percent in the thirteen months beginning June 1937.[221] At its peak, the unemployment rate reached 20 percent, not much below the 25 percent maximum in 1932 (Zarnowitz and Moore 1986). It is no wonder that many feared the 1929–33 disaster had returned.

The Federal Reserve made no purchases until fall. The principal reason, again, was beliefs, not lack of information. John H. Williams recognized

218. The bonus payment declined to about $15 million in 1937.

219. Eccles (1951, 260–65) opposed the Treasury's bill on grounds that it discriminated against small companies with low retained earnings. Like the Treasury, he failed to recognize that the tax increased the cost of capital to corporations financing investment from retained earnings. Eccles's public criticism, and proposals for a less regressive undistributed profits tax, was another reason for resentment by Morgenthau and his staff. The tax worked perversely. Dividend payments increased in advance to avoid the tax, then declined (Roose 1954, 236). Businessmen saw the tax as another example of the administration's hostility toward business (Stein 1990, 87). It was repealed in 1938, effective January 1940.

220. In April, Roosevelt criticized high prices in the durable goods industry as a source of "excessively high profits" and ordered a shift in public works spending to avoid these industries (Roose 1954, 236). The statement reflected widespread concern in view of the rapid price rise. Currie had urged Eccles to consider using antitrust action to deter price increases (memo, Currie to Eccles, Board of Governors File, box 1433, December 16, 1936). This policy was adopted in 1938. Adolph Berle had urged it from the beginning.

221. The two more severe recessions are 1929–33 and 1920–21.

the beginnings of hesitation in the economy at the May 4 meeting of the FOMC, before the peak recorded by the NBER.[222] He saw no reason for action, however, and he favored continuing the policy of preventing disorderly markets, if they should occur. Goldenweiser agreed there was no need for action. The economy had slowed, but "he did not see any possibility at this time of a new period of depression setting in" (Minutes, FOMC, May 4, 1937, 6).[223]

Not much had changed when the FOMC met again on June 8 and 9. The committee discussed the business situation and the continued gold inflow. Williams regarded the slowdown of business as "salutary." He agreed with Goldenweiser that the gold inflows were the most serious problem of the moment (Minutes, FOMC, June 9, 1937, 3–5). Goldenweiser remarked that the System had to be in a position to offset gold imports when the Treasury stopped sterilizing, probably a reference to Morgenthau's reluctance to continue borrowing to sterilize gold inflows (3).

Before Eccles left for summer vacation, he called a meeting of the FOMC executive committee to propose purchases of $200 million to $300 million to offset the seasonal increase in demand for base money.[224] Harrison opposed "increasing our portfolio merely for the purpose of taking care of a seasonal demand for loans and currency. . . . [He] preferred to . . . have the banks borrow and show bills payable" (Harrison Papers, file 2140.2, August 27, 1937, 2–3). In making this argument, he showed the continuing influence of Riefler-Burgess—the need to get the banks in debt to the reserve banks. He argued that pressure on bank reserves in New York reflected the lower rates charged by correspondent banks. He proposed "reduction in discount rates at reserve banks outside New York."

The first steps to ease policy came from Chicago and Atlanta. These banks reduced their discount rates to 1.5 percent on August 20. The Board approved, and Eccles urged Harrison to reduce the New York rate at the next directors' meeting. Ever cautious, Harrison opposed the change as "too early." He believed they should wait for the Treasury to complete its financing. Pressed by the Board, however, he agreed. New York lowered its rate to 1 percent effective August 27, with one dissent (Harrison Papers, file 2140.2, August 27, 1937, 3; Minutes, New York Directors, August 26,

222. "Since the last meeting of the Committee, the movement had leveled out with some reduction of prices both at home and abroad . . . [T]here seemed to be much less likelihood of a runaway movement than was the case a month or two ago" (Minutes, FOMC, May 4, 1937, 3).

223. The Federal Advisory Council found "some recession in business activity in some districts" but "the recession was apparently temporary in character" (Board Minutes, May 18, 1937, 4–5).

224. This was the first executive committee meeting held in the new Board of Governors building (August 18). The building opened formally on October 20, 1937.

1937, 11). By the end of the first week of September, all reserve banks outside New York had lowered their discount rates to 1.5 percent. These were almost the last changes in discount rates until after World War II.[225]

The FOMC voted on September 11 to undertake open market purchases of up to $300 million during the fall and to ask the Treasury to desterilize $200 million to $300 million of inactive gold. The Treasury agreed and acted promptly. The actions were taken more for seasonal than for cyclical reasons, to offset expected seasonal changes in the demand for reserves. After years of inactivity, this was a return to the 1920s policy of seasonal accommodation to prevent interest rates from firming during the harvest and Christmas seasons. Estimates presented at the meeting suggested that the banking system's excess reserves would fall below $400 million before Christmas, and New York banks would use all of their excess reserves.[226]

Only a few months earlier, the FOMC had been reluctant to let the Treasury undertake monetary action by desterilizing gold. Eccles, who appears to have felt most strongly about the issue, was not present at the September meeting. In his absence, Goldenweiser noted that "action by the Treasury also might be interpreted as violating the principle that the Federal Reserve System has primary responsibility for credit conditions and has adequate instruments for handling it" (Minutes, FOMC, September 11, 1937, 5). He urged the System to act on its own. The minutes do not record much discussion of the issue; they report that the committee recognized that "while the System could act alone . . . the most desirable action would be the suggested joint action" (12).

The Federal Reserve had been inactive so long that it needed new criteria to guide operations. Goldenweiser (ibid., 6) recalled that in the past the rule of thumb was that borrowing by New York banks in excess of $50 million suggested tightness and less than $50 million suggested ease. That rule was no longer applicable. In its place he proposed to use excess reserves in place of borrowing; $250 million of excess reserves in New York and $700 million to $800 million for the country could be the threshold for judging ease and tightness.[227] The committee did not discuss the pro-

225. The qualification recognizes the reduction of the Boston bank's discount rate to 1 percent in September 1939 and reduced rates on industrial loans for defense production.

226. See table 6.6 above. At the time, excess reserves were above $3 billion. Contrary to the forecast, excess reserves rose, so the System made few purchases.

227. The staff had estimated the level of excess reserves at which banks would begin to borrow from the reserve banks. A staff memo in February 1937 estimated that the banks wanted to hold $100 million of excess reserves, a clear recognition that not all excess reserves were redundant. At the time, excess reserves were $2.5 billion, but there is no attempt in the memo (or elsewhere that I have seen) to explain why actual excess reserves remained so far above the estimate of desired excess reserves.

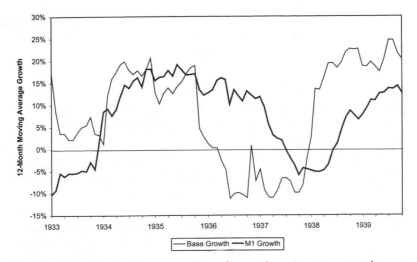

Chart 6.4 Adjusted St. Louis base versus M_1, twelve-month moving average growth.

posal, but it reveals that the events of the 1930s had little effect on the Riefler-Burgess framework. Only the numerical magnitudes had changed.

In his biography, Eccles reports that he expressed concern to the president about the economy as early as March. His concern at that time was that rising prices and wages would prevent the economy from reaching full use of capacity (Eccles 1951, 296–97). In August, he urged the president to encourage housing construction.[228] None of these concerns appear in the September 11 minutes. Williams again recognized that the economy had slowed, but he was uncertain whether a recession had started (Minutes, FOMC, September 11, 1937, 6–8). Harrison noted that bank credit was available, so the "causes of the present situation were not in the monetary field" (9) The implication was that there was no need for policy action.

Once again, the monetary base and the money stock tell a different story. Chart 6.4 shows the growth rates of the adjusted monetary base and the money stock from 1936 to 1939.[229] Growth of the monetary base turned negative after gold sterilization in December 1936. The base fell throughout 1937, much of the time at a 7 to 11 percent rate. The money stock lagged behind; although its growth rate fell throughout 1937, the money stock be-

228. Eccles (1951, 361) defends himself against the charge at the time that the increases in reserve requirements and the undistributed profits tax had caused the depression. These beliefs appear to have been held most vigorously by advocates of a balanced budget who may have wished to avoid criticism of fiscal tightening in 1937.

229. The adjustment corrects the base for changes in reserve requirements by reducing (or increasing) reserves by the dollar value of reserve requirement changes.

gan to fall only in August, two months after the start of the recession. Money growth remained negative until the early months of the recovery. With inflation (deflator) rising at a 6 percent average for the first three quarters, real money balances fell. In fourth quarter 1937 the situation changed; the price level fell and the base rose, so the real value of base money increased as real rates of interest rose. Again, as in 1920–21, the rise in the real value of the base and money dominated the effect on economic activity of rising real rates of interest.

Although the recession began in June, the FOMC made no purchases until November. Even a sharp stock market break, reducing the stock price index by 26 percent from late August to mid-October, did not induce a response. At last, on November 9, the FOMC executive committee voted to begin purchases at once and to purchase $50 million by the end of the month, using the authority of the September meeting. Eccles again wanted purchases because the Treasury threatened to act on its own by desterilizing gold. Harrison opposed purchases but voted in favor (Harrison Papers, file 2140.2, November 6, 1937). Perhaps because excess reserves rose and there was no evidence of seasonal tightening, the system bought only $38 million in November.[230] On November 16, Harrison and Eccles agreed to stop purchases after checking with Morgenthau. The System made no further purchases until March 1938.

Williams explained why the Federal Reserve purchased so little and stopped so soon. He described the period as a small depression but with "continued monetary ease," and "for that reason, a policy of monetary ease could not be counted on as a major corrective" (Minutes, FOMC, November 29, 1997, 3). "Those in authority should not sit back and do nothing. . . . steps should be taken to devise a means of encouraging private investment" (4). But he made few suggestions about what should be done, opposed any increase in government spending, and stressed the impor-

---

230. Unlike earlier recessions, the Federal Reserve learned about the severity of the recession slowly. At the October 8 meeting of the Federal Advisory Council, participants talked about a tendency toward decline and suggested that only steel, textiles, and construction were below September 1936 levels. The council expected that the fourth quarter "would be satisfactory" although below earlier anticipations (Board Minutes, October 8, 1937, 4). By mid-December the Advisory Council recognized that there had been a sharp business recession. Some plants had been closed. Others produced for inventory only. The tone remained relatively optimistic about recovery in the near future (Board Minutes, December 14, 1937, 6). This contrasts with statistics on industrial production. The Board's index shows a decline from 106 in September to 83 in December (22 percent). The Miron-Romer (1989) index shows a modest decline in this period (1.2 percent) and a very large decline in January 1938 (23 percent), with further declines cumulating to 44 percent by July 1938. Kindleberger (1986, 271) reports that on several measures the recession destroyed half the recovery from the 1932 lows.

tance of a balanced budget and other fiscal measures: reduction of the undistributed profits tax, the capital gains tax, and the surtax.

Goldenweiser agreed that monetary policy had been easy since early 1932. The increases in reserve requirements had not reversed the easy money policy; the recession was due to (unspecified) nonmonetary causes. He agreed with Williams that the third increase in reserve requirements should have come earlier (ibid., 6). He saw no reason for "any major monetary action at this time" (9). The System remained inactive.

The committee voted unanimously to continue the authorization to purchase for seasonal adjustment agreed on in September. Not a single dissenting voice suggested that the committee should purchase for expansion. Once again, the level of money market interest rates misled the FOMC. The members failed to see that falling prices meant that real rates of interest had increased as deflation and recession took hold.[231] Using nominal interest rates instead of monetary growth as an indicator of the policy stance gave the wrong signal in 1937 just as it had in 1929–33. Even growth of bank loans would have told the Federal Reserve that policy was restrictive; in the year ending June 1938, total bank loans fell 7.5 percent, reflecting restrictive monetary policy and the recession.[232]

Kindleberger (1986), Roose (1954), and Eccles (1951) describe the recession as principally an inventory recession. Eccles is representative of this view. He denied any monetary influence and attributed the 1937–38 cycle to four causes: (1) the buildup of business inventories at a time when (2) government spending declined; (3) the introduction of Social Security tax payments ($2 billion); and (4) labor disturbances that threatened to raise future production costs (Eccles 1951, 294–95). Instead of the $4 billion deficit in 1936, the Treasury had a cash surplus of $66 million in the first nine months of 1937.[233]

Chart 6.5 shows two measures of the change in inventories during these years. The sharp peaks in fourth quarter 1936 and second or third quarter

---

231. The meeting made a small adjustment in the allocation formula to increase earnings at banks that might have difficulty covering expenses and dividends. After 1933, the reserve banks did not pay franchise tax to the Treasury. Earnings above dividends and expense increased earned surplus.

232. Investments fell also, so total bank earning assets declined.

233. Morgenthau's figures are slightly different. He has a cash deficit (excluding gold and silver purchases) of $288 million for the first nine months compared with a $2.8 billion deficit in the same period of 1936 (Blum 1959, 383). Morgenthau worked tirelessly to get the budget balanced and, to Eccles's consternation, made a speech in New York on November 10, 1937, promising to balance the 1939 budget. Among the cabinet, James A. Farley and Henry Wallace endorsed his view, and Roosevelt also adhered to it until late in the recession.

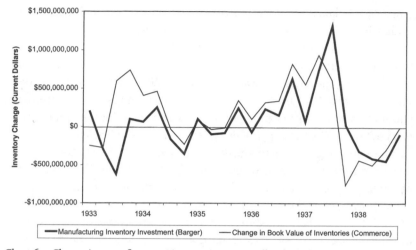

Chart 6.5 Change in manufacturers' inventories, seasonally adjusted.

1937 are clearly visible. The change in inventories, however, is small relative to the change in GNP or final sales.

A more plausible interpretation is that the very large decline in final sales made inventories seem excessive. Chart 6.6 shows that rapid money growth in 1935 preceded the increased growth of final sales in 1936. The deceleration of money in 1937 preceded the sharp decline in final sales, and the resumption of money growth preceded the resumption of growth in final sales. On this interpretation, gold inflows caused an acceleration of the monetary base followed, as in chart 6.4, by an acceleration of money and, as in chart 6.6, by faster growth of final sales. Fiscal changes, especially bonus payments, reinforced these effects. At peak deceleration in the summer of 1937, the monetary base declined at an 11 percent annual rate. Final sales (and real GDP) reached their trough at the end of 1937.[234]

Contemporary observers within and outside the administration gave considerable weight to the president's "antibusiness" rhetoric and actions. Although the undistributed profits tax did not produce more than about $400 million in revenue in fiscal years 1936 to 1938 (much below projections), the revenue aspect seems to have been less important than the

234. Eccles (1951, 299) appears to change his argument without noticing: "Soon thereafter the inflated price bubble burst *for want of purchasing power to sustain it,* and the slump started in earnest" (emphasis added). This recognizes a monetary effect. Consistent with his belief that monetary policy was impotent in recessions, Eccles's proposals for responding to the recession never mention Federal Reserve actions. He urged the president to lower mortgage down payments and interest rates on loans from the Federal Housing Administration (302).

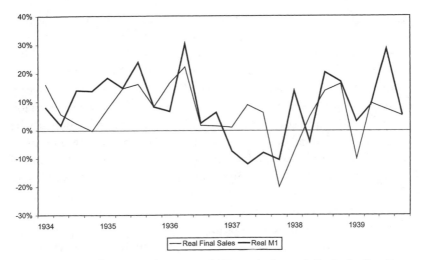

Chart 6.6 Real final sales growth versus real M_1 growth. Quarterly final sales from Barger 1942.

president's message (March 3, 1936) citing the large growth of corporate profits in the 1920s as a source of disturbance. Regulation of foreign exchange and the capital markets by the Securities and Exchange Commission also gave rise to concerns.[235]

End of the Recession

The Federal Reserve did little to correct the mistakes that contributed to the recession. Since short-term market interest rates remained low, it regarded its policy as easy. It continued to express more concern about future inflation than about current deflation. It took expansive actions when prodded by the administration and to avoid criticism for hindering the expansion program that the administration finally adopted.

Although the recession started in May 1937, policy did not change until 1938, when Morgenthau and the Treasury pressed for an end to gold sterilization and reductions in the reserve requirement ratios. Eccles continued to urge increased government spending and a larger deficit. Repeal of the undistributed profits tax relieved some of the real or psychological effects its passage had generated.

In November 1937, when Morgenthau first proposed to end gold steril-

235. Harrison reports, as an example, a conversation with George Whitney, a partner in J. P. Morgan. Whitney attributed the recession "largely to the Government's attitude about taxes and business regulation and the rapidly growing fear of business that it will not be allowed to make a profit" (Harrison Papers, file 2610.1, November 12, 1937). Jacob Viner partly endorsed these views (Blum 1959, 384).

ization, Eccles opposed on the grounds that "Roosevelt might grab the idea as a panacea for solving all economic problems. He considered excess reserves plentiful and contended that neither desterilization nor loosening of reserve requirements would actually ease credit" (Blum 1959, 393).

Morgenthau persevered. On February 8 he met with Roosevelt, deeply concerned about the continuing recession and the effect of the recession on other democratic countries. Despite his concerns about deficits, he wanted to spend an additional $250 million in the remaining months of the fiscal year to increase WPA employment by 650,000. He believed falling prices encouraged delays in private spending, so he proposed to end gold sterilization. Roosevelt accepted both suggestions (Blum 1959, 400). Morgenthau's diary explains that Morgenthau ended sterilization, in part, to prevent more government spending.[236]

Eccles hesitated to approve unlimited gold purchases. The gold purchase program announced on February 14 limited the monetary base increase to $100 million a quarter, retroactive to January 1.[237] Chart 6.4 (above) shows the immediate large change in the growth rate of the monetary base. In the second quarter, final sales rose modestly but inventories declined, so real GDP did not rise until the third quarter.

Eccles regarded the gold program as Morgenthau's plan. He was at best cool to the idea (Blum 1959, 406). Gold purchases expanded money without increasing Federal Reserve earnings, but his principal concern was the size of excess reserves. At the March 1 FOMC meeting, he favored continuing the program of selling long-term bonds and buying bills. The committee discussed open market sales to reduce excess reserves. This action would have neutralized Morgenthau's program, in effect resterilizing gold. Eccles concluded: "No useful purpose would be achieved by reducing the total amount of securities held in the System open market account." He did not propose purchases (Minutes, FOMC, March 1, 1938, 6–7).

Again in April, the Roosevelt administration, not the Federal Reserve, acted to spur the recovery that by then was under way. Morgenthau leaves no doubt about the reason for action. On March 25, while Roosevelt was on vacation in Georgia, the stock market fell sharply. The proponents of spending within the administration seized the opportunity to convince the

236. If nothing was done, they "would get instead a transcontinental highway or $8 billion of extraordinary expenses" (Blum 1959, 405).

237. This implied an annual rate of base growth of 4 percent. The Anderson and Rasche 1999 measure of the base increased 4.6 percent for the quarter; all of the change occurred in March. Morgenthau checked the plan with the British (under the Tripartite Agreement discussed below). The British agreed but asked why the United States did not reduce reserve requirements.

president that more spending would help the economy and the Democratic Party.[238] After much internal wrangling, and Morgenthau's threat to resign over the budgetary consequences, Roosevelt announced a new recovery plan on April 18.[239] Spending for construction and welfare increased by about $2 billion. On the monetary side, the Federal Reserve reduced reserve requirement ratios, and the Treasury desterilized $1.4 billion, all the remaining gold sterilized since December 1936. The reduction in reserve requirement ratios released an estimated $750 million, reversing the May 1, 1937, increase for central reserve and reserve city banks (to 22.75 percent and 17.5 percent) and lowering to 12 percent and 5 percent the requirement for country banks and all time deposits. The Board's minutes refer to the change as part of the president's program (Board Minutes, April 15, 1938, 1–2).[240] The very rapid expansion of the monetary base is apparent in chart 6.4 (above). Estimated excess reserves rose to $3.9 billion when desterilization was complete. Within a few months, the money stock began a sustained increase.

238. On April 5, Roosevelt told the cabinet: "The situation was bad not only for the country but also for the Democratic Party, which might lose the fall election if conditions continued as they were" (Blum 1959, 418). The reaction of the stock market was probably more closely related to foreign than to domestic conditions. The Harrison Papers (file 2140.3, March 21, 1938) discuss growing concerns about a European war after Hitler annexed Austria that month.

239. This program is cited as the first United States example of a planned increase in spending and the deficit to stimulate the economy. Some writers describe the decision as a major change in Roosevelt's thinking about fiscal policy (see Stein 1969, 109–14). Stein does not mention the political argument for spending. Currie, who served as Roosevelt's economic adviser during the war, does not share Stein's view. He claimed (1971, 3) that Roosevelt understood compensatory changes in spending and taxes only in 1940. I am indebted to Roger Sandilands for a copy of Currie's letter. Currie and others may have based their view on Roosevelt's opposition to increased spending in the 1939 budget, but it is also true that, in the fall of 1938—possibly to placate Morgenthau—Roosevelt appointed a conservative businessman, John W. Hanes, as undersecretary of the treasury, responsible for fiscal decisions (Blum 1965, 15–16).

240. The preliminary draft of the announcement stated: "While there were ample excess reserves to meet any probable needs . . . many people were under the impression that the Board's action . . . increasing reserve requirements was unduly deflationary; . . . the System is in a position, in the opinion of a substantial portion of the public at least, of resisting the recovery program; and that for that reason the Board could not be motivated exclusively by the economic factors in the situation and disregard the psychological factors" (Policy Records, Board of Governors File, box 291, April 15, 1938). All this was eliminated in the final draft, which talked about a "concerted effort by the Government." It appears, however, in the FOMC minutes for April 21 (7), which described the reduction of reserve requirements as "in the best interests of the Federal Reserve System."

Discussion of the effects of the 1937 reserve requirement increases was highly contentious. In February, Goldenweiser was relieved of all other duties and ordered to rewrite the annual report to make the discussion of reserve changes more appealing to the Board (Board Minutes, February 25, 1938). The FOMC rejected Williams's report on reserve requirement changes three times.

The Federal Reserve was reluctant to permit all the sterilized gold to increase reserves at once; the Treasury felt otherwise. The Treasury wanted to issue gold certificates in exchange for Federal Reserve deposits, then use the deposits to retire Treasury bills as they came due. This would increase excess reserves quickly, pressuring the banks to expand credit. The Federal Reserve preferred to have the Treasury use its deposits to pay for gold purchases, thereby spreading the increase in excess reserves over a longer period. On April 19 the executive committee of the FOMC agreed to present its case to Morgenthau in terms of disorderly debt markets. Reducing the stock of short-term government securities would reduce yields and could create disorderly markets. The Treasury dismissed the argument.

The president's announcement of the new program sparked a rally in the Treasury market. Already low yields on short-term securities fell to zero out to a maturity of eighteen months (Minutes, FOMC, April 21, 1938, 7). Desterilization and the reduction in reserve requirements appear to dominate any effect of a larger deficit; the market viewed the monetary ease as more than sufficient to absorb any additional debt resulting from the deficit or increased private spending and borrowing.

The FOMC's April 21–22 meeting gave most attention to the problem of replacing Treasury bills and notes with market yields at zero or below.[241] With a large increase of excess reserves currently and prospectively available, yields on Treasury securities had fallen at all maturities. The FOMC's principal concern was "disorderly markets"; rates had declined rapidly and could reverse.[242] The members did not want either to criticize the administration's program or to accept responsibility for correcting disorderly markets.

Eccles told Morgenthau about these problems. He reported to the FOMC that Morgenthau was sympathetic but would not agree to stop retiring $50 million in Treasury bills a week. The most he offered was to reconsider the subject later. Divided and uncertain about what to do, the

241. Treasury bills have large denominations that make them useless in transactions. At an equal nominal rate of zero, the real yield on currency—the own or nonpecuniary yield—is the higher of the two. Also, Cecchetti (1988) shows that the negative yields were the price paid for "exchange privileges." Certain coupon securities carried rights to purchase new issues of these securities. Adjusted for this option, rates on notes are positive but close to zero. Treasury bills did not have the exchange privilege. Bankers urged their customers to withdraw deposits and buy bills (even with very low yields) to save the cost of deposit insurance, one-twelfth of 1 percent.

242. Yields on long-term government securities declined from 2.62 in April to 2.51 in May and June (Board of Governors of the Federal Reserve System 1943, 471).

FOMC voted to replace maturing Treasury bills with notes out to a two-year maturity, if it could be done without paying a premium (negative yield).[243]

The following week the committee reconsidered the same issues. Harrison wanted authority to replace maturing issues with longer-term securities if useful for maintaining orderly markets and authority to purchase or sell securities to prevent disorderly markets. Eccles opposed sales as counter to the administration program. He proposed to continue replacing securities as long as yields were not negative. Harrison's motion was defeated eight to three; Eccles's proposal then passed unanimously.[244] Unlike the situation in the 1920s, the Board had control.

In September, long-term Treasury yields rose as the economy recovered and despite foreign buying of United States securities at the time of the Czech (Munich) crisis. The Treasury bought $37 million of notes and bonds. The Federal Reserve made smaller purchases, offset by sales of bills. Pressure from the Treasury to keep yields low lessened a bit after the Munich agreement. With Eccles absent, Harrison urged the executive committee on September 15 to let up to $700 million in bills run off without replacement if necessary. This would have reversed the April reduction in reserve requirements and offset Treasury purchases to hold rates down. The committee defeated the proposal. It voted instead to replace government bonds with Treasury bills to put the System in a position to offset monetary expansion without taking portfolio losses.[245]

The December meeting reconsidered the same issue, the problem of replacing bills as they matured without paying a premium to buy bills. The

243. Failure to replace maturing securities reduced the open market portfolio. The System was reluctant to offset or cancel the reserves released by the reduction in reserve requirements so as not to appear in opposition to the president's recovery program.

244. At the May 31 meeting, the FOMC decided that meetings with the secretary of the treasury were not official FOMC meetings, so they did not have to be reported in the minutes.

245. The September 15 meeting accepted the resignation of W. Randolph Burgess as manager of the System Open Market Account. Burgess resigned as vice president of the New York bank on September 13 to become vice chairman of National City Bank. He returned in the 1950s as treasury undersecretary in the Eisenhower administration. Allan Sproul became account manager. Appointment of a new manager led to a brief discussion of the conduct of open market operations. Harrison mused that "he had come to question whether the Committee had not gone into the market too frequently to try to moderate movements which, in some cases, were merely temporary. . . . He suggested that better results might be obtained in the future if the Committee were less responsive to minor fluctuations." The suggestion had no visible effect. The System continued and later intensified its concern for short-term changes. Governor Ransom suggested that the System "enter the market in the early stages of a situation which might develop into a disorderly rise or fall." He offered no suggestion about how that perennial problem could be solved (Minutes, Executive Committee, FOMC, September 15, 1938, 3).

FOMC asked Morgenthau to increase the size of weekly bill issues, but he preferred to encourage lower bond yields by keeping bill yields near zero. Over Eccles's objection, the FOMC voted to let bills run off without replacement if they could not be replaced without paying a premium. A background memo prepared for the December 30 meeting showed the problem worsening. The System had to buy an increasing amount of notes to prevent a decline in its portfolio. In its announcement after the December 30–31 meeting, the FOMC noted that its portfolio might show some fluctuation solely because the System was unable to replace maturing bills. The committee assured the public that "no change in Federal Reserve policy is contemplated at this time" (Press Release, FOMC, Board of Governors File, box 1452, December 31, 1938).[246]

GOLD AND EXCHANGE RATES, 1935–40

Gold and exchange rate policies, culminating in the 1934 devaluation, provided the main stimulus to domestic recovery in the first two years of the Roosevelt administration. The permanent increase in the gold price to $35 an ounce permitted gold holders to exchange gold for United States goods and assets on more favorable terms. As gold flowed to the United States, the principal countries remaining on the gold standard—France, Belgium, Italy, and Switzerland—came under increasing deflationary pressure.

By 1935 advocates of stable exchange rates, to revive international trade, had become more active. In the Treasury, Jacob Viner argued that side. Harrison favored allowing the British Exchange Equalization Account to buy and sell gold directly with the Treasury to help stabilize the pound.[247] These ideas appealed to Morgenthau, who wanted to build a democratic alliance against Hitler and hoped that monetary cooperation would help achieve that goal (Blum 1959, 140–41). But Morgenthau hesitated, because Roosevelt was suspicious of British intentions and believed Harrison was influenced too much by the British.

---

246. In December the staff considered means of improving operations of the government securities market. The suggestions included allowing each reserve bank to deal in government securities in its own district (a return to conditions in the early 1920s), making open market operations continuous instead of intermittent, and having the manager report directly to the executive committee of the FOMC instead of to the New York reserve bank, an issue that would return many times (Board of Governors File, box 1433, December 9, 1938). The committee's use of press releases, and its concerns about market reactions, contrasts with its traditional secrecy. The System became aware of anticipations as a strong influence on markets without explicit recognition of why these changes could be helpful.

247. Under Treasury rules, only countries that remained on the gold standard could deal with the Treasury. This excluded Britain.

The dollar weakened early in 1935 when the Supreme Court was about to decide the gold clause cases. United States gold clause bonds went to a premium. Harrison discussed with Morgenthau and Undersecretary T. J. Coolidge what actions the Treasury planned or had under way through the Exchange Stabilization Fund.[248] He wanted the Treasury to develop a policy instead of operating from day to day. Morgenthau agreed to talk to Roosevelt, who controlled the decision (Harrison Papers, file 2012.6, February 18, 1935).

At about this time, Morgenthau asked John H. Williams to suggest a policy. Williams proposed informal discussions with the British. Something had to be done, he believed, because United States gold and silver policies drained gold and silver from all other countries, making both standards untenable. Harrison agreed. Morgenthau relayed the conversation to the president, but Roosevelt would consider cooperation only if the British asked for help (Harrison Papers, file 2013.2, March 2, 1935).[249]

With the pound continuing to weaken against the dollar and the franc, the Bank of France proposed to extend credit of $330 million (Fr 5 billion) if the British would agree to defend the pound and would state, informally, the level they intended to hold. The French asked the New York reserve bank to join in the support operation if the French government approved. Morgenthau discussed the issue with the president, who was ambivalent. The United States offered "sympathetic support" and expressed hope that the pound would not go below $4.86, the old parity (Harrison Papers, Memo J. E. Crane to Files, file 2012.6, March 6, 1935).

The pound continued to fall, reaching $4.776 on average for March. Morgenthau did not pursue the issue of support operations. Instead, he invited some advisers on foreign exchange and domestic prices to dinner on March 5. The topic was further devaluation of the dollar against gold to raise commodity prices. Former governor Eugene Meyer was in favor, but he gave no reason.[250] George Warren and Herman Oliphant favored devaluation. Oliphant wanted the president to announce a price level objective. Harrison, Williams, Viner, and undersecretary Coolidge opposed. Viner

248. T. J. Coolidge served as special assistant to the secretary from March to May 1934 before he became undersecretary, where he served until February 1936. The Treasury had been selling pounds to buy French francs, while the British did the opposite, selling francs and buying pounds.

249. Harrison urged a conversation among technical central bank experts to avoid politics. The Treasury responded that those days were gone; exchange policy was now run in the Treasury (Harrison Papers, file 2013.2, March 2, 1935, 5).

250. Eccles was governor at the time but was not present. Meyer was no longer in the System. J. E. Crane was a deputy governor of the New York reserve bank concerned with foreign exchange operations. He was present at the dinner and summarized the discussion in a memo to Harrison, who was present also. Herman Oliphant was the Treasury counsel at the time and one of Morgenthau's principal advisers.

and Harrison argued that the administration's objective should be to increase business activity and reduce unemployment. Profits, not just prices,
were the key to recovery. Williams supported this position and warned
against further competitive devaluations. With his council divided, Morgenthau did not pursue the idea.

The next move, again, came from France. Still wanting to stay on the
gold standard, and willing to deflate as necessary, the Bank of France requested permission to sell gold to the United States.[251] Morgenthau agreed
to buy up to $150 million on May 31 and to release the dollars for immedi-
ate use in New York or Paris (Harrison Papers, file 2012.5, June 3, 1935).
This support helped to convince the French government that the United
States would cooperate.

Conversations with the British and the French continued sporadically
throughout 1935. Roosevelt, who did not trust the British, was particularly
wary of Neville Chamberlain, then chancellor of the exchequer. He blamed
Chamberlain for the system of empire preference that gave British exports
an advantage in British colonies. And he blamed the British for the failure
of the London Monetary and Economic Conference. They blamed him
(Blum 1959, 141). Despite these antipathies, Morgenthau remained eager
to engage the British and the French in stabilization measures as a means
of strengthening democratic governments against Hitler. He believed that
exchange rate stability would improve prospects for expansion in all three
countries. By 1936 the United States economy was expanding rapidly, attracting gold from the rest of the world; faster expansion abroad would
slow the inflow.[252]

Late in April 1936 Poland, one of the remaining members of the gold
bloc, imposed exchange controls and embargoed gold, effectively leaving
the gold standard. The pound fell slightly. Morgenthau used the opportunity to convince Roosevelt to permit him to begin conversations with the
British about stabilization. Since the president's authority to devalue had
expired at the end of January, the United States was less able to threaten independent action. The British eventually replied to his overture, and to
Morgenthau's insistence on greater transparency in their actions, by stat-

251. One reason for pressure on the franc-gold price was the continued gold drain to the
United States. The more immediate cause was the crumbling of the Latin Monetary Union,
the last gold bloc. Belgium devalued in April. Italy, the Netherlands, and Switzerland did not
devalue until the following year, 1936, but Italy adopted extensive exchange controls, contrary
to gold standard rules.

252. Contemporary Federal Reserve explanations of the inflow gave primary responsibility to relatively strong United States expansion and uncertainty about devaluation by the
gold bloc countries. It did not mention the $35 gold price (memo, Despres to Sproul, Sproul
Papers, December 5, 1935).

ing their aims. They wanted to return, eventually, to a reformed gold standard, but they were not ready to commit to such a move. They wanted to retain the right to devalue if necessary. Within that framework, they welcomed cooperation. Morgenthau was pleased by these conditions. He suggested further discussions between the two treasuries, avoiding the central banks (Blum 1959, 142–43).

The French elections of May 1936 accelerated the conversation. A coalition of leftist parties, known as the Popular Front and including the Communist Party, came to power under the leadership of a Socialist, Leon Blum. Their platform did not put forward a clear monetary program. The Socialists were willing to consider devaluation, but the Communists opposed (Kindleberger 1986, 252). Morgenthau favored devaluation of the franc by 15 percent but opposed a French gold embargo. Several of his advisers were willing to accept a 25 percent devaluation (Harrison Papers, file 2012.6, June 9, 1936).

The British used the market disturbance resulting from French strikes, the election, and concerns about devaluation to request authority to purchase gold directly from the United States Treasury. Morgenthau, as usual, took the issue to Roosevelt, who objected. But Morgenthau managed to convince the president of the importance of a French devaluation followed by stabilization of the pound, franc, and dollar. The next day Roosevelt agreed to let Morgenthau sound out the British on a program to let the franc devalue by 25 percent without any retaliation by the United States or Britain (Blum 1959, 145–47).

France was the stumbling block. In a pattern later followed by socialist governments in Chile, France, Peru, and elsewhere, Blum and his finance minister, Vincent Auriol, believed they could raise wages and reduce the workweek to forty hours without devaluing. To add to their mistakes, they allowed firms to borrow from the Bank of France at a 3 percent interest rate to cover the additional employment costs. The government guaranteed the loans.

The program increased costs and raised prices. In the Blum government's first year, French wholesale prices rose 47 percent. Blum and Auriol had pledged to maintain the franc's gold parity, but they left room for an adjustment in its value as part of an international agreement. In fact, they had few choices. Faced with a continuing loss of gold, they could devalue or resort to exchange controls. Morgenthau's offer of assistance, and his use of sanctions against Germany, convinced the new government that a cooperative agreement was possible.[253] They sent a special repre-

253. Germany used currency manipulation—discounts of the mark for purchases in Germany, export subsidies, and other policies—to expand exports. The Treasury claimed these actions violated the 1930 Tariff Act, so they required retaliation. The State Department

sentative to meet Morgenthau to discuss international monetary relations.[254]

The Tripartite Agreement

To remain on the gold standard, France and the gold bloc had followed deflationary policies in 1934–35. By the summer of 1935, French wholesale prices were 51 percent of their 1929 average. The policy would have worked had it been followed long enough, but the cost was high, and the policy had become unpopular. There were two problems. First, devaluation of the dollar and the increased United States gold price drained gold from France. Second, as a consequence of continued deflation, the gold bloc countries faced increasing unemployment or lower wages at a time of recovery in Britain, Germany, and the United States.[255]

Beginning in summer 1935, repeated efforts to deflate by balancing the budget, reducing wages and pensions, and other means failed to stop inflation. Chart 6.7 shows that French prices began to rise absolutely and relative to prices abroad. Eichengreen (1992, 367–74) describes the response; successive governments blamed the unbalanced budget. They promised to do better.[256] If fiscal stringency did not work, many said, the answer was more stringency.

In the year before the Blum government took office, French wholesale prices rose 15 percent. By September 1936 the French price level was back to 67 percent of the 1929 average. This compares with 86 percent and 78 percent for the United States and Britain. In August, before the franc devaluation, the real dollar-franc exchange rate was 4.8 cents, about 20 percent above the 1929 rate.

The Blum government hesitated to act. The final push came after renewed weakness of the franc against the dollar and the pound in August 1936. The French wanted the dollar and pound to remain fixed if they de-

---

objected, but the solicitor general found for the Treasury. Roosevelt agreed. On June 4, the United States ordered countervailing duties (Blum 1959, 149–53).

254. Governor Montagu Norman usually took his vacation in Maine. In June 1936 he expressed interest in coming to Washington during July to confer with Morgenthau and Eccles. Morgenthau talked to Roosevelt, who was concerned that, since no agreement was contemplated, the press would decide that the meeting had failed to reach agreement. Part of the concern may have been an unwillingness to have a policy "failure" so close to the presidential election (Harrison Papers, Conversations with Other Officers of the Bank of England, file 3117.4, June 29, 1936).

255. Eichengreen (1992, 357–74) gives a good account of the problems within the gold bloc. Even before the Popular Front, a French government had tried reflation instead of deflation. As noted in the text, French prices began to rise in 1935 before the election.

256. Eichengreen (1992, 367) notes that in 1935 France lost 20 percent of its gold reserves, the Netherlands 25 percent, and Switzerland 40 percent.

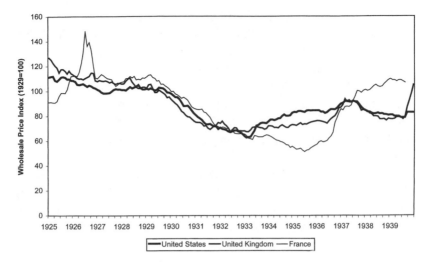

Chart 6.7 Wholesale price indexes (1929 = 100).

valued the franc, and they wanted an agreement to return to the gold standard. Neither the United States nor Britain would agree to fix rates permanently. Roosevelt, Morgenthau knew, would not agree to return to the gold standard.

The French government's position was weak. It had paid out more than one-fourth of its gold stock in nine months and counted on devaluation to provide enough profit on its remaining gold to balance its budget. Morgenthau offered only a general agreement to avoid retaliation following a French devaluation. He did not mention the gold standard. The British response was similar. The final agreement accepted the main points of the United States statement, although each government used its own wording.[257] The agreement provided funding for a French stabilization fund from half the proceeds of the devaluation. Each country agreed to stabilize exchange rates, one day at a time, by announcing in the morning the price at which it would exchange its currency for gold at the end of the day.[258] The British did not insist that the United States agree to sell gold to stabilization funds, but it did agree to do so on October 12. Belgium, the Netherlands, and Switzerland chose to comply with the agreement. Switzerland

257. The Blum government hesitated to state that it would devalue the franc. It preferred to float the franc but in the end agreed to a devaluation of 25 percent to 34.3 percent with the pound at $5.00 ± 0.10. Roosevelt insisted the pound must be above $4.86 as the United States election approached. Blum (1959, 160–73) gives the details of the discussion and negotiation. The British did not mention $4.86 and did not agree to keep the pound fixed, but they agreed not to force devaluation.

258. The Bank for International Settlements called the arrangement a daily gold settlement system.

and the Netherlands devalued by 28 percent and 20 percent, respectively. Italy also devalued by an additional 33 percent to bring its devaluation to 40 percent since the United States devaluation in 1934.

Morgenthau did not mention the agreement to Eccles or the Federal Reserve until it was final. Like Roosevelt, he wanted to put governments, not bankers, in charge of monetary policy. The Tripartite Agreement was another step in that program. Unlike the 1920s, when Strong and the New York bank ran international monetary policy, the Treasury was now in charge.[259]

Morgenthau was euphoric about the outcome. He believed the agreement was a major step toward peace, economic stability, and prosperity. The Treasury staff shared his enthusiasm, as is common among those who have participated in a long and difficult negotiation.[260] Major newspapers lauded the agreement (Blum 1959, 173; Eichengreen 1992, 380). Harrison was cautious. He probably expressed the view of those who wanted to restore the gold standard when he told Morgenthau that "a stabilization fund to keep the franc within a 10 percent range only added one more flexible exchange [rate]" (Harrison Papers, file 2012.6, September 25, 1936).

In fact, the agreement was more symbolic than substantive. The franc and some of the currencies allied in the former gold bloc devalued their nominal exchange rates by 15 percent to 30 percent of their 1929 values. The dollar and the pound remained close to their predepression nominal parity. Britain and the United States agreed not to respond immediately to the French devaluation, a modest sign of cooperation.

One measure of the agreement is the effect on exchange rates. Table 6.7 shows estimates of exchange rates adjusted for changes in wholesale price levels, a measure of so-called real exchange rates, at selected dates. The top row shows bilateral real exchange rates before the start of the Great Depression. Rows 2 and 3 show these rates after the 1931 British devaluation and the 1934 United States devaluation. Row 4 follows the Tripartite Agreement.

Devaluation restored the 1929 real franc exchange rate for the dollar

259. Eccles's book does not mention the agreement. Harrison was informed and acted as an adviser to Morgenthau, but he could not talk to Eccles or Ransom. When the countries reached an agreement, he called the principal New York bankers, at Morgenthau's request, to ask that they avoid speculating against the three currencies.

260. The Bank of England was enthusiastic also, judging from correspondence between H. A. Siepmann at the bank and Allan Sproul at New York. These men exchanged personal letters, sharing views and information. Siepmann's letter dated October 27, 1936, for example, is sixteen pages of handwritten comments that end by noting that he did not inform the bank's governor of their correspondence (Sproul Papers, Bank of England, November 6, 1936).

Table 6.7   Real Exchange Rates, Selected Dates

DATE	DOLLAR-POUND	DOLLAR-FRANC
June 1929	4.75	0.042
October 1931	3.90	0.040
February 1934	4.71	0.053
October 1936	4.60	0.041

and devalued the real rate for the pound by 3 percent. What a cumbersome and costly way to correct the misalignment of exchange rates after the restoration of the gold standard in the 1920s![261]

The adjustment that the agreement made possible did not produce stability. Chart 6.7 shows that between September 1936 and the start of the United States recession in June 1937, French prices continued to rise relative to United States and British prices; the franc depreciated in real value against the dollar and the pound.

After the Agreement

Harrison telephoned to ask for cooperation from the major bankers on Friday evening, after agreement was reached. Apparently they did not all relay the message to their traders. On Saturday morning the pound began to sink, falling from $5.02 to $4.91. The proximate reason was an order from the Russian State Bank to Chase National Bank to sell £1.2 million for dollars. Morgenthau viewed this as an attempt to subvert his agreement: "He was not going to have the Reds or Communists ruining this program" (Harrison Papers, file 2012.6, September 26, 1936, 9). He ordered Harrison to buy the pounds immediately for the Exchange Stabilization Fund, and he threatened to announce publicly that "the Reds were making an attack on the pound in order to draw it down and spoil the program" (10).[262]

The agreement did not specify who could buy or sell gold at the Treasury. Morgenthau tried to clarify the issue at a press conference in October, but he misstated the policy. By limiting transactions to governments only,

261. The agreement has always had greatest appeal to proponents of currency stabilization policies. See, for example, Kindleberger 1986, 258–59, or Eichengreen 1992, 381–82. See chart 6.1 (above) for more detail on real exchange rates.

262. When Morgenthau called the Chase to get permission to announce the transaction, he learned that the total was £1.2 million, of which £300,000 had been sold on the thin Saturday market before the Exchange Stabilization Fund intervened. After Morgenthau made the announcement, with Roosevelt's permission, at a Saturday press conference, Winthrop Aldrich, president of Chase, informed him that the transaction was a commercial transaction by the Russians to obtain dollars to repay a loan to Sweden. Morgenthau did not dispute the explanation but remained skeptical (Blum 1959, 173–74). And he was happy to show that the bankers, not the government, were doing business with the Russians.

he was more restrictive than he intended, but he would not issue a corrected statement until after the November election (Harrison Papers, file 2012.6, October 13, 1936). Finally, on November 24 the Treasury announced that it would sell gold to treasuries or fiscal agents acting for treasuries (including stabilization funds) that would sell gold to the United States. This statement relaxed the restriction on the Treasury to deal only with gold standard countries, in effect since January 1934. Britain, France, Switzerland, the Netherlands, and Belgium became trading partners.

In 1937 the French began to respond to German rearmament by increasing military spending. The increased spending added to the burden of the Popular Front's social programs and the devaluation. By February the franc was under pressure, falling against the dollar and the pound. Harrison began conversations with the British about stabilization of exchange rates, and the Treasury began intergovernment discussions. At $2.5 billion, French gold holdings were at the lowest level since the 1931 British devaluation. The French suggested that the United States buy $5 million to $10 million worth of francs but not convert them into gold until after the summer tourist season. Morgenthau was shocked. The suggestion "made him break out in a cold sweat" (Blum 1959, 456). The loan would probably have violated the Johnson Act, passed in 1934, prohibiting loans to any foreign government that had defaulted on its war debt.

The French thought they would have to impose exchange controls, violating the Tripartite Agreement. At Neville Chamberlain's urging, bankers arranged a private loan to France, so the agreement continued. The Blum government survived (ibid.).[263]

By March 1937 the franc was under pressure again. The French wanted to arrange a defense loan, payable in dollars, francs, and pounds. The announcement created a storm in Washington, and Morgenthau had to testify that the Treasury viewed the loan as a violation of the Johnson Act, hence illegal (Harrison Papers, file 1610.1, March 8 and 9, 1937; Blum 1959, 461–62).

So it continued, with intermittent disturbances followed by brief periods of calm. Again, as in 1927–29, the main problem was never mentioned: exchange rates were misaligned and, as charts 6.1 and 6.7 show, inconsistent with the relative movements of wholesale prices in the principal countries.

Rumors spread in April that, to slow gold flows, the United States planned to revalue the dollar against gold. Gold flowed to the United States

---

263. Both the United States and Britain wanted the Blum government to survive. Both saw Blum as the strongest antifascist likely to form a government. Morgenthau and Roosevelt also liked his social policies (Blum 1959, 456–57).

from private speculators and the exchange stabilization funds of smaller countries (Kindleberger 1986, 265). The franc weakened again in nominal and real terms. On April 9 President Roosevelt denied any knowledge of a plan to change the gold price. The franc continued to weaken, but the rate of decline slowed temporarily (Harrison Papers, file 2012.7, April 10, 1937).

The Blum government fell in June 1937. The new government promptly devalued the franc by 15 percent but agreed to hold the new range, 3.80 to 3.96 cents, and not seek a competitive devaluation. It wanted only to offset the costs to French industry of the Blum government's social legislation.

Morgenthau accepted the devaluation as within the Tripartite Agreement because the French avoided new controls and announced a buying and selling rate at which they would sell gold. He was able to persuade the British to agree also, although they privately warned the French to avoid a further devaluation (Blum 1959, 478).

For the next year, several French governments, plans, and discussions produced no result. To save the remnants of the agreement, Morgenthau offered to let the French use "temporary" exchange controls (ibid., 500). In May 1938 France again devalued the nominal exchange rate to 175 francs to the pound and 2.8 cents per franc. The more critical real exchange rate was now 3.6 cents per franc, about 12 percent lower than at the start of the agreement. The British did not want to accept the new parity, but they feared even more ending the Tripartite Agreement while facing the prospect of war to stop German and Italian expansionist actions.

Discussions continued about how to use the agreement as a political measure to strengthen the democratic governments. For practical purposes, the agreement ended before the May 1938 devaluation. After Munich, in September 1938, preparations for war increased in Britain and France. Both currencies fell against the dollar in nominal and real terms. The United States continued to regard the agreement as in effect.

What Was Achieved?

Proponents of international cooperation point out that exchange rate variability declined after the agreement. Eichengreen (1992, 382) shows that afterward monthly exchange rates were more stable in leading countries (except France).

This is a modest benefit to put beside the economic cost. The agreement could work only if the new nominal exchange rates were (close to) full equilibrium rates, consistent with stable real exchange rates. Differences in price levels and in economic policies leave little doubt that this was not so. Within six months the real dollar-pound exchange changed by 6 percent.

Try as they did, Morgenthau and Chamberlain could not make cooperation produce stability. The British insisted that the agreement was limited to daily, or short-term, exchange rates and a pledge to avoid using devaluation to improve relative positions.[264] That meant uncertainty about future exchange rates remained. Countries remained free to pursue policies that would result in devaluation. Indeed, the French were engaged in such policies at the time. Instead of criticizing the policies as inconsistent with the agreement, Morgenthau and Roosevelt praised and encouraged them as a French version of Roosevelt's New Deal.

The policies failed. French industrial production had increased 9 percent in the year ending March 1936. Under the Popular Front, production fell; increased costs of production, particularly labor costs, aborted a recovery that was under way, much the same as happened in the United States under the NIRA in summer 1933. Prices rose, requiring devaluation. The agreement postponed devaluation, delaying adjustment. A floating rate would have devalued the currency to reflect the cost increase; the fixed rate forced the adjustment to come through changes in prices, output, and employment.[265]

The agreement had two basic flaws. The first was failure to distinguish between real and nominal exchange rates. Fixing nominal exchange rates forced adjustment of misalignment through price changes. The discussions leading up to the agreement, and after, show no recognition of this central point. Second was the belief that international cooperation was a viable alternative to exchange rate adjustment. Exchange rates and prices were misaligned in the mid-thirties, just as at the end of the twenties. Belief in the gold standard remained strong, however. Prominent economists like Viner and Williams, who advised Morgenthau, and many businessmen and politicians believed that fixing exchange rates under some type of gold standard was evidence of adjustment and a source of stability. What better way to restore stability than to fix exchange rates?

In retrospect, we know now that the agreement ended the major principle of the gold standard—that countries should avoid devaluation as a means of adjustment whatever the cost. If the British devaluation was the

264. They did not fully agree on what the Tripartite Agreement required. As late as December 1937, Sproul and Siepmann exchanged views on such basic questions as the size of permissible fluctuations, responsibility for maintaining stability of the bilateral rate, and the conditions requiring gold shipments (Siepmann to Sproul, Sproul Papers, Bank of England, December 15, 1937).

265. France is the only major country in the 1930s, and possibly the only country, that saw output fall after devaluation. This suggests the extent of misalignment in countries such as the United States, Belgium, and Britain.

first step, the French, Dutch, and Swiss devaluations represent rejection of the principle by the last countries with strong commitments to the gold standard. After 1931–36, devaluation was no longer unthinkable.

As a political measure, the agreement had greater merit. Morgenthau was eager to show the Germans and Italians that the democracies would work together toward a common goal. And Roosevelt overcame some of his suspicions about the British, so he was better prepared to cooperate in a wartime alliance.

POLICY AND WAR PREPARATIONS, 1939–41

The probability of a European war rose and fell in the late 1930s. The first explicit mention of preparations by the reserve banks came at the time of the Munich agreement, on September 8, 1938. The New York directors discussed their policy toward loans on government securities in the event of a war. They reached no decision, but they reopened the subject at the Conference of Reserve Bank Presidents (Presidents Conference) later that month. The main issues were the rates at which the reserve banks would lend on government securities and whether the rates would be higher for nonmember banks, individuals, and corporations. The presidents recommended making their discount rates (1 percent to 1.5 percent) the applicable rates for member banks but using a slightly higher rate for nonmember banks and others (Board Minutes, September 21, 1938, 1–2). The political problem in Europe eased, so they did not make a decision.

By early 1939, real GNP rose above its prerecession peak, with prices slowly falling. Falling prices and economic recovery, plus the threat of a European war, increased the gold flow from $113 million in the first half of 1938 to $1.3 billion in the second half. More than $3 billion followed in 1939.[266] Sterilization had ended, so the monetary base rose 23 percent in 1938 and 20 percent in 1939. Interest rates and risk premiums fell as excess reserves rose.

At the end of 1938, excess reserves were above $3 billion, higher than in August 1936, when the System first increased reserve requirements. A year later, excess reserves were above $5 billion. The gold reserve percentage reached 83.5 percent, the highest level since World War I, but not yet a

---

266. People shipped gold by parcel post. Many of the shipments came from France, although the sender may have lived elsewhere. The Bank of England tried to stop or slow the shipments by getting insurance companies to raise insurance rates, but the insurance business shifted to Swiss companies. In 1938 shipments averaged £1 million per month. By February 1939 shipments reached £4 million per month (telephone conversation with the Bank of England, Sproul Papers, Bank of England, March 13, 1939).

peak. Although excess reserves were again greater than the open market portfolio, the Federal Reserve remained inactive.[267]

Conflict continued between the Treasury and the Federal Reserve over whether to increase the size of the weekly Treasury bill auction. The System wanted a higher bill rate so it would not have to extend portfolio maturity. It hoped that an increased supply of bills would lower the price and raise the yield. Higher short-term rates were expected to raise long-term interest rates, permitting the System to reverse the approximately $100 million (4 percent) increase in the portion of its portfolio with five years or more to maturity.[268] The Treasury opposed. Morgenthau liked the low yields on Treasury bills, so he turned down the request. To prevent a fall in long-term rates, Morgenthau sold $10 million from the Treasury trust accounts. He invited the System to participate in the sale, but it declined because markets were not disorderly. The "strength of the market was due to fundamental causes which would not be reached by the action suggested" (Minutes, Executive Committee, FOMC, March 13, 1939, 2). The fundamental causes were the government's silver purchase policy and the gold inflow at the time of the March 1939 German occupation of western Czechoslovakia.[269]

Concerns about a European war remained high. Pressed by the Treasury for a policy to prevent market disorder in the event of war, the executive committee agreed to share purchases equally with the Treasury until the Treasury had invested all of the balances in the trust accounts, approximately $100 million. After that, the System would purchase on its own up to $500 million, a 20 percent increase in its portfolio.

Eccles made his reasoning clear. After the Treasury exhausted the trust funds, any additional Treasury purchases would come from the Exchange Stabilization Fund, "which would create in the Treasury an open market portfolio of Government securities. . . . This would be undesirable" (Minutes, Executive Committee FOMC, March 14, 1939, 2). He preferred to operate alone, after consultation with the Treasury (3).

Harrison, cautious as usual, agreed to the proposal but asked for a com-

---

267. In March the New York bank acknowledged defeat in its efforts to establish a bill market comparable to the London market, as Strong and Warburg had planned. The directors abolished the bill department and merged bill and securities (governments) operations (Minutes, New York Directors, vol. 45, March 2, 1939, 21).

268. The Federal Reserve did not want to take the risk of a rise in longer-term yields, but it also did not want to sacrifice income.

269. A background memo suggested that the decline in long-term rates resulted from $390 million of purchases by New York banks. The banks wanted to increase their income, so they sold notes and bills and purchased bonds (Board of Governors File, box 1452, March 17, 1939).

mitment to sell the securities after the emergency passed: "There should be no objection . . . solely on the ground that no sales should be made before conditions warranted a change in the present easy money policy" (ibid., 3–4). The committee agreed only to keep an open mind about sales.[270] The following week, the full FOMC authorized the proposed purchase policy.

The presidents and governors again discussed discount policy in the event of a European war. Late in April, the reserve banks agreed to make loans to member and nonmember banks at the discount rate, if collateralized by government securities valued at par. The New York rate was 1 percent, with 1.5 percent at all other banks. The Board approved the policy but agreed not to announce it until a war began.[271] This changed as war approached in late August; the Board wanted to announce the policy as part of a general statement describing its powers and its willingness to serve as lender of last resort. Only the Cleveland bank objected to not waiting for the war to start. By the time the discussion finished, war had started. The Board issued the statement on September 1.

Gold flows increased. As war approached, safety of capital and, later, payment for war materials supplemented the United States gold price as a driving force. By the end of 1940, the United States Treasury owned almost 80 percent of the world's monetary gold (Schwartz 1982, tables SC6 and SC8). The inflow would have slowed without policy action as Treasury gold holdings approached 100 percent of the world's monetary gold stock.

Policy changed first. In March 1941 Congress approved "lend-lease," under which countries allied against Germany or at war with Japan could obtain materials in the United States on loan from the United States.[272]

Before lend-lease, Britain purchased supplies by selling $2.5 billion in

270. After this discussion, the committee discussed how to maintain an orderly market in the event of a major disturbance. Committee members were aware of some dynamic effects of policy. Harrison argued against fixed, or pegged, interest rates because they would encourage market participants to "dump their holdings," since most of them had profits. He proposed an adjustable peg, under the current market. Each day a new price would be set. He did not consider, however, why the adjustable peg would not generate the same expectations and sales by market participants. The committee agreed to the procedure (Minutes, Executive Committee, FOMC, March 14, 1939, 4–5).

271. Only Chicago opposed; it wanted a 4 percent rate for nonmembers. Federal Reserve officials regarded these rates as low, as they were in an absolute sense. Rates on prime commercial paper and banker's acceptances were lower still. The System had inadvertently returned to a penalty rate.

272. The act was initially an amendment to the Neutrality Act, but hostility to foreign aid was strong in the Foreign Relations Committees, so the majority leaders introduced the bill (Blum 1965, 216–17). The act also contained a section authorizing negotiations about the postwar economy. Discussions leading to the Bretton Woods Agreements began under this title.

gold and United States securities formerly held by British citizens. To appease Congress, Morgenthau insisted that they also sell direct investments in United States companies. Lend-lease substituted United States government debt for gold as payment for war material.

Almost immediately, the gold inflow slowed. After rising at a 22 percent annual rate from the start of the European war to first quarter 1941, the base fell at a 4 percent rate for the next three quarters.[273] The banking system's excess reserves reached a peak of $6.5 billion in January 1941. By December, excess reserves had fallen to $3.4 billion.

Criticism of Easy Money

With the economy expanding strongly in the spring of 1939, excess reserves far larger than the (stagnant) open market portfolio, and interest rates on Treasury bills at 0.25 percent or less, the Federal Reserve began considering what it could or should do. Harrison raised the possibility of open market sales in discussions with the New York directors. The directors believed that sales were appropriate (Minutes, New York Directors, vol. 45, June 1, 1939, 94).

Earlier, the Federal Advisory Council had asked the Board at its February meeting to reexamine the effects of "cheap money." The Board rejected the suggestion on grounds that there had been many studies, so not much more could be learned. The council was more forceful in June. The easy money policy, in effect since 1929 (sic), they wrote, expected to stimulate business by making borrowing cheap. The policy had failed. The reasons were that low interest rates reduced saving, weakened the capital position of the banks by reducing their earnings, and made the public and Congress indifferent to the size of the government's debt. The council urged the Board to abandon the policy of extreme easy money (Board Minutes, June 6, 1939, 6–7).

Governor Ransom asked what the council wanted the Board to do. One member proposed open market sales and increased reserve requirements to raise interest rates: "Nothing would be more effective than the resumption of the coinage and circulation of gold and . . . no further devaluation of the dollar." He said that the System should advocate this policy (ibid., 7). Other members agreed on the importance of higher interest rates and pointed to the British agreement to have a minimum 0.5 percent rate on

273. Since gold flows had been the driving force in growth of the monetary base, base growth turned negative in second quarter 1941. Despite rising government expenditure, the economy slowed in the second half of 1941. The Federal Reserve made no open market purchases. In the fourth quarter, industrial production, real GNP, and stock prices fell.

Treasury bills at auctions. Several participants urged open market sales of $100 million to show that the System recognized that rates were too low.

Goldenweiser gave the Board's view. Policy had not forced easy money. Low rates had been brought about by an active policy in 1932. Since that time the System had been passive, except for the increase in reserve requirements in 1936–37. This was "not a policy of restraint, but a preliminary precautionary action to bring the System in touch with the market" (ibid., 12–13). Low rates reflected gold flows, silver policy, and business conditions. The System could make some minor adjustments, but even if the FOMC sold its entire portfolio, excess reserves would be plentiful and would continue to increase: "The System would be deprived of its ability to do anything in the future . . . and would have no source of income with which to pay its expenses" (14).

Goldenweiser's defense of inaction did not convince the bankers. They differed only on the rate at which securities should be sold. Several emphasized that market participants believed long-term rates would continue to fall, so they saw little risk in buying bonds. A signal that the System disapproved of the easy money policy, or was concerned about low bank profits, would change perceptions. Some expressed concern about bank losses and possible failures if war in Europe raised rates in the United States.

The bankers' arguments were largely self-serving, the search for an argument to justify higher portfolio earnings. Goldenweiser's response again showed the persistence of the Riefler-Burgess framework. The Federal Reserve could do nothing. With total member bank borrowing below $5 million and excess reserves above $4 billion and rising, the System was "disconnected" from the market.

Both sides shared a "lending" approach. Neither suggested an aggressive policy of buying long-term bonds, corporate bonds, and other securities to change the relative prices of assets and output and encourage expansion.[274] The bankers would have opposed purchases of long-term securities because, temporarily, their earnings would have declined.

The meeting authorized reductions in the open market portfolio to maintain orderly market conditions. This action was in the direction the bankers wanted. Between June 21 and August 16, the FOMC sold $100 million. Bond yields rose by 0.1 percent. These were the first net sales in any week since March 1933.

---

274. Eccles came closest to this position. He wanted the Treasury to stop the sale of long-term bonds not only to avoid capital losses at banks but to force investors to buy corporates "and thus encourage the private capital market" (memo Harrison to Rouse, Harrison Papers, file 2140.4, August 16, 1939).

War Starts

As Europe moved toward war at the end of August 1939, the Federal Reserve at first was alert to market disturbances, but not active. On August 25 Britain suspended gold payments, formally ending the Tripartite Agreement.[275] The pound fell from $4.53 to $4.44, but the bond market opened unchanged. Harrison met with city bankers to urge them not to sell bonds. During the week to September 1, the System purchased $6.8 million as rates fell.

Eccles reminded Harrison that they had authorization to purchase up to $500 million in the event of a disturbance if war started. This pledge had been made to the president, and he wanted assurance that Harrison would carry it out. Harrison was characteristically hesitant to take decisive action or to disagree with Eccles. With yields at 2.27 percent, they agreed that bonds would not fall below par, about 2.75 percent—a decline of approximately $6 per bond (Harrison Papers, file 2140.4, August 30, 1939, 5–7). On September 1 and 2, the System purchased $139 million as prices fell (System Open Market Account, Board of Governors File, box 1452, September 13, 1939).

Bond prices continued to fall. On September 5 Harrison talked to an excited Eccles, who shifted between proposals to let the market fall and to support it on the way down. Harrison proposed buying at declining yields, pointing out that bondholders were shifting to the equity market and that corporate bonds had fallen more than governments, so governments were out of line.[276]

Between August 30 and September 13, the FOMC bought $800 million, half for the Treasury accounts. Bond yields rose about 0.5 percent. The Federal Reserve continued the policy of following market prices down until, at a meeting in the Treasury on September 12, Morgenthau urged it to let prices "go down faster and with less expenditure of money." He had to sell some new issues soon, and he wanted the market to reach bottom (Harrison Papers, file 2140.5, September 16, 1939).[277]

---

275. The Bank of England sold dollars in large volume during August. New York Federal Reserve records report $235 million from August 10 to August 24, with the daily amounts increasing. The bank told the Federal Reserve of its decision to float the pound the night before the public announcement (Sproul Papers, Bank of England, August 1939).

276. Harrison reports Eccles as saying: "Why try to stabilize at all, why not let it go down 2 or 3 points? I [Harrison] said that was our judgment [to let it open ¹/₂ point down] and if he did not like it, he [Eccles] could take a vote and we would abide by that" (Harrison Papers, file 2140.5, September 5, 1939, 1).

277. With Eccles absent, the executive committee split two to two, so no change was made. The Board members voted to keep the gradual policy. Harrison was angry when the

The System's aggressive purchases, to slow the rise in interest rates, contrast sharply with its passivity throughout the depression. There are only two previous periods in which weekly rates of purchase were closely comparable to the $800 million purchased jointly with the Treasury in three weeks at the war's start. One was in the fall of 1929 when, despite the Board, New York purchased $157 million in two weeks. The other was at the peak of the purchase policy in spring 1932, when the System purchased $640 million in seven weeks.

Three main reasons explain the 1939 purchases. First, the FOMC had discussed for months the policy it should follow in the event of a European war. Eccles had committed to an expansive policy in meetings with the president and the Treasury. The reserve banks had agreed in advance to purchases of up to $500 million for the System account. Second, the objective was to stabilize the money or bond market in the face of an external disturbance. This objective was widely shared and uncontroversial. Unlike New York's effort in October 1929, there were no issues about the inevitable consequences of stock market speculation dividing New York and Washington. Third, low rates were interpreted as "easy" policy, rising rates as evidence of tightening. Neither the Federal Reserve nor the Treasury distinguished between real and nominal rates, so they did not mention, and probably did not recognize, that the war changed real expected returns and risk premiums.

The Federal Reserve agreed to lend to member and nonmember banks at the prevailing discount rate. This was a major change—the first time the System publicly accepted responsibility for systemwide liquidity.[278] As Walter Bagehot had urged, it announced its policy in advance. Although there is no mention of the deposit insurance system, by lowering the risk to the Federal Reserve of lending to nonmember banks, deposit insurance may have contributed to this change.

At the September 18 FOMC meeting, Eccles presented three issues: the speed at which the bond market should decline, the size of purchases during declines, and the timing of purchases. He favored strong resistance to prevent bonds from going below par value (Minutes, FOMC, September 18, 1939, 6.

For the first time in many years, Eccles asked for individual views. The committee was divided. Harrison repeated Morgenthau's view that the System had been too active. He preferred to let the market decline while avoiding disorder by placing bids below current prices. This would revive the

news of the split appeared in the papers. The Treasury believed the committee had opposed action to embarrass the secretary (Harrison Papers, file 2140.5, September 22, 1939, 12–13).

278. New York agreed to hold clearing balances for nonmember banks in 1935 (Minutes, New York Directors, August 22, 1935, 1134).

private securities market and help the Treasury. Roy A. Young (Boston) and John S. Sinclair (Philadelphia) expressed views similar to Harrison's. George Hamilton (Kansas City) wanted aggressive purchases if bonds fell below par, because the public expected it. Most of the others preferred to continue the policy of purchasing to prevent rapid decline and opposed pegging yields.

The committee voted to buy up to $500 million additional if needed to maintain an orderly market. Within a week, the System was able to sell as yields reached a peak and declined. The decline in yields continued for the rest of the year. Sales and retirements brought the account below $2.5 billion by year end, and lower than before purchases began. Bond yields ended the year at 2.30 percent, 0.16 percent above the lowest rates of the year and 0.44 percent below the peak.

The FOMC resumed the quiet life. The December 13 meeting concluded that the System should confine its activity to smoothing the market by buying or selling on a sliding scale when there were few other bids. Again, it explicitly resolved not to peg interest rates.

The policy statement at the December meeting, withdrawing from active play, reflected earlier discussions with the Federal Advisory Council. The council again unanimously approved a statement opposing the "easy money" policy and urging the Federal Reserve to allow bonds to be priced by the market, "free of official intervention" (Board Minutes, October 10, 1939, 2). It approved of actions to prevent a disorderly market but opposed the prevailing actions—sales to force rates back to earlier levels.

Discussion at this meeting was a prelude to discussion of "bills only" in the 1950s. Governor Ransom asked, What is an orderly market? Several members acknowledged that they could not define "orderly." The best the group did was to define an orderly market either as "a natural self-supporting market" that, if perturbed, maintained the new price without panic buying or selling or as a market in which bids and offers were not too far from the last sale (ibid., 4–5). A market was not orderly if there was a single buyer or seller "whose one purpose was to maintain a market" (14).

The members stated forcefully that they opposed "easy money," and they disliked the System's requirement that buyers and sellers had to give their names during the market break.[279] They again suggested a return to the 1920s policy of letting individual reserve banks buy and sell government securities with district banks.

---

279. This requirement remained in effect for only a few days. The idea was to prevent speculative selling. Several bankers argued that it also prevented buying, so the effect was ambiguous at best. The bankers' discussion mentions some of the rumors spread by security dealers to increase transactions volume (Board Minutes, October 10, 1939).

Eccles's main comment is similar to Goldenweiser's statement at the June meeting. He denied that the System influenced the interest rate structure. Any influence was temporary, he said.[280] The System had not bought to maintain "easy money"; the dominating factors were the gold flow and the level of excess reserves.

Three lasting procedural and administrative changes were made at the end of 1939. Although he was a member of the executive committee, Hugh Leach (Richmond) was not included in the frequent telephone conversations between New York and Washington. In response to his complaint, Harrison ordered the manager of the System Open Market Account to call Leach every day at about noon to keep him informed. This is the origin of the daily conference call that continues to the present (Harrison Papers, file 2140.6, November 29, 1939).

Early in November the New York bank nominated Robert Rouse to replace Allan Sproul as manager of the System Open Market Account.[281] At about the same time, the bank adopted new rules limiting trading to "recognized dealers."

Search for a Policy Guide

By March 1940, the pace of decline had slowed. Goldenweiser and Williams regarded the decline as a correction of heavy inventory building after the war started. They proposed no policy action, and none was taken (Minutes, FOMC, March 20, 1940).

The main decision was to undertake a study of the role of open market operations under prevailing conditions—conditions of relatively large and growing excess reserves and minuscule yields on Treasury bills. The study produced the first statement of guiding principles in many years (Memo, Despres to Goldenweiser, Board of Governors File, box 1433, April 29, 1940).[282]

The report began by repeating the explanation of how open market operations worked in the 1920s, made familiar by Riefler and Burgess. The new elements were the large volume of excess reserves and the relatively small supply of short-term assets issued by government and corporations. Monetary policy could work in this environment by changing the interest

280. For several years the FOMC had been trading bonds for shorter-term securities, at times with the announced intention of changing relative yields. Eccles's statement suggests that he concluded that these operations had only temporary effects.

281. Rouse joined the New York bank as assistant vice president on July 1, 1939. He became a vice president when he became manager.

282. Emile Despres was an international economist at the New York bank and later a professor at Stanford University.

rate structure—the relation of short- to long-term rates. Changes in money were irrelevant: "Any volume of expenditure in the markets for goods and services can be financed by any quantity of money" (ibid., 2). The memo illustrated how changes in short-term interest rates induced changes in borrowing, money holding, and spending. The discussion emphasized mainly borrowing costs.[283]

The memo then made a significant break with standard beliefs: "Excess reserves are truly 'excess' only in the legal sense. In an economic sense, they meet the banking system's demand for liquidity which was formerly met by its holding of short-term assets. The willingness of banks to hold their present portfolios of Government securities at existing yields is dependent on the present supply of reserves" (ibid., 4). Goldenweiser's marginal comment: "That I think is doubtful."

The memo applied similar analysis to money holdings. The argument reflected contemporary understanding of Keynes's 1936 *General Theory*. There were fewer alternatives to cash than in the twenties. Money holders had shifted into long-term bonds, but their willingness to hold bonds depended on expectations about future interest rates, and thus on Federal Reserve policy: "If the market believes that the System is prepared to furnish vigorous support to the government security market, holders of high-grade securities will be less disposed to press their holdings on the market" (ibid., 5). By signaling its intentions, the System could shift holders between cash (money) and bonds, with significant effects on long-term rates.

The conclusion was that excess reserves and low short-term rates did not remove the possibility of controlling inflation. With short-term rates near zero, the System had much greater influence over long-term rates than in the past, so it could operate directly on the margin between money and long-term assets (ibid., 5). The memo concluded by urging a policy to promote "expansion now and stability later."

Entrenched views were too strong to overcome. The System continued its inactivity, and the Federal Advisory Council continued its concern for the System's "easy money" policy. At the Board's suggestion, the council developed a statement of the causes of easy money and what might be done. The council wanted the statement published in the next issue of the *Federal Reserve Bulletin*.

The council's statement gave seven main causes of "easy money." Placed first was the Board's easy money policy and "its continuous advocacy" of that policy. The Board had not "set up warning signals against the evil ef-

---

283. Goldenweiser's handwritten comment is, "Availability is more important than cost" (Memo, Despres to Goldenweiser, Board of Governors File, box 1433, April 29, 1940, 4).

fects of the extreme to which it has been carried and of the dangers of its continuance" (Board Minutes, May 21, 1940, 8). The policy began at the end of 1929 and had not been reversed. Instead, bill rates had been pushed to zero, and the System had bought long-term debt (a speculative asset). The government's spending program and deficits also contributed by making the Treasury a proponent of low interest rates, dollar devaluation, silver purchases, and the Johnson Act (prohibiting loans to foreign governments that had defaulted on war debts). Finally, the statement cited the continued gold inflow and discontinued sterilization policy.

The council proposed open market sales, purchases only to offset disorderly markets, sale of Treasury issues to nonbank investors, and jawboning by the Federal Reserve against easy money policy. The quality of the council's understanding is suggested by its simultaneous call for a return to a full gold standard, followed in the very same sentence by a request to resume gold sterilization.[284]

The only proposal that appealed to Eccles came near the end—an increase in legal reserve requirements. He told the council he could think of nothing more injurious to the position of the council than publication of its views. The Board would respond to the statement, bringing the conflict before the public. He urged them to cooperate in a joint statement that might get Congress to act.

Several members of the Board denied responsibility for "easy money." Criticisms of the Board and the administration aside, there was general agreement on the need to end easy money by reducing excess reserves. Governor Szymczak raised the usually unspoken issue. If the System reduced its bond portfolio, "it would be without sufficient earnings and would be forced to go to Congress for appropriations" (Board Minutes, May 21, 1940, 17). Eccles added that only a small amount could be sold before earnings fell below expenses. And he reminded the council that it had publicly opposed giving the Board authority to increase reserve requirements when the Banking Act of 1935 came before Congress.

The outcome was an agreement to work on a joint statement and to invite the reserve banks to join the discussion. In December the Board, the council, and the presidents of the reserve banks agreed on three main recommendations: (1) authority to double reserve requirement ratios from the current maximum to 28 percent, 40 percent, and 52 percent for the three classes of banks; (2) decisions about reserve requirements to be transferred from the Board to the FOMC, where the reserve banks, hence

---

284. The council ended its statement by reciting its opposition to many "artificial" devices. The list includes devaluation, pump priming, taxing undistributed profits, and easy money. These policies had failed, they said.

the member banks, had more influence; and (3) reserve requirements to apply to member and nonmember banks. Eccles explained that he had agreed to the second change to avoid opposition from commercial banks.[285] The discussion and recommendations show no recognition of Emile Despres's memo to Goldenweiser. Excess reserves were treated uniformly as an inflationary threat, "excess" in the economic as well as the legal and accounting sense.

The final draft offered the recommendations as part of defense policy, necessary to prevent inflation from hindering mobilization. In addition to the powers to change reserve requirements, the memo called for repeal of the silver policy, the Thomas amendment authorizing the president to issue greenbacks, and the president's authority to devalue the dollar. These provisions removed several of the irritants that bankers disliked. The memo also suggested that, as production expanded, a rising share of government spending should be financed by taxation.

The Board sent the statement to Morgenthau, who angered Eccles by doing nothing for ten days and failed to endorse the statement or comment on it publicly when it was sent to Congress at the end of December. When long-term bond yields rose (from 1.88 to 1.97), Morgenthau blamed Eccles and declared the increase in interest rates "not warranted" (Eccles 1951, 355). In response to a question, he suggested that Congress was unlikely to act on the statement. He would give his opinion of the policy only if Congress took the proposal seriously (Sproul Papers, Monetary Policy, 1940–41, January 9, 1941). Eccles complained to Roosevelt without effect.[286]

Morgenthau's only policy proposal asked Congress to make interest on all government securities taxable. Dismissal of the joint proposal started a new period of hard feelings and intermittent feuding between the Federal Reserve and the Treasury and between Eccles and Morgenthau. Eccles described the Board's response to Morgenthau's statements as "a mood of impotence and frustration" (Eccles, 1951, 355).

285. Eccles's acceptance of a large role for the reserve banks reversed his position at the time of the 1935 banking act. President Young (Boston) wanted to add to the statement that it was a change from the "easy money" policy, but other presidents opposed. Goldenweiser suggested that the limit be raised to three times present requirements, but it was not adopted.

286. Morgenthau's reaction should not have surprised Eccles. Eccles, Harrison, and Edward E. Brown, chairman of the Federal Advisory Council, presented the statement to Morgenthau on December 19. Morgenthau's response was that issuing the statement might raise interest rates. He promised only to discuss the issue with the president, and he urged Eccles to discuss the matter with Lauchlin Currie, who was then on the White House staff as economic adviser. In conversation with Morgenthau, Roosevelt dismissed both the idea and Eccles: "This is so unimportant, the Federal Reserve system is so unimportant, nobody believes anything that Marriner Eccles says or pays any attention to him" (Blum 1965, 298). Later Roosevelt assured Eccles that everything would "work out all right" (Eccles 1951, 357).

The bankers' criticisms and reconsideration of policy actions had a modest effect on decisions. The FOMC was much less active at the time of the German invasion of the Netherlands, Belgium, and France and the fall of France in May and June.[287] The FOMC authorized sales at the May meeting, to prevent disorderly conditions. It made a few sales in June, as interest rates fell. During the autumn, sales increased. Between September and December the FOMC sold $250 million, more than 10 percent of the portfolio. By December, members expressed concern about whether the portfolio would be large enough to pay the reserve banks' expenses and dividends. Authority to prevent disorderly markets replaced the authority to sell (Minutes, FOMC, December 18, 1940, 10). The FOMC made no further purchases or sales until the United States entered the war a year later. During most of this period, long-term bond yields remained between 1.9 percent and 2 percent. The gold stock rose above $22 billion, and excess reserves reached $5 billion. On November 1, 1941, with inflation above 10 percent, the Board reversed the 1938 reduction in reserve requirement ratios, returning to the maximum values and removing approximately $1.5 billion of excess reserves.

Disputes ended when the United States entered the war. In December 1941 the Board adopted a statement assuring the public and the administration that it was "prepared to use its powers to assure that an ample supply of funds is available at all times for financing the war effort and maintaining conditions in the United States Government security market that are satisfactory from the standpoint of the Government's requirements" (Minutes, FOMC, Board of Governors File, box 1433, April 4, 1950).

Controls and Regulations

Treasury intransigence about interest rates helped to shift the Federal Reserve's focus toward selective controls. Soon after President Roosevelt declared an emergency. He used his emergency powers to order controls on consumer credit in summer 1941. The Board issued regulation W setting rules for credit allocation and down payment requirements, effective

287. German conquests raised the issue of ownership of gold earmarked and held for foreign central banks. An executive order, issued on April 10, 1940, extended the president's authority, under the Trading with the Enemy Act (1917) and the Emergency Banking Act of 1933, to license all transfers between banking institutions in the United States and abroad. The order explicitly protected Norwegian and Danish gold from transfer to Germany. It was extended later to include other countries. On April 19 the order was extended to include transfer of stocks, bonds, or any property in which a foreign state or national had an interest (Board Minutes, April 23, 1940, 12–14). In May the board agreed to assist the Vatican by accepting deposit of its gold under earmark at the New York bank (Board Minutes, May 22, 1940, 1–3).

September 1, 1941. Eccles believed the controls would help the defense effort by restraining consumer spending, particularly spending on durable goods. He expected in this way to reduce inflationary pressure.

The Board's announcement of credit controls warned about what was ahead—price controls, rationing, and allocation: "Our people can not spend their increased incomes and go into debt for more and more things today without precipitating a price inflation that would recoil ruinously upon all of us" (Board Minutes, September 1, 1941, 2–3). The Board's announcement recognized that credit controls are "a supplemental instrument to be used in conjunction with the broader, more basic fiscal and other governmental powers in combating price inflation" (3).

Controls were supposed to work by restricting demand. They work only if the public does not spend on other goods or services but saves instead, and if it uses the saving to finance government spending. Credit controls alone have little effect on aggregate demand.

To Eccles's credit, he did not rely only on controls. He strongly urged higher taxes and higher interest rates to finance defense and wartime spending (Hyman 1976, 278–81). Morgenthau opposed. The two protagonists changed sides. Eccles, who had favored government investment and larger deficits to increase output and employment, now wanted smaller deficits and increased taxes. Morgenthau, who had abhorred deficits in the 1930s, welcomed them as an inexpensive way of financing defense and wartime spending.

Earlier the Board had made the facilities of the Federal Reserve System available to finance construction of defense plants. The Board set rates as low as 1.5 percent, the discount rate at most reserve banks, for loans to finance these facilities. The maximum rate was 4 percent (Board Minutes, October 7, 1940, 2–3).

PERSONNEL AND ORGANIZATIONAL CHANGES

Harrison left the New York Bank at the end of 1940 to become president of New York Life Insurance Company. Although his resignation was effective on July 1, the Board asked him to postpone his departure until the end of the year.[288] Allan Sproul succeeded Harrison as president of the New York reserve bank, and Leslie Rounds replaced Sproul as first vice presi-

---

288. There is a hint in the New York directors' minutes that Harrison was annoyed by the board's refusal to approve his salary increase for 1940. Discussions of senior officers' salaries became more contentious in the late 1930s.

289. Sproul began service as head of research at the San Francisco reserve bank in 1920. In 1924 he became secretary of the bank. He moved to New York, as secretary, in 1930, then became, in turn, assistant to Harrison, account manager, and first vice president. He re-

dent.[289] At the same time, Owen Young completed his long service as director and chairman of the bank's board. Under the 1935 act, he could serve only six years.

Under the Banking Act of 1935, Boston and New York shared a seat on the FOMC. In practice, Boston ceded the seat to New York by agreeing each year that Roy Young would serve as Harrison's alternate. Harrison's resignation reopened the issue. A committee of Boston and New York directors recommended that Boston should be moved to a different group so that Young (and his successor) could serve as a member of the FOMC. New York would hold a permanent seat. This required an amendment to section 12A of the Federal Reserve Act.

Pending the legislative change, the directors agreed to have Sproul serve for the first year and Young (or his successor William Paddock) serve in the second year. The Board was unwilling to sponsor the legislation, so it was not presented (Minutes, New York Directors, May 1941). Perhaps because of the war, Boston agreed to suspend the agreement in 1942, so Sproul continued as a member of the FOMC with Paddock as alternate.

In August 1942, Congress amended section 12A to make New York's president a permanent member of the FOMC with its first vice president as his (or her) alternate. Boston moved to a three-year rotation. Cleveland and Chicago shared the only remaining two-year alternation.[290]

To cooperate with the defense effort, the Board approved a letter to the president in June 1940, offering use of the facilities of the Board and the reserve banks and the services of the System. The offer included the directors of the reserve banks, members of the Federal Advisory Council, and the System's staff. The Council on National Defense used the facilities.[291]

---

mained as president until June 1956. Sproul's initial salary was unchanged at $32,500. In March 1941 he was appointed to a five-year term at a salary of $45,000 (approximately $500,000 in the late 1990s).

290. In 1940 the Board discussed employment of married women whose husbands worked. It declined to reappoint a woman draftsman to a permanent position because she was married to a man who was employed (not at the Board). Governor Ransom was the only member to argue that "women should have the same right to a career as men" (Board Minutes, June 27, 1940, 2–4).

291. To Eccles's consternation, one user of the System's resources wanted to take them over for the duration of the war. In December 1941, a meeting of the chief military advisers to the United States and British governments took place in the Federal Reserve's boardroom. The United States Joint Chiefs admired the Board's building and proposed to move in. They suggested the Board could move to Maryland. The meetings are known as the Arcadia Conference. Twelve meetings were held. Eccles successfully defended the Board's territory by ceding some space to the military. As in most matters of great urgency, the president decided the issue. The Board remained in its home. See Hyman 1976, 282–84, for a more complete account of the incident.

RECOVERY FROM DEPRESSION

In 1940 more than 8 million people, 14.6 percent of the labor force, were counted as unemployed. As Darby (1976) noted, some of these people were on work relief or other government work programs. Allowing for Darby's suggested correction reduces the unemployment rate to 9.5 percent.[292] The usual interpretation of these data is that until wartime spending began, economic policies were unsuccessful. Since gold inflows provided substantial growth of money and low market interest rates, this interpretation suggests that monetary policy was weak or impotent. Table 6.8 gives selected data for the period.

The data show that the labor force grew by 7 million persons, but employment was the same in 1940 as in 1929 and below 1929 in all the intervening years. The economy did not absorb, net, any of the increase in population and labor force, facts that Morgenthau recognized at the time (Blum 1965, 24). Further, hours of work were about 14 percent smaller at the end of the period. Real GNP rose modestly, less than 2 percent, and per capita real GNP rose only $50 for the eleven-year period as a whole.

The experience raises two central questions: First, why after more than ten years was the recovery incomplete before war and defense spending restored high employment and more complete use of resources? Second, why was economic activity more responsive to government spending for war and defense than for public works and relief?

The Roosevelt administration did not have a uniform answer. At first the administration seemed optimistic that its program would work. By 1937–38, doubts set in. Within the government, many concluded that monopoly pricing by utilities, construction firms, and large manufacturers slowed the recovery. Morgenthau believed that "the best way to stimulate building was to knock down building costs" (Blum (1959, 414). For a change, Eccles agreed: "Big business was exploiting the bad times [in 1938] to drive for repeal of New Deal reforms" (ibid.). The president told Congress in 1938: "One of the primary causes of our present difficulties lies in the disappearance of competition in many industrial fields, particularly in basic manufacture where concentrated economic power is most evident and where rigid prices and fluctuating payrolls are general" (quoted in Cox 1981, 179). To counter monopoly power, the administration began an active antitrust campaign, and Congress ordered an investigation of pricing

---

292. As new opportunities developed in 1940–41, workers made substantial shifts out of work relief. This suggests that counting this employment as equivalent to private employment overstates employment.

Table 6.8   Income, Output, Employment, and Hours, Selected Dates, 1929–40

DATE	LABOR FORCE	EMPLOYMENT	NUMBER UNEMPLOYED	LABOR HOURS PER WEEK IN MANUFACTURING	REAL GNP ($)
1929	49.2	47.6	1.6	44.2	203.6
1933	51.6	38.8	12.8	38.1	141.5
1937	54.0	46.3	7.7	38.6	203.2
1938	54.6	44.2	10.4	35.6	192.9
1940	56.2	47.5	8.1	38.1	227.2

Source: Economic Report of the President, February 1971.
Note: Labor force, employment, and unemployed are in millions. Real GNP is in billions of 1958 dollars.

practices to show how monopoly power hurt consumers and delayed or prevented recovery.[293]

Alvin Hansen (1938) explained the incomplete recovery as the result of secular stagnation. Investment opportunities had declined, and the economy was mature. This explanation extended the Keynesian argument for government spending and deficits as a cure for the problems of the time.

Many businessmen took the opposite view. Government deficits were part of the problem. Morgenthau and some others in the administration, including at times the president, held firmly to this view. They believed that deficits promoted lack of confidence and fear of inflation.[294] At the Federal Reserve, Harrison held strongly to this view, as did much of the banking community in New York.[295] One variant, found in Williams's memos to Harrison, is that low-risk government debt permitted banks to earn a profit without taking lending risk. Hence bank lending remained low.

The argument about harmful effects of deficits is difficult to reconcile with the facts. The total increase in government debt from 1932 to 1940 was $23.8 billion. Even if the entire decline in private debt ($8.5 billion) is considered to have been "crowded out" in these eight years, the increase in outstanding debt is relatively small. Most of the increase ($16.4 billion) oc-

293. The Temporary National Economic Committee (TNEC) was organized to study concentration. Adolph Berle had proposed antimonopoly policy as a means to recovery in 1933. Berle's argument requires increasing monopoly power, not just its presence.

294. Morgenthau also believed that a low interest rate was evidence of public confidence in government.

295. This argument carried some weight in Congress. In 1939 Congress defeated some of the administration's spending proposals. Assistant Treasury Secretary Hanes told Harrison: "Business must show that it has the power to recover through private spending before Congress reconvenes; otherwise, it is very likely that the next Congress, convening in an election year, will resort to unbridled public spending" (Harrison Papers, file 2150.2, August 16, 1939). Hanes added: "The action of both Houses in turning down the President's spending program . . . was intended as a very definite evidence of a change in the trend and an attempt to give business its chance" (ibid.). Harrison agreed but did not think the action went far enough.

curred during the years of rapid recovery, 1932 to 1936. In the five following years, 1940 to 1945, government debt increased $207.7 billion without provoking concerns that prevented expansion. In fact, bankers responded positively to the president's declaration of an emergency and his announcement of increased defense spending. Within a few days, the same bankers who had opposed deficits and repeatedly urged a balanced budget told Harrison about "their existing desire and ample capacity to finance the credit requirements . . . which might arise from the preparedness program" (Minutes, New York Directors, June 13, 1940, 95).[296]

Businessmen did not limit their criticism and antagonism to deficits. There were frequent complaints about high tax rates, the undistributed profits tax, regulation of securities markets, licensing of foreign exchange, and devaluation. In fact, corporate income tax rates rose sharply under the Hoover administration to forestall criticism of unbalanced budgets. The Roosevelt administration did little to increase these rates before 1938. Chart 6.8 compares the maximum corporate tax rate for the period with average marginal tax rates paid by individuals. The highest corporate and individual tax rates (note the different scales) are at the end of the period, so they cannot explain both the sluggish recovery earlier and the robust wartime expansion.[297] Although the increased marginal tax rates in the 1930s were a deterrent, any deterrent effect was dominated by other factors, including the pace of recovery.

Personal income tax rates rose a bit more than corporate rates under the New Deal, but until 1941 the average marginal personal tax rate remained in the range 3 to 5 percent. From the 1940s to the 1980s, the average marginal rate was 20 to 25 percent.[298]

The different explanations for the sluggish recovery offered in the late 1930s show that many contemporary observers accepted the conclusion that the recovery was slow. Here it seems useful to distinguish between early and later views, between explanations applicable to the entire period, like complaints about the New Deal, and those that were offered after 1937–38, when there is more of a puzzle about the absence of full recovery.

296. The New York bankers asked Harrison to send a letter to the National Defense Advisory Commission in Washington to affirm their interest in lending for industrial expansion and preparedness.

297. At an income of $10,000, relatively high in the 1930s, a taxpayer paid an average effective rate of 0.9 percent in 1928, 6.0 percent in 1932, and 5.6 percent in 1938. At $100,000 the rates are 14.9 percent in 1928, 30.2 percent in 1932, and 33.4 percent in 1938 (Bureau of the Census 1960, 217).

298. The undistributed profits tax is not included, but that tax was more a nuisance than a revenue raiser. Excess profits tax was levied also, but average corporate tax payments remained at about 14 percent of corporate income.

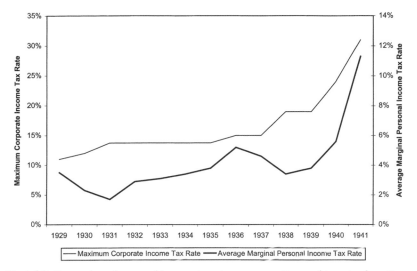

Chart 6.8 Corporate and personal income tax rates, 1929–41. Personal tax rates from Barro and Sahasakul 1983; corporate tax rates from Economic Almanac 1953–54.

Table 6.9 uses real GNP data from Balke and Gordon (1986) to compare the speed of recovery from deep recessions. These data suggest that, relative to the length and severity of the decline, the speed of recovery was not very different from 1933 to 1937 than it was in the 1890s or 1920–21. Recovery from the 1929–33 depression was not especially slow in the early years; real GNP rose 17.5 percent and 9.8 percent, respectively, in 1935 and 1936. Table 6.10 shows growth of real GNP from Balke and Gordon (1986) and total return on common stocks from Ibbotson and Sinquefeld (1989). These data suggest that much of the problem lies in the period after 1937.

Two striking features of table 6.10 are that stock prices fell after the 1937–38 recession despite the recovery and output recovered at a relatively rapid rate. By 1940, real GNP had passed the 1929 or 1937 level. We know from table 6.8, however, that average labor hours in manufacturing were no higher in 1940 than in 1933, and more workers were counted as unemployed in 1940 than in 1937.

Other Explanations

Kindleberger's explanation emphasizes international external policy and policy coordination:

> The explanation in this book is that the 1929 depression was so wide, so deep, and so long because the international economic system was rendered unstable by British inability and U.S. unwillingness to assume responsibility for stabilizing it by discharging five functions: (1) maintaining an open

Table 6.9   Recoveries from Deep Recessions

RECESSION	QUARTERS TO TROUGH	QUARTERS TO 50 PERCENT RECOVERY	QUARTERS TO 90 PERCENT RECOVERY	QUARTERS TO 100 PERCENT RECOVERY
1893.1–1893.4	3	10	10	10
1895.4–1896.4	4	7	7	8
1920.1–1920.4	3	4	6	7
1929.3–1933.1	14	22	29	40

Source: Data from Balke and Gordon 1986.

Table 6.10   Real Growth and Stock Returns, 1933–41 (percent)

YEAR	GROWTH	STOCK RETURNS	YEAR	GROWTH	STOCK RETURNS
1933	2.8	49.3	1938	7.4	27.7
1934	6.2	–4.5	1939	8.9	–2.7
1935	17.5	43.6	1940	6.0	–11.8
1936	9.8	30.3	1941	8.7	–13.3
1937	–7.8	–36.7			

Source: Data from Balke and Gordon 1986 and from Ibbotson and Sinquefeld 1989.
Note: All growth rates are fourth quarter to fourth quarter except 1933, last three quarters only.

market for distress goods; (2) providing counter-cyclical or at least stable, long-term lending; (3) policing a relatively stable system of exchange rates; (4) ensuring the coordination of macroeconomic policies; (5) acting as a lender of last resort . . . in financial crises. (Kindleberger 1986, 289)

Let us accept the relevance of tariffs as a factor disrupting trade in 1929–31. United States trade barriers fell after 1934, and most research suggests that the aggregate effect of the 1929 increase was small.[299] The failure of the Federal Reserve to serve as lender of last resort is generally accepted as an explanation of 1931–33 but has less relevance for the late 1930s after development of deposit insurance in 1934.

The remaining items put most of the burden of explanation on international factors, particularly exchange rate variability and absence of policy coordination. Kindleberger does not mention the misalignment of real exchange rates, discussed earlier, before and during the depression.

The problem in the 1930s, as on other occasions, was that unemployment and misaligned exchange rates required countries to choose. High employment, freedom of capital, trade, and exchange, and price and exchange rate stability could not be achieved simultaneously. Some countries sacrificed fixed exchange rates and capital mobility to increase domestic

299. In Meltzer 1976 I point to the role of the 1929 Smoot-Hawley Tariff and retaliation for its effects on trade, but mainly on gold flows. Most research suggesting a small effect ignores the pronounced effect on farm exports, distress, bankruptcies, and bank failures in farm states.

employment. President Roosevelt's choice, in 1933–34, of domestic expansion over international stability was a major reason for United States recovery in 1934–36. International cooperation to maintain fixed exchange rates required a different set of choices. France, Belgium, Switzerland and the rest of the gold bloc made this choice until 1935. Results were poor. Deflation continued.

Policy coordination can solve problems of misalignment only if countries are willing to adjust their tax, spending, and monetary policies to benefit their partners. Given the political difficulties that many countries, including France and the United States, faced in adjusting spending and tax policies for domestic reasons, the required cooperation was unlikely.

It was also unnecessary. Exchange rate changes were a readily available substitute. To argue that exchange rate changes led to competitive devaluations misses the point. There is every reason to expect that countries seeking relative advantage through devaluation would have chosen other policies to gain relative advantage, as Germany did.

The main difficulty with Kindleberger's argument is that it misstates the central problem. The sluggish decline in United States unemployment was mainly a result of domestic policy. The decline in the United States was larger and deeper than in the principal European countries, but the recovery after 1933 was also more robust. Chart 6.9 shows comparative data for real GNP growth in six advanced countries.

The recovery of German GNP, based on armaments and autarky, is the only one that surpasses that of the United States, and only for a few years. Until the policy mistakes of 1937, real GNP growth in the United States seemed certain to pass the 1929 level. Relative to the other developed countries, the United States recovery until 1937 was strong, not weak.

Unemployment rates tell a different story. The reported unemployment rate declined more slowly in the United States than in Europe and was much higher in 1939.[300] Insufficient international cooperation cannot explain this difference. Policy mistakes in 1937 are again part of the explanation, but the United States unemployment rate remained relatively high before the 1937–38 recession, despite its relatively strong recovery. Chart 6.10 shows these data.

Wages and Profits

Recent research on wages and employment during the recovery concludes that New Deal wage and labor policy acted as a negative shock to the supply

300. Correcting for part or all of the relief workers, as in Darby 1976, would alter this statement only slightly. Unemployment in Switzerland and the United Kingdom had fallen to about 6 percent in 1939. Darby's measure is 9.5, slightly above Sweden.

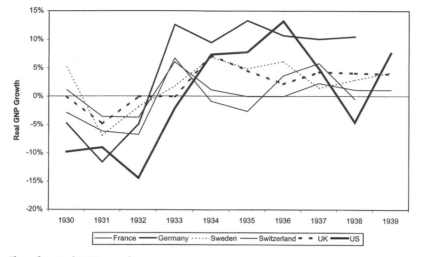

Chart 6.9 Real GNP growth, 1930–39.

of output by raising wages and encouraging labor unions. In 1933 and 1934, as we have seen, the NIRA established codes that raised wages in many industries. Subsequently the Wagner Act (1935) strengthened trade unions and led to the organization of labor in the steel, automobile, rubber, and other manufacturing industries. Strikes and occupation of plants achieved settlements that recognized unions and further raised wages. In 1938 the Fair Labor Standards Act introduced a minimum wage and maximum hours of work.

When demand rose rapidly, as in 1935–36, profits rose despite higher wages. Hourly wages in manufacturing continued to increase in 1937 and 1938 despite the recession and the reduction in hours of work. Chart 6.11 shows that after 1938, growth of profits is much slower absolutely and relative to wages.[301] Further, stock prices fell in 1939, 1940, and 1941, and prices of large company shares fell relative to small company shares, suggesting that profits were not expected to increase strongly, particularly at larger companies most subject to government and union pressures.[302]

301. The profit series from Barger 1942 is not comparable in coverage to the Commerce Department Series, so I have not attempted to combine the two series and have omitted 1939, the transition year.

302. Silver and Sumner (1995) find strong support for the negative effect of wage policy on output. Their findings show considerable difference in the effect of wage growth on growth of industrial production in the 1920s and 1930s. They attribute the large negative effect in the 1930s to New Deal wage policy. As noted above, Weinstein (1981) estimates that NRA codes raised real wages in manufacturing 12 percent a year in 1933 and 1934. Bordo, Erceg, and Evans (1997, charts 14 and 18) show the very rapid rise in real wages and the sluggish increase in hours worked noted earlier.

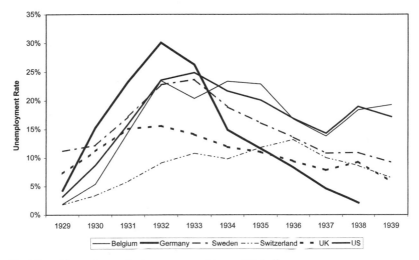

Chart 6.10 Unemployment rates, 1929–39. Source: Mitchell 1992.

Chart 6.11 compares rates of change of nominal profits and nominal wages from 1935 to 1941. Note the difference in scales. Growth of profits declined well before the 1937 recession and (based on a different data series) increased more slowly after the recession. The economy entered the recession with rising wage growth and falling profit growth. After the recession, wage growth continued to increase, contributing to the low level of optimism about future profit growth that stock prices reflected at the time.

Productivity growth appears to be a principal factor affecting stock prices, most likely by changing the growth rate of expected future earnings. Chart 6.12 shows that the two series move together from 1933 to 1938. Thereafter they diverge; productivity growth exceeds growth of stock prices after 1938. Stock price changes for this period support the finding in chart 6.11 based on the less reliable profits data. Together the two charts suggest that after the 1937–38 recession, both profit growth and expected future profits fell.

Real wages remained above average productivity through most of 1933–40. New Deal labor policies were a common complaint. If the data for manufacturing in chart 6.13 are representative of the economy, two periods dominate these years. The first, 1933–35, corresponds to the NRA period but also to the start of recovery. The second, 1937–38, includes the wages and hours legislation and mandatory minimum wages. It follows the period of militant union organizing. Following both periods, productivity remained below real wages.

The data on productivity and real wages correspond broadly to the patterns shown by profits after 1936. There are too few observations to pre-

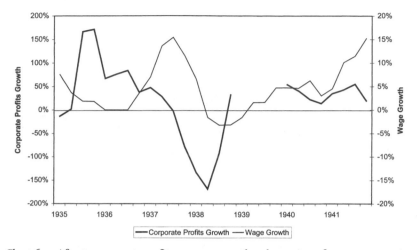

Chart 6.11 After-tax corporate profits versus average hourly earnings, four-quarter moving average rates of change: 1934–38, data from Barger 1942; 1939–41, data from Department of Commerce.

cisely separate current and lagged effects of cyclical and New Deal changes. Nevertheless, the evidence is consistent with a number of studies suggesting that New Deal labor legislation increased unemployment rates by raising costs of employing labor (Weinstein 1981; Silver and Sumner 1995; Cole and Ohanian 1999).

New Deal labor policies emphasized demand. Proponents of these policies expected higher wages, and higher incomes, to stimulate demand through the income effect. In labor markets, as in agricultural markets, the policies ignored or minimized the effect of relative price changes, later called supply-side changes.

Political calculation and economic beliefs are not easily separated in the policy process. Particularly after 1936, the president and parts of his administration reinforced the concerns of businessmen with rhetoric suggesting that additional costly changes were more likely than a retreat from the policies that increased costs of production and lowered profits.

For the postwar years 1962 to 1984, Fallick and Hassett (1998), building on Rose 1987, test the hypothesis that unionization is a tax on capital. They find that, on average, union certification is equivalent to a thirty percentage point increase in the corporate tax rate. Applied to the 1930s, this finding suggests that rising unionism, encouraged first by the NIRA and later by the Wagner Act, may explain both rising real wages and the sluggish growth of investment in the 1930s. The possible effect is large; union membership rose from 11 percent of the labor force in 1933 to 27 percent in 1941. The largest jump came in 1937 (Freeman 1998, 292).

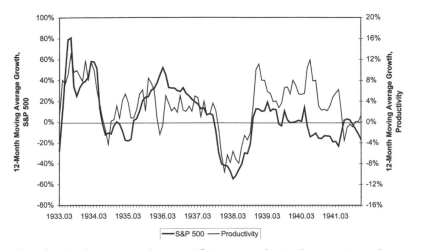

Chart 6.12 Productivity growth versus S&P 500 growth, March 1933 to December 1941. Source: National Bureau of Economic Research database index of output per man-hour, manufacturing.

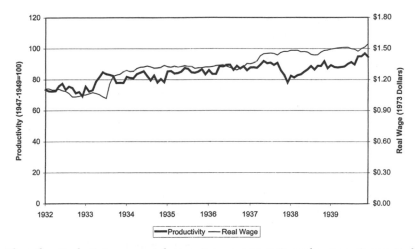

Chart 6.13 Productivity versus real wage, January 1932 to December 1939. Source: Real wages in manufacturing from Bureau of Labor Statistics, 1932–59; productivity from National Bureau of Economic Research, 1932–51.

Chart 6.13 shows that real wages again rose rapidly in 1941. Yet unemployment fell, and most explanations based on the stifling effect of New Deal policies, taxation, and regulation do not apply to the defense and war period. Nor do they apply to the postwar period, when high rates of taxation and many regulations remained. If New Deal regulations are part of the explanation for the thirties, by the end of the decade their effect was probably more on prices and exchange rates than on profits. And by 1940

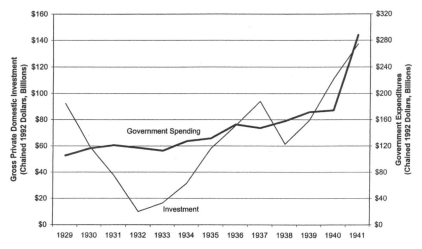

Chart 6.14 Real gross private domestic investment and government expenditures, 1929–41. Source: Bureau of Economic Analysis.

the president and most of his administration sought cooperation. Antibusiness rhetoric declined.

Frequent unanticipated changes in policy may have been important also. The New Deal had little coherence and little continuity. Roosevelt was proud of his commitment to experimentation and not much concerned with consistency. The NIRA and the AAA sought to raise prices. The antimonopoly rhetoric and the antitrust drive aimed to prevent price increases or to lower prices. The administration shifted also on balanced budgets, the role of gold, devaluation, and many other issues. Policy changes, reinforced by changing rhetoric, maintained a state of flux in which long-term planning was difficult.[303] As Alvin Hansen remarked at the time, "Businessmen avoided as much as possible long-term capital commitments" (quoted in Roose 1954, 174).

In contrast, defense (and later wartime) spending was both larger and expected to continue longer. President Roosevelt's declaration of an emergency in June 1940 was the beginning of a sustained program. A permanent expansion replaced temporary experiments. Output and employment responded to the permanent change and perhaps to the changes in rhetoric and practice. To manage the defense buildup, the president appointed

303. Higgs (1997) makes a persuasive case for heightened uncertainty about what the administration intended. There was also concern with what it did, for example, abrogating the gold clause in contracts, regulating small details, and prosecuting even very small businesses that violated the NRA codes or later legislation.

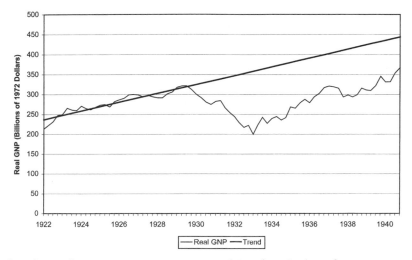

Chart 6.15 Real GNP versus 1922.1 to 1929.4 trend. Data from Gordon 1982.

leading Republicans—Frank Knox and Henry Stimson—to the cabinet, and leading businessmen to the new defense agencies.[304] Chart 6.14 shows the increase in real government spending and private investment. The slope of the real investment line increases in 1940 and 1941.

Chart 6.15 shows one measure of the incomplete recovery. Trend real output growth, at the rate calculated for 1922 to 1929 (based on Balke and Gordon's quarterly data), put 1940 output about 15 percent below the capacity output that would have been achieved if the 1920s trend (2.7 percent) had continued in the 1930s.[305] One reason for using the 2.7 percent growth rate is that recovery from the depths of the recession was rapid to the end of 1936, 11 to 12 percent a year. If the economy had avoided the policy errors that produced the 1937–38 recession, real GNP, on this path, would have reached the 2.7 percent trend line by the end of 1938. No doubt this is an overestimate. Growth would likely have slowed as it approached the old trend. Nevertheless, much of the gap between actual and potential output would have closed before wartime spending began.

304. Recall that Harrison met with New York bankers in the summer of 1940. Many of these men led the criticism of New Deal taxes and deficits. Now faced with much higher tax rates and larger prospective deficits, they wanted Harrison to express their interest in financing defense plants.

305. Admittedly this is a relatively high growth rate, well above the approximate 2 percent average generally used as the trend. I have used the higher rate intentionally for the calculation that follows. At 2 percent growth, the shortfall is less than 10 percent in 1940.

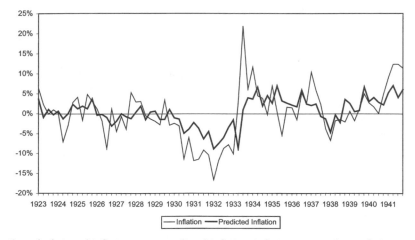

Chart 6.16 Actual inflation versus predicted inflation: inflation regressed on inflation (−1) and M_1 (−1): 1929.4 to 1941.4 forecast based on 1923.1 to 1929.3 regression.

The conclusion I draw is that the 1937–38 recession is part of the explanation for the failure of the economy to fully recover. New Deal labor, and other policies, played a role. That these policies did not prevent recovery of profits, employment, and production after 1940 suggests that, if the deep 1937–38 recession had been avoided, the lasting effect of New Deal policies would have been mainly on the price level and the real exchange rate.

Money and Inflation

Money growth had a major role in the recovery and in the 1937–38 recession. Although the Federal Reserve took few actions, gold flows and gold sterilization changed the rates of growth of money and base money. Chart 6.6 (p. 529) plots the relation between quarterly values of growth in real final sales and growth of real money balances. The association is strong, although there are some large exceptions.[306] The chart suggests that money growth continued to affect spending during the recovery. The chapter appendix shows some statistical analysis.

Finally, chart 6.16 shows the relation between actual inflation and the inflation predicted for 1930 to 1941 using estimates computed from the 1920s. The prediction captures the thrust of actual inflation, again suggesting that the relation of money growth to inflation remained in the 1930s. The chapter appendix shows the underlying relation.

306. McCallum (1990) shows that an adaptive rule for the monetary base captures the main features of the decline and recovery of nominal GNP.

CONCLUSION

The two outstanding features of economic performance from 1933 to 1941 are the strong recovery of output, interrupted by a deep recession in 1937–38 and the weak recovery of employment and investment spending. Together these features tell a consistent story about economic policy.

The main policy stimulus to output came from the rise in money, an unplanned and for the most part undesired consequence of the 1934 devaluation of the dollar against gold. Later in the decade, German mobilization and annexation of the Rhineland, Austria, and Czechoslovakia, the rising threat of war, and war itself supplemented the $35 gold price as a cause of the rise in gold and money.

The United States was on the gold standard after 1934 in the sense that changes in the monetary base were dominated by gold movements and the Treasury agreed to buy or sell gold at a fixed price.[307] At first the Treasury agreed to sell gold only to countries on the gold standard. Later, after few countries remained on the gold standard, it bought and sold gold with other foreign governments and their agencies, but not with United States citizens.

In practice, the Treasury bought all gold offered at the $35 price and issued gold certificates to the Federal Reserve. With market interest rates low and excess reserves accumulating rapidly, the Federal Reserve and the Treasury became concerned about inflation. One response was to return to the gold sterilization policy that the Federal Reserve followed during much of the 1920s. A second response was to remove excess reserves by raising reserve requirements for member banks. In 1935 the Federal Reserve received new powers to increase reserve requirement ratios without presidential approval. In 1936 and 1937 it put the new powers to use.

The two discretionary monetary actions, coming within a brief period and supplemented by the end of the soldiers' bonus, caused a reversal of the rapid economic recovery. The economy returned to recession in 1937–38.

As in 1920–21 and 1929–33, the Federal Reserve took no responsibility for the recession, denied that higher reserve requirements had contributed, and took no expansive actions until late in the recession. The administration increased relief payments but did not initiate countercyclical policy until spring 1938.[308]

---

307. Silver purchases also added to the monetary base, but their contribution was much smaller.

308. Eccles, his principal aide Goldenweiser, and most of the Board denied that the increase in reserve requirement ratios had done more than absorb redundant excess reserves. This view was not unchallenged. A staff memo by Emile Despres later argued the opposite side

The principal force for recovery from the 1937–38 recession came from the decline in prices that raised the real value of the money stock and, later, from the rise in the nominal money stock. As in 1921, both real money balances and real interest rates rose; again the expansive effect of real balances outweighed the contractive effect of real interest rates. With the release of gold from sterilization and a modest reduction in reserve requirement ratios, the nominal stock also rose, followed by a rise in spending.

Although Federal Reserve officials believed that monetary policy was impotent, and this view was widely held in the academic profession, the evidence suggests very strong effects of real money balances on real output during the recovery. (See chart 6.6, for example.) For the period 1933 to 1941 as a whole, there is very little change in monetary velocity. Using Balke and Gordon's (1986) quarterly data, real GNP and the price deflator rose at a compound annual rate of 6.6 and 2.5 percent, respectively. The monetary base rose at a 9.7 percent annual rate, so monetary base velocity changed relatively little over the period.[309] This is consistent with the small change in interest rates, particularly long-term rates. (See appendix chart 6.A1.)

Marriner Eccles headed the Federal Reserve Board from 1934 to 1935 and the Board of Governors after March 1936. Eccles was much more interested in fiscal actions, housing, and advising President Roosevelt on these and other issues than in conducting monetary policy. The Federal Reserve took very few discretionary actions. Except for doubling reserve requirements in 1936–37, it was passive through most of these years. Despite the mutual antipathy between Eccles and Treasury Secretary Morgenthau, the Treasury usually led and the Federal Reserve followed.

A main reason the Treasury could lead in monetary matters was that most of the profit from the 1934 revaluation of gold went to establish the Exchange Stabilization Fund. Morgenthau threatened to use the fund, and the Treasury trust funds, to engage in open market operations. The Federal Reserve disliked these actions, disliked being a junior partner, and feared that the Treasury would take over its functions. Morgenthau, on his side, distrusted Eccles and regarded most Federal Reserve officials as bankers of questionable loyalty to the administration. He wanted interest rates to remain low so he could market government debt on favor-

and urged that a vigorous monetary policy of expansion could be used to end the recession. Goldenweiser opposed this view, and it does not appear to have had any effect on decisions.

309. Starting in first quarter 1934 avoids the revaluation of the gold stock and the bank holiday. This conclusion would not change greatly if official (annual) data are used instead. For 1933 to 1941, nominal GNP, as reported by the Commerce Department, rose approximately 10 percent a year compared with the 9.7 percent rate of base money growth.

able terms; and he was willing to use his trust funds as a threat so that he could choose the monetary policy he wanted. These efforts were generally successful.

Treasury pressure is not a full explanation for Federal Reserve passivity and subservience to the Treasury. Board members and the Board's principal staff believed that monetary policy was impotent. One reason is that nominal or market interest rates were low. A second reason is that excess reserves rose.

At first the appearance of excess reserves puzzled the staff and the governors. Gradually they modified the Riefler-Burgess doctrine to include excess reserves. Excess reserves replaced borrowing as the main indicator of the thrust of monetary policy and the position of the financial system. In the 1920s, the Federal Reserve considered borrowing of $500 million neutral; policy was neither easy nor tight at that level. With borrowing almost eliminated, the level of excess reserves and short-term interest rates became the principal measures of policy thrust. Both measures suggested that policy remained easy throughout the decade. Hence there was no reason for action.

One of Morgenthau's achievements, which he valued highly for political and economic reasons, is known as the Tripartite Agreement. The agreement fixed exchange rates between the British pound, the French franc, and the dollar. Morgenthau believed the agreement showed that the democracies could cooperate politically to achieve a common end. Economically, it fixed exchange rates daily; the parties could change rates with one day's notice.

In fact, the agreement had little economic effect. The principal reasons are that countries pursued independent policies often unrelated to the exchange rate goal and that after adjusting for differences in inflation, nominal exchange rates were misaligned. The agreement to fix nominal or market rates meant that the French government had to deflate its economy further. After years of high unemployment and repeated cuts in spending on social services and pensions, most French voters were unwilling to accept additional austerity. Even before the agreement was made, a centrist coalition had started an expansive policy. Its successor, a socialist government with Communist support, pursued expansive policies more aggressively. These policies were inconsistent with the Tripartite Agreement, so the agreement could not, and did not, accomplish much economically.

The period between 1933 and 1940 is known as the New Deal, the name President Franklin Roosevelt gave to his administration. The New Deal introduced many programs to redistribute income and initiate welfare state measures. These programs succeeded politically; the administration was reelected by a large majority in 1936 and a smaller but decisive majority in 1940.

At the time, and afterward, many economists regarded the New Deal as a failure or as less than successful (Arndt 1966; Hansen 1938; Kindleberger 1986; Morgenthau, in Blum 1965, 124). A principal reason was continued high unemployment. Between 1929 and 1940, the figure of 6.5 million new entrants in the labor force is about the same as the net increase in the number unemployed. Hours of work declined.

New Deal programs raised real and nominal wages faster than productivity or encouraged these increases. By 1940 per capita real output had returned to the 1929 level, but real wages in manufacturing were 44 percent higher than in 1929. The early New Deal prescribed wage increases through NIRA codes. When the Supreme Court declared NIRA unconstitutional in 1935, other legislation encouraged union organizing, a shorter workweek, a minimum wage, and other measures to raise wages. Similar measures in France after 1936 had a similar effect; wages and prices rose while employment fell.

Although New Deal measures help to explain the sluggish growth of employment and the persistence of unemployment during the 1930s, the long-term effect of these measures was on the price level and the exchange rate. Once the United States entered the war, employment rose rapidly.

The New Deal had a lasting effect on the organization of the Federal Reserve. The Banking Act of 1935 changed the locus of power in the Federal Reserve System by strengthening the role and powers of the (renamed) Board of Governors in Washington. Without ever reaching an explicit, collective judgment, Congress and the Roosevelt administration appear to have concluded that the policies pursued by the reserve banks, particularly New York, had encouraged speculation, leading to the 1929 stock market collapse, bank failures, and depression. Centralization of responsibility and authority in the Board, and measures to prevent security market speculation, were the chosen solutions.

Subservience to the Treasury during the recovery, and in the war that followed, limited the effect of the legislation for a time. The Treasury took control of international economic policy. Both New York and the Board had a limited role. The Board gained nominal control of open market operations and the power to approve appointment of reserve bank presidents. The new powers changed the System's internal organization and operations in the 1930s. Major effects on policy had to wait for the postwar years.

APPENDIX: STATISTICAL RELATIONS

This appendix shows the regressions underlying chart 6.16, gives some related equations, and reproduces the chart on base velocity, highlighting the data for the 1930s recovery.

Chart 6.A1 compares base velocity to a long-term interest rate as in chapters 4 and 5. The chart notes the points for 1933–41 in relation to the long-term position of the curve. Base velocity declined as interest rates declined. Both reached the lowest values in recorded United States history.

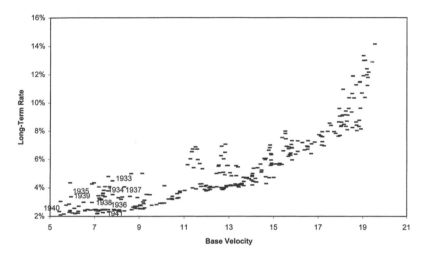

Chart 6.A1 Base velocity versus long-term Treasury bond rate, 1919.1 to 1995.2.

Table 6.A1 Relation of Money Growth to Real GNP Growth and Inflation
(*t*-statistics in parentheses)

	DEPENDENT VARIABLE			
	REAL GNP GROWTH (1934.1–1941.4)	REAL GNP GROWTH	INFLATION RATE (1923.1–1941.4)	INFLATION RATE (1923.1–1929.3*)
Real M₁ growth	0.54	0.72		
Lagged one quarter	(2.13)	(3.61)		
Nominal M₁ growth			0.17	0.36
Lagged one quarter			(2.64)	(2.56)
Inflation		0.53	0.07	
Lagged one quarter		(5.13)	(0.36)	
AR(1)		−0.44		
		(2.51)		
R^2	0.10	0.28	0.45	0.18
DW	2.60	2.20	2.11	2.08

*Used to forecast 1929.4–1941.4, chart 6.16.

SEVEN

Under Treasury Control, 1942 to 1951

The period from 1942 to March 1951 divides almost equally into years of war and years of peacetime expansion. For Federal Reserve policy, the period can be treated as a whole, a repeat with different details and a different outcome of the experience during and after World War I. Once again the Federal Reserve put itself at the service of the wartime Treasury, and once again it had difficulty extricating itself from the Treasury's grasp after the war. And again it took almost as much time to free postwar monetary policy as to fight the war.

The Federal Reserve summarized its "primary duty" in wartime as "the financing of military requirements and of production for war purposes" (Board of Governors of the Federal Reserve System 1947). In practice, this meant continuation of the historically low interest rates carried over from the 1930s. Principal efforts to control spending and inflation fell to administration tax policy and, during wartime, to price and wage controls and the rationing of several commodities. The Federal Reserve supplemented these policies mainly by regulating credit used to purchase consumer durable goods. Wartime allocation of materials and conversion of factories to military production restricted the supply of durable goods; consumer credit controls aimed to restrict demand at the controlled prices. After the war, Congress removed controls (1947), but it soon restored them (1948). In the early postwar years, the Federal Reserve used margin requirements to limit securities purchases. Credit controls proved difficult to administer and ineffective against inflation.

Eccles described his work in wartime as "a routine administrative job. . . . [T]he Federal Reserve merely executed Treasury decisions" (Eccles 1951, 382). When his term ended in February 1944, he offered to resign but agreed to remain if the president would commit to consolidation of banking regulation and supervision under a single agency. His reappointment as a member of the Board ran to 1958, as chairman to 1948.[1]

The Treasury relied more heavily on taxation than in World War I. Tax receipts rose from less than $9 billion (7 percent of GNP) in the 1941 fiscal year to more than $45 billion (21 percent of GNP) in 1945, but expenditures rose more. Public debt increased by $200 billion in the same four-year period (approximately 25 percent of GNP). Secretary Morgenthau's passionate attachment to low interest rates meant that in practice the Federal Reserve's "primary duty" was to market the debt at prevailing interest rates and, as in World War I, assist in the periodic war loan drives.[2] To carry out this policy, beginning in April 1942, the System fixed ceiling rates on government securities at 0.375 percent for Treasury bills and 2.5 percent for long-term bonds, with intermediate rates on intermediate maturities. This pattern of rates became a main source of difficulty. With all rates expected to remain fixed, banks, financial institutions, and the public increased profits by buying higher-yielding long-term bonds and selling short-term bills in the market, where they were acquired by the System.

The war ended with wartime rates still in place. As in 1919, the Treasury was reluctant to let rates change, first because it wanted to float a Victory Loan, later because it was unwilling to increase the cost of debt service. Unlike 1919–20, no one at the Federal Reserve was willing to challenge the Treasury's position. Eccles gave three reasons. First, like the Treasury, he was concerned about the budgetary cost. Economists in and outside government cited the large outstanding debt, the higher cost to the Treasury, and potential losses to bondholders from higher interest rates as impediments to the use of orthodox policies. Eccles shared this view. Second, higher interest rates would increase bank earnings, an outcome consid-

1. The president's wartime powers included authority to reorganize government agencies. According to Eccles, Roosevelt agreed to consolidate the banking agencies but soon afterward rejected Eccles's proposal. Eccles did not resign. Eccles's service dates from 1934, but he was reappointed to a twelve-year term in 1936 after reorganization. Since he had not served a full term, he could be reappointed for fourteen years. The other members at the time were Governors Ronald Ransom, John K. McKee, Ernest G. Draper, M. S. Szymczak, and Rudolph M. Evans.

2. There is no evidence supporting Toma's (1997) argument that the low-interest policy was intended to maximize the government's seigniorage. Under the rules adopted in 1933, the Federal Reserve did not transfer any surpluses to the Treasury to compensate for its subscription to the initial stock of the Federal Deposit Insurance Corporation. This rule changed in 1947 to the present rule, under which the Federal Reserve pays 90 percent of its net earnings to the Treasury. A reader familiar with Secretary Morgenthau's excessive concern about small changes in interest rates in the 1930s, when debt issues were relatively small (chapter 6), would not seek another explanation for wartime interest rate pegs when the size of debt issue increased by about 20 percent of GNP.

ered politically unacceptable. Third, Eccles believed there was no political support for higher interest rates. He was unwilling to make the case, certain he would lose to the Treasury, and skeptical that inflation could be controlled without raising interest rates so high that a postwar depression would be likely.[3]

An unspoken fourth reason was also present. The dominant view of professional economists at the time was that the task of monetary policy was to promote budgetary finance. Fiscal or budgetary policy was believed to have much more powerful effects on prices and economic activity than changes in the quantity of money or interest rates. In addition, many economists believed the war would be followed by a return to unemployment and slow growth, as in the 1930s. This view was based in part on historical precedent—most wars had been followed by recessions—but even more on Keynesian analyses showing that private spending would be too small to sustain full employment (Samuelson 1943).

Woodlief Thomas, of the Board's senior staff, set out the prevailing view on the role of money. His essay emphasizes the role of unmeasured magnitudes such as "availability" and "turnover" as more important influences on the economy than money. Changes in money did not cause changes in output or aggregate income (Thomas 1941, 324–25). The Federal Reserve had limited influence on the stock of money (304–5), and the stock of money was less important than its rate of turnover, or velocity of circulation (330).

Nevertheless, the Federal Reserve had statutory responsibility for monetary control. Because it could be blamed for inflation, it became increasingly restive under tight Treasury control. It claimed that restrictions on interest rates converted the Federal Reserve into an "engine of inflation." Morgenthau's resignation in 1945 did nothing to change the Treasury's stance. His successors, Fred M. Vinson and John W. Snyder, were no less concerned about maintaining the wartime pattern of interest rates.

Fears of a postwar depression soon disappeared as a reason for low in-

---

3. Eccles repeated this belief many times. One example is his 1946 testimony on the continuation of price controls after the war ended. On that occasion, Eccles testified that "it would be quite unsatisfactory, it seems to me, to try to meet the present problem by what was considered the usual or the orthodox way of dealing with inflationary forces, which was through increasing the discount rate, raising interest rates. Now, the reason for not following this course is that it would increase the cost of carrying the public debt, which is already very high, and it would likewise increase the earnings of the banking system which are also high. Such a policy would be a very unsatisfactory way to deal with this problem. I am sure that the Treasury would have considerable objection, as Congress and the public would, to increasing the interest burden on the Federal debt for the benefit of the banking system" (House Committee on Banking and Currency 1946, 183).

terest rates, but other reasons remained. Although Eccles continued to oppose confrontation, he was not passive. He favored raising reserve requirements, mandating that banks must hold a secondary reserve of Treasury bills, higher tax rates to produce a budget surplus, selective credit
controls, and during the transition, price and wage controls.

At first there was little opposition within the System to many of these
ideas. After the transition, Allan Sproul, president of the New York Federal
Reserve bank, began to advocate a more active monetary policy. Although
generally reluctant to clash openly with Eccles and the Treasury or reopen
the 1920s split between the New York bank and the Board, Sproul became
the principal spokesman for a more independent monetary policy. When
Eccles's term as chairman ended in 1948, Sproul's influence increased
under the new chairman, Thomas B. McCabe.

Little changed until two events altered the political balance. First Congress, under the leadership of Senator Paul Douglas, opposed the Treasury's position. Second, the start of the Korean War, in June 1950, heightened public concern about renewed inflation. The result was an agreement
with the Treasury in March 1951, known as the Treasury–Federal Reserve
Accord (the accord), that permitted the Federal Reserve to implement a
more independent policy.

In fact, early postwar monetary policy was far from an "engine of inflation." By the end of 1948 prices were falling, and long-term interest rates
were below the Treasury–Federal Reserve maximums. The decline in
prices was soon followed by a decline in output and a mild recession. Chart
7.1 shows growth of output and inflation from 1942 to 1951. The large spike
in inflation in third quarter 1946 (and some of the increase in the previous
two quarters) reflects the removal of wartime price and wage controls in
that quarter.

Reliance on selective controls, to limit general price level increases,
shows the System's inability or unwillingness to use more general measures. But it also reflects the lingering effects of the real bills doctrine. Buyers of durables could borrow in ways other than the particular way that controls restricted, just as buyers of stock had done when the Board tried to
control stock purchases by restricting credit to the stock market. Discussions at the time did not explain how inflation—a sustained rate of increase in a broad-based price index—could be controlled by limiting the
use of credit to purchase particular goods and services.[4] To prevent "spec-

---

4. As late as 1980, the Carter administration imposed selective credit controls seeking to
end a general inflation.

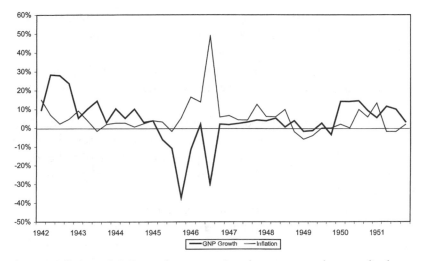

Chart 7.1 Inflation and GNP growth, 1942–51. Growth rates measured as annualized quarterly rates of change.

ulative" accumulation of inventories of consumer goods, the Federal Reserve urged bankers to curtail lending to firms with rising inventories.

In June 1950 the United States went to war again. Spending to fight the Korean War brought nominal government spending back to its peak wartime level. President Truman chose to finance the war out of current revenues, so the cash budget had a surplus. After a brief spurt, inflation remained modest. Despite pegged interest rates, growth rates of the monetary base and the money stock were modest also, in part because gold outflows increased.

Korean War finance shows that wartime inflation can be avoided if policymakers choose to do so. President Truman's budget policy did not force interest rates to rise, and it did not require the Federal Reserve to increase money growth to prevent the rise. In the two years beginning June 1950, the monetary base rose about 7 percent, a 3.5 percent annual rate. In the same period the consumer price index rose 11 percent, but by far the larger part of the rise occurred as a one-time price level change driven on one side by fear of a return to wartime shortages when the war started and on the other by the expectation that money growth always increases to finance wartime deficits. When the administration chose a balanced budget, expectations of inflation collapsed.

The principal international financial event of the period was the attempt to reconstruct the international monetary system as a fixed exchange rate system and, at the end of the period, the start of the gold outflow from the

United States. At first the Federal Reserve and the administration welcomed the loss of gold as a necessary step in the reconstruction of a more viable international monetary framework. A decade later, concerns about the United States gold loss became the subject of an increasingly active discussion about the viability of the monetary standard based on gold and the dollar.[5]

The architects of the early postwar international monetary standard, the Bretton Woods system, believed that the failure of surplus countries to adjust was one of two major flaws in the interwar gold standard of the 1920s. The other was competitive devaluation, or beggar-thy-neighbor policies. The Bretton Woods Agreement established the International Monetary Fund as a public intermediary in the international monetary system. The fund's key features were (1) an agreement to lend and borrow to adjust "temporary" imbalances in international payments and (2) a structural adjustment arrangement to correct "permanent" imbalances by changing exchange rates while preventing competitive devaluations.

Countries with a "temporary" current account deficit could use the fund to borrow from countries in surplus. This provision sought to avoid the problem that the United States and France created by failing to expand and inflate in response to gold inflows at the end of the 1920s. Their decisions forced deficit countries to contract without triggering an equilibrating expansion in the surplus countries. Under Bretton Woods rules, deficit countries did not have to contract. They could borrow the funds accumulated by the surplus countries.

The structural adjustment provisions permitted countries to correct persistent or permanent imbalances by adjusting exchange rates. A major problem with this provision was that central banks and governments could not distinguish temporary from persistent imbalances ex ante or even for some time after deficits appeared. A related problem was that fund rules did not make it clear what should happen when the principal reserve currency country—the United States—ran persistent trade or current account deficits.

Reliance on gold as a principal reserve asset of the fund and the member countries gave the appearance of a gold-based system. This appearance probably strengthened the belief that inflation would remain modest and thus contributed to the slow adjustment of inflationary anticipations in the 1960s. In practice the system was based mainly on the dollar, and there proved to be no binding restrictions on the supply of dollars under the Bretton Woods system.

5. I return to this discussion, and proposals for change, in volume 2.

The principal designers of the International Monetary Fund were John Maynard Keynes of Great Britain and Harry Dexter White of the United States. Keynes spent the war years, until his death in 1946, at the British Treasury. White was an economist at the United States Treasury. In contrast to the 1920s, when Governors Benjamin Strong and Montagu Norman were the principal architects of the postwar international monetary arrangements, power and influence over international monetary arrangements rested firmly in the two treasuries. Here, too, central banks had a subsidiary role.

At the New York bank, John H. Williams became one of the principal opponents, so he was kept from membership on the United States delegation. The Federal Reserve never formally considered the Bretton Woods Agreement and was not asked to do so. As the system developed, however, Williams's proposal for an international system, based on the dollar, soon supplanted many of the features of the Keynes-White plan.

THE ADMINISTRATION'S WARTIME PROGRAM

There are both similarities and differences in the financing programs for the two world wars. Table 7.1 shows that interest rates remained lower and rose less in World War II, and the measured rate of inflation was lower also. Price controls distort the timing of price changes for the period. When controls were removed, in third quarter 1946, the deflator rose at a 45 percent annual rate, releasing most of the changes suppressed by wartime controls.

The first observation for each war is for the quarter in which the United States entered the war—second quarter 1917 and fourth quarter 1941. Second is the observation for the quarter in which the war ended—fourth quarter 1918 and third quarter 1945. Third is the observation for the postwar quarter in which wartime inflationary pressures began to recede, as measured by the rate of growth of the monetary base. Annualized rates of change for money and prices are computed from the first to the third date shown in the table.

Financing World War II was a much larger task. The cost of the war was substantially larger both absolutely and relative to GNP.[6] Real GNP was approximately two and a half times greater in the later war, and the level of the deflator was similar in both periods, but government debt increased nearly ten times as much, as the table shows. The larger increase in debt occurred despite the larger share of taxes and faster growth of base money

6. Feinstein, Temin, and Toniolo (1997) put the cost of the two wars at 13 percent and 45 percent of United States GNP at the time. For Germany, they estimated the costs as 53 percent and 76 percent.

Table 7.1   Money, Prices, Debt, and Interest Rates in Wartime

DATE	MONETARY BASE (BILLIONS OF DOLLARS)	MONEY (M₁) (BILLIONS OF DOLLARS)	DEFLATOR	INTEREST RATE (SHORT-TERM, PERCENT)	PUBLIC DEBT[a] (BILLIONS OF DOLLARS)
		World War I			
1917.1	4.8	16.4	26.2	4.12	1.2
1918.4	6.5	20.8	33.2	5.81	12.4
1920.3	7.3	2.5	40.7	7.97	24.3
Change (%) annual rate	11.6	10.2	12.5		
		World War II			
1941.4	17.9	48.2	32.1	0.69	49.0
1945.3	36.3	101.8	36.9	0.75	258.7
1946.3	37.2	107.7	45.6	0.81	269.4
Change (%) annual rate	15.4	16.9	7.4		

[a]End of preceding fiscal year (June 30), Bureau of the Census 1960, 720.

in World War II. Also, the Federal Reserve chose a different method of supplying reserves and supporting the Treasury market. In World War I, the Federal Reserve System did not have an open market policy. Banks obtained reserves by borrowing at the discount window using Treasury securities as collateral. In World War II, the System supplied reserves principally by open market purchases. Since the Federal Reserve supported a pattern of rates, it became the residual buyer. This left control of reserve changes to the banks' decisions, much the same as in World War I.

With long- and short-term interest rates comparatively lower in the 1940s, the demand for real money balances was higher. In World War I, base money, money, and prices rose at about the same rate, 10 to 12 percent. Real balances declined slightly. In World War II, base money and money rose at about the same rate (16 percent), but prices rose at less than half that rate, reflecting the rising demand for cash balances. The rise in real cash balances financed spending and inflation at the end of the war and therefore became a cause for concern.

Beginning in 1942, the government severely curtailed automobile production and took all residual production. Production of other durables was curtailed also; spending declined and saving increased. Part of the saving was held as money because higher mobility of the population increased the demand for currency (Cagan 1965).

Chart 7.2 shows the relation of base velocity to a long-term interest rate and highlights quarterly data from 1942 to first quarter 1951. The chart suggests that much of the quarterly movement in wartime and postwar velocity (the reciprocal of average cash balances) is consistent with the long-term relationship. Velocity was historically low, and average cash balances were correspondingly high, principally because long-term interest rates remained close to the 2.5 percent maximum.

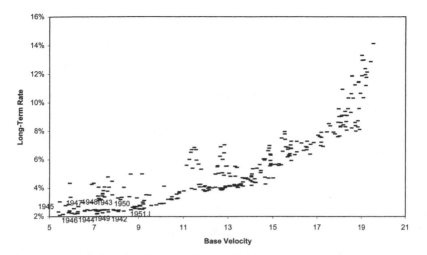

Chart 7.2 Base velocity versus long-term Treasury bond rate, 1919.1 to 1995.2.

Chart 7.3 looks at the war and postwar period on a finer scale. The positive relation remains, but the effect of the 2.5 percent interest rate ceiling is now visible. Observations at the ceiling rate, mainly in 1943 and 1944, suggest that the ceiling was binding in these years. Extrapolating from the linear relationship, the data suggest that without the ceiling, interest rates and velocity would have been higher and average cash balances correspondingly lower during part of the war years. For much of the period, however, the ceiling rate seems not to have affected money holding.[7]

The opposite side of the much larger rise in cash balances was the much smaller increase in the public's share of the debt. Morgenthau's Treasury urged individuals to purchase debt, but he was unwilling to pay them to do so. The Treasury issued series E war bonds at prices as low as $18.75 per bond and war savings stamps for as little as 10 cents, which could cumulate to a bond purchase. The Treasury encouraged corporations, schools, and other institutions to sell bonds and stamps through payroll deduction and appeals to patriotism. These actions were not enough to offset the low interest rates paid on the debt. The nonbank public acquired a smaller portion of the debt in World War II than in World War I. Commercial banks acquired 40 percent of debt held outside the government and the reserve banks. Although many citizens and corporations pledged to buy bonds during bond drives, they sold many of the bonds to banks after the bond drive ended.

7. Base velocity is computed as the ratio of GNP from Balke and Gordon 1986 to high-powered money from Anderson and Rasche 1999.

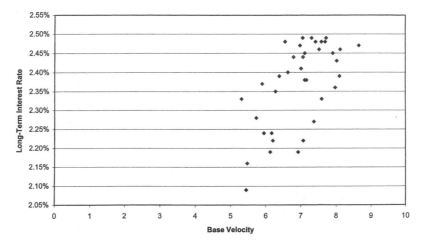

Chart 7.3 Base velocity versus long-term interest rate, quarterly, 1942.1 to 1952.1; not seasonally adjusted.

Secretary Morgenthau set three major objectives for war finance (Blum 1967, 14–15). He wanted to finance 50 percent of the war by direct taxation, to finance most of the rest by voluntary purchases of bonds, and to maintain low interest rates. He believed that low interest rates would minimize the cost of the war. He succeeded in his third objective, came close to his first, and managed to avoid most of the pressures from Congress and other parts of the administration calling for compulsory bond purchases.[8]

For calendar years 1942–45, total government spending was $306 billion, revenues were $138 billion, and GNP was $740 billion. These periods correspond to the war years, with a few additional months of demobilization and reconversion to peacetime resource use at the end. Based on these data, tax collections were 45 percent of spending, only $15 billion short of Morgenthau's goal.[9]

8. J. M. Keynes advocated a compulsory saving scheme as part of a British plan for war finance. Many of Keynes's followers in the United States wanted to adopt Keynes's program. Morgenthau opposed it, in part because the United States economy started the war with output far below capacity, in part because he was able to market the debt at historically low interest rates (Blum 1965, 297, 299). In World War I, the Treasury assigned a quota for banks' purchases. The quota was a minimum subscription for each bank (Sproul Papers, Monetary Policy, 1940–41).

9. Eccles (1951, 381) includes the prewar defense spending in his calculation. For July 1940 to December 1945 he reports spending as $380 billion financed by $153 billion of taxes (40 percent), and $228 billion of borrowing and money creation. Nonbank investors acquired about $130 billion but sold some of their bonds to commercial banks after the bond drives. Elsewhere, Eccles gives contemporary data for June 1940 to June 1946, the period including prewar preparation. Total cost was $398 billion, 44 percent paid by taxation, 56 percent by borrowing and money creation (Board Minutes, November 26, 1947, 4).

Tax Policy

Morgenthau had little success getting Congress to approve his tax policy. Despite a Democratic majority in both houses, he did not fully meet his revenue goal or get his preferred tax policy. By 1944, relations between Congress and the administration became so strained that, with large majorities, both houses of Congress overrode the president's veto of a tax bill for the first time in United States history. The administration did not try again to change tax rates during the war.

The main sources of conflict were the level of rates and the distribution of the tax burden. Many congressmen favored a sales tax. Morgenthau opposed on equity grounds; the sales tax would put more of the burden on low-income earners, a group he tried to shelter. At the opposite end of the income distribution, Roosevelt favored a limit of $25,000 on individual after-tax income, $50,000 for families. This proposal had so little appeal that Congress did not consider it seriously.

The 1943 tax bill made a lasting change in the tax system by introducing withholding at the source. Before 1943, taxpayers paid taxes in March on the previous year's income. Withholding shifted most tax collection to the current year, a pay-as-you-go system for wage earners and some others. Withholding greatly simplified enforcement, as the number of taxpayers expanded to include 40 million to 50 million returns on incomes as low as $600 a year.[10]

Morgenthau at first opposed the withholding plan because Congress proposed to forgive all 1942 tax liabilities (due in March 1943) when withholding began. His main objection was that, with progressive taxation and high wartime rates, high-income taxpayers (and wartime profiteers) would benefit most. He was able to limit tax forgiveness and introduce some progressivity. The bill forgave $50 or 75 percent of the lower of 1942 or 1943 tax liabilities. Withholding began on July 1, 1943.

Morgenthau recognized inflation as a tax on households. He claimed he preferred direct taxation to inflation, but he would not allow interest rates to rise.[11] However, he proposed some fiscal changes to reduce household income. One of his proposals would have raised the Social Security tax on

---

10. The proposal was advocated in 1941 by Beardsley Ruml, head of R. H. Macy's department store and chairman of the New York Federal Reserve bank. Hence it was often referred to as the Ruml plan.

11. Using the average values of the monetary base and GNP for the war years, the government taxed nearly 10 percent of the base through inflation. The base was about 5 percent of GNP and 15 percent of government spending, so the inflation tax on the base is about 0.5 percent of GNP and 1.5 percent of government spending.

labor income during the war, with the proceeds returned after the war, if needed, as unemployment compensation (Blum 1965, 313). Perhaps without fully recognizing the change, Morgenthau had become a proponent of countercyclical fiscal policy.

At the Federal Reserve Marriner Eccles saw the war as a major shift in demand that had to be met by substantial tax increases. In 1940–41 he agreed with the Keynesians who argued that, given the high unemployment at the start of the war, the country could increase both "guns and butter." By 1942 he was concerned that the administration and Congress would be slow to recognize that the problem was no longer an excess supply of goods. There was an excess supply of money and excess demand for goods (Eccles 1951, 346–47).[12]

Debt Finance

Morgenthau foresaw that the war would require an unprecedented volume of borrowing. The Treasury and the Federal Reserve agreed on the desirability of ceiling rates of interest, high tax rates, and selling bonds mainly to the nonbank public. Morgenthau described relations with the Federal Reserve as "more harmonious during the war than they had ever been during the years of the New Deal" Blum (1967, 15). Board members shared this view.

Differences about substance remained, however (Board Minutes, April 9, 1942, 8). Eccles and some others preferred a mandated program—forced saving—to Morgenthau's mainly voluntary bond purchase program. The Board offered proposals in each of the eight bond drives intended to increase sales to nonbanks, restrict speculation in bonds, and limit the role of banks to short maturities. The Treasury accepted few of these suggestions.

There were other differences about debt finance. Although the Treasury agreed on the aim of selling as many bonds as possible to nonbank investors during bond drives, it was less concerned than the Federal Reserve about whether the purchasers held the bonds after the drive. Getting the bonds sold at prevailing rates was its overriding interest.

Three main problems arose. First, with interest rates lower on short-

12. Eccles cites a conversation with Roosevelt in December 1940, just after Roosevelt had announced the lend-lease program to help Britain. Roosevelt understood that technically it made no difference to the economy whether we lent the British money or lent them goods. But he believed the public would favor lending goods but oppose lending money. "If we made a dollar loan to the British, it would seem to our people that we were giving the British money, of which we were short, instead of goods which were in surplus" (quoted in Eccles 1951, 348).

term than on long-term debt, the Treasury faced an upward-sloping yield curve. Bank and nonbank holders sold shorter-term securities and reinvested in longer-term bonds. Second, as in World War I, the Treasury permitted a "borrow and buy" policy. To ensure that bond drives were successful, banks lent money to finance bond purchases at interest rates below the bonds' yield. Many banks agreed to buy the bonds from their customers after the drive. Since the buyers could profit by buying the bonds, they oversubscribed the new issue. This gave the appearance of public subscription but depended on bank financing. Third, Treasury certificates with one year or less to maturity were troublesome throughout. The Treasury first offered certificates in 1942 at a yield of 0.8 percent. The rate was above the rate required by the market, so prices rose to a premium. As the certificates approached maturity, they sold at a premium over Treasury bills. Banks sold them to the Federal Reserve at a profit. The Federal Reserve tried repeatedly to get the yield reduced to 0.75 percent on new issues or to shorten the maturity and lower the rate, but the Treasury would not change (Minutes, FOMC, March 1, 1944, at 11:40, 1).

Officially, the Treasury opposed the borrow and buy policy. In practice, it did little to prevent it (Eccles 1951, 361). As a result, nonbank purchasers acquired $147 billion of government securities (including nonmarketable war bonds) but held only $93 billion. Corporations subscribed to about $60 billion in bond drives but increased their holdings only $19 billion.

Commercial banks financed bond purchases by selling Treasury bills and other low-yielding securities to the Federal Reserve. With bill rates pegged and ceiling rates set on all other Treasury securities, the banks moved to the higher end of the yield curve. To limit bank purchases of long-term debt, many of the bonds were made "bank restricted." Small and medium-sized banks complained that mutual savings banks and savings and loans could buy the restricted bonds and thus were able to offer higher returns to savers. In 1944 the rules changed to permit commercial banks to purchase restricted securities during bond drives up to 10 percent of their savings deposits (Board Minutes, December 7, 1943, 2–4). Overall, bank purchases were limited to $10 billion during all bond drives. Bank holdings increased by $57 billion, however (Eccles 1951, 362).[13]

As in World War I, debt finance was much less successful than claimed after the war bond drives. The monetary base doubled in the four years ending fourth quarter 1945, an 18 percent compound average annual rate

13. The Federal Reserve minutes for the period return repeatedly to the topic of "educating" the public about the importance of holding the bonds they purchased. The problem was not ignorance but knowledge of opportunities.

of increase. Purchases of Treasury securities account for almost all of the $18 billion increase in the base.[14]

Eccles proposed a three-part alternative. First, he wanted more of the debt made ineligible for bank purchases. This limited the profits that non-banks could make by buying bonds at a favorable price during bond drives and reselling them to banks after the drive. Second, Eccles thought more of the debt should be in nonmarketable securities to supplement the (non-marketable) series E, F, and G bonds sold to individuals. The Treasury accepted part of this proposal, issuing a nonmarketable short- term bond. They did not issue a nonmarketable long-term bond, mainly because they did not want to pay the additional cost. Third, Eccles wanted to limit bank eligible issues to the residual amount required to finance the budget. He urged Morgenthau to sell banks only short-term securities with low yields. This "would have prevented the excessive profits which many banks were able to make" (Eccles (1951, 365).

To support Eccles's suggestions, the executive committee of the FOMC voted to recommend a long-term program. On January 28, 1942, it sent a memo to the Treasury that proposed (1) tap issues (on demand) to absorb surplus funds of nonbank corporations; (2) a 2.5 percent rate on securities with fifteen or more years to maturity; and (3) flexible rates on shorter maturities, bounded between 0.25 percent and 0.5 percent for Treasury bills.

As on many subsequent occasions, the Treasury did not accept most of the FOMC's suggestions. It was not interested in a long-term plan. Morgenthau preferred to remain opportunistic, and he was not concerned with rate flexibility or higher interest rates. He accepted only the fixed 2.5 percent maximum rate. At war's end, he was proud of his achievement—financing more than $200 billion at an average cost of 1.94 percent. In World War I, he noted, the average interest cost was 4.22 percent (Blum 1967, 30).[15]

In all, there were seven war bond drives and a Victory Loan drive between November 1942 and December 1945. Judging from discussions by the New York Federal Reserve directors and the open market committee, problems with "speculators" increased in the later drives. The bank put limits on the volume of discounting and issued warnings to member

14. As shown in table 7.1, the rate of base growth slowed in 1946. Morgenthau blamed "speculative practices" for the sales by nonbank investors. In contrast, Eccles recognized Treasury practices as the cause. Suspicious of bankers, Morgenthau argued that Eccles's program (see text) would have raised interest rates, increasing the profits of banks and Federal Reserve banks (Blum 1967, 29).

15. Morgenthau was so pleased with his achievement that he concluded the Treasury should have a larger role in monetary and financial policy. He advocated returning the secretary to the Board of Governors (Blum 1967, 31).

banks not to participate in these activities (Minutes, New York Directors, November 16, 1944, 48; July 5, 1945, 8; October 25, 1945, 96).

The warnings did not reduce the undesired activities. The open market committee was reluctant to change course at the end of the war until the Treasury completed the last (Victory) bond drive in the fall of 1945. But it agreed unanimously to discuss with the Treasury "policies which should be adopted for the reconversion and postwar periods" (Minutes, FOMC, October 17, 1945, 5).

Price and Wage Controls

Unable to persuade the Congress to pass all its proposed tax increases, the administration turned to price and wage controls to prevent wartime inflation. In July 1941 the president asked for selective controls on prices, but the bill did not pass in the Senate. After the war started, Congress approved the Emergency Price Control Act in January 1942, authorizing selective controls.

In March the president appointed a committee to consider the inflation problem. The committee concluded that selective price controls would fail. It recommended controls on rents, profits, wage rates, and prices and a $50,000 a year limit on incomes of corporate executives and professionals.[16] Workers would have an incentive to increase income by working more hours (at overtime rates). Morgenthau opposed wage controls, but he favored limiting profits to 6 percent of invested capital (Blum 1965, 314).

In April and July 1942 the administration tried selective price controls. Prices rose at a 4.8 percent annual rate in that year's first three quarters. The administration considered that rate too high. The president requested authority to freeze prices and wages, warning Congress that if the bill was not passed by October 1, he would issue an executive order. The Stabilization Act gave the president broad authority to control prices and wages. A former senator, Justice James Byrnes resigned from the Supreme Court to administer the Office of Economic Stabilization. Controls remained until the fall of 1946, when Congress repealed the authority it granted in 1942.[17]

16. The committee also recommended compulsory saving and lower tax exemptions to absorb purchasing power. In the Treasury, Undersecretary Randolph Paul and Harry Dexter White also favored compulsory saving (Blum 1967, 43).

17. Two modest policy benefits during the war were the end of the wasteful policy of purchasing Canadian silver and a reduction of the purchase price for Mexican silver to 35 cents an ounce, slightly below the world market price. The reason for these changes was to release silver for wartime use in photography and armaments. The Treasury continued to purchase domestically produced silver at 71.11 cents an ounce, as required by law (Blum 1967, 12).

THE FEDERAL RESERVE IN WARTIME

In a prescient 1942 memo, the staff of the Philadelphia reserve bank analyzed the problem the Federal Reserve faced in wartime. Although the war was less than a year old, the bank's staff projected that by the end of 1944 the government debt would reach $200 billion. Banks would hold between $85 billion and $100 billion; bank reserves would have to increase by $14 billion to $18 billion to support the purchases (Memo, Supply of Reserve Funds, Board of Governors File, box 1452, October 8, 1942). The memo concluded that open market purchases were the best method of supplying the reserves (ibid., 7).

With discount rates at 0.5 percent and open market rates on Treasury bills below 0.375 percent, banks preferred to sell bills rather than discount. The main wartime decision of the Federal Reserve was to keep this structure unchanged.

Pegged Rates

On April 30, 1942, the Federal Reserve announced its commitment to purchase all ninety-day Treasury bills offered "on a discount basis at the rate no higher than 0.375 percent per annum" (Board of Governors File, box 1441, April 30, 1942). It did not fix rates on other government securities explicitly, but it established a pattern of rates that it maintained throughout the war and beyond. It held one-year rates at 0.875 percent. At the longest end, it held the rate on bonds with twenty-five years or more to initial maturity to a maximum of 2.5 percent, as noted earlier. During the war and early postwar period, the duration of the longest-term bonds declined, but the maximum yield remained fixed.

The announcement put maximum Treasury bill rates above the rates prevailing at the time. During 1941 and early 1942, the Treasury bill rate had increased gradually from 0.02 percent to 0.25 percent. At the long-term end, bond yields had increased from 2 percent in much of 1941 to 2.5 percent in January 1942. The announcement had no effect on the long-term yield.[18]

The Federal Reserve did not vote to fix yields on all securities for the duration of the war. Memos written in early 1942 are explicit about rates on

---

18. The Treasury's initial interest was not in an explicit peg. They asked the System to keep large excess reserves in the market, preferably by reducing reserve requirement ratios. When the Federal Reserve objected, the Treasury proposed the 0.375 percent bill rate. The FOMC approved the agreement unanimously. The agreement to support the "pattern of rates" was made in March. "The general market to be maintained on about the present curve of rates, but this does not mean special support for issues that may be out of line" (Minutes, FOMC, May 8, 1942, 3). The agreement provided for more flexibility than the Treasury allowed and much less than the FOMC anticipated.

the shortest and longest maturities. Conversations with bankers and other active market participants show some concern that the 2.5 percent long-term rate might be too low; Federal Reserve officials wanted to increase the prevailing 0.25 percent rate on short-term bills. But the uniform opinion was that "the cost of war is a social cost and its risks should be borne by the public at large, not by any one group, such as those who have bought government securities" (Letter Sproul to Bell, Sproul Papers, Monetary Policy 1940–41, March 16, 1942, 2). "The Treasury, representing the public at large, should assume the risk of a change in credit conditions."[19] (ibid., March 10, 1942, 3).[20]

Households would get nonmarketable securities that they could redeem at the Treasury at a fixed price. This decision avoided the problem of imposing losses on the general public, a concern based on experience after World War I. Banks would be large holders of marketable debt, so it would be "necessary . . . for the Federal Reserve and the Treasury to protect that market, not only during the war, but during the post-war period" (ibid., March 16, 1942, 2). Sproul recognized that protecting the market meant that government debt would "have some attributes of a demand obligation." The problem was to manage the debt "in the way least likely to contribute to . . . inflation" (2).[21]

A few days later, Sproul's letter to Eccles summarized the agreement with the Treasury. At the short end, the Federal Reserve agreed to support the market "when the rate on Treasury bills reaches $^1/_4$ of 1 percent, and support[ing] with increasing strength as the rate approaches $^3/_8$ of 1 percent" (Sproul to Eccles, Sproul Papers, FOMC 1942, March 21, 1942). The general market would be kept "on about the present curve of rates but this . . . does not mean that we must hold the 2's of 1951–55 or the 2$^1/_2$'s of 1967–72, or any other issue, at par, or any other fixed price" (ibid.). The

19. This is a very different rationale than Eccles gave: "It would have been wrong for the government to pay increasing rates of interest for the use of the funds it helped to create" (Eccles 1951, 350). The same statement could be made at any time about any supply of base money. It expresses a preference for relying on inflation to tax wealth instead of relying on explicit taxation.

20. The memos do not mention that the benefits of victory would go to both future and current generations, justifying some sharing of the social costs through taxation to retire the debt after the war.

21. Sproul proposed interest rates starting at 0.375 percent for up to six months, rising by 0.25 percent to 1.375 percent at two and a half years, then by 0.125 percent to 2 percent at five years. The Treasury proposed a lower short-term rate and a steeper slope starting at 0.25 percent and progressing by 0.25 percent to 2.5 percent at five years. By June some in the System recognized that a fixed pattern of rates increasing with maturity gave holders an opportunity to "play the pattern of rates" by buying long, letting the price rise as maturity shortened, taking the profit, and then repeating the operation. The (unsigned) memo proposed letting rates fluctuate to reduce certainty (Sproul Papers, FOMC, June 1, 1942).

System maintained this position for a time, but it was unable to get the Treasury to agree.[22]

Even granting that the Federal Reserve had no choice but to finance the war at fixed rates, it was a mistake to accept the prevailing structure of interest rates. That structure reflected market anticipations in April 1942 about future economic expansion and inflation. The positive slope of the yield curve, expressing rates by maturity of the debt, suggests that the market anticipated that output, inflation, and therefore interest rates would rise over time. The fixed pattern of rates was inconsistent with this anticipation, so it invited debt holders to sell low-yield securities and buy at higher yields. Since the peg made all government securities equally liquid, or nearly so, the Federal Reserve's decision was the cause of its principal problems for the next nine years. First, banks could lend to their customers for short periods at rates below the rates on long-term debt. As debts matured, bond prices rose to a premium. Holders sold, took capital gains, and purchased longer-term debt. Although the Treasury disliked both practices, it was unwilling to consider any changes in the structure of rates during the war. Second, banks followed the same pattern, selling bills with yields of 0.375 percent to the Federal Reserve and buying longer maturities with higher yields. By 1945 the Federal Reserve had acquired almost all of the outstanding bills: "They ceased to be a market instrument" (Eccles 1951, 359).

In the late 1930s, the Federal Reserve urged the Treasury to increase the supply of short-term debt. The Treasury refused. With the short-term rate fixed, the Treasury could now reduce interest cost by issuing a relatively large volume of short-term debt. At prevailing rates and policies, the market wanted more long-term debt. By fixing the structure of interest rates, the Federal Reserve sacrificed its ability to change the composition of the debt held by the public. Market demand dictated the amount and composition of its purchases and sales.

In 1944 some members of the open market committee began to shift their position. They asked the Treasury to increase bill rates to 0.5 percent by lengthening the initial term to four months (Minutes, FOMC, March 1, 1944, 5). Eccles opposed the request on the improbable grounds that large banks would use the additional revenue to absorb exchange charges on checks. Small banks would increase these charges, weakening the banking system (Board Minutes, March 8, 1944, 2).

22. In June the Federal Reserve repeated that the pattern of rates "does not involve fixed or pegged prices for individual issues, but means maintenance of prices *within a range which may include prices below par as well as above par*" (Sproul Papers, FOMC, June 27, 1942, 4). The Federal Reserve did not refer to this position in the postwar years.

Despite the comments about flexibility he made in 1942, Eccles favored the fixed rate structure throughout the war to reduce financing costs and to prevent owners of Treasury securities from profiting from war finance. He opposed a proposal to extend the maturity of the debt by selling more three- to four-year securities and fewer bills because "there was no reason why they [banks] should receive $1^{1}/_{4}$ or $1^{1}/_{2}$ percent" (Board Minutes, Meeting of the Federal Advisory Council, December 4, 1944, 9). "It was highly desirable that the proportion of outstanding Government debt in the form of bills and certificates (under one year) should continue" (11). He regretted only that banks did not buy more short-term securities. It was a mistake, he thought, not to restrict them to these short-term issues in 1941 (13). The banks had too much profit.[23]

With its chairman firmly holding views of this kind, the Federal Reserve did not seek changes in interest rates during the war. Even if it had sought higher rates, it would have faced two obstacles. Morgenthau opposed any increase. And populists in Congress claimed the interest cost was too high. Congressman Wright Patman (Texas), a member of the House Banking Committee, denied that he wanted "printing press money." He wanted lower interest rates: "If money must be created on the government's credit, the taxpayers should not be compelled to pay interest on it" (Board of Governors File, box 141, July 1942).[24]

The Board and the banks understood the inflationary consequences of pegging rates, but they did not oppose the policy during the war. Those most concerned about inflation urged higher income tax rates, sales or expenditure taxes, or compulsory savings to absorb purchasing power. To improve understanding of the problem and disseminate information more widely, Eccles urged the reserve banks to expand their research staffs and coordinate their efforts through a System committee (Board Minutes, March 2, 1943, 2–7).[25]

Open Market and Other Purchases

With rates fixed, the FOMC had little to do. It approved new limits on the size of the account and authorizations to purchase and sell. It spent much of its time discussing problems associated with bond drives, banks playing

23. He said that since the banks had a franchise from the government to create money in the form of checks, the banking system was vulnerable to the trend throughout the world to socialize banking (Sproul Papers, FOMC, June 27, 1942, 17).

24. The quotation comes from a June 1942 letter to a Dallas newspaper signed by Congressman Wright Patman. The news clipping is in the Board's files.

25. Eccles's proposal called for a staff member at the Board "to direct the coordination of the work of the Board and the Federal Reserve Banks." This brought a quick response from Allan Sproul of New York opposing direction by the Board.

Table 7.2   System Purchases of Government Securities, 1942–45

| YEAR | PURCHASES | |
	DOLLARS (BILLIONS)	PERCENTAGE CHANGE
1942	3.9	174.5
1943	5.8	86.5
1944	7.3	63.3
1945	5.4	28.7
Total	22.4	

the pattern of rates, and the possibility of lending to banks instead of buying securities or using repurchase agreements instead of discounts and outright purchases.

Banks held more than $6.5 billion of excess reserves early in 1941. At first they purchased securities by reducing excess reserves. The decline was most rapid in New York, slowest at country banks.[26] By August, New York banks had all but eliminated their excess reserves (Minutes, FOMC, August 8, 1942). To provide reserves, the Federal Reserve removed all restrictions on the amount of short-term securities (bills and certificates) in the System Open Market Account by the end of 1942. Limits on the amount of longer-term securities remained.

Table 7.2 shows the rates of purchase from 1942 to 1945. By the end of the war, short-term government securities had become the Federal Reserve's principal asset. The pre–World War I problem of a portfolio insufficient to offset a gold inflow or, in the 1930s, excess reserves greater than the portfolio, would not return. Financing World War II left the Federal Reserve balance sheet and the monetary base dominated by the open market portfolio. This result was very different from the founders' plan; the System had become an indirect source of government finance.

It soon became a direct source as well. On March 27, 1942, the second War Powers Act authorized Federal Reserve banks to acquire direct or guaranteed obligations of the United States by purchase from the Treasury. Eccles supported the bill enthusiastically. At one point he suggested that the FOMC should view the change as a new method of distribution: "Instead of having to . . . price an issue at a figure which would attract heavy oversubscriptions, the securities could be taken by the System and sold to the market as it could absorb them" (Board Minutes, February 3, 1942, 4).

Other Board members accepted the change as a wartime measure

---

26. At the end of the war, excess reserves of all member banks were about $1 billion. The low yield on Treasury bills and the small size of many country banks probably explain the sacrifice of pecuniary returns. The FOMC considered reducing the discount rate to encourage banks to increase borrowing and reduce excess reserves, but it did not act (Minutes, FOMC, August 3, 1942, 14–17).

needed to ensure that Treasury issues would not fail to find buyers at established rates and to furnish funds for short periods around tax dates. Sproul, who was at the meeting, did not oppose the amendment. He criticized the Board's failure to discuss the subject with the president before it was included in the War Powers bill, and he opposed Eccles's suggestion that the reserve banks distribute government securities. He accepted direct purchases as a temporary measure to help the Treasury around tax dates or in an emergency.[27]

The change repealed a section of the Banking Act of 1935 that prohibited the System from purchasing government securities except in the open market. A few months later, the Board told the account manager to combine direct purchases from the Treasury with open market purchases in the weekly statement. The War Powers Act expired six months after the war ended; initial authority for direct purchases expired in December 1944. The Board requested renewal for two more years; later the authority became permanent.

Despite the low interest rates on short-term debt, war finance greatly increased earnings of the reserve banks. Net earnings rose from an average of $11 million for 1937–41 to more than $92 million in 1945. The Federal Reserve had been relieved of payments to the United States Treasury after 1933 in exchange for the capital provided to establish the Federal Deposit Insurance Corporation.[28] By September 1942, Vice Governor Ronald Ransom anticipated that the government would reinstate the franchise tax if earnings rose (Board Minutes, September 15, 1942, 2). He was correct but premature. Congress imposed a tax equal to 90 percent of annual net earnings in 1946. The tax offset a substantial portion of the interest payments on Treasury debt held by the reserve banks.[29]

27. In the course of the discussion Eccles offered his interpretation of central bank independence: "The kind of independence a central bank should have was an opportunity to express its views in connection with the determination of policy, and that after it had been heard it should not try to make its will prevail but should cooperate in carrying out the program agreed upon by the Government. . . . [A]ny other kind of independence would be an impractical position which would result in the loss of authority and influence that it otherwise might have" (Board Minutes, February 3, 1942, 8).

28. The System paid a modest amount to the Treasury from 1936 to 1946 for interest received on industrial loans. The largest annual payment was $327,000.

29. There were other lasting changes. The large increase in wartime debt and in trading led to changes in the market for government securities. The FOMC and the Board considered proposals to use the reserve banks instead of government dealers to make markets in government securities. The reserve banks opposed suggestions that the Treasury sell all government securities to the reserve banks, which would market the debt to the public. Instead, the New York bank agreed to license government security dealers. In exchange, the dealers agreed to provide detailed portfolio and transactions data (Minutes, FOMC, February 29, 1944, 6–8). Another change increased the roles of reserve bank economists at the FOMC.

Reserve Requirements

With the bill rate at 0.375 percent in 1942 and income taxable at high wartime rates, banks outside New York and Chicago did not bother to invest in bills or send excess reserves to correspondent banks. The Treasury wanted to reduce reserve requirement ratios for urban banks to release reserves for purchases of Treasury securities.

The Banking Act of 1935 did not permit the Board to change reserve requirements for only one class of banks. Congress approved the additional authority on July 7, 1942. The change was contentious within the System. The Federal Advisory Council opposed the change, and initially so did the Board. Eccles described the reduction as "a grave mistake" (Board Minutes, February 16, 1942, 2–3). Prodded by the Treasury, once the legislation passed, the Federal Reserve reduced required reserve ratios at central reserve city banks in three steps, from 26 percent to 24 percent on August 19, 22 percent on September 14, and 20 percent on October 3. Together the three reductions released $1.2 billion, about 6 percent of the monetary base at the time.

The New York and Chicago banks bought Treasury bills, as expected. The principal effect of the change was not on reserves or the monetary base but on the earnings of the banks and reserve banks. With interest rates rigidly fixed, banks as a group determined the aggregate amount of reserves by buying or selling Treasury bills. Further, New York and Chicago banks could create more deposits and add more to earning assets per dollar of reserves or base money. Contrary to Eccles's aim, the reserve banks had smaller earnings and the banks had more.[30]

The three changes brought required reserve ratios for the two central reserve cities to equality with reserve city banks for the first time in Federal Reserve history. There were no further changes in reserve requirement ratios during the war. The only other wartime change removed reserve requirements on war loan deposits as an inducement to banks to buy securities by increasing Treasury deposits during bond drives.

Until the war, only New York had sent an economist to the meeting. During the war, all banks were invited to adopt this practice. Discussion at FOMC meetings continued to be dominated by Eccles, Sproul, and economists at the Board and the New York bank, however.

30. The Board did not fully understand the limited effect of the change. On April 9, 1944, it unanimously approved a letter to a Mississippi banker who had written to request a reduction in the reserve requirement ratio for country banks from 14 percent to 7 percent. The Board explained in part that "reserves supplied through open market operations . . . go in the first instance directly to the particular banks needing them" (Board Minutes, June 9, 1944, 4–5). The letter then went on to cite other reasons, including the greater ease of monetary control after the war. There was no mention of earnings.

Discount and Other Rates

Discount rates ranged from 1 to 1.5 percent when the war started. After some prodding from the Board, on April 11, 1942, the reserve banks agreed to a uniform discount rate of 1 percent. In addition to the basic discount rates, the Federal Reserve set a preferential rate for loans collateralized by short-term government securities and a rate on direct loans to military contractors made under its authority to lend to individuals and businesses. The latter provision, a depression measure, was used to finance production of war materials. The amount outstanding on June and December reporting dates never exceeded $35 million (lent in 1936). During World War II, the total outstanding was about $10 million. Almost all the loans were for one year or less (Board Minutes, 1976, 492).[31]

Analysis at the Philadelphia reserve bank correctly noted that banks would obtain reserves at lowest cost and would hold debt with higher rates and longer terms to maturity. With discount rates above Treasury bill rates, discounting remained small. The memo criticized preferential rates for loans collateralized by government securities. Preferential rates would not affect the volume of borrowing, only the collateral used to borrow and the maturity of bank-held debt (Board of Governors File, box 1452, October 8, 1942, 7–10).

The Philadelphia bank's memo was critical of preferential discount rates on other grounds also. The memo rejected the real bills doctrine: "The experience with preferential rates in the last war and the postwar period on the whole was not satisfactory. The general conclusion of Reserve officials and analysts is that the particular paper used to secure an advance has no relation at all to the use that the bank will make of the funds it secures" (ibid., 9).

Despite this correct analysis, the Board adopted a preferential discount rate of 0.5 percent for discounts secured by short-term governments. The main argument for the preferential rate was that it would induce banks to hold more short-term bills instead of higher-yielding bonds. George L. Harrison said that it would be easier to eliminate the preferential rate, when it was time to reverse policy, than to increase the general discount rate (Board Minutes, October 7, 1942, 9).[32]

---

31. The New York Federal Reserve bank set the rate on direct loans to war contractors at 4 percent to 6 percent. The Board wanted the rate reduced to from 2.5 percent to 4 percent. The compromise was to lower the rate schedule to from 4 percent to 5 percent (Minutes, New York Directors, May 7 and June 4, 1942).

32. Harrison, former governor of the New York bank, was a member of the Federal Advisory Council. His memory of 1919–20 was faulty. The Treasury was willing to increase the general discount rate before it was willing to raise the preferential rate. See chapter 3.

Harrison underestimated the Treasury. In June 1945 Sproul proposed an increase in the preferential rate to 0.75 percent. All the presidents concurred, but the rate remained at 0.5 percent (Minutes, FOMC, June 20, 1945, 9). The following month, the New York bank directors asked to eliminate the preferential discount rate. The Treasury remained unwilling, so the rate stayed (Minutes, New York Directors, July 19, 1945, 20).

Bankers grumbled occasionally about Treasury tax and interest rate policies. When the opportunity arose, members of the Federal Advisory Council argued for higher rates on short-term securities to get banks to hold more of them. The most strenuous plea came from a member who argued that banks could not be expected to finance the war if they were "'bled white' through the maintenance of low interest rates and application of high taxes" (Board Minutes, April 9, 1942, 13).[33]

Selective Credit Controls

Unable to control money or interest rates, the Board turned first to controls on consumer credit and later to controls on real estate, stock market, and other forms of lending and borrowing. Some of these actions were taken to show that it was "doing something" to control inflation, some in the belief that it had to use existing authority before Congress would grant additional powers, and some at the urging of other agencies.

The Board adopted regulation W to reduce the demand for durable goods. The original order required a 20 percent down payment and limited loans to a maximum of eighteen months. Wartime revisions and amendments extended the range of goods covered, raised the required down payment, and reduced the maximum term.[34] Experience with regulation established once again that efforts to control a complex economy produce unforeseen consequences leading to both extensions and exclusions from

33. Between 1941 and 1945, member bank income after taxes rose from $390 million to $788 million, about a 50 percent increase in real terms. (Since prices were controlled, the price index is biased downward. Using the 1945 price index, the gain is 60 percent; using 1946, after controls were removed, the gain was 43 percent.) To help the Treasury sell debt to the public, the Board discussed lowering the maximum rate that commercial banks could pay on time deposits from 2.5 percent to 1.5 percent. Eccles, Ransom, and Leo Crowley (chairman of the FDIC) favored the change, but it was not made. One reason is that banks feared they would lose savings deposits to nonbank thrift institutions, a problem that returned in the 1960s.

34. By spring 1942, the list included new and used goods, shoes, hats, and haberdashery. Monthly charge accounts were covered also. The regulations became so detailed that the Board agreed to exempt the Boy Scouts and railroad employees required to use a precision watch (Board Minutes, June 29, 1942, 9; August 12, 1942, 1).

earlier regulations.[35] Since credit is fungible, restrictions on one type of credit shifted demand to less regulated forms and encouraged innovation to circumvent regulations.[36]

By 1943 the Board began to discuss extending credit regulation to include real estate, securities, and traded commodities. Eccles explained to the reserve bank presidents that "the Board was not seeking the authority . . . but was willing to accept it" (Board Minutes, June 29, 1943, 21). Eccles preferred to increase taxes and forgo additional regulation, but he accepted the new responsibility to retain credit control under the Federal Reserve System: "Some of the Presidents indicated agreement with Chairman Eccles's attitude and expressed doubt as to the ability of any agency successfully to discharge the responsibility" (22).

Enforcement differed across the country because each reserve bank chose the extent of enforcement. Vice Chairman Ransom complained at one point that the Board had chosen a middle course between strict and lax enforcement. Strict enforcement "would antagonize the people whose support was necessary," and lax enforcement would foster the "impression that the System did not care whether the provisions of the regulation were observed" (ibid., 23).

Years later, W. Randolph Burgess summarized matters: "Looking back at the experience with the control of consumer credit, it would be very hard to make a case that what was done . . . was useful, and it certainly made a great deal of work for a great many people, at a time when there was a shortage of manpower and a heavy surplus of irritating red-tape and procedures to interfere with essential war work" (Letter Burgess to Sproul, Sproul Papers, Board of Governors, Joint Committee on Economic Report, October 7, 1949, 2).

Common stock prices had fallen a total of more than 20 percent from 1939 to 1941. Stock prices rose 20 percent in 1942 but remained below their 1938 value (Ibbotson and Sinquefeld 1989). In March 1943 the Board began discussing increases in margin requirements on securities. The volume of trading had increased to about one million shares a day, making

35. The Board had to decide such weighty matters as Should reupholstered furniture be treated like new furniture? Should loans for funeral expenses be exempted? Medical and dental expenses? (Board Minutes, August 12, 1942, 1).

36. Studies of the effect of selective controls on housing and durable goods find no evidence of their effectiveness. For housing, see Kane 1977 and Meltzer 1974. For durables, see Hamburger and Zwick 1977, 1979. These studies apply to later periods, but their findings are applicable to the war. A principal finding is that credit controls have clear effect on the form in which lenders extend credit, but there is no evidence of an effect on the allocation of resources or total spending.

some of the staff uneasy. Earlier, the Board had issued regulations T and U to set margin requirements as authorized by the 1934 Securities Exchange Act. Some staff members urged a preemptive strike against speculation, but the Board decided not to act (Board Minutes, March 15, 1943, 2–4). Prices continued to rise. By the end of 1944, the stock price index was almost 40 percent above the 1936 peak.

On February 5, 1945, the Board increased margin requirements to 50 percent. Eccles argued that there was no evidence of excessive use of credit in the stock market, but the Board approved the increase to show that it was concerned about future inflation (Board Minutes, February 2, 1945, 3–9).

Three weeks later, Eccles reported that the Economic Stabilization Board had suggested a 100 percent margin requirement. Eccles saw no need for the change, but Chairman Vinson of the Stabilization Board thought that Congress would not authorize new powers to control inflation until existing powers had been used. Eccles suggested that Vinson send a letter to the Federal Reserve asking for the increase in margin requirements (Board Minutes, February 23, 1945, 7–8). Vinson sent the letter, but the Board delayed a decision.

By a vote of five to one, the Board agreed to let Eccles tell the Economic Stabilization Board that the System favored an increase only to 70 percent. Governor John K. McKee opposed because the government's anti-inflation program was incomplete, and not much credit had been used for purchasing and carrying securities (Board Minutes, May 3, 1945, 7–8).[37]

The Federal Advisory Council agreed unanimously that speculation in real estate and stocks should be discouraged, but it saw little evidence of inflationary pressure in asset markets: "Farm lands are about where they were in 1913. . . . There has been a good deal of speculation in the larger apartment buildings and hotels and in some kinds of commercial buildings, but even there the prices are below the cost of reproduction. Stock prices are not above the 1936–37 levels, in spite of the fact that in the interim most corporations have added very materially to their assets" (Board Minutes, May 14, 1945, 2).

By late June 1945, with the war almost over, the Economic Stabilization Board agreed to recommend credit controls on real estate, higher margin requirements on stock transactions, and a longer holding period for capital gains. It considered an increase in the capital gains tax rate. It could not

37. John K. McKee was appointed to the FOMC in February 1936. He served ten years, leaving in April 1946.

decide whether new construction should be exempt from real estate controls. Eccles believed that the new credit controls would be ineffective and should not be used unless Congress passed a tax increase (Board Minutes, June 21, 1945, 18–19).

Pressed by the administration, the Board voted to increase margin requirements on new purchases of securities to 75 percent effective July 5. The Board also required that the proceeds of security sales be used to bring the margin on the whole portfolio toward the new requirements before cash could be distributed to the owner. Governor McKee again opposed the increase.

The new requirements were unpopular with the public and with many bankers and securities dealers. In September the Federal Advisory Council urged the Board to consider returning to a 50 percent margin. Eccles thought it was premature to consider a reduction. Effective January 2, 1946, the Board increased the margin requirement to 100 percent; all transactions had to be for cash.

Other Wartime Changes

Rapid growth of the Federal Reserve's portfolio and the monetary base, and a small gold outflow, lowered the System's gold reserve ratio toward the legal limit—40 percent of notes in circulation and 35 percent of deposits at Federal Reserve banks. By mid-1944 the System's gold reserve ratio had fallen to 55 percent (from 91 percent in November 1941).

The FOMC minutes first mention the problem in May 1944. The committee voted to reallocate Treasury bills in the System account to prevent the ratio at any reserve bank from falling below 45 percent. Members agreed to buy Treasury bills from the reserve banks with low ratios and to change the allocation of open market purchases (Minutes, FOMC, May 4, 1944, 14–15). Several banks sold Treasury bills to other reserve banks for gold certificates, and the Federal Open Market Committee revised the securities allocation formula to adjust for differences in gold reserves.

The System's gold reserve ratio continued to fall. In July the executive committee considered asking Congress to reduce the ratio to a uniform 25 percent against notes and deposits. Eccles favored eliminating the requirement, but the committee thought the public was not ready to remove all ties to gold. The executive committee voted to put off any decision until after the election.

Legislation introduced in January, and passed in June, lowered the gold reserve requirement to 25 percent and extended the "temporary" authority, first granted in 1932, to use government securities as collateral for Federal

Table 7.3   Gold Reserve Ratios, June 1945 (percent)

BANK	RATIO	BANK	RATIO
Boston	24.9	Chicago	65.3
New York	50.1	St. Louis	28.8
Philadelphia	25.4	Minneapolis	22.9
Cleveland	32.6	Kansas City	31.0
Richmond	38.2	Dallas	22.0
Atlanta	44.9	San Francisco	59.4

Source: Minutes, Executive Committee, FOMC, June 20, 1945, 5.

Reserve notes.[38] The FOMC responded by lowering from 45 percent to 35 percent the gold reserve ratio at which the individual reserve banks would cease to participate in open market purchases. Table 7.3 shows that even after the legal change, several of the reserve banks did not meet the requirement.

Eccles attempted to coordinate the research functions at the reserve banks under the direction of the Board's research division. The issue had arisen first in 1936, after the Banking Act of 1935 became law. It arose again in 1943, under the guise of having a "steering committee" to give direction to research work. The reserve banks resisted and, on both occasions, prevented the Board's staff from acquiring authority over the banks' staffs (Sproul Papers, Memorandums and Drafts, December 17, 1943). Eccles tried again, claiming that the Board had the right to approve persons appointed to supervisory positions in the banks' research departments, but he did not prevail over the protests of the banks' officers and directors (Minutes, New York Directors, August 17, 1944, 267).

To supplement wartime price controls, the government ordered coupon rationing of gasoline, food, shoes, and other consumer goods. Purchasers presented coupons along with cash to complete transactions. Processing ration coupons became the responsibility of commercial banks and Federal Reserve banks beginning in January 1943.

The army decided early in 1942 to move Japanese and Nisei living in the western states into camps. After the administration approved the order, Japanese and Nisei had to leave their homes and businesses. The Treasury had responsibility for protecting the property they left behind. The

38. When the bill was introduced, Senator Elmer Thomas wrote asking the Board to append his bill authorizing all banks and other financial institutions to carry government obligations at par value. It declined (Board Minutes, January 26, 1945, 2). The Board also requested repeal of the Thomas amendment authorizing the president to issue $3 billion of currency (Board Minutes, March 15, 1945, 202). At about this time, Congress considered a proposal to have the General Accounting Office audit the Federal Reserve, as it had done in the System's early years (Minutes, New York Directors, February 5, 1945, 170). This issue returned many times.

Federal Reserve banks administered the program for the Treasury (Blum 1967, 3–4).[39]

POSTWAR PLANNING

Planning postwar economic policies began long before the war ended. Interwar experience convinced many businessmen, economists, and others that it would be unwise, and probably unacceptable, to return to the high unemployment rates and instability that characterized the interwar period. Keynes's *General Theory* (1936) seemed to provide an economic rationale for activist government policies to expand or slow domestic economic activity.[40] His plan for international monetary cooperation, prepared during the war, made a major contribution to the development of the postwar Bretton Woods institutions. Earlier, in his *Treatise on Money* (1930), he had made the case for international monetary reform, based on a more flexible gold standard. These topics moved to the forefront in planning for the postwar world.

Discussion of postwar planning shows significant changes in policy views since the 1920s. Two changes eventually altered the role of United States monetary policy. First was the commitment to economic stabilization. This commitment was a long step away from the Federal Reserve's denial in the 1920s that its actions affected the price level or the pace of economic activity. Second was the primacy given to domestic over international considerations. The proponents of these changes assigned a very modest role to monetary policy and the Federal Reserve. As the perceived influence of monetary policy changed in the 1950s and 1960s, full employment and domestic stability became dominant policy concerns by the 1960s. Although not fully recognized at the time, the heightened emphasis given to domestic concerns in many countries was incompatible with plans for an international monetary system based on gold and fixed exchange rates.

Domestic Plans

In spring 1943 the System began to study postwar reconversion. One set of issues was transitional. For example, when the military canceled contracts, small and medium-sized firms would need loans to convert to peacetime

---

39. The unique private-public structure of the Federal Reserve left unresolved whether property such as the Board of Governors building was taxable by the District of Columbia. The District agreed to treat the property as government property provided each of the reserve banks disclaimed ownership (Minutes, New York Directors, January 13, 1944, 21).

40. In fact Keynes (1936) says very little about activist policies. Keynes's support for such policies antedates his book and is more explicit in his policy tracts. See Meltzer 1988.

production just as regulation V loans to finance military procurement ended. The System appointed a committee to study transitional lending (Board Minutes, April 29, 1943, 5–7; June 20, 1943, 5–7). In May 1944 the Board authorized a series of studies of postwar policies. A sample of the ideas gives the flavor of many economists' opinions at the time.

The Board's economic adviser, Emanuel A. Goldenweiser, recommended the "continuation of wage and price controls, rationing and allocation, as well as licensing exports . . . [as] a prime condition of a successful transition from a war to a peace economy" (Board of Governors of the Federal Reserve System 1945, 1:3). Goldenweiser proposed that the government offer employment to any unemployed worker to sustain consumption. He favored keeping selective credit controls, margin requirements, and "all the powers over the general volume and cost of money that they have had in the past, and they should have additional authority over member bank reserves" (1:15). The "additional authority" is probably a reference to a secondary reserve requirement of securities to prevent banks from selling Treasury bills to the reserve banks.

Unemployment was a main concern. The second study in the Board's series warned of another 1929 collapse and unemployment of 6 to 8 million during reconversion to peacetime (ibid., 1:18–49).[41] Postwar experience turned out very differently. Reconversion occurred quickly. After a brief adjustment, economic activity rose rapidly. Unemployment remained low.

Like Goldenweiser, Eccles believed that price controls should be retained until postwar output increased enough to satisfy demand. He testified that "price controls, rationing, curbs on consumer credit or stock market credit, and similar devices, admittedly deal only with effects and not with basic causes of inflationary pressures" (House Committee on Banking and Currency 1946, 171).[42] Nevertheless, he believed that an opportunity to control inflation was lost with repeal of the excess profits tax in 1945, termination of the War Labor Board, and failure to increase the capital gains tax at the end of the war (Board Minutes, November 19, 1945, 10–11). He did not mention that these wartime measures distorted allocation and slowed investment. Nor did he recognize that price and wage controls caused many low-priced goods to disappear and encouraged producers to lower quality as a substitute for raising prices. Similarly, wage controls encouraged both labor

41. There is nothing in the studies about the need to restore monetary control by eliminating the interest rate peg. Volume 8, devoted to Federal Reserve policy, is given over mainly to a historical review of past options.

42. "To the extent that we can deal effectively with the money supply and production factors, we will be getting at the root causes of the inflationary problems confronting the country today" (House Committee on Banking and Currency 1946, 171).

"hoarding" and shortages and the substitution of noncash benefits for cash payments.[43] Neither he nor his staff recognized that deregulation and correct price signals would speed the transition and reduce waste.[44]

Congress did not concur. It responded to the general dissatisfaction with wartime controls, rationing, and black markets by removing most controls by fall 1946. The immediate effect was a short-lived surge in the reported price index, as reported prices adjusted to reflect hidden or deferred changes (see chart 7.1 above). Consumer prices rose at a 29 percent annual rate between June and November, with the largest rise in July. By January 1947 the monthly increase had fallen to zero.[45] After these adjustments, price levels were 33 percent above the level at the start of the war, a 6.5 percent annual rate of increase.

Lauchlin Currie, on the White House staff, and Keynesian economists at Commerce, Treasury, and other agencies believed that a severe postwar depression was likely. They bolstered their argument by showing that private spending would not expand enough to replace military spending as a source of employment. Much of the shortfall was a consumption "gap"—the difference between predicted consumption spending and spending consistent with full employment. And because the consumption gap would be large, private investment would remain low and unemployment high.[46] Beginning in 1944, Keynesian economists urged gradual release of materials from military use to smooth postwar readjustment. The military opposed the change while the war continued, and nothing was done. Interest in peacetime conversion rose when the European war ended in April 1945. The National Resources Planning Board advocated a comprehensive social welfare program, pollution abatement, public transport systems, and other government programs.

Nothing in Keynesian analysis favored government spending instead of

43. World War II wage controls, and tax deductibility, produced a long-term inefficiency—health care benefits paid by employers who deduct the cost. This distortion increases the demand for health insurance and limits opportunities for individual workers or families to choose the health insurance they prefer.

44. Eccles had a mixed view of price and wage controls. He supported the call for controls in 1942, but he saw them as at best a supplement to taxation that removed private command of resources. At the same time, he seems aware of the conflicts set off by controls—whether costs could be controlled as effectively as, or more effectively than, prices, problems such as setting rents, concerns about excess profits, and so on. See Eccles 1951, 370–72. Morgenthau favored controls on prices but not on wages. He said that labor was not a commodity, so wages should not be treated like other prices.

45. Price controls expired in June 1946. Congress voted for rapid decontrol, but President Truman vetoed the bill, so controls ended when they expired. In early August, Congress renewed controls (but not food subsidies). This was followed almost immediately by meat shortages. Almost all controls were abolished by executive order on November 11, 1946.

46. This section is based on Jones 1972.

tax reduction as a way for government to influence the transition from war to peace. Largely as a matter of belief, administration economists and their outside advisers favored government spending.[47] System economists were divided.[48]

President Roosevelt adopted part of the Keynesian program. His last State of the Union message to Congress set a goal of 60 million postwar jobs. At the time, there were 55 million people in the civilian labor force and an additional 11.4 million in the armed forces, but some of these were women who were expected to leave the labor force after the war. The statement was seen as a loose commitment to "full employment."

Roosevelt's statement was soon followed by a proposed Full Employment Act that became the Employment Act of 1946.[49] The original proposal recognized a person's right to employment and the government's responsibility to provide full employment. To achieve this end, the proposal

47. Principal among them were Seymour Harris (1943), Alvin Hansen of Harvard, and Paul Samuelson of MIT (1943). Others such as Herbert Stein of the Committee for Economic Development preferred lower taxes. Stein's influential essay became the basis for policies advocated by the Committee for Economic Development, a business-sponsored group.

48. At a meeting of the Board and the presidents to discuss the Board's studies of postwar problems, John H. Williams was highly critical of a study by Richard Musgrave, a member of the Board's staff. The study showed that the budget would not be balanced if government spending remained low. The argument, based on a Keynesian model, proposed that the government absorb the excess savings. Williams countered that Musgrave had neglected the crowding out of private spending. Some government spending makes "private business work better, but when you get up to this level, you are bound to ask what these expenditures are doing to the private economy. It is inevitable that it will take its place to an increasing degree" (Board Minutes, March 2, 1945, 5). Williams's remarks anticipated major controversies about the effects of government spending, deficits, and debt in the 1960s and 1970s. Williams added, "[Economists] are interested in large and even growing public expenditures. I think there is a lot to be looked into on that point before we accept it as a guide for postwar policy" (Board Minutes, March 2, 1945, 6). Seymour Harris (1943) wrote: "These [Keynesian] economists are impressed with the failure of the capitalism of the twenties to provide full employment and are impatient with economic theory that fails to discuss conditions of disequilibrium and underemployment. Keynesian influences will be especially evident in the parts of the volume devoted to the discussion of full employment and fiscal policy" (5). In the same volume Paul Samuelson (1943, 53) wrote: "All our findings lead to the conclusion that there is a serious danger of underestimating the magnitude of the problem of maintaining continuing full employment in the postwar period."

49. See Murray 1945. The standard reference to the act is Bailey 1950. The bill was pushed by Leon Keyserling. Later George Terborgh of the Machinery and Allied Products Institute rejected the Hansen-Samuelson argument. "Nothing in the purely economic or technical situation indicates that private investment will have to be propped up by public investment not desired for its own sake. Indeed, the situation is so favorable for a boom after the inevitable transition period" (Sproul Papers, Board of Governors, Correspondence 1943–44). The quotations are from a speech by Terborgh, 14–15. One of the first members of the Council of Economic Advisers and its second chairman, Keyserling had been a legislative assistant to Senator Robert Wagner of New York, one of the sponsors. Keyserling was a principal developer of "the Fair Deal," President Truman's economic program. See Brazelton 1997.

called for some national planning: a National Production and Employment Budget would forecast the state of the economy and the levels of employment and output consistent with full employment. The president would recommend actions needed to close any "gap" between expected and full employment.

Discussion of the bill shows the large shift in opinion that had occurred in a decade. The bill had three Republican senators as sponsors and more than one hundred sponsors in the House, including Congresswoman Clare Booth Luce, a prominent conservative and the wife of a prominent publisher. Few in Congress criticized the commitment to an expanding economy or the idea that government spending could affect the economy. The right to a job and a commitment to full employment were more contentious. Opponents pointed to the risk of inflation, the possibility of continuous budget deficits, and the possible use of the act to promote "national planning," price controls, or other restrictions on freedom.

The act that emerged was a compromise, but it gave more to the opponents than to the original proponents.[50] Gone were the commitments to full employment and mandatory computation of the "gap." The legislation called only for "maximum employment, production, and purchasing power," a phrase that was undefined, therefore open to whatever interpretation an administration or Congress might put on it. Gone also was a legislated commitment to forecasts of economic activity, although forecasting became standard procedure in all administrations.[51]

The act created a Council of Economic Advisers in the Office of the President to help the president decide on economic policy. The intention may have been to keep the council as a professional body, free of politics. In practice the council, as a staff agency, had a weaker position than many of the current and future line agencies representing business, labor, environmental, educational, consumer, and other interest groups. The role of the council has varied with the president's interest in receiving its advice and the relationship between the council's chairman and the president.[52]

The Board's reaction was generally positive and supportive of the origi-

50. For a contrary view, see Keyserling 1972. According to Keyserling, the act allowed economic planning but was not carried out because of the unwillingness of government (and Keynesian economists) to propose income redistribution.

51. Forecasters' failure to foresee rapid postwar recovery instead of a return to high unemployment did not strengthen their case. See Stein 1990, 202. On the inaccuracy of economic forecasts, see Meltzer 1987.

52. The Reagan administration considered abolishing the council because of differences between one of its chairmen and other presidential advisers over budget deficits. Since the council was authorized in the Employment Act, demission required legislation. The administration chose not to raise the issue.

nal bill. Woodlief Thomas, assistant director of research at the Board, read the bill as an attempt to "legislate the Keynes-Eccles-Hansen-Beveridge theory of economic stabilization" (Memo Thomas to Ransom, Board of Governors File, box 198, February 12 and 4, 1945). Thomas saw enactment of a particular economic theory as a danger, but the act did not do that. The bill, he said, was "a statement of goals, not an outline of policies" (ibid.).

Eccles had favored countercyclical use of fiscal policy since the early 1930s. He came to Washington early in the New Deal to promote that policy. In a letter to Senator Robert Wagner, he accepted the objectives of the bill but emphasized the primary role of the private sector in providing employment. He urged Wagner to substitute for full employment "maintaining economic stability at as high a level of employment and production as can be continuously maintained" (Eccles to Wagner, Board of Governors File, box 198, June 16, 1945). Although he discussed the Federal Reserve, he did not mention monetary policy as a tool for reaching the objectives of the act.

Neglect of monetary policy was not an oversight. The conventional view among economists at the time was that monetary policy had, at most, modest effects on output and prices.[53] These beliefs justified the passive monetary policy that the System chose mainly for political reasons. When conventional views changed in later years, the Federal Reserve accepted major responsibility for moderating recessions and controlling inflation.

International Plans

Planning for postwar international monetary cooperation began before the United States entered the war. Section 7 of the lend-lease agreement, under which Britain and others obtained military supplies and equipment "on credit," provided that the United States could waive postwar repayment if the British agreed to eliminate trade "discrimination" and reduce tariffs. Discrimination was not further defined, but the objectives it expressed included elimination of the prewar system of imperial preference that bound Britain to its empire and favored British exports.

Avoidance of bilateral agreements and imperial preference was a major goal of the State Department. Secretary of State Cordell Hull favored a multilateral system centered on "most favored nation" clauses that gave each signatory the lowest tariff rate agreed with any other country. The British

---

53. This position dominated research at the time. See Villard 1948 and Ackley 1961, and for a Federal Reserve view see Thomas 1941. For a contrary view see Friedman 1956 and Warburton 1966. Assigning a more powerful influence to monetary policy would have required the Federal Reserve to accept more responsibility for the Great Depression, but it would have moderated, or even prevented, the Great Inflation after 1965.

accepted section 7 out of wartime desperation. They did not like it (Presnell 1997).

In the course of negotiations leading to the lend-lease agreement, Keynes broadened the terms of reference to include finance and exchange rates. The two treasuries then took the lead in negotiations, shifting emphasis from trade issues to finance. By September 1941 Keynes had developed a proposal for an international clearing union that could create a currency for member central banks to use in settling payments imbalances. After adjustment, Keynes's proposal became the British government proposal in April 1943, when formal bilateral discussions began.

Keynes (1924) had developed the basic analysis much earlier. Each country acting alone can achieve either stable prices or a fixed exchange rate but not both. To achieve both, there must be international cooperation or agreement. The gold standard is one type of agreement; each country accepts the rules of the standard, defining currency value in grams of gold, agreeing to buy and sell gold at a fixed price, and allowing money and prices to rise or fall with gold movements. If member countries followed these rules, exchange rates would remain fixed and inflation or deflation would be limited to changes around the world price level, the latter set by world demand for and output of gold. Large productivity shocks might disrupt countries' efforts to maintain employment and stable prices, but prices and output would eventually adjust as required by the fixed exchange rate.

The rules, however, required procyclical policies—allowing gold inflows to inflate the economy during expansions and to accept contraction, unemployment, and deflation when gold flowed out. With the growth of industrialization, labor unions, and the spread of the voting franchise, voters and governments were less willing to follow such rules in the 1920s. Many proposals to eliminate or reduce procyclicality had been made, but none had been adopted.[54]

In December, a week after the United States entered the war, Morgenthau asked Harry Dexter White to "prepare a memorandum on the establishment of an inter-Allied stabilization fund" as the basis for postwar international monetary arrangements (Blum 1967, 228–29).[55] Morgen-

54. Chapter 4 discusses attempts in the United States to enact Irving Fisher's proposal for a "compensated" gold dollar and to establish domestic price stability as the principal policy goal.

55. White was director of monetary research and later assistant secretary of the treasury. The United States proposal that became the basis of the International Monetary Fund is often referred to as the White plan. Keynes's plan called for a clearing union to adjust current account balances of debtors and creditors. White envisaged a permanent fund that could lend to debtor countries. White's version was the basis of the Bretton Woods Agreement.

thau's diary suggests that, although the United States had insisted on title 7, he had no more than a vague idea about expanding the prewar Tripartite Agreement to avoid competitive devaluation.[56]

The British were particularly interested in preventing a return of their interwar problem, when efforts to expand their economy by lowering interest rates were followed by a current account deficit and an outflow of gold that reduced the money stock and forced contraction and deflation.[57] White, and others at the United States Treasury, also favored a more flexible system. He too proposed a middle way between fixed and fluctuating rates with rules for lending and borrowing. Exchange rates would be fixed but adjustable; countries with a balance of payments surplus (like the United States in the 1920s) would lend to countries with deficits (like Britain in the 1920s). Unlike Keynes's plan, the new international institution could not create money.

The plan envisaged that deficit countries would not be forced to contract and deflate for balance of payments purposes. They would maintain imports from the rest of the world instead of reducing purchases and spreading contraction. To enforce lending, member countries agreed to impose costs on surplus countries that would neither expand imports nor lend to countries in deficit. Thus deficit and surplus countries alike would benefit from increased flexibility.[58] Both Keynes and White limited their proposals to financing trade and current account deficits. To the extent that they considered lending and borrowing on capital account, it was the responsibil-

56. Blum (1967, 228) speaks of "a kind of New Deal for a New World" and avoiding past difficulties caused by "private bankers, pursuing selfish ends" (229). Gardner 1956 is a comprehensive history of the origins of the fund. Several papers in Bordo and Eichengreen 1993 are a useful supplement. I limit my discussion principally to Treasury and Federal Reserve responses and actions. Keynes visited the United States in fall 1941 and possibly discussed his plan informally before White began work.

57. Keynes's dislike of the classical gold standard and what he called laissez-faire was no longer heretical in Britain by the 1940s. The established view was that the maldistribution of gold had made the system untenable. The accepted conclusion was that Britain should manage domestic policy to maintain full employment (Ikenberry 1993; Presnell 1997). Fluctuating rates were anathema to bankers and policymakers. An influential study by Nurkse (1944) concluded that fluctuating exchange rates caused destabilizing speculation in exchange rates and the prices of traded commodities. Nurkse's argument and evidence were later successfully challenged by Friedman (1953), but Nurkse's view remains widely held by bankers and governments.

58. This benefit could be achieved if all fluctuations were temporary, or cyclical, so that members could borrow in recessions and repay in recoveries, but the authors did not specify how to distinguish cyclical or temporary changes from permanent changes. Countries were allowed to devalue up to 10 percent without approval by the fund, and by more than 10 percent with prior approval. Devaluation was to be used to adjust to a "fundamental" disequilibrium. The fund was never able to define "fundamental" or to enforce the requirement that countries could not devalue by more than 10 percent without agreement.

ity of the proposed International Bank for Reconstruction and Development, later called the World Bank.[59]

Countries could pursue the domestic policies of their choice, a main British aim and another major departure from classical gold standard rules. Countries could correct policy errors by changing the exchange rate, with the consent of the new agency, the International Monetary Fund. The fund would also prevent multiple currency practices, discriminatory bilateral arrangements, and competitive devaluations. Eventually countries would maintain current account convertibility, a main aim of the United States.

Many in the banking community and the Federal Reserve wanted to return to the gold standard. White dismissed these proposals: "There isn't the slightest chance of getting other countries to return to the gold standard" (White to the Board and Reserve Bank Presidents, Minutes, FOMC, March 2, 1945, 20). The only chance for agreement was to combine stability of exchange rates with the flexibility to change them with the fund's approval. Other countries would agree to this mixture of stability and flexibility if it was part of an agreement that gave each country some assurance that it could borrow in an emergency: "We must give them time to balance their payments in such a way that they will not hurt the rest of the world" (25). Adjustment might take two, three, five, or even ten years.

The Reserve Board began to consider the Keynes and White plans in May–June 1943. Their first concern was the amount of new bank reserves that the United States would have to create. To eliminate all restrictions on current account financing, as Keynes proposed, required an expansion of $25 billion to $30 billion of United States base money. An expansion of this magnitude would double the amount of base money then outstanding. Board members wanted either power to control the domestic effect of such a large increase or a limit on the size of the increase (Board Minutes, May 29 and June 1, 1943). The Board also favored a provision, suggested by the Canadian representatives, that if the amount of foreign exchange balances at the fund increased beyond a preset limit, the member would gain voting power (ibid., June 1, 1943, 4). This would permit a surplus country to even-

59. White explained to the Federal Reserve Board that the World Bank would be responsible for capital transfers. "Many of the loans will be risky and there will be some losses. That is one of the reasons why we insisted that the Bank be an international bank rather than to take the risks by ourselves. We felt that the benefits would be world-wide and that other countries should bear part of the risk" (White to the Board and Reserve Bank Presidents, Board Minutes, March 2, 1945, 17). The Bank was also expected to remove the impediment to economic development arising because risk-averse private lenders restricted lending to developing countries or charged excessive risk premiums. Although no evidence was presented, this conclusion was widely held.

tually limit borrowing and expansion of its money stock. The British would not accept this proposal. They remembered the policies of surplus countries (the United States and France) in the 1920s and did not intend to repeat the experience.

As the plan developed, the Board's discussion of substantive issues ceased. Board staff participated actively in meetings organized by the Treasury, but few of the issues they raised came before the Board. The Board never considered the merits of alternative proposals and objections to the plan by leading bankers and the New York reserve bank.

The Board's consideration of the proposals that became the Bretton Woods Agreement is remarkable for the failure to discuss substance. This was not its initial intention. On March 7, 1944, Governor Menc S. Szymczak proposed that the Board approve the joint statement of a committee of international experts provided the Board would participate in the selection and control of the United States representative to the fund (Board Minutes, March 7, 1944, 1).[60] The Board did not act. The following day the Federal Advisory Council, meeting with the Board, supported the principle of exchange rate stabilization under an international agency but mentioned no details. A week later, Szymczak asked whether the Board wanted to suggest changes in the plan.[61] There was "general agreement . . . that if a plan were to come into existence it would not be possible for the Board to propose any fundamental changes" (Board Minutes, March 13, 1944, 2). The only decision was that a majority of the Board wanted "a voice in the selection of the American member of the board of directors" (3). "Reference was made to the fact that discussion of the plan up to this point had been strictly on a staff level and that none of the interested heads of agencies of the Government had in any way committed himself to what had been done" (4). The Board agreed to wait and not take a position until other agencies did. It instructed Goldenweiser, one of the Board's representatives at the technical discussions, to say that the Board's representatives did not speak for the Board.

60. Menc S. Szymczak, who served from 1933 to 1961, was a professor of business administration at DePaul University in Chicago when he was appointed to the Board. He had been active in Chicago area banking and had served also as comptroller of the city of Chicago. He was the Board's expert on international economics and participated in some of the Treasury meetings preparatory to the Bretton Woods Conference. Later he served as director in charge of rehabilitation of the German economy, on leave from the Board. His long service is explained by appointment to a twelve-year term in 1936 followed by a fourteen-year term beginning in 1948. He resigned six months before his term expired (Katz 1992).

61. Before the meeting, each of the members received a copy of the Joint Statement of Experts, a synthesis of the Keynes and White plans, and a statement of the positions taken by the Board's staff in the discussions.

This was either subterfuge or myopia. The Treasury was moving rapidly toward agreement on the plan. Morgenthau called a meeting in mid-April to discuss next steps. Eccles reported to the Board that Morgenthau had asked whether the Board would make a commitment to the plan. Eccles said no, the discussions had been at the staff level, and "it was understood that no commitments had been made or were expected at this time. I said it had been my understanding that the principals would meet and consider the report of the technicians, after which there would be an opportunity to discuss the matter, and that no such meeting had been called" (Board Minutes, April 18, 1944, 2). White, who was present, did not agree. The conference "would not go outside of the statement of principles" (1).[62] The Board hesitated, neither endorsing nor opposing the plan.[63] Instead it adopted a statement saying that "no governments are committed by action of the technicians. It now becomes necessary for the executive branch of the Government to consider the proposal of the technical experts and to determine what course of action in this matter should be undertaken and ultimately what program should be recommended to Congress" (Board Minutes, April 24, 1944, 2). The Board voted five to one to approve the statement. McKee abstained because he said the statement had no value.

Late in May the president announced an international conference to begin July 1 at Bretton Woods, New Hampshire. Governor Szymczak told the Board that, on June 15, technical experts from twelve countries would meet to prepare the conference agenda. Eccles, who was not present at the Board meeting, had agreed to be a member of the United States delegation. Some of the Board's staff would serve as members of the conference staff.[64]

The Board members agreed that the main issue they faced was how the Board wished to counsel Eccles as their representative (Board Minutes, May 31, 1944, 3). Governor McKee asked for a meeting with the reserve bank presidents to hear objections from President Sproul and to discuss the plans "point by point" (3).

The meeting was held on June 6, but the "point by point" discussion did

62. Goldenweiser was present also. He told Eccles that agreement with the statement of principles meant a commitment to a major part of the plan.

63. This was not true of the New York bank. Sproul was opposed, and his vice president, John H. Williams, had made several public statements in opposition. The New York board of directors voted unanimously in October 1943 and June 1944 to endorse the position taken by Sproul and Williams (Minutes, New York Directors, June 19, 1944, 208–9). At Morgenthau's request, Eccles agreed to suggest to Sproul that Williams desist from criticism.

64. Szymczak reported that White had agreed that John H. Williams could come as an assistant to Eccles if Eccles wished. Later he insisted that Williams could participate only if he accepted the Joint Statement of Experts as the basis for discussion. He was sure Williams would not agree to the statement.

not occur. The main reason was that Eccles was now a member of the United States delegation, and the conference was only a few weeks away. Eccles did not attend the meeting; it was chaired by Vice Chairman Ransom, who opened the meeting by limiting discussion "to the question of how to make the international fund serve the best interests of this country, including the Federal Reserve System, rather than the question whether the international fund should be created or some other mechanism devised" (Board Minutes, June 6, 1944, 2–3). This limitation prevented Williams and Sproul from proposing an alternative. Governor Szymczak proposed removing additional topics from discussion. The meeting should discuss issues that had not yet been decided at the technical level, how the proposed arrangement would affect the United States economy and Federal Reserve operations, and how to raise the United States contribution to the fund. This was opposite to the position he had taken a few months earlier.

The most substantive discussion came after Goldenweiser distributed copies of the plan agreed to by United States, British, and Russian experts. The opening paragraph said in part: "No government is formally committed. In practice, the governments are committed, except that Congress can refuse to ratify" (Board Minutes (June 6, 1944, 4).[65] Sproul responded that "the plan as indicated is the wrong way to approach the problem" (8). He recommended that the conference concentrate on the immediate postwar problem of providing borrowing and lending arrangements for the transition from war to peace. Ransom replied that the international conference would not consider alternative proposals. It would be limited to discussion of the prepared joint statement. Sproul's reply summarized what had happened. He was now faced with the outcome of "the procedure which had been followed of discussions at the technical level, with no commitments . . . leading inevitably to the position where, without having expressed its views or having been able to develop its point of view, the System would be committed to a program on which it was stated there was to be no variation except as to details" (9). Sproul threatened to oppose the program when it came before Congress.[66]

---

65. The proposal Goldenweiser distributed contained many of the provisions in the final agreement. The fund would have $8 billion from countries in the United Nations. Country quotas would be paid 25 percent in gold. Quota sizes had not been set. The fund was limited to financing trade; capital movements were explicitly excluded from fund lending. Exchange controls on current account were to be removed in three to five years, but capital restrictions were permitted.

66. Williams asked whether all countries agreed at the technical level. Goldenweiser replied that he knew only about England and Russia. He agreed that the fund "was wholly inadequate" for the postwar transition. It would have to be part of a program of lending and relief (Board Minutes, June 6, 1944, 11).

Those who spoke in favor of the plan did not discuss it. They spoke in favor of international cooperation and the need for monetary stability. Sproul and Williams, supported by Governor McKee, wanted to limit agreement to a transitional arrangement. Most of their arguments did not attack the plan directly; they argued that it was not appropriate at that time.

Sproul, Williams, and many bankers disliked the plan partly for the lack of attention to transitional problems. They saw, correctly, that the fund's resources were inadequate for the task of reestablishing an international payments system. At the time of the Tripartite Agreement, they had accepted the principle that exchange rates had to be set collectively. For the longer term, they preferred a system, like the Tripartite Agreement, based on gold and fixed exchange rates. They viewed the British commitment to full employment as inconsistent with stable exchange rates. They were skeptical about Britain's willingness to end imperial preference, and they believed that Britain's transition to peacetime stability would take more than three years. Although Sproul and Williams did not express their distaste for an international organization, they must have seen the plan as a further weakening of New York's influence on international economic policy.[67]

A central concern of the opponents was often implicit in their remarks. The agreement reversed a central principle of the classical gold standard. Countries on the gold standard had to adjust domestic policies to maintain their exchange rate. The agreement allowed international policy to adjust to domestic policy. If a country adopted a full employment policy that was incompatible with its exchange rate, it could borrow from the fund to cover its current account balance or, if the problem persisted, it could devalue. This central principle was acceptable to the British and the Americans, so much of their negotiation was concerned with how the principle would be carried out in practice. This involved the size of the fund, how much could be borrowed, what happened if a country's surplus became large relative to the fund, and so on.

Williams addressed part of the transitional arrangement at the meeting: "This is a stabilization plan with all the stabilization measures left out" (Board Minutes, June 6, 1944, 16). The British press, he said, was exultant: "Lord Keynes is said to have said that this plan is the opposite of the gold standard. If this is so, I think that we should declare that this cannot be the opposite of the gold standard" (16). Later he added: "The essence of monetary stability is to stabilize the major currency and all else flows from that.

---

67. Williams's proposal tried to solve the transition problem by permitting different speeds of adjustment to convertibility. At first the United States, Britain, and a few others would adopt stable exchange rates. Other countries would have more time to adjust. At the time, as much as 50 percent of all trade was denominated in pounds sterling.

If you do that, it is much easier to permit of exchange controls and exchange rate variations for the younger countries. That does not really affect stability" (17).

Alvin Hansen replied that countries were unwilling to deflate. Without the plan, the international system would lack discipline. The issue was internal, not external, stability. Turning to the unmentioned concerns about British postwar policy, Hansen was hopeful. The plan, he said, "would exercise moral restraint against unsound policies" (ibid., 20).[68]

Karl Bopp (Philadelphia) pointed out that if the fund had existed in the 1930s, it would not have prevented any devaluation that took place. But he favored international cooperation. Unlike Williams, he believed that exchange rate adjustment was important because it was unlikely that countries would set postwar exchange rates correctly.

The meeting concluded without reaching agreement on the plan or discussing most of its provisions. Those present agreed only on the importance of the System's being consulted on the choice of the United States director and having reports sent to the chairman of the Board of Governors as well as the secretary of the treasury and the secretary of state.

At the June 19 meeting, with McKee absent, the Board unanimously approved Eccles as the Board's representative at the conference and gave him full discretion to act for the Board. In an attempt to silence Sproul and Williams, the Board agreed that "public expressions of differences of opinion within the System would tend to impair effective representation at the international conference and to destroy any influence that the System might have" (Board Minutes, June 19, 1944, 8).

The meeting at Bretton Woods lasted three weeks. At its end, forty-four countries agreed to the plans for the International Monetary Fund (IMF) and the World Bank. In contrast to the 1920s, representatives of the United States and British treasuries ran the meeting. Central bankers had a modest role.[69] In contrast to the League of Nations agreement, the United States

68. In correspondence with Jacob Viner, Keynes wrote that he favored price stability as a goal and was skeptical of the alleged advantages of devaluation. The main occasion for devaluation, he wrote, was when efficiency wages increased relative to wages abroad. Viner replied that the wage criterion "accepts the business agent of the powerful unions as the ultimate and unlimited sovereign over monetary policy." See Meltzer 1988, 241.

69. Morgenthau led the American delegation. It included Fred M. Vinson, Dean Acheson of the State Department, Harry Dexter White, and four members of Congress. Eccles was the only representative of the Federal Reserve, but Edward E. Brown, president of the First National Bank of Chicago and chairman of the Federal Advisory Council, was a member. Senator Robert A. Taft was omitted because he was opposed. The British delegation, led by Keynes, also included only one representative of the Bank of England. Williams refused to accept the restriction that his comments remain within the framework established by the proposal, so he did not attend.

delegation included key members of Congress. White's assistant, Edward Bernstein, described the work of the conference as modest: "Everything of importance had been discussed and settled in the two years of discussion before the Conference" (Black 1991, 47).[70] This refers more to the IMF than to the World Bank. The bank agreement was much less developed before the meeting because there was less controversy about the main provisions, and no agreement about the bank would have been approved if countries had not agreed on the fund.[71]

The Federal Reserve Board's principal effort after the conference was to include an international financial council in the bill authorizing United States participation in the fund and the bank.[72] The proposed council, with the Board represented, would supervise, approve, or reject decisions by United States representatives to the bank and the fund before any action could be taken. The Treasury agreed to an informal arrangement but would not include the council in the legislation.[73]

---

70. Bernstein served as chief technical adviser of the United States delegation and chairman of the Committee on Unsettled Questions. Later he became the IMF's first director of research.

71. At one point Morgenthau (Blum 1967, 432) thought that a single board of directors should coordinate the work of the fund and the bank. Proposals of this kind reappeared many times.

72. Eccles and the Board also attempted to silence the proposal's critics at the New York bank. On September 19 Eccles read a statement that he proposed to give to the presidents. The statement reviewed the discussions held the previous spring, then concluded: "The public expression of an adverse attitude, if any, on the part of any of the Federal Reserve Banks and their officers would be likely to impair the usefulness of the System in relation to the problems growing out of the conference" (Board Minutes, September 19, 1944, 6). Eccles explained that by attending the conference he had committed the Board to support the plan. Only McKee argued against the statement. He could accept a statement saying that no one could speak for or against the agreement, but not a one-sided statement. The Board approved the statement with McKee voting against. When the Board met with the Presidents Conference, the statement was the last (eleventh) item on the agenda. Eccles read the prepared statement. Sproul responded that on an issue of this importance, until it became law, "he had a duty to express his views and that if . . . such an expression [was] damaging to the System then he would have to decide whether to leave the System, but he could not agree with the view that the officers of the System from here on should be muzzled" (Board Minutes, September 22, 1944, 31). President John N. Peyton (Minneapolis) supported Sproul. Eccles retreated. He thought it would harm the System, but they were at liberty to express conflicting views.

73. The Board obtained assurance from White that he would discuss the Board's request with Senator Wagner, chairman of the Senate Banking Committee, and other committee members. Since the proposal originated with the American Bankers Association, Morgenthau regarded it as additional evidence that the Federal Reserve represented the bankers. He had held that view for some time, so it did not take much to convince him (Blum (1967, 428). The Board's effort was an attempt to restore some of the System's responsibility for international monetary policy. At the same meeting, the Board voted to end the Treasury's Exchange Stabilization Fund, scheduled to expire on June 30, 1945. The Board asked that the Stabilization Fund terminate when the subscription to the International Monetary Fund became due.

The Board's resolution supporting ratification of the agreements included a provision asking Congress to create the council. It did not condition its support on the creation of the council, and it revised its earlier statement to remove the explicit reference to its membership on the council. The council "would not only advise the American governors and directors on the Fund and the Bank of its views with respect to the financial and monetary policies of the United States" but would also be authorized to act for the United States in matters that required approval under the agreements.[74] The Board approved the resolution, with Governor McKee abstaining (Board Minutes, March 21, 1945, 1–5). To reduce bankers' resistance, the Treasury supported the proposal.

The System remained divided on the proposal for the fund. Except for McKee, the governors supported the plan. At the New York bank, Sproul and Williams favored the bank but opposed the fund, usually stating their opposition as a matter of timing, not principle. Other presidents remained undecided or neutral. White attributed opposition or ambivalence to the influence of the American Bankers Association, which opposed both the fund and the bank.

In its haste to pass the bill, so as to show the international commitment of the United States before the San Francisco meeting to create the United Nations, the House did not ask Board members to testify. On June 21, Sproul and Williams testified at the Senate hearings.[75]

---

74. Congress gave the Treasury main responsibility for the bank and the fund. The United States executive directors are assistant secretaries of the treasury. The secretary is the United States delegate, and the chairman of the Board of Governors is his alternate.

75. Board members were enraged. On September 25 they discussed voting to censure Sproul. Their counsel advised them that they did not have a case. They knew his intention in advance and had authorized his right to appear more than a year before (in September) when the Board had tried but failed to silence the opponents. The Board then discussed statements by Chairman Beardsley Ruml, of the New York bank, and his use of this position as a platform from which to criticize the Bretton Woods Agreement. Eccles said that Ruml should not be reappointed when his term expired. Eccles also thought that the Board should dismiss John H. Williams because his "part time job [as vice president and research director] left him free to make public statements." They agreed only to prepare a statement of policy about public statements by bank officials (Board Minutes, September 25, 1945, 7–10). The Board prepared a letter to Chairman Ruml stating that Sproul's actions were "inappropriate and unwise." The Board "could not countenance" that degree of independence. Nothing could be done about the past, but in the future they must function as a system. The governors could not agree, so they voted to have Eccles speak to Sproul (Board Minutes, October 16, 1945, 3–4).

In December, Eccles reported on his conversations with Sproul and Ruml. Sproul replied that the directors of the New York bank would not accept the Board's position. Sproul made no commitment to be bound by the Board's positions. Eccles replied by threatening not to renew his appointment as president. Sproul repeated that he would not commit to a different position (Board Minutes, December 7, 1945, 4–7). Then Eccles discussed Williams's part-time appointment and his freedom to express his views outside the bank. Again, Sproul dis-

OBJECTIONS TO THE INTERNATIONAL MONETARY FUND
The Board's concern was out of keeping with the New York spokesmen's testimony. Both Sproul and Williams favored the World Bank and international cooperation. They did not explicitly oppose the fund; they opposed starting it at a time when there was no hope of restoring multilateral trade.[76] Their testimony went beyond their support for the fund. Williams, especially, proposed an alternative.

Their principal concern was Britain. The British still had imperial preference and were signing bilateral clearing agreements, contrary to the spirit of multilateral clearing. They could not redeem sterling balances, so these balances would overhang the fund. Sproul and Williams did not object to exchange controls on capital movements, but they doubted that controls on trade and payments would be removed in the foreseeable future. This violated the agreement and, of greater concern, increased the demand for dollars as the principal convertible currency. The fund would gain inconvertible currencies, lose dollars, and fail. Initially, the fund would hold only $2.75 billion, so the risk of running out of dollars was high.

Exchange rate flexibility was also a concern. The agreement permitted devaluation, so exchange rates were not really fixed. A country could follow social or economic policies leading to "fundamental disequilibrium," then devalue its currency "if it seems to advance its interests" (Senate Committee on Banking and Currency 1945, 305). Further, the agreement was very explicit about the obligations of creditor countries, much less so about debtor countries. Since countries could devalue, they could force the adjustment on others instead of accepting it themselves. Countries would not agree on whether a devaluation was to gain competitive advantage or to respond to a "fundamental problem."

Williams was concerned particularly about Britain's large export sector and its precarious financial position.

> The gist of the agreement is that if this country will create and maintain the conditions necessary for multilateral trade in a free exchange market, England will undertake, after a transition period of 3 to 5 years during which ex-

---

agreed. He was unable to control Williams's public statements. This did not satisfy Eccles, so he threatened not to renew Williams's appointment.

Eccles was no more successful with Ruml than with Sproul. Ruml agreed only that he would stay within the policy statements made by the Board; he said he would state his views on other public issues.

76. Sproul's Senate Banking Committee testimony is in Senate Committee on Banking and Currency 1945, 301–17. Williams's is in ibid., 318–34. Eccles tried to prevent the testimony. He told Morgenthau that "he did not think the Banks should be asked to express their views on the Agreements, particularly since at least one of the Banks was opposed" (Board Minutes, February 23, 1945, 4).

change controls and bilateral currency arrangements are permitted, to relinquish her controls and join a multilateral exchange system. The agreement, however, carefully states that, even after the 5-year period, the member country shall be the judge of whether the conditions are right for relaxing its controls. (Ibid., 323)

Williams argued, also, that the proposed system was more complicated then necessary. He advocated a "key currency" approach, with the dollar and the pound as the key currencies. Once Britain restored convertibility, other countries could fix their exchange rates to one of the key currencies. The main problem at the time was the British transition and the large volume of inconvertible sterling balances left from the war.

Both Sproul and Williams questioned whether the United States should enter the agreement when there was great uncertainty about what Britain and others would do and when, if ever, they would do it.[77] White's statements that adjustment loans might be made with five or ten years' duration suggested that he too believed the transition would be long and difficult.

Potential dangers are not the same as flaws. Opponents who favored delay faced two major obstacles: the belief that, after the interwar experience, the United States had to show that it would support a multilateral approach and the conviction that the best time to get agreement was now. White did not disagree with many of the criticisms. He argued that reopening the agreement would not produce a better agreement.

Williams's strongest argument was that in three to five years Britain would not be ready for multilateral trade and the elimination of current account restrictions. He estimated that the British war debt was $12 billion and rising, and that the country faced current account deficits of $1.2 billion to $2 billion a year for many years after the war. These arguments lost some of their persuasive power when the United States later agreed to a $3.75 billion loan to make the transition succeed.[78] But Williams was right about the difficulties Britain would have in the postwar period. He erred

77. "A set of vested interests and a network of discriminatory trade and currency practices will have grown up which it may prove difficult to break down" (Senate Committee on Banking and Currency 1945, 323). "The agreement may institutionalize exchange controls" (306). Bankers and others opposed the agreements because they gave away United States gold and supported deficit finance abroad, and because Keynes supported them. The American Bankers Association, and other bank associations, testified in opposition (James 1996, 64–65).

78. The French also borrowed $800 million to help in the transition. This loan came from the Export-Import Bank, so it did not require congressional approval. William McChesney Martin Jr., head of the Export-Import Bank and later chairman of the Board of Governors, opposed the loan. The Treasury insisted, and the loan was made (Black 1991, 56).

only in being insufficiently pessimistic about British policy and prospects and the problem of maintaining convertibility. The pound did not become a fully convertible currency until 1979.

Major newspapers supported New York's position and either opposed the agreement or wanted major changes. Senator Robert A. Taft (Ohio) led the opposition in Congress. Taft saw the World Bank in much the same way as Morgenthau described it to White at the start of negotiations—a new type of deficit finance, an extension of President Roosevelt's New Deal into a new class of problems to the benefit of other countries (Blum 1967, 429).[79]

On June 8 the House approved the agreement by a wide margin. Ratification by the Senate was more difficult. The Treasury worked for passage by offering rosy forecasts and minimizing the difficulties of transition from war to peace (ibid., 436). Late in July, the Senate approved the agreement by a two-thirds majority.

The British loan agreement, signed in December 1945, imposed many of the restrictions Williams wanted. After the loan's ratification in July 1946, Britain agreed to ratify the Bretton Woods Agreement. It agreed to make the pound convertible within a year and relinquished the long transition to convertibility permitted under Bretton Woods. Trade discrimination against the United States had to end by December 1946.[80] In return, the United States lent $3.75 billion at 2 percent interest, repayable over fifty years beginning in 1951 and settled lend-lease obligations of approximately $17 billion for about 4 percent of the claim. Since the loan was fixed in nominal value, United States inflation eased repayment; British inflation and devaluation increased the cost.

The Bretton Woods Agreement Act directed the Treasury to pay the $2.75 million subscription to the International Monetary Fund in installments. The Exchange Stabilization Fund contributed $1.8 billion of the profit on the 1934 revaluation of gold. The Treasury paid the remaining $950 million in dollars and non-interest-bearing notes, payable from tax

79. Blum (1967, 427) lists the *Wall Street Journal*, *New York Times*, *World Telegram*, and others as opponents. Morgenthau believed that criticism of the fund was misplaced. The fund would be open only to countries capable of keeping exchange rates stable, and its loans would be only for short-term trade finance. (429). Proponents included the national labor unions, the Independent Bankers Association, and most economists.

80. The fund began operations in March 1946 under the leadership of Camille Gutt, a Belgian. Britain removed restrictions, as promised, in July 1947, followed by the postwar British exchange crisis in August. Under the "scarce currency" clause of the IMF agreement, the British could continue trade discrimination if the fund declared the dollar "scarce." A main reason for the early postwar discussion of the dollar shortage was to have the dollar declared "scarce." The clause was never invoked.

revenues. The $950 million was an ordinary expenditure. To fund the $1.8 billion, the Treasury transferred $1 billion in gold to the IMF and, in February 1947, sold $800 million in gold certificates to the Federal Reserve.[81]

Despite the emphasis on trade and avoidance of discrimination in the lend-lease agreement, countries did not adopt a trade agreement at the Bretton Woods Conference. In fact, the British delegation was under orders not to discuss trade policy, so the conference limited its statement to a recommendation favoring cooperation in trade matters. However, the British loan agreement also committed the British to participate in a trade conference. This was a major change from Keynes's policy of separating trade and payments, then neglecting trade. The conference, held in Havana, Cuba, from December 1947 to March 1948, brought back the conflict between the United States, at the time the proponent of open, multilateral trade, and the British, still attached to preferential arrangements with its empire.

The conference agreed that preferences would end within five years, but the agreement had so many exceptions that the United States Congress would not approve it. The Truman administration withdrew the agreement, and it was never ratified (Presnell 1997, 227). Instead, countries adopted the General Agreement on Tariffs and Trade (GATT), negotiated separately. Originally a transitional arrangement, GATT became the postwar trade organization until it was replaced by the World Trade Organization fifty years later.

The International Bank for Reconstruction and Development (World Bank) created much less controversy at the Bretton Woods Conference. The consensus was that private international lending would remain small after the many loan defaults in the 1930s. The plan was that the World Bank would lend directly and encourage private capital lending by guaranteeing part of the loans. John McCloy, the first governor, thought the bank would concentrate on reconstruction of wartime damage, then close (Dominguez 1993, 377).

The bank started slowly. The Marshall Plan took over much of its original task of reconstruction. By the 1980s, private capital movements had increased. Contrary to the belief under which the bank was organized, most postwar financial problems in developing countries came about because of too much lending, not too little, particularly short-term lending.

---

81. The Treasury issued $1.75 billion of special non-interest-bearing notes to the IMF, in effect borrowing back and deferring payment of part of its subscription. It then used the $800 million balance obtained from issuing gold certificates to retire $500 million in debt from the reserve banks and $300 million to offset an outflow of gold in January (Fforde 1954, 194). These operations neutralized the effect on the monetary base.

The bank specialized at first in loans to developing countries and technical assistance. Countries soon learned to offer the bank projects with the highest expected return. Although aware that money is fungible, the bank made few efforts to assess its role in financing or learn about the marginal projects that its loans permitted countries to undertake.[82]

Summary on Postwar Planning

Early Keynesian models based their predictions of postwar depression, and a return to prewar unemployment rates, on estimates of consumer spending. Some market indicators gave a different forecast. For example, measures of risk, such as the spread between Baa and Aaa bonds, fell below 1 percent in 1944 and continued to fall as the yields on riskier bonds declined. By early 1946, the spread was below 0.5 percent, the lowest value reached by the series up to that time. There is no sign in these or similar data of an expected return to depression, unemployment, and bankruptcies.

Investors remained cautious, however. Wars have typically been followed by depressions. Stock prices fell in 1946 as profits declined. For the next five years, capitalization of profits remained low relative to past (or future) experience. Chart 7.4 shows the relation of corporate profits to market capitalization, the inverse of the capitalization rate. The relatively low capitalization rate (high value of the ratio) from 1947 to 1951 suggests that wealth owners did not anticipate continuation of robust profit growth.

In the event, the Keynesian models were inaccurate, the bond market forecasts correct. There was no postwar depression. Instead, the United States had a sharp eight-month recession as war plants closed or converted to peacetime production. The National Bureau of Economic Research dates the peak of wartime expansion to February 1945, two months before the end of the European war and six months before the end of the Asian war. By November the economy began to recover.

Though brief, the recession produced a large drop in output. Strikes for higher wages added to the loss. Industrial production fell 38 percent, but the peak unemployment rate reached only 4.3 percent of the labor force (Zarnowitz and Moore 1986).[83]

Internationally, the World Bank and the International Monetary Fund

---

82. Later the bank broadened its scope to include poverty reduction, environmental concerns, women's rights, and other projects popular with contemporary political groups in the United States. Keynes had feared that locating the bank in Washington would expose it to pressures from United States domestic politics. James (1996, 72) quotes Keynes's comment that the United States wanted to move control of international economic policy from Congress to the new institutions where it had a large voice.

83. For 1945 as a whole, production (1992 = 100) fell from 25.9 to 21.2, a drop of 18 percent. The wartime peak in industrial production came in 1944 and was not surpassed until 1950.

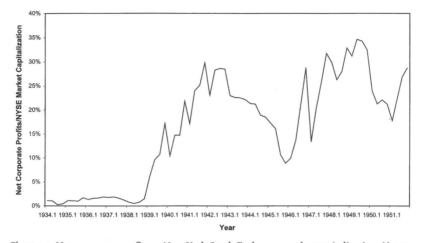

Chart 7.4 Net corporate profits to New York Stock Exchange market capitalization. Net corporate profits from National Bureau of Economic Research, 1934–38; Bureau of Economic Analysis, 1939–51.

did very little to smooth the transition from war to peace (Presnell 1997; Bernstein and Black 1991). As Williams and Sproul had insisted, the fund and the bank could not cope with the transition. After Roosevelt's death, Morgenthau and White resigned. The new secretary, Fred M. Vinson, recognized that the fund had limited resources. The British loan and, by 1948, the Marshall Plan provided sufficient capital transfer to Western Europe to permit these countries to import both nondurables and the capital equipment needed for reconstruction. The United States operated unilaterally, outside the institutions it had worked to establish.

James (1996, 60) summarizes the failure of the Morgenthau-White international economic policy and the substitution of a policy that recognized the reality of American power.

> The U.S.S.R. withdrew. In the United Kingdom and the United States bitter conflicts were fought out over the ratification of the Bretton Woods Agreement. The United States adopted more and more a dollar-centered view of the world, more compatible with a different intellectual tradition than that which had led to Bretton Woods. Over the next two decades, the United States often in practice behaved as if a dollar exchange standard had been created in 1944. . . . The United Kingdom clung desperately to the role of the pound sterling as an international currency and, as a consequence, became an obstacle to economic liberalization.[84]

84. Morgenthau and his aides worked hard and made several concessions to get the USSR to join the International Monetary Fund. Russia did not join until after the collapse of the Soviet Union in the late 1980s.

One of the anomalies of the period is that the American Bankers Association and most large New York banks vigorously opposed the IMF agreement. They could not, and did not, foresee the evolution of the fund. In the 1980s and 1990s, one of the fund's main tasks was lending to countries experiencing capital outflow to permit them to service debts to large banks in New York and other financial centers.

POSTWAR POLICIES, BELIEFS, AND ACTIONS

Fred M. Vinson left the Treasury after a year to accept appointment to the Supreme Count. His replacement was John W. Snyder, a Missouri banker and friend of President Truman who had served during wartime in several government agencies. Snyder remained secretary until the Eisenhower administration took office in January 1953.

Economic policy remained under the control of the Treasury. On the fiscal side, at the war's end, government purchases, mainly military spending, declined from $97.3 billion to $29.9 billion in the four quarters ending in second quarter 1946. Tax rates remained close to peak wartime levels. After a short postwar recession the economy grew, so tax receipts stabilized and the budget had a surplus.

After World War I, the budget shifted from a $13 billion deficit in 1919 to a $500 million surplus in 1921. The larger effort in World War II produced both a larger deficit and a larger swing—from a $54 billion deficit in fiscal 1945 to surpluses of $700 million in fiscal 1947 and $8 billion in fiscal 1948. Part of the surplus was used to reduce tax rates in November 1945 and April 1948. The highest income tax rate in World War I was 66.3 percent on an income of $1 million. By 1922 that rate was 55 percent, and a few years later, 24 percent. In World War II the highest rate, 90 percent at $1 million, fell to 84 percent in 1946–47 and 77 percent in 1944–49. Thereafter the rate rose to 87 percent during and after the Korean War.[85]

Despite pegged interest rates, pent-up demand, and fiscal stimulus from lower tax rates, inflation remained in the 4 to 6 percent range (deflator) through most of 1947 and 1948. By 1949 prices were stable or falling. This is one of the very few times in the postwar years to date that the price level declined.

Treasury operations were a main reason for reduced money growth and lower inflation. The Treasury used the proceeds of the Victory Loan in 1946

---

85. The 1948 act permitted income splitting, so it reduced the rate applicable to many married, high-income taxpayers. The act, passed over President Truman's veto, increased the standard deduction and reduced rates for all taxpayers by $5 billion, about 11.5 percent of receipts.

Table 7.4   Postwar Changes in Composition and Distribution of
Government Debt

CHANGE IN COMPOSITION[a] (BILLIONS OF DOLLARS)		CHANGE IN DISTRIBUTION[b] (BILLIONS OF DOLLARS)	
Bills	−4.9	Government agencies	10.3
Certificates	−12.0	Federal Reserve	1.0
Notes	−16.0	Commercial banks	−28.3
Bonds	−10.2	Corporations	−7.4
Nonmarketables		All others	−0.6
Treasury special issues	10.9	Total	−24.9
Saving bonds	7.0		
Total	−25.2		

Source: Board of Governors of the Federal Reserve System 1976.
[a]February 1946 to February 1949.
[b]December 1945 to December 1948.

and its surpluses in 1947 and 1948 to retire debt.[86] Gross public debt reached a local peak at $279.2 billion in February 1946. In the next three years, gross debt declined about 10 percent, $28 billion. Table 7.4 shows the change in the distribution of the debt by type of securities and by ownership.

One of the Treasury's aims was to reduce the debt held in the banking system. As the table shows, it succeeded by selling the Victory Loan, consisting of securities ineligible for bank purchase, and by retiring notes and certificates held mainly by banks. The Victory Loan placed nearly $11 billion (net) with nonbank holders.

The administration retired outstanding debt after reducing spending in 1946, 1947, and 1948 and running $13 billion in cash budget surpluses, mainly in the 1947 and 1948 calendar years.[87] The surplus, an excess of Treasury receipts over expenditures, reduced the public's money balances. Using the surplus to retire debt held by the public restored those balances. Reducing debt held by commercial banks increased bank reserves and permitted banks to increase loans. Table 7.5 shows the changes in bank assets during this period. The most deflationary policy retired debt held by the reserve banks. This policy reduced the monetary base and did not restore the public's money balances.

86. The Victory Loan raised $21 billion between December 1945 and February 1946. Gross public debt declined $20 billion from February through December 1946, so the net effect was to cancel the Victory Loan. As in the text, the reduction was mainly in notes and certificates, held mainly by banks, so the combined effect shifted debt ownership from banks to nonbank holders. The Treasury's effort to sell bank-ineligible securities was less successful than the text suggests. During the Victory Loan, commercial banks purchased $7 billion in the market, almost all of it from nonbank investors.

87. The Treasury also sold $11 billion of nonmarketable special issues to its trust accounts to fund its obligations, and the public added $7 billion to its holdings of government savings bonds.

Table 7.5 Member Bank Loans and Investments, December 1945 and 1948 (millions of dollars)

	TOTAL LOANS AND INVESTMENTS	TOTAL LOANS	TOTAL INVESTMENTS
December 1945	107,183	22,775	84,408
December 1948	95,616	36,060	59,556
Change	−11,567	13,285	−24,852

Source: Board of Governors of the Federal Reserve System 1976, 60–61.

Market yields changed very little during the period. After a short-lived decline to 2.08 percent during winter 1946, yields on long-term bonds remained between 2.15 and 2.25 percent until late in 1947. Thereafter, yields rose slowly toward 2.45 percent. These yields give no hint that the public anticipated sustained inflation. Growth of the monetary base and money suggest that inflation would remain low. Table 7.6 shows that, after an initial surge that includes the removal of price controls, the rate of inflation slowed in 1948. By the end of 1948, prices were falling. All of the 5.8 percent inflation in 1950 came after the start of the Korean War. During the years of low inflation and falling prices, the monetary base and money fell. Treasury debt retirement, not Federal Reserve policy, was the main influence on monetary growth and inflation. The Federal Reserve urged the Treasury to pursue deflationary policies, but it had little influence on decisions.

Since the Treasury used its surplus to retire debt, it had less reason to be concerned about interest rates. In similar circumstances in the 1920s, Secretary Andrew Mellon pressed the Federal Reserve to avoid actions that lowered rates. Secretaries Vinson and Snyder were more concerned about rolling over maturing obligations, so they continued to insist that wartime interest rates be maintained.[88]

Unlike the bond market, the government saw a threat of inflation. President Truman called a special session of Congress in fall 1947 to restore price and wage controls, renew consumer credit controls, and introduce controls on commodity speculation. The Federal Reserve asked for secondary reserve requirements, a new power.[89] Congress did not approve any of these requests at the time, but in August 1948 it restored consumer credit controls on installment loans for one year to show its concern about inflation at election time. Although installment credit had not increased rapidly, the Board reimposed regulation W effective September 20, 1948.

88. When bond yields fell to 2.08 percent in the winter of 1946, Chairman Brown of the Advisory Council asked Eccles whether the Treasury was concerned that rates were far below the ceiling. Eccles replied that the Treasury had no financing in prospect and so was unconcerned (Board Minutes, April 24, 1946, 11).

89. The Federal Reserve proposal is discussed in the next section.

Table 7.6   Budget Surplus, Growth of Monetary Base, Money, and Prices
1946–51 (fourth quarter to fourth quarter)

YEAR	MONETARY BASE (%)	M$_1$ (%)	CONSUMER PRICES (%)	CASH SURPLUS (BILLIONS OF DOLLARS)
1946	1.6	4.8	16.6	0.05
1947	1.0	4.8	8.5	5.66
1948	–1.6	–1.2	2.9	8.02
1949	–1.5	–0.1	–2.1	–1.30
1950	0.1	4.3	5.8	0.45
1951	4.1	5.0	5.8	1.23

Source: Surplus from *Federal Reserve Bulletin;* consumer prices is for all items, 1982–84 base, from Department of Labor.

Prices rose after the start of the Korean War in June 1950. The twelve-month change in consumer prices increased from –0.5 percent in June to 5.8 percent in December. President Truman disliked budget deficits; he proposed to fight the war with a balanced budget. In September Congress increased individual and corporate income tax rates and levied some new excise taxes on durable goods purchases. In January 1951 an excess profits tax passed Congress, retroactive to July 1950. An additional round of tax rate increases for individuals and corporations passed in October 1951. The net effect, as shown in table 7.6 above, was to continue surpluses in the cash budget despite the large increase in military spending. Total outlays rose $30 billion from 1950 to 1952 (calendar years), an increase of 71 percent. Revenues rose almost as much, so the budget had a surplus in 1951 and a modest deficit in 1952.

President Truman's determination to finance the war by taxation may have convinced the public that the wartime price increases were a one-time change, not the start of sustained inflation. Although measured inflation rates were more than double the interest rate on long-term Treasury bonds, rates on long-term bonds remained below the 2.5 percent ceiling. Between late June and December 1950, the long-term rate rose only from 2.34 percent to 2.39 percent. Short-term rates rose slightly more—from 1.17 percent to 1.37 percent on new issues of Treasury bills. Growth of the monetary base remained low throughout. These data suggest that the Federal Reserve's concern about inflation was misplaced. Its error, repeated by many economists at the time and subsequently, was a failure to distinguish one-time price level changes from the sustained rate of change that constitutes inflation.

The period provides evidence on the role of money in inflation. The surge in the price level was nonmonetary; recalling wartime shortages, rationing, and allocation of scarce materials, consumers and producers bought goods and ordered larger inventories. Prices rose, but base money growth remained low or negative. Within a few months, the price level stabilized.

The dominant view in the academic profession and the Board of Governors was that the price increases were evidence of inflation, but that monetary policy could do little to prevent inflation.[90] Eccles's strong belief was that the budget was a much more important instrument for responding to depression or inflation. Unlike many of the Keynesian economists who had joined him in urging larger deficits during the 1930s, Eccles urged budget surpluses after the war. He forecast postwar inflation, not depression, so he recommended tax increases at every opportunity and supported other policies including maintenance of price and wage controls and consumer credit controls until peacetime production was restored (Eccles 1951, 409).[91] The Board's staff and its members reflected the views of contemporary economists, as they had in the past and would in the future. They minimized or denied the effect of money growth on inflation. Such views now seem extreme, but they dominated professional writing in the 1940s and 1950s.[92]

A central belief at the time was that the large wartime increase in government debt had rendered traditional monetary policy useless. Banks did not borrow from reserve banks, so discount policy could not be effective. Eccles described the discount rate as "largely irrelevant" because banks could sell government securities (ibid., 420): "A moderate rise in yields on government securities would not prevent and would only slightly restrain banks from selling securities in order to make loans. On the other hand, an increase in rates large enough to exercise effective restraint on banks may have to be too great or too abrupt to be consistent with the maintenance of stable conditions in the government securities market" (420).

90. "The notion that inflation is a monetary phenomena and that it can be prevented by refusing to allow the quantity of money to increase is to mistake a symptom for a cause" (Robinson and Wilkinson 1985). See also Kaldor 1982.

91. The Board formally disapproved of tax reduction in 1947 and notified the president (Board Minutes, June 9, 1947, 1–2). Eccles also proposed, and the Board agreed unanimously, to recommend to President Truman that he sign the Taft-Hartley Act. The Board recognized that labor relations was not its field but agreed that strikes and labor unrest would disrupt production and raise prices. The letter was approved and sent (Board Minutes, October 17, 1947, 1–5).

92. Three sources will suggest how broadly these views were held in the academic community. Henry Villard (1948) was commissioned by the American Economic Association to survey monetary theory. The paper was published in the association's *Survey of Contemporary Economics*. The Committee on the Working of Monetary System (1959), known as the Radcliffe Committee, denied any role for a policy of monetary control in Britain. As late as 1965, the American Economic Association's *Readings in Business Cycles* has no role for money (Gordon and Klein 1965). Citations of popular textbooks such as Ackley 1961 or of econometric models of the period provide additional evidence.

Eccles had always chafed under Morgenthau's control of interest rates and monetary policy. In the 1930s the Treasury had exercised control by threatening to use the Exchange Stabilization Fund and other Treasury accounts to buy securities. Eccles and the Board believed they were in a weak position to pursue an independent policy or counter the Treasury. The Federal Reserve held a small securities portfolio relative to the gold inflows, so it had no way to control the monetary base had it chosen to do so. These problems vanished with the wartime growth of debt and the Federal Reserve's portfolio. Now the argument was that the large debt made traditional monetary policy tools and techniques useless.[93]

Further, market-determined interest rates would confront the Treasury with "an impossible debt-management problem" (ibid.). The Treasury would be at the mercy of the market and subject to chaotic swings in interest rates. Therefore Eccles restricted his recommendations for monetary policy and debt management to modest increases in short-term rates on bills and certificates, more reliance on selling debt to the public, and new powers to control bank reserves. Since the Federal Reserve owned most of the outstanding Treasury bills and (pegged) long rates exceeded short rates, the main effect of a rise in the bill rate would be the increased interest cost as the bill rate rose and other rates moved in response.

The New York Federal Reserve Bank, and many bankers, held a different view. Directors of the New York bank began pressing for higher rates on Treasury certificates late in 1944. In December they arranged to meet with Secretary Morgenthau to convey their views (Minutes, New York Directors, December 28, 1944, 112). In January 1945 they discussed the difficulty of maintaining the existing yield curve (pattern of rates) when holders were free to shift from one maturity to another (ibid., January 18, 1945, 139).

Allan Sproul, president of the New York bank, spoke out against the prevailing view. In a December 1946 speech he argued publicly that small changes in interest rates would have beneficial effects by changing bond values and by introducing uncertainty about future market rates. Uncertainty would remove the belief that reserves could be obtained on demand without loss of principal. He believed this would have a modest effect on

93. This belief in the impotence of monetary policy was so widely held that it is rare to find a memo suggesting the opposite. One such memo, by Walter Salant, warned that the swing in opinion since the 1920s went too far. Monetary policy was not totally impotent, Salant wrote, and experience did not support total impotence. Drawing on Currie 1934, he argued that policy had not been easy during most of 1929–33 or in 1937–38. He concluded with a double negative: there is no reason to believe that monetary policy "cannot exert a significant expansive influence" (Salant 1948, 8). The memo, dated May 21, concerns mainly policy in recession. At the time, Salant was on the staff of the Council of Economic Advisers. He sent me a copy of the memo.

the banks' decisions to expand. Sproul did not claim that monetary policy could have more than a secondary role in controlling inflation, but he wanted to adjust market yields to reflect the change from war to peace and the increased risk of inflation (Sproul 1947).

At times Sproul pressed for a policy change. He was one of the first to urge the Treasury to relax the ceiling on long-term interest rates. In 1950, before the Korean War renewed concern about inflation, he told his System colleagues: "There cannot be a purposeful monetary policy unless the Federal Reserve System is able to pursue alternating programs of restraint, neutrality, and ease. . . . The terms of Treasury offerings for new money, and for refunding issues, must be affected" (Board of Governors File, box 1433, April 4, 1950).

Vinson remained at the Treasury about a year. His successor, John W. Snyder, knew very little about monetary or fiscal policies. Morgenthau's staff continued to serve Vinson and later Snyder. Its priority was minimizing the current budget cost of financing the debt.[94] Further, by maintaining the pattern of rates the Treasury staff kept control of interest rates away from the Federal Reserve. Though nominally an independent agency, the Federal Reserve remained under Treasury control.

Issues and Views

In May 1947 the Board unanimously approved the text of a long letter that Eccles sent to Thomas B. McCabe.[95] McCabe had expressed concern about inflation and Federal Reserve policy. Eccles's reply shows the ambivalence that characterized policy at the time. Concern about inflation had to be balanced by concern that an effective policy would require a steep rise in interest rates.[96] "It was not possible by any practicable means, except higher taxes, to contract either current income or accumulated buying power in the form of liquid asset holdings" (Eccles to McCabe, Board Minutes, May 28, 1947, 7).

---

94. Eccles describes the clash with Snyder as arising from conflicting responsibilities, not personalities (Eccles 1951, 421). Casimir Sienkiewicz, who worked in the System from 1920 to 1947, is less charitable. He described the Treasury as under the control of its staff. "Mr. Snyder did not really know very much about the problem he should have been coping with" (interview with Casimir Sienkiewicz, CHFRS, March 18, 1954, 3).

95. At the time, McCabe was chairman of the Philadelphia Federal reserve bank. In 1948, he succeeded Eccles as chairman of the Board of Governors.

96. "Every member of the Open Market committee is aware of the disastrous consequences that would follow if the system were to attempt to force rates up to levels that would be effectively restrictive on private borrowing" (Board to McCabe, Board Minutes, May 28, 1947, 8). The letter spells out the "disastrous consequences" as substantial losses on bank (and other) portfolios, increased cost to the Treasury, and loss of any freedom of action by the Board, a reference to the political consequences the Board most feared.

The issues at the time were in several respects a replay of earlier issues in a different context. Contemporary writers, within and outside the Federal Reserve, expressed concern about whether monetary policy could operate with a large debt. This concern was both economic and political. A rise in interest rates sufficient to stop inflation would lower bond prices below par (initial offering price), imposing losses on all holders. Reserve officials and some senior staff could recall the political response in 1920–21 to higher interest rates and the public's losses on war bonds.[97]

Vestiges of the real bills doctrine remained. Board members feared that speculative credit would increase: "It is too much to expect that further increases in bank credit will be confined to productive loans, the more likely outcome, in the absence of repressive measures, will be an increase in speculative credit" (Minutes, FOMC, October 14, 1947, 4). Under the real bills doctrine, speculative use of credit would be evidence of inflation. Even the New York reserve bank, which had rejected the real bills doctrine in the 1920s, expressed concerns about "speculative purchasing and carrying of securities" and opposed loans for that purpose (Minutes, FOMC, June 10, 1946, 10).

Eccles's reasons for opposing an increase in interest rates are a mixture of economic and political considerations that seem inconsistent. He too referred to 1920–21 and argued that rates could not be changed until the public supported the move (ibid., 10–11). At times he opposed an increase in interest rates because a small increase would have little effect.[98] But he also claimed that the effect on the prices of government bonds would be too great.[99]

Eccles's economic views seem confused. In the 1930s he saw no reason for Federal Reserve action because monetary policy was ineffective when interest rates were low in a recession. In 1946, a period of anticipated ex-

---

97. "Mr. Evans stated that he was opposed to increasing the rate on certificates because the burden of such an increase would fall on the farmers, and the small businessmen, and the taxpayers. He recalled the situation after World War I, when the Federal Reserve was blamed for increasing interest rates, tightening credit, and causing a fall in prices, and he said that in some places the Federal Reserve system was still held responsible" (Minutes, FOMC, May 2, 1947). Rudolph M. Evans served as a member of the Board of Governors from March 1942 to August 1954. He held the "agricultural seat" after the resignation of Chester C. Davis in April 1941.

98. "Chairman Eccles did not think that a higher rate of interest—unless it was a very much higher rate—would have any substantial effect in curbing the demand for credit for private purposes" (Minutes, FOMC, June 10, 1946, 10).

99. A partial resolution of the apparent inconsistency is that there was a large debt outstanding, so a small change in interest rates would have a larger effect on private wealth than heretofore. Williams used the same argument, however, to claim that a small change "would have a greater retarding effect than in the past" (Minutes, FOMC, June 10, 1946, 13).

pansion, part of his argument was that policy would have little effect unless the Federal Reserve undertook large-scale operations and raised interest rates substantially. He saw no way of stopping an expansion of private
credit by rate action except by rates high enough to seriously affect the government securities market, and if such action were taken by the System "it
would be received in much the same way as action to increase rates was received following the last war" (ibid.). But he also claimed that using the
modest budget surplus to retire Treasury debt had increased bond interest
rates in fall 1946. He urged additional retirements and favored rate increases on (nonmarketable) savings bonds to encourage purchases and reduce redemptions[100] (Minutes, FOMC, October 3, 1946, 13, 17).

Differences of opinion between New York and the Board were similar
to the differences in 1928–29. New York, under the leadership of Allan
Sproul, periodically pushed for higher interest rates. The Board preferred
alternative methods of controlling credit. As in 1928–29, the Board was
more concerned about the political response to higher interest rates and
the effects on commerce and agriculture. Hence it favored control of specific uses of credit instead of more general policies. The Board's political
concern is clear in the letter to McCabe: "If the Secretary of the Treasury
were confronted with any such consequences as would be produced by the
System's abandonment of support of the Government bond market, he
would no doubt take the issue directly to the President who, in turn, would
take it to the Congress if the Open Market Committee remained adamant.
There can hardly be any doubt as to what the result would be" (Eccles to
McCabe, Board Minutes, May 28, 1947, 9).[101] During the rest of his term
as chairman, Eccles held to this view. In his memoir, he recognized that he
erred in not taking a more independent position (Eccles 1951, 425).

The Federal Reserve's failure to act raised legal as well as political issues.
The Board's counsel advised "that the System would not be relieved of responsibility because the Treasury did not want the System to take action
which it [the Board] believed . . . should be taken" (Minutes, FOMC, January 23, 1946, 12). Without political support, the Board believed it had to
take the legal risk.

---

100. The reasoning is wrong. Debt retirements raise bond prices and lower interest rates,
not the reverse.

101. This is a political argument, but the Board was also skeptical about the economic effects. The letter ends as follows: "Outside of the monetary cranks, no one at all informed on
the subject would suggest that in the great complex of economic forces there is some simple
monetary device that could preserve or restore economic equilibrium" (Board to McCabe,
Board Minutes, May 28, 1947, 10). Eccles also expressed concern about large bank earnings
if interest rates rose (Minutes, FOMC, January 23, 1946).

The Postwar Recession

An eight-month recession began in February and ended in October 1945. Data available at the time show a decline in nominal GNP of $20 billion (9.7 percent) between the first and fourth quarters of 1945. Prices rose, and real GNP fell almost 14 percent.

Resources shifted to peacetime use. Government spending declined more than $39 billion, nearly twice the decline in GNP, but spending on gross private capital formation rose from $3.6 billion to $15 billion in the same period. Private investment and consumption continued to increase and government spending continued to fall. By third quarter 1946, almost a year after the recession ended, private capital spending exceeded government spending for the first time since 1941.

Monetary actions were limited, so they had limited influence. Monetary base growth remained high during 1945 and fell with the budget deficit after the recession ended. Interest rates remained in a narrow range throughout the recession.

A major concern at the time was that readjustment to a peacetime economy would, via the Keynesian multiplier, bring a sharp decline in private consumption and investment. The data on nominal GNP and government spending suggest that the ratio of the two changes was about 1/2, far below estimates of the multiplier then in use.

First Steps, 1946–47

The Federal Reserve limited its initial postwar efforts to raising short-term rates on Treasury bills and certificates, ending the preferential discount rate for loans secured by governments, and asking for new powers. It wanted the Treasury to use its cash balance to reduce outstanding marketable short-term debt and issue more nonmarketable long-term debt to the public. During the war, the Treasury had sold nonmarketable series E bonds in small denominations to small savers and series F and G bonds in larger denominations. The public could buy and redeem these bonds on demand, but banks and financial institutions could not hold them. The System wanted to increase the amount outstanding and raise the limits on the amount a buyer could own (Board Minutes, February 18, 1946, 3–14).

Efforts to eliminate the preferential discount rate began before the war in Asia ended. In a letter to Vinson, who had just become treasury secretary, Sproul advised him that the System had two options under consideration. First was elimination of the preferential discount rate of 0.5 percent (for loans collateralized by government securities with one year or less to maturity). Second was an increase in the interest rate from 0.5 percent to

0.75 percent. The System's concern, he wrote, was the "abuses" that had developed. The use of bank credit to finance government security purchases and "great speculative" activity occurred "in an atmosphere somewhat reminiscent of the late 1920s" (Sproul to Vinson, Sproul Papers, FOMC, July 31, 1945, 1). The letter assured Vinson that the System would support the government securities market "into the indefinite future" and that the "Treasury would continue to borrow . . . at no more than the rates it is now paying" (1). The Treasury would not agree to the changes, so the preferential rate remained.

Sproul tried again in December 1945, after the Treasury had sold the Victory Loan. This letter repeated the earlier arguments and added new ones. The preferential rate was inflationary. It encouraged banks to expand credit and made it profitable for them to borrow from the reserve banks. Also, with the war ended and no further new borrowing likely, the earlier rationale was gone (Sproul Papers, FOMC, December 12, 1945, 2–3).[102] Secretary Vinson's reply rejected the proposal. Throughout the winter, Vinson refused to accept the change, arguing that it would increase interest rates; the Federal Reserve repeated its arguments without success.

In late March, Sproul warned Eccles that the New York directors would vote to eliminate the preferential rate at the next meeting, April 4. Eccles asked for two additional weeks' delay because the Treasury had agreed to use part of its cash balance to retire $4.8 billion of securities in March and April.

Further, to ease the Treasury's concern, the Board notified Secretary Vinson that it would keep unchanged the 0.875 percent rate on certificates when it approved the elimination of the preferential rate on certificates (Board Minutes, March 15 and April 12, 1946). Vinson objected that the reserve banks' action would raise interest rates. He continued to oppose the change.[103]

The Treasury's position was more extreme than after World War I, when it insisted on no change in interest rates as long as it had to undertake large-scale financing. By spring 1946 the Treasury had current and prospective surpluses in its cash budget. It could now retire debt, but it continued to oppose even the slightest change in wartime monetary arrangements.

---

102. The quotations are from Sproul's draft. Eccles sent the letter to Vinson the following day.

103. Total member banks borrowing was about $200 million to $300 million at the time but had reached $600 million earlier, the highest level since the early 1930s. The Treasury contributed to anti-inflation policy by running a surplus of $754 million in fiscal 1946 and retiring debt of $10 billion. The difference between the two is explained by costs of the IMF, World Bank, and veterans' loans not spent that year ($3.9 billion), use of trust funds to purchase debt ($5 billion), and sale of savings bonds ($1.1 billion) to retire debt.

Treasury intransigence annoyed the Federal Reserve. In a strongly worded letter, the Board claimed that eliminating the preferential borrowing rate would stop further monetization of government debt without raising interest rates.[104] The Board assured him again that it would act to keep the certificate rate from rising (Board Minutes, April 19, 1946, 9). The guarantee of the 0.875 percent certificate rate irritated Sproul because it bound the System unconditionally (Memo, Sproul to Ruml, Sproul Papers, FOMC, July 19, 1946, 1–3).

On April 23 the Board approved actions by directors at New York, Philadelphia, and San Francisco to discontinue the preferential rate effective April 25. The announcement emphasized that the rate was a wartime measure and that the Board did not favor higher rates. Weekly average short-term rates in the New York market remained unchanged, but average discounts fell by $100 million in the following week and, on monthly average, by $300 million from March to May.

It had taken eight months since the end of the war to achieve this first, very modest change in wartime monetary policy. Another year passed before the System could raise the 0.375 percent bill rate. Moreover, the System continued to discount banker's acceptances at 0.5 percent.[105]

Eccles told the FOMC that the Board was committed to the Treasury's interest rate policy until Congress and the public would accept higher interest rates. To gain support, he agreed to discuss the problem and the need for higher reserve requirement ratios and other new powers in the Board's annual report, so that the public would be aware of the Board's position. Sproul wanted to reopen the rate issue with Secretary John W. Snyder, who had just replaced Vinson. With respect to the new powers that Eccles wanted, Sproul noted that to be effective the System had to make credit less easily available and therefore more costly. Higher rates could not be avoided.

Sproul opposed an increase in reserve requirements on central reserve city banks.[106] His program at the time called for "some modest increase in short rates while maintaining the $2^1/_2$ percent rate on long-term bonds."

104. Banks could still sell bills yielding 0.375 percent. The Federal Reserve was the principal and usually the only buyer.

105. The volume was small, however. Eccles questioned the manager (Robert Rouse) about the acceptance rate at the June 10 FOMC meeting. Sproul responded that the New York bank wanted to "go slow," a strange argument given his interest in raising rates. The rate was raised to 0.75 percent in July and 1 percent in August (Board of Governors of the Federal Reserve System 1976, 636). Sproul's argument recalls the New York reserve bank's policy of nurturing the acceptance market in the 1920s.

106. A letter to Eccles explained that, with interest rates unchanged, banks would sell securities to restore their ability to lend (Sproul to Eccles, Sproul Papers, Memorandums and Drafts, May 6, 1946). Eccles's reply argued that they had to use their existing powers or Congress would not grant additional ones. However, he argued also that the increase in require-

Other specific actions that he favored included using the budget surplus to retire long-term debt and increased sales of savings bonds and bank-restricted 2.5 percent long-term bonds.

Eccles disagreed about interest rates. It was not useful to overemphasize the importance of credit policy in discussions with the Treasury. He concluded a very lively exchange by repeating that "there was nothing that the System could do to unfreeze the rate structure, and that the best thing it could do would be to present the problem to Congress and point out . . . [that] the use of those powers under present circumstances [was] entirely inappropriate" (Minutes, FOMC, June 10, 1946).

The Board's annual report for 1945 emphasized the "inherent limitations of the System's existing statutory powers, under present conditions, or the inevitable repercussions on the economy generally and on the Government's financing operations in particular of the exercise of such existing powers to the degree necessary to be an effective anti-inflationary influence" (Board of Governors of the Federal Reserve System, *Annual Report, 1945*, 1). Further, the Board argued that letting holders shift substantially into longer-term debt "would be undesirable because it would increase the cost to the Government of carrying the public debt" (5).[107]

For the rest of 1946, the FOMC made recommendations to the Treasury for debt retirement and for new issues that would place more of the debt in private, nonbank hands. After the Board failed to get legislative approval of secondary (security) reserve requirements, it concentrated on legislation to increase maximum reserve requirement ratios, consumer credit controls, and margin requirements for purchasing and holding stock.[108]

---

ments would force banks to sell short-term securities. They could then not sell these securities to increase bank loans (Eccles to Sproul, Sproul Papers, Memorandums and Drafts, May 17, 1946).

107. The Board proposed three changes in powers: authority to set a maximum amount of long-term debt (public and private) that a bank could hold relative to its deposits; power to set a secondary reserve of short-term securities that a bank must hold as a percentage of its deposits; and authority to increase reserve requirement ratios. The Board recognized that with excess reserves low, an increase in reserve requirement ratios would raise interest rates as banks sold assets. The Federal Reserve would acquire the securities to prevent higher rates. This is the first time I have found the Board clear on this point (Board of Governors of the Federal Reserve System, *Annual Report*, 1945, 8). Elsewhere the report recommended that the Treasury issue more nonmarketable debt, a recommendation the Board and Eccles made many times. The 1946 annual report repeats the same argument but omits reference to the cost of financing the debt when discussing the importance of lengthening the maturity structure of the publicly held debt (Board of Governors of the Federal Reserve System, *Annual Report*, 1946, 6).

108. In October the executive committee authorized the manager to engage in direct purchases and sales of United States securities with the International Monetary Fund and the World Bank. It rejected a request from the bank that the Federal Reserve stabilize the market for World Bank debt (Minutes, Executive Committee, FOMC, October 3, 1946, 10–11).

By October Sproul had become more cautious, citing a slowdown in business activity, the Treasury's debt retirement program, aggressive bank bidding for government bonds, and a rise in short-term rates of interest (Minutes, FOMC, October 3, 1946, 17). The last was "weak medicine" against inflation, but he was reluctant to be more aggressive with the economy weakening.

Meanwhile he proposed that the System prepare for its next moves—elimination of the 0.375 percent bill rate and 0.875 percent certificate rate. Increases in these rates would increase System earnings at the same time that Treasury borrowing costs increased. Since the System held most of the 0.375 percent bills, it cou!d offset some of the Treasury's higher costs by restoring the franchise tax on earnings it had paid until 1933.[109] At the next meeting, in December, the executive committee decided to put Sproul's proposal into a memorandum for Secretary Snyder.

The Board considered three methods of paying interest to the Treasury: restoring the franchise tax; charging interest on Federal Reserve notes not backed by gold certificates; and eliminating charges for performing fiscal operations (Board Minutes, February 28, 1947, 38). A majority of the reserve bank presidents favored the franchise tax, provided the reserve banks maintained an adequate surplus. Eccles's concern was that a request for legislation would raise questions about the size of Federal Reserve earnings, the size (6 percent) of dividends paid to member banks, the amount of expenses, and the issue of ownership (39). Sproul responded that the questions could be answered, but he did not persuade Eccles.

The legal staff found an alternative. Under paragraph 4 of section 16 of the act, the Board could charge the reserve banks interest on their outstanding notes. After Eccles discussed the proposal with members of the House and Senate banking committees, the Board approved the tax in April.[110] The tax was supposed to provide enough revenue to transfer 90 percent of the System's earnings to the Treasury.

Eccles and Sproul discussed the interest charge on notes with Secretary Snyder. Snyder agreed to the tax on note issues but delayed the increase in the 0.375 percent rate. Although Eccles argued that the decision about rates was the Federal Reserve's responsibility, the System did not act until the Treasury approved (Meeting, Executive Committee, FOMC, June 5,

---

109. Eccles proposed an alternative—exchange the System's 0.375 percent bills for a lower yielding bill. Sproul opposed giving the Treasury control of the rates paid to the reserve banks (Minutes, FOMC, October 3, 1946, 18).

110. Questions were raised about the Board's authority. The section of the act provided for the tax to restrict the note issue. Counsel ruled that the authority was broader, citing a 1920 discussion by Governor W. P. G. Harding.

1947, 4). Treasury Undersecretary Albert Wiggins explained the Treasury's hesitancy. A rise in the bill rate would cause existing certificates to fall in price.[111]

On April 23, 1947, the Board voted to charge interest on the difference between the average daily amount of Federal Reserve notes outstanding and the average daily amount of gold certificates held by the reserve banks. Rates were not uniform at all reserve banks. New York and San Francisco paid more than twice the interest rate at St. Louis. In aggregate, the interest payments transferred 90 percent of the earnings of the reserve banks to the Treasury, about $60 million at the time.[112]

It took nine months to go from first proposal to action. On July 3, 1947, the System withdrew its commitment to the 0.375 percent rate. Beginning July 10, the Treasury issued ninety-day bills at rising rates. By September the bill rate was 0.79 percent, close to the 0.875 percent yield on nine- to twelve-month Treasury certificates. The rate continued to rise, forcing reconsideration of the rate on certificates as Sproul had hoped.[113] Two years after the war ended, the Federal Reserve had taken the first small steps toward market-determined rates on short-term securities, but with long-term rates pegged, bill rates had not increased enough to attract banks to hold them (Meeting, Executive Committee, FOMC, August 6, 1947, 6–9).

Regulations 1946–47

Through most of 1945–46 the System could not agree to take even small steps to increase interest rates. Yet it recognized its responsibility for inflation and knew that Congress and the public would hold it accountable. Unwilling to act effectively, or pessimistic about its ability to do so, it turned to regulatory actions.[114]

111. One member of the Board objected to the proposed increase in rates on certificates. It would have no noticeable effect on inflation. The banks would gain, and the System would be blamed for raising interest rates paid by farmers and small businessmen (Minutes, FOMC, June 5, 1947, 7–8).

112. This amount can be compared with the $149 million paid as franchise tax from inception to 1932. Wartime inflation and the large increase in debt held by the reserve banks account for the change in order of magnitude. At the end of 1946, the reserve banks had a $440 million surplus and capital of $374 million.

113. In 1943 Congress amended the Federal Reserve Act to permit direct purchases of government securities from the Treasury up to a $5 billion maximum holding. This power expired with the War Powers Act in March 1947. Congress renewed the authority as a temporary measure, later made permanent. At about the same time, at the Board's request, Congress repealed a section of the Emergency Banking Act of 1933 that gave the Treasury authority to regulate and prohibit banking transactions (Board Minutes, March 3, 1947, 3–6).

114. Some of the actions were entirely cosmetic. For example, when President Truman asked all departments and agencies to reduce spending so as to increase the budget surplus, Eccles proposed cutting the Board's expenditure and asked the reserve banks to do the same

RESERVE CITIES   In August 1945 the Board approved a change in regulation D to require member banks with branches in reserve cities to maintain reserves based on the reserve city classification. This opened a long-dormant issue about the criteria for classifying cities as reserve cities. The Board could not at first agree on criteria, so none were adopted.[115]

The Board later chose two explicit criteria: the proportion of interbank demand deposits held at member banks in each city to total Systemwide interbank deposits or the proportion of interbank demand deposits at member banks to total demand deposits at member banks in the city. Designations would be renewed or changed every three years.[116] The new rule took effect on March 1, 1948 (Board Minutes, December 19, 1947, 2–7). New York and Chicago continued as central reserve cities. All other cities with Federal Reserve banks or their branches continued as reserve cities.

CONSUMER CREDIT   The president authorized regulation of consumer credit, under the Board's regulation W, by proclamation under the Trading with the Enemy Act of 1917. Six months after the war ended, many wartime restrictions and regulations expired. The Trading with the Enemy Act was permanent, but the grant of emergency powers to the president expired, and with it the authority to control terms and conditions for consumer credit.

President Truman endorsed continued regulation, and so did the Conference of Reserve Bank Presidents, in a divided vote (Board Minutes, October 4, 1946, 19). The Republicans controlled Congress after the Novem-

---

even though they were not part of the budget and, at the time, did not pay a tax to the Treasury (Board Minutes, August 2, 1946, 3).

115. The classification system was archaic, carried over from the National Banking Act when central reserve and reserve cities had held the principal reserves of country banks as correspondent balances. Under the Federal Reserve Act, banks continued to serve as correspondents, but most reserves were held at Federal Reserve banks. In discussion with the Federal Advisory Council, Eccles favored uniform reserve requirements for all banks, a position that was inconsistent with his efforts to get congressional approval of an increase in reserve requirements for central reserve city banks only (Board Minutes, May 20, 1946, 6). Some bankers opposed eliminating the reserve city classification because they claimed banks would lose correspondent deposits. There was nearly general agreement that the classification system had lost its logical basis. The problem was that no one could suggest an appropriate revision (1–7). In 1930–31, 1932, and 1934, the System considered basing reserve requirement ratios on activity. Congress turned down these requests. It returned to these proposals in 1945, when it considered three classes of deposits—interbank, other demand, and time. The revised system would count vault cash as reserves (Sproul Papers, Memorandums and Drafts, 1945, October 1, 1945). The System offered the proposal again in 1948, with ratios of 30, 20, and 7 percent for the three types of deposit (ibid., April 22, 1948).

116. If all the member banks in a city chose to continue an existing reserve city classification, the Board agreed to maintain the classification.

ber 1946 election. They wanted to end all wartime regulation and controls. Many merchants who had to enforce controls agreed, but the Board wanted to retain controls, citing the need to control spending. It failed to recognize that aggregate spending could not be controlled by restricting credit for purchasing particular goods. Households could borrow in other ways.

The Board claimed that by restricting consumer credit regulation W limited total credit outstanding and thereby reduced total spending. Since the Federal Reserve would not raise interest rates and banks no longer held idle reserves, the Board omitted from its argument the step by which credit control reduced banks' demand for reserves and the monetary base at prevailing interest rates. Without a change in interest rates or reserves, controls did not change the amounts of money and bank credit.[117]

The reserve bank presidents had the job of enforcing regulation W. They claimed that enforcement would be easier if Congress authorized regulation instead of relying on an executive order. The Board's annual report for 1946 asked for such legislation. President Truman supported legislation, but he warned that if Congress did not legislate, he would vacate the executive order and allow authority for consumer credit regulation to lapse (Board Minutes, June 6, 1947, 22).

Congress ended controls in August, effective November 1.[118] The Board sent a letter, approved unanimously, urging merchants to exercise self-restraint and reduce prices instead of lengthening credit terms to attract new customers. Data for consumer credit show no evidence of acceleration after controls ended.

SECONDARY RESERVE REQUIREMENTS At the October FOMC meeting, Woodlief Thomas of the Board's staff led a discussion of three op-

117. The Board confused relative and absolute changes in demand. "It has not seemed to the Board that any change in the regulation [W] would be advisable at the present time. With employment and incomes high and the supply of spendable funds excessive, credit beyond that now available would only waste itself in stimulating undesirable price rises and retarding needed price adjustments" (Board to T. Schlesinger, Board Minutes, May 13, 1947, 14–15). Schlesinger was vice president of Allied Stores Corporation. Other letters from congressmen and their constituents questioned the legality of peacetime regulation. In its 1946 annual report, the Board made its error explicit. "It [regulation W] can restrict excessive demands for credit by limiting the borrowing capacity of prospective purchasers of goods without operating, as general instruments of credit policy must do, by increasing the cost of credit to the Government or to industry" (Board of Governors of the Federal Reserve System, *Annual Report*, 1946, 8).

118. The Board's press release, a mixture of annoyance and economic error, is remarkable for its implicit criticism of Congress. "The continuance of strong inflationary pressures has confirmed the belief of the Board that this is no time for the relaxation of terms by banks, finance companies and installment dealers" (Board Minutes, November 24, 1947, 6).

tions for slowing or preventing inflation: permit a gradual further increase in short-term rates to observe whether credit demand slows; adopt a policy of controlling bank reserves, a return to earlier procedures; and push more vigorously for passage of the Board's legislative program. John H. Williams followed Thomas's discussion by arguing against control of money and credit. These methods "might operate to bring about a deflation through reducing production" (Minutes, FOMC, October 6, 1947, 7). As usual, Eccles opposed rate increases or control of reserves as ineffective. Sproul disagreed. He urged the System "to accommodate itself to the powers it already had and not continue to refer to powers that it might have had" (10). He urged also that the System not exaggerate the amount of bank credit expansion.[119]

The committee agreed on a six-point program that included increasing short-term rates to 1.125 percent by the end of the year (1947), raising discount rates and reserve requirements for central reserve city banks, and moral suasion to call bankers' attention to the dangers of rapid credit growth. The FOMC voted eleven to one to approve the program and authorized Eccles and Sproul to discuss the program with the Treasury. Governor Rudolph M. Evans opposed. He saw no evidence that higher interest rates would reduce credit expansion.

Eccles did not endorse the System's program when asked in November about recommendations to slow the rise in prices. His main proposal called for a secondary reserve requirement, originally proposed in the Board's 1945 annual report, that made all banks (including nonmember banks) hold a reserve consisting of government securities with less then two years to maturity. The FOMC would have authority to vary the requirement up to 25 percent of gross demand deposits.[120] His only other proposal was to reinstate consumer credit controls.

119. This was a response to Eccles's use of rising bank loans to make his case for control, neglecting sales of securities that limited total credit expansion. Eccles argued, also, that a further increase in interest rates would have little effect on the demand to borrow—another example of "elasticity pessimism" (Minutes, FOMC, October 6, 1947, 4).

120. Governor Draper opposed the plan. He had not received any advance notice, nor had other governors. There had been no analysis. He thought the plan was too drastic. Nevertheless, he voted in favor to make the vote unanimous (Board Minutes, November 5, 1947, 5). The reason for haste in presenting the plan was that Eccles had been asked by the White House to recommend policies for the president's speech to a special session of Congress. Bankers opposed the plan as "impractical, socialistic, and unnecessarily drastic" (Eccles 1951, 428). Snyder opposed and had the proposal replaced in Truman's message by a general statement favoring a reduction in credit. Snyder nevertheless agreed to support the Board's proposal for consumer credit controls (430–31), and to refrain from testifying against the secondary reserve plan. When asked his opinion, however, he said that "he didn't think it would work" (432).

Concerns about inflation were well founded at the time. A very large increase in the gold stock during the third and fourth quarters of the year temporarily raised the growth rate of the monetary base. From June to December, consumer prices rose at a 12 percent annual rate. The burst of inflation was short-lived, however. It ended before Congress could act on the president's proposals for new controls on consumer credit, commodity speculation, price and wage controls, stronger rent controls, and new powers for the Federal Reserve over reserve requirements. Congress did not approve any of the new controls.[121]

The arguments made by proponents and opponents of controls show the reasoning at the time. Bankers argued that there was no need for additional controls. At a meeting with the Board, the Federal Advisory Council rejected Eccles's argument that bank credit expansion was excessive. There was no evidence of excessive growth of money: "As bank loans have increased, the banks have decreased their investments" (Board Minutes, November 18, 1947, 3). In a sharply worded statement, the council pointed out that the growth of bank loans reflected demands by businesses and households, not speculative actions by the banks. It cited some of the many ways government policy encouraged borrowing: the Reconstruction Finance Corporation guaranteed risky loans; foreign aid programs raised farm prices and encouraged expansion; and mortgage guarantees for war veterans and others increased construction and mortgage lending. The council challenged the Federal Reserve to control bank reserves using the powers it had instead of seeking new ones, and it opposed the request for secondary reserves as impractical and as a transfer of power from individual bankers and their directors to the Federal Reserve.

The council's argument did not change Eccles's views. Testifying before the Joint Committee on the Economic Report a week later, he urged Congress to give the System additional powers. He told the committee that "there is no easy, simple, or single remedy. We are already in the advanced stages of this disease" (Board Minutes, November 26, 1947, 3).[122] The problem was not just inflation. Ultimately, inflation would be followed by deflation: "The higher prices rise and credit expands, the greater the subsequent liquidation and downward pressure on prices is bound to be" (5–6).

This is an extraordinary statement for the head of a central bank. Not only did he fail to recognize his ability to prevent inflation using existing

---

121. Contemporary observers point out that the administration knew that Congress, under a Republican majority, would reject the program. The president wanted to blame Congress for inaction. Congress provided more stimulus by reducing tax rates in April 1948 and overriding the president's veto of the tax bill (Fforde 1954, 163–64).

122. The verbatim statement is part of the Board Minutes.

powers, he treated deflation as an inevitable consequence of the preceding inflation, just as the System had done in 1929–33. The new powers the Board had gained in 1933 and 1935 did not affect his analysis or argument. Although he asked Congress to restore consumer credit controls (ibid., 7) and to establish secondary reserve requirements, the only general control he recommended was to adjust fiscal policy so as to use "the largest possible budgetary surplus" to retire government debt (6). He opposed the tax cut that the Republicans in Congress favored.

Although he favored using the budget surplus to reduce the money stock, the usual methods of monetary control could not be used, Eccles said, because (1) the cost of servicing the large outstanding debt would rise, requiring higher taxes; (2) the increase in interest rates would have to be very large, "substantially above the present relatively low levels" (ibid., 10); (3) the Treasury would not know at what price it could sell its securities, and (4) there would be massive liquidation of government bond holdings, including series E, F, and G bonds held by households. Despite these dire consequences, he added, if Congress favored ending wartime policy, "we would welcome such an expression from the Congress" (9). This was hardly a likely outcome after his warnings.

Eccles's statement had several errors. First, he neglected the effect of inflation on interest rates. The statement presumed that the structure of rates could be held indefinitely, with only a few additional powers. Second, he endorsed a comment by a New York banker that raising interest rates to control inflation would be highly inflationary. Removing the interest rate peg, he said, "would be the most dramatically inflationary move that could be made at this time . . . so catastrophic as to make present fears appear as one raindrop in a storm" (ibid., 10). Third, after removing the peg, the System would remain powerless to offset increases in bank reserves from gold inflows.[123] Fourth, to control credit expansion, the System would have to sell securities in competition with private credit demands and gold inflows: "Private borrowers might outbid us for these reserves" (10).

Eccles used the experience in 1928–29 to bolster his argument: "We are convinced that the remedy of letting interest rates on Government debt go up on the theory that this would bring an end to inflationary borrowing is dubious at best, as has been demonstrated in past monetary history, notably in the 20s when high rates were unsuccessful in restraining specula-

---

123. This statement denies that the System could sterilize gold inflows, as in the 1920s. At best the statement is misleading. The System held more than $22 billion in securities at the time, a sum larger than the combined monetary gold stock of all countries other than the United States.

tion in the stock markets, real estate, or otherwise" (ibid., 12). This is a misstatement of history. The Board had opposed interest rate increases in 1928–29. Although Eccles had often said that a large increase in interest rates would be required to stop inflation, he had not previously based his case on the disaster scenario he sketched for Congress. Nor did he mention Sproul's contrary view.[124]

Doing nothing was dangerous too, he warned. To make the case for a special security reserve requirement, Eccles exaggerated the risks of excessive expansion. He assumed that banks might sell half of the $70 billion in government securities to the Federal Reserve. The increase in bank reserves would support a $200 billion increase in credit and money, six times the increase in reserves.[125] The money stock, currency, and demand deposits would increase from $112 billion to more than $300 billion, and gold inflows would add an additional $2 billion to $3 billion to reserves. Further, he told the committee, other holders of securities could sell up to $70 billion of securities to the Federal Reserve.

The Board's solution was to increase the demand for government debt by imposing a security reserve of up to 25 percent against demand deposits and 10 percent against time deposits. It would phase in the new requirement gradually. At the maximum percentages, Eccles said, the new requirements would reduce credit expansion by about 60 percent. Further, banks would reduce the supply of loans, so lending rates would rise without increasing rates on Treasury debt: "Hence, the cost of restraining credit would be borne by private borrowers who are incurring additional debt, and not by the government which is reducing its debt" (ibid., 14). Eccles and the Board did not explain why banks would not sell debt and make loans if loan rates rose relative to rates on government bonds.

Bankers regarded the reserve banks as more concerned for their interests than the Board. To reduce bankers' criticisms, Eccles proposed giving the FOMC power to set secondary reserve requirements. He concluded by

124. After reading Eccles's proposal to the president, asking for a secondary reserve requirement, Sproul telegraphed: "It would be most unfortunate if in our zeal to acquire new powers which might not be granted we were unnecessarily to minimize the effectiveness of our present policy, exaggerate the role of monetary factors . . . and expose the System to the risk of being held responsible for not checking or remedying a situation due primarily to nonmonetary causes. In the circumstances I want to reaffirm that as a member of the Federal Open Market Committee I cannot regard myself as in any way committed to what is proposed" (Sproul Papers, Memorandums and Drafts, 1947, November 13, 1947).

125. The money multiplier of six appears to be based on the average reserve requirement ratio with no allowance for a spillover from deposits into currency. At the time the average base money multiplier was about three.

submitting the Federal Advisory Council's statement opposing secondary reserves.

The Board approved Eccles's statement unanimously and voted to send a copy to all banks and banking supervisors. It also unanimously approved a lengthy reply to the Federal Advisory Council and voted to send a statement of its views to the Joint Committee on the Economic Report. The reply to the council argued that if interest rates increased, the System would have to supply more, rather than fewer reserves.[126]

A puzzling feature about this period is that interest rates rose very little, a repeat of the experience during and after World War I. As inflation rose from 4 percent to more than 10 percent during the second half of the year, rates on prime commercial paper rose from 1 to 1.25 percent and rates on three- to five-year Treasury securities rose from 1.25 to 1.5 percent. Although long-term interest rates rose modestly in autumn 1947, long-term Treasury bonds were at 2.36 percent at the time of Eccles's testimony.[127]

One partial explanation of the puzzle is that the public did not expect inflation to persist.[128] The "peg" on rates contributed to the lack of response, but despite the interest rate ceiling, money growth remained modest. For the year as a whole, the base increased less than 1 percent. The money stock rose slightly faster, 4.9 percent for the year.

The Federal Reserve recognized that using the Treasury's surplus to retire debt from the reserve banks reduced the stock of money. Hence, despite a $2 billion increase in the gold stock, Treasury operations left the monetary base little changed for the year. As long as money growth remained low, the public was right to interpret the higher rates of inflation reported for July to September 1947 as temporary and unsustainable.

The Bretton Woods Agreement fixed the dollar to gold at $35 an ounce. At the time, many considered this arrangement a type of gold standard, involving a commitment by the United States to a fixed gold exchange rate.

126. The reply argues that an "attempt to use those [the System's established] powers would increase sales of Government securities in the market by banks and others. If the System refused to purchase any more securities, bond prices would decline sharply. The threat of such a policy would induce a wave of selling. . . . The Reserve System would have to purchase securities in order to meet the drains on the Treasury, and new reserves would therefore be created" (Board Minutes, November 26, 1947, 22–23).

127. The Treasury sold securities from the trust accounts in May to raise long-term rates toward the ceiling. This annoyed the FOMC members because they had not been notified in advance.

128. Friedman and Schwartz (1963), suggest that the public expected postwar deflation. A related explanation is that on the margin, bondholders believed that inflation would be followed "inevitably" by deflation. Such explanations compound the problem. Why did expectations of a future deflation, at an uncertain date, overwhelm evidence of current inflation?

Although United States citizens could not buy gold from the Treasury, foreign banks could.[129]

Further, by the fall of 1947 the United States government was committed to aiding European recovery by lending and transferring funds abroad. This limited the gold inflow at the time. With neither a budget deficit nor a large capital inflow to expand domestic money, the risk of persistent inflation may have seemed slight.

This explanation is partial. It can explain why rates on long-term securities did not reflect reported rates of inflation. It does not explain why short-term rates, adjusted for measured inflation, remained negative during and immediately after the war.

MARGIN REQUIREMENTS Stock prices rose rapidly at the end of the war. Urged on by the chairman of the Securities and Exchange Commission, the Board increased stock market margin requirements to 100 percent on future purchases effective January 21, 1946. Eccles explained to President Truman that "elements were present . . . which might result in a speculative movement exceeding even 1929" (Board Minutes, January 17, 1946, 2). He believed that raising margin requirements was a poor substitute for an increase in the capital gains tax or control of bank credit. In their absence, margin requirements would have a modest effect against speculative use of credit. The peak in stock prices and trading volume came in May. In February 1947, with the Standard and Poor's index 16 percent below its peak, the Board reduced margin requirements to 75 percent. Trading volume remained between 25 million and 30 million shares a month, and the Standard and Poor's index continued to decline until May.

The Board's announcement, lowering margin requirements effective February 1, 1947, recognized that the adjustment to a peacetime economy was far along. Despite many strikes, industrial production rose rapidly in the second half of 1946. Ten million demobilized veterans found jobs. Shortages of most goods had ended.

Eccles favored a further reduction of margin requirements for banks, but not for brokers and dealers. He also favored a change in the law to eliminate all broker margin accounts and to leave regulation of banks' margin loans to the bank supervisory agencies. The Board did not propose legislation, however. The new requirements remained in effect until March 30, 1949, when the Board reduced the margin requirement to 50 percent.

129. Surprisingly, Board and FOMC minutes make no mention of the commitment under Bretton Woods or its possible effect on inflation. The slow response of interest rates to inflation occurred again in the 1950s and 1960s. This is consistent with the view that, at the time, creditors believed inflation was temporary, although there is no direct evidence.

Beginning of Restraint

The October 1947 meeting was a turning point. Although Eccles had not presented the System's program in his testimony to Congress, the FOMC resumed discussion of higher rates. There was general agreement that the special session of Congress had created anxiety in the market. Bond yields had increased as banks reversed the way they played "the pattern of rates." They now sold long-term securities and, at the increased rates on bills and certificates, bought short-term securities.

The directive issued at the October meeting reflected the change at the Federal Reserve. Instead of referring to particular prices or interest rates to be maintained, the directive now called for "maintenance of stable and orderly conditions in the government securities market" and for "relating the supply of funds more closely to the needs of commerce and business." The new directive looked more to the economy and less to the Treasury market. It left open the meaning of "stable and orderly," but by referring to the "needs of commerce," it pointed the System back toward the 1920s and away from the years under Treasury control. And by referring to an orderly market, the FOMC tried to end its commitment to the pattern of rates. Only the commitment to the long-term rate remained.

The change was easier to state than to put into practice, but some changes were made. The Treasury agreed in November to use its surplus to retire Treasury bills held by the reserve banks instead of paying out cash to retire debt held by the commercial banks or the public.[130] The Board joined with other regulators to warn lenders and borrowers that "our country is experiencing a boom of dangerous proportions" (Board Minutes, November 21, 1947, 3). Its letter urged bankers to " exercise extreme caution in their lending policies" and to curtail loans for speculation in real estate, commodities, or securities.[131] As in the 1920s, the letter did not advise banks how to identify such loans.[132]

The December meeting took a more effective step. It agreed that long-

130. Between November 1 and June 30 the Treasury retired $6.8 billion, of which $4.9 billion came from reserve banks.

131. The warning was aimed especially at insurance companies to try to stop their sales of long-term bonds. Banks complained about competition from insurance companies in the loan market, claiming that they exercised restraint but insurers did not.

132. A further change brought an end to the practice of exempting Treasury war loan accounts at commercial banks from reserve requirements. The exemption was a wartime measure, taken in 1943 to increase banks' returns from bond sales. War loan accounts served as a depository for receipts from sales of Treasury new issues. Removing the exemption in 1947 forced a small increase in required bank reserves. A secondary effect was a reduction in the contractive effect of a shift in Treasury deposits from commercial to reserve banks.

Table 7.7   Bond Market Support, 1947–48

DATE	SYSTEM HOLDINGS (BILLIONS OF DOLLARS)		INTEREST RATE (%)	
	OVER FIVE YEARS	UNDER ONE YEAR	BONDS	CERTIFICATES
October 1947	0.4	21.5	2.27	0.97
March 1948	5.1	15.3	2.44	1.09

Source: Board of Governors of the Federal Reserve System 1976.

term yields should be allowed to rise to the 2.5 percent ceiling once the Treasury completed its January refunding. Governor Szymczak suggested letting bonds go below par, but the FOMC decided to hold bonds at or above par value until the Treasury agreed to a higher rate.

Also in December, Eccles opened a discussion of discount rates by reporting that the Board was now ready to consider an increase in rates.[133] Eccles favored 1.25 percent, above the rate on one-year certificates. Sproul favored 1.125 percent. On January 12, discount rates were set at 1.25 percent, the first change in almost six years. The 1.25 percent rate equaled the rate on securities held by banks that would mature in the next five years. Eccles wanted short-term rates at that level to encourage banks to hold short-term and sell longer-term securities.

The new program worked more quickly than expected. Banks, insurance companies, and other holders of long-term debt perceived these changes as a first step toward increased rates on long-term bonds. Bonds no longer seemed as riskless as before, so banks, insurance companies, and others sold bonds and bought bills and certificates. The Federal Reserve now faced the question, Should it allow bonds to go below par?

Its actions give the answer. Table 7.7 shows the large volume of System purchases of long-term debt, and sales of short-term debt, between October 1947 and March 1948. To support the market, the System purchased as rates fell. In addition, the Treasury bought about $1 billion for the trust accounts.

The Treasury continued to run a surplus. Instead of holding the surplus (in war loan accounts) at commercial banks, the Treasury withdrew its balances to the Federal Reserve banks, then used them to retire short-term debt as it matured. The shift in Treasury balances from commercial banks

133. The issue was first discussed in July, after the increase in bill rates. The Board postponed consideration until rates on certificates rose. In October, after the Treasury accepted the 1.125 percent rate on one-year certificates, the Board considered raising discount rates to 1.25 percent. It decided to observe the response to the higher certificate rates before acting. The Board renewed discussion on December 5 and 19, but it again delayed action because of seasonal demands and to give the market time to adjust to recent changes in rates.

to the reserve banks reduced bank reserves, as expected at the time. The monetary base declined in the first two quarters of 1948.[134]

The principal disagreement at the FOMC meeting was about how quickly tightening should proceed. Eccles was more aggressive than Sproul. He argued that the Treasury's cash position presented "an opportunity to exert enough pressure on the reserve position of member banks to curb to a substantial extent the volume of capital expansion that otherwise would take place, that such expansion was undesirable at the present time because of the shortage of labor and materials" (Minutes, Executive Committee, FOMC, January 20, 1948, 15). Sproul did not disagree on the desirability of reducing bank reserve growth, but he believed the committee should spread its effort over months rather than weeks. He suggested that Eccles wanted a bold program so that he could tell Congress that the System had used its existing powers and needed new authority (17).[135]

The difference was not resolved at the January meeting, so the FOMC's letter to Secretary Snyder included both views, along with a recommendation to raise the certificate rate from 1.125 percent to 1.25 percent at the March refunding. The Treasury used a decline in commodity prices in February to postpone the rate change.

The decline in commodity prices concerned the FOMC also. At the February 27 meeting, Sproul interpreted the decline as a temporary correc-

---

134. Rouse's memo to the FOMC estimated that the shift in Treasury balances in the first quarter would reduce bank reserves by $7.3 billion before offsets from gold inflows and other (estimated) changes (Minutes, Executive Committee, FOMC, January 20, 1948, 11). Rouse was the account manager. His report also shows the relative changes in bond prices at the end of 1947. Some long-term bonds fell as much as $4.50. These were large changes. The Treasury accepted them, unlike Secretary Morgenthau, who had treated almost any price decline as a crisis. Rouse reported that almost all the bond price decline occurred on December 24, "when the new support level was adopted" (5). Later the Treasury blamed the Federal Reserve for the disturbance in the bond market.

135. Sproul made his argument for a gradual approach in a lengthy January 13 letter to Senator Taft. The letter responded to speeches Taft made criticizing monetary policy as too expansive. He emphasized the need to avoid depression while achieving deflation. In a prelude to the position Sproul and others took during the recession that started later that year, Sproul wrote: "We are all a little enchanted, of course, with the idea of a modest downturn which would relieve some existing pressures and forestall worse disturbances later. But no one has yet found a sure way of bringing just a little depression, and I think our present program of modest restraints involving a combination of debt management and credit policy is the best course to follow in trying to achieve that objective" (Sproul to Taft, Sproul Papers, January 13, 1948, 3). Sproul's letter may have convinced Senator Taft to choose a different target. Soon after, Taft chaired the committee that responded to the 1948 economic report. The response does not repeat the criticism. It blames inflation on the government's "huge programs" of foreign aid, public works, and domestic assistance and criticizes Eccles's proposals for credit controls, secondary reserve requirements, and price and wage controls (Joint Committee on the Economic Report 1948, 3–6).

tion, not the start of recession and deflation. Nevertheless he proposed a less restrictive policy than he had urged in the fall: no further reductions in the Treasury's war loan accounts at commercial banks; receipts from taxes held in the war loan accounts; continued run-off of System bill holdings at the rate of $100 million a week; and reducing to eleven months the maturity of the 1.125 percent certificate issued in April, to signal that certificate rates would rise in June. The FOMC approved Sproul's program. Governor Evans voted no on the recommendation to raise certificate rates. Once again he objected that the rate increase would be ineffective against inflation and would increase bank earnings. He preferred the secondary reserve plan. Eccles explained that the purpose was to flatten the yield curve so that banks and others would stop playing the pattern of rates (Minutes, FOMC, February 27, 1948, 12–13).[136]

For the first time, the committee agreed unanimously that it would not prevent interest rate increases even if some bonds went below par. "At the appropriate time" Eccles would advise Secretary Snyder that "the only commitment the System had made was, under existing and prospective conditions, to maintain the 2.5 percent long-term rate and not that it would support all issues of Government securities at par" (16).[137]

By March, holders apparently had become convinced that the System would maintain the price of long-term bonds above par. Selling slowed, and System purchases ended. During 1948, long-term Treasury yields remained between 2.41 and 2.45 percent. Although still operating under the Treasury's strictures, for the first time since the 1930s the Federal Reserve had managed a sudden shift in market sentiment following a policy change. The Treasury had a smaller role, supporting the System's operation by purchasing for the trust accounts.

New Leadership

Leadership at the Federal Reserve changed after the war. Emanuel A. Goldenweiser retired as research director in January 1946. Governor John K. McKee retired the following month, but he remained at the Board until his successor, James K. Vardaman Jr., arrived in April. Eccles's former assistant, Lawrence Clayton, joined the Board in February 1947. Vice Chairman

136. Although not yet confirmed by the Senate, chairman-designate McCabe was present at the meeting.

137. Since 1944, the System had licensed a limited number of dealers in governments to trade with the System. Small dealers, who were excluded, complained that their business was hurt because the Federal Reserve had become the principal buyer in the market. They claimed the conditions to become a licensed dealer were too burdensome. The executive committee decided to keep the requirements unchanged (Minutes, Executive Committee, FOMC, March 1 and April 21, 1948). No major change was made for many years.

Ronald Ransom died at the end of 1947. A month later, President Truman notified Marriner Eccles that he would not reappoint him as chairman when his third term expired on February 1, 1948. The new chairman was Thomas B. McCabe. Truman offered Eccles the vice chairmanship of the Board, and Eccles accepted.[138]

President Truman gave no reason for removing Eccles as chairman. In his memoirs, Eccles made a strong circumstantial case that Truman wanted election year support of the Giannini family that controlled Bank of America and Transamerica Corporation.[139] There was ample reason for the Giannini family to want Eccles removed. The Federal Reserve had tried to obtain legislation to limit further expansion by their holding company, Transamerica Corporation.[140] After years of investigation, the Board began a proceeding under the Clayton Act to prevent Transamerica from expanding further. Eccles believed he had been removed in the expectation that the investigation would end.

Transamerica may have contributed to Eccles's dismissal, but there were other possible reasons. Eccles's relations with the banking industry had never been friendly. Bankers and Secretary Snyder strongly opposed his call for secondary reserve requirements. Despite Snyder's objections, Eccles testified in favor of his proposal. Moreover, he had become friendly with Republican Senators Robert A. Taft and Charles W. Tobey and critical of the administration's budgets. He openly favored increased taxation to prevent inflation. His working relationship with Secretary Snyder was never comfortable. It probably did not help that the Board raised discount rates and allowed bond rates to rise in December and January. These changes came at the same time that President Truman's budget message to Congress supported maintaining the pattern of rates on government bonds.[141]

138. McCabe was the chairman of Scott Paper Company. He had served as a board member and as chairman of the Philadelphia reserve bank. The Senate approved his appointment on April 12, and he took office as chairman on April 15, 1948. He served until March 31, 1951. President Truman did not announce Eccles's appointment as vice chairman. In April, Eccles withdrew his name in a sharply worded letter to the president (Eccles 1951, 442).

139. This summary is based on Eccles 1951, 434–56. Eccles's personal and family interest in banking in an adjacent region are part of the circumstances of the case. Eccles's book denies any connection, although he acknowledges that the charge was made at the time (1951, 454). On the other side, Secretary Snyder was a friend of the Gianninis, and the bank's general counsel had been counsel to a Senate committee that Truman chaired. Eccles's account of the events shows that he ignored several strong hints from Secretary Snyder to stop investigating Transamerica.

140. The proposed legislation was the Bank Holding Company Act of 1947. The legislation did not pass until 1956.

141. Eccles's testimony to Senator Douglas's subcommittee by letter in December 1949 suggests that relations between the Federal Reserve and the Treasury had deteriorated. Almost every meeting of the FOMC advised the Treasury on debt management policy, but the

Although his term as chairman ended on February 1, Eccles continued as chairman pro tem until McCabe took office on April 15. He continued to take an active role in System policy and later played an important role in removing the ceiling rate on long-term bonds. He left the Board in July 1951.

A Deflationary Interlude

The inflation rate slowed at the start of 1948. By year end prices were falling. Quarterly average values of the consumer price index show several quarters of deflation beginning in fourth quarter 1948. Inflation did not return until the start of the Korean War in June 1950.

At first prices fell rapidly. Early in 1950 the decline slowed. At the end of the deflation interlude, the consumer price index had returned to the level reached in first quarter 1948. Table 7.8 shows these data.

Both Treasury and Federal Reserve actions contributed to the deflation. The Treasury continued to use its surplus to retire debt from the reserve banks and to purchase debt for the trust accounts. This policy reduced the public's holding of government debt without increasing the monetary base.

Falling output soon followed falling prices. The National Bureau of Economic Research puts the economy's cyclical peak in November 1948 and the trough eleven months later, in October 1949. Industrial production (1992 = 100) fell about 9 percent from peak to trough. The unemployment rate reached a peak of 7.9 percent.

With the interest rate peg in effect, the Federal Reserve could not prevent inflation, but it was entirely capable of stopping deflation. The monetary base shows no sign of expansionary actions. Interest rates rose modestly as the monetary base declined. The rate on four- to six-month commercial paper, representative of short-term rates, increased by 0.5 percent in the year before the recession. It remained unchanged (at 1.56 percent) through July 1949, eight months after the cyclical peak.

As in 1921 and 1938, deflation had two positive effects. First the gold inflow increased. Between fourth quarter 1947 and the peak in Federal

---

suggestions were not often taken. Eccles recognized that the Federal Reserve had lost its independence: "It can hardly be said that the Federal Reserve System retains any effective influence in its own right over the supply of money in the country" (Eccles 1951, 460). Eccles offered three alternatives. The first continued prevailing arrangements. Credit and monetary restraint would depend on the Treasury's willingness to accept higher interest rates. The second expanded the Board's power over reserve requirements for *all* banks; he included secondary reserve requirements as one option. The third proposal restored independence. The Treasury would be required to consult with the Federal Reserve about debt management policy and interest rates. Eccles warned the subcommittee that interest rates would rise (Eccles 1951, 461–62).

Table 7.8   Money, Prices, Output, and Debt, 1947–50

| | | | | | HELD BY | | |
DATE	BASE GROWTH	CONSUMER PRICES	REAL GNP	GROSS[a] DEBT	AGENCIES	RESERVE BANKS	PRIVATE OWNERS
1947.4	5.2%	7.4%	4.4%	$255.7	$34.4	$22.6	$198.7
1948.1	−14.7	0	4.0				
1948.2	−3.2	11.2	5.4	251.2	35.8	21.4	194.1
1948.3	−7.6	6.6	0.6				
1948.4	17.2	−7.1	4.0	251.7	37.3	23.3	191.1
1949.1	−12.8	−3.9	−1.7				
1949.2	7.5	0.6	−1.3	251.7	38.3	19.3	194.1
1949.3	−4.2	0	−2.6				
1949.4	4.3	−3.9	−3.5	256.2	39.4	18.9	197.9
1950.1	5.8	−1.1	15.0				
1950.2	−0.8	4.5	14.9	256.1	37.8	18.3	199.9

Note: Dollar amounts are billions.
[a]Gross public debt includes guaranteed securities. Data for debt are for June and December. Other data are quarterly averages at annual rates.

Reserve gold holdings—third quarter 1949—the gold stock rose 9.5 percent, slowing the decline in the nominal stock of base money.[142] Second, falling prices raised the real value of the monetary base, creating an excess supply of real balances and a demand for goods and services.

CHANGES IN RESERVE REQUIREMENTS   Early in 1948 the Board again considered an increase in a reserve requirement ratio to slow loan growth. At the time, reserve requirement ratios for reserve city and country banks were at their maximum values, 20 percent and 14 percent, respectively, but central reserve city banks, at 20 percent, were below their 26 percent maximum. The Board voted unanimously to raise reserve requirements at central reserve city banks to 22 percent, effective February 27.

The Board's staff estimated that the change would absorb $530 million of reserves at New York and Chicago banks. This is an overstatement based on faulty analysis. The true estimate of the effect is approximately zero.[143] Banks sold government securities to acquire additional reserves and slightly increased borrowing. The main effect was a transfer of income (on government securities) from commercial banks to the reserve banks.

142. Earlier, the Board sent a letter to all reserve bank presidents requesting them to notify banks that they should discourage individuals and businesses from buying gold at premium prices. The letter was a response to rumors that the dollar would be revalued against gold (Board Minutes, July 22, 1947, 10).

143. The qualification allows for a secondary effect on the profitability of loan demand. Central reserve city banks had to hold higher reserves against the deposits created when making new loans. With interest rates unchanged, loans were less profitable. Market interest rates remained unchanged.

Since the Board had voted before the Federal Advisory Council met, the council did not oppose the February 27 increase. The members expressed concern, however, about the recent decline in commodity prices and the possibility of a recession. They wanted a halt to restrictive policy, maintenance of the 2.5 percent rate, no further increases in discount rates or reserve requirement ratios at central reserve city banks, and no additional powers for the Federal Reserve. The council thought "it would be a good thing if the situation could develop into a mild recession, but . . . the members of the Council felt that it might develop into a very severe recession if not into a depression" (Board Minutes, February 17, 1948, 9). Chairman Eccles agreed that "a recession at this time would be in the best interests of the country and that the longer such a development was delayed the greater would be the downward adjustment that eventually would have to come" (10).[144]

The Board was eager to get the council to agree on a joint program to send to Congress, as in 1940. The bankers were reluctant, so their emphasis on the possibility of a deep recession may have been an expression of dissent.[145] Eccles argued that whether inflation continued or ended in recession, the Board and the commercial banks would be blamed for what happened. They had a common interest. He agreed that discount rates could not be raised, but his reason was not concern about recession. First the Treasury had to increase the coupon on the one-year certificate to 1.25 percent. That would not be done in current circumstances. Council chairman Edward E. Brown responded that banks were so "jittery" that a change to 1.25 percent might cause additional selling of government securities.

The next three years are a unique period in the use of reserve requirements as a policy instrument. The System made nineteen changes, up and down, in these ratios. Many were small. Table 7.9 shows the level of reserve requirements on February 1, 1948, and the adjustments in the next three years. The last column shows the weighted average, or effective, ratio. This ratio changed very little from year to year. The largest change, in 1950, resulted from a shift in deposits from demand to time accounts.

After the changes in reserve requirement ratios, banks increased their use of the discount window to adjust reserves. Discounting had started to revive during the war but remained below $100 million, on a sustained basis, until August 1944. After 1946, discounts remained between $100 mil-

144. The language shows how little had changed since the early 1930s. Recessions were still seen as the "inevitable consequence" of prior inflation. Although the Employment Act was now law, the Federal Reserve had not changed its analysis.

145. Although interest rate remained low, the bankers no longer complained about easy money as they did in 1940.

Table 7.9   Actual and Effective Reserve Requirement Ratios, 1948–51 (percent)

DATE	CENTRAL RESERVE CITIES		RESERVE CITIES		COUNTRY		YEAR	EFFECTIVE AVERAGE[a]
	DEMAND	TIME	DEMAND	TIME	DEMAND	TIME		
1948								
February 1	20	6	20	6	14	6	1948	15.71
February 27	22							
June 11	24							
September 16					16			
September 24	26	7.5	22	7.5		7.5		
1949								
May 1					15		1949	15.87
May 5	24	7	21	7		7		
June 30		6	20	6		6		
July 1					14			
August 1					13			
August 11	23.5	5	19.5	5		5		
August 16					12		1950	14.22
August 18	23		19					
August 25	22.5		18.5					
September 1	22		18					
1951								
January 11	23	6	19	6		6	1951	15.86
January 16					13			
January 25	24		20					
February 1					14			

[a]Based on call report data for June 30.

lion and $300 million. Discounts typically increased after an increase in reserve requirement ratios, reviving the adjustment pattern that Strong, Riefler, and Burgess had observed in the 1920s.

After February 1948, the Board and the FOMC discussed additional increases in reserve requirement ratios at New York and Chicago. Governor Evans was often the leading proponent. Eccles remained cautious, despite strong output growth and continued inflation early in 1948. The Board and the FOMC repeatedly urged the Treasury to increase the certificate rate to 1.25 percent, so they could raise the discount rate, but the Treasury ignored or rejected the advice and the rate stayed at 1.125 percent throughout the spring and summer.[146]

146. An example of the Treasury's argument against raising the certificate rate from 1.125 percent to 1.25 percent is that "the Secretary [Snyder] felt that if the rate were raised at this time it would not be as effective as at some future time when, if inflationary pressures were increased, the rate could well be raised" (Minutes, Executive Committee, FOMC, May 20, 1948, 2). Snyder explained that the actual decision to reject the System's advice was made after discussions with "bankers from various parts of the country." A majority had told him to make no change (11).

The System remained divided over whether future inflation or deflation posed the greater risk. After the Treasury rejected its suggestion of a 1.25 percent certificate rate for the July refunding, Sproul and Szymczak looked to the September refunding. Eccles urged the committee not to act without Treasury agreement, but it ignored him and voted to permit an increase in short-term rates before the September refunding if inflation increased during the summer. It wanted to force the Treasury to raise the rate to 1.25 percent. This was a significant change, since the committee had earlier declined to increase rates until the Treasury agreed.

Spending for foreign aid began to rise, beginning with the Greek-Turkish aid bill in 1947 and the Marshall Plan in 1948. Looking forward, the members worried that the budget surplus would decline and with it debt retirement (see table 7.8 above). Effective action against inflation would end.[147] At the meeting of the Federal Advisory Council in April, the Board recalled the 1940 proposal to Congress, sponsored jointly by the council and the System, calling for a statutory increase in maximum reserve requirement ratios for all banks. The council was reluctant to increase banks' costs. It noted that there were both inflationary and deflationary tendencies at work, so it preferred to wait until the future became clearer. It urged the System to use existing powers by raising the discount rate or reserve requirements at central reserve city banks.[148]

Several bankers spoke against the proposal to increase maximum reserve requirements. Their principal arguments were that a request to Congress for higher reserve requirement ratios would at once induce banks to shift assets from long- to short-term securities. If the proposal was adopted, banks would have more difficulty raising capital and would take more risk to compensate for lower earnings. Membership in the System would be discouraged, particularly if the higher reserve requirements applied to all banks, as the Board wished. They were particularly opposed to Eccles's recent testimony calling for higher cash reserve requirement ratios and a secondary securities reserve.[149]

147. For fiscal years ending June 1947, 1948, 1949, and 1950, spending for national security and international affairs was (in billions): $20.9, $16.3, $19, $17.7.

148. The council showed signs of changing beliefs about the effectiveness of monetary policy: "Relatively slight changes in open market policy . . . can greatly influence bank operations, the security markets and business" (Board Minutes, April 27, 1948, 7).

149. Eccles had testified at a congressional hearing on April 13; he reported on the progress made against inflation but warned that the money supply was "excessive" and that proposed tax reduction would add $5 billion to purchasing power and reduce future budget surpluses and debt reduction. Increased military spending added a new large source of inflation both directly and through its effects on private sector attitudes. A shift from budgetary surplus to "deficit . . . would eliminate the only remaining important anti-inflationary influence" (Board Minutes, April 2, 1948, 18, with transcript of Eccles's April 13 testimony). He

Chairman McCabe asked the bankers what they would do if inflation rose. They responded that, unlike the Board, they did not expect that to happen. However, they favored maintaining the 2.5 percent ceiling rate, partly out of concern that a fall in government security prices would lower bank capital (Board Minutes, April 27, 1948, 19).

The Board continued to prepare for an increase in the reserve requirement ratio at central reserve city banks. The main issue had become not whether the change should be made but when. A principal consideration was to find a time when the change would have greatest effect on inflationary psychology, but there was concern also to use existing powers. Congress had again rejected the request for additional powers, and one of the reasons given was that Board had not used its existing powers fully.

On June 1, 1948, the Board voted to increase to 24 percent the reserve requirement ratio at central reserve city banks, effective June 11. McCabe was absent, and Szymczak opposed the timing of the increase. He argued that New York and Chicago banks had no excess reserves, so the increase would simply shift $500 million of government securities from banks to the reserve banks. McCabe wrote a letter that was read at the meeting urging the Board to delay the change for a month. He believed the change would be more effective if accompanied by a rise in the certificate rate (Board Minutes, June 1, 1948, 5–6).[150]

To prepare for the 1948 election and give the appearance of decisive action, President Truman called a special session of Congress in August. He asked for price controls, rationing, rent control, an excess profits tax, repeal of the Taft-Hartley Act, and regulation of commodity markets. He also asked Congress to increase spending on Social Security and education, more government aid for housing, and increases in the minimum wage and farm price supports. The aim was to return to the wartime control program while redistributing income toward traditional Democratic constituencies. The Federal Reserve asked for renewed controls on consumer credit and higher statutory maximum reserve requirement ratios as part of the program.

---

asked again for new powers to increase reserve requirements at all commercial banks and secondary reserve requirements. He described the latter as "essential" in the event of larger deficits (20). None of his forecasts were correct.

150. Like Szymczak, McCabe argued that the banks would sell securities to the Federal Reserve, so there would be no effect on lending or inflation. This was a correct forecast, of course; in the two weeks following the effective date, New York and Chicago banks sold securities. Interest rates remained unchanged, and the monetary base (adjusted for the change in reserve requirements) continued to fall at about a 1 to 2 percent annual rate. The action was criticized in the press as an attempt by Eccles to push through an increase against the Treasury's wishes while McCabe was absent.

Congress rejected most of the program, but by joint resolution it approved renewal of consumer credit controls until June 30, 1949, and an increase in maximum reserve requirement ratios for member banks. In September the Board set minimum down payments of 33.33 percent for automobiles and 20 percent for other durables.

The president's proposals suggest the haphazard way the administration thought about the substance of economic policy. Proposals for higher wages accompanied a proposal for price control, and encouragement of home building accompanied controls to discourage purchases of household durables and furniture. The increased mortgage credit, if approved, would have substituted for consumer credit.[151]

On August 2 Chairman McCabe and Governor Evans testified on parts of the president's proposal. McCabe repeated the familiar arguments supporting legislation authorizing higher reserve requirement ratios. He referred several times to the problem of controlling inflation while maintaining the 2.5 percent rate, but he insisted that it should be maintained "to insure orderly conditions in that market, not primarily because of an implied commitment to wartime investors that their savings would be protected, nor to aid the Treasury in refunding maturing debt, but because of the widespread repercussions that would ensue . . . if the vast holdings of public debt were felt to be of unstable value" (House Committee on Banking and Currency 1948, 89).[152] McCabe urged that the Board's powers be extended to include nonmember banks, but he offered no evidence of relative expansion by nonmember banks and gave more attention to increased lending at insurance companies than at banks.[153]

Several times, members of Congress asked McCabe whether long-term rates had to rise for effective control of inflation. The Board had discussed

151. The administration, not the Board, initiated the decision to reimpose consumer credit controls (Board Minutes, July 20, 1948, 3). The Board sent Woodlief Thomas to participate in a meeting on July 23 at which the White House staff presented the details of the president's message to Congress. The Board authorized Thomas to say that the Board favored consumer credit controls, to last three years, and authority to increase reserve requirement ratios "in such form as it might wish." If required to be specific, Thomas was authorized to ask for ten percentage points for demand and four percentage points for time deposits above current maximum rates. He was told not to raise the issue of whether the change applied to all banks or only to member banks (Board Minutes, July 23, 1948, 6).

152. This statement is clearly disingenuous and misleading, since the Federal Reserve would not change the 2.5 percent rate without Treasury approval, and the Treasury was concerned about interest costs on the debt. McCabe recognized the Treasury's concern later in his testimony (House Committee on Banking and Currency 1948, 95).

153. The Board's proposal was part of the program for the special session of Congress in August 1948. The bill authorized state bank supervisors to enforce reserve requirements against nonmember banks. The Senate bill limited the change in reserve requirements to member banks.

the possibility that this question would arise at its July 30 meeting, but it did not reach a conclusion. McCabe did not want to confront the Treasury and tried to avoid the issue by saying that "it was vitally necessary to support the $2^1/_2$ percent bonds" (ibid., 101).[154]

Chairman Jesse P. Wolcott and other members questioned McCabe and Evans about the reason for credit controls. McCabe tried to shift responsibility to Congress, suggesting that Congress should order an end to pegged rates. Wolcott demurred.[155] He challenged McCabe and Evans to explain how credit controls would reduce demand, pointing out that people could take out larger home mortgages to offset larger down payments on cars and other durables. Other members cited examples showing that credit controls did not curtail demand for durables. McCabe and Evans had no answers.

During the summer of 1948, the Board continued to press the Treasury to raise short-term interest rates on its refundings and to use its balances to retire Treasury bills. On July 16 McCabe gave Snyder the draft of a letter outlining the Board's concerns. The Board again referred to its "statutory responsibility" to control inflation, warned of higher inflation ahead, and expressed concern that the Treasury had failed to increase the rate on certificates at the April and June refundings. The letter warned that credit demands remained strong and that insurance companies and other holders of long-term bonds were likely to sell as much as $1.5 billion of such debt to the System in the second half of 1948. To offset these prospective purchases, the System had to be able to sell an equal amount in the short-term market.

The letter again proposed higher rates on certificates and higher discount rates. The Federal Reserve pledged again to support the long-term market, and it asked the Treasury to continue retiring short-term debt from

154. Congressman Jesse P. Wolcott was the committee chairman. "The Chairman: Then you mean . . . that it is going to be your continued policy . . . to buy Governments in the open market? Mr. McCabe: I would not say that it is our policy forever. I say for the foreseeable future. . . . The Chairman: That is to support our debt. Mr. McCabe: That is to support our debt; yes, sir. The Chairman: Then you are saying that it is necessary to continue inflation in order to carry the national debt? Mr. McCabe: I would not like to put it that way, sir" (House Committee on Banking and Currency 1948, 101).

155. "The Chairman: There have been orthodox ways of controlling it [credit] heretofore. . . . I do not know why we have to supplement those with consumer credit controls at the present time, anymore than we did before. Mr. McCabe: . . . [I]f it is the wisdom of this Congress that the Federal Reserve should not support the Government bond market, then I think Congress should so direct the Federal Reserve. . . . The Chairman: I do not think we are going to direct you not to support the government bond market. I do not think we are going to direct you to support the Government bond market at a particular figure" (House Committee on Banking and Currency 1948, 109).

Table 7.10   Minimum and Maximum Reserve Requirement Ratios, 1948

DEPOSITS	MINIMUM	MAXIMUM
Demand		
Central reserve city	13	30 (26)
Reserve city	10	24 (20)
Country	7	18 (14)
Time		
All member banks	3	7.5 (6)

Note: Previous maximum shown in parentheses.

the reserve banks. While awaiting the Treasury's response, the Board began to discuss a further increase in reserve requirements, to 26 percent, at central reserve city banks.

In July the annualized monthly rate of increase in consumer prices reached 15 percent, and the twelve-month rate reached 9.3 percent. The Treasury agreed to an additional 0.25 percent increase in the discount rate, to 1.5 percent, a 1.25 percent rate on one-year certificates, and an increase in the bill rate. In return, Snyder asked the Board to again reaffirm its support for the 2.5 percent long-term rate and to postpone a decision about reserve requirements until September (Letter, Snyder to Board, Board Minutes, August 10, 1948, 3). The Board promptly notified the reserve banks that they could raise discount rates. All banks voted for an increase. Open market rates on short-term securities rose. Two years after the war's end, the spread between short- and long-term rates was down to 1.25 percent.[156]

Table 7.10 shows the minimum and maximum rates fixed in August 1948. These rates applied only to member banks and were temporary until June 30, 1949. Congress refused again to authorize the Federal Reserve to set reserve requirements for nonmember banks.[157]

At the Board's August 24 meeting, Governor Vardaman announced that he intended to propose increases in reserve requirement ratios for demand and time deposits at the first meeting after Labor Day. McCabe spoke in favor of the increase as part of a more general program developed jointly with the executive committee of the FOMC. Vardaman and Szymczak preferred

156. The account manager, Rouse, explained how the market worked at the time. The Federal Reserve was the residual buyer at the end of the day. If it allowed prices on certificates or bonds to move by more than $1/_{32}$, the market would offer all maturities to learn whether the support price had changed. This made it difficult to move to a more flexible rate policy. This description makes clear that the market was no longer confident that the peg would remain indefinitely.

157. Out of more than fourteen thousand banks in 1948, eleven withdrew from membership in 1948 and four in 1949. Admissions to membership were twenty-seven in 1948 and fifteen in 1949. More than two thousand banks had not agreed to par collection at the time, so they were not eligible for membership.

immediate action. Eccles was not present but sent a letter proposing increases, effective within the next two weeks, and expressing concern that, having been granted additional authority, the Board would hesitate to use it (Board Minutes, September 7, 1948, 7–14). The discussion reached an informal agreement that the Board would increase reserve requirements by two percentage points for demand and 1.5 percentage points for time deposits and would notify Secretary Snyder of its intention. The only formal decision was to postpone the vote until after the meeting of the FOMC executive committee the following day.

At that meeting, President Clifford S. Young of the Chicago bank gave the correct analysis: "The increase would not do much good as an anti-inflationary move because banks would only sell securities which the System would buy in order to give them the reserves to meet the increased requirements" (Minutes, Executive Committee, FOMC, September 8, 1948, 6). Sproul, on the other hand, thought the change was too big. It would "churn the market unnecessarily" as banks sold governments to meet the higher requirements (6). McCabe favored lowering the support price for long-term bonds to the 2.5 percent rate, a reduction of only $25 on a $1,000 bond, but Sproul opposed using the same argument that had been used against him—that such a move would "create apprehension as to whether the entire support program was going to be continued." They would then have to buy large amounts (9).[158] McCabe urged a drop in other support prices with an announcement that the 2.5 percent rate would be maintained, but Sproul cautioned that they had done that successfully in December 1947 and could not repeat the promise a second time after imposing losses on bondholders in December. He wanted to be rid of pegged rates, and he disliked further commitments to support them, but he did not favor the small step McCabe proposed (10). Sproul also opposed McCabe's suggestion that the bill rate be allowed to fluctuate more freely. With a fixed rate on certificates at 1.25 percent and the bill rate at 1.08 percent, there was little to be gained.

The Board met the same afternoon and voted unanimously to increase reserve requirement ratios, as previously agreed, for demand and time deposits. The staff estimated that the change would absorb $1.9 billion in reserves. On average the system portfolio rose $1.54 billion, and the gold stock rose $130 million, canceling most of the restrictive effect. Banks and others responded by selling long-term and buying short-term securities.

---

158. A notable feature of these discussions is the unwillingness to pay a one-time cost to improve control and reduce certainty about the 2.5 percent rate. This problem remained long after the peg was removed.

Short-term interest rates remained unchanged, and the monetary base continued to decline.[159]

New York now had a more important role than at any time since the 1920s. Sproul took the lead in shaping the September decision. McCabe deferred to Sproul's views, whereas Eccles had not.

The 1948–49 Recession

Industrial production fell in August and September, rose in October, then fell sharply in November. The consumer price index reached a peak in August, remained unchanged in September, and fell in October. The fall was precipitate, from a 15 percent annualized rate of increase in July to unchanged in September.

The Board and the FOMC were unprepared and at first did not respond to the recession. The only mention of a decline referred to an eventual, inevitable recession if inflation continued. At a meeting of the System Research Advisory Committee in late September, Woodlief Thomas, the director of research, forecast a substantial increase in expenditure and income and continued price increases (Sproul Papers, Board of Governors, Memorandums and Drafts, September 27, 1948). He urged actions to slow the expansion. The Board's staff forecast 10 percent growth of GNP in the last three quarters of 1948 and the first quarters of 1949 (ibid., September 30, 1948).

The recession eventually forced the System to face facts it had tried hard to avoid; it could not control inflation and was reluctant to respond to recession. Consumer credit controls, changes in stock market margin requirements, or adjustment of reserve requirement, with interest rates unchanged, accomplished little. Interest rates and money growth were set by markets, not by the System.

Realization grew slowly and spread even more slowly. More than halfway through the recession, the Board and the FOMC continued to press the Treasury to raise short-term interest rates, despite sustained declines in industrial production and consumer prices. Two closely related reasons help to explain why policy was slow to change. First, the principals regarded the recession as temporary, and for many it was a welcome interlude. The problem of greater concern was long-term inflation. Second, market interest rates were at historical lows, so they believed policy was easy. No one mentioned the effect of falling prices on real interest rates, a repeat of behavior in previous periods of deflation.

---

159. The volume of security sales was so heavy that the manager had to make three requests to increase the ceiling on purchases during September.

The New York bank was more perceptive than the Board about the start of the recession. At the October FOMC meeting, John H. Williams predicted that the economy was about to enter a mild recession, while inflation "was in the process of wearing itself out" (Minutes, FOMC, October 4, 1948, 5). He favored additional increases in short-term rates and no change in long-term rates.

His comments about recession had no impact, perhaps because the FOMC welcomed a mild recession. The main topic at the meeting was an increase in certificate rates to 1.5 percent as soon as possible but before the January refunding. The increase would permit the Treasury bill rate to rise toward the certificate rate and increase commercial banks' bill purchases. Sproul proposed that the Federal Reserve should present its plan to the Treasury without seeking approval or disapproval. Following the FOMC meeting, Sproul and McCabe met with Snyder, but they waited for approval and did not act. A month later, in mid-November, over Federal Reserve objections, Secretary Snyder announced that the certificate rate would remain unchanged through January. Short-term rates remained the same until May 1949.

Stymied by the Treasury's reluctance to increase rates, the Board discussed a further increase in reserve requirement ratios but did nothing. Banks objected to the further increase as costly to them and ineffective against inflation.

President Truman's reelection surprised many bankers, businessmen, and others. The Federal Advisory Council ignored the deflationary policy but blamed the election for "a very profound change in business sentiment" (Board Minutes, November 16, 1948, 2). The council reported that businessmen were concerned about an excess profits tax, higher corporate tax rates, and new price controls. It warned that these policies would slow the economy. The risk of recession had increased. There would be a pause; construction and expansion would slow. The length and depth of the slowdown depended on the administration's programs.

Long-term bond yields fell after the election, at least partly in response to recession and deflation. Insurance companies had been heavy sellers before the election. They now began to buy, so the Federal Reserve reversed course, selling long-term and buying short-term securities.[160] The Treasury also changed its operations after the election. Instead of retiring bills from the Federal Reserve, it began to retire bills held by commercial banks.

---

160. Between May and November 1948, Federal Reserve holdings of governments with ten years to maturity increased by $4.3 billion. In the next six months to May 1949, during the recession, its holdings decreased by $2.3 billion.

The effect on the stock of debt was of course the same, but the monetary base and the money stock increased.

The FOMC discussed the Treasury's new procedure at its November 30 meeting and concluded that the Treasury was trying to reduce the outstanding stock of bills to the point where the rate could be set free. Although the FOMC preferred to keep pressure on bank reserves, it did not object that the new procedure increased reserves. It decided also to reduce the premium above par on long-term debt. There was no mention of recession.

After his reelection, President Truman asked the Board for its legislative program. The Board suggested several changes: (1) extend the temporary powers to raise reserve requirements and impose consumer credit control beyond June 30, 1949; (2) enact new legislation giving the Board power to regulate bank holding companies; (3) authorize the Federal Reserve to guarantee loans by banks to businesses; and (4) ease membership requirements by reducing capital requirements for branches of state banks (Board Minutes, November 30, 1948, 4–6). Later the Board modified its request. It asked to maintain new maximum reserve requirements only if they applied to member and nonmember banks. None of the proposals had much to do with inflation (or deflation), and none became law.

At its December 1 meeting, the Board reviewed material to be included in the president's economic report. The draft showed no awareness of recession or deflation. The principal recommendations called for a larger budget surplus, achieved by raising tax rates and reducing spending to retire debt at reserve banks (Board Minutes, December 1, 1948, 3–5). On the critical issue of the bond price support, the Board recognized "a serious dilemma," but it offered no new solution and did not recommend increasing long-term rates (5).[161]

The Board asked the reserve bank presidents to comment on consumer credit controls and reserve requirements. The presidents favored credit controls, and some wanted to make them permanent. A majority opposed further increases in reserve requirements. They reported that "banks continued to hold the view that the only effect of an increase was to transfer Government securities from the banks to the Federal Reserve banks" (ibid., 6). They noted that bankers talked about withdrawing from membership, but none had done so.

---

161. Although the recession had started, the administration's budget ignored evidence of recession and deflation. The budget asked for higher taxes on profits and estates and a surtax on incomes, and it assumed continued growth. It requested more spending for defense and education. By mid-February, when Chairman McCabe testified on the budget, he recognized that a mild readjustment was occurring, but he continued to urge his legislative program to control inflation.

The Board responded by making two changes in its proposals for the State of the Union message. It proposed paying interest on the additional required reserves.[162] And it limited its request for authority to regulate reserve requirements for nonmember banks to those that offered deposit insurance, thereby exempting the smallest, nonmember banks (Board Minutes, December 17, 1948, 5).[163]

At the turn of the year, the FOMC continued to press gently for a 0.125 percent increase in short-term rates. One of the main objectives at the time was to reduce the spread between short- and long-term rates so that holders would have no incentive to play the pattern of rates. Sproul reported that the Treasury would resume its former practice of retiring debt from the reserve banks and, despite declining economic activity, was open to the idea of increasing short-term rates at the March and April refundings (Minutes, Executive Committee, FOMC, January 4, 1949, 5–7).

The January 1949 meeting was the first time the FOMC discussed how it could end support of the long-term market. Sproul proposed refunding outstanding long-term debt into higher-yielding issues that would not require support (ibid., 8). The Treasury did not agree until 1951.

The Federal Advisory Council opposed the Board's legislative program. It reminded the Board that increases in reserve requirements had no effect on inflation. The council also opposed interest payments on reserves and extension of the Board's authority to include nonmember banks (Board Minutes, February 15, 1949, 3).[164]

February's minutes show the first clear recognition that a recession had started. The council "was definitely of the opinion that the country was in a recession . . . that the business decline was spreading (ibid., 3–4). McCabe challenged this view: "In spite of the decline in business activity, there was more optimism than had been expressed by the Council" (5).[165]

---

162. The president's staff objected to including insured banks on the grounds that the recommendation was too "controversial" for the State of the Union message. The Board agreed to delete the sentence from the speech provided it remained in the Economic Report of the President (Board Minutes, December 22, 1948, 5).

163. Several Board members accepted payment of interest on reserves reluctantly. Governors Szymczak, Evans, Vardaman, and Clayton preferred a secondary reserve of securities but regarded that proposal as unacceptable to Congress.

164. State banks could convert to national charters, but national banks could not convert to state charters. The increase in maximum reserve requirement ratios may have stimulated interest in removing this restriction. The Board opposed the change unless Congress approved its request to place nonmember banks under its reserve requirements. The so-called membership problem continued to occupy the Board until the 1980s (Board Minutes, March 17, 1949, 2–4).

165. During the general discussion, Eccles responded that the increase in reserve requirements "did nothing more than immobilize reserves received by the banking system as

Council members demurred and used the recession to argue against the Board's program. In a statement reminiscent of Miller or Young in the 1920s, Eccles showed that he had forgotten why he came to Washington in 1933: "The business decline that was now occurring was an inevitable result of the unprecedented inflation during the past two or three years, that the longer the unbalance and distortion in the economy continued the more disastrous the deflationary adjustments would be . . . and that some adjustment was necessary and desirable [sic] if the economy was to return to a period of stability" (13–14).[166]

A widening rift between the Federal Reserve and the Treasury developed at the March 2, 1949, FOMC meeting. Secretary Snyder's letter, responding to the committee's request for an increase in short-term rates, stimulated an active discussion during which several members gave their views. Three issues were in contention at the time. First, the secretary again rejected the proposed 0.125 percent increase in certificate rates. Second, he cautioned the System to reconsider its policy of allowing rates on Treasury bills to rise because it would force a rise in the certificate rate.[167] Third, the Treasury would not commit to retire debt from the reserve banks. It preferred to retain its freedom to choose the source of open market retirements. The System saw this as a threat to its role.

FOMC members differed about whether interest rates should be raised. Some of the Board's staff and Governor Clayton opposed the increase in rates as inappropriate in a recession. Some noted that prices had fallen (since October). Sproul described the decline as "a healthy readjustment." He proposed to continue pressure to increase the bill rate, while avoiding an increase in the discount rate, to "improve the interest rate structure . . . and avoid the appearance of more or less permanently pegged rates at both ends of the rate pattern" (Minutes, FOMC, March 1, 1949, 12).

The FOMC adopted Chairman McCabe's suggestion that it ask Secretary Snyder to increase the rate but to be less insistent than in the past. To show its awareness of conditions in the economy, the committee included the words "in the light of changing economic conditions" in its directive. The vote, however, was to raise rates. Some members may have voted for the increase knowing that the Treasury would reject it.

---

a result of the System's support policy and, therefore, was entirely justified for that reason" (Board Minutes, February 15, 1949, 8). Despite the recession, Eccles favored the rate increase.

166. The council also favored an increase in short-term rates despite the clear recognition of recession and deflation, but it opposed an increase in the discount rate.

167. Snyder irritated the FOMC by writing that the 1.25 percent certificate rate should remain until "a different rate can be mutually agreed upon" (Minutes, FOMC, March 1, 1949, 6). The FOMC recognized that it would not act unilaterally, but it disliked the presumption that the Treasury had veto power. It voted to so inform Snyder (7).

In March, four months after the peak, with industrial production down almost 6 percent, the Board made its first public acknowledgment of recession. By a vote of five to one, it reduced down payment requirements on furniture and appliances to 15 percent (from 20 percent) but kept the 33.33 percent down payment on autos. The maximum maturity on all loans increased to twenty-one months (from fifteen or eighteen months). Eccles opposed the change as "premature." Further, he thought it encouraged families to go heavily into debt on "too easy terms at high prices" (Board Minutes, March 2, 1949, 2–3).

At the end of the month, by unanimous vote, the Board reduced stock market margin requirements from 75 percent to 50 percent, effective March 30.[168] The purpose was to stimulate investment without reducing open market rates. The decline in output continued at a steeper pace. The Board continued to press for a rise in short-term rates and new issues of long-term debt restricted to nonbank holders. The staff continued to view falling prices as helpful and to regard future inflation as a more serious concern than current deflation (Minutes, FOMC, March 1, 1949, 4).

Sproul explained the System's dilemma in an April memo. Wholesale prices and industrial production were 8 percent below their previous peaks. Factory man-hours had fallen 9 percent. Bank credit had declined "rapidly and substantially." The economic and credit situation called for lower interest rates; the problem was that the Treasury might not permit a reversal after the economy recovered. He proposed a resolution calling for greater interest rate flexibility that would allow "the short rate to move up and down from the new level with some freedom while trying to find a long rate . . . which will float by itself without too great deviations either up or down" (Sproul Papers, FOMC, April 1949, 2–3).

On April 21, the Board began discussing a reduction in reserve requirements. Interest in an expansive action conflicted with a desire to have Congress renew temporary authority for higher maximum reserve requirements. Facts overcame politics. A key fact was the size of the contraction of bank credit, described as one of the most severe on record (Board Minutes, April 28, 1949, 7). Effective May 1 and 5, the Board reduced reserve requirement ratios by two percentage points at central reserve city banks, one percentage point at other banks, and one-half percentage point on all time deposits (see table 7.9 above). The relative size of the changes reflected the relative size of the decline in bank credit in the year to date. In

---

168. Before acting, the Board informed the Securities and Exchange Commission (SEC). The SEC did not object.

all, the staff estimated that the changes liberated $1.2 billion of reserves.[169] The Treasury issued $100 million in long-term debt to absorb part of the reserves without lowering rates unduly. In May the System sold $1.3 billion, offsetting the effect of the reduction on the monetary base.

Open market rates remained unchanged except for a modest (0.005) decline in the ninety-day bill yield. The Board's policy now aimed to "twist the yield curve" by raising short-term rates while slowly reducing long-term rates.[170] The Treasury was unwilling to permit higher short-term rates, so the System was forced to sell long-term, bonds to prevent a steep decline and buy short-term to prevent a rise (Minutes, Executive Committee, FOMC, May 3, 1949, 2).

The Federal Advisory Council praised the Board for reducing consumer credit controls but questioned why controls were needed when durable goods were in excess supply. Governor Vardaman sided with the bankers: controls had been authorized to reduce inflation; inflation had ended. Some manufacturers wanted the controls retained to regulate trade practices but, Vardaman said, that was not authorized in the law (Board Minutes, May 17, 1949, 13–14).

The council again opposed supplementary reserve requirements and asked the Board why it did not reduce requirement ratios below the former maximum values. McCabe questioned the members about the effect on interest rates. W. Randolph Burgess, a member of the council, said there would be little if any effect if the Board sold securities and the Treasury issued medium-term bonds to fill gaps in the maturity structure.

By early June, several in the System began to express concern that the recession was spreading. Their policy of pressing for higher short-term rates and resisting lower long-term rates prevented any effective monetary response to the decline. FOMC members who wanted a more expansive

169. The Board decided to ask for renewal of authority to change reserve requirements, to make the supplemental reserve requirements permanent, and to extend the requirements to all insured banks that received demand deposits (thereby exempting mutual savings banks). The members wanted the maximum requirements increased by 10 percentage points for demand and 4 percentage points for time deposits, as initially requested in the State of the Union address, but they realized this was not likely to pass. They prepared two bills, one with the higher ratios they wanted and one renewing authority beyond June 30 with maximum increases of 4 percentage points and 1.5 percentage points above former statutory ratios. The Board also asked for a two-year extension of consumer credit controls instead of the permanent authority it preferred (Letter McCabe to Maybank, Board Minutes, May 5, 1949, 2–3). The chairman of the Federal Advisory Council testified against the bill.

170. "Twisting the yield curve" was the name given in the early 1960s to a policy of raising the interest rate on short-term debt and lowering the rate on long-term debt. As this experience shows, the policy had been tried before.

policy agreed that the Treasury would not oppose rate reduction. Later, they hoped, rates could be raised if necessary and policy would be more flexible.

Sproul took the lead in urging flexibility, but Eccles and McCabe joined him. Eccles said that future policy should maintain an orderly market without supporting a pattern of rates. He favored a symbolic reduction in the discount rate and in reserve requirements. Sproul agreed that the time had come to ease the money market to combat deflation, but he insisted that the change to an independent policy should be permanent, not tied to a current reduction in rates.

Congress did not renew supplementary reserve requirements or consumer credit controls. Both expired on June 30, so demand deposit reserve requirement ratios returned to 26, 20, and 14, with 6 percent for time deposits. The Board considered additional reductions near the end of June but postponed its decision until the Treasury agreed to a general program that included an end to the peg on short-term rates.

POLICY CHANGES Seven months of recession, and a growing sense of its impotence, had moved the System toward a new policy. On June 21, Mc-Cabe and Sproul met with Snyder to propose lower rates on bills and certificates. The Federal Reserve would remove the peg at the short end but retain it at the long end. It would announce the change publicly. Privately they assured Snyder that rates would probably fall and would not be allowed to rise when the peg was removed. Snyder liked the proposal but was hesitant to announce the change.

By July the consumer price index had fallen in six of the preceding nine months and was below the previous year's level. To stop the deflation, the Board's staff proposed that reserve requirements be reduced by three percentage points on demand deposits and one point on time deposits, to release $2.6 billion of required reserves. The proposed reductions were an addition to the reserves released by the expiration of supplementary reserve requirement ratios. The Board also reduced the discount rate by 0.25 percent (Board Minutes, June 21, 1949, 16).[171]

As the System began a more activist policy, it restored the indicators of ease and restraint it had used in the 1920s. Riefler played a major role in drafting and presenting the proposal, so it is not surprising that the proposal discussed policy in terms of excess or free reserves (excess reserves minus member bank borrowing). Reducing reserve requirements, he said,

---

171. Eccles said that although he favored the proposal, it "implied that credit policy had a greater influence on the economic situation than the facts warranted" (Board Minutes, June 28, 1949, 2).

increased excess reserves and put downward pressure on market rates, easing policy.

Although the proposal called for a Board decision, it was the main subject of the June 28 FOMC meeting. The committee held the most active policy discussion in many years. What seems remarkable in hindsight is that opinion was divided about the need for change. Of those who are recorded, Presidents C. E. Earhart (San Francisco), Ray M. Gidney (Cleveland), and Hugh Leach (Richmond) were most aggressive; they favored ending the peg for both short- and long-term rates and announcing the change as a permanent change whether rates moved up or down. Governor Evans, at the opposite pole, favored letting rates decline but wanted the Board's public statement to reaffirm the commitment to the 2.5 percent rate as a maximum. Keeping the 2.5 percent rate "was one of the major accomplishments of the postwar period" (Minutes, FOMC, June 28, 1949, 8).

Snyder's support for lower rates seemed to give the opportunity Sproul had waited for. He favored letting rates fall, but he was reluctant to announce that rates would be more flexible henceforth. He wanted to limit the public announcement to a statement that the FOMC would maintain orderly conditions, omitting words about stable rates but not making a permanent commitment to market-determined rates (ibid., 22).

McCabe hesitated also. He "felt it would be catastrophic if long-term government bonds were allowed to drop below par" (ibid., 11). He proposed avoiding the issue in his letter to Secretary Snyder by reaffirming that the "programs and policies to be pursued would be decided upon after full discussion and mutual understanding" (10). This formulation did not assert independence or accept a Treasury veto. It was ambiguous enough to gain unanimous consent.

The committee next had to decide what it would announce publicly and what it intended to do about the $800 million that would be released when the supplementary reserve requirements expired in two days. There was general agreement that the System would not absorb the $800 million by open market sales but, instead, would allow banks to lower market rates. Riefler wanted to supplement the $800 million by a further reduction in reserve requirement ratios. Reverting to the Riefler-Burgess framework of the 1920s, "he was not interested in lower short-term rates as such. . . . [He] was prepared to accept them as the inevitable consequence of bank reserve positions that would put banks under some pressure as lenders" (ibid., 18–19). Sproul emphasized market rates, not free reserves. He thought $800 million of additional reserves was a sufficient increase to reduce rates. The presidents agreed with Sproul. Only President W. S. McLarin Jr. (Atlanta) favored the staff position.

The public announcement, approved unanimously, emphasized the "needs of commerce, business, and agriculture," and the "general business and credit situation." It added that "under present conditions the maintenance of a relatively fixed pattern of rates has the undesirable effect of absorbing reserves from the market at a time when the availability of credit should be increased." This formulation left open whether the decision to drop the peg was temporary or permanent.[172] The committee's hesitation proved costly when it wanted to increase rates. Because it failed to tell Snyder and the market what it wanted to do, it weakened its claim that the June 1949 change permitted rate increases later.

Stock prices reached their cyclical low in mid-June, 13 percent below the October 1948 peak. The announced change in policy may have contributed to a rise in stock prices; the July average is more than 5 percent above June. The actual change in policy was slight. Contrary to its discussion, the System sold securities, withdrawing $800 million of reserves in July. Bill, certificate, and bond rates declined in July, with long-term bonds reaching the lowest rate in two years, 2.27 percent in late July. Gold continued to flow in, increasing the monetary base. The decline in rates was not steep enough to compensate for ongoing deflation, so real rates of interest continued to rise.

The following day, urged on by McCabe, the Board again discussed an additional reduction in reserve requirements. All other governors opposed, preferring to observe the full effects of the expiration of supplementary reserve requirements.[173] Ten days later, and continuing through July, Board members and staff frequently suggested additional action, including reductions in the discount rates and in reserve requirement ratios. Several governors were on vacation, so discussions remained informal.

172. Leading banks welcomed the June 28 action as the end "of the fixed rates . . . and of the close relationship of System open market policies to Treasury financing policies that had existed since the war" (Minutes, FOMC, August 5, 1949, 2).

173. Eccles cited the overnight drop in Treasury bill yields from 1.16 percent to 1.10 percent following the Board's announced policy change. Yields fell to 1.02 percent by the end of July, then rose back to 1.10 percent by late December.

Eccles drafted a long statement after the June 29 meeting. He proposed releasing the statement to the public, but only four governors agreed to the statement. McCabe, Vardaman, and Draper did not sign. Part of the statement shows the mistaken interpretation of low nominal interest rates as evidence of monetary ease. The relevant section reads: "Since we have had easy money conditions with relatively low rates all along in the money market, it should not be supposed that still easier conditions with lower rates will completely correct or cure a deflationary trend, although they may encourage greater use of the existing money supply. . . . To the extent that the Reserve System becomes a reluctant seller of its holdings of Government securities, banks may be more disposed to make productive loans to private borrowers. . . . Monetary policy by itself cannot make lenders lend or borrowers borrow. . . . It cannot by itself bring about the very necessary price and other readjustments within the economy" (Board Minutes, June 29, 1949, 17–18).

By August the Board was ready to reduce reserve requirement ratios by two percentage points on demand deposits in a series of steps (Board Minutes, August 4, 1949, 10). The following day the FOMC agreed to absorb the reserves released by the Board's action so as to hold bill and certificate rates within their current ranges. Although discount rates were now above market rates on Treasury bills and certificates, McCabe proposed postponing any rate reduction. Discussion of a discount rate reduction continued throughout the fall, but discount rates remained unchanged.[174]

Several FOMC members asked the reasons for the August reduction in reserve requirement ratios. The Board did not give a credit or monetary reason. The reasons given were that the System wanted to make clear that it was no longer concentrating its efforts on controlling inflation; that requirements could be raised later, if needed; and that increased ownership of government securities would increase bank earnings.[175]

The August 5 meeting raised issues that would not be resolved for a decade. New York pressed for flexibility in the range of short-term rates and authority to purchase and sell at all maturities. It claimed that it was difficult to forecast how much of any increase in reserves would be held as excess reserves, so the account manager needed to respond to the market. As usual during discussions in this period, Robert Rouse, manager of the System Open Market Account, Woodlief Thomas, the Board's chief economist, and Winfield Riefler, adviser to the chairman, took an active role not limited to staff or operating duties. Sproul's was the dominant voice, Eccles's a close second. McCabe remained relatively passive, looking for compromise and unwilling to challenge the Treasury. Most of the bank presidents were recorded infrequently or not at all.

Rouse suggested a further reduction in reserve requirements so that they could be raised later if inflation developed. The committee members rejected this proposal, recognizing at last that they could act through open market purchases (or sales) if they were willing to let market rates change.

---

174. The New York directors voted to reduce the discount rate to 1.25 percent, effective September 19. At first the Board postponed action pending discussion with the Federal Advisory Council (Board Minutes, September 16, 1949, 8). One reason for hesitation was signs of recovery, but the Board also cited the British devaluation that week. The Federal Advisory Council opposed the reduction, as did several presidents (Minutes, FOMC, September 21, 1949, 6–7). They preferred to keep the discount rate as a penalty rate (Board Minutes, September 20, 1949, 2–3). New York tried again in October, but the Board refused again. Governor Eccles cited the explosion of a Russian atomic bomb as a reason for opposing the reduction. The Russian action would cause United States defense spending to increase, with inflationary consequences.

175. Chairman McCabe read a letter from Leslie Rounds of the New York reserve bank citing the low prices of bank stocks in relation to book values (Minutes, FOMC, August 5, 1949, 7).

For the first time, there was general recognition that the System could not control the size of excess reserves while maintaining a fixed level of interest rates. It gave up using excess reserves as a target. Instead, it set a target for Treasury bill rates at 0.94 to 1.06, about the prevailing range.

END OF THE RECESSION   The National Bureau of Economic Research dates the end of the recession in October. Industrial production increased at a 12 percent annual rate in August and again in September. October's decline reflected strikes in that month. In November and December production rose at a 25 percent annual rate, and third quarter GNP rose 2.5 percent.

The FOMC executive committee recognized the turn in November. Renewed fears of inflation replaced concerns about recession and deflation. Using a phrase that recurred many times in the next fifty years, the minutes referred to "the largest peacetime deficits in the history of the United States at a time of very high levels [sic] of production and employment" (Minutes, Executive Committee, FOMC, November 18, 1949, 2). The members agreed that interest rates should rise and now asserted more forcefully that the flexible policy adopted the previous June allowed rates to change up as well as down. The committee unanimously approved an increase in bill rates by 0.07, a range for bills from 1.00 to 1.14 percent and for certificates 1.10 to 1.16 percent.

The minutes show that the Treasury would not agree to flexible rates. It wanted to sell certificates at 1.125 percent. Since the System was unwilling to challenge the Treasury in the marketplace, it could only petition and advise but was not free to act.

Much of the committee's discussion in this period concerned advice on Treasury debt management. Sproul and McCabe continued to meet with Snyder, or to petition him by mail, seeking higher rates at Treasury refundings. Occasionally the advice was accepted; most often it was not.

The System did not limit its advice to rates for new issues and refundings.[176] It expressed concern about the decline in the maturity of the debt, a reflection both of the passage of time and of Treasury policy. The rate structure did not permit the Treasury to sell longer maturities. As notes and bonds matured, the Treasury substituted bills and certificates. Five years after the war, Treasury notes had declined from a peak of $20 billion

---

176. The System also responded to requests from the president for legislative proposals and for statements to be included in the January 1950 Economic Report. The principal legislation sought at the time was regulation of bank holding companies. It asked also for renewal of authority to purchase a limited volume of securities directly from the Treasury, authority over nonmember banks, and modification of limits on the cost of new Federal Reserve buildings.

to less than $4 billion. The stock of bonds outstanding also continued to fall as bonds matured. There were no new bond issues until 1952, after the interest rate peg was removed.

WHY DID THE RECESSION END? The Federal Reserve was slow to respond to deflation and recession but quick to dampen recovery. Until June, seven months after the recession started, the System did little, none of it effective. Yet it raised rates in November, one month into the recovery. This behavior raises two questions. Why was policy action, and the recognition of a need for action, asymmetric? Did policy actions contribute to recovery?

The minutes suggest some answers. Many policymakers believed the economy would expand because of pent-up wartime domestic and foreign demand. Also, the System had struggled to raise interest rates and was reluctant to give up some of its "progress" toward higher rates and a flatter term structure. It acted only after Secretary Snyder accepted greater flexibility in principle, with some concern about whether the Treasury would permit flexibility both ways. This was a legitimate concern, given the Board's experience, and it soon proved to be correct. Further, Eccles and other Board members remained skeptical about the effectiveness of monetary policy. This view was widely held by officials and economists within the System and outside.

At another level was the belief that had done much harm in the Great Depression—failure to distinguish between nominal and real rates. With market rates from 1 to 2.5 percent, officials thought monetary policy was easy. John H. Williams offered a classic restatement of this view: "The System had not had a tight money policy . . . any effort to ease money conditions to counter the recession would be starting from an already easy situation, and he felt that the System was likely to be frozen into a low-interest rate situation about which it might not be able to do anything" (Minutes, FOMC, May 3, 1949, 4).

Prices were falling at the time, so real interest rates rose. The rise increased the cost of investing in new capital relative to the cost of buying existing assets and increased the return to holding money. But falling prices raised the real value of money balances and the excess supply of money.

Chart 7.5 compares the change in real base money to the ex post real rate of interest on long-term bonds. Both series reflect the common influence of falling prices, hence they are roughly parallel in the months preceding the 1948–49 recession and during the recession.[177]

---

177. Inflation in chart 7.5 is based on the deflator from Balke and Gordon 1986. The interest rate is the yield on long-term Treasury bonds with ten years or more to maturity.

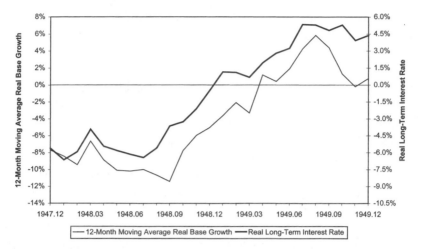

Chart 7.5 Twelve-month moving average real base growth versus real long-term interest rate, December 1947 to December 1949.

The chart suggests that monetary policy in 1948–49 is qualitatively similar to that in 1920–21. Both recessions followed an inflation that drove down the real interest rate and the real value of the monetary base. The real value of the monetary base reached a trough two months before the 1948–49 recession started, and it turned positive in April, six months before the recession's trough. Industrial production started to rise in July, three months later. As in 1920–21 and 1937–38, but to a lesser extent, gold inflows under a fixed exchange rate contributed to the increase in real balances.

Real interest rates give a very different picture of events. Ex post real rates were lowest before the recession and highest before the recovery. The fall in real rates did not prevent the recession, and the rise did not prevent recovery. As in 1920–21 and 1937–38, the effects of real rates on economic activity appear to have been dominated by the response to rising real balances.

Two of the deflationary recessions, 1937–38 and 1948–49, provide evidence on the frequently stated proposition that monetary action becomes ineffective at low nominal interest rates. The data suggest that nominal interest rates near zero did not make monetary policy ineffective or irrelevant. Between November 1948 and July 1949, the rate on new issues of Treasury bills remained between 1.13 and 1.16 percent. In July the rate fell to about 1.05 percent, where it remained for most of the summer and fall. Changes in the rate of deflation dominated the small changes in the growth of the base and the level of nominal rates.

The deflationary recessions provide evidence, also, on the process by which monetary policy affects output. The fall in market prices raised the public's stock of real balances above the desired amount, just as if the Federal Reserve had increased base money at a constant price level. The public used its excess real balances to purchase assets, goods, and services. These purchases stimulated production directly and by changing asset prices relative to the prices of new production, thereby increasing the demand for new production. The rise in real interest rates worked in the opposite direction, but it was less powerful.

RECOVERY, EXPANSION, AND INFLATION

Industrial production passed its prerecession peak in April 1950. Consumer prices started to rise but remained near 1948 levels. The Federal Reserve took no action. Throughout the winter and spring of 1950, FOMC meetings considered, in detail, whether the Treasury should sell tap issues on demand, long-term nonmarketable debt, or bank eligible debt. The committee again offered advice on Treasury refundings and new debt issues. Typically the advice called for a slight increase in rates with the hope that the System could follow by raising its buying and selling rates for bills and certificates. The opposite was also true. Unless the Treasury was willing to increase its offering rate, the System could not raise open market rates. If it pushed the market rate above the offering rate, it expected large open market sales by private holders, who were expected to sell outstanding debt and buy new issues.[178]

The System remained unwilling to confront the Treasury publicly and was frustrated by its failure. As long as Secretary Snyder insisted on a 1.125 percent offering rate for new issues or refundings, the System had to either insist on independence or remain subservient. Fearing the consequences of the first course, it remained with the second.

The government budget heightened the members' concerns. After three (fiscal) years of surplus, in the 1950 fiscal year the budget had a deficit. Instead of net debt reductions, the Treasury sold more than $3 billion of new issues. Defense spending and foreign aid rose. There seemed to be no prospect of soon again using a budget surplus to reduce the monetary base.

The Treasury permitted very modest increases in short-term rates in February and May and a larger increase in June, without any negative market reaction. The long-term rate remained between 2.38 and 2.43 for the entire period, and the stock market index rose 13 percent between December and June as recovery gained momentum.[179]

178. In March 1950 the FOMC authorized reserve banks to enter into repurchase agreements with nonbank government securities dealers to provide reserves temporarily. These were the first such operations since the 1920s.

179. Real GNP rose at an annualized 15 percent rate in the first half of 1950 (Balke and Gordon 1986).

Table 7.11   Rates Set at FOMC Meetings, December 1949 to June 1950

MEETING[a]	BILL RATES	MONETARY CERTIFICATE RATES	BASE GROWTH[b] (%)
12/13/49	1.04–1.12	1.08–1.12	–1.3
1/6/50	1.04–1.12	1.08–1.12	–1.8
2/6/50	1.06–1.14	1.09–1.17	–0.1
3/1/50	1.06–1.14	1.09–1.17	0.4
4/12/50	1.06–1.14	1.09–1.17	–1.7
5/3/50	1.06–1.14	1.12–1.19	0.7
6/14/50	1.12–1.19	1.12–1.24	–1.6
After July 1	1.10–1.36		

[a]Includes executive committee meetings.
[b]Twelve-month moving average.

Table 7.11 shows the interest rates set at each meeting between December and June. In June the staff suggested that the economy showed signs of an unsustainable boom. Real estate and commodity prices had increased. Reported rates of inflation were 5 percent or higher in May and June.

The return of expansion and inflation turned attention back to monetary policy. At the May 3 meeting of the executive committee, Sproul proposed to confront the Treasury. Referring to the June 1949 decision to permit flexibility, he "saw no reason why the System should, and every reason why it should not, make statements about support or non-support of the Government securities market at par or any other price" (Minutes, Executive Committee, FOMC, May 3, 1950, 5). In June he continued to press for a firmer policy, including an increase in certificate rates to 1.25 percent followed by an increase in discount rates, as "a signal to the whole financial community and to the public that there has been a change in our policy in the light of the changed business and credit situation" (Minutes, FOMC, June 13, 1950, 4).[180] He wanted to continue selling long-term bonds from the System account and, if the problem arose, to let these bonds go below par.

Eccles gave Sproul limited support. He continued to urge new issues of long-term nonmarketable bonds. Although he favored an increase in bill and certificate rates, he opposed an increase in discount rates and was not yet ready to allow long-term bonds to go below par value. The FOMC remained unwilling to confront the Treasury over long-term rates. It agreed to let the long-term rate rise until long-term bonds were at 100.75 and to

180. Sproul went on to assert that there was no difference between the effect of selling marketable and nonmarketable bonds. This is the first clear rejection of the view held by Eccles and others that it was less inflationary to sell nonmarketable issues.

have the executive committee meet again if that happened. The committee, however, increased short-term rates in two steps, immediately to a maximum of 1.24 percent, and after the Treasury refunding to 1.36 percent, consistent with a 1.375 percent certificate rate.

The Treasury did not accept the System's advice or accede to its threat to raise rates. It continued to issue Treasury bills at 1.15 percent and certificates at 1.25 percent. Open market rates on bills remained unchanged and were only 0.05 percent higher on certificates, at the lower end of the System's support range.

The issue remained unresolved when the Treasury came to market. Snyder refused to raise offering rates. The System was unwilling to allow the new issues to fail, so it purchased heavily, offsetting part of the purchases with sales of bills. For the month of June, System holdings in the one- to five-year range rose nearly $2 billion, and total holdings of governments rose $942 million (5.4 percent). In the market, certificate rates rose by 0.05 percent to 1.23 percent in the week ending June 3. System purchases kept rates at this level through the refunding and beyond. The first skirmish with the Treasury ended with the System supporting the rates set by the Treasury.

Reform of Reserve Requirements

In the months before the start of the Korean War, both the Board and Congress again considered eliminating geographical location as the basis for reserve requirements. Classification into reserve city and country classes caused repeated problems. Not all banks in reserve cities held correspondent deposits of country banks, and some large country banks served as correspondents. The Board exempted from reserve city status banks on the periphery of a reserve city that did not hold correspondent balances, but it recognized that this was not entirely satisfactory.

After discussions with interested groups, the Board proposed the system based on type of deposit it first developed in the 1930s. Reserve requirement ratios would be 26 percent for interbank deposits, 15 percent for demand deposits, and 4 percent for time deposits. The requirements would apply to all commercial banks, not just members. The proposal did not attract support from bankers. Country banks would face increases, so they were strongly opposed. Banks that held a large volume of interbank deposits also opposed. Reserve city banks would have lower requirements for demand deposits, but they did not trust the Board to administer the requirements objectively: "The Federal Reserve System would go to almost any end to get banks to join the System and in so doing would take steps that would injure the business of the correspondent banks" (Board Minutes, October 3, 1950, 4). Bankers told the Board that to get banks to accept the proposed changes, it would have to reduce reserve requirement ratios. With concern about inflation rising, the Board was unwilling to consider anything that would increase the credit multiplier. The proposal remained on the System agenda but was never implemented.[181]

The Korean War

The Korean War began on June 26, 1950. The almost immediate economic response was a surge in domestic demand and prices. The economy was recovering rapidly, with real incomes rising. Memories of wartime shortages of durable goods remained strong. Also, war periods in the United States had always been financed by deficit spending and money growth. The public anticipated a repetition. When it did not occur and money growth did not rise, inflation concerns vanished. In the first two quarters of 1950, real GNP rose at a 14.9 percent annual rate. Third quarter GNP increased slightly faster, and consumer prices accelerated from a 4.5 percent rate of increase in the second quarter to 10 percent in the third.

The Korean War inflation is one of the few examples of expectationally driven price increases. Concerns about shortages and possible rationing increased demand, and an anticipated reallocation of resources from civilian to military uses reduced expected supply. Growth of the monetary base or M_1 was modest in the first nine months of war. The federal budget shifted from a $3 billion deficit to a $6 billion surplus, driven mainly by a large increase in personal and corporate tax rates. Government revenues increased by $12 billion in fiscal year 1952, a 30 percent increase.[182] Tax revenues reached $51 billion, the highest level up to that time. Income tax rates were near (or above) peak World War II rates.

The Federal Reserve could not know at the time that the first year of war would be financed by taxes. Its concern was that wartime deficits would bring back inflation. Unlike the decision in 1942 to finance the war at prevailing, low interest rates, to many in the System the war gave greater urgency to the need for higher interest rates. This view was widely but not uniformly held.

The eight months from the start of the Korean War to the end of Feb-

---

181. In May President Truman nominated Edward L. Norton to be a member of the Board of Governors. In July he named Oliver S. Powell. Norton was from Alabama. He served from September 1, 1950, to February 1, 1952, completing Ernest Draper's unexpired term. Powell had been a vice president of the Minneapolis reserve bank. He served from September 1, 1950, to June 30, 1952.

182. As another sign of the Federal Reserve's role in government policy at the time, the Treasury asked the Federal Reserve to present its ideas about the tax program. McCabe designated Riefler as its representative (Board Minutes, July 18, 1950, 2).

ruary 1951 brought a growing rift between the Treasury and the Federal Reserve. Faced with the prospect of having to finance expected wartime deficits and to roll over large parts of the $250 billion marketable debt, the Treasury became less willing to increase short-term rates or acknowledge Federal Reserve responsibilities for restraining inflation. Since Snyder was a longtime close friend of President Truman, he was confident that the president would rebuff a Federal Reserve appeal.

THE DOUGLAS HEARINGS

That left matters to Congress. In fall 1949 a subcommittee of the Joint Committee on the Economic Report (later the Joint Economic Committee) under the chairmanship of Senator Paul Douglas (Illinois) held hearings on monetary, credit, and fiscal policies.[183] The hearings gave the Federal Reserve a public forum in which to make its case under the sympathetic questioning of Senator Douglas, Senator Ralph E. Flanders (Vermont), and Congressman Jesse P. Wolcott (Michigan). While there is no way to directly connect the hearings to the System's subsequent behavior, System policy discussions changed in 1950, before the Korean War started. Many in the System believed that the Treasury's reluctance to let rates rise during the recovery broke the 1949 agreement under which it reduced rates in the recession. Nevertheless, the FOMC remained unwilling to act without Treasury agreement.

Eccles had often said that the System could not act independently without congressional support. The hearings gave the first public evidence of that support.[184] McCabe, Sproul, and Eccles testified for the Federal Reserve. Snyder spoke for the Treasury. Other witnesses included Leon Keyserling, chairman of the Council of Economic Advisers, the heads of other financial agencies, and representatives of labor, agriculture, and finance.

Secretary Snyder denied there was a conflict. The Treasury had final responsibility for debt management. The Federal Reserve had principal responsibility for credit and monetary policy, but debt management required the cooperation of the Federal Reserve: "I have been very happy with that cooperation. I think it has been splendid" (Subcommittee on Monetary, Credit and Fiscal Policies 1950a, 408). He refused to be drawn into a dis-

---

183. Paul Douglas was a distinguished economist who had been an economics professor at the University of Chicago before his election to the Senate. As is often the case, senators who had little understanding of the technical issues relied on a colleague's expertise, so Douglas's opposition to pegged rates carried considerable weight.

184. Eccles's book does not emphasize the role of the Douglas committee, but he later recognized that congressional support helped the Federal Reserve to regain its independence (CHFRS, May 18, 1954, 2).

cussion of possible conflicts. Most of his testimony discussed the difficulty of managing a large debt and the Treasury's successful management. At one point he compared his record favorably with debt management after World War I, when government bonds went below par value.

Snyder denied that the Treasury was unwilling to let interest rates change: "The Treasury Department has never taken an inflexible position" (ibid., 409). Senator Flanders responded by reading from a letter Eccles sent to the committee to supplement his testimony. Discussing the Board and the FOMC, Eccles wrote: "Under present circumstances the talents and efforts of these men are largely wasted. Views of the Federal Reserve Board and the Open Market Committee regarding debt-management policies are seldom sought by the Treasury before decisions are reached. . . . Decisions are apparently made by the Treasury largely on the basis of a general desire to get money as cheaply as possible" (410).[185] Snyder would not comment publicly, but he agreed to meet privately with McCabe, Sproul, Eccles, and the members of the subcommittee.[186] Later in his testimony, however, he denied that the Treasury's decisions were based on the desire to borrow cheaply (425).

The System did not speak with a single voice. Its three spokesman differed in both tone and substance. McCabe was most conciliatory, Eccles characteristically the most outspoken. On substance, however, Sproul was the strongest proponent of an independent central bank, McCabe most willing to accommodate the needs of the Treasury.

Differences in style and presentation reflected differences in personality. Substantive differences show that after forty years, political and financial interests had not been fully harmonized. McCabe and Eccles saw the Federal Reserve as mainly a government institution regulating the financial industry and carrying out government policy. Sproul saw the Federal Reserve mainly as a financial institution, blending private and public control. The difference had always been one of degree or mix; although the mix

185. In a later hearing, Snyder described the consultative role of the Federal Reserve in debt management. Until 1943, Secretary Morgenthau called on a large number of experts for advice on the pricing, timing, and maturity of new debt issues. He included presidents of reserve banks among the experts. Eccles and Sproul objected to this procedure on the grounds that advice from the presidents should come through them. Citing the statutory responsibility of the FOMC, the Board asked the Treasury to recognize the chairman and vice chairman of the FOMC as the representatives of the FOMC. The Treasury agreed. This procedure continued in effect under Secretaries Vinson and Snyder (Subcommittee on General Credit Control and Debt Management 1951, 78–79).

186. There is no record of the discussion at this meeting. Snyder was either misleading or not well informed. He denied that there had been a recession in 1948–49 (Subcommittee on Monetary, Credit and Fiscal Policies 1950a, 412) and claimed that the United States was on a gold bullion standard (422).

had changed in the 1930s, the difference between New York and Washington continued.

The testimony brought out several changes in analysis and outlook. Unlike the 1920s, all System spokesmen accepted responsibility for countercyclical policy and recognized that System actions affected prices, output, and employment. Although there were occasional references to "speculative" uses of credit, these have a much less prominent role.

Witnesses offered reform proposals, including abolishing the Board and vesting all monetary powers in the FOMC. At the opposite extreme, Eccles repeated his earlier wish for a five-person Board without reserve bank participation in open market decisions. Such perennial issues as required membership, uniform reserve requirements for all commercial banks, and coordination with other banking and financial regulators reappeared. Members of the subcommittee and the witnesses considered whether some type of domestic policy council would help to coordinate policy actions. The three System spokesmen differed on these issues, reflecting their views on the role of government.

The main focus remained on Federal Reserve–Treasury conflicts and whether there was a legal obligation or commitment to prevent bonds from going below par value. Snyder denied any legal obligation. It was a policy, not a binding commitment. McCabe denied that the FOMC had been pressured by the Treasury to support the 2.5 percent long-term rate (ibid., 465). There were "widely varying shades of judgment" about appropriate policy. His view was that the System had to avoid the "repercussions that would ensue throughout the economy if the vast holding of the public debt were felt to be of unstable value" (465). The Treasury had been slow to accept higher short-term rates, but McCabe did not challenge the ceiling on the long-term rate.[187]

McCabe quoted from the June 1949 announcement that interest rates would be more flexible: "I regard June 28, 1949 as a most important date. It signified removal of the strait-jacket in which monetary policy had been operating for nearly a decade" (ibid., 471). The public debt was now sufficiently settled in the hands of stable holders that monetary actions could be more flexible. Coordination would continue to be required: "A splendid degree of cooperation exists between the Treasury and the Federal Reserve" (472).[188]

187. Unlike Sproul, McCabe argued that raising reserve requirement ratios had been useful. Sproul argued correctly that the changes simply shifted securities between the Federal Reserve and banks without effects on money or credit.

188. Douglas gently but repeatedly challenged McCabe. Coordination and cooperation, he said, are vague terms, often covering up disagreement. The June 1949 agreement came in

Sproul asked Congress to issue a directive to the Treasury requiring it to carry out debt management within a structure of rates "appropriate to the economic situation" (ibid., 431). He described policy coordination as "better than might have been expected . . . but agreed action . . . has most often been too little and too late so far as the aims of an effective monetary program were concerned" (431). Neither he nor members of the committee mentioned that the Employment Act gave the Treasury some of the guidance that Sproul wanted.[189]

Like Strong in the 1921 hearings, Sproul showed far greater sophistication about the working of monetary policy than Board spokesmen and many economists of that period. Interest rate changes did more than change borrowing costs, as in the simple Keynesian framework of that period or the Board's view: "I think in dealing with the interest rate, you are dealing both with expectations as to the future business situation and as to future profits. . . . I think you have an effect far beyond what I admit is the minor cost of interest in the carrying out of any business undertaking" (ibid., 436). Sproul rejected the prevailing view that monetary policy was either ineffective or too powerful to use in an economy with a large outstanding debt. Monetary policy could be used effectively to maintain a satisfactory degree of economic stability. The large debt was not a deterrent to effective policy, as many believed. Small changes in interest rates could be helpful if they were supported by stabilizing fiscal, labor, and debt management policies.[190] The main limitation was political. With great insight, he forecast a central feature of the policy of the 1960s and 1970s. Large changes in interest rates were impractical. People would not submit to that sort of discipline because it required reduced production and employment: "I do not think that is the kind of climate we live in" (438). On the critical issue of whether there was an implied or explicit commitment to bondholders, Sproul was firm. No such commitment had ever been made or discussed. A contrary statement by the chairman of the Federal Deposit Insurance Corporation was "grossly mistaken" (439).[191]

---

a period of recession and called for a reduction in interest rates. The Treasury would, of course, agree to that. "Does it follow that . . . the Treasury will go along with primary regard to the general business and credit situation in other periods?" (Subcommittee on Monetary, Credit and Fiscal Policies, 493–94).

189. Sproul recommended uniform reserve requirements for commercial banks and was willing to open the discount window to nonmember banks as compensation.

190. Douglas asked Sproul to comment on a statement he had sent to the Board: "The problem of the budget is not merely that of deficits and surpluses but also one of size. . . . Carried beyond some point, a large budget destroys incentives throughout the whole community" (Subcommittee on Monetary, Credit and Fiscal Policies, 438). Sproul agreed.

191. Sproul testified that reserve requirements, margin requirements, and other controls should be decided by the FOMC. He strongly defended the regional character of the System

The start of Eccles's testimony repeated the themes he had emphasized throughout—the need for additional powers over nonmember banks and secondary reserve requirements. Eccles argued, with customary force, that the policy of fixed rates of interest rendered the System powerless to control the supply of money. The process of making decisions continued, but the Treasury controlled the substance of decisions (ibid., 223). Congress had to choose one of three courses. It could retain the present arrangement under which the Treasury controlled monetary policy and the Federal Reserve advised the Treasury; give the Federal Reserve additional powers as a partial substitute for open market and discount powers; or restore the Federal Reserve's powers to carry out the mandate of the Employment Act and compel the Treasury to take account of the mandate when managing the debt (225).[192]

Eccles did not argue for a change in the 2.5 percent interest rate. Nor did he argue that the Federal Reserve should force the Treasury to increase interest rates. Federal Reserve independence did not go that far. His statement explains some of the reason for a long delay in implementing an anti-inflation policy in the 1970s: "Congress appropriates the money; they levy the taxes; they determine whether or not there should be deficit financing. The Treasury then is charged with the responsibility of raising whatever funds the Government needs to meet its requirements. . . . I do not believe it is consistent to have an agent so independent that it can undertake, if it chooses, to defeat the financing of a large deficit, which is a policy of the Congress" (ibid., 231). Chairman William McChesney Martin Jr. also held this view in the 1950s and 1960s.

None of the three Federal Reserve witnesses criticized the 2.5 percent ceiling or asked Congress to remove the ceiling. That recommendation was made most forcefully by a banker, W. Randolph Burgess.[193] In contrast

---

and its importance for decision making (Subcommittee on Monetary, Credit and Fiscal Policies, 444–45). The System should continue to combine the political influence from Washington with financial concerns (445). In a letter to McCabe, he endorsed Eccles's proposal (see below) that Congress should require the Treasury to consult with the FOMC about debt management (Sproul to McCabe, Sproul Papers, Board of Governors, Douglas Hearings, December 16, 1949).

192. McCabe was reluctant to have Congress mandate consultation between the Federal Reserve and the Treasury about interest rates and debt management. His concern was political. He thought that "it would be inexpedient to inject language as explicit as is embodied in this directive into the political arena of Congressional debate" (Letter McCabe to Senator Douglas, Sproul Papers, Board of Governors, Douglas Hearings, December 22, 1949, 6–7). His concern was that the populists in Congress would use the opportunity to mandate low interest rates.

193. W. Randolph Burgess was chairman of the executive committee, National City Bank. He had been a vice president of the New York reserve bank in the 1920s and 1930s and was a member of the System's Federal Advisory Council.

to Eccles, Burgess argued that the Federal Reserve did not need new powers. The System's problems arose from insufficient independence, "The wise executive will yield to the Reserve System a substantial measure of independence of action so that its judgments can be objective and free from political bias" (ibid., 178). Open market operations and discount rate changes are powerful tools, Burgess said: "If we will act to restore the prestige of the Federal Reserve System, to give it greater independence and better cooperation from other Government agencies, I believe it does not need any new powers" (179).

Burgess distinguished between real and nominal values, a subject that Reserve officials never mentioned. He compared the relative fixity of interest rates to the loss of value from inflation.[194] His testimony also made the strongest argument for allowing interest rates to change. Unlike Snyder, McCabe, and Eccles, who argued that losses on the debt had major consequences that made interest increases too socially costly to impose, Burgess testified that "a moderate decline in bond prices is nothing very serious" (ibid., 182). Small savers were protected from capital losses. The Treasury, mindful of experience in the 1920s, had offered nonmarketable savings bonds, redeemable at the Treasury at a fixed price, including interest, that could only increase in nominal value. Then, he added: "The responsibility of the United States government for the buying power of the savings bonds . . . is fully as important as the cash redemption of these bonds at the price you sell them" (184).[195]

The subcommittee's report was a victory for the Federal Reserve. The subcommittee opposed subordination of monetary policy to debt management. It supported Sproul's and Burgess's view that monetary policy could be used flexibly, with fiscal and other policies, to achieve the goals of the Employment Act. New powers were not necessary if existing powers were used flexibly. (Subcommittee on Monetary, Credit, and Fiscal Policies, 1950a).[196]

---

194. "Since the war the buying power of those bonds has been reduced very substantially (Subcommittee on Monetary, Credit and Fiscal Policies 1950a 181). "Let's not get our attention focused solely on the dollar price of things. Let's think in terms of the buying power" (184).

195. Burgess had served as account manager, so he could describe how the System could permit small changes in interest rates. He favored "orderly markets" operated according to the judgment of the manager and the FOMC.

196. The subcommittee recommended a new coordinating body in the federal government consisting of heads of four agencies, the Treasury, Federal Reserve, Budget, and Council of Economic Advisers. The group would discuss issues of common interest. The Kennedy administration tried a council of this kind, called the Quadriad, but it did not last.

Policy Actions before the Accord

Conflict over refunding rates on certificates at the end of June was a main topic at the FOMC executive committee meeting on July 10. The Federal Reserve had voted to raise rates, without Treasury concurrence. Snyder called the System's bluff. By refusing to raise rates on the new issue, he had forced it either to let the issue fail or to hold the rate by purchasing enough to clear the market. Snyder blamed the large purchases by the Federal Reserve on leaks to the press about differences between the Federal Reserve and the Treasury. The Federal Reserve regarded the differences as real and known to market watchers. The issue for the members was whether to stay with the June policy decision to discontinue purchases of short-term securities until rates reached 1.375 percent.

The July meeting was the first meeting after the start of war in Korea. The members viewed the war and increased military spending as an additional inflationary threat. Yet they decided to take no action to increase interest rates and resolved only to draft another letter to Secretary Snyder explaining the problems they faced and asking again for a tap issue of long-term bonds, ineligible for bank purchase.[197] They believed a tap issue would absorb saving, thereby satisfying part of the market demand for long-term issues. The letter explained that, as in World War II, banks were "playing the pattern of rates," selling short-term and buying long-term securities. To keep long-term rates from falling further, the System sold long-term debt. It also purchased short-term debt to prevent yields from rising. Since the Treasury would not raise its offering rates, the System felt unable to let market rates rise.[198] A long-term Treasury bond would absorb market demand, reducing the Federal Reserve's need to sell long term bonds and buy short term. This would firm short-term rates, a System objective that the Treasury did not share.

Snyder's reply again emphasized the need for stable market rates as the first priority. Although he did not mention the proposed tap issue, he opposed "experimentation" and emphasized the importance of leaving short-term rates unchanged.[199] After canvassing the opinions of all the presi-

197. A tap issue permits buyers to purchase from the Treasury on demand. The main reason Sproul gave for not raising short-term rates was that it might generate uncertainty, leading to further consumer buying and inventory building.

198. The only other action at the meeting was to propose reimposition of consumer credit controls.

199. Snyder explained later that in view of the uncertainties about war finance and the unprecedented size of the debt at the outbreak of the war, he wanted the Federal Reserve to maintain rates unchanged. He pointed out that far from monetizing debt and acting as an in-

dents, the executive committee renewed its request for a tap issue (Minutes, Executive Committee, FOMC, July 21, 1950). It also postponed a decision on the New York bank's request to increase the discount rate to 1.75 percent pending discussion with the Treasury.[200]

On August 18 the Board approved discount rate increases at New York and Boston, the first changes in two years. Within the week, all other reserve banks raised their discount rates to 1.75 percent. In announcing the increase, a joint statement of the FOMC and the Board declared that they were willing "to use all the means at their command to restrain further expansion of bank credit consistent with the policy of maintaining orderly conditions in the Government securities market" (Board Minutes, August 18, 1950, 3–4). The FOMC met on the same day. It supported the decision by voting to let short-term market rates rise to 1.375 percent immediately.

Before announcing the rate increases, McCabe and Sproul met with Snyder and his staff. Instead of asking the Treasury to agree, McCabe and Sproul told Snyder of their concerns about the growth of credit and inflation and their decision to raise short-term rates. They promised to maintain orderly markets. Snyder made no comment. "Chairman McCabe asked him if he was in accord with what we had done. The Secretary said we had told him what we had done and there was nothing he could say." McCabe promised to read the announcement to Snyder when he returned to the Board (Sproul Papers, Meetings with Secretary Snyder, August 18, 1950).

The meeting was brief. "A few minutes after our return, a call came through from Secretary Snyder. He told Chairman McCabe that he was announcing his September–October financing immediately, and that he was offering the market a 13-month $1^3/4$ percent note. . . . Chairman McCabe said that the announcement . . . would be in direct conflict with our announcement, that it would create confusion, and that it ran counter

---

flationary force, the Federal Reserve had reduced its portfolio by $4.5 billion in 1949 and continued the reduction in the first half of 1950 (Subcommittee on General Credit Control and Debt Management 1951, 66).

200. The New York directors had discussed an increase in the discount rate on July 6, but they postponed action, at Sproul's urging, until they had more information about the cost of the Korean War. On July 20, with Sproul absent, they voted for a 0.25 percent increase in the rate (Minutes, New York Directors, July 6 and 20, 1950). The letter from the New York directors also urged the Board to increase short-term market rates, get the Treasury to issue a long-term bond, and control consumer and real estate credit. The New York directors renewed their request on July 27. Again the Board deferred action pending discussion with the Treasury (Board Minutes, July 28, 1950, 2–3). The following week the Board approved a statement to all banks, issued jointly with federal and state banking regulators. The statement asked banks "to decline to make loans . . . used for speculative purposes" (Board Minutes, August 3, 1950, 7). The real bills tradition continued.

Table 7.12   System Portfolio and Gold Certificates, July 1950 to February 1951 (billions of dollars)

DATE	90 DAYS AND UNDER	91 DAYS TO ONE YEAR	1–5 YEARS	5–10 YEARS	OVER 10 YEARS	TOTAL	GOLD
July 1950	6.3	3.7	5.1	0.04	2.7	18.0	24.2
August	9.6	4.6	1.7	0.02	2.4	18.4	23.9
September	6.4	3.9	6.6	—ᵃ	2.6	19.6	23.6
October	0.8	9.2	6.2	—ᵃ	3.0	19.2	23.4
November	1.8	13.3	1.4	—ᵃ	3.1	19.7	23.2
December	3.6	11.8	1.8	—ᵃ	3.5	20.8	22.9
January 1951	1.7	12.2	4.0	0.99	2.6	21.5	22.5
February	1.5	12.2	4.3	0.99	2.8	21.9	22.2
Change July–February						3.9	–2.0

Source: Board of Governors of the Federal Reserve System 1976, 488.
ᵃLess than 10 million.

to any ideas of restraining inflation by credit measures" (ibid., 3). McCabe then called the president to read the announcement of the rate increase and to inform him of the conflict with the Treasury announcement.

Neither side retreated. The System again faced a choice of supporting the Treasury issue or letting it fail. Sproul later explained that "failure" meant that the Federal Reserve had to buy most of the maturing short-term issue, $8 billion of the $13 billion refunded. To offset the purchase, the System sold $7 billion of other securities, absorbing the difference in interest rates as a portfolio loss.[201] Sproul affirmed that the Treasury had been informed about the increase in the discount rate before making its announcement (Subcommittee on General Credit Control and Debt Management 1951, 518–19). Table 7.12 shows the large swings in bill and certificate holdings one year and under, and in one- to five-year maturities, between August and November.

Total system holdings increased $3.9 billion, approximately 22 percent in seven months. Gold losses offset about half of the increase; an increase in reserve requirements in December offset the other half. The net effect was a 3.2 percent ($620 million) annual rate of increase in the monetary base for the seven-month period ending in February 1951.[202]

Minutes of the August 18 FOMC meeting show the heightened antagonism that marked the Federal Reserve–Treasury relationship during this period. The Federal Reserve continued to urge the Treasury to issue a long-term, nonbank 2.5 percent tap issue. The Treasury continued to refuse,

201. Private holders exchanged less than 6 percent of the maturing issue; $2.25 billion was redeemed in cash, the largest change of that kind experienced to that time.

202. The $620 million increase includes all transactions affecting the base. Data on the base are from the Anderson-Rasche series (St. Louis Federal Reserve bank), so they are adjusted for the change in reserve requirement ratios in January 1951.

claiming there was not enough demand. The System challenged the Treasury's data with its own estimates of demand, but it could not get Treasury staff to discuss the differences. Phrases like "the bitter experience of recent years," "unwillingness of the Treasury to sop up nonbank funds," or "spirited discussion" leading to "an impasse" appear in letters to the Treasury and in the discussion at FOMC meetings (Minutes, FOMC, August 18, 1950, 4–6). Secretary Snyder continued to talk about stable rates; System representatives referred to stable markets.[203]

The FOMC held four more meetings between August and December, and the executive committee met separately twice during this period. Nothing changed. The System recommended a long-term tap issue, pressed for higher rates at refundings, and discussed its inability to persuade Secretary Snyder or his aides.

The Federal Reserve had support from members of Congress and from the Federal Advisory Council. When voting on the Defense Production Act in August, Senators Paul Douglas (Illinois), J. William Fulbright (Arkansas), and Ralph E. Flanders (Vermont) urged the Treasury and the Federal Reserve to reduce credit expansion. The Federal Advisory Council urged the Board to press its case with the Treasury, to seek Treasury cooperation but, if that failed, to take its case to the president. As a last resort, the members should resign if they felt the issues were of sufficient importance (Board Minutes, September 13, 1950, 4–7). In November, Edward E. Brown, chairman of the Federal Advisory Council, suggested letting the 2.5 percent bond go below par value (Board Minutes, November 21, 1950, 15). Eccles objected.

McCabe continued to seek a compromise with the Treasury. He urged caution, and he continued to consult Snyder before taking any action. Sproul seems to have decided that the Treasury would not agree to any rate increases. He told his colleagues in September, "We ought to proceed immediately with open market operations that would permit the short-term rate to rise" (Minutes, Executive Committee, FOMC, September 27, 1950, 3). He proposed a one-year rate of 1.75 percent, an increase of almost 0.5 percent. When McCabe and Sproul again made their case to Snyder, Snyder urged delay. The only suggestion he offered was voluntary credit restraint.[204]

203. On August 10, McCabe told Snyder that the System had purchased $400 million in the past three months. "He then asked the secretary just how far he thought the System could go in providing hot money. The secretary replied that 'it wasn't a question he should try to answer . . . and that in the natural course of things reserves needed to be supplied to the market'" (Minutes, FOMC, August 18, 1950, 7).

204. The FOMC minutes report his views (referring to the August decision) as follows: "There was a big question in his mind whether the recent increase of $1/8$ percent had any value whatever. . . . Both the Secretary and Mr. Bartelt [assistant secretary] brought up the cost to

The FOMC voted unanimously to let the one-year rate increase to 1.75 percent but to postpone the increase until after a further meeting between McCabe, Sproul, and Snyder. The long-term rate would remain at 2.5 percent or slightly below. On completion of the rate increase, the FOMC suggested that the Board increase reserve requirement ratios by two percentage points on demand deposits.

Not much happened. Secretary Snyder and his aides thought inflation might be ending. On October 5, he promised an answer by October 9. Although this meeting was more cordial, it was no more decisive. The FOMC executive committee could not agree on a response. McCabe and Evans wanted to wait for Snyder's response. Sproul and Eccles wanted to increase rates but would defer putting the change into effect until October 10, after Snyder's reply. On a two to two vote, the committee took no action.

The FOMC met again the following week. Snyder had taken a strong position against a rate increase, citing the harmful effect on sales of series E savings bonds. The committee voted to put the rate increase into the market, to let the one-year rate rise to 1.75 percent, provided the long-term 2.5 percent bond remained above par value. And it repeated its recommendation that the Board increase reserve requirement ratios by two percentage points. The Board discussed a change in reserve requirement ratios throughout the fall but did not act until December.[205]

In a letter to Snyder explaining the decision to increase rates, McCabe pointed for the first time to the effects of inflation on real values and purchasing power. He did not mention the effect on interest rates, but he reminded Snyder that "any resultant increase in the costs of carrying the public debt will be directly saved, many times over, if it helps to curb the rising costs of Government procurement" (Minutes, Executive Committee, FOMC, October 11, 1950, 7). He assured Snyder again that the 2.5 percent rate would remain as a ceiling for long-term bonds.

Table 7.13 shows the levels of short-term interest rates from August to February. The System's actions did not get the one-year rate to 1.75 percent, but they permitted short-term commercial paper rates to rise by 0.30 percent between August and October and an additional 0.24 percent between October and February. Rates on government securities changed by lesser

---

the government of an increase in the short-term rate, asking in different ways what proof we had of the effectiveness of the increase. He seemed pretty emphatic that any further increase in the short-term rate would be a step of very doubtful character" (Minutes, FOMC, September 28, 1950, 8). Compare this statement with his testimony at the Douglas hearings the year before denying that he insisted on low interest rates.

205. On October 2 the Board voted to dispense with the requirement that the chairman sign the minutes of Board meetings. This requirement had been in place since 1914.

Table 7.13   Market Interest Rates, August 1950 to February 1951 (percent)

MONTH	PRIME FOUR- TO SIX-MONTH COMMERCIAL PAPER	THREE-MONTH TREASURY BILLS	NINE- TO TWELVE-MONTH GOVERNMENTS	THREE- TO FIVE-YEAR GOVERNMENTS
August	1.42	1.20	1.26	1.45
September	1.65	1.30	1.33	1.55
October	1.72	1.31	1.40	1.65
November	1.69	1.36	1.47	1.62
December	1.72	1.34	1.46	1.64
January	1.86	1.34	1.47	1.66
February	1.96	1.36	1.60	1.67
Change	0.54	0.16	0.34	0.22

Source: Board of Governors of the Federal Reserve System 1976.

amounts, and long-term rates remained nearly constant at about 2.38 percent. To forestall Federal Reserve activism, the Treasury preannounced its December and January refunding on November 22. Acceding to the Federal Reserve's request, and after the usual consultations with advisory committees, the Treasury offered to refund $7.9 billion in maturing bonds and certificates into a five-year, 1.75 percent Treasury note.[206]

The initial market response was favorable, but market sentiment quickly changed after the Chinese entered the Korean War. The Federal Reserve supported the issue by buying $2.7 billion of the maturing issues, partly offset by sales of $1.3 billion.[207] The result was a large increase in the System's portfolio in December, as shown in table 7.12 above. "Throughout the whole period . . . a premium was maintained on the new issue despite the fact that prices on many outstanding issues continued to move lower" (Subcommittee on General Credit Control and Debt Management (1951, 520).

On December 21, McCabe reported to the Board that he had again discussed an increase in reserve requirement ratios with Secretary Snyder. Snyder had questioned the effectiveness of the action, since the Federal Reserve would have to purchase securities that banks sold to meet the increase. He did not object, however.[208] The Board voted an increase of two

206. Rates on three- to five-year issues had remained between 1.60 percent and 1.68 percent in October and November. The rate on November 18 was 1.60 percent.

207. Holders converted only 51 percent of the maturing issue into the new offering. They exchanged 14.5 percent of the old issues for cash. At the time, the average cash redemption was about 5 percent (Subcommittee on General Credit Control and Debt Management 1951, 72).

208. McCabe also discussed the action with Charles Wilson, director of the Office of Defense Mobilization, Senators A. Willis Robertson (Virginia) and Burnet R. Maybank (South Carolina), and Leon Keyserling. None objected, perhaps because they recognized that it would have no effect on market rates.

percentage points for demand deposits and one percentage point for time deposits, effective in the second half of January. The Board's statement highlighted growth of credit and "an excessive rise in the money supply" (Board Minutes, December 21, 1950, 6).

The action moved an estimated $2 billion into required reserves. The move had been discussed so long and with so many groups that banks had accumulated more than $1 billion of excess reserves in advance. The following week the executive committee, on Sproul's recommendation, voted to keep interest rates unchanged, so the change in reserve requirement ratios again had no effect on the monetary base. In January bank reserves and the monetary base increased.

Looking back on these events more than a year later, the Board wrote:

> It was not possible during the period of August 1950 through February 1951 to carry out adequately the August 18 decision to undertake a limited program of general credit restraint. Immediately after the System in mid-August 1950 began to strengthen its efforts to curb inflation through monetary and credit action, it became necessary to buy Government securities in volume in support of an exceptionally large Treasury refinancing program. After the refunding was out of the way, short-term yields tended to adjust upward further in response to pressures in the credit market. The increase permitted, however, was very small. Under the circumstances, the policy of credit restraint could not be followed far enough to make the discount rate effective. Beginning in mid-November, both short-term and long-term yields on Government securities were again firmly pegged until the Treasury–Federal Reserve accord in early March. (Subcommittee on General Credit Control and Debt Management 1951, 365)

This summary, like similar statements about credit expansion made at the time, either is based on an error of interpretation or is deliberately misleading. It is true that bank loans increased rapidly during this period. Total bank credit and money increased modestly, at noninflationary rates. Table 7.14 shows the values of money, loans, and bank credit for the period. These data appear to support the Treasury view that monetization of debt had not occurred. In fact, monetization did occur, but its effect was largely offset by loss of gold.

Only the data for loans show rapid expansion. Banks sold government securities to finance most of their loan growth. The Federal Reserve and the Treasury trust accounts made heavy net purchases, but the gold outflow offset most of the effect on the monetary base. The base, M_1 and M_2, rose modestly. Once again the Federal Reserve appears to have been mis-

Table 7.14   Money, Credit, and Bank Loans, August 1950 to March 1951 (billions of dollars)

| DATE | MONEY | | DATE | BANK CREDIT[a] | |
	M₁	M₂		LOANS	LOANS PLUS INVESTMENTS
August 1950	115.0	151.7	8/16/50	26.6	67.8
March 1951	117.1	153.7	2/28/51	31.8	69.1
Change (%)	1.8	1.3		19.6	1.9

Source: Board of Governors of the Federal Reserve System 1976.
[a]Weekly reporting banks.

led by its focus on nominal interest rates and bank lending and its neglect of monetary aggregates.

What about inflation? The data tell an unusual story for wartime. Inflation soared at the turn of the year. The consumer price index rose at a 19 percent annual rate for three months, December 1950 through February 1951. The rate of price change then fell back to about 1 percent (annual rate) from March through June 1951. The GNP deflator shows a similar pattern, 14 percent in first quarter 1951, −2.9 percent in the second quarter. Low rates of inflation continued for the next year or longer.

The surge in the measured rate of inflation appears to be a one-time change in the price level. For the Federal Reserve, the timing was ideal. The inflation it had warned about appeared with a vengeance just as its conflict with the Treasury became both more open and more intense.

Other Actions

The Board did not confine its action to the modest changes in interest rates and reserve requirement ratios. President Truman, Secretary Snyder, and the Board agreed to bring back consumer credit controls and supplement them with controls on real estate credit, authorized under the Defense Production Act of 1950. The Board delegated regulation of credit for real estate construction to the Housing and Home Finance Administrator. On September 18 the Board restored consumer credit controls, setting minimum down payments and maximum length of contract. The following month, it introduced real estate credit controls with the cooperation of the Federal Housing Administrator and tightened controls on consumer credit.

Although Secretary Snyder and the Board referred to credit controls as important parts of the anti-inflation program during the Korean War, at times the Board recognized that controls were "of secondary importance" though "effective in their respective spheres of operation" (Letter to President Truman, Board Minutes, December 1, 1950, 8).

The Board's staff had a different, and more correct, appraisal.

Industry lawyers proved to be highly adept at developing arrangements that effectively circumvented the letter of Reg *W* [consumer credit]. Fed regulators found themselves lagging far behind industry lawyers, first in ferreting out the loopholes, and then in devising measures to close them. Similar enforcement problems developed in the administration of Regulation *X* [real estate credit].

This generally negative experience with mandatory credit allocation programs strongly influenced Fed attitudes. Each time Congress has subsequently proposed new programs for direct credit regulation, Fed officials have taken a negative view of their feasibility. (Stockwell 1989, 19)

The Board also raised stock market margin requirements by twenty-five percentage points, to 75 percent, in January 1951. It had discussed, and dismissed, the change several times during the fall, usually on the grounds that stock market credit had not increased rapidly. A rise of more than 7 percent in stock prices between December and January, with increased trading volume, led the Board to respond.

THE END OF PEGGED RATES

Between August and December 1950, conflict between the Federal Reserve and the Treasury intensified and became open. Although the FOMC continued to advise on debt management and McCabe continued to discuss Federal Reserve concerns, there was less talk about cooperation and coordination and growing determination at the Federal Reserve to free monetary policy from Treasury control.

The Treasury's decision to accept the FOMC's advice by offering a four-year note in November to extend the maturity of the debt deepened the conflict. The issue's failure to attract buyers required the Federal Reserve to support the market by buying a large part. The Treasury blamed the System's advice for the failure and charged that rate increases had accomplished nothing useful. Federal Reserve talk and actions had unsettled securities markets, raised rates, and increased the cost of debt finance to the Treasury and the taxpayers.

The Federal Reserve accused the Treasury of announcing refundings far in advance to prevent the System from carrying out its responsibilities to control credit and money. It had become resentful of Treasury dominance, particularly after the Treasury ignored the modest 0.125 percent increase in interest rates in August. And of greater substance, System officials were skeptical about the administration policy to control wartime inflation. Sproul in particular doubted that the resources for war could be obtained without restricting private demand more than the Treasury contemplated. In his view, the administration's program relied too much on credit, wage, and price controls and too little on higher interest rates to restrict demand and control inflation. Sproul made these views known at a meeting with Snyder and McCabe early in January 1951.[209] He again urged higher short-term interest rates, to flatten the yield curve and stop debt owners from playing the pattern of rates, and higher rates on long-term debt, to permit the Treasury to sell debt without System support. Still, Sproul stopped short of asking for a long-term rate above 2.5 percent. He limited his demands to letting the bond price fall to par.[210]

Discussions between McCabe, Sproul, and Snyder could not resolve the differences over power, responsibility, and policy. On January 17 Snyder and McCabe met with President Truman in an effort to resolve differences and restore cooperation after failed attempts in August and November to market government securities. McCabe's account of the meeting does not mention short-term rates, the immediate issue in dispute. The president said he would like the 2.5 percent long-term rate to remain "if possible."[211] McCabe replied that "we have some doubt as to whether a long-term bond can maintain itself at the $2^1/_2$ percent rate. Secretary Snyder said that he thought it could and that he would meet the situation when he came to it. . . . The Secretary said that we ought to let the public know that we are going to maintain it" (Sproul Papers, January 18, 1951, 2). McCabe replied that the FOMC had sent the secretary a letter several weeks earlier giving its views, and he could not commit the FOMC beyond that letter.[212]

Snyder has a different, though not wholly contradictory, account. At the meeting with President Truman, Snyder later reported to Congress, "The President, the Chairman and I agreed that market stability was desirable, and the Chairman again assured the President that he need not be con-

209. Sproul and McCabe reported on the meeting. Their statements and reports of Snyder's response are in Minutes, Executive Committee, FOMC, January 31, 1951, 4–9.

210. Sproul also warned about savings bond redemptions. Ten-year series E bonds sold to small savers in 1941 were due to mature. Sproul urged the Treasury to increase rates and revitalize the selling organization to reduce redemptions. McCabe told the FOMC that the Federal Reserve staff had worked out a program for refunding E bonds but that Treasury staff had listened to their suggestions but ignored them (ibid., 9).

211. The quotations are not direct. They are quoted from Chairman McCabe's telephone discussions with Allan Sproul as reported by Sproul and available in Sproul's papers in the Archives of the Federal Reserve Bank of New York. Other quotations in this section are from the same source but are based on Sproul's notes of meetings he attended. The notes refer to the president as "the Chief."

212. The latter was sent after the October FOMC meeting. Although Snyder is not quoted as asking for a renewal of the 1942 policy statement fixing interest rates for the duration of the war, it seems clear that this was his aim.

cerned with the 2¹/₂ percent long-term rate" (Subcommittee on General Credit Control and Debt Management 1952, 73).[213] Snyder responded to McCabe's complaints about the size of recent purchases by blaming the Federal Reserve for creating uncertainty about future interest rates.

According to McCabe, Snyder did not mention a speech to the financial community in New York that he planned to give the following day. The speech first discussed the importance of avoiding inflation and the desirability of financing the Korean engagement out of current taxes. He then forecast a $16.5 billion deficit for fiscal 1952.[214] Snyder dismissed small increases in interest rates as ineffective. To control inflation, the government would rely on a return to wartime policies, allocation of materials for defense, selective credit control, and wage and price control. Then he said: "The Treasury has concluded, after a joint conference with President Truman and Chairman McCabe, . . . that the refunding and new money issues will be financed within the pattern of that [2.5 percent] rate" (Sproul Papers, FOMC, January 31, 1951; Eccles 1951, 484).[215]

The speech was a turning point. Federal Reserve officials were incensed that Snyder's speech had publicly committed them to a policy many of them no longer supported. Some, who had continued to support the 2.5 percent rate, changed their position. The speech seemed to convince

213. McCabe reported his statement as: "The Chief [president] said he is concerned about maintenance of the 2¹/₂ percent rate. The Chairman replied the market has been acting well recently, that what support has been necessary has been given, and that he could *not see anything to be concerned about*" (Sproul Papers, January 18, 1951, 1; emphasis added). McCabe went on to refer to the letter he had sent to Snyder giving the FOMC's position. This was not the first time President Truman intervened directly with the Federal Reserve. In early December he called Chairman McCabe at home. Referring to a newspaper article reporting that the Federal Reserve was "undercutting" the Treasury, he "hoped we would stick rigidly to the pegged rates on the longest bonds" (Minutes, Executive Committee, FOMC, January 31, 1951, 9). McCabe explained how many bonds they had bought (at the time of the failed note offering) and said they had bought the bonds at a premium, rewarding the sellers. President Truman ended with: "I hope the Board will realize its responsibilities and not allow the bottom to drop from under our securities. If that happens that is exactly what Mr. Stalin wants" (10). McCabe responded by assuring the president that they would "do all in our power to insure the successful financing of the Government's needs" (10). After reporting to the president on the amount purchased to support the recent financing ($2.5 billion gross, $1 billion net), McCabe did not commit to announcing a firm peg. Instead, he asked to talk to the president about the risks and costs of such an announcement. The president subsequently sent some news clippings with a letter urging the Federal Reserve to stabilize the long-term rate.

214. The actual deficit was $1.5 billion followed by a $6.5 billion deficit in fiscal 1953. Tax rates were increased to reduce the deficit.

215. Sproul's notes on the speech, taken at the time, do not record the reference to Truman and McCabe that caused subsequent excitement (Sproul Papers, Snyder Talk, January 18, 1951, 2).

them that the Treasury took their support for granted and would not change its position.[216]

Four factors worked to the benefit of the System. First, it found support within the administration. Second, the financial press took its side. Third, some congressional leaders, especially in the Senate, wanted a more independent policy. Fourth, as noted earlier, economic activity and inflation were rising rapidly. Nominal GNP growth in 1950 was above 15 percent. Fourth quarter growth in GNP continued at that pace. Industrial production increased more than 20 percent in 1950. In December, consumer prices rose 14 percent. These data bolstered the Federal Reserve's arguments with each of the groups that now supported its position.

Support within the administration became clear when McCabe met with President Truman on January 19 to correct the impression left by Snyder's speech. The president told him he had not known about the speech in advance. McCabe warned the president about inflation. He then read a memo he had sent to mobilization director Charles Wilson warning about the effects of inflation on defense costs. The president said he would talk to Wilson. Wilson supported the System's view that inflation was a problem and that he wanted to avoid rising defense costs (Sproul Papers, January 19, 1951, 4; Minutes, Executive Committee, FOMC, January 31, 1951, 14).[217]

Strong support in the financial press bolstered the System's position in Washington. One of the leading financial journalists, writing in the *New York Times*, gave his opinion of Snyder's speech:

> In the opinion of this writer, last Thursday constituted the first occasion in history on which the head of the Exchequer of a great nation had either the effrontery or the ineptitude, or both, to deliver a public address in which he has so far usurped the function of the central bank as to tell the country what

216. The usually conciliatory McCabe described his position as "untenable." He had not committed, and could not commit, the FOMC. Governors Evans, Norton, and Szymczak were cautious, believing the System would lose a public confrontation. McCabe hesitated, pointing out that the statement had not committed the FOMC, only referred to consultations. Sproul protested. The press and the financial community regarded the statement as a commitment. He urged McCabe to tell President Truman that the System was not committed to the 2.5 percent rate. He did not want a press release or immediate public statement. They should inform the public in their speeches and public statements later. Governor Szymczak called Sproul later in the day to say he agreed, adding that McCabe had received a letter from Secretary Snyder reaffirming the importance of keeping the 2.5 percent rate. Eccles also called, agreed with Sproul, and advised that he would testify at the Joint Committee on the Economic Report the following Thursday (Sproul Papers, January 19, 1951, 2–5).

217. McCabe also pointed out that before taking any decisions, he advised and consulted with all relevant parts of the government, especially the Treasury. Snyder did not reciprocate when setting interest rates on debt issues. The president agreed to talk to Snyder and urge him to be more cooperative.

kind of monetary policy it was going to be subjected to. For the moment at least, the fact that the policy enunciated by Mr. Snyder was, as usual, thoroughly unsound and inflationary, was overshadowed by the historic dimensions of this impertinence. (Quoted in Eccles 1951, 485)

Press coverage of this kind, especially if widespread, undermines the position of officials in political Washington. Politicians who cannot have a well-founded, independent position on every issue are often influenced by public opinion as reflected in the press. This is particularly true when the criticism finds support among members of Congress who are viewed as knowledgeable about the subject.

In this controversy, many members of Congress regarded Senator Douglas as an expert. He firmly supported the Federal Reserve and the need to control inflation by controlling money growth.[218] Douglas was not alone. Senators A. Willis Robertson (Virginia) and Burnet R. Maybank (South Carolina), both influential members of the Banking Committee, worked to avoid public hearings, at which populist senators would side with the Treasury. They too supported the System's position and opposed the Treasury. On the Republican side, Senator Taft, a minority member, invited Eccles to present the Federal Reserve's position to the Joint Committee on the Economic Report. Eccles changed his earlier position and criticized the bond support policy as inflationary.

The FOMC was scheduled to meet on January 31. At Secretary Snyder's suggestion, President Truman invited the entire committee to meet with him. The White House announced the meeting to the press, so it drew considerable attention. It was the first and only meeting of this kind ever held. It shows how much independence had been lost since President Wilson's decision not to interject political consideration into Federal Reserve proceedings.

Before meeting the president, the FOMC discussed its options. McCabe suggested three alternatives: agree to maintain the 2.5 percent ceiling rate; agree to support the rate conditionally and to discuss a change with the president and the secretary if economic conditions changed; or resign if unwilling to make any commitment.

Sproul disagreed. He found the first two alternatives unacceptable, the third an admission of failure. He proposed asking Congress for new instructions, thereby shifting the onus of continued inflation onto Congress

218. In a Senate speech a month later, Douglas warned of the destructive power of inflation and compared it to wartime destruction. Then he added: "In the eyes of those who want to destroy democracy and capitalistic institutions it is a cheap way of achieving their collapse" (quoted in Eccles 1951, 481).

if it failed to support the Federal Reserve (Minutes, FOMC, January 31, 1951, 15–19). No one suggested letting the market adjust. That would continue conflict with the Treasury, an unacceptable outcome for both sides.

The committee did not make a choice. The members could not agree on the language for a written statement of their position. They agreed only that Chairman McCabe would speak for the group. Agreement was not unanimous. Governor Vardaman said he would offer his own view, that the committee should be "guided by whatever request was made by the President as Commander-in Chief" (Minutes, FOMC, January 31, 1951, 21).[219]

The substance of the meeting with the president was less important than its aftermath.[220] The president talked about the seriousness of the wartime emergency and the importance of maintaining confidence in government securities. He recalled his experience in 1920 when the value of government bonds fell to 80 before rising to a premium. He thanked the committee members for their past cooperation, then told them that he wanted to finance the war with taxes and that he would ask for $16.5 billion of new revenues to balance the fiscal 1952 budget (Minutes, FOMC, January 31, 1951, 25).

McCabe explained that the Federal Reserve shared his concern about maintaining the government's credit, but that it had responsibility for economic stability. Its decisions were made by a committee of public-spirited men who might, however, disagree. He did not touch on the dispute with the Treasury, nor did the president. He promised to continue consultation with the secretary. If they failed to reach agreement, he would discuss the issue with the president.

The president said that was "entirely satisfactory." He concluded the meeting by again stressing the importance of maintaining confidence in the government's credit and in the securities market. The president said the White House would issue a statement saying that "we discussed the general emergency situation, the defense effort, budget and taxes, and that he had stressed the need for public confidence in the Government's credit" (ibid., 27).

The meeting with the president smothered the conflict in ambiguity.

219. Governor Vardaman then read a memo he had presented to the Board the previous day. The memo criticized McCabe and the other members for opposing the Treasury. The decision about interest rates and debt finance was the secretary's. "This Board has nothing further to say on the question involved other than to state quite firmly and clearly that the Board will support to the fullest extent of its authority the program as officially promulgated by the United States Treasury" (Board Minutes, January 30, 1951, 7–8).

220. The text is based on a memo prepared by Governor Evans after the meeting, probably based on notes made during the meeting, and on Eccles 1951, 487–90.

Everyone seemed to agree, but no one changed position. Some members of the FOMC complained that they had wasted an opportunity.

Press reports at the time said that the FOMC voted eight to four against a motion to support the 2.5 percent rate. This is an error. There is no mention of a vote, only a statement by McCabe that the price of the long-term bond would remain $100^{21}/_{32}$. Although Snyder was not present when the FOMC met with the president, the Treasury began to tell the press its version of what had taken place. In the Treasury's version, the Federal Reserve had agreed to support Treasury issues and maintain the 2.5 percent rate. These stories infuriated Sproul and other Federal Reserve officials. But there was more to come. As Sproul and McCabe discussed the Treasury's leaks to the press and debated whether to respond, McCabe received a letter from the president thanking the FOMC for its cooperation and for its "assurance that you would fully support the Treasury . . . financing program" (Minutes, FOMC, February 6, 1951, 3). McCabe then said that there were two courses of action: one, get the president to take back the letter or, two, deny that the FOMC had given any such assurances.

At noon on February 1, the White House released a press statement that took the Federal Reserve by surprise. Instead of the bland statement that President Truman had given at the meeting, the White House press office announced: "The Federal Reserve Board has pledged its support to President Truman to maintain the stability of Government securities as long as the emergency lasts." Soon after, a statement from the Treasury said that the White House announcement meant that interest rate levels would be maintained during the Korean emergency.

These efforts to force the System to remain subservient accomplished in a few days what most of the members had been unwilling to consider in the previous five and a half years. The Treasury had lied publicly. In Sproul's words, "publicity concerning yesterday's meeting with the President . . . doesn't accord with the facts" (Sproul Papers, February 1, 1951, 1).

At the February 2 Board meeting, McCabe circulated the letter from the president and asked for discussion of a response. The Board decided that McCabe should ask to meet with the president to show him Governor Evans's summary of the January 31 meeting. Then McCabe would ask the president to withdraw the letter. Before a meeting could be arranged, the White House released the letter to the press late on Friday afternoon.[221]

That was too much for Eccles.[222] After thinking about his response

---

221. Eccles (1951, 492) claims the Treasury drafted the letter.

222. Eccles (1951, 495) had decided to resign and return to Utah. He held his letter of resignation until after the controversy ended. He left the Federal Reserve on July 14, 1951. His last days were among his best. Eccles recognized that what he did next was irregular and im-

overnight, he released a copy of Evans's memo, summarizing the January 31 meeting at the White House, that the Board had agreed to unanimously. The memo, published in the press on February 4, showed that the White House and the Treasury had released false information to give the impression that the Federal Reserve had capitulated. The press and much public opinion supported the Federal Reserve.

The FOMC met on February 6–8. Sproul proposed a confidential response to the president and another to Secretary Snyder. The letter to the president was polite, but firm and carefully reasoned. The committee stressed its responsibility to control inflation and argued that control of inflation was essential for achieving the president's goal of maintaining confidence in the "integrity of the dollar and therefore in Government securities" (Minutes, FOMC, February 6–8, 1951, 26). The letter reminded the president of his own frequent statements on the importance of controlling inflation. Confidence would be destroyed, however, "by a flood of newly created dollars [that] will overwhelm whatever price, wage, and similar controls, including selective credit controls, that might be contrived" (26).

The letter then explained the differences between 1941 and 1951 to show why higher interest rates must be part of the 1951 program. The FOMC did not want high interest rates: "We favor the lowest rate of interest on Government securities that will cause true investors to buy and hold these securities" (ibid., 27). Then, at last, the committee took up the president's press statements and releases: "The inevitable result [of supporting bond prices] is more and more money and cheaper and cheaper dollars. This means less and less public confidence. Mr. President, you did not ask us in our recent meeting to commit ourselves to continue on this dangerous road. Such a course would seriously weaken the financial stability of the United States and encourage a further flight from money into goods" (27).[223] The letter closed with an assurance that the FOMC would seek to work out an agreement with the secretary to protect both the credit of the United States and the purchasing power of the dollar.[224]

---

proper. At the FOMC meeting on February 6, only Sproul supported Eccles's action, although he agreed that it was improper to discuss publicly what happened at meetings with the president. No other member of the FOMC took a position (Minutes, FOMC, February 6, 1951, 10). Sproul described the conflict with the Treasury as "violent," the FOMC record of the meeting with the president as "fair and accurate," and the White House statement and the president's letter as inaccurate and a misrepresentation (9–10).

223. The letter then reminded the president of the difference between the bonds he bought in World War I and the series E bonds sold to the general public in World War II. The latter were protected against loss of nominal value.

224. The Board approved the letter eleven to one. Vardaman dissented on grounds that the committee had not adopted a program. He agreed to have his dissent recorded along with his reason, but McCabe said he would not include the dissent when he sent the letter to the

The importance of the letter lay not so much in what it said to the president as in what it said about the FOMC. The committee was now on record favoring an anti-inflationary policy, even if that meant that long-term rates would rise. Money growth had to be controlled. It is of interest, also, that nowhere does the letter, or the discussion, suggest that if inflation persisted interest rates would rise.[225]

The committee turned next to the letter it would send to the secretary. By unanimous vote, it approved a letter outlining a coordinated program to control inflation and finance Treasury borrowing. The Federal Reserve offered to hold the price of long-term debt above par "for the present." If this required a substantial increase in reserves, the Treasury could issue a "longer-term bond with a coupon sufficiently attractive" to investors. Holders of outstanding long-term bonds would be permitted to exchange them for the new bond. This exchange would remove any debt overhang. The Federal Reserve would maintain an orderly market for short-term securities but would not maintain fixed interest rates. Returning to its 1920s procedures, "banks would be expected to obtain needed reserves primarily by borrowing" (ibid., 30–31).[226]

All that remained was to work out an agreement with the Treasury. On February 7, Senators Robertson and Maybank asked McCabe and Sproul to meet with Snyder. They both agreed, but they refused to accept Snyder's suggestion that bankers and outsiders should be present. Snyder agreed to think about it. The first meeting was held the following day.

At the February 8 meeting, both sides repeated their grievances. Snyder was angry. He claimed that McCabe had agreed to support the 2.5 percent

---

president. Vardaman wanted to remain on good terms with the president and the administration, so he insisted that the staff tell the president's press secretary he had dissented. There were several exchanges with other Board members at about this time accusing Vardaman of leaking confidential information to the press and the administration. Vardaman denied these charges. He also sided with the White House and Treasury interpretation that McCabe had agreed to support government bonds at the January 31 meeting (Board Minutes, February 6, 1951, 1–6). He was the only one.

225. The change in attitudes is reflected in a long statement that Governor Eccles made at the time. "We are almost solely responsible for this inflation. It is not deficit financing that is responsible because there has been a surplus in the Treasury right along; the whole question of having rationing and price controls is due to the fact that we have this monetary inflation, and this Committee is the only agency in existence that can curb and stop the growth of money" (Board Minutes, February 6, 1951, 18). Later he added: "I believe we have been derelict; . . . I think I have not made the record I should have. . . . If we had had a row [in 1946–47] I could have resigned" (19).

226. The committee also approved a motion to ask the president to fire any Board member who leaked information about meetings. There is a reference to a member who had called the *Wall Street Journal* and also offered to confer with members of Congress. This is apparently a reference to Governor Vardaman.

rate at the January 17 meeting with President Truman. He charged that the FOMC had given him an ultimatum in August 1950 and that he had not been asked to express a view. Sproul criticized Snyder for not conducting a dialogue, for listening to the Federal Reserve's position but refusing to discuss his plans. The only progress that was made came at the end, when McCabe read a letter to Snyder outlining the Federal Reserve's position on future monetary and debt management policy. The secretary "expressed strong reservations." He thought they should just let markets settle down, but he agreed to study the letter and meet again (ibid., 34).[227]

The FOMC proposal became the basis for the Treasury–Federal Reserve Accord. The Federal Reserve agreed to remove support of the 2.5 percent rate gradually. It would regain its independence only after the market stabilized at a new level of interest rates. The Treasury would assist the adjustment by offering to refund outstanding 2.5 percent bonds at a higher interest rate and would absorb the cost of removing the excess supply of bonds.

Two days later, Secretary Snyder told McCabe he was going into the hospital for eye surgery. He expected to be away for two weeks and asked that the status quo be maintained during that time. McCabe told Snyder that "unless there was someone at the Treasury who could work out a prompt and definitive agreement with us as to a mutually satisfactory course of action, we would have to take unilateral action" (Subcommittee on General Credit Control and Debt Management (1951, 520).[228] Secretary Snyder then appointed assistant secretaries Edward F. Bartelt and William McChesney Martin Jr. to negotiate with the Federal Reserve.[229] The System appointed Riefler, Thomas, and Rouse.[230]

227. McCabe questioned Snyder about why he had not mentioned his January 18 speech in New York when they met with the president on January 17. Snyder said that the president knew what he planned to do, but McCabe replied that the president had denied any knowledge of the speech. Snyder agreed to keep McCabe informed in the future, but McCabe was not mollified. The meeting permitted both sides to complain and respond to the other side's complaints, but it made no progress toward agreement.

228. To support the long-term rate at a slight premium (2.4 percent) the System bought (net) $700 million in the first two weeks of February. Market pressure slowed after mid-February. For the month as a whole, the System purchased (net) $400 million, of which $200 million had ten or more years to maturity (Board of Governors of the Federal Reserve System 1976, 488, 536). Holdings of long-term bonds were $2 billion lower than a year earlier.

229. Sproul's papers (February 10, 1951, 2) report a conversation with McCabe. McCabe wanted to agree to a postponement, but Sproul was opposed. McCabe said, "As long as the Treasury [sic] is supporting the longest term restricted $2^1/_2$ there wouldn't be anything for us to do. I said yes, there is continued purchase of short-term securities to prevent the rate from going above $1^1/_2$ percent for one year—we ought to quit that right away." They agreed to discuss their next move at the executive committee meeting on February 12.

230. The Federal Reserve came under almost immediate pressure to delay discussion and withdraw its letter to the president. Senator Maybank and others urged delay. They re-

Snyder's stay in the hospital lasted a month. He asked for more time before reaching agreement so that the discussions at the technical level, led by Martin and Riefler, could consider alternatives other than those proposed by the Federal Reserve. McCabe declined because, he said, the FOMC continued to buy government bonds in "very substantial amounts" (Minutes, Executive Committee, FOMC, February 26, 1951, 3).

One reason the Federal Reserve's position hardened was that the staff had almost completed the technical discussions with the Treasury. At meetings between Riefler, Martin, and their associates between February 20 and 23, the Federal Reserve insisted on ending the monetization of long-term debt, a rise in short-term rates to 1.75 percent, and reliance on member bank discounting to supply reserves.[231] The Treasury team agreed to all of this. It asked only that the Federal Reserve maintain discount rates at 1.75 percent until December to facilitate Treasury planning of future issues. Riefler proposed, also, that the Treasury issue a 2.75 percent nonmarketable long-term bond in exchange for the 2.5 percent bonds of 1967–72. The bond would not be redeemable before maturity but could be exchanged for a marketable 1.5 percent five-year note (Minutes, FOMC, March 1–2, 1951, 4–11).

The main difference between the two sides had been reduced to different speculations about what would happen if they agreed on the program

---

ported that Congressman Wright Patman "was very critical of the Federal Reserve" and eager to conduct public hearings on the controversy (Minutes, FOMC, February 14, 1951, 2). McCabe asked other members of the executive committee. Sproul favored sending the letter but not releasing it to the press. He opposed a commitment to maintain rates. Young (Chicago) and Evans agreed with Sproul about the letter but were willing to postpone action on interest rates. Eccles sided with Sproul. McCabe told the senators that the System was buying long-term bonds at a premium above par. This, he said, encouraged additional sales, further increasing reserves.

At its next meeting, the executive committee voted unanimously not to withdraw the letter to the president. Negotiations with the Treasury were under way based on the System's recommendations in their letter to the secretary, so the committee decided not to raise rates provided it was not required to purchase heavily to support the rate structure. If it had to buy, McCabe would discuss the decision with Martin and Bartelt before acting.

The Board asked the Federal Advisory Council for support. The council was reluctant to take a stand. Meeting with the Board on February 20, the council recognized the threat of inflation, but it concluded "that small changes in interest rates will not have any important effect on the volume of loans made" (Board Minutes, February 20, 1951, 3). Citing the large government debt outstanding, it called for "a flexible attitude" by the Treasury and the Federal Reserve. (At the time, commercial banks held about $9 billion of government securities with five or more years to maturity, and insurance companies held about $15 billion.) McCabe tried to get a stronger statement, but the bankers were unwilling. Eccles took them to task and accused them of lacking courage, but he did not sway them.

231. Riefler's case for discounting is along the lines of his book (Riefler 1930). Banks were reluctant to borrow, so increased borrowing is contractive.

and how to lessen the market response. "The Federal Reserve's position was firm that this could be done without repercussions in the money market while the Treasury view has been that it could be minimized through direct controls which were preferable to increases in interest rates" (Martin memo in Minutes, FOMC, March 1–2, 1951, 11).[232]

With agreement nearly in hand, the Federal Reserve wanted to avoid additional delay. The members were in no mood to compromise when the president called a meeting at the White House on February 26 to discuss a program to prevent inflation. McCabe and Sproul represented the Federal Reserve. In Snyder's absence Treasury Undersecretary Edward H. Foley and Martin represented the Treasury.[233]

The president began the meeting by reading a lengthy statement about the need to reconcile stability of the government securities market with restriction of private credit. He sketched a comprehensive program of controls, spending reductions, tax increases, credit restraint, and debt management. Clark described the Federal Reserve's policy as disastrous for the economy and the government's credit. Foley talked about the possible destruction of confidence if government securities prices fell. Sproul described the System's statutory responsibility and claimed that the System's proposals would strengthen confidence in the market rather than weaken it.

The president again referred to his post–World War I experience with Liberty bonds and said he did not want that experience repeated. Sproul replied that fluctuations in securities prices would not affect World War II savings bonds (Sproul Papers, February 27, 1951, 1–3).

Wilson agreed that something had to be done to slow the growth of bank credit. The president appointed him to take responsibility in Snyder's absence by chairing a committee to study ways to reconcile credit control and debt management. The president asked that the Federal Reserve maintain current interest rates during the study period, until March 15. The White House released a press statement following the meeting. This time it did not announce the Federal Reserve's commitment.

232. The Treasury team was able to reconcile acceptance of the Federal Reserve's proposal with Snyder's January 18 speech because Snyder had not discussed an exchange issue. The non marketable 2.75 percent bonds "would be consistent with the $2\frac{1}{2}$ percent rate as announced by the Secretary on January 18" (Martin memo in Minutes, FOMC, March 1–2, 1951, 11).

233. Also present in addition to President Truman: Charles Wilson, director of defense mobilization, Charles Murphy, special counsel to the president, Leon Keyserling, John D. Clark, and Roy Blough of the Council of Economic Advisers, and Harry McDonald, chairman of the Securities and Exchange Commission.

That evening McCabe and Sproul told Wilson that the meeting "had all the appearances of another delaying action. . . . The FOMC could not commit itself to the maintenance of fixed rates" (Sproul Papers, February 27, 1951, 3). Wilson said he understood their position and doubted that his committee could resolve the issue.

Two days later, after additional discussion, Martin told Riefler that "from the standpoint of the Treasury, the matter was sufficiently in hand so that it could be presented to the Federal Open Market Committee as a basis for discussion" (ibid., 12). The discussions now moved from the technical level to the policy level.

Martin and Bartelt met with the FOMC to present the Treasury's counterproposal. They asked for three principal changes, based on conversations with Secretary Snyder. The first required the Federal Reserve banks to keep discount rates unchanged until the end of the calendar year. The second asked the Federal Reserve to maintain the existing premium on long-term bonds until the Treasury sold the 2.75 percent long-term bond. The commitment had a ceiling of $600 million in open market purchases to be shared with the Treasury. The third was mainly cosmetic; to appear consistent with Snyder's January 18 speech, the joint statement would say that nonmarketable saving bonds would be available at unchanged interest rates.

After Martin and Bartelt left, the FOMC discussed the proposal. It declared itself unable to commit reserve bank directors to hold the discount rate. And it was reluctant to maintain the premium on the 2.5 percent bonds during the refunding.

The final agreement said that the Board "will approve no change in the discount rate during the rest of the calendar year without prior consultation with Treasury" (ibid., 37). The FOMC agreed to a maximum of $200 million of purchases of the 2.5 percent bonds during the refunding and until April 15.

The Board then approved the following statement, subject to approval by the secretary: "The Treasury and the Federal Reserve System have reached full accord with respect to debt-management and monetary policies to be pursued in furthering their common purpose to assure the successful financing of the government's requirements and, at the same time, to minimize monetization of the public debt" (Board Minutes, March 2, 1951, 1–2). The rest of the statement discussed the conversion of long-term debt, the commitment to support rates during the conversion, and the agreement to let short-term rates rise and to maintain an orderly market.

The FOMC approved the agreement the same day. Secretary Snyder approved it the following day. The joint statement was published on March 4, 1951.[234]

For the first time since 1934, the Federal Reserve could look forward to conducting monetary actions without approval of the Treasury. The accord ended ten years of inflexible rates, following seven years of inactive and inflexible policies. The System now faced the task of rediscovering how to operate successfully.

On March 9 McCabe resigned. His efforts at conciliation had lost support on both sides. Although his term as a member ran until 1956, President Truman told McCabe that "his services were no longer satisfactory, and he quit" (President Truman in Snyder's memoirs as quoted in Kettl 1986, 75). He left the System on March 31, after confirmation of his successor. The president named William McChesney Martin Jr. as chairman.[235] Martin served for almost nineteen years beginning April 2, 1951, the longest term of any chairman to this time.[236]

The accord was a major achievement for the country. It was not inevitable. The Truman administration could have appealed to patriotism, to the exigencies of war and to populist sentiment against higher interest rates to keep the support program in place. That decision would have required an earlier end to the Bretton Woods system, a different history than the one we know.

---

234. The 2.75 percent bond was exchanged successfully in April 1951. Press reports of the accord did not treat the agreement as a major change in policy or independence. See Keech 1995.

235. Concerned that Martin's appointment meant the Treasury would dominate, Senator Douglas voted against him (Stein 1990, 277). Snyder proposed Martin. Truman and his staff preferred Harry McDonald, chairman of the Securities and Exchange Commission. McDonald was not from an open Federal Reserve district, so he was ineligible (Kettl 1986, 75).

236. Martin was forty-five years old at the time. His father had served as the first chairman and, after 1928, as governor (president) of the St. Louis reserve bank. He had taken graduate courses in economics at Columbia and had studied law. He worked as a broker after graduation. In 1938, at thirty-one, Martin became the first paid president of the New York Stock Exchange after a personal scandal sent his predecessor, Richard Whitney, to jail. He served as president of the Export-Import Bank after World War II and as assistant secretary of the Treasury from 1949 until his appointment as chairman. When he met President Truman before his appointment to the Board, the president retold the story of his loss on government securities in 1920–21. He hoped that would not happen again. Martin's answer was: "I'll do my best, Mr. President" (taken from some unpublished remarks by Robert Solomon on October 27, 1998). There are many stories about Martin's strength of character and integrity. One that he told concerned his possible appointment by President Roosevelt as chairman of the Securities and Exchange Commission. Martin describes Roosevelt as very cheerful until Martin told him that he would gladly accept the chairmanship "but that he thought Mr. Roosevelt should know that there were three members of the commission that he could not get on with." The president's mood changed, and he did not appoint Martin (CHFRS, May 19, 1955, 3).

The Immediate Aftermath

The announcement of the accord lifted uncertainty from the securities markets. Considering the strength with which Secretary Snyder had resisted the change, the initial response of interest rates and stock prices seems modest. By the standards of the time, however, the changes in short- and medium-term rates are relatively large; the nine- to twelve-month certificate rate increased as much in March as in the seven months following the August 1950 decision to allow rates to rise to 1.75 percent. Table 7.15 shows rates in the weeks following the announcement and at the end of the month.

The refunding into 2.75 percent nonmarketable bonds in mid-April did not greatly change the yield on long-term debt. After the refunding, the yield rose to 2.62 percent on April 19. Federal Reserve purchases during March may have eased the transition to a freer market. It is difficult to separate open market purchases at that time from the normal seasonal change in bank reserves over the (then) March 15 tax date.[237] The monetary base rose more than 5 percent in the second quarter, the largest six-month rate of increase since 1945. As noted earlier, the consumer price index rose very little (0.3 percent) in the next three months. Interest rates were no higher on June 30 than on March 31, suggesting that most of the adjustment had occurred within the month. In June the Treasury carried out a refunding by selling nine-and-one-half-month certificates at 1.875 percent, a yield Sproul described as "generous" (Sproul Papers, FOMC, June 7, 1951).

In less than two years, General Dwight D. Eisenhower became president, with George Humphrey as secretary of the Treasury and W. Randolph Burgess as his deputy. Burgess had testified strongly against pegged rates in 1949. He favored an independent monetary policy. The Federal Reserve was once again independent within the government.[238]

---

237. The seasonally adjusted growth of the St. Louis monetary base is smaller in March than in February or April. Monthly numbers contain relatively large random components, suggesting caution in drawing conclusions.

238. This phrasing was used by Martin, and it is often attributed to him. I believe it originated in Sproul's 1952 letter to Congressman Wright Patman amplifying his testimony in hearings on monetary policy and management of the public debt. Sproul responded to questions about why monetary policy should be independent if defense policy or foreign policy was not. His reply included the following: "I think it should be continuously borne in mind that whenever stress is placed on the need for the 'independence' of the Federal Reserve, *it does not mean independence from the government but independence within the government*" (Sproul 1980, 144; emphasis added).

Table 7.15   Interest Rates, March 1951 (percent)

WEEK ENDING	THREE-MONTH BILLS[a]	NINE TO TWELVE MONTHS	THREE TO FIVE YEARS	LONG TERM
March 3	1.390	1.60	1.69	2.40
March 10	1.406	1.72	1.78	2.44
March 31	1.507	1.94	2.03	2.51

Source: Board of Governors of the Federal Reserve System 1976.
[a]New issues.

Why So Little and So Long?

The Treasury's warnings about disaster proved empty. A rise of 0.25 percent in long-term bond rates, and about 0.34 percent in medium-term issues, restored equilibrium. There was neither panic nor destruction of confidence in the government's credit. Apparently, existing market rates had not been far from equilibrium rates. The puzzles are to explain why interest rates rose so little and why the Federal Reserve was so slow in regaining independence.

The principal reason for the modest adjustment was that, despite the Federal Reserve's repeated concern, inflation remained low. It is true that consumer prices rose, on average, 7 percent a year from 1946 through 1951. Most of the rise was an adjustment to the end of wartime controls. Much more relevant is that the consumer price index at the start of the Korean War was the same as in April 1948. In between, prices had fallen and gradually returned to their earlier level.

Again, despite its protests, the Federal Reserve had not become an "engine of inflation," the description Eccles was fond of using. The principal reason is not hard to find. The government budget was in surplus most of the time; the net budget surplus for fiscal years 1947 to 1951 was approximately $8 billion. Federal government civilian employment declined from a World War II peak of 3.4 million to 2.1 million in 1950. And President Truman committed repeatedly to fighting the Korean War with a balanced budget. Further, gold flows reduced monetary expansion after 1948. The gold stock reached a peak in September 1949, near the end of the deflation. By the time of the accord, gold holdings had declined 10 percent from their peak. Almost all of the decline came after the start of the Korean War.

With a modest budget surplus, no gold inflow, and given interest rates, money growth depends mainly on growth of private spending and the portion financed by the banking system. The monetary base was about the same in March 1951 as in December 1945. Without sustained growth of money per unit of output, the public had no reason to expect continued inflation, and there is no evidence in market data that it did.

With hindsight, it seems clear that the Federal Reserve could have

ended pegged rates much earlier, without harm to the economy, if its officials had been more forceful. Their delay was more for political than for
economic reasons, and resistance to change was usually stronger in Washington than in New York.

System officials believed they had no friends in high political office.
Secretary Snyder was a Missouri banker, a longtime friend of the president. Although he denied it in the 1949 Douglas hearings, his principal
concern was to borrow and refund debt at low interest rates. Until the Douglas hearings, the Federal Reserve had little overt congressional support to
end pegged rates. And there was considerable opposition from the more
populist members of Congress.[239]

Through most of the early postwar period, the Federal Reserve lacked a
leader who was willing to push the issue forward. During his chairmanship, Eccles preferred to seek new powers over reserve requirements and
to pursue his long-standing goal of gaining authority over nonmember
banks. Reliance on credit controls, margin requirements, and other nonmonetary arrangements reflects an effort to show that the Federal Reserve
recognized its legal responsibility to prevent inflation, in part a mistaken
belief that the Federal Reserve could control inflation without raising interest rates and controlling money.

Although political concerns were paramount, faulty economic analysis
had a prominent role. Eccles did not believe that monetary policy could
control inflation without very large increases in interest rates. Like many
private and public sector economists at the time, he believed that fiscal
policy was powerful and monetary policy was weak or impotent. On many
occasions he expressed concern about the size of the change in interest
rates required to control inflation. This too reflected political and economic
concerns. Memories of 1920–21, when discount rates rose to 7 percent (in

239. I worked for the House Banking Committee in 1964 and had several opportunities
to discuss some of these issues with the chairman, Congressman Wright Patman (Texas).
Patman regarded the period of pegged interest rates as akin to a golden age of monetary
policy. His slightly more muted views are on the record in many hearings, including the 1952
hearings on monetary policy and debt management that he chaired. These hearings, coming
after the accord, gave opponents of the accord a chance to voice their complaints. By the time
he held the hearings, the Treasury was not eager to reopen the issue. The subcommittee recommended many changes in the System, including required reserves for nonmember banks,
appointment of labor representatives on reserve bank boards, six-year terms for governors
(with reappointment), elimination of geographical requirements for governors, four-year
term for the chairman, coterminous with the president's term, an advisory council to coordinate policy, and an annual audit of the Board's accounts. It opposed selective credit controls
except in "special circumstances," favored "mutual discussion" to resolve conflicts between
the Federal Reserve and the Treasury, and pointed to the Employment Act as the policy mandate (Subcommittee on General Credit Control and Debt Management 1952, 2–7).

a period of high inflation), haunted the Federal Reserve, Secretary Snyder, and President Truman. Since no official at the time distinguished between nominal and real rates of interest, concern that interest rates would rise again to 6 percent or 7 percent deterred action. The existence of a large stock of debt—ten times the size of the federal debt after World War I—reinforced other concerns about higher rates. A substantial increase in market rates would lower the value of existing debt, causing losses to the public and financial institutions.

Neither Federal Reserve nor other economists had developed a framework linking debt, money, and interest rates to output and prices. The common belief, repeated many times by officials and economists, was that the large outstanding debt changed the possibility of using monetary policy.[240] It was not until the Korean War that Federal Reserve spokesmen pointed out that if inflation rose, the budget saving from holding interest rates low would be more than offset by the rising cost of government purchases.

The System began to change its view near the end of Eccles's term as chairman. Sproul was often the most forceful proponent of change. Since McCabe was a much weaker chairman than Eccles, leadership shifted to New York. It was Sproul who pushed for the 1949 decision to make policy more flexible and the August 1950 decision to raise interest rates without Treasury approval. And it was Sproul who appeared most determined, in the eight months of conflict that preceded the accord, to regain full independence from Treasury domination. But even Sproul was slow to state opposition to the 2.5 percent rate until concern about wartime inflation and political and press support opened an opportunity in 1951.

GOLD AND INTERNATIONAL ISSUES

The 1949 Douglas Committee hearings also reviewed the role of gold in the monetary system. The hearings came soon after several European countries, led by Britain, devalued against the dollar. Some members questioned whether the president or secretary could change the price of gold without the approval of the International Monetary Fund or Congress. The

---

240. One explanation for the delay in changing policy is fear of capital losses at banks. This argument is valid as one part of the concern at the time, within and outside the Federal Reserve, about using monetary policy actively in the presence of a large outstanding debt. It finds support in the emphasis given to issuing debt that banks could not buy, although the proposals were not defended on that ground. The argument is incomplete, however. I believe the Federal Reserve would have changed policy after June 1949, and possibly in December 1947, if it had believed that Congress and the public would support its decision.

fund had the right to approve a devaluation, but Congress had retained authority to set the gold price of the dollar.[241]

The Federal Reserve gave little attention to international monetary issues during this period. Gold holdings were large at the end of the war compared with any previous experience. They continued to increase once the initial postwar United States inflation ended. Deflation in the United States and concerns about devaluation of some European currencies added to the gold inflow. Despite exchange controls in most of Europe, the United States gold stock increased more than 22 percent, to $24.6 billion, in the four years following the end of the war in August 1945.

The peak in the United States gold stock came in 1949 when Britain, the sterling area, and Scandinavia devalued by 30 percent, with smaller devaluations by Germany, France, Belgium, and Portugal. Purchasing power parity calculations suggest that the devaluations substantially overvalued the dollar against the British pound and the Swedish krona (Friedman and Schwartz 1963, 771).[242] By the following September, the United States gold stock was 4.4 percent lower. A larger decline began after the start of the Korean War.

Chart 7.6 shows the real value of gold from 1934 to 1951 in 1982–84 prices. As commodity prices rose, the price of gold in constant dollars fell. By 1951 the $35 gold price, set in 1934, had fallen by almost 50 percent in real terms.

There was only a slight echo of the Federal Reserve's earlier concerns about gold inflows in the early postwar years. Gold movements were small relative to changes in the government budget. Gold inflows reinforced demand for new powers to raise reserve requirements, but the demand would almost certainly have been made in any case.

Aside from a few technical adjustments, the Bretton Woods agencies leave no mark in the System's minutes for the period. The principal reason is that these agencies were inactive at the time. James (1996, 83) describes the IMF as "moribund," a view apparently shared by the fund's first two managing directors (83–84).

---

241. Section 5 of the Bretton Woods Agreement Act, enabling the United States to join the fund and the World Bank, provided that "neither the President nor any person or agency shall propose to the International Monetary Fund any change in the par value of the United States dollar or approve any change in par values unless Congress by law authorizes such action." When President Nixon stopped the sale of gold in August 1971, he did not get the prior approval of Congress or order a change in par value. He claimed authority under the same Trading with the Enemy Act that President Roosevelt used to stop gold sales in March 1933.

242. The British devaluation lifted the purchasing power of the pound relative to the dollar far more than Britain's 1931 devaluation. To a lesser extent this is true of the Swedish krona.

Chart 7.6 Real price of gold per troy ounce, January 1934 to December 1951, base period 1982–84.

The IMF's minor role reflected both errors in the original plan and changed views in the United States and abroad.[243] Roosevelt and Morgenthau were gone. Their multilateral, internationalist views did not survive in the emerging postwar struggle with the Soviet Union. The Truman administration shifted toward a unilateral policy (James 1996, 60, 62). After 1947 the Marshall Plan, providing unilateral aid, became the principal source of European aid.

Even if there had not been a Cold War, it seems unlikely that the IMF and the World Bank would have taken a large role. They had limited resources, and the misalignment of exchange rates was much greater than the IMF's resources could handle. John H. Williams of the New York reserve bank, W. Randolph Burgess, and Allan Sproul had foreseen the problem. Their writings and testimony in 1945–46 opposed the Keynes-White plan as premature and inadequate for the circumstances they expected after the war. Williams especially argued for a "key currencies" approach, based on the dollar and the pound sterling. He believed that the increased postwar demand for dollars could not be satisfied from the fund's resources.

The so-called dollar shortage—the excess demand for dollars by foreigners—reflected the misaligned exchange rates agreed to at Bretton Woods. These rates did not take adequate account of the wartime differences in inflation and the destruction of capital and living standards.[244] By

243. James (1996, chap. 3) summarizes changing views in Russia, Britain, and elsewhere.

244. The pound was set at $4.035, its prewar value, whereas the French franc was devalued by about 60 percent in 1946 and the Belgian franc by about 75 percent.

raising concerns about devaluation, and despite currency controls, discussion of the "dollar shortage" probably contributed to capital flight from Europe to the United States. After the 30 percent devaluation of the British pound in September 1949, followed by a 22 percent devaluation of the German mark and other devaluations, discussion of the dollar shortage ended.

Unlike the postwar 1920s, this time the Federal Reserve had a modest, insignificant role in international monetary affairs. Authority and responsibility shifted to the Treasury, where it has remained through most of the postwar era.

CONCLUSION

From the start of United States participation in World War II to the accord of March 1951, debt management policy dominated monetary policy. To a considerable degree, the period continued the Morgenthau policy of 1934–41: keep interest rates low to minimize the cost of selling and refunding debt. The Federal Reserve willingly supported this policy in wartime. After the war, it feared postwar deflation and depression. The problem seemed much greater after 1945 because the increased stock of debt fostered concern that higher interest rates would impose capital losses, weaken the financial system, curtail lending, and bring back deflation and depression. Many in the System believed that an independent policy was impossible. Table 7.16 shows the wartime rise in debt and the postwar change in ownership.

At its peak, gross debt was much larger than gross national product. Almost 27 percent of the debt was in bills and certificates with less than one year to maturity. The Treasury may have been right in 1945–46 to be concerned about the task of managing the debt while avoiding the (widely predicted) postwar depression that had been the norm after earlier wars. It was wrong, however, when it refused to agree to the very modest changes in interest rates that the Federal Reserve wanted and to insist on continuing wartime interest rates long after the threat of postwar depression had passed.

Table 7.16 shows that the Treasury used budget surpluses to retire debt. In addition, Congress used part of the surplus to reduce taxes by more than $20 billion, overriding President Truman's veto. However, tax rates remained high by historical standards, thereby contributing to the budget surplus. In addition, the Treasury purchased more than $12 billion of debt for its accounts.

Commercial banks had been the largest wartime buyers; they became the largest postwar sellers. The Federal Reserve was a net seller also. Instead of serving as "engine of inflation," as Eccles and others often de-

Table 7.16   Size and Ownership of Marketable Debt, 1941–50 (billions of dollars)

DATE	GROSS DEBT	TREASURY ACCOUNTS	FEDERAL RESERVE	COMMERCIAL BANKS	INSURANCE COMPANIES	INDIVIDUALS
December 1941	64.3	9.5	2.3	21.4	8.2	13.5
December 1945	278.7	27.0	24.3	90.8	24.0	64.1
December 1949	256.2	39.4	18.9	66.8	20.1	66.3
December 1950	255.5	39.2	20.8	61.8	18.7	66.3

Source: Board of Governors of the Federal Reserve System 1976, 882.
Note: Detail does not add to total because some owners are omitted and nonmarketable debt is part of gross debt but not part of the detail.

scribed its role, monetary actions were often deflationary; the monetary base and the money stock fell, and the consumer price index fell more than at any time in the postwar years. Chart 7.7 shows that the base and the money stock rose rapidly during the war, grew more slowly after the war, and declined in 1948–49 in advance of the recession and during its early months.

Converted to constant dollars, base growth remained nearly constant during the war, then collapsed at the end of the war when controls were removed and prices fully reflected earlier wartime inflation. Thereafter, real money balances fell until 1949. With nominal long-term interest rates almost constant, the movement of real interest rates shows mainly the rise and fall of measured inflation. Chart 7.8 shows highly negative ex post real interest rates at the end of the war; the one-time effect of removing price controls in 1946 overstates the decline, however. Negative real rates encouraged holding money for its real return. Negative real base growth reduced spending and aggregate demand.

As in several earlier recessions and recoveries, real base growth and real interest rates are positively related during recession and recovery, reflecting the common effect of inflation. Although the two series move together, they have opposite implications. Rising real interest rates produced by deflation imply that policy has become more restrictive; rising real balances may suggest an excess supply of money. In the 1948–49 recession, the effects of the real base again dominated the effects of real interest rates on output and economic activity, a repeat of experience in 1920–21 and 1937–38.[245]

Historically low nominal interest rates of the early postwar years, and the continued negative real long-term rates from 1946 to 1949, show that monetary policy—measured by the growth rate of money—was not impo-

245. The influence of the real base represents more than the conventional real balance effect. In Brunner and Meltzer 1976, 1993, the response includes relative price changes of assets to output in addition to the standard wealth effect. These changes induce an excess supply of real balances and an increase in spending.

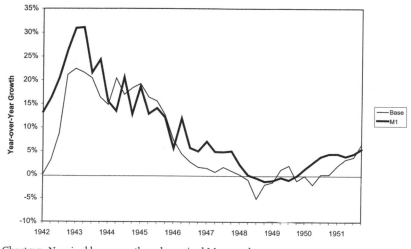

Chart 7.7 Nominal base growth and nominal M_1 growth, 1942.1 to 1951.4.

Chart 7.8 Real base growth versus real interest rate; data smoothed using four-quarter moving average.

tent even at the prevailing interest rates. Relative prices, including stock prices, and prices of existing real assets continued to respond to current and prospective rates of money growth and inflation. In 1947 and 1948, with real base growth negative, the total return to common stocks was 5 to 6 percent; when real base growth turned positive in 1949, stock prices rose more than 18 percent, and the recession ended.

In 1942, the Federal Reserve volunteered to keep the long-term rate on

Treasury bonds at 2.5 percent, fix short-term rates, and hold the pattern of rates prevailing at the time. After the war it did not insist on, or even propose, a free market in Treasury debt. It believed, correctly, that the spread between short- and long-term rates was much too large to encourage banks and others to hold short-term debt. Its goal through most of the period before the Korean War was to raise short-term rates enough to stop holders from selling short-term bills and buying long-term debt.

Most members of the FOMC shared this goal. They differed about how to achieve it. The Board, led by Eccles, preferred to increase reserve requirement ratios, use selective credit controls to ration credit, and require banks to hold secondary reserves of government securities. Influenced by political pressures from the Treasury, and reinforced by his own beliefs, Eccles hoped to control credit expansion without increasing interest rates. The reserve banks, particularly New York, acquiesced in some of these policies or supported them. They argued correctly that none of these actions would be effective unless interest rates rose. Although New York urged a slow and deliberate policy, it took advantage of opportunities to change short-term rates when they arose in December 1947, June 1949, and after the start of the Korean War.

Policy differences between New York and the Board have some aspects of a repeat, in different form, of the policy dispute in 1928–29. As before, the Board most often favored some type of credit or monetary control that did not require higher interest rates. New York argued for higher interest rates as a necessary step to control money growth and inflation. And as in 1928–29, the Federal Reserve ignored deflation in 1948–49.

Both the Board and the reserve banks had political and economic concerns. The main political concern was to avoid an open fight with the Treasury. The two main economic concerns were (1) that an increase in interest rates large enough to prevent postwar inflation would run the risk of reproducing the 1920–21 deflation and deep recession and (2) the mistaken belief that historically low nominal interest rates indicated an easy monetary policy. As in 1928–29, the Board and the FOMC paid less attention to money growth and price changes than to nominal interest rates.

Eccles and several of the Board's economists, like many private sector economists, did not believe that small changes in interest rates had much effect on economic activity and prices. In the 1930s, Eccles accepted the phrase "pushing on a string" to describe the alleged impotence of expansive policies. In the postwar years he had similar reservations about contractive policies, unless carried far enough to run the risk of deflation. In both periods many economists, influenced by early Keynesian analysis, shared this view. There was no attempt to reconcile the conflicting beliefs that monetary policy was weak or impotent with the expressed concern that allowing interest rates to rise would risk deflation and depression. And along with these divergent views, a third view was often repeated: that deflation must inevitably occur to purge the effects of the previous inflation.

Before the start of the Federal Reserve System, bankers expressed concern about political dominance by a Board located in Washington. The Banking Act of 1935 shifted power from the reserve banks, particularly New York, to Washington. The sixteen years from 1935 to 1951 did little to dispel the early concerns. Resistance to the Treasury was stronger in the reserve banks, particularly New York, than in Washington. After Thomas B. McCabe replaced Marriner Eccles as chairman in 1948, Allan Sproul was able to gradually increase New York's influence over the direction of Federal Reserve policy and, three years later, to insist on an end to pegged interest rates and a restoration of some of the System's independence. But Sproul too was cautious, unwilling to push hard for independence until the threat of Korean War inflation made action seem imperative and support in Congress made success more likely.

Restoration of independence was not simply a victory for the reserve banks over the Board. Eccles played an important role, as did Senator Paul Douglas and other members of the congressional banking committees. High-handed actions by the Treasury and President Truman helped to marshal support for the System in the financial press and in Congress.

The FOMC had little to do during the long period when open market policy remained subordinate to Treasury debt management. The committee spent much of its time giving advice to the Treasury about the types of debt to sell, advice that the Treasury usually ignored. The Board also recommended tax changes, wage and price controls, and other policies unrelated to its mission. Within the System, the role of the account manager changed. Since the account manager had more information about the debt markets than the members did, his influence increased. Often he took the lead, making recommendations to the FOMC and, beyond his role, recommending changes in reserve requirement ratios. This shift in the manager's role remained for years after the accord.

The long period when the FOMC was inactive did not eliminate the Riefler-Burgess doctrine as a guide to policy action. When the FOMC became more active, it reverted to its earlier operating procedure. Riefler was again at the Board, and Sproul used that framework to discuss monetary policy. Discussions at the FOMC before the accord, and the accord itself, refer to future policy actions as intended to "immediately reduce or discontinue purchases of short-term securities and permit the short-term market to adjust to a position at which banks would depend upon borrowing at the Federal Reserve to make needed adjustments of their reserves" (Krooss 1969, 4:3056).

Monetary policy was not the only friction between Washington and New York. Eccles and Sproul disagreed about the International Monetary Fund. The New York bank opposed the multilateral system developed at Bretton Woods. It favored a key currency system based on the dollar and the British pound. Although the Board had no role in the design of the postwar international system, the Treasury gained its support by appointing Eccles to the delegation for the Bretton Woods meeting.

The war opened a wide gap in the relative size and strength of the United States economy. Net exports and, despite controls, capital inflow continued the gold inflow that the war and the lend-lease program of allied war finance interrupted. Low inflation—even deflation—budget surpluses, and an expanding economy attracted foreign investment. Recovery in Europe, foreign aid policies like the Marshall Plan, and the start of the Korean War reversed the inflow. By 1950 the deflated price of gold was back to the predevaluation level. Large outflows began in 1950. For the next two decades, gold and the balance of payments deficit would become matters of increased attention and concern.

EIGHT

Conclusion:
The First Thirty-seven Years

Monetary history reveals the fact that folly has frequently been paramount; for it describes many fateful mistakes. On the other hand, it would be too much to say that mankind has learned nothing from these mistakes.
—Wicksell 1935, 4

The Federal Reserve began operations in 1914 as a peculiar hybrid, a partly public, partly private institution, intended to be independent of political influence with principal officers of the government on its supervisory board, endowed with central banking functions, but not a central bank. Each of the twelve semiautonomous reserve banks set its own discount rates, subject to the approval of the Federal Reserve Board in Washington, made its own policy decisions, and set its own standards for what was eligible for discounting. Even branches of reserve banks initially had some independent powers.

The new system had two principal monetary powers. It could buy and sell gold, thereby changing interest rates and money, and it could set the rate at which member banks discounted eligible paper. Other activities and responsibilities included centralizing the country's gold reserve, developing a domestic market for bills of exchange, acting as lender of last resort in a crisis, and eliminating large seasonal increases in interest rates during the autumn, when the agricultural harvest moved through the commodity markets.

The Federal Reserve had little discretion. The founders intended the gold standard to work automatically. Discounting was at the discretion of the member banks. The Federal Reserve could decide the timing of discount rate changes, but the rules of the gold standard limited the range within which it could set the discount rate. It could set the rate at which it bought acceptances, but despite its efforts, the acceptance market did not become large and active.

The original structure, organization, and methods of operation did not survive. Establishment of the Federal Reserve helped to create a national financial market that undermined the system of separate discount rates. Banks used the correspondent banking system to borrow in markets with lower rates. By the early 1920s, the System had moved toward more uniform discount rates; although differences between districts continued, they were smaller, and rate schedules became more uniform.

Wars, the growing role of the federal government, and other external forces contributed to the major changes in structure and organization in the years to 1951. Flaws in the original plan and different conceptions about the roles and responsibilities of the Board and the reserve banks combined with these external events to force changes. Different beliefs about the roles of the reserve banks and the Board, and rivalry over power and influence, worked to delay change and disperse power.

By 1951 the Federal Reserve System had become a central bank with its headquarters in Washington. The accord with the Treasury in March of that year released the Federal Reserve from Treasury control and began the evolution toward the modern Federal Reserve. Although struggles over power and influence continued, the Board of Governors had final control over decisions. The semiautonomous regional banks were now part of a unified system. The Federal Open Market Committee (FOMC) made binding portfolio decisions for the reserve banks. Open market purchases and sales of government securities replaced discounting as the principal means of implementing policy. The discount rate had a minor role.

The System's founders would not have liked or even recognized the Federal Reserve that existed in 1951. Gold no longer had an important role. Activist policies, based on collective judgment, determined money, interest rates, and prices. A small, mostly passive institution had become the most important central bank in the world.

The Federal Reserve's founders wanted to base currency or note issue on discounts of commercial paper to free currency from dependence on government securities. They believed that the new arrangement would permit currency and money to expand and contract with the needs of trade and the public's demand. In the Great Depression a change, believed to be temporary, permitted the Federal Reserve once again to issue currency backed by government securities. Eventually the change became permanent. Government securities became the Federal Reserve's principal asset.

Discounts of commercial paper and bills of exchange had only a modest and inconsequential role.

Volume 1 tells how and why these changes occurred in response both to external events and to flaws in the original plan. It is also a record of the achievements and failures of the first thirty-seven years.

ACHIEVEMENTS AND FAILURES

Looking back from 1951, few would conclude that the Federal Reserve had achieved the hopes of its founders and early proponents. The Great Depression, though at the time not considered a failure of monetary policy, was the deepest and longest in United States history. The Federal Reserve had not prevented thousands of bank failures, the collapse of the financial system, and the devaluation of the dollar. The dominant view in 1951 regarded monetary policy as unimportant for economic stabilization, but it recognized that the Federal Reserve had failed to maintain financial stability. Deposit insurance, stock market regulation, and separation of commercial and investment banking, among other New Deal measures, showed that the public, through its representatives, no longer trusted the Federal Reserve alone to maintain a stable and solvent financial system.

Central bankers and most economists in the 1920s regarded the gold standard as essential for monetary stability. The Federal Reserve achieved one of its major goals when Britain and France followed Germany back to a fixed exchange rate with their currencies convertible into gold. Other countries pegged to gold also; by 1928 all major trading countries, and many others, had adopted a gold exchange standard. The Federal Reserve and other central bankers considered restoration of a type of gold standard one of the major achievements of the 1920s.

Although central bankers and governments wanted the gold standard restored, several were reluctant to accept its implications. Three problems arose. First, after restoration, exchange rates in major trading countries were incompatible with domestic price stability. The British overvalued the pound; the French undervalued the franc. Britain would not deflate after 1925; France would not inflate after 1927, so price changes could not adjust real exchange rates to remove these differences, as the gold standard required. Second, countries would not permit dynamic adjustment to work. Gold flowed to the United States through much of the decade and to France at the end of the decade. Both countries sterilized most gold flows to prevent prices from rising. With receiving countries sterilizing, the countries paying gold had to deflate or leave the standard. The gold standard had an unwelcome deflationary bias. As countries returned to the gold standard, the increased demand for monetary gold stocks added to deflationary pressure.

Third, under the gold exchange standard the United States and Britain held their reserves in gold. Other countries held dollar or pound sterling balances. France, especially, regarded its status as second-rate. As in the 1960s, the rules permitted the Bank of France to convert its reserves into gold. France's gold purchases, and sales of dollars and pounds, added to the deflationary pressures imposed by the return to gold. Unwilling to follow the rules or give up the standard, countries resisted steps to restore equilibrium real exchange rates. In retrospect, the breakdown of the gold standard seems inevitable; at the time, it seemed calamitous.

As the world economy moved toward deflation and depression. The Federal Reserve's principal concern was inflation. To contemporary economists, this concern is puzzling because the price level fell slowly from 1927 to 1929, then more rapidly. Federal Reserve officials did not base their concern about inflation on price changes or sluggish money growth. To most of them, rising stock prices and growing use of borrowing to purchase shares was all the evidence of inflation they needed. Their interpretation relied on the real bills doctrine—the belief that credit extended for common stocks, real estate, government securities, or commodity speculation created inflation because the additional credit did not give rise to additional output.

Deflationary policies contributed to the start of the 1929 recession. When the Federal Reserve raised the New York discount rate in August 1929, part of the world was in recession. Although it was not known at the time, the United States economy was at a peak. The Great Depression had started.

There is no single cause of the Great Depression or a unique monetary shock. A series of financial shocks followed—bank failures, Britain's departure from the gold standard followed by other departures, and financial failures in the United States. Most Federal Reserve officials favored a passive policy. They viewed the depression as the inevitable consequence of excessive speculation in stocks financed by credit creation. On their view, the proper response was to purge the economic system of its excesses—excesses made more serious by credit expansion unrelated to real bills. Monetary or credit expansion to end the depression would require purchases of government securities. On the real bills interpretation, such purchases prevented the inevitable adjustment and purge of previous excesses.

If the Federal Reserve had maintained monetary growth, the country and the world would have avoided years of depression. Failure to act during the Great Depression was the Federal Reserve's largest error, but far from its only one. Failure to expand can be explained as the result of prevailing beliefs about the inevitability of a downturn following the stock market boom. Nothing in theory or central banking practice can explain why the Federal Reserve did not respond to the failure of thousands of banks. Most of the banking failures from 1929 to 1932, and the final collapse in the winter of 1933, could have been avoided. The failing banks included many member banks. After years of recession, banks had little eligible paper to borrow against. The Federal Reserve, following the real bills doctrine, saw no reason to expand. This was a destructive and mistaken interpretation of banking theory. In *Lombard Street,* his classic work on banking, Walter Bagehot quotes the spokesman for the Bank of England in the 1825 panic: "We lent it . . . by every possible means and in modes we had never adopted before . . . in short, by every possible means consistent with the safety of this Bank, and we were not on some occasions over-nice" (Bagehot 1962, 25).

Bagehot's work was known at the time. Senior officials referred to him, but they did not follow his advice. They tried to protect the gold reserve and, at crucial times, did not function as a system. Individual reserve banks refused to participate in open market purchases to protect their banks' gold holdings. A design failure and a failure of leadership permitted individual banks to opt out of System purchases. There was too much autonomy built into the 1913 Federal Reserve Act, and the Board failed to use its powers to force the reserve banks to expand together.

Ideas were important too. The original Federal Reserve Act wrote the real bills doctrine into law. At the Federal Reserve Board, and at several reserve banks, officials followed this doctrine. They considered real bills— commercial credit—to be the only correct foundation for credit expansion. If banks did not borrow, they believed it was wrong to expand credit. This policy gives rise to procyclical policy action: credit and money expand when output expands and contract when output contracts. The gold standard, too, makes policy action procyclical.

The Federal Reserve's attachment to the real bills doctrine was not peculiar. Economists, bankers, congressional leaders, and many others accepted the theory and believed the Federal Reserve was right to follow it. There were few critics at the time.

Early in the nineteenth century, one of the founders of economics, Henry Thornton (1962) recognized the principal flaw in the real bills doctrine: controlling the quality of credit did not ensure control of the quantity. At the Federal Reserve, Benjamin Strong rediscovered this proposition in the 1920s. Neither the discovery nor the rediscovery convinced real bills proponents.

Strong's conclusion reflected experience in the postwar recession of 1920–21. After the Federal Reserve convinced the Treasury to end wartime restrictions on interest rates, the nominal discount rate rose to 7 percent in New York. Use of marginal discount rates at regional banks raised interest rates far above that level. Discounting continued to increase, in part because banks could borrow at preferential rates using Treasury securities as collateral. But that was not the lesson drawn by Strong and others.

The 1920–21 experience affected subsequent developments in two ways. First, the Federal Reserve became convinced that the traditional British central banking procedures would not work in the larger, more diverse circumstances of the United States. Second, and closely related, complaints from agricultural and commercial interests, particularly in the South and West, aroused congressional concerns. Topmost among the political concerns was the fear that the Federal Reserve would operate for the benefit of Wall Street and large banks and against the interests of farmers, ranchers, and the general public. Federal Reserve policy in the 1920–21 recession seemed to confirm these fears.

Failure to distinguish between real and nominal interest rates was another, no less important error. As prices fell, real interest rates rose. Federal Reserve officials, and outsiders, failed to distinguish between the two rates, a distinction recognized early in the nineteenth century by Henry Thornton and later developed more fully by Irving Fisher. Although there are occasional references to the possibility that a low nominal interest rate did not necessarily connote an easy policy, none of those making these comments offered a clear analysis of the effect of falling prices on real interest rates and exchange rates.

Failure to distinguish clearly between real and nominal interest rates is puzzling. Fisher was professionally active in the 1920s and 1930s. He warned about the high cost of deflation and urged officials to pay attention to measures of deposits and money. In the 1920s Fisher worked to get Congress to mandate price stability as the Federal Reserve's goal. The Federal Reserve opposed the legislation, and it did not pass.

The Federal Reserve also ignored Walter Bagehot's analysis of the role of a lender of last resort. At times Board members and governors referred to Bagehot's *Lombard Street,* but they did not follow his doctrine: In a financial crisis, lend freely at a penalty interest rate; do not try to protect the gold reserve.

Theories, or beliefs, go a long way toward explaining why the Federal Reserve did not avoid crises in 1920–21, 1929–33, and 1937–38. The beliefs that officials used to interpret events, and the interpretations they reached, were conventional at the time. The Federal Reserve Act used the gold standard and the real bills doctrine as guiding principles. Faith in the gold standard and belief in its stabilizing power constituted a cornerstone of the orthodoxy of the time, an orthodoxy that was widely shared by leading members of the business, banking, and academic communities. It would have required a strong, forceful leader to recognize the need to abandon orthodox beliefs. A divided Federal Reserve could not supply that leadership. It is highly uncertain that even a strong leader could have overcome the firmly held beliefs that led to the mistakes of 1929–33 and 1937–38.

Between 1930 and 1933, the Federal Reserve did little to prevent the collapse of the United States financial system and thousands of bank failures. President Herbert Hoover and Secretary Andrew Mellon proposed a National Monetary Commission and, soon after, the Reconstruction Finance Corporation (RFC) to prevent failures from spreading. Initially the Federal Reserve was wary of these efforts, concerned that it would have to lend to insolvent banks or to institutions like the RFC that lent to insolvent banks. By June 1932, the Federal Reserve wanted the RFC to be more active. In part this change of view reflects two opposing influences. One was the System's desire to limit or end bank failures and the large increases in the demand for currency by concerned depositors. The other was the firm belief that it could, or should, do nothing to prevent bank failures.

Financial collapse in the winter of 1933 was not inevitable. President Hoover appealed to the Federal Reserve to offer guidance. Hoover also appealed to President-Elect Roosevelt to support a bank holiday. Hoover believed he lacked authority to act, and Roosevelt was unwilling to accept responsibility when he lacked authority.

Political maneuvering and hesitancy do not explain the Federal Reserve's failure to act. Chapter 5 offers three plausible explanations. First, some members of the Open Market Policy Conference believed that the very large open market operations in 1932 accomplished little. Additional operations would do no more. Failures, they believed, were the inevitable consequence of bad decisions and speculative excesses that had to be purged before stability could return. Second, some reserve banks, notably Boston and Chicago, refused to participate in additional purchases during the summer of 1932. They would likely have refused again, if asked, in the winter of 1933. Third, some reserve banks may have feared that open market purchases would be offset, in part, by a loss of gold. Protecting the gold reserve by refusing to lend was one of the main errors of central banking practice that Bagehot warned against.

Reliance on discounting gave monetary policy a procyclical bias. In the severe recessions of 1920–21 and 1937–38, the Federal Reserve imposed deflation. The 1920–21 recession resulted from a decision to restore the prewar dollar–British pound exchange rate by deflating prices in both countries. Britain had experienced more inflation, so it had to deflate most to restore the prewar exchange rate. Deflation by Britain alone, however, would not have removed the effects of wartime finance on the United States stocks of money and credit, contrary to the real bills doctrine. The decision delayed Britain's return to the gold standard and raised the social cost. The two governments did not repeat this mistake after World War II.

The decision to deflate together also raised the social cost in the United States. The 1920–21 recession is the only recession in Federal Reserve history that has short-term nominal interest rates higher at the trough of the recession than at the previous peak. Severe deflation made real interest rates higher still.

The Federal Reserve took no action to end the recession. Rising real interest rates, however, attracted gold, raising the stock of base money. The counterpart of rising real interest rates was a rising stock of real balances. As prices fell and gold flowed in, real money balances rose rapidly. When the public's real balances exceeded the amount it wished to hold, spending increased and the recession ended.

The pattern of rising real money balances and rising real interest rates contributed to ending recession in 1937–38 and 1948–49. This dynamic did not work to restore prosperity in 1929–33 because the Federal Reserve allowed the nominal stock of money to decline so much that real money balances fell despite the expansive effect of deflation on the stock of real balances. Bank failures, and fears of additional failures, contributed to the decline in real balances. Efforts to shift from deposits to currency drained reserves from the banking system. The Federal Reserve's failure to offset the loss of reserves added to bank insolvency and brought about the result the public feared.

Theory or beliefs also contributed to the Federal Reserve's reluctance to end pegged interest rates after World War II. Many economists and businessmen claimed that a large outstanding government debt limited the size of permissible interest rate changes. Marriner Eccles, Federal Reserve chairman at the time, repeated frequently that, to be effective, interest rate increases had to be large. Large increases, however, imposed large losses on debt owners (with gains to the Treasury). Unwilling to impose large losses, Eccles sought other ways to reduce spending growth.

His proposals show the absence of careful analysis at the time. Eccles often favored higher reserve requirement ratios, secondary reserve requirements to force banks to hold more (low yield) Treasury bills, and controls requiring higher down payments and shorter duration of consumer loans. With interest rates fixed (or pegged), increases in reserve requirement ratios transferred incomes from banks to the government. Banks sold securities to meet the additional requirement. To keep interest rates unchanged, the Federal Reserve supplied the additional reserves by buying the securities that banks sold.

Congress never agreed to secondary reserve requirements. Such requirements would force banks to hold more government securities, reducing their profits. With unchanged growth of base money and government debt, the total supply of credit would remain unchanged. Portfolio composition of the principal institutions would differ. Banks would own more Treasury bills; other lenders would acquire loans that the banks would forgo.

The Federal Reserve was not alone in these errors. Many in the academic profession, and other economists, made similar statements.

The Federal Reserve had some notable successes during its first four decades. Evidence of success and acceptance was the agreement in 1927 to replace the Federal Reserve's twenty-year charter with a permanent one. The new charter evoked little of the passion and attention so much in evidence in 1913. The relatively stable price level and stable interest rates from 1922 to 1929 lay behind acceptance of the Federal Reserve and its increased congressional support. Strict adherents to the real bills doctrine criticized the use of open market operations to supplement discounting of real bills. They saw open market operations as a departure from the letter and spirit of the law. These criticisms found little congressional support as long as the System avoided major recessions or a return of financial crises accompanied by failures and surging interest rates.

Before 1914, United States interest rates rose sharply during the scramble for liquidity that became a standard feature of a financial panic. The Federal Reserve avoided financial panics between 1914 and 1928. Interest rates rose much less in the 1920–21, 1923–24, and 1926–27 recessions than in the 1890s or in 1907–8. Also, before 1914 interest rates had a large seasonal element. The Federal Reserve removed the seasonal swing using discount policy and acceptance and open market purchases. This fulfilled one of the founders' main reasons for creating the institution.

The Federal Reserve helped to finance both world wars; it provided credit and money by lending to commercial banks at fixed interest rates or by open market purchases. In addition, the System acted as the principal bond salesman for the Treasury, using its network of regional and branch banks, and its relations with the leading commercial banks, to place the bonds. The Federal Reserve's decision to allow banks to profit from bond sales to the nonbank public gave banks a powerful incentive to cooperate in the financing.

During the 1920s, the System undertook pathbreaking research and the development of new statistical series to support its work. The absence of an operative gold standard immediately after World War I, and widespread criticism of discount policy and discount rates in the 1920–21 recession, encouraged consideration of operating procedures and market signals about the need for policy action. Concern for market signals, in turn, required the development of new data series and fostered the use of new analytical techniques. By the mid-1920s, System economists had constructed measures of production, inventories, department store sales, and other variables. These are the forerunners of the data series that markets and policymakers rely on to this day. Developing these series and combining them required skillful use of index number theory.

In its 1923 annual report, the System discussed a general framework that sought to reconcile the passive stance implied by the real bills doctrine with more active use of open market operations. The new framework tried to achieve the Bank of England's control of discounting without relying very much on the discount rate. Also, it tried to satisfy both advocates of the real bills doctrine and their opponents. Subsequently, economists at the Board and the New York bank developed a more explicit framework to guide policy decisions. This framework, though based on observations by many people, was mainly the work of Winfield Riefler and W. Randolph Burgess. Their work implied that the Federal Reserve could control the volume of member bank borrowing with fewer and smaller changes in interest rates. Open market purchases supplied reserves and encouraged banks to repay borrowing, offer more loans, and reduce interest rates; open market sales drove banks to borrow, restrict lending, and raise interest rates. The emphasis satisfied real bills advocates. Quantitative control through the use of open market operations satisfied Strong and others who no longer believed that the quality of credit restricted the quantity.

The new framework brought together open market operations, discounting, discount policy, and credit expansion as part of a theory of central banking. The theory required the strong proposition that banks did not borrow to profit from higher market rates. This proposition removed the need for an unpopular penalty rate, set above the rate on prime commercial paper. Experience in 1928–29, when the Federal Reserve tried to control the volume of discounts without increasing the discount rate, rejected the proposition but failed to change it. Federal Reserve officials continued to claim that banks did not borrow for profit. They found it necessary, however, to inform bankers that borrowing was a privilege and not a right of membership and to impose administrative restrictions to limit the amount and duration of borrowing. This was a long step away from the original idea that the Federal Reserve's main function was to discount for member banks.

The Riefler-Burgess framework combined banks' reluctance to borrow with another proposition that did not distinguish between individual banks and the banking system: "Banks disliked being continuously in debt and hence tended to contract credit when the level of indebtedness was increased and to expand credit when the level of indebtedness was reduced. Because of the tradition against continuous borrowing, when the Federal Reserve System sold securities, the resulting increase in indebtedness tended to cause banks to control credit" (Subcommittee on General Credit Control and Debt Management 1951, 283).

This reasoning does not explain why open market sales would contract total bank credit. Why didn't other banks borrow when an individual bank repaid its indebtedness? The proper answer would have required the Federal Reserve to develop a framework linking its operations to market interest rates and the supply of bank reserves or monetary base.

The tenth annual report and the Riefler-Burgess framework covered over, but did not resolve, differences between opponents and proponents of the real bills doctrine. The conflict emerged first in the 1924 and 1927 recessions when, under the leadership of Benjamin Strong of the New York bank, the System expanded credit and the monetary base both to help the British and to encourage recovery from domestic recessions. The conflict became more open in 1929, when the Board wanted to control borrowing by discouraging speculative credit and New York and some other reserve banks wanted to raise the discount rate.

The Riefler-Burgess framework retained a central role in the Federal Reserve's analysis of monetary developments until the 1950s. The staff adjusted the framework to reflect new developments, notably the increase in excess reserves during the 1930s.

The 1923 annual report, books by Riefler and Burgess, speeches by Strong and Adolph C. Miller (a prominent Board member from 1914 to 1936), and other statements and publications moved toward greater openness about procedures and analysis. Nineteenth-century central banks were secretive about what they did and why they did it. Gold standard rules were known, of course, but central banks often did not follow the rules automatically. One of Bagehot's (1962) main criticisms of the Bank of England in the nineteenth century is that it failed to preannounce its policy response to financial panics. The movement toward transparency was slow, but by the end of the twentieth century, all leading central banks had moved decisively toward greater openness.

Other major accomplishments included extension of the par collection system, development of the payments system, and a national money market. Interest rates and discount rates became more uniform within the country as banks' size increased and new money market instruments were developed. The founders failed in their attempts to create a broad national acceptance market to replace reliance on stock market call loans as a money market instrument. By the 1930s, Treasury bills and certificates served this function. Wartime increases in government debt made the government securities market the market of choice for short-term reserve adjustment. By the 1950s, the government securities market and the market for federal funds (bank reserves) achieved one of the founders' goals in a way they did not envisage. These markets replaced the call money market as the market in which banks adjusted reserve positions. Monetary operations and bank adjustment were freed from dependence on stock market activity.

The lasting achievements of the early years include the development of a high-quality professional staff. Although research on central banking lagged in the 1930s and 1940s, Federal Reserve staff pioneered in research on topics such as the measurement of government deficits and the effects of budget deficits on the economy. In areas such as supervision, regulation, and banking law, Federal Reserve staff made important contributions. Two notable examples are legislation closing the banking system for the 1933 bank holiday and the Banking Act of 1935.

In the early years, international monetary policy was a central bank responsibility. Central bankers dealt with their counterparts abroad. In the 1920s the New York reserve bank and its governor, Benjamin Strong, negotiated and granted loans to foreign central banks to help restore the gold standard and to coordinate actions. Governments borrowed in the marketplace, assisted by investment bankers.

Although central banks attempted policy coordination, the Federal Reserve was explicit that it would not change its course for the benefit of another country if the change required inflation or deflation at home. This restricted the role of coordination. Some economists assign a large role to insufficient policy coordination. They claim that governments could have maintained the gold standard and prevented worldwide deflation and depression by acting together in the 1920s and 1930s.

This claim neglects exchange rate misalignment, particularly the misalignment of real exchange rates. Lending and borrowing or simultaneous intervention in exchange markets had a limited role at best. In the 1920s, countries on the gold standard had to accept inflation or deflation to adjust real exchange rates. Surplus countries would not inflate; deficit countries were reluctant to deflate after the mid-1920s. The remaining solution was to devalue or revalue against gold and other currencies. Britain left the gold standard in 1931. Other countries followed.

In the 1930s, the Treasury replaced the Federal Reserve as the principal negotiator of international financial agreements. Secretary Henry Morgenthau signed the Tripartite Agreement with Britain and France. The agreement sought to stabilize exchange rates between the three countries, but again real exchange rates were misaligned, and countries followed independent policies. French policy, especially, was inconsistent with the agreement, necessitating devaluations of the franc that violated the spirit of the agreement.

Again in the 1940s, the Treasury negotiated an international monetary agreement. The Bretton Woods Agreement attempted to formalize international policy coordination. Member countries agreed to fix exchange rates but retained the right to devalue (with international approval) to correct structural imbalances. The agreement tried to reconcile domestic and international stability and provide a means by which surplus countries could lend to deficit countries.

The agreement divided the Federal Reserve. The Board sided with the Treasury, favoring the agreement. The leaders of the New York bank opposed. They preferred a return to the gold standard, not adjustable exchange rates. Neither side had much influence on the agreement. The Treasury took control and retained it.

INDEPENDENCE AND CONTROL

The Federal Reserve's independence was so well established in the first twenty years of its existence that President Hoover was reluctant to even ask its advice during the financial crisis at the end of his administration. Within a few years, this independence was lost. From 1934 to 1951, the Treasury Department severely restricted Federal Reserve actions. When William McChesney Martin Jr. became chairman of the Board of Governors in 1951, one of his tasks was to reestablish the independence of the Federal Reserve System from the executive branch, particularly the Treasury.

Independence

One of the anomalies of the 1930s and 1940s is that the Treasury had more influence over the Federal Reserve after the secretary left the Board. Secretary Morgenthau permitted Congress to eliminate his statutory position as chairman of the Federal Reserve Board, but he acquired another means of influencing the Federal Reserve. He held most of the profit from devaluing the dollar against gold in the Exchange Stabilization Fund. He used the

fund, and other Treasury trust funds, to buy and sell gold or foreign exchange, and he could threaten the Federal Reserve with his power to
supply reserves and lower interest rates. Occasionally he did just that.

Morgenthau's threats and influence were not the only reason the System failed to resist Treasury control. Eccles believed that monetary policy
was powerless, since interest rates were at historically low levels. His
greater interest was fiscal policy. He wanted to advise the president and
participate in budget and legislative decisions. His principal interest in
Federal Reserve independence in the 1930s surfaced when Morgenthau
threatened to act in place of the Federal Reserve.

Wartime Treasury influence or control had a different origin. The Federal Reserve agreed in 1942 to finance the war at low nominal interest
rates, as central banks traditionally have done. Regaining independent authority to set interest rates after World War II proved difficult, just as it had
after World War I. Regaining independence of decisions and actions required political support from the administration, the Congress, or the public. Political support began to form in 1949 under the leadership of Senator Paul Douglas. Support strengthened after the Korean War started in
1950. Heavy-handed action by Treasury Secretary John W. Snyder and support for an anti-inflation policy in Congress helped the Federal Reserve get
an agreement that allowed interest rates to rise provided they rose slowly
during the transition to greater independence.

Independence was never thought to be absolute. Independence prevented an administration from deciding unilaterally to use monetary expansion to gain temporary political advantage or to finance too much of the
budget at the central bank. Allan Sproul, president of the New York reserve
bank from 1941 to 1956, recognized the nuances hiding in the term "independence":

> I don't suppose that anyone would still argue that the central banking system
> should be independent of the Government of the country.[1] The control,
> which such a system exercises, over the volume and value of money is a right
> of Government, and is exercised on behalf of Government, with powers del-
> egated by the Government. But there is a distinction between independence
> from Government and independence from political influence in a narrower
> sense. The powers of the central banking system should not be the pawn of
> any group or faction or party, or even any particular administration, subject
> to political pressures and its own passing fiscal necessities. It is clear that in
> war or in any other great emergency, the policy of the central banking system
> must support the national plan of action. It seems to me equally clear that in

1. The European Monetary System suggests that this statement is no longer true.

less emergent circumstances it is wise for government to set-up barriers or buffers of protection of the central banking system from narrow political influence. (Letter to Robert R. Bowie, Sproul Papers, Memorandums and Drafts, September 1, 1948, 2)

This statement of general principles seems well crafted. However, it does not say what happens if the government and the Federal Reserve disagree about the importance of the emergency. Secretary Snyder argued that "the President has the right, and the duty, to discuss disputes without attempting to dictate to the Board of Governors but by full and complete consultation with the Board" (Subcommittee on General Credit Control and Debt Management, Answers to Questions 1951, 31).

The secretary also favored creating a "discussion group" consisting of the secretary of the treasury, the chairman of the Board of Governors, the director of the budget, the chairman of the Council of Economic Advisers, and the chairman of the Securities and Exchange Commission (ibid., 31).[2] The Federal Reserve's statement did not mention a coordinating body. It favored a more independent role. When conflicts arise "each agency involved shares the responsibility for finding ways to resolve the conflict" (264).

The meaning assigned to "independence" did not progress much subsequently. Resolution of its conflict with the Treasury did not settle what a central bank should do if the government ran large or regular deficits in peacetime. FOMC members recognized that Congress approved the spending plan and deficit finance. A central bank could not, and they believed should not try to, reverse congressional decisions. But that appeal to democratic rule did not answer the question, How much should the central bank raise interest rates, or permit them to increase? It took years of sustained inflation to force attention to that question. In the 1950s the Federal Reserve hoped it could avoid the issue by joining a coordinating body of the four leading economic agencies known as the quadriad during the Kennedy administration. The quadriad continued through the early 1970s until replaced by less formal arrangements.

In both world wars, the Federal Reserve surrendered its independence to assist in war finance. Each time it found that regaining independence

---

2. The Treasury also pointed out that section 10 of the 1913 Federal Reserve Act gave the Treasury power to override the Board in the event of conflict (Subcommittee on General Credit Control and Debt Management 1951, 28). The wording is: "Wherever any power vested by this Act in the Federal Reserve Board or the Federal Reserve agent appears to conflict with the powers of the Secretary of the Treasury, such powers shall be exercised subject to the supervision and control of the Secretary" (Krooss 1969, 4:2450). The section protects the Treasury against any interpretation of the Federal Reserve Act that limited the Treasury's authority. The Treasury's interpretation seems extreme.

was difficult and long delayed. It did not learn from its experience after World War I to negotiate an end to pegged interest rates before it made a commitment in 1942. It did not foresee that raising interest rates would be unpopular after the war. It worked hard to gain public support for independence among journalists, academics, bankers, and the public, and within the government by undertaking unpopular duties that Congress and the executive branch did not want to do. Only after the Korean War started and concern about inflation rose did the Federal Reserve muster the popular and congressional support necessary to sustain an independent policy.

Control

President Wilson's compromise, establishing semiautonomous reserve banks and a supervisory Federal Reserve Board, did not resolve the issue of control. Conflicts arose not only because the act dispersed control but because, from the start, officials had different ideas about how the new System should function. New York bankers especially wanted a central bank, under their leadership. The Board often tried to stretch the term "supervise" until it meant "decide."

Benjamin Strong avoided the Board's control by responding to the interests of other reserve banks. Several of the governors thought of their activity as banking, and they wanted their banks to profit. The act granted a dividend on the shares held by member banks, so earnings had to be sufficient to pay the dividend. In the early years some reserve banks—particularly the smaller banks in predominantly agricultural regions—did not have enough discounted paper to pay expenses and the dividend. Strong offered to pool the income on acceptances and then on government securities. By adjusting the allocation formula, he helped the smaller banks solve their problem. In return, they supported his decisions.

In 1919 the Board was able to get the acting attorney general to interpret its power to include changing discount rates even if a reserve bank opposed the change. The Board used the power again in 1927 when it ordered Chicago to reduce its rate.

By the mid-1920s, discounting had a much-reduced role compared with the original plan. Open market operations became the instrument of choice for affecting interest rates and member bank borrowing. Board members could reject the reserve banks' decision, but they could not order the banks to buy or sell. That decision remained with the directors until changed by the 1935 act. The 1935 act not only placed all Board members on the Federal Open Market Committee, for the first time it gave the Board a majority of the votes.

During the years of depression and war, the Board was slow to use its powers. Regular open market operations did not begin until the Federal Reserve was again independent.

In 1927 Strong decided to help Britain remain on the gold standard by lowering interest rates, without first consulting the Board or other governors. The Board and some of the governors later concluded that Strong erred. They blamed the decision for the stock market boom and blamed Strong for the mistake. The Banking Act of 1933 stripped New York of its dominant role. After devaluation of the dollar, control shifted to the Treasury.

WHAT REMAINED IN 1951?

Much of the original plan and organization did not survive to 1951. Gold remained part of reserves, but the dollar, not gold, became the world currency. The Federal Reserve neither thought nor acted as if interest rates and money creation depended on capital flows. Monetary policy became discretionary. In the 1920s the Federal Reserve sterilized part of the gold inflows. In the 1950s it ignored them as a reason for policy action. Increasingly, domestic objectives became the main guide to action.

Vestiges of the real bills doctrine remained part of Federal Reserve thinking. Credit controls such as regulation of down payment requirements and length of loan reflected the mistaken idea that the Federal Reserve could control inflation and the quantity of money by controlling the type or quality of credit. Later these ideas faded away, encouraged both by the difficulty of administering controls and by their ineffectiveness as an anti-inflation policy.

Open market operations in government securities had much earlier replaced the discounting of eligible commercial paper as the principal means of intervening. These operations were more efficient. They did not require decisions about what was eligible, and they did not require the Federal Reserve to accept credit risk. The Federal Reserve determined the size and timing of purchases and sales.

One of the Federal Reserve Act's major innovations removed government securities as collateral behind Federal Reserve notes. The intent was to make note issues more "elastic," capable of expanding and contracting with commerce, agriculture, and trade. When borrowing declined in the 1930s, the Federal Reserve had to use more than the required percentage of gold as backing for its notes. The Glass-Steagall Act of 1932 reversed the original innovation by permitting the Federal Reserve to use government securities in place of eligible paper as backing for its note issue. Originally a temporary measure, after several renewals the use of government securities as collateral became permanent. Later, Congress removed the required gold backing.

The change in collateral behind notes symbolizes the decline in the real bills doctrine as a guiding principle. The doctrine required procyclical monetary expansion: the Federal Reserve provided additional currency and reserves as the economy expanded and withdrew currency and reserves in economic contractions. The revised Federal Reserve Act, in 1935, retained "the needs of commerce" as a policy objective but added "the general credit situation." The Employment Act of 1946 did not impose a clear objective on the Federal Reserve, but it emphasized employment and production. Maintaining production and employment required countercyclical policies.

The 1946 legislation suggests the change in public attitudes about the role of government. The change affected the Federal Reserve by endorsing its transformation from a largely passive authority to an activist policymaker. The 1913 Federal Reserve Act gave little scope for discretionary action. By the 1950s, a generation trained in Keynesian analysis rose to prominence at the Federal Reserve and elsewhere in society. Its members believed that budget policy would have the senior role. The role of monetary policy was secondary, supportive of fiscal actions, but useful as a means of keeping interest rates from rising. The emphasis on interest rates fit well with traditional practices.

POLICY LESSONS FROM THE EARLY YEARS

The wide range of monetary experience—wartime inflation, deflation, economic expansion in the 1920s, depression in the 1930s—provides evidence of the relative roles of money and interest rates in the transmission of central bank actions. In some cases money growth falls as interest rates rise or money growth rises as interest rates fall. Since changes in money growth change interest rates, binary comparisons cannot distinguish in these cases whether the transmission of monetary impulses operates principally through changes in interest rates or through changes in money operating through other relative prices and real wealth.

Previous chapters showed that at times interest rates and money growth moved in opposite directions. In 1937–38 and 1947–48, deflation occurred with the short-term interest rate near zero. In both cases the economy recovered without much expansive action by the Federal Reserve. Deflation increased real money balances and real interest rates. The increase in real money balances dominated the effect of the higher real interest rate; output and economic activity increased. These experiences contradict the be-

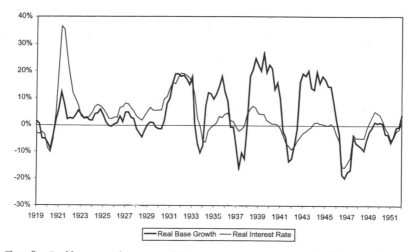

Chart 8.1 Real base growth versus real interest rate, 1919.1 to 1952.1. Real base growth measured year over year.

lief that monetary policy becomes ineffective when the short-term interest rate remains close to zero.

The 1920–22 experience was similar. The short-term interest rate was not zero in this case, but the economy experienced severe deflation. As prices fell, real balances and real interest rates rose. Falling prices also attracted gold from abroad, increasing the monetary base. The ex post real interest rate on government bonds reached 37 percent at its peak. Nevertheless, economic activity and output recovered, consistent with the increase in real balances but contrary to the rise in the real interest rate.

Chart 8.1 shows changes of the real monetary base and the real interest rate during most of the early Federal Reserve history. Growth of the base is measured year to year. The year-to-year change in the GDP deflator measures the rate of price change subtracted from the Treasury long-term rate to convert nominal rates to real rates. The very high real interest rates in 1921 and 1931–32 reflect the severe deflation at these times.

Real base growth is negative before the Great Depression and in its early years. Ex post real interest rates were comparatively high, above the average for the period shown in chart 8.1 but consistent with cyclical peaks in the 1920s. Both measures suggest that monetary policy was restrictive in 1928–29, contrary to the interpretation made at the time. The data for the late 1920s suggest that a productivity-based expansion, as industry adopted new technologies, was ended at least partly by a deflationary monetary policy.

At the start of the depression, real base growth remained low and ex post real interest rates rose. Base growth rose in 1931 and remained high under the impact of the currency drain. The real interest rate is a better predictor than real base growth for this exceptional period.[3]

Notable also is the collapse of real base growth in 1937 and renewed expansion in 1938. The real interest rate and real base growth moved together in the early postwar years. The common movement reflects the rate of price change, highly positive in 1946, modestly negative in 1948–49, briefly positive at the start of the Korean War in 1950–51. After each of these periods, economic activity moved in the direction implied by base growth.

We can summarize these data in three propositions:

Proposition 1: when growth of real balances rises sharply, expansion follows whatever happens to the real interest rate. Some examples are 1921, 1934–36, 1939–41, and 1943–45. An exception is 1931–33.

Proposition 2: when real balances decline, or their growth is comparatively slow, the economy goes into recession even if the real interest rate is comparatively low or negative. Examples are 1920, 1923, 1926, 1929, 1933, 1937, and 1947. An exception is 1941.

Proposition 3: if the real interest rate is comparatively high, the economy expands if real balances rise and does not expand if they fall. Examples are 1921, 1925, 1927, and 1938–39. Again, 1931–33 is an exception.

These comparisons suggest that the Federal Reserve erred by ignoring the information in the growth rates of real and nominal balances. For short periods, changes in real balances may have little information. The data suggest, however, that attention to money growth would have enabled the Federal Reserve to avoid its largest errors.

The errors the Federal Reserve made in the years 1913 to 1951 were not unique to the System. The few critics of the real bills doctrine and the gold standard were out of step with the dominant views of the period. Many shared the belief that the Federal Reserve could not have prevented the Great Depression or reduced its duration. Historically low nominal interest rates were considered relevant evidence. The view that monetary policy was akin to "pushing on a string" antedates Keynes's liquidity trap.

Similarly, many bankers and economists as well as ordinary citizens believed that the gold standard was the correct way to harmonize international monetary policy. Efforts to restore the gold standard in the 1920s,

3. The real money stock, M_1/p, fell.

and to fix exchange rates within a gold-based system, met little opposition. Many opponents of the Bretton Woods Agreement criticized its differences from a gold standard.

The gradual dissemination of Keynesian ideas in the 1940s slowly transformed the consensus view. Keynes's emphasis on the role of interest rates and neglect of money fit well with the views widely held by central bankers and in time displaced them. The change to activist, discretionary monetary policy that produced the Great Inflation of the 1970s had not yet occurred by 1951, but important changes had been made. The Federal Reserve gained scope for a more independent, discretionary policy. The United States had an ample supply of gold and, like other parts of the government, a mandate to maintain a high level of employment.

Increasingly, the public looked to government to manage the economy. Within a few years, governments would look to their central bankers to take a leading role in making the macroeconomic policies that first produced the Great Inflation and then learned how to control it.

The shift toward government responsibility required a change in the intellectual consensus on two issues: the roles of gold and government budget deficits. Although some populists opposed the gold standard in the nineteenth century, by 1900 most contemporary opinion in the industrial countries, and many others, viewed the gold standard as the proper way to restrict monetary policy and prevent long-term inflation. The gold standard was a main issue in several presidential elections in the United States. Each time, the gold standard candidate won.

This consensus no longer existed in the 1950s. The population had become more urban and more educated, the country more industrialized, and the workforce more unionized. The public in many countries favored policies that stabilized output, even if the currency value changed.

The belief that balanced budgets should be the norm except in wartime gave way to a loose commitment to cyclically balanced budgets. When private spending declined, government deficits could replace private spending until employment rose.

Weak attachment to the old standards of financial rectitude left the financial system without a belief system that central bankers could appeal to. The new consensus eliminated what had gone before without offering a clear set of rules. At the next stage in the evolution of central banks and governments, the major problem was to learn how to operate in the new, more discretionary environment.

REFERENCES

Ackley, Gardiner. 1961. *Macroeconomic theory.* New York: Macmillan.

Aftalion, Albert. 1931. *Selected documents on the distribution of gold.* Geneva: League of Nations.

Anderson, Clay. 1965. *A half century of Federal Reserve policymaking.* Philadelphia: Federal Reserve Bank.

———. 1966. *Evolution of the role and functioning of the discount mechanism.* Steering Committee for the Fundamental Reappraisal of the Discount Mechanism. Washington, D.C.: Board of Governors of the Federal Reserve System.

Anderson, Gary, William F. Shughart II, and Robert Tollison. 1988. A public choice theory of the great contraction. *Public Choice,* October, 3–23.

Anderson, Richard G., and Robert H. Rasche. 1999. Eighty years of observations on the adjusted monetary base. *Review* (Federal Reserve Bank of St. Louis) 81 (January–February): 3–22.

Arndt, H. W. 1966. *The economic lessons of the nineteen thirties.* New York: Kelley.

Awalt, Francis G. 1969. Recollections of the banking crisis in 1933. *Business History Review* 43 (autumn): 347–71.

Bach, George L. 1967. Criteria for the conduct of monetary policy. In *Monetary process and policy: A symposium,* ed. G. Horwich. Homewood, Ill.: Richard D. Irwin.

———. 1971. *Making monetary and fiscal policy.* Washington, D.C.: Brookings Institution.

Bagehot, Walter. 1962. *Lombard Street: A Description of the Money Market.* 1873. Reprint, Homewood, Ill.: Richard D. Irwin.

Bailey, Stephen K. 1950. *Congress makes a law: The story behind the Employment Act of 1946.* New York: Columbia University Press.

Balke, Nathan S., and Robert J. Gordon. 1986. Historical data. In *The american business cycle: Continuity and change,* ed. Robert J. Gordon, 781–850. Chicago: University of Chicago Press for the National Bureau of Economic Research.

Barber, William J. 1996. *Designs within disorder: Franklin D. Roosevelt, the economists, and the shaping of American economic policy, 1933–1945.* Cambridge: Cambridge University Press.

Barger, Harold. 1942. *Outlay and income in the United States, 1921–1938.* New York: National Bureau of Economic Research.

Barro, Robert J., and Chaipat Sahasakul. 1983. Measuring the average marginal tax rate from the individual income tax. *Journal of Business* 56 (October): 419–52.

Baruch, Bernard M. 1933. Statement. In *Investigation of economic problems.* Hearings before the Committee on Finance, United States Senate, part 1, February 13 and 14. Washington, D.C.: Government Printing Office.

Beckhart, Benjamin H. 1972. *Federal Reserve System*. New York: American Institute of Banking.

Benston, George J. 1964. Interest payments on demand deposits and bank investment behavior. *Journal of Political Economy* 72 (October): 431–49.

———. 1990. *The separation of investment and commercial banking*. London: Macmillan.

Berg, Claes, and Lars Jonung. 1998. Pioneering price level targeting: The Swedish experience, 1931–37. Paper presented at the Conference on Monetary Policy Rules, Stockholm, June.

Bernanke, Ben. 1983. Nonmonetary effects of the financial crisis in the propagation of the Great Depression. *American Economic Review* 73 (June): 257–76.

———. 1994. The macroeconomics of the Great Depression: A comparative approach. *Journal of Money, Credit, and Banking* 27 (1): 1–28.

Bernanke, Ben, and Harold James. 1991. The gold standard, deflation, and financial crisis in the Great Depression: An international comparison. In *Financial markets and financial crises*, ed. R. G. Hubbard, 33–68. Chicago: University of Chicago Press.

Bernstein, Edward M., and Stanley W. Black. 1991. *A Levite among the priests: Edward M. Bernstein and the origin of the Bretton Woods system*. Boulder, Colo.: Westview Press.

Blum, John M. 1959. *From the Morgenthau diaries: Years of crisis, 1928–1938*. Boston: Houghton Mifflin.

———. 1965. *From the Morgenthau diaries: Years of urgency, 1938–1941*. Boston: Houghton Mifflin.

———. 1967. *From the Morgenthau diaries: Years of war, 1941–1945*. Boston: Houghton Mifflin.

Board Minutes. See Board of Governors of the Federal Reserve System. Various dates. Board Minutes.

Board of Governors File. See Board of Governors of the Federal Reserve System. 1913–54.

Board of Governors of the Federal Reserve System. Various dates. *Annual report*. Washington, D.C.: Government Printing Office.

———. Various dates. Board Minutes. Unpublished. Cited in text as Board Minutes.

———. Various dates. Minutes of the Open Market Committee. Unpublished. Washington, D.C., Library, Board of Governors of the Federal Reserve System.

———. 1913–54. Central subject file. Washington, D.C., National Archives II. Unpublished. Cited in text as Board of Governors File.

———. 1943. *Banking and monetary statistics*. Washington, D.C.: Board of Governors of the Federal Reserve System.

———. 1945. *Postwar economic studies*, August.

———. 1947. *The Federal Reserve System: Its purposes and functions*. 2d ed. Washington, D.C.: Board of Governors of the Federal Reserve System.

———. 1959. *The federal funds market*. Washington, D.C.: Board of Governors of the Federal Reserve System.

———. [1962?] *Industrial Production 1957–59 Base*. Washington, D.C.: Board of Governors of the Federal Reserve System.

———. Various dates. Weekly review of periodicals. Unpublished.

———. 1976. *Banking and monetary statistics, 1941–1970*. Washington, D.C.: Board of Governors of the Federal Reserve System.

Bomhoff, Eduard. 1983. *Monetary uncertainty*, Amsterdam: North-Holland.

Bordo, Michael. 1994. Review of *Golden Fetters*. *Journal of International Economics*, February, 193–97.

Bordo, Michael, Ehsan Chaudri, and Anna Schwartz. 1995. Could stable money have averted the great contraction? *Economic Inquiry*, July, 484–505.

Bordo, Michael, and Barry Eichengreen, eds. 1993. *A retrospective on the Bretton Woods system:*

Lessons for international monetary reform. Chicago: University of Chicago Press for the National Bureau of Economic Research.

Bordo, Michael, Christopher Erceg, and Charles Evans. 1997. Money, sticky wages and the Great Depression. Working Paper 6021. National Bureau of Economic Research, June.

Bordo, Michael, and Angela Redish. 1988. Costs and benefits of exchange rate stability. *Contemporary Policy Issues* 6 (April).

Bordo, Michael, and Anna J. Schwartz, eds. 1984. *A retrospective on the classical gold standard, 1821–1931.* Chicago: University of Chicago Press for the National Bureau of Economic Research.

Brazelton, W. Robert. 1997. Retrospectives: The economics of Leon Hirsch Keyserling. *Journal of Economic Perspectives* 11 (autumn): 189–97.

Brown, William A. 1940. *The international gold standard reinterpreted, 1914–34,* vol. 1. New York: National Bureau of Economic Research.

Brunner, Karl. 1968. Introduction. In *Supply and control of money in the United States,* by Lauchlin Currie. 1934. Reprint, New York: Russell and Russell.

———, ed. 1981. *The Great Depression revisited.* Boston: Martinus Nijhoff.

Brunner, Karl, and A. H. Meltzer. 1964a. Evolving Federal Reserve conceptions concerning the money supply process. Unpublished. Carnegie Mellon University.

———. 1964b. *The Federal Reserve's attachment to the free reserve concept.* Washington, D.C.: House Committee on Banking and Currency. Reprinted in *Monetary economics,* ed. Karl Brunner and A. H. Meltzer. London: Blackwell, 1989.

———. 1968a. Liquidity traps for money, bank credit and interest rates. *Journal of Political Economy* 76 (January–February): 1–37.

———. 1968b. What did we learn from the monetary experiences of the United States in the Great Depression? *Canadian Journal of Economics* 1:334–48.

———. 1976. An aggregative theory for a closed economy. In *Monetarism,* ed. Jerome L. Stein, 69–103. Amsterdam: North-Holland.

———. 1993. *Money and the economy: Issues in monetary analysis.* Cambridge: Cambridge University Press for the Raffaele Mattioli Foundation.

Bureau of the Census. 1960. *Historical statistics of the United States.* Washington, D.C.: Government Printing Office.

Burgess, W. Randolph. 1936. *The Reserve banks and the money market.* 2d ed. New York: Harper.

———. 1964. Reflections on the early development of open market policy. *Monthly Review* (Federal Reserve Bank of New York), November, 219–26.

Cagan, P. 1965. *Determinants and effects of changes in the stock of money, 1875–1960.* New York: Columbia University Press for the National Bureau of Economic Research.

Calomiris, Charles W. 1993. Financial factors in the Great Depression. *Journal of Economic Perspectives* 7 (spring): 61–85.

———. 1997. Statement. Subcommittee on Financial Institutions and Regulatory Relief, Senate Committee on Banking, Housing and Urban Affairs, March 20.

Calomiris, Charles W., and Joseph Mason. 1997. Contagion and bank failures during the Great Depression: The June 1932 Chicago banking panic. *American Economic Review* 87 (December): 863–83.

———. 2000. Causes of U.S. bank distress during the Great Depression. Working Paper 7919. National Bureau of Economic Research, September.

Calomiris, Charles W., and David Wheelock. 1996. The neutrality of reserve requirement changes in the 1930s. Photocopy, School of Business, Columbia University.

Calomiris, Charles W., and Eugene N. White. 1994. The origins of federal deposit insurance. In *The regulated economy: A historical approach to political economy,* ed. Claudia Goldin and Gary D. Libecap, 145–88. Chicago: University of Chicago Press for the National Bureau of Economic Research.

Cecchetti, G. 1988. The case of the negative nominal interest rates: New estimates of the term structure of interest rates during the Great Depression. *Journal of Political Economy* 96 (November–December): 1111–41.

Chandler, Lester. 1958. *Benjamin Strong, central banker.* Washington, D.C.: Brookings Institution.

Chernow, Ron. 1993. Father of the Fed. *Audacity,* fall, 34–45.

CHFRS. See Committee on the History of the Federal Reserve System.

Clapham, John. 1944. *The Bank of England: A history.* Cambridge: Cambridge University Press.

———. 1945. *The Bank of England: A history.* Cambridge: Cambridge University Press.

Clarke, Stephen V. O. 1967. *Central bank cooperation: 1924–31.* New York: Federal Reserve Bank of New York.

Clay, Henry. 1957. *Lord Norman.* London: Macmillan.

Coelho, P., and G. J. Santoni. 1991. Regulatory capture and the monetary contraction of 1932: A comment on Epstein and Ferguson. *Journal of Economic History,* March, 182–89.

Cole, Harold, and Lee Ohanian. 1999. The Great Depression in the United States from a neoclassical perspective. *Quarterly Review* (Federal Reserve Bank of Minneapolis), winter, 2–24.

Committee on the History of the Federal Reserve System. 1954–55. Memoranda concerning the history and source materials. CHFRS, unpublished memoranda. Washington, D.C., Brookings Institution.

Committee on the Working of the Monetary System. 1959. *Report.* London: Her Majesty's Stationery Office.

Cox, Charles C. 1981. Monopoly explanations of the Great Depression and public policies toward business. In *The Great Depression revisited,* ed. Karl Brunner, 174–207. Boston: Martinus Nijhoff.

Crabbe, Leland. 1989. The international gold standard and U.S. monetary policy from World War I to the New Deal. *Federal Reserve Bulletin,* June, 423–39.

Currie, Lauchlin. 1934. The failure of monetary policy to prevent the depression of 1929–32. *Journal of Political Economy* 42 (April): 145–77.

———. 1968. *The supply and control of money in the United States.* With *A proposed revision of the monetary system of the United States,* submitted to the secretary of the Treasury, September 1934. New York: Russell and Russell.

———. 1971. Letter to Alan Sweezy, August 5. Unpublished.

Darby, Michael R. 1976. Three-and-a-half million U.S. employees have been mislaid, or An explanation of unemployment, 1934–41. *Journal of Political Economy* 84 (February): 1–16.

D'Arista, Jane W. 1994. *The evolution of U.S. finance.* Vol. 1, *Federal Reserve monetary policy, 1915–35.* Armonk, N.Y.: M. E. Sharpe.

Dominguez, Kathryn. 1993. The role of international organizations in the Bretton Woods system. In *A retrospective on the Bretton Woods system: Lessons for international monetary reform,* ed. Michael Bordo and Barry Eichengreen, 357–97. Chicago: University of Chicago Press for the National Bureau of Economic Research.

Dornbusch, Rudiger, and Jacob A. Frenkel. 1984. The gold standard and the Bank of England in the crisis of 1847. In *A retrospective on the classical gold standard,* ed. Michael D. Bordo and Anna J. Schwartz, 233–64. Chicago: University of Chicago Press for the National Bureau of Economic Research.

Dowd, Kevin. 1991. The evolution of central banking in England, 1821–90. In *Unregulated banking: Chaos or order?* ed. Forrest Capie and Geoffrey E. Wood. London: Macmillan.

Dunne, G. T. 1963. A Christmas present for the president. *Business Horizons,* winter.

Dykes, Ellen S., and Michael Whitehouse. 1989. The establishment and evolution of the Federal Reserve Board: 1913–23. *Federal Reserve Bulletin,* April, 227–42.

Eccles, Marriner. 1933. Testimony. In *Investigation of economic problems.* Hearings before the

Senate Finance Committee, February 13 and 14. Washington, D.C.: Government Printing Office.

———. 1934–37. *Addresses, statements, and letters of Marriner S. Eccles*. Washington, D.C. Board of Governors of the Federal Reserve System.

———. 1951. *Beckoning frontiers: Public and personal recollections*. New York: Alfred A. Knopf.

Economic Almanac. 1953–54. *Public Finance*, 530–31.

Eichengreen, Barry. 1992. *Golden fetters: The gold standard and the Great Depression*. New York: Oxford.

Eichengreen, Barry, and Peter M. Garber. 1991. Before the US accord: US monetary-financial policy, 1945–51. In *Financial markets and financial crises*, ed. R. Glenn Hubbard, 175–205. Chicago: University of Chicago Press.

Epstein, G., and T. Ferguson. 1984. Monetary policy, loan liquidation, and industrial conflict: The Federal Reserve and open market operations of 1932. *Journal of Economic History*, December, 957–83.

Fallick, Bruce C., and Kevin A. Hassett. 1998. Investment and union certification. *Journal of Labor Economics* 17 (July): 570–82.

Federal Open Market Committee (FOMC). See Board of Governors of the Federal Reserve System. Various dates. Minutes of the Open Market Committee.

Federal Reserve Agents Conference. Various dates. Washington, D.C., Board of Governors of the Federal Resesrve System. Unpublished.

Federal Reserve Bank of Boston. 1928–31. *Proceedings of the annual meeting of stockholders*. Boston: Federal Reserve Bank, November.

Federal Reserve Bank of New York. Various dates. Minutes of directors' meetings. Federal Reserve Bank of New York. Cited in text as Minutes, New York Directors.

Federal Reserve Board. See Board of Governors of the Federal Reserve System.

Federal Reserve Governors Conference. Various dates. Washington, D.C., Board of Governors of the Federal Reserve System. Unpublished. Cited in text as Governors Conference.

Feinstein, Charles H., Peter Temin, and Gianni Toniolo. 1997. *The European economy between the wars*. Oxford: Oxford University Press.

Fforde, John S. 1954. *The Federal Reserve System, 1945–1949*. Oxford: Clarendon Press.

Field, Alexander J. 1984. Asset exchanges and the transaction demand for money, 1919–29. *American Economic Review* 74 (March): 43–59.

Fisher, Irving. 1896. Appreciation and interest. *Publications of the American Economic Association* 9 (4): 331–442.

———. 1920. *The purchasing power of money*. Rev. ed. New York: Macmillan.

———. 1930a. *The stock market crash and after*. New York: Macmillan.

———. 1930b. *The theory of interest*, New York: Macmillan. Reprint, New York: A. M. Kelley, 1961.

———. 1933. The debt-deflation theory of great depressions. *Econometrica* 1 (October): 337–57.

———. 1934. Discussion. *Annals of the American Academy of Political and Social Science*, January, 150–51.

———. 1946. Letter to Clark Warburton dated July 23, 1946. Unpublished.

FOMC. See Board of Governors of the Federal Reserve System. Various dates. Minutes of the Open Market Committee.

Freeman, Richard B. 1998. Spurts in union growth: Defining moments and social processes. in *The defining moments*, ed. Michael D. Bordo, Claudia Goldin, and Eugene N. White. Chicago: University of Chicago Press for the National Bureau of Economic Research.

Fremling, Gertrud. 1985. Did the United States transmit the Great Depression to the rest of the world? *American Economic Review* 75 (December): 1181–85.

Friedman, Milton. 1953. The case for flexible exchange rates. In *Essays on positive economics*, ed. Milton Friedman, 157–203. Chicago: University of Chicago Press.

———. 1992. *Money mischief*. New York: Harcourt, Brace.

————, ed. 1956. *Studies in the quantity theory of money.* Chicago: University of Chicago Press.

Friedman, Milton, and Anna J. Schwartz. 1963. *A monetary history of the United States, 1867–1960.* Princeton: Princeton University Press for the National Bureau of Economic Research.

————. 1970. *Monetary statistics of the United States.* New York: Columbia University Press for the National Bureau of Economic Research.

Frost, Peter A. 1966. The banks' demand for reserves. *Journal of Political Economy* 79 (July–August): 805–25.

Fusfeld, Daniel. 1956. *The economic thought of Franklin D. Roosevelt and the origins of the New Deal.* New York: Columbia University Press.

Galbraith, John Kenneth. 1955. *The great crash, 1929.* Boston: Houghton Mifflin.

Gandolfi, A. E., and J. R. Lothian. 1977. Did monetary forces cause the Great Depression? *Journal of Money, Credit and Banking* 9:679–91.

Gardner, Richard N. 1956. *Sterling-dollar diplomacy.* Oxford: Clarendon Press.

Gayer, Arthur D., W. W. Rostow, and Anna J. Schwartz. 1978. *The growth and fluctuation of the British economy, 1790–1850.* 1953. Reprint, Oxford: Clarendon Press.

Glass, Carter. 1927. *An adventure in constructive finance.* Garden City, N.Y.: Doubleday, Page.

Goldenweiser, Emanuel A. 1951. *American monetary policy.* New York: McGraw-Hill for the Committee for Economic Development.

Golembe, Carter. 1960. The deposit insurance legislation of 1933. *Political Science Quarterly,* June, 181–200.

Gordon, Robert A., and Lawrence R. Klein, eds. 1965. *Readings in business cycles.* Homewood, Ill.: Richard D. Irwin.

Governors Conference. See Federal Reserve Governors Conference.

Greef, Albert O. 1938. *The commercial paper house in the United States.* Cambridge: Harvard University Press.

Hamburger, Michael, and Burton Zwick. 1977. Installment credit controls, consumer expenditures and the allocation of real resources. *Journal of Finance* 32 (December): 1557–69.

————. 1979. The efficacy of selective credit policies: An alternative test. *Journal of Money, Credit, and Banking* 11 (February): 106–10.

Hamilton, James D. 1987. Monetary factors in the Great Depression. *Journal of Monetary Economics* 19:145–69.

Hansen, Alvin H. 1938. *Full recovery or stagnation.* New York: W. W. Norton.

Hardy, Charles O. 1932. *Credit policies of the Federal Reserve System.* Washington, D.C.: Brookings Institution.

Harris, Seymour E. 1933. *Twenty years of Federal Reserve policy.* 2 vols. Cambridge: Harvard University Press.

————. 1943. Introduction. In *Postwar economic problems,* ed. Seymour E. Harris, 1–7. New York: McGraw-Hill.

Harrison, George L. Various dates. The George L. Harrison Papers. Unpublished. Department of Special Collections, Columbia University and Archives, Federal Reserve Bank of New York.

Haubrich, J. G. 1990. Nonmonetary effects of financial crises: Lessons from the Great Depression. *Journal of Monetary Economics,* March, 223–52.

Hawtrey, Ralph. 1924. The tenth annual report of the Federal Reserve Board. *Economic Journal* 34 (June): 283–86.

————. 1932. *The art of central banking.* London: Longmans.

————. 1962. *A century of bank rate.* New York: Kelley.

Hegeland, Hugo. 1951. *Studies in the quantity theory of money.* Göteborg: Elanders.

Hetzel, Robert L. 1985. The rules versus discretion debate over monetary policy in the 1920s. *Economic Review* (Federal Reserve Bank of Richmond) 71 (November–December): 3–14.

———. 1987. Henry Thornton: Seminal monetary theorist and father of the modern central bank. *Economic Review* (Federal Reserve Bank of Richmond) 73 (July–August): 3–16.

Higgs, Robert. 1997. Regime uncertainty: Why the Great Depression lasted so long and why prosperity resumed after the war. *Independent Review* 1 (spring): 561–90.

Hoover, Herbert. 1952. *The Great Depression: 1929–1941.* Vol. 3 of *The memoir of Herbert Hoover.* New York: Macmillan.

House Committee on Banking and Currency. 1922–23. *Stabilization of purchasing power of money.* 67th Cong., 4th sess. Washington, D.C.: Government Printing Office.

———. 1926. *Hearings: Stabilization.* Washington, D.C.: Government Printing Office.

———. 1928. *Stabilization.* H.R. 11806, 69th Cong., 1st sess. Washington, D.C.: Government Printing Office.

———. 1935. *Hearings on the Banking Act of 1935.* 74th Cong., 1st sess. Washington, D.C.: Government Printing Office.

———. 1946. 1946 Extension of the Emergency Price Control and Stabilization Acts of 1942, as amended. February 25, 169–208.

———. 1948. *Inflation control.* Hearing on S.J. Res. 157 (July 29–August 4). Washington, D.C.: Government Printing Office.

Howson, Susan. 1975. *Domestic monetary management in Britain, 1919–38.* Cambridge: Cambridge University Press.

Hyman, Sidney. 1976. *Marriner S. Eccles: Private entrepreneur and public servant.* Stanford: Graduate School of Business, Stanford University.

Ibbotson, Roger, and Rex Sinquefeld. 1989. *Stocks, bonds, bills, and inflation: Historical returns, 1926–1987.* Charlottesville, Va.: Institute of Chartered Financial Analysts.

Ikenberry, G. John. 1993. The political origins of Bretton Woods. In *A retrospective on the Bretton Woods system: Lessons for international monetary reform,* ed. Michael Bordo and Barry Eichengreen, 155–82. Chicago: University of Chicago Press for the National Bureau of Economic Research.

James, Harold. 1996. *International monetary cooperation since Bretton Woods.* Washington, D.C.: International Monetary Fund; New York: Oxford University Press.

Joint Commission of Agricultural Inquiry. 1921. *The 1920 recession.* 67th Cong., 1st sess. Washington, D.C.: Government Printing Office.

Joint Committee on the Economic Report. 1948. *Joint economic report.* 80th Cong., 2d sess. (May 18). Washington, D.C.: Government Printing Office.

Jones, Byrd L. 1972. The role of Keynesians in wartime policy and postwar planning. *American Economic Review, Papers and Proceedings* 62 (May): 125–33.

Kaldor, Nicholas. 1982. *The scourge of monetarism.* London: Oxford University Press.

Kane, Edward J. 1977. Good intentions and unintended evil: The case against selective credit allocation. *Journal of Money, Credit, and Banking* 9 (February): 55–69.

Kane, Edward J., and Berry Wilson. 1998. A contracting-theory interpretation of the origins of deposit insurance. *Journal of Money, Credit and Banking* 30 (3, pt. 2): 573–95.

Katz, Bernard S., ed. 1992. *Biographical dictionary of the Board of Governors of the Federal Reserve System.* New York: Greenwood.

Keech, William. 1995. Central bank independence as a choice variable: The case of the Fed-Treasury accord. Carnegie Mellon University. Unpublished.

Kennedy, Susan E. 1973. *The Banking Act of 1933.* Lexington: University of Kentucky Press.

Kettl, Donald F. 1986. *Leadership at the Fed.* New Haven: Yale University Press.

Keynes, John Maynard. 1924. *Monetary reform.* New York: Harcourt, Brace.

———. 1930. *A treatise on money.* 2 vols. New York: Harcourt, Brace.

———. 1931. *Essays in persuasion.* London: Macmillan.

———. 1936. *The general theory of employment, interest and money.* New York: Harcourt, Brace.

Keyserling, Leon H. 1972. Discussion. *American Economic Review, Papers and Proceedings* 62 (May): 134–38.

Kindleberger, Charles, P. 1986. *The world in depression, 1929–1939.* Rev. ed. Berkeley: University of California Press.

Krooss, Herman. 1969. *Documentary history of banking and currency in the United States.* 4 vols. New York: Chelsea House in Association with McGraw-Hill.

Laidler, David. 1988. British monetary orthodoxy in the 1870s. *Oxford Economic Papers* 40:74–109.

———. 1992. Wage and price stickiness in macroeconomics: An historical perspective. Photocopy. University of Western Ontario.

———. 1993. Hawtrey, Harvard, and the origins of the Chicago tradition. *Journal of Political Economy* 101 (December): 1068–1103.

———. 1999. *Fabricating the Keynesian revolution.* Cambridge: Cambridge University Press.

League of Nations. 1930. *Interim report of the Gold Delegation of the Financial Committee.* Geneva: League of Nations.

———. 1932. *Report of the Gold Delegation of the Financial Committee.* Geneva: League of Nations.

Leffingwell, Russell C. 1921. Discussion. *American Economic Review* 11 (March): 30–36.

Mankiw, N. G., J. A. Miron, and D. N. Weil. 1987. The adjustment of expectations to a change in regime: A study of the founding of the Federal Reserve. *American Economic Review* 77 (June): 358–74.

Margo, Robert A. 1993. Employment and unemployment in the 1930s. *Journal of Economic Perspectives* 7 (spring): 61–86.

Mason, Joseph R. 1994. The determinants and effects of reconstruction finance corporations loans to banks during the Great Depression. Photocopy. University of Illinois.

McCallum, Bennett. 1990. Could a monetary base rule have prevented the Great Depression? *Journal of Monetary Economics* 26 (August): 3–26.

McCalmont, David. 1963. The sharing of gold reserves among Federal Reserve banks. Ph.D. diss., Ohio State University.

McCloskey, Donald N., and J. Richard Zecher. 1984. The success of purchasing power parity: Historical evidence and its implications for macroeconomics. In *A retrospective on the classical gold standard, 1821–1931,* ed. Michael Bordo and Anna J. Schwartz, 121–50. Chicago: University of Chicago Press.

Meltzer, Allan H. 1974. Credit availability and economic decisions: Some evidence from the mortgage and housing markets. *Journal of Finance* 29 (June): 763–78.

———. 1976. Monetary and other explanations of the start of the Great Depression. *Journal of Monetary Economics* 2:455–72.

———. 1987. Limits of short-run stabilization policy: Presidential address to the Western Economic Association. *Economic Inquiry* 25 (January): 1–13.

———. 1988. *Keynes's monetary theory: A different interpretation.* Cambridge: Cambridge University Press.

Meltzer, Allan H., and R. Rasche. 1994. The demand for money revisited. Photocopy. Carnegie Mellon University.

Miller, Adolph C. 1921. Federal Reserve policy. *American Economic Review* 11 (June): 177–206.

———. 1925a. Federal Reserve discount policy and the diversion of credit into speculative channels. *Trust Companies* 41 (November): 589–91.

———. 1925b. Restoration of the British gold standard. In Addresses and statements, vol. 2. Board of Governors of the Federal Reserve System. Multilithed.

———. 1928. Will open market operations be discontinued? *American Bankers Association Journal* 21 (July): 11–12, 75–76.

———. 1931. Statement. In *Operation of the national and Federal Reserve banking system,* Senate Committee on Banking and Currency, January 23.

———. 1935. Responsibility for Federal Reserve policies, 1927–29. *American Economic Review* 25 (September): 442–58.

————. 1936. The Banking Act of 1935. In Addresses and statements, ed. Adolph Miller, vol. 2. Board of Governors of the Federal Reserve System. Multilithed.

Mints, Lloyd, W. 1945. *A history of banking theory*. Chicago: University of Chicago Press.

Minutes, New York Directors. See Federal Reserve Bank of New York. Various dates. Minutes of directors' meetings.

Minutes, Open Market Committee. See Board of Governors of the Federal Reserve System. Various dates. Minutes of the Open Market Committee.

Miron, Jeffrey, A. 1986. Financial panics, the seasonality of the nominal interest rate, and the founding of the Fed. *American Economic Review* 76 (March): 125–40.

Miron, Jeffrey A., and Christina D. Romer. 1989. A new monthly index of industrial production, 1884–1940. Working Paper 3172. National Bureau of Economic Research.

Mishkin, Frederick S. 1976. Illiquidity, consumer durable expenditure, and monetary policy. *American Economic Review* 66 (September): 642–54.

Mitchell, Brian R. 1992. *International historical statistics: Europe, 1750–1988*. 3d ed. New York: Stockton Press.

————. 1993. *International historical statistics: The Americas, 1750–1988*. 2d ed. New York: Stockton Press.

Moley, Raymond. 1939. *After seven years*. New York: Harper.

Moore, Thomas G. 1966. Stock market margin requirements. *Journal of Political Economy* 74 (April): 158–67.

Moreau, Émile. 1954. *Souvenirs d'un gouverneur de la Banque de France*. Paris: Genin, Librairie des Medicis.

Murray, James E. 1945. National policy and program for continuing full employment. *Congressional Record*. 79th Cong., 1st sess., January 22, 1–7.

Myers, Margaret. 1931. *The New York money market: Origins and development*. New York: Columbia University Press.

Nurkse, Ragnar. 1944. *International currency experience*. Geneva: League of Nations.

Ohanian, Lee E. 2001. Why did productivity fall so much during the Great Depression? Staff Report 285, Federal Reserve Bank of Minneapolis.

Parthemos, James. 1990. The Federal Reserve Bank of Richmond: Governor Seay and the issues of the early years. *Economic Review* (Federal Reserve Bank of Richmond) 76 (January–February): 7–17.

Patrick, Sue. 1993. *Reform of the Federal Reserve System in the early 1930s*. New York, Garland.

Patterson, James T. 1972. *Mr. Republican: A biography of Robert A. Taft*. Boston: Houghton Mifflin.

Pearson, F. A., W. I. Myers, and A. R. Gans. 1957. Warren as presidential advisor. *Farm Economics* 211 (December): 5598–5676.

Phillips, Ronnie J. 1995. *The Chicago Plan and New Deal banking reform*. Armonk, N.Y.: M. E. Sharpe.

Presnell, L. S. 1997. What went wrong? The evolution of the IMF, 1941–1961. *Banca Nazionale del Lavoro Quarterly Review* 50:213–39.

Rajan, Raghuram. 1992. A theory of the costs and benefits of universal banking. Working Paper 346. University of Chicago, Center for Research on Security Prices.

Reed, Harold. 1930. *Federal Reserve Policy, 1921–30*, New York: McGraw-Hill.

Reserve Bank Organizing Committee. 1914. *First choice vote for Reserve bank cities*. Washington, D.C.: Government Printing Office.

Riefler, W. W. 1930. *Money rates and money markets in the United States*. New York: Harper.

————. 1956. Open market investment policy, excerpts 1923–31. 2 vols. Washington, D.C., Board of Governors of the Federal Reserve System. Unpublished.

Rist, Charles. 1940. *History of monetary and credit theory from John Law to the Present Day*. Trans. Jane Degras. New York: Macmillan.

Robbins, Lionel. 1934. *The Great Depression*. London: Macmillan.

Robinson, Joan (with F. Wilkinson). 1985. Ideology and logic. In *Keynes's relevance today*, ed. F. Vicarelli, 73–98. Philadelphia: University of Pennsylvania Press.

Rockoff, Hugh. 1993. The meaning of money in the Great Depression. Historical Paper 52, National Bureau of Economic Research, December.

Romer, Christina D. 1992. What ended the Great Depression? *Journal of Economic History* 52 (December): 757–84.

Roose, Kenneth D. 1954. *The economics of recession and revival: An interpretation of 1937–38*. New Haven: Yale University Press.

Rose, Nancy L. 1987. Labor, rent sharing and regulation: Evidence from the trucking industry. *Journal of Political Economy* 95 (December): 1146–78.

Saint-Etienne, Christian. 1984. *The Great Depression, 1929–1938*. Stanford, Calif.: Hoover Institution.

Salant, Walter S. 1948. Memo to Stabilization Devices Committee. Unpublished. Author's files.

Samuelson, Paul A. 1943. Full employment after the war. In *Postwar economic problems*, ed. Seymour E. Harris, 27–55. New York: McGraw-Hill.

Sandilands, Roger J. 1990. *The life and political economy of Lauchlin Currie*. Durham, N.C.: Duke University Press.

Sayers, R. S. 1957. *Central banking after Bagehot*. Oxford: Clarendon Press.

Scammell, W. M. 1968. *The London discount market*, New York: St. Martin's Press.

Schacht, Hjalmar. 1955. *My first seventy-six years*. Trans. Diana Pyke. London: Wingate.

Schumpeter, Joseph A. 1955. *A history of economic analysis*, New York: Oxford University Press.

Schwartz, Anna J. 1982. Statistical compendium to *The report of the Commission on the Role of Gold in the Domestic and International Monetary Systems*. Vol. 1 Washington, D.C.: U.S. Treasury Department.

———. 1987a. Banking school, currency school, free banking school. In *New Palgrave dictionary of economics*. London: Macmillan.

———. 1987b. Real and pseudo financial crises. In *Money in historical perspective*, ed. Anna J. Schwartz, 271–88. Chicago: University of Chicago Press for the National Bureau of Economic Research.

———. 1997. From obscurity to notoriety: A biography of the Exchange Stabilization Fund. Money, Credit and Banking Lecture. *Journal of Money, Credit and Banking* 29 (May): 135–53.

Selgin, George. 1995. The check tax and the great contraction. University of Georgia. Unpublished.

Senate Committee on Banking and Currency. 1931. *Operation of the national and Federal Reserve banking systems*, 71st Cong., 3d sess. Washington, D.C.: Government Printing Office.

———. 1934. *Gold Reserve Act of 1934*. Hearings on S. 2366, January 19–23. Washington, D.C.: Government Printing Office.

———. 1935. *Banking Act of 1935*. Hearings. 74th Cong., 1st sess. Washington, D.C.: Government Printing Office.

——— 1945. *Hearings on H.R. 3314, The Bretton Woods Agreement Act*. Washington, D.C.: Government Printing Office, June 12–28.

Silberling, N. S. 1919. British prices and business cycles, 1779–1850. *Review of Economics and Statistics* 1 (October): 282–97.

Silver, Stephen, and Scott Sumner. 1995. Nominal and real wage cyclicality during the interwar period. *Southern Economic Journal*, January, 588–601.

Sirkin, Gerald. 1975. The stock market of 1929 revisited: A note. *Business History Review* 49 (summer): 223–31.

Sprague, O. M. W. 1921. The discount policy of the Federal Reserve banks. *American Economic Review* 11 (March): 16–29.

Sproul, Allan. Various dates. Files of Allan Sproul, Federal Reserve Bank of New York. Unpublished. Cited in text as Sproul Papers.

———. 1947. Speech to the New Jersey State Bankers Association. *Monthly Review* (Federal Reserve Bank of New York), January, 1–6.

———. 1980. *Selected papers of Allan Sproul.* Ed. Lawrence Ritter. New York: Federal Reserve Bank.

Stein, Herbert. 1969. *The fiscal revolution in America.* Chicago: University of Chicago Press.

———. 1990. *The fiscal revolution in America.* Rev. ed. Washington, D.C.: AEI Press.

Stockwell, Eleanor, ed. 1989. *Working at the Board, 1920–1970.* Washington, D.C.: Board of Governors of the Federal Reserve System.

Strong, Benjamin. 1927. Testimony of Governor Strong. In *Stabilization.* Hearings before the Committee on Banking and Currency, 69th Cong., 1st sess. Washington, D.C.: Government Printing Office.

———. 1930. *Interpretations of Federal Reserve policy in the speeches and writings of Benjamin Strong.* Ed. W. R. Burgess. New York: Harper.

Subcommittee on General Credit Control and Debt Management. 1951. *Questions on general credit control and debt management.* Joint Committee on the Economic Report, 82d Cong., 2d sess. Washington, D.C.: Government Printing Office.

———. 1952. *Monetary policy and the management of the public debt.* 82d Cong., 2d sess. (June 27). Washington, D.C.: Government Printing Office.

Subcommittee on Monetary, Credit, and Fiscal Policies. 1950a. *Monetary, credit, and fiscal policies.* Hearings. Joint Committee on the Economic Report. 81st Cong., 2d sess. (November–December). Washington, D.C.: Government Printing Office.

———. 1950b. *Monetary, credit, and fiscal policies: Report.* Joint Committee on the Economic Report. 81st Cong., 2d sess. Washington, D.C.: Government Printing Office.

Sumner, Scott. 1995. Bold and persistent experimentation: Macroeconomic policy during 1933. Photocopy, Bentley College.

Tallman, Ellis W., and Jon R. Moen. 1990. Lessons from the panic of 1907. *Review* (Federal Reserve Bank of Atlanta) 75 (May–June): 2–13.

———. 1995. Private sector responses to the panic of 1907: A comparison of New York and Chicago. *Economic Review* (Federal Reserve Bank of Atlanta) 80 (March–April): 1–9.

Tavlas, George S. 1997. Chicago, Harvard, and the doctrinal foundations of monetary economics. *Journal of Political Economy* 105 (February): 153–77.

Telser, Lester G. 1996. On the Great Depression. Working Paper 130. Center for the Study of the Economy and the State, University of Chicago.

Temin, Peter. 1976. *Did monetary forces cause the Great Depression?* New York: Norton.

Temple, Alan H. 1928. If I were running the Reserve banks. *Commerce and Finance* 34 (August 22): 1771.

Thomas, Woodlief. 1935. Use of credit in security speculation. *American Economic Review* 25 (March): 21–30.

———. 1941. Money system of the United States. In *Banking studies,* 295–319. Washington, D.C.: Board of Governors of the Federal Reserve System.

Thornton, Henry. 1962. *An inquiry into the nature and effects of the paper credit of Great Britain.* 1802. Reprint, New York: Kelley.

Timberlake, Richard H., Jr. 1978. *The origins of central banking in the United States.* Cambridge: Harvard University Press.

Todd, Walker F. 1994. The Federal Reserve Board before Marriner Eccles (1931–1934). Working Paper. Federal Reserve Bank of Cleveland.

———. 1995. *From constitutional republic to corporate state: The Federal Reserve Board, 1931–1934.* Charlotte, N.C.: Committee for Monetary Research and Education.

Toma, Mark. 1982. Inflationary bias of the Federal Reserve System. *Journal of Monetary Economics* 10:163–90.

————. 1997. *Competition and monopoly in the Federal Reserve System.* Cambridge: Cambridge University Press.

U.S. Department of Commerce, Bureau of the Census. 1966. *Long term economic growth, 1860–1965.* Washington, D.C.: U.S. Department of Commerce.

U.S. Treasury Department. 1915. *Annual report of the secretary of the Treasury for the year 1915.* Washington, D.C.: U.S. Treasury Department.

Upham, Cyril, and Edwin Lamke. 1934. *Closed and distressed banks.* Washington, D.C.: Brookings Institution.

Villard, Henry. 1948. Monetary theory. In *A survey of contemporary economics,* ed. Howard S. Ellis, 314–51. Philadelphia: Blakiston for the American Economic Association.

Viner, Jacob. 1924. *Canada's balance of international indebtedness, 1900–1913.* Cambridge: Harvard University Press.

————. 1965. *Studies in the theory of international trade.* 1937. Chicago: University of Chicago Press. Reprint, New York: Kelley.

Wallace, Robert F. 1956. The use of the progressive discount rate by the Federal Reserve System. *Journal of Political Economy* 64 (February): 59–68.

Warburg, Paul M. 1930. *The Federal Reserve System, its origins and growth.* 2 vols. New York: Macmillan.

Warburton, Clark. 1948. Bank reserves and business fluctuations. *Journal of the American Statistical Association* 43 (December): 547–58.

————. 1966. *Depression, inflation, and monetary policy: Selected papers, 1945–53.* Baltimore: Johns Hopkins University Press.

Weinstein, Michael. 1981. Some macroeconomic impacts of the National Industrial Recovery Act. In *The Great Depression revisited,* ed. Karl Brunner, 262–281. Boston: Martinus Nijhoff.

Westerfield, Ray B. 1933. The Banking Act of 1933. *Journal of Political Economy* 41 (December): 721–49.

Wheelock, David. 1990. Member bank borrowing and the Fed's contractionary monetary policy during the Great Depression. *Journal of Money, Credit and Banking* 22 (November): 409–26.

————. 1992. Monetary policy in the Great Depression: What the Fed did and why. *Review* (Federal Reserve Bank of St. Louis) 74 (March–April): 3–28.

————. 1995. Regulation, market structure, and the bank failures of the Great Depression. *Review* (Federal Reserve Bank of St. Louis) 77 (March): 27–38.

White, Eugene N. 1997. The legacy of deposit insurance: The growth, spread, and cost of insuring financial intermediaries. Working Paper 6063. National Bureau of Economic Research, June.

Wicker, Elmus R. 1965. Federal Reserve monetary policy, 1922–33: A reinterpretation. *Journal of Political Economy* 73 (August): 325–43.

————. 1966. *Federal Reserve monetary policy, 1917–1933.* New York: Random House.

————. 1969. Brunner and Meltzer on Federal Reserve monetary policy during the Great Depression. *Canadian Journal of Economics* 2:318–21.

————. 1996. *The banking panics of the Great Depression.* Cambridge: Cambridge University Press.

————. 2000. The Bagehot-Coe legacy: The role of the New York Clearing House during banking panics. Photocopy, Indiana University, April.

Wicksell, Knut. 1935. *Lectures on political economy.* London: Routledge.

Wood, Elmer. 1939. *English theories of central banking control, 1819–1858.* Cambridge: Harvard University Press.

Yohe, William P. 1982. The mysterious career of Walter W. Stewart, especially 1922–30. *History of Political Economy* 14 (4): 583–607.

————. 1990. The intellectual milieu at the Federal Reserve Board in the 1920s. *History of Political Economy* 22 (3): 465–88.

Young, Allyn A. 1929. Downward price trend probable, due to hoarding of gold by central banks. *Annalist* 33 (January 18): 96–97.

Zarnowitz, Victor, and Geoffrey Moore. 1986. Major changes in cyclical behavior. In *The American business cycle: Continuity and change,* ed. Robert J. Gordon, 519–72. Chicago: University of Chicago Press for the National Bureau of Economic Research.

DATA SOURCES

Discounts and advances: from National Bureau of Economic Research (NBER) Macro History Online Database. Series is "Bills Discounted, Federal Reserve Banks" and is not seasonally adjusted; units are million of dollars. NBER documentation states that the data came from the following sources:

    1914–28: Federal Reserve Board, *Annual Report, 1928*
    1929–33: Federal Reserve Board, *Annual Report, 1933*
    1934–41: Federal Reserve Board, *Banking and Monetary Statistics, 1943*
    1942–69: *Federal Reserve Bulletin*

Quoting documentation: "Data are monthly averages of daily figures. Data represent discounts and advances mainly to member banks; at times some rediscounts for non-member banks are also included. Small amounts of loans on foreign gold which have been included with bills discounted in the 1934 Annual Report and in *Banking and Monetary Statistics* are excluded here, except in 1934."

Gold stock: Data are from NBER Macro History Online Database. Series is "Monetary Gold Stock" and is not seasonally adjusted; units are billions of dollars. NBER documentation states that the data come from the *Federal Reserve Bulletin* and from *Banking and Monetary Statistics*. Figures for 1914 to July 1917 are end-of-month data; data for August 1917–70 are monthly averages of daily figures. Quoting documentation: "Between January 31, 1934 and February 1, 1934, the gold stock was increased 2.98 billion dollars, of which 2.81 billion was the increment resulting from reduction in the weight of the gold dollar and the remainder was gold which had been purchased by the Treasury previously but not added to the gold stock."

Monetary base: Units are billions of dollars; data are seasonally adjusted. Data come from the following sources:

    January 1914 to October 1914: Data are from Friedman and Schwartz, *A Monetary History of the United States, 1867–1960*, and are "High Powered Money." Friedman and Schwartz document their definition as currency held by the public plus vault cash. Seasonal adjustment by Friedman and Schwartz.

    November 1914 to December 1918: Data are from Friedman and Schwartz, *A Monetary History of the United States, 1867–1960* and are "High Powered Money." Friedman and

Schwartz document their definition as currency held by the public plus vault cash plus bank deposits at Federal Reserve banks. Seasonal adjustment by Friedman and Schwartz.

January 1919 to March 1951: Data are from Anderson and Rasche 1999; Federal Reserve Bank of St. Louis. Series is adjusted by adding the dollar amount of reserves liberated or impounded by changes in reserve requirement ratios. The data are seasonally adjusted using the multiplicative procedure in Micro-TSP.

1959 to present: Data are from St. Louis Federal reserve bank's Adjusted Monetary Base, seasonally adjusted by the St. Louis Federal Reserve bank.

M_1: Units are billions of dollars; data are seasonally adjusted. Data come from the following sources:

1914–45: Data are from NBER Macro History Online Database. Series is "Adjusted Demand Deposits, All Commercial Banks, plus Currency Held by Public, Seasonally Adjusted." Documentation states that the series was calculated by NBER as sum of "Adjusted Demand Deposits, All Banks" and "Currency Held by the Public." Seasonal adjustment was performed by NBER. Quoting documentation: "Data for 1914–1917 and May 1921–1945 refer to figures for the Wednesday nearest the end of the month. Data for January 1918–April 1921 refer to the Friday nearest the end of the month."

1946–47: Data are from NBER Macro History Online Database. Series is "Adjusted Demand Deposits, All Commercial Banks, plus Currency Held by Public, Seasonally Adjusted." Documentation states that the series was calculated by NBER as sum of "Adjusted Demand Deposits, All Banks" and "Currency Held by the Public." Documentation states that the data come from an unpublished Federal Reserve Board table; seasonal adjustment was performed by NBER. Quoting documentation: "Data represent middle of the month, being averages of two half-monthly figures that are based on daily figures."

1948–58: Data are from NBER Macro History Online Database. Series is "Adjusted Demand Deposits, All Commercial Banks, plus Currency Held by Public, Seasonally Adjusted." Documentation states that the data come from an unpublished Federal Reserve Board table; seasonal adjustment was performed by NBER. Quoting documentation: "Data represent middle of the month, being averages of two half-monthly figures that are based on daily figures."

1959 to present: Data are from the St. Louis Federal Reserve bank's FRED online database and are M_1, seasonally adjusted. Seasonal adjustment by the Board of Governors.

Long-term interest rate: Data are from the St. Louis Federal Reserve bank's FRED online database and are "Long-Term U.S. Government Bond Yield (10 Years or More) Including Flower Bonds; Averages of Daily Figures."

Commercial paper rate, 1914 to January 1937: Data are from the NBER Macro History Online Database. Series is "Commercial Paper Rates, New York City." NBER documentation states that the data come from F. R. MacAulay, *The Movement of Interest Rates, Bond Yields, and Stock Prices in the U.S. since 1856*, NBER no. 33 (New York: National Bureau of Economic Research 1938).

February 1937–42: Data are from the NBER Macro History Online Database. Series is "Commercial Paper Rates, New York City." NBER documentation states that the data were computed by the NBER using weekly data from *Bank and Quotation Record, Commercial and Financial Chronicle*.

1943 to March 1971: Data are from Board of Governors.

The documentation states that the data represent prime sixty- to ninety-day double-name commercial paper rates for 1914 to 1934 and prime four- to six-month double and single names 1924 to March 1971.

April 1971 to present: Data are from the St. Louis Federal Reserve bank's FRED online database and are defined as the thirty-day prime commercial rate, average of daily figures.

Term spread: Calculated as the difference between the Treasury bond rate and the commercial paper rate.

Discount rate: Discount rate. Series represents the following:

November 1914–21: Data are from NBER Macro History Online Database and are "Discount Rates, Federal Reserve Bank of New York"; documentation states that the data come from *Discount Rates of Federal Reserve Banks, 1914–1921,* Federal Reserve Board.

1922–41: Data are from NBER Macro History Online Database and are "Discount Rates, Federal Reserve Bank of New York; documentation states that the data come from Federal Reserve Board annual reports.

1942 to July 1969: Data are from NBER Macro History Online Database and are "Discount Rates, Federal Reserve Bank of New York; documentation states that the data come from the *Federal Reserve Bulletin.* Quoting documentation: "Data are computed by NBER by taking simple averages of rates for commercial, agricultural, and livestock paper, and weighting them by the number of days each rate was in force. Data are for all classes and maturities of discount bills."

August 1969 to present: Transformed data from the St. Louis Federal Reserve bank's FRED online database. Original data are "Discount Rate Changes (Date and Rate)." Data are transformed by weighting the rates by the number of days each rate was in force.

Aaa rate: Data are from the St. Louis Federal Reserve bank's FRED online database and are "Corporate Aaa Bond Rate, Average of Daily Figures."

Acceptances: Banker's acceptance rates. From the following sources:

1917–40: Data are from the NBER Macro History Online Database and are "Banker's Acceptance Rates, New York City." Quoting documentation: "Data represent prime bankers' acceptances, ninety days. Data for 1917–1950 are averages of weekly prevailing rates calculated on the basis of frequency of a single rate or a range of rates occurring during the month."

1941 to present: Data are from the St. Louis Federal Reserve bank's FRED online data base and are "Bankers Acceptance Rates, Ninety Days."

Time spread: Calculated as the difference between the Aaa rate and the banker's acceptance rate.

Baa rate: Data are from the St. Louis Federal Reserve bank's FRED online database and are "Corporate Baa Bond Rate, Average of Daily Figures."

Risk spread: Calculated as the difference between the Baa rate and the Aaa rate.

Real GNP: data are from the following sources:

1914–46: Data are from Balke and Gordon (1986). Since Balke and Gordon's data do not correspond to official data that were revised subsequent to their publication, real GNP was calculated as Balke and Gordon's nominal GNP deflated by a revision of their deflator as described below.

1947 to present: Data are from the St. Louis Federal Reserve bank's FRED online database. Nominal GNP was deflated by the GNP deflator as described below.

Deflator: Data from the following sources.

1914–46: Data are a revision of data from Balke and Gordon (1986). Since Balke and Gordon's data do not correspond to official data that were revised subsequent to their publication, inflation rates were calculated (as log ratios) using the data. Using 1946.4 to 1947.1 as a splicing point, a new series was then calculated from official data by iterating backward using Balke and Gordon's inflation rates.

1947 to present: Data are from the St. Louis Federal Reserve bank's FRED online database and are the GNP deflator.

Index of industrial production, monthly January 1919 to March 1951, seasonally adjusted. From Board of Governors Web site.

Consumer price index, monthly, January 1914 to March 1951, not seasonally adjusted. From Bureau of Labor Statistics Web site.

INDEX

Italic page numbers refer to tables and charts. In subentries, Federal Reserve System is abbreviated as FRS.

ket crash, 289–90, 296n.28; on real
bills, 70, 158, 246; and recession after
stock market crash, 293–94; and recession of 1923–24, 198; in second year of
Great Depression, 339, 340; on Strong
and the British, 211

call money market: bill market to replace
under FRS, 70, 71, 76, 263; call loans as
money market instrument, 736; interest
rates after stock market crash, 285; interest rates in 1928, 229, 230; interest
rates in 1929, 242, 243, 252, 265, 283; in
nineteenth-century Britain, 37; preventing interior banks from sending money
to, 207; in response to stock market
crash, 244; Warburg on, 54

Calomiris, Charles W., 313, 323, 425n.19,
431n.34, 518

Canada, 255, 262, 396–97

capital gains tax, 604–5, 608, 651

Case, J. Herbert: on bank holiday for New
York, 386n.134; becomes chairman at
New York, 296n.30; on Bullock proposal on discount rate, 183; on Committee on Centralized Purchases and Sales,
146; on gold reserve ratio, 166; on New
York acceptance purchases binding
other banks, 108n.87; New York bank's
1927–29 policy defended by, 251–52; as
OMIC deputy chair, 199; on open market operation centralization, 151; in Public and Manufacturers' bank merger,
323, 324; and recession after stock market crash, 298; and recession of 1923–
24, 200, 200n.97; in stock price conflict, 227–28, 229; on Strong and discount rate in 1929, 195; on tenth annual
report, 156, 157, 159

Cecchetti, G., 532n.241

central banks: FRS becoming, 5, 486, 726;
governments taking control of, 2; international policy as responsibility of, 736;
as lenders of last resort, 1, 4, 22, 23, 49,
50n, 64, 730; organizing principles of
modern, 2; as privately owned before
1913, 1–2; as secretive in nineteenth century, 735; theory and practice before Federal Reserve Act, 19–64. See also Bank of
England; Bank of France; Federal
Reserve System

Central Republic Bank (Chicago), 368,
368n.104

Chamberlain, Neville, 536, 542, 544

Chandler, Lester, 153n, 166n, 172, 203n.105

Chase National Bank, 128, 431, 431n.33,
44In.50, 541, 541n.262

Chaudri, Ehsan, 393n.147, 394

Chicago, Federal Reserve Bank of. See Federal Reserve Bank of Chicago

China, 461, 462

Churchill, Winston, 171, 171n.48

City of Glasgow Bank, 47

Clark, John D., 710n.233

Clarke, Stephen V. O., 262, 273n, 336n.65,
405n

Clayton, Lawrence, 655, 670n.163, 671

Clayton Act of 1914, 656

clearinghouse certificates, 380, 384, 385,
385n.132

commercial banking: investment banking
separated from, 417, 430, 431–32, 727;
proposal for reserve requirements to apply to all banks, 683; ration coupons
processed by, 606; reserve requirement
increase of 1948 transferring income
from, 658; restricted securities during
bond drives, 591; war debt acquired by,
587, 719; war loan accounts, 652n.132,
653–54

Committee for the Nation, 443, 443n.56,
454

Committee of Governors on the Centralized
Execution of Purchases and Sales of
Government Securities, 146–48, 150,
151, 199

Committee on the High Price of Bullion
(Britain), 32

commodity prices: central bankers' meeting
of 1927 considering, 177; decline in
1930, 299; decline in 1933, 437, 448,
452n.71, 454; decline in 1948, 654–55;
rise in 1932, 373; rise in 1933, 450; Warren's charts of weekly, 449, 451

Commons, John R., 189n.82, 191, 426

compensated gold dollar, 182–83, 444,
444n.60

comptroller of the currency: as FDIC director, 432n.36; as FRS Board member, 4,
74, 429, 485, 485n.147, 500

consumer credit controls: expiration of in
1949, 674; Federal Advisory Council
criticizing, 673; postwar, 579, 644–45,
647, 663, 663n.151, 698; reserve bank
presidents on, 669; wartime, 557–58

consumer durable goods, 579, 582, 602,
632, 663, 672